# The Oxford ESL Dictionary

OXFORD
UNIVERSITY PRESS

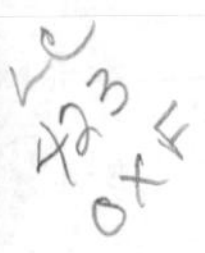

OXFORD
UNIVERSITY PRESS

Great Clarendon Street, Oxford OX2 6DP

Oxford University Press is a department of the University of Oxford.
It furthers the University's objective of excellence in research, scholarship, and education by publishing worldwide in

Oxford New York

Auckland Bangkok Buenos Aires Cape Town Chennai
Dar es Salaam Delhi Hong Kong Istanbul Karachi Kolkata
Kuala Lumpur Madrid Melbourne Mexico City Mumbai
Nairobi São Paulo Shanghai Taipei Tokyo Toronto

OXFORD and OXFORD ENGLISH are registered trade marks of Oxford University Press in the UK and in certain other countries


First published 2004

Library of Congress Cataloging-in-Publication Data
Oxford ESL dictionary.
p. cm.
Includes bibliographical references.
ISBN 0-19-431683-1 (pbk.) – ISBN 0-19-431628-9 (pbk. and cd-rom pack) – ISBN 0-19-431674-2 (workbook)
1. English language–Dictionaries. 2. English language–Textbooks for foreign speakers. I. Title: Oxford English as a second language dictionary.
PE1628.O8685 2004
423–dc22 2004006849



Illustrations by Richard Lewington; Martin Shovel; Michael Woods.
Original photography © Oxford University Press 2004
The publisher would like to thank Corel and Hemera Technologies Inc. for permission to reproduce photographs: © Oxford University Press 2004
Maps © Oxford University Press

ISBN 0 19 431683 1 (dictionary)
ISBN 0 19 431628 9 (dictionary with CD-ROM)
ISBN 0 19 431674 2 (workbook)

Data capture and processing by Oxford University Press
Printed in Hong Kong

# Contents

# Guide to the dictionary

## Finding and spelling words

A star shows **important words**.

★**pow·er**[1] /ˈpaʊər/ ***noun***
▸ABILITY| **1** [C,U] the ability to do sth: *The ambassador promised to do everything in her power to make sure the hostages were not harmed.* ◇ *He has great powers of observation.*
▸ENERGY| **2** [U] force or strength: *The ship was helpless against the power of the storm.* **3** [U] energy that is used for making machines work, giving light, heat, etc.: *nuclear power* ◇ *the power supply*
▸INFLUENCE| **4** [U] control or influence over other people: *The military government came to power after a long struggle.* ◇ *the power of the unions* ◇ *He sacrificed everything for power and money.* ◇ *to have sb in your power*
▸AUTHORITY| **5** [C] the right or authority to do sth: *Do the police have the power to stop cars without a good reason?*

**Shortcuts** help you to **find the right meaning** more quickly.

**Another possible spelling** is given in parentheses.

**ac·knowl·edg·ment** (*also* **ac·knowl·edge·ment**) /əkˈnɑlɪdʒmənt/ ***noun*** **1** [U] the act of acknowledging sth: *I have received no acknowledgment for all the work I did.* **2** [C] a letter, etc. stating that sth has been received **3** [C] a few words of thanks that an author writes at the beginning or end of a book to the people who have helped him/her

Words with the **same spelling** have different numbers.

**glim·mer**[1] /ˈglɪmər/ ***noun*** [C] **1** a weak unsteady light **2** a weak sign of sth: *a glimmer of hope*
**glim·mer**[2] /glɪmər/ ***verb*** [I] to give out a weak unsteady light

**Dots** show how to divide words into syllables.

**la·dy·bug** /ˈleɪdibʌg/ ***noun*** [C] a small insect that is red or orange with black spots

## Words and phrases related to the main word

**Idioms** are shown in a section marked by the sign IDM.

The arrow → shows that the meaning of an idiom is explained at the word following the arrow.

IDM **a breath of fresh air** → BREATH
**in the air** probably going to happen soon: *A feeling of change was in the air.*
**in the open air** → OPEN[1]

**Phrasal verbs** are shown in a section marked by the sign PHR V.

PHR V **take after sb** to look or behave like an older member of your family
**take sth apart** to separate sth into the different parts it is made of
**take sth away** to cause a feeling, etc. to disappear: *This asprin will take the pain away.*

**Derivatives** of the main word (= words with the same spelling but a different part of speech; or the main word plus an ending such as *-ly, -ness,* etc.) are shown after a ▶ sign.

**eager** /ˈigər/ ***adj.*** full of desire or interest: *He is eager to meet you.* ◇ *eager for success* ▶ **eagerly** ***adv.*** ▶ **eagerness** ***noun*** [U]

## Meaning

The **meaning** of words and phrases is given in simple English using words that are easy to understand. If there is more than one meaning, all the meanings are listed after numbers.

**swarm**[1] /swɔrm/ ***noun*** [C] **1** a large group of insects, especially bees, moving around together **2** a large number of people together

The **example sentences** help you to understand the word and show how it is used in English.

★**be·low**[1] /bɪˈloʊ/ ***prep.*** at or to a lower position or level than sb/sth: *Do not write below this line.* ◇ *It hurts here – just below my knee.* ◇ *The temperature fell below freezing.* ◇ *Her test score was below average.* ◇ *He drives way below the speed limit.*

Words with the **same meaning** are given.

**glas·ses** /ˈglæsəz/ (*also* **eyeglasses**) ***noun*** [pl.] two pieces of glass in a frame that a person wears in front of his/her eyes (in order to be able to see better)

a **figurative** use of the word (= not using a word in its true sense, but in an imaginative way in order to give a special effect)

**chunk** /tʃʌŋk/ ***noun*** [C] a large or thick piece of sth: *chunks of ice floating in the lake* ◇ (*figurative*) *A big chunk of my income goes toward paying bills.*

## Grammar

the **part of speech** (= whether it is a noun, verb, etc.)

**slurp** /slərp/ ***verb*** [I,T] (informal) to drink noisily: *I hate the way he slurps when he drinks coffee.* ▶ **slurp** ***noun*** [C]

**slush** /slʌʃ/ ***noun*** **1** [U] snow that has partly melted and that is often very wet and dirty **2** [C,U] a drink that is made from crushed ice with a fruit flavor ▶ **slush·y** ***adj.***

**countable and uncountable nouns**
These letters tell you whether the noun can be counted [C] or not [U].

★**e·mo·tion** /ɪˈmoʊʃn/ ***noun*** **1** [C] a strong feeling such as love, anger, fear, jealousy, etc. **2** [U] strength of feeling: *His voice was filled with emotion.*

a **singular noun**

**ruck·us** /ˈrʌkəs/ ***noun*** [sing.] (*informal*) a noisy argument or disturbance

**a plural noun**

★**pre·mis·es** /ˈprɛməsəz/ ***noun*** [pl.] (*formal*) a building and the land that surrounds it: *Smoking is not allowed on the premises.*

an **irregular plural** form

★**to·ma·to** /təˈmeɪt̬oʊ/ ***noun*** [C] (*pl.* **to·ma·toes**) a soft red fruit that is often eaten raw in salads or cooked as a vegetable: *tomato juice*

**irregular forms of verbs**

**transitive and intransitive verbs**
These letters tell you whether a verb is transitive [T] (= followed by an object) or intransitive [I] (= never followed by an object).

★**hide**[1] /haɪd/ ***verb*** (*pt* **hid** /hɪd/; *pp* **hidden** /ˈhɪdn/) **1** [T] to put or keep sb/sth in a place where he/she/it cannot be seen: *Where should I hide the money?* ◇ *The scar is partially hidden by hair.* ◇ *The trees hid the house from view.* **2** [I] to be or get in a place where you cannot be seen or found: *Quick, run and hide!* ◇ *Tammy was hiding under the bed.* **3** [T] **hide sth (from sb)** to keep sth secret so that other people do not know about it: *She tried to hide her disappointment from them.*

The **last letter** of the word **is doubled** before you add *-ing* or *-ed*.

**hum**[1] /hʌm/ ***verb*** **(hum·ming; hummed)** **1** [I] to make a continuous low noise like the noise bees make: (figurative) *The classroom was humming with activity.*

the **comparative** and **superlative** forms (regular forms are not given)

★**good**[1] /gʊd/ ***adj.*** **(bet·ter /ˈbɛt̮ər/, best /bɛst/)** ▸HIGH QUALITY **1** of a high quality or standard: *a good book/movie/concert* ◇ *The hotel was really good.*

★**hap·py** /ˈhæpi/ ***adj.*** **(hap·pi·er; hap·pi·est)** **1** feeling, showing or giving pleasure or satisfaction: *a happy childhood* ◇ *a happy family* ◇ *a happy smile*

★**scis·sors** /ˈsɪzərz/ ***noun*** [pl.] a tool for cutting things that consists of two flat sharp blades that are joined together

a note giving **grammatical information**

**HELP** **Scissors** is a plural noun: *These scissors are blunt.* We CANNOT say "a scissors"; we must use the word **pair**: *I need a new pair of scissors.*

## Using words

how a word is used in a sentence (sb = somebody; sth = something)

★**blame**[1] /bleɪm/ ***verb*** [T] **1** **blame sb (for sth); blame sth on sb** to think or say that a certain person or thing is responsible for sth bad that has happened:

the particular **preposition** that is used after a word

**de·pend·ent**[2] /dɪˈpɛndənt/ ***adj.*** **dependent (on sb/sth)** needing sb/sth to support you: *The industry is heavily dependent on government contracts.*

The adjective cannot be used before a noun; it must always follow a verb like *be, seem, etc.*

★**a·wake**[1] /əˈweɪk/ ***adj.*** (not before a noun) not sleeping: *I was awake most of the night, worrying.* ◇ *The kids are always wide* (= completely) *awake at 6 o'clock in the morning.*

The adjective can only be used before a noun.

**lone** /loʊn/ ***adj.*** (only before a noun) without any other people; alone: *a lone swimmer*

**words used in particular situations**
Word may be labeled *(formal)* (used in formal, especially written English), *(written)* (literary or not used in spoken English), *(informal)* (used in informal conversation and not usually written in essays, etc.), *(slang)* (very informal and often used especially by younger people).

**awe·some** /ˈɔsəm/ ***adj.*** **1** (*formal*) impressive and sometimes frightening: *an awesome task* **2** (*informal*) very good; excellent: *We went to an awesome party at Dave's house.* ◇ *Wow! That's totally awesome!*

## Choosing the right word/vocabulary building

**build**[2] /bɪld/ ***noun*** [C,U] the shape and size of sb's body: *She has a very athletic build.* ◇ *Police are looking for a young man of slim build.*

a note explaining the **difference between words** that might be confused

**HELP** Compare **build** and **figure**. **Build** usually describes size in connection with strength and muscle and is used for both men and women. **Figure** usually describes shape, especially whether it is attractive or not, and is usually used only for women.

★**a·part·ment** /ə'pɑrtmənt/ ***noun*** [C] (*abbr.* **apt.**) a set of rooms that is used as a home (usually on one floor in a larger building): *a three-bedroom apartment.*

a note giving **related vocabulary**

**HELP** You **rent** an apartment from a **landlord** or from a company that owns the apartment. The landlord **rents** the apartment **out** to you, the **tenant**. The money you have to pay is called **rent**. ➲ Look also at **condominium**.

**sane** /sem/ ***adj.*** **1** (used about a person) mentally normal; not crazy: *With a job like mine, it's incredible that I'm still sane!* **2** (used about a person or an idea, a decision, etc.) sensible; showing good judgment: *I had to accept the offer. It was the only sane thing to do.*

members of a **word family**

OPP **insane** ➲ noun **sanity**

**nude**[1] /nud/ ***adj.*** not wearing any clothes

**synonyms**

SYN **bare, naked**

## Pronunciation

the **pronunciation** of each word

★**en·gi·neer**[1] /ˌɛndʒə'nɪr/ ***noun*** [C] **1** a person whose job is to use science and math in practical ways, e.g. to design machines, roads, bridges, etc., or to plan processes in factories, etc.: *a civil/chemical/mechanical engineer*

where the **stress** falls on a word

**ˌmass ˈmedia** ***noun*** [pl.] the means of communicating with large numbers of people, i.e. newspapers, television and radio

## Canadian English

Look at the U.S. word after the = (equals) sign to find the meaning of a **Canadian word**.

**eaves·trough** /'ivztrɔf/ ***noun*** [C] (Cdn) = GUTTER (1)

## Quiz answers

***Answers to Dictionary quiz – page viii***

1 potatoes
2 a baby or a very young child
3 spend money
4 the receiver
5 dishonest
6 shadow
7 commence
8 an adjective
9 uncountable
10 swore
11 facto**ries**
12 occu**rr**ing
13 the "p"
14 **hot** dog
15 three (have an hour, etc. to kill; kill time; kill two birds with one stone)
16 five (burn (sth) down; burn (sb/yourself) out; burn sth out; burn up; burn sth up)
17 smuggler; smuggling
18 elegance
19 a Norwegian
20 million

# Dictionary quiz

This quiz shows how the ***Oxford ESL Dictionary*** can help you.
You'll find the answers to all these questions in the dictionary.

| Questions | |
|---|---|
| 1 What are **hash browns** made of?<br>2 Who would wear a **diaper**?<br>3 What doesn't a **cheapskate** like to do? | **Meanings**<br>The dictionary explains what words mean in language that is easy to understand, and the example sentences show you how to use the word correctly. |
| 4 What's the name of the part of a **telephone** that you pick up when you want to make a phone call?<br>5 What's the opposite of **honest**?<br>6 *I could see the **shade** of a man outside the window.*<br>In this sentence, the word **shade** is wrong. What's the correct word? | **Vocabulary**<br>There are notes (shown by the ➲ symbol and NOTE icon) that give useful extra vocabulary associated with a word and explain the difference between words that people often confuse. |
| 7 Which word in this sentence would you NOT use in an informal situation:<br>—*What time does the meeting commence?* | **Style**<br>The dictionary tells you if a word is formal or informal, and it often suggests another word that you can use in most situations. |
| 8 Is the word **meek** a noun, a verb or an adjective?<br>9 Is the word **luggage** countable or uncountable?<br>10 What's the past tense form of **swear**? | **Grammar**<br>The dictionary tells you whether a word is a noun, verb, adjective, etc. and whether nouns are countable or uncountable. It also gives irregular forms (e.g. irregular past tenses of verbs). |
| 11 How do you spell the plural of **factory**?<br>12 How do you spell the -ing form of the verb **occur**? | **Spelling**<br>You can use the dictionary to check how a word is spelled. It also tells you about small spelling changes in other forms of the word (e.g. irregular plurals). |
| 13 Which letter is silent in the word **receipt**?<br>14 Which part of **hot dog** receives the main stress? | **Pronunciation**<br>This dictionary gives the pronunciation of words, and at the bottom of each page there is a key that shows you how to read the phonetic spelling. Look also at the marks that show you where the main stress of the word is. |
| 15 How many idioms are there that have the word **kill** in them?<br>16 How many phrasal verbs can you make with the word **burn**? | **Idioms and phrasal verbs**<br>These are given in two separate sections after the main meanings of the word. (Look also at the "Phrasal verbs" study page – on pages A**4** – **5**.) |
| 17 What two nouns can you form from the word **smuggle**?<br>18 What's the noun formed from **elegant**? | **Words formed from other words**<br>Derivatives (**loudly** and **loudness** are derivatives of **loud**) are given after the main meanings of the word. |
| 19 What do you call a person who comes from **Norway**?<br>20 What number does the prefix **mega-** indicate? | **Extra Information**<br>At the back of the dictionary you will find a list of irregular verbs, a list of prefixes and suffixes, maps and a list of geographical names. |

*Answers on page vii*

# A a

**A, a**[1] /eɪ/ ***noun*** [C,U] (*pl.* A's; a's /eɪz/) **1** the first letter of the English alphabet: *"Andy" begins with (an) "A."* **2** the highest grade given for a test or piece of work: *I got an "A" on my essay.*
IDM **earn/get straight A's** → STRAIGHT[1]

★**a**[2] /ə; *strong form* eɪ/ (*also* **an** /ən; *strong form* æn/) ***indefinite article***

NOTE The form **an** is used before a vowel sound.

**1** one: *I'll have a cup of coffee.* ◇ *an apple and a pear* **2** (used when you are talking about sth in general, not one particular example of it): *A lion is a dangerous animal.* **3** (used with sb's name to show that the speaker does not know the person): *There's a Ms. Mills here to see you.* **4** (used for showing that sb/sth is a member of a group, class or profession): *She's a Muslim.* ◇ *Their car's a Volvo.* ◇ *She's a senator.* **5** (used with some expressions of quantity): *a lot of money* ◇ *a few cars* **6** (used with prices, rates, measurements) each: *They cost 50¢ a pound.* ◇ *He was traveling at about 80 miles an hour.*

**a·back** /ə'bæk/ ***adv.***
IDM **be taken aback** to be surprised or shocked: *I was completely taken aback when I saw the bill from the mechanic.*

**aba·cus** /'æbəkəs/ ***noun*** [C] (*pl.* **aba·cuses** /-kəsɪz/) a frame with small balls, arranged in rows, which can be moved backward and forward to help people to count, add and subtract

★**a·ban·don** /ə'bændən/ ***verb*** [T] **1** to leave sb/sth that you are responsible for, usually permanently: *an abandoned car* **2** to stop doing sth without finishing it or without achieving what you wanted to do: *The search for the missing sailors was abandoned after two days.* ▶ **a·ban·don·ment *noun*** [U]

**a·bashed** /ə'bæʃt/ ***adj.*** ashamed and embarrassed because of having done sth bad

**ab·bey** /'æbi/ ***noun*** [C] a building where monks or nuns live or used to live

**abbr.** (*also* **abbrev.**) = ABBREVIATION

**ab·bre·vi·ate** /ə'brivieɪt/ ***verb*** [T] **1** to make a word or phrase shorter by leaving out some letters **2** to make a story, a piece of writing or speech shorter: *the abbreviated version of the story*

**ab·bre·vi·a·tion** /əˌbrivi'eɪʃn/ ***noun*** [C] a short form of a word or phrase: *In this dictionary, "sth" is the abbreviation for "something."*

**ab·di·cate** /'æbdɪkeɪt/ ***verb*** [I,T] to give sth up, especially power or a position: *The queen abdicated and her son became king.* ◇ *to abdicate responsibility* (= to refuse to be responsible for sth) ▶ **ab·di·ca·tion** /ˌæbdɪ'keɪʃn/ ***noun*** [C,U]

**ab·do·men** /'æbdəmən/ ***noun*** [C] a part of the body between the chest and the legs, in which the stomach is contained ▶ **ab·dom·i·nal** /æb'dɑmɪnl; əb-/ ***adj.*** ➲ Look at **abs**.

**ab·duct** /əb'dʌkt; æb-/ ***verb*** [T] to take hold of sb and take him/her away illegally: *He has been abducted by a terrorist group.* ▶ **ab·duc·tion** /-'dʌkʃn/ ***noun*** [C,U]

**a·bet** /ə'bɛt/ ***verb*** [T] (**a·bet·ting; a·bet·ted**)
IDM **aid and abet** → AID[2]

**ab·hor** /əb'hɔr; æb-/ ***verb*** [T] (**ab·hor·ring; ab·horred**) (*formal*) to hate sth very much: *All civilized people abhor the use of torture.* ▶ **ab·hor·rence** /-'hɔrəns; -'hɑrəns/ ***noun*** [U] ▶ **ab·hor·rent** /-'hɔrənt; -'hɑrənt/ ***adj.***

**a·bide** /ə'baɪd/ ***verb*** (*formal*)
IDM **can't/couldn't abide sb/sth/doing sth** to dislike sth very much: *I can't abide getting up early.*
PHR V **abide by sth** to obey a law, etc.; to do what you have agreed or decided: *You must abide by the rules of the game.*

★**a·bil·i·ty** /ə'bɪləṭi/ ***noun*** [C,U] (*pl.* **a·bil·i·ties**) the mental or physical power or skill that makes it possible to do sth: *A person of his ability will have no difficulty getting a job.*

**a·blaze** /ə'bleɪz/ ***adj.*** (not before a noun) burning strongly; completely on fire: *Within ten minutes, the whole house was ablaze.*

★**a·ble** /'eɪbl/ ***adj.*** **1 be able to do sth** (used as a modal verb) to have the ability, power, opportunity, time, etc. to do sth: *Will you be able to come to a meeting next week?* ◇ *I was able to solve the problem quickly.*

NOTE In the passive, **can/could** is used, not **be able to**: *The arrangement can't be changed.*

**2** (*formal*) intelligent; doing your job well: *an able politician* ▶ **a·bly** /'eɪbli/ ***adv.***

**able-bodied** /ˌeɪbl' bɑdid/ ***adj.*** strong and healthy: *All the able-bodied young men from our town were drafted into the army.*

**ABM** /ˌeɪ bi 'ɛm/ ***noun*** [C] (*Cdn*) automated banking machine; a machine inside or outside a bank, in a shopping center, etc. from which you can get money at any time of day by putting in a special card

**ab·nor·mal** /æb'nɔrml/ ***adj.*** different from what is normal or usual, in a way that worries you or that is unpleasant: *I don't want to have children. Is that abnormal?* ◇ *abnormal weather conditions* ▶ **ab·nor·mal·i·ty** /ˌæbnɔr'mæləṭi; ˌæbnər-/ ***noun*** [C,U] (*pl.* **ab·nor·mal·i·ties**) ▶ **ab·nor·mal·ly *adv.***

**a·board** /ə'bɔrd/ ***adv., prep.*** on or into a train, ship or aircraft: *We went aboard the ship.* ◇ *Welcome aboard Flight 397 to Caracas.*

**a·bol·ish** /ə'bɑlɪʃ/ ***verb*** [T] to put an end to or stop a law or system officially: *When was capital punishment abolished here?* ▶ **ab·o·li·tion** /ˌæbə'lɪʃn/ ***noun*** [U]: *the abolition of slavery in the U.S.*

**a·bom·i·na·ble** /ə'bɑmənəbl/ ***adj.*** (*formal*) very bad; very unpleasant: *abominable behavior*

A

**ab·o·rig·i·nal** /ˌæbəˈrɪdʒənl/ ***adj.*** **1** of or belonging to the original inhabitants of a place: *aboriginal tribes* **2 Aboriginal** of or belonging to the race of people who were the original inhabitants of Australia

**Ab·o·rig·i·ne** /ˌæbəˈrɪdʒəni/ ***noun*** [C] a member of the race of people who were the original inhabitants of Australia

**a·bort** /əˈbɔrt/ ***verb*** [I,T] **1** to remove a baby (a fetus) from a pregnant woman so that it does not develop further and will not be born **2** to end sth before it is complete: *to abort a bombing mission*

**a·bor·tion** /əˈbɔrʃn/ ***noun*** **1** [C,U] an operation on a pregnant woman so that she will not have a baby: *to have an abortion* ◇ *Abortion is illegal in that country.* **2** [C] an event which causes a pregnant woman to lose her baby accidentally: *a spontaneous abortion*

**a·bor·tive** /əˈbɔrt̬ɪv/ ***adj.*** not completed successfully: *an abortive attempt*

**a·bound** /əˈbaʊnd/ ***verb*** [I] **1** to exist in large numbers: *Restaurants abound in this part of the city.* **2 abound with sth** to contain large numbers of sth

★**a·bout**[1] /əˈbaʊt/ ***adv.*** (*informal*) **1** (*also* **around**) a little more or less than; approximately: *It's about three miles from here to the center of town.* ◇ *I got home about 7:30.* **2** almost; nearly: *Dinner's just about ready.*

IDM **be about to do sth** to be going to do sth very soon: *The show's about to start.*

**be not about to do sth** not to be willing to do sth: *I'm not about to let a little rain spoil our picnic!*

★**a·bout**[2] /əˈbaʊt/ ***prep.*** **1** on the subject of: *a book about Spain* ◇ *I don't like it, but there's nothing I can do about it.* **2** in the character of sb: *There's something about him that I don't quite trust.*

IDM **how/what about...?** **1** (used when asking for information about sb/sth or for sb's opinion or wish): *I'm going to have chicken. How about you?* ◇ *What about Ruth? Have you heard from her lately?* **2** (used when making a suggestion): *How about going to a movie tonight?*

**aˌbout-ˈface** ***noun*** [C] a turn in the opposite direction; a change of opinion

★**a·bove**[1] /əˈbʌv/ ***adv., prep.*** **1** in a higher place: *The people in the apartment above make a lot of noise.* ◇ *I live in the hills above the city.* ➲ picture at **over**. **2** (*formal*) in an earlier part (of sth written): *the items mentioned above* **3** more than a number, amount, price, etc.: *children age 11 and above* ◇ *A score of 70 and above will get you a B on the test.* ◇ *You have to get above 50% to pass.* ◇ *above-average temperatures* **4** too good, etc. to do sth: *She's not above telling a few lies if it makes life easier.* **5** with a higher rank: *The person above me is the department manager.*

IDM **above all** most importantly: *Above all, stay calm!*

**a·bove**[2] /əˈbʌv/ ***adj.*** mentioned before in a piece of writing: *If you answered "yes" to the above questions, go on to number 6.* ▶ **ˌthe aˈbove** ***noun*** [U, pl.]: *Which of the above best describes your personality?*

**ab·ra·sive** /əˈbreɪsɪv/ ***adj.*** **1** rough and likely to scratch: *Do not use abrasive cleaning products on the bathtub.* **2** (used about a person) rude and fairly aggressive

**a·breast** /əˈbrɛst/ ***adv.*** (used after a number) next to or level with each other and going in the same direction: *The soldiers marched two abreast.*

IDM **be/keep abreast of sth** to have all the most recent information about sth

**a·bridge** /əˈbrɪdʒ/ ***verb*** [T] to make sth (usually a book) shorter by removing parts of it ▶ **a·bridged** ***adj.***: *an abridged version of a novel* OPP **unabridged** ▶ **a·bridg·ment** (*also* **abridgement**) ***noun*** [C,U]

★**a·broad** /əˈbrɔd/ ***adv.*** in or to another country or countries: *My mother has never been abroad.* ◇ *They found it difficult to get used to living abroad.*

**a·brupt** /əˈbrʌpt/ ***adj.*** **1** sudden and unexpected: *an abrupt change of plan* **2** (used about a person's behavior) fairly rude and unfriendly ▶ **a·brupt·ly** ***adv.*** ▶ **a·brupt·ness** ***noun*** [U]

**abs** /æbz/ ***noun*** [pl.] (*informal*) the muscles of the stomach (= the abdominal muscles)

**ab·scess** /ˈæbsɛs/ ***noun*** [C] a swelling on or in the body, containing a poisonous liquid (**pus**)

**ab·scond** /əbˈskɑnd; æb-/ ***verb*** [I] (*formal*) to run away from a place where you should stay, sometimes with sth that you should not take: *She absconded with all the company's money.*

★**ab·sence** /ˈæbsəns/ ***noun*** **1** [C,U] a time when sb is away from somewhere; the fact of being away from somewhere: *frequent absences due to illness* ◇ *His absence from the team will definitely weaken it.* **2** [U] the fact of sth not being there; a lack of sth: *The first thing I noticed about the place was the absence of noise.*

**ab·sent** /ˈæbsənt/ ***adj.*** **1** not present somewhere: *He was absent from work.* **2** thinking about sth else, and so not paying attention: *an absent stare* ▶ **ab·sent·ly** ***adv.***

**ab·sen·tee** /ˌæbsənˈti/ ***noun*** [C] a person who should be present but is not

**ab·sen·tee·ism** /ˌæbsənˈtiɪzəm/ ***noun*** [U] the problem of workers or students often not going to work or school

**ˌabsent-ˈminded** ***adj.*** often forgetting or not noticing things, because you are thinking about sth else ▶ **ˌabsent-ˈmindedly** ***adv.*** ▶ **ˌabsent-ˈmindedness** ***noun*** [U]

★**ab·so·lute** /ˈæbsəlut; ˌæbsəˈlut/ ***adj.*** **1** complete; total: *We are aiming at absolute perfection!* ◇ *The whole trip was an absolute disaster.* **2** certain; definite: *We don't have absolute proof that this suspect committed the robbery.* **3** not measured in comparison with sth else: *Food prices have increased in absolute terms.*

★**ab·so·lute·ly** ***adv.*** **1** /ˈæbsəlutli/ completely; totally: *What you're saying is absolutely wrong.* ◇ *I absolutely refuse to believe that.* ◇ *He made absolutely no effort* (= no effort at all) *to help me.* **2** /ˌæbsəˈlutli/ (used when you are agreeing with sb) yes; certainly: *"It's a good idea, isn't it?" "Oh, absolutely!"*

**ab·solve** /əbˈzɑlv/ ***verb*** [T] **absolve sb (from/of sth)** to state formally that sb is free from guilt or blame: *The driver was absolved from any responsibility for the train crash.*

A

★**ab·sorb** /əb'sɔrb; -'zɔrb/ ***verb*** [T] **1** to take in and hold sth (a liquid, heat, etc.): *a drug that is quickly absorbed into the bloodstream* **2** to take sth into the mind and understand it: *I found it impossible to absorb so much information so quickly.* **3** to take sth into sth larger, so that it becomes part of it: *Over the years many towns have been absorbed into the metropolitan area.* **4** to hold sb's attention completely or interest sb greatly: *History is a subject that absorbs her.* ▸ **ab·sorp·tion** /əb'sɔrpʃn; -'zɔrp-/ ***noun*** [U]

**ab·sorbed** /əb'sɔrbd; -'zɔrbd/ ***adj.*** with sb's attention completely held: *He was absorbed in his work and didn't hear me come in.*

**ab·sorb·ent** /əb'sɔrbənt; -'zɔr-/ ***adj.*** able to take in and hold liquid: *an absorbent cloth*

**ab·sorb·ing** /əb'sɔrbɪŋ; -'zɔr-/ ***adj.*** so interesting that it holds the attention completely: *an absorbing story*

**ab·stain** /əb'steɪn/ ***verb*** [I] **abstain (from sth)** **1** to stop yourself from doing sth that you enjoy: *to abstain from eating fattening food* ➲ noun **abstinence** **2** (in a vote) to say that you are not voting either for or against sth: *Two people voted in favor, two voted against and one abstained.* ➲ noun **abstention**

**ab·sten·tion** /əb'stɛnʃn/ ***noun*** [C,U] the act of not voting either for or against sth

**ab·sti·nence** /'æbstənəns/ ***noun*** [U] stopping yourself from having or doing sth that you enjoy: *The doctor advised total abstinence from alcohol.*

**ab·stract**[1] /əb'strækt; æb-; 'æbstrækt/ ***adj.*** **1** existing only as an idea, not as a physical or real thing: *I find it hard to think about abstract ideas like the meaning of life.* **2** (used about art) not showing things as they really look: *an abstract painting* ➲ Compare **representational**.

**ab·stract**[2] /'æbstrækt/ ***noun*** [C] **1** an example of ABSTRACT[1] (2) art: *an exhibit of abstracts* **2** a much shorter version of an article, a book, etc. giving the main points or ideas from it; a summary

**IDM** **in the abstract** without mentioning particular people, objects, etc.: *I find it hard to think about a problem in the abstract.*

**ab·surd** /əb'sərd/ ***adj.*** that should be laughed at; ridiculous; not seeming sensible: *That's totally absurd! I can't possibly do all this work in one day.* ▸ **ab·surd·i·ty** /əb'sərdət̬i/ ***noun*** [C,U] (*pl.* **ab·surd·i·ties**) ▸ **ab·surd·ly** ***adv.***: *The rules of the game are absurdly complicated.*

**a·bun·dance** /ə'bʌndəns/ ***noun*** [U, sing.] a very large quantity of sth

**a·bun·dant** /ə'bʌndənt/ ***adj.*** existing in very large quantities; more than enough: *abundant supplies of food* ▸ **a·bun·dant·ly** ***adv.***

★**a·buse**[1] /ə'byuz/ ***verb*** [T] **1** to use sth in the wrong way, e.g. dishonestly: *He was accused of abusing his position for personal gain.* **2** to treat sb badly, often violently: *The girl had been sexually abused by her father.* **3** to say rude things to sb

**a·buse**[2] /ə'byus/ ***noun*** **1** [C,U] using sth in the wrong way: *an abuse of power* ◇ *the dangers of drug abuse* **2** [U] bad, usually violent treatment of sb: *child abuse* **3** [U] rude words, used to insult another person: *The other driver leaned out of the car and hurled abuse at me.*

**a·bu·sive** /ə'byusɪv; -zɪv/ ***adj.*** **1** treating sb badly, often violently: *an abusive husband* **2** using rude language to insult sb: *an abusive remark*

**a·bys·mal** /ə'bɪzməl/ ***adj.*** very bad; of very poor quality ▸ **a·bys·mal·ly** ***adv.***

**abyss** /ə'bɪs/ ***noun*** [C] (*formal*) a very deep hole that seems to have no bottom

★**ac·a·dem·ic**[1] /ˌækə'dɛmɪk/ ***adj.*** **1** connected with the educational activities of schools, colleges and universities: *The academic year begins in September.* **2** connected with subjects of interest to the mind rather than technical or practical subjects: *academic subjects such as history* ▸ **ac·a·dem·i·cal·ly** /-kli/ ***adv.***

**ac·a·dem·ic**[2] /ˌækə'dɛmɪk/ ***noun*** [C] a person who teaches and/or does research at a university or college

**a·cad·e·my** /ə'kædəmi/ ***noun*** [C] (*pl.* **a·cad·e·mies**) **1** a private school, or a school for special training: *a military academy* **2** (*also* **Academy**) a society of people who are important in art, science or literature: *the National Academy of Sciences*

**AˌcademyA'ward™** (*also* **Oscar**) ***noun*** [C] one of the awards given every year by the U.S.Academy of Motion Picture Arts and Sciences for achievement in the making of movies

**A·ca·di·an** /ə'keɪdiən/ ***noun*** [C] **1** a French-speaking Canadian from New Brunswick, and parts of Quebec near it, Nova Scotia or Prince Edward Island **2** (in the U.S.) a person from Louisiana whose family originally came from the French colony of Acadia in what is now Nova Scotia

**ac·cel·er·ate** /ək'sɛləreɪt/ ***verb*** [I,T] to go faster; to make sth go faster or happen more quickly: *I accelerated and left the other cars behind.* ▸ **ac·cel·er·a·tion** /əkˌsɛlə'reɪʃn/ ***noun*** [U]

**ac·cel·er·a·tor** /ək'sɛləreɪt̬ər/ (*also informal* **gas pedal**) ***noun*** [C] the pedal in a car, etc. that you press in order to increase speed

**ac·cent** /'æksɛnt/ ***noun*** **1** [C,U] a particular way of pronouncing words that is connected with the country, area or social group that you come from: *a strong Southern accent* **2** [C] the act of emphasizing a word or part of a word by pronouncing it with greater force: *In the word "because", the accent is on the second syllable.* **3** [C] (in writing) a mark, usually above a letter, that shows that it has to be pronounced in a certain way **4** [C, usually sing.] the particular importance that is given to sth: *In all our products the accent is on quality.*

**ac·cen·tu·ate** /ək'sɛntʃueɪt/ ***verb*** [T] to make sth easier to notice

★**ac·cept** /ək'sɛpt/ ***verb***

➤ OFFER/INVITATION **1** [I,T] to take sth willingly that sb offers you: *Do I have to pay cash or will you accept a check?* ◇ *Why won't you accept my advice?*

➤ AGREE **2** [I,T] to say yes to sth or to agree to sth: *Thank you for your invitation. I am happy to accept.* ◇ *I'd be pleased to accept your offer.*

➤ RESPONSIBILITY **3** [T] to admit or recognize that sth bad is true: *They refused to accept responsibility for the accident.*

A

➤ DIFFICULT SITUATION **4** [T] to recognize that sth cannot be changed: *It is hard to accept the death of a child.*
➤ BELIEVE **5** [T] to believe sth: *I just don't accept that – it simply isn't true.* ◇ *She didn't accept that I was telling the truth.*
➤ RECEIVE AS SUITABLE **6** [T] to take sth because it is suitable; to decide that sb/sth is suitable: *The vending machine won't accept my five-dollar bill.* ◇ *I had a letter saying that I had been accepted for the fall semester.* OPP Look at **refuse**[1] and **reject**.

★**ac·cept·a·ble** /ək'sɛptəbl/ *adj.* **1** allowed, often by people in general: *One or two mistakes are acceptable but no more than that.* **2** satisfactory; good enough: *We hope that you will consider our offer acceptable.* OPP **unacceptable** ▶ **ac·cept·a·bil·i·ty** /ək,sɛptə'bɪləṭi/ *noun* [U] ▶ **ac·cept·a·bly** /ək'sɛptəbli/ *adv.*

**ac·cep·tance** /ək'sɛptəns/ *noun* [C,U] the act of accepting or being accepted: *a letter of acceptance from the university* ◇ *the acceptance of a difficult situation* (= seeing that it cannot be changed) ◇ *He quickly gained acceptance in the group* (= the other people thought of him as equal to them).

★**ac·cess**[1] /'æksɛs/ *noun* [U] **1 access (to sth)** a way of entering or reaching a place: *Access to the attic is through this door.* **2 access (to sth)** the chance or right to use or have sth: *Do you have access to a fax machine?* **3 access (to sb)** permission, especially legal or official, to see sb: *They are divorced, but he has regular access to the kids.*

**ac·cess**[2] /'æksɛs/ *verb* [T] to get or use sth, especially with a computer: *This software makes it easy to access information in the database.*

**ac·ces·si·ble** /ək'sɛsəbl/ *adj.* **1** possible to be reached or entered: *Because of the snow, the farm was not accessible by car.* **2** easy to get, use or understand OPP **inaccessible** ▶ **ac·ces·si·bil·i·ty** /ək,sɛsə'bɪləṭi/ *noun* [U]

**ac·ces·so·ry** /ək'sɛsəri/ *noun* [C] (*pl.* **ac·ces·so·ries**) **1** an extra item that is added to sth and is useful or attractive but not essential: *The car has accessories such as an electronic alarm.* **2** [usually pl.] a small item that is worn or carried with the main items of clothing (e.g. shoes, jewelry, a purse, etc.) **3 accessory (to sth)** (in law) a person who helps sb to do sth illegal

★**ac·ci·dent** /'æksədənt; -dɛnt/ *noun* [C] an unpleasant event that happens unexpectedly and causes damage, injury or death: *I hope they haven't had an accident.* ◇ *a car accident* ◇ *a fatal accident* (= when sb is killed) ◇ *I didn't mean to kick you – it was an accident.*

IDM **by accident** by chance; without being planned: *We met each other again completely by accident.*

**ac·ci·den·tal** /,æksə'dɛnṭl/ *adj.* happening by chance; not having been planned ▶ **ac·ci·den·tal·ly** /,æksə'dɛnṭəli/ *adv.*

'**accident-prone** *adj.* frequently having accidents, and therefore more likely to have them than other people

**ac·claim** /ə'kleɪm/ *verb* [T] to praise sb/sth greatly: *The novel has been acclaimed as a modern classic.* ▶ **ac·claim** *noun* [U]: *The movie received widespread critical acclaim.*

**ac·cli·mate** /'ækləmeɪt/ *verb* [I,T] **acclimate (yourself/sb/sth) (to sth)** to get used to a new climate, a new situation, etc. so that it is not a problem anymore: *It took me a long time to get acclimated to the heat when I went to live in Africa.* ▶ **ac·cli·ma·tion** /,æklə'meɪʃn/ *noun* [U]

**ac·col·ade** /'ækəleɪd/ *noun* [C] a comment, prize or sth else that shows that people approve of what you have done

**ac·com·mo·date** /ə'kɑmədeɪt/ *verb* [T] **1** to have enough space for sb/sth (especially a certain number of people): *The van can accommodate up to eight people.* **2** to provide sb with a place to stay, live or work: *During the conference you will be accommodated in a nearby hotel.* **3** to do or provide what sb wants or needs: *If you have any special requests, our employees will do their best to accommodate you.*

**ac·com·mo·dat·ing** /ə'kɑmə,deɪṭɪŋ/ *adj.* (used about a person) willing to do or provide what sb wants

★**ac·com·mo·da·tion** /ə,kɑmə'deɪʃn/ *noun* **1** [U] (*also* **accommodations** [pl.]) a place where people can stay for a short time, e.g. in a hotel, and the services they can receive there: *first-class hotel accommodations* **2** [U] (*formal*) the process of changing to suit sb else's needs: *This government will not make any accommodation to terrorists.* **3** [C] (*formal*) an agreement which tries to satisfy both sides in an argument: *We managed to reach an accommodation with the other party.*

**ac·com·pa·ni·ment** /ə'kʌmpənimənt/ *noun* **1** [C] something that naturally or pleasantly goes with sth else (especially food or drinks): *This sauce is the perfect accompaniment to grilled meat.* **2** [C,U] music that is played with singing or the main instrument: *a violin piece with a piano accompaniment*

★**ac·com·pa·ny** /ə'kʌmpəni/ *verb* [T] (*pres. part.* **ac·com·pa·ny·ing**; *3rd person sing. pres.* **ac·com·pa·nies**; *pt, pp* **ac·com·pa·nied**) **1** to go with sb to a place: *Children must be accompanied by an adult.* **2** to happen or exist at the same time as, or because of, sth: *A huge ad campaign accompanied the movie's release.* **3** to give or send sth together with sth else, in addition to it: *The letter was accompanied by a check for $50.* **4** to play music for a singer or another instrument: *She accompanied him on the guitar.*

**ac·com·plice** /ə'kɑmplɪs/ *noun* [C] a person who helps sb to do sth bad, especially a crime

**ac·com·plish** /ə'kɑmplɪʃ/ *verb* [T] to succeed in doing sth requiring effort and/or skill; to achieve sth: *Very little was accomplished at the meeting.*

**ac·com·plished** /ə'kɑmplɪʃt/ *adj.* skilled: *an accomplished pianist*

**ac·com·plish·ment** /ə'kɑmplɪʃmənt/ *noun* **1** [U] the act of completing sth successfully **2** [C] something impressive that sb has achieved; a skill that sb has

**ac·cord**[1] /ə'kɔrd/ *noun* [C] (*formal*) an agreement, e.g. between countries: *the Helsinki accords on human rights*

A

IDM **in accord** in agreement about sth
**of/on your own accord** without being forced or asked: *He wasn't fired from his job; he left of his own accord.*

**ac·cord²** /ə'kɔrd/ ***verb*** [T] (*formal*) to give sth to sb: *The diplomats were accorded every courtesy during their visit.*

**ac·cor·dance** /ə'kɔrdns/ ***noun***
IDM **in accordance with sth** in a way that follows or obeys sth: *to act in accordance with instructions*

**ac·cord·ing·ly** /ə'kɔrdɪŋli/ ***adv.*** **1** in a way that is suitable after what has happened: *I realized that I was in danger and acted accordingly.* **2** (*formal*) therefore; for that reason: *We accept full responsibility for the error. Accordingly, we are refunding your money.*

★**according to** /ə'kɔrdɪŋ tə/ ***prep.*** **1** as stated by sb; as shown by sth: *According to Mick, it's a great movie.* ◇ *More people now have a high standard of living, according to the statistics.* **2** in a way that matches, follows or depends on sth: *Everything went according to plan* (= as we had planned it). ◇ *The salary will be determined according to education and experience.*

**accordion**

**ac·cor·di·on** /ə'kɔrdiən/ ***noun*** [C] a musical instrument with keys like those on a piano. You hold an accordion in both hands and play it by pulling the two sides apart and then pushing them together, while pressing the keys with your fingers.

**ac·cost** /ə'kɔst; -'kɑst/ ***verb*** [T] to approach and talk to a stranger in a way that is considered bad or frightening

★**ac·count¹** /ə'kaʊnt/ ***noun*** [C] **1** a report or description of sth that has happened: *She gave the police a full account of the robbery.* **2** the arrangement by which a bank holds your money for you: *a bank account* ◇ *to open/close an account* ◇ *I'd like to deposit this check into my account.*

> NOTE We use a **checking account** to pay for things with a **check**. We can save money in a **savings account**.

**3** an arrangement with a store, company, etc. that allows you to pay for goods or services at a later date: *Please mention your account number if you have a question about your bill.* **4** [usually pl.] a record of all the money that a person or business has received or paid out: *He manages the store and his wife takes care of the accounts.*
IDM **by all accounts** according to what everyone says: *By all accounts, she's a very good doctor.*
**on account of** (*informal*) because of: *Our flight was delayed on account of bad weather.*
**on no account; not on any account** (*formal*) not for any reason: *On no account should prisoners be left without supervision.*
**take sth into account; take account of sth** to consider sth, especially when deciding or judging sth: *We'll take your comments into account.*

**ac·count²** /ə'kaʊnt/ ***verb***
PHR V **account for sth** **1** to explain or give a reason for sth: *How can we account for these changes?* ◇ *My boss asked me to account for all the money I had spent* (= to say what I had spent it on). **2** to supply the amount that is mentioned: *Sales to Europe accounted for 80% of our total sales last year.*

**ac·count·a·ble** /ə'kaʊnt̬əbl/ ***adj.*** expected to give an explanation of your actions, etc.; responsible: *She is too young to be held accountable for what she did.* ▸ **ac·count·a·bil·i·ty** /əˌkaʊntə'bɪlət̬i/ ***noun*** [U]: *The new law requires greater accountability from the police.*

**ac·count·ant** /ə'kaʊntnt/ ***noun*** [C] a person whose job is to keep or examine the financial records of a business, etc.

**ac·count·ing** /ə'kaʊnt̬ɪŋ/ ***noun*** [U] the profession of an accountant: *a career in accounting*

**ac·cred·i·ta·tion** /əˌkrɛdə'teɪʃn/ ***noun*** [C,U] the official approval that says a school, etc. meets certain requirements: *The school must show that it has adequate library resources to receive accreditation.*

**ac·cred·it·ed** /ə'krɛdɪt̬əd/ ***adj.*** (used about a course, school, etc.) having official approval that says it meets certain requirements: *an accredited language course*

**ac·cu·mu·late** /ə'kyumyəleɪt/ ***verb*** **1** [T] to collect a number or quantity of sth over a period of time: *Over the years, I've accumulated hundreds of CDs.* **2** [I] to increase over a period of time: *Dust soon accumulates if you don't clean for a week or so.* ▸ **ac·cu·mu·la·tion** /əˌkyumyə'leɪʃn/ ***noun*** [C,U]

**ac·cu·ra·cy** /'ækyərəsi/ ***noun*** [U] the quality of being exact and correct OPP **inaccuracy**

★**ac·cu·rate** /'ækyərət/ ***adj.*** careful and exact; without mistakes: *an accurate description of the house* ◇ *That clock isn't very accurate.* OPP **inaccurate** ▸ **ac·cu·rate·ly** ***adv.***

**ac·cu·sa·tion** /ˌækyə'zeɪʃn/ ***noun*** [C,U] a statement that says that sb has done sth wrong: *He said that false accusations had been made against him.*

★**ac·cuse** /ə'kyuz/ ***verb*** [T] **accuse sb (of sth)** to say that sb has done sth wrong or broken the law: *I accused her of cheating.* ◇ *He was accused of murder.*

**ac·cus·ing** /ə'kyuzɪŋ/ ***adj.*** that shows that you think sb has done sth wrong: *He gave me an accusing look.* ▸ **ac·cus·ing·ly** ***adv.***

**ac·cus·tomed** /ə'kʌstəmd/ ***adj.*** **1 accustomed to sth** if you are accustomed to sth, you are used to it and it is not strange for you: *She's accustomed to traveling a lot in her job.* ◇ *They had grown accustomed to life in the country.* **2** (*formal*) usual; regular: *He was sitting in his accustomed seat.*

**ace¹** /eɪs/ ***noun*** [C] **1** a playing card which has a single shape on it. An ace has either the lowest or the highest value in a game of cards: *the ace of spades* ➲ Look at the note at **card**. **2** (*informal*) a person who is very good at a particular activity **3** (in tennis) the first stroke of a game (a serve) that the person playing against you cannot hit back

**ace²** /eɪs/ ***adj.*** (only *before* a noun) very good: *an ace newspaper reporter*

**ache¹** /eɪk/ ***noun*** [C, usually sing.] (usually in compounds) a pain that lasts for a long time: *to have a*

A

*headache/a toothache/an earache/a stomachache* ◇ *Old people suffer from a lot of aches and pains.*

**ache²** /eɪk/ ***verb*** [I] to feel a continuous pain: *His legs ached after playing soccer for two hours.*

★**a·chieve** /əˈtʃiv/ ***verb*** [T] **1** to gain sth, usually by effort or skill: *You have achieved the success you deserve.* **2** to get sth done; to complete sth: *They have achieved a lot in a short time.*

★**a·chieve·ment** /əˈtʃivmənt/ ***noun*** **1** [C] something that is done successfully, especially through hard work or skill: *She considered the book her greatest achievement.* **2** [U] the act of finishing sth successfully; the feeling that you get when you have finished sth successfully: *Climbing the mountain gave him a sense of achievement.*

**Achil·les heel** /əˌkɪliz ˈhil/ ***noun*** [C] a weak point or a fault in sb/sth

**Achil·les ten·don** /əˌkɪliz ˈtɛndən/ (*also* **Achil·les**) ***noun*** [C] the strong strip of tissue inside your leg that connects the muscles at the back of the lower part of your leg (**calf**) to the back part of your foot (**heel**)

★**ac·id¹** /ˈæsɪd/ ***noun*** [C,U] (in chemistry) a liquid substance that can dissolve metal and may burn your skin or clothes: *hydrochloric acid* ➲ Look at **alkali** and **base¹** (7).

**ac·id²** /ˈæsɪd/ ***adj.*** **1** (used about a fruit, etc.) with a sharp, sour taste **2** (*also* **a·cid·ic**) containing an acid: *an acid solution* ➲ Look at **alkaline** and **base¹** (7).

**a·cid·i·ty** /əˈsɪdət̬i/ ***noun*** [U] the quality of being acid

ˌ**acid ˈrain** ***noun*** [U] rain that is polluted by acid substances from the chimneys of factories and that causes damage to trees, buildings and rivers

★**ac·knowl·edge** /əkˈnɑlɪdʒ/ ***verb*** [T] **1** to accept or admit that sth is true or exists: *He acknowledged the fact that he had been wrong.* ◇ *They wouldn't acknowledge defeat.* ◇ *It is acknowledged that he is the country's greatest writer.* ◇ *He is acknowledged to be the country's greatest writer.* **2** to show that you have seen sb by raising your hand, smiling, etc.: *She refused to acknowledge him and walked straight past.* **3** to say that you have received a letter, etc.: *I would appreciate it if you could acknowledge my letter.* **4** to show or say that you are grateful for sth: *I would like to acknowledge all the help I have received from my family.*

**ac·knowl·edg·ment** (*also* **ac·knowl·edge·ment**) /əkˈnɑlɪdʒmənt/ ***noun*** **1** [U] the act of acknowledging sth: *I have received no acknowledgment for all the work I did.* **2** [C] a letter, etc. stating that sth has been received **3** [C] a few words of thanks that an author writes at the beginning or end of a book to the people who have helped him/her

**ac·ne** /ˈækni/ ***noun*** [U] a type of skin disease, usually affecting young people, that causes a lot of red spots (**pimples**) on the face and neck

**a·corn** /ˈeɪkɔrn/ ***noun*** [C] a small nut that is the fruit of the oak tree

**a·cous·tic** /əˈkustɪk/ ***adj.*** **1** connected with sound or the sense of hearing **2** (of a musical instrument) not electric: *an acoustic guitar* ➲ picture at **guitar**.

**a·cous·tics** /əˈkustɪks/ ***noun*** [pl.] **1** the qualities of a room, etc. that make it good or bad for you to hear music, etc.: *The theater has excellent acoustics.* **2** [with sing. verb] the scientific study of sound

**ac·quaint** /əˈkweɪnt/ ***verb*** [T] (*formal*) **acquaint sb/yourself with sth** to make sb/yourself familiar with or aware of sth: *She took a few minutes to acquaint herself with the layout of the house.*

**ac·quain·tance** /əˈkweɪntns/ ***noun*** **1** [C] a person that you know but who is not a close friend **2** [U] **acquaintance with sb/sth** a slight knowledge of sb/sth: *I made his acquaintance* (= got to know him) *at a party.*

**ac·quaint·ed** /əˈkweɪnt̬əd/ ***adj.*** (not before a noun) **1 acquainted (with sb)** knowing sb, but usually not very closely: *We had a chance to get acquainted with our new neighbors at the party.* **2 acquainted with sth** (*formal*) knowing sth: *Are you acquainted with the facts of this case?*

**ac·qui·esce** /ˌækwiˈɛs/ ***verb*** [I] (*formal*) **acquiesce (in/to sth)** to accept sth without argument, although you may not agree with it ► **ac·qui·es·cence** /-ˈɛsns/ ***noun*** [U]

★**ac·quire** /əˈkwaɪər/ ***verb*** [T] to get or obtain sth: *The company has acquired shares in a rival business.* ◇ *She acquired a southern accent while living in New Orleans.* ◇ *He's acquired a reputation for being difficult to work with.*

**ac·qui·si·tion** /ˌækwəˈzɪʃn/ ***noun*** **1** [C] something that you have obtained or bought, especially sth you are pleased with: *This painting is my latest acquisition.* **2** [U] the act of obtaining sth: *the acquisition of wealth*

**ac·quit** /əˈkwɪt/ ***verb*** [T] (**ac·quit·ting**; **ac·quit·ted**) **1 acquit sb (of sth)** to declare formally that a person is not guilty of a crime: *The jury acquitted her of murder.* OPP **convict** **2 acquit yourself...** (*formal*) to behave in the way that is mentioned: *He acquitted himself extremely well in his first game as a professional.* ► **ac·quit·tal** /əˈkwɪt̬l/ ***noun*** [C,U]

**a·cre** /ˈeɪkər/ ***noun*** [C] a measure of land; 0.405 of a hectare: *a farm of 200 acres/a 200-acre farm*

**ac·ro·bat** /ˈækrəbæt/ ***noun*** [C] a person who performs difficult movements of the body or difficult balancing acts (e.g. walking on a wire), especially in a circus ► **ac·ro·bat·ic** /ˌækrəˈbæt̬ɪk/ ***adj.***

**ac·ro·bat·ics** /ˌækrəˈbæt̬ɪks/ ***noun*** [U] (the art of performing) acrobatic acts

**ac·ro·nym** /ˈækrənɪm/ ***noun*** [C] a short word that is made from the first letters of a group of words: *TOEFL is an acronym for Test of English as a Foreign Language.*

★**a·cross** /əˈkrɔs/ ***adv., prep.*** **1** from one side of sth to the other: *The stream was too wide to jump across.* ◇ *I drew a line across the page.* ◇ *A smile spread across his face.* **2** on the other side of sth: *There's a bank across the street.*

> NOTE We can use **across** or **over** to mean "on or to the other side": *I ran across/over the field.* But when we talk about crossing something high, we usually use **over**: *I can't climb over that wall.* With "room" we usually use **across**: *I walked across the room to the door.*

**3** measuring from side to side: *The river was about 20 meters across.*

IDM **across the board** involving or affecting all groups, members, cases, etc.: *a 10% pay increase across the board*

★**a'cross from** *prep.* directly on the other side of a space between sth and sth else; facing sb/sth: *Our house is right across from the high school.* ◇ *He sat across from me at the table.* ◇ *We sat across from each other.* ➲ picture at **front**.

**a·cryl·ic** /əˈkrɪlɪk/ *noun* [U] a material that is made artificially by a chemical process and used in making sweaters and other clothes, paints, and some types of plastics ▶ **a·cryl·ic** *adj.*: *an acrylic sweater*

**ACT** /ˌeɪ si ˈti/ *abbr.* American College Test; an exam that some high school students take in the U.S. before they go to college: *to take the ACT* ➲ Look at **SAT**.

★**act**[1] /ækt/ *verb* **1** [I] to do sth; to take action: *There's no time to lose – you must act now.* ◇ *The School Board has to act on the teachers' suggestions.* ◇ *The man we met on the plane to Tokyo was kind enough to act as our guide* (= to perform the function of guide). **2** [I] to behave in the manner stated: *Don't act like a fool.* **3** [I,T] to perform or have a part in a play or movie: *I've never acted before.* ◇ *He has always wanted to act the part of Hamlet.*

PHR V **act sth out** to perform a story, ceremony, etc.: *Each group can act out their scene in front of the class.*

**act up** (*informal*) to behave badly: *The children were bored in the grocery store and began to act up, so their mother took them home.*

★**act**[2] /ækt/ *noun* [C]

➤STH THAT SB DOES **1** a thing that you do: *In a typical act of generosity they refused to accept any money.*

> NOTE **Act** and **action** can have the same meaning: *It was a brave act/action.* **Act**, not **action**, can be followed by **of**: *It was an act of bravery.* **Activity** is used for something that is done regularly: *I like outdoor activities such as walking and bike riding.* **Deed** is a formal and old-fashioned word and often refers to very important acts: *Robin Hood was famous for his brave deeds.* It is the word usually used with **good**: *I wanted to pay back the good deed he had done.*

➤IN PLAY/ENTERTAINMENT **2** (often **Act**) one of the main divisions of a play or an opera: *How many scenes are there in Act 4?* **3** a short piece of entertainment that is usually part of a show or circus: *Ladies and gentlemen, please welcome our next act, the Roncalli brothers.*

➤LAW **4** (often **Act**) (*formal*) a law made by Congress, the state legislature or Parliament: *an act of Congress/Parliament*

➤PRETENDING **5** (*informal*) a piece of behavior that hides your true feelings: *She seems very happy, but she's just putting on an act.*

IDM **get your act together** (*informal*) to get organized so that you can do sth

**in the act (of doing sth)** while doing sth, especially sth wrong: *She caught him in the act of looking through her papers.*

**act·ing**[1] /ˈæktɪŋ/ *noun* [U] the art or profession of performing in plays or movies

**act·ing**[2] /ˈæktɪŋ/ *adj.* doing the job mentioned for a short time: *Mr. Wong will be the acting principal while Mrs. Richards is away.*

★**ac·tion** /ˈækʃn/ *noun*

➤WHAT SB DOES **1** [U] doing things, often for a particular purpose: *Now is the time for action.* ◇ *I didn't like the movie – there wasn't much action in it.* **2** [C] something that you do: *The doctor's quick action saved the child's life.* ◇ *They should be judged by their actions, not by what they say.* ➲ Look at the note at **act**[2].

➤IN STORY/PLAY **3** [sing.] the most important events that are happening, especially in a story or play: *The action is set in Germany.* ◇ *This is where the action is on a Saturday night.*

➤EFFECT **4** [sing.] the effect that one substance has on another: *the harmful action of acid rain on buildings*

➤IN WAR **5** [U] the fighting that takes place in battle: *Their son was killed in action.*

➤LEGAL PROCESS **6** [C,U] the process of settling an argument in a court of law: *They decided not to take legal action against the newspaper.*

IDM **course of action** → COURSE

**in action** in operation; while working or doing sth: *We will have a chance to see their new team in action next week.*

**into action** into operation: *We'll put the plan into action immediately.*

**take action** to do sth in order to solve a problem, etc.: *The Governor promised to take action to reduce unemployment in the state.*

**ac·ti·vate** /ˈæktəveɪt/ *verb* [T] to make sth start working: *A slight movement can activate the car alarm.*

★**ac·tive** /ˈæktɪv/ *adj.* **1** able and willing to do things; energetic: *My grandfather is very active for his age.* ◇ *Students should take an active part in school life.* ◇ *He was on* ***active duty*** *for five years during the war* (= he served in the armed forces). **2** that produces an effect; that is in operation: *What is the active ingredient in this medicine?* ◇ *an active volcano* (= one that can still erupt) **3** (used about the form of a verb or a sentence when the subject of the sentence performs the action of the verb): *In the sentence "The dog bit him," the verb is active.*

> NOTE You can also say: "The verb is in the active." ➲ Look at **passive**.

**ac·tiv·ist** /ˈæktəvɪst/ *noun* [C] a person who works to make changes in society: *a gay rights activist*

★**ac·tiv·i·ty** /ækˈtɪvət̬i/ *noun* (*pl.* **ac·tiv·i·ties**) **1** [U] a situation in which there is a lot of action or movement: *The house was full of activity on the morning of the wedding.* OPP **inactivity** **2** [C] something that you do, usually regularly and for enjoyment: *outdoor activities* ➲ Look at the note at **act**[2].

★**ac·tor** /ˈæktər/ *noun* [C] a person whose job is to act in a play, movie or television program

**ac·tress** /ˈæktrəs/ *noun* [C] a woman whose job is to act in a play, movie or television program

★**ac·tu·al** /ˈæktʃuəl/ *adj.* real; that happened, etc. in fact: *The actual damage to the car was not as great as we had thought it might be.* ◇ *Our goal for last year was $3 million, but our actual sales were much*

A

*higher.* ◇ *The teacher said our reports had to be about an actual company, not one we made up.*

★**ac·tu·al·ly** /ˈæktʃuəli; ˈækʃəli/ ***adv.*** **1** really; in fact: *You don't actually believe her, do you?* ◇ *I can't believe that I'm actually going to England!* **2** although it may seem strange or surprising: *He actually expected me to cook his dinner for him!* ◇ *Well, actually, I know a lot about computers – my dad's a programmer.*

NOTE In English **actual** and **actually** do NOT mean "(existing) at the present time." We use **currently** or **right now** instead: *He's currently working for the government.* ◇ *I'm studying for my final exams right now.*

**ac·u·punc·ture** /ˈækyəˌpʌŋktʃər/ ***noun*** [U] a way of treating an illness or stopping pain by putting thin needles into parts of the body

**a·cute** /əˈkyut/ ***adj.*** **1** severe; very great: *an acute shortage of food* ◇ *acute pain* **2** (used about an illness) reaching a dangerous stage quickly: *acute appendicitis* ➲ Compare **chronic**. **3** (used about feelings or the senses) very strong: *Dogs have an acute sense of smell.* **4** showing that you are able to understand things quickly and clearly: *The report contains some acute observations on the situation.* ▶ **a·cute·ly** ***adv.***: *They are acutely aware of the problem.*

**aˌcute ˈangle** ***noun*** [C] an angle of less than 90° ➲ picture at **angle**.

**A.D.** /ˌeɪ ˈdi/ (*also* **AD**) ***abbr.*** Anno Domini; used in dates for showing the number of years after the time when Christians believe Jesus Christ was born: *A.D. 44* SYN **C.E.** ➲ Compare **B.C.** and **B.C.E.**

★**ad** /æd/ ***noun*** [C] (*informal*) = ADVERTISEMENT: *I saw your ad in the local paper.*

**ad·age** /ˈædɪdʒ/ ***noun*** [C] a well-known phrase expressing sth that is usually true about people or the world: *As the old adage says, you can lead a horse to water but you can't make it drink.*

**ad·a·mant** /ˈædəmənt/ ***adj.*** (used about a person) very sure; not willing to change your mind: *He was adamant that he had not made a mistake.* ▶ **ad·a·mant·ly** ***adv.***

**Adam's apple** /ˈædəmz ˌæpl/ ***noun*** [C] the lump at the front of the throat that sticks out, especially in men, and moves up and down when you swallow

★**a·dapt** /əˈdæpt/ ***verb*** **1** [I] **adapt (to sth)** to change your behavior because the situation you are in has changed: *He was quick to adapt to the new system.* **2** [T] to change a book, etc. so that it can be shown as a movie, etc.: *a play that has been adapted for television* **3** [T] **adapt sth (for sth)** to change sth so that you can use it in a different situation: *The van was adapted for use by a person in a wheelchair.*

**a·dapt·a·ble** /əˈdæptəbl/ ***adj.*** able and willing to change to suit new conditions: *You have to be adaptable if you want to live in a foreign country.*

**ad·ap·ta·tion** /ˌædəpˈteɪʃn; ˌædæp-/ ***noun*** **1** [C] a play or movie that is based on a novel, etc.: *a television adaptation of one of Shakespeare's plays* **2** [C,U] the state or process of adapting: *a period of adaptation*

**a·dapt·er** /əˈdæptər/ ***noun*** [C] **1** a device for connecting pieces of equipment that were not originally designed to be connected: *You'll need an adapter if you want to use your hair dryer in Europe.* **2** a device that allows more than one plug to be connected to the electricity supply at one point (**socket**)

★**add** /æd/ ***verb*** **1** [I,T] **add (sth) (to sth)** to put sth together with sth else, so that you increase the size, number, value, etc.: *Next, add some milk to the mixture.* ◇ *They invited a magician to the party, just to add to the fun.* **2** [T] to put numbers or amounts together so that you get a total: *If you add 3 and 3 together, you get 6.* ◇ *Add $8 to the total, to cover postage and handling.* OPP **subtract**

NOTE We often use the word **plus** when we add two numbers: *2 plus 2 is 4.*

**3** [T] to say sth more: *"Don't forget to write to us," she added.*

PHR V **add sth on (to sth)** to include: *10% will be added on to your bill as a penalty for late payment.*

**add up** to seem as if it could be true: *I'm sorry, but your story just doesn't add up.*

**add (sth) up** to find the total of several numbers: *The waiter hadn't added up the check correctly.*

**add up to sth** to have as a total: *The bill should add up to about $40.*

**ad·dict** /ˈædɪkt/ ***noun*** [C] a person who cannot stop taking or doing sth, especially sth harmful: *a drug addict* ◇ *After a long day at the mall we would sometimes joke that we were turning into shopping addicts!*

**ad·dict·ed** /əˈdɪktəd/ ***adj.*** **addicted (to sth)** unable to stop taking or doing sth, especially sth harmful: *He is addicted to heroin.* ◇ *He's addicted to football.*

**ad·dic·tion** /əˈdɪkʃn/ ***noun*** [C,U] the condition of being unable to stop taking or doing sth harmful: *the problem of teenage drug addiction*

**ad·dic·tive** /əˈdɪktɪv/ ***adj.*** (used about a drug, etc.) causing sb to be unable to stop taking or doing it

★**ad·di·tion** /əˈdɪʃn/ ***noun*** **1** [U] the process of adding sth, especially of adding up two or more numbers ➲ Look at **subtraction**. **2** [C] **addition (to sth)** a person or thing that is added to sth: *They have a new addition to the family* (= another child).

IDM **in addition (to sth)** as well as (sth): *She speaks five foreign languages in addition to English.*

★**ad·di·tion·al** /əˈdɪʃənl/ ***adj.*** added; extra: *a small additional charge for the use of the swimming pool* ▶ **ad·di·tion·al·ly** /əˈdɪʃənəli/ ***adv.***

**ad·di·tive** /ˈædət̬ɪv/ ***noun*** [C] a substance that is added in small amounts for a special purpose: *food additives* (= to add color or flavor)

★**ad·dress**[1] /əˈdrɛs; ˈædrɛs/ ***noun*** [C] **1** the information needed for mail to arrive at the place where you live or work; usually the number of the house and the name of the street and town: *Let me give you my home/business address.* ◇ *She no longer lives at this address.* ◇ *Please inform the office of any change of address.* ◇ *an address book* (= a small book that you keep the addresses of people you know in) ◇ *My e-mail address is george@msu.edu.*

**2** a formal speech that is given to an audience ➲ Look also at **public address system**.

**ad·dress²** /əˈdrɛs; ˈædrɛs/ ***verb*** [T] **1 address sth (to sb/sth)** to write (on a letter, etc.) the name and address of the person you are sending it to: *The package was returned because it had been wrongly addressed.* **2** to make an important or formal speech to a crowd or audience: *The President will address the nation tonight.* **3** to consider sth (especially a problem) and try to deal with it: *We will address the issue at the next meeting.* **4** to talk or write to sb using a particular name or title: *She prefers to be addressed as "Ms."* **5 address sth to sb** (*formal*) make a remark, etc. to sb: *He addressed his criticisms mainly to the new members.*

**a·dept** /əˈdɛpt/ ***adj.*** **adept (at sth)** very good or skillful at sth

★**ad·e·quate** /ˈædɪkwət/ ***adj.*** (*formal*) **1** enough for what you need: *The food they eat is barely adequate to keep them alive.* **2** good enough; acceptable: *Your work is adequate, but I'm sure you could do better.* OPP **inadequate** ▸ **ad·e·qua·cy** /ˈædɪkwəsi/ ***noun*** [U] ▸ **ad·e·quate·ly** ***adv.***: *The work was done adequately but not well.* ◇ *The mystery has never been adequately explained.*

**ad·here** /ədˈhɪr/ ***verb*** [I] (*formal*) **1 adhere (to sth)** to stick firmly: *Make sure that the paper adheres firmly to the wall.* **2 adhere to sth** to continue to support an idea, etc.; to follow a rule: *This rule has never been strictly adhered to.* ▸ **ad·her·ence** /ədˈhɪrəns/ ***noun*** [U]: *His adherence to his principles cost him his job.*

**ad·he·sive¹** /ədˈhisɪv; -zɪv/ ***noun*** [C,U] a substance that makes things stick together: *a fast-drying adhesive*

**ad·he·sive²** /ədˈhisɪv; -zɪv/ ***adj.*** that can stick, or can cause two things to stick together: *He sealed the package with adhesive tape.*

**ad·ja·cent** /əˈdʒeɪsnt/ ***adj.*** situated next to or close to sth: *There was a fire in the adjacent building.* ◇ *She works in the office adjacent to mine.*

**ad·jec·ti·val** /ˌædʒɛkˈtaɪvl/ ***adj.*** that contains or is used like an adjective: *an adjectival phrase*

**ad·jec·tive** /ˈædʒɪktɪv/ ***noun*** [C] (*grammar*) a word used with a noun that tells you more about it: *The adjective "hot" can come either before or after a noun, i.e. you can say "that is hot soup" or "that soup is hot."*

**ad·join·ing** /əˈdʒɔɪnɪŋ/ ***adj.*** joining sth or situated next or nearest to sth: *A scream came from the adjoining room.*

**ad·journ** /əˈdʒərn/ ***verb*** [I,T] (*formal*) to stop sth (a meeting, a trial, etc.) for a short period of time and start it again later: *This court will adjourn until tomorrow.* ◇ *The meeting was adjourned until the following week.* ▸ **ad·journ·ment** ***noun*** [C,U]: *The lawyers asked for an adjournment.*

**ad·ju·di·cate** /əˈdʒudəkeɪt/ ***verb*** [I,T] (*formal*) to act as an official judge in a competition or to decide who is right when two sides disagree about sth

**ad·ju·di·ca·tor** /əˈdʒudəˌkeɪt̬ər/ ***noun*** [C] (*formal*) a person who acts as a judge, especially in a competition

★**ad·just** /əˈdʒʌst/ ***verb*** **1** [T] to change sth slightly, especially because it is not in the right position: *The brakes on the car need to be adjusted.* ◇ *The figures have been adjusted to take inflation into account.* **2** [I] **adjust (to sth)** to get used to new conditions or a new situation: *She found it hard to adjust to working at night.* ▸ **ad·just·ment** ***noun*** [C,U]

**ad·just·a·ble** /əˈdʒʌstəbl/ ***adj.*** that can be adjusted: *an adjustable mirror*

**ad lib** /ˌæd ˈlɪb/ ***adj.***, ***adv.*** done or spoken without preparation: *She had to speak ad lib because she couldn't find her notes.* ▸ **ad-lib** ***verb*** [I,T] (**ad-·lib̲b̲ing; ad-·lib̲b̲ed**)

**ad·min·is·ter** /ədˈmɪnəstər/ ***verb*** [T] **1** to control or manage sth: *The system is very complicated and difficult to administer.* **2** (*formal*) to give sb sth (especially medicine): *The doctor administered a pain-killing drug.*

★**ad·min·is·tra·tion** /ədˌmɪnəˈstreɪʃn/ ***noun*** **1** [U] the control or management of sth (e.g. a system, an organization or a business): *The administration of a large project like this is very complicated.* **2** [sing.] the group of people who organize or control sth: *the hospital administration* **3** (often **the Administration**) [C] the President of the U.S. and the people and departments working closely with the President; the government of a country: *the Kennedy Administration*

**ad·min·is·tra·tive** /ədˈmɪnəstreɪt̬ɪv/ ***adj.*** connected with the organization and management of a country or business, etc.: *Washington is the country's administrative center.* ◇ *an administrative assistant*

**ad·min·is·tra·tor** /ədˈmɪnəstreɪt̬ər/ ***noun*** [C] a person whose job is to organize or manage a system, a business, etc.: *Ask the system administrator to give you a password for the computers.*

**ad·mi·ra·ble** /ˈædmərəbl/ ***adj.*** deserving admiration or praise: *an admirable example of good planning* ▸ **ad·mi·ra·bly** /ˈædmərəbli/ ***adv.***: *She dealt with the problem admirably.*

**ad·mi·ral** /ˈædmərəl/ ***noun*** [C] an officer of very high rank in the navy who commands a group (a fleet) of ships

★**ad·mi·ra·tion** /ˌædməˈreɪʃn/ ***noun*** [U] a feeling that you have when you like and respect sb/sth very much: *I have great admiration for his work.*

★**ad·mire** /ədˈmaɪər/ ***verb*** [T] to respect or like sb/sth very much; to look at sb/sth with pleasure: *Everyone admired the way he dealt with the problem.* ◇ *I've always admired her.* ◇ *We walked around the house, admiring the furniture and decorations.* ▸ **ad·mir·er** ***noun*** [C]

**ad·mir·ing** /ədˈmaɪrɪŋ/ ***adj.*** feeling or expressing admiration: *an admiring look* ▸ **ad·mir·ing·ly** ***adv.***

**ad·mis·sion** /ədˈmɪʃn/ ***noun*** **1** [C,U] permission to enter a school, club, public place, etc.: *All those who were not wearing a necktie were refused admission to the club.* ◇ *Admissions to universities have increased by 15% this year.* **2** [U] the amount of money that you pay to enter a place: *The museum charges $3 admission.* **3** [C] a statement that something, usually bad, is true: *I viewed her silence as an admission of guilt.*

★**ad·mit** /ədˈmɪt/ ***verb*** (**ad·mit̲t̲ing; ad·mit̲t̲ed**) **1** [I,T] **admit to sth/doing sth; admit (that...)**: *He*

A

*refused to admit to the theft.* ◇ *You should admit your mistake.* ◇ *I have to admit that I was wrong.* ◇ *"I was wrong," he admitted.* ◇ *She admitted to having broken the lamp.* OPP **deny** **2** [T] **admit sb/sth (into/to sth)** to allow sb/sth to enter; to take sb into a place: *a ticket that admits a member plus one guest to the gallery* ◇ *He wasn't admitted to the hospital; they just treated him and sent him home.*

**ad·mit·tance** /əd'mɪtns/ ***noun*** [U] being allowed to enter a place (especially a private one); the right to enter: *The journalist tried to gain admittance to the legislature.*

**ad·mit·ted·ly** /əd'mɪt̬ədli/ ***adv.*** it must be admitted (that): *The work is very interesting. Admittedly, I do get awfully tired.*

**ad·o·les·cence** /ˌædə'lɛsns/ ***noun*** [U,C] the period of a person's life between being a child and becoming an adult, i.e. between the ages of about 13 and 17

**ad·o·les·cent** /ˌædə'lɛsnt/ ***noun*** [C] a young person who is no longer a child and not yet an adult: *the problems of adolescents* ➲ Look at **teenager**. ▸ **ad·o·les·cent** ***adj.***: *an adolescent daughter*

★**a·dopt** /ə'dɑpt/ ***verb*** **1** [I,T] to take a child into your family and treat him/her as your own child by law **2** [T] to take and use sth: *She decided not to adopt her husband's name when she got married.* ◇ *All his suggestions have been adopted.* ▸ **a·dopt·ed** ***adj.***: *an adopted child* ▸ **a·dop·tion** ***noun*** [C,U]: *the adoption of a new foreign trade policy* ◇ *How many teen mothers* ***put*** *their babies* ***up for adoption*** (= let other people adopt their babies)? ◇ *The number of adoptions has risen in the past year* (= the number of children being adopted).

**a·dop·tive** /ə'dɑptɪv/ ***adj.*** (usually *before* a noun) an adoptive parent or family is one that has legally made a child part of their family

**a·dor·a·ble** /ə'dɔrəbl/ ***adj.*** (used for expressing affection for a child or animal) very attractive

**a·dore** /ə'dɔr/ ***verb*** [T] **1** to love and admire sb/sth very much: *Kim adores her older sister.* **2** to like sth very much: *I adore strawberries.* ▸ **ad·o·ra·tion** /ˌædə'reɪʃn/ ***noun*** [U]

**a·dorn** /ə'dɔrn/ ***verb*** [T] to add sth in order to make a thing or person more attractive or beautiful: *a building adorned with flags*

**a·dren·a·line** /ə'drɛnl·ɪn/ ***noun*** [U] a substance that your body produces when you are very angry, frightened or excited and that makes your heart beat faster

**a·drift** /ə'drɪft/ ***adj.*** (not before a noun) not tied to anything or controlled by anybody (used about a boat)

**ADSL** /ˌeɪ di ɛs 'ɛl/ ***abbr.*** asymmetric digital subscriber line; a system for connecting a computer to the Internet so that information can move very quickly

★**a·dult** /ə'dʌlt; 'ædʌlt/ ***noun*** [C] a person or animal that is fully grown: *This movie is suitable for both adults and children.* ▸ **a·dult** ***adj.***: *She was born here but has spent her adult life in Chile.*

**a·dul·ter·y** /ə'dʌltəri/ ***noun*** [U] sexual relations between a person who is married and sb who is not that person's wife/husband: *to commit adultery*

**a·dult·hood** /ə'dʌlthʊd/ ***noun*** [U] the state of being an adult; the time that you are an adult: *Adulthood brings new privileges, but also new responsibilities.*

★**ad·vance**[1] /əd'væns/ ***verb*** **1** [I] to move forward: *The army advanced toward the city.* OPP **retreat** **2** [I,T] to make progress or help sth make progress: *Our research has not advanced much recently.*

★**ad·vance**[2] /əd'væns/ ***noun*** **1** [C, usually sing.] forward movement: *the army's advance toward the border* **2** [C,U] progress in sth: *advances in computer technology* **3** [C] an amount of money that is paid to sb before the time when it is usually paid **4** [pl.] sb who makes advances toward another person attempts to start a sexual relationship with that person: *unwanted sexual advances*

> NOTE When we use **advances** in this way it usually indicates an inappropriate way of behaving.

IDM **in advance (of sth)** before a particular time or event: *You should buy your tickets for the concert well in advance.*

★**ad·vanced** /əd'vænst/ ***adj.*** **1** of a high level: *an advanced English class* **2** highly developed: *a country that is not very advanced industrially*

★**ad·van·tage** /əd'vænt̬ɪdʒ/ ***noun*** **1** [C] **an advantage (over sb)** something that may help you to do better than other people: *Her secretarial experience gave her an advantage over the other people applying for the job.* ◇ *Our team had the advantage of playing on our home field.* **2** [C,U] something that helps you or that will bring you a good result: *the advantages and disadvantages of a plan* ◇ *There are advantages to having a cordless phone; for example, you can do other things while you talk.* OPP **disadvantage**

IDM **take advantage of sth** **1** to make good or full use of sth: *Take advantage of these discount prices while they last.* **2** to make unfair use of sb or of sb's kindness, etc. in order to get what you want: *You shouldn't let him take advantage of you like this.*

**ad·van·ta·geous** /ˌædvæn'teɪdʒəs; -vən-/ ***adj.*** that will help you or bring you a good result

**ad·vent** /'ædvɛnt/ ***noun*** [sing.] **1** (*written*) the arrival or coming of sb/sth: *Before the advent of the computer, a project like this would have been impossible.* **2** (*also* **Advent**) (in the Christian year) the four weeks before Christmas

★**ad·ven·ture** /əd'vɛntʃər/ ***noun*** [C,U] an experience or event that is very unusual, exciting or dangerous: *She left home to travel, hoping for excitement and adventure.* ◇ *an adventure story*

**ad·ven·tur·ous** /əd'vɛntʃərəs/ ***adj.*** **1** (*also* **ad·ven·ture·some** /əd'vɛntʃərsəm/) (used about a person) liking to try new things or have adventures **2** involving adventure: *For a more adventurous vacation, try mountain climbing.*

**ad·verb** /'ædvərb/ ***noun*** [C] a word that adds information to a verb, adjective, phrase or another adverb: *In the sentence "Please speak slowly," "slowly" is an adverb.* ◇ *"Happily," "well," "always," "very" and "too" are all adverbs.*

A

**ad·ver·bi·al** /əd'vərbiəl/ ***adj.*** used like an adverb: *an adverbial phrase* (e.g. "in the afternoon")

**ad·ver·sar·y** /'ædvər,sɛri/ ***noun*** [C] (*pl.* **ad·ver·sar·ies**) (*formal*) an enemy, or an opponent in a competition

**ad·verse** /əd'vərs; 'ædvərs/ ***adj.*** (*formal*) making sth difficult for sb; not favorable: *Our flight was canceled because of adverse weather conditions.* ▶ **ad·verse·ly** ***adv.***

**ad·ver·si·ty** /əd'vərsəṭi; æd-/ ***noun*** [C,U] (*pl.* **ad·ver·si·ties**) (*formal*) difficulties or problems: *to show strength in the face of adversity*

★**ad·ver·tise** /'ædvərtaɪz/ ***verb*** **1** [I,T] to put information in a newspaper, on television, on a poster, etc. in order to persuade people to buy sth, apply for a job, etc.: *a billboard advertising a new brand of cookies* ◇ *It's very expensive to advertise on television.* **2** [I] **advertise for sb/sth** to say publicly in a newspaper, on a sign, etc. that you need sb to do a particular job, want to buy sth, etc.: *The office is advertising for a part-time assistant.* ▶ **ad·ver·tis·ing** ***noun*** [U]: *The magazine gets a lot of money from advertising.* ◇ *an advertising campaign*

★**ad·ver·tise·ment** /,ædvər'taɪzmənt/ ***noun*** [C] (*also informal* **ad**) a piece of information in a newspaper, on a poster, etc. that tries to persuade people to buy sth, apply for a job, etc.: *to put an ad in the paper*

NOTE An advertisement on TV or on the radio is called a **commercial**.

★**ad·vice** /əd'vaɪs/ ***noun*** [U] an opinion that you give sb about what he/she should do or how he/she should behave: *She* ***took*** *her doctor's* ***advice*** *and quit smoking.* ◇ *You should get some legal advice* (= ask a lawyer to tell you what to do). ◇ *Let me give you some advice...*

NOTE **Advice** is an uncountable noun, so we CANNOT say "an advice" or "some advices." We can say *a piece of advice* and *a lot of advice*.

**ad·vis·a·ble** /əd'vaɪzəbl/ ***adj.*** (*formal*) that sb would recommend that you do; sensible: *It is advisable to reserve a seat.*

★**ad·vise** /əd'vaɪz/ ***verb*** **1** [I,T] **advise (sb) (to do sth)**; **advise (sb) (against sth/against doing sth)** to tell sb what you think he/she should do: *I would strongly advise you to take the job.* ◇ *The newspaper article advised against buying a house in that area.* ◇ *He did what the doctor advised.* ◇ *She advises the President on economic affairs.* **2** [T] (*formal*) to inform sb: *Passengers are advised that flight 365 to Montreal is now ready for boarding.*

**ad·vis·er** (*also* **advisor**) /əd'vaɪzər/ ***noun*** [C] a person who gives advice to a student, company, government, etc.: *an adviser on economic affairs* ◇ *My advisor says I need to take another math class in order to graduate.*

**ad·vi·so·ry**[1] /əd'vaɪzəri/ ***adj.*** giving advice only; not having the power to make decisions: *an advisory committee*

**ad·vi·so·ry**[2] /əd'vaɪzəri/ ***noun*** [C] (*pl.* **ad·vi·so·ries**) a report or warning that gives information about a dangerous situation: *a weather advisory*

**ad·vo·cate**[1] /'ædvəkeɪt/ ***verb*** [T] (*formal*) to recommend or say that you support a particular plan or action: *The candidate advocated a reform of the tax system.*

**ad·vo·cate**[2] /'ædvəkət/ ***noun*** [C] **advocate (of sth)** a person who supports a particular plan, action, or group of people: *an advocate of nuclear disarmament* ◇ *civil rights advocates*

**aer·i·al** /'ɛriəl/ ***adj.*** **1** from or in the air: *an aerial attack on the city* ◇ *aerial warfare* **2** taken from an aircraft: *an aerial photograph of the town*

**aer·o·bics** /ɛ'roʊbɪks; ə-/ ***noun*** [U] energetic physical exercises that increase the amount of oxygen in your blood. People often do aerobics to music: *to do aerobics* ◇ *an aerobics class* ▶ **aer·o·bic** ***adj.***: *aerobic exercise*

**aer·o·dy·nam·ic** /,ɛroʊdaɪ'næmɪk/ ***adj.*** having smooth, curved edges that help sth to move fast and use less fuel: *the car's sleek, aerodynamic shape*

**aer·o·dy·nam·ics** /,ɛroʊdaɪ'næmɪks/ ***noun*** [U] the scientific study of the way that things move through the air

**aer·o·sol** /'ɛrəsɔl/ ***noun*** [C] a liquid substance which is kept under pressure in a container. When you press a button the liquid comes out in a fine spray: *an aerosol deodorant*

**aer·o·space** /'ɛroʊspeɪs/ ***noun*** [U] the science that deals with the earth's atmosphere and outer space and the technology used in building planes, spacecraft, etc.

**aes·thet·ic** (*also* **esthetic**) /ɛs'θɛṭɪk; ɪs-/ ***adj.*** involving people's sense of beauty: *The columns are there for purely aesthetic reasons* (= only to look beautiful). ▶ **aes·thet·i·cal·ly** (*also* **esthetically**) /-kli/ ***adv.***: *to be aesthetically pleasing*

**aes·thet·ics** (*also* **esthetics**) /ɛs'θɛṭɪks; ɪs-/ ***noun*** [U] the branch of philosophy that studies the principles of beauty, especially in art: *function and aesthetics in architecture*

**a·far** /ə'fɑr/ ***adv.*** (*formal*)

IDM **from afar** from a long distance away: *The lights of the city were visible from afar.*

★**af·fair** /ə'fɛr/ ***noun*** **1** [C] an event or situation, often an unpleasant one: *The whole affair has been extremely depressing.* ◇ *The family reunion was a three-day-long affair.* **2** **affairs** [pl.] important personal, business, national, etc. matters: *The organization should have control of its own financial affairs.* ◇ *current affairs* (= the political and social events that are happening at the present time) **3** [sing.] something private that you do not want other people to know about: *What happened between us is my affair. I don't want to discuss it.* **4** [C] a sexual relationship between two people who are not married to each other, especially if one of them is married to sb else: *He's having an affair with his boss.*

IDM **state of affairs** → STATE[1]

★**af·fect** /ə'fɛkt/ ***verb*** [T] **1** to influence or cause sb/sth to change in a particular way: *Her personal problems seem to be affecting her work.* ◇ *Loud music can affect your hearing.* ➲ Look at the note at **influence**. **2** to cause sb to feel very sad, angry, etc.: *The whole community was affected by the terrible tragedy.*

NOTE Notice that **affect** is a verb and **effect** is a

A

noun: *Smoking can affect your health.* ◇ *Smoking can have a bad effect on your health.*

**af·fect·ed** /əˈfɛktəd/ ***adj.*** (used about a person or a person's behavior) not natural or sincere: *an affected laugh* ▸ **af·fec·ta·tion** /ˌæfɛkˈteɪʃn/ ***noun*** [C,U]

★**af·fec·tion** /əˈfɛkʃn/ ***noun*** [U] **affection (for/toward sb/sth)** a feeling of loving or liking sb/sth: *Mark felt great affection for his sister.*

**af·fec·tion·ate** /əˈfɛkʃənət/ ***adj.*** showing that you love or like sb very much: *a very affectionate child* ▸ **af·fec·tion·ate·ly** ***adv.***: *He looked at her affectionately.*

**af·fi·da·vit** /ˌæfəˈdeɪvət/ ***noun*** [C] a written statement that you swear is true, and that can be used as evidence in a court of law

**af·fil·i·ate** /əˈfɪliət/ ***noun*** [C] a company, organization, etc. that is connected to a larger organization: *local affiliates of the major TV networks*

**af·fil·i·at·ed** /əˈfɪlieɪt̬əd/ ***adj.*** **affiliated (with sth)** (used about an organization) connected with a larger organization: *the AFL-CIO and its affiliated unions*

**af·fil·i·a·tion** /əˌfɪliˈeɪʃn/ ***noun*** [C,U] a connection made by affiliating: *The group has affiliations with the Democratic Party.*

**af·fin·i·ty** /əˈfɪnət̬i/ ***noun*** [C,U] (*pl.* **af·fin·i·ties**) **1 affinity (for/with sb/sth)** a strong feeling that you understand sb/sth and like him/her/it: *Sam was brought up on a farm and had a great affinity for nature.* **2 affinity (with sb/sth)**; **affinity (between A and B)** a similar quality in two or more people or things: *His music has certain affinities with Brahms.*

**af·firm** /əˈfərm/ ***verb*** [T] (*formal*) **1** to say clearly that you hold a particular belief: *The people affirmed their country's right to independence.* **2** to say that sth is a fact: *She affirmed that he would resign.* ▸ **af·fir·ma·tion** /ˌæfərˈmeɪʃn/ ***noun*** [C,U]

**af·fir·ma·tive** /əˈfərmət̬ɪv/ ***adj.*** (*formal*) meaning "yes": *an affirmative answer* ➲ We can also say "an answer **in the affirmative**." OPP **negative**

**afˌfirmative ˈaction** ***noun*** [U] a policy or program that helps to give members of different races, people with disabilities, women, etc. a better chance of getting jobs, going to college, etc. than they had in the past: *the university's affirmative action policy*

**af·flict** /əˈflɪkt/ ***verb*** [T] (usually passive) (*formal*) to cause sb/sth to suffer pain, sadness, etc.: *He had been afflicted with a serious illness since childhood.*

**af·flic·tion** /əˈflɪkʃn/ ***noun*** [C,U] a thing that causes suffering: *Poor sight and hearing are common afflictions of old age.*

**af·flu·ent** /ˈæfluənt/ ***adj.*** having a lot of money: *an affluent neighborhood* ▸ **af·flu·ence** ***noun*** [U] /ˈæfluəns/

★**af·ford** /əˈfɔrd/ ***verb*** [T] **1** (usually after *can, could* or *be able to*) to have enough money or time to be able to do sth: *We couldn't afford a TV in those days.* **2 can't/couldn't afford** to not be able to do sth or let sth happen because it would have a bad result for you: *We can't afford to lose this contract. The future of the company depends on it.* ▸ **af·ford·a·bil·i·ty** /əˌfɔrdəˈbɪlət̬i/ ***noun*** [U]: *The car's big advantage is its affordability.* ▸ **af·ford·a·ble** /əˈfɔrdəbl/ ***adj.***: *the need for more affordable housing in cities*

**af·front** /əˈfrʌnt/ ***noun*** [C] something that you say or do that is insulting to another person or thing

**a·field** /əˈfild/ ***adv.***

IDM **far afield** → FAR[2]

**a·float** /əˈfloʊt/ ***adj.*** (not before a noun) **1** on the surface of the water; not sinking **2** (used about a business, an economy, etc.) having enough money to survive: *We will need to borrow ten million dollars to keep the company afloat.*

**AFN** /ˌeɪ ɛf ˈɛn/ ***abbr.*** Armed Forces Network; the part of the U.S. military that provides television and radio programs

★**a·fraid** /əˈfreɪd/ ***adj.*** (not before a noun) **1 afraid (of sb/sth)**; **afraid (of doing sth/to do sth)** having or showing fear; frightened: *Why are some people afraid of spiders?* ◇ *Sue is afraid of going out after dark.* ◇ *I was too afraid to answer the door.* **2 afraid (that...)**; **afraid (of doing sth)** worried about sth: *We were afraid that you would be upset.* ◇ *to be afraid of offending sb*

IDM **I'm afraid (that...)** (used for saying politely that you are sorry to say sth): *I'm afraid I can't come on Sunday.*

NOTE Compare **afraid** and **frightened**. You can only use **afraid** after a noun, but you can use **frightened** before or after a noun: *a frightened animal* ◇ *The animal was afraid/frightened.*

**a·fresh** /əˈfrɛʃ/ ***adv.*** (*formal*) again, in a new way: *to start afresh*

**Af·ri·can-A·mer·i·can** /ˌæfrɪkən əˈmɛrɪkən/ ***noun*** [C] an American citizen whose family was originally from Africa ▸ **Af·ri·can-A·mer·i·can** ***adj.***

NOTE Some North Americans whose ancestors originally came from Africa do not like to be called **Black**. They prefer to be called **African-Americans** or **African-Canadians**: *a biography of an African-American scientist.* **Afro-American** is a similar term, but it is considered old-fashioned nowadays. When used as a noun, **Black** is usually considered offensive.

**ˌAfrican-Caˈnadian** ***noun*** [C] a Canadian citizen whose family was originally from Africa ▸ **ˌAfrican-Caˈnadian** ***adj.*** ➲ Look at the note at **African-American**.

★**af·ter**[1] /ˈæftər/ ***prep.*** **1** later than sth: *Shelley called just after six o'clock.* ◇ *the week/month/year after next* ◇ *After finishing my homework, I went out for a walk.* **2 ...after...** repeated many times or continuing for a long time: *day after day of hot weather* ◇ *I've told the kids time after time not to do that.* **3** following or behind sb/sth: *Shut the door after you.* ◇ *The dog ran after its owner.* **4** following in order: *C comes after B in the alphabet.* **5** because of sth: *After the way he behaved, I won't invite him here again.* **6** (used when telling the time) later than: *We left at a quarter after five.* **7** looking for or trying to catch or get sb/sth: *The police were after him.* ◇ *The company is going after younger consumers.* **8** (used when sb/sth is given the name of another person or thing): *The street is called Washington Street, after the first American President.*

IDM **after all 1** (used when sth happens that you did not expect to happen, or when you discover that sth that you thought was not true is, in fact, true): *So you decided to come after all!* (= I thought you weren't going to come) **2** (used for reminding sb of a certain fact): *She can't understand. After all, she's only two.*

★**af·ter²** /ˈæftər/ ***conj.*** at a time later than sth: *They arrived at the station after the train had left.* ◇ *After we had finished our dinner, we sat outside on the patio.*

★**af·ter³** /ˈæftər/ ***adv.*** at a later time: *That was in 1998. Soon after, I heard that he had cancer.* ◇ *They lived happily ever after* (= forever).

NOTE It is more common to use **afterward** or **afterwards** at the end of a sentence: *We played tennis and then went to Angela's house afterward.*

**af·ter·ef·fect** /ˈæftərɪˌfɛkt/ ***noun*** [C] an unpleasant result of sth that comes some time after it has happened: *the aftereffects of a serious illness*

**af·ter·math** /ˈæftərmæθ/ ***noun*** [sing.] a situation that is the result of an important or unpleasant event: *the aftermath of a war*

★**af·ter·noon** /ˌæftərˈnun/ ***noun*** [C,U] the part of a day between noon and about six o'clock: *I'll see you tomorrow afternoon.* ◇ *She arrived at four o'clock in the afternoon.* ◇ *Tom works two afternoons a week.* ◇ *Are you busy Friday afternoon?* ◇ *an afternoon snack* ◇ *Where were you the afternoon of February 26th?*

IDM **good afternoon** (*formal*) (used when you see sb for the first time in the afternoon) ➲ Look at the note at **morning**.

**af·ter·shave** /ˈæftərʃeɪv/ ***noun*** [C,U] a liquid with a pleasant smell that men put on their faces after shaving

**af·ter·shock** /ˈæftərʃɑk/ ***noun*** [C] a sudden movement of the earth's surface which follows another, more violent movement like this (**an earthquake**): *a series of moderate aftershocks*

**af·ter·thought** /ˈæftərθɔt/ ***noun*** [C, usually sing.] something that you think of or add to sth else at a later time: *He did the grocery shopping and then bought some flowers on the way home as an afterthought.*

★**af·ter·ward** /ˈæftərwərd/ (*also* **afterwards** /ˈæftərwərdz/) ***adv.*** at a later time: *I met her at a party and saw her again soon afterward.* ◇ *Afterward, Nick said he hadn't enjoyed the movie.*

★**a·gain** /əˈgɛn/ ***adv.*** **1** once more; another time: *Could you say that again, please?* ◇ *Don't ever do that again!* **2** in the place or condition that sb/sth was in before: *It's great to be home again.* ◇ *I hope you'll soon feel well again.* **3** in addition: *"Is that enough?" "No, I'd like half as much again, please* (= one-and-a-half times the original amount).

IDM **again and again** many times: *He said he was sorry again and again.*

**(but) then again** → THEN

**(every) now and again/then** → NOW¹

**yet again** → YET¹

★**a·gainst** /əˈgɛnst/ ***prep.*** **1** touching or leaning on sb/sth for support: *Put the broom over there against the wall.* **2** in the opposite direction from sth: *We had to pedal against the wind.* **3** opposing sb/sth in a game, competition, war, etc.: *We're playing against the Cardinals Saturday.* **4** not agreeing with or supporting sb/sth: *Are you for or against the plan?* ◇ *I felt like everybody was against me.* **5** what a law, rule, etc. says you must not do: *It's against the law to buy cigarettes before you are sixteen.* **6** to protect yourself from sb/sth: *Take these pills as a precaution against malaria.*

★**age¹** /eɪdʒ/ ***noun*** **1** [C,U] the length of time that sb has lived or that sth has existed: *She learned to drive at the age of sixteen.* ◇ *Children of all ages will enjoy this game.* ◇ *He needs some friends his own age.* ◇ (*formal*) *Most students here are between eighteen and twenty-two years of age.*

NOTE When you want to ask about somebody's age, you usually say *How old are you?* and the answer can be *I'm sixteen* or *I'm sixteen years old* but NOT *I'm sixteen years* and NOT *I have sixteen years.* Here are some examples of other ways of talking about age: *I'm almost seventeen.* ◇ *a girl of sixteen* ◇ *a sixteen-year-old girl.* Children often say: *I'm six, going on seven.*

**2** [U] one of the periods of sb's life: *a problem that often develops in middle age* ◇ *the 20-30 age group* (= the group of people who are between 20 and 30 years old) **3** [U] the state of being old: *a face lined with age* ➲ Look at **youth**. **4** [C] a particular period of history: *We are now living in the computer age.* ◇ *the history of art through the ages* **5** [pl.] (*informal*) a very long time: *It took me ages to find a parking place.*

IDM **under age** not old enough by law to do sth

**age²** /eɪdʒ/ ***verb*** [I,T] (*pres. part.* **ag·ing**; *pt, pp* **ag·ed** /eɪdʒd/) to become or look old; to cause sb to look old: *My father seems to have aged a lot recently.*

★**ag·ed** /eɪdʒd/ ***adj.*** **1** (not before a noun) of a particular AGE (1): *The woman had three children, aged 3, 5 and 10.* **2 the aged** /ˈeɪdʒəd/ ***noun*** [pl.] old people

**age·ism** (*also* **ag·ism**) /ˈeɪdʒɪzəm/ ***noun*** [U] unfair treatment of people because they are considered too old ▸ **age·ist** (*also* **ag·ist**) /ˈeɪdʒɪst/ ***adj.***, ***noun*** [C]: *an ageist hiring policy*

★**a·gen·cy** /ˈeɪdʒənsi/ ***noun*** [C] (*pl.* **a·gen·cies**) **1** a business that provides a particular service: *an advertising agency* **2** a government department: *the Central Intelligence Agency*

**a·gen·da** /əˈdʒɛndə/ ***noun*** [C] a list of all the subjects that are to be discussed at a meeting: *What's the next item on the agenda?*

★**a·gent** /ˈeɪdʒənt/ ***noun*** [C] **1** a person whose job is to do business for a company or for another person: *Our company's agent in Rio will meet you at the airport.* ◇ *Most actors and musicians have their own agents.* ◇ *a travel agent* ◇ *a real estate agent* **2** an officer in certain government departments: *an FBI agent* ◇ *Customs agents seized a shipment of drugs at the airport.* **3** a person who tries to find out secret information especially about the government of another country: *an undercover agent* ➲ Look at **spy**.

**ag·gra·vate** /ˈægrəveɪt/ ***verb*** [T] **1** to make sth worse or more serious: *The country's food problems*

A

were aggravated by the hot dry summer. SYN **exacerbate** **2** (*informal*) to make sb angry or annoyed ▸ **ag·gra·va·tion** /ˌægrəˈveɪʃn/ ***noun*** [C,U]

**ag·gres·sion** /əˈgrɛʃn/ ***noun*** [U] **1** the act of starting a fight or war without reasonable cause: *This is an intolerable act of aggression against my country.* **2** angry feelings or behavior that make you want to attack other people: *People often react to this kind of situation with fear or aggression.*

★**ag·gres·sive** /əˈgrɛsɪv/ ***adj.*** **1** ready or likely to fight or argue: *an aggressive dog* ◇ *Some people get aggressive after drinking alcohol.* **2** using or showing force or pressure in order to succeed: *an aggressive salesman* ▸ **ag·gres·sive·ly** ***adv.***

**ag·gres·sor** /əˈgrɛsər/ ***noun*** [C] a person or country that attacks sb/sth or starts fighting first

**ag·ile** /ˈædʒl; -dʒaɪl/ ***adj.*** able to move quickly and easily ▸ **a·gil·i·ty** /əˈdʒɪləṭi/ ***noun*** [U]

**ag·i·tate** /ˈædʒəteɪt/ ***verb*** [I] **agitate (for/against sth)** to make other people feel very strongly about sth so that they want to do sth to help you achieve it: *to agitate for reform* ▸ **ag·i·ta·tion** /ˌædʒəˈteɪʃn/ ***noun*** [U]

**ag·i·tat·ed** /ˈædʒəˌteɪṭəd/ ***adj.*** worried or excited: *She became more and more agitated when her son did not appear.*

**ag·nos·tic** /ægˈnɑstɪk; əg-/ ***noun*** [C] a person who believes that you cannot know whether or not God exists

★**a·go** /əˈgoʊ/ ***adv.*** in the past; back in time from now: *Patrick left ten minutes ago* (= if it is twelve o'clock now, he left at 11:50). ◇ *That was a long time ago.* ◇ *How long ago did this happen?*

> NOTE **Ago** is used with the simple past tense and not the present perfect tense: *I arrived in North America three months ago.*
> ➲ Compare **ago** and **before**. **Ago** means "before now" and **before** means "before then" (i.e. before a particular time in the past): *Anne married Evan two years ago.* ◇ *She had left her first husband six years before* (= six years before she married Evan).

**ag·o·nize** /ˈægənaɪz/ ***verb*** [I] to worry or think about sth for a long time: *to agonize over a difficult decision*

**ag·o·nized** /ˈægənaɪzd/ ***adj.*** showing extreme pain or worry: *an agonized cry*

**ag·o·niz·ing** /ˈægənaɪzɪŋ/ ***adj.*** causing extreme worry or pain: *an agonizing decision* ◇ *an agonizing headache*

**ag·o·ny** /ˈægəni/ ***noun*** [C,U] (*pl.* **ag·o·nies**) great pain or suffering: *to scream in agony*

**ag·o·ra·pho·bi·a** /ˌægərəˈfoʊbiə; əˌgɔrə-/ ***noun*** [U] a strong fear of open spaces or of crowded public places ▸ **ag·o·ra·pho·bic** /-ˈfoʊbɪk/ ***adj.***

★**a·gree** /əˈgri/ ***verb***

▸SHARE OPINION **1** [I,T] **agree (with sb/sth)**; **agree (that...)** to have the same opinion as sb: *"I think we should talk to the manager about this." "Yes, I agree."* ◇ *I agree with Paul.* ◇ *Do you agree that we should go by train?* ◇ *No, I don't agree.* OPP **disagree**

▸SAY YES **2** [I] **agree (to sth)** to say yes to sth: *I asked if I could go home early and she agreed.* ◇ *Andy has agreed to loan me his car for the weekend.* OPP **refuse**[1]

▸MAKE AN ARRANGEMENT **3** [I] **agree (to do sth)**; **agree (on sth)** to make an arrangement or agreement with sb: *They agreed to meet again the following day.* ◇ *Can we agree on a price?* ◇ *We agreed that Leah would contact us if she needed help.*

▸ACCEPT **4** [I] **agree with sth** to think that sth is right: *I don't agree with experiments on animals.*

▸BE THE SAME **5** [I] to be the same as sth: *The two accounts of the accident do not agree.* ◇ *In French the adjective must agree with the noun in number and gender.*

PHR V **agree with sb** to be pleasant for sb or good for sb's health: *No, thanks. Onions don't agree with me.*

**a·gree·a·ble** /əˈgriəbl/ ***adj.*** (*formal*) **1** pleasant; nice OPP **disagreeable** **2** ready to agree: *Would you be agreeable to our suggestion?* **3** acceptable; that can be agreed on: *a proposal that is agreeable to both sides in a dispute*

★**a·gree·ment** /əˈgrimənt/ ***noun*** **1** [C] a contract or decision that two or more people have made together: *Please sign the rental agreement and return it to us.* ◇ *The leaders reached an agreement after five days of talks.* **2** [U] the state of agreeing with sb/sth: *She nodded her head in agreement.* OPP **disagreement** **3** [U] (*grammar*) the fact that two or more words have the same form, e.g. if the subject of a verb is plural, the verb must also be plural: *subject-verb agreement*

**ag·ri·cul·ture** /ˈægrəkʌltʃər/ ***noun*** [U] keeping animals and growing crops for food; farming: *the U.S. Department of Agriculture* ▸ **ag·ri·cul·tur·al** /ˌægrəˈkʌltʃərəl/ ***adj.***: *agricultural land*

**ah** /ɑ/ ***interjection*** (used for expressing surprise, pleasure, etc.): *Ah yes. I see it now.* ◇ *Ah, what a beautiful day!*

**a·ha** /ɑˈhɑ/ ***interjection*** (used when you suddenly find or understand sth): *Aha! Now I understand.*

★**a·head** /əˈhɛd/ ***adv., adj.*** **ahead (of sb/sth)** **1** in front of sb/sth: *I could see the other car about half a mile ahead of us.* ◇ *Look straight ahead and don't turn around!* **2** before or in advance of sb/sth: *Jane and Nicole arrived a few minutes ahead of us.* ◇ *New York is three hours ahead of Los Angeles.* **3** into the future: *He's got a difficult time ahead of him.* ◇ *You have to plan ahead and not leave all the details for the last minute.* **4** doing better than another person or team in a game, competition, etc.: *The third goal put Toronto ahead.* **5** more advanced than sb/sth else: *The Japanese are way ahead of us in their research.*

**AI** /ˌeɪ ˈaɪ/ ***abbr.*** = ARTIFICIAL INTELLIGENCE

★**aid**[1] /eɪd/ ***noun*** **1** [U] help: *to walk with the aid of a cane* ◇ *to go to sb's aid* (= to go and help sb) ➲ Look at **first aid**. **2** [C] a person or thing that helps you: *a hearing aid* **3** [U] money, food, etc. that is sent to a country or people in order to help them: *aid to developing countries* ◇ *the Red Cross and other international aid agencies*

IDM **in aid of sb/sth** (*Cdn*) in support of sb/sth: *a concert in aid of refugee families*

**aid**[2] /eɪd/ ***verb*** [T] (*formal*) to help sb

IDM **aid and abet** to help sb to do sth that is against the law: *to be accused of aiding and abetting a robbery*

**aide** /eɪd/ ***noun*** [C] a person who is an assistant to sb important in the government, etc.: *the President's top aides*

**AIDS** /eɪdz/ ***noun*** [U] an illness which destroys the body's ability to fight infection: *an AIDS victim* ◇ *Thousands of people have died of AIDS.*

NOTE "AIDS" is short for **Acquired Immune Deficiency Syndrome**.

**ail·ing** /ˈeɪlɪŋ/ ***adj.*** not in good health; weak: (*figurative*) *an ailing economy*

**ail·ment** /ˈeɪlmənt/ ***noun*** [C] (*formal*) an illness (that is not very serious)

★**aim**[1] /eɪm/ ***noun*** **1** [C] something that you intend to do or achieve: *Our aim is to open offices in Knoxville and Memphis before the end of the year.* ◇ *His only aim in life is to make money.* **2** [U] the act of pointing sth at sb/sth before trying to hit him/her/it with it: *The hunter took aim at a deer nearby.* ◇ *Her aim was good and she hit the target.*

★**aim**[2] /eɪm/ ***verb*** **1** [I] **aim to do sth; aim at/for sth** to intend to do or achieve sth: *We aim to leave after breakfast.* ◇ *The company is aiming at a 25% increase in profit.* ◇ *You should always aim for perfection in your work.* **2** [T] **aim sth at sb/sth** to direct sth at a particular person or group: *The advertising campaign is aimed at young people.* **3** [I,T] **aim (sth) (at sb/sth)** to point sth at sb/sth before trying to hit him/her/it with it: *She picked up the gun, aimed, and fired.*
IDM **be aimed at sth** to be intended to achieve sth: *The new laws are aimed at reducing pollution in cities.*

**aim·less** /ˈeɪmləs/ ***adj.*** having no purpose: *an aimless discussion* ▶ **aim·less·ly** ***adv.***

**ain't** /eɪnt/ (*informal*) *short for* AM NOT, IS NOT, ARE NOT, HAS NOT, HAVE NOT

NOTE **Ain't** is not considered correct English.

★**air**[1] /ɛr/ ***noun*** **1** [U] the mixture of gases that surrounds the earth and that people, animals and plants breathe: *the pure mountain air* ◇ *The air was polluted by smoke from the factory.* **2** [U] the space around and above things: *to throw a ball high into the air* **3** [U] travel or transportation in an aircraft: *to travel by air* ◇ *an air ticket* **4** [C] **an air (of sth)** the impression that sb gives or the impression you get of a place, event, etc.: *a confident air* ◇ *There was a general air of confusion outside the company office.* **5** [U] = AIR CONDITIONING: *a house with central air*
IDM **a breath of fresh air** → BREATH
**in the air** probably going to happen soon: *A feeling of change was in the air.*
**in the open air** → OPEN[1]
**on (the) air** broadcasting on the radio or television: *This radio station is on the air 24 hours a day.*
**vanish, etc. into thin air** → THIN[1]

**air**[2] /ɛr/ ***verb***
➤CLOTHES **1** [I,T] **air (sth) (out)** to put clothes, etc. in a warm place or outside in the fresh air to make sure they are completely dry; to be put in this place: *Put the sleeping bag on the clothesline to air.*
➤A ROOM **2** [I,T] **air (sth) (out)** to make a room, etc. fresh by letting air into it; to become fresh in this way: *Open the window to air the room out.*
➤OPINIONS **3** [T] to tell people what you think about sth: *The discussion gave people a chance to air their views.*
➤RADIO/TV PROGRAM **4** [I,T] to broadcast sth or to be broadcast on television or the radio: *The interview is scheduled to air Monday evening.* ◇ *The next episode will be aired in two weeks.*

**ˈair bag** (*also* **air·bag**) ***noun*** [C] a bag in a car that suddenly fills with air during an accident in order to protect the driver or a passenger

**ˈair base** ***noun*** [C] a military center from which an air force operates

**air·borne** /ˈɛrbɔrn/ ***adj.*** flying or floating in the air: *Do not leave your seat until the plane is airborne.* ◇ *airborne dust particles* ◇ *the 506th Airborne Infantry Regiment*

**ˈair-conˌditioned** ***adj.*** having air conditioning: *air-conditioned offices*

**ˈair conˌditioner** ***noun*** [C] a piece of equipment that keeps the air in a room, building, etc. cool and dry

**ˈair conˌditioning** ***noun*** [U] the system that keeps the air in a room, building, etc. cool and dry: *Close the window – the air conditioning is on.*

★**air·craft** /ˈɛrkræft/ ***noun*** [C] (*pl.* **air·craft**) any vehicle that can fly in the air, e.g. an airplane, a helicopter, etc.

**ˈaircraft ˌcarrier** ***noun*** [C] a ship that carries military aircraft and that has a long flat area where they can take off and land

**air·fare** /ˈɛrfɛr/ ***noun*** [C,U] the amount of money that you pay to travel by plane

**air·field** /ˈɛrfild/ ***noun*** [C] an area of land where airplanes can land or take off. An airfield is smaller than an airport.

**ˈair force** ***noun*** [C] the part of a country's military organization that fights in the air ➲ Look at **army**, **Marine Corps** and **navy**.

**ˈair gun** = AIR RIFLE

**air·less** /ˈɛrləs/ ***adj.*** not having enough fresh air: *The room was hot and airless.*

**air·line** /ˈɛrlaɪn/ ***noun*** [C] a company that provides regular flights for people or goods in airplanes: *an airline pilot*

**air·lin·er** /ˈɛrlaɪnər/ ***noun*** [C] a large airplane that carries passengers

**air·mail** /ˈɛrmeɪl/ ***noun*** [U] the system of sending letters, packages, etc. to other countries by airplane

★**air·plane** /ˈɛrpleɪn/ (*also* **plane**) ***noun*** [C] a vehicle with wings and one or more engines that can fly through the air: *the noise of an airplane flying overhead* ◇ *I went to Calgary by plane.*

★**air·port** /ˈɛrpɔrt/ ***noun*** [C] a place where aircraft can land and take off and that has buildings for passengers to wait in: *Jill went to meet her friend at the airport.* ◇ *Los Angeles International Airport*

**ˈair raid** ***noun*** [C] an attack by military airplanes

A

**ˌair ˌrifle** (*also* **ˈair gun**) ***noun*** [C] a gun that uses air pressure to fire small metal balls (**pellets**) ➲ Look at **BB gun**.

**air·space** /ˈɛrspeɪs/ ***noun*** [U] the part of the sky that is above a country and that belongs to that country by law

**air·strip** /ˈɛrstrɪp/ ***noun*** [C] (*also* **ˈlanding strip**) a narrow piece of cleared land that an aircraft can land on

**air·tight** /ˈɛrtaɪt/ ***adj.*** that air cannot get into or out of: *Keep the cookies in an airtight container.*

**ˌair ˌtraffic conˈtroller** ***noun*** [C] a person whose job is to organize routes for airplanes, and to tell pilots by radio when they can land and take off

**air·y** /ˈɛri/ ***adj.*** (**air·i·er**; **air·i·est**) having a lot of fresh air: *a light and airy room*

**aisle** /aɪl/ ***noun*** [C] a passage between the rows of seats in a church, a theater, an airplane, etc.: *Would you like a window seat or an aisle seat?*

**a·jar** /əˈdʒɑr/ ***adj.*** (not before a noun) slightly open (used about a door)

**a·kin** /əˈkɪn/ ***adj.*** **akin to sth** similar to or like sth

**à la mode** /ˌɑ lə ˈmoʊd; ˌæ lə ˈmoʊd/ ***adj.***, ***adv.*** served with ice cream: *apple pie à la mode*

★**a·larm**[1] /əˈlɑrm/ ***noun*** **1** [C] a machine that warns you of danger, e.g. by ringing a loud bell: *a burglar alarm* ◇ *a fire alarm* **2** [C] = ALARM CLOCK **3** [U] a sudden feeling of fear or worry: *There's no cause for alarm.*

IDM **a false alarm** → FALSE

**raise/sound the alarm** to warn people about sth dangerous: *I hammered on all the doors to raise the alarm.*

**a·larm**[2] /əˈlɑrm/ ***verb*** [T] to make sb/sth feel suddenly frightened or worried: *The news of the escaped prisoner alarmed the local people.* SYN **perturb**

**aˈlarm clock** (*also* **alarm**) ***noun*** [C] a clock that you can set to make a noise at a particular time to wake you up: *My alarm clock goes off at seven o'clock.* ◇ *She set the alarm for six-thirty.* ➲ picture at **clock**.

**a·larmed** /əˈlɑrmd/ ***adj.*** **alarmed (at/by sth)** frightened or worried: *Government officials are alarmed at the recent rise in unemployment.*

**a·larm·ing** /əˈlɑrmɪŋ/ ***adj.*** that makes you frightened or worried: *The rainforests are disappearing at an alarming rate.* ▸ **a·larm·ing·ly** ***adv.***

**a·las** /əˈlæs/ ***interjection*** (*formal*) (used for expressing sadness about sth)

**al·be·it** /ɔlˈbiət; æl-/ ***conj.*** (*formal*) although: *He finally agreed, albeit reluctantly, to go.*

**al·bi·no** /ælˈbaɪnoʊ/ ***noun*** [C] (*pl.* **al·bi·nos**) a person or animal with very white skin, white hair and pink eyes

**al·bum** /ˈælbəm/ ***noun*** [C] **1** a collection of pieces of music that have been recorded on one CD, cassette or record **2** a book in which you can keep stamps, photographs, etc. that you have collected

★**al·co·hol** /ˈælkəhɔl; -hɑl/ ***noun*** [U] **1** the colorless liquid in drinks such as beer, whiskey and wine that can make you drunk **2** the drinks (e.g. beer, whiskey, wine) that contain alcohol

★**al·co·hol·ic**[1] /ˌælkəˈhɔlɪk; -ˈhɑlɪk/ ***adj.*** containing alcohol: *alcoholic drinks* OPP **non-alcoholic**

NOTE Drinks without alcohol are also called **soft drinks**.

**al·co·hol·ic**[2] /ˌælkəˈhɔlɪk; -ˈhɑlɪk/ ***noun*** [C] a person who is dependent on alcohol and drinks a large amount of it every day

NOTE A person who does not drink alcohol at all is a **teetotaler**.

**al·co·hol·ism** /ˈælkəhɔlɪzəm; -hɑl-/ ***noun*** [U] the medical condition that is caused by regularly drinking a large amount of alcohol

**al·cove** /ˈælkoʊv/ ***noun*** [C] a small area in a room where one part of the wall is farther back than the rest of the wall

**al·der·man** /ˈɔldərmən/ ***noun*** [C] (*pl.* **al·der·men**) an elected member of the city council in some North American cities

**ale** /eɪl/ ***noun*** [U] a type of beer

**a·lert**[1] /əˈlərt/ ***adj.*** **alert (to sth)** watching, listening, etc. for sth with full attention: *Security guards must be alert at all times.* ◇ *to be alert to possible changes*

**a·lert**[2] /əˈlərt/ ***noun*** [C] a warning of possible danger: *a bomb alert*

IDM **on the alert (for sth)** ready or prepared for danger or an attack: *The public was warned to be on the alert for possible tornadoes.*

**a·lert**[3] /əˈlərt/ ***verb*** [T] **alert sb (to sth)** to warn sb of danger or a problem

**al·fal·fa** /ælˈfælfə/ ***noun*** [U] a plant that is used for feeding farm animals. People sometimes eat the young plants (**sprouts**) as a vegetable, especially in salads

**al·gae** /ˈældʒi/ ***noun*** [pl., with sing. or pl. verb] very simple plants that grow mainly in water: *If you don't clean your swimming pool, algae will grow in it.*

**al·ge·bra** /ˈældʒəbrə/ ***noun*** [U] a type of mathematics in which letters and symbols are used to represent numbers

**a·li·as**[1] /ˈeɪliəs/ ***noun*** [C] a false name, e.g. one that is used by a criminal

**a·li·as**[2] /ˈeɪliəs/ ***adv.*** (used for giving sb's false name): *Mrs. Phillips, alias Maria Jones*

**al·i·bi** /ˈæləbaɪ/ ***noun*** [C] (*pl.* **al·i·bis**) a statement by sb that says you were in a different place at the time of a crime and so cannot be guilty of the crime: *He had a good alibi for the night of the robbery.*

**a·li·en**[1] /ˈeɪliən/ ***noun*** [C] **1** (*formal*) a person who is not a citizen of the country in which he/she lives or works: *an illegal alien* **2** a creature that comes from another planet

**a·li·en**[2] /ˈeɪliən/ ***adj.*** **1** of another country; foreign: *an alien land* **2** very strange and completely different from your normal experience: *The idea of eating meat was alien to her.*

**al·ien·ate** /ˈeɪlyəneɪt; ˈeɪliə-/ ***verb*** [T] **1** to make people feel that they cannot share your opinions anymore: *The President's new policies on welfare have alienated many of his supporters.* **2** **alienate sb (from sb/sth)** to make sb feel that he/she does not belong somewhere or is not part of sth: *Many young people feel alienated from the rest of society.* ▸ **al·ien·a·tion** ***noun*** [U] /ˌeɪlyəˈneɪʃn; ˈeɪliə-/

**a·light**[1] /əˈlaɪt/ ***adj.*** on fire; burning: *The kerosene had been set alight* (= made to start burning) *by a cigarette.*

> NOTE **Alight** cannot be used before a noun, but you can use **burning** before a noun: *The whole building was alight.* ◇ *a burning building.*

**a·light**[2] /əˈlaɪt/ ***verb*** [I] (*formal*) **1 alight (in/on/upon sth)** (used about a bird or an insect) to land in or on sth after flying to it **2 alight (from sth)** to get off a bus, train, etc.

PHR V **alight on/upon sth** to think, find or notice sth, especially by chance: *Her eyes alighted on a bundle of documents.*

**a·lign** /əˈlaɪn/ ***verb*** [T] **1 align sth (with sth)** to arrange things in a straight line or so that they are parallel to sth else: *to align the wheels of a car* **2 align yourself with sb** to say that you support the opinions of a particular group, country, etc.: *Canada has aligned itself with the United States over this issue.* ➲ Look at **non-aligned**.

**a·lign·ment** /əˈlaɪnmənt/ ***noun*** **1** [U] arrangement in a straight line or parallel to sth else **2** [C,U] an agreement between political parties, countries, etc. to support the same thing: *the alignment of Japan with the West*

**a·like**[1] /əˈlaɪk/ ***adj.*** (not before a noun) like one another; the same: *The two children are very alike.*

**a·like**[2] /əˈlaɪk/ ***adv.*** in the same way: *We try to treat all our employees alike.* ◇ *The musical has been a success with adults and children alike.*

**al·i·mo·ny** /ˈæləmoʊni/ ***noun*** [U] money that you have to pay by law to your former wife or husband after a divorce

★**a·live** /əˈlaɪv/ ***adj.*** **1** not dead; living: *The young woman was still alive when the ambulance reached the hospital.*

> NOTE **Alive** can only be used after a noun, but you can use **living** before a noun: *Are her parents still alive?* ◇ *Does she have any living relatives?*

**2** full of life: *In the evening the town really comes alive.* **3** continuing to exist: *Many old traditions are still alive in this area of the country.*

**al·ka·li** /ˈælkəlaɪ/ ***noun*** [C,U] any of the chemical substances which have a pH value of more than 7 ➲ Look at **acid** and **base**[1]. ▸ **al·ka·line** /ˈælkəlɪn; -laɪn/ ***adj.***

★**all**[1] /ɔl/ ***det., pronoun*** **1** the whole of a thing: *All (of) the food is gone.* ◇ *They ate all of it.* ◇ *They ate it all.* ◇ *This money is all yours.* ◇ *All of it is yours.* **2** the whole of the period of time: *It rained all day.* ◇ *He worked hard all his life.* **3** every one of a group: *All (of) my kids can swim.* ◇ *My kids can all swim.* ◇ *She's read all (of) these books.* ◇ *She's read them all.* ➲ Look at **y'all**. **4** everything that; the only thing that: *I wrote down all I could remember.* ◇ *All I've eaten today is a slice of toast.*

IDM **above all** → ABOVE[1]

**after all** → AFTER[1]

**in all** in total: *There were ten of us in all.*

**(not) at all** in any way: *I didn't enjoy it at all.*

**on all fours** with your hands and knees on the ground; crawling: *The kids went through the tunnel on all fours.*

**you all** → YOU

★**all**[2] /ɔl/ ***adv.*** **1** completely; very: *He has lived all alone since his wife died.* ◇ *I didn't watch that program – I forgot all about it.* **2** (in sports) for each side: *The score was two all.*

IDM **all along** from the beginning: *I knew you were joking all along.*

**all but 1** almost; very nearly: *With this delay, it'll be all but impossible to meet our deadline.* **2** everybody or everything except sb/sth: *All but $500 of the stolen money has been found.*

**all over**; **all over the place** everywhere: *We looked all over for Monica's watch.*

**all the better, harder, etc.** better, harder, etc. than before: *It will be all the more difficult with two people missing.*

**not all that...** (*informal*) not very: *The movie wasn't all that good.*

**Al·lah** /ˈɑlə; ˈælə/ ***noun*** the Muslim name for God

**ˌall-Aˈmerican** ***adj.*** **1** having qualities that people think are typically American: *Todd is a real all-American boy: he's bright, works hard and is good at sports.* **2** having members who were chosen as the best in the U.S. in a particular sport, etc.: *the all-American girls' high school basketball team*

**ˌall-aˈround** ***adj.*** (only *before* a noun) **1** able to do many different things well: *an excellent all-around musician* **2** including many different things; general: *The school provides a good all-around education.*

**al·lay** /əˈleɪ/ ***verb*** [T] (*formal*) to make sth less strong: *to allay sb's fears*

**ˌall-Caˈnadian** ***adj.*** **1** (used especially about an athlete) chosen as one of the best in, or representing the whole of, Canada **2** having qualities that people think are typically Canadian

**the ˌall ˈclear** ***noun*** [sing.] a signal telling you that danger is over

**al·lege** /əˈlɛdʒ/ ***verb*** [T] (*formal*) to say that sb has done sth wrong, but without proving that this is true: *The woman alleged that Williams had attacked her with a knife.* ▸ **al·le·ga·tion** /ˌæləˈgeɪʃn/ ***noun*** [C]: *to make allegations of police corruption* ▸ **al·leged** /əˈlɛdʒd/ ***adj.***: *the alleged murderer* (= people say this person is a murderer but nobody has proved that this is true) ▸ **al·leg·ed·ly** /əˈlɛdʒədli/ ***adv.***: *The former manager allegedly stole thousands of dollars from the company.*

**al·le·giance** /əˈlidʒəns/ ***noun*** [U] (*formal*) support for or loyalty toward a leader, government, belief, etc. ➲ Look at **the Pledge of Allegiance**.

**al·ler·gic** /əˈlərdʒɪk/ ***adj.*** **1 allergic (to sth)** having an allergy: *I can't drink cow's milk. I'm allergic to it.* **2** caused by an allergy: *an allergic reaction to house dust*

**al·ler·gy** /ˈælərdʒi/ ***noun*** [C] (*pl.* **al·ler·gies**) **an allergy (to sth)** a medical condition that makes you sick when you eat, touch or breathe sth that does not normally make other people sick: *an allergy to cats/shellfish/pollen*

**al·le·vi·ate** /əˈlivieɪt/ ***verb*** [T] to make sth less

A

strong or bad: *The doctor gave me a shot to alleviate the pain.* ▶ **al·le·vi·a·tion** /ə,livi'eɪʃn/ ***noun*** [U]

**al·ley** /'æli/ ***noun*** [C] a narrow passage between or behind buildings

**al·li·ance** /ə'laɪəns/ ***noun*** [C] an agreement between people, groups, countries, etc. to work together and support each other: *to form/make an alliance* ➲ Look at **ally**.

**al·lied** /'ælaɪd; ə'laɪd/ ***adj.*** **1** (used about organizations, countries, etc.) having an agreement to work together and support each other: *allied forces* **2 allied (to sth)** connected with sth; similar: *nursing and allied health professions*

**al·li·ga·tor** /'æləgeɪt̬ər/ (*also informal* **gator**) ***noun*** [C] a large animal with a long body and sharp teeth that lives in the lakes and rivers of the southern U.S. and China. An alligator is similar to a crocodile.

**al·lo·cate** /'æləkeɪt/ ***verb*** [T] **allocate sth (to sb/sth); allocate sth (for sth)** to give sth to sb as his/her share or to decide to use sth for a particular purpose: *Federal funding is allocated to each department.* ◇ *We need to allocate some extra time for the final stage of the project.*

**al·lo·ca·tion** /,ælə'keɪʃn/ ***noun*** [C,U] giving sth for a particular purpose; the amount that is given: *the allocation of resources for cancer research*

**al·lo·phone** /'æləfoʊn/ ***noun*** [C] (*Cdn*) a person who comes to live in Canada, especially Quebec, from another country (**an immigrant**), whose first language is neither French nor English ▶ **al·lo·phone** ***adj.***: *Within French-speaking Quebec, anglophone, allophone and Aboriginal minorities also exist.*

**al·lot** /ə'lɑt/ ***verb*** [T] (**al·lot·ting; al·lot·ted**) **allot sth (to sb/sth)** to give sb money, a piece of work, etc. as his/her share or to decide to allow a certain amount of time for sth: *Different tasks were allotted to each member of the class.* ◇ *We all finished the exam in the allotted time.*

**,all 'out** ***adj., adv.*** using all your strength, etc.: *We're going all out for the championship.* ◇ *an all-out effort*

★**al·low** /ə'laʊ/ ***verb*** [T]

➤LET SB/STH DO STH **1 allow sb/sth to do sth; allow sth** to give permission for sb/sth to do sth or for sth to happen: *Children under sixteen are not allowed to buy cigarettes.* ◇ *Photography is not allowed inside the museum.*

NOTE Compare **allow**, **permit** and **let**. **Allow** can be used in both formal and informal English. The passive form **be allowed to** is especially common. **Permit** is a formal word and is usually used only in written English. **Let** is an informal word, and very common in spoken English. You **allow sb to do sth** but **let sb do sth** (no "to"). **Let** cannot be used in the passive: *Visitors are not allowed/permitted to smoke in this area.* ◇ *Smoking is not allowed/permitted.* ◇ *I'm not allowed to smoke in my bedroom.* ◇ *My dad won't let me smoke in my bedroom.*

**2** to give permission for sb/sth to be or go somewhere: *I'm only allowed to go out on Friday and Saturday nights.* **3 allow sb sth** to let sb have sth: *We're only allowed half an hour for our lunch break.*

➤MAKE POSSIBLE **4 allow sb/sth to do sth** to make it possible for sb/sth to do sth: *Working part-time would allow me to spend more time with my family.*

➤TIME/MONEY/FOOD, ETC. **5 allow sth (for sb/sth)** to provide money, time, etc. for sb/sth: *You should allow about 30 minutes for each question on the test.*

PHRV **allow for sb/sth** to think about possible problems when you are planning sth and include extra time, money, etc. for them: *The trip should take about two hours, allowing for heavy traffic.*

**al·low·ance** /ə'laʊəns/ ***noun*** [C] **1** an amount of sth that you are allowed: *Most flights have a 70 pound baggage allowance.* **2** an amount of money that you receive for a particular purpose: *Laura gets a weekly allowance of $5 from her parents.* ◇ *a travel allowance*

IDM **make allowances for sb/sth** to think about possible problems when you are planning sth and include extra time, money, etc. for them: *The design of the new school should make allowances for future increases in the student population.*

**al·loy** /'ælɔɪ/ ***noun*** [C,U] a metal that is formed by mixing two types of metal together, or by mixing metal with another substance: *Brass is an alloy of copper and zinc.*

★**all 'right** (*also informal* **al·right**) ***adj., adv., interjection*** **1** good or good enough; satisfactory: *Is everything all right?* **2** safe; not hurt; well: *The kids are all right. Don't worry.* ◇ *Do you feel all right?* **3** (showing you agree): *"You go first." "Oh, all right."*

NOTE Some people consider the informal spelling **alright** to be unacceptable in formal writing.

**'all-star** ***adj.*** (only *before* a noun) including many famous actors, players, etc.: *a movie with an all-star cast*

**,all-ter,rain 'vehicle** ***noun*** [C] = ATV

**al·lude** /ə'lud/ ***verb*** [I] **allude to sb/sth** (*formal*) to speak about sb/sth in an indirect way: *When he mentioned "certain problems," what was he alluding to?*

**al·lu·sion** /ə'luʒn/ ***noun*** [C,U] an act of speaking about sth indirectly: *The play is full of allusions to classical mythology.*

★**al·ly** /'ælaɪ; ə'laɪ/ ***noun*** [C] (*pl.* **al·lies**) **1** a person who helps and supports you, especially when other people are against you: *the President's political allies* **2** a country that has an agreement to support another country, especially in a war: *France and its European allies* ➲ Look at **alliance**. **3 the Allies** [pl.] the group of countries including Canada, the U.S. and Britain that fought together in the First and Second World Wars

**al·ma ma·ter** (*also* **Alma Mater**) /,ælmə 'mɑt̬ər; ,ɑl-/ ***noun*** [sing.] the school or university that sb went to: *I always enjoy going back to my alma mater, Ohio State.*

**al·might·y** /ɔl'maɪt̬i/ ***adj.*** **1** having the power to do anything: *Almighty God* **2** (only *before* a noun) (*informal*) very great: *Suddenly we heard the most almighty crash.* **3 the Almighty** ***noun*** [sing.] God

**al·mond** /'ɑmənd/ ***noun*** [C] an oval nut that is

often used in cooking: *almond cookies* ➲ picture at **nut**.

★**al·most** /ˈɔlmoʊst/ ***adv.*** not quite; very nearly: *By nine o'clock almost everybody had arrived.* ◇ *Careful! You almost spilled my drink!* ◇ *The show is almost over.*

**a·lo·ha** /əˈloʊhɑ/ ***interjection*** (used in Hawaii as a way of saying "hello" or "goodbye")

★**a·lone** /əˈloʊn/ ***adj.***, ***adv.*** **1** without any other person: *The old man lives alone.* ◇ *Are you alone? Can I talk to you for a minute?* ◇ *I don't like walking home alone after dark.*

NOTE **Alone**, **lonely** and **lonesome** all mean that you are not with other people. **Lonely** and **lonesome** mean that you are unhappy about this, but **alone** does not usually suggest either happiness or unhappiness. **Alone** cannot be used before a noun. You can also use **on your own** and **by yourself** to mean "alone." These expressions are more informal and very common in spoken English.

**2** (after a noun or pronoun) only: *You alone can help us.* ◇ *The food alone cost $40. The wine was extra.*

IDM **leave sb/sth alone** → LEAVE[1]
**let alone** → LET

★**a·long**[1] /əˈlɔŋ/ ***prep.*** **1** from one end to or toward the other end of sth: *I walked slowly along the beach.* **2** in a line that follows the side of sth long: *Wild flowers grew along both sides of the river.* **3** at a particular point on or beside sth long: *Our house is about halfway along Hope Street.*

★**a·long**[2] /əˈlɔŋ/ ***adv.*** **1** forward: *We moved along slowly with the crowd.* **2** with sb: *We're going out for lunch. Why don't you come along?*

IDM **all along** → ALL[2]
**along with sb/sth** together with sb/sth: *Along with hundreds of others, she lost her job when the factory closed.*

**a·long·side** /əˌlɔŋˈsaɪd/ ***adv.***, ***prep.*** **1** next to or along the side of sth: *a field with a small creek running alongside* ◇ *We parked alongside Ben's car.* **2** together with sb/sth: *the opportunity to work alongside experienced musicians*

**a·loof** /əˈluf/ ***adj.*** **1** not friendly or open to other people; distant **2** not involved in sth; apart: *The Bishop can no longer remain aloof from the problem.*

**a·loud** /əˈlaʊd/ ***adv.*** in a normal speaking voice that other people can hear; not silently: *to read aloud from a book* ➲ Look at **out loud**.

**al·pha** /ˈælfə/ ***noun*** (*symbol* Α, α) the first letter of the Greek alphabet ➲ Look at the note at **fraternity**.

**al·pha·bet** /ˈælfəbɛt/ ***noun*** [C] the set of letters that you use when you are writing a particular language, especially when they are arranged in a fixed order: *There are 26 letters in the English alphabet.*

**al·pha·bet·i·cal** /ˌælfəˈbɛt̬ɪkl/ ***adj.*** arranged in the same order as the letters of the alphabet: *The poems are listed in alphabetical order.* ▸ **al·pha·bet·i·cal·ly** /-kli/ ***adv.***

★**al·read·y** /ɔlˈrɛdi/ ***adv.*** **1** (used for talking about sth that has happened before now or before a particular time in the past, especially if it happened earlier than you expected): *"Would you like some lunch?" "No thanks, I've already eaten."* ◇ *We got there at 6:30, but Martin had already left.* ◇ *Sarah was already awake when I went into her room.* **2** (used in negative sentences and questions for expressing surprise) so early; as soon as this: *Have you finished already?* ◇ *You can't be leaving already!*

★**al·right** /ɔlˈraɪt/ ***adv.***, ***adj.***, ***interjection*** (*informal*) = ALL RIGHT

NOTE Some people find this spelling unacceptable in formal writing.

★**al·so** /ˈɔlsoʊ/ ***adv.*** (not with negative verbs) in addition; too: *Mark Wilson paints in his spare time. He also speaks Chinese.* ◇ *The food is wonderful, and also very cheap.*

NOTE **Too** is less formal than **also** and is very common in spoken English. **Also** usually goes before a main verb or after "is," "are," "were," etc.: *She also enjoys reading.* ◇ *He has also been to Australia.* ◇ *She is also intelligent.* **As well** is more formal than **also**. **Too** and **as well** usually go at the end of a phrase or sentence: *We're flying to Brazil, and we hope to visit Argentina too/as well.* Do not confuse **also** with **even**: *Even (NOT also) in the middle of summer, the nights can be cold.*

IDM **not only ... but also** → ONLY[2]

**al·tar** /ˈɔltər/ ***noun*** [C] the holy table in a church or temple

**al·ter** /ˈɔltər/ ***verb*** **1** [I,T] (*formal*) to make sth different in some way, but without changing it completely; to become different: *They've altered the plans for the new building.* ◇ *This does not alter the fact that the company is having serious financial difficulties.* ◇ *The town seems to have altered very little in the last twenty years.* **2** [T] to make changes to a piece of clothing so that it will fit you better: *This skirt is too big; I'll have to alter it.*

**al·ter·a·tion** /ˌɔltəˈreɪʃn/ ***noun*** [C,U] a small change in sb/sth: *He bought a new suit but it's still at the store for alterations.* ◇ *The airline will inform you of any alteration in the time of departure.*

**al·ter·nate**[1] /ˈɔltərnət/ ***adj.*** **1** one of every two: *He works alternate weeks* (= he works the first week, he doesn't work the second week, he works again the third week, etc.) **2** (used about two types of events/things) happening or following regularly one after the other: *There will be alternate periods of sun and showers tomorrow.* **3** that you can use, do, etc. instead of sth else: *an alternate entrance to a building* ▸ **al·ter·nate·ly** ***adv.***

**al·ter·nate**[2] /ˈɔltərneɪt/ ***verb*** **1** [I] **alternate with sth**; **alternate between A and B** (used about two types of events, things, etc.) to happen or follow regularly one after the other: *It's exciting music. Quiet passages alternate with sudden bursts of sound.* ◇ *She seemed to alternate between hating him and loving him.* **2** [T] **alternate A with B** to cause two types of events or things to happen or follow regularly one after the other: *He alternated periods of work with periods of rest.* ▸ **al·ter·na·tion** /ˌɔltərˈneɪʃn/ ***noun*** [C,U]

★**al·ter·na·tive**[1] /ɔlˈtərnət̬ɪv/ ***adj.*** **1** (only *before* a noun) that you can use, do, etc. instead of sth else: *an alternative site for a new building* **2** not traditional; not following or accepting the usual options, styles, etc.: *alternative music* ◇ *alternative*

A

lifestyles ▸ **al·ter·na·tive·ly** *adv.*: *You can pay in full now or, alternatively, in five monthly installments.*

**al·ter·na·tive**[2] /ɔl'tərnət̬ɪv/ *noun* [C] one of two things that you can choose between: *The senator suggested community service as an alternative to imprisonment.*

NOTE **Alternative** is often used for talking about more than two things: *There are several alternatives available to us right now.*

★ **al·though** /ɔl'ðoʊ/ *conj.* **1** (used for introducing a statement that makes the main statement in a sentence seem surprising): *Although she was tired, she stayed up to watch the late night movie on TV.* **2** (used for introducing a statement that modifies the main statement) and yet; but: *There will be heavy rain in many parts of the city tonight, although it is unlikely to reach the metro area until morning.*

NOTE You can also use **though** but it is less formal than **although**. **Even** can be used with **though** for emphasis, but not with **although**: *She didn't want to go to the party, although/though/even though she knew all her friends would be there.* **Though**, but not **although**, can be used at the end of a sentence: *She knew all her friends would be there. She didn't want to go, though.*

**al·ti·tude** /'æltətud/ *noun* **1** [sing.] the height of sth above sea level: *The plane climbed to an altitude of 30,000 feet.* **2** [usually pl.] a place that is high above sea level: *You need to carry oxygen when you are climbing at high altitudes.*

**al·to** /'æltoʊ/ *noun* [C] (*pl.* **al·tos**) the lowest normal singing voice for a woman, the highest for a man; a woman or man with this voice

★ **al·to·geth·er** /ˌɔltə'gɛðər/ *adv.* **1** completely: *That's an altogether different situation.* ◇ *At the age of 55, he stopped working altogether.* **2** including everything: *We've got about $65 altogether.* **3** when you consider everything; generally: *Altogether, I would call the project a success.*

NOTE **Altogether** is not the same as **all together**. **All together** means "everything or everybody together": *Put your books all together on the table.* ◇ *Let's sing. All together now!*

**a·lu·mi·num** /ə'lumənəm/ (*symbol* **Al**) *noun* [U] a light silver-colored metal that is used for making cooking equipment, etc.: *aluminum foil*

**a·lum·na** /ə'lʌmnə/ *noun* [C] (*pl.* **a·lum·nae** /ə'lʌmni/) (*formal*) a woman former student of a school, college or university

**a·lum·ni** /ə'lʌmnaɪ/ *noun* [pl.] former students of a school, college or university

**a·lum·nus** /ə'lʌmnəs/ (*also informal* **alum**) *noun* [C] (*pl.* **a·lum·ni** /ə'lʌmnaɪ/) (*formal*) a former male student of a school, college or university

★ **al·ways** /'ɔlweɪz/ *adv.* **1** at all times; regularly: *Why is the bus always late when I'm in a hurry?* **2** all through the past until now: *I've always liked music.* **3** forever: *I will always remember this moment.* **4** (with continuous tenses) again and again, usually in an annoying way: *She's always complaining about something.* **5** (used with "can" or "could" for suggesting sth that sb could do, especially if nothing else is possible): *If you don't have enough money, I could always loan you some.*

NOTE **Always** does not usually go at the beginning of a sentence. It usually goes before the main verb or after "is," "are," "were," etc.: *He always wears those shoes.* ◇ *I have always wanted to visit Egypt.* ◇ *Tammy is always late.* However, **always** can go at the beginning of a sentence when you are telling somebody to do something: *Always stop and look before you cross the street.*

**Alz·hei·mer's dis·ease** /'ɑltshaɪmərz dɪˌziz; 'ælts-/ (*also* **Alzheimer's**) *noun* [U] a serious disease, especially affecting older people, that prevents the brain from functioning normally and causes loss of memory, loss of ability to speak clearly, etc.

**A.M.** (*also* **a.m.**) /ˌeɪ 'ɛm/ *abbr.* before noon: *10 A.M.* (=10 o'clock in the morning)

**am** → BE[1,2]

**a·mass** /ə'mæs/ *verb* [T] to collect or put together a large quantity of sth: *We've amassed a lot of information on the subject.*

**am·a·teur**[1] /'æmətʃər/ *noun* [C] **1** a person who takes part in a sport or an activity for pleasure, not for money or as a job: *Only amateurs can take part in the tournament; no professionals will be allowed.* **2** (usually used when being critical) a person who does not have skill or experience when doing sth: *The repair work on this house was obviously done by a bunch of amateurs.*

**am·a·teur**[2] /'æmətʃər/ *adj.* **1** done, or doing sth, for pleasure (not for money or as a job): *an amateur photographer* **2** (*also* **amateurish**) done without skill or experience

★ **a·maze** /ə'meɪz/ *verb* [T] to surprise sb very much; to seem incredible to sb: *Sometimes your behavior amazes me!* ◇ *It amazes me that anybody could be so stupid!* ▸ **a·maze·ment** *noun* [U]: *He looked at me in amazement.* ◇ *To my amazement, I got an A on the test.*

★ **a·mazed** /ə'meɪzd/ *adj.* extremely surprised; feeling that you cannot believe sth: *She was amazed to discover the truth about her husband.* ◇ *I was amazed by the change in his attitude.*

★ **a·maz·ing** /ə'meɪzɪŋ/ *adj.* causing you to be very surprised: *She has shown amazing courage.* ◇ *I have an amazing story to tell you.* ▸ **a·maz·ing·ly** *adv.*: *It's an amazingly expensive country to visit.*

**am·bas·sa·dor** /æm'bæsədər; əm-/ *noun* [C] a diplomat of high rank who represents his/her country in a foreign country: *the United States Ambassador to Canada*

NOTE The ambassador lives and works in an **embassy**.

**am·ber** /'æmbər/ *noun* [U] **1** a hard clear yellow-brown substance used for making jewelry or ornaments **2** a yellow-brown color ▸ **am·ber** *adj.*

**am·bi·gu·i·ty** /ˌæmbə'gyuət̬i/ *noun* [C,U] (*pl.* **am·bi·gu·i·ties**) the possibility of being understood in more than one way; sth that can be understood in more than one way

**am·big·u·ous** /ˌæmˈbɪgyuəs/ ***adj.*** having more than one possible meaning: *That's an awfully ambiguous statement – what exactly do you mean?* ▸ **am·big·u·ous·ly** ***adv.***

★**am·bi·tion** /æmˈbɪʃn/ ***noun*** **1 ambition (to be/do sth)** [U] strong desire to be successful, to have power, etc.: *One problem with young people today is their lack of ambition.* **2** [C] something that you very much want to have or do: *It's always been her ambition to travel around the world.*

**am·bi·tious** /æmˈbɪʃəs/ ***adj.*** **1 ambitious (to be/do sth)** having a strong desire to be successful, to have power, etc.: *I'm not particularly ambitious – I'm content with my life the way it is.* **2** difficult to achieve or do because it takes a lot of work or effort: *The company has announced ambitious plans for expansion.*

**am·biv·a·lent** /æmˈbɪvələnt/ ***adj.*** having or showing a mixture of feelings or opinions about sth or sb: *I've always felt somewhat ambivalent about having children.* ▸ **am·biv·a·lence** ***noun*** [U]

**am·bu·lance** /ˈæmbyələns/ ***noun*** [C] a special vehicle for taking sick or injured people to the hospital

**am·bush** /ˈæmbʊʃ/ ***noun*** [C] a surprise attack from a hidden position ▸ **am·bush** ***verb*** [T]

**a·men** (*also* **A·men**) /eɪˈmɛn; ɑˈmɛn/ ***interjection*** (used at the end of a prayer by Christians and Jews) let this be so: *In the name of the Father, the Son and the Holy Ghost, Amen.*

**a·me·na·ble** /əˈminəbl; əˈmɛn-/ ***adj.*** willing to accept sth; willing to be guided: *I'm amenable to any suggestions you might have.*

**a·mend** /əˈmɛnd/ ***verb*** [T] to change sth slightly, often in order to make it better: *The law needs to be amended.*

**a·mend·ment** /əˈmɛndmənt/ ***noun*** **1** [C,U] a change or improvement that is made to a law or a document; the process of changing a law or a document: *She made several minor amendments to her paper.* **2** (often **Amendment**) [C] a statement of a change to the Constitution of the U.S: *The 19th Amendment gave women the right to vote.*

**a·mends** /əˈmɛndz/ ***noun*** [pl.]
**IDM make amends (for sth)** to do sth for sb, that shows that you are sorry for sth bad that you have done before: *I bought her a present to make amends for the horrible things I had said to her.*

**a·men·i·ty** /əˈmɛnət̬i/ ***noun*** [C] (*pl.* **a·men·i·ties**) something in a place that helps to make being there pleasant or easy: *The health club offers a sauna, beauty salon, cafeteria and many other amenities.*

★**A·mer·i·can**[1] /əˈmɛrɪkən/ ***adj.*** from or connected with the U.S: *Have you met Bob? He's American.* ◇ *American history* ➲ Look also at **Latin American**.

★**A·mer·i·can**[2] /əˈmɛrɪkən/ ***noun*** [C] a person who comes from the U.S: *His wife is an American.* ➲ Look also at **African-American** and **Asian-American**.

**Aˈmerican cheese** (*U.S.*) ***noun*** [U] a kind of soft cheese which is orange in color and is usually sold in thin slices wrapped in plastic

**Aˌmerican ˈIndian** ***adj.***, ***noun*** [C] = NATIVE AMERICAN

**a·mi·a·ble** /ˈeɪmiəbl/ ***adj.*** friendly and pleasant ▸ **a·mi·a·bly** ***adv.***

**am·i·ca·ble** /ˈæmɪkəbl/ ***adj.*** made or done in a friendly way, without argument: *I'm sure we can find an amicable way of settling the dispute.* ▸ **am·i·ca·bly** ***adv.***

**a·mid** /əˈmɪd/ (*also* **a·midst** /əˈmɪdst/) ***prep.*** (*formal*) in the middle of; among: *Amid all the confusion, the thieves got away.*

**a·miss** /əˈmɪs/ ***adj.***, ***adv.*** (not before a noun) wrong; not as it should be: *When I walked into the room, I could sense that something was amiss.*

**am·mu·ni·tion** /ˌæmyəˈnɪʃn/ ***noun*** [U] **1** the supply of bullets, etc. that you need to fire from a weapon: *The troops surrendered because they had run out of ammunition.* **2** information that can be used against sb in an argument

**am·ne·sia** /æmˈniʒə/ ***noun*** [U] a medical condition in which sb partly or completely loses his/her memory

**am·nes·ty** /ˈæmnəsti/ ***noun*** [C] (*pl.* **am·nes·ties**) **1** a time when a government forgives crimes, especially political crimes **2** a time when people can admit that they have done sth illegal or wrong, without fear of punishment: *The library has announced an amnesty on overdue books.*

★**a·mong** /əˈmʌŋ/ (*also* **a·mongst** /əˈmʌŋst/) ***prep.*** **1** surrounded by; in the middle of: *I often feel nervous when I'm among strangers.* ◇ *The modern skyscraper looks out of place among all the old buildings.* ◇ *I found the missing letter among a heap of old newspapers.* ➲ picture at **between**[1]. **2** in the group or number of: *She is among the town's wealthiest residents.* ◇ *Among the city's attractions are a number of important museums.* **3** to each one (of a group): *On his death, his money will be divided among his children.* **4** inside (a group): *Discuss it among yourselves and let me know your decision.* ➲ Look at the note at **between**[1].

**a·mor·al** /eɪˈmɔrəl; -ˈmɑr-/ ***adj.*** not following any moral rules and not caring about right and wrong: *Guy was greedy, amoral and dishonest.* ➲ Look also at **immoral** and **moral**. ▸ **a·mo·ral·i·ty** /ˌeɪməˈræləṭi/ ***noun*** [U]

★**a·mount**[1] /əˈmaʊnt/ ***noun*** [C] **1** the amount of sth is how much of it there is; a quantity of sth: *I spent a huge amount of time preparing for the exam.* ◇ *I have a certain amount of sympathy for her.* **2** a total or a sum of money: *You are requested to pay the full amount within seven days.*

**a·mount**[2] /əˈmaʊnt/ ***verb*** [I] **amount to sth** **1** to add up to sth; to total sth: *The cost of the repairs amounted to $5,000.* **2** to be the same as sth: *No matter whether I tell her today or tomorrow, it amounts to the same thing.*

**amp** /æmp/ ***noun*** [C] **1** (*also formal* **ampere** /ˈæmpɪr/) (*symbol* **A**) a unit for measuring electric current **2** (*informal*) = AMPLIFIER: *a guitar amp*

**am·per·sand** /ˈæmpərsænd/ ***noun*** [C] the symbol (&) used to mean "and": *She works for AT&T.*

**am·phet·a·mine** /æmˈfɛṭəmin/ ***noun*** [C,U] a type of drug that makes your heart beat faster and that makes you feel excited. Amphetamines are sometimes taken illegally.

A

**am·phib·i·an** /æmˈfɪbiən/ ***noun*** [C] any animal that can live both on land and in water: *frogs, toads and other amphibians* ➲ Compare **reptile**.

**am·ple** /ˈæmpl/ ***adj.*** **1** enough or more than enough: *We have ample time to make a decision.* ◇ *I'm not sure how much the trip will cost, but I should think $500 will be ample.* **2** large; having a great deal of space ▸ **am·ply** /ˈæmpli/ ***adv.***: *The report amply demonstrates whose fault it was.*

**am·pli·fi·er** /ˈæmpləˌfaɪər/ (*also informal* **amp**) ***noun*** [C] a piece of electrical equipment for making sounds louder or signals stronger

**am·pli·fy** /ˈæmpləfaɪ/ ***verb*** [T] (*pres. part.* **am·pli·fy·ing**; *3rd person sing. pres.* **am·pli·fies**; *pt, pp* **am·pli·fied**) **1** to increase the strength of a sound, using electrical equipment **2** to add details to sth in order to explain it more fully ▸ **am·pli·fi·ca·tion** /ˌæmpləfəˈkeɪʃn/ ***noun*** [U]

**am·pu·tate** /ˈæmpyəteɪt/ ***verb*** [I,T] to cut off a person's arm or leg (or part of it) for medical reasons: *His leg was so badly injured that it had to be amputated.* ▸ **am·pu·ta·tion** /ˌæmpyəˈteɪʃn/ ***noun*** [C,U]

★**a·muse** /əˈmyuz/ ***verb*** [T] **1** to make sb laugh or smile; to seem funny to sb: *His jokes always amused her.* **2** to make time pass pleasantly for sb; to stop sb from getting bored: *I did some crossword puzzles to amuse myself on the trip.* ◇ *I brought a few toys to amuse the kids.*

**a·mused** /əˈmyuzd/ ***adj.*** if you are amused you think that sth is funny and it makes you want to laugh or smile: *You might think it's funny, but I'm not amused.* ◇ *I was amused to hear his account of what happened.*

IDM **keep sb amused** to make sb pass the time pleasantly, without getting bored: *These magazines should keep you amused while you're waiting for me to finish in the kitchen.*

**a·muse·ment** /əˈmyuzmənt/ ***noun*** **1** [U] the feeling caused by sth that makes you laugh or smile, or by sth that entertains you and that stops you from being bored: *There was a look of amusement on his face.* ◇ *Much to the students' amusement, the teacher fell off his chair.* **2** [C] a machine, game, etc. that you can play on for enjoyment

**aˈmusement park** ***noun*** [C] an open area with games for people to play and machines for them to ride on (**rides**): *The "Wild West Train" was my favorite ride at the amusement park.*

★**a·mus·ing** /əˈmyuzɪŋ/ ***adj.*** causing you to laugh or smile: *an amusing story*

**an** → A²

**an·aes·thet·ic** = ANESTHETIC

**an·aes·thet·ist** = ANESTHETIST

**an·aes·the·tize** = ANESTHETIZE

**an·a·gram** /ˈænəgræm/ ***noun*** [C] a word or phrase that is made by arranging the letters of another word or phrase in a different order: *"Worth" is an anagram of "throw."*

**a·nal·o·gy** /əˈnælədʒi/ ***noun*** [C] (*pl.* **a·nal·o·gies**) **an analogy (between A and B)** a comparison between two things that shows a way in which they are similar: *You could make an analogy between the human body and a car engine.*

IDM **by analogy** if you explain sth by analogy to sth else, you compare it to the other thing and show how it is similar

★**a·nal·y·sis** /əˈnæləsɪs/ ***noun*** (*pl.* **a·nal·y·ses** /-siz/) **1** [C,U] the careful examination of the different parts or details of sth: *Some samples of the water were sent to a laboratory for analysis.* ◇ *They carried out an analysis of the causes of the problem.* **2** [C] the result of such an examination: *Your analysis of the situation is different from mine.*

**an·a·lyst** /ˈænəlɪst/ ***noun*** [C] a person whose job is to analyze things as an expert: *a political analyst*

**an·a·lyt·ic** /ˌænəˈlɪt̬ɪk/ (*also* **an·a·lyt·i·cal** /-kl/) ***adj.*** looking carefully at the different parts of sth in order to understand or explain it: *analytic techniques*

★**an·a·lyze** /ˈænəlaɪz/ ***verb*** [T] to look at or think about the different parts or details of sth carefully in order to understand or explain it: *The water samples are now being analyzed in a laboratory.* ◇ *to analyze statistics* ◇ *She analyzed the situation and then decided what to do.*

**an·ar·chist** /ˈænərkɪst/ ***noun*** [C] a person who believes that there should be no government or laws in a country, especially one who takes action to achieve this

**an·ar·chy** /ˈænərki/ ***noun*** [U] a situation in which people do not obey rules and laws; a situation in which there is no government in a country

**a·nat·o·my** /əˈnæt̬əmi/ ***noun*** (*pl.* **a·nat·o·mies**) **1** [U] the scientific study of the structure of human or animal bodies **2** [C] the structure of a living thing: *the anatomy of the frog* ▸ **an·a·tom·i·cal** /ˌænəˈtɑmɪkl/ ***adj.***

★**an·ces·tor** /ˈænsɛstər/ ***noun*** [C] a person in your family who lived a long time before you, from whom you are descended: *My ancestors settled in this country two hundred years ago.*

**an·ces·try** /ˈænsɛstri/ ***noun*** [C,U] (*pl.* **an·ces·tries**) all of a person's ancestors, when you think of them as a group: *He was of Irish ancestry.*

**an·chor¹** /ˈæŋkər/ ***noun*** [C] **1** a heavy metal object at the end of a chain or rope that you drop into the water from a boat in order to keep the boat in one place **2** (*also* **an·chor·man, an·chor·wom·an**) (*pl.* **an·chor·men; an·chor·wom·en**) a person whose job is to read the news on TV and to introduce news reports from other people: *a network news anchor*

**an·chor²** /ˈæŋkər/ ***verb*** **1** [I,T] to drop an ANCHOR¹; to stop a boat from moving by using an ANCHOR¹: *We anchored the boat in the harbor and went ashore.* **2** [T] to fasten sth firmly so that it is held in place and cannot move: *They anchored the tent with strong ropes.* **3** [T] to read the news on TV and introduce news reports from other people: *She anchors the 11 o'clock news broadcast.*

★**an·cient** /ˈeɪnʃənt/ ***adj.*** **1** belonging to or connected with the distant past: *ancient civilizations* **2** having existed for a long time: *This ceremony is an ancient Native American tradition.* **3** (*informal*) very old: *I can't believe he's only 30 – he looks ancient!*

★**and** /ənd; ən; *also* n; *especially after* t; *and* d; *strong*

A

*form* ænd/ ***conj.*** **1** (used to connect words or parts of sentences) also; in addition to: *bread and butter* ◇ *one woman, two men and three children* ◇ *a boy and a girl* ◇ *an apple and a pear* ◇ *Do it slowly and carefully.* ◇ *We sang and danced all night.*

NOTE When the two things are closely linked, you do not need to repeat the "a," etc.: *a knife and fork* ◇ *my mother and father*

**2** (used when you are saying numbers) plus: *Twelve and six is eighteen.* ◇ *It cost me a hundred and sixty dollars.*

NOTE When you are saying large numbers, *and* is often used after the word "hundred": *We say 2,264 as two thousand, two hundred (and) sixty-four.*

**3** then; following this or that: *Come in and sit down.* **4** as a result of this or that; because of this or that: *It was a terrible shock and he was very upset.* ◇ *Say that again and I'll lose my temper.* **5** (used between repeated words to show that sth is increasing or continuing): *The situation is getting worse and worse.* ◇ *I shouted and shouted, but nobody answered.* **6** (used instead of "to" after certain verbs, e.g. "go," "come," "try"): *Go and answer the door for me, will you?* ◇ *I'll try and find out what's going on.* ◇ *Why don't you come and stay with us for the weekend?*

**an·ec·dote** /ˈænɪkdoʊt/ ***noun*** [C] a short interesting story about a real person or event

**a·ne·mi·a** /əˈnimiə/ ***noun*** [U] a medical condition in which there are not enough red cells in the blood ▸ **a·ne·mic** /əˈnimɪk/ ***adj.***

**an·es·the·si·ol·o·gist** /ˌænəsˌθiziˈɑlədʒɪst/ ***noun*** [C] a doctor who studies the use of anesthetics

**an·es·thet·ic** (*also* **anaesthetic**) /ˌænəsˈθɛt̬ɪk/ ***noun*** [C,U] a substance that stops you from feeling pain, e.g. when a doctor is performing an operation on you: *You'll be under anesthetic during the operation.* ◇ *a local anesthetic* (= one that only affects part of the body and does not make you unconscious) ◇ *a general anesthetic* (= one that makes you unconscious)

**a·nes·thet·ist** (*also* **anaesthetist**) /əˈnɛsθət̬ɪst/ ***noun*** [C] a person who is trained to give anesthetics to patients

**a·nes·the·tize** (*also* **anaesthetize**) /əˈnɛsθətaɪz/ ***verb*** [T] to give an anesthetic to sb

**a·new** /əˈnu/ ***adv.*** (*formal*) again; in a new or different way

**an·gel** /ˈeɪndʒl/ ***noun*** [C] **1** (especially in the Christian religion) a spirit that lives with God in Heaven. In pictures, angels are often dressed in white, with wings **2** a person who is very kind or easy to love: *Be an angel and wash these clothes for me, will you?* ◇ *The baby was a perfect little angel – she slept all afternoon.*

**an·gel·ic** /ænˈdʒɛlɪk/ ***adj.*** looking or acting like an angel ▸ **an·gel·i·cal·ly** ***adv.*** /-kli/

★**an·ger**[1] /ˈæŋgər/ ***noun*** [U] the strong feeling that you have when sth has happened or sb has done sth that you do not like: *He could not hide his anger at the news.* ◇ *She was shaking with anger.* ➲ adjective angry

**an·ger**[2] /ˈæŋgər/ ***verb*** [T] to cause sb to become angry: *It angers me that such things can be allowed to happen.*

**angles**

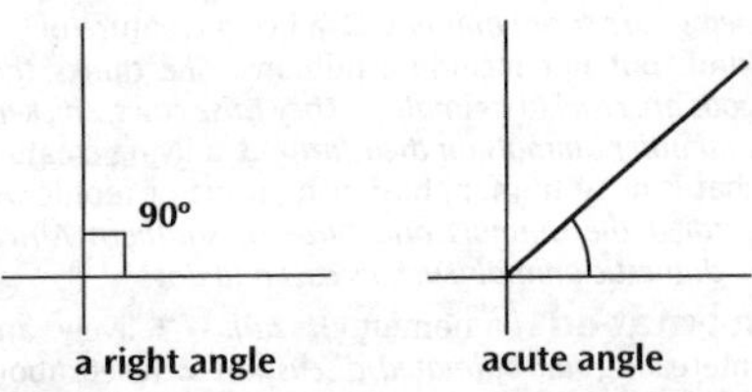


★**an·gle**[1] /ˈæŋgl/ ***noun*** [C] **1** the space between two lines or surfaces that meet, measured in degrees: *a right angle* (= an angle of 90°) ◇ *at an angle of 40°* ◇ *The three angles of a triangle add up to 180°.* **2** the direction from which you look at sth: *Viewed from this angle, the building looks bigger than it really is.* ◇ *If we look at the problem from another angle, it might be easier to solve it.*

IDM **at an angle** not straight: *This hat is meant to be worn at an angle.*

**an·gle**[2] /ˈæŋgl/ ***verb*** [I] to try and make sb give you sth, without asking for it directly: *She was angling for a free ticket to the game.*

**an·gler** /ˈæŋglər/ ***noun*** [C] (*formal*) a person who catches fish as a hobby

**An·gli·can** /ˈæŋglɪkən/ ***noun*** [C] a member of the official church of England, or of a related church in another English-speaking country

**An·glo** /ˈæŋgloʊ/ ***noun*** [C] (*pl.* **An·glos**) **1** (*especially US*) a white, English-speaking person whose family originally came from Europe, especially northern Europe **2** (*Cdn informal*) = ANGLOPHONE ▸ **An·glo** ***adj.***: *relations between Hispanic and Anglo students* ◇ *a group of Anglo students from Montreal*

**Anglo-** /æŋgloʊ/ ***prefix*** (in compounds) English or British; connected with England or Britain (and another country or countries): *Anglo-American relations*

**an·glo·phone** /ˈæŋgləfoʊn/ ***noun*** [C] (*Cdn*) an English-speaking person ▸ **an·glo·phone** ***adj.***

**An·glo-Sax·on** /ˌæŋgloʊ ˈsæksən/ ***noun*** [C] **1** a person whose ancestors were English **2** an English person of the period before the French came to power in England in 1066 (**the Norman Conquest**) ▸ **An·glo-Sax·on** ***adj.***: *Anglo-Saxon kings*

★**an·gry** /ˈæŋgri/ ***adj.*** (**an·gri·er**; **an·gri·est**) **angry (with sb) (at/about sth)**; **angry (at sb) (about sth)** feeling or showing anger: *Calm down – there's no need to get angry.* ◇ *My parents will be really angry if I get home late.* ◇ *I'm angry at them for letting me down at the last minute.* ▸ **an·gri·ly** /-əli/ ***adv.***

**angst** /ɑŋst; æŋst/ ***noun*** [U] a feeling of anxiety and sadness about your life

**an·guish** /ˈæŋgwɪʃ/ ***noun*** [U] great pain or suffering, especially of a mental kind: *The newspaper reported on the mother's anguish at the death of her son.* ▸ **an·guished** ***adj.***: *There was an anguished expression in his eyes.*

**an·gu·lar** /ˈæŋgyələr/ ***adj.*** with sharp points or

corners: *an angular face* (= one where you can see the bones clearly)

★**an·i·mal** /ˈænəml/ ***noun*** [C] **1** a living creature that is not a plant: *the animal kingdom* ◇ *Human beings are social animals.* **2** a living creature of this kind, but not including humans: *She thinks that zoos are cruel to animals.* ◇ *They raise cows, chickens and other animals on their farm.* **3** a living creature that is not a human, bird, fish, insect or reptile: *He studied the animals and birds of southern Africa.* ◇ *domestic animals such as cats and dogs*

**an·i·mat·ed** /ˈænəmeɪt̬əd/ ***adj.*** **1** lively and interesting: *an animated discussion* **2** (used about movies) using a technique by which drawings appear to move: *an animated cartoon*

**an·i·ma·tion** /ˌænəˈmeɪʃn/ ***noun*** [U] **1** the state of being lively: *She spoke with great animation on the subject.* **2** the technique of making movies, videos and computer games with drawings that appear to move

★**an·kle** /ˈæŋkl/ ***noun*** [C] the part of the body where the foot joins the leg: *I tripped and sprained my ankle.* ➲ picture on study page **A32**.

**an·nex**[1] /əˈnɛks; ˈænɛks/ ***verb*** [T] to take possession and control of another country or region: *Many people think that the dictator plans to annex the two neighboring countries.* ▸ **an·nex·a·tion** /ˌænɪkˈseɪʃn; ˌænɛk-/ ***noun*** [C,U]: *the annexation of Austria by Nazi Germany*

**an·nex**[2] /ˈænɛks/ ***noun*** [C] a building that is joined to or near a larger one

**an·ni·hi·late** /əˈnaɪəleɪt/ ***verb*** [T] to destroy or defeat sb/sth completely: *The army was annihilated in the battle.* ▸ **an·ni·hi·la·tion** /əˌnaɪəˈleɪʃn/ ***noun*** [U]: *Modern weapons have placed mankind in danger of annihilation.*

★**an·ni·ver·sa·ry** /ˌænɪˈvərsəri/ ***noun*** [C] (*pl.* **an·ni·ver·sa·ries**) a day that is exactly a year or a number of years after a special or important event: *the hundredth anniversary of the country's independence* ◇ *a twenty-fifth wedding anniversary* ➲ Look at **birthday**.

**an·no·tat·ed** /ˈænəteɪt̬əd/ ***adj.*** (used about a book, etc.) with notes added to it that explain and give extra information about the contents: *an annotated bibliography*

★**an·nounce** /əˈnaʊns/ ***verb*** [T] **1** to make sth known publicly, in an official way: *We are pleased to announce the opening of our new store.* ◇ *The winners will be announced in next week's paper.* **2** to say sth in a loud voice or in an aggressive way: *She stormed into my office and announced that she was quitting.*

**an·nounce·ment** /əˈnaʊnsmənt/ ***noun*** **1** [C] a statement that tells people about sth: *I have an important announcement to make.* **2** [U] the act of telling people about sth: *The announcement of the award winners will be broadcast live on TV.*

**an·nounc·er** /əˈnaʊnsər/ ***noun*** [C] a person who introduces or gives information about programs on radio or television

★**an·noy** /əˈnɔɪ/ ***verb*** [T] to make sb fairly angry: *It really annoys me when you act like that.*

**an·noy·ance** /əˈnɔɪəns/ ***noun*** **1** [U] the feeling of being annoyed: *To her annoyance, the neighbor's dog barked all night long.* **2** [C] something that annoys sb: *Low-flying planes are an annoyance in this area.*

★**an·noyed** /əˈnɔɪd/ ***adj.*** angry or fairly angry: *She's annoyed at herself for making such a stupid mistake.* ◇ *He's annoyed that nobody believes him.* ◇ *I was annoyed to see that they had left the door open.*

★**an·noy·ing** /əˈnɔɪɪŋ/ ***adj.*** making you feel fairly angry: *That constant hammering noise is really annoying.*

★**an·nu·al** /ˈænyuəl/ ***adj.*** **1** happening or done once a year or every year: *the company's annual report* ◇ *an annual event* **2** for the period of one year: *Her annual income is $30,000.* ▸ **an·nu·al·ly** ***adv.***: *China produces about 60 tons of gold annually.*

**a·nom·a·lous** /əˈnɑmələs/ ***adj.*** (*formal*) different from what is normal or expected: *He is in an anomalous position as the only part-time employee in the firm.*

**a·nom·a·ly** /əˈnɑməli/ ***noun*** [C] (*pl.* **a·nom·a·lies**) **anomaly (in sth)** a thing, situation, etc. that is different from what is normal or expected: *the many anomalies in the tax system*

**an·o·nym·i·ty** /ˌænəˈnɪmət̬i/ ***noun*** [U] the situation where a person's name is not known

**a·non·y·mous** /əˈnɑnəməs/ ***adj.*** **1** (used about a person) with a name that is not known or made public: *An anonymous caller told the police that the robbery was going to take place.* **2** done, written, given, etc. by sb whose name is not known or made public: *He received an anonymous letter.* ▸ **a·non·y·mous·ly** ***adv.***

**an·o·rex·i·a** /ˌænəˈrɛksiə/ (*also formal* **anorexia nervosa** /-nərˈvoʊsə/) ***noun*** [U] an illness that makes sb believe he/she is fat and so stop eating, which can cause a dangerous loss of weight ▸ **an·o·rex·ic** /ˌænəˈrɛksɪk/ ***adj.***, ***noun*** [C]

★**an·oth·er** /əˈnʌðər/ ***det.***, ***pronoun*** **1** one more; an additional thing or person: *Would you like another drink?* ◇ *They have three kids already and now they're going to have another.* ◇ *Is this another one of your stupid jokes?* **2** a different thing or person: *I'm sorry, but I can't see you tomorrow. Could we arrange to meet another day?* ◇ *They spent hours at the exhibit, walking from one display to another.*

IDM **one after another/the other** → ONE[1]

**one another** → ONE[2]

★**an·swer**[1] /ˈænsər/ ***verb*** [I,T] **1** to say or write sth back to sb who has asked you sth: *I asked her what the matter was, but she didn't answer.* ◇ *I asked you a question; now please answer me.* ◇ *Answer all the questions on the form.* ◇ *When I asked him how much he earned, he answered that it was none of my business.*

NOTE **Answer** and **reply** are the most common verbs used for speaking or writing in reaction to questions, letters, etc.: *I asked him a question, but he didn't answer.* ◇ *I sent my application, but they haven't replied yet.* Note that you **answer** a person, a question or a letter (no "to"), but you **reply to** a letter. **Respond** is less common and more formal with this meaning: *Applicants must respond within seven days.* It is more commonly used with the meaning of "reacting in a way that is desired": *Despite all the doctor's efforts, the patient did not respond to treatment.*

**2** to do sth as a reply: *I rang their doorbell but nobody answered.* ◇ *He hasn't answered my letter yet* (= written a letter back to me).

PHR V **answer for sb/sth** to accept responsibility or blame for sb/sth: *Somebody will have to answer for all the damage that has been caused.*

★**an·swer²** /ˈænsər/ ***noun*** [C] **answer (to sb/sth) 1** something that you say, write or do as a reply: *The answer to your question is that I don't know.* ◇ *I wrote to them two weeks ago, and I'm still waiting for an answer.* ◇ *I knocked on the door and waited, but there was no answer.* **2** a solution to a problem: *I didn't have any money, so the only answer was to borrow some.* **3** something that is written or said, trying to give the correct information asked for on a test or exam: *What was the answer to the last question?* ◇ *to choose the right/wrong answer*

**an·swer·a·ble** /ˈænsərəbl/ ***adj.*** **answerable to sb (for sth)** having to explain and give good reasons for your actions to sb; responsible to sb

**ˈan·swer·ing maˌchine** ***noun*** [C] a machine that answers the telephone and records messages from callers: *I called his house and left a message on his answering machine.*

**ant** /ænt/ ***noun*** [C] a very small insect with no wings that lives in large groups and works very hard ➲ picture at **insect**.

**an·tag·o·nism** /ænˈtæɡənɪzəm/ ***noun*** [C,U] **antagonism (toward sb/sth)**; **antagonism (between A and B)** a feeling of hate and of being opposed to sb/sth

**an·tag·o·nist** /ænˈtæɡənɪst/ ***noun*** [C] a person who opposes sb and tries to make him/her angry or annoyed

**an·tag·o·nis·tic** /ænˌtæɡəˈnɪstɪk/ ***adj.*** **antagonistic (toward sb/sth)** unfriendly; showing that you disagree with sb/sth

**an·tag·o·nize** /ænˈtæɡənaɪz/ ***verb*** [T] to make sb angry or to annoy sb: *She tends to antagonize people with her outspoken remarks.*

**Ant·arc·tic** /æntˈɑrktɪk; -ˈɑrt̬ɪk/ ***adj.*** connected with the coldest, most southern parts of the world (Antarctica): *an Antarctic expedition* ➲ Look at **Arctic**. ➲ picture at **earth**.

**an·te·bel·lum** /ˌæntiˈbɛləm/ ***adj.*** connected with the period of time before the beginning of the Civil War in the U.S., in 1861: *one of the finest antebellum mansions in the South*

**an·te·lope** /ˈæntəloʊp/ ***noun*** [C] (*pl.* **an·te·lope** or **an·te·lopes**) an animal with horns that has long, thin legs, looks like a deer and can run very fast. It is found especially in Africa.

**an·ten·na** /ænˈtɛnə/ ***noun*** [C] **1** (*pl.* **an·ten·nas**) a long metal stick on a building, car, etc. that receives radio or television signals ➲ Picture on study page **A31**. **2** (*pl.* **an·ten·nae** /-ni/) one of the two long thin parts on the heads of insects and some animals that live in shells. It is used for feeling things.

**an·them** /ˈænθəm/ ***noun*** [C] a serious song, especially one that is sung on special occasions: *the national anthem* (= the special song of a country)

**an·thol·o·gy** /ænˈθɑlədʒi/ ***noun*** [C] (*pl.* **an·thol·o·gies**) a book that contains pieces of written work or poems, often on the same subject, by different authors: *an anthology of love poetry*

**an·thrax** /ˈænθræks/ ***noun*** [U] a serious disease that affects sheep and cows and sometimes people, and can cause death

**an·thro·pol·o·gy** /ˌænθrəˈpɑlədʒi/ ***noun*** [U] the study of human beings, especially of their origin, development, customs and beliefs

**an·ti·bi·ot·ic** /ˌæntɪbaɪˈɑt̬ɪk/ ***noun*** [C] a medicine which is used for destroying bacteria and curing infections: *The doctor gave me some antibiotics for a chest infection.*

**an·ti·bod·y** /ˈæntɪˌbɑdi/ ***noun*** [C] (*pl.* **an·ti·bod·ies**) a substance that the body produces in the blood to fight disease

★**an·tic·i·pate** /ænˈtɪsəpeɪt/ ***verb*** [T] to expect sth to happen (and to prepare for it): *to anticipate a problem* ◇ *Strong winds are anticipated in the northern part of the state this weekend.* ◇ *I anticipate that the situation will get worse.*

**an·tic·i·pa·tion** /ænˌtɪsəˈpeɪʃn/ ***noun*** [U] **1** the state of expecting sth to happen (and preparing for it): *We bought a lot of groceries in anticipation of the blizzard.* **2** the state of feeling excited about sth that is going to happen: *An air of anticipation filled the town before the centennial celebration.*

**an·ti·cli·max** /ˌæntiˈklaɪmæks/ ***noun*** [C,U] an event, etc. that is less exciting than you had expected or than what has already happened: *The ending of the movie was a big anticlimax.*

**an·tics** /ˈæntɪks/ ***noun*** [pl.] funny, strange or silly ways of behaving: *The audience roared with laughter at the clown's antics.*

**an·ti·de·pres·sant** /ˌæntidɪˈprɛsnt; ˌæntaɪ-/ ***noun*** [C] a drug used to treat depression ▸ **an·ti·de·pres·sant** ***adj.*** (only *before* a noun): *antidepressant drugs*

**an·ti·dote** /ˈæntɪdoʊt/ ***noun*** [C] **1** a medical substance that is used to prevent a poison or a disease from having an effect: *an antidote to snake bites* **2** anything that helps you to deal with sth unpleasant: *Many people find music a marvelous antidote to stress.*

**an·ti·freeze** /ˈæntɪfriz/ ***noun*** [U] a liquid that you add to the water in the cooling system of a car, etc. to prevent it from freezing

**an·ti·pas·to** /ˌæntiˈpɑstoʊ/ ***noun*** [C] (*pl.* **an·ti·pas·ti** /-ti/) (in Italian cooking) a small amount of food such as cheese, olives or meat, which you eat before the main part of a meal SYN **appetizer**

**an·tip·a·thy** /ænˈtɪpəθi/ ***noun*** [U] **antipathy (to/toward sb/sth)** (a strong feeling of) dislike: *I experienced a feeling of antipathy toward him.*

**an·ti·per·spi·rant** /ˌæntiˈpərspərent/ ***noun*** [C,U] a substance that people use, especially under their arms, to prevent or reduce sweat ➲ Look also at **deodorant**.

**an·ti·quat·ed** /ˈæntɪkweɪt̬əd/ ***adj.*** (of things or

A

ideas) old-fashioned and no longer suitable for modern conditions

**an·tique**[1] /æn'tik/ ***adj.*** very old and therefore unusual and valuable: *an antique vase/table*

**an·tique**[2] /æn'tik/ ***noun*** [C] an old and valuable object, e.g. a piece of furniture: *He collects antiques.* ◇ *an antique shop* (= one that sells antiques) ◇ *That vase is an antique.*

**an·tiq·ui·ty** /æn'tɪkwət̬i/ ***noun*** (*pl.* **an·tiq·ui·ties**) **1** [U] a time hundreds of years ago, especially the time of the Egyptians, Greeks or Romans: *myths and legends from antiquity* **2** [C, usually pl.] a building, work of art or other object that remains from ancient times: *Greek/Roman antiquities* **3** [U] great age: *priceless objects of great antiquity*

**an·ti-Se·mit·ic** /ˌæntisə'mɪt̬ɪk; ˌæntaɪ-/ ***adj.*** connected with hatred of Jewish people: *anti-Semitic remarks/incidents*

**an·ti-Se·mi·tism** /ˌænti'sɛmətɪzəm; ˌæntaɪ-/ ***noun*** [U] hatred or unfair treatment of Jewish people

**an·ti·sep·tic** /ˌæntə'sɛptɪk/ ***noun*** [C,U] a liquid or cream that prevents a cut, etc. from becoming infected: *Put some antiseptic on that scratch.* ▸ **an·ti·sep·tic *adj.***: *antiseptic cream*

**an·ti·so·cial** /ˌænti'soʊʃəl; ˌæntaɪ-/ ***adj.*** **1** not considered acceptable by other people or the rest of society: *antisocial behavior/activities* ◇ *Some people regard smoking as antisocial.* **2** not willing to be with other people; unfriendly: *We don't go out much. I guess we're pretty antisocial.*

**an·tith·e·sis** /æn'tɪθəsɪs/ ***noun*** [C,U] (*pl.* **an·tith·e·ses** /-siz/) (*formal*) **1** the opposite of sth: *Love is the antithesis of selfishness.* **2** a contrast between two things: *There is an antithesis between the needs of the state and the needs of the people.*

**ant·ler** /'æntlər/ ***noun*** [C, usually pl.] a horn on the head of a male deer: *a pair of antlers* ➲ pictures at **deer** and **elk**.

**an·to·nym** /'æntənɪm/ ***noun*** [C] a word that is opposite in meaning to another word: *"Old" has two possible antonyms: "young" and "new."* ➲ Compare **synonym**.

**ant·sy** /'æntsi/ ***adj.*** (*informal*) impatient; not able to keep still

**a·nus** /'eɪnəs/ ***noun*** [C] (*pl.* **a·nus·es**) (*formal*) the hole through which solid waste substances leave the body

★**anx·i·e·ty** /æŋ'zaɪət̬i/ ***noun*** [C,U] (*pl.* **anx·i·e·ties**) a feeling of worry or fear, especially about the future: *a feeling/a state of anxiety* ◇ *There are anxieties over the effects of unemployment.*

★**anx·ious** /'æŋkʃəs/ ***adj.*** **1 anxious (about/for sb/sth)** worried and afraid: *I started to get anxious when they still hadn't arrived at 9 o'clock.* ◇ *an anxious look/expression* **2** causing worry and fear: *For a few anxious moments, we thought we'd missed the plane.* **3 anxious about/for sth**; **anxious to do sth** wanting sth very much; eager for sth: *Police are anxious to find the owner of the white car.* ◇ *The Democratic candidate is anxious for a victory in next week's election.* ▸ **anx·ious·ly *adv.***

★**an·y**[1] /'ɛni/ ***det., pronoun*** **1** (used in negative sentences and in questions, also after *if/whether*) some: *We didn't have any lunch.* ◇ *I don't know any Canadians.* ◇ *He asked if we had any questions.* ◇ *I wanted some cookies, but there aren't any.* ◇ *I don't like any of his books.* ➲ Look at the note at **some**. **2** (used for saying that it does not matter which thing or person you choose): *Take any book you want.* ◇ *Any teacher would say the same.* ◇ *Come around any time – I'm usually in.* ◇ *I'll take any that you don't want.*

★**an·y**[2] /'ɛni/ ***adv.*** (used in negative sentences and questions) at all; to any degree: *I can't run any faster.* ◇ *Is there any more milk in the fridge?* ➲ Look at **anymore**.

★**an·y·bod·y** /'ɛniˌbʌdi; -ˌbɑdi/ (*also* **anyone**) ***pronoun*** **1** (usually in questions or negative statements) any person: *I didn't know anybody at the party.* ◇ *Is there anybody here who can speak Japanese?*

> NOTE The difference between **somebody** and **anybody** is the same as the difference between **some** and **any**. ➲ Look at the notes at **some** and **somebody**.

**2** any person, it does not matter who: *Anybody* (= all people) *can learn to swim.* ◇ *Can anybody come? Or are there special invitations?*

**an·y·how** /'ɛnihaʊ/ ***adv.*** (*informal*) = ANYWAY

**an·y·more** /ˌɛni'mɔr/ ***adv.*** (used at the end of negative sentences and questions) now; any longer: *She doesn't live here anymore.* ◇ *Why doesn't he speak to me anymore?*

★**an·y·one** /'ɛniwʌn/ ***pronoun*** = ANYBODY

**an·y·place** /'ɛnipleɪs/ ***adv.*** (*informal*) = ANYWHERE

★**an·y·thing** /'ɛniθɪŋ/ ***pronoun*** **1** (usually in questions or negative statements) one thing (of any kind): *The fog was so thick that I couldn't see anything at all.* ◇ *Did you buy anything?* ◇ *That's amazing – I've never seen anything like it!* ◇ *"I'd like a cheeseburger." "Anything else?"* (= any other thing?)

> NOTE The difference between **something** and **anything** is the same as the difference between **some** and **any**. ➲ Look at the note at **some**.

**2** any thing or things; it does not matter what: *I'm starving! I'll eat anything.* ◇ *I'll do anything you say.*
IDM **anything but** definitely not: *What a surprise – the meeting was anything but dull.*
**or anything** (*informal*) or sth else of a similar type: *If you ever want to go to the movies or anything, give me a call.*

**an·y·time** /'ɛnitaɪm/ ***adv.*** at any time or times; it does not matter when: *Feel free to call us anytime.* ◇ *We can go anytime you want.*

★**an·y·way** /'ɛniweɪ/ (*also informal* **anyhow**) ***adv.*** **1** (used to add an extra point or reason) in any case: *Mexico will be very hot in August, and anyway we can't afford a vacation this summer.* **2** (used when saying or writing sth which contrasts in some way with what has gone before) however: *Sorry I can't come to your party, but thanks anyway.* **3** (used for correcting sth you have just said and making it more accurate) at least: *Everybody wants to be rich – well, most people anyway.* **4** (used after a pause in order to change the subject or go back to

A

a subject being discussed before): *Anyway, that's enough about my problems. How are you doing?*

★**an·y·where** /ˈɛniwɛr/ (*also informal* **anyplace**) ***adv.*** **1** (usually in questions or negative statements) in, at or to any place: *I can't find my keys anywhere.* ◇ *Is there a post office anywhere near here?* ◇ *You can't buy the book anywhere else* (= in another place).

NOTE The difference between **somewhere** and **anywhere** is the same as the difference between **some** and **any**. ➲ Look at the note at **some**.

**2** any place; it does not matter where: *"Where should we go to eat?" "Oh, anywhere is fine."*

★**a·part** /əˈpɑrt/ ***adv.*** **1** away from sb/sth or each other; not together: *They always argue, so it's best to keep them apart.* **2** away from each other by the distance mentioned: *Plant the potatoes two feet apart.* **3** into pieces: *The material was so old that it just fell/came apart in my hands.* ◇ *Their relationship was clearly falling apart* (= about to end).

IDM **take sth apart** to separate sth into pieces: *He took the whole bicycle apart.*

**tell A and B apart** to see the difference between A and B: *It's very difficult to tell the twins apart.*

★**aˈpart from** (*also* **aˈside from**) ***prep.*** **1** except for: *I'm done with my homework, apart from some reading we have to do.* ◇ *There's nobody here apart from me.* **2** as well as; in addition to: *Apart from their penthouse in New York City, they have a house in Florida.*

★**a·part·ment** /əˈpɑrtmənt/ ***noun*** [C] (*abbr.* **apt.**) a set of rooms that is used as a home (usually on one floor in a larger building): *a three-bedroom apartment.*

NOTE You **rent** an apartment from a **landlord** or from a company that owns the apartment. The landlord **rents** the apartment **out** to you, the **tenant**. The money you have to pay is called **rent**. ➲ Look also at **condominium**.

★**aˈpartment ˌbuilding** (*also* **aˈpartment house**) ***noun*** [C] a large building that contains many separate apartments

**ap·a·thet·ic** /ˌæpəˈθɛt̬ɪk/ ***adj.*** lacking interest or a desire to act: *Don't be so apathetic!*

**ap·a·thy** /ˈæpəθi/ ***noun*** [U] the feeling of not being interested in or enthusiastic about anything

**ape** /eɪp/ ***noun*** [C] a type of animal like a large monkey with no tail or only a very short tail: *Chimpanzees and gorillas are apes.*

**a·piece** /əˈpis/ ***adv.*** each: *He gave the children $1 apiece.*

**a·pol·o·get·ic** /əˌpɑləˈdʒɛt̬ɪk/ ***adj.*** feeling or showing that you are sorry for sth you have done: *He was very apologetic about his son's bad behavior.* ◇ *I wrote him an apologetic letter.* ▸ **a·pol·o·get·i·cal·ly** /-kli/ ***adv.***

★**a·pol·o·gize** /əˈpɑlədʒaɪz/ ***verb*** [I] **apologize (to sb) (for sth)** to say that you are sorry for sth you have done: *I sincerely apologize for taking so long to reply to your letter.* ◇ *You'll have to apologize to your teacher for forgetting to do your homework.*

NOTE When you apologize, the actual words you use are usually **"I'm sorry."**

**a·pol·o·gy** /əˈpɑlədʒi/ ***noun*** [C,U] (*pl.* **a·pol·o·gies**) **apology (to sb) (for sth)** a spoken or written statement that you are sorry for sth you have done, etc.: *The minister demanded a public apology from her colleague for making false statements.* ◇ *a letter/note of apology*

**A·pos·tle** /əˈpɑsl/ ***noun*** [C] one of the twelve men chosen by Christ to spread his teaching

**a·pos·tro·phe** /əˈpɑstrəfi/ ***noun*** [C] **1** the sign (') used for showing that you have left a letter out of a word (as in "I'm," "can't," "we'll," etc.) **2** the sign (') used for showing who or what sth belongs or relates to as in "John's chair," "the boy's room" or "the car's rear window."

**ap·pall** /əˈpɔl/ ***verb*** [T] (**ap·pal̲l̲·ing**; **ap·pal̲l̲ed**) (usually passive) to shock sb deeply: *We were appalled by the poverty and starvation we saw everywhere.*

**ap·pall·ing** /əˈpɔlɪŋ/ ***adj.*** shocking or terrible: *appalling cruelty* ◇ *Conditions in the prison are appalling.*

★**ap·pa·ra·tus** /ˌæpəˈræt̬əs/ ***noun*** (*pl.* **ap·pa·ra·tus** or **ap·pa·ra·tus·es**) **1** [C,U, usually sing.] a set of tools, instruments or equipment used for doing a job or an activity: *the scientific apparatus necessary for carrying out experiments* **2** [sing.] the complex structure of an organization: *the nation's military and political apparatus*

**ap·par·el** /əˈpærəl/ ***noun*** [U] (*formal*) clothing: *manufacturers of women's apparel*

★**ap·par·ent** /əˈpærənt; -ˈpɛr-/ ***adj.*** **1** (only *before* a noun) perhaps not true or real although seeming to be so: *His apparent interest in the proposal didn't last very long.* **2 apparent (to sb)** clear; easy to see: *It was apparent to everyone that the man could not be trusted.* ◇ *For no apparent reason, she suddenly burst into tears.*

★**ap·par·ent·ly** /əˈpærəntli; -ˈpɛr-/ ***adv.*** **1** according to what people say (but perhaps not true): *Apparently, he's already been married twice.* **2** according to how sth seems or appears (but perhaps not true): *She was apparently undisturbed by the news.* SYN **seemingly**

★**ap·peal¹** /əˈpil/ ***verb*** **1** [I] **appeal to sb (for sth/to do sth)**; **appeal for sth** to make a serious request for sth you need or want very much: *Relief workers in the disaster area are appealing for more help and supplies.* ◇ *She appeared on television to appeal to the kidnappers for her child's safe return.* **2** [I] **appeal (to sb)** to be attractive or interesting (to sb): *The idea of living in the country doesn't appeal to me at all.* **3** [I] **appeal to sth** to influence sb's feelings or thoughts so that he/she will do sth you want: *to appeal to sb's honor/sense of justice* ◇ *We aim to appeal to people's generosity.* **4** [I,T] **appeal sth**; **appeal (to sb) (against sth)** to ask sb in authority to change a decision: *He decided to appeal his conviction.* ◇ *They plan to appeal to the Supreme Court against the lower court's decision.*

★**ap·peal²** /əˈpil/ ***noun*** **1** [C] a serious request for sth you need or want very much: *Blood banks have issued an urgent appeal for donors.* ◇ *a television/*

A

*radio appeal* (= a television or radio program asking for help or money for a particular cause) **2** [C] **appeal to sth** a written or spoken statement that tries to influence sb's feelings or thoughts so that he/she will do what you want: *a powerful appeal to our sense of national pride* **3** [C] a formal request to sb in authority to change a decision: *The judge turned down the defendant's appeal.* **4** [U] attraction or interest: *I can't understand the appeal of stamp collecting.*

**ap·peal·ing** /ə'pilɪŋ/ ***adj.*** attractive or interesting: *The thought of a vacation in Hawaii is very appealing!*

★**ap·pear** /ə'pɪr/ ***verb*** [I]
➤BE SEEN **1** to be seen; to come into sight: *The bus appeared around the corner.*
➤BEGIN TO EXIST **2** to begin to exist: *The disease is thought to have appeared in Africa.*
➤OF BOOK/PROGRAM **3** to be published or printed: *The article appeared in the paper on Friday.*
➤IN MOVIE/PLAY **4** to present yourself in public to speak, perform, act, etc.: *I've been asked to appear in court.* ◇ *She is currently appearing in a Broadway musical.*
➤LOOK/SEEM **5** to seem: *She appears to be very happy in her job.* ◇ *It appears that you were given the wrong information.* ◇ *"Do you think he will resign?" "It appears so."* ➲ adjective **apparent**

★**ap·pear·ance** /ə'pɪrəns/ ***noun*** **1** [U] the way that sb/sth looks: *A different hairstyle can completely change your appearance.* ◇ *He gives the appearance of being extremely confident.* **2** [C] an act of appearing in public, especially on stage, television, etc.: *The program will feature appearances by a number of top stars.* **3** [sing.] the arrival of sb/sth: *I was surprised by her unexpected appearance at the party.* **4** [sing.] the beginning (of sth never seen or used before): *the appearance of television in many homes in the 1950s*

**ap·pen·di·ci·tis** /ə,pɛndə'saɪt̬əs/ ***noun*** [U] an illness in which the APPENDIX (1) becomes extremely painful and usually has to be removed

**ap·pen·dix** /ə'pɛndɪks/ ***noun*** [C] (*pl.* **ap·pen·di·ces** /-dəsiz/ or **ap·pen·dix·es**) **1** a small tube inside your body which is attached to the intestine **2** a section at the end of a book, etc. that gives extra information

**ap·pe·tite** /'æpətaɪt/ ***noun*** **1** [C,U] the desire for food: *a good/healthy appetite* ◇ *My two teenage sons have enormous appetites!* ◇ *Some fresh air and exercise should* ***give you an appetite*** (= make you hungry). ◇ *Symptoms of this illness include a headache, fever and* ***loss of appetite****.* **2** [C,U] a strong desire: *his insatiable appetite for new electronic gadgets*
IDM **whet sb's appetite** → WHET

**ap·pe·tiz·er** /'æpətaɪzər/ ***noun*** [C] a small amount of food that you eat as the first part of a meal

**ap·pe·tiz·ing** /'æpətaɪzɪŋ/ ***adj.*** (used about food, etc.) attractive and tempting: *an appetizing smell*

**ap·plaud** /ə'plɔd/ ***verb*** **1** [I,T] to clap your hands in order to show that you like sb/sth: *The audience applauded loudly.* ◇ *The team was applauded as it left the field.* **2** [T] to praise sb/sth: *Many citizens applauded the decision to lower taxes.*

**ap·plause** /ə'plɔz/ ***noun*** [U] the pleasure and approval of a group of people, shown by them clapping their hands: *The performance received enthusiastic applause from the audience.*
IDM **a round of applause** → ROUND²

★**ap·ple** /'æpl/ ***noun*** [C] a hard, round fruit with smooth green, red or yellow skin: *an apple tree* ◇ *apple juice* ➲ Look also at **the Big Apple**.

**ˌapple 'cider** ***noun*** [U] = CIDER

**ap·plet** /'æplət/ ***noun*** [C] (*computing*) a program which is run from within another program, for example from within a Web browser

**ap·pli·ance** /ə'plaɪəns/ ***noun*** [C] a piece of equipment for a particular purpose in the house: *electrical appliances*

**ap·pli·ca·ble** /'æplɪkəbl; ə'plɪkəbl/ ***adj.*** (not before a noun) **applicable (to sb/sth)** that concerns or relates to sb/sth: *This part of the form is only applicable to married women.*

**ap·pli·cant** /'æplɪkənt/ ***noun*** [C] a person who applies for sth, especially a job

★**ap·pli·ca·tion** /ˌæplə'keɪʃn/ ***noun*** **1** [C,U] **application (to sb) (for sth)** a formal written request, especially for a job or a place in a school, club, etc.: *We are accepting applications for the position of assistant manager.* ◇ *an* ***application form*** (= a special form that you use to apply for a job, etc.) **2** [C,U] a/the practical use (of sth): *the application of educational theory to the classroom* **3** [U] **application (of sth)** the action of putting or spreading sth onto a surface: *This cream is for external application only.* **4** [C] (*computing*) a computer program that you use to perform a specific function or several functions: *a word-processing application*

**ap·plied** /ə'plaɪd/ ***adj.*** (used about a subject) having a practical use: *applied mathematics* (e.g. as used in engineering)

★**ap·ply** /ə'plaɪ/ ***verb*** (*pres. part.* **ap·ply·ing**; *3rd person sing. pres.* **ap·plies**; *pt, pp* **ap·plied**)
➤FOR JOB/COURSE **1** [I] **apply (to sb) (for sth)** to ask for sth in writing: *I'm going to apply for that job they advertised.*
➤BE RELEVANT **2** [I] **apply (to sb/sth)** to concern sb/sth or relate to sb/sth: *This information applies to all children born after 2000.*
➤USE **3** [T] to use a word, a name, etc. to refer to sb/sth: *I don't think the word "antique" can be applied to this old table, do you?* **4** [T] **apply sth (to sth)** to make practical use of sth: *new technology which can be applied to solving problems in industry*
➤PAINT/CREAM **5** [T] **apply sth (to sth)** to put or spread sth onto a surface: *Apply the cream to the infected area twice a day.*
➤WORK HARD **6** [T] **apply yourself/sth (to sth/to doing sth)** to make yourself concentrate on sth: *to apply your mind to sth* ◇ *He really applied himself to his studies.*

★**ap·point** /ə'pɔɪnt/ ***verb*** [T] **1** **appoint sb (sth/as sth/to sth)** to choose sb for a job, etc.: *The committee has appointed a new chairperson.* ◇ *He's been appointed (as) the new school superintendent.* **2** **appoint sth (for sth)** (*formal*) to arrange or decide on sth: *the date appointed for the next meeting*

★**ap·point·ment** /ə'pɔɪntmənt/ ***noun*** **1** [C,U] **appointment (with sb)** an arrangement to see sb at a particular time: *a doctor's/dentist's appointment* ◇ *I'd like to make an appointment to see the manager.* ◇ *to keep/cancel an appointment* ◇ *visits are by appointment only* (= at a time that has been arranged in advance). **2** [U] **appointment (to sth)** the act of choosing sb for a job: *Many people criticized the appointment of such a young man to the post.* **3** [C] a job or position of responsibility

**ap·prais·al** /ə'preɪzl/ ***noun*** [C,U] an opinion about the value or quality of sb/sth; a judgment

**ap·praise** /ə'preɪz/ ***verb*** [T] to form an opinion about the value or quality of sb/sth

**ap·pre·cia·ble** /ə'priʃəbl/ ***adj.*** noticeable or important: *There has been an appreciable drop in the rate of inflation.*

⋆**ap·pre·ci·ate** /ə'priʃieɪt/ ***verb*** **1** [T] to enjoy sth or to understand the value of sth: *The art of Van Gogh was not appreciated during his own lifetime.* **2** [T] to understand sth (a problem, situation, etc.): *I don't think you appreciate how serious this situation is.* **3** [T] to be grateful for sth: *Thanks for your help. We really appreciate it.* **4** [I] to increase in value over a period of time: *Houses in this area have appreciated faster than elsewhere.*

**ap·pre·ci·a·tion** /əˌpriʃi'eɪʃn/ ***noun*** **1** [U] understanding and enjoyment (of the value of sth): *I'm taking an introductory course in music appreciation.* **2** [U] the feeling of being grateful for sth: *Please accept these flowers as a token* (= a sign) *of my appreciation.* **3** [U, sing.] an understanding of what sth involves: *The visit gave him a new appreciation of the problems facing poor people.* **4** [U] an increase in value: *the yen's appreciation against the dollar*

**ap·pre·cia·tive** /ə'priʃət̬ɪv/ ***adj.*** **1** feeling or showing pleasure or admiration: *"You look nice tonight," he said, with an appreciative smile.* **2 appreciative (of sth)** grateful for sth: *He was very appreciative of our efforts to help.*

**ap·pre·hend** /ˌæprɪ'hɛnd/ ***verb*** [T] (used about the police) to catch and arrest sb: *The suspects were apprehended as they tried to board a plane to the Bahamas.*

**ap·pre·hen·sion** /ˌæprɪ'hɛnʃn/ ***noun*** [C,U] (*formal*) worry or fear about sth in the future: *feelings of apprehension*

**ap·pre·hen·sive** /ˌæprɪ'hɛnsɪv/ ***adj.*** worried or afraid: *to be/feel apprehensive* ◇ *The students were apprehensive about their upcoming exams.*

**ap·pren·tice** /ə'prɛntɪs/ ***noun*** [C] a person who works for sb for low wages, in order to learn an occupation or skill: *an apprentice electrician*

**ap·pren·tice·ship** /ə'prɛntəʃɪp/ ***noun*** [C,U] the state or time of being an apprentice

⋆**ap·proach**[1] /ə'proʊtʃ/ ***verb*** **1** [I,T] to come near or nearer to sb/sth: *The date of her wedding was approaching.* ◇ *When you approach the town, you will see a gas station on your left.* **2** [T] to speak to sb, usually in order to ask for sth: *I'm going to approach my boss about a raise.* **3** [T] to begin to deal with sth (a problem, a situation, etc.): *What is the best way to approach this problem?* **4** [T] to almost reach sth (a certain standard, level, etc.): *at a depth approaching 50 feet under water*

**ap·proach**[2] /ə'proʊtʃ/ ***noun*** **1** [C] a way of dealing with sb/sth: *Parents don't always know what approach to take with teenagers.* **2** [sing.] the act of coming nearer (to sb/sth): *The plane's engine stalled during its approach to the runway.* **3** [C] a road or path, etc. leading to sth: *the approach to the town*

**ap·proach·a·ble** /ə'proʊtʃəbl/ ***adj.*** friendly and easy to talk to: *She's nice, but her husband's not very approachable.* OPP **unapproachable**

⋆**ap·pro·pri·ate**[1] /ə'proʊpriət/ ***adj.*** **appropriate (for/to sth)** suitable or right: *This card is very appropriate for the occasion, isn't it?* ◇ *Take whatever action you think is appropriate.* OPP **inappropriate** ▸ **ap·pro·pri·ate·ly** ***adv.***

**ap·pro·pri·ate**[2] /ə'proʊprieɪt/ ***verb*** [T] (*formal*) **1 appropriate sth (for/to sth)** to decide to use sth, especially money, for a particular purpose: *Congress has appropriated over $150 million for cancer research.* **2** to take or use sth for your own purposes, usually without permission or illegally: *He admitted that he had appropriated some facts from another writer's article.*

**ap·pro·pri·a·tion** /əˌproʊpri'eɪʃn/ ***noun*** [C] a thing, especially a sum of money, that is appropriated: *The proposal includes an appropriation of $72 million for loans to small businesses.*

⋆**ap·prov·al** /ə'pruvl/ ***noun*** [U] feeling, showing or saying that you think sth is good; agreement: *Everybody gave their approval to the proposal.* ◇ *She was always anxious to win her mother's approval.*

⋆**ap·prove** /ə'pruv/ ***verb*** **1** [I] **approve (of sb/sth)** to be pleased about sth; to like sb/sth: *Her parents don't approve of her friends.* OPP **disapprove** **2** [T] to agree to sth or to accept sth as correct: *We need to get an accountant to approve these figures.*

**ap·prov·ing** /ə'pruvɪŋ/ ***adj.*** showing support or admiration for sth: *"Good job," he said with an approving smile.* ▸ **ap·prov·ing·ly** ***adv.***

**ap·prox·i·mate** /ə'prɑksəmət/ ***adj.*** (*abbr.* **approx.**) almost correct but not completely accurate: *The approximate time of arrival is 3 o'clock.* ◇ *I can only give you an approximate idea of the cost.*

⋆**ap·prox·i·mate·ly** /ə'prɑksəmətli/ ***adv.*** (*abbr.* **approx.**) about: *It's approximately fifty miles from here.*

**ap·prox·i·ma·tion** /əˌprɑksə'meɪʃn/ ***noun*** [C] a number, answer, etc. which is nearly, but not exactly, right

**a·pri·cot** /'eɪprɪkɑt; 'æp-/ ***noun*** [C] a small, round, yellow or orange fruit with soft flesh and a large hard part (a **pit**) inside

**A·pril** /'eɪprəl/ ***noun*** [C,U] (*abbr.* **Apr.**) the fourth month of the year, coming before May ➲ For examples of the use of the months in sentences, look at **January**.

**ˌApril 'Fool's Day** ***noun*** [sing.] April 1

> NOTE On this day it is traditional for people to play tricks on each other, especially by inventing silly stories and trying to persuade other people that they are true.

**a·pron** /'eɪprən/ ***noun*** [C] a piece of clothing that you wear over the front of your usual clothes in

A

order to keep them clean, especially when cooking ➲ picture at **overall**.

**apt** /æpt/ ***adj.*** **1** suitable: *a very apt description* **2 apt to do sth** having a tendency to do sth; likely to do sth: *You'd better remind me. I'm apt to forget.*

**apt.** ***abbr.*** = APARTMENT

**ap·ti·tude** /ˈæptətud/ ***noun*** [C,U] **aptitude (for sth/for doing sth)** (a) natural ability: *She has an aptitude for learning languages.*

**apt·ly** /ˈæptli/ ***adv.*** suitably: *The hotel was aptly named "Ocean View"* (= because it had a view of the ocean).

**a·quar·i·um** /əˈkwɛriəm/ ***noun*** [C] (*pl.* **a·quar·i·ums** or **a·quar·i·a** /-riə/) **1** a glass container filled with water, in which fish and water animals are kept **2** a building, often in a zoo, where fish and water animals are kept

**A·quar·i·us** /əˈkwɛriəs/ ***noun*** [C,U] the eleventh sign of the zodiac, the Water Carrier; a person who was born under this sign

**a·quat·ic** /əˈkwæt̬ɪk; əˈkwɑt̬ɪk/ ***adj.*** **1** (used about an animal or a plant) living in water **2** (used about a sport) performed on or in water

**Ar·ab** /ˈærəb/ ***noun*** [C] a member of a race of people who now live in many parts of the Middle East and North Africa ▸ **Ar·ab** ***adj.***: *Arab countries*

**Ar·a·bic** /ˈærəbɪk/ ***noun*** [sing.] the language that is spoken by Arab people and the religious language of Islam

**ar·a·ble** /ˈærəbl/ ***adj.*** (used about land) suitable for growing crops

**ar·bi·trar·y** /ˈɑrbətrɛri/ ***adj.*** not based on any principle or reason; not thinking about the wishes of the other people involved: *The choice he made seemed completely arbitrary.* ▸ **ar·bi·trar·i·ly** ***adv.*** /ˌɑrbəˈtrɛrəli/

**ar·bi·trate** /ˈɑrbətreɪt/ ***verb*** [I,T] to settle an argument between two people or groups by finding a solution that both can accept

**ar·bi·tra·tion** /ˌɑrbəˈtreɪʃn/ ***noun*** [U] the process of settling an argument between two people or groups by a third person (who has been chosen by them): *The baseball players and the team owners decided to go to arbitration.*

**ar·bi·tra·tor** /ˈɑrbətreɪt̬ər/ ***noun*** [C] a person who is chosen to settle an argument between two people or groups, in formal discussions

**arc** /ɑrk/ ***noun*** [C] a curved line, part of a circle

**ar·cade** /ɑrˈkeɪd/ ***noun*** [C] **1** a large room with machines and games that you put coins into to play: *a video game arcade* **2** a large covered passage or area with stores along one or both sides; a passage with arches: *a shopping arcade*

**arches**

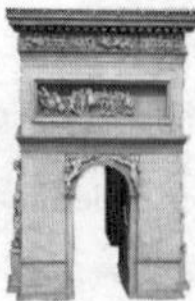

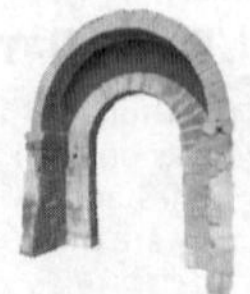

**arch¹** /ɑrtʃ/ ***noun*** [C] **1** a structure made with two columns joined over the top in a curve. An arch may support a bridge or the roof of a large building or it may be above a door or a window. **2** a monument in the shape of an arch: *the Gateway Arch in St. Louis* **3** the middle part of the inside of your foot

**arch²** /ɑrtʃ/ ***verb*** [I,T] to make a curve: *The cat arched its back and hissed.*

**ar·chae·o·log·i·cal** (*also* **archeological**) /ˌɑrkiəˈlɑdʒɪkl/ ***adj.*** connected with archaeology

**ar·chae·ol·o·gist** (*also* **archeologist**) /ˌɑrkiˈɑlədʒɪst/ ***noun*** [C] an expert in archaeology

**ar·chae·ol·o·gy** (*also* **archeology**) /ˌɑrkiˈɑlədʒi/ ***noun*** [U] the study of ancient civilizations, based on objects or parts of buildings that are found in the ground

**ar·cha·ic** /ɑrˈkeɪɪk/ ***adj.*** old-fashioned; no longer in common use

**arch·bish·op** /ˌɑrtʃˈbɪʃəp/ ***noun*** [C] a priest in some branches of the Christian church who is in charge of all the priests and churches in a large area of a country: *the Archbishop of Philadelphia*

**arch·er·y** /ˈɑrtʃəri/ ***noun*** [U] the sport of shooting arrows using a curved piece of wood (a bow) that is held together by a string

**ar·chi·tect** /ˈɑrkətɛkt/ ***noun*** [C] a person whose job is to design buildings

**ar·chi·tec·tur·al** /ˌɑrkəˈtɛktʃərəl/ ***adj.*** connected with the design of buildings

**ar·chi·tec·ture** /ˈɑrkəˌtɛktʃər/ ***noun*** [U] **1** the study of how buildings are planned and built **2** the style or design of a building or buildings: *the architecture of the fifteenth century* ◇ *modern architecture*

**ar·chives** /ˈɑrkaɪvz/ ***noun*** [pl.] (*also* [C] **archive** /ˈɑrkaɪv/) a collection of historical documents, etc. that record the history of a place or an organization; the place where they are kept: *In the city archives, they found letters written by George Washington.* ◇ *archive material on the First World War*

**Arc·tic** /ˈɑrktɪk; ˈɑrt̬ɪk/ ***adj.*** **1** connected with the region around the North Pole (the most northern point of the world) ➲ picture at **earth**. **2 arctic** very cold: *A blast of arctic air swept across the prairies today.*

**the Arctic** /ˈɑrktɪk; ˈɑrt̬ɪk/ ***noun*** [sing.] the area around the North Pole

**the ˌArctic ˈCircle** ***noun*** [sing.] the line of latitude 66° 33′N ➲ Look at **Antarctic**.

**ar·dent** /ˈɑrdnt/ ***adj.*** showing strong feelings, especially a strong liking for sb/sth: *He was an ardent supporter of the Democrats.* ▸ **ar·dent·ly** ***adv.***

**ar·du·ous** /ˈɑrdʒuəs/ ***adj.*** full of difficulties; needing a lot of effort over a period of time: *an arduous journey*

**are, aren't** → BE[1,2]

★**ar·e·a** /ˈɛriə/ ***noun*** **1** [C] a part of a town, a country or the world: *Housing is very expensive in the San Francisco area.* ◇ *The wettest areas are in the south of the country.* ◇ *The high winds scattered debris over a wide area.* ➲ Look at the note at **district**. **2** [C,U] the size of a surface, that you can calculate by multiplying the length by the width: *The area of the office is 150 square feet.* ◇ *The office is 150 square feet in area.* **3** [C] a space used for a particular activity: *I'd* *rather sit in the non-smoking area.* **4** [C] a particular part of a subject or activity: *Training is one area of the business that we could improve.*

**'area code** *noun* [C] a set of three numbers at the beginning of telephone numbers in the U.S. and Canada, that you must use when you are calling from outside the area: *The area code for Chicago is 312.*

**a·re·na** /ə'rinə/ *noun* [C] **1** an area with seats around it where public events (sports, games, concerts, etc.) are held **2** where a particular activity happens: *She was well respected in the international political arena.*

**ar·gu·a·ble** /'ɑrgyuəbl/ *adj.* **1** that can be argued; probably true: *It is arguable that no one should have to go without health insurance.* **2** not certain; that you do not accept without question: *Whether it is a good idea to invest so much money is highly arguable.*

**ar·gu·a·bly** /'ɑrgyuəbli/ *adv.* probably; you can argue that: *She is arguably the nation's greatest living actress.*

★**ar·gue** /'ɑrgyu/ *verb* **1** [I] **argue (with sb) (about/over sth)** to say things (often angrily) that show that you do not agree with sb about sth: *The people next door are always arguing.* ◇ *I never argue with my husband about money.* **2** [I,T] **argue that...; argue (for/against sth)** to give reasons that support your opinion about sth: *John argued that buying a new computer was a waste of money.* ◇ *He argued against buying a new computer.*

★**ar·gu·ment** /'ɑrgyumənt/ *noun* **1** [C,U] **argument (with sb) (about/over sth)** an angry discussion between two or more people who disagree with each other: *Sue had an argument with her father about politics.* ◇ *He accepted the decision without argument.* **2** [C] the reason(s) that you give to support your opinion about sth: *His argument was that if they bought a smaller car, they would save money.* ◇ *The defense attorney began her closing arguments yesterday.*

**ar·gu·men·ta·tive** /ˌɑrgyu'mɛntət̬ɪv/ *adj.* often involved in or enjoying arguments

**ar·id** /'ærɪd/ *adj.* (used about land or climate) very dry; with little or no rain

**Ar·ies** /'ɛriz/ *noun* [C,U] the first sign of the zodiac, the Ram; a person who was born under this sign

★**a·rise** /ə'raɪz/ *verb* [I] (*pt* **a·rose** /ə'roʊz/; *pp* **a·ris·en** /ə'rɪzn/) to begin to exist; to appear: *If any problems arise, let me know.*

**ar·is·toc·ra·cy** /ˌærə'stɑkrəsi/ *noun* [C] (*pl.* **ar·is·toc·ra·cies**) the people of the highest social class in some countries, who often have special titles

**a·ris·to·crat** /ə'rɪstəkræt/ *noun* [C] a member of the highest social class in some countries, often with a special title ▸ **a·ris·to·crat·ic** /əˌrɪstə'kræt̬ɪk/ *adj.*

**a·rith·me·tic** /ə'rɪθmətɪk/ *noun* [U] the branch of mathematics that involves counting with numbers (adding, subtracting, multiplying and dividing) ➲ Look at **algebra** and **math**.

★**arm**[1] /ɑrm/ *noun* [C] **1** the limb at each side of the human body from the shoulder to the hand: *He was carrying a newspaper under his arm.* ◇ *They waved*

**arm**

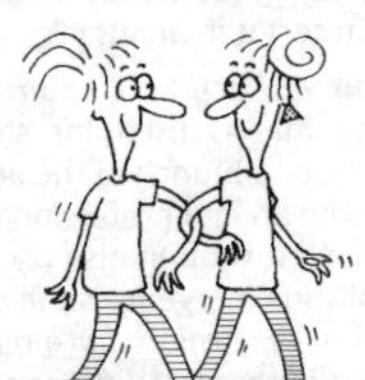

arm in arm

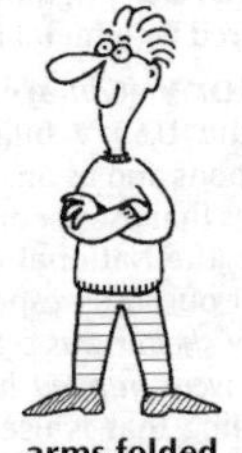

arms folded

*their arms in the air and shouted at us.* ◇ *I put my arm around her.* ➲ picture on study page A32. **2** the part of a piece of clothing that covers your arm; a sleeve: *He had a hole in the arm of his sweater.* **3** something shaped like an arm: *the arm of a chair* (= where you rest your arm) ➲ Look also at **arms**.

IDM **arm in arm** with your arm linked together with sb else's arm: *The two friends walked arm in arm.*

**cost/pay an arm and a leg** (*informal*) to cost/pay a large amount of money: *I had to pay an arm and a leg for these plane tickets.*

**cross/fold your arms** to cross your arms in front of your chest: *She folded her arms and waited.* ◇ *James was sitting with his arms crossed.*

**twist sb's arm** → TWIST[1]

**with open arms** → OPEN[1]

★**arm**[2] /ɑrm/ *verb* [I,T] to prepare sb/yourself to fight by supplying weapons: *The country is beginning to arm itself for war.* ➲ Look at **armed** and **arms**.

**ar·ma·dil·lo** /ˌɑrmə'dɪloʊ/ *noun* [C] (*pl.* **ar·ma·dil·los**) a small animal that lives in the southern U.S. and Central and South America. Its body is covered in a shell of hard plates for protection.

**armadillo**

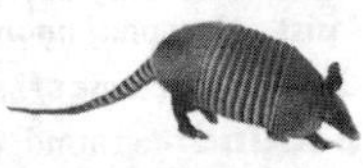

**ar·ma·ments** /'ɑrməmənts/ *noun* [pl.] weapons and military equipment

**arm·band** /'ɑrmbænd/ *noun* [C] a piece of material that you wear around your sleeve: *People often used to wear black armbands at funerals.*

**arm·chair** /'ɑrmtʃɛr/ *noun* [C] a soft comfortable chair with sides that support your arms ➲ picture at **chair**[1].

★**armed** /ɑrmd/ *adj.* carrying a gun or other weapon; involving weapons: *The escaped prisoners are considered armed and dangerous.* ◇ *armed robbery* ◇ *the armed forces* (= the Army, Navy, Air Force and Marine Corps) ◇ (*figurative*) *They came to the meeting armed with all the latest information.*

**arm·ful** /'ɑrmfʊl/ *noun* [C] the amount that you can carry in your arms: *She was carrying an armful of books.*

**arm·hole** /'ɑrmhoʊl/ *noun* [C] the opening in a piece of clothing that your arm goes through

**ar·mi·stice** /'ɑrməstɪs/ *noun* [C] an agreement between two countries who are at war that they will stop fighting

**ar·mor** /'ɑrmər/ *noun* [U] clothing, often made of metal, that soldiers wore in earlier times to protect themselves: *a suit of armor*

A

**ar·mored** /ˈɑrmərd/ *adj.* (used about a vehicle) covered with metal to protect it in an attack

**ar·mor·y** (*Cdn* **ar·mour·y**) /ˈɑrməri/ *noun* [C] **1** (in the U.S.) a building that is used for storing weapons and as an office for a branch of the armed forces that uses people who are not professional soldiers (**the National Guard**). It is often also used for other purposes, especially in emergencies: *An emergency shelter was set up in the armory for motorists who were trapped by the blizzard.* **2** (in Canada) a building that is used for storing weapons and for training people who are not professional soldiers (**militia**)

**arm·pit** /ˈɑrmpɪt/ *noun* [C] the part of the body under the arm at the point where it joins the shoulder ➲ picture on study page **A32**.

**arms** /ɑrmz/ *noun* [pl.] weapons, especially those that are used in war: *a reduction in nuclear arms*

IDM **be up in arms** to be very angry; to be protesting about sth: *The workers were up in arms over the news of possible layoffs.*

★**ar·my** /ˈɑrmi/ *noun* [C, with sing. or pl. verb] (*pl.* **ar·mies**) the military forces of a country that are trained to fight on land; a large group of soldiers: *the United States Army* ◇ *She joined the army at the age of eighteen.* ◇ *an army officer* ➲ Look at **air force** and **navy**.

**a·ro·ma** /əˈroʊmə/ *noun* [C] a smell (usually one that is pleasant)

**a·ro·ma·ther·a·py** /əˌroʊməˈθɛrəpi/ *noun* [U] the use of natural oils with special smells to control pain or help people relax, especially by rubbing them into the body (**massage**) ▸ **a·ro·ma·ther·a·pist** /-ˈθɛrəpɪst/ *noun* [C]

**a·rose** *past tense of* ARISE

★**a·round**[1] /əˈraʊnd/ *adv.* **1** in or to various places or directions: *I don't plan to buy anything – I'm just looking around.* ◇ *This is our office – David will show you around* (= show you the different parts of it). **2** moving so as to face in the opposite direction: *Turn around and go back the way you came.* **3** on all sides; forming a circle: *The back yard is very large with a hedge all around.* ◇ *Gather around so that you can all see.* **4** measured on all sides: *That old tree must be at least 10 feet around.* **5** present or available: *I went to the house, but there was nobody around.* ◇ *That isn't a new book. It's been around for ages.* **6** (used for activities with no real purpose): *"What are you doing?" "Nothing, just puttering around."* ◇ *John likes messing around with cars.* **7** here and there, in different positions: *clothes lying around all over the floor* **8** (*also* **about**) (at) approximately: *It's around three hours' drive from here.* ◇ *I'll see you around seven* (= at about 7 o'clock).

★**a·round**[2] /əˈraʊnd/ *prep.* **1** in various directions inside an area; in different places in a particular area: *They wandered around the town, looking in some of the stores.* **2** in a circle or following a curving path: *The athlete ran around the track ten times.* ◇ *Go around the corner and it's the first house on the left.* ◇ *She had a bandage around her leg.* ◇ (*figurative*) *There doesn't seem to be any way around the problem.* **3** near a place: *Is there a bank around here?*

**a·rouse** /əˈraʊz/ *verb* [T] to cause a particular reaction in people: *His actions have aroused a lot of criticism.* ▸ **a·rous·al** /əˈraʊzl/ *noun* [U]

**ar·raign** /əˈreɪn/ *verb* [T] (usually passive) to bring an accused person into court and formally announce the crime or crimes that he/she is accused of: *Both suspects in the case will be arraigned on murder charges tomorrow.* ▸ **ar·raign·ment** *noun* [C,U]

★**ar·range** /əˈreɪndʒ/ *verb* **1** [T] to put sth in order or in a particular pattern: *The books were arranged in alphabetical order.* ◇ *She arranged the flowers in a vase.* **2** [I,T] to make plans and preparations so that sth can happen in the future: *Isabel's parents arranged a big party for her birthday.* ◇ *He arranged for Peter to stay with friends in Toronto.* ◇ *She arranged to meet Stuart after work.*

★**ar·range·ment** /əˈreɪndʒmənt/ *noun* **1** [C, usually pl.] plans or preparations for sth that will happen in the future: *We're just making the final arrangements for the concert.* **2** [C,U] something that you have agreed or settled with sb else; the act of doing this: *They made an arrangement to share the cost of the food.* ◇ *Use of the swimming pool will be by prior arrangement only.* **3** [C] a group of things that have been placed in a particular pattern: *a flower arrangement*

**ar·ray** /əˈreɪ/ *noun* [C] a large collection of things, especially one that is impressive and is seen by other people: *The store offers a wide array of imported foods.*

**ar·rears** /əˈrɪrz/ *noun* [pl.] money that should have been paid by an earlier date: *property tax arrears*

IDM **in arrears** owing money: *The company is $2 million in arrears on its taxes.*

★**ar·rest**[1] /əˈrɛst/ *verb* [T] (used about the police) to take sb prisoner in order to question him/her about a crime

★**ar·rest**[2] /əˈrɛst/ *noun* **1** [C] the act of arresting sb: *The police made ten arrests after the riot.* **2** [C,U] (*medical*) the action or an act of sth stopping: *He died of cardiac arrest* (= his heart stopped beating). ◇ *respiratory arrest* (= when a person stops breathing)

IDM **be under arrest** to have been arrested by the police: *He was under arrest for murder.*

★**ar·ri·val** /əˈraɪvl/ *noun* **1** [U] the act of reaching the place to which you were traveling: *On our arrival we were told that our rooms had not been reserved.* ◇ *Amtrak apologizes for the late arrival of this train.* **2** [C] people or things that have arrived: *We brought in extra chairs for the late arrivals.* ◇ *Residents near the airport have complained about the number of late-night arrivals and departures.*

★**ar·rive** /əˈraɪv/ *verb* [I] **1** to reach the place to which you were traveling: *We arrived home at about midnight.* ◇ *What time does the flight arrive in Toronto?* ◇ *They arrived at the airport ten minutes late.* ◇ *Has my letter arrived yet?* **2** to come or happen: *The day of the wedding had finally arrived.* ◇ *Paula's baby arrived* (= was born) *two weeks late.*

PHR V **arrive at** to reach sth: *After months of discussions, they finally arrived at a decision.*

**ar·ro·gant** /ˈærəgənt/ *adj.* thinking that you are better and more important than other people and not caring about their feelings; too proud ▶ **ar·ro·gance** /'ærəgəns/ ***noun*** [U] ▶ **ar·ro·gant·ly** ***adv.***

**ar·row** /'æroʊ/ ***noun*** [C] **1** a thin piece of wood or metal, with one pointed end and feathers at the other end, that is shot from a curved piece of wood that is held in shape by a string (a **bow**): *Native Americans traditionally hunted with bows and arrows.* **2** the sign (→) which is used to show direction: *The arrow is pointing right.*

**ar·se·nal** /'ɑrsənl/ ***noun*** [C] a collection of weapons; a place where weapons are made or stored: *the nation's nuclear arsenal* ◇ *(figurative) The police had a whole arsenal of evidence against the suspect.*

**ar·son** /'ɑrsn/ ***noun*** [U] the crime of setting fire to a building on purpose

**ar·son·ist** /'ɑrsənɪst/ ***noun*** [C] a person who commits the crime of arson

★**art** /ɑrt/ ***noun*** **1** [U] the producing of beautiful things such as paintings, drawings, etc.; the objects that are produced: *an art class* ◇ *the art of the Italian Renaissance* ◇ *modern art* ◇ *an art gallery* ➲ Look also at **state-of-the-art** and **work of art**. **2** [C, usually sing.] a skill or sth that requires skill: *There's an art to writing a good letter.* **3 the arts** [pl.] activities such as painting, writing literature or writing and performing music: *The government is threatening to cut funding for the arts.* **4 arts** [pl.] subjects such as history or languages that you study at a school, college or university: *a Bachelor of Arts degree in anthropology* ◇ *the university's Faculty of Arts and Sciences*

NOTE It is more common to call these subjects the **humanities**. ➲ Look also at **fine arts** and **liberal arts**.

**ar·ter·y** /'ɑrt̬əri/ ***noun*** [C] (*pl.* **ar·ter·ies**) one of the tubes which take blood from the heart to other parts of the body ➲ Look at **vein**.

**ar·thri·tis** /ɑr'θraɪt̬əs/ ***noun*** [U] a disease which causes swelling and pain in the joints of your body (where you bend your arms, fingers, etc.)

**ar·ti·choke** /'ɑrt̬ɪtʃoʊk/ ***noun*** [C] a plant whose flower looks like pointed leaves. The bottoms of the leaves and the center (**heart**) of the flower can be eaten as a vegetable. ➲ picture on study pages **A28-29**.

★**ar·ti·cle** /'ɑrt̬ɪkl/ ***noun*** [C] **1** a thing or object, especially one of a set: *Articles of clothing were lying all over the room.* **2** a piece of writing in a newspaper or magazine: *I read an interesting article in today's paper.* **3** a part of a legal document: *Article One of the United States Constitution* **4** (*grammar*) the words "a/an" (the indefinite article) or "the" (the definite article)

**ar·tic·u·late**[1] /ɑr'tɪkyələt/ ***adj.*** good at expressing your ideas clearly

**ar·tic·u·late**[2] /ɑr'tɪkyəleɪt/ ***verb*** [I,T] to say sth clearly or to express your ideas or feelings

**ar·ti·fact** (*Cdn. also* **artefact**) /'ɑrt̬əfækt/ ***noun*** [C] (*technical*) an object that is made by a person, especially sth of historical or cultural interest

★**ar·ti·fi·cial** /ˌɑrt̬ə'fɪʃl/ ***adj.*** not genuine or natural but made by people: *artificial flowers* ▶ **ar·ti·fi·cial·ly** ***adv.***: *This drug cannot be produced artificially.*

**ˌartificial inˌsemi'nation** ***noun*** [U] a scientific technique to introduce male seeds (**sperm**) into a female so that babies or young can be produced without sex

**ˌartificial in'telligence** ***noun*** [U] (*abbr.* **AI**) (*computing*) (the study of) the way in which computers can be made to copy intelligent human behavior

**ar·til·ler·y** /ɑr'tɪləri/ ***noun*** [U] a number of large guns on wheels; the part of the army which uses them

★**art·ist** /'ɑrt̬ɪst/ ***noun*** [C] somebody who produces art, especially paintings or drawings: *I like that picture – who is the artist?* ◇ *an exhibition of paintings by the American artist, Andrew Wyeth*

★**ar·tis·tic** /ɑr'tɪstɪk/ ***adj.*** **1** connected with art: *the artistic director of the theater* **2** showing a skill in art: *Helen is very artistic – her drawings are excellent.* ▶ **ar·tis·ti·cal·ly** /-kli/ ***adv.***

**art·ist·ry** /'ɑrt̬əstri/ ***noun*** [U] the skill of an artist

**art·work** /'ɑrtwərk/ ***noun*** **1** [U] photographs and pictures prepared for books, advertisements and magazines **2** [C] a work of art, especially one in a museum

**a·ru·gu·la** /ə'rugələ/ ***noun*** [U] a plant with long green leaves that have a strong flavor and that are eaten in salads

★**as** /əz; *strong form* æz/ ***conj.***, ***prep.***, ***adv.*** **1** while sth else is happening: *The phone rang just as I was leaving the house.* ◇ *As she walked along the street, she thought about her father.* **2 as...as** (used for comparing people or things): *Tom's almost as tall as I am.* ◇ *It's not as cold as it was yesterday.* **3 as...as** (used with "much" or "many" for comparing people or things): *She earns twice as much as her husband.* ◇ *I don't have as many books as you do.* **4** (used for talking about sb's job): *He works as a bus driver for the school district.* **5** (used for describing sb/sth's role): *Think of me as your friend, not as your boss.* **6** (used for describing sb/sth in an unusual role or function): *I went to the party dressed as a police officer.* ◇ *You could use this white sheet as a tablecloth.* **7** in a particular way, state, etc.: *Please do as I tell you.* ◇ *Leave the room as it is. Don't move anything.* **8** (used at the beginning of a comment about what you are saying): *As you know, I've decided to leave at the end of the month.* **9** because: *I didn't buy the dress, as I decided it was too expensive.*

IDM **as for** (used when you are starting to talk about a different person or thing): *Jane's in Paris right now. As for Andrew, I have no idea where he is.*

**as if**; **as though** (used for saying how sb/sth appears): *She looks as if she's just gotten out of bed.* ◇ *He behaved as though nothing had happened.*

**as it were** (*formal*) (used for saying that sth is only true in a certain way): *She felt, as it were, a stranger in her own house.*

**as of** starting from a particular time: *As of next week, Tim Shaw will be managing this department.*

**as to** about a particular thing: *I was given no instructions as to how to begin.*

**ASAP** (*also* **asap**) /ˌeɪ ɛs eɪ 'pi/ ***abbr.*** as soon as possible

**as·bes·tos** /æs'bɛstəs; æz-/ ***noun*** [U] a soft gray material which does not burn and which was often

A

used in the past to protect against heat. It can cause serious diseases if you breathe it in.

**as·cend** /ə'sɛnd/ *verb* [I,T] (*formal*) to go or come up ▸ **as·cend·ing** *adj.*: *The questions are arranged in ascending order of difficulty* (= the most difficult ones are at the end). ➲ Look at **descend**.

**as·cent** /ə'sɛnt/ *noun* [C] **1** the act of climbing or going up: *the first ascent of Mount Everest* **2** a path or slope leading upward: *There was a steep ascent before the path became flat again.* ➲ Look at **descent**.

**as·cer·tain** /ˌæsər'teɪn/ *verb* [T] (*formal*) to find out: *It was difficult to ascertain who was telling the truth.*

**as·cribe** /ə'skraɪb/ *verb* [T] (*formal*) **ascribe sth to sb/sth** to say that sth was written by or belonged to sb, or that sth was caused by sth: *This piece of music was ascribed to Bach, although we now believe it was written by another composer.* ◇ *The company ascribed the price increases to a shortage of raw materials.*

**ash** /æʃ/ *noun* **1** [C,U] (*also* **ashes** [pl.]) the gray or black powder which is left after sth has burned: *They found the ring in the ashes of the fire.* ◇ *The volcano produced huge clouds of ash.* **2 ashes** [pl.] what is left after a dead person has been burned **3** [C] a type of tree that is found in North America and Europe

★**a·shamed** /ə'ʃeɪmd/ *adj.* **ashamed (of sth/sb/yourself)**; **ashamed (that...)**; **ashamed (to...)** (not before a noun) feeling sorry or embarrassed about sb/sth or about yourself or sth you have done: *She was ashamed of her old clothes.* ◇ *He was ashamed of himself for having made such an unkind remark.* ◇ *She felt ashamed that she hadn't visited her aunt more often.* ◇ *He knew that it was his fault, but he was ashamed to admit his mistake.*

**a·shore** /ə'ʃɔr/ *adv.* onto the land: *The passengers went ashore for an hour while the ship was in port.*

**ash·tray** /'æʃtreɪ/ *noun* [C] a small dish for cigarette ashes

**A·sian** /'eɪʒn/ *noun* [C] a person from Asia, especially the eastern part ▸ **A·sian** *adj.*: *Asian cuisine*

**ˌAsian A'merican** *noun* [C] an American person whose family was originally from Asia, especially the eastern part ▸ **ˌAsian-A'merican** *adj.*

★**a·side** /ə'saɪd/ *adv.* **1** on or to one side; out of the way: *She took Richard aside to tell him her secret.* **2** to be kept separately, for a special purpose: *They are setting aside $100 a month for their summer vacation.*

**a'side from** *prep.* = APART FROM

★**ask** /æsk/ *verb*

▸QUESTION **1** [I,T] **ask (sb) (about sb/sth)** to put a question to sb in order to find out some information: *We need to ask about the price.* ◇ *Do you mind if I ask a dumb question?* ◇ *I'll ask the salesman how much the jacket is.* ◇ *Did you ask Sarah about the bike?* ◇ *She asked whether I wanted tea or coffee.* ◇ *"What time is it?" he asked.* ◇ *He asked what time it was.* ◇ *He asked me the time.* ◇ *I got lost coming here and I had to ask somebody the way.* ◇ *I saw Mrs. Vasquez today. She asked about you* (= asked about your health, etc.).

▸REQUEST **2** [I,T] **ask (sb) for sth**; **ask sth (of sb)**; **ask sb to do sth**; **ask (sb) that...** to request sb to give you sth or do sth for you: *She asked for a cup of coffee.* ◇ *Don't ask John for money – he doesn't have any.* ◇ *You are asking too much of him – he can't possibly do all that!* ◇ *Call this number and ask for Mrs. Smith* (= ask to speak to Mrs. Smith). ◇ *I asked him if he would drive me home.* ◇ *I asked him to drive me home.* ◇ *We ask that everyone remain seated.* ➲ Look at the note at **recommend** (2).

▸MONEY **3** [T] to say the price that you want for sth: *They're asking $2,000 for their car.*

▸PERMISSION **4** [I,T] to request permission to do sth: *I'm sure she'll let you go if you ask.* ◇ *He asked to use our phone.* ◇ *We asked permission to go early.* ◇ *We asked if we could go home early.*

▸INVITE **5** [T] **ask sb (to sth)** to invite sb: *They asked six friends to dinner.* ◇ *He asked Eileen out* (= asked her to go out with him) *this Saturday.*

IDM **ask for trouble/it** to behave in a way that will almost certainly cause trouble: *Not wearing a seat belt is just asking for trouble.*

**if you ask me** if you want my opinion: *If you ask me, she's too young to travel alone.*

**a·skew** /ə'skyu/ *adv., adj.* (not before a noun) not in a straight or level position

★**a·sleep** /ə'slip/ *adj.* (not before a noun) not awake; sleeping: *The baby is asleep.* ◇ *She was fast/sound asleep and I couldn't wake her up.* ◇ *to fall asleep*

> NOTE Notice that you cannot use **asleep** before the noun. **Sleeping** can be used before or after the noun: *a sleeping child.* ➲ Look at the note at **sleep**[2].

**as·par·a·gus** /ə'spærəgəs/ *noun* [U] a plant with long green stems that you can cook and eat as a vegetable ➲ picture on study page **A28-29**.

★**as·pect** /'æspɛkt/ *noun* [C] one of the qualities or parts of a situation, idea, problem, etc.: *information on many aspects of modern life*

**as·phalt** /'æsfɔlt/ *noun* [U] a thick black substance that is used for making the surface of roads, etc.

**as·phyx·i·ate** /əs'fɪksieɪt/ *verb* **1** [T] (usually passive) (used about gas, smoke, etc.) to cause sb to die or become very sick by making him/her unable to breathe: *He was asphyxiated by the smoke while he was asleep.* **2** [I] to die or become very sick because you are unable to breathe: *She asphyxiated on the fumes from the car's exhaust.* ▸ **as·phyx·i·a·tion** /əsˌfɪksi'eɪʃn/ *noun* [U]

**as·pi·ra·tion** /ˌæspə'reɪʃn/ *noun* [C,U] (often plural) a strong desire to have or do sth: *She has aspirations to become an opera singer.*

**as·pire** /ə'spaɪər/ *verb* [I] **aspire to sth/to do sth** (*formal*) to have a strong desire to have or do sth: *She aspired to become president of the company.*

**as·pi·rin** /'æsprən/ *noun* [C,U] (*pl.* **as·pi·rins** or **as·pi·rin**) a type of medicine that reduces pain and fever: *I took two aspirin(s)* (= two aspirin pills).

**as·pir·ing** /əs'paɪrɪŋ/ *adj.* (only *before* a noun) having a strong desire to become sth: *an aspiring ballet dancer*

A

**ass** /æs/ ***noun*** [C] (*taboo, slang*) the part of the body that you sit on; your butt

**as·sail·ant** /ə'seɪlənt/ ***noun*** [C] (*formal*) a person who attacks sb

**as·sas·sin** /ə'sæsn/ ***noun*** [C] a person who kills a famous or important person for money or for political reasons

**as·sas·si·nate** /ə'sæsəneɪt/ ***verb*** [T] to kill a famous or important person for money or for political reasons ➲ Look at the note at **kill**. ▶ **as·sas·si·na·tion** /əˌsæsə'neɪʃn/ ***noun*** [C,U]: *an assassination attempt*

**as·sault** /ə'sɔlt/ ***noun*** [C,U] **assault (on sb/sth)** a sudden attack on sb/sth: *Assaults on the police are becoming more common.* ▶ **as·sault** ***verb*** [T]: *a prison sentence for assaulting a police officer*

**as·sem·ble** /ə'sɛmbl/ ***verb*** **1** [I,T] to come together in a group; to gather or collect: *The leaders assembled in Washington for the summit meeting.* ◇ *I've assembled all the information I need for my essay.* **2** [T] to fit the parts of sth together: *We spent all day trying to assemble our new bookcase.*

★**as·sem·bly** /ə'sɛmbli/ ***noun*** (*pl.* **as·sem·blies**) **1** [C,U] a large group of people who come together for a particular purpose: *There will be an assembly* (= a meeting for all the students and teachers of a school) *in the auditorium this afternoon.* ◇ *the United Nations General Assembly* **2** [U] the act of fitting the parts of sth together: *the assembly of cars by robots*

**as'sembly line** ***noun*** [C] a line of people and machines in a factory that fit the parts of sth together in a fixed order: *the assembly line workers at the Toyota car plant*

**as·sent** /ə'sɛnt/ ***noun*** [U] (*formal*) agreement: *The committee gave its assent to the proposed changes.*

**as·sert** /ə'sərt/ ***verb*** [T] **1** to say sth clearly and firmly: *He asserted that the allegations were untrue.* **2** to behave in a way that makes other people listen to you and take notice of you: *You ought to assert yourself more.* ◇ *to assert your authority*

**as·ser·tion** /ə'sərʃn/ ***noun*** **1** [U] the act of asserting sth/yourself: *the assertion of power* **2** [C] something that you say firmly and clearly, but that you do not prove is true: *his confident assertion that he would win*

**as·ser·tive** /ə'sərṭɪv/ ***adj.*** expressing your opinion clearly and firmly so that people listen to you and take notice of you: *to speak in an assertive manner* OPP **submissive** ▶ **as·ser·tive·ly** ***adv.*** **as·ser·tive·ness** ***noun*** [U]

**as·sess** /ə'sɛs/ ***verb*** [T] **1** to judge or form an opinion about sth: *It's too early to assess the effects of the price increases.* **2** to estimate or decide the amount or value of sth: *The value of the house was assessed at $75,000.* ◇ *to assess the cost of repairs* **3** to decide the amount of money that sb should pay as a punishment: *to assess a fine*

**as·sess·ment** /ə'sɛsmənt/ ***noun*** [C,U] the act of judging or forming an opinion about sb/sth: *to make a careful assessment of a situation*

**as·set** /'æsɛt/ ***noun*** [C] **1 an asset (to sb/sth)** a person or thing that is useful to sb/sth: *She's a great asset to the organization.* ◇ *It's an asset to be able to speak a foreign language.* **2** [usually pl.] something of value that a person, company, etc. owns: *The court ordered the company to sell off its remaining assets.*

**as·sign** /ə'saɪn/ ***verb*** [T] **1 assign sth to sb** to give sth to sb for him/her to use or do **2 assign sb to sth** to give sb a particular job or type of work to do: *She was assigned to the accounting department.* ◇ *A detective was assigned to the case.*

**as·sign·ment** /ə'saɪnmənt/ ***noun*** [C,U] a job or type of work that you are given to do: *to give students a homework assignment* ◇ *a reporter on assignment in Moscow*

**as·sim·i·late** /ə'sɪməleɪt/ ***verb*** **1** [I,T] to become, or to allow sb/sth to become, part of a larger thing or group: *Many immigrants have difficulty in assimilating into their new culture.* ◇ *to assimilate people from other cultures* **2** [T] to learn and understand sth: *to assimilate new information/ideas* ▶ **as·sim·i·la·tion** /əˌsɪmə'leɪʃn/ ***noun*** [U]

★**as·sist** /ə'sɪst/ ***verb*** [I,T] **assist (sb) (in/with sth)**; **assist (sb) (in doing sth)** (*formal*) to help: *Dozens of police officers assisted in the search for the missing girl.*

★**as·sis·tance** /ə'sɪstəns/ ***noun*** [U] (*formal*) **1** help: *Our center provides assistance to recent immigrants in finding housing and employment.* **2** money that is given, especially by the government, to help sb: *financial assistance for college students* ◇ *people living on public assistance* (= money that the government gives to poor people)

★**as·sis·tant** /ə'sɪstənt/ ***noun*** [C] (*abbr.* **asst.**) a person who helps sb of higher rank: *The director is away today. Would you like to speak with her assistant?* ◇ *the assistant manager*

**asˌsistant pro'fessor** ***noun*** [C] a teacher at a college or university who is lower in rank than a professor and an associate professor

**assn.** ***abbr.*** = ASSOCIATION (2)

**as·so·ci·ate¹** /ə'soʊʃiət; -siət/ ***adj.*** (*abbr.* **assoc.**) (only *before* a noun) of a slightly lower rank or status: *associate members of the organization*

**as·so·ci·ate²** /ə'soʊʃiət; -siət/ ***noun*** [C] a person that you meet and get to know through your work: *a business associate*

★**as·so·ci·ate³** /ə'soʊʃiˌeɪt; -siˌeɪt/ ***verb*** **1** [T] **associate sb/sth (with sb/sth)** to connect sb/sth with sb/sth else (in your mind): *illnesses associated with smoking* ◇ *Somehow, I don't associate Iowa with skiing.* **2** [I] **associate with sb** to spend time with sb: *I prefer not to associate with colleagues outside work.* **3** [T] **associate yourself with sth** to say that you support sth or agree with sth: *I do not want to associate myself with any organization that promotes violence.*

**asˌsociate pro'fessor** ***noun*** [C] a teacher at a college or university who is higher in rank than an assistant professor, but lower than a professor

**as'sociate's degree** (*also* **as'sociate degree**) ***noun*** [C] a degree that you get after studying for two years at a college or university in the U.S.

★**as·so·ci·a·tion** /əˌsoʊsi'eɪʃn; -ʃi'eɪʃn/ ***noun*** **1** [U] the act of joining or working with another person or group: *We work in association with our London office.* **2** (*abbr.* **assn.**; **assoc.**) [C] a group of

A

people or organizations who join or work together for a particular purpose: *a trade association* ◇ *the American Medical Association* **3** [C,U] the act of connecting sb/sth to sb/sth else in your mind

**as·sort·ed** /əˈsɔrt̬əd/ ***adj.*** of different types; mixed: *a box of assorted chocolates*

**as·sort·ment** /əˈsɔrtmənt/ ***noun*** [C] a group of different things or of different types of the same thing; a mixture: *You'll find a wide assortment of souvenirs in our gift shop.*

**asst.** ***abbr.*** = ASSISTANT

★**as·sume** /əˈsum/ ***verb*** [T] **1** to accept or believe that sth is true even though you have no proof; to expect sth to be true: *I assume that you have the necessary documents.* ◇ *You'll be going to the meeting, I assume?* ◇ *In your calculations, assume x is a number greater than zero.* **2** to falsely pretend to have or be sb/sth: *to assume a false name* **3** to begin to use power or to have a powerful position: *to assume control of sth* ◇ *to assume a position of responsibility*

**as·sump·tion** /əˈsʌmpʃn/ ***noun*** **1** [C] something that you accept is true even though you have no proof: *Our figures are based on the assumption that the rate of inflation will be 5%.* ◇ *a reasonable/false assumption* **2** [U] **assumption of sth** the act of taking power or of starting an important job: *the assumption of power by the army*

**as·sur·ance** /əˈʃʊrəns/ ***noun*** [C,U] (*formal*) a promise that sth will certainly happen or be true: *News reporters gave assurances that the hurricane would move away from the coast.* ◇ *a company's quality assurance procedures*

★**as·sure** /əˈʃʊr/ ***verb*** [T] **1 assure sb (of sth/ that...)** to promise sb that sth will certainly happen or be true, especially if he/she is worried: *I assure you that it is perfectly safe.* ◇ *Let me assure you of my full support.* **2** to make sth sure or certain: *The new road will assure adequate supplies of food to the region.*

**as·ter·isk** /ˈæstərɪsk/ ***noun*** [C] the sign (*) that you use to call attention to sth in a piece of writing

**as·ter·oid** /ˈæstərɔɪd/ ***noun*** [C] any one of the many small planets which go around the sun

**asth·ma** /ˈæzmə/ ***noun*** [U] a medical condition that causes difficulty in breathing: *a new medication for asthma sufferers*

**asth·mat·ic** /æzˈmæt̬ɪk/ ***noun*** [C] a person who suffers from asthma ▸ **asth·mat·ic** ***adj.***

**a·ston·ish** /əˈstɑnɪʃ/ ***verb*** [T] to cause sb to be very surprised: *She astonished everybody by announcing her engagement.* ▸ **a·ston·ished** ***adj.***: *The chancellor was said to be astonished by the decision.*

**a·ston·ish·ing** /əˈstɑnɪʃɪŋ/ ***adj.*** very surprising: *astonishing news* ▸ **a·ston·ish·ing·ly** ***adv.***: *an astonishingly high price*

**a·ston·ish·ment** /əˈstɑnɪʃmənt/ ***noun*** [U] very great surprise: *To my absolute astonishment, the plan was a huge success.* ◇ *A look of astonishment crossed her face.* ◇ *He dropped his book in astonishment.*

**a·stound** /əˈstaʊnd/ ***verb*** [T] (usually passive) to cause sb to be very surprised: *We were astounded at how well he performed.*

**a·stound·ing** /əˈstaʊndɪŋ/ ***adj.*** very surprising: *an astounding success*

**a·stray** /əˈstreɪ/ ***adv.*** away from the right way: *Teenagers are easily led astray* (= persuaded to do bad things by other people).

**a·stride** /əˈstraɪd/ ***adv.***, ***prep.*** with one leg on each side of sth: *to sit astride a horse*

**as·trol·o·ger** /əˈstrɑlədʒər/ ***noun*** [C] a person who is an expert in astrology

**as·trol·o·gy** /əˈstrɑlədʒi/ ***noun*** [U] the study of the positions and movements of the stars and planets and the way that they are supposed to affect people and events ➲ Look at **astronomy** and also at **horoscope** and **zodiac**.

**as·tro·naut** /ˈæstrənɔt; -nɑt/ ***noun*** [C] a person who travels in a spaceship

**as·tron·o·mer** /əˈstrɑnəmər/ ***noun*** [C] a person who is an expert in astronomy

**as·tro·nom·i·cal** /ˌæstrəˈnɑmɪkl/ ***adj.*** **1** connected with astronomy **2** very large, often too large (describing a price, number, amount, etc.): *the astronomical prices of housing*

**as·tron·o·my** /əˈstrɑnəmi/ ***noun*** [U] the scientific study of the sun, moon, stars, etc. ➲ Look at **astrology**.

**as·tute** /əˈstut/ ***adj.*** very intelligent; good at judging people or situations

**a·sy·lum** /əˈsaɪləm/ ***noun*** **1** [U] protection that a government gives to people who have left their own country for political reasons: *political asylum* **2** [C] (*old-fashioned*) a hospital for people who are mentally ill

★**at** /ət; *strong form* æt/ ***prep.*** **1** (showing the position of sth or where sth happens): *at the bottom/top of the page* ◇ *He was standing at the door.* ◇ *Turn left at the next intersection.* ◇ *We were at home all weekend.* ◇ *Are the kids still at school?* ◇ *at the theater* ◇ *"Where's Peter?" "He's at Sue's."* (= at Sue's house) ◇ *You can reach me at 637-2335, extension 354* (= using this telephone number). **2** (showing when sth happens): *I start work at 9 o'clock.* ◇ *at night* ◇ *at Easter* ◇ *She got married at 18* (= when she was 18). **3** in the direction of sb/sth: *What are you looking at?* ◇ *He pointed a gun at the police officer.* ◇ *Don't shout at me!* **4** because of: *I was surprised at her behavior.* ◇ *We laughed at his jokes.* **5** (showing what sb is doing or what is happening): *They were hard at work.* ◇ *The two countries were at war.* **6** (showing the amount, price, rate, speed, etc. of sth): *Bake at 350° for 25 minutes.* ◇ *We were traveling at about 50 miles per hour.* **7** (used with adjectives that show how well sb/sth does sth): *She's not very good at French.* ◇ *I'm terrible at baseball.*

IDM **at any rate** → RATE[1]

**ate** *past tense of* EAT

**a·the·ism** /ˈeɪθiɪzəm/ ***noun*** [U] the belief that there is no God

**a·the·ist** /ˈeɪθiɪst/ ***noun*** [C] a person who believes that there is no God

**ath·lete** /ˈæθlit/ ***noun*** [C] a person who is a member of a sports team or who regularly plays a sport or sports

A

**ath·let·ic** /æθ'lɛt̮ɪk/ *adj.* **1** connected with athletes or athletics **2** (used about a person) having a strong, healthy body and able to play many sports well

**ath·let·ics** /æθ'lɛt̮ɪks/ *noun* [U] any sports that people compete in ➲ picture on study page **A32**.

**At·lan·tic Can·a·da** /ət,læntɪk 'kænədə/ *noun* [sing.] (*also* [pl.] **the At,lantic 'provinces**) the Canadian provinces of New Brunswick, Nova Scotia, Prince Edward Island and Newfoundland and Labrador ➲ Look also at the **Maritimes**.

**At'lantic ,Time** *noun* [U] (in Canada) the standard time system that is used in a zone which includes the Maritime provinces and parts of Labrador and East Quebec

> NOTE **Atlantic Standard Time** is four hours behind **Greenwich Mean Time**, and **Atlantic Daylight Time** is three hours behind **Greenwich Mean Time**.

**at·las** /'ætləs/ *noun* [C] (*pl.* **at·las·es**) a book of maps

**ATM** /,eɪ ti 'ɛm/ (*also* **'cash machine**) *noun* [C] automated teller machine; a machine inside or outside a bank, in a shopping center, etc. from which you can get money at any time of day by putting in a special card

★**at·mos·phere** /'ætməsfɪr/ *noun* **1** [C, usually sing.] **the atmosphere** the mixture of gases that surrounds the earth or any other star, planet, etc.: *the earth's atmosphere* **2** [C, U] the mood or feeling of a place or situation: *There was a tense atmosphere during the final minutes of the game.*

**at·mos·pher·ic** /,ætməs'fɪrɪk/ *adj.* connected with the ATMOSPHERE (1)

★**at·om** /'æt̮əm/ *noun* [C] the smallest part into which an element can be divided ➲ Look at **molecule** and **nucleus**.

**a·tom·ic** /ə'tɑmɪk/ *adj.* of or concerning an atom or atoms: *atomic physics* ➲ Look at **nuclear**.

**a,tomic 'bomb** (*also* **'atom bomb**) *noun* [C] a bomb that explodes using the energy that is produced when an atom or atoms are split

**a,tomic 'energy** *noun* [U] the energy that is produced when an atom or atoms are split. Atomic energy can be used to produce electricity. ➲ Look also at **nuclear**.

**a,tomic 'number** *noun* [C] the number of protons in the center of an atom (**nucleus**), which is characteristic of a chemical element. Elements are placed in the periodic table according to their atomic numbers.

**a·tro·cious** /ə'troʊʃəs/ *adj.* very bad or unpleasant: *atrocious crimes*

**a·troc·i·ty** /ə'trɑsət̮i/ *noun* [C,U] (*pl.* **a·troc·i·ties**) (an act of) great cruelty: *Both sides were accused of committing atrocities during the war.*

★**at·tach** /ə'tætʃ/ *verb* [T] **1 attach sth (to sth)** to fasten or connect sth to sth: *A note was attached to the document with a paper clip.* **2 attach sb to sb/sth** (*formal*) to make sb join another person or group: *Tom was attached to the embassy in Beijing for three years.* **3 attach sth to sb/sth** to think that sb/sth has a particular quality: *Don't attach too much importance to what they say.* ◇ *No blame was attached to him.*

IDM **(with) no strings attached** → STRING[1]

**at·tached** /ə'tætʃt/ *adj.* **attached to sb/sth** liking sb/sth very much: *He's become very attached to you.*

**at·tach·ment** /ə'tætʃmənt/ *noun* **1** [C] something that can be fastened to sth else: *a camera with a flash attachment* **2** [C,U] **attachment (to/for sb/sth)** the feeling of liking sb/sth very much: *an emotional attachment* ◇ *I feel a strong attachment to this house.* **3** [C] a document that you send to sb with an e-mail message

★**at·tack**[1] /ə'tæk/ *noun* **1** [C,U] **an attack (on sb/sth)** an act of trying to hurt or defeat sb/sth by using force: *The rebel forces launched an attack on the capital.* ◇ *to be under attack* (= to be attacked by sb/sth) **2** [C,U] **attack (on sb/sth)** an act of saying strongly that you do not like or agree with sb/sth: *an outspoken attack on the President's policy* **3** [C] a short period when you suffer badly from a disease, medical condition, etc.: *an attack of asthma/bronchitis* ➲ Look also at **heart attack**. **4** [C] an act of trying to score a point, goal, etc. in a sports game: *The Giants made several strong attacks but failed to score a touchdown.* ◇ *The home team went on the attack again.*

★**at·tack**[2] /ə'tæk/ *verb* **1** [I,T] to try to hurt or defeat sb/sth by using force: *The enemy attacked at night.* ◇ *to be attacked by a wild animal* **2** [T] to say strongly that you do not like or agree with sb/sth: *The senator attacked the press for misleading the public.* **3** [T] to damage or harm sb/sth: *a virus that attacks the nervous system* **4** [I,T] to try to score a point in a sports game

**at·tack·er** /ə'tækər/ *noun* [C] a person who attacks sb/sth

**at·tain** /ə'teɪn/ *verb* [T] to succeed in getting or achieving sth, especially after great effort: *to attain your objectives*

**at·tain·a·ble** /ə'teɪnəbl/ *adj.* that can be attained

**at·tain·ment** /ə'teɪnmənt/ *noun* **1** [U] the act of achieving sth: *the attainment of the teacher's goals* **2** [C,U] a level of skill or achievement: *to measure students' educational attainment*

★**at·tempt**[1] /ə'tɛmpt/ *verb* [T] to try to do sth that is difficult: *The prisoner was shot while attempting to escape.* ◇ *She was accused of attempted murder* (= she didn't succeed). ◇ *Don't attempt to argue with him.*

★**at·tempt**[2] /ə'tɛmpt/ *noun* [C] **1 attempt (to do sth/at doing sth)** an act of trying to do sth: *He managed to hit the target on the first attempt.* ◇ *They failed in their attempt to reach the North Pole.* **2 attempt (on sb/sth)** an act of trying to attack or beat sb/sth: *an attempt on sb's life* (= to kill sb)

★**at·tend** /ə'tɛnd/ *verb* **1** [T] to go to or be present at a place: *Do you attend church regularly?* ◇ *I won't be able to attend tonight's meeting.* ◇ *Our kids attend the local high school.* **2** [I] **attend to sb/sth** (*formal*) to give your care, thought or attention to sb/sth: *Please attend to this matter immediately.*

**at·ten·dance** /ə'tɛndəns/ *noun* [U] **1** being

A

present somewhere: *Attendance at lectures is not mandatory.* **2** the number of people who go to or are present at a place: *Attendance at the club's meetings has decreased in recent months.*

IDM **take attendance** to check who is present and who is absent at a place, and to mark this information on a list of names

**at·ten·dant¹** /ə'tɛndənt/ ***noun*** [C] a person who takes care of a public place or a business: *a gas station attendant* ➲ Look also at **flight attendant**.

**at·ten·dant²** /ə'tɛndənt/ ***adj.*** (only *before* a noun) (*formal*) that goes with or results from sth: *unemployment and all its attendant social problems*

★**at·ten·tion¹** /ə'tɛnʃn/ ***noun*** [U] **1** the act of watching, listening to or thinking about sb/sth carefully: *The bride is always the center of attention* (= the person that everybody is watching). ◇ *I shouted in order to attract her attention.* ◇ *to hold sb's attention* (= to keep them interested in sth) **2** special care or action: *The hole in the roof needs urgent attention.* ◇ *to require medical attention* ◇ *Mark your letter **for the attention of** M. Nolan, Sales Dept.* (= Write "attn. M. Nolan, Sales Dept." on the envelope of the letter to show who should deal with it.) **3** a position in which a soldier stands up straight and still: *to stand at attention*

IDM **bring sth to sb's attention; call/draw sb's attention to sth** to make sb aware of sth

**catch sb's attention/eye; get sb's attention** to make sb notice sth: *I tried to get the waiter's attention.*

**come to sb's attention** (*formal*) to be seen or heard by sb: *It has come to my attention that you have missed a lot of classes.*

**pay attention** → PAY²

**at·ten·tion²** /ə'tɛnʃn/ ***interjection*** (used for asking people to listen to sth carefully): *Attention, please! The boat will be leaving in five minutes.*

**at·ten·tive** /ə'tɛntɪv/ ***adj.*** watching, listening to or thinking about sb/sth carefully: *The waiters in that restaurant were very attentive.* ◇ *an attentive audience* ▸ **at·ten·tive·ly** ***adv.***: *to listen attentively to sth*

**at·tic** /'æṭɪk/ ***noun*** [C] the space or room under the roof of a house

★**at·ti·tude** /'æṭətud/ ***noun*** **1** [C] **attitude (to/toward sb/sth)** the way that you think, feel or behave: *social attitudes and beliefs* ◇ *She has a very positive attitude toward her work.* **2** [U] confident, sometimes aggressive behavior that shows you do not care about other people's opinions and that you want to do things in an individual way: *a band with attitude* ◇ *You'd better get rid of that attitude, buster.*

**attn.** ***abbr.*** (written on an envelope, a package etc.) for the attention of: *attn. A. Waters*

★**at·tor·ney** /ə'tərni/ (*also* at,torney at 'law) ***noun*** [C] (*pl.* **at·tor·neys**) a lawyer ➲ Look also at **district attorney** and **Crown attorney**.

**at·tor·ney gen·er·al** ***noun*** [C] (*pl.* **at·tor·neys gen·er·al** or **at·tor·ney gen·er·als**) **1** the chief lawyer for the U.S. or for a particular state, appointed by the government **2 At·tor·ney Gen·er·al** (*Cdn*) the chief lawyer for Canada or for a particular province or territory and who also acts as legal advisor to the government

★**at·tract** /ə'trækt/ ***verb*** [T] **1** (usually passive) **attract sb (to sb/sth)** if you are attracted by sth, it interests you and makes you want it; if you are attracted by sb, you like or admire him/her: *I had always been attracted by the idea of working abroad.* ◇ *What first attracted me to her was her sense of humor.* **2** to cause sb/sth to come somewhere or give attention to sth: *to attract sb's attention* ◇ *Moths are attracted to light.* ◇ *The new movie has attracted a lot of publicity.*

★**at·trac·tion** /ə'trækʃn/ ***noun*** **1** [U] attracting or being attracted: *I can't understand the attraction of fishing.* ◇ *sexual attraction* **2** [C] something that attracts sb/sth: *Washington D.C. offers all kinds of tourist attractions.* ◇ *One of the attractions of the job is having a company car.*

★**at·trac·tive** /ə'træktɪv/ ***adj.*** **1** that pleases or interests you; that you like: *an attractive idea* **2** pretty, beautiful or handsome: *an attractive room* ◇ *an attractive man/woman* ▸ **at·trac·tive·ly** ***adv.*** ▸ **at·trac·tive·ness** ***noun*** [U]

**at·trib·ute¹** /ə'trɪbyut/ ***verb*** [T] **attribute sth to sb/sth** to believe that sth was caused or done by sb/sth: *Jamal attributes his success to hard work.* ◇ *a poem attributed to Shakespeare*

**at·trib·ute²** /'ætrəbyut/ ***noun*** [C] a quality or feature of sb/sth: *physical attributes*

**atty.** ***abbr.*** = ATTORNEY

**ATV** /,eɪ ti 'vi/ ***noun*** [C] the abbreviation for "all-terrain vehicle"; a kind of car with one seat and four wheels with very thick tires, designed to be used on rough ground without roads

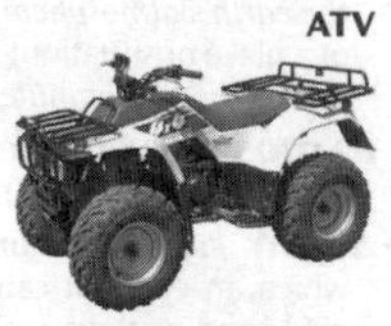
ATV

**a·typ·i·cal** /eɪ'tɪpɪkl/ ***adj.*** not typical or usual: *atypical behavior* OPP **typical**

**au·burn** /'ɔbərn/ ***adj.*** (usually used about hair) reddish-brown

**auc·tion¹** /'ɔkʃn/ ***noun*** [C,U] a public sale at which items are sold to the person who offers to pay the most money: *The house will be sold by auction.*

**auc·tion²** /'ɔkʃn/ ***verb*** [T] **auction sth (off)** to sell sth at an auction

**auc·tion·eer** /,ɔkʃə'nɪr/ ***noun*** [C] a person whose job is to direct an auction and sell the goods

**au·di·ble** /'ɔdəbl/ ***adj.*** that can be heard: *Her speech was barely audible.* OPP **inaudible** ▸ **au·di·bly** /-əbli/ ***adv.***: *to sigh audibly*

★**au·di·ence** /'ɔdiəns/ ***noun*** [C] **1** the group of people who are watching or listening to a play, concert, speech, the television, etc.: *The audience was wild with excitement.* ◇ *Television can reach an audience of millions.* **2** a formal meeting with a very important person: *an audience with the Pope*

**au·di·o** /'ɔdioʊ/ ***adj.*** connected with the recording of sound: *audio equipment* ◇ *audiotape*

**au·di·o·vis·u·al** /,ɔdioʊ'vɪʒuəl/ ***adj.*** (*abbr.* **AV**) using both sound and pictures: *A VCR is an excellent audiovisual aid in the classroom.*

**au·dit**[1] /'ɔdət/ ***noun*** [C] an official examination of the accounts and tax records of a person, company, etc. to see that they are correct: *a tax audit*

**au·dit**[2] /'ɔdət/ ***verb*** [T] **1** to officially examine the accounts and tax records of a person, company, etc., to see that they are correct **2** to attend a course at a college or university but without taking any exams or receiving credit ▸ **au·di·tor** /'ɔdət̬ər/ ***noun*** [C]

**au·di·tion** /ɔ'dɪʃn/ ***noun*** [C] a short performance by a singer, actor, musician, etc. to find out if he/she is good enough to be in a play, show, concert, etc.

**au·di·to·ri·um** /ˌɔdə'tɔriəm/ ***noun*** [C] (*pl.* **au·di·to·ri·ums** or (*formal*) **au·di·to·ri·a**) a large room like a theater where people sit and watch a performance, etc.: *School assemblies are always held in the auditorium.*

**Au·gust** /'ɔgəst/ ***noun*** [C,U] (*abbr.* **Aug.**) the eighth month of the year, coming before September ➲ For examples of the use of the months in sentences, look at **January**.

★**aunt** /ænt; ɑnt/ ***noun*** [C] the sister of your father or mother, or the wife of your uncle: *Aunt Ann*

**au·ra** /'ɔrə/ ***noun*** [C] (*formal*) the quality that sb/sth seems to have: *The small town had an aura of peace and tranquility.*

**au·ral** /'ɔrəl/ ***adj.*** of or concerning the ear or hearing: *an aural comprehension test* ➲ Look at **oral**.

**au·ro·ra bo·re·al·is** /əˌrɔrə bɔri'æləs/ ***noun*** [sing.] = THE NORTHERN LIGHTS

**aus·pi·ces** /'ɔspəsəz; -siz/ ***noun*** [pl.]

IDM **under the auspices of sb/sth** with the help and support of sb/sth: *The visit was arranged under the auspices of the local church.*

**aus·pi·cious** /ɔ'spɪʃəs/ ***adj.*** (*formal*) that seems likely to lead to success: *an auspicious occasion*

**aus·tere** /ɔ'stɪr/ ***adj.*** **1** not having pleasures or luxuries: *The nuns lead simple and austere lives.* **2** very plain and simple; without decoration ▸ **aus·ter·i·ty** /ɔ'stɛrət̬i/ ***noun*** [U]

**au·then·tic** /ɔ'θɛntɪk/ ***adj.*** that you know is true or genuine: *an authentic Van Gogh painting* ▸ **au·then·tic·i·ty** /ˌɔθɛn'tɪsət̬i/ ***noun*** [U]: *to check the authenticity of a document*

★**au·thor**[1] /'ɔθər/ ***noun*** [C] a person who writes a book, play, etc.: *a well-known author of detective novels* ▸ **au·thor·ship** ***noun*** [U]: *The authorship of the play is unknown.*

**au·thor**[2] /'ɔθər/ ***verb*** [T] to be the author of a book, a report, etc.: *The senator authored a new bill on traffic safety.*

**au·thor·i·tar·i·an** /əˌθɔrə'tɛriən; əˌθɑr-/ ***adj.*** not allowing people the freedom to decide things for themselves: *The authoritarian government crushed all signs of opposition.* ◇ *authoritarian parents*

**au·thor·i·ta·tive** /ə'θɔrəˌteɪt̬ɪv; ə'θɑr-/ ***adj.*** **1** having authority; demanding or expecting that people obey you: *an authoritative tone of voice* **2** that you can trust because it/he/she has a lot of knowledge and information: *They will be able to give you authoritative advice on the problem.*

★**au·thor·i·ty** /ə'θɔrət̬i; ə'θɑr-/ ***noun*** (*pl.* **au·thor·i·ties**)
➤ORGANIZATION **1** [C] (often plural) a person, group or government department that has the power to give orders, make official decisions, etc.: *the city housing authority* ◇ *The French authorities refused permission for the plane to land.*
➤POWER **2** [U] the power and right to give orders and make others obey: *Children often begin to question their parents' authority at a very early age.* ◇ *You need to get this signed by a person in authority* (= who has a position of power). **3** [U] **authority (to do sth)** the right to act in a particular way: *Do the police have the authority to question anybody they want?*
➤KNOWLEDGE **4** [U] a quality that sb has which makes it possible to influence and control other people: *He spoke with authority and everybody listened.*
➤EXPERT **5** [C] a person with special knowledge: *She's an authority on ancient Egypt.*

**au·thor·i·za·tion** /ˌɔθərə'zeɪʃn/ ***noun*** [U] official permission for sth: *I can't give you that information without authorization.*

**au·thor·ize** /'ɔθəraɪz/ ***verb*** [T] to give official permission for sth or for sb to do sth: *Any new buildings have to be authorized by the city council.* ◇ *He authorized his secretary to sign letters in his absence.*

**au·tis·tic** /ɔ'tɪstɪk/ ***adj.*** having a serious mental illness which makes it very difficult to form relationships with other people

**au·to** /'ɔt̬oʊ/ ***noun*** [C] (*pl.* **au·tos**) (*formal*) a car: *auto insurance* ➲ It is more common to say **car**.

**au·to·bi·og·ra·phy** /ˌɔt̬əbaɪ'ɑgrəfi/ ***noun*** [C,U] (*pl.* **au·to·bi·og·ra·phies**) the story of a person's life written by that person ➲ Look at **biography**. ▸ **au·to·bi·o·graph·i·cal** /ˌɔt̬əˌbaɪə'græfɪkl/ ***adj.***: *an autobiographical novel*

**au·to·graph**[1] /'ɔt̬əgræf/ ***noun*** [C] the signature of a famous person: *We waited at the stage door to get the dancer's autograph.*

**au·to·graph**[2] /'ɔt̬əgræf/ ***verb*** [T] to put your signature on or in sth: *a painting autographed by the artist*

**au·to·mate** /'ɔt̬əmeɪt/ ***verb*** [T] (usually passive) to make sth operate by machine, without needing people: *The system in the factory has been fully automated.*

**ˌautomated 'banking maˌchine** ***noun*** [C] (*Cdn*) = ABM

**ˌautomated 'teller maˌchine** ***noun*** [C] = ATM

★**au·to·mat·ic**[1] /ˌɔt̬ə'mæt̬ɪk/ ***adj.*** **1** (used about a machine) that can work by itself without direct human control: *an automatic garage door opener* ◇ *a car with automatic transmission* OPP Look at **manual**. **2** (used about actions) done without thinking or like a machine; unconscious: *Practice this exercise until it becomes automatic.* **3** certain to happen because it is part of a normal process: *Cheating will result in automatic failure in this class.* ▸ **au·to·mat·i·cal·ly** /-kli/ ***adv.***: *The lights come on automatically when it gets dark.*

**au·to·mat·ic**[2] /ˌɔt̬ə'mæt̬ɪk/ ***noun*** [C] an automatic machine or gun: *The weapon used in the robbery was a .357 automatic.*

A

**au·to·ma·tion** /ˌɔtəˈmeɪʃn/ *noun* [U] the use of machines, instead of people, to do work

**au·to·mo·bile** /ˌɔtəməˈbil; ˈɔtəməbil/ *noun* [C] (*formal*) a car: *the automobile industry*

**au·to·mo·tive** /ˌɔt̬əˈmoʊt̬ɪv/ *adj.* connected with cars, trucks, etc.: *automotive parts and accessories*

**au·ton·o·mous** /ɔˈtɑnəməs/ *adj.* having the right to govern or control its own affairs: *The people in this region want to be completely autonomous.*

**au·ton·o·my** /ɔˈtɑnəmi/ *noun* [U] the right of an organization, region, etc. to govern or control its own affairs

**au·top·sy** /ˈɔtɑpsi/ *noun* [C] (*pl.* **au·top·sies**) an examination of a dead body to find out the cause of death: *to perform an autopsy*

★**au·tumn** /ˈɔt̬əm/ *noun* [C,U] (*formal*) fall; the season between summer and winter

**aux·il·ia·ry**[1] /ɔgˈzɪləri; -ˈzɪlyəri/ *adj.* (only *before* a noun) giving extra help: *auxiliary personnel/troops* ◇ *auxiliary equipment*

**aux·il·ia·ry**[2] /ɔgˈzɪləri; -ˈzɪlyəri/ (*also* **auxiliary verb, helping verb**) *noun* [C] (*pl.* **aux·il·ia·ries**) (*grammar*) a verb (e.g. *be*, *do* or *have*) that is used with a main verb to show tense, etc. or to form questions

**AV** /ˌeɪ ˈvi/ *abbr.* = AUDIOVISUAL: *AV equipment*

**Av.** *abbr.* = AVENUE

**a·vail** /əˈveɪl/ *noun* [U]

IDM **to little/no avail** without success: *They searched everywhere, but to no avail.*

**a·vail·a·bil·i·ty** /əˌveɪləˈbɪlət̬i/ *noun* [U] the state of being available: *the availability of health care in rural areas*

★**a·vail·a·ble** /əˈveɪləbl/ *adj.* **1** (used about things) that you can get, buy, use, etc.: *Are there still tickets available for the concert?* ◇ *Her latest novel is now available in bookstores everywhere.* ◇ *The available evidence was not sufficient to prove that he was guilty.* **2** (used about people) free to be seen, talked to, etc.: *The senator was not available for an interview.*

**av·a·lanche** /ˈævəlæntʃ/ *noun* [C] a very large amount of snow that slides quickly down the side of a mountain: *Two skiers are still missing after yesterday's avalanche.* ◇ (*figurative*) *The company received an avalanche of complaints.*

**a·vant-garde** /ˌævɑŋ ˈgɑrd; ˌɑvɑŋ-/ *adj.* (used especially about art and literature) extremely new and modern

**Ave.** *abbr.* = AVENUE

**a·venge** /əˈvɛndʒ/ *verb* [T] to punish sb for hurting you, your family, etc. in some way: *He wanted to avenge his father's murder.* ➲ Look at **revenge**.

**av·e·nue** /ˈævənu/ *noun* [C] **1** (*abbr.* **Av.**; **Ave.**) a street in a town or city: *I live at 12 Tennyson Avenue.* ◇ *at the corner of Sixth Avenue and 72nd Street* **2** a way of doing or getting sth: *We must explore every avenue open to us* (= try every possibility).

★**av·er·age**[1] /ˈævrɪdʒ/ *noun* **1** [C] the number you get when you add two or more figures together and then divide the total by the number of figures you added: *The average of 14, 3 and 1 is 6* (= 18 divided by 3 is 6). **2** [C] the AVERAGE (1) of grades that a student receives on tests, written work, etc.: *If I get an A on the next quiz, that will bring my average up to a B +.* ➲ Look also at **grade point average**. **3** [sing., U] the normal standard, amount or quality: *Temperatures this week have been well below the average for this time of year.* ◇ *On average, Americans consume more fat than people from Asian countries do.*

★**av·er·age**[2] /ˈævrɪdʒ/ *adj.* **1** (only *before* a noun) (used about a number) found by calculating the AVERAGE[1] (1): *What's the average age of your students?* **2** normal or typical: *an average income* ◇ *children of above/below average intelligence* **3** not very good: *I was just an average student in math.*

**av·er·age**[3] /ˈævrɪdʒ/ *verb* [T] to do, get, etc. a certain amount as an average: *If we average 50 miles an hour, we should get there at about 4 o'clock.*

PHRV **average out (to sth)** to result in an average (of sth): *The meal averaged out to about $20 each.*

**a·verse** /əˈvərs/ *adj.* **averse to sth** (*formal*) (often with a negative) against or opposed to sth: *She is not averse to trying out new ideas.*

**a·ver·sion** /əˈvərʒn/ *noun* [C] **1** [usually sing.] **an aversion (to sb/sth)** a feeling of great dislike: *Many children have an aversion to vegetables.* **2** a thing that you greatly dislike: *Math was always an aversion of mine.*

**a·vert** /əˈvərt/ *verb* [T] to prevent sth unpleasant; to avoid sth: *The accident could have been averted.*

**avian influenza** /ˌeɪviən ɪnfluˈɛnzə/ (*also informal* **ˈbird flu, ˈchicken flu**) *noun* [U] a serious disease that affects birds, especially chickens, and that can be spread from birds to humans

**a·vi·a·tion** /ˌeɪviˈeɪʃn/ *noun* [U] the flying or building of aircraft: *the aviation industry*

**av·id** /ˈævəd/ *adj.* (only *before* a noun) enthusiastic and eager: *an avid golfer* ▶ **av·id·ly** *adv.*: *He read avidly as a child.*

**av·o·ca·do** /ˌɑvəˈkɑdoʊ; ˌævə-/ *noun* [C] (*pl.* **av·o·ca·dos**) a fruit shaped like a pear with tough dark green skin and a large hard part (**pit**) inside

★**a·void** /əˈvɔɪd/ *verb* [T] **1 avoid (doing sth)** to prevent sth from happening: *He always tried to avoid an argument if possible.* ◇ *She has to avoid eating fatty food* (= she must make an effort not to eat it). **2** to keep away from (sb/sth): *I leave home at 7 o'clock to avoid the rush hour.* ◇ *She's been trying to avoid her boyfriend recently.* ▶ **a·void·ance** /əˈvɔɪdns/ *noun* [U]

**a·void·a·ble** /əˈvɔɪdəbl/ *adj.* that can be prevented; unnecessary: *Many deaths from heart disease are avoidable.* OPP **unavoidable**

**aw** /ɔ/ *interjection* (used for expressing affection, sympathy, disappointment, etc.): *Aw, what a cute baby!* ◇ *Aw, that's too bad.*

**a·wait** /əˈweɪt/ *verb* [T] (*formal*) **1** to wait for sb/sth: *Please await further instructions.* **2** to be going to happen to sb: *We were unaware of the danger that awaited us.*

★**a·wake**[1] /əˈweɪk/ *adj.* (not before a noun) not sleeping: *I was awake most of the night, worrying.* ◇ *The kids are always wide* (= completely) *awake at 6 o'clock in the morning.* ◇ *They were so tired that they couldn't stay awake.* OPP **asleep**

**a·wake²** /əˈweɪk/ ***verb*** (*pt* **a·woke** /əˈwoʊk/; *pp* **a·wok·en** /əˈwoʊkən/) (*formal*) **1** [I,T] to wake up; to make sb/sth wake up: *I awoke to find that it was already 9 o'clock.* ◇ *A sudden loud noise awoke us all.*

NOTE **Wake up** is less formal and more common than **awake**.

**2** [T] to make sb have a particular feeling, attitude, etc.: *His words awoke fear and hatred in the boy.*

**a·wak·en** /əˈweɪkən/ ***verb*** **1** [I,T] (*formal*) to wake up; to make sb/sth wake up: *I awakened to find the others already up.* ◇ *We were awakened by a knock at the door.*

NOTE **Wake up** is much more common and less formal than **awaken**.

**2** [T] (*formal*) to produce a particular feeling, attitude, etc. in sb: *The movie awakened memories of her childhood.*
PHRV **awaken sb to sth** to make sb become aware of sth: *The letter awakened me to the seriousness of the situation.*

**a·wak·en·ing** /əˈweɪkənɪŋ/ ***noun*** **1** [C, usually sing.] an occasion when you realize sth or become aware of sth: *It was a **rude** (= unpleasant)**awakening** when I suddenly found myself unemployed.* **2** [C,U] the act of beginning to understand or feel sth; the act of sth starting or waking: *the awakening of an interest in environmental issues*

★**a·ward¹** /əˈwɔrd/ ***noun*** [C] **1** a prize, etc. that sb gets for doing sth well: *This year, the awards for best actor and actress went to two newcomers to Hollywood.* **2** an amount of money given to sb as the result of a court decision: *She received an award of $5,000 for damages.*

★**a·ward²** /əˈwɔrd/ ***verb*** [T] **award sth (to sb)** to give sth to sb as a prize, payment, etc.: *She was awarded first prize in the music competition.* ◇ *The court awarded $100,000 each to the workers injured in the accident.*

★**a·ware** /əˈwɛr/ ***adj.*** **1 aware (of sb/sth); aware (that)** knowing about or realizing sth; conscious of sb/sth: *I am aware of the difficulties you face.* ◇ *I am aware that you will face difficulties.* ◇ *She suddenly felt aware of somebody watching her.* ◇ *There is no other entrance, as far as I am aware.* OPP **unaware** **2** interested and informed: *to be politically aware*

**a·ware·ness** /əˈwɛrnəs/ ***noun*** [U] knowledge, consciousness or interest: *People's awareness of healthy eating has increased in recent years.*

**a·wash** /əˈwɑʃ; əˈwɔʃ/ ***adj.*** **awash in/with sth** having too much of sth: *The city was awash with rumors.*

★**a·way** /əˈweɪ/ ***adv.***

NOTE For the special uses of **away** in phrasal verbs, look at the entries for the verbs. For example **give sth away** is in the phrasal verb section at **give**.

**1 away (from sb/sth)** to a different place or in a different direction: *Go away! I'm busy!* ◇ *I asked him a question, but he just looked away.* **2** at a distance from a place: *My parents live five miles away.* ◇ *The town is two miles away from the ocean.* **3 away (from sth)** (used about people) not present; absent: *My neighbors are away on vacation right now.* ◇ *Tom was away from school for two weeks with the measles.* **4 away (from sth)** in the future: *Our summer vacation is only three weeks away.* **5** into a safe place: *Put your books away now.* ◇ *They cleared away the dishes* (= off the table). ➲ Compare these examples with *throw sth away* (= put it in the garbage can). **6** (used about a football, etc. team) at the other team's field, stadium, etc.: *Our team's playing away on Saturday.* **7** until it disappears completely: *The noise slowly died away.* ◇ *The picture has almost faded away.* **8** continuously, without stopping: *They chatted away for hours.*
IDM **right away** → RIGHT²

**awe** /ɔ/ ***noun*** [U] a feeling of respect and either fear or admiration: *We watched in awe as the rocket took off into space.* ◇ *As a boy he was very much in awe of his uncle.*

**ˈawe-inˌspiring** ***adj.*** causing a feeling of respect and fear or admiration

**awe·some** /ˈɔsəm/ ***adj.*** **1** (*formal*) impressive and sometimes frightening: *an awesome task* **2** (*informal*) very good; excellent: *We went to an awesome party at Dave's house.* ◇ *Wow! That's totally awesome!*

**aw·ful¹** /ˈɔfl/ ***adj.*** **1** very bad or unpleasant: *We had an awful vacation. It rained every day.* ◇ *What an awful thing to say!* **2** terrible; very serious: *I have some awful news for you.* **3** (only *before* a noun) (*informal*) very great or large: *I'm in an awful hurry. See you later.* ◇ *We've got an awful lot of work to do.*

**aw·ful²** /ˈɔfl/ ***adv.*** (*informal*) very; extremely: *Joe is awful smart.*

**aw·ful·ly** /ˈɔfli/ ***adv.*** very; very much: *I'm awfully sorry.*

★**awk·ward** /ˈɔkwərd/ ***adj.*** **1** making you feel embarrassed: *an awkward silence* **2** not convenient, difficult: *My mother always calls at an awkward time.* ◇ *an awkward question* **3** without grace or skill: *an awkward gesture* ◇ *an awkward teenage boy* ▶ **awk·ward·ly** ***adv.*** **awk·ward·ness** ***noun*** [U]

**a·woke** *past tense of* AWAKE¹

**a·wok·en** *past participle of* AWAKE¹

**a·wry** /əˈraɪ/ ***adv.*** wrong, not in the way that was planned: *Our plans went awry.*

**ax¹** (*also* **axe**) /æks/ ***noun*** [C] a tool with a wooden handle and a metal blade used for cutting wood, etc.: *He chopped the tree down with an ax.* ➲ picture at **garden**.

**ax²** (*also* **axe**) /æks/ ***verb*** [T] **1** to remove or end sth: *Hundreds of jobs have been axed.* **2** to reduce sth greatly: *School budgets are to be axed.*

**ax·is** /ˈæksəs/ ***noun*** [C] (*pl.* **ax·es** /ˈæksiz/) **1** an imaginary line through the middle of an object that turns: *The earth rotates on its axis.* ➲ picture at **earth**. **2** a fixed line used for marking measurements on a graph: *the horizontal/vertical axis*

**ax·le** /ˈæksl/ ***noun*** [C] a bar that connects a pair of wheels on a vehicle

# B b

**B, b** /bi/ ***noun*** [C,U] (*pl.* **B's**; **b's** /biz/) **1** the second letter of the English alphabet: *"Bill" begins with (a) "B."* **2** the second-highest grade given for a test or a piece of work, lower than an "A": *I got a "B" on my essay.*

**b.** ***abbr.*** born: *Cynthia Waters, b. 1937*

**B.A.** /ˌbi ˈeɪ/ ***abbr.*** Bachelor of Arts; a degree that you receive when you complete a program of study at a college or university ➲ Compare **B.S.** ➲ For more information on the North American educational systems, look at study pages **A8-A9**.

**baa** /bɑ; bæ/ ***noun*** [C] the sound that a sheep or lamb makes

**bab·ble¹** /ˈbæbl/ ***verb*** [I] **1** to talk quickly, especially about unimportant things, or in a way that is difficult to understand: *What are you babbling about?* **2** to make the sound of water running over stones: *a babbling brook*

**bab·ble²** /ˈbæbl/ ***noun*** [U] **1** the sound of many voices talking at the same time: *I could hear a babble of voices coming from downstairs.* **2** the sound of water running over stones

**babe** /beɪb/ ***noun*** [C] **1** (*slang*) (used when talking to sb close to you, for example your husband or wife, as a way of showing affection): *Hey babe, how's it going?*

> NOTE Many women are offended if a man they don't know very well uses this word toward them.

**2** an attractive young woman or man **3** (*old-fashioned*) a baby

**ba·boon** /bæˈbun/ ***noun*** [C] a large African or Asian monkey with a long face like a dog's

★**ba·by¹** /ˈbeɪbi/ ***noun*** [C] (*pl.* **ba·bies**) **1** a very young child: *I've got some great news. I'm going to have a baby!* ◇ *She's expecting a baby early next year.* ◇ *When's the baby due?* (= when will it be born?) ◇ *a baby boy/girl* **2** a very young animal or bird: *a baby rabbit* **3** (*slang*) (used when talking to sb, especially sb that you love) ➲ Look at the note at **babe** (1).

**ba·by²** /ˈbeɪbi/ ***verb*** [T] (*pres. part.* **ba·by·ing**; *3rd person sing. pres.* **ba·bies**; *pt, pp* **ba·bied**) to treat sb with too much care, as if he/she were a baby

**ˈbaby boom** ***noun*** [C, usually sing.] a period of time when a lot of babies are born. In North America, this usually means the time between the end of World War II and about 1964.

**ˈbaby ˌboomer** (*also* **boom·er**) ***noun*** [C] a person who was born during a baby boom

**ˈbaby ˌcarriage** ***noun*** [C] a small vehicle on four wheels for a baby to go out in, pushed by a person on foot ➲ picture at **stroller**.

**ˈbaby ˌshower** ***noun*** [C] → SHOWER¹ (5)

**ba·by·sit** /ˈbeɪbisɪt/ ***verb*** [I,T] (**ba·by·sit·ting**; *pt, pp* **ba·by·sat**) to take care of a child for a short time while the parents are out: *We have friends who babysit for us if we go out in the evening.* ▶ **ba·by·sit·ter** /ˈbeɪbisɪt̬ər/ (*also* **sitter**) ***noun*** [C]: *We can't come tonight. We couldn't find a babysitter.* ➲ Look at **day-care**.

**ˈbaby talk** ***noun*** [U] the words or sounds a baby says when it is learning to talk; the special language adults sometimes use when talking to babies

**ˈbaby tooth** ***noun*** [C] (*pl.* **baby teeth**) any of the first set of teeth young children get that drop out and are replaced by others

**bach·e·lor** /ˈbætʃlər; ˈbætʃələr/ ***noun*** [C] **1** a man who has never been married

> NOTE Nowadays it is more common to say "a **single** man" or "He's **single**."

**2** (used in the name of a college or university degree that you get after studying for four years): *a Bachelor of Arts/Science* ◇ *I have a bachelor's degree in biology.* ➲ Look at the note at **degree**. **3** (*Cdn*) = BACHELOR APARTMENT

**ˈbachelor aˌpartment** ***noun*** [C] (*Cdn*) an apartment consisting of a single large room serving as bedroom and living room, with a separate bathroom

**ˈbachelor ˌparty** ***noun*** [C] a party that a man has with his male friends just before he gets married, often the night before

★**back¹** /bæk/ ***noun*** [C]

➤PART OF THE BODY **1** the part of a person's or animal's body between the neck and the hips: *Do you sleep on your back or on your side?* ◇ *She was standing with her back to me, so I couldn't see her face.* ◇ *He swung himself up onto the horse's back.*

➤PART FURTHEST FROM THE FRONT **2** the part or side of sth that is farthest from the front: *Dan couldn't see the chalkboard because he was sitting at the back of the class.* ◇ *Jane sat next to the driver, and I sat in the back of the car.* ◇ *You can take the front seat and I'll sit* ***in back***. ◇ *The back of the house looks much nicer than the front.* ◇ *There's some information about the author at the back of the book.* ◇ *You need to sign the back of the check in order to cash it.*

➤OF CHAIR **3** the part of a chair that you lean against when you sit down: *Don't climb on the back of the couch!*

IDM **behind sb's back** without sb's knowledge or agreement: *They criticized her behind her back.*

**get off sb's back** (*informal*) to stop bothering or annoying sb: *I wish she'd get off my back!*

**in the back of your mind** in your thoughts, but not the main thing that you are thinking about: *Even when I'm at work, that problem is in the back of my mind.*

**know sth inside out/like the back of your hand** → KNOW

**a pat on the back** → PAT²

★**back²** /bæk/ ***adj.*** **1** (only *before* a noun) farthest

B

from the front: *Did you lock the back door?* ◇ *the back row of the theater* ◇ *back teeth* **2** owed for a time in the past: *back taxes*

IDM **on the back burner** (*informal*) (used about an idea, a plan, etc.) left to be done or considered later: *We'll have to put that project on the back burner until our financial situation improves.*

★**back³** /bæk/ ***adv.*** **1** in or to a place or state that sb/sth was in before: *Bye! I'll be back around 6 o'clock* (= back home again). ◇ *When is Joe coming back from Australia?* ◇ *Go back to sleep.* ◇ *Can I have my pen back, please?* **2** away from the direction you are facing or moving in: *She walked away without looking back.* ◇ *Could everyone move back a little, please?* **3** away from sth; under control: *The police were unable to keep the crowds back.* ◇ *She tried to hold back her tears.* **4** in return or in reply: *He said he'd call me back in an hour.* **5** in or into the past; ago: *I met him a few years back, in Vancouver.* ◇ *Think back to your first day in school.*

IDM **back and forth** from one place to another and back again, all the time: *Traveling back and forth to work takes up a lot of time.* ◇ *The dog ran back and forth, barking.*

★**back⁴** /bæk/ ***verb*** **1** [I,T] to move backward or to make sth move backward: *I'll have to back into that parking space.* ◇ *She backed the car into the parking space.* **2** [T] to give help or support to sb/sth: *We can go ahead with the project if the bank will agree to back us.* **3** [T] to bet money that a particular horse, team, etc. will win in a race or game

PHR V **back away (from sb/sth)** to move backward because you are afraid, shocked, etc.: *He began to back slowly away from the snake.*

**back down** to stop insisting that you are right: *You have the right to a raise; don't back down now.*

**back out (of sth)** to decide not to do sth that you had promised to do: *You promised you would come with me. You can't back out of it now!*

**back up** to move backward, especially in a car, etc.: *Back up slowly – there might be another car coming.*

**back sb/sth up** to support sb; to say or show that sth is true: *I'm going to say exactly what I think at the meeting. Will you back me up?* ◇ *All the evidence backed up what the man had said.*

**back sth up 1** (*computing*) to make a copy of a computer program, etc. in case the original one is lost or damaged: *If you don't back up your files, you risk losing data.* **2** to move a car, etc. backward: *Back the truck up a little so that other people can get past.*

**back·ache** /ˈbækeɪk/ ***noun*** [C,U] a continuous pain in the back: *to have a backache*

**back·bit·ing** /ˈbækbaɪṱɪŋ/ ***noun*** [U] unpleasant and unkind talk, usually about sb who is not present

**back·board** /ˈbækbɔrd/ ***noun*** [C] the board behind the basket in the game of basketball ➲ picture at **basketball**.

**back·bone** /ˈbækboʊn/ ***noun*** **1** [C] the line of bones down the back of your body SYN **spine** **2** [sing.] the main strength or support: *Volunteer workers are the backbone of the organization.*

**back·coun·try** /ˈbækkʌntri/ ***noun*** [U] an area away from roads and towns

**back·drop** /ˈbækdrɑp/ ***noun*** [C] **1** a painted piece of fabric that is hung behind the stage in a theater as part of the scenery **2** (*written*) the scenery surrounding an event: *The mountains provided a dramatic backdrop for our picnic.* **3** (*written*) the general conditions in which an event takes place, which sometimes help to explain that event: *It was against this backdrop of racial tension that the civil war began.*

**back·er** /ˈbækər/ ***noun*** [C] a person who gives support or money to another person, a project, etc.

**back·fire** /ˈbækˌfaɪər/ ***verb*** [I] to have an unexpected and unwanted result, often the opposite of what was intended: *This decision could easily backfire on us.*

**back·gam·mon** /ˈbækˌgæmən/ ***noun*** [U] a game for two people played on a board marked with long thin triangles

★**back·ground** /ˈbækgraʊnd/ ***noun*** **1** [C] the type of family and social class you come from and the education and experience you have: *We get along really well together in spite of our different backgrounds.* ◇ *a middle-class background* **2** [sing., U] the facts or events that are connected with a situation: *The talks are taking place against a background of increasing tension.* ◇ *I need some background information.* **3** [sing.] the part of a view, scene, picture, etc. which is farthest away from the person looking at it: *You can see the mountains in the background of the picture.* ➲ Look at **foreground**. **4** [sing.] a position where sb/sth can be seen/heard, etc. but is not the center of attention: *The singer's husband prefers to stay in the background.* ◇ *I could hear a baby crying in the background.* ◇ *The restaurant kept playing the same background music again and again.*

**back·hand** /ˈbækhænd/ ***noun*** [sing.] a way of hitting the ball in tennis, etc. that is made with the back of your hand facing forward ➲ Compare **forehand**.

**back·hand·er** /ˈbækhændər/ ***noun*** [C] a secret and illegal payment made to sb in exchange for a favor SYN **bribe**

**back·ing** /ˈbækɪŋ/ ***noun*** [U] help or support to do sth, often in the form of money: *financial backing*

**back·lash** /ˈbæklæʃ/ ***noun*** [sing.] a strong reaction against a political or social event or development

**back·log** /ˈbæklɔg; -lɑg/ ***noun*** [C, usually sing.] an amount of work, etc. that has not yet been done and needs to be done: *I have a huge backlog of mail to answer.*

**back·pack¹** /ˈbækpæk/ (*also* **rucksack**) ***noun*** [C] a bag that you use for carrying things on your back. You often use a backpack when you are walking, camping, going to school, etc. ➲ picture at **luggage**.

**back·pack²** /ˈbækpæk/ ***verb*** [I] to go walking, traveling, etc. with a backpack: *Before I start university, I'm going to spend a year backpacking around Europe.* ▶ **back·pack·er** /ˈbækpækər/ ***noun*** [C]: *We met a lot of other backpackers at the youth hostel.*

ˈ**back rub** ***noun*** [C] the act of rubbing and pressing sb's back to reduce pain or make him/her relax

ˌ**back ˈseat** ***noun*** [C] a seat in the back of a vehicle

B

IDM **take a back seat** to allow sb else to play a more active and important role in a particular situation than you do

**back·side** /'bæksaɪd/ ***noun*** [C] the part of the body that you sit on; your buttocks

**back·slash** /'bækslæʃ/ ***noun*** [C] a mark (\), used in computer commands ➲ Compare **forward slash**.

**back·slid·ing** /'bækslaɪdɪŋ/ ***noun*** [U] the situation when sb stops behaving well and returns to his/her former bad behavior

**back·space** /'bækspeɪs/ ***verb*** [I] to move backward on a line when you are writing on a computer or typing: *the backspace key* (= the key that allows you to backspace on a computer)

**back·stage** /ˌbæk'steɪdʒ/ ***adv.*** behind the stage in a theater, where the actors get dressed, etc.

**back·stroke** /'bækstroʊk/ ***noun*** [U] a style of swimming that you do on your back: *Can you do the backstroke?*

**'back talk** ***noun*** [U] (*informal*) a way of answering that shows no respect for sb in authority

**ˌback to 'back** ***adv.*** **1** happening one after the other: *They played two games back to back.* **2** (used about two people) sitting or standing next to each other, usually with their backs touching: *The girls stood back to back to see who was taller.*

**ˌback-to-'back** ***adj.*** happening one after the other: *Students who schedule back-to-back classes can come to campus less often.*

**back·track** /'bæktræk/ ***verb*** [I] **1** to go back the same way you came: *We got lost on the way through the woods and had to backtrack.* **2** to change your mind about a plan, promise, etc. that you have made: *The administration continues to backtrack on environmental protection.*

**back·up** /'bækʌp/ ***noun*** **1** [U] extra help or support: *Her success is partly due to the backup she gets from her team.* **2** [C] an extra thing or a copy of sth that you can use if the original one is lost or damaged: *Always make a backup of your computer files.* ◇ *We have a generator to use as a backup when the lights go out.*

★**back·ward¹** /'bækwərd/ ***adj.*** **1** (only *before* a noun) directed toward the back: *a backward step/glance* **2** not modern; not aware of other cultures, etc.: *Transportation is very difficult in the more backward areas of the country.*

**back·ward²** /'bækwərd/ (*also* **back·wards** /'bækwərdz/) ***adv.*** **1** away from the front; toward the back: *Could everybody take a step backward?* ◇ *He fell backward and hit the back of his head.* ◇ *We seem to be going backward, not forward.* **2** in a way that is opposite to usual; with the end first: *"Dog" written backward spells "god."* **3** with the back where the front should be: *You've got your sweater on backward!* **4** toward an earlier time: *The movie was about some people who traveled backward in time.*

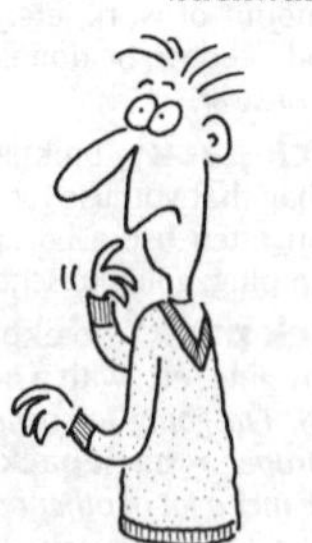
backward

**back·wa·ter** /'bækwɔt̬ər; -wɑt̬ər/ ***noun*** [C] **1** a part of a river away from the main part, where the water only moves slowly **2** a place that is away from the places where most things happen, and is therefore not affected by events, progress, new ideas, etc.: *a sleepy/quiet/rural backwater*

**back·woods** /ˌbæk'wʊdz/ ***noun*** [pl.] a place that is away from any big towns and from the influence of modern life

**back·yard** /ˌbæk'yɑrd/ ***noun*** [C] an area behind a house with grass, plants, etc.: *You kids can go and play in the backyard.* ◇ (*figurative*) *I won't let them build a prison in my backyard* (= near my home)*!*

**ba·con** /'beɪkən/ ***noun*** [U] thin pieces of salted or smoked meat from the back or sides of a pig: *a hearty breakfast of pancakes, bacon and eggs.* ➲ Look at the note at **meat**.

★**bac·te·ri·a** /bæk'tɪriə/ ***noun*** [pl.] very small living things that can only be seen with a microscope. Bacteria exist in large numbers in air, water, soil, plants and the bodies of people and animals. Some bacteria cause disease. ➲ Look at **germ** and **virus**.

★**bad¹** /bæd/ ***adj.*** (**worse** /wərs/, **worst** /wərst/)
➤UNPLEASANT **1** not good or pleasant: *The weather forecast for tomorrow is bad.* ◇ *I'm in a bad mood today.* ◇ *I felt really bad about leaving her standing in the rain.*
➤SERIOUS **2** severe or serious: *The traffic was really bad on the way to work.* ◇ *She went home with a bad headache.* ◇ *a bad mistake*
➤POOR QUALITY **3** of poor quality; of a low standard: *Many accidents are caused by bad driving.* ◇ *The company's problems are the result of bad management.*
➤NOT GOOD AT STH **4 bad (at sth/at doing sth)** not able to do sth well or easily; not skillful or reliable: *a bad teacher/driver/cook* ◇ *I've always been bad at sports.* ◇ *He's really bad at keeping us informed* (= we can't rely on him to give us information).
➤FOOD **5** (used about food) not fresh or suitable to eat; rotten: *Smell this meat – I think it's gone bad.*
➤NOT HEALTHY **6** (used about parts of the body) not healthy; painful: *He has a bad heart.*
➤WICKED **7** (used about a person or behavior) not good; morally wrong: *Wayne isn't a bad kid – he just needs a lot of supervision.* ◇ *In cowboy movies, the bad guys always wear black hats.*
➤HARMFUL **8** (not before a noun) **bad for sb/sth** likely to damage or hurt sb/sth: *Smoking's bad for you.*
➤NOT APPROPRIATE **9 bad (for sth/to do sth)** difficult or unsuitable: *This is a bad time to call – everybody's in a meeting.*

> NOTE Some young people like to use the word **bad** to mean "very good": *Man! That is one bad car!* When it is used as a slang word in this way, **bad** has the comparative and superlative forms **badder** and **baddest**.

IDM **not bad; not too bad** (*informal*) fairly good: *"How was your vacation?" "Not bad."* ◇ *He earned $100 – not too bad for four hours' work!*
**too bad** (*informal*) → TOO

**bad**[2] /bæd/ ***adv.*** (*informal*) badly: *Are you hurt bad?* ◇ *I need a drink bad!*

NOTE Many people consider this use of the word **bad** incorrect.

**badge** /bædʒ/ ***noun*** [C] a small piece of metal with a design or words on it which you pin onto your clothing. A badge can show position, rank, membership in a club, that you have achieved sth, etc.: *a police officer's badge* ◇ *a merit badge in cooking*

**badg·er** /ˈbædʒər/ ***noun*** [C] an animal with black and white stripes on its head that lives in holes in the ground and comes out at night

ˌ**bad** ˈ**hair day** ***noun*** [C] (*informal*) a day on which everything seems to go wrong

ˌ**bad** ˈ**language** ***noun*** [U] words that are used for swearing: *You'll get into trouble if you use bad language.*

★**bad·ly** /ˈbædli/ ***adv.*** (**worse**; **worst**) **1** in a way that is not satisfactory; not well: *"Can you speak French?" "Well, only very badly."* ◇ *Some apartment houses are very badly built.* ◇ *She did pretty badly on the test.* **2** greatly or severely: *He was badly hurt in the accident.* **3** very much: *She badly needed a vacation.*

**bad·min·ton** /ˈbædmɪntn/ ***noun*** [U] a game for two or four people in which players hit a type of light ball with feathers over a high net, using rackets: *to play badminton*

**bad-mouth** /ˈbædmaʊθ; -maʊð/ ***verb*** [T] (*informal*) to say unpleasant things about sb: *No one wants to hire somebody who badmouths their former employer.*

**baf·fle** /ˈbæfl/ ***verb*** [T] to be impossible for sb to understand; to confuse greatly: *His illness baffled the doctors.* ◇ *We were completely baffled by Jerry's strange remarks.* ▶ **baf·fling** ***adj.***: *English is a baffling language.*

★**bag**[1] /bæg/ ***noun***

➤CONTAINER **1** [C] a container made of paper, plastic, cloth or leather that is open at the top, often with handles, in which you can carry things: *Would you like me to put these in a bag for you?* ◇ *I'll store the leftovers in a plastic bag.* ◇ *Do you need help carrying your grocery bags to the car?* ◇ *a brown paper bag* ◇ *a shopping/garbage bag* ➲ Look also at **sack**. **2** [C] a container made of paper or plastic that is closed at the top; a package: *a bag of candy/potato chips/sugar* ➲ picture at **container**. **3** [C] a suitcase or other piece of luggage: *Each passenger is allowed to check in two bags on this flight.* ◇ *Let me carry the bags up to your room.*

➤UNDER EYES **4 bags** [pl.] dark circles or loose folds of skin under the eyes, because of old age or lack of sleep

➤UNPLEASANT WOMAN **5** [C] (*slang*) an unpleasant woman: *an old bag*

IDM **let the cat out of the bag** → CAT[1]

**bag**[2] /bæg/ ***verb*** [T] (**bag·ging**; **bagged**) to put sth into a bag: *to bag groceries*

**ba·gel** /ˈbeɪgl/ ***noun*** [C] a hard bread roll that is shaped like a ring ➲ picture at **bread**.

**bag·gage** /ˈbægɪdʒ/ ***noun*** [U] bags and suitcases that you carry your clothes, etc. in when you travel: *We loaded our baggage into the car.* ◇ *Baggage should be checked in* (= given to an airline employee at a counter) *at least an hour before the flight.* ➲ Look also at **luggage**.

**Bag·gie™** /ˈbægi/ ***noun*** [C] (*pl.* **Bag·gies**) a small bag made of clear plastic that is used for storing sandwiches, etc.

**bag·gy** /ˈbægi/ ***adj.*** (**bag·gi·er**; **bag·gi·est**) (used about a piece of clothing) hanging loosely on the body: *baggy jeans*

ˈ**bag lady** ***noun*** [C] (*pl.* ˈ**bag ladies**) a woman who has no home and who walks around carrying her possessions with her in shopping bags

**bag·pipes** /ˈbægpaɪps/ ***noun*** [pl.] a musical instrument, popular in Scotland, that is played by blowing air through a pipe into a bag and then pressing the bag so that the air comes out of other pipes

**bagpipes**

**bail**[1] /beɪl/ ***noun*** [U] **1** money that is handed over to a court so that a person accused of a crime can be free until the trial: *She was released on $2,000 bail.* ◇ *The judge set bail at $10,000.* **2** permission for sb who is accused of a crime to be free until the trial if a sum of money is handed over to the court: *The judge felt that he was a dangerous man and ordered him to be held without bail.*

**bail**[2] /beɪl/ ***verb***

PHR V **bail sb out 1** to obtain sb's freedom by paying his/her BAIL[1] (1): *After she had been charged, her parents bailed her out.* **2** to rescue sb or sth from a difficult situation (especially by providing money)

**bail·iff** /ˈbeɪlɪf/ ***noun*** [C] a guard in a court of law

**bail·out** /ˈbeɪlaʊt/ ***noun*** [C] (*informal*) an act of giving money to help a business or an organization which has financial problems and may otherwise stop operating (**go bankrupt**)

**bait** /beɪt/ ***noun*** [U] **1** food or sth that looks like food that is put onto a hook to catch fish, or placed in a trap to catch animals or birds **2** something that is used for tempting or attracting sb: *Free offers are often used as bait to attract customers.*

★**bake** /beɪk/ ***verb*** [I,T] **1** to cook in an oven in dry heat: *I could smell bread baking in the oven.* ◇ *On his birthday, she baked him a cake.* ◇ *Would you like baked potatoes or French fries?* ➲ Look at the note at **cook**. **2** to become or to make sth hard by heating it: *The hot sun baked the earth.*

**bak·er** /ˈbeɪkər/ ***noun*** [C] a person who bakes and sells bread, cake, etc.

IDM **a baker's dozen** a group or set of thirteen

**bak·er·y** /ˈbeɪkəri/ ***noun*** [C] (*pl.* **bak·er·ies**) a place where bread, cakes, etc. are baked to be sold

ˈ**bake sale** ***noun*** [C] an event in which cakes, etc. are baked and sold to make money, usually for a school group or charity

**bake·shop** /ˈbeɪkʃɑp/ (*also* ˈ**bake shop**) ***noun*** [C] = BAKERY

B

'**baking ˌpowder** *noun* [U] a mixture of powders that are used to make cakes rise and become light as they are baked

'**baking ˌsoda** *noun* [U] = BICARBONATE OF SODA

★**bal·ance**[1] /'bæləns/ *verb*

➤KEEP STEADY **1** [I,T] to be or to put sb/sth in a steady position in which weight is evenly spread: *I had to balance on the top step of the ladder to paint the ceiling.* ◇ *Carefully, she balanced a glass on top of the pile of plates.*

➤MONEY **2** [I,T] to have equal totals of money spent and money received: *I must have made a mistake – the accounts don't balance.* **3** [T] to add up the amounts of money spent and received in an account and to make sure that the totals are correct: *to balance a checkbook*

➤BE/KEEP EQUAL **4** [T] **balance sth (out) (with sth)** to have or give sth equal value, importance, etc. in relation to other parts: *It's difficult to balance the demands of a career with caring for an elderly relative.* ◇ *The loss in the first half of the year was balanced out by the profit in the second half.*

➤COMPARE **5** [T] **balance sth against sth** to consider and compare one matter in relation to another: *In planning the new highway, we have to balance the benefit to drivers against the damage to the nearby neighborhoods.*

★**bal·ance**[2] /'bæləns/ *noun* **1** [U] the state of being in a steady position in which weight is evenly spread: *You need a good sense of balance to ride a motorcycle.* **2** [sing.] **(a) balance (between A and B)** a situation in which different or opposite things are of equal importance, size, etc. or are in the correct proportions: *The course provides a good balance between oral and written work.* ◇ *Humans have upset the environmental balance of the world.* **3** [C] (*technical*) an instrument used for weighing things ➲ Look at **scale**. **4** [C] the amount of money in sb's bank account: *I asked the bank teller for my balance.* **5 the balance** [sing.] the amount that still has to be paid: *You can pay a 10% deposit now, with the balance due in one month.*

IDM **in the balance** uncertain: *Following poor profits, the company's future is hanging in the balance.*

**keep/lose your balance** to remain/not to remain steady and upright: *It's difficult to keep your balance on this icy sidewalk.* ◇ *She tripped, lost her balance and fell down.*

**(catch/throw sb) off balance** (to find or put sb) in an unsteady position from which it is easy to fall: *A strong gust of wind caught me off balance and I almost fell down.*

**strike a balance** → STRIKE[2]

**bal·anced** /'bælənst/ *adj.* **1** including all different sides, opinions, etc. equally; fair: *a balanced report* **2** having equal totals of money spent and money received: *Do you think Congress will be able to propose a balanced budget this year?* **3** consisting of parts that are in the correct or pleasing proportions: *A balanced diet plays an important part in good health.*

ˌ**balance of 'payments** *noun* [sing.] the difference between the amount a country pays for imports and the amount it receives for exports in a particular period of time

ˌ**balance of 'power** *noun* [sing.] a situation in which power is evenly divided among the various sides, parties, groups, etc. involved

'**balance sheet** *noun* [C] a written record of money received and money paid out, showing the difference between the totals of each

**bal·co·ny** /'bælkəni/ *noun* [C] (*pl.* **bal·co·nies**) **1** a platform built on an upstairs outside wall of a building, with a wall or rail around it: *Our hotel room had a balcony where we could sit and look at the lake.* **2** an area of seats upstairs and near the back of a theater

**balcony**

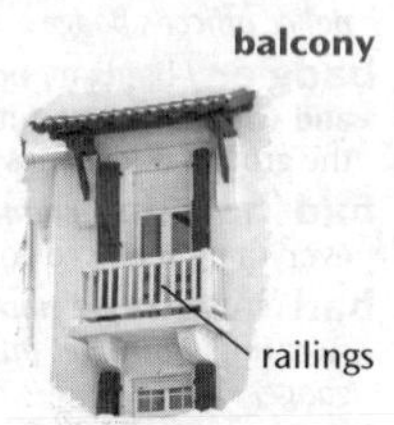


**bald** /bɔld/ *adj.* (used about people) having little or no hair on the head: *He went bald when he was only 30.* ◇ *He has a bald patch on the top of his head.* ➲ picture at **hair**.

ˌ**bald 'eagle** *noun* [C] a type of large bird with brown feathers on its body and white feathers on its head. It is an official symbol of the U.S.

**bald eagle**

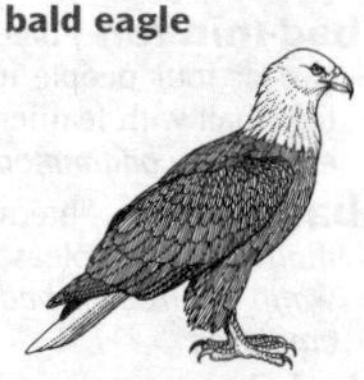

**bald·ing** /'bɔldɪŋ/ *adj.* starting to lose the hair on your head: *a balding man in his fifties*

**bale** /beɪl/ *noun* [C] a large quantity of sth (hay, cloth, etc.) tied together in a bundle so that it can be transported

**balk** /bɔk/ *verb* [I] **balk (at sth)** to be unwilling to do or agree to sth because it seems difficult, dangerous or unpleasant: *Several people were interested in buying my car, but they all balked at the price.*

★**ball** /bɔl/ *noun* [C] **1** a round or egg-shaped object that you hit, kick, throw, etc. in games and sports: *a tennis ball* ◇ *a golf ball* ◇ *a football* ◇ *The kids were playing with a ball in the back yard.* ◇ *The ball bounced over the fence.* **2** any object that has this shape or has been formed into this shape: *a ball of yarn* ◇ *The cat curled up into a ball and went to sleep.* ◇ *The kids threw snowballs at each other.* ◇ *We had spaghetti and meatballs for dinner.* **3** [usually pl.] (*taboo, informal*) = TESTICLE **4** a large formal party at which people dance

IDM **(be) on the ball** (*informal*) (to be) aware of what is happening and able to react to or deal with it quickly: *With so many new developments, you really have to be on the ball.*

**get/start the ball rolling** to start sth (an activity, conversation, etc.) that involves or is done by a group: *I made the first comments in our discussion to get the ball rolling.*

**have a ball** (*informal*) to enjoy yourself very much: *We had a ball on vacation last month.*

**play ball** → PLAY[1]

**bal·lad** /'bæləd/ *noun* [C] a long song or poem in simple language, telling a story

**bal·le·ri·na** /ˌbæləˈrinə/ ***noun*** [C] a woman who dances in ballets

**bal·let** /bæˈleɪ/ ***noun*** **1** [U] a style of dancing that tells a story with music but without words: *I like opera, but I'm not very fond of ballet.* ◇ *a ballet dancer* **2** [C] a performance or work that consists of this type of dancing

**ˈball game** (*also* **ball·game**) ***noun*** [C] a baseball game

IDM **a (whole) different/new ball game** (*informal*) a completely different kind of situation: *After living in a small town for so long, living in the big city is a whole new ball game for me.*

**ˈball ˌhockey** ***noun*** [U] (*Cdn*) a version of hockey played in a gymnasium or in an arena without ice, or on any other paved surface (e.g. a tennis court, road, etc.) using a ball in place of a puck

**bal·lis·tic** /bəˈlɪstɪk/ ***adj.*** connected with the scientific study of things that are shot or fired through the air, such as bullets

IDM **go ballistic** (*informal*) to become very angry: *He went ballistic when I told him I'd wrecked his car.*

**bal·loon** /bəˈlun/ ***noun*** [C] **1** a small colored rubber bag that you blow air or a gas into and use as a toy or for decoration: *We hung balloons around the room for the party.* ◇ *The boy cried when his balloon popped.* **2** (*also* ˌ**hot-ˈair balloon**) a large bag that is filled with gas or hot air so that it can rise into and fly through the air, carrying people in a basket attached below it: *They crossed the Atlantic in a balloon.*

**bal·lot** /ˈbælət/ ***noun*** **1** [C] a piece of paper that is used in voting: *She put an "X" next to the candidate's name on the ballot.* **2** [U,C] the system of voting with ballots; an occasion when people vote in this way: *to vote by secret ballot* ◇ *No candidate received an absolute majority of the votes in the first ballot.*

**ˈballot box** ***noun*** **1** [C] a box in which people put their BALLOTS (1) after voting **2 the ballot box** [sing.] the system of voting in an election: *The people made their wishes known through the ballot box.*

**ball·park** /ˈbɔlpɑrk/ ***noun*** [C] a field or sports center where baseball is played: *We spent the afternoon at the ballpark.*

IDM **in the ballpark** approximately correct: *The cost of the repairs was in the ballpark of 2 million dollars.*

**a ballpark figure, estimate, etc.** a number, etc. that is approximately correct

**ball·point pen** /ˌbɔlpɔɪnt ˈpɛn/ (*also* **ballpoint** /ˈbɔlpɔɪnt/) ***noun*** [C] a pen with a very small metal ball at the end that rolls ink onto paper

**ball·room** /ˈbɔlrum/ ***noun*** [C] a large room used for formal dancing

**ba·lo·ney** /bəˈloʊni/ ***noun*** [U] **1** (*informal*) nonsense: *What a bunch of baloney!* **2** = BOLOGNA

**bam·boo** /ˌbæmˈbu/ ***noun*** [C,U] a tall tropical plant of the grass family. Young bamboo shoots can be eaten; the hard, hollow stems are used for making furniture, etc.: *a bamboo chair*

★**ban** /bæn/ ***verb*** (**ban<u>n</u>ing; ban<u>n</u>ed**) [T] **1** to forbid sth officially, often by law: *The government has banned the import of products containing ivory.* **2 ban sb from sth/from doing sth** to officially forbid sb to do sth, often by law: *Prisoners are banned from voting in elections.* ▸ **ban** ***noun*** [C] **a ban (on sth/sb)**: *There is a ban on smoking in this office.*

**ba·nal** /bəˈnæl; ˈbeɪnl/ ***adj.*** (*formal*) not original or interesting: *a banal comment*

**ba·nan·a** /bəˈnænə/ ***noun*** [C] a long curved fruit that has yellow skin and that can be eaten: *a bunch of bananas* ➲ picture on study page **A28-29**.

**baˌnana ˈsplit** ***noun*** [C] a sweet dish made from a banana that is cut in half along its length and filled with ice cream, sweet sauces and nuts

★**band** /bænd/ ***noun*** [C] **1** a thin, flat, narrow piece of material used for fastening sth, or put around sth, often to hold it together: *The cards were held together by a rubber band.* ◇ *He was wearing a white hat with a black band around it.* **2** a line of a color or design that is different from the one on either side of it: *She wore a red sweater with a green band across the middle.* **3** a group of people who have joined together with a common purpose: *The attack was made by a small band of rebels.* **4** a group of musicians: *a brass/jazz/rock band* **5** (*Cdn*) an Indian community that is officially recognised by the federal government

**bandage**

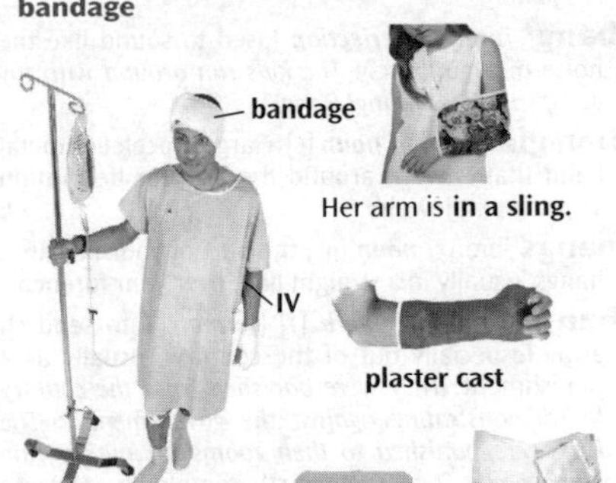

Her arm is **in a sling.**

He is **on an IV.** **Band-Aid™** **dressing**

**band·age¹** /ˈbændɪdʒ/ ***noun*** [C] a long piece of soft material that is wrapped around a wound or an injury

**band·age²** /ˈbændɪdʒ/ ***verb*** [T] to put a bandage on a wound or around a part of the body: *She played the game with a bandaged knee.*

**Band-Aid™** /ˈbændeɪd/ ***noun*** [C] **1** a small piece of sticky material that is used to cover a cut, etc. on the body ➲ picture at **bandage** **2** an effort to improve a bad situation that does not do anything about the real source of the problem: *The loan was just a temporary Band-Aid – we needed more help than that to keep our business running.*

**ban·dan·na** /bænˈdænə/ ***noun*** [C] a piece of brightly colored fabric worn around the neck or head ➲ picture on study page **A30**.

**ˈband ˌcouncil** ***noun*** [C] (*Cdn*) a local form of Aboriginal government in Canada, consisting of an elected chief and councilors

**ban·dit** /ˈbændət/ ***noun*** [C] an armed robber, usually in a wild place

**band·wag·on** /ˈbændwægən/ ***noun***
IDM **jump on the bandwagon** → JUMP[1]

**band·width** /ˈbændwɪdθ; -wɪtθ/ ***noun*** [U] (*computing*) a measurement of the amount of information that a particular computer network or Internet connection can send in a particular time. It is often measured in bits per second.

**bang[1]** /bæŋ/ ***verb*** [I,T] **1** to make a loud noise by hitting sth hard, closing sth, or putting sth down: *The man downstairs banged on his ceiling to complain about the noise.* ◇ *Somewhere in the house, I heard a door bang.* ◇ *She stormed out of the room, banging the door behind her.* ◇ *He banged his fist on the table and started shouting.* **2** to knock against sth by accident: *As I was crossing the room in the dark, I banged into a table.* ◇ *Be careful not to bang your head on the ceiling. It's pretty low.*
PHR V **bang sth up** (*informal*) to damage sth by knocking it against sth else: *I banged up my knee when I fell off my bike.*

**bang[2]** /bæŋ/ ***noun*** [C] **1** a sudden, short, very loud noise: *Witnesses heard three loud bangs and saw the gunman run down an alley.* **2** a short, strong knock or blow: *Give the nail a couple of bangs with the hammer.* **3 a bang** (*informal*) a feeling of great pleasure and enjoyment: *I get a real bang out of Larry's jokes!*

**bang[3]** /bæŋ/ ***interjection*** (used to sound like the noise of a gun, etc.): *The kids ran around with toy guns, shouting, "Bang! Bang!"*

**ban·gle** /ˈbæŋgl/ ***noun*** [C] a large bracelet or metal band that is worn around the arm for decoration ➲ picture at **jewelry**.

**bangs** /bæŋz/ ***noun*** [pl.] the part of your hair that hangs, usually in a straight line, over your forehead

**ban·ish** /ˈbænɪʃ/ ***verb*** [T] (*formal*) **1** to send sb away (especially out of the country), usually as a punishment: *They were banished from the country for demonstrating against the government.* ◇ *The kids were banished to their rooms for making too much noise.* **2** to remove sth completely; to force out: *She banished all hope of winning from her mind.*

**ban·is·ter** /ˈbænəstər/ ***noun*** [C] (often plural) a rail supported by vertical bars at the side of a staircase, that you hold on to when you are going upstairs or downstairs

**ban·jo** /ˈbændʒoʊ/ ***noun*** [C] (*pl.* **ban·jos**) a musical instrument with a long thin neck, a round body and four or more strings, played with the fingers

banjo

★**bank[1]** /bæŋk/ ***noun*** [C]
➤FOR MONEY **1** an organization that keeps money safely for its customers; the office or building of such an organization. You can take money out, save, borrow or exchange money at a bank: *Is there a bank near here where I can cash some traveler's checks?* ◇ *He went to the bank and withdrew some money from his account.* ◇ *She got a loan from the bank to buy a new car.*
➤STH COLLECTED/STORED **2** a supply of things that you keep to use later: *a data bank* ◇ *a blood bank*
➤OF RIVER/CANAL **3** the ground along the side of a river or canal: *People were fishing along the banks of the river.* ◇ *We rowed to the bank and got out of the boat.*
➤SLOPE **4** any area of sloping ground: *There were grassy banks on either side of the freeway.*
➤OF CLOUD/SNOW, ETC. **5** (used about certain features of weather) a mass of sth: *a bank of clouds*

**bank[2]** /bæŋk/ ***verb*** [I] to keep your money at a particular bank: *I bank at the First National Bank.*
PHR V **bank on sb/sth** to expect and trust sb to do sth, or sth to happen: *You can try to get a ticket, but I wouldn't bank on succeeding.*

**bank·er** /ˈbæŋkər/ ***noun*** [C] a person who owns or has an important job in a bank

**bank·ing** /ˈbæŋkɪŋ/ ***noun*** [U] the type of business done by banks: *She decided on a career in banking.*

**bank·rupt[1]** /ˈbæŋkrʌpt/ ***adj.*** not having enough money to pay your debts: *The company went bankrupt last year.*

**bank·rupt[2]** /ˈbæŋkrʌpt/ ***verb*** [T] to cause sb/sth to become bankrupt

**bank·rupt·cy** /ˈbæŋkrəpsi; -rəptsi/ ***noun*** [C,U] (*pl.* **bank·rupt·cies**) the state when a person or an organization is BANKRUPT[1]: *During this period of economic difficulty, bankruptcies are becoming more common.* ◇ *to file for bankruptcy* ◇ *to declare bankruptcy*

**ˈbank ˌstatement** ***noun*** [C] a printed record of all the money paid into and out of a customer's bank account within a particular period

**ˈbank ˌteller** ***noun*** [C] → TELLER

**ban·ner** /ˈbænər/ ***noun*** [C] a long piece of cloth with words or signs on it, that can be hung up or carried through the streets on poles: *The demonstrators carried banners saying "Stop the War."*

**ban·quet** /ˈbæŋkwət/ ***noun*** [C] a formal dinner for a large number of people, usually as a special event at which speeches are made

**ban·ter[1]** /ˈbæntər/ ***noun*** [U] friendly remarks and jokes: *He enjoyed exchanging banter with the customers.*

**ban·ter[2]** /ˈbæntər/ ***verb*** [I] **banter (with sb)** to joke with sb: *He bantered with reporters and posed for photographers.*

**bap·tism** /ˈbæptɪzəm/ ***noun*** [C,U] a ceremony in which a person becomes a member of the Christian church by being placed briefly under water or having drops of water put onto his/her head. Often he/she is also formally given a name.

**Bap·tist** /ˈbæptɪst/ ***noun*** [C], ***adj.*** (a member) of a Protestant church that believes that baptism should only be for people who are old enough to understand the meaning of the ceremony and should be done by placing the person fully under water

**bap·tize** /ˈbæptaɪz/ ***verb*** [T] to perform the ceremony of baptism: *Were you baptized as a child?* ◇ *He was baptized "James Harry."*

★**bar[1]** /bɑr/ ***noun*** [C]
➤FOR DRINKS/FOOD **1** a place where you can buy and drink (especially alcoholic) drinks: *We had a drink in the bar before our meal.* **2** a small restaurant that serves drinks or light meals: *a*

*snack bar* **3** a long, narrow, high table or counter where drinks are served: *She went to the bar and ordered a drink.* ◇ *We sat on stools at the bar.*
▸ OF METAL/WOOD **4** a long, thin, straight piece of metal, often placed across a window or door, etc. to make it strong or to prevent people from passing through it: *the bars of a prison cell*
▸ OF CHOCOLATE/SOAP **5** a small block of solid material, longer than it is wide: *a bar of soap* ➲ Look also at **candy bar**.
▸ THAT PREVENTS STH **6** a thing that prevents you from doing sth: *Lack of education is not always a bar to success in business.*
IDM **behind bars** (*informal*) in prison

**bar²** /bɑr/ ***verb*** [T] (**bar·ring**; **barred**) **1** to fasten sth with a BAR¹ (4) or bars: *The heavy door was barred and bolted.* **2** to stop sb from going through or into a place: *A policeman barred the entrance to the embassy.* **3 bar sb from sth/from doing sth** to forbid sb officially to do, use or enter sth: *He was barred from the club for fighting.*

**bar·bar·i·an** /bɑrˈbɛriən/ ***noun*** [C] a wild, uncivilized person

**bar·bar·ic** /bɑrˈbærɪk; -ˈbɛrɪk/ ***adj.*** very cruel and violent: *barbaric punishments* ◇ *barbaric treatment of prisoners* ▸ **bar·ba·rism** /ˈbɑrbərɪzəm/ ***noun*** [U]: *acts of barbarism*

**bar·bar·i·ty** /bɑrˈbærət̮i; -ˈbɛr-/ ***noun*** [C,U] (*pl.* **bar·bar·i·ties**) behavior that deliberately causes extreme pain or suffering to others: *The barbarity of the old regime was eventually exposed.*

**bar·be·cue¹** /ˈbɑrbɪkyu/ ***noun*** [C] (*abbr.* **BBQ**) an outdoor party at which food is cooked on a metal frame (a **grill**) over an open fire: *Let's have a barbecue.*

**bar·be·cue²** /ˈbɑrbɪkyu/ ***verb*** [T] to cook food outdoors on a metal frame (a **grill**) over an open fire, often with a special sauce: *barbecued ribs*

**barbed wire** /ˌbɑrbd ˈwaɪər/ ***noun*** [U] strong wire with sharp points on it: *a barbed wire fence*

**bar·ber** /ˈbɑrbər/ ***noun*** [C] a man who cuts men's hair: *My hair's too long. It's time I went to the barber.* ◇ *a barbershop* (= where a barber works)

**bar·bit·ur·ate** /bɑrˈbɪtʃərət/ ***noun*** [C] a powerful drug that makes you feel calm and relaxed or puts you to sleep. There are several types of barbiturate: *He died from an overdose of barbiturates.*

**ˈbar chart** (*also* **ˈbar graph**) ***noun*** [C] a diagram which uses narrow bands of different heights to show different amounts, so that they can be compared ➲ picture at **graph**.

**ˈbar code** ***noun*** [C] a pattern of thick and thin parallel lines on a book, product in a store, etc. It contains information that a computer can read. SYN **Universal Product Code**

**bare** /bɛr/ ***adj.*** **1** (used about part of the body) not covered by clothing: *bare arms* ◇ *a bare chest* ◇ *She killed him with her bare hands* (= without a weapon). SYN **naked** and **nude**. **2** without anything covering it: *They had taken the painting down, so the walls were all bare.* **3** empty; without its usual contents: *bare bookshelves* **4** minimum, basic and no more: *We were so poor that we didn't even have the bare necessities of life.* ◇ *Just give me the bare facts as quickly as you can.*

**bare·faced** /ˈbɛrfeɪst/ ***adj.*** (only *before* a noun) showing that you do not care about offending sb or about behaving badly: *a barefaced lie*

**bare·foot** /ˈbɛrfʊt/ ***adj.***, ***adv.*** with nothing (e.g. shoes, socks, etc.) on the feet: *I was barefoot because my shoes and socks had gotten wet.* ◇ *We walked barefoot along the beach.*

**bare·ly** /ˈbɛrli/ ***adv.*** just; hardly; almost not: *We barely had enough money to pay for our tickets.* ◇ *She's barely older than you.*

**barf** /bɑrf/ ***verb*** [I] (*slang*) to bring food up from the stomach and out of the mouth SYN **vomit** ▸ **barf** ***noun*** [U]

**bar·gain¹** /ˈbɑrgən/ ***noun*** [C] **1** something that is cheaper or at a lower price than usual: *At that price, it's a real bargain!* ◇ *I found some good bargains at the garage sale.* **2** an agreement between people or groups about what each of them will do for the other or others: *I hope he keeps his side of the bargain.* ➲ Look also at **plea bargain**.

**bar·gain²** /ˈbɑrgən/ ***verb*** [I] **bargain (with sb) (about/over/for sth)** to discuss the form of an agreement, a price, etc.: *I'm sure that if you bargain with him, he'll drop the price.* ◇ *to bargain over the price*
PHR V **bargain for sth** to expect sth or to be prepared for sth: *When I agreed to take care of Al's dog, I got more than I'd bargained for.*

**ˌbargain ˈbasement** ***noun*** [C] a part of a large store, usually on the floor below street level, where goods are sold at reduced prices: *bargain-basement prices*

**ˈbargaining chip** ***noun*** [C] a fact or thing that a person or a group of people can use to get an advantage for themselves when they are trying to reach an agreement with another group

**barge¹** /bɑrdʒ/ ***noun*** [C] a long narrow boat with a flat bottom that is used for transporting goods or people on a canal, river, etc.

**barge²** /bɑrdʒ/ ***verb*** [I] to move in a rough way, pushing people or things out of the way: *Don't just barge into my room without knocking!*

**ˈbar graph** ***noun*** [C] = BAR CHART

**bar·i·tone** /ˈbærətoʊn/ ***noun*** [C] a male singing voice that is fairly low, between tenor and bass

**bark¹** /bɑrk/ ***noun*** [U] the hard outer covering of a tree ➲ picture at **tree**.

**bark²** /bɑrk/ ***verb*** **1** [I] **bark (at sb/sth)** (used about dogs) to make a loud, short noise or noises: *Their dog always barks at strangers.* **2** [I,T] **bark (sth) (out) (at sb)** to speak to sb in a loud voice with an angry or aggressive tone: *The boss came in, barked some orders and left again.* ▸ **bark** ***noun*** [C]: *The dog next door has a very loud bark.*

**bar·ley** /ˈbɑrli/ ***noun*** [U] **1** a plant similar to grass that produces grain that is used for food or for making beer and other drinks **2** the grain produced by this plant

**bar mitz·vah** /ˌbɑr ˈmɪtsvə/ ***noun*** [C] a ceremony in the Jewish religion for a boy who is about

13 years old, after which he is considered an adult ➲ Look at **bat mitzvah**.

B

**barn** /bɑrn/ *noun* [C] a large building on a farm in which crops or animals are kept

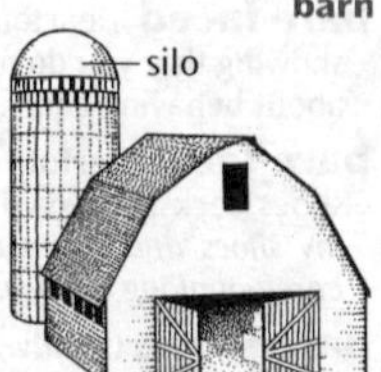


'**barn dance** *noun* [C] an informal social event at which people dance traditional dances such as square dances, etc.

**barn·yard** /'bɑrnyɑrd/ *noun* [C] an area of land with a fence around it near a barn, in which animals are kept

**ba·rom·e·ter** /bə'rɑmət̬ər/ *noun* [C] **1** an instrument that measures air pressure and indicates changes in weather **2** something that indicates the state of sth (a situation, a feeling, etc.): *The stock market is a barometer of the nation's economy.*

**bar·on** /'bærən/ *noun* [C] a person who controls a large part of a particular industry or type of business: *an oil baron*

**bar·racks** /'bærəks/ *noun* [C] (*pl.* **bar·racks**) a building or group of buildings in which soldiers live

**bar·rage** /bə'rɑʒ/ *noun* [C] **1** a continuous attack with a large number of guns in a particular direction **2** a large number of questions, remarks, etc., aimed at a person very quickly: *The mayor faced a barrage of questions from reporters.*

**bar·rel¹** /'bærəl/ *noun* [C] **1** a large, round container for liquids, that has a flat top and bottom and is often wider in the middle: *a barrel of wine* ◇ *How much is oil per barrel?* **2** the long metal tube of a gun, through which the bullet passes when it is fired

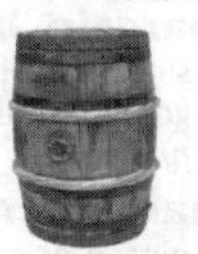
barrel

**bar·rel²** /'bærəl/ *verb* [I] (*informal*) to move very fast in a particular direction, especially in a way that you cannot control: *He came barreling down the hill and smashed into a phone booth.*

**bar·ren** /'bærən/ *adj.* **1** (used about land) not good enough to grow crops on **2** (used about trees or plants) not producing fruit or seeds

**bar·rette** /bə'rɛt/ *noun* [C] a small piece of metal or plastic used by women and girls to hold their hair in place

**bar·ri·cade¹** /'bærəkeɪd/ *noun* [C] an object or a line of objects that is placed (usually quickly) across a road, entrance, etc. to stop people from getting through: *The demonstrators put up barricades to keep the police away.*

**bar·ri·cade²** /'bærəkeɪd/ *verb* [T] to block sth with a barricade: *Rioters barricaded the road with cars.*

★**bar·ri·er** /'bæriər/ *noun* [C] **1** an object that keeps people or things apart or prevents them from moving from one place to another: *The police put up barriers to stop the crowd from getting on to the road.* **2** something that causes problems or makes it impossible for sth to happen: *Old-fashioned attitudes are a barrier to progress.* ◇ *When you live in a foreign country, the language barrier is often the most difficult problem to overcome.* ◇ *trade barriers*

**bar·ring** /'bɑrɪŋ/ *prep.* (*formal*) **1** except for: *Barring an initial delay, the new system caused no problems.* **2** if there is/are not: *Barring any unforeseen problems, the transition is expected to occur next month.*

**bar·ri·o** /'bæriou; 'bɑr-/ *noun* [C] (*pl.* **bar·ri·os**) (in the U.S.) a part of a city or town where most of the people speak Spanish

**bar·ris·ter** /'bærəstər/ *noun* [C] (*Cdn*) a lawyer who argues cases before the courts

**bar·tend·er** /'bɑrtɛndər/ *noun* [C] a person who serves drinks from behind a bar

**bar·ter** /'bɑrt̬ər/ *verb* [I,T] **barter (sth) (for sth)** to exchange goods or services for other goods or services, not for money: *In remote parts of the country, people bartered vegetables for tools.* ▶ **bar·ter** *noun* [U]: *a barter system*

★**base¹** /beɪs/ *noun* [C]

➤LOWEST PART **1** the lowest part of sth, especially the part on which it stands or at which it is attached to sth: *the base of a statue* ◇ *I felt a terrible pain at the base of my spine.*

➤ORIGINAL SITUATION **2** a starting point from which sth develops or is made: *The car's base price is $16,800, but that doesn't include taxes or optional equipment.*

➤OF SUPPORT/INCOME/POWER **3** a strong foundation on which sth is built or maintained: *The country needs a strong economic base.* ◇ *More affluent residents will increase the city's tax base.*

➤MAIN PLACE **4** a place used as a center from which activities are done or controlled: *Detectives are using the local school as a base for their investigation.*

➤OF THE MILITARY **5** a military center from which forces operate: *an army/air base*

➤BASEBALL **6** (in baseball) one of the four points that a runner must touch

➤CHEMISTRY **7** a chemical substance with a pH value of more than 7

IDM **off base** not correct or accurate: *Your estimate of the cost of the project was way off base.*
**touch base (with sb)** → TOUCH¹

★**base²** /beɪs/ *verb* [T] **1 base sth on sth** to form or develop sth from a particular starting point or source: *This movie is based on a true story.* **2** (usually passive) **base sb/sth in...** to make one place the center from which sb/sth can work or move around: *I'm based in New York, although my job involves a lot of travel.*

**base·ball** /'beɪsbɔl/ *noun* **1** [U] a team game that is popular in the U.S. and Canada in which players hit a ball with a bat and run around four points (bases) on a field. They have to touch all four bases in order to score a point (run). **2** [C] the hard round ball that is used in this game

NOTE There are nine players on a baseball team. The **pitcher pitches** (= throws) the ball to a **batter** from the other team. If the batter tries to hit the ball but misses it, this is called a **strike**. After three strikes the batter is **out** and the next batter comes to bat. If a batter manages to hit the ball so far that it goes out of the field, this is a **home run** and the batter is allowed to touch all four bases.

B

**baseball**

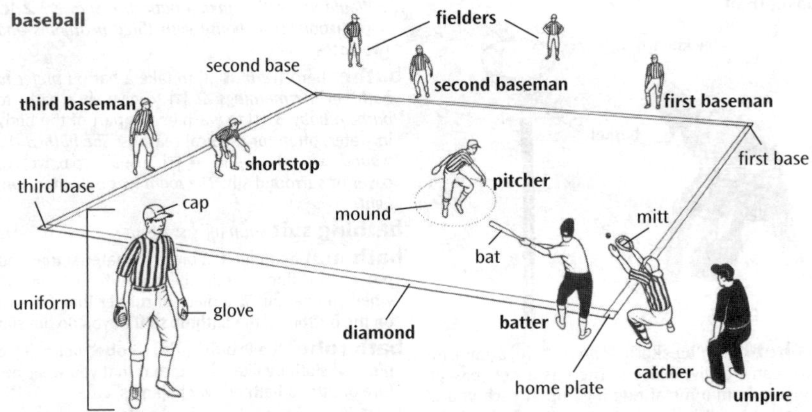


**ˈbaseball cap** *noun* [C] a type of hat with a long curved part sticking out at the front (a **bill**), worn by baseball players

**baseball cap**

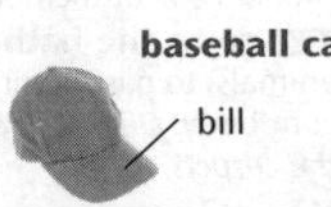


**baseball cap**

**base·ment** /ˈbeɪsmənt/ *noun* [C] the lowest room or rooms of a building which are partly or completely below ground level: *The toy department is in the basement of the store.* ◇ *a basement apartment*

**ba·ses** *plural of* BASIS

**bash**[1] /bæʃ/ *verb* [T] (*informal*) **1** to hit sb/sth very hard **2** to criticize sb/sth strongly: *The candidate continued to bash her opponent's policies.*

**bash**[2] /bæʃ/ *noun* [C] **1** a hard blow or an act of hitting **2** (*informal*) a party: *The Johnsons invited us to a big bash.*

**bash·ful** /ˈbæʃfl/ *adj.* shy and embarrassed

★**ba·sic** /ˈbeɪsɪk/ *adj.* **1** forming a starting point or basis on which other ideas rest: *The basic question is, can we afford it?* **2** simplest or most elementary; including only what is most necessary: *This course teaches basic skills in first aid.* ◇ *The basic pay is $200 a week – with extra for overtime.* ◇ *The rooms in the hotel are very basic – they have no showers or televisions.* **3** (*technical*) (used about chemical substances) having a pH value of more than 7 ➲ Look at **acid**[2](2) and **alkaline**.

**ba·si·cal·ly** /ˈbeɪsɪkli/ *adv.* looking at what is most important or basic in a person or an object or in a particular situation: *She seems to me to be basically a very nice person.* ◇ *The design of the new car is basically the same as the old one.* ◇ *Basically, all I want is to be left alone.*

**ba·sics** /ˈbeɪsɪks/ *noun* [pl.] the things that you need most or that are the most important: *You can get all the basics at the local store.*

**ba·sil** /ˈbeɪzl; ˈbæzl/ *noun* [U] a plant with green leaves that smell sweet and are used in cooking as an herb ➲ picture on study page A28-29.

**ba·sin** /ˈbeɪsn/ *noun* [C] **1** a large round open container that is used for holding liquids **2** an area of land from which water flows into a river: *the Great Basin of Nevada and western Utah*

★**ba·sis** /ˈbeɪsəs/ *noun* [C] (*pl.* **ba·ses** /ˈbeɪsiz/) **1** the way sth is done or organized: *They meet on a regular basis.* ◇ *The changes have been introduced on a voluntary basis.* **2** the principle or reason which lies behind sth: *We made our decision on the basis of your reports.* **3** a starting point, from which sth can develop: *Her diaries formed the basis of her autobiography.*

**bask** /bæsk/ *verb* [I] to sit or lie in a place where you can enjoy the warmth: *to bask in the sunshine* ◇ (*figurative*) *He basked in the admiration of his fans.*

**baskets**

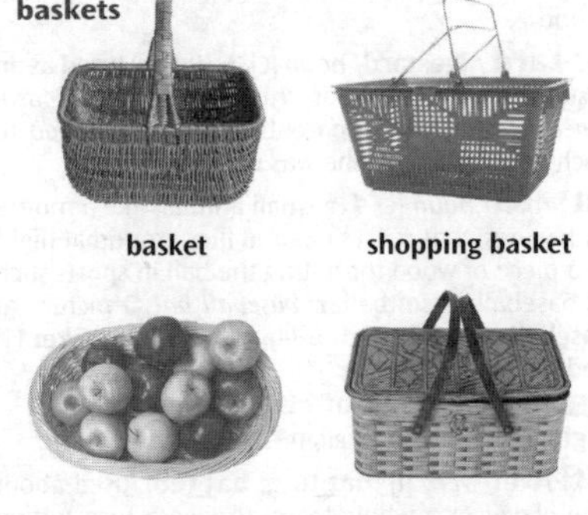


★**bas·ket** /ˈbæskət/ *noun* [C] **1** a container for carrying or holding things, made of strips of light material such as wire or thin wood that are woven together: *a picnic basket* ◇ *a waste basket* **2** a net that hangs from a metal ring high up at each end of a basketball court **3** a point that is scored in basketball by throwing the ball through one of the nets: *to make/shoot a basket* ➲ picture at **basketball**.

IDM **put all your eggs in one basket** → EGG[1]

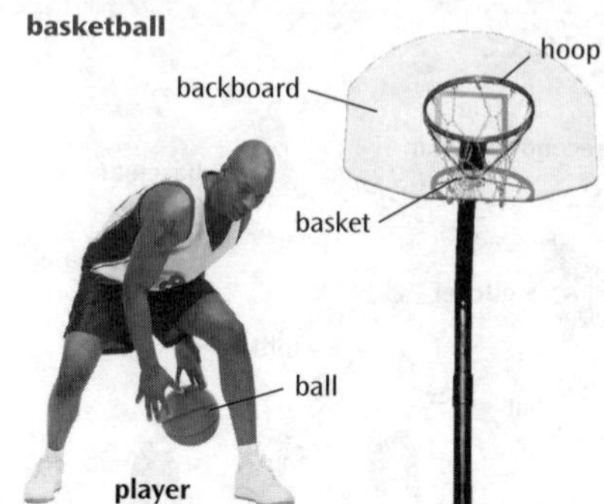


**bas·ket·ball** /ˈbæskətbɔl/ ***noun*** **1** [U] a game for two teams of five players. There is a net (**basket**) hanging from a metal ring high up at each end of the court and the players try to throw a ball through the other team's net in order to score points (**baskets**). **2** [C] the large round ball that is used in this game

**bass¹** /beɪs/ ***noun*** **1** [C] the lowest male singing voice; a singer with this kind of voice **2** [U] the lowest part in music **3** [C] = DOUBLE BASS **4** [C] (*also* ˌ**bass guiˈtar**) an electric guitar which plays very low notes ➲ picture at **guitar**.

**bass²** /beɪs/ ***adj.*** producing a deep sound; connected with the lowest part in music: *a bass drum* ◇ *Can you sing the bass part in this song?*

**bass³** /bæs/ ***noun*** [C] (*pl.* **bass** or **bass·es**) a type of fish that is caught for food or for sport. Some types of bass live in the ocean, and other types live in lakes and rivers.

**bas·soon** /bəˈsun/ ***noun*** [C] a musical instrument of the woodwind family which makes a very deep sound

**bas·tard** /ˈbæstərd/ ***noun*** [C] **1** (*taboo*) (used as an insult) an unpleasant or cruel person **2** (*old-fashioned*) a child whose parents were not married to each other when he/she was born

**bat¹** /bæt/ ***noun*** [C] **1** a small animal, like a mouse with wings, that comes out and flies around at night **2** a piece of wood for hitting the ball in sports such as baseball or softball: *a baseball bat* ➲ picture at **baseball**. ➲ Look at **club¹**(4), **paddle¹**(2), **racket** (1) and **stick¹**(2).

IDM **like a bat out of hell** (*informal*) very fast
**right off the bat** → RIGHT²

**bat²** /bæt/ ***verb*** [I] (**bat·ting**; **bat·ted**) (used about one player or a whole team) to take a turn hitting the ball in sports such as baseball

IDM **not bat an eye** to show no reaction

**batch** /bætʃ/ ***noun*** [C] a number of things or people that belong together as a group: *to bake a batch of cookies* ◇ *The guide waited for the next batch of tourists.*

**bat·ed** /ˈbeɪt̬əd/ ***adj.***

IDM **with bated breath** excited or afraid, because you are waiting for sth to happen

★**bath** /bæθ/ ***noun*** (*pl.* **baths** /bæθs; bæðz/) **1** [sing.] an act of washing your whole body when you sit or lie in a bathtub filled with water: *to take a bath* ◇ *Would you rather take a bath or a shower?* **2** [C] = BATHROOM (1): *a house with three bedrooms and two baths*

**bathe** /beɪð/ ***verb*** **1** [I] to take a bath: *I prefer to bathe in the mornings.* **2** [T] to give sb a bath: *to bathe a baby* **3** [T] to wash or put part of the body in water, often for medical reasons: *She bathed the wound with antiseptic.* **4** [T] (usually passive) to cover or surround sth: *The room was bathed in sunlight.*

ˈ**bathing suit** ***noun*** [C] = SWIMSUIT

ˈ**bath mat** ***noun*** [C] **1** a piece of material that you put on the floor beside the bathtub to stand on when you get out **2** a piece of rubber that you put on the bottom of the bathtub so that you do not slip

**bath·robe** /ˈbæθroʊb/ (*also* **robe**) ***noun*** [C] a piece of clothing like a loose coat that you wear before or after a bath or over pajamas, etc.

★**bath·room** /ˈbæθrum/ ***noun*** [C] a room with a toilet and usually a bathtub and/or shower and a sink ➲ Look at the note at **toilet**.

IDM **go to the bathroom** (used about people or animals) to pass liquid or solid waste material from your body: *Oh, no! The dog went to the bathroom on the carpet!*

NOTE This is a polite way of talking about what you do on the toilet.

**bath·tub** /ˈbæθtʌb/ (*also informal* **tub**) ***noun*** [C] a large container for water in which you sit to wash your body: *Can you answer the phone? I'm in the bathtub!* ➲ picture at **overflow**.

**bat mitz·vah** /ˌbɑt ˈmɪtsvə; ˌbɑs-/ ***noun*** [C] a ceremony in the Jewish religion for a girl who is about 13 years old, after which she is considered an adult ➲ Look at **bar mitzvah**.

**ba·ton** /bəˈtɑn/ ***noun*** [C] **1** a short thin stick used by the person who directs an orchestra **2** a stick that a runner in some races passes to the next person in the team **3** a metal stick that a person who marches in front of a band holds and sometimes throws into the air and catches **4** a short thick stick that a police officer carries as a weapon

**bat·tal·ion** /bəˈtælyən/ ***noun*** [C] a large unit of soldiers that forms part of another larger unit in the army

**bat·ter¹** /ˈbæt̬ər/ ***verb*** [I,T] to hit sb/sth hard, many times: *The wind battered against the window.* ◇ *High winds battered the coast again yesterday.* ◇ *The parents were accused of battering the child.*

**bat·ter²** /ˈbæt̬ər/ ***noun*** **1** [U] a thin mixture of flour, eggs, milk and usually oil, used to make pancakes, etc. or to cover food such as fish before frying: *cake batter* ➲ Look at **dough**. **2** [C] a person who hits the ball in baseball ➲ picture at **baseball**.

**bat·tered** /ˈbæt̬ərd/ ***adj.*** **1** no longer looking new; damaged or out of shape: *a battered old hat* **2** having been hit many times, usually over a period of time: *a shelter for battered women*

★**bat·ter·y** /ˈbæt̬əri/ ***noun*** [C] (*pl.* **bat·ter·ies**) a device that provides electricity for a radio, car, etc.: *I need some new batteries for my Walkman.* ◇ *He couldn't start the car because the battery was dead.*

B

★**bat·tle**[1] /ˈbæt̬l/ ***noun*** **1** [C,U] a fight, especially between armies in a war: *the Battle of Gettysburg* ◇ *They won the first battle, but still they lost the war.* ◇ *to die/be killed in battle* **2** [C] a struggle of any kind: *After three years, she lost her battle against cancer.*

IDM **a losing battle** → LOSE

**bat·tle**[2] /ˈbæt̬l/ ***verb*** [I,T] **battle (sb/sth) (for sth); battle (with/against sb/sth) (for sth)** to fight hard; to struggle: *The rebels battled (with) police for control of the region.* ◇ *These programs are aimed at battling poverty in the inner city.* ◇ *The two brothers were battling for leadership of the family business.*

**bat·tle·field** /ˈbæt̬lfild/ (*also* **bat·tle·ground** /ˈbæt̬lgraʊnd/) ***noun*** [C] the place where a battle is fought

**bat·tle·ship** /ˈbæt̬lʃɪp/ ***noun*** [C] the largest type of ship used in war

**bawl** /bɔl/ ***verb*** [I,T] to shout or cry loudly

**bay** /beɪ/ ***noun*** [C] **1** a part of the coast where the land forms a curve inward: *Hudson Bay* ◇ *The harbor was in a sheltered bay.* **2** a part of a building, aircraft or area that has a particular purpose: *the loading bay of the factory*

IDM **hold/keep sb at bay** to stop sb who is chasing you from coming near; to stop sb/sth from reaching you

**bay·o·net** /ˌbeɪəˈnɛt; ˈbeɪənət/ ***noun*** [C] a knife that can be attached to the end of a gun

**bay·ou** /ˈbaɪu; ˈbaɪoʊ/ ***noun*** [C] a small river with many curves that flows slowly through an area of wet land with a lot of plants in the southern U.S.

ˈ**Bay Street** ***noun*** [sing.] a street in Toronto, Canada, where many important banks, law firms and other businesses are located

ˌ**bay ˈwindow** ***noun*** [C] a window in a part of a room that sticks out from the wall of a house ➲ Picture on study page **A31**.

**ba·zaar** /bəˈzɑr/ ***noun*** [C] **1** (in countries in the Middle East) a market **2** a sale where the money that is made usually goes to charity: *a church bazaar*

**BB gun** /ˈbibi gʌn/ ***noun*** [C] a type of gun (air rifle) which uses air pressure to shoot small pieces of metal (BBs)

**BBQ** /ˈbɑrbɪkyu/ ***abbr.*** = BARBECUE[1]

**B.C.** (*also* **BC**) /ˌbi ˈsi/ ***abbr.*** before Christ; used in dates to show the number of years before the time when Christians believe Jesus Christ was born: *300 B.C.*

**B.C.E.** /ˌbi si ˈi/ (*also* **BCE**) ***abbr.*** before the Common Era (= before the birth of Christ) SYN **B.C.** ➲ Compare **A.D.** and **C.E.**

★**be**[1] /bi/ ***auxiliary verb*** **1** (used to form the continuous tense of verbs): *You're sitting on my book.* ◇ *We were listening to the radio.* ◇ *Is he coming?* ◇ *How long have we been waiting?* **2** (used to form the passive): *This cheese is made in Wisconsin.* ◇ *We were taken to the police station.* ◇ *The car has been repaired.* **3** (used to show that sth must happen or that sth has been arranged): *You are to leave here at 10 o'clock at the latest.* ◇ *They are to be married in June.* **4** (used to show that sth is possible but not very likely): *If they were to offer me the job, I'd probably take it.*

| be | |
|---|---|
| *present tense* | *past tense* |
| I **am** (I**'m**) | I **was** |
| you **are** (you**'re**) | you **were** |
| he/she/it **is** (he**'s**/she**'s**/it**'s**) | he/she/it **was** |
| we **are** (we**'re**) | we **were** |
| you **are** (you**'re**) | you **were** |
| they **are** (they**'re**) | they **were** |
| *past participle* | **been** |
| *present participle* | **being** |
| *negative short forms* | **aren't, isn't, wasn't, weren't** |

★**be**[2] /bi/ ***verb*** **1** (used with *there* to say that sb/sth exists or is in in a particular place): *Is there life after death?* ◇ *I tried calling them but there was no answer.* ◇ *There are some people outside.* ◇ *There are a lot of trees in our yard.* **2** (used when you are naming people or things, describing them or giving more information about them): *That's Jane over there.* ◇ *I'm Alan.* ◇ *Sue is 18. She's in college.* ◇ *He's a doctor.* ◇ *What's that?* ◇ *Where are the scissors?* ◇ *"What color is your car?" "It's green."* ◇ *It's 6 o'clock.* ◇ *How much was your ticket?* ◇ *The show was excellent.* **3** (only used in the perfect tenses) to go to a place (and return): *Have you ever been to Japan?*

IDM **be yourself** to act naturally: *Don't be nervous; just be yourself and the interview will be fine.*

**-to-be** (in compounds) future: *his wife-to-be*

★**beach** /bitʃ/ ***noun*** [C] the piece of sandy or rocky land next to the ocean: *a nice sandy beach* ◇ *to lie on the beach*

**bea·con** /ˈbikən/ ***noun*** [C] a fire or light on a hill, a tower or near the coast, that is used as a signal

**bead** /bid/ ***noun*** [C] **1** a small ball of wood, glass or plastic with a hole in the middle for threading a string through ➲ picture at **jewelry**. **2** a drop of liquid: *There were beads of sweat on his forehead.*

**bea·gle** /ˈbigl/ ***noun*** [C] a small dog with short legs, used in hunting

★**beak** /bik/ ***noun*** [C] the hard pointed part of a bird's mouth ➲ picture at **eagle**.

**beak·er** /ˈbikər/ ***noun*** [C] a glass container with a flat bottom, used by scientists for pouring liquids

**beam**[1] /bim/ ***noun*** [C] **1** a long piece of wood, metal, concrete, etc. that is used to support weight, e.g. in the floor or ceiling of a building **2** a line of light: *the beam of a car's headlights* ◇ *a laser beam*

**beam**[2] /bim/ ***verb*** **1** [I] to send out light and warmth: *The sun beamed down on them.* **2** [I] to smile happily: *Beaming with pleasure, she stepped forward to receive her prize.* **3** [T] to broadcast a signal: *The program was beamed live by satellite to many different countries.*

**bean** /bin/ ***noun*** [C] **1** the seeds or seed containers (pods) from a plant that are eaten as vegetables: *green beans* ◇ *a can of baked beans* (= beans in a

B

tomato sauce) **2** similar seeds from other plants: *coffee beans*

**bean·bag** /ˈbinbæg/ ***noun*** [C] **1** a very large bag made of fabric and filled with small pieces of plastic, used for sitting on **2** a small bag made of fabric filled with dried beans and used especially in children's games

ˈ**bean sprouts** ***noun*** [pl.] seeds that are just beginning to grow, often eaten raw

**bear**[1] /bɛr/ ***noun*** [C] a large, heavy wild animal with thick fur: *a black bear* ◇ *a polar bear* ➲ Look at **grizzly bear** and **teddy bear**.

★**bear**[2] /bɛr/ ***verb*** (*pt* **bore** /bɔr/; *pp* **borne** /bɔrn/)

➤SUPPORT WEIGHT **1** [T] to support sth: *Twelve pillars bear the weight of the roof.*

➤CARRY **2** [T] (*formal*) to carry sth: *The waiters came in bearing trays of food.* ◇ (*figurative*) *In her position as governor, she bears a great deal of responsibility.* ◇ (*figurative*) *Customers will bear the full cost of the improvements.*

➤SUFFER **3** [T] to suffer sth without complaining or giving in: *She bore her illness bravely.* ◇ *The heat is too much to bear.* ◇ *These figures won't bear close examination* (= when you look closely, you will find mistakes).

➤NOT BE SUITABLE **4** [T] (with *can/could* in negative sentences or in questions) to dislike strongly; to hate: *Joanne can't bear people who are late.* ◇ *She can't bear waiting for people.* ◇ *How can you bear to listen to that music?*

➤CHILD **5** [T] (*formal*) to give birth to children: *She bore four children, all sons.*

NOTE A more common expression is "She has had four children." When you talk about a person's own birth, you use "to be born": *Olivia was born in 2000.* ◇ *The baby will be born next spring.*

➤OF TREES/PLANTS **6** [T] to produce flowers or fruit: *The tree in our yard bears more apples than we can eat.* ◇ (*figurative*) *Our plan is beginning to bear fruit – these are the first signs of success.*

➤SHOW **7** [T] to show the mark of sth: *The coins bear a moose's head.* ◇ *He still bears the scars of his accident.* ◇ *She bears a strong resemblance to her mother* (= she looks very much like her).

➤NEGATIVE FEELING **8** [T] (*formal*) to have a feeling: *I offended him once and he bore a grudge against me for years.*

➤TURN **9** [I] **bear left/right** to turn or go in the direction that is mentioned: *At the fork in the road, bear left.*

IDM **bear/take the brunt of sth** → BRUNT

**bear in mind (that)** to remember that: *Bear in mind that the weather here can change very quickly.*

PHR V **bear down on sb/sth** **1** to press on sb/sth: *Bear down on it with all your strength so it doesn't move.* **2** to move quickly toward sb/sth in a determined or threatening way

**bear sb/sth out** to show that sb is right or that sth is true: *The figures bear him out.* ◇ *The figures bear out what he says.*

**bear up (against/under sth)** to remain as cheerful as possible during a difficult time

**bear with sb/sth** to be patient with: *Please bear with us while we sort out these technical problems.*

**bear·a·ble** /ˈbɛrəbl/ ***adj.*** that you can accept or deal with, although unpleasant: *She was the only thing that made life bearable.* OPP **unbearable**

**beards**

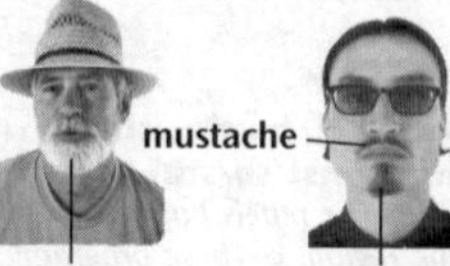
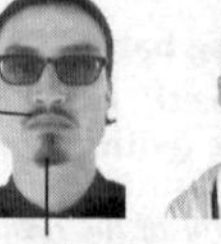
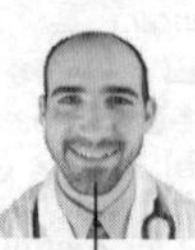


**beard** /bɪrd/ ***noun*** [C] the hair which grows on a man's cheeks and chin: *He has a beard.* ◇ *He's growing a beard.* ◇ *He shaved his beard off.*

**beard·ed** /ˈbɪrdəd/ ***adj.*** with a beard

ˈ**bear hug** ***noun*** [C] an act of showing affection for sb by holding him/her very tightly and strongly in your arms

**bear·ing** /ˈbɛrɪŋ/ ***noun*** **1** [U,C, sing.] **(a) bearing on sth** a relation or connection to the subject being discussed: *Her comments **had no bearing on** our decision.* **2** [C] a direction measured by an instrument with a needle that always points north (a **compass**)

IDM **get your bearings** to find out where you are by becoming familiar with your surroundings

**lose your bearings** → LOSE

ˌ**bear ˈmarket** ***noun*** [C] a period during which people are selling SHARES[1] (2) rather than buying, because they expect the prices to fall ➲ Compare **bull market**.

**beast** /bist/ ***noun*** [C] **1** (*old-fashioned* or *formal*) an animal, especially a large or dangerous one: *a wild beast* **2** an unpleasant or cruel person

★**beat**[1] /bit/ ***verb*** (*pt* **beat**; *pp* **beat·en** /ˈbitn/) **1** [I,T] to hit sb/sth many times, usually very hard: *The man was beating a dog with a stick.* ◇ *The rain was beating down on the roof of the car.* **2** [T] to mix sth quickly with a fork, etc.: *Beat the eggs and sugar together.* **3** [I,T] to make a regular sound or movement: *Her heart beat faster as she ran.* ◇ *We could hear drums beating.* ◇ *The bird beat its wings and tried to fly away.* **4** [T] to defeat sb; to be better than sth: *He always beats me at tennis.* ◇ *We're hoping to beat the world record.* ◇ *You can't beat a hot cup of coffee.*

IDM **beat around the bush** to talk about sth without mentioning the main point

**beat it!** (*informal*) go away immediately: *We don't want you guys around here, so beat it!*

**(it) beats me** (*informal*) I don't know: *"Where's Andy?" "Beats me – I haven't seen him all day."*

**beat time (to sth)** to move sth (a stick, your foot or your hand) following the rhythm of a piece of music

**off the beaten path/track** in a place where people do not often go

PHR V **beat sb/sth off** to fight until sb/sth goes away: *The muggers tried to take his wallet, but he managed to beat them off.*

**beat sb out of sth** (*informal*) get sth from sb by cheating or taking full advantage of a situation: *He beat me out of $500.*

**beat sb to sth** to get somewhere or do sth before

sb else: *She beat me back to the house.* ◇ *I wanted to call him first, but Michael beat me to it.*

**beat sb up** to attack sb by hitting or kicking him/her many times

**beat up on sb** to hit sb hard, especially sb who is young or weak: *I've heard people say that he used to beat up on his wife.*

**beat yourself up (about/over sth)** to blame yourself too much for sth bad that has happened: *Don't beat yourself up over a stupid mistake.*

**beat**[2] /bit/ ***noun*** **1** [C] a single stroke or hit that comes at regular intervals in a series; the sound it makes: *a heartbeat* ◇ *the beat of the drum* **2** [sing.] the strong rhythm that a piece of (especially pop or rock) music has **3** [sing.] the route along which a police officer regularly walks: *Having more police on the beat helps reduce crime.*

**beat·ing** /ˈbit̬ɪŋ/ ***noun*** [C] **1** a punishment that you give to sb by hitting him/her: *He got a beating from his dad when he was caught stealing.* **2** a defeat: *The team took a real beating at the tournament.*

**beau·ti·cian** /byuˈtɪʃn/ ***noun*** [C] (*old-fashioned*) a person whose job is to improve the way people look, e.g. by giving them beauty treatments ➲ Look also at **hairdresser**.

★**beau·ti·ful** /ˈbyut̬əfl/ ***adj.*** attractive; giving pleasure to the senses: *The view from the top of the hill was really beautiful.* ◇ *What a beautiful day – the weather's perfect!* ◇ *He has a beautiful voice.* ◇ *A beautiful perfume filled the air.* ◇ *a beautiful woman*

NOTE **Beautiful** is usually used for women and girls. It is stronger than **pretty**, which is also used for women and girls only. Men are described as **handsome** or **good-looking**.

▶ **beau·ti·ful·ly** /-fli/ ***adv.***: *He plays the piano beautifully.* ◇ *She was beautifully dressed.*

★**beau·ty** /ˈbyut̬i/ ***noun*** (*pl.* **beau·ties**) **1** [U] the quality that gives pleasure to the senses; the state of being beautiful: *the beauty of Victoria's coast* ◇ *Brahms wrote music of great beauty.* **2** [C] an especially good example of sth: *Look at this tomato – it's a beauty!* **3** [C] (*old-fashioned*) a beautiful woman: *She grew up to be a beauty.*

ˈ**beauty saˌlon** (*also* ˈ**beauty ˌparlor**) ***noun*** [C] a place where you can pay to have your hair cut or have beauty treatments

**bea·ver** /ˈbivər/ ***noun*** [C] **1** an animal with brown fur, a long, broad tail and sharp teeth, which it uses to cut down trees to build barriers (dams) across rivers. It is an official symbol of Canada. **2 Beaver** (*Cdn*) a member of the SCOUTS[1] (1) at the youngest level (age 5-7) in Canada

beaver

**be·came** *past tense of* BECOME

★**be·cause** /bɪˈkɔz; -ˈkʌz/ ***conj.*** for the reason that: *They didn't go for a walk because it was raining.*

★**beˈcause of** ***prep.*** by reason of, as a result of: *They didn't go for a walk because of the rain.*

**beck·on** /ˈbɛkən/ ***verb*** [I,T] to show sb (often with a movement of your finger or hand) that you want him/her to come closer: *She beckoned me over to speak to her.* ◇ (*figurative*) *When Doug retired, the sunny beaches of California beckoned.*

★**be·come** /bɪˈkʌm/ ***verb*** [I] (*pt* **be·came** /bɪˈkeɪm/; *pp* **be·come**) to begin to be sth: *She became president of the company in 2003.* ◇ *Jo wants to become a pilot.* ◇ *They became friends.* ◇ *It became clear that they wanted to stay.* ◇ *He is becoming stronger every day.* ◇ *This neighborhood has become more dangerous in the last few years.*

NOTE **Get** is also used with adjectives in this sense: *He's getting stronger every day.* ◇ *This neighborhood has gotten more dangerous in the last few years.* **Get** is very common in conversation and is less formal than **become**.

PHRV **become of sb/sth** to happen to sb/sth: *What became of Eileen? – I haven't seen her for years!*

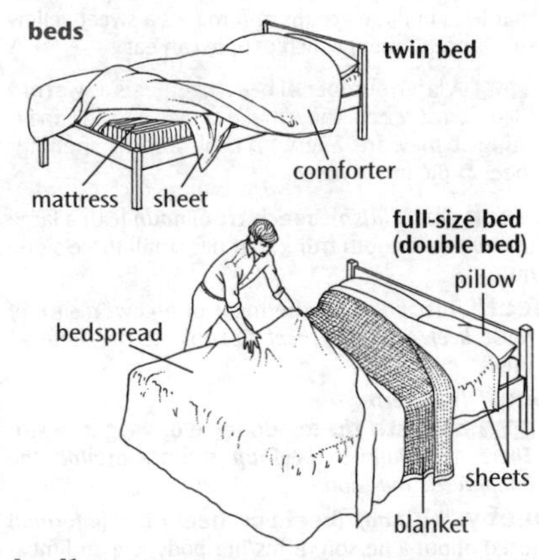


★**bed**[1] /bɛd/ ***noun*** **1** [C,U] a piece of furniture that you lie on when you sleep: *The kids sleep in bunk beds.* ◇ *What time do you usually go to bed?* ◇ *I was already in bed when he called.* ◇ *It's time for bed.* ◇ *to get into/out of bed*

NOTE There are four standard sizes of beds: **twin** (wide enough for one person), **full** or **double**, **queen** and **king** (the widest).

**2** [C] the ground at the bottom of a river or the ocean ➲ Look also at **flower bed**.

IDM **get up on the wrong side of the bed** to be in a bad mood for the whole day for no particular reason

**go to bed with sb** (*informal*) to have sex with sb

**make the/your bed** to arrange the sheets, etc. so that they are smooth and the bed is ready for sb to sleep in

**bed**[2] /bɛd/ ***verb***

PHRV **bed down** to make yourself comfortable and sleep somewhere: *We bedded down for the night in the back of the van.*

**bed·clothes** /ˈbɛdkloʊz; -kloʊðz/ ***noun*** [pl.] the covers, sheets, blankets, etc. that you put on a bed

**bed·ding** /ˈbɛdɪŋ/ ***noun*** [U] everything that you put on a bed and need for sleeping

B

**bed·pan** /ˈbɛdpæn/ ***noun*** [C] a container used as a toilet by a person who is too sick to get out of bed

**be·drag·gled** /bɪˈdrægld/ ***adj.*** made wet, dirty or messy by rain, mud, etc.: *bedraggled hair/clothes*

**bed·rid·den** /ˈbɛdrɪdn/ ***adj.*** having to stay in bed all the time because of sickness, injury or old age

★**bed·room** /ˈbɛdrum/ ***noun*** [C] a room that is used for sleeping in: *You can sleep in the spare bedroom.* ◇ *a two-bedroom apartment*

**bed·side** /ˈbɛdsaɪd/ ***noun*** [usually sing.] the area next to a bed: *She sat at his bedside all night long.* ◇ *a bedside table*

**bed·spread** /ˈbɛdsprɛd/ ***noun*** [C] an attractive cover for a bed that you put on top of the sheets and other covers ➲ picture at **bed**[1].

**bed·time** /ˈbɛdtaɪm/ ***noun*** [C,U] the time that you normally go to bed

**bee** /bi/ ***noun*** [C] a black and yellow striped insect that lives in large groups and makes a sweet yellow substance (**honey**) which people can eat

> NOTE A large number of bees together is a **swarm**. Bees **buzz** when they make a noise. They may **sting** if they are angry. ➲ Look also at **spelling bee**. ➲ picture at **insect**.

**beech** /bitʃ/ (*also* **ˈbeech tree**) ***noun*** [C,U] a large tree with a smooth trunk that has small three-sided nuts

★**beef**[1] /bif/ ***noun*** [U] the meat of a cow: *a slice of roast beef* ◇ *ground beef* ➲ Look at the note at **meat**.

**beef**[2] /bif/ ***verb***

PHRV **beef sth up** to add force or weight to sth: *There are plans to beef up security around the billionaire's mansion.*

**beef·y** /ˈbifi/ ***adj.*** (**beef·i·er**; **beef·i·est**) (*informal*) (used about a person or his/her body) big and muscular: *beefy men/arms*

**bee·hive** /ˈbihaɪv/ (*also* **hive**) ***noun*** [C] a type of box that people keep bees in, or a round structure that bees build and live in

**bee·keep·er** /ˈbikipər/ ***noun*** [C] a person who owns and takes care of bees ▸ **bee·keep·ing** ***noun*** [U]

**been** /bɪn/ *past participle of* BE, GO

> NOTE **Been** is used as the past participle of both **be** and **go**: *I've never been seriously ill.* ◇ *I've never been to Mexico.*

**beep**[1] /bip/ ***noun*** [C] a short high noise, e.g. made by a piece of electronic equipment

**beep**[2] /bip/ ***verb*** [I] to make a short high noise: *Why is the computer beeping?*

**beep·er** /ˈbipər/ ***noun*** [C] = PAGER

★**beer** /bɪr/ ***noun*** **1** [U] a type of alcoholic drink that is made from grain **2** [C] a type or glass of beer: *This bar serves a wide range of beers.* ◇ *We stopped for a couple of beers on the way home.* ➲ Look also at **root beer**.

**bees·wax** /ˈbizwæks/ ***noun*** [U] a yellow sticky substance that is produced by bees and is used especially for making candles and polish for wood

**beet** /bit/ ***noun*** [C] a plant with a dark red root that is cooked and eaten as a vegetable ➲ picture on study page **A28-29**.

**bee·tle** /ˈbiṭl/ ***noun*** [C] an insect that has hard coverings for its wings and often a black shiny body. There are many different types of beetle. ➲ picture at **insect**.

**be·fall** /bɪˈfɔl/ ***verb*** [I,T] (*pt* **be·fell** /bɪˈfɛl/; *pp* **be·fall·en** /bɪˈfɔlən/) (*written*) (used about sth bad) to happen to sb

★**be·fore**[1] /bɪˈfɔr/ ***prep.*** **1** earlier than sb/sth: *You can call me anytime before 10 o'clock.* ◇ *the week before last* ◇ *Ellen worked in Montreal before moving here.* ◇ *They should be here before long* (= soon). **2** in front/ahead of sb/sth (in an order): *"M" comes before "N" in the alphabet.* ◇ (*figurative*) *A very difficult task lies before us.* ◇ (*figurative*) *a company that puts profit before safety* **3** when sb is present: *You will appear before the court in the morning.* **4** (*formal*) in a position in front of sb/sth: *They knelt before the throne.*

★**be·fore**[2] /bɪˈfɔr/ ***conj.*** **1** earlier than the time that: *Turn the lights off before you leave.* **2** rather than; so that sth bad does not happen: *I'd die before I apologized to him!* ◇ *Pick up your toys before somebody steps on them.*

★**be·fore**[3] /bɪˈfɔr/ ***adv.*** at an earlier time: *I think we've met somewhere before.* ◇ *It was nice yesterday, but it rained the day before.*

**be·fore·hand** /bɪˈfɔrhænd/ ***adv.*** at an earlier time than sth: *We prepared most of the food for the party beforehand.*

**be·friend** /bɪˈfrɛnd/ ***verb*** [T] (*formal*) to act as a friend to sb; to be kind to sb

**beg** /bɛg/ ***verb*** (**beg·ging**; **begged**) **1** [I] **beg for sth (from/of sb)** to ask sb for food, money, etc., e.g. because you are very poor: *There are people begging for food on the streets of New York.* **2** [I,T] **beg (sb) for sth** to ask sb for sth strongly, or with great emotion: *He begged for forgiveness.* ◇ *We begged him to let the kids go.*

IDM **I beg your pardon** (*formal*) **1** I'm sorry: *I beg your pardon. I picked up your bag by mistake.* **2** (used for asking sb to repeat sth because you did not hear it correctly): *"Hi, I'm Bob." "I beg your pardon?" "Bob."*

**be·gan** *past tense of* BEGIN

**beg·gar** /ˈbɛgər/ ***noun*** [C] a person who lives by asking people for money, food, etc. on the streets

★**be·gin** /bɪˈgɪn/ ***verb*** (*pres. part.* **be·gin·ning**; *pt* **be·gan** /bɪˈgæn/; *pp* **be·gun** /bɪˈgʌn/) **1** [I] to take place from a particular time; to start: *What time does the concert begin?*

> NOTE **Begin** and **start** are very similar in meaning, but **start** is more often used in informal speech. They can be followed by *to* or by the *-ing* form of a verb: *The baby began to cry/crying.* ◇ *The baby started to cry/crying.* When **begin** or **start** are themselves in the *-ing* form, they must be followed by *to*: *The baby was just beginning/starting to cry.* In some meanings, only **start** can be used: *I couldn't start the car.* ◇ *We'll have to start* (= leave) *early if we want to be there by 8 o'clock.* **Commence** is much more formal than **begin** or **start** and is not usually used in conversation.

B

**2** [I,T] to do or make a start on the first part of sth; to start: *Should I begin or do you want to?* ◇ *Please begin at page 10.* ◇ *I began* (= started reading) *this book last month and I still haven't finished it.* ◇ *He sat down and began to cry.* ◇ *Children usually begin school at age 5.* ◇ *We began writing to each other in 2000.* ◇ *I would like to begin by thanking everybody for coming.* **3** [I] to form the first part of sth: *My name begins with "W," not "V."* ◇ *This is where the neighbors' yard begins.*

IDM **to begin with 1** (used for giving your first reason for sth): *There's no way we can go. To begin with it's too far, and we can't afford it either.* **2** at first: *To begin with, they were very happy.*

**be·gin·ner** /bɪˈgɪnər/ ***noun*** [C] a person who has just begun learning sth

★**be·gin·ning** /bɪˈgɪnɪŋ/ ***noun*** [C,U] the first part of sth; the time when or place where sth starts: *The beginning of the movie isn't very interesting.* ◇ *I read the article from beginning to end.* ◇ *We're going away at the beginning of next month.*

**be·grudge** /bɪˈgrʌdʒ/ ***verb*** [T] (often used in negative sentences) **1** to feel unhappy that sb has sth because you do not think that he/she deserves it: *You surely don't begrudge him his happiness.* **2** to feel unhappy about having to do, pay or give sth: *I begrudge every second I spent trying to help him.* ◇ *Many people begrudge paying so much money for a second-rate service.*

**begun** *past participle of* BEGIN

★**be·half** /bɪˈhæf/ ***noun***

IDM **on/in behalf of sb; on/in sb's behalf 1** for sb; as the representative of sb: *Mary couldn't be there, so her husband accepted the prize on her behalf.* ◇ *I will be acting on behalf of my client.* **2** in order to help sb; for sb: *We collected money on behalf of refugee families.*

★**be·have** /bɪˈheɪv/ ***verb*** **1** [I] **behave well, badly, etc. (toward sb)** to act in a particular way: *Liz has been behaving very strangely recently.* ◇ *He behaved very badly toward his father.* ◇ *He behaves as if he were the boss.* **2** [I,T] **behave (yourself)** to act in the correct or proper way: *Now, you kids behave yourselves while we're away!*

**-beˈhaved** /bɪˈheɪvd/ ***combining form*** behaving in a particular way: *a well-behaved child*

★**be·hav·ior** /bɪˈheɪvyər/ ***noun*** [U] the way that you act or behave: *Her behavior has been very strange recently.* ◇ *"I will not tolerate this kind of behavior," said the teacher.*

★**be·hind**[1] /bɪˈhaɪnd/ ***prep.*** **1** in, at or to the back of sb/sth: *There's a small shed behind the house.* ◇ *The sun went behind a cloud.* ◇ *Look behind you before you drive away.* ◇ (*figurative*) *It's time you put your problems behind you* (= forgot about them). **2** later or less good than sb/sth: *The flight is twenty minutes behind schedule.* ◇ *Jane is behind the rest of the class in math.* **3** supporting or agreeing with sb/sth: *Most people are behind the President's policies.* **4** causing or starting sth: *What is the reason behind his sudden change of opinion?*

IDM **behind sb's back** → BACK[1]

★**be·hind**[2] /bɪˈhaɪnd/ ***adv.*** **1** in, at or to the back of sb/sth: *You go ahead. I'll follow behind in a few minutes.* ◇ *Try not to look behind.* ◇ *He ran off, but the police were close behind.* **2** in the place where sb/sth is or was: *Oh, no! I left the tickets behind* (= at home). **3 behind (in/with sth)** later or less good than sb/sth: *We are a month behind with the rent.* ◇ *The Bears were behind at halftime.* ➲ Look at **ahead**.

**be·hind**[3] /bɪˈhaɪnd/ ***noun*** [C] (*informal*) the part of your body that you sit on ➲ Look at **bottom** (5) and **butt**.

**beige** /beɪʒ/ ***adj.***, ***noun*** [U] (of) a light brown color

**be·ing** /ˈbiɪŋ/ ***noun*** **1** [U] the state of existing: *The organization came into being* (= started) *two years ago.* **2** [C] a living person or thing: *a human being* ◇ *a strange being from another planet*

**be·lat·ed** /bɪˈleɪt̬əd/ ***adj.*** coming late: *a belated apology* ▶ **be·lat·ed·ly** ***adv.***: *They realized, somewhat belatedly, that they had made a big mistake.*

**belch** /bɛltʃ/ ***verb*** **1** [I] to let air out from your stomach through your mouth with a sudden noise, e.g. because you have eaten a lot ➲ Look also at **burp**. **2** [T] to send out smoke, etc.: *The volcano belched smoke and ashes.* ▶ **belch *noun*** [C]: *He gave a loud belch.*

**be·lie** /bɪˈlaɪ/ ***verb*** [T] (*pres. part.* **be·ly·ing**; *3rd person sing. pres.* **be·lies**; *pt, pp* **be·lied**) to give a false or untrue idea of sth: *His smiling face belied his true feelings.*

★**be·lief** /bɪˈlif/ ***noun*** (*pl.* **be·liefs**) **1** [sing., U] **belief (in sb/sth)** a feeling that sb/sth is true, good or right, or that sb/sth really exists: *She has lost her belief in God.* ◇ *Her salary has increased beyond belief* (= very much). ➲ Look at **disbelief**. **2** [sing., U] **belief (that...)** something you accept as true; what you believe: *It's my belief that people are basically good.* ◇ *There is a general belief that things will soon get better.* ◇ *Contrary to popular belief* (= unlike what many people think), *snakes do not really have slimy skin.* **3** [C] an idea that sb has about religion, politics, etc.: *Divorce is against their religious beliefs.*

**be·liev·a·ble** /bɪˈlivəbl/ ***adj.*** that can be believed OPP **unbelievable**

★**be·lieve** /bɪˈliv/ ***verb*** (not in the continuous forms) **1** [T] to feel sure that sth is true or that sb is telling the truth: *He says he didn't take the money, but I don't believe him.* ◇ *Nobody believes a word she says.* ◇ *When she said she was leaving, I just couldn't believe it.* **2** [T] **believe (that)...** to think or suppose: *I believe they moved to Halifax.* ◇ *This is yours, I believe.* ◇ *The escaped prisoner is believed to be in this area.* **3** [I] to have religious faith

IDM **believe it or not** it may be surprising but it is true: *Believe it or not, he's a dancer.*

PHR V **believe in sb/sth** to be sure that sb/sth exists: *Do you believe in God?*

**believe in sb/sth; believe in doing sth** to think that sb/sth is good or right: *I believe in the value of education.* ◇ *He doesn't believe in eating meat.*

**be·liev·er** /bɪˈlivər/ ***noun*** [C] a person who has religious faith

IDM **be a (great/firm) believer in sth** to think that sth is good or right: *She is a great believer in exercise.*

**be·lit·tle** /bɪˈlɪt̬l/ ***verb*** [T] to make sb/sth seem unimportant or not very good

B

★**bell** /bɛl/ ***noun*** [C] **1** a hollow metal object, usually shaped like a cup, that makes a ringing sound when it is hit: *the sound of church bells* **2** an object that makes a ringing sound, or the sound that it makes, often used as a signal: *a doorbell* ◇ *Ring the bell and see if they're home.* ◇ *There's the bell for the end of class.*

IDM **ring a bell** → RING²

ˈ**bell-ˌbottoms** ***noun*** [pl.] pants with legs that become very wide below the knee ▶ ˈ**bell-ˌbottomed** ***adj.***

**bell·hop** /ˈbɛlhɑp/ (*also* **bell·boy** /ˈbɛlbɔɪ/) ***noun*** [C] a person, especially a young man, employed in a hotel to carry cases, open doors for people, etc.

**bel·low** /ˈbɛloʊ/ ***verb*** **1** [I] to make a deep low sound, like a bull **2** [I,T] to shout in a loud deep voice ▶ **bel·low** ***noun*** [C]

ˌ**bell** ˈ**pep·per** ***noun*** [C] = PEPPER¹ (2) ➲ picture on study page **A28-29**.

**bel·ly** /ˈbɛli/ ***noun*** [C] (*pl.* **bel·lies**) (*informal*) the stomach, or the part of the body between the chest and the legs: *a full/empty belly*

IDM **go belly-up** (used about a business) to have financial problems and fail

ˈ**belly ˌbutton** ***noun*** [C] (*informal*) = NAVEL

ˈ**belly dance** ***noun*** [C] a dance, originally from the Middle East, in which a woman moves her stomach and her hips around

**bel·ly·flop** /ˈbɛliflɑp/ (*also* ˈ**belly flop**) ***noun*** [C] (*informal*) a bad dive into water, in which the front of the body hits the water flat

★**be·long** /bɪˈlɔŋ/ ***verb*** [I] **1 belong to sb** to be owned by sb: *Who does this pen belong to?* ◇ *Don't take anything that doesn't belong to you.* **2 belong to sth** to be a member of a group or organization: *Do you belong to any political party?* **3** to have a correct or usual place: *The plates belong in the cupboard.* ◇ *I don't think this paragraph really belongs here.* ◇ *It took quite a long time before we felt as if we belonged in the neighborhood* (= until we felt at home).

**be·long·ings** /bɪˈlɔŋɪŋz/ ***noun*** [pl.] the things that you own that can be moved, i.e. not land and buildings: *The tourists lost all their belongings in the fire.*

**be·lov·ed** /bɪˈlʌvd/ ***adj.*** (*formal*) much loved: *He was a man who was beloved by all who knew him.* ◇ *They sang about their beloved homeland.*

> NOTE When "beloved" comes before a noun, the pronunciation is /bɪˈlʌvəd/.

★**be·low¹** /bɪˈloʊ/ ***prep.*** at or to a lower position or level than sb/sth: *Do not write below this line.* ◇ *It hurts here – just below my knee.* ◇ *The temperature fell below freezing.* ◇ *Her test score was below average.* ◇ *He drives way below the speed limit.* ➲ Look at the note at **under**. ➲ picture at **under**.

★**be·low²** /bɪˈloʊ/ ***adv.*** at or to a lower position or level: *For further explanation of this point, please see below* (= a later part of the book, etc.). ◇ *winter temperatures of 30° and below*

★**belt¹** /bɛlt/ ***noun*** [C] **1** a thin piece of cloth, leather, etc. that you wear around your waist: *I need a belt to keep these pants up.* ◇ *He was wearing a belt with a huge silver buckle.* ➲ Look also at **seat belt**. **2** a long strip of rubber, etc. in a circle, that is used for carrying things or for making parts of a machine move: *The suitcases were carried along on a conveyor belt.* ◇ *the fan belt of a car* **3** an area of land that has a particular quality: *the Bible belt*

IDM **below the belt** (*informal*) in a way that is unkind or not fair: *That remark really hit below the belt.*

**tighten your belt** → TIGHTEN

**under your belt** (*informal*) that you have already done or achieved: *Woods has four tournament wins under his belt.*

**belt²** /bɛlt/ ***verb*** [T] (*informal*) to hit sb hard

PHR V **belt sth out** (*informal*) to sing sth very loudly and with a lot of force: *She can really belt out a song.*

**belt·way** /ˈbɛltweɪ/ ***noun*** [C] (*especially US*) **1** a wide road that goes all around the edge of a city so that traffic does not have to go through the center of the city **2 Beltway** the central part of the Washington D.C. area, where many people are involved in politics: *A lot of people within the Beltway think that the President will have to raise taxes this year.*

**be·mused** /bɪˈmyuzd/ ***adj.*** not knowing what to think or do; confused

**bench** /bɛntʃ/ ***noun*** [C] **1** a long wooden or metal seat for two or more people, often outdoors: *a park bench* **2** a long narrow table that people work at, e.g. in a factory, court of law or laboratory: *a carpenter's bench*

**bench·mark** /ˈbɛntʃmɑrk/ ***noun*** [C] something which can be measured and used as a standard that other things can be compared with: *Tests at the age of seven can provide a benchmark against which the child's progress at school can be measured.*

**bend**

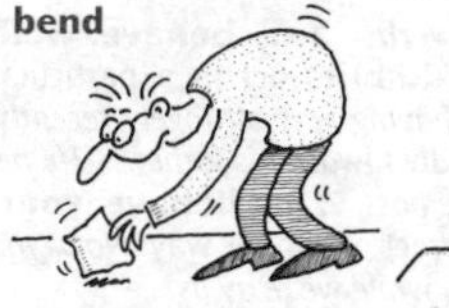

bending down (*also* bending over)

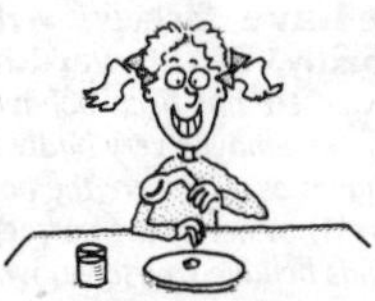

bending a spoon

★**bend¹** /bɛnd/ ***verb*** (*pt, pp* **bent** /bɛnt/) **1** [T] to make sth that was straight into a curved shape, or to make sth that was upright lean forward: *Bend your knees when you pick up something heavy.* ◇ *to bend a piece of wire into an S shape* ◇ *She sat with her head bent forward.* **2** [I] to be or become curved: *The road bends to the left here.* **3** [I] to move your body forward and downward: *He bent down to tie his shoelaces.* ◇ *She bent forward to hear what I was saying.*

IDM **bend the rules** to change the rules a little in order to allow sth for a particular reason

★**bend²** /bɛnd/ ***noun*** [C] a curve or turn, e.g. in a road: *a sharp bend in the road*

★**be·neath¹** /bɪˈniθ/ ***prep.*** **1** in, at or to a lower position than sb/sth; under: *It's wonderful to feel the grass beneath my feet.* ◇ *He seemed like a nice person, but there was a lot of anger beneath the surface.* ➲ Look at the note at **under**. **2** not good enough for sb: *She felt that washing dishes for other people was beneath her.*

**be·neath²** /bɪˈniθ/ ***adv.*** (*formal*) in, at or to a lower position: *From the top of the tower, we gazed down on the city beneath.*

**ben·e·fac·tor** /ˈbɛnəfæktər/ ***noun*** [C] a person who helps or gives money to a person or an organization

**ben·e·fi·cial** /ˌbɛnəˈfɪʃl/ ***adj.*** **beneficial (to sb/sth)** having a good or useful effect: *a beneficial influence on the economy*

**ben·e·fi·ci·ar·y** /ˌbɛnəˈfɪʃiɛri; -ˈfɪʃəri/ ***noun*** [C] (*pl.* **ben·e·fi·ci·ar·ies**) **beneficiary (of sth) 1** a person who gains as a result of sth: *Who will be the main beneficiary of the cuts in income tax?* **2** a person who receives money or property when sb dies

★**ben·e·fit¹** /ˈbɛnəfɪt/ ***noun*** **1** [U] the advantage or good or useful effect of sth: *Most parents want to give their children the benefit of a good education.* ◇ *A change in the law would be to everyone's benefit.* ◇ *I can't see the benefit of doing things this way.* **2** [C] a thing that has a good or useful effect: *the benefits of modern technology* **3** [C,U] money that the government gives to people who are sick for a long time, injured at work, unemployed, etc.: *unemployment benefit payments* **4** [C] (*also* **fringe benefit**) an extra payment or service that is given to an employee in addition to his/her salary: *Our generous employee benefits package includes health insurance and three weeks' paid vacation.* **5** [C] a concert, party, show, etc. that is held in order to raise money to help a charity, an organization, etc.: *a benefit concert to raise money for victims of the earthquake*

IDM **for sb's benefit** especially to help, please, etc. sb: *For the benefit of newcomers, I will explain the plan again.*

**give sb the benefit of the doubt** to believe that what sb says is true because there is no clear proof that it is not

★**ben·e·fit²** /ˈbɛnəfɪt/ ***verb*** (**ben·e·fi̱t·ing**; **ben·e·fi̱t·ed** or **ben·e·fi̱t·ting**; **ben·e·fi̱t·ted**) **1** [T] to have a good or useful effect: *The new tax laws will benefit people on low wages.* **2** [I] **benefit (from sth)** to receive an advantage from sth: *We've certainly benefited from the changes in the law.*

**be·nev·o·lent** /bəˈnɛvələnt/ ***adj.*** (*formal*) kind, friendly and helpful to others ▸ **be·nev·o·lence** /-ləns/ ***noun*** [U]

**be·nign** /bəˈnaɪn/ ***adj.*** **1** (used about people) kind or gentle **2** (used about a disease, etc.) not causing death: *a benign tumor* ➲ Compare **malignant**.

★**bent¹** *past tense, past participle of* BEND¹

**bent²** /bɛnt/ ***adj.*** **bent on sth/on doing sth** wanting to do sth very much, so that you cannot accept not doing it: *She seems bent on becoming an actress, no matter how hard it is.*

IDM **be/get bent out of shape** (*slang*) to become very angry or upset: *The boss got totally bent out of shape about my mistake.*

**be·queath** /bɪˈkwiθ; -ˈkwið/ ***verb*** [T] (*formal*) **bequeath sth (to sb)** to arrange for sth to be given to sb after you die: *He bequeathed $1,000 to his church.* ➲ **Leave** is a more common word.

**be·quest** /bɪˈkwɛst/ ***noun*** [C] (*formal*) something that you arrange to be given to sb after you have died: *He left a bequest to each of his grandchildren.*

**be·reaved** /bɪˈrivd/ ***adj.*** **1** having had a relative or close friend die **2 the bereaved** ***noun*** [C] a person whose relative or close friend has died recently ➲ The plural is also **the bereaved**.

**be·reave·ment** /bɪˈrivmənt/ ***noun*** **1** [U] the state of having lost a relative or close friend because he/she has died: *the pain of an emotional crisis such as divorce or bereavement* **2** [C] the death of a relative or close friend: *A family bereavement meant that he could not attend the conference.*

**be·ret** /bəˈreɪ/ ***noun*** [C] a soft flat round hat

**ber·ry** /ˈbɛri/ ***noun*** [C] (*pl.* **ber·ries**) a small soft fruit with seeds: *Those berries are poisonous.*

**ber·serk** /bərˈzərk; -ˈsərk/ ***adj.***

IDM **go berserk** (*informal*) to become extremely angry and violent and unable to control yourself: *Then this guy just went berserk and started screaming.*

**berth** /bərθ/ ***noun*** [C] a place where a ship can be tied up in a harbor

**be·set** /bɪˈsɛt/ ***verb*** (*pres. part.* **be·set·ting**; *pt, pp* **be·set**) [T] (usually passive) (*formal*) to affect sb/sth in an unpleasant or harmful way: *The team had been beset by injuries all season.* ◇ *It's one of the most difficult problems besetting our modern way of life.*

★**be·side** /bɪˈsaɪd/ ***prep.*** at the side of, or next to sb/sth: *Come and sit beside me.* ◇ *He kept his bag close beside him at all times.*

IDM **beside yourself (with sth)** not able to control yourself because of a very strong emotion: *Jennifer was almost beside herself with grief.*

**be·sides¹** /bɪˈsaɪdz/ ***prep.*** in addition to or as well as sb/sth: *There will be six people coming, besides you and Uli.*

**be·sides²** /bɪˈsaɪdz/ ***adv.*** in addition; also: *I thought the hotel was too expensive. Besides, it was very close to the freeway.*

**be·siege** /bɪˈsidʒ/ ***verb*** [T] **1** to surround a building, city, etc. with soldiers **2** (especially of sth unpleasant or annoying) to surround sb/sth in large numbers: *The actor was besieged by fans and reporters.*

**be·sot·ted** /bɪˈsɑṭəd/ ***adj.*** **besotted (by/with sb/sth)** loving sb/sth so much that you do not behave in a sensible way: *He is completely besotted with his new girlfriend.*

**best¹** /bɛst/ ***adj.*** (the superlative of *good*) of the highest quality or level; most suitable: *Who's your best friend?* ◇ *His latest book is by far his best.* ◇ *It's best to call early.* ◇ *Who in the class is best at math?* ◇ *What's the best way to get to the airport from here?* ◇ *The best thing to do is to forget all about it.*

IDM **your best bet** (*informal*) the best thing for you to do in a particular situation: *There's nowhere to park downtown. Your best bet is to take the bus.*

**the best/better part of sth** → PART¹

**best²** /bɛst/ ***adv.*** (the superlative of *well*) **1** in the most excellent way: *She works best in the morning.* **2** to the greatest degree; most: *Which of these dresses do you like best?* ◇ *one of America's best-loved TV stars* ◇ *Mother knows best.*

B

IDM **as best you can** as well as you can, even if it is not perfectly

**best**[3] /bɛst/ ***noun*** [sing.] **1** something that is of the highest quality or level: *When you pay that much for a meal, you expect the best.* ◇ *I'm not in the best of health.* ◇ *The best we can hope for is that the situation doesn't get any worse.* ➲ Look at **second-best**. **2 the best** [with sing. or pl. verb] a person that is best: *Even the best of us make mistakes sometimes.*
IDM **all the best** (*informal*) (used when you are saying goodbye to sb and wishing him/her success): *All the best! Keep in touch, OK?*
**at best** if everything is as favorable as possible; taking the most hopeful view: *At best, it'll be ready by the end of March.*
**at its/your best** in its/your best state or condition: *This is an example of Beckett's work at its best.* ◇ *No one is at their best first thing in the morning.*
**bring out the best/worst in sb** to show sb's best/worst qualities: *The crisis really brought out the best in Tony.*
**do/try your best** to do all or the most that you can: *It doesn't matter whether you win or not. Just do your best.*
**look your best** to look as beautiful or attractive as possible
**make the best of sth** to accept a difficult situation and try to be as happy as possible

**ˌbest ˈman** ***noun*** [C] a man who helps and supports the man who is getting married (groom) at his wedding ➲ Look at the note at **wedding**.

**best·sell·er** /ˌbɛstˈsɛlər/ ***noun*** [C] a book or other product that has been bought by large numbers of people

**ˌbest-ˈselling** ***adj.*** very popular: *a best-selling novel*

★**bet**[1] /bɛt/ ***verb*** [I,T] (*pres. part.* **bet·ting**; *pt, pp* **bet**) **bet (sth) (on sth)** to risk some money on the result of sth (e.g. a horse race). If you are wrong about the result, you have to pay some money: *Which horse did you bet on?* ◇ *I bet him $10 he couldn't stop smoking for a week.*
IDM **I bet (that)...** (*informal*) I'm sure that...: *I bet he feels stupid.*
**you bet** (*informal*) (a way of saying, "Yes, of course!"): *"Are you coming too?" "You bet!"*

**bet**[2] /bɛt/ ***noun*** [C] an act of betting: *Did you have a bet on that race?* ◇ *to win/lose a bet*
IDM **your best bet** → BEST[1]

**be·ta** /ˈbeɪt̬ə/ ***noun*** [C] (*symbol* Β, β) the second letter of the Greek alphabet ➲ Look at the note at **fraternity**.

**ˈbeta ˌblocker** ***noun*** [C] a drug used to control heart rhythm, treat severe chest pain and reduce high blood pressure

**bet·cha** /ˈbɛtʃə/ (*informal*) a way of writing "bet you" to show that sb is speaking in an informal way: *I betcha I get a better grade on the test than you do.*

> NOTE Do not write "betcha" yourself (unless you are copying sb's speech) because it might be marked as a mistake.

**be·tray** /bɪˈtreɪ/ ***verb*** [T] **1** to be disloyal to a person or thing; to harm a person or organization that trusts you: *When parents get divorced, the children often feel betrayed.* ◇ *to betray your country* **2** to make facts about sb/sth known to an enemy; to make a secret known: *She betrayed them to the secret police.* ◇ *He refused to betray the information.* **3** to show a feeling or quality that you would like to keep hidden: *Her steady voice did not betray the emotion she was feeling.* ► **be·tray·al** /bɪˈtreɪəl/ ***noun*** [C,U]

★**bet·ter**[1] /ˈbɛt̬ər/ ***adj.*** **1** (the comparative of *good*) **better (than sth)** of a higher quality or level or more suitable: *I think her second novel was much better than her first.* ◇ *He's better at chemistry than physics.* ◇ *It's a long way to drive. It would be better to fly.* **2** less sick or fully recovered from an illness: *I feel a little better today.* ◇ *You can't go swimming until you're better.*
IDM **the bigger, smaller, faster, slower, etc. the better** used to say that sth should be as big, small, etc. as possible: *As far as the connection speed is concerned, the faster the better.*
**have seen better days** to be in poor condition: *Our car has sure seen better days, but we can't afford a new one this year.*

★**bet·ter**[2] /ˈbɛt̬ər/ ***adv.*** (the comparative of *well*) **better (than sb/sth)** to a greater or higher degree: *I think you could have done this better.* ◇ *Sylvie speaks English better than I do.* ◇ *She is much better known than her sister.* ◇ *I like the red one better than the blue one.*
IDM **the best/better part of sth** → PART[1]
**(be) better off 1** to be in a more pleasant or suitable situation: *You look terrible. You'd be better off at home in bed.* **2** with more money: *We're much better off now that both of us work.*
**you, etc. had better** you should; you would be wise to: *I think we'd better go before it gets dark.*
**know better** → KNOW
**think better of (doing) sth** → THINK

★**bet·ter**[3] /ˈbɛt̬ər/ ***noun*** [sing.] something that is of higher quality: *The hotel wasn't too bad, but I've certainly seen better.*
IDM **get the better of sb/sth** to defeat or be stronger than sb/sth: *When we have an argument, she always gets the better of me.*

**between/among**

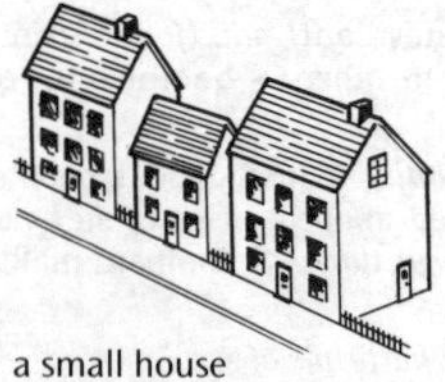

a small house **between** two large ones

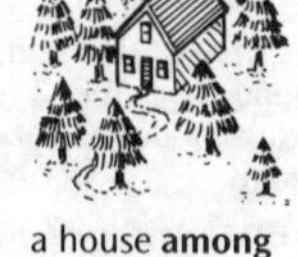

a house **among** some trees

★**be·tween**[1] /bɪˈtwin/ ***prep.*** **1** in the space that separates two things, people, etc.; somewhere in the middle: *I was sitting between Anne and Derek.* ◇ *a town between Los Angeles and San Diego* **2** from one place to another and back again: *There aren't any direct flights between here and Toronto.* ◇ *the trip between home and the office* **3** involving or linking two people, groups or things: *There's some sort of disagreement between them.* ◇ *There may be a* *connection between the two crimes.* **4** (used about two amounts, distances, ages, times, etc.) at a point that is greater or later than the first and smaller or earlier than the second; somewhere in the middle: *She must be between about thirty and thirty-five.* ◇ *They said they would arrive between 4 and 5 o'clock.* ◇ *a cost of between $200 and $300* **5** choosing one and not the other (of two things): *to choose between two jobs* ◇ *What's the difference between "some" and "any?"* **6** by putting together the actions, efforts, etc. of two or more people: *We've got over a thousand dollars saved up between us.* **7** giving each person a share: *The money was divided equally between the two children.* ◇ *We ate all the candy between us.*

NOTE **Between** is usually used of two people or things: *She was sitting between her mother and father.* ◇ *between the ages of 12 and 14.* **Among** is always used for more than two people or things considered as a group, rather than as individuals: *You're among friends here.*

**be·tween²** /bɪ'twin/ (*also* ˌ**in be'tween**) ***adv.*** in the space or period of time that separates two things, points, people, times, etc.: *We can't get to the beach this way. There's a highway in between.* ◇ *I have a meeting at 10:00 and one at 11:00, but I should manage to see you in between.*

**bev·er·age** /'bɛvrɪdʒ; 'bɛvərɪdʒ/ ***noun*** [C] (*formal*) (used especially on menus) a drink

**be·ware** /bɪ'wɛr/ ***verb*** [I] (only in the imperative or infinitive) **beware (of sb/sth)** (used for giving a warning) to be careful: *Beware of the dog!* (written on a sign) ◇ *We were told to beware of pickpockets in the city.*

**be·wil·dered** /bɪ'wɪldərd/ ***adj.*** confused: *He seemed bewildered by all the activity around him.*

**be·wil·der·ing** /bɪ'wɪldərɪŋ/ ***adj.*** making you feel confused and unable to decide what to do: *a bewildering array of choices*

★**be·yond¹** /bɪ'yɑnd/ ***prep.*** **1** on the other side of: *beyond the distant mountains* **2** farther than; later than: *Does the expressway continue beyond Miami?* ◇ *Most people don't work beyond the age of 65.* **3** out of the range or reach of sth (so that sth is not possible): *The house was beyond what I could afford.* ◇ *The car was completely beyond repair.* ◇ *His success was beyond all our expectations* (= more than we expected). ◇ *The fact that she is guilty is beyond doubt* (= there is no doubt about it). **4** except for or apart from: *I haven't heard anything beyond a few rumors.*

IDM **be beyond sb** (*informal*) to be impossible for sb to understand or imagine: *Why she wants to go and live there is beyond me.*

**be·yond²** /bɪ'yɑnd/ ***adv.*** on the other side or farther along: *We could see the mountains and the ocean beyond.*

**bi·as¹** /'baɪəs/ ***noun*** [C,U, usually sing.] (*pl.* **bi·as·es**) **1** [C] an opinion, feeling or attitude that is not fair and not based on facts: *a bias against recent immigrants* **2** [C,U] giving one side in an argument an advantage over the other; not being neutral: *The organization has been accused of political bias.*

**bi·as²** /'baɪəs/ ***verb*** [T] to influence sb/sth, especially unfairly; to give an advantage to one group, etc.: *The jury members must not let these news reports bias them against the defendant.*

**bi·ased** /'baɪəst/ ***adj.*** giving advantage to one group, etc.: *Good newspapers should not be biased toward a particular point of view.* ◇ *Is our legal system biased in favor of the rich and powerful?* ◇ *a biased* (= unfair) *report*

**bib** /bɪb/ ***noun*** [C] a piece of cloth or plastic that a baby or small child wears under the chin to protect its clothes while it is eating

**bi·ble** /'baɪbl/ ***noun*** [C] **1 the Bible** the holy book of the Christian people, made up of the Old and New Testaments **2 the Bible** the holy book of the Jewish people **3** a very useful and important book about a particular topic: *This is the amateur chef's bible.* ▸ **bib·li·cal** (*also* **Biblical**) /'bɪblɪkl/ ***adj.***

**bib·li·og·ra·phy** /ˌbɪbli'ɑgrəfi/ ***noun*** [C] (*pl.* **bib·li·og·ra·phies**) **1** a list of the books and articles that a writer used when he/she was writing a particular book **2** a list of books on a particular subject

ˌ**bib 'overalls** ***noun*** [pl.] = OVERALLS

**bi·car·bon·ate** /baɪ'kɑrbənət/ ***noun*** [U] a salt containing a double amount of a gas (**carbon dioxide**)

**biˌcarbonate of 'soda** (*also* **'baking ˌsoda**) ***noun*** [U] (*technical*) (*symbol* $NaHCO_3$) a chemical compound in the form of a white powder that dissolves and is used in baking to make cakes, etc. rise and become light, and in making soft drinks and some medicines

**bi·cen·ten·ni·al** /ˌbaɪsɛn'tɛniəl/ ***noun*** [C] the day or year two hundred years after sth happened or began: *The bicentennial of the American Revolution was celebrated on July 4, 1976.*

**bi·ceps** /'baɪsɛps/ ***noun*** [C] (*pl.* **bi·ceps**) the large muscle at the front of the top part of your arms

**bick·er** /'bɪkər/ ***verb*** [I] to argue about unimportant things: *The boys were bickering about whose turn it was to use the computer.*

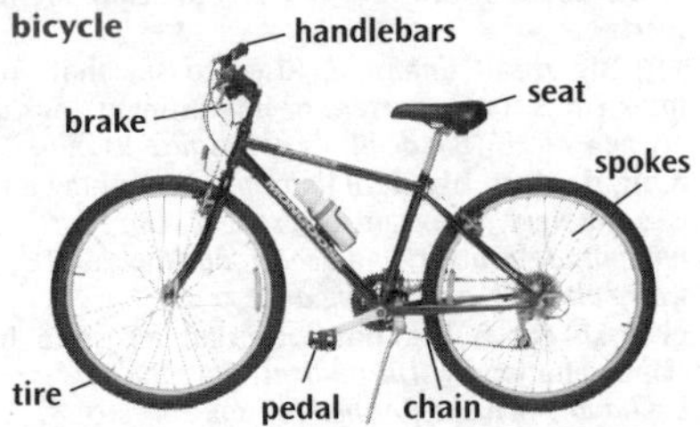


★**bi·cy·cle** /'baɪsɪkl/ (*also informal* **bike**) ***noun*** [C] a vehicle with two wheels that you sit on and ride by moving your legs: *to ride a bicycle* ◇ *to go somewhere on your bicycle*

★**bid¹** /bɪd/ ***verb*** (**bid·ding**; *pt, pp* **bid**) **1** [I,T] **bid (sth) (for/on sth)** to offer a sum of money in order to buy sth: *to bid for/on sth at an auction* ◇ *Somebody* ***bid*** *$5,000* ***for*** *the painting.* **2** [I] to offer to do work or provide a service for sb for a particular price: *A Canadian company will be* ***bidding for*** *the contract.* **3** [T] **bid to do sth** (used especially in newspapers) to try to do, get or achieve sth: *The*

B

*new president promises reform as he bids to win broader support.*

**bid²** /bɪd/ ***noun*** [C] **1** an offer to pay a sum of money in order to buy sth: *We made a bid of $500 for the painting at the auction.* ◇ *a higher/lower bid* **2** a formal offer to supply goods or do work at a certain price: *to submit a bid for a project* **3** an attempt to do, obtain, etc. sth: *her bid to win the championship* ◇ *His bid for power had failed.*

**bid³** /bɪd/ ***verb*** [T] (**bid·ding**; *pt* **bid** or **bade** /beɪd; bæd/; *pp* **bid** or **bid·den** /ˈbɪdn/) (*formal*) **bid (sb) good morning, farewell, etc.** to say "good morning," etc. to sb: *It has been a pleasure to visit your great city, but now I must bid you a fond farewell.*

**bid·der** /ˈbɪdər/ ***noun*** [C] a person who offers a sum of money in order to buy sth: *The house was sold to the highest bidder* (= the person who offered the most money).

★**big¹** /bɪg/ ***adj.*** (**big·ger**; **big·gest**)

➤ LARGE **1** large; not small: *a big house/town/salary* ◇ *This dress is too big for me.* ◇ *a big eater/spender* (= sb who eats/spends a lot)

➤ IMPORTANT **2** great or important: *They had a big argument yesterday.* ◇ *That was the biggest decision I've ever had to make.* ◇ *some of the big names in Hollywood*

> NOTE **Big** and **large** can both be used when talking about size or number. **Large** is more formal and is not usually used for describing people: *a big/large house* ◇ *a big boy.* **Great** is mostly used when talking about the importance, quality, etc. of a person or thing. It can also be used with uncountable nouns to mean "a lot of": *a great occasion* ◇ *a great musician* ◇ *great happiness/care*

➤ OLDER **3** (only *before* a noun) (*informal*) older: *my big sister*

➤ POPULAR **4** (*informal*) popular with the public: *Video games are big again this year.*

➤ ENTHUSIASTIC **5 big on sb/sth** (*informal*) enthusiastic about sb/sth: *I've never been really big on sports.*

IDM **Big deal!** (*informal*) (used to say that you think sth is not important or interesting): *"Look at my new bike!" "Big deal! It's not as nice as mine."*

**a big deal/no big deal** (*informal*) something that is/is not very important or exciting: *The Fourth of July parade is a very big deal in our town.* ◇ *Don't worry about it – it's no big deal.*

**give sb/get a big hand** to clap for sb/to be clapped for loudly: *The audience gave the little girl a big hand when she finished her song.*

**big²** /bɪg/ ***adv.*** (*informal*) in a grand or ambitious way: *You have to think big if you want to be successful in this job.*

**big·a·my** /ˈbɪgəmi/ ***noun*** [U] the crime of being married to two people at the same time

**the ˌBig ˈApple** ***noun*** [sing.] (*informal*) New York City: *I've lived in the Big Apple for 20 years.* ➲ Look at the note at **White House**.

**ˌbig ˈcheese** ***noun*** [C] (*informal*) an important or powerful person: *If you want to take the afternoon off, you'll have to ask the big cheese* (= the boss).

**the ˌBig ˈDipper** ***noun*** [sing.] a group of seven bright stars that can only be seen from the northern half of the world

**the ˈbig league** ***noun*** [C] **1** the most important division(s) of a sport, especially baseball, with the best professional teams **2** [usually pl.] the highest level of an activity, a business, etc. that you reach when you are very successful: *The company has already joined the big leagues with its popular computer games.* ▶ **ˈbig-league** ***adj.***: *a big-league baseball player* ◇ *big-league politics*

**big·ot** /ˈbɪgət/ ***noun*** [C] a person who has very strong and unreasonable opinions and who refuses to change them or listen to other people ▶ **big·ot·ed** ***adj.***

**ˈbig shot** ***noun*** [C] (*informal*) a person who thinks he/she is more important or powerful than he/she really is: *He acts like a big shot, but nobody listens to him.*

**the ˈbig time** ***noun*** [sing.] the highest level of an activity, especially entertainment, that you reach when you are very successful: *This is the role that could help her make it to the big time in Hollywood.*

**ˈbig time** ***adv.*** (*slang*) very much: *You screwed up big time, Wayne!*

**ˈbig-time** ***adj.*** (only before a noun) important or famous: *big-time drug dealing* ◇ *big-time politicians*

**bike** /baɪk/ ***noun*** [C] (*informal*) a bicycle or a motorcycle: *Mary has just learned to ride a bike.* ◇ *Bike riders should stay off the sidewalk.* ◇ *Let's go for a bike ride.*

**bi·ki·ni** /bɪˈkini/ ***noun*** [C] a piece of clothing, in two pieces, that women wear for swimming

**bi·lin·gual** /ˌbaɪˈlɪŋgwəl/ ***adj.*** **1** able to speak two languages equally well: *Our kids are bilingual in English and Spanish.* **2** having or using two languages: *a bilingual dictionary*

★**bill¹** /bɪl/ ***noun***

➤ FOR PAYMENT **1** [C] a piece of paper that shows how much money you owe for goods or services: *to pay a bill* ◇ *a telephone bill*

> NOTE In restaurants in the U.S., the bill is called a **check**: *Could I have the check, please?* In Canada, you can ask for either the **check** or a **bill** in restaurants.

➤ MONEY **2** [C] a piece of paper money: *a ten-dollar bill* ➲ picture at **money**.

➤ LAW **3** [C] a plan for a possible new law: *The bill was discussed in Congress.* ◇ *The bill was passed/defeated.* ➲ For more information on the U.S. political system, look at study page **A10**.

➤ AT THEATER **4** [sing.] the program of entertainment offered in a show, concert, etc.: *Diana Ross headed the bill.* ◇ *There's a double bill* (= two different movies) *of horror movies at the theater tonight.*

➤ OF BIRDS **5** [C] the hard pointed or curved part of a bird's mouth SYN **beak**

➤ ON HAT **6** [C] the pointed front part of a hat that is above your eyes: *He wears his baseball cap with the bill facing backward.*

IDM **foot the bill** → FOOT²

**bill²** /bɪl/ ***verb*** [T] **1 bill sb (for sth)** to send sb a BILL¹ (1) for sth: *I've been billed for several items that I didn't order.* **2** to announce to the public with an

B

advertisement, etc.: *The show is billed as a musical comedy.*

**bill·board** /ˈbɪlbɔrd/ ***noun*** [C] a large board near a street or road where advertisements are put

**bill·fold** /ˈbɪlfoʊld/ ***noun*** [C] = WALLET

**bil·liards** /ˈbɪlyərdz/ ***noun*** [pl.] a game played on a big table covered with cloth. You use a long stick (a cue) to hit balls against each other and into holes at the corners and sides of the table: *to have a game of/ play billiards* ➲ Look at pool[1](4).

**bil·lion** /ˈbɪlyən/ ***number*** 1,000,000,000: *billions of dollars*

NOTE Notice that when you are counting, you use billion without "s": *nine billion dollars.*

**bil·lion·aire** /ˌbɪlyəˈnɛr/ ***noun*** [C] a person who has a billion dollars; an extremely rich person

**the ˌBill of ˈRights** ***noun*** [sing.] the first ten additions (amendments) to the basic law of the United States (the Constitution), which guarantee certain basic rights to citizens, such as freedom of speech and freedom of religion ➲ For more information on the U.S. political system, look at study page **A10**.

**bil·low** /ˈbɪloʊ/ ***verb*** [I] to rise or move slowly in the wind, like waves: *curtains billowing in the breeze*

**bil·ly club** /ˈbɪli klʌb/ ***noun*** [C] a short wooden stick used as a weapon by police officers

**bin** /bɪn/ ***noun*** [C] a large container that is used for storing or holding things: *Put those empty cans in the recycling bin.*

**bind[1]** /baɪnd/ ***verb*** [T] (*pt, pp* **bound** /baʊnd/) **1 bind A (to B); bind A and B (together)** to tie or fasten with string or rope: *They bound the prisoner's hands behind his back.* ◇ (*figurative*) *The two men were bound together by the strength of their beliefs.* **2 bind sb (to sth)** to cause or force sb to do sth: *to be bound by a law/an agreement* ◇ *The contract binds you to completion of the work within two years.* **3** (usually passive) to fasten sheets of paper into a cover to form a book: *The book was bound in leather.*

**bind[2]** /baɪnd/ ***noun*** [sing.]
IDM **in a bind** (*informal*) in a difficult situation that you do not know how to get out of: *I was in a real bind when I couldn't find my house key.*

**bind·er** /ˈbaɪndər/ ***noun*** [C] a hard cover for holding loose sheets of paper together

**bind·ing[1]** /ˈbaɪndɪŋ/ ***noun*** **1** [C] the part of a cover that holds the pages of a book together **2** a device on a ski that holds the heel and toe of your boot in place and releases the boot automatically if you fall ➲ picture at **snowboard**.

**bind·ing[2]** /ˈbaɪndɪŋ/ ***adj.*** making it necessary for sb to do sth he/she has promised or to obey a law, etc.: *This contract is **legally binding**.*

**binge[1]** /bɪndʒ/ ***noun*** [C] (*informal*) a period of eating or drinking too much: *to go on a drinking binge*

**binge[2]** /bɪndʒ/ ***verb*** [I] (**binge·ing** or **bing·ing**; **binged**) **binge (on sth)** to eat or drink too much, especially without being able to control yourself: *to binge on junk food*

**bin·go** /ˈbɪŋgoʊ/ ***noun*** [U] a game in which each player has a different card with twenty-five numbers on it. The person in charge of the game calls numbers out, and the winner is the first player to have five of his/her numbers in a row called out.

**binoculars**

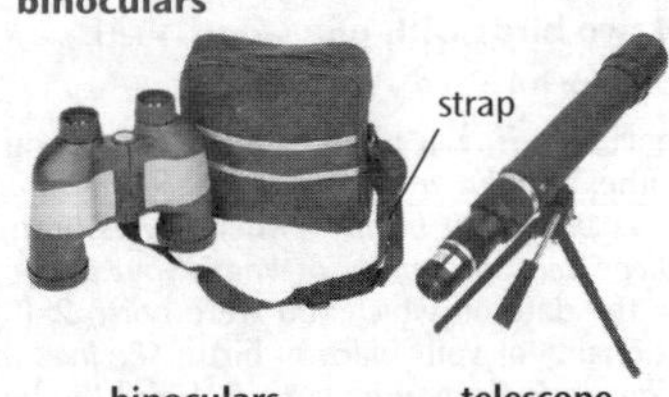


**bin·oc·u·lars** /bɪˈnɑkyələrz/ ***noun*** [pl.] an instrument with two tubes which you look through in order to make objects that are far away seem nearer: *a pair of binoculars* ➲ Look at **telescope**.

**bi·o·chem·is·try** /ˌbaɪoʊˈkɛməstri/ ***noun*** [U] the study of the chemistry of living things

**bi·o·de·grad·a·ble** /ˌbaɪoʊdɪˈgreɪdəbl/ ***adj.*** that can decay naturally: *biodegradable packaging*

**bi·og·ra·pher** /baɪˈɑgrəfər/ ***noun*** [C] a person who writes a story of sb else's life

**bi·o·graph·i·cal** /ˌbaɪəˈgræfɪkl/ ***adj.*** containing information about sb's life

**bi·og·ra·phy** /baɪˈɑgrəfi/ ***noun*** [C,U] (*pl.* **bi·og·ra·phies**) the story of a person's life written by sb else: *a biography of Lincoln* ➲ Look at **autobiography**.

**bi·o·log·i·cal** /ˌbaɪəˈlɑdʒɪkl/ ***adj.*** **1** connected with the scientific study of animals, plants and other living things: *biological research* **2** involving the use of living things to destroy or damage other living things: *biological weapons*

**bioˌlogical ˈclock** ***noun*** [C] (*technical*) a mechanism in plants and animals that controls regular physical activities such as sleeping: (*figurative*) *At 35, Kate's biological clock was ticking* (= she was beginning to think that she would soon be too old to have children).

**bi·ol·o·gist** /baɪˈɑlədʒɪst/ ***noun*** [C] a person who is an expert in biology

**bi·ol·o·gy** /baɪˈɑlədʒi/ ***noun*** [U] the scientific study of living things

**birch** /bərtʃ/ ***noun*** [C,U] a type of tree with a smooth trunk and thin branches

**bird**

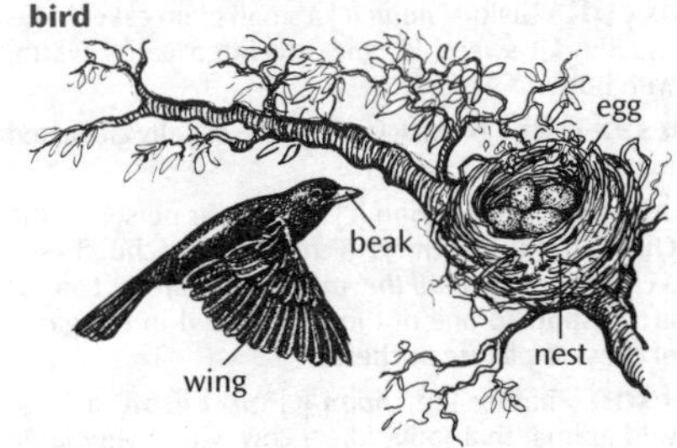

B

★**bird** /bərd/ ***noun*** [C] a creature with feathers and wings that can (usually) fly

NOTE Birds **fly** and **sing**. They build **nests** and **lay** eggs. ➲ picture on **page 63**.

IDM **kill two birds with one stone** → KILL[1]

**bird flu** ***noun*** [U] = AVIAN INFLUENZA

★**birth** /bərθ/ ***noun*** **1** [C,U] being born; coming out of a mother's body: *a difficult birth* ◇ *The baby weighed six pounds at birth* (= when it was born). ◇ *She's been deaf since birth.* ◇ *What's your date of birth?* (= the date on which you were born) **2** [U] your nationality or your place of birth: *She lives in the U.S. but she's German by birth.* **3** [sing.] the beginning of sth: *the birth of an idea*

IDM **give birth (to sb/sth)** to produce a baby: *She gave birth to her second child at home.*

'**birth certificate** ***noun*** [C] an official piece of paper that states the date and place of a person's birth

'**birth control** ***noun*** [U] ways of controlling or limiting the number of children you have ➲ Look at **contraception**.

'**birth date** ***noun*** [C] the date on which sb was born

★**birth·day** /ˈbərθdeɪ/ ***noun*** [C] the day in each year that is the same date as the one when you were born: *My birthday's (on) November 15.* ◇ *my eighteenth birthday* ◇ *a birthday present* ◇ *a birthday card*

NOTE An **anniversary** is not the same as a **birthday**. An anniversary is the day in each year that is the same date as an important past event: *our wedding anniversary* ◇ *the fiftieth anniversary of the sinking of the Titanic* (= exactly fifty years after it happened). When it is a person's birthday we say **Happy Birthday**! If we know the person well, we send a special card to him/her or give him/her a present. Your eighteenth birthday is an important occasion when you legally become an adult.

**birth·mark** /ˈbərθmɑrk/ ***noun*** [C] a permanent mark on your body, that you are born with

**birth·place** /ˈbərθpleɪs/ ***noun*** **1** [C] the house or area where a person was born **2** [sing.] the place where sth began: *in Greece, the birthplace of the Olympic Games*

**birth·rate** /ˈbərθreɪt/ ***noun*** [C] the number of babies born in a particular group of people during a particular period of time: *The birthrate is falling/rising.*

**bis·cuit** /ˈbɪskət/ ***noun*** [C] a small plain cake that is usually not sweet. Biscuits are often eaten warm, with butter.

**bi·sex·u·al** /ˌbaɪˈsɛkʃuəl/ ***adj.*** sexually attracted to both men and women

**bish·op** /ˈbɪʃəp/ ***noun*** [C] **1** a senior person in the Christian church, who is in charge of the churches in a city or a district: *all the Anglican bishops* ➲ Look at **archbishop**. **2** one of the pieces used in the game of chess ➲ picture at **chess**.

**bi·son** /ˈbaɪsn; -zn/ ***noun*** [C] (*pl.* **bi·son**) a large wild animal that looks like a cow with a very large head, curved horns and thick fur on its head and neck: *a herd of bison* SYN This type of animal is often called a **buffalo**.

★**bit**[1] /bɪt/ ***noun*** [C] **1** a small piece or amount of sth: *There were bits of broken glass all over the floor.* ◇ *I think these strawberries need a little bit more sugar.* ◇ *Could you give me a bit of advice?* **2** (*technical*) the smallest unit of information that is stored in a computer's memory, represented by the numbers 0 or 1

IDM **a bit 1** slightly: *I'll be a bit late tonight.* **2** a short time or distance: *Could you move forward a bit?* ➲ It is more common to say **a little** or **a little bit**.

**bit by bit** slowly or a little at a time

**a bit of a** (used to say that sth is really larger, worse, etc. than you want to say it is): *I have a little bit of a problem...* ◇ *It was a bit of a surprise to see him standing in the doorway!*

**quite a bit** → QUITE

**to bits** into small pieces: *Two cars were blown to bits by the explosion.*

**bit**[2] *past tense of* BITE[1]

**bitch**[1] /bɪtʃ/ ***noun*** [C] **1** (*slang*) a very unpleasant woman: *She's a real bitch.* ◇ *You bitch!* (= used to insult a woman) **2** (*slang*) a thing that causes problems or difficulties: *Parking downtown's a real bitch.* **3** (*formal*) a female dog

**bitch**[2] /bɪtʃ/ ***verb*** [I] (*slang*) **bitch (about sth)** to complain in a very critical way: *You're always bitching about the other people at work.*

**bitch·y** /ˈbɪtʃi/ ***adj.*** (**bitch·i·er**; **bitch·i·est**) saying unpleasant and unkind things about other people: *a bitchy remark*

★**bite**[1] /baɪt/ ***verb*** (*pt* **bit** /bɪt/; *pp* **bit·ten** /ˈbɪtn/) **1** [I,T] **bite (sb/sth)**; **bite into sth** to cut or attack with the teeth: *Does your dog bite?* ◇ *The dog bit me.* ◇ *He bit into the burger hungrily.* ➲ picture at **lick**. **2** [T] (used about insects or snakes) to make a small hole in your skin and cause pain: *He was bitten by a snake.*

NOTE Wasps and bees do not **bite** you. They **sting** you.

IDM **bite sb's head off** to answer sb in a very angry way, often for no good reason: *I was just asking, you don't have to bite my head off!*

**bite the bullet** to start to deal with an unpleasant or difficult situation which cannot be avoided

**bite**[2] /baɪt/ ***noun*** **1** [C] a piece of food that you can put into your mouth: *to take a big bite of an apple* **2** [C] a painful place on the skin made by an insect, snake, dog, etc.: *a mosquito bite* **3** [sing.] (*informal*) some food: *Would you like a bite to eat before you go?*

**bit·ing** /ˈbaɪṭɪŋ/ ***adj.*** (used about sth you say) unkind and critical: *a biting comment*

**bit·ten** *past participle of* BITE[1]

★**bit·ter** /ˈbɪṭər/ ***adj.*** **1** (used about a person) very unhappy or angry about sth that has happened; disappointed: *She was very bitter about the divorce.* **2** causing unhappiness or anger for a long time; difficult to accept: *His son has been a bitter disappointment to him.* **3** caused by anger or hatred: *a bitter argument* **4** (used about cold weather) extreme: *Because of the bitter cold, we stayed indoors.*

**5** having a sharp, unpleasant taste; not sweet: *bitter coffee*

**bit·ter·ly** /ˈbɪt̬ərli/ ***adv.*** **1** (used for describing strong negative feelings or cold weather) extremely: *bitterly disappointed* ◇ *a bitterly cold winter* **2** in a BITTER (1) way: *"I've lost everything," he said bitterly.*

**bit·ter·ness** /ˈbɪt̬ərnəs/ ***noun*** [U] anger and unhappiness as a result of sth bad happening

**bi·zarre** /bɪˈzɑr/ ***adj.*** very strange: *The story had a bizarre ending.*

★**black¹** /blæk/ ***adj.***

➤COLOR **1** of the darkest color possible, the color of the night sky

➤PEOPLE **2** (often **Black**) belonging to a race of people with dark skin, originally from Africa: *the Black population of America* ◇ *Black culture* ➲ Look at **African-American**.

➤TEA/COFFEE **3** (used about coffee) without milk or cream: *black coffee with sugar*

➤DEPRESSING **4** (used about a situation) without hope; depressing: *The economic outlook is pretty black.*

➤HUMOR **5** funny in a cruel or unkind way: *The movie is a black comedy.*

➤ANGRY **6** very angry: *a black mood* ◇ *to give sb a black look*

IDM **black and blue** covered with dark marks on the skin that were caused by hitting: *Her whole face was black and blue.*

**black and white** (used about television, photographs, etc.) showing no colors except black, white and gray

▶ **black·ness** ***noun*** [U]

★**black²** /blæk/ ***noun*** **1** [U] the darkest color, like the night sky: *People usually wear black* (= black clothes) *at funerals.* **2** (usually **Black**) [C] a person who belongs to a race of people with dark skin, originally from Africa: *South African Blacks*

NOTE This is sometimes considered offensive when used as a noun. ➲ Look at the note at **African-American**.

IDM **(be) in the black** having some money in the bank ➲ Look at **in the red** at **red²**.

**in black and white** in writing or in print: *I won't believe the news until I see it in black and white.*

**black³** /blæk/ ***verb***

PHR V **black out** to lose consciousness for a short time: *I remember losing control of the car and then I blacked out.*

**black·ber·ry** /ˈblækˌbɛri/ ***noun*** [C] (*pl.* **black·ber·ries**) a small black or dark purple fruit that grows on bushes ➲ picture on study page **A28-29**.

**black·bird** /ˈblækbərd/ ***noun*** [C] a common bird. The male is black and the female is usually brown.

**black·board** /ˈblækbɔrd/ (*also* **board**, **chalkboard**) ***noun*** [C] a piece of dark board that you write or draw on with chalk, especially in a classroom

**ˌblack ˈbox** (*also* **ˈflight reˌcorder**) ***noun*** [C] a small machine in a plane that records all the details of each flight and is useful for finding out the cause of an accident

**black·en** /ˈblækən/ ***verb*** [T] **1** to make sth black: *wood blackened by fire* **2** to make sth seem bad, by saying unkind things about it: *to blacken sb's name*

**ˌblack ˈeye** ***noun*** [C] an area of dark-colored skin that can form around sb's eye if he/she is hit in the face by sb/sth: *He got a black eye in the fight.*

**black·head** /ˈblækhɛd/ ***noun*** [C] a small spot on the skin with a black center

**black·jack** /ˈblækdʒæk/ ***noun*** [U] a card game that is usually played for money, in which players try to get cards with a total value of 21

**black·list** /ˈblæklɪst/ ***noun*** [C] a list of people who are considered bad or dangerous: *to be on sb's blacklist* ▶ **black·list** ***verb*** [T]

**ˌblack ˈmagic** ***noun*** [U] a type of magic that is used for evil purposes

**black·mail** /ˈblækmeɪl/ ***noun*** [U] the crime of forcing a person to give you money or do sth for you, usually by threatening to make known sth that he/she wants to keep secret ▶ **black·mail** ***verb*** [T]: *He was blackmailed into paying an enormous amount of money.* ▶ **black·mail·er** ***noun*** [C]

**ˌblack ˈmarket** ***noun*** [C] the buying and selling of goods or foreign money in a way that is not legal: *to buy/sell sth on the black market*

**black·out** /ˈblækaʊt/ ***noun*** [C] **1** a time when the electricity supply to an area is cut off SYN **power outage** **2** a period when you lose consciousness for a short time: *to have a blackout*

**black·smith** /ˈblæksmɪθ/ ***noun*** [C] (*old-fashioned*) a person whose job is to make and repair things made of metal, especially horses' shoes

**ˌblack ˈwidow** ***noun*** [C] a very poisonous spider which is black with red or orange marks

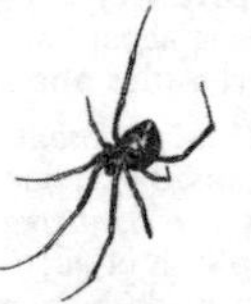
**black widow**

**blad·der** /ˈblædər/ ***noun*** [C] the part of the body where waste liquid (urine) collects before leaving the body

★**blade** /bleɪd/ ***noun*** [C] **1** the flat, sharp part of a knife, a pair of scissors, etc. ➲ picture at **pocket knife**. **2** one of the flat, wide parts that spin around on an airplane, etc.: *a propeller blade* **3** a long, thin leaf of grass: *a blade of grass*

★**blame¹** /bleɪm/ ***verb*** [T] **1** **blame sb (for sth)**; **blame sth on sb** to think or say that a certain person or thing is responsible for sth bad that has happened: *The teacher blamed me for the accident.* ◇ *Some people blame the changes in the climate on pollution.* **2** **not blame sb (for sth)** to think that sb is not wrong to do sth: *"I'd like to quit this job and start my own company." "I don't blame you."* (= I can understand why) ◇ *I don't blame you for feeling angry.*

IDM **be to blame (for sth)** to be responsible for sth bad: *The police say that careless driving was to blame for the accident.*

★**blame²** /bleɪm/ ***noun*** [U] **blame (for sth)** responsibility for sth bad: *to take the blame for sth* ◇ *The report puts the blame on inflation.*

**bland** /blænd/ ***adj.*** **1** (used about food) mild or lacking in taste **2** ordinary or uninteresting: *a fairly bland style of writing* **3** showing no strong feelings or interest: *a bland smile* ▶ **bland·ly** ***adv.***

B

**blank¹** /blæŋk/ ***adj.*** **1** without writing or anything else on it: *a blank cassette* ◇ *a blank piece of paper* ◇ *a blank diskette* **2** without feelings, understanding or interest: *a blank expression on his face* ◇ *My mind went blank when I saw the test questions* (= I couldn't think or remember anything).

**blank²** /blæŋk/ ***noun*** [C] an empty space: *Fill in the blanks in the following exercise.* ◇ (*figurative*) *I couldn't remember his name – my mind was a complete blank.*
IDM **draw a blank** → DRAW²

**ˌblank ˈcheck** ***noun*** [C] a check that has been signed but that has an empty space so that the amount to be paid can be filled in later

**blan·ket¹** /ˈblæŋkət/ ***noun*** [C] a cover made of wool, etc. that is put on beds to keep people warm: (*figurative*) *A fresh blanket of snow covered the fields.* ➲ picture at **bed¹**.
IDM **a wet blanket** → WET¹

**blan·ket²** /ˈblæŋkət/ ***adj.*** (only *before* a noun) affecting everybody or everything: *a **blanket ban** on journalists reporting the case*

**blan·ket³** /ˈblæŋkət/ ***verb*** [T] to cover sth completely: *The countryside was blanketed in snow.*

**blank·ly** /ˈblæŋkli/ ***adv.*** with a BLANK¹ (2) expression

**blare** /blɛr/ ***verb*** [I,T] **blare (sth) (out)** to make a loud, unpleasant noise: *The radio was blaring in the room next to ours.* ◇ *The loudspeaker blared out a warning.* ▸ **blare *noun*** [sing.]: *the blare of a siren*

**blas·phe·my** /ˈblæsfəmi/ ***noun*** [U] writing or speaking about God in a way that shows a lack of respect ▸ **blas·phe·mous** /ˈblæsfəməs/ ***adj.***

**blast¹** /blæst/ ***noun*** **1** [C] an explosion, especially one caused by a bomb: *The windows of the nearby stores were shattered in the blast.* **2** [C] a sudden strong rush of air: *a blast of cold air* **3** [C] a loud sound made by a musical instrument such as a horn: *a few blasts on his trumpet* **4** [sing.] (*informal*) a time when you enjoy yourself very much: *Why don't you come along to the party? It'll be a blast!*

**blast²** /blæst/ ***verb*** [T] **1** to make a hole, a tunnel, etc. in sth with an explosion: *They had to blast their way through the mountainside.* **2** to criticize or attack sb very strongly: *The governor blasted journalists for publishing secret information.*
PHR V **blast off** (used about a spacecraft) to leave the ground; to take off

**ˈblast ˌfurnace** ***noun*** [C] a large enclosed fire that is used for melting metal, glass, etc.

**blast·off** /ˈblæstɔf/ ***noun*** [U] the time when a spacecraft leaves the ground

**bla·tant** /ˈbleɪtnt/ ***adj.*** (used about actions that are considered bad) very clear or obvious: *a blatant attempt to buy votes* ◇ *a blatant lie* ▸ **bla·tant·ly *adv.***

**blaze¹** /bleɪz/ ***noun*** **1** [C] a large and often dangerous fire: *It took firefighters four hours to put out the blaze.* **2** [sing.] **a blaze of sth** a very bright display of light or color: *She suddenly appeared on stage in a blaze of light.* ◇ (*figurative*) *The new theater opened in **a blaze of publicity*** (= the newspapers/television gave it a lot of attention).

**blaze²** /bleɪz/ ***verb*** [I] to burn with bright strong flames: *a blazing log fire*

**blaz·er** /ˈbleɪzər/ ***noun*** [C] a jacket, especially one that you wear indoors over a shirt, etc.: *Members of the school band wear special blazers with the school's emblem on them.*

**bleach¹** /blitʃ/ ***verb*** [T] to make sth white or lighter in color (by using a chemical or by leaving it in the sun)

**bleach²** /blitʃ/ ***noun*** [C,U] a strong chemical substance used for making clothes, etc. whiter or for cleaning things

**bleach·ers** /ˈblitʃərz/ ***noun*** [pl.] an area with wide seats (**benches**), usually without backs, where people sit to watch a sports game, etc.: *We sat in the bleachers.*

**bleak** /blik/ ***adj.*** **1** (used about a situation) bad; not encouraging or hopeful: *a bleak future for the next generation* **2** (used about a place) cold, bare and gray: *the bleak prairies in the winter* **3** (used about the weather) cold and gray: *a bleak winter day* ▸ **bleak·ly *adv.***

★**bleed** /blid/ ***verb*** [I] (*pt, pp* **bled** /blɛd/) to lose blood: *He was bleeding badly from a cut on his head.* ◇ *Is your finger bleeding?*

**bleed·ing** /ˈblidɪŋ/ ***noun*** [U] blood flowing from a cut, etc.: *She wrapped a scarf around her arm to try to stop the bleeding.*

**blem·ish¹** /ˈblɛmɪʃ/ ***noun*** [C] a mark that spoils the way sth looks: *makeup to hide pimples and other blemishes*

**blem·ish²** /ˈblɛmɪʃ/ ***verb*** [T] (*formal*) to spoil sth

**blend¹** /blɛnd/ ***verb*** **1** [T] **blend A with B; blend A and B (together)** to mix: *Blend the red and the blue paint together to make purple.* **2** [I] **blend (into sth)** to be difficult to tell apart from sth else: *These animals' ability to blend into their surroundings provides a natural form of defense.*
PHR V **blend in (with sth)** to look or sound good with sth else because the two things are similar: *new buildings that don't blend in with their surroundings*

**blend²** /blɛnd/ ***noun*** [C] a mixture: *a blend of wool and cotton* ◇ *He had the right blend of enthusiasm and experience.*

**blend·er** /ˈblɛndər/ ***noun*** [C] an electric machine that is used for blending foods, especially liquids, or for cutting food into very small pieces ➲ Look at **food processor** and **mixer**. ➲ picture at **mixer**.

**bless** /blɛs/ ***verb*** [T] (*pt, pp* **blessed** /blɛst/) to ask for God's help and protection for sb/sth: *At the end of the marriage service, the minister will bless the young couple.*
IDM **be blessed with sth/sb** to be lucky enough to have sth/sb: *We've been blessed with three wonderful children.*
**bless you!** (what you say to a person who has just sneezed)

**bless·ed** /ˈblɛsəd/ ***adj.*** **1** (in religious language) holy: *the Blessed Virgin Mary* **2** (in religious language) lucky; fortunate: *Blessed are the pure in heart.* **3** giving great pleasure: *The cool breeze brought blessed relief from the heat.*

**bless·ing** /ˈblɛsɪŋ/ ***noun*** [C] **1** a thing that you are grateful for or that brings happiness: *It's a great blessing that we have two healthy children.* ◇ *a blessing in disguise* (= something which seems unlucky but turns out to be a good thing) ◇ *to count your blessings* **2** [usually sing.] approval or support: *They got married without their parents' blessing.* **3** [usually sing.] (a prayer asking for) God's help and protection: *to ask for God's blessing* ◇ *The priest gave a blessing.*

**blew** *past tense of* BLOW[1]

★**blind[1]** /blaɪnd/ ***adj.*** **1** unable to see: *a blind person* ◇ *to be completely/partially blind*

NOTE We often describe a person as **visually impaired** rather than **blind**. If a person is not completely blind, but cannot see well even if he/she wears glasses, we can say that he/she is **legally blind**.

**2 blind (to sth)** not willing to notice or understand sth: *He was completely blind to her faults.* **3** without reason or thought: *her blind acceptance of fate* ◇ *He drove down the freeway in a blind panic.* **4** impossible to see around or impossible to see from a certain position: *The accident happened at a blind intersection.* **5 the blind** ***noun*** [pl.] people who cannot see: *ways of making buildings accessible to the blind*

IDM **turn a blind eye (to sth)** to pretend not to notice sth

▸ **blind·ly** ***adv.*** ▸ **blind·ness** ***noun*** [U]

**blind[2]** /blaɪnd/ ***verb*** [T] **1** to make sb unable to see: *Her grandfather had been blinded in an accident* (= permanently). ◇ *For a minute I was blinded by the lights of the oncoming car* (= for a short time). **2 blind sb (to sth)** to prevent sb from being aware of sth

**blind[3]** /blaɪnd/ ***noun*** [C, usually pl.] a covering for a window which is made of many long, narrow strips of metal, plastic, or other material: *to open/close the blinds* ◇ *vertical blinds* ➲ Look also at **Venetian blind**.

**ˌblind ˈdate** ***noun*** [C] an arranged meeting between two people who have never met before to see if they like each other enough to begin a romantic relationship

**blind·fold[1]** /ˈblaɪndfoʊld/ ***verb*** [T] to cover a person's eyes with a piece of cloth, etc. so that he/she cannot see

**blind·fold[2]** /ˈblaɪndfoʊld/ ***noun*** [C] a piece of cloth, etc. that is used for covering sb's eyes

**ˈblind spot** ***noun*** [C] **1** if you have a blind spot about sth, you cannot understand or accept it **2** the part of the road that you cannot see when driving a car, i.e. the part which is just behind you

**blink** /blɪŋk/ ***verb*** **1** [I,T] to shut your eyes and open them again very quickly: *Oh no! You blinked just as I took the picture!* ➲ Look at **wink**. **2** [I] (used about a light) to come on and go off again quickly ▸ **blink** ***noun*** [C]

**blip** /blɪp/ ***noun*** [C] **1** a small point of light on a screen: *a radar blip* **2** a small problem that does not last for long: *We hope that this price increase is just a temporary blip.*

**bliss** /blɪs/ ***noun*** [U] perfect happiness: *fifteen years of domestic bliss with his wife, Mary* ▸ **bliss·ful** /-fl/ ***adj.*** ▸ **bliss·ful·ly** ***adv.***

**blis·ter[1]** /ˈblɪstər/ ***noun*** [C] a small painful area of skin that looks like a bubble and contains clear liquid. Blisters are usually caused by rubbing or burning: *These shoes give me blisters.*

**blis·ter[2]** /ˈblɪstər/ ***verb*** [I,T] to get or cause BLISTERS[1]

**blis·ter·ing** /ˈblɪstərɪŋ/ ***adj.*** **1** very great or severe: *the blistering summer heat* **2** showing great anger: *a blistering attack on her political enemies*

**blitz** /blɪts/ ***noun*** [C] a sudden great effort or attack, especially a military attack from the air: *The company launched a $30 million TV advertising blitz.*

**bliz·zard** /ˈblɪzərd/ ***noun*** [C] a very bad storm with a lot of snow and strong winds ➲ Look at the note at **storm**.

**bloat·ed** /ˈbloʊt̬əd/ ***adj.*** unusually large and full because of liquid, food or gas inside: *I felt really bloated after all that food.*

**blob** /blɑb/ ***noun*** [C] a small piece of a thick liquid: *a blob of paint/cream/ink*

**bloc** /blɑk/ ***noun*** [C, with sing. or pl. verb] a group of countries, political parties, people, etc. who have similar political ideas and who act together: *former Communist bloc countries* ◇ *the importance of the Hispanic voting bloc*

★**block[1]** /blɑk/ ***noun*** [C] **1** a large, heavy piece of sth, usually with flat sides: *a block of wood* ◇ *huge concrete blocks* **2** an area of land in a town which has streets on four sides: *I went for a walk around the block.* ◇ *My best friend lives three blocks away from us.* ➲ Look at the note at **avenue**. **3** [usually sing.] a thing that makes movement or progress difficult or impossible: *a block to further progress in the talks*

IDM **to have a block (about sth)** to be unable to think or understand sth well: *I had a complete mental block. I just couldn't remember his name.*

★**block[2]** /blɑk/ ***verb*** [T] **1 block sth (up)** to make it difficult or impossible for anything or anybody to go through, to see, etc.: *Many roads are completely blocked by snow.* ◇ *The sink's blocked up – call a plumber!* **2** to prevent sth from being done: *The management tried to block the deal.* ◇ *Get out of the way – you're blocking the view!*

PHR V **block sth off** to separate one area from another with sth solid: *This section of the highway has been blocked off by the police.*

**block sth out** to try not to think about sth unpleasant: *She tried to block out the memory of the crash.*

**block·ade** /blɑˈkeɪd/ ***noun*** [C] a situation in which a place is surrounded by soldiers or ships in order to prevent goods or people from reaching it ▸ **block·ade** ***verb*** [T]

**block·age** /ˈblɑkɪdʒ/ ***noun*** [C] a thing that is blocking sth; the state of being blocked: *a blockage in the drain* ◇ *blockages on some major roads*

**block·bust·er** /ˈblɑkˌbʌstər/ ***noun*** [C] a book or movie with an exciting story that is very successful and popular: *He's directed a string of Hollywood blockbusters.*

**ˌblock ˈletters** (*also* **ˌblock ˈcapitals**) ***noun*** [pl.] separate capital letters that are not joined with other letters: *Please write your name in block letters.*

**blog[1]** /blɑg/ ***noun*** [C] (*informal*) (*computing*) (*also* 'weblog) a personal record that sb puts on a page on the Internet (website) giving an account of his/her activities and opinions, and discussing places on the Internet he/she has visited

B

**blog²** /blɑg/ *verb* [I] (**blog'ging**; **blogged**) to keep a blog and regularly send it to other Internet users ▸ **blog·ger** *noun* [C]

**blond** (*also* **blonde**) /blɑnd/ *noun* [C], *adj.* (a person) with light-colored or yellow hair: *Most people in our family have blond hair.*

NOTE When the adjective is used to describe a woman, the spelling **blonde** is used: *She's tall, slim and blonde.* The noun is usually only used for women and is spelled **blonde**: *She's a blonde.*

★**blood** /blʌd/ *noun* [U] the red liquid that flows through the body: *Blood was pouring from a cut on his knee.* ◇ *The heart pumps blood around the body.* ◇ *red and white blood cells* ➲ Look at **bleed**.
IDM **in your blood** a strong part of your character: *A love of the wilderness was in his blood.*
**in cold blood** → COLD¹

**blood·bath** /'blʌdbæθ/ *noun* [C] an act of violently killing many people

'**blood ˌdonor** *noun* [C] a person who gives his/her blood for use in medical operations

**blood·less** /'blʌdləs/ *adj.* without killing or violence: *a bloodless coup*

'**blood ˌpressure** *noun* [U] the force with which the blood travels around the body: *to have high/low blood pressure*

**blood·shed** /'blʌdʃɛd/ *noun* [U] the killing or wounding of people: *Both sides in the war want to avoid any more bloodshed.*

**blood·shot** /'blʌdʃɑt/ *adj.* (used about the white part of the eyes) full of red lines, e.g. when sb is tired

**blood·stained** /'blʌdsteɪnd/ *adj.* having marks of blood on it

**blood·stream** /'blʌdstrim/ *noun* [sing.] the blood as it flows through the body: *drugs injected directly into the bloodstream*

'**blood type** *noun* [C] any of several different types of human blood: *Do you know which blood type you have?*

'**blood ˌvessel** *noun* [C] one of the tubes in the body that blood flows through

**blood·y** /'blʌdi/ *adj.* (**blood·i·er**; **blood·i·est**) **1** involving a lot of violence and killing: *a bloody war* **2** covered with blood: *a bloody knife*

**bloom¹** /blum/ *noun* [C] (*formal*) a flower
IDM **in (full) bloom** (used about plants, trees, etc.) with the flowers fully open: *All the wild plants are in bloom.*

**bloom²** /blum/ *verb* [I] to produce flowers: *This shrub blooms in May.*

**blos·som¹** /'blɑsəm/ *noun* [C] a flower or a mass of flowers, especially on a fruit tree: *The apple tree is covered in blossoms.* ➲ picture at **tree**.

**blos·som²** /'blɑsəm/ *verb* [I] **1** (used especially about trees) to produce flowers **2 blossom (into sth)** to develop well: *Their romance blossomed soon after they had met.*

**blot¹** /blɑt/ *noun* [C] **1** a spot or stain, especially one made by ink on paper **2 a blot on sth** a thing that spoils sb's reputation, character, future, etc.

**blot²** /blɑt/ *verb* [T] (**blot·ting**; **blot·ted**) **1** to make a spot or stain on sth, especially one of ink on paper **2** to dry spots of liquid on sth by pressing it with soft paper or cloth
PHRV **blot sth out** to cover or hide sth: *Heavy fog blotted out the view completely.* ◇ *She kept herself busy, hoping to blot out her unhappy memories* (= trying not to think of them).

**blotch** /blɑtʃ/ *noun* [C] a mark or an area of different color, especially on sb's skin: *The blotches on her face showed that she had been crying.*

**blotch·y** /'blɑtʃi/ *adj.* covered in blotches

★**blouse** /blaʊs/ *noun* [C] a piece of clothing like a shirt, that women wear

**blow/suck**

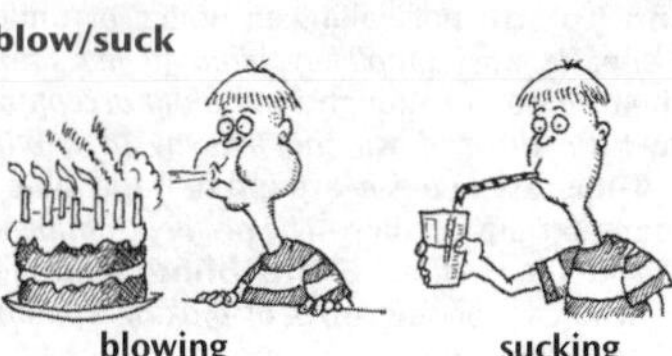

blowing sucking

★**blow¹** /bloʊ/ *verb* (*pt* **blew** /blu/; *pp* **blown** /bloʊn/)
➤ OF WIND **1** [I] (used about wind, air, etc.) to move: *A gentle breeze was blowing through the curtains.*
➤ FROM MOUTH **2** [I] to send air out of the mouth: *Take a deep breath and then blow.*
➤ SHAPE STH **3** [T] to make or shape sth by blowing air out of your mouth: *to blow bubbles*
➤ WHISTLE/INSTRUMENT **4** [I,T] to produce sound from a musical instrument, whistle, etc. by means of air: *The referee's whistle blew at the end of the game.* ◇ *He blew a few notes on the trumpet.* ◇ *All the drivers were blowing their horns.*
➤ OPPORTUNITY **5** [T] (*informal*) to waste an opportunity to succeed in sth: *I think I've blown my chances of a promotion.* ◇ *You really blew it this time, Tim!*
➤ MONEY **6** [T] **blow sth (on sth)** (*informal*) to spend or waste a lot of money on sth: *She blew all her savings on a trip to China.*
➤ ELECTRICITY **7** [I,T] (used about an electric fuse) to stop working suddenly because the electric current is too strong; to make sth do this: *A fuse just blew.* ◇ *Don't turn on everything at once or you'll blow a fuse.*
IDM **blow your mind** (*slang*) to be very surprising, often in a pleasant way: *Wow! That concert totally blew my mind!*
**blow your nose** to clear your nose by blowing strongly through it into a piece of cloth, etc.
**blow the whistle on sb/sth** (*informal*) to tell sb in authority about sth wrong or illegal that sb is doing ➲ Look at **whistle-blower**.
PHRV **blow (sb/sth) down, off, over, etc.** to move or make sth move through the air in the direction mentioned, because of the wind, etc.: *My papers blew all over the sidewalk.* ◇ *The balloons blew away into the sky.* ◇ *The wind suddenly blew my hat off.*
**blow sth out** to make sth stop burning by

blowing air at it: *to blow out the candles on a birthday cake*

**blow over** to go away; to end: *I hope those dark clouds will blow over soon.* ◇ *Our arguments usually blow over fairly quickly.*

**blow up 1** to explode or to be destroyed in an explosion: *The car blew up when the door was opened.* **2** to start suddenly and strongly: *A storm blew up in the night.* ◇ *An argument blew up about money.*

**blow sth up 1** to make sth explode or to destroy sth in an explosion: *The terrorists tried to blow up the plane.* **2** to fill sth with air or gas: *to blow up a balloon* **3** to make a larger copy of sth: *to blow up a picture*

★**blow**[2] /bloʊ/ ***noun*** [C] **1** a hard knock from your hand, a weapon, etc. that hits or is intended to hit sb/sth: *He felt a blow on the back of his head.* ◇ *She aimed a blow at me.* **2 a blow (to sb/sth)** a sudden shock or disappointment: *It was a major blow when I heard that I hadn't gotten the job.* **3** an act of blowing: *Give your nose a blow!*

IDM **a blow-by-blow account, description, etc. (of sth)** an account, etc. of an event that gives all the exact details of it

**deal sb/sth a blow**; **deal a blow to sb/sth** → DEAL[1]

ˈ**blow-dry** ***verb*** [T] (*pt, pp* **blow-dried**) to dry and shape sb's hair using a piece of electrical equipment (a **blow dryer**) that you hold and a brush

**blown** *past participle of* BLOW[1]

**blow·out** /ˈbloʊaʊt/ (*also* ˈ**blow-out**) ***noun*** [C] **1** the sudden bursting of a car tire **2** (*informal*) a large party or social occasion **3** (*informal*) an easy win in a sports game or competition

**BLT** /ˌbi ɛl ˈti/ ***abbr.*** bacon, lettuce and tomato; (used to refer to a sandwich made with these things): *I'll have a BLT and a cup of coffee, please.*

★**blue**[1] /blu/ ***adj.*** **1** having the color of a clear sky on a sunny day: *bright blue eyes* ◇ *light/dark blue* **2** (*informal*) (often used in popular songs) sad

IDM **black and blue** → BLACK[1]

★**blue**[2] /blu/ ***noun*** **1** [C,U] the color of a clear sky on a sunny day: *The room was decorated in vibrant blues and yellows.* ◇ *dressed in blue* (= blue clothes) **2 blues** [pl., with sing. or pl. verb] a type of slow sad music: *a blues singer* **3 the blues** [pl.] (*informal*) the state of feeling sad or depressed: *to have the blues*

IDM **once in a blue moon** → ONCE[1]

**out of the blue** suddenly; without being expected: *The news of his death came right out of the blue.*

**blue·ber·ry** /ˈbluˌbɛri/ ***noun*** [C] (*pl.* **blue·ber·ries**) a small, round, soft, dark blue fruit that grows on a bush: *blueberry muffins* ➲ picture on study page **A28-29**.

ˈ**blue book** ***noun*** [C] a small book, often with a blue cover, that is used by college students for writing their answers to exam questions

ˌ**blue-ˈcollar** ***adj.*** doing or involving physical work with the hands rather than office work: *a blue-collar job* ◇ *blue-collar workers* ◇ *a blue-collar neighborhood* (= where many blue-collar workers live) ➲ Look at **white-collar**.

**blue·grass** /ˈblugræs/ ***noun*** [U] **1** a type of grass with a bluish-green color that grows in parts of North America, especially the state of Kentucky in the U.S. **2** a type of traditional country music that developed among poor people in the southern U.S., and that is usually played on guitars or banjos

**blue·print** /ˈbluprɪnt/ ***noun*** [C] a plan or description of how to make, build or achieve sth

**bluff**[1] /blʌf/ ***verb*** [I,T] to try to convince people of sth that is not really true, usually by appearing very confident: *Don't pay any attention to him – he's just bluffing.* ◇ *They tried to bluff their parents into believing there was no school that day.*

**bluff**[2] /blʌf/ ***noun*** [C] **1** a steep cliff **2** an act of trying to convince people of sth that is not really true: *John keeps threatening to leave home, but I'm sure it's only a bluff!*

**blu·ish** /ˈbluɪʃ/ ***adj.*** (*informal*) slightly blue in color: *bluish green*

**blun·der** /ˈblʌndər/ ***noun*** [C] a stupid mistake: *We haven't made any major blunders yet.*

**blunt**[1] /blʌnt/ ***adj.*** **1** (used about a person, remark, etc.) saying exactly what you think in a very direct way: *I'm sorry to be so blunt, but you're just not good enough.* **2** (used about a knife, pencil, tool, etc.) not sharp: *blunt scissors* ▸ **blunt·ly** ***adv.*** ▸ **blunt·ness** ***noun*** [U]

**blunt**[2] /blʌnt/ ***verb*** [T] to make sth less sharp or less strong

**blur** /blər/ ***noun*** [C, usually sing.] something that you cannot see or remember clearly: *Last night's party is just a blur now.*

**blur·ry** /ˈbləri/ ***adj.*** unclear: *a blurry picture/photograph*

**blurt** /blərt/ ***verb***

PHRV **blurt sth out** to say sth suddenly or without thinking: *We didn't want to tell Mom, but Ann blurted the whole thing out.*

**blush**[1] /blʌʃ/ ***verb*** [I] to become red in the face, especially because you are ashamed or embarrassed: *He blushed with embarrassment.*

**blush**[2] /blʌʃ/ ***noun*** **1** [C, usually sing.] an act of blushing: *She admitted, with a blush, that she had been lying.* **2** [U] = BLUSHER

**blush·er** /ˈblʌʃər/ (*also* **blush**, *old-fashioned* **rouge**) ***noun*** [U] a red powder or cream that is used for giving more color to the cheeks

**Blvd.** ***abbr.*** = BOULEVARD

**B.O.** /ˌbi ˈoʊ/ ***abbr.*** (*informal*) = BODY ODOR

**boa constrictor** /ˈboʊə kənˌstrɪktər/ (*also* **boa** /ˈboʊə/) ***noun*** [C] a large snake that kills animals by squeezing them

**boar** /bɔr/ ***noun*** [C] **1** a male pig **2** a wild pig ➲ Look at the note at **pig**.

★**board**[1] /bɔrd/ ***noun***

➤ PIECE OF WOOD **1** [C] a long, thin, flat piece of wood used for making floors, walls, etc.: *floorboards* **2** [C] a thin flat piece of wood, etc. used for a particular purpose: *an ironing board* ◇ *a diving board* ◇ *a surfboard* ◇ *a chessboard* **3** [C] = BLACKBOARD: *Can everybody see the board all right?*

➤ GROUP OF PEOPLE **4** [C] a group of people who control an organization, a company, etc.: *the board* *of directors* ◇ *She was elected to the local school board.*

➤MEALS **5** [U] the meals that are provided when you live at a college or university, etc.: *The price of tuition does not include room and board.*

➤EXAMS **6 boards** (*also* **Boards**) [pl.] exams that you take to be able to study at a college or to be allowed to practice a certain profession: *after three years of residency, you may take boards in that area.* ◇ *College Boards*

IDM **across the board** → ACROSS

**on board** on a ship or airplane: *All the passengers were safely on board.*

**board²** /bɔrd/ *verb* [I,T] to get on a plane, ship, bus, etc.: *We said goodbye and boarded the train.* ◇ *Flight 143 to London is now boarding* (= ready to take passengers) *at Gate 27.*

PHRV **board sth up** to cover with BOARDS¹ (1): *Nobody lives there now – it's all boarded up.*

**'board game** *noun* [C] any game played on a special board, usually using a small object for each player to move around ➲ picture at **chess**.

**'boarding house** *noun* [C] a private house where you can pay to stay and have meals for a period of time

**'boarding pass** *noun* [C] a card that you must show in order to get on a plane or ship: *Could passengers please have their boarding passes ready for inspection?*

**'boarding school** *noun* [C] a school that students live at during the school year

**board·room** /'bɔrdrum/ *noun* [C] the room where a company's board of directors meets

**board·walk** /'bɔrdwɔk/ *noun* [C] a raised path that is made of boards, usually along a beach

**boast** /boʊst/ *verb* **1** [I,T] to talk with too much pride about sth that you have or can do: *I wish she wouldn't boast about her family so much.* ◇ *He's always boasting that he's the fastest runner in school.* SYN **Brag** is more common in informal speech. **2** [T] (used about a place) to have sth that it can be proud of: *The town boasts over a dozen restaurants.*

**boast·ful** /'boʊstfl/ *adj.* (used about a person or the things that he/she says) showing too much pride

★**boat** /boʊt/ *noun* [C] a small vehicle that is used for traveling across water: *The cave can only be reached by boat/in a boat.* ◇ *a fishing boat* ◇ *a rowboat/motorboat/sailboat*

NOTE Usually **boat** means a small vessel but it can also be used for a large ship, especially one that carries passengers

IDM **be in the same boat** → SAME¹

**'boat ˌpeo·ple** *noun* [pl.] people who have left their own country in boats, usually because of a dangerous political situation: *Vietnamese boat people* ➲ Look at **refugee**.

**bob** /bɑb/ *verb* (**bob·bing**; **bobbed**) [I,T] to move quickly up and down; to make sth do this: *The boats were bobbing up and down in the water.*

**bob·cat** /'bɑbkæt/ *noun* [C] a wild cat

**bob·sled** /'bɑbslɛd/ (*also* **bob·sleigh** /'bɑbsleɪ/) *noun* [C] a small vehicle for two or four people that is used for racing down a special track made of ice

**boats**

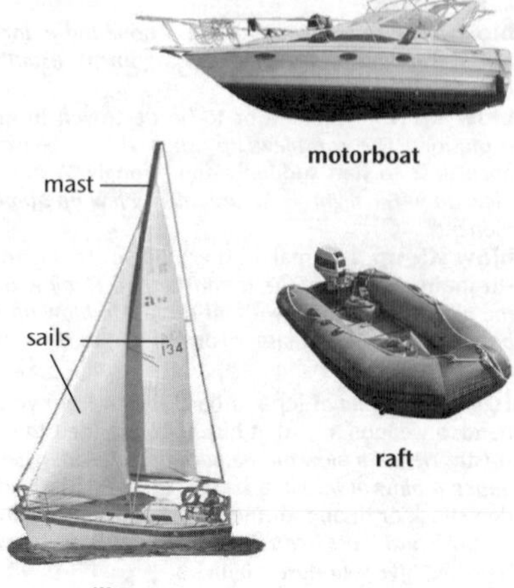


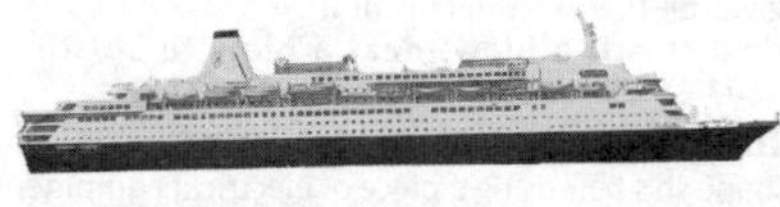


**bode** /boʊd/ *verb*

IDM **bode well/ill (for sb/sth)** to be a good/bad sign for sb/sth

**bod·i·ly** /'bɑdl·i/ *adj.* of the human body; physical: *The AIDS virus is carried in the blood and other bodily fluids.* ◇ *bodily injury*

★**bod·y** /'bɑdi/ *noun* (*pl.* **bod·ies**)

➤OF PERSON/ANIMAL **1** [C] the whole physical form of a person or animal: *the human body* **2** [C] the main part of a body, not including the head, or not including the head, arms and legs: *She had injuries to her head and body.* **3** [C] the body of a dead human or animal: *The police have found a body in the canal.*

➤MAIN PART **4** [sing.] the main part of sth: *The main body of my work involves research in the lab.* ◇ *There's some rust on the car's body panels.*

➤GROUP OF PEOPLE **5** [C] a group of people who work or act together, especially in an official way: *Tanisha has been elected president of the student body.*

➤OBJECT **6** [C] an object: *to remove a **foreign body*** (= something that should not be there) *from a wound*

**bod·y·build·ing** /'bɑdiˌbɪldɪŋ/ *noun* [U] making the muscles of the body stronger and larger through exercise

**bod·y·guard** /'bɑdigɑrd/ *noun* [C] a person whose job is to protect sb: *an armed bodyguard*

**'body ˌlanguage** *noun* [U] showing how you feel by the way you move, stand, sit, etc., rather than by what you say

**'body ˌodor** (*also informal* **B.O.**) *noun* [U] the unpleasant smell of a person's body when it is sweating

B

**ˈbody ˌpiercing** *noun* [U] the making of holes in parts of the body so that rings and other jewelry can be worn in them: *tattooing and body piercing*

**bog** /bɔg/ *noun* [C,U] an area of ground that is very soft and wet

**bogged down** /ˌbɑgd ˈdaʊn; ˌbɔgd-/ *adj.* **1** if a vehicle is bogged down, it has sunk into mud, etc. and cannot move **2** if a person is bogged down in sth, he/she cannot make any progress: *We got bogged down in a long discussion and didn't have time to make any decisions.*

**bo·gus** /ˈboʊgəs/ *adj.* pretending to be real or genuine: *He tried to cash a bogus check/cheque.*

★**boil**[1] /bɔɪl/ *verb* **1** [I] (used about a liquid) to reach a high temperature where bubbles rise to the surface and the liquid changes to a gas: *Water boils at 212°F, or 100°C.* ◇ *The pot's boiling* (= the water inside the pot). **2** [T] to heat a liquid until it boils and let it keep boiling: *Boil all drinking water for five minutes.* **3** [I,T] to cook in boiling water: *Put the potatoes on to boil.* ◇ *to boil an egg* **4** [I] (used about a person) to feel very angry: *She was boiling with rage.*

PHR V **boil down to sth** to have sth as the most important point: *What it all boils down to is that you don't want to spend too much money.*

**boil over 1** (used about a liquid) to boil and flow over the sides of a pan: *Don't let the soup boil over.* **2** (used about an argument or sb's feelings) to become more serious or angry

**boil**[2] /bɔɪl/ *noun* [sing.] an act or period of boiling

IDM **bring sth to a boil** to heat sth until it boils **come to a boil** to begin to boil

**boil·er** /ˈbɔɪlər/ *noun* [C] **1** a metal container used for providing hot water and heat in a building: *the boiler room* **2** a large metal container used for producing steam in an engine

**boil·ing** /ˈbɔɪlɪŋ/ (*also* ˌ**boiling** ˈ**hot**) *adj.* (*informal*) very hot: *Open a window – it's boiling hot in here.*

**ˈboiling point** *noun* [C] the temperature at which a liquid starts to boil

**bois·ter·ous** /ˈbɔɪstərəs/ *adj.* (used about a person or his/her behavior) noisy and full of energy: *Their kids are very nice, but they can get a little too boisterous.*

**bok choy** /ˌbɑk ˈtʃɔɪ/ *noun* [U] a type of Chinese cabbage with long green leaves and thick white stems ➲ picture on study page **A28-29**.

**bold** /boʊld/ *adj.* **1** (used about a person or his/her behavior) brave and confident; not afraid: *Not many people are bold enough to say exactly what they think.* ◇ *We need somebody with bold new ideas.* **2** that you can see clearly: *bold colors* **3** (used about printed words) in thick, dark letters: *The title is written in bold type.* ▶ **bold·ly** *adv.* ▶ **bold·ness** *noun* [U]

**bo·lo·gna** (*also* **baloney**) /bəˈloʊni/ *noun* [U] a food that is made of different types of cooked meats that have been chopped into tiny pieces and formed into a large roll (a sausage): *a bologna sandwich*

**bol·ster** /ˈboʊlstər/ *verb* [T] to support or encourage sb/sth; to make sth stronger: *His remarks did nothing to bolster my confidence.*

**bolt**[1] /boʊlt/ *noun* [C] **1** a small piece of metal (shaped like a screw without a point) that is used with another piece of metal (a **nut**) for fastening things together. The nut screws onto the bolt. ➲ picture at **nail**. **2** a bar of metal that you can slide across the inside of the door in order to fasten it **3** a sudden flash of light in the sky during a storm: *a bolt of lightning* ◇ *a lightning bolt*

**bolt**[2] /boʊlt/ *verb* **1** [T] to fasten one thing to another using a BOLT[1] (1): *All the tables have been bolted to the floor so that nobody can steal them.* **2** [T] to fasten a door, etc. with a BOLT[1] (2): *Make sure that the door is locked and bolted.* **3** [I] to run away very suddenly, usually in fear or in order to escape: *The horse suddenly bolted when it heard the gunfire.*

★**bomb**[1] /bɑm/ *noun* **1** [C] a container that is filled with material that will explode when it is thrown or dropped, or when a device inside it sets it off: *The bomb went off without warning.* ◇ *The terrorists planted the bomb in a garbage can.* ◇ *Several tons of bombs were dropped on the city.* **2 the bomb** [sing.] nuclear weapons: *How many countries have the bomb now?* **3** [C] (*informal*) a complete failure: *The movie was a bomb at the box office.*

★**bomb**[2] /bɑm/ *verb* **1** [T] to attack a city, etc. with bombs **2** [I,T] (*informal*) to fail: *The play bombed on Broadway.* ◇ *I really bombed the final exam.*

**bom·bard** /bɑmˈbɑrd/ *verb* [T] to attack a place with bombs or guns: *They bombarded the city until the enemy surrendered.* ◇ (*figurative*) *The reporters bombarded the mayor with questions.* ▶ **bom·bard·ment** /-mənt/ *noun* [C,U]: *to come under enemy bombardment*

**ˈbomb disˌposal** *noun* [U] the removing or exploding of bombs in order to make an area safe: *a bomb disposal expert*

**bomb·er** /ˈbɑmər/ *noun* [C] **1** a type of airplane that drops bombs **2** a person who throws bombs or leaves them to explode in a public place

**bomb·shell** /ˈbɑmʃɛl/ *noun* [C, usually sing.] an unexpected piece of news, usually about sth unpleasant

**bo·na fide** /ˈboʊnə faɪd; ˈbɑnə-/ *adj., adv.* (*formal*) real or genuine

**bond**[1] /bɑnd/ *noun* [C] **1** something that links two or more people or groups of people together, such as a feeling of friendship: *Our two countries are united by bonds of friendship.* **2** a certificate that you can buy from a government or company that promises to pay you interest on the money you have lent: *savings bonds*

**bond**[2] /bɑnd/ *verb* [I,T] **1 bond (A and B) (together)**; **bond (A) to B** to join two things firmly together; to join firmly to sth else: *This new adhesive bonds a variety of surfaces in seconds.* ◇ *It cannot be used to bond wood to metal.* ◇ *The atoms bond together to form a molecule.* **2 bond (with sb)** to develop or create a relationship of trust with sb: *Mothers who are depressed sometimes fail to bond with their children.*

★**bone**[1] /boʊn/ *noun* **1** [C] one of the hard parts inside the body of a person or animal that are covered with flesh and skin: *He broke a bone in his hand.* ◇ *The dog is chewing on a bone.* ◇ *This fish has a lot of bones in it.* **2** [U] the substance that bones are made of

B

IDM **make no bones about (doing) sth** to do sth without hesitating or feeling worried about it: *She made no bones about telling him exactly what she thought about him.*

**bone²** /boʊn/ ***verb*** [T] to take the BONES¹ (1) out of sth: *to bone a fish/chicken*

**ˈbone ˌmar·row** (*also* **marrow**) ***noun*** [U] the soft substance that is inside the bones of a person or an animal

**bon·fire** /ˈbɑnfaɪər/ ***noun*** [C] a large fire that you build outside to burn garbage, etc.

**bon·kers** /ˈbɑŋkərz; ˈbɔŋ-/ ***adj.*** (*slang*) (not before a noun) crazy

**bon·net** /ˈbɑnət/ ***noun*** [C] a type of hat for babies that covers the sides of the face and is fastened with strings under the chin

**bo·nus** /ˈboʊnəs/ ***noun*** [C] (*pl.* **bo·nu·ses**) **1** a payment that is added to what is usual: *to receive an annual bonus* **2** something good that you get in addition to what you expect: *If you answer this extra question correctly, you'll get two bonus points on your test score.*

**bon·y** /ˈboʊni/ ***adj.*** (**bon·i·er**; **bon·i·est**) so thin that you can see the shape of the bones: *long bony fingers*

**boo** /bu/ ***interjection, noun*** [C] (*pl.* **boos**) **1** a sound you make to show that you do not like sb/sth: *The candidate's speech was met with boos from the audience.* **2** a sound you make to frighten or surprise sb: *He jumped out from behind the door and shouted, "Boo!"* ▸ **boo** ***verb*** [I,T]: *The crowd booed when they sang.*

**boo-boo** /ˈbubu/ ***noun*** [C] (*pl.* **boo-boos**) (*informal*) a silly mistake: *to make a boo-boo*

**boo·by trap** /ˈbubi træp/ ***noun*** [C] something dangerous, like a bomb, which is hidden inside sth that seems harmless ▸ **boo·by-trap** ***verb*** [T]: *The car had been booby-trapped.*

★**book¹** /bʊk/ ***noun***

➤ PRINTED WORK **1** [C] a number of sheets of paper, fastened together inside a cover, with words printed on them for people to read: *I'm reading a book on astrology.* ◇ *She's writing a book about her childhood experiences.* ◇ *Do you have any books by Toni Morrison?* ◇ *Open your books, please.* ◇ *to publish a book* ◇ *a library book* ◇ *a cookbook* ◇ *This book is also available on CD-ROM.* ◇ *a book report*

➤ FOR WRITING IN **2** [C] a number of pieces of paper, fastened together inside a cover, for people to write on: *an address book* ➲ Look at **notebook**.

➤ OF STAMPS/TICKETS/MATCHES, ETC. **3** [C] a small number of things fastened together in the form of a book: *a book of stamps*

➤ SECTION OF BIBLE, ETC. **4** [C] any of the main divisions of a large written work: *the books of the Bible*

➤ ACCOUNTS **5 books** [pl.] the records that a company, etc. keeps of the amount of money it spends or receives: *We employ an accountant to keep the books.* ◇ *to balance the books*

IDM **by the book** exactly according to the rules: *He always does things by the book.*

★**book²** /bʊk/ ***verb*** **1** [I,T] to arrange to have or do sth at a particular time: *It's wise to book well in advance.* ◇ *Have you booked a table, sir?* ◇ *All the hotels in town are* ***booked up*** (= completely full). ◇ *I'm sorry, but the doctor is* ***fully booked*** *and isn't taking new patients.* **2** [T] to arrange for sb to have a seat on an airplane, etc.: *I've booked you on the next flight.* **3** [T] to arrange for a singer, etc. to perform on a particular date: *We've booked a jazz band for the party.* **4** [T] to make an official record, e.g. at a police station, of sb's name and sth that he/she has done wrong: *The police booked her for drunk driving* (= charged her with drunk driving). ◇ *The protesters were* ***booked for investigation of*** *trespassing.*

**book·case** /ˈbʊkkeɪs/ ***noun*** [C] a piece of furniture with shelves to keep books on

**book·keep·er** /ˈbʊkˌkipər/ ***noun*** [C] a person who keeps the accounts of the money that a company, etc. spends or receives ▸ **book·keep·ing** ***noun*** [U]: *to do the bookkeeping*

**book·let** /ˈbʊklət/ ***noun*** [C] a small thin book, usually with a soft cover, that gives information about sth

**book·mark** /ˈbʊkmɑrk/ ***noun*** [C] **1** a narrow card, etc. that you put between the pages of a book so that you can find the same place again easily **2** (*computing*) a record of the address of a file, a page on the Internet, etc. that enables you to find it quickly ▸ **book·mark** ***verb*** [T]: *Do you want to bookmark this site?*

**book·store** /ˈbʊkstɔr/ ***noun*** [C] a store that sells books ➲ Look at **library**.

**book·worm** /ˈbʊkwərm/ ***noun*** [C] a person who likes reading books very much

**boom¹** /bum/ ***noun*** [C] **1** a period in which sth increases or develops very quickly: *There was a boom in car sales in the 1990s.* ◇ *a boom year for exports* ➲ Look also at **baby boom**. **2** a loud, deep, hollow sound: *We heard a huge boom followed by silence.*

**boom²** /bum/ ***verb*** **1** [I] to grow very quickly in size or value: *Business is booming.* **2** [I,T] **boom (sth) (out)** to make a loud, deep, hollow sound: *guns booming in the distance* ◇ *The loudspeaker boomed out instructions to the crowd.*

**ˈboom box** ***noun*** [C] (*informal*) a large radio with a cassette or CD player that can be carried around and that can be played very loudly

**boom·er** /bumər/ ***noun*** [C] = BABY BOOMER

**boo·mer·ang** /ˈbuməræŋ/ ***noun*** [C] a curved piece of wood that returns to you when you throw it in the right way, used for hunting by the first people who lived in Australia

**boon** /bun/ ***noun*** [C] a thing that is very helpful and that you are grateful for

**boon·docks** /ˈbundɑks/ (*also* **boon·ies** /ˈbuniz/) ***noun*** [pl.] (*informal*) an area far away from cities or towns

**boost¹** /bust/ ***verb*** [T] **1** to increase sth in number, value or strength: *If we lower the price, that should boost sales.* ◇ *The good grade on her essay boosted her confidence.* **2** to push or lift sb up from behind below: *Boost me up to the window so I can see inside.*

**boost²** /bust/ ***noun*** [C] **1** an increase; sth that encourages people: *The fall in the value of the dollar has led to a boost in exports.* ◇ *The President's visit* *gave a boost to the soldiers' morale.* **2** an act of lifting sb up and forward: *Give me a boost over the fence.*

★**boot**[1] /but/ ***noun*** [C] **1** a type of shoe that covers your foot and ankle and sometimes part of your leg: *a pair of old boots* ◇ *ski/hiking/winter boots* ➲ pictures at **shoe** and **ski**. **2** = DENVER BOOT

**boot**[2] /but/ ***verb*** [T] to kick sth/sb hard: *He booted the ball over the fence.*

PHR V **boot sb out (of sth)** (*informal*) to force sb to leave a place: *He got booted out of the club.*

ˈ**boot camp** ***noun*** [C] a training camp for new members of the armed forces, where they have to work hard

**booth** /buθ/ ***noun*** [C] (*pl.* **booths** /buθs; buðz/) **1** a small enclosed place with thin walls that divide it from the rest of the room or area: *a ticket/voting booth* ➲ Look also at **phone booth**. **2** a place to sit in a restaurant with a table between two long seats that are attached to the floor

**boot·leg** /ˈbutlɛg/ ***adj.*** (only *before* a noun) made and sold illegally: *a bootleg CD*

**boo·ty** /ˈbuṭi/ ***noun*** [U] things that are taken by thieves or captured by soldiers in war

**booze** /buz/ ***noun*** [U] (*informal*) alcoholic drink

★**bor·der**[1] /ˈbɔrdər/ ***noun*** [C] **1** a line that divides two countries, etc.; the land close to this line: *The refugees escaped across/over the border.* ◇ *We crossed the border into Mexico.* ◇ *the Canadian border* ◇ *the border between France and Italy* ◇ *Italy's border with France*

NOTE We use **border** to talk about the line that divides two countries, states or provinces: *The river forms the border between the two countries.* **Line** can also be used for the line that divides states, provinces, countries, or smaller areas: *the state/county line.* **Boundary** is also used for the line that divides smaller areas: *This fence marks the boundaries of our property.* **Frontier** is used for areas where people are just beginning to live: *frontier towns of the Wild West.*

**2** a band or strip around the edge of sth, often for decoration: *a white tablecloth with a blue border*

**bor·der**[2] /ˈbɔrdər/ ***verb*** [T] **1** to share a border with another country or state: *Which states border Canada?* **2** to form a line along or around the edge of sth: *The road was bordered with trees.*

PHR V **border on sth** **1** to be next to sth: *Our back yard borders on the school grounds.* **2** to be almost the same as sth: *His ideas bordered on madness.*

**bor·der·line** /ˈbɔrdərlaɪn/ ***noun*** [sing.] the line that marks a division between two different cases, conditions, etc.: *The novel is on the borderline between fiction and nonfiction.* ◇ *He's a borderline case – he may pass the exam or he may fail.*

★**bore**[1] /bɔr/ ***verb*** **1** [T] to make sb tired and uninterested: *I hope I'm not boring you.* ◇ *Those old jokes bore me.* **2** [I,T] to make a round hole or passage through sth: *The drill can bore through solid rock.* ◇ *They are boring a tunnel through the mountain.*

**bore**[2] /bɔr/ ***noun*** **1** [C] a person who talks or behaves in an uninteresting way: *He's a real bore.* **2** [sing.] (*informal*) something that you have to do that you find uninteresting: *It's such a bore having to study every day.*

**bore**[3] /bɔr/ *past tense of* BEAR[2]

★**bored** /bɔrd/ ***adj.*** feeling uninterested and tired because sth is not exciting or because you do not have anything to do: *I'm bored. There's nothing to do at home.* ◇ *The kids get bored on long car trips.* ◇ *The play was terrible. We were bored stiff* (= extremely bored).

**bore·dom** /ˈbɔrdəm/ ***noun*** [U] the state of being bored: *People say that many young people turn to crime out of boredom.*

★**bor·ing** /ˈbɔrɪŋ/ ***adj.*** uninteresting; dull: *a boring movie* ◇ *boring work*

★**born**[1] /bɔrn/ ***verb* be born** to come into the world by birth; to start existing: *Where were you born?* ◇ *My parents were born in Korea, but they grew up in the U.S.* ◇ *I'm going to give up work after the baby is born.* ◇ *Their baby was born deaf.* ◇ *The idea of free education for all was born in the eighteenth century.* ◇ *His unhappiness was* ***born out of*** *a feeling of frustration.*

**born**[2] /bɔrn/ ***adj.*** having a natural ability to do the task mentioned: *She's a born leader.*

**-born** /bɔrn/ ***combining form*** born in the place or state mentioned: *Samuel Beckett, the Irish-born writer, lived in Paris for most of his life.*

ˌ**born-aˈgain** ***adj.*** having found new, strong faith in a religion: *a born-again Christian*

**borne** /bɔrn/ *past participle of* BEAR[2]

**-borne** /bɔrn/ ***combining form*** carried by: *insect-borne diseases*

**bor·ough** /ˈbəroʊ/ ***noun*** [C] a town, or an area within a large city, especially New York City, that has some form of local government: *the borough of Queens in New York City*

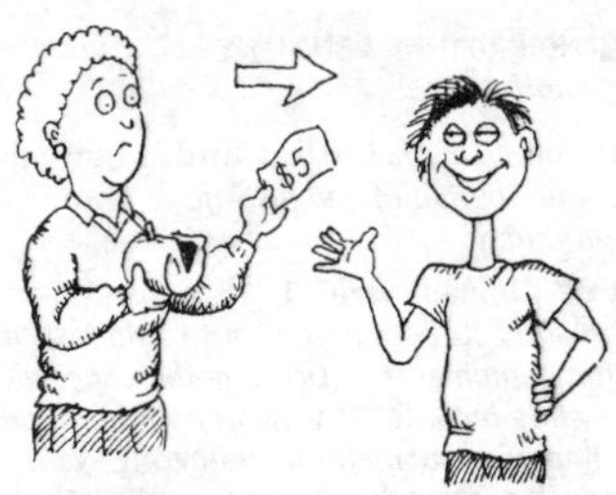


She's **lending/ loaning** her son some money. He's **borrowing** some money from his mother.

★**bor·row** /ˈbɑroʊ; ˈbɔr-/ ***verb*** [I,T] **borrow (sth) (from/off sb/sth)** **1** to take or receive sth from sb/sth that you intend to give back, usually after a short time: *I had to borrow from the bank to pay for my car.* ◇ *They borrowed $10,000 to buy a new car.* ◇ *Could I borrow your pen for a minute?* ◇ *Can I borrow $10? I'll pay you back next week.* ◇ *He's always borrowing off his mother.* ◇ *I borrowed a book from the library.*

NOTE Be careful not to confuse **borrow** with its opposites **lend** and **loan**.

**2** to take sth and use it as your own; to copy: *That idea is borrowed from another book.*

**bor·row·er** /ˈbɑroʊər; ˈbɔr-/ ***noun*** [C] a person who borrows

**bos·om** /ˈbʊzəm/ ***noun*** (*formal*) [C] (usually singular) a person's chest, especially a woman's breasts: *She clutched the child to her bosom.*

★**boss¹** /bɔs/ ***noun*** [C] a person whose job is to give orders to others at work; an employer; a manager: *I'm going to ask the boss for a day off work.* ◇ *OK. You're the boss* (= you make the decisions).

**boss²** /bɔs/ ***verb*** [T] **boss sb (around)** to give orders to sb, especially in an annoying way: *I wish you'd quit bossing me around.*

**boss·y** /ˈbɔsi/ ***adj.*** (**boss·i·er**; **boss·i·est**) liking to give orders to other people, often in an annoying way ▸ **boss·i·ly** ***adv.*** ▸ **boss·i·ness** ***noun*** [U]

**bo·tan·i·cal** /bəˈtænɪkl/ ***adj.*** connected with the scientific study of plants: *a botanical garden* (= a type of park where plants are grown for scientific study)

**bot·a·nist** /ˈbɑtn·ɪst/ ***noun*** [C] a person who studies plants

**bot·a·ny** /ˈbɑtn·i/ ***noun*** [U] the scientific study of plants

**botch** /bɑtʃ/ ***verb*** [T] **botch sth (up)** (*informal*) to do sth badly or to ruin sth because you are not very skillful: *a botched* (= unsuccessful) *robbery attempt*

★**both¹** /boʊθ/ ***det.***, ***pronoun*** the two; the one as well as the other: *Both women/Both the women/Both of the women were French.* ◇ *I talked to the women. Both of them were French/They were both French.* ◇ *I liked them both.* ◇ *We were both very tired.* ◇ *Both of us were tired.* ◇ *They have both seen the movie.* ◇ *I have two sisters. They both live in Florida/Both of them live in Florida.* ◇ *Both of my sisters live in Florida.*

NOTE Note that we CANNOT say: *the both women* or: *my both sisters.*

★**both²** /boʊθ/ ***adv.*** **both... and...** not only... but also...: *I like both him and his wife.* ◇ *I was both hungry and thirsty.*

★**both·er** /ˈbɑðər/ ***verb*** **1** [T] to disturb or annoy sb: *I'm sorry to bother you, but could I speak with you for a moment?* ◇ *Don't bother Sue with that now – she's busy.* **2** [T] to worry sb: *You don't look very happy. Is something bothering you?* **3** [I,T] **bother (to do sth)**; **bother with sth** (usually negative) to make the effort to do sth: *"Should I make you something to eat?" "No, don't bother – I'm not hungry."* ◇ *He didn't even bother to say thank you.* ◇ *Don't bother with the dishes. I'll do them later.* ◇ *Don't bother waiting for me – I'll catch up with you later.*

**Bo·tox™** (*also* **bo·tox**) /ˈboʊtɑks/ ***noun*** [U] a substance that makes muscles relax. It is sometimes injected into the skin around sb's eyes to remove lines and make the skin look younger. ▸ **Bo·tox** ***verb*** (usually passive): *Do you think she's been Botoxed?*

★**bot·tle¹** /ˈbɑt̬l/ ***noun*** [C] **1** a glass or plastic container with a narrow neck for keeping liquids in: *a beer bottle* ◇ *an empty bottle* ➲ picture at **container**. **2** the amount of liquid in a bottle: *a bottle of beer*

**bot·tle²** /ˈbɑt̬l/ ***verb*** [T] to put sth into bottles: *After three or four months, the wine is bottled.*

PHRV **bottle sth up** to not allow yourself to express strong emotions: *It's not good to keep your feelings bottled up.*

**bot·tled** /ˈbɑt̬ld/ ***adj.*** that you can buy in bottles: *bottled water*

**bot·tle·neck** /ˈbɑt̬lnɛk/ ***noun*** [C] something that slows down progress

★**bot·tom¹** /ˈbɑt̬əm/ ***noun***

▸LOWEST PART **1** [C, usually sing.] the lowest part of sth: *The house is at the bottom of a hill.* ◇ *Look at the picture at the bottom of page 23.* ◇ *I think I have a pen in the bottom of my bag.* **2** [C] the flat surface on the outside of an object, on which it stands: *There's a label on the bottom of the box.*

▸LOWEST POSITION **3** [sing.] the least important position in relation to other people: *She started at the bottom and now she's president of the company.*

▸OF RIVER/POOL **4** [sing.] the ground under the ocean, a river, a swimming pool, etc.: *The water was so clear that we could see the bottom.*

▸PART OF BODY **5** [C] the part of your body that you sit on: *I fell down and landed on my bottom.* ➲ Look also at **butt**.

▸CLOTHING **6** [usually pl.] the lower part of a piece of clothing that is in two parts: *pajama bottoms* ◇ *a bikini bottom*

IDM **be at the bottom of sth** to be the real cause of sth: *I'm sure Kate Mills is at the bottom of all this.* **get to the bottom of sth** to find out the real cause of sth

PHRV **bottom out** (of prices, a bad situation, etc.) to stop getting worse: *The recession is finally showing signs of bottoming out.*

★**bot·tom²** /ˈbɑt̬əm/ ***adj.*** in the lowest position: *the bottom shelf*

IDM **the bottom line 1** the amount of money that a company earns or loses: *Our boss doesn't care about employee safety – he's only interested in the bottom line.* **2** the most important or final point in an argument, etc.: *The bottom line is that the company will go bankrupt if we don't give our customers what they want.*

**bought** *past tense, past participle of* BUY¹

**boul·der** /ˈboʊldər/ ***noun*** [C] a very large rock

**boul·e·vard** /ˈbʊləvɑrd/ ***noun*** **1** [C] a wide street in a town or city **2 Boulevard** (*abbr.* **Blvd.**) [sing.] (used in the names of some streets in towns and cities): *1270 Sunset Blvd., Los Angeles*

**bounce** /baʊns/ ***verb***

▸MOVE OFF SURFACE **1** [I,T] (used about a ball, etc.) to move away quickly after it has hit a hard surface; to make a ball do this: *In tennis, the ball can only bounce once before you hit it back.* ◇ *The stone bounced off the wall and hit her.* ◇ *A small boy came down the street, bouncing a ball.*

▸MOVE UP AND DOWN **2** [I] to jump up and down continuously: *The kids were bouncing on their beds.*

▸CHECK **3** [I] (used about a check) to be returned by a bank without payment because there is not enough money in the account **4** [T] to write a check without having enough money in the bank account: *to bounce a check*

➤COMPUTING **5** [I,T] (*computing*) if an e-mail bounces or the system bounces it, it returns to the person who sent it because the system cannot deliver it

PHR V **bounce back** to recover from a failure, disappointment, etc. and return quickly to your normal life with the same energy as before

▶ **bounce** *noun* [C,U]

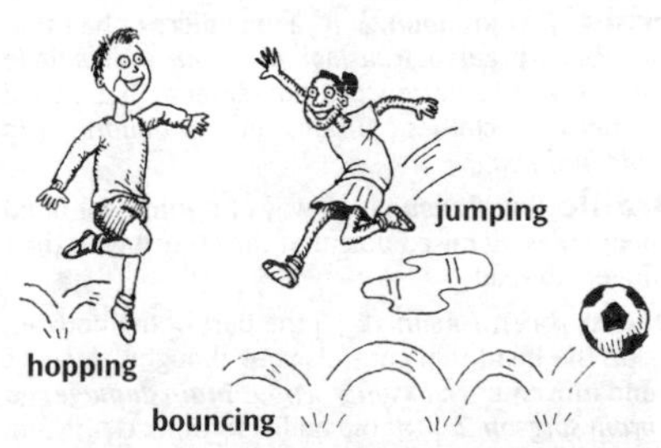


**bounc·er** /ˈbaʊnsər/ *noun* [C] a person whose job is to stand at the entrance to a bar, etc., to stop people who are not wanted from going in, and to throw out anyone who makes trouble inside

★**bound**[1] /baʊnd/ *adj.* **1 bound to do sth** certain to do sth: *You've done so much studying that you're bound to get an "A" on the test.* ◇ *There are bound to be problems in a situation like this.* **2** (not before a noun) having a legal or moral duty to do sth: *She was not legally bound to pay for the damage.* ◇ *Agents are bound by an oath of secrecy.* **3 bound (for…)** traveling or leading to a particular place: *a ship bound for Australia* ◇ *the southbound lanes of the freeway*

IDM **bound up with sth** very closely connected with sth

**bound**[2] /baʊnd/ *verb* [I] to run quickly with jumping movements: *The big dog bounded up to us.*

**bound**[3] *past tense, past participle of* BIND[1]

**bound·a·ry** /ˈbaʊndri; -dəri/ *noun* [C] (*pl.* **bound·a·ries**) **1** a line that marks the limits of a place and divides it from other places: *The highway is the boundary between the two counties.* **2** the farthest limit of sth: *Scientists continue to push back the boundaries of human knowledge.* ➲ Look at the note at **border**.

**bound·less** /ˈbaʊndləs/ *adj.* having no limit: *boundless energy*

**bounds** /baʊndz/ *noun* [pl.] limits that cannot or should not be passed: *Price increases must be kept within reasonable bounds.*

IDM **out of bounds** (*sports*) outside the area of play

**bou·quet** /boʊˈkeɪ; bu-/ *noun* [C] a bunch of flowers that is arranged in an attractive way: *a bouquet of roses*

**bour·bon** /ˈbərbən/ *noun* [C,U] a type of whiskey that is made mainly in the U.S.

**bour·geois** /ˌbʊrˈʒwɑ; ˈbʊrʒwɑ/ *adj.* typical of middle-class people in society: *bourgeois attitudes/ideas/values*

NOTE This word is used in a critical way.

**the bour·geoi·sie** /ˌbʊrʒwɑˈzi/ *noun* [sing.] the class of people in society who are interested mainly in money and social position

NOTE This word is used in a critical way.

**bout** /baʊt/ *noun* [C] **1** a short period of great activity: *a bout of hard work* **2** a period of illness: *I'm just recovering from a bout of the flu.*

**bou·tique** /buˈtik/ *noun* [C] a small store that sells expensive clothes, etc.

**bo·vine** /ˈboʊvaɪn/ *adj.* (*technical*) connected with cows: *bovine diseases*

**bow**[1] /baʊ/ *verb* **1** [I,T] to bend your head or the upper part of your body forward and down, as a sign of respect: *All the actors came onto the stage and bowed.* ◇ *He bowed his head respectfully.* **2 bow to sb/sth** [I] to accept or obey sb/sth: *I do not think that Congress should bow to pressure from big corporations.*

PHR V **bow out (of sth)** to leave an important position or stop taking part in sth: *After 12 years on the committee, she decided to bow out.*

**bow**[2] /baʊ/ *noun* [C] **1** an act of BOWING[1] (1): *The actors came back to take another bow.* **2** the front part of a ship ➲ Look at **stern**[2].

**bow**[3] /boʊ/ *noun* [C] **1** a knot with two loops and two loose ends that you use when you are tying shoes, wrapping presents, etc.: *He tied the ribbon into a bow.* ◇ *She had a bow in her hair.* ➲ picture at **knot**. **2** a weapon for shooting arrows. A bow is a curved piece of wood or similar material that is held in shape by a tight string. **3** a long thin piece of wood with horse hair stretched along it that you use to play a violin, etc. ➲ picture at **violin**.

**bow·el** /ˈbaʊəl/ *noun* [C, usually pl.] one of the tubes that takes waste food from the stomach so that it can pass out of the body

★**bowl** /boʊl/ *noun* [C] **1** a deep round dish, usually without a lid, that is used for holding food or liquid: *a sugar bowl* ◇ *a mixing bowl* **2** the amount of sth that is in a bowl: *a bowl of cereal* ➲ picture at **plate**.

**bowl·ing** /ˈboʊlɪŋ/ *noun* [U] a game in which you roll a heavy ball along a special track (**lane**) toward a group of wooden objects (**pins**) and try to knock down as many of them as you can: *Let's **go bowling**.* ◇ *a bowling alley* (= a building with many lanes for bowling) ◇ *bowling shoes*

**bow tie** /ˈboʊ taɪ/ *noun* [C] a tie in the shape of a BOW[3] (1), that is worn by men, especially on formal occasions

★**box**[1] /bɑks/ *noun* [C]

➤CONTAINER **1** a square or rectangular container for solid objects. A box often has a lid: *I opened the lid and looked inside the box.* ➲ picture at **container**. **2** a BOX (1) and the things inside it: *a box of candy/tissues*

➤SHAPE **3** an empty square or rectangle on a form in which you have to write sth: *Write your full name in the box below.*

➤FOR MAIL **4** a place in a post office or in an office where letters, packages, etc. are kept until they are picked up by the person that they were sent to ➲ Look also at **post office box**.

B

▸IN SPORT **5** an enclosed area that is used for a particular purpose: *the penalty box next to a hockey rink*
▸IN THEATER/SPORTS CENTER, ETC. **6** an enclosed area in a theater, sports center, etc. in which a small group of people can sit and watch the event: *box seats in the stadium*

**box²** /bɑks/ ***verb*** **1** [I,T] to fight in the sport of boxing: *He used to box at school.* **2** [T] to put sth into a BOX¹ (1): *a boxed set of CDs*

**box·er** /ˈbɑksər/ ***noun*** **1** [C] a person who BOXES² (1) as a sport, often professionally **2 boxers** (*also* **ˈboxer shorts**) [pl.] men's underpants that are loose and cover the body from the waist to the top of the legs

**box·ing** /ˈbɑksɪŋ/ ***noun*** [U] a sport in which two people fight by hitting each other with their hands inside large gloves: *the world heavyweight boxing champion* ◇ *boxing gloves*

**ˈBoxing Day** ***noun*** [sing.] a holiday celebrated on December 26 or the first weekday after Christmas in Canada and other parts of the COMMONWEALTH (1)

**ˈbox ˌoffice** ***noun*** [C] the place in a theater, etc. where the tickets are sold

★**boy¹** /bɔɪ/ ***noun*** **1** [C] a male child: *They have three children – two boys and a girl.* **2 the boys** [pl.] (*informal*) a group of male friends

**boy²** /bɔɪ/ ***interjection*** (*informal*) (used for expressing a strong feeling): *Boy, it's hot today!* ◇ *Oh boy! I can't wait to open my presents!*

**boy·cott** /ˈbɔɪkɑt/ ***verb*** [T] to refuse to buy things from a particular company, take part in an event, etc. because you strongly disapprove of it: *Several countries boycotted the Olympic Games in protest.* ▸ **boy·cott *noun*** [C]

★**boy·friend** /ˈbɔɪfrɛnd/ ***noun*** [C] a man or boy with whom a person has a romantic and/or sexual relationship

**boy·hood** /ˈbɔɪhʊd/ ***noun*** [U] the time of being a boy: *his boyhood friends* (= from when he was a boy)

**boy·ish** /ˈbɔɪɪʃ/ ***adj.*** like a boy: *a boyish smile*

**ˈBoy Scout** ***noun*** [C] (*U.S.*) = SCOUT¹ (1)

**bra** /brɑ/ ***noun*** [C] a piece of clothing that women wear under their other clothes to support their breasts

**brace¹** /breɪs/ ***noun*** **1** [C] an apparatus that is designed to support weak or injured parts of the body: *a neck/leg brace* **2 braces** [pl.] wires that are attached to sb's teeth in order to make them straight

**brace²** /breɪs/ ***verb*** **1** [T] **brace sth/yourself** to make your body stiff or press it against sth in order to prepare yourself, e.g. if sth is going to hit you, or to stop yourself from falling: *He braced himself as he began to slip on the ice.* **2** [I,T] **brace (yourself) (for sth)** to prepare yourself for sth difficult or unpleasant: *You'd better brace yourself for some bad news.*

**brace·let** /ˈbreɪslət/ ***noun*** [C] a piece of jewelry (e.g. a metal chain or band) that you wear around your wrist or arm ➲ picture at **jewelry**.

**brack·et** /ˈbrækət/ ***noun*** [C] **1** [usually pl.] one of two marks, [ ], that you put around extra information in a piece of writing ➲ Look at **parentheses**. **2** a piece of metal or wood that is attached to a wall and used as a support for a shelf, lamp, etc. **3** a group of people whose ages, incomes, etc. are between two limits: *to be in a high income bracket* ◇ *a magazine for people in the 30-40 age bracket.*

**brag** /bræg/ ***verb*** [I,T] (**brag·ging**; **bragged**) to talk too proudly about sth: *She's always bragging about how much she earns.*

**braid¹** /breɪd/ ***verb*** [T] to twist three or more long thin pieces of hair, rope, etc. over and under each other to make one thick piece

**braid²** /breɪd/ ***noun*** **1** [C] a long piece of hair that has been braided: *You look nice with your hair **in braids**.* **2** [U] a narrow piece of material that is used to decorate clothes, curtains, etc.: *a uniform with gold braid on it*

**Braille** /breɪl/ ***noun*** [U] a way of printing for blind people, using raised dots that they touch with their fingers to read

★**brain** /breɪn/ ***noun*** **1** [C] the part of the body inside the head that controls your thoughts, feelings and movements: *to suffer serious **brain damage*** ◇ *a brain surgeon* **2** [C,U] the ability to think clearly; intelligence: *He doesn't **have the brains** to be a doctor.* **3** [C] (*informal*) a very intelligent person: *He's one of the best brains in the country.* ◇ *Gee, Harriet, you're such a brain!* **4 the brains** [sing.] the person who plans or organizes sth: *She's the real brains in the organization.*

IDM **rack your brains** → RACK²

**brain·child** /ˈbreɪntʃaɪld/ ***noun*** [sing.] the idea or invention of a particular person: *The festival was the brainchild of a young teacher.*

**ˈbrain-dead** ***adj.*** **1** suffering from serious damage to the brain and needing a machine to stay alive **2** (*informal*) unable to think clearly; stupid: *He's brain-dead from watching too much TV.*

**brain·storm** /ˈbreɪnstɔrm/ ***verb*** [I,T] to try to come up with as many ideas as possible about a problem or project, often together with other people: *Let's brainstorm the areas we have to cover before we start writing the report.*

**brain·wash** /ˈbreɪnwɑʃ; -wɔʃ/ ***verb*** [T] to force sb to believe sth by using strong mental pressure: *TV commercials try to brainwash people into buying things that they don't need.* ▸ **brain·wash·ing *noun*** [U]

**brake¹** /breɪk/ ***noun*** [usually pl.] **1** the part of a vehicle that makes it go slower or stop: *She put her foot on the brake and just managed to stop in time.* ◇ *These brakes don't work.* ➲ picture at **bicycle**. **2** something that makes sth else slow down or stop: *The government must try to **put the brakes on** inflation.*

**brake²** /breɪk/ ***verb*** [I] to use the BRAKE¹ (1) in a car to stop it or make it go more slowly: *The driver braked suddenly.*

**bran** /bræn/ ***noun*** [U] the brown outer parts of grains that have been separated from the flour: *oat/wheat bran*

★**branch¹** /bræntʃ/ ***noun*** [C] **1** one of the main parts of a tree that grows from its central stem (trunk) and often has leaves, flowers or fruit on it: *I climbed the tree and sat on a branch.* ➲ picture at tree. **2** an office, a store, etc. that is part of a larger organization: *The company I work for has branches in Paris, Milan and New York.* ◇ *the bank's downtown branch* **3** a part of an academic subject: *Psychiatry is a branch of medicine.*

**branch²** /bræntʃ/ ***verb***
**PHRV branch off** (used about a road) to leave a larger road and go off in another direction: *The road branches off to the left ahead.*
**branch out (into sth)** to start doing sth new and different from the things you usually do: *He started as a poet but branched out into songwriting.*

★**brand¹** /brænd/ ***noun*** [C] **1** the name of a product that is made by a particular company: *the **leading brand** of detergent* **2** a particular type of sth: *a strange brand of humor*

**brand²** /brænd/ ***verb*** [T] **1** to mark an animal with a hot iron to show who owns it **2 brand sb (as sth)** to say that sb has a bad character so that people have a bad opinion of him/her: *She was branded as a troublemaker after she complained about the pay.*

**bran·dish** /ˈbrændɪʃ/ ***verb*** [T] to wave sth in the air in an aggressive or excited way: *to brandish a knife*

ˈ**brand name** ***noun*** [C] the name that a company gives to a product that it produces

**brand-new** /ˌbrænˈnu; ˌbrænd-/ ***adj.*** completely new

**bran·dy** /ˈbrændi/ ***noun*** [C,U] a strong alcoholic drink that is made from wine

**brash** /bræʃ/ ***adj.*** too confident and direct: *a brash young salesman*

**brass** /bræs/ ***noun*** **1** [U] a yellow metal that is a mixture of a red-colored metal (**copper**) and a white-colored metal (**zinc**): *brass buttons* **2** [C,U] the group of musical instruments that are made of BRASS (1), e.g. the trumpet, the trombone, etc. ➲ picture at **trumpet**. [U]: *the brass section in an orchestra* ◇ *a brass band* ◇ *The brasses need to play more softly in this section.*

**brat** /bræt/ ***noun*** [C] a child who behaves badly and annoys you

★**brave¹** /breɪv/ ***adj.*** ready to do things that are dangerous or difficult without showing fear: *"This might hurt a little, so try and be brave," said the dentist.* ▶ **brave·ly *adv.*** ▶ **brav·er·y** /ˈbreɪvəri/ ***noun*** [U]: *After the war he received a medal for bravery.*

**brave²** /breɪv/ ***verb*** [T] to face sth dangerous or difficult without showing fear: *She braved the rain and went out into the street.*

**bra·vo** /ˈbrɑvoʊ; ˌbrɑˈvoʊ/ ***interjection*** a word that you shout to show that you like sth that sb has done, e.g. an actor's performance in a play

**brawl** /brɔl/ ***noun*** [C] a noisy fight among a group of people, usually in a public place: *a drunken brawl outside a bar*

**Bra·zil nut** /brəˈzɪl nʌt/ ***noun*** [C] a nut with a very hard shell; Brazil nuts can be eaten ➲ picture at **nut**.

**breach¹** /britʃ/ ***noun*** (*formal*) **1** [C,U] an act that breaks an agreement, a law, etc.: *Giving private information about clients is a breach of confidence.* ◇ *She was dismissed from the company for breach of contract.* **2** [C] a break in friendly relations between people, groups, etc.: *a breach between two countries* **3** [C] an opening in a wall, etc. that defends or protects sb/sth: *The waves made a breach in the sea wall.*

**breach²** /britʃ/ ***verb*** [T] **1** to break an agreement, a law, etc.: *He accused the corporation of breaching international law.* **2** to make an opening in a wall, etc. that defends or protects sb/sth

**bread**

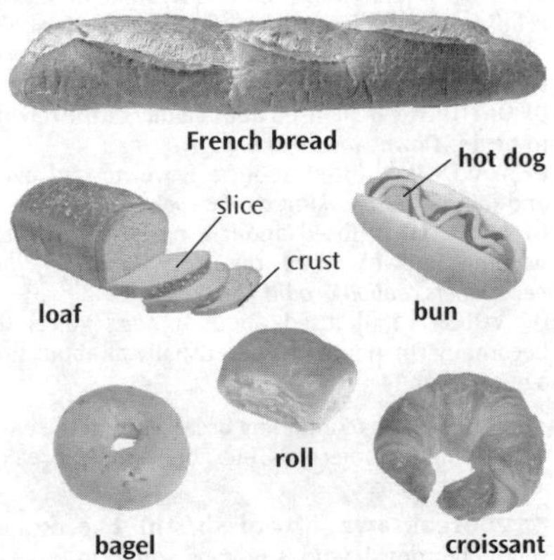


★**bread** /brɛd/ ***noun*** [U] a type of food. To make bread you mix together flour and water, and often a substance to make the bread rise (yeast), and bake the mixture in an oven: *a piece/slice of bread* ◇ *fresh/stale bread* ◇ *Would you like some bread and butter?*

> **NOTE** A **loaf** of bread is bread that has been shaped and cooked in one piece. **Rolls** and **buns** are small round pieces of bread that are the right size for one person to eat. **White bread** is made from flour that has had the outside part of the grain taken off. **Whole-wheat** bread is made from flour that contains all the grain.

**breadth** /brɛdθ/ ***noun*** **1** [C,U] the distance between the two sides of sth: *We measured the length and breadth of the garden.*

> **NOTE** **Width** is more common than **breadth** in this meaning.

**2** [U] the wide range of sth: *I was amazed by the breadth of her knowledge.* ➲ adjective **broad**

**bread·win·ner** /ˈbrɛdwɪnər/ ***noun*** [C, usually sing.] the person who earns the money that his/her family needs

★**break¹** /breɪk/ ***verb*** (*pt* **broke** /broʊk/; *pp* **broken** /ˈbroʊkən/)
➤IN PIECES **1** [I,T] to separate, or make sth separate, into two or more pieces: *She dropped the vase onto the floor and it broke.* ◇ *I'm sorry I broke one of your dinner plates.* ◇ *He broke his leg in a car accident.*
➤STOP WORKING **2** [I,T] (used about a machine, etc.) to stop working; to stop a machine, etc. from working: *My watch broke last week.* ◇ *Be careful with my camera – I don't want you to break it.*

B

➤ LAW/PROMISE **3** [T] to do sth that is against the law, or to not keep a promise, etc.: *A police officer told me that I was breaking the law.* ◇ *to break a contract* ◇ *Don't worry – I never break my promises.*
➤ A RECORD **4** [T] **break a record** to do sth better or faster than anyone has ever done before: *She broke the world record for the 100 meters.*
➤ STOP FOR A SHORT TIME **5** [I] to stop doing sth for a short time: *to break for lunch*
➤ END STH **6** [T] to interrupt sth so that it ends suddenly: *Suddenly, the silence was broken by the sound of a bird singing.*
➤ DESTROY **7** [T] to make sth end by force or strong action: *Smoking is a very difficult habit to break.* ◇ *Two days of talks failed to break the deadlock between the countries.*
➤ OF DAY/DAWN **8** [I] (used about a day or the dawn) to begin: *Dawn was breaking.*
➤ OF WAVES **9** [I] (used about a wave) to curl over and fall: *waves breaking on the rocks*
➤ OF NEWS **10** [I] (used about a piece of news) to become known: *When the story broke in the newspapers, nobody could believe it.*
➤ OF VOICE **11** [I] (used about a boy's voice) to become permanently deeper, usually at about the age of 13 or 14

NOTE For idioms containing **break**, look at the entries for nouns, adjectives, etc. For example, **break even** is at **even**.

PHR V **break away (from sb/sth) 1** to escape suddenly from sb who is holding you **2** to leave a group, an organization, etc. in order to form a new one: *The region broke away from the rest of the country and declared independence.*
**break down 1** (used about a vehicle or machine) to stop working: *My car broke down on the way to work this morning.* **2** (used about a system, discussion, etc.) to fail: *Talks between the two countries have completely broken down.* **3** to lose control of your feelings and start crying: *to break down in tears*
**break sth down** to make a substance separate into parts or change into a different form in a chemical process: *Food is broken down in our bodies by the digestive system.*
**break in** to enter a building by force, usually in order to steal sth: *The burglars broke in through a window.*
**break into sth 1** to enter a building by force, usually in order to steal sth **2** to start doing sth suddenly: *to break into a smile* ◇ *to break into a run*
**break off** to suddenly stop doing or saying sth: *He broke off in the middle of a sentence.*
**break (sth) off** to remove a part of sth by force; to come off in this way: *Could you break off a piece of chocolate for me?* ◇ *Oh no, part of my tooth just broke off!*
**break sth off** to end a relationship suddenly: *They broke off their engagement after a bad argument.* ◇ *to break off diplomatic relations with another country*
**break out** (used especially about fighting, wars, fires, etc.) to start suddenly: *Riots broke out in the prison.* ◇ *Applause broke out in the courtroom.*
**break out in sth** to suddenly become covered in sth: *His face broke out in a rash.* ◇ *He broke out in a cold sweat* (for example, through fear).
**break out (of sth)** to escape from a prison, etc.
**break up** (used about events that involve a group of people) to come to an end: *The meeting broke up just before lunch.*
**break up (with sb)** to end a relationship with a wife, husband, girlfriend or boyfriend: *My marriage broke up when I was 25.* ◇ *She broke up with her boyfriend.*
**break (sth) up** to separate into parts: *The ship broke up on the rocks.*
**break sth up** to end an event by separating the people who are involved in it: *The police arrived and broke up the fight.*
**break with sth** to end a relationship or connection with sb/sth: *to break with tradition/the past*

★**break²** /breɪk/ ***noun*** [C]
➤ OF AN OBJECT **1** a place where sth has been broken: *a break in a pipe*
➤ OPENING/SPACE **2** an opening or space in sth: *Wait for a break in the traffic before you cross the street.*
➤ SHORT STOP/PAUSE **3** a short period of rest: *Let's take a break.* ◇ *a lunch/coffee break* ➲ Look at the note at **pause**.
➤ CHANGE IN SITUATION **4 break (in sth)**; **break (with sb/sth)** a change from what usually happens or an end to sth: *a break with tradition* ◇ *The incident led to a break in diplomatic relations.*
➤ OPPORTUNITY **5** an arrangement or a change that is favorable to sb: *tax breaks for small businesses* ◇ *Give him a break. Everybody makes mistakes when they start a new job.*
IDM **give me a break!** (*informal*) stop annoying me or making problems for me: *Oh, give me a break. That's not true and you know it.*

**break·danc·ing** /ˈbreɪkˌdænsɪŋ/ ***noun*** [U] a very active style of dancing, often performed in the street ▶ **break·dance** /ˈbreɪkdæns/ ***verb*** [I] ▶ **break·danc·er** /ˈbreɪkˌdænsər/ ***noun*** [C]

**break·down** /ˈbreɪkdaʊn/ ***noun*** [C] **1** a time when a vehicle, machine, etc. stops working: *We had a breakdown on the highway.* **2** the failure or end of sth: *The breakdown of the talks means that a strike is likely.* **3** = NERVOUS BREAKDOWN **4** a list of all the details of sth: *I would like a complete breakdown of how the money was spent.*

★**break·fast** /ˈbrɛkfəst/ ***noun*** [C,U] the meal that you have when you get up in the morning: *to have breakfast* ◇ *to eat a big breakfast*

ˈ**break-in** ***noun*** [C] the act of entering a building, car, computer system, etc. by force, especially in order to steal sth: *The police say there have been several break-ins in this area.*

**break·through** /ˈbreɪkθru/ ***noun*** [C] an important discovery or development: *a major breakthrough in cancer research* ◇ *The agreement represents a breakthrough in relations between the two countries.*

**break·up** /ˈbreɪkʌp/ ***noun*** [C] **1** the end of a relationship between two people: *the breakup of a marriage* **2** the separation of a group or organization into smaller parts: *the breakup of the Soviet Union* **3** (*also* (*especially Cdn*) ˌ**spring** ˈ**breakup**) the breaking of a frozen river, etc. into blocks of ice at the time when the weather gets warmer in spring:

*Everyone had their boats ready to launch after the spring breakup.*

★**breast** /brɛst/ ***noun*** [C] **1** one of the two soft round parts of a woman's body that can produce milk **2** (used especially in literature) the upper part of the front of your body: *to clasp sb to your breast* **3** the front part of the body of a bird

**breast·feed** /ˈbrɛstfid/ ***verb*** [I,T] (*pt, pp* **ˈbreast·fed** /ˈbrɛstfɛd/) to feed a baby with milk from the BREAST (1)

**breast·stroke** /ˈbrɛststroʊk; ˈbrɛstroʊk/ ***noun*** [U] a style of swimming on your front in which you start with your hands together, push both arms forward and then pull them outward and back through the water

★**breath** /brɛθ/ ***noun*** **1** [U] the air that you take into and blow out of your lungs: *to have bad breath* (= breath which smells unpleasant) **2** [C] an act of taking air into or blowing air out of your lungs: *Take a deep breath.*

IDM **a breath of fresh air** the clean air that you breathe outside, especially when compared to the air inside a room or building: *Let's go for a walk. I need a breath of fresh air.* ◇ (*figurative*) *Her happy face is like a breath of fresh air in that miserable place.*

**catch your breath** → CATCH[1]

**hold your breath** to stop breathing for a period of time, e.g. when swimming underwater or because of fear or excitement: *We all held our breath as we waited for her reply.*

**(be) out of/short of breath** to be breathing very quickly, e.g. after physical exercise

**say sth, speak, etc. under your breath** to say sth very quietly, usually because you do not want people to hear what you are saying

**take your breath away** to surprise sb very much: *The spectacular view took our breath away.* ➲ adjective breathtaking

**with bated breath** → BATED

**breath·a·lyze** /ˈbrɛθəlaɪz/ ***verb*** [T] (usually passive) to check how much alcohol a driver has drunk by making him/her breathe into a Breathalyzer: *Both drivers were breathalyzed at the scene of the accident.*

**Breath·a·lyz·er™** /ˈbrɛθəlaɪzər/ ***noun*** [C] a device used by the police to measure the amount of alcohol in a driver's breath

★**breathe** /brið/ ***verb*** [I,T] to take air, etc. into your lungs and blow it out again: *She was unconscious but still breathing.* ◇ *to breathe in/out* (= to take air in/to blow air out) ◇ *I hate sitting in bars breathing other people's cigarette smoke.*

IDM **not breathe a word (of/about sth) (to sb)** to not tell sb about sth that is secret: *If you breathe a word of this to my mother, I'll never speak to you again!*

▸ **breath·ing** /ˈbriðɪŋ/ ***noun*** [U]: *heavy/irregular breathing*

**breath·er** /ˈbriðər/ ***noun*** [C] (*informal*) a short rest: *to take a breather*

**breath·less** /ˈbrɛθləs/ ***adj.*** **1** breathing quickly or with difficulty, e.g. after physical exercise **2** not able to breathe because you are so excited, frightened, etc.: *to be breathless with excitement* ▸ **breath·less·ly** ***adv.***

**breath·tak·ing** /ˈbrɛθteɪkɪŋ/ ***adj.*** very exciting, beautiful, etc.: *breathtaking mountain scenery* ▸ **breath·tak·ing·ly** ***adv.***

★**breed[1]** /brid/ ***verb*** (*pt, pp* **bred** /brɛd/) **1** [I] (used about animals or plants) to produce young animals or plants: *Many animals won't breed in zoos.* **2** [T] to keep animals or plants in order to produce young from them: *cattle that are bred to produce high yields of milk* **3** [T] to cause sth: *This kind of thinking breeds intolerance and violence.*

**breed[2]** /brid/ ***noun*** [C] a type of animal: *a breed of cattle*

**breed·er** /ˈbridər/ ***noun*** [C] a person who BREEDS[1] (2) animals or plants: *a dog breeder*

**ˈbreed·ing ground** ***noun*** [C] **1** a place where wild animals go to BREED[1] (1) **2** a place where sth can develop: *a breeding ground for crime*

**breeze** /briz/ ***noun*** **1** [C] a light wind: *A warm breeze was blowing.* **2 a breeze** [C, sing.] something that is very easy to do: *If you study hard enough, the test should be a breeze.*

**breez·y** /ˈbrizi/ ***adj.*** (**breez·i·er**; **breez·i·est**) **1** a little windy **2** informal and cheerful: *a fashion magazine written in a breezy style*

**brev·i·ty** /ˈbrɛvət̬i/ ***noun*** [U] the state of being short or quick ➲ adjective **brief**

**brew[1]** /bru/ ***verb*** [T] **1** to make beer **2** to make tea or coffee by adding hot water: *to brew a pot of coffee*

IDM **be brewing** (used about sth bad) to develop or grow: *There's trouble brewing.*

**brew[2]** /bru/ ***noun*** [C,U] a drink that is made by brewing: *home brew* (= beer that is made at sb's home)

**brew·er·y** /ˈbruəri/ ***noun*** [C] (*pl.* **brew·er·ies**) a place where beer is made

**bribe** /braɪb/ ***noun*** [C] money, etc. that sb gives to another person, such as an official, to persuade him/her to do sth, especially sth dishonest: *to offer a bribe to sb* ◇ *to accept/take bribes* ▸ **bribe** ***verb*** [T] **bribe sb (with sth)**: *They got a visa by bribing an official.*

**brib·er·y** /ˈbraɪbəri/ ***noun*** [U] the giving or taking of bribes

**bric-a-brac** /ˈbrɪkəbræk/ ***noun*** [U] small objects of little value used for decoration: *second-hand stores selling cheap bric-a-brac*

★**brick** /brɪk/ ***noun*** [C,U] a hard block of baked clay that is used for building houses, etc.: *a house built of red brick* ◇ *a truck carrying a load of bricks*

**brick·lay·er** /ˈbrɪkˌleɪər/ ***noun*** [C] a person whose job is to build walls with bricks

**bri·dal** /ˈbraɪdl/ ***adj.*** (only *before* a noun) connected with a bride or a wedding: *the bridal suite in a hotel*

**ˈbridal ˌshower** ***noun*** [C] → SHOWER[1] (5)

**bride** /braɪd/ ***noun*** [C] a woman on or just before her wedding day: *the bride and groom* ➲ Look at the note at **wedding**.

B

**bride·groom** /ˈbraɪdgrum/ ***noun*** [C] (*formal*) = GROOM[1]

**brides·maid** /ˈbraɪdzmeɪd/ ***noun*** [C] a woman or girl who helps the bride at her wedding ➲ Look at the note at **wedding**.

★**bridge**[1] /brɪdʒ/ ***noun*** **1** [C] a structure that carries a road, railroad, etc. across a river, valley, road or railroad: *a bridge over the Mississippi River* **2** [C] the high part of a ship where the captain and the people who control the ship stand **3** [U] a card game for four people

**bridge**[2] /brɪdʒ/ ***verb*** [T] to build or form a bridge over sth

IDM **bridge a/the gap** to fill a space between two people, groups or things or to bring them closer together

**bri·dle** /ˈbraɪdl/ ***noun*** [C] the leather straps that you put over a horse's head so that you can control it when you are riding it ➲ picture at **horse**.

★**brief**[1] /brif/ ***adj.*** short or quick: *a brief phone call* ◇ *Please be brief. We don't have much time.* ➲ noun brevity

**brief**[2] /brif/ ***noun*** **1** [C] a short statement or document that gives information and that is often a summary of a longer document: *a news brief* ◇ *Each attorney must submit a brief before the trial.* **2 briefs** [pl.] a type of underpants

**brief**[3] /brif/ ***verb*** [T] to give sb information or instructions about sth: *The mayor has been fully briefed on what questions to expect.*

**brief·case** /ˈbrifkeɪs/ ***noun*** [C] a flat case that you use for carrying papers, etc., especially when you go to work ➲ picture at **luggage**.

**brief·ing** /ˈbrifɪŋ/ ***noun*** [C,U] instructions or information that you are given before sth happens: *a press/news briefing* (= where information is given to journalists)

★**brief·ly** /ˈbrifli/ ***adv.*** **1** for a short time; quickly: *We met briefly to discuss Marsha's report.* **2** using only a few words: *I'd like to comment very briefly on that last statement.*

**bri·gade** /brɪˈgeɪd/ ***noun*** [C] **1** a unit of soldiers in the army **2** a group of people who work together for a particular purpose

★**bright** /braɪt/ ***adj.*** **1** having a lot of light: *a bright, sunny day* ◇ *eyes bright with happiness* **2** (used about a color) strong: *a bright yellow sweater* **3** intelligent, or able to learn things quickly: *a bright idea* ◇ *a bright child* **4** likely to be pleasant or successful: *The future looks bright.* **5** cheerful, happy: *You seem very bright and cheerful today.* ▸ **bright·ly** ***adv.***: *brightly-colored clothes* ▸ **bright·ness** ***noun*** [U]

**bright·en** /ˈbraɪtn/ ***verb*** [I,T] **brighten (sth) (up)** to become brighter or happier; to make sth brighter: *His face brightened when he saw her.* ◇ *to brighten up sb's day* (= make it happier)

★**bril·liant** /ˈbrɪlyənt/ ***adj.*** **1** having a lot of light; very bright: *brilliant sunshine* **2** very intelligent; showing a lot of intelligence: *a brilliant young scientist* ◇ *That's a brilliant idea!* ▸ **bril·liance** /-yəns/ ***noun*** [U] ▸ **bril·liant·ly** ***adv.***

**brim**[1] /brɪm/ ***noun*** [C] **1** the top edge of a cup, glass, etc.: *The cup was filled to the brim.* **2** the bottom part of a hat, that is wider than the rest

**brim**[2] /brɪm/ ***verb*** [I] (**brim·ming**; **brimmed**) **brim (with sth)** to be full of sth: *His eyes were brimming with tears.*

**bring/take**

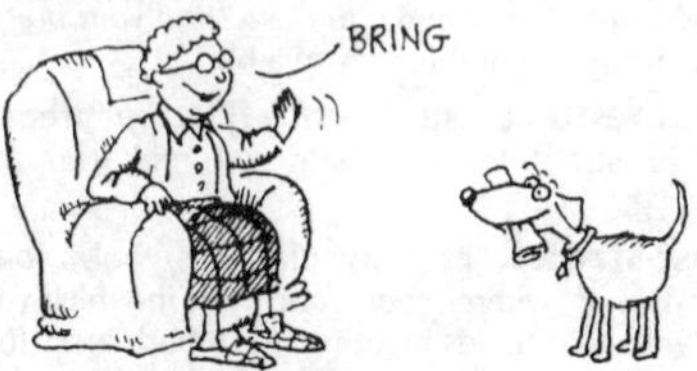

**"Bring me my newspaper!"**

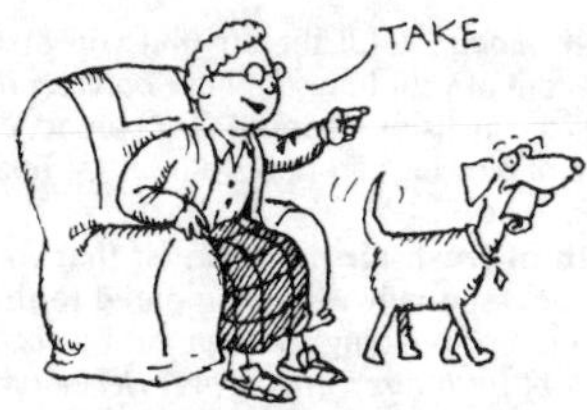

**"Take it into the kitchen!"**

★**bring** /brɪŋ/ ***verb*** [T] (*pt, pp* **brought** /brɔt/) **1** to come to a place with sb/sth: *The weather can be chilly here, so bring a jacket with you.* ◇ *Is it all right if I bring a friend to the party?* ◇ *Bring us two coffees, please.* ◇ (*figurative*) *He will bring valuable skills and experience to the team.* **2** to cause or result in sth: *The sight of her brought a smile to his face.* ◇ *Money doesn't always bring happiness.* **3** to cause sb/sth to be in a certain place or condition: *Their screams brought people running from all directions.* ◇ *Add water to the mixture and bring it to a boil.* ◇ *to bring sth to an end* **4** to force yourself to do sth: *The movie was so scary that I couldn't bring myself to watch it.*

PHR V **bring sth about** to cause sth to happen: *to bring about changes in people's lives*

**bring sb around** to cause sb to become conscious again

**bring sb/sth back** to return sb/sth: *You can borrow the video if you bring it back tomorrow morning.*

**bring sth back 1** to cause sth that existed before to be introduced again: *Nobody wants to bring back the days of child labor.* **2** to cause sb to remember sth: *The pictures brought back memories of his childhood.*

**bring sb sth back** to return with sth for sb: *My sister went to Spain on vacation and brought me back a T-shirt.*

**bring sb/sth down** to cause sb/sth to be defeated or to lose a position of power: *to bring down a government*

**bring sth down** to make sth lower in level: *to bring down the price of sth*

**bring sth forward** to suggest sth for discussion

**bring sb in** to ask or appoint sb to do a particular job: *A specialist was brought in to set up the new computer system.*

**bring sth in 1** to introduce sth: *Congress has brought in a new law on air bags in cars.* **2** to obtain or earn something valuable or important: *He wasn't a very warm father, but he brought money in every week.* ◇ *The firm is happy with the new associate; she's bringing in lots of new clients.* **3** to give a decision in a court of law: *The jury brought in a verdict of guilty.*

**bring sth on** to cause sth: *Her headaches are brought on by stress.*

**bring sth out** to produce sth or cause sth to appear: *When is the company bringing out its next new model?* ◇ *A crisis can sometimes bring out the best in people.*

**bring sb up** to take care of a child until he/she is an adult and to teach him/her how to behave: *After her parents were killed the child was brought up by her uncle.*

**bring sth up** to introduce sth into a discussion or conversation: *I intend to bring the matter up at the next meeting.*

**brink** /brɪŋk/ ***noun*** [sing.] the edge at the top of a high place: (*figurative*) *The new president brought the company back from the brink of disaster.*

IDM **be on the brink (of sth/of doing sth)** to be about to do or experience sth exciting or dangerous

**brisk** /brɪsk/ ***adj.*** **1** quick or using a lot of energy; busy: *They set off at a brisk pace.* **2** (used about wind and the weather) cold but pleasantly fresh: *a brisk wind* ▸ **brisk·ly** ***adv.***

**bris·tle¹** /ˈbrɪsl/ ***noun*** [C] **1** a short thick hair on an animal **2** one of the short thick hairs of a brush

**bris·tle²** /ˈbrɪsl/ ***verb*** [I] **1** (used about hair or an animal's fur) to stand up straight because of fear, anger, cold, etc. **2 bristle (with sth)** to show that you are angry **3 bristle (at sth)** to react (to sth) in an angry way: *The politician bristled at suggestions that he had accepted bribes.*

**brit·tle** /ˈbrɪt̬l/ ***adj.*** hard but easily broken: *brittle fingernails*

**broach** /broʊtʃ/ ***verb*** [T] to start talking about a particular subject, especially one which is difficult or embarrassing: *Have you broached the subject of the money he owes us?*

★**broad** /brɔd/ ***adj.*** **1** large in size from one side to the other; wide: *a broad river valley*

> NOTE **Wide** is more often used than **broad** when you are talking about the distance between one side of something and the other: *The gate is four yards wide.* ◇ *The table is too wide to go through the door.* **Broad** is often used about geographical features: *a broad expanse of desert* and in particular phrases such as: *broad shoulders.* ➲ noun **breadth** OPP **narrow**

**2** without a lot of detail; general: *Just give me a broad outline of your plan.* **3** felt or believed by a lot of people: *There seems to be broad support for stronger anti-pollution laws.*

IDM **in broad daylight** during the day, i.e. not at night: *He was attacked in broad daylight.*

**broad·band** /ˈbrɔdbænd/ ***noun*** [U] a communications system that allows large amounts of information for several different purposes to pass through a single cable at the same time, for example telephone and Internet access ▸ **broad·band** ***adj.***

★**broad·cast¹** /ˈbrɔdkæst/ ***verb*** (*pt, pp* **broad·cast**) [I,T] to send out radio or television programs: *The local radio station broadcasts 24 hours a day.* ◇ *The Olympics are broadcast live via satellite.*

**broad·cast²** /ˈbrɔdkæst/ ***noun*** [C] something that is sent out by radio or television: *a news broadcast*

**broad·cast·er** /ˈbrɔdkæstər/ ***noun*** [C] **1** a person who speaks on serious subjects on the radio or on television **2** a radio or television station

**broad·en** /ˈbrɔdn/ ***verb*** [I,T] to become broader; to make sth broader: *The river broadens beyond the bridge.* ◇ (*figurative*) *Travel* ***broadens the mind*** (= it makes you understand other people better).

**broad·ly** /ˈbrɔdli/ ***adv.*** **1** (used to describe a way of smiling): *to* ***smile broadly*** (= to have a very big, wide smile) **2** generally: *Broadly speaking, the plan will work as follows...*

**broc·co·li** /ˈbrɑkəli/ ***noun*** [U] a plant with dark green flower heads that can be cooked and eaten as a vegetable ➲ picture on study page **A28-29**.

**bro·chure** /broʊˈʃʊr/ ***noun*** [C] a thin book with pictures in it that gives you information about sth: *a travel brochure*

**broil** /brɔɪl/ ***verb*** **1** [T] to cook sth under a heat source in an oven, or on a system of metal bars (a grill) over flames: *broiled salmon* ➲ Look at the note at **cook**. **2** [I,T] to become or to make sth very hot: *I'm broiling in this heavy coat!*

**broil·er** /ˈbrɔɪlər/ ***noun*** [C] a device in an oven that cooks food with heat from above: *Put the fish under the broiler for eight minutes.*

**broke¹** *past tense of* BREAK¹

**broke²** /broʊk/ ***adj.*** (not before a noun) (*informal*) having no money: *I can't go out tonight. I'm completely broke.*

**bro·ken¹** *past participle of* BREAK¹

**bro·ken²** /ˈbroʊkən/ ***adj.***

➤ DAMAGED **1** damaged or in pieces; not working: *Watch out! There's broken glass on the floor.* ◇ *The washing machine's broken.* ➲ picture at **chip²**.

➤ NOT CONTINUOUS **2** not continuous; interrupted: *a broken line*

➤ PROMISE/AGREEMENT **3** not kept: *a broken promise*

➤ LANGUAGE **4** (used about a foreign language) spoken slowly with a lot of mistakes: *to speak in broken English*

➤ RELATIONSHIP **5** (used about a family or a home) no longer together: *Many of the kids come from broken homes.* **6** (used about a relationship, etc.) that has ended because the people no longer want to stay together: *a broken marriage*

ˌ**broken-ˈdown** ***adj.*** in a very bad condition: *a broken-down old pickup truck*

**bro·ker** /ˈbroʊkər/ ***noun*** [C] **1** a person who arranges the buying and selling of things such as property, insurance, etc. for other people: *an insurance broker* **2** = STOCKBROKER

**bron·chi·tis** /brɑŋˈkaɪt̬əs/ ***noun*** [U] an illness of the tiny tubes in the lungs, that causes a very bad cough

**bron·co** /ˈbrɑŋkoʊ/ ***noun*** [C] (*pl.* **bron·cos**) a wild horse of the western U.S: *a bucking bronco in the rodeo*

B

**bronze** /brɑnz/ *noun* **1** [U] a brown-colored metal that is made from a combination of a red-colored metal (copper) and a silver-colored metal (tin) **2** [U] the color of BRONZE (1) **3** [C] = BRONZE MEDAL ▸ **bronze** *adj.*

ˌ**bronze ˈmedal** *noun* [C] a round piece of bronze that you get as a prize for coming third in a race or a competition ➲ Look at **gold medal** and **silver medal**.

**brood¹** /brud/ *noun* [C] all the young birds that belong to one mother

**brood²** /brud/ *verb* [I] **brood (about/over sth)** to worry, or to think a lot about sth that makes you sad: *to brood over a failure*

**brook** /brʊk/ *noun* [C] a small stream

**broom** /brum/ *noun* [C] a brush with a long handle that you use for sweeping the floor ➲ picture at **brush¹**.

**broom·stick** /ˈbrumstɪk/ *noun* [C] the handle of a broom. In stories witches sometimes fly on broomsticks.

**broth** /brɔθ/ *noun* [U] thin soup: *chicken broth*

**broth·el** /ˈbrɑθl; ˈbrɔθl/ *noun* [C] a place where men can go and pay to have sex

★**broth·er** /ˈbrʌðər/ *noun* [C] **1** a man or boy who has the same parents as another person: *Michael and Jim are brothers.* ◇ *Michael is Jim's brother.* ◇ *a younger/an older brother* ➲ Look at **half-brother** and **stepbrother**.

NOTE Notice that there is not a common English word that means "both brothers and sisters": *Do you have any brothers and sisters?* The word **sibling** is very formal.

**2** a man who is a member of a Christian religious community (a **monastery**): *Brother John* **3** (*informal*) a boy or man who is your friend or who is from the same social class, race, etc. as you

**broth·er·hood** /ˈbrʌðərhʊd/ *noun* **1** [U] a feeling of great friendship and loyalty between people: *the brotherhood of all humans* (= a feeling of friendship among all the people in the world) **2** [C] an organization that is formed for a particular, usually religious, purpose

ˈ**brother-in-ˌlaw** *noun* [C] (*pl.* ˈ**brothers-in-ˌlaw**) **1** the brother of your husband or wife **2** the husband of your sister

**broth·er·ly** /ˈbrʌðərli/ *adj.* of or like a brother: *brotherly love*

**brought** *past tense, past participle of* BRING

**brow** /braʊ/ *noun* [C] **1** [usually pl.] = EYEBROW **2** (*formal*) = FOREHEAD: *Sweat was pouring from his brow.*

★**brown¹** /braʊn/ *adj.* having the color of soil or wood: *brown shoes* ◇ *dark brown hair*

★**brown²** /braʊn/ *noun* [C,U] the color of soil or wood: *the yellows and browns of the trees in the fall* ◇ *You don't look nice in brown* (= in brown clothes).

**brown³** /braʊn/ *verb* [I,T] to become or cause sth to become brown: *Heat some oil and brown the chicken on both sides.*

**brown·ie** /ˈbraʊni/ *noun* [C] **1** a type of small, heavy chocolate cake that often contains nuts **2 Brownie** a young girl who is a member of the junior branch of the Girl Scouts organization in the U.S. or the Girl Guides organization in Canada

ˈ**brownie point** *noun* [usually pl.] (*informal*) if you do sth to earn brownie points you do it to make sb in authority have a good opinion of you: *The kids were trying to **score** as many **brownie points** as they could before their dad got home.*

**brown·ish** /ˈbraʊnɪʃ/ *adj.* slightly or fairly brown: *She has brownish eyes.*

**brown·stone** /ˈbraʊnstoʊn/ *noun* [C,U] a type of brown-colored stone that is used to make buildings; a house that is made of this type of stone, especially in the eastern U.S: *We live in a three-story brownstone.*

**browse** /braʊz/ *verb* [I] **1** to spend time pleasantly, looking around a store, without a clear idea of what you are looking for: *I spent hours browsing in the local bookstore.* **2 browse through sth** to look through a book or magazine without reading every part or studying it carefully: *I enjoyed browsing through the catalogue, but I didn't order anything.*

**brows·er** /ˈbraʊzər/ *noun* [C] a computer program that lets you look at words and pictures that you choose from other computer systems by receiving information through telephone wires: *an Internet browser*

**bruise¹** /bruz/ *noun* [C] a dark mark on the skin caused by a blow that injures but does not break the skin: *He didn't break any bones, but he suffered cuts and bruises on his face.* SYN A bruise on your eye is a **black eye**.

**bruise²** /bruz/ *verb* **1** [T] to cause a bruise or bruises: *I fell down and bruised my knee.* ◇ *She had a badly bruised face.* **2** [I] to get a bruise or bruises: *I have the sort of skin that bruises easily.*

**brunch** /brʌntʃ/ *noun* [C,U] a late morning meal that is eaten instead of breakfast and lunch: *The hotel serves Sunday brunch from 10:00 to 12:00.*

**brunt** /brʌnt/ *noun*

IDM **bear/take the brunt of sth** to suffer the main force of sth: *The West Coast bore the brunt of the storm.*

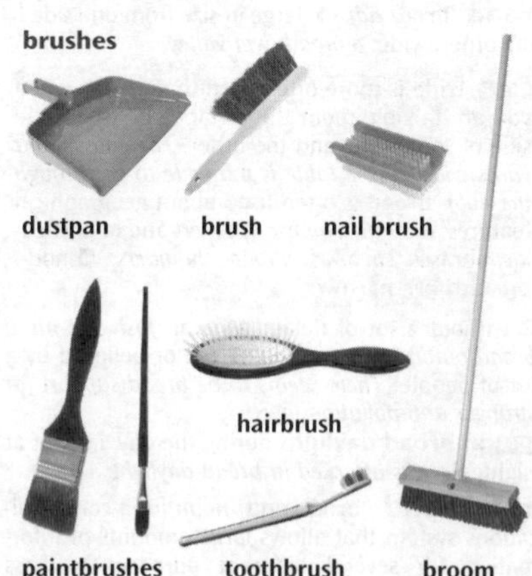


★**brush¹** /brʌʃ/ *noun* **1** [C] an object that is used for cleaning things, painting, arranging your hair, etc.: *I scrubbed the kitchen floor with a brush.* ◇ *a toothbrush* ◇ *a paintbrush* ◇ *a hairbrush* **2** [sing.] an act of sweeping, cleaning, etc. with a brush or with your hand: *Give your coat a quick brush.* **3** [U] a thick covering of bushes and small trees; land that is covered in bushes and small trees: *brush fires*

IDM **a brush with sth** an unexpected and often unpleasant meeting or association with sth: *a brush with death* ◇ *This isn't Jill's first brush with the law – she's been arrested before.*

★**brush**[2] /brʌʃ/ *verb* **1** [T] to clean, sweep, etc. with a brush: *Make sure you brush your teeth twice a day.* ◇ *She was brushing her hair in front of a mirror.* ➲ Look at the note at **clean**[2]. **2** [I,T] to touch sb/sth lightly when passing: *Her hand brushed his cheek.* ◇ *Leaves brushed against the car as we drove along the narrow road.*

PHRV **brush sb/sth aside 1** to refuse to pay attention to sb/sth: *She brushed aside the protests and continued with the meeting.* **2** to get past sb/sth: *He hurried along, brushing aside the reporters who tried to stop him.*

**brush sth away**; **brush sth off (sth)** to remove sth with a brush or with the hand, as if using a brush: *I brushed the dust off my jacket.*

**brush sth up/brush up on sth** to study or practice sth in order to get back knowledge or skill that you had before and have lost: *She took a course to brush up (on) her Spanish.*

**Brussels sprout** /ˈbrʌsl spraʊt/ *noun* [C, usually pl.] a green vegetable that looks like a very small cabbage ➲ picture on study page **A28-29**.

**bru·tal** /ˈbrut̬l/ *adj.* very cruel and violent: *a brutal murder* ◇ *a brutal dictatorship* ▸ **bru·tal·ly** *adv.*: *The girl had been brutally attacked.* ◇ *He was brutally honest and told her that he didn't love her anymore.*

**bru·tal·i·ty** /bruˈtæləṭi/ *noun* [C,U] (*pl.* **bru·tal·i·ties**) very cruel and violent behavior: *complaints of police brutality*

**B.S.** /ˌbi ˈɛs/ *abbr.* Bachelor of Science; a degree that you receive when you complete a program of study at a college or university ➲ Compare **B.A.**

**BS** (*also* **bs**) /ˌbi ˈɛs/ *abbr.* (*taboo, slang*) = BULLSHIT[1]: *He's full of BS.*

**BTW** (*also* **btw**) *abbr.* (*informal*) used in writing, especially e-mails and text messages, to mean "by the way"

**bubbles**

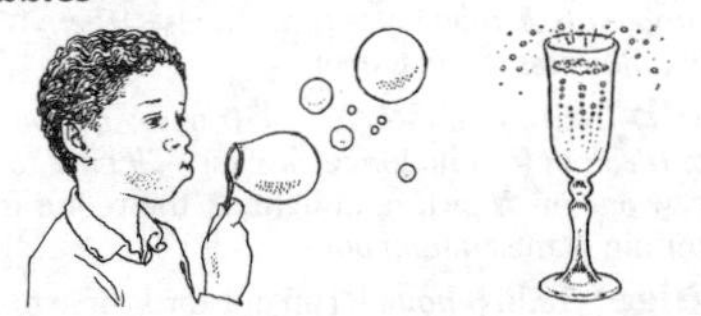

★**bub·ble**[1] /ˈbʌbl/ *noun* [C] a hollow ball containing air or gas, in liquid or floating in the air: *The kids were blowing soap bubbles.*

**bub·ble**[2] /ˈbʌbl/ *verb* [I] to produce BUBBLES[1] or to rise with bubbles: *Bake the pizza until the cheese starts to bubble.* ◇ *The clear water bubbled up out of the ground.*

ˈ**bubble bath** *noun* **1** [U] a liquid soap that smells pleasant and makes a lot of bubbles when it is added to bath water **2** [C] a bath with bubble bath in the water

ˈ**bubble gum** *noun* [U] chewing gum that can be blown into BUBBLES[1] out of the mouth

**bub·bly** /ˈbʌbli/ *adj.* **1** full of BUBBLES[1]: *a bubbly drink* **2** (used about a person) lively and happy: *She has a naturally bubbly personality.*

**buck**[1] /bʌk/ *noun* [C] **1** (*informal*) a dollar: *Could you loan me a few bucks?* ◇ *I paid 50 bucks for that thing!* **2** (*pl.* **buck** or **bucks**) a male deer ➲ Look at the note at **deer**. ➲ picture at **deer**.

IDM **pass the buck** → PASS[2]

**buck**[2] /bʌk/ *verb* **1** [I,T] (used about a horse) to jump into the air with all four feet off the ground, and sometimes throw a rider to the ground: *Wayne's horse suddenly bucked him off.* ◇ *a bucking bronco* **2** [T] to resist or oppose sb/sth: *Sales in the city bucked the national downward trend, rising by 5%.*

**buck·et** /ˈbʌkət/ (*also* **pail**) *noun* [C] **1** a round, open container, usually made of metal or plastic, with a handle, that is used for carrying or holding liquids or sand **2** the amount that a BUCKET (1) contains: *How many buckets of cement do you think we'll need?*

**bucket**

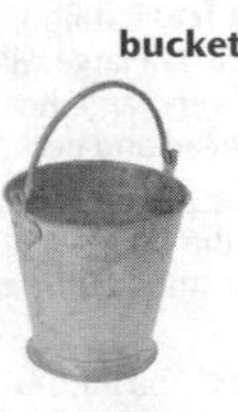

**buck·le**[1] /ˈbʌkl/ *noun* [C] a piece of metal or plastic at the end of a belt or strap that is used for fastening it

**buck·le**[2] /ˈbʌkl/ *verb* [I,T] **1** to fasten or be fastened with a buckle **2** to bend because of heat, force, weakness, etc.: *Some train tracks buckled in the heat.*

PHRV **buckle up** to fasten your seat belt in a car or in an airplane: *I want everyone to buckle up before I start the car.*

ˌ**buck** ˈ**naked** *adj.* (*informal*) (of a person) not wearing any clothes at all

**bud** /bʌd/ *noun* [C] **1** a small lump on a tree or plant that opens and develops into a flower or leaf: *rosebuds* ➲ picture at **tree**. **2** (*informal*) = BUDDY

IDM **nip sth in the bud** → NIP

**Bud·dhism** /ˈbudɪzəm; ˈbʊd-/ *noun* [U] an Asian religion that was founded in India by Buddha

**Bud·dhist** /ˈbudɪst; ˈbʊd-/ *noun* [C] a person whose religion is Buddhism ▸ **Bud·dhist** *adj.*: *a Buddhist temple*

**bud·ding** /ˈbʌdɪŋ/ *adj.* wanting or starting to develop and be successful: *Do you have any tips for budding young photographers?*

**bud·dy** /ˈbʌdi/ (*also* **bud**) *noun* [C] (*pl.* **bud·dies**) (*informal*) **1** a friend, especially a male friend **2** used to speak to a man you do not know: *"Where to, buddy?" the driver asked.*

**budge** /bʌdʒ/ *verb* [I,T] **1** to move or cause sth to move a little: *I tried to loosen the screw, but it just wouldn't budge.* ◇ *We couldn't budge the car when it got stuck in the mud.* **2** to change or cause sb to change a firm opinion: *Neither side in the dispute is* *prepared to budge.* ◇ *Once he's made up his mind, nothing will budge him.*

★**budg·et[1]** /ˈbʌdʒət/ ***noun*** [C] a plan of how to spend an amount of money over a particular period of time; the amount of money that is mentioned: *What's your monthly budget for food?* ◇ *the country's defense budget* ◇ *an advertising budget of $2 million* ◇ *to balance a budget* (= to make the money that goes out of the budget equal to the money that comes in)

**budg·et[2]** /ˈbʌdʒət/ ***verb*** [I,T] **budget (sth) (for sth)** to plan carefully how much money to spend on sth: *Don't forget to budget for possible increased costs.* ◇ *Costs for the new building are already far greater than the $10 million originally budgeted.*

**budg·et[3]** /ˈbʌdʒət/ ***adj.*** (only before a noun) very cheap: *a budget meal*

**buff** /bʌf/ ***noun*** [C] (*informal*) a person who knows a lot about a particular subject and is very interested in it: *a history/movie buff*

**buf·fa·lo** /ˈbʌfəloʊ/ ***noun*** [C] (*pl.* **buf·fa·lo** or **buf·fa·loes**) **1** a large wild animal that looks like a cow with a very large head, curved horns and thick fur on its head and neck: *a herd of buffalo* **2** = BISON

**buff·er** /ˈbʌfər/ ***noun*** [C] a thing or person that reduces the unpleasant effects of sth or that protects against sth: *a buffer zone between the two sides in a battle*

**buf·fet[1]** /bəˈfeɪ; bʊ-/ ***noun*** [C] **1** a long table in a restaurant, etc. with food on it, from which people serve themselves: *There are several kinds of pasta on the buffet.* **2** a meal (usually at a party or a special occasion) at which food is placed on a long table and people serve themselves: *a buffet lunch*

**buf·fet[2]** /ˈbʌfət/ ***verb*** [T] to knock or push sth in a rough way from side to side: *The boat was buffeted by the rough waves.*

**bug[1]** /bʌg/ ***noun*** [C] **1** a small insect **2** an illness that is not very serious and that people get from each other: *I don't feel very well – I think I've got the bug that's going around.* **3** something wrong in a system or machine, especially a computer: *There's a bug in the software.* **4** a tiny hidden microphone that secretly records people's conversations

**bug[2]** /bʌg/ ***verb*** [T] (**bug·ging**; **bugged**) **1** (*informal*) to annoy or worry sb: *You look like something's bugging you. What's wrong?* **2** to hide a tiny microphone somewhere so that people's conversations can be recorded secretly: *Be careful what you say. This room is bugged.*

IDM **bug off!** (*informal*) (a rude way to tell sb to go away)

**bug·gy** /ˈbʌgi/ ***noun*** [C] (*pl.* **bug·gies**) a type of old-fashioned vehicle without an engine, that is pulled by a horse: *a horse-drawn buggy*

★**build[1]** /bɪld/ ***verb*** (*pt, pp* **built** /bɪlt/) **1** [T] to make sth by putting pieces, materials, etc. together: *They built a new bridge across the river.* ◇ *The house is built of wood.* **2** [I] to put new buildings in a place: *There's plenty of land to build on around here.* **3** [T] to develop or increase sth: *We're trying to build a safer community for our children.* ◇ *This book claims to help people to build their self-confidence.*

PHR V **build sth in**; **build sth into sth** to make sth a part of sth else: *A large number of safety features are built into the system.* ➲ Look also at **built-in**.

**build on sth** to use sth as a base from which you can make further progress: *Now that we're beginning to make a profit, we should build on this success.*

**build sth on sth** to base sth on sth: *a society built on the principles of freedom and democracy*

**build up** to become greater in amount or number; to increase: *The traffic starts to build up at this time of day.*

**build sth up 1** to make sth seem more important or greater than it really is: *I don't think it's a very serious matter – it's just been built up in the newspapers.* **2** to increase or develop sth over a period: *You'll need to build up your strength again after the operation.*

**build[2]** /bɪld/ ***noun*** [C,U] the shape and size of sb's body: *She has a very athletic build.* ◇ *Police are looking for a young man of slim build.*

NOTE Compare **build** and **figure**. **Build** usually describes size in connection with strength and muscle and is used for both men and women. **Figure** usually describes shape, especially whether it is attractive or not, and is usually used only for women.

**build·er** /ˈbɪldər/ ***noun*** [C] **1** a company or person that builds sth, usually houses and other buildings: *a master builder* **2** (in compounds) a computer program, a book, etc. which helps you to build, create, or develop sth: *a résumé/vocabulary builder*

★**build·ing** /ˈbɪldɪŋ/ ***noun*** **1** [C] a structure, such as a house, church or school, that has a roof and walls: *There are a lot of very old buildings in this town.* **2** [U] the process or business of making BUILDINGS (1): *building materials* ◇ *the building industry*

**build·up** /ˈbɪldʌp/ ***noun*** [C, usually sing.] **1 a buildup (of sth)** an increase of sth over a period: *The buildup of tension in the area has made war seem more likely.* **2 a buildup (to sth)** a period of preparation or excitement before an event: *The players started to get nervous in the buildup to the big game.*

**built** *past tense, past participle of* BUILD[1]

**-built** /bɪlt/ ***combining form*** having a body with a particular shape and size: *a tall well-built man*

ˌ**built-ˈin** ***adj.*** **1** (used about furniture) built so it is fastened to a wall and cannot be moved: *built-in cupboards* **2** made a part of sth else: *There is built-in unfairness in the system.*

**bulb** /bʌlb/ ***noun*** [C] **1** = LIGHT BULB: *The bulb just burned out* (= it no longer works) – *I'll have to put a new one in.* ➲ picture at **light**. **2** the round root of certain plants: *a tulip bulb*

**bulge[1]** /bʌldʒ/ ***noun*** [C] an outward curve or lump on sth that is usually flat

**bulge[2]** /bʌldʒ/ ***verb*** [I] **1** to stick out from sth that is usually flat; to swell outward: *My stomach is starting to bulge. I ought to get more exercise.* **2 bulge with sth** to be full of sth: *His bags were bulging with presents for the kids.*

**bulg·ing** /ˈbʌldʒɪŋ/ ***adj.*** **1** sticking out: *He had a* *thin face and bulging eyes.* **2** very full: *She came home with bulging grocery bags.*

**bulk** /bʌlk/ ***noun*** **1** [U] the large size or amount of sth: *The dresser isn't especially heavy – it's its bulk that makes it hard to move.* **2** [C] a very large body: *He slowly lifted his vast bulk out of the chair.* **3** **the bulk (of sth)** [sing.] the main part of sth; most of sth: *The bulk of the work has been done – there's only a little left.*

IDM **in bulk** in large quantities: *If you buy in bulk, it is 10% cheaper.*

**bulk·y** /ˈbʌlki/ ***adj.*** (**bulk·i·er**; **bulk·i·est**) large and heavy and therefore difficult to move or carry: *a bulky package*

**bull** /bʊl/ ***noun*** [C] **1** an adult male of the cow family ➲ Look at the note at **cow**. ➲ picture at **cow**. **2** the male of certain other animals, e.g. the elephant and the whale

**bull·dog** /ˈbʊldɔg/ ***noun*** [C] a strong dog with short legs, a large head and a short, thick neck

**bull·doze** /ˈbʊldoʊz/ ***verb*** [T] to make ground flat or knock down a building with a bulldozer: *The old buildings were bulldozed and new ones were built.*

**bull·doz·er** /ˈbʊldoʊzər/ ***noun*** [C] a large, powerful tractor with a wide piece of metal at the front, used for clearing ground or knocking down buildings

★**bul·let** /ˈbʊlət/ ***noun*** [C] a small piece of metal with a pointed end that is shot from a gun: *The bullet hit her in the arm.* ◇ *a bullet wound*

IDM **bite the bullet** → BITE[1]

**bul·le·tin** /ˈbʊlətn/ ***noun*** [C] **1** a short news report on TV or radio; an official statement about a situation: *a news bulletin* **2** a short newspaper that an organization produces: *the monthly church bulletin*

ˈ**bulletin board** ***noun*** [C] a board on a wall for putting papers, signs, etc. on

**bul·let·proof** /ˈbʊlətpruf/ ***adj.*** made of a strong material that stops bullets from passing through it: *Police officers wear bulletproof vests.*

**bull·fight** /ˈbʊlfaɪt/ ***noun*** [C] a traditional public entertainment, especially in Spain, Portugal and Latin America, in which bulls are fought and usually killed ▸ **bull·fight·er** /ˈbʊlfaɪţər/ ***noun*** [C] ▸ **bull·fight·ing** /ˈbʊlfaɪţɪŋ/ ***noun*** [U]

**bul·lion** /ˈbʊlyən/ ***noun*** [U] bars of gold or silver: *The price of gold bullion has risen by more than 10%.*

ˌ**bull ˈmarket** ***noun*** [C] a period during which people are buying SHARES[1] (2) because share prices are rising ➲ Compare **bear market**.

**bull's-eye** (*also* **bullseye**) /ˈbʊlzaɪ/ ***noun*** [C] **1** the center of a target that you aim at when you are shooting or throwing sth ➲ picture at **dart**. **2** a shot that hits this target

**bull·shit**[1] /ˈbʊlʃɪt/ (*also* **bull**) (*abbr.* **BS**) ***noun*** [U] (*taboo, slang*) nonsense: *That's bullshit! I don't believe a word of it.*

**bull·shit**[2] /ˈbʊlʃɪt/ ***verb*** [I,T] (*pres. part.* **bull·shit·ting**; *pt, pp* **bull·shit·ted**) to lie or to say sth in a way that is not serious, especially in order to deceive sb: *She's just bullshitting.* ◇ *Don't try to bullshit me!* ▸ **bull·shit·ter** ***noun*** [C]

**bul·ly**[1] /ˈbʊli/ ***noun*** [C] (*pl.* **bul·lies**) a person who uses his/her greater strength or power to hurt or frighten people who are weaker

**bul·ly**[2] /ˈbʊli/ ***verb*** [I,T] (*pres. part.* **bul·ly·ing**; *3rd person sing. pres.* **bul·lies**; *pt, pp* **bul·lied**) to use your strength or power to hurt or frighten sb who is weaker: *Tony was bullied a lot in school because he was small.*

PHR V **bully sb into doing sth** to force sb to do sth by frightening him/her

**bum**[1] /bʌm/ ***noun*** [C] (*informal*) **1** a person who has no home and lives by begging ➲ A more polite expression is **a homeless person**. **2** a lazy or useless person **3** (in compounds) a person who spends all of his/her time on a certain activity, instead of on serious work: *a beach bum* ◇ *a ski bum*

**bum**[2] /bʌm/ ***verb*** [T] (*pres. part.* **bum·ming**; *pt, pp* **bummed**) **bum sth (off sb)** (*informal*) to get sth from sb by begging: *It's too late to catch a bus – we'll have to bum a ride home.* ◇ *Can I bum a cigarette off you?*

PHR V **bum around** (*informal*) to travel around or to spend your time doing nothing in particular: *We spent the summer bumming around (in) Europe.*

**bum sb out** (*slang*) to make sb feel very disappointed: *It really bums me out when that happens!*

**bum·mer** /ˈbʌmər/ ***noun*** [C] (*slang*) a disappointing situation: *What a bummer! I couldn't get tickets to the concert.*

**bump**[1] /bʌmp/ ***verb*** **1** [I] **bump against/into sb/sth** to hit sth solid by accident when you are moving: *She bumped into a lamppost because she wasn't looking where she was going.* **2** [T] **bump sth (against/on sth)** to hit sth against or on sth by accident when moving it: *I bumped my knee on the edge of the table.* **3** [I] to move in an uneven way as if going over bumps: *We bumped along the gravel road.*

PHR V **bump into sb** to meet sb by chance: *I bumped into a old friend today.*

**bump**[2] /bʌmp/ ***noun*** [C] **1** a sudden strong blow caused by sth hard hitting sth else; the sound of such a blow: *She fell and hit the ground with a bump.* ◇ *We heard a loud bump from upstairs.* **2** a lump on the body, often caused by a blow **3** a part of a flat surface that is raised above the rest of it: *There are a lot of bumps in the road, so drive carefully.*

**bump·er**[1] /ˈbʌmpər/ ***noun*** [C] the bar fastened to the front and back of a car, etc. to reduce the effect if it hits sth

**bump·er**[2] /ˈbʌmpər/ ***adj.*** larger than usual: *The unusually good weather has produced a bumper crop this year.*

ˈ**bumper** ˌ**sticker** ***noun*** [C] a small sign with a message on it, usually a political opinion or a joke, which people stick on the back of their cars: *That car must be old; it has a bumper sticker that says "Vote for Reagan!"*

**bump·y** /ˈbʌmpi/ ***adj.*** (**bump·i·er**; **bump·i·est**) **1** (used about a surface) having a lot of BUMPS[2] (3): *a bumpy road* **2** (used about a trip) rough and uncomfortable; not smooth: *Because of the stormy weather, it was a very bumpy flight.*

**bun** /bʌn/ ***noun*** [C] **1** a small bread roll: *a hamburger/hot dog bun* ➲ picture at **bread**. **2** hair

B

fastened tightly into a round shape at the back of the head: *She wears her hair in a bun.* ➲ picture at **braid**. **3** (*informal*) one of the two parts of the body which you sit on: *If you go out dressed like that you'll freeze your buns off!*

★**bunch¹** /bʌntʃ/ ***noun*** [C] **1** a number of things, usually of the same type, fastened or growing together: *a bunch of flowers* ◇ *a bunch of bananas* ◇ *a bunch of keys* **2** [with sing. or pl. verb] (*informal*) a large group of people or things; a large amount of sth: *A whole bunch of us went out for pizza after work.* ◇ *I have a bunch of work to do today.*

NOTE We usually use **bunch** with a singular verb when we are thinking of the whole group together: *That bunch of bananas is too green to eat.* But if we use a phrase like *a bunch of...* with a plural noun or pronoun, we usually use a plural verb: *A bunch of my friends are going to the movies tonight.*

**bunch²** /bʌntʃ/ ***verb*** [I,T] **bunch (sth/sb) (up/together)** to stay together in a group; to form sth into a group or bunch: *The runners bunched up as they came around the final bend.* ◇ *He kept his papers bunched together in his hand.*

**bun·dle¹** /ˈbʌndl/ ***noun*** [C] a number of things tied or wrapped together: *a bundle of letters with a rubber band around them*

**bun·dle²** /ˈbʌndl/ ***verb*** **1** [T] **bundle sth (up)** to make or tie sth into a bundle or bundles: *I bundled up the old newspapers and threw them away.* **2** [I,T] **bundle (sb) (up)** to dress warmly: *It's cold outside – be sure to bundle up.* **3** [T] to put or push sb or sth quickly and in a rough way in a particular direction: *He was arrested and bundled into a police car.*

**bun·ga·low** /ˈbʌŋgəloʊ/ ***noun*** [C] a type of house that is usually small and square, with a covered platform (**porch**) in front

**bun·gee** /ˈbʌndʒi/ (*also* **ˈbungee ˌcord**) ***noun*** [C] a thick elastic rope with hooks at each end that you can use to hold a package, box, etc. together

**ˈbungee ˌjumping** ***noun*** [U] a sport in which you jump from a high place, e.g. a bridge, with a thick elastic rope tied around your feet

**bun·gle** /ˈbʌŋgl/ ***verb*** [I,T] to do sth badly: *The men fled after bungling a bank robbery.*

**bunk** /bʌŋk/ ***noun*** [C] **1** a bed that is fastened to a wall (e.g. on a ship or in a prison) **2** one of a pair of narrow beds built as a unit with one above the other: *I sleep in the top bunk and my brother sleeps in the bottom one.*

**ˈbunk bed** ***noun*** [C, usually pl.] a pair of narrow beds built as a unit with one above the other

**bun·ker** /ˈbʌŋkər/ ***noun*** [C] **1** a strongly built underground shelter that gives protection in a war **2** an area of sand on a golf course, where it is difficult to hit the ball

**bun·ny** /ˈbʌni/ ***noun*** [C] (*pl.* **bun·nies**) (used by and to children) a rabbit: *Small children believe that the Easter bunny brings them candy on Easter morning.*

**buoy¹** /ˈbui; bɔɪ/ ***noun*** [C] a floating object, fastened to the bottom of the ocean or a river, that shows ships and boats where dangerous places are

**buoy²** /ˈbui; bɔɪ/ ***verb*** [T] **1 buoy sb (up)** to keep sb cheerful: *His encouragement buoyed her up during that difficult period.* **2 buoy sth (up)** to keep sth high by supporting it: *Stock prices were buoyed by news of a takeover.*

**buoy·ant** /ˈbɔɪənt/ ***adj.*** **1** (used about a material) floating or able to float **2** (used about economic and business life) successful, with a lot of activity: *Despite the recession, the real estate market remained buoyant.* **3** (used about prices) rising or keeping at a high level **4** happy and cheerful: *The team was in a buoyant mood after their win.* ▶ **buoy·an·cy** /-ənsi/ ***noun*** [U]: *the buoyancy of the economy*

★**bur·den¹** /ˈbərdn/ ***noun*** [C] **1** a heavy load that is difficult to carry **2** a responsibility or difficult task that causes a lot of work or worry: *Having to make all the decisions is a terrible burden for me.* ◇ *I don't want to be a burden on my kids when I'm old.*

**bur·den²** /ˈbərdn/ ***verb*** [T] **burden sb/yourself (with sth)** to give sb/yourself a responsibility or task that causes a lot of work or worry: *If I were you, I wouldn't burden myself with other people's problems.*

**bu·reau** /ˈbyʊroʊ/ ***noun*** [C] **1** = DRESSER **2** one of certain government departments: *the Federal Bureau of Investigation* **3** an organization or a company that provides information: *a reporter from the magazine's Vancouver bureau*

**bu·reauc·ra·cy** /byʊˈrɑkrəsi/ ***noun*** (*pl.* **bu·reauc·ra·cies**) **1** [C,U] a system of government by a large number of officials in various departments **2** [U] (often used in a critical way) the system of official rules that an organization has for doing sth, that people often think are too complicated: *With all the bureaucracy involved, it takes forever to get a visa.*

**bu·reau·crat** /ˈbyʊrəkræt/ ***noun*** [C] (often used in a critical way) an official in an organization or in a government department

**bu·reau·crat·ic** /ˌbyʊrəˈkræt̬ɪk/ ***adj.*** connected with a bureaucracy, especially when it follows official rules too closely: *a complex bureaucratic procedure*

**burg·er** /ˈbərgər/ ***noun*** [C] = HAMBURGER

**-burger** /ˈbərgər/ ***combining form*** **1** a hamburger with sth else on top: *a cheeseburger* **2** something that is cooked like and looks like a hamburger, but is made of sth else: *a fishburger*

**bur·glar** /ˈbərglər/ ***noun*** [C] a person who enters a building illegally in order to steal: *The burglars broke in by smashing a window.* ➲ Look at the note at **thief**.

**ˈburglar aˌlarm** ***noun*** [C] a piece of equipment, usually fastened on a wall, that makes a loud noise if a thief enters a building

**bur·glar·ize** /ˈbərglərɑɪz/ ***verb*** [T] to enter a building illegally in order to steal from it: *Our house was burglarized while we were out.*

**bur·gla·ry** /ˈbərgləri/ ***noun*** [C,U] (*pl.* **bur·gla·ries**) the crime of entering a building illegally in order to steal: *There was a burglary at the house next door last week.* ◇ *He is in prison for burglary.*

**bur·i·al** /ˈbɛriəl/ ***noun*** [C,U] the ceremony when a dead body is put in the ground (**buried**): *The burial* *took place on Friday.* ◇ *The victims of the disaster were flown home for burial.* ➲ Look at the note at **funeral**.

**bur·ly** /ˈbərli/ ***adj.*** (used about a person, usually a man, or sb's body) strong and heavy

★**burn**[1] /bərn/ ***verb*** (*pt, pp* **burned** /bərnd/ or **burnt** /bərnt/)

➤FIRE **1** [T] to destroy, damage or injure sb/sth with fire or heat: *People who live in town aren't allowed to burn their trash.* ◇ *It was a terrible fire and the whole building was burned to the ground* (= was completely destroyed). ◇ *The water was so hot that I burned my hands.* ◇ *The people inside the building were all burned to death.* **2** [I] to be destroyed, damaged or injured by fire or heat: *If you leave the cake in the oven for much longer, it will burn.* ◇ *I can't spend too much time in the sun because I burn easily.* **3** [T] to produce a hole or mark in or on sth by burning: *He dropped his cigarette and it burned a hole in the carpet.* **4** [I] to be on fire: *Firemen raced to the burning building.*

➤OF A LIGHT **5** [I] to produce light: *I don't think he went to bed at all – I could see his light burning all night.*

➤OF PART OF BODY **6** [I] to feel unpleasantly hot: *You must have a temperature – your forehead's burning.*

➤CD, ETC. **7** [T] to put information onto a CD, etc.

➤TRICK/CHEAT **8** [T] (usually passive) (*informal*) to hurt sb by tricking or cheating him/her, or treating him/her badly: *He got burned in his last relationship and says he never wants to have a girlfriend again.*

➤FEEL EMOTION/DESIRE **9** [I] (*written*) **burn (with sth)** to be filled with a very strong feeling: *She was burning with indignation.*

PHR V **burn (sth) down** (used about a building) to destroy or be destroyed completely by fire: *The fire could not be brought under control and the school burned down.*

**burn (sb/yourself) out** to use all your energy or ruin your health, especially by working too hard over a long period of time: *You're going to burn yourself out if you don't stop working so hard.* ◇ *She burned out on drugs.*

**burn sth out** (usually passive) to completely destroy sth by burning: *the burnt-out wreck of a car*

**burn up** to be destroyed by fire or strong heat: *The space capsule burned up when it entered the earth's atmosphere.*

**burn sth up** to destroy sth by fire: *She burned up all the letters from her former boyfriend.*

**burn**[2] /bərn/ ***noun*** [C] an injury or piece of damage caused by fire or heat: *He has been treated for burns to his face and hands.* ◇ *the burn unit of a hospital*

**burn·er** /ˈbərnər/ ***noun*** [C] one of the round parts on the top of a stove, on which you can put pans ➲ picture at **stove**.

IDM **on the back burner** → BACK[2]

**burn·out** /ˈbərnaʊt/ ***noun*** [U,C] the state of being very tired or sick because you have worked too hard

**burnt**[1] *past tense, past participle of* BURN[1]

★**burnt**[2] /bərnt/ ***adj.*** that has been burned: *burnt toast*

**burp** /bərp/ ***verb*** [I] to make a noise with the mouth when air rises from the stomach and is forced out: *He sat back when he had finished his meal and burped loudly.* ▶ **burp** ***noun*** [C]: *a loud burp*

**bur·ri·to** /bəˈriţoʊ/ ***noun*** [C] (*pl.* **bur·ri·tos**) a Mexican dish that is made with a thin, flat piece of bread (a **tortilla**) filled with beans, meat, etc. and rolled up

**bur·row**[1] /ˈbəroʊ/ ***noun*** [C] a hole in the ground made by certain animals (e.g. rabbits) in which they live

**bur·row**[2] /ˈbəroʊ/ ***verb*** **1** [I,T] to dig a hole in the ground **2** [I] to search for sth, using your hands as if you were digging: *She burrowed in her purse for her keys.*

★**burst**[1] /bərst/ ***verb*** (*pt, pp* **burst**) **1** [I,T] to break open suddenly and violently, usually because there is too much pressure inside; to cause this to happen: *My shopping bag burst as I was leaving the grocery store.* ◇ *You'll burst that balloon if you blow it up any more.* ◇ *The balloon burst with a loud bang.* ◇ (*figurative*) *"Would you like some more to eat?" "No, thanks. If I have any more, I'll burst!"* ◇ *If it rains much more, the river will burst its banks.* **2** [I] **burst (with sth)** (only in the *-ing* forms) to be so full that it is in danger of breaking open: *I packed so many clothes that my suitcases were bursting.* ◇ (*figurative*) *He was bursting with happiness on his wedding day.*

PHR V **burst in on sb/sth** to interrupt sb/sth by arriving suddenly: *I'm sorry to burst in on you like this, but there's an urgent phone call.*

**burst into sth** to start doing sth suddenly: *On hearing the news she **burst into tears*** (= started crying). ◇ *The truck hit a wall and **burst into flames*** (= started burning).

**burst into, out of, through, etc.** to move suddenly in a particular direction, often using force: *She burst into the manager's office and demanded to speak to him.*

**burst out 1** to start doing sth suddenly: *He looked so ridiculous that I **burst out laughing**.* **2** to say sth suddenly and with strong feeling: *Finally she burst out, "I can't stand it anymore!"*

**burst**[2] /bərst/ ***noun*** [C] **1** an occasion when sth bursts or explodes; a crack caused by an explosion: *a burst in a water pipe* **2** a short period of a particular activity, that often starts suddenly: *With a burst of speed, she left the other runners behind.* ◇ *He prefers to work in short bursts.* ◇ *There were several bursts of applause during her speech.*

★**bur·y** /ˈbɛri/ ***verb*** [T] (*pres. part.* **bur·y·ing**; *3rd person sing. pres.* **bur·ies**; *pt, pp* **bur·ied**) **1** to put a dead body in a grave: *She wants to be buried next to her mother.* ◇ *Elvis is buried at Graceland.* **2** to put sth in a hole in the ground to cover it up: *Our dog always buries its bones in the yard.* ◇ *All kinds of dangerous materials are buried in garbage dumps.* **3** (usually passive) to cover or hide: *At last I found the picture, buried at the bottom of a drawer.* ◇ *The state was buried under a foot of snow after yesterday's blizzard.* ◇ (*figurative*) *Sally's always got her nose buried in a book.*

IDM **bury the hatchet** to end a period of being enemies and become friendly: *It's time to bury the hatchet and start working together.*

★**bus**[1] /bʌs/ ***noun*** [C] (*pl.* **bus·es** also **bus·ses**) a big public vehicle that takes passengers from one place to another along a fixed route: *to get on/off the bus* ◇ *We'll have to hurry up if we want to catch the 9 o'clock bus.* ◇ *It's too difficult to park your car downtown. It's better to take the bus.* ◇ *I ride the bus to work every day.*

NOTE You can get on or off a local bus at a **bus stop**. Large cities also have **bus stations** where you can get on a bus to another city. You need to pay the exact **fare** when you get on a city bus. Most **school buses** are yellow. Students can ride them to and from school without paying a fare. Note that we travel **by bus** or **on the bus**: *"How do you get to work?" "On the bus."*

**bus²** /bʌs/ ***verb*** [T] (*pres. part.* **bus·ing** or **bus·sing**; *3rd person sing. pres.* **bus·es** or **bus·ses**; *pt, pp* **bused** or **bussed**) to transport sb by bus: *The passengers were bused from the airport terminal to the plane.* ◇ *Students from the country were bused in to schools in the city.*

NOTE In some large U.S. cities, students are bused to schools that are far away from their own neighborhoods so that students from different races can go to school together.

**bus·boy** /ˈbʌsbɔɪ/ ***noun*** [C] a person who works in a restaurant and whose job is to clear the dirty dishes, bring customers water, etc.

**bush¹** /bʊʃ/ ***noun*** **1** [C] a plant like a small, thick tree with many low branches: *a rose bush* ◇ *The house was surrounded by thick bushes.* **2** (often **the bush**) [U, sing.] wild land that is not cultivated, especially in Africa and Australia

IDM **beat around the bush** → BEAT¹

**bush·el** /ˈbʊʃl/ ***noun*** [C] **1** (in Canada) a unit for measuring grain and fruit (equal in volume to 8 gallons or 36.4 liters) **2** (in the U.S.) a unit for measuring grain and fruit (equal in volume to 64 pints or 35.2 liters)

**bush·y** /ˈbʊʃi/ (**bush·i·er**; **bush·i·est**) ***adj.*** growing thickly: *bushy hair* ◇ *bushy eyebrows*

**bus·i·er, bus·i·est, bus·i·ly** → BUSY¹

★**busi·ness** /ˈbɪznəs/ ***noun***

➤TRADE **1** [U] buying and selling as a way of earning money: *She's interested in a career in international business.* ◇ *They are very easy to do business with.* ◇ *He teaches English for Business.* **2** [U] the amount of goods and services that are bought and sold: *Business has been good for this time of year.*

➤WORK **3** [U] the work that you do as your job: *The manager will be away on business next week.* ◇ *a business trip*

➤COMPANY **4** [C] a company, a store, a factory, etc. that produces or sells goods or provides a service: *She started a marketing business of her own.* ◇ *Small businesses are finding it hard to survive these days.*

➤BEING A CUSTOMER **5** the fact of a person buying goods or services at a store or business: *Thanks for your business! Please come again.*

➤RESPONSIBILITY **6** [U] something that concerns a particular person: *The friends I choose are my business, not yours.* ◇ *Our business is to collect the information, not to comment on it.* ◇ *"How much did it cost?" "It's none of your business!"* (= I don't want to tell you. It's private.)

➤EVENT **7** [sing.] a situation or an event: *The divorce was a messy business.* ◇ *I found the whole business very depressing.*

IDM **get down to business** to start the work that must be done: *Let's just have a cup of coffee before we get down to business.*

**go out of business** to have to close because there is no more money available: *The store went out of business because it couldn't compete with the new shopping mall.*

**have no business doing sth** to have no right to do sth: *You have no business reading my letters without asking me.*

**mind your own business** → MIND²

**ˈbusiness adminiˌstration** ***noun*** [U] the study of how to control and manage a BUSINESS (4): *She's studying for a master's degree in business administration.*

**ˈbusiness card** (*also* **card**) ***noun*** [C] a small card printed with sb's name and information about his/her job and company

**busi·ness·like** /ˈbɪznəslaɪk/ ***adj.*** efficient and practical: *She has a very businesslike manner.*

**busi·ness·man** /ˈbɪznəsmæn/ (*also* **busi·ness·wom·an** /ˈbɪznəswʊmən/) ***noun*** [C] (*pl.* **busi·ness·men** /-mən/, **busi·ness·wom·en** /-wɪmən/) **1** a person who works in BUSINESS (1), especially in a top position **2** a person who is skillful at dealing with money: *My brother can advise you on your investments – he's a better businessman than I am.*

**bust¹** /bʌst/ ***noun*** [C] **1** a model in stone, etc. of a person's head, shoulders and chest **2** a woman's breasts; the measurement around a woman's chest: *That style of blouse doesn't look good on someone with a big bust.* **3** an act of arresting sb by the police, etc.: *a drug bust* **4** (*informal*) a failure

**bust²** /bʌst/ ***verb*** [T] **1** (*slang*) to break or damage sth so that it cannot be used **2** **bust sb (for sth)** (*informal*) (used about the police, etc.) to suddenly enter a place and catch sb doing sth illegal or wrong: *He got busted for possession of drugs.* ◇ *The teacher busted her for smoking in the restroom.*

IDM **bust a gut (doing/to do sth)** (*informal*) to make a great effort to do sth: *I bust a gut to get you out of this mess!*

**bust³** /bʌst/ ***adj.***

IDM **go bust** (*informal*) (used about a business) to have to close because it has lost so much money: *During the recession, thousands of businesses went bust.*

**bust·er** /ˈbʌstər/ ***noun*** [C] (*informal*) **1** used to speak to a man or boy in a way that shows you are angry with him: *Watch where you're going, buster!* **2** (usually in compounds) a person or thing that stops or gets rid of sth: *The new Attorney General is trying to build a reputation as a crime buster*

**bus·tle¹** /ˈbʌsl/ ***verb*** [I] **bustle (with sth)** to be full of sth (people, noise, activity, etc.): *It was the week before Christmas and the streets were bustling with shoppers.*

**bus·tle²** /ˈbʌsl/ ***noun*** [U] excited and noisy activity: *She loved the hustle and bustle of city life.*

★**bus·y¹** /ˈbɪzi/ ***adj.*** (**bus·i·er**; **bus·i·est**) **1** **busy (at/with sth)**; **busy (doing sth)** having a lot of work or tasks to do; not free; working on sth: *Mr.*

*Smith is busy until 4 o'clock, but he could see you after that.* ◇ *Don't disturb him. He's busy.* ◇ *She's busy with her preparations for the party.* ◇ *We're busy decorating the guest room before our visitors arrive.* **2** (used about a period of time) full of activity and things to do: *I've had a pretty busy week.* **3** (used about a place) full of people, movement and activity: *Main Street was so busy that I could hardly move.* **4** (used about a telephone) in use: *The line's busy right now. I'll try again later.* ◇ *a busy signal*

IDM **get busy** start working: *We'll have to get busy if we're going to be ready in time.*

▸ **bus·i·ly** /ˈbɪzəli/ ***adv.***: *When I came in she was busily writing something at her desk.*

**bus·y**[2] /ˈbɪzi/ ***verb*** [T] (*pres. part.* **bus·y·ing**; *3rd person sing. pres.* **bus·ies**; *pt, pp* **bus·ied**) **busy yourself with sth**; **busy yourself doing sth** to keep yourself busy; to find sth to do

**bus·y·work** /ˈbɪziwərk/ ***noun*** [U] (*informal*) work that has no real purpose and that is just supposed to keep sb busy

★**but**[1] /bət; *strong form* bʌt/ ***conj.*** **1** (used for introducing an idea that contrasts with or is different from what has just been said): *The weather will be sunny but cold.* ◇ *Theirs is not the first but the second house on the left.* ◇ *James doesn't have a car, but his sister does.* **2** however; and yet: *She's been studying Italian for five years, but she doesn't speak it very well.* ◇ *I'd love to come, but I can't make it until 8 o'clock.* **3** (used with an apology): *I'm sorry, but I can't stay any longer.* **4** (used for introducing a statement that shows that you are surprised or annoyed or that you disagree): *"Here's the money I owe you." "But that's not right – it was only $6."*

IDM **but then (again)** → THEN

**but**[2] /bət; *strong form* bʌt/ ***prep.*** except: *I haven't told anyone but you about this.* ◇ *We've had nothing but trouble with this washing machine!*

IDM **but for sb/sth** (*formal*) except for or without sb/sth: *We wouldn't have managed but for your help.*

**butch** /bʊtʃ/ ***adj.*** (used especially about a woman) acting or dressing like a man

**butch·er** /ˈbʊtʃər/ ***noun*** [C] **1** a person who sells meat: *The butcher cut me four lamb chops.* ◇ *She went to the butcher shop for some sausages.* **2** a person who kills many people in a cruel way

**but·ler** /ˈbʌtlər/ ***noun*** [C] the most important male servant in a big house, especially in former times

**butt**[1] /bʌt/ ***noun*** [C] **1** (*informal*) the part of your body that you sit on: *Get up off your butt and do some work!* ◇ *I took two steps on the ice and fell right on my butt.* ◇ *Get your butt in here* (= come in here) *right now!* **2** a person who is often laughed at or talked about in an unkind way: *Fat children are often the butt of other children's jokes.* **3** the thicker, heavier end of a gun: *the butt of a rifle* **4** a short piece of a cigarette or cigar that is left when it has been smoked

**butt**[2] /bʌt/ ***verb*** [T] to hit or push sb/sth with the head

PHR V **butt in (on sb/sth)** (*informal*) to interrupt sb/sth or to join in sth without being asked: *You shouldn't butt in like that when somebody else is talking.*

**butt out** (*informal*) to stop interfering in other people's affairs: *I'm talking to Molly about something personal, so just butt out, Jerry!*

**butte** /byut/ ***noun*** [C] a hill that is flat on top and is separate from other high ground

★**but·ter**[1] /ˈbʌt̬ər/ ***noun*** [U] a soft yellow fat that is made from cream and is put on bread, etc. or used in cooking: *Would you rather have butter or margarine?* ◇ *First, melt a little butter in the pan.*

**but·ter**[2] /ˈbʌt̬ər/ ***verb*** [T] to spread butter on bread, etc.: *Can you butter the bread when it comes out of the toaster?* ◇ *hot buttered popcorn*

ˈ**butter bean** ***noun*** [C] = LIMA BEAN

**but·ter·fly** /ˈbʌt̬ərflaɪ/ ***noun*** [C] (*pl.* **but·ter·flies**) an insect with a long, thin body and four brightly colored wings: *Caterpillars develop into butterflies.* ➲ picture at **insect**.

IDM **to have butterflies (in your stomach)** (*informal*) to feel very nervous before doing sth

**but·ter·milk** /ˈbʌt̬ərmɪlk/ ***noun*** [U] the liquid that is left when butter has been separated from milk

**but·ter·scotch** /ˈbʌt̬ərskɑtʃ/ ***noun*** [U] a type of hard pale brown candy made by boiling butter and brown sugar together: *chocolate cake with butterscotch icing*

**but·tock** /ˈbʌt̬ək/ ***noun*** [C, usually pl.] (*formal*) one of the two parts of the body which you sit on ➲ Look at **bun** (3).

★**but·ton**[1] /ˈbʌtn/ ***noun*** [C] **1** a small, often round, piece of plastic, wood or metal that you use for fastening your clothes: *One of the buttons on my jacket came off.* ◇ *a coat/shirt button* ◇ *This blouse is too tight. I can't fasten the buttons.* **2** a small part of a machine, etc. that you press in order to operate sth: *Press this button to ring the bell.* ◇ *Which button turns the volume down?* ◇ *Position the cursor where you want it and click with the left mouse button.* ◇ *the buttons on a telephone* ➲ picture at **telephone**. **3** a round, flat piece of plastic or metal with pictures, etc. on it that people fasten to their clothes: *The volunteers gave out campaign buttons with the candidate's picture on them.* ◇ *She was wearing a button that said "Have a nice day."* ➲ Look also at **belly button**.

**but·ton**[2] /ˈbʌtn/ ***verb*** [T] **button sth (up)** to fasten sth with BUTTONS[1] (1): *He buttoned up his coat.* OPP **unbutton**

**but·ton·hole** /ˈbʌtnhoʊl/ ***noun*** [C] a hole in a piece of clothing that you push a BUTTON[1] (1) through in order to fasten it

★**buy**[1] /baɪ/ ***verb*** [T] (*pt, pp* **bought** /bɔt/) **1** to get sth by paying money for it: *I'm going to buy a new dress for the party.* ◇ *We bought this book for you in New York.* ◇ *Can I buy you a cup of coffee?* ◇ *He bought the car from a friend.* ◇ *Did you buy this sofa new?* ◇ *He bought the necklace as a present for his wife.* **2** (*informal*) to believe sth: *The boss is never going to buy that excuse!*

IDM **buy time** to do sth in order to delay an event/a decision: *They made excuses in order to buy time to finish the project.*

PHR V **buy sb off** to pay sb money to make him/her do what you want, especially sth wrong or illegal

**buy sb/sth out** to pay sb for his/her share in a business: *When Sarah discovered she couldn't work with her partner, she bought him out.* ◇ *I'd like to buy out his share in the business.*
**buy sth up** to buy all or as much as possible of sth: *Foreign investors have bought up most of the real estate in the area.*

**buy²** /baɪ/ ***noun*** [C] an act of buying sth or a thing that you can buy: *I think your house was a very good buy* (= worth the money that you paid).

★**buy·er** /ˈbaɪər/ ***noun*** [C] **1** a person who is buying sth or may buy sth: *I think we've found a buyer for our house!* **2** a person whose job is to choose and buy goods that are to be sold in a large store

**buy·out** /ˈbaɪaʊt/ ***noun*** [C] an act of getting control of a company by buying all of it or a big enough part of it: *Rumors of a possible buyout caused the company's stock price to rise.*

**buzz¹** /bʌz/ ***verb*** [I] to make the sound that bees, etc. make when flying: *A large fly was buzzing against the window.*

**buzz²** /bʌz/ ***noun*** **1** [C] the sound that a bee, etc. makes when flying: *the buzz of insects* **2** [sing.] the low sound made by many people talking at the same time: *I could hear the buzz of conversation in the next room.* **3** [sing.] (*informal*) a strong feeling of pleasure, excitement or achievement: *She* ***gets a buzz from*** *all the responsibility she has in her new job.* ◇ *One drink* ***gives me a buzz;*** *two drinks put me to sleep.*

**buzz·er** /ˈbʌzər/ ***noun*** [C] a piece of equipment that makes a buzzing sound: *Press the buzzer in the lobby and I'll let you in.*

**buzz·word** /ˈbʌzwərd/ ***noun*** [C] a word or phrase, especially one connected with a particular subject, that has become fashionable and popular and is used a lot: *A lot of people use the latest buzzwords without knowing what they mean.*

★**by¹** /baɪ/ ***adv.*** **1** past: *We stopped to let the ambulance get by.* ◇ *If we sit here, we can watch the boats sail by.* ◇ *Time seemed to be going by very slowly.* **2** near: *There's a nice restaurant close by.*
IDM **by and large** → LARGE¹

★**by²** /baɪ/ ***prep.*** **1** beside; very near: *Come and sit by me.* ◇ *We stayed at a resort by the ocean.* **2** past: *He walked straight by me without speaking.* **3** not later than; before: *I'll be home by 7 o'clock.* ◇ *He should have called by now/by this time.* ◇ *By this time tomorrow you'll be married!* **4** (usually without *the*) during a period of time; in particular circumstances: *She attends classes by day and works as a waitress by night.* ◇ *The power went off so we had to work by candlelight.* **5** (after a passive verb) (used for showing who or what did or caused sth): *He was hit by a car.* ◇ *The event was organized by local people.* ◇ *I was deeply shocked by the news.* ◇ *The building was designed by Frank Lloyd Wright.* ◇ *Who was the book written by?/Who is the book by?* **6** through doing sth: *You can get hold of me by calling this number.* **7** using sth: *Will you be paying by credit card?* ◇ *The house is heated by electricity.* ◇ *"How do you go to work?" "By bus, usually."* ◇ *by bus, car, plane, bicycle, etc.* **8** as a result of; due to: *I went to the wrong house by mistake/accident.* ◇ *I met an old friend by chance.* **9** according to: *It's 8 o'clock by my watch.* ◇ *By law you have to attend school from the age of five.* **10** (used for multiplying or dividing): *4 multiplied by 5 is 20.* ◇ *6 divided by 2 is 3.* **11** (used for showing the measurements of an area): *The table is six feet by three feet* (= six feet long and three feet wide). **12** (with *the*) in quantities or periods of: *Gasoline is sold by the gallon.* ◇ *I get paid by the hour.* ◇ *Copies of the book have sold by the million.* **13** in groups or units of: *They came in one by one.* ◇ *Workers cleared away the debris piece by piece.* ◇ *Day by day she was getting better.* **14** to the amount of: *Prices have gone up by 10 percent.* ◇ *I missed the bus by a few minutes.* **15** (used with a part of the body or an article of clothing) holding: *He grabbed me by the arm.* **16** with regard to: *She's French by birth.* ◇ *He's a doctor by profession.* ◇ *By nature she's a very gentle person.*
IDM **by the way** (used for adding sth to the conversation) on a new subject: *Oh, by the way, I saw Cindy downtown yesterday.*

**bye¹** /baɪ/ (*also* **bye-bye** /ˈbaɪbaɪ; ˌbaɪˈbaɪ/) ***interjection*** (*informal*) goodbye: *Bye! See you tomorrow.*

**bye²** /baɪ/ ***noun*** [C] (*sports*) a situation in which a player or team does not have an opponent in one part of a competition and continues to the next part as if he/she/they had won: *The Cavaliers got a bye in the first round.*

**BYOB** /ˌbi waɪ oʊ ˈbi/ (*especially Cdn* **BYO**) ***abbr.*** "bring your own bottle" or "bring your own beer/ booze"; written on an invitation to say that the guests should bring their own drink: *Since college students don't have much money, parties are usually BYOB.*

**by·pass¹** /ˈbaɪpæs/ ***noun*** [C] **1** a road that traffic can use to go around a city, instead of through it **2** a medical operation to create a new passage for blood to flow through, especially near the heart: *to have heart bypass surgery*

**by·pass²** /ˈbaɪpæs/ ***verb*** [T] to go around or to avoid sth using a BYPASS¹ (1): *Let's try to bypass the downtown area.* ◇ (*figurative*) *It's no good trying to bypass the problem.*

**by·prod·uct** (*also* **by-product**) /ˈbaɪprɑdʌkt/ ***noun*** [C] **1** something that is formed during the making of sth else **2** something that happens as the result of sth else

**by·stand·er** /ˈbaɪstændər/ ***noun*** [C] a person who is standing near and sees sth that happens, without being involved in it: *Several innocent bystanders were hurt when the two gangs attacked each other.*

**byte** /baɪt/ ***noun*** [C] (*computing*) a unit of information that can represent one item, such as a letter or a number. A byte usually consists of a series of eight smaller units (**bits**). ➲ Look at **megabyte**.

# Cc

**C, c** /si/ ***noun*** [C,U] (*pl.* **C's**; **c's** /siz/) **1** the third letter of the English alphabet: *"Come" begins with (a) "C."* **2** a grade that is given for a test or a piece of work that is average in quality. A "C" is lower than a "B": *I got a "C" on my essay.*

**C** (*also* **C.**) ***abbr.*** Celsius; Centigrade

**c.** ***abbr.*** (*written*) **1** cup; cups: *Add 2 c. flour and mix well.* **2** (*also* **C**) century **3** (*also* **c, ca.**) (especially before dates) about; approximately (from Latin *circa*) **4** (*symbol* ¢) cent(s)

**cab** /kæb/ ***noun*** [C] **1** = TAXI[1]: *Let's take a cab home.* **2** the part of a truck, etc. where the driver sits

**cab·a·ret** /ˌkæbəˈreɪ/ ***noun*** [C,U] an entertainment with singing, dancing, etc. in a restaurant or nightclub

**cab·bage** /ˈkæbɪdʒ/ ***noun*** [C,U] a large round vegetable with thick green, or sometimes dark red leaves, often eaten cooked: *We're growing cabbages in the garden.* ◇ *a head of cabbage* ➲ picture on study page **A28-29**.

**cab·bie** (*also* **cab·by**) /ˈkæbi/ ***noun*** [C] (*pl.* **cab·bies**) (*informal*) a person who drives a taxi

**cab·in** /ˈkæbən/ ***noun*** [C] **1** a small wooden house in the country: *a log cabin in the woods* **2** one of the parts of an airplane, at the front or where the passengers sit: *A member of the cabin crew will be happy to help you.* ◇ *the first-class cabin* **3** a small room on a ship or boat, where a passenger sleeps: *Phil had to stay in our cabin for most of the cruise because he was seasick.*

**cab·i·net** /ˈkæbənət/ ***noun*** [C] **1** an object like a box with shelves or drawers, used for storing things: *a medicine cabinet* ◇ *kitchen cabinets* ◇ *a filing cabinet* **2** (usually **the Cabinet**) the most important leaders of departments or senior ministers in the government, who have regular meetings with the President/Prime Minister: *a Cabinet meeting/member* ➲ For more information on the Canadian political system, look at study page **A11**.

**ca·ble** /ˈkeɪbl/ ***noun*** **1** [C] a very strong, thick rope or chain, etc. **2** [C,U] a set of wires covered with plastic, etc. for carrying electricity or signals: *a telephone cable* ◇ *underground electrical cable* **3** [C] (*old-fashioned*) = TELEGRAM **4** [U] = CABLE TELEVISION

**ˈcable car** ***noun*** [C] **1** a vehicle that runs on tracks and is pulled by a moving CABLE (1): *We took a ride on a cable car in San Francisco.* **2** a vehicle that hangs from and is pulled by a moving cable and that carries passengers up and down a mountain

**ˌcable ˈtelevision** (*also* **ˌcable TˈV, cable**) ***noun*** [U] a system of sending television programs by CABLE (2), which you have to pay for every month

**cache** /kæʃ/ ***noun*** [C] **1** a hidden store of things such as weapons: *an arms cache* **2** (*computing*) a part of a computer's memory that stores copies of data that is often needed while a program is running, so that this data can be found quickly

**cack·le** /ˈkækl/ ***noun*** [C] **1** the loud sound that a chicken makes after laying an egg **2** a loud, unpleasant laugh ▸ **cack·le** ***verb*** [I]

**cac·tus** /ˈkæktəs/ ***noun*** [C] (*pl.* **cac·ti** /ˈkæktaɪ/ or **cac·tus·es**) a type of plant that grows in hot, dry areas, especially deserts. A cactus has a thick stem and sharp points (**spines**) but no leaves.

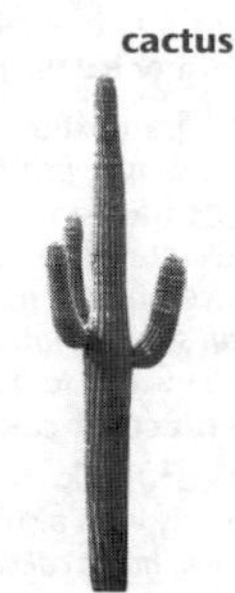
**cactus**

**CAD** /kæd; si eɪ ˈdi/ ***abbr.*** **1** computer-aided design; the use of computers to design machines, buildings, vehicles, etc. **2** Canadian dollars

**CAD·CAM** (*also* **CAD/CAM**) /ˈkædkæm/ ***abbr.*** computer-aided design, computer-aided manufacturing; the use of computers to design and make buildings, vehicles, etc.

**cad·die** /ˈkædi/ (*also* **cad·dy** (*pl.* **cad·dies**)) ***noun*** [C] a person who helps a golf player during a game by carrying his or her equipment (**clubs**)

**cad·dy** /ˈkædi/ ***noun*** [C] (*pl.* **cad·dies**) **1** a container for storing or carrying things that you use for a specific purpose: *a shower/sewing caddy* **2** = CADDIE

**ca·det** /kəˈdɛt/ ***noun*** [C] a young person who is training to be in the military forces or the police

**Cae·sar·e·an sec·tion** /sɪˌzɛriən ˈsɛkʃn/ ***noun*** [C] (*Cdn*) = CESAREAN SECTION

**ˌCaesar ˈsalad** /ˌsizər ˈsæləd/ ***noun*** [C] a salad made with cheese, small pieces of fried bread (**croutons**) and a sauce (**dressing**) with a strong flavor

**ca·fé** (*also* **cafe**) /kæˈfeɪ; kæ-/ ***noun*** [C] a small restaurant that serves drinks and light meals

**caf·e·te·ri·a** /ˌkæfəˈtɪriə/ ***noun*** [C] a type of restaurant where people choose individual items of food and carry them to their tables: *the school cafeteria*

**caf·feine** /kæˈfin/ ***noun*** [U] the substance found in coffee and tea that makes you feel more awake and lively ➲ Look at **decaffeinated**.

**caf·fè lat·te** (*also* **caf·fe lat·te, lat·te**) /ˌkɑfeɪ ˈlɑteɪ; ˌkæfeɪ-/ ***noun*** [C] (*pl.* **lat·tes**) a drink made by adding a small amount of strong coffee to a cup of hot milk ➲ Look at the note at **coffee**.

**cage** /keɪdʒ/ ***noun*** [C] a box made of bars or wire, or a space surrounded by wire or metal bars, in which a bird or animal is kept so that it cannot escape: *The parrot escaped from its cage.* ▸ **caged** /keɪdʒd/ ***adj.***: *He felt like a caged animal in the tiny office.*

**Ca·jun**[1] /ˈkeɪdʒən/ ***noun*** [C] a person from a state in the south of the U.S. (Louisiana) whose family in the past were French and who speaks a form of French, also called Cajun

**Ca·jun²** /ˈkeɪdʒən/ ***adj.*** connected with the Cajuns, their language, music or cooking: *Cajun music* ◇ *a Cajun recipe for catfish*

C

⋆**cake¹** /keɪk/ ***noun*** **1** [C,U] a sweet food made by mixing flour, eggs, butter, sugar, etc. together and baking the mixture in the oven: *a birthday cake* ◇ *I saved you a slice of our wedding cake.* ◇ *a chocolate cake* ◇ *a fruit cake* ◇ *The bride and groom cut the cake.* ◇ *Would you like another piece of cake?* ◇ *a piece of birthday cake*

NOTE After **making** or **baking** a cake we often **frost** or **ice** the top and sides of it.

**2** [C] a mixture of other food, cooked in a round, flat shape: *fish cakes* ◇ *rice cakes*

IDM **have your cake and eat it too** to enjoy the advantages of sth without its disadvantages; to have both things that are available: *Rick thinks he can stay out late every night and still get good grades – he wants to have his cake and eat it too.*

**a piece of cake** → PIECE¹

**cake²** /keɪk/ ***verb*** [T] (usually passive) to cover sth thickly with a substance that becomes hard when it dries: *boots caked in/with mud*

**ca·lam·i·ty** /kəˈlæməṭi/ ***noun*** [C,U] (*pl.* **ca·lam·i·ties**) a terrible event that causes a lot of damage or harm

**cal·ci·um** /ˈkælsiəm/ ***noun*** [U] (*symbol* **Ca**) a chemical substance that is found in foods such as milk and cheese and that helps to make bones and teeth strong

⋆**cal·cu·late** /ˈkælkyəleɪt/ ***verb*** [T] **1** to find sth out by using mathematics: *I've been calculating the costs involved and it's too expensive.* ◇ *It's difficult to calculate how long the project will take.* **2** to consider or expect sth: *We calculated that the advantages would be greater than the disadvantages.*

**cal·cu·lat·ed** /ˈkælkyəˌleɪṭəd/ ***adj.*** done on purpose, with careful planning: *a calculated attempt to damage his opponent's reputation*

IDM **be calculated to do sth** to be intended or designed to do sth: *His remark was clearly calculated to annoy me.*

**cal·cu·la·tion** /ˌkælkyəˈleɪʃn/ ***noun*** **1** [C,U] finding an answer by using mathematics: *Several of his calculations are wrong.* ◇ *Calculation of the exact cost is impossible.* **2** [U] (*formal*) careful thought and planning in order to achieve your own, selfish aims: *His actions were clearly the result of deliberate calculation.*

**cal·cu·la·tor** /ˈkælkyəleɪṭər/ ***noun*** [C] a small electronic machine that is used for calculating figures: *a pocket calculator*

**cal·en·dar** /ˈkæləndər/ ***noun*** [C] **1** a list, often in the form of a book, that shows the days, weeks and months of a particular year: *She had circled the important dates on her calendar in red.* ◇ *There was a calendar hanging on the back of the door.* ◇ *I'll write that down in my appointment calendar.* **2** a system for dividing time into fixed periods and for marking the beginning and end of a year: *the Muslim calendar* ◇ *Our school's academic calendar is divided into four quarters.* **3** a list of dates and events in a year that are important in a particular area of activity: *The party's convention is a major event on the campaign calendar.*

**ˌcalendar ˈmonth** ***noun*** [C] **1** = MONTH (1) **2** a period of time from a particular date in one month to the same date in the next one

**ˌcalendar ˈyear** ***noun*** [C] = YEAR (2)

**calf** /kæf/ ***noun*** [C] (*pl.* **calves** /kævz/) **1** a young cow ➲ The meat from a calf is called **veal.** ➲ Look at the note at **meat** and the picture at **cow. 2** the young of some other animals, e.g. elephants **3** the back of your leg, below your knee ➲ picture on study page **A32**.

**cal·i·ber** /ˈkæləbər/ ***noun*** **1** [C, usually sing.] the width of the inside of a tube, especially the long tube (**barrel**) of a gun: *a .22 caliber rifle* **2** [sing., U] the quality or ability of a person or thing: *The company's employees are of the highest caliber.*

⋆**call¹** /kɔl/ ***noun***

➤LOUD SOUND **1** [C] a loud sound that is made to attract attention; a shout: *a call for help* ◇ *That bird's call is easy to recognize.*

➤ON TELEPHONE **2** (*also* **ˈphone call**) [C] an act of telephoning or a conversation on the telephone: *Were there any calls for me while I was out?* ◇ *I'll give you a call this weekend.* ◇ *The manager is on line 2. Will you take the call?* ◇ *a local call* ◇ *a long-distance call*

➤VISIT **3** [C] a short visit, especially to the house or business of a customer: *Doctors used to make house calls when people were sick.* ◇ *I'm sorry, but the technician is out on a call right now.*

➤REQUEST/DEMAND **4** [C] a request or demand for sth: *There have been calls for the president to resign.*

➤NEED **5** [C,U] **call for sth** a need for sth: *The doctor said there was no call for concern.*

➤DANCING **6** [C] the order that sb shouts to tell the dancers what to do next in a traditional kind of dance (**square dancing**)

➤DECISION **7** [C] a decision; the right to decide sth: *I don't mind Chinese or Italian food for dinner;* ***it's your call.***

IDM **a close call/shave** → CLOSE¹

**(be) on call** (to be) ready to work if necessary: *Dr. Young will be on call this weekend.*

⋆**call²** /kɔl/ ***verb***

➤SHOUT **1** [I,T] **call (out) to sb**; **call (sth) (out)** to say sth loudly or to shout in order to attract attention: *"Hello, is anybody there?" she called.* ◇ *I could hear a voice calling for help.* ◇ *He called out the names and the winners stepped forward.* ◇ *Call the kids. Breakfast is ready.*

➤TELEPHONE **2** [I,T] to telephone (sb/sth): *Who's calling, please?* ◇ *Thank you for calling.* ◇ *I'll call you tomorrow.* ◇ *We're right in the middle of dinner. Can I call you back later?*

➤GIVE NAME **3 be called** to have as a name: *This type of apple is called "Golden Delicious."* ◇ *What was that town called?*

➤DESCRIBE **4** [T] to name or describe a person or thing in a certain way: *My name is Elizabeth, but my friends call me Liz.* ◇ *Can you really call this picture "art?"* ◇ *It was mean to call her fat.* ◇ *Are you calling me a liar?*

➤ORDER SB TO COME **5** [T] to order or ask sb to

come to a certain place: *Can you call everybody in for lunch?* ◇ *The President called his advisers to the White House.* ◇ *I think we had better call the doctor.*

➤ MEETING/STRIKE, ETC. **6** [T] to arrange for sth to take place at a certain time: *to call a meeting/an election/a strike*

➤ DANCING **7** [I,T] to shout orders telling the dancers what they should do next in a traditional kind of dance (**square dancing**)

IDM **call it a day** (*informal*) to decide to stop doing sth: *Let's call it a day. I'm exhausted.*

**call it quits** (*informal*) to decide to stop doing sth: *We finally called it quits when it started raining.*

**call/draw sb's attention to sth** → ATTENTION

PHR V **call for sth** to demand or need sth: *Critics of the senator are calling for her to resign.* ◇ *The crisis calls for immediate action.* ◇ *This calls for a celebration!* ◇ *His nasty comment was not called for* (= there was no need for it).

**call sb in** to ask sb to come and help you: *I can't figure out what's wrong with the copier – we'd better call in the technician.*

**call sth off** to cancel sth: *The baseball game was called off because of rain.*

**call on sb** to ask sb to speak or answer a question: *I just hope the teacher doesn't call on me – I forgot to read the assignment!*

**call sb out** to ask or tell sb to go somewhere: *The police were called out to control the riot.*

**call sb up 1** to telephone sb: *She called me up to tell me the good news.* **2** to order the army, etc. to go somewhere and work, fight, etc.: *Twenty National Guard units have been called up to help fight the forest fires.*

**call sth up** to look at sth that is stored in a computer: *The bank teller can call up your balance on screen.*

**call·er** /'kɔlər/ **noun** [C] **1** a person who telephones sb: *I don't know who the caller was. He hung up without giving his name.* **2** the person who shouts orders telling the dancers what they should do next in a traditional dance (**square dancing**)

ˌ**caller I'D noun** [U] a telephone service that lets you see who is calling when the telephone rings

ˈ**calling card noun** [C] a card which allows you to make a call from any telephone and later the call is charged to your home telephone number

ˈ**call-in show** (*also* ˈ**call-in ˌprogram**) **noun** [C] a radio or television program during which you can ask a question or give your opinion by telephone: *a live radio call-in show*

**cal·lous** /'kæləs/ **adj.** not caring about the suffering of other people

ˌ**call ˈwaiting noun** [U] a telephone service that tells you if sb is trying to call you when you are using the phone

★**calm¹** /kɑm/ **adj. 1** not worried or angry; quiet: *Try to stay calm – there's no need to panic.* ◇ *She spoke in a calm voice.* ◇ *The city is calm again after last night's riots.* **2** without big waves: *a calm sea* **3** without much wind: *calm weather* ▸ **calm·ly adv.**: *Len told the police very calmly exactly what he had seen.* ▸ **calm·ness noun** [U]

★**calm²** /kɑm/ **noun** [U, sing.] a period of time or a state when everything is peaceful: *Attacks were reported after months of relative calm.*

★**calm³** /kɑm/ **verb** [I,T] **calm (sb/sth) (down)** to become or to make sb quiet or calm: *Calm down! Shouting at everybody won't help.* ◇ *She calmed the horses by talking quietly to them.* ◇ *He read the kids a story to calm them down.*

C

★**cal·o·rie** /'kæləri/ **noun** [C] **1** a unit for measuring the energy that a certain amount of food will produce **2** a unit for measuring heat

**calves** *plural of* CALF

**cam·cord·er** /'kæmkɔrdər/ **noun** [C] a camera that you can carry with you and use to record pictures and sound on a video cassette

**came** *past tense of* COME

hump camel

★**cam·el** /'kæml/ **noun 1** [C] an animal that lives in the desert and has a long neck and either one or two humps on its back. It is used for carrying people and goods. **2** [U] a light brown color

★**cam·er·a** /'kæmrə; -ərə/ **noun** [C] a piece of equipment that you use for taking photographs or moving pictures: *I need more film for my camera.* ◇ *a security camera in a bank* ◇ *a digital/video camera*

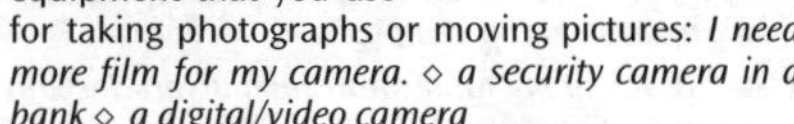

**cam·er·a·man** /'kæmrəmæn/ (*also* **cam·er·a·wom·an** /'kæmrəwʊmən/) **noun** [C] (*pl.* **cam·er·a·men**; **cam·er·a·wom·en**) a person whose job is to operate a camera for a movie or a television company

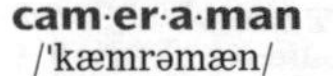

camera flash lens

NOTE It is also common to say **camera operator** or **cameraperson**, especially if you do not know if you are speaking about a man or a woman.

**cam·ou·flage¹** /'kæməflɑʒ/ **noun** [U] materials or colors that soldiers use to make themselves and their equipment less easy to see

**cam·ou·flage²** /'kæməflɑʒ/ **verb** [T] to make sb/sth difficult to see in a particular place

★**camp¹** /kæmp/ **noun** [C,U] a place where people live in tents or small houses for a short time: *a summer camp* ◇ *a Boy Scout camp* ◇ *a training camp* (= for soldiers) ◇ *We returned to camp tired after our long hike.* ◇ *The climbers **set up camp** at the foot of the mountain.*

**camp²** /kæmp/ **verb** [I] **camp (out)** to sleep outdoors, especially in a tent: *The kids like to camp out in the back yard.*

NOTE **Go camping** is a common way of talking about camping for pleasure: *They went camping in Banff last year.*

★**cam·paign¹** /kæm'peɪn/ **noun** [C] **1** a plan to do a number of things in order to achieve a special aim: *an advertising campaign* ◇ *Bush's presidential* *campaign* (= his campaign to be elected President) **2** a planned series of attacks in a war

**cam·paign²** /kæm'peɪn/ ***verb*** [I] **campaign (for/against sb/sth)** to take part in a CAMPAIGN¹ (1) in order to make sth happen or to prevent sth: *They campaigned against whaling for over 15 years.* ▶ **cam·paign·er** ***noun*** [C]: *a campaigner for equal rights for women*

**camp·er** /'kæmpər/ ***noun*** [C] **1** a person who camps **2** a large vehicle in which you can sleep, cook, etc. and that you can drive around while you are on vacation, or a similar vehicle that can be pulled by a car or small truck ➲ Look also at **trailer** (2) and **RV**.

**camp·fire** /'kæmpfaɪər/ ***noun*** [C] an outdoor fire made by people who are sleeping outside or living in a tent

**camp·ground** /'kæmpgraʊnd/ (*also* **camp·site** /'kæmpsaɪt/) ***noun*** [C] a place where you can camp

**camp·ing** /'kæmpɪŋ/ ***noun*** [U] sleeping or spending a vacation in a tent: *Camping is cheaper than staying in hotels.* ◇ *a camping trip*

**cam·pus** /'kæmpəs/ ***noun*** [C,U] (*pl.* **cam·pus·es**) the area of land where the main buildings of a college or university are: *the college campus* ◇ *About half the students live **on campus** – most of the others have apartments off campus.*

★**can¹** /kən; *strong form* kæn/ ***modal verb*** (*negative* **can·not** /'kænɑt; kə'nɑt/, *short form* **can't** /kænt/, *pt* **could** /kəd/, *strong form* /kʊd/, *negative* **could not**, *short form* **could·n't** /'kʊdnt/) **1** (used for showing that it is possible for sb/sth to do sth or that sb/sth has the ability to do sth): *I can catch a bus from here.* ◇ *Can you ride a bike?* ◇ *He can't speak French.* ◇ *She couldn't answer the question.*

> NOTE **Can** has no infinitive or participle forms. To make the future and perfect tenses, we use **be able to**: *One day people will be able to travel to Mars.* ◇ *He's been able to swim for almost a year.* **Could have** is used when we say that somebody had the ability to do something but did not do it: *She could have passed the test, but she didn't try.*

**2** (asking or giving permission): *Can I have a drink, please?* ◇ *He asked if he could have a drink.* ◇ *You can't go swimming today.*

> NOTE When we are talking about general permission in the past, **could** is used: *I could do anything I wanted when I stayed with my grandma.* When we are talking about one particular occasion, we do not use **could**: *They were allowed to visit him in the hospital yesterday.* Some people do not like the use of **can** in questions asking permission to do something. They prefer to use **may**: *May I go to the bathroom?*

**3** (asking sb to do sth): *Can you help me carry these books?* **4** (offering to do sth): *Can I help you find anything?* **5** (talking about sb's typical behavior or a typical effect): *You can be really annoying sometimes.* ◇ *Bee stings can be very painful.* **6** (used in the negative for saying that you are sure sth is not true): *That can't be the last slice of bread – I just bought a fresh loaf today.* ◇ *You can't possibly be hungry. You only just had lunch.* **7** (used with the verbs "feel," "hear," "see," "smell," "taste")

> NOTE These verbs are not used in the continuous forms. If we want to talk about seeing, hearing, etc. at a particular moment, we use **can**: *I can smell something burning.* NOT *I'm smelling...*

★**can²** /kæn/ ***noun*** [C] **1** a metal container for food that is sealed so that the food stays fresh: *a can of soup* ◇ *a can of beer* ◇ *an empty soda can* ➲ picture at **container**. **2** a metal or plastic container that is used for holding or carrying liquid: *an oil can* ◇ *a can of oil* ◇ *a watering can* ➲ picture at **spray**. **3 the can** (*slang*) the fact of being fired from your job: *Harold got the can yesterday.* **4 the can** (*slang*) prison

IDM **can of worms** (*informal*) if you open up a can of worms, you start doing sth that will cause a lot of problems and be very difficult

**can³** /kæn/ ***verb*** [T] (**can·ning**; **canned**) **1** to put food into a can in order to keep it fresh for a long time **2** (*informal*) to say that sb can no longer work for you (because of bad work, bad behavior, etc.): *Joe got canned from his job for stealing from the company.* ▶ **canned** ***adj.***: *canned fruit/goods*

**Can·a·da** /'kænədə/ ***noun*** [sing.] the second largest country in the world, covering all the northern half of North America, with the exception of Alaska, and which is divided into 10 provinces and 3 territories

**ˌCanada ˌCustoms and 'Revenue ˌAgency** ***noun*** [sing.] → CCRA

**'Canada Day** ***noun*** [sing.] (in Canada) a national holiday held on July 1 to celebrate the original joining together of provinces to form Canada in 1867

**ˌCanada 'Pension Plan** ***noun*** [sing.] (*abbr.* **CPP**) (in Canada) a system for saving money to live on in old age, which both workers and their employers pay into and which is administered by the government

**Ca·na·di·an** /kə'neɪdiən/ ***adj.*** from or connected with Canada: *Have you met Heather? She's Canadian.* ◇ *Canadian history* ▶ **Ca·na·di·an** ***noun*** [C]: *He married a Canadian.*

**the CaˌnadianˌBill of 'Rights** ***noun*** [sing.] an official written statement which guarantees certain basic human rights to Canadian citizens, such as life, freedom, equality, etc.

**the CaˌnadianˌCharter ofˌRights and 'Freedoms** ***noun*** [sing.] an official document that is part of Canada's constitution which guarantees basic political, legal and language rights, as well as the rights of Aboriginals

**Caˌnadian 'football** ***noun*** [C] a game that is played by two teams of twelve players who wear special protective equipment and try to throw, carry or kick an oval ball to the opposing team's end of the field ➲ Look at the note at **football**.

**the Caˌnadian 'Forces** ***noun*** [pl.] the official name of the Canadian military, consisting of the army, navy and air force

**Caˌnadian 'French** ***noun*** [U] the French language as it is written and spoken by French-speaking (francophone) Canadians

★**ca·nal** /kə'næl/ ***noun*** [C] a channel that is cut

through land so that boats or ships can travel along it or so that water can flow to an area where it is needed: *the Panama Canal*

**ca·nar·y** /kəˈnɛri/ ***noun*** [C] (*pl.* **ca·nar·ies**) a small yellow bird that sings and is often kept in a cage as a pet

★**can·cel** /ˈkænsl/ ***verb*** [T] (**can·cel·ing**; **can·celed** or **can·cel̲·ling**; **can·cel̲led**) **1** to decide that sth that had been planned or arranged will not happen: *Because of the bad weather, the picnic was canceled.* ➲ Look at **postpone**. **2** to stop sth that you asked for or agreed to: *We need to cancel the reservation.* ◇ *I would like to cancel my order for these books.*

PHR V **cancel (sth) out** to be equal or have an equal effect: *What I owe you is the same as what you owe me, so our debts cancel each other out.*

**can·cel·la·tion** (*also* **cancelation**) /ˌkænsəˈleɪʃn/ ***noun*** [C,U] the act of canceling sth: *After the snowstorm, we listened to the list of school cancellations on the radio.* ◇ *The cancellation of the game was a great disappointment.*

**Can·cer** /ˈkænsər/ ***noun*** [C,U] the fourth sign of the zodiac, the Crab; a person who was born under this sign

★**can·cer** /ˈkænsər/ ***noun*** [C,U] a very serious disease in which cells in the body grow in an uncontrolled way: *She has lung cancer.* ◇ *He died of cancer.* ▸ **can·ce·rous** /ˈkænsərəs/ ***adj.***

**can·did** /ˈkændəd/ ***adj.*** honest and open; saying exactly what you think ➲ noun **candor** ▸ **can·did·ly** ***adv.***

**can·di·da·cy** /ˈkændədəsi/ ***noun*** [U] being a candidate

★**can·di·date** /ˈkændədət; -deɪt/ ***noun*** [C] a person who applies for a job or wants to be elected to or chosen for a particular position: *a candidate for the job*

**candles**

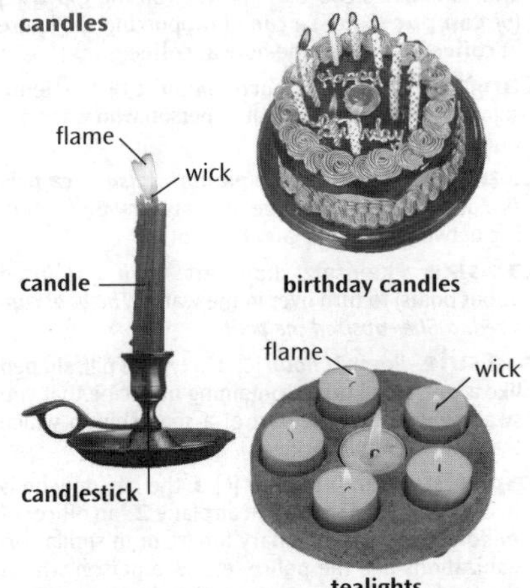


★**can·dle** /ˈkændl/ ***noun*** [C] a round stick of wax with a piece of string (a **wick**) through the middle that you can burn to give light: *to light/blow out a candle*

**can·dle·light** /ˈkændl·laɪt/ ***noun*** [U] the light that a candle produces: *They had dinner by candlelight.*

**can·dle·stick** /ˈkændlstɪk/ ***noun*** [C] a holder for a candle or candles ➲ picture at **candle**.

**can·dor** /ˈkændər/ ***noun*** [U] the quality of being honest; saying exactly what you think ➲ adjective **candid**

★**can·dy** /ˈkændi/ ***noun*** [C,U] (*pl.* **can·dies**) (a small piece of) sweet food made with sugar or chocolate: *You eat too much candy.* ◇ *a piece of candy*

ˈ**candy bar** ***noun*** [C] a piece of sweet food, usually made of or covered in chocolate, that is long and thin and that you buy wrapped in paper or plastic

**cane** /keɪn/ ***noun*** **1** [C] a stick that you use to lean on if you have difficulty walking: *My grandmother walks with a cane.* ➲ picture at **crutch**. **2** [C,U] the long, hollow stem of certain plants, such as the sugar plant

**ca·nine** /ˈkeɪnaɪn/ ***adj.*** connected with dogs or like a dog

**can·is·ter** /ˈkænəstər/ ***noun*** [C] a small metal container

**can·na·bis** /ˈkænəbəs/ ***noun*** [U] (*formal*) a plant whose leaves some people dry and smoke. Cannabis is illegal in the U.S., Canada and many other countries. ➲ Look at **marijuana**.

**can·ni·bal** /ˈkænəbl/ ***noun*** [C] a person who eats other people ▸ **can·ni·bal·ism** /-bəlɪzəm/ ***noun*** [U]

**can·non** /ˈkænən/ ***noun*** [C] (*pl.* **can·nons** or **cannon**) **1** a large old-fashioned gun that was used for firing stone or metal balls (**cannonballs**) **2** a large modern gun on a ship, tank, airplane, etc. ➲ Look also at **loose cannon**.

**can·not** /ˈkænɑt; kəˈnɑt/ = CAN NOT

**ca·noe**[1] /kəˈnu/ ***noun*** [C] a light, narrow boat for one or two people that you can move through the water using a flat piece of wood (a **paddle**) ➲ Look at **kayak**.

**ca·noe**[2] /kəˈnu/ ***verb*** [I] (*pres. part.* **ca·noe·ing**; *3rd person sing. pres.* **ca·noes**; *pt, pp* **ca·noed**) to travel in a CANOE[1]

NOTE We can say "He is learning to canoe" or "They canoed down the river," but when we are talking about spending time in a canoe, it is more usual to say **go canoeing**: *We're going canoeing on the lake tomorrow.*

ˈ**can ˌopener** ***noun*** [C] a kitchen tool for opening cans of food ➲ picture at **kitchen**.

**can·o·py** /ˈkænəpi/ ***noun*** [C] (*pl.* **can·o·pies**) a cover, often a piece of cloth, that hangs above sth: *a bed with a canopy over it*

**can't** *short for* CAN NOT

**can·ta·loupe** (*also* **cantaloup**) /ˈkæntl·oʊp/ (*also* ˈ**cantaloupe ˌmelon**) ***noun*** [C] a type of large fruit (**melon**) with a green skin and orange flesh ➲ picture on study page **A28-29**.

**can·teen** /kænˈtin/ ***noun*** [C] a small container for carrying water and other drinks, used by people who are camping, etc.

**can·vas** /ˈkænvəs/ ***noun*** **1** [U] a type of strong cloth that is used for making tents, sails, bags, etc.

2 [C] a piece of CANVAS (1) for painting a picture on; the painting itself

**can·vass** /'kænvəs/ ***verb*** **1** [T] to find out what people's opinions are about sth: *to canvass voters before an election* **2** [I,T] to go around an area trying to persuade people to vote for a particular person or political party in an election

**can·yon** /'kænyən/ ***noun*** [C] a deep valley with very steep sides: *the Grand Canyon in Arizona*

**can·yon·eer·ing** /ˌkænyə'nɪrɪŋ/ (*especially Cdn* **can·yon·ing** /'kænyənɪŋ/) ***noun*** [U] a sport in which you follow mountain streams into deep valleys (canyons) by climbing down with ropes or by being carried along by the fast-flowing water

★**cap**[1] /kæp/ ***noun*** [C] **1** a type of soft hat: *a baseball cap* ➲ Look also at **baseball cap** and **stocking cap**. **2** a hat that is worn for a particular purpose: *a shower cap* **3** a covering for the end or top of sth: *Please put the cap back on the bottle.* ◇ *Take the lens cap off before you take the picture!* ➲ Look at the note at **top**[1]. **4** an upper limit on sth, especially money: *Congress is discussing a cap on corporate taxes.* ◇ *They plan to put a cap on the number of new employees that can be hired.*

**cap**[2] /kæp/ ***verb*** [T] (**cap·ping**; **capped**) **1** to cover the top of sth: *mountains capped with snow* ◇ *Every dentist knows how to cap a tooth.* **2** to follow sth with sth bigger or better **3** to put a limit on sth, especially money: *plans to cap taxes*

**ca·pa·bil·i·ty** /ˌkeɪpə'bɪləṭi/ ***noun*** [C,U] (*pl.* **ca·pa·bil·i·ties**) the quality of being able to do sth: *How many countries have nuclear capability* (= have a nuclear bomb)? ◇ *People are often not aware of their own capabilities.*

★**ca·pa·ble** /'keɪpəbl/ ***adj.*** **1** having a lot of skill; good at doing sth: *She's a very capable teacher.* ◇ *We need a capable person to organize the concert.* **2 capable of (doing) sth** able to do sth; having the power to do sth: *He's capable of passing the test if he tries harder.* ◇ *That car is capable of 180 miles per hour.* ◇ *I do not believe that she's capable of stealing* (= she is not the sort of person who would steal). OPP **incapable**

★**ca·pac·i·ty** /kə'pæsəṭi/ ***noun*** (*pl.* **ca·pac·i·ties**) **1** [sing., U] the greatest amount that a container or space can hold: *The gas tank has a capacity of 20 gallons.* ◇ *The stadium was filled* ***to capacity***. **2** [sing., U] the amount that a factory or machine can produce: *The power plant is working at full capacity.* **3** [sing.] **capacity (for sth)** the ability to understand or do sth: *He has the mental capacity of a three-year-old child.* **4** [C] the official position that a person has: ***In his capacity as*** *chairman of the committee, he approved the plan.*

**cape** /keɪp/ ***noun*** [C] **1** a piece of clothing with no sleeves that hangs from your shoulders **2** a piece of land that sticks out into the ocean: *the Cape of Good Hope*

**ca·per** /'keɪpər/ ***noun*** [C] the small green flower bud of a Mediterranean bush, preserved in vinegar and used to flavor dishes and sauces

★**cap·i·tal**[1] /'kæpəṭl/ ***noun*** **1** [C] the town or city where the government of a country or state is: *Madrid is the capital of Spain.* ◇ *Minneapolis is the biggest city in Minnesota, but St. Paul is the state capital.* ➲ Look at **capitol**. **2** [C] (*also* **capital letter**) the large form of a letter that is used at the beginning of a name or sentence: *Write your name in capitals.* **3** [U] an amount of money that you use to start a business or to invest so that you earn more money on it: *When she had enough capital, she bought some new equipment.* ◇ *The corporation has been trying to raise extra capital.*

**cap·i·tal**[2] /'kæpəṭl/ ***adj.*** **1** (only *before* a noun) written in the large form that we use at the beginning of a name, a sentence, etc.: *"David" begins with a capital "D."* **2** connected with punishment by death: *a capital offense* (= a crime for which sb can be sentenced to death) ◇ *capital punishment* (= punishment by death)

**cap·i·tal·ism** /'kæpəṭəlɪzəm/ ***noun*** [U] the economic system in which businesses are owned and run for profit by individuals and not by the government ➲ Look at **communism** and **socialism**. ▸ **cap·i·tal·ist** ***noun*** [C], ***adj.***

**cap·i·tal·ize** /'kæpəṭəlaɪz/ ***verb*** [T] to write sth as a CAPITAL[2] (1) letter: *Remember to capitalize the first letters of names.*

PHR V **capitalize on sth** to use sth to your advantage: *We can capitalize on the mistakes that our rivals have made.*

**cap·i·tol** /'kæpəṭl/ ***noun*** [C] **1** (*also* **Capitol**) the building where a state's government meets: *the state capitol building* **2 the Capitol** [sing.] the building in Washington, D.C., where the U.S. Congress meets ➲ For more information on the U.S. political system, look at study page **A10**.

**ca·pit·u·late** /kə'pɪtʃəleɪt/ ***verb*** [I] (*formal*) to stop fighting and say that you have lost; to give in to sb and do what he/she wants ▸ **ca·pit·u·la·tion** /kəˌpɪtʃə'leɪʃn/ ***noun*** [C,U]

**cap·puc·ci·no** /ˌkæpə'tʃinoʊ; ˌkɑ-/ ***noun*** **1** [U] a type of coffee made with milk which has been heated with steam so that it has bubbles (foam) and sometimes chocolate powder on the top **2** [C] (*pl.* **cap·puc·ci·nos**) a cup of cappuccino ➲ Picture at **coffee**. ➲ Look at the note at **coffee**.

**Cap·ri·corn** /'kæprɪkɔrn/ ***noun*** [C,U] the tenth sign of the zodiac, the Goat; a person who was born under this sign

**ca·pri pants** /kə'pri pænts/ (*also* **ca·pris** /kə'priz/) ***noun*** [pl.] a type of pants for women ending between the knee and the foot

**cap·size** /'kæpsaɪz; kæp'saɪz/ ***verb*** [I,T] (used about boats) to turn over in the water: *The boat capsized.* ◇ *She capsized the boat.*

**cap·sule** /'kæpsl/ ***noun*** [C] **1** a type of pill, shaped like a very small tube, containing medicine that you swallow whole **2** the part of a spaceship in which the crew live and work

★**cap·tain** /'kæptən/ ***noun*** [C] **1** the person who is in command of a ship or an airplane **2** an officer of middle rank in the military forces, or in similar organizations like the police, etc. **3** a person who is the leader of a group or team: *Who's the captain of the football team?*

**cap·tion** /'kæpʃn/ ***noun*** [C] the words that are written above or below a picture, cartoon, etc. to explain what it is about

**cap·ti·vate** /ˈkæptəveɪt/ *verb* [T] to attract and hold sb's attention ▸ **cap·ti·vat·ing** *adj.* /-veɪt̬ɪŋ/

**cap·tive¹** /ˈkæptɪv/ *noun* [C] a prisoner

**cap·tive²** /ˈkæptɪv/ *adj.* kept as a prisoner; (of animals) kept in a cage, zoo, etc.
IDM **hold sb captive** to keep sb as a prisoner and not allow him/her to escape
**take sb captive** to catch sb and hold him/her as your prisoner

NOTE It is also possible to say **hold sb prisoner** and **take sb prisoner**.

**cap·tiv·i·ty** /kæpˈtɪvət̬i/ *noun* [U] the state of being kept as a captive: *Wild animals are often unhappy in captivity.*

**cap·tor** /ˈkæptər/ *noun* [C] (*formal*) a person who takes or keeps a person as a prisoner

★**cap·ture¹** /ˈkæptʃər/ *verb* [T] **1** to take a person or animal prisoner: *The lion was captured and taken back to the zoo.* **2** to take or win sth from your enemy by force: *The town has been captured by the rebels.* **3** to succeed in representing sth in words, pictures, etc.: *This poem captures the atmosphere of the carnival.*

**cap·ture²** /ˈkæptʃər/ *noun* [U] a time when a person, animal or thing is captured

**cars**

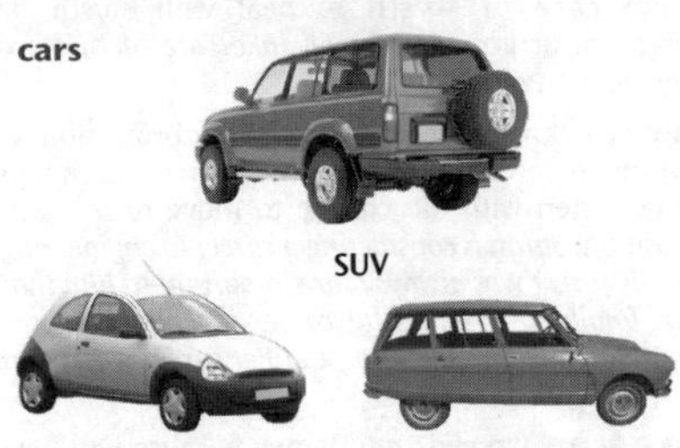


★**car** /kɑr/ *noun* [C] **1** (*also* **automobile**, **auto**) a vehicle with an engine and four wheels that up to five or six people can ride in: *a new/used car* ◇ *Where can I park the car?* ◇ *He's having the car serviced tomorrow.* ◇ *They had a car accident.* ◇ *She gave me a ride in her car.* ◇ *to get into/out of a car* ◇ *a sports car*

NOTE Note that we go **by car**. We can also say **in the car**: *Do you prefer to travel by bus or by car?* ◇ *I come to work in the car.*

**2** one of the separate parts of a train: *a dining car* ◇ *a subway car* ◇ *Some freight trains are over 100 cars long.*

**car·a·mel** /ˈkærəml; ˈkɑrml/ *noun* [C,U] a type of sticky brown candy that is made from boiled sugar, butter, and cream or milk

**car·at** /ˈkærət/ *noun* [C] a unit of measurement used to describe how heavy jewels are: *a 2-carat diamond ring* ➲ Look at **karat**.

**car·bo·hy·drate** /ˌkɑrboʊˈhaɪdreɪt/ *noun* [C,U] one of the substances in food, e.g. sugar, that gives your body energy: *Athletes need a diet that is high in carbohydrates and low in fat.* ◇ *Bread, potatoes and rice all contain carbohydrates.*

**car·bon** /ˈkɑrbən/ *noun* [U] (*symbol* **C**) a chemical substance that is found in all living things, and in a pure form in diamonds and in an impure form in coal

**car·bon·at·ed** /ˈkɑrbəneɪt̬əd/ *adj.* (used about a drink) containing many small bubbles

**ˌcarbon ˈcopy** *noun* [C] (*pl.* **ˌcarbon ˈcopies**) **1** (*abbr.* **cc.**) a copy of a letter, etc. that was made by using a special type of paper with a dark substance on one side (**carbon paper**) **2** a person or thing that is very similar to sb/sth else

**carbon dioxide** /ˌkɑrbən daɪˈɑksaɪd/ *noun* [U] (*symbol* $CO_2$) a gas that has no color or smell that people and animals breathe out of their lungs

**carbon monoxide** /ˌkɑrbən məˈnɑksaɪd/ *noun* [U] (*symbol* **CO**) the poisonous gas that is produced when carbon is burned in a small amount of air. Motor vehicles produce a lot of carbon monoxide.

**car·bu·re·tor** /ˈkɑrbəreɪt̬ər/ *noun* [C] the piece of equipment in a car's engine that mixes gasoline and air

**car·cass** /ˈkɑrkəs/ *noun* [C] the dead body of an animal ➲ Look at **corpse**.

**cards**

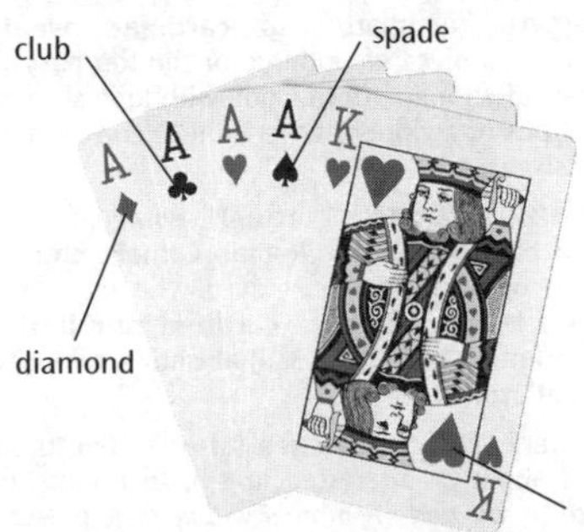


★**card¹** /kɑrd/ *noun* **1** [C] a piece of thick paper or plastic that has information on it: *Here is my business card with my address and telephone number on it.* ◇ *a membership/credit card* ◇ *an identity card* **2** [C] a piece of thick paper with a picture on it that you use to send greetings or a message to sb: *a Christmas/birthday card* ◇ *a get well card* (= one that you send to sb who is sick) ◇ *We got a card* (= a postcard) *from Diana in Portugal.* **3** (*also* **playing card**) [C] one of a set of 52 small pieces of thick paper with shapes or pictures on them that are used for playing games: *a deck of cards* **4 cards** [pl.] games that are played with cards: *Let's play cards.* ◇ *Let's play a game of cards.* ◇ *I never win at cards!*

NOTE A **deck** of cards is divided into four **suits**, two red (**hearts** and **diamonds**) and two black (**clubs** and **spades**). Each suit has an **ace**, a **king**, a **queen**, a **jack** and nine other cards, numbered from 2 to 10. Before we play cards we **shuffle** and **deal** the cards.

**5** a small electronic device that is part of a computer or added to it, and lets it do certain tasks: *a network/sound card*

IDM **in the cards** (*informal*) likely to happen: *The merger has been in the cards for a long time now.*

**lay/put your cards on the table** to tell sb honestly what your plans, ideas, etc. are

**play your cards right** to deal successfully with a particular situation so that you achieve some advantage or the result that you want

**card²** /kɑrd/ ***verb*** [I,T] (*informal*) to ask sb to show an identification card, especially to prove that he/she is old enough to buy or drink alcohol: *We got carded outside the club and they wouldn't let us in.* ◇ *A lot of students buy their beer at the supermarket because they usually don't card there.*

★**card·board** /'kɑrdbɔrd/ ***noun*** [U] very thick paper that is used for making boxes, etc.: *The computer paper was delivered in large cardboard boxes.*

**'card ˌcatalog** ***noun*** [C] a set of cards that contain information on names, books, subjects, etc. and that are kept in order in boxes, drawers, etc. especially in a library

**card·hold·er** /'kɑrdhoʊldər/ ***noun*** [C] a person who has a card that he/she can use to pay for things (a credit card) and whose name appears on the card

**car·di·ac** /'kɑrdiæk/ ***adj.*** (*medical*) connected with the heart or heart disease

**car·di·gan** /'kɑrdɪgən/ (*also* **ˌcardigan 'sweater**) ***noun*** [C] a piece of clothing for the top part of the body, often made from wool, with long sleeves and buttons or a zipper at the front ➲ Look at the note at **sweater**.

**car·di·nal** /'kɑrdn·l; 'kɑrdnəl/ ***noun*** [C] **1** a priest of high rank in the Roman Catholic church **2** a type of North American bird. The male has bright red feathers. **3** (*also* **ˌcardinal 'number**) a whole number, e.g. 1, 2, 3, that shows quantity ➲ Look at **ordinal**.

★**care¹** /kɛr/ ***verb*** **1** [I,T] **care (about sth)** to be worried about or interested in sth; to mind: *I'm going to be late and my mother will be furious, but I don't care.* ◇ *Money is the thing that she cares about most.* ◇ *I don't care what you do.* **2** [I] **care for sth; care to do sth** (*formal*) to like or want sth: *Would you care for a drink?* ◇ *Would you care to leave a message, sir?*

> NOTE **Care for** in this sense is used in questions and always with "would."

**3 care for sb/sth** to like sb/sth: *I don't care for that color very much.* ◇ *Do you think she still cares for him even though he married someone else?*

IDM **I, etc. couldn't care less** (*informal*) it does not matter to me, etc. at all: *"Your jacket isn't very clean." "Well, to tell you the truth, I couldn't care less."*

> NOTE Some people also say **I could care less** in informal situations, but many people consider this form incorrect.

**who cares?** (*informal*) nobody is interested; it is not important to anyone: *"I wonder who'll win the game." "Who cares?"*

PHR V **care for sb** to help sb who is sick or old and do things for him/her: *Who cared for her while she was sick?*

★**care²** /kɛr/ ***noun*** **1** [U] **care (in doing sth)** thinking about what you are doing so that you do it well or do not have an accident: *This box contains glasses – please handle it with care.* **2** [U] taking care of people so that they have things they need; responsibility for sb/sth: *The children were put into foster care.* ◇ *medical care* ◇ *She's in intensive care* (= the part of the hospital for people who are very seriously sick or injured). **3** [U] keeping sth in good condition: *information on the care and maintenance of antique furniture* ◇ *health care* ◇ *skin care products* **4** [C,U] (*formal*) worry, anxiety: *When we were young, we didn't have a care in the world.* ◇ *It was a happy life, free from care.*

IDM **(in) care of sb; c/o** words used on an envelope when you are writing to sb at another person's address: *Mary Jenkins, c/o Mrs. Brown, 10 Riverside Drive, Seattle.* ◇ *You can write to the author in care of his publisher.*

**take care (to do sth)** to be careful: *Goodbye and take care!* ◇ *Take care not to spill your coffee.*

**take care of yourself/sb/sth** to keep yourself/sb/sth safe from injury, illness, damage, etc.: *You should take better care of yourself. You look tired.* ◇ *Could you take care of the cat while we are away on vacation?* ◇ *She always takes great care of her books.*

**take care of sb/sth** to deal with sb/sth; to organize or arrange sth: *I'll take care of the food for the party.*

★**ca·reer** /kə'rɪr/ ***noun*** [C] **1** a job or profession for which you are trained and which you do for a long time, often with the chance to move to a higher position: *Sarah is considering a career in engineering.* ◇ *His career was always more important to him than his family.* ◇ *a successful career in politics* **2** your working life: *She spent most of her career working in India.*

**care·free** /'kɛrfri/ ***adj.*** happy because you have no problems or worries

★**care·ful** /'kɛrfl/ ***adj.*** **1 careful (with sth)** thinking about what you are doing so that you do not have an accident or make mistakes, etc.: *Be careful! There's a car coming.* ◇ *Please be very careful with those glasses.* ◇ *That ladder doesn't look very safe. Be careful you don't fall.* ◇ *I was careful not to say anything about the money.* ◇ *Don't worry – she's a careful driver.* **2** showing care and attention to details: *I'll need to give this matter some careful thought.* ▸ **care·ful·ly** ***adv.***: *Please listen carefully.* ▸ **care·ful·ness** ***noun*** [U]

**care·giv·er** /'kɛrgɪvər/ ***noun*** [C] someone, especially a family member, who looks after a child or a sick or an old person, usually in that person's home: *She enrolled in a support group for caregivers.*

★**care·less** /'kɛrləs/ ***adj.*** **careless (about/with sth)** not thinking enough about what you are doing so that you make mistakes, lose or damage things, etc.: *Here's another careless mistake – you forgot the period at the end of the sentence.* ◇ *an accident caused by careless driving* ▸ **care·less·ly** ***adv.***: *She threw her coat carelessly on the chair.* ▸ **care·less·ness** ***noun*** [U]

**'care ˌpackage** ***noun*** [C] a package of good things to eat sent by friends or family to sb who lives away from home, especially college students or people in the military, etc.

**ca·ress** /kə'rɛs/ ***verb*** [T] to stroke sb in a gentle and loving way: *He caressed her hand and looked into her eyes.* ▸ **ca·ress *noun*** [C]

**care·tak·er** /'kɛrteɪkər/ ***noun*** [C] a person whose job is to take care of a building, land, etc., especially when the owner is away

★**car·go** /'kɑrgoʊ/ ***noun*** [C,U] (*pl.* **car·goes** or **car·gos**) the goods that are carried in a ship or an aircraft: *a cargo plane* (= that carries goods, but not passengers)

**'cargo pants *noun*** [pl.] loose-fitting informal pants with many pockets, including some on the side of the legs ➲ picture on study page **A30**.

**Car·ib·be·an** /ˌkærɪ'biən; kə'rɪbiən/ ***noun*** [sing.] **the Caribbean** the area in the Caribbean Sea where Jamaica, Puerto Rico and other islands are located ▸ **Car·ib·be·an *adj.***: *the Caribbean islands*

**car·i·bou** /'kærəbu/ ***noun*** [C] (*pl.* **car·i·bou** or **car·i·bous**) a type of large deer that lives in the Arctic regions of North America ➲ Look at **reindeer**.

**car·i·ca·ture** /'kærəkətʃər; -tʃʊr/ ***noun*** [C] a picture or description of sb that makes his/her appearance or behavior funnier and more extreme than it really is: *She drew a really funny caricature of our English teacher.* ◇ *Many of the people in the book are caricatures of the author's friends.*

**car·ing** /'kɛrɪŋ/ ***adj.*** showing that you care about other people: *He is a very caring person and will make a wonderful doctor.*

**car·jack·ing** /'kɑrdʒækɪŋ/ ***noun*** [C,U] the crime of taking control of sb's car or forcing him/her to give you his/her car, especially using a gun or other weapon ▸ **car·jack *verb*** [T] ▸ **car·jack·er *noun*** [C]

**car·nage** /'kɑrnɪdʒ/ ***noun*** [U] the violent killing of a large number of people: *a scene of carnage*

**car·na·tion** /kɑr'neɪʃn/ ***noun*** [C] a white, pink or red flower with a pleasant smell

**car·ni·val** /'kɑrnəvl/ ***noun*** [C] a public festival that may include a parade in the streets, music, dancing, or other types of entertainment: *the carnival in Rio* ◇ *The town is holding its annual winter carnival this weekend.*

**car·ol** /'kærəl/ ***noun*** [C] a Christian religious song that people sing at Christmas: *to sing Christmas carols*

**car·ou·sel** /ˌkærə'sɛl/ ***noun*** [C] **1** = MERRY-GO-ROUND **2** (at an airport) a moving belt that carries luggage for passengers to pick up

★**car·pen·ter** /'kɑrpəntər/ ***noun*** [C] a person whose job is to make and repair wooden objects

**car·pen·try** /'kɑrpəntri/ ***noun*** [U] the skill or work of a carpenter

★**car·pet** /'kɑrpət/ ***noun*** **1** [C,U] (a piece of) thick, flat material that is used for covering floors and stairs: *We need new carpet in the bedroom.* ◇ *All the carpets in the house had to be replaced.* ➲ Look at **rug**. **2** [C] a thick layer of sth that covers the ground: *The fields were under a carpet of snow.* ▸ **car·pet·ed *adj.*** /-pət̬əd/: *All the rooms are carpeted.*

**car·pet·ing** /'kɑrpət̬ɪŋ/ ***noun*** [U] carpet that has usually been cut to the exact shape of room: *wall-to-wall carpeting* (= that is the exact size and shape of a room and that has been fastened to the floor)

**car·pool** /'kɑrpul/ ***noun*** [C] an arrangement where several people travel together to work, school, etc. in one car and usually share the costs of traveling ▸ **car·pool *verb*** [I]: *There would be less traffic if more people carpooled and used public transportation.*

**car·port** /'kɑrpɔrt/ ***noun*** [C] a shelter for a car that is made of a roof supported by posts and which is often built beside or against the side of a house ➲ Look at **garage**.

**car·riage** /'kærɪdʒ/ ***noun*** [C] an elegant old-fashioned vehicle with wheels that is pulled by horses ➲ Look also at **baby carriage**.

**car·ri·er** /'kæriər/ ***noun*** [C] **1** (in business) a company that transports people or goods: *The airport is served by all the major U.S. airlines and several foreign carriers.* ◇ *a long-distance carrier* (= that provides equipment and service for long-distance telephone calls) **2** a military vehicle or ship that is used for transporting soldiers, planes, weapons, etc.: *an armored personnel carrier* ◇ *an aircraft carrier* **3** a person or animal that can give an infectious disease to others but does not show the signs of the disease: *Some insects are carriers of tropical diseases.* **4** a box or container that is used for carrying things: *a pet carrier* ➲ Look also at **letter carrier**.

★**car·rot** /'kærət/ ***noun*** [C,U] a long thin orange vegetable that grows under the ground: *a pound of carrots* ◇ *half a cup of grated carrot* ➲ picture on study page **A28-29**.

★**car·ry** /'kæri/ ***verb*** (*pres. part.* **car·ry·ing**; *3rd person sing. pres.* **car·ries**; *pt, pp* **car·ried**)

➤TAKE WITH YOU **1** [T] to hold sb/sth in your hand, arms or on your back while you are moving from one place to another: *Could you carry this bag for me? It's really heavy.* ◇ *She was carrying a backpack on one shoulder.*

> NOTE You use **wear**, not **carry**, to talk about having clothes, jewelry, etc. on your body: *He was wearing a black jacket.*

**2** [T] to have sth with you as you go from place to place: *I never carry much cash with me when I go downtown.* ◇ *Do the police carry guns in your country?*

➤TRANSPORT **3** [T] to transport sb/sth from one place to another: *A plane carrying two hundred passengers crashed yesterday.* ◇ *The waves carried the boat to the shore.*

➤DISEASE **4** [T] to have an infectious disease that can be given to others, usually without showing any signs of the disease yourself: *Rats carry all sorts of diseases.*

➤HAVE AS QUALITY/FEATURE **5** [T] to have sth as a punishment or a result: *The crime carries a penalty of up to 10 years in prison.*

➤APPROVAL/SUPPORT **6** [T] (usually passive) to accept a proposal in a meeting because a majority of people vote for it: *The motion was carried by 12 votes to 9.*

➤OF SOUND **7** [I] (used about a sound) to reach a

long distance: *You'll have to speak louder if you want your voice to carry to the back of the room.*
IDM **be/get carried away** to be so excited that you forget what you are doing: *I got so carried away watching the game that I forgot how late it was.*
**carry weight** to have great influence on the opinion of sb else: *Nick's views carry a lot of weight with our manager.*
PHRV **carry it/sth off** to succeed in doing sth difficult: *He felt nervous before he started his speech but he carried it off very well.*
**carry on (with sth); carry sth on** to continue: *I know it's hard, but we have to try our best to carry on.* ◇ *They ignored me and carried on with their conversation.* ◇ *She intends to carry on her father's work after he retires.*
**carry sth on** to take part in sth: *I can't carry on a normal conversation when you're making that noise.*
**carry sth out 1** to do sth that you have been ordered to do: *The soldiers carried out their orders without question.* **2** to do or perform sth, e.g. a test, repair, etc.: *I think we should wait until more tests have been carried out.* ◇ *The landlord is responsible for carrying out repairs to the building.*

**'carry-on** ***noun*** [C] a small bag or case that you take with you when you go into an airplane: *Only one carry-on is allowed.*

**car·ry·out** /'kæriaʊt/ ***noun*** [C,U] (*especially US*) = TAKEOUT

**'car seat** ***noun*** [C] **1** a special safety seat for a child to use when riding in a car **2** a seat in a car

**carts**

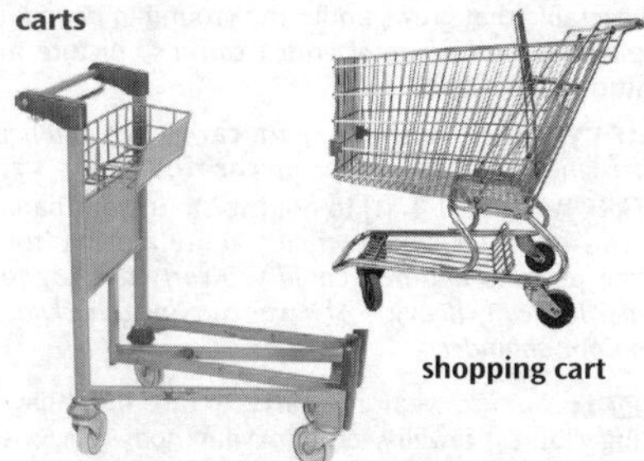

**shopping cart**

**luggage cart**
(*also* **baggage cart**)

**cart**[1] /kɑrt/ ***noun*** [C] **1** a vehicle with two or four wheels that is used for transporting people or things: *a horse and cart* ◇ *a golf cart* **2** a piece of equipment on wheels that you use for moving things: *a shopping/luggage cart*

**cart**[2] /kɑrt/ ***verb*** [T] (*informal*) to take or carry sth somewhere, often with difficulty: *We left our luggage at the hotel because we didn't want to cart it around all day.* ◇ *Six of the women were carted off to the police station.*

**car·ti·lage** /'kɑrt̬əlɪdʒ/ ***noun*** [C,U] a strong substance that surrounds the places where your bones join together

**car·ton** /'kɑrtn/ ***noun*** [C] a small container, usually made of cardboard: *a carton of milk, eggs, etc.* ➲ picture at **container**.

**car·toon** /kɑr'tun/ ***noun*** [C] **1** a funny drawing, especially one in a newspaper or magazine that makes a joke about a current event **2** a movie or television program that tells a story by using moving drawings instead of real people and places: *a Bugs Bunny cartoon*

**car·toon·ist** /kɑr'tunɪst/ ***noun*** [C] a person who draws cartoons

**car·tridge** /'kɑrtrɪdʒ/ ***noun*** [C] **1** a small tube that contains explosive powder and a bullet. You put a cartridge into a gun when you want to fire it. **2** a case containing sth that is used in a machine, for example film for a camera, ink for a printer, etc. Cartridges are put into the machine and can be removed and replaced when they are finished or empty.

**carve** /kɑrv/ ***verb*** **1** [T] **carve sth (out of sth)** to cut wood or stone in order to make an object or to put a pattern or writing on it: *Grandpa enjoys carving miniature animals out of wood.* ◇ *He carved his initials into the desk.* ◇ *to carve a pumpkin* (= into a jack-o'-lantern) *at Halloween* **2** [I,T] to cut a piece of cooked meat into slices: *Can you carve while I serve the vegetables?* ◇ *to carve a turkey*

**carv·ing** /'kɑrvɪŋ/ ***noun*** [C,U] an object or design that has been carved: *There are ancient carvings on the walls of the cave.*

**cas·cade** /kæ'skeɪd/ ***noun*** [C] **1** a waterfall **2** something that hangs or falls in a way that seems similar to a waterfall: *The balcony was covered in a cascade of flowers.* ▶ **cas·cade** ***verb*** [I]: *Water cascaded down the mountainside.*

★**case** /keɪs/ ***noun***
➤SITUATION **1** [C] a particular situation or a situation of a particular type: *In some cases, people have had to sell their homes to pay for medical care.* ◇ *Most of us can sing pretty well – or, in Susie's case, very well.* ◇ *There's no secret to success in this business. It's just a case of hard work.* **2 the case** [sing.] the true situation: *The man said he had graduated from Harvard, but we discovered later that this was not the case.*
➤OF DISEASE **3** [C] an example of an illness; a person who is suffering from an illness: *Cases of the disease are very unusual in this country.* ◇ *The most serious cases were taken to the hospital immediately.*
➤POLICE INVESTIGATION **4** [C] a crime that is being investigated by the police: *a murder case*
➤IN COURT OF LAW **5** [C] something that is decided in a court of law; a trial: *The case will come to trial in a few months.*
➤ARGUMENTS **6** [C, usually sing.] the facts and reasons that support one side in a discussion or legal matter: *She made a case for buying new equipment, but the others disagreed.*
➤CONTAINER **7** [C] (especially in compounds) a container or cover for sth: *a pencil case* ◇ *a pillowcase* ◇ *She put her sunglasses back in the case.* **8** [C] a large box, and often the things inside it: *They delivered three cases of supplies yesterday.* ◇ *It's cheaper to buy them by the case.*
IDM **in any case** whatever happens or has happened: *He didn't say anything about it at the meeting and in any case it's too late now.*
**in case** because sth might happen: *I think I'll take an umbrella in case it rains.* ◇ *Take my number in*

*case you need to call me.* ◇ *I wasn't planning to buy anything, but I took my credit card just in case.*
**in case of sth** if sth happens: *In case of fire, break this glass.*
**in that case** if that is the situation: *"I'm busy on Tuesday." "Oh well, in that case we'll have to meet another day."*

**case·load** /ˈkeɪsloʊd/ ***noun*** [C] all the people that a doctor, lawyer, etc. is responsible for at one time: *a heavy caseload*

**ˌcase ˈstudy** ***noun*** [C] (*pl.* **case studies**) a study of the development of a person, company or group of people

**case·work·er** /ˈkeɪswərkər/ ***noun*** [C] a person whose job is to help a particular person or family in the community with special needs or social problems ▶ **case·work** ***noun*** [U]

★**cash¹** /kæʃ/ ***noun*** [U] **1** money in the form of coins or paper money and not checks, credit cards, etc.: *How would you like to pay – cash or credit card?* ◇ *How much cash do you have with you?*

NOTE We use **cash** when we are talking about coins and paper money, but **change** when we are talking about coins only.

**2** (*informal*) money in any form: *I'm a little short of cash this month, so I can't afford to go out much.*

**cash²** /kæʃ/ ***verb*** [T] to exchange a check, traveler's check, etc. for coins and paper money: *I'm just going to the bank to cash my paycheck.*
PHR V **cash in (on sth)** to take advantage of a situation: *I'm just going to the bank to cash my paycheck.*

**ˈcash cow** ***noun*** [C] a part of a business that always makes a profit and that provides money for the rest of the business

**cash·ew** /ˈkæʃu; kæˈʃu/ (*also* **ˈcashew nut**) ***noun*** [C] a small curved nut from a tropical tree, used in cooking and often eaten with salt on it ➲ picture at **nut**.

**ˈcash flow** ***noun*** [C,U] the movement of money into and out of a business as goods are bought and sold: *a healthy cash flow* (= having the money to make payments when necessary) ◇ *cash flow problems*

**cash·ier** /kæˈʃɪər/ ***noun*** [C] the person in a store, an office, etc. that customers pay money to or get money from

**ˈcash machine** ***noun*** [C] = ATM

**cash·mere** /ˌkæʒˈmɪr; ˌkæʃ-/ ***noun*** [U] a type of wool that is very fine and soft

**ˈcash ˌregister** (*also* **register**) ***noun*** [C] a machine in a store that is used to add together the cost of things that you buy. A cash register has a drawer where money is kept.

**ca·si·no** /kəˈsinoʊ/ ***noun*** [C] (*pl.* **ca·si·nos**) a place where people play card games and other types of games in which you can win or lose money

**cas·ket** /ˈkæskət/ (*also* **coffin**) ***noun*** [C] a box in which a dead body is buried ➲ Look at the note at **funeral**.

**cas·se·role** /ˈkæsəroʊl/ ***noun*** **1** [C,U] a type of food that you make by cooking meat and vegetables in liquid for a long time in the oven: *chicken casserole* **2** [C] a large dish with a lid for cooking casseroles in

**cas·sette** /kəˈsɛt/ ***noun*** [C] a flat case with magnetic tape inside that you use to record and play music and other sounds: *to listen to a cassette* ◇ *to record/play a cassette*

NOTE Another word for **cassette** is **tape**. When you want to go back to the beginning of a cassette you **rewind** it. When you want to go forward, you **fast forward** it. The machine that you use for recording and playing cassettes can be called a **cassette player** or a **tape recorder**. ➲ Look at **video**.

**cast¹** /kæst/ ***noun*** [C] **1** all the actors in a play, movie, etc.: *The movie has an all-star cast.* **2** a covering made of soft, wet material that quickly becomes hard (**plaster**), that is kept around a broken bone until it heals: *Her arm is in a cast.* ➲ picture at **bandage**.

**cast²** /kæst/ ***verb*** [T] (*pt, pp* **cast**) **1** (often passive) to choose an actor for a particular role in a play, movie, etc.: *She always seems to be cast in the same sort of role.* **2** to make an object by pouring hot liquid metal into a shaped container (a **mold**): *a statue cast in bronze* **3** (*old-fashioned*) to throw sth: *She cast a stone into the river.*
IDM **cast doubt on sth** to make people unsure about sth: *The newspaper report casts doubts on the truth of his statement.*
**cast an eye/your eye(s) over sb/sth** to read or look at sb/sth quickly in order to check that it is correct, in good condition, etc.: *Can you just cast an eye over my essay before I hand it in?*
**cast a shadow (across/over sth)** to cause a shadow to appear somewhere: *The tree cast a long shadow across the yard.*
**cast a shadow (over sth)** to stop people from enjoying sth fully: *The accident cast a shadow over the rest of the trip.*
**cast a/your vote** to vote: *Union members will cast their votes on the new agreement today.*
PHR V **cast sb/sth aside** to make yourself free of sb/sth or to leave sb/sth behind because you do not want it anymore: *She cast aside her fear of water and bravely jumped into the pool.*

**caste** /kæst/ ***noun*** [C,U] one of the social classes into which Hindus are divided, especially in India, or the system of dividing people in this way

**ˌcast-ˈiron** ***adj.*** made of a hard type of iron that has been shaped by pouring hot liquid metal into a hollow form (a **mold**): (*figurative*) *a cast-iron alibi* (= one that people cannot doubt)

★**cas·tle** /ˈkæsl/ ***noun*** [C] **1** a large building with high walls and towers that was built in the past to defend people against attack: *a medieval castle* **2** = ROOK ➲ picture at **chess**.

**cas·trate** /ˈkæstreɪt/ ***verb*** [T] to remove part of the sexual organs of a male animal or person ▶ **castra·tion** /kæˈstreɪʃn/ ***noun*** [U]

**ca·su·al** /ˈkæʒuəl/ ***adj.*** **1** (used about clothes) not formal: *On Fridays we're allowed to wear casual clothes to work.* **2** not involving or showing deep feelings: *She tried to appear casual* (= relaxed and not worried) *as he walked toward her.* ◇ *She has a very casual attitude toward her work – I think she should try harder.* ◇ *It was only a casual remark, so I* *don't know why he got so mad.* ◇ *The two species may appear similar to the casual observer, but in fact they are very different.* **3** happening by chance; not planned: *The AIDS virus is not spread through casual contact.* ▶ **ca·su·al·ly** /ˈkæʒəli/ ***adv.***: *Dress casually – it won't be a formal party.* ◇ *She walked in casually and said, "I'm not late, am I?"*

C

**ca·su·al·ty** /ˈkæʒəlti; -ʒuəl-/ ***noun*** [C] (*pl.* **ca·su·al·ties**) **1** a person who is killed or injured in a war or an accident: *The army retreated after suffering heavy casualties.* **2** a person or thing that suffers as a result of sth else: *Many small companies have been casualties of the country's economic problems.*

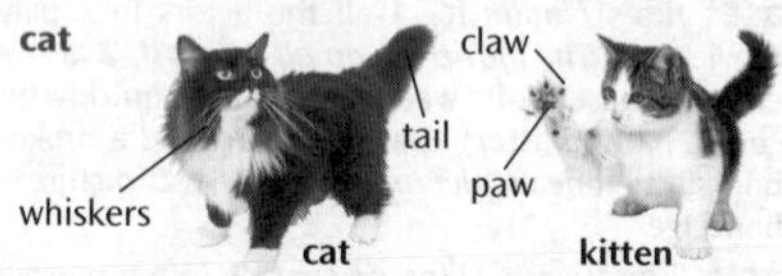


★**cat**[1] /kæt/ ***noun*** [C] **1** a small furry animal with four legs and a tail. People often keep cats as pets. **2** any larger wild animal that is related to a cat, e.g. a lion or tiger: *We went to the zoo to see the big cats.*

NOTE A young cat is called a **kitten**. When a cat makes a soft sound of pleasure, it **purrs**. When it makes a louder sound, it **meows**.

IDM **let the cat out of the bag** to tell a secret carelessly or by mistake: *I wanted it to be a surprise, but my sister let the cat out of the bag.*

**cat·a·log**[1] (*especially Cdn* **catalogue**) /ˈkæt̬l·ɔg; -lɑg/ ***noun*** [C] **1** a book that contains information about all the things you can buy from a company: *a mail-order catalog* **2** a list, often in the form of a book, of all the courses at a college or university, all the paintings in an art show, etc.: *the full course catalog* ➲ Look also at **card catalog**. **3** a series, especially of bad things: *a catalog of disasters*

**cat·a·log**[2] (*especially Cdn* **catalogue**) /ˈkæt̬l·ɔg; -lɑg/ ***verb*** [T] (*pres. part.* **cat·a·log·ing** or **cat·a·log·uing**; *pt, pp* **cat·a·loged** or **cat·a·logued**) to list things in a CATALOG[1]: *She started to catalog all the new library books.*

**cat·a·lyst** /ˈkæt̬əlɪst/ ***noun*** [C] **1** (*technical*) a substance that makes a chemical reaction happen faster, but that is not changed itself **2** a person or thing that causes a change: *The newspaper article served as a catalyst for change in the city government.*

**cat·a·pult** /ˈkæt̬əpʌlt/ ***verb*** [T] to throw sb/sth suddenly and with great force: *When the car crashed, the passengers were catapulted through the windows.* ◇ (*figurative*) *The success of his first movie catapulted him to fame.*

**cat·a·ract** /ˈkæt̬ərækt/ ***noun*** [C] a diseased area that can grow on a person's eye and cause difficulty in seeing

**ca·tas·tro·phe** /kəˈtæstrəfi/ ***noun*** [C] a sudden event that causes great suffering or damage; a disaster: *Major catastrophes like floods and earthquakes happen regularly in that part of the world.* ◇ *a financial catastrophe* ▶ **cat·a·stroph·ic** /ˌkæt̬əˈstrɑfɪk/: *The war had a catastrophic effect on the whole country.*

★**catch**[1] /kætʃ/ ***verb*** (*pt, pp* **caught** /kɔt/)

➤HOLD **1** [T] to take hold of sth that is moving, usually with your hand or hands: *She threw the ball and he caught it in one hand.* ◇ *The dog caught the ball in its mouth.*

➤CAPTURE **2** [T] to capture sb/sth that you have been chasing or looking for: *Two police officers ran after the thief and caught him at the end of the street.* ◇ *The murderer still hasn't been caught.* ◇ *to catch a fish*

➤SB DOING STH **3** [T] to discover sb who is doing sth bad: *I caught her taking money from my purse.*

➤BUS/TRAIN/PLANE **4** [T] to get on a form of public transportation: *I took the bus downtown.* ◇ *to catch a train/plane*

➤BE IN TIME **5** [T] to be in time for sth; not to miss sb/sth: *We arrived just in time to catch the beginning of the movie.* ◇ *I'll call her now. I might just catch her before she leaves the office.*

➤HEAR/UNDERSTAND **6** [T] to hear or understand sth that sb says: *Sorry, I didn't quite catch what you said. Could you say it again?*

➤BECOME STUCK **7** [I,T] to become or cause sth to become accidentally attached to or trapped in sth: *His jacket caught on a nail.* ◇ *I caught my finger in the drawer as I shut it.* ◇ *I'm sorry I'm late. I got caught in the traffic.*

➤ILLNESS **8** [T] to get an illness: *I have a bad cold. I must have caught it from somebody at work.*

IDM **catch sb's attention/eye** → ATTENTION

**catch your breath** to rest after physical exercise so that your breathing returns to normal: *I just need a minute to catch my breath.*

**catch fire** to start burning, often accidentally: *Nobody knows how the building caught fire.*

**catch sb off guard** to surprise and often confuse sb because he/she is not prepared: *The question caught me off guard and I didn't know what to say.*

**catch sb red-handed** to find sb just as he/she is doing sth wrong: *A police officer noticed the broken window and caught the burglars red-handed.*

**catch sight/a glimpse of sb/sth** to see sb/sth for a moment: *I caught sight of the man at the end of the street.* ◇ *We waited outside the theater, hoping to catch a glimpse of the actress.*

PHRV **catch on** (*informal*) **1** to understand or realize sth: *Sometimes she's a little slow to catch on.* **2** to become popular or fashionable: *The idea never really caught on in this country.*

**catch up (with sb)** **1** to reach sb/sth who is ahead of you: *Jackie was walking very fast and I had to run to catch up with her.* **2** to reach the same level as sb/sth else: *Our economy is developing fast and we should soon catch up with other countries in the western world.*

**catch up on sth** to spend time doing sth that you have not been able to do until now: *I'll have to go into the office this weekend to catch up on my work.*

**be/get caught up in sth** to be or get involved in sth, usually without intending to: *I got caught up in all the excitement about the championship game.*

**catch**[2] /kætʃ/ ***noun*** [C] **1** an act of taking hold of sth that is moving, usually with your hand or hands **2** the amount of fish that sb has caught: *The fishermen brought their catch to the harbor.* **3** a device for fastening sth and keeping it closed: *The catch on my necklace is broken.* **4** a hidden disadvantage to sth that seems attractive: *I can't believe you're selling that for such a low price – what's the catch?*

IDM (a) **Catch-22; a Catch-22 situation** a difficult situation from which you cannot escape because you need to do one thing before doing a second, and you cannot do the second thing before doing the first: *I can't get a job because I don't have any work experience, but how can I get work experience without getting a job? It's a Catch-22 situation.*

**'catch-all** *noun* [C] **1** a thing for holding many small objects **2** a group or a description that includes different things and that does not state clearly what is included or not ▸ **'catch-all** *adj.* (only before a noun): *a catch-all phrase/term*

**catch·er** /'kætʃər/ *noun* [C] (*sports*) (in baseball) the player who stands behind the person who should hit the ball (**the batter**) and catches the balls that he/she does not hit ➲ picture at **baseball**.

**catch·phrase** /'kætʃfreɪz/ *noun* [C] a popular phrase that may be connected with a politician, entertainer, etc. who used it and made it famous

**catch·y** /'kætʃi/ *adj.* (**catch·i·er; catch·i·est**) (used about a tune or song) easy to remember

**cat·e·gor·i·cal** /ˌkæt̬ə'gɔrɪkl; -'gɑr-/ *adj.* completely definite: *The answer was a categorical "no."* ▸ **cat·e·gor·i·cal·ly** /-kli/: *The spokesperson categorically denied the rumor.*

**cat·e·go·rize** /'kæt̬əgəraɪz/ *verb* [T] to divide people or things into groups; to say that sb/sth belongs to a particular group ➲ Look also at **label**[2](2) and **pigeonhole**[2](1).

★**cat·e·go·ry** /'kæt̬əˌgɔri/ *noun* [C] (*pl.* **cat·e·go·ries**) a group of people or things that are similar to each other: *There were two categories in the contest: teams and individuals.* ◇ *These books are divided into categories according to subject.*

**ca·ter** /'keɪt̬ər/ *verb* **1** [I] **cater to sb/sth** to provide what sb/sth needs or wants: *We need a hotel that caters to small children.* ◇ *a show that caters to people's love of celebrity gossip* **2** [I,T] **cater (sth); cater (for sb/sth)** to provide and serve food and drinks for a social event: *the company that catered our wedding reception*

**ca·ter·er** /'keɪt̬ərər/ *noun* [C] a person or business that provides food and drinks for social events

**ca·ter·ing** /'keɪt̬ərɪŋ/ *noun* [U] the activity or business of providing food and drinks for social events: *the hotel and catering industry*

**cat·er·pil·lar** /'kæt̬əpɪlər; 'kæt̬ər-/ *noun* [C] an animal like a small hairy worm with legs, that changes into a butterfly or moth ➲ picture at **insect**.

**cat·fish** /'kætfɪʃ/ *noun* [C,U] (*pl.* **cat·fish**) a large fish that lives in lakes and rivers and is eaten as food. Catfish have long thin things like hairs near their mouths.

**ca·the·dral** /kə'θidrəl/ *noun* [C] a large church that is the most important one in a district

**Cath·o·lic** /'kæθlɪk; -θəlɪk/ *noun* [C], *adj.* (a member) of the Christian church which has the Pope as its head: *She's (a) Catholic.* ➲ Look at **Protestant**.

**Ca·thol·i·cism** /kə'θɑləsɪzəm/ *noun* [U] the beliefs of the Catholic Church

**CAT scan** /'kæt skæn/ (*also* **CT scan** /ˌsi 'ti skæn/) *noun* [C] (*medical*) a medical examination that uses a computer to produce an image of the inside of sb's body from X-RAY or ULTRASOUND pictures

**cat·sup** /'kætsəp; 'kɛtʃəp/ *noun* [U] (*U.S.*) = KETCHUP

**cat·tle** /'kæt̬l/ *noun* [pl.] male and female cows, e.g. on a farm: *a herd of cattle* (= a group of them) ➲ Look at the note at **cow**.

**Cau·ca·sian** /kɔ'keɪʒn/ *noun* [C], *adj.* (of) a member of the race of people who have white or light-colored skin ➲ **White** is more common nowadays.

**cau·cus** /'kɔkəs/ *noun* (*pl.* **cau·cus·es**) **1** [C] (in politics) a group of people with a special set of interests or responsibilities who meet to make decisions or work to make something happen: *the Congressional Black Caucus* **2** [C] (in the U.S.) an event in which people decide who will be a political party's candidate in a later election: *20 states will hold precinct caucuses on Tuesday to choose delegates to the parties' national conventions.* ➲ Look at **primary**[2]. **3** [C] (in Canada) the members of a legislative assembly belonging to a political party **4** [C,U] a meeting of a caucus: *Before the meeting, representatives met* ***in caucus****.*

**caught** *past tense, past participle of* CATCH[1]

**cau·li·flow·er** /'kɔlɪˌflaʊər; 'kɑlɪ-/ *noun* [C,U] a large vegetable with green leaves and a round white center that you eat when it is cooked ➲ picture on study page **A28-29**.

★**cause**[1] /kɔz/ *noun* **1** [C] a thing or person that makes sth happen: *The police do not know the cause of the accident.* ◇ *Smoking is one of the causes of heart disease.* **2** [U] **cause (for sth)** reason: *I don't think you have any real cause for complaint.* **3** [C] an aim or principle that a group of people believe in and support: *We are all committed to the cause of racial equality.* ◇ *I don't mind giving money to a good cause.*

IDM **a lost cause** → LOST[2]

★**cause**[2] /kɔz/ *verb* [T] to make sth happen: *The fire was caused by careless smoking.* ◇ *High winds caused many trees to fall during the night.* ◇ *Is your leg causing you any pain?*

**'cause** /kəz/ *conj.* (*informal*) because

> NOTE This word is common in spoken English, but in formal writing we must use **because**.

**caus·tic** /'kɔstɪk/ *adj.* **1** (used about a substance) able to burn or destroy things by chemical action **2** (used about a comment or type of humor) cruel and unkind

**cau·tion**[1] /'kɔʃn/ *noun* [U] great care, because of possible danger: *Caution: Dangerous Intersection Ahead* (= on a road sign). ◇ *Use caution when working with strong chemicals.*

**cau·tion**[2] /'kɔʃn/ *verb* [I,T] to warn sb about sth: *He cautioned me not to speak to reporters about the case.* ◇ *The President's advisers have cautioned against reacting too strongly to the news.* ◇ *Dixon was cautioned by his boss for arriving late.*

**cau·tious** /'kɔʃəs/ *adj.* taking great care to avoid possible danger: *I'm very cautious about expressing*

C

*my opinions in public.* ◇ *a cautious approach to a difficult problem* ◇ *She's a very cautious driver.* ▸ **cau·tious·ly** *adv.*

**cav·al·ry** /ˈkævlri/ *noun* [sing.] **1** the part of the army that fights in heavily protected vehicles **2** the group of soldiers who fought on horses in the past

**cave**[1] /keɪv/ *noun* [C] a large hole in the side of a cliff or hill, or under the ground: *prehistoric paintings on a cave wall*

**cave**[2] /keɪv/ *verb*

PHRV **cave in 1** to fall in: *The roof of the tunnel had caved in and we couldn't go any farther.* **2** to suddenly stop arguing or opposing sth: *He finally caved in and agreed to our plan.*

**cav·ern** /ˈkævərn/ *noun* [C] a large, deep cave

**cav·i·ar** (*also* **caviare**) /ˈkæviɑr/ *noun* [U] the eggs of a large fish that are eaten as food. Caviar is usually very expensive.

**cav·i·ty** /ˈkævət̬i/ *noun* [C] (*pl.* **cav·i·ties**) **1** a hole in a tooth: *You'll get cavities if you eat too much candy.* **2** an empty space inside sth solid, especially inside your body: *sinus cavities*

**CBC** /ˌsi bi ˈsi/ *abbr.* Canadian Broadcasting Corporation

**CBS** /ˌsi bi ˈɛs/ *abbr.* Columbia Broadcasting System

**cc** /ˌsi ˈsi/ *abbr.* **1** carbon copy; (used on business letters and e-mails to show that a copy is being sent to another person): *to Sandra Garcia, cc Richard Waters* **2** cubic centimeter(s): *an 850cc engine*

**CCRA** /ˌsi si ɑr ˈeɪ/ (*also* **ˌRevenue ˈCanada**) *noun* [sing.] Canada Customs and Revenue Agency; the department of the Canadian government that deals with personal income tax, and with taxes on goods that are bought and sold

★**CD** /ˌsi ˈdi/ (*also* **compact disc**) *noun* [C] a small, round piece of hard plastic, like a record, on which sound is recorded or information is stored. You play a CD on a special machine: *a CD player*

**CD-ROM** /ˌsi di ˈrɑm/ *noun* [U] compact disc read-only memory; a compact disc that can be used in a computer and has a lot of information recorded on it. The information cannot be changed or removed.

**C.E.** (*also* **CE**) /ˌsi ˈi/ *abbr.* Common Era SYN **A.D.** ➲ Compare **B.C.** and **B.C.E.**

★**cease** /sis/ *verb* [I,T] (*formal*) to stop or end: *Fighting in the area has now ceased.* ◇ *That organization has ceased to exist.* ◇ *500 people lost their jobs when the company ceased operations.*

**cease·fire** /ˈsisfaɪər/ (*also* **ˈcease-fire**) *noun* [C] an agreement between two groups to stop fighting each other SYN **truce**

**ce·dar** /ˈsidər/ *noun* **1** [C] a type of tall tree that has very thin sharp leaves (**needles**) and red wood with a sweet smell **2** [U] the wood from the cedar tree: *a cedar chest*

**cede** /sid/ *verb* [T] (*formal*) to give land or control of sth to another country or person

★**ceil·ing** /ˈsilɪŋ/ *noun* [C] **1** the top surface of the inside of a room: *We painted the walls pink and the ceiling white.* ◇ *a room with a high/low ceiling* **2** a top limit on wages, prices, etc.: *to put a ceiling on welfare spending*

★**cel·e·brate** /ˈsɛləbreɪt/ *verb* **1** [I,T] to do sth special and enjoyable on an important day or because of an important event: *When I got the job, we celebrated by opening a bottle of champagne.* ◇ *Mrs. Halford celebrated her 80th birthday yesterday.* **2** [T] (used about a priest) to lead a religious ceremony: *to celebrate Mass*

**cel·e·brat·ed** /ˈsɛləbreɪt̬əd/ *adj.* (*formal*) famous: *a celebrated actress*

★**cel·e·bra·tion** /ˌsɛləˈbreɪʃn/ *noun* [C,U] the act or occasion of doing sth enjoyable because sth good has happened or because it is a special day: *New Year's Eve celebrations* ◇ *Her son's visit was cause for celebration.*

**ce·leb·ri·ty** /səˈlɛbrət̬i/ *noun* [C] (*pl.* **ce·leb·ri·ties**) a famous person

**cel·er·y** /ˈsɛləri/ *noun* [U] a vegetable with long green stems that is eaten raw in salads and sometimes used in cooking: *a stalk of celery* ➲ picture on study page **A28-29**.

**cel·i·bate** /ˈsɛləbət/ *adj.* (*formal*) remaining unmarried or never having sexual relations, often because of religious beliefs ▸ **cel·i·ba·cy** /ˈsɛləbəsi/ *noun* [U]: *to practice celibacy*

★**cell** /sɛl/ *noun* [C] **1** the smallest living part of an animal or a plant body: *The human body consists of billions of cells.* ◇ *red blood cells* **2** a small room in a prison or police station in which a prisoner is locked

**cel·lar** /ˈsɛlər/ *noun* [C] an underground room, especially one that is used for storing things: *a wine cellar* ◇ *a storm/hurricane cellar* ➲ Look at **basement**.

**cel·list** /ˈtʃɛlɪst/ *noun* [C] a person who plays the cello

**cel·lo** /ˈtʃɛloʊ/ *noun* [C] (*pl.* **cel·los**) a musical instrument like a large violin. You sit down to play it and hold it between your knees.



**cel·lo·phane** /ˈsɛləfeɪn/ *noun* [U] thin transparent material that is used for wrapping things

**cel·lu·lar** /ˈsɛlyələr/ *adj.* consisting of CELLS (1): *cellular tissue*

★**ˌcellular ˈphone** (*also informal* **cell·phone**, **ˈcell phone**) *noun* [C] a telephone that you can carry around with you and that works by using radio signals

**cel·lu·lite** /ˈsɛlyəlaɪt/ *noun* [U] a type of fat that some people get below their skin, which stops the surface of the skin looking smooth

**Cel·si·us** /ˈsɛlsiəs/ (*also* **centigrade**) *adj.* (*abbr.* **C**) the name of a scale for measuring temperatures, in which water freezes at 0° and boils at 100°: *The temperature tonight will fall to 7°C.*

NOTE We say "seven degrees Celsius." **Celsius** is the system of measuring temperature used in Canada. In the U.S., Celsius is mainly used in science and **Fahrenheit** is the scale used to talk about the weather, body temperature, etc.

**ce·ment**[1] /səˈmɛnt/ *noun* [U] a gray powder that becomes hard after it is mixed with water and left to dry. It is used in building for sticking bricks or stones together or for making very hard surfaces. ➲ Look at the note at **concrete**[2].

**ce·ment**[2] /sə'mɛnt/ ***verb*** [T] **1** to stick things together **2** to make a relationship very strong: *This agreement has cemented the relationship between our two companies.*

**cem·e·ter·y** /'sɛmə,tɛri/ ***noun*** [C] (*pl.* **cem·e·ter·ies**) a place where dead people are buried ➲ Look at **graveyard**.

**cen·sor** /'sɛnsər/ ***noun*** [C] an official who examines books, movies, plays, etc. and removes any parts that might offend people, or who examines letters, newspaper reports, etc. and removes any parts which contain secret information: *The network's censors wouldn't allow the comedian to say those words on TV.* ▸ **cen·sor *verb*** [T]: *The journalists said that all the information they sent back to the U.S. was being censored.* ▸ **cen·sor·ship *noun*** [U]: *government censorship of radio and TV programs*

**cen·sure** /'sɛnʃər/ ***verb*** [T] (*formal*) to tell sb, in a strong and formal way, that he/she has done sth wrong: *The attorney was censured for not revealing the information earlier.* ▸ **cen·sure *noun*** [U] (*formal*): *a letter of censure*

**cen·sus** /'sɛnsəs/ ***noun*** [C] (*pl.* **cen·sus·es**) an official count of the people who live in a country, including information about their ages, jobs, etc.: *to take a census*

★**cent** /sɛnt/ ***noun*** [C] (*symbol* ¢) a unit of money that is worth 1/100 of a dollar or of the main unit of money in some other countries

NOTE A coin that is worth one cent is called a **penny**. Look also at **nickel**, **dime** and **quarter**.

**cen·ten·ni·al** /sɛn'tɛniəl/ ***noun*** [C] the year that comes exactly one hundred years after an important event or the beginning of sth: *1986 was the centennial of the Statue of Liberty.* ◇ *centennial celebrations* ➲ Look at **bicentennial**.

★**cen·ter**[1] /'sɛntər/ ***noun***

➤MIDDLE **1** [C, usually sing.] the middle point or part of sth: *There was a vase of flowers in the center of the table.* ◇ *The parade went right through the center of town.* ◇ *a chocolate with a caramel center* ➲ Look at the note at **middle**.

➤BUILDING/PLACE **2** [C] a building or place where a particular activity or service is based: *a shopping center* ◇ *the campus health center* ◇ *New York is a major financial center.*

➤OF ATTENTION **3** [C] a person or thing that receives a lot of attention: *She always likes to be the center of attention.*

➤IN POLITICS **4 the center** [sing.] a political position that is not extreme: *The candidate's views place her firmly in the center.*

➤IN SPORT **5** [C] (*sports*) a player whose position is in the middle of the field, etc. in sports such as football and basketball ➲ picture at **soccer**. ➲ picture at **tennis**.

**cen·ter**[2] /'sɛntər/ ***verb***

PHR V **center on/around sb/sth** to have sb/sth as its center: *His life centers on his family.*

**cen·ti·grade** /'sɛntəgreɪd/ ***adj.*** = CELSIUS

**cen·ti·me·ter** /'sɛntə,miṭər/ ***noun*** [C] (*abbr.* **cm**) a measure of length. There are 100 centimeters in a meter: *The insect was about two centimeters long.*

★**cen·tral** /'sɛntrəl/ ***adj.*** **1** (usually *before* a noun) in the center of sth: *a town in central Manitoba* ◇ *the countries of Central America* (= between Mexico and Colombia) ◇ *the building's central staircase* **2** (only *before* a noun) (used about an office, group, etc.) having control of all other parts of an organization: *All packages are transported to the city's central post office.* **3** controlled from one main point: *central air conditioning* **4** most important; main: *The story's central character is a fifteen-year-old girl.* ◇ *This point is central to my argument.*

**,Central 'Daylight Time** ***noun*** [U] (*abbr.* **CDT**) the time system used in the central part of the U.S. and Canada from April to October, when the clocks are set one hour ahead of *Central Standard time* ➲ Look at **daylight-saving time**.

**cen·tral·ize** /'sɛntrəlaɪz/ ***verb*** [T] to make sth come under central control: *We plan to centralize our customer services to make them more efficient.*

**cen·tral·ly** /'sɛntrəli/ ***adv.*** in or from the center: *a centrally located city* (= near the center of a region or country) ◇ *the centrally planned economies of Communist countries*

**,central 'processing ,unit** ***noun*** [C] (*computing*) (*abbr.* **CPU**) the part of a computer that controls all the other parts of the system

**,Central 'Standard Time** ***noun*** [U] (*abbr.* **CST**) the time system used in the central part of the U.S. and Canada from October to April when clocks are set one hour behind standard time ➲ Look at **Standard Time**.

**'Central Time** ***noun*** [U] (*abbr.* **CT**) the standard time system that is used in the central part of the U.S. and Canada ➲ Compare **Eastern Time**, **Mountain Time** and **Pacific Time**.

★**cen·tu·ry** /'sɛntʃəri/ ***noun*** [C] (*pl.* **cen·tu·ries**) **1** a particular period of 100 years that is used for giving dates: *the 20th century* (= the period between the years 1901 and 2000) **2** any period of 100 years: *People have been making wine in that area for centuries.*

**CEO** /,si i 'oʊ/ ***abbr.*** = CHIEF EXECUTIVE OFFICER

**ce·ram·ic** /sə'ræmɪk/ ***adj.*** made of clay that has been made hard by baking it: *ceramic tiles*

**ce·ram·ics** /sə'ræmɪks/ ***noun*** [U] the art of making and decorating clay pots, etc.

**ce·re·al** /'sɪriəl/ ***noun*** [C,U] food that is made from plants such as corn or wheat and that is often eaten with milk for breakfast: *a bowl of cereal*

**cer·e·bral** /sə'ribrəl; 'sɛrəbrəl/ ***adj.*** connected with the brain: *He died of a cerebral hemorrhage.*

**cerebral palsy** /,sɛrəbrəl 'pɔlzi/ ***noun*** [U] a disease that causes a person to lose control of his/her movements because of brain damage before or during birth

**cer·e·mo·ni·al** /,sɛrə'moʊniəl/ ***adj.*** relating to a ceremony: *a ceremonial occasion*

★**cer·e·mo·ny** /'sɛrəmoʊni/ ***noun*** (*pl.* **cer·e·mo·nies**) **1** [C] a formal public or religious event: *the opening ceremony of the Olympic Games* ◇ *a wedding ceremony* **2** [U] formal behavior, speech,

C

actions, etc. that are expected on special occasions: *The foreign ambassador was welcomed with great ceremony.*

★**cer·tain** /ˈsərtn/ ***adj.*** **1** (not before a noun) **certain (that...)**; **certain (of sth)** completely sure; without any doubts: *Police are now certain that the explosion was not an accident.* ◇ *The events may be connected, but we cannot be certain.* ◇ *Scientists are not yet certain what causes this to happen.* ◇ *Officials are not absolutely certain of the effects of this decision.* SYN **Sure** is more common than **certain** in informal speech. **2 certain (that...)**; **certain (to do sth)** sure to happen or to do sth; definite: *It is almost certain that unemployment will increase this year.* ◇ *The principal is certain to agree.* ◇ *Nothing is certain right now. Wait and see.* ◇ *If sales do not increase, the company will face certain bankruptcy.* ➲ Look at the note at **sure**. **3** (only *before* a noun) (used for talking about a particular thing or person without naming him/her/it): *You can only contact me at certain times of the day.* ◇ *There are certain reasons why that information is not available.* **4** (only *before* a noun) noticeable but difficult to describe: *There was a certain amount of fear in his voice.*

IDM **for certain** without doubt: *I don't know for certain how many people will come.*

**make certain (that...)** to do sth in order to be sure that sth else happens: *They're doing everything they can to make certain they win.*

★**cer·tain·ly** /ˈsərtnli/ ***adv.*** **1** without doubt; definitely: *The number of students will certainly increase after 2003.* ◇ *I certainly don't think you should tell him now.* **2** (*formal*) (used in answer to questions) of course: *"Excuse me, ma'am. Could I ask you a question?" "Certainly."* ◇ *"Senator, could you please comment on this report?" "Certainly not!"*

**cer·tain·ty** /ˈsərtnti/ ***noun*** (*pl.* **cer·tain·ties**) **1** [U] the state of being completely sure about sth: *We can't say with certainty that there is life on other planets.* OPP **uncertainty** **2** [C] something that is sure to happen: *It's now almost a certainty that Oakland will play in the World Series.*

**cer·tif·i·cate** /sərˈtɪfəkət/ ***noun*** [C] an official piece of paper that says that sth is true or correct: *a birth certificate*

ˌ**certified ˈmail** ***noun*** [U] a postal service that you pay extra for. The person who receives a letter that was sent by certified mail must sign his/her name on a special form (a receipt).

ˌ**certified ˌpublic acˈcountant** ***noun*** [C] (*abbr.* **CPA**) a fully trained and qualified accountant (= a person whose job is to keep or examine the financial records of a business, etc.)

**cer·ti·fy** /ˈsərt̬əfaɪ/ ***verb*** [T] (*pres. part.* **cer·ti·fy·ing**; *3rd person sing. pres.* **cer·ti·fies**; *pt, pp* **cer·ti·fied**) **1** to say formally that sth is true or correct: *We need someone to certify that this statement is accurate.* **2** to give sb a certificate to show that he/she has successfully completed a course of training for a particular profession: *a certified diving instructor*

**Ce·sar·e·an sec·tion** (*Cdn. also* **Caesarean section**) /sɪˌzɛriən ˈsɛkʃn/ (*also* **C-section**) ***noun*** [C] an operation to remove a baby from its mother's body when a normal birth would be impossible or dangerous

**CFC** /ˌsi ɛf ˈsi/ ***noun*** [C] chlorofluorocarbon; a type of gas found, for example, in cans of spray, which is harmful to the earth's atmosphere ➲ Look at **ozone layer**.

**CFL** /ˌsi ɛf ˈɛl/ ***abbr.*** Canadian Football League; the organization of professional football teams in Canada ➲ Compare **NFL** in the U.S.

★**chain**[1] /tʃeɪn/ ***noun*** **1** [C,U] a line of metal rings that are joined together: *They used heavy chains to pull the car out of the snow.* ◇ *a bicycle chain* ◇ *She was wearing a silver chain around her neck.* ◇ *a 4-foot length of chain* ➲ pictures at **bicycle** and **jewelry**. **2** [C] a number of things in a line: *a chain of islands/an island chain* **3** [C] a group of stores, hotels, etc. that are owned by the same person or company: *a chain of restaurants/a restaurant chain* ◇ ***a chain store*** (= one store that is part of a chain) **4** [C] a number of connected events that happen one after another: *The book examines the complex chain of events that led to the Russian Revolution.*

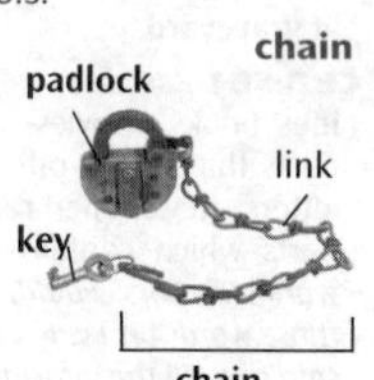


**chain**[2] /tʃeɪn/ ***verb*** [T] **chain sb/sth (to sth)**; **chain sb/sth (up)** to fasten sb/sth to sth else with a chain: *The neighbor's dog has been chained up in the yard all day.*

ˈ**chain ˌletter** ***noun*** [C] a letter or an e-mail sent to several people asking them to make copies of the letter and send them on to more people

ˌ**chain reˈaction** ***noun*** [C] a series of events or chemical changes, each of which causes the next one: *If the factory closes, it could set off a chain reaction of other business closures in the area.*

**chain·saw** /ˈtʃeɪnsɔ/ ***noun*** [C] a tool made of a chain with sharp teeth set in it, that is driven by a motor and used for cutting wood

ˈ**chain-smoke** ***verb*** [I] to smoke cigarettes continuously, lighting one cigarette after another ▶ ˈ**chain-ˌsmoker** ***noun*** [C]

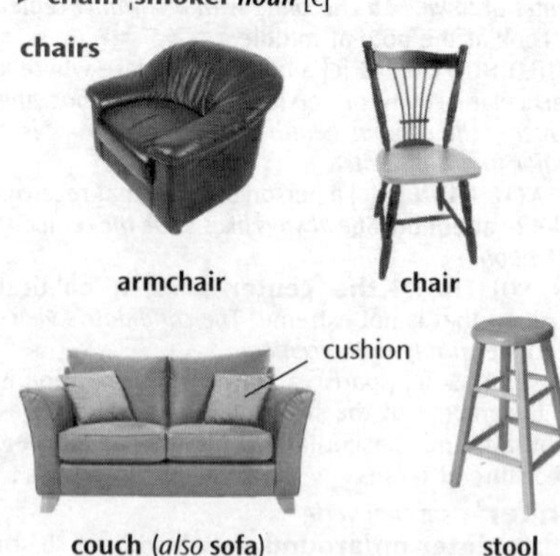


★**chair**[1] /tʃɛr/ ***noun*** [C] **1** a piece of furniture for one person to sit on. It has a seat, a back and usually

four legs. It sometimes has two arms: *a kitchen chair* ◇ *an armchair* ◇ *a wheelchair* ➲ Look also at **electric chair**. **2** (*also* **chairman**, **chairperson**, **chairwoman**) [usually sing.] the person who controls a meeting, leads a committee, etc.: *Rosa is the new chair of the County Historical Society.* **3** a professor who is the head of a department at a college or university: *the chair of economics at Princeton University*

**chair²** /tʃɛr/ ***verb*** [T] to be the chairman or chairwoman of a meeting, a committee, etc.: *Mr. Tran has been appointed to chair the school's finance committee.*

★**chair·man** /ˈtʃɛrmən/ ***noun*** [C] (*pl.* **chair·men**) **1** the head of a committee, company or other organization: *the Chairman of IBM* **2** = CHAIR¹ (2)

**chair·man·ship** /ˈtʃɛrmənʃɪp/ ***noun*** [sing.] being the chairman of sth; the time during which sb is chairman of sth

★**chair·per·son** /ˈtʃɛrˌpərsn/ ***noun*** [C] (*pl.* **chair·per·sons**) = CHAIR¹ (2)

★**chair·wom·an** /ˈtʃɛrˌwʊmən/ (*pl.* **chair·wom·en**) ***noun*** [C] = CHAIR¹ (2)

**cha·let** /ʃæˈleɪ/ ***noun*** [C] a house or hut that is made of wood, especially in a mountain area

**chalk¹** /tʃɔk/ ***noun*** [U] a small stick of white or colored powder that has been pressed together, which is used for writing or drawing on a blackboard: *a piece of chalk*

**chalk²** /tʃɔk/ ***verb***

IDM **chalk sth up to experience** (*informal*) used to say that you should think of a failure as being sth that you can learn from: *Let's chalk that defeat up to experience and start thinking about the next game.*

PHR V **chalk up sth** (*informal*) to succeed in getting sth: *The team has chalked up five wins this summer.*

**chalk sth up to sth** (*informal*) to say that sth is caused by sth: *We'll have to chalk the extra expense up to bad luck* (= bad luck is the reason we had the extra expense).

**chalk·board** /ˈtʃɔkbɔrd/ ***noun*** [C] = BLACKBOARD

★**chal·lenge¹** /ˈtʃæləndʒ/ ***noun*** **1** [C,U] something new and difficult that forces you to make a lot of effort, but that is often exciting and interesting: *Starting my own business was a real challenge.* ◇ *After over 15 years at her old job, Laura wanted a new challenge.* ◇ *The government's next big challenge will be to reduce unemployment.* **2** [C] **a challenge (to sb) (to do sth)** an invitation from sb to fight/play/argue against him/her: *She issued her opponents a challenge to find a better solution.*

★**chal·lenge²** /ˈtʃæləndʒ/ ***verb*** [T] **1 challenge sb (to sth)** to invite sb to fight, play, argue, etc. against you: *They challenged us to a softball game this Saturday.* **2** to question whether sth is true or right: *Several officials challenged the reports of bribery.*

**chal·lenged** /ˈtʃæləndʒd/ ***adj.*** (in compounds) having a particular type of difficulty in doing sth that most other people can do: *to be visually/mentally/physically challenged* ➲ Look at the note at **handicapped**.

NOTE **Challenged** can also be used in a joking way about a problem which most people do not consider to be serious: *help for the **financially challenged*** (= people who do not have much money).

**chal·leng·er** /ˈtʃæləndʒər/ ***noun*** [C] a person who takes part in a competition, because he/she wants to win a title or position that sb else already has

**chal·leng·ing** /ˈtʃæləndʒɪŋ/ ***adj.*** forcing you to make a lot of effort, but often also exciting and interesting: *a challenging job*

★**cham·ber** /ˈtʃeɪmbər/ ***noun*** [C] **1** a large room that is used for formal meetings: *a city council chamber* ◇ *a judge's private chambers* **2** a room that is used for a particular purpose: *a gas chamber* (= where people are killed with poisonous gas) **3** an enclosed space in the body, in a plant or in a machine: *the chambers of the heart* ◇ *the chamber of a gun* (= the part that holds the bullets)

**ˈchamber ˌmusic** ***noun*** [U] classical music that is written for a small group of instruments

**ˌchamber of ˈcommerce** ***noun*** [C] (*pl.* **chambers of commerce**) an organization of businesses and store owners in a city or an area, that encourages the development of business

**cha·me·le·on** /kəˈmilyən/ ***noun*** [C] a type of small reptile (a lizard) that can change color according to what is around it

**cham·pagne** /ʃæmˈpeɪn/ ***noun*** [U] a French white wine that has a lot of bubbles in it and is often very expensive

★**cham·pi·on¹** /ˈtʃæmpiən/ ***noun*** [C] **1** a person, team, etc. that has won a competition: *a world champion* ◇ *a champion swimmer* **2** (*formal*) a person who speaks and fights for a particular group, idea, etc.: *a champion of equal rights for women*

**cham·pi·on²** /ˈtʃæmpiən/ ***verb*** [T] (*formal*) to support or fight for a particular group or idea: *to champion the cause of human rights*

**cham·pi·on·ship** /ˈtʃæmpiənˌʃɪp/ ***noun*** [C] **1** a competition or series of competitions to find the best player or team in a sport or game: *to win the world championship* **2** the position or title of a CHAMPION (1)

★**chance¹** /tʃæns/ ***noun*** **1** [C,U] **chance of (doing) sth; chance (that...)** (a) possibility: *The plan didn't really have a chance of succeeding.* ◇ *I think there's a good chance that she'll be the next President.* ◇ *He has very little chance of winning.* ◇ *Is there any chance of getting tickets for tonight's concert?* **2** [C] **chance (to do sth)** an opportunity: *Could you mail this letter for me if you get a chance?* ◇ *Be quiet and give her a chance to explain.* ◇ *I think you should tell him now. You might not get another chance.* ◇ *Even though he made a serious mistake, I think he deserves a second chance.* ➲ Look at the note at **occasion**. **3** [C] a risk: *We might lose some money, but that's a chance we'll have to take.* **4** [U] luck or fortune (= sth that you cannot control): *You should plan ahead – don't just leave everything to chance.* ◇ *I discovered these old pictures by chance while I was looking for something else in the attic.*

IDM **by any chance** (used for asking sth politely)

perhaps or possibly: *Are you by any chance going downtown this afternoon?*
**chances are (that)...** (*informal*) it is probable that...: *Chances are that it will rain tomorrow.*
**stand a chance (of doing sth)** to have a possibility of achieving sth: *The other team was a lot better than us – we didn't stand a chance of winning.*

C

**chance²** /tʃæns/ ***verb*** [T] (*informal*) to risk sth: *Should we take umbrellas or should we chance it* (= risk getting wet)*?*

**chan·cel·lor** /ˈtʃænsələr/ ***noun*** [C] **1** the head of government in some countries: *the German chancellor* **2** the head of some universities: *the chancellor of the University of Massachusetts*

**chan·cer·y** /ˈtʃænsəri/ ***noun*** [C] (*U.S.*) (*also* often ˈ**chancery court**) a COURT¹ (1) in some parts of the U. S. that decides cases which are related to financial matters

**chan·de·lier** /ˌʃændəˈlɪr/ ***noun*** [C] a large light that hangs from the ceiling and that has many light bulbs or candles

★**change¹** /tʃeɪndʒ/ ***verb***
➤BECOME/MAKE DIFFERENT **1** [I,T] to become different or to make sb/sth different: *This town has changed a lot since I was young.* ◇ *Our plans have changed. We leave in the morning.* ◇ *His fame has not changed him at all.* **2** [I,T] **change (sb/sth) to/into sth**; **change (from sth) (to/into sth)** to become sth different; to make sb/sth take a different form: *to change from a caterpillar into a butterfly* ◇ *Honestly – I didn't see the traffic light change to red!* ◇ *to change water into ice*
➤REPLACE **3** [T] to take, have or use sth instead of sth else: *to change jobs* ◇ *to change a light bulb* ◇ *to change direction* ◇ *Can I change my appointment from Wednesday to Thursday?*
➤BUS/TRAIN/PLANE **4** [I,T] to get out of one bus, airplane, etc. and get into another: *Does this bus go all the way to the airport or do we have to change?* ◇ *She has to change planes in Dallas.*
➤CLOTHES **5** [I,T] **change (out of sth) (into sth)** to take off your clothes and put different ones on: *He changed his shirt.* ◇ *I'm going straight to the party from work, so I'll change when I get there.* ◇ *She changed out of her swimsuit and into a dress.*
➤BABY **6** [T] to put clean things onto sb/sth: *It's your turn to change the baby* (= to put a clean diaper on him/her).
➤MONEY **7** [T] **change sth (for/into sth)** to give sb money and receive the same amount back in money of a different type: *Can you change a twenty-dollar bill?* ◇ *I'd like to change a hundred dollars into Swiss francs.*
IDM **change hands** to pass from one owner to another
**change your mind** to change your decision or opinion: *I'll have the green one. No, I changed my mind. I want the red one.*
**change/trade places (with sb)** → PLACE¹
**change the subject** to start talking about sth different
**change your tune** (*informal*) to change your opinion or feelings about sth
PHR V **change over (from sth) (to sth)** to stop doing or using one thing and start doing or using sth else: *Our office has changed over to a new computer system.*

★**change²** /tʃeɪndʒ/ ***noun***
➤DIFFERENCE **1** [C,U] **change (in/to sth)** the process of becoming or making sth different: *There was little change in the patient's condition overnight.* ◇ *After two very cold winters, people were talking about a change in the climate.*
➤STH NEW AND INTERESTING **2** [C] **change (of sth)** something that you take, have or use instead of sth else: *We need to notify the bank of our change of address.* ◇ *Bring **a change of clothes** in case it rains and you get wet.*
➤MONEY **3** [U] coins or bills of lower value that together make up the same value as a larger coin or bill: *Do you have change for a dollar?* ◇ *Passengers should have the exact fare; drivers cannot **make change**.* **4** [U] coins: *He needs some change for the phone.* **5** [U] the money that you get back if you pay more than the amount sth costs: *If a cake costs $8 and you pay with a $10 bill, you will get $2 in change.*
IDM **a change of heart** a change in your opinion or the way that you feel
**for a change** in order to do sth different from usual: *We always stay home in the evenings. Let's go out tonight for a change.*

**change·o·ver** /ˈtʃeɪndʒˌoʊvər/ ***noun*** [C] a change from one system to another

★**chan·nel¹** /ˈtʃænl/ ***noun*** [C] **1** a television station: *My favorite program is on Channel 10 at 7:30.* ◇ *Go ahead and change the channel.* **2** a narrow area of water between two seas or oceans **3** an open passage along which liquids can flow: *a drainage channel* **4** a way or route along which news, information, etc. is sent: *We are working through diplomatic channels to free the hostages.*

**chan·nel²** /ˈtʃænl/ ***verb*** [T] to make sth move along a particular path or route: *Water is channeled from the river to the fields.* ◇ (*figurative*) *You should channel your energies into something constructive.*

**chant¹** /tʃænt/ ***noun*** [C] a word or phrase that is sung or shouted many times: *A chant of "We're number one!" went around the stadium.*

**chant²** /tʃænt/ ***verb*** [I,T] to sing or shout a word or phrase many times: *The protestors marched past, chanting slogans.*

**Cha·nu·kah** /ˈxɑnəkə/ ***noun*** [C,U] = HANUKKAH

**cha·os** /ˈkeɪɑs/ ***noun*** [U] a state of great disorder; confusion: *The meeting ended in chaos when demonstrators burst into the room.* ◇ *The accident has caused total chaos on the highway.*

**cha·ot·ic** /keɪˈɑt̬ɪk/ ***adj.*** in a state of chaos: *With no one in charge the situation became chaotic.*

**chap·el** /ˈtʃæpl/ ***noun*** **1** [C] a small part of a large church that can be used for private prayer **2** [C] a small building or room in a prison, hospital, college, etc. that is used as a church **3** [C,U] a church for some Protestant groups: *a Baptist chapel* **4** [C,U] a regular religious meeting for all the students and teachers at some schools: *We have to attend chapel every morning.*

**chap·er·one** /ˈʃæpəroʊn/ ***noun*** [C] an older person who goes to social events for young people to watch them and to make sure that they behave correctly ▶ **chap·er·one** ***verb*** [T]

**chap·lain** /ˈtʃæplən/ ***noun*** [C] a priest who works in a hospital, school, prison, in the army, etc.

★**chap·ter** /ˈtʃæptər/ ***noun*** [C] **1** one of the parts into which a book is divided: *Please read Chapter 2 for tomorrow.* ◇ *In the opening chapter, the author sets the scene of the novel.* **2** a local branch of a club, an organization, etc.

★**char·ac·ter** /ˈkærəktər/ ***noun***
➤ QUALITIES/FEATURES **1** [C,U, sing.] the quality that makes sb/sth different from other people or things; the nature of sb/sth: *Although they are twins, their characters are really different.* ◇ *The new shopping center has completely changed the character of downtown.* ◇ *Modern houses often seem to lack character* (= they all seem the same). **2** [U] a person's inner strength: *The game developed into a test of character rather than just physical strength.* ◇ *Dad said that this camping trip would help build my character.* **3** [C] a person who is very amusing, or who has an unusual personality: *Neil's a real character.*
➤ STRANGE/INTERESTING PERSON **4** [C] (*informal*) a person: *There was a suspicious-looking character hanging around outside, so I called the police.*
➤ IN BOOK/PLAY/MOVIE **5** [C] a person in a book, story, etc.: *The main character in the book is a boy who finds a dead body.*
➤ SYMBOL/LETTER **6** [C] a letter or sign that you use when you are writing or printing: *Chinese characters*
IDM **in character/out of character** typical/not typical of sb/sth

★**char·ac·ter·is·tic**[1] /ˌkærəktəˈrɪstɪk/ ***noun*** [C] a quality that is typical of sb/sth and that makes him/her/it different from other people or things: *The chief characteristic of reptiles is that they are cold-blooded.*

**char·ac·ter·is·tic**[2] /ˌkærəktəˈrɪstɪk/ ***adj.*** **characteristic (of sb/sth)** typical (of sb/sth): *This piece is characteristic of the artist's early paintings.* OPP **uncharacteristic** ▶ **char·ac·ter·is·ti·cal·ly** /-kli/ ***adv.***: *"No," he said, in his characteristically direct manner.*

**char·ac·ter·ize** /ˈkærəktəraɪz/ ***verb*** [T] **1** (often passive) to be typical of sb/sth: *The 1990s were characterized by big business deals.* **2 characterize sb/sth as sth** to describe the nature of sb/sth or to show a person's character in a particular way: *Diplomats characterized the meeting as friendly and positive.*

**cha·rade** /ʃəˈreɪd/ ***noun*** **1 charades** [U] a game that is played at a party, etc. in which one person or team acts out a word for others to guess **2** [C] a situation or event that is clearly false but in which people pretend to do or be sth: *They pretend to be friends, but it's all a charade. Everyone knows they hate each other.*

**char·coal** /ˈtʃɑrkoʊl/ ***noun*** [U] a black substance that is produced when you burn wood in an oven with very little air. Charcoal can be used for drawing or as a fuel: *a charcoal grill* (= that uses charcoal for fuel)

**Char·don·nay** /ˌʃɑrdnˈeɪ/ ***noun*** [U,C] a type of white wine or the type of grape from which it is made: *Would Chardonnay go well with this fish?* ◇ *This is a fine Chardonnay.*

★**charge**[1] /tʃɑrdʒ/ ***noun*** **1** [C,U] the price that you must pay for sth: *There is no charge for our information booklet.* ◇ *We deliver free of charge.* ◇ *There is a small admission charge.* ➲ Look at the note at **price**. **2** [C] = CHARGE CARD: *Will that be cash or charge?* **3** [C] an official statement that says that sb has done sth which is against the law: *All the charges against him were dropped and he was free to go.* **4** [C] a sudden attack where sb/sth runs directly at sb/sth else: *The bull made a charge toward the gate.*
IDM **in charge (of sb/sth)** in control or command (of sb/sth): *Who is in charge of the office while Alan's gone?* ◇ *I'd like to speak to the person in charge.*
**press charges (against sb)** → PRESS[1]
**take charge (of sth)** to take control of or responsibility for sth

**charge**[2] /tʃɑrdʒ/ ***verb***
➤ MONEY **1** [I,T] **charge (sb/sth) for sth** to ask sb to pay a particular amount of money: *Do you charge for delivery?* ◇ *We charge $40 per night for a single room.* ◇ *How much did they charge you for that?* **2** [T] to buy sth by using a special plastic card (a **credit card**) instead of money: *"Will you be paying cash for this?" "No, I'll charge it."*
➤ OF CRIME/STH WRONG **3** [T] **charge sb (with sth)** to accuse sb officially of doing sth that is against the law: *Six men have been charged with attempted robbery.*
➤ RUSH/ATTACK **4** [I,T] to attack sb/sth by running directly at him/her/it: *The bull put its head down and charged.* ◇ (*figurative*) *The kids charged down the stairs and out the back door.*
➤ ELECTRICITY **5** [T] to put electricity into sth: *to charge a battery*

ˈ**charge account** ***noun*** [C] an arrangement with a store or business that allows you to pay for goods at a later date: *to open a charge account at a department store*

ˈ**charge card** (*also* **charge**) ***noun*** [C] a small plastic card that you can use to get goods or services without using money. You usually receive a bill once a month for what you have bought ➲ Look at **credit card**.

**char·i·ot** /ˈtʃæriət/ ***noun*** [C] an open vehicle with two wheels, that was pulled by a horse or horses in ancient times

**cha·ris·ma** /kəˈrɪzmə/ ***noun*** [U] the power that some people have to attract and influence people ▶ **char·is·mat·ic** /ˌkærəzˈmæt̬ɪk/ ***adj.***: *a charismatic politician*

**char·i·ta·ble** /ˈtʃærət̬əbl/ ***adj.*** **1** kind; generous: *Some people accused him of lying, but a more charitable explanation was that he had made a mistake.* OPP **uncharitable** **2** connected with a CHARITY (1): *Charitable contributions can be deducted from your income tax.*

★**char·i·ty** /ˈtʃærət̬i/ ***noun*** (*pl.* **char·i·ties**) **1** [C,U] an organization that collects money to help people who are poor, sick, etc. or to do work that will be of benefit to society: *to raise money for charity* ◇ *He supports a charity that helps the handicapped.* **2** [U] kindness toward other people: *to act out of charity*

C

★**charm**[1] /tʃɑrm/ ***noun*** **1** [C,U] the quality of being pleasant or attractive: *The charm of the island lies in its unspoiled beauty.* ◇ *One of his charms was his ability to tell funny stories.* **2** [C] something that you wear because you believe it will bring you good luck: *a necklace with a good-luck charm on it*

★**charm**[2] /tʃɑrm/ ***verb*** [T] to please sb; to influence people by your power to attract them: *She charmed the judges at the contest with her bright smile.*

**charm·ing** /ˈtʃɑrmɪŋ/ ***adj.*** very pleasing or attractive: *He wrote a charming poem for his grandmother's birthday.* ◇ *What a charming little boy!*

**charred** /tʃɑd/ ***adj.*** black and partly burned by fire

★**chart**[1] /tʃɑrt/ ***noun*** **1** [C] a drawing that shows information in the form of a diagram, etc.: *a temperature chart* ◇ *This chart shows the company's profits over the last three years.* ➲ picture at **graph**. **2** [C] a map of the ocean or the sky: *navigation charts* **3 the charts** [pl.] an official list of the pop and rock songs that have sold the most copies of records, CDs, etc.

★**chart**[2] /tʃɑrt/ ***verb*** [T] **1** to make a map of one area of the ocean or sky: *an uncharted coastline* **2** to follow or record sth carefully and in detail: *Analysts have been charting the company's financial progress.*

**char·ter**[1] /ˈtʃɑrt̬ər/ ***noun*** [C,U] **1** an official written statement of the rights, beliefs and purposes of an organization or a particular group of people: *The club's charter does not permit women to become members.* **2** an official document from a government or another authority, that allows a company, university, town, etc. to exist, and that gives it certain rights **3** the renting of a ship, airplane, etc. for a particular purpose or for a particular group of people: *a charter flight* **4 the Charter** (*Cdn*) = THE CANADIAN CHARTER OF RIGHTS AND FREEDOMS

**char·ter**[2] /ˈtʃɑrt̬ər/ ***verb*** [T] **1** to rent a ship, airplane, etc. for a particular purpose or for a particular group of people **2** to give a CHARTER[1] (2) to an organization or a particular group of people

ˌ**charter ˈmember** ***noun*** [C] one of the first members of an organization, etc., especially one who helped start it

★**chase**[1] /tʃeɪs/ ***verb*** [I,T] to run after sb/sth in order to catch him/her/it: *The dog chased the cat up a tree.* ◇ *The police car chased the stolen van down the highway.*

★**chase**[2] /tʃeɪs/ ***noun*** [C] the act of following sb/sth in order to catch him/her/it; chasing or being chased: *an exciting car chase*

IDM **give chase** to begin to run after sb/sth in order to try to catch him/her/it: *The robber ran off and the police officer gave chase.*

**chasm** /ˈkæzəm/ ***noun*** [C] **1** a long deep hole in the ground **2** [sing.] (*formal*) a very big difference between two people or groups, for example because they have different attitudes

**chas·sis** /ˈtʃæsi; ˈʃæsi/ ***noun*** [C] (*pl.* **chas·sis** /ˈtʃæsiz; ˈʃæsiz/) the metal frame of a vehicle onto which the other parts fit

**chas·ti·ty** /ˈtʃæstət̬i/ ***noun*** [U] the state of never having had a sexual relationship: *The nuns took a vow of chastity.*

**chat**[1] /tʃæt/ ***noun*** [C] a friendly informal conversation: *I had a nice chat with Sandy this afternoon.*

**chat**[2] /tʃæt/ ***verb*** [I] (**chat̲ting**; **chat̲ted**) to talk to sb in a friendly, informal way: *The senator chatted briefly with some visitors in her office.*

ˈ**chat room** ***noun*** [C] an area on the Internet where people can communicate with each other, usually about one particular topic

**chat·ter**[1] /ˈtʃæt̬ər/ ***verb*** [I] **1** to talk quickly or for a long time about sth unimportant: *The kids chattered away continuously.* **2** (used about your teeth) to knock together because you are cold or frightened

**chat·ter**[2] /ˈtʃæt̬ər/ ***noun*** [U] continuous fast talk, usually about sth unimportant: *Most of the stuff on the radio is just idle chatter.*

**chauf·feur** /ʃoʊˈfər/ ***noun*** [C] a person whose job is to drive a car for sb else: *a chauffeur-driven limousine* ▶ **chauf·feur *verb*** [T]: *Every Saturday I have to chauffeur the kids around to sports practice.*

**chau·vin·ism** /ˈʃoʊvənɪzəm/ ***noun*** [U] **1** = MALE CHAUVINISM **2** a strong belief that your country is better and more important than all others

**chau·vin·ist** /ˈʃoʊvənɪst/ ***noun*** [C] a person who believes in or shows chauvinism

★**cheap**[1] /tʃip/ ***adj.*** **1** low in price; costing little money: *Oranges are cheap at this time of year.* ◇ *It's cheaper to buy a round-trip ticket than two one-way tickets.* OPP **expensive** **2** charging low prices: *There's a cheap restaurant right around the corner.* ➲ Look also at **inexpensive**. It has a less negative meaning than senses 1 and 2 of **cheap**. **3** of low quality: *The cheap thing broke before I even got it home!* **4** (*informal*) not willing to spend money: *Her boyfriend is so cheap – he never takes her out to eat.*

**cheap**[2] /tʃip/ ***adv.*** (*informal*) for a low price: *You can eat pretty cheap in the snack bars on campus.*

**cheap·ly** /ˈtʃipli/ ***adv.*** for a low price: *These items can be produced more cheaply in the Far East.*

**cheap·skate** /ˈtʃipskeɪt/ ***noun*** [C] (*informal*) a person who does not like to spend money and often acts in an unreasonable way in order to avoid spending money: *What a cheapskate – Bob bought his girlfriend a fake diamond ring!*

★**cheat**[1] /tʃit/ ***verb*** [I] **1** to act in a dishonest or unfair way in order to get an advantage for yourself: *Len got caught cheating on the test.* ◇ *to cheat at cards* **2 cheat (on sb)** to not be faithful to your husband, wife or regular partner by having a secret sexual relationship with sb else: *He's cheating on his wife.*

PHR V **cheat sb (out) of sth** to take sth from sb in a dishonest or unfair way: *They tried to cheat the old lady out of her savings.*

★**cheat**[2] /tʃit/ ***noun*** [C] a person who tries to get money, etc. by acting in a dishonest or unfair way: *The government is trying to crack down on tax cheats.*

**cheat·er** /ˈtʃit̬ər/ ***noun*** [C] a person who cheats on a test, etc.: *Cheaters will automatically receive an "F" on the final exam.*

★**check**[1] /tʃɛk/ ***verb***

➤EXAMINE **1** [I,T] to examine or look at sth in order to make sure that it is safe, correct, in good condition, whether it has changed, etc.: *He wasn't sure whether he had locked the door, so he went back to check.* ◇ *Check your work carefully for mistakes before you hand it in.* ◇ *Don't forget to check your e-mail* (= to see if you have new messages). ◇ *Can you check that we have everything on the list?* ◇ *She looked at her calendar to check what time her appointment was.*

➤MAKE MARK **2** [T] to write a mark (✓) on a form, etc. to show your choice, to show that sth is done, etc.: *Check the box next to the right answer.*

➤COATS/BAGS **3** [T] to give sth to sb at an airport, a restaurant, etc. so that it can be kept in a safe place or taken to another place: *All bags must be checked at the counter.*

➤CONTROL **4** [T] (*formal*) to stop or go more slowly; to make sb/sth stop or go more slowly: *A tight bandage should check the flow of blood from a wound.*

PHR V **check in (at...); check into...** to go to a hotel/airline desk and say that you have arrived: *Passengers should check in two hours before their departure time.*

**check sth off** to put a check mark (✓) next to names or items on a list: *The cartons were all checked off as they were unloaded.*

**check on sb/sth** to find out more information about sb/sth: *Could you please check on the status of my order?* ◇ *I'll just check on the baby and make sure he's all right.*

**check out (of...)** to pay your bill and leave a hotel

**check sb/sth out 1** (*slang*) to look at sb/sth, especially because it is interesting: *Wow! Check this out, you guys!* ◇ *Check out Darla's cool new jacket!* **2** to find out more information about sb/sth, especially to find out if sth is true or not: *We need to check out these rumors about possible pay cuts.*

**check sth out 1** to examine or test sth to make sure it works correctly: *The car is back from the repair shop, so let's check it out on the highway!* **2** to record that sth has been borrowed or bought: *to check out a book from the library* ◇ *It took a long time for the cashier to check my groceries out.*

**check sth over** to examine sth to make sure it is correct: *Check your work over carefully before you hand it in.*

**check up on sb/sth** to make sure sb/sth is working correctly, behaving well, etc.: *I wish Mom wouldn't keep checking up on me every five minutes!*

★**check**[2] /tʃɛk/ ***noun*** **1** [C] **a check (on sth)** a close look at sth to make sure that it is safe, correct, in good condition, etc.: *We conduct regular checks on our products to make sure that they are of high quality.* ◇ *a safety check* ◇ *a security check* ➲ Look also at **reality check**. **2** (*especially Cdn* **cheque**) [C,U] a piece of paper printed by a bank that you can fill out, sign and use to pay for things: *She wrote a check for $40.* ◇ *I went to the bank to cash a check.* ◇ *If there isn't enough money in your account, your check will* **bounce** (= the bank will not pay it). ◇ *Can I pay by check?* ➲ Look also at **paycheck**. **3** [C, usually sing.] a bill for food in a restaurant: *Miss, could I have the check, please?* **4** [C] = CHECK MARK: *Put a check next to the right answer.* **5** [sing.] (in the game of chess) the situation in which a player must move to protect his/her king ➲ Look at **checkmate. 6** [C] an act of going more slowly or stopping, or of making sb/sth go more slowly or stop: *A cold spring will provide a natural check on the number of insects.*

IDM **hold/keep sth in check** to stop sth from advancing or increasing too quickly: *government measures to keep inflation in check*

**check·book** /ˈtʃɛkbʊk/ ***noun*** [C] a book of CHECKS[2] (2) from a bank

**checked** /tʃɛkt/ (*also* **checkered**) ***adj.*** with a pattern of squares: *a red-and-white checked tablecloth* ➲ Picture at study page **A30**.

**check·er** /ˈtʃɛkər/ ***noun*** [C] (*especially US*) a person whose job is to use a machine (**a cash register**) to add up the cost of the things that sb is buying, and to take his/her money: *a supermarket checker*

**check·er·board** /ˈtʃɛkərbɔrd/ ***noun*** [C] a square board with 64 smaller squares in two colors on it, that you play checkers on

**check·ered** /ˈtʃɛkərd/ ***adj.*** = CHECKED ➲ Picture at study page **A30**.

**check·ers** /ˈtʃɛkərz/ ***noun*** [U] a game for two players that you play on a board with 64 squares on it (a **checkerboard**) using round pieces in two different colors: *to play checkers* ◇ *a game of checkers*

ˈ**check-in** ***noun*** [C] **1** the act of checking in at an airport: *Our check-in time is 10:30 a.m.* **2** the place where you check in at an airport: *the check-in desk*

ˈ**checking acˌcount** ***noun*** [C] a bank account from which you can pay for things or take out money by writing a CHECK[2] (2): *to open/close a checking account* ➲ Look at **savings account**.

**check·list** /ˈtʃɛklɪst/ ***noun*** [C] a list of things that you must do or have

ˈ**check mark** (*also* **check**) ***noun*** [C] a mark (✓) that shows your choice, that sth has been done, or that sth is correct: *She put a check mark next to the names of the people who had paid.*

**check mark**

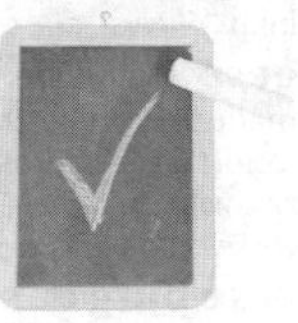

**check·mate** /ˈtʃɛkmeɪt/ (*also* **mate**) ***noun*** [sing.] (in the game of chess) the situation in which you cannot protect your king and so have lost the game ➲ Look at **check**[2](5).

**check·out** /ˈtʃɛkaʊt/ ***noun*** [C] the place in a store where you pay for the things you have bought

**check·point** /ˈtʃɛkpɔɪnt/ ***noun*** [C] a place where all people and vehicles must stop and be checked: *an army checkpoint*

ˌ**checks and ˈbalances** ***noun*** [pl.] (especially in the U.S.) a system of government that means that no one part of the government is strong enough to make decisions if the other parts do not agree

**check·up** /ˈtʃɛkʌp/ ***noun*** [C] a general medical examination to find out whether you are healthy: *You should visit your dentist for a checkup twice a year.*

C

**ched·dar** (*also* **Cheddar**) /ˈtʃɛdər/ ***noun*** [U] a type of hard cheese that is orange, white or yellow

★**cheek** /tʃik/ ***noun*** [C] one of the two parts of your face that are on each side of your nose and mouth and below your eyes: *Their cheeks were red when they came in out of the cold.* ◇ *Tears rolled down her cheeks.* ➲ Look also at **tongue-in-cheek**.

**cheek·bone** /ˈtʃikboʊn/ ***noun*** [C] the bone that is below your eye

**cheer**[1] /tʃɪr/ ***verb*** [I,T] to shout to show that you like sth or to encourage sb who is taking part in a competition, sport, etc.: *The crowd clapped and cheered.* ◇ *Everyone cheered the winner as he crossed the finish line.*

PHR V **cheer sb on** to cheer sb in order to encourage him/her to do better: *As the runners started the last lap, the crowd cheered them on.*

**cheer (sb) up** to become or to make sb happier: *Cheer up! Things aren't that bad.* ◇ *This good news should cheer him up.*

**cheer**[2] /tʃɪr/ ***noun*** [C] a loud shout to show that you like sth or to encourage sb who is taking part in a competition, sport, etc.: *There were a lot of cheers when the team came onto the field.*

★**cheer·ful** /ˈtʃɪrfl/ ***adj.*** happy: *Tom seems very cheerful despite his illness.* ◇ *a cheerful smile* ▶ **cheer·ful·ly** ***adv.***

**cheer·lead·er** /ˈtʃɪrlidər/ ***noun*** [C] **1** a person who wears a special uniform and who shouts, dances, etc. in front of the audience at a sports game in order to encourage the audience to shout in support of the players **2 cheerleader (for sb/sth)** a person who supports a person, policy, etc. and who encourages others to support the same person or thing: *one of the biggest cheerleaders for the party's economic policies*

**cheers** /tʃɪrz/ ***interjection*** (*informal*) (used to express good wishes before you have an alcoholic drink): *"Cheers!" she said, raising her wine glass.*

★**cheese** /tʃiz/ ***noun*** **1** [U] a type of solid food that is made from milk. Cheese is usually white or yellow in color: *a cheese sandwich* ◇ *Sprinkle the top of the pizza with grated cheese.* **2** [C] a type of cheese: *a wide selection of cheeses* ➲ Look also at **big cheese**.

**cheese·burg·er** /ˈtʃiz,bərgər/ ***noun*** [C] a sandwich made of chopped meat in a flat, round shape (a **hamburger**) with a slice of cheese on top

**cheese·cake** /ˈtʃizkeɪk/ ***noun*** [C,U] a type of cake that is made from soft white cheese, eggs and sugar on a base made of crushed cookies

**chee·tah** /ˈtʃiṭə/ ***noun*** [C] a large wild animal of the cat family that comes from Africa and can run very fast

**Cheez·ies™** /ˈtʃiziz/ ***noun*** [pl.] (*Cdn*) a type of crunchy, cheese-flavored snack food

**chef** /ʃɛf/ ***noun*** [C] a person who works as the chief cook in a hotel, restaurant, etc.

**ˈchef's ˌsalad** ***noun*** [C] a large salad consisting of lettuce, tomato and other vegetables with slices of cheese and meat such as chicken or ham, on top

★**chem·i·cal**[1] /ˈkɛmɪkl/ ***adj.*** connected with chemistry; produced by processes that involve changing the structure of a substance: *a chemical reaction* ◇ *the chemical industry* ◇ *a ban on the use of chemical weapons* ◇ *She's being treated for chemical dependency* (= being addicted to drugs). ▶ **chem·i·cal·ly** /-kli/ ***adv.***

★**chem·i·cal**[2] /ˈkɛmɪkl/ ***noun*** [C] a substance that is used or produced in a chemical process: *You must wear eye protection when handling dangerous chemicals.*

**chem·ist** /ˈkɛmɪst/ ***noun*** [C] a person who is a specialist in chemistry

★**chem·is·try** /ˈkɛməstri/ ***noun*** [U] **1** the scientific study of the structure of substances and what happens to them in different conditions or when mixed with each other: *We did an experiment in chemistry class today.* ◇ *a chemistry laboratory* **2** the structure of a particular substance and the way that it may change under different conditions

**che·mo·ther·a·py** /ˌkimoʊˈθɛrəpi/ (*also informal* **chemo** /ˌkimoʊ/) ***noun*** [U] the treatment of disease, especially cancer, with the use of chemical substances: *chemotherapy treatments* ➲ Look at **radiotherapy**.

**cheque** /tʃɛk/ ***noun*** [C] (*Cdn*) = CHECK[2] (2)

**cher·ish** /ˈtʃɛrɪʃ/ ***verb*** [T] **1** to love sb/sth and take care of him/her/it: *The ring was her most cherished possession.* **2** to keep a thought, feeling, etc. in your mind and think about it often: *We cherish the time we spend with our grandchildren.*

**cher·ry** /ˈtʃɛri/ ***noun*** **1** [C] (*pl.* **cher·ries**) a small round black or red fruit that grows on a tree and that has a small hard part (**pit**) inside it **2** [C] (*also* ˈ**cherry tree**) the tree that produces cherries: *a flowering cherry* ➲ picture on study page **A28-29**. **3** [U] the wood from the cherry tree: *a table made of cherry*

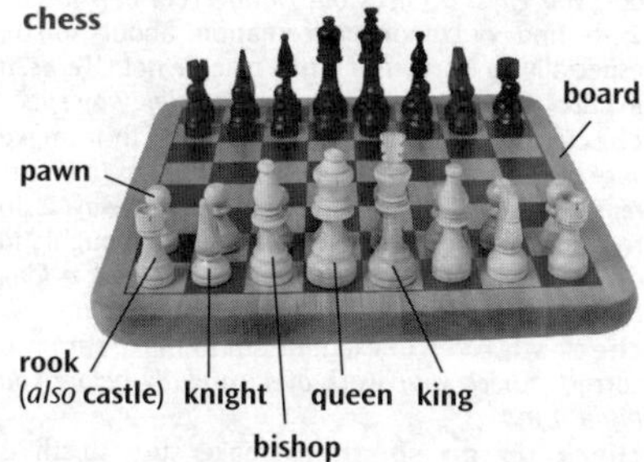


**chess** /tʃɛs/ ***noun*** [U] a game for two people that is played on a board with 64 black and white squares (a **chessboard**). Each player has sixteen pieces which can be moved according to fixed rules.

★**chest** /tʃɛst/ ***noun*** [C] **1** a container, usually with a lid that is fastened on one side, that is used for storing or transporting things: *a jewelry chest* ◇ *We'll pack the food for the picnic in the ice chest.* ◇ *The aspirin is in the medicine chest* (= the cabinet where you keep the medicines) *in the bathroom.* **2** the upper part of the front of your body: *What is your chest measurement?* ◇ *This jacket has a 40-inch chest.* ◇ *to have a hairy chest* ◇ *Linda went to the doctor, complaining of chest pains.* ➲ picture on study page **A32**.

IDM **get sth off your chest** (*informal*) to talk

about sth that you have been thinking about or that has been worrying you

**ches·ter·field** /'tʃɛstərfild/ ***noun*** [C] (*Cdn*) a couch or sofa

**chest·nut** /'tʃɛsnʌt/ ***noun*** [C] **1** (*also* **'chestnut tree**) a tree with large leaves that produces smooth reddish-brown nuts in shells with sharp points **2** one of the nuts from the chestnut tree. You can eat some chestnuts. ➲ picture at **nut**.

★**chew** /tʃu/ ***verb*** [I,T] to break up food in your mouth with your teeth before you swallow it: *You should chew your food carefully.*

PHRV **chew sb out** (*slang*) to criticize or speak to sb in an angry way, because he/she has done sth wrong: *The boss really chewed him out for showing up late.*

**'chewing gum** ***noun*** [U] = GUM (2)

**chew·y** /'tʃui/ ***adj.*** (**chew·i·er**; **chew·i·est**) (used about food) difficult to break up with your teeth before it can be swallowed: *chewy chocolate chip cookies*

**chi** /kaɪ/ ***noun*** [C] (*symbol* X, χ) the twenty-second letter of the Greek alphabet ➲ Look at the note at **fraternity**.

**chic** /ʃik/ ***adj.*** fashionable; elegant

**chick** /tʃɪk/ ***noun*** [C] **1** a young bird, especially a young chicken **2** (*informal*) a young woman or girl

> NOTE This word is used by some men. Many women dislike it.

★**chick·en**[1] /'tʃɪkən/ ***noun*** **1** [C] a bird that people keep for its eggs and its meat **2** [U] the meat of this bird: *roast chicken* ◇ *a chicken sandwich*

> NOTE Notice that chicken is the general word for the bird and its meat. A male chicken is called a **rooster**, a female is called a **hen** and a young bird is called a **chick**.

**3** [C] (*informal*) a person who is afraid of sth or has not got much courage: *He called me a chicken because I didn't want to swim in the ocean.*

**chick·en**[2] /'tʃɪkən/ ***verb***

PHRV **chicken out (of sth)** (*informal*) to decide not to do sth because you are afraid: *Come on! You said you'd give a speech – you can't chicken out now!*

**'chicken feed** ***noun*** [U] (*informal*) an amount of money that is not large enough to be important

**chicken flu** ***noun*** [U] = AVIAN INFLUENZA

**chicken pox** /'tʃɪkən pɑks/ ***noun*** [U] a disease, especially of children. When you have chicken pox you have a high temperature and get red spots on your skin that itch a lot.

**chick·pea** /'tʃɪkpi/ ***noun*** [C] = GARBANZO

★**chief**[1] /tʃif/ ***noun*** [C] **1** the leader or ruler of a group of people: *Native American tribal chiefs* **2** the person who has command or control over an organization: *the chief of police* **3** (*Cdn*) the leader of a Canadian Aboriginal community

★**chief**[2] /tʃif/ ***adj.*** (only *before* a noun) **1** most important; main: *One of the chief reasons for his decision was money.* **2** (often **Chief**) of the highest rank: *She was recently appointed Chief Medical Examiner.*

**ˌchief ex'ecutive** ***noun*** [C] **1 the Chief Executive** the President of the U.S. **2** (*also* **ˌchief exˌecutive 'officer**) (*abbr.* **CEO**) the leader of a large company or organization

**ˌchief 'justice** (*also* **ˌChief 'Justice**) ***noun*** [C] the most important judge in a court of law, especially the Supreme Court

**chief·ly** /'tʃifli/ ***adv.*** mainly; mostly: *His success was due chiefly to hard work.*

**chi·hua·hua** /tʃɪ'wɑwə/ ***noun*** [C] a very small dog with smooth hair

★**child** /tʃaɪld/ ***noun*** [C] (*pl.* **chil·dren** /'tʃɪldrən/) **1** a boy or girl; a human who is not yet fully grown: *A group of children were playing in the park.* ◇ *a six-year-old child* ◇ *child abuse*

> NOTE **Kid** is more common in informal English.

**2** a son or daughter of any age: *She has two children, but both are married and have moved away.* ◇ *He is married with three children.*

> NOTE An **only child** is a child who has no brothers or sisters. A couple may **adopt** a child who is not their own son or daughter (for example if the child's parents are dead). A **foster child** stays for a certain period of time with a family that is not his/her own.

**child·birth** /'tʃaɪldbərθ/ ***noun*** [U] the act of giving birth to a baby: *His wife died **in childbirth**.*

**child·care** /'tʃaɪldkɛr/ ***noun*** [U] the service of taking care of children while their parents are at work: *It's difficult to find affordable childcare these days.*

★**child·hood** /'tʃaɪldhʊd/ ***noun*** [C,U] the time when you are a child: *Harriet had a very unhappy childhood.* ◇ *childhood memories*

**child·ish** /'tʃaɪldɪʃ/ ***adj.*** like a child

> NOTE If you say that people or their behavior are **childlike**, you mean that they are like children in some positive way: *childlike innocence* ◇ *his childlike enthusiasm for the project.* If you say that an adult's behavior is **childish**, you are criticizing it because you think it is silly and that he/she should be more mature: *Don't be so childish! You can't always have everything you want.*

▸ **child·ish·ly** ***adv.***: *to giggle childishly*

**child·less** /'tʃaɪldləs/ ***adj.*** having no children: *a childless couple*

**child·like** /'tʃaɪldlaɪk/ ***adj.*** like a child ➲ Look at the note at **childish**.

**chil·dren** /'tʃɪldrən/ ***noun*** [U] *plural of* CHILD

**'child supˌport** ***noun*** [U] money that a parent who does not live with his/her children must pay to support them

**chil·i** /'tʃɪli/ ***noun*** [C,U] (*pl.* **chil·ies**) **1** [C,U] (*also* **'chili pepper**) a small green or red vegetable that is used in cooking to give food a strong hot taste ➲ picture on study page **A28-29**. **2** (*also* **chil·i con car·ne** /ˌtʃɪli kɑn 'kɑrni/) [U] a hot-tasting dish of meat and red beans: *a bowl of chili*

**chill**[1] /tʃɪl/ ***verb*** [I,T] to become or to make sb/sth colder: *It's better to chill white wine before you serve it.*

C

**chill²** /tʃɪl/ ***noun*** [sing.] an unpleasant coldness: *There's a chill in the air.* ◇ (*figurative*) *A chill of fear went down my spine.*

**chill·ing** /ˈtʃɪlɪŋ/ ***adj.*** frightening: *a chilling ghost story*

**chill·y** /ˈtʃɪli/ ***adj.*** (**chill·i·er**; **chill·i·est**) unpleasantly cold: *It's a chilly morning. You need a coat on.* ◇ (*figurative*) *The movie got a chilly reception from critics.*

**chime¹** /tʃaɪm/ ***verb*** [I] (used about a bell) to ring
PHR V **chime in (with sth)** (*informal*) to interrupt a conversation and add your own comments

**chime²** /tʃaɪm/ ***noun*** [C] the sound of a bell or a clock chiming

**chim·ney** /ˈtʃɪmni/ ***noun*** [C] (*pl.* **chim·neys**) the passage through which smoke, etc. can get out of a building. A chimney in a house usually goes up from a fire or heating system, behind the walls and to a hole in the roof: *Smoke poured out of the factory chimneys.* ➲ Picture on study page **A31**.

**chim·pan·zee** /ˌtʃɪmpænˈzi/ (*also informal* **chimp** /tʃɪmp/) ***noun*** [C] a type of small ape that lives in Africa

★**chin** /ˈtʃɪn/ ***noun*** [C] the part of your face that is below your mouth: *He sat listening with his chin in his hand.*

**chi·na** /ˈtʃaɪnə/ ***noun*** [U] **1** the substance of which cups, plates, etc. can be made. China is made from fine white baked clay: *a china vase* **2** cups, saucers, plates, etc. that are made from CHINA (1): *The dinner was served on fine china.*

**chi·nos** /ˈtʃinoʊz/ ***noun*** [pl.] informal pants made from strong cotton: *a polo shirt and a pair of chinos*

**chip**

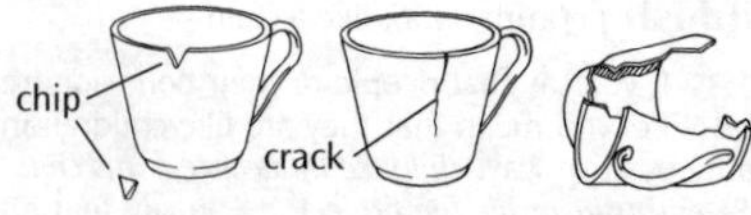


★**chip¹** /tʃɪp/ ***noun*** [C] **1** a small piece of wood, stone, glass, etc. that has broken off sth **2** a place where a piece has broken off sth: *This dish has a chip in it.* **3** a thin piece of food that has been fried in oil, dried and covered with salt: *potato chips* ◇ *tortilla chips* ◇ *Help yourself to some chips and dip.* **4** a flat round piece of plastic that you use instead of money when you are playing some games **5** (*also* **microchip**, **computer chip**, **silicon chip**) a very small piece of a special material (**silicon**) that is used inside a computer, etc. to make it work **6** (*Cdn*) = FRENCH FRY
IDM **have a chip on your shoulder** (*informal*) to be angry about sth for a long time, especially because you think you have been treated unfairly

**chip²** /tʃɪp/ ***verb*** [I,T] (**chip·ping**; **chipped**) to lose or to knock a small piece off the edge or surface of sth: *I fell off my bike and chipped my tooth.*

**chip·munk** /ˈtʃɪpmʌŋk/ ***noun*** [C] a small animal with a long tail and brown fur with black and white stripes

**chi·ro·prac·tor** /ˈkaɪrəpræktər/ ***noun*** [C] a person whose job is to treat pain in people's bodies by pressing on and moving their bones, especially in sb's back

**chirp** /tʃərp/ ***noun*** [C] the short high sound that a small bird makes ► **chirp** ***verb*** [I]

**chis·el** /ˈtʃɪzl/ ***noun*** [C] a tool with a sharp end that is used for cutting or shaping wood, stone, etc. ➲ picture at **tool**.

**chives** /tʃaɪvz/ ***noun*** [pl.] a plant with purple flowers and long thin leaves that are used in cooking. Chives taste similar to onions. ➲ picture on study page **A28-29**.

**chlo·rine** /ˈklɔrin; klɔˈrin/ ***noun*** [U] (*symbol* **Cl**) a greenish-yellow gas with a strong smell, that is used for making water safe to drink or to swim in

**chlo·ro·fluor·o·car·bon** /ˌklɔrəˌflɔroʊˈkɑrbən; -ˌflʊroʊ-/ ***noun*** [C] = CFC

**chlo·ro·form** /ˈklɔrəfɔrm/ ***noun*** [U] (*symbol* $CHCl_3$) a colorless liquid used in the past in medicine, etc. to make people unconscious, for example before an operation

**chlo·ro·phyll** /ˈklɔrəfɪl/ ***noun*** [U] the green substance in plants that absorbs light from the sun to help them grow

★**choc·o·late¹** /ˈtʃɑklət; ˈtʃɔk-/ ***noun*** **1** [U] a sweet brown substance that you usually buy in the form of a hard block (a **bar**). Chocolate is made from cocoa beans: *milk chocolate* (= sweet and light in color) ◇ *dark chocolate* (= more bitter and darker in color) **2** [C] a small candy that is made from chocolate with a nut or another sweet substance inside: *a box of assorted chocolates* ➲ Look also at **hot chocolate**.

**choc·o·late²** /ˈtʃɑklət/ ***adj.*** **1** made with chocolate: *chocolate cake* ◇ *a chocolate donut* **2** dark brown

ˌ**chocolate ˈchip** ***noun*** [C] a small piece of CHOCOLATE¹ (1) used in baking ► ˌ**chocolate-ˈchip** ***adj.***: *chocolate-chip cookies/ice cream*

★**choice¹** /tʃɔɪs/ ***noun*** **1** [C] **choice (between A and B)** an act of choosing between two or more people or things: *to make the right/wrong choice* ◇ *David faced a difficult choice between moving to a different city and losing his job.* ◇ *You can have first choice of the candy* (= you can choose first). **2** [U] the right or chance to choose: *All the hotels were full so we had no choice but to stay at Lisa's house.* ◇ *to have freedom of choice* **3** [C,U] two or more things from which you can or must choose: *There's a choice of six different movies every night.* **4** [C] a person or thing that has been chosen: *Who's your choice for governor?*
IDM **by choice** because you want to; of your own free will: *Rick didn't leave his job by choice – he was fired.*

**choice²** /tʃɔɪs/ ***adj.*** of good quality: *choice beef*

**choir** /ˈkwaɪər/ ***noun*** [C] a group of people who sing together: *Dennis sings in the church choir.* ◇ *The choir meets on Thursdays to rehearse.*

**choke** /tʃoʊk/ ***verb*** [I,T] to be or to make sb unable to breathe because sth is stopping air from getting into the lungs: *The child swallowed a pen cap and choked to death.* ◇ *The smoke was choking us.*

PHR V **choke sth back** to hide or control a strong emotion: *to choke back tears*

**chol·er·a** /ˈkɑlərə/ ***noun*** [U] a serious disease that makes it difficult for you to keep food in your body. Cholera is most common in hot countries and can be carried by water.

**cho·les·ter·ol** /kəˈlɛstərɔl/ ***noun*** [U] a substance that is found in the bodies of people and animals, and that helps to carry fats. Too much cholesterol is thought to be a cause of heart disease: *to have a high/low cholesterol level*

★**choose** /tʃuz/ ***verb*** [I,T] (*pt* **chose** /tʃoʊz/; *pp* **cho·sen** /ˈtʃoʊzn/) **1 choose (between A and/or B); choose sb/sth as sth** to pick or select the person or thing that you prefer: *Choose carefully before you make a final decision.* ◇ *Amy had to choose between getting a job or going to college.* ◇ *You can choose three questions out of the five on the exam.* ◇ *There were too many things to choose from.* ◇ *The viewers chose this program as their favorite.* **2** to decide or prefer to do sth: *You are free to leave whenever you choose.* ◇ *They chose to resign rather than work for the new manager.*

★**chop¹** /tʃɑp/ ***verb*** [T] (**chop·ping**; **chopped**) **chop sth (up) (into sth)** to cut sth into small pieces with an ax or knife: *They chopped the logs into firewood.* ◇ *finely chopped herbs* ◇ *Chop the onions up into small pieces.*

PHR V **chop sth down** to cut a tree, etc. at the bottom so that it falls down

**chop sth off (sth)** to remove sth from sth by cutting it with an ax or knife: *to chop a branch off a tree*

**chop²** /tʃɑp/ ***noun*** [C] **1** an act of chopping sth **2** a thick slice of meat, usually from a pig: *a pork chop* ➲ Look at **steak**.

**chop·per** /ˈtʃɑpər/ ***noun*** [C] (*informal*) = HELICOPTER

**chop·py** /ˈtʃɑpi/ ***adj.*** (**chop·pi·er**; **chop·pi·est**) **1** (used especially about the ocean, etc.) having a lot of small waves or uneven movement **2** (used about writing or speech) using many very short sentences and changing topics too often

**chop·sticks** /ˈtʃɑpstɪks/ ***noun*** [pl.] two thin sticks that people in China, Japan, etc. use for picking up food

**cho·ral** /ˈkɔrəl/ ***adj.*** written for or involving a group of singers (a choir)

**chord** /kɔrd/ ***noun*** [C] two or more musical notes that are played at the same time

IDM **strike a chord** → STRIKE²

**chore** /tʃɔr/ ***noun*** [C] a job that is not interesting but that you must do: *household chores*

**cho·re·o·graph** /ˈkɔriəɡræf/ ***verb*** [T] to design and arrange the movements of a dance

**cho·re·og·ra·pher** /ˌkɔriˈɑɡrəfər/ ***noun*** [C] a person whose job is to plan the movements for a dance

**cho·re·og·ra·phy** /ˌkɔriˈɑɡrəfi/ ***noun*** [U] the arrangement of movements for a dance

**cho·rus** /ˈkɔrəs/ ***noun*** [C] **1** a large group of people who sing together **2** (*also* **refrain**) the part of a song that is repeated at the end of each verse: *The audience joined in for the chorus.* **3** a piece of music for a large group to sing **4** something that a lot of people say together: *a chorus of cheers/boos/criticism* **5** a group of singers and dancers in a show

**chose** *past tense of* CHOOSE

**cho·sen** *past participle of* CHOOSE

**chow¹** /tʃaʊ/ ***noun*** [U] (*slang*) food

**chow²** /tʃaʊ/ ***verb*** [I,T] **chow (down) on sth**; **chow (sth) down** (*slang*) to eat sth quickly because you are very hungry or because you like it very much: *After the game, we chowed down on burgers and hot dogs.*

**chow·der** /ˈtʃaʊdər/ ***noun*** [U] a thick soup made with vegetables and usually fish ➲ Look at **clam chowder**.

**Christ** /kraɪst/ (*also* **Jesus, Jesus Christ**) ***noun*** the man who Christians believe is the son of God and who established the Christian religion

**chris·ten** /ˈkrɪsn/ ***verb*** [T] to give sb/sth a name: *Dad christened his new boat "The Wanderer."* ◇ *There have been so many accidents on this road that they've christened it "Suicide Alley."* ➲ Look at **baptize**.

**chris·ten·ing** /ˈkrɪsnɪŋ/ ***noun*** [C] the ceremony when sb is christened ➲ Look at **baptism**.

**Chris·tian** /ˈkrɪstʃən; ˈkrɪʃtʃən/ ***noun*** [C] a person whose religion is Christianity: *Christians all over the world will join in prayers for peace today.* ▸ **Chris·tian** ***adj.***: *the Christian Church/faith/religion*

**Chris·ti·an·i·ty** /ˌkrɪstʃiˈænət̬i/ ***noun*** [U] the religion that is based on the teachings of Jesus Christ: *to be converted to Christianity*

**Christ·mas** /ˈkrɪsməs/ (*also informal* **Xmas**) ***noun*** [C,U] Christmas Day, or the period of time before and after this holiday: *Merry Christmas!* ◇ *Where are you spending Christmas this year?* ◇ *the Christmas season*

ˈ**Christmas card** ***noun*** [C] a card with a picture on the front and a greeting inside that people send to their friends and relatives at Christmas

ˈ**Christmas ˌcarol** ***noun*** [C] = CAROL

ˌ**Christmas ˈDay** (*also* **Christmas**) ***noun*** [C] the day on which Christians celebrate the birth of Christ each year. For most Christians Christmas Day is December 25.

ˌ**Christmas ˈEve** ***noun*** [C] the day before Christmas Day, December 24

ˈ**Christmas tree** ***noun*** [C] a tree with thin sharp leaves (**an evergreen tree**), or an artificial tree, which people bring into their homes and decorate with bright lights and colored balls

**chrome** /kroʊm/ ***noun*** [U] hard shiny metal that is used for covering other metals: *a chrome bumper on a car*

**chro·mo·some** /ˈkroʊməsoʊm; -zoʊm/ ***noun*** [C] the part of the cells of living things that contains the information for producing new cells

**chron·ic** /ˈkrɑnɪk/ ***adj.*** (used about a disease or a problem) that continues for a long time: *chronic bronchitis* ◇ *There is a chronic shortage of housing in the city.* ▸ **chron·i·cal·ly** /-kli/ ***adv.***

**chron·i·cle** /ˈkrɑnɪkl/ ***noun*** [C] a record of events that happened in the past

**chron·o·log·i·cal** /ˌkrɑnəˈlɑdʒɪkl/ ***adj.*** arranged in the order in which the events happened: *a list of events arranged in chronological order* ▸ **chron·o·log·i·cal·ly** /-kli/ *adv.*

**chry·san·the·mum** /krɪ'sænθəməm/ *noun* [C] a large garden flower that is shaped like a ball and grows in bright colors

C

**chub·by** /'tʃʌbi/ *adj.* (**chub·bi·er**; **chub·bi·est**) slightly fat; round: *chubby cheeks*

**chuck·le** /'tʃʌkl/ *verb* [I] to laugh quietly: *Bruce chuckled to himself as he read the letter.* ▸ **chuck·le** *noun* [C]: *He put down the phone with a chuckle.*

**chug** /tʃʌg/ *verb* (**chug·ging**; **chugged**) **1** [I] to move making the sound of an engine running slowly: *The boat chugged down the river.* **2** [T] (*slang*) to drink sth completely, without stopping: *Each of those guys chugged a whole pitcher of beer!*

**chum** /tʃʌm/ *noun* [C] (*informal, old-fashioned*) a friend

**chunk** /tʃʌŋk/ *noun* [C] a large or thick piece of sth: *chunks of ice floating in the lake* ◇ (*figurative*) *A big chunk of my income goes toward paying bills.*

**chunk·y** /'tʃʌŋki/ *adj.* (**chunk·i·er**; **chunk·i·est**) **1** short and slightly fat **2** containing thick pieces: *chunky peanut butter*

★**church** /tʃərtʃ/ *noun* **1** [C,U] a building where Christians go to pray: *Services are held in this church every Sunday morning at 10.* ◇ *They are getting married in a beautiful old church.* ◇ *the church steeple* ◇ *Do you go to church regularly?*

> NOTE Notice that when you are talking about going to a ceremony (a service) in a church you say "in church," "to church" or "at church" without "**a**" or "**the**": *Was Mrs. Stevens in church today?*

**2** (*also* **Church**) [C] a particular group of Christians: *the Catholic/Methodist/Southern Baptist church*

**church·go·er** /'tʃərtʃgoʊər/ *noun* [C] a person who goes to church regularly

**churn** /tʃərn/ *verb* **1** [T] to beat milk or cream so that it turns into butter **2** [I,T] **churn (sth) (up)** to move, or to make sth move with great force: *The hurricane churned up huge waves along the coast.*

PHRV **churn sth out** (*informal*) to produce large numbers of sth very quickly: *Some authors of romance novels can churn out a new book every month.*

**chute** /ʃut/ *noun* [C] a passage down which you can drop or slide things so that you do not have to carry them: *a laundry chute*

**chutz·pah** /'hʊtspə; 'xʊt-/ *noun* [U] (*informal*) behavior, or a person's attitude that is rude or shocking but so confident that people may feel forced to admire it ➲ Look also at **nerve** (5).

**the CIA** /ˌsi aɪ 'eɪ/ *noun* [sing.] (*U.S.*) the Central Intelligence Agency; the U.S. government organization that tries to get secret political and military information about other countries ➲ Look at the note at **White House**.

**cia·bat·ta** /tʃə'bɑtə/ *noun* [U,C] a type of Italian bread; a wide flat loaf of this

**ci·der** /'saɪdər/ *noun* [U,C] **1** (*also* ˌ**sweet 'cider**) a drink made from the juice of apples that does not contain alcohol: *The children had cider and cookies at the party.* **2** (*also* ˌ**hard 'cider**) an alcoholic drink made from the juice of apples

**ci·gar** /sɪ'gɑr/ *noun* [C] a roll of dried tobacco leaves that people smoke. Cigars are larger and more expensive than cigarettes: *cigar smoke*

★**cig·a·rette** /ˌsɪgə'rɛt; 'sɪgərɛt/ *noun* [C] a roll of tobacco in a tube of thin white paper that people smoke: *a pack of cigarettes* ◇ *to smoke a cigarette* ◇ *She lit another cigarette.* ◇ *John put out his cigarette.*

**ci·lan·tro** /sɪ'læntroʊ; -'lɑn-/ *noun* [U] = CORIANDER ➲ picture on study page **A28-29**.

**cin·der** /'sɪndər/ *noun* [C] a very small piece of coal, wood, etc. that has been burning and may still be hot

★**cin·e·ma** /'sɪnəmə/ *noun* [U] (*formal*) the art and industry of making movies: *one of the most important directors in Latin American cinema* ➲ Look also at **movie**.

**Cin·e·plex**™ /'sɪnəplɛks/ *noun* [C] = MULTIPLEX

**cin·na·mon** /'sɪnəmən/ *noun* [U] a brown powder that is used for giving flavor to sweet food

**cir·ca** /'sərkə/ *prep.* (*abbr.* **c, ca.**) (*formal*) (used with dates) about: *The vase was made circa 600 B.C.*

★**cir·cle**[1] /'sərkl/ *noun* [C] **1** a line that curves around to form the shape of a ring. Every point on the line is the same distance from the center: *The kids were drawing circles and squares on a piece of paper.* ◇ *We all stood in a circle and held hands.* ➲ picture at **shape**. **2** a flat, round area: *She cut out a circle of paper.* **3** a group of people who are friends, or who have the same interest or profession: *He has a large circle of friends.* ◇ *Her name was well known in artistic circles.*

IDM **a vicious circle/cycle** → VICIOUS

**cir·cle**[2] /'sərkl/ *verb* **1** [I,T] to move, or to move around sth, in a circle, especially in the air: *The plane circled the town several times before it landed.* **2** [T] to draw a circle around sth, e.g. on a test: *There are three possible answers to each question. Circle the correct one.*

**cir·cuit** /'sərkət/ *noun* [C] **1** a complete circular path that an electric current can flow around ➲ Look also at **closed-circuit television**. **2** a number of events that people take part in, moving around from place to place: *Now that Senator Wilson is retired, he's traveling the college lecture circuit* (= giving lectures at many different colleges). **3** an area that a judge travels around, hearing court cases in several different cities: *the 9th U.S. Circuit Court of Appeals*

**'circuit ˌbreaker** *noun* [C] a small piece of equipment that stops the flow of electricity if there is too much power in a circuit ➲ Look at **fuse**[1](3).

**'circuit ˌtraining** *noun* [U] a type of training in sport in which different exercises are each done for a short time

**cir·cu·lar**[1] /'sərkyələr/ *adj.* **1** round and flat; shaped like a circle: *a circular table* **2** (used about a trip, etc.) going around in a circle: *The bus will take you on a circular tour of Boston.*

**cir·cu·lar**[2] /'sərkyələr/ *noun* [C] a printed letter, notice or advertisement that is sent to a large number of people: *an advertising circular*

**cir·cu·late** /ˈsərkyəleɪt/ ***verb*** **1** [I,T] to go from one person to another; to pass information from one person to another: *Stories were circulating about the mayor's private life.* ◇ *We circulated a copy of the report to each department.* **2** [I,T] (used about a substance) to move or make sth move around continuously: *Blood circulates around the body.*

**cir·cu·la·tion** /ˌsərkyəˈleɪʃn/ ***noun*** **1** [U] the passing of sth from one person or place to another: *the circulation of news/information/rumors* ◇ *Old silver dollar coins are no longer in circulation* (= being used by people). **2** [C] the number of copies of a newspaper, magazine, etc. that are sold each time it is produced: *This newspaper has a circulation of over a million.* **3** [sing.] the movement of blood around the body: *Grandma says she has poor circulation, so her hands and feet get cold easily.*

**cir·cum·cise** /ˈsərkəmsaɪz/ ***verb*** [T] to cut off the skin at the end of a person's sexual organ, for religious or (in the case of a man) medical reasons ▸ **cir·cum·ci·sion** /ˌsərkəmˈsɪʒn/ ***noun*** [C,U]

**cir·cum·fer·ence** /sərˈkʌmfrəns/ ***noun*** [C,U] the distance around a circle or sth circular: *The circumference of the moon is about 6,800 miles.* ◇ *The moon is about 6,800 miles in circumference.*

**cir·cum·stance** /ˈsərkəmstæns/ ***noun*** **1** [C, usually pl.] the facts and events that affect what happens in a particular situation: *We need to know the exact circumstances surrounding the accident.* ◇ *I'm not sure what I would do under those circumstances.* ◇ *the unusual circumstances surrounding her death* ◇ *We can only make exceptions to the rules in special circumstances.* **2 circumstances** [pl.] (*formal*) the amount of money that you have: *The company has promised to repay the money when its financial circumstances improve.*

IDM **under no/any circumstances** never, for any reason: *Under no circumstances will this government cooperate with terrorists.* ◇ *Late papers will not be accepted under any circumstances.*

**under the circumstances** as the result of a particular situation: *Well, it's not an ideal solution, but it's the best we can do under the circumstances.*

**cir·cum·stan·tial** /ˌsərkəmˈstænʃl/ ***adj.*** containing information and details that strongly suggest that sth is true but do not prove it: *circumstantial evidence*

**cir·cus** /ˈsərkəs/ ***noun*** [C] a show performed in a large tent by a company of people and often animals: *We saw clowns, acrobats, lions and elephants at the circus.*

**ci·ta·tion** /saɪˈteɪʃn/ ***noun*** [C] **1** an official warning that you get after you have done sth wrong, that often means that you have to go to court: *Police officers will issue citations to drivers who park here without a permit.* ◇ *a traffic citation* **2** an official report that praises sb for sth he/she has done: *a citation for bravery* **3** [C,U] a reference in a speech or piece of writing to sth that sb else has said or written: *Her thesis contained citations to all the important works on that topic.*

**cite** /saɪt/ ***verb*** [T] (*formal*) **1** to mention sth as an example to support what you are saying: *She cited the high unemployment figures as an example of the government's bad management.* **2** to name sb officially in a legal case: *He was cited in the divorce proceedings.*

★**cit·i·zen** /ˈsɪt̬əzn/ ***noun*** [C] **1** a person who is legally accepted as a member of a particular country: *She was born in Japan, but became a Canadian citizen in 2003.* ◇ *a British citizen* **2** a person who lives in a town or city: *Many of the citizens of New York leave the city for the beach during the summer.* ➲ Look at **senior citizen**.

**cit·i·zen·ship** /ˈsɪt̬əzənʃɪp/ ***noun*** [U] the state of being a citizen of a particular country: *After living in Spain for twenty years, he decided to apply for Spanish citizenship.*

**cit·rus** /ˈsɪtrəs/ (*also* ˈ**citrus fruit**) ***noun*** [C,U] (a) fruit such as an orange or a lemon

★**cit·y** /ˈsɪt̬i/ ***noun*** (*pl.* **cit·ies**) **1** [C] a large and important town: *Venice is one of the most beautiful cities in the world.* ◇ *Many people are worried about housing conditions in our inner cities* (= the central parts where there are often social problems). **2** [C] a town or CITY (1) that has specific rights and borders that were decided by the state government: *the city council* ◇ *a bar just outside the city limits* **3 the city** [sing.] the government of a CITY (2) and the related offices that provide services for the people who live there: *I work for the city.* ◇ *The city picks up our trash once a week.*

ˌ**city** ˈ**hall** (*also* often **City Hall**) ***noun*** **1** [C] the building where the offices of a city's government are **2** [U] the government of a city: *Our neighborhood is ready to fight city hall in order to get our streets repaired.*

ˌ**city** ˈ**slicker** ***noun*** [C] (*informal*) a person who behaves in a way that is typical of people who live in big cities

**civ·ic** /ˈsɪvɪk/ ***adj.*** of a city or town: *civic pride* (= feeling proud because you belong to a particular town or city)

ˌ**civic** ˈ**center** ***noun*** [C] a large building where public meetings, sports events, performances, etc. are held: *Graduation this year will be held at the civic center.*

ˌ**civic** ˈ**holiday** ***noun*** [C] (*Cdn*) a holiday that is taken on the first Monday in August in all of Canada apart from Quebec, Alberta and Prince Edward Island

**civ·ics** /ˈsɪvɪks/ ***noun*** [U] the study of the rights and responsibilities of citizens and the way government works

★**civ·il** /ˈsɪvl/ ***adj.*** **1** polite, but not very friendly: *I know you don't like the director, but please try and be civil to him.* **2** (only *before* a noun) connected with the public, not with the army or a church: *civil aviation* ◇ *We got married in a civil ceremony* (= not a religious one). **3** (in law) relating to the rights of ordinary people, and not criminal offenses: *a civil case*

ˌ**civil engiˈneering** ***noun*** [U] the design, building and repair of roads, bridges, etc.; the study of this as a subject ▸ ˌ**civil engiˈneer** ***noun*** [C]

**ci·vil·ian** /səˈvɪlyən/ ***noun*** [C] a person who is not in the police or military forces: *Two soldiers and one civilian were killed when the bomb exploded.* ◇ *He left the army and returned to civilian life.*

C

**civ·i·li·za·tion** /ˌsɪvələˈzeɪʃn/ ***noun*** **1** [C,U] a society that has its own highly developed culture and way of life: *the civilizations of ancient Greece and Rome* ◇ *Western civilization* **2** [U] an advanced state of social and cultural development, or the process of reaching this state: *China had reached a higher level of civilization than Europe at that time.* ◇ *The civilization of the human race has taken thousands of years.*

**civ·i·lized** /ˈsɪvəlaɪzd/ ***adj.*** **1** (used about a society) having a high level of social and cultural development: *In a civilized society there should not be people sleeping on the streets.* **2** polite and reasonable: *a civilized conversation*

**ˌcivil ˈliberties** ***noun*** [pl.] a citizen's legal right to such rights as freedom of speech, freedom of religion, etc.

**ˌcivil ˈrights** ***noun*** [pl.] the legal right to freedom and equality for citizens of every race, sex, religion, etc.: *the continuing struggle for civil rights for black Americans*

**ˌcivil ˈservant** ***noun*** [C] a person who works in the civil service: *People who are elected to a job in the government are called "elected officials" and not civil servants.*

**the ˌcivil ˈservice** ***noun*** [sing.] the government departments in a country, state, province, etc., except the military, and the people who work for them: *He had a long career in the civil service.*

**ˌcivil ˈwar** ***noun*** **1 the Civil War** [sing.] (*U.S.*) the war that was fought from 1861 to 1865 between the northern and the southern states. The two groups of states fought about whether it was right to own slaves. **2** [C,U] a war between different groups of people who live in the same country

**clad** /klæd/ ***adj.*** (not before a noun) (*formal*) dressed: *Many people were clad only in pajamas as they escaped from the burning building.*

★**claim¹** /kleɪm/ ***verb*** [T] **1** to say that sth is true, without having any proof: *The bus driver claimed that she had not seen the bike rider.* ◇ *Eric claims the book belongs to him.* ◇ *She claims to be the oldest person in the country.* ◇ *No one has claimed responsibility for the bomb attack.* **2** to ask for sth because you think you should have it or that it belongs to you: *The police are keeping the animal until somebody claims it.* ◇ *If you are disabled, you can claim a special deduction on your taxes.* **3** (*formal*) to cause death: *The earthquake claimed thousands of lives.*

★**claim²** /kleɪm/ ***noun*** [C] **1** a statement that sth is true, but that does not have any proof: *I don't believe the President's claim that he can reduce unemployment by the end of the year.* **2 claim (for sth)** a demand for sth that you think you have a right to: *to make an insurance claim* ◇ *After the accident he decided to submit a claim for damages.* **3 claim (on/to sth)** the right to have sth: *You will have to prove your claim to the property in court.*
IDM **stake a/your claim** → STAKE²

**claim·ant** /ˈkleɪmənt/ ***noun*** [C] a person who makes an official CLAIM²(2) for sth: *The insurance form has a space at the bottom for the signature of the claimant* (= the person who is asking for money from the insurance company).

**clam¹** /klæm/ ***noun*** [C] a type of shellfish that lives in water and has a shell in two parts that can open and close: *fried clams*

**clam²** /klæm/ ***verb*** (**clam<u>m</u>ing**; **clam<u>m</u>ed**)
PHR V **clam up** (*informal*) to stop talking and refuse to speak: *She always clams up when I ask her about her past.*

**clam·bake** /ˈklæmbeɪk/ ***noun*** [C] an outdoor party for eating clams and other seafood

**ˈclam ˌchowder** ***noun*** [U] a kind of soup made with clams and potatoes

**clam·my** /ˈklæmi/ ***adj.*** (**clam·mi·er**; **clam·mi·est**) damp and sticky: *clammy hands*

**clam·or¹** /ˈklæmər/ ***verb*** [I] **clamor for sth** to demand sth in a loud or angry way: *The public is clamoring for answers to all these questions.*

**clam·or²** /ˈklæmər/ ***noun*** [sing.] a loud, angry discussion or argument: *We could hear the clamor of angry voices.*

**clamp¹** /klæmp/ ***noun*** [C] a tool that you use to hold two things together very tightly

**clamp²** /klæmp/ ***verb*** [T] **1** to fasten two things together with a CLAMP¹: *Clamp the two pieces together until the glue dries.* ◇ *Clamp the board to the table so that it doesn't move.* **2** to put or hold sth very firmly in a particular place
PHR V **clamp down on sb/sth** (*informal*) to take strong action against sb/sth in order to stop or control sth: *The police are clamping down on people who drink and drive.*

**clamp·down** /ˈklæmpdaʊn/ ***noun*** [C] strong action in order to stop or control sth: *a clampdown on tax evasion*

**clan** /klæn/ ***noun*** [C] **1** a group of families who are related to each other **2** (*informal*) a large family or a group of people with a close relationship: *When the Robinson clan gets together at Thanksgiving, there's a big crowd.*

**clan·des·tine** /klænˈdestən/ ***adj.*** (*formal*) secret and often not legal

**clang** /klæŋ/ ***noun*** [C] a loud ringing sound that is made when a metal object hits sth: *The huge metal door closed with a clang.* ▶ **clang** ***verb*** [I,T]

**clank** /klæŋk/ ***noun*** [C] a loud sound that is made when a metal object (e.g. a heavy chain) hits sth ▶ **clank** ***verb*** [I,T]

**clap¹** /klæp/ ***verb*** (**clap<u>p</u>ing**; **clap<u>p</u>ed**) **1** [I,T] to put your hands together quickly in order to make a loud sound, usually to show that you like sth: *The audience clapped as soon as the singer walked onto the stage.* ◇ *Everybody was clapping their hands in time to the music.* **2** [T] to put sth onto sth quickly and firmly: *"Oh no, I shouldn't have said that," she said, clapping a hand over her mouth.*

**clap²** /klæp/ ***noun*** [C] a sudden loud noise of thunder: *a clap of thunder*

**clap·board** /ˈklæbərd; ˈklæpbɔrd/ ***noun*** [C,U] a long, narrow board that is used to cover the outside walls of a house or other building

**clar·i·fi·ca·tion** /ˌklærəfəˈkeɪʃn/ ***noun*** [C,U] an explanation that makes sth clear and easier to understand: *We'd like some clarification on exactly what your company intends to do.*

**clar·i·fy** /ˈklærəfaɪ/ ***verb*** [T] (*pres. part.* **clar·i·fy·ing**; *3rd person sing. pres.* **clar·i·fies**; *pt, pp* **clar·i·fied**) to make sth become clear and easier to understand: *I hope that what I say will clarify the situation.*

**clar·i·net** /ˌklærəˈnɛt/ ***noun*** [C] a musical instrument that is made of wood. You play a clarinet by blowing through it.

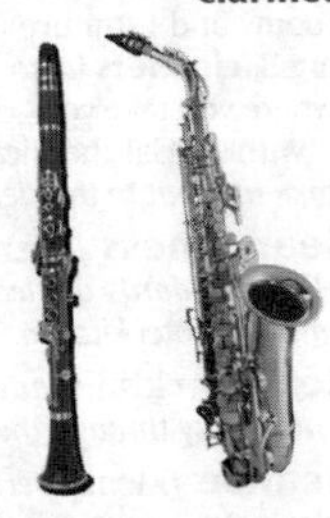

**clarinet**

**clarinet saxophone**

**clar·i·ty** /ˈklærət̬i/ ***noun*** [U] the quality of being clear and easy to understand: *clarity of expression*

**clash¹** /klæʃ/ ***verb*** **1** [I] **clash (with sb) (over sth)** to fight or disagree seriously about sth: *A group of demonstrators clashed with police.* ◇ *Congress and the President have clashed again over defense cuts.* **2** [I] **clash (with sth)** (used about colors, etc.) not to match or look nice together: *I don't think you should wear that tie – it clashes with your shirt.* **3** [I,T] (used about two metal objects) to hit together with a loud noise; to cause two metal objects to do this: *Their swords clashed.*

**clash²** /klæʃ/ ***noun*** [C] **1** a fight or serious disagreement: *a clash between police and demonstrators* **2** a big difference: *a clash of opinions* ◇ *There was a personality clash between the two men.* **3** a loud noise, made by two metal objects hitting each other: *the clash of cymbals*

**clasp¹** /klæsp/ ***noun*** [C] an object, usually of metal, which fastens or holds sth together: *the clasp on a necklace/purse*

**clasp²** /klæsp/ ***verb*** [T] to hold sb/sth tightly: *She clasped her hands together in her lap.*

★**class** /klæs/ ***noun***

➤IN EDUCATION **1** [C] a group of students who are taught together: *Jane and I are in the same class at school.* ◇ *The whole class is going to the theater tonight.* **2** [C] a group of students who are or were in the same year of their studies at the same time: *the class president* ◇ *the class of 2002* (= who finished high school/college in 2002) **3** [C,U] a lesson: *Classes begin at 9 o'clock in the morning.* ◇ *We watched an interesting video in class* (= during the lesson) *yesterday.* **4** [C] a course in a particular subject: *I'm taking four classes this semester.* ◇ *My cooking class starts next Wednesday evening.*

➤IN SOCIETY **5** [C,U] a group of people who are at the same social and economic level: *members of the middle class* ◇ *middle-class families*

➤GROUP OF PEOPLE/ANIMALS **6** [C] a group of things of a similar type: *There are several different classes of insects.*

➤SKILL/STYLE **7** [U] (*informal*) high quality or style: *Barry has absolutely no class.*

➤IN TRAIN/PLANE **8** [C,U] (especially in compounds) of a certain level of quality or comfort: *the most expensive class of service* ➲ Look also at **first-class** and **second-class**.

IDM **cut/skip class** (*informal*) to stay away from class without permission: *Rick skipped math class twice last week.*

**ˌclass ˈaction** (*also* **ˌclass ˈaction suit**) ***noun*** [C] a type of court case (lawsuit) that is started by a group of people who have a problem in common

★**clas·sic¹** /ˈklæsɪk/ ***adj.*** **1** typical: *This painting is a* ***classic example*** *of the French Impressionist style.* ◇ *It was a classic case of bad management.* **2** (used about a book, play, etc.) important and having a value that will last: *classic Hollywood movies from the 1930s and '40s*

★**clas·sic²** /ˈklæsɪk/ ***noun*** **1** [C] a famous book, play, etc. which has a value that will last: *All of Charles Dickens' novels are classics.* **2 Classics** [U] the study of ancient Greek and Roman language and literature

**clas·si·cal** /ˈklæsɪkl/ ***adj.*** **1** (used about music) serious and having a value that lasts: *I prefer classical music to rock or jazz.* **2** traditional, not modern: *classical ballet* ◇ *classical scientific methods* **3** relating to ancient Greece or Rome: *classical architecture*

**clas·si·cal·ly** /ˈklæsɪkli/ ***adv.*** **1** in a traditional way: *a classically trained pianist* **2** typically: *These symptoms are classically associated with food poisoning.*

**clas·si·fi·ca·tion** /ˌklæsəfəˈkeɪʃn/ ***noun*** **1** [U] the process of putting sb/sth into a group with other people or things of a similar type: *the classification of different species of butterflies* **2** [C] a group or CLASS (6) into which sb/sth is put

**clas·si·fied** /ˈklæsəfaɪd/ ***adj.*** officially secret: *classified information*

**ˌclassified ˈadvertisement** (*also informal* **ˌclassified ˈad**, **ˈwant ad**) ***noun*** [C] a small advertisement that you put in a newspaper if you want to buy or sell sth, employ sb, find an apartment, etc.

**clas·si·fy** /ˈklæsəfaɪ/ ***verb*** [T] (*pres. part.* **clas·si·fy·ing**; *3rd person sing. pres.* **clas·si·fies**; *pt, pp* **clas·si·fied**) **classify sb/sth (as sth)** to put sb/sth into a group with other people or things of a similar type: *The books in a library are usually classified according to subject.*

**class·mate** /ˈklæsmeɪt/ ***noun*** [C] a person who is in the same CLASS (1,2) as you in school or college

**class·room** /ˈklæsrum/ ***noun*** [C] a room in a school, college, etc. where classes are taught

**class·y** /ˈklæsi/ ***adj.*** (**class·i·er**; **class·i·est**) (*informal*) of high quality or style; expensive: *She took me to a classy restaurant downtown.*

**clat·ter** /ˈklæt̬ər/ ***noun*** [sing.] a series of short loud repeated sounds that is made when hard objects hit against each other: *the clatter of computer keyboards in an office* ▶ **clat·ter** ***verb*** [I]: *The dishes clattered in the cupboard when he slammed the door.*

**clause** /klɔz/ ***noun*** [C] **1** a paragraph in a legal document **2** (*grammar*) a group of words that includes a subject and a verb. A clause is usually only part of a sentence: *The sentence, "After we had finished eating, we watched a video," contains two clauses.*

**claus·tro·pho·bi·a** /ˌklɔstrəˈfoʊbiə/ ***noun*** [U] great fear of being in a small or closed space

**claus·tro·pho·bic** /ˌklɔstrəˈfoʊbɪk/ ***adj.***

C

**1** afraid of being in a small or closed space: *I always feel claustrophobic in elevators.* **2** (used about sth that makes you feel afraid of being in a small or closed space): *a claustrophobic little room*

**claw** /klɔ/ ***noun*** [C] **1** one of the pointed nails on the feet of some animals and birds: *Cats have sharp claws.* **2** the part of a leg on some types of insects and sea animals that they use to hold things

**clay** /kleɪ/ ***noun*** [U] heavy earth that is soft when it is wet and becomes hard when it is baked or dried: *The students were modeling heads out of clay.* ◇ *clay pots*

★**clean¹** /klin/ ***adj.*** **1** not dirty: *Are your hands clean?* ◇ *I think I'll put on a clean shirt.* **2** (used about animals and people) having clean habits: *Cats are very clean animals.* **3** (used about humor) not about sex, etc.; not dirty: *a clean joke* **4** having no record of offenses: *a clean driving record* **5** (*informal*) no longer using illegal drugs: *I've been clean for two years now.*

IDM **a clean slate** a record of your work or behavior that does not show any mistakes or bad things that you have done: *Students with low grades from high school have the chance to start with a clean slate in college.*

**a clean sweep 1** a complete victory in a sports competition, election, etc. that you get by winning all the different parts of it: *The Russians made a clean sweep of all the gymnastics events.* **2** a complete removal of things or people that you think are no longer necessary: *The new director plans to make a clean sweep and fire everyone in this department.*

★**clean²** /klin/ ***verb*** **1** [T] to remove dirt and marks from sth: *to clean the bathtub/the windows/the kitchen floor*

> NOTE **Clean** is a general word for removing dirt from something. If you **wash** something, you clean it with water and often soap. You can **wipe** a surface by rubbing it with a wet cloth; you **dust** a surface by rubbing it with a dry cloth. If you **brush** something, you clean it with a brush that has a short handle; if you **sweep** the floor, you use a broom with a long handle.

**2** [T] to put sth into good order; to make sth neat: *Why don't you ever clean your room? It's a mess!* **3** [I] to make the inside of a house, office, etc. free from dust and dirt: *Mr. Burrows comes in to clean in the evenings.*

PHR V **clean sth out 1** to clean the inside of sth thoroughly: *I'm going to clean out all the kitchen cabinets next week.* **2** to empty sth completely: *We have to clean out our lockers on the last day of school.*

**clean (sth) up 1** to remove all the dirt from a place that is very dirty: *I'm going to clean up the kitchen before Mom and Dad get back.* **2** to put sth into good order; to make sth neat: *Will you please clean up all this junk that's on the floor?* **3** to remove sth that has just been spilled: *Oh no, you spilled juice on Mom's new carpet! You'd better clean it up!*

**clean³** /klin/ (*informal*) ***adv.*** completely: *We're clean out of coffee!*

**ˌclean-ˈcut** ***adj.*** (used about men) looking clean, neat and honest: *a clean-cut young man*

**clean·er** /ˈklinər/ ***noun*** **1** [C] a substance or an instrument that you use for cleaning sth: *liquid floor cleaners* ◇ *a carpet cleaner* ➲ Look at **vacuum cleaner**. **2** [C] a person whose job is to clean the rooms and furniture inside a house or other building **3 cleaners** (*also* **dry cleaners**) [pl.] a business where you take your clothes to be cleaned, especially with special chemicals instead of water: *Could you take my coat to the cleaners?*

**clean·li·ness** /ˈklɛnlinəs/ ***noun*** [U] being clean: *High standards of cleanliness are extremely important in a hotel kitchen.*

**clean·ly** /ˈklinli/ ***adv.*** easily or smoothly: *The knife cut cleanly through the rope.*

**cleanse** /klɛnz/ ***verb*** [T] to make sth thoroughly clean: *to cleanse a cut*

**cleans·er** /ˈklɛnzər/ ***noun*** [C,U] a substance that you use for cleaning sth: *skin cleanser* ◇ *Do not use abrasive cleansers on the bathtub.*

**clean-shav·en** /ˌklin ˈʃeɪvn/ ***adj.*** (used about men) not having a beard or a mustache

★**clear¹** /klɪr/ ***adj.***

➤TRANSPARENT **1** easy to see through: *clear glass* ◇ *The water was so clear that we could see the bottom of the lake.*

➤EASY TO SEE/HEAR **2** easy to see, hear or understand: *We get a very clear picture on our new TV set.* ◇ *His voice wasn't very clear over the phone.* ◇ *She gave me clear directions on how to get there.*

➤WITHOUT MARKS **3** free from marks: *a clear sky* (= without clouds) ◇ *clear skin* (= without pimples)

➤NOT BLOCKED **4** free from things that are blocking the way: *The highway patrol says that most roads are now clear of snow.*

➤WITHOUT CONFUSION/DOUBT **5 clear (to sb)** easy to see; obvious: *There are clear advantages to the second plan.* ◇ *It was clear to me that he was not telling the truth.* ◇ *The answer to the problem is absolutely clear.* **6 clear (about/on sth)** sure or definite; without any doubts: *I'm not quite clear about the arrangements for tomorrow.* **7** not confused: *Clear thinking is very important in this job.* ◇ ***a clear understanding*** *of the situation*

➤CONSCIENCE **8** free from guilt: *It wasn't your fault. You can have a completely clear conscience.*

IDM **crystal clear** → CRYSTAL

**make yourself clear; make sth clear/plain (to sb)** to speak so that there can be no doubt about what you mean: *"I do not want you to go to that concert," said my mother. "Do I make myself clear?"* ◇ *He made it very clear that he was not happy with the decision.*

★**clear²** /klɪr/ ***adv.*** **1** = CLEARLY (1): *We can hear you* ***loud and clear*** *from here.* **2 clear (of sth)** away from sth; not touching sth: *They managed to pull the victims clear of the car wreckage.* **3** (*informal*) completely: *Jim just kicked his foot clear through the door!*

IDM **keep/stay/steer clear (of sb/sth)** to avoid sb/sth: *You'd better steer clear of Vanessa – she's in a bad mood today.*

★**clear³** /klɪr/ ***verb***

➤REMOVE STH/SB **1** [T] to remove sth that is not

wanted or needed from a place: *to clear the roads of snow/to clear snow from the roads* ◇ *It's your turn to* ***clear the table*** (= to take away the dirty plates after a meal). ◇ *Can I help you clear away the dishes?* **2** [T] to make people leave a place: *After the bomb warning, the police cleared the building.*
➤ OF SMOKE, ETC. **3** [I] (used about fog, smoke, etc.) to disappear: *The fog slowly cleared and the sun came out.*
➤ GET OVER/PAST **4** [T] to jump over or get past sth without touching it: *Sara didn't hit the ball very hard, so it barely cleared the net.*
➤ GET/GIVE OFFICIAL PERMISSION **5** [T] to go through a process, especially of getting permission for sth to happen: *The bill has cleared the House and the Senate and will soon be signed into law.* **6** [T] to give permission for sth to happen: *At last the plane was cleared for takeoff.*
➤ MONEY **7** [I] (used about a check) to go through the system that transfers money from one account to another: *The check will take three days to clear.*
➤ PROVE SB INNOCENT **7** [T] **clear sb (of sth)** to prove that sb is not guilty of a crime or mistake: *Hector was finally cleared of murder and has been released from prison.*

IDM **clear the air** to help people feel better in a difficult situation by talking openly about worries, doubts, etc.: *If you discuss your feelings with her, it will help to clear the air between you.*

**clear your throat** to cough slightly in order to make it easier to speak: *He cleared his throat and then began his speech.*

PHR V **clear sth out** to clean sth and throw away things that you do not want: *I really need to clear out the kitchen cabinets.*

**clear up** (used about the weather or an illness) to get better: *We can go out for a walk if it clears up later on.* ◇ *The doctor told him to stay at home until his cold cleared up.*

**clear (sth) up** to make sth neat and clean: *Make sure you clear up all your stuff before you leave.*

**clear sth up** to find the solution to a problem, mystery, etc.: *There was a slight misunderstanding, but we've cleared it up now.*

**clear·ance** /'klɪrəns/ ***noun*** **1** [U] the removing of sth that is old or not wanted: *The store is having a clearance sale* (= reducing the price of things in order to sell all of them quickly). **2** [U] the distance between an object and sth that is passing under or beside it, e.g. a ship or vehicle: *There was not enough clearance for the bus to pass under the bridge safely.* **3** [C,U] official permission for sb/sth to do sth: *Only people with a top-level security clearance may enter the nuclear research lab.*

**ˌclear-'cut** ***adj.*** definite and easy to see or understand: *It was a clear-cut case of police corruption.*

**clear·ing** /'klɪrɪŋ/ ***noun*** [C] a small area without trees in the middle of woods or a forest

★**clear·ly** /'klɪrli/ ***adv.*** **1** in a way that is easy to see, hear or understand: *It was so foggy that we couldn't see the road clearly.* **2** in a way that is not confused: *I'm so tired that I can't think clearly.* **3** obviously; without doubt: *She clearly doesn't want to speak to you anymore.*

**cleav·age** /'klivɪdʒ/ ***noun*** [C,U] the space between a woman's breasts

**clef** /klɛf/ ***noun*** [C] (in music) a sign (𝄞,𝄢) at the beginning of a line of written music that shows the range of the notes ➲ picture at **music**.

**clench** /klɛntʃ/ ***verb*** [T] to close or hold tightly: *He clenched his teeth in pain.* ◇ *She clenched her fists and looked as if she were about to hit him.*

**cler·gy** /'klərdʒi/ ***noun*** [pl.] the people who perform religious ceremonies in the Christian church: *a member of the clergy*

**cler·gy·man** /'klərdʒimən/ ***noun*** [C] (*pl.* **cler·gy·men** /-mɛn/) a man who is a member of the clergy

**cler·gy·wom·an** /'klərdʒiwʊmən/ ***noun*** [C] (*pl.* **cler·gy·wom·en** /-wɪmən/) a woman who is a member of the clergy

**cler·i·cal** /'klɛrɪkl/ ***adj.*** **1** connected with the work of a clerk in an office: *clerical work* **2** of or concerning the clergy

**clerk** /klərk/ ***noun*** [C] **1** (*also* **'salesclerk**) a person who sells things to people in a store **2** a person whose job is to do written work or keep records or accounts in an office, a bank, a court of law, etc. **3** (*also* **'desk clerk**) a person whose job is dealing with people arriving at or leaving a hotel: *Leave your keys with the desk clerk.*

★**clev·er** /'klɛvər/ ***adj.*** **1** (used about things, ideas, etc.) showing skill or intelligence: *a clever device* ◇ *a clever plan* **2** (used about a person) able to find a way of doing sth easily, especially in order to trick people: *a clever criminal* ▸ **clev·er·ly** ***adv.***

**cli·ché** /kli'ʃeɪ/ ***noun*** [C] a phrase or idea that has been used so many times that it no longer has any real meaning or interest: *the old cliché that life begins at 40*

**click**[1] /klɪk/ ***noun*** [C] a short sharp sound: *the click of a light switch*

**click**[2] /klɪk/ **1** ***verb*** [I,T] to make a short sharp sound; to cause sth to do this: *The door clicked shut.* ◇ *He clicked the switch.* **2** [I,T] (*computing*) **click (on sth)** to choose a particular function or item on a computer screen, etc. by pressing one of the buttons on a mouse: *Click on the icon to select a document.* ◇ ***Right click*** (= click the right mouse button) *and select "copy."* ➲ Look at **double-click**.

★**cli·ent** /'klaɪənt/ ***noun*** [C] **1** someone who receives a service from a professional person

> NOTE Be careful. **Client** cannot be used for people in shops or restaurants. Those people are **customers**. **Clientele** is a general, formal word that includes both **clients** and **customers**.

**2** (*computing*) one of a number of computers that is connected to a computer that stores shared information (a server)

**cli·en·tele** /ˌklaɪən'tɛl/ ***noun*** [U] the group of people who regularly go to a particular store, hotel, etc.

> NOTE This word is more formal than alternatives such as **customers** or **guests**.

**cliff** /klɪf/ ***noun*** [C] a high, very steep area of rock

★**cli·mate** /'klaɪmət/ ***noun*** [C] **1** the normal weather conditions of a particular region: *a dry/humid/tropical climate* ◇ *What are the effects of global warming on our climate?* **2** the general opinions, etc. that people have at a particular time: *What is the current climate of opinion regarding the death penalty?* ◇ *the political climate*

**cli·mat·ic** /klaɪˈmæt̬ɪk/ ***adj.*** of climate: *a conference to discuss climatic change*

C

**cli·max¹** /ˈklaɪmæks/ ***noun*** [C] the most important and exciting part of a book, play, piece of music, event, etc.: *the novel's climax in the final chapter* ◇ *The election victory marked the climax of her political career.*

**cli·max²** /ˈklaɪmæks/ ***verb*** [I] to reach a CLIMAX¹

★**climb¹** /klaɪm/ ***verb*** **1** [I,T] to move up to the top of sth: *The cat climbed to the top of the tree.* ◇ *to climb a tree/mountain/rope* ◇ *She climbed the stairs to the attic.* ◇ *to climb up a ladder* **2** [I] to move, with difficulty, in the direction mentioned: *I managed to climb out of the window.* **3** [I] to go up mountains, etc. as a sport **4** [I] to rise to a higher position: *The plane climbed steadily.* ◇ *The road climbed steeply up the side of the mountain.* ◇ (*figurative*) *The value of the dollar against the British pound has climbed to a record level.*

**climb²** /klaɪm/ ***noun*** [C] **1** an act of climbing up a mountain, etc.: *The cabin could only be reached by a three-hour climb.* **2** an increase in value, amount, or position: *the stock market's rapid climb*

**climb·er** /klaɪmər/ ***noun*** [C] a person who climbs mountains or rocks as a sport

**clinch** /klɪntʃ/ ***verb*** [T] to settle or decide sth finally, e.g. an argument or business agreement: *to clinch a victory*

**cling** /klɪŋ/ ***verb*** [I] (*pt, pp* **clung** /klʌŋ/) **1 cling (on) to sb/sth; cling together** to hold on tightly to sb/sth: *to cling to a rope* ◇ *They clung together for warmth.* **2** to continue to believe that sth is true, often when it is not reasonable to do so: *They were still clinging to the hope that the girl would be found alive.* **3** to stick firmly to sth: *Her wet clothes clung to her body.*

**clin·ic** /ˈklɪnɪk/ ***noun*** [C] **1** a building where you go to see a doctor for examination or treatment, if you are not sick enough to go to the hospital **2** a medical center or a part of a hospital where you go to receive special medical treatment: *a family planning clinic* ◇ *a drug rehabilitation clinic*

**clin·i·cal** /ˈklɪnɪkl/ ***adj.*** connected with the examination and treatment of patients at a clinic or hospital: *Clinical trials of the new drug have proven successful.*

**clin·i·cal·ly** /ˈklɪnɪkli/ ***adv.*** according to medical examination: *to be clinically dead*

**clink** /klɪŋk/ ***noun*** [sing.] the short sharp sound that objects made of glass, metal, etc. make when they touch each other: *the clink of glasses* ▶ **clink** ***verb*** [I,T]

**clip¹** /klɪp/ ***noun*** [C] **1** a small object, usually made of metal or plastic, used for holding things together: *a paper clip* ◇ *clip earrings* ➲ picture at **jewelry**. **2** a short section of a movie or video: *a video clip* ◇ *They showed a clip from his speech on the news.*

**clip²** /klɪp/ ***verb*** (**clip·ping**; **clipped**) **1** [I,T] to be fastened with a CLIP¹ (1); to fasten sth to sth else with a clip: *Clip the papers together.* ◇ *These earrings just clip on.* **2** [T] to cut sth, especially by cutting small parts off: *to clip the hedge*

ˈ**clip art** ***noun*** [U] (*computing*) pictures and symbols that are stored in computer programs or on websites which you can copy into your own computer documents: *This site offers hundreds of free clip-art images for teachers.*

**clip·board** /ˈklɪpbɔrd/ ***noun*** [C] **1** a small board with a CLIP¹ (1) at the top to hold papers on it, used by sb who wants to write while standing or moving around **2** (*computing*) a place where information from a computer file is stored temporarily until it is added to another file

**clip·pers** /ˈklɪpərz/ ***noun*** [pl.] a small metal tool used for cutting things (e.g. hair or fingernails): *a pair of nail clippers*

**clip·ping** /ˈklɪpɪŋ/ ***noun*** [C] a piece that has been cut out from a newspaper, magazine, etc.: *newspaper clippings*

**clique** /klik; klɪk/ ***noun*** [C] a small group of people with the same interests who do not want others to join their group

**cloak** /kloʊk/ ***noun*** **1** [C] a type of loose coat without sleeves, worn especially in the past **2** [sing.] a thing that hides sth else: *a project hidden under a cloak of secrecy*

**cloak·room** /ˈkloʊkrum/ ***noun*** [C] a room in a public building where people can leave coats, bags, etc. for a time

**clob·ber** /ˈklɑbər/ ***verb*** [T] (*informal*) to hit sb hard

**clocks**

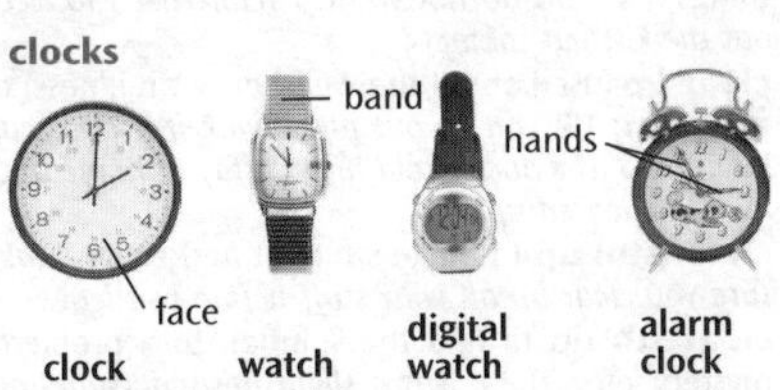


★**clock¹** /klɑk/ ***noun*** [C] an instrument that shows you what time it is, often found on the wall of a house or building (not worn like a watch): *an alarm clock* ◇ *That clock is five minutes slow* (= it says 10:55 when it is really 11 o'clock). ◇ *The clock is five minutes fast* (= it says 6:05 when it is really 6 o'clock). ◇ *The clock struck midnight.* ➲ Look also at **time clock**.

IDM **around the clock** all day and all night: *They are working around the clock to repair the bridge.*

**clock²** /klɑk/ ***verb*** [T] **clock sb/sth (at sth)** (usually passive) to measure the speed of sb/sth: *Winds were clocked at 80 miles per hour during the storm.*

**clock·wise** /ˈklɑkwaɪz/ ***adv., adj.*** in the same direction as the hands of a clock: *Turn the handle clockwise.* ◇ *to move in a clockwise direction* OPP **counterclockwise**

**clock·work** /ˈklɑkwərk/ ***noun*** [U]

IDM **like clockwork** smoothly and without any problems: *The plan went like clockwork.*

**clog¹** /klɑg/ ***noun*** [C] a type of shoe made completely of wood or with a thick wooden bottom: *a pair of clogs*

**clog**[2] /klɑg/ ***verb*** (**clog·ging; clogged**) [I,T] **clog (sth) (up) (with sth)** to block sth or become blocked: *The drain is clogged up with leaves.* ◇ *You clogged up the sink again.* ◇ *The roads were clogged with traffic.*

**clone**[1] /kloʊn/ ***noun*** [C] **1** an identical copy of a plant or animal that is produced by artificial methods **2** *(computing)* a computer that is designed to work in the same way as another, usually more expensive, computer: *an IBM clone*

**clone**[2] /kloʊn/ ***verb*** [T] to produce a CLONE[1] of sth

★**close**[1] /kloʊs/ ***adj.***

➤NEAR **1** (not before a noun) **close (to sb/sth); close (together)** near: *Is our hotel close to the beach?* ◇ *It's close to midnight.* ◇ *The edges are fairly close together.*

➤RELATIONSHIP **2** (used about a friend, etc.) known very well and liked: *They invited only close friends to the wedding.* **3** near in a family relationship: *a close relative*

➤COMPETITION, ELECTION, ETC. **4** (used about a competition, etc.) only won by a small amount: *a close race*

➤CAREFUL **5** careful; thorough: *On close examination, you could see that the 20-dollar bill was a forgery.*

IDM **a close call/shave** a bad thing that almost happened: *I wasn't hurt, but it was a pretty close call.*

**keep a close eye/watch on sb/sth** → EYE[1]

▶ **close·ly** ***adv.***: *to watch sb closely* ◇ *The insect closely resembles a stick.* ▶ **close·ness** ***noun*** [U]

★**close**[2] /kloʊs/ ***adv.*** near: *The child stood close to his mother.* ◇ *to follow close behind someone* ◇ *I held her close* (= tightly).

IDM **close by (sb/sth)** at a short distance from sb/sth: *She lives close by.*

**close to** almost: *He was born close to a hundred years ago.*

**close up (to sb/sth)** at or from a very short distance to sb/sth: *You can't tell it's a forgery until you look at it close up.*

★**close**[3] /kloʊz/ ***verb*** [I,T] **1** to shut: *The door closed quietly.* ◇ *to close a door/window/cupboard* ◇ *Close your eyes – I have a surprise for you.* **2** to be, or to make sth, not open to the public: *What time do the banks close?* ◇ *The police closed the street to traffic.* **3** to come or bring sth to an end: *Registration for fall classes closes at 4:00.* ◇ *Detectives have closed the case on the missing girl.*

PHR V **close (sth) down** to stop all business or work permanently, at a store or factory: *The factory has had to close down because of the recession.* ◇ *Health inspectors have closed the restaurant down.*

**close in (on sb/sth)** to come nearer and gradually surround sb/sth, especially in order to attack: *The army is closing in on the enemy troops.*

★**close**[4] /kloʊz/ ***noun*** [sing.] the end, especially of a period of time or an activity: *the close of trading on the stock market*

IDM **bring sth/come/draw to a close** to end: *The chairman brought the meeting to a close.* ◇ *The guests began to leave as the evening drew to a close.*

**closed** /kloʊzd/ ***adj.*** **1** not open; shut: *Keep your mouth closed.* **2** (usually before a noun) not open to everyone: *a closed meeting of the board of directors*

ˌ**closed-ˈcaptioned** ***adj.*** (used about a television program) having the words that people say written at the bottom of the screen (**captions**) that can only be seen by people who have a special machine (**a decoder**) connected to their television: *This program is closed-captioned for the hearing impaired.*

ˌ**closed-ˌcircuit ˈtelevision** ***noun*** [C,U] a type of television system that sends signals only to televisions that are directly connected to the system by wires, usually in the same building

**close·out** /ˈkloʊzaʊt/ ***noun*** [C] a sale in which a store reduces the prices of things in order to sell all of them quickly: *a closeout sale*

★**clos·et**[1] /ˈklɑzət/ ***noun*** [C] an area for storing things, with a door, that is built behind the wall of a room: *a walk-in closet*

IDM **come out of the closet** to admit sth openly that you kept secret before, especially because of shame or embarrassment: *Homosexuals in public life are now coming out of the closet.*

**clos·et**[2] /ˈklɑzət/ ***adj.*** (only *before* a noun) (used to describe people who want to keep some fact about themselves secret): *For years he was a closet drinker.*

ˈ**close-up** ***noun*** [C] a photograph or movie of sb/sth that you take from a very short distance away

**clo·sure** /ˈkloʊʒər/ ***noun*** **1** [C,U] the permanent closing, e.g. of a business: *Auto workers are protesting against plant closures.* ◇ *The company is threatened with closure.* **2** [U] the feeling that a difficult or unhappy period of time is over so that you do not have to think about it anymore

**clot**[1] /klɑt/ ***noun*** [C] a lump formed by blood as it becomes thick

**clot**[2] /klɑt/ ***verb*** (**clot·ting; clot·ted**) [I,T] to form or cause sth to form CLOTS[1]

★**cloth** /klɔθ/ ***noun*** (*pl.* **cloths** /klɔθz; klɔðz/) **1** [U] a material made of cotton, wool, etc. that you use for making clothes, curtains, etc.: *a yard of cloth* **2** [C] a piece of CLOTH (1) that you use for a particular purpose: *a tablecloth* ◇ *Where can I find a cloth to wipe this up?* ➲ Look also at **washcloth**.

**clothe** /kloʊð/ ***verb*** [T] *(formal)* to provide clothes for sb: *to feed and clothe a child*

**clothed** /kloʊðd/ ***adj.*** **clothed (in sth)** dressed: *He was clothed only in his underwear.* ◇ *Luckily I was fully clothed when they came in.*

★**clothes** /kloʊz; kloʊðz/ ***noun*** [pl.] the things that you wear, e.g. pants, shirts, dresses, coats, etc. (when thought of all together): *Take off those wet clothes.* ◇ *She was wearing new clothes.*

> NOTE Remember that clothes is always plural. We can use an **item/piece/article of clothing** to describe a single thing that you wear: *A sweatshirt is an informal item of clothing.* ➲ Look also at **garment**.

**clothesline**

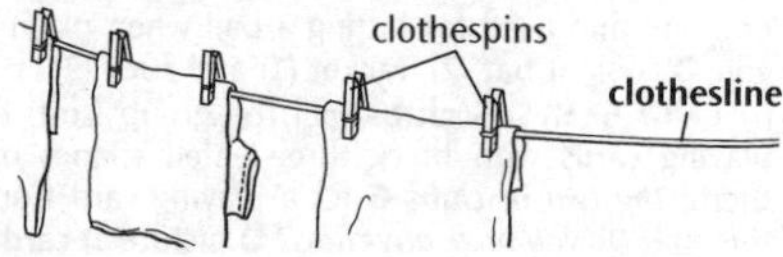

C

**clothes·line** /ˈkloʊzlaɪn; ˈkloʊðz-/ ***noun*** [C] a thin rope that you hang clothes on so that they can dry ➲ picture on **page 123**.

**clothes·pin** /ˈkloʊzpɪn; ˈkloʊðz-/ ***noun*** [C] a type of small wooden or plastic object used for fastening clothes to a clothesline ➲ picture on **page 123**.

★**cloth·ing** /ˈkloʊðɪŋ/ ***noun*** [U] the clothes that you wear: *You will need waterproof clothing.*

NOTE **Clothing** is more formal than **clothes**.

★**cloud¹** /klaʊd/ ***noun*** **1** [C,U] a mass of very small drops of water that floats in the sky and is often gray or white: *The sun disappeared behind a cloud.* ◇ *A band of thick cloud is spreading from the west.* **2** [C] a mass of smoke, dust, sand, etc.: *Clouds of smoke were pouring from the burning building.*

**cloud²** /klaʊd/ ***verb*** **1** [T] to make sth less clear or easy to understand: *We shouldn't let other factors cloud the issue in our discussion.* **2** [T] to make sth less enjoyable; to spoil sth: *The festival was clouded by violence between rival gangs.*

PHRV **cloud over 1** (*also* **cloud up**) (used about the sky) to become full of clouds **2** (used about a person's face) to start to look sad

**cloud·less** /ˈklaʊdləs/ ***adj.*** (used about the sky, etc.) clear; without any clouds

**cloud·y** /ˈklaʊdi/ ***adj.*** (**cloud·i·er**; **cloud·i·est**) **1** (used about the sky, etc.) full of clouds **2** (used about liquids, etc.) not clear: *cloudy water*

**clout** /klaʊt/ ***noun*** [U] influence and power: *Our mayor can use his political clout to bring more industries to our area.*

**clove** /kloʊv/ ***noun*** [C] **1** the small dried flower of a tropical plant, used to give a special flavor in cooking **2** one of the small separate sections of the round underground part (**bulb**) of garlic ➲ picture on study page **A28-29**.

**clo·ver** /ˈkloʊvər/ ***noun*** [C] a small plant with pink or white flowers and leaves with three parts to them

NOTE Sometimes clover leaves have four parts and it is thought to be very lucky if you find one of these.

**clown¹** /klaʊn/ ***noun*** [C] a person who wears funny clothes and makes people laugh

**clown²** /klaʊn/ ***verb*** [I] **clown (around)** to act in a funny or foolish way, like a clown: *Quit clowning around and get some work done!*

★**club¹** /klʌb/ ***noun***

➤FOR ACTIVITY/SPORT **1** [C] a group of people who meet to share an interest; the place where they meet: *to join a club* ◇ *to be a member of a club* ◇ *a social club* ◇ *the school's chess club*

➤MUSIC/DANCING **2** [C] a place where you can go to dance, drink, etc. until late at night

➤WEAPON **3** [C] a heavy stick, usually with one end that is thicker than the other, used as a weapon

➤IN GOLF **4** [C] a long stick that is specially shaped at one end and used for hitting a ball when playing golf ➲ Look at **bat¹**(2), **racket** (1) and **stick¹**(2).

➤IN CARD GAMES **5 clubs** [pl.] the group (suit) of playing cards with black three-leafed shapes on them: *the two of clubs* **6** [C] a playing card from this suit: *Do you have any clubs?* ➲ picture at **card¹**.

**club²** /klʌb/ ***verb*** (**club·bing**; **clubbed**) **1** [T] to hit sb/sth hard with a heavy object, especially a CLUB¹(3): *to club somebody to death* **2** [I] to enjoy yourself, dance, etc. at a CLUB¹(2)

NOTE We usually say **go clubbing**.

**ˌclub ˈsandwich** ***noun*** [C] a sandwich made with three pieces of bread and layers of meat (usually chicken and bacon), tomato and lettuce between them

**cluck** /klʌk/ ***noun*** [C] the noise made by a chicken ▸ **cluck** ***verb*** [I]

**clue** /klu/ ***noun*** [C] a piece of information that helps you solve a problem, answer a question, etc.: *The police were looking for clues to his disappearance.* ◇ *the clues for solving a crossword puzzle* ➲ picture at **crossword puzzle**.

IDM **not have a clue** (*informal*) to know nothing; to be unable to help or understand: *I don't have a clue where you left your watch.*

**clue·less** /ˈkluləs/ ***adj.*** (*slang*) stupid; not knowing anything about sth: *Fred is totally clueless about music.*

**clump** /klʌmp/ ***noun*** [C] a lump of something or a group of things that are stuck together, without a regular shape: *a clump of dirt* ◇ *a clump of grass*

**clum·sy** /ˈklʌmzi/ ***adj.*** (**clum·si·er**; **clum·si·est**) **1** (used about a person) careless or awkward and likely to drop things or do things badly **2** (used about a remark, etc.) not showing enough understanding of the feelings of other people; likely to upset or offend people: *He made a clumsy apology.* ◇ *her clumsy attempts at humor* **3** large, awkward to use, and not attractive in design: *a clumsy piece of furniture*

**clung** *past tense, past participle of* CLING

**clus·ter¹** /ˈklʌstər/ ***noun*** [C] a group of people, plants or things that stand or grow close together: *a cluster of buildings* ◇ *a cluster of grapes*

**clus·ter²** /ˈklʌstər/ ***verb***

PHRV **cluster/be clustered around sb/sth** to form a group around sb/sth: *The tourists clustered around their guide.*

**clutch¹** /klʌtʃ/ ***verb*** [T] to hold sth tightly, especially because you are afraid or excited: *He clutched his mother's hand in fear.* ◇ *The girl ran off, clutching her prize.*

**clutch²** /klʌtʃ/ ***noun*** **1** [C] an act of seizing or clutching: *to make a clutch at sth* **2 clutches** [pl.] the power or control of a person or group: *He fell into the enemy's clutches.* **3** [C] the part of some cars that you press with your foot before you change gear; the apparatus that it is connected to: *to press/release the clutch*

**clut·ter¹** /ˈklʌt̬ər/ ***noun*** [U] things that are where they are not wanted or needed and make a place messy: *Who left all this clutter on the table?*

**clut·ter²** /ˈklʌt̬ər/ ***verb*** [T] **clutter sth (up)** to cover or fill sth with a lot of objects in a messy way: *I think these pictures clutter up the design of the page.* ▸ **clut·tered** ***adj.***: *a cluttered office*

**cm** ***abbr.*** = CENTIMETER

**CNN** /ˌsi ɛn ˈɛn/ ***abbr.*** (*U.S.*) Cable News Network; a broadcasting company that sends television news programs all over the world

**Co.** ***abbr.*** = COMPANY

**c/o** /ˌsi ˈoʊ/ ***abbr.*** (used for addressing a letter to sb who is staying at another person's house) care of: *Jill Wallace, c/o The Schmidts, 245 Walnut Street, Springfield, MO*

★**coach¹** /koʊtʃ/ ***noun*** [C] a person who trains people to compete in certain sports: *a football/basketball/hockey coach* ➲ Look also at **manager** (3).

**coach²** /koʊtʃ/ ***verb*** [I,T] to train or teach sb, especially to compete in a sport or pass an examination: *She is coached by a former Olympic champion.*

★**coal** /koʊl/ ***noun*** **1** [U] a type of black mineral that is dug (**mined**) from the ground and is burned to give heat and energy: *a lump of coal* ◇ *a coal mine* ◇ *a coal miner* **2 coals** [pl.] burning pieces of coal

**co·a·li·tion** /ˌkoʊəˈlɪʃn/ ***noun*** [C] an association of people, groups, political parties, etc. who are working together, often for a short period of time: *the National Coalition for the Homeless* ◇ *a coalition government* (= formed by two or more political parties working together)

**coarse** /kɔrs/ ***adj.*** **1** consisting of large, not fine pieces; rough, not smooth: *coarse salt* ◇ *coarse fabric* **2** (used about a person or sb's behavior) rude, likely to offend people; having bad manners: *His coarse remarks about women offended her.* ▶ **coarse·ly** ***adv.***: *Chop the onion coarsely* (= into pieces which are not too small).

★**coast¹** /koʊst/ ***noun*** [C] the area of land that is next to or close to the ocean: *Vacationers reported seeing sharks just off the coast.* ◇ *We went for an afternoon drive along the coast.* ◇ *the West Coast* (= next to the Pacific Ocean) ◇ *the East Coast* (= next to the Atlantic Ocean)

**coast²** /koʊst/ ***verb*** [I] **1** to move (especially down a hill) without using power **2** to achieve sth without much effort: *They coasted to victory.*

**coast·al** /ˈkoʊstl/ ***adj.*** at or near a coast: *coastal areas* ◇ *fishing in coastal waters*

**ˈcoast guard** (*also* **ˈCoast Guard**) ***noun*** [sing.] **1** (in the U.S.) the military force that watches the ocean near the coast in order to warn or help ships that are in danger or to stop illegal activities **2** (in Canada) a government organization that watches the ocean near the coast and major lakes in order to rescue people in trouble, break ice, warn ships that are in danger and to stop illegal activities

**coast·line** /ˈkoʊstlaɪn/ ***noun*** [C] the edge or shape of a coast: *a rocky coastline*

★**coat¹** /koʊt/ ***noun*** [C] **1** a piece of clothing with long sleeves, that you wear on top of other clothes to keep warm: *Put your winter coat on – it's cold outside.* ◇ *Take off your coat and sit down.* ➲ Look also at **overcoat** and **raincoat**. **2** the fur or hair covering an animal's body: *a dog with a smooth coat* **3** a layer of sth covering a surface: *The walls will probably need two coats of paint.*

**coat²** /koʊt/ ***verb*** [T] **coat sth (with/in sth)** to cover sth with a layer of sth: *peanuts coated with milk chocolate*

**ˈcoat check** ***noun*** [C] a room in a public building where people can leave coats, bags, etc. for a time and sb watches them to make sure they are safe

**coat·ing** /ˈkoʊt̬ɪŋ/ ***noun*** [C,U] a thin layer of sth that covers sth else: *caramels with chocolate coating*

**coax** /koʊks/ ***verb*** [T] to persuade sb gently: *They coaxed the cat out of the basket.*

**cob** /kɑb/ ***noun*** [C] the long, round, hard part of the corn plant that grains (**kernels**) of corn grow on: *corn on the cob* (= that has been cooked with the kernels still attached to the cob)

**cob·ble·stone** /ˈkɑblstoʊn/ ***noun*** [C] a rounded stone used (in the past) for covering the surface of streets: *cobblestone streets*

**co·bra** /ˈkoʊbrə/ ***noun*** [C] a poisonous snake found in Africa and Asia

**cob·web** /ˈkɑbwɛb/ (*also* **spider web**) ***noun*** [C] a net of threads made by a spider in order to catch insects

**Co·ca-Co·la™** /ˌkoʊkə ˈkoʊlə/ (*also* **Coke™**) ***noun*** [C,U] a brown, sweet, nonalcoholic drink

**co·caine** /koʊˈkeɪn/ ***noun*** [U] (*also informal* **coke**) an illegal drug, usually in the form of a white powder, that some people take for pleasure but which it is difficult to stop using

**cock·pit** /ˈkɑkpɪt/ ***noun*** [C] **1** the part of an aircraft where the pilot sits **2** the part of a racing car in which the driver sits

**cock·roach** /ˈkɑkroʊtʃ/ (*also* **roach**) ***noun*** [C] a large dark brown insect, often found in dirty rooms or damp places

**cock·tail** /ˈkɑkteɪl/ ***noun*** **1** [C] an alcoholic drink made from a mixture of drinks: *a cocktail party* **2** [C,U] a mixture of small pieces of food, usually served as the first part of a meal: *Would you like some fruit cocktail?* ◇ *shrimp cocktail*

**cock·y** /ˈkɑki/ ***adj.*** (*informal*) too proud and confident, in a way that annoys other people: *It's great that you won the game, but don't get too cocky about it.*

**co·coa** /ˈkoʊkoʊ/ ***noun*** [U] **1** (*also* **cocoa powder**) a dark brown powder made from the seeds of a tropical tree and used in making chocolate **2** (*also* **hot chocolate**) a hot drink made from this powder mixed with milk: *a cup of cocoa*

**co·co·nut** /ˈkoʊkənʌt/ ***noun*** [C,U] the large brown fruit of a tropical tree. Coconuts have very hard, hairy shells and are filled with a white liquid that you can drink. The white substance inside the shell is often eaten in candy and cakes.

**co·coon** /kəˈkun/ ***noun*** [C] a covering of silk threads that some insects make to protect themselves before they become adults ➲ picture at **insect**.

**COD** /ˌsi oʊ ˈdi/ ***abbr.*** (*written*) cash on delivery or collect on delivery; a way of paying for goods that you have ordered when you receive them

**cod** /kɑd/ ***noun*** [C,U] (*pl.* **cod**) a large ocean fish that you can eat

★**code¹** /koʊd/ ***noun*** **1** [C,U] a system of words, letters, numbers, etc. used instead of other words, letters, etc. so that messages, information, etc. can be kept secret: *They succeeded in breaking/cracking/deciphering the enemy code* (= in finding out what it was). ◇ *They wrote letters to each other in code.* **2** [C] a group of numbers, letters, etc. that is used for identifying sth: *a bar code* (= a pattern of lines printed on goods, that a computer can read) ➲ Look also at **area code** and **Zip code** or, in Canada, **postal code**. **3** [C] a set of rules for behavior: *a code of practice* (= a set of standards agreed and accepted by a particular profession) ◇ *the city building code* (= the rules and standards for constructing buildings in a city) ◇ *a dress code* (= a set of rules about what clothes sb may wear in a particular place)

**code²** /koʊd/ ***verb*** [T] **1** to put or write sth in CODE¹ (1): *coded messages* **2** to use a particular system for identifying things: *The files are color-coded: blue for North America, green for South America.*

**co·ed** (*also* **co-ed**) /ˌkoʊˈɛd/ ***adj.*** for both boys and girls or men and women: *a coed volleyball team* ◇ *Oberlin College went coed in 1837.* ➲ Compare **single-sex**.

**co·ed·u·ca·tion·al** /koʊˌɛdʒəˈkeɪʃənl/ ***adj.*** (*formal*) (used about a school) with both boys and girls together in the same classes ➲ Compare **single-sex**.

**co·erce** /koʊˈərs/ ***verb*** [T] (*formal*) to force sb to do sth, e.g. by threatening him/her ▸ **co·er·cion** /koʊˈərʒn; -ʃn/ ***noun*** [U]

**co·ex·ist** /ˌkoʊɪgˈzɪst/ ***verb*** [I] to exist together at the same time or in the same place: *Is it possible for these different ethnic groups to coexist peacefully?* ▸ **co·ex·is·tence** ***noun*** [U]

**coffee**

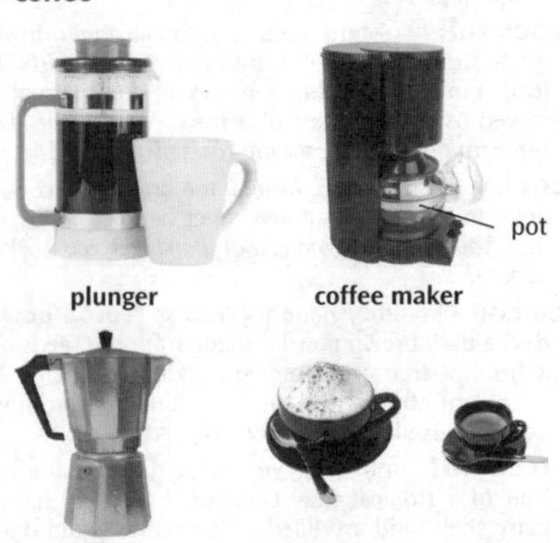


plunger · coffee maker · percolator · cappuccino · espresso

★**cof·fee** /ˈkɔfi; ˈkɑ-/ ***noun*** **1** [U] the roasted seeds (beans) of a tropical tree, made into powder and used for making a drink: *Coffee is the country's biggest export.* **2** [U] a drink made by adding hot water to coffee beans that have been made into powder: *Would you like tea or coffee?* ◇ *a cup of coffee* **3** [C] a cup of this drink: *I'll have a donut and a large coffee with cream and sugar.*

NOTE **Black coffee** is made without milk. **Decaffeinated coffee**, also called **decaf**, has had the caffeine taken out. Coffee can be **weak** or **strong**. **Instant coffee** is made by pouring hot water onto coffee powder. Other kinds of coffee include **espresso**, a strong coffee which is served in small cups, and **cappuccino** and **caffè latte**, which are made by adding warm milk to **espresso**. If milk with little or no fat is used, it is called **skinny**.

**ˈcoffee bean** ***noun*** [C] the bean of the coffee plant which is roasted and then made into a powder (ground) and then used to make a drink of coffee

**ˈcoffee break** ***noun*** [C] a short period of rest when you stop working and drink coffee: *Let's take a coffee break.*

**ˈcoffee cake** ***noun*** [C] a simple kind of cake with brown sugar on top, which people often eat with coffee

**ˈcoffee ˌgrinder** ***noun*** [C] a machine which turns roasted coffee beans into a powder

**cof·fee·house** /kɔfihaʊs; ˈkɑ-/ (*also* **coffee house**) ***noun*** [C] a small restaurant where people go to talk and drink coffee

**ˈcoffee ˌmaker** ***noun*** [C] a machine which heats water and pours it over a powder made from coffee beans to make coffee

**ˈcoffee pot** ***noun*** [C] a tall covered container for making or serving coffee

**ˈcoffee shop** ***noun*** [C] a small informal restaurant where people go to have fast, cheap meals, coffee and other drinks (but no alcohol)

**ˈcoffee ˌtable** ***noun*** [C] a small low table, usually in a living room

**ˈcoffee-table ˌbook** ***noun*** [C] a large, expensive book with many pictures, which people leave on their coffee table to be looked at

**cof·fin** /ˈkɔfən/ ***noun*** [C] = CASKET ➲ Look at the note at **funeral**.

**cog** /kɑg/ ***noun*** [C] one of the tooth-shaped parts on the edge of a wheel in a piece of machinery. The cogs fit into those on another wheel so that, as it moves, the other wheel moves too.

**co·hab·it** /koʊˈhæbət/ ***verb*** [I] **cohabit with sb** (*formal*) to live together and have a sexual relationship without being married: *Statistics demonstrate that younger people tend to cohabit before marriage.* ▸ **co·hab·i·ta·tion** /koʊˌhæbəˈteɪʃn/ ***noun*** [U]

**co·her·ent** /koʊˈhɪrənt/ ***adj.*** connected in a way that makes sense; clear and easy to understand: *a coherent plan* ▸ **co·her·ence** ***noun*** [U] ▸ **co·her·ent·ly** ***adv.***

**co·he·sion** /koʊˈhiʒn/ ***noun*** [U] the ability to stay or fit together well: *What the team lacks is cohesion – all the players play as individuals.*

**coil¹** /kɔɪl/ ***verb*** [I,T] to wind sth into a round shape: *The snake coiled itself around a tree.* ◇ *He coiled up the cord and put it into his tool bag.*

**coil²** /kɔɪl/ ***noun*** [C] a length of rope, wire, etc. that has been wound into a round shape: *a coil of rope*

★**coin¹** /kɔɪn/ ***noun*** [C] a piece of money made of metal ➲ picture at **money**.

**coin²** /kɔɪn/ ***verb*** [T] to invent a new word or phrase: *Who was it who coined the phrase, "every cloud has a silver lining?"*

**co·in·cide** /ˌkoʊɪnˈsaɪd/ ***verb*** [I] **coincide (with sth)** **1** (used about events) to happen at the same time as sth else: *The candidate's visit is timed to* *coincide with local elections.* **2** to be exactly the same or very similar: *Our views coincide completely.*

**co·in·ci·dence** /koʊ'ɪnsədəns/ ***noun*** [C,U] the surprising fact of two or more similar things happening at the same time by chance; an occasion when this happens: *By pure coincidence, I found myself sitting next to an old friend from school.* ◇ *It's no coincidence that my necklace disappeared the same day Wendy came to visit – I bet she took it!*

**co·in·ci·den·tal** /koʊˌɪnsə'dɛntl/ ***adj.*** resulting from two similar or related events happening at the same time by chance ▶ **co·in·ci·den·tal·ly** ***adv.***

**Coke™** /koʊk/ ***noun*** [C,U] = COCA-COLA

**coke** /koʊk/ ***noun*** [U] (*slang*) = COCAINE

**co·la** /'koʊlə/ ***noun*** [C,U] a brown, sweet nonalcoholic drink such as Coca-Cola™ or Pepsi-Cola™; a glass, can, etc. of this

**col·an·der** /'kɑləndər; 'kʌl-/ ***noun*** [C] a metal or plastic bowl with a lot of small holes in it, used for draining water from food

⋆**cold¹** /koʊld/ ***adj.*** **1** having a low temperature; not hot or warm: *If I were you, I'd put a coat on. It's cold outside.* ◇ *I'm not going into the lake – the water's too cold.* ◇ *Should I turn the heat on? I'm cold.*

NOTE Compare **cold**, **hot**, **cool**, and **warm**. **Cold** indicates a lower temperature than **cool** and may describe a temperature that is unpleasantly low: *a terribly cold winter.* **Cool** means "fairly cold" and may describe a pleasantly low temperature: *It's boiling hot outside, but it's nice and cool in here.* **Hot** indicates a higher temperature than **warm** and may describe a temperature that is unpleasantly high: *I can't drink this yet – it's too hot.* **Warm** means "fairly hot" and may describe a pleasantly high temperature: *You won't need your jacket – it's nice and warm outside.*

**2** (used about food or drink) not heated or cooked; having become cool after being heated or cooked: *I don't feel like coffee – I'd rather have a cold drink.* ◇ *Eat your soup before it gets cold.* **3** (used about a person or sb's behavior) very unfriendly; not showing kindness, sympathy, etc.: *She gave him a cold, hard look.*

IDM **cold turkey** suddenly, instead of getting used to sth gradually: *I quit smoking cold turkey.*

**get/have cold feet** (*informal*) to become/be afraid to do sth: *She started to get cold feet as her wedding day approached.*

**give sb the cold shoulder** to treat sb in an unfriendly way

**in cold blood** in a cruel way and without pity: *to kill sb in cold blood*

⋆**cold²** /koʊld/ ***noun*** **1** [sing., U] lack of heat; low temperature; cold weather: *More bitter cold is forecast for the Northeast today.* ◇ *We had to stand out in the cold and wait for the bus.* **2** [C,U] a common illness of the nose and throat. When you have a cold, you have a sore throat and often cannot breathe through your nose: *I think I'm getting a cold – I've been sneezing all day.* ◇ *Wear a hat when you go out or you'll catch cold.*

**cold-blood·ed** /ˌkoʊld 'blʌdəd/ ***adj.*** **1** having a blood temperature that changes with the temperature of the surroundings: *Reptiles are cold-blooded.* ➲ Compare **warm-blooded**. **2** cruel; having or showing no pity: *cold-blooded killers*

ˈ**cold-ˌcalling** ***noun*** [U] the practice of telephoning sb that you do not know, in order to sell him/her sth ▶ ˌ**cold 'call** ***noun*** [C]

ˈ**cold cuts** ***noun*** [pl.] cooked meat that has been cut into thin slices and is served cold

**cold·ly** /'koʊldli/ ***adv.*** in an unfriendly way; in a way that shows no kindness or sympathy: *He looked at her coldly and did not reply.*

ˈ**cold sore** ***noun*** [C] a small painful spot on the lips or inside the mouth caused by an infection (a virus)

**cole·slaw** /'koʊlslɔ/ ***noun*** [U] a salad made with raw cabbage and other vegetables that have been cut into very thin pieces and mixed with mayonnaise

**col·lab·o·rate** /kə'læbəreɪt/ ***verb*** [I] **1 collaborate (with sb) (on sth)** to work together (with sb), especially to create or produce sth: *She collaborated with another author on the book.* **2 collaborate (with sb)** to help the enemy forces who have taken control of your country

NOTE This use of **collaborate** shows disapproval.

▶ **col·lab·o·ra·tion** /kəˌlæbə'reɪʃn/ ***noun*** [U]

**col·lab·o·ra·tor** /kə'læbəreɪṭər/ ***noun*** [C] **1** a person who works together with sb else, especially in order to create or produce sth **2** a person who helps the enemy forces who have taken control of his/her country

**col·lage** /kə'lɑʒ; koʊ-/ ***noun*** **1** [C] a picture made by fastening pieces of paper, cloth, photographs, etc. onto a surface **2** [U] the art of making these pictures

⋆**col·lapse¹** /kə'læps/ ***verb*** [I] **1** to fall down or inward suddenly: *A lot of buildings collapsed in the earthquake.* **2** (used about a person) to fall down and perhaps become unconscious: *The winner collapsed at the end of the race.* **3** to fail or break down suddenly or completely: *Many investors lost millions of dollars when the stock market collapsed.*

⋆**col·lapse²** /kə'læps/ ***noun*** **1** [sing., U] a sudden fall: *the collapse of the roof under the weight of snow* **2** [C,U] sudden or complete failure: *economic collapse*

**col·lar** /'kɑlər/ ***noun*** [C] **1** the part of a shirt, coat, dress, etc. that fits around the neck and is often folded over ➲ picture at **shirt**. **2** a band of leather that is put around an animal's neck (especially a dog or cat) ➲ Look also at **blue-collar** and **white-collar**.

**col·lar·bone** /'kɑlərboʊn/ ***noun*** [C] one of the two bones that connect the chest bones to the shoulder

**col·lat·er·al¹** /kə'læṭərəl/ ***noun*** [U] property or sth valuable that you promise to give to sb if you cannot pay back money that you borrow

**col·lat·er·al²** /kə'læṭərəl/ ***adj.*** (*formal*) connected with sth else but in addition to it and less important: *The Pentagon denied that there had been any collateral damage* (= injury to people or buildings that were not the aim of the attack) *during the bombing raid.*

⋆**col·league** /'kɑlig/ ***noun*** [C] (*formal*) a person

that you work with in a job, especially in a profession

NOTE Nowadays it is more common to say **co-worker**, especially among younger people.

C

★**col·lect¹** /kəˈlɛkt/ ***verb*** **1** [T] to bring a number of things, or a large amount of sth, together: *All the test booklets will be collected at the end of the exam.* ◇ *My computer screen collects a lot of dust.* **2** [I] to come together; to gather: *Dirt and leaves always collect in the gutters after a storm.* **3** [I,T] to ask for sth, especially money, from a number of people: *Hello, I'm collecting for a local charity. Would you like to make a contribution?* ◇ *We've collected over 200 signatures on our petition so far.* ◇ *to collect taxes* **4** [T] to gather a number of objects of a particular type over a period of time as a hobby: *He used to collect stamps.* **5** [T] **collect yourself/sth** to get control of yourself, your feelings, thoughts, etc.: *She collected herself and went back into the room as if nothing had happened.* ◇ *I tried to collect my thoughts before the test.*

**col·lect²** /kəˈlɛkt/ ***adj.***, ***adv.*** (used about a telephone call) to be paid for by the person who receives the call: *a collect call* ◇ *She called me collect.*

★**col·lec·tion** /kəˈlɛkʃn/ ***noun*** **1** [C,U] the act of getting sth from a place or from people: *Garbage collection is on Thursdays in this neighborhood.* **2** [C] a group of objects of a particular type that sb has collected as a hobby: *a stamp collection* **3** [C] a number of poems, stories, letters, articles, etc. published in one book: *a collection of modern poetry* **4** [C] the act of asking for money from a number of people (for charity, in church, etc.): *a collection for the homeless* ◇ *The department took a collection to buy him a present when he retired.* **5** [C] a group of people or things; a pile: *a large collection of papers on the desk*

**col·lec·tive** /kəˈlɛktɪv/ ***adj.*** shared by a group of people together; not individual: *collective responsibility* ▶ **col·lec·tive·ly** ***adv.***: *We made the decision collectively at a meeting.*

**col·lec·tor** /kəˈlɛktər/ ***noun*** [C] (often in compounds) a person who collects things: *a stamp collector* ◇ *a tax collector*

★**col·lege** /ˈkɑlɪdʒ/ ***noun*** **1** (*U.S.*) [C,U] a university where you can study for a degree after you finish high school: *a private/public college* ◇ *college students* ◇ *a college campus* ◇ *He first got interested in politics when he was **in college**.*

NOTE We talk about **college**, without **the**, when we mean that somebody is attending it as a student: *He's at college in California.* ◇ *She's going to college in September*, but not if somebody goes there for any other reason: *I went to an art exhibit at the college last night.* ➲ Look also at **community college** and at **university**.

**2** [C] one of the main divisions of some large universities: *The history department is part of the College of Arts and Sciences.* **3** [C,U] (*Cdn*) a place where you can study for higher or more specialized qualifications after you finish high school

NOTE The difference between a **college** in Canada and one in the United States is that most Canadian colleges are not universities, and so you cannot earn a degree there, although some colleges do offer university-level classes. ➲ For more information about the education system in North America, look at study pages **A8-9**.

**col·le·giate¹** /kəˈlidʒət/ ***adj.*** (only *before* a noun) connected with a college or colleges: *collegiate sports teams*

**col·le·giate²** /kəˈlidʒət/ ***noun*** [C] (*Cdn*) (*also* **col,legiate ˈinstitute**) (in some provinces) a public high school ➲ For more information on the Canadian educational system, look at study page **A9**.

**col·lide** /kəˈlaɪd/ ***verb*** [I] **collide (with sb/sth)** to crash; to hit sb/sth very hard while moving: *Energy is released when the two atoms collide.* ◇ *The truck collided with a bus but fortunately nobody was injured.*

**col·lie** /ˈkɑli/ ***noun*** [C] a type of dog with a long pointed nose and hair that can be either long or short. They are popular as pets and are also used to control sheep on farms.

**col·li·sion** /kəˈlɪʒn/ ***noun*** [C] a crash; an occasion when things or people collide: *It was a head-on collision and the driver was killed instantly.*

**col·lo·qui·al** /kəˈloʊkwiəl/ ***adj.*** (used about words, phrases, etc.) used in conversation, not in formal situations or formal writing ▶ **col·lo·qui·al·ly** /-kwiəli/ ***adv.***

**co·logne** /kəˈloʊn/ ***noun*** [U] a type of perfume that is not very strong

**co·lon** /ˈkoʊlən/ ***noun*** [C] **1** a punctuation mark (:) used before a list, an explanation, an example, etc. **2** the large tube below the stomach that carries solid waste material out of the body: *colon cancer*

**colo·nel** /ˈkərnl/ ***noun*** [C] an officer with a high rank in the army

**co·lo·ni·al** /kəˈloʊniəl/ ***adj.*** **1** (*also often* **Colonial**) connected with the original 13 British COLONIES (1) that became the U.S: *people who lived in Colonial times* (= before 1776, when the U.S. became independent) **2** connected with or owning a COLONY (1): *Spain used to be a major colonial power.*

**co·lo·ni·al·ism** /kəˈloʊniəlɪzəm/ ***noun*** [U] the practice of keeping countries as colonies

**col·o·nist** /ˈkɑlənɪst/ ***noun*** [C] **1** a person who lived in one of the 13 original British COLONIES (1) before the U.S. became independent in 1776 **2** a person who goes to live in a COLONY (1) when it is first established as one

**col·o·nize** /ˈkɑlənaɪz/ ***verb*** [T] to take control of a place as a COLONY (1); to establish a colony in a place ▶ **col·o·ni·za·tion** /ˌkɑlənəˈzeɪʃn/ ***noun*** [U]: *the colonization of Latin America by Spain and Portugal*

**col·o·ny** /ˈkɑləni/ ***noun*** (*pl.* **col·o·nies**) **1** [C] a country or area that is ruled by another, more powerful country: *the 13 original colonies* (= that became the United States) ◇ *Kenya used to be a British colony.* **2** [C] a group of people with the same interests, profession, etc. living together in the same place: *an artists' colony* **3** [C] a group of the same type of animals, insects or plants living or growing in the same place: *a colony of ants*

★**col·or¹** (*Cdn* **col·our**) /ˈkʌlər/ ***noun*** **1** [C,U] the quality that makes sth red, green, yellow, etc.: *"What color is your car?" "Red."* ◇ *Brown isn't my favorite color.* ◇ *a dark/light color* ◇ *a bright color* ◇ *a deep/pale color* ◇ *Those flowers will give the room a little color.* ◇ *Our school colors are blue and gold.*

NOTE We say that a thing **is** a certain color, not that it **has** a color.

**2** [U] the use of all the colors, not just black and white: *All the pictures in the book are in color.* ◇ *a color TV set* **3** [U, sing.] redness in your face, particularly showing how healthy you are: *Playing outdoors in the fresh air sure gave you some color.* **4** [C,U] the color of a person's skin, showing the person's race: *people of all colors and religions* **5** [U] interesting or exciting details: *These descriptions give the story some real color.*

IDM **of color** (only *after* a noun) (used about a person) belonging to a race that does not have white skin: *Persons of color are especially encouraged to apply for this position.* ◇ *a collection of poetry by women of color*
**with flying colors** → FLYING[1]

**col·or²** (*Cdn* **col·our**) /'kʌlər/ ***verb*** [T] **1** to put color on sth, e.g. by painting it: *Color the picture with your crayons.* ◇ *The area colored yellow on the map is desert.* **2** to influence thoughts, opinions, etc.: *You shouldn't let one bad experience color your attitude toward everything.*

**col·or·blind** (*also* **color-blind**) /'kʌlərblaɪnd/ ***adj.*** **1** unable to distinguish between certain colors, especially red and green **2** treating people of all races equally: *the dream of a colorblind society*

★**col·ored** /'kʌlərd/ ***adj.*** **1** having color; a particular color: *She always writes letters on colored paper.* ◇ *a coffee-colored dress* ◇ *brightly-colored lights* **2** (used about a person) belonging to a race that does not have white skin

NOTE This meaning of **colored** is old-fashioned and is now considered offensive.

**col·or·fast** /'kʌlərfæst/ ***adj.*** material that is colorfast will not change or lose color when it is washed

**col·or·ful** (*Cdn* **col·our·ful**) /'kʌlərfl/ ***adj.*** **1** with bright colors; full of color: *a colorful shirt* **2** full of interest or excitement: *a colorful story* ◇ *He's a pretty colorful character.*

**col·or·ing** /'kʌlərɪŋ/ ***noun*** [C,U] a substance that is used for giving a particular color to sth, especially food

**col·or·less** /'kʌlərləs/ ***adj.*** **1** without color: *a colorless liquid, like water* **2** dull and uninteresting: *a colorless description*

**'color scheme** ***noun*** [C] the way in which colors are arranged, especially in a room

**co·los·sal** /kə'lɑsl/ ***adj.*** extremely large; huge: *a colossal building/amount*

**colt** /koʊlt/ ***noun*** [C] a young male horse

★**col·umn** /'kɑləm/ ***noun*** [C] **1** a tall solid vertical post made of stone, supporting or decorating a building or standing alone **2** something that has the shape of a COLUMN (1): *a column of smoke* **3** one of the vertical sections into which a printed page, especially in a newspaper, is divided **4** a series of numbers written one under the other: *to add up a column of figures* **5** a piece of writing in a newspaper or magazine that is part of a regular series or written by the same writer: *the gossip column* **6** a long line of people, vehicles, etc., one following behind another: *a column of troops*

C

**col·um·nist** /'kɑləmnɪst/ ***noun*** [C] a journalist who writes regular articles in a newspaper or magazine: *a gossip columnist* ◇ *a political columnist*

**co·ma** /'koʊmə/ ***noun*** [C] a state of deep unconsciousness, often lasting for a long time and caused by serious illness or injury: *She went into a coma and died a few days later.*

**com·a·tose** /'koʊmətoʊs; 'kɑ-/ ***adj.*** **1** deeply unconscious; in a coma **2** extremely tired and without energy; sleeping deeply

**comb¹** /koʊm/ ***noun*** [C] a piece of metal or plastic with a row of teeth that you use for making your hair neat

**comb²** /koʊm/ ***verb*** [T] **1** to make your hair neat using a comb **2 comb (through) sth (for sb/sth)** to search sth thoroughly: *Police are combing the area for the escaped prisoners.*

**com·bat¹** /'kɑmbæt/ ***noun*** [U] fighting, especially in war: *unarmed combat* (= without weapons) ◇ *He got a medal for bravery in combat.*

**com·bat²** /kəm'bæt; 'kɑmbæt/ ***verb*** [T] to fight against sth; to try to stop, reduce or defeat sth: *This administration will do everything in its power to combat crime.*

★**com·bi·na·tion** /ˌkɑmbə'neɪʃn/ ***noun*** **1** [C,U] a number of people or things mixed or joined together; a mixture: *He left the job for a combination of reasons.* ◇ *The coach still hasn't found the right combination of players.* ◇ *This medication may be dangerous when taken in combination with alcohol.* **2** [C] a series of numbers or letters used to open a lock: *Can you remember the combination?*

**combi'nation lock** ***noun*** [C] a type of lock which can only be opened by using a particular series of numbers or letters

★**com·bine¹** /kəm'baɪn/ ***verb*** **1** [I,T] **combine (with sb/sth); combine A and B/A with B** to join or mix two or more things together: *The two businesses combined to form one corporation.* ◇ *Bad planning, combined with bad luck, led to the company's collapse.* **2** [T] **combine A and B/A with B** to do two or more things at the same time or have two or more qualities at the same time: *to combine business with pleasure* ◇ *This car combines speed and reliability.*

**com·bine²** /'kɑmbaɪn/ ***noun*** [C] a farm machine that both cuts grain and separates the seed from the stem

**com·bined** /kəm'baɪnd/ ***adj.*** done by a number of people joining together, resulting from the joining of two or more things: *The combined efforts of the police and fire departments prevented a major disaster.* ◇ *I use that room as a guest bedroom and office combined* (= it is used as both).

**com·bus·tion** /kəm'bʌstʃən/ ***noun*** [U] the process of burning

★**come** /kʌm/ ***verb*** [I] (*pt* **came** /keɪm/; *pp* **come**) **1** to move to or toward the person who is speaking

C

or the place that sb is talking about: *Come here!* ◇ *Come (and) look at this.* ◇ *I hope you can come to my party.* ◇ *They're coming to stay for a week.* ◇ *The kids came running into the room.* **2** to arrive or reach a place: *What time are you coming home?* ◇ *Did the newspaper come yet?* ◇ *The news came as a complete surprise.* ◇ *The time has come to say goodbye.* **3** to have a particular position: *March comes after February.* **4** to be available: *This blouse comes in a choice of four colors.* **5** to be produced by or from sth: *Wool comes from sheep.* **6** to become: *My shoelace came untied.* **7** **come to do sth** (used for talking about how, why or when sth happened): *How did you come to lose your passport?* **8** (usually used with *to/into* and a noun) to reach a particular state: *We were all sad when summer vacation came to an end.* ◇ *My dream of going to Hawaii finally came true last month.*

IDM **come and go** to be present for a short time and then go away: *The pain in my ear comes and goes.*

**come easily, etc. to sb** to be easy, etc. for sb to do: *Apologizing does not come easily to her.*

**how come...?** (*informal*) why or how: *How come you're back so early?* ◇ *How come I didn't get one too?*

**to come** (used after a noun) in the future: *You'll regret it in years to come.*

**when it comes to sth/to doing sth** when it is a question of sth: *When it comes to good cooking, Rick's fried chicken is hard to beat.*

PHR V **come about** to happen: *How did this situation come about?*

**come across** to make an impression of a particular type: *Elizabeth comes across as being fairly shy.*

**come across sb/sth** to meet or find sb/sth by chance: *I came across this book at a garage sale.*

**come along 1** to arrive or appear: *She won't get married until the right man comes along.* **2** to make progress or improve: *Your English is coming along nicely.*

**come apart** to break into pieces: *This old coat is coming apart at the seams.*

**come around 1** (used about an event that happens regularly) to happen: *The end of summer vacation always comes around very quickly.* **2** = COME TO

**come around (to sth)** to change your opinion so that you agree with sb/sth: *They finally came around to our way of thinking.*

**come back 1** to return: *I don't know what time I'll be coming back.* **2** to become popular or fashionable again: *Flared pants are coming back again.*

**come back to sb** to be remembered: *At first my mind went blank when she asked me a question, but then everything started to come back to me.*

**come before sb/sth** to be more important than sb/sth else: *Mark feels his family comes before his career.*

**come between sb and sb** to damage the relationship between two people: *Arguments over money came between the two brothers.*

**come by sth** to get sth: *Fresh strawberries are hard to come by in the winter.*

**come down 1** to fall down: *The power lines came down in the storm.* **2** to become lower: *The price of land has come down in the past year.*

**come down to sth/to doing sth** (*informal*) to have as the main feature or most important fact: *It all comes down to having the right experience for the job.*

**come down to sth** to reach down to a particular point: *Her hair comes down to her waist.*

**come down with sth** to become sick with sth: *I think I'm coming down with the flu.*

**come forward** to offer help: *The police are asking witnesses to come forward.*

**come from...** to live in or have been born in a place: *Where do you come from originally?*

**come from (doing) sth** to be the result of sth: *"I'm tired." "That comes from all the partying you've done lately."*

**come in 1** (used about the tide) to move toward the land **2** (used about news or information) to be received: *Reports are coming in of a shooting downtown.* **3** to finish a race, contest, etc. in a particular position: *Kelly came in first in the 400-meter dash.*

**come of sth/of doing sth** to be the result of sth: *We've written to several companies asking for help, but nothing has come of it yet.*

**come off 1** to be able to be removed: *Does the collar come off?* **2** to give a certain impression, especially a negative one: *She* ***comes off as*** *rude, but she's really a warm person when you get to know her.* **3** (*informal*) to be successful: *The deal seems unlikely to come off.*

**come off (sth)** to become removed from sth: *One of the legs came off this table.* ◇ *A button came off when I was putting my shirt on.*

**come off it** (*informal*) (used to disagree with sb or to tell sb to change his/her attitude, ideas, etc.): *Come off it! That's never going to happen and you know it!*

**come on 1** (used about a machine or a piece of equipment) to start to work: *All the lights suddenly came on in the neighbors' house.* **2** (used about a television or radio program, etc.) to start: *The local news comes on at 6:00.* **3** to begin: *I think I feel a sneeze coming on.* **4** to start to act, play in a sports game, etc.: *They played the same music every time the bad guy came on.* ◇ *A substitute came on in the second quarter.* **5** **come on!** (*informal*) (used for telling sb to hurry up): *Come on! It's time to go.* **6** **come on!** (*informal*) (used for telling sb to stop acting silly, stop telling lies, try harder, etc.): *Oh, come on! Do you expect me to believe that?* ◇ *Come on, you guys! You can do better than that.*

**come out 1** to appear: *The rain stopped and the sun came out.* ◇ *The report came out in 2003.* **2** to become known: *It was only after his death that the truth came out.* **3** to be produced or published: *When is her new book coming out?* **4** to tell sb for the first time that you are sexually attracted to people of the same sex as yourself

**come out (of sth)** to be removed from sth: *Red wine stains don't come out easily.*

**come out with sth** to say or produce sth: *The committee came out with a new report on the economy.*

**come over (to...)** to visit a person or place: *Why don't you come over to our house on Saturday?*

**come over (to...) (from...)** to move from one

place to another: *My great-grandfather came over to New York from Germany in 1921.*

**come over sb** (used about a feeling) to affect sb: *A feeling of despair came over me.*

**come through** (used about news, information, etc.) to arrive: *Election results are just starting to come through.*

**come through (sth)** to escape injury or death in a dangerous situation, an illness, etc.: *to come through a heart attack*

**come to**; **come around** to become conscious again

**come to sth 1** to equal or total a particular amount: *The bill for the meal came to $35.* **2** to reach a bad situation: *We will sell the house to pay our debts if we have to, but we hope it won't come to that.*

**come under sth 1** to be included in a particular section, department, etc.: *Serious crimes do not come under the jurisdiction of this court.* **2** to be the object of criticism, an attack, etc.: *Our principal has come under intense pressure to resign.*

**come up 1** to be about to happen in the future: *I have an important meeting coming up next week.* **2** to be discussed: *The subject of religion came up.* **3** (used about a plant) to appear above the soil **4** (used about the sun and moon) to rise

**come up against sb/sth** to find a problem or difficulty that you have to deal with: *We have come up against stiff competition from foreign manufacturers.*

**come up to sth 1** to reach up as far as a particular point: *The water in the pool came up to our knees.* **2** to be as good as usual or as necessary: *This piece of work does not come up to your usual standard.*

**come up with sth** to find an answer or solution to sth: *Engineers have come up with new ways of saving energy.*

**come·back** /ˈkʌmbæk/ ***noun*** [C] **1** a return to a position of strength or importance that you had before: *The former world champion is hoping to* ***make a comeback****.* **2** (*informal*) a quick reply to a critical remark **3** a way of holding sb responsible for sth wrong which has been done to you: *You agreed to the contract, so now you have no comeback.*

**co·me·di·an** /kəˈmidiən/ (*also* **comic**) ***noun*** [C] a person whose job is to entertain people and make them laugh, e.g. by telling jokes

**com·e·dy** /ˈkɑmədi/ ***noun*** (*pl.* **com·e·dies**) **1** [C] an amusing play, movie, etc. that has a happy ending ➲ Look at **tragedy**. **2** [U] the quality of being amusing or making people laugh: *There is a hint of comedy in all her novels.*

**ˈcome-on** ***noun*** [usually sing.] (*informal*) an object or action which is intended to attract sb or to persuade sb to do sth: *He said he really liked my hair this way, but I think it was just a come-on.*

**com·et** /ˈkɑmət/ ***noun*** [C] an object that looks like a bright star and that moves around the sun

**come·up·pance** /kʌmˈʌpəns/ ***noun*** [sing.] (*informal*) a punishment for sth bad that you have done, that other people feel you really deserve: *I was glad to see that the bad guy* ***got his comeuppance*** *at the end of the movie.*

★**com·fort**[1] /ˈkʌmfərt/ ***noun*** **1** [U] the state of having everything your body needs, or of having a pleasant life and being relaxed: *to travel in comfort* ◇ *This furniture is not designed for comfort.* **2** [U] help or kindness to sb who is suffering: *I tried to offer a few words of comfort.* **3** [sing.] a person or thing that helps you when you are very sad or worried: *You've been a real comfort to me.* **4** [C] something that makes your life easier or more pleasant: *After a week of camping, we really appreciated the comforts of home.* ➲ Look at **discomfort**.

★**com·fort**[2] /ˈkʌmfərt/ ***verb*** [T] to try to make sb feel less worried or unhappy: *to comfort a crying child*

★**com·fort·a·ble** /ˈkʌmftəbl; ˈkʌmfərt̬əbl/ ***adj.*** **1** (*also informal* **comfy**) allowing you to feel relaxed and providing you with everything your body needs: *Our hotel room was large and comfortable.* ◇ *a comfortable temperature* (= not too hot or too cold) ◇ *Sit down and make yourselves comfortable.* OPP **uncomfortable 2** not having or causing worry, pain, difficulty, etc.: *He did not feel comfortable in the presence of so many women.* **3** having or providing more than enough money for all your needs: *They enjoyed a very comfortable lifestyle.* ◇ *a comfortable income* ▶ **com·fort·a·bly** ***adv.***: *You can't live comfortably on such low wages.*

**com·fort·er** /ˈkʌmfərt̬ər/ ***noun*** [C] a thick cover filled with feathers or another soft material that is placed on top of the sheets and blankets on a bed ➲ picture at **bed**[1].

**com·fy** /ˈkʌmfi/ ***adj.*** (**com·fi·er**; **com·fi·est**) (*informal*) comfortable (1): *a comfy chair*

**com·ic**[1] /ˈkɑmɪk/ ***adj.*** that makes you laugh; funny: *a comic scene in a serious play*

**com·ic**[2] /ˈkɑmɪk/ ***noun*** **1** [C] = COMEDIAN **2** (*also* **ˈcomic book**) [C] a magazine that tells stories through pictures **3 the comics** [pl.] the section of a newspaper that contains comic strips

**com·i·cal** /ˈkɑmɪkl/ ***adj.*** that makes you laugh

**ˈcomic strip** ***noun*** [C] a series of pictures that tell a story, e.g. in a newspaper, etc.

**com·ing** /ˈkʌmɪŋ/ ***noun*** [sing.] the arrival of sth: *The coming of the railroad meant more trade for these towns.*

IDM **comings and goings** activities that people do in a particular place, such as arriving, leaving, etc.: *Our neighbor sits on her porch and watches all the comings and goings on the block.*

**com·ma** /ˈkɑmə/ ***noun*** [C] the punctuation mark (,) used for dividing parts of a sentence or items in a list

★**com·mand**[1] /kəˈmænd/ ***verb*** **1** [I,T] to tell or order sb to do sth: *The men did as their officer had commanded.* **2** [T] to control or be in charge of sb/sth: *to command a ship/an army* **3** [T] to deserve and get sth: *The conductor commanded great respect.*

★**com·mand**[2] /kəˈmænd/ ***noun*** **1** [C] an order: *The captain's commands must be obeyed without question.* **2** [C] an instruction that is given to a computer **3** [U] control over sb/sth: *Who is in command of the expedition?* ◇ *General Weston has numerous advisers under his command.* ◇ *to take command of a situation* **4** [C] a division of an army, a navy, etc.

that has a specific function **5** [sing.] the state of being able to do or use sth: *She has a good command of French.*

IDM **at your command** available for you to use: *We'll need all the resources at our command in order to solve this problem.*

C

**com·man·deer** /ˌkɑmən'dɪr/ ***verb*** [T] to take control or possession of sth for military use

**com·mand·er** /kə'mændər/ ***noun*** [C] a person who controls or is in charge of sb/sth

**com·mand·ing** /kə'mændiŋ/ ***adj.*** **1** (used about a person who COMMANDS[1] (2) sb/sth): *Who is your commanding officer?* **2** having or showing power or authority: *to speak in a commanding tone of voice* **3** strong: *Martha holds a commanding lead over her rival in the election polls.*

**com·mand·ment** (*also* **Commandment**) /kə'mændmənt/ ***noun*** [C] (*formal*) one of the ten important rules in the Bible that Christian people should obey

**com·man·do** /kə'mændoʊ/ ***noun*** [C] (*pl.* **com·man·dos** or **com·man·does**) one of a group of soldiers who are trained to make quick attacks in enemy areas

**com·mem·o·rate** /kə'mɛməreɪt/ ***verb*** [T] to keep a special event in people's memories; to exist in order to make people remember a special event: *a statue commemorating all the soldiers who died in the Vietnam War* ▶ **com·mem·o·ra·tion** /kəˌmɛmə'reɪʃn/ ***noun*** [C,U]: *The ceremony was held in commemoration of the 150th anniversary of the town's founding.*

**com·mence** /kə'mɛns/ ***verb*** [I,T] (*formal*) **commence (sth/doing sth)** to begin to happen; to begin sth ➲ Look at the note at **begin**.

**com·mence·ment** /kə'mɛnsmənt/ ***noun*** **1** [usually sing.] (*formal*) a beginning **2** [C,U] an official ceremony at which students who have finished high school, college, etc. receive their degrees

**com·mend** /kə'mɛnd/ ***verb*** [T] (*formal*) to say that sb/sth is very good: *Dean was commended for his excellent work.*

**com·mend·a·ble** /kə'mɛndəbl/ ***adj.*** (*formal*) that you must praise: *She played a commendable role in the negotiations.*

★**com·ment**[1] /'kɑmɛnt/ ***noun*** [C,U] **comment (about/on sth)** something that you say or write that gives your opinion or feeling about sth: *The governor was not available for comment.* ◇ *Please use the space below to write any additional comments.*

IDM **no comment** (used in reply to a question when you do not want to say anything at all): *"Senator, how do you feel about these latest developments?" "No comment."*

★**com·ment**[2] /'kɑmɛnt/ ***verb*** [I,T] **comment (on sth)** to give your opinion or feeling about sth: *Several people commented on how nice the yard looked.* ◇ *Somebody commented that it didn't seem very fair.*

**com·men·tar·y** /'kɑmənˌtɛri/ ***noun*** [C,U] (*pl.* **com·men·tar·ies**) **1** a spoken description on the radio or television of sth as it is happening: *the commentary on a football game* **2** a written explanation or discussion of sth: *a magazine containing a mixture of news and commentary*

**com·men·tate** /'kɑmənteɪt/ ***verb*** [I] **commentate (on sth)** to give a spoken description on the radio or television of sth as it is happening

**com·men·ta·tor** /'kɑmənteɪt̬ər/ ***noun*** [C] **1** a person who commentates on sth: *a sports commentator* **2** a person who gives his/her opinion about sth on the radio, on television or in a newspaper: *a political commentator*

**com·merce** /'kɑmərs/ ***noun*** [U] the activities that are involved in buying and selling things: *international commerce* ➲ Look also at **chamber of commerce**.

★**com·mer·cial**[1] /kə'mərʃl/ ***adj.*** **1** connected with buying and selling goods: *commercial activities* **2** making a profit: *Although it won a lot of awards, the movie was not a commercial success.* ▶ **com·mer·cial·ly** /-ʃəli/: *These products are still being developed and are not yet commercially available.*

★**com·mer·cial**[2] /kə'mərʃl/ ***noun*** [C] an advertisement on the radio or on television ➲ Look also at **infomercial**.

**com·mer·cial·ize** /kə'mərʃəlaɪz/ ***verb*** [T] to try to make a profit out of sth, even if it means spoiling it: *The holidays have become too commercialized in recent years.*

★**com·mis·sion**[1] /kə'mɪʃn/ ***noun*** **1** [C] an official organization that controls or watches an industry or other activity and makes rules for it: *the Federal Trade Commission* **2** [C] (*U.S.*) a group of people who are elected to manage affairs for a city or county: *the Fulton County Commission* **3** [C,U] money that you get for selling sth: *Agents get 10% commission on everything they sell* (= 10% of the value of the things they sell). **4** [C] an act of asking sb to do a piece of work for you: *He received a commission to write a play for the festival.*

**com·mis·sion**[2] /kə'mɪʃn/ ***verb*** [T] to ask sb to do a piece of work: *to commission an architect to design a building*

**com·mis·sion·er** /kə'mɪʃənər/ ***noun*** [C] **1** a member of a COMMISSION[1] (1,2) **2** an official who is in charge of a government department: *the city police commissioner* ◇ *the state education commissioner* ➲ For more information on the North American political systems, look at study pages **A10-A11**.

★**com·mit** /kə'mɪt/ ***verb*** [T] (**com·mit·ting; com·mit·ted**) **1** to do sth bad or illegal: *to commit a crime* ◇ *After years of mental illness, Frank committed suicide.* **2** (*formal*) to send sb to a prison, mental hospital, etc.: *He was committed to a psychiatric hospital for five years.* **3** **commit sb/yourself (to sth/to doing sth)** to promise to do sth: *I can't commit myself to helping you tomorrow. I'm still not sure if I will be free.* **4** to decide to use sth for a particular purpose: *We've already committed over $4 million to the project.* **5** **commit yourself (on sth)** to say openly what you think or believe: *When asked for her opinion, she refused to commit herself.* ➲ Look at **noncommittal**.

★**com·mit·ment** /kə'mɪtmənt/ ***noun*** **1** [U] **commitment (to sth)** the state of giving a lot of your time and attention to sth because you believe it is right or important: *We are looking for a teacher with* *enthusiasm and commitment.* ◇ *commitment to an ideal* **2** [C] something that you have promised to do; a responsibility: *Marriage is a great commitment.* ◇ *The mayor was unable to attend the ceremony due to a previous commitment.* ◇ *Japan has made a commitment to respect the new agreement.*

**com·mit·ted** /kəˈmɪt̬əd/ ***adj.*** giving a lot of your time and attention to sth because you believe it is right or important: *a committed supporter of women's rights*

★**com·mit·tee** /kəˈmɪt̬i/ ***noun*** [C] a group of people who have been chosen to discuss sth or decide on sth: *They have set up a committee to look into ways of attracting new businesses to the city.* ◇ *to be/sit on a committee* ◇ *a member of a committee* ◇ *The planning committee meets twice a week.*

**com·mod·i·ty** /kəˈmɑdət̬i/ ***noun*** [C] (*pl.* **commod·i·ties**) something that you buy or sell, especially farm products, minerals, etc.: *Salt was once a very valuable commodity.*

★**com·mon¹** /ˈkɑmən/ ***adj.*** **1** happening or found often or in many places; usual: *These days it's fairly common for people to change careers several times.* ◇ *The word is no longer in common use.* ◇ *The daisy is a common wild flower.* **2 common (to sb/sth)** shared by or belonging to two or more people or groups, or by most or all people: *The Mexicans and the Spanish share a common language.* ◇ *This type of behavior is common to most children of that age.* ◇ *We have a common interest in computers.* **3** (only before a noun) not special; ordinary: *The officers had much better living conditions than the common soldiers.*

IDM **be common knowledge** to be known by a lot of people: *It's common knowledge that he took the money – why does he pretend he didn't?*

★**com·mon²** /ˈkɑmən/ ***noun***

IDM **have sth in common (with sb/sth)** to share sth with sb/sth else: *They seem to be good friends, although they have few interests in common.* ◇ *to have a lot in common with sb*

**in common with sb/sth** like sb/sth: *This company, in common with many others, is losing a lot of money.*

**ˌcommon ˈground** ***noun*** [U] beliefs, interests, etc. that two or more people or groups share: *We will try to find some common ground during the negotiations.*

**ˌcommon-law ˈwife** (*also* **ˌcommon-law ˈhusband**) ***noun*** [C] a person who has been living with a person of the opposite sex for a long time but who is not married to him/her. A common-law wife/husband usually has the same rights as an official wife/husband.

**com·mon·ly** /ˈkɑmənli/ ***adv.*** often; usually: *These insects are commonly known as midges.*

**com·mon·place** /ˈkɑmənpleɪs/ ***adj.*** not very exciting or unusual; ordinary: *Fax machines have become commonplace in recent years.*

**ˌcommon ˈsense** ***noun*** [U] the ability to make good sensible decisions because of your experience of life, not because of what you have learned at school or from books: *Safety precautions are basically just common sense.*

**com·mon·wealth** /ˈkɑmənwɛlθ/ ***noun*** **1** [sing.] **the Commonwealth** the group of countries that once formed the British Empire and that try to work and to trade together in a friendly way: *Canada is a member of the Commonwealth.* **2** (usually **the Commonwealth**) [C, usually sing.] the official legal description of certain U.S. states: *the Commonwealth of Virginia* **3** [C] the official legal description of certain regions that are part of the U.S. but are not states: *Puerto Rico remains a U.S. commonwealth, not a state.*

**com·mo·tion** /kəˈmoʊʃn/ ***noun*** [sing., U] great noise or excitement: *People looked out of their windows to see what all the commotion was about.* SYN **rumpus**

**com·mu·nal** /kəˈmyunl; ˈkɑmyənl/ ***adj.*** shared by a group of people: *four bedrooms with a communal kitchen and bathroom*

**com·mune** /ˈkɑmyun/ ***noun*** [C] a farm or a small community where a group of people, not from the same family, live together and share their property and responsibilities

★**com·mu·ni·cate** /kəˈmyunəkeɪt/ ***verb*** [I,T] to make information or your opinions, feelings, etc. known to sb: *Parents often have difficulty communicating with their teenage children* (= understanding them and being understood). ◇ *They communicate by sign language.* ◇ *to communicate news by satellite*

★**com·mu·ni·ca·tion** /kəˌmyunəˈkeɪʃn/ ***noun*** **1** [U] the act of communicating: *There is little real communication between father and daughter.* ◇ *verbal/nonverbal communication* ◇ *Radio is the only means of communication in remote areas.* **2** [C] (*formal*) a message: *a communication from our chairman* **3 communications** [sing., U] the study of communicating in an effective way: *Toni plans to major in communications when she goes to college.* **4 communications** [pl.] the methods that are used for traveling to and from a place or for sending messages between places: *The phone lines are down, so communications are very difficult.*

IDM **be in communication with sb/sth** (*formal*) to be in regular contact with sb/sth: *The astronauts are in direct communication with the control center in Houston.*

**com·mu·ni·ca·tive** /kəˈmyunəˌkeɪt̬ɪv; -kət̬ɪv/ ***adj.*** willing to talk or give information: *Leslie seems shy and not very communicative.* OPP **uncommunicative**

**com·mun·ion** /kəˈmyunyən/ ***noun*** **Communion** (*also* **Holy Communion**) [U] the ceremony in the Christian Church in which people share bread and wine as symbols of Christ's body and blood: *to take/go to Communion* ◇ *a Communion wafer*

**com·mu·ni·qué** /kəˌmyunəˈkeɪ; -ˈmyunəkeɪ/ ***noun*** [C] an official statement, especially from a government, a political group, etc.

**com·mu·nism** /ˈkɑmyənɪzəm/ ***noun*** [U] the political and economic system or theory in which the government owns and controls the means of production and in which everybody is supposed to be equal

➲ When we are talking about a particular society or political party which is organized according to the principles of communism, we often use a capital "C" for **communism** and **communist**: *He was a member of the Communist Party.*

**com·mu·nist** /ˈkɑmyənɪst/ ***noun*** [C] a person who believes in or supports communism ▶ **com·mu·nist** ***adj.***: *communist sympathies*

C

⋆**com·mu·ni·ty** /kəˈmyunət̮i/ ***noun*** (*pl.* **com·mu·ni·ties**) **1 the community** [sing.] the group of people who live in a particular place or area: *She was given an award for her work with young people in the community.* ◇ *Recent increases in crime have disturbed the whole community.* **2** [C] a town: *The storm caused severe damage in several communities in the region.* **3** [C] a group of people who have sth (e.g. nationality, interests, type of work, etc.) in common: *the Asian community in Vancouver* ◇ *the business community*

**comˈmunity ˌcenter** ***noun*** [C] a building where local people can take part in classes, meetings, etc.

**comˌmunity ˈcollege** (*also* **ˈjunior college**) ***noun*** [C] a college that is mainly for students from the local community and that offers programs that are two years long. Some students go to another college or university after they have finished studying at a community college.

**comˌmunity ˈproperty** ***noun*** [U] property that is considered to belong equally to a married couple: *The judge decided that the condo was community property.*

**com·mute** /kəˈmyut/ ***verb*** [I] to travel from home to work by car, bus, train or subway every day: *A lot of people commute into Detroit from nearby suburbs.* ▶ **com·mut·er** /kəˈmyut̮ər/ ***noun*** [C]: *The subways are always full of commuters at this time of day.* ◇ *a commuter train*

**comp¹** /kɑmp/ ***noun*** [C] **1** a free meal, ticket, etc. that you are given and do not have to pay for: *He got two comps for next week's game.* **2** (*informal*) = COMPENSATION ➲ Look at **comp time**.

**com·pact¹** /ˈkɑmpækt; kəmˈpækt/ ***adj.*** small, neat and taking up little space: *a compact camera* ◇ *The compact design of this iron makes it ideal for travel.*

**com·pact²** /ˈkɑmpækt/ ***noun*** [C] **1** a small car **2** a small flat box that contains a mirror and powder, etc. for the face

**ˌcompact ˈdisc** ***noun*** [C] = CD

**com·pan·ion** /kəmˈpænyən/ ***noun*** [C] a person or animal with whom you spend a lot of time or go somewhere: *a traveling companion* ◇ *His dog is his only companion.* ◇ *Witnesses saw the victim walking with two female companions shortly before the murder.*

**com·pan·ion·ship** /kəmˈpænyənʃɪp/ ***noun*** [U] friendship or company: *A lot of people get married for companionship.*

⋆**com·pa·ny** /ˈkʌmpəni/ ***noun*** (*pl.* **com·pa·nies**) **1** [C] a business organization selling goods or services: *an insurance company* ◇ *You should contact the telephone company to complain about your phone bill.* ◇ *She applied to several companies for a job.* ◇ *The company is planning to build a new factory in Colorado.*

➲ In names, **company** is written with a capital letter. The abbreviation is **Co.**: *the Walt Disney Company* ◇ *Milton & Co.*

**2** [U] a visitor or visitors: *Sorry, but I can't talk now. We've got company.* **3** [U] being with a person: *I always enjoy her company because she always has funny stories to tell.* ◇ *She was very good company* (= pleasant to be with) *and I really enjoyed our evening together.* **4** [C] a group of actors, singers, dancers, etc.: *a ballet company*

IDM **keep sb company** to go or be with sb so that he/she is not alone: *She was nervous, so I went with her to keep her company.*

**part company** → PART³

**com·pa·ra·ble** /ˈkɑmpərəbl/ ***adj.*** **comparable (to/with sb/sth)** of a similar standard or size; that can be compared with sb/sth: *A comparable house in Iowa would be a lot cheaper.*

**com·par·a·tive¹** /kəmˈpærət̮ɪv/ ***adj.*** **1** compared with sth else or with what is usual or normal: *Good soil and a warm climate give this region a comparative advantage over other farming areas.* **2** involving comparing things of the same kind: *a comparative study of government systems* **3** (*grammar*) (used about the form of an adjective or adverb) expressing a greater amount, quality, size, etc.: *"Hotter" is the comparative form of "hot."*

**com·par·a·tive²** /kəmˈpærət̮ɪv/ ***noun*** [C] (*grammar*) the form of an adjective or adverb that expresses a greater amount, quality, size, etc.: *"Worse" is the comparative of "bad."*

**com·par·a·tive·ly** /kəmˈpærət̮ɪvli/ ***adv.*** as compared with sth else or with what is usual: *The disease is comparatively rare nowadays.* ◇ *Most of the houses are old, but this one was built comparatively recently.*

⋆**com·pare** /kəmˈpɛr/ ***verb*** **1** [T] **compare A and B; compare A with/to B** to consider people or things in order to find ways in which they are similar or different: *If you compare the old and the new models, you'll see the changes we made.* ◇ *When the police compared the two letters, they realized that they had been written by the same person.* ◇ *Write an essay comparing lifestyles in the United States and Canada.* **2** [T] **compare A to B** to say that things or people are similar in a way or ways: *When it was built, people compared the stadium to a huge tent.* **3** [I] **compare (with sb/sth)** to be of the same quality as sb/sth: *Her last album was fantastic, but this one just doesn't compare.* ◇ *Nothing compares with the taste of bread fresh from the oven.*

**com·pared** /kəmˈpɛrd/ ***adj.*** **compared to/with** in comparison with; considered in relation to: *Compared to the place where I grew up, this town is exciting.* ◇ *I'm a very patient person, compared with him.*

⋆**com·par·i·son** /kəmˈpærəsn/ ***noun*** [C,U] an act of comparing; a statement in which people or things are compared: *Put the new one and the old one side by side for comparison.* ◇ *A comparison of this year's figures with last year's shows that the economy is improving.* ◇ *It's hard to make comparisons between Jason's painting and Catherine's because he's been learning so much longer.*

IDM **by/in comparison (to/with sb/sth)** when

compared: *When she told me about her problems I realized that mine were small by comparison.* ◇ *He's pretty tall in comparison to some of the older boys.* ◇ *In comparison with many other people, they're fairly well-to-do.*
**draw a comparison/a parallel** → DRAW[1]

**com·part·ment** /kəm'pɑrtmənt/ ***noun*** [C] one of the separate sections into which certain containers are divided: *The drugs were discovered in a secret compartment in his suitcase.* ◇ *the glove compartment* (= the space where you can keep maps, etc. in a car)

**compasses**

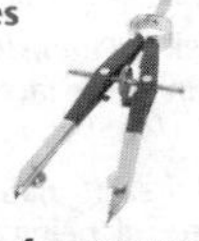

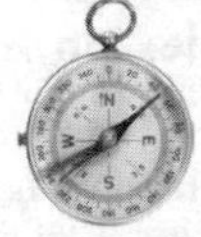


**a pair of compasses** **compass**

**com·pass** /'kʌmpəs/ ***noun*** [C] **1** an instrument for finding direction, with a needle that always points north: *a ship's compass* ◇ *They had to find their way back to the camp using a map and a compass.* **2** a V-shaped instrument that is used for drawing circles, etc.

**com·pas·sion** /kəm'pæʃn/ ***noun*** [U] **compassion (for sb)** sympathy or pity for sb who is suffering

**com·pas·sion·ate** /kəm'pæʃənət/ ***adj.*** having or showing sympathy or pity for sb who is suffering

**com·pat·i·ble** /kəm'pæṭəbl/ ***adj.*** **compatible (with sb/sth)** suitable to live together or to be used together: *As a couple, they are simply not compatible.* ◇ *Is this software compatible with my computer?* OPP **incompatible** ▸ **com·pat·i·bil·i·ty** /kəm,pæṭə'bɪləṭi/ ***noun*** [U]

**com·pa·tri·ot** /kəm'peɪtriət/ ***noun*** [C] a person who comes from the same country as another

**com·pel** /kəm'pɛl/ ***verb*** [T] (**com·pel**l**ing**; **com·pel**l**ed**) (*formal*) to force sb to do sth: *I felt compelled to tell her what I really thought of her.*

**com·pel·ling** /kəm'pɛlɪŋ/ ***adj.*** **1** forcing sb to do sth; convincing: *The fingerprints provided compelling evidence of his guilt.* ◇ *I felt that there was no compelling reason to stay, so I left.* ➲ noun compulsion **2** very exciting; holding your attention: *a compelling drama*

**com·pen·sate** /'kɑmpənseɪt/ ***verb*** **1 compensate (sb) (for sth)** [I,T] to pay sb money because you have injured him/her or lost or damaged his/her property: *To compensate for the loss of my luggage, the airline sent me a check.* **2 compensate (for sth)** [I] to remove or reduce the bad effect of sth; to make up for sth: *His willingness to work hard compensates for his lack of skill.*

**com·pen·sa·tion** /,kɑmpən'seɪʃn/ ***noun*** **compensation (for sth) 1** [U] money that you pay to sb, especially because you have injured him/her or lost or damaged his/her property: *She demanded compensation from the company for the injury she suffered while working there.* ◇ *unemployment compensation* **2** [C,U] a fact or action that removes or reduces the bad effect of sth: *Being a parent can be difficult, but there are compensations* (= good things about it). ◇ *Angie developed a very outgoing personality as compensation for her learning difficulties.*

★**com·pete** /kəm'pit/ ***verb*** [I] **compete (against/with sb) (for sth)** to try to win or achieve sth, or to try to be better than sb else: *The world's best athletes compete in the Olympic Games.* ◇ *The teams are competing for the state championship.* ◇ *When they were kids, they always used to compete with each other.* ◇ *They had to compete against several larger companies to get the contract.*

**com·pe·tence** /'kɑmpəṭəns/ ***noun*** [U] having the ability or skill that is needed: *This job requires competence in several computer applications.* OPP **incompetence**

**com·pe·tent** /'kɑmpəṭənt/ ***adj.*** **1** having the ability or skill needed for sth: *a highly competent player* ◇ *She is competent at her job.* ◇ *He is not competent to be a manager.* OPP **incompetent** **2** satisfactory but not excellent: *a competent, but not particularly exciting, performance* ▸ **com·pe·tent·ly** ***adv.***

★**com·pe·ti·tion** /,kɑmpə'tɪʃn/ ***noun*** **1** [C] an organized event in which people try to win sth: *She entered a competition in the newspaper and won a car.* ◇ *He finished second in an international piano competition.* **2** [U] a situation where two or more people are trying to achieve the same thing or gain an advantage: *There was fierce competition among the players for places on the team.* ◇ *She is in competition with three other people for the scholarship.* ◇ *Competition from the national chains means that many small stores have had to close.* **3** [U, sing.] the other people, companies, etc. who are trying to achieve the same as you: *If we are going to succeed, we must offer a better product than our competition.* ◇ *laws to protect domestic industries from foreign competition*

★**com·pet·i·tive** /kəm'pɛṭəṭɪv/ ***adj.*** **1** involving people competing against each other: *The travel industry is a highly competitive business.* ◇ *competitive sports* **2** able to be as successful as or more successful than those competing: *They are trying to make the company competitive in the international market.* ◇ *Our prices are highly competitive* (= as low as or lower than those of the others). **3** (used about people) eager to win or to be more successful than others: *She's a very competitive player.* ▸ **com·pet·i·tive·ly** ***adv.***

**com·pet·i·tor** /kəm'pɛṭəṭər/ ***noun*** [C] a person, company, product, etc. that is competing with another or others: *All competitors must wear a number in the race.* ◇ *Two local companies are our main competitors.*

**com·pi·la·tion** /,kɑmpə'leɪʃn/ ***noun*** **1** [U] the act of compiling: *The compilation of the encyclopedia took many years.* **2** [C] something that has been compiled: *The album is a compilation of the band's previous hits.*

**com·pile** /kəm'paɪl/ ***verb*** [T] to collect information and arrange it in a list, book, etc.: *to compile a list of addresses*

**com·pla·cent** /kəm'pleɪsnt/ ***adj.*** feeling so satisfied with yourself or with the situation that you think (perhaps wrongly) that there is no need to worry: *He had won his matches so easily that he was*



C

C

*in danger of becoming complacent.* ▸ **com·pla·cen·cy** /kəm'pleɪsnsi/ ***noun*** [U]: *We have achieved a high standard but there is no cause for complacency. We can still improve.*

★**com·plain** /kəm'pleɪn/ ***verb*** **1** [I,T] **complain (about sth); complain (that...)** to say that you are not satisfied with or happy about sth: *I wish you would quit complaining.* ◇ *People are always complaining about the weather.* ◇ *We complained to the hotel manager that the room was too noisy.* ➲ Look at the notes at **grumble** and **protest**. **2** [I] **complain of sth** to say that you have a pain or illness: *He went to the doctor, complaining of chest pains.*

★**com·plaint** /kəm'pleɪnt/ ***noun*** **complaint (about sth); complaint (that...)** **1** [U] an act or acts of complaining: *I wrote a letter of complaint to the manager about the service I had received.* ◇ *a cause for complaint* **2** [C] a statement that you are not satisfied with sth: *You should make a complaint to the company that made the machine.* **3** [C] an illness or disease: *a heart complaint* ◇ *minor complaints*

**com·ple·ment**[1] /'kɑmpləmənt/ ***noun*** [C] **1** a thing that goes together well with sth else: *A light sauce is the perfect complement to this dessert.* **2** the total number that makes a group complete: *Without a full complement of players, the team will not be able to take part in the game.* **3** (*grammar*) a word or words, especially a noun or adjective, used after a verb such as "be" or "become" and describing the subject of that verb: *In "He's friendly" and "He's a fool," "friendly" and "fool" are complements.*

**com·ple·ment**[2] /'kɑmpləmənt/ ***verb*** [T] to go together well with: *The colors of the furniture and the carpet complement each other.*

**com·ple·men·ta·ry** /ˌkɑmplə'mɛntəri; -'mɛntri/ ***adj.*** going together well with sth; adding sth which the other thing does not have: *They work well together because their skills are complementary: he's practical and she's creative.*

★**com·plete**[1] /kəm'plit/ ***adj.*** **1** having or including all parts; with nothing missing: *I gave a complete list of the stolen items to the police.* ◇ *a complete set of Twain's novels* ◇ *The book explains the complete history of the place.* **2** (not before a noun) finished or ended: *The investigation should be complete by Friday.* **3** (only *before* a noun) as great as is possible; total; in every way: *the complete reorganization of the department* ◇ *It was a complete waste of time.*

★**com·plete**[2] /kəm'plit/ ***verb*** [T] **1** to make sth whole: *We need two more players to complete the team.* ◇ *I finally managed to complete my collection.* **2** to finish sth; to bring sth to an end: *When the building has been completed, it will look impressive.* ◇ *He completed medical school in June, 2002.* **3** to fill out sth (e.g. a form): *Please complete the following questionnaire in capital letters.* ◇ *Completed application forms should be received by December 9.*

★**com·plete·ly** /kəm'plitli/ ***adv.*** as much as is possible; totally; in every way: *The building was completely destroyed by fire.* ◇ *We're trying a completely new method.*

**com·ple·tion** /kəm'pliʃn/ ***noun*** [U] the act of completing or the state of being complete: *The new freeway is due for completion within two years.*

★**com·plex**[1] /kəm'plɛks; 'kɑmplɛks/ ***adj.*** made up of several connected parts and often difficult to understand; complicated: *a complex system of taxation* ◇ *You won't find a simple solution when the problem is so complex.*

**com·plex**[2] /'kɑmplɛks/ ***noun*** [C] **1** a group or set of things, especially buildings, designed for a particular purpose: *a high-rise apartment complex* **2** a mental problem that causes sb to worry or be upset about sth: *He has a complex about his height.* ◇ *an inferiority complex*

**com·plex·ion** /kəm'plɛkʃn/ ***noun*** [C] the natural color and quality of the skin or the face: *a dark complexion* ◇ *a healthy complexion*

**com·plex·i·ty** /kəm'plɛksəṭi/ ***noun*** (*pl.* **com·plex·i·ties**) **1** [U] the state of being complex: *an issue of great complexity* **2** [C] one of the many details that make sth complicated: *I don't have time to explain the complexities of the chemical process now.*

**com·pli·ant** /kəm'plaɪənt/ ***adj.*** (*formal*) **compliant (with sth)** working or done in agreement with particular rules, orders, etc.: *The Web page is compliant with all applicable standards.* ▸ **com·pli·ance** /-əns/ ***noun*** [U]: *A hard hat must be worn at all times* ***in compliance with*** *safety regulations.*

**com·pli·cate** /'kɑmpləkeɪt/ ***verb*** [T] to make sth difficult to understand: *Let's not complicate things by adding too many details.*

★**com·pli·cat·ed** /'kɑmpləkeɪṭəd/ ***adj.*** difficult to understand; made up of many parts: *a novel with a very complicated plot* ◇ *a complicated mathematical calculation* ◇ *I can't tell you all the details now – it's too complicated.*

**com·pli·ca·tion** /ˌkɑmplə'keɪʃn/ ***noun*** [C] **1** something that complicates sth: *Unless there are any unexpected complications, I'll be arriving next month.* ◇ *A further complication in the project was the delay in receiving the raw materials.* **2** a new illness that you get when you are already sick

**com·plic·i·ty** /kəm'plɪsəṭi/ ***noun*** [U] being involved, with sb else, in a crime

**com·pli·ment**[1] /'kɑmpləmənt/ ***noun*** **1** [C] **a compliment (on sth)** a statement or action that praises or expresses admiration for sb: *People have often paid her compliments on her piano playing.* **2** **compliments** [pl.] (*formal*) greetings or good wishes given in a message: *Please help yourself to coffee and donuts, compliments of the hotel management* (= without charge).

**com·pli·ment**[2] /'kɑmpləmɛnt/ ***verb*** [T] **compliment sb (on sth)** to praise or express admiration for sb: *She complimented them on their good manners.*

**com·pli·men·ta·ry** /ˌkɑmplə'mɛntəri; -'mɛntri/ ***adj.*** **1** praising or expressing admiration for sb: *He made several complimentary remarks about her work.* **2** given free of charge: *a complimentary beverage with dinner*

**com·ply** /kəm'plaɪ/ ***verb*** [I] (*pres. part.* **com·ply·ing**; *3rd person sing. pres.* **com·plies**; *pt, pp* **com·plied**) **comply (with sth)** (*formal*) to obey an order or request: *All office buildings must comply with fire and safety regulations.*

**com·po·nent**[1] /kəm'poʊnənt/ ***noun*** [C] one of the parts that together form sth, especially a machine: *stereo components* ◇ *Fresh fruit and vegetables are essential components of a good diet.*

**com·po·nent**[2] /kəm'poʊnənt/ ***adj.*** being one of the parts that together form sth: *the component parts of an engine*

**com·pose** /kəm'poʊz/ ***verb*** **1** [I,T] to write music: *Mozart composed 41 symphonies.* **2** [T] to produce a piece of writing, using careful thought: *I sat down and composed a letter to the editor of the paper.* **3** [T] to be the parts that form sth: *the elements that compose the book's central theme* **4** [T] **compose yourself/sth** to make yourself, your feelings, etc. become calm and under control: *The news came as such a shock that it took me a while to compose myself.* ◇ *She tried to compose her thoughts and answer calmly.*

**com·posed** /kəm'poʊzd/ ***adj.*** **1 composed of sth** made up of sth; having sth as its parts: *The committee is composed of politicians from both parties.* **2** calm, in control of your feelings: *Although he felt very nervous, he managed to appear composed.*

**com·pos·er** /kəm'poʊzər/ ***noun*** [C] a person who writes music professionally

**com·pos·ite** /kəm'pɑzət/ ***adj.*** consisting of different parts, substances or materials

**com·po·si·tion** /ˌkɑmpə'zɪʃn/ ***noun*** **1** [C] a piece of music that has been written by sb: *"Finlandia" is probably Sibelius' best-known composition.* **2** [U] the act of composing a piece of music or writing **3** [U] the skill or technique of writing music: *She studied both music theory and composition.* **4** [C] (*old-fashioned*) a short piece of writing done as part of an educational course or exam: *Write a composition of about 500 words on one of the following subjects.* ➲ **Essay** is more common nowadays. **5** [U] the parts that form sth: *the chemical composition of a substance* ◇ *the composition of the population*

**com·post** /'kɑmpoʊst/ ***noun*** [U] a mixture of decaying substances, such as plants and waste material, that is added to soil to help plants to grow: *a compost pile/heap*

**com·po·sure** /kəm'poʊʒər/ ***noun*** [U] the state of being calm and having your feelings under control

★**com·pound**[1] /'kɑmpaʊnd/ ***noun*** [C] **1** something that consists of two or more things or substances combined: *a chemical compound* **2** (*grammar*) a word or phrase consisting of two or more parts that combine to make a single meaning: *"Roommate" and "round-trip" are compounds.* **3** an area of land with a group of buildings on it, surrounded by a wall or fence

**com·pound**[2] /kəm'paʊnd/ ***verb*** [T] to make sth (a problem, etc.) worse

**com·pre·hend** /ˌkɑmprɪ'hɛnd/ ***verb*** [T] (*formal*) to understand sth completely: *She's too young to comprehend what happened.*

**com·pre·hen·si·ble** /ˌkɑmprɪ'hɛnsəbl/ ***adj.*** easy to understand: *The book is written in clear, comprehensible language.* OPP **incomprehensible**

**com·pre·hen·sion** /ˌkɑmprɪ'hɛnʃn/ ***noun*** **1** [U] the ability to understand or the act of understanding: *How such a strange thing could happen is beyond my comprehension.* OPP **incomprehension** **2** [U] an exercise that tests how well you understand spoken or written language: *The first part of the test is reading comprehension.*

**com·pre·hen·sive** /ˌkɑmprɪ'hɛnsɪv/ ***adj.*** including everything or nearly everything that is connected with a particular subject: *a guide book giving comprehensive information on the area* ◇ *comprehensive medical insurance*

**com·press** /kəm'prɛs/ ***verb*** [T] **compress sth (into sth) 1** to press sth together so that it takes up less space **2** to express sth briefly or in a shorter form ▸ **com·pres·sion** /kəm'prɛʃn/ ***noun*** [U]

**com·prise** /kəm'praɪz/ ***verb*** [T] **1** to consist of; to have as parts or members: *The metropolitan area comprises five counties.* ◇ *a committee comprising businesspeople, local politicians and clergy members* **2** to be the parts or members that make up sth; to form: *Women comprise 62% of all employees.*

★**com·pro·mise**[1] /'kɑmprəmaɪz/ ***noun*** [C,U] **a compromise (on sth); a compromise (between A and B)** an agreement that is reached when each side allows the other side part of what it wanted: *Unless the union and the management can reach a compromise on pay, there will be a strike.* ◇ *It's difficult to find a compromise between the protection of the environment and our need for more technology.* ◇ *"There can be no compromise on the subject of terrorism," a senator said.*

★**com·pro·mise**[2] /'kɑmprəmaɪz/ ***verb*** **1** [I] **compromise (with sb) (on sth)** to reach an agreement by which each side gets sth it wants and allows the other side to have sth it wants **2** [T] **compromise yourself** to put yourself in a position in which other people can criticize you for not being honest: *He compromised himself by accepting money from them.* **3** [T] to do sth that is harmful to sth: *She refused to compromise her principles by signing the letter.*

**'comp time** ***noun*** [U] time off work that is given because you have worked more hours than usual in the period before

**com·pul·sion** /kəm'pʌlʃn/ ***noun*** **1** [U] forcing sb to do sth or being forced to do sth: *There is no compulsion to take part. You can decide yourself.* ➲ The verb is **compel**. **2** [C] a strong desire that you cannot control, often to do sth that you should not do

**com·pul·sive** /kəm'pʌlsɪv/ ***adj.*** **1** (used about a bad or harmful habit) caused by a strong desire that you cannot control: *compulsive eating* **2** (used about a person) having a bad habit that he/she cannot control: *a compulsive gambler*

**com·pul·so·ry** /kəm'pʌlsəri/ ***adj.*** that must be done, by law, rules, etc.: *Education is compulsory for children under age 16.* ◇ *The United States does not have compulsory military service.*

➲ Look also at **mandatory**. It is similar in meaning. Something that you do not have to do is **voluntary**.

C

**com·pu·ta·tion·al** /ˌkɑmpyʊˈteɪʃənl/ ***adj.*** (usually before a noun) using or connected with computers: *computational linguistics/theory/skills*

**com·pute** /kəmˈpyut/ ***verb*** [T] (*formal*) to calculate sth: *Losses were computed at $5 million.* ▶ **com·pu·ta·tion** /ˌkɑmpyʊˈteɪʃn/ ***noun*** [C,U]

⋆**com·put·er** /kəmˈpyuṭər/ ***noun*** [C] an electronic machine that can store and arrange information, make calculations and control other machinery: *The bills are all processed by computer.* ◇ *a computer program* ◇ *a computer programmer* ◇ *computer software/hardware/graphics* ◇ *computer games* ◇ *First of all, the details are entered into a computer.* ➲ Look also at **personal computer**.

**com·put·er·ize** /kəmˈpyuṭəraɪz/ ***verb*** [T] to deal with sth by computer; to store information in a computer: *We have now computerized the library catalog.*

**comˌputer-ˈliterate** ***adj.*** able to use computers well

**comˌputer ˈscience** ***noun*** [U] the study of computers and how they can be used: *a degree in computer science*

**com·put·ing** /kəmˈpyuṭɪŋ/ ***noun*** [U] the skill of using computers: *She took a course in computing.*

**com·rade** /ˈkɑmræd/ ***noun*** [C] **1** (used by members of a socialist party when they talk about or to each other): *Comrades, we will fight against injustice!* **2** (*formal*) a friend or companion, especially one with whom you share a difficult experience: *an old army comrade*

**con¹** /kɑn/ ***verb*** [T] (**con·ning**; **conned**) **con sb (into doing sth/out of sth)** (*informal*) to cheat sb, especially in order to get money: *He conned her into investing in a company that didn't really exist.*

**con²** /kɑn/ ***noun***

IDM **the pros and cons** → PRO²

**con·cave** /kɑnˈkeɪv; ˈkɑnkeɪv/ ***adj.*** (used about a surface) curving inward ➲ Look at **convex**.

**con·ceal** /kənˈsil/ ***verb*** [T] **conceal sth/sb (from sb/sth)** to hide sth/sb; to prevent sth/sb from being seen or discovered: *She tried to conceal her anger from her friend.* ◇ *The video was recorded with a concealed camera.* ▶ **con·ceal·ment** ***noun*** [U]: *the concealment of the facts of the case*

**con·cede** /kənˈsid/ ***verb*** [T] **1** to admit that sth is true, often unwillingly: *When it was clear that he would lose the election, he conceded defeat.* ◇ *She conceded that the problem was mostly her fault.* **2 concede sth (to sb)** to allow sb to take sth, often unwillingly: *They lost the war and had to concede territory to their enemy.* ◇ *Despite conceding two late touchdowns, they still won.* ➲ noun **concession**

**con·ceit** /kənˈsit/ ***noun*** [U] too much pride in yourself, too high an opinion of your abilities and importance

**con·ceit·ed** /kənˈsiṭəd/ ***adj.*** too proud of yourself, your abilities, your importance, etc.: *He's so conceited – he thinks he's the best at everything!*

**con·ceiv·a·ble** /kənˈsivəbl/ ***adj.*** possible to imagine or believe: *I made every conceivable effort to succeed.* OPP **inconceivable** ▶ **con·ceiv·a·bly** -əbli/ ***adv.***: *She might just conceivably be telling the truth.*

**con·ceive** /kənˈsiv/ ***verb*** **1** [I,T] to form a baby (fetus) inside a woman's body: *Tests showed that she was unable to conceive.* ◇ *Their first child was conceived soon after they got married.* **2** [T] (*formal*) to form or think of sth (an idea, a plan, etc.); to imagine sth: *He conceived the idea for the novel during his trip through India.* **3** [I,T] **conceive of sb/sth (as sth)** to think of sb/sth in a particular way: *He started to conceive of the world as a dangerous place.* ➲ noun conception

⋆**con·cen·trate¹** /ˈkɑnsntreɪt/ ***verb*** [I,T] **1 concentrate (sth) (on sth/doing sth)** to give all your attention or effort to sth: *How can you concentrate on your work with so much noise going on?* ◇ *It is important to concentrate on the road when you are driving.* ◇ *I tried to concentrate my thoughts on the problem.* **2** to come together or to bring people or things together in one place: *The general concentrated most of his tanks on the border.*

**con·cen·trate²** /ˈkɑnsntreɪt/ ***noun*** [C,U] a substance that has been made stronger by having water taken out of it: *orange juice concentrate*

**con·cen·trat·ed** /ˈkɑnsntreɪṭəd/ ***adj.*** **1** aimed at one particular point: *With another concentrated attack we should break through the enemy's defenses.* **2** made stronger by the removal of some liquid: *This is concentrated orange juice. You have to add water before you drink it.*

⋆**con·cen·tra·tion** /ˌkɑnsnˈtreɪʃn/ ***noun*** **1** [U] **concentration (on sth)** the act of giving all your attention or effort to sth: *This type of work requires total concentration.* ◇ *She lost her concentration when she heard a door slam.* **2** [C] **concentration (of sth)** a large amount of people or things in one place: *There are high concentrations of bacteria in the drinking water here.*

**ˌconcenˈtration camp** ***noun*** [C] a prison (usually a number of buildings inside a high fence) where political prisoners are kept in very bad conditions: *Millions of Jews died in Nazi concentration camps.*

⋆**con·cept** /ˈkɑnsɛpt/ ***noun*** [C] **concept (of sth/that...)** an idea; a basic principle: *The basic concepts of physics can be difficult to understand.* ◇ *The concept that "big is beautiful" is no longer as popular as it was.* ◇ *Their success was due to their radical new concept for customer service.*

**con·cep·tion** /kənˈsɛpʃn/ ***noun*** [C,U] **1** the beginning of a new life inside a female person or animal: *an embryo 14 days after conception* ➲ verb conceive **2** an idea or a plan: *We have no real conception of what people suffered during the Middle Ages.*

⋆**con·cern¹** /kənˈsərn/ ***verb*** [T] **1** to affect or be of importance to sb: *The destruction of the world's forests concerns everybody in some way.* ◇ *This doesn't concern you. Just go away.* ◇ *The closure of the factory came as a shock to all those concerned.* ◇ *It is important that no risks be taken where safety is concerned.* **2 concern yourself with sth** to give your attention to sth: *You don't need to concern yourself with the plans for the party. We'll take care of everything.* **3** to worry sb: *What concerns the experts most is the level of pollution in our cities.*

IDM **as/so far as sb/sth is concerned** → FAR²

**to be concerned with sth** to be about sth: *Tonight's program is concerned with the effects of the law on ordinary people.*

★**con·cern²** /kən'sərn/ ***noun*** **1** [U] **concern (for/about/over sb/sth)**; **concern (that...)** worry: *Following the crash there is growing concern over the safety of air travel.* ◇ *Don't worry. There is no cause for concern.* **2** [C,U] something that affects you or is important to you: *Edward's family problems are not my concern.* ◇ *He showed great concern for the homeless.* **3** [C] a company or business: *a large industrial concern*

★**con·cerned** /kən'sərnd/ ***adj.*** **concerned (about/for sth)**; **concerned (that...)** worried or anxious: *If you are concerned about your baby's health, you should consult a doctor immediately.* OPP **unconcerned**

★**con·cern·ing** /kən'sərnɪŋ/ ***prep.*** about; on the subject of: *She refused to answer questions concerning her private life.*

★**con·cert** /'kɑnsərt/ ***noun*** [C] a performance of music: *a rock concert* ◇ *The concert was held in Central Park.* ◇ *The orchestra is giving concerts in Cleveland, Columbus and Cincinnati.*

**con·cert·ed** /kən'sərt̬əd/ ***adj.*** done by a group of people working together: *We must all make a concerted effort.*

**con·cer·to** /kən'tʃɛrt̬oʊ/ ***noun*** [C] (*pl.* **con·cer·tos**) a piece of music for an orchestra with one instrument playing an important part (a solo): *Tchaikovsky's piano concerto*

**con·ces·sion** /kən'sɛʃn/ ***noun*** **1** [C,U] **concession (to sb/sth)** something that you agree to do or give up in order to end an argument: *The school district has been forced to make concessions to the teachers' union.* ➲ verb **concede** **2** [C] = CONCESSION STAND **3** [C] a special right to do sth that is given or sold to sb/sth: *The government has granted gambling concessions to several Native American tribes.*

**con'cession stand** ***noun*** [C] a place in a public building, sports center, theater, etc. where food, drink and souvenirs are sold: *For some people, a baseball game is just an excuse to make endless trips to the concession stand.*

**con·cierge** /kɑn'syɛrʒ; kən-/ ***noun*** [C] the person in a hotel whose job is to give guests information or help them find a restaurant, order a taxi, etc.: *I'll ask the concierge if she can get us tickets to the theater.*

**con·cil·i·a·tion** /kənˌsɪli'eɪʃn/ ***noun*** [U] the process of ending a disagreement: *All attempts at conciliation have failed and civil war seems inevitable.*

**con·cil·i·a·to·ry** /kən'sɪliəˌtɔri/ ***adj.*** intended to end a disagreement: *a conciliatory speech*

**con·cise** /kən'saɪs/ ***adj.*** giving a lot of information in a few words; short: *He gave a clear and concise summary of what had happened.* ▸ **con·cise·ly** ***adv.***

★**con·clude** /kən'klud/ ***verb*** **1** [I,T] (*formal*) to end or to bring sth to an end: *I'd like to conclude by thanking our guest speaker.* ◇ *The orchestra concluded its concert with a piece by Copland.* **2** [T] **conclude sth from sth** to reach a belief or opinion as a result of thought or study: *From their studies the archaeologists concluded that the area was the site of an ancient burial ground.* **3** [T] **conclude sth (with sb)** to arrange or agree to sth formally: *to conclude a treaty/business deal*

★**con·clu·sion** /kən'kluʒn/ ***noun*** **1** [C, usually sing.] the end: *The conclusion of the novel was a big surprise.* ◇ *to bring sth to a conclusion* ◇ *The conclusion is just as important a part of your essay as the introduction.* **2** [C] **the conclusion (that...)** a belief or opinion that you reach after considering sth carefully: *We came to the conclusion that he was right.* ◇ *What conclusions can you draw from her remarks?* ◇ *The jury reached the conclusion that the defendant was guilty.* **3** [U] an act of arranging or agreeing to sth formally: *The summit ended with the conclusion of a free-trade treaty.*

IDM **a foregone conclusion** → FOREGONE

**in conclusion** finally; lastly: *In conclusion, I would like to wish you continued success in the future.*

**jump/leap to conclusions** to form an opinion about sth without thinking about it carefully enough

**con·clu·sive** /kən'klusɪv/ ***adj.*** that shows sth is definitely true or real: *conclusive proof of sb's guilt* OPP **inconclusive** ▸ **con·clu·sive·ly** ***adv.***: *Tests can now prove conclusively who is the father of a child.*

**con·coct** /kən'kɑkt/ ***verb*** [T] **1** to make sth by mixing different things together **2** to make up or invent sth (an excuse, a story, etc.) ▸ **con·coc·tion** /kən'kɑkʃn/ ***noun*** [C,U]

**con·course** /'kɑŋkɔrs/ ***noun*** [C] a large hall or space inside a building such as a train station or an airport

★**con·crete¹** /kɑn'krit; 'kɑŋkrit/ ***adj.*** **1** that can be touched, felt, etc.; real: *a concrete object* **2** definite; particular: *Can you give me a concrete example of the behavior you're complaining about?* ▸ **con·crete·ly** ***adv.***

★**con·crete²** /'kɑnkrit; 'kɑŋ-/ ***noun*** [U] a hard substance made from cement mixed with sand, water, small stones (**gravel**), etc., that is used in building: *a slab of concrete*

> NOTE Many people also use the word **cement** to refer to this substance: *cement blocks.*

**con·cur** /kən'kər/ ***verb*** [I] (**con·cur·ring**; **con·curred**) (*formal*) **concur (with sb/sth) (in sth)** to agree

**con·cur·rent** /kən'kərənt/ ***adj.*** existing or happening at the same time as sth else ▸ **con·cur·rent·ly** ***adv.***: *He will serve both his prison sentences concurrently.*

**con·cus·sion** /kən'kʌʃn/ ***noun*** [C] an injury to the brain that was caused by a blow to the head: *She suffered a concussion in a car accident.*

**con·demn** /kən'dɛm/ ***verb*** [T] **1** **condemn sb/sth (for/as sth)** to say strongly that you think sb/sth is very bad or wrong: *The President has been condemned for trying to cut funding for education.* ◇ *A government spokesman condemned the bombing as a cowardly act of terrorism.* **2** **condemn sth (as sth)** to say officially that sth is not good enough to use: *The building was condemned and had to be demolished.* **3** **condemn sb (to sth/to do sth)** to say what sb's punishment will be: *The murderer was condemned to die in the electric chair.* ◇

C

(*figurative*) *Their poor education condemns them to a lifetime of poverty.*

**con·dem·na·tion** /ˌkɑndəmˈneɪʃn/ ***noun*** [C,U] the act of condemning sth; a statement that condemns sth: *The airport bombing brought condemnation from all around the world.*

**con·den·sa·tion** /ˌkɑndənˈseɪʃn/ ***noun*** [U] small drops of liquid that are formed when warm air touches a cold surface: *condensation on the windows*

**con·dense** /kənˈdɛns/ ***verb*** **1** [I,T] to change from gas to liquid; to make a gas change to liquid: *Steam condenses into water when it touches a cold surface.* ➲ Look at **evaporate**. **2** [I,T] to become or to make sth thicker: *condensed mushroom soup* **3** [T] **condense sth (into sth)** to make a piece of writing shorter: *We'll have to condense these three chapters into one.*

**con·de·scend** /ˌkɑndəˈsɛnd/ ***verb*** [I] **1** to do sth that you believe is below your level of importance: *Sarah only condescends to speak to me when she wants me to do something for her.* **2 condescend (to sb)** to behave toward sb in a way that shows that you think you are better or more important than him/her: *The teacher must be able to explain things at the right level for the children without condescending to them.* ▶ **con·de·scend·ing** ***adj.***: *a condescending smile*

**con·di·ment** /ˈkɑndəmənt/ ***noun*** [C] a sauce, salt, etc., that is used to give flavor to food, or that is eaten with food: *Mustard, ketchup and other condiments are available after the cash registers.*

★**con·di·tion¹** /kənˈdɪʃn/ ***noun*** **1** [sing., U] the state that sb/sth is in: *The car is five years old but it is still in very good condition.* ◇ *He looks really sick. He is certainly not in a condition to drive home.* **2** [C] something that must happen so that sth else can happen or be possible: *One of the conditions of the job is that you agree to work on Sundays.* ◇ *We agreed to the conditions that the negotiators set.* **3 conditions** [pl.] a situation or circumstances: *The prisoners were kept in terrible conditions.* ◇ *poor housing conditions* ◇ *The weather conditions were very favorable for the flight.* **4** [C] an illness: *to have a heart condition*

IDM **on the condition (that...)** only if: *I agreed to help on the condition that I got half the profit.*

**under no condition; not under any condition(s)** (*formal*) not at all; for no reason: *Under no condition can the press find out about this new project.*

**con·di·tion²** /kənˈdɪʃn/ ***verb*** [T] **1** to affect or control the way that sb/sth behaves: *Boys are conditioned to feel that they shouldn't cry in public.* ◇ *to be conditioned by your environment* **2** to keep sth in a good CONDITION¹ (1): *a shampoo that moisturizes and conditions your hair*

**con·di·tion·al** /kənˈdɪʃənl/ ***adj.*** **1 conditional (on/upon sth)** if sth is conditional on sth else, it can only happen if this other thing happens first; the one thing depends on the other: *This job offer is conditional on your graduating from high school this spring.* ◇ *conditional approval of a business deal* **2** (*grammar*) (used about a phrase or sentence) expressing a condition: *A conditional clause usually begins with "if" or "unless."* ▶ **con·di·tion·al·ly** /-ʃənəli/ ***adv.***

**con·di·tion·er** /kənˈdɪʃənər/ ***noun*** [C,U] a substance that keeps sth in a good condition: *hair conditioner*

**con·do** /ˈkɑndoʊ/ ***noun*** [C] (*pl.* **con·dos**) (*informal*) = CONDOMINIUM

**con·do·lence** /kənˈdoʊləns/ ***noun*** [C, usually pl., U] an expression of sympathy to sb whose relative or close friend has just died: *Please accept my* ***condolences on*** *your sister's death.*

**con·dom** /ˈkɑndəm/ (*also informal* **rubber**) ***noun*** [C] a rubber covering that a man wears over his penis during sex to prevent his partner from becoming pregnant or as protection against disease

**con·do·min·i·um** /ˌkɑndəˈmɪniəm/ (*also informal* ˈ**condo**) ***noun*** [C] (*pl.* **con·do·min·i·ums** or (*informal*) **con·dos**) an apartment or apartment building owned by the people who live in it

**con·done** /kənˈdoʊn/ ***verb*** [T] to accept sth; not to consider sth to be wrong: *I can never condone violence – in any circumstances.*

**con·dor** /ˈkɑndɔr; -dər/ ***noun*** [C] a very large bird that lives in the SW U.S. and in Latin America, and that eats dead animals

**con·du·cive** /kənˈdusɪv/ ***adj.*** **conducive (to sth)** helping or making sth likely to happen: *This hot weather is not conducive to hard work.*

★**con·duct¹** /kənˈdʌkt/ ***verb*** [T] **1** to carry out or organize sth: *Tests are being conducted to find the cause of the accident.* **2** to stand in front of an orchestra and direct the musicians: *The orchestra was conducted by Ozawa.* **3** to allow heat or electricity to pass along or through sth: *Rubber does not conduct electricity.* **4 conduct yourself well, badly, etc.** (*formal*) to behave in a particular way **5** to lead or guide sb/sth: *A tour of the museum is conducted every hour.*

★**con·duct²** /ˈkɑndʌkt/ ***noun*** [U] **1** a person's behavior: *Ron was fired from the bank for unprofessional conduct.* ◇ *a code of conduct* (= a set of rules for behavior) ➲ Look at **misconduct**. **2 conduct of sth** the act of controlling or organizing sth: *She was criticized for her conduct of the bank's financial dealings.*

**con·duc·tor** /kənˈdʌktər/ ***noun*** [C] **1** a person who stands in front of an orchestra and directs the musicians **2** a person who collects the tickets on a train **3** a substance that allows heat or electricity to pass through or along it: *Water is a good conductor.*

**cone** /koʊn/ ***noun*** [C] **1** a solid shape that has a round base and gets narrower, making a point at the top ➲ picture at **cube**. **2** an object of this shape: *an ice cream cone* ◇ *orange traffic cones along the side of the road* **3** the hard fruit of a pine or a fir tree: *a pine cone* ➲ picture at **tree**.

**con·fec·tion·er's sug·ar** (*also* **confectioners' sugar**) /kənˈfɛkʃənərz ˌʃʊgər/ ***noun*** [U] (*U.S.*) fine white powder made from sugar, that is mixed with water to make a sweet layer to put on top of a cake (icing)

**con·fed·er·a·cy** /kənˈfɛdərəsi/ ***noun*** **1 the Confederacy** [sing.] the 11 southern states that separated from the U.S. in 1860-61 and fought against the northern states in the Civil War ➲ Look at the note at **White House**. **2** [C] (*pl.* **con·fed·er·a·cies**) a union of states, groups of people or political parties with the same aim

**con·fed·er·ate**[1] /kən'fɛdərət/ ***noun*** [C] **1 Confederate** a person who supported the CONFEDERACY (1) **2** a person who helps sb, especially to do sth illegal or secret: *Rokovssky was his confederate in the assassination plot.*

**con·fed·er·ate**[2] /kən'fɛdərət/ ***adj.*** **1** joined by an official agreement **2 Confederate** connected with the CONFEDERACY (1): *the Confederate flag*

**con·fed·er·a·tion** /kən,fɛdə'reɪʃn/ ***noun*** [C] **1** an organization of smaller groups which have joined together: *a confederation of independent republics* **2 Confederation** (in Canada) the joining together of provinces and territories forming Canada, which began July 1, 1867

**con·fer** /kən'fər/ ***verb*** (**con·fer·ring**; **con·ferred**) **1** [I] **confer (with sb) (on/about sth)** to discuss sth with sb before making a decision: *The President is conferring with his aides.* **2** [T] **confer sth (on sb)** to give sb a special right or advantage: *The university plans to confer honorary degrees on two distinguished authors.*

★**con·fer·ence** /'kɑnfrəns; -fərəns/ ***noun*** [C] **1** a meeting for discussion, often one held every year where representatives of a particular profession, organization, etc. meet for several days to hear speeches and vote on the matters discussed: *an international conference on global warming* ◇ *a press conference* (= when a politician, etc. talks to reporters) ➲ Look also at **convention**. **2** a group of sports teams that compete against each other: *The Canuks won the western conference final.*

'**conference call** ***noun*** [C] a telephone call in which several people in different places take part at the same time

**con·fess** /kən'fɛs/ ***verb*** [I,T] **1 confess (to sth/ to doing sth)**; **confess (sth) (to sb)** to say that you have done sth bad or wrong: *The young woman confessed to the murder of her boyfriend/to murdering her boyfriend.* ◇ *Frank confessed that he had stolen the car.* ◇ *They confessed to their mother that they had spent all the money.* ◇ *I have to confess I didn't understand a word of that speech!* **2 confess (sth) (to sb)** to tell a priest or God what you have done that is bad or wrong: *to confess a sin*

**con·fes·sion** /kən'fɛʃn/ ***noun*** [C,U] an act of confessing sth: *The suspect made a full confession to the police.* ◇ *She goes to confession* (= with a priest) *twice a year.*

**con·fes·sion·al** /kən'fɛʃənl/ ***noun*** [C] a private enclosed place in a church where people CONFESS (2) to a priest

**con·fet·ti** /kən'fɛṭi/ ***noun*** [U] small pieces of colored paper that people throw at parties, festivals or after weddings

**con·fide** /kən'faɪd/ ***verb*** [T] **confide sth to sb** to tell sb sth that is secret: *She did not confide her love to anyone – not even to her best friend.*

**PHR V** **confide in sb** to talk to sb whom you trust about sth that is secret or private

★**con·fi·dence** /'kɑnfədəns/ ***noun*** **1** [U] **confidence (in sb/sth)** trust or strong belief in sb/sth: *I have every confidence in Kim's ability to do the job.* ◇ *They don't have much confidence in him.* ◇ *The public is losing confidence in the government's ability to improve the economy.* **2** [U] the feeling that you are sure about your own abilities, opinion, etc.: *I didn't have the confidence to tell her I thought she was wrong.* ◇ *to be full of confidence* ◇ *"Of course we will win," the coach said with confidence.* ➲ Look at **self-confidence**.

**IDM** **in confidence** as a secret: *People with information about the crime can talk in confidence to the police.*

★**con·fi·dent** /'kɑnfədənt/ ***adj.*** **confident (about/of sth)**; **confident (that...)** feeling or showing that you are sure about your own abilities, opinions, etc.: *Kate feels confident about her chances of passing the test.* ◇ *to be confident of success* ◇ *David has a very confident manner.* ➲ Look at **self-confident**. ▸ **con·fi·dent·ly** ***adv.***: *She stepped confidently onto the stage and began to sing.* ◇ *We confidently expect an improvement in sales next year.*

**con·fi·den·tial** /,kɑnfə'dɛnʃl/ ***adj.*** secret; not to be shown or told to other people: *The letter was marked "private and confidential."* ▸ **con·fi·den·ti·al·i·ty** /,kɑnfə,dɛnʃi'æləṭi/ ***noun*** [U] ▸ **con·fi·den·tial·ly** /,kɑnfə'dɛnʃəli/ ***adv.***

**con·fine** /kən'faɪn/ ***verb*** [T] **1 confine sb/sth (in/to sth)** to keep a person or animal in a particular place, usually a small place: *The prisoners are confined to their cells for long periods at a time.* **2 confine sb/sth/yourself to sth** to stay within the limits of sth: *Please confine your questions and comments to the topic we are discussing.*

**con·fined** /kən'faɪnd/ ***adj.*** (used about a space) very small: *Sailors on submarines must get used to living in confined spaces.*

**con·fine·ment** /kən'faɪnmənt/ ***noun*** [U] being kept in a small space: *to be kept in solitary confinement*

**con·fines** /'kɑnfaɪnz/ ***noun*** [pl.] (*formal*) the limits or outer edges of sth: *Patients are not allowed beyond the confines of the hospital grounds.*

★**con·firm** /kən'fərm/ ***verb*** [T] **1** to say or show that sth is true; to make sth definite: *Please confirm our agreement in writing.* ◇ *Seeing the two of them together confirmed our suspicions.* ◇ *Can you confirm that you will be able to attend?* **2** to accept sb as a full member of a Christian church: *He was baptized as a baby and confirmed at the age of 13.*

**con·fir·ma·tion** /,kɑnfər'meɪʃn/ ***noun*** **1** [C,U] a statement that confirms sth: *We are waiting for confirmation of the report.* ◇ *You will receive a written confirmation of your reservation.* **2** [C] a religious service at which a person is CONFIRMED (2)

**con·fis·cate** /'kɑnfəskeɪt/ ***verb*** [T] to take sth away from sb as a punishment: *Any cigarettes found in school will be confiscated.* ▸ **con·fis·ca·tion** /,kɑnfə'skeɪʃn/ ***noun*** [C,U]

★**con·flict**[1] /'kɑnflɪkt/ ***noun*** [C,U] **1** a fight or an argument: *an armed conflict* ◇ *Sheila's aggressive personality often brought her into conflict with her boss.* **2** a difference between two or more ideas, wishes, etc.: *Don't you see any conflict between being a vegetarian and wearing leather shoes?*

IDM **conflict of interest** a situation in which a person's private interests (for example, his/her own business or company) have an unfair influence on his/her duties in an official position (for example, as a politician)

C

★**con·flict²** /kən'flɪkt/ ***verb*** [I] **1 A and B conflict; A conflicts with B** to disagree with or be different from sb/sth: *The statements of the two witnesses conflict.* ◇ *John's statement conflicts with yours.* ◇ *The two studies came up with conflicting results.* **2 conflict (with sth)** to happen at the same time so that you must choose one thing: *Sorry, I can't come to the meeting on Wednesday. It conflicts with my history class.*

**con·form** /kən'fɔrm/ ***verb*** [I] **conform (to sth) 1** to obey a rule or law; to come up to a particular standard: *This building does not conform to fire regulations.* **2** to behave in the way that other people and society expect you to behave: *Kids are under a lot of pressure to conform when they are in high school.*

**con·form·i·ty** /kən'fɔrməṭi/ ***noun*** [U] (*formal*) behavior which conforms to rules and customs

★**con·front** /kən'frʌnt/ ***verb*** [T] **1 confront sth; confront sb with sb/sth** to think about, or to make sb think about, sth that is difficult or unpleasant: *to confront a problem/difficulty* ◇ *When the police confronted him with the evidence, he confessed.* **2** to stand in front of sb, e.g. because you want to fight him/her: *The unarmed demonstrators were confronted by a row of soldiers.*

**con·fron·ta·tion** /ˌkɑnfrən'teɪʃn/ ***noun*** [C,U] a fight or an argument

★**con·fuse** /kən'fyuz/ ***verb*** [T] **1** to make sb unable to think clearly or to know what to do: *He confused everybody with his pages of facts and figures.* **2 confuse A and/with B** to mistake sb/sth for sb/sth else: *I often confuse Lee with his brother. They look very much alike.* ◇ *Don't confuse "complement" with "compliment."* **3** to make sth unclear: *The situation is confused by the fact that so many organizations are involved.*

★**con·fused** /kən'fyuzd/ ***adj.*** **1** not able to think clearly: *When he regained consciousness, he was dazed and confused.* **2** difficult to understand because it is not in good order: *Following the attempted coup, the political situation was confused and unstable.*

**con·fus·ing** /kən'fyuzɪŋ/ ***adj.*** difficult to understand: *I can't figure out these instructions – they're too confusing.*

★**con·fu·sion** /kən'fyuʒn/ ***noun*** [U] **1** the state of not being able to think clearly or to know what to do: *He stared in confusion at the crowd of people in front of his house.* **2** a state of disorder: *In the panic and confusion, two people were trampled to death.* ◇ *Their unexpected visit threw all our plans into confusion.* **3** the act of mistaking sb/sth for sb/sth else: *To avoid confusion, all luggage should be labeled with your name and destination.* **4** the state of being uncertain or unclear: *There is still a great deal of confusion as to the true facts.*

**con·gen·ial** /kən'dʒinyəl/ ***adj.*** (*formal*) pleasant: *We have a very congenial atmosphere in our office.*

**con·gen·i·tal** /kən'dʒɛnəṭl/ ***adj.*** (used about a disease) beginning at and continuing since birth: *a congenital heart defect*

**con·gest·ed** /kən'dʒɛstəd/ ***adj.*** so full of sth that nothing can move: *The streets of New York are congested with traffic.* ◇ *I had a terrible cold last week – my head and chest were all congested.*

**con·ges·tion** /kən'dʒɛstʃən/ ***noun*** [U] the state of being very full of sth: *severe traffic congestion* ◇ *medicine to relieve coughing and nasal congestion*

**con·glom·er·ate** /kən'glɑmərət/ ***noun*** [C] a large firm made up of several different companies

**con·grat·u·late** /kən'grætʃəleɪt; -'grædʒə-/ ***verb*** [T] **congratulate sb (on sth)** to praise sb or tell sb that you are pleased about sth he/she has done: *I congratulated Sue on graduating from college.* ◇ *They sent a card to congratulate the couple on their engagement.*

**con·grat·u·la·tions** /kənˌgrætʃə'leɪʃnz; -ˌgrædʒə-/ ***noun*** [pl.] (used for praising sb or telling sb that you are pleased about sth he/she has done): ***Congratulations on*** *the birth of your baby boy!* ◇ *Congratulations! Your painting has won first prize.*

**con·gre·gate** /'kɑŋgrəgeɪt/ ***verb*** [I] to come together in a crowd

**con·gre·ga·tion** /ˌkɑŋgrə'geɪʃn/ ***noun*** [C] a group of people who go to a particular church

**con·gress** /'kɑŋgrəs/ ***noun*** **1 Congress** [sing.] the group of people who are elected to make the laws for the U.S: *a member of Congress* ◇ *to run for Congress* (= in order to be elected)

NOTE The U.S. Congress is made up of the **Senate** and the **House of Representatives**. ➲ For more information on the U.S. political system, look at study page **A10**.

**2** [C] (in some countries) the group of people who are elected to make the laws: *the Brazilian congress* **3** [C] a large formal meeting or series of meetings: *the Communist Party congress in Beijing* ➲ Look at **conference** and **convention**.

**con·gres·sion·al** /kən'grɛʃənl; kəŋ-/ ***adj.*** connected with Congress: *a congressional committee*

**con·gress·man** /'kɑŋgrəsmən/ ***noun*** [C] (*feminine* **con·gress·wom·an** /'kɑŋgrəsˌwʊmən/) (*pl.* **con·gress·men**; **con·gress·wom·en**) a member of the U.S. Congress, especially the House of Representatives

NOTE A member of the Senate is usually called a **senator**.

**con·jec·ture** /kən'dʒɛktʃər/ ***noun*** [C,U] guessing or a guess about sth without real proof or evidence

**con·ju·gate** /'kɑndʒəgeɪt/ ***verb*** [T] to give the different forms of a verb ▶ **con·ju·ga·tion** /ˌkɑndʒə'geɪʃn/ ***noun*** [C,U]

**con·junc·tion** /kən'dʒʌŋkʃn/ ***noun*** [C] a word that is used for joining other words, phrases or sentences: *"And," "but" and "or" are conjunctions.*

IDM **in conjunction with sb/sth** together with sb/sth: *Various charities are working in conjunction with the United Nations to help the disaster victims.*

**con·jure** /'kɑndʒər/ ***verb*** [T] **conjure sth (up)** to cause a picture to appear in your mind: *Hawaiian* *music conjures up images of sunshine, flowers and sandy beaches.*

**ˈcon man** *noun* [C] (*pl.* **con men**) (*also* **ˈcon artist**) (*informal*) a person who tricks others into giving him money, etc.

★**con·nect** /kəˈnɛkt/ *verb* **1** [I,T] **connect (sth) (to/with sth)** to be joined or linked to sth; to join or link sth to sth else: *You need the right software to be able to connect to the Internet.* ◇ *The printer is connected to the computer.* ◇ *The new subway line will connect the southern suburbs directly with downtown.* ◇ *The phone company hasn't connected our phone line yet.* OPP **disconnect** **2** [T] (usually passive) **connect sb/sth (to/with sb/sth)** to associate sb/sth with sb/sth; to consider sb/sth to be related to sb/sth else: *There was no evidence that she was connected with the crime.* ◇ *Doctors believe that the increase in asthma is connected to pollution levels.* **3** [I] **connect (with sth)** (used about a bus, train, plane, etc.) to arrive at a particular time so that passengers can change to another bus, train, plane, etc.: *I hope we won't miss our connecting flight in Chicago!* **4** [T] **connect sb (to/with sb)** to link sb by telephone: *Please stay on the line while we connect you to the next available representative.* **5** [I] **connect (with sb)** to understand sb well and have a good relationship with him/her: *If he wants to win the election, he'll have to connect with middle-class voters.*

★**con·nec·tion** /kəˈnɛkʃn/ *noun* **1** [C,U] **connection between A and B; connection with/to sth** connecting or being connected: *There is a clear connection between crime and drug addiction.* ◇ *Is there any connection between the two organizations?* ◇ *What is your connection with the school? Do you work here?* **2** [C] a place where two wires, pipes, etc. join together: *The radio doesn't work. There must be a loose connection somewhere.* **3** [C] a bus, train, plane, etc. that leaves soon after another arrives: *Our plane was late so we missed our connection.* **4** [C, usually pl.] a person that you know who is important or of high rank: *Chris got a good job because of his mother's connections.*

IDM **in connection with sb/sth** (*formal*) about or concerning: *I am writing to you in connection with your application.*

**con·nois·seur** /ˌkɑnəˈsər; -ˈsʊr/ *noun* [C] a person who knows a lot about art, good food, music, etc.: *a connoisseur of modern art*

**con·no·ta·tion** /ˌkɑnəˈteɪʃn/ *noun* [C] an impression that a word gives in addition to its meaning: *"Spinster" means a single woman, but it has negative connotations.*

**con·quer** /ˈkɑŋkər/ *verb* [T] **1** to take control of an area by winning a war: *Napoleon's ambition was to conquer the whole of Europe.* ◇ (*figurative*) *The young singer conquered the hearts of audiences all over the world.* **2** to defeat an enemy, an army, etc.; to overcome sth: *The Spanish conquered the Incas.* ◇ *She's trying to conquer her fear of flying.* ▸ **con·quer·or** /ˈkɑŋkərər/ *noun* [C]

**con·quest** /ˈkɑŋkwɛst/ *noun* **1** [C, U] an act of conquering sth: *the Spanish conquest of South America* ◇ *the conquest of Mount Everest* **2** [C] an area of land that has been taken by war

**con·science** /ˈkɑnʃəns/ *noun* [C,U] your own feeling about whether what you are doing is right or wrong: *a clear/a guilty conscience*

IDM **have sth on your conscience** to feel guilty because of sth that you have done that was wrong

**con·sci·en·tious** /ˌkɑnʃiˈɛnʃəs/ *adj.* **1** (used about people) careful to do sth correctly and well: *He's a very conscientious worker.* **2** (used about actions) done with great care and attention: *conscientious work* ▸ **con·sci·en·tious·ly** *adv.*

**consciˌentious obˈjector** *noun* [C] a person who refuses to join the army, etc. because he/she believes it is morally wrong to kill other people

★**con·scious** /ˈkɑnʃəs/ *adj.* **1** able to see, hear, feel, etc. things; awake: *She was badly injured but conscious and able to tell the doctor what had happened.* OPP **unconscious** **2** **conscious of sth/that...** noticing or aware of sth: *He suddenly became conscious that someone was following him.* ◇ *She didn't seem conscious of the danger.* **3** that you do on purpose or for a particular reason: *We made a conscious effort to treat both kids fairly.* SYN **deliberate** OPP **unconscious** **4** being particularly interested in or aware of sth: *Teenagers are very fashion-conscious.* ▸ **con·scious·ly** *adv.*: *I have never consciously harmed another human being.*

**con·scious·ness** /ˈkɑnʃəsnəs/ *noun* **1** [U] the state of being CONSCIOUS (1); being able to see, hear, feel, etc. things: *As he fell, he hit his head and lost consciousness.* ◇ *She regained consciousness after two weeks in a coma.* **2** [U, sing.] the state of being aware of sth: *growing consciousness of the need to save energy*

**con·script** /kənˈskrɪpt/ *verb* [T] = DRAFT² (2)

**con·se·crate** /ˈkɑnsəkreɪt/ *verb* [T] to make a place, an object or a person holy in a special ceremony: *Four new bishops were consecrated in the cathedral.* ▸ **con·se·cra·tion** /ˌkɑnsəˈkreɪʃn/ *noun* [C,U]

**con·sec·u·tive** /kənˈsɛkyət̬ɪv/ *adj.* coming or happening one after the other: *We have had three consecutive rainy weekends.* ▸ **con·sec·u·tive·ly** *adv.*

**con·sen·sus** /kənˈsɛnsəs/ *noun* [sing., U] agreement among a group of people: *to reach a consensus after a long discussion* ◇ *There is no general consensus among experts about the causes of global warming.*

**con·sent**¹ /kənˈsɛnt/ *verb* [I] **consent (to sth)** to agree to sth; to allow sth to happen

**con·sent**² /kənˈsɛnt/ *noun* [U] agreement; permission: *The child's parents had to give their consent to the operation.*

★**con·se·quence** /ˈkɑnsəkwɛns/ *noun* **1** [C] something that follows as a result or effect of sth else: *The bridge was unsafe and, as a consequence, was closed and repaired.* ◇ *The error had tragic consequences.* **2** [U] (*formal*) importance: *It is of no consequence.*

**con·se·quent** /ˈkɑnsəkwɛnt/ *adj.* (*formal*) following as the result of sth else: *The economy has benefited from new jobs and the consequent drop in the unemployment rate.* ▸ **con·se·quent·ly** *adv.*:

*She didn't work hard enough and consequently failed the exam.*

★**con·ser·va·tion** /ˌkɑnsərˈveɪʃn/ ***noun*** [U] **1** not allowing sth to be wasted, damaged or destroyed: *the conservation of energy* **2** the protection of the natural world: *Conservation groups are protesting against the plan to build a road through the forest.* ➲ verb conserve

C

**con·ser·va·tion·ist** /ˌkɑnsərˈveɪʃənɪst/ ***noun*** [C] a person who believes in the protection of the natural world

**con·ser·va·tism** /kənˈsərvətɪzəm/ ***noun*** [U] the dislike of new ideas and change

**con·ser·va·tive¹** /kənˈsərvət̬ɪv/ ***adj.*** **1** not liking change; traditional: *They have very conservative tastes. This design is too modern for them.* **2** supporting a free market, low taxes and traditional ideas about family life, sex, etc. ➲ Compare **liberal**. **3 Conservative** (*Cdn*) connected with the Conservative Party, a political party in Canada **4** (used about a guess, estimate, etc.) cautious, not extreme; fairly low: *I would say the damage will cost about $4,000 to repair – and that's a conservative estimate.* ▸ **con·ser·va·tive·ly** ***adv.***: *We have estimated the costs conservatively.*

**con·ser·va·tive²** /kənˈsərvət̬ɪv/ ***noun*** [C] a CONSERVATIVE¹ (1,2) person

**the Conˈservative ˌParty** ***noun*** [sing.] (in Canada) one of three main political parties, on the political right

NOTE A member or supporter of the **Conservative Party** is called a **Tory**. ➲ Look also at the **Liberal Party** and the **New Democratic Party**. ➲ For more information about the political system in Canada, look at study page **A11**.

**con·ser·va·to·ry** /kənˈsərvəˌtɔri/ ***noun*** [C] (*pl.* **con·ser·va·to·ries**) **1** a school where students can go to study music or acting **2** a building with a glass roof and walls in which plants are grown and shown to the public

**con·serve** /kənˈsərv/ ***verb*** [T] to avoid wasting sth: *Higher charges will encourage people to conserve water.* ➲ noun conservation

★**con·si·der** /kənˈsɪdər/ ***verb*** [T] **1 consider sb/sth (for/as sth); consider doing sth** to think about sb/sth, often before making a decision: *We must consider the matter carefully before we make our choice.* ◇ *They are considering him for the part of Romeo.* ◇ *She had never considered nursing as a career.* ◇ *He is still considering what material to include in the book.* ◇ *We're considering going to Hawaii for our vacation.* **2** to have sth as your opinion; to think about sb/sth in a particular way: *He considered that the risk was too great.* ◇ *He considered the risk (to be) too great.* **3** to remember or pay attention to sth: *I can't just quit my job. I have to consider my family.* ◇ *Be tactful. Consider how other people feel.*

★**con·sid·er·a·ble** /kənˈsɪdərəbl/ ***adj.*** great in amount or size: *We had considerable difficulty in getting tickets for the flights we wanted.* ◇ *A considerable number of people preferred the old building to the new one.* ▸ **con·sid·er·a·bly** /-əbli/ ***adv.***: *This apartment is considerably larger than our last one.*

**con·sid·er·ate** /kənˈsɪdərət/ ***adj.*** careful not to upset people; thinking of others: *It was very considerate of you to offer to drive me home.* OPP **inconsiderate**

★**con·sid·er·a·tion** /kənˌsɪdəˈreɪʃn/ ***noun*** **1** [U] (*formal*) an act of thinking about sth carefully or for a long time: *I have given some consideration to the idea but I don't think it would work.* ◇ *After careful consideration, we regret that we cannot offer you the position.* ◇ *Several options are currently under consideration.* **2** [U] **consideration (for sb/sth)** the quality of thinking about other people's wishes and feelings: *You should keep your music turned down low out of consideration for your neighbors.* **3** [C] something that you think about when you are making a decision: *If he changes his job, the salary will be an important consideration.*

IDM **take sth into consideration** to think about sth when you are forming an opinion or making a decision

**con·sid·er·ing** /kənˈsɪdərɪŋ/ ***prep., conj.*** (used for introducing a surprising fact) when you think about or remember sth: *He coped with the long trip well, considering his age.* ◇ *Considering you've only been studying for a year, you speak English very well.*

**con·sign** /kənˈsaɪn/ ***verb*** [T] (*formal*) to put sb/sth in, or to send sb/sth to, a particular place

**con·sign·ment** /kənˈsaɪnmənt/ ***noun*** [C] goods that are being sent to sb/sth: *We sent a consignment of old books to a used book store.*

★**con·sist** /kənˈsɪst/ ***verb***

PHRV **consist of sth** to be made up of sth: *The band consists of a singer, two guitarists, a bass player and a drummer.*

**con·sis·ten·cy** /kənˈsɪstənsi/ ***noun*** (*pl.* **con·sis·ten·cies**) **1** [U] the quality of being CONSISTENT (1); always having the same standard, opinions, etc.: *Your work lacks consistency. Sometimes it's excellent, but at other times it's full of mistakes.* OPP **inconsistency** **2** [C,U] the degree of thickness or firmness that a substance has: *The mixture should have a thick, sticky consistency.*

**con·sis·tent** /kənˈsɪstənt/ ***adj.*** **1** always having the same opinions, standard, behavior, etc.; not changing: *You have to be consistent. If you punish Jason, you should punish Paul for doing the same thing.* **2 consistent (with sth)** agreeing with or similar to sth: *Your statement is not consistent with what the other witnesses said.* ▸ **con·sis·tent·ly** ***adv.***: *We must try to maintain a consistently high standard.*

**con·so·la·tion** /ˌkɑnsəˈleɪʃn/ ***noun*** **1** [U] making sb feel better when he/she is sad: *It was some consolation to me to know that I wasn't the only one who had failed the final exam.* ◇ *a consolation prize* (= for sb who has lost a contest/game) **2** [C] a person or thing that consoles you: *Having his children near him was a great consolation when his wife died.*

**con·sole¹** /kənˈsoʊl/ ***verb*** [T] to make sb happier when he/she is very sad or disappointed; to comfort sb

**con·sole²** /ˈkɑnsoʊl/ ***noun*** [C] **1** a board or surface that contains the controls for a machine or a piece of electronic equipment: *rows of computer* *consoles at the space center* **2** a type of cupboard or box for a TV or stereo that stands on the floor

**con·sol·i·date** /kən'sɑlədeɪt/ ***verb*** [I,T] **1** to combine several things into one: *We plan to close several smaller branches and consolidate our operations here in Chicago.* **2** to become or to make sth firmer or stronger: *an attempt by party members to consolidate their power* ▸ **con·sol·i·da·tion** /kən,sɑlə'deɪʃn/ ***noun*** [U]

**con·so·nant** /'kɑnsənənt/ ***noun*** [C] **1** a sound that you make by partly stopping the air as it comes out through your mouth **2** a letter that represents this sound: *The letters "t," "m," "s" and "b" are all consonants.* ➲ Look at **vowel**.

**con·sor·ti·um** /kən'sɔrʃiəm; -ʃəm; -t̬iəm/ ***noun*** [C] (*pl.* **con·sor·ti·ums** or **con·sor·ti·a** /-ʃiə; -ʃə; -t̬iə/) a group of companies that work closely together for a particular purpose

**con·spic·u·ous** /kən'spɪkyuəs/ ***adj.*** easily seen or noticed: *As a tall, blonde woman, she was very conspicuous in China.* OPP **inconspicuous** ▸ **con·spic·u·ous·ly** ***adv.***: *He was conspicuously dressed in a large hat.*

**con·spir·a·cy** /kən'spɪrəsi/ ***noun*** [C,U] (*pl.* **con·spir·a·cies**) **conspiracy (to do sth)**; **conspiracy (against sb/sth)** a secret plan by a group of people to do sth bad or illegal: *Investigators have uncovered a conspiracy to defraud the bank of thousands of dollars.* ◇ *conspiracies against the president*

**con·spir·a·tor** /kən'spɪrət̬ər/ ***noun*** [C] a person who plans sth, especially a crime, together with other people

**con·spir·a·to·ri·al** /kən,spɪrə'tɔriəl/ ***adj.*** **1** connected with, or like, a conspiracy **2** a way of behaving that shows that you share a secret with sb: *"I know you understand," he said and gave a conspiratorial wink.*

**con·spire** /kən'spaɪər/ ***verb*** [I] **1** to plan sth, especially a crime, together with other people: *A group of thieves were conspiring to rob the bank.* **2 conspire (against sb/sth)** to work together to produce a particular, usually bad, result for sb/sth: *When we both lost our jobs in the same week, we felt that everything was conspiring against us.*

**constable** /'kɑnstəbl/ (*also* **po'lice ,constable**) ***noun*** [C] (in Canada) a police officer of the lowest rank

★**con·stant** /'kɑnstənt/ ***adj.*** **1** happening or existing all the time or again and again: *The constant noise gave me a headache.* ◇ *There were constant interruptions, so we didn't get the work finished.* **2** that does not change: *You use less gas if you drive at a constant speed.*

**con·stant·ly** /'kɑnstəntli/ ***adv.*** always; again and again: *The situation is constantly changing.*

**con·stel·la·tion** /,kɑnstə'leɪʃn/ ***noun*** [C] a number of stars that are considered as a group

**con·ster·na·tion** /,kɑnstər'neɪʃn/ ***noun*** [U] surprise and worry or fear: *We stared at each other in consternation.*

**con·sti·pat·ed** /'kɑnstəpeɪt̬əd/ ***adj.*** not able to pass waste material easily from the bowels: *If you are constipated, you should eat more fiber and fresh fruit.* ▸ **con·sti·pa·tion** /,kɑnstə'peɪʃn/ ***noun*** [U]

**con·stit·u·en·cy** /kən'stɪtʃuənsi/ ***noun*** [C] (*pl.* **con·stit·u·en·cies**) **1** (*especially Cdn*) a group of voters in a particular area that elects its own representative to parliament, Congress, etc.; the district or area represented in this way **2** a particular group of people in society who are likely to support a person, an idea or a product

**con·stit·u·ent** /kən'stɪtʃuənt/ ***noun*** [C] **1** a person who lives in the district for which a particular representative in government is responsible **2** one of the parts of sth

**con·sti·tute** /'kɑnstətut/ ***verb*** [T] (*formal*) (not in the continuous tenses) to make up or form sth: *Women constitute a high proportion of part-time workers.* ◇ *The presence of the troops constitutes a threat to peace.*

**con·sti·tu·tion** /,kɑnstə'tuʃn/ ***noun*** [C] **1** (*also* often **Constitution**) the basic laws or rules of a country, state or organization: *this country's constitution* ◇ *the Tennessee state constitution* **2** the condition of your body and its ability to fight disease: *to have a strong/weak constitution*

**con·sti·tu·tion·al** /,kɑnstə'tuʃənl/ ***adj.*** **1** in agreement with or allowed by the CONSTITUTION (1) of a country or state: *The Supreme Court will decide whether the law is constitutional.* OPP **unconstitutional** **2** connected with a CONSTITUTION (1): *a constitutional amendment* ▸ **con·sti·tu·tion·al·ly** /,kɑnstə'tuʃənəli; -'tuʃnəli/ ***adv.***: *constitutionally guaranteed rights*

**con·sti·tu·tion·al·i·ty** /,kɑnstə,tuʃə'næləti/ ***noun*** [U] the fact that a law, etc. is acceptable according to a CONSTITUTION (1)

**con·strain** /kən'streɪn/ ***verb*** [T] (*formal*) to set limits on sth, especially sb's freedom; to force sb to do sth

**con·straint** /kən'streɪnt/ ***noun*** [C] a limit on sth, or on your freedom to do sth: *There are always some financial constraints on a project like this.*

**con·strict** /kən'strɪkt/ ***verb*** [T] **1** to make sth tighter or narrower; to reduce sth **2** to limit a person's freedom to do sth

★**con·struct** /kən'strʌkt/ ***verb*** [T] to build or make sth: *Early houses were constructed out of logs.*

NOTE **Construct** is more formal than **build**.

★**con·struc·tion** /kən'strʌkʃn/ ***noun*** **1** [U] the act or method of building or making sth: *A new bridge is now under construction.* ◇ *He works in the construction industry.* ◇ *We had to take a detour because of the road construction in town.* **2** [C] something that has been built or made: *The new pyramid was a construction of glass and steel.* **3** [C] the way that words are used together in a phrase or sentence: *a complex sentence construction* ◇ *Which of these constructions is more common – "to dress" or "to get dressed?"*

**con'struction ,paper** ***noun*** [U] a type of heavy paper that comes in bright colors and that can be cut into shapes to make pictures, designs, etc.

**con'struction site** ***noun*** [C] an area of land where sth is being built

**con·struc·tive** /kən'strʌktɪv/ ***adj.*** useful or helpful: *She made a number of constructive criticisms to help us to improve our work.* ▸ **con·struc·tive·ly** ***adv.***

**con·strue** /kən'stru/ ***verb*** [T] (usually passive) **construe sth (as sth)** (*formal*) to understand the meaning of a word, a sentence, or an action in a particular way: *Her words could hardly be construed as an apology.*

**con·sul** /'kɑnsl/ ***noun*** [C] an official who works in a foreign city helping people from his/her country who are living or visiting there ➲ Look at **ambassador**.

**con·su·late** /'kɑnsələt/ ***noun*** [C] the office of a consul

★**con·sult** /kən'sʌlt/ ***verb*** **1** [T] **consult sb/sth (about sth)** to ask sb or to look sth up in a book, etc. to get information or advice: *You should consult a doctor if the symptoms get worse.* ◇ *He consulted the map to find the shortest route.* **2** [I] **consult with sb** to discuss sth with sb

**con·sult·ant** /kən'sʌltnt/ ***noun*** [C] a person who gives advice to people on business, law, etc.: *a management consultant* ◇ *Diane quit her old job and now works as a computer consultant.*

**con·sul·ta·tion** /ˌkɑnsl'teɪʃn/ ***noun*** **1** [U] discussing sth or looking sth up in a book to get information or advice **2** [C,U] a meeting at which sth is discussed: *Diplomats met for consultations on the hostage crisis.* ◇ *The measures were introduced without consultation.*

**con·sult·ing** /kən'sʌltɪŋ/ ***noun*** [U] giving advice to people on business, computers, etc.: *I'm thinking about a career in computer consulting.*

**con·sume** /kən'sum/ ***verb*** [T] (*written*) **1** to use sth, especially fuel, energy or time: *25 per cent of the world's population consumes 80 per cent of the planet's resources.* **2** to eat or drink sth **3** (used about fire) to completely destroy sth **4** (used about an emotion) to affect sb very strongly: *She was consumed by grief when her son was killed.*

★**con·sum·er** /kən'sumər/ ***noun*** [C] a person who buys things or uses services: *Consumers should complain if they are not satisfied with the service they receive.* ◇ *the rights of the consumer* ◇ *Consumer spending has risen in the past few months.*

**con·sum·ing** /kən'sumɪŋ/ ***adj.*** (only *before* a noun) that takes up a lot of your time and attention: *Music is her consuming passion.* ➲ Look also at **time-consuming**.

**con·sump·tion** /kən'sʌmpʃn/ ***noun*** [U] **1** the act of using, eating, etc. sth: *This fish is unfit for **human consumption*** (= for people to eat). **2** the amount of fuel, etc. that sth uses: *a car with low fuel consumption*

★**con·tact**[1] /'kɑntækt/ ***noun*** **1** [U] the state of touching sb/sth: *Don't let the wires come into contact with each other.* **2** [U] meeting, talking to or writing to sb else: *We are in close contact with our office in Ontario.* ◇ *I've lost contact with most of my old classmates.* ◇ *They are trying to make contact with the kidnappers.* ◇ *Tom has not been in contact since he moved to Minneapolis.* ◇ *Tom broke off contact with his family after an argument.* **3** [C] a person that you know who may be able to help you: *I have some useful business contacts in Canada.* **4** [C] = CONTACT LENS

★**con·tact**[2] /'kɑntækt/ ***verb*** [T] to call, write to, etc. sb: *Is there a phone number where I can contact you?*

**'contact lens** (*also* **contact**) ***noun*** [C] a small piece of plastic that fits onto your eye to help you to see better

**contact lens**

**con·ta·gious** /kən'teɪdʒəs/ ***adj.*** (used about a disease) that you can catch by touching sb/sth: *Smallpox is a contagious disease.* ◇ (*figurative*) *contagious laughter* ➲ Look at **infectious**.

★**con·tain** /kən'teɪn/ ***verb*** [T] **1** to have sth inside (or as part of) itself: *Each box contains 24 cans.* ◇ *food containing fiber* **2** to keep sth within limits: *efforts to contain inflation* ◇ *The kids couldn't contain themselves – they burst out laughing.* ◇ *She found it hard to contain her anger.*

NOTE **Contain** or **include**? **Contain** is used when we are talking about objects which have other things inside them: *a jar containing olives* ◇ *The package contained six books.* **Include** is used to show that several things are part of a whole or thought to belong to something: *The price of the car does not include sales tax.* ◇ *a team of seven people including a cameraman and a doctor*

★**con·tain·er** /kən'teɪnər/ ***noun*** [C] **1** a box, bottle, package, etc. in which sth is kept: *a plastic container* ◇ *a watertight container* **2** a large metal box that is used for transporting goods: *The cargo containers were loaded onto the plane.* ➲ picture on **page 147**.

**contam·i·nate** /kən'tæməneɪt/ ***verb*** [T] to add a substance which will make sth dirty, harmful or dangerous: *The town's drinking water was contaminated with poisonous chemicals.* ▶ **con·tam·i·na·tion** /kənˌtæmə'neɪʃn/ ***noun*** [U]: *There was widespread radioactive contamination after the accident at the nuclear power plant.*

**con·tem·plate** /'kɑntəmpleɪt/ ***verb*** [T] **1** to think about sth or the possibility of doing sth: *The idea was too horrible to contemplate.* ◇ *Before her illness she had never contemplated retiring.* **2** to look at sb/sth, often quietly or for a long time

**con·tem·pla·tion** /ˌkɑntəm'pleɪʃn/ ***noun*** [U] **1** looking at sth quietly **2** thinking deeply about sth

**con·tem·pla·tive** /kən'tɛmplət̬ɪv/ ***adj.*** **1** thinking quietly and seriously about sth: *She was in a contemplative mood.* **2** spending time thinking deeply about religious matters: *the contemplative life* (= life in a religious community)

★**con·tem·po·rar·y**[1] /kən'tɛmpəˌrɛri/ ***adj.*** **1** of the present time; modern: *contemporary music/art* **2** belonging to the same time as sb/sth else: *These letters give us a contemporary account of life in colonial America.*

**con·tem·po·rar·y**[2] /kən'tɛmpəˌrɛri/ ***noun*** [C] (*pl.* **con·tem·po·rar·ies**) a person who lived or did sth at the same time as sb else: *Telemann, a contemporary of Bach*

**con·tempt** /kən'tɛmpt/ ***noun*** [U] **1 contempt (for sb/sth)** the feeling that sb/sth does not deserve to be respected or is unimportant: *They had shown a contempt for the values she thought*

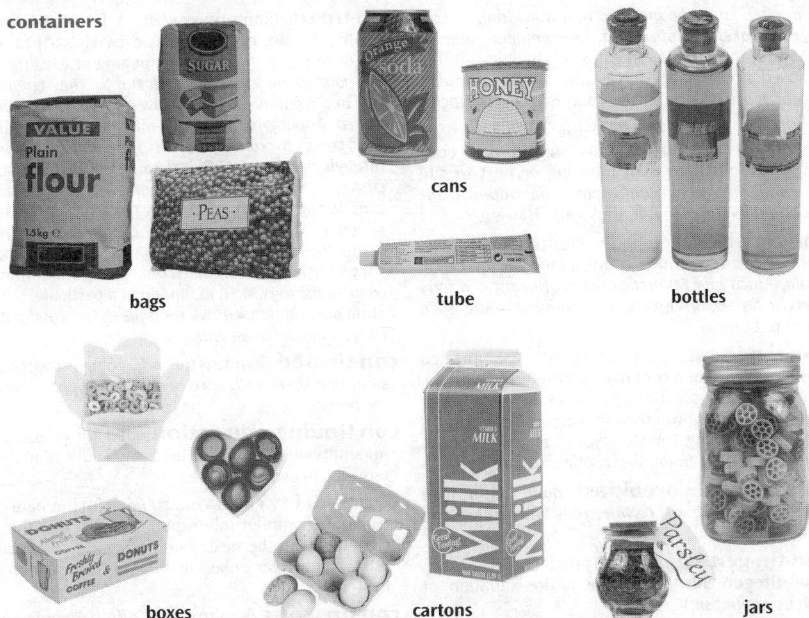


important. **2** = CONTEMPT OF COURT: *She was held **in contempt** for refusing to testify.*

**con,tempt of 'court** (*also* **contempt**) ***noun*** [U] the crime of refusing to obey an order made by a court of law; not showing respect for a court or judge: *Any person who disregards this order will be found in contempt of court.*

**con·temp·tu·ous** /kən'tɛmptʃuəs/ ***adj.*** **contemptuous (of sb/sth)** feeling or showing that you have no respect for sb/sth: *She gave him a contemptuous look.* ◇ *You're contemptuous of everything I do.*

**con·tend** /kən'tɛnd/ ***verb*** **1** [I] **contend with/against sb/sth; contend for sth** to struggle to overcome sth or to win sth: *She's had a lot of problems to contend with.* ◇ *Two athletes are contending for first place.* **2** [T] (*formal*) to declare or argue that sth is true: *He contended that he had never met the murdered girl.*

**con·tend·er** /kən'tɛndər/ ***noun*** [C] a person who takes part in a competition: *There were three contenders for the position.*

★**con·tent**[1] /kən'tɛnt/ ***adj.*** (not before a noun) **content (with sth); content to do sth** satisfied with what you have: *She is perfectly content to stay home and take care of her children.*

**con·tent**[2] /kən'tɛnt/ ***verb*** [T] **content yourself with sth** to accept sth even though it was not exactly what you wanted: *The museum was closed, so we contented ourselves with a walk around the park.*

★**con·tent**[3] /'kɑntɛnt/ ***noun*** **1 contents** [pl.] the thing or things that are inside sth: *Add the contents of this packet to a quart of cold milk and mix well.* ◇ *The table of contents tells you what is inside a book.* **2** [sing.] the main subject, ideas, etc. of a book, article, television program, etc.: *The content of the essay is good, but there are too many grammatical mistakes.* **3** [sing.] the level or amount of a particular substance that sth contains: *Many processed foods have a high sugar content.*

**con·tent·ed** /kən'tɛntəd/ ***adj.*** happy or satisfied: *The baby gave a contented smile.* ▶ **con·tent·ed·ly** ***adv.***: *The cat purred contentedly.*

**con·ten·tion** /kən'tɛnʃn/ ***noun*** **1** [U] the situation of competing for sth: *Four players are still in contention for the championship.* **2** [U] arguing; disagreement **3** [C] your opinion; sth that you declare to be true: *It is our client's contention that the fire was an accident.*

**con·ten·tious** /kən'tɛnʃəs/ ***adj.*** likely to cause argument: *a contentious issue*

**con·tent·ment** /kən'tɛntmənt/ ***noun*** [U] the state of being happy or satisfied: *a sigh of contentment*

★**con·test**[1] /'kɑntɛst/ ***noun*** [C] a competition to find out who is the best, strongest, most beautiful, etc.: *to enter a talent contest* ◇ *The election will be a contest between an unpopular incumbent and an energetic newcomer.*

**con·test**[2] /kən'tɛst/ ***verb*** [T] **1** to say that sth is wrong or that it was not done correctly: *They contested the decision, saying that the judges had not been fair.* **2** to take part in a competition or try to win sth: *a hotly contested championship fight*

**con·tes·tant** /kən'tɛstənt/ ***noun*** [C] a person who takes part in a contest: *Four contestants appear on the game show every day.*

★**con·text** /'kɑntɛkst/ ***noun*** [C,U] **1** the words that come before or after a word, phrase, sentence, etc. and that help you to understand its meaning: *You* *can often guess the meaning of a word from its context.* ◇ *Taken out of context, his comment made no sense.* **2** the situation in which sth happens or that caused sth to happen: *The increase in unemployment must be seen in the context of our changing economy.*

**con·tig·u·ous** /kən'tɪgyuəs/ ***adj.*** (*formal*) **contiguous (with/to sth)** touching or next to sth: *The bruising was not contiguous to the wound.* ◇ *the* ***contiguous states*** (= not Alaska and Hawaii)

★**con·ti·nent** /'kɑntənənt; 'kɑntn·ənt/ ***noun*** [C] one of the seven main areas of land on the Earth: *Asia, Africa and Antarctica are continents.* ◇ *a ferry service linking Britain and the continent* (= the main part of Europe)

**con·ti·nen·tal** /ˌkɑntə'nɛntl/ ***adj.*** **1** connected with or typical of a continent **2** connected with the main part of a CONTINENT (1): *Prices are often higher in Alaska and Hawaii than in the continental United States.* **3** coming from or typical of various European countries: *traditional continental cuisine*

**ˌcontiˌnental 'breakfast** ***noun*** [C] a light breakfast of bread or sweet rolls with coffee and fruit juice

**con·tin·gen·cy** /kən'tɪndʒənsi/ ***noun*** [C] (*pl.* **con·tin·gen·cies**) a possible future situation or event: *contingency plans*

**con·tin·gent¹** /kən'tɪndʒənt/ ***noun*** [C] **1** a group of people at a meeting or event who have sth in common, especially the place they come from, that is not shared by other people at the event: *A strong contingent of local residents was there to block the proposal.* **2** a group of soldiers that are part of a larger force: *the French contingent in the UN peacekeeping force*

**con·tin·gent²** /kən'tɪndʒənt/ ***adj.*** **contingent (on/upon sth)** (*formal*) dependent on sth that may or may not happen: *Any further payments are contingent upon satisfactory completion dates.* ◇ *Students' continued enrollment is contingent on their maintaining a minimum grade point average.*

**con·tin·u·al** /kən'tɪnyuəl/ ***adj.*** happening again and again: *His continual phone calls started to annoy her.* ▸ **con·tin·u·al·ly** ***adv.***: *She continually criticizes his behavior.*

> NOTE **Continual** or **continuous?** We use **continuous** to describe an action or state that goes on without stopping: *There has been a continuous improvement in his work.* ◇ *After climbing continuously for three hours, we were exhausted.* **Continual** is used to describe something that happens repeatedly, especially something that annoys you: *I have had continual problems with my car.*

**con·tin·u·ance** /kən'tɪnyuəns/ ***noun*** **1** [U] (*formal*) the state of continuing to exist or function: *No one is in favor of the continuance of war.* **2** [C] (in law) a decision that a court case should be heard later: *The judge refused his motion for a continuance.*

**con·tin·u·a·tion** /kənˌtɪnyu'eɪʃn/ ***noun*** **1** [sing., U] continuing to do sth without stopping; starting to do sth again after you have stopped **2** [sing.] something that continues sth else or makes it longer: *a continuation of recent trends*

★**con·tin·ue** /kən'tɪnyu/ ***verb*** **1** [I,T] **continue (doing/to do sth)**; **continue (with sth)** to go on, or to make sth go on, happening or existing: *If the pain continues, see your doctor.* ◇ *They ignored me and continued their conversation.* ◇ *He continued working/to work late into the night.* ◇ *Are you going to continue with your music lessons through the summer?* **2** [I,T] to begin to do or say sth again after you had stopped: *The meeting will continue after lunch.* ◇ *I'm sorry I interrupted. Please continue.* ◇ *The next day we continued our trip across the country.* **3** [I,T] to go further or to make sth go further: *We continued along the path until we came to the river.* **4** [I] to remain in a particular situation or condition: *He will continue as principal until the end of the school year.*

**con·tin·ued** /kən'tɪnyud/ ***adj.*** going on without stopping: *There are reports of continued fighting near the border.*

**conˌtinuing edu'cation** ***noun*** [U] education for adults which is outside the formal education system, e.g. in evening classes

**con·ti·nu·i·ty** /ˌkɑntə'nuəṭi/ ***noun*** [U] the state of continuing without interruption; linking one thing smoothly with the next: *Jean has agreed to remain as manager of the project in order to ensure continuity.*

★**con·tin·u·ous** /kən'tɪnyuəs/ ***adj.*** happening or existing without stopping: *a period of continuous economic growth* ◇ *a continuous process* ◇ *There was a continuous line of cars stretching for miles.* ▸ **con·tin·u·ous·ly** ***adv.***: *It has rained continuously here for three days.* ➲ Look at the note at **continual**.

**con'tinuous tense** (*also* **progressive tense**) ***noun*** [C] (*grammar*) the form of a verb such as "I am waiting" or "It was raining" which is made from a part of "be" and a verb ending in "-ing" and is used to describe an action that continues for a period of time

**con·tort** /kən'tɔrt/ ***verb*** [I,T] to move or to make sth move into an unnatural shape: *His face contorted/was contorted with pain.* ▸ **con·tor·tion** /kən'tɔrʃn/ ***noun*** [C]

**con·tour** /'kɑntʊr/ ***noun*** [C] the outline or shape of the outer surface of sth: *I could just make out the contours of the house in the dark.*

**con·tra·band** /'kɑntrəbænd/ ***noun*** [U] goods that are illegally taken into or out of a country: *contraband goods* ◇ *to smuggle contraband*

**con·tra·cep·tion** /ˌkɑntrə'sɛpʃn/ ***noun*** [U] the means of preventing a woman from becoming pregnant: *Your doctor will be happy to advise you about contraception.* ◇ *a reliable form of contraception*

**con·tra·cep·tive** /ˌkɑntrə'sɛptɪv/ ***noun*** [C] a pill or an object that prevents a woman from becoming pregnant: *an oral contraceptive* ▸ **con·tra·cep·tive** ***adj.***: *a contraceptive pill*

★**con·tract¹** /'kɑntrækt/ ***noun*** [C] a written legal agreement: *They signed a three-year contract with a major record company.* ◇ *The company has just won a contract to supply machinery to the government.* ◇ *an employment contract*

★**con·tract²** /kən'trækt/ ***verb*** **1** [I,T] to become or to make sth smaller or shorter: *"I'm" is the* *contracted form of "I am."* ◇ *Metals contract as they cool.* OPP **expand 2** [T] to get an illness or a disease: *She contracted pneumonia.*

**con·tract**[3] /'kɑntrækt/ ***verb*** [I,T] to make a written legal agreement with sb to do sth or to have sb work for you: *His company has been contracted by the government to produce military uniforms.*

**con·trac·tion** /kən'trækʃn/ ***noun*** **1** [U] the process of getting smaller or of making sth smaller **2** [C] a contracted form of a word or words: *"Mustn't" is a contraction of "must not."* **3** [C] a strong tightening of muscles that happens to a woman as her baby is born

**con·trac·tor** /'kɑntræktər; kən'træktər/ ***noun*** [C] a person or company that does work, especially building work, by CONTRACT[1]: *The general contractor is in charge of hiring people to remodel our house.*

**con·trac·tu·al** /kən'træktʃuəl/ ***adj.*** connected with or included in a CONTRACT[1]

**con·tra·dict** /ˌkɑntrə'dɪkt/ ***verb*** **1** [I,T] to say that sth is wrong or untrue; to say the opposite of sth: *I didn't dare contradict him, but I think he was wrong.* **2** [T] (used about a statement, fact, etc.) to be different from or opposite to sth: *These instructions seem to contradict previous ones.*

**con·tra·dic·tion** /ˌkɑntrə'dɪkʃn/ ***noun*** **1** [C] a statement or fact that is opposite to or different from another: *There were a number of contradictions in what he told the police.* **2** [C,U] **(a) contradiction (between A and B)** the fact of two things being opposite to or not matching each other: *There is a contradiction between his public and private personalities.* ◇ *This letter is in complete contradiction to their previous one.*

**con·tra·dic·to·ry** /ˌkɑntrə'dɪktəri/ ***adj.*** being opposite to or not matching sth else: *Contradictory reports appeared in the newspapers.*

**con·trap·tion** /kən'træpʃn/ ***noun*** [C] a strange or complicated piece of equipment

**con·trar·y**[1] /'kɑnˌtrɛri/ ***adj.*** **contrary to sth** completely different from sth; opposite to sth; against sth: *He's really very nice, contrary to what people say about him.*

**con·trar·y**[2] /'kɑnˌtrɛri/ ***noun***

IDM **on the contrary** the opposite is true; certainly not: *"You look as if you're not enjoying yourself." "On the contrary, I'm having a great time."*

**to the contrary** saying the opposite: *Unless I hear anything to the contrary, I will assume that the arrangements haven't changed.*

★**con·trast**[1] /kən'træst/ ***verb*** **1** [T] **contrast (A and/with B)** to compare people or things in order to show the differences between them: *It's interesting to contrast the various styles of architecture here.* ◇ *The book contrasts his poor childhood with his later life as a millionaire.* **2** [I] **contrast with sb/sth** to be clearly different when compared: *The red cushions contrast dramatically with the black sofa.* ◇ *This comment contrasts sharply with his previous remarks.*

★**con·trast**[2] /'kɑntræst/ ***noun*** **contrast (to/with sb/sth); contrast (between A and B) 1** [U] comparison between two people or things that shows the differences between them: *In contrast to previous years, we've had a very successful summer.* ◇ *He was friendly and talkative; she, by contrast, said nothing.* **2** [C,U] a clear difference between two things or people that is seen when they are compared: *There is a tremendous contrast between the climate in the valley and the climate in the hills.* **3** [C] something that is clearly different from sth else when the two things are compared: *This house is a real contrast to your old one!*

★**con·trib·ute** /kən'trɪbyut/ ***verb*** **1** [I,T] to give a part of the total, together with others: *Would you like to contribute toward our collection for famine relief?* ◇ *He didn't contribute anything to the conversation.* ◇ *We contributed $5 each toward a retirement present for her.* **2** [I] to help to produce sth; to play a part in sth: *Every member of the team contributed to the victory.* **3** [I,T] to write articles for a magazine or newspaper

★**con·tri·bu·tion** /ˌkɑntrə'byuʃn/ ***noun*** [C,U] something that you give or do together with others; the act of giving your share: *All contributions to the fund are tax-deductible.* ◇ *He made a significant contribution to the country's struggle for independence.*

**con·trib·u·tor** /kən'trɪbyət̬ər/ ***noun*** [C] a person who contributes to sth

**con·trib·u·to·ry** /kən'trɪbyəˌtɔri/ ***adj.*** helping to cause or produce sth: *a contributory factor*

**con·trived** /kən'traɪvd/ ***adj.*** clearly artificial or invented, not natural: *The ending of the movie seemed pretty contrived.*

★**con·trol**[1] /kən'troʊl/ ***noun*** **1** [U] **control (of/over sb/sth)** power over sth; the ability to organize, direct or guide sb/sth: *Students took control of the president's office.* ◇ *He lost control of the car and crashed.* ◇ *There's nothing I can do about the problem – it's outside my control.* ◇ *I was late because of circumstances beyond my control.* **2** [C,U] **(a) control (on/over sth)** a limit on sth; a way of keeping sb/sth within certain limits: *price controls* ◇ *crowd control* **3** [C] one of the parts of a machine that is used for operating it: *the controls of an airplane* **4** [sing.] the place from which sth is operated or where sth is checked: *We went through passport control and then got onto the plane.*

IDM **be in control (of sth)** to be in command of sth; to have the power or ability to deal with sth: *Who is in control of the project?*

**be/get out of control** to be/become impossible to deal with or guide: *The demonstration got out of control and fighting broke out.*

**under control** being dealt with, directed or run successfully: *It took several hours to bring the fire under control.* ◇ *She finds it difficult to keep her feelings under control.*

★**con·trol**[2] /kən'troʊl/ ***verb*** [T] (**con·trol<u>l</u>ing**; **con·trol<u>l</u>ed**) **1** to have power over sb/sth or the ability to organize, direct or guide sb/sth: *One family controls the company.* ◇ *Police struggled to control the crowd.* ◇ *I couldn't control myself any longer and burst out laughing.* **2** to keep sth within certain limits: *measures to control inflation*

**con'trol freak** ***noun*** [C] (*informal*) a person who always wants to be in control of his/her own and others' lives, and to organize how things are done

C

**con,trolled 'substance** *noun* [C] (*technical*) an illegal drug: *to be arrested for possession of a controlled substance*

**con·trol·ler** /kən'troʊlər/ *noun* [C] a person who directs sth ➲ Look at **air traffic controller**.

**con'trol ,tower** *noun* [C] a building at an airport from which the movements of aircraft are controlled

**con·tro·ver·sial** /,kɑntrə'vərʃl/ *adj.* causing public discussion and disagreement: *a controversial TV program* ◇ *a controversial new law*

**con·tro·ver·sy** /'kɑntrəvərsi/ *noun* [C,U] (*pl.* **con·tro·ver·sies**) public discussion and disagreement about sth: *The plans to build a nuclear power plant caused a great deal of controversy.*

**con·va·lesce** /,kɑnvə'lɛs/ *verb* [I] to spend time getting your health and strength back after an illness: *She is convalescing at home after her operation.* ▸ **con·va·les·cence** /'lɛsns/ *noun* [sing., U]

**con·va·les·cent** /,kɑnvə'lɛsnt/ *adj.* connected with resting and getting better over a period of time after an illness: *a convalescent home*

**con·vene** /kən'vin/ *verb* [I,T] to come together or to bring people together for a meeting, etc.

**con·ven·ience** /kən'vinyəns/ *noun* **1** [U] the quality of being suitable or practical for a particular purpose: *For your convenience, we offer a free delivery service.* **2** [C, usually pl.] a piece of equipment or a service that is useful and that makes life easier: *All apartments are equipped with modern conveniences such as dishwashers and cable TV.*

**con'venience food** *noun* [C,U] food that you buy ready to eat or which needs very little preparation

**con'venience store** *noun* [C] a store that sells food, magazines and other small items, and stays open longer than other stores

★**con·ven·ient** /kən'vinyənt/ *adj.* **1** suitable or practical for a particular purpose; not causing difficulty: *I'm willing to meet you on any day that's convenient for you.* ◇ *It isn't convenient to talk right now – I'm in the middle of a meeting.* **2** close to sth; in a useful position: *a parking garage convenient to the downtown shopping area* OPP **inconvenient** ▸ **con·ven·ient·ly** *adv.*: *She had conveniently forgotten that she owed me some money.* ◇ *Our offices are conveniently located near two major freeways.*

**con·vent** /'kɑnvɛnt; -vənt/ *noun* [C] a place where women (**nuns**) live in a religious community ➲ Look at **monastery**.

★**con·ven·tion** /kən'vɛnʃn/ *noun* **1** [C] a large meeting or conference: *Dr. Kwan is giving a speech at the association's annual convention.* ◇ *the Democratic Party Convention* ◇ *a convention center* (= a large building where conventions are held) **2** [C,U] a traditional way of behaving or of doing sth: *A speech by the best man is one of the conventions of a wedding.* ◇ *By convention, the top two students give speeches at the graduation ceremony.* **3** [C] a formal agreement, especially between nations: *the Geneva Convention*

★**con·ven·tion·al** /kən'vɛnʃənl/ *adj.* following what is traditional or considered to be normal, sometimes too closely: *conventional attitudes* ◇ *The house was built with conventional materials but in a totally new style.* ◇ *I like him, but he's so conventional* (= boring, because of this). OPP **unconventional** ▸ **con·ven·tion·al·ly** /-ʃənəli/ *adv.*: *He always dresses conventionally.*

**con·verge** /kən'vərdʒ/ *verb* [I] **converge (on sb/sth)** to move toward or meet at the same point from different directions: *People from the whole area converge on the town during the annual festival.* ◇ *The paths converge at the bottom of the hill.*

★**con·ver·sa·tion** /,kɑnvər'seɪʃn/ *noun* [C,U] informal talk: *I had a long conversation with her about her plans for the future.* ◇ *His job is his only topic of conversation.* ◇ *They sat in the corner, deep in conversation.* ◇ *She finds it difficult to make conversation* (= to think of things to say).

**con·ver·sa·tion·al** /,kɑnvər'seɪʃənl/ *adj.* **1** not formal; as used in conversation: *a casual and conversational tone* ◇ *I learned conversational Spanish in evening classes.* SYN **colloquial** **2** (only before a noun) connected with conversation: *Men have a more direct conversational style.* ▸ **con·ver·sa·tion·al·ly** *adv.*: *"Have you been here long?" he asked conversationally.*

**con·verse** /kən'vərs/ *verb* [I] (*formal*) to talk informally; to have a conversation

**con·ver·sion** /kən'vərʒn; -ʃn/ *noun* **(a) conversion (from sth) (into/to sth)** **1** [C,U] (a) change from one form, system or use to another: *a conversion table for miles and kilometers* **2** [C,U] becoming a member of a new religion: *conversion to Catholicism*

★**con·vert**[1] /kən'vərt/ *verb* [I,T] **1** **convert (sth) (from sth) (into/to sth)** to change from one form, system or use to another: *a sofa that converts into a double bed* ◇ *How do you convert pounds into kilograms?* ◇ *They're converting the warehouse into an apartment building.* **2** **convert (sb) (from sth) (to sth)** to change to, or persuade sb to change to a new religion: *As a young man, he converted to Islam.* ◇ *to convert people to Christianity*

**con·vert**[2] /'kɑnvərt/ *noun* [C] **a convert (to sth)** a person who has been persuaded to become a member of a particular religion

**con·vert·i·ble**[1] /kən'vərṭəbl/ *adj.* able to be changed into another form: *convertible currencies* (= those that can be exchanged for other currencies)

**con·vert·i·ble**[2] /kən'vərṭəbl/ *noun* [C] a car with a roof that can be folded down or taken off

**con·vex** /'kɑnvɛks/ *adj.* having a surface that curves outward: *a convex lens* OPP **concave**

**con·vey** /kən'veɪ/ *verb* [T] **convey sth (to sb)** to make ideas, thoughts, feelings, etc. known to sb; to communicate sth: *The video conveys a lot of information, but in a fun way.* ◇ *The President tried to convey a message of hope in his speech.*

**conveyor belt** /kən'veɪər bɛlt/ *noun* [C] a continuous moving belt that carries objects from one place to another, e.g. in a factory

**con·vict**[1] /kən'vɪkt/ *verb* [T] **convict sb (of sth)** to declare in a court of law that sb is guilty of a crime: *He was convicted of armed robbery and sent to prison.* ◇ *a convicted criminal* OPP **acquit**

**con·vict²** /ˈkɑnvɪkt/ (*formal*) ***noun*** [C] a person who has been found guilty of a crime and put in prison

**con·vic·tion** /kənˈvɪkʃn/ ***noun*** **1** [C,U] an occasion when sb is found guilty of a crime in a court of law; the act of finding sb guilty in this way: *He has several previous convictions for burglary.* **2** [C] a very strong opinion or belief: *religious convictions* **3** [U] being certain and able to convince others about what you are doing: *He played without conviction and lost easily.*

★**con·vince** /kənˈvɪns/ ***verb*** [T] **1** **convince sb (of sth/that...)** to succeed in making sb believe sth: *She convinced him of the need to go back.* ◇ *I couldn't convince her that I was right.* **2** **convince sb (to do sth)** to persuade sb to do sth: *The salesman convinced them to buy it.*

**con·vinced** /kənˈvɪnst/ ***adj.*** completely sure about sth: *He's convinced of his ability to win.* ◇ *I'm convinced that she said it, but she denies it.*

**con·vinc·ing** /kənˈvɪnsɪŋ/ ***adj.*** **1** able to make sb believe sth: *Her explanation for her absence wasn't very convincing.* **2** (used about a victory) complete; clear: *a convincing win* ▶ **con·vinc·ing·ly** ***adv.***: *She argued convincingly that the law should be changed.* ◇ *He won the race convincingly.*

**con·voy** /ˈkɑnvɔɪ/ ***noun*** [C] a group of vehicles or ships traveling together: *a convoy of trucks*

**con·vul·sion** /kənˈvʌlʃn/ ***noun*** [C, usually pl.] a sudden violent movement of the body that you cannot control: *Children sometimes have convulsions when their temperature goes up.*

**coo** /ku/ ***verb*** [I] **1** to make the sound that a dove or pigeon makes **2** to speak in a soft, gentle voice: *He went to the crib and cooed over the baby.*

★**cook¹** /kʊk/ ***verb*** **1** [I,T] to prepare food for eating by heating it: *My mother taught me how to cook.* ◇ *He cooked us a meal.* **2** [I] (used about food) to be prepared for eating by being heated: *I could smell something cooking in the kitchen.*

NOTE Food can be cooked in various ways: by **boiling** in a pan of hot water; by **frying** in a frying pan with hot oil or fat; or by **broiling** under a broiler, which heats the food from above. We can **toast** bread in a toaster to make it crisp and brown. Cakes and bread are **baked** in the oven, but we use the word **roast** for cooking meat or potatoes in the oven.

PHR V **cook sth up** (*informal*) to invent sth that is not true: *She cooked up an excuse for not arriving on time.*

★**cook²** /kʊk/ ***noun*** [C] a person who cooks: *My sister is an excellent cook.* ◇ *He works as a cook in a hotel restaurant.*

**cook·book** /ˈkʊkbʊk/ ***noun*** [C] a book of recipes and instructions for cooking

★**cook·ie** /ˈkʊki/ ***noun*** [C] (*pl.* **cook·ies**) **1** a type of cake that is thin, hard and sweet: *chocolate chip cookies* **2** (*informal*) a person: *She's a smart/tough cookie.* **3** (*computing*) a computer file with information in it that is sent to the central computer (server) each time a person uses a NETWORK (4) or the Internet

IDM **that's the way the cookie crumbles** (*informal*) that is the situation and we cannot change it, so we must accept it

**ˈcookie sheet** ***noun*** [C] a flat metal tray used for baking food on

**cook·ing** /ˈkʊkɪŋ/ ***noun*** [U] **1** the preparation of food for eating: *Cooking is one of her hobbies.* ◇ *a Chinese cooking class*

NOTE A common way of talking about the activity of preparing food is **do the cooking**: *In our house, I do the cleaning and my husband does the cooking.*

**2** food produced by cooking: *He missed his mother's cooking when he left home.*

**cook·out** /ˈkʊkaʊt/ ***noun*** [C] an event where food is cooked and eaten outdoors: *We have a lot of cookouts in our back yard during the summer months.*

★**cool¹** /kul/ ***adj.*** **1** fairly cold; not hot or warm: *It was a cool evening, so I put on a sweater.* ◇ *This product should be stored in a cool place.* ◇ *What I'd like is a nice cool drink.* ➲ Look at the note at **cold.** **2** (*informal*) very good; excellent: *What a cool car!* ◇ *"There's a party at Dave's tonight." "Cool!"* **3** calm; not excited or affected by strong emotions: *She always manages to remain cool under pressure.* **4** unfriendly; not showing interest: *When we first met, she was fairly cool toward me, but later she became friendlier.* **5** (*informal*) fashionable; popular: *A lot of kids think that smoking makes them look cool.* **6** (*informal*) (used to say that sth is acceptable and not a problem for you): *"Can you come at 10:30 tomorrow?" "That's cool."* ◇ *I was surprised she got promoted, but I'm cool with it.* ▶ **cool·ness** ***noun*** [U]

★**cool²** /kul/ ***noun*** [sing.]

IDM **keep/lose your cool** to remain calm/to stop being calm and become angry, nervous, etc.

★**cool³** /kul/ ***verb*** **1** [I,T] **cool (sth/sb) (down/off)** to lower the temperature of sth/sb; to become COOL¹ (1): *Let the soup cool (down).* ◇ *After the game we needed to cool off.* ◇ *A nice cold drink will cool you right down.* **2** [I] (used about feelings) to become less strong: *It took a long time for tensions to cool after the riot.*

IDM **Cool it!** (*informal*) be calm: *Cool it, you guys! There's no reason to fight about this.*

PHR V **cool (sb) down/off** to become or make sb calmer

**cool·er** /ˈkulər/ ***noun*** [C] **1** a box with ice in it that is used for keeping food or drinks cool: *We need three coolers to hold all the drinks for the picnic.* **2** a drink with ice and usually wine in it: *a wine cooler*

**cool·ly** /ˈkulli/ ***adv.*** in a calm way; without showing much interest or excitement: *At first she was very angry; then she explained the problem coolly.* ◇ *Employees reacted coolly to the company's proposal.*

**coop** /kup/ ***verb***

PHR V **coop sb/sth up (in sth)** to keep sb/sth inside a small space: *The kids were cooped up indoors all day because the weather was so bad.*

**co·op·er·ate** /koʊˈɑpəreɪt/ ***verb*** [I] **1** to work with sb else to achieve sth: *Our company is cooperating with a Mexican firm on this project.* **2** to be helpful by doing what sb asks you to do: *If everyone cooperates by following the instructions, there will be*

C

*no problem.* ◇ *to cooperate with an investigation* (e.g. by giving information to the police)

**co·op·er·a·tion** /koʊˌɑpəˈreɪʃn/ ***noun*** [U] **1 co-operation (with sb)** working together with sb else to achieve sth: *international cooperation to protect the ozone layer* ◇ *This device was developed in co-operation with a Korean company.* **2** willingness to be helpful by doing what sb asks you to do: *The police asked the public for their cooperation in the investigation.*

**co·op·er·a·tive¹** /koʊˈɑprət̬ɪv/ ***adj.*** **1** done by people working together: *a cooperative business venture* **2** helpful; doing what sb asks you to do: *My boss was very cooperative and let me take some time off.* OPP **uncooperative**

**co·op·er·a·tive²** /koʊˈɑprət̬ɪv/ ***noun*** [C] a business or organization that is owned and run by all of the people who work for it: *an agricultural cooperative*

**co·or·di·nate¹** /koʊˈɔrdənət/ ***noun*** [C] one of the two sets of numbers and/or letters that are used for finding the position of a point on a map

**co·or·di·nate²** /koʊˈɔrdəneɪt/ ***verb*** [T] to organize different things or people so that they work together efficiently: *It is her job to coordinate the various departments.*

**co·or·di·na·tion** /koʊˌɔrdəˈneɪʃn/ ***noun*** [U] **1** the organization of different things or people so that they work together efficiently **2** the ability to control the movements of your body properly: *You need good hand-eye coordination to play badminton well.*

**co·or·di·na·tor** /koʊˈɔrdəneɪt̬ər/ ***noun*** [C] a person who is responsible for organizing different things or people so that they work together efficiently: *a project coordinator*

★**cop¹** /kɑp/ ***noun*** [C] (*informal*) a police officer

**cop²** /kɑp/ ***verb*** (**cop·ping**; **copped**) (*informal*)
PHRV **cop out (of sth)** to avoid sth that you should do, because you are afraid or lazy: *You guys promised you'd help me – you can't cop out now!*

**cope** /koʊp/ ***verb*** [I] **cope (with sb/sth)** to deal successfully with a difficult matter or situation: *She sometimes finds it difficult to cope with all the pressure at work.*

★**cop·i·er** /ˈkɑpiər/ ***noun*** [C] (*also* ˈ**copy maˌchine**, *formal* ˈ**photocopier**) a machine that makes copies of documents on paper

ˈ**cop-out** (*also* **copout**) ***noun*** [C] (*informal*) a way of avoiding sth that you should do: *Using temporary workers is just a cop-out – the company ought to hire more qualified personnel.*

**cop·per** /ˈkɑpər/ ***noun*** [U] (*symbol* **Cu**) a common reddish-brown metal: *water pipes made of copper* ◇ *copper wire*

**cop·u·late** /ˈkɑpyəleɪt/ ***verb*** [I] (*formal*) (used especially about animals) to have sex ▶ **cop·u·la·tion** /ˌkɑpyəˈleɪʃn/ ***noun*** [U]

★**cop·y¹** /ˈkɑpi/ ***noun*** [C] (*pl.* **cop·ies**) **1** something that is made to look exactly like sth else: *The painting isn't an original, of course – it's only a copy.* ◇ *to make a copy of a computer file* **2** (*also formal* **photocopy**) a piece of paper that looks exactly like another piece of paper, page in a book, etc. and that is made by a special machine (a **copier**) that can photograph sth quickly: *Can you make 20 copies of this for me?* **3** a book, newspaper, record, etc. of which many have been printed or produced: *I managed to buy the last copy of the book left in the store.*

★**cop·y²** /ˈkɑpi/ ***verb*** (*pres. part.* **cop·y·ing**; *3rd person sing. pres.* **cop·ies**; *pt, pp* **cop·ied**) **1** [T] **copy sth (down/out)** to write down sth exactly as it is written somewhere else: *The students copied what was written on the board.* ◇ *I copied down the address on the brochure.* ◇ *I copied out the letter more neatly.* **2** [T] to make a copy of a video, computer information, etc.: *It is illegal to copy videos.* **3** (*also formal* **photocopy**) [T] to make a copy of a piece of paper, page in a book, etc., using a special machine (a **copier**) **4** [T] to do or try to do the same as sb else; to imitate sb/sth: *She copies everything her friends do.* **5** [I] **copy (from sb)** to cheat by writing what sb else has written: *He was caught copying from his neighbor during the test.*

**cop·y·cat¹** /ˈkɑpikæt/ ***noun*** [C] (*informal*) (used especially by children about and to a person who copies what sb else does because he/she has no ideas of his/her own)

**cop·y·cat²** /ˈkɑpikæt/ ***adj.*** (only *before* a noun) (used especially about crimes) similar to and seen as copying an earlier well-known crime, etc.: *The copycat phenomenon is a danger to which the media may be contributing.*

ˈ**copy machine** ***noun*** [C] = COPIER

**cop·y·right** /ˈkɑpiraɪt/ ***noun*** [C,U] the legal right to be the only person who may print, copy, perform, etc. a piece of original work, such as a book, a song or a computer program

**cor·al** /ˈkɔrəl; ˈkɑrəl/ ***noun*** [U] a hard red, pink or white substance formed from the bones of very small sea animals, often used for making jewelry: *a coral reef* (= a line of rock in the ocean formed by coral) ◇ *a coral necklace*

**cord** /kɔrd/ ***noun*** **1** [C,U] (a piece of) strong, thick string **2** [C,U] electric wire inside a plastic tube, used for carrying electricity to electrical equipment

> NOTE At the end of a cord there is a **plug** which you put into an **outlet**.

**cor·dial** /ˈkɔrdʒəl/ ***adj.*** (*formal*) friendly: *a cordial greeting* ◇ *a cordial meeting* ▶ **cor·dial·ly** /ˈkɔrdʒəli/ ***adv.***

**cord·less** /ˈkɔrdləs/ ***adj.*** without a CORD (2): *a cordless phone*

**cor·don¹** /ˈkɔrdn/ ***noun*** [C] a line or ring of police or soldiers that prevents people from entering or leaving an area

**cor·don²** /ˈkɔrdn/ ***verb***
PHRV **cordon sth off** to close an area by surrounding it with a ring of police or soldiers: *The street where the shooting happened was quickly cordoned off.*

**cor·du·roy** /ˈkɔrdərɔɪ/ ***noun*** [U] a thick soft cotton cloth with raised lines on it, used for making clothes: *a corduroy jacket*

★**core** /kɔr/ ***noun*** **1** [C] the hard center of certain fruits, containing seeds: *an apple core* **2** [sing.] the

central or most important part of sth: *Our core business is installing computer systems, but we also offer computer training.* ◇ *the core vocabulary of a language* (= the most common and important words) **3** [C] the central part of a planet: *the earth's core*
IDM **to the core** completely; in every way: *The system is rotten to the core* (= bad in every part).

**co·ri·an·der** /ˈkɔriændər; ˌkɔriˈæn-/ (*also* **ci·lan·tro**) *noun* [U] a plant whose leaves and seeds are used in cooking ➲ picture on study page **A28**.

**cork** /kɔrk/ *noun* **1** [U] a light but tough substance which comes from the outside of a type of tree. It floats on water. **2** [C] a round piece of CORK (1) that you push into the end of a bottle to close it, especially a bottle of wine

**cork·screw** /ˈkɔrkskru/ *noun* [C] a tool that you use for pulling CORKS (2) out of bottles ➲ picture at **kitchen**.

**corn** /kɔrn/ *noun* **1** [U] a tall plant that produces yellow grains (**kernels**) in a large mass (**an ear**) which can be eaten as a vegetable: *corn on the cob* (= that has been cooked with the kernels still attached to the cob) **2** [C] a small, painful area of hard skin on the toe

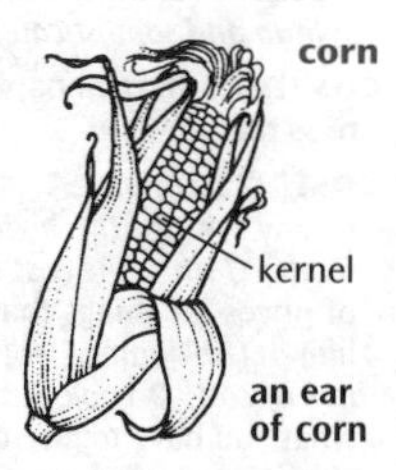


**corn·bread** /ˈkɔrnbrɛd/ *noun* [U] a kind of flat bread made with cornmeal

★**cor·ner¹** /ˈkɔrnər/ *noun* [C] **1** a place where two lines, edges, surfaces or roads meet: *in a corner of the room* ◇ *Write your address in the upper right-hand corner.* ◇ *The office is on the corner of Fifth Avenue and 35th Street.* ◇ *There's a mailbox around the corner on Walnut Street.* **2** a quiet or secret place or area: *a remote corner of Alaska* **3** a difficult situation which you cannot escape from: *to get yourself into a corner*
IDM **cut corners** → CUT¹
**(just) around the corner** (used about an event or a date) very near: *Dad's birthday is just around the corner – have you bought him a present yet?*

**corner**

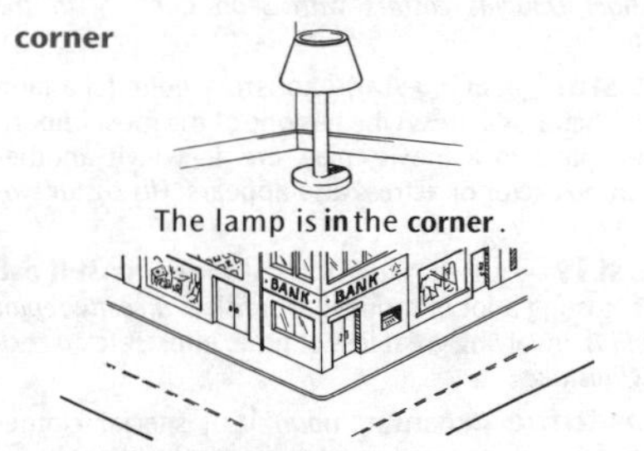

The lamp is **in** the **corner**.
The bank is **on** the **corner**.

**cor·ner²** /ˈkɔrnər/ *verb* [T] to get a person or an animal into a position from which it is difficult or impossible to escape: *He cornered me at the party and started telling me about his problems.*
IDM **corner the market (on sth)** to get control in some area of business so that there is no room for anybody else to have any success: *We hope to corner the market on healthy snacks.*

**corn·flakes** /ˈkɔrnfleɪks/ *noun* [pl.] food made of small pieces of dried corn and eaten with milk for breakfast: *a bowl of cornflakes*

**corn·meal** /ˈkɔrnmil/ *noun* [U] a kind of flour made from pieces of corn which have been crushed

**corn·starch** /ˈkɔrnstɑrtʃ/ *noun* [U] fine white powder made from corn, used especially for making sauces thicker

**corn·y** /ˈkɔrni/ *adj.* (**corn·i·er**; **corn·i·est**) (*informal*) too ordinary or familiar to be interesting or amusing: *a corny joke*

**cor·o·nar·y** /ˈkɔrənɛri/ *adj.* connected with the heart: *coronary artery disease*

**cor·o·na·tion** /ˌkɔrəˈneɪʃn/ *noun* [C] a ceremony at which sb becomes a king or queen

**cor·o·ner** /ˈkɔrənər/ *noun* [C] an official whose job is to find out the causes of death of people who have died in violent or unusual ways

**corp.** *abbr.* = CORPORATION

**cor·po·ral** /ˈkɔrpərəl/ *noun* [C] **1** (in the U.S.) a person of low rank in the Army or Marine Corps **2** (in Canada) a person of low rank in the Canadian Army or Air Force

**ˌcorporal ˈpunishment** *noun* [U] the punishment of people by hitting them, especially the punishment of children by parents or teachers

★**cor·po·rate** /ˈkɔrpərət/ *adj.* connected with a large company: *corporate responsibility*

**cor·po·ra·tion** /ˌkɔrpəˈreɪʃn/ *noun* [C] (*abbr.* **corp.**) a large business company: *multinational corporations* ➲ Look also at **incorporated**.

**corps** /kɔr/ *noun* [C] (*pl.* **corps** /kɔrz/) **1** a part of an army with special duties: *the medical corps* ➲ Look also at **Marine Corps**. **2** a group of people involved in a special activity: *the press corps* ➲ Look also at **Peace Corps**.

**corpse** /kɔrps/ *noun* [C] a dead body, especially of a person

**cor·ral** /kəˈræl/ *noun* [C] a piece of land with a fence around it where people keep cows, horses, etc. on a farm

★**cor·rect¹** /kəˈrɛkt/ *adj.* **1** with no mistakes; right or true: *Good job! All your answers were correct.* ◇ *Be sure you put the correct address on the envelope.* **2** (used about behavior, manners, dress, etc.) suitable according to normal customs and ideas: *What's the correct form of address for a priest?* OPP **incorrect** ➲ Look also at **politically correct**. ▸ **cor·rect·ly** *adv.* ▸ **cor·rect·ness** *noun* [U]

★**cor·rect²** /kəˈrɛkt/ *verb* [T] **1** to make a mistake, fault, etc. right or better: *to correct a spelling mistake* ◇ *to correct a test* (= to mark the mistakes in it) **2** to point out the mistakes or faults of sb: *He's always correcting me when I say something wrong.*

**cor·rec·tion** /kəˈrɛkʃn/ *noun* [C,U] (an act of) making sth right or changing sth: *Make your corrections in red ink.* ◇ *Some parts of the report needed correction.*

**corˈrection ˌfluid** *noun* [U] a white liquid that you use to cover mistakes that you make when you

C

are writing or typing, and that you can write on top of

**cor·rec·tive** /kəˈrɛktɪv/ ***adj.*** intended to put right sth that is wrong: *to take corrective action*

**cor·re·la·tion** /ˌkɔrəˈleɪʃn; ˌkɑr-/ ***noun*** [C,U] a relationship or connection: *a correlation between salt intake and high blood pressure*

**cor·re·spond** /ˌkɔrəˈspɑnd; ˌkɑr-/ ***verb*** [I] **1 correspond (to/with sth)** to be the same as sth; to match sth: *Does the name on the envelope correspond with the name inside the letter?* **2 correspond (to sth)** to be similar or equal (to sth): *Canadian provinces correspond to American states.* **3 correspond (with sb)** to write letters to and receive them from sb: *They corresponded for a year while he was in prison.*

**cor·re·spon·dence** /ˌkɔrəˈspɑndəns; ˌkɑr-/ ***noun*** **1** [U] the act of writing letters; the letters that sb writes: *Please address all correspondence to the editor.* **2** [C,U] a close connection or relationship: *There is no correspondence between the two sets of figures.*

**cor·res·pon·dent** /ˌkɔrəˈspɑndənt; ˌkɑr-/ ***noun*** [C] **1** a person who provides news or writes articles for a newspaper, etc.: *our Middle East correspondent, Andy Jenkins* **2** (*formal*) a person who writes letters

**cor·re·spond·ing** /ˌkɔrəˈspɑndɪŋ; ˌkɑr-/ ***adj.*** (only *before* a noun) related or similar: *Sales are up 10% compared with the corresponding period last year.* ▸ **cor·re·spond·ing·ly** ***adv.***

**cor·ri·dor** /ˈkɔrədɔr; -dər; ˈkɑr-/ ***noun*** [C] a long narrow passage in a building, with doors that open into rooms, etc.: *to walk along a corridor*

**cor·rob·o·rate** /kəˈrɑbəreɪt/ ***verb*** [T] (*formal*) to support a statement, idea, etc. by providing new evidence: *The witness corroborated her statement about the night of the murder.* ▸ **cor·rob·o·ra·tion** /kəˌrɑbəˈreɪʃn/ ***noun*** [U]

**cor·rode** /kəˈroʊd/ ***verb*** [I,T] (used about metals) to become weak or to be destroyed by chemical action; to cause a metal to do this: *Parts of the car were corroded by rust.* ▸ **cor·ro·sive** /kəˈroʊsɪv/ ***adj.***

**cor·ro·sion** /kəˈroʊʒn/ ***noun*** [U] the process of being destroyed by chemical action; the damage caused when sth is corroded

**cor·ru·gat·ed** /ˈkɔrəgeɪt̬əd; ˈkɑr-/ ***adj.*** (used about metal or cardboard) shaped into folds; not smooth and flat: *corrugated iron*

**cor·rupt**[1] /kəˈrʌpt/ ***adj.*** **1** not honest, moral or legal: *corrupt business practices* ◇ *corrupt politicians who accept bribes* **2** (*computing*) containing changes or faults, and no longer in the original state: *corrupt software* ◇ *The text on the disk seems to be corrupt.*

**cor·rupt**[2] /kəˈrʌpt/ ***verb*** [I,T] **1** to cause sb/sth to become dishonest or to have lower moral standards: *Does television corrupt the minds of young people?* **2** (*computing*) to cause mistakes to appear in a computer file, etc. with the result that the information in it is no longer correct: *The program has somehow corrupted the system files.* ◇ *The disk will corrupt if it is overloaded.*

**cor·rup·tion** /kəˈrʌpʃn/ ***noun*** [U] behavior that is not honest or legal, especially by people in official positions: *accusations of corruption among senior police officers*

**cos·met·ic**[1] /kɑzˈmɛt̬ɪk/ ***noun*** [C] a substance that you put on your face or hair to make yourself look more attractive: *I only use cosmetics that are not tested on animals.*

**cos·met·ic**[2] /kɑzˈmɛt̬ɪk/ ***adj.*** **1** used or done in order to improve your appearance: *cosmetic products/surgery* **2** done in order to improve only the appearance of sth, without changing it in any other way: *changes in government policies which are purely cosmetic*

**cos·mic** /ˈkɑzmɪk/ ***adj.*** of the whole universe

**cos·mo·pol·i·tan** /ˌkɑzməˈpɑlətn/ ***adj.*** **1** containing people from all over the world: *a cosmopolitan city* **2** having, or influenced by, wide experience of other countries and cultures: *a cosmopolitan and sophisticated young woman*

**cos·mos** /ˈkɑzmoʊs; -məs/ ***noun*** [sing.] **the cosmos** the universe

★**cost**[1] /kɔst/ ***noun*** **1** [C,U] the money that you have to pay for sth: *the high cost of insurance after September 11th* ◇ *the* ***cost of living*** (= the general level of prices for things that you need to live a normal life) ◇ *The damage will have to be repaired, regardless of cost.* ➲ Look at the note at **price**. **2** [sing., U] what you have to give or lose in order to obtain sth else: *He achieved great success, but only* ***at the cost of*** *a happy family life.*

IDM **at all costs; at any cost** using all the means that are necessary to achieve sth: *We must win at all costs.*

★**cost**[2] /kɔst/ ***verb*** [T] (*pt, pp* **cost**) **1** to have the price of: *These apples cost 80¢ a pound.* ◇ *How much does it cost?* ◇ *It cost me $10 to have my watch repaired.* **2** to make you lose sth: *That one mistake cost him his job.*

IDM **cost/pay an arm and a leg** → ARM[1]

**co·star**[1] (*also* **co-star**) /ˈkoʊstɑr/ ***verb*** (**co·starring** or **co·star·ring; co·starred** or **co·starred**) **1** [T] (used of a movie, play, etc.) to have two or more famous actors as its stars: *a movie costarring Michael Douglas and Sean Connery* **2** [I] (used of actors) to be one of two or more stars in a movie, play, etc.: *Michael Douglas costars with Sean Connery in the movie.*

**co·star**[2] (*also* **co-star**) /ˈkoʊstɑr/ ***noun*** [C] a famous actor or actress who has one of the most important parts in a movie, play, etc. in which another famous actor or actress also appears: *His costar was Halle Berry.*

**cost·ly** /ˈkɔstli/ ***adj.*** (**cost·li·er; cost·li·est**) **1** costing a lot of money; expensive: *a costly repair bill* **2** involving great loss of time, effort, etc.: *a costly mistake*

**cos·tume** /ˈkɑstum/ ***noun*** [C,U] special clothes that people wear to a party or in the theater, on television, etc. in order to look like a different person or an animal, etc.: *a Halloween costume* ◇ *a costume drama* (= a TV or film production in which the actors wear costumes typical of the time in history in which the action takes place)

ˈ**costume ˌjewelry** ***noun*** [U] large heavy jewelry

that can look expensive but is made with cheap materials

**ˈcostume ˌparty** ***noun*** [C] a party where all the guests wear special clothes, in order to look like a different person, an animal, etc.

**co·sy** /ˈkoʊzi/ ***adj.*** (**co·si·er**; **co·si·est**) (*Cdn*) = COZY

**cot** /kɑt/ ***noun*** [C] a narrow bed, especially one that folds to make it easier to store

**cot·tage** /ˈkɑṭɪdʒ/ ***noun*** [C] a small and often old house, especially in the country: *We spent the weekend at our summer cottage on the lake.*

**ˌcottage ˈcheese** ***noun*** [U] a type of soft white cheese in small lumps

★**cot·ton** /ˈkɑtn/ ***noun*** [U] **1** a natural cloth or thread; the tall plant that produces it: *This shirt is 60% cotton and 40% polyester.* ◇ *cotton fields in Mississippi* **2** soft, white hairs of the cotton plant in a mass, used for cleaning the skin or for putting cream, medicine, etc. on the skin: *a cotton ball*

**ˌcotton ˈcandy** ***noun*** [U] a type of candy in the form of a mass of sticky threads made from melted sugar and served on a stick, especially at FAIRS[3] (1)

**couch** /kaʊtʃ/ (*also* **sofa**) ***noun*** [C] a comfortable seat with a back and arms. It is long enough for two or more people to sit on: *Don't let the dog sit on the couch!*

NOTE **Sofa** is more formal than **couch**. ➲ picture at **chair**[1].

**ˈcouch poˌta·to** ***noun*** [C] (*pl.* **couch potatoes**) (*informal*) a person who is very lazy and who watches a lot of television

**cou·gar** /ˈkugər/ ***noun*** [C] = MOUNTAIN LION

★**cough**[1] /kɔf/ ***verb*** [I] to send air out of your throat and mouth with a sudden loud noise, especially when you have a cold, have sth in your throat, etc.: *I could hear him coughing all night.* ➲ picture at **sneeze**.

PHR V **cough sth up** to send sth out of your throat and mouth with a sudden loud noise: *He was coughing up blood.*

**cough (sth) up** (*informal*) to give money unwillingly: *Come on, cough up what you owe me!*

★**cough**[2] /kɔf/ ***noun*** [C] **1** an act or the sound of coughing: *He gave a nervous cough before he started to speak.* **2** an illness or infection that makes you cough a lot: *She's had a bad cough for weeks.* ◇ *coughs and colds*

**could** /kəd; *strong form* kʊd/ ***modal verb*** (*negative* **could not**; *short form* **could·n't** /ˈkʊdnt/) **1** (used as the past form of "can" when you report what sb says): *She said that she couldn't come.* **2** (used for saying that sth is, will be, or was possible): *I could do it now if you want.* ◇ *Couldn't you come earlier?* (= I wish you could) ◇ *He could have gone to college, but he didn't want to.* ◇ *I can't find my purse. I could have left it at the bank.* ◇ *You could have said you were going to be late!* (= I wish that you had)

NOTE If something was possible on one occasion in the past, use **was/were able to**: *The firefighters were able to rescue the children.* But in negative sentences **could not** can be used too: *The firefighters couldn't rescue the children.*

**3** (used for saying that sb had the ability in the past to do sth): *I could run two miles without stopping when I was younger.* ◇ *My grandma could cook really well.* **4** (used for asking permission politely): *Could I possibly borrow your car?* **5** (used for asking sb politely to do sth for you): *Could you open the door? My hands are full.* **6 I could/could have** I would like/have liked to do sth: *I could scream, I'm so mad.* ◇ *I was so mad I could have screamed.* **7** (used with the verbs "feel," "hear," "see," "smell," "taste")

NOTE These verbs are not used in the continuous tenses. If we want to talk about seeing, hearing, etc. at a particular moment in the past, we use **could**: *We could hear the birds singing.* (NOT *We were hearing...*)

★**coun·cil** /ˈkaʊnsl/ ***noun*** [C] **1** a group of people who are elected to manage affairs for a town, city, etc.: *The city council has decided to build a new road.* ◇ *council members* **2** a group of people chosen to give advice, manage affairs, etc. for a particular organization or area of activity: *a student council*

**coun·cil·or** /ˈkaʊnsələr/ ***noun*** [C] a member of a council

NOTE It is more common to say **council member**.

**coun·sel**[1] /ˈkaʊnsl/ ***verb*** [T] **1** (*formal*) to advise or recommend: *Mr. Dean's lawyers counseled him against making public statements.* **2** to give professional advice to sb with a problem

**coun·sel**[2] /ˈkaʊnsl/ ***noun*** **1** [C] (*pl.* **coun·sel**) a lawyer who speaks in a court of law: *the counsel for the defense/prosecution* **2** [U] (*formal*) advice

**coun·sel·ing** /ˈkaʊnsəlɪŋ/ ***noun*** [U] professional advice given to people with problems: *Many students come to us for counseling.* ◇ *psychiatric counseling*

**coun·sel·or** /ˈkaʊnsələr/ ***noun*** [C] a person whose job is to give advice: *a student counselor*

★**count**[1] /kaʊnt/ ***verb*** **1** [I] to say numbers one after another in order: *Close your eyes and count (up) to 20.* ◇ *to count from 1 to 100* **2** [T] **count sth (up)** to calculate the total number or amount of sth: *Count up the number of mistakes and subtract from 50.* **3** [I] **count (for sth)** to be important or valuable: *Your opinion really counts.* **4** [I] **count (as sth)** to be accepted: *"I won!" shouted Tom. "But you cheated, so it doesn't count," replied Sarah.* ◇ *Will my driver's license count as identification?* **5** [T] to consider to be: *You should count yourself lucky to have a good job.* **6** [T] to include sb/sth when you are calculating an amount or number: *There should be about 15 people at our party, not counting ourselves.*

PHR V **count against sb** to be considered as a disadvantage: *Do you think my age will count against me?*

**count on sb/sth** to expect sth with confidence; to rely on sb/sth: *As an artist you can't always count on a steady income.* ◇ *Can I count on you to help me?*

**count sb/sth out 1** to count things slowly, one by one: *She carefully counted out $100 in five-dollar bills.* **2** (*informal*) to not include sb/sth: *If you're going swimming, you can count me out!*

**count**[2] /kaʊnt/ ***noun*** [C] **1** [usually sing.] an act of counting or a number that you get after counting: *At the latest count, there were nearly 2 million unemployed.* **2** [usually pl.] a point that is made in a discussion, argument, etc.: *I proved her wrong on all counts.* **3** an official statement that sb has done sth which is against the law: *He was charged with two counts of robbery and one count of drug possession.*

C

IDM **keep/lose count (of sth)** to know/not know how many there are of sth: *I've lost count of the number of times he's told that joke!*

**count·a·ble** /ˈkaʊntəbl/ ***adj.*** that can be counted OPP **uncountable**

ˌ**countable noun** (*also* ˈ**count noun**) ***noun*** [C] (*grammar*) a noun that can be used in the plural, and with words like "a," "many" and "few": *Countable nouns are marked [C] in this dictionary.*

**count·down** /ˈkaʊntdaʊn/ ***noun*** [C] the act of saying numbers backward to zero just before sth important happens: *the countdown to takeoff* ◇ (*figurative*) *The candidates are making dozens of speeches in the countdown to the election.*

★**coun·ter**[1] /ˈkaʊntər/ ***noun*** [C] a long, flat surface like a table in a kitchen, restaurant, store, etc., where food is prepared or customers are served: *Just put that stuff on the kitchen counter.* ◇ *the jewelry counter in a department store*

IDM **over the counter** (used about medicine) that can be bought in a store without a special form (**prescription**) from a doctor: *cough syrup that is available over the counter* ◇ *over-the-counter medications*

**coun·ter**[2] /ˈkaʊntər/ ***verb*** [I,T] to answer or react to sb/sth with a different opinion or a return attack: *He countered our criticism with a powerful defense of his actions.*

**coun·ter**[3] /ˈkaʊntər/ ***adv.*** **counter to sth** (*formal*) in the opposite direction of sth: *Events seemed to be going counter to our expectations.*

**coun·ter·act** /ˌkaʊntəˈrækt/ ***verb*** [T] to reduce the effect of sth by acting against it: *medication to counteract the side effects of cancer treatment*

**coun·ter·at·tack** /ˈkaʊntərətæk/ ***noun*** [C] an attack made in reaction to an enemy's attack ▸ **coun·ter·attack** ***verb*** [I,T]

**coun·ter·clock·wise** /ˌkaʊntərˈklɑkwaɪz/ ***adv.***, ***adj.*** in the opposite direction of the movement of a clock: *Turn the lid counterclockwise/in a counterclockwise direction.*

**coun·ter·feit** /ˈkaʊntərfɪt/ ***adj.*** not genuine, but copied so that it looks like the real thing: *counterfeit money*

**coun·ter·part** /ˈkaʊntərpɑrt/ ***noun*** [C] a person or thing that has a similar position or function to sb/sth else: *She's my counterpart in our London office* (= she does the same job there that I do here).

**coun·ter·pro·duc·tive** /ˌkaʊntərprəˈdʌktɪv/ ***adj.*** having the opposite effect of the one you want

**count·less** /ˈkaʊntləs/ ***adj.*** (*formal*) (only *before* a noun) very many: *The earthquake killed 2,000 people and left countless others homeless.*

★**coun·try** /ˈkʌntri/ ***noun*** (*pl.* **coun·tries**) **1** [C] an area of land with its own people, government, etc.: *Argentina, Brazil and other South American countries* ◇ *There was snow over the northern part of the country last night.*

> NOTE **Land** is more formal or literary: *explorers who set out to discover new lands.* Look also at **nation**.

**2 the country** [sing.] the people who live in a COUNTRY (1): *a survey to find out what the country really thinks* **3 the country** [sing.] land which is away from towns and cities: *Do you live in the city or the country?* ◇ *country life*

> NOTE The word **country** is used for emphasizing that an area of land is away from towns, etc.: *city workers who like to get out into the country on weekends.* The word **countryside** also refers to areas of land that are away from towns, but it emphasizes the natural features such as hills, rivers, trees, etc. that you find there: *beautiful countryside* ◇ *the destruction of the countryside by new roads.* **Landscape** refers to everything you see when you look across an area of land either in the town or the country: *a dreary landscape of factories and chimneys* ◇ *a landscape of forests and lakes*

**4** [U] an area of land (especially considering its physical features): *miles of open country* ◇ *hilly country* **5** [U] (*informal*) = COUNTRY MUSIC

ˌ**country and** ˈ**western** ***noun*** [U] = COUNTRY MUSIC

ˈ**country club** ***noun*** [C] a club in the country, or on the edge of a town, where people can play sports and go to social events

**coun·try·man** /ˈkʌntrimən/ ***noun*** [C] (*feminine* **coun·try·wom·an** /ˈkʌntriwʊmən/; *pl.* **coun·try·men**; *pl.* **coun·try·wom·en**) a person from your own country

ˌ**country** ˈ**music** (*also* **country**, **country and western**) ***noun*** [U] a type of popular music that is based on traditional music from the southern and western parts of the U.S.

★**coun·try·side** /ˈkʌntrisaɪd/ ***noun*** [U, sing.] **the countryside** land which is away from towns and cities, consisting of farms, woods, etc.: *the French countryside* ◇ *The countryside in Colorado is very beautiful.* ➲ Look at the note at **country**.

★**coun·ty** /ˈkaʊnti/ ***noun*** [C] (*pl.* **coun·ties**) **1** (*U.S.*) a district within a state, which has its own government: *the Cook County sheriff* ◇ *a county courthouse* **2** any district in some countries or provinces that has its own government, legal system, etc.

**coup** /ku/ ***noun*** [C] (*pl.* **coups** /kuz/) **1** (*also* **coup d'ét·at** /ˌku deɪˈtɑ/) (*pl.* **coups d'ét·at** /ˌku deɪˈtɑ/) a sudden and often violent change of government organized by a small group of people: *a coup to overthrow the President* ◇ *an attempted coup* (= one which did not succeed) **2** a clever and successful thing to do: *It was a real coup for us to get the governor to speak at our school.*

★**cou·ple**[1] /ˈkʌpl/ ***noun*** [C] two people who are married, living together, etc.: *A very nice couple moved in next door to us.* ◇ *a married couple*

IDM **a couple of people/things 1** two people/things: *I need a couple of glasses.* **2** a few (not saying an exact number): *I saw her a couple of months ago.*

**cou·ple²** /ˈkʌpl/ ***verb*** [T] (usually passive) to join or link sb/sth to sb/sth else: *The fog, coupled with the amount of traffic on the roads, made driving very difficult.*

**cou·pon** /ˈkupɑn; ˈkyu-/ ***noun*** [C] **1** a small piece of paper which you can use to buy goods at a lower price, or which you can collect and then exchange for goods: *a coupon worth $1 off your next purchase* **2** a small form in a newspaper or magazine which you fill out with your name and address and send off, in order to get information or to enter a competition: *To place your order, simply fill out the coupon at the bottom of this page.*

★**cour·age** /ˈkərɪdʒ/ ***noun*** [U] the ability to control fear in a situation that may be dangerous or unpleasant: *It took real courage to go back into the burning building.* ◇ *She showed great courage through her long illness.*

**cou·ra·geous** /kəˈreɪdʒəs/ ***adj.*** having or showing courage; brave ▸ **cou·ra·geous·ly *adv.***

**cou·ri·er** /ˈkəriər; ˈkʊr-/ ***noun*** [C] a person whose job is to carry letters, important papers, etc., especially when they are urgent

★**course** /kɔrs/ ***noun*** **1** [C] **a course (in/on sth)** a complete series of lessons: *I enrolled in an English course.* ◇ *a course in self-defense* ◇ *How many courses are you taking this semester?* **2** [C] one of the parts of a meal: *a three-course lunch* ◇ *I had chicken for the main course.* **3** [C] an area where golf is played or where certain types of race take place: *a golf course* ◇ *a racecourse* (= where horse races take place) **4** [C] **a course (of sth)** a series of medical treatments: *The doctor put her on a course of radiation therapy.* **5** [C,U] the route or direction that sth, especially an airplane, ship or river, takes: *We changed course and sailed toward land.* ◇ *to be on/off course* (= going in the right/wrong direction) ◇ (*figurative*) *I'm* ***on course*** (= making the right amount of progress) *to finish this work by the end of the week.* **6** [sing.] the development of sth over a period of time: *events that changed the course of history* ◇ ***In the normal course of events*** (= the way things normally happen) *such problems do not arise.* **7** (*also* **course of action**) [C] a way of acting in or dealing with a particular situation: *It was the only course left open to us in those circumstances.*

IDM **in the course of sth** during sth: *He mentioned it in the course of conversation.*

**in due course** → DUE[1]

**of course** naturally; certainly: *Of course, having children has changed their lives a lot.* ◇ *"Can I use your phone?" "Of course you can."* ◇ *"You're not mad at me, are you?" "Of course not."*

**course·book** /ˈkɔrsbʊk/ ***noun*** [C] = TEXTBOOK

★**court¹** /kɔrt/ ***noun*** **1** [C,U] a place where trials take place in front of a judge or a jury, to decide whether a person has broken the law: *a civil/criminal court* ◇ *A man has been charged and will appear in court tomorrow.* **2 the court** [sing.] the people in a court, especially the judge or judges: *Only one attorney may address the court at a time.* ◇ *The court ruled that the law was unconstitutional.* ➲ Look also at **supreme court**. **3** [C,U] an area where certain ball games are played: *a tennis/basketball court* ➲ picture at **tennis**.

IDM **take sb to court** to take legal action against sb in a court of law: *She took the company to court for breaking the contract.*

**court²** /kɔrt/ ***verb*** **1** [T] to try to gain sb's support by paying special attention to him/her: *Politicians from all parties will be courting voters this week.* **2** [T] to do sth that might lead to sth bad: *America is courting ecological disaster if it continues to ignore global warming.*

**cour·te·ous** /ˈkərt̬iəs/ ***adj.*** polite and pleasant, showing respect for other people: *The salesclerk was courteous and helpful.* OPP **discourteous** ▸ **cour·te·ous·ly *adv.***

**cour·te·sy** /ˈkərt̬əsi/ ***noun*** (*pl.* **cour·te·sies**) **1** [U] polite and pleasant behavior that shows respect for other people: *She didn't even have the courtesy to say that she was sorry.* **2** [C] (*formal*) a polite action or remark: *The two presidents exchanged courtesies before their meeting.*

IDM **courtesy of sb** with the permission or because of the kindness of sb: *These pictures are being shown courtesy of ABC-TV.*

**court·house** /ˈkɔrthaʊs/ ***noun*** [C] a building where courts of law and other offices of a county are located

**court-mar·tial¹** /ˈkɔrt ˌmɑrʃl/ ***noun*** [C] (*pl.* **courts-martial** or **court-martials**) a military court that deals with matters of military law; a trial that takes place in such a court: *His case will be heard by a court-martial.*

**court-mar·tial²** /ˈkɔrt ˌmɑrʃl/ ***verb*** [T] to put sb on trial in a military court

**ˌcourt of apˈpeals** (*also* **ˌcourt of apˈpeal**; *especially Cdn* **ˌCourt of Apˈpeal**, **ˌCourt of Apˈpeals**) (*pl.* **courts of appeal**) ***noun*** [C] a court of law that people can go to in order to try and change decisions that have been made by a lower court

★**ˌcourt of ˈlaw** ***noun*** [C] (*pl.* **courts of law**) a place where a judge or jury decides legal matters (e.g. whether a person is innocent or guilty)

**ˌcourt ˈorder** ***noun*** [C] a decision that is made in a court of law about what must happen in a particular situation: *They didn't send their daughter to school until a court order forced them to.*

**court·room** /ˈkɔrtrum/ ***noun*** [C] a room where trials or other law cases are held

**court·yard** /ˈkɔrtyɑrd/ ***noun*** [C] an area of ground, without a roof, that has walls or buildings around it, e.g. in a public building, or between houses or apartment buildings

**cous·cous** /ˈkuskus/ ***noun*** [U] a type of North African food made from crushed wheat; a dish made of meat and/or vegetables with couscous

★**cous·in** /ˈkʌzn/ (*also* **ˌfirst ˈcousin**) ***noun*** [C] the child of your aunt or uncle: *Have you met Alison? We're cousins.*

NOTE The same word is used for both male and female cousins.

**cove** /koʊv/ ***noun*** [C] a small bay on the coast: *a sandy cove*

★**cov·er¹** /ˈkʌvər/ ***verb*** [T] **1 cover sb/sth (up) (with sth)** to put sth on or in front of sth in order to hide or protect it: *Could you cover the food and put it in the refrigerator?* ◇ *She couldn't look*

C

*anymore and covered her eyes.* ◇ *She was asleep on the couch, so he covered her up with a blanket.* **2** to be across or over the surface of sth: *Snow covered the ground.* **3 cover sb/sth in/with sth** to form a layer on sb/sth: *A car went through the puddle and covered me with mud.* **4** to fill or be spread over a certain area: *The smoke from the fire now covers about 15,000 square miles.* **5** to include or to deal with sth: *Part-time workers are not covered by the law.* ◇ *The course covered both North and South American history.* **6** to travel a certain distance: *We covered about 500 miles that day.* **7** to be enough money for sth: *Will $20 cover your expenses?* **8** (used about the media) to report on or show sth: *All the papers covered the election in depth.* **9 cover sb/sth against/for sth** to protect sb/sth by insurance: *The insurance policy covers us for any damage to our property.* ◇ *The policy even covers your lawn furniture* (= it is insured).

PHR V **cover (sth) up** to prevent people from hearing about a mistake or sth bad: *The police have been accused of trying to cover up the facts of the case.*

**cover up for sb** to hide a person's mistakes or crimes in order to protect him/her: *His wife covered up for him when the police questioned them.*

★**cov·er²** /ˈkʌvər/ ***noun*** **1** [C] something that is put on or over sth, especially in order to protect it: *a plastic cover for a computer* **2** [C] the outside part of a book or magazine: *I can't remember the title of the book, but I know it has a green cover.* ◇ *I read the magazine from cover to cover* (= from beginning to end). **3 the covers** [pl.] the blankets, sheets, etc. that cover sb in bed: *She pulled the covers off him and said: "Get up!"* **4** [U] shelter or protection from the weather, damage, etc.: *When the storm started, we took cover in a hotel lobby.* ◇ *The soldiers had no cover and were easy targets.* **5** [C, usually sing.] **a cover (for sth)** something that hides the real nature of sth, especially sth illegal: *The whole company was just a cover for all kinds of criminal activities.*

IDM **under cover of sth** hidden by sth; not noticed because of sth: *They attacked under cover of darkness.*

**cov·er·age** /ˈkʌvərɪdʒ; ˈkʌvrɪdʒ/ ***noun*** [U] **1** the act or amount of reporting on or showing an event in the media: *TV coverage of the Olympic Games* **2 coverage (for sth)** insurance against sth, so that if sth bad happens you get money or help in return: *The policy provides coverage for theft.*

**cov·er·alls** /ˈkʌvərɔlz/ ***noun*** [pl.] a piece of clothing that covers your body, arms and legs and that you wear over your clothes to keep them clean when you are working ➲ picture at **overalls**.

**cov·ered** /ˈkʌvərd/ ***adj.*** **1 covered in/with sth** having a layer or a large amount of sth on sb/sth: *The victim was lying on the floor, covered in blood.* ◇ *The bookshelves were covered with dust.* **2** having a cover, especially a roof: *The pioneers traveled west in covered wagons.*

★**cov·er·ing** /ˈkʌvərɪŋ/ ***noun*** [C] something that covers the surface of sth: *A thick covering of snow lay on the ground.*

ˈ**cover ˌletter** ***noun*** [C] a letter that you send with a package or with other documents, explaining them or giving more information about them

**cov·ert** /ˈkoʊvərt; ˈkʌv-; ˌkoʊˈvərt/ ***adj.*** done secretly, not openly: *a covert police operation* ▶ **cov·ert·ly** ***adv.***

ˈ**cover-up** (*also* **cov·er·up**) ***noun*** [C] an act of preventing sth bad or dishonest from becoming known: *Several newspapers claimed that there had been a government cover-up.*

**cows**

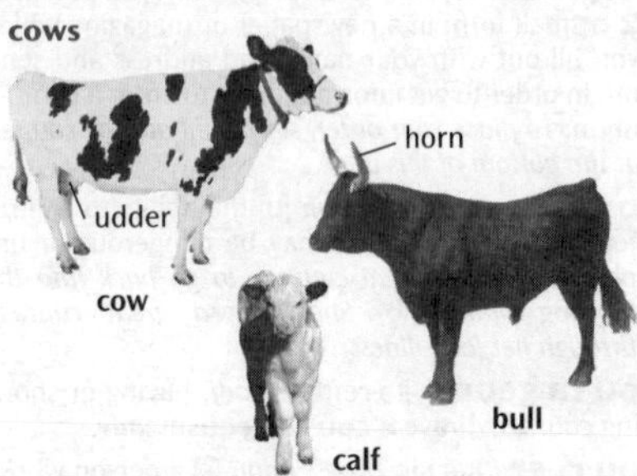


★**cow** /kaʊ/ ***noun*** [C] **1** a large female animal that is kept on farms to produce milk: *to milk a cow* ◇ *a herd of cows*

> NOTE **Cow** is often used for both male and female members of the **cattle** family. The special word for a male is **bull**. A young cow is a **calf**. A number of cows together can be called **cattle**. ➲ Look at the note at **meat**.

**2** the adult female of certain large animals, e.g. the elephant

IDM **have a cow** (*slang*) to be very anxious, nervous, impatient, etc.: *All right, I'm coming! Don't have a cow!*

**cow·ard** /ˈkaʊərd/ ***noun*** [C] (used when disapproving) a person who has no courage and is afraid in dangerous or unpleasant situations: *I was too much of a coward to argue.* ▶ **cow·ard·ly** ***adj.***

**cow·ard·ice** /ˈkaʊərdəs/ ***noun*** [U] a lack of courage

**cow·boy** /ˈkaʊbɔɪ/ ***noun*** [C] a man whose job is to take care of cattle, especially in western North America: *cowboy boots* ➲ picture at **shoe**.

**cow·er** /ˈkaʊər/ ***verb*** [I] to move back or into a low position because of fear: *The dog cowered under the table.*

**cow·girl** /ˈkaʊgərl/ ***noun*** [C] a woman whose job is to take care of cattle, especially in western North America

**co·work·er** (*also* **co-worker**) /ˈkoʊwərkər/ ***noun*** [C] a person that you work with in a job

**coy·o·te** /kaɪˈoʊt̬i; ˈkaɪoʊt/ ***noun*** [C] a wild animal that looks like a dog and lives mainly in western North America

**co·zy** /ˈkoʊzi/ ***adj.*** (**co·zi·er**; **co·zi·est**) warm and comfortable: *a cozy room with a fireplace*

**CPA** /ˌsi pi ˈeɪ/ ***abbr.*** = CERTIFIED PUBLIC ACCOUNTANT

**CPP** /ˌsi pi ˈpi/ ***abbr.*** = CANADA PENSION PLAN

**CPU** /ˌsi pi ˈyu/ ***abbr.*** = CENTRAL PROCESSING UNIT

**crab** /kræb/ ***noun*** [C] a sea animal with a flat body covered by a shell and five pairs of curved legs. The front two legs have long claws on them. Crabs move sideways. ➲ picture at **shellfish**.

★**crack**[1] /kræk/ ***noun*** **1** [C] a line on the surface of sth where it has broken, but not into separate pieces: *a pane of glass with a crack in it* ➲ picture at **chip**[1]. **2** [C] a narrow opening: *The wind blew through the cracks in the roof.* **3** [C] a sudden loud, sharp sound: *There was a crack and he realized that he had broken his leg.* **4** [C] an amusing, often critical, remark; a joke: *She **made a crack** about his clothes.* **5** [U] an illegal drug which is a very strong form of cocaine. It is very difficult to stop using crack: *to smoke crack* ◇ *a crack addict*

IDM **at the crack of dawn** very early in the morning

**fall/slip through the cracks** to not be noticed, helped, or checked by anybody: *We need to make sure that no abused children fall through the cracks in the social services.*

★**crack**[2] /kræk/ ***verb*** **1** [I,T] to break so that a line appears, but without breaking into pieces; to make sth do this: *Don't put boiling water into that glass – it'll crack.* ◇ *You can crack this kind of glass, but you can't break it.* **2** [T] to break sth open: *Crack two eggs into a bowl.* **3** [I,T] to make a sudden loud, sharp sound; to cause sth to make this sound: *The cowboy cracked his whip.* **4** [I] to stop being able to deal with pressure and so lose control: *She cracked under the strain of all her problems.* **5** [T] (*informal*) to solve a problem: *Police have finally cracked the murder case.* **6** [T] (*informal*) to reach a difficult goal: *We're hoping to crack the Asian markets with these two new products.* **7** [T] to tell or make a joke

PHRV **crack down (on sb/sth)** (used about people in authority) to start dealing severely with bad or illegal behavior: *The police have started to crack down on drug dealers.*

**crack up** (*informal*) **1** to suddenly start laughing: *I crack up every time I watch this video.* **2** to be unable to deal with pressure and so lose control and become mentally ill: *He cracked up when his wife left him.*

**crack·down** /ˈkrækdaʊn/ ***noun*** [C] action to stop bad or illegal behavior: *a police crackdown on street crime*

**crack·er** /ˈkrækər/ ***noun*** [C] a type of thin flat dry bread that is often salty: *cheese and crackers*

**crack·le** /ˈkrækl/ ***verb*** [I] to make a series of short, sharp sounds: *The radio started to crackle and then it stopped working.* ▸ **crack·le *noun*** [sing.]: *the crackle of dry wood burning*

**cra·dle**[1] /ˈkreɪdl/ ***noun*** [C] a small bed for a baby. Cradles can often be moved from side to side.

**cra·dle**[2] /ˈkreɪdl/ ***verb*** [T] to hold sb/sth carefully and gently in your arms: *He cradled her head in his arms until the ambulance came.*

**craft** /kræft/ ***noun*** [C] **1** a job or activity for which you need skill with your hands: *an arts and crafts exhibition* ◇ *the craft of basket making* ➲ Look at **handicraft**. **2** any job or activity for which you need skill: *He regards acting as a craft.* **3** (*pl.* **craft**) a boat, aircraft or spaceship: *There were a few fishing craft in the harbor.*

**crafts·man** /ˈkræftsmən/ ***noun*** [C] (*pl.* **crafts·men**) a person who makes things skillfully, especially with the hands: *All the furniture we sell is individually made by craftsmen.*

**crafts·man·ship** /ˈkræftsmənʃɪp/ ***noun*** [U] the skill used by sb to make sth of high quality, especially with the hands

**craft·y** /ˈkræfti/ ***adj.*** (**craft·i·er**; **craft·i·est**) intelligent and skillful at getting or achieving things by deceiving people or using indirect methods

**crag·gy** /ˈkrægi/ ***adj.*** **1** having a lot of steep, rough rock **2** (used about a man's face) strong, with deep lines, especially in an attractive way

**cram** /kræm/ ***verb*** (**cram·ming**; **crammed**) **1** [T] to push people or things into a small space: *I managed to cram all my clothes into the bag, but I couldn't zip it up.* ◇ *We only spent two days in New York, but we crammed in a lot of sightseeing.* **2** [I] to move, with a lot of other people, into a small space: *He only had a small car, but we all crammed into it.* **3** [I] to study very hard and learn a lot in a short time before an examination: *She's cramming for her final exams.*

**crammed** /kræmd/ ***adj.*** **crammed (with sth)** very full or too full: *This book is crammed with useful information.* ◇ *Orlando is crammed with tourists at that time of year.*

**cramp** /kræmp/ ***noun*** [C] a sudden pain that you get in a muscle, that makes it difficult to move: *One of the swimmers got a cramp and we had to pull him out of the water.* ◇ *stomach cramps*

**cramped** /kræmpt/ ***adj.*** not having enough space: *There were five of us living in a cramped apartment.*

**cran·ber·ry** /ˈkrænˌbɛri/ ***noun*** [C] (*pl.* **cran·ber·ries**) a small red berry with a sour taste: *turkey with cranberry sauce* ➲ picture on study page **A28-29**.

**crane**[1] /kreɪn/ ***noun*** [C] a large machine with a long metal arm that is used for moving or lifting heavy objects

**crane**[2] /kreɪn/ ***verb*** [I,T] to stretch your neck forward in order to see or hear sth: *We all craned forward to get a better view.*

**cra·ni·um** /ˈkreɪniəm/ ***noun*** [C] (*pl.* **cra·ni·ums**; **cra·ni·a**) the bone structure that forms the head and surrounds and protects the brain SYN **skull**

**crank**[1] /kræŋk/ ***verb***

PHRV **crank sth out** (*informal*) to produce large numbers of sth very quickly: *My computer printer can crank out 12 pages a minute.*

**crank sth up** (*informal*) to make sth stronger, louder, work harder, etc.: *It's too hot in here – crank up the air conditioner.* ◇ *This is an awesome song – crank it up!*

**crank**[2] /kræŋk/ ***noun*** [C] a person with strange ideas or who behaves in a strange way: *Lots of cranks called the police confessing to the murder.*

**crank·y** /ˈkræŋki/ ***adj.*** (**crank·i·er**; **crank·i·est**) bad-tempered: *The kids were getting tired and cranky.*

**cran·ny** /ˈkræni/ ***noun*** [C] (*pl.* **cran·nies**) a small opening in a wall, a rock, etc.

IDM **every nook and cranny** → NOOK

**crap**[1] /kræp/ ***noun*** [U] (*slang*) **1** nonsense: *I don't want to listen to any more of that crap.* **2** something that is of poor quality: *This piece of crap broke the first time I used it!* **3** solid waste from the body

NOTE Some people find this word offensive.

▸ **crap·py** /'kræpi/ ***adj.***

**crap²** /kræp/ ***verb*** [I] (**crap·ping**; **crapped**) (*slang*) to push out solid waste material from the body

NOTE Some people find this word offensive.

★ **crash¹** /kræʃ/ ***noun*** [C] **1** a sudden loud noise made by sth breaking, hitting sth, etc.: *I heard a crash and ran outside.* **2** an accident when a car or other vehicle hits sth and is damaged: *She was injured in a serious car crash.* ◇ *a plane crash with no survivors* **3** an occasion when there is a failure in the business world: *the stock market crash of 1987*

★ **crash²** /kræʃ/ ***verb*** **1** [I,T] to have an accident in a vehicle; to cause a vehicle to have an accident: *He braked too late and crashed into the car in front.* **2** [I] to fall or move suddenly, making a loud noise: *The tree crashed through the window.* ◇ *waves crashing on the beach* **3** [I] (used about a business or a financial organization) to fail suddenly **4** [I] (used about a computer) to stop working suddenly: *We lost the data when the computer crashed.* **5** [T] (*informal*) to go to a private party without being invited: *to crash a party*

**ˌcrash 'course** ***noun*** [C] a course in which you learn the basic information about sth in a short period of time: *I took a crash course in Japanese before I went to work in Tokyo.*

**ˌcrash 'diet** ***noun*** [C] a diet that you follow to reduce your weight as much as possible in a short period of time: *She had to lose ten pounds in two weeks to fit into her new dress, so she* ***went on a crash diet****.*

**'crash ˌhelmet** ***noun*** [C] a hat made of very strong material and worn when riding a motorcycle to protect the head

**'crash-land** ***verb*** [I,T] if an airplane crash-lands or a pilot crash-lands it, the pilot lands it in a dangerous way in an emergency, usually because it is damaged and cannot land normally ▸ **ˌcrash 'landing** ***noun*** [C]: *The pilot warned the passengers to prepare for a crash landing.*

**crate** /kreɪt/ ***noun*** [C] a large box, usually made of wood, in which goods are transported or stored: *We had to pack everything into crates when we moved to our new house.* ◇ *a crate of apples*

**cra·ter** /'kreɪt̬ər/ ***noun*** [C] **1** a large hole in the ground: *The bomb left a large crater.* ◇ *craters on the moon* **2** the hole in the top of a volcano

**crave** /kreɪv/ ***verb*** [T] to want and need to have sth very much: *He craves attention from other people.*

**crav·ing** /'kreɪvɪŋ/ ***noun*** [C] **craving (for sth)** a strong desire for sth: *When she was pregnant, she had cravings for a lot of strange foods.*

**craw·fish** /'krɔfɪʃ/ ***noun*** [C] (*pl.* **craw·fish**) = CRAYFISH

**crawl¹** /krɔl/ ***verb*** [I] **1** to move slowly with your body on or close to the ground, or on your hands and knees: *An insect crawled across the floor.* ◇ *Their baby has just started to crawl.* **2** (used about vehicles) to move very slowly: *The traffic crawls along the expressway during rush hour.*

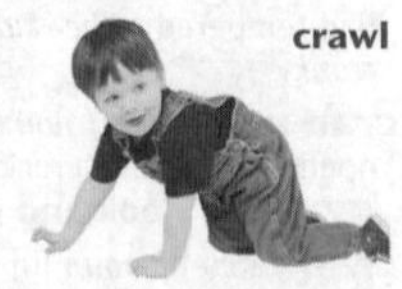
crawl

IDM **be crawling with sth** to be completely full of or covered with sb/sth that is moving and that is considered unpleasant: *The kitchen was crawling with insects.* ◇ *The resort is crawling with tourists.*

**crawl²** /krɔl/ ***noun*** [sing.] **1** a very slow speed: *The traffic slowed to a crawl.* **2** (often **the crawl**) a style of swimming which you do on your front. When you do the crawl, you move first one arm and then the other over your head, turn your face to one side so that you can breathe and kick up and down with your legs.

**cray·fish** /'kreɪfɪʃ/ (*also* **craw·fish**) ***noun*** [C] (*pl.* **cray·fish**) a shellfish that lives in rivers or lakes and can be eaten

**cray·on** /'kreɪɑn; -ən/ ***noun*** [C,U] a soft, thick, colored pencil made of wax, used for drawing or writing, especially by children

**craze** /kreɪz/ ***noun*** [C] **a craze (for sth) 1** a strong interest in sth, that usually only lasts for a short time: *There was a craze for that kind of music years ago.* **2** something that a lot of people are very interested in: *Scooters are the latest craze among teenagers.*

★ **cra·zy** /'kreɪzi/ ***adj.*** (**cra·zi·er**; **cra·zi·est**) **1** with a sick mind; mentally ill

NOTE It is not polite to use **crazy** or **insane** to describe a person who is not mentally normal. We use the expression **mentally ill**.

**2** very silly or foolish: *I think that's a crazy idea.* ◇ *You must be crazy to turn down such a great offer.* **3** very angry: *These kids are driving me crazy!* **4 crazy about sth** very interested in sth; liking sth very much: *He's always been crazy about horses.* **5 crazy about sb** very much in love with sb **6** showing great excitement: *The fans went crazy when their team scored the first touchdown.*

IDM **like crazy** → LIKE²

▸ **cra·zi·ness** ***noun*** [U]

**creak** /krik/ ***verb*** [I] to make the noise of wood bending or of sth not moving smoothly: *The floorboards creaked when I walked across the room.* ▸ **creak** ***noun*** [C] ▸ **creak·y** ***adj.***: *creaky stairs*

★ **cream¹** /krim/ ***noun*** **1** [U] the thick yellowish-white liquid that is the fatty part of milk and that rises to the top of it: *coffee with cream* ◇ *strawberries and cream* ◇ *whipped cream* (= cream that has been beaten) ➲ Look also at **ice cream**. **2** [C,U] a substance that you rub into your skin to keep it soft or as a medical treatment

IDM **the cream of the crop** the best part of sth or the best people in a group

★ **cream²** /krim/ ***adj.*** a yellowish-white color

**cream³** /krim/ ***verb*** [T] (*informal*) to defeat sb heavily: *The Bulls creamed the Lakers 121-73.* ◇ *Our team got creamed in the tournament.*

**ˌcream 'cheese** ***noun*** [U] a type of soft white cheese that has a mild flavor

**cream·er** /'krimər/ ***noun*** [U] a liquid or powder that you can put in coffee, etc. instead of cream or milk: *non-dairy creamer*

**cream·y** /'krimi/ ***adj.*** (**cream·i·er**; **cream·i·est**)

C

**1** containing cream: *a creamy sauce* **2** thick, smooth and soft; looking or feeling like cream: *Beat the mixture until it is light and creamy.*

**crease**[1] /kris/ ***noun*** [C] **1** a line on paper, material, a piece of clothing, etc. that is caused by not treating it carefully: *When I unrolled the poster, there was a crease in it.* **2** a neat line that is put on paper, material, a piece of clothing, etc. intentionally: *He had a sharp crease in his pants.*

**crease**[2] /kris/ ***verb*** [I,T] to get CREASES[1] (1,2); to make sth get creases: *Hang up your jacket or it will crease.* ◇ *Be careful not to crease the paper.*

★**cre·ate** /kri'eɪt/ ***verb*** [T] to cause sth new to happen or exist: *a plan to create new jobs in the area* ◇ *The Bible says that God created the world.* ◇ *All these changes will simply create confusion.*

★**cre·a·tion** /kri'eɪʃn/ ***noun*** **1** [U] the act of causing sth new to happen or exist: *the creation of new independent states* **2** (usually **the Creation**) [sing.] the act of making the whole universe, as described in the Bible **3** [C] something that sb has made or produced, especially using skill or imagination: *This dish is a new creation – I didn't use a recipe.*

**cre·a·tive** /kri'eɪt̬ɪv/ ***adj.*** **1** using skill or imagination to make or do new things: *She's a fantastic designer – she's so creative.* ◇ *We need some creative thinking to solve this problem.* **2** connected with producing new things, especially works of art: *His creative life went on until he was well over 80.* ▶ **cre·a·tive·ly** ***adv.***: *They don't have a very big house, but they use the space creatively.*

**cre·a·tiv·i·ty** /ˌkrieɪ'tɪvət̬i/ ***noun*** [U] the ability to make or produce new things, especially using skill or imagination: *teaching that encourages children's creativity*

**cre·a·tor** /kri'eɪt̬ər/ ***noun*** **1** [C] a person who makes or produces sth new, especially using skill or imagination: *He was the creator of some of the best-known characters in literature.* **2 the Creator** [sing.] God

★**crea·ture** /'kritʃər/ ***noun*** [C] a living thing such as an animal, a bird, a fish or an insect, but not a plant: *a living creature* ◇ *creatures from other planets*

**cre·den·tials** /krə'dɛnʃlz/ ***noun*** [pl.] **1** something that shows that a person is qualified or suitable for sth: *He has the perfect credentials for the top job.* **2** a document that proves that sb is who he/she claims to be, or that he/she is qualified to do sth

**cred·i·bil·i·ty** /ˌkrɛdə'bɪlət̬i/ ***noun*** [U] the quality of being able to be believed or trusted and taken seriously: *The CEO had lost all credibility and had to resign.*

**cred·i·ble** /'krɛdəbl/ ***adj.*** (*formal*) **1** that you can believe: *a credible witness in a court case* **2** that you can trust or take seriously: *a credible alternative to nuclear energy* ➲ Look at **incredible**. ▶ **cred·i·bly** /-əbli/ ***adv.***

★**cred·it**[1] /'krɛdət/ ***noun*** **1** [U] the system of buying goods or services and not paying for them until later: *I bought the television* ***on credit.*** ◇ *interest-free credit* (= payment over a period of time without any extra charges) **2** [C,U] a sum of money that a bank, etc. lends: *The company was not able to get any further credit and went bankrupt.* **3** [U] praise for sth good that a person has done: *He got all the credit for the success of the project.* ◇ *She didn't do very well, but at least* ***give her credit for*** *trying.* ◇ *Even though your answer wasn't completely correct, I can give you partial credit for it.* **4** [C] a unit of study at a school, college or university: *My math class is worth three credits.* ◇ *108 credits are required for graduation.* ➲ For more information on the U.S. educational system, look at study page **A8**. **5 credits** [pl.] the list of the names of the people who made a movie or TV program, shown at the beginning or end of the movie **6** [sing.] **a credit to sb/sth** a person or thing that gives honor: *She is a wonderful girl and a credit to her school.*

IDM **(be) to sb's credit** (used for showing that you approve of sth that sb has done, although you have criticized sth else): *The company, to its credit, apologized and refunded my money.*

**have sth to your credit** to have finished sth that is successful: *She has three best-selling novels to her credit.*

**cred·it**[2] /'krɛdət/ ***verb*** [T] **1 credit sb/sth for/with sth** to accept or believe that sb/sth has a particular quality or is responsible for sth: *Rap artists are credited with making people aware of the problems in inner cities.* **2 credit sth to sth** to say or believe that sth is the result of sth: *She credited her success to a lot of hard work.* **3** to record that money has been added to an account: *Has the money been credited to my account yet?*

**'credit card** ***noun*** [C] a small plastic card that allows sb to get goods or services without using money. You usually receive a bill once a month for what you have bought, and you can choose to pay all or part of the bill: *Do you take credit cards here?* ➲ Look also at **charge card**.

**'credit ˌlimit** ***noun*** [C] the highest amount of money that you are allowed to spend or borrow using your credit card: *Before she went on vacation, Maggie asked the bank for a higher credit limit.*

**cred·i·tor** /'krɛdət̬ər/ ***noun*** [C] a person or company to whom money is owed

**'credit ˌrating** ***noun*** [C] a judgment made by a bank, etc., about how likely sb is to pay back money that he/she borrows, and how safe it is to lend money to him/her: *A good credit rating is important if you want to buy a house.*

**'credit ˌunion** ***noun*** [C] an organization similar to a bank, that is owned by the people who keep their money in it, and which lends money to its members at low rates of interest: *One benefit of working for that company is their employees' credit union.*

**creed** /krid/ ***noun*** [C] a set of beliefs or principles (especially religious ones) that strongly influence sb's life

**creek** /krik; krɪk/ ***noun*** [C] a small river or stream

**creep**[1] /krip/ ***verb*** [I] (*pt, pp* **crept** /krɛpt/) **1** to move very quietly and carefully, often with your body in a low position, so that nobody will notice you: *The cat crept silently toward the bird.* **2** to move forward or higher slowly: *Inflation crept up by 0.1% in the last quarter.*

PHRV **creep in** to begin to appear: *I could hear a note of sadness creeping into her voice.*

C

**creep²** /krip/ *noun* [C] (*informal*) an annoying or disgusting person

IDM **give sb the creeps** (*informal*) to give sb an unpleasant feeling; to make sb feel frightened: *There's something about the way he laughs that gives me the creeps.*

**creep·y** /ˈkripi/ *adj.* (**creep·i·er**; **creep·i·est**) (*informal*) that makes you feel nervous and frightened: *a creepy smile*

**cre·mate** /ˈkrimeɪt; krɪˈmeɪt/ *verb* [T] to burn the body of a dead person as part of a funeral service

**cre·ma·tion** /krɪˈmeɪʃn/ *noun* [C,U] an act of cremating a dead person ➲ Look at the note at **funeral**.

**cre·ma·to·ri·um** /ˌkriməˈtɔriəm/ *noun* [C] (*pl.* **cre·ma·to·ri·ums** or **cre·ma·to·ri·a** /-ˈtɔriə/) a place where dead people are cremated

**crème brû·lée** /ˌkrɛm bruˈleɪ/ *noun* [C,U] (*pl.* **crèmes brû·lées**) (from French) a cold sweet dish (dessert) made from cream, with burnt sugar on top

**Cre·ole** /ˈkrioʊl/ (*also* **cre·ole**) *noun* [C], *adj.* = CAJUN

**crept** *past tense, past participle of* CREEP¹

**cres·cen·do** /krəˈʃɛndoʊ/ *noun* [C] (*pl.* **cres·cen·dos**) a noise or piece of music that is very loud or that gets louder and louder

**cres·cent** /ˈkrɛsnt/ *noun* [C] the shape of the moon in its first and last stages; a curved shape that is pointed at both ends ➲ picture at **shape**.

**crest** /krɛst/ *noun* [C] **1** the white part at the top of a wave **2** the top of a hill **3** a group of attractive feathers on the top of a bird's head

**cre·vasse** /krəˈvæs/ *noun* [C] a deep crack in thick ice

**crev·ice** /ˈkrɛvəs/ *noun* [C] a narrow crack in a rock, wall, etc.

**crew** /kru/ *noun* [C] **1** all the people who work on a ship/an airplane: *The captain and his crew hope you had a pleasant flight.* **2** a group of people who work together: *a camera crew* (= people who film things for television, etc.)

**ˈcrew cut** (*also* **ˈcrew·cut**) *noun* [C] a very short hairstyle for men

**crib** /krɪb/ *noun* [C] a bed for a baby or young child, with high sides to stop it from falling out

**ˈcrib death** *noun* [U,C] = SIDS

**crick** /krɪk/ *noun* [sing.] a pain in your neck, back, etc. that makes it difficult for you to move easily: *I have a crick in my neck.*

**crick·et** /ˈkrɪkət/ *noun* [C] an insect that makes a loud noise by rubbing its wings together

★**crime** /kraɪm/ *noun* **1** [C] something which is against the law and which people are punished for, e.g. by being sent to prison: *to commit a crime* ◇ *serious crimes such as murder and armed robbery* ➲ Look also at **hate crime**. **2** [U] illegal behavior in general: *an increase in violent crime* ◇ *to lead a life of crime* ◇ ***crime prevention** measures* **3** (usually **a crime**) [sing.] something that is morally wrong: *It is a crime to waste food when people are starving.*

★**crim·i·nal¹** /ˈkrɪmənl/ *adj.* **1** (only *before* a noun) connected with crime: *Vandalism is a criminal offense.* ◇ *criminal law* **2** morally wrong: *a criminal waste of taxpayers' money*

★**crim·i·nal²** /ˈkrɪmənl/ *noun* [C] a person who has committed a crime: *convicted criminals*

**crim·son** /ˈkrɪmzn/ *adj.*, *noun* [U] (of) a dark red color ➲ Look at **maroon** and **scarlet**.

**cringe** /krɪndʒ/ *verb* [I] **1** to move away from sb/sth because you are frightened: *The dog cringed in terror when the man raised his arm.* **2** to feel embarrassed: *terrible home videos that make you cringe in embarrassment*

**crin·kle** /ˈkrɪŋkl/ *verb* [I,T] **crinkle (sth) (up)** (to cause sth) to have thin folds or lines in it: *His face crinkled into a smile.* ▸ **crink·ly** /ˈkrɪŋkli/ *adj.*: *a type of soft crinkly material*

**crip·ple¹** /ˈkrɪpl/ *noun* [C] (*old-fashioned*) a person who cannot walk well because his/her legs or back have been injured: *The accident left her a cripple at the age of 20.* ◇ (*figurative*) *an emotional cripple*

> NOTE This is an old-fashioned word and is now considered offensive. A more polite way of expressing the same meaning today is to say that somebody is **disabled** or that he/she has a **disability**.

**crip·ple²** /ˈkrɪpl/ *verb* [T] **1** (usually passive) (*old-fashioned*) to cause sb to be a CRIPPLE¹: *He was crippled in a car accident.* **2** to damage sth badly: *The recession has crippled the automobile industry.*

**crip·pling** /ˈkrɪplɪŋ/ *adj.* that causes very great damage; that has a very harmful effect: *crippling debts*

★**cri·sis** /ˈkraɪsəs/ *noun* [C,U] (*pl.* **cri·ses** /ˈkraɪsiz/) a time of great danger or difficulty; the moment when things change and either improve or get worse: *the international crisis caused by the invasion* ◇ *a friend you can rely on in times of crisis*

★**crisp¹** /krɪsp/ *adj.* **1** hard and dry: *Store the crackers in an airtight container to keep them crisp.* **2** firm and fresh or new: *a crisp apple/salad* ◇ *a crisp new $10 bill* **3** (used about the air or weather) cold and dry: *a crisp winter morning* **4** (used about the way sb speaks) quick, clear but not very friendly: *a crisp reply*

**crisp·y** /ˈkrɪspi/ *adj.* (**crisp·i·er**; **crisp·i·est**) = CRISP¹ (1,2): *crispy onion rings*

**criss·cross** /ˈkrɪskrɔs/ *adj.* (only *before* a noun) with many lines that cross over each other: *a crisscross pattern* ▸ **criss·cross** *verb* [I,T]: *the trails that crisscross the park*

★**cri·te·ri·on** /kraɪˈtɪriən/ *noun* [C] (*pl.* **cri·te·ri·a** /-riə/) the standard that you use when you make a decision or form an opinion about sb/sth: *What are the criteria for deciding who gets financial aid?*

★**crit·ic** /ˈkrɪt̬ɪk/ *noun* [C] **1** a person who says what he/she thinks is bad or wrong with sb/sth: *He is a long-standing critic of the present transportation policy.* **2** a person whose job is to give his/her opinion about a play/movie/book/work of art: *a movie critic* (= in a newspaper, etc.)

★**crit·i·cal** /ˈkrɪt̬ɪkl/ *adj.* **1 critical (of sb/sth)** saying what is wrong with sb/sth; disapproving: *The report was very critical of the condition of the country's highways.* ◇ *to make some critical remarks* **2** (only *before* a noun) describing the good and bad points of a play, movie, book, work of art, etc.: *a critical guide to this month's new movies* **3** dangerous or serious: *The patient is in a critical condition.* **4** very important; at a time when things can suddenly become better or worse: *The talks between the two leaders have reached a critical stage.* ► **crit·i·cal·ly** /-ɪkli/ ***adv.***: *a critically ill patient* ◇ *a critically important decision*

★**crit·i·cism** /ˈkrɪt̬əsɪzəm/ ***noun*** **1** [C,U] (an expression of) what you think is bad about sb/sth: *severe criticism of the city council's plans* ◇ *My main criticism is that it is too expensive.* **2** [U] the act of describing the good and bad points of a play, movie, book, work of art, etc.: *literary criticism*

★**crit·i·cize** /ˈkrɪt̬əsaɪz/ ***verb*** [I,T] **criticize (sb/sth) (for sth)** to say what is bad or wrong with sb/sth: *The doctor was criticized for not sending the patient to the hospital.* ◇ *Stop criticizing!*

**cri·tique¹** /krɪˈtik/ ***noun*** [C] a piece of writing that describes the good and bad points of sb/sth

**cri·tique²** /krɪˈtik/ ***verb*** [T] to describe the good and bad points of sb/sth

**crit·ter** /ˈkrɪt̬ər/ ***noun*** [C] (*informal*) a creature; an animal: *Those little critters sure can run fast!*

**croak¹** /kroʊk/ ***noun*** [C] a deep low sound, like the noise that a frog makes

**croak²** /kroʊk/ ***verb*** **1** [I,T] to make a noise like a croak, e.g. because you have a cold and are losing your voice **2** [I] (*slang*) to die: *She married a millionaire who was just about to croak.*

**cro·chet** /kroʊˈʃeɪ/ ***verb*** [I,T] (*pt, pp* **cro·chet·ed** /-ʃeɪd/) to make clothes, blankets, etc. by using wool or thick cotton and one needle with a hook at one end: *to crochet a shawl* ➲ Look at **knit**.

**croc·o·dile** /ˈkrɑkədaɪl/ ***noun*** [C] a large, long animal with hard skin that lives in rivers in hot regions. A crocodile is a dangerous animal because it has a large mouth with a lot of sharp teeth in it. It is a reptile. ➲ Look at **alligator**.

**crois·sant** /krəˈsɑnt; krwɑˈsɑn/ ***noun*** [C] a type of light bread roll, shaped in a curve, that is often eaten with butter ➲ picture at **bread**.

**cro·ny** /ˈkroʊni/ ***noun*** [C] (*pl.* **cro·nies**) (*informal*) (often used in a critical way) a friend

**crook** /krʊk/ ***noun*** [C] **1** (*informal*) a dishonest person; a criminal **2** a bend or curve in sth: *the crook of your arm* (= the inside of your elbow)

**crook·ed** /ˈkrʊkəd/ ***adj.*** **1** not straight or even: *That picture is crooked. I'll straighten it for you.* ◇ *crooked teeth* **2** (*informal*) not honest: *a crooked politician*

★**crop¹** /krɑp/ ***noun*** **1** [C] all the grain, fruit, vegetables, etc. that grow or are collected at one time or place: *this year's wheat crop* ◇ *Another year of crop failure would mean starvation for many people.* **2** [C, usually pl.] plants that are grown on farms for food: *Corn and soybeans are the main crops here.* **3** [sing.] a number of people or things which have appeared at the same time: *the new crop of freshmen*

IDM **the cream of the crop** → CREAM¹

**crop²** /krɑp/ ***verb*** [T] (**crop·ping**; **cropped**) to cut sth very short: *cropped hair*

PHR V **crop up** to appear suddenly, when you are not expecting it: *Some problems have cropped up.*

★**cross¹** /krɔs/ ***noun*** [C] **1** a vertical piece of wood with another piece of wood across it, on which people were killed as a punishment in former times, or sth shaped like this that is used as a symbol of the Christian religion: *Christ's death on the cross* ◇ *The priest made the sign of the cross* (= by moving his right hand in front of his face and chest in the shape of a cross). ➲ Look at **crucifix**. **2** [usually sing.] **a cross (between A and B)** something (especially a plant or an animal) that is a mixture of two different types of things: *a fruit which is a cross between a peach and an apple*

★**cross²** /krɔs/ ***verb*** **1** [I,T] **cross (over) (from sth/to sth)** to go from one side of sth to the other: *to cross the street* ◇ *Where did you cross the border?* **2** [I] (used about lines, roads, etc.) to pass across each other: *The two roads cross just north of the town.* ◇ (*figurative*) *Our letters crossed in the mail.* **3** [T] to put sth across or over sth else: *to cross your legs* **4** [T] **cross yourself** to make the sign of a cross in front of your face and chest as a symbol of the Christian religion **5** [T] to refuse to do what sb wants you to do; to oppose sb: *He's an important man. It could be dangerous to cross him.* **6** [T] **cross sth with sth** to produce a new type of plant or animal by mixing two different types: *If you cross a horse with a donkey, you get a mule.*

IDM **cross my heart (and hope to die)** (*informal*) (used for emphasizing that what you are saying is true)

**cross your fingers** to hope that things will happen in the way that you want; to wish for good luck: *There's nothing more we can do now – just cross our fingers and hope for the best.*

> NOTE If people say they are **crossing their fingers** or **keeping their fingers crossed**, it doesn't mean that they are really doing this with their hands. It means that they are wishing somebody luck or hoping very much that something good will happen.

**cross your mind** (used about a thought, an idea, etc.) to come into your mind: *It never even crossed my mind that she was lying.*

PHR V **cross sth off (sth)** to remove sth from a list, etc. by drawing a line through it: *Cross Dave's name off the guest list – he can't come.*

**cross sth out** to draw a line through sth that you have written because you have made a mistake, etc.: *to cross out a spelling mistake*

**cross³** /krɔs/ ***adj.*** angry or annoyed: *I was really cross with her for leaving me with all the work.* ◇ *What are you so cross about?*

**ˌcross-ˈcountry** ***adj., adv.*** across fields, etc.; not using main roads: *a cross-country run* ◇ *cross-country skiing* ➲ picture at **ski**.

**ˌcross-exˈamine** ***verb*** [T] to ask sb a lot of questions (e.g. in a court) in order to find out the truth about sth: *to cross-examine a witness in court* ► **ˌcross-exˌamiˈnation** ***noun*** [C,U]

**ˈcross-eyed** ***adj.*** having one or both of your eyes looking toward your nose

**cross·fire** /ˈkrɔsfaɪər/ ***noun*** [U] **1** the shooting of guns from two or more places so that the bullets cross each other: *Two children were shot when they were caught in the crossfire between rival gangs.* **2** a situation in which two people or groups are arguing and in which sb else becomes involved against his/her will

**cross·ing** /ˈkrɔsɪŋ/ ***noun*** [C] **1** the act of going or traveling across sth: *Most illegal border crossings are made at night.* **2** a place where roads or railroad tracks cross each other: *Buses must come to a full stop at railroad crossings.* **3** a place where you can cross over sth: *The guards stopped us at the border crossing and searched our car.*

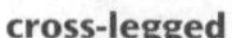

**cross-legged**

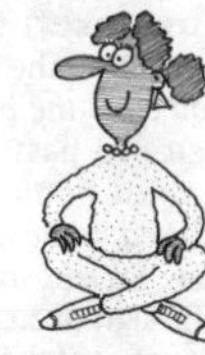

**cross-legged**

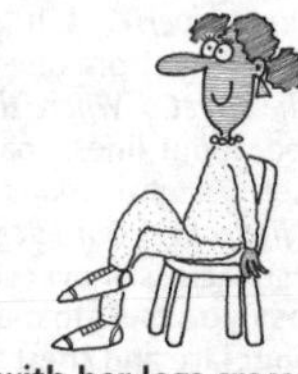

**with her legs crossed**

**cross-legged** /ˈkrɔs ˌlɛgəd; -lɛgd/ ***adj., adv.*** sitting on the floor with your legs pulled up in front of you and with one leg or foot over the other: *to sit cross-legged*

ˈ**cross-ˌref·er·ence** ***noun*** [C] a note in a book, etc. that tells you to look in another place in the book for more information

**cross·roads** /ˈkrɔsroʊdz/ ***noun*** [C] (*pl.* **crossroads**) a place where two or more roads cross each other: *When you come to the next crossroads, turn right.* ◇ (*figurative*) *The nation is* ***at a crossroads*** *– the next election will determine the country's future.*

ˈ**cross ˌsection** (*also* ˈ**cross-ˌsection**) ***noun*** [C] **1** a picture of what the inside of sth would look like if you cut through it: *a diagram of a cross section of the human brain* **2** a group of people that are typical of a larger group: *The students in our program represent a cross section of society.*

ˈ**cross street** ***noun*** [C] a street that crosses another street, usually at an angle of 90°: *Our office is at 198 Madison Avenue – the nearest cross street is 35th St.*

**cross·town** /ˈkrɔstaʊn/ ***adj.*** (only *before* a noun) going from one side of a town or city to the other side: *a crosstown bus/highway*

ˈ**cross-ˌtraining** ***noun*** [U] doing more than one sport or physical activity regularly, to improve your physical condition generally: *His tennis game has improved a lot since he started cross-training.* ▶ ˈ**cross-ˌtrainer** ***noun*** [C]

**cross·walk** /ˈkrɔswɔk/ ***noun*** [C] a place where people can cross a street

**crossword puzzle**

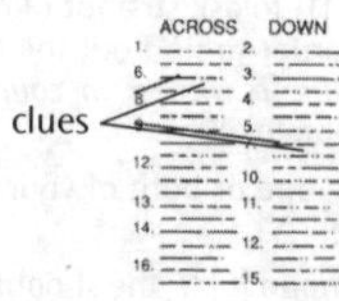



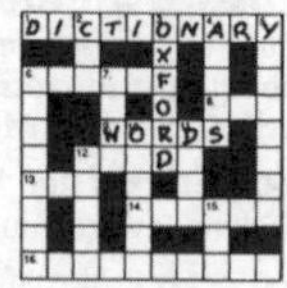



**cross·word** /ˈkrɔswərd/ (*also* ˈ**crossword ˌpuzzle**) ***noun*** [C] a word game with black and white squares where you write the words in the white squares, either across or down. The correct words are the answers to special questions (clues): *to do a crossword*

**crotch** /krɑtʃ/ ***noun*** [C] the place where a person's legs, or pant legs, join at the top

**crouch** /kraʊtʃ/ ***verb*** [I] to bend down so that your body is close to the ground and lean forward slightly: *The cat crouched in front of the hole waiting for the mouse to appear.* ◇ *He crouched down behind the couch.* ➲ picture at **kneel**.

**crou·ton** /ˈkrutɑn/ ***noun*** [C] a small piece of cold, crisp fried bread served in soup or on a salad

**crow**[1] /kroʊ/ ***noun*** [C] a large black bird that makes a loud noise

**IDM** **as the crow flies** (used for describing distances) in a straight line: *It's a mile as the crow flies, but three miles by car.*

**crow**[2] /kroʊ/ ***verb*** [I] **1** to make a loud noise, such as a male chicken (a rooster) makes, e.g. early in the morning **2 crow (about sth)** (*informal*) to speak too proudly about sth

**crow·bar** /ˈkroʊbɑr/ ***noun*** [C] a long iron bar that is used for forcing sth open

★**crowd**[1] /kraʊd/ ***noun*** **1** [C] a large number of people in one place: *A large crowd gathered to hear the President speak.* ◇ *He pushed his way through the crowd.* ◇ *There were crowds of people waiting outside the theater.* **2 the crowd** [sing.] most people: *to follow the crowd* (= to do what everybody else does) **3** [C] (*informal*) a group of people who know each other: *Bob, Mike and Joe will be there – the usual crowd.*

**crowd**[2] /kraʊd/ ***verb*** **1** [I] **crowd around (sb)** (used about a lot of people) to come together in one place: *Fans crowded around the singer, hoping to get his autograph.* **2** [T] (used about a lot of people) to fill an area: *Groups of tourists crowded the main streets.*

**PHR V** **crowd into sth**; **crowd in** to go into a small place and make it very full: *Somehow we all crowded into their small living room.*

**crowd sb/sth into sth**; **crowd sb/sth in** to put a lot of people into a small place: *Ten prisoners were crowded into one small cell.*

★**crowd·ed** /ˈkraʊdəd/ ***adj.*** full of people: *The mall was crowded with holiday shoppers.* ◇ *a crowded bus*

★**crown**[1] /kraʊn/ ***noun*** **1** [C] a round ornament made of gold and jewels, that a king or queen wears on his/her head on official occasions **2 the Crown** [sing.] (*Cdn*) the king or queen, especially when considered as the head of the government; the federal or provincial government in Canada **3** [C] an artificial covering for the top part of a tooth that has been damaged **4** [sing.] the top of your head or of a hat

**crown**[2] /kraʊn/ ***verb*** [T] **1** to put a CROWN[1] (1) on the head of a new king or queen in an official ceremony: *Queen Elizabeth of England was crowned in 1952.* ◇ (*figurative*) *the newly crowned American champion* **2 crown sth (with sth)** (*formal*) to cover the top of sth: *The mountain was crowned with snow.* **3** to be a good or successful end to sth: *years of hard work that were finally crowned with success*

ˌ**Crown atˈtorney** ***noun*** [C] (*pl.* **Crown**

**attorneys**) (*also* ˌ**Crown ˈcounsel**, ˌ**Crown ˈprosecutor**) (*Cdn*) a lawyer who works for the CROWN (2) and whose job is to prove in a court of law that sb is guilty of a crime

**ˈCrown corpoˌration** *noun* [C] (*Cdn*) a large business company (**corporation**) that is owned by the federal or provincial government

**ˌCrown ˈcounsel** *noun* [C] (*Cdn*) = CROWN ATTORNEY

**crown·ing** /ˈkraʊnɪŋ/ *adj.* (only *before* a noun) the best or most important: *Winning the championship was the crowning moment of her career.*

**ˈCrown land** *noun* [U] (in Canada) land that is owned by the federal or provincial government

**ˌCrown ˈprosecutor** *noun* [C] (*Cdn*) = CROWN ATTORNEY

⋆**cru·cial** /ˈkruʃl/ *adj.* **crucial (to/for sth)** very important: *Early diagnosis of the illness is crucial for successful treatment.* ▶ **cru·cial·ly** /-ʃəli/ *adv.*: *a crucially important decision/meeting*

**cru·ci·fix** /ˈkrusəfɪks/ *noun* [C] a small model of a cross with a figure of Jesus on it

**cru·ci·fix·ion** /ˌkrusəˈfɪkʃn/ *noun* [C,U] the act of crucifying sb: *the Crucifixion of Christ*

**cru·ci·fy** /ˈkrusəfaɪ/ *verb* [T] (*pres. part.* **cru·ci·fy·ing**; *3rd person sing. pres.* **cru·ci·fies**; *pt, pp* **cru·ci·fied**) to kill sb by nailing or tying him/her to a cross

**crud** /krʌd/ *noun* [U] (*informal*) any dirty or unpleasant substance

**crud·dy** /krʌdi/ *adj.* (**crud·di·er**; **crud·di·est**) (*informal*) bad, dirty, or of low quality: *We got really cruddy service in that restaurant last time.*

**crude** /krud/ *adj.* **1** in its natural state: *crude oil* **2** done or made in a simple way; not skillful: *The method was crude but very effective.* **3** rude, talking or acting in a way that would offend many people: *He always tells such crude jokes!* ▶ **crude·ly** *adv.*

⋆**cru·el** /kruəl/ *adj.* (**cru·el·er** or **cru·el·ler**; **cru·el·est** or **cru·el·lest**) causing physical or mental pain or suffering to sb/sth; unkind: *I think it's cruel to keep animals in cages.* ◇ *a cruel punishment* ▶ **cru·el·ly** /ˈkruəli/ *adv.*

**cru·el·ty** /ˈkruəlti/ *noun* (*pl.* **cru·el·ties**) **1** [U] **cruelty (to sb/sth)** cruel behavior: *cruelty to children* **2** [C, usually pl.] a cruel act: *the cruelties of war*

**cruise¹** /kruz/ *verb* [I] **1** to travel by boat, visiting a number of places, as a vacation: *to cruise around the Caribbean* **2** to travel by car, plane, etc. staying at the same speed: *cruising at 65 miles an hour* **3** to travel, usually slowly, by car, without intending to go to a particular place: *kids cruising up and down Main Street on Friday night*

**cruise²** /kruz/ *noun* [C] a vacation in which you travel on a ship and visit a number of different places: *After they retired, they went on a Caribbean cruise.*

**ˈcruise conˌtrol** *noun* [U] a system in a car that keeps the car going at the same speed, so that the driver does not need to use his/her feet

**cruis·er** /kruzər/ *noun* [C] **1** a police car **2** a large military ship

**crumb** /krʌm/ *noun* [C] a very small piece of bread, cake or cookie

**crum·ble** /ˈkrʌmbl/ *verb* [I,T] **crumble (sth) (into/to sth)**; **crumble (sth) (up)** (to cause sth) to break into very small pieces: *The walls of the old church are beginning to crumble.* ◇ (*figurative*) *Support for the policy is starting to crumble.*

**crum·my** /ˈkrʌmi/ *adj.* (**crum·mi·er**; **crum·mi·est**) (*informal*) bad or unpleasant: *a crummy little basement apartment*

**crum·ple** /ˈkrʌmpl/ *verb* [I,T] **crumple (sth) (into sth)**; **crumple (sth) (up)** (to cause sth) to be folded or pressed in a messy way: *The front of the car crumpled when it hit the wall.* ◇ *to crumple a piece of paper into a ball*

**crunch¹** /krʌntʃ/ *verb* **1** [T] **crunch (on) sth** to make a loud noise when you are eating sth hard: *to crunch on an apple* **2** [I] to make a loud noise like the sound of sth being walked on and crushed: *The snow made a crunching noise under our feet.*

**crunch²** /krʌntʃ/ *noun* **1** [sing.] an act or noise of CRUNCHING¹: *the crunch of their boots on the snow* **2** [C] a situation when there is not enough money, time, etc.: *a financial crunch* ◇ *We are experiencing the city's worst housing crunch in 20 years*

**crunch·y** /ˈkrʌntʃi/ *adj.* (**crunch·i·er**; **crunch·i·est**) hard and crisp, so that it makes a noise when you eat it or step on it: *a crunchy apple*

**cru·sade** /kruˈseɪd/ *noun* [C] **1 Crusade** one of the wars that European Christians fought with Muslims in the Middle Ages to win back land in the area that is now Israel **2** a fight for sth that you believe to be good or against sth that you believe to be bad: *a crusade against drugs*

**cru·sad·er** /kruˈseɪdər/ *noun* [C] a person who takes part in a crusade

⋆**crush¹** /krʌʃ/ *verb* [T] **1** to press sb/sth hard so that he/she/it is broken, damaged or injured: *Don't pack the eggs at the bottom of the bag or they'll get crushed.* ◇ *to be crushed to death* **2 crush sth (up)** to break sth hard into very small pieces or a powder: *First, crush the garlic and fry in olive oil.* **3** to defeat sb/sth completely: *The army was sent in to crush the rebellion.*

**crush²** /krʌʃ/ *noun* **1** [C] **a crush (on sb)** (*informal*) a strong feeling of love and admiration for sb that does not usually last for a long time: *to have a crush on your teacher* **2** [sing.] a large group of people in a small space: *There was a crush of reporters in the lobby of the courthouse.*

**crush·ing** /ˈkrʌʃɪŋ/ *adj.* (only *before* a noun) that defeats sb/sth completely or upsets sb/sth a lot: *a crushing defeat* ◇ *a crushing blow to the country's economy*

**crust** /krʌst/ *noun* [C,U] **1** the hard part on the outside of a loaf of bread, a pie, etc.: *I cut the crusts off the bread.* ➲ picture at **bread**. **2** [C] a hard layer on the outside of sth: *the earth's crust*

**crus·ta·cean** /krʌˈsteɪʃn/ *noun* [C] (*technical*) any creature with a soft body that is divided into sections, and a hard outer shell. Most crustaceans live in water: *Crabs, shrimp and lobsters are crustaceans.* ➲ Compare **shellfish**.

**crust·y** /ˈkrʌsti/ *adj.* (**crust·i·er**; **crust·i·est**) **1** having a hard CRUST (1): *crusty bread* **2** (*informal*) bad-tempered and impatient: *a crusty old professor*

**crutch** /krʌtʃ/ *noun* [C] a type of stick that you put

under your arm to help you walk when you have hurt your leg or foot: *to be on crutches* (= to walk using crutches)

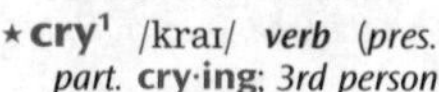
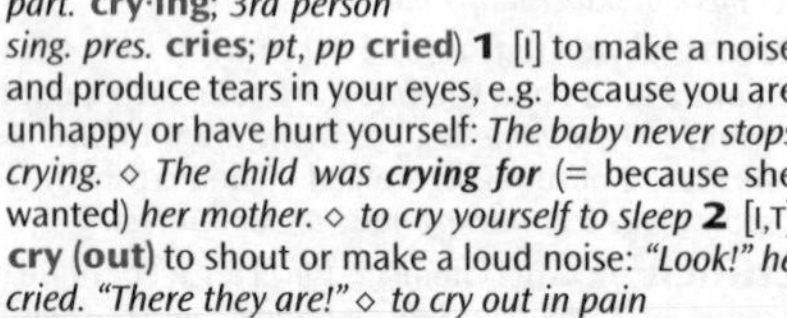


**crux** /krʌks/ ***noun*** [sing.] the most important or difficult part of a problem: *Now we come to the crux of the problem.*

★**cry**[1] /kraɪ/ ***verb*** (*pres. part.* **cry·ing**; *3rd person sing. pres.* **cries**; *pt, pp* **cried**) **1** [I] to make a noise and produce tears in your eyes, e.g. because you are unhappy or have hurt yourself: *The baby never stops crying.* ◇ *The child was* ***crying for*** (= because she wanted) *her mother.* ◇ *to cry yourself to sleep* **2** [I,T] **cry (out)** to shout or make a loud noise: *"Look!" he cried. "There they are!"* ◇ *to cry out in pain*

PHRV **cry out for sth** to need sth very much: *The school district is crying out for good teachers.*

★**cry**[2] /kraɪ/ ***noun*** (*pl.* **cries**) **1** [C] a shout or loud noise: *the cry of a seagull* ◇ *a cry of pain/fear/joy* **2** [sing.] an act of CRYING[1] (1): *After a good cry I felt much better.*

IDM **a far cry from sth/from doing sth** → FAR[1]

**cry·ing** /ˈkraɪɪŋ/ ***adj.*** (only *before* a noun) very great (usually used when talking about a bad situation, etc.): *There's a crying need for more doctors.* ◇ *It's a crying shame that so many people can't find jobs.*

**cryp·tic** /ˈkrɪptɪk/ ***adj.*** having a hidden meaning that is not easy to understand; mysterious: *a cryptic message/remark*

**crys·tal** /ˈkrɪstl/ ***noun*** **1** [U] a transparent rock or mineral **2** [U] very high-quality glass: *a crystal vase* **3** [C] a regular shape that some mineral substances form when they are solid: *salt crystals*

IDM **crystal clear** very easy to understand: *The meaning is crystal clear.*

**ˌcrystal ˈball** ***noun*** [C] a glass ball in which some people believe you can see what is going to happen in the future

**crys·tal·lize** /ˈkrɪstəlaɪz/ ***verb*** [I,T] **1** (used about thoughts, plans, beliefs, etc.) to become or make sth become clear and fixed: *Our ideas began to crystallize into a definite plan.* ◇ *The final chapter crystallizes all the main issues.* **2** (*technical*) to form or make sth form into CRYSTALS (3): *The salt crystallizes as the water evaporates.*

**C-section** /ˈsi ˌsɛkʃn/ ***noun*** [C] = CESAREAN SECTION

**CT** ***abbr.*** (*written*) = CENTRAL TIME

**CT scan** /ˌsi ˈti skæn/ ***noun*** [C] = CAT SCAN

**cu.** ***abbr.*** = CUBIC

**cub** /kʌb/ ***noun*** [C] **1** a young fox, bear, lion, tiger or wolf **2 Cub** a boy or girl in the second level (ages 8-10) of the SCOUTS[1] (1) in Canada

**cube**[1] /kyub/ ***noun*** [C] **1** a solid shape that has six equal square sides: *ice cubes* **2** the number that you get if you multiply a number by itself twice: *the cube of 5 ($5^3$) is 125 (= 5 x 5 x 5).*

**cube**[2] /kyub/ ***verb*** [T] (usually passive) to multiply a number by itself twice: *Four cubed ($4^3$) is 64 (= 4 x 4 x 4).*

**cube**

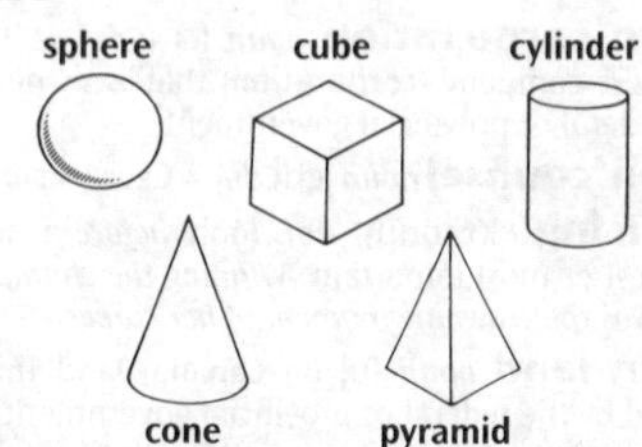


**cu·bic** /ˈkyubɪk/ ***adj.*** (*abbr.* **cu.**) measured by multiplying the length by the width by the height of sth: *If a box is 2 ft. long, 2 ft. wide and 2 ft. high, its volume is 8 cubic feet.*

**cu·bi·cle** /ˈkyubɪkl/ ***noun*** [C] a small separate section of a larger room, e.g. part of an office with low walls around it

**ˈCub Scout** ***noun*** [C] a member of the junior level (ages 8-10) in the Boy Scouts organization in the U.S. ➲ Look at **scout**[1].

**cu·cum·ber** /ˈkyukʌmbər/ ***noun*** [C,U] a long, thin vegetable with dark green skin and a soft white part inside that is often used in salads ➲ Look also at **pickle**. ➲ Picture on study page **A28-29**.

**cud·dle** /ˈkʌdl/ ***verb*** [I,T] to hold sb/sth closely in your arms as a sign of love

**cud·dly** /ˈkʌdli/ (**cud·dli·er**; **cud·dli·est**) ***adj.*** soft and pleasant to hold close to you: *a cuddly teddy bear*

**cue** /kyu/ ***noun*** [C] **1** a word or gesture that is the signal for sb else to say or do sth, especially in a play: *When Julia puts the tray on the table, that's your cue to come on stage.* **2** an example of how to behave: *I wasn't sure how to behave at a Japanese wedding, so I took my cue from my hosts.* **3** a long, thin wooden stick, used to hit the ball in games like pool and billiards

IDM **(right) on cue** at exactly the moment expected

**cuff** /kʌf/ ***noun*** [C] **1** the end part of a sleeve, which often fastens at the wrist ➲ picture at **shirt**. **2** the bottom part of a pants leg that is folded up on the outside ➲ Look also at **handcuffs**.

**cuff·link** (*also* **ˈcuff link**) /ˈkʌflɪŋk/ ***noun*** [usually pl.] one of a pair of small objects used instead of buttons to fasten a shirt sleeve together at the wrist

**cui·sine** /kwəˈzin/ ***noun*** [U] a style of cooking: *Italian cuisine*

NOTE A less formal word is **cooking**.

**cul-de-sac** /ˈkʌl də sæk/ ***noun*** [C] (*pl.* **cul-de-sacs**) a street that is closed at one end

**cu·li·nar·y** /ˈkʌləˌnɛri/ ***adj.*** connected with cooking

**cull** /kʌl/ ***verb*** [T] to gather or select information, ideas, etc., from different sources

**cul·mi·nate** /ˈkʌlməneɪt/ ***verb*** [I] (*formal*) **culminate in sth** to reach a final result or high point: *The team's efforts culminated in victory in the* *national championships.* ▸ **cul·mi·na·tion** /ˌkʌlməˈneɪʃn/ **noun** [sing.]: *The joint space mission was the culmination of years of research.*

**cu·lottes** /ˈkulɑts; kuˈlɑts/ **noun** [pl.] women's pants that stop at the knee and are made to look like a skirt

**cul·pa·ble** /ˈkʌlpəbl/ **adj.** (*formal*) responsible and deserving blame for having done sth wrong: *The accident came about through culpable negligence.*

**cul·prit** /ˈkʌlprət/ **noun** [C] a person who has done sth wrong

**cult** /kʌlt/ **noun** [C] **1** a type of religion or religious group, especially one that is considered unusual **2** (usually used before another noun) a person or thing that has become popular with a particular group of people: *His books have become cult favorites among young people.*

**cul·ti·vate** /ˈkʌltəveɪt/ **verb** [T] **1** to prepare and use land for growing crops: *to cultivate the soil* **2** to grow crops: *Olives have been cultivated for centuries in Mediterranean countries.* **3** to try hard to develop sth that could be useful to you: *He cultivated links with colleagues in Europe.* ▸ **cul·ti·va·tion** /ˌkʌltəˈveɪʃn/ **noun** [U]

**cul·ti·vat·ed** /ˈkʌltəveɪţəd/ **adj.** **1** well educated, with good manners **2** (used about land) used for growing plants for food or to sell **3** (used about plants) grown on a farm, not wild

⋆**cul·tur·al** /ˈkʌltʃərəl/ **adj.** **1** connected with the customs, ideas, art, etc. of a society: *cultural identities* ◇ *the nation's cultural diversity* **2** connected with art, music, literature, etc.: *The city has a rich cultural life, with many theaters, concert halls and art galleries.* ➲ Look also at **multicultural**. ▸ **cul·tur·al·ly** /-rəli/ **adv.**

⋆**cul·ture** /ˈkʌltʃər/ **noun** **1** [C,U] the customs, ideas, civilization, etc. of a particular society or group of people: *the language and culture of the Aztecs* ◇ *The international conference aims to bring together people from many different cultures.* **2** [U] achievement in or understanding of art, literature, ideas, etc.: *New York has always been a center of culture.*

**cul·tured** /ˈkʌltʃərd/ **adj.** well-educated, showing a good knowledge of the arts, etc.: *a cultured manner, mind, person, etc.*

ˈ**culture shock** **noun** [U] a feeling of confusion, etc. that you may experience when you go to a country that is very different from your own

**cum·ber·some** /ˈkʌmbərsəm/ **adj.** **1** heavy and difficult to carry, use, wear, etc. **2** (used about a system, etc.) slow; too complicated to be efficient: *cumbersome rules and regulations*

**cum lau·de** /kʊm ˈlaʊdə; -di; kʌm ˈlɔdə/ **adj.**, **adv.** (in the U.S.) at the third of the three highest levels of achievement that students can reach when they finish high school or college: *She graduated cum laude from Pennsylvania State University.* ➲ Look also at **magna cum laude** and **summa cum laude**.

**cu·mu·la·tive** /ˈkyumyələţɪv/ **adj.** increasing steadily in amount, degree, etc.: *a cumulative effect*

**cun·ning** /ˈkʌnɪŋ/ **adj.** skillful at deceiving people: *a cunning liar* ◇ *a cunning trick* ▸ **cun·ning·ly** **adv.**

⋆**cup**[1] /kʌp/ **noun** [C] **1** a small deep container with a round base and usually a handle, used for drinking liquids: *a cup and saucer* ◇ *a cup of coffee* ➲ picture at **cup**. **2** (*abbr.* **c.**) a unit of measurement used in cooking. A cup of liquid is equal to 0.237 liter: *Add half a cup of sugar and two cups of flour.* **3** (in sports) a large metal CUP (1) given as a prize; the competition for such a cup: *the World Cup soccer tournament* **4** an object shaped like a CUP (1): *a set of measuring cups*

IDM **not sb's cup of tea** not what sb likes or is interested in: *Horror movies just aren't my cup of tea.*

**cups**

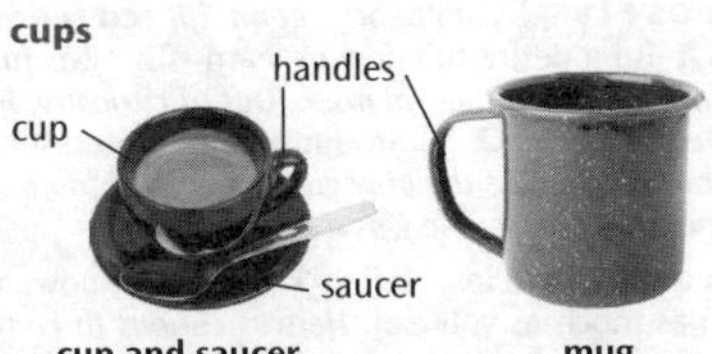


**cup**[2] /kʌp/ **verb** (**cup·ping**; **cupped**) [T] to form sth, especially your hands, into the shape of a cup: *I cupped my hands to take a drink from the stream.* ◇ *to cup your hand behind your ear*

⋆**cup·board** /ˈkʌbərd/ **noun** [C] a piece of furniture, usually with shelves inside and a door or doors at the front, used for storing food, etc.: *a kitchen cupboard* ➲ Look also at **cabinet** and **closet**.

**cup·cake** /ˈkʌpkeɪk/ **noun** [C] a small round cake for one person

**cur·a·ble** /ˈkyʊrəbl/ **adj.** that can be cured: *a curable disease* OPP **incurable**

**cu·ra·tor** /kyʊˈreɪţər; ˈkyʊrəţər/ **noun** [C] a person whose job is to take care of the things that are kept in a museum, an art gallery, etc.

**curb**[1] /kərb/ **noun** [C] **1** a line of stones or cement that forms a raised border along the side of a street: *kids sitting on the curb* ➲ Picture on study page **A31**. **2 a curb (on sth)** something that controls or puts a limit on sth else: *to put a curb on government spending*

**curb**[2] /kərb/ **verb** [T] to control or set a limit on sth: *a plan to curb inflation*

**curb·side**[1] /ˈkərbsaɪd/ **noun** [U] the side of the street near the CURB[1] (1): *to stand at the curbside*

**curb·side**[2] /ˈkərbsaɪd/ **adj.** happening at the side of the street or in some convenient place: *curbside recycling* ◇ *Does the airport have curbside drop-off and pick-up?*

**curd** /kərd/ **noun** [U] (*also* **curds** [pl.]) a thick soft substance that is formed when milk turns sour and is used to make cheese

**cur·dle** /ˈkərdl/ **verb** [I,T] **1** when a liquid, especially milk, curdles or sth curdles it, it separates into solid and liquid parts **2** if sth curdles your blood or makes your blood curdle, it makes you extremely frightened or shocked

C

★**cure¹** /kyʊr/ ***verb*** [T] **1 cure sb (of sth)** to make sb healthy again: *The treatment cured him of cancer.* ◇ *The doctors couldn't cure her.* **2** to make an illness, injury, etc. end or disappear: *It is still not possible to cure the common cold.* **3** to make certain types of food last longer by drying, smoking or salting them: *cured ham*

★**cure²** /kyʊr/ ***noun*** [C] **1** a medicine or treatment that can cure an illness, etc.: *There is no known cure for AIDS.* **2** a return to good health; the process of being cured: *The new drug brought about a miraculous cure.*

**cur·few** /ˈkərfyu/ ***noun*** [C] a time after which sb is not allowed to go outside his/her home: *The government imposed a curfew.* ◇ *Mom and Dad set a curfew of 10:00 for my brother and me.*

**cu·ri·os·i·ty** /ˌkyʊriˈɑsət̬i/ ***noun*** (*pl.* **cu·ri·os·i·ties**) **1** [U] a desire to know or learn sth: ***I was full of curiosity*** *about their plans.* ◇ ***Out of curiosity****, he opened her letter.* **2** [C] an unusual and interesting person or thing: *As the only girl who played football for the school team, she was a real curiosity.*

**cu·ri·ous** /ˈkyʊriəs/ ***adj.*** **1** eager to know or learn as much as you can: *He was curious to know how the machine worked.* ◇ *I've always been curious about politics.* **2** unusual or strange: *As I was walking home, a curious thing happened.* ▶ **cu·ri·ous·ly** ***adv.***: ***Curiously enough****, we discovered that we had exactly the same name.*

★**curl¹** /kərl/ ***noun*** [C] **1** a piece of hair that curves around: *Her hair fell in curls around her face.* **2** a thing that has a curved round shape: *a curl of blue smoke*

★**curl²** /kərl/ ***verb*** **1** [I,T] to form or to make sth form into a curl or curls: *The pages had curled with age.* ◇ *to curl your hair* **2** [I] to move around in a curve: *The snake curled around his arm.*

PHRV **curl up** to pull your arms, legs and head close to your body: *I like to curl up on the couch and watch TV.* ◇ *The animal curled up into a ball to protect itself.*

**curl·er** /ˈkərlər/ (*also* **roller**) ***noun*** [C] a small plastic or metal tube that you wrap hair around in order to make it curly

**curl·y** /ˈkərli/ ***adj.*** (**curl·i·er**; **curl·i·est**) full of curls; shaped like a curl: *curly hair* OPP **straight** ➲ picture at **hair**.

**cur·ren·cy** /ˈkərənsi/ ***noun*** (*pl.* **cur·ren·cies**) **1** [C,U] the system or type of money that a particular country uses: *foreign currency* ◇ *a weak/strong/stable currency* **2** [U] (*formal*) the state of being believed, accepted or used by many people: *new ideas that soon gained currency*

★**cur·rent¹** /ˈkərənt/ ***adj.*** of the present time; happening now: *current fashions* ◇ *current events*

**cur·rent²** /ˈkərənt/ ***noun*** **1** [C] a continuous flowing movement of water, air, etc.: *to swim against/with the current* ◇ (*figurative*) *a current of anti-government feeling* **2** [U] the flow of electricity through a wire, etc.: *electrical current*

ˌ**current afˈfairs** ***noun*** [pl.] important political or social events that are happening at the present time

★**cur·rent·ly** /ˈkərəntli/ ***adv.*** now: *He is currently working in Spain.*

**cur·ric·u·lum** /kəˈrɪkyələm/ ***noun*** [C] (*pl.* **cur·ric·u·lums** or **cur·ric·u·la** /-lə/) all the subjects that are taught in a school, college or university: *Latin is not part of the curriculum at our school.* ◇ *The school's science curriculum includes biology, chemistry and physics.*

**cur·ric·u·lum vi·tae** /kəˌrɪkyələm ˈvitaɪ; -ˈvaɪt̬i/ (*abbr.* **CV**; **c.v.**) (*also* **ré·su·mé**) ***noun*** [C] a written record of your education, qualifications and employment, which you send when you are applying for a job

NOTE In North America, **curriculum vitae** is used mostly by college and university teachers; for other jobs, the word **résumé** is usually used.

**cur·ry** /ˈkəri/ ***noun*** [C,U] (*pl.* **cur·ries**) a hot-tasting dish of meat, vegetables, etc. usually served with rice: *some Indian vegetable curry* ◇ *a hot/mild curry*

ˈ**curry ˌpowder** ***noun*** [C] a mixture of strongly flavored substances (**spices**) in powder form, that is used to make curry

**curse¹** /kərs/ ***noun*** [C] **1** a word used for expressing anger; a swear word **2** a word or words expressing the wish that sth terrible will happen to sb: *In the story, the witch put a curse on the prince.* ◇ *The family seemed to be under a curse* (= lots of bad things happened to them). **3** something that causes great harm: *the curse of drug addiction*

**curse²** /kərs/ ***verb*** **1** [I,T] to swear at sb/sth; to use rude language to express your anger: *He dropped the box, cursed, and started to pick up the contents.* **2** [T] to use a CURSE¹ (2) against sb/sth: *She cursed his family.*

**cur·sor** /ˈkərsər/ ***noun*** [C] a small sign on a computer screen that you can move to indicate a particular position

**cur·so·ry** /ˈkərsəri/ ***adj.*** quick and brief; done in a hurry: *a cursory glance at the newspaper*

**curt** /kərt/ ***adj.*** (used about a person's manner or behavior) appearing rude because very few words are used, or because sth is done in a very quick way: *a curt reply/nod* ◇ *His tone was curt and unfriendly.*

**cur·tail** /kərˈteɪl/ ***verb*** [T] (*formal*) to make sth shorter or smaller; to reduce sth

**curtains**

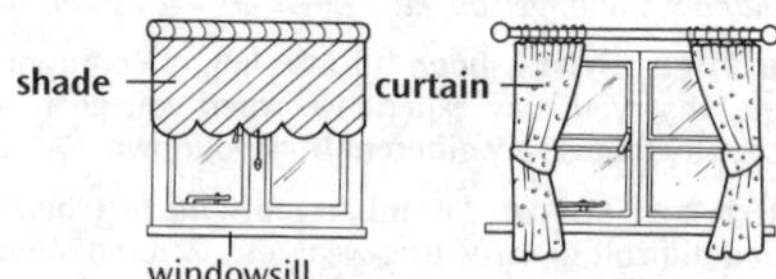


★**cur·tain** /ˈkərtn/ ***noun*** [C] **1** a piece of material that you can move sideways to cover a window, etc.: *Could you close the curtains?* ◇ *a shower curtain* ◇ *The curtain goes up at 7 p.m.* (= in a theater, the play begins). ➲ Look also at **drapery**. **2** a thing that covers or hides sth: *a curtain of mist*

**curt·sy¹** (*also* **curtsey**) /ˈkərtsi/ ***noun*** [C] (*pl.* **curt·sies** or **curt·seys**) a movement made by a woman as a sign of respect, done by bending the knees, with one foot behind the other

**curt·sy²** /ˈkərtsi/ (*also* **curtsey**) *verb* (*pres. part.* **curt·sy·ing** or **curt·sey·ing**; *3rd person sing. pres.* **curt·sies** or **curt·seys**; *pt, pp* **curt·sied** or **curt·seyed**) [I] to make a CURTSY¹

★**curve¹** /kərv/ *noun* [C] **1** a line that bends around: *a curve on a graph* **2** [usually sing.] a system in which letter grades are given to students based on how well they have done in comparison with other students, not based on a fixed standard: *Prof. Jenkins grades on a curve.* **3** = CURVEBALL

IDM **throw sb a curve** to confuse sb by doing or saying sth he/she is not expecting: *One of the journalists threw the senator a curve.*

★**curve²** /kərv/ *verb* [I,T] to bend or to make sth bend in a CURVE¹ (1): *The bay curved around to the south.* ◇ *a curved line*

**curve·ball** /ˈkərvbɔl/ (*also* **curve**) *noun* [C] in the sport of baseball, a ball that moves in a CURVE¹ (1) when it is thrown and is therefore more difficult to hit

**cush·ion¹** /ˈkʊʃn/ *noun* [C] **1** a thick pad or a bag filled with soft material that you can sit on: *I found my keys under the cushions on the couch.* ➲ Picture at **chair¹**.

NOTE A cushion on a bed is a **pillow**.

**2** something that acts or is shaped like a CUSHION (1): *a cushion of air*

**cush·ion²** /ˈkʊʃn/ *verb* [T] **1** to make a blow, etc. less painful: *The snow cushioned his fall.* **2** to reduce the bad effect of sth: *government programs that help to cushion the blow of unemployment*

**cush·y** /ˈkʊʃi/ *adj.* (**cush·i·er**; **cush·i·est**) very easy, needing little effort: *a cushy job*

**cus·tard** /ˈkʌstərd/ *noun* [U] a soft, sweet food made from milk, eggs and sugar, that is baked in an oven

**cus·to·di·an** /kəˈstoʊdiən/ (*also* **janitor**) *noun* [C] a person whose job is to clean a large building and to do small repairs: *a school custodian*

**cus·to·dy** /ˈkʌstədi/ *noun* [U] **1** the legal right or duty to take care of sb/sth: *After the divorce, the mother was given custody of the children.* **2** the state of being guarded, or kept in prison temporarily, especially by the police: *The man was arrested and kept in police custody until his trial.*

**custom-** /ˈkʌstəm/ *prefix* (in compounds) specially done for a particular customer: *a custom-made suit* ◇ *custom-designed furniture*

★**cus·tom¹** /ˈkʌstəm/ *noun* [C,U] a way of behaving which a particular group or society has had for a long time: *the Native American custom of smoking a peace pipe at ceremonies* ◇ *according to local custom* ➲ Look at the note at **habit**.

**cus·tom²** /ˈkʌstəm/ *adj.* (only *before* a noun) specially made or built for a particular customer: *custom kitchen cabinets*

**cus·tom·ar·y** /ˈkʌstəˌmɛri/ *adj.* according to custom; usual: *Is it customary to send Christmas cards in your country?* ▶ **cus·tom·ar·i·ly** /ˌkʌstəˈmɛrəli/ *adv.*

★**cus·tom·er** /ˈkʌstəmər/ *noun* [C] a person who buys goods or services: *a regular customer* ◇ *The salesclerk was helping a customer.*

**cus·toms** (*also* **Customs**) /ˈkʌstəmz/ *noun* [U] **1** the government department that inspects, and collects taxes (**duties**) on, goods that are brought into the country **2** the place at an airport, etc. where government officials check your luggage to see whether you are bringing goods into the country illegally: *We went straight through customs with nothing to declare.* ◇ *a customs officer*

★**cut¹** /kʌt/ *verb* (*pres. part.* **cut·ting**; *pt, pp* **cut**) **1** [I,T] to make an opening, wound or mark in sth using a sharp tool, e.g. a pair of scissors or a knife: *Be careful not to cut yourself on that broken glass!* ◇ *This knife doesn't cut very well.* **2** [T] to remove sth or a part of sth, using a knife, etc.: *She cut two slices of bread.* **3** [T] **cut sth (in/into sth)** to divide sth into pieces with a knife, etc.: *She cut the cake into eight pieces.* ◇ *He cut the rope in two.* ◇ *Cut the sandwich in half* (= into two equal pieces). **4** [T] to make sth shorter by using scissors, etc.: *I cut my own hair.* ◇ *to have your hair cut* (= at the salon) ◇ *to cut the grass* **5** [T] to make or form sth by removing material with a sharp tool: *She cut a hole in the card and pushed the string through.* ◇ *They cut a path through the jungle.* **6** [T] to reduce sth or make it shorter; to remove sth: *to cut taxes* ◇ *Several employees' hours have been cut because of budget problems.*

IDM **cut/skip class** → CLASS

**cut corners** to do sth quickly and not as well as you should

**cut in line** to go to the front of a line of people without waiting for your turn, or to join a line of people in the middle and not at the end

**have your work cut out for you** → WORK¹

PHR V **cut across sth** to go beyond the limits of: *The question of aid for the earthquake victims cuts across national boundaries.*

**cut across, along, through, etc. (sth)** to go across, etc. sth, in order to shorten your trip: *It's a lot quicker if we cut across the field.*

**cut sth back**; **cut back (on sth)** to reduce sth: *to cut back on public spending*

**cut sth down 1** to make sth fall down by cutting it: *to cut down a tree* **2** to shorten sth: *I have to cut my essay down to 2,000 words.*

**cut sth down**; **cut down (on sth)** to reduce the quantity or amount of sth; to do sth less often: *You should cut down on fatty foods.*

**cut in (on sb/sth)**; **cut into sth** to interrupt sb/sth: *to cut into a conversation*

**cut sb off** (often passive) to stop or interrupt sb's telephone conversation: *We were cut off before I could give her my message.*

**cut sb/sth off** (often passive) to stop the supply of sth to sb: *If you don't pay your gas bill, they'll cut you off.* ◇ *The electricity was cut off.*

**cut sth off** to block a road, etc. so that nothing can pass: *We must cut off all possible escape routes.*

**cut sb/sth off (from sb/sth)** (often passive) to prevent sb/sth from moving from a place or contacting people outside: *The farm was cut off from the highway by heavy snow.*

**cut sth open** to open sth by cutting: *She fell and cut her head open.*

**cut sth out 1** to remove sth or to form sth into a particular shape by cutting: *to cut out a dress from a piece of cloth* **2** to leave sth out: *Cut out the*

*boring details!* **3** (*informal*) (often in orders) to stop saying or doing sth, usually sth annoying: *Cut that out and leave me alone!* ◇ *Cut it out! That hurts!* **4** (*informal*) to stop doing or using sth: *You'll only lose weight if you cut out junk food from your diet.*
**cut sth out (of sth)** to remove sth from sth larger by cutting: *He cut the advertisement out of the newspaper.*
**be cut out for sth; be cut out to be sth** to have the qualities to be able to do sth; to be suitable for sth/sb: *You're not cut out to be a soldier.* ◇ *David and Janet are cut out for each other.*
**cut sth up** to cut sth into small pieces with a knife, etc.

★**cut²** /kʌt/ ***noun*** [C] **1** a wound or an opening made with a knife, etc.: *He had a deep cut on his forehead.* **2** an act of cutting: *to have a cut and blow-dry* (= at a hair salon) **3 a cut (in sth)** a reduction in size, amount, etc.: *a cut in government spending* ◇ *tax cuts* **4** a piece of meat from a particular part of an animal **5** (*informal*) a share, especially in profits

**cut·back** /ˈkʌtbæk/ ***noun*** [C] a reduction in amount or number: *budget cutbacks* ◇ *The management had to make cutbacks in personnel.*

**cute** /kyut/ ***adj.*** attractive; good-looking: *Your little girl is so cute!* ◇ *Check out those cute guys over there!* ◇ *a cute dress* ➲ Look at the note at **pretty**¹.

**cu·ti·cle** /ˈkyuţɪkl/ ***noun*** [C] an area of hard skin at the base of the nails on the fingers and toes

**cut·ler·y** /ˈkʌtləri/ ***noun*** [U] the instruments, especially sharp knives, that you use to cut and eat food

**cut·let** /ˈkʌtlət/ ***noun*** [C] a small, flat piece of meat that is usually covered in flour or very small bits of bread (crumbs) and fried or baked

**cut·off** (*also* **cut-off**) /ˈkʌţɔf/ ***noun*** [C] the level or time at which sth stops: *The cutoff date for applications is May 12.*

**ˈcut-rate** ***adj.*** sold at a reduced price; selling goods that are often of poor quality at low prices: *cut-rate plane fares* ◇ *a cut-rate store*

**cut·ter** /ˈkʌţər/ ***noun*** [C] (*also* **cut·ters** [pl.]) a tool that you use for cutting through sth, e.g. metal: *a pair of wire cutters*

**cut·throat** /ˈkʌtθroʊt/ ***adj.*** caring only about success and not worried about hurting anybody: *cutthroat business practices*

**cut·ting** /ˈkʌţɪŋ/ ***noun*** [C] a piece cut off from a plant that you use for growing a new plant

**ˈcutting ˌboard** ***noun*** [C] a piece made of wood or plastic used for cutting meat or vegetables on ➲ picture at **kitchen**.

**ˌcutting ˈedge** ***noun*** [sing.] the most advanced position in a field of study: *Our firm is right at the cutting edge of cancer research.* ◇ *cutting-edge technology*

**CV** (*also* **c.v.**) /ˌsi ˈvi/ ***abbr.*** = CURRICULUM VITAE

**cy·a·nide** /ˈsaɪənaɪd/ ***noun*** [U] a poisonous chemical

**cyber-** /ˈsaɪbər/ ***prefix*** (in nouns and adjectives) connected with electronic communication networks, especially the Internet

**cy·ber·ca·fé** (*also* **cy·ber·ca·fe**) /ˈsaɪbərkæˌfeɪ/ ***noun*** [C] = INTERNET CAFÉ

**cy·ber·space** /ˈsaɪbərspeɪs/ ***noun*** [U] the imaginary place where electronic messages exist while they are being sent from one computer to another

★**cy·cle¹** /ˈsaɪkl/ ***noun*** [C] **1** a series of events, etc. that happen repeatedly in the same order: *the life cycle of a frog* **2** a bicycle or motorcycle: *a cycle shop*
IDM **a vicious circle/cycle** → VICIOUS

★**cy·cle²** /ˈsaɪkl/ ***verb*** [I] to ride a bicycle, especially as a sport

> NOTE **Ride a bike** is a common way of talking about cycling for pleasure: *We like to ride our bikes on weekends.*

**cy·cli·cal** /ˈsaɪklɪkl; æpstress:sɪk-/ (*also* **cy·clic** /ˈsaɪklɪk; æpstress:sɪk-/) ***adj.*** following a repeated pattern

**cy·clist** /ˈsaɪklɪst/ ***noun*** [C] a person who rides a bicycle, especially as a sport

**cy·clone** /ˈsaɪkloʊn/ ***noun*** [C] a violent wind that moves in a circle, causing a storm ➲ Look at the note at **storm**. Look also at **tornado**.

**cyl·in·der** /ˈsɪləndər/ ***noun*** [C] **1** a shape or an object with circular ends and straight sides ➲ picture at **cube**. **2** a cylinder-shaped part of an engine, e.g. in a car: *a six-cylinder engine*

**cy·lin·dri·cal** /səˈlɪndrɪkl/ ***adj.*** having the shape of a cylinder

**cym·bal** /ˈsɪmbl/ ***noun*** [C, usually pl.] one of a pair of round metal plates used as a musical instrument. Cymbals make a loud ringing sound when you strike them together or hit them with a stick. ➲ picture at **drum**.

**cy·nic** /ˈsɪnɪk/ ***noun*** [C] a person who believes that people only do things for selfish reasons: *Don't be such a cynic. He did it to help us, not for the money.* ▸ **cyn·i·cal** /ˈsɪnɪkl/ ***adj.***: *She has a cynical view of politics.* ◇ *a cynical remark* ▸ **cyn·i·cal·ly** /-kli/ ***adv.*** ▸ **cyn·i·cism** /ˈsɪnəsɪzəm/ ***noun*** [U]

**Cy·ril·lic** /sɪˈrɪlɪk/ ***adj.*** the Cyrillic alphabet is used in languages such as Russian

**cyst** /sɪst/ ***noun*** [C] a swelling filled with liquid in the body or under the skin

# D d

**D, d** /di/ ***noun*** [C,U] (*pl.* **D's**; **d's** /diz/) **1** the fourth letter of the English alphabet: *"David" begins with (a) "D."* **2** a grade that is given for a test or piece of work that is not very good. A "D" is the lowest grade with which you can pass: *I got a "D" on my essay.*

**D** ***abbr.*** (*U.S.*) = DEMOCRAT

**d.** ***abbr.*** (used in writing) died: *Abraham Lincoln, b. 1809, d. 1865*

**D.A.** (*also* **DA**) /ˌdi ˈeɪ/ ***abbr.*** (*U.S.*) = DISTRICT ATTORNEY

**dab**[1] /dæb/ ***verb*** (**dab·bing**; **dabbed**) [I,T] to touch sth lightly, usually several times: *He dabbed the cut with a cotton ball.*

PHR V **dab sth on/off (sth)** to put sth on or to remove sth with a light stroke or strokes: *to dab some antiseptic on a wound*

**dab**[2] /dæb/ ***noun*** [C] **1** a light touch: *She gave her eyes a dab with a handkerchief.* **2** a small quantity of sth that is put on a surface: *a dab of paint/perfume*

**dab·ble** /ˈdæbl/ ***verb*** [I] to become involved in sth in a manner that is not very serious: *to dabble in politics*

**dachs·hund** /ˈdɑkshʊnt; -hʊnd/ ***noun*** [C] (*also* ˈ**wiener dog**) a small dog with a long body, long ears and very short legs

★**dad** /dæd/ ***noun*** [C] (*informal*) father: *Is that your dad?* ◇ *Come on, Dad!*

**dad·dy** /ˈdædi/ ***noun*** [C] (*pl.* **dad·dies**) (*informal*) (used by children) father: *I want my daddy!* ◇ *Give Daddy a kiss.*

**daf·fo·dil** /ˈdæfədɪl/ ***noun*** [C] a tall yellow flower that grows early in the spring

**dag·ger** /ˈdægər/ ***noun*** [C] a type of knife with a point and two sharp edges used as a weapon, especially in former times: *He plunged a dagger into her heart.*

★**dai·ly**[1] /ˈdeɪli/ ***adj.***, ***adv.*** done, made or happening every day: *a daily routine/delivery/newspaper* ◇ *Our airline flies to Japan daily.*

**dai·ly**[2] /ˈdeɪli/ ***noun*** [C] (*pl.* **dai·lies**) a newspaper that is published every day, or every day except Saturday and Sunday

**dai·ry**[1] /ˈdɛri/ ***noun*** [C] (*pl.* **dai·ries**) a company that buys and sells milk, butter, cheese, etc.

**dai·ry**[2] /ˈdɛri/ ***adj.*** (only *before* a noun) **1** made from milk: *dairy products such as butter, cheese and ice cream* **2** connected with the production of milk rather than meat: *the dairy industry* ◇ *a dairy cow*

ˈ**dairy cattle** ***noun*** [pl.] cows which are kept for their milk, not their meat

ˈ**dairy farm** ***noun*** [C] a farm that produces mainly milk and milk products

**dai·sy** /ˈdeɪzi/ ***noun*** [C] (*pl.* **dai·sies**) a small white flower with a yellow center, which usually grows wild on grass, or a larger flower grown in gardens

**dam** /dæm/ ***noun*** [C] a wall built across a river to hold back the water and form a lake (**a reservoir**) behind it

★**dam·age**[1] /ˈdæmɪdʒ/ ***noun*** **1** [U] **damage (to sth)** harm or injury caused when sth is broken or spoiled: *The earthquake caused widespread damage.* ◇ *The driver suffered severe brain damage in the accident.* **2** **damages** [pl.] money that you can claim from sb if he/she damages sth of yours or hurts you: *The jury awarded him $2 million in damages.*

★**dam·age**[2] /ˈdæmɪdʒ/ ***verb*** [T] to spoil or harm sth, e.g. by breaking it: *The roof was damaged by the storm.*

**dam·ag·ing** /ˈdæmədʒɪŋ/ ***adj.*** having a bad or harmful effect

**dame** /deɪm/ ***noun*** [C] (*old-fashioned, slang*) a woman

> NOTE Nowadays many people consider this word offensive because it does not show respect toward women.

**damn**[1] /dæm/ ***verb*** **1** [I,T] (*informal*) (used to show that you are angry or annoyed): *Damn that stupid driver!* ◇ *Damn! I left my wallet at home.*

> NOTE **Darn** is not as strong as **damn**.

**2** [T] to describe sth as very bad: *The movie was damned by all the critics.* **3** [T] (used about God) to send sb to hell

**damn**[2] /dæm/ ***noun***

IDM **not give a damn (about sb/sth)** (*informal*) to not care at all: *I don't give a damn what he thinks about me.*

> NOTE Some people find this expression offensive. Look also at **darn**[2].

**damned**[1] /dæmd/ (*also* **damn** /dæm/) ***adj.*** (only *before* a noun) (*informal*) (used for showing that you are angry or annoyed): *Some damned fool parked too close to me.*

> NOTE **Darned** is not as strong as **damned**.

**damned**[2] /dæmd/ (*also* **damn** /dæm/) ***adv.*** (*informal*) (used for emphasizing that sth is good or bad) very: *Don't be so damned dumb!* ◇ *You guys played pretty damn well today.*

> NOTE **Darned** is not as strong as **damned**.

**damn·ing** /ˈdæmɪŋ/ ***adj.*** very unfavorable; showing that sb/sth is bad or guilty: *The most damning evidence against her was a fingerprint on the weapon.*

**damp** /dæmp/ ***adj.*** a little wet: *The grass is a little damp. Sit on the blanket.* ◇ *Wipe the surface with a damp cloth.* ► **damp·ness** /ˈdæmpnəs/ ***noun*** [U]

**damp·en** /ˈdæmpən/ ***verb*** [T] **1** to make sth less

strong or urgent: *Even the bad weather did not dampen their enthusiasm for the trip.* **2** to make sth a little wet: *He dampened his hair to try to stop it from sticking up.*

D

★**dance**[1] /dæns/ ***noun*** **1** [C] a series of steps and movements which you do to music: *What type of dance is this? A waltz?* **2** [C] a social meeting at which people dance with each other: *There's usually a dance at the end of the semester.* **3** [U] dancing as a form of art or entertainment: *She's very interested in modern dance.*

★**dance**[2] /dæns/ ***verb*** **1** [I,T] to move around to the rhythm of music by making a series of steps: *to dance the waltz* **2** [I] to move in a lively way, usually up and down: *She was dancing up and down with excitement.*

★**danc·er** /ˈdænsər/ ***noun*** [C] a person who dances, often as a job: *a ballet dancer* ◇ *She's a good dancer.*

★**danc·ing** /ˈdænsɪŋ/ ***noun*** [U] moving to music: *Will there be dancing at the party?* ◇ *ballet dancing*

**dan·de·li·on** /ˈdændəlaɪən/ ***noun*** [C] a small wild plant with a bright yellow flower, that often grows in grass around people's houses

**dan·druff** /ˈdændrəf/ ***noun*** [U] small pieces of dead skin in the hair, which look like white dust

★**dan·ger** /ˈdeɪndʒər/ ***noun*** **1** [U] the chance that sb/sth may be hurt, killed or damaged or that sth bad may happen: *Danger! Falling rocks!* (= on a sign) ◇ *The men kept on running until they thought they were out of danger.* **2** [C] **a danger (to sb/sth)** a person or thing that can cause injury, pain or damage: *Drunk drivers are a danger to everyone on the road.*

★**dan·ger·ous** /ˈdeɪndʒərəs/ ***adj.*** likely to cause injury or damage: *a dangerous animal/road/illness* ◇ *The strong currents in the ocean here are extremely dangerous for swimmers.* ▶ **dan·ger·ous·ly** ***adv.***: *He was standing dangerously close to the edge of the cliff.*

**dan·gle** /ˈdæŋgl/ ***verb*** [I,T] to hang or swing freely; to hold sth so that it hangs in this way: *She sat on the dock with her legs dangling over the water.*

**Dan·ish** /ˈdeɪnɪʃ/ (*also* ˌ**Danish ˈpastry**) (*pl.* ˌ**Danish ˈpastries**) ***noun*** [C] a type of round, sweet bread, usually with fruit, jam or sweet cheese in the center

**dank** /dæŋk/ ***adj.*** (used especially about a place) wet, cold and unpleasant: *a dark dank cave*

**dare**[1] /dɛr/ ***verb*** **1** [I] (usually in negative sentences) to be brave enough to do sth: *I don't dare ask her to loan me any more money.* ◇ *We were so scared that we didn't dare go into the room.* ◇ *Who would dare to criticize her in public?* ◇ *Nobody dared (to) speak.*

> NOTE In this sense, **dare** can be followed by an infinitive with or without "to."

**2** [T] to try to persuade sb to do sth in order to prove how brave he/she is: *Can you jump off that wall? Go on, I dare you!* ◇ *He dared his friend to put a worm on the teacher's desk.*

> NOTE In this sense, **dare** is used with an infinitive with "to."

IDM **don't you dare** (used for telling sb very strongly not to do sth): *Don't you dare tell my parents about this!*

**how dare you** (used when you are angry about sth that sb has done): *How dare you speak to me like that!*

★**dare**[2] /dɛr/ ***noun*** [C, usually sing.] something you do because sb asks you to, to prove how brave you are: *"Why did you try to swim across the river?" "It was a dare."*

**dare·dev·il** /ˈdɛrdɛvl/ ***noun*** [C] a person who is willing to take risks, often foolishly

**dar·ing** /ˈdɛrɪŋ/ ***adj.*** willing to take risks or to do or say things which other people might not; brave; bold: *a daring attack*

★**dark**[1] /dɑrk/ ***noun*** [sing.] **the dark** the state of having no light: *He's afraid of the dark.* ◇ *Why are you sitting alone in the dark?*

IDM **before/after dark** before/after the sun goes down

**(be/keep sb) in the dark (about sth)** (be/keep sb) in a position of not knowing (about sth): *Don't keep me in the dark. Tell me!*

★**dark**[2] /dɑrk/ ***adj.*** **1** with no light or very little light: *It was a dark night, with no moon.* **2** (used about a color) nearer black than white; not light: *dark blue* **3** (only *before* a noun) sad; without hope: *the dark days leading up to the start of the war* **4** (only *before* a noun) mysterious or slightly threatening: *He seemed friendly, but there was a dark side to his character.*

**dark·en** /ˈdɑrkən/ ***verb*** [I,T] to become or to make sth darker: *The sky suddenly darkened and it looked like it was going to rain.*

ˌ**dark ˈglass·es** ***noun*** [pl.] = SUNGLASSES

**dark·ness** /ˈdɑrknəs/ ***noun*** [U] the state of being dark: *We sat in complete darkness, waiting for the lights to come back on.*

**dark·room** /ˈdɑrkrum/ ***noun*** [C] a room that can be made completely dark so that film can be taken out of a camera and photographs can be produced there

**dar·ling** /ˈdɑrlɪŋ/ ***noun*** [C] (used for speaking to sb that you love): *Darling, I'm home!* ◇ *How was your day at school, darling?*

**darn**[1] /dɑrn/ ***verb*** **1** [I,T] (*informal*) (used to show that you are angry or annoyed): *Darn it! I can't make this stupid thing work.* ◇ *There's no milk for my coffee. Darn!* **2** [T] to fix a hole in clothes by sewing across it in one direction and then in the other

**darn**[2] /dɑrn/ ***noun***

IDM **not give a darn (about sb/sth)** (*informal*) to not care at all: *I don't give a darn what the neighbors say.*

**darned**[1] /dɑrnd/ (*also* **darn** /dɑrn/) ***adj.*** (only *before* a noun) (*informal*) (used for showing that you are angry or annoyed): *Those darned kids stole my garbage can!*

**darned**[2] /dɑrnd/ (*also* **darn** /dɑrn/) ***adv.*** (*informal*) (used for emphasizing that sth is good or bad) very: *You did a darned good job today.* ◇ *It's just too darn hot!*

**dart**[1] /dɑrt/ ***noun*** **1** [C] an object like a small arrow. It is thrown or shot as a weapon or in a game: *First, they tranquilize the tiger with a special dart.*

**2 darts** [U] a game in which you throw darts at a round board with numbers on it (a **dartboard**): *to play darts*

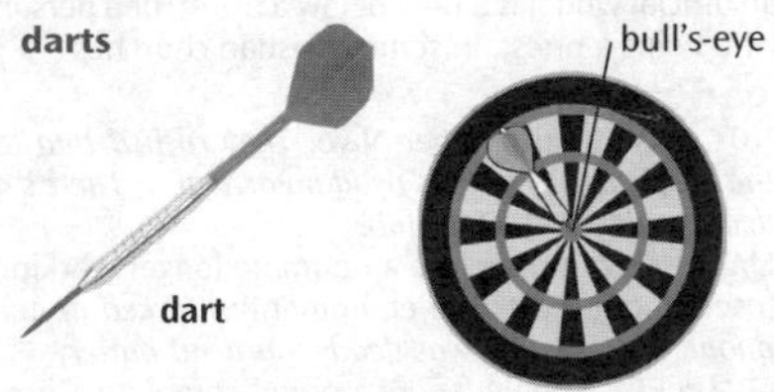


**dart²** /dɑrt/ ***verb*** [I] to move suddenly and quickly in a certain direction: *A rabbit darted across the field.*

**dash¹** /dæʃ/ ***noun*** **1** [sing.] a short, quick act of running: *We made a dash for the bus and just got on.* ◇ *Tonya finished third in the 200-meter dash.* **2** [C, usually sing.] a small amount of sth that you add to sth else: *a dash of lemon juice* **3** [C] a small horizontal line (—) used in writing, especially for adding extra information ➲ Look at **hyphen**. **4** [C] = DASHBOARD

**dash²** /dæʃ/ ***verb*** **1** [I] to go or run suddenly and quickly: *We all dashed for shelter when it started to rain.* **2** [T] to ruin or destroy sb's hopes, dreams, etc.: *The accident dashed his hopes of becoming a pianist.* **3** [I,T] to hit sth with great force; to throw sth so that it hits sth else very hard: *She dashed her racket to the ground.*

PHR V **dash sth off** to write or draw sth very quickly

**dash·board** /ˈdæʃbɔrd/ (*also* **dash**) ***noun*** [C] the part in a car in front of the driver where most of the switches, etc. are

**DAT** /dæt; ˌdi eɪ ˈti/ ***abbr.*** digital audio tape

★**da·ta** /ˈdeɪt̬ə; ˈdæt̬ə/ ***noun*** [U, pl.] facts or information: *to collect data* ◇ *The data is/are still being analyzed.*

NOTE **Data** was originally the plural form of a Latin noun, but it is now often used as an uncountable noun: *The data we have is not very interesting.*

**da·ta·base** /ˈdeɪt̬əbeɪs; ˈdæt̬ə-/ ***noun*** [C] a large amount of data that is stored in a computer and can easily be used, added to, etc.

**ˈdata ˌmining** ***noun*** [U] (*computing*) looking at large amounts of information that has been collected on a computer and using it to provide new information

**ˌdata ˈprocessing** ***noun*** [U] (*computing*) a series of actions that a computer performs on data in order to find, change or classify information

**ˈdata proˌtection** ***noun*** [U] legal restrictions that keep information stored on computers private and that control who can read it or use it

★**date¹** /deɪt/ ***noun***

➤PARTICULAR DAY **1** [C] a particular day of the month or of the year: *What's the date today?* ◇ *What date is it today?* ◇ *What's your date of birth/your birth date?*

➤PARTICULAR TIME **2** [sing.] a particular time: *We can discuss this at a later date.*

➤ROMANTIC MEETING **3** [C] an appointment to meet sb, especially a boyfriend or girlfriend: *I'm going out on a date with Tom on Friday night.* ➲ Look also at **blind date**. **4** [C] a person that you have made an appointment to meet, especially a boyfriend or girlfriend: *Sarah introduced us to her date at the party.*

➤FRUIT **5** [C] a small, sweet, dark brown fruit that comes from a tree which grows in hot countries

IDM **out of date** unfashionable; no longer useful: *out-of-date methods/machinery* ◇ *This textbook is completely out of date.*

**to date** (*formal*) until now: *We've had very few complaints to date.*

**up to date** with all the latest information: *In this report, we'll bring you up to date with the latest news from the area.* ◇ *We need to keep our records up to date.* ➲ Look also at **up-to-date**.

★**date²** /deɪt/ ***verb***

➤FIND AGE **1** [T] to discover or guess how old sth is: *to date a skeleton/a rock*

➤WRITE DATE **2** [T] to write the day's date on sth: *The letter is not dated, so we can't tell when it was written.*

➤OF CLOTHES/WORDS **3** [I,T] to seem, or to make sb/sth seem, unfashionable: *We chose a simple style so that it wouldn't date as quickly.*

➤HAVE RELATIONSHIP **4** [I,T] to meet a girlfriend or boyfriend regularly

➤PERIOD OF EXISTENCE **5** [I] **date back to...**; **date from...** to have existed since...: *The house dates back to the Revolutionary War.*

**date·book** /ˈdeɪtbʊk/ ***noun*** [C] a book in which you write down things that you have to do, remember, etc.: *I'll check my datebook and see if I'm free on Thursday.*

**dat·ed** /ˈdeɪt̬əd/ ***adj.*** unfashionable: *a very dated hairstyle*

★**daugh·ter** /ˈdɔt̬ər/ ***noun*** [C] a female child: *I have two sons and one daughter.* ◇ *Janet's daughter is a doctor.*

**ˈdaughter-in-law** ***noun*** [C] (*pl.* **daughters-in-law**) the wife of your son

**daunt** /dɔnt/ ***verb*** [T] (usually passive) to frighten or to worry sb by being too big or difficult: *I was daunted by the sudden responsibility.*

**daunt·ing** /ˈdɔnt̬ɪŋ/ ***adj.*** making you feel frightened or making you worry by being too big or difficult: *We faced the daunting task of cleaning up after the flood.*

**dawn¹** /dɔn/ ***noun*** **1** [C,U] the early morning, when light first appears in the sky: *before/at dawn* **2** [sing.] the beginning: *the dawn of civilization*

IDM **the crack of dawn** → CRACK¹

**dawn²** /dɔn/ ***verb*** [I] to begin to grow light, after the night: *The day dawned bright and cold.* ◇ (*figurative*) *A new era of peace is dawning.*

PHR V **dawn on sb** to become clear to sb: *Suddenly it dawned on her. "Of course!" she said. "You're Mike's brother!"*

★**day** /deɪ/ ***noun*** **1** [C] a period of 24 hours, of which seven make up a week: *"What day is it today?" "Tuesday."* ◇ *We went to Hawaii for ten days.* ◇ *I saw that movie a few days ago.* ◇ *The next day was Saturday.* ◇ *the day before* ◇ *New Year's Day* **2** [C,U] the period of time after the sun rises and before it sets: *The days were warm, but the nights were freezing.* ◇ *Have a nice day! See you tonight.* ◇ *It's been raining all day.* ➲ adjective and adverb **daily 3** [C] the hours of the day when you work: *She has to work an eight-hour day.* **4** [C] (*also* **days**) a particular period of time: *in Shakespeare's day* ◇ *in the days of Shakespeare* ◇ *In the old days, most houses didn't have electricity.*

D

IDM **by day/night** during the day/night: *These animals sleep by day and hunt by night.*
**call it a day** → CALL[2]
**the day after tomorrow** not tomorrow, but the next day
**the day before yesterday** not yesterday, but the day before
**day by day** every day; as time passes: *Day by day, she was getting a little bit stronger.*
**day in, day out** every day, without any change: *He sits at his desk working, day in, day out.*
**from day to day; from one day to the next** within a short period of time: *Things change so quickly that we never know what will happen from one day to the next.*
**have a field day** → FIELD DAY
**make sb's day** (*informal*) to make sb very happy
**one day; some day** at some time in the future: *Some day we'll go back and see all our old friends.*
**the other day** a few days ago; recently: *I bumped into him in town the other day.*
**the present day** → PRESENT[1]
**these days** in the present age; nowadays: *More and more couples are getting divorced these days.*

**day·break** /ˈdeɪbreɪk/ ***noun*** [U] the time in the early morning when light first appears: *at daybreak*

**ˈday camp** ***noun*** [C,U] a place where younger children go during the day in the summer vacation to be outside, do activities, play games etc. ➲ Look at **summer camp**.

**day·care** /ˈdeɪkɛr/ ***noun*** [U] the service of taking care of small children while their parents are working; a place that offers this service: *a daycare center* ◇ *My wife takes the kids to daycare every morning.*

**day·dream** /ˈdeɪdrim/ ***noun*** [C] thoughts that are not connected with what you are doing; often pleasant scenes in your imagination: *He stared out of the window, lost in a daydream.* ▶ **day·dream *verb*** [I]

**day·light** /ˈdeɪlaɪt/ ***noun*** [U] the light that there is during the day: *The colors look a lot different in daylight.* ◇ *daylight hours*
IDM **in broad daylight** → BROAD

**ˌdaylight-ˈsaving time** ***noun*** [U] the period of time from April to October when clocks in most parts of the U.S. and Canada are set one hour ahead of standard time

**day·time** /ˈdeɪtaɪm/ ***noun*** [U] the period of time after the sun rises and before it sets: *These flowers open in the daytime and close up again at night.*

**daze** /deɪz/ ***noun***
IDM **in a daze** in a confused state

**dazed** /deɪzd/ ***adj.*** confused; not showing normal reactions: *He had a dazed expression on his face.*

**daz·zle** /ˈdæzl/ ***verb*** [T] (usually passive) to impress sb very much: *He had been dazzled by her beauty.*

**daz·zling** /ˈdæzlɪŋ/ ***adj.*** very bright or impressive: *a dazzling light* ◇ *a dazzling performance*

**dea·con** /ˈdikən/ (*feminine* **dea·con·ess**) ***noun*** [C] an official who has a rank below a priest, or a person who helps a priest, in some Christian churches

★**dead[1]** /dɛd/ ***adj.***
➤NOT ALIVE **1** no longer alive: *They rushed him to the hospital, but he was dead on arrival.* ◇ *There's a dead spider in the bathtub.*
➤MACHINE **2** (not before a noun) no longer working (used about a piece of equipment): *I picked up the phone, but the line was dead.* ◇ *a dead battery*
➤COMPLETE **3** (only *before* a noun) complete: *There was dead silence when she finished speaking.*
➤PLACE **4** without movement, activity or interest: *This town is completely dead after 11 o'clock at night.*
➤NOT USED **5** no longer used; over and finished: *Latin is a dead language.*
IDM **a dead end 1** a street that is only open at one end **2** a point, situation, etc. from which you can make no further progress: *a dead-end job* (= one that offers no chance of promotion)
**drop dead** → DROP[1]

**dead[2]** /dɛd/ ***noun* the dead** [pl.] people who have died: *A church service was held in memory of the dead.*
IDM **in the dead of night** in the middle of the night, when it is very dark and quiet

**dead·beat** /ˈdɛdbit/ ***noun*** [C] (*informal*) **1** a lazy person; a person with no job and no money, who is not part of normal society **2** a person who tries to avoid paying money that he/she owes **3** (*also* **ˌdeadbeat ˈdad**) a father who does not live with his children and does not pay his ex-wife any money to take care of them (**child support**)

**dead·en** /ˈdɛdn/ ***verb*** [T] to make sth less strong, painful, etc.: *They gave her drugs to try and deaden the pain.*

**ˌdead ˈheat** ***noun*** [C] a situation in a race or contest when two or more people are at the same level: *The two candidates are in a dead heat in the polls.*

**dead·line** /ˈdɛdlaɪn/ ***noun*** [C] a time or date before which sth must be done: *A journalist is used to having to **meet deadlines**.* ◇ *The deadline for our history paper is Friday.*

**dead·lock** /ˈdɛdlɑk/ ***noun*** [C, U] a situation in which an agreement between two sides cannot be reached

**dead·ly[1]** /ˈdɛdli/ ***adj.*** (**dead·li·er; dead·li·est**) **1** causing or likely to cause death: *a deadly poison* **2** very great: *They're deadly enemies.*

**dead·ly[2]** /ˈdɛdli/ ***adv.*** extremely; very: *I'm not joking – I'm deadly serious!*

**dead·pan** /ˈdɛdpæn/ ***adj.*** looking or sounding completely serious, without any expression or emotion, often when you are joking: *deadpan humor*

**deaf** /dɛf/ ***adj.*** **1** unable to hear anything or unable to hear very well: *You'll have to speak louder. My father's going deaf.*

NOTE We often describe a person as **hearing-impaired** rather than **deaf**.

**2 the deaf *noun*** [pl.] deaf people: *sign language for the deaf* ▶ **deaf·ness *noun*** [U]

**deaf·en·ing** /ˈdɛfənɪŋ/ ***adj.*** very loud: *a deafening noise*

★**deal**[1] /dil/ ***verb*** [I,T] (*pt, pp* **dealt** /dɛlt/) **1 deal sth (out); deal (sth) (to sb)** to give cards to players in a game of cards: *Start by dealing seven cards to each player.* **2** to sell illegal drugs: *He was arrested for dealing heroin.*

IDM **deal sb/sth a blow; deal a blow to sb/sth** to give sb a shock, etc.: *This news dealt a terrible blow to my father.*

PHRV **deal in sth** to buy and sell sth; to trade in sth: *She deals in antique furniture.*

**deal with sb** to behave toward sb; to handle sb: *He's a difficult man. Nobody really knows how to deal with him.*

**deal with sth 1** to act in a suitable way in order to solve a problem, complete a task, etc.; to handle sth: *I'm not sure how to deal with the situation at work.* **2** to have sth as its subject: *This chapter deals with writing letters.*

★**deal**[2] /dil/ ***noun*** **1** [C] an agreement or arrangement, especially in business: *We **made a deal with** a Korean company.* ◇ *I got a terrific deal on these tires today* (= I bought them for a low price). **2** [sing.] (*informal*) a situation: *What's the deal with Bob? He's in a rotten mood.* ◇ *Here's the deal: Diane says she can help us, but only for a short time.*

IDM **big deal** → BIG[1]

**a good/great deal (of sth)** (used with uncountable nouns) a lot (of sth): *I spent a great deal of time on this report.*

**strike a deal (with sb)** → STRIKE[2]

**deal·er** /ˈdilər/ ***noun*** [C] **1** a person whose business is buying and selling things: *a dealer in gold and silver* ◇ *a drug dealer* **2** the person who gives the cards to the players in a game of cards

**deal·er·ship** /ˈdilərʃɪp/ ***noun*** [C] a business that sells a particular type of product: *a used car dealership*

**deal·ing** /ˈdilɪŋ/ ***noun*** **1** [U] buying and selling: *drug dealing* **2 dealings** [pl.] relations, especially in business: *We are investigating his financial dealings with known criminals.*

**dealt** *past tense, past participle of* DEAL[1]

**dean** /din/ ***noun*** [C] an important official at a college or university: *the dean of students*

ˈ**dean's list** ***noun*** [C] a list of the names of students at a college or university who have earned high grades: *Susan made the dean's list* (= her name was put on the list) *every semester.*

★**dear**[1] /dɪr/ ***adj.*** **1** (used at the beginning of a letter before the name or title of the person you are writing to): *Dear Sarah, ...* ◇ *Dear Sir or Madam, ...* **2 dear (to sb)** loved by or important to sb: *She's one of my dearest friends.* ◇ *It was a subject that was very dear to him.*

**dear**[2] /dɪr/ ***noun*** [C] (*informal*) (used for speaking to sb you know well or love): *Did you have a nice day, dear?*

**dear**[3] /dɪr/ ***interjection*** (*old-fashioned*) (used for expressing disappointment, sadness, surprise, etc.): *Oh dear! I spilled the wine.*

**dear·ly** /ˈdɪrli/ ***adv.*** **1** very much: *He loves her dearly.* **2** (*formal*) at great cost: *I've already paid dearly* (= suffered a lot) *for that mistake.*

**dearth** /dərθ/ ***noun*** [sing.] **a dearth (of sth)** (*formal*) a lack of sth; not enough of sth: *There was a dearth of reliable information on the subject.*

★**death** /dɛθ/ ***noun*** **1** [C,U] the end of sb/sth's life; dying: *He continued to write until his death.* ◇ *There were two deaths and many other people were injured.* ◇ *The police do not know the cause of death.* ◇ *There was no food and people were starving to death.* **2** [U] the end (of sth): *the death of communism*

IDM **put sb to death** (usually passive) to kill sb, usually as a punishment: *The general had ordered the prisoners to be put to death.*

**sick to death of sb/sth** → SICK

**the ˈdeath penalty** ***noun*** [sing.] the punishment of being killed

ˌ**death ˈrow** ***noun*** [U] the part of a prison for people who will be killed as a punishment for crimes they have committed, especially in the U.S: *prisoners **on death row***

ˈ**death toll** ***noun*** [C] the number of people killed in a disaster, war, etc.

**de·bat·a·ble** /dɪˈbeɪt̬əbl/ ***adj.*** not certain; something that you could argue about

★**de·bate**[1] /dɪˈbeɪt/ ***noun*** **1** [C] a formal argument or discussion of a question at a public meeting or in Congress, etc. At the end there may be a vote: *a debate in the legislature on tax reform* **2** [C,U] a discussion; talk expressing different opinions: *There's been a lot of debate about the cause of acid rain.*

★**de·bate**[2] /dɪˈbeɪt/ ***verb*** [I,T] **1** to discuss sth in a formal way or at a public DEBATE[1] (1) **2** to think about or discuss sth before deciding what to do: *They debated (about) whether to go or not.*

**de·bris** /dəˈbri; ˈdeɪ-/ ***noun*** [U] pieces from sth that has crashed to the ground or been destroyed: *debris from the plane crash*

★**debt** /dɛt/ ***noun*** **1** [C] a sum of money that you owe sb: *She borrowed a lot of money and she's still paying off the debt.* ◇ *the national debt* (= that the government owes to other countries and organizations) **2** [U] the state of owing money: *After he lost his job, he got into debt.* **3** [C, usually sing.] (*formal*) something that you owe sb, e.g. because he/she has helped or been kind to you: *He acknowledged his debt to his family and friends for their support.*

IDM **be in debt/out of debt** to owe/not owe money

**be in sb's debt** (*formal*) to feel grateful to sb for sth that he/she has done for you

**debt·or** /ˈdɛt̬ər/ ***noun*** [C] a person who owes money

**de·but** (*also* **début**) /deɪˈbyu/ ***noun*** [C] the first appearance in public of an actor, etc.: *She **made her debut** at Carnegie Hall in 1989.*

★**de·cade** /ˈdɛkeɪd/ ***noun*** [C] a period of ten years

**dec·a·dent** /ˈdɛkədənt/ ***adj.*** having low standards, especially moral ones, and an interest only in pleasure and enjoyment rather than serious things: *a decadent lifestyle* ▸ **dec·a·dence** ***noun*** [U]

**de·caf** /ˈdikæf/ ***noun*** [U] coffee that has had most or all of the caffeine removed: *Regular or decaf?*

D

D

**de·caf·fein·at·ed** /ˌdiˈkæfəneɪt̮əd/ ***adj.*** (used about coffee or tea) with most or all of the caffeine removed

**de·cap·i·tate** /dɪˈkæpəteɪt/ ***verb*** [T] (*formal*) to cut off a person's head

★ **de·cay¹** /dɪˈkeɪ/ ***verb*** [I] **1** to become bad or fall apart: *The old farm buildings had been left to decay.* ◇ *Children's teeth will decay if they eat too much candy.* **2** to become weaker or less efficient: *The Roman Empire had by then begun to decay.*

★ **de·cay²** /dɪˈkeɪ/ ***noun*** [U] the process of decaying, or the state reached after decaying: *tooth decay* ◇ *Many of the old houses had fallen into decay.*

**de·ceased** /dɪˈsist/ ***adj.*** (*formal*) dead: *He inherited the house from his deceased parents.*

**the de·ceased** /dɪˈsist/ ***noun*** [sing.] a person who has died, especially one who has died recently: *Many friends of the deceased were present at the funeral.*

**de·ceit** /dɪˈsit/ ***noun*** [U] dishonest behavior; trying to make sb believe sth that is not true

**de·ceit·ful** /dɪˈsitfl/ ***adj.*** dishonest, and intending to make sb believe sth that is not true ▶ **de·ceit·ful·ly** ***adv.*** ▶ **de·ceit·ful·ness** ***noun*** [U]

★ **de·ceive** /dɪˈsiv/ ***verb*** [T] **deceive sb/yourself (into doing sth)** to try to make sb believe sth that is not true: *Her story didn't deceive me – I knew it was a lie.* ◇ *You're deceiving yourself if you think there's an easy solution to the problem.* ➲ noun **deception** or **deceit**

**De·cem·ber** /dɪˈsɛmbər/ ***noun*** [C,U] (*abbr.* **Dec.**) the twelfth month of the year, coming before January ➲ For examples of the use of the months in sentences, look at **January**.

**de·cen·cy** /ˈdisənsi/ ***noun*** [U] moral or correct behavior: *She had the decency to admit that it was her fault.*

**de·cent** /ˈdisənt/ ***adj.*** **1** satisfactory; of an acceptable standard: *All she wants is a decent job with decent pay.* **2** (used about people or behavior) honest and respectable: *All decent people are appalled by such terrible crimes.* **3** not likely to embarrass or offend sb: *I can't come to the door – I'm not decent* (= I'm not dressed). OPP **indecent** ▶ **de·cent·ly** ***adv.***

**de·cep·tion** /dɪˈsɛpʃn/ ***noun*** [C,U] deceiving or being deceived; a trick: *He had obtained the secret papers by deception.*

**de·cep·tive** /dɪˈsɛptɪv/ ***adj.*** likely to give a false impression or to make sb believe sth that is not true: *The water is deceptive. It's much deeper than it looks.* ▶ **de·cep·tive·ly** ***adv.***: *She made the task sound deceptively easy.*

**de·ci·bel** /ˈdɛsəbl; -bɛl/ ***noun*** [C] a measurement of how loud a sound is

★ **de·cide** /dɪˈsaɪd/ ***verb*** **1** [I,T] to think about two or more possibilities and choose one of them: *There are so many to choose from – I can't decide!* ◇ *She decided against borrowing the money.* ◇ *They decided on a name for the baby.* ◇ *He decided that it was too late to go.* ◇ *You'll have to decide what to do.* ◇ *We decided not to invite Isabel.* **2** [T] to influence sth so that it produces a particular result: *Your votes will decide the winner.* ➲ noun **decision** ➲ adjective **decisive**

**de·cid·ed** /dɪˈsaɪdəd/ ***adj.*** clear; definite: *There has been a decided improvement in his work.* ▶ **de·cid·ed·ly** ***adv.***: *The new office is decidedly better than the old one.*

**de·cid·u·ous** /dɪˈsɪdʒuəs/ ***adj.*** (used about a tree) of a type that loses its leaves every year ➲ Look at **evergreen**.

**dec·i·mal¹** /ˈdɛsəml/ ***adj.*** based on or counted in units of ten

**dec·i·mal²** /ˈdɛsəml/ ***noun*** [C] part of a number, written after a dot (a **decimal point**) and expressed in tenths, hundredths, etc.: *Three quarters expressed as a decimal is 0.75.*

**de·ci·pher** /dɪˈsaɪfər/ ***verb*** [T] to succeed in reading or understanding sth that is not clear: *It's impossible to decipher his handwriting.*

★ **de·ci·sion** /dɪˈsɪʒn/ ***noun*** **1** [C,U] **a decision (on/about sth); a decision (to do sth); a decision (that...)** a choice or judgment that you make after thinking about various possibilities: *"Have you made a decision yet?" "No, I'm still thinking about it."* ◇ *I realize now that I made the wrong decision.* ◇ *It took us several hours to reach a decision.* ◇ *There were good reasons for his decision to leave.* **2** [U] being able to decide clearly and quickly

**de·ci·sive** /dɪˈsaɪsɪv/ ***adj.*** **1** making sth certain or final: *the decisive battle of the war* **2** having the ability to make clear decisions quickly: *It's no use hesitating. Be decisive.* ▶ **de·ci·sive·ly** ***adv.***

★ **deck** /dɛk/ ***noun*** [C] **1** one of the floors of a ship: *The restaurant is on the upper deck.* **2** a complete set of playing cards ➲ Look at the note at **card**. **3** a platform, usually made of wood, that is attached to the back of a house: *Let's go sit out on the deck.* ➲ Look also at **patio**, **porch** and **veranda**.

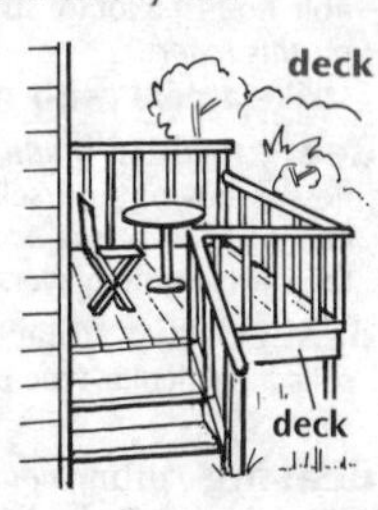


IDM **on deck** on the floor of a ship which is in the open air: *I'm going out on deck for some fresh air.*

**dec·la·ra·tion** /ˌdɛkləˈreɪʃn/ ***noun*** **1** [C,U] a statement: *a strong declaration of support* ◇ *Fighting has started without declaration of war.* ◇ *the Declaration of Independence* (= the official document, written in 1776, that said that the United States was an independent country) **2** [C] a written statement giving information on goods or income on which you have to pay tax: *If you're sending a package abroad, you have to fill out a customs declaration form.*

★ **de·clare** /dɪˈklɛr/ ***verb*** [T] **1** to announce sth or to make sth known, especially in an official or forceful way: *to declare war on another country* ◇ *The republic has declared its independence.* ◇ *"I've had enough of this," she declared.* **2** to give information about goods or income on which you have to pay taxes: *You must declare all your income on this form.*

★ **de·cline¹** /dɪˈklaɪn/ ***verb*** **1** [I,T] (*formal*) to refuse, usually politely: *Thank you for the invitation, but unfortunately I have to decline.* ◇ *The candidate declined to make a statement.* **2** [I] to become weaker, smaller or less good: *declining profits* ◇ *The standard of education has declined in this country.*

★**de·cline²** /dɪˈklaɪn/ ***noun*** [C,U] **(a) decline (in sth)** a process or period of becoming weaker, smaller or less satisfactory: *a decline in sales* ◇ *As an industrial power, the country is in decline.*

**de·code** /diˈkoʊd/ ***verb*** [T] to find the meaning of sth that is in code OPP **encode**

**de·cod·er** /diˈkoʊdər/ ***noun*** [C] a device that changes an electronic signal into a form that people can understand, such as sound and pictures: *a satellite/video decoder* ◇ *A decoder is required for certain television programs.*

**de·com·pose** /ˌdikəmˈpoʊz/ ***verb*** [I,T] to decay or to make sth decay: *The body was so badly decomposed that it couldn't be identified.*

**dé·cor** (*also* **decor**) /deɪˈkɔr; ˈdeɪkɔr/ ***noun*** [U, sing.] the furniture and decoration in a place

★**dec·o·rate** /ˈdɛkəreɪt/ ***verb*** [T] **decorate sth (with sth)** to add sth in order to make a thing more attractive to look at: *Decorate the cake with cherries and nuts.* ◇ *to decorate a Christmas tree*

★**dec·o·ra·tion** /ˌdɛkəˈreɪʃn/ ***noun*** **1** [C,U] something that is added to sth in order to make it look more attractive: *We put up decorations for Jason's birthday party.* **2** [C] a military award that sb wears on his/her uniform

**dec·o·ra·tive** /ˈdɛkərət̬ɪv/ ***adj.*** attractive to look at; added to sth to make it prettier: *The cloth had a decorative lace edge.*

**de·coy** /ˈdikɔɪ/ ***noun*** [C] a person or object that is used to lead sb/sth in the wrong direction

★**de·crease¹** /dɪˈkris; ˈdikris/ ***verb*** [I,T] to become or to make sth smaller or less: *Profits have decreased by 15%.* ◇ *Decrease your speed when you are approaching an intersection.* OPP **increase**

★**de·crease²** /ˈdikris/ ***noun*** [C,U] **(a) decrease (in sth)** a process of becoming or making sth smaller or less; a reduction: *a decrease in the number of students* ◇ *a 10% decrease in sales* OPP **increase**

**de·cree¹** /dɪˈkri/ ***noun*** [C] an official order given by a government, a ruler, etc.

**de·cree²** /dɪˈkri/ ***verb*** [T] (*pt, pp* **de·creed**) (used about a government, a ruler, etc.) to give an official order

**de·crep·it** /dɪˈkrɛpɪt/ ***adj.*** old and in very bad condition

**ded·i·cate** /ˈdɛdəkeɪt/ ***verb*** [T] **1** to give all your energy, time, efforts, etc. to sth: *He dedicated his life to helping the poor.* **2 dedicate sth to sb** to say that sth is in honor of sb: *She dedicated the book she had written to her brother.*

**ded·i·cat·ed** /ˈdɛdəkeɪt̬əd/ ***adj.*** **1** giving a lot of your energy, time, efforts, etc. to sth that you believe to be important: *dedicated nurses and doctors* **2** (only *before* before a noun) made or used for only one specific task: *a dedicated fax line*

**ded·i·ca·tion** /ˌdɛdəˈkeɪʃn/ ***noun*** **1** [U] being willing to give your time and energy to sth: *I admire her dedication to her career.* **2** [C] a message at the beginning of a book or before a piece of music is played, saying that it is for a particular person

**de·duce** /dɪˈdus/ ***verb*** [T] to form an opinion using the facts that you already know: *From his name, I deduced that he was Polish.* ➲ noun **deduction**

**de·duct** /dɪˈdʌkt/ ***verb*** [T] **deduct sth (from sth)** to take sth such as money or points away from a total amount: *Pension payments are deducted from your salary.* ◇ *Points will be deducted for sloppy work.*

**de·duct·i·ble¹** /dɪˈdʌktəbl/ ***adj.*** that can be taken away from a total amount or number: *tax-deductible business expenses*

**de·duct·i·ble²** /dɪˈdʌktəbl/ ***noun*** [C] an amount of money that sb must pay before his/her insurance pays the rest of the cost of sth: *My house insurance policy has a $500 deductible.*

**de·duc·tion** /dɪˈdʌkʃn/ ***noun*** [C,U] **1** something that you work out from facts that you already know; the skill of reasoning in this way: *It was a brilliant piece of deduction by the detective.* **2 deduction (from sth)** taking away an amount or number from a total; the amount or number taken away from the total: *What is your total income after deductions?* (= when taxes/insurance are taken away)

**deed** /did/ ***noun*** [C] (*formal*) something that you do; an action: *Deeds are more important than words.*

**deem** /dim/ ***verb*** [T] (*formal*) to consider sth: *He did not even deem it necessary to apologize.*

★**deep¹** /dip/ ***adj.***

➤TOP TO BOTTOM **1** going a long way down from top to bottom: *the deep end of a swimming pool* ◇ *to dig a deep hole* ◇ *a coat with deep pockets* ➲ noun **depth**

➤FRONT TO BACK **2** going a long way from front to back: *deep shelves*

➤MEASUREMENT **3** measuring a particular amount from top to bottom or from front to back: *The water is only three feet deep at this end of the pool.*

➤SOUNDS **4** (used about sounds) low: *a deep voice*

➤COLORS **5** (used about colors) dark; strong: *a deep red*

➤EMOTIONS **6** strongly felt; serious: *Please accept my deepest sympathy on this sad occasion.* ◇ *The country is in a deep recession.*

➤BREATH **7** (used about a breath) taking in or letting out a lot of air: *Take a few deep breaths.*

➤INVOLVED **8** concentrating on or involved in sth: *She was deep in thought.* ◇ *to be in a deep coma/sleep/trance*

➤UNDERSTANDING **9** thorough, able to deal with the difficult parts of sth: *His books show a deep understanding of human nature.* ➲ noun **depth**
▶ **deep·ly** ***adv.***: *a deeply unhappy person* ◇ *to breathe deeply*

★**deep²** /dip/ ***adv.*** a long way down or inside sth: *The ship sank deep into the sea.* ◇ *They talked deep into the night.*

IDM **deep down** in what you really think or feel: *I tried to appear optimistic, but deep down I knew there wasn't any hope.*

**deep·en** /ˈdipən/ ***verb*** [I,T] to become or to make sth deep or deeper: *The river deepens here.* ◇ *This bad news deepened the atmosphere of depression.*

**ˌdeep-ˈfried** ***adj.*** (used about food) cooked in oil that covers it completely: *deep-fried chicken pieces* ▶ **ˌdeep-ˈfry** ***verb*** [T]

ˌ**deep-'rooted** (*also* ˌ**deep-'seated**) ***adj.*** strongly felt or believed and therefore difficult to change: *deep-seated prejudices*

**the ˌDeep 'South** ***noun*** [sing.] an area in the southeastern U.S., including Louisiana, Mississippi, Alabama, Georgia and South Carolina

**deer** /dɪr/ ***noun*** [C] (*pl.* **deer**) a large wild grass-eating animal. The male has horns shaped like branches (**antlers**).

NOTE A male deer is called a **buck**. The female is a **doe** and a young deer a **fawn**. **Venison** is the meat from deer.

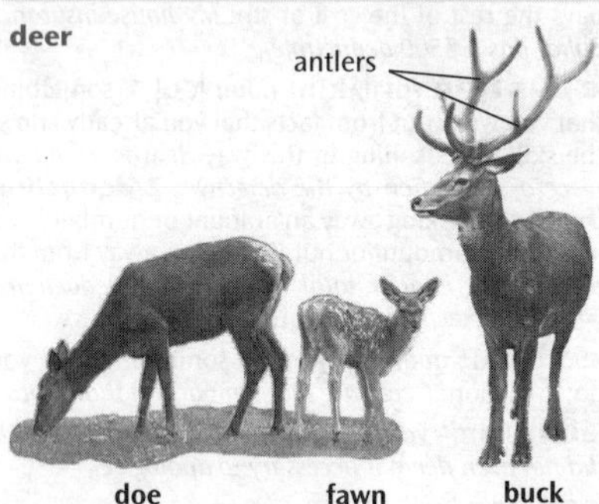


**de·face** /dɪˈfeɪs/ ***verb*** [T] to spoil the way sth looks by writing on or marking the surface of it: *Vandals defaced the statue with graffiti.*

**de·fault¹** /dɪˈfɔlt/ ***noun*** **1** [sing.] (*computing*) a course of action taken by a computer when it is not given any other instruction **2** [C,U] not doing sth that you should do by law: *Defaults on student loans* (= people failing to pay them back) *have increased in recent years.*

IDM **by default** because nothing happened, not because of successful effort: *They won by default because the other team didn't show up.*

**de·fault²** /dɪˈfɔlt/ ***verb*** [I] not to do sth that you should do by law: *If you default on the loan payments* (= you don't pay them), *the car will be taken back.*

★**de·feat¹** /dɪˈfit/ ***verb*** [T] **1** to win a game, a fight, a vote, etc. against sb: *In the last game, Ohio State defeated Michigan by 14 points to 6.* **2** to prevent sth from succeeding: *The local residents are determined to defeat the city's building plans.* **3** to be too difficult for sb to do or understand: *I've tried to figure out what's wrong with the car, but it defeats me.*

★**de·feat²** /dɪˈfit/ ***noun*** **1** [C] an occasion when sb is defeated: *This season they have had two victories and three defeats.* **2** [U] defeating or being defeated: *She refused to admit defeat and kept on trying.*

**def·e·cate** /ˈdɛfəkeɪt/ ***verb*** [I] (*formal*) to pass solid waste materials from the bowels

NOTE It is more common to say **go to the bathroom**. ➲ Look also at **poop**.

**de·fect¹** /ˈdifɛkt; dɪˈfɛkt/ ***noun*** [C] something that is wrong with or missing from sb/sth: *a speech defect* ◇ *defects in the education system* ▸ **de·fec·tive** /dɪˈfɛktɪv/ ***adj.***: *The accident was caused by a defective bolt.*

**de·fect²** /dɪˈfɛkt/ ***verb*** [I] to leave your country, a political party, etc. and go to or join an opposing one: *a spy who defected from a communist country* ▸ **de·fec·tion** ***noun*** [C,U]

★**de·fend** /dɪˈfɛnd/ ***verb***

➤PROTECT AGAINST ATTACK **1** [T] **defend sb/sth (against sb/sth)** to act, especially to fight, to protect sb/sth: *Would you be able to defend yourself if someone attacked you on the street?*

➤SUPPORT **2** [T] **defend sb/sth (against sb/sth)** to say or write sth to support sb/sth: *The candidate went on television to defend her policy.*

➤LAW **3** [T] (in law) to speak for sb who is accused of sth in a court of law

➤IN SPORTS **4** [I,T] to try to stop the other team or player from scoring: *They defended well and managed to hold onto their lead.*

➤IN COMPETITIONS **5** [T] to try to win a game so that you remain champion: *She successfully defended her title.*

**de·fen·dant** /dɪˈfɛndənt/ ***noun*** [C] a person who is accused of sth in a court of law

**de·fend·er** /dɪˈfɛndər/ ***noun*** [C] a person who defends sb/sth, especially in sports ➲ picture at **soccer**. ➲ Look also at **public defender**.

★**de·fense¹** (*Cdn* **de·fence**) /dɪˈfɛns/ ***noun***

➤PROTECTION AGAINST ATTACK **1** [U] **defense (against sth)** action to protect sb/sth from attack: *Would you fight in defense of your country?* **2** [C] **a defense (against sth)** something that protects sb/sth from sth or that is used for fighting against attack: *to build up a country's defenses* ◇ *the body's defenses against disease* **3** [U] the military equipment, forces, etc. for protecting a country: *the Defense Department* ◇ *Defense spending can be cut if fewer weapons are needed.*

➤SUPPORT **4** [C,U] something that you say or write to support sb/sth that is being attacked or accused: *He made a strong defense of the President's policy.* ◇ *I must say in her defense that I have always found her very reliable.*

➤LAW **5** [C] (in law) an argument in support of the accused person in a court of law: *His defense was that he was only carrying out orders.* **6 the defense** [sing.] (in law) the accused person in a court of law and the lawyer or lawyers who are acting for him/her: *The defense claims that many of the witnesses were lying.* ◇ *a defense attorney*

**de·fense²** /ˈdifɛns; dɪˈfɛns/ ***noun*** [C,U, usually sing.] (in sports) the players who try to prevent the other team from scoring points; the action of these players: *The Vikings' defense was unable to stop Jackson's spectacular touchdown pass.*

**de·fense·less** /dɪˈfɛnsləs/ ***adj.*** unable to defend yourself against attack

**de·fen·sive¹** /dɪˈfɛnsɪv/ ***adj.*** **1** used or intended for protecting sb/sth from attack: *The troops took up a defensive position.* **2** showing that you feel that sb is accusing or criticizing you: *When I asked him about his new job, he became very defensive and tried to change the subject.*

**de·fen·sive²** /dɪˈfɛnsɪv/ ***noun***

IDM **on the defensive** ready to defend yourself against attack or criticism

**de·fer** /dɪˈfər/ ***verb*** [T] (**de·fer̲r̲ing**; **de·fer̲r̲ed**) (*formal*) to leave sth until a later time

**def·er·ence** /ˈdɛfərəns/ ***noun***

IDM **in deference to sb/sth** (*formal*) because you respect and do not wish to upset sb: *In deference to her father's wishes, she didn't mention the subject again.*

**de·fi·ance** /dɪˈfaɪəns/ ***noun*** [U] open refusal to obey: *As an act of defiance, they continued to play loud music.*

IDM **in defiance of sb/sth** openly refusing to obey sb/sth

**de·fi·ant** /dɪˈfaɪənt/ ***adj.*** showing open refusal to obey ▸ **de·fi·ant·ly** ***adv.***

**de·fi·cien·cy** /dɪˈfɪʃənsi/ ***noun*** (*pl.* **de·fi·cien·cies**) **1** [C,U] a condition of not having enough of sth; a lack: *a vitamin C deficiency* **2** [C] (*formal*) something that is not good enough or that is wrong with sb/sth: *The problems were caused by deficiencies in the design.*

**de·fi·cient** /dɪˈfɪʃənt/ ***adj.*** **1 deficient (in sth)** not having enough of sth: *food that is deficient in minerals* **2** not good enough or not complete

**def·i·cit** /ˈdɛfəsɪt/ ***noun*** [C] the amount by which the money you receive is less than the money you have spent: *the federal budget deficit*

★**de·fine** /dɪˈfaɪn/ ***verb*** [T] **1** to say exactly what a word or idea means: *How would you define "happiness?"* **2** to explain the exact nature of sth clearly: *Something is worrying me, but I can't define exactly what it is.*

★**def·i·nite** /ˈdɛfənət/ ***adj.*** **1** fixed and unlikely to change; certain: *I'll give you a definite answer in a couple of days.* **2** clear; easy to see or notice: *There has been a definite change in her attitude recently.*

**ˌdefinite ˈarticle** ***noun*** [C] (*grammar*) the name used for the word "the" ➲ Compare **indefinite article**.

★**def·i·nite·ly** /ˈdɛfənətli/ ***adv.*** certainly; without doubt: *We definitely can't afford such a high price.* ◇ *This is definitely not what I expected!* ◇ *"Are you coming along tonight?" "Definitely!"*

★**def·i·ni·tion** /ˌdɛfəˈnɪʃn/ ***noun*** [C,U] a statement of the exact meaning of a word or idea

**de·fin·i·tive** /dɪˈfɪnət̬ɪv/ ***adj.*** in a form that cannot be changed or that cannot be improved: *This is the definitive version of the document.* ▸ **de·fin·i·tive·ly** ***adv.***

**de·flate** /dɪˈfleɪt; di-/ ***verb*** **1** [I,T] to become or to make sth smaller by letting the air or gas out: *The balloon slowly deflated and began to come down.* OPP **inflate** **2** [T] to make sb feel less confident, proud or excited

**de·fla·tion** /dɪˈfleɪʃn; di-/ ***noun*** [U] **1** a reduction in the amount of money in a country's economy so that prices fall or remain the same **2** the action of air being removed from sth OPP **inflation**

**de·flect** /dɪˈflɛkt/ ***verb*** **1** [I,T] to change direction after hitting sb/sth; to make sth change direction in this way: *The ball was deflected off the rim and into the hoop.* **2** [T] to turn sb or sb's attention away from sth: *The senator hoped to deflect criticism of his financial dealings.*

**de·for·es·ta·tion** /diˌfɔrəˈsteɪʃn; -ˌfɑr-/ ***noun*** [U] cutting down trees over a large area: *Deforestation is a major cause of global warming.*

**de·form** /dɪˈfɔrm/ ***verb*** [T] to change the shape of sth so that it is unnatural

**de·formed** /dɪˈfɔrmd/ ***adj.*** having an unnatural or ugly shape

**de·for·mi·ty** /dɪˈfɔrmət̬i/ ***noun*** (*pl.* **de·for·mi·ties**) [C,U] the state of being deformed; a part of the body that is deformed: *The drug caused women to give birth to babies with severe deformities.*

**de·fraud** /dɪˈfrɔd/ ***verb*** [T] to get sth from sb by cheating

**de·frost** /ˌdɪˈfrɔst/ ***verb*** **1** [T] to remove the ice from sth: *to defrost a fridge* (= by turning it off so that the ice melts) **2** [I,T] (used about frozen food) to return to a normal temperature; to make food do this: *Defrost the chicken thoroughly before cooking.*

**deft** /dɛft/ ***adj.*** (used especially about movements) skillful and quick ▸ **deft·ly** ***adv.***

**de·funct** /dɪˈfʌŋkt/ ***adj.*** no longer existing or in use

**de·fuse** /ˌdiˈfyuz/ ***verb*** [T] **1** to remove the part of a bomb that would make it explode: *Army experts defused the bomb safely.* **2** to make a situation calmer or less dangerous: *She defused the tension by changing the subject.*

**de·fy** /dɪˈfaɪ/ ***verb*** [T] (*pres. part.* **de·fy·ing**; *3rd person sing. pres.* **de·fies**; *pt, pp* **de·fied**) **1** to openly refuse to obey sb/sth: *She defied her parents and continued seeing him.* ➲ noun **defiance** ➲ adjective **defiant** **2 defy sb to do sth** to tell sb to do sth that you believe to be impossible: *I defy you to prove me wrong.* **3** to make sth impossible or very difficult: *It's such a beautiful place that it defies description.*

**de·gen·er·ate**[1] /dɪˈdʒɛnəreɪt/ ***verb*** [I] to fall to a less satisfactory standard; to become worse: *It degenerated from a pleasant discussion into an ugly argument.* ▸ **de·gen·er·a·tion** /dɪˌdʒɛnəˈreɪʃn/ ***noun*** [U]

**de·gen·er·ate**[2] /dɪˈdʒɛnərət/ ***adj.*** having moral standards that have fallen to a very low level: *a degenerate popular culture*

**de·gen·er·ate**[3] /dɪˈdʒɛnərət/ ***noun*** [C] a person with very low moral standards, especially for sexual behavior

**de·gen·er·a·tive** /dɪˈdʒɛnərət̬ɪv/ ***adj.*** (*technical*) (of an illness) getting worse or likely to get worse as time passes: *degenerative diseases such as Alzheimer's*

**deg·ra·da·tion** /ˌdɛgrəˈdeɪʃn/ ***noun*** [U] **1** degrading sb or being degraded: *the degradation of women* **2** causing the condition of sth to become worse: *environmental degradation*

**de·grade** /dɪˈgreɪd/ ***verb*** [T] to make people respect sb less: *It's the type of movie that really degrades women.* ▸ **de·grad·ing** ***adj.***: *Having to ask other people for money is degrading.*

★**de·gree** /dɪˈgri/ ***noun*** **1** [C] a measurement of temperature: *Water boils at 212 degrees Fahrenheit*

D

*(212°F) or 100 degrees Celsius (100° C).* ◇ *three degrees below zero/minus three degrees (-3°)* **2** [C] a measurement of angles: *a 45-degree (45°) angle* ◇ *An angle of 90 degrees is called a right angle.* ➲ picture at **angle**. **3** [C,U] (used about feelings or qualities) a certain amount or level: *There is always some degree of risk involved in mountain climbing.* ◇ *Our lives have changed to a considerable degree.* ◇ *I sympathize with her to some degree.* **4** [C] a qualification gained by successfully completing a program at a university: *A university degree is one of the requirements for the job.* ◇ *He has a bachelor's degree in economics.*

NOTE There are many different types of degrees given by North American colleges and universities. The first degree that most people receive is a **bachelor's degree**, which is usually given after four years of study. In the U.S., community colleges also award **associate's degrees** to students who have studied for two or three years. ➲ Look also at **master's degree** and **Ph.D.** ➲ For more information about the education systems in the United States and Canada, look at study pages **A8-9**.

**de·hy·drate** /ˌdiˈhaɪdreɪt/ ***verb*** **1** [T] (usually passive) to remove all the water from food so that it can be kept longer: *dehydrated vegetables* **2** [I,T] to lose or to take water from the body: *If you run for a long time in the heat, you start to dehydrate.* ▶ **de·hy·dra·tion** /ˌdihaɪˈdreɪʃn/ ***noun*** [U]

**de·i·ty** /ˈdeɪət̬i; ˈdiət̬i/ ***noun*** [C] (*pl.* **de·i·ties**) (*formal*) a god or goddess

**dé·jà vu** /ˌdeɪʒɑ ˈvu/ ***noun*** [U] the feeling that you have previously experienced sth which is happening to you now: *I had a strong sense of déjà vu as I entered the room.*

★**de·lay¹** /dɪˈleɪ/ ***verb*** **1** [T] to make sb/sth slow or late: *The plane was delayed for several hours because of bad weather.* **2** [I,T] **delay (sth/doing sth)** to decide not to do sth until a later time: *I was forced to delay the trip until the following week.*

★**de·lay²** /dɪˈleɪ/ ***noun*** [C,U] a situation or period of time where you have to wait: *Delays are likely on the roads because of heavy traffic.* ◇ *Because of the storm, all flights are subject to delay.*

**del·e·gate¹** /ˈdɛləgət/ ***noun*** [C] a person who has been chosen to speak or make decisions for a group of people, especially at a meeting: *delegates at the party's national convention*

**del·e·gate²** /ˈdɛləgeɪt/ ***verb*** [I,T] to give sb with a lower job or rank a particular task to carry out: *You can't do everything yourself. You need to learn how to delegate.*

**del·e·ga·tion** /ˌdɛləˈgeɪʃn/ ***noun*** **1** [U] giving sb with a lower job or rank a particular task to perform **2** [C] a group of people who have been chosen to speak or make decisions for a larger group of people, especially at a meeting: *The American delegation walked out of the meeting in protest.*

**de·lete** /dɪˈlit/ ***verb*** [T] **1** to cross out or leave out part of sth that is written: *If you do not attend class during the first week, your name will be deleted from the class list.* **2** (*computing*) to remove sth (e.g. a word, a sentence, a document, etc.) that is stored in a computer: *Don't delete that file!*

**de·le·tion** /dɪˈliʃn/ ***noun*** **1** [U] the act of deleting sth **2** [C] part of sth written or printed (e.g. a word, a sentence, a paragraph, etc.) that is deleted

**del·i** /ˈdɛli/ ***noun*** [C] (*informal*) = DELICATESSEN: *the deli counter at the grocery store*

★**de·lib·er·ate¹** /dɪˈlɪbərət; -brət/ ***adj.*** **1** done on purpose; planned: *Was it an accident or was it deliberate?* **2** done slowly and carefully, without hurrying: *She spoke in a calm, deliberate voice.*

**de·lib·er·ate²** /dɪˈlɪbəreɪt/ ***verb*** [I,T] (*formal*) to think about or discuss sth thoroughly before making a decision: *The jury deliberated for two days before announcing their verdict.*

★**de·lib·er·ate·ly** /dɪˈlɪbərətli; -brətli/ ***adv.*** **1** on purpose; intentionally: *I didn't break it deliberately – it was an accident.* **2** slowly and carefully, without hurrying

**de·lib·er·a·tion** /dɪˌlɪbəˈreɪʃn/ ***noun*** **1** [C,U] discussion or thinking about sth: *After much deliberation, I decided to reject the offer.* **2** [U] slowness and carefulness; lack of hurry: *He spoke with great deliberation.*

**del·i·ca·cy** /ˈdɛlɪkəsi/ ***noun*** (*pl.* **del·i·ca·cies**) **1** [C] a type of food that is considered particularly good: *Try this dish – it's a local delicacy.* **2** [U] using or needing particular care or skill so as not to offend sb: *She approached the issue with great delicacy.* **3** [U] the quality of being fine, light or detailed: *the delicacy of the antique china cups*

★**del·i·cate** /ˈdɛlɪkət/ ***adj.*** **1** fine or thin; easy to damage or break: *delicate skin* ◇ *delicate china teacups* **2** (used about colors, flavors, etc.) light and pleasant; not strong: *a delicate shade of pale blue* **3** requiring skillful treatment and care: *a very delicate operation* **4** (*old-fashioned*) frequently sick or easily made sick: *He was a delicate child and often in the hospital.*

**del·i·cate·ly** /ˈdɛlɪkətli/ ***adv.*** **1** lightly, gently or finely: *delicately painted vases* **2** with skillful and careful movement: *She stepped delicately over the broken glass.* **3** carefully so as not to offend sb or to cause problems: *a delicately balanced agreement*

**del·i·ca·tes·sen** /ˌdɛlɪkəˈtɛsn/ (*also informal* **deli**) ***noun*** [C] a store that sells foods such as meat, cheese and salads that are ready to eat and do not need to be cooked

**de·li·cious** /dɪˈlɪʃəs/ ***adj.*** having a very pleasant taste or smell: *What are you cooking? It smells delicious.*

**de·light¹** /dɪˈlaɪt/ ***noun*** **1** [U] great pleasure; joy: *She laughed with delight as she opened the present.* **2** [C] something that gives sb great pleasure: *The story is a delight to read.*

★**de·light²** /dɪˈlaɪt/ ***verb*** [T] to give sb great pleasure: *She delighted the audience by singing all her old songs.*

PHR V **delight in sth/in doing sth** to get great pleasure from sth: *He delights in playing tricks on people.*

**de·light·ed** /dɪˈlaɪt̬əd/ ***adj.*** **delighted (about/at/with sth); delighted (to do sth/that...)** extremely pleased: *"How do you feel about winning today?" "Delighted."* ◇ *She was delighted about* *getting the job/that she got the job.* ◇ *"Would you like to come for dinner?" "Thanks – I'd be delighted to."*

**de·light·ful** /dɪ'laɪtfl/ ***adj.*** giving sb great pleasure: *a delightful view* ◇ *He has a delightful sense of humor.* ▸ **de·light·ful·ly *adv.***

**de·lin·quen·cy** /də'lɪŋkwənsi/ ***noun*** [U] bad or criminal behavior, usually among young people

**de·lin·quent** /də'lɪŋkwənt/ ***adj.*** (usually used about a young person) behaving badly and often breaking the law: *delinquent children* ▸ **de·lin·quent *noun*** [C]: *a juvenile delinquent*

**de·lir·i·ous** /dɪ'lɪriəs/ ***adj.*** **1** speaking or thinking in a crazy way, often because of a fever **2** extremely happy ▸ **de·lir·i·ous·ly *adv.***

★**de·liv·er** /dɪ'lɪvər/ ***verb*** **1** [I,T] to take sth (goods, letters, etc.) to the place requested or to the address on it: *Your order will be delivered within five days.* **2** [T] to help a mother to give birth to her baby: *The doctor who delivered the baby said she was lucky to be alive.* **3** [T] to give sth (a speech, a warning, etc.): *She delivered a long lecture to the employees about efficiency.* **4** [I] **deliver (on sth)** (*informal*) to do or give sth that you have promised: *He's made a lot of promises, but can he deliver?*

★**de·liv·er·y** /dɪ'lɪvəri/ ***noun*** (*pl.* **de·liv·er·ies**) **1** [U] the act of taking sth (goods, letters, packages, etc.) to the place or person who has ordered it or whose address is on it: *Please allow 28 days for delivery.* ◇ *a delivery truck* **2** [C] an occasion when sth is delivered: *Mail deliveries may be delayed because of the blizzard.* **3** [C] something (letters, packages, etc.) that is delivered **4** [C] the process of giving birth to a baby: *an easy delivery*

**del·ta** /'dɛltə/ ***noun*** [C] **1** an area of flat land shaped like a triangle where a river divides into smaller rivers flowing toward the ocean **2** (*symbol* Δ, δ) the fourth letter of the Greek alphabet ➲ Look at the note at **fraternity**.

**del·uge**[1] /'dɛlyudʒ/ ***noun*** [C] **1** a sudden very heavy fall of rain; a flood **2** a very large number of things that happen or arrive at the same time: *The program was followed by a deluge of complaints from the public.*

**del·uge**[2] /'dɛlyudʒ/ ***verb*** [T] (usually passive) to send or give sb/sth a very large quantity of sth, all at the same time: *They were deluged with applications for the job.*

**de·lu·sion** /dɪ'luʒn/ ***noun*** [C,U] a false belief: *He seems to be under the delusion that he's popular.*

**de·luxe** /dɪ'lʌks/ ***adj.*** of extremely high quality and more expensive than usual: *a deluxe hotel*

**delve** /dɛlv/ ***verb*** [I] **delve into sth** to search inside sth: *She delved into the bag and brought out a tiny box.*

★**de·mand**[1] /dɪ'mænd/ ***noun*** **1** [C] **a demand (for sth/that...)** a strong request or order that must be obeyed: *a demand for changes in the law* ◇ *I was amazed by their demand that I leave immediately.* ➲ Look at the note at **recommend** (2). **2** [U, sing.] **demand (for sth/sb)** the desire or need for sth among a group of people: *We don't stock that product anymore because there is no demand for it.* ◇ *the effects of supply and demand on retail prices*

IDM **in demand** wanted by a lot of people: *Air conditioners are always in demand at the beginning of summer.*

**make demands on sb/sth** to require a large amount of effort from sb or a lot of sth: *Being the club leader makes a lot of demands on my free time.*

★**de·mand**[2] /dɪ'mænd/ ***verb*** [T] **1** to ask for sth in a way that shows you expect to get it: *I walked into the office and demanded to see the manager.* ◇ *She demanded that I pay her immediately.* ◇ *Your behavior was disgraceful and I demand an apology.* ➲ Look at the note at **recommend** (2). **2** to ask a question in a rude way: *"What are you doing here?" he demanded.* **3** to require or need sth: *a sport that demands skill as well as strength*

**de·mand·ing** /dɪ'mændɪŋ/ ***adj.*** **1** (used about a job, task, etc.) requiring a great deal of effort, care, skill, etc.: *It will be a demanding schedule – I have to go to six cities in six days.* **2** (used about a person) constantly wanting attention or expecting very high standards of people: *a demanding child/boss*

**de·mise** /dɪ'maɪz/ ***noun*** [sing.] **1** (*formal*) the death of a person: *the President's demise* **2** the unsuccessful end of sth: *Poor business decisions led to the company's demise.*

**dem·o** /'dɛmoʊ/ ***noun*** [C] (*pl.* **dem·os**) (*informal*) = DEMONSTRATION (2): *This is just a demo version of the software – the real program will have even more functions.*

**de·moc·ra·cy** /dɪ'mɑkrəsi/ ***noun*** (*pl.* **de·moc·ra·cies**) **1** [U] a system in which the government of a country is elected by its citizens **2** [C] a country that has this system: *How long has that country been a democracy?* **3** [U] the right of everyone in an organization, etc. to vote on matters that affect them and to be treated equally: *There is a need for more democracy in the company.* ➲ For more information on the North American political systems, look at study pages **A10-A11**.

**Dem·o·crat** /'dɛməkræt/ (*abbr.* **D**) ***noun*** [C] (*U.S.*) a member or supporter of the Democratic Party of the U.S. ➲ For more information on the U.S. political system, look at study page **A10**. ➲ Look at **Republican**.

**dem·o·crat·ic** /ˌdɛmə'krætɪk/ ***adj.*** **1** based on the system of democracy: *democratic elections* ◇ *a democratic government* **2** having or supporting equality for all members: *a fully democratic society* **3 Democratic** connected with the Democratic Party of the U.S: *the Democratic senator from Illinois* ▸ **dem·o·crat·i·cal·ly** /-kli/ ***adv.***: *a democratically elected government*

**the ˌDemoˌcratic ˈParty** ***noun*** [sing.] one of the two main political parties in the U.S.

> NOTE The other main party is the **Republican Party**. ➲ For more information about the political system in the U.S., look at study page **A10**.

**de·mol·ish** /dɪ'mɑlɪʃ/ ***verb*** [T] **1** to knock sth down (e.g. a building): *The old houses were demolished and a shopping mall was built in their place.* **2** to destroy sth (an idea, a belief, etc.): *She demolished his argument in one sentence.*

**dem·o·li·tion** /ˌdɛmə'lɪʃn/ ***noun*** [C,U] the act of knocking down or destroying sth

**de·mon** /'dimən/ ***noun*** [C] an evil spirit

D

D

★**dem·on·strate** /ˈdɛmənstreɪt/ **verb** **1** [T] to show clearly that sth exists or is true; to prove sth: *The prison escape demonstrates the need for greater security.* **2** [T] to show and explain to sb how to do sth or how sth works: *The crew demonstrated the use of lifejackets just after takeoff.* **3** [I] **demonstrate (against/for sb/sth)** to take part in a public protest or march in which a crowd of people express their opposition to, or support of, sb/sth: *Enormous crowds have been demonstrating for human rights.*

★**dem·on·stra·tion** /ˌdɛmənˈstreɪʃn/ **noun** **1** [C,U] something that shows clearly that sth exists or is true: *This accident is a clear demonstration of the system's faults.* **2** (*also informal* **demo**) [C,U] an act of showing or explaining to sb how to do sth or how sth works: *The salesclerk gave me a demonstration of what the computer could do.* **3** [C] **a demonstration (against/for sb/sth)** a public protest or march in which a crowd of people show how they oppose or support sb/sth: *Thousands took part in demonstrations for greater political freedom.*

**de·mon·stra·tive** /dəˈmɑnstrət̬ɪv/ **adj.** (used about a person) showing feelings, especially affection, openly

**dem·on·stra·tor** /ˈdɛmənstreɪt̬ər/ **noun** [C] a person who takes part in a public protest or march

**de·mor·al·ize** /dɪˈmɔrəlaɪz; -ˈmɑr-/ **verb** [T] to make sb lose confidence or the courage to continue doing sth: *Repeated defeats demoralized the team.* ▸ **de·mor·al·iz·ing** **adj.**: *The layoffs had a demoralizing effect on the whole company.*

**de·mote** /dɪˈmoʊt/ **verb** [T] (often passive) **demote sb (from sth) (to sth)** to move sb to a lower position or rank, often as a punishment: *After his mistake was discovered, Frank was demoted from office manager to office assistant.* OPP **promote** ▸ **de·mo·tion** **noun** [C,U] OPP **promotion**

**de·mure** /dɪˈmyʊr/ **adj.** (used especially about a girl or young woman) shy, quiet and well behaved

**den** /dɛn/ **noun** [C] **1** the hidden home of certain wild animals, e.g. lions **2** a secret meeting place: *a den of thieves* **3** a room in a house where people go to relax, watch television, etc.

**de·ni·al** /dɪˈnaɪəl/ **noun** **1** [C] a statement that sth is not true: *The mayor issued a denial about his involvement in the scandal.* **2** [U] refusing to believe that sth is true: *I think Mary's still in denial about her son's drug use.* **3** [C,U] **(a) denial (of sth)** refusing to allow sb to have or do sth: *a denial of personal freedom* ➲ verb **deny**

**den·im** /ˈdɛnəm/ **noun** [U] a thick cotton material (often blue) that is used for making clothes, e.g. jeans

**de·nom·i·na·tion** /dɪˌnɑməˈneɪʃn/ **noun** [C] a religious group that is part of a larger religious organization; a particular type of religious group: *Various denominations hold services in the hospital chapel.*

**de·nom·i·na·tor** /dɪˈnɑməneɪt̬ər/ **noun** [C] (in math) the number below the line in a FRACTION (2) showing how many parts the whole is divided into: *Four is the denominator in ¾.* ➲ Compare **numerator**.

**de·note** /dɪˈnoʊt/ **verb** [T] (*formal*) to indicate or be a sign of sth; to mean sth: *What does* [U] *denote in this dictionary?*

**de·nounce** /dɪˈnaʊns/ **verb** [T] to say publicly that sth is wrong; to be very critical of a person in public: *The President denounced the bombing as a cowardly act of terrorism.* ➲ noun **denunciation**

**dense** /dɛns/ **adj.** **1** containing a lot of things or people close together: *dense forests* ◇ *areas of dense population* **2** difficult to see through: *dense fog* **3** (*informal*) unintelligent; stupid: *How can you be so dense?* ▸ **dense·ly** **adv.**: *densely populated*

**den·si·ty** /ˈdɛnsət̬i/ **noun** (*pl.* **den·si·ties**) **1** [U] the number of things or people in a place in relation to its area: *the density of the population* **2** [C,U] (*technical*) the relation of the weight of a substance to the space it occupies

**dent**[1] /dɛnt/ **noun** [C] a hollow place in the surface of sth hard, especially metal, that is the result of sth hitting or pressing against it: *This can has a dent in it.*

**dent**[2] /dɛnt/ **verb** [T] to damage sth by hitting it and making a hollow place in it: *I hit a wall and dented the front of the car.*

**den·tal** /ˈdɛntl/ **adj.** connected with teeth: *dental care*

ˌ**dental hyˈgienist** (*also* **hy·gien·ist**) **noun** [C] a person who works with a dentist and whose job is to clean people's teeth and give them advice about keeping them clean

★**den·tist** /ˈdɛntɪst/ **noun** [C] a person whose job is to take care of people's teeth: *You should go to the dentist for a checkup.* ◇ *I have a dentist's appointment tomorrow.*

**den·tures** /ˈdɛntʃərz/ **noun** [pl.] teeth that are made of plastic, etc., worn by a person who has lost his/her natural teeth

**de·nun·ci·a·tion** /dɪˌnʌnsiˈeɪʃn/ **noun** [C,U] an expression of strong disapproval of sb/sth in public: *a strong denunciation of the invasion* ➲ verb **denounce**

ˌ**Denver ˈboot** (*also* **boot**) **noun** [C] a device that is attached to the wheel of a car that has been parked illegally, so that it cannot be driven away

★**de·ny** /dɪˈnaɪ/ **verb** [T] (*pres. part.* **de·ny·ing**; *3rd person sing. pres.* **de·nies**; *pt, pp* **de·nied**) **1 deny sth/doing sth/that...** to state that sth is not true: *The mayor denied reports that he had accepted bribes.* ◇ *She denied telling lies/that she had told lies.* **2 deny sb sth; deny sth (to sb)** to refuse to allow sb to have sth: *She was denied permission to remain in the country.* ➲ noun **denial**

**de·o·dor·ant** /diˈoʊdərənt/ **noun** [C,U] a chemical substance that you put onto your body to destroy or prevent bad smells

**de·part** /dɪˈpɑrt/ **verb** [I] (*formal*) to leave a place, usually at the beginning of a trip: *Tour buses depart from Kennedy Plaza every hour.* ➲ noun **departure** ➲ Look at the note at **leave**[1].

★**de·part·ment** /dɪˈpɑrtmənt/ **noun** [C] (*abbr.* **dept.**) **1** one of the sections into which an organization (e.g. a school or a business) is divided: *The book department is on the second floor.* ◇ *She works in the personnel department.* **2** a division of the government responsible for a particular area of activity: *the Department of Defense*

**de·part·men·tal** /ˌdipɑrtˈmɛntl/ ***adj.*** concerning a department: *a departmental meeting*

**deˈpartment store** ***noun*** [C] a large store that is divided into departments selling many different types of goods

★**de·par·ture** /dɪˈpɑrtʃər/ ***noun*** [C,U] **1** leaving or going away from a place: *Arrivals and departures are shown on screens around the airport.* ◇ *Passengers should check in at least one hour before departure.* **2** an action which is different from what is usual or expected: *a departure from normal practice*

★**de·pend** /dɪˈpɛnd/ ***verb***

IDM **it/that depends** (used alone or at the beginning of a sentence) it is not certain; it is influenced or decided by sth: *"Can you loan me some money?" "That depends. How much do you want?"* ◇ *I don't know whether I'll see him. It depends what time he gets here.*

PHR V **depend on sb/sth** to be sure that sb/sth will help you; to trust sb/sth to do sth: *If you ever need any help, you know you can depend on me.* ◇ *You can't depend on the buses. They're always late.*

**depend on sb/sth (for sth)** to need sb/sth to provide sth: *I depend on my parents for advice.* ◇ *Our organization depends on donations from the public.*

**depend on sth** to be decided or influenced by sb/sth: *His whole future depends on these exams.* ◇ *The starting salary will be between $25,000 and $30,000, depending on education and experience.*

**de·pend·a·ble** /dɪˈpɛndəbl/ ***adj.*** that can be trusted: *The bus service is usually very dependable.*

**de·pend·ence** /dɪˈpɛndəns/ ***noun*** [U] **dependence on sb/sth** the state of needing sb/sth: *The country wants to reduce its dependence on imported oil.*

**de·pend·en·cy** /dɪˈpɛndənsi/ ***noun*** [U] the state of being dependent on sb/sth; the state of being unable to live without sth, especially a drug: *a drug dependency clinic*

**de·pend·ent**[1] /dɪˈpɛndənt/ ***noun*** [C] a person who depends on sb else for money, a home, food, etc.: *The insurance provides coverage for you and all your dependents.*

**de·pend·ent**[2] /dɪˈpɛndənt/ ***adj.*** **dependent (on sb/sth)** needing sb/sth to support you: *The industry is heavily dependent on government contracts.* ◇ *dependent children*

**de·pict** /dɪˈpɪkt/ ***verb*** [T] **1** to show sb/sth in a painting or drawing: *a painting depicting a country scene* **2** to describe sb/sth in words: *The novel depicts rural life a century ago.*

**de·plane** /diˈpleɪn/ ***verb*** [I] to get off an airplane: *We landed and deplaned.* SYN **disembark**

**de·plete** /dɪˈplit/ ***verb*** [T] to reduce the amount of sth: *We are depleting the world's natural resources.* ▸ **de·ple·tion** /dɪˈpliʃn/ ***noun*** [U]: *the depletion of the ozone layer*

**de·plor·a·ble** /dɪˈplɔrəbl/ ***adj.*** morally bad and deserving disapproval ▸ **de·plor·a·bly** /-əbli/ ***adv.***

**de·plore** /dɪˈplɔr/ ***verb*** [T] (*formal*) to feel or state that sth is morally bad: *I deplore such dishonest behavior.*

**de·ploy** /dɪˈplɔɪ/ ***verb*** [T] **1** to put soldiers or weapons in a position where they can be used **2** to arrange people or things so that they can be used efficiently ▸ **de·ploy·ment** ***noun*** [U]: *the deployment of troops*

**de·port** /dɪˈpɔrt/ ***verb*** [T] to send a foreigner out of a country officially: *A number of illegal immigrants have been deported.* ▸ **de·por·ta·tion** /ˌdipɔrˈteɪʃn/ ***noun*** [C,U]: *The illegal immigrants face deportation.*

**de·pose** /dɪˈpoʊz/ ***verb*** [T] to remove a ruler or leader from power: *There was a revolution and the dictator was deposed.*

★**de·pos·it**[1] /dɪˈpɑzət/ ***verb*** [T] **1** to put money into an account at a bank: *She deposited $20 a week into her savings account.* **2** to put sth valuable in an official place where it is safe until needed again: *Valuables can be deposited in the hotel safe.* **3** to put sth down somewhere: *He deposited his bags on the floor and sat down.* **4** to leave sth lying on a surface, as the result of a natural or chemical process: *mud deposited by a flood*

**de·pos·it**[2] /dɪˈpɑzət/ ***noun*** [C] **1** a sum of money put into a bank account; the paying of a sum of money into a bank account: *to make a deposit* **2 a deposit (on sth)** a sum of money which is the first payment for sth, with the rest of the money to be paid later: *Once you have paid a deposit, the merchandise will be held for you.* **3 a deposit (on sth)** a sum of money that you pay when you rent sth and that you get back when you return it or finish using it without damage: *The rent is $500 a month, plus a $500 deposit.* **4** a substance that has been left on a surface or has developed in the ground as the result of a natural or chemical process: *mineral deposits*

**dep·o·si·tion** /ˌdɛpəˈzɪʃn/ ***noun*** **1** [C] (in law) a formal statement, taken from sb who has promised to tell the truth and used in court **2** [U,C] the act of removing sb, especially a ruler, from power

**de·pot** /ˈdipoʊ/ ***noun*** [C] **1** a place where military supplies are stored **2** (*old-fashioned*) a small bus or train station, especially in the country or a small town

**de·pre·ci·ate** /dɪˈpriʃieɪt/ ***verb*** [I] to lose value, especially as a result of use or age ▸ **de·pre·ci·a·tion** /dɪˌpriʃiˈeɪʃn/ ***noun*** [C,U]

★**de·press** /dɪˈprɛs/ ***verb*** [T] **1** to make sb unhappy: *The thought of going to work tomorrow really depresses me.* **2** (used especially in connection with business) to cause sth to become less successful or profitable: *The reduction in the number of tourists has depressed local business.*

★**de·pressed** /dɪˈprɛst/ ***adj.*** very unhappy, often for a long period. If you are depressed, you may be suffering from the medical condition of depression: *He's been very depressed ever since he lost his job.*

★**de·press·ing** /dɪˈprɛsɪŋ/ ***adj.*** making sb feel sad or without hope: *The outlook for the future of the company is very depressing.*

**de·pres·sion** /dɪˈprɛʃn/ ***noun*** **1** [U] a feeling of unhappiness and lack of hope that lasts for a long time. Depression can be a medical condition and may have physical symptoms. **2** [C] a period when the economic situation is bad, with little business activity and many people without a job: *the Great Depression of the 1930s* **3** [C] a hollow part in the surface of sth: *a depression in the ground*

**de·prive** /dɪˈpraɪv/ ***verb*** [T] **deprive sb/sth of sth** to prevent sb/sth from having sth; to take away sth from sb: *to deprive people of their rights as citizens* ◇ *The prisoners were deprived of food.* ▸ **dep·ri·va·tion** /ˌdɛprəˈveɪʃn/ ***noun*** [C,U]: *people suffering from sleep deprivation*

**de·prived** /dɪˈpraɪvd/ ***adj.*** not having enough of the basic things in life, such as food, money, etc.: *He came from a deprived background.*

**dept.** ***abbr.*** = DEPARTMENT

★**depth** /dɛpθ/ ***noun*** **1** [C,U] the distance down from the top surface of sth; the measurement of how deep sth is: *What's the depth of the swimming pool?* ◇ *The hole should be one inch in depth.* ➲ picture at **length**. **2** [C,U] the distance from the front to the back: *the depth of a shelf* **3** [U] (used about emotions, knowledge, etc.) the amount that a person has: *the depth of his feelings for her*

IDM **in depth** looking at all the details: *to discuss a problem in depth*

**out of your depth** in a situation that is too difficult for you: *When they started discussing politics, I felt totally out of my depth.*

**dep·u·ta·tion** /ˌdɛpyəˈteɪʃn/ ***noun*** [C] (*formal*) a small group of people who are asked or allowed to act or speak for another larger group

**dep·u·ty** /ˈdɛpyət̮i/ ***noun*** [C] (*pl.* **dep·u·ties**) **1** a person with the second-highest rank in a particular organization. A deputy does the work of his/her boss if the boss is absent: *the deputy chief of police* **2** (*U.S.*) a person who works for a county's police force (**the sheriff's department**): *Sheriff's deputies are investigating a series of thefts from farms.* ◇ *Deputy Sheriff Karen Thompson*

**de·rail** /dɪˈreɪl/ ***verb*** [I,T] (used about a train) to come off a railroad track; to cause a train to do this ▸ **de·rail·ment** ***noun*** [C,U]: *Several people were injured in a derailment near Springfield this morning.*

**de·ranged** /dɪˈreɪndʒd/ ***adj.*** thinking and behaving in a way that is not normal, especially because of mental illness

**der·e·lict** /ˈdɛrəlɪkt/ ***adj.*** no longer used and in bad condition: *a derelict house*

**de·ride** /dɪˈraɪd/ ***verb*** [T] (*formal*) to say that sb/sth is ridiculous; to laugh at sth in a cruel way ▸ **de·ri·sion** /dəˈrɪʒn/ ***noun*** [U]: *Her comments were met with howls of derision.*

**der·i·va·tion** /ˌdɛrəˈveɪʃn/ ***noun*** [C,U] the origin or development of sth, especially a word: *a word of Greek derivation*

**de·riv·a·tive¹** /dəˈrɪvətɪv/ ***adj.*** copied from sth or influenced by sth and therefore not new or original: *a derivative action movie*

**de·riv·a·tive²** /dəˈrɪvət̮ɪv/ ***noun*** [C] **1** a form of sth (especially a word) that has developed from the original form: *"Sadness" is a derivative of "sad."* **2** a substance that has been developed from another substance: *The new medication is a derivative of Vitamin A.*

★**de·rive** /dɪˈraɪv/ ***verb*** **1** [T] (*formal*) to get sth (especially a feeling or an advantage) from sth: *I derive great satisfaction from my work.* **2** [I,T] to come from sth; to have sth as its origin: *The town derives its name from a Native American word for "clear water."*

**der·ma·tol·o·gy** /ˌdərməˈtɑlədʒi/ ***noun*** [U] the scientific study of skin diseases ▸ **der·ma·tol·o·gist** /-dʒɪst/ ***noun*** [C]

**de·rog·a·to·ry** /dəˈrɑgəˌtɔri/ ***adj.*** expressing a lack of respect for, or a low opinion of sth: *derogatory comments about the standard of my work*

**de·scend** /dɪˈsɛnd/ ***verb*** [I,T] (*formal*) to go down to a lower place; to go down sth: *The plane started to descend, and a few minutes later we landed.* ◇ *She descended the stairs slowly.* OPP **ascend**

IDM **be descended from sb** to have as a relative or relatives in the distant past: *He says he's descended from a Russian prince.*

**de·scen·dant** /dɪˈsɛndənt/ ***noun*** [C] a person who is related to sb who lived a long time ago: *She's a descendant of freed slaves.* ➲ Look at **ancestor**.

**de·scent** /dɪˈsɛnt/ ***noun*** **1** [C] a movement down to a lower place: *The pilot informed us that we were about to begin our descent.* **2** [U] family origins, especially in connection with a particular country: *He is of Italian descent.*

★**de·scribe** /dɪˈskraɪb/ ***verb*** [T] **describe sb/sth (as sth)** to say what sb/sth is like, or what happened: *Can you describe the bag you lost?* ◇ *It's impossible to describe how I felt.* ◇ *The thief was described as tall, thin and about twenty years old.* ◇ *Would you describe yourself as confident?*

★**de·scrip·tion** /dɪˈskrɪpʃn/ ***noun*** **1** [C,U] a picture in words of sb/sth or an account of sth that happened; the ability to describe sb/sth: *The man gave the police a detailed description of the burglar.* **2** [C] a type or kind of sth: *There were animals of every description at the fair.*

**de·scrip·tive** /dɪˈskrɪptɪv/ ***adj.*** **1** that describes sb/sth: *a piece of descriptive writing* **2** that describes sb/sth in a skillful and interesting way: *She gave a highly descriptive account of the trip.*

**de·seg·re·gate** /ˌdiˈsɛgrəgeɪt/ ***verb*** [T] to end a system of separating people of different races in a place: *a plan to desegregate the city's public schools* ➲ Look also at **segregate** and **integrate**. ▸ **de·seg·re·ga·tion** /diˌsɛgrəˈgeɪʃn/ ***noun*** [U]

**de·sert¹** /dɪˈzərt/ ***verb*** **1** [T] to leave sb/sth, usually forever: *He deserted his wife and went to live with another woman.* **2** [I,T] (used especially about sb in the armed forces) to leave without permission: *He deserted from the army because he didn't want to fight.*

★**des·ert²** /ˈdɛzərt/ ***noun*** [C,U] a large area of land, usually covered with sand, that has very little water and very few plants: *the Gobi Desert*

**de·sert·ed** /dɪˈzərt̮əd/ ***adj.*** empty, because all the people have left: *The streets are practically deserted on Sunday nights.*

**de·sert·er** /dɪˈzərt̮ər/ ***noun*** [C] a person who leaves military duty without permission

★**de·serve** /dɪˈzərv/ ***verb*** [T] (not used in the continuous tenses) to earn sth, especially a suitable reward or punishment, for sth that you have done: *We've done a lot of work and we deserve a break.* ◇ *He deserves to be punished severely for such a crime.*

**de·serv·ing** /dɪˈzərvɪŋ/ ***adj.*** that deserves help: *The scholarship will be awarded to a deserving student with good grades.*

★**de·sign**[1] /dɪˈzaɪn/ ***noun*** **1** [C] a drawing that shows how sth should be made: *The architect showed us her design for the new theater.* **2** [U] the way in which sth is planned and made or in which the parts of sth are arranged: *Design flaws have been discovered in the car.* **3** [U] the process and skill of making drawings that show how sth should be made: *to study industrial design* ◇ *graphic design* **4** [C] a pattern of lines, shapes, etc. that decorate sth: *a T-shirt with a geometric design on it*

★**de·sign**[2] /dɪˈzaɪn/ ***verb*** **1** [I,T] to plan and make a drawing of how sth will be made: *She designs the interiors of office buildings.* **2** [T] to invent, plan and develop sth for a particular purpose: *The bridge wasn't designed for such heavy traffic.*

**des·ig·nate** /ˈdɛzɪgneɪt/ ***verb*** [T] (*formal*) **1** to say officially that sth has a particular character or name; to describe sth in a particular way: *This has been designated a historic site.* **2** to choose or name sb for a particular job or position: *the man designated to succeed the president* **3** to show or mark sth: *These arrows designate the emergency exits.*

**ˌdesignated ˈdriver** ***noun*** [C] a person in a group who agrees not to drink alcohol and to drive the other members of the group home from a bar/party

**ˌdesignated ˈhitter** ***noun*** [C] (in baseball) a person chosen to hit the ball instead of another player (the pitcher)

**de·sign·er** /dɪˈzaɪnər/ ***noun*** [C] a person whose job is to make drawings showing how sth will be made: *a fashion designer* ◇ *designer clothing* (= made by a famous designer)

**de·sir·a·ble** /dɪˈzaɪrəbl/ ***adj.*** **1** wanted, often by many people; worth having: *a desirable neighborhood* (= one that many people would like to live in) ◇ *Experience is desirable but not essential for this job.* **2** sexually attractive

★**de·sire**[1] /dɪˈzaɪər/ ***noun*** [C,U] **(a) desire (for sth/to do sth) 1** the feeling of wanting sth very much; a strong wish: *the desire for a peaceful solution to the crisis* ◇ *I have no desire to visit that place again.* **2** the wish for sexual relations with sb

★**de·sire**[2] /dɪˈzaɪər/ ***verb*** [T] **1** (*formal*) to want: *They have everything they could possibly desire.* **2** to find sb/sth sexually attractive

★**desk** /dɛsk/ ***noun*** [C] **1** a type of table, often with drawers, that you sit at to write or work: *The students took their books out of their desks.* ◇ *a computer that fits easily onto any desk* **2** a table or place in a building where a particular service is provided: *Brochures are available at the information desk.*

**ˈdesk clerk** ***noun*** [C] = CLERK (3)

**desk·top** /ˈdɛsktɑp/ ***noun*** [C] **1** the flat surface on the top of a desk: *a desktop computer* (= one that fits on the top of a desk) **2** (*computing*) the background picture on a computer screen: *Use the mouse to move the icons on the desktop.*

**ˌdesktop ˈpublishing** ***noun*** [U] (*abbr.* **DTP**) (*computing*) the use of a small computer and a machine for printing, to produce books, magazines and other printed material

**des·o·late** /ˈdɛsələt/ ***adj.*** **1** (used about a place) sad, empty and depressing: *desolate wasteland* **2** (used about a person) lonely, very unhappy and without hope

**des·o·la·tion** /ˌdɛsəˈleɪʃn/ ***noun*** [U] **1** the state of being empty because all the people have left: *All the factories closed, leaving the town in a state of desolation.* **2** the feeling of being lonely and without hope: *He felt utter desolation when his wife died.*

**de·spair**[1] /dɪˈspɛr/ ***noun*** [U] the state of having lost all hope: *I felt like giving up in despair.* ◇ *Despair drove him to attempt suicide.*

**de·spair**[2] /dɪˈspɛr/ ***verb*** [I] **despair (of sb/sth)** to lose all hope and to feel that there will be no improvement: *We began to despair of ever getting out of debt.*

**des·per·ate** /ˈdɛspərət; -prət/ ***adj.*** **1** out of control and willing to do anything to change the situation you are in because it is so terrible: *I only took this job because I was desperate.* **2** done with little hope of success, as a last thing to try when everything else has failed: *I made a desperate attempt to persuade her to change her mind.* **3 desperate (for sth/to do sth)** wanting or needing sth very much: *Let's go into a coffee shop. I'm desperate for something to drink.* **4** terrible, very serious: *There is a desperate shortage of doctors in rural areas.* ▸ **des·per·ate·ly** ***adv.***: *She desperately needs a heart transplant in order to survive.*

**des·per·a·tion** /ˌdɛspəˈreɪʃn/ ***noun*** [U] the feeling or state of being desperate: *She wanted to scream in desperation.*

**des·pi·ca·ble** /dəˈspɪkəbl/ ***adj.*** deserving to be hated: *a despicable liar* ◇ *a despicable act of terrorism*

**de·spise** /dɪˈspaɪz/ ***verb*** [T] to hate sb/sth; to consider sb/sth worthless: *I despise him for lying about me to other people.*

★**de·spite** /dɪˈspaɪt/ ***prep.*** (used to show that sth happened although you would not expect it): *Despite having very little money, they enjoy life.* ◇ *The project went ahead despite public opposition.*

**de·spon·dent** /dɪˈspɑndənt/ ***adj.*** without hope; expecting no improvement

**des·sert** /dɪˈzərt/ ***noun*** [C,U] something sweet that is eaten after the main part of a meal: *What would you like for dessert – ice cream or fresh fruit?*

**des·ti·na·tion** /ˈdɛstəˈneɪʃn/ ***noun*** [C] the place where sb/sth is going or being sent: *I finally reached my destination two hours late.*

**des·tined** /ˈdɛstənd/ ***adj.*** **1 destined for sth/to do sth** sure to or intended to be, have or do sth: *I think she is destined for success.* ◇ *He was destined to become one of the country's leading politicians.* **2 destined for...** on a trip or moving toward a particular place: *They were destined for a new life in a new country.*

**des·ti·ny** /ˈdɛstəni/ ***noun*** (*pl.* **des·ti·nies**) **1** [U] a power that people believe influences their lives; fate **2** [C] the things that happen to you in your life, especially things that you do not control: *She felt that it was her destiny to be a great singer.*

**des·ti·tute** /ˈdɛstətut/ ***adj.*** not having the things that are necessary in life, such as money, food, a home, etc. ▶ **des·ti·tu·tion** /ˌdɛstəˈtuʃn/ ***noun*** [U]

D

★**de·stroy** /dɪˈstrɔɪ/ ***verb*** [T] **1** to damage sth so badly that it can no longer be used or no longer exists: *The building was destroyed by fire.* ◇ *The defeat destroyed his confidence.* **2** to kill an animal, especially because it is injured or dangerous: *The horse broke its leg and had to be destroyed.*

**de·stroy·er** /dɪˈstrɔɪər/ ***noun*** [C] **1** a person or thing that destroys sth **2** a small warship

★**de·struc·tion** /dɪˈstrʌkʃn/ ***noun*** [U] destroying or being destroyed: *the destruction of the rainforests*

**de·struc·tive** /dɪˈstrʌktɪv/ ***adj.*** causing a lot of damage: *destructive weapons* ◇ *the destructive effects of alcohol and drugs*

**de·tach** /dɪˈtætʃ/ ***verb*** [T] **detach sth (from sth)** to separate sth from sth it is attached to: *Detach the form at the bottom of the page and send it to this address...* ▶ **de·tach·a·ble** ***adj.***

**de·tached** /dɪˈtætʃt/ ***adj.*** not being or not feeling personally involved

**de·tach·ment** /dɪˈtætʃmənt/ ***noun*** **1** [U] the fact or feeling of not being personally involved **2** [C] a group of soldiers who have been given a particular task away from the main group

★**de·tail¹** /ˈditeɪl; dɪˈteɪl/ ***noun*** [C,U] a small individual fact, point or piece of information: *Just give me the basic facts. Don't worry about the details.* ◇ *For more details on how to join the club, call this number...* ◇ *The work involves close attention to detail.*
IDM **go into detail(s)** to talk or write about the details of sth: *I can't go into detail now because it would take too long.*
**in detail** including the details; thoroughly: *We haven't discussed the matter in detail yet.*

**de·tail²** /dɪˈteɪl; ˈditeɪl/ ***verb*** [T] to give a full list of sth; to describe sth fully: *He detailed all the equipment he needed for the job.*

★**de·tailed** /dɪˈteɪld; ˈditeɪld/ ***adj.*** having many details or giving a lot of attention to details: *a detailed description of the accident*

**de·tain** /dɪˈteɪn/ ***verb*** [T] (*formal*) to stop sb from leaving a place; to delay sb: *He was detained by immigration officials at the airport.* ➲ noun **detention**

**de·tect** /dɪˈtɛkt/ ***verb*** [T] to notice or discover sth that is difficult to see, feel, etc.: *Traces of blood were detected on his clothes.* ▶ **de·tec·tion** /dɪˈtɛkʃn/ ***noun*** [U]: *The crime escaped detection for many years.*

**de·tec·tive** /dɪˈtɛktɪv/ ***noun*** [C] a person, especially a police officer, who tries to solve crimes and find the person who is guilty

**de·tec·tor** /dɪˈtɛktər/ ***noun*** [C] an instrument that is used for detecting sth: *a smoke detector*

**de·ten·tion** /dɪˈtɛnʃn/ ***noun*** [U] **1** the act of stopping a person from leaving a place, especially by keeping him/her in prison, often for political reasons ➲ verb **detain** **2** the punishment of having to stay at school after the school day is finished: *I got detention for skipping class.*

**de·ter** /dɪˈtər/ ***verb*** [T] (**de·ter·ring**; **de·terred**) **deter sb (from doing sth)** to make sb decide not to do sth: *Even the high prices didn't deter people from buying tickets.*

**de·ter·gent** /dɪˈtərdʒənt/ ***noun*** [C,U] a chemical liquid or powder that is used for cleaning things

**de·te·ri·o·rate** /dɪˈtɪriəreɪt/ ***verb*** [I] to become worse: *The political tension is deteriorating into civil war.* ▶ **de·te·ri·o·ra·tion** /dɪˌtɪriəˈreɪʃn/ ***noun*** [C,U]

★**de·ter·mi·na·tion** /dɪˌtərməˈneɪʃn/ ***noun*** **1** [U] the quality of having firmly decided to succeed in doing sth, even if it is very difficult or people are against you: *You need great determination to succeed in business.* **2** (*formal*) [C,U] the act of deciding or calculating sth: *The board will make a determination today as to which students will be awarded scholarships.* ◇ *the determination of payments on insurance claims*

**de·ter·mine** /dɪˈtərmən/ ***verb*** [T] **1** to decide or calculate sth: *The results of the tests will determine what treatment you need.* **2** to find sth out: *an attempt to determine the exact position of the enemy submarine*

★**de·ter·mined** /dɪˈtərmənd/ ***adj.*** having firmly decided to succeed in doing sth, even if it is difficult or people are against you: *He is determined to drop out of school, even though his parents want him to stay.*

**de·ter·min·er** /dɪˈtərmənər/ ***noun*** [C] (*grammar*) a word that comes before a noun to show how the noun is being used: *"Her," "most" and "those" are all determiners.*

**de·ter·rent** /dɪˈtərənt/ ***noun*** [C] something that is intended to stop you from doing sth: *Their punishment will be a deterrent to others.* ▶ **de·ter·rent** ***adj.***

**de·test** /dɪˈtɛst/ ***verb*** [T] (*formal*) to hate or dislike sb/sth very much: *They absolutely detest each other.*

**det·o·nate** /ˈdɛtn·eɪt/ ***verb*** [I,T] to explode or to make sth explode

**de·tour** /ˈditʊr/ ***noun*** [C] **1** a different route which traffic can take when a road is closed **2** a longer route that you take from one place to another in order to avoid sth or in order to see or do sth: *On our way to the lake, we made a detour to visit Aunt Joan.*

**de·tox** /ˈditɑks/ ***noun*** [U] (*informal*) **1** the process of removing harmful substances from your body by only eating and drinking particular things: *a 28-day detox plan* **2** = DETOXIFICATION: *a detox clinic* ◇ *He's gone into detox.*

**de·tox·i·fi·ca·tion** /diˌtɑksəfəˈkeɪʃn/ (*also informal* **de·tox**) ***noun*** [U] treatment given to people to help them stop drinking alcohol or taking drugs: *a detoxification unit*

**de·tract** /dɪˈtrækt/ ***verb*** [I] **detract from sth** to make sth seem less good or important: *These criticisms in no way detract from the team's achievements.*

**det·ri·ment** /ˈdɛtrəmənt/ ***noun***
IDM **to the detriment of sb/sth** harming or

damaging sb/sth: *The new law will be to the detriment of public safety.*

**det·ri·men·tal** /ˌdɛtrəˈmɛntl/ ***adj.*** harmful: *Too much alcohol is detrimental to your health.*

**de·val·ue** /ˌdiˈvælyu/ ***verb*** [T] to reduce the value of the money of one country in relation to the value of the money of other countries: *The peso has been devalued against the dollar.* ▸ **de·val·u·a·tion** /ˌdivælyuˈeɪʃn/ ***noun*** [U]

**dev·as·tate** /ˈdɛvəsteɪt/ ***verb*** [T] to destroy sth or damage it badly: *a land devastated by war* ▸ **dev·as·ta·tion** /ˌdɛvəˈsteɪʃn/ ***noun*** [U]: *a scene of total devastation*

**dev·as·tat·ed** /ˈdɛvəsteɪt̬əd/ ***adj.*** **1** completely destroyed **2** shocked or very upset: *The community was devastated by the killings.*

**dev·as·tat·ing** /ˈdɛvəsteɪt̬ɪŋ/ ***adj.*** **1** that destroys sth completely: *a devastating explosion* **2** that shocks or upsets sb very much: *The factory shutdown was a devastating blow to the workers.*

★**de·vel·op** /dɪˈvɛləp/ ***verb***

➤ GROW BIGGER/STRONGER **1** [I,T] to grow slowly, increase, or change into sth else; to make sb/sth do this: *to develop from a child into an adult* ◇ *a plan to help children develop their natural talents*

➤ DISEASE/PROBLEM **2** [T] to begin to have sth: *to develop cancer*

➤ BECOME SERIOUS/IMPORTANT **3** [I] to begin to happen or be noticeable: *His symptoms developed soon after we got home.* ◇ *Trouble is developing at the border.*

➤ PHOTOGRAPHS **4** [T] to make pictures from a piece of film by using special chemicals: *to develop a roll of film*

➤ BUILD HOUSES **5** [T] to build houses, stores, factories, etc. on a piece of land: *This site is being developed for offices.*

**de·vel·oped** /dɪˈvɛləpt/ ***adj.*** having advanced political and economic systems and a high standard of living: *a highly developed economy*

**de·vel·op·er** /dɪˈvɛləpər/ ***noun*** [C] a person or company that plans new projects, such as buildings: *a real estate developer* ◇ *a software developer*

**de·vel·op·ing** /dɪˈvɛləpɪŋ/ ***adj.*** (used about a country, an area, etc.) trying to develop or improve its economy: *assistance to developing nations*

★**de·vel·op·ment** /dɪˈvɛləpmənt/ ***noun*** **1** [U] developing or being developed: *the history of Japan's development from a feudal to an industrial society* ◇ *a child's intellectual development* **2** [C] a new event: *a number of new developments in the situation in the Middle East* **3** [C,U] a new product or the act of making a new product: *a technological development* ◇ *research and development* **4** [C] a piece of land on which houses, stores, factories, etc. have been built: *a new housing development*

**de·vi·ate** /ˈdivieɪt/ ***verb*** [I] to change the way you think or behave, or to start to behave in a way that is not acceptable to other people: *He never deviated from his principles.*

**de·vi·a·tion** /ˌdiviˈeɪʃn/ ***noun*** [C,U] a difference from what is usual or expected, or from what is approved of by society: *a deviation from our usual way of doing things*

★**de·vice** /dɪˈvaɪs/ ***noun*** [C] **1** a tool or piece of equipment made for a particular purpose: *a security device which detects movement* ◇ *labor-saving devices such as washing machines and vacuum cleaners* ➲ Look at the note at **tool**. **2** a trick or plan: *Critics dismissed the speech as a political device for winning support.*

**dev·il** /ˈdɛvl/ ***noun*** [C] **1 the Devil** the most powerful evil being, according to the Christian religion ➲ Look at **Satan**. **2** an evil being or spirit **3** (*informal*) a person, especially a child, who behaves badly and causes trouble: *Those little devils threw an egg at my car!*

**de·vi·ous** /ˈdiviəs/ ***adj.*** intelligent but not honest or direct: *I wouldn't trust him – he can be very devious.*

**de·vise** /dɪˈvaɪz/ ***verb*** [T] to invent a plan, system, etc.: *Scientists have devised a new method of preserving vitamins in foods.*

**de·void** /dɪˈvɔɪd/ ***adj.*** (*formal*) **devoid of sth** not having a particular quality; without sth: *to be devoid of hope*

★**de·vote** /dɪˈvoʊt/ ***verb*** [T] **devote yourself/sth to sb/sth** to give a lot of time, energy, etc. to sb/sth: *She wanted to devote herself full-time to her music.* ◇ *Schools should devote more time to science.*

★**de·vot·ed** /dɪˈvoʊt̬əd/ ***adj.*** loving sb/sth very much: *a devoted husband*

**dev·o·tee** /ˌdɛvəˈti; -teɪ/ ***noun*** [C] a person who likes sb/sth very much: *Devotees of science fiction will enjoy this new movie.*

**de·vo·tion** /dɪˈvoʊʃn/ ***noun*** [U] **devotion (to sb/sth) 1** great love: *a mother's devotion to her children* **2** the act of giving a lot of your time, energy, etc. to sb/sth: *devotion to duty* **3** great religious feeling

**de·vour** /dɪˈvaʊər/ ***verb*** [T] to eat sth quickly and with enjoyment

**de·vout** /dɪˈvaʊt/ ***adj.*** very religious: *a devout Muslim family*

**dew** /du/ ***noun*** [U] small drops of water that form on plants, leaves, etc. during the night

**dex·ter·i·ty** /dɛkˈstɛrət̬i/ ***noun*** [U] skill at doing things, especially with your hands ▸ **dex·ter·ous** (*also* **dex·trous**) /ˈdɛkstrəs/ ***adj.***

**di·a·be·tes** /ˌdaɪəˈbit̬iz; -ˈbit̬əs/ ***noun*** [U] a serious disease in which a person's body cannot control the level of sugar in the blood

**di·a·bet·ic** /ˌdaɪəˈbɛt̬ɪk/ ***noun*** [C] a person who suffers from diabetes ▸ **di·a·bet·ic** ***adj.***: *diabetic children*

**di·ag·nose** /ˌdaɪəgˈnoʊs/ ***verb*** [T] to find out what is wrong or what illness a person has: *His illness was diagnosed as bronchitis.*

**di·ag·no·sis** /ˌdaɪəgˈnoʊsəs/ ***noun*** [C,U] (*pl.* **di·ag·no·ses** /-ˈnoʊsiz/) an act of diagnosing sth: *The doctor's diagnosis turned out to be right.* ◇ *What's your diagnosis of the situation?*

**di·ag·o·nal** /daɪˈægənl/ ***adj.*** **1** (used about a straight line) not vertical or horizontal; sloping **2** going from one corner to the opposite corner of a square, rectangle, etc. ➲ picture at **vertical**.

D

▸ **di·ag·o·nal·ly** /-nəli/ ***adv.***: *I was sitting diagonally across from Diane at the table.*

★**di·a·gram** /ˈdaɪəgræm/ ***noun*** [C] a simple picture that is used to explain how sth works or what sth looks like: *a diagram of the body's digestive system*

**di·al¹** /ˈdaɪəl; daɪl/ ***noun*** [C] **1** the round part of a clock, watch or other piece of equipment that gives you information about the time or about a measurement. A dial has numbers and an arrow on it: *a dial for showing air pressure* **2** the round part on a piece of equipment that you turn to change sth **3** the round part with holes in it on some telephones. You put your finger in one of the holes and turn the dial to call a number.

**di·al²** /ˈdaɪəl/ ***verb*** [I,T] to move the DIAL¹ (3) or push the buttons on a telephone in order to call a particular telephone number: *to dial the wrong number*

**di·a·lect** /ˈdaɪəlɛkt/ ***noun*** [C,U] a form of a language that is spoken in one part of a country: *a local dialect*

ˈ**dialog box** (*Cdn* ˈ**dialogue box**) ***noun*** [C] (*computing*) a box that appears on a computer screen asking the user to choose what he/she wants to do next: *Select an option from the dialog box.*

**di·a·logue** (*also* **dialog**) /ˈdaɪəlɔg; -lɑg/ ***noun*** [C,U] **1** (a) conversation between people in a book, play, etc. **2** (a) discussion between people who have different opinions: *a dialogue between the political parties*

ˈ**dial tone** ***noun*** [C] the sound that you hear when you pick up a telephone before you begin to dial

**di·am·e·ter** /daɪˈæmət̬ər/ ***noun*** [C] (the length of) a straight line that goes from one side to the other of a circle, passing through the center ➲ Compare **radius**.

★**di·a·mond** /ˈdaɪmənd; ˈdaɪə-/ ***noun*** **1** [C,U] a hard, bright precious stone which is very expensive and is used for making jewelry and in industry. A diamond usually has no color. **2** [C] a flat shape that has four sides of equal length and points at two ends ➲ picture at **shape**. **3** [C] a field where baseball is played ➲ picture at **baseball**. **4 diamonds** [pl.] the group (suit) of playing cards with red shapes like DIAMONDS (2) on them: *the seven of diamonds* ➲ picture at **card¹**. **5** [C] one of the cards from this suit: *If you don't have any diamonds, you can play a trump.*

ˌ**diamond ˌanniˈversary** ***noun*** [C] the 60th anniversary of a wedding ➲ Look at **golden anniversary** and **silver anniversary**.

**di·a·per** /ˈdaɪpər; ˈdaɪə-/ ***noun*** [C] a piece of soft, thick cloth or paper that a baby or very young child wears around its bottom and between its legs: *Does her diaper need to be changed?* ◇ *disposable diapers* (= that you throw away when they have been used)

**di·a·phragm** /ˈdaɪəfræm/ ***noun*** [C] **1** the muscle between your lungs and your stomach that helps you to breathe **2** a thin piece of rubber that a woman puts inside her body before having sex to stop her from becoming pregnant

**di·ar·rhe·a** /ˌdaɪəˈriə/ ***noun*** [U] (*also informal* **the runs**) an illness that causes you to pass waste material (feces) from your bowels very often and in a more liquid form than usual: *diarrhea and vomiting*

★**di·a·ry** /ˈdaɪəri/ ***noun*** [C] (*pl.* **di·a·ries**) a book in which you write down what happens to you each day: *Do you keep a diary?*

**dice** /daɪs/ (*also* **die** /daɪ/) ***noun*** [C] (*pl.* **dice**) a small cube with a different number of spots (from one to six) on each side, used in certain games: *Throw the dice to see who goes first.*

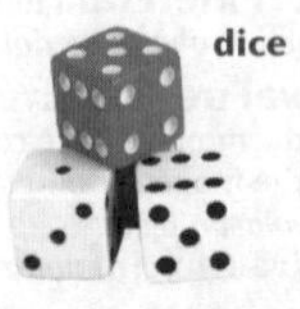
dice

**dic·tate** /ˈdɪkteɪt/ ***verb*** **1** [I,T] to say sth aloud so that sb else can write or type it: *to dictate a letter to a secretary* **2** [I,T] to tell or order sb to do sth: *Parents can't dictate to their children how they should run their lives.* **3** [T] to decide or influence sth: *an attempt by large corporations to dictate the country's economic policy*

**dic·ta·tion** /dɪkˈteɪʃn/ ***noun*** [C,U] spoken words that sb else must write or type: *We had a dictation test in English today* (= in which we had to write down what the teacher said).

**dic·ta·tor** /ˈdɪkteɪt̬ər/ ***noun*** [C] a ruler who has total power in a country, especially one who used force to gain power and who rules the country unfairly

**dic·ta·tor·ship** /dɪkˈteɪt̬ərʃɪp; ˈdɪkteɪt̬ər-/ ***noun*** [C,U] government by a dictator; a country that is ruled by a dictator: *a military dictatorship*

★**dic·tion·ar·y** /ˈdɪkʃəˌnɛri/ ***noun*** [C] (*pl.* **dic·tion·ar·ies**) a book that lists the words of a language in alphabetical order and that tells you what they mean in the same or another language: *to look up a word in a dictionary* ◇ *a bilingual/monolingual dictionary* ◇ *a French-English dictionary*

**did** *past tense of* DO¹·²

**diddly-squat** /ˈdɪdl·i skwɑt; ˈdɪdli-/ (*also* **squat**) ***pronoun*** (*informal*) (used with a negative to emphasize that you mean "nothing"): *He doesn't know diddly-squat about teaching.*

**did·n't** *short for* DID NOT

★**die¹** /daɪ/ ***verb*** (*pres. part.* **dy·ing**; *3rd person sing. pres.* **dies**; *pt, pp* **died**) **1** [I] to stop living: *Thousands of people have died from this disease.* ◇ *to die of a heart attack* ◇ *to die for what you believe in* ◇ (*figurative*) *Our love will never die.* **2** [I] (used about a machine) to stop working: *The pilot managed to land the plane safely after one of the engines died.* **3** [T] to have a particular kind of death: *to die a natural death*

IDM **be dying for sth/to do sth** to want sth/to do sth very much: *I'm dying for a cup of coffee.*

**die hard** to change or disappear only slowly or with difficulty: *Old attitudes toward women die hard.*

PHR V **die away** to slowly become weaker before stopping or disappearing: *The sound of the engine died away as the car drove off.*

**die down** to slowly become less strong: *Let's wait until the storm dies down before we go out.*

**die out** to disappear: *The use of horses on farms died out a long time ago.*

**die²** /daɪ/ ***noun*** [C] (*pl.* **dice** /daɪs/) = DICE

**die·sel** /ˈdizl; ˈdisl/ ***noun*** **1** (*also* ˈ**diesel engine**)

[C] an engine in buses, trucks, and some cars that uses heavy oil **2** [U] the heavy oil that is used in these engines: *a taxi that runs on diesel* ➲ Compare **gasoline**.

★**di·et**[1] /ˈdaɪət/ ***noun*** **1** [C,U] the food that a person or animal usually eats: *The peasants live on a diet of rice and vegetables.* ◇ *Poor diet is a cause of ill health.* **2** [C] certain foods that a person is allowed to eat for a special reason: *a low-fat diet* ◇ *a kosher diet* ◇ *diet cola* (= that has no sugar in it)

IDM **be/go on a diet** to eat only certain foods or a small amount of food because you want to lose weight: *I won't have any cake today. I'm on a diet.*

**di·et**[2] /ˈdaɪət/ ***verb*** [I] to try to lose weight by eating less food or only certain kinds of food: *You've lost some weight. Have you been dieting?*

**dif·fer** /ˈdɪfər/ ***verb*** [I] **1 differ (from sb/sth)** to be different: *How does this car differ from the other model?* **2 differ (with sb) (about/on sth)** to have a different opinion: *Although I differ with Sue on some issues, we get along well.*

★**dif·fer·ence** /ˈdɪfrəns/ ***noun*** **1** [C] **difference (between A and B)** the way that people or things are not the same or the way that sb/sth has changed: *the differences between men and women* **2** [C,U] **difference (in sth) (between A and B)** the amount by which people or things are not the same or by which sb/sth has changed: *There's not much difference in price between the two brands.* ◇ *We put down a 30% deposit and have to pay the difference* (= the rest of the money) *when the work is finished.* **3** [C] a disagreement that is not very serious: *All couples have their differences from time to time.*

IDM **make a, some, etc. difference (in/to sb/sth)** to have an effect (on sb/sth): *A week of vacation made a big difference to her health.*

**not make any difference (to sb/sth); make no difference** to not be important (to sb/sth): *"Do you want the red one or the blue one?" "Oh, it doesn't make any difference."*

★**dif·fer·ent** /ˈdɪfrənt/ ***adj.*** **1 different (from/than sb/sth)** not the same: *Football is very different from soccer.* ◇ *We always stay home on Saturdays – let's do something different this weekend.*

> NOTE Some people do not like the use of **different than**, especially in formal writing. However, **different...than** is often used with longer phrases: *The company shipped me a different item than what I had ordered.*

**2** separate; individual: *This coat is available in three different colors.* ▶ **dif·fer·ent·ly** ***adv.***: *I think you'll feel differently about it tomorrow.*

**dif·fer·en·ti·ate** /ˌdɪfəˈrɛnʃieɪt/ ***verb*** **1** [I,T] **differentiate between A and B; differentiate A (from B)** to see how things are different: *It is hard to differentiate between these two species of fungus.* **2** [T] **differentiate sth (from sth)** to make one thing different from another: *What differentiates him from previous presidents?* **3** [T] to treat one person or group differently from another: *We don't differentiate between the two groups – we treat everybody alike.*

★**dif·fi·cult** /ˈdɪfɪkəlt/ ***adj.*** **1** not easy to do or understand: *a difficult test* ◇ *Dean found it difficult to pass the driving test.* ◇ *It was difficult for Dean to pass the driving test.* ◇ *I'm in a difficult situation.* **2** (used about a person) not friendly, reasonable or helpful: *a difficult customer*

★**dif·fi·cul·ty** /ˈdɪfɪkəlti/ ***noun*** (*pl.* **dif·fi·cul·ties**) **1** [U] **difficulty (doing sth/in doing sth)** the state of being difficult or of not being able to do sth easily: *We didn't have any difficulty selling our car.* **2** [C, usually pl.] (*formal*) something that is difficult to do or understand; a problem: *Students who encounter difficulties in applying for financial aid should speak to a counselor.*

**dif·fuse**[1] /dɪˈfyus/ ***adj.*** **1** spread over a wide area: *diffuse light* ◇ *a diffuse community* **2** not clear or easy to understand; using a lot of words: *a diffuse style of writing*

**dif·fuse**[2] /dɪˈfyuz/ ***verb*** (*formal*) **1** [I,T] to spread sth or become spread widely in all directions: *Technologies diffuse rapidly.* **2** [I,T] to make light shine less brightly by spreading it in many directions: *The light from the full moon was diffused by clouds.*

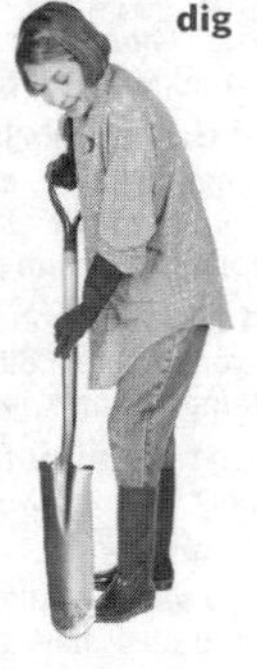
dig

★**dig**[1] /dɪg/ ***verb*** (*pres. part.* **dig·ging**; *pt, pp* **dug** /dʌg/) [I,T] to move earth and make a hole using your hands/a tool/a machine: *The kids are busy digging in the sand.* ◇ *to dig a hole* ◇ *to dig for gold*

PHR V **dig in** (*informal*) to begin to eat sth in an enthusiastic way: *The food's ready – let's dig in!*

**dig sth in; dig sth into sth** to push sth into sb/sth: *She dug her fingernails into my arm.*

**dig sb/sth out (of sth) 1** to get sb/sth out of sth by digging: *Rescue workers dug the survivors out of the rubble.* **2** to get or find sb/sth by searching: *Bill went into the attic and dug out some old pictures.*

**dig sth up 1** to remove sth from the earth by digging: *to dig up potatoes* **2** to make a hole or take away soil by digging: *Workers are digging up the road in front of our house.* **3** to find information by searching or studying: *Newspapers dug up some embarrassing facts about his private life.*

**dig**[2] /dɪg/ ***noun*** [C] **1** a hard push: *to give sb a dig in the ribs* (= with your elbow, etc.) **2** something that you say to upset sb: *The others kept making digs at him because of the way he spoke.*

**di·gest** /daɪˈdʒɛst; dɪ-/ ***verb*** [T] to change food in your stomach so that it can be used by the body ▶ **di·ges·tive** /daɪˈdʒɛstɪv; dɪ-/ ***adj.***: *the digestive system*

**di·ges·tion** /daɪˈdʒɛstʃən; dɪ-/ ***noun*** [C,U] the process of digesting food

**dig·it** /ˈdɪdʒət/ ***noun*** [C] any of the numbers from 0 to 9: *a four-digit code number* ◇ *a six-digit salary* (= $100,000 or more) ➲ Look also at **double-digit**.

**dig·i·tal** /ˈdɪdʒət̮l/ ***adj.*** **1** using information in the form of many separate electronic signals: *digital sound recordings on CD* ◇ *digital TV* **2** showing information, e.g. time, by numbers alone: *a digital*

D

*display screen* ◇ *a digital clock/watch* ➲ picture at **clock**.

ˌ**digital ˈcamera** ***noun*** [C] a camera that makes pictures by storing digital information instead of using film

**dig·i·tize** /ˈdɪdʒətaɪz/ ***verb*** [T] (*computing*) to change data into a digital form that can be easily read and processed by a computer: *a digitized map*

**dig·ni·fied** /ˈdɪgnəfaɪd/ ***adj.*** behaving in a calm, serious way that makes other people respect you: *dignified behavior* OPP **undignified**

**dig·ni·ty** /ˈdɪgnət̬i/ ***noun*** [U] **1** calm, serious behavior that makes other people respect you: *to behave with dignity* **2** the quality of being serious or formal: *the quiet dignity of the funeral service*

**di·gress** /daɪˈgrɛs; dɪ-/ ***verb*** [I] (*formal*) to stop talking or writing about the main subject under discussion and start talking or writing about another, possibly less important, one ▸ **di·gres·sion** ***noun*** [C,U]: *After several digressions, he finally got to the point.*

**dike** /daɪk/ ***noun*** [C] a wall made of earth, etc. used for preventing a river or an ocean from flooding

**di·lap·i·dat·ed** /dəˈlæpədeɪt̬əd/ ***adj.*** (used about a building, furniture, etc.) old and broken: *a dilapidated apartment building* ▸ **di·lap·i·da·tion** /dəˌlæpɪˈdeɪʃn/ ***noun*** [U]

**di·lem·ma** /dəˈlɛmə/ ***noun*** [C] a situation in which you have to make a difficult choice between two or more things: *to face a moral dilemma*

**dil·i·gent** /ˈdɪlɪdʒənt/ ***adj.*** (*formal*) showing care and effort in your work or duties ▸ **dil·i·gent·ly** ***adv.***

**dill** /dɪl/ ***noun*** [U] a plant with yellow flowers whose leaves and seeds have a strong taste and are used in cooking as a herb

ˌ**dill ˈpickle** ***noun*** [C] a kind of vegetable (cucumber) which is covered with a liquid with a strong flavor (vinegar) and the leaves of the dill plant

**di·lute** /dɪˈlut; daɪ-/ ***verb*** [T] **dilute sth (with sth)** to make a liquid weaker by adding water or another liquid ➲ Look at **concentrate**.

**dim**[1] /dɪm/ ***adj.*** (**dimmer**; **dimmest**) **1** not bright or easily seen; not clear: *The light was too dim to read by.* ◇ *dim memories* **2** not favorable or likely to succeed: *The team's chances of winning the championship appear very dim.* ◇ *the dim prospects for this year's harvest* ▸ **dim·ly** ***adv.***: *a dimly lit room*

**dim**[2] /dɪm/ ***verb*** [I,T] (**dimming**; **dimmed**) to become or make sth DIM[1] (1): *to dim the lights*

★**dime** /daɪm/ ***noun*** [C] a coin used in the U.S. and Canada that is worth ten cents

IDM **a dime a dozen** (*informal*) very common and so not interesting or special: *Aspiring actors are a dime a dozen in Los Angeles.*

**di·men·sion** /dəˈmɛnʃn/ ***noun*** **1** [C,U] a measurement of the length, width or height of sth **2 dimensions** [pl.] the size of sth including its length, width and height: *to measure the dimensions of a room* ◇ (*figurative*) *the full dimensions of a problem* **3** [C] something that affects the way you think about a problem or situation: *Global warming has added a new dimension to the problem of hunger in the world.* **4 -dimensional** (in compounds) having the number of dimensions mentioned: *a three-dimensional object*

ˈ**dime store** (*also* **five and dime**) ***noun*** [C] (*old-fashioned*) = FIVE-AND-DIME STORE

ˈ**dime-store** ***adj.*** cheap and of poor quality

**di·min·ish** /dəˈmɪnɪʃ/ ***verb*** [I,T] (*formal*) to become or to make sth smaller or less important: *The bad news did nothing to diminish her enthusiasm for the plan.*

**di·min·u·tive** /dəˈmɪnyət̬ɪv/ ***adj.*** (*formal*) very small

**dim·ple** /ˈdɪmpl/ ***noun*** [C] a small round hollow area on your chin, cheek, etc. which can often be seen when you smile

**dim sum** /ˌdɪm ˈsʌm/ ***noun*** [U] a meal of Chinese food consisting of many small dishes, often eaten at lunch time

**din** /dɪn/ ***noun*** [sing.] (*formal*) a loud unpleasant noise that continues for a long time: *We had to shout over the din of the helicopters.*

**dine** /daɪn/ ***verb*** [I] (*formal*) to eat dinner: *We dined at an exclusive French restaurant.*

PHRV **dine out** to eat in a restaurant

**din·er** /ˈdaɪnər/ ***noun*** [C] **1** (*formal*) a person who is eating at a restaurant **2** a restaurant which serves simple, cheap food in an informal atmosphere

**din·ghy** /ˈdɪŋi/ ***noun*** [C] (*pl.* **din·ghies**) a small open boat, often used to take people to or from a larger boat

**din·gy** /ˈdɪndʒi/ ***adj.*** (**din·gi·er**; **din·gi·est**) dirty and not bright or cheerful: *a dark and dingy room*

ˈ**dining** ˌ**room** ***noun*** [C] a room where you eat meals

★**din·ner** /ˈdɪnər/ ***noun*** **1** [C,U] the main meal of the day, eaten either at noon or in the evening: *What's for dinner, Mom?* ◇ *That was a great dinner you cooked.* ◇ *It's dinnertime/time for dinner.*

NOTE People from different parts of the country and different backgrounds have different ways of talking about their meals. People may call the meal they eat around noon **lunch** or **dinner**. If people eat their main meal of the day in the evening, they may call this meal **dinner**. Some people who eat a lighter meal in the evening prefer to call this meal **supper**. On certain holidays, people may eat a large formal meal called **dinner** in the afternoon: *Thanksgiving dinner.*

**2** [C] a formal occasion in the evening during which a meal is served: *A dinner was given for the celebrity.*

**di·no·saur** /ˈdaɪnəsɔr/ ***noun*** [C] a very large animal that disappeared from the earth (**became extinct**) before the appearance of human beings

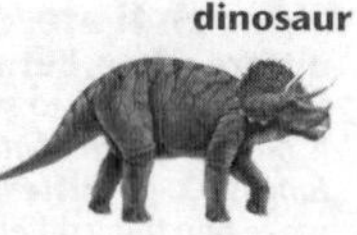
**dinosaur**

**di·o·cese** /ˈdaɪəsɪs; -sis/ ***noun*** [C] an area containing a number of churches, for which a bishop is responsible

**dip**[1] /dɪp/ ***verb*** (**dipping**; **dipped**) **1** [T] **dip sth (into sth)**; **dip sth (in)** to put sth into liquid for a short time: *Julie dipped her toe into the pool to see* *how cold it was.* **2** [I,T] to go down; to lower sth: *The road suddenly dipped down to the river.* ◇ *The temperature dipped below freezing last night.*

PHRV **dip into sth 1** to take money out of sth: *Tim had to dip into his savings to pay for his new suit.* **2** to read parts, but not all, of sth: *I've only dipped into the book. I haven't read it all the way through.*

**dip²** /dɪp/ ***noun*** **1** [C] a drop; a downward movement: *a dip in sales* **2** [C] (*informal*) a quick swim: *We went for a dip in the pool before breakfast.* **3** [C,U] a thick sauce that you eat by dipping pieces of vegetable, etc. into it: *Help yourselves to some chips and dip.* **4** [C] an area of lower ground: *Careful – there's a dip in the road ahead.*

**diph·the·ri·a** /dɪfˈθɪriə; dɪp-/ ***noun*** [U] a serious disease of the throat that makes it difficult to breathe

**diph·thong** /ˈdɪfθɔŋ; ˈdɪp-/ ***noun*** [C] two vowel sounds pronounced together, making one sound: *The /aɪ/ sound in "fine" is a diphthong.*

★**di·plo·ma** /dəˈploʊmə/ ***noun*** [C] the official piece of paper which shows that you have completed a course of study: *a high school diploma* ➲ Look at the note at **degree**.

**di·plo·ma·cy** /dəˈploʊməsi/ ***noun*** [U] **1** the management of the relations between countries **2** skill in dealing with people: *He handled the awkward situation with tact and diplomacy.*

**dip·lo·mat** /ˈdɪpləmæt/ ***noun*** [C] one of the officials who represent his/her country abroad: *a diplomat at the embassy in Rome*

**dip·lo·mat·ic** /ˌdɪpləˈmæt̬ɪk/ ***adj.*** **1** connected with DIPLOMACY (1): *Diplomatic relations between the two countries have been restored.* **2** clever at dealing with people: *He searched for a diplomatic reply so as not to offend her.* ▶ **dip·lo·mat·i·cal·ly** /-kli/ ***adv.***

**dire** /ˈdaɪər/ ***adj.*** (*formal*) very bad or serious; terrible: *dire consequences* ◇ *dire poverty*

★**di·rect¹** /dəˈrɛkt; daɪ-/ ***adj.*** **1** going from one place to another without turning or stopping; straight: *The most direct route is through the center of town.* ◇ *a direct flight to Hong Kong* **2** with nobody/nothing in between; not involving anybody/anything else: *The President is in direct contact with his Cabinet.* ◇ *Keep the plant away from direct sunlight.* **3** saying what you mean; clear: *Politicians never give a direct answer to a direct question.* OPP The opposite for senses **1, 2** and **3** is **indirect** **4** (only *before* a noun) complete; exact: *What she did was in direct opposition to my orders.*

**di·rect²** /dəˈrɛkt; daɪ-/ ***adv.*** **1** not turning or stopping; straight: *Our airline flies direct to Tokyo.* **2** not involving anybody/anything else: *I always deal direct with the manager.*

★**di·rect³** /dəˈrɛkt; daɪ-/ ***verb*** [T] **1 direct sb (to...)** to tell or show sb how to get somewhere: *I was directed to an office at the end of the corridor.* ➲ Look at the note at **lead**³(1). **2** to manage or control sb/sth: *a police officer directing traffic* ◇ *to direct a play/movie* **3 direct sth to/toward sb/sth; direct sth at sb/sth** to turn or aim your attention or actions toward sb/sth: *In recent weeks, the media's attention has been directed toward events in Washington.* ◇ *The ad is directed at young people.* **4** (*formal*) to tell or order sb to do sth: *Take the medication as directed by your doctor.*

★**di·rec·tion** /dəˈrɛkʃn; daɪ-/ ***noun*** **1** [C] the path or line along which a person or thing is moving, looking or pointing: *A woman was seen running in the direction of Seventh Avenue.* ◇ *The wind changed direction.* ◇ *Wait! We're going in the wrong direction.* **2** [C, usually pl.] information or instructions about how to do sth or how to get to a place: *I can give you directions to our house.* **3** [U] management or control: *This department is under the direction of Mrs. Waters.* ◇ *the direction of a play/movie*

D

**di·rec·tive** /dəˈrɛktɪv; daɪ-/ ***noun*** [C] an official order to do sth: *a government directive on safety at work*

★**di·rect·ly** /dəˈrɛktli; daɪ-/ ***adv.*** **1** exactly; in a direct way: *The bank is directly across from the grocery store.* ◇ *He refused to answer my question directly.* OPP **indirectly** **2** (especially in the southern U.S.) immediately; very soon: *Wait where you are. I'll return directly.*

**diˌrect ˈobject** ***noun*** [C] (*grammar*) a noun or phrase that is directly affected by the action of a verb: *In the sentence "Anne bought a book," "a book" is the direct object.* ➲ Look at **indirect object**.

★**di·rec·tor** /dəˈrɛktər; daɪ-/ ***noun*** [C] **1** a person who manages or controls a company or organization: *the Director of Operations of the CIA* **2** a person who tells the actors, camera crew, etc., what to do in a movie, play, etc.

**di·rec·to·ry** /dəˈrɛktəri; daɪ-/ ***noun*** [C] (*pl.* **di·rec·to·ries**) **1** an alphabetical list of names, addresses and telephone numbers **2** (*computing*) a place where a group of files is stored in some types of computers ➲ Look also at **folder**.

**diˈrectory asˌsistance** ***noun*** [U] a telephone service that you can use to find out a person's telephone number

★**dirt** /dərt/ ***noun*** [U] **1** a substance that is not clean: *Wipe that dirt off your face.* **2** earth or soil: *Pack some more dirt around the plant's roots.* ◇ *a dirt road*

**ˌdirt ˈcheap** ***adj., adv.*** (*informal*) very cheap: *I couldn't resist the shoes; they were dirt cheap.* ◇ *I got them dirt cheap.*

**ˌdirt ˈpoor** ***adj.*** extremely poor; not having many of the things necessary for life

★**dirt·y¹** /ˈdərt̬i/ ***adj.*** (**dirt·i·er**; **dirt·i·est**) **1** not clean: *Your hands are dirty. Go and wash them!* ◇ *Fixing the car can be a dirty job* (= it makes you dirty). **2** referring to sex in a way that may upset or offend people: *to tell a dirty joke* **3** unkind and not honest; intended to harm sb: *That's a dirty lie!* ◇ *a dirty trick*

IDM **a dirty word** an idea or thing that you do not like or agree with or that you find offensive: *Students aren't allowed to use dirty words in class.* ◇ (*figurative*) *"Socialism" is a dirty word to many Americans.*

**dirt·y²** /ˈdərt̬i/ ***verb*** [I,T] (*pres. part.* **dirt·y·ing**; *3rd person sing. pres.* **dirt·ies**; *pt, pp* **dirt·ied**) to become or to make sth dirty

D

**dis** (*also* **diss**) /dɪs/ ***verb*** [T] (**dis·sing**; **dissed**) (*slang*) to say sth unkind to sb, showing that you do not respect him/her; to insult sb: *If you keep dissing those guys, you're going to get beaten up!* ➲ Look also at **disrespect**².

**dis·a·bil·i·ty** /ˌdɪsəˈbɪləṭi/ ***noun*** (*pl.* **dis·a·bil·i·ties**) **1** [U] the state of being unable to use a part of your body properly: *physical/mental disability* **2** [C] something that makes you unable to use a part of your body properly: *Because of his disability, he needs constant care.*

**dis·a·ble** /dɪsˈeɪbl/ ***verb*** [T] **1** (often passive) to make sb unable to use a part of his/her body properly: *Many soldiers were disabled in the Vietnam War.* **2** to do sth in order to stop a machine or part of a machine from working: *to disable a function in a computer program*

**dis·a·bled** /dɪsˈeɪbld/ ***adj.*** **1** unable to work or use a part of the body properly: *The car has been adapted for disabled drivers.* **2 the disabled *noun*** [pl.] people who are DISABLED (1): *The hotel has improved facilities for the disabled.*

★**dis·ad·van·tage** /ˌdɪsədˈvæntɪdʒ/ ***noun*** [C] **1** something that may make you less successful than other people: *Your qualifications are good. Your main disadvantage is your lack of experience.* **2** something that is not good or that causes problems: *What are the advantages and disadvantages of nuclear energy?*

IDM **put sb/be at a disadvantage** to put sb/be in a situation where he/she/you may be less successful than other people: *The fact that you don't speak Spanish will put you at a disadvantage in Mexico.*

**to sb's disadvantage** (*formal*) not good or helpful for sb: *The agreement will be to your disadvantage – don't accept it.*

**dis·ad·van·taged** /ˌdɪsədˈvæntɪdʒd/ ***adj.*** in a bad social or economic situation; poor: *extra help for the most disadvantaged members of society*

**dis·ad·van·ta·geous** /ˌdɪsædvænˈteɪdʒəs; -vən-/ ***adj.*** (*formal*) **disadvantageous (to/for sb)** causing sb to be in a worse situation compared to other people: *The deal will not be disadvantageous to your company.*

★**dis·a·gree** /ˌdɪsəˈgri/ ***verb*** [I] **1 disagree (with sb/sth) (about/on sth)** to have a different opinion from sb/sth; to not agree: *Bill often disagrees with his father about politics.* ◇ *They strongly disagreed with the idea.* **2** to be different: *These two sets of statistics disagree.*

**dis·a·gree·a·ble** /ˌdɪsəˈgriəbl/ ***adj.*** (*formal*) unpleasant

★**dis·a·gree·ment** /ˌdɪsəˈgrimənt/ ***noun*** **1** [U] **disagreement (about/on sth)** having a different opinion from sb or not agreeing with sb/sth: *There's a lot of disagreement about what causes people to turn to crime.* **2** [C] an argument: *Diane resigned after a disagreement with her boss.*

**dis·al·low** /ˌdɪsəˈlaʊ/ ***verb*** [T] to not allow or accept sth: *The touchdown was disallowed because the player stepped out of bounds.*

★**dis·ap·pear** /ˌdɪsəˈpɪr/ ***verb*** [I] **1** to become impossible to see; to go away: *He walked away and disappeared into a crowd of people.* ◇ *My purse was here a second ago, and now it's disappeared.* **2** to go to a place where you cannot be found: *She disappeared five years ago and hasn't been heard from since.* **3** to stop existing: *Plant and animal species are disappearing at an alarming rate.* ▶ **dis·ap·pear·ance** /ˌdɪsəˈpɪrəns/ ***noun*** [C,U]: *The mystery of her disappearance was never solved.*

★**dis·ap·point** /ˌdɪsəˈpɔɪnt/ ***verb*** [T] to make sb sad because what he/she had hoped for has not happened or because sb/sth is less good, interesting, etc. than he/she had hoped: *I'm sorry to disappoint you, but you didn't win the prize.*

★**dis·ap·point·ed** /ˌdɪsəˈpɔɪntəd/ ***adj.*** **disappointed (about/at sth); disappointed (in/with sb/sth)** sad because you/sb/sth did not succeed or because sth was not as good, interesting, etc. as you had hoped: *They are very disappointed that they can't stay longer.* ◇ *Connie was deeply disappointed at not being chosen for the team.* ◇ *I'm disappointed in you. I thought you could do better.*

★**dis·ap·point·ing** /ˌdɪsəˈpɔɪntɪŋ/ ***adj.*** making you feel sad because sth was not as good, interesting, etc. as you had hoped: *It has been a disappointing year for the company.* ▶ **dis·ap·point·ing·ly *adv.***: *The amount of money they collected was disappointingly small.*

★**dis·ap·point·ment** /ˌdɪsəˈpɔɪntmənt/ ***noun*** **1** [U] the state of being disappointed: *To his great disappointment, he failed to get the job.* **2** [C] **a disappointment (to sb)** a person or thing that disappoints you: *Our vacation was a big disappointment.*

★**dis·ap·prov·al** /ˌdɪsəˈpruvl/ ***noun*** [U] a feeling that sth is bad or that sb is behaving badly: *to shake your head in disapproval*

★**dis·ap·prove** /ˌdɪsəˈpruv/ ***verb*** [I] **disapprove (of sb/sth)** to think that sb/sth is bad, foolish, etc.: *His parents strongly disapproved of his dropping out of college.* ▶ **dis·ap·prov·ing *adj.***: *After he had told the joke there was a disapproving silence.* ▶ **dis·ap·prov·ing·ly *adv.***: *David frowned disapprovingly when I lit a cigarette.*

**dis·arm** /dɪsˈɑrm/ ***verb*** [T] **1** to take weapons away from sb: *The police caught and disarmed the terrorists.* **2** [T] to make a bomb or weapon safe and unable to explode

**dis·ar·ma·ment** /dɪsˈɑrməmənt/ ***noun*** [U] reducing the number of weapons that a country has: *nuclear disarmament*

**dis·arm·ing** /dɪsˈɑrmɪŋ/ ***adj.*** making sb feel less angry: *a disarming smile*

**dis·as·so·ci·ate** /ˌdɪsəˈsoʊsieɪt; -ʃieɪt/ ***verb*** = DISSOCIATE

★**dis·as·ter** /dɪˈzæstər/ ***noun*** **1** [C] an event that causes a lot of harm or damage: *earthquakes, floods and other natural disasters* **2** [C] a person or thing that is very bad, harmful or unsuccessful: *The school play was a total disaster. Everything went wrong.* **3** [U] failure; a terrible situation: *The drought brought disaster to the area.*

**dis·as·trous** /dɪˈzæstrəs/ ***adj.*** very bad, harmful or unsuccessful: *Our mistake had disastrous results.*

**dis·band** /dɪsˈbænd/ ***verb*** [I,T] to stop existing as a group; to break up

**dis·be·lief** /ˌdɪsbɪˈlif/ ***noun*** [U] not believing sb/sth: *"It can't be true!" he shouted in disbelief.* ▶ **dis·be·lieve** /ˌdɪsbɪˈliv/ ***verb*** [T]: *He seemed to disbelieve me.*

★**disc** /dɪsk/ ***noun*** [C] = DISK ➲ Look also at **compact disc**.

**dis·card** /dɪˈskɑrd/ ***verb*** [T] (*formal*) to throw sth away because it is not useful

**dis·cern** /dɪˈsərn/ ***verb*** [T] (*formal*) to see or notice sth with difficulty: *I discerned a note of anger in his voice.*

**dis·cern·i·ble** /dɪˈsərnəbl/ ***adj.*** (*formal*) that can only be seen or noticed with difficulty: *The shape of a house was just discernible through the mist.*

**dis·cern·ing** /dɪˈsərnɪŋ/ ***adj.*** (*formal*) able to recognize the quality of sb/sth: *The discerning music lover will appreciate the excellence of this recording.*

**dis·charge**[1] /dɪsˈtʃɑrdʒ/ ***verb*** **1** [T] to send sth out (a liquid, gas, etc.): *Smoke and fumes are discharged from the factory and cause air pollution.* **2** [I] to shoot a bullet or explode, especially by accident: *The rifle accidentally discharged, and a bullet struck Andy in the chest.* **3** [T] to allow sb officially to leave; to send sb away: *to discharge sb from hospital/the army*

**dis·charge**[2] /ˈdɪstʃɑrdʒ/ ***noun*** **1** [C,U] the action of sending sb/sth out or away: *The discharge of oil from the leaking tanker could not be prevented.* ◇ *The wounded soldier was given a medical discharge.* **2** [C,U] a substance that has come out of somewhere: *yellowish discharge from a wound*

**dis·ci·ple** /dɪˈsaɪpl/ ***noun*** [C] **1** (*also* **Disciple**) a person who follows a teacher, especially a religious one: *the twelve Disciples of Jesus* **2** a person who follows and believes strongly in a particular idea or set of ideas: *disciples of free-market capitalism*

**dis·ci·pli·nar·y** /ˈdɪsəpləˌnɛri/ ***adj.*** connected with punishment for breaking rules

★**dis·ci·pline**[1] /ˈdɪsəplɪn/ ***noun*** **1** [U] a way of training your mind and body so that you control your actions and obey rules: *military discipline* ◇ *It takes a lot of self-discipline to practice for three hours a day.* **2** [U] the result of such training: *A good teacher must be able to maintain discipline in the classroom.* **3** [C] a subject of study: *academic disciplines*

**dis·ci·pline**[2] /ˈdɪsəplɪn/ ***verb*** [T] **1** to train sb to obey and to behave in a controlled way: *You should discipline yourself to practice the piano every morning.* **2** to punish sb

ˈ**disc ˌjockey** ***noun*** [C] = DJ

**dis·claim** /dɪsˈkleɪm/ ***verb*** [T] to say that you do not have sth; to deny sth: *to disclaim responsibility/knowledge*

**dis·claim·er** /dɪsˈkleɪmər/ ***noun*** [C] **1** an official statement that sb has no knowledge of, or responsibility for, sth: *The TV program carried a disclaimer saying that it was not based on actual events.* **2** an official document that says that sb has no right to do sth: *I had to sign a disclaimer which said that I couldn't sue the hospital if anything went wrong.*

**dis·close** /dɪsˈkloʊz/ ***verb*** [T] (*formal*) to tell sth to sb or to make sth known publicly: *The newspapers did not disclose the victim's name.*

**dis·clo·sure** /dɪsˈkloʊʒər/ ***noun*** [C,U] making sth known; the facts that are made known: *the disclosure of secret information* ◇ *He resigned following disclosures about his private life.*

**dis·co** /ˈdɪskoʊ/ ***noun*** (*pl.* **dis·cos**) **1** [U] a type of music that was popular in the 1970s. Disco music has a strong, fast beat and people dance to it. **2** [C] (*old-fashioned*) a place where people dance to popular music on records, etc. Discos usually have loud music and bright colored lights.

NOTE The word that we usually use nowadays is **club**.

**dis·col·or** /dɪsˈkʌlər/ ***verb*** **1** [I] to change color (often by the effect of light, age or dirt) **2** [T] to change or spoil the color of sth

**dis·com·fort** /dɪsˈkʌmfərt/ ***noun*** **1** [U] a slight feeling of pain: *You may have some discomfort from the wound after the operation.* **2** [C] something that makes you feel uncomfortable or that causes a slight feeling of pain: *The beauty of the scenery made up for the discomforts of the long trip.* **3** [U] a feeling of embarrassment

**dis·con·cert** /ˌdɪskənˈsərt/ ***verb*** [T] to make sb feel anxious, confused or embarrassed: *His answer rather disconcerted her.* ▶ **dis·con·cert·ed** /ˌdɪskənˈsərt̬əd/ ***adj.***

**dis·con·cert·ing** /ˌdɪskənˈsərt̬ɪŋ/ ***adj.*** making sb feel confused or worried: *disconcerting news from the war zone* ▶ **dis·con·cert·ing·ly** ***adv.***

**dis·con·nect** /ˌdɪskəˈnɛkt/ ***verb*** [T] to undo two things that are joined or connected together: *If you don't pay your gas bill, your supply will be disconnected.* ◇ *Disconnect the appliance from the power supply before cleaning it.*

**dis·con·tent** /ˌdɪskənˈtɛnt/ ***noun*** [U] (*formal*) the state of being unhappy or not satisfied with sth

**dis·con·tent·ed** /ˌdɪskənˈtɛntəd/ (*also* **discontent**) ***adj.*** unhappy or not satisfied

**dis·con·tin·ue** /ˌdɪskənˈtɪnyu/ ***verb*** [T] (*formal*) to stop sth or stop producing sth

**dis·cord** /ˈdɪskɔrd/ ***noun*** (*formal*) **1** [U] disagreement or argument **2** [C] two or more musical notes that do not sound pleasant when they are played together

**dis·cor·dant** /dɪsˈkɔrdnt/ ***adj.*** that spoils a general feeling of agreement: *Her criticism was the only discordant note in the discussion.*

**dis·count**[1] /ˈdɪskaʊnt/ ***noun*** [C,U] a reduction in the price or cost of sth: *Employees get a 20% discount on all merchandise.* ◇ *discount prices*

**dis·count**[2] /dɪsˈkaʊnt; ˈdɪskaʊnt/ ***verb*** [T] to consider sth not true or not important: *I think we can discount that idea. It's just not practical.*

ˈ**discount store** ***noun*** [C] a large store that sells many different types of items at low prices

**dis·cour·age** /dɪsˈkərɪdʒ/ ***verb*** [T] **1 discourage sb (from doing sth)** to make sb lose hope or feel less confident about sth: *Don't let these little problems discourage you.* **2 discourage sb from doing sth** to try to stop sb doing sth: *Consumers should be discouraged from throwing glass and cans in the garbage.* OPP **encourage**

**dis·cour·aged** /dɪsˈkərɪdʒd/ ***adj.*** having lost

hope; not feeling confident about sth: *After failing the final exam, Paul felt very discouraged.*

**dis·cour·age·ment** /dɪs'kərɪdʒmənt/ ***noun*** [C,U] discouraging or being discouraged; something that discourages you

**dis·course** /'dɪskɔrs/ ***noun*** **1** [C,U] (*formal*) a long and serious discussion of a subject in speech or writing: *a discourse on issues of gender and sexuality ◇ He was hoping for some lively political discourse at the meeting.* **2** [U] the use of language in speech and writing in order to produce meaning; language that is studied, usually in order to see how the different parts of a text are connected: *spoken/written discourse ◇ discourse analysis*

D

★**dis·cov·er** /dɪs'kʌvər/ ***verb*** [T] **1** to find or learn sth that nobody knew or had found before: *Who discovered the source of the Mississippi? ◇ Scientists are hoping to discover the cause of the epidemic.* **2** to find or learn sth new or unexpected or sth that you did not know before: *I think I discovered why the computer won't print out. ◇ We recently discovered that a famous writer used to live in this house.*

**dis·cov·er·er** /dɪ'skʌvərər/ ***noun*** [C] a person who discovers sth

★**dis·cov·er·y** /dɪ'skʌvəri/ ***noun*** (*pl.* **dis·cov·er·ies**) **1** [U] finding sth: *The discovery of X-rays changed the history of medicine.* **2** [C] something that has been discovered: *scientific discoveries*

**dis·cred·it** /dɪs'krɛdət/ ***verb*** [T] to cause sb/sth to lose people's trust; to damage the reputation of sb/sth

**dis·creet** /dɪ'skrit/ ***adj.*** careful not to attract attention and so cause embarrassment or difficulty for sb: *She was too discreet to mention the argument in front of Neil.* ➲ noun **discretion** OPP **indiscreet** ▶ **dis·creet·ly** ***adv.***

**dis·crep·an·cy** /dɪ'skrɛpənsi/ ***noun*** [C,U] (*pl.* **dis·crep·an·cies**) a difference between two things that should be the same: *There is a discrepancy between these two sets of figures.*

**dis·cre·tion** /dɪ'skrɛʃn/ ***noun*** [U] **1** care not to attract attention and so cause embarrassment or difficulty for sb: *This is confidential, but I know I can rely on your discretion.* ➲ adjective **discreet** **2** the freedom and ability to make decisions by yourself: *You need to decide what is best. Use your discretion.*

IDM **at sb's discretion** depending on what sb thinks or decides: *Pay raises are awarded at the discretion of the manager.*

**dis·crim·i·nate** /dɪ'skrɪməneɪt/ ***verb*** **1** [I] **discriminate (against sb)** to treat one person or group worse than others: *It is illegal to discriminate against any ethnic or religious group.* **2** [I,T] **discriminate (between A and B)** to see or make a difference between two people or things: *Does the tax law discriminate between commercial and residential properties?*

**dis·crim·i·na·tion** /dɪˌskrɪmə'neɪʃn/ ***noun*** [U] **1 discrimination (against sb)** treating one person or group worse than others: *sexual, racial, religious, etc. discrimination* **2** the state of being able to judge what is good/true

**dis·cus** /'dɪskəs/ ***noun*** [C] a heavy round flat object that is thrown as a sport

★**dis·cuss** /dɪ'skʌs/ ***verb*** [T] **discuss sth (with sb)** to talk or write about sth seriously or formally: *I need to discuss the matter with my parents before I make a decision. ◇ The article discusses the need for a change in the law.*

★**dis·cus·sion** /dɪ'skʌʃn/ ***noun*** [C,U] a time when you talk about sth: *After a great deal of discussion, we all agreed to share the cost. ◇ a long discussion on the meaning of life*

IDM **under discussion** being talked about: *The proposal is still under discussion in Congress.*

**dis·dain** /dɪs'deɪn/ ***noun*** [U] (*formal*) the feeling that sb/sth is not good enough and does not deserve to be respected

★**dis·ease** /dɪ'ziz/ ***noun*** [C,U] an illness of the body in humans, animals or plants: *an infectious disease ◇ Rats and flies spread disease.* ▶ **dis·eased** ***adj.***: *His diseased kidney had to be removed.*

> NOTE **Illness** and **disease** can be used in a similar way. However, we use **disease** to describe a type of illness which has a name and is recognized by certain symptoms. Diseases may be caused by bacteria, viruses, etc., and you can often catch them and pass them on to others. **Illness** is used to describe the general state of being sick and the time during which you are not well.

**dis·em·bark** /ˌdɪsəm'bɑrk/ ***verb*** [I] (*formal*) to get off a ship or an aircraft OPP **embark** ▶ **dis·em·bar·ka·tion** /ˌdɪsɛmbɑr'keɪʃn/ ***noun*** [U]

**dis·en·chant·ed** /ˌdɪsən'tʃæntəd/ ***adj.*** having lost your good opinion of sb/sth ▶ **dis·en·chant·ment** ***noun*** [U]: *There is increasing disenchantment among voters with the government's policies.*

**dis·fig·ure** /dɪs'fɪgyər/ ***verb*** [T] to spoil the appearance of sb/sth

**dis·grace**[1] /dɪs'greɪs/ ***noun*** **1** [U] the state of not being respected by other people, usually because you have behaved badly: *There is no disgrace in finishing third in the race.* **2** [sing.] **a disgrace (to sb/sth)** a person or thing that gives such a bad impression that other people feel ashamed: *The sidewalks are covered with trash. It's a disgrace!*

IDM **(be) in disgrace** (to be) in a position where other people do not respect you, usually because you have behaved badly

**dis·grace**[2] /dɪs'greɪs/ ***verb*** [T] **1** to cause disgrace to sb/yourself **2** to cause sb to lose his/her position of power: *the disgraced leader*

**dis·grace·ful** /dɪs'greɪsfl/ ***adj.*** very bad, making other people feel ashamed: *Your behavior last night was absolutely disgraceful.* ▶ **dis·grace·ful·ly** ***adv.***

**dis·grun·tled** /dɪs'grʌntld/ ***adj.*** fairly angry; disappointed and annoyed

**dis·guise**[1] /dɪs'gaɪz/ ***verb*** [T] **disguise sb/sth (as sb/sth)** to change the appearance, sound, etc. of sb/sth so that people cannot recognize him/her/it: *They disguised themselves as fishermen and escaped in a boat. ◇ to disguise your voice ◇ (figurative) His smile disguised his anger.*

**dis·guise**[2] /dɪs'gaɪz/ ***noun*** [C,U] clothes or items such as false hair, glasses, etc. that you wear to change your appearance so that nobody recognizes you

IDM **in disguise** wearing or using a disguise

★**dis·gust¹** /dɪsˈgʌst/ ***noun*** [U] a strong feeling of dislike or disapproval: *She looked around the filthy room **with disgust**. ◇ The movie was so bad that we walked out **in disgust**.*

**dis·gust²** /dɪsˈgʌst/ ***verb*** [T] to cause a strong feeling of dislike or disapproval: *Cruelty toward animals really disgusts me.*

★**dis·gust·ed** /dɪsˈgʌstəd/ ***adj.*** feeling strong dislike or disapproval: *We were **disgusted at** the standard of service we received.*

★**dis·gust·ing** /dɪsˈgʌstɪŋ/ ***adj.*** causing a strong feeling of dislike or disapproval: *What a disgusting smell!* ▸ **dis·gust·ing·ly** ***adv.***

★**dish¹** /dɪʃ/ ***noun*** **1** [C] a shallow container for food. You can use a dish to cook sth in the oven, to serve food on the table or to eat from: *I'll have a dish of ice cream for dessert.* ➲ picture at **plate**. **2** [C] a type of food prepared in a particular way: *The **main dish** was lasagna. It was served with a selection of **side dishes**.* **3 the dishes** [pl.] all the plates, cups, etc. that you use during a meal: *Will you put the dishes away in the cupboard?* **4** [C] (*also* **satellite dish**) a large round object that you place outside your house or another building in order to receive television pictures by satellite

IDM **do/wash the dishes** to wash the plates, cups, etc. that you used during a meal

**dish²** /dɪʃ/ ***verb***

PHR V **dish sth out** (*informal*) to give away a lot of sth

**dish sth up** (*informal*) to serve food

**dis·heart·ened** /dɪsˈhɑrtnd/ ***adj.*** disappointed; without hope or confidence

**dis·heart·en·ing** /dɪsˈhɑrtn·ɪŋ/ ***adj.*** making you lose hope or confidence

**di·shev·eled** /dɪˈʃɛvld/ ***adj.*** (used about a person's appearance) messy

★**dis·hon·est** /dɪsˈɑnəst/ ***adj.*** not honest or truthful ▸ **dis·hon·est·ly** ***adv.*** ▸ **dis·hon·es·ty** ***noun*** [U]

**dis·hon·or** /dɪsˈɑnər/ ***noun*** [U, sing.] (*formal*) the state of no longer being respected; shame ▸ **dis·hon·or·a·ble** /-nərəbl/ ***adj.***

**dish·tow·el** (*also* **dish towel**) /ˈdɪʃtaʊəl/ ***noun*** [C] a small towel used for drying cups, plates, knives, etc. after they have been washed

**dish·wash·er** /ˈdɪʃwɑʃər; -wɔʃ-/ ***noun*** [C] **1** an electric machine that washes plates, cups, knives, forks, etc. **2** a person whose job is to wash the plates, cups, knives, forks, etc. in a restaurant

**dis·il·lu·sion** /ˌdɪsəˈluʒn/ ***verb*** [T] to destroy sb's belief in or good opinion of sb/sth

**dis·il·lu·sioned** /ˌdɪsəˈluʒnd/ ***adj.*** disappointed because sb/sth is not as good as you first thought: *She's disillusioned with law school.*

**dis·il·lu·sion·ment** /ˌdɪsəˈluʒnmənt/ ***noun*** [U] disappointment because sb/sth is not as good as you first thought

**dis·in·fect** /ˌdɪsənˈfɛkt/ ***verb*** [T] to clean sth with a liquid that destroys bacteria: *to disinfect a toilet ◇ to disinfect a wound*

**dis·in·fec·tant** /ˌdɪsənˈfɛktənt/ ***noun*** [C,U] a substance that destroys bacteria and is used for cleaning: *to mop the floor with disinfectant*

**dis·in·te·grate** /dɪsˈɪntəgreɪt/ ***verb*** [I] to break into many small pieces: *The plate hit the floor and disintegrated.*

**dis·in·te·gra·tion** /dɪsˌɪntəˈgreɪʃn/ ***noun*** [U] the act of breaking or dividing into many parts: *the disintegration of families*

**dis·in·ter·est·ed** /dɪsˈɪntrəstəd; -ˈɪntərɛstəd/ ***adj.*** fair; not influenced by personal feelings: *disinterested advice* ➲ Look at **uninterested**. It has a different meaning.

**dis·joint·ed** /dɪsˈdʒɔɪntəd/ ***adj.*** (used especially about ideas, writing or speech) not clearly linked and therefore difficult to follow

**disk** /dɪsk/ ***noun*** [C] **1** (*also* **disc**) a round flat object **2** (*computing*) a flat piece of plastic that stores information for use by a computer ➲ Look at **floppy disk** and **hard disk**. **3** (*also* **disc**) one of the pieces of thin strong material (**cartilage**) between the bones in your back

ˈ**disk drive** ***noun*** [C] a piece of electrical equipment, often a part of a computer, that passes information to or from a computer disk

**disk·ette** /dɪsˈkɛt/ ***noun*** [C] (*old-fashioned*) = FLOPPY DISK

ˈ**disk ˌjockey** ***noun*** [C] = DJ

★**dis·like¹** /dɪsˈlaɪk/ ***verb*** [T] to think that sb/sth is unpleasant: *I really dislike flying. ◇ What is it that you dislike about living here?*

★**dis·like²** /dɪsˈlaɪk/ ***noun*** [U, sing.] **dislike (of/for sb/sth)** the feeling of not liking sb/sth: *She couldn't hide her dislike for him. ◇ He seems to have a strong dislike of hard work.*

IDM **likes and dislikes** → LIKE⁵

**dis·lo·cate** /dɪsˈloʊkeɪt; ˈdɪsloʊkeɪt/ ***verb*** [T] to put a bone out of its correct position: *He dislocated his shoulder.* ▸ **dis·lo·ca·tion** /ˌdɪsloʊˈkeɪʃn/ ***noun*** [C,U]

**dis·lodge** /dɪsˈlɑdʒ/ ***verb*** [T] to make sb/sth move from a fixed position

**dis·loy·al** /dɪsˈlɔɪəl/ ***adj.*** doing or saying sth that is against sb/sth that you should support; not loyal ▸ **dis·loy·al·ty** /-ˈlɔɪəlti/ ***noun*** [C,U] (*pl.* **dis·loy·al·ties**)

**dis·mal** /ˈdɪzməl/ ***adj.*** **1** depressing; causing sadness: *dismal surroundings ◇ a dismal failure* **2** of low quality; poor: *the team's dismal record of 2 wins and 15 losses*

**dis·man·tle** /dɪsˈmæntl/ ***verb*** [T] to separate sth into the parts it is made from: *The photographer dismantled his equipment and packed it away.*

**dis·may¹** /dɪsˈmeɪ/ ***noun*** [U] a strong feeling of worry and shock: *Several people expressed dismay at the news of the murder.*

**dis·may²** /dɪsˈmeɪ/ ***verb*** [T] (usually passive) to give sb a strong feeling of worry and shock: *I am dismayed by the growing use of drugs in our nation's cities.*

**dis·mem·ber** /dɪsˈmɛmbər/ ***verb*** [T] to tear or cut a body apart

★**dis·miss** /dɪsˈmɪs/ ***verb*** [T] **1** (*formal*) to order an employee to leave his/her job: *He was dismissed for refusing to obey orders.*

D

**NOTE** **Fire** is a less formal word for **dismiss**.

**2** to allow sb to leave: *The lecture ended and the professor dismissed the class.* **3** to remove sb/sth from your mind; to stop thinking about sb/sth completely: *Dismiss any thoughts of failure from your mind.* **4 dismiss sb/sth (as sth)** to say or think that sb/sth is not important or is not worth considering seriously: *He dismissed the idea as nonsense.*

D

**dis·miss·al** /dɪsˈmɪsl/ ***noun*** **1** [C,U] ordering sb or being ordered to leave a job: *a case of unfair dismissal* **2** [U] refusing to consider sb/sth seriously: *She was hurt at their dismissal of her suggestion.*

**dis·mis·sive** /dɪsˈmɪsɪv/ ***adj.*** saying or showing that you think that sb/sth is not important or is not worth considering seriously: *The boss was dismissive of my efforts.*

**dis·o·be·di·ent** /ˌdɪsəˈbidiənt/ ***adj.*** not willing to obey; refusing to do what you are told to do ▶ **dis·o·be·di·ence** /-iəns/ ***noun*** [U]

**dis·o·bey** /ˌdɪsəˈbeɪ/ ***verb*** [I,T] to refuse to do what you are told to do; not to obey: *He was punished for disobeying orders.*

**dis·or·der** /dɪsˈɔrdər/ ***noun*** **1** [U] a messy, confused or disorganized state: *His financial affairs are in complete disorder.* **2** [U] violent behavior by a large number of people **3** [C,U] an illness in which the mind or part of the body is not working correctly: *a stomach disorder* ◇ *eating disorders*

**dis·or·dered** /dɪsˈɔrdərd/ ***adj.*** messy, confused or disorganized

**dis·or·der·ly** /dɪsˈɔrdərli/ ***adj.*** **1** very messy **2** (used about people or behavior) out of control and violent; causing trouble in public: *They were arrested for disorderly conduct.*

**dis·or·gan·i·za·tion** /dɪsˌɔrgənəˈzeɪʃn/ ***noun*** [U] a lack of organization

**dis·or·gan·ized** /dɪsˈɔrgənaɪzd/ ***adj.*** not organized; badly planned

**dis·o·ri·ent** /dɪsˈɔriənt/ ***verb*** [T] (usually passive) to make sb lose all sense of direction or become confused about where he/she is: *The street signs were very confusing and I soon became disoriented.* ▶ **dis·o·ri·en·ta·tion** /dɪsˌɔriənˈteɪʃn/ ***noun*** [U]

**dis·own** /dɪsˈoʊn/ ***verb*** [T] to decide or say that you are no longer associated with sb/sth: *When he was arrested, his family disowned him.*

**dis·par·age** /dɪˈspærɪdʒ/ ***verb*** [T] (*formal*) to talk about sb/sth in a critical way or to say that sb/sth is of little value or importance

**dis·par·ag·ing** /dɪˈspærɪdʒɪŋ/ ***adj.*** very critical of sth: *disparaging remarks*

**dis·patch¹** /dɪˈspætʃ/ ***verb*** [T] (*formal*) to send sb/sth somewhere, especially for a special purpose: *Medical workers and supplies have been dispatched to the area.*

**dis·patch²** /dɪˈspætʃ; ˈdɪspætʃ/ ***noun*** [C] an official message or news report

**dis·pel** /dɪˈspɛl/ ***verb*** [T] (**dis·pel·ling**; **dis·pelled**) to make sth disappear; to remove sth from sb's mind: *His reassuring words dispelled all her fears.*

**dis·pen·sa·ble** /dɪˈspɛnsəbl/ ***adj.*** not necessary: *I suppose I'm dispensable. Anybody could do my job.* ➲ **indispensable**

**dis·pense** /dɪˈspɛns/ ***verb*** [T] **1** (*formal*) to give out: *a machine that dispenses hot and cold drinks* **2** (*formal*) to prepare and give out medicines

**PHRV** **dispense with sb/sth** to get rid of sb/sth that is not necessary: *They decided to dispense with luxuries and live a simple life.*

**dis·pen·ser** /dɪˈspɛnsər/ ***noun*** [C] a machine or container from which you can get sth: *a paper towel dispenser*

**dis·perse** /dɪˈspərs/ ***verb*** [I,T] to separate and go in different directions; to break sth up: *When the meeting was over, the group dispersed.* ◇ *Police arrived and quickly dispersed the crowd.*

**dis·pir·it·ed** /dɪˈspɪrət̬əd/ ***adj.*** having lost confidence or hope; depressed

**dis·place** /dɪsˈpleɪs/ ***verb*** [T] **1** to force sb/sth to move from the usual or correct place: *Thousands of people were displaced from their homes by the flood.* **2** to remove and take the place of sb/sth: *She hoped to displace Hingis as the top player in the world.*

★**dis·play¹** /dɪˈspleɪ/ ***verb*** [T] **1** to put sth in a place where people will see it or where it will attract attention: *Posters for the concert were displayed all over the city.* **2** to show sth (e.g. a feeling or personal quality): *She displayed no interest in the discussion.*

★**dis·play²** /dɪˈspleɪ/ ***noun*** [C] **1** a public event in which sth is shown in action: *a fireworks display* **2** an arrangement of things for people to see: *We're going to set up a display of our new products at the convention.* **3** behavior that shows a particular feeling or quality: *a display of aggression* **4** (*computing*) words, pictures, etc. that can be seen on a computer screen

**IDM** **on display** in a place where people will see it and where it will attract attention: *The bones were put on display at the museum.*

**dis·please** /dɪsˈpliz/ ***verb*** [T] (*formal*) to annoy sb or to make sb angry or upset

**dis·pleas·ure** /dɪsˈplɛʒər/ ***noun*** [U] (*formal*) the feeling of being annoyed or not satisfied

**dis·pos·a·ble** /dɪˈspoʊzəbl/ ***adj.*** intended to be thrown away after being used once or for a short time: *a disposable razor*

**dis·pos·al** /dɪˈspoʊzl/ ***noun*** **1** [U] the act of getting rid of sth: *the disposal of chemical waste* **2** [C] = GARBAGE DISPOSAL

**IDM** **at sb's disposal** available for sb's use at any time: *We are using all the means at our disposal to develop a cure for this disease.*

**dis·pose** /dɪˈspoʊz/ ***verb***

**PHRV** **dispose of sb/sth** to throw away or sell sth; to get rid of sb/sth that you do not want

**dis·pro·por·tion·ate** /ˌdɪsprəˈpɔrʃənət/ ***adj.*** larger or smaller than is acceptable or expected ▶ **dis·pro·por·tion·ate·ly** ***adv.***

**dis·prove** /ˌdɪsˈpruv/ ***verb*** [T] to show or prove that sth is not true

**dis·pute¹** /dɪˈspyut/ ***noun*** [C,U] disagreement or argument between people: *There was some dispute about whose fault it was.* ◇ *a pay dispute*

**IDM** **in dispute** in a situation of arguing or being

argued about: *The exact number of victims is still in dispute.*

**dis·pute²** /dɪˈspyut/ ***verb*** [T] to argue about sth or to suggest that sth is not true: *The coach disputed the referee's call.*

**dis·qual·i·fy** /dɪsˈkwɑləfaɪ/ ***verb*** [T] (*pres. part.* **dis·qual·i·fy·ing**; *3rd person sing. pres.* **dis·qual·i·fies**; *pt, pp* **dis·qual·i·fied**) **disqualify sb (from sth/from doing sth)** to officially forbid sb to do sth or to take part in sth, usually because he/she has broken a rule or law: *The runner was disqualified for taking illegal drugs.* ▸ **dis·qual·i·fi·ca·tion** /dɪsˌkwɑləfəˈkeɪʃn/ ***noun*** [C,U]

**dis·re·gard¹** /ˌdɪsrɪˈgɑrd/ ***verb*** [T] to pay no attention to sb/sth: *These are the latest instructions. Please disregard any you received before.*

**dis·re·gard²** /ˌdɪsrɪˈgɑrd/ ***noun*** [U, sing.] **(a) disregard (for/of sb/sth)** lack of attention to, interest in or care for sb/sth: *He rushed into the burning building with complete disregard for his own safety.*

**dis·re·pair** /ˌdɪsrɪˈpɛr/ ***noun*** [U] a bad condition, existing because repairs have not been made: *Over the years the building fell into a state of disrepair.*

**dis·rep·u·ta·ble** /dɪsˈrɛpyət̬əbl/ ***adj.*** not deserving to be trusted; having a bad reputation

**dis·re·pute** /ˌdɪsrɪˈpyut/ ***noun*** [U] the situation when people no longer respect sb/sth: *Such unjust jury verdicts bring the legal system into disrepute.*

**dis·re·spect¹** /ˌdɪsrɪˈspɛkt/ ***noun*** [U] behavior or words that show that you do not respect sb/sth ▸ **dis·re·spect·ful** /-fl/ ***adj.*** ▸ **dis·re·spect·ful·ly** ***adv.***

**dis·re·spect²** /ˌdɪsrɪˈspɛkt/ ***verb*** [T] (*informal*) to say or do sth which shows that you do not respect sb/sth: *Why do so many kids disrespect their parents these days?* ➲ Look also at **dis**.

**dis·rupt** /dɪsˈrʌpt/ ***verb*** [T] to disturb a process or system: *The strike severely disrupted flights.* ▸ **dis·rup·tion** /dɪsˈrʌpʃn/ ***noun*** [C,U] ▸ **dis·rup·tive** /dɪsˈrʌptɪv/ ***adj.***: *The child was taken out of class because of his disruptive behavior.*

**diss** /dɪs/ ***verb*** [T] (*slang*) = DIS

**dis·sat·is·fac·tion** /dɪˌsæt̬əsˈfækʃn; dɪs-/ ***noun*** [U] the feeling of not being satisfied or pleased: *There is some dissatisfaction among teachers with their workload.*

**dis·sat·is·fied** /dɪˈsæt̬əsfaɪd/ ***adj.*** **dissatisfied (with sb/sth)** not satisfied or pleased: *complaints from dissatisfied customers*

**dis·sect** /dɪˈsɛkt; daɪ-/ ***verb*** [T] to cut up a dead body, a plant, etc. in order to examine its structure ▸ **dis·sec·tion** /dɪˈsɛkʃn; daɪ-/ ***noun*** [C,U]

**dis·sent¹** /dɪˈsɛnt/ ***noun*** [U] (*formal*) disagreement with official or generally agreed ideas or opinions: *There is some dissent among Republicans on these issues.*

**dis·sent²** /dɪˈsɛnt/ ***verb*** [I] **dissent (from sth)** (*formal*) to have opinions that are different from those that are officially held

**dis·sent·ing** /dɪˈsɛntɪŋ/ ***adj.*** showing or feeling DISSENT¹: *the dissenting opinion given by one of the judges*

**dis·ser·ta·tion** /ˌdɪsərˈteɪʃn/ ***noun*** [C] a long piece of writing on a topic on which you have done research, as part of the highest university degree (a Ph.D.) ➲ Look at **thesis**.

**dis·serv·ice** /dɪˈsərvəs; dɪs-/ ***noun*** [U, sing.] **(a) disservice to sb/sth** an action that is unhelpful or has a negative effect

**dis·si·dent** /ˈdɪsədənt/ ***noun*** [C] a person who expresses disagreement with the actions or ideas of a government or an organization

**dis·sim·i·lar** /dɪˈsɪmələr; dɪs-/ ***adj.*** **dissimilar (from/to sb/sth)** unlike; not similar; different

**dis·so·ci·ate** /dɪˈsoʊsieɪt; -ʃieɪt/ (*also* **disassociate** /ˌdɪsəˈsoʊsieɪt; -oʊʃi-/) ***verb*** [T] **dissociate sb/sth/yourself from sth** to say or believe that a thing or a person is not connected with another, or that you do not agree with sth: *She dissociated herself from the views of the extremists in her party.*

★**dis·solve** /dɪˈzɑlv/ ***verb*** [I,T] to become liquid or to make sth become liquid: *Sugar dissolves in water.* ◇ *Dissolve two tablets in cold water.*

**dis·suade** /dɪˈsweɪd/ ***verb*** [T] **dissuade sb (from doing sth)** to persuade sb not to do sth: *I tried to dissuade her from calling him.*

★**dis·tance¹** /ˈdɪstəns/ ***noun*** **1** [C,U] the amount of space between two places or points: *It's only a short distance from my home to work.* ◇ *The map tells you the distances between the major cities.* ◇ *We still have some distance to go.* ◇ *The house is within walking distance of the stores.* **2** [sing.] a point that is a long way from sb/sth: *At this distance I can't read the sign.* ◇ *From a distance, the farm looks very nice.*

IDM **in the distance** far away: *I could hear voices in the distance.*

**keep your distance (from sb/sth) 1** to avoid going too close to sb/sth: *Remember to keep your distance from the car in front of you.* **2** to avoid becoming too friendly with sb or too involved in a situation: *I tried to keep my distance from the gangs at school.*

**dis·tance²** /ˈdɪstəns/ ***verb*** [T] **1** to make sb feel less friendly toward sb/sth: *Her wealth and success have distanced her from her old friends.* **2 distance yourself from sb/sth** to show that you are not involved or connected with sb/sth: *She was careful to distance herself from the views of her colleagues.*

**dis·tant** /ˈdɪstənt/ ***adj.*** **1** a long way away in space or time: *to travel to distant parts of the world* ◇ *in the not too distant future* (= quite soon) **2** (used about a relative) not closely related: *a distant cousin* **3** (used about a competition, etc.) losing by a large amount: *Lopez won the race, with Wilson finishing a distant second.* **4** not very friendly: *He can sometimes seem very cold and distant.* **5** seeming to be thinking about sth else: *She had a distant look in her eyes.*

**dis·taste** /dɪsˈteɪst/ ***noun*** [U, sing.] **(a) distaste (for sb/sth)** dislike; the feeling that sb/sth is unpleasant or unacceptable: *She viewed politics with distaste.* ◇ *He seems to have a distaste for hard work.*

**dis·taste·ful** /dɪsˈteɪstfl/ ***adj.*** causing the feeling of dislike; unpleasant or unacceptable

**dis·till** /dɪˈstɪl/ ***verb*** [T] to heat a liquid until it becomes steam and then collect the liquid that forms when the steam cools: *distilled water*

D

**dis·till·er·y** /dɪˈstɪləri/ *noun* [C] (*pl.* **dis·till·er·ies**) a factory where strong alcoholic drink is made by the process of distilling

**dis·tinct** /dɪˈstɪŋkt/ *adj.* **1** clear; easily seen, heard or understood: *There has been a distinct improvement in your work recently.* ◇ *I had the distinct impression that she was lying.* **2 distinct (from sth)** clearly different: *Her books fall into two distinct groups: the novels and the travel stories.* ◇ *This region, as distinct from other parts of the country, relies heavily on tourism for its income.*

★**dis·tinc·tion** /dɪˈstɪŋkʃn/ *noun* [C,U] **1 (a) distinction (between A and B)** a clear or important difference between things or people: *We must make a distinction between classical and popular music here.* **2** the quality of being excellent; fame for what you have achieved: *a violinist of great distinction* ◇ *She has the distinction of being the only player to win the championship five times.* ◇ *Becky graduated from high school with distinction.*

IDM **draw/make a distinction between A and B** to show how two things are different: *It's important to draw a distinction between legal and illegal drugs.*

**dis·tinc·tive** /dɪˈstɪŋktɪv/ *adj.* clearly different from others and therefore easy to recognize: *the U. N. forces wearing their distinctive light blue helmets* ▸ **dis·tinc·tive·ly** *adv.*

**dis·tinct·ly** /dɪˈstɪŋktli/ *adv.* **1** clearly: *I distinctly heard her say that she couldn't come.* **2** very; particularly: *The town has a distinctly southern atmosphere.*

★**dis·tin·guish** /dɪˈstɪŋgwɪʃ/ *verb* **1** [I,T] **distinguish between A and B**; **distinguish A from B** to recognize the difference between things or people: *He doesn't seem able to distinguish between what's important and what isn't.* ◇ *People who are colorblind often can't distinguish red from green.* **2** [T] **distinguish A (from B)** to make sb/sth different from others; to show the difference between people or things: *Each zebra's unique pattern of stripes distinguishes it from others in the herd.* ◇ *distinguishing features* (= things by which sb/sth can be recognized) **3** [T] to see, hear or recognize with effort: *I heard voices, but I couldn't distinguish what they were saying.* **4** [T] **distinguish yourself** to do sth which causes you to be noticed and admired: *She distinguished herself in track and field events.*

**dis·tin·guish·a·ble** /dɪˈstɪŋgwɪʃəbl/ *adj.* **1** possible to distinguish as different from sb/sth else: *The male bird is distinguishable from the female by the color of its beak.* **2** possible to see, hear or recognize with effort: *The letter is so old that the signature is barely distinguishable.*

**dis·tin·guished** /dɪˈstɪŋgwɪʃt/ *adj.* important and respected: *distinguished guests*

**dis·tort** /dɪˈstɔrt/ *verb* [T] **1** to change the shape or sound of sth so that it seems unnatural: *Her face was distorted with grief.* **2** to change sth and show it falsely: *Television footage gives a distorted view of the conflict.* ▸ **dis·tor·tion** /dɪˈstɔrʃn/ *noun* [C,U]

**dis·tract** /dɪˈstrækt/ *verb* [T] to take sb's attention away from sth: *Could you please stop talking? You're distracting me (from my work).*

**dis·trac·tion** /dɪˈstrækʃn/ *noun* [C,U] something that takes your attention away from what you were doing or thinking about: *I find it hard to work at home because there are so many distractions.*

**dis·traught** /dɪˈstrɔt/ *adj.* extremely sad and upset

**dis·tress¹** /dɪˈstrɛs/ *noun* [U] **1** the state of being very upset or unhappy or of suffering great pain: *Their distress on hearing the bad news was obvious.* ◇ *He was in such distress that I didn't want to leave him on his own.* **2** the state of being in great danger and needing immediate help: *The ship's captain radioed that it was in distress.*

**dis·tress²** /dɪˈstrɛs/ *verb* [T] (often passive) to make sb very upset or unhappy: *I didn't mean to distress you.* ▸ **dis·tressed** *adj.*: *She was too distressed to talk.*

**dis·tress·ing** /dɪˈstrɛsɪŋ/ *adj.* causing sb to be very upset or unhappy

**dis·trib·ute** /dɪˈstrɪbyut/ *verb* [T] **1 distribute sth (to/among sb/sth)** to give things to a number of people; to divide sth up and give the parts to people or place them in various positions: *Protesters were distributing leaflets in the street.* ◇ *Tickets will be distributed to all club members.* ◇ *Make sure that the weight is evenly distributed.* **2 distribute sth (to sb/sth)** to transport and supply sth to various people or places: *They distributed emergency food supplies to the areas that were most in need.*

★**dis·tri·bu·tion** /ˌdɪstrəˈbyuʃn/ *noun* **1** [sing., U] the act of giving sth: *the distribution of food packages to needy families* **2** [sing., U] the way sth is divided among people; the pattern in which sth is found: *the uneven distribution of wealth* ◇ *a map to show the distribution of rainfall in India* **3** [U] the transport and supply of goods, etc. to various people or places: *The country produces enough food, but distribution is a problem.*

**dis·trib·u·tor** /dɪˈstrɪbyət̬ər/ *noun* [C] a person or company that transports and supplies goods to a number of stores and companies

★**dis·trict** /ˈdɪstrɪkt/ *noun* [C] **1** an official division of a city, state, country, etc.: *a school district* **2** a part of a town or city that is of a particular type: *a business district* ◇ *the city's financial district*

NOTE A **district** may be part of a town, city, state or country, and it may have fixed boundaries: *a judicial district.* A **region** is larger, usually part of a country or state and may not have fixed boundaries: *the industrial regions of the country.* An **area** is also a general term and is used with the same meaning as **region**: *the poorer areas of a town* ◇ *an agricultural area of the country.* We use **part** more often when we are talking about a specific section of a town, city, state or country: *Which part of St. Louis do you live in?* ◇ *The rain will affect mainly the northern and western parts of the province.*

ˌ**district atˈtorney** (*abbr.* **D.A.**) or (*abbr.* **DA**) *noun* [C] (*U.S.*) a lawyer who works for the government of a city, county, etc. in the U.S. and whose job is to prove in a court of law that sb is guilty of a crime

ˌ**district ˈcourt** *noun* [C,U] (*U.S.*) a court of law for a particular area in the U.S., in which cases involving national (federal) laws, and not state or local laws, are considered

**dis·trust** /dɪs'trʌst/ ***noun*** [U, sing.] **(a) distrust (of sb/sth)** the feeling that you cannot believe sb/sth; lack of trust ▶ **dis·trust** ***verb*** [T]: *She distrusts him because he lied to her once before.* ▶ **dis·trust·ful** ***adj.***

★**dis·turb** /dɪ'stərb/ ***verb*** [T] **1** to interrupt and possibly annoy sb while he/she is doing sth or sleeping; to spoil a peaceful situation: *I'm sorry to disturb you but there's a phone call for you.* ◇ *Keep the noise down! You'll disturb the neighbors.* **2** to cause sb to worry: *It disturbed her to think that he might be unhappy.* **3** to change sth from its normal position or condition: *I noticed a number of things had been disturbed and realized that there had been a burglary.*

**dis·tur·bance** /dɪ'stərbəns/ ***noun*** **1** [C,U] an interruption; something that stops you from concentrating, sleeping, etc. **2** [C] an occasion when people behave violently or make a lot of noise in public: *Further disturbances have been reported in the downtown area.*

**dis·turbed** /dɪ'stərbd/ ***adj.*** having mental or emotional problems: *The suspect was described as mentally disturbed.*

**dis·turb·ing** /dɪ'stərbɪŋ/ ***adj.*** causing sb to worry: *These disturbing developments suggest that war is a possibility.*

**dis·use** /dɪs'yus/ ***noun*** [U] the state of not being used anymore: *The farm buildings had fallen into disuse.*

**ditch**[1] /dɪtʃ/ ***noun*** [C] a long narrow hole that has been dug into the ground, especially along the side of a road or field for water to flow through: *The car left the road and ended up in a ditch.*

**ditch**[2] /dɪtʃ/ ***verb*** [T] (*informal*) to get rid of or leave sb/sth: *The suspect ditched his gun in a field before he fled.*

**dit·to** /'dɪt̬oʊ/ ***adv.*** (*informal*) (used to say that something is the same as sth that you have already mentioned): *We should get rid of those old chairs – ditto the couch in the basement.*

**dive**[1] /daɪv/ ***verb*** [I] (*pt* **dived** or **dove** /doʊv/; *pp* **dived**) **1** to jump into water with your head first: *to dive off rocks into the ocean* ◇ *A passerby dived in and saved the drowning man.* **2 dive (for sth)** to go under water, often to search for sth: *people diving for pearls* **3** to move downward steeply and quickly through the air: *The engines failed and the plane dived.* **4** to move quickly in a particular direction, especially downward: *He dove under the table and hid there.*

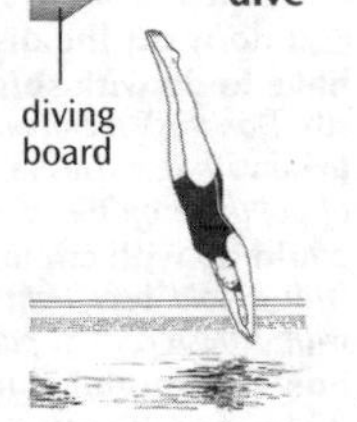


**dive**[2] /daɪv/ ***noun*** [C] **1** an act of diving into the water **2** a quick movement in a particular direction, especially down or across: *a desperate dive to catch the ball*

IDM **take a dive** (*informal*) to fall or go down suddenly: *Stock prices took a huge dive yesterday.*

**div·er** /'daɪvər/ ***noun*** [C] a person who goes under water using special equipment: *Police divers searching the lake found the body.*

**di·verse** /də'vərs; daɪ-/ ***adj.*** very different from each other: *people with diverse social backgrounds*

**di·ver·si·fy** /də'vərsəfaɪ; daɪ-/ ***verb*** [I,T] (*pres. part.* **di·ver·si·fy·ing**; *3rd person sing. pres.* **di·ver·si·fies**; *pt, pp* **di·ver·si·fied**) (used especially about a business) to increase the range of activities, products, etc.: *To remain successful in the future, the company will have to diversify.* ◇ *to diversify your investments* ▶ **di·ver·si·fi·ca·tion** /də͵vərsəfə'keɪʃn/ ***noun*** [C, U]

**di·ver·sion** /də'vərʒn; daɪ-/ ***noun*** **1** [C,U] the act of changing the direction or purpose of sth: *the diversion of a river to prevent flooding* ◇ *the illegal diversion of government funds to terrorist groups* **2** [C] something that takes your attention away from sth: *Two girls created a diversion while the third stole several necklaces.*

**di·ver·si·ty** /də'vərsət̬i; daɪ-/ ***noun*** [U] the wide range or variety of sth: *the racial and ethnic diversity of the population*

**di·vert** /də'vərt; daɪ-/ ***verb*** [T] **divert sb/sth (from sth) (to sth)** to change the direction or purpose of sb/sth: *All traffic is being diverted around the accident site.* ◇ *Government money was diverted from defense to education and training.*

**di·vide** /də'vaɪd/ ***noun*** [C, usually sing.] **a divide (between A and B)** a difference between two groups of people that separates them from each other: *the divide between the rich and the poor*

★**di·vide**[1] /də'vaɪd/ ***verb***

➤SEPARATE **1** [I,T] **divide (sth) (up) (into sth)** to separate (sth) into different parts: *The egg divides into two cells.* ◇ *a book divided into ten sections* ◇ *The house was divided into apartments.* **2** [T] **divide sth (up) (between/among sb)** to separate sth into parts and give a share to each of a number of people: *The robbers divided the money among themselves.* ◇ *When he died, his property was divided up among his children.* **3** [T] **divide sth (between A and B)** to use different parts or amounts of sth for different purposes: *They divide their time between their two homes.* **4** [T] to separate two places by being a boundary or area between them: *The Charles River divides Boston from Cambridge.*

➤CAUSE DISAGREEMENT **5** [T] to cause people to disagree: *The question of immigration has divided the country.*

➤MATHEMATICS **6** [T] **divide sth by sth** to calculate how many times a number will go into another number: *10 divided by 5 is 2.*

**di͵vided 'highway** ***noun*** [C] a road that has an area of grass or a fence down the middle to separate the traffic that is going in one direction from the traffic that is going in the other direction

**div·i·dend** /'dɪvədɛnd/ ***noun*** [C] a part of a company's profits that is paid to the people who own stock in it

**di·vine** /də'vaɪn/ ***adj.*** connected with God or a god ▶ **di·vine·ly** ***adv.***

**div·ing** /'daɪvɪŋ/ ***noun*** [U] the activity or sport of diving into water or swimming under water: *The* *resort has facilities for sailing, water skiing and diving.* ➲ Look also at **scuba diving**.

**'diving board** ***noun*** [C] a board at the side of a swimming pool from which people can dive into the water ➲ picture at **dive**[1].

**di·vis·i·ble** /də'vɪzəbl/ ***adj.*** that can be divided: *9 is divisible by 3.*

D

★**di·vi·sion** /də'vɪʒn/ ***noun***

➤INTO SEPARATE PARTS **1** [U] the dividing of sth into separate parts: *the division of the class into two teams* **2** [U, sing.] the sharing of sth: *a fair/an unfair division of the profits*

➤MATH **3** [U] dividing one number by another: *the teaching of multiplication and division*

➤DISAGREEMENT **4** [C] a disagreement or difference in thought, way of life, etc.: *deep divisions within the Democratic Party*

➤DIFFERENCE **5** [C] something that divides or separates: *There is no great division between being a teenager and being an adult.*

➤PART OF ORGANIZATION **6** [C] a part or section of an organization: *the company's sales division*

**di·vi·sive** /də'vaɪsɪv/ ***adj.*** (*formal*) likely to cause disagreements or arguments between people: *a divisive policy*

★**di·vorce**[1] /də'vɔrs/ ***noun*** [C,U] the legal end of a marriage: *to get a divorce* ◇ *One in three marriages ends in divorce.*

★**di·vorce**[2] /də'vɔrs/ ***verb*** [T] **1** to legally end your marriage to sb

> NOTE It is more common to say **to get divorced** than **to divorce**: *My parents got divorced when I was three.* However when only one partner wants a divorce, we say **to divorce**: *She divorced her first husband after suffering years of abuse.*

**2 divorce sb/sth from sth** to separate sb/sth from sth: *His ideas are divorced from reality.* ▶ **divorced** ***adj.***: *No, I'm not married – I'm divorced.*

**di·vulge** /də'vʌldʒ; daɪ-/ ***verb*** [T] (*formal*) to tell sb sth secret: *The reporter refused to divulge her sources.*

**Dix·ie** /'dɪksi/ ***noun*** [sing.] (*informal*) the southeastern states of the U.S.

**diz·zy** /'dɪzi/ ***adj.*** (**diz·zi·er**; **diz·zi·est**) feeling as if everything is spinning around and that you might fall: *to feel/get dizzy* ▶ **diz·zi·ness** ***noun*** [U]: *He had been to the doctor complaining of headaches and dizziness.*

**DJ** /'didʒeɪ/ (*also* **'disc ˌjockey**, **'disk ˌjockey**) ***noun*** [C] a person who plays and introduces music on the radio or in a dance club

**DNA** /ˌdi ɛn 'eɪ/ ***noun*** [U] the chemical in the cells of animals and plants that carries information about what they will be like, look like, etc. (their genetic structure): *DNA testing*

**do**[1] /du/ ***auxiliary verb*** (*negative* **do not**; *short form* **don't** /doʊnt/; *3rd person sing. pres.* **does** /dəz; *strong form* dʌz/; *negative* **does not**; *short form* **does·n't** /'dʌznt/; *pt* **did** /dɪd/; *negative* **did not**; *short form* **did·n't** /'dɪdnt/) **1** (used with other verbs to form questions and negative sentences, also in short answers and tag questions): *Do you know John?* ◇ *He doesn't live in Portland.* ◇ *"Do you agree?" "No, I don't/Yes, I do."* ◇ *She works in Montreal, doesn't she?* ◇ *He didn't say that, did he?* **2** (used for emphasizing the main verb): *"Why didn't you buy any milk?" "I did buy some – it's in the fridge."* **3** (used to avoid repeating the main verb): *He earns a lot more than I do.* ◇ *She's feeling a lot better than she did last week.*

| do | |
|---|---|
| *present tense* | *past tense* |
| I **do** | I **did** |
| you **do** | you **did** |
| he/she/it **does** | he/she/it **did** |
| we **do** | we **did** |
| you **do** | you **did** |
| they **do** | they **did** |
| *past participle* | **done** |
| *present participle* | **doing** |
| *negative short forms* | **don't, doesn't, didn't** |

★**do**[2] /du/ ***verb*** (*pres. part.* **do·ing**; *3rd person sing. pres.* **does** /dʌz/; *pt* **did** /dɪd/; *pp* **done** /dʌn/)

➤ACTION **1** [T] to perform an action: *What are you doing?* ◇ *We didn't do much yesterday.* ◇ *Please do as you're told.* ◇ *It's not fair but what can we do about it* (= how can we change it)? ◇ *What is the government doing about the national debt?* ◇ *What do you do* (= what is your job)? ◇ *I don't know what I did with the keys* (= where I put them).

➤TASK/ACTIVITY **2** [T] to carry out a particular activity: *Barbara always does* (= styles) *my hair.* ◇ *Did he do his homework?* ◇ *Who does the cooking in your house?* ◇ *I do the laundry every Saturday.* ◇ *Did you get your essay done* (= finished)?

➤SUCCEED/PROGRESS **3** [I] to make progress or develop: *How are you doing* (= how are you)? ◇ *"How's your daughter doing at school?" "She's doing well* (= she is successful)*."*

➤SPEED **4** [T] to travel at a certain speed: *This car can do 120 miles per hour.* **5** [T] to produce sth: *The copy machine does 60 copies a minute.*

➤HAVE AN EFFECT **6** [T] to have a particular effect: *A vacation will do you good.* ◇ *The storm did a lot of damage.*

➤BE SUITABLE/ENOUGH **7** [I,T] to be good enough: *I don't need much money – $10 will do.*

IDM **do/wash the dishes** → DISH[1]

**have to do with sb/sth** to be connected with sb/sth: *Don't ask me about the accident. I had nothing to do with it.* ◇ *This report has to do with the effects of pollution on the environment.*

**could do with sth** to want or need sth: *I could do with a cold beer right now.* ◇ *The house could do with a fresh coat of paint.*

**how do you do?** → HOW[1]

**make do with sth** → MAKE[1]

PHR V **do away with sth** to get rid of sth: *It's time to do away with old stereotypes about women drivers.*

**do sb in** (*informal*) to kill sb: *All those cigarettes he smoked throughout his life finally did him in.*

**do sth over** to do sth again, usually becuse you did not do it well enough the first time: *The camera broke during the filming, so they had to do the whole scene over.* ◇ *If I had to do it all over again* (= repeat my life) *I wouldn't change a thing.*

**do without (sth)** to manage without having sth:

*If there isn't any coffee left, we'll just have to do without.*

**do**[3] /du/ ***noun***

IDM **do's and don'ts** (*informal*) rules that tell you what you should do and what you should not do in a particular situation: *Here are some basic do's and don'ts for successful job interviews...*

**D.O.B.** ***abbr.*** (*written*) date of birth

**Do·ber·man** /ˈdoʊbərmən/ (*also* **Doberman pinscher** /ˌdoʊbərmən ˈpɪnʃər/) ***noun*** [C] a large dog with short dark hair, often used for guarding buildings

**doc·ile** /ˈdɑsl/ ***adj.*** (used about a person or an animal) quiet and easy to control

**dock**[1] /dɑk/ ***noun*** **1** [C] a wooden platform at the edge of a lake, river, etc. that you can walk on and tie a boat to: *Fishing from the dock is not allowed.* **2** [C,U] an area of a port where ships stop to be loaded, unloaded, repaired, etc.

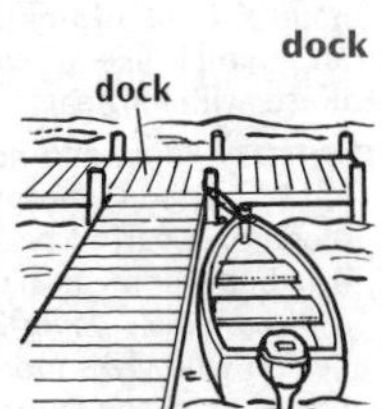


**dock**[2] /dɑk/ ***verb*** **1** [I,T] (used about a ship) to sail into a DOCK[1] (2): *The ship had docked/was docked at Tampa.* **2** [I] **dock (with sth)** (used about a spacecraft) to join together with another spacecraft in space **3** [T] to take away part of sb's wages, especially as a punishment: *They docked $20 from my paycheck for taking the morning off without asking.*

**dock·et** /ˈdɑkət/ ***noun*** [C] a list of the cases that will take place in a court of law

★**doc·tor**[1] /ˈdɑktər/ ***noun*** [C] (*abbr.* **Dr.**) **1** a person who has been trained in medical science and who treats people who are sick: *Our family doctor is Dr. Young.* ◇ *I have a doctor's appointment at 10 o'clock.*

NOTE We can say **go to the doctor** or **go to the doctor's** (= the doctor's office or clinic). A doctor **sees**, **examines** or **treats** his/her **patients**. He/she may **prescribe treatment** or **medication**. This is written on a **prescription**. We also use the title "Doctor" when we speak to dentists.

**2** a person who has received the highest degree from a university: *Doctor of Philosophy* ➲ Look also at **Ph.D.**

**doc·tor**[2] /ˈdɑktər/ ***verb*** [T] **1** to change sth that should not be changed in order to gain some advantage: *The police were accused of doctoring evidence.* **2** to add sth harmful to food or drink

**doc·tor·ate** /ˈdɑktərət/ ***noun*** [C] the highest university degree ➲ Look also at **Ph.D.** ▶ **doc·tor·al** /-tərəl/ ***adj.***

**doc·trine** /ˈdɑktrən/ ***noun*** [C,U] a belief or a set of beliefs that is taught by a church, political party, etc.

★**doc·u·ment** /ˈdɑkyəmənt/ ***noun*** [C] **1** an official piece of writing which gives information, proof or evidence: *Her lawyer asked her to read and sign a number of documents.* **2** (*computing*) a file such as a letter, a picture, etc., that is stored in a computer or on a disk

**doc·u·men·ta·ry** /ˌdɑkyəˈmɛntəri; -ˈmɛntri/ ***noun*** [C] (*pl.* **doc·u·men·ta·ries**) a movie or television or radio program that gives facts or information about a particular subject: *a documentary on/about life in Arctic*

**dodge** /dɑdʒ/ ***verb*** **1** [I,T] to move quickly in order to avoid sb/sth: *I ran across the road, dodging the traffic.* **2** [T] to avoid doing or thinking about sth such as a duty, etc.: *He was accused of dodging* (= not paying) *his income taxes for years.*

**doe** /doʊ/ ***noun*** [C] a female deer or rabbit ➲ picture at **deer**.

**does** → DO[1,2]

★**dog**[1] /dɔg/ ***noun*** [C] an animal that many people keep as a pet, or for working on farms, hunting, etc.

NOTE A dog can **bark**, **growl**, **whine** and **wag** its tail. ➲ Look also at **hot dog**.

**dog**[2] /dɔg/ ***verb*** [T] (**dog·ging**; **dogged**) (often passive) to follow closely and often cause problems for sb: *Her career has been dogged by bad luck.*

**dog-eared** /ˈdɔgɪrd/ ***adj.*** (used about a book or piece of paper) in bad condition and having the corners of the pages turned down because it has been used a lot

**dog·ged** /ˈdɔgəd/ ***adj.*** refusing to give up even when sth is difficult: *I was impressed by his dogged determination to succeed.* ▶ **dog·ged·ly** ***adv.***: *She doggedly refused all offers of help.*

**dog·gy bag** (*also* **doggie bag**) /ˈdɔgi bæg/ ***noun*** [C] a small bag or box for food that you do not finish eating at a restaurant, that you can take home with you

**dog·ma** /ˈdɔgmə/ ***noun*** [C,U] a belief or set of beliefs that people are expected to accept as true without questioning

**dog·mat·ic** /dɔgˈmæt̬ɪk/ ***adj.*** insisting that sth is true or right; not prepared to consider other opinions

ˈ**dog tag** ***noun*** [C] (*slang*) a small piece of metal that soldiers wear around their necks with their name and number on it

**dol·drums** /ˈdoʊldrəmz/ ***noun*** [pl.]

IDM **in the doldrums** (*informal*) **1** not active or busy: *Business has been in the doldrums but should improve later in the year.* **2** sad or depressed

**dole** /doʊl/ ***verb*** (*informal*)

PHRV **dole sth out** to give sth, especially food, money, etc. to a number of people, in small amounts

**dole·ful** /ˈdoʊlfl/ ***adj.*** sad or unhappy: *She looked at him with doleful eyes.* ▶ **dole·ful·ly** ***adv.***

**doll** /dɑl/ ***noun*** [C] a child's toy that looks like a small person or a baby

★**dol·lar** /ˈdɑlər/ ***noun*** **1** [C] (*symbol* $) a unit of money in the U.S., Canada, Australia, etc.: *Melissa earns $24,000 a year.* ◇ *a five-dollar bill* ◇ *Grandpa sent me a check for $25.*

NOTE There are 100 **cents** in a dollar.

**2** [C] a bill or coin that is worth one DOLLAR (1): *I found a dollar lying on the sidewalk.* **3 the dollar** [sing.] the value of the U.S. dollar on international money markets: *The dollar has fallen against the yen.*

**doll·house** /ˈdɑlhaʊs/ ***noun*** [C] a small toy house that children use when they play with dolls

**dol·phin** /ˈdɑlfən/ ***noun*** [C] an intelligent animal that lives in the ocean and looks like a large fish. Dolphins usually swim in large groups.

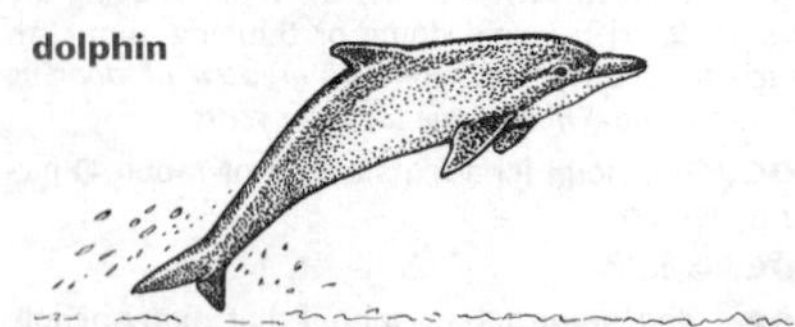
dolphin

**do·main** /doʊˈmeɪn/ ***noun*** [C] **1** an area of knowledge or activity: *I don't know the answer – that's really outside my domain.* ◇ *This issue is now **in the public domain*** (= the public knows about it). **2** (*computing*) a set of Internet addresses which end with the same group of letters: *I can't remember his whole e-mail address, but the domain is "osu.edu."*

**dome** /doʊm/ ***noun*** [C] a round roof on a building

★**do·mes·tic** /dəˈmɛstɪk/ ***adj.*** **1** connected with the home or family: *domestic responsibilities* **2** (used about a person) enjoying doing things in the home, such as cooking and cleaning: *No, I don't know how to bake cookies – I'm not really very domestic.* **3** not international; of or inside a particular country: *domestic flights* (= within one country) **4** (used about animals) kept as pets or on farms; not wild: *domestic animals such as cats and dogs*

**do·mes·ti·cat·ed** /dəˈmɛstəkeɪt̬əd/ ***adj.*** (used about animals) used to living near people and being controlled by them

**dom·i·nance** /ˈdɑmənəns/ ***noun*** [U] control or power: *Japan's dominance of the car industry*

**dom·i·nant** /ˈdɑmənənt/ ***adj.*** the strongest or most important: *Norman's mother was the dominant influence in his life.*

★**dom·i·nate** /ˈdɑməneɪt/ ***verb*** **1** [I,T] to have strong control or influence; to be the most important person or thing in sth: *The Raiders' offense dominated throughout the second half of the game.* ◇ *She always tends to dominate the conversation at dinner parties.* **2** [T] (used about a building or place) to look down on or over sth: *The Space Needle dominates Seattle's skyline.*

**dom·i·na·tion** /ˌdɑməˈneɪʃn/ ***noun*** [U] strong control, power or influence

**dom·i·neer·ing** /ˌdɑməˈnɪrɪŋ/ ***adj.*** having a very strong character and wanting to control other people

**dom·i·no** /ˈdɑmənoʊ/ ***noun*** [C] (*pl.* **dom·i·noes**) one of a set of small flat pieces of wood or plastic that are used for playing a game (**dominoes**). Each domino has a different number of spots on one side of it.

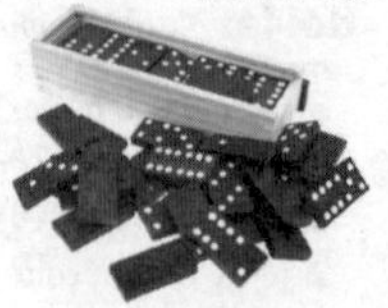
dominoes

**do·nate** /ˈdoʊneɪt; doʊˈneɪt/ ***verb*** [T] to give money or goods to an organization, especially one for people or animals who need help: *She donated a large sum of money to the Cancer Society.*

**do·na·tion** /doʊˈneɪʃn/ ***noun*** [C] a gift of money or goods to an organization, especially one for people or animals who need help: *Would you like to make a small donation to the Red Cross?*

**done**[1] *past participle of* DO[2]

**done**[2] /dʌn/ ***adj.*** (not before a noun) **1** finished: *I have to go out as soon as this job is done.* **2** (used about food) cooked enough: *The meat's ready, but the vegetables still aren't done.* ➲ Look also at **well-done**.

IDM **over (and done) with** → OVER[2]

**don·key** /ˈdɑŋki; ˈdɔŋ-/ ***noun*** [C] (*pl.* **don·keys**) an animal like a small horse, with long ears

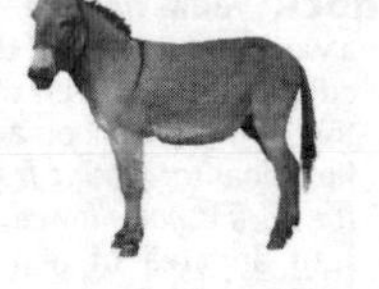
donkey

**do·nor** /ˈdoʊnər/ ***noun*** [C] **1** a person who gives blood or a part of his/her own body for medical use: *a blood/kidney donor* **2** a person who gives money or goods to an organization that needs it, especially an organization for helping other people

**don't** → DO[1,2]

**do·nut** ***noun*** [C] = DOUGHNUT

**doo·dle** /ˈdudl/ ***verb*** [I] to draw lines, patterns, etc. without concentrating, especially when you are bored or thinking about sth else ▶ **doo·dle** ***noun*** [C]

**doom** /dum/ ***noun*** [U] death or a terrible event in the future which you cannot avoid: *a sense of doom* (= that something bad is going to happen)

**doomed** /dumd/ ***adj.*** certain to fail or to suffer sth bad: *The plan was doomed from the start.* ◇ *a doomed love affair*

★**door** /dɔr/ ***noun*** [C] **1** a piece of wood, glass, etc. that you open and close to get in or out of a room, building, car, etc.: *to open/shut/close the door* ◇ *Don't forget to lock the door when you leave the house.* ◇ *Please don't slam the door.* ◇ *Can you get the door* (= open it and see who is there) *for me?* ◇ *I could hear someone knocking on the door.* ◇ *Go and see who's at the door.* ◇ *the front/back door* **2** the entrance to a building, room, car, etc.: *I peeked through the door and saw her sitting there.*

IDM **door to door** from house to house: *The candidate went door to door to ask people to vote for her.* ◇ *a door-to-door salesperson* (= a person who visits people in their homes to try and sell them things)

**next door (to sb/sth)** in the next house, room, etc.: *Do you know the people (who live) next door?* ◇ *You'll find the bathroom next door to your bedroom.*

**door·bell** /ˈdɔrbɛl/ ***noun*** [C] a bell on the outside of a house which you ring when you want to go in

**door·knob** /ˈdɔrnɑb/ ***noun*** [C] a round handle on a door that you turn to open the door

**door·mat** /ˈdɔrmæt/ ***noun*** [C] **1** a piece of material in front of a door which you can wipe your shoes on to clean them before going inside **2** (*informal*) a person who allows other people to treat him/her badly without complaining

**door·step** /ˈdɔrstɛp/ ***noun*** [C] a step in front of a door, usually outside a building

IDM **on your doorstep** very near to you: *The beach was practically on our doorstep.*

**door·way** /ˈdɔrweɪ/ ***noun*** [C] an entrance into a building, room, etc.: *She was standing in the doorway.*

**dope**[1] /doʊp/ ***noun*** (*informal*) **1** [U] a drug that is not legal, especially marijuana: *to smoke dope* **2** [C] a stupid person: *What a dope!*

**dope**[2] /doʊp/ ***verb*** [T] to give a drug secretly to a person or animal, especially to make him/her/it sleep

**dop·ey** (*also* **dopy**) /ˈdoʊpi/ ***adj.*** (**dop·i·er**; **dop·i·est**) **1** tired and not able to think clearly, especially because of drugs, alcohol or lack of sleep **2** (*informal*) stupid; not very intelligent

**dork** /dɔrk/ ***noun*** [C] (*slang*) a person who you think is boring and stupid because he/she behaves in a strange way and wears unfashionable clothes ▸ **dork·y** /ˈdɔrki/ ***adj.***

**dorm** /dɔrm/ ***noun*** [C] (*informal*) = DORMITORY: *a dorm room*

**dor·mant** /ˈdɔrmənt/ ***adj.*** not active for some time: *a dormant volcano*

**dor·mi·to·ry** /ˈdɔrməˌtɔri/ (*also informal* **dorm**, *formal* **residence hall**) ***noun*** [C] (*pl.* **dor·mi·to·ries**) a building at a college or university where students live

**dos·age** /ˈdoʊsɪdʒ/ ***noun*** [C, usually sing.] the amount of a medicine you should take over a period of time: *The recommended dosage is one tablet every four hours.*

**dose** /doʊs/ ***noun*** [C] **1** an amount of medicine that you take at one time: *How large a dose should I take?* **2** (*informal*) an amount of sth, especially sth bad: *Rick got a dose of reality when his first credit card bill arrived in the mail.* ◇ *I can only stand my mother-in-law in small doses.*

★**dot**[1] /dɑt/ ***noun*** [C] **1** a small, round mark: *The letters i and j have dots over them.* ➲ Look also at **polka dot**. **2** something that looks like a DOT (1): *The airplane was just a dot in the sky.*

IDM **on the dot** (*informal*) at exactly the right time or at exactly the time mentioned: *Classes start at 9 o'clock on the dot.*

**dot**[2] /dɑt/ ***verb*** [T] (**dot·ting**; **dot·ted**) to mark sth with a DOT[1] (1)

IDM **be dotted with** to have many things or people in or on it: *a hillside dotted with sheep*

**dot-com** (*also* **dot·com**) /ˌdɑtˈkɑm/ ***noun*** [C] a company that sells goods and services on the Internet, especially one whose address ends ".com": *The weaker dot-coms have collapsed.* ◇ *a dot-com millionaire*

**dote** /doʊt/ ***verb*** [I] **dote on sb/sth** to have or show too much love for sb/sth and think he/she/it is perfect: *He dotes on his youngest son.*

**dot·ing** /ˈdoʊt̬ɪŋ/ ***adj.*** very or too loving: *doting parents*

**dot·ted line** /ˌdɑt̬əd ˈlaɪn/ ***noun*** [C] a line of dots which show where sth is to be written on a form, etc.: *Just sign your name on the dotted line.* ➲ picture at **line**.

★**dou·ble**[1] /ˈdʌbl/ ***adj.*** **1** twice as much or as many (as usual): *a double helping of ice cream* **2** having two equal or similar parts: *double doors* ◇ *a double burger* (= with two pieces of meat in it) **3** made for or used by two people or things: *a double garage* ◇ *a double bed*

**dou·ble**[2] /ˈdʌbl/ ***det.*** twice as much or as many (as usual, as sb/sth, etc.): *His income is double hers.* ◇ *We'll need double the amount of food.*

**dou·ble**[3] /ˈdʌbl/ ***adv.*** in twos or two parts: *When I saw her with her twin sister I thought I was seeing double.*

★**dou·ble**[4] /ˈdʌbl/ ***noun*** **1** [U] twice the (usual) number or amount: *I only ordered a small serving of French fries, but they gave me double.* **2** [C] a person who looks very much like another: *I thought it was you I saw at the grocery store. You must have a double.* **3 doubles** [pl.] (in some sports, e.g. tennis) with two pairs of people playing: *the men's doubles championship* ➲ Compare **single**[2](3).

★**dou·ble**[5] /ˈdʌbl/ ***verb*** **1** [I,T] to become or to make sth twice as much or as many: *The price of houses has almost doubled.* ◇ *Think of a number and double it.* **2** [I] **double as sth** to have a second use or function: *The small room doubles as a study.*

PHR V **double (sb) over/up** (to cause sb) to bend the body: *to be doubled up in pain* ◇ *to double over with laughter*

**dou·ble bass** /ˌdʌbl ˈbeɪs/ (*also* **bass**) ***noun*** [C] the largest instrument of the violin family, that you play standing up or sitting down

ˌ**double ˈbed** ***noun*** [C] (*Cdn*) a bed big enough for two people to sleep in, especially one measuring 137 x 190cm (53.5 x 75 inches) ➲ Look at the note and the picture at **bed**[1].

**dou·ble-breast·ed** /ˌdʌbl ˈbrɛstəd/ ***adj.*** (used about a coat or jacket) having the front parts cross over each other, with two rows of buttons ➲ Compare **single-breasted**.

ˌ**double-ˈcheck** ***verb*** [I,T] to check sth again, or with great care

ˌ**double-ˈclick** ***verb*** [I,T] **double-click (on sth)** to choose a particular function or item on a computer screen, etc. by pressing one of the mouse buttons twice quickly

ˌ**double-ˈcross** ***verb*** [T] to cheat sb who believes that he/she can trust you

ˌ**double-ˌdecker ˈbus** /ˌdʌbl ˌdɛkər ˈbʌs/ (*also* ˌ**double-ˈdeck·er**) ***noun*** [C] (*pl.* **double-decker buses**) a bus with two floors

ˌ**double-ˈdigit** ***adj.*** (only *before* a noun) connected with a number from 10 to 99: *double-digit inflation*

**dou·ble-head·er** (*also* **dou·ble head·er**) /ˌdʌbl ˈhɛdər/ ***noun*** [C] (in sport, especially baseball) two games that are played on the same day, the second immediately after the first

ˌ**double ˈnegative** ***noun*** [C] the use of two negative words, such as "no" or "not," in one sentence. This is considered incorrect according to the rules of English: *The sentence "She doesn't have no friends," contains a double negative.*

ˌ**double-ˈpark** *verb* [I,T] to park (a car) illegally in the middle of a street, beside another car that is already parked at the edge of the street

**dou·bly** /ˈdʌbli/ *adv.* **1** in two ways: *He was doubly blessed with both good looks and talent.* **2** more than usually: *I made doubly sure that the door was locked.*

D

★**doubt**[1] /daʊt/ *noun* [C,U] (a feeling of) being uncertain: *I am starting to have some serious doubts about my relationship with Jeff.* ◇ *You'll definitely pass. There's no doubt about it.* ◇ *There was some doubt as to whether she was the right person for the job.*

NOTE Be careful – **doubt** is not the same as **question**. We use **doubt** when we are not certain about sth: *I have some doubts about the fairness of this new policy.* We use **question** when we are asking for information about sth: *I have some questions about the homework assignment.*

IDM **beyond/without a shadow of a doubt** → SHADOW[1]
**cast doubt on sth** → CAST[2]
**give sb the benefit of the doubt** → BENEFIT[1]
**in doubt** not sure or definite
**no doubt** (used when you expect sth to happen but you are not sure that it will) probably: *No doubt she'll write when she has time.*
**without (a) doubt** definitely: *It was without doubt the coldest winter for many years.*

★**doubt**[2] /daʊt/ *verb* [T] to think that sth is unlikely or to feel uncertain (about sth): *She never doubted* (= she was always sure) *that he was telling the truth.* ◇ *I doubt whether/if I'll have time to go shopping today* (= I don't think I'll be able to go). ◇ *He had never doubted her support.*

**doubt·ful** /ˈdaʊtfl/ *adj.* **1** unlikely or uncertain: *It's doubtful whether/if we'll finish in time for the meeting.* ◇ *It was doubtful that he was still alive.* **2 doubtful (about sth/about doing sth)** (used about a person) not sure: *He still felt doubtful about his decision.* ▶ **doubt·ful·ly** *adv.*: *"I suppose it'll be all right," she said doubtfully.*

**doubt·less** /ˈdaʊtləs/ *adv.* (*formal*) almost certainly: *The talks will doubtless promote better relations between the two countries.*

**dough** /doʊ/ *noun* [U] **1** a thick mixture of flour, water and sometimes fat and sugar. It is used for baking into bread, etc.: *cookie dough* ➲ Look also at **batter**[2]. **2** (*informal, old-fashioned*) money

**dough·nut** (*also* **donut**) /ˈdoʊnʌt/ *noun* [C] a small cake in the shape of a ring or a ball, made from sweet dough cooked in fat

**dour** /ˈdaʊər; dʊr/ *adj.* (used about a person's manner or expression) cold and unfriendly

**douse** /daʊs/ *verb* [T] **1** to cover sb/sth with liquid: *to douse yourself in perfume* (= wear too much of it) **2** (*formal*) to stop a fire, etc. from burning: *The firemen managed to douse the blaze.*

**dove**[1] /dʌv/ *noun* [C] a type of white or gray bird that is often used as a sign of peace

**dove**[2] /doʊv/ *past tense of* DIVE[1]

**dow·dy** /ˈdaʊdi/ *adj.* (**dow·di·er**; **dow·di·est**) (used about a person or the clothes he/she wears) dull and unfashionable

★**down**[1] /daʊn/ *adv.* **1** to or at a lower level or place; not up: *We sat and watched the sun go down.* ◇ *Can you get that book down from the top shelf?* ◇ *"Where's Mary?" "She's down in the basement."* **2** from a standing or vertical position to a sitting or horizontal one: *I think I'll sit/lie down.* **3** to or in the south: *We went down to Florida on our vacation.* **4** (used for showing that the level, amount, strength, etc. of sth is less or lower): *Do you mind if I turn the heat down a little?* **5** (written) on paper: *Put these dates down in your calendar.* **6** as a first payment: *We bought the car for just $500 down.* **7 down to sb/sth** even including: *Everybody was invited, from the president down to the custodians.*

IDM **be/come down to sb** to be sb's responsibility: *It's all down to you, Pat – if you make this basket, we'll win the game!* ◇ *When my father died, it came down to me to take care of the family's affairs.*
**be down to sth** to have only the amount mentioned left: *I can't loan you any money – I'm down to my last $5.*
**come down with sth** to be or become sick with sth: *I think I'm coming down with the flu.*
**down and out** having no money, job or home
**down under** (*informal*) (in) Australia: *He comes from down under.*

★**down**[2] /daʊn/ *prep.* **1** along: *"Where's the nearest gas station?" "Go down this road and take the first right."* **2** from the top toward the bottom of sth: *Her hair hung down her back.* ◇ *The snow began to slide down the mountain.* **3** at or to a lower or further part of sth: *We sailed down the river.*

**down**[3] /daʊn/ *verb* [T] (*informal*) to finish a drink quickly: *He downed two beers and left.*

**down**[4] /daʊn/ *noun* [U] very soft feathers: *a down comforter*

IDM **ups and downs** → UP[3]

**down**[5] /daʊn/ *adj.* **1** sad: *You're looking a little down today.* **2** lower than before: *Unemployment figures are down for the third month in a row.* **3** (used about computers) not working

**down·beat** /ˈdaʊnbit/ *adj.* (*informal*) **1** dull or depressing; not having much hope for the future: *The overall mood of the meeting was downbeat.* OPP **upbeat** **2** not showing strong feelings or enthusiasm

**down·cast** /ˈdaʊnkæst/ *adj.* **1** (used about eyes) looking down **2** (used about a person) sad and without hope

**down·er** /ˈdaʊnər/ *noun* **1** [usually pl.] (*informal*) a type of drug (a **barbiturate**) that relaxes you or makes you want to sleep **2** [C] an experience that makes you sad: *That movie was a real downer!*

**down·fall** /ˈdaʊnfɔl/ *noun* [sing.] **1** a loss of power or success: *The senator's downfall seemed inevitable.* **2** a thing that causes a loss of power or success: *Alcohol proved to be her downfall.*

**down·grade** /ˈdaʊngreɪd/ *verb* [T] to reduce sb/sth to a lower level or position of importance

**down·heart·ed** /ˌdaʊnˈhɑrt̬əd/ *adj.* feeling depressed or sad

**down·hill** /ˌdaʊnˈhɪl/ *adj.*, *adv.* (going) down a slope; toward the bottom of a hill: *It's an easy walk.*

*The road runs downhill most of the way.* ◇ *Do you go downhill or cross-country skiing?* ➲ picture at **ski**.
IDM **go downhill** to get worse: *Their relationship has been going downhill for quite a while.*

**down·load[1]** /ˈdaʊnloʊd/ ***verb*** [T] (*computing*) to move data to a smaller computer system from a larger one OPP **upload**

**down·load[2]** /ˈdaʊnloʊd/ ***noun*** [C] data (e.g. a program, song, document, etc.) which is downloaded from another computer system OPP **upload**

**ˌdown ˈpayment** ***noun*** [C] a first payment for sth that you buy, with the rest of the price to be paid later: *I finally saved enough money to make a down payment on a new car.*

**down·pour** /ˈdaʊnpɔr/ ***noun*** [C, usually sing.] a heavy, sudden fall of rain

**down·right[1]** /ˈdaʊnraɪt/ ***adj.*** (only *before* a noun) (used about sth bad or unpleasant) complete: *Our trip was a downright disaster.*

**down·right[2]** /ˈdaʊnraɪt/ ***adv.*** completely or thoroughly: *That road is downright dangerous!*

**down·side** /ˈdaʊnsaɪd/ ***noun*** [C, usually sing.] the disadvantages or less positive aspects of sth: *All good ideas have a downside.*

**down·size** /ˈdaʊnsaɪz/ ***verb*** [I,T] (used about a large company) to reduce the number of people working, in order to save money: *Several hundred jobs were lost when the company downsized its operations.* ▶ **down·siz·ing** ***noun*** [U]: *the era of corporate downsizing*

**down·spout** /ˈdaʊnspaʊt/ ***noun*** [C] a pipe that carries rainwater away from the roof of a building to a DRAIN[1] or to the ground

**down·stairs** /ˌdaʊnˈstɛrz/ ***adv.*** **1** down the stairs: *He fell downstairs and broke his arm.* **2** to a lower floor: *Dad's downstairs in the basement.* OPP **upstairs** ▶ **down·stairs** /ˈdaʊnstɛrz/ ***adj.***: *the downstairs bathroom*

**down·stream** /ˌdaʊnˈstrim/ ***adv.*** in the direction in which a river flows: *The boat floated downstream.* OPP **upstream**

**Down syn·drome** /ˈdaʊn ˌsɪndroʊm/ (*also* **Down's syn·drome**) /ˈdaʊnz ˌsɪndroʊm/ ***noun*** [U] a medical condition in which a person is born with a wide, flat face, sloping eyes and a mental ability that is below average

**ˌdown-to-ˈearth** ***adj.*** sensible and practical; not too silly

**down·town** /ˌdaʊnˈtaʊn/ ***adj., adv.*** in or to the central area of a city or large town, especially where there are many stores and businesses: *downtown Milwaukee* ◇ *I need to go downtown and get some stuff for the party.*

NOTE In New York City, **downtown** is used to describe the southern part of Manhattan, where the streets have low numbers in their names. ➲ Look also at **uptown**.

**down·trod·den** /ˈdaʊntrɑdn/ ***adj.*** (used about a person) made to suffer bad treatment or living conditions by people in power, but being too tired, poor, sick, etc. to change things

**down·turn** /ˈdaʊntərn/ ***noun*** [usually sing.] **a downturn (in sth)** a drop in the amount of business that is done; a time when the economy becomes weaker: *a downturn in sales/business* OPP **upturn**

★**down·ward[1]** /ˈdaʊnwərd/ ***adj.*** (only *before* a noun) toward the ground or a lower level: *a downward movement* ◇ *There is still a downward trend in the stock market.*

★**down·ward[2]** /ˈdaʊnwərd/ (*also* **downwards** /ˈdaʊnwərdz/) ***adv.*** toward the ground or a lower level: *They stood a few feet apart, staring downward and refusing to speak.* OPP **upward(s)**

**dow·ry** /ˈdaʊri/ ***noun*** [C] (*pl.* **dow·ries**) an amount of money or property which, in some countries, a woman's family gives to the man she is marrying

**doz.** ***abbr.*** = DOZEN: *3 doz. eggs*

**doze** /doʊz/ ***verb*** [I] to sleep lightly and/or for a short time: *He was dozing in front of the television.*
PHR V **doze off** to go to sleep, without meaning to: *I'm sorry – I must have dozed off for a minute.*

★**doz·en** /ˈdʌzn/ ***noun*** (*abbr.* **doz.**) **1** [C] (*pl.* **dozen**) twelve or a group of twelve: *I need to buy a dozen eggs.* ◇ *half a dozen* (= six) ◇ *two dozen sheep* **2 doz·ens** [pl.] (*informal*) very many: *I've tried calling her dozens of times.*
IDM **a dime a dozen** → DIME

**Dr.** ***abbr.*** **1** = DOCTOR[1] **2** = DRIVE[2] (3)

**drab** /dræb/ ***adj.*** (**drab·ber**; **drab·best**) dull and not interesting or attractive: *a drab gray office building*

★**draft[1]** /dræft/ ***noun*** **1** [C] a piece of writing, etc. which will probably be changed and improved; not the final copy: *the first draft of a speech* ◇ *a rough draft of an essay* **2** [C] a current of air that comes into a room: *Can you shut the door? There's a draft in here.* **3 the draft** [sing.] (*especially US*) the system of making sb join the army, etc.: *young men who tried to avoid the draft during the Vietnam War* **4** [sing.] a process of picking players for professional sports teams from college teams once every year
IDM **on draft** (used about beer, etc.) taken from a large container (a **barrel**): *This beer is not available on draft* (= it is only available in bottles or cans).

**draft[2]** /dræft/ ***verb*** [T] **1** to make a first or an early copy of a piece of writing: *I'll draft a letter and show it to you before I type it.* **2** (usually passive) to order sb to join the armed forces: *He was drafted into the army.*

**draft[3]** /dræft/ ***adj.*** (used about beer, etc.) served from a large container (a **barrel**) rather than in a bottle or can: *draft beer*

**draft·y** /ˈdræfti/ ***adj.*** (**draft·i·er**; **draft·i·est**) having currents of air blowing through it: *a drafty old house*

**drag[1]** /dræg/ ***noun*** **1** [sing.] (*informal*) a thing that is boring or annoying: *Having to stay home on a Saturday night is a real drag.* **2 a drag on sth** [sing.] something that slows the progress of sth else: *High interest rates continue to be a drag on the economy.* **3** [C] (*informal*) an act of breathing in cigarette smoke: *He took a long drag on his cigarette.* **4** [U] (*informal*) the wearing of women's clothes by a man, especially as part of a show, etc. ➲ Look also at **main drag**.

★**drag[2]** /dræg/ ***verb*** (**drag·ging**; **dragged**) **1** [T] to pull sb/sth along with difficulty: *The box was so* *heavy we had to drag it along the floor.* ➲ picture at **drag**. **2** [T] to force or to make sb come or go somewhere: *She dragged the child up the steps by her arm.* ◇ *Can I drag you away from your desk for a minute?* **3** [I] **drag (on)** to be boring or to seem to last a long time: *The speeches dragged on for hours.* **4** [T] to move some text, etc., across the screen of a computer using a mouse

D

PHR V **drag sth out** to make sth last longer than necessary: *Let's not drag this decision out – should we go or not?*

**drag sth out (of sb)** to force or persuade sb to give you information that you want

**drag·on** /ˈdræɡən/ **noun** [C] (in stories, etc.) an imaginary animal with wings, which can breathe out fire

**drag·on·fly** /ˈdræɡənflaɪ/ **noun** [C] (*pl.* **drag·on·flies**) an insect with a long thin body, usually brightly colored, and two pairs of large transparent wings. Dragonflies are often seen over the water.

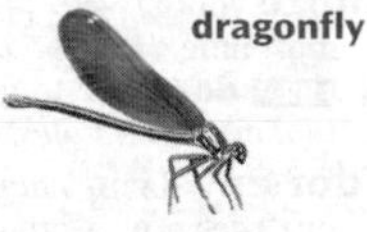
dragonfly

**drain¹** /dreɪn/ **noun** [C] a pipe or hole that dirty water, etc. goes down to be carried away: *Just pour the rest of that stuff down the drain.*

IDM **a drain on sb/sth** something that uses up time, money, strength, etc.: *The cost of college tuition is a big drain on our budget.*

**(go) down the drain** (*informal*) (to be) wasted: *All that hard work has gone down the drain.*

**drain²** /dreɪn/ **verb** **1** [I,T] to flow away; to make a liquid flow: *The sink's clogged – the water won't drain away at all.* ◇ *The mechanic drained the oil from the engine.* **2** [I,T] to become dry as liquid flows away; to make sth dry in this way: *Drain the spaghetti and serve.* **3** [T] to drink all the liquid (in a glass, etc.): *She drained her glass in one gulp.* **4** [I] (used about a feeling) to become weaker and weaker until it disappears: *He felt his anger drain away.* **5** [T] **drain sb/sth (of sth)** to make sb/sth weaker, poorer, etc. by slowly using all the strength, money, etc. available

**drain·age** /ˈdreɪnɪdʒ/ **noun** [U] a system used for draining water, etc. away from a place: *a drainage ditch*

**drain·board** /ˈdreɪnbɔrd/ (*also* **drain·er** /ˈdreɪnər/) **noun** [C] a flat surface in the kitchen where cups, plates, etc. are left to dry after being washed

**drain·pipe** /ˈdreɪnpaɪp/ **noun** [C] a pipe that carries water or liquid waste away from a building

**drake** /dreɪk/ **noun** [C] a male duck ➲ picture at **duck**.

★**dra·ma** /ˈdrɑmə/ **noun** **1** [C] a play for the theater, radio or television: *a contemporary drama* **2** [U] plays as a form of writing; the performance of plays: *He wrote some drama as well as poetry.* ◇ *a drama student* **3** [C] an exciting event **4** [U] excitement: *...and to add to all the drama, the lights went out!*

★**dra·mat·ic** /drəˈmæt̬ɪk/ **adj.** **1** noticeable or sudden: *a dramatic change* **2** exciting or impressive: *a dramatic scene.* **3** (used about a person, a person's behavior, etc.) showing feelings, etc. in a very obvious way because you want other people to notice you or pay attention to you: *Calm down. There's no need to be so dramatic about everything!* **4** connected with plays or the theater: *Shakespeare's dramatic works* ▶ **dra·mat·i·cal·ly** /-kli/ **adv.**: *"I can't go on," she said dramatically.*

**dram·a·tist** /ˈdrɑmətɪst; ˈdræ-/ **noun** [C] a person who writes plays

**dram·a·tize** /ˈdrɑmətaɪz; ˈdræ-/ **verb** **1** [T] to make a book, an event, etc. into a play: *The novel has been dramatized for television.* **2** [I,T] to make sth seem more exciting or important than it really is: *The newspaper was accused of dramatizing the situation.* ▶ **dram·a·ti·za·tion** /ˌdrɑmət̬əˈzeɪʃn; ˌdræ-/ **noun** [C,U]

**drank** *past tense of* DRINK¹

**drape** /dreɪp/ **verb** [T] **1 drape sth around/over sth** to put a piece of cloth, clothing, etc. loosely on sth: *He quickly draped a towel around his waist.* **2 drape sb/sth (in/with sth)** (usually passive) to cover sb/sth (with cloth, etc.): *The stadium was draped with red, white and blue flags.*

**drap·er·y** /dreɪpəri/ (*also* **drape** /dreɪp/) **noun** [C, usually pl.] (*pl.* **drap·er·ies**) a long curtain that is made of heavy cloth

**dras·tic** /ˈdræstɪk/ **adj.** **1** strong, effective and usually quick: *The situation requires drastic action.* **2** very noticeable or serious: *a drastic rise in crime* ▶ **dras·tic·al·ly** /-kli/ **adv.**: *Home prices have fallen drastically over the last two years.*

★**draw¹** /drɔ/ **verb** (*pt* **drew** /dru/; *pp* **drawn** /drɔn/)

➤MAKE PICTURES **1** [I,T] to make a picture or diagram of sth with a pencil, pen, etc.: *I'll draw you a map of how to get there.*

➤PULL **2** [T] **draw sth out of/from sth** to pull sth smoothly out of its present position: *She drew the letter out of her pocket and handed it to me.* **3** [T] to pull sb/sth gently into a new position: *He drew me by the hand into the room.* **4** [T] (used about horses, etc.) to pull sth along: *The carriage was drawn by six horses.*

➤CURTAINS **5** [T] to close curtains, drapes, etc.: *I couldn't see inside the window because the curtains were drawn.*

➤WEAPON **6** [T] to pull a gun, sword or knife out of its holder, quickly and in order to attack sb: *The police officer drew his gun.*

➤MOVE **7** [I] (*formal*) to move in the direction mentioned: *The President's limousine drew into/out of the White House grounds.*

➤GET INFORMATION/REACTION **8** [T] **draw sth from sb/sth** to gain sth from sb/sth: *This information has been drawn from a number of sources.* **9** [T] **draw sth (from sb)** to produce a reaction or response to the thing mentioned: *The advertisement has drawn interest from people all over the country.*

➤CONCLUSION **10** [T] **draw sth (from sth)** to learn sth from study, experience, etc.: *Can we draw any conclusions from this survey?*

➤ATTRACT **11** [T] **draw sb (to sb/sth)** to attract or interest sb: *The musicians drew a fairly large crowd.*

IDM **bring sth/come/draw to an end** → END¹

**call/draw sb's attention to sth** → ATTENTION

**draw a blank** to fail to find an answer: *Detectives investigating the case have drawn a blank so far.*
**draw a comparison/a parallel** to show how two things compare or are similar: *The program drew an interesting comparison between education in Japan and in North America.*
**draw/make a distinction between A and B** → DISTINCTION
**draw the line at sth** to say "no" to sth even though you are prepared to be helpful in other ways: *I do most of the cooking but I draw the line at doing the dishes afterward!*
**draw straws** to decide sth by chance: *They drew straws to see who should stay behind.*
PHR V **draw sth out** to make sth last longer than usual or necessary: *There's no need to draw this discussion out any longer.*
**draw up** (used about a car, etc.) to drive up and stop in front of or near sth: *A police car drew up outside the building.*
**draw sth up** to prepare a document, list, etc. and write it out: *Our lawyer is going to draw up the contract.*

**draw²** /drɔ/ ***noun*** [C] **1** a person or thing that attracts interest or attention: *The young star is a big draw at the box office.* **2** a result of a game or competition in which both players or teams get the same score so that neither of them wins: *The game ended in a draw.*

NOTE It is more common to say **tie**.

**draw·back** /ˈdrɔbæk/ ***noun*** [C] a disadvantage or problem: *His lack of experience is a major drawback.*

★**draw·er** /drɔr/ ***noun*** [C] a container which forms part of a piece of furniture, such as a desk, that you can pull out to put things in or take things out: *There's some paper in the top drawer of my desk.*

★**draw·ing** /ˈdrɔɪŋ/ ***noun*** **1** [C] a picture made with a pencil, pen, etc. **2** [U] the art of drawing pictures: *She's good at drawing and painting.*

ˈ**drawing board** ***noun*** [C] a large flat board used for holding a piece of paper while a drawing or plan is being made: *an architect's drawing board*
IDM **(go) back to the drawing board** to start thinking about a new way of doing sth after an earlier plan or idea has failed: *They rejected our proposal, so it's back to the drawing board.*

**drawl** /drɔl/ ***verb*** [I,T] to speak slowly, making the vowel sounds very long ▸ **drawl *noun*** [sing.]

**drawn¹** /drɔn/ ***adj.*** (used about a person or his/her face) looking tired, worried or sick: *He looked pale and drawn after the long journey.*

**drawn²** *past participle of* DRAW¹: *The curtains were drawn.*

ˌ**drawn-ˈout** ***adj.*** lasting longer than necessary: *long, drawn-out negotiations*

**draw·string** /ˈdrɔstrɪŋ/ ***noun*** [C] a piece of string sewn inside the material at the top of a bag, pair of pants, etc. that can be pulled tighter in order to make the opening smaller: *They fasten with a drawstring.*

**drawstring**

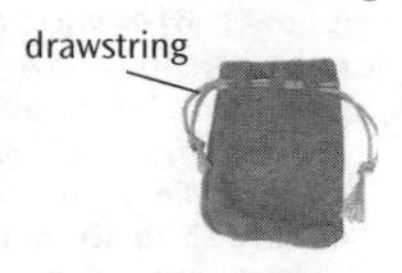


**dread¹** /drɛd/ ***noun*** [U, sing.] great fear: *He lived in dread of the same thing happening to him one day.* ◇ *a secret dread of what might happen*

**dread²** /drɛd/ ***verb*** [T] to be very afraid of or worried about sth: *I'm dreading my final exams.* ◇ *She dreaded having to tell him what had happened.* ◇ ***I dread to think** what my dad will say.*

**dread·ed** /ˈdrɛdəd/ ***adj.*** terrible; causing you to feel afraid or worried

**dread·ful** /ˈdrɛdfl/ ***adj.*** very bad, unpleasant or poor in quality: *There's been a dreadful* (= very serious) *accident.* ▸ **dread·ful·ly *adv.***

**dread·locks** /ˈdrɛdlɑks/ ***noun*** [pl.] hair worn in long thick pieces that look like rope

**dreadlocks**

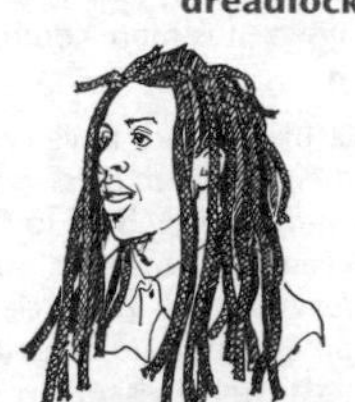

★**dream¹** /drim/ ***noun*** **1** [C] a series of events or pictures which happen in your mind while you are asleep: *I had a strange dream last night.* ◇ *In my dream I was flying a helicopter.* ➲ Look at **nightmare**. **2** [C] an event or situation that you want very much to happen, although it is not very likely that it will: *His dream was to give up his job and live on an island.* ◇ *a dream house* (= one that you would like very much to own)

★**dream²** /drim/ ***verb*** [I,T] (*pt, pp* **dreamed** /drimd/ or **dreamt** /drɛmt/) **1** to see or experience pictures and events in your mind while you are asleep: *I dreamed about the house that I lived in as a child.* ◇ *I woke up to find that I wasn't really rich. I had only dreamed it.* ◇ *I dreamed that I was running but I couldn't get away.* **2** to imagine sth that you would like to happen: *I've always dreamed about winning lots of money.* ◇ *I never dreamed that I would be so lucky!* ➲ Look at **daydream**.
IDM **I, etc. would not dream of sth** I, etc. would definitely not do sth, under any circumstances: *"Don't tell anybody." "Of course not. I wouldn't dream of it."*
PHR V **dream sth up** (*informal*) to think of sth such as a plan, etc. especially sth unusual or slightly foolish: *Which one of you dreamed up that idea?*

**dream·er** /ˈdrimər/ ***noun*** [C] a person who thinks a lot about ideas, plans, etc. which may never happen instead of concentrating on what is really happening

**dream·y** /ˈdrimi/ ***adj.*** (**dream·i·er**; **dream·i·est**) (used about a person or his/her expression) having or showing thoughts that are far away from the real world: *a dreamy look/expression*

**drea·ry** /ˈdrɪri/ ***adj.*** (**drea·ri·er**; **drea·ri·est**) dull, boring or depressing: *dreary weather*

**dredge** /drɛdʒ/ ***verb*** [T] to clear the mud, etc. from the bottom of a river or harbor using a special machine
PHR V **dredge sth up** to mention again sth bad from the past that it would be better to forget: *The newspaper had dredged up all sorts of embarrassing details about her private life.*

**drench** /drɛntʃ/ ***verb*** [T] (usually passive) to make

D

sb/sth completely wet: *We got totally drenched in the storm.*

★**dress**[1] /drɛs/ ***noun*** **1** [C] a piece of clothing worn by a girl or a woman. It covers the body from the shoulders to the knees or below and often covers the arms. **2** [U] clothes for either men or women: *formal/informal dress* ◇ *evening dress*

D

★**dress**[2] /drɛs/ ***verb*** **1** [I,T] to put clothes on sb or yourself: *He dressed quickly and left the house with a minute to spare.* ◇ *If you don't get dressed soon, we'll be late.* ◇ *My husband dressed the kids while I got breakfast ready.* ◇ *Hurry up, Kelly! Aren't you dressed yet?*

NOTE It is more common to say **get dressed** than **dress.**

**2** [I] to put or have clothes on, in the way or style mentioned: *to dress well/badly* ◇ *to be well dressed/badly dressed* **3** [I] to put on formal clothes for the evening: *In the past, wealthy families always dressed for dinner.* **4** [T] to clean and put a bandage, etc. on a wound: *to dress a wound*

IDM **(be) dressed in sth** wearing sth: *The people at the funeral were all dressed in black.*

PHR V **dress up 1** to put on special or unusual clothes for fun or for a play: *The kids decided to dress up as pirates.* **2** to put on nice clothes, usually for a special occasion: *You don't need to dress up for the party.*

ˈ**dress code** ***noun*** [C] a set of rules explaining what types of clothes people are allowed to wear in a particular place: *Our company's dress code requires all employees to wear business suits.*

**dress·er** /ˈdrɛsər/ ***noun*** [C] a piece of furniture with drawers in it that is used for storing clothes

**dress·ing** /ˈdrɛsɪŋ/ ***noun*** **1** [C,U] = SALAD DRESSING **2** [U] = STUFFING (1) **3** [C] a covering that you put on a wound to protect it and keep it clean ➲ picture at **bandage**.

ˈ**dressing room** ***noun*** [C] **1** a room where actors change their clothes and get ready to go on stage, TV etc. **2** = FITTING ROOM

**drew** *past tense of* DRAW[1]

**drib·ble** /ˈdrɪbl/ ***verb*** **1** [I,T] (used about a liquid) to move downward in a thin stream; to make a liquid move in this way: *The paint dribbled down the side of the can.* **2** [I,T] (used in basketball or soccer) to make a ball move forward by using many short hits or kicks: *to dribble a basketball*

**dried**[1] *past tense, past participle of* DRY[2]

**dried**[2] /draɪd/ ***adj.*** (used about food) with all the liquid removed from it: *dried fruit*

**dri·er** /ˈdraɪər/ ***adj.*** → DRY[1]

**drift**[1] /drɪft/ ***verb*** [I] **1** to be carried or moved along by wind or water: *The boat drifted out to sea.* **2** (used about snow or sand) to be moved into piles by wind or water: *The snow drifted up to six feet deep in some places.* **3** to move slowly or without any particular purpose: *She drifted into acting almost by accident.* ◇ *At one time they were close friends, but over the years they drifted apart.*

**drift**[2] /drɪft/ ***noun*** **1** [C] a slow movement toward sth: *the country's drift into economic decline* **2** [sing.] the general meaning of sth: *I couldn't understand every word, but I got the drift of what he was saying.* **3** [C] = SNOWDRIFT

**drill**[1] /drɪl/ ***noun*** **1** [C] a tool or machine that is used for making holes in things: *a dentist's drill* ➲ picture at **tool**. **2** [U] exercise in marching, etc. that soldiers do **3** [C] something that you repeat many times in order to learn sth **4** [C,U] practice for what you should do in an emergency: *a fire drill*

**drill**[2] /drɪl/ ***verb*** [I,T] **1** to make a hole in sth with a DRILL[1] (1): *to drill a hole in sth* ◇ *to drill for oil* **2** to teach sb by making him/her repeat sth many times

★**drink**[1] /drɪŋk/ ***verb*** (*pt* **drank** /dræŋk/; *pp* **drunk** /drʌŋk/) **1** [I,T] to take liquid into your body through your mouth: *You've lost a lot of fluid. You need to keep drinking.* ◇ *I never drink coffee.* **2** [I] to drink alcohol: *Don't drink and drive.*

PHR V **drink to sb/sth** to wish sb/sth good luck by raising your glass before you drink: *We all drank to the future of the bride and groom.* ➲ Look at **toast**[2].

★**drink**[2] /drɪŋk/ ***noun*** [C,U] **1** liquid for drinking: *Can I have a drink?* ◇ *a drink of milk* ◇ *food and drink* **2** alcoholic drink: *a strong drink* ◇ *He turned to drink when his problems became too much for him.*

**drink·er** /ˈdrɪŋkər/ ***noun*** [C] a person who drinks alcohol: *a heavy drinker*

**drink·ing** /ˈdrɪŋkɪŋ/ ***noun*** [U] drinking alcohol: *Her drinking became a problem.*

ˈ**drinking box** // ***noun*** [C] (*Cdn*) a small cardboard carton of juice, etc. that is packaged with a drinking straw that can be pushed through a small hole in the top

ˈ**drinking** ˌ**fountain** (*also* **water fountain, fountain**) ***noun*** [C] a piece of equipment connected to the water supply in a public building, that produces a stream of water that you can drink from

ˈ**drinking** ˌ**water** ***noun*** [U] water that is safe to drink

**drip**[1] /drɪp/ ***verb*** (**drip·ping**; **dripped**) **1** [I] (used about a liquid) to fall in small drops: *Water was dripping down through the roof.* **2** [I,T] to have drops of liquid falling: *The faucet is dripping.* ◇ *Her finger was dripping blood.*

**drip**[2] /drɪp/ ***noun*** **1** [C] a drop of liquid that falls down from sb/sth: *Be sure to wipe up any paint drips immediately.* **2** [sing.] the act or sound of water dripping: *the drip of a leaky faucet*

★**drive**[1] /draɪv/ ***verb*** (*pt* **drove** /droʊv/; *pp* **driv·en** /ˈdrɪvn/)

➤VEHICLE **1** [I,T] to control or operate a car/train/bus: *Can you drive?* ◇ *to drive a car/train/bus/truck* **2** [I,T] to go or take sb somewhere in a car, etc.: *I usually drive to work.* ◇ *We drove Nancy to the airport.*

➤MACHINE **3** [T] to make a machine work by giving it power: *What drives the wheels in this engine?*

➤MAKE SB DO STH **4** [T] to cause sb to be in a particular state or to do a particular thing: *That noise is driving me crazy.* ◇ *to drive sb to despair* ◇ *His loneliness drove him to commit suicide.* **5** [T] to force sb to act in a particular way: *The urge to survive drove them on.* ◇ *You shouldn't drive yourself so hard.*

➤MAKE SB/STH MOVE **6** [T] to force people or animals to move in a particular direction: *The farmer drove the sheep into the pen.*
➤HIT/PUSH **7** [T] to force sth into a particular position by hitting it: *to drive a post into the ground*
IDM **drive sb up the wall** (*informal*) to make sb extremely angry: *These kids have been driving me up the wall all day!*
PHRV **drive off** (used about a car, driver, etc.) to leave
**drive sb/sth off** to force sb/sth to go back or away: *The defenders drove off each attack.*

★**drive²** /draɪv/ ***noun***
➤IN/OF VEHICLE **1** [C] a trip in a car: *The shopping mall is only a five-minute drive away.* ◇ *Let's go out for a drive through the country.* **2** [U] the position of the gears of a car, etc. with automatic transmission in which the engine is sending power to the wheels so that the car can move forward: *Don't turn off the ignition while the car is still **in drive**.* ➲ Look at **neutral²**, **park¹**(4) and **reverse²**(2).
➤OUTSIDE HOUSE **3** [C] a private road that leads to a large house
➤EFFORT **4** [C] a strong effort by a group of people in order to achieve sth: *a sales drive*
➤DESIRE/ENERGY **5** [C,U] a strong natural need or desire: *a strong sex drive* **6** [U] the energy and determination you need to succeed in doing sth
➤IN SPORTS **7** [C] a long hard hit or kick: *She has a strong forehand drive* (= in tennis).
➤COMPUTING **8** [C] the part of a computer that reads and stores information on disks or tapes: *a 224 MB hard drive* ◇ *a CD drive* ➲ Look also at **disk drive**.
➤STREET **9** (*abbr.* **Dr.**) [sing.] (used in the name of some streets): *We live at 1120 Lakeside Drive.*

ˈ**drive-by** ***adj.*** (only *before* a noun) (used about an attack, etc.) done by sb who is going past in a car: *drive-by shootings/killings*

ˈ**drive-in** ***noun*** [C] a place where you can go to eat, watch a movie, etc. in your car

**driv·en** *past participle of* DRIVE¹

★**driv·er** /ˈdraɪvər/ ***noun*** [C] a person who drives a vehicle: *One passenger died in the accident, but the driver was unhurt.*

ˈ**driver's ˌlicense** ***noun*** [C] an official card that says you are allowed to drive a car, etc. You get this card after you have passed a written examination and a driver's test.

ˈ**drive-through** (*also informal* ˈ**drive-thru**) ***noun*** [C] a part of a restaurant, bank, or other business where you can buy sth or receive a service without getting out of your car

**drive·way** /ˈdraɪvweɪ/ ***noun*** [C] a small private road or an area wth a hard surface that goes from a street to sb's house: *I see Ann's car in the driveway – she must be home.* ➲ Picture on study page **A31**.

★**driv·ing¹** /ˈdraɪvɪŋ/ ***noun*** [U] the act of controlling a car, etc.: *She was arrested for reckless driving.*

**driv·ing²** /ˈdraɪvɪŋ/ ***adj.*** very strong: *driving rain* ◇ *Who's the **driving force** behind this plan?*

ˌ**driving under the** ˈ**influence** ***noun*** [U] (*abbr.* **DUI**) (*also* ˌ**driving while in**ˈ**toxicated**) (*abbr.* **DWI**) driving after drinking too much alcohol: *He was arrested for DUI.*

**driz·zle** /ˈdrɪzl/ ***noun*** [U] light rain that has many small drops ▸ **driz·zle** ***verb*** [I] ➲ Look at the note at **weather**.

**drone¹** /droʊn/ ***verb*** [I] **1** to make a continuous low sound: *I could hear the TV droning in the background.* **2** to talk in a flat or boring voice

**drone²** /droʊn/ ***noun*** [C] **1** [usually sing.] a continuous low sound **2** a person who does a lot of boring work and who other people think is not very important: *low-paid office drones*

**drool** /drul/ ***verb*** [I] **1** to let liquid (saliva) come out from your mouth: *Oh, no – the baby just drooled on my new blouse!* **2 drool (over sb/sth)** to show in a foolish way how much you like or admire sb/sth: *teenagers drooling over pictures of their favorite rock stars*

**droop** /drup/ ***verb*** [I] to bend or hang downward, e.g. because of weakness: *The flowers were drooping without water.* ▸ **droop·ing** /ˈdrupɪŋ/ ***adj.***: *drooping shoulders* ◇ *a drooping mustache*

★**drop¹** /drɑp/ ***verb*** (**drop·ping**; **dropped**)

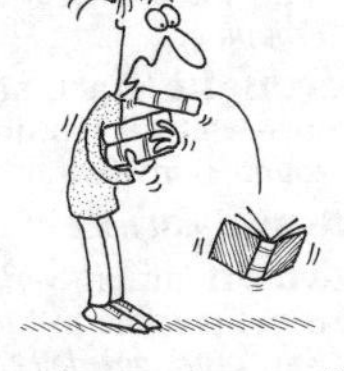


**1** [T] to allow sth to fall: *That vase was very expensive. Whatever you do, don't drop it!* **2** [I] to fall: *The soldier climbed over the wall and dropped safely to the ground.* **3** [I] to become weaker or lower; to make sth weaker or lower: *The temperature will drop below freezing overnight.* **4** [T] to no longer include sb/sth in sth: *Joe has been dropped from the team.* **5** [T] to not continue sth: *I'm going to drop my geography course* (= stop studying it). ◇ *Drop everything – I need your help right now!* ◇ *All the charges against you have been dropped – you're free to go home.*
IDM **drop dead** (*informal*) **1** to die suddenly **2** (used to tell sb that you are very angry with him/her)
**drop sb a line** to write a letter to sb: *I hope you'll drop us a line when you get a chance.*
**drop names** to mention the names of famous or important people you know or have met in order to impress other people ➲ Look also at **name-drop**.
PHRV **drop back**; **drop behind (sb)** to move into a position behind sb else, because you are moving more slowly: *Toward the end of the race she dropped behind the other runners.*
**drop by/in**; **drop in on sb** to visit sb informally or without having told him/her you were coming: *We were in the area, so we thought we'd drop in and see you.*
**drop off** (*informal*) to fall into a light sleep: *I must have dropped off in front of the television.*
**drop sb/sth off** to stop your car, etc. so that sb can get out, or in order to take sth out: *Drop me off at the corner, please.* ◇ *I'll drop off the package at your house.*
**drop out (of sth)** to leave or stop doing sth before you have finished: *His injury forced him to drop out of the tournament.* ◇ *to drop out of school*

★**drop²** /drɑp/ ***noun*** **1** [C] a small round mass of liquid: *I thought I felt a drop of rain.* **2 drops** [pl.] liquid medicine that you put into your eyes, ears or nose **3** [C] a small piece of candy or a small, sweet piece of medicine: *cough drops* **4** [sing.] a vertical distance down from a place: *It's a drop of 100 feet from the top of the cliff.* **5** [sing.] a smaller amount or level of sth: *We were forced to accept a drop in salary.*

**ˌdrop-ˈdead** *adv.* (*informal*) (used before an adjective to emphasize that sb/sth is attractive in a very noticeable way): *drop-dead gorgeous/handsome*

D

**ˈdrop-down ˌmenu** *noun* [C] (*computing*) a MENU (2) that appears on a computer screen when you choose it, and that stays there until you choose one of the functions on it ➲ Compare **pull-down menu**.

**drop·out** /ˈdrɑpaʊt/ *noun* [C] **1** a person who leaves school, college, university, etc. before finishing his/her studies: *high school dropouts* **2** a person who does not accept the rules of society and who wants to live in a way that is different from one that most people consider is acceptable

**drop·pings** /ˈdrɑpɪŋz/ *noun* [pl.] waste material from the bodies of small animals or birds: *rabbit droppings*

**drought** /draʊt/ *noun* [C,U] a long period of weather which is too dry: *Drought has affected many countries in Africa.*

**drove** *past tense of* DRIVE[1]

**drown** /draʊn/ *verb* [I,T] to die in water because it is not possible to breathe; to make sb die in this way: *The girl fell into the river and drowned.* ◇ *Twenty people were drowned in the floods.*

PHR V **drown sb/sth out** (used about a sound) to be so loud that you cannot hear sb/sth else: *His answer was drowned out by the music.*

**drow·sy** /ˈdraʊzi/ *adj.* (**drow·si·er**; **drow·si·est**) very sleepy: *The heat made me feel drowsy.* ▶ **drow·si·ly** /-əli/ *adv.* ▶ **drow·si·ness** *noun* [U]

★**drug**[1] /drʌg/ *noun* [C] **1** a chemical which is used as a medicine: *Some drugs can only be obtained with a prescription from a doctor.* **2** a chemical which people use to give them pleasant or exciting feelings. It is against the law in many countries to use drugs: *illegal drugs such as heroin and cocaine* ◇ *a drug dealer* ◇ *I think Rob is* ***on drugs*** (= I think he uses drugs). ◇ (*slang*) *to do drugs* (= to use illegal drugs)

**drug**[2] /drʌg/ *verb* [T] (**drug·ging**; **drugged**) to give a person or animal a chemical to make him/her/it tired or unconscious: *The lion was drugged before the start of the trip.*

**ˈdrug addict** *noun* [C] a person who cannot stop taking drugs

**ˈdrug adˌdiction** (*also* **ˈdrug deˌpendency**) *noun* [U] the state of being a drug addict

**drug·store** /ˈdrʌgstɔr/ *noun* [C] a store that sells medicine, soap, shampoo, film, etc.

★**drum**[1] /drʌm/ *noun* [C] **1** a round hollow musical instrument, with plastic or skin stretched across the ends. You play a drum by hitting it with your hands or with sticks: *She plays the drums in a band.* **2** a round hollow container: *an oil drum*

**drum**[2] /drʌm/ *verb* (**drum·ming**; **drummed**) **1** [I] to play a DRUM[1] (1) or drums **2** [I,T] to make a noise like a DRUM[1] (1) by hitting sth many times: *to drum your fingers on the table* (= because you are annoyed/impatient)

PHR V **drum sth into sb** to make sb remember sth by repeating it many times: *Safety rules should be drummed into children from an early age.*

**drum sth up** to try to get more of sth: *to drum up more support for a candidate*

**drums**

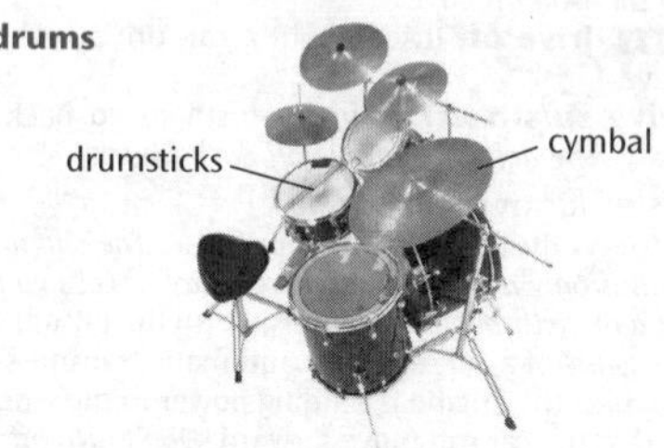


**drum·mer** /ˈdrʌmer/ *noun* [C] a person who plays a DRUM[1] (1) or drums

**drum·stick** /ˈdrʌmstɪk/ *noun* [C] **1** a stick used for playing the drums ➲ picture at **drum**. **2** the lower leg of a chicken or similar bird that is cooked and eaten as food: *a chicken/turkey drumstick*

**drunk**[1] *past participle of* DRINK[1]

★**drunk**[2] /drʌŋk/ *adj.* having drunk too much alcohol: *You're drunk!* ◇ *drunk drivers*

**drunk**[3] /drʌŋk/ *noun* [C] (*informal*) a person who is drunk, or who often gets drunk

**drunk·en** /ˈdrʌŋkən/ *adj.* (only *before* a noun) **1** showing the effects of too much alcohol: *drunken singing* **2** having drunk too much alcohol: *drunken drivers* ▶ **drunk·en·ness** *noun* [U]

★**dry**[1] /draɪ/ *adj.* (**dri·er**; **dri·est**) **1** without liquid in it or on it; not wet: *The laundry isn't dry yet.* ◇ *The paint is dry now.* ◇ *Rub your hair dry with a towel.* ◇ *In the hot weather the stream* ***ran dry***. **2** having little or no rain: *a hot, dry summer* **3** (used about wine) not sweet **4** dull or boring **5** (used of a remark, etc.) amusing, although it sounds serious: *a dry sense of humor* **6** (used about a place) not allowing alcohol to be sold or drunk: *a dry graduation party* ▶ **dry·ness** *noun* [U]

★**dry**[2] /draɪ/ *verb* [I,T] (*pres. part.* **dry·ing**; *3rd person sing. pres.* **dries**; *pt, pp* **dried**) **dry (off)**; **dry sth (off)** to become dry; to make sth dry: *Leave your swimsuit in the sun to dry.* ◇ *to dry your hands on a towel* ◇ *to dry yourself off after a bath*

PHR V **dry (sth) out** (to cause sth wet) to become very dry or too dry: *Don't allow the soil to dry out.*

**dry up 1** (used about a river, etc.) to have no more water in it **2** to stop being available: *Because of the recession a lot of construction work has dried up.*

**ˈdry-clean** *verb* [T] to clean clothes using special chemicals, without using water

**ˈdry ˌcleaners** *noun* = CLEANER (3)

**dry·er** /ˈdraɪər/ *noun* [C] a machine that you use for drying sth: *a hair dryer* ◇ *a clothes dryer*

**ˈdry goods** *noun* [pl.] **1** fabrics and things that are made out of fabric, such as clothes and sheets **2** (*Cdn*) types of foods that are solid and dry, such as tea, coffee and flour

ˌ**dry ˈice** ***noun*** [U] the solid form of a gas (**carbon dioxide**) that is used for keeping food, etc. cold and producing special effects in the theater

ˌ**dry ˈland** ***noun*** [U] land, not the ocean

**dry·ly** (*also* **drily**) /ˈdraɪli/ ***adv.*** in a DRY[1] (5) way: *"I can hardly contain my excitement," Peter said dryly* (= he was not excited at all).

ˌ**dry ˈrun** ***noun*** [C] (*informal*) = TRIAL RUN

**DST** ***abbr.*** (*written*) = DAYLIGHT-SAVING TIME

**DTP** /ˌdi ti ˈpi/ ***abbr.*** = DESKTOP PUBLISHING

**du·al** /ˈduəl/ ***adj.*** (only *before* a noun) having two parts; double: *the dual role of mother and working woman ◇ to have dual citizenship*

**dub** /dʌb/ ***verb*** [T] (**du<u>b</u>·bing**; **du<u>bb</u>ed**) **1** to give sb/sth a new or amusing name (a **nickname**): *Ronald Reagan was dubbed "The Great Communicator."* **2** to change the sound in a movie so that what the actors said originally is spoken by actors using a different language: *I don't like foreign movies when they're dubbed into English. I prefer subtitles.*

**du·bi·ous** /ˈdubiəs/ ***adj.*** **1 dubious (about sth/about doing sth)** not sure or certain: *I'm very dubious about whether we're doing the right thing.* **2** (only *before* a noun) having little value: *They have the dubious distinction of being the first team to lose 15 games in a row.* **3** that may not be honest or safe: *dubious financial dealings*

**duch·ess** (*also* **Duchess**) /ˈdʌtʃəs/ ***noun*** [C] **1** the wife of a duke **2** a woman who is of the same rank as a duke

**ducks**

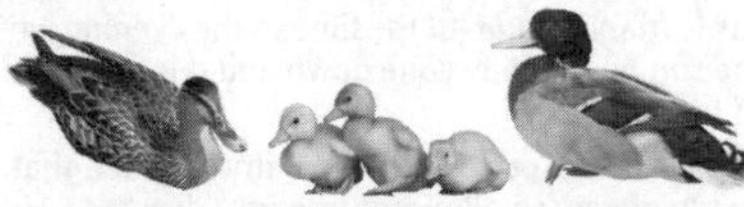


**duck[1]** /dʌk/ ***noun*** **1** [C] a common bird that lives on or near water. Ducks have short legs, special (**webbed**) feet for swimming and a wide beak.

> NOTE A male duck is called a **drake** and a young duck is a **duckling**. A duck **waddles** and **quacks**.

**2** [U] the meat of a duck ➲ Look also at **lame duck**.

**duck[2]** /dʌk/ ***verb*** **1** [I,T] to move your head down quickly so that you are not seen or hit by sb/sth: *I saw the ball coming toward me and ducked.* **2** [T] (*informal*) to try to avoid sth difficult or unpleasant: *The coach ducked several important questions during the interview.*

**duct** /dʌkt/ ***noun*** [C] a tube that carries liquid, gas, etc.: *They got into the building through the air duct.*

**dud** /dʌd/ ***noun*** [C] (*informal*) a thing that is useless or that does not work correctly

**dude** /dud/ ***noun*** [C] (*slang*) a boy or young man: *Hey, dude, what's happening? ◇ Do you know those dudes over there?*

★**due[1]** /du/ ***adj.*** **1** (not before a noun) expected or planned to happen or arrive: *What time is the plane due? ◇ Their first child is due* (= is expected to be born) *in August.* **2** (not before a noun) having to be paid, finished, etc.: *The rent is due on the first of each month.* **3** that is owed to you because it is your right to have it: *Make sure you claim any refund that is due to you.* **4 due to sb/sth** caused by or because of sb/sth: *His illness is probably due to stress.*

> NOTE Some careful speakers only use **due to** after the verb **to be**: *The strike was due to poor working conditions.* However, **due to** is often used in the same way as **owing to** and **because of**: *Due to/Owing to/Because of the bad weather, many flights have been canceled.*

**5 due for sth** deserving or expecting to have sth: *I think I'm due for a raise.* **6** (only *before* a noun) (*formal*) suitable or right: *With all due respect, ma'am, I can't let you into the chairman's office.*

IDM **in due course** (*formal*) at some time in the future: *All applicants will be informed of our decision in due course.*

**due[2]** /du/ ***adv.*** (used before "north," "south," "east" and "west") exactly: *The airplane was flying due east.*

**du·el[1]** /ˈduəl/ ***noun*** [C] **1** a fight or an angry competition **2** a formal type of fight with guns or swords which was used in the past to settle an argument between two men: *to challenge sb to a duel*

**du·el[2]** /ˈduəl/ ***verb*** [I,T] **duel (with sb/sth)** to fight or compete (against sb/sth): *Environmentalists are dueling with real estate developers over plans to build a new shopping mall.*

ˌ**due ˈprocess** ***noun*** [U] the correct way in which action should be taken in a court of law, by the police, etc. in order to protect sb's rights

**dues** /duz/ ***noun*** [pl.] money that you must pay to be a member of an organization, a club, etc.: *to pay your union dues*

**du·et** /duˈet/ ***noun*** [C] a piece of music for two people to sing or play

**duf·fel bag** (*also* **duf·fle bag**) /ˈdʌfl bæg/ ***noun*** [C] a bag made of cloth with two round ends, that you can carry clothes, etc. in

**dug** *past tense, past participle of* DIG[1]

**dug·out** /ˈdʌgaʊt/ ***noun*** [C] **1** (in baseball) an area at the side of the field that is partly underground, with a roof, where the players can wait for their turn to play **2** (*also* ˌ**dugout caˈnoe**) a small, narrow boat that is made by cutting out a long space in a thick, round part of a tree (a **log**)

**DUI** /ˌdi yu ˈaɪ/ ***abbr.*** = DRIVING UNDER THE INFLUENCE

**duke** (*also* **Duke**) /duk/ ***noun*** [C] (in some countries) a man with a very high social rank: *the Duke of York* ➲ Look at **duchess**.

★**dull** /dʌl/ ***adj.*** **1** not interesting or exciting: *Life is never dull in the city.* **2** not loud, sharp or strong: *Her head hit the floor with a dull thud. ◇ a dull pain* **3** not bright: *dull, drab colors* ▸ **dull·ness** ***noun*** [U]

**du·ly** /ˈduli/ ***adv.*** (*formal*) (only *before* a verb or a participle) in the correct or official way: *a duly authorized government representative*

**dumb** /dʌm/ ***adj.*** **1** stupid: *What a dumb thing to do!* **2** (*old-fashioned*) not able to speak: *to be deaf and dumb ◇* (*figurative*) *They were struck dumb with amazement.*

> NOTE This use of **dumb** is considered offensive

nowadays. If a person is unable to speak, we can say that he/she is **mute** or **speech-impaired**.

**dumb·found·ed** /dʌm'faʊndəd/ ***adj.*** very surprised

**dum·my**[1] /'dʌmi/ ***noun*** [C] (*pl.* **dum·mies**) **1** a model of the human body used for showing clothes in a store window or while you are making clothes: *a department store dummy* **2** (*informal*) a stupid person: *You dummy! What did you do that for?* ◇ *Of course I know how to program the VCR – I'm no dummy!* **3** something that is made to look like sth else but that is not the real thing

**dum·my**[2] /'dʌmi/ ***adj.*** (only *before* a noun) made to look like sth else but not the real thing

**dump**[1] /dʌmp/ ***verb*** [T] **1** to take sth that you do not want to a place, especially a place which is not suitable, and leave it there: *Nuclear waste should not be dumped in the ocean.* **2** to put something down quickly or in a careless way: *The kids dumped their coats and bags in the hall and ran off to play.* **3** (*informal*) to leave sb in a rude and sudden way: *Jill dumped her boyfriend after they'd been together for two years.*

**dump**[2] /dʌmp/ ***noun*** [C] **1** a place where garbage or waste material from factories, etc. is left: *the municipal garbage dump* **2** (*informal*) a place that is very dirty, messy or unpleasant: *Your room is a total dump!*

**dump·ling** /'dʌmplɪŋ/ ***noun*** [C] a small ball of fat and flour (**dough**) that is boiled and usually eaten with meat

**dumps** /dʌmps/ ***noun*** [pl.]

IDM **down in the dumps** (*informal*) unhappy or depressed

**Dump·ster™** (*also* **dumpster**) /'dʌmpstər/ ***noun*** [C] a very large metal container for garbage, that is usually used outdoors

**'dump truck** ***noun*** [C] a vehicle for carrying earth, stones, etc. in a container which can be lifted up for the load to fall out ➲ picture at **truck**.

**dune** /dun/ (*also* **'sand dune**) ***noun*** [C] a low hill of sand by the ocean or in the desert

**dung** /dʌŋ/ ***noun*** [U] waste material from the bodies of large animals

**dun·geon** /'dʌndʒən/ ***noun*** [C] an underground prison, e.g. in a castle

**dunk** /dʌŋk/ ***verb*** **1** [T] to push sb's head under water for a short time, especially when playing **2** [T] to put sth into liquid for a short time: *to dunk a cookie in your coffee* **3** [I,T] (in basketball) to jump very high and put the ball through the basket with great force from above ➲ Look also at **slam-dunk**.

**du·o** /'duoʊ/ ***noun*** [C] (*pl.* **du·os**) two people who do sth together, especially playing music or singing

**Du·o-Tang™** /'duoʊ tæŋ/ ***noun*** [C] (*Cdn*) a cardboard folder with three metal fasteners in the center which you push through the holes in loose pieces of paper in order to keep them together

**dupe** /dup/ ***verb*** [T] to trick sb: *The woman was duped into carrying the drugs.*

**du·plex** /'duplɛks/ ***noun*** [C] a house that is divided into two separate homes, usually with a separate door for each one

**du·pli·cate**[1] /'dupləkət/ ***adj.*** (only *before* a noun) exactly the same as sth else: *a duplicate key* (= a copy of another key)

**du·pli·cate**[2] /'dupləkət/ ***noun*** [C] something that is exactly the same as sth else

IDM **in duplicate** with two copies (e.g. of an official piece of paper) that are exactly the same: *The form must be submitted in duplicate.*

**du·pli·cate**[3] /'dupləkeɪt/ ***verb*** [T] **1** to make an exact copy of sth ➲ Compare **replicate**. **2** to do sth that has already been done: *We don't want to duplicate the work of other departments.* ▸ **du·pli·ca·tion** /ˌduplə'keɪʃn/ ***noun*** [U]

**du·ra·ble** /'dʊrəbl/ ***adj.*** that is able to last a long time: *a durable fabric* ▸ **du·ra·bil·i·ty** /ˌdʊrə'bɪləṭi/ ***noun*** [U]

**du·ra·tion** /dʊ'reɪʃn/ ***noun*** [U] the time that sth lasts: *Please remain seated for the duration of the flight.*

**du·ress** /dʊ'res/ ***noun*** [U]

IDM **under duress** because of the threat of force being used; not willingly: *He signed the confession under duress.*

★**dur·ing** /'dʊrɪŋ/ ***prep.*** **1** for all of a period of time: *The audience must remain seated during the performance.* **2** on more than one occasion in a period of time: *During the summer vacation we went swimming every day.* **3** at some point in a period of time: *Grandpa had a stroke during the night.*

NOTE Notice that you use **during** to say when something happens and **for** to say how long something lasts: *I went shopping during my lunch break. I was out for about 25 minutes.*

**dusk** /dʌsk/ ***noun*** [U] the time in the evening when the sun has already gone down and it is nearly dark ➲ Look at **dawn**.

★**dust**[1] /dʌst/ ***noun*** [U] a fine dry powder that is made of very small pieces of earth, dirt, etc.: *There is dust everywhere in our house.* ◇ *chalk dust* ◇ *The truck drove off in **a cloud of dust**.* ◇ *a speck* (= small piece) *of dust*

★**dust**[2] /dʌst/ ***verb*** [I,T] to remove DUST[1] from furniture, etc. with a cloth: *Let me dust those shelves before you put the books on them.* ➲ Look at the note at **clean**[2].

**dust·pan** /'dʌstpæn/ ***noun*** [C] a flat container with a handle into which you brush dust or dirt from the floor ➲ picture at **brush**[1].

**dust·y** /'dʌsti/ ***adj.*** (**dust·i·er**; **dust·i·est**) having a lot of DUST[1]: *This shelf has gotten very dusty.*

**Dutch** /dʌtʃ/ ***adj.*** of or connected with the Netherlands, its people or its language

IDM **go dutch**; **go Dutch** (*informal*) to share the cost of sth, especially a meal, equally: *When we were students and went out to dinner, we always went dutch.*

**du·ti·ful** /'duṭɪfl/ ***adj.*** doing everything that you are expected to do; willing to obey and to show respect: *a dutiful son* ▸ **du·ti·ful·ly** ***adv.***

★**du·ty** /'duṭi/ ***noun*** (*pl.* **du·ties**) **1** [C,U] something that you have to do because people expect you to do it or because you think it is right: *a sense of moral duty* ◇ *It's your duty to take care of your parents when they get older.* **2** [C,U] the tasks that you do when you are at work: *the duties of a police officer ◇ Colonel Hamilton is retired from active military duty.* **3** [C] a tax that you pay, especially on goods that you bring into a country

IDM **on/off duty** (used about doctors, nurses, police officers, etc.) to be working/not working: *Sergeant Smith is on duty from 8 to 4. ◇ What time does she go off duty?* ➲ Look also at **heavy-duty**.

**ˌduty-ˈfree** ***adj., adv.*** (used about goods) that you can bring into a country without paying tax: *a duty-free shop at the airport ◇ How much wine can you bring into the U.S. duty-free?*

**DVD** /ˌdi vi ˈdi/ ***noun*** [C] a disk on which large amounts of information, especially photographs and video, can be stored, for use on a computer (an abbreviation for "digital videodisc" or "digital versatile disk"): *Do you have a **DVD player**? ◇ Let's buy that movie **on DVD**, not on a video.*

**dwarf**[1] /dwɔrf/ ***noun*** [C] (*pl.* **dwarfs** or **dwarves** /dwɔrvz/) **1** a person, animal or plant that is much smaller than the usual size **2** (in children's stories) a very small person, often with special powers: *Snow White and the Seven Dwarfs*

**dwarf**[2] /dwɔrf/ ***verb*** [T] (used about a large object) to make sth seem very small in comparison: *The skyscraper dwarfs all the other buildings around it.*

**dwell** /dwɛl/ ***verb*** [I] (*pt, pp* **dwelt** /dwelt/ or **dwelled**) (*old-fashioned, formal*) to live or stay in a place

PHR V **dwell on/upon sth** to think, speak or write about sth for a long time: *I don't want to dwell on the past. Let's think about the future.*

**dwell·er** /ˈdwɛlər/ ***noun*** [C] (often in compounds) a person or animal that lives in the place mentioned: *apartment dwellers*

**dwell·ing** /ˈdwɛlɪŋ/ ***noun*** [C] (*formal*) the place where a person lives; a house

**DWI** /ˌdi ˌdʌblyu ˈaɪ/ ***abbr.*** = DRIVING WHILE INTOXICATED ➲ Look at **driving under the influence**.

**dwin·dle** /ˈdwɪndl/ ***verb*** [I] to become smaller or weaker: *Their savings dwindled away to nothing.*

**dye**[1] /daɪ/ ***verb*** [T] (*pres. part.* **dye·ing**; *3rd person sing. pres.* **dyes**; *pt, pp* **dyed**) to color sth, especially by putting it into a liquid: *Does she dye her hair? ◇ I'm going to dye this blouse black.*

**dye**[2] /daɪ/ ***noun*** [C,U] a substance, usually added to a liquid, that changes the color of sth, e.g. cloth, hair

**dy·ing** → DIE

**dyke** /daɪk/ ***noun*** [C] (*slang*) a woman who is sexually attracted to other women

NOTE This word can be offensive. Look at **lesbian**.

**dy·nam·ic** /daɪˈnæmɪk/ ***adj.*** **1** (used about a person) full of energy and ideas; active **2** (used about a force or power) that causes movement ▸ **dy·na·mism** /ˈdaɪnəmɪzəm/ ***noun*** [U]

**dy·na·mite** /ˈdaɪnəmaɪt/ ***noun*** [U] a type of explosive substance, used especially in mining: *a stick of dynamite*

**dy·na·mo** /ˈdaɪnəmoʊ/ ***noun*** [C] (*pl.* **dy·na·mos**) (*informal*) a person who is full of energy

**dy·nas·ty** /ˈdaɪnəsti/ ***noun*** [C] (*pl.* **dy·nas·ties**) a series of rulers who are from the same family: *the Ming dynasty*

**dys·en·ter·y** /ˈdɪsənˌtɛri/ ***noun*** [U] a serious disease which causes a severe form of diarrhea

**dys·func·tion** /dɪsˈfʌŋkʃn/ ***noun*** [C,U] failure to work correctly; a time when sth does not work correctly

**dys·func·tion·al** /dɪsˈfʌŋkʃənl/ ***adj.*** (used about a family, a relationship between people, etc.) not happy or behaving according to the normal rules of society: *children growing up in dysfunctional families*

**dys·lex·i·a** /dɪsˈlɛksiə/ ***noun*** [U] a problem in sb's brain that causes difficulties in reading and spelling ▸ **dys·lex·ic** /dɪsˈlɛksɪk/ ***noun*** [C], ***adj.***

# Ee

**E, e** /i/ ***noun*** [C,U] (*pl.* **E's**; **e's**) the fifth letter of the English alphabet: *"Egg" begins with (an) "E."*

**E** (*also* **E.**) ***abbr.*** = EAST, EASTERN

**e-** /i/ ***prefix*** connected with the use of the Internet for sending information, doing business, etc.: *e-commerce* ➲ Look also at **e-business** and **e-mail**.

★**each** /itʃ/ ***det., pronoun*** every one of two or more things or people in a group, when you think about them individually: *Each class lasts an hour. ◇ Each of the classes lasts an hour. ◇ The classes each last an hour. ◇ He gave each child a present. ◇ He gave each of the children a present. ◇ He gave the children a present each.*

★**ˌeach ˈother** ***pronoun*** (used for saying that sb feels, does or has the same thing as another person/other people in the group): *They loved each other very much. ◇ We looked at each other.*

**ea·ger** /ˈigər/ ***adj.*** full of desire or interest: *He is eager to meet you. ◇ eager for success* ▸ **ea·ger·ly** ***adv.*** ▸ **ea·ger·ness** ***noun*** [U]

**ea·gle** /ˈigl/ ***noun*** [C] a very large bird that can see very well. It eats small birds and animals. ➲ Look also at **bald eagle**. ➲ picture on **page 214**.

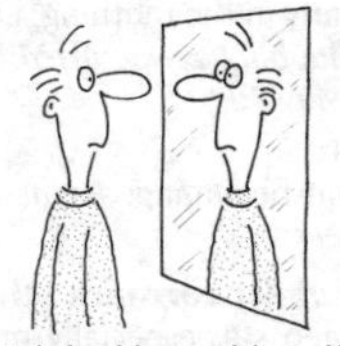

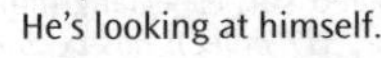

He's looking at himself.

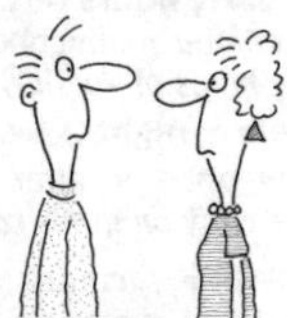

They're looking at **each other**.

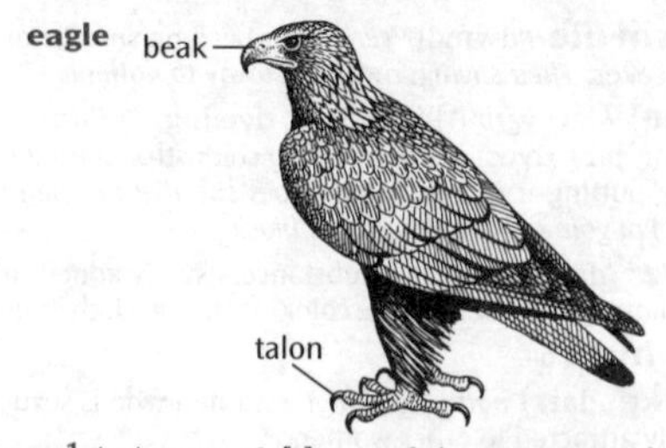




★**ear**[1] /ɪr/ ***noun*** **1** [C] one of the two parts of the body of a person or an animal that are used for hearing: *Elephants have large ears.* ◇ *He pulled his hat down over his ears.* ◇ *Whisper in my ear!* **2** [sing.] **an ear (for sth)** an ability to recognize or appreciate sounds, especially in music or language: *an ear for music* **3** [C] the part of a grain plant, especially a corn plant, where the grains grow ➲ picture at **corn**.

IDM **be all ears** (*informal*) to be waiting with interest to hear what sb has to say: *"Do you know what he said?" "Go ahead – I'm all ears!"*

**go in one ear and out the other** (*informal*) (used about information, etc.) to be forgotten quickly: *Everything I tell my students goes in one ear and out the other.*

**play (sth) by ear** to play a piece of music, etc. from memory and without using written notes

**play it by ear** (*informal*) to decide what to do as things happen, instead of planning in advance

**be up to your ears/eyes/neck in sth** → UP[1]

**wet behind the ears** → WET[1]

**ear·ache** /ˈɪreɪk/ ***noun*** [C] a pain in your ear: *I have an earache.*

**ear·drum** /ˈɪrdrʌm/ ***noun*** [C] a thin piece of skin inside the ear that is tightly stretched and that allows you to hear sound

**ear·lobe** /ˈɪrloʊb/ (*also* **lobe**) ***noun*** [C] the round soft part at the bottom of your ear

★**ear·ly** /ˈərli/ (**ear·li·er**; **ear·li·est**) ***adj.***, ***adv.*** **1** near the beginning of a period of time, a piece of work, a series, etc.: *Come in the early afternoon.* ◇ *I have to get up early on weekday mornings.* ◇ *He died in his early twenties.* ◇ *The project is still in its early stages.* ◇ *The tunnel should be finished early next year.* **2** before the usual or expected time: *She arrived five minutes early for her interview.* ◇ *Spring is early this year.* ◇ *She's an early riser* (= she gets up early in the morning).

IDM **at the earliest** not before the date or time mentioned: *I can fix it by Friday at the earliest.*

**an early bird** a person who gets up, arrives, etc. very early: *You're an early bird this morning!*

**the early hours** very early in the morning, i.e. the hours after midnight: *The burglary occurred in the early hours of Tuesday, May 10.*

**an early night** → NIGHT

**early on** soon after the beginning: *He achieved fame early on in his career.*

**ear·mark** /ˈɪrmɑrk/ ***verb*** [T] **earmark sth (for sth/sb)** to choose or keep sth, especially money, for a particular purpose: *$17 million has been earmarked for highway improvements.*

**ear·muffs** /ˈɪrmʌfs/ ***noun*** [pl.] coverings for your ears that are made of thick material connected by a curved band, that you wear in cold weather to keep your ears warm: *a pair of earmuffs*

★**earn** /ərn/ ***verb*** [T] **1** to get money by working: *How much does a dentist earn?* ◇ *I earn $30,000 a year.* ◇ *He earns his living as an artist.* ◇ *How much interest will my savings earn* (= produce) *in the bank?* **2** to get sth that you deserve: *You've earned a vacation.*

**earn·er** /ˈərnər/ ***noun*** [C] **1** a person who earns money for a job he/she does: *a high/low earner* **2** an activity or a business that makes a profit: *Tourism is the country's biggest foreign currency earner.*

**ear·nest**[1] /ˈərnəst/ ***adj.*** serious or determined: *They were having a very earnest discussion.* ▶ **ear·nest·ly** ***adv.***

**ear·nest**[2] /ˈərnəst/ ***noun***

IDM **in earnest** happening more seriously or with more force than before: *Work began in earnest on the project.*

**earn·ings** /ˈərnɪŋz/ ***noun*** [pl.] the money that a person earns by working: *Average earnings have increased by 5%.*

**ear·phones** /ˈɪrfoʊnz/ ***noun*** [pl.] a piece of equipment that fits over or in the ears and is used for listening to music, the radio, etc.

**ear·plug** /ˈɪrplʌg/ ***noun*** [C, usually pl.] a piece of soft material that you put into your ears to keep out noise or water

**ear·ring** /ˈɪrɪŋ/ ***noun*** [C] a piece of jewelry that is worn in or on the lower part of the ear: *Do these earrings clip on or are they for pierced ears?* ➲ picture at **jewelry**.

**ear·shot** /ˈɪrʃɑt/ ***noun*** [U]

IDM **(be) out of/within earshot** (to be) where a person cannot/can hear: *Wait until he's out of earshot before you say anything about him.*

ˈ**ear-ˌsplitting** ***adj.*** extremely loud

**the earth**

**northern hemisphere**

axis
North Pole
tropic of Cancer
Arctic Circle
tropic of Capricorn
equator
line of longitude
South Pole
line of latitude
Antarctic Circle

**southern hemisphere**

★**earth** /ərθ/ ***noun*** **1** (*also* **the earth, the Earth**) [sing.] the world; the planet on which we live: *life on earth* ◇ *The earth is protected by the ozone layer.* **2** [sing., U] the surface of the world; land: *The satellite fell toward earth.* ◇ *The earth shook.* **3** [U] soil: *The* *bulldozer piled up a huge mound of earth.* ➲ Look at the note at **ground**.

IDM **how, why, where, who, etc. on earth** (*informal*) (used for emphasizing sth or expressing surprise): *Where on earth have you been?*

**earth·ly** /ˈərθli/ ***adj.*** **1** (often used in questions and negatives for emphasis) possible: *There's **no earthly reason** why you shouldn't go.* **2** connected with this world, not heaven: *The monks gave up all their earthly possessions.*

**earth·quake** /ˈərθkweɪk/ (*also informal* **quake**) ***noun*** [C] a sudden violent movement of the earth's surface: *Thousands of people were left homeless by the earthquake.*

ˈ**earth-ˌshattering** ***adj.*** having a very great effect and of great importance: *an earth-shattering discovery*

**earth·worm** /ˈərθwərm/ ***noun*** [C] a common type of worm that lives in the soil

**ear·wax** /ˈɪrwæks/ ***noun*** [U] = WAX (2)

★**ease¹** /iz/ ***noun*** [U] a lack of difficulty: *She answered the questions with ease.* ➲ Look at **easy**.

IDM **(be/feel) at ease** to be/feel comfortable, relaxed, etc.: *They were all so kind and friendly that I felt completely at ease.*

★**ease²** /iz/ ***verb*** **1** [I,T] to become or make sth less painful or severe: *These pills will help ease the pain.* ◇ *The tension between the two countries has eased.* **2** [T] to cause sth to move slowly and gently: *He eased his truck into a narrow parking space.*

PHR V **ease up 1** to work less hard: *Ease up a little or you'll make yourself sick!* **2** to become less severe: *Let's wait until the rain eases up.*

**ea·sel** /ˈizl/ ***noun*** [C] a wooden frame that holds a blackboard or a picture that is being painted

★**eas·i·ly** /ˈizəli/ ***adv.*** **1** without difficulty: *I can easily call up and check the time.* **2** without doubt: *It's easily his best novel.*

★**east¹** /ist/ ***noun*** [sing.] (*abbr.* **E**; **E.**) **1** (*also* **the east**) one of the four main points of the compass; the direction you look toward in order to see the sun rise: *Which way is east?* ◇ *a cold wind from the east* ◇ *Which state is to the east of Indiana?* ➲ picture at **north**. **2 the east**; **the East** the part of any country, city, etc. that lies further to the EAST (1) than the other parts: *The oldest American universities are in the East.* ➲ Look at **Far East** and **Middle East**.

★**east²** /ist/ (*also* **East**) ***adj.*** in or toward the east, or from the east: *the East Coast* (= next to the Atlantic Ocean) ◇ *an east wind* ◇ *East Vancouver*

★**east³** /ist/ ***adv.*** to or toward the east: *They headed east.* ◇ *We live east of the city.*

**east·bound** /ˈistbaʊnd/ ***adj.*** traveling or leading toward the east: *The eastbound lanes of the highway are closed.*

**Eas·ter** /ˈistər/ ***noun*** [U] the Sunday in March or April when Christians celebrate Christ's return to life

ˈ**Easter egg** ***noun*** [C] an egg that has been boiled inside its shell and decorated, that you give as a present at Easter

**east·er·ly** /ˈistərli/ ***adj.*** **1** to, toward or in the east: *They traveled in an easterly direction.* **2** (used about winds) coming from the east: *cold easterly winds*

★**east·ern** /ˈistərn/ ***adj.*** **1** of, in or from the east of a place: *eastern Canada* ◇ *the eastern shore of the lake* **2** (*also* **Eastern**) from or connected with the countries of Asia: *Eastern philosophy*

ˌ**Eastern ˈDaylight Time** ***noun*** [U] (*abbr.* **EDT**) the time system used in the eastern part of the U.S. and Canada from April to October, when the clocks are set one hour ahead of Eastern Standard time ➲ Look at **daylight-saving time**.

ˌ**Eastern ˈStandard Time** ***noun*** [U] (*abbr.* **EST**) the time system used in the eastern part of the U.S. and Canada from October to April when clocks are set one hour behind standard time ➲ Look at **Standard Time**.

ˈ**Eastern Time** ***noun*** [U] (*abbr.* **ET**) the standard time system that is used in the eastern part of the U.S. and Canada ➲ Compare **Central Time**, **Mountain Time** and **Pacific Time**.

ˌ**East ˈIndian** ***noun*** [C] a person whose family originally came from the Indian subcontinent ▶ ˌ**East ˈIndian** ***adj.***

**east·ward¹** /ˈistwərd/ ***adj.*** toward the east: *to travel in an eastward direction*

**east·ward²** /ˈistwərd/ (*also* **eastwards** /ˈistwərdz/) ***adv.*** toward the east: *The Amazon flows eastward.*

★**eas·y¹** /ˈizi/ ***adj.*** (**eas·i·er**; **eas·i·est**) **1** not difficult: *an easy question* ◇ *It isn't easy to explain the system.* ◇ *The system isn't easy to explain.* **2** without any pain, trouble or worry: *an easy drive to work* ◇ *Life is easy when you've got plenty of money.* ➲ Look at **ease** and **easily**.

**eas·y²** /ˈizi/ ***adv.*** (**eas·i·er**; **eas·i·est**)

IDM **easier said than done** more difficult to do than to talk about: *"You should get her to help you." "That's easier said than done."*

**easy does it** (*informal*) (used to tell sb to do sth, or move sth, slowly and carefully)

**go easy on sb/sth** (*informal*) **1** to be gentle or less strict with sb: *Go easy on him; he's just a child.* **2** to avoid using too much of sth: *Go easy on the salt; it's bad for your heart.*

**over easy/medium/hard** → OVER²

**take it easy** (*informal*) to relax and not work too hard or worry too much: *My doctor advised me to take it easy for a while.*

ˈ**easy chair** ***noun*** [C] a large comfortable chair with arms

**eas·y·go·ing** /ˌiziˈgoʊɪŋ/ ***adj.*** (used about a person) calm, relaxed and not easily worried: *Her parents are very easygoing. They let her do what she wants.*

★**eat** /it/ ***verb*** (*pt* **ate** /eɪt/; *pp* **eat·en** /ˈitn/) **1** [I,T] to put food into your mouth, then chew and swallow it: *Did you eat all the cookies?* ◇ *Eat up your lunch, Joe* (= Finish it all). ◇ *She doesn't eat right. No wonder she's so thin.* **2** [I] to have a meal: *What time should we eat?*

IDM **eat your heart out!** (*informal*) (used to say that sb, especially a famous person, should be jealous because sb else thinks that he/she can do

sth better): *I scored 42 points in one game – eat your heart out, Shaquille O'Neal!*
**eat your words** to admit that what you said was wrong
**have your cake and eat it too** → CAKE
PHR V **eat sth away/eat away at sth** to damage or destroy sth gradually: *The ocean waves had eaten away at the cliff.*
**eat out** to have a meal in a restaurant: *Would you like to eat out tonight?*

E

**eat·er** /ˈit̬ər/ ***noun*** [C] a person who eats in a particular way: *My uncle's a big eater* (= he eats a lot).

**eat·er·y** /ˈit̬əri/ ***noun*** [C] (*pl.* **eat·er·ies**) (*informal*) a restaurant

ˈ**eating disˌorder** ***noun*** [C] one of several medical conditions which involve not being able to eat in a normal and healthy way: *Anorexia is a serious eating disorder.*

**eaves·drop** /ˈivzdrɑp/ ***verb*** [I] (**eaves·dropping**; **eaves·dropped**) to listen secretly to other people talking: *They caught her eavesdropping on their conversation.*

**eaves·trough** /ˈivztrɔf/ ***noun*** [C] (*Cdn*) = GUTTER (1)

**ebb** /ɛb/ ***verb*** [I] **1** (used about the water in the ocean) to flow away from the land **2** (used about a feeling, etc.) to become weaker: *My enthusiasm for the idea began to ebb.*

**eb·on·y** /ˈɛbəni/ ***noun*** [U] a hard black wood

**e-busi·ness** /ˈiˌbɪznəs/ ***noun*** **1** [U] (*also* **e-commerce**) doing business by means of the Internet: *E-business is expected to grow quickly in the coming years.* **2** [C] a company that sells goods or services on the Internet

**ec·cen·tric**[1] /ɪkˈsɛntrɪk/ ***adj.*** (used about people or their behavior) strange or unusual: *People said he was crazy, but I think he was just slightly eccentric.* ▸ **ec·cen·tric·i·ty** /ˌɛksɛnˈtrɪsət̬i/ ***noun*** [C,U] (*pl.* **ec·cen·tric·i·ties**)

**ec·cen·tric**[2] /ɪkˈsɛntrɪk/ ***noun*** [C] an eccentric person: *She is quite an eccentric.*

**ec·cle·si·as·ti·cal** /ɪˌkliziˈæstɪkl/ ***adj.*** connected with the Christian church: *ecclesiastical law*

**ECG** /ˌi si ˈdʒi/ (*also* **EKG**) ***noun*** [C] (*medical*) the abbreviation for "electrocardiogram"; a medical test that measures and records electrical activity of the heart

**ech·o**[1] /ˈɛkoʊ/ ***noun*** [C] (*pl.* **ech·oes**) a sound that is repeated as it is sent back off a surface such as the wall of a cave: *If you shout across the valley, you'll hear an echo of your own voice.*

**ech·o**[2] /ˈɛkoʊ/ ***verb*** **1** [I] (used about a sound) to be repeated; to come back as an echo: *Their footsteps echoed in the empty church.* **2** [T] to repeat sth that sb else has said: *Citizens' groups have echoed the governor's call for tougher drug laws.* **3** [I] **echo (with sth)** (used about places) to be full of a particular sound: *The valley echoed with their laughter.*

**é·clair** (*also* **ec·lair**) /eɪˈklɛr; i-/ ***noun*** [C] a long thin cake for one person, made of light pastry, filled with cream and usually with chocolate on top: *a chocolate éclair*

**e·clipse**[1] /ɪˈklɪps/ ***noun*** [C] **1** an occasion when the moon passes between the earth and the sun or the earth's shadow falls on the moon, cutting off all or some of the light: *a total/partial eclipse of the sun* **2** the loss of a person's importance, success, etc.

**e·clipse**[2] /ɪˈklɪps/ ***verb*** [T] **1** (used about the moon, etc.) to cause an eclipse of the sun, etc. **2** (used about a person) to make another person seem less interesting, important, etc.

**eco-** /ˈikoʊ/ ***prefix*** connected with the environment: *eco-friendly* ◇ *eco-warriors* (= people who protest about damage to the environment)

**e·col·o·gist** /ɪˈkɑlədʒɪst/ ***noun*** [C] a expert in ecology

**e·col·o·gy** /ɪˈkɑlədʒi/ ***noun*** [U] the relations between living things and their surroundings; the study of this subject ▸ **ec·o·log·i·cal** /ˌikəˈlɑdʒɪkl; ˌɛkə-/ ***adj.***: *an ecological disaster* ◇ *Environmentalists have tried to make people aware of ecological issues.* ▸ **ec·o·log·i·cal·ly** ***adv.***

**e-com·merce** /ˈi ˌkɑmərs/ ***noun*** [U] = E-BUSINESS (1)

★**ec·o·nom·ic** /ˌɛkəˈnɑmɪk; ˌikə-/ ***adj.*** (only *before* a noun) connected with the supply of money, trade, industry, etc.: *economic policy* ◇ *The country faces growing economic problems.* ➲ Compare **economical**. It has a different meaning. ▸ **ec·o·nom·i·cal·ly** /-kli/ ***adv.***: *The country was very underdeveloped economically.*

**ec·o·nom·i·cal** /ˌɛkəˈnɑmɪkl; ˌikə-/ ***adj.*** not costing much time, money, fuel, etc.; using sth carefully: *an economical car to drive* ◇ *The company felt it wouldn't be economical to expand.* ➲ Compare **economic**. It has a different meaning. ▸ **ec·o·nomi·cal·ly** /-kli/ ***adv.***: *The business could be run more economically.*

**ec·o·nom·ics** /ˌɛkəˈnɑmɪks; ˌikə-/ ***noun*** [U] the study or principles of the way money, trade and industry are organized: *a bachelor's degree in economics* ◇ *the economics of a company* ➲ Look also at **home economics**.

**e·con·o·mist** /ɪˈkɑnəmɪst/ ***noun*** [C] an expert in economics

**e·con·o·mize** /ɪˈkɑnəmaɪz/ ***verb*** [I] **economize (on sth)** to save money, time, resources, etc.; to use less of sth

★**e·con·o·my**[1] /ɪˈkɑnəmi/ ***noun*** (*pl.* **e·con·o·mies**) **1** [C] (*also* **the economy**) the operation of a country's money supply, trade and industry: *The economy of the country is based on agriculture.* ◇ *There are signs of improvement in the economy.* ◇ *the economies of the United States and Canada* **2** [U] careful spending of money, time, resources, etc.; trying to save, not waste sth: *For reasons of economy, please turn off all unnecessary lights.*

**e·con·o·my**[2] /ɪˈkɑnəmi/ ***adj.*** (only *before* a noun) that helps you to save money because it is cheaper to use: *You should buy the large economy-size box of detergent – it costs less per ounce than the small box.* ◇ *an economy car* ◇ *an economy-class airline ticket*

**e·co·sys·tem** /ˈikoʊˌsɪstəm/ ***noun*** [C] all the plants and living creatures in a particular area considered in relation to their physical environment

**e·co·tour·ism** /ˌikoʊˈtʊrɪzəm/ ***noun*** [U] organized vacations that are designed so that the tourists damage the environment as little as possible, especially when some of the money they pay is used to protect the local environment and animals: *Ecotourism is financing rainforest preservation.* ▸ **e·co·tour·ist** /ˌikoʊˈtʊrɪst/ ***noun*** [C]

**ec·sta·sy** /ˈɛkstəsi/ ***noun*** [U] a feeling or state of great happiness: *to be in ecstasy*

**ec·stat·ic** /ɪkˈstæt̬ɪk/ ***adj.*** extremely happy

**ec·u·men·i·cal** /ˌɛkyəˈmɛnɪkl/ ***adj.*** connected with the idea of uniting all the different parts of the Christian Church

**ec·ze·ma** /ˈɛksəmə; ˈɛgzəmə; ɪgˈzimə/ ***noun*** [U] a disease which makes the skin red and sore

**ed·dy** /ˈɛdi/ ***noun*** [C] (*pl.* **ed·dies**) a circular movement of water, wind, dust, etc.

★**edge**[1] /ɛdʒ/ ***noun*** [C] **1** the place where sth, especially a surface, ends; the limit: *the edge of a table* ◇ *The leaves were brown and curling at the edges.* ◇ *I stood at the water's edge.* **2** the sharp cutting part of a knife, etc. ➲ Look also at **cutting edge**.

IDM **an/the edge on/over sb/sth** a slight advantage over sb/sth: *She knew she had an edge over the other candidates.*

**(be) on edge** (to be) nervous, excited or quick to become angry: *I'm a little on edge because I get my report card today.* ➲ Look at **edgy**. It has a similar meaning.

**edge**[2] /ɛdʒ/ ***verb*** **1** [I,T] **edge (sth/your way) across, along, away, back, etc.** to move (sth) slowly and carefully across, etc.: *The burglar edged his way along the roof.* ◇ *We edged closer to get a better view.* ◇ *She edged her chair up to the window.* **2** [I] to increase or decrease by a small amount: *Unemployment edged up by 0.2% to 4.6% in January.* **3** [T] (usually passive) **edge sth (with sth)** to arrange sth along the edge of sth else: *The cloth was edged with lace.*

**edge·wise** /ˈɛdʒwaɪz/ ***adv.***

IDM **get a word in edgewise** → WORD[1]

**edg·y** /ˈɛdʒi/ ***adj.*** (*informal*) nervous, worried or quick to become upset: *You seem awfully edgy. What's bothering you?*

**ed·i·ble** /ˈɛdəbl/ ***adj.*** good or safe to eat: *Are these mushrooms edible?* OPP **inedible**

**ed·i·fice** /ˈɛdəfəs/ ***noun*** [C] (*formal*) a large impressive building: *an imposing edifice from the 19th century*

**ed·it** /ˈɛdət/ ***verb*** [T] **1** to prepare a piece of writing to be published, making sure that it is correct, the right length, etc. **2** to prepare a movie or a television or radio program by arranging filmed material in a particular order **3** to be in charge of a newspaper, magazine, etc.

★**e·di·tion** /ɪˈdɪʃn/ ***noun*** [C] **1** the form in which a book is published: *a paperback/hardcover edition* **2** one of a series of television or radio programs: *And now for this week's edition of the nation's top news program...* **3** the number of copies of a book, etc. that are printed at the same time: *the morning edition of a newspaper*

★**ed·i·tor** /ˈɛdət̬ər/ ***noun*** [C] **1** a person whose job is to prepare a book, television or radio program **2** the person who is in charge of a newspaper or part of a newspaper: *Who is the editor of the school newspaper?*

**ed·i·to·ri·al**[1] /ˌɛdəˈtɔriəl/ ***noun*** [C] an article in a newspaper, usually written by the editor, giving an opinion on an important subject

**ed·i·to·ri·al**[2] /ˌɛdəˈtɔriəl/ ***adj.*** connected with the work of an editor, especially in a newspaper: *the editorial pages*

★**ed·u·cate** /ˈɛdʒəkeɪt/ ***verb*** [T] to teach or train sb, especially in school: *Young people should be educated to care for their environment.* ◇ *All their children were educated at private schools.*

**ed·u·cat·ed** /ˈɛdʒəkeɪt̬əd/ ***adj.*** having learned a lot of things to a high standard: *a highly educated woman*

★**ed·u·ca·tion** /ˌɛdʒəˈkeɪʃn/ ***noun*** [C, usually sing., U] the teaching or training of people, especially in schools, etc. to improve their knowledge and develop their skills: *elementary and secondary education* ◇ *She received an excellent education.*

★**ed·u·cational** /ˌɛdʒəˈkeɪʃənl/ ***adj.*** connected with or providing education: *an educational toy/visit/experience*

**ed·u·ca·tor** /ˈɛdʒəkeɪt̬ər/ ***noun*** [C] (*formal*) a teacher

**EEG** /ˌi i ˈdʒi/ ***noun*** [C] (*medical*) the abbreviation for "electroencephalogram", a medical test that measures and records electrical activity in the brain

**eel** /il/ ***noun*** [C] a long fish that looks like a snake

**ee·rie** /ˈɪri/ ***adj.*** strange and frightening ▸ **ee·ri·ly** ***adv.***

★**ef·fect**[1] /ɪˈfɛkt/ ***noun*** **1** [C,U] **(an) effect (on sb/sth)** a change that is caused by sth; a result: *the effects of acid rain on the lakes and forests* ◇ *His words had a strong effect on me.* ◇ *Her shouting had little or no effect on him.* ➲ Look at **aftereffect** and **side effect**. **2** [C,U] the impression that a speaker, book, movie, etc. gives: *How does the artist create the effect of moonlight?* ◇ *He likes to say things just for effect* (= to impress people). **3 effects** (*formal*) your personal possessions

IDM **come into effect** (used especially about laws or rules) to begin to be used; to come into operation

**in effect 1** (used to describe how a situation really is, especially if it appears to be different): *Although they haven't made an official announcement, she is, in effect, the new director.* **2** (used about a rule, a law, etc.) in operation; in use: *The new rules will be in effect starting next season.*

**take effect 1** (used about a drug, etc.) to begin to work; to produce the desired result: *The anesthetic took effect immediately.* **2** (used about a law, etc.) to come into operation: *The cease-fire takes effect at midnight.*

**to this/that effect** with this/that meaning: *I told him to leave her alone, or words to that effect.*

**ef·fect**[2] /ɪˈfɛkt/ ***verb*** [T] (*formal*) to cause sth to happen; to have sth as a result: *to effect a change* ➲ Look at **affect**. It has a different meaning.

★**ef·fec·tive** /ɪˈfɛktɪv/ ***adj.*** **1** producing the result that you want: *Scientists are looking for an effective way to reduce energy consumption.* ◇ *a medicine that is effective against the common cold*

OPP **ineffective** **2** real or actual, although perhaps not official: *The soldiers gained effective control of the town.* ▸ **ef·fec·tive·ness** ***noun*** [U]

★**ef·fec·tive·ly** /ɪˈfɛktɪvli/ ***adv.*** **1** in an effective way: *She dealt with the situation effectively.* **2** (used to describe how a situation really is, especially if it appears to be different): *It meant that, effectively, they had lost.*

**ef·fem·i·nate** /ɪˈfɛmənət/ ***adj.*** (used about a man or his behavior) like a woman

E

★**ef·fi·cient** /ɪˈfɪʃnt/ ***adj.*** able to work well without making mistakes or wasting time and energy: *Our secretary is very efficient.* ◇ *You need to find a more efficient way of organizing your time.* ◇ *a fuel-efficient car* (= one that does not use much fuel) OPP **inefficient** ▸ **ef·fi·cien·cy** /ɪˈfɪʃnsi/ ***noun*** [U] ▸ **ef·fi·cient·ly** ***adv.***

**ef·flu·ent** /ˈɛfluənt/ ***noun*** [U] liquid waste, especially chemicals produced by factories

★**ef·fort** /ˈɛfərt/ ***noun*** **1** [U] the use of strength or energy: *They have put a lot of effort into their group project.* ◇ *He made no effort to contact his parents.* **2** [C] something that is done with difficulty or the use of energy: *It was a real effort to stay awake during class.*

**ef·fort·less** /ˈɛfərtləs/ ***adj.*** (apparently) needing little or no effort ▸ **ef·fort·less·ly** ***adv.***

★**EFL** /ˌi ɛf ˈɛl/ ***abbr.*** English as a Foreign Language; (the subject of) the English language when it is taught in countries where most people do not speak English ➲ Compare **ESL**.

**e.g.** /ˌi ˈdʒi/ ***abbr.*** for example

**e·gal·i·tar·i·an** /ɪˌɡæləˈtɛriən/ ***adj.*** (used about a person, system, society, etc.) following the principle that everyone should have equal rights

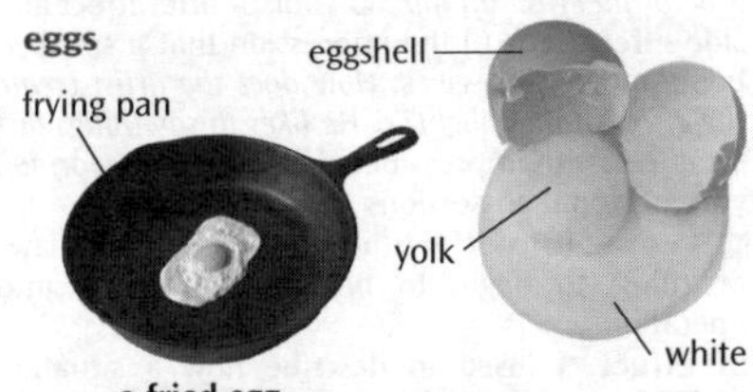

a fried egg

★**egg¹** /ɛɡ/ ***noun*** **1** [C] an oval object with a hard shell that contains a young bird, reptile or insect

> NOTE A female bird **lays** her eggs and then **sits on** them until they **hatch**.

**2** [C,U] an egg from a chicken, etc., used as food: *We had bacon and eggs for breakfast.*

> NOTE Eggs may be **hard-boiled** (until the yolk is solid), **soft-boiled** (so that the yolk is still soft), **fried**, **poached** (cooked in water without their shells) or **scrambled**. Eggs can be **fried** in several different ways. ➲ Look at **over easy/medium/hard** and **sunny-side up**.

**3** [C] the small cell in a female animal or a woman that can join with a male cell (a **sperm**) to make a baby

IDM **have/get egg on your face** (*informal*) to be made to look stupid: *They were left with egg on their faces when only ten people showed up.*

**put all your eggs in one basket** to risk everything by depending completely on one thing, plan, etc.

**egg²** /ɛɡ/ ***verb***

PHR V **egg sb on (to do sth)** to encourage sb to do sth (bad or dangerous)

**egg·plant** /ˈɛɡplænt/ ***noun*** [C,U] a long vegetable with dark purple skin ➲ picture on study page **A28-29**.

ˈ**egg roll** ***noun*** [C] a type of Chinese food consisting of a tube of thin pastry filled with vegetables and/or meat and fried until it is crisp

**egg·shell** /ˈɛɡʃɛl/ ***noun*** [C,U] the hard outside part of an egg ➲ picture at **egg**.

**e·go** /ˈiɡoʊ/ ***noun*** [C] (*pl.* **e·gos**) the (good) opinion that you have of yourself: *It was a blow to her ego when she lost her job.*

**e·go·cen·tric** /ˌiɡoʊˈsɛntrɪk/ ***adj.*** interested only in yourself; selfish

**e·go·tism** /ˈiɡətɪzəm/ ***noun*** [U] thinking about yourself too much; selfishness ▸ **e·go·tis·ti·cal** /ˌiɡəˈtɪstɪkl/ ***adj.***

**eh** /eɪ/ ***interjection*** (*informal*) (used for asking sb to agree with you): *"Good party, eh?"*

**EI** /ˌi ˈaɪ/ ***abbr.*** (*Cdn*) = EMPLOYMENT INSURANCE

**eight** /eɪt/ ***number*** 8; one more than seven ➲ For examples of how to use numbers in sentences, look at **six**.

**eight-** /eɪt/ ***prefix*** (in compounds) having eight of sth: *an eight-hour workday*

**eight·een** /eɪˈtin/ ***number*** 18; one more than seventeen ➲ For examples of how to use numbers in sentences, look at **six**. ▸ **eight·eenth** /ˌeɪˈtinθ/ ***pronoun, det., adv.*** ➲ Look at the examples at **sixth**.

**eighth¹** /eɪtθ/ ***pronoun, det., adv.*** 8th; next after seventh ➲ Look at the examples at **sixth**.

**eighth²** /eɪtθ/ ***noun*** [C] the fraction ⅛; one of eight equal parts of sth

ˈ**eighth note** ***noun*** [C] (*symbol* ♪) (in music) a note that lasts half as long as a quarter note ➲ picture at **music**.

**eight·y** /ˈeɪt̬i/ ***number*** 80; one more than seventy-nine ➲ For examples of how to use numbers in sentences, look at **sixty**. ▸ **eight·i·eth** /ˈeɪt̬iəθ/ ***pronoun, det., adv.*** ➲ Look at the examples at **sixth**.

★**ei·ther¹** /ˈiðər; ˈaɪðər/ ***det., pronoun*** **1** one or the other of two; it does not matter which: *There's cake or ice cream. You can have either.* ◇ *You can ask either of us for advice.* ◇ *Either of us is willing to help.*

> NOTE **Either** is used with a singular verb, but in spoken informal English a plural verb can be used after **either of** and a plural noun: *Either of us are willing to help.*

**2** both: *It is a pleasant road, with trees on either side.*

★**ei·ther²** /ˈiðər; ˈaɪðər/ ***conj.*** **either...or...** (used when you are giving a choice, usually of two things): *You can get the jacket in either black or blue.* ◇ *Either you leave or I do.* ◇ *You can either write or call.*

★**ei·ther**[3] /ˈiðər; ˈaɪðər/ ***adv.*** **1** (used after two negative statements) also: *I don't like Pat and I don't like Nick very much either.* ◇ *"I can't remember his name." "I can't either."*

> NOTE In the last example, we can also say **neither can I** or **me neither**. In very informal situations, some people also say **me either**.

**2** (used for emphasizing a negative statement): *The restaurant is pretty good – and it's not too expensive either.*

**e·jac·u·late** /ɪˈdʒækyəleɪt/ ***verb*** [I] to send out liquid (semen) from the male sex organ (penis) ▸ **e·jac·u·la·tion** /ɪˌdʒækyəˈleɪʃn/ ***noun*** [C,U]

**e·ject** /ɪˈdʒɛkt/ ***verb*** **1** [T] to push or send sb/sth out of a place (usually with force): *The protesters were ejected from the building.* **2** [I] to make an emergency exit from an airplane

**eke** /ik/ ***verb***

IDM **eke out a living** to manage to live with very little money

**EKG** /ˌi keɪ ˈdʒi/ (*also* **ECG**) ***noun*** [C] (*medical*) the abbreviation for "electrocardiogram"; a medical test that measures and records electrical activity of the heart

**e·lab·o·rate**[1] /ɪˈlæbərət; -brət/ ***adj.*** very complicated; done or made very carefully: *elaborate plans*

**e·lab·o·rate**[2] /ɪˈlæbəreɪt/ ***verb*** [I] **elaborate (on sth)** (*formal*) to give details about sth

**e·lapse** /ɪˈlæps/ ***verb*** [I] (*formal*) (used about time) to pass

**e·las·tic**[1] /ɪˈlæstɪk/ ***noun*** **1** [U] material with rubber in it which can stretch **2** [C] (*especially Cdn*) = RUBBER BAND

**e·las·tic**[2] /ɪˈlæstɪk/ ***adj.*** **1** (used about material, etc.) able to return to its original size after being stretched **2** (*figurative*) able to be changed; not fixed: *Our rules are fairly elastic.*

**e·lat·ed** /ɪˈleɪt̬əd/ ***adj.*** (*formal*) very happy and excited ▸ **e·la·tion** /ɪˈleɪʃn/ ***noun*** [U]

★**el·bow**[1] /ˈɛlboʊ/ ***noun*** [C] **1** the place where the arm bends in the middle **2** the part of the sleeve of a coat, jacket, etc. that covers the ELBOW (1) ➲ picture on study page **A32**.

IDM **rub elbows/shoulders with sb** → RUB[1]

**el·bow**[2] /ˈɛlboʊ/ ***verb*** [T] to push sb/sth with the elbows: *She elbowed me out of the way to get to the food first.*

ˈ**elbow grease** ***noun*** [U] the effort used in physical work, especially in cleaning or polishing sth: *Using the right tool can save a lot of elbow grease.*

ˈ**elbow room** ***noun*** [U] enough space to move freely

**eld·er**[1] /ˈɛldər/ ***adj.*** (*formal*) (only *before* a noun) older (of two members of a family): *my elder sister*

> NOTE **Older** is more common and less formal than **elder**.

**eld·er**[2] /ˈɛldər/ ***noun*** **1** [sing.] (*formal*) the older of two people: *Who is the elder of the two?*

> NOTE **Older** is more common and less formal than **elder**.

**2 elders** [pl.] older people

★**eld·er·ly** /ˈɛldərli/ ***adj.*** (used about a person) old

> NOTE This is a polite way of saying "old." You can use **the elderly** to refer to old people in general: *health care for the elderly.*

**eld·est** /ˈɛldəst/ ***adj.***, ***noun*** [C] (*formal*) oldest (of three or more members of a family): *Their eldest child is a boy.*

> NOTE **Oldest** is more common and less formal than **eldest**.

★**e·lect** /ɪˈlɛkt/ ***verb*** **1** [T] **elect sb (to sth)**; **elect sb (as sth)** to choose a President, Prime Minister, senator, representative, an MP, etc. by voting: *He was elected to Congress in 2001.* ◇ *The committee elected her as their representative.* **2** [I] **elect to do sth** (*formal*) to decide to do sth

★**e·lec·tion** /ɪˈlɛkʃn/ ***noun*** [C,U] (the time of) choosing a member of Congress, Parliament, a Prime Minister, President, etc. by voting: *I will not be running for election again.* ◇ *After many years of dictatorship, the government finally allowed free elections.*

> NOTE In the U.S., **presidential elections** are held every four years in November. Sometimes state and local elections are held at other times. In Canada, national and provincial elections are held every 3-5 years. Voters choose from a list of **candidates** who are usually members of **political parties**. ➲ Look at study pages **A10-A11**.

**e·lec·tive**[1] /ɪˈlɛktɪv/ ***noun*** [C] a school or college course that you can choose to take if you want to: *I'm taking three core courses plus two electives this semester.* ➲ For more information on the U.S. educational system, look at study page **A8**.

**e·lec·tive**[2] /ɪˈlɛktɪv/ ***adj.*** (used about a job, position, etc.) for which there is an election

**e·lec·tor·al** /ɪˈlɛktərəl/ ***adj.*** connected with elections or an election: *the electoral process*

**the eˌlectoral ˈcollege** (*also* **the Eˌlectoral ˈCollege**) ***noun*** [sing.] (*U.S.*) a group of people who represent all the people that vote in each state, who meet to choose the next President and Vice President

**e·lec·tor·ate** /ɪˈlɛktərət/ ***noun*** [C] all the people who can vote in a district, state, country, etc.

★**e·lec·tric** /ɪˈlɛktrɪk/ ***adj.*** **1** producing or using electricity: *an electric current* ◇ *an electric drill* **2** (*figurative*) very emotional: *The atmosphere in the room was electric.*

★**e·lec·tri·cal** /ɪˈlɛktrɪkl/ ***adj.*** of or about electricity: *an electrical appliance* (= a machine that uses electricity) ◇ *an electrical engineer* (= a person who produces electrical systems and equipment)

**the eˈlectric ˌchair** ***noun*** [sing.] a special chair that is used for putting criminals to death with a very strong electric current: *to be sent to the electric chair*

**e·lec·tri·cian** /ɪˌlɛkˈtrɪʃn/ ***noun*** [C] a person whose job is to install and repair electrical systems and equipment

★**e·lec·tric·i·ty** /ɪˌlɛkˈtrɪsət̬i/ ***noun*** [U] a type of energy that provides heat, light and power to work machines, etc.: *Turn that light off. We don't want to waste electricity.*

E

NOTE Electricity is usually **generated** in **power plants**. It may also be produced by **generators** or by **batteries** (e.g. in portable radios or flashlights).

**e͵lectric ˈshock** (*also* **e͵lectrical ˈshock, shock**) ***noun*** [C] the effect on the body when an electric current goes through it: *That light switch isn't safe. I got an electric shock when I touched it.*

**e·lec·tri·fy** /ɪˈlɛktrəfaɪ/ ***verb*** [T] (*pres. part.* **e·lec·tri·fy·ing**; *3rd person sing. pres.* **e·lec·tri·fies**; *pt, pp* **e·lec·tri·fied**) **1** to supply sth with electricity: *an electrified fence* **2** (*figurative*) to make sb excited

**e·lec·tro·car·di·o·gram** /ɪˌlɛktroʊˈkɑrdiəgræm/ ***noun*** [C] (*abbr.* **ECG**; **EKG**) (*medical*) a medical test that measures and records electrical activity of the heart

**e·lec·tro·cute** /ɪˈlɛktrəkyut/ ***verb*** [T] (usually passive) to kill sb with an electric current that passes through the body: *A worker was electrocuted while trying to repair a power cable.* ▸ **e·lec·tro·cu·tion** /ɪˌlɛktrəˈkyuʃn/ ***noun*** [U]

**e·lec·trode** /ɪˈlɛktroʊd/ ***noun*** [C] one of two points (**terminals**) where an electric current enters or leaves a battery, etc.

**e·lec·tro·en·ceph·a·lo·gram** /ɪˌlɛktroʊɪnˈsɛfələgræm/ ***noun*** [C] (*medical*) = EEG

**e·lec·tron** /ɪˈlɛktrɑn/ ***noun*** [C] a very small piece of matter with a negative electric charge that is found in all atoms ➲ Look also at **neutron** and **proton**.

★**e·lec·tron·ic** /ɪˌlɛkˈtrɑnɪk; ˌilɛk-/ ***adj.*** using electronics: *electronic equipment* ◇ *This dictionary is available in electronic form* (= on a computer disk). ▸ **e·lec·tron·i·cal·ly** /-kli/ ***adv.***

**elec͵tronic ˈmail** ***noun*** [U] = E-MAIL

**e·lec·tron·ics** /ɪˌlɛkˈtrɑnɪks/ ***noun*** [U] the technology of using electricity and very small parts (**chips**) in equipment such as computers, radios, etc.: *the electronics industry*

★**el·e·gant** /ˈɛləgənt/ ***adj.*** showing style or good design: *She looked very elegant in her new dress.* ◇ *an elegant coat* ▸ **el·e·gance** /ˈɛləgəns/ ***noun*** [U] ▸ **el·e·gant·ly** ***adv.***

★**el·e·ment** /ˈɛləmənt/ ***noun***

➤ PART/AMOUNT **1** [C] one important part of sth: *Cost is an important element when we're thinking about our vacation.* **2** [C, usually sing.] **an element of sth** a small amount of sth: *There was an element of truth in what he said.*

➤ GROUP OF PEOPLE **3** [C] people of a certain type: *the criminal element in our society*

➤ CHEMISTRY **4** [C] one of the most basic chemical substances, e.g. iron, oxygen, gold, etc.

➤ ELECTRICAL PART **5** [C] the part of an electric oven, an electric heater, etc. that produces heat

➤ WEATHER **6 the elements** [pl.] (*formal*) (bad) weather

IDM **in your element/out of your element** in a situation where you feel comfortable/uncomfortable

**el·e·men·ta·ry** /ˌɛləˈmɛntəri; -ˈmɛntri/ ***adj.*** **1** at or in the beginning stages: *an elementary course in English* **2** basic; not difficult: *elementary physics*

**eleˈmentary school** (*also* **ˈgrade school**, (*U.S. old-fashioned*) **ˈgrammar school**) ***noun*** [C] a school for children who are about five to twelve years old ➲ For more information on the North American educational systems, look at study pages **A8-A9**.

**elephant**

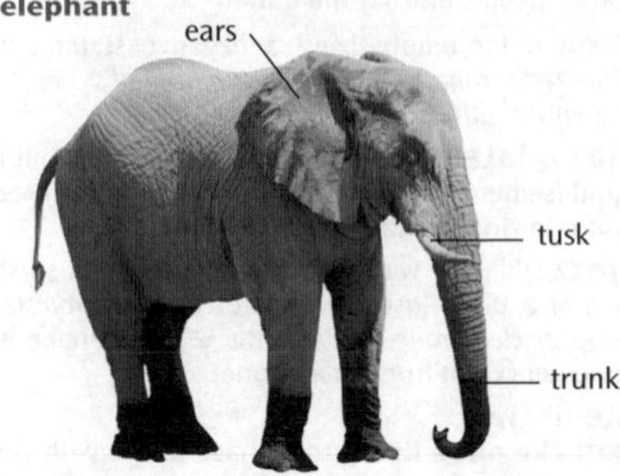


**el·e·phant** /ˈɛləfənt/ ***noun*** [C] a very large gray animal with two long curved teeth (**tusks**) and a long nose (a **trunk**)

**el·e·vate** /ˈɛləveɪt/ ***verb*** [T] (*formal*) to raise sb/sth to a higher place or position: *an elevated highway* ◇ *He was elevated to the Board of Directors.*

**el·e·va·tion** /ˌɛləˈveɪʃn/ ***noun*** **1** [C,U] (*formal*) elevating or being elevated **2** [C] the height of a place (above sea level): *The city is at an elevation of 5,000 feet.*

★**el·e·va·tor** /ˈɛləveɪt̬ər/ ***noun*** [C] a machine in a building that is used for carrying people or goods from one floor to another: *It's on the fifth floor, so we'd better* ***take the elevator.***

**e·lev·en** /ɪˈlɛvən/ ***number*** 11, one more than ten ➲ For examples of how to use numbers in sentences, look at **six**. ▸ **e·lev·enth** /ɪˈlɛvənθ/ ***pronoun, det., adv.*** ➲ Look at the examples at **sixth**.

**elf** /ɛlf/ ***noun*** [C] (*pl.* **elves** /ɛlvz/) (in stories) a small creature with pointed ears who has magic powers

**e·lic·it** /ɪˈlɪsət/ ***verb*** [T] **elicit sth (from sb)** (*formal*) to get information, facts, a reaction, etc. from sb

**el·i·gi·ble** /ˈɛlɪdʒəbl/ ***adj.*** **eligible (for sth/to do sth)** having the right qualifications for sth; suitable: *In Canada, you are eligible to vote when you are eighteen.* ◇ *an eligible young man* (= a man who might be a suitable husband)

**e·lim·i·nate** /ɪˈlɪməneɪt/ ***verb*** [T] **1** to remove sb/sth that is not wanted or needed: *We must try and eliminate waste.* **2** (often passive) to stop sb from going further in a competition, etc.: *The team was eliminated in the first round of the playoffs.* ▸ **e·lim·i·na·tion** /ɪˌlɪməˈneɪʃn/ ***noun*** [U]: *They picked a restaurant by* ***process of elimination*** (= by eliminating the ones they did not like and picking what was left).

**e·lite** /ɪˈlit; eɪ-/ ***noun*** [C, with sing. or pl. verb] a social group that is thought to be the best or most important because of its power, money, intelligence, etc.: *the ruling elite* ◇ *an intellectual elite* ▸ **e·lite** ***adj.*** (only *before* a noun): *an elite military unit*

**e·lit·ism** /ɪˈlit̬ɪzəm; eɪ-/ ***noun*** [U] **1** a way of organizing a system, society, etc. so that only a few people (an elite) have power or influence: *Many people believe that private education encourages elitism.* **2** the feeling of being better than other people that being part of an elite encourages ▸ **e·lit·ist** /-t̬ɪst/ *noun* [C], *adj.*

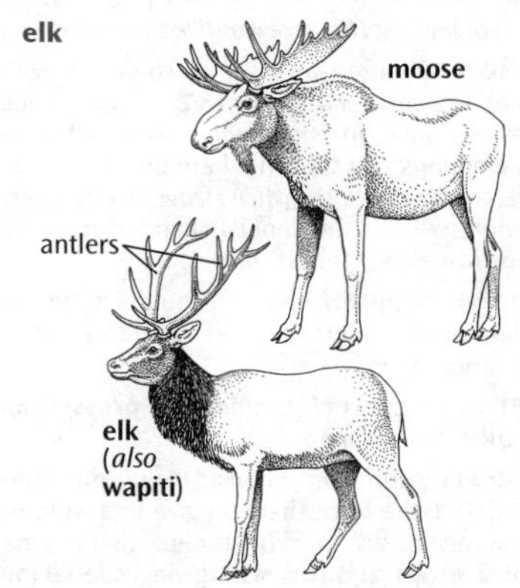


**elk** /ɛlk/ (*also* **wap·i·ti**) *noun* [C] (*pl.* **elk** or **elks**) a large deer that lives in North America

**elm** /ɛlm/ (*also* **'elm tree**) *noun* [C] a tall tree with broad leaves

**e·lon·gat·ed** /ɪ'lɔŋgeɪt̬əd/ *adj.* long and thin

**e·lope** /ɪ'loʊp/ *verb* [I] **elope (with sb)** to run away secretly to get married

**el·o·quent** /'ɛləkwənt/ *adj.* (*formal*) able to speak well and influence other people ▸ **el·o·quence** /'ɛləkwəns/ *noun* [U] ▸ **el·o·quent·ly** *adv.*

★**else** /ɛls/ *adv.* (used after words formed with *any-*, *no-*, *some-* and after question words) **1** in addition: *What else would you like?* ◇ *Does anybody else* (= any other person) *know about this?* **2** different: *There's nothing on TV. Let's find something else to do.* ◇ *This isn't mine. It must be somebody else's* (= belong to another person). ◇ *You'll have to pay. Nobody else* (= no other person) *will.* **3** apart from: *Everybody else* (= everybody apart from me) *has gone.*

IDM **or else 1** otherwise; if not: *You'd better go to bed now or else you'll be tired in the morning.* ◇ *He either forgot or else decided not to come.* **2** (*informal*) (used to express a threat or a warning): *Give us the money or else!*

★**else·where** /'ɛlswɛr/ *adv.* (*formal*) in or to another place: *If she doesn't like it here, she can go elsewhere.* ◇ *He's traveled a lot – in Europe and elsewhere.*

**e·lude** /ɪ'lud/ *verb* [T] (*formal*) **1** to escape (from sb/sth) (sometimes by using a trick) **2** to be difficult or impossible to remember: *I remember his face, but his name eludes me.*

**e·lu·sive** /ɪ'lusɪv/ *adj.* not easy to find, catch or remember

**elves** *noun* [C] *plural of* ELF

**'em** /əm/ *pronoun* (*informal*) = THEM

**e·ma·ci·at·ed** /ɪ'meɪʃieɪt̬əd/ *adj.* (used about a person) thin and weak because of illness, lack of food, etc.

★**'e-mail**[1] (*also* **e·mail**) /'imeɪl/ (*also* **elec,tronic 'mail**) *noun* **1** [U] the system of sending electronic messages from one computer to another: *The results were sent* **by e-mail**. **2** [C,U] a message or messages sent by e-mail: *He sent me more than 20 e-mails.* ◇ *I read my e-mail before I start work in the morning.*

**'e-mail**[2] (*also* **e·mail**) /'imeɪl/ *verb* [I,T] to send a message to sb by e-mail: *I'll e-mail you with the information.*

**e·man·ci·pate** /ɪ'mænsəpeɪt/ *verb* [T] to give sb the same legal, social and political rights as other people ▸ **e·man·ci·pa·tion** /ɪˌmænsə'peɪʃn/ *noun* [U]

**em·bank·ment** /ɪm'bæŋkmənt/ *noun* [C] a thick wall of earth, stone, etc. that is built to stop a river from overflowing or to carry a road or railroad

**em·bar·go** /ɪm'bɑrgoʊ/ *noun* [C] (*pl.* **em·bar·goes**) an official order to stop trade with another country: *to impose an oil embargo* ◇ *to lift/remove the embargo on foreign oil*

**em·bark** /ɪm'bɑrk/ *verb* [I]

PHR V **embark on sth** (*formal*) to start sth (new): *I'm embarking on a completely new career.*

★**em·bar·rass** /ɪm'bærəs/ *verb* [T] to make sb feel ashamed or uncomfortable: *Why do you always embarrass me in front of my friends?* ▸ **em·bar·rass·ing** *adj.*: *an embarrassing mistake* ▸ **em·bar·rass·ing·ly** *adv.*

★**em·bar·rassed** /ɪm'bærəst/ *adj.* feeling ashamed or uncomfortable: *He was too embarrassed to talk about what had happened.*

★**em·ba·r·rass·ment** /ɪm'bærəsmənt/ *noun* **1** [U] the feeling you have when you are embarrassed **2** [C] a person or thing that makes you embarrassed

★**em·bas·sy** /'ɛmbəsi/ *noun* [C] (*pl.* **em·bas·sies**) (the official building of) a group of people (**diplomats**) headed by an ambassador, who are sent to live in a foreign country and represent their government there ➲ Look at **consulate**.

**em·bed** /ɪm'bɛd/ *verb* [T] (**em·bed·ding**; **em·bed·ded**) (usually passive) to fix sth firmly and deeply (in sth else): *The ax was embedded in the piece of wood.*

**em·ber** /'ɛmbər/ *noun* [C, usually pl.] a piece of wood or coal that is not burning, but is still red and hot after a fire has died

**em·bez·zle** /ɪm'bɛzl/ *verb* [T] to steal money, etc. that you are responsible for (e.g. in a business or an organization) ▸ **em·bez·zle·ment** *noun* [U]

**em·blem** /'ɛmbləm/ *noun* [C] an object or a symbol that represents sth: *a T-shirt with the team's emblem on it*

**em·bod·y** /ɪm'bɑdi/ *verb* [T] (*pres. part.* **em·bod·y·ing**; *3rd person sing. pres.* **em·bod·ies**; *pp, pt* **em·bod·ied**) (*formal*) **1** to be a very good example of sth: *To me she embodies all the best qualities of a teacher.* **2** (often passive) to include or contain sth: *the ideas and values embodied in the U.S. Constitution*

**em·brace**[1] /ɪm'breɪs/ *verb* **1** [I,T] (*written*) to take sb into your arms as a sign of love or affection

NOTE **Hug** is less formal.

**2** [T] (*formal*) to accept sth eagerly: *She embraced Christianity in her later years.*

**em·brace²** /ɪmˈbreɪs/ ***noun*** [C] the act of EMBRACING¹ (1) sb: *a warm embrace*

**em·broi·der** /ɪmˈbrɔɪdər/ ***verb*** [T] to decorate cloth by sewing with small stitches

**em·broi·der·y** /ɪmˈbrɔɪdəri/ ***noun*** [U] decorative sewing with small stitches; something that has been embroidered

E

**em·bry·o** /ˈɛmbrioʊ/ ***noun*** [C] (*pl.* **em·bry·os** /-oʊz/) an animal or a plant in the early stages of development before birth ➲ Look at **fetus**. ▸ **em·bry·on·ic** /ˌɛmbriˈɑnɪk/ ***adj.***

**em·cee¹** /ˌɛmˈsi/ ***noun*** [C] a person who introduces the different performers in a show at a theater or on television and talks to the audience

**em·cee²** /ˌɛmˈsi/ ***verb*** [T] (*pres. part.* **em·cee·ing**; *pt, pp* **em·ceed**) to act as an EMCEE¹ at a show

**em·er·ald¹** /ˈɛmərəld/ ***noun*** [C] a bright green precious stone

**em·er·ald²** /ˈɛmərəld/ (*also* **ˌemerald ˈgreen**) ***adj.*** bright green

⋆**e·merge** /ɪˈmərdʒ/ ***verb*** [I] **emerge (from sth)** **1** to appear or come from somewhere (unexpectedly): *A man emerged from the shadows.* ◇ (*figurative*) *She is likely to emerge as the top candidate for the job.* **2** to become known: *During investigations, it emerged that he was lying about his age.* ▸ **e·mer·gence** /-dʒəns/ ***noun*** [U]

⋆**e·mer·gen·cy** /ɪˈmərdʒənsi/ ***noun*** [C,U] (*pl.* **e·mer·gen·cies**) a serious event that needs immediate action: *In an emergency, dial 911 for help.* ◇ *The government has declared a state of emergency.* ◇ *an emergency exit*

**eˈmergency brake** ***noun*** [C, usually sing.] **1** (*also* **parking brake**) a device in a car, etc. that is used when the car is not moving to prevent it from rolling down a hill **2** a device in a train, etc. that you can pull in an emergency to stop the train from moving

⋆**eˈmergency room** ***noun*** [C] (*abbr.* **ER**) the part of a hospital where people who have been injured in accidents or who are very sick are taken for immediate treatment

**em·i·grant** /ˈɛməgrənt/ ***noun*** [C] a person who has gone to live in another country ➲ Compare **immigrant**.

⋆**em·i·grate** /ˈɛməgreɪt/ ***verb*** [I] to leave your own country to go and live in another one: *They emigrated to Australia twenty years ago.* ▸ **em·i·gra·tion** /ˌɛməˈgreɪʃn/ ***noun*** [C,U] ➲ Compare **immigrate** and **immigration**.

**em·i·nent** /ˈɛmənənt/ ***adj.*** (*formal*) (used about a person) famous and important: *an eminent scientist*

**em·i·nent·ly** /ˈɛmənəntli/ ***adv.*** (*formal*) obviously; very: *She is eminently qualified for the job.*

**e·mit** /ɪˈmɪt/ ***verb*** [T] (**e·mit·ting**; **e·mit·ted**) (*formal*) to send out sth (a smell, a sound, smoke, heat, light, etc.) ▸ **e·mis·sion** /ɪˈmɪʃn/ ***noun*** [C,U]: *controls on hazardous emissions from factories*

**e·mo·ti·con** /ɪˈmoʊt̬ikɑn/ ***noun*** [C] a symbol that you can use in an e-mail to show your feelings about what you are writing

NOTE Common emoticons are :-) to show a smile, :-( for a frown and ;-) for a wink. You shouldn't use an emoticon in a formal e-mail.

⋆**e·mo·tion** /ɪˈmoʊʃn/ ***noun*** **1** [C] a strong feeling such as love, anger, fear, jealousy, etc. **2** [U] strength of feeling: *His voice was filled with emotion.*

⋆**e·mo·tion·al** /ɪˈmoʊʃənl/ ***adj.*** **1** connected with the emotions: *emotional problems* **2** causing strong feelings: *He gave an emotional speech.* **3** having strong emotions and showing them openly: *She always gets really emotional when I leave.* ◇ *He's a very emotional person* (= his moods change suddenly). ▸ **e·mo·tion·al·ly** /-ʃənəli/ ***adv.***

**em·pa·thy** /ˈɛmpəθi/ ***noun*** [U] the ability to imagine how another person is feeling and so understand his/her mood

**em·per·or** /ˈɛmpərər/ (*feminine* **em·press**) ***noun*** [C] the ruler of an empire

⋆**em·pha·sis** /ˈɛmfəsəs/ ***noun*** [C,U] (*pl.* **em·pha·ses** /-əsiz/) **1** the force that you give to a word or phrase when you are speaking to show that it is important **2 emphasis (on sth)** (giving) special importance or attention (to sth): *There's a lot of emphasis on science at our school.* ◇ *We should really put a greater emphasis on getting our facts right.*

⋆**em·pha·size** /ˈɛmfəsaɪz/ ***verb*** [T] **emphasize (that...)** to put emphasis on sth; stress: *They emphasized that healthy eating is important.* ◇ *They emphasized the importance of healthy eating.*

**em·phat·ic** /ɛmˈfæt̬ɪk/ ***adj.*** having or using emphasis: *an emphatic refusal* ▸ **em·phat·i·cal·ly** /-kli/ ***adv.***

⋆**em·pire** /ˈɛmpaɪər/ ***noun*** [C] **1** a group of countries that is governed by one country: *the Roman Empire* ➲ Look at **emperor** and **empress**. **2** a group of companies or businesses that is controlled by one parent company or by one person or group: *a publishing empire*

**em·pir·i·cal** /ɪmˈpɪrɪkl; ɛm-/ ***adj.*** (*formal*) based on experiments or practical experience rather than ideas or theories: *empirical evidence/knowledge/research*

⋆**em·ploy** /ɛmˈplɔɪ/ ***verb*** [T] **1 employ sb (in/on sth)**; **employ sb (as sth)** to pay sb to work for you: *He is employed in a chocolate factory.* ◇ *She is employed as a truck driver.* ◇ *They employ 600 workers.* ➲ Look at **unemployed**. **2 employ sb/sth (in/on) sth** (*formal*) to use sb/sth: *a factory that employs modern techniques in the manufacturing process*

⋆**em·ploy·ee** /ɛmˈplɔɪi; ˌɛmplɔɪˈi/ ***noun*** [C] a person who works for sb: *These restrooms are for employees only.* ◇ *federal and state employees* (= of the federal and state governments)

⋆**em·ploy·er** /ɛmˈplɔɪər/ ***noun*** [C] a person or company that employs other people: *My health insurance is paid for by my employer.*

⋆**em·ploy·ment** /ɛmˈplɔɪmənt/ ***noun*** [U] **1** the state of having a paid job: *She is looking for employment.* ◇ *It is difficult to find employment in rural areas.* ➲ Look at **unemployment** and at the note at **work¹**. **2** (*formal*) the use of sth: *the employment of force*

**em'ployment ˌagency** ***noun*** [C] (*pl.* **employment agencies**) a business that helps people to find work

**em'ployment inˌsurance** ***noun*** [U] (*abbr.* **EI**) (*Cdn*) a type of insurance system that is run by the Canadian government, which pays money regularly to people who are out of work

**em·pow·er** /ɪm'paʊər/ ***verb*** [T] to give sb power or authority (to do sth), or to make sb feel that he/she can do more things ▶ **em·pow·er·ment** ***noun*** [U]

**em·press** /'ɛmprəs/ ***noun*** [C] **1** a woman who rules an empire **2** the wife of an emperor

★**emp·ty¹** /'ɛmpti/ ***adj.*** **1** having nothing or nobody inside it: *an empty box* ◇ *The bus was half empty.* ◇ *That house has been empty for months.* **2** without meaning or value: *It was **an empty threat*** (= it was not meant seriously). ◇ *My life feels empty now that the kids have left home.* ▶ **emp·ti·ness** ***noun*** [U]

★**emp·ty²** /'ɛmpti/ ***verb*** (*pres. part.* **emp·ty·ing**; *3rd person sing. pres.* **emp·ties**; *pt, pp* **emp·tied**) **1** [T] **empty sth (out)** to make sth empty: *Just empty your cup into the sink.* ◇ *Empty your pockets out.* **2** [T] **empty sth (out) (into/onto sth)** to take sth from a container and put it somewhere else: *Empty that milk into the sink. It's sour.* ◇ *The boy emptied out all his toys onto the floor.* **3** [I] to become empty: *The theater emptied very quickly once the movie was over.*

**ˌempty-'handed** ***adj.*** bringing or taking nothing: *She went out to buy a new dress but returned empty-handed.*

**em·u·late** /'ɛmyəleɪt/ ***verb*** [T] (*formal*) to try and do sth as well as, or better than, sb SYN A less formal word is **copy**.

★**en·a·ble** /ɛ'neɪbl/ ***verb*** [T] **enable sb/sth to do sth** to make sb/sth able to do sth (by giving him/her/it power, authority, etc.): *Computer technology enables us to predict the weather more accurately.*

**e·nam·el** /ɪ'næml/ ***noun*** [U] **1** a hard, shiny substance used for protecting or decorating metal, etc.: *enamel paint* **2** the hard white outer covering of a tooth

**en·chant·ed** /ɪn'tʃæntəd/ ***adj.*** **1** (especially in children's stories) under the influence of special magic words (a spell): *an enchanted forest* **2** pleased or delighted: *The little girl was competely enchanted with the dollhouse.*

**en·chant·ing** /ɪn'tʃæntɪŋ/ ***adj.*** very nice or pleasant; delightful

**en·chi·la·da** /ˌɛntʃə'lɑdə/ ***noun*** [C] a Mexican dish consisting of a special kind of flat bread (a tortilla) filled with meat and/or cheese and covered with a spicy sauce

IDM **the big enchilada** (*informal*) the most important person or thing

**the whole enchilada** (*informal*) the whole thing; everything: *When she gets married, she wants a white gown, six bridesmaids, flowers – the whole enchilada.*

**en·cir·cle** /ɪn'sərkl/ ***verb*** [T] (*formal*) to make a circle around sth; to surround sth: *The building was completely encircled by police.*

**encl.** (*also* **enc.**) ***abbr.*** (*written*) (used on business letters to show that another document is being sent in the same envelope) = ENCLOSURE (2)

★**en·close** /ɪn'kloʊz/ ***verb*** [T] **1 enclose sth (in/with sth)** to surround sth with a wall, fence, etc.: *The yard is enclosed by a tall fence.* ◇ *He gets very nervous in enclosed spaces.* **2** to put sth in an envelope, package, etc.: *Can I enclose a letter with this package?*

**en·clo·sure** /ɪn'kloʊʒər/ ***noun*** [C] **1** a piece of land that is enclosed by a wall, fence, etc. **2** (*abbr.* **encl.**) something that is enclosed in an envelope, package, etc.

**en·core¹** /'ɑnkɔr/ ***interjection*** (called out by an audience that wants the performers in a play, concert, etc. to perform sth extra)

**en·core²** /'ɑnkɔr/ ***noun*** [C] an extra performance at the end of a play, concert, etc.

★**en·coun·ter¹** /ɪn'kaʊntər/ ***verb*** [T] **1** (*formal*) to meet sb unexpectedly **2** to experience sth (a danger, difficulty, etc.): *I've never encountered any discrimination at work.* SYN **Meet with** is used as a synonym for encounter in this sense.

**en·coun·ter²** /ɪn'kaʊntər/ ***noun*** [C] an unexpected (often unpleasant) meeting

★**en·cour·age** /ɪn'kərɪdʒ/ ***verb*** [T] **1 encourage sb/sth (in sth/to do sth)** to give hope, support or confidence to sb: *The teacher encouraged her students to ask questions.* ◇ *His friends encouraged him in his attempt to stop smoking.* OPP **discourage**

> NOTE Note that we say **discourage sb from doing sth**: *The teacher discouraged her students from asking questions.*

**2** to make sth happen more easily: *The city wants to encourage investment in the area.* ▶ **en·cour·age·ment** ***noun*** [C,U] ▶ **en·cour·ag·ing** ***adj.***

**en·croach** /ɪn'kroʊtʃ/ ***verb*** [I] (*formal*) **encroach (on/upon sth) 1** to use more of sth than you should: *Students' extracurricular activities must not encroach on the time their studies demand.* **2** to slowly begin to cover more and more of an area: *The growing town began to encroach upon the surrounding countryside.*

**en·cy·clo·pe·di·a** /ɛnˌsaɪklə'pidiə/ ***noun*** [C] (*pl.* **en·cy·clo·pe·di·as**) a book or set of books that gives information about many subjects, arranged in alphabetical order (i.e. from A to Z). Some encyclopedias are also available on CD-ROM so they can be used in a computer.

★**end¹** /ɛnd/ ***noun*** [C] **1** the furthest or last part of sth; the place or time where sth stops: *the end of a road/room/piece of string* ◇ *Go to the end of the line.* ◇ *My house is at the end of the street.* ◇ *The man on the other end of the phone spoke so quietly that I didn't catch his name.* ◇ *There are some seats at the far end of the room.* ◇ *I'm going on vacation at the end of October.* ◇ *He promised to give me an answer by the end of the week.* ◇ *She couldn't wait to hear the end of the story.*

> NOTE **End** is sometimes used before another noun: *the end house* ◇ *the end seat.* ➲ Look at the noun **finish**. It is used to mean **end** only in connection with races and competitions. ➲ Look also at **rear end**.

**2** (*formal*) an aim or purpose: *They were prepared to do anything to achieve their ends.*
IDM **at an end** (*formal*) finished or used up: *Her career is at an end.*
**at the end of your rope** having no more patience or strength
**bring sth/come/draw to an end** (to cause sth) to finish: *The summer is coming to an end.*
**a dead end** → DEAD[1]
**end to end** in a line with the ends touching: *They put the tables end to end.*
**in the end** at last; finally: *He wanted to get home early, but in the end it was midnight before he left.*
**loose ends** → LOOSE
**make ends meet** to have enough money for your needs: *It's hard for us to make ends meet.*
**odds and ends** → ODDS
**on end** (used about time) continuously: *He sits and reads for hours on end.*
**put an end to sth** to stop sth from happening any more
**the short end of the stick** → SHORT[1]

★**end**[2] /ɛnd/ ***verb*** [I,T] **end (in/with sth)** (to cause sth) to finish: *The road ends here.* ◇ *How does this story end?* ◇ *Most adverbs in English end in "-ly."* ◇ *I think we'd better end this conversation now.*
PHRV **end up (as sth); end up (doing sth)** to find yourself in a place/situation that you did not intend or expect: *We got lost and ended up in a bad part of town.* ◇ *She had always wanted to be a writer but ended up as a teacher.* ◇ *There was nothing to eat at home so we ended up ordering a pizza.*

**en·dan·ger** /ɪn'deɪndʒər/ ***verb*** [T] to cause danger to sb/sth: *Smoking endangers your health.*

**en·dan·gered** /ɪn'deɪndʒərd/ ***adj.*** (used about animals, plants, etc.) in danger of disappearing from the world (**becoming extinct**): *The panda is an endangered species.*

**en·dear·ing** /ɪn'dɪrɪŋ/ ***adj.*** very pleasing and easy to like: *Mike's playful sense of humor is one of his most endearing qualities.*

**en·deav·or**[1] /ɪn'dɛvər/ ***verb*** [I] (*formal*) **endeavor (to do sth)** to try: *She endeavored to make the best of a very difficult situation.*

**en·deav·or**[2] /ɪn'dɛvər/ ***noun*** [C,U] (*formal*) effort, or an act of trying to do sth: *remarkable advances in every area of human endeavor* ◇ *We wish you every success in your future endeavors.*

★**end·ing** /'ɛndɪŋ/ ***noun*** [C] **1** the end (of a story, play, movie, etc.): *a story with a happy ending* **2** (*grammar*) the last part of a word, which can change: *When nouns end in -ch or -sh or -x, the plural ending is -es, not -s.*

**end·less** /'ɛndləs/ ***adj.*** without end: *Our plane was delayed for hours and the wait seemed endless.* ▸ **end·less·ly** ***adv.***

**en·dorse** /ɪn'dɔrs/ ***verb*** [T] **1** to give (official) support or agreement to a candidate or a plan, statement, decision, etc.: *The auto workers' union has endorsed the Democratic candidate for President.* **2** to say in an advertisement that you use and like a product: *professional athletes who endorse sneakers on TV* **3** to sign your name on the back of a check ▸ **en·dorse·ment** ***noun*** [C,U]

'**end ˌproduct** ***noun*** [C] something that is produced by a particular process or activity: *The two alternative processes arrive at the same end product.*

**en·dur·ance** /ɪn'dʊrəns/ ***noun*** [U] the ability to endure(1) sth: *The competition will test your strength and endurance.*

**en·dure** /ɪn'dʊr/ ***verb*** (*formal*) **1** [T] to suffer sth painful or uncomfortable: *She endured ten years of loneliness.* **2** [I] to last; to continue: *Mozart died long ago, but his music endures.*

**en·dur·ing** /ɪn'dʊrɪŋ/ ***adj.*** lasting for a long time: *enduring memories* ◇ *an enduring relationship* ◇ *the game's enduring appeal*

'**end zone** ***noun*** [C] an area at each end of a football field, where players must carry the ball in order to score points (**touchdowns**) ➲ picture at **football**.

★**en·e·my** /'ɛnəmi/ ***noun*** (*pl.* **en·e·mies**) **1** [C] a person who hates and tries to harm sb/sth: *The former friends became* ***bitter enemies****.* ◇ *He has* ***made*** *several* ***enemies*** *since his arrival at the school.* ➲ noun enmity **2 the enemy** the army or country that your country is fighting against: *The enemy is attacking at dawn.*

**en·er·get·ic** /ˌɛnər'dʒɛt̬ɪk/ ***adj.*** full of or needing ENERGY(1): *Running is a very energetic form of exercise.* ▸ **en·er·get·i·cal·ly** /-kli/ ***adv.***

**en·er·gize** /'ɛnərdʒaɪz/ ***verb*** [T] to give energy to sb/sth: *Her speech energized the audience members.*

★**en·er·gy** /'ɛnərdʒi/ ***noun*** (*pl.* **en·er·gies**) **1** [U] the ability to be very active or do a lot of work without getting tired: *Children are usually full of energy.* ◇ *This flu has left me with no energy at all.* **2 energies** [pl.] the effort and attention which you give to doing sth: *She devoted all her energies to helping the homeless.* **3** [U] the power that comes from coal, electricity, gas, etc. that is used for driving machines, etc.: *nuclear energy*

**en·force** /ɪn'fɔrs/ ***verb*** [T] **1** to make sure that laws, etc. are obeyed: *How will they enforce the new law?* **2** to force sth to be done or to happen: *Enforcing discipline by using threats is not often successful.* ▸ **en·force·ment** ***noun*** [U] ➲ Look also at **law enforcement**.

★**en·gage** /ɪn'geɪdʒ/ ***verb*** [T] **1** to fill sb's thoughts, time, interest, etc.: *You need to engage the students' attention right from the start.* **2** to make parts of a machine fit together: *Be sure that the emergency brake is engaged before leaving the car.*
PHRV **engage in sth** to take part in sth: *to engage in illegal activities*

★**en·gaged** /ɪn'geɪdʒd/ ***adj.*** **1 engaged (to sb)** having agreed to get married: *We just got engaged.* ◇ *Susan is engaged to Jim.* **2** (*formal*) (used about a person) busy or occupied with sth: *Sorry, I can't come. I'm* ***otherwise engaged****.*

**en·gage·ment** /ɪn'geɪdʒmənt/ ***noun*** [C] **1** an agreement to get married; the time when you are engaged: *Their engagement was announced in the paper.* ◇ *Their engagement only lasted for six months.* ◇ *He broke off their engagement.* **2** (*formal*) an arrangement to go somewhere or do sth at a fixed time; an appointment

**en'gagement ring** ***noun*** [C] a ring, usually with

precious stones in it, that a man gives to a woman when they get ENGAGED (1)

★**en·gine** /'ɛndʒən/ ***noun*** [C] **1** the part of a machine that changes energy (from oil, electricity, etc.) into movement: *This engine runs on diesel.* ◇ *an automobile engine* ➲ Look at the note at **motor**. **2** (*also* **locomotive**) a machine that pulls a train

★**en·gi·neer¹** /ˌɛndʒə'nɪr/ ***noun*** [C] **1** a person whose job is to use science and math in practical ways, e.g. to design machines, roads, bridges, etc., or to plan processes in factories, etc.: *a civil/chemical/mechanical engineer* **2** a person whose job is to drive a train

**en·gi·neer²** /ˌɛndʒə'nɪr/ ***verb*** [T] **1** (*formal*) to arrange for sth to happen by careful (secret) planning: *Her promotion was engineered by her father.* **2** (often passive) to change the structure of sth, often in order to make it work or develop in a different way: *strawberry plants that have been genetically engineered to produce bigger fruit*

★**en·gi·neer·ing** /ˌɛndʒə'nɪrɪŋ/ ***noun*** [U] (the study of) the work that is done by an ENGINEER¹ (1): *a degree in engineering* ➲ Look also at **genetic engineering**.

**Eng·lish¹** /'ɪŋglɪʃ/ ***noun*** **1** [U] the language that is spoken in the U.S., Canada, Britain and in some other countries: *Do you speak English?* ◇ *I've been learning English for five years.* ◇ *How do you say "perro" in English?* **2 the English** [pl.] the people of England

**Eng·lish²** /'ɪŋglɪʃ/ ***adj.*** from or connected with England: *My friend Simon is English.* ◇ *English history*

**NOTE** Be careful. The people of Scotland (the Scots) and of Wales (the Welsh) are **British**, not English. ➲ Look at the note at **United Kingdom**.

ˌ**English 'Canada** ***noun*** [sing.] the areas of Canada where English-speaking Canadians (anglophones) are in the majority ➲ Compare **French Canada**.

**en·grave** /ɪn'greɪv/ ***verb*** [T] **engrave B on A/ engrave A with B** to cut patterns or words on metal, stone, etc.: *His name is engraved on the plaque.* ◇ *The plaque is engraved with his name.*

**en·grav·ing** /ɪn'greɪvɪŋ/ ***noun*** [C] a picture that is printed from an engraved metal plate

**en·grossed** /ɪn'groʊst/ ***adj.*** **engrossed (in sth)** very interested in sth so that you forget other things: *She was completely engrossed in her book.*

**en·gulf** /ɪn'gʌlf/ ***verb*** [T] **engulf sb/sth (in sth)** to surround or cover sb/sth completely (with sth): *Flames quickly engulfed the entire house.*

**en·hance** /ɪn'hæns/ ***verb*** [T] (*formal*) to improve sb/sth or to make sb/sth look better: *computer techniques that enhance images* ◇ *the skilled use of make-up to enhance your best features* ▶ **en·hance·ment** ***noun*** [C,U]

**e·nig·ma** /ɪ'nɪgmə/ ***noun*** [C] (*pl.* **e·nig·mas**) a person, thing or situation that is strange or difficult to understand ▶ **en·ig·ma·tic** /ˌɛnɪg'mætɪk/ ***adj.***

★**en·joy** /ɪn'dʒɔɪ/ ***verb*** [T] **1 enjoy sth/enjoy doing sth** to get pleasure from sth: *I really enjoyed that meal.* ◇ *Do you enjoy your work?* ◇ *He enjoys listening to music while he's driving.* **2 enjoy yourself** to be happy; to have a good time: *I enjoyed myself at Sue's party last night – did you?*

★**en·joy·a·ble** /ɪn'dʒɔɪəbl/ ***adj.*** giving pleasure: *We spent an enjoyable few days at the beach.*

★**en·joy·ment** /ɪn'dʒɔɪmənt/ ***noun*** [C,U] pleasure, or a thing which gives pleasure: *She gets a lot of enjoyment from traveling.*

**en·large** /ɪn'lɑrdʒ/ ***verb*** [I,T] (to cause sth) to become larger: *I'm going to have this picture enlarged.*

**en·large·ment** /ɪn'lɑrdʒmənt/ ***noun*** [C,U] making sth larger or sth that has been made larger: *an enlargement of a picture*

**en·light·en** /ɪn'laɪtn/ ***verb*** [T] to give sb more information about sth so that he/she knows the truth

**en·list** /ɛn'lɪst/ ***verb*** **1** [I,T] to join the army, navy or air force; to make sb a member of the army, etc. **2** [T] to get help, support, etc.: *We need to enlist the support of everybody who works here.*

**en·mi·ty** /'ɛnməṭi/ ***noun*** [U] the feeling of hatred toward an enemy

**e·nor·mi·ty** /ɪ'nɔrməṭi/ ***noun*** [sing.] (*formal*) the level of seriousness of sth; how bad sth is

★**e·nor·mous** /ɪ'nɔrməs/ ***adj.*** very large or very great: *an enormous building* ◇ *enormous pleasure* ◇ *There is an enormous amount of work involved in this.* ▶ **e·nor·mous·ly** ***adv.***

★**e·nough¹** /ɪ'nʌf/ ***det., pronoun*** **1** as much or as many of sth as necessary: *We've saved enough money to buy a computer.* ◇ *Not everybody can have a book – there aren't enough.* ◇ *Are there enough chairs?* ◇ *If enough of you are interested, we'll arrange a trip to the theater.* **2** as much or as many as you want: *Don't give me any more work. I have enough already.*

**IDM** **have had enough (of sth)** to be tired of sth and annoyed by it: *I've had enough of living in the city* (= I don't want to live in the city anymore).

★**e·nough²** /ɪ'nʌf/ ***adv.*** (used *after* verbs, adjectives and adverbs) to the necessary degree; sufficiently: *You don't practice enough.* ◇ *He's not old enough to travel alone.* ◇ *Does she speak Italian well enough to get the job?* ◇ *Are those shoes big enough for you, or do you need a larger size?*

**IDM** **fair enough** → FAIR²

**funnily, strangely, etc. enough** it is funny, etc. that...: *Funnily enough, I thought exactly the same thing myself.*

**sure enough** → SURE²

**en·raged** /ɪn'reɪdʒd/ ***adj.*** very angry

**en·rich** /ɪn'rɪtʃ/ ***verb*** [T] to improve the quality, flavor, etc. of sth: *These cornflakes are enriched with vitamins.*

**en·roll** /ɪn'roʊl/ ***verb*** [I,T] **enroll (sb) (in/as sth)** to become or to make sb a member of a club, school, etc.: *I enrolled in my local swimming class.* ◇ *They enrolled 100 new students last year.*

**en·roll·ment** /ɪn'roʊlmənt/ ***noun*** [C,U] the number of people who are members of a school, club, etc.: *Enrollment in this course is limited to twenty people.*

**en route** /ˌɑn'rut; ˌɛn-/ ***adv.*** **en route (from...)**

(**to...**) on the way: *The car broke down when we were en route to work.*

**en·sue** /ɪn'su/ **verb** [I] (*formal*) to happen after (and often as a result of) sth else

★**en·sure** /ɪn'ʃʊr/ (*also* **insure**) **verb** [T] (*formal*) to make sth certain to happen: *regulations to ensure that water supplies are safe to drink* ◇ *a plan that would ensure a victory in the election* SYN A less formal expression is **make sure (that)....**

E

**en·tail** /ɪn'teɪl/ **verb** [T] (*formal*) to make sth necessary; to involve sth: *This is going to entail a lot of hard work.* ◇ *What exactly does the job entail?*

**en·tan·gled** /ɪn'tæŋgəld/ **adj.** caught in sth: *The bird was entangled in the net.*

★**en·ter**[1] /'ɛntər/ **verb** **1** [I,T] (*formal*) to come or go into a place: *Don't enter without knocking.* ◇ *They all stood up when he entered the room.* ◇ (*figurative*) *We have just entered a new phase in international relations.*

NOTE Note that **enter** is used without a preposition. **Come into** and **go into** are much more common. ➲ Look also at **entrance**, **entrant** and **entry**.

**2** [T] **enter sth** to put your name on the list for an exam, a race, a competition, etc.: *I entered the Boston Marathon last year, but I didn't finish.* **3** [T] **enter sth (in/into/on sth)** to put names, numbers, etc. in a list, book, computer, etc.: *Your name has not been entered in our records.* ◇ *Enter your 4-digit code and press the "return" key.* **4** [T] to become a member of a school, a college, a profession, an institution, etc.: *She entered politics in 2000.*

PHR V **enter into sth (with sb)** to begin sth: *to enter into an agreement with another company*

**en·ter**[2] /'ɛntər/ **noun** = RETURN[2] (5)

**en·ter·prise** /'ɛntərpraɪz/ **noun** **1** [C] something (e.g. a plan or a project) that is new and difficult: *It's a very exciting new enterprise.* **2** [U] the courage that you need to start a new and difficult project: *We need men and women of enterprise and energy.* **3** [C,U] a business; the way business is organized: *a new industrial enterprise* ◇ *The government supports private enterprise.*

**en·ter·pris·ing** /'ɛntərpraɪzɪŋ/ **adj.** having ENTERPRISE (2): *an enterprising young manager* OPP **unenterprising**

★**en·ter·tain** /ˌɛntər'teɪn/ **verb** **1** [T] to interest and amuse sb: *He entertained us with jokes all evening.* ◇ *I find it very hard to keep my class entertained on a Friday afternoon.* **2** [I,T] to welcome sb as a guest; to give sb food and drink: *They entertain a lot./They do a lot of entertaining.*

★**en·ter·tain·er** /ˌɛntər'teɪnər/ **noun** [C] a person who ENTERTAINS (1) as a job

**en·ter·tain·ing** /ˌɛntər'teɪnɪŋ/ **adj.** interesting and amusing

★**en·ter·tain·ment** /ˌɛntər'teɪnmənt/ **noun** [U] things to do that interest and amuse people: *There isn't much entertainment for young people in this town.* ◇ *live entertainment* (= people singing/dancing in front of an audience)

**en·thrall** /ɪn'θrɔl/ **verb** [T] to hold sb's interest and attention completely: *He was enthralled by her story.* ▸ **en·thrall·ing** **adj.**

★**en·thu·si·asm** /ɛn'θuziæzəm/ **noun** [U] **enthusiasm (for/about sb/sth)** a strong feeling of eagerness or interest: *Jan showed great enthusiasm for the new project.*

**en·thu·si·ast** /ɛn'θuziæst/ **noun** [C] a person who is very interested in an activity or a subject: *She is a jazz enthusiast.*

★**en·thu·si·as·tic** /ɪnˌθuzi'æstɪk/ **adj.** full of enthusiasm ▸ **en·thu·si·as·ti·cal·ly** /-kli/ **adv.**

**en·tice** /ɪn'taɪs/ **verb** [T] to persuade sb to do sth by offering something nice: *Advertisements try to entice people into buying more things than they need.* ▸ **en·tice·ment** **noun** [C,U]

**en·tic·ing** /ɪn'taɪsɪŋ/ **adj.** attractive and making you want to do sth

★**en·tire** /ɪn'taɪər/ **adj.** (only *before* a noun) whole or complete: *the entire world* ◇ *We invited the entire class to the party.*

NOTE **Entire** is stronger than **whole**.

★**en·tire·ly** /ɪn'taɪərli/ **adv.** completely: *I entirely agree with you.*

**en·tire·ty** /ɪn'taɪrəṭi; ɛn'taɪərṭi/ **noun** [U]

IDM **in its entirety**; **in their entirety** (*formal*) as a whole: *We need to consider the problem in its entirety.*

★**en·ti·tle** /ɪn'taɪṭl/ **verb** [T] to give sb the right to have or do sth: *I think I'm entitled to a day off – I've worked hard enough.*

**en·ti·tled** /ɪn'taɪṭld/ **adj.** (used about books, plays, etc.) with the title: *The first song on the album is entitled "Common People."*

**en·ti·tle·ment** /ɪn'taɪṭlmənt/ **noun** **1** [C,U] **entitlement (to sth/to do sth)** a person's right to have or do sth: *employees' entitlements to paid vacation time* **2** (*also* **en'titlement ˌprogram**) [C] a government system or plan that makes money, food, etc. available to people because they are poor, over a certain age, etc.

**en·ti·ty** /'ɛntəṭi/ **noun** [C] (*pl.* **en·ti·ties**) something that exists separately from sth else: *The city and county governments are separate entities.*

★**en·trance** /'ɛntrəns/ **noun** **1** [C] the door, gate or opening where you go into a place: *I'll meet you at the entrance to the theater.* ➲ Look also at **entry** (3). It has a similar meaning. **2** [C] **entrance (into/onto sth)** the act of coming or going in: *He made a dramatic entrance onto the stage.* ➲ **Entry** can be used with the same meaning. **3** [U] **entrance (to sth)** the right to enter a place: *They were refused entrance to the nightclub.* ◇ *an entrance fee* SYN **entry** ➲ Look also at **admission** and **admittance**. **4** [U] **entrance (into/to sth)** the right to join a club, an institution, etc.: *You may not need to take an entrance exam to get into a university.* ➲ Look at **admission**.

**'entrance ramp** (*also* **'on-ramp**) **noun** [C] a road that leads onto a freeway or highway ➲ Look at the note at **freeway**.

**en·trant** /'ɛntrənt/ **noun** [C] a person who enters a competition, etc.

**en·trée** (*also* **entree**) /ˈɑntreɪ/ ***noun*** [C] the main course of a meal, especially in a restaurant

**en·tre·pre·neur** /ˌɑntrəprəˈnər; -ˈnʊr/ ***noun*** [C] a person who starts a business and often takes risks in order to become successful ▶ **en·tre·pre·neur·i·al** /ˌɑntrəprəˈnʊriəl/ ***adj.***: *entrepreneurial talent*

**en·trust** /ɪnˈtrʌst/ ***verb*** [T] **entrust A with B/entrust B to A** (*formal*) to make sb responsible for sth that is given to him/her: *I entrusted Rachel with the arrangements for the party./I entrusted the arrangements for the party to Rachel.*

★**en·try** /ˈɛntri/ ***noun*** (*pl.* **en·tries**)
➤ GOING IN **1** [C] **entry (into sth)** the act of coming or going in; entering(1): *The thieves forced an entry into the building.* SYN **entrance** **2** [U] **entry (to sth)** the right to enter a place: *an entry visa* SYN **entrance** ➲ Look at **admission** and **admittance**.
➤ DOOR/GATE **3** [C] a door, gate, passage, etc. where you enter a building, etc.; an entrance hall: *We stood in the entry of the building until the rain stopped.* SYN **Entrance** and **entryway** have similar meanings.
➤ WRITTEN INFORMATION **4** [C] **entry (in sth)** one item that is written down in a list, calendar, account book, dictionary, etc.: *You'll find "briskly" at the entry for "brisk."*
➤ IN COMPETITION **5** [C] **entry (for sth)** a person or thing that is entered for a competition, etc.: *There were 50 entries for the best apple pie at the fair.*

**ˈentry-ˌlevel** ***adj.*** (only *before* a noun) for people who are just beginning their career or some other activity: *an entry-level job*

**en·try·way** /ˈɛntriweɪ/ ***noun*** [C] an area, usually with a roof or a covering, that you go through to enter a place

**en·vel·op** /ɛnˈvɛləp/ ***verb*** [T] (*formal*) to cover or surround sb/sth completely (in sth): *The hills were enveloped in mist.*

★**en·ve·lope** /ˈɛnvəloʊp; ˈɑn-/ ***noun*** [C] the paper cover for a letter

> NOTE After writing a letter, you **address** the envelope, **seal** it and stick a stamp in the top right-hand corner. Sometimes when you answer an advertisement you are asked to send a **self-addressed stamped envelope**, i.e. an envelope that is addressed to yourself with a stamp on it.

**en·vi·ous** /ˈɛnviəs/ ***adj.*** **envious (of sb/sth)** feeling or showing that you want sth that sb else has: *She was envious of her sister's success.*

★**en·vi·ron·ment** /ɛnˈvaɪərnmənt/ ***noun*** **1** [C,U] the conditions in which you live, work, etc.: *A bad home environment can affect a child's progress in school.* **2 the environment** [sing.] the natural world, e.g. land, air, water, etc. in which people, animals and plants live: *We need stronger laws to protect the environment.* ▶ **en·vi·ron·men·tal** /ɛnˌvaɪərnˈmɛntl/ ***adj.***: *environmental science* ▶ **en·vi·ron·men·tal·ly** /-ˈmɛntəli/ ***adv.***: *environmentally sensitive areas*

**en·vi·ron·men·tal·ist** /ɛnˌvaɪərnˈmɛntəlɪst/ ***noun*** [C] a person who wants to protect the ENVIRONMENT (2)

**environˌmentally ˈfriendly** (*also* **enˌvironment-ˈfriendly**) ***adj.*** not harming the environment: *products with environmentally friendly packaging* ◇ *More people should try environmentally friendly ways of getting to work.*

**en·vi·rons** /ɪnˈvaɪrənz; -ˈvaɪərnz/ ***noun*** [pl.] (*formal*) a place and the area surrounding it: *things to do in Ontario and its environs* ◇ *A meeting was called to discuss changes to the campus and its environs.*

**en·vis·age** /ɪnˈvɪzɪdʒ/ ***verb*** [T] (*formal*) to imagine what will happen in the future: *I don't envisage any problems with this.*

**en·vi·sion** /ɛnˈvɪʒən/ ***verb*** [T] (*formal*) to think of sth as being possible in the future; to imagine sth: *I don't envision any problems.*

**en·voy** /ˈɛnvɔɪ; ˈɑn-/ ***noun*** [C] a person who is sent by a government with a message to another country

**en·vy¹** /ˈɛnvi/ ***noun*** [U] **envy (of sb/sth)** the feeling that you have when sb else has sth that you want: *It was difficult for her to hide her envy of her friend's success.* ➲ adjective **envious**
IDM **the envy of sb** the thing that causes sb to feel envy: *The city's school system is the envy of many of its neighbors.*
**green with envy** → GREEN¹

**en·vy²** /ˈɛnvi/ ***verb*** [T] (*pres. part.* **en·vy·ing**; *3rd person sing. pres.* **en·vies**; *pt, pp* **en·vied**) **envy sb/sth** to want sth that sb else has; to feel ENVY¹: *I've always envied your good luck.* ◇ *I don't envy the people who have to clean up after the party* (= I'm glad that I don't have to clean up).

**en·zyme** /ˈɛnzaɪm/ ***noun*** [C] a substance, usually produced by plants and animals, which helps a chemical change happen or happen more quickly, without being changed itself

**ep·ic¹** /ˈɛpɪk/ ***noun*** [C] a long book, poem, movie, etc. that describes exciting adventures

**ep·ic²** /ˈɛpɪk/ ***adj.*** of or like an EPIC¹: *an epic struggle*

**ep·i·cen·ter** /ˈɛpəˌsɛntər/ ***noun*** [C, usually sing.] the point on the Earth's surface that is directly over the point inside the Earth where a sudden, violent movement (an **earthquake**) begins

**ep·i·dem·ic** /ˌɛpəˈdɛmɪk/ ***noun*** [C] a large number of cases of people or animals suffering from the same disease at the same time: *A flu epidemic broke out in February.*

**ep·i·lep·sy** /ˈɛpəlɛpsi/ ***noun*** [U] a disease of the brain that can cause a person to become unconscious (sometimes with violent uncontrolled movements)

**ep·i·lep·tic¹** /ˌɛpəˈlɛptɪk/ ***adj.*** connected with or suffering from epilepsy: *an epileptic seizure* ◇ *She's epileptic.*

**ep·i·lep·tic²** /ˌɛpəˈlɛptɪk/ ***noun*** [C] a person who suffers from epilepsy

**the E·pis·co·pal Church** /ɪˌpɪskəpl ˈtʃərtʃ/ ***noun*** [sing.] a Protestant church that is connected with the official church of England

**E·pis·co·pa·lian** /ɪˌpɪskəˈpeɪliən/ ***adj.*** connected with the Episcopal Church ▶ **E·pis·co·pa·lian** ***noun*** [C]

**ep·i·sode** /ˈɛpəsoʊd/ ***noun*** [C] **1** one separate event in sb's life, a novel, etc.: *That's an episode in my life I'd rather forget.* **2** one part of a TV or radio drama that is broadcast in several parts (a series): *Don't miss tomorrow's exciting episode!*

**ep·i·taph** /ˈɛpətæf/ ***noun*** [C] words that are written or said about a dead person, especially words written on a gravestone

**e·pit·o·me** /ɪˈpɪt̬əmi/ ***noun*** [sing.] a perfect example of sth: *Paula is the epitome of the successful businesswoman.*

**e·pit·o·mize** /ɪˈpɪt̬əmaɪz/ ***verb*** [T] to be typical of sth

**ep·och** /ˈepək/ ***noun*** [C] a period of time in history (that is important because of special events, features, etc.)

**ep·si·lon** /ˈɛpsəlɑn/ ***noun*** [C] (*symbol* Ε, ϵ) the fifth letter of the Greek alphabet ➲ Look at the note at **fraternity**.

★**e·qual¹** /ˈikwəl/ ***adj.*** the same in size, amount, value, number, status, etc.: *They are equal in weight.* ◇ *They are of equal weight.* ◇ *Divide it into two equal parts.* ◇ *Employees will receive a bonus equal to one week's salary.* ◇ *Women are demanding equal pay for equal work.* ◇ *Our company adopted an Equal Opportunities policy* (= rules to make sure that people are treated equally). OPP **unequal**

IDM **on equal terms (with sb)** with the same advantages and disadvantages (as sb else)

**e·qual²** /ˈikwəl/ ***noun*** [C] a person who has the same ability, rights, etc. as you do: *to treat sb as an equal*

**e·qual³** /ˈikwəl/ ***verb*** [T] **1** to be or mean the same as sth: *44 plus 17 equals 61 is written: 44 + 17 = 61.* ◇ *Some people believe that money equals happiness.* **2 equal sb/sth (in sth)** to be as good as sb/sth: *He ran an excellent race, equaling the club record in the 400 meters.*

**e·qual·i·ty** /ɪˈkwɑlət̬i/ ***noun*** [U] the situation in which everybody has the same rights and advantages; being equal: *Absolute equality is probably impossible to achieve.* ◇ *racial equality* (= between people of different races) OPP **inequality**

**e·qual·ize** /ˈikwəlaɪz/ ***verb*** [I,T] to make things equal in size, level, etc.: *efforts to equalize the academic performance of boys and girls*

★**e·qual·ly** /ˈikwəli/ ***adv.*** **1** to the same degree or extent: *They both worked equally hard.* **2** in equal parts: *His money was divided equally among his three children.*

**e·quate** /ɪˈkweɪt/ ***verb*** [T] **equate sth (with sth)** to consider one thing as being the same as sth else: *It is a mistake to equate wealth with happiness.*

**e·qua·tion** /ɪˈkweɪʒn/ ***noun*** [C] (in mathematics) a statement that two quantities are equal: *Solve the equation 2x + 5 = 11.*

**the e·qua·tor** (*also* **the Equator**) /ɪˈkweɪt̬ər/ ***noun*** [sing.] the imaginary line around the earth at an equal distance from the North and South Poles: *on the equator* ➲ picture at **earth**.

**e·ques·tri·an** /ɪˈkwɛstriən/ ***adj.*** (*formal*) connected with horse riding

**e·quip** /ɪˈkwɪp/ ***verb*** [T] (**e·quip·ping**; **e·quipped**) **equip sb/sth (with sth) 1** (usually passive) to supply sb/sth with what is needed (for a particular purpose): *We will equip all schools with new computers in the next year.* ◇ *The schools in the suburbs are much better equipped than the ones in large cities.* ◇ *The car comes equipped with air conditioning and automatic transmission.* **2** to prepare sb for a particular task: *We were just not equipped to deal with the problem.*

★**e·quip·ment** /ɪˈkwɪpmənt/ ***noun*** [U] the things that are needed for carrying out a particular activity: *office equipment* ◇ *sports equipment* ◇ *Standard equipment in the car includes power steering and an airbag.*

> NOTE Note that **equipment** is uncountable. We have to say "a piece of equipment" if we are talking about one item: *a very useful piece of kitchen equipment.*

★**e·quiv·a·lent¹** /ɪˈkwɪvələnt/ ***adj.*** **equivalent (to sth)** equal in value, amount, meaning, importance, etc.: *The price of imported cars is higher than that of equivalent American models.* ◇ *Is the Canadian House of Commons roughly equivalent to the House of Representatives?* ▶ **e·quiv·a·lence** /-ləns/ ***noun*** [U] ▶ **e·quiv·a·len·cy** /-lənsi/ ***noun*** [C,U] (*pl.* **e·quiv·a·len·cies**)

**e·quiv·a·lent²** /ɪˈkwɪvələnt/ ***noun*** [C] something that is EQUIVALENT¹: *There is no English equivalent to the French "bon appetit."*

**ER** /ˌi ˈɑr/ ***abbr.*** = EMERGENCY ROOM

**e·ra** /ˈɪrə; ˈɛrə/ ***noun*** [C] a period of time in history (that is special for some reason): *We are living in the era of the computer.* ◇ *the Prohibition era*

**e·rad·i·cate** /ɪˈrædəkeɪt/ ***verb*** [T] (*formal*) to destroy sth completely ▶ **e·rad·i·ca·tion** /ɪˌrædəˈkeɪʃn/ ***noun*** [U]

**e·rase** /ɪˈreɪs/ ***verb*** [T] to remove sth (a pencil mark, a recording on tape, etc.): *Be sure to erase any mistakes completely.*

**e·ras·er** /ɪˈreɪsər/ ***noun*** [C] a piece of rubber or other material that you use to remove writing made with a pencil, chalk, etc.

**e·rect¹** /ɪˈrɛkt/ ***adj.*** **1** standing straight up; upright: *He stood with his head erect.* **2** (used about the male sexual organ) stiff and upright because of sexual excitement

**e·rect²** /ɪˈrɛkt/ ***verb*** [T] (*formal*) to build sth or to put sth in an upright position: *to erect a statue* ◇ *Huge TV screens were erected so that everybody could see what was going on.*

**e·rec·tion** /ɪˈrɛkʃn/ ***noun*** **1** [U] (*formal*) the act of putting sth in an upright position or of building sth **2** [C] the hardening of the male sexual organ in sexual excitement: *to get/have an erection*

**er·go·nom·ic** /ˌərgəˈnɑmɪk/ ***adj.*** designed to improve people's working conditions and to help them work more efficiently: *the ergonomic design and installation of computer screens* ▶ **er·go·nom·ic·al·ly** ***adv.***

**e·rode** /ɪˈroʊd/ ***verb*** [T] (usually passive) (used about the ocean, the weather, etc.) to destroy sth slowly: *The cliff has been eroded by the ocean waves.* ◇ (*figurative*) *Freedom of speech is being eroded.* ▶ **e·ro·sion** /ɪˈroʊʒn/ ***noun*** [U]: *the erosion of the coastline by the ocean*

**e·rot·ic** /ɪˈrɑt̬ɪk/ ***adj.*** causing sexual excitement: *an erotic video/poem*

**err** /ɛr; ər/ ***verb*** [I] (*formal*) to be or do wrong; to make mistakes: *It is better to **err on the side of caution*** (= it is better to be too careful rather than not careful enough).

**er·rand** /ˈɛrənd/ ***noun*** [C] a short trip to take or get sth for sb, e.g. to buy sth from a store: *to run an errand*

**er·rat·ic** /ɪˈræt̬ɪk/ ***adj.*** (used about a person's behavior, or about the quality of sth) changing without reason; that you cannot rely on: *Phil's moods became more erratic when he was under a lot of stress.* ▸ **er·rat·i·cal·ly** /-kli/ ***adv.***

★**er·ror** /ˈɛrər/ ***noun*** **1** [C] a mistake: *an error of judgment* ◇ *to make an error*

NOTE **Error** is more formal than **mistake**. There are some expressions, e.g. *error of judgment, human error* where only **error** can be used.

**2** [U] the state of being wrong in behavior or belief: *The letter was sent to you in error.* ◇ *The accident was the result of human error.*

IDM **trial and error** → TRIAL

**e·rupt** /ɪˈrʌpt/ ***verb*** [I] **1** (used about a volcano) to explode and throw out fire, rock that has melted (lava), etc. **2** (used about violence, anger, etc.) to start suddenly: *The demonstration erupted into violence.* **3** (used about people) to suddenly become very angry ▸ **e·rup·tion** /ɪˈrʌpʃn/ ***noun*** [C,U]

**es·ca·late** /ˈɛskəleɪt/ ***verb*** [I,T] **1** (to cause sth) to become stronger or more serious: *The demonstrations are escalating into violent protest in several cities.* **2** (to cause sth) to become greater or higher; to increase: *The cost of housing has escalated in recent years.* ▸ **es·ca·la·tion** /ˌɛskəˈleɪʃn/ ***noun*** [C,U]

**es·ca·la·tor** /ˈɛskəleɪt̬ər/ ***noun*** [C] a moving staircase in a store, etc.

★**es·cape**[1] /ɪˈskeɪp/ ***verb*** **1** [I] **escape (from sb/sth)** to get away from a place where you do not want to be; to get free: *to escape from prison* **2** [I] (used about gases or liquids) to find a way out of a container, etc. **3** [I,T] to be safe from sth; to avoid sth: *The two passengers were killed, but the driver escaped unhurt.* ◇ *to escape criticism* **4** [T] to be forgotten or not noticed by sb: *Her name escapes me.* ◇ *to escape sb's notice* (= not be noticed by sb)

★**es·cape**[2] /ɪˈskeɪp/ ***noun*** **1** [C,U] **escape (from sth)** the act of ESCAPING[1] (1,2,3): *Escape from Alcatraz Prison was impossible.* ◇ *She had **a narrow escape** when a truck crashed into her car* (= she was nearly killed or seriously hurt). **2** [C] a way, or sth that you can use, to escape: *a fire escape* **3** [U, sing.] something that helps you forget your daily life: *For him, listening to music is a means of escape.* ◇ *an escape from reality* **4** (*also* **es'cape key**) (*computing*) a button on a computer keyboard that you press to stop a particular operation or leave a program: *Press escape to get back to the main menu.*

**es·caped** /ɪˈskeɪpt/ ***adj.*** having ESCAPED[1] (1) from a place: *The escaped prisoners have not been recaptured.*

**es·cort**[1] /ˈɛskɔrt/ ***noun*** [C] **1** a person or vehicle (or group of people and vehicles) that goes with and protects sb/sth, or that goes with sb/sth as an honor: *a police escort* ◇ *He arrived **under** military **escort**.* **2** (*formal*) a companion for a particular social event

**es·cort**[2] /ɛsˈkɔrt/ ***verb*** [T] **1** to go with sb as an escort: *The governor's limousine was escorted by several police cars.* **2** to take sb somewhere: *Philip escorted her to the door.*

**Es·ki·mo** /ˈɛskəmoʊ/ ***noun*** [C] (*pl.* **Es·ki·mo** or **Es·ki·mos**) (*old-fashioned*) a member of a race of Aboriginal peoples living in Alaska, northern Canada, Greenland and Siberia

NOTE In Canada, the term **Eskimo** is considered offensive nowadays and is no longer used. These people are now officially referred to as **Inuit**, and their language as **Inuktitut**.

**ESL** /ˌi ɛs ˈɛl/ ***abbr.*** English as a Second Language; (the subject of) the English language when it is taught in countries where most people speak English, e.g. the U.S., Canada, or Britain, to people whose native language is not English ➲ Look at **EFL**.

★**es·pe·cial·ly** /ɪˈspɛʃəli/ ***adv.*** **1** (*abbr.* **esp.**) to an unusual degree; in particular: *She loves animals, especially dogs.* ◇ *The car is pretty small, especially if you have a big family.* **2** for a particular purpose: *I made this especially for you.*

NOTE **Specially** is also possible with this meaning. It is less formal.

**3** very (much): *Donna gave me an especially large piece of cake.* ◇ *"Do you like jazz?" "Not especially."*

**es·pi·o·nage** /ˈɛspiənɑʒ/ ***noun*** [U] the system of finding out secret information about another country or organization ➲ Look at **spy**.

**es·pres·so** /ɛˈsprɛsoʊ/ (*pl.* **es·pres·sos**) ***noun*** **1** [U] strong black coffee made by forcing steam through ground coffee **2** [C] a cup of espresso: *Two espressos, please.* ➲ Picture at **coffee**. ➲ Look at the note at **coffee**.

**es·say** /ˈɛseɪ/ ***noun*** [C] a short piece of writing about one subject: *Your assignment for Monday is to write a 250-word essay on this painting.*

NOTE A **paper** is usually longer than an **essay**.

**es·sence** /ˈɛsns/ ***noun*** [sing.] the basic or most important quality of sth: *The essence of the problem is that there is not enough money available.*

★**es·sen·tial**[1] /ɪˈsɛnʃl/ ***adj.*** absolutely necessary; that you must have or do: *Essential medical supplies will be delivered to the area by plane.* ◇ *Math is essential for a career in computers.* ◇ *It is essential that you have a high school diploma for this job.* ◇ *It is absolutely essential to have a passport to travel to the U.S.*

**es·sen·tial**[2] /ɪˈsɛnʃl/ ***noun*** [C, usually pl.] something that is necessary or very important: *food and other essentials such as clothing and heating*

★**es·sen·tial·ly** /ɪˈsɛnʃəli/ ***adv.*** basically; really: *The problem is essentially one of money.*

★**es·tab·lish** /ɪˈstæblɪʃ/ ***verb*** [T] **1** to start sth (especially an organization or institution): *The school was established in 1875.* **2** to make sth exist: *We need to establish good relations with the local residents.* **3** **establish sb/sth (as sth)** to place sb/sth in a position permanently: *She has been trying to* *get/become established as a novelist for several years.* **4** to decide sth: *We need to establish our aims before we can go any further.* **5** to make certain of sth; to prove sth: *The police are not able to establish where he was at the time of the murder.*

★**es·tab·lish·ment** /ɪˈstæblɪʃmənt/ ***noun*** **1** [C] (*formal*) a store or business **2 the establishment** [sing.] the people in positions of power in a country, who usually do not support change **3** [U] the act of starting or creating sth that is intended to last for a long time: *The speaker announced the establishment of a new college.*

E

★**es·tate** /ɪˈsteɪt/ ***noun*** [C] **1** a large area of land in the country that is owned by one person or family: *We visited George Washington's estate, Mount Vernon.* **2** all the money and property that sb leaves when he/she dies ➲ Look also at **real estate**.

**es·teem** /ɪˈstim/ ***noun*** [U] (*formal*) great respect; a good opinion of sb: *to hold sb in high esteem*

**es·thet·ic** = AESTHETIC

★**es·ti·mate¹** /ˈɛstəmət/ ***noun*** [C] **1** a guess or judgment about the size, cost, etc. of sth, before you have all the facts and figures: *Can you give me a rough estimate of how many people will be at the meeting?* **2** a written statement giving a price for a particular job that sb will do, e.g. building or fixing sth

★**es·ti·mate²** /ˈɛstəmeɪt/ ***verb*** [T] to calculate the size, cost, etc. of sth approximately, before you have all the facts and figures: *She estimated that the work would take three months.* ◇ *The police estimated the crowd at 10,000.* ◇ *Work on the new bridge will cost an estimated five million dollars.*

**es·ti·ma·tion** /ˌɛstəˈmeɪʃn/ ***noun*** [U] (*formal*) opinion or judgment

**es·tranged** /ɪˈstreɪndʒd/ ***adj.*** **1** no longer living with your husband/wife: *He's estranged from his wife.* ◇ *her estranged husband* **2** no longer friendly toward sb who used to be close to you, especially a member of your family

**e·ta** /ˈeɪt̬ə/ ***noun*** [C] (*symbol* Η, η) the seventh letter of the Greek alphabet ➲ Look at the note at **fraternity**.

**etc.** ***abbr.*** et cetera; and so on, and other things of a similar kind: *cars, trucks, vans, etc.*

**e·ter·nal** /ɪˈtərnl/ ***adj.*** without beginning or end; lasting forever: *eternal life* (= after death) ▸ **e·ter·nal·ly** /-əli/ ***adv.***: *I'll be eternally grateful if you could help me.*

**e·ter·ni·ty** /ɪˈtərnət̬i/ ***noun*** **1** [U] time that has no end; the state or time after death **2 an eternity** [sing.] (*informal*) a period of time that seems endless: *It seemed like an eternity before the ambulance came.*

**E·ther·net** /ˈiθərnɛt/ ***noun*** [U] (*computing*) a system for connecting a number of computer systems to form a NETWORK (4)

**eth·i·cal** /ˈɛθɪkl/ ***adj.*** **1** connected with ETHICS (2): *an ethical problem* **2** morally correct: *She did not break the law but her behavior was not ethical.* OPP **unethical**

**eth·ics** /ˈɛθɪks/ ***noun*** **1** [U] the study of what is right and wrong in human behavior: *Ethics is a branch of philosophy.* **2** [pl.] beliefs about what is morally right and wrong: *The medical profession has its own code of ethics.*

**eth·nic** /ˈɛθnɪk/ ***adj.*** connected with or typical of a racial group or groups, or of a group from a particular country or region: *ethnic minorities* ◇ *ethnic food/music*

**ˌethnic ˈcleansing** ***noun*** [U] the policy of forcing the people of a particular race or religion to leave an area or a country

**et·i·quette** /ˈɛt̬ɪkɛt; -kət/ ***noun*** [U] the rules of polite and correct behavior

**et·y·mol·o·gy** /ˌɛt̬əˈmɑlədʒi/ ***noun*** (*pl.* **et·y·mol·o·gies**) **1** [U] the study of the origins and history of words and their meanings **2** [C] an explanation of the origin and history of a particular word

**eu·phe·mism** /ˈyufəmɪzəm/ ***noun*** [C,U] (using) a polite word or expression instead of a more direct one when you are talking about sth that is unpleasant or embarrassing: *"Go to the bathroom" is a euphemism for "urinate."*

**eu·pho·ri·a** /yuˈfɔriə/ ***noun*** [U] (*formal*) a strong feeling of happiness

**eu·ro** /ˈyʊroʊ/ (*pl.* **eu·ros**) ***noun*** [C] (*symbol* €) the unit of money used by some countries in the European Union

**Eu·ro·pe·an¹** /ˌyʊrəˈpiən/ ***adj.*** of or from Europe: *European languages*

**Eu·ro·pe·an²** /ˌyʊrəˈpiən/ ***noun*** [C] a person from a country in Europe

**the ˌEuropean ˈUnion** (*abbr.* **EU**) ***noun*** [sing.] an economic and political association of certain European countries

**eu·tha·na·sia** /ˌyuθəˈneɪʒə/ ***noun*** [U] the painless killing of sb who is very old or suffering from a disease that cannot be cured

**e·vac·u·ate** /ɪˈvækyueɪt/ ***verb*** [T] (often passive) to move people from a dangerous place to somewhere safer; to leave a place because it is dangerous: *The town had to be evacuated when the river flooded its banks.* ▸ **e·vac·u·a·tion** /ɪˌvækyuˈeɪʃn/ ***noun*** [C,U]

**e·vade** /ɪˈveɪd/ ***verb*** [T] **1** to get out of the way of or to escape from sb/sth: *They managed to evade capture and escaped to Canada.* **2** to avoid sth: *He was accused of evading income tax.* ➲ noun evasion

**e·val·u·ate** /ɪˈvælyueɪt/ ***verb*** [T] (*formal*) to study the facts and then give your opinion about the meaning of sth or about how good sth is: *We evaluated the situation very carefully before we made our decision.* ▸ **e·val·u·a·tion** /ɪˌvælyuˈeɪʃn/ ***noun*** [C,U]

**e·van·gel·i·cal** /ˌivænˈdʒɛlɪkl/ ***adj.*** (of certain Protestant churches) believing that religious ceremony is not as important as faith in Jesus Christ and study of the Bible

**e·van·gel·ist** /ɪˈvændʒəlɪst/ ***noun*** [C] a person who tells other people about Jesus Christ and the Bible and tries to persuade them to become Christians ▸ **e·van·gel·ism** /ɪˈvændʒəlɪzm/ ***noun*** [U]

**e·vap·o·rate** /ɪˈvæpəreɪt/ ***verb*** [I] **1** (used about a liquid) to change into steam or a gas and disappear: *The water evaporated in the sunshine.* ➲ Look at **condense**. **2** (used about feelings) to disappear:

*All her hopes evaporated when she heard the news.*
▶ **e·vap·o·ra·tion** /ɪˌvæpəˈreɪʃn/ ***noun*** [U]

**e·va·sion** /ɪˈveɪʒn/ ***noun*** [C,U] an action, statement, etc. that is used for avoiding sth unpleasant: *He has been sentenced to two years' imprisonment for income tax evasion.* ➲ verb evade

**e·va·sive** /ɪˈveɪsɪv/ ***adj.*** trying to avoid sth; not direct: *Ann gave an evasive answer.*

**eve** /iv/ ***noun*** [C] the day or evening before a religious festival, important event, etc.: *Christmas Eve* (= December 24)

★**e·ven¹** /ˈivən/ ***adj.*** **1** flat, level or smooth: *an even surface* **2** not changing; regular: *This wine must be stored at an even temperature.* **3** (used about a competition, etc.) with one side being as good as the other: *an even contest* OPP The opposite for senses **1,2** and **3** is **uneven**. **4** (used about numbers) that can be divided by two: *4, 6, 8, 10, etc. are even numbers.* OPP **odd**

IDM **be/get even (with sb)** to hurt or harm sb who has hurt or harmed you

**break even** to make neither a loss nor a profit

▶ **e·ven·ly** ***adv.***: *The game was very evenly balanced.*

★**e·ven²** /ˈivən/ ***adv.*** **1** (used for emphasizing sth that is surprising): *It isn't very warm here even in the summer.* ◇ *Even the kids helped in the yard.* ◇ *He didn't even open the letter* (= so he certainly didn't read it). ◇ *I have been so busy that I haven't even had time to read the newspaper.* ◇ *I like her a lot, even though she can be really annoying.* ➲ Look at the note at **although**. **2** (used when you are comparing things, to make the comparison stronger): *It is even more difficult than I expected.* ◇ *We are even busier than we were yesterday.*

IDM **even if** (used for saying that what follows "if" makes no difference): *I wouldn't do it, even if you paid me a thousand dollars.*

**even so** (used for introducing a new idea, fact, etc. that is surprising) in spite of that; nevertheless: *There are a lot of spelling mistakes; even so, it's a very good essay.*

★**eve·ning** /ˈivnɪŋ/ ***noun*** [C,U] the part of the day between the afternoon and the time that you go to bed: *What are you doing this evening?* ◇ *We were out yesterday evening.* ◇ *I went to the movies Saturday evening.* ◇ *Tom usually goes swimming Wednesday evenings.* ◇ *Most people watch television in the evening.* ◇ *an evening class* (= a course for adults that takes place in the evening)

IDM **good evening** (*formal*) (used when you see sb for the first time in the evening): *Good evening, ladies and gentlemen, and welcome to the show.*

NOTE When you use the adjectives *early* or *late* before "evening" you must use the preposition **in**: *It started to rain in the early evening.* ◇ *They arrived in the late evening.* With other adjectives, we often use **on**: *After sunset on a clear evening, the temperature can drop quickly.* But with days of the week, we do not usually use **on**: *My Spanish class starts Monday evening.* No preposition is used before *this, tomorrow, last* or *yesterday*: *I'll wash the dishes this evening.* ◇ *I'll call Liz tomorrow evening.* ◇ *We went to Omar's house last evening.* ◇ *They weren't home yesterday evening.* ➲ Look also at the notes at **morning** and **night**.

★**e·vent** /ɪˈvɛnt/ ***noun*** [C] **1** something that happens, especially sth important or unusual: *a historic event* ◇ *The events of the past few days have made things very difficult for the government.* **2** one of the races, competitions, etc. in a sports program: *The next event is the 800 meters.*

IDM **in any event** whatever happens: *I hope to see you soon, but in any event I'll call you on Sunday.*

**in the event of sth** (*formal*) if sth happens: *In the event of fire, leave the building as quickly as possible.*

**e·vent·ful** /ɪˈvɛntfl/ ***adj.*** full of interesting or important events OPP **uneventful**

**e·ven·tu·al** /ɪˈvɛntʃuəl/ ***adj.*** (only *before* a noun) happening as a result; happening at last: *It is impossible to say what the eventual cost will be.*

★**e·ven·tu·al·ly** /ɪˈvɛntʃəli/ ***adv.*** in the end; at last: *He eventually persuaded his parents to buy him a motorcycle.*

★**ev·er** /ˈɛvər/ ***adv.*** **1** (used in questions and negative sentences, when you are comparing things, and in sentences with "if") at any time: *Do you ever wish you were famous?* ◇ *She hardly ever* (= almost never) *goes out.* ◇ *Today is hotter than ever.* ◇ *This is the best meal I've ever had.* ◇ *If you're ever in Dallas, give me a call.* **2** (used in questions with verbs in the perfect tenses) at any time up to now: *Have you ever been to Spain?*

NOTE Notice that when you answer a question like this, you do not use "ever." You say, "Yes, I have" or "No, I haven't" (or "No, never"). ➲ Look also at **whatever**, **whenever**, **however**, etc.

**3 ever-** (in compounds) always; continuously: *the ever-growing problem of pollution*

IDM **(as) bad, good, etc. as ever** (as) bad, good, etc. as usual or as you expected: *In spite of his problems, Andrew is as cheerful as ever.*

**ever after** (used especially at the end of stories) from that moment on for always: *The prince married the princess and they lived happily ever after.*

**ever since (...)** all the time from (...) until now: *She has had a car ever since she learned to drive.*

**ev·er·green** /ˈɛvərgrin/ ***noun*** [C], ***adj.*** (a tree, etc.) with green leaves all year ➲ Look at **deciduous**.

**ev·er·last·ing** /ˌɛvərˈlæstɪŋ/ ***adj.*** (*formal*) lasting forever: *everlasting life*

★**eve·ry** /ˈɛvri/ ***det.*** **1** (used with singular nouns) all the people or things in a group of three or more: *She knows every student in the school.* ◇ *There are 400 students in the school, and she knows every one of them.* ◇ *I've read every book in this house.* ◇ *You were out every time I called.* **2** all that is possible: *You have every chance of success.* ◇ *She had every reason to be angry.* **3** (used for saying how often sth happens): *We see each other every day.* ◇ *Take the medicine every four hours* (= at 8:00/12:00/4:00). ◇ *Our team practices every other day* (= on Monday/Wednesday/Friday). ◇ *One in every three marriages ends in divorce.*

IDM **every last**; **every single** (used to emphasize the importance of each individual unit): *I can't*



E

*believe you ate every last cookie in the box!* ◇ *The candidate shook hands with every single person in the room.*

**(every) now and then** → NOW[1]

**(every) once in a while** → ONCE[1]

**every so often** occasionally

★**eve·ry·bod·y** /ˈɛvriˌbɑdi; -ˌbʌdi/ (*also* **every-one** /ˈɛvriwʌn/) ***pronoun*** [with sing. verb] every person; all people: *Is everybody here?* ◇ *The police questioned everyone who was at the party.* ◇ *I'm sure everybody else* (= all the other people) *will agree with me.*

> NOTE **Everyone** is only used about people and is not followed by "of." **Every one** means "each person or thing" and is often followed by "of": *Every one of his records has been successful.* ➲ Look also at the note at **somebody**.

**eve·ry·day** /ˈɛvrideɪ/ ***adj.*** (only *before* a noun) normal and usual: *The computer is now part of everyday life.* SYN **workaday**

**eve·ry·place** /ˈɛvripleɪs/ ***adv.*** (*informal*) = EVERYWHERE

★**eve·ry·thing** /ˈɛvriθɪŋ/ ***pronoun*** [with sing. verb] **1** each thing; all things: *Sam lost everything in the fire.* ◇ *Everything is very expensive in this store.* ◇ *We can leave everything else* (= all the other things) *at my parents' house.* **2** the most important thing: *Money isn't everything.*

★**eve·ry·where** /ˈɛvriwɛr/ ***adv.*** in or to every place: *I've looked everywhere, but I still can't find it.*

**e·vict** /ɪˈvɪkt/ ***verb*** [T] to force sb (officially) to leave the house or land where he/she is living: *They were evicted for not paying the rent.* ▸ **e·vic·tion** /ɪˈvɪkʃn/ ***noun*** [C,U]

★**ev·i·dence** /ˈɛvədəns/ ***noun*** [U] something that gives a reason for believing sth: *There was no evidence of a struggle in the room.* ◇ *There was not enough evidence to prove him guilty.* ◇ *Her statement to the police was used as evidence against him.*

> NOTE Note that **evidence** is uncountable. We use **piece** if we are talking about single items that are evidence: *One piece of evidence is not enough to prove that somebody is guilty.*

IDM **be in evidence** (*formal*) to be seen; to be noticeable: *The effects of last year's flood are still in evidence.*

**ev·i·dent** /ˈɛvədənt/ ***adj.*** clear (to the eye or mind); obvious: *It was evident that the damage was very serious.*

**ev·i·dent·ly** /ˈɛvədəntli/ ***adv.*** **1** it appears that: *Evidently he has decided to leave.* **2** it is obvious that: *She was evidently extremely shocked at the news.*

★**e·vil**[1] /ˈivl/ ***adj.*** very bad; causing trouble or harm: *evil crimes*

★**e·vil**[2] /ˈivl/ ***noun*** [C,U] (*formal*) something that is very bad: *The play is about the good and evil in all of us.* ◇ *Drugs and alcohol are two of the evils of modern society.*

IDM **the lesser of two evils** → LESSER

**e·voke** /ɪˈvoʊk/ ***verb*** [T] (*formal*) to produce a memory, feeling, etc.: *For me, that music always evokes long summer evenings.* ◇ *Her article evoked a lot of interest.*

**ev·o·lu·tion** /ˌɛvəˈluʃn/ ***noun*** [U] **1** the development of living things over many thousands of years from simple early forms: *Darwin's theory of evolution* **2** the process of change and development: *Political evolution is a slow process.*

**e·volve** /ɪˈvɑlv/ ***verb*** **1** [I] (used about living things) to develop from simple early forms **2** [I,T] (*formal*) to develop or to make sth develop: *His style of painting has evolved gradually over the past 20 years.* ◇ *The twins have evolved a language of their own.*

**ewe** /yu/ ***noun*** [C] a female sheep ➲ picture at **sheep**.

**ex**[1] /ɛks/ ***noun*** [C] (*informal*) a former husband, wife, partner in a relationship, etc.: *My ex and I are still good friends.*

**ex**[2] /ɛks/ ***abbr.*** (*Cdn*) = EXHIBITION (2)

**ex-** /ɛks/ ***prefix*** (in compounds) former; of an earlier time: *Monica's ex-husband* ◇ *an ex-girlfriend*

> NOTE We use **ex-** when a relationship has ended sooner than it should have, or in a negative way. When a relationship comes to a natural end, we say **former** or **old**: *The company was receiving threatening letters from an ex-employee.* ◇ *The company sometimes invites former employees back to work as consultants.* ◇ *I saw my old teacher today.*

**ex·ac·er·bate** /ɪgˈzæsərbeɪt/ ***verb*** [T] (*written*) to make sth worse, especially a disease or problem: *His aggressive reaction only exacerbated the situation.* ◇ *The symptoms may be exacerbated by certain drugs.* SYN **aggravate** ▸ **ex·ac·er·ba·tion** ***noun*** [C,U]

★**ex·act**[1] /ɪgˈzækt/ ***adj.*** **1** (completely) correct; accurate: *He's in his mid-fifties. Well, 56 to be exact.* ◇ *I can't tell you the exact number of people who are coming.* ◇ *She's the exact opposite of her sister.* **2** able to work in a way that is completely accurate: *You need to be very exact when you calculate the costs.*

**ex·act**[2] /ɪgˈzækt/ ***verb*** [T] (*formal*) to demand and get sth

**ex·act·ing** /ɪgˈzæktɪŋ/ ***adj.*** needing or demanding a lot of care and attention; difficult: *Our product must meet the client's exacting standards.*

★**ex·act·ly** /ɪgˈzæktli; -ˈzækli/ ***adv.*** **1** (used for emphasizing sth) just: *You arrived at exactly the right moment.* ◇ *I found exactly what I wanted.* **2** (used when you are asking for, or giving, completely correct information): *Where exactly do you live?* ◇ *He took exactly one hour to finish.* **3** (used for agreeing with a statement) yes; you are right: *"I don't think she's old enough to travel on her own." "Exactly."*

IDM **not exactly** (*informal*) **1** not really; not at all: *He's not exactly the most careful driver I know.* **2** (used as an answer to say that sth is almost true): *"So you think I'm wrong?" "No, not exactly, but ..."*

★**ex·ag·ger·ate** /ɪgˈzædʒəreɪt/ ***verb*** [I,T] to make sth seem larger, better, worse, etc. than it really is: *Don't exaggerate. I was only two minutes late, not twenty.* ◇ *The problems have been greatly exaggerated.*

**ex·ag·ger·a·tion** /ɪɡˌzædʒəˈreɪʃn/ ***noun*** [C,U] making sth seem bigger, etc. than it really is; sth that does this: *It's an exaggeration to say that all the students are lazy.*

★**ex·am** /ɪɡˈzæm/ ***noun*** [C] (*also formal* **examination**) a written, spoken or practical test of what you know or can do, especially at the end of a course: *a final exam* ◇ *the exam scores*

NOTE A **test** is less formal and usually less important than an exam.

★**ex·am·i·na·tion** /ɪɡˌzæməˈneɪʃn/ ***noun*** **1** [C,U] the act of looking at sth carefully: *They made a thorough examination of the car before buying it.* ◇ ***On close examination****, it was found that the passport was false.* **2** [C] (*formal*) = EXAM

★**ex·am·ine** /ɪɡˈzæmən/ ***verb*** [T] **1 examine sb/sth (for sth)** to look at sb/sth carefully in order to find out sth: *The detective examined the room for clues.* ◇ *I'm going to have my teeth examined next week.* **2 examine sb (in/on sth)** (*formal*) to test what sb knows or can do: *You will be examined on everything that has been studied in the course.*

**ex·am·in·er** /ɪɡˈzæmənər/ ***noun*** [C] a person whose job is to check business records, etc. to make sure that they are correct: *a bank examiner* ➲ Look also at **medical examiner**.

★**ex·am·ple** /ɪɡˈzæmpl/ ***noun*** [C] **1** a thing that shows a general rule about what sth is like: *I don't quite understand you. Can you give me an example of what you mean?* ◇ *This is a typical example of a Picasso painting.* **2** a person or thing or a type of behavior that is good and should be copied: *Joe's bravery should be an example to us all.*

IDM **follow sb's example/lead** → FOLLOW

**for example** (used for giving an illustration of what you are talking about): *In many countries – Italy, for example – family life is much more important than here.* ◇ *There are lots of ways to lose weight. For example, use skim milk instead of whole milk.*

NOTE The short form, which is always used *before* the illustration you are giving, is **e.g.**

IDM **set a good, bad, etc. example (for sb)** to behave in a way that should/should not be copied: *Professional athletes who use drugs set a bad example for kids.*

**ex·as·per·ate** /ɪɡˈzæspəreɪt/ ***verb*** [T] to make sb angry; to annoy sb: *She was exasperated by the lack of progress.* ▸ **ex·as·per·at·ing** /-reɪt̬ɪŋ/ ▸ **ex·as·per·a·tion** /ɪɡˌzæspəˈreɪʃn/ ***noun*** [U]: *She finally threw the book across the room in exasperation.*

**ex·ca·vate** /ˈɛkskəveɪt/ ***verb*** [I,T] **1** to dig a hole in the ground **2** to uncover objects or buildings from the past by digging in an area of land: *The remains of a Native American village have been excavated in a valley near the river.* ▸ **ex·ca·va·tion** /ˌɛkskəˈveɪʃn/ ***noun*** [C,U]: *Excavations on the site have revealed several ancient burial grounds.*

**ex·ceed** /ɪkˈsid/ ***verb*** [T] **1** to be greater than sth: *The price must not exceed $100.* **2** to go beyond what is allowed or necessary: *to exceed the speed limit* ➲ noun excess ➲ adjective excessive

**ex·ceed·ing·ly** /ɪkˈsidɪŋli/ ***adv.*** very: *an exceedingly difficult problem*

**ex·cel** /ɪkˈsɛl/ ***verb*** [I] (**ex·cel̲l̲ing**; **ex·cel̲l̲ed**) (*formal*) **excel in/at sth** to be very good at sth

**ex·cel·lence** /ˈɛksələns/ ***noun*** [U] the quality of being very good: *The school is a center of academic excellence.*

**ex·cel·lent** /ˈɛksələnt/ ***adj.*** very good; of high quality: *He speaks excellent French.* ▸ **ex·cel·lent·ly** ***adv.***

★**ex·cept**[1] /ɪkˈsɛpt/ ***prep.*** **except (for) sb/sth**; **except (that...)** not including sb/sth; apart from the fact that: *The museum is open every day except Tuesdays.* ◇ *Everyone except Tony is going on the trip.* ◇ *I can answer all of the questions except for the last one.* ◇ *It was a good hotel except that it was a little noisy.*

**ex·cept**[2] /ɪkˈsɛpt/ ***verb*** [T] (often passive) **except sb/sth (from sth)** (*formal*) to leave sb/sth out; to not include sb/sth

★**ex·cep·tion** /ɪkˈsɛpʃn/ ***noun*** [C] a person or thing that is not included: *Most of his songs are terrible, but this one is an exception.* ◇ *There's an exception to every rule.*

IDM **to make an exception (for sb/sth)** to treat sb/sth differently: *We don't usually allow kids under 14 in, but we'll make an exception in your case.*

**with the exception of** except for; apart from: *He has won every major tennis championship with the exception of Wimbledon.*

**without exception** in every case; including everybody/everything: *Everybody without exception must take the test.*

**ex·cep·tion·al** /ɪkˈsɛpʃənl/ ***adj.*** very unusual; unusually good: *You will only be allowed to leave early in exceptional circumstances.* ◇ *exceptional skill* ▸ **ex·cep·tion·al·ly** /-ʃənəli/ ***adv.***: *exceptionally difficult*

**ex·cerpt** /ˈɛksərpt/ ***noun*** [C] a short piece taken from a book, movie, piece of music, etc.

**ex·cess**[1] /ɪkˈsɛs; ˈɛksɛs/ ***noun*** **1** [sing.] more of sth than is needed or usual; too much of sth: *An excess of fat in your diet can lead to heart disease.* **2 excesses** [pl.] behavior or actions that people think are too harmful or extreme

IDM **in excess of** more than: *Her debts are in excess of $1,000.*

**to excess** too much; much more than people think is normal or acceptable: *After his wife left him, he began drinking to excess.*

**ex·cess**[2] /ˈɛksɛs/ ***adj.*** (only *before* a noun) more than is usual or allowed; extra: *There are high charges for* ***excess baggage*** *on planes.*

**ex·ces·sive** /ɪkˈsɛsɪv/ ***adj.*** too much; too great: *I think $200 for a dress is excessive.* ▸ **ex·ces·sive·ly** ***adv.***: *I think you are being excessively pessimistic about this.*

★**ex·change**[1] /ɪksˈtʃeɪndʒ/ ***noun*** **1** [C,U] giving or receiving sth in return for sth else: *a useful exchange of information* ◇ *We can offer free room and board in exchange for some help in the house.* **2** [C] an (angry) conversation or argument **3** [U] the relation in value between kinds of money used in different countries: *What's the* ***exchange rate/rate of***

E

*exchange for dollars?* ◇ *The exchange rate is one dollar to one hundred yen.* ➲ Look at **foreign exchange** and **stock exchange**. **4** [C] a visit by a person or group of people to another country and often a return visit by a similar person or group from that country: *an exchange student*

★**ex·change²** /ɪks'tʃeɪndʒ/ ***verb*** [T] **exchange A for B; exchange sth (with sb)** to give or receive sth in return for sth else: *I would like to exchange this skirt for a bigger one.* ◇ *Kari and Linda exchanged addresses with the boys.* ◇ *They exchanged glances* (= they looked at each other).

**ex·cit·a·ble** /ɪk'saɪt̬əbl/ ***adj.*** easily excited

**ex·cite** /ɪk'saɪt/ ***verb*** [T] **1** to cause strong feelings (e.g. of happiness or nervousness): *Don't excite the baby too much or we'll never get him to sleep.* **2** to cause a reaction in sb: *The program excited great interest.*

★**ex·cit·ed** /ɪk'saɪt̬əd/ ***adj.*** feeling very happy because you are looking forward to sth happening; not calm: *Are you getting excited about your vacation?* ◇ *We're all really excited to be moving into our new house.* ▸ **ex·cit·ed·ly** ***adv.***

★**ex·cite·ment** /ɪk'saɪtmənt/ ***noun*** [U] the state of being excited; a feeling of pleasure, especially because sth interesting is happening or will happen: *The children could not hide their excitement before the trip.* ◇ *There was a lot of excitement in the room as the winner's name was announced.*

★**ex·cit·ing** /ɪk'saɪt̬ɪŋ/ ***adj.*** causing strong feelings of pleasure and interest: *That's very exciting news.* ◇ *San Francisco is one of the most exciting cities in America.* OPP **unexciting**

**ex·claim** /ɪk'skleɪm/ ***verb*** [I,T] to say sth suddenly because you are surprised, angry, etc.: *"I just don't believe it!" he exclaimed.*

**ex·cla·ma·tion** /ˌɛksklə'meɪʃn/ ***noun*** [C] a sound or word that expresses sudden pain, anger, surprise, etc.: *"Ouch!" is an exclamation.*

ˌ**excla'mation point** ***noun*** [C] a mark (!) that is written after an exclamation

★**ex·clude** /ɪk'sklud/ ***verb*** [T] **1 exclude sb/sth (from sth)** to prevent sb/sth from getting in: *Women are excluded from the temple.* ◇ *Many health insurance companies exclude people with previous illnesses from coverage.* **2** to decide that sth is not true: *The police had excluded the possibility that the child had run away.* **3** to leave sb/sth out; to not include sb/sth: *These statistics exclude people over 70.*

**ex·clud·ing** /ɪk'skludɪŋ/ ***prep.*** not including: *The price of the car is $14,995, excluding taxes and registration.*

**ex·clu·sion** /ɪk'skluʒn/ ***noun*** [U] keeping or leaving sb/sth out

**ex·clu·sive¹** /ɪk'sklusɪv/ ***adj.*** **1** expensive and not welcoming people who are thought to be from a low social class: *an exclusive restaurant* ◇ *a home in an exclusive neighborhood* **2** (only *before* a noun) for only one person, group, etc.; not to be shared: *an exclusive interview with Tom Cruise* (= on only one television or radio station).

**ex·clu·sive²** /ɪk'sklusɪv/ ***noun*** [C] a newspaper story that is given to and published by only one newspaper

**ex·clu·sive·ly** /ɪk'sklusɪvli/ ***adv.*** only; not involving anybody/anything else: *The swimming pool is reserved exclusively for members of the club.*

**ex·cre·ment** /'ɛkskrəmənt/ ***noun*** [U] (*formal*) the solid waste matter that is passed from the body through the bowels SYN **feces**. An informal word is **poop**.

**ex·cru·ci·at·ing** /ɪk'skruʃieɪt̬ɪŋ/ ***adj.*** (used about pain, etc.) very bad

**ex·cur·sion** /ɪk'skərʒn/ ***noun*** [C] a short trip (that a group of people make for pleasure): *to go on a weekend excursion to Atlantic City*

**ex·cus·a·ble** /ɪk'skyuzəbl/ ***adj.*** that can be forgiven OPP **inexcusable**

★**ex·cuse¹** /ɪk'skyus/ ***noun*** [C] **excuse (for sth/for doing sth)** a reason (that may be true or untrue) that you give in order to explain your behavior: *There's no excuse for bad manners.* ◇ *He always finds a good excuse for not helping with the housework.*

★**ex·cuse²** /ɪk'skyuz/ ***verb*** [T] **1 excuse sb/sth (for sth/for doing sth)** to forgive sb/sth: *Please excuse the mess – I haven't had time to clean up.* **2** to explain sb's bad behavior and make it seem less bad: *Nothing can excuse such behavior.* **3 excuse yourself** to say politely that you need to leave a place: *She excused herself and got up from the table.* **4 excuse sb (from sth)** to free sb from a duty, responsibility, etc.: *I was excused from gym class today because I hurt my knee.*

NOTE The expression **excuse me** is used when you interrupt somebody or when you want to start talking to somebody that you don't know: *Excuse me, can you tell me the way to the post office?* We can also use **excuse me** to apologize for something, such as sneezing, yawning, etc.: *Did I step on your toe? Excuse me.* **Excuse me** can be used as a question, for asking sb to repeat what he/she just said because you did not hear or understand it: *"Is this your bag?" "Excuse me?" "I asked if this was your bag."* ➲ Look also at **pardon³** and **sorry**.

**ex·e·cute** /'ɛksəkyut/ ***verb*** [T] **1** to kill sb as an official punishment: *He was executed for murder.* **2** (*formal*) to perform a task, etc. or to carry out a plan

**ex·e·cu·tion** /ˌɛksə'kyuʃn/ ***noun*** **1** [C,U] the act of killing sb as an official punishment **2** [U] (*formal*) carrying out a plan, order, etc.

**ex·e·cu·tion·er** /ˌɛksə'kyuʃənər/ ***noun*** [C] a person whose job is to EXECUTE (1) criminals

★**ex·ec·u·tive¹** /ɪg'zɛkyət̬ɪv/ ***adj.*** **1** (used in connection with people in business, government, etc.) concerned with managing, making decisions, carrying out plans, etc.: *an executive vice president of the company* **2** connected with the part of the government that makes decisions about running the country: *The President is the head of the executive branch of the federal government.* **3** (used about goods, buildings, etc.) designed to be used by important businesspeople: *an executive briefcase*

★**ex·ec·u·tive²** /ɪg'zɛkyət̬ɪv/ ***noun*** [C] a person who has an important position in a business: *She's a senior executive in a computer company.*

**ex·em·pla·ry** /ɪɡˈzɛmpləri/ *adj.* very good; that can be an example to other people: *exemplary behavior*

**ex·em·pli·fy** /ɪɡˈzɛmpləfaɪ/ *verb* (*pres. part.* **ex·em·pli·fy·ing**; *3rd person sing. pres.* **ex·em·pli·fies**; *pt, pp* **ex·em·pli·fied**) [T] to be a typical example of sth

**ex·empt¹** /ɪɡˈzɛmpt/ *adj.* **exempt (from sth)** free from having to do sth or pay sth: *Are city employees exempt from the new law?* ◇ *tax-exempt contributions to charity*

**ex·empt²** /ɪɡˈzɛmpt/ *verb* [T] **exempt sb/sth (from sth)** (*formal*) to say officially that sb does not have to do sth or pay sth ▸ **ex·emp·tion** /ɪɡˈzɛmpʃn/ *noun* [C,U]

★**ex·er·cise¹** /ˈɛksərsaɪz/ *noun*

➤ACTIVITY/MOVEMENTS **1** [U] use of the body in a way that will keep you healthy: *The doctor advised him to get regular exercise.* ◇ *Swimming is a good form of exercise.* **2** [C] (often plural) a movement or activity that you do in order to keep healthy or to train sth: *You need to do some exercises to improve your technique.*

➤QUESTIONS **3** [C] a piece of work that is intended to help you learn or practice sth: *an exercise on phrasal verbs* ◇ *a grammar exercise*

➤FOR A PARTICULAR AIM **4** [C] an action or a series of actions that have a particular aim: *The senator's speech was really just an exercise in public relations.*

➤USE OF POWER/RIGHT **5** [U] (*formal*) the use of sth (e.g. a power, right, etc.)

➤FOR SOLDIERS **6** [C] a series of activities by soldiers to practice fighting: *military exercises*

★**ex·er·cise²** /ˈɛksərsaɪz/ *verb* **1** [I] to do some form of physical movement in order to stay fit and healthy: *It is important to exercise regularly.* **2** [T] to make use of sth (e.g. a power, right, etc.): *You should exercise your right to vote.*

**ex·ert** /ɪɡˈzərt/ *verb* [T] **1** to make use of sth (e.g. influence, strength, etc.): *Parents exert a powerful influence on their children's opinions.* **2 exert yourself** to make an effort: *You won't make any progress if you don't exert yourself a little more.*

**ex·er·tion** /ɪɡˈzərʃn/ *noun* [C,U] using your body in a way that takes a lot of effort; sth that you do that makes you tired: *At his age physical exertion was dangerous.*

**ex·hale** /ɛksˈheɪl; ɛkˈseɪl/ *verb* [I,T] to breathe out the air, smoke, etc. in your lungs: *He sat back and exhaled deeply.* OPP **inhale**

**ex·haust¹** /ɪɡˈzɔst/ *noun* **1** [C] a pipe (especially at the back of a car) through which waste gas escapes from an engine or machine **2** [U] the waste gas that escapes from an engine or machine

**ex·haust²** /ɪɡˈzɔst/ *verb* [T] **1** to make sb very tired: *Getting up so early every morning exhausted him.* **2** to use sth up completely; to finish sth: *All the supplies of food have been exhausted.* **3** to say everything you can about a subject, etc.: *Well, I think we've exhausted that topic.*

**ex·haust·ed** /ɪɡˈzɔstəd/ *adj.* very tired

**ex·haust·ing** /ɪɡˈzɔstɪŋ/ *adj.* making sb very tired: *Teaching young children is exhausting work.*

**ex·haus·tion** /ɪɡˈzɔstʃən/ *noun* [U] great tiredness

**ex·haus·tive** /ɪɡˈzɔstɪv/ *adj.* including everything possible: *an exhaustive list*

**ex·hib·it¹** /ɪɡˈzɪbət/ *noun* [C,U] an object or a collection of objects that is shown in a museum, etc.: *a special exhibit of works by local artists* ◇ *The kids loved the panda exhibit at the zoo.* ◇ *Her paintings will be* ***on exhibit*** *in Montreal through April 30.*

**ex·hib·it²** /ɪɡˈzɪbət/ *verb* [T] **1** to show sth to the public: *His paintings have been exhibited in the local art gallery.* **2** (*formal*) to show sth (e.g. a feeling or quality): *The refugees are exhibiting signs of exhaustion and stress.*

★**ex·hi·bi·tion** /ˌɛksəˈbɪʃn/ *noun* [C] **1** a collection of objects that are shown to the public: *Have you seen the Picasso exhibition?* **2** (*Cdn*) (*abbr.* **ex**) a large regional FAIR³ (1), where you can ride on machines, look at farm animals, buy products people have made, etc.

**ˌexhiˈbition game** *noun* [C] a sports game that is not part of a serious competition

**ex·hib·i·tor** /ɪɡˈzɪbət̬ər/ *noun* [C] a person who shows his/her work to the public

**ex·hil·a·rate** /ɪɡˈzɪləreɪt/ *verb* [T] (usually passive) to make sb feel very happy, excited, etc.: *We felt exhilarated by our walk along the beach.* ▸ **ex·hil·a·rat·ing** *adj.* ▸ **ex·hil·a·ra·tion** /ɪɡˌzɪləˈreɪʃn/ *noun* [U]

**ex·ile¹** /ˈɛɡzaɪl; ˈɛks-/ *noun* **1** [U] the state of being forced to live outside your own country (especially for political reasons): *to go* ***into exile*** ◇ *They lived* ***in exile*** *for many years.* **2** [C] a person who is forced to live outside his/her own country (especially for political reasons): *political exiles* ➲ Look at **refugee**.

**ex·ile²** /ˈɛɡzaɪl; ˈɛks-/ *verb* [T] (usually passive) to send sb to live in another country (especially for political reasons): *The king was exiled after the revolution.*

★**ex·ist** /ɪɡˈzɪst/ *verb* [I] **1** to be real; to be found in the real world; to live: *Does God exist?* ◇ *I don't think that word exists, does it?* ◇ *Fish cannot exist out of water.* **2 exist (on sth)** to manage to live: *I don't know how she exists on so little money.*

★**ex·is·tence** /ɪɡˈzɪstəns/ *noun* **1** [U] the state of existing: *This is the oldest human skeleton in existence.* ◇ *The country of Liberia came into existence in 1821.* **2** [sing.] a way of living; life: *They lead a miserable existence in a tiny shack in the mountains.*

**ex·ist·ing** /ɪɡˈzɪstɪŋ/ *adj.* (only *before* a noun) that is already there or being used; present: *Under the existing law, you are not allowed to work in this country.*

**ex·it¹** /ˈɛɡzət; ˈɛksət/ *noun* [C] **1** a door or way out of a public building: *an emergency exit* **2** the act of leaving sth: *When he saw her coming, he made a quick exit.* **3** a place where traffic can turn off a freeway, etc.: *Take Exit 3 and go south on Lake Shore Drive.*

**ex·it²** /ˈɛɡzət; ˈɛksət/ *verb* [I] to go out or away

**ˈexit poll** *noun* [C] a process of predicting who will win an election by asking some people who they have voted for when they leave the buildings where they voted

**'exit ramp** (*also* **'off-ramp**) ***noun*** [C] a road that leads off a freeway ➲ Look at the note at **freeway**.

**ex·on·er·ate** /ɪg'zɑnəreɪt/ ***verb*** [T] (often passive) (*formal*) to free sb from blame, responsibility etc.

**ex·or·bi·tant** /ɪg'zɔrbət̬ənt/ ***adj.*** (*formal*) (used about the cost of sth) much more expensive than it should be

E

**ex·ot·ic** /ɪg'zɑt̬ɪk/ ***adj.*** unusual or interesting because it comes from a different country or culture: *exotic plants/animals*

★**ex·pand** /ɪk'spænd/ ***verb*** [I,T] to become bigger or to make sth bigger: *Metals expand when they are heated.* ◇ *We hope to expand our business this year.* OPP **contract**

PHR V **expand on sth** to give more details of a story, plan, point of view, etc.

**ex·panse** /ɪk'spæns/ ***noun*** [C] a large open area (of land, ocean, sky, etc.)

**ex·pan·sion** /ɪk'spænʃn/ ***noun*** [U] the action of expanding or the state of being expanded: *The rapid expansion of the university has caused a lot of problems.*

**ex·pan·sive** /ɪk'spænsɪv/ ***adj.*** **1** broad in size or range: *the university's expansive campus* ◇ *an expansive survey of music* **2** (*formal*) (used about a person) willing to talk a lot; friendly

**ex·pa·tri·ate** /ˌɛks'peɪtriət/ ***noun*** [C] a person who lives outside his/her own country

★**ex·pect** /ɪk'spɛkt/ ***verb*** [T] **1** to think or believe that sb/sth will come or that sth will happen: *She was expecting a letter from the bank this morning, but it didn't come.* ◇ *We expect that more people will buy computers this year.* ◇ *He expected it to be hot in Hawaii and it was.* ◇ *"I'm really disappointed – she forgot my birthday." "Well, what did you expect?"* (= it's not surprising) ◇ *She's* ***expecting a baby*** *in the spring* (= she's pregnant). ➲ Look at the note at **wait**[1]. **2 expect sth (from sb); expect sb to do sth** to hope that you will get sth from sb or that he/she will do what you want: *He expects a high standard of work from everyone.* ◇ *Factory workers are often expected to work at night.*

**ex·pec·tan·cy** /ɪk'spɛktənsi/ ***noun*** [U] the state of expecting sth to happen; hope: *a look/feeling of expectancy* ➲ Look at **life expectancy**.

**ex·pec·tant** /ɪk'spɛktənt/ ***adj.*** **1** expecting sth good; hopeful: *an expectant audience* ◇ *expectant faces* **2** pregnant; waiting for a baby: *Expectant mothers should drink plenty of milk.* ▸ **ex·pec·tant·ly** ***adv.***

★**ex·pec·ta·tion** /ˌɛkspɛk'teɪʃn/ ***noun*** (*formal*) **1** [C,U] the belief that sth will happen: *There's no expectation of any increase in our profits yet.* **2** [C, usually pl.] hope for the future: *They had* ***high expectations*** *for their daughter, but she didn't really live up to them.*

**ex·pe·di·ent** /ɪk'spidiənt/ ***adj.*** (*formal*) (used about an action) useful or necessary for a particular purpose, but not always fair or right: *The government decided that it was expedient not to increase taxes until after the election.* ▸ **ex·pe·di·en·cy** ***noun*** [U]

**ex·pe·dite** /'ɛkspədaɪt/ ***verb*** [T] (*formal*) to make a process happen more quickly: *We have developed rapid order processing to expedite deliveries to customers.* SYN **speed sth up**

**ex·pe·di·tion** /ˌɛkspə'dɪʃn/ ***noun*** [C] a long trip for a special purpose: *a scientific expedition to Antarctica*

**ex·pel** /ɪk'spɛl/ ***verb*** [T] (**ex·pel·ling**; **ex·pelled**) **1** to force sb to leave a school, country, club, etc.: *The student was expelled for bringing a knife to school.* ◇ *The government has expelled all foreign journalists from the country.* ➲ Look also at **suspend** (3). **2** to send sth out by force: *to expel air from the lungs* ➲ noun **expulsion**

**ex·pend** /ɪk'spɛnd/ ***verb*** [T] (*formal*) to spend or use money, time, care, etc. in doing sth: *I have expended a lot of time and energy on that project.*

**ex·pend·a·ble** /ɪk'spɛndəbl/ ***adj.*** (*formal*) not considered important or worth saving: *In a war, human life is expendable.*

**ex·pen·di·ture** /ɪk'spɛndətʃər/ ***noun*** [C,U] (*formal*) the act of spending or using money, etc.; an amount of money, etc. which is spent: *Government expenditure on education is very low in this country.* ◇ *The President has cut military expenditure by 5%.* ◇ *an expenditure of $2,000*

★**ex·pense** /ɪk'spɛns/ ***noun*** **1** [C,U] the cost of sth in time or money: *Maintaining a second home is a great expense.* ◇ *The house was restored* ***at great expense*** *(= at a high cost).* ◇ ***No expense was spared*** *to make the party a success.* **2 expenses** [pl.] money that is spent for a particular purpose: *You can deduct your business travel expenses from your income tax.*

IDM **at sb's expense 1** with sb paying; at sb's cost: *My trip is at the company's expense.* **2** against sb, so that he/she looks silly: *They were always making jokes at Paul's expense.*

**at the expense of sth** harming or damaging sth: *He was a successful businessman, but it was at the expense of his family life.*

★**ex·pen·sive** /ɪk'spɛnsɪv/ ***adj.*** costing a lot of money: *Houses are very expensive in this area.* ◇ *It's too expensive.* OPP **inexpensive** or **cheap** ▸ **ex·pen·sive·ly** ***adv.***

★**ex·pe·ri·ence**[1] /ɪk'spɪriəns/ ***noun*** **1** [U] the things that you have done; the knowledge or skill that you get from seeing or doing sth: *She has five years' teaching experience.* ◇ *You need a lot of experience in this job.* ◇ *I know from experience what will happen.* **2** [C] something that has happened to you (often something unusual or exciting): *She wrote a book about her experiences in Africa.* ◇ *It's an experience that shouldn't be missed.*

**ex·pe·ri·ence**[2] /ɪk'spɪriəns/ ***verb*** [T] to have EXPERIENCE[1] (1) of sth; to feel sth: *It was the first time I had ever experienced failure.* ◇ *to experience pleasure/pain/difficulty*

**ex·pe·ri·enced** /ɪk'spɪriənst/ ***adj.*** having the knowledge or skill that is necessary for sth: *He's not a very experienced driver.* OPP **inexperienced**

★**ex·per·i·ment**[1] /ɪk'spɛrəmənt/ ***noun*** [C] a scientific test that is done in order to prove sth or to get new knowledge: *a chemistry experiment* ◇ *Researchers often perform experiments on animals.*

◇ *It's difficult to conduct experiments on how people learn languages.* ◇ *I'm going to try riding my bike to work – it's just part of an experiment in ways to save energy.*

**ex·per·i·ment²** /ɪk'spɛrəmənt/ ***verb*** [I] **experiment (on sth) /(with sth)** to do an experiment or to test sth: *Is it really necessary to experiment on animals?* ◇ *teenagers who experiment with* (= try) *illegal drugs*

**ex·per·i·men·tal** /ɪkˌspɛrə'mɛntl/ ***adj.*** connected with experiments or new ideas: *experimental treatments for AIDS* ◇ *The government approved the new drug for use on an experimental basis.* ▶ **ex·per·i·men·tal·ly** /-təli/ ***adv.***

★**ex·pert¹** /'ɛkspərt/ ***noun*** [C] **an expert (at/in/on sth)** a person who has special knowledge or skill: *He's an expert on the history of rock music.* ◇ *She's a computer expert.* ◇ *Let me try – I'm an expert at parking cars in small spaces.*

★**ex·pert²** /'ɛkspərt/ ***adj.*** **expert (at/in/on sth)** with special knowledge or skill: *He's an expert cook.* ◇ *I think we should get expert advice on the problem.* ▶ **ex·pert·ly** ***adv.***

**ex·per·tise** /ˌɛkspər'tiz/ ***noun*** [U] special knowledge or skill: *She has shown real expertise in dealing with difficult customers.*

**ex·pi·ra·tion** /ˌɛkspə'reɪʃn/ (*Cdn. also* **expiry**) ***noun*** [U] the end of a period when you can use sth: *the library's account expiration policy*

**expi'ration date** (*Cdn. also* **ex'piry date**) ***noun*** [C] **1** the date printed on containers of food after which the food should not be eaten: *Check the expiration date on the milk before you buy it.* **2** the date after which an offer, agreement, etc. is no longer open: *Coupons can't be used after their expiration date.*

**ex·pire** /ɪk'spaɪər/ ***verb*** [I] (*formal*) (used about sth that only lasts for a certain period of time) to come to the end of the time when you can use it: *My passport expired. I'll have to get it renewed.*

**ex·pi·ry** /ɪk'spaɪri; 'ɛkspəri/ (*Cdn*) = EXPIRATION

★**ex·plain** /ɪk'spleɪn/ ***verb*** [I,T] **1** to make sth clear or easy to understand: *A dictionary explains the meaning of words.* ◇ *She explained how I should fill out the form.* ◇ *I don't understand this. Can you explain it to me?* **2** to give a reason for sth: *I know I'm half an hour late, but please let me explain.* ◇ *That explains why she was looking so miserable.* ◇ *The manager explained to the customers why the goods were not available.*

★**ex·pla·na·tion** /ˌɛksplə'neɪʃn/ ***noun*** **1** [U] making sth clear or giving a reason for sth: *That idea doesn't need much explanation.* **2** [C] something that makes a situation clear or understandable: *He could not give a satisfactory explanation for his behavior.*

**ex·plan·a·to·ry** /ɪk'splænəˌtɔri/ ***adj.*** giving an explanation: *There are some explanatory notes at the back of the book.* ◇ *The instructions are self-explanatory* (= they don't need explaining).

**ex·ple·tive** /'ɛksplət̬ɪv/ ***noun*** [C] (*formal*) a word, especially a strong word that may offend people, that you use when you are angry or in pain SYN **swear word**

**ex·plic·it** /ɪk'splɪsət/ ***adj.*** **1** clear, not making anything difficult to understand: *I gave you explicit instructions not to touch anything.* ◇ *She was very explicit about her feelings on the subject.* **2** not hiding anything: *a sexually explicit movie* ▶ **ex·plic·it·ly** ***adv.***: *The law explicitly states which kinds of drugs are illegal.*

★**ex·plode** /ɪk'sploʊd/ ***verb*** [I,T] to burst with a loud noise: *The bomb exploded without warning.* ◇ *The bomb was taken away and the police exploded it at a safe distance from the houses.* ◇ (*figurative*) *My dad exploded* (= became very angry) *when I told him how much the car would cost to repair.* ➲ noun explosion

**ex·ploit¹** /ɪk'splɔɪt/ ***verb*** [T] **1** to use sth or to treat sb unfairly or selfishly: *Developing countries are often exploited by the richer nations.* **2** to develop sth or make the best use of sth: *Solar energy is a source of power that needs to be exploited more fully.*

**ex·ploit²** /'ɛksplɔɪt/ ***noun*** [C] a brave or adventurous action

**ex·ploi·ta·tion** /ˌɛksplɔɪ'teɪʃn/ ***noun*** [U] exploiting or being exploited: *They're only paying $3 an hour? That's exploitation!*

**ex·plo·ra·tion** /ˌɛksplə'reɪʃn/ ***noun*** [C,U] the act of exploring: *space exploration*

**ex·plo·r·a·to·ry** /ɪk'splɔrəˌtɔri/ ***adj.*** done in order to find sth out: *The doctors are doing some exploratory tests to try and find out what's wrong.*

★**ex·plore** /ɪk'splɔr/ ***verb*** [I,T] to travel around a place, etc. in order to learn about it: *They went on an expedition to explore the Amazon River.* ◇ *scientists exploring near the base of the volcano* ◇ (*figurative*) *We need to explore* (= look carefully at) *all the possibilities before we decide.*

**ex·plor·er** /ɪk'splɔrər/ ***noun*** [C] a person who travels around a place in order to find out about it

★**ex·plo·sion** /ɪk'sploʊʒn/ ***noun*** [C] the sudden and violent bursting and loud noise that happen when sth like a bomb explodes: *The explosion may have been caused by a gas leak.* ◇ (*figurative*) *the population explosion* (= the sudden increase in the number of people in a country or in the world)

**ex·plo·sive¹** /ɪk'sploʊsɪv/ ***adj.*** **1** capable of exploding and therefore dangerous: *Hydrogen is extremely explosive.* **2** causing strong feelings or having dangerous effects: *The situation is explosive. We need to do everything we can to calm people down.*

**ex·plo·sive²** /ɪk'sploʊsɪv/ ***noun*** [C] a substance that can explode: *Dynamite is a powerful explosive.*

★**ex·port¹** /ɪk'spɔrt; 'ɛkspɔrt/ ***verb*** [I,T] to send goods, etc. to another country, usually for sale: *India exports tea and cotton.* OPP **import**

★**ex·port²** /'ɛkspɔrt/ ***noun*** **1** [U] sending goods to another country for sale: *Most of our products are manufactured for export.* ◇ *the export trade* **2** [C, usually pl.] something that is sent to another country for sale: *What are the main exports of Brazil?* OPP **import**

**ex·port·er** /ɪk'spɔrt̬ər; 'ɛkspɔrt̬ər/ ***noun*** [C] a person, company or country that exports goods:

*Japan is the largest exporter of electronic products.* OPP **importer**

★**ex·pose** /ɪk'spoʊz/ ***verb*** [T] **1** to make it possible to see sth that is usually hidden: *He liked to wear his shirt open to expose his chest.* ◇ *The rocks are exposed at low tide.* ◇ *He was arrested for exposing himself* (= showing his sexual organs) *in the park.* **2** to put sb/sth or yourself in a situation that could be difficult or dangerous: *Thousands of people were exposed to radiation when the nuclear reactor exploded.* **3** to make the truth about a bad person or situation known to the public: *This is an injustice which needs to be exposed.* ◇ *The letter has been exposed as a forgery.* **4** (in photography) to allow light to reach the film in a camera

**ex·po·sé** /ˌɛkspoʊ'zeɪ/ ***noun*** [C] an account of the facts of a situation that is shocking or has deliberately been kept secret: *a damning exposé of police corruption*

**ex·posed** /ɪk'spoʊzd/ ***adj.*** not covered or protected: *The cord had been damaged, leaving the wires exposed.* ◇ *High winds and blowing snow are likely in exposed areas tonight.*

**ex·po·si·tion** /ˌɛkspə'zɪʃn/ ***noun*** [C] an occasion when new products are shown to the public

**ex·po·sure** /ɪk'spoʊʒər/ ***noun***

➤TO STH HARMFUL **1** [U] **exposure to sth** seeing or being in contact with sth, and possibly being affected by it: *Does exposure to violence on TV make children more aggressive?*

➤MEDICAL CONDITION **2** [U] a harmful condition when a person becomes very cold because he/she has been outside in very bad weather: *The mountain climbers all died of exposure.*

➤SHOWING TRUTH **3** [C,U] the act of making sth public; the thing that is made public: *The congressman resigned because of the exposures about his private life.*

➤ON TV/IN NEWSPAPERS, ETC. **4** [U] attention from newspapers, television, etc.; publicity: *The Pope's visit has been given a lot of exposure in the media.*

➤FILM IN CAMERA **5** [C] the amount of film that is EXPOSED (4) when you take one photograph: *How many exposures are there on this film?* (= how many photographs can I take?)

★**ex·press**[1] /ɪk'sprɛs/ ***verb*** [T] **1** to show sth such as a feeling or an opinion by words or actions: *I found it very hard to express what I felt about her.* **2 express yourself** to speak or write: *I don't think she expresses herself very well in that article.*

**ex·press**[2] /ɪk'sprɛs/ ***adj.*** (only *before* a noun) **1** going or sent quickly: *express delivery* ◇ *an express bus* **2** (used about a wish, command, etc.) clearly and openly stated: *It was her express wish that they have the picture after her death.*

**ex·press**[3] /ɪk'sprɛs/ ***adv.*** by a special service that does sth faster than usual: *We'd better send the package express if we want it to get there on time.*

★**ex·pres·sion** /ɪk'sprɛʃn/ ***noun*** **1** [C] a number of words that belong together: *You don't quite have the right expression here.* ◇ *a slang expression* ◇ *"Ballpark figure" is often a difficult expression for foreign students to understand.* **2** [C] the look on a person's face that shows what he/she is thinking or feeling: *He had a puzzled expression on his face.* **3** [C,U] putting feelings or thoughts into words or actions; an example of doing this: *Freedom of expression* (= freedom to say what you think) *is a basic human right.* ◇ *These flowers are an expression of our gratitude.* ◇ *She read the poem with a great deal of expression* (= showing feeling for the meaning of it).

**ex·pres·sive** /ɪk'sprɛsɪv/ ***adj.*** showing feelings or thoughts: *That is a very expressive piece of music.* ▶ **ex·pres·sive·ly** ***adv.***

**ex·press·ly** /ɪk'sprɛsli/ ***adv.*** (*formal*) **1** clearly; definitely: *The law expressly prohibits the sale of alcohol to people under 21.* **2** for a special purpose; specially: *These scissors are expressly designed for left-handed people.* SYN A less formal word is **specifically**.

**ex·press·way** /ɪk'sprɛsweɪ/ ***noun*** [C] = FREEWAY

**ex·pul·sion** /ɪk'spʌlʃn/ ***noun*** [C,U] making sb leave a place or an institution (when he/she does not want to go): *There have been three expulsions from school this year.* ➲ verb **expel**

**ex·qui·site** /ɪk'skwɪzət; 'ɛkskwəzət/ ***adj.*** very beautiful and pleasing: *an exquisite diamond ring* ◇ *The dancers' costumes were absolutely exquisite.*

★**ex·tend** /ɪk'stɛnd/ ***verb*** **1** [T] to make sth longer or larger (in space or time): *They are planning to extend the expressway as far south as New Orleans.* ◇ *Could you extend your visit for a few days?* **2** [I] (usually used about space, land, time, etc.) to continue or stretch: *How far does your property extend?* ◇ *This project will extend well into next year.* **3** [T] to stretch out a part of the body: *She extended her hand to her new colleague.* **4** [T] (*formal*) to offer or give sth (such as an invitation or a welcome): *The whole town extended a warm welcome to the team.*

**exˌtended 'family** ***noun*** [C] a family group with a close relationship among the members that includes not only parents and children but also uncles, aunts, grandparents, etc. ➲ Look at **nuclear family**.

★**ex·ten·sion** /ɪk'stɛnʃn/ ***noun*** **1** [C] a new part which is added to a building, etc.: *a planned extension to the hospital* **2** [U,C] the act of making sth longer or larger; the thing that is made longer and larger: *A four-mile extension to Route 7 is planned.* ◇ ***hair extensions*** (= pieces of artificial hair that are added to your hair to make it longer) **3** [C] an extra period of time that is given to you, especially by an official: *I applied for an extension of my work permit.* ◇ *I asked the professor for an extension on my English paper.* **3** [C] (*abbr.* **ext.**) a telephone that is connected to a central phone in a house or to a central point (a **switchboard**) in a large office building: *What's your extension number?* ◇ *My phone number is 555-1800, extension 342.*

**ex'tension cord** ***noun*** [C] an extra length of electric wire, used when the wire on an electrical device is not long enough

★**ex·ten·sive** /ɪk'stɛnsɪv/ ***adj.*** large in area or amount: *an extensive search for the missing boy* ◇ *Most of the buildings suffered extensive damage in the earthquake.* ▶ **ex·ten·sive·ly** ***adv.***

★**ex·tent** /ɪk'stɛnt/ ***noun*** [U] the area or size of sth: *I was amazed at the extent of his knowledge.* ◇ *The full extent of the damage is not yet known.*

IDM **to a certain/to some extent** (used to show that sth is only partly true): *I agree with you to a certain extent, but there are still a lot of points I disagree on.*
**to a great/large extent** (used to show that sth is mostly true): *The increase in crime has been caused to a large extent by gangs and drugs.*
**to what extent** how much: *I'm not sure to what extent I believe her.*

**ex·te·ri·or**[1] /ɪk'stɪriər/ ***adj.*** (only *before* a noun) on the outside: *the exterior walls of a house* OPP **interior**

**ex·te·ri·or**[2] /ɪk'stɪriər/ ***noun*** [C, usually sing.] the appearance of sb/sth; the outside of sth: *The exterior of the house is fine, but inside it isn't in very good condition.* OPP **interior**

**ex·ter·mi·nate** /ɪk'stərməneɪt/ ***verb*** [T] to kill a large group of people, animals, insects, etc. ▶ **ex·ter·mi·na·tion** /ɪkˌstərmə'neɪʃn/ ***noun*** [U]

★**ex·ter·nal** /ɪk'stərnl/ ***adj.*** **1** connected with the outside of sth: *The cream is **for external use** only* (= to be used on the skin). **2** coming from another place: *Several external factors were blamed for the company's failure.* OPP **internal**

**ex·tinct** /ɪk'stɪŋkt/ ***adj.*** **1** (used about a type of animal, plant, etc.) no longer existing: *Tigers are nearly extinct in the wild.* **2** (used about a volcano) no longer active ▶ **ex·tinc·tion** /ɪk'stɪŋkʃn/ ***noun*** [U]: *The panda is in danger of extinction.*

**ex·tin·guish** /ɪk'stɪŋgwɪʃ/ ***verb*** [T] (*formal*) to cause sth to stop burning: *The fire was extinguished very quickly.* ◇ *The flight attendant asked everyone to extinguish their cigarettes.* SYN A less formal expression is **put sth out**.

**ex·tin·guish·er** /ɪk'stɪŋgwɪʃər/ ***noun*** [C] = FIRE EXTINGUISHER

**ex·tort** /ɪk'stɔrt/ ***verb*** [T] **extort sth (from sb)** to get sth, especially money, by using threats, violence, etc.

**ex·tor·tion** /ɪk'stɔrʃn/ ***noun*** [U] getting sth, especially money, by using threats, violence, etc.

★**ex·tra**[1] /'ɛkstrə/ ***adj., adv.*** more than is usual: *I'll need some extra money for the weekend.* ◇ *"What size is this sweatshirt?" "Extra large."* ◇ *The bed costs $495, and delivery is extra.* ◇ *They charge $1 extra if you pay by credit card.* ◇ *I tried to be extra nice to him yesterday because it was his birthday.*

★**ex·tra**[2] /'ɛkstrə/ ***noun*** [C] **1** something that is or costs extra: *All these fancy little extras added a lot to the price of the car.* **2** a person in a movie, etc. who has a small unimportant part, for example in a crowd

**ex·tract**[1] /ɪk'strækt/ ***verb*** [T] to take or get sth out (with force or difficulty): *to extract gold and other precious metals from rock* ◇ *I wasn't able to extract an apology from her.*

**ex·tract**[2] /'ɛkstrækt/ ***noun*** **1** [C] a part of a book, piece of music, etc. An extract has often been specially chosen to show sth: *We're reading extracts from modern American novels this semester.* **2** [U] a substance (usually a liquid) that is taken from a plant or food and that has a strong smell or taste of that plant or food: *Add 1 teaspoon of vanilla extract.*

**ex·trac·tion** /ɪk'strækʃn/ ***noun*** **1** [U] the act of taking or getting sth out **2** [C] the removal of a tooth **3** [U] (*formal*) family origin: *He's a Canadian of Italian extraction.*

**ex·tra·cur·ric·u·lar** /ˌɛkstrəkə'rɪkyələr/ ***adj.*** not part of the normal program of studies (the curriculum) in a school or college: *The school offers many extracurricular activities such as sports/music/drama.*

**ex·tra·dite** /'ɛkstrədaɪt/ ***verb*** [T] to send a person who may be guilty of a crime from the country or state in which he/she is living to the country or state which wants to put him/her on trial for the crime: *The suspected terrorists were captured in Mexico and extradited to the United States.* ▶ **ex·tra·di·tion** /ˌɛkstrə'dɪʃn/ ***noun*** [C,U]

**ex·traor·di·nar·y** /ɪk'strɔrdəˌnɛri/ ***adj.*** **1** unusually good, large, etc.: *She had an extraordinary ability to learn new languages.* ◇ *They spent an extraordinary amount of time on the project.* **2** very strange (and not what you would expect in a particular situation): *The law allows special actions to be taken under extraordinary circumstances.* ▶ **extraor·di·nar·i·ly** /ɪk'strɔrdəˌnɛrəli/ ***adv.***: *He was an extraordinarily talented musician.*

**ex·tra·ter·res·tri·al**[1] /ˌɛkstrətə'rɛstriəl/ ***noun*** [C] (in stories) a creature that comes from another planet; a creature that may exist on another planet

**ex·tra·ter·res·tri·al**[2] /ˌɛkstrətə'rɛstriəl/ ***adj.*** connected with life existing outside the planet Earth: *extraterrestrial beings/life*

**ex·trav·a·gant** /ɪk'strævəgənt/ ***adj.*** **1** spending or costing too much money: *He stole from the company in order to finance his extravagant lifestyle.* ◇ *an extravagant present* **2** (used about ideas, behavior, etc.) not controlled, not realistic: *The advertisements made extravagant claims about the product.* ▶ **ex·trav·a·gance** /-gəns/ ***noun*** [C,U] ▶ **ex·trav·a·gant·ly** ***adv.***

★**ex·treme**[1] /ɪk'strim/ ***adj.*** **1** (only *before* a noun) as far away as possible; at the very beginning or at the very end: *Barrow is in the extreme north of Alaska.* **2** (only *before* a noun) the greatest or strongest possible: *Use extreme caution when driving on icy roads.* **3** (used about a person and his/her political opinions) not usual or moderate: *She holds extreme views on immigration.* ◇ *the extreme left/right*

NOTE This word is used in a disapproving way in this sense.

**ex·treme**[2] /ɪk'strim/ ***noun*** [C] something that is completely different from or opposite to sth else: *Alex used to be very shy, but now he's gone to the opposite extreme.*

★**ex·treme·ly** /ɪk'strimli/ ***adv.*** very: *It was an extremely difficult decision.*

**ex·trem·ist** /ɪk'strimɪst/ ***noun*** [C] a person who has EXTREME[1] (3) political opinions ▶ **ex·trem·ism** ***noun*** [U]

**ex·trem·i·ty** /ɪk'strɛməṭi/ ***noun*** [C] (*pl.* **ex·trem·i·ties**) **1** the furthest point of sth **2** **extremities** [pl.] the hands and feet: *Her heart was not pumping enough blood to her extremities.*

**ex·tri·cate** /'ɛkstrəkeɪt/ ***verb*** [T] to free sb/sth/yourself from a difficult situation or position: *I finally managed to extricate myself from the*



E

*meeting by saying that I had to pick up my kids from school.*

**ex·tro·vert** /ˈɛkstrəvərt/ ***noun*** [C] a person who is enthusiastic and cheerful and who prefers being with other people to being alone OPP **introvert** ▸ **ex·tro·vert·ed** /-vərt̬əd/ ***adj.***

**ex·u·ber·ant** /ɪɡˈzubərənt/ ***adj.*** (used about a person and his/her behavior) full of energy and excitement ▸ **ex·u·ber·ance** /-rəns/ ***noun*** [U]

**ex·ude** /ɪɡˈzud/ ***verb*** **1** [I,T] if you exude a particular quality or feeling, or it exudes from you, people can easily see that you have it: *She exuded self-confidence.* ◇ *Her rage positively exuded from her.* **2** [I,T] if sth exudes a liquid or smell, or a liquid or smell exudes from somewhere, the liquid, etc. comes out slowly: *The plant exudes a sticky fluid.* ◇ *An awful smell exuded from the creature's body.*

★**eye**[1] /aɪ/ ***noun*** [C] **1** one of the two organs of the body that we use to see with: *She opened/closed her eyes.* ◇ *He is blind in one eye.* ◇ *She has blue eyes.* ◇ *an eye operation* ➲ picture on study page **A32**.

> NOTE If somebody hits you in the eye you might get a **black eye**. When you close both eyes very quickly and open them again, you **blink**. To close one eye quickly and open it again is to **wink**.

**2** the power of seeing: *He has sharp eyes* (= he can see very well). ◇ *She has an eye for detail* (= she notices small details). **3** the part at one end of a needle that the thread passes through **4** the center of a large storm, where the winds are calm: *the eye of the hurricane/tornado*

IDM **be up to your ears/eyes/neck in sth** → UP[1]

**cast an eye/your eye(s) over sb/sth** → CAST[2]

**catch sb's attention/eye** → ATTENTION

**in the eyes of sb/in sb's eyes** in the opinion of sb: *She was still a child in her mother's eyes.*

**keep a close eye/watch on sb/sth; keep an eye on sb/sth** to make sure that sb/sth is safe; to watch sb/sth carefully: *Could you please keep an eye on the house while we are away?*

**keep an eye open/out (for sb/sth); keep your eyes open (for sb/sth)** to watch or look out for sb/sth: *I lost my ring – could you keep an eye out for it?*

**the naked eye** → NAKED

**not bat an eye** → BAT[2]

**see eye to eye with sb** to agree with sb; to have the same opinion as sb: *We're good friends, but we don't always see eye to eye on political matters.*

**set eyes on sb/sth** to see sb/sth: *He loved the house the moment he set eyes on it.*

**turn a blind eye** → BLIND[1]

**eye**[2] /aɪ/ ***verb*** [T] (*pres. part.* **eye·ing** or **ey·ing**; *pt, pp* **eyed**) to look at sb/sth closely: *She eyed him with suspicion.*

**eye·ball**[1] /ˈaɪbɔl/ ***noun*** [C] the whole of the eye (including the part which is hidden inside the head)

**eye·ball**[2] /ˈaɪbɔl/ ***verb*** [T] (*informal*) to look at sb/sth in a way that is very direct and not always polite or friendly

**eye·brow** /ˈaɪbraʊ/ (*also* **brow**) ***noun*** [C] the line of hair that is above your eye: *to pluck your eyebrows*

IDM **raise your eyebrows** → RAISE[1]

ˈ**eye-ˌcatching** ***adj.*** interesting or attractive to look at: *an eye-catching design*

ˈ**eye ˌcontact** ***noun*** [U] a look directly into sb else's eyes: *When she wouldn't* ***make eye contact*** *with him, he knew she was lying.*

**eye·glass·es** /ˈaɪɡlæsəz/ ***noun*** [pl.] = GLASSES

**eye·lash** /ˈaɪlæʃ/ (*also* **lash**) ***noun*** [C] one of the hairs that grow on the edges of your eyelids

**eye·lid** /ˈaɪlɪd/ (*also* **lid**) ***noun*** [C] the piece of skin that you can move to close your eye

**eye·lin·er** /ˈaɪlaɪnər/ ***noun*** [U] makeup that you use to draw a line around your eyes

ˈ**eye ˌopener** ***noun*** [C] something that makes you realize the truth about sth: *That TV program about the greenhouse effect was a real eye opener.*

ˈ**eye ˌshadow** ***noun*** [U] colored powder that you use to decorate your eyelids

**eye·sight** /ˈaɪsaɪt/ ***noun*** [U] the ability to see: *good/poor eyesight*

**eye·sore** /ˈaɪsɔr/ ***noun*** [C] something that is ugly and unpleasant to look at: *All this garbage in the streets is a real eyesore.*

**eye·wit·ness** /ˌaɪˈwɪtnəs; ˈaɪwɪtnəs/ ***noun*** [C] = WITNESS[1] (1)

**e-zine** /ˈi zin/ ***noun*** [C] a magazine that is published on the Internet, and not printed on paper

# Ff

**F, f** /ɛf/ ***noun*** [C,U] (*pl.* **F's**; **f's**) **1** the sixth letter of the English alphabet: *"Father" begins with (an) "F."* **2** the lowest grade that is given for a test or a piece of work. An "F" means that the person has failed: *I got an "F" on my last history test.*

**F** ***abbr.*** = FAHRENHEIT: *98.6° F*

**fa·ble** /ˈfeɪbl/ ***noun*** [C] a short story that teaches a lesson (a moral) and that often has animals as speaking characters: *Aesop's fables*

**fab·ric** /ˈfæbrɪk/ ***noun*** **1** [C,U] (a type of) cloth: *cotton fabrics* **2** [sing.] the basic structure of sth: *The Industrial Revolution changed the fabric of society.*

**fab·ri·cate** /ˈfæbrɪkeɪt/ ***verb*** [T] (often passive) to invent false information, a false story, etc., on purpose, to make people believe sth that is not true: *The evidence was totally fabricated.* ▸ **fab·ri·ca·tion** ***noun*** [C,U]: *Her story was a complete fabrication.*

**fab·u·lous** /ˈfæbyələs/ ***adj.*** **1** (*informal*) very good; excellent **2** (used about beauty, wealth, etc.) very great

**fa·çade** (*also* **facade**) /fəˈsɑd/ ***noun*** [C] **1** the front wall of a large building that you see from the outside **2** something that gives you the wrong impression about a situation: *His good mood was just a façade.*

★**face[1]** /feɪs/ ***noun*** [C] **1** the front part of your head and the expression on it: *Go and wash your face.* ◇ *She has a very pretty face.* ◇ *He came in with a smile on his face.* ◇ *the children's happy faces* **2** the front or one side of sth: *the north face of the mountain* ◇ *He put the cards face up/down on the table.* ◇ *a clock face* ➲ picture at **clock**.

IDM **face to face (with sb/sth)** close to and looking at sb/sth: *She turned the corner and came face to face with the principal.*

**keep a straight face** → STRAIGHT[1]

**lose/save face** to lose/keep yourself from losing the respect of other people: *He did not want to lose face by making a mistake in front of his boss.*

**make faces/a face (at sb)** to make an expression that shows that you dislike sb/sth: *When she saw what was for dinner, she made a face.*

**make faces** to make rude expressions with your face: *The children made faces behind the teacher's back.*

**to sb's face** openly and directly: *I wanted to say that I was sorry to her face, not on the phone.* OPP **behind sb's back**

★**face[2]** /feɪs/ ***verb*** [T] **1** to have or turn the face or front toward sb/sth: *The porch faces south.* ◇ *Can you all face the front, please?* **2** to have to deal with sth unpleasant; to deal with sb in a difficult situation: *They faced a lot of problems when they moved to a new house.* ◇ *I can't face another argument.* ◇ *Face it – you're never going to be a professional athlete.* ◇ *He couldn't face going to work yesterday – he felt too sick.* ◇ *I didn't know how to face my mother after I'd wrecked her car.* **3** to need attention from sb: *There are several problems facing the country.* **4** (often passive) to force somebody to deal with a situation, etc.: *We are faced with a difficult decision.*

IDM **let's face it** (*informal*) we must accept it as true: *Let's face it – not everybody is going to pass the test.*

PHRV **face up to sth** to accept a difficult or unpleasant situation and do sth about it: *She faced up to the fact that she had no money and went out and got a job.*

ˈ**face cloth** ***noun*** [C] (*Cdn*) = WASHCLOTH

**-faced** /feɪst/ ***combining form*** with a particular type of face: *red-faced* ◇ *a bare-faced lie* (a direct lie, told with no embarrassment)

**face·less** /ˈfeɪsləs/ ***adj.*** without individual character: *faceless government employees*

ˈ**face·lift** (*also* ˈ**face-lift**) /ˈfeɪslɪft/ ***noun*** [C] a medical operation that makes your face look younger: (*figurative*) *The monument is scheduled for a $5 million facelift next year.*

ˈ**face-ˌsaving** ***adj.*** done to stop yourself from looking silly or losing other people's respect: *to make a face-saving excuse*

**fac·et** /ˈfæsət/ ***noun*** [C] **1** one part of sth: *There are many facets to this argument* (= points that must be considered). **2** one side of a precious stone

**fa·ce·tious** /fəˈsiʃəs/ ***adj.*** trying to be amusing at an unsuitable time or about an unsuitable subject: *He kept making facetious remarks during the lecture.* ▸ **fa·ce·tious·ly** ***adv.***

ˌ**face ˈvalue** ***noun*** [C,U] the cost or value that is shown on stamps, coins, etc.

IDM **take sb/sth at face value** to accept sb/sth as it, he, etc. appears to be: *Don't take his story at face value.*

**fa·cial[1]** /ˈfeɪʃl/ ***adj.*** of or for the face: *a facial expression*

**fa·cial[2]** /ˈfeɪʃl/ ***noun*** [C] a beauty treatment in which a person's face is cleaned using creams, steam, etc. in order to improve the quality of the skin

**fa·cil·i·tate** /fəˈsɪləteɪt/ ***verb*** [T] (*formal*) to make sth possible or easier

★**fa·cil·i·ty** /fəˈsɪləṭi/ ***noun*** (*pl.* **fa·cil·i·ties**) **1 facilities** [pl.] a service, piece of equipment, etc. that makes it possible to do sth: *Our town has excellent sports facilities* (a big stadium/swimming pool). **2** [C] a building where a particular type of service is provided: *a health care facility* ◇ *a storage facility* **3** [C] an extra feature that a machine, etc. may have: *This program has a facility for checking spelling.*

**fac·sim·i·le** /fækˈsɪməli/ ***noun*** [C,U] an exact copy of a picture, piece of writing, etc. ➲ Look at **fax**.

★**fact** /fækt/ ***noun*** **1** [C] something that you know has happened or is true: *It is a scientific fact that light travels faster than sound.* ◇ *We need to know all the facts before we can decide.* ◇ *I know for a fact that Peter wasn't sick yesterday.* ◇ *The fact that I am older than you makes no difference at all.* ◇ *You need to face the facts and accept that he has gone.* **2** [U] true things; reality: *The movie is based on fact.* OPP **fiction**

IDM **as a matter of fact** → MATTER[1]

**the fact (of the matter) is (that)...** the truth is that...: *I would love a car, but the fact is that I just can't afford one.*

**facts and figures** (*informal*) detailed information: *Here are some facts and figures on new housing developments in the city:...*

**a fact of life** a true situation that you cannot ignore, even if it is unpleasant: *It's just a fact of life that some children come from poor families.*

**the facts of life** the details of sexual behavior and how babies are born

**hard facts** → HARD[1]

**in fact 1** (used for emphasizing that sth is true) really; actually: *I thought the lecture would be boring, but in fact it was pretty interesting.* **2** (used for introducing more detailed information): *It was cold. In fact, it was freezing.*

**fac·tion** /ˈfækʃn/ ***noun*** **1** [C] a small group of people within a larger one whose members have some different aims and beliefs to those of the larger group: *rival factions within the administration* **2** [U] disagreement, etc. that exists between small groups of people within an organization or political party: *a party divided by faction and intrigue* **3** [U] movies, books, etc. that combine fact with imagined events (**fiction**)

★**fac·tor** /ˈfæktər/ ***noun*** [C] **1** one of the things that influences a decision, situation, etc.: *His unhappiness at home was a major factor in his decision to* *move away.* **2** (in mathematics) a whole number by which a larger number can be divided: *2, 3, 4 and 6 are factors of 12.*

★**fac·to·ry** /ˈfæktəri; -tri/ ***noun*** [C] (*pl.* **fac·to·ries**) a large building or group of buildings where goods are manufactured or put together in large quantities (by machine): *a car factory* ◇ *factory workers*

**fac·tu·al** /ˈfæktʃuəl/ ***adj.*** based on or containing facts: *a factual account of the events* ➲ Look at **fictional**.

**fac·ul·ty** /ˈfæklti/ ***noun*** [C] (*pl.* **fac·ul·ties**) **1** [usually sing.] the people who teach at a school, college, or university: *This dining room is only for members of the faculty, staff and administration.* ◇ *a faculty meeting* **2** one of the natural abilities of a person's body or mind: *At 85, he still had all his mental faculties.*

**fad** /fæd/ ***noun*** [C] (*informal*) a fashion, interest, etc. that will probably not last long

**fade** /feɪd/ ***verb*** **1** [I] to become lighter in color or less strong or fresh: *Jeans fade when you wash them.* ◇ *The sun was setting and the light was fading fast.* **2** [T] to make sth fade: *Look how the sun has faded these curtains.* **3** [I] **fade (away)** to disappear slowly (from sight, hearing, memory, etc.): *The cheering of the crowd faded away.* ◇ *The smile faded from his face.*

**fag** /fæg/ ***noun*** (*slang*) a man who is sexually attracted to other men

> NOTE This word is extremely offensive. Look at **gay**.

**Fahr·en·heit** /ˈfærənhaɪt/ ***noun*** [U] (*abbr.* **F**) the name of a scale which measures temperatures: *Water freezes at 32 degrees Fahrenheit (32°F).*

> NOTE In everyday situations in the U.S., temperatures are almost always given in **Fahrenheit**. In Canada they are usually given in **Celsius**.

★**fail**[1] /feɪl/ ***verb***

➤ NOT SUCCEED **1** [I,T] to be unsuccessful in sth: *She failed her driving test.* ◇ *I feel that I've failed – I'm 25 and I still don't have a steady job.* ➲ Look at **pass** and **succeed**. **2** [T] (used about a teacher, etc.) to decide that sb is unsuccessful in a test, on a piece of work, etc.: *The teachers failed 10 percent of the students who took the exam.* OPP **pass**

➤ NOT DO STH **3** [I] **fail to do sth** to not do sth: *Jimmy failed to arrive on time.* ◇ *She never fails to do her homework.*

➤ NOT BE ENOUGH **4** [I,T] to not be enough or not do what people are expecting or wanting: *If the crops fail, people will starve.* ◇ *Words fail me!* (= I don't know how to express my feelings) ◇ *I think the government has failed us.*

➤ OF HEALTH/SIGHT **5** [I] (used about health, eyesight, etc.) to become weak: *His health is failing.*

➤ OF MACHINES/PARTS OF THE BODY **6** [I] to stop working: *My brakes failed on the hill, but I managed to stop the car.*

**fail**[2] /feɪl/ ***noun*** [U]

IDM **without fail** always, even if there are difficulties: *The school bus always comes at 8 o'clock without fail.*

**fail·ing**[1] /ˈfeɪlɪŋ/ ***noun*** [C] a weakness or fault: *She's not very patient – that's her only failing.*

**fail·ing**[2] /ˈfeɪlɪŋ/ ***adj.*** showing that sb/sth has failed; no longer functioning correctly: *Five students received failing grades on the test.*

**fail·ing**[3] /ˈfeɪlɪŋ/ ***prep.*** (*formal*) if sth is not possible: *We hope to solve the problem today, or, failing that, to develop a plan to solve it soon.*

★**fail·ure** /ˈfeɪlyər/ ***noun*** **1** [U] lack of success: *All my efforts ended in failure.* **2** [C] a person or thing that is unsuccessful: *I was a failure as a mother.* **3** [C,U] **failure to do sth** not doing sth that people expect you to do: *I was very disappointed at his failure to come to the meeting.* **4** [C,U] an example of sth not working or functioning properly: *She died of heart failure.* ◇ *a power failure*

**faint**[1] /feɪnt/ ***adj.*** **1** (used about things that you can see, hear, feel, etc.) not strong or clear: *a faint light in the distance* ◇ *There is still a faint hope that they will find more people alive.* **2** (used about people) on the point of losing consciousness; very weak: *I feel faint – I'd better sit down.* **3** (used about actions, etc.) done without much effort: *He made a faint protest.*

IDM **not have the faintest idea** not to know at all: *I don't have the faintest idea where they went.*

**faint**[2] /feɪnt/ ***verb*** [I] to lose consciousness: *She fainted from shock and loss of blood.*

★**fair**[1] /fɛr/ ***adj.***

➤ TREATING PEOPLE EQUALLY **1** **fair (to sb)** treating each person or side equally, according to the law or the rules, etc.: *That's not fair – he made the same number of mistakes as I did and he got a better grade.* ◇ *It wasn't fair to her to ask her to stay so late.* ◇ *a fair trial*

➤ ACCEPTABLE/APPROPRIATE **2** right, according to what people generally accept as right: *a fair price* ◇ *I think it's fair to say that the number of homeless people is increasing.* OPP The opposite for senses **1** and **2** is **unfair**.

➤ AVERAGE **3** not better, bigger, etc. than average: *They have a fair chance of success.* ◇ *It is a fair-sized house.* ◇ *How would you describe the service here: excellent, good, fair or poor?*

➤ HAIR/SKIN **4** (used about the skin or hair) light in color: *He has a fair complexion and gets sunburned easily.*

➤ WEATHER **5** (used about the weather) good, without rain

IDM **fair game** a person or thing that is easy to criticize or that people think should be criticized: *The silly behavior of celebrities makes them fair game for comedians.*

**fair play** equal treatment of both/all sides according to the rules: *Special privileges for some people violate our sense of fair play.*

**have (more than) your (fair) share of sth** → SHARE[1]

▶ **fair·ness** ***noun*** [U]

**fair**[2] /fɛr/ ***adv.*** in a FAIR[1] (1) way: *You have to play fair in all team games.*

IDM **fair and square** in an honest and FAIR[1] (1) way: *Quit complaining – she won the game fair and square.*

**fair enough** (used for showing that you think that what sb has said is right, even if you do not like it):

*"I washed the dishes every night last week – I'm not doing them again." "Okay, fair enough. I'll do them tonight."*

**fair**[3] /fɛr/ ***noun*** [C] **1** a public event which is organized by people who live in a particular area. At a fair you can ride on machines, look at farm animals and products that people have made, or try to win prizes in games: *My pumpkin pie won first prize at the county fair.* **2** a large exhibition of commercial or industrial goods: *a trade fair*

**ˌfair ˈgame** ***noun*** [U] if a person or thing is said to be fair game, it is considered acceptable to play jokes on him/her, criticize him/her/it, etc.: *The younger teachers were considered fair game by most of the kids.*

**fair·ground** /ˈfɛrgraʊnd/ ***noun*** [C] a large outdoor area where FAIRS[3] (1) are held

★**fair·ly** /ˈfɛrli/ ***adv.*** **1** in a FAIR[1] (1) way: *I felt that the teacher didn't treat us fairly.* OPP **unfairly** **2** more than a little, but not extremely: *fairly tall* ◇ *We need to leave fairly soon.* ➲ Look at the note at **rather**.

**fair·y** /ˈfɛri/ ***noun*** [C] (*pl.* **fair·ies**) (in stories) a small creature with magical powers

fairy

wing

**ˈfairy tale** ***noun*** [C] a story that is about fairies, magic, etc.: *Grimm's fairy tales*

**fait ac·com·pli** /ˌfeɪt̬ əkɑmˈpli; ˌfet̬ ɑkɔmˈpli/ ***noun*** [C] (*pl.* **faits ac·com·plis**) something that has already happened or been done and that you cannot change: *We got married secretly and then presented our parents with a fait accompli.*

★**faith** /feɪθ/ ***noun*** **1** [U] **faith (in sb/sth)** strong belief (in sb/sth); trust: *I have great faith in your ability to do the job* (= I'm sure that you can do it). ◇ *I have lost faith in him.* **2** [U] strong religious belief **3** [C] a religion: *the Christian faith*

IDM **in good faith** with honest reasons for doing sth: *I bought the car in good faith. I didn't know it was stolen.*

★**faith·ful** /ˈfeɪθfl/ ***adj.*** **1** not changing; loyal: *a faithful friend* ◇ *He was always faithful to his wife* (= he didn't have sex with anyone else). OPP **unfaithful** **2** true to the facts; accurate: *a faithful description* ▸ **faith·ful·ly** ***adv.*** ▸ **faith·ful·ness** ***noun*** [U]

**fa·ji·ta** /fəˈhit̬ə; fɑ-/ ***noun*** [C] a Mexican dish made with a kind of bread (**tortilla**) filled with meat or fish, vegetables and sauces

**fake**[1] /feɪk/ ***noun*** [C] **1** a work of art, etc. that seems to be real or genuine but is not: *That's not a real diamond necklace. It's just a fake!* **2** a person who pretends to be sb/sth else in order to deceive people

**fake**[2] /feɪk/ ***adj.*** not real or genuine: *a fake passport*

**fake**[3] /feɪk/ ***verb*** [T] **1** to copy sth in order to deceive people: *He faked his father's signature.* **2** to pretend that you are feeling sth that you are not: *I faked surprise when he told me the news.*

**fal·con** /ˈfælkən; ˈfɔl-/ ***noun*** [C] a bird that kills and eats other animals. Falcons can be trained to hunt.

★**fall**[1] /fɔl/ ***verb*** [I] (*pt* **fell** /fɛl/; *pp* **fall·en** /ˈfɔlən/)

▸ DROP DOWN **1** to drop down toward the ground: *He fell off the ladder onto the grass.* ◇ *Don't walk along that ledge – you might fall.* ◇ *October came and the leaves started to fall.* ◇ *The rain was falling steadily.*

▸ STOP STANDING **2 fall (down/over)** to suddenly stop standing: *She slipped on the ice and fell.* ◇ *The little boy fell down and hurt his knee.* ◇ *The tree fell over onto my car.*

▸ HAPPEN/OCCUR **3** (*formal*) to come or happen: *My birthday falls on a Sunday this year.* ◇ *In the word "interesting," the stress falls on the first syllable.*

▸ OF HAIR/MATERIAL **4** to hang down: *Her hair fell down over her shoulders.*

▸ DECREASE **5** to become lower or less: *The temperature is falling.* ◇ *The price of coffee has fallen again.*

▸ DIE IN BATTLE **6** to be killed (in battle)

▸ BE DEFEATED **7** to be defeated: *The senator fell from power because of the scandal.*

▸ BECOME **8** to change into a different state; to become: *He fell asleep on the sofa.* ◇ *I need to get some new shoes – these ones are falling to pieces.*

▸ BELONG TO A GROUP **9** to belong to a particular group, type, etc.: *Animals fall into two groups: those with backbones and those without.*

IDM **fall flat** → FLAT[2]

**fall in love** → LOVE[1]

**fall short (of sth)** → SHORT[2]

**fall/slip through the cracks** → CRACK[1]

PHRV **fall apart** to break (into pieces): *My car is falling apart.*

**fall back on sb/sth** to use sb/sth when you are in difficulty: *If my new business isn't a success, we can always fall back on my wife's income.*

**fall for sb** (*informal*) to fall in love with sb

**fall for sth** (*informal*) to be tricked into believing sth that is not true: *He makes excuses and she falls for them every time.*

**fall out (with sb)** to argue or fight (with sb)

**fall through** to fail or not happen: *Our trip to Japan fell through.*

★**fall**[2] /fɔl/ ***noun***

▸ ACT OF FALLING **1** [C] an act of FALLING[1] (1,2): *She had a bad fall while she was skiing.*

▸ OF SNOW/ROCKS **2** [C] **a fall (of sth)** the amount of sth that has fallen or the distance that sth has fallen: *a heavy fall of snow*

▸ DECREASE **3** [C] a decrease (in value, quantity, etc.): *There has been a sharp fall in the price of oil.* OPP **rise**

▸ DEFEAT **4** [sing.] **the fall of sth** a (political) defeat: *the fall of the Roman Empire*

▸ SEASON **5** [C, usually sing.] (*also formal* **autumn**) the season of the year that comes between summer and winter: *I visited Europe in the fall of 2003.* ◇ *fall weather*

▸ WATER **6** [C, usually pl.] a waterfall: *Niagara Falls*

**fal·la·cy** /ˈfæləsi/ ***noun*** (*pl.* **fal·la·cies**) [C,U] (*formal*) a false or mistaken belief or argument: *It's a fallacy to believe that money brings happiness.*

**fall·en** *past participle of* FALL[1]

**fal·li·ble** /ˈfæləbl/ ***adj.*** able or likely to make mistakes: *Even our new computerized system is fallible.* OPP **infallible** ▸ **fal·li·bil·i·ty** /ˌfæləˈbɪləṭi/ ***noun*** [U]

**fall·out** /ˈfɔlaʊt/ ***noun*** [U] dangerous waste matter that is carried in the air after a nuclear explosion: (*figurative*) *the political fallout* (= bad effects) *from the scandal*

★**false** /fɔls/ ***adj.***

➤NOT TRUE **1** not true; incorrect: *I think the information you were given is false.*

➤NOT NATURAL **2** not real; artificial: *false hair/teeth/eyelashes*

➤WRONG/MISTAKEN **3** based on wrong information or beliefs: *I got a completely false impression of him from our first meeting.*

➤NOT GENUINE **4** made or done incorrectly in order to deceive people: *This suitcase has a false bottom.* ◇ *a false name*

➤NOT SINCERE **5** not faithful; not loyal: *a false friend*

IDM **a false alarm** a warning about a danger that does not happen

**under false pretenses** pretending to be or to have sth in order to deceive people: *The journalist got the information under false pretenses – she claimed to be the senator's secretary.*

**fal·si·fy** /ˈfɔlsəfaɪ/ ***verb*** [T] (*pres. part.* **fal·si·fy·ing**; *3rd person sing. pres.* **fal·si·fies**; *pt, pp* **fal·si·fied**) (*formal*) to change a document, information, etc. in order to deceive other people

**fal·ter** /ˈfɔltər/ ***verb*** [I] **1** to become weak or move in a weak, unsteady way: *As she began to speak, her voice faltered.* ◇ *The engine faltered and stopped.* **2** to lose confidence and hesitate: *Agassi faltered and missed the ball.*

★**fame** /feɪm/ ***noun*** [U] being known or talked about by many people: *She achieved fame at a young age.* ➲ Look also at **hall of fame**.

**famed** /feɪmd/ ***adj.*** well-known (for sth): *Colorado is famed for its ski resorts.* ➲ Look at **famous**, which is the more usual word.

★**fa·mil·iar** /fəˈmɪlyər/ ***adj.*** **1** (not before a noun) **familiar with sth** having a good knowledge of sth: *Are you familiar with Chinese music?* **2 familiar (to sb)** well-known (to sb): *Chinese music isn't very familiar to people in America.* ◇ *It was a relief to see a familiar face in the crowd.* OPP The opposite for senses **1** and **2** is **unfamiliar**.

**fa·mil·iar·i·ty** /fəˌmɪliˈærəṭi; fəˌmɪlˈyærəṭi/ ***noun*** [U] good knowledge of sth: *His familiarity with the area was an advantage.*

**fa·mil·iar·ize** /fəˈmɪlyəraɪz/ ***verb*** [T] to inform sb/yourself about sth: *I want to familiarize myself with the plans before the meeting.*

★**fam·i·ly** /ˈfæmli; ˈfæməli/ ***noun*** (*pl.* **fam·i·lies**) **1** [C] a group of people who are closely related to each other and who usually live together: *There are four people in my family.* ◇ *the Wilson family* ◇ *We are planning to start a family next year* (= to have our first baby).

NOTE Sometimes we use "family" to mean "parents and their children" (a **nuclear family**); sometimes we use it to include other relatives, e.g. grandparents, aunts, uncles, etc. (an **extended family**). **Family** can be used before another noun to describe things that are suitable for or that can be used by the whole family: *family entertainment* ◇ *a family car*

**2** [C,U] (a group of) people who are related to sb: *Do you have any family in the area?* ◇ *a family reunion* **3** [C] a group of animals, plants, etc. that are related to each other: *Lions belong to the cat family.*

IDM **run in the family** to be found very often in a FAMILY (2): *Red hair runs in the family.*

ˌ**family ˈdoctor** (*also* ˌ**family phyˈsician**, ˌ**family pracˈtitioner**) ***noun*** [C] a doctor who treats common health problems in people of all ages

ˈ**family name** ***noun*** [C] the name that is shared by members of a family; a person's last name ➲ Look at the note at **name**.

ˌ**family ˈplanning** ***noun*** [U] controlling the number of children in a family by using birth control ➲ Look at **contraception**.

ˈ**family room** ***noun*** [C] a room in a house, usually with informal furniture, where a family can watch television, listen to music, etc.

ˌ**family ˈtree** ***noun*** [C] a diagram that shows the relationships between different members of a family

ˌ**family ˈvalues** ***noun*** [pl.] qualities such as hard work, strong religious belief, strict discipline, moral behavior and traditional roles for men and women

**fam·ine** /ˈfæmən/ ***noun*** [C,U] a lack of food in a large area that can cause the death of many people: *There is a severe famine in many parts of Africa.* ◇ *The long drought was followed by famine.*

**fam·ished** /ˈfæmɪʃt/ ***adj.*** (*informal*) very hungry: *When's lunch? I'm famished!* SYN **starving**

★**fa·mous** /ˈfeɪməs/ ***adj.*** **famous (for sth)** well-known to many people: *a famous singer* ◇ *New York is famous for its museums and art galleries.* ➲ Look at **infamous** and **notorious**, which mean "famous for being bad." ▸ **fa·mous·ly** ***adv.***: *As Benjamin Franklin famously said, "A penny saved is a penny earned."*

**fans**

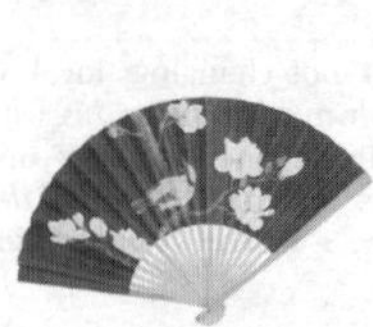

fan

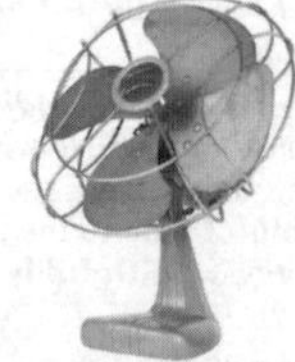

desk fan

★**fan**[1] /fæn/ ***noun*** [C] **1** something that is used for making a (cool) wind, e.g. an object made of paper, feathers, etc. in the shape of half a circle, or an electric machine with large blades that turn around very quickly **2** a person who admires and is very enthusiastic about a sport, a movie star, a singer, etc.: *football fans* ◇ *He's a Mariah Carey fan.* ◇ *I'm not a big fan of modern jazz* (= I don't like it very much).

**fan**[2] /fæn/ ***verb*** [T] (**fan·ning**; **fanned**) **1** to cool sb/sth/yourself by moving the air with a FAN[1] (1) or sth like a fan: *She used a newspaper to fan her face.* **2** to make a fire burn more strongly: *The strong wind really fanned the flames.*

PHR V **fan out** to spread out: *The police fanned out across the field.*

**fa·nat·ic** /fəˈnæt̬ɪk/ ***noun*** [C] a person who is too enthusiastic about sth (especially about religion or politics): *a religious fanatic* ◇ *She's a health food fanatic.*

**fa·nat·i·cal** /fəˈnæt̬ɪkl/ ***adj.*** feeling very strongly or being too enthusiastic about sth: *He's fanatical about keeping things neat.* ▸ **fa·nat·i·cal·ly** /-kli/ ***adv.*** ▸ **fa·nat·i·cism** /-t̬əsɪzəm/ ***noun*** [C,U]

**ˈfan club** ***noun*** [C] an organization for people who are FANS[1] (2) of a famous person

**fan·cy** /ˈfænsi/ ***adj.*** not simple or ordinary: *a fancy restaurant* ◇ *I just want a regular pair of blue jeans – nothing fancy.*

**fan·fare** /ˈfænfɛr/ ***noun*** **1** [C] a short loud piece of music played on trumpets that is used for introducing sb/sth **2** [C,U] an exciting event or behavior that attracts people's attention: *The tax cut was announced with a great deal of fanfare.*

**fang** /fæŋ/ ***noun*** [C] a long sharp tooth of a dog, poisonous snake, etc.

**fan·ny** /ˈfæni/ ***noun*** [C] (*pl.* **fan·nies**) (*informal*) the part of your body that you sit on

**ˈfanny pack** ***noun*** [C] a small bag worn around the waist to keep money, etc. in

**fan·ta·size** /ˈfæntəsaɪz/ ***verb*** [I,T] to imagine sth that you would like to happen: *He liked to fantasize about winning a gold medal in the Olympics.*

**fan·tas·tic** /fænˈtæstɪk/ ***adj.*** **1** very good; excellent: *She's a fantastic swimmer.* ◇ *You passed your test. Fantastic!* **2** strange and difficult to believe: *fantastic creatures from other worlds* ▸ **fan·tas·ti·cal·ly** /-kli/ ***adv.***

**fan·ta·sy** /ˈfæntəsi/ ***noun*** [C,U] (*pl.* **fan·ta·sies**) a situation that is not true, that you just imagine: *My fantasy is to become a famous actress.* ◇ *They live in a world of fantasy.* ➲ Look at the note at **imagination**.

**fan·zine** /ˈfænzin/ ***noun*** [C] a magazine that is written by and for people (**fans**) who like a particular sports team, singer, etc., or for people who like books, movies, etc. about how the future might be (science fiction)

**FAQ** /fæk; ˌɛf eɪ ˈkyu/ ***noun*** [C] a document on the Internet that contains the most *frequently asked questions* about a subject and the answers to these questions

★**far**[1] /fɑr/ ***adj.*** (**far·ther** /ˈfɑrðər/ or **fur·ther** /ˈfərðər/, **far·thest** /ˈfɑrðəst/ or **fur·thest** /ˈfərðəst/) (only *before* a noun) more distant (used about one of two ends, sides, etc.): *My friend lives at the far end of the street.* ◇ *In the far north, days are short during the winter.*

IDM **a far cry from sth/from doing sth** an experience that is very different from sth/doing sth

★**far**[2] /fɑr/ ***adv.*** (**far·ther** /ˈfɑrðər/ or **fur·ther** /ˈfərðər/, **far·thest** /ˈfɑrðəst/ or **fur·thest** /ˈfərðəst/) **1** (at) a distance: *Do you live far from Seattle?* ◇ *How far did we walk yesterday?* ◇ *Call me if you need me; I won't be far away.*

> NOTE **Far** in this sense is usually used in negative sentences and questions. In positive sentences we say **a long way**: *It's a long way from here to the ocean.* Some sentences have a negative meaning although they are positive in form. **Far** can be used in them: *Let's drive there. It's way too far to walk.*

**2** a long time: *This story began far back in 1850.* ◇ *We danced far into the night.* **3** (before comparative adjectives) very much: *She's far more intelligent than I thought.* ◇ *It's far wetter in Vancouver than in Saskatoon.*

IDM **as far as** to the place mentioned but not farther: *We walked as far as the river and then turned back.*

**as/so far as** to the degree that: *As far as I know, she's not coming, but I may be wrong.*

**as far as I can see/tell** (used for introducing your opinion): *As far as I can tell, the accident was John's fault, not Ann's.*

**as far as sb is concerned** in sb's opinion: *As far as I'm concerned, there's nothing left to say on the subject.*

**as/so far as sth is concerned**; **as far as sth goes** on the subject of sth; as sth is affected or influenced by sth: *As far as school work goes, he's not very good.*

**by far** (used for emphasizing comparative or superlative words) by a large amount: *Jane is by far the best student in the class.*

**far afield** far away, especially from where you live or from where you are staying: *We decided to rent a car in order to explore farther afield.*

**far from sth/from doing sth** almost the opposite of sth: *The future of the company is far from certain* (= it's very uncertain).

**far from it** (*informal*) certainly not; just the opposite: *"Were there a lot of people at the concert?" "Far from it – the place was almost empty."*

**few and far between** → FEW[1]

**go too far** to be too extreme: *He's always been mean, but this time he's gone too far.*

**so far** until now: *So far the weather has been good but it might change.*

**so far, so good** (*informal*) everything has gone well up to now

**far·a·way** /ˈfɑrəˌweɪ/ ***adj.*** **1** distant: *He told us stories of faraway countries.* **2** (used about a look in a person's eyes) as if you are thinking of sth else: *She stared out of the window with a faraway look in her eyes.*

**farce** /fɑrs/ ***noun*** [C] **1** something important or serious that is not organized well or treated with respect: *The election was a farce. Everybody already knew what the result would be.* **2** a funny play for the theater that is full of silly situations

**fare**[1] /fɛr/ ***noun*** **1** [C] the amount of money you pay to travel by bus, plane, taxi, etc.: *How much is the fare to Toledo?* ◇ *He didn't even have enough money for the bus fare into town.* **2** [U] (*formal*) food, especially food served in a restaurant

**fare**[2] /fɛr/ ***verb*** [I] (*formal*) to be successful/unsuccessful in a particular situation: *How did you fare on the test* (= Did you do well or badly)?



F

**the ˌFar ˈEast** *noun* [sing.] China, Japan and other countries in eastern Asia

**fare·well** /ˌfɛrˈwɛl/ *interjection* (*old-fashioned*) goodbye
IDM **bid sb farewell** → BID[1]
▸ **fare·well** *noun* [C]: *a farewell party*

**ˌfar-ˈfetched** *adj.* not easy to believe: *It's a good book, but the story's too far-fetched.*

**ˌfar-ˈflung** *adj.* **1** a long distance away: *expeditions to the far-flung corners of the earth* **2** spread over a wide area: *a newsletter that helps to keep all our far-flung alumni in touch*

F

★**farm[1]** /fɑrm/ *noun* [C] an area of land with fields and buildings that is used for growing crops and keeping animals: *My grandparents live on a farm.* ◇ *farm buildings* ◇ *a pig farm*

**farm[2]** /fɑrm/ *verb* [I,T] to use land for growing crops or keeping animals: *They farm 1,200 acres south of town.*

**ˈfarm belt** *noun* [C] an area where there are a lot of farms

★**farm·er** /ˈfɑrmər/ *noun* [C] a person who owns or manages a farm

**ˈfarmers' ˌmarket** *noun* [C] a place in a town or city where farmers and other people bring food that they have grown or made and sell it directly to other people

**farm·house** /ˈfɑrmhaʊs/ *noun* [C] the house on a farm where the farmer lives

★**farm·ing** /ˈfɑrmɪŋ/ *noun* [U] managing a farm or working on it: *Farming is extremely hard work.*

**farm·yard** /ˈfɑrmyɑrd/ *noun* [C] an area that is surrounded by farm buildings

**ˌfar-ˈreaching** *adj.* having, or going to have, a great influence on a lot of other things: *far-reaching changes*

**far·sight·ed** /ˈfɑrˌsaɪt̬əd/ *adj.* **1** able to see things clearly only when they are far away OPP **nearsighted** **2** being able to see what will be necessary and making plans for it OPP **shortsighted**

**fart** /fɑrt/ *verb* [I] (*informal*) to suddenly let gas from the stomach escape from your anus ▸ **fart** *noun* [C]

**far·ther** /ˈfɑrðər/ *adj., adv.* more distant in space or time; a greater distance: *Los Angeles is farther from New York than Boston is.* ◇ *I can swim farther than you.*

NOTE **Farther** is the comparative of **far.** ➲ Look at the note at **further.**

**far·thest** /ˈfɑrðəst/ (*also* **furthest**) *adj., adv.* most distant in space or time; the greatest distance: *the farthest corner of the country* ◇ *Who can swim farthest?*

NOTE **Farthest** is the superlative of **far.**

**fas·ci·nate** /ˈfæsəneɪt/ *verb* [T] to attract or interest sb very much: *He fascinated the kids with his magic tricks.* ◇ *I was fascinated by that movie.* ▸ **fas·ci·nat·ing** *adj.* ▸ **fas·ci·na·tion** /ˌfæsəˈneɪʃn/ *noun* [C,U]

**fas·cism** (*also* **Fascism**) /ˈfæʃɪzəm/ *noun* [U] an extreme political system in which one very powerful ruler (a dictator) controls the social and economic systems of a country and often expresses hatred of people from other countries or races: *the rise of fascism in the 1930s* ▸ **fas·cist** (*also* **Fascist**) /ˈfæʃɪst/ *noun* [C], *adj.*

★**fash·ion** /ˈfæʃn/ *noun* **1** [C,U] the style of dressing or behaving that is the most popular at a particular time: *men's fashions* ◇ *a fashion show/model* **2** [U, sing.] the way you do sth: *It should be possible to connect the parts in some fashion.* ◇ *Over 60% of women approved of the plan, and men responded in a similar fashion.*
IDM **come into/be in fashion** to become or to be popular as a style: *Jeans are always in fashion.*
**go/be out of fashion** to become or to be unpopular as a style: *This simple blazer will never go out of fashion.*

★**fash·ion·a·ble** /ˈfæʃn·əbl; ˈfæʃnəbl/ *adj.* following the latest popular style: *a fashionable woman/suit/restaurant/idea* OPP **unfashionable** or **old-fashioned.** ▸ **fash·ion·a·bly** /-əbli/ *adv.*

★**fast[1]** /fæst/ *adj.* **1** able to move or act at great speed: *a fast car/horse/worker*

NOTE There is no noun formed from **fast.** Use **speed**: *The car was traveling very fast./The car was traveling at a high speed.* Look at the note at **quick.**

**2** (used about a clock or watch) showing a time that is later than the real time: *I'm early – my watch must be fast.* ◇ *The clock is five minutes fast.* OPP **slow**

★**fast[2]** /fæst/ *adv.* **1** quickly: *Don't drive so fast.* **2** firmly or deeply: *fast asleep* ◇ *Our car was stuck fast in the mud.*

**fast[3]** /fæst/ *verb* [I] to eat no food for a certain time, usually for religious reasons or in order to lose weight: *Muslims fast during Ramadan.* ▸ **fast** *noun* [C]

★**fas·ten** /ˈfæsn/ *verb* **1** [T] to connect, join or shut and lock sth firmly: *Please fasten your seat belts.* **2** [I] to become closed or connected: *My blouse fastens at the back.* **3** [T] **fasten sth (on/to sth)**; **fasten A and B (together)** to attach sth to sth, or two things together: *Fasten this tag onto your suitcase.* ◇ *How can I fasten these pieces of wood together?*

**fas·ten·er** /ˈfæsn·ər; ˈfæsnər/ *noun* [C] something that fastens things together

**ˌfast ˈfood** *noun* [U] food that can be cooked and eaten quickly in a restaurant or taken away from the restaurant: *a fast-food restaurant*

**ˌfast-ˈforward** *verb* [I,T] (used about a tape or video) to go forward or to make sth go forward quickly, without playing it ➲ Look at the note at **cassette.**

**ˈfast lane** *noun* [C] the part of a wide road or freeway that is for the fastest cars
IDM **life in the fast lane** → LIFE

**ˈfast track** *noun* [sing.] a quick way to achieve sth, e.g. a high position in a job ▸ **ˈfast-track** *adj.*: *the fast-track route to promotion* ◇ *fast-track graduates*

★**fat[1]** /fæt/ *adj.* (**fat·ter**; **fat·test**) **1** (used about bodies) covered with too much flesh: *You'll get fat if you eat too much.*

NOTE It is not polite to describe a person as **fat.**

Less direct words are **plump**, **heavy** or **overweight**. ➲ Look also at **obese**.

OPP thin **2** (used about a thing) thick or full: *a fat wallet/book*

★**fat²** /fæt/ ***noun*** **1** [U] the greasy substance under the skins of animals and people: *I don't like meat with too much fat on it.* ➲ adjective fatty **2** [C,U] the greasy substance we obtain from animals, plants or seeds and use for cooking: *You have too much fat in your diet.* ◇ *Vegetable fats are healthier than animal fats.*

**fa·tal** /ˈfeɪṭl/ ***adj.*** **1** causing or ending in death: *a fatal accident* **2** causing trouble or a bad result: *the fatal flaw in his plan* ▸ **fa·tal·ly** ***adv.***

**fa·tal·i·ty** /feɪˈtæləṭi; fə-/ ***noun*** [C] (*pl.* **fa·tal·i·ties**) a person's death caused by an accident or in war, etc.: *There were no fatalities in the fire.*

ˈ**fat cat** ***noun*** [C] a person who earns, or has a lot of money, especially compared to people who do not earn so much

**fate** /feɪt/ ***noun*** **1** [U] the power that some people believe controls everything that happens: *It was fate that brought them together again after 20 years.* **2** [C] your future or something that happens to you: *Both men suffered the same fate – they both lost their jobs.*

**fate·ful** /ˈfeɪtfl/ ***adj.*** having an important effect on the future: *a fateful decision*

★**fa·ther¹** /ˈfɑðər/ ***noun*** [C] **1** a person's male parent: *John looks exactly like his father.* **2** a man who starts sth important: *The Wright brothers are the fathers of air travel.* **3 Father** the title of certain priests: *Father O'Reilly*

**fa·ther²** /ˈfɑðər/ ***verb*** [T] to become a father: *to father a child*

**fa·ther·hood** /ˈfɑðərhʊd/ ***noun*** [U] the state of being a father: *How are you enjoying fatherhood?*

ˈ**father-in-law** ***noun*** [C] (*pl.* **fathers-in-law**) the father of your husband or wife

**fa·ther·ly** /ˈfɑðərli/ ***adj.*** like or typical of a father: *a piece of fatherly advice*

ˈ**Father's Day** ***noun*** [C] the third Sunday in June, when fathers receive cards and gifts from their children

**fath·om** /ˈfæðəm/ ***verb*** [T] to understand sth: *I can't fathom why she did that.*

**fa·tigue** /fəˈtig/ ***noun*** [U] **1** great tiredness **2** weakness in metals caused by a lot of use

**fat·ten** /ˈfætn/ ***verb*** [T] **fatten sb/sth (up)** to make sb/sth fatter: *He's fattening the pigs up for slaughter.*

**fat·ten·ing** /ˈfætn·ɪŋ; ˈfætnɪŋ/ ***adj.*** (used about food) that makes people fat: *You shouldn't eat too much chocolate. It's very fattening.*

**fat·ty** /ˈfæṭi/ ***adj.*** (**fat·ti·er**; **fat·ti·est**) (used about food) having a lot of fat in or on it

★**fau·cet** /ˈfɔsət/ (*also* **tap**) ***noun*** [C] a type of handle that you turn to let water out of a pipe: *Go and turn the bathroom faucet off – I can hear it dripping.* ➲ picture at **plug**.

★**fault¹** /fɔlt/ ***noun*** **1** [C] something wrong or not perfect in a person's character or in a thing: *One of my faults is that I'm always late.* ◇ *a fault in the car's brakes* ➲ Look at the note at **mistake**. **2** [U] responsibility for a mistake: *"We're going to be late." "Well, it's not my fault – I was ready on time."* ◇ *It will be your own fault if you don't pass your test.* **3** [C] a large crack in the surface of the Earth: *earthquakes near the San Andreas fault*

IDM **be at fault** to be wrong or responsible for a mistake: *The other driver was at fault – he didn't stop at the traffic light.*

**find fault** → FIND¹

**fault²** /fɔlt/ ***verb*** [T] to find a fault or mistake in sb/sth: *It was impossible to fault her English.*

**fault·less** /ˈfɔltləs/ ***adj.*** without any mistakes; perfect: *The pianist gave a faultless performance.*

**fault·y** /ˈfɔlti/ ***adj.*** (used especially about electricity or machinery) not working correctly; having a FAULT¹ (1): *a faulty switch* ◇ *faulty reasoning*

**fau·na** /ˈfɔnə/ ***noun*** [U] all the animals of an area or a period of time: *the flora and fauna of South America* ➲ Look at **flora**.

**faux pas** /ˌfoʊ ˈpɑ/ ***noun*** [C] (*pl.* **faux pas** /ˌfoʊ ˈpɑz/) something you say or do that is embarrassing or offends people

★**fa·vor¹** /ˈfeɪvər/ ***noun*** **1** [C] something that helps sb: *Would you do me a favor and mail this letter for me?* ◇ *Can I ask you a favor – could you babysit for us tonight?* **2** [U] liking or approval: *In the end, the politician won the crowd's favor.* **3** [C] = PARTY FAVOR

IDM **be/fall out of favor (with sb)** to have/lose the approval of sb: *The politician fell out of favor with the voters after he made a racist comment.*

**in favor of sb/sth** in agreement with sb/sth: *Are you in favor of gun control?*

**in sb's favor** to the advantage of sb: *The committee decided in their favor.*

**fa·vor²** /ˈfeɪvər/ ***verb*** [T] **1** to support sb/sth; to prefer sb/sth: *Which suggestion did they favor?* **2** to treat one person very well and so be unfair to others: *Does the legal system favor wealthy citizens?*

**fa·vor·a·ble** /ˈfeɪvərəbl; ˈfeɪvrəbl/ ***adj.*** **1** showing liking or approval: *Did you get a favorable report on your work?* ◇ *He made a favorable impression on his new boss.* **2** (often used about the weather) suitable or helpful: *Conditions are favorable for skiing today.* OPP The opposite for both senses is **unfavorable**. ▸ **fa·vor·a·bly** /-əbli/ ***adv.***

★**fa·vor·ite¹** /ˈfeɪvrət; ˈfeɪvərət/ ***adj.*** liked more than any other: *What is your favorite color?* ◇ *My favorite singer is Whitney Houston.*

**fa·vor·ite²** /ˈfeɪvrət; ˈfeɪvərət/ ***noun*** [C] **1** a person or thing that you like more than any others: *This restaurant is a big favorite of mine.* ◇ *That sweater is my husband's favorite.* **2 the favorite** (especially in sports) the person, team, or thing that is expected to win **3** a page on the Internet that you like and whose address you save so that you can return to it easily: *The library's home page is in my **favorites** folder.*

**fa·vor·it·ism** /ˈfeɪvrətɪzəm; ˈfeɪvərət-/ ***noun*** [U] giving unfair advantages to the people that you like best

**fawn** /fɔn/ ***noun*** [C] a young deer ➲ Look at the note and the picture at **deer**.

F

**fax**[1] /fæks/ ***noun*** **1** [C,U] a copy of a letter, etc. which you can send by telephone lines using a special machine: *I need an answer today. Send them a fax!* ◇ *They contacted us by fax.* **2** [C] (*also* **'fax machine**) the machine that you use for sending FAXES (1): *Do you have a fax?* ◇ *What's your fax number?*

**fax**[2] /fæks/ ***verb*** [T] **fax sth (to sb)**; **fax sb (sth)** to send sb a fax: *We will fax our order to you tomorrow.* ◇ *I faxed her a copy of the letter.*

**faze** /feɪz/ ***verb*** [T] to make sb anxious or nervous: *Jeff always stays calm – nothing seems to faze him.*

**the FBI** /ˌɛf bi 'aɪ/ ***noun*** [sing.] the Federal Bureau of Investigation; the department of the U.S. government which investigates serious crimes that are against national (**federal**) law ➲ Look at the note at **White House**.

★**fear**[1] /fɪr/ ***noun*** [C,U] the feeling that you have when sth dangerous, painful or frightening might happen: *He was shaking with fear after the accident.* ◇ *She showed no fear.* ◇ *My fears for his safety were unnecessary.*

★**fear**[2] /fɪr/ ***verb*** **1** [I,T] to be afraid of sb/sth great or important: *We all fear illness and death.* ◇ *We'll get there in time – never fear!* (= don't worry). **2** [T] to feel that something bad might happen: *The mayor fears that she will lose the next election.* ➲ Look at **afraid** and at the note at **frightened**.

PHR V **fear for sb/sth** to be worried about sb/sth: *Parents often fear for the safety of their children.*

**fear·ful** /'fɪrfl/ ***adj.*** **fearful (of sth/of doing sth)**; **fearful (that)** anxious or afraid about sth: *You should never be fearful of starting something new.* ➲ Look at **frightened** and the note at **afraid**. These words are much more common. ▸ **fear·ful·ly** ***adv.***

**fear·less** /'fɪrləs/ ***adj.*** not afraid; brave ▸ **fear·less·ly** ***adv.*** ▸ **fear·less·ness** ***noun*** [U]

**fea·si·ble** /'fizəbl/ ***adj.*** possible to do: *a feasible plan* SYN **practicable** ▸ **fea·si·bil·i·ty** /ˌfizə'bɪləti/ ***noun*** [U]

**feast** /fist/ ***noun*** [C] a large, special meal (sometimes to celebrate sth) ▸ **feast** ***verb*** [I]

**feat** /fit/ ***noun*** [C] something you do that shows great strength, skill or courage: *That new bridge is a real feat of engineering.*

★**feath·er** /'fɛðər/ ***noun*** [C] one of the light, soft things that grow in a bird's skin and cover its body

IDM **ruffle (sb's) feathers** → RUFFLE[1]

**feath·er·y** /'fɛðəri/ ***adj.*** soft and light; like a feather: *feathery leaves/snowflakes*

★**fea·ture**[1] /'fitʃər/ ***noun*** [C] **1** an important or noticeable part of sth: *Lakes are a main feature of the landscape of Ontario.* ◇ *Noise is a feature of city life.* ◇ *improved safety features on a car* **2** a part of the face: *Her eyes are her best feature.* **3** an important newspaper or magazine article, especially one that is meant to be interesting or entertaining: *a feature on popular pets* **4** (*also* **feature film**) a full-length movie with a story

★**fea·ture**[2] /'fitʃər/ ***verb*** **1** [T] to include sb/sth as an important part: *Tonight's program features an interview with actor Brad Pitt.* **2** [I] **feature in sth** to have a part in sth: *Does marriage feature in your future plans?*

**Feb·ru·ar·y** /'fɛbyuˌɛri; 'fɛbru-/ ***noun*** [C,U] (*abbr.* **Feb.**) the second month of the year, coming before March ➲ For examples of the use of the months in sentences, look at **January**.

**fe·ces** /fisiz/ ***noun*** [pl.] (*formal*) solid waste matter that is passed from the body through the bowels ➲ **Feces** is used mainly in a medical context. ➲ Look also at **excrement**. SYN An informal word is **poop**.

**Fed** /fɛd/ ***noun*** [C] (*informal*) an officer of the Federal Bureau of Investigation or another federal organization

**fed**[1] /fɛd/ *past tense, past participle of* FEED[1]

★**fed·er·al** /'fɛdərəl/ ***adj.*** **1** having a system of government in which the individual states of a country have control over their own affairs, but are controlled by a central government for national decisions, etc.: *a federal republic* **2** (within a federal system, especially the U.S. and Canada) connected with national government rather than the local government of an individual state or province: *state and federal income taxes* ◇ *a federal judge* ◇ *the federal government* ➲ For more information on the North American political systems, look at study pages **A10-A11**.

**the ˌFederal ˌBureau of Investi'gation** ***noun*** [sing.] = THE FBI

**the ˌFederal Re'serve** (*also* **the Federal Reserve System**) ***noun*** [sing.] the central bank system of the U.S. government that controls the supply of money

**fed·er·a·tion** /ˌfɛdə'reɪʃn/ ***noun*** [C] a group of people, organizations, states, etc. that have joined together: *The American Federation of Teachers*

**fed up** /ˌfɛd'ʌp/ ***adj.*** (not before a noun) (*informal*) bored or unhappy; tired of sth: *What's the matter? You look really fed up.* ◇ *I'm fed up with waiting for the phone to ring.*

★**fee** /fi/ ***noun*** [C] **1** (usually plural) the money you pay for professional advice or services from doctors, lawyers, universities, etc.: *Some attorneys charge extremely high fees for their services.* **2** the cost of an examination, club membership, entrance, etc.: *How much is the entrance fee?* ➲ Look at the note at **pay**[1].

**fee·ble** /'fibl/ ***adj.*** **1** with no energy or power; weak: *a feeble old man* **2** not able to convince sb: *a feeble argument*

★**feed**[1] /fid/ ***verb*** (*pt, pp* **fed** /fɛd/) **1** [T] to give food to a person or an animal: *Don't forget to feed the dog.* ◇ *I can't come yet. I haven't fed the baby.* ◇ *I cooked enough to feed us all week.* ➲ Look also at **fed up**. **2** [I] (used about animals) to eat: *What do horses feed on in the winter?* **3** [T] to put sth, such as supplies or information, into sth else: *Can you feed this information into the computer?*

**feed**[2] /fid/ ***noun*** [U] food for animals: *cattle feed*

**feed·back** /'fidbæk/ ***noun*** [U] information about sth that you have done or made which tells you how good or successful it is: *We need some more feedback from the people who use our textbooks.*

**feed·ing** /ˈfidɪŋ/ ***noun*** [C] a meal for an animal or a baby: *It's almost time for the baby's feeding.*

★**feel¹** /fil/ ***verb*** (*pt, pp* **felt** /fɛlt/)
➤WELL/SICK/HAPPY/SAD, ETC. **1** [I] (usually with an adjective) to be in the state that is mentioned: *to feel cold/sick/tired/happy* ◇ *How are you feeling today?* ◇ *You'll feel better in the morning.*
➤GIVE/HAVE IMPRESSION **2** [I] **feel (to sb) (like sth/sb)** to give an impression of sth: *The cavity in my tooth feels a lot bigger than it is.* ◇ *My new coat feels like leather, but it's not.* **3** [I] **feel as if/as though/like** to have or give the impression that: *He felt as if he had been there before.* ◇ *My head feels as though it will burst.* ◇ *I feel like I'm going to throw up!*

NOTE **It** is often used as the subject of **feel** in this sense: *It feels as if it is going to snow soon.* **Feel like** is very common in informal English, but some people do not like to use this phrase in formal writing.

➤TOUCH **4** [T] to learn about sth by touching it with your hands: *Feel this material. Is it silk or cotton?* ◇ *I felt her forehead and knew that she had a temperature.*
➤BE/BECOME AWARE OF **5** [T] to be aware of sth: *I felt something crawling up my back.* ◇ *I could feel myself dropping off to sleep.*
➤THINK/BELIEVE **6** [T] to believe or think: *I felt (that) it was a mistake not to ask her advice.*
➤BE STRONGLY AFFECTED **7** [T] to suffer from sth: *Do you feel the cold in winter?* ◇ *She felt the loss badly when her mother died.*
➤SEARCH WITH HANDS **8** [I] **feel (around) (for sb/sth)** to try to find something with your hands instead of your eyes: *She felt around in the dark for the light switch.*
IDM **be/feel sorry for sb** → SORRY¹
**feel like sth/doing sth** to want sth or to want to do sth: *Do you feel like going out?*
PHR V **feel for sb** to understand sb's feelings and situation and to feel sorry for him/her: *I really felt for him when his wife died.*

**feel²** /fil/ ***noun*** [sing.] **1 the feel** the impression something gives you when it is touched; the impression an experience gives you: *You can tell it's wool by the feel.* **2** an act of touching sth in order to learn about it: *Let me have a feel.*
IDM **get/have a feel for sth** to get or have a natural understanding or ability for sth: *Barbara has a good feel for trends in business.*

ˈ**feel-good** ***adj.*** making you feel happy and pleased about life: *a feel-good movie*

★**feel·ing** /ˈfilɪŋ/ ***noun***
➤STH THAT YOU FEEL **1** [C] **a feeling (of sth)** something that you feel in your mind or body: *a feeling of hunger/happiness/fear/success*
➤EMOTIONS **2 feelings** [pl.] a person's emotions: *I don't want to hurt his feelings* (= make him unhappy). ◇ *to show/hide your feelings*
➤ABILITY TO FEEL **3** [U] the ability to feel in your body: *After the accident, he lost all feeling in his legs.*
➤IDEA/BELIEF **4** [sing.] a belief or idea that you cannot explain exactly: *I had a feeling that something terrible would happen.*
➤SYMPATHY/LOVE **5** [U] sympathy or understanding: *She doesn't have much feeling for music.*
IDM **bad/ill feeling(s)** unhappy relations between people: *The decision caused a lot of bad feelings at the factory.*
**have mixed feelings about sb/sth** → MIXED

**feet** ***noun*** [C] *plural of* FOOT¹

**feist·y** /ˈfaɪsti/ ***adj.*** (**feist·i·er**; **feist·i·est**) (used about a person) having a lot of energy and liking to argue or fight

**fe·line** /ˈfilaɪn/ ***adj.*** of or like a cat

**fell¹** *past tense of* FALL¹

**fell²** /fɛl/ ***verb*** [T] (*formal*) to cut down a tree

★**fel·low¹** /ˈfɛloʊ/ ***noun*** [C] **1** (*informal*) a man: *What's that fellow over there doing?* **2** a person who has received an award of money in order to study at a university, etc.: *Jill is a research fellow in the biology department.*

★**fel·low²** /ˈfɛloʊ/ ***adj.*** (only *before* a noun) another or others like yourself in the same situation: *Her fellow students were all older than she was.*

**fel·low·ship** /ˈfɛloʊʃɪp; ˈfɛlə-/ ***noun*** **1** [U] friendly relations with others **2** [C] a group or society, especially a Christian religious group **3** [C] an award of money that makes it possible for sb to study at a university, etc.

**fel·on** /ˈfɛlən/ ***noun*** [C] a person who is guilty of a felony: *a convicted felon*

**fel·o·ny** /ˈfɛləni/ ***noun*** [C] (*pl.* **fel·o·nies**) a serious crime, e.g. murder: *to be charged with a felony* ➲ Look at **misdemeanor**.

**felt¹** *past tense, past participle of* FEEL¹

**felt²** /fɛlt/ ***noun*** [U] a type of soft cloth made from wool, etc. which has been pressed flat

ˌ**felt-tip ˈpen** (*also* ˈ**felt-tip**) ***noun*** [C] a type of pen with a tip made of FELT²

★**fe·male¹** /ˈfimeɪl/ ***adj.*** of the sex that can give birth to young: *Please state sex: male or female* (e.g. on a form).

★**fe·male²** /ˈfimeɪl/ ***noun*** [C] a female animal: *Is your dog a male or a female?*

NOTE **Female** and **male** are used only to describe the sex of a creature. To describe the qualities we think of as typical of females and males, we use **feminine** and **masculine**.

**fem·i·nine** /ˈfɛmənən/ ***adj.*** **1** of or like a woman: *My daughter always dresses like a boy. She hates looking feminine.* ➲ Look at **masculine** and the note at **female. 2** (*grammar*) (*abbr.* **fem.**) (in English) of the forms of words used to describe females: *"Lioness" is the feminine form of "lion."* **3** (*grammar*) (*abbr.* **fem.**) (in certain languages) belonging to a certain grammatical class: *The German word "Blume" is feminine.* ➲ Look at **masculine** and **neuter.** ▶ **fem·i·nin·i·ty** /ˌfɛməˈnɪnət̬i/ ***noun*** [U]

**fem·i·nism** /ˈfɛmənɪzəm/ ***noun*** [U] the belief that women should have the same rights and opportunities as men

**fem·i·nist** /ˈfɛmənɪst/ ***noun*** [C] a person who believes in and supports the aims of feminism

★**fence¹** /fɛns/ ***noun*** [C] a line of wooden or metal posts joined by wood, wire, metal, etc. to divide land or to keep animals in or out: *a fence around*

F

*the back yard* ◇ *an electric fence* ◇ *a barbed-wire fence* ➲ picture at **fence**.

IDM **be/sit on the fence** to be unwilling or unable to decide between two things

**fence²** /fɛns/ ***verb*** **1** [T] to surround land with a fence **2** [I] to fight with a long thin sword as a sport

PHRV **fence sb/sth in** to surround sb/sth with a fence: *They fenced in their back yard to make it more private.*

**fence sth off** to separate one area from another with a fence: *Several streets were fenced off while police searched for the bomb.*

F

**fenc·ing** /ˈfɛnsɪŋ/ ***noun*** [U] the sport of fighting with swords

**fend** /fɛnd/ ***verb***

PHRV **fend for yourself** to take care of yourself without having to rely on help from other people: *It's time Ben left home and learned to fend for himself.*

**fend sth/sb off** to defend yourself from sth/sb: *He fended off the dog with a stick.*

**fend·er** /ˈfɛndər/ ***noun*** [C] the part of the outside of a car, truck, etc. that is over the top of the wheels

**ˈfender-ˌbender** (*also* **ˈfender ˌbender**) ***noun*** [C] (*informal*) a car accident that does not cause much damage

**feng shui** /ˌfʌŋ ˈʃweɪ/ ***noun*** [U] a way of organizing a home, office, etc., so that all the parts seem to fit well with each other

**fer·ment¹** /fərˈmɛnt/ ***verb*** [I,T] to (make sth) change chemically: *The wine is starting to ferment.*

**fer·ment²** /ˈfərmɛnt/ ***noun*** [U] (*formal*) a state of uncertainty and change: *Central African nations are in ferment and no one is sure what will happen next.*

**fern** /fərn/ ***noun*** [C] a green plant with no flowers and a lot of long thin leaves

**fe·ro·cious** /fəˈroʊʃəs/ ***adj.*** very fierce and violent ▸ **fe·ro·cious·ly** ***adv.***

**fe·roc·i·ty** /fəˈrɑsət̬i/ ***noun*** [U] violent cruelty

**Fer·ris wheel** /ˈfɛrəs wil/ ***noun*** [C] (at an outdoor festival, etc.) a machine like a large vertical wheel with seats attached to its outside edge, that people can sit in and ride as it goes around

**fer·ry¹** /ˈfɛri/ ***noun*** [C] (*pl.* **fer·ries**) a boat that transports people and goods over short distances: *You can take the ferry from Vancouver Island to the mainland.* ◇ *a ferry terminal*

**fer·ry²** /ˈfɛri/ ***verb*** [T] (*pres. part.* **fer·ry·ing**; *3rd person sing. pres.* **fer·ries**; *pt, pp* **fer·ried**) to carry people or goods by boat, airplane, car, etc. from one place to another: *We share the job of ferrying the kids to school.*

**fer·tile** /ˈfərt̬l/ ***adj.*** **1** (used about land, plants, animals and people) able to produce crops, fruit or young OPP **infertile** **2** (used about a person's mind) full of ideas: *a fertile imagination*

**fer·til·i·ty** /fərˈtɪlət̬i/ ***noun*** [U] the state of being fertile: *drugs that can increase a woman's fertility* (= her chances of having a child) OPP **infertility**

**fer·til·ize** /ˈfərt̬l·aɪz/ ***verb*** [T] **1** to put a male seed into an egg, a plant or a female animal so that it starts to develop fruit or young **2** to put natural or artificial substances on soil in order to make it more fertile ▸ **fer·til·i·za·tion** /ˌfərt̬l·əˈzeɪʃn/ ***noun*** [U]

**fer·til·iz·er** /ˈfərt̬l·aɪzər/ ***noun*** [C,U] a natural or chemical substance that is put on land to make plants grow better

**fer·vent** /ˈfərvənt/ ***adj.*** showing strong feelings: *She's a fervent believer in women's rights.* ▸ **fer·vent·ly** ***adv.***

**fer·vor** /ˈfərvər/ ***noun*** [U] strong feeling

**fest** /fɛst/ ***noun*** [C] (*informal*) = FESTIVAL (2)

**fes·ter** /ˈfɛstər/ ***verb*** [I] **1** (used about a cut or wound) to become infected **2** (used about a bad situation, feeling or thought) to become worse or more painful

★**fes·ti·val** /ˈfɛstəvl/ ***noun*** [C] **1** a day or time when people celebrate sth (especially a religious event): *Hanukkah is an important Jewish festival.* **2** (*also informal* **fest**) a large public celebration that is often held regularly in one place: *a jazz festival*

**fes·tive** /ˈfɛstɪv/ ***adj.*** happy, because people are enjoying themselves: *a festive occasion*

**fes·tiv·i·ty** /fɛˈstɪvət̬i/ ***noun*** (*pl.* **fes·tiv·i·ties**) **1** [U] being happy and celebrating **2** **fes·tiv·i·ties** [pl.] happy events when people celebrate sth: *The festivities went on until dawn.*

**fetch** /fɛtʃ/ ***verb*** **1** [I,T] (usually used about a dog) to go for and bring back sth that sb has thrown: *If I throw this ball, my dog will fetch it.* ◇ *I taught my dog to fetch.* **2** [T](*formal* or *old-fashioned*) to go for and bring back sb/sth: *Residents of the village still have to fetch their water from a well.* **3** [T] (used about goods) to be sold for the price mentioned: *The painting could fetch up to $2 million at the auction.*

**fe·tus** /ˈfit̬əs/ ***noun*** [C] (*pl.* **fe·tus·es**) a young human or animal that is still developing in its mother's body

NOTE An **embryo** is at an earlier stage of development.

**feud** /fyud/ ***noun*** [C] a long and serious argument between two people or groups ▸ **feud** ***verb*** [I]

**feu·dal** /ˈfyudl/ ***adj.*** relating to the system of feudalism

**feu·dal·ism** /ˈfyudl·ɪzəm/ ***noun*** [U] the social system which existed in the Middle Ages in Europe, in which people worked and fought for a person who owned the land, and received land and protection from him

★**fe·ver** /ˈfivər/ ***noun*** **1** [C,U] a condition of the body when it is too hot because of illness: *A high fever can be dangerous, especially in small children.* ◇ *Symptoms include dizziness, fever and diarrhea.*

NOTE When somebody's body is very hot, we can also say he/she **has a temperature**.

**2** [sing.] (*figurative*) a state of nervous excitement

**fe·ver·ish** /ˈfivərɪʃ/ ***adj.*** **1** showing the signs of a fever **2** showing great excitement: *to work at a feverish pace*

**fe·ver·ish·ly** /ˈfivərɪʃli/ ***adv.*** very quickly and excitedly

★**few¹** /fyu/ ***det.***, ***adj.***, ***pronoun*** (used with a plural noun and a plural verb) not many: *Few people live* *to be 100. ◇ There are fewer cars here today than yesterday. ◇ The few people I asked thought the same as I do. ◇ Few of the players played really well. ◇ Very few of the books were new.*

IDM **few and far between** (*informal*) not happening very often; not very common: *Our visits to the theater are few and far between. ◇ Real gentlemen are few and far between these days.*

★**few²** /fyu/ **a few** ***det., pronoun*** (used with a plural noun and a plural verb) a small number of; some: *a few people ◇ a few letters ◇ Only a few of the people who applied were suitable. ◇ She's written lots of books, but I've only read a few (of them). ◇ I knew a few* (= some) *of the people there.* ➲ Compare with: *I knew few of the people* (= not many).

IDM **quite a few** → QUITE

**fi·an·cé** /ˌfiɑnˈseɪ; fiˈɑnseɪ/ ***noun*** [C] a man to whom a woman is engaged to be married: *This is my fiancé Dave. We got engaged a few weeks ago.*

**fi·an·cée** /ˌfiɑnˈseɪ; fiˈɑnseɪ/ ***noun*** [C] a woman to whom a man is engaged to be married: *Can I introduce you to my fiancée?*

**fi·as·co** /fiˈæskoʊ/ ***noun*** [C] (*pl.* **fi·as·coes** or **fi·as·cos**) the ridiculous failure of an organized event: *Our last party was a complete fiasco.*

**fib¹** /fɪb/ ***noun*** [C] (*informal*) something you say that is not true; a small lie: *to tell a fib*

**fib²** /fɪb/ ***verb*** [I] (**fib·bing; fibbed**) (*informal*) to say untrue things; to tell a FIB¹: *to fib about your age* ➲ Look at **lie¹**. **Fib** is used when the lie does not seem very important.

**fi·ber** /ˈfaɪbər/ ***noun*** **1** [C] one of the thin threads which form a natural or artificial substance: *cotton fibers ◇ a muscle fiber* **2** [C,U] material or a substance made from fibers

> NOTE **Natural** fibers are, for example, cotton and wool. **Man-made** or **synthetic** fibers are nylon, polyester, etc.

**3** [U] the part of plants (used as food) that your body cannot digest and that are thought to be good for it: *Whole wheat bread is high in fiber.*

**fi·ber·glass** /ˈfaɪbərglæs/ ***noun*** [U] a hard material made from plastic and glass fibers, used for making small boats, parts of cars, etc.

**fi·ber op·tics** /ˌfaɪbər ˈɑptɪks/ ***noun*** [U] the use of thin fibers of glass, etc. for sending information in the form of light signals ▸ **fi·ber-op·tic** ***adj.***: *fiber-optic cables*

**fick·le** /ˈfɪkl/ ***adj.*** always changing your mind or your feelings

**fic·tion** /ˈfɪkʃn/ ***noun*** [U] stories, novels, etc. which describe events and people that do not really exist: *I don't read much fiction.*

> NOTE Fiction is one type of **literature**. ➲ Look at **drama** and **poetry**. OPP **non-fiction** ➲ Look also at **fact**.

**fic·tion·al** /ˈfɪkʃənl/ ***adj.*** only existing in fiction: *The book gave a fictional account of a doctor's life.* ➲ Look at **factual**.

**fic·ti·tious** /fɪkˈtɪʃəs/ ***adj.*** invented; not real: *They used fictitious names in the newspaper article.*

**fid·dle¹** /ˈfɪdl/ ***noun*** [C] (*informal*) a violin

> NOTE We use **fiddle** especially when we are talking about country music.

**fid·dle²** /ˈfɪdl/ ***verb*** [I] **fiddle (around) (with sth)** to play with sth carelessly, nervously or without thinking: *He sat nervously, fiddling with a paper clip.*

**fi·del·i·ty** /fɪˈdɛləṭi/ ***noun*** [U] (*formal*) the quality of being faithful OPP **infidelity** SYN A less formal word is **faithfulness**.

**fidg·et** /ˈfɪdʒət/ ***verb*** [I] **fidget (with sth)** to move about or play with sth in a restless way because you are nervous, bored, etc.: *Stop fidgeting! ◇ The students were fidgeting with their pens while they waited for the bell to ring.* ▸ **fidg·et·y** ***adj.***

★**field¹** /fild/ ***noun***

▸AREA OF LAND **1** [C] an area of land on a farm that is used for growing crops or for feeding animals: *a cornfield ◇ a field of corn ◇ farmers working in the fields* **2** [C] an area of land used for sports, games or some other activity: *a baseball, football/soccer field ◇ an airfield* (= where airplanes land and take off) *◇ a battlefield* ➲ picture at **football**. ➲ Look also at **track and field**. **3** [C] an area of land where oil, coal or other minerals are found: *an oil field*

▸SUBJECT/ACTIVITY **4** [C] an area of study or knowledge: *He's an expert in the field of economics. ◇ That question is outside my field.*

▸AREA AFFECTED BY STH **5** [C] an area affected by or included in sth: *a magnetic field ◇ It's outside my field of vision* (= I can't see it).

▸IN COMPETITION **6 the field** [sing.] all the people, animals, companies, etc. who are competing against each other in a race, in business, etc.: *We have a huge lead over the rest of the field.*

**field²** /fild/ ***verb*** **1** [I,T] (to be ready) to catch and throw back the ball (in baseball)

> NOTE When one team is **fielding**, the other is **batting**.

**2** [T] to choose a group of candidates for an election, a team for a sports game, soldiers for an army, etc.: *In spite of injuries, they managed to field a good team.* **3** [T] to answer a difficult question, a telephone call, etc. without having time to prepare your answer: *The governor spoke about taxes and then fielded questions from the audience.*

ˈ**field day** ***noun*** [C] a special day at a school when there are no classes and students compete in sports activities

IDM **have a field day** to have a time of great excitement, especially because you have an opportunity to make sb appear silly or stupid: *The newspapers always have a field day when there's a political scandal.*

**field·er** /ˈfildər/ ***noun*** [C] in baseball, a member of the team who tries to catch the ball after it has been hit (batted) ➲ picture at **baseball**.

ˈ**field goal** ***noun*** [C] (in football) a goal scored by kicking the ball over the bar of the goal

ˈ**field ˌhockey** ***noun*** [U] a game that is played on a field by two teams of eleven players who try to hit a small hard ball into a goal, using a curved wooden stick

ˈ**field house** ***noun*** [C] **1** a building at a sports field where people can change their clothes, take a shower, etc. **2** a building where events in a certain sport (athletics) are held, with seats for people to watch

ˈ**field trip** *noun* [C] a trip that a group of people, especially a class, go on in order to learn about sth: *Our class is going on a field trip to the state capitol building.*

**field·work** /ˈfildwərk/ *noun* [U] research or study that is done in the real world and not in a school, university, etc.

**fiend** /find/ *noun* [C] **1** a devil or a very cruel person **2** (*informal*) a person who is unusually interested in one particular thing: *a sports fiend*

**fiend·ish** /ˈfindɪʃ/ *adj.* **1** very fierce or cruel **2** clever and complicated: *a fiendish plan*

**fierce** /fɪrs/ *adj.* **1** angry and aggressive: *a fierce dog* **2** very strong: *fierce competition for jobs* ➲ noun ferocity ▸ **fierce·ly** *adv.*

**fier·y** /ˈfaɪəri/ *adj.* **1** looking like fire **2** (used about a person's character or temper) quick to become angry

**fi·es·ta** /fiˈɛstə/ *noun* [C] a party, especially one that has some connection with Spanish, or with the countries that speak Spanish

**fif·teen** /ˌfɪfˈtin/ *number* 15, one more than fourteen ➲ For examples of how to use numbers in sentences, look at **six**. ▸ **fif·teenth** /ˌfɪfˈtinθ/ *pronoun*, *det.*, *adv.* ➲ Look at the examples at **sixth**.

**fifth**[1] /fɪfθ/ *pronoun*, *det.*, *adv.* 5th, next after fourth ➲ Look at **five** and at the examples at **sixth**.

**fifth**[2] /fɪfθ/ *noun* [C] the fraction ⅕; one of five equal parts of sth ➲ Look at the examples at **sixth**.

**fif·ty** /ˈfɪfti/ *number* 50, one more than forty-nine ➲ For examples of how to use numbers in sentences, look at **sixty**. ▸ **fif·ti·eth** /ˈfɪftiəθ/ *pronoun*, *det.*, *adv.* ➲ Look at the examples at **sixth**.

ˌ**fifty-ˈfifty** *adj.*, *adv.* (*informal*) equal or equally (between two people, groups, etc.): *You have a fifty-fifty chance of winning.* ◇ *We'll split the money fifty-fifty.*

**fig** /fɪg/ *noun* [C] (a type of tree with) a soft sweet fruit full of small seeds that grows in warm areas and is often eaten dried

**fig.** *abbr.* **1** = FIGURE[1] (7): *See diagram in fig. 2.* **2** = FIGURATIVE

★**fight**[1] /faɪt/ *verb* (*pt*, *pp* **fought** /fɔt/) **1** [I,T] **fight (against/with sb/sth) (about/over sth)** to use physical strength/guns/weapons against sb/sth: *What were the boys fighting each other about?* ◇ *Have you been fighting with your sister again?* **2** [I] **fight (about/over sth)** to argue: *It's not worth fighting about money.* **3** [I,T] **fight (against sth)** to try very hard to stop or prevent sth: *to fight a fire, a decision, etc.* ◇ *to fight against crime/disease* **4** [I] **fight (for sth/to do sth)** to try very hard to get or keep sth: *to fight for your rights*

PHRV **fight back** to protect yourself by fighting with actions or with words: *If he hits you again, fight back!*

★**fight**[2] /faɪt/ *noun* **1** [C] an act of fighting or a struggle: *Don't get into a fight at school, okay?* ◇ *the administration's fight against inflation* **2** [C] a very angry argument: *I had a big fight with my parents last night.* **3** [U] the desire to continue trying or struggling: *I've had some bad luck, but I've still got plenty of fight left in me.*

IDM **pick a fight** → PICK[1]

**fight·er** /ˈfaɪt̬ər/ *noun* [C] **1** a person who fights in war or in sports (especially a boxer) **2** (*also* **fighter plane**) a small fast aircraft that is used for shooting down enemy aircraft

**fight·ing** /ˈfaɪt̬ɪŋ/ *noun* [U] an occasion when people fight: *The fighting between the two gangs continued past midnight.*

**fig·u·ra·tive** /ˈfɪgyərət̬ɪv/ *adj.* (*abbr.* **fig.**) (used about a word or an expression) not used with its exact meaning but used for giving an imaginative description or a special effect: *"He exploded when he heard the news" is a figurative use of the verb "to explode."* OPP **literal** ▸ **fig·u·ra·tive·ly** *adv.*

★**fig·ure**[1] /ˈfɪgyər/ *noun* [C]

➤NUMBER **1** a written sign for a number (0 to 9): *Write the numbers in figures, not words.* **2** an amount (in numbers) or a price: *The unemployment figures are lower this month.* ◇ *That figure of $10,000 is just a rough estimate.*

➤PERSON **3** a well-known or important person: *an important political figure* **4** a person (that you cannot see very clearly): *Two figures were coming toward us in the dark.*

➤IN PAINTING/PICTURE **5** a person (in a picture or photograph): *There were two figures on the right of the picture that I didn't recognize.*

➤SHAPE OF BODY **6** the shape of the human body, especially a woman's body: *She's almost 50, but she still has the figure of a teenager.* ◇ *I'll lose my figure* (= I'll get fat) *if I eat too much chocolate.* ➲ Look at the note at **build**.

➤PICTURE/DIAGRAM **7** (*abbr.* **fig.**) a diagram or illustration used in a book to explain sth: *Figure 3 shows the major cities of Italy.*

IDM **facts and figures** → FACT

★**fig·ure**[2] /ˈfɪgyər/ *verb* **1** [T] **figure (that)** (*informal*) to think or guess sth: *I figured he was here because I saw his car outside.* **2** [T] to calculate sth: *to figure your income taxes* **3** [I] **figure (in sth)** to be included in sth; to be an important part of sth: *Women don't figure much in his novels.*

IDM **go figure** (*informal*) used to say that you are surprised about sth: *So Phil finally got married? Go figure!*

**it/that figures** (*informal*) that is what I expected

PHRV **figure sb/sth out** to find an answer to sth or to understand sb

ˌ**figure ˈeight** *noun* [C] something in the shape of an 8

ˌ**figure of ˈspeech** *noun* [C] (*pl.* **figures of speech**) a word or expression used not with its original meaning but in an imaginative way to make a special effect ➲ Look at **figurative**.

**file**[1] /faɪl/ *noun* [C] **1** a collection of papers or information kept in a box or a cover: *Which file is that letter in?* **2** a collection of information or material on one subject that is stored in a computer or on a disk: *to open/close a file* **3** a metal tool with a rough surface that is used for making rough surfaces smooth: *a nail file*

IDM **in single file** → SINGLE[1]

**on file** kept in a file: *We have all the information you need on file.*
**the rank and file** → RANK[1]

★**file**[2] /faɪl/ ***verb*** **1** [T] **file sth (away)** to put sth in a FILE[1] (1): *File these letters under "Job Applications."* **2** [T] to send a form, report, etc. to a place where it is officially recorded: *to file criminal charges against sb* ◇ *Your income tax return must be filed in April.* **3** [I,T] to use a FILE[1] (3) to cut sth or make sth smooth: *to file your fingernails* **4** [I] **file in, out, past, etc.** to walk or march in a line
IDM **file suit (against sb)** to send an official document to a court of law, saying that you intend to ask for money from sb because he/she did sth bad to you or said sth bad about you: *She filed suit against her former employer for discrimination.*

**fi·let** (*also* **fillet**) /fɪˈleɪ/ ***noun*** [C,U] (a piece of) fish with no bones in it

★**fill** /fɪl/ ***verb*** **1** [I,T] **fill (sth/sb) (with sth)** to make sth full or to become full: *The candidate's supporters completely filled the auditorium.* ◇ *The news filled him with excitement.* ◇ *The room filled with smoke within minutes.* **2** [T] to occupy a position or time: *That teaching position has just been filled* (= somebody has gotten the job).
PHR V **fill sth in** to write information on a form, etc.: *Please fill in your name and address here.* ◇ *to fill in the blanks on a quiz*
**fill sth out** to complete a form, etc. by writing information on it: *to fill out a questionnaire*
**fill (sth) up** to become or to make sth completely full: *There weren't many people at first, but then the room filled up.* ◇ *I need to fill up the car* (= with gasoline) *before we start on our trip.*

**fil·let** ***noun*** [C,U] = FILET

**fill·ing** /ˈfɪlɪŋ/ ***noun*** **1** [C] the material that a dentist uses to fill a hole in a tooth: *a gold filling* **2** [C,U] food put inside a sandwich, pie, cake, etc. to make it taste good ➲ picture at **pie**.

ˈ**filling ˌstation** ***noun*** [C] (*old-fashioned*) = GAS STATION

★**film**[1] /fɪlm/ ***noun*** **1** [C,U] a roll of thin plastic that you use in a camera to take photographs: *a 35 millimeter film* ◇ *I need to buy a new roll of film.* ◇ *black-and-white film* ◇ *color film* ◇ *Fast film is better in this light.*

> NOTE You **load** a film into a camera and **rewind** it when it is finished. When the film is **developed**, you can have **prints** made from the **negatives**.

**2** [C] a movie

> NOTE **Film** is usually used for serious works with important artistic value. **Movie** is usually used for more popular works: *a French avant-garde film* ◇ *the latest action movie starring Sylvester Stallone.*

**3** [usually sing.] a thin layer of a substance or material: *a film of oil*

★**film**[2] /fɪlm/ ***verb*** [I,T] to make a movie of an event, a story, etc. with a camera: *The show was filmed on location in New York.*

**fil·ter**[1] /ˈfɪltər/ ***noun*** [C] **1** a piece of paper or other material with many small holes in it that is used for holding back solid substances from a liquid or gas that passes through it: *a coffee filter* ◇ *an oil filter* **2** a piece of colored glass that is used with a camera to hold back some types of light

**fil·ter**[2] /ˈfɪltər/ ***verb*** **1** [T] to pass a liquid through a FILTER[1] (1): *Do you filter your water?* **2** [I] **filter in, out, through, etc.** to move slowly: (*figurative*) *News of her illness filtered through to her friends.*

**filth** /fɪlθ/ ***noun*** [U] **1** disgusting dirt: *The room was covered in filth.* **2** extremely offensive words, pictures, etc. usually in books, magazines or movies

**filth·y** /ˈfɪlθi/ ***adj.*** (**filth·i·er**; **filth·i·est**) **1** very dirty: *They got completely filthy playing football in the rain.* **2** (used about language, books, movies, etc.) extremely unpleasant, often about sex

**fin** /fɪn/ ***noun*** [C] a part of a fish, shaped like a thin wing. Fish use fins for swimming.

★**fi·nal**[1] /ˈfaɪnl/ ***adj.*** **1** (only *before* a noun) last (in a series): *This will be the final lesson of our course.* ◇ *I don't want to miss the final episode of that series.* **2** not to be changed: *The judge's decision is always final.*
IDM **the last/final straw** → STRAW

**fi·nal**[2] /ˈfaɪnl/ ***noun*** [C] **1** (*also* **finals**) the last game or match in a series of competitions or sports events: *Do you think the Lakers will make it to the NBA finals this year?* ◇ *The finals of the swimming championship will be held in Niagara Falls.* ➲ Look at **semifinal**. **2** (*also* **final exam**) an examination that you take at the end of a course: *I'm studying hard for my finals.* ◇ *I'm taking my history final tomorrow.*

**fi·nal·e** /fɪˈnæli; -ˈnɑli/ ***noun*** [C] the last part of a piece of music, an opera, a show, etc.

**fi·nal·ist** /ˈfaɪnl·ɪst/ ***noun*** [C] a person who is in the FINAL[2] (1) of a competition ➲ Look at **semifinalist**.

**fi·nal·ize** /ˈfaɪnl·aɪz/ ***verb*** [T] to make firm decisions about plans, dates, etc.: *Have you finalized your vacation plans yet?*

★**fi·nal·ly** /ˈfaɪnl·i/ ***adv.*** **1** after a long time or delay: *It was getting dark when the plane finally took off.* **2** (*formal*) (used at the beginning of a sentence when you have a list of things to say, especially in a speech) as a last point: *Finally, I would like to say how much we all enjoyed this evening.*

★**fi·nance**[1] /ˈfaɪnæns; fəˈnæns/ ***noun*** **1** [U] the management of (public) money: *the Senate Finance Committee* ◇ *an expert in finance* **2** **finances** [pl.] the money a person, company, country, etc. has available to spend: *What are our finances like right now?* (= How much money do we have?)

★**fi·nance**[2] /ˈfaɪnæns; fəˈnæns/ ***verb*** [T] to provide the money to pay for sth: *Your trip will be financed by the company.*

★**fi·nan·cial** /fəˈnænʃl; faɪ-/ ***adj.*** connected with money: *The business got into financial difficulties.* ◇ *If you plan to go to college, you'll probably have to apply for financial aid.* ▶ **fi·nan·cial·ly** ***adv.***

★**find**[1] /faɪnd/ ***verb*** [T] (*pt, pp* **found** /faʊnd/) **1** to get back sth that you have lost: *Did you find the pen you lost?* ◇ *I can't find my new sweater anywhere.* **2** to discover sth or get sth that you want (after a search): *After six months, she finally found a job.* ◇ *Did you manage to find a good hotel?* ◇ *Scientists still haven't found a cure for colds.* ◇ *I hope you find an answer to your problem.*

➲ Notice the expressions **find time**, **find the money**: *I never seem to find time to write letters these days.* ◇ *We'd like to go on vacation, but we can't find the money.*

**3** to discover sth by chance: *Tom found a $20 bill in the park.* ◇ *We went into the house and found her lying on the floor.* **4** to think or to have an opinion about sth (because of your own experience): *I find that book very difficult to understand.* ◇ *We didn't find the movie at all funny.* ◇ *How are you finding life as a student?*

NOTE When we are expressing an opinion, we say **I think that...** NOT **I find that...**

IDM **find fault (with sb/sth)** to look for things that are wrong with sb/sth and complain about them

PHR V **find (sth) out** to get some information by asking or studying: *Did you find out how much the tickets cost?*

**find sb out** to discover that sb has done sth wrong: *He used a false name for years before he was found out.*

**find²** /faɪnd/ ***noun*** [C] a thing or a person that is unusually good or valuable: *This little gadget was a real find.*

**find·er** /ˈfaɪndər/ ***noun*** [C] a person who finds sth

**find·ing** /ˈfaɪndɪŋ/ ***noun*** [C] (usually plural) something that is discovered by research or investigation: *the findings of a survey/a report/a committee*

★**fine¹** /faɪn/ ***adj.***

➤ VERY GOOD **1** (only *before* a noun) of very good quality, beautiful: *a fine piece of work* ◇ *That's the finest painting I've ever seen by that artist.*

➤ ACCEPTABLE/SATISFACTORY **2** good enough: *"Do you want some more cream in your coffee?" "No, thanks, that's fine."* ◇ *Don't cook anything special – a sandwich will be fine.* ◇ *The hotel rooms were fine but the food was terrible.* **3** in good health, or happy and comfortable: *"How are you?" "Fine, thanks."* ◇ *"Do you want to trade places?" "No, thanks. I'm fine here."*

NOTE We do not use meanings **2** and **3** in questions or in the negative form, so you CANNOT say "Are you fine?" or "This isn't fine."

➤ THIN **4** very thin: *shampoo for fine hair* ◇ *a fine pencil* OPP **thick**

➤ WITH SMALL GRAINS **5** made of very small pieces, grains, etc.: *Salt is finer than sugar.* OPP **coarse**

➤ DETAIL/DISTINCTIONS **6** difficult to see; very detailed: *The difference in meaning between those two words is very fine.* ◇ *I couldn't understand the finer points of his argument.*

**fine²** /faɪn/ ***adv.*** (*informal*) very well: *Don't worry – you'll do just fine.*

**fine³** /faɪn/ ***noun*** [C] a sum of money that you have to pay for breaking a law or rule: *a parking fine* ◇ *You'll get a fine if you park your car there.* ◇ *He'll have to either pay a heavy fine or go to prison.*

**fine⁴** /faɪn/ ***verb*** [T] **fine sb (for sth/for doing sth)** to make sb pay a sum of money because he/she has broken a law or rule: *He was fined $50 for speeding.*

ˌ**fine ˈarts** ***noun*** [pl.] subjects such as painting, drawing, music, or making movies that you study at a school, college or university

**fine·ly** /ˈfaɪnli/ ***adv.*** **1** into small pieces: *finely chopped onions* **2** very delicately: *a finely tuned instrument*

ˌ**fine ˈprint** ***noun*** [U] a part or parts of a legal contract, document, etc. that contain important details that you might not notice: *Make sure you read the fine print before you sign anything.*

★**fin·ger¹** /ˈfɪŋgər/ ***noun*** [C] one of the five parts at the end of each hand (or a glove): *little finger, ring finger, middle finger, index finger, thumb* ◇ *Children learn to count on their fingers.* ➲ picture on study page **A32**.

NOTE Sometimes we think of the **thumb** as one of the fingers; sometimes we contrast it: *Hold the pen between your finger and thumb.* The "fingers" on our feet are called **toes**.

IDM **give sb the finger** (*informal*) to make an offensive sign to sb by holding up your middle finger, to show that you are angry at him/her

**keep your fingers crossed** to hope that sb/sth will be successful or lucky: *Good luck on the test – I'll keep my fingers crossed for you!* ➲ Look also at **cross your fingers** at **cross²**.

**point a/the finger at sb/sth** → POINT²

**snap your fingers** → SNAP¹

**fin·ger²** /ˈfɪŋgər/ ***verb*** [T] **1** to touch or feel sth with your fingers: *Gary sat fingering his beard, saying nothing.* **2** **finger sb (as/for sth)** (*informal*) to tell the police that sb did sth illegal

**fin·ger·nail** /ˈfɪŋgərneɪl/ (*also* **nail**) ***noun*** [C] the hard part on the end of each finger: *Your fingernails are filthy!*

**fin·ger·print** /ˈfɪŋgərprɪnt/ ***noun*** [C] **1** the mark made by the skin of a finger, used for identifying people: *The burglar left his fingerprints all over the house.* ◇ *The police took the suspect's fingerprints.* **2** a mark on a wall, door, book, etc. made by a dirty finger

**fin·ger·tip** /ˈfɪŋgərtɪp/ ***noun*** [C] the end of a finger

IDM **have sth at your fingertips** to have sth ready for quick and easy use: *They asked some difficult questions but luckily I had all the facts at my fingertips.*

★**fin·ish¹** /ˈfɪnɪʃ/ ***verb*** **1** [I,T] **finish (sth/doing sth)** to come or bring sth to an end or to reach the end of sth: *The U.S. sprinters finished first, second and third.* ◇ *Finish your work quickly!* ◇ *Did you finish typing that letter?* **2** [T] **finish sth (off/up)** to eat, drink or use the last part of sth: *Finish your milk, Tommy!* **3** [T] **finish sth (off/up)** to complete the last details of sth or make sth perfect: *She stayed up all night to finish up the article she was writing.*

PHR V **finish sb/sth off** (*informal*) to kill sb/sth: *The cat pounced and finished off the mouse.* ◇ (*figurative*) *It was losing his job that really finished him off* (= depressed him).

★**fin·ish²** /ˈfɪnɪʃ/ ***noun*** [C] **1** (used especially about a race) the end: *The last race was a very close finish* (= the runners at the front were close together at the end of the race). OPP **start** **2** (used especially about wood and furniture) the feel or look that sth has when it has been polished, etc.: *This table has a beautiful finish.*

**fin·ished** /ˈfɪnɪʃt/ ***adj.*** **1** (not before a noun) **finished (with sb/sth)** having stopped doing sth, using sth or dealing with sb/sth: *Aren't you finished in there yet? Hurry up!* ◇ *I'll borrow that book when you're finished with it.* **2** (not before a noun) not able to continue: *If we don't improve profits this quarter, we're finished.* **3** made; completed: *the finished product/article*

**fir** /fər/ (*also* **ˈfir tree**) ***noun*** [C] a straight tree that keeps its thin sharp leaves (**needles**) in the winter

★**fire**[1] /ˈfaɪər/ ***noun*** **1** [U] hot bright flames produced by sth that is burning: *Many animals are afraid of fire.* **2** [C,U] burning that destroys things and is out of control: *Firefighters struggled for three hours to put out the fire.* ◇ *forest fires* ◇ *You need to insure your house against fire.* ◇ *The furniture* ***caught fire*** (= started burning) *within seconds.* ◇ *Did someone set fire to that pile of wood?* ◇ *Help! The frying pan's on fire!* **3** [C] burning wood or coal to warm people or cook food: *They lit a fire to keep warm.* ◇ *It's cold – don't let the fire go out!* ◇ *Let's roast chestnuts over the fire.* **4** [U] shooting from guns: *The soldiers were under fire from all sides.*
IDM **open fire** → OPEN[3]

★**fire**[2] /ˈfaɪər/ ***verb*** **1** [I,T] **fire (sth) (at sb/sth)**; **fire (sth) into sth** to shoot with a gun or shoot bullets, etc. from a gun: *"Fire!" shouted the officer.* ◇ *Can you hear the guns firing?* ◇ *He fired his gun at the ceiling.* ◇ *They fired rubber bullets into the crowd.* **2** [T] to say that sb can no longer work for you (because of bad work, bad behavior, etc.): *He was fired for always being late.* **3** [T] **fire sth at sb** to ask questions, or make remarks, quickly and aggressively: *If you stop firing questions at me, I might be able to answer!* **4** [T] **fire sb with sth** to produce a strong feeling in sb: *Her speech fired me with determination.*

**ˈfire aˌlarm** ***noun*** [C] a bell or other signal to warn people that there is a fire: *If the fire alarm goes off, leave the building immediately.*

**fire·arm** /ˈfaɪərɑrm/ ***noun*** [C, usually pl.] a gun that you can carry: *The prison guards carry firearms.*

**fire·crack·er** /ˈfaɪərˌkrækər/ ***noun*** [C] a very small container filled with chemicals, that explodes with a sudden loud noise when you set fire to it

★**ˈfire deˌpartment** ***noun*** [C] an organization of people trained to put out (= stop) fires: *Dial 911 to call the fire department.*

**ˈfire ˌengine** (*also* **ˈfire truck**) ***noun*** [C] a special truck that carries equipment for fighting large fires

**ˈfire esˌcape** ***noun*** [C] a special staircase on the outside of a building that people can run down if there is a fire

**ˈfire exˌtinguisher** (*also* **extinguisher**) ***noun*** [C] a metal container with water or chemicals inside that you use for fighting small fires

**fire·fight·er** /ˈfaɪərˌfaɪt̬ər/ ***noun*** [C] a person whose job is to fight fires

NOTE People of both sexes now work in most jobs, so nowadays it is usually not necessary to use different words for men and women doing the same job. Some people, especially women, consider names of jobs that mention a person's sex old-fashioned or offensive. For example, instead of **policeman** or **policewoman** we can say **police officer**. Instead of **mailman** we can say **letter carrier**, and instead of **stewardess** we can say **flight attendant**.

**ˈfire ˌhydrant** (*also* **hydrant**) ***noun*** [C] a piece of metal equipment on a sidewalk, connected to a pipe from which water can be taken for putting out fires

**fire·man** /ˈfaɪərmən/ ***noun*** [C] (*pl.* **fire·men** /-mən/) a man whose job is to fight fires ➲ Look at the note at **firefighter**.

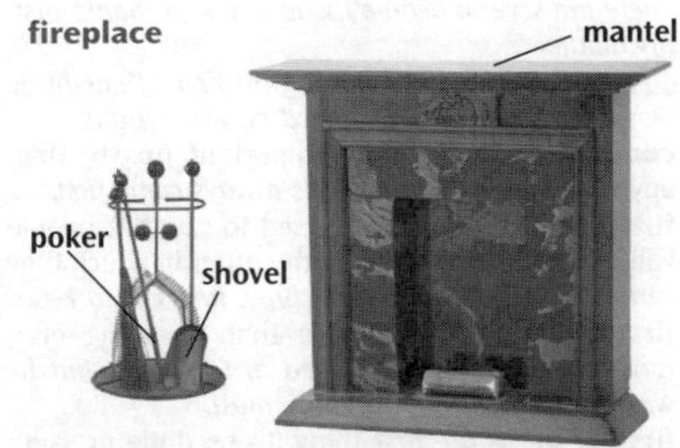


**fire·place** /ˈfaɪərpleɪs/ ***noun*** [C] the open place in a room (at the bottom of a chimney) where you light a fire

**ˈfire ˌsta·tion** ***noun*** [C] a building where fire engines are kept and firefighters wait to be called

**fire·wall** /ˈfaɪərwɔl/ ***noun*** [C] (*computing*) a part of a computer system that protects the system by stopping people from getting information that they shouldn't have, while letting them get the information they should have

**fire·wood** /ˈfaɪərwʊd/ ***noun*** [U] wood used for burning on fires

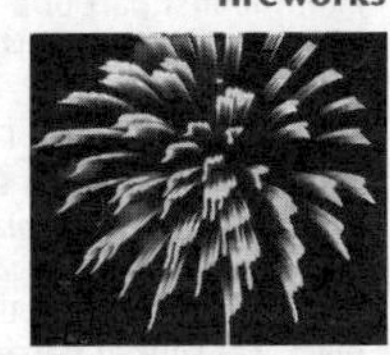


**fire·work** /ˈfaɪərwərk/ ***noun*** [C, usually pl.] a small container with chemicals inside that burns or explodes with colored lights and loud noises, used for entertainment: *a fireworks display*

**ˈfir·ing squad** ***noun*** [C] a group of soldiers who have been ordered to shoot and kill a prisoner

★**firm**[1] /fərm/ ***noun*** [C] a business company: *a law firm* (= that lawyers work for)

★**firm**[2] /fərm/ ***adj.*** **1** able to stay the same shape when pressed; fairly hard: *a firm mattress* **2** strong or steady or not likely to change: *She kept a firm grip on her mother's hand.* ◇ *Do you have a firm date for your wedding yet?* ◇ *We made a firm decision – we're not going to change it now.* ◇ *I have a firm offer of a job in New York.* **3** **firm (with sb)** insisting that people do what you want: *He's very firm with his kids.* ▸ **firm·ly** ***adv.*** ▸ **firm·ness** ***noun*** [U]

★**first**[1] /fərst/ ***det.*** coming before all others; that has not happened before: *his first day at school* ◇ *their first baby* ◇ *You won first prize!* ◇ *first impressions*

F

◇ *The first time she went skiing, she broke her leg.* ◇ *King Charles I* (= King Charles the First)

IDM **at first glance/sight** when first seen or examined: *At first glance, it looked like solid gold.* ◇ *When I met Andy, it was love at first sight.*

**first thing** as early as possible: *I'll call her first thing tomorrow morning.*

★**first²** /fərst/ ***adv.*** **1** before any others: *Sue arrived first at the party.* ◇ *Our team finished first in the race* (= we won). ◇ *Do you want to go first or second?* **2** before doing anything else: *I'll come out later. I have to finish my homework first.* **3** for the first time: *Where did you first meet your husband?* **4** at the beginning: *When I first started my job, I hated it.* **5** (used for introducing the first thing in a list): *There are several people I would like to thank: first, my mother.*

IDM **at first** at the beginning: *At first I thought he was joking, but then I realized he was serious.*

**come first** to be more important (to sb) than anything else: *Her family has always come first.*

**first come, first served** used to say that people will be seen, helped, etc. in the order in which they came: *Tickets are on a first come, first served basis.*

**first and foremost** more than anything else; most importantly: *He worked in television, but he was a stage actor first and foremost.*

**first of all** as the first thing (to be done or said): *First of all, make sure your hands are clean.*

**first³** /fərst/ ***noun, pronoun*** **1** [C] (*pl.* **first**) the first person or thing, people or things: *Are we the first to arrive?* ◇ *They enjoyed the vacation – their first in ten years.* **2** [sing.] an important event that is happening for the first time: *This operation is a first in medical history.*

★ˌ**first 'aid** ***noun*** [U] medical help that you give to sb who is hurt or sick before the doctor arrives

ˌ**first 'base** ***noun*** [sing.] **1** (in baseball) the first point (base) on the field that a player must touch after hitting the ball ➲ picture at **baseball** **2** (*informal*) the first part of a project, process, etc.: *If the boss is in a bad mood, you won't even get to first base with your proposal.* ▸ **first base·man** /ˌfərst 'beɪsmən/ ***noun*** [C] ➲ picture at **baseball**.

ˌ**first 'class** ***noun*** [U] **1** the most comfortable and expensive area on a plane, train, etc.: *The seats in first class are a lot bigger than these.* **2** the class of mail, especially for letters, that is delivered most quickly ➲ Look at **parcel post**.

ˌ**first-'class** ***adj.*** (usually *before* a noun) **1** excellent, of the best quality: *a first-class player* **2** giving or using the best or most expensive type of service: *the first-class section of an airplane* ◇ *How much does a first-class stamp cost?* ▸ ˌ**first 'class** ***adv.***: *to travel first class* ◇ *If you send the package first class, it will get there sooner.*

ˌ**first 'cousin** ***noun*** [C] = COUSIN

ˌ**first-de'gree** ***adj.*** (only *before* a noun) (used about crimes) of the worst or most serious kind: *He was charged with first-degree murder.*

ˌ**first 'floor** (*also* **ground floor**) ***noun*** [C] the floor of a building on street level: *I live in an apartment on the first floor/a first-floor apartment.*

**first·hand** /ˌfərst'hænd/ ***adj., adv.*** (used about information, experience, a story, etc.) heard, seen or learned directly, not from other people: *He gave me a firsthand account of the accident* (= he had seen it). ◇ *I've experienced the problem firsthand, so I know exactly how you feel.*

ˌ**first 'lady** ***noun*** [usually sing.] (*pl.* **first ladies**) **1 First Lady** the wife of the President of the U.S. or of the governor of a state **2** the woman who is thought to be the best in a particular profession, sport, etc.: *the first lady of country music*

★'**first name** ***noun*** [C] the name that is given to a person when he/she is born: *"What's Mrs. Brown's first name?" "Alice, I think."* ➲ Look at the note at **name¹**.

IDM **be on a first-name basis (with sb)** to know sb well enough to call him/her by his/her first name

ˌ**First 'Nations** ***noun*** [pl.] (*Cdn*) the Aboriginal peoples of Canada, not including the Inuit or Metis

**the ˌfirst 'person** ***noun*** [sing.] **1** (*grammar*) the words such as "I," "me," "we," and the verb forms that go with them: *"I am" is the first person singular of the verb "to be."* **2** the style of telling a story as if it happened to you: *The author writes in the first person* (= he/she writes, "I..."). ➲ Look at the note at **White House**.

ˌ**first-'rate** ***adj.*** excellent; of the best quality

**fis·cal** /'fɪskl/ ***adj.*** (only *before* a noun) connected with money that the government receives and spends: *the government's fiscal policies*

ˌ**fiscal 'year** ***noun*** [C] a period of twelve months that a company or government uses to calculate its accounts, taxes, etc.

★**fish¹** /fɪʃ/ ***noun*** (*pl.* **fish** or **fish·es**) **1** [C] an animal that lives, breathes and swims in water: *How many fish did you catch?* ◇ (*formal*) *exotic fishes* (= types or species of fish) *of the Caribbean.*

> NOTE The plural form **fish** is more common. **Fishes** is used in formal or technical English when we are talking about different types of fish.

**2** [U] fish (1) as food: *fresh fish*

★**fish²** /fɪʃ/ ***verb*** [I] **1 fish (for sth)** to try to catch fish with rods, nets, etc.: *He's fishing for trout.*

> NOTE When we are talking about spending time fishing, we usually say **go fishing**: *They often go fishing on weekends.*

**2 fish (around) for sth** to search for sth in water or in a deep or hidden place: *She fished (around) for her keys in the bottom of her bag.*

PHRV **fish for sth** to try to get sth you want in an indirect way: *to fish for a compliment*

**fish sth out (of sth)** to take or pull sth out (of sth) especially after searching for it: *After the accident, they fished the car out of the river.* ◇ *She fished a pair of socks out of the bottom of the drawer.*

**fish·er·man** /'fɪʃərmən/ ***noun*** [C] (*pl.* **fish·er·men** /'fɪʃərmən/) a person who catches fish as a job or as a sport

★**fish·ing** /'fɪʃɪŋ/ ***noun*** [U] catching fish as a job, sport or hobby: *Fishing is a major industry in New England.*

'**fishing rod** (*also* '**fishing pole**) ***noun*** [C] a long thin stick with a long string and a hook on it for catching fish

**'fish stick** *noun* [C] a small square or long piece of fish that is covered in very small pieces of dried bread: *a box of frozen fish sticks*

**fish·y** /fɪʃi/ *adj.* (**fish·i·er**; **fish·i·est**) **1** (*informal*) seeming suspicious or untrue: *The police thought his story sounded pretty fishy.* **2** of or like a fish, especially in taste or smell: *a fishy smell*

**fist** /fɪst/ *noun* [C] a hand with the fingers closed together tightly: *She clenched her fists.*

★**fit**[1] /fɪt/ *adj.* (**fit·ter**; **fit·test**) **1 fit for sb/sth; fit to do sth** good enough; suitable: *These houses are not fit (for people) to live in.* ◇ *a meal fit for a king* **2** in good physical health (especially because of exercise): *He keeps physically fit by jogging five miles a day.* ➲ The expression **in (good) shape** is more common than **fit** in this sense.

★**fit**[2] /fɪt/ *verb* (*pres. part.* **fit·ting**; *pt, pp* **fit** or, especially in the passive **fit·ted**)
➤RIGHT SIZE/TYPE **1** [I,T] to be the right size or shape for sb/sth: *These jeans don't fit.* ◇ *This dress doesn't fit me anymore.* ◇ *This key doesn't fit the lock.* ◇ *My car won't fit into your garage.* **2** [T] **fit sb/sth in/into/on/onto sth** to find enough space for sb/sth: *Can you fit one more person in the car?* ◇ *I can't fit all these books onto the shelf.*
➤PUT STH SOMEWHERE **3** [T] to put or fasten sth in the right place: *I can't fit these pieces of the model together.* **4** [T] **fit sth with sth** (often passive) to put or attach sth, such as a part or a piece of equipment, onto or into sth: *a car that has been fitted with an alarm*
➤BE/MAKE SUITABLE **5** [T] to be or make sb/sth right or suitable: *The punishment should fit the crime.*
PHR V **fit sb/sth in; fit sb/sth in/into sth** to find time to see sb or to do sth: *The doctor managed to fit me in this morning.* ◇ *You're tired because you're trying to fit too much into one day.*
**fit in (with sb/sth)** to be able to live, work, etc. in an easy and natural way (with sb/sth): *The new girl found it difficult to fit in (with the other kids) at school.* ◇ *I can easily change my plans to fit in with yours.*

**fit**[3] /fɪt/ *noun* **1** [sing.] (usually after an adjective) the way in which sth (e.g. a piece of clothing) fits: *a good/bad/tight fit* **2** [C] (*old-fashioned*) a sudden loss of consciousness with movements that are not controlled and sometimes violent ➲ **Seizure** is more common nowadays. **3** [C] a sudden (usually short) attack of illness: *a fit of coughing* **4** [C] a sudden period of activity or violent feeling: *a fit of laughter/energy* ◇ *a fit of anger*
IDM **have/throw a fit** (*informal*) to suddenly become very angry, shocked, etc.: *Dad'll have a fit when he finds out we got arrested!*

**fit·ness** /'fɪtnəs/ *noun* [U] **1** the condition of being FIT[1] (2): *physical fitness* **2 fitness for sth/to do sth** the quality of being suitable: *The managers were not sure about his fitness for the job.*

**fit·ting** /'fɪṭɪŋ/ *adj.* (*formal*) right; suitable

**'fitting room** *noun* [C] a room in a store where you can try on clothes to see if you want to buy them

**five** /faɪv/ *number* 5; one more than four ➲ Look also at **fifth** (= 5th). For examples of how to use numbers in sentences, look at **six**.

**five-** /faɪv/ *prefix* (used in compounds) having five of the thing mentioned: *a five-day week* ◇ *a five-hour flight*

**,five-and-'dime** (*also* **,five-and-'dime store, dime store**) *noun* [C] a store that sells a range of cheap goods

★**fix**[1] /fɪks/ *verb* [T] **1** to repair: *The electrician's coming to fix the light switch.* **2** to decide or arrange sth: *The price has been fixed at $30.* ◇ *Have you fixed a date for the party?* **3 fix sth (for sb)** to prepare sth (especially food or drink) for sb: *Can I fix you a drink/a drink for you?* **4** (usually passive) (*informal*) to arrange the result of sth in a way that is not honest or fair: *The race was fixed* (= the result was arranged before it happened).
IDM **be fixing to do sth** (*informal*) (used especially in the southern U.S.) to get ready to do sth: *I'm fixing to go to the post office. Do you need any stamps?*
**fix your hair** to arrange your hair so that it looks attractive
PHR V **fix sth up** to repair or improve sth so that it is suitable to use: *My brother likes to fix up old cars.*
**fix sb up (with sth)** (*informal*) to arrange for sb to have sth: *I can fix you up with a job and a place to stay.*

**fix**[2] /fɪks/ *noun* [C] **1** [usually sing.] (*informal*) a difficult situation: *I was in a real fix – I'd locked my keys inside the car.* **2** (*slang*) an injection of a drug such as heroin

**fix·a·tion** /fɪk'seɪʃn/ *noun* [C] a feeling (about sb/sth) that is too strong and not normal

★**fixed** /fɪkst/ *adj.* **1** firmly attached in a place so that it will not move: *All the seats are fixed to the floor.* **2** already decided: *a fixed date/rent/price* **3** not changing: *He has such fixed ideas that you can't discuss anything with him.* ◇ *a fixed income*

**fix·ture** /'fɪkstʃər/ *noun* [C] **1** [usually pl.] a piece of furniture or equipment that is attached inside a house or building and sold with it: *a light fixture* **2** a person or thing that always seems to be at a particular place and has become connected with that place in people's minds: *Mr. Carlson is a permanent fixture in the coffee shop.*

**fizz**[1] /fɪz/ *verb* [I] to produce many small bubbles and/or make a soft sound

**fizz**[2] /fɪz/ *noun* [U] the bubbles in a liquid and the sound they make: *This cola has lost its fizz.*

**fiz·zle** /'fɪzl/ *verb*
PHR V **fizzle out** to end in a weak or disappointing way: *The party started well, but it fizzled out around 11:00.*

**fizz·y** /'fɪzi/ *adj.* (**fiz·zi·er**; **fiz·zi·est**) (used about a drink) containing many small bubbles

**flab·ber·gast·ed** /'flæbərgæstəd/ *adj.* (*informal*) extremely surprised

**flab·by** /'flæbi/ *adj.* (**flab·bi·er**; **flab·bi·est**) **1** (used about a person) having too much soft loose flesh **2** (used about muscles, arms, legs, etc.) too soft

**flack** /flæk/ *noun* **1** [U] = FLAK **2** [C] (*informal*) a person who represents a company and gives information about it to the public, especially to people who work for newspapers, television, etc.

★**flag**[1] /flæg/ *noun* [C] a piece of cloth with a pattern

F

or picture on it, often attached to a pole (flagpole) or rope and used as a symbol of a country, club, etc. or as a signal: *a flag flying over the state capitol* ◇ *All the kids were waving flags.*

**flag²** /flæg/ *verb* [I] (**flag·ging**; **flagged**) to become tired or less strong or active

PHR V **flag sb/sth down** to wave to sb in a car to make him/her stop: *to flag down a cab*

**fla·grant** /ˈfleɪgrənt/ *adj.* (only *before* a noun) easily seen to be bad and shocking: *a flagrant violation of the law*

**flag·ship** /ˈflægʃɪp/ *noun* [C] **1** the most important ship in a group of military ships **2** [usually sing.] the most important in a group of products, stores, etc.: *Macy's flagship store in New York City*

**flail** /fleɪl/ *verb* [I,T] to wave or swing around without control: *The insect's legs were flailing in the air.* ◇ *The drowning child flailed his arms above his head.*

**flair** /flɛr/ *noun* **1** (a) **flair for sth** [sing.] a natural ability to do sth well: *She has a flair for languages* (= she's good at learning them). **2** [U] the quality of being interesting or having style: *a poster designed with her usual flair*

**flak** (*also* **flack**) /flæk/ *noun* [U] criticism: *The President will take some flak for the comment he made today.*

**flake¹** /fleɪk/ *noun* [C] **1** a small thin piece of sth: *snowflakes* ◇ *corn flakes* **2** (*slang*) a person who acts in a strange or crazy way and forgets things easily

**flake²** /fleɪk/ *verb* [I] **flake (off)** to come off in FLAKES¹ (1): *The paint is flaking off the wall.*

**flak·y** /ˈfleɪki/ *adj.* (**flak·i·er**; **flak·i·est**) **1** made of FLAKES¹ (1) or that can easily break into flakes: *flaky pie crust* ◇ *dry, flaky skin* **2** (*slang*) behaving in a strange or crazy way and forgetting things easily

**flam·boy·ant** /flæmˈbɔɪənt/ *adj.* **1** (used about a person) acting in a loud, confident way so that other people will notice **2** very easily noticed: *flamboyant colors* ▸ **flam·boy·ance** /-ˈbɔɪəns/ *noun* [U] ▸ **flam·boy·ant·ly** *adv.*

★**flame** /fleɪm/ *noun* [C,U] an area of bright burning gas that comes from sth that is on fire: *the flame of a candle* ◇ *The house was in flames when the fire engine arrived.* ◇ *The car rolled down a hill and burst into flames* (= suddenly began to burn strongly). ◇ *a huge ball of flame* ➲ Picture at **candle**.

**flam·ing** /ˈfleɪmɪŋ/ *adj.* (only *before* a noun) burning brightly: *a flaming torch*

**fla·min·go** /fləˈmɪŋgoʊ/ *noun* [C] (*pl.* **fla·min·gos** or **fla·min·goes**) a large bird that lives near water in warm areas and has long thin legs, a long neck and bright pink feathers

**flam·ma·ble** /ˈflæməbl/ *adj.* able to burn easily SYN **Inflammable** OPP **nonflammable**

**flank¹** /flæŋk/ *noun* [C] (used about an animal or an army ready for battle) the side

**flank²** /flæŋk/ *verb* [T] (often passive) to be at the side or sides of: *The governor was flanked by bodyguards.*

**flan·nel** /ˈflænl/ *noun* [U] a type of soft wool or cotton cloth

**flap¹** /flæp/ *noun* [C] **1** a piece of material that is attached to sth at one side only, often covering an opening: *a tent flap* ◇ *a pocket flap* **2** [usually sing.] (*informal*) a state of worry or nervous excitement: *the latest flap over tax increases*

**flap²** /flæp/ *verb* (**flap·ping**; **flapped**) [I,T] to move sth up and down or from side to side; to move in this way, especially in the wind: *The sails were flapping in the wind.* ◇ *The bird flapped its wings and flew away.*

**flap·jack** /ˈflæpdʒæk/ *noun* [C] = PANCAKE

**flare¹** /flɛr/ *verb* [I] **1** to burn with a sudden bright flame **2** (used about a person's temper, anger, violence, etc.) to start suddenly or become worse: *Tempers flared at Tuesday's school board meeting.*

PHR V **flare up 1** (used about a fire) to suddenly burn more fiercely **2** (used about violence, anger, pain, a person's temper, etc.) to start suddenly or become worse: *My arthritis is flaring up again.*

**flare²** /flɛr/ *noun* [C] **1** a sudden bright light or flame **2** a thing that produces a bright light or flame, used especially as a signal

**flared** /flɛrd/ *adj.* (used about pants and skirts) becoming wider toward the bottom

★**flash¹** /flæʃ/ *noun* [C] **1** a sudden bright light that comes and goes quickly: *a flash of lightning* **2** a sudden ability (to guess, understand or imagine sth): *In a flash of inspiration, I saw what the answer must be.* **3** a bright light that you use with a camera for taking photographs when the light is not good; the apparatus for producing this light: *The light's not very good. You'll need the flash.* ◇ *My new camera has a built-in flash.* ➲ picture at **camera**.

★**flash²** /flæʃ/ *verb* **1** [I,T] to produce a sudden bright light or to make sth produce it: *The neon lights were flashing on and off all night.* ◇ *That truck driver's flashing his lights at us* (in order to tell us sth). **2** [I] to move very fast: *I saw something flash past the window.* ◇ *Thoughts kept flashing through my mind and I couldn't sleep.* **3** [T] to show sth quickly: *The detective flashed his card and went straight in.* **4** [T] to send a particular look toward sb (suddenly, and only for a moment): *He flashed a smile at her and drove away.*

PHR V **flash back** (used about a person's thoughts) to return suddenly to a time in the past: *Something he said made my mind flash back to my childhood.*

**flash·back** /ˈflæʃbæk/ *noun* **1** [C,U] a part of a movie, play, etc. that shows sth that happened before the main story **2** [C] a time when a person's thoughts return suddenly to an event in the past, especially one that was very frightening

ˈ**flash card** (*also* ˈ**flashcard**) *noun* [C] a card with a word or words, numbers, or a picture on it that you look at to help you learn or remember sth

ˌ**flash** ˈ**flood** *noun* [C] a sudden flood of water, usually caused by heavy rain

**flash·light** /ˈflæʃlaɪt/ *noun* [C] a small electric light that you carry in your hand. A flashlight runs on batteries: *Shine the flashlight under the couch and see if you can find my ring.* ➲ picture at **light**.

**flash·y** /ˈflæʃi/ *adj.* (**flash·i·er**; **flash·i·est**) too bright or big and intended to attract attention, especially to make people think that the owner is rich: *a flashy car* ◇ *flashy clothes*

**flask** /flæsk/ *noun* [C] **1** a bottle with a narrow

neck that is used in a laboratory **2** a small flat bottle that is used for carrying alcohol in a pocket

★**flat¹** /flæt/ ***adj.*** (**flat·ter**; **flat·test**)

➤LEVEL **1** smooth and level, with no parts that are raised above the rest: *The countryside in Kansas is extremely flat* (= there are no hills). ◇ *I need a flat surface to write this letter on.* ◇ *a flat roof*

➤NOT HIGH **2** not high or deep: *You need flat shoes for walking.*

➤TIRE **3** (used about a tire) without enough air in it: *I drove over some glass and got a flat tire.*

➤DRINK **4** (used about a drink) not fresh because it has lost its bubbles: *Open a new bottle. This cola is flat.*

➤IN MUSIC **5** (*symbol* ♭) (in music) half a tone lower than the stated note: *a symphony in B flat* ➲ Look at **sharp¹**(10). **6** (in music) lower than the correct note: *That last note was flat. Can you sing it again?* ➲ Look at **sharp¹**(11). ➲ picture at **music**.

➤REFUSAL/DENIAL **7** that will not change; firm (used about sth that you say or decide): *He answered our request with a flat "No."*

➤COST OF STH **8** (used about the cost of sth) that is the same for everybody; that is fixed: *We charge a flat fee of $20, however long you stay.*

➤BUSINESS **9** (used about business, trade, etc.) not increasing or active: *Sales have been flat for the last three months.*

**flat**

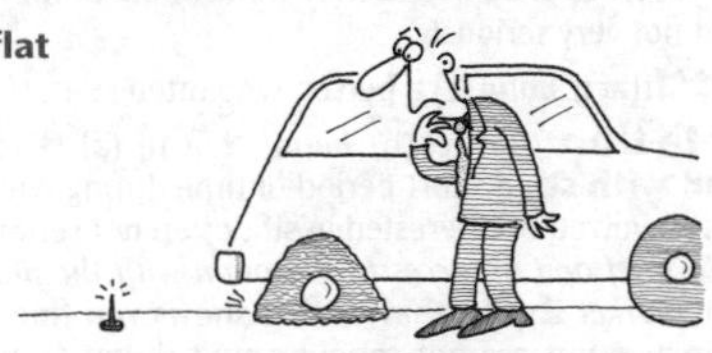

**"Oh, no! I've got a flat tire!"**

★**flat²** /flæt/ ***adv.*** **1** in a level position: *She lay flat on her back in the sunshine.* ◇ *He fell flat on his face in the mud.* **2** lower than the correct note: *You're singing flat.* ➲ Look at **sharp²**(2). **3** (used for emphasizing how quickly sth is done) in exactly the time mentioned and no longer: *She can get up and out of the house in ten minutes flat.*

IDM **fall flat** (used about a joke, a story, an event, etc.) to fail to produce the effect that you wanted **flat out 1** (*informal*) in a direct way; absolutely: *I told the boss flat out that I quit.* ◇ *That's just flat out wrong!* **2** as fast as possible; without stopping: *He's been working flat out for two weeks and he needs a break.*

**flat³** /flæt/ ***noun*** [C] **1** (*symbol* ♭) (in music) a note which is half a step lower than the note with the same letter ➲ Look at **sharp³**. **2** a tire on a car, etc. that has no air in it: *I had a flat on the way to work yesterday.* **3** (*Cdn*) = APARTMENT

**flat·ly** /ˈflætli/ ***adv.*** **1** in a way that shows no interest **2** in a direct way; absolutely: *He flatly denied the allegations.*

**flat·ten** /ˈflætn/ ***verb*** [I,T] **flatten (sth) (out)** to become flat or to make sth flat: *The countryside flattens out as you drive west.* ◇ *The storms flattened crops all over the state.*

**flat·ter** /ˈflæt̬ər/ ***verb*** [T] **1** to praise sb too much because you want to please him/her or because you want to get an advantage for yourself **2** (usually passive) to give pleasure or honor to sb: *I felt very flattered when they gave me the job.*

**flat·ter·ing** /ˈflæt̬ərɪŋ/ ***adj.*** making sb look or sound more attractive or important than he/she really is

**flat·ter·y** /ˈflæt̬əri/ ***noun*** [U] praise that you do not really mean

**flaunt** /flɔnt/ ***verb*** [T] to show sth that you are proud of so that other people will admire it

★**fla·vor¹** /ˈfleɪvər/ ***noun*** [C,U] **1** the taste and smell (of food): *Do you think a little salt would improve the flavor?* ◇ *ten different flavors of yogurt* ◇ *yogurt in ten different flavors* **2** the particular quality or character of sth: *The hotel's architecture gives it a real rustic flavor.*

**fla·vor²** /ˈfleɪvər/ ***verb*** [T] to give flavor to sth: *a strawberry-flavored milkshake* ◇ *I flavored the soup with pepper and parsley.*

**fla·vor·ing** /ˈfleɪvərɪŋ/ ***noun*** [C,U] something that you add to food or drink to give it a particular taste

**flaw** /flɔ/ ***noun*** [C] **1** a mark or crack in an object that means that it is not perfect **2** a mistake in sth that makes it not satisfactory: *a flaw in an argument* **3** a bad quality in sb's character

**flawed** /flɔd/ ***adj.*** with a fault or weakness so that it is not perfect

**flaw·less** /ˈflɔləs/ ***adj.*** perfect

**flea** /fli/ ***noun*** [C] a very small jumping insect without wings that lives on animals, e.g. cats and dogs. Fleas bite people and animals and make them scratch.

**ˈflea ˌmarket** ***noun*** [C] a sale, often in an outdoor place, where people sell old and used goods

**fleck** /flɛk/ ***noun*** [C] a tiny mark on sth; a tiny piece of sth

**flee** /fli/ ***verb*** [I,T] (*pt, pp* **fled** /flɛd/) to run away or escape from sth: *When the hunter fired his gun, the deer turned and fled.* ◇ *The man whom the police want to interview has fled the country.*

**fleece¹** /flis/ ***noun*** **1** [C] the wool coat of a sheep; this coat when it has been removed from a sheep (by **shearing**) ➲ picture at **sheep**. **2** [C,U] a soft warm material that feels like sheep's wool; a jacket or similar clothing that is made from this material: *a fleece lining* ◇ *a bright red fleece* ➲ picture on study page **A30**.

**fleece²** /flis/ ***verb*** [T] to take a lot of money from sb by charging him/her too much: *Some local stores have been fleecing tourists.*

**fleet** /flit/ ***noun*** [C] **1** a group of ships or boats that are sailing together **2** a group of vehicles (especially taxis, buses or aircraft) that are traveling together or owned by one person or company

**fleet·ing** /ˈflit̬ɪŋ/ ***adj.*** passing quickly; lasting only a short time: *I just caught a fleeting glimpse of the burglar.*

★**flesh** /flɛʃ/ ***noun*** [U] **1** the soft part of a human or animal body (around the bones and under the skin)

NOTE **Flesh** that we eat is called **meat**.

**2** the part of a fruit or vegetable that is soft and can be eaten

**flew** *past tense of* FLY²

**flex** /flɛks/ ***verb*** [T] to bend or move a leg, arm, muscle, etc. in order to exercise it

**flex·i·ble** /ˈflɛksəbl/ ***adj.*** **1** able to bend easily without breaking **2** that can change or be changed in order to suit different situations or conditions OPP **inflexible** ▸ **flex·i·bil·i·ty** ***noun*** [U]

**flick¹** /flɪk/ ***verb*** **1** [I,T] to move, or to make sth move, with a quick sudden movement: *The frog's tongue flicked out and caught the fly.* ◇ *She flicked the switch and the light came on.* **2** [T] to hit sb/sth lightly and quickly

PHR V **flick sth away**; **flick sth off sth** to remove sth with a quick movement of your hand or finger

**flick/flip through sth** to turn over the pages of a book, magazine, etc. quickly

**flick²** /flɪk/ ***noun*** [C] **1** a quick sudden movement or light hit **2** (*informal*) a movie

**flick·er¹** /ˈflɪkər/ ***verb*** [I] **1** (used about a light or a flame) to burn or shine in a weak or unsteady way: *The candle flickered and went out.* **2** to move lightly and quickly up and down or backward and forward: *His eyelids flickered for a second and then he lay still.*

**flick·er²** /ˈflɪkər/ ***noun*** [C, usually sing.] **1** a flickering movement **2** a slight feeling of sth: *a flicker of hope*

**flies** /flaɪz/ *plural of* FLY²

★**flight** /flaɪt/ ***noun***

➤ JOURNEY BY AIR **1** [C] a trip in an airplane, etc.: *The captain and crew hope that you enjoyed the flight.* ◇ *a direct flight* ◇ *a scheduled flight* ◇ *a charter flight* ◇ *a manned space flight to the moon*

➤ AIRPLANE **2** [C] an airplane that takes you on a particular trip: *Flight number 340 to New York is boarding now* (= is ready for passengers to get on it).

➤ FLYING **3** [U] the action of flying: *It's unusual to see swans **in flight*** (= when they are flying).

➤ RUNNING AWAY **4** [C,U] the act of running away or escaping

➤ OF STAIRS **5** [C] a number of stairs or steps leading up or down: *a flight of stairs*

**ˈflight atˌtendant** ***noun*** [C] a person whose job is to help the passengers on an airplane and serve them drinks, etc. ➲ Look at the note at **firefighter**.

**ˈflight deck** ***noun*** [C] **1** an area at the front of a large plane where the pilot sits to use the controls and fly the plane **2** a long flat surface on top of a ship that carries aircraft (an aircraft carrier) where they take off and land

**ˈflight path** ***noun*** [C] the route taken by an aircraft through the air: *The pilot was instructed to change his flight path.*

**ˈflight reˌcorder** ***noun*** [C] = BLACK BOX

**flim·sy** /ˈflɪmzi/ ***adj.*** (**flim·si·er**; **flim·si·est**) **1** (used about material) too light and thin **2** (used about an object) not strong; easily broken **3** weak; not convincing you that it is true: *He gave a flimsy excuse for his absence.*

**flinch** /flɪntʃ/ ***verb*** [I] to make a slight movement backward because of sth painful or frightening

**fling¹** /flɪŋ/ ***verb*** [T] (*pt, pp* **flung** /flʌŋ/) to throw sb/sth suddenly or with great force: *She flung her book on the floor and rushed out.*

**fling²** /flɪŋ/ ***noun*** [C] (*informal*) a short period of fun and pleasure

**flint** /flɪnt/ ***noun*** [U] very hard gray stone that produces small flames (sparks) when you strike it against metal or other stone

**flip** /flɪp/ ***verb*** (**flip·ping**; **flipped**) **1** [I,T] to turn with a quick movement: *She flipped the book open and started to read.* **2** [T] to throw sth into the air and make it turn over: *Let's flip a coin to see who starts.* **3** (*also* **flip out**) [I] (*informal*) to become very angry or excited

PHR V **flick/flip through sth** → FLICK¹

**flip-flop** /ˈflɪp flɑp/ ***noun*** [C] (*also* **thong**) a type of open shoe (sandal) that has a piece of rubber, leather, etc. which goes between the big toe and the toe next to it: *a pair of flip-flops*

**flip·pant** /ˈflɪpənt/ ***adj.*** not serious or respectful enough about things that are important

**flip·per** /ˈflɪpər/ ***noun*** [C] **1** a flat limb that some sea animals use for swimming **2** a rubber shoe shaped like an animal's FLIPPER (1) that people wear so that they can swim better (especially underwater): *a pair of flippers*

**flirt¹** /flərt/ ***verb*** [I] **1** to behave in a way that suggests you find sb attractive and are trying to attract him/her: *Who was that guy Suzy was flirting with at the party?* **2** **flirt with sth** to think about doing sth (but not very seriously)

**flirt²** /flərt/ ***noun*** [C] a person who often FLIRTS¹ (1)

**flir·ta·tion** /flərˈteɪʃn/ ***noun*** **1** [C,U] **(a) flirtation with sth** a short period of time during which sb is involved or interested in sth, often not seriously: *a brief and unsuccessful flirtation with the property market* **2** [U] behavior that shows you find sb attractive but are not serious about them: *Frank's attempts at flirtation bored her.*

**flir·ta·tious** /flərˈteɪʃəs/ (*also* **flirt·y** /ˈflərṭi/) ***adj.*** behaving in a way that shows a sexual attraction to sb that is not serious: *a flirtatious young woman* ◇ *a flirtatious smile*

**flit** /flɪt/ ***verb*** [I] (**flit·ting**; **flit·ted**) to fly or move quickly from one place to another

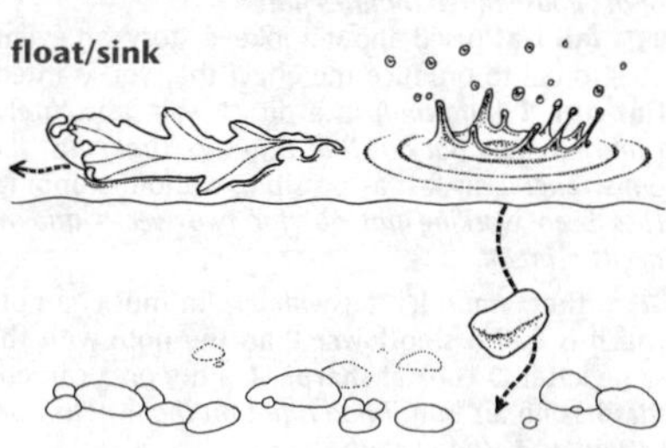

floating sinking

★**float¹** /floʊt/ ***verb*** [I] **1** to stay on the surface of a liquid and not sink; to move gently on the surface of a liquid: *Cork floats in water.* ◇ *There was something floating near the bank of the river.* **2** to move slowly through the air: *A leaf floated gently down to the ground.*

**float²** /floʊt/ ***noun*** [C] **1** a truck or other vehicle that is decorated and used in a procession (a parade **2** a drink that has a balla scoop) of ice cream floating in it: *a root beer float* **3** a light floating object used on a fishing line or net

**flock¹** /flɑk/ ***noun*** [C] **1** a group of birds, sheep or goats ➲ Look at **herd**. **2** a large number of people: *Flocks of tourists visit Florida every summer.*

**flock²** /flɑk/ ***verb*** [I] to gather or go somewhere in large numbers: *People are flocking to the fair this weekend.*

**flog·ging** /ˈflɑgɪŋ; ˈflɔgɪŋ/ ***noun*** [C,U] hitting sb with a whip or stick as a punishment

★**flood¹** /flʌd/ ***verb*** **1** [I,T] to fill a place with water; to be filled or overflow with water: *The river burst its banks and flooded the valley.* ◇ *Our basement flooded after last week's storm.* **2** [T] **flood sb/sth (with sth)** to go or send sth somewhere in large numbers: *The station has been flooded with complaints from angry viewers.* ◇ *Angry viewers flooded the station with complaints.* **3** [I] **flood across, in, into, through, etc.** to arrive in large numbers: *Entries for the contest have been flooding in.* ◇ *Refugees flooded across the border.* **4** [I,T] (used about a thought, feeling, etc.) to fill sb's mind suddenly: *At the end of the day, all his worries came flooding back.*

★**flood²** /flʌd/ ***noun*** [C] **1** (*also* **floods**) [pl.] a large amount of water (from a river, the ocean, etc.) that covers an area which should be dry: *Many people have been forced to leave their homes because of the floods.* ➲ Look also at **flash flood**. **2** a large number or amount: *She received a flood of letters after the accident.*

**flood·light** /ˈflʌdlaɪt/ ***noun*** [C] a powerful light that is used for lighting sports grounds, the outside of public buildings, etc.

**flood·lit** /ˈflʌdlɪt/ ***adj.*** lit by floodlights: *a floodlit stadium*

★**floor** /flɔr/ ***noun*** **1** [C, usually sing.] the flat surface that you walk on indoors: *Don't come in – there's broken glass on the floor!* ◇ *There aren't enough chairs, so some people will have to sit on the floor.* ◇ *to sweep the floor* ◇ *a wooden floor* ➲ Look at the note at **ground¹**. **2** [C, usually sing.] the ground or surface at the bottom of the ocean, a forest, etc.: *the ocean floor* **3** [C] a level in a building: *The restrooms are on the second floor.*

> **NOTE** In North America, the floor that is at street level is called the **first floor** or the **ground floor**.

**4 the floor** [sing.] the area in a large room where the members of an official committee, etc. sit: *a fierce debate on the Senate floor*

**floor·board** /ˈflɔrbɔrd/ ***noun*** [C] one of the long wooden boards used to make a floor

**flop¹** /flɑp/ ***verb*** [I] (**flop·ping**; **flopped**) **1** to move or fall in a heavy or an awkward way: *I was so tired that all I could do was flop down onto the couch and watch TV.* **2** (used about a book, movie, album, etc.) to be unsuccessful with the public

**flop²** /flɑp/ ***noun*** [C] something that is not a success; a failure: *Her first novel was very successful, but her second was a flop.*

**flop·py** /ˈflɑpi/ ***adj.*** (**flop·pi·er**; **flop·pi·est**) soft, loose and hanging downward; not stiff: *a floppy hat*

ˌ**floppy ˈdisk** (*also* **floppy**, **diskette**) ***noun*** [C] a square piece of plastic that can store information for a computer: *Don't forget to back up your files onto a floppy disk.* ➲ Look also at **hard disk**.

**flo·ra** /ˈflɔrə/ ***noun*** [pl.] all the plants growing in a particular area: *He's studying the flora and fauna* (= the plants and animals) *of South America.* ➲ Look at **fauna**.

**flo·ral** /ˈflɔrəl/ ***adj.*** decorated with a pattern of flowers, or made with flowers

**flo·rist** /ˈflɔrɪst; ˈflɑr-/ ***noun*** [C] a person who has a store that sells flowers

**floss** /flɔs; flɑs/ (*also* ˈ**dental floss**) ***noun*** [U] a kind of special thread that you use for cleaning between your teeth ▸ **floss** ***verb*** [I,T]: *Be sure to brush and floss regularly.*

**floun·der¹** /ˈflaʊndər/ ***verb*** [I] **1** to move with difficulty or to struggle (e.g. when you are trying not to sink in water) **2** to find it difficult to speak or act in a suitable way (usually in an awkward situation)

**floun·der²** /ˈflaʊndər/ ***noun*** [C,U] (*pl.* **floun·der** or **floun·ders**) a type of flat fish that you can eat

★**flour** /ˈflaʊər/ ***noun*** [U] a fine powder made from wheat or other grain and used for making bread, cakes, cookies, etc.

**flour·ish¹** /ˈflərɪʃ/ ***verb*** **1** [I] to be strong and healthy; to develop in a successful way: *These plants flourish in a sunny position.* ◇ *a flourishing new community* **2** [T] to wave sth in the air so that people will notice it

**flour·ish²** /ˈflərɪʃ/ ***noun*** [C, usually sing.] a movement that you make to attract attention

**flout** /flaʊt/ ***verb*** [T] (*formal*) to refuse to obey or accept sth: *to flout the rules of the organization* ◇ *to flout sb's advice*

★**flow¹** /floʊ/ ***verb*** [I] **1** to move in a smooth and continuous way (like water): *This river flows south into the Gulf of Mexico.* ◇ *a fast-flowing stream* ◇ *It was three hours before the traffic began to flow normally after the accident.* ◇ *People have been steadily flowing out of the country since the trouble began.* **2** (used about hair and clothes) to hang down in a loose way: *a long flowing dress*

★**flow²** /floʊ/ ***noun*** [sing.] **1** a steady, continuous movement of sth/sb: *There's a steady flow of young people from rural areas to urban areas.* **2** a supply of sth: *Press hard on the wound to stop the flow of blood.* ◇ *a flow of information between the school and the parents*

ˈ**flow chart** (*also* ˈ**flow** ˌ**diagram**) ***noun*** [C] a diagram that shows the connections between the different stages of a process or parts of a system: *a flow chart showing what happens to the product between manufacture and final delivery*

★**flow·er¹** /ˈflaʊər/ ***noun*** [C] **1** the beautiful colored part of a plant or tree from which seeds or fruit grow

> **NOTE** A flower consists of several **petals**. It grows from a **bud** on the end of a **stem**.

**2** a plant that is grown for its flowers; a FLOWER (1) and its stem: *She grows a lot of flowers but no vegetables.* ◇ *a beautiful bunch of flowers*

**NOTE** We **pick** flowers and **arrange** them in a vase. Flowers that are given or carried on a special occasion are called a **bouquet**.

**flow·er**[2] /ˈflaʊər/ ***verb*** [I] to produce FLOWERS[1] (1): *This plant flowers in late summer.*

**ˈflower bed** ***noun*** [C] a piece of ground where flowers are grown

**flow·ered** /ˈflaʊərd/ ***adj.*** covered or decorated with flowers: *a flowered dress/hat/tablecloth* ➲ picture on study page **A30**.

**flow·er·pot** /ˈflaʊərpɑt/ ***noun*** [C] a pot in which a plant can be grown

**flow·er·y** /ˈflaʊəri/ ***adj.*** (used about a style of speaking or writing) using long, difficult words

**flown** *past participle of* FLY[2]

**flu** /flu/ (usually **the flu**) (*also formal* **influenza**) ***noun*** [sing., U] an illness that is like a bad cold but more serious. You usually have a fever and your arms and legs are sore: *The whole family has the flu.* ◇ *They're in bed with the flu.* ◇ *The flu is going around* (= a lot of people have it).

**fluc·tu·ate** /ˈflʌktʃueɪt/ ***verb*** [I] **fluctuate (between A and B)** (used about prices and numbers, or people's feelings) to change frequently from one thing to another: *The number of students fluctuates between 100 and 150.* ◇ *Many people find that their moods fluctuate with the weather.* ▸ **fluc·tu·a·tion** /ˌflʌktʃuˈeɪʃn/ ***noun*** [C,U]

**flu·ent** /ˈfluənt/ ***adj.*** **1 fluent (in sth)** able to speak or write a language easily and accurately: *After a year in France she was fluent in French.* **2** (used about speech, reading or writing) expressed in a smooth and accurate way: *He speaks fluent German.* ▸ **flu·en·cy** /-ənsi/ ***noun*** [U] ▸ **flu·ent·ly** ***adv.***

**fluff** /flʌf/ ***noun*** [U] **1** the soft new fur on young animals or birds **2** material in an article, essay, etc. that is not necessary or important: *The report was mostly fluff.*

**fluff·y** /ˈflʌfi/ ***adj.*** (**fluff·i·er**; **fluff·i·est**) very soft and light: *a fluffy kitten* ◇ *fluffy snow*

**flu·id**[1] /ˈfluəd/ ***noun*** [C] a substance that can flow; a liquid: *The doctor told her to drink plenty of fluids.* ◇ *body fluids*

**flu·id**[2] /ˈfluəd/ ***adj.*** **1** able to flow like a liquid **2** (used about plans, etc.) able or likely to be changed

**ˌfluid ˈounce** (*also* **ounce**) ***noun*** [C] (*abbr.* **fl oz**; **fl. oz.**) a measure of liquid; 0.0296 of a liter. There are 16 fluid ounces in a pint and 32 fluid ounces in a quart.

**fluke** /fluk/ ***noun*** [C, usually sing.] (*informal*) something good that happens by accident, not because you have been intelligent or skillful: *The result was not a fluke. The better team won.*

**flung** *past tense, past participle of* FLING[1]

**flunk** /flʌŋk/ ***verb*** (*informal*) **1** [I,T] to fail a test or a course: *Carl flunked math and now he has to go to summer school.* ◇ *I thought I was going to flunk, but I got a B!* **2** [T] to give sb a failing grade on a test, in a course, etc.: *Prof. Hall claims that he never flunks a student.*

**PHR V** **flunk out (of sth)** (*informal*) to be forced to leave a school, college, etc. because your grades are not good enough: *to flunk out of school*

**fluo·res·cent** /flɔˈrɛsnt; flʊ-/ ***adj.*** **1** shining with a particular kind of hard white light: *a fluorescent light fixture* **2** very bright; seeming to shine: *fluorescent pink socks*

**fluor·ide** /ˈflɔraɪd; ˈflʊ-/ ***noun*** [U] a chemical substance that can be added to water or toothpaste to help keep teeth strong and healthy

**flur·ry** /ˈfləri/ ***noun*** [C] (*pl.* **flur·ries**) **1** a small amount of snow that comes suddenly **2** a short sudden burst of activity or feelings: *a flurry of excitement*

**flush** /flʌʃ/ ***verb*** **1** [T] to clean a toilet by pressing or pulling a handle that sends a stream of water into the toilet: *Please remember to flush the toilet.* **2** [I] (used about a toilet) to be cleaned with a stream of water: *The toilet won't flush.* **3** [T] **flush sth away, down, etc.** to get rid of sth in a stream of water, especially in the toilet: *You can't flush diapers down the toilet – they'll clog it.* **4** [I] (used about a person or his/her face) to become red: *Susan flushed and could not hide her embarrassment.*

**flus·ter** /ˈflʌstər/ ***verb*** [T] (usually passive) to make sb feel nervous and confused (because there is too much to do or not enough time): *Don't get flustered – there's plenty of time.*

**flute**

flute

recorder

**flute** /flut/ ***noun*** [C] a musical instrument like a pipe that you hold sideways and play by blowing over a hole at one side

**flut·ist** /ˈflut̬ɪst/ ***noun*** [C] a person who plays the flute

**flut·ter**[1] /ˈflʌt̬ər/ ***verb*** **1** [I,T] to move up and down or from side to side quickly and lightly; to make sth move in this way: *The flags were fluttering in the wind.* ◇ *The bird fluttered its wings and tried to fly.* **2** [I] to move lightly through the air: *The dead leaves fluttered to the ground.* **3** [I] when your heart or stomach flutters, you are feeling nervous and excited

**flut·ter**[2] /ˈflʌt̬ər/ ***noun*** [C, usually sing.] a quick, light movement

★ **fly**[1] /flaɪ/ ***verb*** (*pres. part.* **fly·ing**; *3rd person sing. pres.* **flies**; *pt* **flew** /flu/; *pp* **flown** /floʊn/)

➤ OF BIRD/INSECT **1** [I] (used about a bird, insect, airplane, etc.) to move through the air: *Penguins can't fly.* ◇ *a plane flying overhead*

➤ AIRCRAFT/SPACECRAFT **2** [I,T] to travel in or to carry sth in an airplane, etc.: *My daughter is flying (out) to Singapore next week.* ◇ *Supplies of food were flown (in) to the starving people.* **3** [I,T] (used about a pilot) to control an airplane, etc.: *You have to have special training to fly a jumbo jet.* **4** [T] to travel over an area of land or ocean by flying: *How long does it take to fly the Atlantic?*

➤ MOVE QUICKLY/SUDDENLY **5** [I] to move quickly or suddenly: *A brick came flying through the window.*

➤ OF TIME **6** [I] (used about time) to pass quickly: *The* *weekend just flew by, and now it's Monday again.* ◇ *Time flies when you're having fun!*

▸ MOVE FREELY **7** [I,T] to move around in the air; to make sth move around in the air: *The flags are flying.* ◇ *to fly a kite* ➲ noun **flight**

IDM **as the crow flies** → CROW[1]

**fly off the handle** (*informal*) to become very angry

★**fly²** /flaɪ/ ***noun*** [C] (*pl.* **flies**) **1** a small insect with two wings: *flies buzzing around a dead animal* ➲ picture at **insect**. **2** the zipper or buttons on the front of a pair of pants: *Henry, your fly is open.* ◇ *jeans with a button fly* **3** (*also* **'fly ball**) (in baseball) a ball that is hit high into the air: *to hit a fly*

**fly·ing¹** /'flaɪɪŋ/ ***adj.*** able to fly: *flying insects*

IDM **with flying colors** with great success; very well: *Shelley passed the test with flying colors.*

**get off to a flying start** to begin sth well and so get some advantage

**fly·ing²** /'flaɪɪŋ/ ***noun*** [U] traveling in an airplane, etc.: *I don't like flying.*

**ˌflying 'saucer** ***noun*** [C] a round, flat spacecraft that some people say they have seen and that they believe comes from another planet

**FM** /ˌɛf 'ɛm/ ***abbr.*** frequency modulation; one of the systems of broadcasting radio signals ➲ Look at **AM**.

**foal** /foʊl/ ***noun*** [C] a young horse ➲ Look at the note at **horse**.

**foam¹** /foʊm/ ***noun*** [U] **1** a mass of small white bubbles that are formed when air and a liquid are mixed together: *white foam on the tops of the waves* ◇ *The firefighters sprayed chemical foam onto the fire.* **2** (*also* **ˌfoam 'rubber**) soft rubber or plastic that is used inside seats, cushions, etc. ▸ **foam·y** /'foʊmi/ ***adj.***

**foam²** /foʊm/ ***verb*** [I] to produce foam: *The dog was foaming at the mouth.*

**fo·cal point** /'foʊkl pɔɪnt/ ***noun*** **1** [C] = FOCUS¹ (1) **2** [sing.] the center of interest or activity

★**fo·cus¹** /'foʊkəs/ ***noun*** [C] (*pl.* **fo·cus·es**) **1** the point at which rays of light meet or from which they appear to come **2** [usually sing.] the center of interest or attention; special attention that is given to sb/sth: *The mayor has been the focus of a lot of media attention recently.*

IDM **in focus/out of focus** (used about a photograph or sth in a photograph) clear/not clear: *It's too bad that Tony's face is out of focus in this picture.*

★**fo·cus²** /'foʊkəs/ ***verb*** **focus (sth) (on sth) 1** [T] to direct rays of light onto one particular point **2** [I,T] to be or become able to see clearly; to adjust your eyes so that you can see clearly: *Gradually his eyes focused.* ◇ *She focused her eyes on the page.* **3** [I,T] to adjust a camera so that the picture that you are taking will be clear: *I focused on the person in the middle of the group.* **4** [I,T] to give all your attention to sth: *to focus on a problem* ◇ *to focus attention on a problem*

**fod·der** /'fɑdər/ ***noun*** [U] food that is given to farm animals

**foe** /foʊ/ ***noun*** [C] (*formal*) an enemy

**fog** /fɔg; fɑg/ ***noun*** [U] a mass of thick clouds that forms close to or just above the land or ocean. Fog makes it difficult for us to see: *Dense fog is making driving dangerous.* ◇ *The fog had lifted/cleared by noon.*

> NOTE **Fog** is thicker than **mist**. **Haze** is caused by heat. **Smog** is caused by pollution. Look at the note at **weather**.

**fog·gy** /'fɔgi; 'fɑgi/ ***adj.*** (**fog·gi·er**; **fog·gi·est**) used to describe the weather when there is fog: *a foggy morning*

IDM **not have the foggiest idea/notion** not to know at all: *He doesn't have the foggiest notion of what's going on.*

**foil¹** /fɔɪl/ ***noun*** [U] metal that has been rolled or beaten into very thin sheets, often used when you are wrapping or cooking food: *aluminum foil*

**foil²** /fɔɪl/ ***verb*** [T] to prevent sb from succeeding or from carrying out his/her plans; to prevent a plan from succeeding: *The escape attempt was foiled.*

**fold**

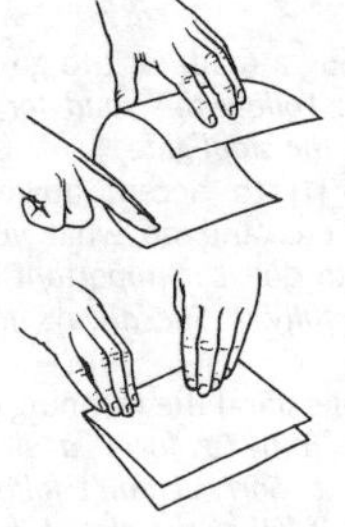

**folding a letter** **folding a chair**

★**fold¹** /foʊld/ ***verb*** **1** [T] **fold sth (up)** to bend one part of sth over another part in order to make it smaller, neater, etc.: *He folded the letter into thirds before putting it into the envelope.* ◇ *Fold up the blanket and put it away.* OPP **unfold 2** [I] **fold (up)** to be able to be folded in order to be easier to carry or to store: *This picnic table folds up flat.* ◇ *a folding chair* **3** [I] (used about a business, a play in the theater, etc.) to close because it is unsuccessful

IDM **cross/fold your arms** → ARM¹

**fold²** /foʊld/ ***noun*** [C] **1** the mark or line where sth has been folded: *Tear the paper along the fold.* **2** a curved shape that is made by a piece of material, etc. that has been folded: *the folds of a dress*

**fold·er** /'foʊldər/ ***noun*** [C] **1** a cardboard or plastic cover that is used for holding papers, etc. **2** a collection of information or files on one subject that is stored in some computers or on some disks ➲ Look at **directory**.

**fo·li·age** /'foʊliɪdʒ/ ***noun*** [U] (*formal*) all the leaves of a tree or plant

★**folk¹** /foʊk/ ***noun*** **1** [pl.] (*also* **folks**) (*informal*) people in general: *Folk around here don't often see foreigners.* ◇ *Some folks are never satisfied.* **2** [pl.] (*also* **folks**) a particular type of people: *country folk* ◇ *Old folks often don't like change.* **3 folks** [pl.] (*informal*) your parents: *How are your folks?*

**folk²** /foʊk/ ***adj.*** traditional in a community; of a

F

traditional style: *Daniel Boone is an American folk hero.* ◇ *an English folk dance*

NOTE **Folk music** is used to describe a type of music which became popular in North America in the 1960's. **Folk singers** who perform this type of music often play guitars and sing about political topics, especially about peace.

**folk·lore** /'foʊklɔr/ ***noun*** [U] (the study of) the traditional stories and beliefs of a community

**folk·sy** /'foʊksi/ ***adj.*** (**folk·si·er**; **folk·si·est**) **1** simple, friendly and informal: *They wanted the store to have a folksy, home-town image.* **2** done or made in a traditional style that is typical of simple customs in the past: *a folksy ballad*

F

★**fol·low** /'fɑloʊ/ ***verb***

➤GO AFTER **1** [I,T] to come, go or happen after sb/sth: *You go first and I'll follow later.* ◇ *The dog followed her wherever she went.* ◇ *The crash was followed by a scream and then there was silence.* ◇ *We had steak followed by fresh fruit.* **2** [T] to go after sb in order to catch him/her: *Go faster! I think the cops are following us!*

➤ROAD/PATH **3** [T] to go along a road, etc.; to go in the same direction as sth: *Follow this road for a mile and then turn right at the stoplight.*

➤ADVICE/INSTRUCTIONS **4** [T] to accept advice, instructions, an example, etc. and do what you have been told or shown to do: *It is important to follow the instructions carefully.* ◇ *She always follows the latest trends.*

➤UNDERSTAND **5** [I,T] to understand the meaning of sth: *Then the molecules join to form a new compound. Do you follow?* ◇ *Sorry, I don't follow you there.* ◇ *The kids couldn't follow the plot of that movie.*

➤WATCH/LISTEN **6** [T] to watch or listen to sb/sth very carefully: *You'll have to follow what he says very carefully if you want to understand it.*

➤BE INTERESTED IN **7** [T] to take an active interest in sth: *Have you been following the tennis tournament?*

➤RESULT **8** [I] **follow (from sth)** to happen as a result (of sth); to be the necessary result (of sth): *It doesn't follow that old people can't lead active lives.*

➤HAPPEN AS PLANNED **9** [T] to happen in the planned or expected way: *The day's events followed the usual pattern.*

IDM **as follows** (used for introducing a list): *The names of the winning candidates are as follows:...*

**follow sb's example/lead** to do what sb else has done or decided to do

**follow suit** to do the same thing that sb else has just done

PHRV **follow through on sth** to continue doing sth until it is finished

**follow sth up 1** to take further action about sth: *You should follow up your letter with a phone call.* **2** to find out more about sth: *We need to follow up the story about the school.*

**fol·low·er** /'fɑloʊər/ ***noun*** [C] a person who follows or supports a person, belief, etc.

★**fol·low·ing¹** /'fɑloʊɪŋ/ ***adj.*** **1** next (in time): *He had a heart attack on Sunday and died the following week.* **2** (in a list) that I will mention now: *Please bring the following items to the meeting: ...*

NOTE We can also use **the following** as a noun: *The following are the winners of the competition:...*

**fol·low·ing²** /'fɑloʊɪŋ/ ***noun*** [sing.] a group of people who support or admire sth: *Baseball has a large following in Japan.*

★**fol·low·ing³** /'fɑloʊɪŋ/ ***prep.*** after; as a result of: *Following the riots, many students were arrested.*

'**follow-through** ***noun*** [C] **1** (in tennis, golf, etc.) the final movement you make after you strike the ball **2** the actions that sb takes in order to complete a plan: *We have a great plan, but it can only succeed if the follow-through is good, too.*

'**follow-up** ***noun*** [C] something that is done to continue sth: *a follow-up to last year's report*

**fol·ly** /'fɑli/ ***noun*** [C,U] (*pl.* **fol·lies**) (*formal*) a foolish act: *It would be folly to throw away all our hard work because of one setback.*

**fond** /fɑnd/ ***adj.*** **1** (not before a noun) **fond of sb/sth**; **fond of doing sth** liking a person or a thing, or liking doing sth: *We're all very fond of Mrs. Simpson.* ◇ *I grew very fond of Turkish food while I was living in Istanbul.* **2** (only *before* a noun) kind and loving: *I have fond memories of both my aunts.*

**fon·dle** /'fɑndl/ ***verb*** [T] to touch or stroke sb/sth in a loving or sexual way: *She accused her boss of trying to fondle her in the hallway.*

**fond·ly** /'fɑndli/ ***adv.*** in a loving way

**fond·ness** /'fɑndnəs/ ***noun*** [U] a liking for sb/sth

★**food** /fud/ ***noun*** **1** [U] something that people, animals or plants take into their bodies in order to keep them alive and healthy: *Plants get food from the soil.* ◇ *a shortage of food* **2** [C,U] a particular type of FOOD (1) that you eat: *baby food* ◇ *frozen foods* ◇ *health foods*

IDM **food for thought** an idea that makes you think seriously and carefully

'**food bank** ***noun*** [C] a place where poor people can go to get free food

'**food chain** ***noun*** [C] (usually **the food chain**) a series of living creatures in which each type of creature feeds on the one below it in the series: *Insects are fairly low down (on) the food chain.*

**food·ie** /'fudi/ ***noun*** [C] a person who is very interested in cooking and eating different kinds of food, especially food of a high quality

'**food ˌpoisoning** ***noun*** [U] an illness that is caused by eating food that is bad

'**food ˌprocessor** ***noun*** [C] an electric machine that can mix food and also cut or slice food into small pieces ➲ picture at **mixer**.

'**food ˌscience** ***noun*** [U] the study of food, what is in it, how it helps people to live and grow (**nutrition**), how to prepare new kinds of food, or to prepare food in new ways, etc.

'**food stamp** ***noun*** [C] (*U.S.*) a small piece of paper (a coupon) that is given to poor people by the government and used instead of money to buy food

**food·stuff** /'fudstʌf/ ***noun*** [C, usually pl.] (*formal*) a substance that is used as food: *There has been a sharp rise in the cost of basic foodstuffs.*

**fool¹** /ful/ ***noun*** [C] a person who is silly or stupid or who acts in a silly or stupid way: *I felt like such a fool*

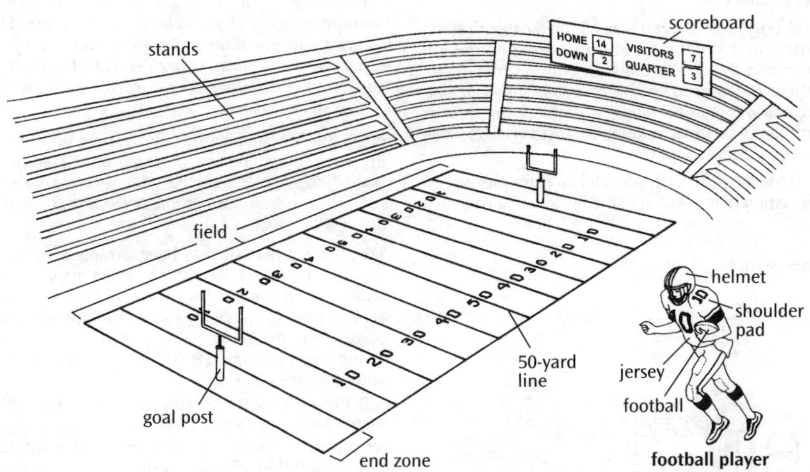


*when I realized my mistake.* ◇ *Only a fool would go out in weather like this.* ➲ Look at **April Fool's Day**.

IDM **make a fool of sb/yourself** to make sb/yourself look foolish or silly

**fool²** /ful/ ***verb*** **1** [T] to trick sb: *Don't be fooled into believing everything the salesman says.* **2** [I] to speak without being serious: *I was only fooling when I said I loved you.*

PHR V **fool around** to behave in a silly or stupid way: *Stop fooling around with that knife or someone will get hurt!*

**fool·har·dy** /ˈfulhɑrdi/ ***adj.*** taking unnecessary risks

**fool·ish** /ˈfulɪʃ/ ***adj.*** **1** silly; not sensible: *I was foolish enough to trust him.* **2** looking silly or feeling embarrassed: *He felt pretty foolish when he couldn't start his motorcycle in front of his friends.* ▶ **fool·ish·ly** ***adv.*** ▶ **fool·ish·ness** ***noun*** [U]

**fool·proof** /ˈfulpruf/ ***adj.*** not capable of going wrong or being wrongly used: *Our security system is absolutely foolproof.*

★**foot¹** /fʊt/ ***noun*** [C] (*pl.* **feet** /fit/)

➤ PART OF BODY **1** the lowest part of the leg, below the ankle, on which a person or animal stands: *She rose to her feet* (= she stood up). ◇ *I've been on my feet* (= standing and walking around) *all day.* ◇ *What size feet do you have?* ◇ *big/small feet* ◇ *wide/narrow feet* ◇ *She sat by the fire and the dog sat at her feet.*

NOTE When you walk somewhere you go **on foot**. The nails on your feet are called **toenails**. If you have no shoes or socks on, you are **barefoot** or **in your bare feet**.

➤ PART OF SOCK **2** the part of a sock, etc. into which you put your foot

➤ BASE/BOTTOM **3** the lowest part on which a piece of furniture, etc. stands: *a typewriter with rubber feet* **4** [sing.] the bottom of sth: *There's a note at the foot of the page.* ◇ *sitting at the foot of the stairs* OPP **top** **5** [sing.] the end of a bed where your feet go OPP **head**

➤ MEASUREMENT **6** (*abbr.* **ft.**) a measure of length; 30.48 centimeters. There are 12 inches in a foot, and 3 feet in a yard: *"How tall are you?" "Five foot two (inches)."* ◇ *a six-foot-high wall* ◇ *We need enough paint to cover 120 square feet.*

NOTE The plural for sense **6** can be **feet** or **foot**.

IDM **get/have cold feet** → COLD¹

**put your foot down** (*informal*) to say firmly that sth must (not) happen: *Susan finally put her foot down and said that the kids could only watch an hour of TV each evening.*

**put your foot in your mouth** (*informal*) to say or do sth that upsets or embarrasses sb

**set foot in/on sth** to visit, enter or arrive at/in a place: *I hope he never sets foot in my house again!*

**stand on your own two feet** to take care of yourself without help; to be independent

**foot²** /fʊt/ ***verb***

IDM **foot the bill (for sth)** to pay (for sth)

★**foot·ball** /ˈfʊtbɔl/ ***noun*** **1** [U] a game that is played by two teams of eleven players in the U.S. (twelve in Canada) who wear special protective equipment and try to carry or kick an oval ball to the end of a field: *a football field/player/game*

NOTE Football players wear **helmets** and **pads** to protect themselves. The most important player on a football team is the **quarterback**, who tries to **pass** (= throw) the ball to other players on his team. Players try to score **touchdowns** by catching the ball in the **end zone** or by carrying it into the **end zone**. A **touchdown** is worth six points. ➲ Look also at **soccer**.

**2** [C] the large, usually brown, oval ball that is used in this game

**foot·bridge** /ˈfʊtbrɪdʒ/ ***noun*** [C] a narrow bridge for people who are walking and not for cars

**foot·hold** /ˈfʊthoʊld/ ***noun*** [C] a place where you can safely put your foot when you are climbing:

*(figurative) We hope to gain a foothold in the European market.*

**foot·ing** /ˈfʊṭɪŋ/ ***noun*** [sing.] **1** being able to stand firmly on a surface: *He lost his footing on the wet floor and fell.* **2** the basis on which sth is established: *The company is now on a solid financial footing and will soon be making a profit.* **3** the level or position of sb/sth (in relation to sb/sth else): *to be on an equal footing with sb*

**foot·note** /ˈfʊtnoʊt/ ***noun*** [C] an extra piece of information that is added at the bottom of a page in a book

F

**footprints**

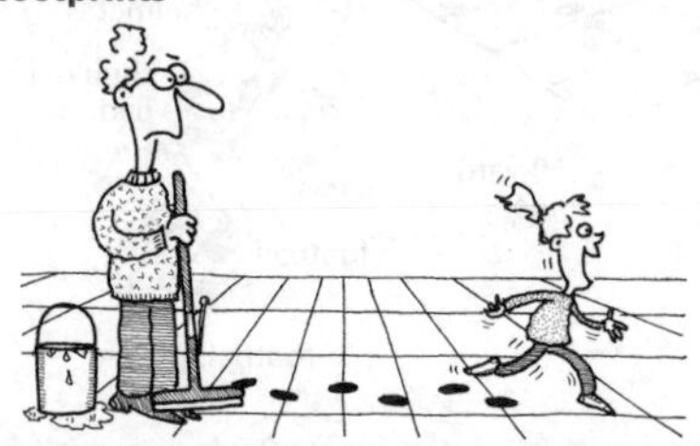

**foot·print** /ˈfʊtprɪnt/ ***noun*** [C] a mark that is left by a foot or a shoe

**foot·step** /ˈfʊtstɛp/ ***noun*** [C] the sound of sb walking: *I heard his footsteps in the hall.*

**foot·wear** /ˈfʊtwɛr/ ***noun*** [U] boots or shoes

**foot·work** /ˈfʊtwərk/ ***noun*** [U] **1** the way in which a person moves his/her feet when playing a sport or dancing **2** the ability to react quickly and skillfully to a difficult situation: *It was going to take some fast political footwork to save the situation.*

**for¹** /fər; *strong form* fɔr/ ***prep.*** **1** (showing the person who will receive sth): *Here is a letter for you.* ◇ *Save a piece of cake for Mary.* ◇ *He made lunch for them.* ◇ *She bought some candy for the kids.* **2** (showing purpose or use): *What's this gadget for?* ◇ *Let's go for a walk.* ◇ *a shampoo for dry hair* ◇ *Let's have eggs for breakfast.* **3** (showing where sb/sth is going to): *passengers on board a flight for Miami* ◇ *They set out for home.* **4** intended to be used by a particular group or in a particular way: *It's a book for children.* ◇ *That chair is for guests.* ◇ *Is that house for sale?* **5** in order to help sb/sth: *What can I do for you?* ◇ *You should take some medicine for your cold.* ◇ *Doctors are fighting for his life.* ◇ *Take care of her for my sake.* **6** (showing the price of sth): *I bought this car for $2,000.* ◇ *She gave me their old TV for nothing.* **7** (showing a reason): *He was sent to prison for murder.* ◇ *The city is famous for its beautiful lakes and parks.* ◇ *"Greg got suspended from school today." "What for?"* ◇ *What did you do that for?* (= Why did you do that?) **8** on the occasion of: *What did they give you for your birthday?* **9** in support of (sb/sth): *Three cheers for the winner!* ◇ *Are you for or against the death penalty?* **10** as a representative of (sb/sth): *Who's the lawyer for the defense?* ◇ *She plays basketball for Boston College.* **11** meaning or representing (sb/sth): *What's the "C" for in "NBC?"* ◇ *What's the Russian word for "window?"* **12** (after a verb) in order to have or get sth: *She asked me for help.* **13** (after an adjective) when you consider what you could expect: *She's tall for her age.* ◇ *It's quite warm for January.* **14** (used when you give one thing and get sth else back): *I want to exchange this sweater for a larger one.* **15** (showing a length of time): *I'm going away for a few days.* ◇ *He was a teacher for 20 years* (= he is not a teacher now). ◇ *He has been a teacher for 20 years* (= he is still a teacher).

> NOTE **Since** is used with a point in time for showing when something began: *He has been a teacher since 1997.* **Ago** is also used for showing when something began: *He became a teacher 20 years ago.*

**16** (showing that sth has been arranged to happen at a particular time): *The appointment is for 10:30.* ◇ *We're planning our vacation for the second week in July.* **17** (showing when sth happens): *I'm warning you for the last time.* ◇ *I met her for the second time yesterday.* **18** (showing a distance): *He walked for ten miles.*

IDM **for all** in spite of: *For all his talk, he really doesn't know what's going on.*

**for good** permanently: *They have left town for good* (= and they will never return).

**for²** /fər; *strong form* fɔr/ ***conj.*** (*formal*) because: *The children could not enter the castle, for they did not know the magic words.*

**for·bid** /fərˈbɪd/ ***verb*** [T] (*pres. part.* **for·bid·ding**; *pt* **for·bade** /fərˈbeɪd/ or **for·bad** /fərˈbæd/; *pp* **for·bid·den** /fərˈbɪdn/) (*formal*) **1 forbid sb to do sth; forbid sb from doing sth** to order sb not to do sth: *My father forbade me to smoke.* **2** to not allow sth: *Eating pork is forbidden by some religions.* ➲ Look at **prohibit** and **permit**.

**for·bid·ding** /fərˈbɪdɪŋ/ ***adj.*** looking unfriendly or frightening: *The steep, rocky path looked very forbidding.*

★**force¹** /fɔrs/ ***noun***

➤PHYSICAL STRENGTH **1** [U] physical strength or power: *The force of the explosion knocked them to the ground.* ◇ *The police used force to break up the demonstration.*

➤STRONG EFFECT **2** [U] power and influence: *His arguments lost some of their force when they were translated into French.*

➤AUTHORITY **3** [C] a person or thing that has power or influence: *The United States is still a major force in international affairs.*

➤PHYSICS **4** [C,U] (*technical*) a power that can cause change or movement: *the force of gravity*

➤OF WIND **5** [C, usually sing.] a measure of wind strength: *hurricane-force winds*

➤GROUP OF PEOPLE **6** [C] a group of people who are trained for a particular purpose: *a highly trained workforce* ◇ *a UN peacekeeping force* ◇ *the police force*

IDM **bring sth/come into force** to start using a new law, etc.; to start being used: *The administration wants to bring new anti-drug legislation into force next year.*

**in force 1** (used about people) in large numbers: *The police were out in force at the protest march.* **2** (used about a law, rule, etc.) being used: *The new laws about seat belts in cars are now in force.*

**join forces (with sb)** → JOIN

★**force²** /fɔrs/ ***verb*** [T] **1** to make sb do sth that he/

she does not want to do: *The bank robber forced us to lie on the floor.* ◇ *She forced herself to speak to him.* **2** to use physical strength to do sth or to move sth: *The window had been forced open.* ◇ *We had to force our way through the crowd.*

**force·ful** /ˈfɔrsfl/ ***adj.*** strong; powerful: *He has a very forceful personality.* ◇ *a forceful speech* ▸ **force·ful·ly *adv.***

**for·ceps** /ˈfɔrsɛps; -səps/ ***noun*** [pl.] a special instrument that looks like a pair of scissors but is not sharp. Forceps are used by doctors and dentists for holding things firmly: *a pair of forceps*

**forc·i·ble** /ˈfɔrsəbl/ ***adj.*** (only *before* a noun) **1** done using (physical) force: *The police made a forcible entry into the building.* **2** (used about ideas, an argument, etc.) strong; convincing: *a forcible reminder*

**forc·i·bly** /ˈfɔrsəbli/ ***adv.*** using force: *The protesters were forcibly removed from the building.*

**fore** /fɔr/ ***noun***

IDM **come to the fore** to get into an important position so that you are noticed by people

**bring sth to the fore** to cause sth to be noticed by people; to emphasize: *to bring an issue to the fore*

**fore·arm** /ˈfɔrɑrm/ ***noun*** [C] the lower part of your arm between your elbow and your wrist

**fore·bod·ing** /fɔrˈboʊdɪŋ/ ***noun*** [U, sing.] a strong feeling that danger or trouble is coming: *a sense of foreboding*

**fore·cast** /ˈfɔrkæst/ ***verb*** [T] (*pt, pp* **fore·cast** or **fore·cast·ed**) to say (with the help of information) what will probably happen in the future: *The market analyst did not forecast the sudden rise in inflation.* ◇ *Rain has been forecast for tomorrow.* ▸ **fore·cast *noun*** [C]: *The weather forecast said it would be sunny tomorrow.*

**fore·close** /fɔrˈkloʊz/ ***verb*** [I,T] **foreclose on sth** (used about a bank, etc.) to take control of sb's property, usually because he/she has not paid back a loan on time ▸ **fore·clo·sure** /fɔrˈkloʊʒər/ ***noun*** [C]

**fore·fa·ther** /ˈfɔrˌfɑðər/ ***noun*** [usually pl.] (*formal*) a person (especially a man) in your family who lived a long time ago: *Our forefathers brought a belief in equality to this country.* SYN **ancestor**

**fore·fin·ger** /ˈfɔrˌfɪŋgər/ ***noun*** [C] = INDEX FINGER

**fore·front** /ˈfɔrfrʌnt/ ***noun*** [sing.] the leading position; the position at the front: *Our department is right at the forefront of scientific research.*

**fore·go** /fɔrˈgoʊ/ ***verb*** [T] (*pt* **fore·went**; *pp* **fore·gone**) = FORGO

**fore·gone** /ˈfɔrgɔn; -gɑn/ ***adj.***

IDM **a foregone conclusion** a result that is or was certain to happen

**fore·ground** /ˈfɔrgraʊnd/ ***noun*** [sing.] **the foreground 1** the part of a view, picture, etc. that appears closest to the person looking at it: *Notice the artist's use of color* ***in the foreground*** *of the picture.* **2** a position where you will be noticed most: *He likes to be in the foreground at every meeting.* ➲ Compare **background**.

**fore·hand** /ˈfɔrhænd/ ***noun*** [C] a stroke in tennis, etc. that is made with the inside of your hand facing forward ➲ Compare **backhand**.

**fore·head** /ˈfɔrɛd; ˈfɑrəd; ˈfɔrhɛd; ˈfɑrhɛd/ (*also* **brow**) ***noun*** [C] the flat part of a person's face above the eyes and below the hair

★**for·eign** /ˈfɔrən; ˈfɑr-/ ***adj.*** **1** belonging to or connected with a country that is not your own: *a foreign country* ◇ *to learn a foreign language* ◇ *a foreign coin* **2** dealing with or involving other countries: *foreign policy* (= government decisions concerning other countries) ◇ *the French Foreign Minister* ➲ Look at the note at **secretary**. **3** (used about an object or a substance) not belonging where it is: *The X-ray showed a foreign body* (= object) *in her stomach.*

**for·eign·er** /ˈfɔrənər; ˈfɑr-/ ***noun*** [C] a person who comes from a country that is not your own

> NOTE This word is often used to show disrespect toward sb from another country, e.g. because you do not approve of his/her customs, etc. A polite way to talk about sb from another country is to mention his/her nationality: *a woman from Mexico* ◇ *students from Asia*. We can also use the phrase **people from other countries** to talk about people who come from countries outside our own.

**ˌforeign exˈchange *noun*** **1** [C,U] the system of buying and selling money from a different country; the place where it is bought and sold: *The dollar dropped against the British pound on the foreign exchange yesterday.* **2** [C] a visit to another country to learn about its culture, language, etc.: *We have a foreign exchange student staying at our house.*

**fore·man** /ˈfɔrmən/ ***noun*** [C] (*pl.* **fore·men** /ˈfɔrmən/) **1** a worker who is in charge of other workers **2** the person on a jury who speaks for all the members

> NOTE Nowadays many people prefer to say **foreperson**, especially when referring to a woman.

**fore·most** /ˈfɔrmoʊst/ ***adj.*** most famous or important; best: *Robert De Niro is among the foremost actors of his generation.*

IDM **first and foremost** → FIRST[2]

**fo·ren·sic** /fəˈrɛnsɪk; -zɪk/ ***adj.*** connected with the law and finding out about a crime: *The police are gathering forensic evidence to try and find out the cause of death.* ◇ *forensic medicine*

**fore·run·ner** /ˈfɔrˌrʌnər/ ***noun*** [C] a person or thing that is an early example or a sign of sth that appears or develops later SYN **precursor**

**fore·see** /fɔrˈsi/ ***verb*** [T] (*pt* **fore·saw** /fɔrˈsɔ/; *pp* **fore·seen** /fɔrˈsin/) to know or guess that sth is going to happen in the future: *Nobody could have foreseen the result of the election.* ➲ Look at **predict** and at **unforeseen**.

**fore·see·a·ble** /fɔrˈsiəbl/ ***adj.*** that can be expected: *These problems were foreseeable.* ◇ *The weather won't change in the foreseeable future* (= as far ahead as we can see).

**fore·sight** /ˈfɔrsaɪt/ ***noun*** [U] the ability to see what will probably happen in the future (and to make wise plans): *My neighbor had the foresight to move to a new house before the new mall was built.* ➲ Look at **hindsight**.

**fore·skin** /ˈfɔrskɪn/ ***noun*** [C] the loose piece of skin that covers the end of the male sexual organ

★**for·est** /ˈfɔrəst; ˈfɑr-/ ***noun*** [C,U] a large area of land that is covered with trees: *tropical rain forests* ◇ *A large part of Canada is covered in forest.* ◇ *a forest fire*

NOTE **Forests** are generally larger than **woods**. **Forest** is used in official names: *Black Hills National Forest.* **The woods** is used as a general expression for an area that is covered with trees: *We went for a walk in the woods.* A **jungle** is a forest in a tropical part of the world.

F

**fore·stall** /fɔrˈstɔl/ ***verb*** [T] (*formal*) to take action to prevent sb from doing sth or sth from happening

**for·est·ry** /ˈfɔrəstri; ˈfɑr-/ ***noun*** [U] the science of planting and taking care of trees in forests

**fore·tell** /fɔrˈtɛl/ ***verb*** [T] (*pt, pp* **fore·told** /fɔrˈtoʊld/) (*formal*) to say what will happen in the future ➲ A more common word is **predict**.

**fore·thought** /ˈfɔrθɔt/ ***noun*** [U] careful thought about, or preparation for, the future

**fore·told** *past tense, past participle of* FORETELL

**for·ev·er** /fəˈrɛvər/ ***adv.*** for all time; permanently: *I wish summer would last forever!* ◇ *I realized that our relationship had ended forever.* ◇ *My sister always takes forever* (= a very long time) *in the bathroom.*

**fore·word** /ˈfɔrwərd/ ***noun*** [C] a piece of writing at the beginning of a book that introduces the book and/or its author

**for·feit** /ˈfɔrfət/ ***verb*** [T] to lose sth or no longer have sth because you have done sth wrong or because you want to achieve an aim: *Because of his violent behavior, he forfeited the right to visit his children.* ◇ *Their team was late, so they had to forfeit the game.*

**for·gave** *past tense of* FORGIVE

**forge** /fɔrdʒ/ ***verb*** [T] **1** to make a copy of sth in order to deceive people: *to forge a signature* **2** to create a relationship with sb/sth: *Our university has forged links with several businesses in the community.*
PHRV **forge ahead** to go forward steadily and gradually: *Despite the problems, we managed to forge ahead and finish the project on time.*

**for·ger·y** /ˈfɔrdʒəri/ ***noun*** (*pl.* **for·ger·ies**) **1** [U] the crime of copying a document, signature, painting, etc. in order to deceive people **2** [C] a document, signature, picture, etc. that has been forged: *The painting that had been sold as a Rembrandt was discovered to be a forgery.*

★**for·get** /fərˈgɛt/ ***verb*** (*pt* **for·got** /fərˈgɑt/; *pp* **for·got·ten** /fərˈgɑtn/) **1** [I,T] **forget about sth** to fail to remember sth; to lose the memory of sth: *"Why didn't you come to the party?" "Oh, no! I completely forgot about it!"* ◇ *You never forget how to ride a bicycle.* ◇ *I forgot what I was going to say.* ◇ *I forgot the telephone number.* ◇ *He forgot that he had invited her to the party.* ◇ *I'll never forget meeting my husband for the first time.* **2** [I,T] to fail to remember to do sth: *Try not to forget about feeding the cat!* ◇ *Don't forget to do your homework!* **3** [T] to fail to bring sth with you: *When my father got to the airport, he realized he'd forgotten his passport.*

NOTE When we are talking about *where* we have forgotten something, we have to use the word **leave**. We CANNOT say: *My father forgot his passport at home.* We have to say: *He left his passport at home.*

**4** [I,T] to stop thinking about sth: *Forget about your work and enjoy yourself!* ◇ *"I'm sorry I shouted at you." "Forget it."* (= Don't worry about it.)

**for·get·ful** /fərˈgɛtfl/ ***adj.*** often forgetting things: *My mother's almost 80 and she's starting to get a little forgetful.*

**for·giv·a·ble** /fərˈgɪvəbl/ ***adj.*** that can be forgiven OPP **unforgivable**

★**for·give** /fərˈgɪv/ ***verb*** [T] (*pt* **for·gave** /fərˈgeɪv/; *pp* **for·given** /fərˈgɪvn/) **1 forgive sth**; **forgive sb (for sth/for doing sth)** to stop being angry with sb or about sth: *I can't forgive his behavior last night.* ◇ *I can't forgive him for his behavior last night.* ◇ *I can't forgive him for behaving like that last night.* **2** (used for apologizing politely): *Forgive me for asking, but where did you get that dress?*

**for·give·ness** /fərˈgɪvnəs/ ***noun*** [U] the act of forgiving

**for·giv·ing** /fərˈgɪvɪŋ/ ***adj.*** ready and willing to forgive

**for·go** (*also* **forego**) /fɔrˈgoʊ/ ***verb*** [T] (*pt* **for·went** /fɔrˈwɛnt/; *pp* **for·gone** /fɔrˈgɔn; -ˈgɑn/) (*formal*) to be willing not to have sth nice or sth that you have a right to: *The defendant has decided to forgo his right to a jury trial.*

**for·got** *past tense of* FORGET

**for·got·ten** *past participle of* FORGET

★**fork**[1] /fɔrk/ ***noun*** [C] **1** a small implement with a handle and two or more points. You use a fork for lifting food to your mouth when eating: *knives, forks and spoons* **2** a place where a road, river, etc. divides into two parts: *When you come to a fork in the road, take the right branch.* ➲ Look also at **pitchfork**.

**fork**[2] /fɔrk/ ***verb*** [I] (used about a road, river, etc.) to divide into two parts
PHRV **fork out** (*informal*) to pay: *I forked out $20 for that book.*
**fork sth over** (*informal*) to give sth (often money) when you do not want to: *I had to fork over the $10 that I owed her.*

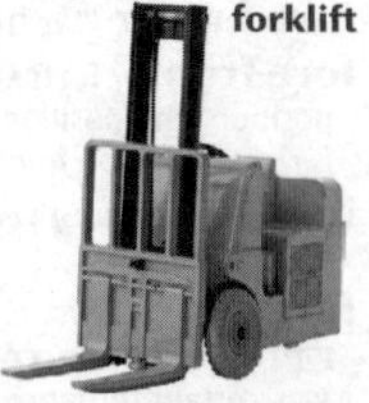
**forklift**

**fork·lift** /ˈfɔrklɪft/ ***noun*** [C] a vehicle with a mechanical device on the front for lifting and moving heavy objects

**for·lorn** /fərˈlɔrn; fɔr-/ ***adj.*** lonely and unhappy; not cared for

★**form**[1] /fɔrm/ ***noun*** **1** [C] a particular type of sth or way of doing sth: *Swimming is an excellent form of exercise.* ◇ *We never eat meat in any form.* ◇ *What form will the meeting take?* (= How will it be organized?) **2** [C,U] the shape of sb/sth: *The articles will be published in book form.* **3** [C] a piece of paper with questions on it and spaces where you give answers and personal information: *a tax form* ◇ *an entry form for a contest* ◇ *to fill out an* application form ◇ Please fill in your name and address on this form. **4** [C] (grammar) a way of spelling or changing a word in a sentence: *the irregular forms of the verbs ◇ The plural form of "mouse" is "mice."*

★**form²** /fɔrm/ ***verb***
➤CREATE **1** [T] to make or organize sth: *They formed an organization called "Citizens for Nature." ◇ In English we usually form the past tense by adding "-ed."*
➤MAKE SHAPE/FORM **2** [T] to take the shape of sth: *The two roads join to form a "Y."* **3** [I,T] to move into the shape or order mentioned: *The police formed a circle around the house.*
➤HAVE FUNCTION/ROLE **4** [T] to be the thing mentioned: *Seminars form the main part of the course.* (= The main part of the course consists of seminars.)
➤START TO EXIST **5** [I,T] to begin to exist or to make sth exist; to begin to have sth: *Buds form on trees in the early spring. ◇ The rain had formed a huge puddle on the street. ◇ We formed a very good impression of the school on our first visit.*

★**for·mal** /'fɔrml/ ***adj.*** **1** (used about language or behavior) used when you want to appear serious or official and when you are in a situation in which you do not know the other people very well: *"Yours sincerely" is a formal way of ending a letter. ◇ a formal occasion* (= one where you must behave politely and wear the clothes that people think are suitable)

NOTE In this dictionary some words and phrases are marked *(formal)* or *(informal)*. This will help you to choose the right word for a particular situation. Often there is an informal or neutral word with a similar meaning to a more formal one.

**2** public and official: *I am going to make a formal complaint to the hospital about the way I was treated.* **3** (only *before* a noun) obtained in a school or college: *My grandfather only had eight years of formal education.* ▶ **for·mal·ly** ***adv.***

**for·mal·i·ty** /fɔr'mæləṭi/ ***noun*** (*pl.* **for·mal·i·ties**) **1** [C] an action that is necessary according to custom or law: *There are certain formalities to go through before we can give you a visa.*

NOTE If an action is **just a formality**, we mean that people think that it is necessary according to custom or law but that it has no real importance or effect otherwise.

**2** [U] careful attention to rules of language and behavior

**for·mat¹** /'fɔrmæt/ ***noun*** [C] the shape of sth or the way it is arranged or produced: *It's the same book but in a different format.*

**for·mat²** /'fɔrmæt/ ***verb*** [T] (**format·ting**; **format·ted**) to arrange sth in a particular format, usually for a computer: *to format a floppy disk*

**for·ma·tion** /fɔr'meɪʃn/ ***noun*** **1** [U] the making or developing of sth: *the formation of a new corporation* **2** [C,U] an arrangement or pattern (especially of soldiers, airplanes, ships, etc.): *Several military planes flew over in formation.* **3** [C] a thing that is formed; the particular way in which it is formed: *rock formations ◇ cloud formations*

**form·a·tive** /'fɔrməṭɪv/ ***adj.*** having an important and lasting influence (on sb's character and opinions): *A child's early years are thought to be the most formative ones.*

★**for·mer¹** /'fɔrmər/ ***adj.*** (only *before* a noun) of an earlier time; previous: *Jimmy Carter, the former President ◇ Their new neighbor is a former teacher. ◇ In former times people often had larger families.*

**for·mer²** /'fɔrmər/ ***adj.***, ***noun*** the first (of two people or things just mentioned): *Of the two hospitals in town, the General and the County, the former* (= the General) *has the better reputation.* ➲ Compare **latter**.

**for·mer·ly** /'fɔrmərli/ ***adv.*** in the past; previously: *the country of Myanmar (formerly Burma) ◇ The hotel was formerly a private house.*

NOTE **Used to** is a more common way of expressing the same meaning: *The hotel used to be a private house.*

**for·mi·da·ble** /'fɔrmədəbl; fər'mɪdəbl/ ***adj.*** **1** causing you to be nervous or frightened: *His mother is a very formidable lady.* **2** difficult to deal with; needing a lot of effort: *Reforming the education system will be a formidable task.*

★**for·mu·la** /'fɔrmyələ/ ***noun*** (*pl.* **for·mu·las** or **for·mu·lae** /'fɔrmyəli/) **1** [C] a group of signs, letters or numbers used in science or math to express a general law or fact: *The formula for carbon monoxide is CO. ◇ What is the formula for converting miles to kilometers?* **2** [C] a list of substances used for making sth; the instructions necessary for making sth: *The formula for the new vaccine has not been made public yet.* **3** [C] a plan of how to get sth or how to do sth: *What is her formula for success?* **4** [U] a kind of milk made for babies

**for·mu·la·ic** /ˌfɔrmyə'leɪɪk/ ***adj.*** made up of fixed patterns of words or ideas: *Traditional stories make use of formulaic language like "Once upon a time..."*

**for·mu·late** /'fɔrmyəleɪt/ ***verb*** [T] **1** to prepare and organize a plan or ideas for doing sth: *The party still has not formulated its policy on defense spending.* **2** to express sth (clearly and exactly)

**for·sake** /fər'seɪk; fɔr-/ ***verb*** [T] (*pt* **for·sook** /fər'sʊk; fɔr-/; *pp* **for·sak·en** /fər'seɪkən; fɔr-/) (*formal*) to leave a person or a place forever (especially when you should stay)

**fort** /fɔrt/ ***noun*** [C] **1** a strong building that is used for military defense **2** (often used in proper names) a place with houses, offices, stores, military equipment, etc. where members of the army, etc. live and work: *Fort Bragg* ➲ Look at **base¹**(5).

**forth** /fɔrθ/ ***adv.***
IDM **and so forth** and other things like those just mentioned: *The kind of job that you'll be doing is taking messages, making coffee and so forth.*
**back and forth** → BACK³

**forth·com·ing** /ˌfɔrθ'kʌmɪŋ/ ***adj.*** **1** going to happen or appear in the near future: *Look in the local paper for a list of forthcoming events.* **2** (not before a noun) offered or given: *If no money is forthcoming, we will not be able to continue the project.* **3** (not before a noun) willing to be helpful, give information, etc.: *Rob was not very forthcoming when his parents asked him about his grades.*

**forth·right** /ˈfɔrθraɪt/ ***adj.*** saying clearly and honestly what you think

**for·ti·eth** /ˈfɔrt̬iəθ/ ***pronoun, det., adv.*** 40th, next after thirty-ninth ➲ Look at the examples at **sixth**.

**for·ti·fy** /ˈfɔrt̬əfaɪ/ ***verb*** [T] (*pres. part.* **for·ti·fy·ing**; *3rd person sing. pres.* **for·ti·fies**; *pt, pp* **for·ti·fied**) **1** to make a place stronger and ready for an attack: *to fortify a city* **2** to improve sth by adding extra substances to it: *This cereal is fortified with vitamins.*

**for·tress** /ˈfɔrtrəs/ ***noun*** [C] a castle or other large building that has been made strong so that it is not easy to attack

**for·tu·nate** /ˈfɔrtʃənət/ ***adj.*** lucky: *You were fortunate to have such good weather for your vacation.* ◇ *It was fortunate that he was at home when you called.* OPP **unfortunate**

**for·tu·nate·ly** /ˈfɔrtʃənətli/ ***adv.*** by good luck; luckily: *Fortunately the traffic wasn't too bad.* ◇ *Jane arrived late but, fortunately for her, everybody was too busy to notice.*

★**for·tune** /ˈfɔrtʃən/ ***noun*** **1** [C] what is going to happen to a person in the future: *Show me your hand and I'll try to tell your fortune.* **2** [C] a very large amount of money: *I always spend a fortune on birthday presents.* **3** [C, usually pl.] the things (both good and bad) that happen to a person, family, country, etc.: *The country's fortunes depend on its industry being successful.* **4** [U] the power that affects what happens in a person's life; luck: *Fortune was not on our side that day* (= we were unlucky).

**ˈfortune ˌteller** ***noun*** [C] a person who tells people's FORTUNES (3)

**for·ty** /ˈfɔrt̬i/ ***number*** 40, one more than thirty-nine ➲ Look at **fortieth**. For examples of how to use numbers in sentences, look at **sixty**.

**fo·rum** /ˈfɔrəm/ ***noun*** [C] a place or meeting where people can exchange and discuss ideas

**for·ward¹** /ˈfɔrwərd/ ***adv.*** **1** (*also* **forwards**) in the direction that is in front of you; toward the front, end or future: *Keep going forward and try not to look back.* ◇ *We seem to be going backward, not forward.* **2** in the direction of progress; ahead: *The new drug is a big step forward in the fight against AIDS.*

> NOTE **Forward** is used after many verbs, e.g. **bring**, **come**, **look**, **put**. For the meaning of the expressions, look at the verb entries.

★**for·ward²** /ˈfɔrwərd/ ***adj.*** **1** (only *before* a noun) toward the front or future: *forward planning* **2** direct and confident: *I don't want to seem too forward, but could I buy you a drink?*

**for·ward³** /ˈfɔrwərd/ ***verb*** [T] to send a letter, etc. to a new address: *The post office is forwarding all our mail.*

**for·ward⁴** /ˈfɔrwərd/ ***noun*** [C] a player in a sport such as basketball or soccer who tries to score points ➲ picture at **soccer**.

**ˌforwarding adˈdress** ***noun*** [C] a new address to which mail should be sent

**ˈforward-ˌlooking** ***adj.*** thinking about or planning for the future; having modern ideas

**ˌforward ˈslash** ***noun*** [C] a mark (/) used in computer commands and in Internet addresses to separate the different parts ➲ Compare **backslash**.

**for·went** *past tense of* FORGO

**fos·sil** /ˈfɑsl/ ***noun*** [C] the remains, or a mark, of a prehistoric animal or plant that has been buried in rock for a very long time and that has become hard

**ˈfossil ˌfuel** ***noun*** [C,U] fuel such as coal or oil, that was formed over millions of years from animals or plants

**fos·sil·ized** /ˈfɑsəlaɪzd/ ***adj.*** **1** having become a fossil: *fossilized leaves* **2** fixed, unable to change or develop

**fos·ter** /ˈfɔstər; ˈfɑs-/ ***verb*** [T] **1** to take a child who needs a home into your family and to care for him/her without becoming the legal parents: *to foster a homeless child*

> NOTE The people who do this are **foster parents**. Their home is a **foster home**. The child is a **foster child**. ➲ Look at **adopt**.

**2** to help or encourage the development of sth (especially feelings or ideas)

**fought** *past tense, past participle of* FIGHT¹

**foul¹** /faʊl/ ***adj.*** **1** disgusting and dirty (often with a bad smell or taste): *foul city air* **2** very bad or unpleasant: *Careful what you say – he's got a foul temper* (= he becomes angry very easily). ◇ *What's in this drink? It tastes foul.* **3** (used about weather) very bad; stormy **4** (used about language) very rude; full of swearing: *That guy's got a really foul mouth* (= he uses a lot of swear words).

**foul²** /faʊl/ ***verb*** **1** [T] to make sth dirty (with garbage, waste, etc.): *rivers fouled by industrial waste* **2** [I,T] (*sports*) to be guilty of a FOUL³ (1)(against another player)

PHR V **foul sth up** to spoil sth: *The weather really fouled up our vacation.*

**foul³** /faʊl/ ***noun*** [C] (*sports*) **1** an action that is against the rules: *to commit a foul on another player* **2** (*also* **ˈfoul ball**) (in baseball) a ball that is hit too far to the left or to the right: *to hit a foul*

**ˌfoul ˈplay** ***noun*** [U] **1** action that is against the rules of a sport **2** violent crime that leads to murder

★**found¹** *past tense, past participle of* FIND¹ ➲ Look also at **lost and found**.

**found²** /faʊnd/ ***verb*** [T] **1** to start an organization, institution, etc. especially by providing money: *The university was founded in 1867.* **2** to begin to build a town or establish a country: *Liberia was founded by freed slaves.* **3** (usually passive) to base sth on sth: *a relationship founded on trust*

★**foun·da·tion** /faʊnˈdeɪʃn/ ***noun*** **1** [U] the act of founding sth (a building, town, organization, etc.) **2** [C,U] the part of a building beneath the ground that forms its base: *The construction workers have just started to lay the foundation of the new school.* **3** [C,U] the idea, principle or fact on which sth is based: *That rumor is completely without foundation* (= it is not true). **4** [C] an organization that provides money for a special purpose, e.g. for research or to help people who have a particular problem: *The National Kidney Foundation* (= researching the causes of kidney disease) **5** [U,C] a skin-colored cream used on the face, usually by women ➲ Look at **makeup**.

**foun·der** /ˈfaʊndər/ ***noun*** [C] a person who founds or establishes sth

**ˌFounding ˈFather** ***noun*** [usually pl.] (*U.S.*) a member of the group of people that helped form the U.S. as a country separate from Britain and who wrote an important document in U.S. history (the Constitution), in 1787

**foun·dry** /ˈfaʊndri/ ***noun*** [C] (*pl.* **foun·dries**) a place where metal or glass is melted and shaped into objects

**foun·tain** /ˈfaʊntn/ ***noun*** [C] **1** an ornament (in a yard, park, etc.) that shoots a stream of water into the air. The water that comes out is also called a fountain. **2** = DRINKING FOUNTAIN

**fountain**

**ˈfountain pen** ***noun*** [C] a type of pen that you fill with ink

**four** /fɔr/ ***number*** 4, one more than three ➲ For examples of how to use numbers in sentences, look at **six**.
IDM **on all fours** → ALL[1]

**four-** /fɔr/ ***prefix*** (in compounds) having four of the thing mentioned: *four-legged animals*

**ˌfour-letter ˈword** ***noun*** [C] one of a type of word (often with four letters) that people think is very rude

**four·teen** /ˌfɔrˈtin/ ***number*** 14, one more than thirteen ➲ For examples of how to use numbers in sentences, look at **six**. ▸ **four·teenth** /ˌfɔrˈtinθ/ ***pronoun, det., adv.*** ➲ Look at the examples at **sixth**.

**fourth** /fɔrθ/ ***pronoun, det., adv.*** 4th, next after third ➲ For ¼ we often use the word **quarter**: *a quarter of an hour* (= fifteen minutes). Look at the examples at **sixth**.

**fourth·ly** /ˈfɔrθli/ ***adv.*** (used to introduce the fourth point in a list): *Fourthly, you must speak clearly.*

**the ˌFourth of Juˈly** ***noun*** [sing.] = INDEPENDENCE DAY

**ˌfour-wheel ˈdrive** (*abbr.* **4WD**) ***adj.*** having an engine that turns all four wheels

**fowl** /faʊl/ ***noun*** [pl.] birds, especially ones that are kept on a farm

**fox** /fɑks/ ***noun*** [C] a wild animal with reddish fur that looks like a dog

NOTE A young fox is a **cub**.

**fox·hole** /ˈfɑkshoʊl/ ***noun*** [C] a hole in the ground that soldiers dig and use for shelter in a battle

**foy·er** /ˈfɔɪər/ ***noun*** [C] an entrance hall in a house, hotel, theater, etc. where people can meet or wait

**frac·tion** /ˈfrækʃn/ ***noun*** [C] **1** a small part or amount: *For a fraction of a second, I thought the car was going to crash.* **2** an exact part of a number: *½ and ¼ are fractions.*

**frac·tion·al·ly** /ˈfrækʃənli/ ***adv.*** to a very small degree; slightly

**frac·ture[1]** /ˈfræktʃər/ ***verb*** [T] to break sth (especially a bone): *She fell and fractured her ankle.* ◇ *a fractured ankle*

**frac·ture[2]** /ˈfræktʃər/ ***noun*** [C] a break in sth hard, especially in a bone: *a fracture of the arm*

**frag·ile** /ˈfrædʒl/ ***adj.*** easily damaged or broken: *This bowl is very fragile. Please handle it carefully.*

**frag·ment[1]** /ˈfrægmənt/ ***noun*** [C] a small piece (that has broken off sth bigger): *fragments of ancient pottery* ◇ (*figurative*) *I only heard a fragment of their conversation.*

**frag·ment[2]** /ˈfrægmɛnt; frægˈmɛnt/ ***verb*** [I,T] (*formal*) to be broken into small pieces; to break sth into small pieces: *The country is becoming increasingly fragmented by civil war.*

**fra·grance** /ˈfreɪgrəns/ ***noun*** [C,U] a pleasant smell

**fra·grant** /ˈfreɪgrənt/ ***adj.*** having a pleasant smell

**frail** /freɪl/ ***adj.*** not strong or healthy: *My grandmother is getting very old and frail.*

**frail·ty** /ˈfreɪlti/ ***noun*** [C,U] (*pl.* **frail·ties**) moral or physical weakness

★**frame[1]** /freɪm/ ***noun*** [C] **1** a border of wood or metal that goes around the outside of a door, picture, window, etc.: *a window frame* **2** [usually pl.] a structure made of plastic or metal that holds the lenses of a pair of glasses ➲ picture at **glasses**. **3** the basic structure of a piece of furniture, building, vehicle, etc. onto which other pieces are added: *the frame of a bicycle* **4** [usually sing.] the shape of a human or animal body: *He has a large frame, but he is not fat.*
IDM **frame of mind** a particular state or condition of your feelings; your mood: *I'm not in the right frame of mind for a party. I'd rather be on my own.*

★**frame[2]** /freɪm/ ***verb*** [T] **1** to put a border around sth (especially a picture or photograph): *Let's have this picture framed.* **2** (*formal*) to express sth in words, in a particular way: *The question was very carefully framed.* **3** (usually passive) to give false evidence against sb in order to make him/her seem guilty of a crime: *The man claimed that he had been framed by the police.*

**frame·work** /ˈfreɪmwərk/ ***noun*** [C] **1** the basic structure of sth that gives it shape and strength: *A greenhouse is made of glass panels fixed in a metal framework.* **2** a system of rules or ideas which help you decide what to do: *The plan may be changed, but it will provide a framework on which we can build.*

**fran·chise** /ˈfræntʃaɪz/ ***noun*** [C] **1** a branch of a chain of restaurants, stores, etc.: *A new burger franchise is going to open on the outskirts of town.* **2** official permission from a company to sell its goods or services in a particular area: *a franchise for a fast-food restaurant*

**fran·co·phone** /ˈfræŋkəfoʊn/ ***noun*** [C] (*Cdn*) a French-speaking person ▸ **fran·co·phone** ***adj.***

**frank** /fræŋk/ ***adj.*** showing your thoughts and feelings openly; saying what you mean; honest: *To be perfectly frank with you, I don't think you'll pass your driver's test.* ▸ **frank·ness** ***noun*** [U]: *She spoke with great frankness about her past life.*

F

**frank·furt·er** /ˈfræŋkfərt̬ər; -fət̬ər/ (*also* **wiener**) ***noun*** [C] a type of sausage usually made from beef or pork ➲ Look at **hot dog**.

**frank·ly** /ˈfræŋkli/ ***adv.*** **1** in a frank manner: *Please tell me frankly what you think about my idea.* **2** speaking openly and honestly: *Quite frankly, I'm not surprised at what happened.*

**fran·tic** /ˈfræntɪk/ ***adj.*** **1** in a very emotional state because you are extremely worried or frightened: *The mother was frantic because she couldn't find her child.* ◇ *frantic cries for help* **2** very busy or rushed; without organization: *a frantic search for the keys* ▸ **fran·ti·cal·ly** /-kli/ ***adv.***: *They have been working frantically all week trying to get things ready in time.*

F

**frat** /fræt/ ***noun*** [C] = FRATERNITY (1)

**fra·ter·nal** /frəˈtərnl/ ***adj.*** (*formal*) of or like brothers; friendly

**fra·ter·ni·ty** /frəˈtərnət̬i/ ***noun*** (*pl.* **fra·ter·ni·ties**) **1** [C] (*also informal* **frat**) a social organization, often only for male students, at colleges and universities

> NOTE A similar student organization for women is called a **sorority**. The names of fraternities and sororities are usually combinations of Greek letters, and **Greek** is used to describe their members, activities, organizations, etc.: *members of Greek organizations* ◇ *How many Greeks are there on this campus?*

**2** [U] the feeling of friendship between people (like that between brothers) **3** [C] a group of people who share the same work or interests: *the legal fraternity*

**fraud** /frɔd/ ***noun*** **1** [C,U] (an act of) deceiving or tricking sb in order to get money, etc. in a way that is against the law: *The accountant was sent to prison for fraud.* ◇ *credit card frauds* **2** [C] a person who deceives or tricks sb by pretending to be sb else

**fraud·u·lent** /frɔdʒələnt/ ***adj.*** (*formal*) done in order to deceive sb; dishonest: *the fraudulent use of stolen credit cards*

**fraught** /frɔt/ ***adj.*** **fraught with sth** filled with sth (bad): *The situation was fraught with danger.*

**fray** /freɪ/ ***verb*** [I,T] (used about cloth, etc.) to become worn so that some threads are loose; to cause cloth to do this: *This shirt is beginning to fray at the cuffs.* ◇ *a frayed cuff* ◇ (*figurative*) *Nerves began to fray toward the end of the game* (= the players started to get nervous).

**freak**[1] /frik/ ***noun*** [C] **1** a very strange or unusual event: *By some strange freak of nature, we had snow in June.* ◇ *a freak accident, storm, etc.* **2** (*informal*) a person who has a very strong interest in sth: *a health freak* **3** a person or animal that is physically abnormal in some way; a person who behaves in a strange way: *Disabled people should never be treated as freaks.*

**freak**[2] /frik/ ***verb*** [I,T] (*informal*) **freak (sb) (out)** to become or make sb suddenly very excited, upset, angry, etc.: *Mom really freaked out when she saw that her favorite vase was broken!* ◇ *Snakes really freak me out.*

**freck·le** /ˈfrɛkl/ ***noun*** [C, usually pl.] a small brown spot on a person's skin: *A lot of people with red hair have freckles.* ▸ **freck·led** ***adj.***: *a freckled face*

★**free**[1] /fri/ ***adj.***

➤NOT PRISONER **1** not in prison or in a cage, etc.: *After twenty years in prison, he was finally set free in 1999.*

➤NOT CONTROLLED **2 free (to do sth)** not controlled by the government, rules, etc.: *a free press* ◇ *You're free to do anything you want.*

➤NO PAYMENT **3** costing nothing: *Admission to the museum is free (of charge).* ◇ *a free sample*

➤WITHOUT STH **4 free from/of sth** not having sth dangerous, bad, etc.: *free from all worries and responsibilities* ◇ *free from pain*

➤NOT BEING USED **5** not being used: *Do you have a room free for Saturday night?*

➤NOT BUSY **6** without appointments; not busy: *I'm sorry, but Mr. Spencer is not free this afternoon.* ◇ *I don't have much free time.*

IDM **of your own free will** because you want to, not because sb forces you

★**free**[2] /fri/ ***adv.*** **1** in a free manner: *There is no place around here where dogs can run free.* **2** without cost or payment: *Children under five usually travel free on the subway.*

★**free**[3] /fri/ ***verb*** [T] **1 free sb/sth (from sth)** to let sb/sth go; to set sb/sth free: *to free a prisoner* ◇ *The protesters freed the animals from their cages.* **2 free sb/sth of/from sth** to take away from sb sth that is bad: *The medicine freed her from pain for a few hours.* **3 free sb/sth (from sth)** to move sb/sth that is stuck or caught: *The fire department took three hours to free the man from the wreckage of his car.* **4 free sb/sth for sth** to make sth available so that it can be used; to put sb in a position in which he/she can do sth: *Cuts in defense spending would free money to spend on education.*

**-free** /fri/ ***combining form*** (used in compounds to form adjectives) without sth: *sugar-free cola*

**ˌfree ˈagent** ***noun*** [C] **1** (*sports*) a player who can decide what team to join and does not have to go through a process that limits the team's choice of players **2** a person who can do what he/she wants because nobody else has the right to tell him/her what to do

**free·bie** /ˈfribi/ ***noun*** [C] sth given to sb that he/she does not have to pay for, usually by a company: *He took all the freebies he found.*

**free·dom** /ˈfridəm/ ***noun*** **1** [U] the state of being free, i.e. of not being in prison or under the control of sb else: *The slaves were granted their freedom after the Civil War.* **2** [C,U] the right to do or say what you want: *You have the freedom to come and go as you please.* ◇ *freedom of speech* ◇ *the rights and freedoms of the individual* ➲ Look at **liberty**. **3 freedom from sth** the state of not having sth bad: *freedom from fear/hunger/pain*

**ˈfreedom ˌfighter** ***noun*** [C] a person who belongs to a group that uses violence to try to remove a government from power

**ˌfree ˈenterprise** ***noun*** [U] the operation of trade and business without government control

**free·hand** /ˈfrihænd/ ***adj.***, ***adv.*** (done) by hand, without the help of an instrument, e.g. a ruler: *a freehand sketch*

**free·lance** /ˈfrilæns/ ***adj.***, ***adv.*** working for several different employers and being paid separately for each piece of work: *a freelance journalist* ◇ *She works freelance.* ▶ **free·lance verb** [I]: *She freelances for the local paper.* ▶ **free·lanc·er** ***noun*** [C]

★**free·ly** /ˈfrili/ ***adv.*** **1** in a way that is not controlled or limited: *He is the country's first freely elected president for 40 years.* ◇ *Traffic is flowing freely this morning.*

NOTE Note that if you travel **free**, it means that you do not have to pay anything. If you can travel **freely**, it means that you can go wherever you want.

**2** willingly, without hesitating: *I freely admit that I made a mistake.*

**ˌfree ˈmarket** ***noun*** [C] an economic system in which the price of goods and services is affected by supply and demand rather than controlled by a government: *to compete in a free market*

**ˌfree-ˈrange** ***adj.*** from animals that are allowed to move around freely: *free-range eggs* ◇ *free-range beef*

**ˌfree ˈspeech** ***noun*** [U] the right to express any opinion in public

**ˌfree ˈtrade** ***noun*** [U] a system of international trade in which there are no rules or taxes which limit imports and exports

**free·ware** /ˈfriwɛr/ ***noun*** [U] (*computing*) computer programs, etc. (**software**) that are offered free for anyone to use ➲ Compare **shareware**.

**free·way** /ˈfriweɪ/ (*also* **expressway**) ***noun*** [C] (*U.S.*) a wide road that is specially built for fast traffic

NOTE A freeway has at least two **lanes** going in each direction. There are no **traffic lights** or **intersections** on freeways. Cars can use **exit ramps** to leave a freeway, and **entrance ramps** to join it. **Interstate** freeways form a system which was built in the United States in the 1960s and 1970s to connect all the states (except Alaska and Hawaii). ➲ Look also at the note at **road**.

★**freeze**[1] /friz/ ***verb*** (*pt* **froze** /froʊz/; *pp* **fro·zen** /ˈfroʊzn/)

➤BECOME ICE **1** [I,T] to become hard (and often change into ice) because of extreme cold; to make sth do this: *Water freezes at 32° Fahrenheit.* ◇ *Leave the heat on when you're away or the pipes will freeze.* ◇ *The ground is frozen solid.* ◇ *I froze the raspberries that we picked.* ◇ *Raspberries freeze well.* ◇ *frozen peas*

➤OF WEATHER **2** [I] (used with "it" to describe extremely cold weather, when water turns into ice): *I think it's going to freeze tonight.*

➤BE VERY COLD **3** [I,T] (to cause a person) to be very cold or to die from cold: *The two men froze to death on the mountain.* ◇ *Turn the heat up a little – my hands are frozen.*

➤STOP MOVING **4** [I] to stop suddenly or become still: *The terrible scream made her freeze with terror.* ◇ *"Freeze!" shouted the gunman and everybody stood completely still.*

➤WAGES/PRICES **5** [T] to keep wages, prices, fares, etc. at a fixed level for a certain period of time: *Spending on defense has been frozen for one year.*

**freeze**[2] /friz/ ***noun*** [C] **1** a period of weather when the temperature stays below 0°C or 32°F (the freezing point) **2** the fixing of wages, prices, fares, etc. at a certain level for a certain period of time

**freez·er** /ˈfrizər/ ***noun*** [C] a piece of electrical equipment in which you can store food for a long time at a temperature below 0°C or 32°F (the freezing point) so that it stays frozen ➲ Look at **refrigerator**.

**freez·ing** /ˈfrizɪŋ/ ***adj.*** (*informal*) very cold (not necessarily below 32° F or 0° C): *Can we turn the heat on? I'm freezing.* ◇ *It's freezing outside.*

**ˈfreezing point** (*also* **freezing**) ***noun*** [C,U] the temperature at which water, etc. freezes: *Last night the temperature fell to six degrees below freezing.*

**freight** /freɪt/ ***noun*** [U] **1** the method of carrying goods from one place to another: *freight costs* **2** things that are carried by train or truck: *a freight train* ➲ Look at **cargo**.

**freight·er** /ˈfreɪt̬ər/ ***noun*** [C] a ship that carries only freight

**ˌFrench ˈbread** ***noun*** [U] white bread in the shape of a long thin stick ➲ picture at **bread**.

**ˌFrench ˈCanada** ***noun*** [sing.] the part of Canada where most French-speaking Canadians (**francophones**) live, especially the province of Quebec ➲ Compare **English Canada**. ▶ **ˌFrench Caˈnadian** ***noun*** [C] ▶ **ˌFrench-Caˈnadian** ***adj.***

**ˌFrench ˈdoor** /ˌfrɛntʃ ˈdɔr/ ***noun*** [C] one of a pair of glass doors that open onto a yard or balcony

**French fry** /ˈfrɛntʃ fraɪ/ ***noun*** [C] (*pl.* **French fries**) (*also* **fry**) a long, thin piece of potato that is fried in hot fat or oil: *a hamburger and French fries* ◇ *Would you like ketchup with your fries?*

**French toast** /ˌfrɛntʃ ˈtoʊst/ ***noun*** [U] bread that has been covered with a mixture of eggs and milk and then fried: *a slice/piece of French toast*

**fren·zied** /ˈfrɛnzid/ ***adj.*** wild and excited: *a frenzied attack*

**fren·zy** /ˈfrɛnzi/ ***noun*** [sing., U] a state of great excitement; a period when a person cannot control his/her actions: *The speaker worked the crowd up into a frenzy.*

**fre·quen·cy** /ˈfrikwənsi/ ***noun*** (*pl.* **fre·quen·cies**) **1** [U] the rate at which sth happens (= the number of times sth happens in a particular period): *Fatal accidents have decreased in frequency in recent years* (= there are fewer of them). **2** [U] the fact that sth happens often: *The frequency of deaths from cancer near the nuclear power plant is being investigated.* **3** [C,U] the rate at which a sound wave or radio wave vibrates: *high-frequency/low-frequency sounds* ◇ *Which frequency does the radio station broadcast on?*

★**fre·quent**[1] /ˈfrikwənt/ ***adj.*** happening often: *a frequent bus service* OPP **infrequent** ▶ **fre·quent·ly** ***adv.***: *Buses run frequently from downtown to the airport.*

**fre·quent**[2] /friˈkwɛnt; ˈfrikwənt/ ***verb*** [T] (*formal*) to go to a place often: *Many famous writers frequented this bar.*

★**fresh** /frɛʃ/ ***adj.***

➤NEW **1** new or different: *They decided to make a fresh start in a different town.* ◇ *a fresh approach to* *a problem* **2** not old (so there has been no time for any change): *There was fresh blood all over the walls.* ◇ *Write down a few notes while the lecture is still fresh in your mind.*

➤FOOD **3** (used about food, flowers, etc.) made or picked not long ago: *fresh bread* OPP **stale** **4** (used about food) not frozen or from a can: *fresh fruit and vegetables*

➤WATER **5** (used about water) not salty; not sea water

NOTE A fish that lives in this type of water is a **freshwater** fish.

F

➤AIR **6** (used about the air) clean and cool: *Open the window and let some fresh air in.*

➤CLEAR/BRIGHT **7** (used about colors, or a person's skin) bright or clear: *a fresh complexion*

➤FULL OF ENERGY **8** not tired: *I'll think about the problem again in the morning when I'm fresh.*

➤RUDE **9** impolite; not showing respect: *Don't you get fresh with me, young man!*

➤JUST FINISHED **10** **fresh from/out of sth** having just finished sth: *Life isn't easy for a young teacher fresh out of college.*

IDM **be fresh out (of sth)** (*informal*) to have just finished your supply of sth: *Sorry. We're fresh out of strawberries.*

▸ **fresh·ness** ***noun*** [U]

**fresh·en** /ˈfrɛʃn/ ***verb*** [T] **freshen sth (up)** to make sth cleaner or brighter: *Some new curtains would freshen up this room.*

PHR V **freshen (yourself) up** to wash and make yourself clean and neat

**fresh·ly** /ˈfrɛʃli/ ***adv.*** newly; recently: *freshly baked bread*

**fresh·man** /ˈfrɛʃmən/ ***noun*** [C] (*pl.* **fresh·men** /ˈfrɛʃmən/) **1** a student who is in the ninth grade in school or in his/her first year at college ➲ Look at **sophomore**, **junior** and **senior**. **2** (*Cdn*) a first-year student at a university or college

**fret** /frɛt/ ***verb*** [I] (*old-fashioned*) (**fret·ting**; **fret·ted**) **fret (about/at/over sth)** to be unhappy or worried about sth: *Don't fret. Everything will be all right.*

**fric·tion** /ˈfrɪkʃn/ ***noun*** [U] **1** the rubbing of one surface or thing against another **2** disagreement between people or groups

**Fri·day** /ˈfraɪdeɪ; -di/ ***noun*** [C,U] (*abbr.* **Fri.**) the day of the week after Thursday and before Saturday ➲ For examples of the use of the days of the week in sentences, look at **Monday**.

**fridge** /frɪdʒ/ ***noun*** [C] (*informal*) = REFRIGERATOR

★**friend** /frɛnd/ ***noun*** [C] **1** a person that you know and like (not a member of your family): *Steve and I are old friends. We went to the same school.* ◇ *We're only inviting close friends and relatives to the funeral.* ◇ *Do you know Irene Pearse? She's my best friend.* ◇ *A friend of mine told me about this restaurant.* ◇ *One of my friends told me about this restaurant.* ➲ Look at **boyfriend** and **girlfriend**. **2** **a friend of/to sth** a helper or supporter of sth: *the friends of the poor*

IDM **be/make friends (with sb)** to be/become a friend (of sb): *Tony is very shy and finds it hard to make friends.*

**friend·less** /ˈfrɛndləs/ ***adj.*** without friends

★**friend·ly** /ˈfrɛndli/ ***adj.*** (**friend·li·er**; **friend·li·est**) **1** behaving in a kind and pleasant way; showing kindness and pleasantness: *Everyone here has been very friendly toward us.* ◇ *a friendly smile* ◇ *a small friendly hotel* **2** **friendly with sb** being the friend of sb: *Nick's gotten quite friendly with the boy next door.* ▸ **friend·li·ness** ***noun*** [U]

**-friendly** /ˈfrɛndli/ ***combining form*** supporting or helping sb/sth: *Our computer is extremely user-friendly.*

★**friend·ship** /ˈfrɛndʃɪp/ ***noun*** **1** [U] the state of being friends: *Our relationship is based on friendship, not love.* **2** [C] a relationship between people who are friends: *lifelong friendships*

ˈ**friendship ˌcentre** (*also* ˌ**native** ˈ**friendship** ˌ**centre**) ***noun*** [C] (*Cdn*) a place, especially in a city, which provides Aboriginal people with counseling and social services

**fright** /fraɪt/ ***noun*** [C,U] a sudden feeling of fear: *That loud bang gave me a real fright.* ◇ *The child cried out in fright.*

★**fright·en** /ˈfraɪtn/ ***verb*** [T] to fill sb with fear: *Sorry, I didn't mean to frighten you.*

PHR V **frighten sb/sth away/off** to cause a person or animal to go away by frightening him/her/it: *The cat frightened the birds away.*

★**fright·ened** /ˈfraɪtnd/ ***adj.*** **1** full of fear or worry: *Frightened children were calling for their mothers.* ◇ *He was frightened at the thought of being alone.* ◇ *I was frightened that they would think I was being rude.* **2** **frightened of sb/sth** fearing a particular person, thing or situation: *When I was little, I was frightened of cats.* ➲ Look at the note at **afraid**.

★**fright·en·ing** /ˈfraɪtn·ɪŋ; ˈfraɪtnɪŋ/ ***adj.*** causing fear: *It was a very frightening situation to be in.* ◇ *It's frightening how quickly time passes.* ◇ *It's frightening that time passes so quickly.*

**fright·ful** /ˈfraɪtfl/ ***adj.*** very bad; causing great fear: *She described the mugging as a frightful experience.*

**frig·id** /ˈfrɪdʒəd/ ***adj.*** **1** very cold: *There will be frigid air coming from the north tomorrow.* **2** (usually used about a woman) disliking sexual activity

**frill** /frɪl/ ***noun*** [C] **1** a special edge for a dress, shirt, etc. which is made by forming many folds in a narrow piece of cloth **2** [usually pl.] something that is not necessary but is decorative or pleasant: *We just want a plain, simple meal – no frills.*

**frill·y** /ˈfrɪli/ (**frill·i·er**; **frill·i·est**) ***adj.*** having many FRILLS (1): *a frilly dress*

**fringe** /frɪndʒ/ ***noun*** [C] **1** a decorative edge on a rug, etc. or on clothes, that is made of loose or hanging threads **2** a place, part or position that is a long way from the center or from what is usual: *the outer fringes of the town*

ˌ**fringe** ˈ**benefit** ***noun*** [C] = BENEFIT² (4)

**Fris·bee™** /ˈfrɪzbi/ ***noun*** **1** [C] a light plastic disk, shaped like a plate, which is thrown between players in a game **2** [U] a game in which players throw and catch a Frisbee: *to play a game of Frisbee*

**frisk** /frɪsk/ ***verb*** **1** [T] to touch sb's body and clothes in order to search for hidden weapons, drugs, etc.: *to frisk a prisoner* **2** [I] (used about an animal or child) to play and jump around in a lively and happy way

**frisk·y** /ˈfrɪski/ ***adj.*** (**frisk·i·er**; **frisk·i·est**) lively and playful

**frit·ter¹** /ˈfrɪt̬ər/ ***verb***

PHR V **fritter sth away (on sth)** to waste time or money on things that are not important

**frit·ter²** /ˈfrɪt̬ər/ ***noun*** [C] a piece of fruit, meat, etc. that has been covered with a mixture of flour, egg and water (**batter**) and then fried in hot fat or oil: *a banana fritter*

**fri·vol·i·ty** /frɪˈvɑlət̬i/ ***noun*** [U] silly behavior or a silly attitude (especially when you should be serious)

**friv·o·lous** /ˈfrɪvələs/ ***adj.*** not serious; silly: *This is a serious issue. Please don't make frivolous remarks.*
▸ **friv·o·lous·ly** ***adv.***

**friz·zy** /ˈfrɪzi/ ***adj.*** (used about hair) with a lot of very small curls

**fro** /froʊ/ ***adv.***

IDM **to and fro** → TO³

**frog** /frɔg; frɑg/ ***noun*** [C] a small animal with smooth skin and long legs that are used for jumping. Frogs live in or near water: *the croaking of frogs*

★**from** /frəm; *strong forms* frʌm; frɑm/ ***prep.*** **1** (showing the place where sb/sth starts or started): *Has the plane from Chicago arrived yet?* ◇ *She comes home from work at 7 o'clock.* ◇ *A child fell from the seventh floor of an apartment building.* **2** (showing the time when sth starts or started): *Peter will be on vacation from Wednesday through Friday.* ◇ *The store is open from 8 a.m. until 8 p.m. every day.* ◇ *We lived in Oregon from 1989 to 2004.* **3** (showing the person who sent, gave, said, etc. sth): *Did you get a birthday card from John?* ◇ *I borrowed this jacket from my sister.* ◇ *a phone call from my father* **4** (showing the origin of sb/sth): *"Where do you come from?" "I'm from Australia."* ◇ *There's a man from the bank here to see you.* **5** (showing the material with which sth is made): *Paper is made from wood.* **6** (showing the distance between two places): *The house is fifty yards from the lake.* **7** (showing the lower limit in a range of prices, figures, etc.): *Our prices start from $2.50 a bottle.* ◇ *Tickets cost from $3 to $11.* **8** (showing the state of sb/sth before a change): *The bus fare has gone up from 75¢ to 85¢.* ◇ *The article was translated from Russian into English.* ◇ *Things have gone from bad to worse.* **9** (showing that sb/sth is taken away): *She borrowed the book from the library.* ◇ *If you subtract 8 from 12, it leaves 4.* **10** (showing sth that you want to avoid): *There was no shelter from the wind.* ◇ *This game will keep you from getting bored.* **11** (showing the reason for sth): *People in the camps are suffering from hunger and cold.* **12** (showing the difference between two people, places or things): *Is Portuguese very different from Spanish?* **13** (showing your position or point of view): *There's a great view from the top of the tower.* ◇ *He always looks at things from his own point of view.*

IDM **from...on** starting at a particular time and continuing forever: *She never spoke to him again from that day on.* ◇ *From now on, you will have to help with the housework.*

★**front¹** /frʌnt/ ***noun***

▸FORWARD PART/POSITION **1** [C, usually sing.] the side or surface of sth that is most usually seen or that is most important: *a dress with buttons down the front* ◇ *the front of a building* (= the front wall) **2** [C, usually sing.] the most forward part of sth or the area that is just outside of or before sb/sth: *Young children should not ride in the front of the car.* ◇ *There is a small porch at the front of the house.*

**in front of/across from**

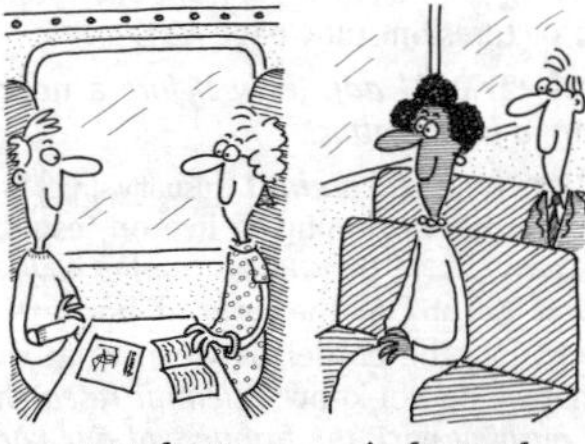

across from     in front of

> NOTE **On the front of** means "on the front surface of sth": *The number is shown on the front of the bus.* **In front of** means "farther forward than another person or thing": *A car stopped in front of the bus.* **At/In the front of** means "in the most forward part inside sth": *The driver sits at the front of the bus.* Look at these sentences too: *The teacher usually stands in front of the class.* ◇ *The noisy students had to sit at the front of the class* (= in the front seats).

▸IN WAR **3 the front** [sing.] the line or area where fighting takes place in a war: *to be sent to the front*

▸HIDING TRUE FEELINGS **4** [sing.] a way of behaving that hides your true feelings: *His brave words were just a front. He was really feeling very nervous.*

▸HIDING STH ILLEGAL **5** [C, usually sing.] a person, group, or thing that hides an illegal or secret activity: *The Mafia set up an export company as a front for its illegal activities.*

▸WEATHER **6** [C] (*technical*) (used when talking about the weather) a line or area where warm air and cold air meet

▸AREA OF ACTIVITY **7** [C] a particular area of activity: *Things are difficult on the domestic front right now.*

IDM **in front** ahead of or further forward than sb/sth: *After three miles, the Kenyan runner was in front.*

**in front of 1** in a position further forward than but close to sb/sth: *The bus stops right in front of our house.* ◇ *Don't stand in front of the TV.* ◇ *The book was open in front of her on the desk.*

> NOTE **In front of** does not mean the same as **across from**.

**2** in the presence of: *I couldn't talk about that in front of my parents.*

**up front** (*informal*) as payment before sth is done: *I want half the money up front and half when the job is finished.*

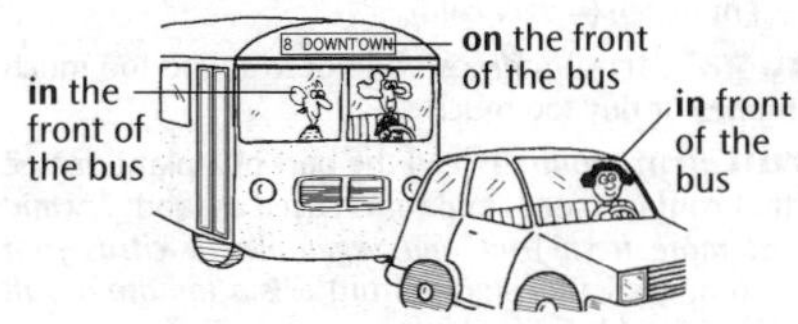

★**front²** /frʌnt/ ***adj.*** (only *before* a noun) of or at the FRONT¹ (1,2): *front teeth* ◇ *the front door/yard/room/walk* ➲ pictures on study page **A31**.

**fron·tal** /ˈfrʌntl/ ***adj.*** (only *before* a noun) from the front: *a frontal attack*

**fron·tier** /frʌnˈtɪr/ ***noun*** **1** [usually sing.] land that people are just beginning to live on, especially in the western U.S. in the 1800s: *frontier towns of the Wild West* ➲ Look at the note at **border¹**. **2 the frontiers** [pl.] the border between what we know and what we do not know: *Scientific research is constantly pushing back the frontiers of our knowledge about the world.*

F

**frost¹** /frɔst/ ***noun*** **1** [C,U] the weather conditions when the temperature falls below the freezing point: *There was a hard frost last night.* **2** [U] a very thin layer of little pieces of ice that is formed on surfaces when the temperature is below the freezing point: *The ground was white with frost.*

**frost²** /frɔst/ ***verb*** [T] to decorate the top of a cake, cookies, etc. with a mixture containing sugar (frosting)

PHRV **frost over/up** to become covered with FROST¹ (2): *The window frosted over/up during the night.*

**frost·bite** /ˈfrɔsbaɪt/ ***noun*** [U] injury to the skin, especially to fingers, toes, etc. that is caused by very low temperatures

**frost·ed** /frɔstəd/ ***adj.*** (used about glass or a window) with a special surface so you cannot see through it

**frost·ing** /ˈfrɔstɪŋ/ ***noun*** [U] a mixture of powdered sugar, butter, flavoring, etc. that is used for decorating cakes, cookies, etc.: *chocolate frosting* ➲ Look at **icing**.

**frost·y** /ˈfrɔsti/ ***adj.*** (**frost·i·er**; **frost·i·est**) **1** very cold, with frost: *a cold and frosty morning* **2** cold and unfriendly: *a frosty welcome*

**froth¹** /frɔθ/ ***noun*** [U] a mass of small white bubbles on the top of a liquid, etc. ▶ **froth·y** ***adj.***: *a frothy drink*

**froth²** /frɔθ/ ***verb*** [I] to have or produce froth: *The mad dog was frothing at the mouth.*

**frown¹** /fraʊn/ ***verb*** [I] to bring your eyebrows together so that you make lines appear on your forehead. You frown when you are angry, worried, or thinking very hard: *"You're late," he said, frowning.*

PHRV **frown on/upon sth** to think that sth is not good; to disapprove of sth: *Smoking is very much frowned upon these days.*

**frown²** /fraʊn/ ***noun*** [C] an act of frowning: *She looked at me with a frown.*

**froze** *past tense of* FREEZE¹

★**fro·zen** /ˈfroʊzn/ *past participle of* FREEZE¹: *The pond is frozen. Let's go skating.* ◇ *frozen vegetables* ◇ *I'm frozen* (= very cold).

**fru·gal** /ˈfrugl/ ***adj.*** careful not to spend too much money or buy too much

★**fruit** /frut/ ***noun*** **1** [C,U] the part of a plant or tree that contains seeds and that is used as food: *Try and eat more fresh fruit and vegetables.* ◇ *citrus fruit* (= oranges/lemons/grapefruit) ◇ *Is a tomato a fruit or a vegetable?* ◇ *fruit juice*

> NOTE When we say "a fruit" we mean "a type of fruit": *Most big supermarkets sell many different tropical fruits.* When we are talking about one individual piece, e.g. a single apple, pear, banana, etc. we must say "a piece of fruit": *What would you like for dessert: ice cream or a piece of fruit?* It is more usual to use the uncountable form: *Would you like some fruit?*

**2** [C] the part of any plant in which the seed is formed **3 the fruits** [pl.] a good result or a reward for what you have done

**fruit·ful** /ˈfrutfl/ ***adj.*** producing good results; useful: *fruitful discussions*

**fru·i·tion** /fruˈɪʃn/ ***noun*** [U] the time when a plan, etc. starts to be successful: *After months of hard work, our efforts were coming to fruition.*

**fruit·less** /ˈfrutləs/ ***adj.*** producing poor or no results; unsuccessful: *a fruitless search*

**frus·trate** /ˈfrʌstreɪt/ ***verb*** [T] **1** to prevent sb from doing sth or sth from happening: *The rescue work has been frustrated by bad weather conditions.* **2** to cause a person to feel angry or dissatisfied because things are not happening as he/she wants: *It's the lack of money that really frustrates him.*

**frus·trat·ed** /ˈfrʌstreɪt̬əd/ ***adj.*** angry or dissatisfied, e.g. because you cannot have or do what you want: *He felt very frustrated at his lack of progress in learning Chinese.*

**frus·trat·ing** /ˈfrʌstreɪt̬ɪŋ/ ***adj.*** making you angry or dissatisfied: *I spent a frustrating morning trying to reach Sandy on the phone.*

**frus·tra·tion** /frʌˈstreɪʃn/ ***noun*** [C,U] a feeling of anger or dissatisfaction, or sth that causes it: *He felt anger and frustration at not being able to help the starving children.* ◇ *Every job has its frustrations.*

★**fry¹** /fraɪ/ ***verb*** [I,T] (*pres. part.* **fry·ing**; *3rd person sing. pres.* **fries**; *pt, pp* **fried** /fraɪd/) to be cooked in hot fat or oil; to cook sth in this way: *to fry an egg* ◇ *a fried egg* ◇ *There was a smell of bacon frying in the kitchen.* ➲ Look at the note at **cook**.

**fry²** /fraɪ/ (*pl.* **fries**) ***noun*** [C] = FRENCH FRY

**ˈfrying pan** (*also* **fry pan**, **skillet**) ***noun*** [C] a flat shallow pan with a long handle that is used for frying food ➲ picture at **pan**.

**fuch·sia** /ˈfyuʃə/ ***noun*** [C,U] a small bush with flowers in two colors of red, purple or white, that hang down

**fudge¹** /fʌdʒ/ ***noun*** [U] a type of soft candy made with milk, butter, sugar and another flavoring

**fudge²** /fʌdʒ/ ***verb*** [I,T] **fudge (on sth)** to give an answer or information that is not completely clear and accurate: *I think he fudged the numbers in his travel expenses a little bit.* ◇ *Never fudge when you answer your teacher.* ◇ *Many people fudge on their income tax deductions.*

★**fuel¹** /ˈfyuəl; fyul/ ***noun*** **1** [U] material that is burned to produce heat or power: *What's the car's fuel consumption?* ◇ *Our fuel bills are very high.* **2** [C] a type of fuel: *I think natural gas is the best fuel for home heating.*

**fuel²** /ˈfyuəl; fyul/ ***verb*** [T] to provide fuel for sth: (*figurative*) *Her comments fueled speculation that she was going to resign.*

**fu·gi·tive** /ˈfyudʒət̮ɪv/ ***noun*** [C] a person who is running away or escaping (e.g. from the police) ➲ Look at **refugee**.

**ful·fill** /fʊlˈfɪl/ ***verb*** [T] **1** to perform or carry out a duty, task, etc.: *She fulfills an advisory role on the committee.* **2** to make sth that you wish for, or have promised, happen: *to fulfill an ambition* ◇ *The government has not yet fulfilled its promises to improve education.* **3** to do, have, or provide what is needed or necessary, especially according to a contract, a rule, etc.: *to fulfill the requirements for a job*

**ful·filled** /fʊlˈfɪld/ ***adj.*** completely satisfied and happy

**ful·fill·ing** /fʊlˈfɪlɪŋ/ ***adj.*** making you feel happy and satisfied: *I find my work very fulfilling.*

**ful·fill·ment** /fʊlˈfɪlmənt/ ***noun*** [U] **1** the act of fulfilling or the state of being fulfilled: *Moving into our own home was the fulfillment of a dream.* **2** the feeling of satisfaction that you have when you have done sth: *Some men find fulfillment in raising a family.*

★**full**[1] /fʊl/ ***adj.***

➤WITH NO EMPTY SPACE **1 full (of sb/sth)** holding or containing as much or as many as possible: *The garbage can needs to be emptied. It's full.* ◇ *a full bottle* ◇ *The bus was full so we had to wait for the next one.* ◇ *"Is there any coffee left?" "Yes, the pot's still half full."* ◇ (*figurative*) *The kids are full of energy.* ◇ (*figurative*) *We need a good night's sleep because we have a full* (= busy) *day tomorrow.*

➤HAVING A LOT **2 full (of sb/sth)** with a lot of people or things in it: *The room was full of people.* ◇ *His work was full of mistakes.*

➤OF FOOD **3 full (up)** having had enough to eat and drink: *No dessert for me. I'm full (up).*

➤COMPLETE **4** (only *before* a noun) complete; not leaving anything out: *I would like a full report on the accident.* ◇ *Full details of today's TV programs are on page 20.* ◇ *He took full responsibility for what had happened.* ◇ *Please give your full address.*

➤AS MUCH AS POSSIBLE **5** (only *before* a noun) the highest or greatest possible: *The roses are in full bloom.* ◇ *a train traveling at full speed*

➤ROUND **6** round in shape: *a full figure*

➤CLOTHES **7** (used about clothes) made with plenty of material: *a full skirt*

➤OF A BED **8** (used about a bed) big enough for two people ➲ Look at the note at **bed**[1].

IDM **be full of yourself** to think that you are very important: *He's been very full of himself ever since he was promoted.*

**have your hands full** → HAND[1]

**in full** with nothing missing; completely: *Your money will be refunded in full* (= you will get all your money back). ◇ *Please write your name in full.*

**in full swing** at the stage when there is a lot of activity: *When we arrived, the party was already in full swing.*

**in full view (of sb/sth)** in a place where you can easily be seen: *In full view of the guards, he tried to escape over the prison wall.* ◇ *in full view of the front windows*

**to the full** as much as possible: *to enjoy life to the full*

**full**[2] /fʊl/ ***adv.*** completely; directly: *All the hotel rooms in town were booked full.* ◇ *You know full well why I asked that question.*

ˌ**full-ˈblown** ***adj.*** fully developed: *to have full-blown AIDS*

**full-fledged** /ˌfʊl ˈflɛdʒd/ ***adj.*** completely trained or completely developed: *Media studies is now a full-fledged academic subject.*

ˌ**full-ˈlength** ***adj.*** **1** (used about a picture, mirror, etc.) showing a person from head to foot **2** (used about a dress, skirt, etc.) reaching the ankles: *a full-length ball gown* **3** not shorter than normal: *a full-length movie/book*

ˌ**full ˈmoon** ***noun*** [sing.] the moon when it appears as a circle OPP **new moon**

ˌ**full-ˈscale** ***adj.*** **1** (used about a plan, drawing, etc.) of the same size as the original object **2** using every means that is available: *a full-scale murder investigation*

ˌ**full-ˈtime** ***adj.***, ***adv.*** for the whole of a normal period of work: *He has a full-time job.* ◇ *He works full-time.* ◇ *We have 800 full-time and 500 part-time employees.* ➲ Look at **part-time**.

★**ful·ly** /ˈfʊli/ ***adv.*** completely; to the highest possible degree: *I'm fully aware of the problem.* ◇ *All our engineers are fully trained.* ◇ *a fully automatic camera*

**fum·ble** /ˈfʌmbl/ ***verb*** [I] to use your hands in an awkward way, especially when you are looking for sth: *She was fumbling in her pocket for her key.*

**fume** /fyum/ ***verb*** [I] to feel or express anger: *By the time they arrived, I was absolutely fuming.* ◇ *"They're almost two hours late," she fumed.*

**fumes** /fyumz/ ***noun*** [pl.] smoke or gases that smell bad and that can be harmful if you breathe them in: *Six people died in the fire when they were overcome by smoke and fumes.*

★**fun**[1] /fʌn/ ***noun*** [U] pleasure and enjoyment; an activity or a person that gives you pleasure and enjoyment: *There isn't much fun in staying home on your own.* ◇ *Staying home on your own isn't much fun.* ◇ *We had a lot of fun at the party last night.* ◇ *The party was a lot of fun.* ◇ *Have fun!* (= Enjoy yourself!) ◇ *Sailing can be good fun if you don't mind getting wet.* ◇ *He was extremely intelligent, but he was also a lot of fun.*

IDM **(just) for fun/for the fun of it** (just) for amusement or pleasure; not seriously: *I don't need English for my work. I am just learning it for fun.*

**(just) in fun** as a joke: *It was said in fun. They didn't mean to upset you.*

**make fun of sb/sth** to laugh at sb/sth in an unkind way; to make other people do this: *The older kids are always making fun of him because of his accent.*

**poke fun at sb/sth** → POKE

★**fun**[2] /fʌn/ ***adj.*** **1** amusing and enjoyable: *a fun evening*

> NOTE Be careful. **Funny** describes something that makes you laugh or that is strange. It is not the same as **fun**: *The party was fun* (= it was enjoyable). ◇ *The movie was funny* (= it made us laugh).

**2** (used about people) amusing and enjoyable to be with: *He's a really fun guy.*

★**func·tion**[1] /ˈfʌŋkʃn/ ***noun*** [C] **1** the purpose or special duty of a person or thing: *One function of the school board is to set salaries.* ◇ *The function of the heart is to pump blood through the body.* **2** an

F

important social event, ceremony, etc.: *The Vice President attends hundreds of official functions every year.* **3** (*computing*) part of a program, etc. that performs a basic operation

★**func·tion²** /ˈfʌŋkʃn/ ***verb*** [I] to work; to be in action: *My new computer isn't functioning very well.* ◇ *Only one engine was still functioning.*

**func·tion·al** /ˈfʌŋkʃənl/ ***adj.*** **1** practical and useful rather than attractive: *cheap, functional furniture* **2** working; being used: *The system is now fully functional.*

**func·tion·al·i·ty** /ˌfʌŋkʃəˈnæləṭi/ ***noun*** **1** [U] the quality in sth of being very suitable for the purpose it was designed for SYN **practicality** **2** [U] the purpose that sth is designed for or expected to perform: *Design processes may be affected by the functionality of the product.* **3** [C,U] (*computing*) the range of functions that a computer or other electronic system can perform

ˈ**function key** ***noun*** [C] one of the buttons (keys) on a computer which are used to perform a particular operation

★**fund¹** /fʌnd/ ***noun*** **1** [C] a sum of money that is collected for a particular purpose: *They contributed $30 to the disaster relief fund.* **2** **funds** [pl.] money that is available and can be spent

★**fund²** /fʌnd/ ***verb*** [T] to provide a project, etc. with money: *The government is funding a new project to help inner-city children.*

★**fun·da·men·tal** /ˌfʌndəˈmɛntəl/ ***adj.*** important or basic; from which everything else develops: *There will be fundamental changes in the way the school is run.* ◇ *There is a fundamental difference between your opinion and mine.* ▸ **fun·da·men·tal·ly** ***adv.***: *The two candidates have fundamentally different views on the issue.*

**fun·da·men·tal·ist** /ˌfʌndəˈmɛntəlɪst/ ***noun*** **1** a person who follows all the teaching of a religion very strictly **2** a Christian who believes that everything in the Bible is absolutely true ▸ **fun·da·men·tal·ist** ***adj.*** ▸ **fun·da·men·tal·ism** ***noun*** [U]

**fun·da·men·tals** /ˌfʌndəˈmɛntəlz/ ***noun*** [pl.] basic facts or principles

ˈ**fund ˌraiser** /ˈfʌnd ˌreɪzər/ ***noun*** [C] **1** a person who collects money for a charity or an organization **2** a social or entertainment event to collect money for a charity or organization ▸ ˈ**fund-ˌraising** ***noun*** [U]

★**fu·ner·al** /ˈfyunərəl/ ***noun*** [C] a ceremony (often in a church or a funeral home) connected with burying or burning (**cremating**) a dead person: *The funeral will be held next week.* ◇ *The mourners at the funeral were all in black.*

> NOTE The body of the dead person is carried in a **casket** or **coffin**, on which there are often **wreaths** of flowers. The casket is buried in a **grave** or is burned (**cremated**).

ˈ**funeral diˌrector** (*also* **mortician**, *old-fashioned* **undertaker**) ***noun*** [C] a person whose job is to prepare dead people's bodies to be buried and to arrange funerals

ˈ**funeral home** (*also* ˈ**funeral ˌparlor**) ***noun*** [C] a place where dead people's bodies are prepared to be buried or burned and where visitors can look at the body

**fun·gus** /ˈfʌŋgəs/ ***noun*** [C,U] (*pl.* **fun·gi** /ˈfʌndʒaɪ; ˈfʌŋgaɪ/ or **fun·gus·es**) a plant that is not green and that does not have leaves or flowers. One type has a thick stem and a big flat top, another type is like a powder. Fungi grow on other plants, decaying wood or food, etc.: *mushrooms and other edible fungi* ◇ *The roses are covered in fungus.* ➲ Look at **mold** and **toadstool**.

**funk** /fʌŋk/ ***noun*** [U] a type of modern dance music with a strong rhythm

**funk·y** /ˈfʌŋki/ ***adj.*** (*informal*) (**funk·i·er**; **funk·i·est**) **1** (used about music) having a strong rhythm that is easy to dance to: *a funky disco beat* **2** fashionable and unusual, in a good way: *She wears really funky clothes.* **3** having an unusual and unpleasant smell: *This milk smells funky – do you think it's okay to drink it?*

**fun·nel¹** /ˈfʌnl/ ***noun*** [C] an object that is wide at the top and narrow at the bottom, used for pouring liquid, powder, etc. into a small opening ➲ picture at **kitchen**.

**fun·nel²** /ˈfʌnl/ ***verb*** [I,T] to move or make sth move through a funnel or a narrow space: *People funneled slowly through the stadium exits.*

ˈ**funnel cloud** ***noun*** [C] a type of dangerous storm with very strong winds that blow in a circle (a **tornado**) that is not touching the ground

**fun·ni·ly** /ˈfʌnl·i/ ***adv.*** **1** (used for expressing surprise at sth strange that has happened): *Funnily enough, my parents weren't at all angry about it.* **2** in a funny way: *She's breathing very funnily.*

★**fun·ny** /ˈfʌni/ ***adj.*** (**fun·ni·er**; **fun·ni·est**) **1** that makes you smile or laugh: *She told us a funny story about taking a cow to church.* ◇ *He's a really funny person* (= he can make people laugh). **2** strange or unusual: *The engine is making a funny noise.* ◇ *It's funny how people never talk in elevators.* ◇ *What a funny little chair!* ◇ *That's funny – he was here a minute ago and now he's gone.* ◇ *Can I sit down for a minute? I feel a little funny* (= a little sick). ➲ Look at the note at **fun²**.

★**fur** /fər/ ***noun*** **1** [U] the soft thick hair that covers the bodies of some animals **2** [C,U] the skin and hair of an animal that is used for making clothes, etc.; a piece of clothing that is made from this: *These boots are lined with fur.* ◇ *a fur coat* ➲ adjective furry

**fu·ri·ous** /ˈfyʊriəs/ ***adj.*** **1 furious (with sb)/(about/at sth)** very angry: *He was furious with her.* ◇ *He was furious at her behavior.* ➲ noun fury **2** very strong; violent: *a furious argument* ▸ **fu·ri·ous·ly** ***adv.***

**fur·nace** /ˈfərnəs/ ***noun*** [C] **1** a piece of equipment in which fuel is burned in order to heat a building: *an oil furnace* ◇ *a gas furnace* **2** = BLAST FURNACE

**fur·nish** /ˈfərnɪʃ/ ***verb*** [T] to put furniture in a room, house, etc.: *The room was comfortably furnished.*

**fur·nished** /ˈfərnɪʃt/ ***adj.*** having furniture: *a furnished apartment* OPP **unfurnished**

**fur·nish·ings** /ˈfərnɪʃɪŋz/ ***noun*** [pl.] the furniture, carpets, curtains, etc. in a room, house, etc.

★**fur·ni·ture** /ˈfərnɪtʃər/ ***noun*** [U] the movable things, e.g. tables, chairs, beds, etc. in a room, house or office: *modern/antique/secondhand furniture*

NOTE Be careful. "Furniture" is an uncountable noun: *We need some new furniture.* If we are talking about an individual item, we must say "a piece of furniture": *The only nice piece of furniture in the room was an antique desk.*

**fur·row** /ˈfəroʊ/ ***noun*** [C] **1** a line in a field that is made by a plow **2** a line in a person's face, especially on the forehead

**fur·ry** /ˈfəri/ ***adj.*** (**fur·ri·er**; **fur·ri·est**) **1** covered with FUR (1): *a small furry animal* **2** having a soft surface like fur: *green furry leaves*

★**fur·ther**[1] /ˈfərðər/ ***adj.*** **1** more; additional: *Are there any further questions?* ◇ *Let us know if you require any further information.* ◇ *The museum is closed until further notice* (= until another announcement is made). **2** more distant or far; farther: *Which is further from school: my house or yours?* ➲ Look at the note at **further**[2](3).

**fur·ther**[2] /ˈfərðər/ ***adv.*** **1** more; to a greater degree: *The board needs time to consider the matter further.* **2** at or to a greater distance in time: *I can't remember any further back than 1990.* **3** at or to a greater distance in space; farther: *It's not safe to go any further.* ◇ *The hospital is further down the road on the left.*

NOTE Some speakers of American English believe that only **farther** should be used when you are talking about distance in space: *I jumped farther than you did.* However, many people also use **further** when talking about distances, especially in informal conversation: *Boston is further/farther from New York than New Haven is.* Only **further** can be used in other senses: *We need a further week to finish the project.*

IDM **further afield** → FAR AFIELD

**fur·ther**[3] /ˈfərðər/ ***verb*** [T] (*formal*) to help sth to be successful: *to further the cause of peace*

**fur·ther·more** /ˈfərðərmɔr/ ***adv.*** (*formal*) in addition; also: *We are donating $6 million to the disaster fund. Furthermore, we will send medical supplies immediately.*

★**fur·thest** /ˈfərðəst/ ***adj.***, ***adv.*** **1** to the greatest degree: *Anne has progressed the furthest of all the children in her class.* **2** = FARTHEST

**fur·tive** /ˈfərt̬ɪv/ ***adj.*** secret, acting as though you are trying to hide sth because you feel guilty: *a furtive glance* ▸ **fur·tive·ly** ***adv.***: *He crept furtively out the front door.*

**fu·ry** /ˈfyʊri/ ***noun*** [U] very great anger: *She was speechless with fury.* ➲ adjective **furious**

**fuse**[1] /fyuz/ ***noun*** [C] **1** a (long) piece of rope, string, etc. that is used for lighting a bomb, etc. **2** a device that makes a bomb, etc. explode at a particular time **3** a small piece of wire in an electrical system, machine, etc. that melts and breaks if there is too much power. This stops the flow of electricity and prevents fire or damage: *You'll blow a fuse if you turn on all the appliances at once.* ◇ *Do you know how to change a fuse?* ➲ Look at **circuit breaker**.

**fuse**[2] /fyuz/ ***verb*** [I,T] to join (sth) together: *Sadness and joy are fused in her poems.*

**fu·se·lage** /ˈfyusəlɑʒ/ ***noun*** [C] the main outer part of an airplane (not the engines, wings or tail)

**fu·sion** /ˈfyuʒn/ ***noun*** [C,U] the joining together of different things: *the fusion of two political systems* ◇ *nuclear fusion* (= a method of releasing nuclear energy)

**fuss**[1] /fʌs/ ***noun*** **1** [sing., U] unnecessary nervous excitement or activity: *The kids brushed their teeth and went to bed without any fuss at all.* ◇ *What's all the fuss about?* **2** [sing.] a time when people are angry: *There will be an awful fuss if my parents find out that I borrowed the car.*

IDM **make, raise, etc. a fuss (about/over sth)** to complain strongly

**make a fuss over sb/sth** to pay a lot of attention to sb/sth

**fuss**[2] /fʌs/ ***verb*** [I] **1** to be worried or excited about small things: *Quit fussing. We're not going to be late.* **2 fuss over sb/sth** to pay too much attention to sb/sth: *to fuss over details*

**fuss·y** /ˈfʌsi/ ***adj.*** (**fuss·i·er**; **fuss·i·est**) (used about people) giving too much attention to small details and therefore difficult to please: *He is a very fussy eater* (= there are many things which he does not eat).

**fu·tile** /ˈfyut̬l/ ***adj.*** (used about an action) having no effect or result; useless: *They made a last futile attempt to persuade him.* ▸ **fu·til·i·ty** /fyuˈtɪlət̬i/ ***noun*** [U]: *the futility of war*

**fu·ton** /ˈfutɑn/ ***noun*** [C] a piece of furniture with a wooden frame and a thin cushion that can be folded and used to sit on, or opened and used as a bed

★**fu·ture**[1] /ˈfyutʃər/ ***noun*** **1** [sing.] the time that will come after the present: *Who knows what will happen in the future?* ◇ *in the near/distant future* (= soon/not soon) ◇ *in the immediate future* (= very soon) **2** [C] what will happen to sb/sth in the time after the present: *The company's future does not look very hopeful.* **3** [U] the possibility of being successful: *I could see no future in this country, so I left to work abroad.* **4** [sing.] (*also* **future tense**) (*grammar*) the tense of a verb that expresses what will happen after the present

★**fu·ture**[2] /ˈfyutʃər/ ***adj.*** (only *before* a noun) of or happening in the time after the present: *She met her future husband when she was still in school.* ◇ *You can keep that book for future reference* (= to look at again later). ◇ *What are your future plans?*

**fu·tur·is·tic** /ˌfyutʃəˈrɪstɪk/ ***adj.*** **1** extremely modern and unusual in appearance, as if belonging to a future time: *futuristic design/furniture* **2** imagining what the future will be like: *a futuristic novel/movie*

**fuzz** /fʌz/ ***noun*** [U] short, thin hairs or threads: *You have some fuzz on your shirt.*

**fuzz·y** /ˈfʌzi/ ***adj.*** (**fuzz·i·er**; **fuzz·i·est**) **1** covered with fuzz: *a fuzzy teddy bear* **2** not clear: *Can you adjust the TV? The picture's kind of fuzzy.*

**FYI** ***abbr.*** (*written*) (used in writing to mean "for your information")

F

# Gg

**G, g** /dʒi/ ***noun*** [C,U] (*pl.* **G's; g's**) the seventh letter of the English alphabet: *"Girl" begins with (a) "G."*

**G** /dʒi/ ***abbr.*** general audience; used to say that a movie can be seen by anyone, including children

**g** ***abbr.*** = GRAM

**ga·ble** /ˈgeɪbl/ ***noun*** [C] the pointed part at the top of an outside wall between two parts of a roof

**gadg·et** /ˈgædʒət/ ***noun*** [C] (*informal*) a small tool or machine

**gag¹** /gæg/ ***noun*** [C] **1** a piece of cloth, etc. that is put in or over sb's mouth in order to stop him/her from talking **2** a joke or funny story

**gag²** /gæg/ ***verb*** (**gag·ging; gagged**) **1** [T] to put a gag in or over sb's mouth: (*figurative*) *The new laws are an attempt to gag the press.* **2** [I] **gag (on sth)** to feel as if you cannot swallow and as if you are going to bring food from your stomach into your throat: *to gag on a piece of raw fish*

**gag·gle** /ˈgægl/ ***noun*** [C] a group of noisy people: *a gaggle of tourists*

**ˈgag ˌorder** ***noun*** [C] an official document which forbids lawyers, journalists, etc. to speak about sth in public: *The judge issued a gag order.*

**gai·e·ty** /ˈgeɪəṭi/ ***noun*** [U] a feeling of happiness and fun ➲ adjective gay

**gai·ly** /ˈgeɪli/ ***adv.*** in a GAY (2) manner

**gain¹** /geɪn/ ***noun*** **1** [C,U] an increase in money; (a) profit or advantage: *Shares in software companies have made big gains on the stock market.* ◇ *Everything he did was for personal gain.* **2** [C] an increase in size, amount or power: *a gain in weight of one pound*

★**gain²** /geɪn/ ***verb*** **1** [T] to get or win sth (especially sth that is wanted or needed): *They managed to gain access to secret information.* ◇ *He has gained an international reputation as an artist.* **2** [T] to get more of sth: *The train was gaining speed.* ◇ *I've gained a lot of weight recently.* **3** [I] **gain by/from (doing) sth** to get an advantage from sth/from doing sth: *Many people will gain from the changes in the law.* ◇ *I have nothing to gain by staying in this job.* **4** [T] (used about a clock or watch) to go too fast and show the incorrect time: *My watch gains five minutes a day.* ➲ When a clock gains time we say it is **fast**. OPP The opposite for **2**, **3** and **4** is **lose**.

IDM **gain ground** to make progress; to become stronger or more popular: *The Republican Party gained some ground in the recent elections.*

PHR V **gain in sth** to get more of sth: *He's gained in confidence in the past year.*

**gain on sb/sth** to get closer to sb/sth that you are trying to catch

**gait** /geɪt/ ***noun*** [sing.] the way that a person or an animal walks

**gal** /gæl/ ***noun*** [C] (*informal, old-fashioned*) a girl or woman

**ga·la** /ˈgeɪlə; ˈgælə/ ***noun*** [C] a special social occasion: *a gala performance for charity*

**gal·ax·y** /ˈgæləksi/ ***noun*** [C] (*pl.* **gal·ax·ies**) a large group of stars and planets in outer space ▸ **ga·lac·tic** /gəˈlæktɪk/ ***adj.***

**gale** /geɪl/ ***noun*** [C] a very strong wind ➲ Look at the note at **storm**.

**gall** /gɔl/ ***noun*** [C] rude behavior showing a lack of respect which is surprising because the person doing it is not embarrassed: *"... and then they had the gall to complain!"*

**gall.** ***abbr.*** = GALLON

**gal·lant** /ˈgælənt/ ***adj.*** (*formal*) **1** brave: *a gallant soldier* **2** /gəˈlænt; -ˈlɑnt; ˈgælənt/ (used about men) polite to and showing special respect for women ▸ **gal·lant·ry** /ˈgæləntri/ ***noun*** [U]

**ˈgall ˌbladder** ***noun*** [C] an organ in the body which holds a substance which helps break down the food you eat (**bile**)

**gal·ler·y** /ˈgæləri/ ***noun*** [C] (*pl.* **gal·ler·ies**) **1** a building or room where works of art are shown to the public: *an art gallery* **2** a raised area around the sides or at the back of a large hall, theater, etc. People can sit in the gallery and watch what is happening below: *the public gallery in the Senate* **3** = PORCH

**gal·ley** /ˈgæli/ ***noun*** [C] the kitchen on a ship or an airplane

**gal·lon** /ˈgælən/ ***noun*** [C] (*abbr.* **gall.**) a unit for measuring liquid. In the U.S. it is equal to about 3.8 liters. In Canada, Britain and other countries, it is equal to about 4.5 liters. ➲ There are 4 **quarts** in a gallon.

**gal·lop¹** /ˈgæləp/ ***verb*** [I] (used about a horse or a rider) to go at the fastest speed, when the horse's four feet all leave the ground together

**gal·lop²** /ˈgæləp/ ***noun*** [sing., C] the fastest speed of a horse, etc.; a time when you ride at this speed: *They went for a gallop over the fields.*

**gal·lows** /ˈgæloʊz/ ***noun*** [C] (*pl.* **gal·lows**) a wooden framework on which criminals are hanged

**ga·lore** /gəˈlɔr/ ***adv.*** (*old-fashioned*) (only *after* a noun) in large numbers: *There will be bargains galore at our super sale on Saturday.*

**gal·va·nize** /ˈgælvənaɪz/ ***verb*** [T] (*written*) **galvanize sb (into sth/into doing sth)** to make sb take action by shocking him/her or by making him/her excited: *The urgency of his voice* ***galvanized them into action.***

**gam·bit** /ˈgæmbət/ ***noun*** [C] a thing that sb does, or sth that sb says at the beginning of a situation or conversation that is intended to give him/her some advantage: *an* ***opening gambit*** (the first thing you say)

★**gam·ble¹** /ˈgæmbl/ ***verb*** [I,T] to risk money on the result of a card game, horse race, etc.: *He spent every evening gambling at poker.* ◇ *She gambled $25 on the last race.*

PHR V **gamble on sth/on doing sth** to act in the hope that sth will happen although it is possible that it will not: *I wouldn't gamble on the weather staying nice like this.*

**gam·ble²** /ˈgæmbl/ ***noun*** [C] something you do that is a risk (i.e. you might win sth but you might also lose): *Setting up this business was a real gamble.*

IDM **take a gamble (on sth)** to take a chance (on sth or on sth happening)

▸ **gam·bler** ***noun*** [C]: *He's always been a gambler.*

▸ **gam·bling** ***noun*** [U]: *an addiction to gambling*

★**game¹** /geɪm/ ***noun*** **1** [C] a form of play or a sport with rules; a time when you play it: *Let's have a game of chess.* ◇ *a game of football/baseball/tennis* ◇ *Our next game is against the Boston Eagles.* ◇ *Tonight's game is between Toronto and Montreal.* ◇ *What an exciting game!* ◇ *The game ended in a tie.* **2** [C] a unit in a match of tennis, etc.: *Hewitt won the first game of the second set.* **3** [C] the set of equipment that you need in order to play a particular (indoor) game: *We usually buy a new board game each year.*

IDM **the name of the game** → NAME¹

**be ahead of the game** to come out of a situation better off than you were before, or than you could have expected to be

**game²** /geɪm/ ***adj.*** (used about a person) ready and willing to do sth new, unusual, difficult, etc.: *I have never been sailing, but I'm game to try.*

**game³** /geɪm/ ***noun*** [U] wild animals or birds that are hunted for sport or food: *Shooting game is popular in Montana.* ◇ *big game* (= lions/tigers that are hunted)

**ˈgame plan** ***noun*** [C] a plan for success in the future, especially in sport, politics or business

**ˈgame show** ***noun*** [C] a television program in which people play games or answer questions in order to win prizes: *a game show host*

**gam·ma** /ˈgæmə/ ***noun*** (*symbol* Γ, γ) the third letter of the Greek alphabet ➲ Look at the note at **fraternity**.

**gam·ut** /ˈgæmət/ ***noun*** [sing.] all the possible kinds of a particular kind of thing

**gan·der** /ˈgændər/ ***noun*** [C] the male of a kind of bird similar to a duck (goose)

**gang¹** /gæŋ/ ***noun*** [C] **1** an organized group of criminals, especially young men: *a gang member* ◇ *to join a gang* ◇ *inner-city gang warfare* **2** a group of prisoners who work together as a team: *a chain gang* (= prisoners who are connected by a chain around their legs) **3** (*informal*) a group of (young) friends: *The whole gang is here tonight.*

**gang²** /gæŋ/ ***verb*** (*informal*)

PHR V **gang up on sb** to join together with other people in order to act against sb: *I felt like all my friends were ganging up on me.*

**gang·bust·ers** /ˈgæŋˌbʌstərz/ ***noun*** [pl.]

IDM **like gangbusters** (*informal*) very quickly: *The economy is growing like gangbusters.*

**gang·land** /ˈgæŋlænd/ ***noun*** [sing.] the world of organized and violent crime: *gangland killings* ◇ *gangland-style shooting*

**gan·gling** /ˈgæŋglɪŋ/ ***adj.*** about a person, tall and thin: *a gangling teenager*

**gan·grene** /ˈgæŋgrin; gæŋˈgrin/ ***noun*** [U] the decay of a part of the body because the blood supply to it has been stopped

**gang·ster** /ˈgæŋstər/ ***noun*** [C] a member of an organization of criminals

★**gap** /gæp/ ***noun*** [C] **a gap (in/between sth) 1** an empty space in sth or between two things: *The sheep got out through a gap in the fence.* ◇ *He has a gap between his two front teeth.* **2** an absence of sth; a space where sth should be: *There were several gaps in his story.* ◇ *I think our new product should fill a gap in the market.* ◇ *Her husband's death left a big gap in her life.* **3** a period of time that is not filled or when you are not doing what you normally do: *I returned to teaching after a gap of about five years.* ◇ *a gap in the conversation* **4** a difference between people or their ideas: *The gap between the rich and the poor is getting wider.* ◇ *the generation gap* (= the difference in opinions between parents and their children)

IDM **bridge a/the gap** → BRIDGE²

**gape** /geɪp/ ***verb*** [I] to stare at sb/sth with your mouth open

**gap·ing** /ˈgeɪpɪŋ/ ***adj.*** (used about a hole) wide open: *There was a gaping hole in the wall after the explosion.*

★**ga·rage** /gəˈrɑʒ; -ˈrɑdʒ/ ***noun*** [C] **1** a building or a part of a house where cars, etc. are kept: *The house has a two-car garage.* ➲ Picture on study page **A31**. **2** a place where you can have your car checked or repaired. It may also sell gasoline, etc.: *to take your car to the garage* ➲ Look at **gas station**.

**gaˈrage sale** ***noun*** [C] a sale, held in sb's garage, of used things that people do not want anymore ➲ Look also at **yard sale** and **rummage sale**.

**garb** /gɑrb/ ***noun*** [U] (*formal*) clothes, especially unusual clothes or those worn by a particular type of person: *military/prison garb*

★**gar·bage** /ˈgɑrbɪdʒ/ (*also* **trash**) ***noun*** [U] **1** things that you do not want anymore; waste material: *Our garbage is picked up every Monday.* ◇ *It's only garbage – throw it away.* **2** the place where you put waste material: *Throw it in the garbage.* **3** (*informal*) something that you think is bad, stupid or wrong: *I don't know why you watch that garbage on TV.*

**ˈgarbage can** (*also* **ˈtrash can**) ***noun*** [C] a container that you put waste material in ➲ picture on **page 282**.

**ˈgarbage disˌposal** (*also* **disposal**) ***noun*** [C] a machine in the kitchen which turns food into small pieces which can be washed away through the pipes

**ˈgarbage man** (*pl.* **garbage men**) ***noun*** [C] a man whose job is to take away the garbage that people put in their garbage cans

**ˈgarbage truck** ***noun*** [C] a vehicle for collecting garbage from outside houses, etc.

**gar·ban·zo** /gɑrˈbɑnzoʊ/ (*also* **garˈbanzo ˌbean**, **ˈchickpea**) ***noun*** [C] (*pl.* **gar·ban·zos**) a hard, round, yellow colored seed that is cooked and eaten as a vegetable

**garden tools**

fork trowel prong pitchfork wheelbarrow rakes hoes fork spade

G

hose watering cans scythe shears ax

**gar·bled** /ˈɡɑrbld/ ***adj.*** (used about a message, story, etc.) difficult to understand; not clear

★**gar·den¹** /ˈɡɑrdn/ ***noun*** [C] **1** a small piece of land (usually near a house) where vegetables or flowers are grown: *My grandfather planted some onions in his garden.* ◇ *a vegetable/flower garden* ◇ *a garden hose* (= that you use in the garden) ➲ Look at **yard** and **lawn**. **2** a public place with flowers, trees and other plants: *the Botanical Garden*

**gar·den²** /ˈɡɑrdn/ ***verb*** [I] to work in a garden: *She's been gardening all afternoon.*

**gar·den·er** /ˈɡɑrdnər/ ***noun*** [C] a person who works in a garden: *to hire a gardener*

**gar·den·ing** /ˈɡɑrdnɪŋ/ ***noun*** [U] taking care of a garden, e.g. planting flowers, digging, etc.: *to do some gardening*

**gar·gle** /ˈɡɑrɡl/ ***verb*** [I] to wash your throat with a liquid (which you do not swallow)

**garbage can**

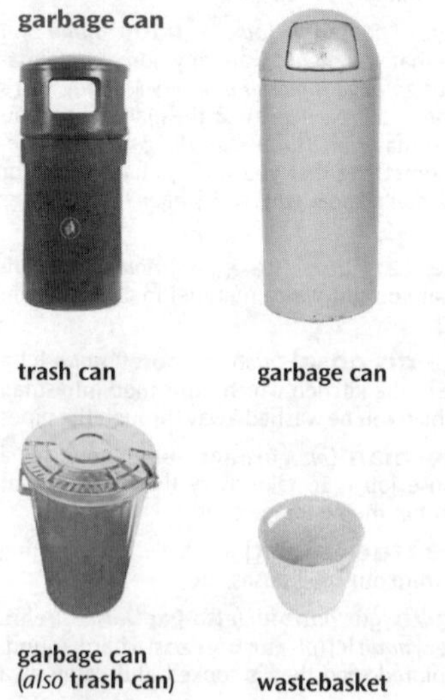

**trash can** **garbage can**

**garbage can** (*also* **trash can**) **wastebasket**

**gar·goyle** /ˈɡɑrɡɔɪl/ ***noun*** [C] an ugly figure of a person or an animal that is made of stone and through which water is carried away from the roof of a building, especially a church, in historical buildings, especially in Europe

**gar·ish** /ˈɡɛrɪʃ/ ***adj.*** too bright or highly decorated

**gar·land** /ˈɡɑrlənd/ ***noun*** [C] a circle of flowers and leaves that is worn on the head or around the neck or is hung in a room as decoration

**gar·lic** /ˈɡɑrlɪk/ ***noun*** [U] a plant with a strong taste and smell that looks like a small onion and is used in cooking: *a clove of garlic* ➲ picture on study page **A28-29**.

**gar·ment** /ˈɡɑrmənt/ ***noun*** [C] (*formal*) one piece of clothing: *This garment must be dry cleaned.*

**gar·nish¹** /ˈɡɑrnɪʃ/ ***verb*** [T] **garnish sth (with sth)** to decorate food or a plate, dish, etc. with small additional amounts of food: *a drink garnished with a slice of lemon*

**gar·nish²** /ˈɡɑrnɪʃ/ ***noun*** [C] a small amount of food that is used to decorate food or a plate, dish, etc.: *Top the potatoes with a garnish of chopped parsley.*

**gar·ri·son** /ˈɡærəsn/ ***noun*** [C] a group of soldiers who are living in and guarding a town or building

**gar·ter** /ˈɡɑrt̬ər/ ***noun*** [C] a band, usually made of elastic, that is worn around the leg to keep up a sock, or the piece of clothing that women wear on their legs with skirts (**stocking**)

★**gas¹** /ɡæs/ ***noun*** (*pl.* **gas·es**)
➤NOT SOLID/LIQUID **1** [C,U] a substance that is like air (i.e. not solid or liquid): *Hydrogen and oxygen are gases.* **2** [U] a GAS (1) or mixture of gases that is used for heating, cooking, etc.: *Does your clothes dryer run on gas or electricity?* ◇ *a gas stove* ◇ *natural gas* ◇ *The explosion was caused by a gas leak.* **3** [U] a poisonous GAS (1) that is used in war ➲ Look also at **tear gas**.
➤IN VEHICLE **4** [U] (*also* **gasoline**) the liquid that is used as fuel for motor vehicles such as cars, trucks, and motorcycles: *a gas pump* ◇ *to fill up the gas tank*

➤IN STOMACH **5** [U] gas (1) that forms in your stomach: *I've got terrible gas.*

**gas²** /gæs/ ***verb*** [T] (**gas·sing**; **gassed**) to poison or kill sb with gas

**'gas ˌchamber** ***noun*** [C] a room that can be filled with poisonous gas in order to kill animals or people

**gas·e·ous** /'gæsiəs; 'gæʃəs/ ***adj.*** (usually before a noun) like or containing a gas: *a gaseous mixture* ◇ *in gaseous form*

**gash** /gæʃ/ ***noun*** [C] a long deep cut or wound: *He had an awful gash in his arm.*

**'gas mask** ***noun*** [C] a piece of equipment that you wear over your face to protect you against poisonous gas

**gas·o·line** /ˌgæsə'lin; 'gæsəlin/ ***noun*** [U] = GAS¹ (4)

**gasp¹** /gæsp/ ***verb*** **1** [I] to breathe quickly and noisily (e.g. when you have been running fast): *At the end of the race, some of the runners were gasping for breath.* **2** [I] **gasp (at sth)** to breathe in suddenly and noisily because you are surprised or in pain: *She gasped in surprise as she read the letter.* **3** [T] to say sth while you are finding it difficult to breathe: *"I can't go on," he gasped. "I've got to sit down."*

**gasp²** /gæsp/ ***noun*** [C] a quick breath (when you are surprised, in pain, etc.): *Suddenly she gave a gasp of surprise.*

**'gas ˌpedal** ***noun*** [C] (*informal*) = ACCELERATOR: *to step on the gas pedal*

★**'gas ˌstation** ***noun*** [C] a place where you can buy gasoline and other things for your car

**gas·tric** /'gæstrɪk/ ***adj.*** (only before a noun) (*medical*) connected with the stomach: *a gastric ulcer* ◇ *gastric flu*

**gas·tro·nom·ic** /ˌgæstrə'nɑmɪk/ ***adj.*** connected with (good) food: *the gastronomic delights of Italy*

★**gate** /geɪt/ ***noun*** [C] **1** a movable structure (like a door) that closes an opening in a wall, fence, etc.: *Please keep the front gate closed.* ➲ picture at **hedge**. **2** (*also* **'gateway**) an opening in a wall, fence, hedge, etc. that is closed by a GATE (1): *Drive through the gates and you'll find the parking lot on the right.* **3** an entrance or exit at an airport: *Flight 139 to Geneva is now boarding at gate 16.*

**gate·crash·er** /'geɪtˌkræʃər/ ***noun*** [C] a person who comes to a party or other event, even though he/she has not been invited

**gate·way** /'geɪtweɪ/ ***noun*** [C] **1** = GATE (2) **2** [sing.] **gateway to sth** the place through which you have to pass through in order to get to somewhere else: (*figurative*) *A good education can be the gateway to success.*

★**gath·er** /'gæðər/ ***verb***

➤COME/BRING TOGETHER **1** [I,T] **gather around (sb/sth)**; **gather sb/sth around (sb/sth)** (used about people) to come together in a group; to make people come together: *A crowd soon gathered at the scene of the accident.* ◇ *The kids were gathered in a group around the teacher's desk.* **2** [T] **gather sth (together/up)** to bring many things together; to collect: *They gathered up all their picnic things and headed home.* ◇ *They have gathered together a lot of information on the subject.* ◇ *I need some time to gather my thoughts before I can give you an answer.*

➤PLANTS/FRUITS **3** [T] to collect plants, fruits, etc.

➤BELIEVE/UNDERSTAND **4** [T] to understand or find out sth (from sb/sth): *I gather from your letter that you have several years' experience in this kind of work.* ◇ *"She's been very sick recently." "So I gather."*

➤CLOTHING **5** [T] to pull material together into small folds and sew it: *a gathered skirt*

➤INCREASE **6** [I,T] to become greater or to make greater; to increase: *The train is gathering speed.* ◇ *In the gathering darkness, it was hard to see the ball.*

**gath·er·ing** /'gæðərɪŋ/ ***noun*** [C] a time when people come together; a meeting: *a family gathering*

**ga·tor** /'geɪt̬ər/ ***noun*** [C] = ALLIGATOR

**gauche** /goʊʃ/ ***adj.*** often saying or doing the wrong thing when dealing with people: *a gauche manner*

**gaud·y** /'gɔdi/ ***adj.*** (**gaud·i·er**; **gaud·i·est**) too bright or highly decorated

**gauge¹** /geɪdʒ/ ***noun*** [C] **1** an instrument for measuring the amount of sth: *a gas gauge on a car* (= to show how much gasoline is left) **2** a measurement of the width of certain things: *a narrow-gauge railroad* ◇ *a 12-gauge shotgun* **3** a fact that you can use to judge a situation, sb's feelings, etc.

**gauge²** /geɪdʒ/ ***verb*** [T] **1** to measure sth **2** to judge a situation, sb's feelings, etc.: *It was difficult to gauge the mood of the audience.*

**gaunt** /gɔnt/ ***adj.*** (used about a person) very thin because of hunger, illness, etc.

**gauze** /gɔz/ ***noun*** [U] thin material (often used for covering wounds)

**gave** *past tense of* GIVE¹

**gawk** /gɔk/ ***verb*** [I] (*informal*) **gawk (at sb/sth)** to look or stare (at sb/sth) in a stupid way (with your mouth open)

**gay** /geɪ/ ***adj.*** **1** sexually attracted to people of the same sex; homosexual: *He told me he was gay.* ◇ *the gay community* **2** (*old-fashioned*) happy and full of fun ➲ noun for sense 2, **gaiety** ➲ adverb for sense 2, **gaily**

**gays** /geɪz/ ***noun*** [pl.] people, especially men, who are sexually attracted to people of the same sex; homosexuals: *a club for lesbians and gays*

> NOTE It is considered very rude and offensive to use the noun form **gay** to refer to a particular person. We use the adjective form instead: *a gay man*

**gaze¹** /geɪz/ ***verb*** [I] to look steadily for a long time: *Stop gazing out the window.*

**gaze²** /geɪz/ ***noun*** [sing.] a long steady look: *The cat kept its gaze fixed on the bird.*

**GB** (*also* **Gb**) ***noun*** [C] (*written*) = GIGABYTE

**GDP** /ˌdʒi di 'pi/ ***noun*** [C] the abbreviation for "gross domestic product"; the total value of all the goods and services produced by a country in one year ➲ Compare **GNP**.

★**gear¹** /gɪr/ ***noun*** **1** [C] one of a set of wheels that fits into another set in order to pass power from one part of a machine to another, e.g. from a car's

G

engine to its wheels: *My bike chain slipped off the gears.* **2** [U] a particular position of the GEARS (1)(on a bicycle, in a car, etc.): *You can't pedal up that hill in fifth gear!*

NOTE A car can be **in** or **out of** gear. You use a **low** gear (**first** gear) when you first start moving and then **shift** gears as you go faster. For the fastest speeds, you use **high** gear. ➲ Look also at the note at **transmission**.

**3** [U] equipment or clothing that you need for a particular activity, etc.: *camping gear* **4** [sing.] (in compounds) an instrument or part of a machine that is used for a particular purpose: *the landing gear of an airplane*

G

**gear**[2] /gɪr/ ***verb***

PHRV **gear sth for/to/toward sth** (often passive) to make sth suitable for a particular purpose: *There is a special course geared toward older students.*

**gear up (for sb/sth); gear sb/sth up (for sb/sth)** to get ready or to make sb/sth ready: *I was all geared up for the party, but it was canceled at the last minute.*

**gear·shift** /ˈgɪrʃɪft/ ***noun*** [C] a stick that is used for changing GEARS[1] (2)(in a car, etc.)

**GED** /ˌdʒi i ˈdi/ ***noun*** [C] general equivalency diploma; an official certificate that people who did not finish high school can get, after taking classes and passing an examination: *I'm going to night school so I can get my GED.*

**gee** /dʒi/ ***interjection*** (*informal*) (used for expressing surprise, pleasure, etc.): *Gee, I'm sorry. I didn't know your dad died.*

**geek** /gik/ ***noun*** [C] (*slang*) a person who is not popular because he/she behaves in a strange way: *Clarence is such a total geek – he never bathes and he picks his nose in class!* ➲ Look at **nerd**. ▸ **geek·y** ***adj.***

**geese** ***noun*** [C] *plural of* GOOSE

**gei·ger count·er** /ˈgaɪgər ˌkaʊntər/ ***noun*** [C] a device for measuring if sth is producing a kind of dangerous ray (radiation)

**gel** /dʒɛl/ ***noun*** [C,U] (often in compounds) a thick substance like jelly that is between a liquid and a solid: *hair gel*

**gel·a·tin** (*also* **gelatine**) /ˈdʒɛlətn; -tən/ ***noun*** [U] **1** = JELL-O™ **2** a powder that is used in making desserts, etc. It is added to liquids to make them firm: *Dissolve one packet of unflavored gelatin in a cup of boiling water.*

**gem** /dʒɛm/ ***noun*** [C] **1** a jewel or precious stone **2** a person or thing that has great value

**Gem·i·ni** /ˈdʒɛmənaɪ; -ni/ ***noun*** [C,U] the third sign of the Zodiac, the Twins; a person who was born under this sign

**Gen.** ***abbr.*** = GENERAL[2]

**gen·der** /ˈdʒɛndər/ ***noun*** [C,U] **1** (*formal*) the classification of people into two sexes: male and female **2** (*grammar*) (in some languages) the classification of nouns, pronouns, etc. into masculine, feminine and neuter; one of these divisions: *There are three genders in German.* ◇ *In French the adjective must agree with the noun in number and gender.*

**gene** /dʒin/ ***noun*** [C] one of the parts of a cell of a living thing which decide its development. Genes are passed from parents to children. In human beings they decide, for example, the size of a child or the color of his/her eyes. ➲ adjective genetic

★**gen·er·al**[1] /ˈdʒɛnərəl; ˈdʒɛnrəl/ ***adj.*** **1** affecting all or most people, places, things, etc.: *a matter of general interest* ◇ *The general feeling is that the situation is improving* (= most people think so). ◇ *the general public* (= most ordinary people) **2** (only *before* a noun) not limited to, or describing, one particular part; not detailed: *Your general health is very good.* ◇ *The introduction gives you a general idea of what the book is about.* ◇ *Let's talk in general terms at first and then get down to details.* **3** not limited to one subject or area of study; not specialized: *Children need a good general education.* ◇ *The quiz tests your general knowledge.* ◇ *a general hospital* **4** (often in compounds) with responsibility for the whole of an organization: *The Secretary General of the United Nations* ◇ *the Surgeon General* (= the chief medical officer for the government) ◇ *a general manager*

IDM **in general** in most cases; usually: *In general, test scores are improving*

**gen·er·al**[2] /ˈdʒɛnərəl; ˈdʒɛnrəl/ ***noun*** [C] (*abbr.* **Gen.**) an army officer of very high rank: *General Roberts*

**ˌgeneral anesˈthetic** ***noun*** [C,U] a substance that is given to a patient in the hospital before an operation so that he/she becomes unconscious and does not feel any pain ➲ Look at **local anesthetic**.

**gen·er·al·i·za·tion** /ˌdʒɛnrələˈzeɪʃn; ˌdʒɛnərəl-/ ***noun*** [C] a general statement about sth that does not consider details

**gen·er·al·ize** /ˈdʒɛnrəlaɪz; ˈdʒɛnərəl-/ ***verb*** [I] **1 generalize (about sth)** to form an opinion using only a small amount of information: *You can't generalize about Italian food after only two meals.* **2 generalize (about sth)** to make a general statement about sth and not look at the details: *You're generalizing. Every case is different.*

**gen·er·al·ized** /ˈdʒɛnrəlaɪzd; ˈdʒɛnərəl-/ ***adj.*** found or happening over a large area; affecting a large number of people: *a generalized effort to reduce poverty*

★**gen·er·al·ly** /ˈdʒɛnərəli; ˈdʒɛnrəli/ ***adv.*** **1** usually: *She generally drives to work.* **2** by most people: *He is generally considered a good doctor.* **3** in a general sense, without looking at the details: *Generally speaking, houses in North America have big back yards.*

**ˌgeneral ˈstore** ***noun*** [C] (*old-fashioned*) a small store, especially in a very small town or in the country, that sells many different types of things

**gen·er·ate** /ˈdʒɛnəreɪt/ ***verb*** [T] **1** to produce power, heat, electricity, etc. **2** to cause sth to exist: *I think this new product will generate a lot of income for the company.*

★**gen·er·a·tion** /ˌdʒɛnəˈreɪʃn/ ***noun*** **1** [U] the act of generating: *the generation of electricity by burning coal* **2** [C] one stage in a family history: *This picture shows three generations of my family* (= children, parents and grandparents). **3** [C] all the people in a group or country who were born at about the same time: *My grandmother's generation didn't have*

*TV when they were young.* ◇ *future generations* ◇ *The younger generation only seems to be interested in money.* **4** [C] a period of about 25 or 30 years (i.e. the time that a person takes to become an adult): *A generation ago, foreign travel was still only possible for a few people.*

**gener'ation gap** ***noun*** [sing.] the difference in behavior, and the lack of understanding, between young people and older people, or between people of two different generations

**ˌGeneration 'X** ***noun*** [U] the group of people who were born between the early 1960s and the middle of the 1970s, who seem to lack a sense of direction in life and to feel that they have no part to play in society

**ˌGeneration 'Y** ***noun*** [U] the group of people who were born in the 1980s and the 1990s, who have grown up using computers, the Internet, etc.

**gen·er·a·tor** /'dʒɛnəˌreɪṭər/ ***noun*** [C] a machine that produces electricity

**ge·ner·ic** /dʒə'nɛrɪk/ ***adj.*** **1** (used about a product) without a special name that was given by the company that made it: *It's cheaper to buy the generic pills.* **2** describing a general type of sth, not one thing in particular: *a diagram of a generic engine*

**gen·er·os·i·ty** /ˌdʒɛnə'rɑsəṭi/ ***noun*** [U] the quality of being generous

**gen·er·ous** /'dʒɛnərəs/ ***adj.*** **1** willing to give more money, help, etc. than is usual or necessary: *It was very generous of your parents to loan us all that money.* **2** larger than usual: *The recipe makes four generous servings.* ▸ **gen·er·ous·ly** ***adv.***: *Please give generously.*

**gen·e·sis** /'dʒɛnəsəs/ ***noun*** [sing.] the beginning or origin of sth

**ge·net·ic** /dʒə'nɛṭɪk/ ***adj.*** connected with the parts of cells in living things that decide their development (genes) or genetics: *The disease is caused by a genetic defect.* ▸ **ge·net·i·cal·ly** /-kli/ ***adv.***

**geˌnetically 'modified** ***adj.*** (*abbr.* **GM**) (used about food, plants, etc.) that has been grown from cells whose units of information (genes) have been changed artificially

**geˌnetic engi'neering** ***noun*** [U] changes made by scientists in the genetic structure of plants and animals

**ge·net·ics** /dʒə'nɛṭɪks/ ***noun*** [U] the scientific study of the way that the development of living things is controlled by features that have been passed on from parents to children ➲ Look at **gene**.

**gen·ial** /'dʒinyəl; 'dʒiniəl/ ***adj.*** (used about a person) pleasant and friendly

**ge·nie** /'dʒini/ ***noun*** [C] (*pl.* **ge·nies**; **ge·ni·i** /-niaɪ/) (in Arabian stories) a spirit with magic powers, especially one that lives in a bottle or a lamp

**gen·i·tals** /'dʒɛnəṭlz/ ***noun*** [pl.] (*formal*) the external sex organs ▸ **gen·i·tal** /'dʒɛnəṭl/ ***adj.***

**gen·ius** /'dʒinyəs/ ***noun*** (*pl.* **gen·ius·es**) **1** [U] very great and unusual ability: *Shakespeare's tragedies show true genius.* **2** [C] a person who has very great and unusual ability, especially in a particular subject: *Einstein was a mathematical genius.* **3** [sing.] **a genius for (doing) sth** great natural ability for (doing) sth: *Our teacher had a genius for explaining difficult things in a simple way.*

**gen·o·cide** /'dʒɛnəsaɪd/ ***noun*** [U] the murder of a nation or race

**ge·nome** /'dʒinoʊm/ ***noun*** [C] the complete set of information units (genes) in a cell or living thing: *the human genome*

**gen·re** /'ʒɑnrə/ ***noun*** [C] a particular type of literature, art, etc.

**gent** /dʒɛnt/ ***noun*** [C] (*informal*) a gentleman

**gen·teel** /dʒɛn'til/ ***adj.*** paying great (perhaps too much) attention to polite manners ▸ **gen·til·i·ty** /dʒɛn'tɪləṭi/ ***noun*** [U]

G

**gen·tile** /'dʒɛntaɪl/ ***noun*** [C] a person who is not Jewish ▸ **gen·tile** ***adj.*** (only before a noun)

★**gen·tle** /'dʒɛntəl/ ***adj.*** **1** (used about people) kind; calm; touching or treating people or things in a careful way so that they are not hurt: *He was a gentle, patient man who loved playing with his grandchildren.* ◇ *"I'll be as gentle as I can," the dentist said.* **2** not rough or violent: *A gentle breeze was blowing through the trees.* ◇ *a gentle* (= not sharp) *curve in the road* ▸ **gen·tle·ness** ***noun*** [U] ▸ **gen·tly** /'dʒɛntli/ ***adv.***: *He touched her gently on the shoulder.* ◇ *The beach slopes gently down to the ocean.*

★**gen·tle·man** /'dʒɛntəlmən/ ***noun*** [C] (*pl.* **gen·tle·men** /-mən/) **1** a man who is polite and who behaves well toward other people and (especially in former times) who is rich and has a high social position: *He is a real gentleman.* **2** (*formal*) (used when speaking to or about a man or men in a polite way): *Ladies and gentlemen!* (e.g. at the beginning of a speech)

★**gen·u·ine** /'dʒɛnyuən/ ***adj.*** **1** a person or thing that is genuine is exactly what he/she/it seems to be; real: *He thought that he had bought a genuine Rolex watch, but it was a cheap fake.* **2** (used about a person or his/her feelings or behavior) honest; real: *She seems genuine enough, but can I trust her?* ▸ **gen·u·ine·ly** ***adv.***: *I'm genuinely interested in a career in teaching.*

**ge·nus** /'dʒinəs/ ***noun*** [C] (*pl.* **gen·er·a** /'dʒɛnərə/) a group into which animals, plants, etc. that have similar characteristics are divided

**ge·og·ra·pher** /dʒi'ɑgrəfər/ ***noun*** [C] a student of or an expert in geography

**ge·og·ra·phy** /dʒi'ɑgrəfi/ ***noun*** [U] **1** the study of the countries of the world, of their natural and physical features and of the cities, industries, etc. that have been made by people **2** the way in which the features of a particular country or place are arranged: *We're studying the geography of Asia.* ▸ **ge·o·graph·ic** /ˌdʒiə'græfɪk/ (*also* **ge·o·graph·i·cal** /-ɪkl/) ***adj.*** ▸ **ge·o·graph·i·cal·ly** /-kli/ ***adv.***

**ge·ol·o·gist** /dʒi'ɑlədʒɪst/ ***noun*** [C] a student of or an expert in geology

**ge·ol·o·gy** /dʒi'ɑlədʒi/ ***noun*** [U] the study of rocks and soil, and of their development ▸ **ge·o·log·i·cal** /dʒiə'lɑdʒɪkl/ ***adj.***

**ge·o·met·ric** /dʒiə'mɛtrɪk/ (*also* **ge·o·met·ri·cal** /-ɪkl/) ***adj.*** **1** of geometry **2** consisting of regular shapes and lines: *a geometric design/pattern* ▶ **ge·o·met·ri·cal·ly** /-kli/ ***adv.***

**ge·om·e·try** /dʒi'ɑmətri/ ***noun*** [U] the study in mathematics of lines, shapes, curves, etc.

**ge·ra·ni·um** /dʒə'reɪniəm/ ***noun*** [C] a garden plant with a mass of red, pink or white flowers

**ger·bil** /'dʒərbl/ ***noun*** [C] a small desert animal like a mouse, that is often kept as a pet

**ger·i·at·ric** /ˌdʒɛri'ætrɪk; ˌdʒɪri-/ ***adj.*** connected with very old people

**ger·i·at·rics** /ˌdʒɛri'ætrɪks; ˌdʒɪri-/ ***noun*** [U] the branch of medicine concerned with diseases and care of old people

G

**germ** /dʒərm/ ***noun*** [C] a very small living thing that causes disease. Germs can only be seen with a microscope: *This disinfectant kills most germs.* ➲ Compare with **bacteria** and **virus**.

**Ger·man mea·sles** /ˌdʒərmən 'mizlz/ (*also* **rubella**) ***noun*** [U] a mild disease that causes red spots all over the body. It may damage an unborn baby if the mother catches it.

**Ger·man shep·herd** /ˌdʒərmən 'ʃɛpərd/ ***noun*** [C] a large dog with thick black and brown hair, that is often trained to work with the police, as a guard dog or as a guide dog for blind people

**ger·mi·nate** /'dʒərməneɪt/ ***verb*** [I,T] (used about a seed of a plant) to start growing; to cause a seed to do this ▶ **ger·mi·na·tion** /ˌdʒərmə'neɪʃn/ ***noun*** [U]

**ger·und** /'dʒɛrənd/ ***noun*** [C] (*grammar*) a noun, ending in -ing, that has been made from a verb: *In the sentence "His hobby is collecting stamps," "collecting" is a gerund.*

**ges·tic·u·late** /dʒɛ'stɪkyəleɪt/ ***verb*** [I] to make movements with your hands and arms in order to express sth

**ges·ture¹** /'dʒɛstʃər; 'dʒɛʃtʃər/ ***noun*** [C] **1** a movement of the hand, head, etc. that expresses sth: *The kid made an obscene gesture and ran away.* **2** something that you do that shows other people what you think or feel: *It would be a nice gesture to invite the neighbors over for dinner.*

**ges·ture²** /'dʒɛstʃər; 'dʒɛʃtʃər/ ***verb*** [I,T] to point at sth, to make a sign to sb: *We saw the manager speak to the boys and gesture toward the door.*

**ge·sund·heit** /gə'zʊnthaɪt/ ***interjection*** used when sb has made a sudden noise through his/her nose (a sneeze) to wish that person good health

★**get** /gɛt/ ***verb*** (*pres. part.* **get·ting**; *pt* **got** /gɑt/; *pp* except in sense 1 **got·ten** /'gɑtn/)

➤HAVE **1** [T] **have/has got** to have sth: *I've got a headache.*

> NOTE We generally do not use **have got** in questions. We usually use **have got** to emphasize the fact that sb has one thing instead of another: *"Does your brother have brown hair?" "No, he's got blond hair."* In very informal spoken English, it is possible to use **got** in questions without **have** or **has**: *"You got any money?" "Yeah, I do./No, I don't.* However, this use is not considered correct in more formal English.

➤STATE/CONDITION **2** [I] to become: *It's getting dark.* ◇ *She got angry.* **3** [I] to be in a certain situation: *He got into trouble with the police.* **4** [I] (used with a past participle) to do sth that you are responsible for: *I'm getting dressed.* ◇ *They got divorced.* **5** [I] (used in a similar way to the passive) to have sth happen to you: *She got bitten by a dog.*

➤RECEIVE/OBTAIN **6** [T] to receive or obtain sth: *I got a letter from my sister.* ◇ *He went shopping and got a suit.* ◇ *She got a job in a travel agency.* ◇ *I'll do it if I get time.* ◇ *Nina gets $10 an hour for working in her family's business.*

➤BRING **7** [T] to go and bring sth back: *Go (and) get me a pen.* ◇ *I'll get the kids from school today.*

➤UNDERSTAND **8** [T] to hear or understand sth: *Sorry, I didn't get that. Can you repeat it?* ◇ *I don't get it. Why did he buy a car when he can't drive?*

➤ILLNESS **9** [T] to catch a disease: *You can get cancer from smoking.*

➤MOVE/TRAVEL **10** [T] to use a form of transportation: *I didn't walk – I got a taxi.* **11** [I] to move somewhere; to reach a place: *We got to San Diego at about 10.* ◇ *What time will we get there?* ➲ Look at **get in**, **on**, **etc.**. **12** [T] to cause sth to be in a particular place: *We couldn't get the piano upstairs.*

➤CATCH/HIT **13** [T] (*informal*) to hurt sb as punishment for sth that he/she did to you: *I'll get you guys for making a fool of me!*

➤PERSUADE/ACHIEVE **14** [T] to cause sb/sth to do sth or to happen: *I got him to agree to the plan.* ◇ *I can't get the TV to work.* ◇ *She finally got the assignment finished.*

> NOTE Note that we also use **get** when we arrange for somebody else to do something: *You need to get the car serviced every 10,000 miles* (= at a service station).

➤OPPORTUNITY **15** [I] **get to do sth** to have the opportunity to do sth: *Did you get to go to the concert?*

IDM **get it** (*informal*) **1** to be punished: *You're gonna get it when Mom sees this mess!* **2** to understand something: *I don't get it...you'd better explain it again.*

**get somewhere/nowhere (with sb/sth)** to make some/no progress: *I'm not getting anywhere with my research.*

> NOTE For other idioms containing **get**, look at the noun and adjective entries, e.g. for **get rid of** look at **rid**.

PHRV **get sth across (to sb)** to succeed in making people understand sth: *The candidate failed to get his policies across to the voters.*

**get ahead** to progress and be successful in sth, especially a career

**get along 1** to make progress: *How are you getting along at school?* **2** to perform in a particular way or to have a good or bad experience in a particular situation: *How did you get along at your interview?*

**get along with sb**; **get along (together)** to have a friendly relationship with sb: *Do you get along well with your coworkers?* ◇ *We're not close friends, but we get along pretty well together.*

**get around 1** to move or travel to and from many places: *Calgary this week, Dallas next week – you sure get around!* **2** (used about news, a story, etc.) to spread; to become known by many people

**get around sth** to find a way of avoiding or overcoming a problem
**get around to sth/doing sth** to find the time to do sth, after a delay: *I've been meaning to reply to that letter, but I haven't gotten around to it yet.*
**get at sb** to say unkind or critical things to sb
**get at sb/sth** to succeed in reaching sb/sth: *You'll need to stand on a chair to get at the top shelf.*
**get at sth** (used only in the continuous tenses) to suggest sth indirectly; to mean sth but not to state it directly: *I'm not quite sure what you're getting at – am I doing something wrong?*
**get away (from…)** to succeed in leaving or escaping from sb or a place: *He kept talking to me and I couldn't get away from him.* ◇ *The thieves got away in a stolen car.*
**get away with sth/with doing sth** to do sth bad and not be punished for it: *He lied, but he got away with it.* ◇ *I don't know how they get away with charging such high prices.*
**get back** to return to the place where you live or work: *When did you get back from vacation?*
**get sth back** to be given sth that you had lost or lent: *Can I borrow this book? You'll get it back next week, I promise.*
**get back to sb** to speak to, write to or call sb later, especially in order to give an answer or deal with sth: *I'll get back to you when I have some more information.*
**get back to sth** to return to doing sth or talking about sth: *I woke up early and couldn't get back to sleep.* ◇ *Let's get back to the point you raised earlier.*
**get behind (on/with sth)** to fail to do or produce sth on time: *We got behind on our rent.*
**get by (on sth)** to manage, often with difficulty, to live, using a certain income: *It's very hard to get by on such a low income.*
**get by (with sth)** to manage by doing or having as little of sth as possible: *I can get by on just five hours' sleep.*
**get sb down** to make sb miserable: *These cold winter days get me down.*
**get sth down** to make a note of sth; to write sth down: *Did you get the address for the contest down?*
**get down to sth/doing sth** to start doing or concentrating on sth: *That's enough small talk – let's get down to business.*
**get in** to reach a place: *What time does your flight get in?*
**get in; get into sth** to climb into a car: *We all got in and Tim drove off.*
**get into sb** (*informal*) (used about a feeling or attitude) to start affecting sb strongly, causing the person to behave in an unusual way: *I wonder what's gotten into him – he isn't usually that mean.*
**get into sth 1** to start a particular activity; to become involved in sth: *How did you first get into the music business?* ◇ *She has gotten into the habit of turning up late.* ◇ *We got into an argument about politics.* **2** (*informal*) to become interested in sth: *She doesn't usually like sports, but recently she's been getting into basketball.*
**get off (sth) 1** to leave a bus, plane, bicycle, etc.; to climb down from a horse **2** to leave work with permission at a particular time: *I might be able to get off early today.*
**get sth off (sth)** to remove sth from sth: *Can you help me get these boots off?*
**get off on sth/doing sth** (*slang*) to get great pleasure or satisfaction from sth/doing sth: *For some reason, he gets off on criticizing people.*
**get (sb) off (with sth)** to receive little or no punishment; to help sb to receive little or no punishment: *If you're lucky, you'll get off with a small fine.* ◇ *Her lawyer was confident that he would get her off.*
**get on 1** to be getting old: *He's getting on – I'm sure he's over 60.* **2** to be getting late: *Time's getting on –we don't want to be late.*

> NOTE **Get on** is only used in the continuous tenses.

**get on/onto sth** to climb onto a bus, plane, bicycle, horse, etc.: *I got onto the wrong bus by mistake.*
**get sth on** to put on a piece of clothing: *Get your shoes on – we're going out now.*
**get onto sb (about sth)** (*informal*) to speak or write to sb about a particular matter, especially because you want him/her to do sth for you: *You should get onto the city council about that hole in the sidewalk.*
**get on with sth** to continue doing sth, especially after an interruption: *Stop talking and get on with your work!*
**get out** (used about a piece of information) to become known, having previously been secret
**get sth out (of sth)** to take sth from its container: *I got my keys out of my bag.*
**get out (of sth)** to leave or escape from a place: *My grandmother doesn't get out of the house much.*
**get out of sth/doing sth** to avoid a duty or doing sth that you have said you will do: *I said I'd go to their party, and I can't get out of it now.*
**get sth out of sb** to obtain sth from sb by force or by persuading him or her: *His parents finally got the truth out of him.*
**get sth out of sb/sth** to gain sth from sb/sth: *I get a lot of pleasure out of music.*
**get over sth** to recover from sth bad, or from an illness: *He still hasn't gotten over his wife's death.* ◇ *It took her a long time to get over her operation.* ◇ *I can't get over how mean he was!* (= I still find it surprising.)
**get sth over with** (*informal*) to do and complete sth unpleasant that has to be done: *I'll be glad to get my visit to the dentist over with.*
**get (sb) through (sth)** to be successful in sth (often sth unpleasant); to help sb to be successful: *She got through her final exams easily.* ◇ *Her kindness got me through those awful days.*
**get through (to sb) 1** to succeed in making a telephone connection with sb: *I couldn't get through to them because their phone was busy all day.* **2** to succeed in making sb understand what you are saying: *They couldn't get through to him that he was completely wrong.*
**get to sb** (*informal*) to affect sb in a bad way: *Don't let their comments get to you – just do your best.*
**get together (with sb)** to meet socially or in order to discuss or do sth: *Let's get together and talk about it.*
**get up** to rise to a standing position; to stand up: *He got up to let an elderly woman sit down.*
**get (sb) up** to get out of bed or make sb get out of

bed: *What time do you have to get up in the morning?* ◇ *Could you get me up at 6 tomorrow?*

**get up to sth** **1** to reach a particular point or stage in sth: *We've gotten up to the last section in our grammar book.* **2** to do sth, especially sth bad: *I wonder what the kids are getting up to.*

**get·a·way** /ˈgɛt̬əweɪ/ ***noun*** [C] an escape (after a crime): *to make a getaway* ◇ *a getaway car*

**ˈget-toˌgether** ***noun*** [C] (*informal*) an informal social meeting or party: *We're having a little get-together Saturday evening.*

**gey·ser** /ˈgaɪzər/ ***noun*** [C] a natural hole in the ground that suddenly sends hot water and steam up into the air with great force

G

**ghast·ly** /ˈgæstli/ ***adj.*** (**ghast·li·er**; **ghast·li·est**) **1** causing fear or shock: *a ghastly accident* **2** very bad, ugly or unpleasant: *a ghastly mistake*

**ghet·to** /ˈgɛt̬oʊ/ ***noun*** [C] (*pl.* **ghet·toes**) a part of a city where many poor people of the same race live in crowded conditions

**ˈghetto ˌblaster** /ˈgɛt̬oʊ ˌblæstər/ (*also* **ˈboom box**) ***noun*** [C] (*informal*) a radio and cassette and/or CD player that can be carried around, especially to play loud music in public

★**ghost** /goʊst/ ***noun*** [C] the spirit of a dead person that is seen or heard by sb who is still living: *I don't believe in ghosts.* ◇ *a ghost story* ▸ **ghost·ly** /ˈgoʊstli/ ***adj.***: *ghostly noises*

**ˈghost town** ***noun*** [C] a town whose inhabitants have all left

**ghost·wri·ter** /ˈgoʊstˌraɪt̬ər/ ***noun*** [C] a person who writes a book, etc. for a famous person (whose name appears as the author)

**GI** /ˌdʒi ˈaɪ/ ***noun*** [C] (*pl.* **GIs**) (*U.S.*) a soldier in the U.S. armed forces

★**gi·ant¹** /ˈdʒaɪənt/ ***noun*** [C] **1** (in children's stories) a person of human shape but very great size and strength **2** something that is very large: *the multinational oil giants* (= very large companies)

★**gi·ant²** /ˈdʒaɪənt/ ***adj.*** extremely large: *a giant new shopping center*

**gib·ber·ish** /ˈdʒɪbərɪʃ/ ***noun*** [U] words that have no meaning or that are impossible to understand: *I was so nervous during the interview that I just spoke gibberish.*

**gibe** /dʒaɪb/ = JIBE¹

**gid·dy** /ˈgɪdi/ ***adj.*** **1** (*old-fashioned*) having the feeling that everything is going around and that you are going to fall; dizzy: *I feel giddy; I have to sit down.* **2** not serious; behaving in a silly way: *After a few drinks she became giddy.*

★**gift** /gɪft/ ***noun*** **1** [C] something that you give to a person; a present: *wedding gifts* ◇ *Their teacher was presented with a gift of flowers and candy.* ◇ *They often give away a free gift with the magazine.* ➲ Look at the note at **present**. **2** [sing.] **a gift (for sth/doing sth)** natural ability: *She has a gift for languages.*

**ˈgift cerˌtificate** ***noun*** [C] a piece of paper that is often given as a gift, that you can exchange at a particular store for goods or services with a certain value

**gift·ed** /ˈgɪftəd/ ***adj.*** having natural ability or great intelligence: *a gifted musician*

**ˈgift wrap** ***noun*** [U] special paper that you use to cover sth that you will give to sb as a present: *Children love colorful gift wrap on their presents.* ▸ **ˈgift wrap *verb*** [T]: *I got his present, but I forgot to ask the store to gift wrap it.* ◇ *Would you like that gift wrapped?*

**gig** /gɪg/ ***noun*** [C] a performance by rock or jazz musicians

**gig·a·byte** /ˈgɪgəbaɪt; ˈdʒɪgə-/ ***noun*** [C] (*abbr.* **GB**; **Gb**) (*computing*) a unit of computer memory, equal to $2^{30}$ (= or about 1 billion) bytes: *an 80-gigabyte hard drive*

**gi·gan·tic** /dʒaɪˈgæntɪk/ ***adj.*** extremely large

**gig·gle¹** /ˈgɪgl/ ***verb*** [I] to laugh in a silly way because you are amused or nervous

**gig·gle²** /ˈgɪgl/ ***noun*** [C] a silly laugh: *I have the giggles* (= I can't stop laughing).

**gill** /gɪl/ ***noun*** [C, usually pl.] one of the parts on the side of a fish's head that it breathes through

**gilt** /gɪlt/ ***noun*** [U] a thin covering of gold

**gim·mick** /ˈgɪmɪk/ ***noun*** [C] something unusual or amusing that is used to attract people's attention (usually so that they buy sth): *They're looking for a new gimmick to advertise the restaurant.*

**gin** /dʒɪn/ ***noun*** [C,U] a colorless alcoholic drink that is made from grain and a particular type of berry: *I'll have a gin and tonic.*

**gin·ger** /ˈdʒɪndʒər/ ***noun*** [U] the hot-tasting root of a plant (used in cooking): *ground ginger*

**ˈginger ale** ***noun*** [U] a non-alcoholic drink that is flavored with ginger, sometimes mixed with alcoholic drinks

**gin·ger·bread** /ˈdʒɪndʒərbrɛd/ ***noun*** [U] a sweet cake or soft cookie made with ginger, often in the shape of a person

**gin·ger·ly** /ˈdʒɪndʒərli/ ***adv.*** very slowly and carefully so as not to cause harm, make a noise, etc.

**ging·ham** /ˈgɪŋəm/ ***noun*** [U] a cotton fabric with a pattern of white and colored checks: *a blue and white gingham dress*

**gin·seng** /ˈdʒɪnsɛŋ/ ***noun*** [U] a root of a plant used in tea and other drinks, medicines, etc.; some people believe this makes you stay young and healthy

**gi·raffe** /dʒəˈræf/ ***noun*** [C] (*pl.* **gi·raffe** or **gi·raffes**) an African animal with a very long neck and legs and dark spots on its skin

**gird·er** /ˈgərdər/ ***noun*** [C] a long iron or steel bar that is used in the construction of bridges, large buildings, etc.

★**girl** /gərl/ ***noun*** [C] **1** a female child: *the little girl who lives next door* ◇ *There are more boys than girls in the class.* **2** a daughter: *They have two boys and a girl.* **3** a young woman: *He was 18 before he became interested in girls.* ◇ *The girl at the checkout was very helpful.* **4 the girls** [pl.] female friends of any age: *a night out with the girls*

★**girl·friend** /ˈgərlfrɛnd/ ***noun*** [C] **1** a girl or woman with whom sb has a romantic and/or sexual relationship **2** a girl or woman's female friend

ˌ**Girl ˈGuide** ***noun*** [C] (*Cdn*) a member of a girls' organization which teaches them to be responsible and help other people. Girl Guides also learn useful skills, go camping, etc.

ˈ**Girl Scout** ***noun*** [C] (*U.S.*) = SCOUT[1] (1)

**the gist** /dʒɪst/ ***noun*** [sing.] the general meaning of sth rather than all the details: *I know a little Spanish, so I was able to get the gist of what he said.*

★**give[1]** /gɪv/ ***verb*** (*pt* **gave** /geɪv/; *pp* **giv·en** /ˈgɪvn/)
➤HAND/PROVIDE **1** [T] **give sb sth; give sth to sb** to hand sth to sb as a present; to allow sb to have sth as a present: *My parents gave me a watch for my birthday.* ◇ *to give money to charity* **2** [T] **give sb sth; give sth to sb** to hand sth to sb so that he/she can look at it, use it or keep it for a time: *Can you give me that book over there?* ◇ *I gave my ticket to the woman at the check-in desk.* **3** [T] **give sb sth; give sth to sb** to provide sb with sth he/she wants, asks for or pays for: *He was thirsty, so I gave him a drink.* ◇ *I hope the doctor will give me some new pills.* ◇ *Can you give me some help with my homework?* **4** [T] **give sth to sb/sth** to spend time, etc. on sb/sth: *I can only give you ten minutes.* ◇ *We'll have to give some more thought to the matter* (= think about it more).
➤PAY **5** [T] **give (sb) sth for sth** to pay: *How much would you give me for my old car?*
➤CAUSE STH **6** [T] **give sb sth** to cause sb/sth to have or feel sth: *The news about his father gave him a big shock.* ◇ *Hard work gives you an appetite.* ◇ *That noise is giving me a headache.* **7** [T] **give sth; give sb sth; give sth to sb/sth** to perform an action: *She gave my hand a squeeze* (= she squeezed it). ◇ *They gave us a warm welcome.* ◇ *He gave me a very long answer.* ◇ *She gave him a kiss.*
➤EVENT/PARTY **8** [T] to perform sth in public: *He gave a very interesting lecture on India.* ◇ *They're giving* (= having) *a party for their son's tenth birthday.*
➤BEND **9** [I] to bend or stretch under pressure: *The branch began to give under his weight.*

IDM **give or take** more or less the number mentioned: *It took us two hours to get here, give or take five minutes.*

> NOTE For other idioms containing **give**, look at the entries for the nouns, adjectives, etc., e.g. **give way** is at **way**.

PHR V **give sb away** (at a wedding in a church) to go with the bride into the church and officially give her to the groom during the marriage ceremony: *Her father gave her away.*

**give sth away** to give sth, often sth that you no longer want, to sb without asking for or receiving money in return: *When she got older, she gave all her toys away.* ◇ *We are giving a shirt away with every suit purchased.*

**give sth away** to show or tell the truth about sth which was secret: *He smiled politely and didn't give away his real feelings.*

**give sb sth back; give sth back (to sb)** to return sth to the person from whom you took or borrowed it: *I should give you back those books you loaned me.*

**give in (to sb/sth)** to stop fighting against sb/sth; to accept that you have been defeated

**give sth off** to send sth (e.g. a smell, heat, etc.) out into the air

**give out** (used about a machine, etc.) to stop working

**give sth out** to hand or pass sth to people: *Could you give out these worksheets to the class?*

**give up** to stop trying to do sth; to accept that you cannot do sth: *Don't give up now – you're improving all the time.* ◇ *I give up. What's the answer?*

**give up on sb** to stop expecting sb to arrive, succeed, improve or recover: *If he doesn't come by noon, we'll give up on him.* ◇ *The doctors had given up on her when she suddenly started to get better.*

**give up sth** to stop doing or having sth that you had done or had regularly before: *to give up smoking* ◇ *Don't give up hope. Things are bound to improve.*

**give yourself/sb up (to sb)** to go to the police when they are trying to catch you: *The suspect gave himself up to the police.*

**give sth up (to sb)** to give sth to sb who needs or asks for it: *He gave up his seat on the bus to an elderly woman.*

**give[2]** /gɪv/ ***noun*** [U] the quality of being able to bend or stretch a little: *These pants don't have enough give in the waist.*

IDM **give and take** the willingness, within a relationship, to move toward another person's point of view because he/she is willing to move toward your point of view: *This dispute can only be settled if there is give and take on both sides.*

**give·a·way** /ˈgɪvəweɪ/ ***noun*** [C] (*informal*) **1** a thing that is free when you buy sth else: *There's usually a giveaway with that magazine.* **2** sth that makes you guess the truth about sb/sth: *She said she didn't know about the money but her face was a **dead giveaway**.*

**giv·en[1]** /ˈgɪvn/ ***adj.*** (only *before* a noun) already stated or fixed: *At any given time, over 10% of students are absent from class.*

**giv·en[2]** /ˈgɪvn/ ***prep.*** taking sth into consideration: *Given that you had very little help, I think you did pretty well.*

ˈ**given name** ***noun*** [C] = FIRST NAME ➲ Look at the note at **name**.

**giz·mo** /ˈgɪzmoʊ/ ***noun*** [C] (*informal*) (*pl.* **giz·mos**) a general word for a small piece of equipment, often one that does sth in a new and clever way

**gla·cial** /ˈgleɪʃl/ ***adj.*** caused by ice or a glacier: *a glacial valley*

**gla·cier** /ˈgleɪʃər/ ***noun*** [C] a mass of ice that moves slowly across land

★**glad** /glæd/ ***adj.*** (**glad·der**; **glad·dest**) (not before a noun) **glad (to do sth/that...)** happy; pleased: *I'm glad to hear he's feeling better.* ◇ *I'm glad (that) he's feeling better.* ◇ *We'd be glad to see you if you're in the area.*

> NOTE **Glad** is not used before a noun, but **happy** CAN be used before the noun it describes: *This kind of music always makes me feel happy.* ◇ *She's such a happy child –she's always laughing.*

**glad·i·a·tor** /ˈglædieɪt̬ər/ ***noun*** [C] (in ancient Rome) a man who fought against another man or a wild animal in a public show

G

**glad·ly** /ˈglædli/ ***adv.*** happily; willingly: *She gladly accepted the invitation to stay at our house.* ◇ *I would gladly give up my job if I could afford to.*

**glam·or·ize** /ˈglæmərɑɪz/ ***verb*** [T] to make sth appear more attractive or exciting than it really is: *Television tends to glamorize violence.*

**glam·or·ous** /ˈglæmərəs/ ***adj.*** attractive or full of glamour: *She didn't look very glamorous without her makeup.* ◇ *a glamorous job* ▸ **glam·or·ous·ly** ***adv.***

**glam·our** (*also* **glamor**) /ˈglæmər/ ***noun*** [U] the quality of seeming to be exciting or attractive: *Young people are often attracted by the glamour of city life.*

**glance¹** /glæns/ ***verb*** [I] to take a quick look: *She glanced around the room to see if they were there.* ◇ *He glanced at her and smiled.* ◇ *The receptionist glanced down the list of names.*

PHR V **glance off (sth)** to hit sth at an angle and move off again in another direction: *Luckily, the bullet glanced off his big belt buckle.*

**glance²** /glæns/ ***noun*** [C] a quick look: *I only had time for a glance at the newspaper.* ◇ *They exchanged glances when no one was looking.* ◇ *She stole* (= sneaked) *a glance at her watch.*

IDM **at a glance** in a form that can be understood by looking quickly at sth: *Here, at a glance, is a summary of the key issues in the election...*

**at first glance/sight** → FIRST¹

**gland** /glænd/ ***noun*** [C] a small part (an organ) of the body that produces a substance that your body uses: *sweat glands* ◇ *the poison glands of a snake* ◇ *swollen glands* (e.g. in your throat)

**glare¹** /glɛr/ ***noun*** **1** [U, sing.] strong light that hurts your eyes: *the glare of the sun on snow* ◇ *the glare of a car's headlights* **2** [C] a (long) angry look

**glare²** /glɛr/ ***verb*** [I] **1** to shine with strong light that hurts your eyes **2 glare (at sb/sth)** to stare at sb angrily: *They stood glaring at each other.*

**glar·ing** /ˈglɛrɪŋ/ ***adj.*** **1** (used about a light, etc.) too strong and bright **2** angry: *glaring eyes* **3** great or very noticeable: *a glaring mistake* ▸ **glar·ing·ly** ***adv.***: *a glaringly obvious mistake*

★**glass** /glæs/ ***noun*** **1** [U] a hard, usually transparent, substance that windows, bottles, etc. are made of: *He cut himself on broken glass.* ◇ *a sheet/pane of glass* ◇ *In case of emergency, break the glass and press the button.* ◇ *a glass jar/dish* **2** [C] a drinking container, usually made of GLASS (1), with no handle; the amount of liquid it contains: *a wine glass/champagne glass* ◇ *Could I have a glass of water, please?* **3** [U] a collection of objects made of GLASS (1)

ˌ**glass ˈceiling** ***noun*** [C, usually sing.] the barrier of attitudes, etc., that stops women, or other groups, from getting the best jobs in a company, etc., although there are no official rules to prevent them from getting these jobs

**glass·es** /ˈglæsəz/ (*also* **eyeglasses**) ***noun*** [pl.] two pieces of glass in a frame that a person wears in front of his/her eyes (in order to be able to see better): *My sister has to wear glasses.* ◇ *I lost my glasses.* ◇ *reading glasses* ◇ *sunglasses*

> NOTE **Glasses** is always plural so we cannot use it with the article *a*. We cannot say: *I need a new glasses.* We can say: *I need a new pair of glasses.*

**glasses**

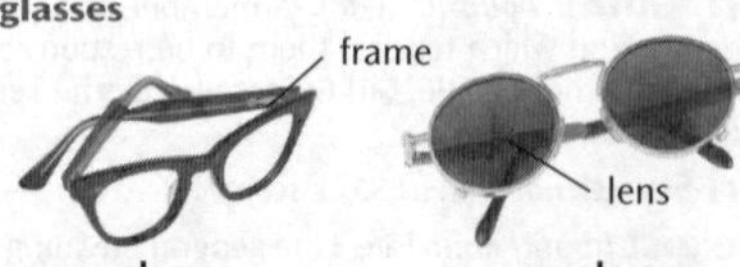


**glass·y** /ˈglæsi/ ***adj.*** (**glass·i·er**; **glass·i·est**) **1** looking like glass: *a glassy lake* **2** (used about the eyes) showing no interest or expression: *a glassy stare*

**glaze¹** /gleɪz/ ***verb*** [T] **1 glaze sth (with sth)** to cover a pot, brick, etc. with a shiny substance (before it is put into an oven) **2** to put a thin, usually sweet sauce on food: *a glazed doughnut* ◇ *glazed carrots*

PHR V **glaze over** (used about the eyes) to show no interest or expression

**glaze²** /gleɪz/ ***noun*** [C,U] **1** (a substance that gives) a shiny surface on a pot, brick, etc. **2** a thin, usually sweet sauce for food

**gleam¹** /glim/ ***noun*** [C, sing.] a soft or bright light (that shines for a short time): *the gleam of moonlight on the water*

**gleam²** /glim/ ***verb*** [I] to shine softly or brightly: *The water of the lake gleamed in the moonlight.*

**gleam·ing** /ˈglimɪŋ/ ***adj.*** shining: *gleaming white teeth*

**glee** /gli/ ***noun*** [U] a feeling of joy or happiness (at sth good that has happened to you or at sth bad that has happened to sb else): *The kids laughed with glee at the clown's tricks.* ▸ **glee·ful** /-fl/ ***adj.*** ▸ **glee·ful·ly** ***adv.***

**glib** /glɪb/ ***adj.*** **1** (used about a person) speaking quickly and cleverly, in a way that will persuade people, but not always telling the truth: *a glib salesman/politician* **2** spoken quickly and without hesitating, but not always true: *a glib answer/excuse* ▸ **glib·ly** ***adv.***

**glide** /glaɪd/ ***verb*** [I] **1** to move smoothly without noise or effort: *The dancers glided across the floor.* ◇ *The yachts went gliding past.* **2** to fly in a glider, or in another aircraft without using an engine

**glid·er** /ˈglaɪdər/ ***noun*** [C] a light airplane without an engine that flies using air currents ➲ Look at **hang glider**.

**glim·mer¹** /ˈglɪmər/ ***noun*** [C] **1** a weak unsteady light **2** a weak sign of sth: *a glimmer of hope*

**glim·mer²** /ˈglɪmər/ ***verb*** [I] to give out a weak unsteady light

**glimpse¹** /glɪmps/ ***noun*** [C] **a glimpse (at/of sth)** a quick incomplete view of sb/sth

> NOTE **Glimpse** is most often used in the phrase **catch a glimpse of**: *I caught a glimpse of myself in the mirror as I walked past.*

**glimpse²** /glɪmps/ ***verb*** [T] to get a quick look at sb/sth (often by chance): *I glimpsed Cathy in the crowd, but I don't think she saw me.*

**glint** /glɪnt/ ***verb*** [I] to shine with small bright flashes of light: *His eyes glinted at the thought of all that money.*

**glis·ten** /ˈglɪsn/ ***verb*** [I] (used about wet surfaces) to shine: *Her eyes glistened with tears.* ◇ *Tears glistened in her eyes.*

**glit·ter** /ˈglɪt̬ər/ ***verb*** [I] to give out many little flashes of light: *The stars glittered in the frosty sky.* ▶ **glit·ter *noun*** [U]: *the glitter of jewelry* ◇ (*figurative*): *the glitter of Broadway*

**glit·ter·ing** /ˈglɪt̬ərɪŋ/ ***adj.*** **1** shining brightly with many little flashes of light: *a glittering Christmas tree* **2** very successful, exciting, etc.: *a glittering career/performance*

**glitz** /glɪts/ ***noun*** [U] (*informal*) the quality of seeming to be exciting and attractive, often in an exaggerated way: *Hollywood glitz and glamour* ▶ **glitz·y** /ˈglɪtsi/ ***adj.***

**gloat** /gloʊt/ ***verb*** [I] **gloat (about/over sth)** to feel or express pleasure at sth good that has happened to you or at sth bad that has happened to sb else: *Don't gloat – you might be in the same position yourself sometime.*

**glob** /glɑb/ ***noun*** [C] (*informal*) a drop or ball of a liquid or melted solid: *There was a big glob of fat in my soup.*

**glob·al** /ˈgloʊbl/ ***adj.*** **1** affecting the whole world: *the global effects of pollution* **2** affecting the whole of a group of facts, possibilities, etc.: *We need to take a global view of the problem.* ▶ **glob·al·ly** /-bəli/ ***adv.***

**glob·al·i·za·tion** /ˌgloʊbələˈzeɪʃn/ ***noun*** [U] (used about a company, etc.) the process of getting bigger and coming to operate around the world

**glob·al·ize** /ˈgloʊbəlaɪz/ ***verb*** [I,T] if sth, for example a company, globalizes or is globalized, it operates all around the world

**ˌglobal ˈvillage** ***noun*** [sing.] the world considered as a single community linked by computers, telephones, etc.

**ˌglobal ˈwarming** ***noun*** [U] the increase in the temperature of the earth's atmosphere caused by the increase of certain gases

**globe** /gloʊb/ ***noun*** **1** [C] a model of the earth, in the shape of a ball, with the continents, etc. painted on it **2 the globe** [sing.] the earth: *to travel (all) over the globe* ◇ *With the help of television, we can see things that are going on on the other side of the globe.*

**globe·trot·ter** /ˈgloʊbˌtrɑt̬ər/ ***noun*** [C] (*informal*) a person who travels to many countries

**gloom** /glum/ ***noun*** [U] **1** a feeling of sadness or hopelessness: *The news brought deep gloom to the community.* **2** (near) darkness: *It was hard to see anything in the gloom.*

**gloom·y** /ˈglumi/ ***adj.*** (**gloom·i·er**; **gloom·i·est**) **1** dark (and depressing): *What a gloomy day!* ◇ *This dark paint makes the room very gloomy.* **2** (making sb feel) sad or depressed: *For many young people graduating from high school, the prospects of finding a job are gloomy.* ◇ *Don't be so gloomy all the time – cheer up!* ▶ **gloom·i·ly** /-əli/ ***adv.*** ▶ **gloom·i·ness *noun*** [U]

**glo·ri·fied** /ˈglɔrəfaɪd/ ***adj.*** (only *before* a noun) described in a way that makes sb/sth seem better, bigger, more important, etc. than he/she/it really is: *The "luxury hotel" turned out to be a glorified motel.*

**glo·ri·fy** /ˈglɔrəfaɪ/ ***verb*** (*pres. part.* **glo·ri·fy·ing**; *3rd person sing. pres.* **glo·ri·fies**; *pt, pp* **glo·ri·fied**) [T] **1** to make sb/sth appear better or more important than he/she/it really is: *Critics claimed that the movie glorified drug abuse.* **2** (*formal*) to praise sb/sth highly

**glo·ri·ous** /ˈglɔriəs/ ***adj.*** **1** having or deserving fame or glory: *a glorious victory* **2** wonderful or excellent: *What glorious weather!* ◇ *a glorious day/view* ▶ **glo·ri·ous·ly *adv.***

**glo·ry** /ˈglɔri/ ***noun*** [U] **1** fame or honor that is won by great achievements: *The winning team was welcomed home in a blaze of glory.* **2** great beauty: *October is the best time to see the New England foliage in all its glory.*

G

**gloss¹** /glɔs; glɑs/ ***noun*** [U, sing.] (a substance that gives) brightness or shine on a surface: *the gloss on wood/hair/silk* ◇ *gloss paint*

**gloss²** /glɔs; glɑs/ ***verb***

PHR V **gloss over sth** to avoid talking about a problem, mistake, etc. in detail

**glos·sa·ry** /ˈglɑsəri; ˈglɔs-/ ***noun*** [C] (*pl.* **glos·sa·ries**) a list of special or unusual words and their meanings (at the end of a book)

**gloss·y** /ˈglɔsi; ˈglɑsi/ ***adj.*** (**gloss·i·er**; **gloss·i·est**) **1** smooth and shiny: *glossy hair* ◇ *glossy photographs* ➲ Look at **matte**. **2** (used about a magazine, etc.) printed on good quality paper and having many color photographs

**glove** /glʌv/ ***noun*** [C] a piece of clothing that covers your hand (and has separate parts for the thumb and each finger): *I need a new pair of gloves for the winter.*

NOTE Common types of gloves are *baseball gloves, boxing gloves, leather gloves, rubber gloves* and *winter gloves*. Look also at **mitten**. ➲ picture at **baseball**.

**ˈglove comˌpartment** (*also* **ˈglove box, glove·box**) ***noun*** [C] a small enclosed space or shelf facing the front seats of a car, used for keeping small things in

**glow¹** /gloʊ/ ***verb*** [I] **1** to give out light and/or heat without smoke or flames: *The TV screen glowed in the dark room.* **2 glow (with sth)** to be warm or red because of excitement, exercise, etc.: *to glow with health/enthusiasm/pride*

**glow²** /gloʊ/ ***noun*** [sing.] **1** a warm light: *the glow of the sky at sunset* **2** a feeling or look of warmth or satisfaction: *a rosy glow on the children's cheeks*

**glow·er** /ˈglaʊər/ ***verb*** [I] **glower (at sb/sth)** to look angrily at sb/sth

**glow·ing** /ˈgloʊɪŋ/ ***adj.*** giving high praise; favorable: *His teacher wrote a glowing report about his work.* ▶ **glow·ing·ly *adv.***

**glu·cose** /ˈglukoʊs/ ***noun*** [U] a type of sugar that is found in fruit

★**glue¹** /glu/ ***noun*** [U] a thick sticky liquid that is used for joining things together: *You can make glue from flour and water.* ◇ *Stick the photo in with glue.*

★**glue²** /glu/ ***verb*** [T] (*pres. part.* **glu·ing**) **glue A (to/onto B)**; **glue A and B (together)** to join a thing or things together with GLUE¹: *Do you think you can glue the handle back onto the mug?*

**IDM glued to sth** (*informal*) giving all your attention to sth and unwilling to leave it: *He just sits there every evening glued to the TV set.*

**glum** /glʌm/ ***adj.*** (*informal*) sad or disappointed: *What are you looking so glum about?* ▶ ***glum·ly adv.***

**glut** /glʌt/ ***noun*** [C, usually sing.] more of sth than is needed: *The oil glut has forced down the price of gasoline.*

**glut·ton** /ˈglʌtn/ ***noun*** [C] **1** a person who eats too much **2 a glutton for sth** (*informal*) a person who is willing to have or do more of sth difficult, unpleasant, etc.: *She's a glutton for punishment –she always takes the hardest jobs.*

**glut·ton·y** /ˈglʌtn·i/ ***noun*** [U] the habit of eating and drinking too much

G

**GM** /ˌdʒi ˈɛm/ ***abbr.*** genetically modified

**gm** ***abbr.*** gram

**GMAT™** /ˌdʒi ɛm eɪ ˈti/ ***noun*** [sing.] Graduate Management Admissions Test; an examination that people who have a first (bachelor's) degree take in order to study for another degree in business

**GMT** /ˌdʒi ɛm ˈti/ ***abbr.*** = GREENWICH MEAN TIME

**gnarled** /nɑrld/ ***adj.*** rough and twisted, because of old age or hard work: *The old man had gnarled fingers.* ◇ *a gnarled oak tree*

**gnash** /næʃ/ ***verb***

**IDM gnash your teeth** to make a noise with your teeth because of anger, pain, worry, etc.

**gnat** /næt/ ***noun*** [C] a very small flying insect that bites

**gnaw** /nɔ/ ***verb*** [I,T] **1 gnaw (at/on) sth** to bite a bone, etc. many times: *The dog lay on the carpet gnawing on a bone.* **2 gnaw (at) sb/sth** to cause sb/sth to feel nervous, worried, etc. all the time: *Fear of the future gnawed away at her all the time.*

**gnome** /noʊm/ ***noun*** [C] (in children's stories, etc.) a little old man with a beard and a pointed hat who lives under the ground

**GNP** /ˌdʒi ɛn ˈpi/ ***noun*** [C] the abbreviation for "gross national product"; the total value of all the goods and services produced by a country in one year, including the total money earned from foreign countries ➲ Compare **GDP**.

★**go**[1] /goʊ/ ***verb*** (*pres. part.* **go·ing**; *3rd person sing. pres.* **goes**; *pt* **went** /wɛnt/; *pp* **gone** /gɔn; gɑn/)

➤ MOVE/TRAVEL **1** [I] to move or travel from one place to another: *We're going downtown.* ◇ *"Is Anita here?" "No, she went home."* ◇ *We still have fifty miles to go.* ◇ *How fast does this car go?*

> NOTE **Been** is often used as the past participle of **go** in this meaning: *Have you ever been to Arizona?*

**2** [I] to travel to a place to take part in an activity or do sth: *Are you going to Dave's party?* ◇ *Do you want to go swimming this afternoon?* ◇ *They went on vacation.* ◇ *We went to watch the game.* ◇ *I'll go make some coffee.*

➤ VISIT/ATTEND **3** [I] to visit or attend a place regularly: *Does Jacob go to school yet?*

➤ LEAVE **4** [I] to leave a place: *I have to go now. It's almost 4 o'clock.*

➤ LEAD **5** [I] to lead to or reach a place or time: *Where does this road go to?* ◇ *This cut on my hand goes pretty deep.*

➤ PLACE/SPACE **6** [I] to have as its usual place: *Where does this vase go?* **7** [I] to fit into a space: *My clothes won't all go in one suitcase.*

➤ PROGRESS **8** [I] to happen in a particular way; to develop: *Hi, Mark. How's it going* (= How are you)? ◇ *My work's going pretty well.*

➤ STATE/CONDITION **9** [I] to become; to reach a particular state: *Her hair is going gray.* ◇ *He went blind when he was 20.* ◇ *The baby just went to sleep.* **10** [I] to remain in the state mentioned: *Many mistakes go unnoticed.*

➤ MACHINE **11** [I] to become worse or stop working correctly: *The brakes on the car suddenly went yesterday.*

➤ SONG/STORY **12** [I] to have certain words or a certain tune: *How does that song go?*

➤ SOUND **13** [T] to make a sound: *Cats go "meow."*

➤ SAY **14** [T] (*informal*) (usually used in the present tense) to say or ask: *...So then I go, "I have to work tonight," and he goes, "How come?"*

> NOTE Many people, especially older people, do not like this use of the word **go**. However, it is very common in informal speech.

➤ TIME **15** [I] (used about time) to pass: *The last hour went very slowly.* ◇ *There's only one minute left to go.*

**IDM as people, things, etc. go** compared to the average person or thing: *As Chinese restaurants go, it wasn't bad.*

**be going to do sth 1** (used for showing what you plan to do in the future): *We're going to sell our car.* **2** (used for saying that you are sure sth will happen): *It's going to rain soon.* ◇ *Oh no! He's going to fall!*

**go all out to do sth** to make a great effort to do sth

**Here goes!** (said just before you start to do sth difficult or exciting)

**to go** (used about food) ready to be taken from a restaurant and eaten in another place: *I'll have a cheeseburger and fries to go.*

> NOTE For other idioms containing **go**, look at the entries for nouns, adjectives, etc., for example **go astray** is at **astray**.

**PHRV go about sth** to continue to do what you usually do: *We went about our normal routine.*

**go about sth/doing sth** to start trying to do sth difficult: *I wouldn't have any idea how to go about building a house.*

**go against sb** to be unfavorable to sb: *The referee's decision went against him.*

**go against sb/sth** to do sth that is opposed to sb/sth: *She went against her parents' wishes and married him.*

**go against sth** to be opposed or opposite to sth; not to be in agreement with sth: *It goes against my principles to use violence.*

**go ahead 1** to take place after being planned: *Although several members were missing, the meeting went ahead without them.* **2** to walk, move, etc. in front of sb else: *Go ahead – I still have to button my coat.*

**go ahead (and do sth)** (used to encourage sb to do sth): *Go ahead and have another piece of cake – there's plenty.*

**go ahead (with sth)** to begin to do sth that you have planned
**go along** to continue: *The course gets more difficult as you go along.*
**go along with sb/sth** to agree with sb/sth: *I'm happy to go along with whatever you suggest.*
**go around 1** (used about a story, a belief, etc.) to pass from person to person: *There's a rumor going around that he's going to resign.* **2** (used about an illness) to pass from person to person in a group or area: *There's a virus going around at work.* **3** (used especially after "enough") to be shared among all the people: *In this area, there aren't enough jobs to go around.*
**go around (doing sth)** to go from place to place in a certain way or while you are doing sth, especially sth that people do not approve of: *You can't go around in your pajamas all day!* ◇ *She's been going around accusing me of stealing the money.*
**go away 1** to leave a person or place: *Go away! Just leave me alone!* **2** to leave the place where you live (e.g. for a vacation) for a period of time of at least one night: *We're going away this weekend and we'll be back on Sunday evening.* **3** to disappear: *I tried to remove the stain in the carpet, but it won't go away.*
**go back (to...)** to return (to a place): *It's a wonderful city and I'd like to go back there some day.*
**go back (to sth) 1** to return to a previous matter or situation: *Let's go back to the subject we were discussing a few minutes ago.* **2** to have its origins in a previous period of time: *A lot of buildings on the East Coast go back to colonial times.*
**go back on sth** to break a promise, an agreement, etc.: *I promised to help them and I can't go back on it now.*
**go back to sth/to doing sth** to start doing again sth that you had stopped doing: *When the kids got a little older, she went back to full-time work.*
**go by 1** (used about time) to pass: *As time went by, her confidence grew.* **2** to pass a place: *She stood at the window watching people go by.*
**go by sth** to obey, follow or be guided by sth: *I wouldn't go by what politicians say.*
**go down 1** (used about an aircraft) to crash: *A military helicopter went down 10 miles from the Air Force base.* **2** (used about a ship, etc.) to sink **3** (used about the sun) to disappear from the sky **4** to become lower in price, level, etc.; to fall: *The price of these computers has gone down in the last two years.* ◇ *The number of people out of work went down last month.*
**go down (with sb)** (used with adverbs, especially "well" or "badly," or in questions beginning with "how") (used about sth that is said, a performance, etc.) to be received by sb: *The play went down well with the critics.*
**go for sb** to attack sb
**go for sb/sth** to be true for a particular person or thing: *We have financial problems, but I suppose the same goes for a lot of people.*
**go for sth** to make a great effort to reach a particular goal: *We know we can win this race, so let's go for it!*
**go into sth 1** to start working in a certain type of job: *After she graduated, she went into nursing.* **2** to look at or describe sth in detail: *I don't have time to go into all the details now.*
**go off 1** to explode: *The soldiers were injured when a bomb went off near them.* **2** to make a sudden loud noise: *I woke up when my alarm clock went off.* **3** (used about lights, heating, etc.) to stop working: *There was a power outage and all the lights went off.*
**go off with sth** to take sth that belongs to sb else: *Who went off with my cup?*
**go on 1** (used about lights, heating, etc.) to start working: *I saw the lights go on in the house across the street.* **2** (used about time) to pass: *As time went on, she became more and more successful.* **3** (used especially in the continuous tenses) to happen or take place: *Can anybody tell me what's going on here?* **4** (used about a situation) to continue without changing: *This is a difficult period, but it won't go on forever.* **5** to continue speaking after stopping briefly: *Go on. What happened next?* **6** (used as an order for encouraging sb to do sth): *Go on, ask her!*
**go on sth** to use sth as information so that you can understand a situation: *There were no witnesses to the crime, so the police had very little to go on.*
**go on (about sb/sth)** to talk about sb/sth for a long time in a boring or annoying way: *She went on and on about the people she works with.*
**go on (with sth)** to continue doing sth, perhaps after a pause or break: *She ignored me and went on with her dinner.*
**go on doing sth** to continue doing sth without stopping or changing: *We don't want to go on living here for the rest of our lives.*
**go out 1** to leave the place where you live or work for a short time, returning on the same day: *Let's go out for a meal tonight* (= to a restaurant). ◇ *I'm going out for a walk, but I won't be long.* **2** (used about the ocean) to move away from the land: *The water was a long way away because the tide had gone out.* **3** to stop being fashionable or in use: *That kind of music went out in the seventies.* ◇ *Teaching methods like that went out years ago.* **4** to stop shining or burning: *Suddenly all the lights went out.*
**go out with sb; go out (together)** to spend time regularly with sb, having a romantic and/or sexual relationship: *He's going out with Jill Brown now.* ◇ *They went out together for five years before they got married.*
**go over sth** to look at, think about or discuss sth carefully from beginning to end: *Go over your work carefully before you hand it in.*
**go over (to...)** to visit sb's home, usually a short distance away: *I'm going over to Jo's for dinner tonight.*
**go through** to be completed successfully: *The deal went through as we had agreed.*
**go through sth 1** to look in or at sth carefully, especially in order to find sth: *I went through all my pockets, but I couldn't find my wallet.* **2** to look at, think about or discuss sth carefully from beginning to end: *Let's go through the arrangements for the trip again.* ◇ *We'll start class by going through your homework.* **3** to suffer a bad experience: *I'd hate to go through such a terrible ordeal again.*
**go through with sth** to do sth bad or difficult that you have decided, agreed or threatened to do:

G

*Do you think she'll go through with her threat to leave him?*
**go together** (used about two or more things) **1** to belong to the same set or group **2** to look good together
**go toward(s) sth** to be used as part of the payment for sth: *The money I got for my birthday went toward my new bike.*
**go under 1** to sink below the surface of water **2** (*informal*) (used about a company) to go out of business: *A lot of businesses are going under in the recession.*
**go up 1** to start burning suddenly and strongly: *The car crashed into a wall and went up in flames.* **2** to become higher in price, level, amount, etc.; to rise: *Gas went up again yesterday.* ◇ *The birthrate has gone up by 10%.*
**go with sth 1** to be included with sth; to happen as a result of sth: *Pressure goes with the job.* **2** to match or be suitable with sth: *What color carpet would go with the walls?*
**go without (sth)** to manage without having sth: *They went without sleep many nights when the baby was sick.*

**go²** /goʊ/ *noun*
IDM **be on the go** (*informal*) to be very active or busy: *I'm exhausted. I've been on the go all day.*
**to have a go (at sth/doing sth)** (*informal*) to try to do sth: *I'm not sure if I can fix it, but I'll have a go.*
**make a go of sth** (*informal*) to be successful in sth: *They're struggling to make a go of their small store.*

**goad** /goʊd/ *verb* [T] **goad sb/sth (into sth/doing sth)** to cause sb to do sth by making him/her angry

**ˈgo-aˌhead** *noun* [sing.] permission to do sth: *We've been given the go-ahead for the new building.*

★**goal** /goʊl/ *noun* [C] **1** your purpose or aim: *I've finally achieved my goal of getting a college degree.* **2** (in soccer, hockey, etc.) the area between two posts which the ball or puck must enter for a point to be scored **3** a point that is scored when the ball goes into the GOAL (2): *The Bruins won by three goals to two.* ◇ *to score a goal*

**goal·keep·er** /ˈgoʊlˌkipər/ (*also* **goal·tend·er** /ˈgoʊlˌtɛndər/ or (*informal*) **goalie** /ˈgoʊli/) *noun* [C] the player who stands in front of the GOAL (2) and tries to stop the other team from scoring a GOAL (3): *The goalkeeper made a terrific save.* ➲ picture at **soccer**.

**ˈgoal post** *noun* [C] one of the two posts that form the sides of a goal. They are joined together by a bar (the crossbar). ➲ picture at **football**.

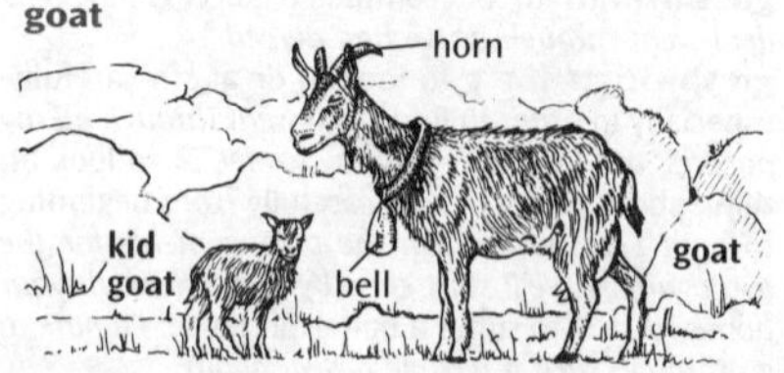


**goat** /goʊt/ *noun* [C] a small animal with horns which lives in mountainous areas or is kept on farms for its milk and meat

NOTE A young goat is called a **kid**.

**goat·ee** /goʊˈti/ *noun* [C] a small pointed beard on a man's chin ➲ picture at **beard**.

**gob** /gɑb/ *noun* [C] (*informal*) **1** a small piece of a thick liquid or of sth soft: *Yuck! There's a gob of toothpaste in the sink.* **2 gobs (of sth)** [pl.] a large amount of sth: *a businessman with gobs of cash*

**gob·ble** /ˈgɑbl/ *verb* [I,T] (*informal*) **gobble sth (up)** to eat quickly and noisily: *He had gobbled up all his food before I even started mine.*

**gob·ble·dy·gook** (*also* **gobbledegook**) /ˈgɑbl-digʊk/ *noun* [U] (*informal*) official language that is hard to understand

**ˈgo-beˌtween** /ˈgoʊ bɪˌtwin/ *noun* [C] a person who takes messages between two people or groups who do not or cannot meet: *He acted as a go-between in the peace negotiations.*

**gob·lin** /ˈgɑblən/ *noun* [C] (in stories) a small ugly creature who plays tricks on people

**ˈgo-cart** *noun* [C] a very small racing car with no roof

★**god** /gɑd/ *noun* **1** (*feminine* **god·dess**) [C] a being or force who is worshipped by a group of people and who is believed to have the power to control nature and human affairs: *Mars was the Roman god of war and Venus was the goddess of love.* **2 God** [sing.] (in Christianity, Islam and Judaism) the creator and ruler of all things: *Do you believe in God?* ◇ *Muslims worship God in a mosque.* ◇ *Dear God, please help us...*

NOTE **God** is used in a number of expressions. (However, some people think that it is wrong to use God's name in this way.) **Oh my God!** expresses surprise or shock: *Oh my God! I won $1,000!* We use **thank God** when we are happy and relieved about something: *Thank God you're here – I was beginning to think you'd had an accident.* The expression **God forbid!** is used when we say that we don't want something to happen: *If, God forbid, anything should happen to us, our children will take over the family business.* We use **for God's sake** when we are asking somebody to do something and want to sound more urgent or when we are angry with somebody: *For God's sake, shut up!* **God (only) knows** is used when we don't know an answer or when we don't understand something: *"What ever happened to our old neighbors?" "God knows!"*

**god·child** /ˈgɑdtʃaɪld/ *noun* [C] (*pl.* **god·chil·dren** /ˈgɑdˌtʃɪldrən/) a person for whom a godparent takes responsibility at a Christian baptism

NOTE A male godchild is a **godson**, and a female godchild is a **goddaughter**.

**god·damn** /ˌgɑdˈdæm/ (*also* **goddam**, **god-damned**) *interjection* used to show that you are angry or annoyed: *You don't have to be so goddamn rude!* ◇ *Where's that goddamned pen?*

NOTE Many people find this word offensive.

**god·dess** /ˈgɑdəs/ *noun* [C] a female god

**god·fa·ther** /ˈgɑdˌfɑðər/ ***noun*** [C, sing.] **1** a man who promises to take responsibility for a child at his/her baptism and to make sure that he/she is educated as a Christian **2** (*also* **Godfather**) a very powerful man in a criminal organization (**the Mafia**)

**god·for·sak·en** (*also* **Godforsaken**) /ˈgɑdfərˌseɪkən/ ***adj.*** (used about a place) depressing or having nothing of interest

**god·moth·er** /ˈgɑdˌmʌðər/ ***noun*** [C, sing.] a woman who promises to take responsibility for a child at his/her baptism and to make sure that he/she is educated as a Christian

**god·par·ent** /ˈgɑdˌpɛrənt; -ˌpær-/ ***noun*** [C, sing.] a person who promises to take responsibility for a child at his/her baptism and to make sure that he/she is educated as a Christian

**god·send** /ˈgɑdsɛnd/ ***noun*** [C, sing.] something unexpected that is a great help to you because it comes just when it is needed: *The lottery win was a real godsend just after I lost my job.*

**go·fer** /ˈgoʊfər/ (*also* **gopher**) ***noun*** [C] (*informal*) a person whose job is to do small, boring tasks for other people in a company

**go-get·ter** /ˌgoʊ ˈgɛt̬ər; ˈgoʊ ˌgɛt̬ər/ ***noun*** [C] a person who works hard to succeed, especially in business

**gog·gles** /ˈgɑglz/ ***noun*** [pl.] special glasses that you wear to protect your eyes from water, wind, dust, etc. ➲ Look at **mask**. ➲ picture at **ski**.

**go·ing[1]** /ˈgoʊɪŋ/ ***noun*** [U] the rate or speed of travel, progress, etc.: *It's been slow going lately.*
IDM **comings and goings** → COMING

**go·ing[2]** /ˈgoʊɪŋ/ ***adj.***
IDM **the going rate (for sth)** the usual cost (of sth): *The going rate for a cleaner is about $6 an hour.*

**ˌgoings-ˈon** ***noun*** [pl.] (*informal*) unusual things that are happening: *The old lady was shocked by the goings-on in the house next door.*

★**gold[1]** /goʊld/ ***noun*** **1** [U] a precious yellow metal that is used for making coins, jewelry, etc.: *Is your bracelet made of gold?* ◇ *solid/pure/22-karat gold* ◇ *a gold chain/ring/watch* **2** [C] = GOLD MEDAL
IDM **(as) good as gold** very well-behaved: *The children were as good as gold while you were out.*

★**gold[2]** /goʊld/ ***adj.*** the color of gold: *The invitation was written in gold letters.*

★**gold·en** /ˈgoʊldən/ ***adj.*** made of gold or like gold: *a golden crown* ◇ *golden hair* ◇ (*figurative*) *a golden* (= excellent) *opportunity*

**ˌgolden ˌanniˈversary** ***noun*** [C] the 50th anniversary of a wedding ➲ Look at **diamond anniversary** and **silver anniversary**.

**gold·fish** /ˈgoʊldfɪʃ/ ***noun*** [C] (*pl.* **gold·fish**) a small orange fish that is kept as a pet in a bowl or pond

**ˌgold ˈmedal** (*also* **gold**) ***noun*** [C] the prize for first place in a sports competition: *How many gold medals did we win in the 2000 Olympics?* ➲ Look at **silver medal** and **bronze medal**.

**ˌgold ˈmedalist** ***noun*** [C] the winner of a gold medal

**ˈgold mine** ***noun*** [C] **1** a place where gold is taken from the earth **2** (*informal*) a business that makes a lot of profit

**ˈgold rush** ***noun*** [C] a situation in which many people hurry to an area where gold has just been discovered in the earth: *the California gold rush of 1849*

★**golf** /gɑlf; gɔlf/ ***noun*** [U] a game that is played outdoors on a large area of grass (**a golf course**) and in which you use a stick (**a golf club**) to hit a small hard ball (**a golf ball**) into a series of holes (usually 18): *to play a round of golf*

**golf·er** /ˈgɑlfər; ˈgɔlfər/ ***noun*** [C] a person who plays golf

**gol·ly** /ˈgɑli/ ***interjection*** (*old-fashioned, informal*) (used for expressing surprise)

**gone[1]** *past participle of* GO[1]

**gone[2]** /gɔn; gɑn/ ***adj.*** (not before a noun) not present any longer; completely used up: *He stood at the door for a moment, and then he was gone.* ◇ *Is the milk all gone?*

**gon·na** /gənə; ˈgɔnə/ (*informal*) (only used before a verb) a way of writing "going to" to show that sb is speaking in an informal way

> NOTE Do not write **gonna** yourself (unless you are copying somebody's speech) because it might be marked as a mistake. **Wanna** (= want to) and **gotta** (= got to) are similar.

**goo** /gu/ ***noun*** [U] (*informal*) a sticky wet substance ▸ **goo·ey** /ˈgui/ (**goo·i·er**; **goo·i·est**) ***adj.*** (*informal*)

★**good[1]** /gʊd/ ***adj.*** (**bet·ter** /ˈbɛt̬ər/, **best** /bɛst/)
➤HIGH QUALITY **1** of a high quality or standard: *a good book/movie/concert* ◇ *The hotel was really good.* ◇ *"Why don't you apply for the job?" "I don't think my English is good enough."* ◇ *The car was in very good condition.*
➤SKILLFUL **2 good at sth**; **good with sb/sth** able to do sth or deal with sb/sth well; successful: *Jane's good at chemistry.* ◇ *He's very good with children.*
➤PLEASANT **3** pleasant or enjoyable: *It's good to be home again.* ◇ *good news/weather* ◇ *Have a good time!*
➤MORALLY RIGHT **4** morally right or well behaved: *She was a very good person – she spent her whole life trying to help other people.* ◇ *Were the kids good while we were out?*
➤KIND **5 good (to sb)** kind; helpful: *They were good to me when I was sick.*
➤HEALTHY **6 good (for sb/sth)** having a positive effect on your health: *Green vegetables are very good for you.*
➤SUITABLE **7** suitable or favorable: *This beach is very good for surfing.* ◇ *I think Paul would be a good person for the job.* ◇ *"When should we meet?" "Thursday would be a good day for me."*
➤NUMBER/QUANTITY **8** (only used before an adjective or noun) great in number, size, length, etc.: *a good many people* (= a lot of people) ◇ *Take a good* (= long and careful) *look at this picture.*
➤AT LEAST **9** (only *before* a noun) at least: *We waited for a good ten minutes.* ◇ *It's a good three miles to the post office.*
➤IN EXCLAMATIONS **10** (used when you are pleased



G

about sth): *"Tom invited us to dinner next week." "Oh, good!"*

IDM **a good/great many** → MANY

**as good as** almost: *The project is as good as finished.*

**in good faith** → FAITH

**good for you** (*informal*) (used for congratulating sb): *Good for you! You should be really proud.*

**good grief, good heavens, etc.** (used for expressing surprise) ➲ Look at the entries for **grief**, etc.

**good morning/afternoon/evening/night** (used for greeting sb) ➲ Look at the entries for **morning**, etc.

G

★**good²** /gʊd/ ***noun*** [U] **1** the quality of being morally right: *the difference between good and evil* ◇ *I'm sure there's some good in everybody.* **2** something that will help sb/sth; advantage: *I know you don't want to go to the hospital, but it's for your own good.* ◇ *What's the good in learning French if you have no chance of using it?* ➲ Look also at **goods**.

IDM **be no good** to be of no use or value: *This work is just no good – you'll have to do it again.* ◇ *These shoes are no good for walking through snow.*

**do you good** to help or be useful to you: *It'll do you good to meet some new people.*

**for good** forever: *I hope they're gone for good this time!*

**good³** /gʊd/ ***adv.*** (*informal*) well; in a good way: *You guys did pretty good today.*

> NOTE Careful speakers do not use **good** as an adverb, but it is common in very informal speech. We use **well** in writing and in more formal, careful speaking.

**the ˌGood ˈBook** ***noun*** [sing.] (*informal*) the Christian Bible

★**good·bye** (*also* **good-bye**) /ˌgʊdˈbaɪ; gəˈbaɪ/ ***interjection*** (said when sb goes or when you go): *Goodbye! See you tomorrow!* ◇ *We said goodbye to Steven at the airport.*

> NOTE **Bye** has the same meaning and is more informal than **goodbye**. **Goodbye** can also be used as a noun: *a sad goodbye at the airport.*

**ˌGood ˈFriday** ***noun*** [C] the Friday before Easter when Christians remember the death of Christ

**ˈgood guy** ***noun*** [C] (*informal*) a good person in a movie, book, etc.

**good·ies** /ˈgʊdiz/ ***noun*** [pl.] (*informal*) small things that are good, especially good things to eat

**ˌgood-ˈlooking** ***adj.*** (usually used about a person) attractive ➲ Look at the note at **beautiful**.

**good-na·tured** /ˌgʊd ˈneɪtʃərd/ ***adj.*** friendly or cheerful

**good·ness** /ˈgʊdnəs/ ***noun*** [U] **1** the quality of being good **2** the quality that helps sb/sth to grow: *This new product has all the goodness of regular yogurt, but only half the fat.*

> NOTE **Goodness** is used in a number of expressions. We say **Goodness!** or **My goodness!** to show that we are surprised. **Thank goodness** expresses happiness and relief: *Thank goodness it stopped raining!* We say **For goodness' sake** when we are asking somebody to do something and want to sound more urgent or when we are angry with somebody: *For goodness' sake, hurry up!*

**ˈgood old boy** (*also* **good ol' boy** /ˈgʊd oʊl bɔɪ/) ***noun*** [C] (*informal*) **1** = REDNECK **2** a man from the southern U.S. who thinks and behaves in traditional ways, and acts like part of the group and not as if he is better than other people

★**goods** /gʊdz/ ***noun*** [pl.] things that are for sale: *a wide range of consumer goods* ◇ *stolen goods* ➲ Look also at **product** and **merchandise**. They are similar in meaning.

**good-tem·pered** /ˌgʊd ˈtɛmpərd/ ***adj.*** not easily made angry

**good·will** /ˌgʊdˈwɪl/ ***noun*** [U] friendly, helpful feelings toward other people: *There is a new atmosphere of goodwill in international politics.*

**good·y-good·y** /ˌgʊdi ˈgʊdi/ (*pl.* **good·y-good·ies**) (*also* **goody-two-shoes**) ***noun*** (*old-fashioned*) [C] (used especially by and about children) a person who behaves very well to please people in authority such as parents or teachers

**goo·ey** ***adj.*** → GOO

**goof¹** /guf/ ***verb*** [I] (*informal*) to make a stupid mistake

PHR V **goof around** (*informal*) to spend time doing silly, unimportant things: *We spent most of the summer just goofing around at the beach.*

**goof off** (*informal*) to avoid doing sth that you should be doing: *Quit goofing off and get back to work!*

**goof²** /guf/ ***noun*** [C] (*informal*) a stupid mistake: *The government's goof could cost taxpayers $10 million.*

**goof·y** /ˈgufi/ ***adj.*** (**goof·i·er**; **goof·i·est**) (*informal*) silly; stupid

**goose** /gus/ ***noun*** (*pl.* **geese** /gis/) [C] a large bird that is like a duck, but larger. Some geese are kept on farms for their meat and eggs.

> NOTE A male goose is called a **gander** and a young goose is a **gosling**.

**ˈgoose bumps** ***noun*** [pl.] (*also* **ˈgoose pimples**) small points or lumps which appear on your skin because you are cold or frightened

**the GOP** /ˌdʒi oʊ ˈpi/ ***abbr.*** (*U.S.*) Grand Old Party; the Republican Party: *a GOP presidential candidate* ➲ Look at the note at **White House**.

**go·pher** /ˈgoʊfər/ ***noun*** [C] a small animal with brown fur that lives in areas where the land is flat, and that digs holes in the ground

**gore** /gɔr/ ***noun*** [U] the blood that comes from a cut or wound: *His new movie is full of gore* (= there are many violent scenes in it). ➲ adjective gory

**gorge¹** /gɔrdʒ/ ***noun*** [C] a narrow valley with steep sides and a stream or river running through it

**gorge²** /gɔrdʒ/ ***verb*** [I,T] **gorge (yourself) (on/with sth)** to eat a lot of food: *At Thanksgiving, people gorge themselves on rich food.*

**gor·geous** /ˈgɔrdʒəs/ ***adj.*** beautiful; wonderful: *You look gorgeous in that dress.* SYN **ravishing** ▸ **gor·geous·ly** ***adv.***

**go·ril·la** /gəˈrɪlə/ ***noun*** [C] a very large black African monkey that is the largest of the monkeys (apes) that are closely related to people

**go·ry** /ˈgɔri/ ***adj.*** (**go·ri·er**; **go·ri·est**) full of violence and blood: *a gory movie* ◇ (*figurative*) *He told me all the gory details about the divorce.*

**gosh** /gɑʃ/ ***interjection*** (*informal*) (used for expressing surprise, shock, etc.)

**gos·ling** /ˈgɑzlɪŋ/ ***noun*** [C] a young goose

**gos·pel** /ˈgɑspl/ ***noun*** **1 Gospel** [C] one of the four books in the Bible that describe the life and teachings of Jesus Christ: *St. Matthew's/Mark's/Luke's/John's Gospel* **2** [U] the truth: *You can't take what he says as gospel.* **3** (*also* **ˈgospel music**) [U] a style of religious music that is especially popular among African-American Christians

**gos·sip** /ˈgɑsəp/ ***noun*** [U] informal talk about other people and their private lives: *Don't believe all the gossip you hear.* ◇ *He loves spreading gossip about his neighbors.* ▶ **gos·sip *verb*** [I]: *I can't stand here gossiping all day.*

**got** *past tense of* GET

**got·ta** /ˈgɑt̬ə/ (*informal*) (only used before a verb) a way of writing "got to" to show that sb is speaking in an informal way

> NOTE Do not write **gotta** yourself (unless you are copying somebody's speech) because it might be marked as a mistake. **Gonna** and **wanna** are similar: *I gotta go* (= I've got to go).

**got·ten** *past participle of* GET

**gouge** /gaʊdʒ/ ***verb*** [T] to charge sb too much money for sth, especially in a way that is not honest or legal: *laws to prevent stores from gouging consumers*

PHRV **gouge sth out** to take sth out with force (usually with a tool or with your fingers)

**gour·met** /gʊrˈmeɪ; ˈgʊrmeɪ/ ***noun*** [C] a person who enjoys food and wine and knows a lot about them: *a gourmet restaurant*

★**gov·ern** /ˈgʌvərn/ ***verb*** **1** [I,T] to rule or control the public affairs of a country, city, etc.: *A group of rebels overthrew the governing party.* **2** [T] (often passive) to influence or control: *Our decision will be governed by the amount of money we have to spend.*

★**gov·ern·ment** /ˈgʌvərmənt; ˈgʌvərnmənt/ ***noun*** **1** [C] the group of people who govern a country, state, city, etc.: *the federal government* (= the national government of the United States) ◇ *government policy/committees* **2** [usually sing.] the offices, services, etc. that belong to the GOVERNMENT (1) and are not part of a company: *government employees* ◇ *I work for the state government.* **3** [U] the act or method of governing: *Six years of weak government had left the economy in ruins.* ▶ **gov·ern·ment·al** /ˌgʌvərˈmɛnt̬l; ˌgʌvərn-/ ***adj.***: *governmental affairs* ◇ *different governmental systems*

★**gov·er·nor** /ˈgʌvənər; ˈgʌvərnər/ ***noun*** [C] a person who is elected to govern a state: *the governor of California* ➲ adjective **gubernatorial** ➲ For more information on the U.S. political system, look at study page **A10**.

**ˌGovernor ˈGeneral** ***noun*** [C] (*pl.* **Governors General**) the representative of the CROWN (2) in Canada and other Commonwealth countries which regard the Queen as the head of state ➲ For more information on the Canadian political system, look at study page **A11**.

**gown** /gaʊn/ ***noun*** [C] **1** a long woman's dress for a special occasion: *a wedding gown* **2** a loose piece of clothing that is worn by judges or students during official ceremonies, or by doctors and nurses during medical operations

**GPA** /ˌdʒi pi ˈeɪ/ ***abbr.*** = GRADE POINT AVERAGE

★**grab** /græb/ ***verb*** (**grab·bing**; **grabbed**) [I,T] to take sth suddenly or roughly: *Jenny grabbed the toy car from her little brother.* ◇ *Don't grab – there's plenty for everybody.* ◇ (*figurative*) *He grabbed the opportunity of a free trip to Hawaii.* ◇ (*figurative*) *I don't have much time, so I'll just grab a burger for lunch.* ➲ Look at **snatch**. It is similar in meaning. ▶ **grab** /græb/ ***noun*** [C]: *A man suddenly made a grab for my necklace.*

**grace** /greɪs/ ***noun*** [U] **1** the ability to move in a smooth and attractive way: *to walk/dance/move with grace* **2** good or favorable treatment of sb, especially by God **3** a short prayer of thanks to God before or after a meal: *Dad always says grace.*

★**grace·ful** /ˈgreɪsfl/ ***adj.*** having GRACE (1) and beauty: *a graceful dancer* ➲ Look at **gracious**. Its meaning is different. ▶ **grace·ful·ly *adv.***: *She accepted the decision gracefully* (= without showing her disappointment). ▶ **grace·ful·ness *noun*** [U]

**gra·cious** /ˈgreɪʃəs/ ***adj.*** (used about a person or his/her behavior) pleasant, kind or polite (to sb of a lower social position): *Mrs. Lowell is always a warm, gracious hostess.* ▶ **gra·cious·ly *adv.*** ▶ **gra·cious·ness *noun*** [U]

**grad** /græd/ ***adj.***, ***noun*** [C] = GRADUATE[1,3]

★**grade**[1] /greɪd/ ***noun*** [C] **1** a letter or number that is given for school work, etc. or in an examination to show how good the work is: *He got good/bad grades this semester.*

> NOTE In North American schools and universities, grades are usually given as letters of the alphabet. The letters used are A (the best grade), B, C, D and F (a failing grade). Sometimes a plus or a minus sign is added after the letter. For example, a B+ is slightly better than a B, and a B– is slightly worse than a B.

**2** one of the levels in a school. Most students begin a new grade each year in the fall: *My daughter is in (the) third grade.*

> NOTE There are 12 numbered grades in American schools. ➲ Look also at study pages **A8-9**.

**3** the quality or place in a series that sb/sth has: *We need to use high-grade materials for this job.* ◇ *grade A fresh eggs* **4** = GRADIENT (1)

IDM **make the grade** (*informal*) to reach the expected standard; succeed

**grade**[2] /greɪd/ ***verb*** [T] **1** to look at school, etc. work that sb has done, mark where there are mistakes and give it a number or letter to show how good it is: *I spent the whole weekend grading papers.* **2** (often passive) to divide things into groups, according to their quality or size: *The books are graded according to level of difficulty.* ◇ *Meat is graded by quality.*

**ˈgrade point average** *noun* [C, usually sing.] (*abbr.* **GPA**) a number that is calculated from the average of all the GRADES¹ (1) that a student has gotten in his/her courses over a period of time: *I graduated with a 3.7 GPA.*

NOTE A student's grade point average is usually calculated using these numbers: A = 4.0, B = 3.0, C = 2.0, D = 1.0 and F = 0.0. ➲ For more information on the U.S. and Canadian educational systems, look at study pages **A8-9**.

**grad·er** /ˈgreɪdər/ *noun* [C] **1** (used after *first, second, third*, etc.) a student who is in the GRADE¹ (2) mentioned: *The play is open to all seventh and eighth graders.* **2** a person who GRADES² (1) students' papers, tests, etc.: *Prof. Cohen is a really tough grader* (= he/she does not give many high grades).

G

**ˈgrade school** *noun* [C,U] = ELEMENTARY SCHOOL

**gra·di·ent** /ˈgreɪdiənt/ *noun* [C] **1** (*also* **grade**) the degree to which the ground goes up or down, especially on a road or railway **2** (*technical*) the rate at which temperature, pressure, etc. changes, or increases and decreases, between one region and another

**ˈgrad school** *noun* [C,U] (*informal*) = GRADUATE SCHOOL

★**grad·u·al** /ˈgrædʒuəl/ *adj.* happening slowly or over a long period of time; not sudden: *There has been a gradual increase in the number of people without jobs.* ▶ **grad·u·al·ly** /-dʒuəli/ *adv.*: *After the storm, things gradually got back to normal.*

**grad·u·ate¹** /ˈgrædʒuət/ (*also informal* **grad**) *noun* [C] a person who has completed his/her studies at a school, college, university, etc.: *a college graduate* ◇ *She's a graduate of Jefferson High School.* ➲ For more information on the U.S. educational system, look at study page **A8**.

**grad·u·ate²** /ˈgrædʒueɪt/ *verb* [I] **1 graduate (from sth)** to finish your studies at a school, college, university, etc. and receive an official piece of paper (a **diploma**) that shows that you have finished: *I graduated from Florida State University with a degree in biology in 2002.* **2 graduate (from sth) to sth** to change (from sth) to sth more difficult, important, expensive, etc.

**grad·u·ate³** /ˈgrædʒuət/ (*also informal* **grad**) *adj.* (only *before* a noun) for or connected with students who already have a first (**bachelor's**) degree and are studying for a further degree: *graduate students* ◇ *graduate courses* ➲ Look at **undergraduate**.

**ˈgraduate school** (*also informal* ˈ**grad school**) *noun* [C,U] the part of a university that is for students who already have a first (**bachelor's**) degree and are studying for a further degree

**grad·u·a·tion** /ˌgrædʒuˈeɪʃn/ *noun* **1** [U] graduating from a school, university, etc. **2** [C] a ceremony in which official pieces of paper (**diplomas**) are given to people who have finished their studies at a school, university, etc.

**graf·fi·ti** /grəˈfiṭi/ *noun* [U] pictures or writing on a wall, etc. in a public place that are rude, funny or political: *The wall was covered in graffiti.*

**graft¹** /græft/ *noun* **1** [C] a piece of living skin, bone, etc. that is attached onto a damaged part of a body in a medical operation: *a skin graft* **2** [C] a piece of a living plant that is attached inside another plant so that it will grow **3** [U] (*informal*) = CORRUPTION

**graft²** /græft/ *verb* [T] **graft sth onto sth** to attach sth as a GRAFT¹ onto a plant, body, etc. ➲ Look at **transplant**.

★**grain** /greɪn/ *noun* **1** [U] the seeds of wheat, rice, etc. as a product: *The U.S. is a major producer of grain.* ◇ *grain exports* **2** [C] a single seed of wheat/rice **3** [C] a very small piece of sth: *a grain of sand, salt, sugar, etc.* ◇ (*figurative*) *There isn't a grain of truth in what you say.* **4** the natural pattern of lines that can be seen or felt in wood, rock, stone, etc.: *to cut a piece of wood with/against the grain*

IDM **take sth with a grain of salt** to believe that sth is probably not true or not completely accurate

**gram** /græm/ *noun* [C] (*abbr.* **g**) a measure of weight. There are 1,000 grams in a kilogram.

**gram·mar** /ˈgræmər/ *noun* **1** [U] the rules of language, e.g. for forming words or joining words together in sentences: *Russian grammar can be difficult for foreign students.* **2** [U] the way in which sb uses the rules of language: *Your vocabulary is good, but your grammar needs improvement.*

**ˈgrammar school** *noun* [C] (*old-fashioned*) (*U.S.*) = ELEMENTARY SCHOOL

**gram·mat·i·cal** /grəˈmæṭɪkl/ *adj.* **1** connected with grammar: *grammatical rules* **2** following the rules of grammar OPP **ungrammatical** ▶ **grammat·i·cal·ly** /-kli/ *adv.*: *a grammatically correct sentence*

★**grand¹** /grænd/ *adj.* looking impressive in size or appearance (also used in names): *the grand opening of a new store* (= a special ceremony) ◇ *the Grand Canyon* ◇ *the Grand Hotel* ➲ noun **grandeur** ▶ **grand·ly** *adv.*

★**grand²** /grænd/ *noun* [C] (*pl.* **grand**) (*slang*) 1,000 dollars: *It'll cost you 50 grand!*

**grand·child** /ˈgræntʃaɪld/ *noun* [C] (*pl.* **grand·chil·dren** /ˈgræntʃɪldrən/) the daughter or son of your child

**grand·daugh·ter** /ˈgrænˌdɔṭər/ *noun* [C] the daughter of your child

**gran·deur** /ˈgrændʒər; -dʒʊr/ *noun* [U] (*formal*) **1** the quality of being large and impressive: *the grandeur of the Swiss Alps* **2** the feeling of being important

**grand·fa·ther** /ˈgrænˌfɑðər/ *noun* [C] the father of one of your parents ➲ Look at the note at **grandparent**.

**ˈgrandfather clock** *noun* [C] a clock that stands on the floor in a tall wooden case

**gran·di·ose** /ˈgrændioʊs; ˌgrændiˈoʊs/ *adj.* bigger or more complicated than necessary: *Their grandiose scheme was completely impractical.*

NOTE Describing something as **grandiose** shows that you do not have a good opinion of it.

**ˌgrand ˈjury** *noun* [C] (*pl.* **grand juries**) (*U.S.*) a group of people who are chosen to decide whether there is enough evidence against an accused person for a trial

**grand·ma** /ˈgrænmɑ; ˈgræmɑ/ *noun* [C] (*informal*) = GRANDMOTHER

**grand·moth·er** /ˈɡrænˌmʌðər/ ***noun*** [C] the mother of one of your parents ➲ Look at the note at **grandparent**.

**grand·pa** /ˈɡrænpɑ; ˈɡræmpɑ/ ***noun*** [C] (*informal*) = GRANDFATHER

**grand·par·ent** /ˈɡrænˌpɛrənt; -ˌpær-/ ***noun*** [C] the father or mother of one of your parents

NOTE If you need to distinguish between one of your mother's parents and one of your father's parents, you can say, for example: *my maternal/paternal grandfather* or *my grandfather on my mother's/father's side*.

**ˌgrand piˈano** ***noun*** [C] a large flat piano (with horizontal strings)

**ˌgrand ˈslam** ***noun*** [C] winning all the important matches or competitions in a particular sport, for example tennis or golf

**grand·son** /ˈɡrænsʌn/ ***noun*** [C] the son of your child

**grand·stand** /ˈɡrændstænd/ ***noun*** [C] rows of seats (covered by a roof) from which you get a good view of a sports competition, etc.

**grand·stand·ing** /ˈɡrænˌstændɪŋ; ˈɡrænd-/ ***noun*** [U] a way of acting or speaking in order to get attention and impress people

**ˌgrand ˈtotal** ***noun*** [C] the amount that you get when you add several totals together

**gran·ite** /ˈɡrænət/ ***noun*** [U] a hard gray rock

**gran·ny** /ˈɡræni/ ***noun*** [C] (*pl.* **gran·nies**) (*informal*) = GRANDMOTHER

**gra·no·la** /ɡrəˈnoʊlə/ ***noun*** [U] food made of grains, nuts, dried fruit, etc. that you eat with milk for breakfast

★**grant**[1] /ɡrænt/ ***verb*** [T] **1** (*formal*) to give sb what he/she has asked for: *He was granted permission to leave early.* **2** to agree (that sth is true): *I grant you that New York is an interesting place, but I still wouldn't want to live there.*

IDM **take sb/sth for granted** to show too little attention to sb/sth; not be grateful enough to a person or thing: *In developed countries, we take running water for granted.* ◇ *She never says thank you – she just takes me for granted.*

**take sth for granted** to accept sth as being true: *We can take it for granted that the new students will have at least an elementary knowledge of English.*

**grant**[2] /ɡrænt/ ***noun*** [C] money that is given (by the government, etc.) for a particular purpose: *a research grant* (= to help pay for a college education) ➲ Look also at **scholarship**.

**grant·ed** /ˈɡræntəd/ ***adv.*** (used for saying that sth is true, before you make a comment about it): *"We've never had any problems before." "Granted, but this year there are 200 more people coming."*

**gran·u·lat·ed** /ˈɡrænyəleɪṭəd/ ***adj.*** in the form of small hard pieces or grains: *granulated sugar*

**gran·ule** /ˈɡrænyul/ ***noun*** [C] a small hard piece or grain of sth

**grapes**

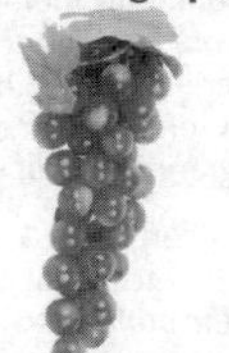

**grape** /ɡreɪp/ ***noun*** [C] a green or purple berry that grows in bunches on a climbing plant (a **vine**) and that is used for making wine: *a bunch of grapes* ◇ *seedless grapes*

NOTE Grapes that have been dried are called **raisins**.

IDM **sour grapes** → SOUR

**grape·fruit** /ˈɡreɪpfrut/ ***noun*** [C] (*pl.* **grape·fruit** or **grape·fruits**) a large round yellow fruit with a thick skin that is like a big orange but with a sour taste

NOTE **Grapefruit** is more common than **grapefruits** as a plural form. ➲ picture on study page **A28-29**.

**grape·vine** /ˈɡreɪpvaɪn/ ***noun***

IDM **hear sth through the grapevine** to hear news that has been passed from one person to another: *"How did you find that out?" "Oh, I just heard it through the grapevine."*

**graphs**

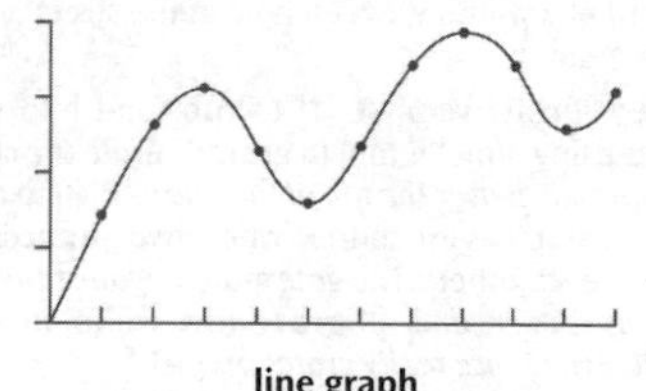

**line graph**

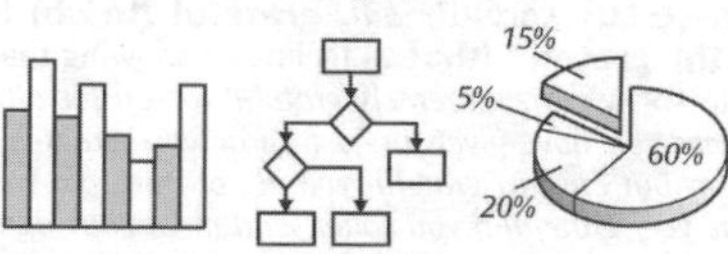


**bar graph/chart** **flow chart** **pie chart**

**graph** /ɡræf/ ***noun*** [C] a mathematical diagram in which a line or a curve shows the relationship between two quantities, measurements, etc.: *a graph showing the number of cars sold each month* ◇ *graph paper* ➲ Look also at **chart**.

**graph·ic**[1] /ˈɡræfɪk/ ***adj.*** **1** (only *before* a noun) connected with drawings, letters, diagrams, etc.: *graphic design* **2** (used about descriptions) clear and giving a lot of detail: *She described the accident in graphic detail.* ◇ *I think there's too much graphic violence on TV.* ▸ **graph·i·cal·ly** /-kli/ ***adv.***

**graph·ic**[2] /ˈɡræfɪk/ ***noun*** [C] a picture or diagram, especially in a computer document or in a book: *a CD-ROM with text and graphics*

**grap·ple** /ˈɡræpl/ ***verb*** [I] **grapple (with sb/sth)** to struggle or fight with a person or a difficult problem: *We have been grappling with this issue all day.*

**grasp**[1] /ɡræsp/ ***verb*** [T] **1** to take hold of sb/sth suddenly and firmly: *Lisa grasped the child firmly by the hand.* ◇ (*figurative*) *to grasp an opportunity* **2** to understand sth: *I don't think you've grasped how serious this is.*

PHRV **grasp at sth** to try to take hold of sth: *He grasped at the swinging rope but missed.*

**grasp**[2] /ɡræsp/ ***noun*** [usually sing.] **1** a firm hold or control over sb/sth: *a strong grasp* **2** the ability to get or achieve sth: *Finally their dream was within their grasp.* **3** understanding: *He has a good grasp of English grammar.*

★**grass** /græs/ ***noun*** **1** [U] the common green plant with thin leaves which covers fields and which often grows around people's houses. Cows, sheep, horses, etc. eat grass: *She lay on the grass and listened to the birds singing.* ◇ *Keep off the grass* (on a sign). ◇ *to mow the grass* ◇ *a blade* (= one leaf) *of grass* ➲ An area of grass around a house is called a **lawn** or a **yard**. Look also at **bluegrass**. **2** [C] one type of GRASS (1): *an arrangement of dried flowers and grasses* **3** (*informal*) = MARIJUANA

G

**grass·hop·per** /ˈgræs,hɑpər/ ***noun*** [C] an insect that lives in long grass and that can jump high in the air

**ˌgrass ˈroots** (*also* **grassroots**) ***noun*** [pl.] the ordinary people in an organization and not those who make decisions: *a grassroots political movement*

**grass·y** /ˈgræsi/ ***adj.*** covered with grass

**grate¹** /greɪt/ ***noun*** [C] a framework of metal bars in front of a window, over a hole in the street, etc.: *a sewer grate*

**grate²** /greɪt/ ***verb*** **1** [T] to rub food into small pieces using a metal tool (a grater): *Grate the cheese and sprinkle it over the top of the pizza.* **2** [I] to make a sharp unpleasant sound (when two surfaces rub against each other): *The gate grated against the sidewalk as it opened.* **3** [I] **grate (on sb)** to annoy or irritate: *Her voice really grates on me!*

★**grate·ful** /ˈgreɪtfl/ ***adj.*** **grateful (to sb) (for sth); grateful (that...)** feeling or showing thanks (to sb): *We are extremely grateful to you for all the help you have given us.* ◇ *I know you wrecked my car, but I'm just grateful you're not hurt.* ◇ *I would be very grateful if you could send me a copy of your brochure.* OPP **ungrateful** The noun is **gratitude**. ▸ **grate·ful·ly** ***adv.***

**grat·er** /ˈgreɪt̬ər/ ***noun*** [C] a piece of kitchen equipment with a rough surface that is used for grating food ➲ picture at **kitchen**.

**grat·i·fi·ca·tion** /ˌgræt̬əfəˈkeɪʃn/ ***noun*** [U] the state of being pleased or satisfied

**grat·i·fy** /ˈgræt̬əfaɪ/ ***verb*** [T] (*pres. part.* **grat·i·fy·ing**; *3rd person sing. pres.* **grat·i·fies**; *pt, pp* **grat·i·fied**) (*formal*) (often passive) to give sb pleasure: *I was gratified to hear that you enjoyed my book.* ▸ **grat·i·fy·ing** ***adj.***

**grat·ing¹** /ˈgreɪt̬ɪŋ/ ***noun*** [C] = GRATE¹

**grat·ing²** /ˈgreɪt̬ɪŋ/ ***adj.*** irritating; (of a sound or sb's voice) unpleasant and harsh to listen to: *the grating sound of fingernails on a blackboard* ◇ *Many people aren't aware of their most grating habits.*

**grat·i·tude** /ˈgræt̬ətud/ ***noun*** [U] **gratitude (to sb) (for sth)** the feeling of being grateful or thankful: *We would like to express our gratitude to David Stewart for all his help and advice.* OPP **ingratitude**

**gra·tu·i·tous** /grəˈtuət̬əs/ ***adj.*** done without any good reason or purpose and often having harmful effects SYN unnecessary: *gratuitous violence on television*

★**grave¹** /greɪv/ ***noun*** [C] the place where a dead body is buried: *The casket was lowered into the grave.* ◇ *I put some flowers on the grave.*

**grave²** /greɪv/ ***adj.*** (*formal*) **1** bad or serious: *These events could have grave consequences for us all.* ◇ *a matter of grave concern* **2** (used about people) sad or serious: *He had a very grave expression on his face.* ➲ noun gravity SYN **Serious** is much more common for both senses.

**grav·el** /ˈgrævl/ ***noun*** [U] very small stones that are used for making roads, paths, etc.

**grave·stone** /ˈgreɪvstoʊn/ ***noun*** [C] = HEADSTONE

**grave·yard** /ˈgreɪvyɑrd/ ***noun*** [C] an area of land (often near a church) where dead people are buried ➲ Look at **cemetery**.

**grav·i·tate** /ˈgrævəteɪt/ ***verb*** [I] (*formal*)
PHR V **gravitate to/toward(s) sth/sb** to move toward sth/sb that you are attracted to: *Many young people gravitate to the cities in search of work.*

**grav·i·ty** /ˈgrævət̬i/ ***noun*** [U] **1** the natural force that makes things fall to the ground when you drop them: *the force of gravity* **2** (*formal*) importance or seriousness: *Politicians are just beginning to realize the gravity of the situation.* ➲ **Seriousness** is more common than gravity in this sense. The adjective is **grave**.

**gra·vy** /ˈgreɪvi/ ***noun*** [U] a sauce that is made from the juices that come out of meat while it is cooking. Gravy is served with meat, potatoes, etc. ➲ Look at **sauce**.

★**gray¹** (*also* **grey**) /greɪ/ ***adj.*** **1** of the color between black and white: *dark/light/pale gray* ◇ *He was wearing a gray suit.* **2** with gray hair: *He's going gray.*

★**gray²** (*also* **grey**) /greɪ/ ***noun*** [C,U] the color between black and white

**gray·ish** (*also* **greyish**) /ˈgreɪɪʃ/ ***adj.*** slightly gray

**graze** /greɪz/ ***verb*** **1** [I] (used about cows, sheep, etc.) to eat grass (that is growing in a field) **2** [T] to pass sth and touch it lightly, perhaps causing slight damage: *Luckily the bullet just grazed his head.*

**grease¹** /gris/ ***noun*** [U] **1** a thick oily substance used, for example, in engines: *engine grease* ◇ *grease marks* **2** oil or fat that has been left in a pan after meat has been cooked: *You'll need very hot water to get all the grease off those pans.*

**grease²** /gris/ ***verb*** [T] to put grease on or in sth: *Grease the pan thoroughly to stop the cake from sticking.*

**greas·y** /ˈgrisi; -zi/ ***adj.*** (**greas·i·er**; **greas·i·est**) covered with or containing a lot of grease: *greasy fingers* ◇ *greasy food* ◇ *greasy hair*

**great-** /greɪt/ ***prefix*** (used before a noun to show a family relationship)

> NOTE The prefix **great** can be added to other words for family members to show another generation: *your great-aunt* (= the aunt of your mother or father) ◇ *your great-nephew* (= the son of your nephew or niece) ◇ *your great-great-grandfather* (= the grandfather of one of your grandparents).

★**great¹** /greɪt/ ***adj.*** **1** (*formal*) large in amount, degree, size, etc.; a lot of: *We had great difficulty in solving the problem.* ◇ *The party was a great success.* ◇ *It gives me great pleasure to introduce tonight's* *guest.* ➲ Look at the note at **big**. **2** particularly important; of unusually high quality: *one of the greatest scientists of the 20th century* ◇ *a great moment in history* **3** (*informal*) good; wonderful: *We had a great time in Florida.* ◇ *It's great to see you again.* ◇ *They were great friends.*

NOTE We sometimes use **great** in a sarcastic way, that is, when something is not good at all: *Oh great! I spilled coffee all over my homework!*

**4** (*informal*) (used to emphasize sth) very: *There was a great big dog in the back yard.*
IDM **go to great lengths to do sth** → LENGTH
**a good/great deal** → DEAL[1]
**a good/great many** → MANY
▸ **great·ness** *noun* [U]

**great²** /greɪt/ *noun* [C, usually pl.] (*informal*) a person or thing of special ability or importance: *He's one of the all-time greats in baseball.*

**ˌgreat-ˈgrandchild** *noun* [C] the daughter or son of your grandchild

**ˌgreat-ˈgrandˌdaughter** *noun* [C] the daughter of one of your grandchildren

**ˌgreat-ˈgrandˌfather** *noun* [C] the father of one of your grandparents

**ˌgreat-ˈgrandˌmother** *noun* [C] the mother of one of your grandparents

**ˌgreat-ˈgrandˌparent** *noun* [C] the father or mother of one of your grandparents

**ˌgreat-ˈgrandson** *noun* [C] the son of one of your grandchildren

**great·ly** /ˈgreɪtli/ *adv.* very much: *She will be greatly missed by friends and family.*

**greed** /grid/ *noun* [U] **greed (for sth)** a strong desire for more food, money, power, etc. than you really need

**greed·y** /ˈgridi/ *adj.* (**greed·i·er**; **greed·i·est**) **greedy (for sth)** wanting more food, money, power, etc. than you really need: *Don't be so greedy – you've already had three pieces of cake.* ▸ **greed·i·ly** /-əli/ *adv.*

★**green¹** /grin/ *adj.* **1** of the color of grass or leaves: *dark/light/pale green* ◇ *olive green* ◇ *These bananas aren't ripe yet – they're still green.* **2** (*informal*) (used about a person) with little experience
IDM **give sb/get the green light** (*informal*) to give sb/get permission to do sth
**green with envy** (*informal*) wanting to have what sb else has: *She was green with envy when she found out how much money I make!*
**have a green thumb** (*informal*) to be able to grow plants well

★**green²** /grin/ *noun* **1** [C,U] the color of grass and leaves: *They were dressed in green.* ◇ *The room was decorated in greens and blues.* **2** **greens** [pl.] green vegetables whose leaves are usually eaten cooked **3** [C] a flat area of very short grass used in games such as golf: *the green at the 18th hole*

**green·back** /ˈgrinbæk/ *noun* [C] (*informal*) a U.S. dollar

**ˌgreen ˈbean** *noun* [C] = STRING BEAN

**ˈgreen card** *noun* [C] (*U.S.*) an official card that shows that sb from another country is allowed to live and work in the U.S: *to apply for a green card*

**green·er·y** /ˈgrinəri/ *noun* [U] attractive green leaves and plants

**green·house** /ˈgrinhaʊs/ *noun* [C] a building made of glass in which plants are grown

**the ˈgreenhouse efˌfect** *noun* [sing.] the warming of the earth's atmosphere as a result of pollution

**ˈgreenhouse gas** *noun* [C] any of the gases that are thought to cause the greenhouse effect, especially carbon dioxide

**green·ish** /ˈgrinɪʃ/ *adj.* slightly green

**ˌgreen ˈlight** *noun* [sing.] permission for a project to start or continue: *The committee gave the new course a green light.*

**ˌgreen ˈonion** *noun* [C,U] a type of small onion with a long green central part and leaves

**Green·wich Mean Time** /ˌgrɛnɪtʃ ˈmin taɪm/ *noun* [U] (*abbr.* **GMT**) the time at Greenwich in London, England on the line of 0° longitude, used for calculating time everywhere in the world

**greet** /grit/ *verb* [T] **1** to welcome sb when you meet him/her; to say hello to sb: *He greeted me with a friendly smile.* **2** **greet sth with sth** (usually passive) to receive sth in a particular way: *The news was greeted with a loud cheer.*

**greet·ing** /ˈgriṭɪŋ/ *noun* [C] **1** the first words you say when you meet sb: *Jan mumbled a quick greeting as she walked past us.* **2** [usually pl.] a good wish: *Greetings from sunny Arizona!*
IDM **season's greetings** → SEASON[1]

**ˈgreeting card** *noun* [C] a card that you send to sb on his/her birthday, on holidays, etc.

**gre·gar·i·ous** /grɪˈgɛriəs/ *adj.* liking to be with other people

**gre·nade** /grəˈneɪd/ *noun* [C] a small bomb that is thrown by hand or fired from a gun: *a hand grenade*

**grew** *past tense of* GROW

**grey** /greɪ/ *adj.* = GRAY[1,2]

**grey·hound** /ˈgreɪhaʊnd/ *noun* [C] a large thin dog that can run very fast and that is used for racing: *greyhound racing*

**grid** /grɪd/ *noun* [C] **1** a pattern of lines that cross each other to form squares **2** a system of squares that are drawn on a map so that the position of any place can be described or found: *a grid reference* **3** the system of cables, etc. taking electricity to all parts of a region

**grid·dle** /ˈgrɪdl/ *noun* [C] a type of flat pan that is used for cooking food on top of a stove ➲ picture at **pan**.

**grid·i·ron** /ˈgrɪdaɪərn/ *noun* [C] the field that football is played on

**grid·lock** /ˈgrɪdlɑk/ *noun* [U] **1** a situation in which there is so much traffic on a city's streets that no cars can move **2** a situation in which no progress can be made because people are not willing to work together or change their opinions: *The President blamed members of the other party for the gridlock in Congress.*

**grief** /grif/ *noun* [U] great sadness (especially because of the death of sb you love)

**IDM good grief** (*informal*) (used for expressing surprise or shock): *Good grief! Look at that!*

**griev·ance** /ˈgrivns/ ***noun*** [C] **a grievance (against sb)** something that you think is unfair and that you want to complain or protest about: *The workers aired* (= expressed) *their grievances at the meeting.*

**grieve** /griv/ ***verb*** [I] **grieve (for sb)** to feel great sadness (especially about the death of sb you love): *He is still grieving for his wife.*

**grill¹** /grɪl/ ***noun*** [C] a framework of metal bars that you put food on to cook over a fire: *Dad's cooking burgers on the grill outside.*

**grill²** /grɪl/ ***verb*** **1** [I,T] to cook on a GRILL¹: *grilled steak* ➲ Look at the note at **cook**. **2** [T] (*informal*) to question sb for a long time: *When she got home her parents grilled her about where she had been.*

**grim** /grɪm/ ***adj.*** (**grim·mer**; **grim·mest**) **1** (used about a person) very serious; not smiling: *His face was grim as he announced the bad news.* **2** (used about a situation, news, etc.) unpleasant or worrying: *We face the grim prospect of even higher inflation.* ◇ *The news is pretty grim.*

**grim·ace** /ˈgrɪməs; grɪˈmeɪs/ ***verb*** [I] to make a GRIMACE¹: *She grimaced with pain.*

**grim·ace¹** /ˈgrɪməs; grɪˈmeɪs/ ***noun*** [C] an expression on your face that shows that you are angry or that sth is hurting you: *a grimace of pain*

**grime** /graɪm/ ***noun*** [U] a thick layer of dirt

**grim·y** /ˈgraɪmi/ ***adj.*** (**grim·i·er**; **grim·i·est**) very dirty

**grin** /grɪn/ ***verb*** [I] (**grin·ning**; **grinned**) to smile broadly (so that you show your teeth): *She grinned at me as she came into the room.* ▸ **grin** ***noun*** [C]: *He came in with a big grin on his face and told us the good news.*

**grind¹** /graɪnd/ ***verb*** [T] (*pt, pp* **ground** /graʊnd/) **1** to crush sth into very small pieces or into a powder, using a machine: *Wheat is ground into flour.* ◇ *ground pepper* ➲ Look also at **ground beef**. **2** to press sth together or into sth firmly: *Some people grind their teeth while they're sleeping.*

**IDM grind to a halt** to stop slowly: *Traffic ground to a halt on I-35 yesterday.*

**grind²** /graɪnd/ ***noun*** **1** [sing.] something that you must do, that is boring, makes you feel tired, etc.: *Riding the subway to work is a real grind.* ◇ *the daily grind* (= the boring things that you must do every day) *at the office* **2** [C] (*informal*) a person who studies too hard

**grind·er** /ˈgraɪndər/ ***noun*** [C] a machine for grinding: *a coffee grinder*

**grip¹** /grɪp/ ***verb*** [T] (**grip·ping**; **gripped**) to take and keep hold of sb/sth firmly: *Don't grip the bat too tight.* ◇ *It's important that the car's tires grip the road well.* ◇ (*figurative*) *The story really gripped my imagination.*

**grip²** /grɪp/ ***noun*** [sing.] **a grip (on sb/sth)** a firm hold (on sb/sth): *I relaxed my grip and he ran away.* ◇ (*figurative*) *a dictator's grip on power*

**IDM come to grips with sth** to start dealing with a problem in an effective way: *We are trying to come to grips with a difficult period in our history.*

**gripe** /graɪp/ ***noun*** [C] (*informal*) a complaint about sth/sb ▸ **gripe** ***verb*** [I]

**grip·ping** /ˈgrɪpɪŋ/ ***adj.*** exciting; holding your attention: *a gripping drama*

**gris·ly** /ˈgrɪzli/ ***adj.*** (used for describing sth that is concerned with death) horrible; terrible: *a series of grisly murders* ➲ Look at **gruesome**. It is similar in meaning.

**Grit** /grɪt/ ***noun*** [C] (*Cdn*) a supporter or member of the Canadian Liberal Party

**grit¹** /grɪt/ ***noun*** [U] **1** small hard bits of dirt or stone: *Be sure to rinse the grit out of the clams.* **2** (*informal*) courage; determination

**grit²** /grɪt/ ***verb*** [T] (**grit·ting**; **grit·ted**)

**IDM grit your teeth** to have courage or determination in a difficult situation: *If things get difficult, you'll have to grit your teeth and keep going.*

**grits** /grɪts/ ***noun*** [pl., with sing. or pl. verb] a soft white or yellow food that is made from corn. Grits are eaten in the southern U.S. and are eaten warm, often with butter or cheese on top.

**griz·zly bear** /ˈgrɪzli bɛr/ (*also* **grizzly**) (*pl.* **griz·zlies**) ***noun*** [C] a type of North American bear that has brown fur

**groan¹** /groʊn/ ***verb*** [I] to make a deep sad sound because you are in pain, or to show that you are unhappy or do not approve of sth: *He groaned with pain.* ◇ *The audience groaned at his terrible jokes.* ▸ **groan** ***noun*** [C]

**groan²** /groʊn/ ***noun*** [C] the sound that you make when you GROAN¹

**gro·cer·ies** /ˈgroʊsəriz; ˈgroʊsriz/ ***noun*** [pl.] food and other small things for the home that are sold in a store

**gro·cer·y store** /ˈgroʊsəri stɔr; ˈgroʊsri-/ ***noun*** [C] a store where groceries are sold ➲ Look at **supermarket**.

**grog·gy** /ˈgrɑgi/ ***adj.*** (**grog·gi·er**; **grog·gi·est**) (*informal*) weak and unable to walk steadily because you feel sick, have not had enough sleep, etc.

**groin** /grɔɪn/ ***noun*** [C] the place where the tops of the legs join the body

**groom¹** /grum/ (*also formal* **bridegroom**) ***noun*** [C] a man on, or just before, his wedding day ➲ Look at the note at **wedding**.

**groom²** /grum/ ***verb*** [T] **1** to clean or take care of an animal by brushing it, etc. **2** (usually passive) to choose and prepare sb for a particular career or job: *He is clearly being groomed for the manager's job.*

**groom·ing** /ˈgrumɪŋ/ ***noun*** [U] the way you take care of your appearance, e.g. by brushing your hair, washing, etc.

**groove** /gruv/ ***noun*** [C] a long deep line that is cut in the surface of sth

**groov·y** /ˈgruvi/ ***adj.*** (*informal*) fashionable, attractive and interesting

**grope** /groʊp/ ***verb*** [I] **1 grope (around) (for sth)** to search for sth using your hands, as you do in the dark: *He groped for the light switch.* **2** (*informal*) to touch sb sexually, especially when he/she does not want you to

**gross**[1] /groʊs/ ***adj.*** **1** (*slang*) very bad; disgusting: *Yuck! This stuff smells really gross.* ◇ *Don't be so gross – keep your mouth closed when you're eating.* **2** (*formal*) obvious or serious: *gross violations of human rights* **3** total: *gross income* (= before taxes, etc. are taken away) OPP **net**

**gross**[2] /groʊs/ ***verb*** [T] to earn an amount of money before taxes, etc. are taken away: *The movie grossed over $12 million last weekend.*

PHR V **gross sb out** (*slang*) to behave in a way that sb finds bad or disgusting: *Could you change the subject? You're really grossing me out.*

**gross·ly** /ˈgroʊsli/ ***adv.*** very, in a way that people think is wrong: *That is grossly unfair.*

**gro·tesque** /groʊˈtɛsk/ ***adj.*** strange or unnatural in a way that is funny or frightening

★**ground**[1] /graʊnd/ ***noun***

➤ SURFACE OF EARTH **1 the ground** [sing.] the solid surface of the earth: *We sat on the ground to eat our picnic.* ◇ *He slipped off the ladder and fell to the ground.*

➤ SOIL **2** [U] an area or type of soil: *rocky ground*

NOTE The **Earth** is the name of the planet where we live. **Land** is the opposite of sea or ocean: *The sailors sighted land./The astronauts returned to Earth.* **Land** is also something that you can buy or sell: *The price of land in Tokyo is extremely high.* When you are outside, the surface under your feet is called **the ground**. When you are inside it is called **the floor**: *Don't sit on the ground. You'll get wet.* ◇ *Don't sit on the floor. I'll get another chair.* Plants grow in **earth**, **soil** or **dirt**.

➤ AREA OF LAND **3** [C] a piece of land that is used for a particular purpose: *a burial ground* ◇ *a playground* **4 grounds** [pl.] land surrounding a large building: *Smoking is not allowed on the school grounds.*

➤ AREA OF KNOWLEDGE/IDEAS **5** [U] an area of interest, study, discussion, etc.: *The lecture went over the same old ground/covered a lot of new ground.*

➤ REASON **6** [C, usually pl.] a reason for sth: *She retired on medical grounds.* ◇ *grounds for divorce*

➤ IN LIQUID **7 grounds** [pl.] the small pieces of solid matter in a liquid that have fallen to the bottom: *coffee grounds*

➤ ELECTRICAL WIRE **8** [C, usually sing.] a wire that makes a piece of electrical equipment safer by connecting it to the GROUND (1)

IDM **above/below ground** above/below the surface of the earth ➲ Look also at **underground**.

**break new ground** to make a discovery or introduce a new method or activity: *Scientists are breaking new ground in the field of genetic engineering.*

**gain ground** → GAIN[2]

**get off the ground** (used about a business, plan, etc.) to make a successful start

**ground**[2] /graʊnd/ ***verb*** [T] **1** to force an airplane, etc. to stay on the ground: *to be grounded by fog* **2** to make a piece of electrical equipment safer by connecting it to the GROUND[1] (1) with a wire **3** to punish a child by not allowing him/her to leave the house for a period of time: *My parents grounded me for two weeks.* ◇ *Get to your room – you're grounded!*

**ground**[3] /graʊnd/ *past tense, past participle of* GRIND[1]: *ground black pepper* ◇ *Our burgers are made with 100% pure ground beef.*

ˈ**ground-ˌbreaking** ***adj.*** making new discoveries; using new methods: *a ground-breaking report/style* ◇ *Many people say the discovery is ground-breaking.*

ˈ**ground crew** (*also* **ground staff**) ***noun*** [C,U] the people in an airport whose job it is to look after an aircraft while it is on the ground

ˌ**ground ˈfloor** ***noun*** [usually sing.] = FIRST FLOOR

IDM **be/get in on the ground floor** to become involved in a plan, project, etc., at the beginning

**ground·hog** /ˈgraʊndhɔg; -hɑg/ ***noun*** [C] = WOODCHUCK ➲ picture at **woodchuck**.

ˈ**Groundhog Day** ***noun*** [C] February 2. On this day, people in North America hold a festival and watch a groundhog come out of its hole in the ground. There is a story that says that if the groundhog does not see its shadow, spring will come early that year. But if the groundhog sees its shadow, there will be six more weeks of winter.

**ground·ing** /ˈgraʊndɪŋ/ ***noun*** [sing.] knowledge of the basic facts or principles of a subject: *This book provides a good grounding in English grammar.*

**ground·less** /ˈgraʊndləs/ ***adj.*** without reason: *Our fears were groundless.* ▸ **ground·less·ly** ***adv.***

**ground·work** /ˈgraʊndwərk/ ***noun*** [U] work that is done in preparation for further work or study

ˌ**ground ˈzero** ***noun*** [U] **1** the beginning; a starting point for an activity: *After two years of work we just seem to be back to ground zero.* **2** the point on the Earth's surface where a bomb explodes **3** the place in New York City where two tall buildings (the World Trade Center) used to stand until the terrorist attack of September 11, 2001 (9/11)

★**group**[1] /grup/ ***noun*** [C] **1** [with sing. or pl. verb] a number of people or things that are together or that are connected: *A group of students are going bowling tonight.* ◇ *Groups of people were standing around in the streets.* ◇ *He is in the 40-50 age group.* ◇ *people of many different social groups* ◇ *a pressure group* (= a political group that tries to influence the government) ◇ *Divide the class into groups.*

NOTE We usually use **group** with a singular verb when we are thinking of the whole group together: *Our drama group meets every Tuesday.* But if we use a phrase like *a group of...* with a plural noun or pronoun, we usually use a plural verb: *A group of students are planning a Halloween party.*

**2** a number of people who play music together: *a jazz group* ➲ Look at **band**. **3** a number of companies that are owned by the same person or organization: *the largest newspaper group in the country* ◇ *the group sales director* ◇ *the Burton group*

**group**[2] /grup/ ***verb*** [I,T] to form or put into one or more GROUPS[1] (1): *Group these words according to their meaning.*

**grov·el** /ˈgrɑvl; ˈgrʌvl/ ***verb*** [I] to try too hard to please sb who is more important than you or who can give you sth that you want: *to grovel for forgiveness*

G

★**grow** /groʊ/ ***verb*** (*pt* **grew** /gru/; *pp* **grown** /groʊn/)
➤INCREASE **1** [I] to increase in size or number; to develop into an adult form: *Look at how much Billy has grown!* ◇ *a growing child* ◇ *You need to invest if you want your business to grow.* ◇ *Kittens soon grow into cats.*
➤OF PLANT **2** [I] (used about plants) to be alive in a particular place: *Palm trees don't normally grow in Canada.*
➤LET STH GROW **3** [T] to cause or allow something to grow: *to grow a beard/mustache* ◇ *My grandfather grows a lot of vegetables in his garden.*
➤BECOME **4** [I] to become (gradually): *It began to grow dark.* ◇ *to grow older/wiser* ➲ **Get** is also possible and is less formal.
➤OF EMOTION/FEELING **5** [I] (used about a feeling, etc.) to develop or become strong: *A close friendship has grown between them.*
PHRV **grow into sth 1** to become (gradually): *She has grown into a very attractive child.* **2** to become big enough to fit clothes, etc.: *The coat is too big for him now, but he will grow into it.*
**grow on sb** to become more pleasing: *I didn't like it at first, but it's a taste that grows on you.*
**grow out of sth** to become too big or too old for sth: *She has grown out of that dress.*
**grow up** to become mature or adult: *What do you want to be when you grow up?* (= what job do you want to do later?) ◇ *Oh, grow up!* (= don't be silly!)

**growl** /graʊl/ ***verb*** [I] (used about dogs and other animals) to make a low noise in the throat to show anger or to give a warning ▸ **growl *noun*** [C]

**grown** /groʊn/ ***adj.*** physically adult or mature: *a full-grown elephant*

ˈ**grown-ˌup *adj.*** (usually before a noun) **1** physically or mentally adult or mature: *They have two grown-up daughters.* **2** for or conected with adults: *My son is too young to watch grown-up movies.*

**grown·up** (*also* **grown-up**) /ˈgroʊnʌp/ ***noun*** [C] an adult person: *Don't use the stove unless a grown-up is there to help you.*

★**growth** /groʊθ/ ***noun* 1** [U] growing or development: *A good diet is very important for children's growth.* ◇ *a growth industry* (= one that is growing) **2** [U, sing.] an increase (in sth): *population growth* ◇ *There has been a sudden growth in the candidate's popularity.* **3** [C] a lump that is not normal, that grows in a person's or an animal's body

**grub**[1] /grʌb/ ***noun* 1** [C] the first form that an insect takes when it comes out of the egg. Grubs are short, fat and white. **2** (*informal*) food

**grub**[2] /grʌb/ ***verb*** [I] **grub (around) (for sth)** to look for sth, especially by digging or by looking through or under other things: *birds grubbing around for worms*

**grub·by** /ˈgrʌbi/ ***adj.*** (**grub·bi·er**; **grub·bi·est**) (*informal*) dirty

**grudge** /grʌdʒ/ ***noun*** [C] **a grudge (against sb)** unfriendly feelings toward sb, because you are angry about what has happened in the past: *She still bears a grudge against me for what happened in high school.* ◇ *to have/hold a grudge against sb*

**gru·el·ing** /ˈgruəlɪŋ; ˈgrulɪŋ/ ***adj.*** difficult and tiring: *a grueling 26-mile race*

**grue·some** /ˈgrusəm/ ***adj.*** (used about sth concerned with death or injury) very bad or shocking: *A gruesome sight awaited the police officers when they arrived at the accident.* ➲ Look at **grisly**. It is similar in meaning.

**gruff** /grʌf/ ***adj.*** (used about a person or a voice) rough and unfriendly ▸ **gruff·ly *adv.***

**grum·ble** /ˈgrʌmbl/ ***verb*** [I] to complain or protest in a slightly angry way; to keep saying that you do not like sth: *The students were always grumbling about food in the cafeteria.*

**grump·y** /ˈgrʌmpi/ ***adj.*** (**grump·i·er**; **grump·i·est**) (*informal*) in a bad mood

**grunt** /grʌnt/ ***verb*** [I,T] to make a noise like a pig (a short low sound in the throat). People grunt when they do not like sth or are not interested and do not want to talk: *She just grunted when I asked her about it.* ▸ **grunt *noun*** [C]

**GST** /ˌdʒi ɛs ˈti/ ***noun*** [U] (*Cdn*) goods and services tax; a tax that is added to the price of goods and services ➲ Look also at **HST** and **PST**.

**gua·ca·mo·le** /ˌgwɑkəˈmoʊli/ ***noun*** [U] a dish made from a fruit (an avocado), which is mixed until it becomes a smooth cream

★**guar·an·tee**[1] /ˌgærənˈti/ ***noun*** [C] **1** a written promise by a company that it will repair or replace a product if it breaks or stops working in a certain period of time: *The watch comes with a two-year money-back guarantee* (= you can get your money back if it stops working within two years). ➲ Look also at **warranty**. **2** a promise that sth will be done or that sth will happen: *There is no guarantee that the treatment will be effective.*

★**guar·an·tee**[2] /ˌgærənˈti/ ***verb*** [T] **1** to give a GUARANTEE[1] (1) on a product: *This washing machine is guaranteed for three years.* **2** to promise that sth will be done or that sth is true: *They guaranteed delivery within one week.* ◇ *The food is guaranteed to be free of additives.* ◇ *I can guarantee that you will have a good time.*

★**guard**[1] /gɑrd/ ***verb*** [T] **1** to keep sb/sth safe from other people; protect: *The building was guarded by men with dogs.* ◇ *agents guarding the President* **2** to watch over sb and prevent him/her from escaping: *The prisoner was closely guarded on the way to the courthouse.*
PHRV **guard against sth** to try to prevent sth or stop sth from happening: *A good diet helps to guard against disease.*

★**guard**[2] /gɑrd/ ***noun* 1** [C] a person who guards sb/sth: *a border guard* ◇ *a security guard* ➲ Look also at **bodyguard**. **2** [U] the state of being ready to prevent attack or danger: *Who is on guard?* ◇ *The prisoner arrived under armed guard.* ◇ *a guard dog* **3** [sing.] a group of soldiers, police officers, etc. who guard sb/sth ➲ Look also at **Coast Guard** and **National Guard**. **4** [C] something that covers sth dangerous or protects sth: *a shin guard*
IDM **catch sb off guard** → CATCH[1]
**on guard (against sth)** prepared for an attack, a surprise, a mistake, etc.: *Visitors to the city should be on guard against pickpockets.*

**guard·ed** /ˈgɑrdəd/ ***adj.*** (used about an answer, a statement, etc.) not saying very much; careful ▸ **guard·ed·ly *adv.***

**guard·i·an** /ˈgɑrdiən/ ***noun*** [C] **1** a person who is responsible for a child who does not live with his/her parents **2** a person or institution that guards or protects sth: *The police are the guardians of law and order.*

**gu·ber·na·to·ri·al** /ˌgubərnəˈtɔriəl/ ***adj.*** (usually before a noun) connected with a governor or the position of a governor of a state

**guer·ril·la** (*also* **guerilla**) /gəˈrɪlə/ ***noun*** [C] a member of a small group of fighters (not an army) who make surprise attacks on the enemy: *guerrilla warfare*

★**guess**[1] /gɛs/ ***verb*** **1** [I,T] to give an answer or opinion about sth without being sure of all the facts: *Can you guess how much this cost?* ◇ *to guess at an answer* ◇ *I'd guess that he's about 45.* **2** [T] to give the correct answer when you are not sure about it; to guess correctly: *He guessed the weight of the package exactly.* ◇ *" You passed the test!" "How did you guess?"*

IDM **I guess** (*informal*) (used when you think that sth is probably true, or when you are not sure about sth) I suppose: *Nobody else is here yet – I guess we'll just have to wait.* ◇ *"Are you ready to go?" "Yeah, I guess so."*

★**guess**[2] /gɛs/ ***noun*** [C] an attempt to give the right answer when you are not sure what it is: *If you don't know the answer, then take a guess!* ◇ *My guess is that they're stuck in traffic.* ◇ *Your guess is as good as mine* (= I don't know).

**guess·ti·mate** /ˈgɛstəmət/ ***noun*** [C] an attempt to calculate sth that is based more on guessing than on information

**guess·work** /ˈgɛswərk/ ***noun*** [U] an act of guessing: *I arrived at the answer by pure guesswork.*

★**guest** /gɛst/ ***noun*** [C] **1** a person that you invite to your home or to a party, etc.: *We are having guests at our house this weekend.* ◇ *wedding guests* ◇ *an unexpected guest* ◇ *an uninvited guest* ➲ Look at **host**. **2** a person that you invite out and pay for at a restaurant, theater, etc. **3** a person who is staying at a hotel, etc.: *This hotel can accomodate 500 guests.* **4** a person who is invited to appear on a television or radio show: *tonight's special guest* ◇ *a guest speaker*

**guid·ance** /ˈgaɪdns/ ***noun*** [U] help or advice: *We need expert guidance on this problem.*

ˈ**guidance** ˌ**counselor** ***noun*** [C] a person who works in a school and whose job it is to give students advice about jobs, further education and personal problems

★**guide**[1] /gaɪd/ ***noun*** [C]

➤PERSON **1** a person whose job is to show cities, museums, etc. to tourists: *a tour guide* **2** a person who shows the way to others where it is difficult or dangerous: *We found a guide who knew the mountains well.*

➤STH THAT HELPS YOU DECIDE **3** something that helps you plan what you are going to do: *As a rough guide, use twice as much water as rice.*

➤BOOK **4** = GUIDEBOOK **5** a book that gives information about a subject: *a guide to French wines*

★**guide**[2] /gaɪd/ ***verb*** [T] **1** to help a person or a group of people to find the right way or direction to go: *He guided us through the busy streets to our hotel.* **2** to have an influence on sb/sth: *I was guided by your advice.* ➲ Look at the note at **lead**[3](1).

**guide·book** /ˈgaɪdbʊk/ (*also* **guide**) ***noun*** [C] a book for tourists, etc. that gives information about interesting places, etc.

**guid·ed** /ˈgaɪdəd/ ***adj.*** led by a GUIDE[1] (1): *a guided tour*

**guide·line** /ˈgaɪdlaɪn/ ***noun*** [C, usually pl.] advice on what to do about sth (that is given by sb in authority): *The government has issued new guidelines on food safety.*

**guil·lo·tine** /ˈgɪlətin; ˈgiətin; ˌgiəˈtin/ ***noun*** [C] a machine with a heavy sharp blade that is dropped from a great height. The guillotine was used (especially in France) for killing criminals by cutting their heads off.

**guilt** /gɪlt/ ***noun*** [U] **1** the feeling that you have when you know that you have done sth wrong: *Now that he was dead, she felt terrible guilt at the way she had behaved.* **2** the fact of having broken a law: *His guilt was not proven, and so he went free.* OPP **innocence**. **3** blame or responsibility for doing sth wrong: *It's difficult to say whether the guilt lies with the parents or the children.*

★**guilt·y** /ˈgɪlti/ ***adj.*** (**guilt·i·er**; **guilt·i·est**) **1 guilty (of sth)** having broken a law; being responsible for doing sth wrong: *She pleaded guilty/not guilty to the crime.* ◇ *to be found guilty of murder* OPP **innocent 2** showing or feeling GUILT (1): *I feel really guilty about not writing to you for so long.* ◇ *a guilty conscience* ▸ **guilt·i·ly** /-əli/ ***adv.***

**guin·ea pig** /ˈgɪni pɪg/ ***noun*** [C] **1** a small furry animal with no tail that is often kept as a pet **2** a person who is used in an experiment

**guise** /gaɪz/ ***noun*** [C] a way in which sb/sth appears, which is often different from usual or hides the truth: *His speech presented racist ideas under the guise of nationalism.*

**gui·tar** /gɪˈtɑr/ ***noun*** [C] a type of musical instrument with strings that you play with the fingers or with a piece of plastic (a **pick**): *an acoustic guitar* (= wooden, with a hollow body) ◇ *an electric guitar* (= using electricity, with a solid plastic body) ➲ Note that we usually say "play **the** guitar."

**guitars**

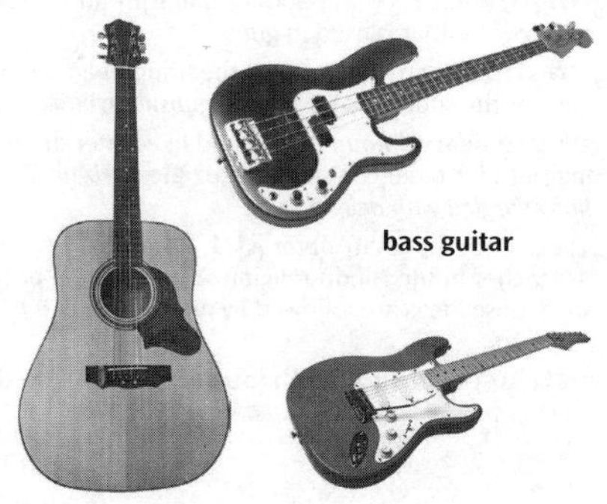


G

**gui·tar·ist** /gɪˈtɑrɪst/ ***noun*** [C] a person who plays the guitar

**gulf** /gʌlf/ ***noun*** [C] **1** a part of the ocean that is almost surrounded by land: *the Gulf of Mexico* **2** an important or serious difference between people or their opinions: *a wide gulf between people of different generations*

**gull** /gʌl/ ***noun*** [C] = SEAGULL

**gul·li·ble** /ˈgʌləbl/ ***adj.*** (used about a person) easily tricked or deceived

**gulp**[1] /gʌlp/ ***verb*** **1** [T] **gulp sth (down)** to eat or drink sth quickly **2** [I] to make a swallowing movement because you are afraid, surprised, etc.

**gulp**[2] /gʌlp/ ***noun*** [C] **1** an act of GULPING[1] **2** the amount that you can swallow when you GULP[1] (1): *He took a gulp of coffee and rushed out.*

**gum** /gʌm/ ***noun*** **1** [C, usually pl.] the hard pink part of the mouth that holds the teeth **2** (*also* **chewing gum**) [U] a sweet, sticky substance that you chew in your mouth but do not swallow ➲ Look also at **bubble gum**.

**gum·ball** /ˈgʌmbɔl/ ***noun*** [C] a small ball of gum

★**gun**[1] /gʌn/ ***noun*** [C] a weapon that is used for shooting. A gun fires bullets from a metal tube (a barrel): *The robber held a gun to my head.* ◇ *activists campaigning for gun control* (= laws that restrict the sale and use of guns)

NOTE Verbs often used with "gun" are **load**, **unload**, **point**, **aim**, **fire**. Different types of gun include a **machine gun**, **rifle** and **shotgun**. **Pistols** and **revolvers** are types of **handguns**.

**gun**[2] /gʌn/ ***verb*** [T] (**gun·ning**; **gunned**)
PHR V **gun sb down** (*informal*) to shoot sb and kill or seriously injure him/her

**gun·boat** /ˈgʌnboʊt/ ***noun*** [C] a small military ship that carries heavy guns

**gun·fire** /ˈgʌnˌfaɪər/ ***noun*** [U] the act of firing a gun or several guns; the sound that it makes: *the distant sound of gunfire*

**gun·man** /ˈgʌnmən/ ***noun*** [C] (*pl.* **gun·men** /-mən/) a man who uses a gun to rob or kill people

**gun·point** /ˈgʌnpɔɪnt/ ***noun***
IDM **at gunpoint** threatening to shoot: *He held the hostages at gunpoint* (= he said that he would shoot them if they did not obey him).

**gun·pow·der** /ˈgʌnˌpaʊdər/ ***noun*** [U] an explosive powder that is used in guns

**gun·shot** /ˈgʌnʃɑt/ ***noun*** [C] the firing of a gun or guns or the sound that it makes: *gunshot wounds*

**gur·gle** /ˈgərgl/ ***noun*** [C] a sound like water draining out of a large container ▶ **gur·gle** ***verb*** [I]: *The baby gurgled with delight.*

**gu·ru** /ˈguru; ˈgʊru/ ***noun*** [C] **1** a spiritual leader or teacher in the Hindu religion **2** (*informal*) a person whose ideas are followed by many people: *a fitness guru*

**gush** /gʌʃ/ ***verb*** [I] **1 gush (out) (from sth)** (used about a liquid) to flow out suddenly and in great quantities: *Blood gushed from the wound.* **2 gush (about/over sb/sth)** to express pleasure or admiration in an exaggerated way ▶ **gush** ***noun*** [C, usually sing.]: *a sudden gush of water*

**gust**[1] /gʌst/ ***noun*** [C] a sudden rush of wind: *A sudden gust of wind blew my hat off.*

**gust**[2] /gʌst/ ***verb*** [I] (used about the wind) to blow in gusts

**gus·to** /ˈgʌstoʊ/ ***noun***
IDM **with gusto** with great enthusiasm: *We all joined in the singing with gusto.*

**gut**[1] /gʌt/ ***noun*** (*informal*) **1 guts** [pl.] the organs inside your body (especially the stomach and the organs below it) **2** [C] the part of the body between the chest and the legs: *Phil punched him right in the gut.* ◇ *a huge beer gut* (=from drinking too much beer) **3 guts** [pl.] courage and determination: *It takes guts to admit that you are wrong.* ◇ *She didn't have the guts to tell them the truth.*

**gut**[2] /gʌt/ ***verb*** [T] (**gut·ting**; **gut·ted**) **1** to remove the GUTS[1] (1) from an animal, fish, etc. **2** to destroy the inside of a building (in a fire): *The warehouse was gutted by fire.*

**gut**[3] /gʌt/ ***adj.*** (only *before* a noun) based on emotion or feeling rather than on reason: *a gut feeling/reaction*

**gut·ter** /ˈgʌt̬ər/ ***noun*** [C] **1** (*especially US*) (*Cdn* **eavestrough**) a long metal or plastic pipe that is attached under the edge of a roof to carry away water **2** a channel between the road and the sidewalk that carries away water

ˈ**gut-ˌwrenching** ***adj.*** (*informal*) very unpleasant; making you feel very upset

★**guy** /gaɪ/ ***noun*** [C] (*informal*) a man or a boy: *He's a nice guy.*
IDM **you guys** → YOU

**gym** /dʒɪm/ ***noun*** **1** [C] (*informal*) = GYMNASIUM **2** [U] a class in school in which you do physical exercises and play sports: *gym shoes* ◇ *I hurt my knee yesterday during gym.*

**gym·na·si·um** /dʒɪmˈneɪziəm/ (*also informal* **gym**) ***noun*** [C] a large room that contains equipment, e.g. bars, ropes, etc. for doing physical exercises

**gym·nast** /ˈdʒɪmnəst; -næst/ ***noun*** [C] a person who is an expert at gymnastics

**gym·nas·tics** /dʒɪmˈnæstɪks/ ***noun*** [U] physical exercises that are done indoors, often using special equipment such as bars and ropes

**gy·ne·col·o·gist** /ˌgaɪnəˈkɑlədʒɪst/ ***noun*** [C] a doctor who has special training in gynecology

**gy·ne·col·o·gy** /ˌgaɪnəˈkɑlədʒi/ ***noun*** [U] the study and treatment of diseases and medical problems that only women have

**gyp·sy** /ˈdʒɪpsi/ ***noun*** [C] (*pl.* **gyp·sies**) a member of a race of people from eastern Europe who spend their lives traveling around from place to place

# H h

**H, h** /eɪtʃ/ ***noun*** [C,U] (*pl.* **H's**; **h's**) the eighth letter of the English alphabet: *"Hat" begins with (an) "H."*

**ha** /hɑ/ ***interjection*** **1** (*also* **hah**) (used for showing that you are surprised or pleased) **2** (*also* **ha! ha!**) (used in written language to show that sb is laughing)

★**hab·it** /ˈhæbət/ ***noun*** **1** [C] something that sb does very often (sometimes almost without thinking about it): *Biting your nails is a bad habit.* ◇ *He has an annoying habit of tapping his pen on his desk.* ➲ adjective **habitual**

NOTE A **habit** is usually something that is done by one person. A **custom** is something that is done by a group, community or nation: *the custom of giving presents at Christmas.*

**2** [U] doing sth regularly: *I think I only smoke out of habit now – I don't really enjoy it.*

IDM **be in/get into the habit of doing sth; make a habit of sth** to do sth regularly: *I've gotten into the habit of going for a jog every morning.* ◇ *I don't make a habit of talking to strange men at parties.*

**kick the habit** to stop doing sth harmful that you have done for a long time

**hab·it·a·ble** /ˈhæbət̬əbl/ ***adj.*** (used about buildings) suitable to be lived in OPP **uninhabitable**

**hab·i·tat** /ˈhæbətæt/ ***noun*** [C] the natural home of a plant or an animal

**hab·i·ta·tion** /ˌhæbəˈteɪʃn/ ***noun*** (*formal*) **1** [U] living in a place: *The caves showed signs of human habitation* (that people had lived there). **2** [C] a place where people live: *Police responded to a report of a burglary in a habitation last night.*

**ha·bit·u·al** /həˈbɪtʃuəl/ ***adj.*** doing sth very often: *a habitual criminal* (= who commits many crimes) ▸ **ha·bit·u·al·ly** ***adv.***

**hack** /hæk/ ***verb*** [I,T] **1** to cut sth using rough strokes with a tool such as a large knife: *He hacked (away) at the branch of the tree until it fell.* ◇ *The explorers hacked their way through the jungle.* **2 hack (into) (sth)** (*informal*) to use a computer to look at (and change) information that is stored on another computer

**hack·er** /ˈhækər/ ***noun*** [C] (*informal*) a person who HACKS (2) into other people's computers without permission

**had**[1] *past tense, past participle of* HAVE[1,2]

**had**[2] /hæd/ ***adj.*** **be had** (*informal*) to be tricked or deceived: *I've been had. This watch I bought doesn't work.*

**hag·gard** /ˈhægərd/ ***adj.*** (used about a person) looking tired or worried

**hag·gle** /ˈhægl/ ***verb*** [I] **haggle (with sb) (over/about sth)** to argue about the price of sth

**hah** /hɑ/ ***interjection*** = HA (1)

**hai·ku** /ˈhaɪku/ (*pl.* **hai·ku**; **hai·kus**) ***noun*** [C] a Japanese poem with three lines and usually 17 syllables

**hail**[1] /heɪl/ ***noun*** [U] frozen rain that falls in small hard balls ➲ Look at the note at **weather**.

**hail**[2] /heɪl/ ***verb*** [T] **1** to call or wave to sb/sth: *She raised her arm to hail the taxi.* **2 hail sb/sth as sth** to say in public that sth is very good: *The book was hailed as a masterpiece.*

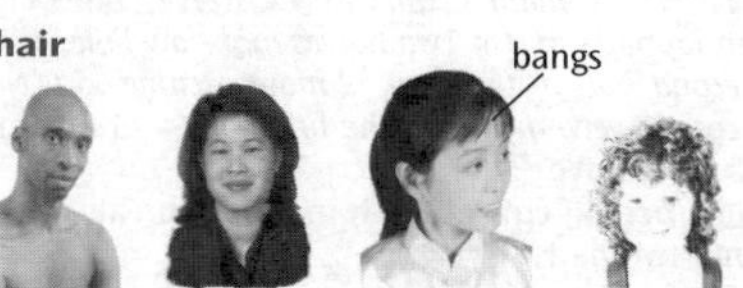

**bald head** **wavy hair** **straight hair** **curly hair**

★**hair** /hɛr/ ***noun*** **1** [C] one of the long thin things that grow on the skin of people and animals: *There's a hair in my soup.* ◇ *The dog left hairs all over the furniture.* **2** [U] the mass of HAIRS (1) on a person's head: *He has short black hair.*

NOTE Some special words for the color of hair are: **auburn**, **blond** and **red**. In order to take care of or style your hair you may **brush**, **comb**, **wash** (or **shampoo**) it and then **blow-dry** it. You may **part** it (or have **a part**) in the middle or on one side. When you go to the **salon** you have your hair **cut**, **styled** or **permed**.

IDM **fix your hair** → FIX[1]

**let your hair down** (*informal*) to relax and enjoy yourself (after being formal): *After the wedding, you can let your hair down at the reception.*

**hair·brush** /ˈhɛrbrʌʃ/ ***noun*** [C] a brush that you use on your hair ➲ picture at **brush**[1].

**hair·cut** /ˈhɛrkʌt/ ***noun*** [C] **1** the cutting of your hair, usually by sb else: *You need a haircut.* **2** the style in which your hair has been cut: *That haircut really looks good on you.*

**hair·do** /ˈhɛrdu/ ***noun*** [C] (*pl.* **hair·dos**) = HAIRSTYLE

**hair·dress·er** /ˈhɛrdrɛsər/ (*also* **hairstylist**) ***noun*** [C] a person whose job is to cut and style people's hair ➲ A **barber** is a hairdresser who only cuts men's hair.

ˈ**hair ˌdryer** ***noun*** [C] a machine that dries hair by blowing hot air through it ➲ Look also at **blow-dry**.

**-haired** /hɛrd/ ***adj.*** (in compounds) having hair of the stated type: *a long-haired rabbit*

**hair·line**[1] /ˈhɛrlaɪn/ ***noun*** [C] the place on a person's forehead where his/her hair starts growing

**hair·line**[2] /ˈhɛrlaɪn/ ***adj.*** (used about a crack in sth) very thin: *a hairline fracture of the bone*

**hair·piece** /ˈhɛrpis/ ***noun*** = TOUPEE

**hair·pin** /ˈhɛrpɪn/ ***noun*** [C] a small thin piece of wire that is folded in the middle, used by women for holding their hair in place

**ˌhairpin ˈcurve** (*also* **ˌhairpin ˈturn**) ***noun*** [C] a very sharp curve in a road, especially a mountain road

**ˈhair-ˌraising** ***adj.*** that makes you very frightened

**ˈhair spray** (*also* **hairspray**) ***noun*** [U] a substance that you spray on your hair to hold it in place

**hair·style** /ˈhɛrstaɪl/ (*also* **hairdo**) ***noun*** [C] the style in which your hair has been cut or arranged

**hair·styl·ist** /ˈhɛrstaɪlɪst/ ***noun*** = HAIRDRESSER

**hair·y** /ˈhɛri/ ***adj.*** (**hair·i·er**; **hair·i·est**) **1** having a lot of hair: *a hairy chest* **2** (*informal*) dangerous or worrying: *We had a pretty hairy drive down the country road in freezing rain.*

H

★**half¹** /hæf/ ***noun*** [C] (*pl.* **halves** /hævz/) one of two equal parts of sth: *Two halves make a whole.* ◇ *The second half of the book is more exciting.* ◇ *O'Neal scored twelve points in the first half* (= of a game). ➲ verb halve

IDM **break, cut, etc. sth in half** to break, etc. sth into two parts

★**half²** /hæf/ ***det., pronoun*** forming one of two equal parts: *Half of this money is yours.* ◇ *He got half his aunt's money when she died.* ◇ *half a gallon/a half-gallon* ◇ *half an hour* ◇ *Half the people in the office leave at 5.*

IDM **half past...** (*formal*) 30 minutes past an hour on the clock: *half past six* (= 6:30)

NOTE It is much more common to say **six-thirty**, etc.

★**half³** /hæf/ ***adv.*** to the extent of half; not completely: *half full* ◇ *The hotel was only half finished.* ◇ *I half thought she might come, but she didn't.* ◇ *He's half German.*

**half-and-half** /ˈhæf n hæf/ ***noun*** [U] a mixture that contains half milk and half cream, that is often used in coffee

**ˌhalf-ˈassed** ***adj.*** (*slang, taboo*) done without care or effort; not well planned

**ˌhalf-ˈbaked** ***adj.*** (*informal*) not well planned or considered: *a half-baked idea*

**ˈhalf ˌbrother** ***noun*** [C] a brother with whom you share one parent

**half-heart·ed** /ˌhæfˈhɑrt̬əd/ ***adj.*** without interest or enthusiasm ▸ **ˌhalf-ˈheart·ed·ly** ***adv.***

**ˈhalf note** ***noun*** [C] (*symbol* 𝅗𝅥) (in music) a note that lasts twice as long as a quarter note ➲ picture at **music**.

**ˈhalf ˌsister** ***noun*** [C] a sister with whom you share one parent

**half·time** /ˈhæftaɪm/ ***noun*** [U] (in sports) the period of time between the two halves of a game

**half·way** /ˌhæfˈweɪ/ ***adj., adv.*** at an equal distance between two places; in the middle of a period of time: *We live halfway between Columbus and Cincinnati.* ◇ *They take a break halfway through the morning.* ◇ *We've reached the halfway point in our project.*

★**hall** /hɔl/ ***noun*** [C] **1** (*also* **ˈhallway**) a room or passage that leads to other rooms in a house or public building: *The restrooms are at the end of the hall, on the right.* ◇ *There is a pay phone in the entrance hall of this building.* ◇ *She ran down the hall and into the classroom.* **2** a building or large room in which meetings, concerts, classes, etc. can be held: *a lecture hall* ◇ *a concert hall* ➲ Look at **city hall**, **residence hall** and **study hall**.

**hall·mark** /ˈhɔlmɑrk/ ***noun*** [C] **1** a characteristic that is typical of sb or sth: *The ability to motivate students is the hallmark of a good teacher.* **2** a mark that is put on objects made of valuable metals, giving information about the quality of the metal and when and where the object was made

**ˌhall of ˈfame** ***noun*** [C] (*pl.* **halls of fame**) a list of people who are very successful in a certain type of activity such as a sport, or a place, similar to a museum, where you can see things connected with these people: *the Baseball Hall of Fame*

**Hal·low·een** /ˌhæləˈwin; ˌhɑ-/ ***noun*** [sing.] October 31

NOTE Halloween is the time when people say that witches and ghosts appear. Children dress up in costumes and go to other houses in their neighborhood. At each house they say, "Trick or treat!" and the people in the houses give them candy. ➲ picture at **mask**.

**hal·lu·ci·na·tion** /həˌlusəˈneɪʃn/ ***noun*** [C,U] seeing sth that is not really there (because you are sick or have taken a drug)

**hall·way** /ˈhɔlweɪ/ ***noun*** = HALL (1)

**ha·lo** /ˈheɪloʊ/ ***noun*** [C] (*pl.* **ha·los** or **hal·oes**) the circle of light that is drawn around the head of a holy person in a painting

**halt¹** /hɔlt/ ***noun*** [sing.] a stop (that does not last very long): *Work came to a halt when the machine broke down.* ◇ *to bring sth to a halt*

IDM **grind to a halt** → GRIND¹

**halt²** /hɔlt/ ***verb*** [I,T] to stop for a short time; to make sth stop

**halve** /hæv/ ***verb*** [T] **1** to divide sth into two equal parts: *First halve the peach and then remove the pit.* **2** to make sth half as big as it was before: *We aim to halve the unemployment rate.*

**ham** /hæm/ ***noun*** [C,U] meat from a pig's back leg that has been smoked, etc. to keep it fresh: *a slice of ham* ◇ *a ham sandwich* ➲ Look at **bacon** and **pork** and at the note at **meat**.

**ham·burg·er** /ˈhæmˌbərgər/ ***noun*** **1** (*also* **burger**) [C] a sandwich that is made with chopped meat that has been formed into a flat round shape, in a soft round bread roll (a bun) **2** [U] meat from cows that has been cut into very small pieces with a special machine

**ham·mer¹** /ˈhæmər/ ***noun*** [C] a tool with a heavy metal head that is used for hitting nails, etc. ➲ picture at **tool**.

**ham·mer²** /ˈhæmər/ ***verb*** **1** [I,T] to hit with a HAMMER¹: *She hammered the nail into the wall.* **2** [I] to hit sth, making a loud noise: *He kept hammering on the door across the hall.*

PHR V **hammer (away) at sb/sth** to repeat a criticism, etc. many times in a very forceful way:

*The candidate kept hammering away at her opponent's voting record.*
**hammer sth into sb** to force sb to remember sth by repeating it many times
**hammer sth out** (*figurative*) to succeed in making a plan or agreement after a lot of difficulty: *Eventually a solution was hammered out.*

**ham·mer·ing** /ˈhæmərɪŋ/ ***noun*** [U] the noise that is made by sb using a hammer or by sb knocking sth many times

**ham·mock** /ˈhæmək/ ***noun*** [C] a bed, made of strong cloth or net, which is hung up at both ends. Hammocks are used on ships or outdoors.

**ham·per**[1] /ˈhæmpər/ ***noun*** [C] a large basket with a lid that you can put dirty clothes in

**ham·per**[2] /ˈhæmpər/ ***verb*** [T] to make sth difficult: *The construction work was hampered by bad weather.*

**ham·ster** /ˈhæmstər/ ***noun*** [C] a small animal that is kept as a pet. Hamsters are like mice but are fatter and do not have a tail. They store food in the sides of their mouths.

★**hand**[1] /hænd/ ***noun***

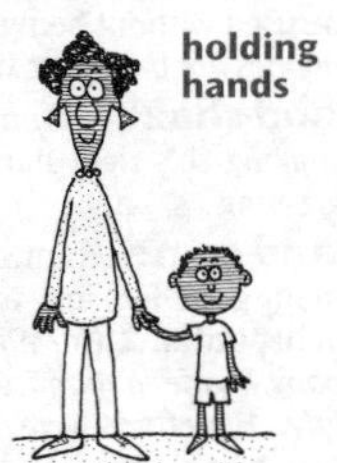


➤PART OF BODY **1** [C] the part of a person's arm below the wrist: *He took the child by the hand.* ◇ *She lifted the hot pan out of the oven with her bare hands.* ◇ *He held the bird gently in the palm of his hand.* ➲ picture on study page **A32**.
➤HELP **2** **a hand** [sing.] some help: *I'll give you a hand with the dishes.*
➤ON CLOCK/WATCH **3** [C] one of the parts on a clock or watch that points to the numbers: *the hour/minute/second hand* ➲ Picture at **clock**.
➤WORKER **4** [C] a person who works with his/her hands: *All hands* (= all sailors) *on deck!* ◇ *He works as a hired hand on a dairy farm.*
➤IN CARD GAMES **5** [C] the set of playing cards that sb has been given in a game of cards
IDM **at hand** **1** near in space or time: *Help is close at hand.* **2** being dealt with at this time: *We need to focus on the task at hand.*
**be an old hand (at sth)** → OLD
**by hand** **1** done by a person and not by machine: *I had to do all the sewing by hand.* **2** not by mail: *The letter was delivered by hand.*
**change hands** → CHANGE[1]
**get, etc. the upper hand** → UPPER
**give sb/get a big hand** → BIG
**hand in hand** **1** holding each other's hands **2** (*figurative*) usually happening together; closely connected
**hands off (sb/sth)** (*informal*) (used for ordering sb not to touch sth or to leave sth alone)
**hands up** **1** (used in a classroom, etc. for asking people to raise one hand and give an answer): *Hands up, who wants to go on the trip this afternoon?* **2** (used by a person with a gun to tell other people to put their hands in the air)
**have your hands full** to be very busy so that you cannot do anything else
**a helping hand** → HELP[1]
**hold sb's hand** to give help or comfort to sb in a difficult situation
**hold hands (with sb)** (used about two people) to hold each other's hands (because you like each other)
**in your/sb's hands** in your/sb's possession, control or care: *The document is no longer in my hands.* ◇ *The matter is in the hands of an attorney.*
**on hand** available to help or to be used: *Several artists will be on hand to discuss their work.*
**on your hands** being your responsibility: *We seem to have a problem on our hands.*
**on the one hand...on the other (hand)** (used for showing opposite points of view): *On the one hand, of course, cars are very useful. But on the other, they cause a huge amount of pollution.*
**out of hand** not under control: *This whole situation has gotten totally out of hand.* OPP Look at **in hand**.
**out of your/sb's hands** not in your/sb's control: *I can't help you – the problem is out of my hands.*
**shake sb's hand/shake hands (with sb)** → SHAKE[1]
**take sth off sb's hands** to help sb by taking a responsibility away from him/her: *I was so glad when Connie offered to take that project off my hands!*
**wash your hands of sb/sth** → WASH[1]

★**hand**[2] /hænd/ ***verb*** [T] to give or pass sth to sb: *Please hand me the scissors.* ◇ *Please hand the scissors to me.* ◇ *Let's hand the picture around the class so everybody can see it.*
IDM **have to hand it to sb** (*informal*) used to say that sb deserves praise for sth: *I don't agree with her methods but I have to hand it to her, they're effective.*
PHR V **hand sth down (to sb)** **1** to pass customs, traditions, etc. from older people to younger ones: *These stories have been handed down from generation to generation.* **2** to pass clothes, toys, etc. from older children to younger ones in the family ➲ Look also at **hand-me-down**. **3** (used about a judge, etc.) to give an official decision in a court of law: *The Supreme Court handed down its ruling on the case yesterday.*
**hand sth in (to sb)** to give sth to sb in authority: *Time's up. Hand in your tests now.* ◇ *Your papers must be handed in by Friday.*
**hand sth out (to sb)** to give sth to many people in a group: *Food was handed out to the starving people.*
**hand sb/sth over (to sb)** to give sb/sth (to sb): *People were tricked into handing over large sums of money.*

**hand·bag** /ˈhændbæg/ ***noun*** [C] = PURSE[1]

**hand·book** /ˈhændbʊk/ ***noun*** [C] a small book that gives useful information and advice about sth

**hand·cuffs** /ˈhændkʌfs/ ***noun*** [pl.] a pair of metal rings that are joined together by a chain and put around the wrists of prisoners

**-hand·ed** /ˈhændəd/ ***combining form*** having, using or made for the stated type of hand(s)[1,2]: *right-handed* ◇ *left-handed scissors*

**hand·ful** /ˈhændfʊl/ ***noun*** **1** [C] **a handful (of sth)** as much or as many of sth as you can hold in one hand: *a handful of sand* **2** [sing.] a small number (of sb/sth): *a handful of people* **3 a handful** [sing.] (*informal*) a person or an animal that is difficult to control: *The little girl is quite a handful.*

**hand·gun** /ˈhændgʌn/ ***noun*** [C] a gun that is small enough to hold in one hand ➲ Look at the note at **gun**[1].

**ˌhand-ˈheld** ***adj.*** (usually before a noun) small enough to be held in the hand while being used: *a hand-held camera/computer* ▸ **hand-held** ***noun*** [C]

**hand·i·cap**[1] /ˈhændikæp/ ***noun*** [C] **1** a physical or mental problem that makes it difficult for you to do some things that other people can do: *people with mental handicaps* ➲ **Disability** is more common nowadays. **2** something that makes doing sth more difficult; a disadvantage: *Not speaking Spanish is going to be a real handicap in my new job.* **3** a disadvantage that is given to a strong competitor in a sports event, etc. so that the other competitors have a better chance

H

**hand·i·cap**[2] /ˈhændikæp/ ***verb*** (**hand·i·capping**; **hand·i·capped**) [T] (usually passive) to give or be a disadvantage to sb: *They were handicapped by their lack of education.*

**hand·i·capped** /ˈhændikæpt/ ***adj.*** **1** having sth serious wrong with you (either physically or mentally) that means that you have difficulties doing things that other people can do: *a handicapped child* ◇ *mentally/visually handicapped*

> NOTE Some people do not like the word **handicapped** and prefer to use expressions such as **disabled people** or **people with disabilities**. We can also use **challenged** or **impaired** in compounds to talk about a specific difficulty that sb has: *physically challenged* ◇ *visually impaired*.

**2** for or connected with HANDICAPPED (1) people: *a handicapped parking space*

**hand·i·crafts** /ˈhændikræfts/ ***noun*** objects that are made with skillful use of the hands as well as artistic ability, e.g. by sewing

**hand·i·work** /ˈhændiwərk/ ***noun*** [U] **1** what you have made or done, especially using your artistic skill: *She put the dress on and stood back to admire her handiwork.* **2** what a particular person or group has done, especially sth bad

**hand·ker·chief** /ˈhæŋkərtʃɪf; -tʃif/ ***noun*** (*pl.* **hand·ker·chiefs** or **hand·ker·chieves** /-tʃivz/) a square piece of cloth that you use for blowing your nose ➲ picture at **sneeze**.

> NOTE The informal word is **hankie**. A handkerchief that is made of soft thin paper is called a **Kleenex** or a **tissue**.

★**han·dle**[1] /ˈhændl/ ***noun*** [C] a part of sth that is used for holding or opening it: *the door handle* ◇ *the handle of a frying pan* ➲ picture at **pan**.
IDM **fly off the handle** → FLY[1]

★**han·dle**[2] /ˈhændl/ ***verb*** [T] **1** to touch sth with, or hold sth in, your hand(s): *Wash your hands before you handle food.* ◇ *Handle with care!* **2** to deal with or to control sb/sth: *This port handles 100 million tons of cargo each year.* ◇ *I have a problem at work and I don't really know how to handle it.*

**han·dle·bar** /ˈhændlbɑr/ ***noun*** [C, usually pl.] the curved metal bar at the front of a bicycle that you hold when you are riding it ➲ picture at **bicycle**.

**hand·made** /ˌhændˈmeɪd/ ***adj.*** made by hand, not by machine

**ˈhand-me-ˌdown** ***noun*** [C] (*pl.* **hand-me-downs**) a thing, such as a piece of clothing, that you no longer want and that you give to sb else in your family: *When I was little, I had to wear my brother's hand-me-downs.* ▸ **ˈhand-me-down** ***adj.*** (only *before* a noun): *a hand-me-down sweater*

**hand·out** /ˈhændaʊt/ ***noun*** [C] **1** food, money, etc. that is given to people who need it badly **2** a printed sheet of paper that is given to a lot of people, e.g. to explain sth in a class

**hand·o·ver** /ˈhændoʊvər/ ***noun*** [C,U] the act of giving sb or sth to sb else, especially in a formal or official way: *the smooth handover of power to the elected government* ◇ *the handover of the hostages*

**hand·picked** /ˌhændˈpɪkt/ ***adj.*** carefully chosen: *the chairman's handpicked successor*

**hand·set** /ˈhænsɛt; ˈhænd-/ ***noun*** [C] = RECEIVER

**ˌhands-ˈfree** ***adj.*** (usually before a noun) able to be used without being held in sb's hand: *Hands-free phones are the safest kind to use while driving.*

**hand·shake** /ˈhændʃeɪk/ ***noun*** [C] the act of shaking sb's right hand with your right hand as a greeting

**hand·some** /ˈhænsəm/ ***adj.*** **1** (used about a man) good-looking; attractive ➲ Look at the note at **beautiful**. **2** (*formal*) large or generous: *The company made a handsome profit.* ▸ **hand·some·ly** ***adv.***: *Her efforts were handsomely rewarded.*

**ˌhands-ˈon** ***adj.*** learned by you doing sth yourself, not watching sb else do it; practical: *hands-on computer experience*

**hand·stand** /ˈhændstænd/ ***noun*** [C] a movement in which you balance on your hands and put your legs straight up in the air

**hand·writ·ing** /ˈhændraɪt̬ɪŋ/ ***noun*** [U] a person's style of writing by hand: *I can't read Joe's handwriting.*

**hand·written** /ˈhændrɪtn/ ***adj.*** written by hand, not typed or printed

**hand·y** /ˈhændi/ ***adj.*** (**hand·i·er**; **hand·i·est**) **1** useful; easy to use: *a handy tip* ◇ *a handy gadget* **2** nearby or easy to reach: *Always keep a first-aid kit handy.* ◇ *Put the printer over there so that it will be handy for everyone.*
IDM **come in handy** to be useful at some time: *Don't throw that box away. It may come in handy.*

**hand·y·man** /ˈhændimæn/ ***noun*** (*pl.* **hand·y·men** /-mɛn/) a person who is good at making or repairing things

★**hang**[1] /hæŋ/ ***verb*** (*pt, pp* **hung** /hʌŋ/)

> NOTE The past tense and past participle **hanged** is only used in sense 2.

**1** [I,T] to fasten sth or be fastened at the top so that the lower part is free or loose: *Hang your coat on the hook.* ◇ *I hung the wash on the line.* ◇ *I left the wash hanging on the line all day.* ◇ (*figurative*) *People were hanging out of windows to see the parade go past.* **2** [I,T] to kill sb by putting a rope around his/her neck and allowing him/her to drop, or to die in this way: *She hanged herself in the attic.* ◇ *He was hanged for murder.* ◇ *He was sentenced to hang for murder.* **3** [I] **hang (above/over sb/sth)** to stay in the air (above/over sb/sth): *Smog hung in the air over the city.* ◇ (*figurative*) *That paper I have to write is hanging over me.*

IDM **hang in there** (*informal*) to have courage in a difficult situation and not stop trying to do sth: *The worst part is over – just hang in there and be patient.*

PHR V **hang around** (*informal*) to stay in or near a place not doing very much: *a bunch of kids hanging around at the mall*

**hang on 1** to not stop making an effort or trying to do sth: *Keep hanging on. We'll get you to the hospital in a few minutes.* **2** to wait for a short time: *Hang on a minute. I'm almost ready.* ◇ *The line is busy. Would you like to hang on or call back later?*

**hang on to sth 1** to hold sth tightly **2** (*informal*) to keep sth: *Let's hang on to the car for another year.*

**hang out** (*slang*) to spend time in a place, often without doing very much: *I usually just hang out with my friends after school.*

**hang sth out** to put wet clothes, etc. outdoors so that they can dry

**hang up (on sb)** to end a telephone conversation by putting down the telephone or pushing a button ➲ Look at the note at **telephone**.

**hang²** /hæŋ/ ***noun***

IDM **get the hang of sth** (*informal*) to learn how to use or do sth: *It took me a long time to get the hang of this computer.*

**han·gar** /ˈhæŋər; ˈhæŋgər/ ***noun*** [C] a big building where airplanes are kept

**hang·er** /ˈhæŋər/ (*also* **ˈclothes hanger, ˈcoat hanger**) ***noun*** [C] a metal, plastic or wooden object with a hook that is used for hanging up clothes in a closet

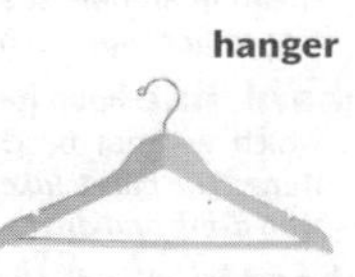
**hanger**

**ˈhang ˌglider** ***noun*** [C] a type of frame with cloth on it, like wings, from which a person can hang and fly through the air ▸ **ˈhang ˌgliding** ***noun*** [U]: *to go hang gliding*

**hang·o·ver** /ˈhæŋoʊvər/ ***noun*** [C] a pain in the head and a feeling of sickness that is caused by drinking too much alcohol the night before

**ˈhang-up** ***noun*** [C] (*informal*) something that worries you a lot: *He has a real hang-up about his height.*

**han·kie** /ˈhæŋki/ ***noun*** [C] (*informal*) = HANDKERCHIEF

**Ha·nuk·kah** (*also* **Chanukah**) /ˈhɑnəkə; ˈxɑ-/ ***noun*** [U] a Jewish religious festival that lasts for eight days in December

**hap·haz·ard** /hæpˈhæzərd/ ***adj.*** without any order or organized plan: *Her system of filing seems to be completely haphazard.* ▸ **hap·haz·ard·ly** ***adv.***

★**hap·pen** /ˈhæpən/ ***verb*** [I] **1** (of an event or situation) to take place: *Can you describe to the police what happened after you left the party?* ◇ *How did the accident happen?*

NOTE **Happen** and **occur** are usually used with events that are not planned. **Occur** is more formal than **happen**. **Take place** suggests that an event is planned: *The wedding took place on Saturday, June 13.*

**2 happen to sb/sth** to be what sb/sth experiences: *What do you think happened to Julie? She should have been here an hour ago.* ◇ *What will happen to the business when your father retires?* **3 happen to do sth** to do sth by chance: *I happened to see him downtown yesterday.* ◇ *She happened to be there yesterday too.*

IDM **as it happens/happened** (used when you are adding to what you have said) by chance; actually: *The deadline for my project is June 5, which, as it happens, is also my birthday.*

**it (just) so happens** → so¹

**what's happening?** (*slang*) (used as a friendly greeting to sb that you know very well): *Hey, dudes, what's happening?*

**hap·pen·ing** /ˈhæpənɪŋ; ˈhæpnɪŋ/ ***noun*** [C, usually pl.] a thing that happens; an event (that is usually strange or difficult to explain): *Strange happenings have been reported in that old hotel.*

NOTE A **happening** is usually something that happens by chance. An **event** is usually something that is planned and suggests something special or important.

★**hap·pi·ly** /ˈhæpəli/ ***adv.*** **1** in a happy way: *They all lived happily ever after.* ◇ *I would happily give up my job if I didn't need the money.* **2** it is lucky that; fortunately: *The police found my purse and, happily, nothing had been stolen.*

★**hap·py** /ˈhæpi/ ***adj.*** (**hap·pi·er**; **hap·pi·est**) **1** feeling, showing or giving pleasure or satisfaction: *a happy childhood* ◇ *a happy family* ◇ *a happy smile* ◇ *The movie is sad, but it has a happy ending.* ◇ *She doesn't feel happy about the salary she was offered.* ◇ *Are you happy with your work?* ◇ *Congratulations! I'm really happy for you.* OPP **unhappy** Look at the note at **glad**. **2** (not before a noun) **happy to do sth** willing; pleased: *I'll be happy to see you any day next week.* **3 Happy** (used in greetings to wish sb an enjoyable time): *Happy Birthday!* ◇ *Happy New Year!* ▸ **hap·pi·ness** ***noun*** [U]: *Money can't buy happiness.*

**ˈhappy hour** ***noun*** [C, U, usually sing.] a time, usually in the early evening, when a bar sells alcoholic drinks at lower prices than usual: *Does the bar near the office have a happy hour?* ◇ *I never miss happy hour on Fridays!*

**ha·rass** /həˈræs; ˈhærəs/ ***verb*** [T] to annoy or put pressure on sb, especially continuously or on many different occasions: *The court ordered him to stop harassing his ex-wife.* ▸ **ha·rass·ment** /-mənt/ ***noun*** [U]: *She accused her boss of* ***sexual harassment***.

**ha·rassed** /həˈræst; ˈhærəst/ ***adj.*** tired and worried because you have too much to do

**har·bor¹** /ˈhɑrbər/ ***noun*** [C,U] a place on the coast where ships can be tied up to shelter from the ocean: *The weather was too rough for the fishing boats to leave the harbor yesterday.*

**har·bor²** /ˈhɑrbər/ ***verb*** [T] **1** to hide or give shelter to sb/sth bad: *They were accused of harboring criminals.* **2** to keep sth secret in your mind for a long time: *She harbored a deep dislike of him for years.*

H

★**hard¹** /hɑrd/ ***adj.***

➤SOLID/STIFF **1** not soft to touch; not easy to break or bend; very firm: *The bed was so hard that I couldn't sleep.* ◇ *Diamonds are the hardest known mineral.*

➤DIFFICULT **2 hard (for sb) (to do sth)** difficult to do or understand; not easy: *The first question on the test was really hard.* ◇ *This book is hard to understand./It is a hard book to understand.* ◇ *It's hard for young people to find good jobs these days.* **3** (used about conditions) bad or unhappy: *He had a hard time when his parents died.*

➤NEEDING/USING EFFORT **4** needing or using a lot of effort: *It's a hard climb to the top of the hill.* ◇ *They say that hard work is good for you.* ◇ *She's a hard worker.*

➤WITHOUT SYMPATHY **5 hard (on sb)** (used about a person) not feeling or not showing kindness or pity; not gentle: *He's way too hard on his kids.*

➤WEATHER **6** (used about the weather) very cold: *The forecast is for a hard winter.* OPP **mild**

➤WATER **7** (used about water) containing particular minerals so that soap does not make many bubbles OPP **soft**

IDM **be hard on sb/sth** to hurt sb/sth or to make things difficult: *Living on very little money can be hard on students.*

**give sb a hard time** (*informal*) to criticize sb or make jokes about him/her, usually in order to make him/her feel embarrassed: *Don't give Bobby such a hard time about being short – he can't help it.*

**hard facts** information that you know is correct: *Reporters still have very few hard facts on this story.*

**hard of hearing** unable to hear well

**have a hard/rough time** → TIME¹

**no hard feelings** used to tell sb you do not feel angry after an argument, etc.: *I hope there are no hard feelings – it was just a joke.*

▸ **hard·ness** ***noun*** [U]

★**hard²** /hɑrd/ ***adv.*** **1** with great effort, energy or attention: *He worked hard all his life.* ◇ *You'll have to try harder than that.* ◇ *She looked hard at the man, but she didn't recognize him.* **2** with great force; heavily: *It was snowing hard.* ◇ *He hit her hard across the face.*

IDM **be hard up (for sth)** (*informal*) to want or need sth, e.g. money, very much: *You must be pretty hard up for entertainment if you're watching that dumb show.*

**die hard** → DIE¹

**ˌhard-and-ˈfast** ***adj.*** (especially after a negative) that cannot be changed: *There are no hard-and-fast rules about this.*

**hard·back** /ˈhɑrdbæk/ ***noun*** [C,U] a book that has a hard, rigid cover: *This book is only available* ***in hardback****.* ◇ *I never buy hardbacks – they're too expensive.* ➲ Compare **paperback**.

**hard·ball** /ˈhɑrdbɔl/ ***noun*** [U] the game of baseball ➲ look at **softball**

IDM **play hardball** behave in a way that shows that you are determined to get what you want: *Successful businesspeople have to know how to play hardball.*

**ˌhard-ˈboiled** ***adj.*** (used about an egg) boiled inside its shell until it is hard inside

**ˌhard-ˈcore** ***adj.*** **1** having a belief or a way of behaving that will not change: *hard-core conservatives* **2** showing or describing sexual activity in a detailed or violent way: *They sell* ***hard-core pornography****.*

**hard·cov·er** /ˈhɑrdkʌvər/ ***noun*** [C] a book that has a hard, rigid cover: *I'm sorry, this book is only available* ***in hardcover****.* ➲ Look at **paperback**.

**ˌhard ˈcurrency** ***noun*** [U] money of a particular country that is easy to exchange for money from another country

**ˈhard drive** (*also* **ˌhard ˈdisk**) ***noun*** [C] a piece of hard plastic used for storing information inside a computer. It can hold more information than a floppy disk.

**ˌhard ˈdrug** ***noun*** [C] powerful and illegal drugs that some people take for pleasure and may become dependent on (**addicted**): *Heroin and cocaine are hard drugs.* ➲ Look at **soft drug**.

**hard·en** /ˈhɑrdn/ ***verb*** **1** [I,T] to become or to make sth hard or less likely to change: *Put the mixture in the freezer to harden.* ◇ *The senator hardened her opposition to the proposal.* **2** [T] (usually passive) **harden sb (to sth)** to make sb less sensitive: *a hardened reporter* ◇ *a hardened criminal*

> NOTE **Harden** is only used when hard means "firm" or "unkind": *The concrete will harden in 24 hours.* ◇ *He hardened himself to the feelings of other people.* **Get harder** is used when hard has another meaning such as "difficult": *Learning a foreign language gets harder as you get older.*

**ˌhard-ˈhitting** ***adj.*** that talks about or criticizes sb/sth in an honest and very direct way: *a hard-hitting campaign/speech* ◇ *hard-hitting journalism*

**ˌhard ˈline** ***noun*** [sing.] a way of thinking or a plan which will not be changed or influenced by anything: *The police take a very hard line against people who drink and drive.*

★**hard·ly** /ˈhɑrdli/ ***adv.*** **1** almost not; with difficulty: *Speak up – I can hardly hear you.* ◇ *She'd hardly gone to sleep when the alarm went off.* ◇ *I can hardly wait for the holidays.* ◇ *It hardly matters whether you are there or not.* ◇ *Winning this money could hardly have come at a better time.*

> NOTE We usually use **hardly** before the main verb in a sentence. Note that **hardly** is *not* the adverb form of **hard**. ➲ Look at **hard²**.

**2** (used especially before "any," "ever," "anybody," etc.) almost none, never, nobody, etc.: *There's hardly any* (= almost no) *coffee left.* ◇ *We hardly ever* (= almost never) *go to the theater these days.* ◇ *Hardly anybody I knew was at the party.*

> NOTE Note that we do not use **hardly** with a negative word.

**3** (used when you are saying that sth is not probable or that it is unreasonable): *She hasn't written for two years – she's hardly likely to write now* (= it's very improbable that she will write now).

**ˈhard-nosed** ***adj.*** not affected by feelings or emotions when trying to get what you want: *hard-nosed journalists/politicians*

**ˌhard-ˈpressed** ***adj.*** **1** having a lot of problems, especially too much work, and too little time or money: *Hard-pressed teachers want smaller classes and more time to plan lessons.* **2 hard-pressed to do sth** finding sth very difficult: *You would be hard-pressed to find a better secretary.*

**ˌhard ˈsell** ***noun*** [sing.] a method of selling sth that puts a lot of pressure on the customer to buy it: *Their salesmen are trained to go for the hard sell.*

**hard·ship** /ˈhɑrdʃɪp/ ***noun*** [C,U] difficulty or problems, e.g. because you do not have enough money; the situation in which these difficulties exist: *families suffering severe financial hardship* ◇ *Not having a car for a week is going to be a real hardship for us.*

**hard·ware** /ˈhɑrdwɛr/ ***noun*** [U] **1** tools and equipment that are used to build or repair things in the house: *a hardware store* **2** the machinery of a computer, not the programs written for it ➲ Look at **software**.

**ˈhard-wired** ***adj.*** **1** (*computing*) built into the permanent system **2** (of an ability, sense, etc.) that you have when you are born and that you don't have to learn: *The ability to feel emotions is hard-wired into us.*

**hard·wood** /ˈhɑrdwʊd/ ***noun*** [C,U] hard, heavy wood from trees of the kind that lose their leaves in the winter: *Environmentalists called for an end to the trade in tropical hardwoods.* ◇ *The house still has the original hardwood floors.*

**ˌhard-ˈworking** ***adj.*** working with effort and energy: *a hard-working student*

**har·dy** /ˈhɑrdi/ ***adj.*** (**har·di·er**; **har·di·est**) (used about people, animals and plants) able to live through cold weather or difficult conditions

**hare** /hɛr/ ***noun*** [C] an animal like a rabbit but bigger, faster and with longer ears and legs

**har·em** /ˈhɛrəm; ˈhær-/ ***noun*** [C] a number of women living with one man, especially in Muslim societies. The part of the building the women live in is also called a harem.

**har·i·cot** /ˈhærɪkoʊ/ (*also* **ˈharicot bean**) ***noun*** [C] (*especially Cdn*) = NAVY BEAN

★**harm**[1] /hɑrm/ ***noun*** [U] hurt or damage: *Peter ate some of those berries, but they didn't do him any harm.* ◇ *The scandal caused a great deal of harm to the company.* ◇ *It was just a joke – she meant no harm.*

★**harm**[2] /hɑrm/ ***verb*** [T] to cause injury or damage; hurt: *Too much sunshine can harm your skin.* ◇ *It wouldn't harm him to work a little harder!*

★**harm·ful** /ˈhɑrmfl/ ***adj.*** causing HARM[1]: *The new drug has no harmful side effects.*

★**harm·less** /ˈhɑrmləs/ ***adj.*** not able to cause harm; safe: *a harmless snake* ▸ **harm·less·ly** ***adv.***

**har·mon·i·ca** /hɑrˈmɑnɪkə/ ***noun*** [C] a small musical instrument that you play by moving it across your lips while you are blowing

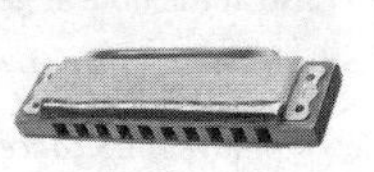

harmonica

**har·mo·nize** /ˈhɑrmənaɪz/ ***verb*** [I,T] to fit in well with other things or to make sth fit in: *That new house was designed to harmonize with the older homes in the street.* ▸ **har·mo·ni·za·tion** /ˌhɑrmənəˈzeɪʃn/ ***noun*** [U]

**har·mo·ny** /ˈhɑrməni/ ***noun*** (*pl.* **har·mo·nies**) **1** [U] a state of agreement (of feelings, interests, opinions, etc.): *There is a lack of harmony within the team.* **2** [C,U] the pleasant combination of different musical notes played or sung together: *They sang in harmony.* ▸ **har·mo·ni·ous** /hɑrˈmoʊniəs/ ***adj.*** ▸ **har·mo·ni·ous·ly** ***adv.***

**har·ness**[1] /ˈhɑrnəs/ ***noun*** [C] **1** a set of leather straps with which a horse is fastened to a cart, etc. and controlled **2** a set of straps that fasten sth to a person's body: *a safety harness*

**har·ness**[2] /ˈhɑrnəs/ ***verb*** [T] **1** to put a HARNESS[1] (1) on a horse or to attach a horse to a cart **2** to control sth so that you can use it to produce electricity

**harp** /hɑrp/ ***noun*** [C] a large musical instrument which has many strings stretching from the top to the bottom of a frame. You play the harp with your fingers.

harp

**har·poon** /hɑrˈpun/ ***noun*** [C] a long thin weapon with a sharp pointed end and a rope attached to it that is thrown or fired when hunting large animals in the ocean

**har·row·ing** /ˈhæroʊɪŋ/ ***adj.*** making people feel very upset: *The program showed harrowing scenes of life in the refugee camps.*

★**harsh** /hɑrʃ/ ***adj.*** **1** not thinking of people's feelings; severe or cruel: *a harsh punishment* ◇ *harsh criticism* ◇ *The judge had some harsh words for the attorney's behavior.* **2** not pleasant to be in: *a harsh climate* **3** (used about light or sound or the way sth feels) too bright, loud or rough: *a harsh light* ▸ **harsh·ly** ***adv.*** ▸ **harsh·ness** ***noun*** [U]

**har·vest**[1] /ˈhɑrvəst/ ***noun*** **1** [C,U] the cutting and picking of crops when they are ripe; the time when this is done: *Farmers always need extra help with the harvest.* ◇ *A storm destroyed the crops a month before harvest.* **2** [C] the crops that have been gathered in; the amount or quality of them: *This year's wheat harvest was very bad.*

**har·vest**[2] /ˈhɑrvəst/ ***verb*** [I,T] to cut, pick or gather a crop

**has** → HAVE[1,2]

**ˈhas-been** ***noun*** [C] (*informal*) a person or thing that is no longer as famous, successful or important as before

**hash browns** /ˈhæʃ braʊnz/ ***noun*** [pl.] a food made from potatoes that have been cut into very small pieces, pressed together into a flat shape and then fried

**hash·ish** /ˈhæʃiʃ; hæˈʃiʃ/ (*also slang* **hash**) ***noun*** [U] an illegal drug that is made from a part of the same plant as marijuana and is usually smoked for pleasure

**ˈhash mark** ***noun*** [C] (*Cdn*) = POUND SIGN

**has·n't** *short for* HAS NOT

**has·sle¹** /ˈhæsl/ ***noun*** [C,U] (*informal*) a thing or situation that is difficult or that causes problems: *It's going to be a real hassle getting to the airport with all this luggage.*

**has·sle²** /ˈhæsl/ ***verb*** [T] (*informal*) to bother or annoy sb by telling him/her to do sth: *I wish she'd quit hassling me about cleaning the house.*

**haste** /heɪst/ ***noun*** [U] (*formal*) doing things too quickly: *In their haste to publish the story, the journalists did not check all the facts.*

IDM **in haste** (*formal*) quickly; in a hurry: *He reacted in haste and was very sorry later on.*

**has·ten** /ˈheɪsn/ ***verb*** (*formal*) **1** [T] to make sth happen or be done earlier or more quickly **2** [I] **hasten to do sth** to be quick to do or say sth

H

**hast·y** /ˈheɪsti/ ***adj.*** (**hast·i·er**; **hast·i·est**) **1 hasty (in doing sth/to do sth)** (used about a person) acting or deciding sth too quickly or without enough thought: *Don't be too hasty. This is an important decision.* **2** said or done too quickly: *He said a hasty "goodbye" and left.* ▸ **hast·i·ly** /-əli/ ***adv.***

★**hat** /hæt/ ***noun*** [C] a covering that you wear on your head, usually when you are outside: *to wear a hat*

IDM **old hat** → OLD

**hatch¹** /hætʃ/ ***noun*** [C] **1** an opening in the deck of a ship for loading and unloading cargo **2** a door in an airplane or spaceship

**hatch²** /hætʃ/ ***verb*** **1** [I] (used about a baby bird, insect, fish, etc.) to come out of an egg **2** [T] to make a baby bird, etc. come out of an egg **3** [I] (used about an egg) to break open and allow the baby bird, etc. inside to get out **4** [T] to think of a plan (usually to do sth bad): *He hatched a plan to avoid paying any income tax.*

**hatch·back** /ˈhætʃbæk/ ***noun*** [C] a small car with a large door at the back that opens upward ➲ picture at **car**.

**hatch·et** /ˈhætʃət/ ***noun*** [C] a small tool with a wooden handle and a metal blade used for cutting wood, etc.

IDM **bury the hatchet** → BURY

★**hate¹** /heɪt/ ***verb*** [T] **1** to have a very strong feeling of dislike (for sb/sth): *I hate grapefruit.* ◇ *I hate to see the countryside ruined.* ◇ *He hates driving at night.* ◇ *I just hate it when she does that!* ➲ Look at **detest** and **loathe**. They express an even stronger feeling. **2** (used as a polite way of apologizing for sth you are going to say) to be sorry: *I hate to disappoint you, but I don't think Val wants to go out with you.*

**hate²** /heɪt/ ***noun*** [U] a very strong feeling of dislike SYN **hatred**

ˈ**hate crime** ***noun*** [C] a crime that sb commits against another person because he/she has a strong dislike of that person's race, religion, etc., or because he/she does not approve of the way that person lives

**hate·ful** /ˈheɪtfl/ ***adj.*** showing or feeling hate: *a hateful remark*

★**ha·tred** /ˈheɪtrəd/ ***noun*** [U] **hatred (for/of sb/sth)** a very strong feeling of dislike SYN **hate**

ˈ**hat trick** ***noun*** [C] (especially in hockey or soccer) three goals scored by the same person in one game: *to score a hat trick*

**haugh·ty** /ˈhɔt̬i/ ***adj.*** proud and thinking that you are better than other people: *She gave me a haughty look and walked away.* ▸ **haugh·ti·ly** ***adv.***

**haul¹** /hɔl/ ***verb*** [T] **1** to pull or drag sth with great effort: *I don't want to haul all that stuff upstairs!* **2** to transport sth in a truck, usually over a long distance

**haul²** /hɔl/ ***noun*** [C, usually sing.] an amount gained, especially of fish in a net or stolen goods in a robbery: *Police seized the largest cocaine haul ever today.*

IDM **the long haul** → LONG¹

**haunt¹** /hɔnt/ ***verb*** [T] **1** (often passive) (used about a ghost of a dead person) to appear in a place regularly: *The ghost of a woman haunts the castle.* ◇ *People say the house is haunted.* **2** (used about sth unpleasant or sad) to be always in your mind: *That memory has haunted me for years.*

**haunt²** /hɔnt/ ***noun*** [C] a place that a person visits regularly: *This bar has always been one of my favorite haunts.*

**haunt·ing** /ˈhɔntɪŋ/ ***adj.*** having a quality that stays in your mind: *a haunting song*

| have | |
|---|---|
| *present tense* | *past tense* |
| I **have** (I've) | I **had** (I'd) |
| you **have** (you've) | you **had** (you'd) |
| he/she/it **has** (he's/she's/it's) | he/she/it **had** (he'd/she'd/it'd) |
| we **have** (we've) | we **had** (we'd) |
| you **have** (you've) | you **had** (you'd) |
| they **have** (they've) | they **had** (they'd) |
| *past participle* | **had** |
| *present participle* | **having** |
| *negative short forms* | **haven't, hasn't, hadn't** |

★**have¹** /həv; əv; v; *strong form* hæv/ ***auxiliary verb*** (used for forming perfect tenses): *I've already seen this program.* ◇ *She's been in the U.S. for six months.* ◇ *Jim hasn't written to me yet.* ◇ *Have you been waiting long?* ◇ *They had already told us the news.*

★**have²** /hæv/ ***verb*** (*3rd person sing. pres.* **has**; *pt, pp* **had**)

➤OWN **1** (*also* **have got**) to own or possess: *I have a new camera.* ◇ *They don't have a car.* ◇ *The apartment has two bedrooms.* ◇ *He's got short dark hair.* ◇ *Do you have any brothers or sisters?*

NOTE We generally do not use **have got** in questions or in negative sentences. We usually use **have got** to emphasize the fact that sb has one thing instead of another: *She doesn't have much money, but at least she's got a steady job.* ➲ Look also at the note at **get**.

➤ILLNESS **2** (*also* **have got**) to be sick with sth: *She's got a bad cold.* ◇ *to have the flu/a headache* ◇ *to have AIDS/cancer*

➤ORDER/DO STH **3** (in a restaurant) to order sth: *I'll have a cheeseburger and a Coke.* ◇ *Okay, who had the chicken?* **4** (used with many nouns to talk about doing sth): *What time do you have breakfast?*

◇ *to have a drink/a cigarette/a cup of coffee/a sandwich* ◇ *to have an argument/a talk/a conversation* ◇ *We're having a meeting next week.*

➤EXPERIENCE **5** (used with many nouns to talk about experiencing sth): *Have a nice day!* ◇ *to have fun/a good time* ◇ *to have problems/difficulties* ◇ *to have an accident/a heart attack/an operation*

➤GIVE BIRTH **6** to give birth to a baby: *Guess what, honey? We're going to have a baby!* ◇ *They kept me in the hospital for a week after I had Josh.*

➤OF A PERSON'S QUALITIES/ABILITIES **7** (*also* **have got**) (used with many abstract nouns): *I have no patience with little kids.* ◇ *to have time to do sth* ◇ *to have power/authority* ➲ Look at the note in sense 2.

➤HAVE STH DONE **8 have sth done** to arrange for sth to be done, usually for payment: *I have my hair cut every six weeks.* ◇ *You should have your eyes tested.* **9 have sth done** (used when sth bad happens to you): *She had her bag stolen on the subway.* ◇ *He had his driver's license taken away.*

➤HAVE SB DO STH **10 have sb do sth** to arrange for or tell sb to do sth: *I'll have Gwen send you a copy of the report.*

IDM **have had it** (*informal*) (used about things that are completely broken, or dead): *This TV set has had it. We'll have to buy a new one.*

**have had it (with sb/sth)** (*informal*) to have no more patience for sb/sth: *I've had it with this stupid job! I'm quitting!*

PHR V **have (got) sth on** to be wearing sth: *She has a green sweater on.* ◇ *What did the man have on?* ➲ Look at the note in sense 2.

**ha·ven** /ˈheɪvn/ ***noun*** [C] a place where people feel safe or where they can rest and be quiet ➲ A **tax haven** is a country where income tax is low.

**have to** /ˈhæftə; ˈhæftʊ; ˈhæftu/ (*also* **have got to**) ***modal verb*** used for saying that sb must do sth or that sth must happen: *I usually have to work on Saturday mornings.* ◇ *Do you have to have a passport to go to Canada?* ◇ *She's got to go to the bank this afternoon.* ◇ *We don't have to* (= it's not necessary to) *go to the party if you don't want to.* ◇ *We had to do a lots of boring exercises.*

**hav·oc** /ˈhævək/ ***noun***

IDM **wreak havoc (on sth)** → WREAK

**hawk** /hɔk/ ***noun*** [C] **1** a type of bird that catches and eats small animals and birds. Hawks can see small things from very far away. **2** (in politics) a person who supports strong action and the use of force rather than peaceful solutions

**hay** /heɪ/ ***noun*** [U] grass that has been cut and dried for use as food for animals: *a bale of hay*

**ˈhay ˌfever** ***noun*** [U] an illness like a bad cold, that especially affects your nose

NOTE People get hay fever if they are **allergic** to the **pollen** of plants.

**hay·wire** /ˈheɪwaɪər/ ***adj.***

IDM **go haywire** (*informal*) to become out of control

**haz·ard** /ˈhæzərd/ ***verb*** [T] to make a guess or to suggest sth even though you know it may be wrong: *I don't know what he paid for the house but I could* ***hazard a guess.***

**haz·ard**[1] /ˈhæzərd/ ***noun*** [C] a danger or risk: *Smoking is a serious health hazard.*

**haz·ard·ous** /hæzərdəs/ ***adj.*** dangerous

**haze** /heɪz/ ***noun*** [U] a thin, low cloud caused by heat, dust or smoke ➲ Look at the note at **fog**.

**ha·zel** /ˈheɪzl/ ***adj.*** (used especially about eyes) light brown in color

**ha·zel·nut** /ˈheɪzlnʌt/ ***noun*** [C] a small nut that you can eat ➲ picture at **nut**.

**haz·y** /ˈheɪzi/ ***adj.*** (**haz·i·er**; **haz·i·est**) **1** not clear; covered by a thin, low cloud: (*figurative*) *I have only a hazy memory of the vacation we spent in France.* **2** (used about a person) uncertain, not expressing things clearly: *She's a little hazy about the details of the trip.*

★**he**[1] /i; *strong form* hi/ ***pronoun*** (the subject of a verb) the male person or animal mentioned earlier: *I talked to John before he left.* ◇ *Look at that little boy – he's going to fall!*

NOTE **He**, **him** and **his** are often used to refer to a member of a group that includes both males and females: *A good teacher prepares his lessons well.* Many people think that this is not fair to women and the use of **he or she**, **him or her**, etc. is becoming more common. In writing **he/she**, **s/he** or **(s)he** can be used: *Ask your doctor. He/she can give you further information.* ◇ *When a baby cries, it means that s/he is tired, hungry or just unhappy.* In informal language **they**, **them** or **their** can be used: *Everybody knows what they want.* ◇ *When somebody asks me a question, I always try to give them a quick answer.* Or the sentence can be made plural: *A baby cries when he/she is tired* becomes: *Babies cry when they are tired.*

**he**[2] /hi/ ***noun*** [sing.] a male animal: *Is your cat a he or a she?*

★**head**[1] /hɛd/ ***noun*** [C]

➤PART OF BODY **1** the part of the body above the neck which has your eyes, nose, mouth and brain in it: *She turned her head to look at him.* ◇ *serious head injuries* ➲ picture on study page **A32**.

NOTE In English-speaking countries, when you **nod** your head, it means "yes" or shows agreement. When you **shake** your head, it means "no" or shows disagreement.

➤MIND **2** a person's mind, brain or mental ability: *Use your head!* (= think!) ◇ *A terrible thought entered my head...* ◇ *He has a good head for numbers.*

➤TOP/FRONT **3** the top, front or most important part or end: *to sit at the head of the table* ◇ *Put your name at the head of the paper.* ◇ *Julia graduated at the head of her class.*

➤OF OBJECT **4** something that is like a HEAD (1) in shape or position: *the head of a hammer*

➤OF GROUP/ORGANIZATION **5** the chief or most important person (in a family, company, country, etc.): *the head of the family* ◇ *The President is welcoming heads of state from all over the world.* ◇ *the head waiter*

➤SIDE OF COIN **6 heads** the side of a coin with the head of a person on it: *Heads or tails? Heads I go first, tails you do.*

➤MEASUREMENT **7 a head** [sing.] the height or length of one head: *a head taller*

➤ONE PERSON **8 a head** [sing.] (for) one person: *Admission is $12 a head.* SYN **per head**

IDM **bite sb's head off** → BITE[1]

**from head to toe/foot** over your whole body: *He was covered in mud from head to toe.*

**go to sb's head 1** to make sb drunk: *Wine always goes straight to my head.* **2** to make sb too proud: *If you keep telling him how smart he is, it will go to his head!*

**head over heels (in love)** completely in love: *Jane's head over heels in love with her new boyfriend.*

**hit the nail on the head** → HIT[1]

**laugh, scream, etc. your head off** to laugh, scream, etc. loudly

**off the top of your head** → TOP[1]

**shake your head** → SHAKE[1]

H

★**head**[2] /hɛd/ ***verb*** **1** [T] to be in charge of or to lead sth: *Do you think that he has the experience necessary to head a department?* **2** [T] to be at the front of a line, top of a list, etc.: *to head a procession* ◊ *Two names headed the list of possible suspects.* **3** [T] (often passive) to give a title or some instructions at the top of a piece of writing: *The report was headed "Private."* **4** [I] to move in the direction mentioned: *The ship headed toward the harbor.* ◊ *Let's head out.*

PHRV **head for** to move toward a place: *It's getting late – I think it's time to head for home.* ◊ (*figurative*) *You're heading for trouble if you go on behaving like that.*

**head·ache** /ˈhɛdeɪk/ ***noun*** [C] **1** a pain in your head: *I have a splitting* (= very bad) *headache.* ➲ Look at the note at **ache**. **2** a person or thing that causes worry or difficulty: *Paying the bills is a constant headache.*

**head·band** /ˈhɛdbænd/ ***noun*** [C] a strip of cloth worn around the head, especially to keep hair or sweat out of your eyes when playing sports

**head·count** /ˈhɛdkaʊnt/ ***noun*** [C] an act of counting the number of people who are at an event, employed by an organization, etc.; the number of people that have been counted in this way: *to do a headcount* ◊ *What's the latest headcount?*

**head·first** /ˌhɛdˈfərst/ ***adv.*** **1** with your head before the rest of your body: *Don't go down the slide headfirst.* **2** too quickly or suddenly: *Don't rush headfirst into a decision.*

**head·ing** /ˈhɛdɪŋ/ ***noun*** [C] the words written as a title at the top of a page or a piece of writing

**head·light** /ˈhɛdlaɪt/ (*also* **headlamp** /ˈhɛdlæmp/) ***noun*** [C] one of the two large bright lights at the front of a car, truck, etc.: *Turn your headlights on – it's getting dark.*

**head·line** /ˈhɛdlaɪn/ ***noun*** **1** [C] the title of a newspaper article printed in large letters above the story **2 the headlines** [pl.] the main news stories that are read on television or the radio

**head·long** /ˈhɛdlɔŋ/ ***adv., adj.*** **1** with your head before the rest of your body **2** too quickly; without enough thought: *He rushed headlong into buying the business.*

**head·mas·ter** /ˈhɛdˌmæstər/ (*feminine* **head·mis·tress** /ˈhɛdˌmɪstrəs/) ***noun*** [C] a man or woman who is in charge of a private school ➲ Look at **principal**[2].

ˌ**head-ˈon** ***adj., adv.*** with the front of one car, etc. hitting the front of another: *There's been a head-on collision between two trucks on the interstate.*

**head·phones** /ˈhɛdfoʊnz/ ***noun*** [pl.] a piece of equipment with two round parts that fit over your ears, connected by a band over the top of your head. Headphones are used for listening to the radio, music, etc.

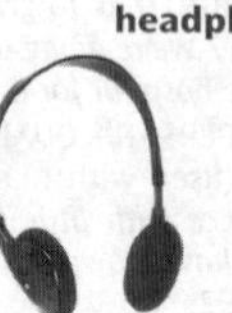
headphones

**head·quar·tered** /ˈhɛdˌkwɔrt̬ərd; -ˌkwɔt̬ərd/ ***adj.*** (not before a noun) having headquarters in a particular place: *Several large companies are headquartered in Cincinnati.*

**head·quar·ters** /ˈhɛdˌkwɔrt̬ərz; -ˌkwɔt̬ərz/ ***noun*** [pl., with sing. or pl. verb] (*abbr.* **HQ**) the central office, etc. of an organization: *Where is/are the company's headquarters?*

**head·set** /ˈhɛdsɛt/ ***noun*** [C] a piece of equipment that you wear on your head that includes a device for listening (**headphones**) and/or a device for speaking into (a **microphone**): *The pilot was talking into his headset.*

ˌ**head ˈstart** ***noun*** [sing.] an advantage that you have from the beginning of a race or competition

**head·stone** /ˈhɛdstoʊn/ (*also* **gravestone**) ***noun*** [C] a large stone used to mark the head of a grave, usually with the dead person's name, etc. on it

**head·strong** /ˈhɛdstrɔŋ/ ***adj.*** doing what you want, without listening to advice from other people

**head·way** /ˈhɛdweɪ/ ***noun***

IDM **make headway** to go forward or make progress in a difficult situation: *It was impossible for the boat to make any headway against the wind.*

**head·y** /ˈhɛdi/ ***adj.*** (*comparative* **head·i·er**; *superlative* **head·i·est**) **1** (usually before a noun) having a strong effect on your senses; making you feel excited and hopeful: *the heady days of youth* ◊ *the heady scent of spices* **2** (not before a noun) (of a person) excited in a way that makes you do things without worrying about the possible results: *She felt heady with success.*

★**heal** /hil/ ***verb*** [I,T] **heal (up)** to become healthy again; to make sth healthy again: *The cut will heal up in a few days if you keep it clean and dry.* ◊ *It takes time to heal a broken leg.* ◊ (*figurative*) *Nothing he said could heal the damage done to their relationship.*

★**health** /hɛlθ/ ***noun*** [U] **1** the condition of a person's body or mind: *Fresh fruit and vegetables are good for your health.* ◊ *in good /poor health* ◊ *health insurance* ◊ *Cigarette packs carry a health warning.* **2** the state of being well and free from illness: *Would you rather have health, wealth or beauty?*

ˈ**health card** ***noun*** [C] (*Cdn*) a card that shows that a person has the right to receive free medical treatment

**ˈhealth care** (*also* **ˈhealthcare**) ***noun*** [U] the services that doctors, nurses, etc. give to people in order to keep them healthy or to make them well if they are sick: *the rising cost of health care* ◇ *the health care industry*

**ˈhealth ˌcenter** ***noun*** [C] a place where doctors, nurses, etc. treat people, that is not part of a hospital: *the campus health center*

**ˈhealth club** ***noun*** [C] a place where people pay to exercise, swim, play sports, etc.

**ˈhealth food** ***noun*** [C,U] natural food that many people think is especially good for your health because it has been made or grown without adding chemicals

**health·ful** /ˈhɛlθfl/ ***adj.*** helping to produce good health: *a healthful diet* ➲ **Healthy** is often used with the same meaning.

**ˈhealth ˌmaintenance ˌorganiˌzation** ***noun*** = HMO

★**health·y** /ˈhɛlθi/ ***adj.*** (**health·i·er**; **health·i·est**) **1** not often sick; strong and well: *a healthy child/animal/plant* **2** showing good health (of body or mind): *healthy skin and hair* **3** helping to produce good health: *a healthy climate* ➲ **Healthful** is often used with the same meaning. OPP The opposite for all senses is **unhealthy**. ▸ **health·i·ly** /-əli/ ***adv.***

**heap¹** /hip/ ***noun*** [C] a large number or amount of sth which is piled up in a messy way: *All his clothes are in a heap on the floor!* ◇ (*figurative*) *a heap of trouble* ➲ Look at the note at **pile**.

**heap²** /hip/ ***verb*** [T] **heap sth (up)** to put things in a pile: *I'm going to heap all the leaves up over there.* ◇ (*figurative*) *to heap praise on sb* (= to give sb a lot of praise)

★**hear** /hɪr/ ***verb*** (*pt, pp* **heard** /hərd/) **1** [I,T] (not used in the *-ing* forms) to receive sounds with your ears: *Can you speak a little louder? I don't hear very well.* ◇ *Sorry I'm late – I didn't hear my alarm clock this morning.*

> NOTE Compare **hear** and **listen**. To **hear** is to receive a sound by chance or in a passive way with your ears; to **listen** is to make a conscious or active effort to hear something: *I always wake up when I hear the neighbors' dog barking.* ◇ *I love listening to music in the evenings.* ◇ *Listen! I have something to tell you.*

**2** [T] (not used in the *-ing* forms) to be told or informed about sth: *I hear that you've been offered a job in Canada.* ◇ *Did you hear about Ken? He got fired yesterday!* **3** [T] (used about a judge, a court, etc.) to listen to the evidence in a trial in order to make a decision about it: *Your case will be heard this afternoon.*

IDM **won't/wouldn't hear of sth** to refuse to allow sth: *I wanted to go to art school, but my parents wouldn't hear of it.*

PHR V **hear from sb** to receive a letter, telephone call, etc. from sb

**hear of sb/sth** (used especially in questions and negatives) to know or receive information about the existence of a person, place, thing, etc.: *Have you ever heard of the Bermuda Triangle?*

**hear·ing** /ˈhɪrɪŋ/ ***noun*** **1** [U] the ability to hear: *Her hearing isn't very good, so you need to speak louder.* **2** [C] a trial in a court of law: *Will there be TV cameras at the hearing?* **3** [C] a chance to give your opinion or explain your position: *If everybody comes to the meeting, it will give all points of view a fair hearing.*

IDM **hard of hearing** → HARD¹

**ˈhearing aid** ***noun*** [C] a small device that makes sound louder, that sb who cannot hear well wears in his/her ear

**ˈhearing-imˌpaired** ***adj.*** unable to hear very well or unable to hear anything

**hear·say** /ˈhɪrseɪ/ ***noun*** [U] things you have heard another person or other people say, which may or may not be true: *Hearsay is not admissable as evidence in court.*

**hearse** /hərs/ ***noun*** [C] a large car used for carrying a dead body in a box (casket) to the funeral

★**heart** /hɑrt/ ***noun***

▸ PART OF BODY **1** [C] the organ inside the chest that sends blood around the body: *When you exercise, your heart beats faster.* ◇ *heart disease*

▸ FEELINGS/EMOTIONS **2** [C] the center of a person's feelings: *She has a kind heart* (= she is kind and gentle). ◇ *In my heart, I knew she was right.*

▸ CENTER **3** [sing.] the most central part of sth; the middle: *Rare plants can be found in the heart of the forest.* ◇ (*figurative*) *Let's get straight to the heart* (= to the most important part) *of the matter.*

▸ SHAPE **4** [C] a symbol that is shaped like a HEART (1), often red or pink and used to show love: *He sent her a card with a big red heart on it.*

▸ IN CARD GAMES **5** **hearts** [pl.] the group (suit) of playing cards with red shapes like HEARTS (4) on them: *I know you have the queen of hearts!* ➲ picture at **card¹**. **6** [C] one of the cards from this suit: *Play a heart, if you have one.*

▸ INTEREST/ATTENTION **7** [U] complete interest or attention: *He's not working well because his heart isn't in the job.*

IDM **at heart** really; in fact: *My father seems strict, but he's a very kind man at heart.*

**break sb's heart** to make sb very sad

**by heart** by remembering exactly; from memory: *to learn a poem by heart* ◇ *I can play three songs by heart.*

**a change of heart** → CHANGE²

**cross my heart** → CROSS²

**do sth to your heart's content** do sth as much as you want: *Finally it was summer vacation and the kids could play at the beach to their hearts' content.*

**lose heart** → LOSE

**not have the heart (to do sth)** to be unable to do sth unkind: *I didn't have the heart to say no.*

**take sth to heart** to be greatly affected or upset by sth

**young at heart** → YOUNG¹

**your heart sinks** to suddenly feel disappointed and sad: *When he heard they had given the job to somebody else, his heart sank.*

**heart·ache** /ˈhɑrt̬eɪk/ ***noun*** [C,U] great sadness or worry; emotional pain

**ˈheart atˌtack** ***noun*** [C] a sudden serious illness when the heart stops working correctly, sometimes causing death: *She had a heart attack.*

H

**heart·beat** /ˈhɑrtbit/ ***noun*** [C] the regular movement of the heart or the sound it makes

IDM **in a heartbeat** immediately, without stopping to think: *"Would you accept that job if they offered it to you?" "In a heartbeat!"*

**heart·break** /ˈhɑrtbreɪk/ ***noun*** [U] very great unhappiness

**heart·break·ing** /ˈhɑrtˌbreɪkɪŋ/ ***adj.*** very sad

**heart·bro·ken** /ˈhɑrtˌbroʊkən/ ***adj.*** extremely sad: *Mary was heartbroken at the news of her friend's death.*

**heart·burn** /ˈhɑrtbərn/ ***noun*** [U] a pain that feels like sth burning in your chest caused by the acid in your stomach that helps break down (**digest**) food

H

**heart·en** /ˈhɑrtn/ ***verb*** [T] (usually passive) to encourage sb; to make sb feel more cheerful OPP **dishearten** ▸ **heart·en·ing** ***adj.*** OPP **disheartening**

**heart·felt** /ˈhɑrtfɛlt/ ***adj.*** deeply felt; sincere: *a heartfelt apology*

**hearth** /hɑrθ/ ***noun*** [C] the place where you have an open fire in the house or the area in front of it

**heart·i·ly** /ˈhɑrṭl·i/ ***adv.*** **1** in a loud cheerful way: *He laughed heartily.* **2** very much; completely: *I heartily recommend that you approve this proposal.*

**heart·land** /ˈhɑrtlænd/ ***noun*** [C] the most central or important part of a country, area, etc.: *The Midwest is America's heartland.*

**ˌheart-to-ˈheart** ***adj.*** (about a conversation, talk, etc.) about the things you really think and feel, without hiding anything: *After a heart-to-heart talk they were able to forgive each other.* ▸ **ˌheart-to-ˈheart** ***noun*** [C]: *It's time we sat down and had a heart-to-heart.*

**heart·warm·ing** /ˈhɑrtˌwɔrmɪŋ/ ***adj.*** causing feelings of happiness and pleasure: *a heartwarming experience/story*

**heart·y** /ˈhɑrṭi/ ***adj.*** (**heart·i·er**; **heart·i·est**) **1** showing warm and friendly feelings: *a hearty laugh* **2** large: *a hearty breakfast ◇ a hearty appetite*

★**heat**[1] /hit/ ***noun***

➤ BEING HOT **1** [U] the feeling of sth hot: *the heat of the sun ◇ This fire doesn't give out much heat.* **2** [sing.] (often with *the*) hot weather: *I like the Alaskan climate because I can't stand the heat.*

➤ SOURCE OF HEAT **3** [sing.] a thing that produces HEAT (1): *Remove the pan from the heat* (= the stove).

➤ IN BUILDING/ROOM **4** [U] a system for heating a house or a building: *Our house has electric heat. ◇ Turn the heat up – I'm freezing!*

➤ STRONG FEELINGS **5** [U] a state or time of anger or excitement: *In the heat of the argument, he said a lot of things he didn't mean.*

➤ RACE **6** [C] one of the first parts of a race or competition. The winners of the heats compete against other winners until the final result is decided: *He won his heat and went through to the finals.*

★**heat**[2] /hit/ ***verb*** [I,T] **heat (sth) (up)** to become or to make sth hot or warm: *Wait for the oven to heat up before you put the cake in. ◇ Old houses are more difficult to heat than newer ones. ◇ a heated swimming pool ◇ The meal is already cooked, but you'll need to heat it up.*

**heat·ed** /ˈhiṭəd/ ***adj.*** (used about a discussion) angry or excited ▸ **heat·ed·ly** ***adv.***

**heat·er** /ˈhiṭər/ ***noun*** [C] a piece of equipment used for heating water or the air in a room, car, etc.: *an electric heater ◇ a water heater*

**ˈheat wave** ***noun*** [C] a period of time when the weather is much hotter than usual

**heave** /hiv/ ***verb*** **1** [I,T] to lift or pull sth heavy, using a lot of effort: *Take hold of this rope and heave! ◇ We heaved the couch up the stairs.* **2** [T] to throw sth heavy **3** [I] to move up and down or in and out in a heavy but regular way: *His chest was heaving with the effort of carrying the cabinet.*

IDM **heave a sigh** to let out a long, deep breath that shows you are sad, tired, relieved, etc.: *He heaved a sigh of relief when he heard the good news.*

★**heav·en** /ˈhɛvn/ ***noun*** **1** [sing.] the place where it is believed that God lives and good people go when they die: *to go to/be in heaven* ➲ Look at **hell**. ➲ **Heaven** (often with a capital H) is used in a number of expressions to mean "God." For the meaning of *for Heaven's sake, Heaven forbid*, etc. look at the entry for **God**. **2 the heavens** [pl.] (*formal*) the sky: *The stars shone brightly in the heavens that night.*

IDM **(good) heavens!** (used to express surprise): *Good heavens! I didn't expect to see you!*

**thank heaven** → THANK

**heav·en·ly** /ˈhɛvnli/ ***adj.*** **1** (only *before* a noun) connected with heaven or the sky: *heavenly music ◇ heavenly bodies* (= the sun/moon/stars) **2** (*informal*) very pleasant; wonderful

★**heav·y**[1] /ˈhɛvi/ ***adj.*** (**heav·i·er**; **heav·i·est**)

➤ WEIGHT **1** weighing a lot, and difficult to lift or move: *This box is too heavy for me to carry.* **2** (used when asking or stating how much sb/sth weighs): *How heavy do you think this bag is?* **3** (used about a person) fat: *Donna's gotten a little heavier since the last time I saw her.*

➤ WORSE THAN USUAL **4** larger or stronger than usual: *heavy rain ◇ heavy traffic ◇ He felt a heavy blow on the back of his head. ◇ a heavy smoker/drinker* (= a person who smokes/drinks a lot) *◇ The sound of his heavy* (= loud and deep) *breathing told her that he was asleep.*

➤ MATERIAL **5** (used about a material or substance) solid or thick: *a heavy coat*

➤ MEAL/FOOD **6** (used about food) difficult for the body to absorb: *He had a heavy meal and dropped off to sleep in the afternoon.*

➤ BUSY **7** full of hard work; (too) busy: *I have a heavy schedule this week.*

➤ SERIOUS/DIFFICULT **8** serious, difficult or boring: *This book is very heavy reading.*

➤ USING A LOT **9 heavy on sth** using a lot of sth: *The traditional North American diet is heavy on red meat and fried foods.*

➤ FULL OF STH **10 heavy with sth** containing a lot of sth: *an airplane heavy with fuel ◇ a speech heavy with symbolism*

▸ **heav·i·ly** /-əli/ ***adv.*** ▸ **heav·i·ness** ***noun*** [U]

**heav·y**[2] /ˈhɛvi/ ***adv.***

IDM **to go heavy on sth** (*informal*) to use a lot of

sth: *I think you went a little too heavy on the perfume.*

**ˌheavy-ˈduty** *adj.* (only *before* a noun) (used about materials, machines, etc.) strong and able to last for a long time: *a heavy-duty truck* ◇ *heavy-duty gloves*

**ˌheavy-ˈhanded** *adj.* **1** not showing much understanding of other people's feelings: *Her heavy-handed approach made her unpopular with her employees.* ◇ **2** using unnecessary force: *heavy-handed police methods*

**ˌheavy ˈindustry** *noun* [C,U] (*pl.* **heavy industries**) an industry that produces materials such as steel or that makes large, heavy objects

**ˌheavy ˈmetal** *noun* [U] a style of very loud rock music that is played on electric instruments

**ˌheavy-ˈset** *adj.* having a broad, heavy body

**heav·y·weight** /ˈhɛviweɪt/ *noun* [C] **1** (in some sports) a person in the heaviest weight group: *a heavyweight boxer/wrestler* **2** (*informal*) an important person who has a lot of power

**He·brew** /ˈhibru/ *noun* **1** a member of an ancient race of people living in what is now Israel and Palestine. Their writings and traditions form the basis of the Jewish religion. **2** the language traditionally used by the Hebrew people, or the modern form of the language which is the official language of Israel ▶ **Hebrew** *adj.*

**heck** /hɛk/ *interjection, noun* [sing.] (*informal*) (used to express or emphasize annoyance or surprise or to emphasize the amount or size of sth): *Oh heck! I missed the bus!* ◇ *How the heck did you know where I was?* ◇ *It's a heck of a long way to drive in one day.*

**heck·le** /ˈhɛkl/ *verb* [I,T] to interrupt a speaker at a public meeting with difficult questions or rude remarks ▶ **heck·ler** /ˈhɛklər/ *noun* [C] ▶ **heck·ling** /ˈhɛklɪŋ/ *noun* [U]

**hec·tic** /ˈhɛktɪk/ *adj.* very busy and full of a lot of things that you have to do quickly: *We had a hectic day at the office.*

**he'd** /hid; *weak form also* id/ *short for* HE HAD; HE WOULD

**hedge**

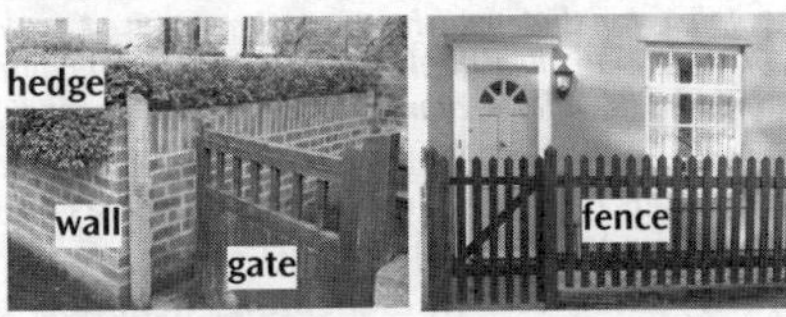


**hedge¹** /hɛdʒ/ *noun* [C] a row of bushes that are planted close together: *I need to trim the hedge.*

**hedge²** /hɛdʒ/ *verb* [I,T] to avoid giving a direct answer to a question, or a direct and complete opinion: *When she asked if he liked her new haircut, he hedged.*

IDM **hedge your bets** to protect yourself against losing or making a mistake by supporting more than one person or opinion

**heed¹** /hid/ *verb* [T] (*formal*) to pay attention to advice, a warning, etc.

**heed²** /hid/ *noun* (*formal*)

IDM **take heed (of sth)** (*formal*) to pay careful attention to what sb says: *You should take heed of your doctor's advice.*

★**heel** /hil/ *noun* [C] **1** the back part of the foot: *These shoes rub against my heels.* ➲ picture on study page **A32**. **2** the part of a sock that covers your HEEL (1) **3** the raised part of a shoe under the HEEL (1) of your foot: *High heels* (= shoes with high heels) *are not practical for long walks.* ➲ picture at **shoe**.

IDM **head over heels (in love)** → HEAD¹

**heft·y** /ˈhɛfti/ *adj.* (**heft·i·er**; **heft·i·est**) (*informal*) strong, heavy or big: *a hefty young man* ◇ *a hefty increase in food prices*

★**height** /haɪt/ *noun*

➤MEASUREMENT **1** [C,U] the measurement from the bottom to the top of a person or thing: *The nurse is going to check your height and weight.* ◇ *She's of medium height.* ◇ *We need a fence that's about six feet in height.* ➲ The adjective is **high**. Look at the note at **tall**. ➲ picture at **length**.

➤BEING TALL **2** [U] being tall: *He's only ten, but he looks older because of his height.*

➤DISTANCE ABOVE GROUND **3** [C,U] the distance that sth is above the ground or sea level: *She survived a fall from a height of 20 feet.*

➤HIGH PLACE **4** [C, usually pl.] a high place or area: *I can't go up there. I'm afraid of heights.*

➤STRONGEST POINT/LEVEL **5** [U] the strongest or most important part of sth: *the height of summer* ◇ *At its height in the 1990s, the company had over 500 employees.* ◇ *He joined the army during the height of the war.*

**height·en** /ˈhaɪtn/ *verb* [I,T] to become or to make sth greater or stronger: *I'm using yellow paint to heighten the sunny effect of the room.*

**hei·nous** /ˈheɪnəs/ *adj.* (*formal*) morally very bad: *a heinous crime* ▶ **hei·nous·ness** *noun* [U]

**heir** /ɛr/ *noun* [C] the person with the legal right to receive (**inherit**) money, property or a title when the owner dies: *He's the heir to a large fortune.* ◇ *Who is the heir to the throne?* (= Who will become king or queen?)

NOTE A female heir is often called an **heiress**, especially when we are talking about somebody who has inherited a very large amount of money.

**heir·loom** /ˈɛrlum/ *noun* [C] something valuable that has belonged to the same family for many years

**heist** /haɪst/ *noun* [C] (*informal*) a crime of stealing sth from a bank, business, etc.: *a jewelry heist*

**held** *past tense, past participle of* HOLD¹

**hel·i·cop·ter** /ˈhɛləkaptər/ (*also informal* **chopper**) *noun* [C] a small aircraft that can go straight up into the air. Helicopters fly with the help of large spinning blades.

**he·li·um** /ˈhiliəm/ (*symbol* **He**) *noun* [U] a chemical element; a very light, colorless gas that does not burn

**he'll** /hil; hɪl; *weak form also* il; ɪl/ *short for* HE WILL

★**hell** /hɛl/ *noun* **1** [sing.] the place that some religions say bad people will go to when they die: *to go* *to/be in hell* ➲ Look at **heaven**. **2** [C,U] (*informal*) a situation or place that is very unpleasant, painful or miserable: *He went through hell when his wife left him.* **3** [U] (*informal*) (used as a swear word to show anger or surprise or to make another expression stronger): *Oh hell, I forgot my money!* ◇ *Go to hell!* (= go away!) ◇ *Who the hell is that at the front door?*

IDM **a/one hell of a...** (*informal*) (used to make an expression stronger or to mean "very"): *That was one hell of a surprise!* ◇ *She's a hell of a nice girl.*

**all hell breaks loose** (*informal*) there is suddenly a lot of noise and confusion: *When he announced he was cutting salaries by 10%, all hell broke loose!*

**from hell** (*informal*) (used to describe a very unpleasant person or thing; the worst that you can imagine): *They are the neighbors from hell.*

**give sb hell** (*informal*) to speak to sb very angrily or to treat sb severely

**(just) for the hell of it** (*informal*) for fun; for no good reason: *I looked at their web page the other day, just for the hell of it.*

**like hell** (*informal*) (used to make an expression stronger): *I'm working like hell* (= very hard) *these days.*

NOTE Be careful. Some people find **hell** offensive when it is used in informal expressions. **Heck** is not as strong as **hell**.

★**hel·lo** /hə'loʊ; hɛ'loʊ/ ***interjection*** (used for greeting sb, to attract sb's attention, or when you are using the telephone): *Hello, how are you?* ◇ *Hello, is anybody there?*

NOTE We usually use **hi**, not **hello**, in less formal situations: *"Rob, this is my friend, Laura Kwan." "Hi, nice to meet you."* However, we always use **hello** when we answer the telephone.

**hell·uv·a** /'hɛləvə/ = HELL OF A

**helm** /hɛlm/ ***noun*** [C] the part of a boat or ship that is used to guide it. The helm can be a handle or a wheel: (*figurative*) *Mr. Perkins has been at the helm* (= in charge) *of the company for 17 years.*

**hel·met** /'hɛlmət/ ***noun*** [C] a type of hard hat that you wear to protect your head: *a crash helmet* ◇ *a football helmet* ➲ picture at **football player**.

★**help**[1] /hɛlp/ ***verb***

➤MAKE EASIER/BETTER **1** [I,T] to do sth for sb in order to be useful or to make a person's work easier: *Can I do anything to help?* ◇ *Could you help me with the cooking?* ◇ *I helped her to organize the party.* ◇ *to help sb off the bus/out of a car/across the street* (= to help sb move in the direction mentioned) **2** [I,T] to make sth better or easier: *If you apologize to him, it might help* (= it might make the situation better). ◇ *These pills should help your headache.*

➤ASSIST CUSTOMER **3** [T] (in a store) to take a customer's order; to show sth to a customer or sell goods, etc.: *Can I help you?* ◇ *Is somebody helping you?* ◇ *Sorry, I'm helping another customer right now.*

➤TAKE FOOD/DRINK **4** [T] **help yourself (to sth)** to take sth (especially food and drink): *Help yourself to a drink!* ◇ *"Can I borrow your pen?" "Yes, help yourself."*

➤STEAL **5** [T] **help yourself to sth** to take sth without asking permission: *Don't just help yourself to my money!*

➤WHEN IN DANGER **6** [I] (used to get sb's attention when you are in danger or difficulty): *Help! I'm going to fall!*

IDM **can/can't/couldn't help sth** to be able/not be able to stop or avoid doing sth: *Try not to move your arm if you can help it.* ◇ *He can't help being so small* (= it's not his fault). ◇ *The accident couldn't be helped* (= it couldn't be avoided, so we must accept that). ◇ *I just couldn't help myself – I had to laugh.* ◇ *It was so funny I couldn't help laughing.*

NOTE It is also possible to say **can't/couldn't help but do sth**: *It was so funny I couldn't help but laugh.*

**a helping hand** some help: *My neighbor is always ready to give me a helping hand.*

PHRV **help (sb) out** to help sb in a difficult situation or to give money to help sb: *My parents promised to help us out with buying the car.*

★**help**[2] /hɛlp/ ***noun*** **1** [U] the act of helping: *Do you need any help?* ◇ *I'll give you all the help I can.* **2** [U, sing.] a person or thing that helps: *This map isn't much help.* ◇ *Your directions were a big help – we found the place easily.*

'**help desk** ***noun*** [C] a service, usually in a company, that gives people information and help, especially if they are having problems with a computer

**help·er** /'hɛlpər/ ***noun*** [C] a person who helps (especially with work)

★**help·ful** /'hɛlpfl/ ***adj.*** giving help: *helpful advice* ◇ *Ask Mr. Brown. He's always very helpful.* OPP **unhelpful** ▸ **help·ful·ly** ***adv.*** ▸ **help·ful·ness** ***noun*** [U]

**help·ing** /'hɛlpɪŋ/ ***noun*** [C] an amount of food that sb serves: *Sarah ate two big helpings of mashed potatoes.*

'**helping verb** ***noun*** [C] = AUXILIARY[2]

**help·less** /'hɛlpləs/ ***adj.*** needing help from other people: *a helpless baby* ▸ **help·less·ly** ***adv.*** ▸ **help·less·ness** ***noun*** [U]

**help·line** /'hɛlplaɪn/ ***noun*** [C] a telephone service that provides advice and information about particular problems: *The university health center runs a helpline for students who are feeling stressed or depressed.* ◇ *I called the helpline about my computer and had to wait for 20 minutes to talk to somebody!*

**hem**[1] /hɛm/ ***noun*** [C] the edge of a piece of cloth (especially on a skirt, dress or pants) that has been turned under and sewn down

**hem**[2] /hɛm/ ***verb*** [T] (**hem·ming**; **hemmed**) to sew a HEM[1] on sth

PHRV **hem sb in** to surround sb and prevent him/her from moving away: *We were hemmed in by the crowd and couldn't leave.*

**hem·i·sphere** /'hɛməsfɪr/ ***noun*** [C] **1** the shape of half a ball; half a sphere **2** one half of the earth: *the northern/southern/eastern/western hemisphere* ➲ Picture at **earth**.

**he·mo·phil·i·a** /ˌhimə'fɪliə; -'fɪlyə/ ***noun*** [U] a disease that causes a person to bleed very heavily from small injuries because the blood does not thicken (clot) properly

**he·mo·phil·i·ac** /ˌhiməˈfɪliæk; -ˈfilyæk/ ***noun*** [C] a person who suffers from hemophilia

**hem·or·rhage** /ˈhɛmrɪdʒ; ˈhɛmərɪdʒ/ ***noun*** [C,U] very heavy bleeding ▸ **hem·or·rhage *verb*** [I]

**hem·or·rhoids** /ˈhɛmrɔɪdz; ˈhɛmərɔɪdz/ ***noun*** [pl.] painful swellings near the hole in your body where solid waste comes out (**the anus**)

**hemp** /hɛmp/ ***noun*** [U] a plant that is used for making rope and rough cloth and for producing the illegal drug marijuana

**hen** /hɛn/ ***noun*** [C] a female bird that is often kept on farms for its eggs or its meat: *Our hens haven't laid many eggs this week.* ➲ Look at the note at **chicken**.

**hence** /hɛns/ ***adv.*** for this reason: (*formal*) *The town was founded by William Clark – hence the name Clarksville.*

**hence·forth** /ˈhɛnsfɔrθ; ˌhɛnsˈfɔrθ/ (*also* **henceforward**) ***adv.*** (*formal*) from now on; in the future

**hench·man** /ˈhɛntʃmən/ ***noun*** [C] (*pl.* **hench·men** /-mən/) a person who follows sb or works for sb and who may do things for him/her that are illegal or violent: *the dictator and his henchmen*

**ˈhen ˌparty *noun*** [C] a party only for women, especially the night before one of the group is to get married

**hep·a·ti·tis** /ˌhɛpəˈtaɪt̬əs/ ***noun*** [U] a serious disease of the liver

★**her¹** /hər; *weak form also* ər/ ***pronoun*** (the object of a verb or preposition) a female person or animal that was mentioned earlier: *He told Sue that he loved her.* ◇ *I have a letter for your mother. Could you give it to her for me?* ◇ (*informal*) *That must be her now.* ➲ Look at **she** and the note at **he**.

★**her²** /hər; *weak form also* ər/ ***det.*** belonging to a female person or animal that was mentioned earlier: *That's her book. She left it there this morning.* ◇ *Lynn broke her leg.*

**her·ald** /ˈhɛrəld/ ***verb*** [T] to be a sign that sb/sth is coming: *The CEO's speech heralded a change in policy.*

**herb** /ərb/ ***noun*** [C] a plant whose leaves, seeds, etc. are used for giving food more flavor or in some types of traditional medicine ➲ Look at **spice**.

**herb·al** /ˈərbl; ˈhərbl/ ***adj.*** made of or using herbs: *herbal tea* ◇ *herbal medicine*

**herd¹** /hərd/ ***noun*** [C] a large number of animals that live and eat together: *a herd of cattle/deer/elephants*

**herd²** /hərd/ ***verb*** [T] to move people or animals forward as if they were in a herd: *The prisoners were herded onto the train.*

★**here¹** /hɪr/ ***adv.*** **1** (after a verb or a preposition) in, at or to the place where you are or which you are pointing to: *I live here.* ◇ *Come (over) here.* ◇ *The school is a mile from here.* ◇ *Please sign here.* **2** (used for introducing or drawing attention to sb/sth): *Here is the ten o'clock news.* ◇ *Here comes the bus.* ◇ *Here we are* (= we have arrived). ◇ *"Are the others coming?" "Yes, here they are now."*

> **NOTE** Note the word order in the last two examples. We say: *Here are the children* and: *Here they are.* Note also the expression: *Here you are* which is used when we are giving something to somebody: *Here you are – this is that book I was talking about.*

**3** at this point: *Here the speaker stopped and looked around the room.* **4** (used for emphasizing a noun): *My friend here saw it happen.* ◇ *I think you'll find this book here very useful.*

**IDM here and there** in various places: *We could see small groups of people here and there along the beach.*

**here goes** (*informal*) (used before doing sth exciting, dangerous, etc.): *I've never done a backward dive before, but here goes!*

**here's to sb/sth** (used for drinking to the health, success, etc. of sb/sth): *Here's to your future happiness!*

**neither here nor there** not important: *What he thinks is neither here nor there; you should make your own decision.*

**here²** /hɪr/ ***interjection*** (used when offering help or when giving sth to sb): *Here, let me help!* ◇ *Here, take this and buy yourself a candy bar.*

**he·red·i·tar·y** /həˈrɛdəˌtɛri/ ***adj.*** passed on from parent to child: *a hereditary disease* ◇ *Do you think intelligence is hereditary?* ➲ verb **inherit**

**he·red·i·ty** /həˈrɛdət̬i/ ***noun*** [U] the passing on of physical or mental features from parent to child ➲ verb **inherit**

**her·e·sy** /ˈhɛrəsi/ ***noun*** [C,U] (*pl.* **her·e·sies**) (*formal*) a (religious) opinion or belief that is against what is generally accepted as true in the group you belong to

**her·e·tic** /ˈhɛrətɪk/ ***noun*** [C] a person who believes a heresy ▸ **he·ret·i·cal** /həˈrɛtɪkl/ ***adj.***

**her·i·tage** /ˈhɛrət̬ɪdʒ/ ***noun*** [C, usually sing.] the traditions, qualities and cultural achievements of a country that have existed for a long time and that have great importance for the country: *Wildlife is an important part of our **national heritage**.* ◇ *We need to preserve our cultural heritage for future generations.* ▸ **her·i·tage *adj.***: *It's important for immigrant children to maintain their heritage language* (= the language traditionally spoken by their families.)

**her·mit** /ˈhərmət/ ***noun*** [C] a person who prefers to live alone, without contact with other people.

**her·ni·a** /ˈhərniə/ (*also* **rupture**) ***noun*** [C,U] the medical condition when an organ inside your body, especially below the stomach, pushes through the wall of muscle which surrounds it

★**he·ro** /ˈhɪroʊ; ˈhiroʊ/ ***noun*** [C] (*pl.* **he·roes**) **1** a person who has done sth brave or good and who is admired and remembered for it: *sports heroes* **2** the most important male character in a book, play, movie, etc. ➲ Look at **villain**. **3** = SUBMARINE (2)

**he·ro·ic** /həˈroʊɪk/ ***adj.*** (used about people or their actions) very brave: *a heroic effort* ▸ **he·ro·i·cal·ly** /-kli/ ***adv.***

**her·o·in** /ˈhɛroʊən/ ***noun*** [U] a very powerful illegal drug that people take especially by putting it directly into their blood with a type of needle (a syringe). It is very difficult to stop using heroin.

H

**her·o·ine** /ˈhɛroʊən/ ***noun*** [C] **1** a woman who has done sth brave or good and who is admired and remembered for it **2** the most important female character in a book, play, movie, etc.

**her·o·ism** /ˈhɛroʊɪzəm/ ***noun*** [U] great courage; being very brave

**her·ring** /ˈhɛrɪŋ/ ***noun*** [C] (*pl.* **her·ring** or **her·rings**) a small silver fish that swims in large groups in the ocean and that is used for food

IDM **a red herring** → RED[1]

**hers** /hərz/ ***pronoun*** of or belonging to her: *I didn't have a pencil, but Jill let me borrow hers.*

★**her·self** /hərˈsɛlf; *weak form also* ərˈsɛlf/ ***pronoun*** **1** (used as the object of a verb or preposition when the female person or animal who does an action is also affected by it): *She hurt herself pretty badly.* ◇ *Val bought herself a burger for lunch.* ◇ *Kim looked at herself in the mirror.* **2** (used for emphasis): *She told me the news herself.* ◇ *Did Sara do this herself?* (= or did sb else do it for her?) **3** in her normal state; healthy: *She's just not herself today* (= she's feeling sick).

IDM **(all) by herself 1** alone: *She lives by herself.* ➲ Look at the note at **alone**. **2** without help: *I don't think she needs any help – she can change a tire by herself.*

**he's** *short for* HE IS, HE HAS

**hes·i·tant** /ˈhɛzətənt/ ***adj.*** **hesitant (to do/about doing sth)** slow to speak or act because you are not sure whether you should or not: *I'm very hesitant about criticizing him too much.* ▸ **hes·i·tan·cy** /-ənsi/ ***noun*** [U] ▸ **hes·i·tant·ly** ***adv.***

★**hes·i·tate** /ˈhɛzəteɪt/ ***verb*** [I] **1** to pause before you do sth or before you make a decision, usually because you are uncertain or worried: *He hesitated before going into the room.* **2 hesitate (to do sth)** to be unwilling to do sth because you are not sure that it is right: *Don't hesitate to call if you have any problems.*

**hes·i·ta·tion** /ˌhɛzəˈteɪʃn/ ***noun*** [C,U] a time when you wait because you are not sure: *He continued speaking after a slight hesitation.*

**het·er·o·sex·u·al** /ˌhɛt̬ərəˈsɛkʃuəl/ ***adj.*** (*formal*) sexually attracted to a person of the other sex (= a man to a woman or a woman to a man) ➲ A less formal word is **straight**. Look also at **bisexual** and **homosexual**. ▸ **het·er·o·sex·u·al** ***noun*** [C]

**hex·a·gon** /ˈhɛksəgɑn/ ***noun*** [C] a shape with six sides ▸ **hex·ag·o·nal** /hɛkˈsægənl/ ***adj.***

**hey** /heɪ/ ***interjection*** (*informal*) (used when you want to attract sb's attention or to show that you are surprised or interested): *Hey, what are you doing?* ◇ *Hey, I like your bike!*

**hey·day** /ˈheɪdeɪ/ ***noun*** [sing.] the period when sb/sth was most powerful, successful, rich, etc.

**hi** /haɪ/ ***interjection*** (*informal*) (used as a greeting when you meet sb) ➲ Look at the note at **hello**.

**hi·ber·nate** /ˈhaɪbərneɪt/ ***verb*** [I] (used about animals) to spend the winter in a state like deep sleep ▸ **hi·ber·na·tion** /ˌhaɪbərˈneɪʃn/ ***noun*** [U]

**hic·cup** /ˈhɪkʌp/ (*also* **hiccough**) ***noun*** **1** [C] a sudden stopping of the breath with a noise like a cough, usually caused by eating or drinking too quickly **2** **(the) hiccups** [pl.] a series of hiccups: *Don't eat so fast, or you'll get the hiccups!* ◇ *I had the hiccups.* ◇ *Do you know of a cure for hiccups?* **3** [C] a small problem or difficulty: *There was a slight hiccup in our plans, but everything's okay now.* ▸ **hic·cup** ***verb*** [I]

**hick** /hɪk/ ***noun*** [C] (*informal*) a person from the countryside or a small town who does not know much about the rest of the world and is not well educated ➲ This word is used in a negative way.

**hick·o·ry** /ˈhɪkəri; ˈhɪkri/ ***noun*** **1** [C] (*pl.* **hick·o·ries**) a North American tree of the walnut family **2** [U] the hard wood of the hickory tree

★**hide[1]** /haɪd/ ***verb*** (*pt* **hid** /hɪd/; *pp* **hid·den** /ˈhɪdn/) **1** [T] to put or keep sb/sth in a place where he/she/it cannot be seen: *Where should I hide the money?* ◇ *The scar is partially hidden by hair.* ◇ *The trees hid the house from view.* **2** [I] to be or get in a place where you cannot be seen or found: *Quick, run and hide!* ◇ *Tammy was hiding under the bed.* **3** [T] **hide sth (from sb)** to keep sth secret so that other people do not know about it: *She tried to hide her disappointment from them.*

**hide[2]** /haɪd/ ***noun*** [C,U] the skin of an animal that will be used for making leather, etc.

**hide-and-seek** /ˌhaɪd n ˈsik/ (*also* **hide-and-go-seek** /ˌhaɪd n goʊ ˈsik/) ***noun*** [U] a children's game in which one person hides and the others try to find him/her

**hid·e·ous** /ˈhɪdiəs/ ***adj.*** very ugly or unpleasant: *a hideous sight* ◇ *a hideous crime* ◇ (*informal*) *a hideous orange dress* ▸ **hid·e·ous·ly** ***adv.***

**hid·ing** /ˈhaɪdɪŋ/ ***noun*** [U]

IDM **be in/go into hiding** to be in or go into a place where you cannot be found: *She escaped from prison and went into hiding.*

**hi·er·ar·chy** /ˈhaɪərɑrki; ˈhaɪrɑrki/ ***noun*** [C] (*pl.* **hi·er·ar·chies**) a system or organization that has many grades or ranks from the lowest to the highest ▸ **hi·er·ar·chi·cal** /ˌhaɪəˈrɑrkɪkl; ˌhaɪˈrɑr-/ ***adj.***

**hi·er·o·glyph·ics** /ˌhaɪərəˈglɪfɪks; ˌhaɪrə-/ ***noun*** [pl.] the system of writing that was used in ancient Egypt in which a type of picture represents a word or sound

★**high[1]** /haɪ/ ***adj.***

➤FROM BOTTOM TO TOP **1** (used about things) measuring a great amount from the bottom to the top: *high cliffs* ◇ *What's the highest mountain in the world?* ◇ *high heels* (= on shoes) ◇ *The fence was so high that we couldn't see over it.* ➲ Look at **height**, **low** and the note at **tall**. **2** having a particular height: *The hedge is three feet high.* ◇ *knee-high boots*

➤FAR ABOVE GROUND **3** at a level which is a long way from the ground, or from sea level: *Keep all medications on a high shelf where children cannot reach them.* ◇ *The fort was built on high ground.*

➤GREATER THAN NORMAL **4** above the usual or normal level or amount: *high prices* ◇ *at high speed* ◇ *a high level of unemployment* ◇ *high-quality goods* ◇ *He has high blood pressure.* ◇ *Oranges are high in vitamin C.*

➤GOOD **5** good or favorable: *Her work is of a very high standard.* ◇ *He has a high opinion of you.*

➤RANK/STATUS **6** having an important position or

rank: *We will have to refer the matter to a higher authority.*
➤IDEALS/PRINCIPLES **7** morally good: *high ideals*
➤SOUND **8** (used about a sound or voice) not deep or low: *She sang the high notes beautifully.*
➤ON ALCOHOL/DRUGS **9 high (on sth)** (*informal*) under the influence of drugs, etc.
➤GEAR IN VEHICLE **10** (used about a gear in a car) that allows a faster speed

★**high²** /haɪ/ ***adv.*** **1** at or to a HIGH¹ (3) position or level: *The sun was high in the sky.* ◇ *I can't jump any higher.* ◇ *The plane flew high overhead.* ◇ *You should aim high.* **2** (used about a sound) at a HIGH¹ (8) level: *How high can you sing?*
IDM **high and low** everywhere: *We searched high and low for the keys.*

**high³** /haɪ/ ***noun*** [C] **1** a high level or point: *Profits reached an all-time high last year.* **2** (used about the weather) the highest temperature in a certain place during a certain time: *Highs tomorrow will be in the mid-80s.* **3** (*slang*) a feeling of great pleasure or happiness that may be caused by a drug, etc. **4 High** (*informal*) (used in the names of schools) *short for* HIGH SCHOOL: *We both went to Central High.*

**high·brow** /ˈhaɪbraʊ/ ***adj.*** connected with people who are interested in serious intellectual things

**ˌhigher eduˈcation** ***noun*** [U] education at a college or university ➲ For more information on the North American educational systems, look at study pages **A8-A9**.

**ˌhigh ˈfive** ***noun*** [C] an action to celebrate victory or to express happiness in which two people raise one arm each and hit their open hands together: *That was great! Give me a high five!*

**ˌhigh-ˈflyer** (*also* **high-flier**) ***noun*** [C] a person who has the desire and the ability to be very successful in his or her job or studies: *academic high flyers*

**the ˈhigh jump** ***noun*** [sing.] the sport in which people try to jump over a bar in order to find out who can jump the highest ➲ Look at **long jump**.

**ˈhigh-ˌlevel** ***adj.*** (only *before* a noun) involving important people: *high-level talks*

**high·light¹** /ˈhaɪlaɪt/ ***noun*** **1** [C] the best or most interesting part of sth: *Highlights of the game will be shown on TV tonight.* **2 highlights** [pl.] areas of lighter color that are put in a person's hair

**high·light²** /ˈhaɪlaɪt/ ***verb*** [T] **1** to give special attention to sth: *The report highlighted the need for improved safety in inner cities.* **2** to mark important parts of a book, document, etc. with a brightly colored pen

★**high·ly** /ˈhaɪli/ ***adv.*** **1** to a high degree; very: *The movie was highly entertaining.* ◇ *The disease is highly contagious.* **2** (very) well or favorably: *I think highly of your work* (= I have a good opinion of it).

**High·ness** /ˈhaɪnəs/ ***noun*** [C] (*pl.* **High·ness·es**) a title used when speaking about or to a member of a royal family: *Good evening, Your Highness.* ◇ *His Royal Highness Prince Charles*

**ˈhigh-ˌpowered** ***adj.*** (only *before* a noun) **1** (used about things) having great power: *a high-powered engine* **2** (used about people) important and successful: *high-powered executives*

**ˌhigh-ˈprofile** ***adj.*** (only *before* a noun) that attracts a lot of attention in the news, on television, etc.: *a high-profile lawsuit*

**ˈhigh-rise** ***adj.*** (only *before* a noun) (used about a building) tall, with many levels: *a high-rise apartment block* ▶ **ˈhigh-rise** (*also* **highrise**) ***noun*** [C]: *a 22-story high-rise*

**ˈhigh school** ***noun*** [C,U] a school that is for children who are about 14 to 18 years old: *Our daughter is already in college, and our son is in high school now.* ◇ *high school students* ◇ *a high school graduate* ◇ *a high school diploma* ➲ Look also at **junior high school** and **senior high school**.

**ˌhigh-ˈstrung** ***adj.*** (used about a person) very nervous or becoming excited very easily

**ˌhigh-ˈtech** ***adj.*** (*informal*) **1** using a lot of modern equipment, especially computers **2** using designs or styles taken from industry, etc.; very modern

**ˌhigh ˈtide** ***noun*** [U] the time when the ocean comes closest to the land

★**high·way** /ˈhaɪweɪ/ ***noun*** [C] a main road (especially between towns or cities) ➲ Look at the note at **road**. Look also at **divided highway**.

**ˈhighway paˌtrol** ***noun*** [U] the police force that is in charge of the main roads in a particular state: *a highway patrol officer*

**hi·jack** /ˈhaɪdʒæk/ ***verb*** [T] to take control of a plane, etc. by force, usually for political reasons: *The plane was hijacked on its flight to Israel.* ▶ **hi·jack·er** ***noun*** [C] ▶ **hi·jack·ing** ***noun*** [C,U]

**hike¹** /haɪk/ ***noun*** [C] **1** a long walk in the mountains or the country **2** (*informal*) a sudden large increase: *a price hike*
IDM **take a hike** (*informal*) a way of telling sb to go away: *"I told you to take a hike! I'm not interested!"*

**hike²** /haɪk/ **1** ***verb*** [I] to go for a long walk in the mountains or the country

> NOTE **Go hiking** is used when you are talking about spending time hiking: *They went hiking in the Rocky Mountains last summer.*

**2** [T] (*informal*) to increase a price, etc. suddenly: *The legislature plans to hike state income taxes.* ▶ **hik·er** ***noun*** [C]

**hi·lar·i·ous** /hɪˈlɛriəs/ ***adj.*** very funny ▶ **hi·lar·i·ous·ly** ***adv.***

**hi·lar·i·ty** /hɪˈlærət̬i; -ˈlɛr-/ ***noun*** [U] great amusement or loud laughter

★**hill** /hɪl/ ***noun*** [C] a high area of land that is not as high as a mountain: *There was a wonderful view from the top of the hill.* ◇ *Tim enjoys walking in the hills.* ◇ *I had to push my bike up the hill – it was too steep to ride.* ➲ Note the words **uphill** and **downhill** (*adj., adv.*): *an uphill climb* ◇ *I like riding downhill on my bike.*

**hill·bil·ly** /ˈhɪlbɪli/ ***noun*** [C] (*pl.* **hill·bil·lies**) (*informal*) a person who is usually not well educated and who comes from a part of the countryside in the southern U.S. where there are many hills

**hill·side** /ˈhɪlsaɪd/ ***noun*** [C] the sloping side of a hill: *a house built on the hillside*

**hill·top** /'hɪltɑp/ ***noun*** [C] the top of a hill

**hill·y** /'hɪli/ ***adj.*** (**hill·i·er**; **hill·i·est**) having many hills: *The landscape is very hilly around here.*

**hilt** /hɪlt/ ***noun*** [C] the handle of a knife, etc.
IDM **to the hilt** to a high degree; completely: *I'll defend you to the hilt.*

★**him** /ɪm; *strong form* hɪm/ ***pronoun*** (the object of a verb or preposition) a male person or animal that was mentioned earlier: *Louise told Joe that she loved him.* ◇ *I have a letter for your father – can you give it to him for me?* ◇ *That must be him now.* ➲ Look at the note at **he**.

★**him·self** /hɪm'sɛlf; *weak form also* ɪm'sɛlf/ ***pronoun*** **1** (used as the object of a verb or preposition when the male person or animal who does an action is also affected by it): *He hurt himself pretty badly.* ◇ *He bought himself a new sweater.* ◇ *John looked at himself in the mirror.* **2** (used for emphasis): *He told me the news himself.* ◇ *The governor himself came to see the damage.* ◇ *Did he write this himself?* (= or did sb else do it for him?) **3** in his normal state; healthy: *He's just not himself today* (= he's feeling sick).
IDM **(all) by himself 1** alone: *He lives by himself.* ➲ Look at the note at **alone**. **2** without help: *He should be able to cook a meal by himself.*

**hind** /haɪnd/ ***adj.*** (only *before* a noun) (used about an animal's legs, etc.) at the back ➲ We also say **back legs**. The legs at the front are **front legs**.

**hin·der** /'hɪndər/ ***verb*** [T] to make it more difficult for sb/sth to do sth: *A lot of scientific work is hindered by lack of money.*

**hin·drance** /'hɪndrəns/ ***noun*** [C] a person or thing that makes it difficult for you to do sth: *Mark wanted to help me, but he was more of a hindrance than a help.*

**hind·sight** /'haɪndsaɪt/ ***noun*** [U] knowing afterward why sth bad happened and how you could have stopped it happening: *It's very easy to criticize with the benefit of hindsight.* ➲ Look at **foresight**.

**Hin·du** /'hɪndu/ ***noun*** [C] a person whose religion is Hinduism ▶ **Hin·du** ***adj.***: *Hindu beliefs*

**Hin·du·ism** /'hɪnduɪzəm/ ***noun*** [U] the main religion of India, which includes a belief in many gods and the belief that, after death, people will return to life in a different form

**hinge¹** /hɪndʒ/ ***noun*** [C] a piece of metal that joins two sides of a box, door, etc. together and allows it to be opened or closed

hinge

**hinge²** /hɪndʒ/ ***verb***
PHR V **hinge on sth** to depend on sth: *The future of the project hinges on the meeting today.*

**hint¹** /hɪnt/ ***noun*** [C] **1** something that you suggest in an indirect way: *She kept looking at her watch as a hint that it was time to go.* ◇ *I don't know the answer – can you give me a hint?* **2** a piece of advice or information: *The magazine had some helpful hints about how to lose weight.* **3** a small amount of sth: *There was a hint of sadness in his voice.*

**hint²** /hɪnt/ ***verb*** [I,T] to suggest sth in an indirect way: *They only hinted at their great disappointment.* ◇ *He hinted that he might be moving to Florida.*

**hip¹** /hɪp/ ***noun*** [C] the part of the side of your body above your legs and below your waist: *He stood there angrily with his hands on his hips.* ◇ *She broke her hip* (= the bone inside her hip) *when she fell.* ➲ picture on study page **A32**.

**hip²** /hɪp/ ***adj.*** (**hip·per**; **hip·pest**) (*informal*) very fashionable or knowing a lot about fashionable clothes, music, etc.

**hip³** /hɪp/ ***interjection***
IDM **hip, hip, hooray** (*old-fashioned*) (used when a group wants to show that it is pleased with sb or with sth that has happened): *"Three cheers for David. He did a great job. Hip, hip..." "Hooray!"*

**'hip-hop** ***noun*** [U] (*informal*) **1** a type of modern dance music with spoken words and a steady beat played on electronic instruments, originally played by young African Americans ➲ Look also at **rap¹**(2). **2** the culture of the young African Americans and others who enjoy this type of music, including special styles of art, dancing, dress, etc.

**hip·pie** (*also* **hippy**) /'hɪpi/ ***noun*** [C] (*pl.* **hip·pies**) a person who does not share the same ideas and values as most people in society. Hippies show that they are different by wearing long hair, colorful clothes, etc. and sometimes by living in groups.

**hip·po·pot·a·mus** /ˌhɪpə'pɑt̮əməs/ ***noun*** [C] (*pl.* **hip·po·pot·a·mus·es** /-məsəz/ or **hip·po·pot·a·mi** /-maɪ/) (*also informal* **hip·po** /'hɪpoʊ/) (*pl.* **hip·pos**) a large African river animal with a large head and short legs and thick dark skin

★**hire** /'haɪər/ ***verb*** [T] to give sb a job: *We hired a new secretary.*

★**his¹** /ɪz; *strong form* hɪz/ ***det.*** belonging to a male person or animal that was mentioned earlier: *That's his book. He left it there this morning.* ◇ *Matthew hurt his shoulder.*

**his²** /hɪz/ ***pronoun*** of or belonging to him: *This is my book, so that one must be his.* ◇ *My dad has a lot of neckties, so I borrowed one of his.* ➲ Look at the note at **he**.

**His·pan·ic¹** /hɪ'spænɪk/ ***adj.*** connected with or coming from a place where Spanish is spoken, especially Latin America: *the Hispanic population of the U.S.*

**His·pan·ic²** /hɪ'spænɪk/ ***noun*** [C] a person who is from a place where Spanish is spoken, especially Latin America, or whose ancestors came from a place where Spanish is spoken

**hiss** /hɪs/ ***verb*** **1** [I] to make a sound like a very long "s" to show that you are angry or do not like sth: *The cat hissed at me.* **2** [T] to say sth in an angry hissing voice: *"Stay away from me!" she hissed.* ▶ **hiss** ***noun*** [C]

**his·to·ri·an** /hɪ'stɔriən/ ***noun*** [C] a person who is an expert in history

**his·tor·ic** /hɪ'stɔrɪk; -'stɑr-/ ***adj.*** famous or important in history: *The astronauts' landing on the moon was a historic occasion.*

★**his·tor·i·cal** /hɪ'stɔrɪkl; -'stɑr-/ ***adj.*** **1** connected with history or the study of history: *There is very little historical evidence about the life of Christ.* ◇ *This house is of great historical interest.* **2** that really lived or happened: *Was Daniel Boone really a historical figure?* ◇ *historical events* ▶ **his·tor·i·cal·ly** /-kli/ *adv.*

★**his·to·ry** /ˈhɪstəri; ˈhɪstri/ *noun* (*pl.* **his·to·ries**) **1** [U] the study of past events and social, political and economic developments: *She has a bachelor's degree in history.* ◇ *History was my favorite subject in school.* ◇ *a history teacher* **2** [U] events of the past (when you are thinking of them as a whole): *History often repeats itself.* ◇ *an important moment in history* ➲ Look at **natural history**. **3** [C] a written description of past events: *a new history of Europe* **4** [C, usually sing.] the series of events or facts that is connected with a person, place or thing: *There is a history of heart disease in our family.*

NOTE **History** is something true that really happened. A **story** is a description of a series of events that may or may not have happened.

★**hit¹** /hɪt/ *verb* (*pres. part.* **hit·ting**; *pt, pp* **hit**) **1** [T] to touch sb/sth with a lot of force: *"Don't hit me," she begged.* ◇ *The old man was hit by a car while he was crossing the street.* ◇ *to hit a ball with a bat* ◇ (*figurative*) *The smell of burning hit her as she entered the room.* ◇ (*figurative*) *Things were going really well until we hit this problem.*

NOTE **Strike** is a more formal word than **hit**. **Beat** means to hit many times: *He was badly beaten in the attack.*

**2** [T] **hit sth (on/against sth)** to knock a part of your body, etc. against sth: *Peter hit his head on the low beam.* **3** [T] to have a bad effect upon sb/sth: *Inner-city areas have been badly hit by unemployment.* ◇ *Her father's death hit her very hard.* **4** [T] to find or reach sth: *If you follow this road, you should hit the freeway in about ten minutes.* ◇ *The price of oil hit a new high yesterday.* **5** [I,T] to attack sb/sth: *We hit the enemy when they least expected it.* ◇ *They waited until night, and then hit.* **6** [T] (*informal*) to experience sth difficult or unpleasant: *We seem to have hit a snag.* ◇ *Everything went well at first, but then we hit trouble.* **7** [T] (*informal*) to come suddenly into your mind: *I couldn't remember where I'd met him and then suddenly it hit me: he works in the bank.* **8** [T] (*informal*) to press sth such as a button to operate a machine, etc.: *Hit the brakes!*

IDM **hit it off (with sb)** (*informal*) to like sb when you first meet him/her: *When I first met Tony's parents, we didn't really hit it off.*

**hit the hay/sack** (*informal*) to go to bed

**hit the jackpot 1** to win a lot of money or a big prize **2** to be very successful or lucky: *We really hit the jackpot with our latest product.*

**hit the nail on the head** to say sth that is exactly right

**hit the road** (*informal*) to leave a place

**hit the roof** → ROOF

PHRV **hit back (at sb/sth)** to attack (with words) sb who has attacked you: *The President hit back at his critics.*

★**hit²** /hɪt/ *noun* [C] **1** the act of hitting sth; a blow: *The ship took a direct hit and sank.* ◇ *What a great hit!* (e.g. in a game of baseball) OPP Look at **miss**. **2** a person or thing that is very popular or successful: *He was a big hit in his last movie.* ◇ *The album was a smash hit.* **3** a result of a search on a computer, especially on the Internet: *When I searched for "tulips" I got over a million hits.* **4** a visit to a page on the Internet: *Since I updated my homepage I've had over a thousand hits.*

**hit-and-run** /ˌhɪt n ˈrʌn/ *adj.* **1** (used about a car driver) causing an accident and not stopping to see if anybody is hurt **2** (used about a car accident) caused by a HIT-AND-RUN (1) driver

**hitch¹** /hɪtʃ/ *verb* **1** [I,T] (*informal*) to get free rides in other people's cars as a way of traveling cheaply: *They hitched a ride in a truck to the next state.* **2** [T] to fasten sth to sth else: *The horses were hitched to the fence.* ◇ *to hitch a trailer to the back of a car*

**hitch²** /hɪtʃ/ *noun* [C] a small problem or difficulty: *The wedding went off without a hitch.*

**hitch·hike** /ˈhɪtʃhaɪk/ *verb* [I] to travel by getting free rides in other people's cars: *He hitchhiked across Europe.* ▶ **hitch·hik·er** *noun* [C]

**hith·er·to** /ˈhɪðərtu; ˌhɪðərˈtu/ *adv.* (*formal*) until now

**HIV** /ˌeɪtʃ aɪ ˈvi/ *noun* [U] human immunodeficiency virus; a very small living thing (a **virus**) that is believed to cause the disease AIDS: *to be HIV-positive* (= to have HIV in your body) ◇ *to be HIV-negative* (= not to have HIV in your body)

**hive** /haɪv/ *noun* [C] = BEEHIVE

**hmm** /hm; m/ *interjection* (used when you are not sure or when you are thinking about sth)

**HMO** /ˌeɪtʃ ɛm ˈoʊ/ (*also* **health maintenance organization**) *noun* [C] (*pl.* **HMOs**) (*U.S.*) a company that gives medical care to people who pay money every month to be members. HMOs control costs by limiting the amount and types of treatment that their doctors and nurses can give to patients.

**hoard¹** /hɔrd/ *verb* [I,T] to collect and store large quantities of sth (often secretly)

**hoard²** /hɔrd/ *noun* [C] a quantity of money, food, etc. that sb has collected and stored (often secretly): *a hoard of treasure*

**hoarse** /hɔrs/ *adj.* **1** (used about a voice) sounding rough and quiet, e.g. because you have a cold: *a hoarse whisper* **2** (used about people) with a hoarse voice: *The fans shouted themselves hoarse.* ▶ **hoarse·ly** *adv.*

**hoax** /hoʊks/ *noun* [C] a trick that is played on sb: *The firefighters answered the call, but it turned out to be a hoax.*

**hob·ble** /ˈhɑbl/ *verb* [I] to walk with difficulty because your feet or legs are hurt: *He hobbled home on his twisted ankle.*

★**hob·by** /ˈhɑbi/ *noun* [C] (*pl.* **hob·bies**) something that you do regularly for pleasure in your free time: *Do you have any hobbies?* ◇ *My favorite hobby is stamp collecting.*

**hock·ey** /ˈhɑki/ (*also* ˈ**ice ˌhockey**) *noun* [U] a game that is played on an area of ice (a **rink**) by two teams of six players that try to hit a small round, flat rubber object (a **puck**) into a goal at each end of the ice with long wooden sticks ➲ picture on study page A32. ➲ Look also at **field hockey** and **ball hockey**.

**hoe** /hoʊ/ *noun* [C] a garden tool with a long handle

H

that is used for turning the soil and for removing weeds ➲ picture at **garden**.

**hog**[1] /hɔg; hɑg/ ***noun*** [C] a pig that is kept for its meat ➲ Look at the note at **pig**.

**hog**[2] /hɔg; hɑg/ ***verb*** [T] (**hog·ging**; **hogged**) (*informal*) to take or keep too much or all of sth in a selfish way: *Don't hog the bathroom when everyone's getting ready to go out!* ◇ *The red car was hogging the middle of the road so no one could pass it.*

**hoist** /hɔɪst/ ***verb*** [T] to raise or lift sth by using ropes, etc.: *to hoist a flag/sail*

★**hold**[1] /hoʊld/ ***verb*** (*pt, pp* **held** /hɛld/)

➤IN HAND/ARMS **1** [T] to take sb/sth and keep him/her/it in your hand, etc.: *He held a gun in his hand.* ◇ *The woman was holding a baby in her arms.* ◇ *He manages to write by holding the pen between his teeth.* ◇ *Hold my hand. This is a busy street.*

➤IN POSITION **2** [T] to keep sth in a certain position: *Hold your head up straight.* ◇ *Hold the camera still or you'll spoil the picture.* ◇ *These two screws hold the shelf in place.*

➤SUPPORT **3** to take the weight of sb/sth: *Don't stand on that chair; I don't think it will hold you.*

➤CONTAIN **4** [I,T] to contain or have space for a particular amount: *The car holds five people.* ◇ *How much does this bottle hold?*

➤SB PRISONER **5** [T] to keep a person in a position or place by force: *The hijackers are holding three men hostage.* ◇ *A suspect is being held at the police station.*

➤HAVE STH **6** [T] to have sth (usually in an official way): *Does she hold an American passport?* ◇ *She holds the world record in the 100 meters.*

➤OPINION **7** [T] to have an opinion, etc.: *They hold the view that we shouldn't spend any more money.* **8** [T] to believe that sth is true about a person: *I hold the parents responsible for the child's behavior.*

➤REMAIN **9** [I] to remain the same: *I hope this weather holds until the weekend.* ◇ *What I said still holds; nothing has changed.*

➤EVENT **10** [T] to organize an event: *They're holding a party for his fortieth birthday.* ◇ *Elections are held every November.*

➤ON TELEPHONE **11** [I,T] (when you are telephoning) to wait until the person you are calling is ready: *That extension is busy right now. Can you hold?*

➤CONVERSATION **12** [T] to have a conversation: *It's impossible to hold a conversation with all this noise.*

IDM **Hold it!** Wait! Don't move!

> NOTE For other idioms containing **hold**, look at the entries for the nouns, adjectives, etc., e.g. **hold your own** is at **own**.

PHRV **hold sb/sth back 1** to prevent sb from making progress **2** to prevent sb/sth from moving forward: *The police tried to hold the crowd back.*

**hold sth against sb** to not forgive sb for sth he or she has done

**hold sth back** not give information: *The police are sure that she is holding something back. She knows a lot more than she is saying.*

**hold on 1** to wait: *Hold on. I'll be with you in a minute.* **2** to manage in a difficult or dangerous situation: *They managed to hold on until an ambulance arrived.*

**hold onto sb/sth** not let go of sb/sth: *The child held onto his mother; he didn't want her to go.*

**hold onto sth** not give or sell sth: *They offered me a lot of money for this painting, but I'm going to hold onto it.*

**hold out** to last (in a difficult situation): *How long will our supply of water hold out?*

**hold sth out** to offer sth by moving it toward sb: *He held out a piece of candy and offered it to the girl.*

**hold out for sth** to continue to ask for sth

**hold sb/sth up** to make sb/sth late: *We were held up by the traffic.*

**hold up sth** to rob sth, using a gun, etc.: *Masked men held up a bank on Main Street yesterday.*

★**hold**[2] /hoʊld/ ***noun*** **1** [C, sing.] the act or manner of holding sb/sth: *to have a firm hold on the rope* ◇ *judo holds*

> NOTE "Hold" is often used with the verbs **catch**, **get**, **grab**, **seize**, **take**, etc.: *Take hold of the other side of this sheet and help me to fold it.* ◇ *I can touch it, but I can't quite get hold of it. It's too far away.*

**2** [sing.] **a hold (on/over sb/sth)** influence or control: *The party has strengthened its hold on Congress.* **3** [C] a place where a climber can put his/her hand or foot when climbing ➲ Look at **foothold**. **4** [C] the part of a ship or an airplane where goods are carried

IDM **get (a) hold of sb/sth 1** to find sth (that will be useful): *Where can I get hold of a good dictionary?* **2** to find sb or make contact with sb: *I've been trying to get hold of the customer service department all morning.*

**on hold 1** (on the telephone) waiting to talk to sb or to continue a conversation: *to put sb on hold* ◇ *They kept me on hold for ten minutes!* **2** (used about a project, etc.) in a state of delay for an uncertain length of time: *Plans to build a new stadium are on hold until we can find more funding.*

**hold·er** /ˈhoʊldər/ ***noun*** [C] (often in compounds) **1** a person who has or holds sth: *the world record holder in the 100 meters* ◇ *holders of Canadian passports* **2** something that contains or holds sth: *a cup holder in the car*

**hold·ing** /ˈhoʊldɪŋ/ ***noun*** [C] **1 holding (in sth)** a number of shares that sb has in a company: *She has a 40% holding in the company.* **2** [usually pl.] an amount of property that is owned by a person, museum, library, etc.: *one of the most important private holdings of Indian art*

**ˈholding ˌcompany** ***noun*** [C] a company that is formed to buy shares in other companies, which it then controls

**hold·o·ver** /ˈhoʊldoʊvər/ ***noun*** [C] a person who keeps a position of power, for example sb who had a particular position in the government and still has it after the next election

**hold·up** /ˈhoʊldʌp/ ***noun*** [C] **1** a delay: *What's the holdup?* **2** an act of robbing sb/sth, by people with guns

★**hole** /hoʊl/ ***noun*** [C] **1** a hollow space in sth solid: *The sidewalk is full of holes.* ◇ *to dig a hole in the ground* **2** an opening or an empty space in sth solid: *There are holes in my socks.* ◇ (*figurative*) *There was a big hole in my life after Jim left.* **3** the place where an animal lives in the ground or in a tree: *a rabbit hole* **4** (in golf) the HOLE (1) in the ground that you must hit the ball into. Each section of a golf course is also called a hole: *an eighteen-hole golf course ◇ Barbara won the seventh hole.*

IDM **in the hole** (*informal*) owing more money then you have: *The company is over $5 million in the hole.*

★**hol·i·day** /ˈhɑlədeɪ/ ***noun*** **1** [C] a special day when government offices, schools, banks and some businesses are closed: *The post office will be closed Monday because it's a holiday. ◇ New Year's Day is a holiday in every state.* **2 the holidays** [pl.] the time in late December and early January that includes Christmas, Hanukkah, New Year's Day, etc.: *Airports across the country are full of people heading home for the holidays.*

> NOTE We say " *Happy holidays!*" to people in December to wish them a nice Christmas, Hanukkah, New Year, etc.

**3** [C,U] (*Cdn*) = VACATION

**hol·ler** /ˈhɑlər/ ***verb*** [I,T] (*informal*) to shout: *"You kids get out of here!" he hollered. ◇ The fans were all screaming and hollering.* ▶ **hol·ler *noun*** [C]

★**hol·low**[1] /ˈhɑloʊ/ ***adj.*** **1** with a hole or empty space inside: *a hollow tree* **2** (used about a sound) seeming to come from a HOLLOW (1) place: *hollow footsteps in the empty house*

IDM **ring hollow** → RING[2]

**hol·low**[2] /ˈhɑloʊ/ ***noun*** [C] an area that is lower than the surrounding land

**hol·low**[3] /ˈhɑloʊ/ ***verb***

PHRV **hollow sth out** to take the inside part of sth out in order to make sth else: *They hollowed out a tree trunk to make a canoe.*

**hol·ly** /ˈhɑli/ ***noun*** [U] a plant that has shiny dark green leaves with sharp points and red berries in the winter. It is often used as a Christmas decoration.

**hol·o·caust** /ˈhɑləkɔst; ˈhoʊlə-/ ***noun*** **1 the Holocaust** [sing.] the killing of large numbers of Jews and other people in central Europe by the Nazis in World War II: *Holocaust victims/survivors* **2** [C] a situation where a great many things are destroyed and a great many people die: *a nuclear holocaust*

**hol·o·gram** /ˈhɑləgræm; ˈhoʊlə-/ ***noun*** [C] an image or picture which appears to stand out from the flat surface it is printed on when light falls on it

**hol·ster** /ˈhoʊlstər/ ***noun*** [C] a leather case for a gun that is attached to a belt or worn under the arm

★**ho·ly** /ˈhoʊli/ ***adj.*** (**ho·li·er**; **ho·li·est**) connected with God or with religion and therefore very special or sacred: *the Holy Bible ◇ holy water ◇ The Koran is the holy book of the Muslims.*

IDM **holy cow** (*informal*) (used to express surprise): *Holy cow! Cruz just scored another goal!*

**ˌHoly Comˈmunion** ***noun*** [U] = COMMUNION (1)

**the ˌHoly ˈGhost** (*also* **the ˌHoly ˈSpirit**) ***noun*** [sing.] one of the three parts of God that Christians believe in. The other two parts are the Father and the Son (Jesus Christ).

**hom·age** /ˈhɑmɪdʒ; ˈɑm-/ ***noun*** [C,U, usually sing.] (*formal*) **homage to sb/sth** something that is said or done to show respect publicly for sb: *Thousands came to **pay/do homage** to the dead leader.*

★**home**[1] /hoʊm/ ***noun***

➤ WHERE YOU LIVE **1** [C,U] the place where you live (with your family) or where you feel that you belong: *She left home at the age of 21. ◇ Children from broken homes* (= whose parents are divorced) *sometimes have learning difficulties.*

> NOTE Be careful. The preposition *to* is not used before "home": *It's time to go home. ◇ She's usually tired when she gets home.* If you want to talk about somebody else's home, you have to say: *at Jane and Andy's* or: *at Jane and Andy's place/house.* Look at the note at **house**.

➤ HOUSE, ETC. **2** [C] a house, an apartment, etc.: *Sales of new homes rose by 3% last year.* ➲ Look also at **mobile home**.

➤ FOR OLD PEOPLE/CHILDREN **3** [C] a place that provides care for a particular type of person: *a retirement home* (= for people who are retired) ➲ Look also at **nursing home**.

➤ WHERE STH BEGAN **4** [sing.] the place where sth began: *Nashville is the home of country music.*

➤ BASEBALL **5** [U] = HOME PLATE

IDM **at home 1** in your house, apartment, etc.: *We bought a computer so that Jackie can work at home. ◇ Nick is 28 years old, but he still lives at home* (= with his parents).

> NOTE With the verbs *be* and *stay*, we usually use **home** without the preposition *at*: *Is anybody home? ◇ I think I'll just stay home tonight.*

**2** as if you were in your own home; comfortable: *Please make yourself at home. ◇ They were warm and welcoming and I felt at home right away.*

**home**[2] /hoʊm/ ***adj.*** (only *before* a noun) **1** connected with HOME[1]: *home cooking ◇ a happy home life* **2** (used in sports) connected with your own sports team or field: *The home team is wearing white, and the visiting team is in red. ◇ The team won all of their home games but lost most of their away games.*

IDM **the home stretch** the last part of a long and often difficult activity, process, competition, etc.: *Both candidates are making a large number of speeches in the home stretch of the campaign.*

★**home**[3] /hoʊm/ ***adv.*** at, in or to your HOME[1] or home country: *We stopped at Jack and Terri's house, but they weren't home. ◇ We should go home soon. ◇ She'll be flying home for the holidays.*

IDM **bring sth home to sb** to make sb understand sth fully: *Looking at those pictures of hungry children really brought home to me how lucky we are.*

**home**[4] /hoʊm/ ***verb***

PHRV **home in on sb/sth** to move toward sb/sth: *The police homed in on the house where the thieves were hiding.*

**home·boy** /ˈhoʊmbɔɪ/ ***noun*** [C] (*slang*) a male friend from the same town as you; a member of a group of young people who go around together (a gang)

**home·com·ing** /ˈhoʊmˌkʌmɪŋ/ ***noun*** **1** [C,U] the arrival home (especially of sb who has been away for a long time) **2** [C] a festival at a high school, college or university which takes place on a weekend in the fall. Many former students return to their old school to watch an important football game and to join in other social events.

**ˌhome ecoˈnomics** (*also informal* **ˌhome ˈec**) ***noun*** [U] a school subject that includes cooking, sewing, etc.

**ˈhome fries** ***noun*** [pl.] a dish made from potatoes which have been boiled, made into small pieces (grated), formed into a flat, round shape and then fried

**home·land** /ˈhoʊmlænd/ ***noun*** [C] the country where you were born or that your parents came from, or to which you feel you belong

**home·less** /ˈhoʊmləs/ ***adj.*** **1** having no home **2 the homeless** ***noun*** [pl.] people without a home ▸ **home·less·ness** ***noun*** [U]

H

**ˌhome ˈloan** ***noun*** [C] = MORTGAGE

**home·ly** /ˈhoʊmli/ ***adj.*** (**home·li·er**; **home·li·est**) (used about a girl or woman) not very attractive

**home·made** /ˌhoʊmˈmeɪd/ ***adj.*** made at home; not bought in a store: *homemade soup*

**home·mak·er** /ˈhoʊmˌmeɪkər/ ***noun*** [C] a person, usually a woman, who cooks, cleans, etc. in his/her own home and does not have another job

**home·own·er** /ˈhoʊmˌoʊnər/ ***noun*** [C] a person who owns his/her home

**ˈhome page** ***noun*** [C] (*computing*) the first page of information about a company, an organization, a person, etc. that can be read on a computer screen when it is connected to an international system of computers (**the World Wide Web**). A home page usually has links to other pages with more information: *Visit our home page at www.oup-usa.org.*

**ˌhome ˈplate** (*also* **home**) ***noun*** [U] (in baseball) the place (**base**) where a player stands when he/she hits the ball and which he/she must touch in order to gain a point (**run**) ➲ picture at **baseball**.

**hom·er** /ˈhoʊmər/ ***noun*** [C] (*informal*) = HOME RUN

**home·room** /ˈhoʊmrum/ ***noun*** [C,U] a room in a school where a group of students must go at the beginning of each day and where a teacher gives them general information about school events and rules

**ˌhome ˈrun** (*also informal* **homer**) ***noun*** [C] (in baseball) a hit that goes so far that the player who hit the ball is allowed to run around all four corners (**bases**) and score a point (**run**): *to hit a home run* ➲ Look at the note at **baseball**.

**home·sick** /ˈhoʊmsɪk/ ***adj.*** sad because you are away from home: *She was very homesick for Japan.* ▸ **home·sick·ness** ***noun*** [U]

**home·town** /ˌhoʊmˈtaʊn/ ***noun*** [C] the town or city where you were born or where you lived when you were a child

**home·work** /ˈhoʊmwərk/ ***noun*** [U] the work that teachers give to students to do away from school: *to do your homework* ◇ (*figurative*) *The mayor had not done his homework and there were several questions that he couldn't answer.* ➲ Look at the note at **housework**.

**hom·ey** (*also* **hom·y**) /ˈhoʊmi/ (*comparative* **hom·i·er**; *superlative* **hom·i·est** /ˈhoʊmiəst/) ***adj.*** pleasant and comfortable, like home: *The hotel had a nice, homey atmosphere.*

**hom·i·cide** /ˈhɑməsaɪd/ ***noun*** [C,U] the illegal killing of one person by another; murder ▸ **hom·i·cid·al** /ˌhɑməˈsaɪdl/ ***adj.***

**hom·o·nym** /ˈhɑmənɪm/ ***noun*** [C] a word that is spelled or pronounced like another word but that has a different meaning

**ho·mo·pho·bi·a** /ˌhoʊməˈfoʊbiə/ ***noun*** [U] a strong dislike and fear of homosexual people ▸ **ho·mo·pho·bic** ***adj.***

**hom·o·phone** /ˈhɑməfoʊn; ˈhoʊ-/ ***noun*** [C] (*grammar*) a word that is pronounced like another word but has a different spelling or meaning: *"Sum" and "some" are homophones.*

**ho·mo·sex·u·al** /ˌhoʊməˈsɛkʃuəl/ ***adj.*** (*formal*) sexually attracted to people of the same sex ➲ A less formal word is **gay**. Look also at **heterosexual**, **bisexual** and **lesbian**. ▸ **ho·mo·sex·u·al** ***noun*** [C] ▸ **ho·mo·sex·u·al·i·ty** /ˌhoʊməsɛkʃuˈæləṭi/ ***noun*** [U]

**hon·cho** /ˈhɑntʃoʊ/ ***noun*** [C] (*pl.* **hon·chos**) (*slang*) a manager or person who is in charge of sb/sth: *the record company's head honcho*

★**hon·est** /ˈɑnəst/ ***adj.*** **1** (used about a person) telling the truth; not cheating or stealing: *Just be honest – do you like this skirt or not?* ◇ *We need somebody who's completely honest for this job.* **2** showing HONEST (1) qualities: *an honest face* ◇ *I'd like your honest opinion.* OPP The opposite for both senses is **dishonest**.

★**hon·est·ly** /ˈɑnəstli/ ***adv.*** **1** in an honest way: *He tried to answer the lawyer's questions honestly.* **2** (used for emphasizing sth): *I honestly don't know where she went.* **3** (used for expressing disapproval): *Honestly! What a mess!*

**hon·es·ty** /ˈɑnəsti/ ***noun*** [U] the quality of being honest OPP **dishonesty**

**hon·ey** /ˈhʌni/ ***noun*** **1** [U] the sweet sticky yellow substance that is made by bees and that people eat: *Would you like honey on your bread?* **2** [C] (*informal*) (a way of speaking to sb that you love): *Honey, I'm home!*

**hon·ey·comb** /ˈhʌnikoʊm/ ***noun*** [C,U] a structure of holes (**cells**) with six sides, in which bees keep their eggs and the substance they produce (**honey**)

**hon·ey·moon** /ˈhʌnimun/ ***noun*** [C] a vacation that is taken by a man and a woman who have just gotten married: *We went to Hawaii on our honeymoon.*

**honk** /hɑŋk; hɔŋk/ ***verb*** [I,T] to sound the horn of a car; to make this sound

★**hon·or**[1] /ˈɑnər/ ***noun*** **1** [sing.] something that gives pride or pleasure: *It was a great honor to give a speech at the convention.* ◇ *He did me the honor of mentioning my name in the book.* **2** [U] the respect from other people that a person, country, etc. gets because of high standards of behavior and moral character: *a man of honor* ◇ *to fight for the honor of your country* ➲ Look at **dishonor**. **3** [C] an award that is given to a person officially, to show great respect or to recognize sth important that he/she has achieved: *She graduated with honors* (= because she had gotten very good grades) *from Madison High School in 2003.* **4 Honor** [U] (used after *Your*, *His*

*or* Her ) (a title that is used when speaking about or to a judge, mayor, or some other official person)
IDM **in honor of sb/sth; in sb/sth's honor** out of respect for sb/sth: *A party was given in honor of the guests from Japan.*

**hon·or²** /ˈɑnər/ ***verb*** [T] **1 honor sb/sth (with sth)** to show great (public) respect for sb/sth or to give sb pride or pleasure: *I am very honored by the confidence you have shown in me.* **2** to keep a promise to do sth

**hon·or·a·ble** /ˈɑnərəbl/ ***adj.*** acting in a way that makes people respect you; having or showing honor: *The only honorable thing to do was to resign.* ◇ *an honorable person* OPP Look at **dishonorable**.
▸ **hon·or·a·bly** ***adv.***

**hon·or·ar·y** /ˈɑnərɛri/ ***adj.*** **1** given as an honor (without the person needing the usual qualifications): *to be awarded an honorary degree* **2** not getting any money for doing a job, and often not doing any real work: *an actor chosen to be the charity's honorary chairman*

**ˈhonor roll** ***noun*** [C, usually sing.] a list of the names of students in a school who have earned high grades

**hon·ors** /ˈɑnərz/ ***adj.*** intended for students with a great deal of ability and who have done well in school in the past: *Because of her good grades in high school, she was able to take honors English at college.*

**ˈhonor ˌsystem** ***noun*** [C] a system that trusts people to behave in a way that is honest: *The cafeteria has an honor system; if there's no cashier, you leave your money next to the cash register.*

**hood** /hʊd/ ***noun*** [C] **1** the part of a coat, etc. that you use to cover your head and neck in bad weather **2** the front part of a car that covers the engine

**hood·lum** /ˈhudləm; ˈhʊd-/ (*also slang* **hood**) ***noun*** [C] (*old-fashioned*) **1** a criminal, especially one who is part of a group (a gang) **2** a violent and noisy young man

**hoof** /hʊf; huf/ ***noun*** [C] (*pl.* **hoofs** or **hooves** /huvz; hʊvz/) the hard part of the foot of horses and some other animals ➲ picture at **horse**.

★**hook¹** /hʊk/ ***noun*** [C] **1** a curved piece of metal, plastic, etc. that is used for catching sth or hanging sth on: *a fish hook* ◇ *Put your coat on the hook over there.* ➲ picture at **hanger**. **2** (used in boxing) a hit or punch that is given with the elbow bent: *a right hook* (= with the right arm)

**hook**

IDM **hook, line and sinker** completely: *What I said was not true, but he fell for it* (= believed it) *hook, line and sinker.*
**off the hook 1** with the part of the telephone that you speak into (the receiver) not in position so that telephone calls cannot be received: *Martha's number is still busy – maybe she left the phone off the hook.* **2** (*informal*) out of a difficult situation: *My dad paid the money I owed and got me off the hook.*
**ring off the hook** → RING²

**hook²** /hʊk/ ***verb*** **1** [I,T] to fasten sth or to be fastened with a HOOK¹ (1) or sth like a hook **2** [T] to catch hold of sth with a HOOK¹ (1) or with sth shaped like a hook
IDM **be/get hooked (on sth)** (*slang*) **1** to like (doing) sth very much: *Brian is hooked on computer games.* **2** to be unable to stop using (**addicted to**) drugs, alcohol, etc.: *to be hooked on gambling*
PHR V **hook (sth) up (to sth)** to connect a machine, etc. to a larger system so that it can work: *You can't call me at my new apartment – the phone isn't hooked up yet.*

**hook·er** /ˈhʊkər/ ***noun*** [C] (*informal*) = PROSTITUTE

**hoo·li·gan** /ˈhulɪgən/ ***noun*** [C] a young person who behaves in an extremely noisy and sometimes violent way in public, usually in a group

**hoop** /hup/ ***noun*** [C] **1** a large metal or plastic ring **2** (in basketball) the metal ring that the net (**basket**) hangs from: *Let's go out and shoot some hoops* (= practice our basketball). ➲ Picture at **basketball**.

**hoo·ray** /hʊˈreɪ/ ***interjection*** (used for expressing great pleasure, approval, etc.): *Hooray, we won!*
IDM **hip, hip, hooray** → HIP³

**hoot¹** /hut/ ***noun*** **1** [C] a loud shout, especially to show disapproval **2** [sing.] (*informal*) something that is very funny: *The party was a real hoot!*
IDM **can't/don't give a hoot** (*informal*) not to care at all about sth: *I don't give a hoot what he thinks.*

**hoot²** /hut/ ***verb*** [I] to make a loud noise: *They hooted with laughter at the suggestion.*

**hooves** ***noun*** [C] *plural of* HOOF

**hop¹** /hɑp/ ***verb*** (**hop·ping; hopped**) [I] **1** (used about a person) to jump on one leg ➲ Picture at **bounce**. **2** (used about an animal or bird) to jump with both or all feet together
PHR V **hop in/into sth; hop out/out of sth** (*informal*) to get in or out of a car, etc. (quickly): *Hop in! I'll give you a ride downtown.*
**hop on/onto sth; hop off sth** to get onto/off a bus, etc. (quickly)

**hop²** /hɑp/ ***noun*** [C] **1** an act of HOPPING¹ (1,2) **2** (*informal*) a short trip: *It's just a short hop from the island to the mainland.*

★**hope¹** /hoʊp/ ***noun*** **1** [C,U] **hope (of/for sth); hope (of doing sth/that...)** the feeling of wanting sth to happen and thinking that it will: *What hope is there for the future?* ◇ *There is no hope of finding anybody else alive.* ◇ *David has high hopes of becoming a doctor.* ◇ *She never gave up hope that he would come back.* **2** [C, usually sing.] a person or thing that gives you HOPE (1): *You've got to help me – you're my only hope.*
IDM **in the hope of sth/that...** because you want sth to happen: *I came here in the hope that we could talk privately.*
**a ray of hope** → RAY

★**hope²** /hoʊp/ ***verb*** [I,T] **hope (for sth); hope to do sth; hope (that) sth will happen** to want sth to happen or be true: *We're hoping for sunny weather tomorrow.* ◇ *I hope (that) you feel better soon.* ◇ *I'm hoping to buy a car this summer.* ◇ *"Is it raining?" "I hope not. I forgot my umbrella."* ◇ *"Are you coming to New York with us?" "I'm not sure yet, but I hope so."*

**hope·ful** /ˈhoʊpfl/ ***adj.*** **1** thinking that sth that you want to happen will happen: *He's very hopeful about the success of the business.* ◇ *The strikers seem hopeful of an improved pay offer.* **2** making you think that sth good will happen: *a hopeful sign*

**hope·ful·ly** /ˈhoʊpfl·i/ ***adv.*** **1** in a hopeful way: *She smiled hopefully at me, waiting for my answer.* **2** I/We hope; if everything happens as planned: *Hopefully, we'll be finished by six o'clock.*

NOTE Some people think this use is not correct.

**hope·less** /ˈhoʊpləs/ ***adj.*** giving no hope that sth will be successful or get better: *This is a hopeless situation. There is nothing we can do.* ▸ **hope·less·ly** ***adv.***: *They were hopelessly lost.* ▸ **hope·less·ness** ***noun*** [U]

**horde** /hɔrd/ ***noun*** [C] a very large number of people: *hordes of shoppers*

**ho·ri·zon** /həˈraɪzn/ ***noun*** [C] **1** the line where the earth and sky appear to meet: *The ship appeared on/disappeared over the horizon.* **2 horizons** [pl.] the limits of your knowledge or experience: *Foreign travel is a good way of expanding your horizons.*

H

★**hor·i·zon·tal** /ˌhɔrəˈzɑntl; ˌhɑr-/ ***adj.*** going from side to side, not up and down; flat or level ➲ picture at **vertical**. ▸ **hor·i·zon·tal·ly** ***adv.***

**hor·mone** /ˈhɔrmoʊn/ ***noun*** [C] a substance in the body that influences growth and development

★**horn** /hɔrn/ ***noun*** [C] **1** one of the hard pointed things that cows, goats, etc. have on their heads ➲ pictures at **cow** and **sheep**. **2** the thing in a car, etc. that gives a loud warning sound: *Don't blow your horn late at night.* ◇ *a fog horn* **3** one of the family of brass musical instruments that you play by blowing into them: *a French horn* ➲ picture at **trumpet**.

**hor·net** /ˈhɔrnət/ ***noun*** [C] a large black and yellow flying insect that has a powerful sting

**horn·y** /ˈhɔrni/ ***adj.*** (**horn·i·er**; **horn·i·est**) (*slang*) sexually excited

**hor·o·scope** /ˈhɔrəskoʊp; ˈhɑr-/ ***noun*** [C] a statement about what is going to happen to a person in the future, based on the position of the stars and planets when he/she was born: *What does my horoscope say for next week?* ➲ Look at **astrology** and **zodiac**.

**hor·ren·dous** /həˈrɛndəs/ ***adj.*** very bad or unpleasant: *a horrendous crime* ▸ **hor·ren·dous·ly** ***adv.***

**hor·ri·ble** /ˈhɔrəbl; ˈhɑr-/ ***adj.*** **1** causing fear or shock: *a horrible murder* **2** very bad or unpleasant: *I've got a horrible feeling that I forgot something.* ▸ **hor·ri·bly** /-əbli/ ***adv.***

**hor·rid** /ˈhɔrəd; ˈhɑrəd/ ***adj.*** very unpleasant or bad: *a horrid experience*

**hor·rif·ic** /həˈrɪfɪk/ ***adj.*** causing fear or shock: *a horrific road accident*

**hor·ri·fy** /ˈhɔrəfaɪ; ˈhɑr-/ ***verb*** [T] (*pres. part.* **hor·ri·fy·ing**; *3rd person sing. pres.* **hor·ri·fies**; *pt, pp* **hor·ri·fied**) to shock sb greatly: *I was horrified by the conditions they were living in.* ▸ **hor·ri·fy·ing** ***adj.***

★**hor·ror** /ˈhɔrər; ˈhɑr-/ ***noun*** **1** [U] a feeling of great fear or shock: *They watched in horror as the building collapsed.* ◇ *a horror movie* (= that shows frightening or shocking things) ◇ (*figurative*) *Jan told us some horror stories about life in her school.* **2** [C] something that makes you feel frightened or shocked: *I'll never forget the horror of what I saw that day.* ◇ *the horrors of war*

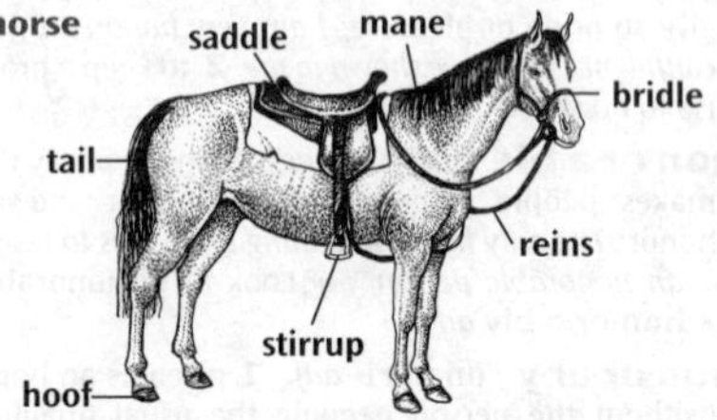


★**horse¹** /hɔrs/ ***noun*** [C] a large animal that is used for riding on or for pulling or carrying heavy loads

NOTE A male horse is a **stallion**, a female horse is a **mare** and a young horse is a **foal**.

**horse²** /hɔrs/ ***verb***

PHR V **horse around** (*informal*) to play or act in a silly, rough way: *Quit horsing around with those knives!*

**horse·back** /ˈhɔrsbæk/ ***noun*** [U]

IDM **on horseback** sitting on a horse: *Police on horseback were controlling the crowds.* ➲ Police on horseback are also called **mounted police**.

**ˈhorseback ˌriding** ***noun*** [U] the sport or hobby of riding a horse: *to go horseback riding*

**horse·pow·er** /ˈhɔrspaʊər/ ***noun*** [C] (*pl.* **horse·pow·er**) (*abbr.* **hp**) a measure of the power of an engine, etc.: *a ten-horsepower engine*

**horse·shoe** /ˈhɔrʃʃu; ˈhɔrsʃu/ ***noun*** **1** [C] a U-shaped piece of metal that is fastened to the bottom of a horse's foot. People believe that horseshoes bring good luck. **2 horseshoes** [U] a game that people play outdoors, in which they throw U-shaped pieces of metal at a small post in the ground

**hor·ti·cul·ture** /ˈhɔrt̬əkʌltʃər/ ***noun*** [U] the study or practice of growing flowers, fruit and vegetables ▸ **hor·ti·cul·tur·al** /ˌhɔrt̬əˈkʌltʃərəl/ ***adj.***

**hose** /hoʊz/ ***noun*** **1** [C,U] a long rubber or plastic tube that is used for getting water from one place to another, in the yard or when there is a fire ➲ picture at **garden**. **2** = PANTYHOSE

**ho·sier·y** /ˈhoʊʒəri/ ***noun*** [U] used especially in stores as a word for socks, hose, (2) etc.

**hos·pice** /ˈhɑspəs/ ***noun*** [C] a special hospital where people who are dying are cared for

**hos·pi·ta·ble** /hɑˈspɪt̬əbl; ˈhɑspɪt̬əbl/ ***adj.*** (used about a person) friendly and helpful to visitors ➲ Look at **inhospitable**.

★**hos·pi·tal** /ˈhɑspɪtl/ ***noun*** [C] a place where sick or injured people are treated: *He was rushed to the hospital in an ambulance.* ◇ *to be admitted to/discharged from the hospital*

NOTE A person who is being treated in a hospital by **doctors** and **nurses** is a **patient**. If you have an accident you are taken first to the **emergency room**.

**hos·pi·tal·i·ty** /ˌhɑspəˈtæləṭi/ ***noun*** [U] being friendly and helpful to guests: *We're very grateful for your hospitality.*

**hos·pi·tal·ize** /ˈhɑspɪṭl·aɪz/ ***verb*** [T] (usually passive) to take sb to a hospital for treatment: *Two men were hospitalized with gunshot wounds.* ▶ **hos·pi·tal·i·za·tion** /ˌhɑspɪṭl·əˈzeɪʃn/ ***noun*** [C,U]

★**host¹** /hoʊst/ ***noun*** [C] **1** a person who receives and entertains visitors: *It's polite to write a thank-you note to your host.* ◇ *the host country for the next Olympic Games* ◇ *We need more host families for international students.* ➲ Look at **hostess**. **2** a person who introduces a television or radio show and talks to the guests **3** (*computing*) the main computer in a system of connected computers (a network) ➲ Look at **server** (2). **4** a company or computer that manages pages on the Internet for another company, organization, etc.

**host²** /hoʊst/ ***verb*** [T] **1** to act as a host or hostess: *a game show hosted by Alex Trebek* ◇ *Have we decided who's hosting Thanksgiving this year?* **2** to supply and manage pages on the Internet for another company, organization, etc.: *We need to find someone who provides web hosting services.*

**hos·tage** /ˈhɑstɪdʒ/ ***noun*** [C] a person who is caught and kept prisoner by a person or group. The hostage may be killed or injured if that person or group does not get what it is asking for: *The hijackers released the women and children but kept the men as hostages.*

IDM **take/hold sb hostage** to catch/keep sb as a hostage

**hos·tel** /ˈhɑstl/ ***noun*** [C] → YOUTH HOSTEL

**host·ess** /ˈhoʊstəs/ ***noun*** [C] **1** a woman who receives and entertains visitors **2** a woman who introduces a television or radio show and talks to the guests **3** a woman whose job is to take you to your table in a restaurant

**hos·tile** /ˈhɑstl; -taɪl/ ***adj.*** very unfriendly toward sb/sth; not having a good opinion of sb/sth: *a hostile crowd* ◇ *They are very hostile to any change.*

**hos·til·i·ty** /hɑˈstɪləṭi/ ***noun*** **1** [U] being unfriendly toward sb/sth: *She didn't say anything, but I could sense her hostility.* **2** [U] thinking that sth is bad: *They didn't try to hide their hostility toward the police.* **3 hostilities** [pl.] fighting in a war: *Negotiations have led to an end to hostilities.*

★**hot** /hɑt/ ***adj.*** (**hot·ter**; **hot·test**) **1** having a high degree of heat; not cold: *Can I open the window? I'm really hot.* ◇ *Be careful. The plates are hot.* ◇ *It's hot today, isn't it?* ◇ *Do you like this hot weather?* ◇ *a hot meal*

> NOTE You can describe the temperature of sth as **freezing (cold), cold, cool, lukewarm** (used about water), **warm, hot** or **boiling (hot)**.

**2** (used about food) causing a burning feeling in your mouth: *hot sauce* **3** (*informal*) very popular with the public, especially because of being new, exciting or interesting: *one of Hollywood's hottest stars* **4** (*informal*) sexually attractive: *I think the new guy in the office is really hot!*

IDM **be hot at sth** (often used with a negative) to know a lot about sth, or to be good at doing sth: *Don't ask me. I'm not very hot at history.*

ˌ**hot-ˈair balˌloon** ***noun*** [C] = BALLOON (2)

**hot·cake** /ˈhɑtkeɪk/ ***noun*** [C] = PANCAKE

IDM **go/sell like hotcakes** to be sold very quickly: *The new Harry Potter book is selling like hotcakes.*

ˌ**hot ˈchocolate** ***noun*** [U] = COCOA (2)

**hot·desk·ing** /ˌhɑtˈdɛskɪŋ/ ***noun*** [U] the practice in an office of giving desks to workers when they are required, rather than giving each worker his/her own desk

> NOTE **Hotdesking** is used especially in companies that allow employees to change their working hours from one day to the next.

ˈ**hot dog** ***noun*** [C] a food, like a type of sandwich, that consists of warm meat in the shape of a tube (a frankfurter) inside a long, soft piece of bread (a bun) ➲ picture at **bread**.

★**ho·tel** /hoʊˈtɛl/ ***noun*** [C] a place where you pay to sleep (and perhaps eat your meals) when you are on vacation or traveling: *to stay at/in a hotel* ◇ *to reserve a hotel room*

> NOTE You reserve a **single room**, a **double room** or a **suite** at a hotel. When you arrive, you **check in** or **register** and when you leave, you **check out**.

**hot·line** /ˈhɑtlaɪn/ ***noun*** [C] a direct telephone line

**hot·ly** /ˈhɑtli/ ***adv.*** **1** angrily or with force: *They hotly denied the newspaper reports.* **2** closely: *The dog ran off, hotly pursued by its owner.*

ˌ**hot poˈtato** ***noun*** [usually sing.] (*informal*) a problem, situation, etc. that is difficult and unpleasant to deal with, and that you try to pass to sb else

ˈ**hot tub** ***noun*** [C] a large container, big enough for several people to sit in, that is filled with warm water which is pumped around to make your body feel relaxed ➲ Look also at **Jacuzzi™**.

**hound¹** /haʊnd/ ***verb*** [T] to follow and disturb sb: *Movie stars are always being hounded by the press.*

**hound²** /haʊnd/ ***noun*** [C] a dog that can run fast and has a good sense of smell, used for hunting

★**hour** /ˈaʊər/ ***noun*** **1** [C] a period of 60 minutes: *He worked for three hours after supper.* ◇ *The program lasts about half an hour.* ◇ *I've been waiting here for hours.* ◇ *I'm going shopping now. I'll be back in about an hour.* ◇ *a four-hour drive* **2 the hour** [sing.] the time when a new hour starts (i.e. 1 o'clock, 2 o'clock, etc.): *The next traffic report is at ten minutes after the hour.* **3 hours** [pl.] the period of time when sb is working or a store, etc. is open: *Office hours are usually from 9 a.m. to 5 p.m.* ◇ *Visiting hours in the hospital are from 2 to 3 p.m.* ◇ *The employees are demanding shorter working hours.* **4** [C,U] a period of time: *I'm going shopping on my lunch hour.* ◇ *The traffic is very bad during rush hour.*

IDM **(at/until) all hours** (at/until) any time: *People come and go at all hours of the day and night next door.* ◇ *I've been working all hours* (= very late) *recently.*

**the early hours** → EARLY

**on the hour** at exactly 1, 2, 3, etc. o'clock: *The buses to downtown leave on the hour.*

**the wee hours** → WEE

**hour·ly¹** /ˈaʊərli/ ***adv.*** every hour: *This medication must be taken hourly.*

H

**hour·ly²** /ˈaʊərli/ ***adj.*** **1** done or happening every hour: *an hourly news bulletin* **2** for an hour: *What is your hourly fee?*

★**house¹** /haʊs/ ***noun*** [C] (*pl.* **hous·es** /ˈhaʊzəz/)
➤BUILDING **1** a building that is made for one family to live in: *a three-bedroom house* ➲ Picture on study page **A31**.

NOTE Your **home** is the place where you live, even if it is not a house: *Let's go home to my apartment.* Your home is also the place where you feel that you belong. A house is just a building: *We just moved into our new house, so it doesn't feel like home yet.* You can **build**, **fix up**, **remodel** or **add on to** a house. You may **rent** a house or **rent it out** to somebody else. If you want to **move** to a new house, you go to a **Realtor**.

**2** [usually sing.] all the people who live in one house: *Don't shout. You'll wake the whole house up.* **3** a building that is used for a particular purpose: *an apartment house* (= that contains several apartments) ◇ *a warehouse* ➲ Look also at **White House**.
➤COMPANY **4** a large firm involved in a particular kind of business: *a fashion/publishing house*
➤PARLIAMENT **5** a group of people who meet to make laws for a country or state: *The Senate is the upper house in the U.S. Congress.* ➲ Look at the note at **Congress**. **6 the House** [sing.] (*U.S.*) = THE HOUSE OF REPRESENTATIVES: *Republicans in the House and Senate voted against the bill.* **7 the House** [sing.] (*Cdn*) = THE HOUSE OF COMMONS
IDM **on the house** paid for by the bar, restaurant, etc. that you are visiting; free: *Your first drink is on the house.*

**house²** /haʊz/ ***verb*** [T] **1** to provide sb with a place to live: *The city is unable to house all homeless families.* **2** to contain or keep sth: *Her office is housed in a separate building.*

**house·boat** /ˈhaʊsboʊt/ ***noun*** [C] a large boat on a river, etc. that sb can live in

**house·bro·ken** /ˈhaʊsˌbroʊkən/ ***adj.*** (used about pets) trained to pass waste liquids (**urine**) and solids (**excrement**) only in appropriate places

★**house·hold** /ˈhaʊshoʊld/ ***noun*** [C] all the people who live in one house and the housework, money, organization, etc. that is needed to take care of them: *Almost all households have a television.* ◇ *the head of the household* ◇ *household expenses* ◇ *household cleaning products*

**house·keep·er** /ˈhaʊsˌkipər/ ***noun*** [C] a person who is paid to clean sb else's house and often cook food, etc.

**house·keep·ing** /ˈhaʊsˌkipɪŋ/ ***noun*** [U] **1** work that is done in a house, such as cleaning, etc. **2** the department in a hotel, a hospital, an office building, etc. that is responsible for cleaning the building, etc.: *Call housekeeping and tell them to bring us some clean towels.*

**the ˌHouse of Asˈsembly** ***noun*** [sing.] (*Cdn*) the building where the government of the province meets in Nova Scotia and Newfoundland and Labrador ➲ For more information about the political system in Canada, look at study page **A11**.

**the ˌHouse of ˈCommons** ***noun*** [sing.] (*Cdn*) **1** the lower house of the Canadian Parliament, made up of elected members **2** the building in which this assembly meets ➲ For more information about the political system in Canada, look at study page **A11**.

**the ˌHouse of ˌRepreˈsentatives** (*also* **the House**) ***noun*** [sing.] one of the two groups of people who are elected to make new laws for the U.S. or for an individual state ➲ For more information on the U.S. political system, look at study page **A10**. ➲ Look at **Congress** and **Senate**, and at the note at **White House**.

**ˌhouse-to-ˈhouse** ***adj.*** going to each house: *The police are making a house-to-house search.*

**house·warm·ing** /ˈhaʊsˌwɔrmɪŋ/ ***noun*** [C] a party that you give when you have just moved into a new home

**house·wife** /ˈhaʊswaɪf/ ***noun*** [C] (*pl.* **house·wives** /-waɪvz/) a woman who spends her time doing housework, cooking, taking care of her family, etc. and who does not have another job ➲ A man who does this is called a **househusband**. A more modern word which can be used for men and women is **homemaker**.

**house·work** /ˈhaʊswərk/ ***noun*** [U] the work that is needed to keep a house clean

NOTE Be careful. The word for work that is given to students by teachers to be done after school hours is **homework**.

★**hous·ing** /ˈhaʊzɪŋ/ ***noun*** [U] houses, apartments, etc. for people to live in: *low-income housing* (= for people with low incomes)

**ˈhousing deˌvelopment** ***noun*** [C] an area where a large number of private houses are planned and built at the same time

**ˈhousing ˌproject** (*also* **ˌpublic ˈhousing ˌproject**, *informal* **project**) ***noun*** [C] an area with a large number of apartments, usually in tall buildings, which are owned by the government for people with low incomes to live in

**hov·er** /ˈhʌvər/ ***verb*** [I] **1** (used about a bird, etc.) to stay in the air in one place **2** to stay at or near one place, level, etc.: *Temperatures hovered around 100° all week.* ◇ *The storm is hovering off the eastern coast of Florida.*

★**how¹** /haʊ/ ***adv.*** **1** (used in questions) in what way: *How do you spell your name?* ◇ *Can you show me how to use this machine?* **2** (used when you are asking about sb's health): *"How is your mother?" "She's feeling a lot better now."*

NOTE You use "how" only when you are asking about a person's health. When you are asking about a person's character or appearance you say **what ... like?**: *"What is your sister like?" "Well, she's taller than I am and she has dark hair."*

**3** (used when you are asking about a thing or a situation): *How was the weather?* ◇ *How is your meal?* **4** (used in questions before an adjective or adverb when you are asking about the degree, amount, age, etc. of sb/sth): *How old are you?* ◇ *How much is that?* ◇ *How long did it take to get* *here?* **5** (used for expressing surprise, shock, thanks, pleasure, etc.): *How nice of you to remember my birthday!* ◇ *How could he have lied to me?*

IDM **how/what about...?** → ABOUT²

**how come...?** → COME

**how do you do?** (*formal*) (used when meeting sb for the first time)

NOTE Be careful. **How are you?** and **How do you do?** are answered very differently: *"How do you do?"* is a very formal old-fashioned greeting and it is answered with the same words: *"How do you do?"* The answer to: *"How are you?"* depends on how you are feeling: *"I'm fine."/"Okay."/"A lot better."*

**how in the world** (used in questions for expressing surprise) in what way; how: *How in the world did you manage to find me here?* ◇ *How in the world can he afford a car like that?*

**how²** /haʊ/ **conj.** the way in which: *I can't remember how to get there.*

**how·dy** /ˈhaʊdi/ **interjection** (*informal, old-fashioned*) (used as an informal greeting): *Howdy, folks!*

★**how·ev·er¹** /haʊˈɛvər/ **adv.** **1** (used for adding a comment on what you have just said) although sth is true: *Sales are low this month. There may, however, be an increase before Christmas.* **2** (*formal*) (before an adjective or adverb) to whatever degree: *We are grateful for any donation, however large or small.* ◇ *They could not succeed however hard they tried.* ➲ The phrase *no matter how...* is more common.

**how·ev·er²** /haʊˈɛvər/ **conj.** used to introduce a statement that contrasts with sth that has just been said: *He was feeling bad; he went to work, however, and tried to concentrate.* ◇ *We thought the figures were correct. However, we have now discovered some errors.*

**howl** /haʊl/ **noun** [C] a long loud cry made by a dog or a wolf: (*figurative*) *The mayor's statement was greeted with howls of protest.* ▸ **howl verb** [I,T]: *The wind howled across the prairie.*

**hr** **abbr.** hour

**HRDC** /ˌeɪtʃ ɑr di ˈsi/ (*also* ˌ**Human** ˌ**Resources** ˌ**Development** ˈ**Canada**) **noun** [U] (*Cdn*) the government department responsible for employment programs

**HST** /ˌeɪtʃ ɛs ˈti/ **noun** [sing.] (*Cdn*) harmonized sales tax; a tax that is added to the price of goods and services in the provinces of Nova Scotia, New Brunswick and Newfoundland and Labrador ➲ Look at **GST** and **PST**.

**HTML** /ˌeɪtʃ ti ɛm ˈɛl/ **abbr.** hypertext markup language; a way of preparing sth you write so that it can be shown on a page on the Internet

**http** /ˌeɪtʃ ti ti ˈpi/ **abbr.** hypertext transfer protocol; a set of rules that allow information to be exchanged between computers through the Internet

**hub** /hʌb/ **noun** [C] the round central part of a wheel

**hud·dle¹** /ˈhʌdl/ **verb** [I] **1** to get close to other people because you are cold or frightened: *The campers huddled (together) around the fire.* **2** to curl your body up and wrap your arms around yourself because you are cold or frightened: *Some of us slept in sleeping bags, while others huddled under blankets.* ▸ **hud·dled adj.**: *We found the children lying huddled together on the ground.*

**hud·dle²** /ˈhʌdl/ **noun** [C] a small group of people or things that are close together: *They all sat in a huddle in front of the computer.*

**hug¹** /hʌg/ **verb** [T] (**hug·ging**; **hugged**) **1** to put your arms around sb to show that you love him/her: *There was a lot of hugging and kissing at the airport before Grandma and Grandpa left.* **2** (used about a ship, car, etc.) to keep close to sth: *to hug the coast*

**hug²** /hʌg/ **noun** [C] an act of hugging: *She gave the child a hug and he stopped crying.*

★**huge** /hyudʒ/ **adj.** very large: *There is a huge amount of work left to be done.* ◇ *a huge building* ▸ **huge·ly adv.**: *The play was hugely successful.*

**huh** /hʌ/ **interjection** (*informal*) **1** (used for asking sb to agree with you): *"Good party, huh?"* **2** (used for asking sb to repeat sth): *"Are you ready?" "Huh?" "I asked if you were ready!"*

**hull** /hʌl/ **noun** [C] the body of a ship

**hum¹** /hʌm/ **verb** (**hum·ming**; **hummed**) **1** [I] to make a continuous low noise like the noise bees make: (*figurative*) *The classroom was humming with activity.* **2** [I,T] to sing with your lips closed: *You can hum the tune if you don't know the words.*

**hum²** /hʌm/ **noun** [C, usually sing.] a humming sound: *the hum of distant traffic*

★**hu·man¹** /ˈhyumən/ **adj.** connected with people, not with animals or machines; typical of people: *the human body* ◇ *The famine caused a terrible loss of human life.* ◇ *A human skeleton was found by the construction workers.* ◇ *The disaster was caused by* ***human error***. ◇ *It's only human to be upset in a situation like that.*

★**hu·man²** /ˈhyumən/ (*also* ˌ**human** ˈ**being**) **noun** [C] a person; a man, woman or child

**hu·mane** /hyuˈmeɪn/ **adj.** having or showing kindness or understanding especially to a person or animal that is suffering: *A civilized society treats mentally handicapped people in a humane way.* OPP **inhumane** ▸ **hu·mane·ly adv.**

ˌ**human** ˈ**interest** **noun** [U] the part of a story in a newspaper, etc. that people find interesting because it describes the experiences, feelings, etc. of the people involved

**hu·man·i·tar·i·an** /hyuˌmænəˈtɛriən/ **adj.** concerned with trying to make people's lives better and reduce suffering

**hu·man·i·ty** /hyuˈmænət̬i/ **noun** [U] **1** all the people in the world, thought of as a group; the human race: *crimes against humanity* **2** the quality of being kind and understanding: *The prisoners were treated with humanity.* OPP **inhumanity** **3** **humanities** [pl.] subjects such as history or languages that you study at a school, college or university: *courses in the arts and humanities*

**hu·man·kind** /ˈhyumənkaɪnd; ˌhyumənˈkaɪnd/ **noun** [U] people in general ➲ Look at **mankind**.

**hu·man·ly** /ˈhyumənli/ **adv.** within human ability: *The doctors did all that was* ***humanly possible*** *to save her* (= nobody could have done more).

**ˌhuman ˈnature** *noun* [U] feelings, behavior, etc. that are common to all people: *It's only human nature to want the best for yourself and your family.*

**the ˌhuman ˈrace** *noun* [sing.] all the people in the world (when you are thinking of them as a group)

**ˌhuman ˈresources** (*also* **personnel**) *noun* [U] the department in a company that is in charge of employing new workers and taking care of all the workers in the company

**ˌhuman ˈrights** *noun* [pl.] the basic freedoms that all people should have, e.g. the right to say what you think, travel freely

**hum·ble**[1] /ˈhʌmbl/ *adj.* **1** not thinking that you are better or more important than other people; not proud: *He became very rich and famous, but he always remained a very humble man.* ➲ noun humility **2** low in social status; unimportant: *She comes from a humble background.* ▸ **hum·bly** *adv.*: *He apologized very humbly for his behavior.*

**hum·ble**[2] /ˈhʌmbl/ *verb* [T] to make sb HUMBLE[1] (1): *He felt humbled by the experience.* ▸ **humbling** /ˈhʌmblɪŋ/ *adj.*: *a humbling defeat*

**hum·drum** /ˈhʌmdrʌm/ *adj.* boring and always the same: *a humdrum existence/job/life*

**hu·mid** /ˈhyuməd/ *adj.* (used about the air or climate) containing a lot of water; damp: *Florida is hot and humid in the summer.* ▸ **hu·mid·i·ty** /hyuˈmɪdət̬i/ *noun* [U]

**hu·mi·dex** /ˈhyumɪdɛks/ *noun* [sing.] (*Cdn*) a scale that measures the level of personal discomfort created by the combination of heat and humidity

**hu·mil·i·ate** /hyuˈmɪlieɪt/ *verb* [T] to make sb feel ashamed: *Did you have to humiliate me in front of all those people?* ▸ **hu·mil·i·at·ing** *adj.*: *a humiliating defeat* ▸ **hu·mil·i·a·tion** /hyuˌmɪliˈeɪʃn/ *noun* [C,U]

**hum·mus** /ˈhʊməs; ˈhʌ-/ *noun* [U] a dish made by mixing a kind of bean (**garbanzo**) with oil and other things to add flavor

★**hu·mor**[1] /ˈhyumər/ *noun* [U] **1** the funny or amusing quality or qualities of sb/sth: *It's an awful situation, but at least you can see the humor in it.* ◇ *It is sometimes hard to understand the humor* (= the jokes) *of another country.* **2** being able to see when sth is funny and to laugh at things: *Rose has a good sense of humor.*

**hu·mor**[2] /ˈhyumər/ *verb* [T] to keep sb happy by doing what he/she wants: *I'm only doing this to humor Dad.*

★**hu·mor·ous** /ˈhyumərəs/ *adj.* amusing or funny: *It's a very humorous book.* ◇ *a humorous speaker* ▸ **hu·mor·ous·ly** *adv.*

**hump** /hʌmp/ *noun* [C] a round lump, e.g. on an animal's back ➲ picture at **camel**.

**hunch**[1] /hʌntʃ/ *noun* [C] (*informal*) a thought or an idea that is based on a feeling rather than on facts or information: *I'm not sure, but I have a hunch that she's got a new job.*

**hunch**[2] /hʌntʃ/ *verb* [I,T] to bend your back and shoulders forward in a round shape: *They sat there, hunched over their desks.*

**hun·dred** /ˈhʌndrəd/ *number* 100; one more than ninety-nine: *two hundred* ◇ *There were a/one hundred people in the room.* ◇ *She's a hundred* (= a hundred years old) *today.*

> NOTE Note that when we are saying a number, e.g. 420, we often put "and" after the word **hundred**: *four hundred (and) twenty.* The plural **hundreds** is used when we mean "many" or "a lot": *The doll cost hundreds of dollars.* ◇ *hundreds of people.*

**hun·dredth**[1] /ˈhʌndrədθ; -ətθ/ *pronoun, det., adv.* 100th; next after ninety-ninth

**hun·dredth**[2] /ˈhʌndrədθ; -ətθ/ *noun* [C] the fraction $^1/_{100}$; one of a hundred equal parts of sth

**hung** *past tense, past participle of* HANG[1]

**hun·ger** /ˈhʌŋgər/ *noun* [U] **1** the wish or need for food: *Hunger is one reason why babies cry.* **2** a lack of food: *to die of hunger* ➲ Look at **thirst**.

> NOTE Be careful. You cannot say *I have hunger* in English. You must say: *I am hungry.*

**ˈhunger strike** *noun* [C,U] a time when people (especially prisoners) refuse to eat because they are protesting about sth

★**hun·gry** /ˈhʌŋgri/ *adj.* (**hun·gri·er; hun·gri·est**) wanting to eat: *I'm hungry. Let's eat soon.* ➲ Look at **thirsty**.

IDM **go hungry** not have any food: *I'd rather go hungry than eat that!*

▸ **hun·gri·ly** /-əli/ *adv.*

**hunk** /hʌŋk/ *noun* [C] **1** a large piece of sth: *a hunk of bread* **2** (*informal*) a man who is considered to be sexually attractive because he is big and strong: *What a hunk!*

★**hunt**[1] /hʌnt/ *verb* [I,T] **1** to chase wild animals, etc. in order to catch or kill them either for sport or for food: *Owls hunt at night.* ◇ *Are tigers still hunted in India?*

> NOTE We often use the expression **go hunting** when we are talking about spending time hunting: *to go duck hunting.*

**2 hunt (for) (sb/sth)** to look or search for sb/sth: *I hunted everywhere for my gloves, but I still can't find them.* ◇ *The police are still hunting the murderer.*

**hunt**[2] /hʌnt/ *noun* [C] **1** [usually sing.] the act of searching or looking for sb/sth: *a job hunt* ◇ *The police have launched a hunt for the missing child.* **2** the act of hunting wild animals, etc.: *a fox hunt*

**hunt·er** /ˈhʌntər/ *noun* [C] a person or animal that hunts: (*figurative*) *a bargain hunter*

★**hunt·ing** /ˈhʌntɪŋ/ *noun* [U] the chasing and killing of wild animals: *Hunting and fishing are Dan's favorite hobbies.* ➲ Look at **shoot**.

**hur·dle** /ˈhərdl/ *noun* **1** [C] a type of light fence that you jump over in a race **2 hurdles** [pl.] a race over HURDLES (1): *the 200-meter hurdles* **3** [C] a problem or difficulty that you must overcome

**hurl** /hərl/ *verb* **1** [T] to throw sth with force **2** [I,T] (*also* **hurl chunks**) (*slang*) = VOMIT

**hur·ray** (*also* **hooray**) /hə'reɪ; hʊ-/ ***interjection*** used for expressing great pleasure, approval, etc.: *Hurray! We won!*

IDM **hip, hip, hurray** → HIP[3]

**hur·ri·cane** /'hərəkən/ ***noun*** [C] a storm with very strong winds and heavy rain, over or near the ocean ➲ Look at the note at **storm**.

**hur·ried** /'hərid/ ***adj.*** done (too) quickly: *a hurried meal* OPP **unhurried** ▸ **hur·ried·ly** ***adv.***

★**hur·ry**[1] /'həri/ ***noun*** [U] a need or wish to do sth quickly: *Take your time. There's no hurry.* ◇ *What's the hurry?*

IDM **in a hurry 1** quickly: *She got up late and left in a hurry.* **2** wanting to do sth soon: *They are in a hurry to get the job done before winter.*

**in no hurry; not in any hurry 1** not needing or wishing to do sth quickly: *We weren't in any hurry, so we stopped to admire the view.* **2** unwilling: *I am in no hurry to repeat that experience.*

★**hur·ry**[2] /'həri/ ***verb*** (*pres. part.* **hur·ry·ing**; *3rd person sing. pres.* **hur·ries**; *pt, pp* **hur·ried**) **1** [I] to move or do sth quickly: *Don't hurry. There's plenty of time.* ◇ *They hurried back home after school.* **2** [T] to cause sb/sth to do sth or to happen more quickly: *He was hurried into a decision.*

PHR V **hurry up** (*informal*) to move or do sth more quickly: *Hurry up or we'll miss our flight.*

★**hurt**[1] /hərt/ ***verb*** (*pt, pp* **hurt**) **1** [T] to cause pain or injury: *Did he hurt himself?* ◇ *I fell and hurt my arm.* ◇ *No one was seriously hurt in the accident.* ◇ (*figurative*) *The tax increase will hurt families on low incomes.*

NOTE Compare **hurt**, **injure** and **wound**. A person may be **wounded** by a knife, sword, gun, etc., usually as a result of fighting: *a wounded soldier*. People are usually **injured** in an accident: *Five people were badly injured in the crash.* **Hurt** and **injured** are similar in meaning but **hurt** is more often used when the damage is not very great: *I hurt my leg when I fell off my bike.*

**2** [I] to produce a feeling of pain: *My leg hurts.* ◇ *It hurts when I lift my leg.* ◇ *These shoes hurt; they're too tight.* **3** [T] to make sb unhappy; to upset sb: *His unkind remarks hurt her deeply.*

IDM **it won't/wouldn't hurt (sb/sth) (to do sth)** (*informal*) it would be a good thing for sb/sth (to do): *It wouldn't hurt you to get some exercise.*

**hurt**[2] /hərt/ ***noun*** [U] (*formal*) mental pain or suffering

**hurt·ful** /'hərtfl/ ***adj.*** unkind; upsetting: *to say hurtful things*

★**hus·band** /'hʌzbənd/ ***noun*** [C] a man that a woman is married to: *a good husband and father* ◇ *Her ex-husband sees the kids once a month.*

**hush** /hʌʃ/ ***noun*** [sing.] silence: *As he rose to speak, a hush fell over the audience.*

**husk·y**[1] /'hʌski/ ***adj.*** (**husk·i·er**; **husk·i·est**) **1** (used about a voice) sounding rough and quiet as if your throat were dry **2** (used about a man or boy) having a strong, wide body

**husk·y**[2] (*also* **huskie**) /'hʌski/ ***noun*** [C] (*pl.* **hus·kies**) a strong dog with thick fur that is used in teams for pulling heavy loads over snow

**hus·tle** /'hʌsl/ ***verb*** **1** [I] (*informal*) to move or do sth quickly and with a lot of energy: *We've got to hustle if we want to win this game!* **2** [T] to push or move sb roughly: *The demonstrators were hustled into police cars.*

**hut** /hʌt/ ***noun*** [C] a small building with one room, usually made of wood or metal

**hy·drant** /'haɪdrənt/ ***noun*** [C] = FIRE HYDRANT

**hy·drau·lic** /haɪ'drɔlɪk/ ***adj.*** worked by water or another liquid moving through pipes, etc.: *hydraulic brakes*

**hy·dro** /'haɪdroʊ/ ***noun*** [U] (*Cdn*) electricity ▸ **hy·dro** ***adj.***: *to pay your hydro bill*

**hy·dro·e·lec·tric** /ˌhaɪdroʊɪ'lɛktrɪk/ ***adj.*** **1** using the power of water to produce electricity: *a hydroelectric dam* **2** (used about electricity) produced by the power of water: *hydroelectric power*

**hy·dro·gen** /'haɪdrədʒən/ ***noun*** [U] (*symbol* **H**) a light colorless gas. Hydrogen and oxygen form water (H2O).

**ˌhydrogen per'oxide** ***noun*** [U] = PEROXIDE

**hy·giene** /'haɪdʒin/ ***noun*** [U] (the rules of) keeping yourself and things around you clean, in order to prevent illness: *High standards of hygiene are essential when you are preparing food.* ◇ *personal hygiene*

**hy·gi·en·ic** /haɪ'dʒɛnɪk; -'dʒinɪk; ˌhaɪdʒi'ɛnɪk/ ***adj.*** clean, without the germs that cause disease: *hygienic conditions* OPP **unhygienic** ▸ **hy·gi·en·i·cal·ly** /-kli/ ***adv.***

**hy·gien·ist** /haɪ'dʒinɪst; -'dʒɛnɪst; 'haɪdʒinɪst/ ***noun*** [C] = DENTAL HYGIENIST

**hymn** /hɪm/ ***noun*** [C] a song of praise to God that Christians sing together in church, etc.

**hype**[1] /haɪp/ ***noun*** [U] (*informal*) advertisements or statements that make sth seem better or more important than it really is: *media hype surrounding the Internet*

**hype**[2] /haɪp/ ***verb*** [T] **hype (sth up)** to advertise sth a lot and exaggerate its good qualities in order to get a lot of public attention for it: *This week his much hyped new movie opens in New York.* ◇ *The meeting was hyped up in the media as a key event.*

**hy·per** /'haɪpər/ ***adj.*** (*informal*) excited and nervous; having too much nervous energy; unable to stay still

**hy·per·ac·tive** /ˌhaɪpər'æktɪv/ ***adj.*** (especially of children and their behavior) too active and only able to keep quiet and still for short periods

**hy·per·link** /'haɪpərlɪŋk/ (*also* **link**) ***noun*** [C] a place in an electronic document on a computer that is connected to another electronic document: *Click on the hyperlink.*

**hy·phen** /'haɪfən/ ***noun*** [C] the punctuation mark (-) used for joining two words together (e.g. *so-called, red-hot*) or to show that a word has been divided and continues on the next line

**hy·phen·ate** /'haɪfəneɪt/ ***verb*** [T] to write with a hyphen: *"Red-hot" is hyphenated.* ▸ **hy·phen·a·tion** /ˌhaɪfə'neɪʃn/ ***noun*** [U]

**hyp·no·sis** /hɪp'noʊsəs/ ***noun*** [U] (the producing of) a state that is like deep sleep where sb's mind and actions can be controlled by another person: *She was questioned under hypnosis.* ▸ **hyp·not·ic**

/hɪp'nɑt̬ɪk/ ***adj.***: *The rhythmic dance had a hypnotic effect on the audience.*

**hyp·no·tize** /'hɪpnətaɪz/ ***verb*** [T] to use hypnosis on sb

**hy·poc·ri·sy** /hɪ'pɑkrəsi/ ***noun*** [U] pretending to feel, believe, etc. sth that is different from what you really feel, etc.; saying one thing and doing another

**hyp·o·crite** /'hɪpəkrɪt/ ***noun*** [C] a person who pretends to have feelings and opinions which he/she does not really have ▸ **hy·po·crit·i·cal** /ˌhɪpə'krɪt̬ɪkl/ ***adj.*** ▸ **hyp·o·crit·i·cal·ly** /-kli/ ***adv.***

**hy·po·der·mic** /ˌhaɪpə'dərmɪk/ ***adj.*** used for putting drugs into the body through the skin: *a hypodermic needle/syringe*

**hy·poth·e·sis** /haɪ'pɑθəsəs/ ***noun*** [C] (*pl.* **hy·poth·e·ses** /-siz/) an idea that is suggested as the possible explanation for sth: *to test a scientific hypothesis*

**hy·po·thet·i·cal** /ˌhaɪpə'θɛt̬ɪkl/ ***adj.*** based on situations that have not yet happened, not on facts: *That's a hypothetical question because we don't know what the situation will be next year.* ▸ **hy·po·thet·i·cal·ly** /-kli/ ***adv.***

**hys·ter·i·a** /hɪ'stɛriə; -'stɪr-/ ***noun*** [U] a state of excitement in which a person or a group of people cannot control their emotions, e.g. cannot stop laughing, crying, shouting, etc.: *mass hysteria*

**hys·ter·i·cal** /hɪ'stɛrɪkl/ ***adj.*** **1** caused by or suffering from hysteria: *hysterical crying* ◇ *She was hysterical with grief.* **2** (*informal*) very funny ▸ **hys·ter·i·cal·ly** /-kli/ ***adv.***

**hys·ter·ics** /hɪ'stɛrɪks/ ***noun*** [pl.] **1** an expression of extreme fear, excitement or anger that makes sb lose control of his/her emotions: *She **went into hysterics** when they told her the news.* ◇ (*informal*) *My father would have hysterics* (be furious) *if he knew I was going out with you.* **2** laughter that you cannot control: *When he heard the joke, he went into hysterics.*

IDM **in hysterics**: *The comedian had the audience in hysterics.*

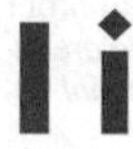

**I, i¹** /aɪ/ ***noun*** [C,U] (*pl.* **I's; i's**) the ninth letter of the English alphabet: *"Island" begins with (an) "I."*

★**I²** /aɪ/ ***pronoun*** (the subject of a verb) the person who is speaking or writing: *I called and said that I was busy.* ◇ *I'm not going to fall, am I?* ◇ *I'm taller than you, aren't I?* ◇ *She and I are planning to go out later.*

**I³** /aɪ/ ***abbr.*** = INTERSTATE¹: *Head east on I-90 for about 25 miles.*

★**ice¹** /aɪs/ ***noun*** [U] water that has frozen solid: *Do you want ice in your drink?* ◇ *I slipped on a patch of ice.* ◇ *The ice on the lake isn't thick enough to walk on.* ◇ *The ice quickly melted in the sunshine.* ◇ *black ice* (= ice on roads, that cannot be seen easily)

**ice²** /aɪs/ ***verb*** [T] to cover a cake with a thin sweet mixture (**icing**)

**ice·berg** /'aɪsbərg/ ***noun*** [C] a very large block of ice that is floating in the ocean: *The ship hit an iceberg and sank.*

IDM **the tip of the iceberg** → TIP¹

**ice·box** /'aɪsbɑks/ ***noun*** [C] **1** (*U.S. old-fashioned*) = REFRIGERATOR **2** (*especially Cdn*) a special box or cupboard containing blocks of ice that is used for keeping something cold, especially food

**'ice cap** ***noun*** [C] a layer of ice permanently covering parts of the earth, especially around the North and South Poles

**ˌice-'cold** ***adj.*** very cold: *ice-cold beer* ◇ *Your hands are ice-cold.*

★**'ice cream** ***noun*** [U] a frozen sweet food that is made from cream

**'ice cube** ***noun*** [C] a small block of ice that you put in a drink to make it cold

**iced** /'aɪst/ ***adj.*** (used about drinks) served very cold, with ice: *iced tea* ◇ *iced coffee*

**'ice ˌhockey** ***noun*** [U] = HOCKEY

**'ice rink** (*also* **rink**) ***noun*** [C] a large area of ice outdoors, or a building containing a large area of ice, that people can skate or play hockey on

**'ice skate¹** (*also* **skate**) ***noun*** [C] a boot with a thick metal blade on the bottom that is used for ice skating ➲ picture at **skate**.

**'ice skate²** (*also* **skate**) ***verb*** [I] to move over ice on ice skates

> NOTE **Go ice skating** is a common way of talking about ice skating for pleasure: *We go ice skating every weekend.*

**i·ci·cle** /'aɪsɪkl/ ***noun*** [C] a pointed piece of ice that is formed by water freezing as it falls or runs down from sth

**ic·ing** /'aɪsɪŋ/ ***noun*** [U] a thin mixture of powdered sugar, water or milk and sometimes butter and flavoring, etc. that is used for decorating cakes: *chocolate icing* ➲ Look at **frosting**.

**'icing ˌsugar** ***noun*** [U] (*Cdn*) = CONFECTIONER'S SUGAR

**i·con** /'aɪkɑn/ ***noun*** [C] **1** a person or thing that is considered to be a symbol of sth: *Elvis Presley and other icons of 1950s popular culture* **2** (*computing*) a small picture or symbol on a computer screen that represents a computer program: *Click on the "print" icon and select the correct paper size.*

**ic·y** /'aɪsi/ ***adj.*** (**ic·i·er; ic·i·est**) **1** very cold: *an icy wind* **2** covered with ice: *icy roads*

**I'd** /aɪd/ *short for* I HAD, I WOULD

**ID** /ˌaɪ'di/ ***noun*** [C,U] (*informal*) = IDENTIFICATION (2)

**ˌI'D card** ***noun*** [C] (*informal*) = IDENTITY CARD

★**i·de·a** /aɪ'diə/ ***noun*** **1** [C] a plan or suggestion: *That's a good idea!* ◇ *He has an idea for a new play.* ◇ *I had the bright idea of getting Jane to help me with my homework.* ◇ *Does anyone have any ideas about* *how to tackle this problem?* ◇ *It was your idea to invite so many people to the party.* **2** [U, sing.] a picture or thought in your mind: *Do you have any idea how much this cost?* ◇ *You have no idea* (= you can't imagine) *how difficult it was!* ◇ *The program gave a good idea of what life was like back then.* **3** [C] an opinion or belief: *She has her own ideas about how to bring up children.* ◇ *If that's your idea of a joke, I don't think it's funny!* **4 the idea** [sing.] the aim or purpose of sth: *The idea of the course is to help people communicate.*

IDM **get the idea** to understand: *It was a mess! Piles of trash everywhere, empty beer bottles... you get the idea.*
**get the idea (that)...** to get the feeling or impression that...: *Where did you get the idea that I was paying for this meal?*
**not have the faintest idea** → FAINT[1]

★**i·de·al[1]** /aɪˈdiəl/ ***adj.*** the best possible; perfect: *In an ideal world, there would be no poverty.*

★**i·de·al[2]** /aɪˈdiəl/ ***noun*** [C] **1** an idea or principle that seems perfect to you and that you want to achieve: *She finds it hard to live up to her parents' high ideals.* ◇ *Christian ideals* **2** [usually sing.] a perfect example of a person or thing: *Fashion magazines present very thin models as the ideal of beauty.*

**i·de·al·ism** /aɪˈdiəlɪzəm/ ***noun*** [U] the belief that people should have high ideals and live according to them, or that the world can be made perfect: *Young people are usually full of idealism.* ➲ Look at **realism**.

**i·de·al·ist** /aɪˈdiəlɪst/ ***noun*** [C] a person who has high ideals (but who is sometimes not very practical) ▸ **i·de·al·is·tic** /ˌaɪdiəˈlɪstɪk/ ***adj.***

**i·de·al·ize** /aɪˈdiəlaɪz/ ***verb*** [T] to imagine or show sth or sb as being better than he/she/it really is: *Old people often idealize the past.*

**i·de·al·ly** /aɪˈdiəli/ ***adv.*** **1** perfectly: *She's ideally suited to the job.* **2** in an ideal situation: *Ideally, no class should have over 25 students.*

**i·den·ti·cal** /aɪˈdɛntɪkl/ ***adj.*** **identical (to/with sb/sth)** exactly the same as: *I can't see any difference between these two pens –they look identical to me.* ▸ **i·den·ti·cal·ly** /-kli/ ***adv.***

**iˌdentical ˈtwin** ***noun*** [C, usually pl.] one of two children who come from the same egg of the mother and so are of the same sex and look exactly alike

**i·den·ti·fi·ca·tion** /aɪˌdɛntəfəˈkeɪʃn/ ***noun*** [C,U] **1** the act of identifying or being identified: *We cannot name the victim until a positive identification of the body has been made.* **2** (*also informal* **ID**) an official card, paper, etc. that proves who you are: *Do you have any identification?* ◇ *They're checking IDs at the door.*

★**i·den·ti·fy** /aɪˈdɛntəfaɪ/ ***verb*** [T] (*pres. part.* **i·den·ti·fy·ing**; *3rd person sing. pres.* **i·den·ti·fies**; *pt, pp* **i·den·ti·fied**) **identify sb/sth (as sb/sth)** to recognize or say who or what sb/sth is: *The police need someone to identify the body.* ◇ *to identify the cause of a problem* ◇ *She has been identified as the main suspect in the case.*

PHRV **identify with sb** to feel that you understand and share what sb else is feeling: *I found it hard to identify with the woman in the movie.*
**identify (yourself) with sb/sth** to be connected with sb/sth

★**i·den·ti·ty** /aɪˈdɛntət̬i/ ***noun*** [C,U] (*pl.* **i·den·ti·ties**) who or what a person or a thing is: *There are few clues to the identity of the killer.* ◇ *The region has its own cultural identity.* ◇ *The arrest was a case of mistaken identity* (= the wrong person was arrested by the police). ◇ *Children of immigrants often suffer from a loss of identity* (= they are not sure which culture they belong to).

**iˈdentity card** (*also informal* **ˌI'D card**) ***noun*** [C] a card, usually with your picture on it, that proves who you are

**i·de·ol·o·gy** /ˌaɪdiˈɑlədʒi/ ***noun*** [C,U] (*pl.* **i·de·ol·o·gies**) a set of ideas which form the basis for a political or economic system: *Marxist ideology* ▸ **i·de·o·log·i·cal** /ˌaɪdiəˈlɑdʒɪkl/ ***adj.***

**id·i·om** /ˈɪdiəm/ ***noun*** [C] a expression with a meaning that you cannot guess from the meanings of the separate words: *The idiom "twist sb's arm" means "force sb to do sth."*

**id·i·o·mat·ic** /ˌɪdiəˈmæt̬ɪk/ ***adj.*** **1** containing an idiom or idioms: *an idiomatic expression* **2** using language in a way that sounds natural: *She speaks good idiomatic English.*

**id·i·ot** /ˈɪdiət/ ***noun*** [C] (*informal*) a stupid or foolish person: *I was an idiot to believe what he said.* ▸ **id·i·ot·ic** /ˌɪdiˈɑt̬ɪk/ ***adj.*** ▸ **id·i·ot·i·cal·ly** /-kli/ ***adv.***

**i·dle** /ˈaɪdl/ ***adj.*** **1** not doing anything; not being used: *The factory stood idle while the machines were being repaired.* **2** not wanting to work hard; lazy **3** (*formal*) (only *before* a noun) not to be taken seriously because it will not have any result: *an idle promise* ▸ **i·dle·ness** ***noun*** [U] ▸ **i·dly** /ˈaɪdli/ ***adv.***

**i·dol** /ˈaɪdl/ ***noun*** [C] **1** a statue that people worship as a god **2** a person (such as a movie star or pop musician) who is admired or loved: *When I was 14, Madonna was my idol.*

**i·dol·ize** /ˈaɪdl·aɪz/ ***verb*** [T] to love or admire sb very much or too much: *He is an only child and his parents idolize him.*

**i·dyl·lic** /aɪˈdɪlɪk; ɪˈdɪlɪk/ ***adj.*** very pleasant and peaceful: *an idyllic Caribbean resort*

**i.e.** /ˌaɪ ˈi/ ***abbr.*** that is; in other words: *a study of people who are obese, i.e. more than 30% overweight*

★**if** /ɪf/ ***conj.*** **1** (used in sentences in which one thing happens or is true, depending on whether another thing happens or is true): *If you see him, give him this letter.* ◇ *We won't go to the beach if it rains.* ◇ *If I had more time, I would learn another language.* ◇ *If I had known about the accident, I would have gone to see her in the hospital.* ◇ *I might see her tomorrow. If not, I'll see her this weekend.* **2** (used after verbs such as "ask," "know," "remember"): *They asked if we wanted to go too.* ◇ *I can't remember if I mailed the letter or not.* ➲ Look at the note at **whether**. **3** (used when you are asking sb to do sth or suggesting sth very politely): *If you would just come this way, sir.* ◇ *If I could add something...* **4** when; every time: *If I try to phone her, she just hangs up.* ◇ *If metal gets hot, it expands.*

IDM **as if** → AS
**even if** → EVEN[2]

**if I were you** (used when you are giving sb advice): *If I were you, I'd leave now.*

**if only** (used for expressing a strong wish): *If only I had a decent car!* ◇ *If only he'd call!*

**ig·loo** /ˈɪglu/ ***noun*** [C] (*pl.* **ig·loos**) a traditional type of small house that is built from blocks of ice by people in the Arctic regions of North America

**ig·nite** /ɪgˈnaɪt/ ***verb*** [I,T] (*formal*) to start burning or to make sth start burning: *A spark from the engine ignited the fuel.*

**ig·ni·tion** /ɪgˈnɪʃn/ ***noun*** **1** [U] starting to burn or making sth start burning: *accidental ignition of a gas tank* **2** [C] the electrical system that starts the engine of a car: *to turn the ignition on/off* ◇ *He had left his key in the ignition.*

**ig·no·min·i·ous** /ˌɪgnəˈmɪniəs/ ***adj.*** (*formal*) making you feel embarrassed: *The team went on to an ignominious defeat.* ▸ **ig·no·min·i·ous·ly** ***adv.***

**ig·no·rance** /ˈɪgnərəns/ ***noun*** [U] lack of information or knowledge (about sth): *The mistake was due to ignorance.* ◇ *widespread ignorance of the new regulations*

**ig·no·rant** /ˈɪgnərənt/ ***adj.*** **1** not knowing about sth: *Many people are ignorant of their rights.* ◇ *I'm pretty ignorant about modern technology.* **2** not educated; stupid

★**ig·nore** /ɪgˈnɔr/ ***verb*** [T] to pay no attention to sb/sth: *I said hi to Debby, but she totally ignored me* (= acted as if she hadn't seen me). ◇ *George ignored his doctor's advice about smoking less.*

> NOTE Be careful. **Ignore** and **be ignorant** are very different in meaning.

**i·gua·na** /ɪˈgwɑnə/ ***noun*** [C] a large tropical American lizard (= a type of reptile)

★**ill**[1] /ɪl/ ***adj.*** **1** (not usually before a noun) not in good health; not well; sick: *I became ill after eating shellfish.* ◇ *terminally ill patients* ◇ *mentally ill*

> NOTE **Ill** is more formal than **sick**. We usually use **ill** with an adverb to describe how sick a person is: *seriously ill.*

**2** (only *before* a noun) bad or harmful: *There should be no ill will* (= bad feelings) *between friends.* ◇ *We suffered no ill effects from all that rich food.*

**ill**[2] /ɪl/ ***adv.*** **1** (often in compounds) badly or wrongly: *You would be ill-advised to drive until you have fully recovered.* **2** (*formal*) only with difficulty; not easily: *They could ill afford the extra money for college tuition.*

IDM **bode well/ill (for sb/sth)** → BODE

**I'll** /aɪl/ *short for* I WILL, I SHALL

★**il·le·gal** /ɪˈligl/ ***adj.*** not allowed by the law; not legal: *It is illegal to own a gun without a license.* ◇ *illegal drugs* ◇ *illegal immigrants* (= people who enter a country illegally) ▸ **il·le·gal·ly** ***adv.***

**il·leg·i·ble** /ɪˈlɛdʒəbl/ ***adj.*** difficult or impossible to read: *The doctor's handwriting is completely illegible.* OPP **legible** ▸ **il·leg·i·bly** /-əbli/ ***adv.***

**il·le·git·i·mate** /ˌɪləˈdʒɪt̬əmət/ ***adj.*** **1** (used about a child) born to parents who are not married to each other **2** not allowed by law; against the rules: *the sale of weapons for illegitimate purposes* ▸ **il·le·git·i·ma·cy** /ˌɪləˈdʒɪt̬əməsi/ ***noun*** [U]

**ill-fat·ed** /ˌɪl ˈfeɪt̬əd/ ***adj.*** unlucky; having an unlucky or unsuccessful result: *a list of the victims aboard the ill-fated flight*

**il·lic·it** /ɪˈlɪsət/ ***adj.*** (used about an activity or substance) not allowed by law or by the rules of society: *the illicit trade in drugs* ◇ *They were having an illicit affair.* OPP **legal**

**il·lit·er·ate** /ɪˈlɪt̬ərət/ ***adj.*** **1** not able to read or write **2** showing that you have little education or knowledge, especially in a particular subject: *computer illiterate* ▸ **il·lit·er·a·cy** /ɪˈlɪt̬ərəsi/ ***noun*** [U]: *adult illiteracy*

★**ill·ness** /ˈɪlnəs/ ***noun*** **1** [U] the state of being physically or mentally ill: *There is a history of mental illness in the family.* **2** [C] a type or period of physical or mental ill health: *Although it is serious, cancer is not always a fatal illness.* ◇ *She died after a long illness.* ➲ Look at the note at **disease**.

**il·log·i·cal** /ɪˈlɑdʒɪkl/ ***adj.*** not sensible or reasonable; not logical: *It seems illogical to pay somebody for doing work that you could do yourself.* ▸ **il·log·i·cal·ly** /-kli/ ***adv.***

**ˌill-ˈtreat** ***verb*** [T] to treat sb/sth badly or in an unkind way: *This cat has been ill-treated* ▸ **ˌill-ˈtreat·ment** ***noun*** [U]

**il·lu·mi·nate** /ɪˈluməneɪt/ ***verb*** [T] (*formal*) **1** to give light to sth or to decorate sth with lights: *The church was illuminated by floodlights.* **2** to explain sth or make sth clear ▸ **il·lu·mi·na·tion** /ɪˌluməˈneɪʃn/ ***noun*** [U]

**il·lu·mi·nat·ing** /ɪˈluməneɪt̬ɪŋ/ ***adj.*** helping to explain sth or make sth clear: *an illuminating discussion*

**il·lu·sion** /ɪˈluʒn/ ***noun*** **1** [C,U] a false idea, belief or impression: *I have no illusions about the situation – I know it's serious.* **2** [C] something that your eyes tell you is there or is true but in fact is not: *That plane seems to be flying very slowly, but that's just an optical illusion.*

IDM **be under an/the illusion (that)** to believe wrongly: *I think he's under the illusion that we're rich.*

**il·lu·so·ry** /ɪˈlusəri; -zə-/ ***adj.*** (*formal*) not real, although seeming to be: *The profits they had hoped for proved to be illusory.*

★**il·lus·trate** /ˈɪləstreɪt/ ***verb*** [T] **1** to explain or make sth clear by using examples, pictures or diagrams: *These statistics illustrate the point that I was making.* **2** to add pictures, diagrams, etc. to a book or magazine: *an illustrated cookbook*

**il·lus·tra·tion** /ˌɪləˈstreɪʃn/ ***noun*** **1** [C] a drawing, diagram or picture in a book or magazine: *color illustrations* **2** [C] an example that makes a point or an idea clear **3** [U] the activity or art of illustrating

**il·lus·tri·ous** /ɪˈlʌstriəs/ ***adj.*** (*formal*) famous and successful

**I'm** /aɪm/ *short for* I AM

★**im·age** /ˈɪmɪdʒ/ ***noun*** [C] **1** the general impression that a person or an organization gives to the public: *Advertising has to create a positive image of the product it is selling.* **2** a mental picture or idea of sb/sth: *Many people have an image of Canada as being cold* *all the time.* **3** a picture or description that appears in a book, movie or painting: *horrific images of war* **4** a copy or reflection: *A perfect image of the building was reflected in the lake.*

**im·age·ry** /ˈɪmɪdʒri/ ***noun*** [U] the use of descriptions and comparisons in language in order to have a strong effect on people's imagination and emotions

**i·mag·i·na·ble** /ɪˈmædʒənəbl/ ***adj.*** (often *after* a noun) that you can think of: *The deli has every imaginable kind of cheese.* ◇ *It was the worst day imaginable!*

★**i·mag·i·nar·y** /ɪˈmædʒəˌnɛri/ ***adj.*** existing only in the mind; not real: *Many children have imaginary friends.*

★**i·mag·i·na·tion** /ɪˌmædʒəˈneɪʃn/ ***noun*** **1** [C,U] the ability to create mental pictures or new ideas: *He has a lively imagination.* ◇ *She's very intelligent, but she doesn't have much imagination.*

> NOTE **Imagination** is a creative quality that a person has. **Fantasy** consists of daydreams about stories and situations that are not related to reality.

**2** [C] the part of the mind that uses this ability: *to use your imagination*

**i·mag·i·na·tive** /ɪˈmædʒənəṭɪv/ ***adj.*** having or showing imagination: *She's always full of imaginative ideas.* ◇ *His writing is highly imaginative.* OPP **unimaginative** ▸ **i·mag·i·na·tive·ly** ***adv.***

★**i·mag·ine** /ɪˈmædʒən/ ***verb*** [T] **1** to form a picture or idea of sth in the mind: *Imagine the colors of the forest in the fall.* ◇ *Imagine that you're lying on a beach.* ◇ *It's not easy to imagine your brother as a doctor.* ◇ *I can't imagine myself working in an office.* ◇ *I can imagine how you felt.* **2** to see, hear or think sth that is not true or does not exist: *There's nobody at the door – you're just imagining things.* **3** to think of sth as probable; to suppose: *I imagine he'll be tired when he gets home.*

**im·ag·ing** /ˈɪmɪdʒɪŋ/ ***noun*** [U] the process of capturing, storing and showing an image on a computer screen: *imaging software/techniques*

**im·bal·ance** /ˌɪmˈbæləns/ ***noun*** [C] a difference or lack of equality: *an imbalance between our import and export trade*

**IMF** /ˌaɪ ɛm ˈɛf/ ***abbr.*** International Monetary Fund. The IMF is part of an international organization (the United Nations) and is concerned with economic activity and economic development.

**IMHO** /ˌaɪ ɛm eɪtʃ ˈoʊ/ ***abbr.*** the abbreviation for "in my humble opinion"; used especially in Internet chat rooms, etc. to say that something is your opinion and other people may not agree

**im·i·tate** /ˈɪməteɪt/ ***verb*** [T] **1** to copy the behavior of sb/sth: *Small children learn by imitating their parents.* **2** to copy the speech or actions of sb/sth, often in order to be amusing: *She could imitate her mother perfectly.*

**im·i·ta·tion** /ˌɪməˈteɪʃn/ ***noun*** **1** [C] a copy (of a real thing): *Some artificial flowers are good imitations of real ones.* ◇ *This suitcase is made of imitation leather* (= of material that is made to look like leather). ➲ Look at **genuine**. **2** [C] a copy (of a person's speech or behavior): *He can do a very good imitations of the teacher.* **3** [U] the act of copying sth: *Good pronunciation of a language is best learned by imitation.*

**im·mac·u·late** /ɪˈmækyələt/ ***adj.*** perfectly clean and neat: *His house is always immaculate.* ◇ *immaculate white shirts* ▸ **im·mac·u·late·ly** ***adv.***

**im·ma·te·ri·al** /ˌɪməˈtɪriəl/ ***adj.*** **immaterial (to sb/sth)** not important: *The judge ruled that the evidence was immaterial and shouldn't be presented to the jury.*

**im·ma·ture** /ˌɪməˈtʃʊr; -ˈtʊr/ ***adj.*** **1** not fully grown or developed; not mature: *an immature body* **2** (used about a person) not behaving in a way that is as sensible as you would expect for a person of that age: *Some students are very immature when they go to university.*

★**im·me·di·ate** /ɪˈmidiət/ ***adj.*** **1** happening or done without delay: *I'd like an immediate answer to my proposal.* **2** (only *before* a noun) existing now and needing attention: *Tell me what your immediate needs are.* **3** (only *before* a noun) nearest in time, position or relationship: *They won't make any changes in the immediate future.* ◇ *He has left most of his money to his immediate family* (= parents, children, brothers and sisters).

★**im·me·di·ate·ly** /ɪˈmidiətli/ ***adv.*** **1** now; without delay: *We need an ambulance immediately!* **2** directly; very closely: *He wasn't immediately involved in the crime.* **3** (*formal*) nearest in time or position: *Who's the girl immediately in front of Dan?* ◇ *What did you do immediately after college?* ➲ It is more common to use **right** with this meaning: *She was sitting right in front of me.*

**im·mense** /ɪˈmɛns/ ***adj.*** very large or great: *immense difficulties* ◇ *She gets immense pleasure from her job.*

**im·mense·ly** /ɪˈmɛnsli/ ***adv.*** extremely; very much: *immensely enjoyable*

**im·men·si·ty** /ɪˈmɛnsəṭi/ ***noun*** [U] very large size or extent

**im·merse** /ɪˈmərs/ ***verb*** [T] **1 immerse yourself (in sth)** to involve yourself deeply in sth so that you give it all your attention: *Rachel's usually immersed in a book.* **2 immerse sth (in sth)** to put sth into a liquid so that it is covered

**im·mi·grant** /ˈɪməgrənt/ ***noun*** [C] a person who has come into a foreign country to live there permanently: *recent immigrants to North America* ◇ *illegal immigrants* (= people who come to live in a country without permission) ◇ *New York has a high immigrant population.* ➲ The U.S. and Canada have many immigrant communities which make them **multicultural societies.** ➲ Compare **emigrant.**

**im·mi·grate** /ˈɪməgreɪt/ ***verb*** [I] to enter a country in order to live there: *His family immigrated to Canada from Taiwan in 1992.* ➲ Look also at **emigrate.**

**im·mi·gra·tion** /ˌɪməˈgreɪʃn/ ***noun*** [U] **1** entering a country in order to live there: *There are more controls on immigration than there used to be.* ◇ *the Immigration and Naturalization Service* **2** the control point at an airport, port, etc. where the documents of people who want to come into a country are checked: *When you leave the plane, you have to go through customs and immigration.*

I

**im·mi·nent** /ˈɪmənənt/ ***adj.*** (usually used about sth bad) almost certain to happen very soon: *Heavy rainfall in the valley means that flooding is imminent.* ▸ **im·mi·nent·ly** ***adv.***

**im·mo·bile** /ɪˈmoʊbl/ ***adj.*** not moving or not able to move ▸ **im·mo·bil·i·ty** /ˌɪməˈbɪləṭi/ ***noun*** [U]

**im·mo·bi·lize** /ɪˈmoʊbəlaɪz/ ***verb*** [T] to prevent sb/sth from moving or working normally: *The airport was completely immobilized by the blizzard.*

★**im·mor·al** /ɪˈmɔrəl; -ˈmɑr-/ ***adj.*** wrong according to the accepted rules of behavior; not moral: *I think experiments on animals are immoral.* ▸ **im·mor·al·i·ty** /ˌɪməˈræləṭi/ ***noun*** [U] ▸ **im·mor·al·ly** ***adv.***

**im·mor·tal** /ɪˈmɔrṭl/ ***adj.*** living or lasting for ever: *Nobody is immortal –we all have to die sometime.* ◇ (*figurative*) *Shakespeare's immortal plays* ▸ **im·mor·tal·i·ty** /ˌɪmɔrˈtæləṭi/ ***noun*** [U]

**im·mor·tal·ize** /ɪˈmɔrṭl·aɪz/ ***verb*** [T] to give lasting fame to sb/sth (especially in a book, movie or painting): *The historic occasion was immortalized in a poem.*

**im·mune** /ɪˈmyun/ ***adj.*** **1 immune (to sth)** protected against a certain disease or illness because you have a resistance to it: *You should be immune to measles if you've had it already.* **2 immune (to sth)** not affected by sth: *You can say what you want – I'm immune to criticism!* **3 immune (from sth)** protected from a danger or punishment: *Are young children immune from prosecution?*

**imˈmune reˌsponse** ***noun*** [C] (*medical*) the reaction of the body to the presence of a substance that can cause disease (**an antigen**)

**imˈmune ˌsystem** ***noun*** [C] the system in your body that protects you from diseases

**im·mu·ni·ty** /ɪˈmyunəṭi/ ***noun*** [U] the ability to avoid or be unaffected by disease/criticism/court cases: *immunity to disease* ◇ *Ambassadors to other countries receive diplomatic immunity* (= protection from being tried in a court of law, etc.).

**im·mu·nize** /ˈɪmyənaɪz/ ***verb*** [T] to make sb immune to a disease, usually by giving an injection of a substance (**vaccine**): *Before visiting certain countries, you will need to be immunized against typhoid.* ➲ Look at **vaccinate**. ▸ **im·mu·ni·za·tion** (*also* **immunisation**) /ˌɪmyənəˈzeɪʃn/ ***noun*** [C,U]

★**im·pact**[1] /ˈɪmpækt/ ***noun*** **1** [C, usually sing.] **an impact (on/upon sb/sth)** an effect or impression: *Her speech made a great impact on the audience.* **2** [U] the action or force of one object hitting another: *The impact of the crash threw the passengers out of their seats.* ◇ *The bomb exploded on impact* (= when it hit something).

**im·pact**[2] /ˈɪmpækt/ ***verb*** [I,T] **impact (on) sb/sth** to have a strong effect on sb/sth, especially in a bad or negative way: *How will the new shopping center impact the businesses downtown?*

> NOTE Many people do not like the use of **impact** as a verb. They prefer to use the verb **affect**.

**im·pair** /ɪmˈpɛr/ ***verb*** [T] to damage or weaken sth: *Ear infections can result in impaired hearing.* ➲ Look at **hearing-impaired** and at the note at **handicapped**.

**im·paired** /ɪmˈpɛrd/ ***adj.*** **1** damaged or not functioning normally: *impaired vision/memory* **2 -impaired** having the type of physical or mental problem mentioned: *hearing-impaired children* ◇ *Nowadays we say someone is "hearing-impaired", not deaf.*

**im·pair·ment** /ɪmˈpɛrmənt/ ***noun*** [C,U] the state of having a physical or mental condition which means that part of your body or brain does not work correctly; a particular condition of this sort

**im·pale** /ɪmˈpeɪl/ **impale sb/sth (on sth)** ***verb*** [T] to push a sharp pointed object through sb/sth: *The boy fell out of a tree and impaled his leg on a stake in the garden below.*

**im·part** /ɪmˈpɑrt/ ***verb*** [T] (*formal*) **1 impart sth (to sb)** to tell or teach: *What kind of values are we imparting to our children?* **2 impart sth (to sth)** to give: *Grilling will impart a smoky flavor to the fish.*

**im·par·tial** /ɪmˈpɑrʃl/ ***adj.*** fair or neutral; not preferring one to another: *A referee must be impartial.* SYN **unbiased** ▸ **im·par·ti·al·i·ty** /ˌɪmˌpɑrʃiˈæləṭi/ ***noun*** [U] ▸ **im·par·tial·ly** /-ʃəli/ ***adv.***

**im·pass·a·ble** /ɪmˈpæsəbl/ ***adj.*** (used about a road, etc.) impossible to travel on because it is blocked: *Flooding and fallen trees have made many roads impassable.*

**im·passe** /ˈɪmpæs/ ***noun*** [usually sing.] a situation in which it is impossible to make any more progress: *Negotiations have reached an impasse.*

**im·pas·sive** /ɪmˈpæsɪv/ ***adj.*** (used about a person) showing no emotion or reaction ▸ **im·pas·sive·ly** ***adv.***

★**im·pa·tient** /ɪmˈpeɪʃnt/ ***adj.*** **1 impatient (with sb/sth)** not able to wait for sb/sth calmly; easily annoyed by sb/sth that seems slow; not patient: *Don't be so impatient –it's your turn next.* ◇ *The passengers are getting impatient due to the delay.* ◇ *It's no good being impatient with small children.* **2 impatient (to do sth)**; **impatient (for sth)** (not before a noun) wanting sth to happen soon: *By the time they are seniors, many young people are impatient to leave high school.* ◇ *At the end of winter, we are often impatient for spring to come.* ▸ **im·pa·tience** /ɪmˈpeɪʃns/ ***noun*** [U]: *He began to explain for the third time with growing impatience.* ▸ **im·pa·tient·ly** ***adv.***

**im·peach** /ɪmˈpitʃ/ ***verb*** [T] to accuse a politician, judge, etc. formally of breaking the law or acting wrongly in his/her job: *The state House of Representatives voted to impeach the governor.* ▸ **im·peach·ment** /-mənt/ ***noun*** [U]

**im·pec·ca·ble** /ɪmˈpɛkəbl/ ***adj.*** perfect; without any mistakes: *impeccable behavior* ◇ *His accent is impeccable.* ▸ **im·pec·ca·bly** /-bli/ ***adv.***

**im·pede** /ɪmˈpid/ ***verb*** [T] (*formal*) to make it difficult for sb/sth to move or make progress: *The completion of the new expressway has been impeded by bad weather conditions.*

**im·ped·i·ment** /ɪmˈpɛdəmənt/ ***noun*** [C] (*formal*) **1** something that makes it difficult for a person or thing to move or progress: *The high tax rate will be a major impediment to new businesses.* **2** something that makes speaking difficult: *a speech impediment*

**im·pend·ing** /ɪmˈpɛndɪŋ/ ***adj.*** (only *before* a

noun) (usually used about sth bad) that will happen soon: *There was a feeling of impending disaster in the air.*

**im·pen·e·tra·ble** /ɪm'pɛnətrəbl/ ***adj.*** **1** impossible to enter or go through: *The jungle was impenetrable.* **2** impossible to understand: *an impenetrable mystery*

**im·per·a·tive¹** /ɪm'pɛrət̬ɪv/ ***adj.*** (*formal*) very important or urgent: *It's imperative that you see a doctor immediately.*

**im·per·a·tive²** /ɪm'pɛrət̬ɪv/ ***noun*** [C, sing.] (*grammar*) the form of the verb that is used for giving orders: *In "Shut the door!" the verb is in the imperative.*

**im·per·cep·ti·ble** /ˌɪmpər'sɛptəbl/ ***adj.*** too small to be seen or noticed: *The difference between the original painting and the copy was almost imperceptible.* OPP **perceptible** ▸ **im·per·cep·ti·bly** /ˌɪmpər'sɛptəbli/ ***adv.***

**im·per·fect** /ɪm'pərfɪkt/ ***adj.*** **1** with mistakes or faults; not perfect: *This is a very imperfect system.* **2** (only *before* a noun) (*grammar*) used for expressing action in the past that is not completed: *In "While I was taking a bath," the verb is in the imperfect tense.*

NOTE We can also use **imperfect** as a noun and say: *The verb is in the imperfect.* It is more usual to call this tense the **past continuous** or **past progressive.**

▸ **im·per·fect·ly** ***adv.***

**im·pe·ri·al** /ɪm'pɪriəl/ ***adj.*** connected with an empire or its ruler: *the imperial palace* ◇ *imperial power*

**im·pe·ri·al·ism** /ɪm'pɪriəlɪzəm/ ***noun*** [U] a political system in which a rich and powerful country controls other countries (**colonies**) which are not so rich and powerful as itself ▸ **im·pe·ri·al·ist** /ɪm'pɪriəlɪst/ ***adj.***

**im·per·son·al** /ɪm'pərsənl/ ***adj.*** **1** not showing friendly human feelings; cold in feeling or atmosphere: *A large organization can be very impersonal to work for.* ◇ *The hotel room was very impersonal.* **2** not referring to any particular person: *Can we try to keep the discussion as impersonal as possible, please?*

**im·per·son·ate** /ɪm'pərsəneɪt/ ***verb*** [T] to copy the actions and way of speaking of a person or to pretend to be a different person: *He was arrested for impersonating a medical doctor.* ▸ **im·per·son·a·tion** /ɪmˌpərsə'neɪʃn/ ***noun*** [C,U] ▸ **im·per·son·a·tor** ***noun*** [C]

**im·per·ti·nent** /ɪm'pərtn·ənt/ ***adj.*** (*formal*) not showing respect; rude: *Previous generations taught their children not to be impertinent.* OPP **polite** or **respectful**, NOT **pertinent** ▸ **im·per·ti·nence** ***noun*** [U] **im·per·ti·nent·ly** ***adv.***

**im·per·vi·ous** /ɪm'pərviəs/ ***adj.*** **1** not allowing water, etc. to pass through **2** not affected or influenced by sth: *impervious to criticism*

**im·pet·u·ous** /ɪm'pɛtʃuəs/ ***adj.*** acting or done quickly and without thinking: *Her impetuous behavior often gets her in trouble.* SYN **impulsive** ▸ **im·pet·u·ous·ly** ***adv.***

**im·pe·tus** /'ɪmpət̬əs/ ***noun*** [sing., U] something that encourages sth else to happen: *I need a fresh impetus to start working on this essay again.*

**im·pinge** /ɪm'pɪndʒ/ ***verb*** [I] **impinge on/upon sth** (*formal*) to have an effect on sth; to interfere with sth: *I'm not going to let my job impinge on my family life.*

**im·plant¹** /ɪm'plænt/ ***verb*** [T] to put sth into the body, usually in a medical operation: *Surgeons implanted an artificial heart into a 64-year-old patient.*

**im·plant²** /'ɪmplænt/ ***noun*** [C] something that is implanted into the body: *breast implants* (= that make the breasts larger)

**im·plau·si·ble** /ɪm'plɔzəbl/ ***adj.*** not easy to believe: *an implausible excuse*

**im·ple·ment¹** /'ɪmpləmənt/ ***noun*** [C] a tool or instrument (especially for work outdoors): *farm implements* ➲ Look at the note at **tool**.

**im·ple·ment²** /'ɪmpləmɛnt/ ***verb*** [T] to start using a plan, system, etc.: *The tax reforms will be implemented next year.* ▸ **im·ple·men·ta·tion** /ˌɪmpləmən'teɪʃn/ ***noun*** [U]

**im·pli·cate** /'ɪmpləkeɪt/ ***verb*** [T] **implicate sb (in sth)** (*formal*) (often passive) to show that sb is involved in sth bad, especially a crime: *The mayor's brother was implicated in the scandal.*

★**im·pli·ca·tion** /ˌɪmplə'keɪʃn/ ***noun*** **1** [C] the effect that sth will have on sth else in the future: *The new law will have serious implications for our work.* **2** [C,U] something that is suggested but that is not said openly: *The implication of her comments was that we had made a bad mistake.* ➲ verb **imply** ➲ Look also at **infer**.

**im·plic·it** /ɪm'plɪsət/ ***adj.*** not expressed directly but understood by the people involved: *an implicit agreement* ➲ Look at **explicit**. ▸ **im·plic·it·ly** ***adv.***

**im·plore** /ɪm'plɔr/ ***verb*** [T] (*formal*) to ask sb for sth or to do sth. You implore sb when the situation is very serious and you need sth very much: *She implored him not to leave her alone.* ◇ *"Don't leave me alone," she implored.* ➲ Look at **beg**. It is similar in meaning.

★**im·ply** /ɪm'plaɪ/ ***verb*** [T] (*pres. part.* **im·ply·ing**; *3rd person sing. pres.* **im·plies**; *pt, pp* **im·plied**) to suggest sth in an indirect way or without actually saying it: *The article implied that the senator was involved in the scandal.* ➲ noun **implication**

**im·po·lite** /ˌɪmpə'laɪt/ ***adj.*** rude; not polite: *I think it was impolite of him to ask you to leave.* ▸ **im·po·lite·ly** ***adv.***

★**im·port¹** /ɪm'pɔrt/ ***verb*** [T] **import sth (from...)**; **import sth (into...)** to buy goods, etc. from a foreign country and bring them into your own country: *This country has to import most of its raw materials.* ◇ *imported goods* ◇ *The U.S. imports cars from Japan/Germany/South Korea.* OPP **export** ▸ **importer** ***noun*** [C]: *Is the U.S. the world's largest importer of oil?* OPP **exporter**

★**im·port²** /'ɪmpɔrt/ ***noun*** **1** [C, usually pl.] goods bought from a foreign country for sale or use in your own country: *What are your country's major imports?* OPP **export** **2** [U] = IMPORTATION: *new import quotas on agricultural products*

★**im·por·tance** /ɪm'pɔrtns/ ***noun*** [U] the state of

being important; value: *The decision was of great importance to the future of the business.*

★**im·por·tant** /ɪmˈpɔrtnt/ ***adj.*** **1** having great value or influence; very necessary: *an important meeting/decision* ◇ *Tomorrow will be the most important day of my life!* ◇ *Is money important for happiness?* ◇ *It's important not to be late.* ◇ *It's important that people learn at least one foreign language.* ◇ *It's important for people to see the results of what they do.* ◇ *It was important to me that you were there.* **2** (used about a person) having great influence or authority: *He was one of the most important writers of his time.* ◇ *I soon got to know who was important in the company and who wasn't.* OPP **unimportant** ▸ **im·por·tant·ly** ***adv.***

**im·por·ta·tion** /ˌɪmpɔrˈteɪʃn/ (*also* **import**) ***noun*** [U] the action of bringing goods from a foreign country to sell or use in your own country: *a ban on the importation of automatic weapons*

★**im·pose** /ɪmˈpoʊz/ ***verb*** **1** [T] to make sth be accepted because you are the person with power: *to impose a tax increase on cigarettes* ◇ *The government should impose restrictions on the use of harmful chemicals.* ◇ *Parents should try not to impose their own ideas on their children.* **2** [I] **impose (on/upon sb/sth)** to ask or expect sb to do sth that may cause extra work or trouble: *I hope I'm not imposing – but could I come and stay at your house next week?* ◇ *I hate to impose on you, but can you loan me $20?*

**im·pos·ing** /ɪmˈpoʊzɪŋ/ ***adj.*** making an impression on people because it is big or important: *I work in a large, imposing building in the center of town.*

**im·po·si·tion** /ˌɪmpəˈzɪʃn/ ***noun*** **1** [U] the action of imposing: *I'm against the imposition of unnecessary rules and regulations on people.* **2** [C] an unfair or bad thing that sb has to accept; sth that causes extra work or trouble: *"Please stay for supper." "Are you sure it's not an imposition?"*

★**im·pos·si·ble** /ɪmˈpɑsəbl/ ***adj.*** **1** not able to be done or to happen; not possible: *It's impossible for me to be there before 12.* ◇ *I find it almost impossible to get up in the morning!* ◇ *That horse is impossible to control.* ◇ *That's impossible!* (= I don't believe it!) **2** very difficult to deal with or to make better: *These kids are just impossible!* ◇ *This is an impossible situation!* ▸ **im·pos·si·bil·i·ty** /ɪmˌpɑsəˈbɪləṭi/ ***noun*** [C,U] (*pl.* **im·pos·si·bil·i·ties**): *the impossibility of reaching an agreement* ◇ *What you are suggesting is a complete impossibility!* ▸ **im·pos·si·bly** /-əbli/ ***adv.***: *impossibly high standards*

**the imˈpossible** ***noun*** [sing.] something that cannot be done: *Don't attempt the impossible!*

**im·pos·tor** /ɪmˈpɑstər/ ***noun*** [C] a person who pretends to be sb else in order to trick other people

**im·po·tent** /ˈɪmpətənt/ ***adj.*** **1** without enough power or influence OPP **powerful** **2** (used about men) not capable of having sex ▸ **im·po·tence** /-təns/ ***noun*** [U]

**im·pound** /ɪmˈpaʊnd/ ***verb*** [T] to take sth and lock it up so that it cannot be used, or so that it can be kept for its owner: *Illegally parked cars will be impounded.* ◇ *Animals that have been impounded can be reclaimed by their owners between 9 a.m. and 5 p.m.*

**im·pov·er·ished** /ɪmˈpɑvərɪʃt/ ***adj.*** extremely poor: *impoverished inner-city neighborhoods*

**im·prac·ti·cal** /ɪmˈpræktɪkl/ ***adj.*** **1** not sensible or reasonable; not practical: *an impractical suggestion* ◇ *It would be impractical to take our bikes on vacation.* **2** (used about a person) not good at doing ordinary everyday jobs: *He's intelligent but completely impractical.*

**im·pre·cise** /ˌɪmprɪˈsaɪs/ ***adj.*** not clear or exact; not precise: *imprecise instructions*

★**im·press** /ɪmˈprɛs/ ***verb*** [T] **1 impress sb (with sth)** to make sb feel admiration and respect: *She's always trying to impress people with her new outfits.* ◇ *It impressed me that he understood immediately what I meant.* **2** (*formal*) **impress sth on/upon sb** to make sth very clear to sb: *I wish you could impress the importance of these tests on John.*

★**im·pres·sion** /ɪmˈprɛʃn/ ***noun*** [C] **1** the effect that a person or thing produces on sb else: *She gives the impression of being older than she really is.* ◇ *I want to create an impression of light and space in the house.* ◇ *Do you think I made a good impression on your parents?* **2** an opinion about sb/sth (that is sometimes unclear or wrong): *What's your impression of the new manager?* ◇ *I'm not sure, but I have the impression that Jane is unhappy.* ◇ *I was under the impression that you were married.* **3** an amusing imitation of the behavior or speech of a well-known person: *My brother does some marvelous impressions of TV stars.* **4** a mark made by pressing an object hard into a surface

**im·pres·sion·a·ble** /ɪmˈprɛʃənəbl/ ***adj.*** (of a person, especially a young one) easily influenced or affected by sb/sth: *children at an impressionable age*

★**im·pres·sive** /ɪmˈprɛsɪv/ ***adj.*** causing a feeling of admiration and respect because of importance/size/excellent quality: *an impressive building, speech, etc.* ◇ *The way he handled the situation was very impressive.* OPP **unimpressive**

**im·print** /ˈɪmprɪnt/ ***noun*** [C] the mark made by pressing an object on a surface: *the imprint of a foot in the sand*

**im·pris·on** /ɪmˈprɪzn/ ***verb*** [T] (often passive) to put or keep in prison: *He was imprisoned for assault with a deadly weapon.* ▸ **im·pris·on·ment** /-mənt/ ***noun*** [U]: *She was sentenced to five years' imprisonment.* ◇ *life imprisonment*

**im·prob·a·ble** /ɪmˈprɑbəbl/ ***adj.*** not likely to be true or to happen; not probable: *an improbable explanation* ◇ *an improbable result* ◇ *It is highly improbable that she will arrive tonight.* ➲ Look at **unlikely**. ▸ **im·prob·a·bil·i·ty** /ɪmˌprɑbəˈbɪləṭi/ ***noun*** [U] ▸ **im·prob·a·bly** /-əbli/ ***adv.***

**im·promp·tu** /ɪmˈprɑmptu/ ***adj.***, ***adv.*** (done) without being prepared or organized: *an impromptu speech*

**im·prop·er** /ɪmˈprɑpər/ ***adj.*** **1** illegal or not honest: *It seems that she had been involved in improper business deals.* **2** not correct or suitable for the situation: *The explosion was caused by improper storage of gasoline.* **3** rude (in a sexual way): *He lost* *his job for making improper suggestions to several of the female employees.* ▶ **im·prop·er·ly** ***adv.***

**im·pro·pri·e·ty** /ˌɪmprəˈpraɪət̬i/ ***noun*** [C,U] (*pl.* **im·pro·pri·e·ties**) (*formal*) the state of being improper; an improper act: *We are certain there were no improprieties in the handling of the deal.*

★**im·prove** /ɪmˈpruv/ ***verb*** [I,T] to become or to make sth better: *I hope the weather will improve later on.* ◇ *Your vocabulary is excellent, but you could improve your pronunciation.*

PHRV **improve on/upon sth** to produce sth that is better than sth else: *I think the movie improved on the book* (= the movie was better than the book). ◇ *Nobody will be able to improve on that score* (= nobody will be able to get a higher score).

★**im·prove·ment** /ɪmˈpruvmənt/ ***noun*** [C,U] **improvement (on/in/over sth)** (a) change which makes the quality or condition of sb/sth better: *There's been a considerable improvement in your mother's condition.* ◇ *These grades are a big improvement over your previous ones.* ◇ *Housing and public transportation are areas which need improvement.* ◇ *Even minor home improvements such as painting can increase the value of your house.*

**im·pro·vise** /ˈɪmprəvaɪz/ ***verb*** [I,T] **1** to make, do, or manage sth quickly or without preparation, using what you have: *If you're short of workers today, you'll just have to improvise* (= manage somehow with the people who are there). **2** to play music, speak or act using your imagination instead of written or remembered material: *I can read music, but I can't improvise, so I can't play jazz.* ◇ *a hilarious improvised comedy act* ▶ **im·prov·i·sa·tion** /ɪmˌprɑvəˈzeɪʃn/ ***noun*** [C,U]

**im·pulse** /ˈɪmpʌls/ ***noun*** [C] **1** a sudden desire to do sth without thinking about the results: *She felt a terrible impulse to steal something.* **2** a single push or signal in a nerve, wire, etc. that causes a reaction: *electrical impulses*

IDM **on impulse** without thinking or planning: *I just bought this cake on impulse when I saw it in the store.*

**im·pul·sive** /ɪmˈpʌlsɪv/ ***adj.*** likely to act suddenly and without thinking; done without careful thought: *an impulsive shopper* ◇ *impulsive behavior* ▶ **im·pul·sive·ly** ***adv.*** ▶ **im·pul·sive·ness** ***noun*** [U]

**im·pure** /ɪmˈpyʊər/ ***adj.*** **1** consisting of more than one substance (and therefore not of good quality); not pure: *impure metals* **2** (*old-fashioned*) (used about thoughts and actions connected with sex) not moral; bad

**im·pu·ri·ty** /ɪmˈpyʊərəti/ ***noun*** (*pl.* **im·pu·ri·ties**) **1** [C, usually pl.] a substance that is present in another substance, making it of poor quality: *impurities in the water* **2** [U] the state of being impure

★**in¹** /ɪn/ ***adv.***

NOTE For special uses with many verbs, e.g. **give in**, look at the verb entries.

**1** to a position within a particular area: *She opened the door and went in.* ◇ *My suitcase is full. I can't get any more in.* ◇ *When does the plane get in?* (= to the airport). **2** at home or at work: *She won't be in until late today.* **3** (used about the movements of the ocean) at the highest point, when the water is closest to the land: *The tide's coming in.* **4** received by sb official: *Entries should be in by March 20.*

IDM **be in for sth**; **be in for it** (*informal*) to be going to experience sth bad: *He's going to be in for a shock when he gets the bill.* ◇ *If Mom finds out about that, you're in for it.*

**be/get in on sth** to have a share in sth; to know about sth that is happening: *I'd like to be in on the new project.*

**have (got) it in for sb** (*informal*) to be unkind to sb because he/she has done sth to upset you: *The boss has had it in for me ever since I refused to work on Thanksgiving.*

★**in²** /ɪn/ ***prep.***

NOTE For special uses with many nouns, e.g. **in time**, look at the noun entries.

**1** (showing place) within the area of sth; enclosed by sth: *a country in Africa* ◇ *a town in Mexico* ◇ *an island in the Pacific* ◇ *in a box* ◇ *I read about it in the newspaper.* ◇ *in bed* ◇ *She put the keys in her pocket.* ◇ *They were working in the garden.* ◇ *His wife's in the hospital.* **2** (showing time) during a period of time: *My birthday is in August.* ◇ *He was born in 1995.* ◇ *You could walk there in about an hour* (= it would take that long to walk there). **3** (showing time) after a period of time: *I'll be finished in ten minutes.* **4** contained in; forming the whole or part of sth: *There are 366 days in a leap year.* **5** (used for giving the rate of sth): *Is it true that one family in four owns a DVD player?* **6** wearing sth: *They were all dressed in black for the funeral.* ◇ *I've never seen you in a suit before.* **7** (used for saying how things are arranged): *We sat in a circle.* **8** (used for saying how sth is written or expressed): *Please write in pen.* ◇ *They were talking in Italian.* **9** (used with feelings): *He looked at me in horror.* **10** (showing the condition or state of sb/sth): *My parents are in poor health.* ◇ *This room is in a mess!* ◇ *Richard's in love.* **11** (showing sb's job or the activity sb is involved in): *He's got a good job in advertising.* ◇ *Her whole family is in politics.* ◇ *He's in the army.* **12** at home or at work: *I phoned him last night but he wasn't in.* ◇ *She won't* ***be in*** *until later today.* **13** received by sb official: *Entries should be in by 20 March.* ◇ *Applications have to be in by Friday.*

**in³** /ɪn/ ***adj.*** (*informal*) fashionable and popular: *Short skirts are going to be in this spring.* ◇ *This is the in place to hang out.*

**in⁴** /ɪn/ ***noun***

IDM **the ins and outs (of sth)** the details and difficulties (involved in sth): *Will somebody explain the ins and outs of the situation to me?*

**in.** ***abbr.*** = INCH(ES): *It's 4ft. 2 in. long.*

★**in·a·bil·i·ty** /ˌɪnəˈbɪləti/ ***noun*** [U] **inability (to do sth)** lack of ability, power or skill: *He has a complete inability to listen to other people's opinions.* ➲ adjective **unable**

**in·ac·ces·si·ble** /ˌɪnækˈsɛsəbl/ ***adj.*** very difficult or impossible to reach or contact: *That beach is inaccessible by car.* ◇ (*figurative*) *His books are inaccessible to* (= cannot be understood by) *the average reader.* ▶ **in·ac·ces·si·bil·i·ty** /ˌɪnækˌsɛsəˈbɪləti/ ***noun*** [U]

**in·ac·cu·ra·cy** /ɪn'ækyərəsi/ ***noun*** (*pl.* **in·ac·cu·ra·cies**) **1** [U] being inaccurate: *The inaccuracy of the statistics was immediately obvious.* **2** [C] an inaccurate statement; a written or spoken mistake: *There are always some inaccuracies in newspaper reports.*

**in·ac·cu·rate** /ɪn'ækyərət/ ***adj.*** not correct; not accurate: *an inaccurate report/description*

**in·ac·tion** /ɪn'ækʃn/ ***noun*** [U] doing nothing; lack of action: *The crisis was blamed on the government's earlier inaction.*

**in·ac·tive** /ɪn'æktɪv/ ***adj.*** doing nothing; not active: *The virus remains inactive in the body.* ▸ **in·ac·tiv·i·ty** /ˌɪnæk'tɪvəti/ ***noun*** [U]

**in·ad·e·quate** /ɪn'ædɪkwət/ ***adj.*** **1** not sufficient; not good enough: *the problem of inadequate housing* **2** (used about a person) not able to deal with a problem or situation, etc.; not confident: *There was so much to learn in the new job that for a while I felt totally inadequate.* ▸ **in·ad·e·qua·cy** /ɪn'ædɪkwəsi/ ***noun*** [C,U] (*pl.* **in·ad·e·qua·cies**): *his inadequacy as a parent* ◇ *The inadequacies in police protection are the result of budget cuts.* ▸ **in·ad·e·quate·ly** /ɪn'ædɪkwətli/ ***adv.***

**in·ad·ver·tent** /ˌɪnəd'vərtənt/ ***adj.*** (used about actions) done without thinking, not on purpose; not intentional ▸ **in·ad·ver·tent·ly** ***adv.***: *She had inadvertently left the letter where he could find it.*

**in·ad·vis·a·ble** /ˌɪnəd'vaɪzəbl/ ***adj.*** not sensible; not showing good judgment: *It is inadvisable to go swimming when you have a cold.* OPP **advisable**

**in·al·ien·a·ble** /ɪn'eiliənəbl; -'eɪlyən-/ ***adj.*** (*formal*) (used about a right) that cannot be taken away from sb

**in·ane** /ɪ'neɪn/ ***adj.*** without any meaning; silly: *an inane remark* ▸ **in·ane·ly** ***adv.***

**in·ap·pro·pri·ate** /ˌɪnə'proʊpriət/ ***adj.*** not suitable: *Her dress was totally inappropriate for the occasion.* ➲ Look at **unsuitable**.

**in·ar·tic·u·late** /ˌɪnɑr'tɪkyələt/ ***adj.*** **1** (used about a person) not able to express ideas and feelings clearly **2** (used about speech) not clear or well expressed OPP **articulate** ▸ **in·ar·tic·u·late·ly** ***adv.***

**in·at·ten·tion** /ˌɪnə'tɛnʃn/ ***noun*** [U] lack of attention: *inattention to detail*

**in·at·ten·tive** /ˌɪnə'tɛntɪv/ ***adj.*** not paying attention: *One inattentive student can disturb the whole class.*

**in·au·di·ble** /ɪn'ɔdəbl/ ***adj.*** not loud enough to be heard ▸ **in·au·di·bly** /ɪn'ɔdəbli/ ***adv.***

**in·au·gu·ral** /ɪ'nɔgyərəl/ ***adj.*** (only *before* a noun) (used about a speech or meeting that marks the beginning of a new organization, leadership, etc.) first: *the President's inaugural speech*

**in·au·gu·rate** /ɪ'nɔgyəreɪt/ ***verb*** [T] **1** to introduce a new official, leader, etc. at a special ceremony: *He will be inaugurated as President next month.* **2** (*formal*) to start, introduce or open sth new (often at a special ceremony) ▸ **in·au·gu·ra·tion** /ɪˌnɔgyə'reɪʃn/ ***noun*** [C,U]

**inc.** (*also* **Inc.**) ***abbr.*** = INCORPORATED

**in·cal·cu·la·ble** /ɪn'kælkyələbl/ ***adj.*** very great; too great to calculate: *an incalculable risk* ◇ *incalculable damage*

**in·ca·pa·ble** /ɪn'keɪpəbl/ ***adj.*** **incapable of sth/doing sth** not able to do sth; not capable of sth/doing sth: *She is incapable of hard work/working hard.*

**in·ca·pac·i·tate** /ˌɪnkə'pæsɪteɪt/ ***verb*** [T] to make sb unable (to work, live normally, etc.): *incapacitated by the tropical heat*

**in·car·cer·ate** /ɪn'kɑrsəreɪt/ ***verb*** [T] (usually passive) to put or keep in prison ▸ **in·car·cer·a·tion** /ɪnˌkɑrsə'reɪʃn/ ***noun*** [U]

**in·car·na·tion** /ˌɪnkɑr'neɪʃn/ ***noun*** [C] a life on earth in a particular form

**in·cen·di·ar·y** /ɪn'sɛndiˌɛri/ ***adj.*** that causes a fire: *an incendiary device*

**in·cense** /'ɪnsɛns/ ***noun*** [U] a substance that produces a sweet smell when burned, used especially in religious ceremonies

**in·censed** /ɪn'sɛnst/ ***adj.*** **incensed (by/at sth)** very angry; furious

**in·cen·tive** /ɪn'sɛntɪv/ ***noun*** [C,U] **incentive (to do sth)** something that encourages you (to do sth): *The company is offering cash incentives to its employees to boost productivity.* ◇ *I get my meals for free, so I have no incentive to cook.*

**in·ces·sant** /ɪn'sɛsnt/ ***adj.*** never stopping: *incessant rain/noise* ➲ Look at **continual**. ▸ **in·ces·sant·ly** ***adv.***

**in·cest** /'ɪnsɛst/ ***noun*** [U] sex between close members of a family, e.g. brother and sister ▸ **in·ces·tu·ous** /ɪn'sɛstʃuəs/ ***adj.***: *an incestuous relationship*

**inch¹** /ɪntʃ/ ***noun*** [C] (*abbr.* **in.**) a measure of length; 2.54 centimeters. There are 12 inches in a foot: *He's 5 feet, 10 inches tall.* ◇ *Three inches of rain fell last night.*

**inch²** /ɪntʃ/ ***verb***

PHR V **inch forward, past, through, etc.** to move slowly and carefully in the direction mentioned: *I inched the car into the space.*

**in·ci·dence** /'ɪnsədəns/ ***noun*** [sing.] the number of times sth (usually sth bad) happens; the rate of sth: *a high incidence of crime/disease/unemployment*

★**in·ci·dent** /'ɪnsədənt/ ***noun*** [C,U] (*formal*) an event (especially one that involves violence, danger, something strange, etc.): *There were a number of violent incidents during the demonstration.* ◇ *We believe the burglary was an isolated incident* (= not part of a series of crimes).

**in·ci·den·tal** /ˌɪnsə'dɛntəl/ ***adj.*** happening as part of sth more important; minor: *Take enough money for food and incidental expenses.*

**in·ci·den·tal·ly** /ˌɪnsə'dɛntəli/ ***adv.*** (used to introduce extra news, information, etc. that the speaker has just thought of): *Incidentally, that new restaurant you told me about is excellent.* ➲ A more informal expression is **by the way**.

**in·cin·er·ate** /ɪn'sɪnəreɪt/ ***verb*** [T] (*formal*) to destroy sth completely by burning

**in·cin·er·a·tor** /ɪn'sɪnəreɪt̬ər/ ***noun*** [C] a container or machine for burning garbage, etc.

**in·ci·sion** /ɪn'sɪʒn/ ***noun*** [C,U] (*formal*) a cut

carefully made into sth (especially into a person's body as part of a medical operation)

**in·cite** /ɪn'saɪt/ ***verb*** [T] **incite sb (to sth); incite sth** to encourage sb to do sth by making him/her very angry or excited: *He was accused of inciting the crowd to violence.* ◇ *to incite a riot* ▸ **in·cite·ment** ***noun*** [C,U]

**in·clem·ent** /ɪn'klɛmənt/ ***adj.*** (*formal*) (used about the weather) not pleasant; cold, wet, etc.

**in·cli·na·tion** /ˌɪnklə'neɪʃn/ ***noun*** [C,U] a feeling that makes sb want to behave in a particular way: *My inclination is to say "no," but what do you think?*

**in·cline** /'ɪnklaɪn/ ***noun*** [C, usually sing.] a slope; an area of sloping ground: *a steep incline*

**in·clined** /ɪn'klaɪnd/ ***adj.*** (not before a noun) **1 inclined to do sth** likely to do sth: *She's inclined to change her mind very easily.* **2 inclined (to do sth)** wanting to behave in a particular way: *I know Andrew well, so I'm inclined to believe what he says.* **3 inclined to do sth** (used to make what is said sound less sure) holding a particular opinion: *I'm inclined to say "yes," but I'll have to ask Molly first.* **4** having a natural ability in the subject mentioned: *to be musically inclined*

★**in·clude** /ɪn'klud/ ***verb*** [T] **1** to have as one part; to contain (among other things): *The price of the room includes one drink in the hotel bar.* ◇ *The crew included one woman.* ➲ Look at **exclude** and at the note at **contain**. **2** to make sb/sth part (of another group, etc.): *We should include the other departments in our discussions.* ◇ *Everyone was disappointed, myself included.* ▸ **in·clu·sion** /ɪn'kluʒn/ ***noun*** [U]: *The inclusion of all that violence in the show was unnecessary.*

★**in·clud·ing** /ɪn'kludɪŋ/ ***prep.*** having as a part: *It costs $17.99, not including sales tax.*

**in·clu·sive** /ɪn'klusɪv/ ***adj.*** including as many types of people or things as possible: *The candidate said his party was aiming to become more friendly and inclusive.*

**in·cog·ni·to** /ˌɪnkɑg'niţoʊ/ ***adj., adv.*** hiding your real name and identity (especially if you are famous and do not want to be recognized): *to travel incognito*

**in·co·her·ent** /ˌɪnkoʊ'hɪrənt/ ***adj.*** not clear or easy to understand; not expressing yourself clearly ▸ **in·co·her·ence** /-əns/ ***noun*** [U] ▸ **in·co·her·ent·ly** ***adv.***

★**in·come** /'ɪnkʌm/ ***noun*** [C,U] the money you receive regularly as payment for your work or from other sources: *It's sometimes difficult for a family to live on one income.*

> NOTE We can talk about a **yearly** or an **annual** income. An income may be **high** or **low**. Your **gross** income is the amount you earn before paying taxes. Your **net** income is your income after taxes. Look at the note at **pay**.

**'income tax** ***noun*** [C,U] the tax that you pay on the money you earn: *federal and income taxes*

**in·com·ing** /'ɪnkʌmɪŋ/ ***adj.*** (only *before* a noun) **1** coming in: *incoming telephone calls* ◇ *incoming missiles* **2** new; recently elected: *incoming freshmen* ◇ *the incoming administration*

**in·com·pat·i·ble** /ˌɪnkəm'pæţəbl/ ***adj.*** **incompatible (with sb/sth)** not able to live or work happily with sb; not able to exist in harmony with sb/sth else: *Their marriage won't last; they're completely incompatible.* ◇ *This software is incompatible with our computer system.* ▸ **in·com·pat·i·bil·i·ty** /ˌɪnkəmˌpæţə'bɪləţi/ ***noun*** [C,U] (*pl.* **in·com·pat·i·bil·i·ties**)

**in·com·pe·tent** /ɪn'kɑmpəţənt/ ***adj.*** lacking the necessary skill to do sth well: *There are too many incompetent people working there.* ◇ *The defendant was found mentally incompetent to stand trial* (= because he/she could not tell the difference between right and wrong). ▸ **in·com·pe·tence** /-təns/ ***noun*** [U] ▸ **in·com·pe·tent·ly** ***adv.***

**in·com·plete**[1] /ˌɪnkəm'plit/ ***adj.*** having a part or parts missing; not total or complete: *The witness could only give an incomplete account of what had happened.* ◇ *Her last novel was left incomplete when she died.* ▸ **in·com·plete·ly** ***adv.***

**in·com·plete**[2] /ˌɪnkəm'plit/ ***noun*** [C] a grade that you get in a course when you have not done all of the work for the course

**in·com·pre·hen·si·ble** /ɪnˌkɑmprɪ'hɛnsəbl/ ***adj.*** impossible to understand: *an incomprehensible explanation* ◇ *I find her attitude incomprehensible.*

**in·con·ceiv·a·ble** /ˌɪnkən'sivəbl/ ***adj.*** impossible or very difficult to believe or imagine

**in·con·clu·sive** /ˌɪnkən'klusɪv/ ***adj.*** not leading to a definite decision or answer: *an inconclusive discussion* ◇ *Results of the tests were inconclusive* (= they didn't prove anything). ▸ **in·con·clu·sive·ly** ***adv.***

**in·con·sid·er·ate** /ˌɪnkən'sɪdərət/ ***adj.*** (used about a person) not thinking or caring about the feelings, or needs of other people: *It was inconsiderate of you not to offer her a ride.* SYN **thoughtless** OPP **considerate**

**in·con·sis·tent** /ˌɪnkən'sɪstənt/ ***adj.*** **1** likely to change (in attitude, behavior, etc.); not reliable: *She's so inconsistent –sometimes her work is good and sometimes it's really awful.* ◇ *inconsistent enforcement of a law* **2 inconsistent (with sth)** not in agreement with sth: *These new facts are inconsistent with the earlier information.* ▸ **in·con·sis·ten·cy** /-tənsi/ ***noun*** [C, U] (*pl.* **in·con·sis·ten·cies**) ▸ **in·con·sis·tent·ly** ***adv.***

**in·con·spic·u·ous** /ˌɪnkən'spɪkyuəs/ ***adv.*** not easily noticed: *inconspicuous colors* ◇ *I tried to make myself as inconspicuous as possible so that no one would ask me a question.* ▸ **in·con·spic·u·ous·ly** ***adv.***

**in·con·ti·nent** /ɪn'kɑntn·ənt; -tənənt/ ***adj.*** unable to control the passing of waste materials from the body ▸ **in·con·ti·nence** /-əns/ ***noun*** [U]

**in·con·ven·ience** /ˌɪnkən'vinyəns/ ***noun*** [C,U] (something that causes) difficulty or problems: *We apologize for any inconvenience caused by the delays this afternoon.* ▸ **in·con·ven·ience** ***verb*** [T]

**in·con·ven·ient** /ˌɪnkən'vinyənt/ ***adj.*** causing difficulty or problems; not convenient: *It's inconvenient for me to drive so far just to pick up a few items.* ▸ **in·con·ven·ient·ly** ***adv.***

**in·cor·po·rate** /ɪn'kɔrpəreɪt/ ***verb*** [T] **incorporate sth (in/into sth)** to make sth part of sth else or to have sth as a part; to include: *I'd like you to incorporate this information into your report.* ◇ *The new car incorporates all the latest safety features.*

**In·cor·po·rat·ed** /ɪnˈkɔrpəreɪt̮əd/ ***adj.*** (*abbr.* **Inc.**) (following the name of a company) formed into a legal organization (**corporation**)

**in·cor·rect** /ˌɪnkəˈrɛkt/ ***adj.*** not right or true; not correct: *an incorrect answer* ▶ **in·cor·rect·ly** ***adv.***: *The envelope was incorrectly addressed.*

★**in·crease[1]** /ɪnˈkris/ ***verb*** [I,T] to become or to make sth larger in number or amount: *The number of people working from home will increase steadily during the next decade.* ◇ *The rate of inflation has increased by 1% to 7%.* ◇ *She increased her speed to pass the truck.* OPP **decrease** or **reduce**

★**in·crease[2]** /ˈɪnkris/ ***noun*** [C,U] **increase (in sth)** a rise in the number, amount or level of sth: *a steady increase in the number of people taking vacations abroad* ◇ *There has been a sharp increase of nearly 50% over last year's figures.* ◇ *Doctors expect some further increase in the spread of the disease.* ◇ *a huge tax increase* ➲ **decrease** or **reduction**

IDM **on the increase** becoming larger or more frequent; increasing: *Attacks by dogs on children are on the increase.*

**in·creas·ing·ly** /ɪnˈkrisɪŋli/ ***adv.*** more and more: *increasingly difficult/important/unhappy*

**in·cred·i·ble** /ɪnˈkrɛdəbl/ ***adj.*** **1** wonderful or fantastic; very great: *He earns an incredible salary.* **2** impossible or very difficult to believe: *It seemed incredible to us that something like that could happen.*

**in·cred·i·bly** /ɪnˈkrɛdəbli/ ***adv.*** extremely: *incredibly strong*

**in·crim·i·nate** /ɪnˈkrɪməneɪt/ ***verb*** [T] to provide evidence that sb is guilty of a crime: *She refused to answer in order to avoid incriminating herself.* ▶ **in·crim·i·nat·ing** /-neɪt̮ɪŋ/ ***adj.***: *The police found several incriminating documents in his desk.*

**in·cu·bate** /ˈɪŋkyəbeɪt/ ***verb*** [I,T] **1** (used about eggs) to keep or be kept warm until the young birds come out (**hatch**) **2** (used about an infectious disease, etc.) to develop: *Some viruses take weeks to incubate.*

**in·cu·ba·tion** /ˌɪŋkyəˈbeɪʃn/ ***noun*** **1** [U] the process of incubating eggs **2** [C] (*also* ˌ**incuˈbation period**) the period between catching a disease and the time when signs of it (**symptoms**) appear

**in·cu·ba·tor** /ˈɪŋkyəbeɪt̮ər/ ***noun*** [C] **1** a heated piece of equipment shaped like a box, that is used in hospitals for keeping small or weak babies alive **2** a similar piece of equipment for keeping eggs warm until they break open (**hatch**)

**in·cum·bent** /ɪnˈkʌmbənt/ ***noun*** [C] a person who is currently in a particular position or job, especially a political one ▶ **in·cum·bent** ***adj.*** (only *before* a noun): *the incumbent vice president*

**in·cur** /ɪnˈkər/ ***verb*** [T] (**in·curred**; **in·cur·ring**) (*formal*) to cause or suffer sth unpleasant as a result of your own actions: *to incur debts/sb's anger*

**in·cur·a·ble** /ɪnˈkyʊrəbl/ ***adj.*** not able to be cured or changed: *an incurable disease* ▶ **in·cur·a·bly** ***adv.***: *incurably ill*

**in·debt·ed** /ɪnˈdɛt̮əd/ ***adj.*** **indebted to sb (for sth)** very grateful to sb: *I am deeply indebted to my family for all their help and support.*

**in·de·cent** /ɪnˈdisnt/ ***adj.*** offending against accepted sexual, moral or social standards of behavior ▶ **in·de·cen·cy** /-nsi/ ***noun*** [C,U] (*pl.* **in·de·cen·cies**) ▶ **in·de·cent·ly** ***adv.***

**in·de·ci·sion** /ˌɪndɪˈsɪʒn/ ***noun*** [U] being unable to decide: *indecision about the future*

**in·de·ci·sive** /ˌɪndɪˈsaɪsɪv/ ***adj.*** **1** (used about a person) not able to make decisions **2** (used about a thing) not having a clear result or a strong effect: *an indecisive election that left no party with an absolute majority* ▶ **in·de·ci·sive·ly** ***adv.***

**in·deed** /ɪnˈdid/ ***adv.*** (*formal*) **1** (used for agreeing with sth that has just been said or for emphasis) really; certainly: *"Have you found out what happened?" "Yes, indeed."* **2** (used for emphasizing a point that has just been made) in fact: *It's important that you come at once. Indeed, it's essential.*

**in·de·fen·si·ble** /ˌɪndɪˈfɛnsəbl/ ***adj.*** (used about behavior, etc.) completely wrong; that cannot be defended or excused

**in·de·fin·a·ble** /ˌɪndɪˈfaɪnəbl/ ***adj.*** difficult or impossible to describe: *an indefinable atmosphere of hostility* ▶ **in·de·fin·a·bly** /-əbli/ ***adv.***

**in·def·i·nite** /ɪnˈdɛfənət/ ***adj.*** not having clear limits or a certain end: *Our plans are still pretty indefinite.*

**inˌdefinite ˈarticle** ***noun*** [C] (*grammar*) the name used for the words "a" and "an" ➲ Look at **definite article**.

**in·def·i·nite·ly** /ɪnˈdɛfənətli/ ***adv.*** for an indefinite period of time (= you do not know how long it will last): *The meeting was postponed indefinitely.*

**in·del·i·ble** /ɪnˈdɛləbl/ ***adj.*** that cannot be removed or washed out: *indelible ink* ◇ (*figurative*) *an indelible impression* ▶ **in·del·i·bly** /-əbli/ ***adv.***

**in·dent** /ɪnˈdɛnt/ ***verb*** [I,T] to start a line of writing further from the left side of the page than the other lines: *to indent the first line of a paragraph*

★**in·de·pend·ence** /ˌɪndɪˈpɛndəns/ ***noun*** [U] **independence (from sb/sth)** (used about a person, country, etc.) the state of being free or not controlled by another person, country, etc.: *In 1776 the United States declared its independence from Britain.* ◇ *financial independence*

ˌ**Indeˈpendence Day** ***noun*** [U] July 4; a national holiday in the U.S. on which Americans celebrate the day in 1776 when America declared itself independent from Britain

★**in·de·pend·ent** /ˌɪndɪˈpɛndənt/ ***adj.*** **1 independent (of sb/sth)** not dependent on or controlled by another person, country, etc.: *Many former colonies are now independent nations.* ◇ *to be independent of your parents* **2** not needing or wanting help: *My son likes traveling on his own – he's very independent for his age.* **3** not influenced by or connected with sb/sth: *an independent candidate for governor* (= one who is not a member of a political party) ◇ *an independent inquiry* ▶ **in·de·pend·ent·ly** ***adv.***: *Scientists working independently of each other have had very similar results in their experiments.*

ˈ**in-depth** ***adj.*** (only before a noun) very thorough;

done with a lot of attention to details: *an in-depth discussion/report/analysis*

**in·de·scrib·a·ble** /ˌɪndɪˈskraɪbəbl/ ***adj.*** too good or bad to be described: *indescribable poverty/luxury* ▶ **in·de·scrib·a·bly** /-əbli/ ***adv.***

**in·de·struc·ti·ble** /ˌɪndɪˈstrʌktəbl/ ***adj.*** that cannot be easily damaged or destroyed

**in·de·ter·mi·nate** /ˌɪndɪˈtərmənət/ ***adj.*** that cannot be identified easily or exactly: *Her eyes were an indeterminate color.* ◇ *She was a tall woman of indeterminate age.* ▶ **in·de·ter·mi·na·cy** ***noun*** [U]

★**in·dex**[1] /ˈɪndɛks/ ***noun*** [C] **1** (*pl.* **in·dex·es**) a list of names or subjects at the end of a book, arranged in the order of the alphabet **2** (*pl.* **in·dex·es** or **in·dic·es** /-dəsiz/) a way of showing how the price, value, rate, etc. of sth has changed: *the consumer price index*

**in·dex**[2] /ˈɪndɛks/ ***verb*** [T] to make an INDEX[1] or include sth in an index

ˈ**index finger** (*also* **forefinger**) ***noun*** [C] the finger next to your thumb

**In·di·an** /ˈɪndiən/ ***noun*** [C], ***adj.*** **1** = NATIVE AMERICAN: *an Indian tribe* **2** (*Cdn*) a Native Canadian who is not Inuit or Metis

NOTE In Canada, Aboriginal people may belong to one of three general categories: **Indian**, **Inuit** and **Metis**.

**3** (a person) from the Republic of India: *Indian food is hot and spicy.*

ˌ**Indian ˈsummer** ***noun*** [C,U] a period of warm weather in late fall

★**in·di·cate** /ˈɪndəkeɪt/ ***verb*** **1** [T] to show or point to sth: *The receptionist indicated where I should sign.* ◇ (*figurative*) *The report indicates a need for more spending on research.* **2** [T] to be or give a sign about sth: *If a horse has its ears forward, that indicates that it is happy.* **3** [T] to say sth briefly and in a general way: *The spokesman indicated that an agreement was likely soon.*

★**in·di·ca·tion** /ˌɪndəˈkeɪʃn/ ***noun*** [C,U] something that shows sth; a sign: *There was no indication of a struggle.* ◇ *There is every indication that he will make a full recovery.*

**in·dic·a·tive** /ɪnˈdɪkət̬ɪv/ ***adj.*** (*formal*) **indicative (of sth)** being or giving a sign of sth: *Is the unusual weather indicative of fundamental changes in the climate?*

**in·di·ca·tor** /ˈɪndəkeɪt̬ər/ ***noun*** [C] something that gives information or shows sth; a sign: *The leading economic indicators point to a strong recovery.*

**in·di·ces** ***noun*** [C] *plural of* INDEX[1] (2)

**in·dict** /ɪnˈdaɪt/ ***verb*** [T] (often passive) (in a court of law) to accuse sb officially of committing a crime: *He was indicted for murder.* ◇ *The grand jury indicted them on charges of theft.*

**in·dict·ment** /ɪnˈdaɪtmənt/ ***noun*** [C] **1** a written paper that officially accuses sb of a crime **2** (*figurative*) something that shows how bad sth is: *The fact that some young people leave school without knowing how to read or write is an indictment of our educational system.*

**in·dif·fer·ence** /ɪnˈdɪfrəns/ ***noun*** [U] a lack of interest or feeling (toward sb/sth): *He treated our suggestion with complete indifference.*

**in·dif·fer·ent** /ɪnˈdɪfrənt/ ***adj.*** **indifferent (to sb/sth)** not interested in or caring about sb/sth: *How can you remain indifferent when children are suffering?* ▶ **in·dif·fer·ent·ly** ***adv.***

**in·dig·e·nous** /ɪnˈdɪdʒənəs/ ***adj.*** (used about people, animals or plants) living or growing in the place where they are from originally

**in·di·gent** /ˈɪndɪdʒənt/ ***adj.*** (*formal*) poor; not having enough money to pay for many things: *medical care for indigent patients*

**in·di·ges·tion** /ˌɪndəˈdʒɛstʃən/ ***noun*** [U] pain in the stomach that is caused by difficulty in digesting food: *Onions give me terrible indigestion.*

**in·dig·nant** /ɪnˈdɪgnənt/ ***adj.*** shocked or angry (because sb has said or done sth that you do not like and do not agree with): *They were indignant that they had to pay more for worse services.* ▶ **in·dig·nant·ly** ***adv.***

**in·dig·na·tion** /ˌɪndɪgˈneɪʃn/ ***noun*** [U] shock and anger: *The brutal crime aroused public indignation.* ◇ *to express indignation*

★**in·di·rect** /ˌɪndɪˈrɛkt; -daɪ-/ ***adj.*** **1** not going in a straight line or using the shortest route; not direct: *We took the indirect route to avoid driving through downtown.* **2** not directly caused by or connected with sth: *an indirect result* **3** not mentioning sth openly: *She gave only an indirect answer to my question.* ▶ **in·di·rect·ly** ***adv.*** ▶ **in·di·rect·ness** ***noun*** [U]

ˌ**indirect ˈobject** ***noun*** [C] (*grammar*) an additional OBJECT[1] (4) that is used after some verbs: *In the sentence, "I wrote her a letter," "her" is the indirect object.*

ˌ**indirect ˈspeech** ***noun*** [U] = REPORTED SPEECH

**in·dis·creet** /ˌɪndɪˈskrit/ ***adj.*** not careful or polite in what you say or do OPP **discreet** ▶ **in·dis·creet·ly** ***adv.***

**in·dis·cre·tion** /ˌɪndɪˈskrɛʃn/ ***noun*** [C,U] behavior that is not careful or polite

**in·dis·crim·i·nate** /ˌɪndɪˈskrɪmənət/ ***adj.*** not carefully chosen or done with careful thought: *the indiscriminate shooting of civilians* ▶ **in·dis·crim·i·nate·ly** ***adv.***

**in·dis·pen·sa·ble** /ˌɪndɪˈspɛnsəbl/ ***adj.*** very important so that it is not possible to be without it; essential or necessary: *A car is indispensable in small towns.*

**in·dis·put·a·ble** /ˌɪndɪˈspyut̬əbl/ ***adj.*** definitely true; that cannot be proved wrong

**in·dis·tinct** /ˌɪndɪˈstɪŋkt/ ***adj.*** not clear; not distinct: *indistinct figures/sounds/memories* ▶ **in·dis·tinct·ly** ***adv.***

**in·dis·tin·guish·a·ble** /ˌɪndɪˈstɪŋgwɪʃəbl/ ***adj.*** **indistinguishable (from sth)** appearing to be the same: *From a distance, the two colors are indistinguishable.*

★**in·di·vid·u·al**[1] /ˌɪndəˈvɪdʒuəl/ ***adj.*** **1** (only *before* a noun) single or particular: *Each individual battery is tested before being packaged.* **2** for or from one person: *Children need individual attention when they are learning to read.*

★**in·di·vid·u·al²** /ˌɪndəˈvɪdʒuəl/ ***noun*** [C] **1** one person: *Are the needs of society more important than the rights of the individual?* ◇ *Two individuals were arrested in connection with the robbery.* **2** (*informal*) a person of the type that is mentioned: *She's a strange individual.*

**in·di·vid·u·al·ism** /ˌɪndəˈvɪdʒuəlɪzəm/ ***noun*** [U] **1** the quality of being different from other people and doing things in your own way: *She owes her success to her individualism and self-confidence.* **2** the belief that individual people in society should have the right to make their own decisions, etc., rather than be controlled by the government: *Capitalism stresses innovation, competition and individualism.*

**in·di·vid·u·al·i·ty** /ˌɪndəˌvɪdʒuˈæləṭi/ ***noun*** [U] the qualities that make sb/sth different from other people/things: *Young people often try to express their individuality by the way they dress.*

**in·di·vid·u·al·ly** /ˌɪndəˈvɪdʒuəli/ ***adv.*** separately; one by one: *The teacher talked to each member of the class individually.*

I

**in·di·vis·i·ble** /ˌɪndəˈvɪzəbl/ ***adj.*** not able to be divided or split into smaller pieces

**In·do-Ca·na·di·an** /ˌɪndoʊ kəˈneɪdiən/ ***noun*** [C] (*Cdn*) a Canadian who was born in the Indian subcontinent, especially India, or whose family originally came from India

**in·doc·tri·nate** /ɪnˈdɑktrəneɪt/ ***verb*** [T] to put ideas or beliefs into sb's mind so that they are accepted without criticism: *For 20 years, the people have been indoctrinated by the government.* ➲ Using the word **indoctrinate** shows that you disapprove of what is happening. ▶ **in·doc·tri·na·tion** /ɪnˌdɑktrəˈneɪʃn/ ***noun*** [U]: *the indoctrination of political prisoners*

**in·door** /ˈɪndɔr/ ***adj.*** (only *before* a noun) done or used inside a building: *indoor sports* ◇ *an indoor swimming pool* ◇ *In those days, many houses had no indoor plumbing* (= water pipes/toilets). OPP **outdoor**

★**in·doors** /ˌɪnˈdɔrz/ ***adv.*** in or into a building: *Let's go/stay indoors.* ◇ *I left my sunglasses indoors.* ➲ Look at **outdoors** and **out of doors**.

**in·duce** /ɪnˈdus/ ***verb*** [T] (*formal*) **1 induce sb to do sth** to make or persuade sb to do sth: *Nothing could induce him to change his mind.* **2** to cause or produce: *a drug that induces sleep*

**in·duce·ment** /ɪnˈdusmənt/ ***noun*** [C,U] sth that is offered to sb to make him/her do sth: *The player was offered a car as an inducement to join the team.*

**in·duct** /ɪnˈdʌkt/ ***verb*** [T] (usually passive) to make sb a member of a group or to give sb a special position or title during an official ceremony: *He was inducted into the baseball hall of fame.*

**in·duc·tion** /ɪnˈdʌkʃn/ ***noun*** [C,U] the process of introducing sb to a new job, skill, organization, etc.; an event at which this takes place: *an induction ceremony*

**in·dulge** /ɪnˈdʌldʒ/ ***verb*** **1** [I] **indulge (in sth)** to allow yourself to have or do sth for pleasure: *There's still some cake left – go ahead and indulge!* ◇ *to indulge in self-pity* **2** [T] satisfy a strong desire for or interest in sth: *After she retired, she had time to indulge her passion for traveling.*

**in·dul·gence** /ɪnˈdʌldʒəns/ ***noun*** **1** [U] the state of having or doing whatever you want: *a life of indulgence* **2** [C] something that you have or do because it gives you pleasure: *A cigar after dinner is my only indulgence.*

**in·dul·gent** /ɪnˈdʌldʒənt/ ***adj.*** allowing sb to have or do whatever he/she wants: *indulgent parents* ▶ **in·dul·gent·ly** ***adv.***

★**in·dus·tri·al** /ɪnˈdʌstriəl/ ***adj.*** **1** (only *before* a noun) connected with INDUSTRY (1): *industrial development* ◇ *industrial workers* **2** having a lot of factories, etc.: *an industrial region/country*

**inˌdustrial ˈarts** (*also* **shop**, **ˈshop class**) ***noun*** [U] a school subject in which students learn to use tools and machines, and to make things out of wood or metal

**in·dus·tri·al·ist** /ɪnˌdʌstriəlɪst/ ***noun*** [C] a person who owns or manages a large industrial company

**in·dus·tri·al·ize** /ɪnˌdʌstriəlaɪz/ ***verb*** [T] to develop INDUSTRIES (2) in a country: *the industrialized nations of the world* ▶ **in·dus·tri·al·i·za·tion** /ɪnˌdʌstriələˈzeɪʃn/ ***noun*** [U]

**inˈdustrial park** ***noun*** [C] an area of land that has small factories and other businesses on it

**in·dus·tri·ous** /ɪnˈdʌstriəs/ ***adj.*** hard-working

★**in·dus·try** /ˈɪndəstri/ ***noun*** (*pl.* **in·dus·tries**) **1** [U] the work of making things in factories: *a good year for North American industry* ◇ *heavy/light industry* **2** [C] all the people, buildings, etc. that are involved in producing sth, providing a service, etc.: *The new high-tech industries are replacing manufacturing industries in many areas.* ◇ *the tourist/catering/entertainment industry*

**in·e·bri·at·ed** /ɪˈnibrieɪṭəd/ ***adj.*** (*formal*) drunk

**in·ed·i·ble** /ɪnˈɛdəbl/ ***adj.*** not suitable to be eaten: *an inedible plant* OPP **edible**

**in·ef·fec·tive** /ˌɪnɪˈfɛktɪv/ ***adj.*** not producing the effect or result that you want

**in·ef·fi·cient** /ˌɪnɪˈfɪʃnt/ ***adj.*** not working or producing results in the best way, so that time and money are wasted: *an inefficient way of working* ◇ *an inefficient use of space* ◇ *Our furnace is very old and extremely inefficient.* ◇ *The new manager is very nice, but he's very inefficient.* ▶ **in·ef·fi·cien·cy** /-nsi/ ***noun*** [U] ▶ **in·ef·fi·cient·ly** ***adv.***

**in·el·i·gi·ble** /ɪnˈɛlɪdʒəbl/ ***adj.*** **ineligible (for sth/to do sth)** without the necessary qualifications to do or get sth: *She was ineligible for financial aid because her family's income was too high.* ◇ *ineligible to vote* ▶ **in·el·i·gi·bil·i·ty** /ɪnˌɛlɪdʒəˈbɪləṭi/ ***noun*** [U]

**in·ept** /ɪˈnɛpt/ ***adj.*** not able to do sth well; having no skill: *weak, inept leadership*

**in·e·qual·i·ty** /ˌɪnɪˈkwɑləṭi/ ***noun*** [C,U] (*pl.* **in·e·qual·i·ties**) (a) difference between groups in society because one has more money, advantages, etc. than the other: *inequality between the sexes*

**in·ert** /ɪˈnərt/ ***adj.*** not able to move or act

**in·er·tia** /ɪˈnərʃə/ ***noun*** [U] the physical force that tends to keep things in the position they are in or to keep them moving in the direction they are traveling: (*figurative*) *The inertia of the system makes change very difficult.*

**in·es·cap·a·ble** /ˌɪnɪˈskeɪpəbl/ ***adj.*** (*formal*) that cannot be avoided: *an inescapable conclusion*

**in·ev·i·ta·ble** /ɪnˈɛvət̬əbl/ ***adj.*** **1** that cannot be avoided or prevented from happening: *With more cars on the road, traffic jams are inevitable.* ◇ *It was inevitable that she would find out the truth one day.* **2 the inevitable** ***noun*** [sing.] something that cannot be avoided or stopped from happening ▸ **in·ev·i·ta·bil·i·ty** /ɪnˌɛvət̬əˈbɪləti/ ***noun*** [U] ▸ **in·ev·i·ta·bly** ***adv.***: *Construction projects on major highways inevitably create huge problems* (= they cannot be avoided).

**in·ex·cus·a·ble** /ˌɪnɪkˈskyuzəbl/ ***adj.*** that cannot be allowed or forgiven: *Their behavior was quite inexcusable.* ◇ *inexcusable delays* SYN **unforgivable**

**in·ex·haust·i·ble** /ˌɪnɪɡˈzɔstəbl/ ***adj.*** that cannot be finished or used up: *Our energy supplies are not inexhaustible.*

**in·ex·pen·sive** /ˌɪnɪkˈspɛnsɪv/ ***adj.*** low in price; not expensive: *an inexpensive camping vacation* ▸ **in·ex·pen·sive·ly** ***adv.***

**in·ex·pe·ri·ence** /ˌɪnɪkˈspɪriəns/ ***noun*** [U] not knowing how to do sth because you have not done it before; lack of experience: *The mistakes were all due to inexperience.*

**in·ex·pe·ri·enced** /ˌɪnɪkˈspɪriənst/ ***adj.*** not having the knowledge that you get from having done sth before; lacking experience: *He's too young and inexperienced to be given such responsibility.*

**in·ex·pli·ca·ble** /ˌɪnɪkˈsplɪkəbl/ ***adj.*** that cannot be explained: *Her sudden disappearance is completely inexplicable.* ▸ **in·ex·pli·ca·bly** ***adv.***

**in·fal·li·ble** /ɪnˈfæləbl/ ***adj.*** **1** (used about a person) never making mistakes or being wrong: *Even the most careful typist is not infallible.* **2** always doing what you want it to do; never failing: *There is no infallible method of birth control.* OPP **fallible** ▸ **in·fal·li·bil·i·ty** /ɪnˌfæləˈbɪləti/ ***noun*** [U]

**in·fa·mous** /ˈɪnfəməs/ ***adj.*** (usually before a noun) famous for being bad: *an infamous dictator* ◇ *The area is infamous for drugs and prostitution.*

**in·fan·cy** /ˈɪnfənsi/ ***noun*** [U] the period when you are a baby: (*figurative*) *Research in this field is still in its infancy.*

**in·fant** /ˈɪnfənt/ ***noun*** [C] a baby: *There is a high rate of infant mortality* (= many children die when they are still babies).

NOTE **Baby** is more common in spoken or informal English.

**in·fan·tile** /ˈɪnfəntaɪl/ ***adj.*** (of behavior) typical of, or connected with, a baby or a very young child and therefore not appropriate for adults or older children: *infantile jokes*

**in·fan·try** /ˈɪnfəntri/ ***noun*** [U] soldiers who fight on foot: *The infantry was supported by heavy gunfire.*

**in·fat·u·at·ed** /ɪnˈfætʃueɪt̬əd/ ***adj.*** having a strong but foolish feeling of love for sb/sth that usually does not last long: *The boy was infatuated with one of his teachers.* ▸ **in·fat·u·a·tion** /ɪnˌfætʃuˈeɪʃn/ ***noun*** [C,U]

★**in·fect** /ɪnˈfɛkt/ ***verb*** [T] (usually passive) to cause sb/sth to have a disease or illness or to become dirty: *We need to clean the wound before it becomes infected.* ◇ *Many thousands of people have been infected with the virus.*

★**in·fec·tion** /ɪnˈfɛkʃn/ ***noun*** **1** [U] making sb sick: *A dirty water supply can be a source of infection.* **2** [C] a disease or illness that is caused by very small living things: *She is suffering from a chest infection.* ◇ *an ear infection*

NOTE Infections can be caused by **bacteria** or **viruses**. An informal word for these is **germs**.

★**in·fec·tious** /ɪnˈfɛkʃəs/ ***adj.*** (used about a disease, illness, etc.) that can be easily passed on to another person: *The flu is very infectious.* ◇ (*figurative*) *infectious laughter* ➲ Look at **contagious**.

**in·fer** /ɪnˈfər/ ***verb*** [T] (**in·fer̲r̲ing; in·fer̲r̲ed**) **infer sth (from sth)** to reach a conclusion from the information you have: *I inferred from our conversation that he was unhappy with his job.* ▸ **in·fer·ence** /ˈɪnfərəns; -frəns/ ***noun*** [C,U]

**in·fe·ri·or** /ɪnˈfɪriər/ ***adj.*** **inferior (to sb/sth)** low or lower in social position, importance, quality, etc.: *I don't like the way he treats new staff as inferior.* ◇ *Cheaper products are generally of inferior quality.* OPP **superior** ▸ **in·fe·ri·or·i·ty** /ɪnˌfɪriˈɔrət̬i; -ˈɑr-/ ***noun*** [U]

**inferiˈority ˌcomplex** ***noun*** [C] a feeling that you are less important, intelligent, successful, etc. than other people

**in·fer·tile** /ɪnˈfərt̬əl; -t̬aɪl/ ***adj.*** **1** (used about a person or animal) not able to have a baby or young animal **2** (used about land) not able to grow strong healthy plants ▸ **in·fer·til·i·ty** /ˌɪnfərˈtɪləti/ ***noun*** [U]: *treatment for infertility*

**in·fest·ed** /ɪnˈfɛstəd/ ***adj.*** **infested (with sth)** (used about a building) with large numbers of unpleasant animals or insects in it: *The warehouse was infested with rats.*

**in·fi·del·i·ty** /ˌɪnfəˈdɛləti/ ***noun*** [C,U] (*pl.* **in·fi·del·i·t·ies**) the act of not being faithful to your wife or husband or partner by having a sexual relationship with sb else SYN A less formal word is **unfaithfulness**.

**in·field** /ˈɪnfild/ ***noun*** [C] in a game of baseball, the group of players who stand in the central area of the field

**in·fight·ing** /ˈɪnfaɪt̬ɪŋ/ ***noun*** [U] the arguments and disagreements between people in the same group who are competing for power: *political infighting within the party*

**in·fil·trate** /ˈɪnfəltreɪt/ ***verb*** [T] to enter an organization, etc. secretly so that you can find out what it is doing: *The police managed to infiltrate the terrorist group.* ▸ **in·fil·tra·tion** /ˌɪnfəlˈtreɪʃn/ ***noun*** [C,U] ▸ **in·fil·tra·tor** /ˈɪnfəltreɪt̬ər/ ***noun*** [C]

**in·fi·nite** /ˈɪnfənət/ ***adj.*** **1** without end or limits: *Supplies of oil are not infinite.* **2** very great: *You need infinite patience for this job.*

**in·fi·nite·ly** /ˈɪnfənətli/ ***adv.*** (used before an adjective or adverb) very much: *Compact discs sound infinitely better than audio cassettes.*

**in·fin·i·tive** /ɪnˈfɪnət̬ɪv/ ***noun*** [C] (*grammar*) the basic form of a verb

NOTE In English the infinitive is sometimes used with and sometimes without *to*: *He can sing.* ◇ *He wants to sing.*

**in·fin·i·ty** /ɪnˈfɪnət̬i/ ***noun*** [U] **1** endless space or time **2** (in mathematics) the number that is larger than any other that you can think of

**in·firm** /ɪnˈfərm/ ***adj.*** sick or weak, e.g. because of old age

**in·fir·ma·ry** /ɪnˈfərməri/ ***noun*** [C] (*pl.* **in·fir·ma·ries**) a part of a university, prison, etc. where sick or injured people can go for treatment

**in·fir·mi·ty** /ɪnˈfərmət̬i/ ***noun*** [C,U] (*pl.* **in·fir·mi·ties**) (*formal*) weakness or illness

**in·flamed** /ɪnˈfleɪmd/ ***adj.*** (used about a part of the body) red and swollen because of some infection

**in·flam·ma·ble** /ɪnˈflæməbl/ ***adj.*** that burns easily: *Natural gas is highly inflammable.* OPP **non-flammable**

NOTE Look also at **flammable**. It has the same meaning and is more common than **inflammable**.

**in·flam·ma·tion** /ˌɪnfləˈmeɪʃn/ ***noun*** [C,U] redness and swelling in a part of the body, because of infection

**in·flat·a·ble** /ɪnˈfleɪt̬əbl/ ***adj.*** that can or must be filled with air: *an inflatable boat*

**in·flate** /ɪnˈfleɪt/ ***verb*** [I,T] (*formal*) to fill sth with air; to become filled with air OPP **deflate**

**in·fla·tion** /ɪnˈfleɪʃn/ ***noun*** [U] a general rise in prices: *High increases in wages cause inflation.* ◇ *the inflation rate/rate of inflation* ◇ *Annual inflation remains at 10%.* ◇ *The government is taking measures to control inflation.* ◇ *They've reduced inflation by 2%.*

**in·flec·tion** /ɪnˈflɛkʃn/ ***noun*** **1** [U] the rise and fall of your voice when you are talking ➲ Compare **intonation**. **2** [U] the act of changing the ending or form of a word to show its grammatical function **3** [C] something that is added to a word that changes its grammatical function, e.g. *-ed*, *-est*

**in·flex·i·ble** /ɪnˈflɛksəbl/ ***adj.*** not able to bend or be bent easily: (*figurative*) *an inflexible attitude* ▸ **in·flex·i·bil·i·ty** /ɪnˌflɛksəˈbɪlət̬i/ ***noun*** [U] ▸ **in·flex·i·bly** ***adv.***

**in·flict** /ɪnˈflɪkt/ ***verb*** [T] **inflict sth (on/upon sb)** to force sb to have sth bad or unwanted: *to inflict severe injuries on sb*

**ˌin-ˈflight** ***adj.*** happening or provided during a trip in a plane: *an in-flight movie*

★**in·flu·ence[1]** /ˈɪnfluəns/ ***noun*** **1** [U] **influence (on/over sb/sth)** the power to affect, change or control sb/sth: *I used my influence with the boss to get things changed.* ◇ *The fact that he's rich and famous had no influence on our decision.* ◇ *Nobody should drive while they are under the influence of alcohol.* **2** [C] **influence (on sb/sth)** a person or thing that affects or changes sb/sth: *His new girlfriend has been a good influence on him.*

★**in·flu·ence[2]** /ˈɪnfluəns/ ***verb*** [T] to have an effect or influence on sb/sth: *You have to decide for yourself. Don't let anyone else influence you.* ◇ *Her style of painting has been influenced by Japanese art.*

NOTE **Affect** and **influence** are often very similar in meaning. **Affect** is usually used when the change is physical and **influence** is more often used to describe a change of feeling or attitude: *Drinking alcohol can affect your ability to drive.* ◇ *Those TV commercials have influenced my attitude toward drinking and driving.*

**in·flu·en·tial** /ˌɪnfluˈɛnʃl/ ***adj.*** having power or influence: *an influential politician* ◇ *He was influential in getting the hostages set free.*

**in·flu·en·za** /ˌɪnfluˈɛnzə/ ***noun*** [U] (*formal*) = FLU

**in·flux** /ˈɪnflʌks/ ***noun*** [C] a sudden arrival of people or things in large numbers: *the influx of tourists from the cities during the summer*

**info** /ˈɪnfoʊ/ ***noun*** [U] (*informal*) information: *Here's some more info on that concert...*

**in·fo·mer·cial** /ˈɪnfoʊmərʃl/ ***noun*** [C] an advertisement on television that is as long as a regular program

★**in·form** /ɪnˈfɔrm/ ***verb*** [T] **inform sb (of/about sth)** to give sb information (about sth): *You should inform the police about the accident.* ◇ *Everyone has been informed of the changes.*

PHR V **inform on sb** to give information, etc. to the police, etc. about what sb has done wrong: *The wife of the killer informed on her husband.*

★**in·for·mal** /ɪnˈfɔrml/ ***adj.*** relaxed and friendly or suitable for a relaxed occasion; not formal: *Don't get dressed up for the party –it'll be very informal.* ◇ *an informal survey* ◇ *informal discussions*

NOTE Some words and expressions in this dictionary are described as *(informal)*. This means that you can use them when you are speaking to friends or people that you know well but that you should not use them in written work, official letters, etc.

▸ **in·for·mal·i·ty** /ˌɪnfɔrˈmælət̬i/ ***noun*** [C,U] (*pl.* **in·for·mal·i·ties**): *an atmosphere of informality* ▸ **in·for·mal·ly** ***adv.***: *Managers met informally* (= unofficially) *with a few employees.*

**in·form·ant** /ɪnˈfɔrmənt/ ***noun*** [C] a person who gives sb knowledge or information: *undercover agents and informants*

★**in·for·ma·tion** /ˌɪnfərˈmeɪʃn/ ***noun*** [U] **information (on/about sb/sth)** knowledge or facts: *For further information, please send for our brochure.* ◇ *Can you give me some information about Spanish classes?* ◇ *to feed information into a computer*

NOTE The word **information** is uncountable so you CANNOT say: *I need an information.* You can, however, talk about **a bit** or **piece** of information.

**in·for·ma·tion su·per·high·way** /ɪnfərˌmeɪʃn supərˈhaɪweɪ; ˈsupərhaɪweɪ/ ***noun*** [sing.] (*computing*) (*also* **superhighway**) a large electronic network such as the Internet, used for sending information such as sound, pictures and video quickly in digital form: *The information superhighway embraces computers, telephones and TVs, linking consumers with services and with each other across the globe.*

**infor,mation ,tech'nology** ***noun*** [U] (*abbr.* **IT**) the study or use of computer systems, etc. for collecting, storing and sending out all kinds of information

**in·form·a·tive** /ɪn'fɔrmət̬ɪv/ ***adj.*** giving useful knowledge or information OPP **uninformative**

**in·formed** /ɪn'fɔrmd/ ***adj.*** having knowledge or information about sth: *The radio keeps me well informed about what is happening.* ◇ *Consumers cannot make informed choices unless they are told all the facts.*

**in·form·er** /ɪn'fɔrmər/ ***noun*** [C] a person who gives the police, etc. information about what sb has done wrong

**in·fra·red** /ˌɪnfrə'rɛd/ ***adj.*** (used about light) that is produced by hot objects but cannot be seen: *infrared radiation* ◇ *an infrared lamp*

**in·fra·struc·ture** /'ɪnfrəˌstrʌktʃər/ ***noun*** [C,U, usually sing.] the basic structures and systems that are needed so that a country or an organization can work well, e.g. roads, transportation, etc.

**in·fre·quent** /ɪn'frikwənt/ ***adj.*** not happening often: *infrequent visits* ▸ **in·fre·quent·ly** ***adv.***

**in·fringe** /ɪn'frɪndʒ/ ***verb*** (*formal*)

PHR V **infringe on/upon sth** to reduce or limit sb's rights, freedom, etc.

▸ **in·fringe·ment** /-mənt/ ***noun*** [C,U]

**in·fu·ri·ate** /ɪn'fyʊrieɪt/ ***verb*** [T] to make sb very angry ▸ **in·fu·ri·at·ing** /-eɪt̬ɪŋ/ ***adj.***: *an infuriating habit* ▸ **in·fu·ri·at·ing·ly** ***adv.***

**in·gen·ious** /ɪn'dʒinyəs/ ***adj.*** **1** (used about a person) good at finding answers to problems or at thinking of new things **2** (used about a thing or an idea) that has been made or planned in an intelligent way, with new ideas: *an ingenious plan* ▸ **ingen·ious·ly** ***adv.*** ▸ **in·ge·nu·i·ty** /ˌɪndʒə'nuət̬i/ ***noun*** [U]

**in·grained** /ɪn'greɪnd/ ***adj.*** deeply fixed; difficult to change: *an ingrained attitude*

**in·gra·ti·ate** /ɪn'greɪʃieɪt/ ***verb*** [T] **ingratiate yourself (with sb)** to make yourself liked by doing or saying things that will please people, especially people who might be useful to you: *He was always trying to ingratiate himself with his teachers.* ▸ **ingra·ti·at·ing** ***adj.***: *an ingratiating smile* ▸ **in·gra·ti·at·ing·ly** ***adv.***

**in·grat·i·tude** /ɪn'grætətud/ ***noun*** [C] the state of not feeling or showing that you are grateful for sth: *Her help was met with ingratitude and unkindness.* OPP **gratitude**

**in·gre·di·ent** /ɪn'gridiənt/ ***noun*** [C] one of the items of food you need to make sth to eat: *The main ingredient of this drink is sugar.* ◇ (*figurative*) *The movie has all the ingredients of success.*

**in·hab·it** /ɪn'hæbət/ ***verb*** [T] to live in a place: *Are the Aleutian Islands inhabited?*

**in·hab·i·tant** /ɪn'hæbətənt/ ***noun*** [C, usually pl.] (*formal*) a person or animal that lives in a place: *the original inhabitants of North America* ➲ Look also at **population**.

**in·hale** /ɪn'heɪl/ ***verb*** [I,T] to breathe in: *to inhale smoke* OPP **exhale**

**in·hal·er** /ɪn'heɪlər/ ***noun*** [C] a small tube containing medicine that sb breathes in through his/her mouth in order to help him/her breathe more easily

**in·her·ent** /ɪn'hɛrənt; -'hɪr-/ ***adj.*** **inherent (in sb/sth)** that is a basic or permanent part of sb/sth and that cannot be removed: *The risk of collapse is inherent in any business.* ▸ **in·her·ent·ly** ***adv.***: *No matter how safe we make them, cars are inherently dangerous.*

**in·her·it** /ɪn'hɛrət/ ***verb*** [T] **inherit sth (from sb) 1** to receive property, money, etc. from sb who has died: *I inherited $12,000 from my grandmother.* **2** to receive a quality, disease, etc. from your parents or family: *She has inherited her father's gift for languages.*

**in·her·i·tance** /ɪn'hɛrətəns/ ***noun*** [C,U] property, money, etc. that you receive from sb who has died: *inheritance tax*

**in·hib·it** /ɪn'hɪbət/ ***verb*** [T] to prevent sth or make sth happen more slowly: *a drug to inhibit the growth of tumors*

**in·hib·it·ed** /ɪn'hɪbət̬əd/ ***adj.*** not able to express your feelings freely or naturally; not relaxed: *I feel inhibited if everyone watches me.* ◇ *inhibited about sex* OPP **uninhibited**

**in·hi·bi·tion** /ˌɪnhɪ'bɪʃn; ˌɪnɪ-/ ***noun*** [C,U] a feeling of being unable to express your feelings freely or naturally or to relax: *She has no inhibitions about speaking in front of a large group of people.*

**ˌin-'house** ***adj.***, ***adv.*** inside a company, an organization, etc.: *an in-house design studio* ◇ *The designs are all done in-house.*

**in·hu·man** /ɪn'hyumən/ ***adj.*** very cruel, not seeming to be human: *inhuman treatment*

**in·hu·mane** /ˌɪnhyu'meɪn/ ***adj.*** very cruel; not caring if people or animals suffer: *the inhumane conditions in which animals are kept in some zoos*

★**in·i·tial**[1] /ɪ'nɪʃl/ ***adj.*** (only *before* a noun) that is at the beginning; first: *My initial reaction was to refuse, but I later changed my mind.* ◇ *the initial stages of our survey*

★**in·i·tial**[2] /ɪ'nɪʃl/ ***noun*** [C, usually pl.] the first letter of a name: *Patricia Anne Morgan's initials are P. A. M.*

**in·i·tial**[3] /ɪ'nɪʃl/ ***verb*** [T] to mark or sign sth with your INITIALS[2]

**in·i·tial·ly** /ɪ'nɪʃl·i/ ***adv.*** at the beginning; at first: *I liked the job initially, but it soon got pretty boring.*

**inˌitial ˌpublic 'offering** ***noun*** [C] → IPO

**in·i·ti·ate** /ɪ'nɪʃieɪt/ ***verb*** [T] **1** (*formal*) to start sth: *to initiate a new training program* **2 initiate sb (into sth)** to bring sb into a group by means of a special ceremony or by giving him/her special knowledge: *to initiate somebody into a secret club* ▸ **in·i·ti·a·tion** /ɪˌnɪʃi'eɪʃn/ ***noun*** [C,U]

★**in·i·tia·tive** /ɪ'nɪʃət̬ɪv/ ***noun*** **1** [C] official action that is taken to solve a problem or improve a situation: *a new government initiative to help people start small businesses* **2** [U] the ability to see and do what needs to be done without help from others: *He'll never get the project started. He has no initiative.*

IDM **seize/take the initiative** to be first to do

I

sth: *Let's take the initiative and start organizing things now.*

★**in·ject** /ɪn'dʒɛkt/ ***verb*** [T] **1** to put a substance into sb/sth with a needle (syringe): *Scientists injected cancer cells into the mice.* **2** to add sth: *They injected a lot of money into the business.* ▸ **in·jec·tion** /ɪn'dʒɛkʃn/ ***noun*** [C,U] **injection (of sth) (into sb/sth)**: *an injection of $2 million into the company*

**in·junc·tion** /ɪn'dʒʌŋkʃn/ ***noun*** [C] **an injunction (against sb)** an official order from a court of law to do/not do sth: *The court* ***granted an injunction*** *against the defendants.* ➲ Look at **restraining order**.

★**in·jure** /'ɪndʒər/ ***verb*** [T] to harm or hurt a person, animal or part of the body: *David was badly injured in the accident.* ◇ *Three people were seriously injured.* ◇ *She fell and injured her back.* ➲ Look at the note at **hurt**.

★**in·jured** /'ɪndʒərd/ ***adj.*** **1** physically or mentally hurt: *an injured leg* **2 the injured** ***noun*** [pl.] people who have been hurt: *The injured were rushed to the hospital.*

★**in·ju·ry** /'ɪndʒəri/ ***noun*** [C,U] (*pl.* **in·ju·ries**) harm or hurt done to a person, animal or part of the body: *They escaped from the accident with only minor injuries.* ◇ *Injury to the head can be extremely dangerous.*

**in·jus·tice** /ɪn'dʒʌstəs/ ***noun*** [C,U] **1** unfairness; a lack of justice: *People are protesting about the injustice of the jury's verdict.* **2** an unfair action or situation: *economic and social injustices* ➲ noun **unjust**

★**ink** /ɪŋk/ ***noun*** [C,U] a colored liquid that is used for writing, drawing, etc.: *Please write in ink, not pencil.*

**in·kling** /'ɪŋklɪŋ/ ***noun*** [sing.] a slight feeling (about sth): *I had an inkling that something was wrong.*

**in·land¹** /'ɪnlənd/ ***adj.*** in the middle of a country away from the coast: *inland areas*

**in·land²** /ˌɪn'lænd/ ***adv.*** in or toward the middle of a country: *The hurricane will weaken as it moves farther inland.*

'**in-laws** ***noun*** [pl.] (*informal*) your husband's or wife's mother and father or other relatives: *My in-laws are coming to lunch on Sunday.*

ˌ**in-line 'skate** ***noun*** [C] = ROLLERBLADE ➲ picture at **skate**.

**in·mate** /'ɪnmeɪt/ ***noun*** [C] one of the people living in an institution such as a prison or mental hospital

**inn** /ɪn/ ***noun*** [C] a small hotel, usually in the country, that often also serves food and drinks

**in·nate** /ɪ'neɪt/ ***adj.*** being a natural quality of sb/sth: *innate ability*

★**in·ner** /'ɪnər/ ***adj.*** (only *before* a noun) **1** (of the) inside: *The inner ear is very delicate.* OPP **outer** **2** (used about a feeling, etc.) that you do not express or show to other people: *Everyone has inner doubts.*

ˌ**inner 'city** ***noun*** [C] (*pl.* **inner cities**) the poor parts of a large city that often have a lot of social problems: *inner-city schools*

**in·ner·most** /'ɪnərmoʊst/ ***adj.*** (only *before* a noun) **1** farthest from the outside **2** (used about a feeling, etc.) most secret or private: *She never told anyone her innermost thoughts.*

**in·ning** /'ɪnɪŋ/ ***noun*** [C] one of nine periods in a game of baseball in which each team has a turn to hit the ball (to bat) ➲ Look at the note at **baseball**.

★**in·no·cent** /'ɪnəsnt/ ***adj.*** **1 innocent (of sth)** not having done wrong; not guilty: *An innocent man was arrested by mistake.* ◇ *to be innocent of a crime* **2** not causing harm or intended to upset sb: *He got very aggressive when I asked an innocent question about his past.* **3** not knowing the bad things in life; believing everything you are told: *young and innocent* ◇ *She was so innocent as to believe that politicians never lie.* ▸ **in·no·cence** /-sns/ ***noun*** [U]: *The accused man protested his innocence throughout his trial.* OPP **guilt** ▸ **in·no·cent·ly** ***adv.***

**in·noc·u·ous** /ɪ'nɑkyuəs/ ***adj.*** (*formal*) not causing harm or intended to upset sb: *I thought it was an innocuous remark, but she got really upset.*

**in·no·vate** /'ɪnəveɪt/ ***verb*** [I] to introduce sth new; to change

**in·no·va·tion** /ˌɪnə'veɪʃn/ ***noun*** [C,U] the introduction of new things, ideas, etc., or something new that has been introduced: *technological innovations in industry* ◇ *a company with a reputation for innovation*

**in·no·va·tive** /'ɪnəveɪt̬ɪv/ ***adj.*** **1** (used about a company, etc.) introducing many new products and ideas **2** (used about a product, an idea, etc.) new; developed using new ways of thinking

**in·no·va·tor** /'ɪnəveɪt̬ər/ ***noun*** [C] a person, company, etc. that introduces changes

**in·nu·en·do** /ˌɪnyu'ɛndoʊ/ ***noun*** [C,U] (*pl.* **in·nu·en·does**; **in·nu·en·dos**) an indirect way of talking about sb/sth, usually suggesting sth bad or rude: *His speech was full of sexual innuendo.*

**in·nu·mer·a·ble** /ɪ'numərəbl/ ***adj.*** too many to be counted

**in·oc·u·late** /ɪ'nɑkyəleɪt/ ***verb*** [T] (*formal*) **inoculate sb (with sth) (against sth)** to inject sb with a mild form of a disease. This protects him/her from getting the serious form: *to be inoculated against tetanus* ➲ Look at **immunize** and **vaccinate**. ▸ **in·oc·u·la·tion** /ɪˌnɑkyə'leɪʃn/ ***noun*** [C,U]

**in·or·di·nate** /ɪn'ɔrdn·ət/ ***adj.*** (*formal*) much greater than usual or expected: *an inordinate amount of time* ▸ **in·or·di·nate·ly** ***adv.***

**in·or·gan·ic** /ˌɪnɔr'gænɪk/ ***adj.*** not made of or coming from living things: *Rocks and metals are inorganic substances.*

**in·pa·tient** /'ɪnpeɪʃnt/ ***noun*** [C] a person who goes to a hospital for medical treatment and stays in the hospital for at least one night ➲ Look at **outpatient**.

**in·put¹** /'ɪnpʊt/ ***noun*** [U] **1 in·put (into/to sth)** what you add to sth to make it better; what you put into sth: *We need some creative input from teachers into this book.* **2** information that is put into a computer: *The computer can process the input in just a few seconds.* ➲ Look at **output**.

**in·put²** /'ɪnpʊt/ ***verb*** [T] (*pres. part.* **in·put·ting**; *pt, pp* **in'put** or **in·put·ted**) to put information into a computer

**in·quest** /'ɪŋkwɛst/ ***noun*** [C] an official investigation that is held when the reason for sb's death is not clear: *to hold an inquest*

**in·quire** /ɪnˈkwaɪər/ ***verb*** (*formal*) [I,T] to ask for information about sth: *I inquired whether the plane had arrived yet.* ◇ *I am writing to inquire about your latest product.*

PHRV **inquire into sth** to study or investigate sth to find out all the facts: *The journalist inquired into the politician's financial affairs.*

**in·quir·ing** /ɪnˈkwaɪərɪŋ/ ***adj.*** interested in learning new things: *We should encourage children to have inquiring minds.*

★**in·quir·y** /ˈɪnkwəri; ɪnˈkwaɪəri/ ***noun*** (*pl.* **in·quir·ies**) **1** [C] **inquiry (about/concerning sb/sth)** (*formal*) a question that you ask about sth: *Thank you for your inquiry about our English language programs.* **2** [C] **inquiry (into sth)** an official investigation to find out about sth or why sth happened: *an inquiry into a plane crash* **3** [U] the act of asking about sth: *His financial dealings are our main area of inquiry.*

**in·quis·i·tive** /ɪnˈkwɪzət̬ɪv/ ***adj.*** very interested in learning about a lot of different things: *He's a very inquisitive child who loves to read.*

**the INS** /ˌaɪ ɛn ˈɛs/ ***noun*** [sing.] the Immigration and Naturalization Service; the government department that gives people permission to enter the U.S. ➲ Look at the note at **White House**.

**in·sane** /ɪnˈseɪn/ ***adj.*** **1** mentally ill or crazy **2** (*informal*) very foolish or stupid; not sensible: *You must be insane to leave your job before you've found another one.* ◇ *$4.00 for a cup of coffee? That's totally insane!* ➲ Look at the note at **crazy**. ▸ **in·sane·ly** ***adv.***: *insanely jealous* ▸ **in·san·i·ty** /ɪnˈsænət̬i/ ***noun*** [U]

**in·sa·tia·ble** /ɪnˈseɪʃəbl/ ***adj.*** not able to be satisfied; very great: *an insatiable desire for knowledge* ◇ *an insatiable appetite*

**in·scribe** /ɪnˈskraɪb/ ***verb*** [T] (*formal*) **inscribe A (on/in B)**; **inscribe B (with A)** to write or cut (carve) words on sth. You inscribe sth when you want it to be a permanent record: *The book was inscribed with the author's name.* ◇ *names inscribed on a trophy*

**in·scrip·tion** /ɪnˈskrɪpʃn/ ***noun*** [C] words that are written or cut on sth: *There was a Latin inscription on the tombstone.*

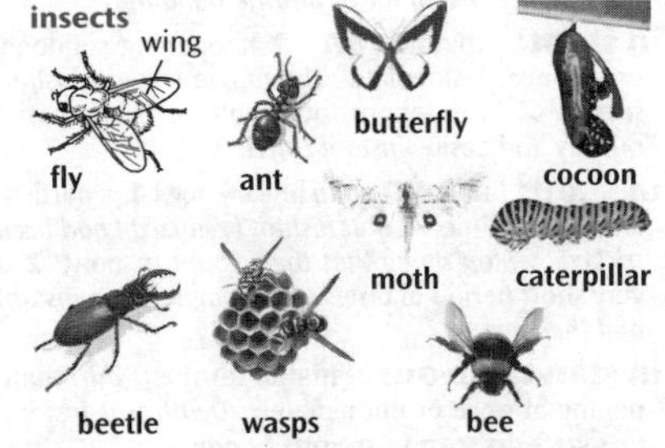


★**in·sect** /ˈɪnsɛkt/ ***noun*** [C] a small animal with six legs and a body which is divided into three parts: *Ants, flies, beetles, butterflies and mosquitoes are all insects.* ◇ *an insect bite/sting*

NOTE Some other small animals, e.g. spiders, are often also called insects although this is technically incorrect. A more informal word for **insect** is **bug**.

**in·sec·ti·cide** /ɪnˈsɛktəsaɪd/ ***noun*** [C,U] a substance that is used for killing insects ➲ Look at **pesticide**.

**in·se·cure** /ˌɪnsəˈkyʊr/ ***adj.*** **1** not supported very well; not safe or secure: *Is that ladder secure?* ◇ *The future of the company looks very insecure.* **2** **insecure (about sb/sth)** feeling anxious and not sure of yourself; not confident: *Some small children feel insecure away from their parents.* ▸ **in·se·cu·ri·ty** /ˌɪnsəˈkyʊrət̬i/ ***noun*** [C,U] (*pl.* **in·se·cu·ri·ties**) [U]: *Their aggressive behavior is really a sign of insecurity.* ◇ *fears and insecurities*

**in·sem·i·na·tion** /ɪnˌsɛməˈneɪʃn/ ***noun*** [U] the act of putting a male's cells (**sperm**) into a female in order to produce a baby ➲ Look also at **artificial insemination**.

**in·sen·si·tive** /ɪnˈsɛnsət̬ɪv/ ***adj.*** **1** not knowing or caring how another person feels and whether you have hurt or upset him/her: *to make an insensitive remark* **2** **insensitive (to sth)** not able to feel sth: *insensitive to pain/* ◇ *cold* ▸ **in·sen·si·tive·ly** ***adv.*** ▸ **in·sen·si·tiv·i·ty** /ɪnˌsɛnsəˈtɪvət̬i/ ***noun*** [U]

**in·sep·a·ra·ble** /ɪnˈsɛpərəbl/ ***adj.*** not able to be separated from sb/sth: *inseparable friends*

**in·sert**[1] /ɪnˈsərt/ ***verb*** [T] (*formal*) to put sth into sth or between two things: *Insert your money and then select an item.* ▸ **in·ser·tion** /ɪnˈsərʃn/ ***noun*** [C,U]

**in·sert**[2] /ˈɪnsərt/ ***noun*** [C] something that is put into sth else: *an advertising insert in a newspaper*

★**in·side**[1] /ɪnˈsaɪd/ ***adv.*** in or to the inner part or surface of sth: *We'd better stay inside until the rain stops.* ◇ *It's getting cold. Let's go inside.* ◇ *Take a look inside and see what's in it.*

★**in·side**[2] /ɪnˈsaɪd/ (*also informal* **inside of**) ***prep.*** **1** in or on the inner part or surface of sb/sth: *Is there anything inside the box?* ◇ *inside a building* **2** (used about time) in less than: *Your photos will be ready inside of an hour.* **3** (*slang*) in prison

★**in·side**[3] /ɪnˈsaɪd/ ***noun*** **1** [C] the inner part or surface of sth: *The insides of the windows need a good cleaning.* ◇ *The door was locked from the inside.* **2** [sing.] (*also* **insides** /ɪnˈsaɪdz/ [pl.]) (*informal*) the inner parts of sth, especially a body or a machine: *Have you ever seen the insides of a computer?*

IDM **inside out** **1** with the inner surface on the outside: *You've got your shirt on inside out.* **2** very well, in great detail: *She knows these streets inside out.*

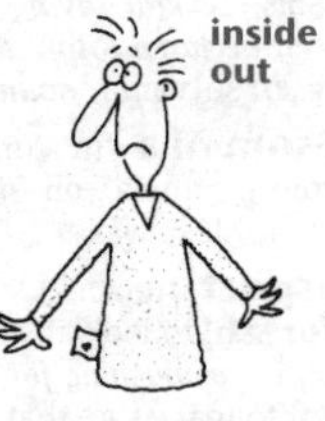


★**in·side**[4] /ˈɪnsaɪd/ ***adj.*** (only before a noun) **1** in or on the inner part or surface of sth: *the inside pocket of a jacket* ◇ *the inside pages of a newspaper* **2** (used about information, etc.) told secretly by sb who belongs

to a group, organization, etc.: *The robbers had some inside information about the bank's security system.*

**in·sid·er** /ˌɪnˈsaɪdər; ˈɪnsaɪdər/ ***noun*** [C] a person who is a member of a group or an organization

ˌ**insider ˈtrading** ***noun*** [U] the crime of buying or selling shares in a company with the help of information known only by those connected with the business

**in·sight** /ˈɪnsaɪt/ ***noun*** [C,U] **insight (into sth)** (an example of) understanding the true nature of sb/sth: *The book gives a good insight into the lives of the poor.* ◇ *You need insight into human nature for this job.*

**in·sig·nif·i·cant** /ˌɪnsɪgˈnɪfɪkənt/ ***adj.*** of little value or importance: *an insignificant detail* ▸ **in·sig·nif·i·cance** /-kəns/ ***noun*** [U] ▸ **in·sig·nif·i·cant·ly** ***adv.***

**in·sin·cere** /ˌɪnsɪnˈsɪr/ ***adj.*** not meaning what you say; not truthful; not sincere: *His apology sounded insincere.* ▸ **in·sin·cere·ly** ***adv.*** ▸ **in·sin·cer·i·ty** /ˌɪnsɪnˈsɛrət̬i/ ***noun*** [U]

**in·sin·u·ate** /ɪnˈsɪnyueɪt/ ***verb*** [T] to suggest sth unkind in an indirect way: *She seemed to be insinuating that our work was below average.* ▸ **in·sin·u·a·tion** /ɪnˌsɪnyuˈeɪʃn/ ***noun*** [C,U]: *to make insinuations about sb's honesty*

**in·sip·id** /ɪnˈsɪpəd/ ***adj.*** not interesting or exciting: *insipid conversation* ◇ *an insipid flavor*

★**in·sist** /ɪnˈsɪst/ ***verb*** [I,T] **1 insist (on sth/on doing sth)** to say or demand that you must have or do sth or that sb else must do sth: *He always insists on the best.* ◇ *Her parents insist that she come home before midnight.* ◇ *Dick insisted on coming too.* ◇ *"Have another piece of cake." "Oh all right, if you insist."* **2 insist (on sth)** to say firmly that sth is true (when sb does not believe you): *She insisted on her innocence.* ◇ *James insisted that the accident wasn't his fault.*

**in·sis·tent** /ɪnˈsɪstənt/ ***adj.*** saying or demanding that you must have or do sth or that sb else must do sth: *Local residents are insistent on having the hazardous waste moved out of the area.* ◇ (*figurative*) *We could not ignore the insistent ringing of the telephone.* ▸ **in·sis·tence** /-əns/ ***noun*** [U] ▸ **in·sis·tent·ly** ***adv.***

**in·so·lent** /ˈɪnsələnt/ ***adj.*** lacking respect; rude: *insolent behavior* ▸ **in·so·lence** ***noun*** [U] ▸ **in·so·lent·ly** ***adv.***

**in·sol·vent** /ɪnˈsɑlvənt/ ***adj.*** (*formal*) (used about a bank, etc.) not having enough money to pay its debts: *Several savings and loan associations have been declared insolvent.* OPP **solvent** ▸ **in·sol·ven·cy** /ɪnˈsɑlvənsi/ ***noun*** [C,U] (*pl.* **in·sol·ven·cies**)

**in·som·ni·a** /ɪnˈsɑmniə/ ***noun*** [U] if you suffer from insomnia you find it difficult to get to sleep and to sleep well

**in·spect** /ɪnˈspɛkt/ ***verb*** [T] **1 inspect sb/sth (for sth)** to look at sth closely or in great detail: *to inspect a machine for faults* **2** to make an official visit to make sure that rules are being obeyed, work is being done correctly, etc.: *All restaurants should be inspected regularly.* ▸ **in·spec·tion** /ɪnˈspɛkʃn/ ***noun*** [C,U]: *Officials carried out inspections of all the airline's planes.* ◇ ***On inspection**, the passport turned out to be false.*

**in·spec·tor** /ɪnˈspɛktər/ ***noun*** [C] **1** an official who inspects(2) sth: *a health and safety inspector* **2** a police officer of middle rank

**in·spi·ra·tion** /ˌɪnspəˈreɪʃn/ ***noun*** [C,U] **inspiration (to/for sb)**; **inspiration (to do sth)** (a person or thing that causes) a feeling of wanting and being able to do sth good, create a work of art, etc.: *The beauty of the mountains was a great source of inspiration to the writer.* ◇ *Her example has been an inspiration to many younger women.*

**in·spire** /ɪnˈspaɪər/ ***verb*** [T] **1** to give sb a feeling of wanting and being able to do sth good, create a work of art, etc.: *His novel was inspired by his relationship with his first wife.* **2 inspire sb (with sth)**; **inspire sth (in sb)** to make sb feel, think, etc. sth: *to be inspired with enthusiasm* ◇ *The guide's nervous manner did not inspire much confidence in us.* ▸ **in·spir·ing** /ɪnˈspaɪərɪŋ/ ***adj.***: *It was not a very inspiring speech.* OPP **uninspiring**

**in·spired** /ɪnˈspaɪərd/ ***adj.*** produced with the help of inspiration: *The pianist gave an inspired performance.* OPP **uninspired**

**in·sta·bil·i·ty** /ˌɪnstəˈbɪlət̬i/ ***noun*** [U] the state of being likely to change: *political instability* ➲ adjective **unstable**

**in·stall** /ɪnˈstɔl/ ***verb*** [T] **1** to put a piece of equipment, etc. in place so that it is ready to be used: *We are waiting to have our new washing machine installed.* ◇ *to install software on a computer* **2** put sb/sth or yourself in a position or place: *He was installed as chairperson yesterday.* ▸ **in·stal·la·tion** /ˌɪnstəˈleɪʃn/ ***noun*** [C,U]

**in·stall·ment** /ɪnˈstɔlmənt/ ***noun*** [C] **1** one of the regular payments that you make for sth. People buy sth in installments when they cannot or do not want to pay the whole amount at once. **2** a single part of a book, television show, etc. that is published or shown regularly over a period of time: *Don't miss next week's exciting installment.*

★**in·stance** /ˈɪnstəns/ ***noun*** [C] an example or case (of sth): *There have been several instances of racial attacks in the area.* ◇ *In most instances the drug has no side effects.*

IDM **for instance** for example: *There are several interesting places to visit around here. Georgetown, for instance, has a lot of historic buildings.*

**in·stant**[1] /ˈɪnstənt/ ***adj.*** **1** happening suddenly or at once; immediate: *The movie was an instant success.* **2** (used about food) able to be prepared quickly and easily: *instant coffee*

**in·stant**[2] /ˈɪnstənt/ ***noun*** [usually sing.] **1** a particular point in time: *At that instant I realized I had been tricked.* ◇ *Stop doing that this instant* (= now)*!* **2** a very short period of time: *Alex thought for an instant and then agreed.*

**in·stan·ta·ne·ous** /ˌɪnstənˈteɪniəs/ ***adj.*** happening at once or immediately: *Death was instantaneous.* ▸ **in·stan·ta·ne·ous·ly** ***adv.***

**in·stant·ly** /ˈɪnstəntli/ ***adv.*** without delay; immediately: *I asked him a question and he replied instantly.*

ˌ**instant ˈreplay** ***noun*** [C] a short part of a sports game on television that is shown again, often at a slower speed, so that people can see an exciting or important moment again

★**in·stead** /ɪnˈstɛd/ ***adv.*** **instead (of sb/sth)** in the place of sb/sth: *I couldn't go so my husband went instead.* ◇ *There's nothing on TV, so let's play a game instead.* ◇ *You should play tennis instead of just watching it on TV.* ◇ *Could I come at 8:00 instead of 7:30?*

**in·step** /ˈɪnstɛp/ ***noun*** [C] **1** the middle part of the foot that forms an arch **2** the part of a shoe that covers this part

**in·sti·gate** /ˈɪnstəgeɪt/ ***verb*** [T] (*formal*) to make sth start to happen ▸ **in·sti·ga·tion** /ˌɪnstəˈgeɪʃn/ ***noun*** [U]

**in·still** /ɪnˈstɪl/ ***verb*** [T] **instill sth (in/into sb)** to make sb think or feel sth: *Parents should try to instill a sense of responsibility into their children.*

**in·stinct** /ˈɪnstɪŋkt/ ***noun*** [C,U] the natural force that causes a person or animal to behave in a certain way without thinking or learning about it: *Birds learn to fly by instinct.* ◇ *I didn't stop to think. I just acted on instinct.* ▸ **in·stinc·tive** /ɪnˈstɪŋktɪv/ ***adj.***: *Your instinctive reaction is to run from danger.* ▸ **in·stinc·tive·ly** ***adv.***

★**in·sti·tute**[1] /ˈɪnstətut/ ***noun*** [C] an academic, etc. organization: *the Massachusetts Institute of Technology*

**in·sti·tute**[2] /ˈɪnstətut/ ***verb*** [T] (*formal*) to set up or start a system, course of action, etc.: *The government has instituted a new job training program.*

★**in·sti·tu·tion** /ˌɪnstəˈtuʃn/ ***noun*** [C] **1** a large organization such as a bank, a university, etc.: *the financial institutions on Wall Street* ◇ *an educational institution* **2** a building where certain people with special needs live and are taken care of: *a mental institution* (= a hospital for the mentally ill) **3** a social custom or habit that has existed for a long time: *the institution of marriage* **4** (*formal*) the act of introducing a system, policy, etc., or of starting a process: *the institution of new safety procedures* ▸ **in·sti·tu·tion·al** /-ʃənl/ ***adj.***

**in·struct** /ɪnˈstrʌkt/ ***verb*** [T] **1 instruct sb (to do sth)** to give an order to sb; to tell sb to do sth: *The soldiers were instructed to shoot above the heads of the crowd.* **2 instruct sb (in sth)** (*formal*) to teach: *Children should be instructed in traffic safety.*

**in·struc·tion** /ɪnˈstrʌkʃn/ ***noun*** **1** [U] **instruction (in sth)** teaching or being taught: *We offer instruction in all styles of dance.* **2** [C, usually pl.] an order or direction that tells you what to do or how to do sth: *The guard was under strict instructions not to let anyone in.* **3 instructions** [pl.] information on how you should use sth, do sth, etc.: *Read the instructions carefully.* ◇ *to follow the instructions*

**in·struc·tive** /ɪnˈstrʌktɪv/ ***adj.*** giving useful information ▸ **in·struc·tive·ly** ***adv.***

**in·struc·tor** /ɪnˈstrʌktər/ ***noun*** [C] a person who teaches: *a driving instructor* ◇ *an instructor at the college*

★**in·stru·ment** /ˈɪnstrəmənt/ ***noun*** [C] **1** a tool that is used for doing a particular job or task: *surgical instruments* ➲ Look at the note at **tool**. **2** something that is used for playing music: *"What instrument do you play?" "The violin."*

NOTE **Musical instruments** may be **stringed** (*violins, guitars*, etc.), **brass** (*horns, trumpets*, etc.) or **woodwind** (*flutes, clarinets*, etc.). **Percussion** instruments include *drums* and *cymbals*.

**3** something that is used for measuring speed, fuel levels, etc. in a car, plane or ship: *the instrument panel of an airplane*

**in·stru·men·tal** /ˌɪnstrəˈmɛntl/ ***adj.*** **1** (not before a noun) **instrumental in doing sth** helping to make sth happen: *She was instrumental in getting him the job.* **2** for musical instruments, without voices: *instrumental music*

**in·sub·or·di·na·tion** /ˌɪnsəˌbɔrdn·ˈeɪʃn/ ***noun*** [U] refusing to obey orders or instructions, especially in the army, etc. ▸ **in·sub·or·di·nate** /ˌɪnsəˈbɔrdn·ət/ ***adj.***

**in·sub·stan·tial** /ˌɪnsəbˈstænʃl/ ***adj.*** not large, solid or strong: *a cabin built of insubstantial materials* OPP **substantial**

**in·suf·fi·cient** /ˌɪnsəˈfɪʃnt/ ***adj.*** **insufficient (for sth/to do sth)** not enough: *We were given insufficient time for the test.*

**in·su·lar** /ˈɪnsələr/ ***adj.*** not interested in, or able to accept, new people or different ideas ▸ **in·su·lar·i·ty** /ˌɪnsəˈlærət̮i/ ***noun*** [U]

**in·su·late** /ˈɪnsəleɪt/ ***verb*** [T] to protect or cover sth with a material that prevents electricity, heat or sound from passing through: *You can save a lot of money on heating if your house is well insulated.*

**in·su·la·tion** /ˌɪnsəˈleɪʃn/ ***noun*** [U] **1** the material used for insulating sth **2** the process of insulating or the state of being insulated: *Foam rubber provides good insulation.*

**in·su·lin** /ˈɪnsələn/ ***noun*** [U] a chemical substance produced in the body that controls the amount of sugar the blood takes up; a similar artificial substance given to people whose bodies do not produce enough naturally: *insulin-dependent diabetes*

★**in·sult**[1] /ɪnˈsʌlt/ ***verb*** [T] to speak or act rudely to sb: *I felt very insulted when I didn't even get an answer to my letter.*

★**in·sult**[2] /ˈɪnsʌlt/ ***noun*** [C] a rude remark or action: *The drivers were yelling insults at each other.* ◇ *Some television commercials are an insult to people's intelligence.*

**in·sult·ing** /ˈɪnsʌltɪŋ/ ***adj.*** rude or offensive: *A lot of women find his behavior very insulting.*

★**in·sur·ance** /ɪnˈʃʊrəns; -ˈʃɔr-/ ***noun*** **1** [U] a contract in which, in return for regular payment, a company or the state agrees to pay a sum of money if sth (e.g. illness, death, loss of or damage to property) happens to sb: *Farmers should always have insurance against crop damage.* ◇ *They had no insurance on their house when it burned down.* ◇ *Our roof was blown off in the storm, but our insurance paid for it.*

NOTE We **take out** an **insurance policy**. An **insurance premium** is the regular amount you pay to the insurance company. We can take out **life**, **health** (or **medical**), **car** (or **auto**), **travel** and **homeowners' insurance**.



I

**2** [U] the business of providing INSURANCE (1) contracts: *He works in insurance.*

**in·sure** /ɪnˈʃʊr; ɪnˈʃɔr/ *verb* [T] **1 insure sb/sth (against sth)** to take out or to provide insurance: *They insured the painting for $10,000 against damage or theft.* ◇ *Are you insured against accident and medical expenses on your trip?* **2** = ENSURE

**in·sur·mount·a·ble** /ˌɪnsərˈmaʊntəbl/ *adj.* (*formal*) (used about a problem, etc.) impossible to solve

**in·sur·rec·tion** /ˌɪnsəˈrɛkʃn/ *noun* [C,U] violent action against the rulers of a country or the government

**in·tact** /ɪnˈtækt/ *adj.* complete; not damaged: *Very few of the buildings remained intact after the earthquake.*

**in·take** /ˈɪnteɪk/ *noun* [C, usually sing.] (used about food, liquid, air, etc.) the amount that sb/sth takes in or the process of taking it in: *If you're driving, you should watch your alcohol intake carefully.*

I

**in·tan·gi·ble** /ɪnˈtændʒəbl/ *adj.* (used about a quality or an idea) difficult to describe, understand or explain

**in·te·gral** /ˈɪntəgrəl/ *adj.* essential (in order to make sth complete): *Lab work is an integral part of the course.*

**in·te·grate** /ˈɪntəgreɪt/ *verb* **1** [T] to end a system of separating people of different races in a place: *plans to integrate public housing in the city* ➲ Look also at **segregate** and **desegregate**. **2** [I,T] **integrate (sb) (into sth/with sth)** to join in and become part of a group or community or to make sb do this: *The school aims to integrate hearing-impaired students into regular classes.* ➲ Look at **segregate**. **3** [T] **integrate sth (into sth)**; **integrate A and B/integrate A with B** to join things so that they become one thing or fit together: *The architect integrated our ideas into the plans for the house.* ▸ **in·te·gra·tion** /ˌɪntəˈgreɪʃn/ *noun* [U]: *racial integration* ➲ Look at **segregation** and **desegregation**.

**in·teg·ri·ty** /ɪnˈtɛgrət̬i/ *noun* [U] the quality of being honest and having firm moral ideas: *He's a person of courage and integrity.*

**in·tel·lect** /ˈɪntəlɛkt/ *noun* [C,U] the power of the mind to think and to learn

**in·tel·lec·tu·al**[1] /ˌɪntəˈlɛktʃuəl/ *adj.* (usually *before* a noun) using or able to use the power of the mind: *The boy's intellectual development was very advanced for his age.* ◇ *intellectual people/interests/discussions*

**in·tel·lec·tu·al**[2] /ˌɪntəˈlɛktʃuəl/ *noun* [C] a person who is interested in ideas, literature, art, etc.: *The café was a well-known meeting place for artists and intellectuals.* ▸ **in·tel·lec·tu·al·ly** *adv.*

★**in·tel·li·gence** /ɪnˈtɛlədʒəns/ *noun* [U] **1** the ability to understand, learn and think: *Examinations are not necessarily the best way to measure intelligence.* ◇ *a person of normal intelligence* ◇ *an intelligence test* **2** important information about an enemy country: *The army gathered intelligence about the enemy's strength.*

★**in·tel·li·gent** /ɪnˈtɛlədʒənt/ *adj.* having or showing intelligence: *All their kids are very intelligent.* ◇ *an intelligent question* OPP **unintelligent** A more informal word for intelligent is **smart**. ▸ **in·tel·li·gent·ly** *adv.*

**in·tel·li·gi·ble** /ɪnˈtɛlədʒəbl/ *adj.* (used especially about speech or writing) possible or easy to understand OPP **unintelligible**

★**in·tend** /ɪnˈtɛnd/ *verb* [T] **1 intend (to do sth)** to plan or mean to do sth: *I spent more money than I had intended.* ◇ *I intended to call, but I totally forgot.* ◇ *I certainly don't intend to wait here all day!* ➲ noun intention **2 intend sth for sb/sth**; **intend sth as sth** (often passive) to plan, mean or make sth for a particular person or purpose: *You shouldn't have read that letter – it wasn't intended for you.* ◇ *This dictionary is intended for intermediate learners of English.* ◇ *His remark was not intended as an insult.* **3 intend sth to do sth**; **intend for sb to do sth** to plan or mean that sb/sth should do sth: *The show was not the success its writers had intended it to be.* ◇ *I never intended for you to do all the work.*

**in·tense** /ɪnˈtɛns/ *adj.* very great, strong or serious: *intense heat* ◇ *intense anger* ◇ *an intense* (= very serious) *young man* ▸ **in·tense·ly** *adv.*: *They obviously dislike each other intensely.* ▸ **in·ten·si·ty** /-sət̬i/ *noun* [U]: *I wasn't prepared for the intensity of his reaction to the news.*

**in·ten·si·fy** /ɪnˈtɛnsəfaɪ/ *verb* (*pres. part.* **in·ten·si·fy·ing**; *3rd person sing. pres.* **in·ten·si·fies**; *pt, pp* **in·ten·si·fied**) [I,T] to become or to make sth greater or stronger: *The government has intensified its anti-smoking campaign.*

**in·ten·sive** /ɪnˈtɛnsɪv/ *adj.* concentrated on a particular activity or area within a limited amount of time: *an intensive investigation* ◇ *The course only lasted a week, but it was very intensive.* ▸ **in·ten·sive·ly** *adv.*

**in,tensive 'care** *noun* [U] special care for patients who are very seriously sick or injured (or the department that gives this care): *Your son has been seriously hurt and is in intensive care.*

**in·tent**[1] /ɪnˈtɛnt/ *noun* [C,U] (*formal*) what sb intends or plans to do; intention: *He was arrested and charged with assault with intent to murder.*

**in·tent**[2] /ɪnˈtɛnt/ *adj.* **1** showing great attention: *He listened to the whole story with an intent expression on his face.* **2 intent on/upon sth/doing sth** determined to do sth or concentrating on sth: *He's always been intent on making a lot of money.* ◇ *She was so intent upon her work that she didn't hear me come in.* ▸ **in·tent·ly** *adv.*

★**in·ten·tion** /ɪnˈtɛnʃn/ *noun* [C,U] what sb intends or means to do; a plan or purpose: *It's not clear what the enemy's intentions are.* ◇ *Our intention was to leave early in the morning.* ◇ *I have no intention of staying indoors on a nice sunny day like this.*

**in·ten·tion·al** /ɪnˈtɛnʃənl/ *adj.* done on purpose, not by chance: *It was an intentional attempt to manipulate the news media.* ◇ *victims of intentional discrimination* OPP **unintentional** ➲ Look also at **deliberate**. It is similar in meaning. ▸ **in·ten·tion·al·ly** /-ʃənəli/ *adv.*: *I can't believe the boys broke the window intentionally.*

**in·ter·act** /ˌɪntərˈækt/ *verb* [I] **1** (used about people) to communicate or mix in a way that has an influence or effect on sb else: *She is studying the* *way babies interact with each other.* **2** (of two things) to have an effect on each other

**in·ter·ac·tion** /ˌɪntərˈækʃn/ ***noun*** [C,U] (an example of) working together or mixing: *An interaction of two chemicals produced the explosion.* ◇ *There is a need for greater interaction among the different departments.*

**in·ter·ac·tive** /ˌɪntərˈæktɪv/ ***adj.*** (*technical*) (used about computers) involving or allowing direct two-way communication between the computer and the person using it: *interactive computer games*

**in·ter·cept** /ˌɪntərˈsɛpt/ ***verb*** [T] to stop or catch sb or sth that is moving from one place to another: *Agents intercepted several messages from the drug dealer to his supplier.* ▶ **in·ter·cep·tion** /ˌɪntərˈsɛpʃn/ ***noun*** [C,U]

**in·ter·change·a·ble** /ˌɪntərˈtʃeɪndʒəbl/ ***adj.*** able to be used in place of each other without making any difference: *Are these two words interchangeable?* ▶ **in·ter·change·a·bly** ***adv.***

**in·ter·com** /ˈɪntərkɑm/ ***noun*** [C] an electrical system for communication between people in different parts of a factory, an airplane, etc.: *Please try to contact Mr. Pearson on/over the intercom.*

**in·ter·con·nect** /ˌɪntərkəˈnɛkt/ ***verb*** [I] to be connected or linked ▶ **in·ter·con·nect·ed** ***adj.***

**in·ter·con·ti·nen·tal** /ˌɪntərˌkɑntəˈnɛntl; -ˌkɑntnˈɛntl/ ***adj.*** between continents: *intercontinental flights*

**in·ter·course** /ˈɪntərkɔrs/ ***noun*** [U] = SEX (3)

**in·ter·de·pend·ent** /ˌɪntərdɪˈpɛndənt/ ***adj.*** depending on each other: *Exercise and good health are generally interdependent.* ▶ **in·ter·de·pend·ence** /-əns/ ***noun*** [U]

★**in·ter·est**[1] /ˈɪntrəst/ ***noun***

➤ WANTING TO KNOW MORE **1** [U, sing.] **an interest (in sb/sth)** a desire to learn or hear more about sb/sth or to be involved with sb/sth: *She's starting to show a great interest in politics.* ◇ *I wish he'd take more interest in his kids.* ◇ *Don't lose interest now!*

➤ HOBBY **2** [C] something that you enjoy doing or learning about: *Tell me about your interests and hobbies.*

➤ ATTRACTION **3** [U] the quality that makes sb curious or attracts sb's attention: *I thought this article might be of interest to you.*

➤ ADVANTAGE **4** [C] something that gives a benefit, profit or advantage to sb: *We have your interests at heart.*

➤ SHARE IN BUSINESS **5** [C] a legal right to share in a business, etc., especially in its profits: *When he retired, he sold his interests in the company.*

➤ MONEY **6** [U] **interest (on sth)** the money that you earn from investments or that you pay for borrowing money: *If you invest your capital wisely, it will earn a lot of interest.* ◇ *We're paying 10% interest on our mortgage right now.* ◇ *The interest rate has never been so high/low.* ◇ *Some companies offer interest-free loans.*

IDM **conflict of interest** → CONFLICT[1]

**in sb's interest(s)** to sb's advantage: *He claimed to be acting in the public interest when he lied in court.*

**in the interest(s) of sth** in order to achieve or protect sth: *In the interest(s) of safety, please fasten your seat belts.*

★**in·ter·est**[2] /ˈɪntrəst/ ***verb*** [T] **1** to make sb want to learn or hear more about sth or to become involved in sth: *Politics is a subject that interests me greatly.* **2** to make sb want to buy, have or do sth: *Can I interest you in our new product line?*

★**in·ter·est·ed** /ˈɪntrəstəd; ˈɪntərɛstəd/ ***adj.*** **1** (not before a noun) **interested (in sth/sb)** wanting to know or hear about sth/sb; or to do or achieve sth: *They weren't interested in my news at all!* ◇ *I was interested to hear that you have a new job. Where is it?* ◇ *All he's interested in is money.* OPP **uninterested** **2** (only *before* a noun) involved in or affected by (a particular situation, etc.): *I think they should have talked to the interested parties* (= people/groups) *before they made that decision.* OPP **disinterested**

★**in·ter·est·ing** /ˈɪntrəstɪŋ; ˈɪntərɛstɪŋ/ ***adj.*** enjoyable and entertaining to do, think about, talk to, etc.; holding your attention: *an interesting person/book/idea/job* ◇ *It's always interesting to hear about other cultures.* OPP **uninteresting** ▶ **in·ter·est·ing·ly** ***adv.***

**in·ter·face**[1] /ˈɪntərfeɪs/ ***noun*** [C] **1** (*computing*) the way a computer program shows information to a user or receives information from a user, and in particular the way the screen looks: *the user interface* **2** (*computing*) an electrical connection or program that joins one device or system to another: *the interface between computer and printer* **3 interface (between A and B)** (*formal*) the point where two subjects, systems, etc. meet and affect each other: *the interface between manufacturing and sales*

**in·ter·face**[2] /ˈɪntərfeɪs/ ***verb*** [I,T] **interface (sth) (with sth); interface A and B** (*computing*) to be connected with sth using an interface; to connect sth in this way: *The new system interfaces with existing telephone equipment.*

**in·ter·fere** /ˌɪntərˈfɪr/ ***verb*** [I] **1 interfere (in sth)** to try to take part in sb's affairs, etc. when you and your help are not wanted: *You shouldn't interfere – let your kids make their own decisions.* **2 interfere (with sb/sth)** to prevent sth or slow down the progress that sb/sth makes: *Every time the telephone rings, it interferes with my work.* **3 interfere (with sth)** to touch or alter sth without permission: *Many people feel that scientists shouldn't interfere with nature.*

**in·ter·fer·ence** /ˌɪntərˈfɪrəns/ ***noun*** [U] **1 interference (in/with sth)** the act of interfering: *I left home because I couldn't stand my parents' interference in my life.* **2** something, such as other signals, that prevents equipment from receiving clear radio, television or telephone signals

**in·ter·im**[1] /ˈɪntərɪm/ ***noun***

IDM **in the interim** in the time between two things happening

**in·ter·im**[2] /ˈɪntərɪm/ ***adj.*** (only *before* a noun) not final or lasting; temporary: *an interim arrangement* (= before sth definite can be decided)

★**in·te·ri·or**[1] /ɪnˈtɪriər/ ***adj.*** (only *before* a noun) inner; on the inside: *interior walls* ◇ *The picture showed an interior view of the house.*

★**in·te·ri·or**[2] /ɪnˈtɪriər/ ***noun*** [C, usually sing.] the inner part; inside: *I'd love to see the interior of their house.* OPP **exterior**

I

**the In'terior Department** *noun* [sing.] the U.S. government department that is in charge of the country's natural resources and the land that the government owns ➲ Look at the note at **White House**.

**in,terior de'signer** *noun* [C] a person whose job is to choose the colors, furniture, carpets, etc., to decorate the inside of a house ▶ **in,terior de'sign** *noun* [U]

**in·ter·jec·tion** /ˌɪntərˈdʒɛkʃn/ *noun* [C] **1** (*formal*) something you say that interrupts sb else **2** (*grammar*) a word or phrase that is used as an expression of surprise, pain, pleasure, etc. (e.g. Oh!, Hey! or Wow!) ➲ Look at **exclamation**.

**in·ter·lude** /ˈɪntərlud/ *noun* [C] a short period of time when an entertainment or activity stops for a break; an interval: *There was a brief interlude in the fighting.*

**in·ter·mar·riage** /ˌɪntərˈmærɪdʒ/ *noun* [U] marriage between people of different races, religions, etc.

**in·ter·me·di·ar·y** /ˌɪntərˈmidiˌɛri/ *noun* [C] (*pl.* **in·ter·me·di·ar·ies**) a person who passes communications between two people or groups, usually in order to help them reach an agreement

**in·ter·me·di·ate** /ˌɪntərˈmidiət/ *adj.* **1** coming between two people or things in position, level, etc. **2** between two stages (beginning and advanced): *an intermediate student/class/course/book/level*

**in·ter·mi·na·ble** /ɪnˈtərmənəbl/ *adj.* lasting for a very long time and therefore boring or annoying: *an interminable delay/wait/speech* SYN **endless** ▶ **in·ter·mi·na·bly** /-bli/ *adv.*

**in·ter·mis·sion** /ˌɪntərˈmɪʃn/ *noun* [C] a break during a play, concert, etc.

**in·ter·mit·tent** /ˌɪntərˈmɪtnt/ *adj.* stopping for a while and then starting again: *There will be intermittent showers.* ▶ **in·ter·mit·tent·ly** *adv.*

**in·tern¹** /ˈɪntərn/ *noun* [C] **1** a doctor who has finished studying in medical school and is receiving practical training in a hospital **2** a person, especially a student, who is working somewhere for a short time in order to learn about a particular job or career ➲ noun **in·tern·ship**

**in·tern²** /ɪnˈtərn/ *verb* [T] (*formal*) to keep sb in prison, especially for political reasons or during a war ▶ **in·tern·ment** /ɪnˈtərnmənt/ *noun* [U]

★**in·ter·nal** /ɪnˈtərnl/ *adj.* **1** of or on the inside (of a place, person or object): *He was rushed to the hospital with internal injuries.* **2** happening or existing inside a particular organization, country, etc.: *The police department conducted an internal investigation.* ◇ *Internal documents showed evidence of bribery.* OPP The opposite for all senses is **external**.

**in·ter·nal·ly** /ɪnˈtərnl·i/ *adv.* on the inside: *This medication is not to be taken internally* (= not to be swallowed).

**the In,ternal 'Revenue ,Service** *noun* [sing.] (*U.S.*) = IRS

★**in·ter·na·tion·al** /ˌɪntərˈnæʃənl/ *adj.* involving two or more countries: *an international agreement/flight/competition* ◇ *international trade/law* ▶ **in·ter·na·tion·al·ly** *adv.*

★**the In·ter·net** /ˈɪntərnɛt/ (*also informal* **the Net**) *noun* [sing.] the international system of computers that makes it possible for you to see information from around the world on your computer and to send information to other computers: *I read about this on the Internet.* ➲ Look at the note at **White House**.

**,Internet ca'fé** (*also* **,Internet ca'fe**) (*also* **'cyberca,fé**) *noun* [C] a place where you can pay to use a computer connected to the Internet and also buy a cup of coffee, other drinks, sandwiches, etc.

**in·tern·ship** /ˈɪntərnʃɪp/ *noun* [C] **1** a period of time when sb, especially a student, works in order to learn about a particular career, or the job that he/she does during that time: *I'm applying for an internship at a software company.* ◇ *a paid/an unpaid internship* **2** a job that an advanced student of medicine, whose training is nearly finished, does in a hospital to get more practical experience

★**in·ter·pret** /ɪnˈtərprət/ *verb* **1** [T] **interpret sth (as sth)** to explain or understand the meaning of sth: *I don't know how to interpret her behavior.* ◇ *How would you interpret this part of the poem?* **2** [I] to translate what sb is saying into another language: *He'll need somebody to interpret for him.*

★**in·ter·pre·ta·tion** /ɪnˌtərprəˈteɪʃn/ *noun* [C,U] **1** an explanation or understanding of sth: *What's your interpretation of these statistics?* **2** the way an actor or a musician chooses to perform or understand a character or piece of music: *The actor's interpretation of Hamlet was severely criticized.*

**in·ter·pret·er** /ɪnˈtərprət̬ər/ *noun* [C] a person whose job is to translate what sb is saying immediately into another language: *The president spoke through an interpreter.* ➲ Look at **translator**.

**in·ter·ra·cial** /ˌɪntərˈreɪʃl/ *adj.* involving people of different races: *interracial dating and marriage*

**in·ter·re·lat·ed** /ˌɪntərɪˈleɪt̬əd/ *adj.* connected with each other

**in·ter·ro·gate** /ɪnˈtɛrəgeɪt/ *verb* [T] **interrogate sb (about sth)** to ask sb questions in a thorough and sometimes aggressive way (in order to get information): *The prisoner was interrogated for six hours.* ▶ **in·ter·ro·ga·tor** *noun* [C]

**in·ter·ro·ga·tion** /ɪnˌtɛrəˈgeɪʃn/ *noun* [C,U] the time when a person is interrogated: *The interrogations took place in a small underground room.* ◇ *The prisoner was led away for interrogation.*

**in·ter·rog·a·tive¹** /ˌɪntəˈrɑgət̬ɪv/ *adj.* **1** (*formal*) asking a question; having the form of a question: *an interrogative tone/gesture/remark* **2** (*grammar*) used in questions: *an interrogative sentence/pronoun/determiner/adverb*

**in·ter·rog·a·tive²** /ˌɪntəˈrɑgət̬ɪv/ *noun* [C] (*grammar*) a word used to make a question: *"Who" "what" and "where" are interrogatives.*

★**in·ter·rupt** /ˌɪntəˈrʌpt/ *verb* **1** [I,T] **interrupt (sb/sth) (with sth)** to make sb stop speaking or doing sth by saying or doing sth yourself: *I'm sorry to interrupt, but there's a phone call for you.* ◇ *Quit interrupting me when I'm talking.* **2** [T] to stop sth or make a break in it: *The program was interrupted by a news bulletin.*

★**in·ter·rup·tion** /ˌɪntəˈrʌpʃn/ *noun* **1** [C] something that prevents an activity or situation from continuing: *I've had so many interruptions this morning that I haven't gotten anything done!* **2** [U] the act of interrupting sb/sth: *I need one whole day without any interruption.*

**in·ter·sect** /ˈɪntərsɛkt; ˌɪntərˈsɛkt/ *verb* [I,T] (used about roads, lines, etc.) to meet and go across each other

**in·ter·sec·tion** /ˌɪntərˈsɛkʃn/ *noun* [C] the place where two or more roads, lines, etc. meet and cross each other: *The accident happened at the intersection of Fifth Avenue and Jefferson Street.*

**in·ter·sperse** /ˌɪntərˈspərs/ *verb* [T] (usually passive) to put things at various points in sth: *His speech was interspersed with jokes.*

**in·ter·state**[1] /ˈɪntərsteɪt/ *noun* [C] (*abbr.* **I**) (*U.S.*) a wide road for fast traffic that is part of a national system of these roads: *Head south on Interstate 95 until you see the sign for Providence.* ➲ Look at the note at **freeway**.

**in·ter·state**[2] /ˈɪntərsteɪt/ *adj.* (*U.S.*) (only *before* a noun) between different states: *interstate commerce*

★**in·ter·val** /ˈɪntərvl/ *noun* [C] a period of time between two events: *I'm trying to leave longer intervals between cigarettes.* ◇ *There were only a few intervals of silence during the discussion.* ➲ Look at the note at **pause**[1].

IDM **at intervals (of...)** with time or with spaces between: *I always write home at regular intervals.* ◇ *The trees should be planted at intervals of two yards.*

**in·ter·vene** /ˌɪntərˈvin/ *verb* [I] **1 intervene (in sth/between A and B)** to act in a way that prevents sth from happening or influences the result of sth: *The police had to intervene between the two groups.* ◇ *to intervene in a dispute* **2** (used about time) to come between: *During the months that intervened, they wrote to each other nearly every day.*

**in·ter·ven·ing** /ˌɪntərˈvinɪŋ/ *adj.* (only *before* a noun) coming or existing between (two events, dates, objects, etc.): *the intervening years*

**in·ter·ven·tion** /ˌɪntərˈvɛnʃn/ *noun* [C,U] an act of intervening, especially to prevent sth from happening: *military intervention in the crisis*

★**in·ter·view**[1] /ˈɪntərvyu/ *noun* [C] **1** a meeting at which a journalist asks sb questions in order to find out his/her opinion, etc. (often shown on television or printed in a newspaper): *an exclusive interview with a popular TV star* ◇ *The actress refused to give an interview.* ◇ *The mayor criticized his opponent in an interview on the local news.* **2** a meeting at which sb is asked questions to find out if he/she is suitable for a job: *Interviews will be held on June 10.* ◇ *They called me for an interview for that job in Washington!*

★**in·ter·view**[2] /ˈɪntərvyu/ *verb* [T] **1 interview sb (about sth)** (used about a journalist, etc.) to ask sb questions in an interview (to find out his/her opinions, etc.) **2 interview sb (for sth)** to ask sb questions in an interview (to find out if he/she is suitable for a job, etc.): *How many applicants did you interview for the job?*

**in·ter·view·er** /ˈɪntərvyuər/ *noun* [C] a person who asks the questions in an interview

**in·tes·tine** /ɪnˈtɛstən/ *noun* [C, usually pl.] the long tube in your body that carries food away from your stomach to the place where it leaves your body: *the small/large intestine* ▶ **in·tes·ti·nal** /ɪnˈtɛstənl/ *adj.*

**in·ti·ma·cy** /ˈɪntəməsi/ *noun* [U] **1** the state of being very close: *Their intimacy grew with the years.* **2** a sexual relationship

**in·ti·mate** /ˈɪntəmət/ *adj.* **1** having a very close relationship: *They're intimate friends.* **2** private and personal: *They told each other their most intimate thoughts and secrets.* **3** connected with sex: *She had had an intimate relationship with the musician.* **4** very detailed: *He has an intimate knowledge of the area.* **5** (used about a place, an atmosphere, etc.) quiet and friendly or small: *a chance to see top Broadway stars in a more intimate setting*

**in·ti·mate·ly** /ˈɪntəmətli/ *adv.* in a close or personal way: *Do you know him intimately?*

**in·tim·i·date** /ɪnˈtɪmədeɪt/ *verb* [T] **intimidate sb (into sth/doing sth)** to frighten sb (often in order to make him/her do sth) ▶ **in·tim·i·da·tion** /ɪnˌtɪməˈdeɪʃn/ *noun* [U]: *The rebel troops controlled the area by intimidation.*

**in·tim·i·dat·ing** /ɪnˈtɪmədeɪṭɪŋ/ *adj.* frightening (because of size or difficulty)

★**in·to** /ˈɪntə; *strong form and before vowels* ˈɪntu/ *prep.* **1** moving to a position inside or in sth: *Come into the house.* ◇ *I'm going into town.* **2** in the direction of sth: *Please speak into the microphone.* **3** to a point at which you hit sth: *I backed the car into a wall.* **4** (showing a change): *We're turning the spare room into a study.* ◇ *She changed into her jeans.* ◇ *The new rules will come into force next year.* **5** (used when you are dividing numbers): *7 goes into 28 four times.*

IDM **be into sth** (*informal*) to be very interested in sth (e.g. as a hobby): *I'm really into canoeing.*

**in·tol·er·a·ble** /ɪnˈtɑlərəbl/ *adj.* too bad or severe to stand or accept: *The living conditions were intolerable.* ◇ *intolerable pain* ➲ verb **tolerate** ▶ **in·tol·er·a·bly** /-əbli/ *adv.*

**in·tol·er·ant** /ɪnˈtɑlərənt/ *adj.* **intolerant (of sb/sth)** not able to accept behavior or opinions that are different from your own ▶ **in·tol·er·ance** /-əns/ *noun* [U]

**in·to·na·tion** /ˌɪntəˈneɪʃn/ *noun* [C,U] the rise and fall of the level of your voice while you are speaking

**in·tox·i·cat·ed** /ɪnˈtɑksəkeɪṭəd/ *adj.* (*formal*) **1** having had too much alcohol to drink; drunk: *He was arrested for driving while intoxicated.* **2** very excited: *She was intoxicated by her success.* ▶ **in·tox·i·ca·tion** /ɪnˌtɑksəˈkeɪʃn/ *noun* [U]

**in·tra·net** /ˈɪntrənɛt/ *noun* [C] (*computing*) a system of computers inside an organization that makes it possible for people who work there to look at the same information and to send information to each other ➲ Compare **Internet**.

**in·tran·si·tive** /ɪnˈtrænsəṭɪv; -ˈtrænz-/ *adj.* (*grammar*) (used about a verb) used without an object

NOTE **Intransitive verbs** are marked [I] in this dictionary.

▸ **in·tran·si·tive·ly** *adv.*

**in·tra·ve·nous** /ˌɪntrəˈvinəs/ *adj.* directly into the body's blood system through a vein: *intravenous drug users* (= who use special needles to put drugs directly into their veins) ➲ Look also at **IV**.

**in·trep·id** /ɪnˈtrɛpəd/ *adj.* (*formal*) (used about people and their actions) brave and without any fear

**in·tri·ca·cy** /ˈɪntrɪkəsi/ *noun* **1 intricacies** [pl.] the complicated details (of sth): *It's difficult to understand all the intricacies of the situation.* **2** [U] the quality of being intricate: *I was impressed by the intricacy of the design.*

**in·tri·cate** /ˈɪntrɪkət/ *adj.* having many small parts put together in a complicated way: *an intricate pattern* ◇ *an intricate plot to the story* ▸ **in·tri·cate·ly** *adv.*

**in·trigue¹** /ɪnˈtrig/ *verb* [T] (often passive) to make sb very interested or curious: *I was intrigued by some of the unusual objects in the exhibit.*

**in·trigue²** /ˈɪntrig; ɪnˈtrig/ *noun* [C,U] the making of a secret plan to do sth bad: *a story of political intrigue and corruption*

**in·trigu·ing** /ɪnˈtrigɪŋ/ *adj.* very interesting; fascinating

**in·trin·sic** /ɪnˈtrɪnzɪk; -sɪk/ *adj.* (only *before* a noun) (*formal*) (used about the value or quality of sth) belonging to sth as part of its nature; basic: *The object has no intrinsic value* (= the material it is made of is not worth anything). ▸ **in·trin·si·cal·ly** /-kli/ *adv.*

★**in·tro·duce** /ˌɪntrəˈdus/ *verb* [T]

➤PEOPLE **1 introduce sb (to sb)** to tell two or more people who have not met before what each others' names are so that they can get to know each other: *"Who's that girl over there?" "Come with me and I'll introduce you to her."* **2 introduce yourself (to sb)** to tell sb what your name is so that you can get to know him/her: *He just walked over and introduced himself to me.*

➤TO AUDIENCE **3** to tell an audience the name of the person, who is going to speak, perform, entertain, etc.: *And now it's time to introduce my next guest on the show...* **4** to announce and give details of a radio or television program: *The program was introduced by Charles Kuralt.*

➤NEW PRODUCT/LAW **5 introduce sth (in/into sth)** to bring in, use, or take sth to a place for the first time: *The new law was introduced in 2004.*

➤NEW EXPERIENCE **6 introduce sb to sth** to make sb begin to learn about sth or do sth for the first time: *This pamphlet will introduce you to the basic aims of our society.*

NOTE There are a number of different ways of introducing one person to another, depending on the occasion: (*informal*) *"John, this is my friend Mary."* ◇ *"Mrs. Smith, this is my daughter, Jane."* ◇ (*formal*) *"Let me introduce you. Dr. Gordon, this is Prof. Phil Jones. Prof. Jones, Dr. Joan Gordon."* An informal response to an introduction is "**Hi**" or "**Nice to meet you**." In a more formal situation you can say "**Hello**" or "**I'm pleased to meet you**." A very formal response is "**How do you do**?" The other person then also replies: "**How do you do**?" When people are introduced, they often **shake hands**.

★**in·tro·duc·tion** /ˌɪntrəˈdʌkʃn/ *noun*

➤BRINGING INTO USE **1** [U] bringing in or using sth for the first time: *the introduction of computers into the classroom*

➤FIRST EXPERIENCE **2** [sing.] **introduction to sth** first experience of sth: *My first job – in a factory – was not a pleasant introduction to work.*

➤OF BOOK/TALK **3** [C] the first part of a book or a talk which gives an explanation of the rest of it

➤TO SUBJECT **4** [C] a book for people who are beginning to study a subject: *An Introduction to English Grammar*

➤OF PEOPLE **5** [C] the act of telling two or more people each others' names for the first time: *I think I'll get my husband to make the introductions – he's better at remembering names!* ◇ *You don't need an introduction, do you?* (= you already know each other)

**in·tro·duc·to·ry** /ˌɪntrəˈdʌktəri/ *adj.* happening or said at the beginning in order to give a general idea of what will follow: *an introductory speech/chapter/remark*

**in·tro·vert** /ˈɪntrəvərt/ *noun* [C] a quiet, shy person who is concerned with his/her own thoughts or feelings OPP **extrovert**

**in·tro·vert·ed** /ˈɪntrəvərţəd/ *adj.* quiet and shy

**in·trude** /ɪnˈtrud/ *verb* [I] **intrude (on/upon sb/sth)** to enter a place or situation without permission or when you are not wanted: *I'm sorry to intrude on your lunch break, but...* ◇ *You're intruding –this is a private party.*

**in·trud·er** /ɪnˈtrudər/ *noun* [C] a person who enters a place without permission and often secretly: *an alarm system to protect your home against intruders*

**in·tru·sion** /ɪnˈtruʒn/ *noun* [C,U] **intrusion (on/upon/into sth)** something that disturbs you or your life when you want to be private ▸ **in·tru·sive** /ɪnˈtrusɪv/ *adj.*

**in·tu·i·tion** /ˌɪntuˈɪʃn/ *noun* [C,U] the feeling or understanding that makes you believe or know sth without any reason or proof: *My intuition tells me something's wrong here.* ▸ **in·tu·i·tive** /ɪnˈtuəţɪv/ *adj.* ▸ **in·tu·i·tive·ly** *adv.*

**In·u·it** /ˈɪnuət; ˈɪnyuət/ *noun* [C] (*pl.* **In·u·it**) *adj.* **1** (members) of a race of Aboriginal peoples from northern Canada and parts of Greenland and Alaska **2** (of or relating to) the language of the Inuit; Inuktitut

**I·nuk·ti·tut** /ɪˈnuktətut/ *noun* [U] (*Cdn*) the language of the Inuit people

**in·un·date** /ˈɪnʌndeɪt/ *verb* [T] (usually passive) **1 inundate sb (with sth)** to give or send sb so many things that he/she can hardly deal with them all: *We were inundated with applications for the job.* **2** (*formal*) to cover with water; to flood: *After the storm the fields were inundated.*

**in·vade** /ɪnˈveɪd/ *verb* **1** [I,T] to enter a country with an army in order to attack, conquer it, etc.: *They invaded the country with tanks and troops.* **2**

[T] to enter in large numbers: *College students invade the Florida beaches every spring.* **3** [T] to come in and disturb: *Door-to-door salespeople invade my privacy.* ▸ **in·vad·er** ***noun*** [C, usually pl.]: *They forced back the invaders.* ➲ Look at **invasion**.

**in·va·lid**[1] /ˈɪnvələd/ ***noun*** [C] a person who has been very sick for a long time and needs sb else to take care of him/her

**in·va·lid**[2] /ɪnˈvæləd/ ***adj.*** **1** not able to be accepted by law; not VALID (1,2): *Your driver's license is invalid.* **2** not correct according to reason; not VALID (3): *an invalid argument*

**in·val·u·a·ble** /ɪnˈvælyəbl; ɪnˈvælyuəbl/ ***adj.*** very useful or valuable: *She has made an invaluable contribution to the project.*

> NOTE Be careful. Invaluable is not the opposite of valuable. The opposite is **worthless**.

**in·var·i·a·bly** /ɪnˈvɛriəbli; -ˈvær-/ ***adv.*** almost always: *She invariably arrives late.*

**in·va·sion** /ɪnˈveɪʒn/ ***noun*** [C,U] a time when the armed forces of one country enter another country in order to attack it: *Germany's invasion of Poland in 1939* ◇ (*figurative*) *Such questions are an invasion of privacy.* ➲ verb **invade**

★**in·vent** /ɪnˈvɛnt/ ***verb*** [T] **1** to think of or make sth for the first time: *Who invented the sewing machine?* ◇ *When was the camera invented?* **2** to make up a story, excuse, etc. that is not true

★**in·ven·tion** /ɪnˈvɛnʃn/ ***noun*** **1** [C] a thing that has been made or designed by sb for the first time: *The microwave oven is a very useful invention.* **2** [U] the act or process of making or designing sth for the first time: *Books had to be written by hand before the invention of printing.*

**in·ven·tive** /ɪnˈvɛntɪv/ ***adj.*** having new and original ideas ▸ **in·ven·tive·ness** ***noun*** [U]

**in·ven·tor** /ɪnˈvɛntər/ ***noun*** [C] a person who INVENTS (1) sth for the first time

**in·ven·to·ry** /ˈɪnvəntɔri/ ***noun*** [C] (*pl.* **in·ven·to·ries**) a detailed list, e.g. of all the items in a store

**in·vert** /ɪnˈvərt/ ***verb*** [T] (*formal*) to put sth in the opposite order or position of the way it should be or usually is

**in·ver·te·brate** /ɪnˈvərt̬əbrət; -breɪt/ ***noun*** [C] any animal with no backbone: *Worms are invertebrates.*

★**in·vest** /ɪnˈvɛst/ ***verb*** **1** [I,T] to buy property or stock in a business, etc. in the hope that you will make a profit: *We invested in the new software company.* ◇ *I usually invest my money in the stock market.* ◇ (*figurative*) *You have to invest a lot of time to learn a language well.* **2** [I] to buy sth (usually sth expensive): *Maybe we should invest in a new lawnmower.*

★**in·ves·ti·gate** /ɪnˈvɛstəgeɪt/ ***verb*** [I,T] to try to find out all the facts about sth: *A murder was reported and the police were sent to investigate.* ◇ *A group of experts are investigating the cause of the crash.* ▸ **in·ves·ti·ga·tor** /-geɪt̬ər/ ***noun*** [C]

★**in·ves·ti·ga·tion** /ɪnˌvɛstəˈgeɪʃn/ ***noun*** [C,U] **investigation (into sth)** [C]: *The airlines are carrying out a thorough investigation into security at airports.* ◇ *The matter is still under investigation.*

**in·ves·ti·ga·tive** /ɪnˈvɛstəgeɪt̬ɪv/ ***adj.*** trying to find out all the facts about sb/sth: *investigative journalism*

★**in·vest·ment** /ɪnˈvɛstmənt/ ***noun*** **1** [U] **investment (in sth)** the act of putting money in a property, business, etc.: *The industry needs new capital investment.* ◇ *foreign investment in the state's economy* **2** [C] **investment (in sth)** an amount of money that has been put in a business, etc.: *We got a good return on our original investment of $10,000.* **3** [C] a thing that you have bought, especially in order to save money or to make a profit: *Those stocks were a good long-term investment.* ◇ *This coat has been a good investment – I've worn it for three years.*

**in·ves·tor** /ɪnˈvɛstər/ ***noun*** [C] a person who INVESTS (1) in sth

**in·vig·or·ate** /ɪnˈvɪgəreɪt/ ***verb*** [I,T] to give new strength or energy to sb/sth: *efforts to invigorate the tourist industry* ▸ **in·vig·or·at·ing** ***adj.***: *an invigorating early-morning run*

**in·vin·ci·ble** /ɪnˈvɪnsəbl/ ***adj.*** too strong or powerful to be defeated or beaten

**in·vis·i·ble** /ɪnˈvɪzəbl/ ***adj.*** not able to be seen: *bacteria that are invisible to the naked eye* ◇ *Frodo put on the magic ring and became invisible.* ◇ (*figurative*) *Children from low-income families are the nation's invisible poor.* ▸ **in·vis·i·bil·i·ty** /ɪnˌvɪzəˈbɪlət̬i/ ***noun*** [U] ▸ **in·vis·i·bly** ***adv.***

★**in·vi·ta·tion** /ˌɪnvəˈteɪʃn/ ***noun*** **2** [U] inviting or being invited: *Admission is by invitation only.* ◇ *a letter of invitation* **1** [C] **an invitation to sb/sth (to sth/to do sth)** a written or spoken request to go somewhere or do sth: *He has been sent an invitation to the opening ceremony.*

> NOTE You can **accept** an invitation or **turn it down**. (**Decline** and **refuse** are more formal.)

★**in·vite** /ɪnˈvaɪt/ ***verb*** [T] **invite sb (to/for sth)** to ask sb to come (to a party, etc.): *We invited the whole family to the wedding.* ◇ *Shall we invite Louise and Pete to the party on Saturday?* ◇ (*figurative*) *You're just inviting trouble if you criticize the boss.*

PHR V **invite sb in** to ask sb to come into your home

**invite sb over** to ask sb to come to your home: *I invited Trevor and his family over for dinner on Sunday.* ➲ Note that **ask** can be used instead of invite in all senses.

**in·vit·ing** /ɪnˈvaɪt̬ɪŋ/ ***adj.*** attractive and pleasant: *The log fire and smell of cooking were very inviting.*

**in·voice** /ˈɪnvɔɪs/ ***noun*** [C] an official paper that lists goods or services that you have received and says how much you must pay for them

**in·vol·un·tar·y** /ɪnˈvɑlənˌtɛri/ ***adj.*** done without wanting or meaning to: *She was charged with involuntary manslaughter.* ▸ **in·vol·un·tar·i·ly** /ɪnˌvɑlənˈtɛrəli/ ***adv.***

★**in·volve** /ɪnˈvɑlv/ ***verb*** [T] **1** to make sth necessary: *The job involves a lot of traveling.* **2** **involve sb/sth in (doing) sth** to cause sb/sth to take part in or be concerned with sth: *a project involving more than 100 people* ◇ *Please don't involve me in your family arguments.* ◇ *I don't want to get involved –*

*figure it out for yourself.* ▸ **in·volve·ment** ***noun*** [C,U]

**in·volved** /ɪn'vɑlvd/ ***adj.*** **1 involved (in sth)** taking part in sth because you are very interested in it: *I'm involved in local politics.* **2** difficult to understand; complicated: *The book has a very involved plot.* **3 involved (with sb)** to be emotionally or sexually connected with sb: *She is involved with an older man.*

**in·ward[1]** /'ɪnwərd/ ***adj.*** (only *before* a noun) inside your mind, not shown to other people: *my inward feelings* OPP **outward**

**in·ward[2]** /'ɪnwərd/ (*also* **inwards**) ***adv.*** toward the inside or center: *Stand in a circle facing inward.* OPP **outward**

**i·o·dine** /'aɪədaɪn; -dɪn/ ***noun*** [U] a dark-colored substance that is found in sea water. A brown liquid containing iodine is sometimes used to clean cuts in your skin.

**i·o·ta** /aɪ'oʊṭə/ ***noun*** (*symbol* Ι, ι) the ninth letter of the Greek alphabet ➲ Look at the note at **fraternity**. IDM **not one/an iota** none at all: *There is not an iota of truth in the story.* ◇ *That won't help one iota.*

**IOU** /ˌaɪ oʊ 'yu/ ***noun*** [C] (*pl.* **IOU's** or **IOUs**) I owe you; a piece of paper that you sign to show that you owe sb some money

**IPA** /ˌaɪ pi 'eɪ/ ***abbr.*** International Phonetic Alphabet

**IPO** /ˌaɪ pi 'oʊ/ ***abbr.*** the abbreviation for "initial public offering"; an occasion when shares in a company are first sold on the stock exchange

**IQ** /ˌaɪ 'kyu/ ***noun*** [C] intelligence quotient; a number that shows how intelligent sb is, according to his/her score on a certain test: *to have a high/low IQ* ◇ *an IQ of 120*

**IRA** /ˌaɪ ɑr 'eɪ; 'aɪrə/ ***noun*** [C] individual retirement account; a special type of bank account in which you can save money without paying taxes on it until you stop working (**retire**) when you are older

**i·rate** /aɪ'reɪt/ ***adj.*** (*formal*) very angry

**i·ris** /'aɪrəs/ ***noun*** [C] the colored part of the eye

**I·rish** /'aɪrɪʃ/ ***adj.*** **1** of Ireland or its people, language, culture, etc.: *Irish folk music* ◇ *Irish whiskey* **2 the Irish** ***noun*** [pl.] the people of Ireland

**iron**

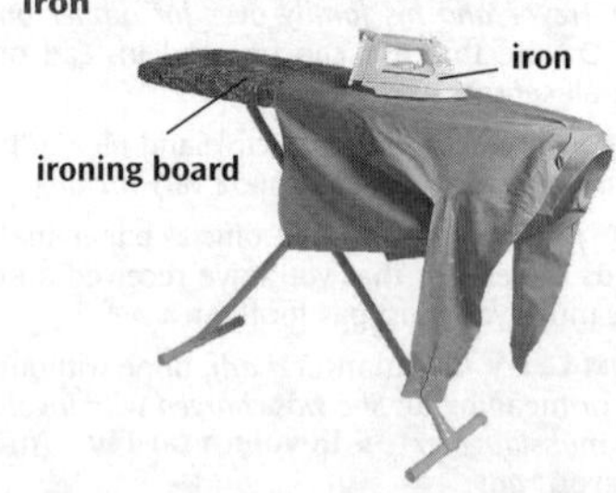


★**i·ron[1]** /'aɪərn/ ***noun*** **1** [U] (*symbol* **Fe**) a common hard gray metal. Iron is used for making steel and is found in small quantities in food and in blood: *an iron bar* ◇ *wrought-iron railings* ◇ *The roof of the shack was made of corrugated iron.* ◇ *a pot made of cast iron* ◇ *iron ore* ◇ (*figurative*) *The general has an iron* (= very strong) *will.* **2** [C] an electrical instrument with a flat bottom that is heated and used to smooth clothes after you have washed and dried them: *Use a hot iron on cotton and a cool iron on polyester.* ◇ *a steam iron*

**i·ron[2]** /'aɪərn/ ***verb*** [I,T] to use an IRON[1] (2) to get the folds out of clothes: *Could you iron this dress for me?* ◇ *That shirt needs to be ironed.*

NOTE **Do the ironing** is often used instead of iron: *I usually do the ironing on Sunday.*

**i·ron·ic** /aɪ'rɑnɪk/ ***adj.*** **1** meaning the opposite of what you say: *"Oh, I'm so pleased," she said in an ironic way.* ➲ Look at **sarcastic**. **2** (used about a situation) strange or amusing because it is unusual or unexpected: *It is ironic that the busiest people are often the most willing to help.* ▸ **i·ron·i·cal·ly** /-kli/ ***adv.***

**'ironing board** ***noun*** [C] a special table that is used for ironing clothes on ➲ picture at **iron**.

**i·ro·ny** /'aɪrəni; 'aɪərni/ ***noun*** (*pl.* **i·ro·nies**) **1** [U] the way of speaking that shows you are joking or that you mean the opposite of what you say: *"Gee, what a generous tip," she said with heavy irony.* **2** [C,U] the unusual or unexpected side of a situation, etc. that seems strange or amusing: *The irony was that he was killed in a car accident soon after the end of the war.*

**ir·ra·tion·al** /ɪ'ræʃənl/ ***adj.*** not based on reason or clear thought: *an irrational fear of worms* ▸ **ir·ra·tion·al·i·ty** /ɪˌræʃə'næləṭi/ ***noun*** [U] **ir·ra·tion·al·ly** ***adv.***

**ir·rec·on·cil·a·ble** /ɪˌrɛkən'saɪləbl/ ***adj.*** (*formal*) (used about people or their ideas and beliefs) so different that they cannot be made to agree

**ir·reg·u·lar** /ɪ'rɛgyələr/ ***adj.*** **1** having parts or sides of different sizes or lengths; not even or regular: *an irregular shape* **2** happening at unequal intervals; not regular: *His visits became more and more irregular.* ◇ *an irregular pulse* **3** not allowed according to the rules or social customs: *It is highly irregular for a doctor to give information about patients without their permission.* **4** not following the usual rules of grammar; not regular: *"Caught" is an irregular past tense form.* ▸ **ir·reg·u·lar·i·ty** /ɪˌrɛgyə'lærəṭi/ ***noun*** [C,U] (*pl.* **ir·reg·u·lar·i·ties**) ▸ **ir·reg·u·lar·ly** ***adv.***

**ir·rel·e·vant** /ɪ'rɛləvənt/ ***adj.*** not connected with sth or important to it: *That's completely irrelevant to the subject under discussion.* ▸ **ir·rel·e·vance** /-əns/ ***noun*** [U] ▸ **ir·rel·e·van·cy** /-ənsi/ ***noun*** [C,U] (*pl.* **ir·rel·e·van·cies**)

**ir·rep·a·ra·ble** /ɪ'rɛpərəbl/ ***adj.*** not able to be repaired or made better: *Acid rain has caused irreparable damage to many forests and lakes.* ▸ **ir·rep·a·ra·bly** ***adv.***

**ir·re·place·a·ble** /ˌɪrɪ'pleɪsəbl/ ***adj.*** (used about sth very valuable or special) not able to be replaced

**ir·re·press·i·ble** /ˌɪrɪ'prɛsəbl/ ***adj.*** full of life and energy: *Her irrepressible humor helped her win her struggle with cancer.* ▸ **ir·re·press·i·bly** ***adv.***

**ir·re·sis·ti·ble** /ˌɪrɪ'zɪstəbl/ ***adj.*** **1** very strong or powerful so that you cannot stop yourself from doing or agreeing with sth: *Their arguments were irresistible – I had to agree.* ◇ *an irresistible urge to* *laugh* **2** very attractive: *The swimming pool is irresistible on a hot day like this.* ⊃ verb resist ▸ **ir·re·sis·ti·bly** /-əbli/ ***adv.***

**ir·re·spon·si·ble** /ˌɪrɪˈspɑnsəbl/ ***adj.*** (used about a person or his/her actions) not thinking about the effect your actions will have; not responsible: *It is irresponsible to let small children go out alone when it's dark.* ▸ **ir·re·spon·si·bil·i·ty** /ˌɪrɪˌspɑnsəˈbɪləṭi/ ***noun*** [U] **ir·re·spon·si·bly** /-əbli/ ***adv.***

**ir·rev·er·ent** /ɪˈrɛvərənt/ ***adj.*** not feeling or showing respect for traditions, important people, etc. ▸ **ir·rev·er·ence** /-əns/ ***noun*** [U] **ir·rev·er·ent·ly** ***adv.***

**ir·re·vers·i·ble** /ˌɪrɪˈvərsəbl/ ***adj.*** not able to be stopped or changed: *Once made, the decision is irreversible.*

**ir·ri·gate** /ˈɪrəgeɪt/ ***verb*** [T] to supply land and crops with water by using pipes, equipment, etc. ▸ **ir·ri·ga·tion** /ˌɪrəˈgeɪʃn/ ***noun*** [U]

**ir·ri·ta·ble** /ˈɪrəṭəbl/ ***adj.*** easily made angry ▸ **ir·ri·ta·bil·i·ty** /ˌɪrəṭəˈbɪləṭi/ ***noun*** [U] ▸ **ir·ri·ta·bly** /-əbli/ ***adv.***

★**ir·ri·tate** /ˈɪrəteɪt/ ***verb*** [T] **1** to make sb angry; to annoy: *It really irritates me the way he keeps repeating himself.* **2** to cause a part of the body to be painful or sore: *Very bright sunlight can irritate your eyes.* ▸ **ir·ri·ta·tion** /ˌɪrəˈteɪʃn/ ***noun*** [C,U]

**the IRS** /ˌaɪ ɑr ˈɛs/ (*also* **the Internal Revenue Service**) ***noun*** [sing.] (*U.S.*) the department of the U.S. government that deals with taxes

**is** → BE[1,2]

**Is·lam** /ɪsˈlɑm; ɪz-/ ***noun*** [U] the religion of Muslim people. Islam teaches that there is only one God and that Muhammad is His Prophet. ▸ **Is·lam·ic** /ɪsˈlæmɪk; ɪz-/ ***adj.***: *Islamic law*

★**is·land** /ˈaɪlənd/ ***noun*** [C] a piece of land that is surrounded by water: *the tropical islands of the Caribbean* ◇ *Robinson Crusoe spent many years living on a desert island.* ◇ *the bridge to Prince Edward Island*

**is·land·er** /ˈaɪləndər/ ***noun*** [C] a person who lives on a small island

**is·n't** /ˈɪznt/ *short for* IS NOT: *It isn't far now.* ◇ *This is enough, isn't it?*

**i·so·late** /ˈaɪsəleɪt/ ***verb*** [T] **isolate sb/sth (from sb/sth)** to put or keep sb/sth apart or separate from other people or things: *Some farms were isolated by the heavy snowfalls.* ◇ *We need to isolate all the animals with the disease so that the others don't catch it.*

**i·so·lat·ed** /ˈaɪsəleɪṭəd/ ***adj.*** **1** not connected with others; separate: *Is this an isolated case or part of a general pattern?* **2** alone or apart from other people or things: *an isolated farmhouse*

**i·so·la·tion** /ˌaɪsəˈleɪʃn/ ***noun*** [U] away from other people or things; a feeling of being alone and lonely: *She lived in complete isolation from the outside world.*

IDM **in isolation (from sb/sth)** alone or separately: *Acting in isolation is not very effective. We need to work together as a team.*

**ISP** /ˌaɪ ɛs ˈpi/ ***abbr.*** Internet service provider; a company that provides you with an Internet connection and services such as e-mail, etc.

★**is·sue**[1] /ˈɪʃu/ ***noun*** [C] **1** a problem or subject for discussion: *I want to* ***raise the issue*** *of overtime pay at the meeting.* ◇ *The government cannot avoid the issue of homelessness any longer.* **2** one in a series of things that are published or produced: *Do you have last week's issue of this magazine?*

IDM **make an issue (out) of sth** to give too much importance to a small problem: *OK, we disagree on this but let's not make a big issue out of it.*

★**is·sue**[2] /ˈɪʃu/ ***verb*** [T] **1** to make sth known or give out sth to the public: *The United Nations issued a report yesterday on the Brazilian rainforests.* **2** to give or supply sth to sb: *The new employees were* ***issued with*** *uniforms.* ◇ *to issue a visa*

**IT** /ˌaɪ ˈti/ ***abbr.*** (*computing*) information technology

★**it** /ɪt/ ***pronoun*** **1** (used as the subject or object of a verb, or after a preposition) an animal or thing mentioned earlier or that is being talked about now: *Look at that car. It's going way too fast.* ◇ *The kids went up to the dog and patted it on the head.* ◇ *This box is heavy. What's inside it?*

> NOTE **It** can also refer to a baby whose sex you do not know: *Is it a boy or a girl?*

**2** (used for identifying a person): *It's your mom on the phone.* ◇ *"Who's that?" "It's the mailman."* ◇ *It's me!* ◇ *It's him!* ◇ *It's Michael!* **3** (used in the position of the subject or object of a verb when the real subject or object is at the end of the sentence): *It's hard for them to talk about their problems.* ◇ *I think it doesn't really matter what time we arrive.* **4** (used in the position of the subject of a verb when you are talking about time, the date, distance, the weather, etc.): *It's almost 8:00.* ◇ *It's Tuesday today.* ◇ *It's about 50 miles north of New York City.* ◇ *It was very cold last weekend.* ◇ *It's raining.* **5** (used when you are talking about a situation): *It gets very crowded here in the summer.* ◇ *I'll come at 7 o'clock if it's convenient.* ◇ *It's too bad they can't come to the party.* **6** (used for emphasizing a part of a sentence): *It's John who's good at cooking, not me.* ◇ *It's your health I'm worried about, not the cost.*

IDM **that's it 1** (used for saying that you have had enough of a situation): *That's it. I'm leaving and I'm not coming back.* **2** that's right: *Just move it a little bit higher – that's it, right there.*

**i·tal·ics** /ɪˈtælɪks/ ***noun*** [U, pl.] the type of writing or printing in which the letters slope to the right: *This sentence and all the example sentences in the dictionary are printed in italics.*

**itch**[1] /ɪtʃ/ ***noun*** [C] the feeling on your skin that makes you want to rub or scratch it

**itch**[2] /ɪtʃ/ ***verb*** [I] to have or cause an ITCH[1]: *My nose is itching.* ◇ *Mosquito bites really itch.* ▸ **itch·y** ***adj.***: *an itchy wool sweater* ▸ **itch·i·ness** ***noun*** [U]

**it'd** /ˈɪṭəd/ *short for* IT HAD, IT WOULD

★**i·tem** /ˈaɪṭəm/ ***noun*** [C] **1** one single thing on a list or in a collection: *Some items arrived too late to be included in the catalog.* ◇ *What is the first item on the agenda?* ◇ *an item of luggage* **2** a single piece of news: *There was an interesting item about Cuba in yesterday's news.*

**i·tem·ize** /ˈaɪt̬əmaɪz/ *verb* [T] to make a list of all the ITEMS (1) in sth: *an itemized bill*

**i·tin·er·ant** /aɪˈtɪnərənt/ *adj.* (only *before* a noun) travelling from place to place: *an itinerant circus family*

**i·tin·er·ar·y** /aɪˈtɪnərɛri/ *noun* [C] (*pl.* **i·tin·er·ar·ies**) a plan of a trip, route, etc.

**it'll** /ˈɪt̬l/ *short for* IT WILL

**it's** /ɪts/ *short for* IT IS; IT HAS

NOTE Be careful. **It's** is a short way of saying *it is* or *it has*. **Its** means "belonging to it": *The bird has broken its wing.*

**its** /ɪts/ *det.* belonging to a thing, animal, etc.: *The cat's had its dinner.* ◇ *The swimming club held its annual meeting last night.*

★**it·self** /ɪtˈsɛlf/ *pronoun* **1** (used as the object of a verb or preposition when the animal or thing that does an action is also affected by it): *The cat was washing itself.* ◇ *The company has gotten itself into financial difficulties.* **2** (used for emphasis): *The town itself is pretty dull, but the surrounding area has spectacular scenery.*

IDM **(all) by itself 1** without being controlled by a person; automatically: *The furnace comes on by itself before we get up.* **2** alone: *The house stood all by itself on top of the hill.* ➲ Look at the note at **alone**.

**IV** /ˌaɪ ˈvi/ *noun* [C] a piece of medical equipment, like a tube, that is used for putting liquid food or medicine directly into a sick person's blood: *She's on an IV in the hospital.* ➲ picture at **bandage**

**I've** /aɪv/ *short for* I HAVE

**IVF** /ˌaɪ vi ˈɛf/ *abbr.* in vitro fertilization; a process for preparing (fertilizing) a human egg outside a woman's body

**i·vo·ry** /ˈaɪvri/ *noun* [U] the hard white substance that an elephant's long teeth (**tusks**) are made of

**i·vy** /ˈaɪvi/ *noun* [U] a climbing plant that has dark leaves with three or five points ➲ Look also at **poison ivy**.

**the ˌIvy ˈLeague** *noun* [sing.] a group of eight private universities in the northeastern U.S. which are very old and are respected for their high social and academic status ➲ Look at the note at **White House**.

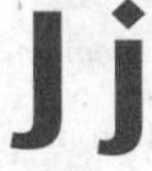

**J, j** /dʒeɪ/ *noun* [C,U] (*pl.* **J's**; **j's**) the tenth letter of the English alphabet: *"Jam" begins with (a) "J."*

**jab** /dʒæb/ *verb* **1** [I,T] **jab (at sb/sth) (with sth)**; **jab sb/sth (with sth)** to push at sb/sth roughly, usually with sth sharp: *He kept jabbing at his potato with his fork.* ◇ *She jabbed me in the ribs with her elbow.* **2** [T] **jab sth into sb/sth** to push sth roughly into sb/sth: *He jabbed his finger into my stomach.* ▸ **jab** *noun* [C]

**jack**[1] /dʒæk/ *noun* [C] **1** a piece of equipment for lifting a car, etc. off the ground, e.g. so that you can change its wheel **2** the card between the ten and the queen in a deck of cards: *the jack of hearts* ➲ Look at the note at **card**. **3** a place where you can connect a telephone or other electronic equipment to the system of telephone wires in a building

**jack**[2] /dʒæk/ *verb*

PHR V **jack sth up 1** to lift a car, etc. using a JACK[1] (1) **2** (*informal*) to increase prices, etc. suddenly by a large amount: *Airlines always jack up their fares during the holidays.*

★**jack·et** /ˈdʒækət/ *noun* [C] **1** a short coat with sleeves: *a tweed sports jacket* ◇ *It's getting chilly – you'd better wear your jacket.* ➲ picture on study page **A30**. ➲ Look also at **life jacket**. **2** a cover for a book or record

**jack·knife**[1] /ˈdʒæknaɪf/ *noun* [C] (*pl.* **jack·knives**) = POCKET KNIFE

**jack·knife**[2] /ˈdʒæknaɪf/ *verb* [I] (used about a truck that is in two parts) to bend in the middle in an uncontrolled way

**jack-o'-lan·tern** /ˈdʒæk ə ˌlæntərn/ *noun* [C] a large round orange vegetable (a **pumpkin**) that has shapes cut into it so that it looks like a face, usually with a light inside. Jack-o'-lanterns are a traditional type of decoration for Halloween.

**jack·pot** /ˈdʒækpɑt/ *noun* [C] the largest prize that you can win in a game

IDM **hit the jackpot** → HIT[1]

**Ja·cuz·zi™** /dʒəˈkuzi/ *noun* [C] a large bathtub with a pump that moves the hot water around, giving a pleasant feeling to your body SYN **spa** (2) ➲ Look also at **hot tub**.

**jad·ed** /ˈdʒeɪdəd/ *adj.* no longer finding things interesting or exciting because you have done or seen them too much

**jag·ged** /ˈdʒægəd/ *adj.* rough and uneven with sharp points: *Be careful not to cut yourself – that metal has a jagged edge.* ◇ *jagged rocks*

**jag·uar** /ˈdʒægwɑr/ *noun* [C] a large spotted wild cat that comes from Central and South America

**jail**[1] /dʒeɪl/ *noun* [C,U] (a) prison: *She was sent to jail for ten years.*

**jail**[2] /dʒeɪl/ *verb* [T] to put sb in prison: *She was jailed for ten years.*

**ja·la·pe·ño** /ˌhɑləˈpeɪnyoʊ; ˌhæ-/ (*also* **ˌjalapeño ˈpepper**) *noun* [C] the small green fruit of a type of pepper plant, that has a very hot taste and is used in Mexican cooking ➲ picture on study page **A28-29**.

★**jam**[1] /dʒæm/ *noun* **1** [U] a sweet substance that you spread on bread, made by boiling fruit and sugar together: *I put jam on my toast.* ◇ *a jar of raspberry jam*

NOTE Note that jam made from oranges is called **marmalade**. ➲ Look also at **jelly**.

**2** [C] a lot of people or things that are crowded together making it difficult to move: *a traffic jam* **3** [C] a situation in which sth is stuck in one position: *There's a paper jam in the copier.* **4** [C] (*informal*) a difficult situation: *We're really in a financial jam.*

**jam²** /dʒæm/ ***verb*** (**jam·ming**; **jammed**) **1** [T] **jam sb/sth in, under, between, etc. sth** to push or force sb/sth into a place where there is not much room: *There were three of us jammed into a phone booth.* ◇ *She managed to jam everything into her suitcase.* **2** [I,T] **jam (sth) (up)** to be stuck in one position or to cause sth to be stuck: *Something is jamming up the machine.* ◇ *Don't stick that pin into the keyhole, or the lock will jam.* **3** [T] **jam sth (up)** to fill sth so that it is difficult to move: *All the fans jammed the stadium exits after the game.* **4** [T] to send out signals in order to stop radio programs, etc. from being received or heard clearly

**jammed** /dʒæmd/ ***adj.*** (not before a noun) stuck in one position or completely full, so that nothing can move: *The parking lot was jammed with shoppers yesterday.*

**Jane Doe** /ˌdʒeɪn ˈdoʊ/ ***noun*** [sing.] **1** used to refer to a woman whose name is not known or is kept secret, especially in a court of law **2** an average woman ➲ Look at **John Doe**.

**jan·i·tor** /ˈdʒænət̬ər/ ***noun*** [C] = CUSTODIAN

**Jan·u·ar·y** /ˈdʒænyuɛri/ ***noun*** [C,U] (*pl.* **Jan·u·ar·ies**) (*abbr.* **Jan.**) the first month of the year, coming before February: *We're going skiing in January.* ◇ *We go skiing every year in January.* ◇ *last/next January* ◇ *the January before last* ◇ *the January after next* ◇ *Christine's birthday is (on) January 17* (we say, "January seventeenth" or sometimes, "the seventeenth of January"). ◇ *The last two Januaries have been extremely cold.* ◇ *January mornings can be very dark.*

**jar¹** /dʒɑr/ ***noun*** [C] **1** a container with a lid, usually made of glass and used for keeping food, etc. in: *a jam jar* ◇ *Can you open this jar for me?* ➲ picture at **container**. **2** the food that a JAR (1) contains: *a jar of honey*

**jar²** /dʒɑr/ ***verb*** (**jar·ring**; **jarred**) [T] to shock or surprise sb by making a sudden movement, noise, etc.: *A mild earthquake jarred local residents awake yesterday.*

**jar·gon** /ˈdʒɑrgən/ ***noun*** [U] special or technical words that are used by a particular group of people and that other people do not understand: *scientific/legal/computer jargon*

**jaun·dice** /ˈdʒɔndəs/ ***noun*** [U] a disease that makes the skin and eyes yellow

**jave·lin** /ˈdʒævlən; ˈdʒævələn/ ***noun*** [C] a long pointed pole that is thrown in sports competitions

**jaw** /dʒɔ/ ***noun*** **1** [C] either of the bones in your face that contain the teeth: *the lower/upper jaw* **2 jaws** [pl.] the mouth (especially of an animal): *The lion was coming toward him with its jaws open.*

★**jazz¹** /dʒæz/ ***noun*** [U] a style of popular music with a strong rhythm, originally played by black Americans: *a jazz band*

**jazz²** /dʒæz/ ***verb***

PHRV **jazz sth up** (*informal*) to make sth brighter, more interesting or lively

**J-cloth** /ˈdʒeɪ klɔθ/ ***noun*** [C] (*Cdn*) a type of light cloth used for cleaning

★**jeal·ous** /ˈdʒɛləs/ ***adj.*** **1** feeling upset because you think that sb loves another person more than you: *Tim gets jealous whenever Sue talks to another boy!* **2 jealous (of sb/sth)** feeling angry or sad because you want to be like sb else or because you want what sb else has: *He's always been jealous of his older brother.* ◇ *I'm really jealous of your new car – how much did it cost?* ▸ **jeal·ous·ly** ***adv.*** ▸ **jeal·ous·y** /ˈdʒɛləsi/ ***noun*** [C,U] (*pl.* **jeal·ous·ies**)

★**jeans** /dʒinz/ ***noun*** [pl.] pants made of strong, usually blue, cotton cloth (**denim**): *These jeans are a little too tight.* ◇ *a pair of jeans* ➲ picture on study page **A30**.

**Jeep™** /dʒip/ ***noun*** [C] a small, strong vehicle that is suitable for traveling over rough ground

**jeer¹** /dʒɪr/ ***verb*** [I,T] **jeer (at) (sb/sth)** to laugh or shout rudely at sb/sth: *The audience jeered the losing team.*

**jeer²** /dʒɪr/ ***noun*** [C] an unkind or rude remark or shout

**jeez** /dʒiz/ ***interjection*** (*slang*) (used for expressing surprise, shock, etc.)

> NOTE Be careful. Some people find this word offensive because it is similar to the name of Jesus Christ.

**Jell-O™** (*also* **Jello**) /ˈdʒɛloʊ/ (*also* **gelatin**) ***noun*** [U] a soft, solid, brightly-colored food that shakes when it is moved. Jell-O usually has a fruit flavor and is often eaten as a dessert.

★**jel·ly** /ˈdʒɛli/ ***noun*** [U] **1** a type of jam made of fruit juice and sugar: *grape jelly* ◇ *a peanut butter and jelly sandwich* **2** a soft solid substance that shakes when it is moved: *My legs felt like jelly before the test* (= not steady because of fear, etc.).

**jel·ly·fish** /ˈdʒɛlifɪʃ/ ***noun*** [C] (*pl.* **jel·ly·fish** or **jel·ly·fish·es**) a sea animal with a body that looks like colorless JELLY (2). Jellyfish sometimes sting.

**jeop·ard·ize** /ˈdʒɛpərdaɪz/ ***verb*** [T] to do sth that may damage sth or put it in a dangerous position

**jeop·ard·y** /ˈdʒɛpərdi/ ***noun***

IDM **in jeopardy** in danger of losing, failing, being injured or damaged, etc.

**jerk¹** /dʒərk/ ***noun*** [C] **1** (*informal*) a person, especially a man or boy, who is stupid, rude or annoying: *Adam's such a jerk!* **2** a sudden pull, push or other movement: *Give the rope a good jerk.*

**jerk²** /dʒərk/ ***verb*** **1** [T] to pull sb/sth suddenly and quickly: *She jerked the door open.* **2** [I] to move with a sudden movement or a series of sudden movements: *The truck jerked from one side to the other over the bumpy road.* ▸ **jerk·y** ***adj.***: *jerky movements* ▸ **jerk·i·ly** /-əli/ ***adv.***

**jer·sey** /ˈdʒərzi/ ***noun*** [C] (*pl.* **jer·seys**) a shirt that is part of a sports uniform: *a football jersey* ➲ picture at **football player**.

**Je·sus** /ˈdʒizəs; ˈdʒizəz/ ***noun*** = CHRIST

★**jet** /dʒɛt/ ***noun*** [C] **1** a fast airplane with an engine that pushes out a stream of hot air and gases at the back **2** a fast, thin stream of water, gas, etc. coming out of a small hole

J

**ˌjet ˈblack** *adj.* very dark black in color

**ˌjet ˈengine** *noun* [C] a powerful engine that makes planes fly by pushing out a current of hot air and gases at the back

**ˈjet lag** *noun* [U] the tired feeling that people often have after a long trip in an airplane to a place where the local time is different ▶ **ˈjet-lagged** *adj.*

**ˈjet ski™** *noun* [C] a vehicle with an engine, like a motorcycle, for riding across water ▶ **ˈjet-ski·ing** *noun* [U] ➲ picture on study page **A32**.

**jet·ty** /ˈdʒɛt̬i/ *noun* [C] (*pl.* **jet·ties**) a stone wall built out into the ocean to protect boats from large waves

★**Jew** /dʒu/ *noun* [C] a person whose family was originally from the ancient land of Israel or whose religion is Judaism ▶ **Jew·ish** /ˈdʒuɪʃ/ *adj.*: *He's Jewish.* ◇ *the Jewish New Year*

★**jew·el** /ˈdʒuəl/ *noun* [C] a valuable stone (e.g. a diamond) or a necklace, ring, etc. with such a stone in it

**jew·el·er** /ˈdʒuələr/ *noun* [C] a person whose job is to buy, sell, make or repair jewelry and watches

**jewelry**

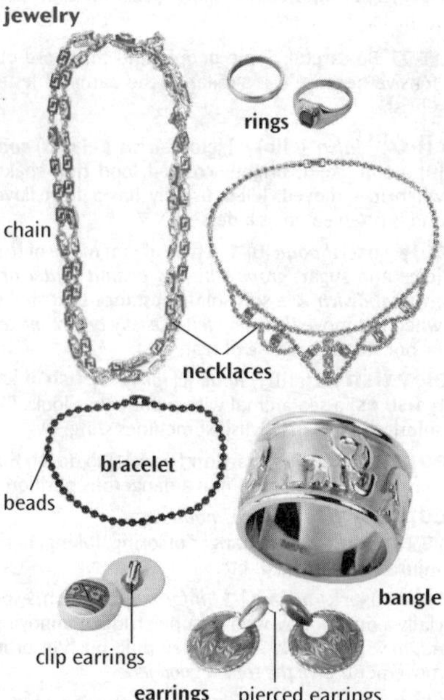


★**jew·el·ry** /ˈdʒuəlri/ *noun* [U] rings and other things made from gold, silver, jewels, etc. that are worn to decorate your body: *a piece of jewelry* ◇ *a jewelry store*

**jibe¹** /dʒaɪb/ (*also* **gibe**) *verb* [I] to say sth that is intended to embarrass sb or make him/her look silly: *He jibed repeatedly at the errors they had made.* ▶ **jibe** *noun* [C]

**jibe²** /dʒaɪb/ **jibe (with sth)** *verb* [I] to be the same as sth or match it: *His statement doesn't jibe with the facts.*

**jif·fy** /ˈdʒɪfi/ *noun*

IDM **in a jiffy** (*informal*) very soon: *I'll be ready in a jiffy.*

**jig** /dʒɪg/ *noun* [C] a kind of quick dance with jumping movements; the music for this dance

**jig·gle** /ˈdʒɪgl/ *verb* [T] to move sth quickly from side to side

**jigsaw puzzle** /ˈdʒɪgsɔ ˌpʌzl/ (*also* **puzzle**) *noun* [C] a picture on cardboard or wood that is cut into small pieces. The pieces are then put together again as a game.

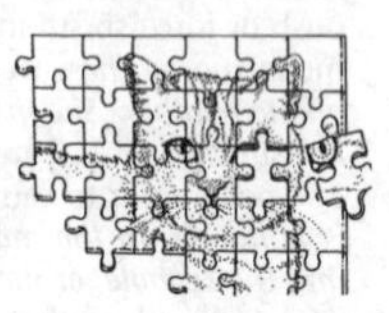

**ji·had** /dʒɪˈhɑd/ *noun* [C] a holy war fought by Muslims against those who reject Islam

**jim·my** /ˈdʒɪmi/ *verb* [T] (*pres. part.* **jim·my·ing**; *3rd person sing. pres.* **jim·mies**; *pt, pp* **jim·mied**) to open a door or window by using a strong metal bar: *None of the neighbors heard the thieves jimmying the door.* ▶ **jim·my** (*pl.* **jim·mies**) *noun* [C]

**jin·gle¹** /ˈdʒɪŋgl/ *noun* **1** [sing.] a noise that sounds like metal objects gently hitting each other: *the jingle of coins* **2** [C] a short simple tune or song, especially one that is used in an advertisement on television or on the radio

**jin·gle²** /ˈdʒɪŋgl/ *verb* **1** [I] to make a gentle noise that sounds like metal objects hitting each other **2** [T] to move sth so that it makes a gentle ringing sound: *He jingled the coins in his pockets.*

**jinx** /dʒɪŋks/ *noun* [C, usually sing.] bad luck; a person or thing that is thought to bring bad luck

**jinxed** /dʒɪŋkst/ *adj.* having or bringing bad luck

**jit·ters** /ˈdʒɪt̬ərz/ *noun* [pl.] (*informal*) extremely nervous or anxious feelings: *Just thinking about the test gives me the jitters!*

**jit·ter·y** /ˈdʒɪt̬əri/ *adj.* (*informal*) nervous or anxious

★**job** /dʒɑb/ *noun* **1** [C] the work that you do to earn money: *My dad told me to go out and get a job.*

> NOTE We **look for, apply for** or **find** a job. A job can be **well-paid/highly-paid** or **badly-paid/low-paid**. A job can be **full-time** or **part-time, permanent** or **temporary**. ➲ Look at the note at **work¹**.

**2** [C] a task or a piece of work that may be paid or unpaid: *I always have a lot of jobs to do around the house on weekends.* **3** [C, usually sing.] a function or responsibility: *It's not his job to tell us what we can and can't do.*

IDM **do a good, bad, etc. job (on sth)** to do or finish sth in a particular way: *The garage did a great job on our car.*

**do the job/trick** (*informal*) to get the result that is wanted

**good/nice job!** (*informal*) (used to praise sb after he/she has done sth very well): *Good job, Amy! You should be proud of yourself.*

**on the job** while working; at work: *He was fired for being drunk on the job.* ◇ *on-the-job training*

**out of a job** without paid work SYN (*formal*) **unemployed**

**ˈjob deˌscription** *noun* [C] a written description

of the exact work and responsibilities of a job: *Bringing you coffee is **not in my job description**!*

**job·less** /ˈdʒɑbləs/ **1** ***adj.*** (used about large numbers of people) without paid work **2 the jobless** ***noun*** [pl.] the people who are without work ▸ **job·less·ness** ***noun*** [U]

**ˈjob seˌcurity** ***noun*** [U] the condition of knowing that you are likely to keep your job: *Study after study has shown that workers with job security are happier and more productive.*

**jock** /dʒɑk/ ***noun*** [C] (*slang*) a person, especially a student, who plays a lot of sports

**jock·ey** /ˈdʒɑki/ ***noun*** [C] (*pl.* **jock·eys**) a person who rides in horse races, especially as a profession ➲ Look at **disc jockey**.

**jog¹** /dʒɑg/ ***verb*** (**jog·ging**; **jogged**) [I] to run slowly, especially as a form of exercise

NOTE We often say **go jogging** rather than **jog**: *I go jogging most evenings.*

IDM **jog sb's memory** to make sb remember sth: *I have a picture here that should jog your memory.*

**jog²** /dʒɑg/ ***noun*** [sing.] a slow run as a form of exercise: *She goes for a jog before breakfast.*

**jog·ger** /ˈdʒɑgər/ ***noun*** [C] a person who goes jogging for exercise

**John Doe** /ˌdʒɑn ˈdoʊ/ ***noun*** [sing.] **1** used to refer to a man whose name is not known or is kept secret, especially in a court of law **2** an average man ➲ Look at **Jane Doe**.

⋆**join** /dʒɔɪn/ ***verb***

›ORGANIZATION **1** [T] to become a member of a club or organization: *James is going to join the army when he leaves school.*

›DO STH WITH SB ELSE **2** [T] to take your place in sth or to take part in sth: *We joined the crowd outside the club.* **3** [I,T] **join (with) sb in doing sth/to do sth; join together in doing sth/to do sth** to take part with sb (in doing sth for sb else): *I know that everybody here joins me in wishing you the best of luck in your new job.* ◇ *The whole class joined together to buy a present for the teacher.*

›MEET **4** [I,T] to meet or unite (with sb/sth): *Do the two rivers join at any point?* ◇ *Where does this road join the main highway?* ◇ *Would you like to join us for a drink?*

›CONNECT **5** [T] **join A with B**; **join A and B (together)** to fasten or connect one thing to another: *The Golden Gate Bridge joins San Francisco with Marin County.* ◇ *The door is made of several sections that are joined together.*

IDM **join forces (with sb)** to work together in order to achieve sth: *Neighborhood residents have joined forces with the police to get rid of drug dealers.*

PHRV **join in (sth/doing sth)** to take part in an activity: *Steve wouldn't join in when everybody else was playing football.*

⋆**joint¹** /dʒɔɪnt/ ***noun*** [C] **1** a part of the body where two bones fit together and are able to bend **2** the place where two or more things are fastened or connected **3** (*informal*) a place such as a bar or restaurant, especially one that is not expensive or elegant: *The band just plays at local beer joints.* **4** (*informal*) a cigarette that contains an illegal drug (**marijuana**)

⋆**joint²** /dʒɔɪnt/ ***adj.*** (only *before* a noun) shared or owned by two or more people: *Do you and your husband have a joint account?* (= at a bank) ◇ *a joint decision* ◇ *the joint chairpersons of the committee* ▸ **joint·ly** ***adv.***

**ˌjoint ˈventure** ***noun*** [C] an agreement between two companies, especially in different countries, to do business together

⋆**joke¹** /dʒoʊk/ ***noun*** **1** [C] something said or done to make you laugh, especially a funny story: *Have you heard the joke about the three men in a taxi?* ◇ *to tell a joke* ◇ *a dirty joke* (= about sex) ◇ *I laughed at her joke even though I didn't get* (= understand) *it.* ➲ A **practical joke** is something you do, not just say. **2** [sing.] a ridiculous person, thing or situation: *The salary he was offered was a joke!*

IDM **play a joke on sb** to trick sb in order to amuse yourself or other people

**take a joke** to accept a trick or sth said about you in fun without getting angry

**joke²** /dʒoʊk/ ***verb*** [I] to say things that are not meant to be serious: *I never joke about religion.*

**jok·er** /ˈdʒoʊkər/ ***noun*** [C] **1** a person who likes to make jokes or play tricks **2** an extra playing card in a deck which can be used instead of any card in some games

**jol·ly** /ˈdʒɑli/ ***adj.*** (**jol·li·er**; **jol·li·est**) (*old-fashioned*) happy and cheerful

**jolt¹** /dʒoʊlt/ ***verb*** [T] to shake sth or make it move suddenly: *The crash jolted all the passengers forward.*

**jolt²** /dʒoʊlt/ ***noun*** [usually sing.] **1** a sudden movement: *The train stopped with a jolt.* **2** a surprise or shock: *His sudden anger gave her quite a jolt.*

**jos·tle** /ˈdʒɑsl/ ***verb*** [I,T] to push against sb in a rough way (often in a crowd)

**jot** /dʒɑt/ ***verb*** (**jot·ting**; **jot·ted**)

PHRV **jot sth down** to make a quick short note of sth: *Let me jot down your address.*

⋆**jour·nal** /ˈdʒərnl/ ***noun*** [C] **1** a magazine, especially one in which all the articles are about a particular subject: *a medical journal* **2** a written account of what you have done each day: *to keep a journal* (= to write regularly in one)

**jour·nal·ism** /ˈdʒərnəl·ɪzəm/ ***noun*** [U] the profession of collecting, writing and publishing news in newspapers and magazines and on television and radio

⋆**jour·nal·ist** /ˈdʒərnəl·ɪst/ ***noun*** [C] a person whose job is to collect, write or publish news, in newspapers and magazines or on television and radio: *a job as a journalist with the local paper* ➲ Look at **reporter**.

⋆**jour·ney** /ˈdʒərni/ ***noun*** [C] (*pl.* **jour·neys**) a long trip from one place to another: *He wrote a book describing his journey through South America.* ➲ Look at the note at **travel**.

**jo·vi·al** /ˈdʒoʊviəl/ ***adj.*** (used about a person) very cheerful and friendly

⋆**joy** /dʒɔɪ/ ***noun*** **1** [U] a feeling of great happiness: *We'd like to wish you joy and success in your life together.* ◇ *to jump/shout for joy* (= because you feel so happy) **2** [C] a person or thing that gives you great pleasure: *That class is a joy to teach.*

J

**joy·ful** /ˈdʒɔɪfl/ *adj.* very happy: *a joyful occasion.* ▸ **joy·ful·ly** *adv.* ▸ **joy·ful·ness** *noun* [U]

**joy·ride** /ˈdʒɔɪraɪd/ *noun* [C] (*informal*) a drive or ride (usually in a stolen car) just for fun and excitement ▸ **ˈjoy·rid·er** *noun* [C] ▸ **ˈjoy·rid·ing** *noun* [U]

**joy·stick** /ˈdʒɔɪstɪk/ *noun* [C] a handle used for controlling movement on a computer, an airplane, etc.

**Jr.** *abbr.* = JUNIOR[1] (2)

**ju·bi·lant** /ˈdʒubɪlənt/ *adj.* (*formal*) extremely happy, especially because of a success: *The fans were jubilant at their team's victory.*

**ju·bi·la·tion** /ˌdʒubɪˈleɪʃn/ *noun* [U] great happiness because of a success

**Ju·da·ism** /ˈdʒudeɪɪzəm; -dɪɪzəm/ *noun* [U] the religion of the Jewish people, which is based on the Old Testament of the Bible

★**judge**[1] /dʒʌdʒ/ *noun* [C] **1** a person whose job is to apply the law and decide what punishment should be given to sb found guilty in a court of law: *The judge sentenced the man to three years in prison.* **2** a person who decides who has won a competition: *The judges included several local celebrities.* ◇ *The judges' decision is final* (= it cannot be changed). **3** a person who has the ability or knowledge to give an opinion about sth: *You're a good judge of character – what do you think of him?*

★**judge**[2] /dʒʌdʒ/ *verb* **1** [I,T] to form or give an opinion about sb/sth; to consider: *Judging from what he said, his work is going well.* ◇ *It's hard to judge how long the project will take.* ◇ *The movie was judged to be too violent for young children.* **2** [T] to decide the result or winner (in a competition): *The principal will judge the contest.* **3** [T] to be critical about sb; to form an unfair opinion about sb: *I wish you'd quit judging my friends!* **4** [I,T] to act as a JUDGE[1] (1), in a court of law: *He said it was the hardest case he had ever had to judge.*

★**judg·ment** /ˈdʒʌdʒmənt/ *noun* **1** [C] an opinion: *What, in your judgment, would be the best course of action?* **2** [C,U] an official decision made by a judge or a court of law: *The man collapsed when the judgment was read out in court.* **3** [U] the ability to form sensible opinions or to make wise decisions

★**ju·di·cial** /dʒuˈdɪʃl/ *adj.* **1** of a judge, a judgment or a court of law: *judicial powers* **2** connected with the part of the government that involves the courts: *the judicial branch of the federal government*

**ju·di·cious** /dʒuˈdɪʃəs/ *adj.* (used about a decision or an action) sensible ▸ **ju·di·cious·ly** *adv.*

**ju·do** /ˈdʒudoʊ/ *noun* [U] a sport from Asia in which two people fight and try to throw each other to the ground ➲ Look at **martial art**.

**jug** /dʒʌg/ *noun* [C] a large container with a small opening and a handle, used for holding liquids: *a jug of cider* ➲ picture at **pitcher**.

**jug·gle** /ˈdʒʌgl/ *verb* **1** [I,T] to keep several objects in the air at the same time by throwing and catching them quickly: *He can dance, sing, juggle – whatever you like!* **2** [T] to try to keep two or more activities, etc. in progress at the same time: *I'll have to juggle my work schedule around so that I'm free on Mondays.* ◇ *She's trying to juggle a career with raising a family.* ▸ **jug·gler** /ˈdʒʌglər/ *noun* [C]

★**juice** /dʒus/ *noun* [C,U] **1** the liquid that comes from fruit and vegetables: *lemon juice* ◇ *I'll have a large orange juice.* **2** [usually pl.] the liquid that comes from a piece of meat when it is cooked

★**juic·y** /ˈdʒusi/ *adj.* (**juic·i·er**; **juic·i·est**) **1** containing a lot of juice: *juicy oranges* **2** (*informal*) interesting because it is connected with sth bad: *Tell me all the juicy details!*

**juke·box** /ˈdʒukbɑks/ *noun* [C] a machine in a cafe or bar that plays music when money is put into it

★**Ju·ly** /dʒʊˈlaɪ/ *noun* [C,U] (*pl.* **Ju·lys**) (*abbr.* **Jul.**) the seventh month of the year, coming before August ➲ For examples of the use of the months in sentences, look at **January**.

**jum·ble** /ˈdʒʌmbl/ *noun* [sing.] a messy group of things; a mess: *a jumble of shoes in the closet* ▸ **jum·bled** /ˈdʒʌmbld/ *adj.*: *a jumbled heap of toys*

**jum·bo** /ˈdʒʌmboʊ/ *adj.* (*informal*) (only *before* a noun) very large

★**jump**[1] /dʒʌmp/ *verb*

➤ MOVE OFF/TO GROUND **1** [I] to move quickly off the ground by pushing yourself up with your legs and feet: *to jump into the air/over a stream/onto a chair* ◇ *How high can you jump?* ◇ *Jump up and down to keep warm.* ➲ Picture at **bounce**. **2** [I] to let your body drop from a high place to a lower place: *She killed herself by jumping off a bridge.* ➲ Look also at **bungee jumping**.

➤ PASS OVER STH **3** [T] to get over sth by JUMPING (1): *The dog jumped the fence and ran off down the road.*

➤ MOVE QUICKLY **4** [I] to move quickly and suddenly: *The telephone rang and she jumped up to answer it.* ◇ *He jumped out of bed when he realized what time it was.* **5** [I] to make a sudden movement because of surprise, fear or excitement: *"Oh, it's only you – you made me jump," he said.*

➤ INCREASE **6** [I,T] **jump (from sth) to sth; jump (by) (sth)** to increase suddenly by a very large amount: *His salary jumped from $30,000 to $50,000 last year.* ◇ *Prices jumped (by) 50% in the summer.*

➤ CHANGE SUDDENLY **7** [I] **jump from sth to sth** to change suddenly from one subject to another: *The book kept jumping from the present to the past.*

IDM **jump on the bandwagon** to copy what other people are doing because it is fashionable or successful

**jump the gun** (*informal*) to do sth or start sth too soon: *Don't jump the gun on this – make sure you get permission first.*

**jump/leap to conclusions** → CONCLUSION

PHR V **jump at sth** to accept an opportunity or an offer eagerly: *I jumped at the chance to be on the committee.*

★**jump**[2] /dʒʌmp/ *noun* [C] **1** an act of jumping: *With a huge jump the horse cleared the fence.* ➲ Look at **high jump** and **long jump**. **2 a jump (in sth)** a sudden increase in amount, price or value

**jump·er** /ˈdʒʌmpər/ *noun* [C] **1** a type of dress without sleeves, that is usually worn over a shirt **2** a person or animal that jumps

**ˈjump rope** (*Cdn. also* **ˈskipping rope**) *noun* [C] a long piece of rope, often with a handle at each end, that is used for jumping over again and again as a game or as a form of exercise

**'jump-start** ***verb*** [T] **1** to start the engine of a car that does not work by using wires to connect its battery to the battery of a car that works **2** (*informal*) to start a process, an activity, etc., or to make sth happen more quickly: *an effort to jump-start the senator's campaign for re-election*

**jump·suit** /'dʒʌmpsut/ ***noun*** [C] a piece of clothing that consists of pants and a jacket or shirt sewn together in one piece, worn especially by women

**jump·y** /'dʒʌmpi/ ***adj.*** (*informal*) nervous or anxious: *Why are you so jumpy today?*

**junc·tion** /'dʒʌŋkʃn/ ***noun*** [C] a place where roads or railroad lines meet or join: *There was an accident at the junction of routes 17 and 21.*

★**June** /dʒun/ ***noun*** [C,U] (*abbr.* **Jun.**) the sixth month of the year, coming before July ➲ For examples of the use of the months in sentences, look at **January**.

★**jun·gle** /'dʒʌŋgl/ ***noun*** [C,U] a thick forest in a hot tropical country: *the jungles of Africa and South America* ➲ Look at the note at **forest**.

**,jungle 'gym** ***noun*** [C] a structure made of metal bars, ropes, steps, etc., joined together for children to climb and play on

★**jun·ior¹** /'dʒunyər/ ***adj.*** **1** connected with students who are in their eleventh year of school or in their third year of college: *the junior class play* **2 Junior** (*abbr.* **Jr.**) (used after the name of a son who has the same first name as his father): *Sammy Davis, Jr.* **3 junior (to sb)** having a low or lower position (than sb) in an organization, etc.: *a junior officer* ◇ *A lieutenant is junior to a captain in the army.* OPP **senior** **4** of or for younger children: *the winner of the junior tournament*

★**jun·ior²** /'dʒunyər/ ***noun*** **1** [C] a student who is in his/her eleventh year in school or his/her third year in college ➲ Look at **freshman**, **sophomore** and **senior**. **2** [sing.] (with *his, her, your*, etc.) a person who is younger than sb else by the number of years mentioned: *She's two years his junior/his junior by two years.* ➲ Look at **senior**.

**,junior 'college** ***noun*** [C] (*U.S.*) = COMMUNITY COLLEGE ➲ For more information on the U.S. education system, look at study page **A8**.

**,junior 'high school** (*also informal* **,junior 'high**) ***noun*** [C,U] a school for students who are about 12 to 15 years old ➲ For more information on the education system, look at study page **A8**.

**junk** /dʒʌŋk/ ***noun*** [U] (*informal*) things that are old or useless or do not have much value: *There's an awful lot of junk up in the attic – we ought to clean it out.*

**'junk food** ***noun*** [U] (*informal*) food that is not healthy but that is ready to eat or easy to prepare: *junk food like potato chips and candy*

**junk·ie** /'dʒʌŋki/ ***noun*** [C] (*informal*) **1** a person who takes a lot of illegal drugs and is unable to stop **2** a person who is extremely interested in sth and does, uses, etc. it a lot: *a sports junkie*

**'junk mail** ***noun*** [U] mail, usually advertisements, that is sent to people but that they do not want

**junk·yard** /'dʒʌŋkyɑrd/ ***noun*** [C] a place where old cars, machines, etc., are collected, so that parts of them, or the metal they are made of, can be sold to be used again

**Ju·pi·ter** /'dʒupəṭər/ ***noun*** [sing.] the planet that is fifth in order from the sun

**ju·ris·dic·tion** /,dʒʊərəs'dɪkʃn/ ***noun*** [U] legal power or authority; the area in which this power can be used: *That matter is outside the jurisdiction of this court.*

**ju·ror** /'dʒʊrər/ ***noun*** [C] a member of a jury

★**ju·ry** /'dʒʊri/ ***noun*** [C] (*pl.* **ju·ries**) a group of twelve people in a court of law who listen to the facts about a crime and decide whether the accused person is guilty or not guilty: *Does the jury have to reach a unanimous decision?* ◇ *The jury returned a guilty verdict.* ➲ Look also at **grand jury**.

★**just¹** /dʒʌst/ ***adv.*** **1** exactly: *That's just what I meant.* ◇ *You're just as smart as he is.* **2** only: *She's just a child.* ◇ *It's not just the money; it's the principle of the thing, too.* ◇ *It was worth it just to see her face as she opened the present.* ◇ *Just a minute! I'm almost ready.* **3** a very short time ago: *She's just been offered a new job.* ◇ *He'd just returned from the Bahamas when I saw him.* ◇ *I just ate a candy bar, so I'm not hungry.* **4 just (about to do sth)**; **just (going to do sth)** at this/that moment; now or very soon: *We were just finishing supper when the phone rang.* ◇ *I was just about to call my mother when she got here.* **5** at exactly the same time (as); when: *Just as I was beginning to enjoy myself, John said it was time to go.* ◇ *Just then the door opened.* **6** (often before *barely*) almost not; hardly: *I could just barely hear what she was saying.* **7** (often with the imperative) (used for getting attention or for emphasis): *Just let me talk for a minute, will you?* ◇ *I just don't want to go to the party.* ◇ *Just imagine how awful she must feel!* **8** really; absolutely: *Our trip was just great.*

IDM **all/just the same** → SAME²

**it is just as well (that)** it is a good thing: *It's just as well that he never found out about it.*

**just about** almost; very nearly: *I'm just about finished.*

**just in case** in order to be completely prepared or safe: *It might be hot in Washington – take your shorts just in case.*

**just now** a very short time ago: *There was a call for you just now.* ◇ *We are just now starting to realize* (= since a very short time ago) *how serious the situation is.*

**just so** neat and correct; exactly as it should be

**would just as soon do sth** (used to say that sb would prefer to do sth): *I'd just as soon forget about that whole evening!*

**just²** /dʒʌst/ ***adj.*** (*formal*) fair and right; reasonable: *I don't think that was a very just decision.* ◇ *a just punishment* OPP **unjust**

★**jus·tice** /'dʒʌstəs/ ***noun*** **1** [U] fair behavior or treatment: *a struggle for justice* **2** [U] the law and the way it is used: *a miscarriage of justice* (= a wrong legal decision) **3** [C] (usually **Chief Justice**) a judge in the highest court (**the Supreme Court**) in the U.S. or Canada

IDM **do justice to sb/sth**; **do sb/sth justice** to treat sb/sth fairly or to show the real quality of sb/sth: *The photograph doesn't do you justice* (= make



J

you look as nice as you are). ◇ *The band couldn't do justice to that difficult piece.*

**ˌjustice of the ˈpeace** (*also* **ˌJustice of the ˈPeace**) **noun** [C] (*abbr.* **JP**) an official who judges less serious cases in a court of law and performs marriage ceremonies, etc.

**jus·ti·fi·a·ble** /ˌdʒʌstəˈfaɪəbl; ˈdʒʌstəfaɪəbl/ **adj.** possible to accept because there is a good reason for it: *His action was entirely justifiable.* OPP **unjustifiable** ▶ **jus·ti·fi·a·bly** /-əbli/ **adv.**: *She was justifiably angry and upset.*

**jus·ti·fi·ca·tion** /ˌdʒʌstəfəˈkeɪʃn/ **noun** [C,U] **justification (for sth/doing sth)** (a) good reason

★**jus·ti·fy** /ˈdʒʌstəfaɪ/ **verb** [T] (*pres. part.* **jus·ti·fy·ing**; *3rd person sing. pres.* **jus·ti·fies**; *pt, pp* **jus·ti·fied**) to give or be a good reason for sth: *Can you justify your decision?* ◇ *Nothing can justify child abuse.*

**just·ly** /ˈdʒʌstli/ **adv.** (*formal*) fairly or correctly

**jut** /dʒʌt/ **verb** (**jut̲·ting**; **jut̲·ted**)

PHR V **jut out** to stand out from sth; to be out of line with the surroundings: *rocks that jut out into the ocean*

★**ju·ve·nile¹** /ˈdʒuvənaɪl; -nl/ **noun** [C] (*formal*) a child or young person who is not yet an adult

★**ju·ve·nile²** /ˈdʒuvənaɪl; -nl/ **adj.** **1** (*formal*) connected with young people who are not yet adults: *juvenile crime* **2** like a child: *Don't be so juvenile!*

**ˌjuvenile deˈlinquent** **noun** [C] a young person who has committed a crime or who behaves like a criminal

**jux·ta·pose** /ˈdʒʌkstəpoʊz; ˌdʒʌkstəˈpoʊz/ **verb** [T] (*formal*) to put two people, things, etc. very close together, especially in order to show a contrast: *The artist achieves a special effect by juxtaposing light and dark.* ▶ **jux·ta·po·si·tion** /ˌdʒʌkstəpəˈzɪʃn/ **noun** [U]

# Kk

**K, k** /keɪ/ **noun** [C,U] (*pl.* **K's**; **k's**) the eleventh letter of the English alphabet: *"Kate" begins with (a) "K."*

**K** /keɪ/ **abbr.** **1** (*informal*) thousand: *She earns $60K a year.* **2** (*computing*) = KILOBYTE, KILOBYTES: *This disk only has 12K of memory free on it.* **3** = KARAT: *a 14K gold ring*

**ka·lei·do·scope** /kəˈlaɪdəskoʊp/ **noun** [C] a toy that consists of a tube containing mirrors and small pieces of colored plastic. When you look into one end of the tube and turn it, you see changing patterns of colors.

**kan·ga·roo** /ˌkæŋgəˈru/ **noun** [C] (*pl.* **kan·ga·roos**) an Australian animal that moves by jumping on its strong back legs and that carries its young in a pocket of skin (a pouch) on its stomach

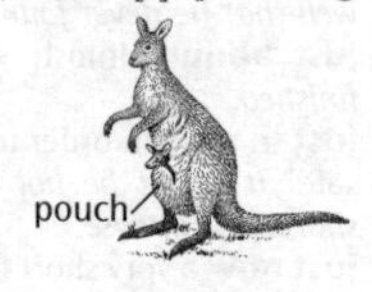


**kap·pa** /ˈkæpə/ **noun** (*symbol* K, κ) the tenth letter of the Greek alphabet ➲ Look at the note at **fraternity**.

**kar·a·o·ke** /ˌkæriˈoʊki; ˌkɛr-/ **noun** [U] a type of entertainment in which a machine plays only the music of popular songs so that people can sing the words themselves

**kar·at** /ˈkærət/ **noun** [C] (*abbr.* **K**) a unit of measurement used to describe how pure gold is: *a 20-karat gold ring*

**ka·ra·te** /kəˈrɑti/ **noun** [U] a style of fighting originally from Japan in which the hands and feet are used as weapons

**kay·ak** /ˈkaɪæk/ **noun** [C] a light narrow boat (canoe) in which the part where you sit is covered over ➲ picture on study page A32

**ke·bab** (*also* **ka·bob**) /kəˈbɑb/ **noun** [C] small pieces of meat, vegetables, etc. that are cooked on a stick (a skewer)

**keel¹** /kil/ **noun** [C] the wooden or metal bar at the bottom of a boat

**keel²** /kil/ **verb**

PHR V **keel over** to fall over sideways: *Several people keeled over in the heat.*

**keen** /kin/ **adj.** (used about one of the senses, a feeling, etc.) good or strong: *Foxes have a keen sense of smell.*

IDM **keen on sb/sth** (often used with a negative) very interested in or having a strong desire for sb/sth: *I'm not very keen on opera music.*

▶ **keen·ly** **adv.**: *We are keenly aware of the problems there.* ▶ **keen·ness** **noun** [U]

★**keep¹** /kip/ **verb** (*pt, pp* **kept** /kɛpt/)

➤ CONTINUE **1** [T] to continue to have sth, permanently or for a period of time: *You can keep that pen – I don't need it anymore.* ◇ *Can I keep the car until next week?* **2** [I] to continue to be in a particular state or position: *You need to keep warm.* ◇ *That boy can't keep still.* ◇ *Keep close to me and we won't get separated.* **3** [T] **keep doing sth** to continue doing sth; to do sth again and again: *Keep going until you get to the church and then turn left.* ◇ *She keeps asking me dumb questions.*

➤ MAKE SB/STH REMAIN **4** [T] to make sb/sth remain in a particular state, place or condition: *Please keep this door closed.* ◇ *He kept his hands in his pockets.* ◇ *It's hard to keep the kids entertained when they can't go outside.* ◇ *I'm sorry to keep you waiting.*

➤ PUT/STORE **5** [T] to have sth in a particular place: *Where do you keep the matches?*

➤ DELAY **6** [T] to delay sb/sth; to prevent sb from leaving: *Finally – you're here! What kept you?*

➤ ANIMALS **7** [T] to have and take care of animals: *They keep ducks on their farm.*

➤PROMISE/ARRANGEMENT **8** [T] to do what you promised or arranged: *Can you keep a promise?* ◇ *She didn't keep her appointment at the dentist.* ◇ *to keep a secret* (= not tell it to anyone)
➤RECORD **9** [T] to write down sth that you want to remember: *Keep a record of how much you spend.*
➤OF FOOD **10** [I] (used about food) to stay fresh: *Onions will keep for months if you store them in a cool place.*

IDM **keep it up** to continue doing sth as well as you are doing it now: *You made very good progress this year. Keep it up!*

NOTE For other expressions using **keep**, look at the entries for the nouns and adjectives, e.g. **keep count** is at **count**.

PHR V **keep at it/sth** to continue to work on/at sth: *Keep at it – we should be finished soon.*
**keep away from sb/sth** to not go near sb/sth, especially to avoid danger: *Keep away from the neighbors' dog.*
**keep sb/sth back** to prevent sb/sth from moving forward: *The police tried to keep the crowd back.*
**keep sth back (from sb)** to refuse to tell sb sth: *I know he's keeping something back; he knows a lot more than he says.*
**keep sth down** to make sth remain at a low level, to stop sth from increasing: *Keep your voice down.* ◇ *We're trying to keep our electricity bill down.* ◇ *Keep it down* (= be quiet) *in there – I'm trying to sleep!*
**keep sb from sth/from doing sth** to prevent sb from doing sth: *His injury kept him from playing in the game yesterday.*
**keep sth from sb** to refuse to tell sb sth
**keep off sth** to not approach or go on sth: *Keep off the grass!*
**keep sth off (sb/sth)** to stop sth from touching or going on sb/sth: *Keep your hands off me!*
**keep on (doing sth)** to continue doing sth; to do sth again and again: *He keeps on interrupting me.*
**keep out (of sth)** to not enter sth: *The sign said "Danger – Keep out!"*
**keep to sth** to continue doing sth: *He didn't keep to the subject* (= he started talking about sth else).
**keep sth up 1** to continue doing sth: *How long can the baby keep up that crying?* ◇ *Your last essay was excellent. Keep up the good work!* **2** to prevent sth from falling down **3** to cause sth to remain at a high level: *We want to keep up standards of education.*
**keep up (with sb)** to move at the same speed as sb: *Can't you walk a little slower? I can't keep up.*
**keep up (with/on sth)** to know about what is happening: *You have to read the latest magazines if you want to keep up.*

**keep²** /kip/ ***noun*** [U] (*old-fashioned*) food and other things that you need for life: *to earn your keep*
IDM **for keeps** (*informal*) forever: *Take it. It's yours for keeps.*

**keep·er** /ˈkipər/ ***noun*** [C] **1** a person who guards or takes care of sth: *a keeper at the zoo* **2** (*informal*) something that is worth keeping, especially a fish that you have just caught: *Wow! This one's a keeper!*

**keep·ing** /ˈkipɪŋ/ ***noun***
IDM **in keeping with sth** correct or expected according to a rule, belief, etc.: *The manager's decision is in keeping with company policy.*

**keg** /kɛg/ ***noun*** [C] a round metal container with curved sides and a flat top and bottom, that is used for holding beer: *a keg party* (= where beer is served from a keg)

**ken·nel** /ˈkɛnl/ ***noun*** [C] a place where dogs can stay while their owners are on vacation.

**kept** *past tense, past participle of* KEEP¹

**ker·nel** /ˈkərnl/ ***noun*** [C] a single piece of grain, especially corn ➲ picture at **corn**.

**ker·o·sene** /ˈkɛrəsin; ˌkɛrəˈsin/ ***noun*** [U] a type of oil that is used in old-fashioned lamps, heaters, etc.

**ketch·up** /ˈkɛtʃəp; kætʃəp/ (*also old-fashioned* **catsup**) ***noun*** [U] a sauce made from tomatoes that is eaten cold with hot or cold food

**ket·tle** /ˈkɛt̬l/ ***noun*** [C] = TEAKETTLE

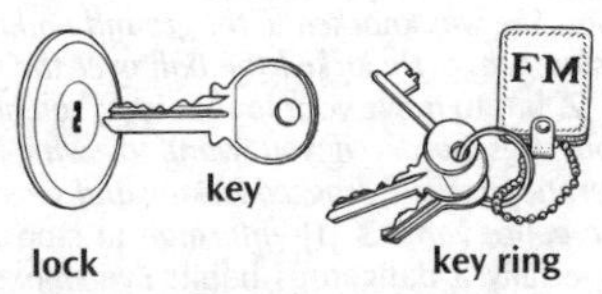


★**key¹** /ki/ ***noun*** [C]
➤FOR LOCK **1** a metal object that is used for locking or unlocking a door, etc.: *Have you seen my car keys anywhere?* ◇ *We need a spare key to the front door.* ◇ *a bunch of keys*
➤MUSIC **2** a set of musical notes that is based on one particular note: *The piece is in the key of A minor.*
➤ON MUSICAL INSTRUMENT/KEYBOARD **3** one of the parts of a piano, keyboard, etc. that you press with your fingers to make it work ➲ picture at **keyboard**.
➤ANSWERS **4** a set of answers to exercises or problems: *The key to the crossword will appear in next week's issue.*
➤ON MAP **5** a list of the symbols and signs used in a map or book, showing what they mean
➤MOST IMPORTANT THING **6** [usually sing.] something that helps you achieve or understand sth: *A good education is the key to success.* ◇ *This letter holds the key to the mystery.*

**key²** /ki/ ***verb*** [T] **key sth (in)** to put information into a computer or give it an instruction by typing on the keyboard: *to key in some data* ◇ *First, key in your password.*

★**key³** /ki/ ***adj.*** very important: *Tourism is a key industry in Florida.* ◇ *When you're writing a paper, organization is key.*

★**key·board** /ˈkibɔrd/ ***noun*** [C] **1** the set of KEYS¹ (3) on a piano, computer, etc. **2** an electrical musical instrument like a small piano

**keyboard**

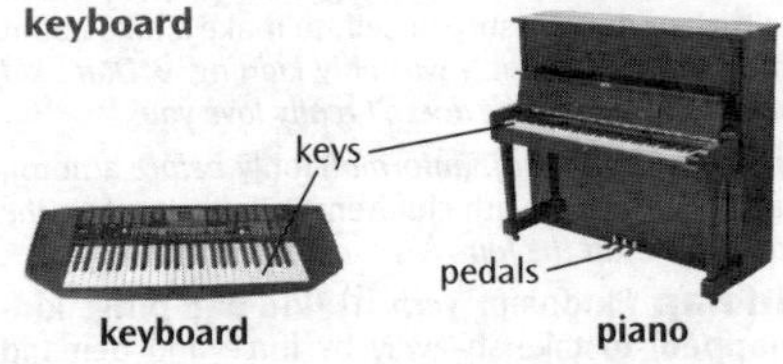

**key·hole** /ˈkihoʊl/ ***noun*** [C] the hole in a lock where you put the key

**key·note** /ˈkinoʊt/ ***adj.*** (only *before* a noun) (used about a speech or a speaker) introducing the most important topic at a large meeting, etc.: *The famous scientist gave the keynote address at the conference.*

**ˈkey ring** ***noun*** [C] a ring on which you keep keys ➲ picture at **key**.

**key·word** /ˈkiwərd/ ***noun*** [C] **1** a word that tells you about the main idea or subject of sth: *When you're studying a language, the keyword is patience.* **2** word that you type into a computer to search for information about a particular subject

**kg.** ***abbr.*** kilogram

**khak·i** /ˈkæki/ ***adj., noun*** [U] (of) a dull greenish-brown color: *khaki pants*

★**kick¹** /kɪk/ ***verb*** **1** [T] to hit or move sb/sth with your foot: *She was knocked to the ground and kicked in the stomach.* ◇ *He kicked the ball over the top of the net.* **2** [I,T] to move your foot or feet: *You have to kick your legs harder if you want to swim faster.* ◇ *The protesters were dragged kicking and screaming into the police vans.* **3** [T] (*informal*) to stop doing sth, especially a dangerous habit: *I've smoked for over twenty years, but I want to kick the habit* (= to stop smoking). ◇ *to kick a drug addiction* **4** [T] **kick yourself** (*informal*) to be annoyed with yourself because you have done sth stupid, missed an opportunity, etc.: *I could kick myself for deciding to take that class! It's way too hard.*

PHR V **kick sth off** to start sth, especially with an exciting event: *The candidate kicked off her election campaign with an appearance at the state capitol building.*

**kick sb out (of sth)** (*informal*) to force sb to leave a place: *He was kicked out of college.*

★**kick²** /kɪk/ ***noun*** **1** [C] an act of KICKING¹ (1,2): *She gave the door a kick and it closed.* **2** [C] (*informal*) a feeling of great pleasure, excitement, etc.: *He gets a real kick out of rock climbing.* ◇ *Some teenagers steal things just for kicks.*

**kick·back** /ˈkɪkbæk/ ***noun*** [C] money paid illegally to sb to influence that person's decision about what he/she or a company will buy: *For years the manager who ordered office supplies took kickbacks from the salesman.* SYN **bribe**

**kick·off** /ˈkɪkɔf/ ***noun*** [C] the start of a game of football: *Kickoff is at 2:30.*

★**kid¹** /kɪd/ ***noun*** [C] **1** (*informal*) a child or young person: *How are your kids?* ➲ **Kid** is much more common than **child** in informal and spoken English. **2** (*informal*) a son or daughter of any age: *Our kids are all grown up and married now.* **3** **kid brother/sister** (*informal*) younger brother/sister **4** a young goat ➲ picture at **goat**.

**kid²** /kɪd/ ***verb*** [I,T] (**kid·ding**; **kid·ded**) (*informal*) to trick or deceive sb/yourself; to make a joke about sth: *I didn't mean it. I was only kidding.* ◇ *Don't kid yourself, Martin –she doesn't really love you.*

**kid·die** /ˈkɪdi/ ***adj.*** (*informal*) (only *before* a noun) for or connected with children: *We only went on the kiddie rides at the fair.*

**kid·nap** /ˈkɪdnæp/ ***verb*** [T] (**kid·nap·ping**; **kid·napped**) to take sb away by force and demand money for his/her safe return: *The child was kidnapped and $50,000 was demanded for her release.* ➲ Look at **hijack**. ▸ **kid·nap·per** ***noun*** [C] ▸ **kid·nap·ping** ***noun*** [C,U]: *The kidnapping took place just outside his home.*

**kid·ney** /ˈkɪdni/ ***noun*** [C] (*pl.* **kid·neys**) one of the two parts of the body that separate waste liquid from the blood

**ˈkidney bean** ***noun*** [C] a type of bean with a red-brown color, shaped like a kidney

★**kill¹** /kɪl/ ***verb*** **1** [I,T] to make sb/sth die: *Smoking kills.* ◇ *She was killed instantly in the crash.*

> NOTE **Murder** means to kill a person on purpose: *This was no accident. The old lady was murdered.* **Assassinate** means to kill for political reasons: *President Kennedy was assassinated.* **Slaughter** and **massacre** mean to kill a large number of people: *Hundreds of people were massacred when the army opened fire on the crowd.* **Slaughter** is also used to talk about killing an animal for food.

**2** [T] (*informal*) to cause sb pain; hurt: *My feet are killing me.* **3** [T] to cause sth to end or fail: *The committee killed the proposal during yesterday's meeting.*

IDM **have an hour, etc. to kill** to have some time when you have nothing to do, usually when you are waiting for sb/sth

**kill time** to do sth uninteresting or unimportant to pass the time

**kill two birds with one stone** to do one thing which will achieve two results

**kill²** /kɪl/ ***noun*** [sing.] the act of killing (an animal): *The lion watched its prey, then moved in for the kill.* ➲ Look also at **road kill**.

**kill·er¹** /ˈkɪlər/ ***noun*** [C] a person, animal or thing that kills: *He's a dangerous killer who may strike again.* ◇ *a serial killer* (= sb who has killed many people) ➲ Look also at **painkiller**.

**kill·er²** /ˈkɪlər/ ***adj.*** (*slang*) (only *before* a noun) extremely difficult to deal with or to do: *We had a killer math test today.*

**kill·ing** /ˈkɪlɪŋ/ ***noun*** [C,U] the act of killing a person or an animal on purpose; a murder: *There have been a number of brutal killings in the area recently.* ◇ *a ban on the killing of whales* ➲ Look also at **mercy killing**.

IDM **make a killing** (*informal*) to make a large amount of money very quickly: *They made a killing on the stock market.*

**kiln** /kɪln; kɪl/ ***noun*** [C] an oven for baking clay and bricks, drying wood and grain, etc.

**ki·lo** /ˈkiloʊ/ ***noun*** [C] (*pl.* **ki·los**) *short for* KILOGRAM

**kil·o·byte** /ˈkɪləbaɪt/ ***noun*** [C] (*abbr.* **K**) (*computing*) a unit for measuring computer memory or information equal to 1,024 bytes

**kil·o·gram** /ˈkɪləgræm/ ***noun*** [C] (*abbr.* **kg.**) a measure of weight; 1,000 grams, or about 2.2 pounds

**kil·o·me·ter** /kɪˈlɑmɪt̬ər; ˈkɪləmit̬ər/ ***noun*** [C] (*abbr.* **km**) a measure of length; 1,000 meters, or about 0.62 miles

**kilt** /kɪlt/ ***noun*** [C] a skirt, usually made of wool, with many folds (**pleats**) and a pattern of colored squares and stripes that cross each other (**plaid**).

Kilts are worn by men in Scotland as part of their traditional national costume.

**kin** /kɪn/ ***noun*** [pl.] members of your family; relatives ➲ Kin is now a formal or old-fashioned word and is rarely used. **Next of kin** however, is still common. It means your closest family member, including your husband or wife, who should be told first if you are injured or killed.

★**kind**[1] /kaɪnd/ ***noun*** [c] a group whose members all have the same qualities: *The concert attracted people of all kinds.* ◇ *The concert attracted all kinds of people.* ◇ *Many kinds of plants and animals are being lost every year.*

NOTE *Kinds of* may be followed by a plural noun or an uncountable noun: *There are so many kinds of cameras on the market that it's hard to know which is best.* ◇ *I'm interested in all different kinds of music.* Sometimes you may hear people say something like: *Those kind/sort of dogs are really dangerous,* but this is still thought by many people not to be correct English.

IDM **a kind of; kind of a** (*informal*) (used for describing sth in a way that is not very clear): *There's a funny kind of smell in here.* ◇ *I had kind of a weird feeling that something was wrong.*

**kind of** (*informal*) a little bit: *I'm kind of worried about the interview.* ◇ *I kind of expected him to come late.*

**one of a kind** → ONE[1]

★**kind**[2] /kaɪnd/ ***adj.*** friendly and thoughtful about what other people want or need: *A present! How kind of you!* ◇ *to be kind to children and animals* OPP **mean** or **unkind** ▸ **kind·ness** ***noun*** [U]: *an act of kindness*

**kin·der·gar·ten** /ˈkɪndərgɑrtn; -gɑrdn/ ***noun*** [C,U] the first year of school for children, before first grade. Children usually begin kindergarten when they are five years old. ➲ Look at **nursery school**. ▸ **kin·der·gart·ner** (*also* **kindergartener**) ***noun*** [C] ➲ For more information on the North American educational systems, look at study pages **A8-A9**.

**kind·ly**[1] /ˈkaɪndli/ ***adv.*** **1** in a KIND[2] way: *The nurse smiled kindly.* **2** (used for asking sb to do sth, especially when you are annoyed) please: *Would you kindly leave me alone?*

**kind·ly**[2] /ˈkaɪndli/ ***adj.*** (**kind·li·er; kind·li·est**) (only *before* a noun) kind and friendly: *a kindly old man*

★**king** /kɪŋ/ ***noun*** [C] **1** (the title of) a man who rules a country. A king is usually the son or close relative of the previous ruler: *the king of Sweden* ◇ (*figurative*) *The lion is the king of the jungle.*

NOTE We say *King Henry VIII* as "King Henry the Eighth." ➲ Look also at **queen**.

**2** one of the four playing cards in a deck with a picture of a king on it: *the king of spades* ➲ Look at the note at **card**. **3** one of the pieces used in the game of chess ➲ picture at **chess**.

**king·dom** /ˈkɪŋdəm/ ***noun*** [C] **1** a country that is ruled by a king or queen: *the Kingdom of Saudi Arabia* **2** one of the parts of the natural world: *the animal kingdom*

ˈ**king-size** (*also* ˈ**king-sized**) ***adj.*** very large: *a king-size bed* ➲ Look at the note at **bed**[1].

**kink** /kɪŋk/ ***noun*** [C] a turn or bend in sth that should be straight: *There's a kink in the hose so the water won't come out.*

**kink·y** /ˈkɪŋki/ ***adj.*** (**kink·i·er; kink·i·est**) **1** (*informal*) connected with strange or unusual sexual activities **2** (used about hair) having many very small curls

★**kiss**[1] /kɪs/ ***verb*** [I,T] to touch sb with your lips as a greeting or to show love or affection: *They sat in the back row of the movie theater, kissing and giggling.* ◇ *He kissed her tenderly on the cheek.* ◇ *They kissed each other goodbye.*

★**kiss**[2] /kɪs/ ***noun*** [C] a touch with the lips: *Give Daddy a goodnight kiss.* ◇ *a kiss on the lips*

**kit** /kɪt/ ***noun*** [C] **1** equipment that you need for a particular activity, situation, etc.: *a first-aid kit* ◇ *a tool kit* **2** a set of parts that you buy and put together in order to make sth: *a kit for a model airplane*

★**kitch·en** /ˈkɪtʃən/ ***noun*** [C] a room where food is prepared and cooked: *We usually eat in the kitchen.* ◇ *a kitchen cupboard*

**kite** /kaɪt/ ***noun*** [C] a toy which is made of a light frame covered with paper or cloth. Kites are flown in the wind on the end of a long piece of string: *Several people were flying kites on the hill.*

**kitchen utensils**

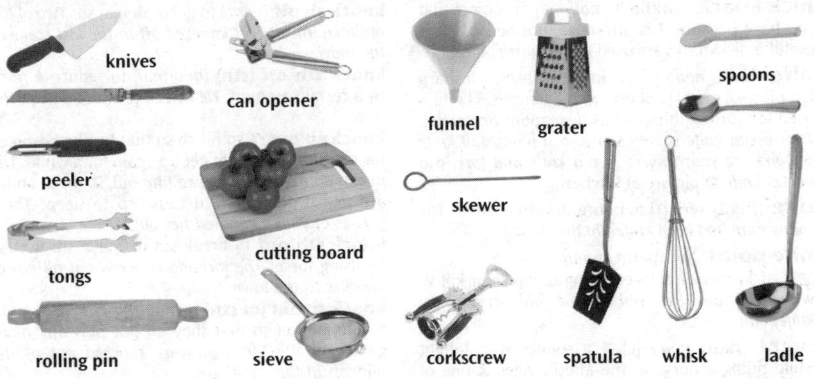

**kit·ten** /ˈkɪtn/ ***noun*** [C] a young cat ➲ Picture at **cat**.

**kit·ty** /ˈkɪṭi/ ***noun*** [C] (*pl.* **kit·ties**) (used especially by children) a cat

**ki·wi** /ˈkiwi/ (*also* ˈ**kiwi fruit**) ***noun*** [C] a fruit with brown skin that is green inside with black seeds ➲ picture on study page **A28-29**.

**Kleen·ex™** /ˈklinɛks/ (*also* **tissue**) ***noun*** [C,U] a thin piece of soft paper that you use for wiping or blowing your nose and throw away after you have used it

**klutz** /klʌts/ ***noun*** [C] (*informal*) a person who often drops things, is not good at sports, etc. ▸ **klutz·y** /ˈklʌtsi/ ***adj.***

**km.** ***abbr.*** kilometer

**knack** /næk/ ***noun*** [sing.] the ability to do sth (difficult): *Knitting isn't difficult once you get the knack of it.*

**knead** /nid/ ***verb*** [T] to press and squeeze sth with your hands: *Knead the bread dough for ten minutes, then let it rise.*

★**knee** /ni/ ***noun*** [C] **1** the place where your leg bends in the middle: *Angie fell and hurt her knee.* ◇ *Come and sit on my knee.* ➲ picture on study page **A32**. **2** the part of a pair of pants, etc. that covers the KNEE (1): *There's a hole in the knee of those jeans.*

**knee·cap** /ˈnikæp/ ***noun*** [C] the bone that covers the front of the knee

ˌ**knee-ˈdeep** ***adj.*** **1** deep enough to reach the knees: *We had to wade through knee-deep water.* **2 knee-deep in sth** (*informal*) very deeply involved in sth: *He was knee-deep in the company's illegal business deals.*

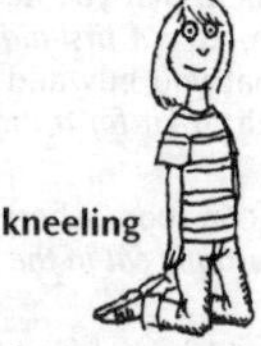

kneeling

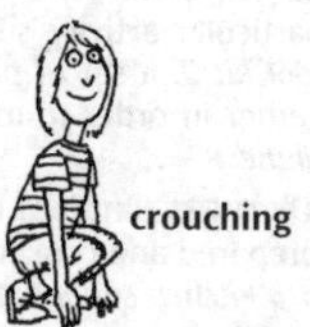

crouching

**kneel** /nil/ ***verb*** [I] (*pt, pp* **knelt** /nɛlt/ or **kneeled**) **kneel (down)** to go down on one or both knees; to be in this position: *Kneel down while I comb your hair.* ◇ *to kneel in prayer*

**knew** *past tense of* KNOW

**knick·knack** /ˈnɪknæk/ ***noun*** [C] an object that you have because it is attractive, not because it is useful. Knickknacks are used to decorate rooms, etc.

★**knife¹** /naɪf/ ***noun*** [C] (*pl.* **knives** /naɪvz/) a sharp flat piece of metal (a **blade**) with a handle. A knife is used for cutting things or as a weapon: *Be careful. That bread knife is very sharp.* ◇ *a blunt/dull knife* ◇ *Don't use your fingers. Use a knife and fork.* ◇ *a pocket knife* ➲ picture at **kitchen**.

**knife²** /naɪf/ ***verb*** [T] to injure sb with a KNIFE¹: *The young man had been knifed in the chest.*

**knife·point** /ˈnaɪfpɔɪnt/ ***noun***

IDM **at knifepoint** threatening to injure or kill sb with a knife: *He robbed the old woman at knifepoint.*

**knight** /naɪt/ ***noun*** [C] **1** a soldier who fought while riding a horse in the Middle Ages **2** one of the pieces used in the game of chess ➲ picture at **chess**.

★**knit** /nɪt/ ***verb*** [I,T] (**knit̲ting**; *pt, pp* **knit** or **knit̲ted**) to make sth (e.g. an article of clothing) with yarn using long NEEDLES (2) or a special machine: *Grandma loves knitting.* ◇ *I'm knitting a sweater for my nephew.*

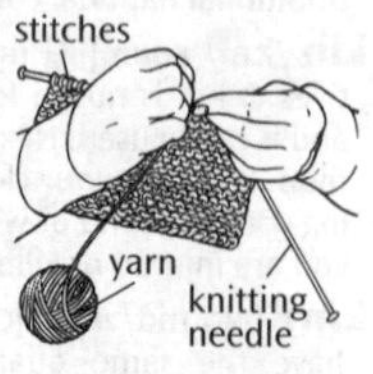


➲ Look also at **close-knit**. ▸ **knit·ting** ***noun*** [U]: *She put down her knitting and yawned.* ◇ *a knitting machine*

ˈ**knitting needle** ***noun*** [C] = NEEDLE (2)

**knives** *plural of* KNIFE¹

**knob** /nɑb/ ***noun*** [C] **1** a round handle on a door, etc. **2** a round button on a machine that controls a part of it

★**knock¹** /nɑk/ ***noun*** [C] a sharp hit or the sound it makes: *I thought I heard a knock at the door.* ◇ (*figurative*) *She has suffered some hard knocks in her life.*

★**knock²** /nɑk/ ***verb*** **1** [T] to hit sb/sth with a sharp blow: *He knocked the vase onto the floor.* ◇ *She fell off her bike and knocked two teeth loose.* ◇ *to knock sb unconscious* **2** [I] to make a noise by hitting sth: *Someone is knocking on the door.* **3** [T] (*informal*) to say bad or unfavorable things about sb/sth: *It's not the best food in the world, but it's free – so don't knock it!*

IDM **knock it off!** (*informal*) (used to tell sb to stop doing sth)

**knock on wood** (an expression that people use, often while knocking on sth made of wood, to prevent good luck from becoming bad luck): *I've been driving for 15 years without an accident – knock on wood!*

**knock your/sb's socks off** (*informal*) to surprise and impress sb: *This new show is really going to knock your socks off.*

PHR V **knock sb down** to cause sb to fall to the ground/floor: *The old lady got knocked down by a car.*

**knock sth down** to destroy a building, etc.: *The old houses will be knocked down to make way for an apartment complex.*

**knock off (sth)** (*informal*) to stop doing work, etc.: *What time do you knock off?*

**knock sb off** (*slang*) to kill or defeat sb: *Two of the main characters get knocked off in the last scene of the movie.*

**knock sth off (sth)** (*informal*) to reduce a price by a certain amount: *He agreed to knock $10 off the price.*

**knock sb out 1** to hit sb so that he/she becomes unconscious or cannot get up again for a while: *The punch on the nose knocked him out.* **2** (used about a drug, alcohol, etc.) to cause sb to sleep: *Three glasses of vodka knocked her out.*

**knock sth out** to break sth or make sth useless by using force: *The tornado knocked out all power supplies to the town.*

**knock sb out (of sth)** to beat a person or team in a competition so that they do not play any more games in it: *Our team was knocked out of the playoffs in the semifinals.*

**knock sb/sth over** to cause sb/sth to fall over: *Be careful not to knock over the drinks.*

**knock·out** /ˈnɑkaʊt/ ***noun*** [C] **1** a blow that causes sb to become unconscious or to be unable to get up again for a while **2** (*informal*) a very attractive woman

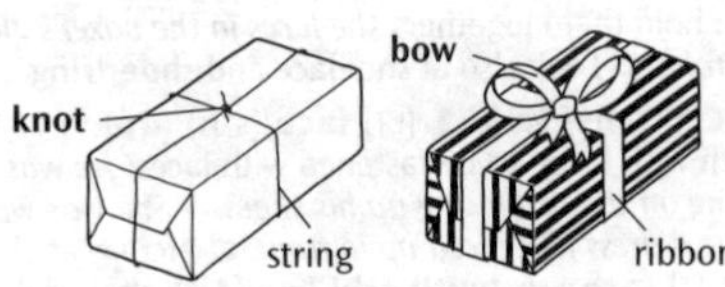


★**knot¹** /nɑt/ ***noun*** [C] a place where two ends or pieces of rope, string, etc. have been tied together firmly: *to tie/untie a knot* ◇ *a tight/loose knot*

**knot²** /nɑt/ ***verb*** [T] (**knot̬·ting; knot̬·ted**) (usually passive) to tie a knot in sth: *She wore her jacket knotted around her waist.*

**knot³** /nɑt/ ***noun*** [C] a measure of the speed of a ship or an airplane; 1.15 miles or 1.85 kilometers per hour

★**know¹** /noʊ/ ***verb*** (*pt* **knew** /nyu; nu/; *pp* **known** /noʊn/) (not in the continuous tenses)

➤ HAVE INFORMATION **1** [I,T] to have knowledge or information in your mind: *I don't know much about sports.* ◇ *Do you know their telephone number?* ◇ *"You've got a flat tire." "I know."* ◇ *Did you know that Jonathan enjoyed painting?* ◇ *Do you know the whole poem by heart?* ◇ *Knowing Sandra, she'll be out with her friends.*

➤ BE FAMILIAR **2** [T] to have met or seen sb before: *We've known each other for years.* ➲ Notice the expression **get to know sb**: *I'd like to get to know John better.* **3** [T] to be familiar with a place: *I don't know this part of the city well.*

➤ EXPERIENCE **4** [T] **know sb/sth (to do sth)** to have seen, heard, etc. sth: *I've known him to go a whole day without eating.* ◇ *It's been known to snow in June.* **5** [T] to have experience of sth: *They have known both wealth and poverty.* ◇ *Many people in western countries don't know what it's like to be hungry.*

➤ GIVE NAME/RECOGNIZE **6** [T] (often passive) to give sth a particular name; to recognize sb/sth as sth: *Istanbul was previously known as Constantinople.* ◇ *She's known as an excellent manager.* ◇ *He knows a genuine antique when he sees one.*

➤ LANGUAGE/SKILL **7** [T] to speak or understand a language: *I don't know much Spanish.* **8** [T] to be able to do sth: *Do you know how to swim?*

> NOTE Be careful. You must use **how to**; you CANNOT say: *I know swim.*

IDM **God/goodness/Heaven (only) knows** **1** I don't know: *They ordered a new car, but goodness only knows how they're going to pay for it.* **2** (used for emphasizing sth): *I hope I get an answer soon. Goodness knows, I've waited long enough.*

**know better (than that/than to do sth)** to have enough sense (not to do sth): *I thought you knew better than to go out in the rain with no coat on.*

**know sth inside out/like the back of your hand** (*informal*) to be very familiar with sth: *I grew up here. I know these woods like the back of my hand.*

**know what you are talking about** (*informal*) to have knowledge of sth from your own experience

**know what's what** (*informal*) to have all the important information about sth

**let sb know** → LET

**you know** (*informal*) **1** (used when the speaker is thinking of what to say next): *Well, you know, it's kind of hard to explain.* **2** (used when the speaker wants to check whether sb understands what he/she is saying): *It just makes me really mad, you know?* ◇ *I bought one of those new bread machines – you know, like the one Mike has.*

PHR V **know of sb/sth** to have information about or experience of sb/sth: *Do you know of a good restaurant nearby?*

**know²** /noʊ/ ***noun***

IDM **in the know** (*informal*) having information that other people do not have: *People in the know say that the governor is going to resign.*

ˈ**know-how** ***noun*** [U] (*informal*) knowledge of or skill in sth: *We are looking for someone with technical know-how in this field.*

**know·ing** /ˈnoʊɪŋ/ ***adj.*** showing that you know a lot about sth: *a knowing look*

**know·ing·ly** /ˈnoʊɪŋli/ ***adv.*** **1** on purpose: *I've never knowingly lied to you.* **2** in a way that shows that you understand: *He smiled knowingly.*

★**knowl·edge** /ˈnɑlɪdʒ/ ***noun*** [U, sing.] information or facts that you have in your mind about sth: *He has extensive knowledge of ancient Egypt.* ◇ *I have a working knowledge of French.* ◇ *To my knowledge they are still living there.* ◇ *She did it without my knowledge.*

IDM **be common knowledge** → COMMON¹

**knowl·edge·a·ble** /ˈnɑlɪdʒəbl/ ***adj.*** having a lot of knowledge; well-informed: *She's very knowledgeable about history.* ▶ **knowl·edge·ably** ***adv.***

**knuck·le** /ˈnʌkl/ ***noun*** [C] one of the places where the fingers join the rest of the hand, or between the bones in a finger

**ko·a·la** /koʊˈɑlə/ (*also* **koala bear**) ***noun*** [C] an Australian animal with thick gray fur that lives in trees and looks like a small bear

**Ko·ran** /kəˈræn; -ˈrɑn/ ***noun*** [sing.] **the Koran** the holy book of the Muslims

**ko·sher** /ˈkoʊʃər/ ***adj.*** (used about food) suitable to be eaten by religious Jews

**kung fu** /ˌkʌŋ ˈfu/ ***noun*** [U] a Chinese style of fighting using the feet and hands as weapons ➲ Look at **martial art**.

**kvetch** /kvɛtʃ; kfɛtʃ/ ***verb*** [I] (*informal*) complain

**kW** ***abbr.*** kilowatt(s); a unit for measuring electrical power: *a 2 kW electric heater*

**Kwan·zaa** /ˈkwɑnzə/ ***noun*** [U] a cultural festival that is celebrated by some African-Americans from December 26 through January 1

# Ll

**L, l** /ɛl/ **noun** [C,U] (*pl.* **L's; l's**) the twelfth letter of the English alphabet: *"Lake" begins with (an) "L."*

**L** *abbr.* large

**l** *abbr.* **1** liter **2 l.** left **3 l.** line

**lab** /læb/ **noun** [C] (*informal*) = LABORATORY

★**la·bel¹** /ˈleɪbl/ **noun** [C] a piece of paper, etc. on an object which gives information about it: *There is a list of all the ingredients on the label.* ◇ (*figurative*) *She hated the label "housewife."*

★**la·bel²** /ˈleɪbl/ **verb** [T] **1** to put a LABEL¹ or labels on sth: *All items of clothing should be clearly labeled with your name.* **2 label sb/sth (as) sth** to describe sb/sth as sth: *The press had labeled him an extremist.* SYN **categorize, pigeonhole**

**la·bor¹** /ˈleɪbər/ **noun** **1** [C,U] work, especially of a hard, physical kind: *manual labor* [C] (*formal*) *These changes are a direct result of her labors.* **2** [U] workers, when thought of as a group: *skilled labor* ◇ ***Labor relations*** (= between workers and managers) have improved in recent years. ◇ *the labor force* **3** [U] the process of giving birth: *She was **in labor** for ten hours.*

★**la·bor²** /ˈleɪbər/ **verb** [I] (*formal*) to work hard, especially on sth that is difficult: *She labored on her book for two years.*

★**lab·o·ra·to·ry** /ˈlæbrətɔri/ **noun** [C] (*pl.* **lab·o·ra·to·ries**) (*also informal* **lab**) a room or building that is used for scientific work or for teaching about science: *a physics laboratory* ➲ Look at **language laboratory**.

ˈ**Labor Day** **noun** [C,U] a holiday on the first Monday in September, when banks, schools and many businesses are closed: *Labor Day weekend* (= the weekend before Labor Day, when many people go on vacation)

**la·bor·er** /ˈleɪbərər/ **noun** [C] a person whose job needs hard physical work: *unskilled laborers*

ˈ**labor-inˌtensive** *adj.* (of a process, job, etc.) needing a lot of people to do it: *labor-intensive production processes*

**la·bo·ri·ous** /ləˈbɔriəs/ *adj.* needing a lot of effort ▸ **la·bo·ri·ous·ly** *adv.*

ˈ**labor-ˌsaving** *adj.* reducing the amount of work needed to do sth: *labor-saving devices such as washing machines and dishwashers*

ˈ**labor ˌunion** **noun** [C] = UNION (3)

**lab·y·rinth** /ˈlæbərɪnθ/ **noun** [C] a complicated set of paths and passages, through which it is difficult to find your way: *a labyrinth of corridors* ➲ Look at **maze**.

**lace¹** /leɪs/ **noun** **1** [U] cloth that is made of very fine threads in beautiful patterns: *lace curtains* ◇ *a collar made of lace* **2** [C] a long piece of string, leather, etc., that is used for tying two parts of an object to hold them together: *The laces in the boxer's glove broke.* ➲ Look also at **shoelace** and **shoestring**.

**lace²** /leɪs/ **verb** **1** [I,T] **lace (sth) (up)** to fasten sth with laces; to be fastened with laces: *He was sitting on the bed lacing up his shoes.* ◇ *She was wearing a dress that laced up in front.* ➲ picture at **shoe**. **2** [T] **lace sth (with sth)** to add alcohol, a drug, poison, etc., to food or a drink: *He laced the punch and everybody got drunk.*

★**lack¹** /læk/ **verb** [T] to have too little or none of sth: *She seems to lack the will to succeed.*

IDM **be lacking** to be needed: *Money is still lacking for the new school building.*

**be lacking in sth** to not have enough of sth: *He's certainly not lacking in intelligence.*

★**lack²** /læk/ **noun** [U, sing.] an absence of sth that is needed: *A lack of food forced many people to leave their homes.*

**lack·lus·ter** /ˈlæklʌstər/ *adj.* dull; not interesting or exciting: *a lackluster performance*

**la·con·ic** /ləˈkɑnɪk/ *adj.* using only a few words to say sth ▸ **la·con·i·cal·ly** /-kli/ *adv.*

**lac·quer** /ˈlækər/ **noun** [U] a type of transparent paint that is put on wood, metal, etc. in order to protect it and make it shiny

**lac·tose** /ˈlæktoʊs/ **noun** [U] a type of sugar found in milk

**lac·y** /ˈleɪsi/ *adj.* of or like lace

**lad·der** /ˈlædər/ **noun** [C] a piece of equipment that is used for climbing up sth. A ladder consists of two long pieces of metal, wood or rope with steps fastened between them: (*figurative*) *to climb the ladder of success*

**ladders**

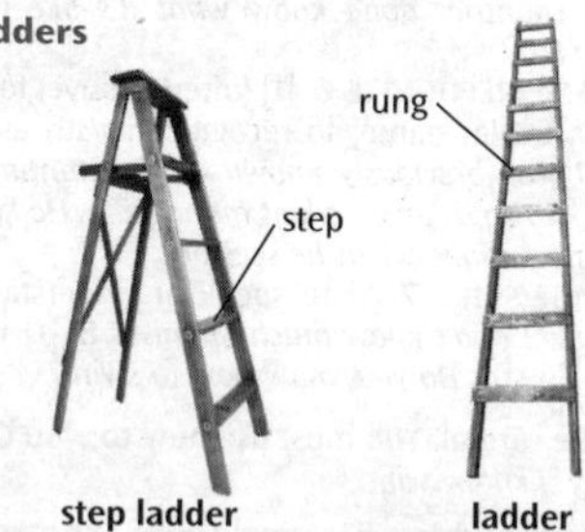


**lad·en** /ˈleɪdn/ *adj.* **laden with sth** having or carrying a lot of sth: *The guests arrived, laden with gifts.* ◇ (*figurative*) *to be laden with guilt*

ˈ**ladies' room** **noun** [C] a room with toilets in it for women in a public building ➲ Look at **men's room**, **restroom** and at the note at **toilet**.

**la·dle¹** /ˈleɪdl/ **noun** [C] a large deep spoon with a long handle, used especially for serving soup ➲ picture at **kitchen**.

**la·dle²** /ˈleɪdl/ ***verb*** [T] to serve food with a ladle

★**la·dy** /ˈleɪdi/ ***noun*** [C] (*pl.* **la·dies**) **1** a woman who is polite and who behaves well to other people: *A real lady does not scream and shout.* ➲ Look at **gentleman**. **2** (a formal or very polite way of saying "woman"): *The old lady next door lives alone.*

> NOTE Many women, especially younger women, do not like this use of **lady** because it seems old-fashioned. They prefer the word **woman**. Look also at **first lady**.

**3** (*informal*) (a rude way of talking to a woman who you do not know): *Hey, lady, why don't you hurry up?*

IDM **ladies and gentlemen** (used when you start making a speech to a large group of people)

**la·dy·bug** /ˈleɪdibʌg/ ***noun*** [C] a small insect that is red or orange with black spots

**lag¹** /læg/ ***verb*** [I] (**lag·ging**; **lagged**) **lag (behind sb/sth)**; **lag (behind)** to go more slowly than sb/sth: *I always lag behind when we go walking.* ◇ (*figurative*) *Tyler has missed a lot of school and is lagging behind the rest of his class.*

**lag²** /læg/ (*also* ˈ**time lag**) ***noun*** [C] a period of time between two events: *There will be a nine-month lag between the opening of the first part of the highway and its completion.* ➲ Look also at **jet lag**.

**la·goon** /ləˈgun/ ***noun*** [C] a lake of salt water that is separated from the sea by sand or rock

**laid** *past tense, past participle of* LAY¹

**laid-back** /ˌleɪd ˈbæk/ ***adj.*** (*informal*) having a relaxed, casual personality or atmosphere: *He's a really laid-back kind of guy.* ◇ *a laid-back style of management*

**lain** *past participle of* LIE²

**lair** /lɛr/ ***noun*** [C] **1** a place where a wild animal sleeps or hides **2** a place where sb goes to hide or to be alone

★**lake** /leɪk/ ***noun*** [C] a large area of water that is surrounded by land: *They went swimming in the lake.* ◇ *Lake Michigan* ◇ *the Great Lakes* ➲ A **pond** is smaller than a lake.

**lamb** /læm/ ***noun*** **1** [C] a young sheep ➲ Look at the note and picture at **sheep**. **2** [U] the flesh of a LAMB (1) when eaten as meat: *lamb chops* ➲ Look at the note at **meat**.

**lamb·da** /ˈlæmdə/ ***noun*** [C] (*symbol* Λ, λ) the eleventh letter of the Greek alphabet ➲ Look at the note at **fraternity**.

**lame** /leɪm/ ***adj.*** **1** not able to walk well because of an injury to the leg: *The horse is lame and cannot work.* ➲ **Lame** is not often used about a person. The verb and noun **limp** are more often used: *He walks with a limp.* ◇ *You're limping. Did you hurt your leg?* **2** (used about an excuse, argument, etc.) not easily believed; weak **3** (*slang*) not interesting, exciting or fashionable: *What a lame party!*

ˌ**lame** ˈ**duck** ***noun*** [C] (*U.S.*) a politician who does not have much real power because his/her period in a political position will end soon

**la·ment** /ləˈmɛnt/ ***verb*** [I,T] (*formal*) to feel or express great sadness (about sth)

**lam·i·nate** /ˈlæməneɪt/ ***verb*** [T] **1** to stick several thin layers of wood, plastic, etc. together **2** to cover sth in thin transparent plastic for protection ▸ **lam·i·nat·ed** ***adj.***

★**lamp** /læmp/ ***noun*** [C] a piece of equipment that uses electricity, gas or oil to produce light: *a table lamp* ➲ picture at **light**.

**lam·poon** /læmˈpun/ ***verb*** [T] to criticize sb/sth publicly in an amusing way that makes him/her/it look ridiculous: *His cartoons lampoon leading politicians.* ▸ **lam·poon** ***noun*** [C]

**lamp·shade** /ˈlæmpʃeɪd/ ***noun*** [C] a cover for a lamp that makes it look more attractive and makes the light softer ➲ picture at **light**.

**LAN** /læn; ˌɛl eɪ ˈɛn/ ***n*** [C] the abbreviation for "local area network"; a system for communicating by computer within a large building

**lance¹** /læns/ ***noun*** [C] a weapon with a long wooden handle and a pointed metal end that was used by people fighting on horses in the past

**lance²** /læns/ ***verb*** [T] to cut open an infected place on sb's body with a sharp knife in order to let out a substance made by the infection (**pus**)

★**land¹** /lænd/ ***noun***

➤SURFACE OF EARTH **1** [U] the solid part of the surface of the earth (= not water): *After three months on a ship, she was glad to reach* ***dry land****.* ➲ Look at the note at **ground**.

➤AREA OF GROUND **2** [C,U] a piece of ground: *They own over 2,000 acres of land.* ◇ *federal lands TP* (= owned by the federal government) **3** [U] ground, soil or earth of a particular kind: *The land is rich and fertile.* ◇ *barren land*

➤COUNTRY/REGION **4** [C] (*formal*) a country: *She died far from her native land.* ➲ Look at the note at **country**. **5** [U, sing.] (*informal*) an area or region that is connected with sth particular in people's minds: *California, the land of sun and fun*

★**land²** /lænd/ ***verb*** **1** [I,T] to come down from the air or bring sth down to the ground: *The bird landed on the roof.* ◇ *The pilot landed the airplane safely.* ◇ *He is due to land at 3 o'clock.* ➲ Look at **take off**. **2** [I,T] to go onto land or put sth onto land from a ship or boat: *Thousands of immigrants landed on Ellis Island in the early 1900s.* ◇ *Dave landed a 5-pound fish.* **3** [T] (*informal*) to get sth after a long effort: *The company just landed a big contract.*

ˈ**land claim** ***noun*** [C] (*Cdn*) a legal claim by an Aboriginal group concerning the use of an area of land

ˌ**landed** ˈ**immigrant** // ***noun*** [C] (*Cdn*) a person from another country who has permission to live permanently in Canada

**land·fill** /ˈlændfɪl/ ***noun*** [C] a place where large amounts of garbage or other waste materials are put into the ground and covered with earth

**land·ing** /ˈlændɪŋ/ ***noun*** [C] **1** coming down onto the ground (in an airplane): *to make an emergency landing* ◇ *a crash landing* ◇ *a safe landing* ➲ Look at **takeoff**. **2** the area at the top of a staircase or between one staircase and another

ˈ**landing strip** ***noun*** [C] = AIRSTRIP

**land·la·dy** /ˈlændˌleɪdi/ ***noun*** [C] (*pl.* **land·la·dies**) a woman who rents a house or an apartment to people for money

**land·locked** /ˈlændlɑkt/ ***adj.*** almost or

completely surrounded by land: *Switzerland is completely landlocked.*

**land·lord** /ˈlændlɔrd/ ***noun*** [C] a person or company that rents a house or an apartment to people for money

**land·mark** /ˈlændmɑrk/ ***noun*** [C] **1** an object (often a building) that can be seen easily from a distance: *The Empire State Building is one of the landmarks on New York's skyline.* **2** an important stage or change in the development of sth: *The French Revolution was a landmark in world history.*

**ˈland mine** ***noun*** [C] a device that is put under the surface of the ground, that explodes when sb walks on it or drives a car over it

**land·scape**[1] /ˈlænskeɪp/ ***noun*** [C] **1** an area of country (when you are thinking about what it looks like): *The prairie landscape is very flat.* ◇ *an urban landscape* ➲ Look at the note at **scenery**. **2** a picture that shows a view of the countryside: *one of Van Gogh's landscapes*

**land·scape**[2] /ˈlænskeɪp/ ***adj.*** (*computing*) (used about a page of a document) printed so that the top of the page is one of the longer sides ➲ Look at **portrait**[2].

**land·slide** /ˈlændslaɪd/ ***noun*** [C] **1** a sudden fall of earth, rocks, etc. down the side of a mountain **2** a result, especially in a political election, in which one person or party receives many more votes than anyone else: *The governor was re-elected in a landslide.*

**lane** /leɪn/ ***noun*** [C] **1** (*abbr.* **Ln.**) (used in the names of some streets in towns and cities): *We live at 1015 Beech Lane.* **2** a part of a wide road for one line of traffic: *You should signal before you change lanes.* ◇ *a four-lane highway* ➲ Look also at **fast lane**. **3** a part of a sports track, swimming pool, etc. for one competitor in a race: *The Kenyan runner is in lane two.* **4** a route or path that is regularly used by ships or airplanes: *shipping lanes*

★**lan·guage** /ˈlæŋgwɪdʒ/ ***noun*** **1** [U] the system of sounds and writing that human beings use to express their thoughts, ideas and feelings: *written language* ◇ *the spoken language* **2** [C] a form of language that is used by a particular group (usually in one country): *a foreign language* ◇ *Latin is a dead language.* **3** [C,U] any system of signs, symbols, movements, etc. that is used to express sth: *sign language* ◇ *computer languages like Fortran* **4** [U] words of a particular type, or words that are used by a particular person or group: *bad language* (= swearing) ◇ *legal language*

**ˈlanguage ˌlaboratory** ***noun*** [C] (*pl.* **language laboratories**) (*also informal* **language lab**) a room that has special equipment, e.g. tape recorders, to help you learn a foreign language

**lank·y** /ˈlæŋki/ ***adj.*** (used about a person) very tall and thin

**lan·tern** /ˈlæntərn/ ***noun*** [C] a type of light that can be carried. A lantern usually consists of a metal frame with glass sides and a lamp or candle inside. ➲ Look also at **jack-o'-lantern**.

**lap**[1] /læp/ ***noun*** [C] **1** the flat area that is formed by the upper part of your legs when you are sitting down: *Come and sit on my lap.* **2** one trip around a race track, across a pool, etc.: *There are three more laps to go in the race.* ➲ Look at the note at **length** (3).

**lap**[2] /læp/ ***verb*** (**lap·ping**; **lapped**) **1** [T] **lap sth (up)** (usually used about an animal) to drink sth using the tongue: *The cat lapped up the cream.* **2** [I,T] (used about water) to make gentle sounds as it splashes against sth: *The waves lapped against the side of the boat.*

PHR V **lap sth up** (*informal*) to listen to or read sth eagerly and accept it as true

**la·pel** /ləˈpɛl/ ***noun*** [C] one of the two parts of the front of a coat or jacket that are folded back

**lapse**[1] /læps/ ***noun*** [C] **1** a short time when you cannot remember sth or you are not thinking about what you are doing: *a lapse of memory* ◇ *The accident was the result of a temporary lapse in concentration.* **2** a short period of bad behavior that is unlike a person's usual behavior **3** a period of time in which you do not do sth, go somewhere, etc.: *She returned to work after a lapse of ten years.* ➲ verb **elapse**

**lapse**[2] /læps/ ***verb***

PHR V **lapse into sth** to go into a particular state: *to lapse into silence/a coma*

**lap·top** /ˈlæptɑp/ (*also* **ˌlaptop comˈputer**) ***noun*** [C] a small computer that is easy to carry around and that can use batteries for power

**lar·ce·ny** /ˈlɑrsəni/ ***noun*** [C,U] (*pl.* **lar·ce·nies**) the crime of stealing sth from sb; an occasion when this takes place: *He was charged with* ***grand/petty larceny*** (= stealing things that are valuable/not valuable)

**lard** /lɑrd/ ***noun*** [U] a white fat from pigs, that is used in cooking

★**large**[1] /lɑrdʒ/ ***adj.*** greater in size or amount than is usual: *I'll have a cheeseburger and a large Coke.* ◇ *Large amounts of money are spent on advertising.* ➲ Look at the note at **big**.

IDM **by and large** mostly; in general: *By and large, the school is very efficient.*

**large**[2] /lɑrdʒ/ ***noun*** [C] (*abbr.* **L**) something that is LARGE[1] or larger than average: *Do you have this shirt in a large?*

IDM **at large 1** (used about a criminal, animal, etc.) free: *The escaped prisoner is still at large.* **2** as a whole; in general: *Society at large is becoming more concerned about the environment.*

★**large·ly** /ˈlɑrdʒli/ ***adv.*** mostly: *His success was largely due to hard work.*

**ˈlarge-scale** ***adj.*** (only *before* a noun) happening over a large area or affecting a lot of people

**lar·va** /ˈlɑrvə/ ***noun*** [C] (*pl.* **lar·vae** /lar·vae; -vi/) an insect at the stage when it has just come out of an egg and looks like a short, fat worm

**lar·yn·gi·tis** /ˌlærənˈdʒaɪt̮əs/ ***noun*** [U] a mild disease of the throat that makes it difficult to speak

**la·sa·gna** /ləˈzɑnyə/ (*also* **la·sa·gne**) ***noun*** [U] an Italian dish made from a mixture of flour and water and sometimes egg (**pasta**), together with meat, vegetables and/or cheese, prepared in the oven

**la·ser** /ˈleɪzər/ ***noun*** [C] (a piece of equipment that produces) a very strong beam of light. Laser beams are used in weapons and medical operations and can also cut hard substances such as metals.

**ˈlaser ˌprinter** ***noun*** [C] a machine that is connected to a computer and that can print documents very clearly

**lash¹** /læʃ/ ***noun*** [C] **1** an act of hitting sb/sth with a whip: *The prisoner was given twenty lashes.* **2** = EYELASH

**lash²** /læʃ/ ***verb*** **1** [I,T] to hit (as if) with a whip: *The rain lashed against the windows.* **2** [T] **lash A to B; lash A and B together** to tie two things together firmly with rope, etc.: *The two boats were lashed together.*

PHR V **lash out (at/against sb/sth)** to suddenly attack sb/sth (with words or by hitting him/her/it): *When he came home drunk his wife lashed out at him.*

**las·so** /ˈlæsoʊ/ ***noun*** [C] (*pl.* **las·sos** or **las·soes**) a long rope with a circle at one end that is used for catching cows and horses ➲ picture at **cowboy**. ▸ **las·so** ***verb*** [T] (*pres. part.* **las·so·ing**; *3rd person sing. pres.* **las·sos** or **las·soes**; *pt, pp* **las·soed**)

★**last¹** /læst/ ***det.*** **1** coming at the end; final: *December is the last month of the year.* ◇ *Would the last person to leave please turn off the lights?* ◇ *She lived alone for the last years of her life.* **2** (only *before* a noun) (used about a time, period, event, etc. in the past that is nearest to the present): *I went shopping last Saturday.* ◇ *The last time I saw her was in San Francisco.*

NOTE **The latest** means "most recent" or "new." **The last** means the one before the present one: *His last novel was a huge success, but the latest one is much less popular.*

**3** (only *before* a noun) only remaining: *This is my last chance to take the test.* ◇ *Who's going to have the last piece of cake?* **4** (only *before* a noun) most unlikely; not suitable: *She's on a diet. Chocolate is the last thing she wants.*

IDM **(have) the last word 1** (to make) the final comment in a discussion or argument **2** (to make) the final decision about sth after a discussion

**the last minute/moment** the final minute/moment before sth happens: *We arrived at the last minute to catch the plane.* ◇ *a last-minute change of plan*

**(as) a last resort** when everything else has failed; the person or thing that helps when everything else has failed: *As a last resort we can always walk home.*

**the last/final straw** → STRAW

**next, second, third, etc. to last** the next, second, third, etc. one from the end: *Y is the second-to-last letter of the alphabet.*

★**last²** /læst/ ***adv.*** **1** at the end; after all the others: *The British athlete came in last.* ◇ *Put the eggs in last so they won't get crushed.* **2** on the occasion in the past that is nearest to the present: *When did you last have your eyes checked?*

IDM **last but not least** (used before the final item in a list) just as important as all the other items: *And last but not least, I'd like to thank you all very much.*

★**last³** /læst/ ***verb*** [I,T] **1** to continue for a period of time: *Do you think this weather will last until the weekend?* ◇ *The meeting lasted for an hour.* **2** to remain in a good condition: *It's only a cheap radio, but it'll probably last a year or so.* **3** (used about the quantity, condition, etc. of sth) to be good enough or sufficient for what sb needs: *The coffee won't last until next week.* ◇ *This old coat will have to last another winter.* ◇ *I only have ten dollars to last me until Saturday.*

**last⁴** /læst/ ***noun*** [C] (*pl.* **last**) **1** a person or thing that is after all the others: *Alex was the last to arrive.* **2 the last (of sb/sth)** the only remaining part of sth: *We finished the last of the milk at breakfast.*

IDM **at (long) last** in the end; finally: *After months of separation they were together at last.*

**last·ing** /ˈlæstɪŋ/ ***adj.*** continuing for a long time: *The children's faces left a lasting impression on me.*

**last·ly** /ˈlæstli/ ***adv.*** finally; last of all: *Lastly, I would like to wish you all a happy new year.*

★**ˌlast ˈname** ***noun*** [C] the name that you share with other people in your family: *"What's your last name?" "Jones."* ➲ Look at the note at **name**.

**ˌlast ˈrites** ***noun*** [pl.] a Christian religious ceremony that a priest performs for and in the presence of a dying person: *to administer/give the last rites to sb* ◇ *to receive the last rites*

**latch¹** /lætʃ/ ***noun*** [C] a small metal bar that is used for fastening a door or a gate. You have to lift the latch in order to open the door.

**latch²** /lætʃ/ ***verb***

PHR V **latch on (to sth); latch onto sth** (*informal*) to understand an idea or what sb is saying: *She latched onto the concept at once.*

**latch on (to sb/sth); latch onto sb/sth** (*informal*) **1** to become attached to sb/sth: *antibodies that latch onto germs* **2** to join sb and stay with him/her, especially when he/she does not want your company

★**late** /leɪt/ ***adj., adv.*** **1** after the usual or expected time: *She was ten minutes late for school.* ◇ *The ambulance arrived too late to save him.* ◇ *to be late with the rent* ◇ *to stay up late* ◇ *The buses are running late today.* **2** near the end of a period of time: *the late nineteenth century* ◇ *His mother's in her late fifties* (= between 55 and 60). ◇ *We got back home late at night.* **3** happening at night: *a late movie* **4** (*formal*) (only *before* a noun) no longer alive; dead: *his late wife*

IDM **a late night** → NIGHT

**late·ly** /ˈleɪtli/ ***adv.*** in the period of time up to now; recently: *I've been feeling really tired lately.* ➲ Look at the note at **recently**.

**lat·er¹** /ˈleɪt̬ər/ ***adv.*** at a time in the future, or more recently than sth in the past: *I'll call you back later.* ◇ *Later, he got a job as a salesman.*

IDM **later (on)** at a later time or in the future: *Later on, you'll probably wish that you'd worked harder in school.*

**see you later** (*informal*) goodbye (until some time in the future)

**sooner or later** → SOON

**lat·er²** /ˈleɪt̬ər/ ***adj.*** (only *before* a noun) coming at a time in the future, or after sth else in the past: *We can discuss that at a later date.* ◇ *The artist's later paintings consist mainly of landscapes.*

**lat·er·al** /ˈlæt̬ərəl/ ***adj.*** (*technical*) (usually before

L

a noun) connected with the side of sth or with movement to the side: *the lateral branches of a tree* ◇ *lateral eye movements* ▶ **lat·er·al·ly** ***adv.***

**lat·est**[1] /ˈleɪt̬əst/ ***noun*** [U] **the latest** the most recent (fashion, news, etc.): *Here is the latest* (= news) *on the space shuttle launch:...* ◇ *They have the very latest in software.*

IDM **at the latest** no later than: *I need your report by Friday at the latest.*

**lat·est**[2] /ˈleɪt̬əst/ ***adj.*** very recent or new: *the latest fashion* ◇ *the latest news* ◇ *the terrorists' latest attack* ➲ Look at the note at **last**[1].

**la·tex** /ˈleɪtɛks/ ***noun*** [U] an artificial substance like rubber, that is used in products such as gloves, paints, etc.

**lath·er** /ˈlæðər/ ***noun*** [U] white bubbles that you get when you mix soap with water

**Lat·in**[1] /ˈlætn/ ***noun*** [U] the language that was used in ancient Rome

**Lat·in**[2] /ˈlætn/ ***adj.*** **1** of or in LATIN[1]: *Latin poetry* **2** connected with, or typical of, Mexico, Central America, or South America

**La·ti·na** /ləˈtinə/ ***noun*** [C] a woman or girl in North America whose family came from Latin America

ˌ**Latin Aˈmerica** ***noun*** [U] Mexico, Central America and South America ▶ ˌ**Latin Aˈmerican** ***noun*** [C], ***adj.***

**La·ti·no** /ləˈtinoʊ/ ***noun*** [C] (*pl.* **La·ti·nos**) a person in North America whose family came from Latin America ▶ **La·ti·no** ***adj.***: *Latino culture*

**lat·i·tude** /ˈlæt̬ɪtud/ ***noun*** [U] the distance of a place north or south of the imaginary line around the middle of the earth (**the equator**) ➲ Latitude is measured in **degrees**. Look at **longitude**. ➲ picture at **earth**.

**la·trine** /ləˈtrin/ ***noun*** [C] a toilet in a camp, etc., especially one made by digging a hole in the ground

**lat·te** /ˈlɑteɪ/ ***noun*** [C] = CAFFÈ LATTE

**lat·ter**[1] /ˈlæt̬ər/ ***noun*** [sing.], ***pronoun*** **the latter** the second of two people or things that are mentioned: *We offer both standard and express delivery – the latter costs $5 extra.* ➲ The first of two people or things that are mentioned is **the former**.

★**lat·ter**[2] /ˈlæt̬ər/ ***adj.*** (*formal*) (only *before* a noun) nearer to the end of a period of time; later: *Interest rates should fall in the latter half of the year.*

★**laugh**[1] /læf/ ***verb*** [I] to make the sounds that show you are happy or amused: *His jokes always make me laugh.* ◇ *to laugh out loud*

PHR V **laugh at sb/sth 1** to show, by laughing, that you think sb/sth is funny: *The kids laughed at the clown.* **2** to show that you think sb is ridiculous: *Don't laugh at him. He can't help the way he speaks.*

★**laugh**[2] /læf/ ***noun*** [C] the sound or act of laughing: *Her jokes got a lot of laughs.* ◇ *She has a really irritating laugh.*

**laugh·a·ble** /ˈlæfəbl/ ***adj.*** deserving to be laughed at; foolish or ridiculous

**laugh·ter** /ˈlæftər/ ***noun*** [U] the sound or act of laughing: *Everyone roared with laughter.*

★**launch** /lɔntʃ/ ***verb*** [T] **1** to send a ship into the water or a rocket, etc. into the sky **2** to start sth new or to show sth for the first time: *The enemy launched an attack at midnight.* ◇ *to launch a new product*

PHR V **launch into sth** to start talking about sth in an enthusiastic or aggressive way: *She launched into an attack on her opponent's policies.*

▶ **launch** ***noun*** [C, usually sing.]: *The shuttle launch has been delayed.*

**Laun·dro·mat™** (*also* **laun·dro·mat**) /ˈlɔndrəmæt/ ***noun*** [C] a type of store where you pay to wash and dry your clothes in machines

★**laun·dry** /ˈlɔndri/ ***noun*** [U] clothes, etc. that need washing or that are being washed: *a laundry basket* ◇ *to do the laundry* (= to wash clothes, etc.)

ˈ**laundry room** ***noun*** [C] a room in an apartment building, etc., with machines for washing and drying clothes

**la·va** /ˈlɑvə/ ***noun*** [U] hot liquid rock that comes out of a volcano

**lav·a·to·ry** /ˈlævətɔri/ ***noun*** [C] (*pl.* **lav·a·to·ries**) a small room, especially in an airplane, that contains a toilet, sink, etc. ➲ Look at the note at **toilet**.

**lav·en·der** /ˈlævəndər/ ***noun*** [U] **1** a garden plant with purple flowers that smells very pleasant **2** a pale purple color ▶ **lav·en·der** ***adj.***

**lav·ish** /ˈlævɪʃ/ ***adj.*** **1** giving or spending generously or in large quantities: *She is very lavish with her presents.* **2** large in amount or number, and often expensive: *a lavish meal*

★**law** /lɔ/ ***noun***

➤RULE **1** [C] an official rule of a country, a state, etc. that says what a person, company, etc. may or may not do: *a law banning the sale of certain automatic weapons*

➤SYSTEM OF RULES **2 the law** [U] a law or the system of laws in a country, etc.: *Stealing is against the law.* ◇ *to break the law* ◇ *to obey the law* ➲ adjective **legal**

➤POLICE **3 the law** [U] the police: *This isn't the first time Dan has been in trouble with the law.*

➤SUBJECT/PROFESSION **4** [U] the law(2) as a subject of study or as a profession: *She is studying law.* ◇ *My brother works for a law firm in Cleveland.* ➲ adjective **legal**

➤IN SCIENCE **5** [C] (in science) a statement of what always happens in certain circumstances: *the laws of mathematics*

IDM **law and order** a situation in which the law is obeyed: *a breakdown of law and order*

ˈ**law-aˌbiding** ***adj.*** (used about a person) obeying the law: *We are all respectable law-abiding citizens.*

ˈ**law enˌforcement** ***noun*** [U] making sure that people obey the laws of a country, etc.: *Law enforcement officials arrested the suspects yesterday.*

**law·ful** /ˈlɔfl/ ***adj.*** (*formal*) allowed or recognized by law: *We will use all lawful means to obtain our demands.* ◇ *his lawful wife* SYN **legal** OPP **unlawful**

**law·less** /ˈlɔləs/ ***adj.*** (used about a person or his/her actions) breaking the law: *a gang of lawless youths* ▶ **law·less·ness** ***noun*** [U]

**law·mak·er** /ˈlɔˌmeɪkər/ ***noun*** [C] (*formal*) a person, e.g. a member of Congress, Parliament, etc., who makes new laws

**lawn** /lɔn/ ***noun*** [C,U] an area of grass in a yard or park that is cut regularly ➲ picture on study page **A31**.

**'lawn ˌmower** (*also* **lawn·mow·er**) /ˈlɔnˌmoʊər/ ***noun*** [C] a machine that is used for cutting the grass in a yard

**law·suit** /ˈlɔsut/ (*also* **suit**) ***noun*** [C] a legal argument in a court of law that is between two people or groups, usually because one person or group thinks the other did sth wrong to them and wants money in order to reduce the bad effect: *to file a lawsuit against sb*

★**law·yer** /ˈlɔyər/ ***noun*** [C] a person who has studied law and whose job is to give advice on legal matters and/or to speak for you in a court of law: *to consult a lawyer*

NOTE A more formal word for **lawyer** is **attorney**, which is used especially in job titles: *a defense attorney*

**lax** /læks/ ***adj.*** not having high standards; not strict: *Their security checks are fairly lax.*

★**lay**[1] /leɪ/ ***verb*** [T] (*pt, pp* **laid** /leɪd/) **1** to put sb/sth carefully in a particular position or on a surface: *He laid the child gently down on his bed.* ◇ *"Don't worry," she said, laying her hand on my shoulder.* **2** to put sth in the correct position, especially on a flat surface or under the ground, for a particular purpose: *They're laying new sewer pipes on our block.* **3** to produce eggs: *Does a snake lay eggs?* **4** (used with some nouns to give a meaning similar to a verb): *They laid all the blame on him* (= they blamed him). ◇ *lay emphasis on sth* (= emphasize it) **5** (often passive) (*slang, taboo*) to have sex with sb: *He went out hoping to* ***get laid*** *that night.*

PHRV **lay sth down** to give sth as a rule: *It's all laid down in the employee handbook.*

**lay off (sb)** (*informal*) to stop annoying sb: *Can't you lay off me for a little while?*

**lay sb off** to stop sb's job, usually because there is not enough work to do: *They laid off 500 workers at the automobile factory.*

**lay sth out** to spread out sth or a group of things so that you can see it/them easily or so that they look nice: *All the food was laid out on a table in the back yard.*

**lay**[2] /leɪ/ ***adj.*** (only *before* a noun) without special training in a particular subject: *a lay preacher*

**lay**[3] *past tense of* LIE[2]

★**lay·er** /ˈleɪər/ ***noun*** [C] a thickness or quantity of sth that is on sth else or between other things: *A thin layer of dust covered everything in the room.* ◇ *It's very cold. You'll need several layers of clothing.* ◇ *the top/bottom layer* ◇ *the inner/outer layer*

**lay·man** /ˈleɪmən/ ***noun*** [C] (*pl.* **lay·men** /-mən/) (*also* **layperson** (*pl.* **lay·people**)) a person who does not have special training in or knowledge of a particular subject: *It's difficult to explain the system in layman's terms* (= in a way that average people can understand).

**lay·off** /ˈleɪɔf/ ***noun*** [C, usually pl.] an act of stopping sb's job because there is not enough work for him/her

**lay·out** /ˈleɪaʊt/ ***noun*** [C, usually sing.] **1** the way in which the parts of sth, such as a building or an area, are arranged **2** the way in which words and pictures, etc., are arranged on a page

**lay·o·ver** /ˈleɪˌoʊvər/ ***noun*** [C] a short stop in a journey by plane

**laze** /leɪz/ ***verb*** [I] **laze (around)** to do very little; to rest or relax

★**la·zy** /ˈleɪzi/ ***adj.*** (**la·zi·er**; **la·zi·est**) **1** (used about a person) not wanting to work: *Don't be lazy. Come and give me a hand.* **2** moving slowly or without much energy: *a lazy river* **3** making you feel that you do not want to do very much: *a lazy summer day* ▸ **la·zi·ly** ***adv.*** ▸ **la·zi·ness** ***noun*** [U]

**lb.** ***abbr.*** = POUND[1] (1)

**LCD** /ˌɛl si ˈdi/ ***abbr.*** liquid crystal display (a way of showing information in electronic equipment so that numbers and letters can be seen on a small screen)

★**lead**[1] /lɛd/ ***noun*** **1** [U] (*symbol* **Pb**) a soft heavy gray metal. Lead is used in pipes, etc. **2** [C,U] the black substance inside a pencil that makes a mark when you write

★**lead**[2] /lid/ ***noun***

›FIRST PLACE **1** [sing.] a position ahead of other people, organizations, etc.: *America has taken the lead in developing computer software.* **2** **the lead** [sing.] the first place or position: *The Canadian athlete has just gone into the lead.* ◇ *Who is in the lead?* **3** [sing.] the distance or amount by which sb/sth is in front of another person or thing: *The company has a lead of several years in the development of the new technology.*

›ACTOR/MUSICIAN **4** [C] the main part or role in a play or show: *Who's playing the lead in the new movie?*

›INFORMATION **5** [C] a piece of information that may help to give the answer to a problem: *The police are following all possible leads to track down the killer.*

IDM **follow sb's example/lead** → FOLLOW

★**lead**[3] /lid/ ***verb*** (*pt, pp* **led** /lɛd/)

›SHOW THE WAY **1** [T] to go with or in front of a person or animal to show the way or to make him/her/it go in the right direction: *The teacher led the class back to the classroom.* ◇ *The receptionist led the way to the office.* ◇ *to lead sb by the hand* ➲ You usually **guide** or **show** a tourist or somebody who needs special help: *He guided the blind woman to her seat.* ◇ *to show visitors around the city*

›OF ROAD/PATH **2** [I] (used about a road or path) to go to a place: *I don't think this path leads anywhere.*

›CAUSE **3** [I] **lead to sth** to have sth as a result: *Eating too much sugar can lead to all kinds of health problems.*

›LIFE **4** [T] to have a particular type of life: *They lead a very busy life.* ◇ *to lead a life of crime*

›BE BEST/FIRST **5** [I,T] **lead (sb/sth) (in sth)** to be the best at sth or to be in first place: *Agassi is leading by two sets to love.* ◇ *Agassi is leading Ferrero by two sets to love.*

›BE IN CONTROL **6** [I,T] to be in control or the leader of sth: *Who is going to lead the discussion?*

›INFLUENCE **7** [T] to influence what sb does or thinks: *He led me to believe he really meant what he said.*

PHRV **lead up to sth** to be an introduction to or cause of sth: *What were the events that led up to the First World War?*

★**lead·er** /ˈlidər/ ***noun*** [C] **1** a person who is the head of sth or in charge of sth: *a weak/strong leader* ◇ *She is a natural leader* (= she knows how to tell other people what to do). **2** the person or team that is best or in first place: *The leader has just finished the third lap.*

**lead·er·ship** /ˈlidərʃɪp/ ***noun*** **1** [U] the qualities that a leader(1) should have **2** [U] the state of being a leader(1): *The company has done well under Mrs. Brown's leadership.* **3** [sing.] a group of leaders(1): *Has the leadership of our country lost touch with ordinary people?*

**lead·ing** /ˈlidɪŋ/ ***adj.*** **1** best or very important: *He's one of the leading experts in this field.* **2** in front or in first place: *Jordan has been the leading point scorer this season.* ◇ *the leading brand of shampoo* (= that sells the most)

★**leaf¹** /lif/ ***noun*** [C] (*pl.* **leaves** /livz/) one of the thin, flat parts of a plant or tree. Leaves are usually green and grow from a branch, but different plants have different shaped leaves: *autumn leaves* ➲ picture at **tree**.

**leaf²** /lif/ ***verb***

PHR V **leaf through sth** to turn the pages of a book, etc. quickly and without looking at them carefully

**leaf·let** /ˈliflət/ ***noun*** [C] a small printed piece of paper that advertises or gives information about sth. Leaflets are usually given free of charge: *I picked up a leaflet about museums in the downtown area.*

**leaf·y** /ˈlifi/ ***adj.*** (**leaf·i·er**; **leaf·i·est**) having many leaves: *cabbage, spinach, lettuce and other leafy vegetables*

★**league** /lig/ ***noun*** [C] **1** a group of sports clubs that compete with each other for a prize: *the National Football League* **2** a group of people, countries, etc. that join together for a particular purpose: *the League of Nations* **3** (*informal*) a standard of quality or achievement: *He is so much better than the others. They're just not in the same league.*

**leak¹** /lik/ ***verb*** **1** [I,T] to allow liquid or gas to get through a hole or crack: *The boat was leaking badly.* **2** [I] (used about liquid or gas) to get out through a hole or crack: *Water is leaking in through the window frame.* **3** [T] **leak sth (to sb)** to give secret information: *The committee's findings were leaked to the press.*

PHR V **leak out** (used about secret information) to become known: *The White House did not want the details to leak out.*

**leak²** /lik/ ***noun*** [C] **1** a small hole or crack that liquid or gas can get through: *There's a leak in the pipe.* ◇ *The roof has sprung a leak.* **2** the liquid or gas that gets through such a hole: *There are oil leaks all over the garage.* **3** the act of giving away information that should be kept secret or secret information that is given out

**leak·age** /ˈlikɪdʒ/ ***noun*** [C,U] an example of leaking; sth that has been leaked: *a leakage of dangerous chemicals*

**leak·y** /ˈliki/ ***adj.*** having a hole or holes through which liquid or gas can get in or out

**lean¹** /lin/ ***adj.*** **1** (used about a person or animal) thin and in good health **2** (used about meat) having little or no fat **3** not producing much: *a lean harvest*

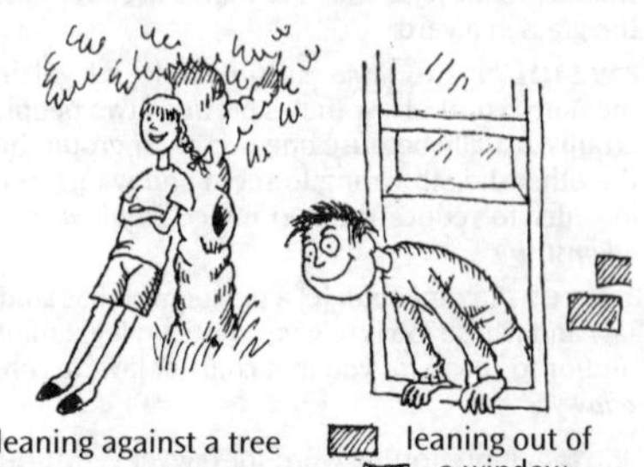

leaning against a tree — leaning out of a window

★**lean²** /lin/ ***verb*** **1** [I] to be in a position that is not straight or upright: *He leaned across the table to pick up the phone.* ◇ *to lean forward/backward/over to one side* **2** [I] **lean against/on sth** to rest against sth so that it gives support: *She had to stop and lean on the gate.* ◇ (*figurative*) *You can rely on me. I'll always be there for you to lean on.* **3** [T] to put sth against sth: *Please don't lean bicycles against this window.*

**leap¹** /lɛpt; lip/ ***verb*** (*pt, pp* **leaped** /lipt/ or **leapt** /lɛpt/) [I] **1** to jump high or a long way: *The horse leaped over the wall.* **2** to move quickly: *I leaped upstairs when I heard the scream.*

IDM **jump/leap to conclusions** → CONCLUSION

PHR V **leap at sth** to accept a chance or offer with enthusiasm: *She leapt at the chance to be on TV.*

**leap²** /lip/ ***noun*** [C] **1** a big jump: *He took a flying leap at the wall but didn't get over it.* **2** a great change (for the better) or an increase in sth: *Penicillin was a great leap forward in the field of medicine.* ◇ *a leap in the price of land*

**leap·frog** /ˈlipfrɔg; -frɑg/ ***noun*** [U] a children's game in which one person bends over and another person jumps over him/her

ˈ**leap year** ***noun*** [C] one year in every four, in which February has 29 days instead of 28

★**learn** /lərn/ ***verb*** **1** [I,T] **learn (sth) (from sb/sth)** to get knowledge, a skill, etc. (from sb/sth): *What did you learn about in school today?* ◇ *Debby is learning to play the piano.* ◇ *to learn a foreign language* ◇ *Where did you learn how to swim?* **2** [I,T] **learn (of/about) sth** (*formal*) to get some information about sth; to find out: *I was sorry to learn of your father's death.* **3** [T] to understand or realize: *We should have learned by now that we can't rely on her.*

IDM **learn (sth) the hard way** to understand or realize sth by having an unpleasant experience rather than by being told: *I had to learn the hard way that "inflammable" is not the opposite of "flammable!"* ◇ *Some people don't like to take advice; they have to learn everything the hard way.*

**learn your lesson** to understand what you must do/not do in the future because you have had an unpleasant experience

**learn·ed** /ˈlərnəd/ ***adj.*** **1** having a lot of knowledge because you have studied and read a lot

**2** connected with, or intended for LEARNED (1) people: *an article in a learned journal*

**learn·er** /ˈlərnər/ ***noun*** [C] a person who is learning: *a dictionary for learners of English*

**learn·ing** /ˈlərnɪŋ/ ***noun*** [U] **1** the process of learning sth: *new methods of language learning* **2** knowledge that you get from studying

ˈ**learning curve** ***noun*** the rate at which you learn a new subject or skill; the process of learning from the mistakes you make

ˈ**learning disaˌbility** ***noun*** [C] mental problems that people have that affect their ability to learn things

**lease**[1] /lis/ ***noun*** [C] an official written agreement (a contract) in which land, a building, etc. is rented to sb else for a certain period of time in return for money, usually paid every month

**lease**[2] /lis/ ***verb*** [T] to pay rent in order to use sth for a certain length of time, or to let sb use sth in this way: *to lease a car*

**leash** /liʃ/ ***noun*** [C] a long chain or piece of leather, rope, etc. that is attached to the collar around a dog's neck and used for keeping the dog under control: *All dogs must be kept on a leash.*

★**least**[1] /list/ ***det., pronoun*** (used as the superlative of *little*) smallest in size, amount, extent, etc.: *He has the least experience of all of us.* ◇ *Sherrie did the most work and John did the least.*

★**least**[2] /list/ ***adv.*** to the smallest extent or degree; less than anybody/anything else: *He's the person who needs help least.* ◇ *I bought the least expensive tickets.*

IDM **at least 1** not less than, and probably more: *It'll cost at least $200.* **2** even if other things are wrong: *It may not be beautiful but at least it's cheap.* **3** (used for correcting sth that you have just said): *I saw him – or at least I think I saw him.* **4** (used for saying that sth is the minimum you expect sb to do): *You could at least say you're sorry!*

**last but not least** → LAST[2]

**least of all** especially not: *Nobody should be worried, least of all you.*

**not in the least** (*formal*) not at all: *It doesn't matter in the least.*

**to say the least** → SAY[1]

★**leath·er** /ˈlɛðər/ ***noun*** [U] the skin of animals which has been specially treated. Leather is used to make shoes, bags, coats, etc.: *a leather jacket*

★**leave**[1] /liv/ ***verb*** (*pt, pp* **left** /lɛft/)

➤GO AWAY **1** [I,T] to go away from sb/sth: *When should we leave for the airport?* ◇ *The train leaves Ottawa at just after ten.* ◇ *He left his mother in tears.* ◇ *Barry left his wife for another woman.*

NOTE Notice that if you leave sb/sth it may be permanently or just for a short time: *He leaves home at 8:00 every morning.* ◇ *He left home and went to live with his girlfriend.* **Depart** is a more formal word and is used about boats, trains, airplanes, etc.: *The 6:15 train for Washington, D.C. departs from Track 3.*

➤SB/STH IN CONDITION/PLACE **2** [T] to cause or allow sb/sth to stay in a particular place or condition: *Leave the door open, please.* ◇ *Don't leave the iron on when you are not using it.* ◇ *Don't leave your friend outside. Ask him in.* **3** [T] to forget to bring sth with you: *I can't find my glasses. I must have left them at work.* **4** [T] to cause sth to remain as a result: *Don't put that cup on the table. It'll leave a mark.* **5** [T] to not use sth: *Leave some cake for me, please.* ◇ *Is there any bread left?* **6** [T] to put sth somewhere: *Val left a message on her answering machine.* ◇ *I left him a note.*

➤STH TO DO LATER **7** [T] to wait until later to do sth: *Let's leave the dishes until tomorrow.*

➤AFTER DEATH **8** [T] to give sth to sb when you die: *In his will he left everything to his three sons.*

➤RESPONSIBILITY TO SB **9** [T] to give the care of sb/sth to another person: *I'll leave it to you to organize the food.* ◇ *He left his assistant in charge when he went on vacation.*

IDM **leave sb/sth alone** to not touch, bother or speak to sb/sth: *She's very upset. Leave her alone for a few minutes.*

**leave sth/a lot, much, etc. to be desired** (*formal*) to be (a lot) less than perfect: *Quite frankly, your work lately has left a lot to be desired.* ◇ *The special effects left something to be desired.*

**leave sb in the lurch** to leave sb without help in a difficult situation

PHR V **leave sb/sth behind** to forget to bring sth with you: *I left my gloves behind and now my hands are cold.*

**leave sb/sth out (of sth)** to not include sb/sth: *This doesn't make sense. I think the typist left out a line.*

**leave sth with sb** to give the responsibility for doing sth to sb else: *Leave it with me and I'll get it taken care of.*

★**leave**[2] /liv/ ***noun*** [C,U] a period of time when you do not go to work, usually for a particular reason: *Peggy has been away on sick leave since her operation.* ◇ *maternity leave* (= for a woman who has just had a baby) ◇ *I'm taking a six-week leave of absence from work.* ➲ Look at the note at **vacation**.

**leaves** *plural of* LEAF[1]

**lec·ture**[1] /ˈlɛktʃər/ ***noun*** [C] **1 a lecture (on/about sth)** a talk or speech to a group of people on a particular subject: *He gave a lecture on the geology of the Pacific.* ◇ *a series of lectures* **2** a serious talk to sb that explains what he/she has done wrong or how he/she should behave

**lec·ture**[2] /ˈlɛktʃər/ ***verb*** **1** [I] **lecture (on sth)** to give a LECTURE[1] or lectures (on a particular subject) **2** [T] **lecture sb (about sth)** to talk seriously to sb about what he/she has done wrong or how he/she should behave: *The police officer lectured the boys about the dangers of playing in the street.*

**lec·tur·er** /ˈlɛktʃərər/ ***noun*** [C] a person who gives lectures

**led** *past tense, past participle of* LEAD[3]

**ledge** /lɛdʒ/ ***noun*** [C] a narrow shelf under a window, or a narrow piece of rock that sticks out on the side of a cliff or mountain

**ledg·er** /ˈlɛdʒər/ ***noun*** [C] a book or electronic document which lists the money which a business, organization, etc. has received or paid out

**lee·way** /ˈliweɪ/ ***noun*** [U] the amount of freedom that you have to change sth or to do sth in the way you want to: *We have some leeway on the deadline.*

L

★**left**[1] /lɛft/ ***adj., adv.*** on or to the side (of your body) that is toward the west when you face north: *Turn left just past the post office.* ◇ *I hurt my left arm.*

★**left**[2] /lɛft/ ***noun*** **1** [U] the left side: *Our house is the next one on the left.* ◇ *...and to your left, you can see the statue of Abraham Lincoln.* **2** [C] a turn to the left, or a street or road on the left: *Make a left at the stoplight.* ◇ *Go past the school and then take the next left.* **3 the left** [sing.] political parties or groups that support socialism: *The left is losing popularity.*

**left**[3] *past tense, past participle of* LEAVE[1]

★**left**[4] /lɛft/ ***adj.*** (not before a noun) remaining; available to use, sell, etc.: *There's only one piece of cake left.* ◇ *We have 50 tickets left to sell.*

IDM **left over** remaining; extra: *After I pay my bills each month, I hardly have any money left over.*

ˌ**left 'field** ***noun*** [sing.] **1** (in baseball) the left part of the field, or the position played by the person who is there **2** (*informal*) an opinion or position that is strange or unusual and a long way from the normal position: *No one else is going to go along with you on that one; you're way out in left field.*

'**left-hand** ***adj.*** (only *before* a noun) of or on the left: *the left-hand side of the road*

ˌ**left-'handed** ***adj.*** **1** (used about a person) using the left hand more easily than the right: *Are you left-handed?* **2** made for left-handed people to use: *left-handed scissors*

**left·o·vers** /'lɛftˌoʊvərz/ ***noun*** [pl.] food that has not been eaten when a meal has finished

'**left-wing** ***adj.*** (only *before* a noun) having political ideas that support government ownership of industries, social change to make everyone more financially equal, etc.: *left-wing politicians*

★**leg** /lɛg/ ***noun*** [C] **1** the part of the body on which a person or animal stands or walks: *A spider has eight legs.* ◇ *long/short legs* ◇ *She sat down and crossed her legs.* ➲ picture on study page **A32**. **2** one of the parts that support a table, chair, etc. **3** the part of a pair of pants, etc. that covers your LEG (1) **4** one part or section of a trip, competition, etc.

IDM **cost/pay an arm and a leg** = ARM[1]

**pull sb's leg** → PULL[1]

**stretch your legs** → STRETCH[1]

**leg·a·cy** /'lɛgəsi/ ***noun*** [C] (*pl.* **leg·a·cies**) a situation that exists because of events that happened in the past: *racial discrimination that is the legacy of slavery*

★**le·gal** /'ligl/ ***adj.*** **1** allowed by law: *It is not legal to own a gun without a license.* OPP **illegal** Look also at **lawful** and **legitimate**. **2** (only *before* a noun) using or connected with the law: *legal advice* ◇ *to take legal action against sb* ◇ *the legal system* ▸ **le·gal·ly** ***adv.***: *Schools are legally responsible for the safety of their students.* ▸ **le·gal·i·ty** /li'gæləṭi/ ***noun*** [U]: *The legality of the agreement is not certain.*

**le·gal·ize** /'ligəlaɪz/ ***verb*** [T] to make sth LEGAL (1)

'**legal pad** ***noun*** [C] a number of sheets of paper with lines on them, fastened together at one end

'**legal-size** (*also* **legal**) ***adj.*** (used about paper) 8½ inches (215.9 mm) wide and 14 inches (355.6 mm) long ➲ Look also at **letter-size**.

**leg·end** /'lɛdʒənd/ ***noun*** **1** [C] an old story that may or may not be true: *the legend of Paul Bunyan* **2** [U] old stories, thought of as a group: *According to legend, Paul Bunyan had an ox named Babe.* **3** [C] a person who is famous for doing sth extremely well: *baseball legend Mickey Mantle*

**leg·en·dar·y** /'lɛdʒəndɛri/ ***adj.*** **1** from a legend or legends: *the legendary heroes of Greek myths* **2** very famous: *Bjorn Borg, the legendary tennis star*

**leg·gings** /'lɛgɪŋz/ ***noun*** [pl.] a piece of clothing, usually worn by women, that fits tightly over both legs and reaches from your waist to your ankles

**leg·i·ble** /'lɛdʒəbl/ ***adj.*** (used about writing or things that are printed) clear enough to be read easily OPP **illegible** ▸ **leg·i·bil·i·ty** /ˌlɛdʒə'bɪləṭi/ ***noun*** [U] ▸ **leg·i·bly** /-əbli/ ***adv.***

**leg·is·late** /'lɛdʒəsleɪt/ ***verb*** [I,T] to make a law or laws (about sth): *It is impossible to legislate morality.*

**leg·is·la·tion** /ˌlɛdʒəs'leɪʃn/ ***noun*** [U] **1** the act of making laws **2** a law or a group of laws: *The government is introducing new legislation to help small businesses.*

**leg·is·la·tive** /'lɛdʒəsleɪṭɪv/ ***adj.*** **1** connected with the act of making laws: *the legislative powers of Congress* **2** connected with the part of the government that makes laws: *the legislative branch of the government* ➲ Look at **executive** and **judicial**. **3** connected with a LEGISLATURE (1)

ˌ**legislative as'sembly** ***noun*** [C] (in Canada) an officially elected group of people (a **legislature**) who have the power to make and change laws, especially within a particular province

ˌ**legislative 'building** ***noun*** [C] (*Cdn*) the building in which the LEGISLATURE (1) of a province meets

**leg·is·la·tor** /'lɛdʒəsleɪṭər/ ***noun*** [C] a person who has been elected to an official government position to make laws

**leg·is·la·ture** /'lɛdʒəsleɪtʃər/ ***noun*** [C] **1** an official group of people who have been elected to the government to make laws: *the Kansas state legislature* **2** (*Cdn*) = LEGISLATIVE BUILDING

**le·git·i·mate** /lɪ'dʒɪṭəmət/ ***adj.*** **1** reasonable or acceptable: *This program is not a legitimate use of taxpayers' money.* **2** allowed by law: *Could he earn so much from legitimate business activities?* ➲ Look at **lawful** and **legal**. ▸ **le·git·i·mate·ly** ***adv.***

**lei·sure** /'liʒər/ ***noun*** [U] the time when you do not have to work; spare time: *leisure activities*

**lei·sure·ly** /'liʒərli/ ***adj.*** without hurry: *to walk at a leisurely pace*

★**lem·on** /'lɛmən/ ***noun*** [C,U] a yellow fruit with sour juice that is used for giving flavor to food and drinks: *a slice of lemon* [C] ➲ picture on study page **A28-29**.

**lem·on·ade** /ˌlɛmə'neɪd/ ***noun*** [C,U] a drink that is made from fresh lemon juice, sugar and water

★**lend** /lɛnd/ ***verb*** [T] (*pt, pp* **lent** /lɛnt/) **1** to allow sb to use sth for a short time or to give sb money that must be paid back after a certain period of time: *Could you lend me $5 until Friday?* ◇ *He lent me his bicycle.* ◇ *He lent his bicycle to me.* ➲ Picture at **borrow**.

NOTE In informal spoken English, many people use **loan** with this meaning: *He loaned me his bike.* However, some people do not like this use of **loan**, especially in formal or written English. If a bank, etc. lends you money, you must **pay it back/repay** it over a fixed period of time with extra payments (called **interest**).

**2 lend sth (to sth)** (*formal*) to add or give: *to lend advice/support* ◇ *The flowers lent a touch of color to the room.* ▸ **lend·er** ***noun*** [C]

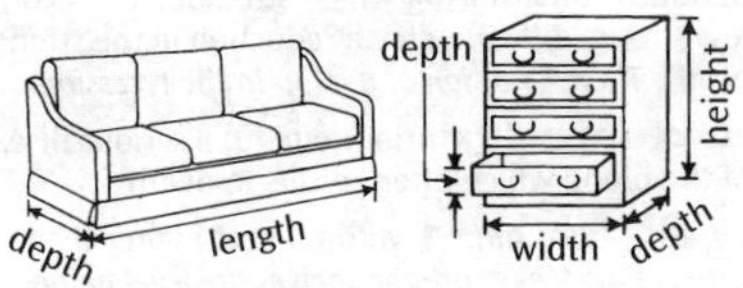


★**length** /lɛŋkθ; lɛŋθ/ ***noun*** **1** [U] the distance or amount that sth measures from one end to the other; how long sth is: *to measure the length of a room* ◇ *It took an hour to walk the length of Rodeo Drive.* ◇ *The tiny insect is only one millimeter in length.* **2** [U] the amount of time that sth takes or lasts: *Many people complained about the length of time they had to wait.* **3** [C] the LENGTH (1) of a swimming pool, path, etc.: *I can swim a length in twenty seconds.* ◇ *They meet and walk five lengths of the mall every morning during the winter.*

NOTE Look at **lap**. If you swim, walk, etc., back and forth along a straight line, you can say that you have **done laps** or **lengths**; if you move around a closed shape, like a circular track, you can only call that a **lap**.

**4** [C] a piece of sth (that is long and thin): *a length of material/rope/string* **5** [C,U] the number of pages in a book, a letter, etc.

IDM **at length** for a long time or in great detail: *We discussed the matter at great length.*

**go to great lengths to do sth** to make more effort than usual in order to achieve sth

**length·en** /ˈlɛŋkθən; ˈlɛŋθən/ ***verb*** [I,T] to become longer or to make sth longer

**length·wise** /ˈlɛŋkθwaɪz; ˈlɛŋθ-/ ***adv.*** in a direction along the length of sth: *Fold the paper lengthwise.*

**length·y** /ˈlɛŋkθi; ˈlɛŋθi/ ***adj.*** (**length·i·er**; **length·i·est**) very long: *lengthy discussions* ◇ *Recovery from the illness will be a lengthy process.*

**le·ni·ent** /ˈliniənt/ ***adj.*** (used about a punishment or person who punishes) not strict or severe ▸ **le·ni·ency** /-ənsi/ ***noun*** [U] ▸ **le·ni·ent·ly** ***adv.***

**lens** /lɛnz/ ***noun*** [C] (*pl.* **lens·es**) a piece of glass, etc. that has one or more curved surfaces. Lenses are used in glasses, cameras, telescopes, microscopes, etc.

NOTE You may wear **contact lenses** to help you see better. You may use a **zoom** or **telephoto lens** on your camera. ➲ pictures at **glasses** and **camera**.

**Lent** /lɛnt/ ***noun*** [U] the period of 40 days before Easter, when some Christians stop doing or eating certain things in order to remember how Jesus Christ suffered during his life

**lent** *past tense, past participle of* LEND

**len·til** /ˈlɛntl/ ***noun*** [C] the small orange or brown seed of a plant that is like a bean. Lentils are dried and then cooked and eaten.

**Le·o** /ˈlioʊ/ ***noun*** [C,U] (*pl.* **Le·os**) the fifth sign of the zodiac, the Lion; a person who was born under this sign

**leop·ard** /ˈlɛpərd/ ***noun*** [C] a large wild animal of the cat family that has yellow fur with dark spots. Leopards live in Africa and southern Asia.

**le·o·tard** /ˈliətɑrd/ ***noun*** [C] a piece of clothing that fits close to the body and arms but does not cover the legs. Leotards are worn by dancers, people doing exercises, etc.

**lep·er** /ˈlɛpər/ ***noun*** [C] **1** a person who has leprosy **2** a person who has done sth that other people do not like or approve of and who, as a result, is avoided by others

**lep·ro·sy** /ˈlɛprəsi/ ***noun*** [U] a serious infectious disease that affects the skin, nerves, etc. and can cause parts of the body to fall off

**les·bi·an** /ˈlɛzbiən/ ***noun*** [C] a woman who is sexually attracted to other women ▸ **les·bi·an** ***adj.***: *a lesbian relationship* ▸ **les·bi·an·ism** ***noun*** [U] ➲ Look at **gay** and **homosexual**.

★**less**[1] /lɛs/ ***det.***, ***pronoun*** (used with uncountable nouns) a smaller amount (of): *It took less time than I thought.* ◇ *I'm too fat – I should try to eat less.*

NOTE Many people use **less** with plural nouns: *less cars*, but **fewer** is the form which is still considered to be correct: *fewer cars.*

★**less**[2] /lɛs/ ***adv.*** to a smaller extent; not so much (as): *He's less intelligent than his brother.* ◇ *It rains less in Arizona than in Oregon.* ◇ *People work less well when they're tired.*

IDM **less and less** becoming smaller and smaller in amount or degree: *I seem to have less and less time for my hobbies.*

**more or less** → MORE[2]

**less·en** /ˈlɛsn/ ***verb*** [I,T] to become less; to make sth less: *This medicine will lessen the pain.*

**less·er** /ˈlɛsər/ ***adj.***, ***adv.*** (only *before* a noun) not as great/much as: *He is guilty, and so, to a lesser extent, is his wife.* ◇ *a lesser-known artist*

IDM **the lesser of two evils** the better of two bad things

★**les·son** /ˈlɛsn/ ***noun*** [C] **1** a period of time when you learn or teach sth, usually not in school: *She teaches piano lessons.* ◇ *a driving lesson*

NOTE We usually use **class** to talk about a period of time in school: *This class is over at 9:55.*

**2** something that you have learned or that must be learned: *I hope we can learn some lessons from this disaster.*

★**let** /lɛt/ ***verb*** [T] (*pres. part.* **let·ting**; *pt, pp* **let**)

➤ALLOW **1** to allow or permit sb/sth to do sth; to allow sth to happen: *My parents let me stay out until 11 o'clock.* ◇ *He wanted to take the day off, but his boss wouldn't let him.*

NOTE You cannot use **let** in the passive in sense **1**. You must use **allow** or **permit** and **to**: *They let her take the test again.* ◇ *She was allowed to take the test again.* ➲ Look at the note at **allow**.

**2** to allow sb/sth to move in a particular direction:

L

*Open the windows and let some fresh air in.* ◇ *They let him out of prison yesterday.*
➤ OFFERING HELP **3** (used for offering help to sb): *Let me help you carry your bags.*
➤ MAKING REQUESTS **4** (used for making requests or giving instructions): *Don't help him. Let him do it himself.* ◇ *If she refuses to come home with us now, let her walk home.*
➤ MAKING SUGGESTIONS **5 let's** (used for making suggestions about what you and other people can do): *Let's go to the movies tonight.*

NOTE The negative is **let's not**: *Let's not go to that awful restaurant again.*

IDM **let alone** and certainly not: *We haven't decided where we're going yet, let alone made any reservations.*
**let sb go** to make sb leave his/her job, usually because there is not enough work: *We're going to have to let 20 people go.*
**let sb/sth go**; **let go of sb/sth** to stop holding sb/sth: *Let me go. You're hurting me!* ◇ *I tried to take the book, but he wouldn't let go of it.*
**let it go** (*informal*) to decide not to argue or worry about sth
**let sb know** to tell sb sth: *If you need any help, let me know.* ◇ *I'll let you know how much the bill is.*
**let me see**; **let's see** (used when you are thinking or trying to remember sth): *Where did I put the car keys? Let's see. I think I left them by the phone.*
**let's say** for example: *You could work two mornings a week, let's say Tuesday and Friday.*
**let yourself go** to allow yourself to behave as you wish; to feel free: *Just relax. Let yourself go!*
**let yourself/sth go** to allow yourself/sth to become messy, dirty, fat, etc.: *She used to be so pretty, but after her husband died she just let herself go.*
PHRV **let sb down** not to do sth that you promised to do for sb; to disappoint sb
**let sb off** not to punish sb, or to give sb a lighter punishment than usual: *He expected to go to prison, but they let him off with a fine.*
**let sth out** to tell people sth that was secret: *Who let the story about the mayor's debts out?*
**let sth out/down** to make clothes larger/longer: *These pants are too tight. I'll have to let them out.*
**let up** to become less strong: *We'd better wait until the rain lets up.*

**le·thal** /ˈliθl/ ***adj.*** able to cause death or great damage ▶ **le·thal·ly *adv.***

★**let·ter** /ˈlɛt̬ər/ ***noun*** [C] **1** a written or printed sign that represents a sound in a language: *"Z" is the last letter of the English alphabet.*

NOTE Letters may be written or printed as **capitals**, (also **upper case**), or **small** letters (also **lower case**): *Is "east" written with a capital or a small "e?"*

**2** a written or printed message. A letter is usually put in an envelope and sent to sb by mail: *I wrote Denise a letter, but I haven't mailed it yet.*

NOTE When you have written a letter you put it in an **envelope**, **address** it, **put/stick** a **stamp** on it and then **mail** it.

ˈ**letter ˌcarrier *noun*** [C] a person whose job is to collect and deliver letters, packages, etc.

ˈ**letter-size** (*also* **letter**) ***adj.*** (used about paper) 8½ inches (215.9 mm) wide and 11 inches (279.4 mm) long ➲ Look also at **legal-size**.

**let·tuce** /ˈlɛt̬əs/ ***noun*** [U] a plant with large green leaves that are eaten raw in salads: *a head of lettuce* ➲ picture on study page **A28-29**.

**let·up** /ˈlɛt̬ʌp/ ***noun*** [U, sing.] **letup (in sth)** a period of time during which sth stops or becomes less strong, difficult, etc.; a reduction in the strength of sth: *There's no sign of a letup in the recession.*

**leu·ke·mi·a** /luˈkimiə/ ***noun*** [U] a serious disease of the blood which often results in death

★**lev·el**[1] /ˈlɛvl/ ***adj.*** **1** with no part higher than any other; flat: *Make sure the shelves are level before you nail them to the wall.* ◇ *a level teaspoon of sugar* **2 level (with sth)** at the same height, standard or position: *The boy's head was level with his father's shoulder.*

★**lev·el**[2] /ˈlɛvl/ ***noun*** [C] **1** the height or position of sth in relation to sth else: *We are at 500 feet above sea level.* ◇ *at ground level* ◇ *an intermediate-level student* ◇ *top-level discussions* **2** the amount, size or number of sth (compared to sth else): *a high level of unemployment* ◇ *low levels of pollution* **3** one of several floors in a building: *The new shopping mall has 180 stores on three levels.*

**lev·el**[3] /ˈlɛvl/ ***verb*** [T] to destroy a building, etc., by knocking it to the ground: *The tornado leveled several barns in the county.*
PHRV **level sth against/at sb/sth** to make a serious criticism of sb or accuse sb of doing sth wrong: *Several criminal charges have been leveled against the mayor.*
**level off/out** to become flat, equal or level: *Stock prices rose sharply yesterday, but today they have leveled off* (= stayed at one level).

ˈ**level-ˌheaded *adj.*** able to act calmly in a difficult situation

**lev·er** /ˈlɛvər; ˈlivər/ ***noun*** [C] **1** a bar or tool that is used to lift or open sth when you put pressure or force on one end **2** a handle that you pull or push in order to make a machine, etc. work: *a gear shift lever in a car*

**lev·er·age** /ˈlɛvərɪdʒ; ˈli-/ ***noun*** [U] power or influence over other people or groups

**lev·y** /ˈlɛvi/ ***verb*** [T] (*pt, pp* **lev·ied**) **levy sth (on sb)** to officially demand and collect money, etc.: *The new tax will be levied on chemical manufacturers.* ▶ **lev·y *noun*** [C] (*pl.* **lev·ies**): *an additional property tax levy*

**li·a·bil·i·ty** /ˌlaɪəˈbɪlət̬i/ ***noun*** (*pl.* **li·a·bil·i·ties**) **1** [U] **liability (for sth)** the state of being responsible (for sth): *The airline admitted liability for the crash.* **2** [C] a person or thing that can cause a lot of problems, cost a lot of money, etc.: *The senator's stupid comments have made him a real liability to the party.*

**li·a·ble** /ˈlaɪəbl/ ***adj.*** (not before a noun) **1 liable (for sth)** responsible (in law) (for sth): *Should tobacco companies be held liable for smokers' health problems?* **2 liable to do sth** likely to do sth, especially sth bad: *We're all liable to have accidents when we are very tired.*

**li·aise** /liˈeɪz/ ***verb*** [I] **liaise (with sb/sth)** to work closely with a person, group, etc. and give him/her/it regular information about what you are doing

**li·ai·son** /li'eɪzɑn; 'lɪəˌzɑn/ ***noun*** **1** [U] communication between two or more people or groups that work together **2** [C] a person who helps to pass information between two or more people or groups that are working together **3** [C] a sexual relationship between two people who are not married to each other

**li·ar** /'laɪər/ ***noun*** [C] a person who tells lies (= who says or writes things that are not true): *She called me a liar.* ➲ Look at the verb and noun lie.

**li·bel** /'laɪbl/ ***noun*** [C,U] something false that is written or printed about sb that would make other people think badly of him/her: *The singer is suing the newspaper for libel.* ➲ Look at **slander.** ▶ **li·bel·ous** ***adj.***

**lib·er·al¹** /'lɪbərəl; 'lɪbrəl/ ***adj.*** **1** willing to accept different opinions or kinds of behavior; tolerant **2** supporting political and social changes to make people more equal, and willing to accept different ideas about family life, sex, etc. ➲ Look at **conservative. 3 Liberal** connected with the Liberal Party, a political party in Canada **4** generous; large: *We were given liberal quantities of food and drink.* ▶ **lib·er·al·ism** /-ɪzəm/ ***noun*** [U]

**lib·er·al²** /'lɪbərəl; 'lɪbrəl/ ***noun*** [C] **1** a person who is LIBERAL¹ (1,2) in his/her way of thinking **2 Liberal** (in Canada) a member or supporter of the Liberal Party

**ˌliberal 'arts** ***noun*** [pl.] subjects such as history, languages, literature, etc. (and not technical subjects) that you study in college

**lib·er·al·ly** /'lɪbərəli; 'lɪbrəli/ ***adv.*** freely or generously

**the 'Liberal ˌParty** // ***noun*** [sing.] (in Canada) one of the three most important political parties, in favor of some political and social change, but not extreme

NOTE A member or supporter of the Liberal Party is sometimes called a **Grit.** ➲ Look also at the **New Democratic Party** and the **Conservative Party.** ➲ For more information about the Canadian political system, look at study page **A11**.

**lib·er·ate** /'lɪbəreɪt/ ***verb*** [T] **liberate sb/sth (from sth)** (*formal*) to set sb/sth free: *France was liberated in 1945.* ◇ *to liberate people from poverty* ▶ **lib·er·a·tion** /ˌlɪbə'reɪʃn/ ***noun*** [U]: *The women's liberation movement wants equal rights for women.*

**lib·er·at·ed** /'lɪbəreɪt̬əd/ ***adj.*** not sharing traditional opinions or ways of behaving

**lib·er·ty** /'lɪbərt̬i/ ***noun*** [C,U] (*pl.* **lib·er·ties**) the freedom to go where you want, do what you want, etc.: *religious liberty* ◇ *We must defend our civil liberties* (= the rights we have as citizens).

IDM **be at liberty to do sth** (*formal*) to be free or allowed to do sth: *I am not at liberty to tell you how I got this information.*

**Li·bra** /'librə/ ***noun*** [C,U] the seventh sign of the zodiac, the Balance; a person who was born under this sign

**li·brar·i·an** /laɪ'brɛriən/ ***noun*** [C] a person who works in or is in charge of a library

★**li·brar·y** /'laɪbrɛri/ ***noun*** [C] (*pl.* **li·brar·ies**) **1** a room or building that contains a collection of books, etc. that can be looked at or borrowed: *My library books are due back tomorrow.*

NOTE Most cities in the United States and Canada have a **public library** where you can borrow books, usually without having to pay anything, and read magazines and newspapers.

**2** a private collection of books, etc.

**lice** *plural of* LOUSE

★**li·cense¹** (*Cdn* **li·cence**) /'laɪsns/ ***noun*** **1** [C] an official paper, card, etc. that shows you are allowed to do or have sth: *a driver's license* ◇ *a fishing license* **2** [U] (*formal*) freedom to do sth: *The soldiers were given license to kill if they were attacked.*

**li·cense²** (*Cdn. also* **li·cence**) /'laɪsns/ ***verb*** [T] to give official permission for sth: *a licensed gun owner*

**'license plate** ***noun*** [C] a sign on the front and back of a car, truck, etc. with numbers and letters on it ➲ Look also at **vanity plate.**

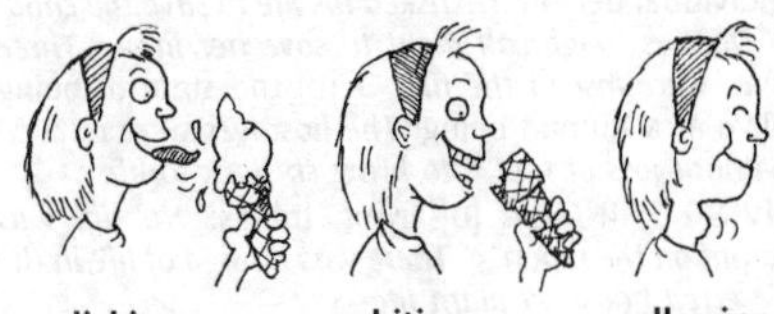

licking biting swallowing

**lick** /lɪk/ ***verb*** [T] to move your tongue across sth: *The child licked the spoon clean.* ▶ **lick** ***noun*** [C]: *Let me have a lick of your ice cream.*

**lic·o·rice** /'lɪkərɪʃ/ ***noun*** [U] a type of black candy with a strong flavor

★**lid** /lɪd/ ***noun*** [C] **1** the top part of a box, pot, etc. that can be lifted up or taken off ➲ picture at **pan.** ➲ Look at the note at **top. 2** = EYELID

★**lie¹** /laɪ/ ***verb*** [I] (*pres. part.* **ly·ing**; *pt, pp* **lied**) **lie (to sb) (about sth)** to say or write sth that you know is not true: *He lied about his age in order to join the army.* ◇ (*figurative*) *The camera cannot lie.*

★**lie²** /laɪ/ ***noun*** [C] a statement that you know is not true: *to tell a lie*

NOTE You tell a **white lie** in order not to hurt sb's feelings. ➲ Look also at **liar** and **fib.**

★**lie³** /laɪ/ ***verb*** [I] (*pres. part.* **ly·ing**; *pt* **lay** /leɪ/; *pp* **lain** /leɪn/) **1** to be or put yourself in a flat or horizontal position (so that you are not standing or sitting): *He lay on the sofa and went to sleep.* ◇ *to lie on your back/side/front* ◇ *The book lay open in front of her.*

NOTE Remember that **lie** cannot be used with an object. If you put an object in a flat position, you **lay** it down.

**2** to be or remain in a certain state or position: *Snow lay thick on the ground.* ◇ *The hills lie to the north of the town.* ◇ *The final decision lies with the chief executive officer.* ◇ *They are young and their whole lives lie ahead of them.* **3 lie (in sth)** to exist or to be found somewhere: *The problem lies in deciding when to stop.*

IDM **lie in wait (for sb)** to hide somewhere waiting to attack, surprise or catch sb

PHR V **lie around** to relax and do nothing: *Don't just lie around all day – do some work!*

**lie back** to relax and do nothing while sb else works, etc.

**lie down** (used about a person) to be or put yourself in a flat or horizontal position so that you can rest: *I'm feeling dizzy – I have to lie down.*

**'lie deˌtector** *noun* [C] = POLYGRAPH

**lieu·ten·ant** /lu'tɛnənt; (*Cdn*) lɛf'tɛnənt/ *noun* [C] a junior officer in the army or navy, or a police officer of middle rank

**lieuˌtenant-'governor** *noun* [C] (in Canada) the representative of the CROWN (2) in a province ➲ For more information on the Canadian political system, look at study page **A11**.

★**life** /laɪf/ *noun* (*pl.* **lives** /laɪvz/)

➤ STATE OF LIVING **1** [U] the quality that people, animals or plants have when they are not dead: *Life on earth began in a very simple form.* ◇ *Do you believe in life after death?* **2** [C] the existence of an individual person: *He risked his life to save the child.* ◇ *Doctors fought all night to save her life.* ◇ *Three lives were lost in the fire.* **3** [U] the state of being alive as a human being: *The hostages were rescued without loss of life.* ◇ *to bring sb back to life*

➤ LIVING THINGS **4** [U] living things: *No life was found on the moon.* ◇ *There was no sign of life in the deserted house.* ◇ *plant life*

➤ PERIOD OF TIME **5** [C] the period between your birth and death or between your birth and the present: *He worked as a doctor all his life.* ◇ *to ruin sb's life* **6** [U] the things that you may experience during your LIFE (5): *Life can be hard for a single parent.* ◇ *I'm not happy with the situation, but **that's life**.* **7** [U] the period between the present and your death: *She was sent to prison for life.* ◇ *life membership in a club*

➤ WAY OF LIVING **8** [C,U] a way of living: *They came to America to start a new life.* ◇ *They lead a busy life.* ◇ *married life*

➤ ENERGY/EXCITEMENT **9** [U] activity; liveliness: *Young kids are full of life.* ◇ *This town comes to life in the evenings.*

IDM **the facts of life** → FACT

**get a life** (*slang*) (often imperative) to stop being boring and annoying; to have a better sense of what things are important: *I can't believe you're still worried about paying an extra dollar for that book. You need to get a life!*

**life in the fast lane** (*informal*) a way of living that involves exciting activities and spending a lot of money

**lose your life** → LOSE

**real life** → REAL[1]

**take your (own) life** to kill yourself

**a walk of life** → WALK[2]

**a/sb's way of life** → WAY[1]

**ˌlife-and-'death** (*also* **ˌlife-or-'death**) *adj.* (only *before* a noun) very serious or dangerous: *a life-or-death situation*

**life·boat** /'laɪfboʊt/ *noun* [C] **1** a small boat that is carried on a large ship and that is used by people to escape from the ship if it is in danger of sinking **2** a special boat that is used for rescuing people who are in danger in the ocean

**'life ˌcycle** *noun* [C] the series of forms or stages of development that a plant, animal, etc. goes through from the beginning of its life to the end

**'life exˌpectancy** *noun* [C,U] (*pl.* **life expectancies**) the number of years that a person is likely to live

**life·guard** /'laɪfgɑrd/ *noun* [C] a person at a beach or swimming pool whose job is to rescue people who are in difficulties in the water

**'life inˌsurance** *noun* [U] a type of insurance that pays a certain amount of money to sb's family after he/she dies

**'life ˌjacket** (*also* **'life vest**) *noun* [C] a plastic or rubber jacket with no sleeves that can be filled with air. A life-jacket is worn by sb to stop him/her from sinking in water.

**life·less** /'laɪfləs/ *adj.* **1** dead: *Police pulled her lifeless body from the river.* **2** without LIFE (9) or energy

**life·like** /'laɪflaɪk/ *adj.* looking like the real person or thing: *a lifelike baby doll*

**life·line** /'laɪflaɪn/ *noun* [C] something that sb needs in order to survive in a difficult situation: *For many old people, their telephone is a lifeline.*

**life·long** /'laɪflɔŋ/ *adj.* (only *before* a noun) for all of your life: *a lifelong friend*

**life preˌserver** *noun* [C] an object, shaped like a ring, that is made from light material which will float. A life preserver is thrown to a person who has fallen into water to stop him/her from sinking.

**'life-size** (*also* **'life-sized**) *adj.* (only *before* a noun) of the same size as the real person or thing: *a life-size statue*

**'life span** *noun* [C] the length of time that sb/sth lives, works, lasts, etc.

**life·style** /'laɪfstaɪl/ *noun* [C] the way that you live: *After I got divorced, my whole lifestyle changed.*

**'life supˌport** *noun* [U] medical equipment that keeps sb alive when he/she cannot breathe, etc. alone: *She spent two weeks in the hospital on life support.*

**life·time** /'laɪftaɪm/ *noun* [C] the period of time that sb is alive: *It's a chance of a lifetime. Don't miss it!*

**'life vest** *noun* [C] = LIFE JACKET

★**lift**[1] /lɪft/ *verb*

➤ RAISE **1** [T] **lift sb/sth (up)** to move sb/sth to a higher level or position: *He lifted the child up onto his shoulders.* ◇ *Lift your arm very gently and see if it hurts.*

➤ MOVE SB/STH **2** [T] to take hold of sb/sth and move him/her/it to a different position: *She lifted the suitcase down from the rack.*

➤ REMOVE LAW/RULE **3** [T] to end or remove a rule, law, etc.: *The ban on imports has been lifted.*

➤ STEAL/COPY **4** [T] **lift sth (from sb/sth)** (*informal*) to steal or copy sth: *Most of his essay was lifted straight from the textbook.* ➲ Look at **shoplift**.

➤ OF MIST/CLOUDS **5** [I] (used about clouds, fog, etc.) to rise up or disappear: *The mist lifted toward the end of the morning.*

PHR V **lift off** (used about a rocket or spacecraft) to rise straight up from the ground

★**lift²** /lɪft/ ***noun*** **1** [sing.] a feeling of happiness or excitement: *Her words of encouragement gave the whole team a lift.* **2** [C] a free ride in a car, etc.: *Can you give me a lift to the store?* **3** [sing.] an act of lifting or being lifted

**lift·off** /ˈlɪftɔf/ ***noun*** [C] the start of the flight of a rocket or spacecraft: *Only ten seconds to liftoff!*

**lig·a·ment** /ˈlɪɡəmənt/ ***noun*** [C] a strong band in a person's or animal's body that holds the bones, etc. together

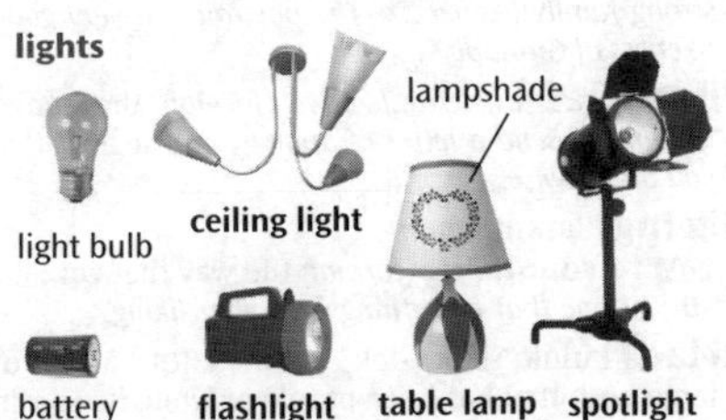


★**light¹** /laɪt/ ***noun***

➤FROM SUN/LAMPS **1** [U] the brightness that allows you to see things: *the light of the sun* ◇ *The light was too bad for us to read by.*

NOTE You may see things by **sunlight**, **moonlight**, **firelight**, **candlelight**, **lamplight**, etc.

**2** [C] something that produces LIGHT (1), e.g. a lamp: *the lights of the city in the distance* ◇ *a neon light* ◇ *That car's lights aren't on.*

NOTE A light can be **on** or **off**: *Why are all the lights on?* You **turn** or **switch** a light **on**, **off** or **out**: *Should I turn the light on? It's getting dark in here.* ◇ *Please switch the lights off before you leave.*

➤FOR TRAFFIC **3** [C] one of three colored lights, or a set of these lights (red, yellow and green) that control traffic: *Slow down – there's a red light ahead.*

➤FOR CIGARETTE **4** [C] something, e.g. a match, that can be used to light a cigarette, start a fire, etc.: *Can you give me a light?*

IDM **come to light** to be found or become known

**give sb/get the green light** → GREEN¹

**in a good, bad, etc. light** (used about the way that sth is seen or described by other people) well, badly, etc.: *The newspapers often portray his behavior in a bad light.*

**in the light of** because of; considering: *We might have to change our decision in the light of what you just said.*

**set light to sth** to cause sth to start burning

**shed light on sth** → SHED

★**light²** /laɪt/ ***adj.***

➤NOT DARK **1** having a lot of LIGHT¹ (1); not dark: *In the summer it's still light at 9 o'clock.* ◇ *a light room*

➤OF A COLOR **2** (used about a color) pale; not dark: *a light blue sweater*

➤NOT HEAVY **3** not of great weight; not heavy: *Carry this bag – it's the lightest.* ◇ *I've lost weight – I'm five pounds lighter than I used to be.* ◇ *light clothes* (= for summer)

➤NOT GREAT **4** not great in amount, degree, etc.: *Traffic downtown is light on Sundays.* ◇ *a light prison sentence* ◇ *a light wind* ◇ *a light breakfast*

➤GENTLE **5** not using much force; gentle: *a light touch on the shoulder*

➤OF WORK, ETC. **6** (used about work, etc.) easy to do: *light exercise*

➤NOT SERIOUS **7** not very serious or hard to understand: *light reading*

➤OF SLEEP **8** not deep: *I've always been a light sleeper.*

➤OF FOOD/DRINKS **9** (*informal*) (*also* **lite**) (used especially on food packages, in restaurants, etc.) containing less fat, alcohol, or other unhealthy substances that can make people gain weight: *light cheesecake*

▶ **light·ness** ***noun*** [U]

★**light³** /laɪt/ ***verb*** (*pt, pp* **lit** or **light·ed**) **1** [I,T] to begin to burn or to make sth do this: *This match won't light.* ◇ *to light a fire*

NOTE **Lighted** is usually used as an adjective before the noun. **Lit** is used as the past participle of the verb: *Candles were lit in memory of the dead.* ◇ *The church was full of lighted candles.*

**2** [T] to give light to sth: *The room was lit with one 40-watt bulb.*

PHR V **light up** (used about sb's face, eyes, etc.) to become bright with happiness or excitement

**light⁴** /laɪt/ ***adv.*** **1** without much luggage: *to travel light* **2** without a lot of fat or oil: *to cook/eat light*

ˈ**light bulb** (*also* **bulb**) ***noun*** [C] the glass part of an electric lamp that gives out light: *a 60-watt light bulb*

**light·en** /ˈlaɪtn/ ***verb*** [I,T] **1** to become lighter in weight or to make sth lighter: *to lighten a load* **2** to become brighter or to make sth brighter

**light·er** /ˈlaɪt̬ər/ ***noun*** [C] an object which produces a small flame for lighting cigarettes, etc.

**light·heart·ed** /ˌlaɪtˈhɑrt̬əd/ ***adj.*** **1** without problems; happy **2** funny; amusing

**light·house** /ˈlaɪthaʊs/ ***noun*** [C] a tall building with a light at the top that guides ships or warns them of dangerous rocks, etc.

**light·ing** /ˈlaɪt̬ɪŋ/ ***noun*** [U] the quality or type of lights used in a room, building, etc.: *Soft lighting helps to make people more relaxed.*

★**light·ly** /ˈlaɪtli/ ***adv.*** **1** in a LIGHT² (5) way: *He touched her lightly on the arm.* **2** not seriously; without serious thought: *We should not take her remarks lightly – this is an important matter.*

**light·ning** /ˈlaɪtnɪŋ/ ***noun*** [U] a bright flash of light that appears in the sky during a thunderstorm: *The tree was struck by lightning.*

**light·weight** /ˈlaɪtweɪt/ ***noun*** [C], ***adj.*** **1** (a boxer) weighing between 126 and 135 pounds **2** (a person or thing) weighing less than usual: *a lightweight suit for the summer*

**lik·a·ble** (*also* **like·a·ble**) /ˈlaɪkəbl/ ***adj.*** (used about a person) easy to like; pleasant

★**like¹** /laɪk/ ***verb*** (not in the continuous tenses) **1** [T] to find sb/sth pleasant; to be fond of sb/sth: *He's nice. I like him a lot.* ◇ *Do you like their new house?* ◇ *I like my coffee with milk.* ◇ *I like playing tennis./I* *like to play tennis.* ◇ *She didn't like it when I shouted at her.* OPP **dislike** **2** [T,I] to want sth: *How do you like your steak done, sir?* ◇ *I'd* ***like for*** *us to be friends.*

NOTE **Would like** is a more polite way to say "want": *Would you like to come to lunch on Sunday?* ◇ *I would like some more cake, please.* ◇ *I'd like to speak to the manager.* **Would like** is always followed by the infinitive (to + verb), never by the *-ing* form.

IDM **like the look/looks/sound of sb/sth** to have a good impression of sb/sth after seeing or hearing about him/her/it

★**like²** /laɪk/ ***prep.*** **1** similar to sb/sth: *He looks like his father.* ◇ *Their car is like ours.* ◇ *With a coat of paint it will look like new.*

NOTE If you want somebody to give a description of something you ask: ***What's it like?*** ◇ *Tell me about your town. What's it like?* ◇ *What's your town like?* OPP **unlike**

**2** showing what is usual or typical for sb: *It was just like him to be late.*

NOTE Notice the difference in meaning between **as** and **like** when used about a person's job, occupation, etc.: *Jeff acted as our leader* (= he was our leader). ◇ *Jeff acted like our leader* (= but he was not really our leader).

**3** in the same way or manner as sb/sth: *Stop behaving like kids.* ◇ *That's not right. Do it like this.* **4** for example: *They enjoy most team games, like football and baseball.*

IDM **like crazy** (*informal*) very much, fast, hard, etc.: *We had to pedal like crazy to get up the hill.*

**like³** /laɪk/ ***conj.*** **1** in the same way or manner as sb/sth: *She can't draw like her sister can.* ◇ *Well, like I said before, it's not going to be easy.* **2** (*informal*) as if: *She acts like she's the boss.* ◇ *I felt like I was going to die.*

**like⁴** /laɪk/ ***adv.*** (*informal*) (used to fill a pause while the speaker is thinking of what to say next, or before an example): *It was, like, really scary, you know?*

IDM **be like...** (not in the continuous tenses) (used to tell what sb said or thought): *I asked Paul if he could help us and he was like, forget it.*

NOTE Many people, especially older people, do not approve of this use of **like**. However, it is very common in informal spoken English.

**like⁵** /laɪk/ ***noun*** **1 likes** [pl.] the things that you like: *After 20 years of marriage, she knows all his* ***likes and dislikes****.* **2** [sing.] a person or thing that is similar to sb/sth else: *to* ***compare like with like*** ◇ *pollution from farms, factories* ***and the like***

**like⁶** /laɪk/ ***adj.*** (*formal*) having similar qualities to another person or thing: *We're* ***of like mind*** (= we have the same opinion).

**-like** /laɪk/ ***combining form*** in the manner of; similar to: *ladylike* ◇ *lifelike*

**like·li·hood** /ˈlaɪklihʊd/ ***noun*** [U] probability: *There seems very little likelihood of success.*

★**like·ly¹** /ˈlaɪkli/ ***adj.*** (**like·li·er**; **like·li·est**) **1** probable or expected: *Do you think it's likely to rain?* ◇ *The boss is not likely to agree.* ◇ *It's not likely that the boss will agree.* **2** probably suitable: *a likely candidate for the job*

**like·ly²** /ˈlaɪki/ ***adv.***

IDM **most/very likely** very probably: *They left very late. They'll most likely miss the start of the movie.*

**lik·en** /ˈlaɪkən/ ***verb*** [T] (*formal*) **liken sth to sth** to compare sth with sth else: *She likened the process to "using a hammer to crack an egg."*

**like·ness** /ˈlaɪknəs/ ***noun*** [C,U] (an example of) being alike or similar in appearance: *There is a strong family likeness.* ◇ *The portrait is a very good likeness of Grandpa.*

**like·wise** /ˈlaɪkwaɪz/ ***adv.*** (*formal*) the same: *I intend to send a letter of apology and suggest that you do likewise.*

**lik·ing** /ˈlaɪkɪŋ/ ***noun***

IDM **to your liking** (*formal*) the way that you like sth: *I hope that everything is to your liking.*

**li·lac** /ˈlaɪlɑk; -læk; -lək/ ***noun*** **1** [C,U] a tree or large bush that has large purple or white flowers in spring. The flowers are also called lilacs. **2** [U] a pale purple color

**lil·y** /ˈlɪli/ ***noun*** [C] (*pl.* **lil·ies**) a type of plant that grows from a bulb and that has large white or colored flowers

**li·ma bean** /ˈlaɪmə bin/ ***noun*** [C] a type of light green flat bean

**limb** /ˈlaɪmə bin/ ***noun*** [C] **1** a leg or an arm of a person **2** one of the main branches of a tree

IDM **go out on a limb** to put yourself in a position in which you do not have the support of other people

**lime** /laɪm/ ***noun*** **1** [C] a small green fruit that tastes like a lemon ➲ picture on study page **A28-29.** **2** [U] (*also* ˌ**lime ˈgreen**) a bright yellowish-green color

**lime·light** /ˈlaɪmlaɪt/ ***noun***

IDM **in the limelight** getting a lot of attention from the public: *The singer was in the limelight wherever he went.*

**lim·er·ick** /ˈlɪmərɪk/ ***noun*** [C] a humorous short poem

★**lim·it¹** /ˈlɪmət/ ***noun*** [C] **1** a point or line that marks the end or edge of sth: *No alcohol is sold within the city limits* (= inside the city). **2** the greatest amount of sth that is possible, allowed, etc.: *What's the speed limit on this road?* ◇ *a limit on government spending*

IDM **off limits** not to be entered, touched, discussed, etc.: *My desk is off limits to my kids.* ◇ *We only talk about work – her personal life is off limits.* **within limits** as long as it is not too much, great, etc.: *I don't mind how much it costs – within limits.*

★**lim·it²** /ˈlɪmət/ ***verb*** [T] **limit sb/sth (to sth)** to keep sb/sth within or below a certain amount, size, degree or area: *laws to limit pollution by manufacturers* ◇ *In China, families are limited to just one child.*

**lim·i·ta·tion** /ˌlɪməˈteɪʃn/ ***noun*** **1** [C,U] controlling sth or making sth smaller; a condition that puts a limit on sth: *There are certain limitations on what* *we can do.* **2** [pl.] **limitations** what you cannot do: *It is important to know your own limitations.*

★**lim·it·ed** /ˈlɪməṭəd/ ***adj.*** small in number or amount: *Reserve early because there are only a limited number of seats available.*

**lim·ou·sine** /ˈlɪməzin; ˌlɪməˈzin/ (*also informal* **limo** /ˈlɪmoʊ/) (*pl.* **lim·os**) ***noun*** [C] a long expensive car that usually has a sheet of glass between the driver and the passengers in the back

**limp**[1] /lɪmp/ ***adj.*** not stiff or strong: *a limp handshake*

**limp**[2] /lɪmp/ ***verb*** [I] to walk in an uneven way, e.g. because you have hurt your leg or foot: (*figurative*) *After the accident the ship limped back to the harbor.* ▶ **limp *noun*** [sing.]: *to walk with a bad limp*

**LINC** /lɪŋk/ ***noun*** [U] (*Cdn*) Language Instruction for Newcomers to Canada; a program run by the Canadian government which offers free language classes to people from other countries who come to live in Canada

★**line**[1] /laɪn/ ***noun***

➤LONG THIN MARK **1** [C] a long thin mark on the surface of sth: *A solid line in the middle of the road means "no passing."* ◇ *to draw a line*

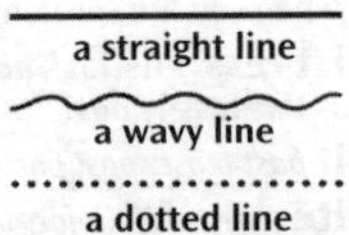


NOTE A line may be **horizontal**, **vertical**, **diagonal**, **parallel** to sth, etc. ➲ picture at **graph**.

**2** [C] a LINE (1) on the ground that marks the side or end of a sports field, etc.: *The ball was definitely over the line.* ◇ *the finish line of a race* ➲ picture at **tennis**.

➤DIVISION **3** [C] an imaginary LINE (1) that marks the boundary between two states, counties, etc.: *the Montana-Idaho state line* ◇ *The neighbors built a brick wall right on our property line.*

➤ROW **4** [C] a row of things, words on a page, etc.: *a neat line of china dolls on a shelf* ◇ *a five-line poem* ◇ *Start each paragraph on a new line.* **5** a row of people, cars, etc. that are waiting for sth or to do sth: *We had to wait in line for hours to get tickets.* ◇ *The line stretched around the block.*

➤ROPE/STRING **6** [C] a piece of rope or string: *He hung out the clothes on the line.* ◇ *a fishing line*

➤WIRE **7** [C] a telephone or electricity wire or connection: *I'm sorry – the line is busy. Can I take a message?* ◇ *The strong winds blew down many power lines.*

➤WORDS **8 lines** [pl.] the words that are spoken by an actor in a play, etc.: *to learn your lines*

➤DIRECTION/ARGUMENT **9** [sing.] a direction or course of thought or action: *a line of argument* ◇ *He can't even walk in a straight line.*

➤TRANSPORTATION **10** [C] a company that provides transportation by air, ship, etc.: *a Greek shipping line*

➤PRODUCT **11** [C] a type of product in a store, etc.: *a new line in environmentally-friendly detergents*

➤ROUTE **12** [C] a route that people move along or send messages, goods, etc. along: *lines of communication* ◇ *Before you travel on the subway, check which line you need.*

➤SOLDIERS **13** [C] the place where an army is fighting: *a spy working behind enemy lines*

IDM **along the same lines** in the way that is mentioned: *We both think along the same lines, so we work well together.*

**along/down the line** (*informal*) at some time: *Somewhere along the line we picked up too many responsibilities.* ◇ *We'll have to sort that out at some point further down the line.*

**the bottom line** → BOTTOM[2]

**cut in line** → CUT[1]

**draw the line at sth/doing sth** → DRAW[1]

**drop sb a line** → DROP[1]

**hook, line and sinker** → HOOK[1]

**in line for sth** likely to get sth: *She's next in line for promotion.*

**in line with sth** similar to sth and fitting in with it

**out of line** (used about sb's behavior) not acceptable or polite: *That remark was totally out of line!*

**stand in line** → STAND[1]

**line**[2] /laɪn/ ***verb*** [T] **1** (often passive) to mark sth with LINES[1] (1): *lined paper* ◇ *a face lined with age* **2** to make or form a LINE[1] (4) along sth: *Crowds lined the streets to see the parade.* ◇ *a tree-lined avenue* **3** (often passive) to cover the inside surface of sth with a different material: *fur-lined boots*

PHR V **line up (for sth)** to form a line (for sth)

**line sth up** to arrange or plan sth: *What do you have lined up for the weekend?*

**lined** /laɪnd/ ***adj.*** **1** covered in lines: *a face lined with age* ◇ *lined paper* **2 -lined** (used in compounds) having the object or material mentioned all along the side(s) or all over the inside surface: *a tree-lined avenue* ◇ *fur-lined boots*

ˈ**line** ˌ**dancing** ***noun*** [U] a type of dancing in which people stand in lines and do sets of steps at the same time

**lin·en** /ˈlɪnɪn/ ***noun*** **1** [U] a type of strong cloth that is made from a natural substance (flax) **2 linens** [pl.] sheets, tablecloths, etc., which often used to be made of LINEN (1): *bed linens*

**lin·er** /ˈlaɪnər/ ***noun*** [C] a large ship that carries people, etc. long distances

ˈ**line-up** ***noun*** [usually sing.] **1** the people who are going to take part in an event: *an impressive line-up of speakers* ◇ *the team's starting line-up* (the people who will play first in the game) **2** a set of items, events, etc. arranged to follow one another: *A horror movie completes this evening's TV line-up.* **3** a row of people, including one who is suspected of a crime, who are shown to a person to see if he or she can recognize the criminal

**lin·ger** /ˈlɪŋgər/ ***verb*** [I] **1** to stay somewhere for a long time: *lingering effects of the floods* **2** (*formal*) to take a long time doing sth: *to linger over a meal*

**lin·ge·rie** /ˌlɑnʒəˈreɪ; ˌlɑndʒəˈreɪ/ ***noun*** [U] women's underwear that is usually very delicate and elegant

**lin·guist** /ˈlɪŋgwɪst/ ***noun*** [C] a person who studies or teaches language(s); a person who is good at learning foreign languages

**lin·guis·tic** /lɪŋˈgwɪstɪk/ ***adj.*** of language or linguistics

**lin·guis·tics** /lɪŋˈgwɪstɪks/ ***noun*** [U] the scientific study of language

**lin·ing** /ˈlaɪnɪŋ/ *noun* [C,U] material that covers the inside surface of sth: *I tore the lining of my coat.*

★**link**[1] /lɪŋk/ *noun* [C] **1** one ring in a chain ➲ picture at **chain**[1]. **2** a person or thing that connects two other people or things: *There is a strong link between smoking and heart disease.* ◇ *Economic links with South Africa were broken for many years.* **3** a means of moving or communicating between two places: *a downtown-airport bus link* **4** = HYPERLINK

★**link**[2] /lɪŋk/ *verb* [T] **link A to/with B; link A and B (together)** to make or suggest a connection between two or more people or things: *Air pollution has been linked to asthma.* ◇ *This evidence could link him with several robberies.*

PHRV **link up (to/with sb/sth)** to join together (with sb/sth), especially by computer

**li·no·le·um** /lɪˈnoʊliəm/ *noun* [U] a type of smooth, hard covering for floors

**lint** /lɪnt/ *noun* [U] small pieces of thread that come off clothing, etc. and form into balls

★**li·on** /ˈlaɪən/ *noun* [C] a large animal of the cat family that lives in Africa and parts of southern Asia. Male lions have a large amount of hair around their head and neck (a mane).

> NOTE A female lion is called a **lioness** and a young lion is called a **cub**. The noise a lion makes is a **roar**.

★**lip** /lɪp/ *noun* [C] **1** one of the two soft red parts above and below your mouth: *to kiss somebody on the lips*

> NOTE You have a **top/upper** lip and a **bottom/lower** lip.

**2** the edge of a cup or of sth that is shaped like a cup

IDM **purse your lips** → PURSE[2]

ˈ**lip-read** *verb* [I,T] (*pt, pp* **lip-read** /-rɛd/) to understand what sb is saying by looking at the movements of his/her lips

**lip·stick** /ˈlɪpstɪk/ *noun* [C,U] a substance that is used for giving color to your lips: *to put on some lipstick* ◇ *a new lipstick*

**li·queur** /lɪˈkər; -ˈkʊr/ *noun* [U] a strong alcoholic (usually sweet) drink that is often drunk in small quantities after a meal

★**liq·uid** /ˈlɪkwəd/ *noun* [C,U] a substance, e.g. water, that is not solid and that can flow or be poured ▸ **liq·uid** *adj.*: *The patient can only be given liquid food.*

**liq·ui·date** /ˈlɪkwədeɪt/ *verb* [T] to close down a business because it has no money left ▸ **liq·ui·da·tion** /ˌlɪkwəˈdeɪʃn/ *noun* [U]: *to go into liquidation* (= of a business)

**liq·uor** /ˈlɪkər/ *noun* [U] (*also* **spirits** [pl.]) strong alcoholic drinks

ˈ**liquor store** *noun* [C] a store where you can buy alcohol, including beer and wine

**lisp** /lɪsp/ *noun* [C] an incorrect way of speaking in which "s" sounds like "th": *He speaks with a slight lisp.* ▸ **lisp** *verb* [I,T]

★**list**[1] /lɪst/ *noun* [C] a series of names, figures, items, etc. that are written or printed one after another: *a shopping list* ◇ *an alphabetical list* ◇ *Your name is third on the waiting list.*

★**list**[2] /lɪst/ *verb* [T] to make a list of sth; to put or include sth on a list: *to list items in alphabetical order* ◇ *Her number is not listed in the phone book.*

★**lis·ten** /ˈlɪsn/ *verb* [I] **1 listen (to sb/sth)** to pay attention to sb/sth in order to hear him/her/it: *Now please listen carefully to what I have to say.* ◇ *to listen to the radio/music* ➲ Look at the note at **hear**. **2 listen (to sb/sth)** to pay attention to or believe what sb says, etc.: *I try to give them advice but they never listen to what I tell them.* ◇ *Now, listen, you two – I want you to behave!*

PHRV **listen for sth** to wait to hear sth: *to listen for a knock on the door*

**listen up** (*informal*) (used to tell people to pay attention to what you are going to say): *Okay, listen up, everybody – I have an important announcement to make.*

**lis·ten·er** /ˈlɪsn·ər/ *noun* [C] a person who listens: *He is a good listener* (= he pays attention to you when you are speaking).

**list·less** /ˈlɪstləs/ *adj.* tired and without energy ▸ **list·less·ly** *adv.*

**lit** *past tense, past participle of* LIGHT[3]

**lite** /laɪt/ *adj.* (*informal*) = LIGHT[2] (9): *lite beer*

**li·ter** (*Cdn* **li·tre**) /ˈliṭər/ *noun* [C] (*abbr.* **l**) a measure of liquid, used commonly in Canada, and used especially in science in the U.S: *She drinks 2 litres of water every day.* ◇ *One liter of fluid evaporated.*

> NOTE In the U.S., it is more common. to measure liquids in **quarts**. One quart is equal to 0.946 liter.

**lit·er·a·cy** /ˈlɪṭərəsi/ *noun* [U] the ability to read and write ➲ Look at **illiteracy**.

**lit·er·al** /ˈlɪṭərəl/ *adj.* **1** (used about the meaning of a word or phrase) original or basic: *The word "gay" isn't used very much in its literal sense anymore.* ➲ Look at **figurative** and **metaphorical**. **2** (used about a translation, etc.) translating each word separately without looking at the general meaning

**lit·er·al·ly** /ˈlɪṭərəli/ *adv.* **1** in a LITERAL (2) way: *You shouldn't take his comments literally.* **2** (*informal*) (used for emphasizing sth): *We were literally frozen to death* (= we were very cold). ➲ Many people consider this use of **literally** incorrect.

**lit·er·ar·y** /ˈlɪṭərɛri/ *adj.* of or concerned with literature: *a literary journal*

**lit·er·ate** /ˈlɪṭərət/ *adj.* **1** able to read and write OPP **illiterate** **2** well-educated

★**lit·er·a·ture** /ˈlɪṭərətʃər; -tʃʊr/ *noun* [U] **1** writing that is considered to be a work of art. Literature includes novels, plays and poetry: *French literature* **2** printed material on a particular subject: *The company sent out new product literature.*

**lit·i·ga·tion** /ˌlɪṭəˈgeɪʃn/ *noun* [U] the process of bringing a legal case to a court of law, especially when one person or group is trying to get money from another

ˈ**litmus test** *noun* [C] **1** (*technical*) a test made with a special kind of paper (**litmus paper**) to see whether a substance is an acid or a base **2** a situation or event that reveals the real nature of sb or sth: *The litmus test for dedicated students is whether they are willing to study on Saturday night.*

**lit·ter**[1] /ˈlɪt̬ər/ ***noun*** **1** [U] pieces of paper, cans, etc. that are left in a public place **2** [C] all the young animals that are born to one mother at the same time: *a litter of six puppies*

**lit·ter**[2] /ˈlɪt̬ər/ ***verb*** [I,T] to make sth messy with LITTER[1]: *The streets were littered with beer bottles.* ◇ *Do Not Litter* (= on a sign)

**lit·ter·bug** /ˈlɪt̬ərbʌg/ ***noun*** [C] (*informal*) a person who drops litter in a public place

★**lit·tle**[1] /ˈlɪt̬l/ ***adj.*** **1** not big; small: *There's a little hole in my sock.* ◇ *your little finger/toe* (= the smallest one on your hand/foot)

NOTE **Little** is often used with another adjective: *a little old lady* ◇ *a sweet little kitten* ➲ Look at the note at **small**.

**2** (used about distance or time) short: *Do you mind waiting a little while?* ◇ *It's only a little farther.* **3** young: *a little girl/boy* ◇ *my little brother* **4** not important: *a little problem*

★**lit·tle**[2] /ˈlɪt̬l/ ***det.*** (with uncountable [U] nouns) **1** not much or not enough: *They have very little money.* ◇ *There is little hope that she will recover.* ➲ Look at **less** and **least**. **2 a little** (*also* **a little bit of**) by a small amount of sth: *I like a little sugar in my coffee.*

★**lit·tle**[3] /ˈlɪt̬l/ ***pronoun*** **1** (also as a noun after *the*) a small amount; not enough: *We studied Latin in school, but I remember very little.* ◇ *The little I know of him has given me a good impression.* **2 a little** (*also* **a little bit**) a small amount: *"Is there any butter left?" "Yes, just a little."*

IDM **after/for a little (bit)** after/for a short distance or time: *You should rest for a little.*

★**lit·tle**[4] /ˈlɪt̬l/ ***adv.*** **1** not much or not enough: *I slept very little last night.* ◇ *a little-known author* **2 a little** (*also* **a little bit**) by a small amount: *This skirt is a little (bit) too tight.*

IDM **little by little** slowly: *After the accident, her strength returned little by little.*

ˈ**Little League** ***noun*** [sing.] a series of baseball teams for children

★**live**[1] /lɪv/ ***verb***

➤BE ALIVE **1** [I] to be or remain alive: *You can't live without water.* ◇ *She doesn't have long to live.* ◇ *to live to the age of 100*

➤IN A PLACE **2** [I] to have your home: *Where do you live?* ◇ *I lived in Texas for three years.*

➤HAVE A TYPE OF LIFE **3** [I,T] to spend your life in a certain way: *to live a quiet life* ◇ *They have plenty of money and live well.*

➤HAVE ENOUGH MONEY **4** [I] to be able to buy the things that you need: *Many families don't have enough to live.*

➤ENJOY LIFE **5** [I] to enjoy all the opportunities of life fully: *I want to live a little before settling down and getting married.*

PHRV **live sth down** to make people forget sth bad or embarrassing that has happened to you: *They lost 10–0? They'll never live it down!*

**live off sb/sth** to depend on sb/sth in order to live: *Barry lives off frozen food.* ◇ *She could get a job but she'd rather live off her parents.*

**live on** to continue to exist: *Mozart is dead, but his music lives on.*

**live on sth 1** to have sth as your only food: *to live on bread and water* **2** to have sth as your income: *I don't know how they live on $8,000 a year!*

**live together 1** to live in the same house as sb **2** to live in the same house, etc. as sb and have a sexual relationship with him/her

**live up to sth** to be as good as expected: *Children sometimes find it hard to live up to their parents' expectations.*

**live with sb** = LIVE TOGETHER: *He's 30 years old and still lives with his parents.*

**live with sth** to accept sth unpleasant that you cannot change: *I know it's not the best solution, but we'll just have to live with it.*

★**live**[2] /laɪv/ ***adj.***

➤NOT DEAD **1** having life; not dead: *Have you ever touched a real live snake?* ➲ Look at **alive** and **living**[1].

➤BULLETS/BOMBS, ETC. **2** (used about a bomb, etc.) that has not yet exploded, or that can explode: *The police used live ammunition when they fired on the crowd.*

➤ELECTRICITY **3** (used about a wire, etc.) carrying electricity. If you touch sth that is live you will get an electric shock.

➤OF BROADCAST/PERFORMANCE **4** (used about a radio or TV program) seen or heard as it is happening: *live coverage of the championships* **5** recorded from a concert, etc., i.e. not made in a studio: *a live recording of Bob Dylan's last concert*

★**live**[3] /laɪv/ ***adv.*** appearing on television or on the radio at the same time as it is happening: *The concert will be broadcast live from New York.*

ˈ**lived-in** ***adj.*** (usually of a place) that has been used so much that it does not look new: *With three small children, their home had that lived-in look.*

ˈ**live-in** ***adj.*** (about a person) who lives with you: *a live-in girlfriend* ◇ *a live-in nurse*

**live·li·hood** /ˈlaɪvlihʊd/ ***noun*** [C, usually sing.] the way that you earn money: *to lose your livelihood*

★**live·ly** /ˈlaɪvli/ ***adj.*** (**live·li·er**; **live·li·est**) full of energy, interest, excitement, etc.: *lively kids* ◇ *There was a lively debate on the route of the new highway.* ◇ *a lively imagination*

**li·ven** /ˈlaɪvn/ ***verb***

PHRV **liven (sb/sth) up** to become lively or to make sb/sth lively: *Once the band started to play, the party livened up.*

**liv·er** /ˈlɪvər/ ***noun*** **1** [C] the part of your body that cleans your blood **2** [U] the liver of an animal when it is cooked and eaten as food

**lives** *plural of* LIFE

**live·stock** /ˈlaɪvstɑk/ ***noun*** [U] animals that are kept on a farm, e.g. cows, pigs, sheep, etc.

**liv·ing**[1] /ˈlɪvɪŋ/ ***adj.*** **1** alive now: *He has no living relatives.* **2** (used about a language, etc.) still used OPP The opposite for both meanings is **dead**.

**liv·ing**[2] /ˈlɪvɪŋ/ ***noun*** **1** [C, usually sing.] a means of earning money to buy the things you need: *What do you do for a living?* **2** [U] your way or quality of life: *The cost of living has risen in recent years.* ➲ Look at **standard of living**.

L

ˈ**living room** *noun* [C] the room in a house where people sit, relax, watch TV, etc. together

**liz·ard** /ˈlɪzərd/ *noun* [C] a small reptile with four legs, rough skin and a long tail. A lizard has a long tongue that it uses to catch insects.

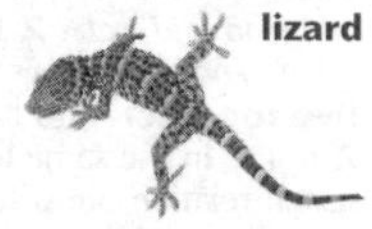


**lla·ma** /ˈlɑmə/ *noun* [C] a South American animal kept for its soft wool or for carrying loads

**Ln.** *abbr.* = LANE

★**load**[1] /loʊd/ *noun* [C] **1** something (heavy) that is being or is going to be carried: *The ship was carrying a full load of oil.* **2** (often in compounds) the quantity of sth that can be carried in a machine, car, etc.: *a truckload of sand* ◇ *busloads of tourists* **3 loads (of sth)** [pl.] (*informal*) a lot (of sth): *loads of cash*

IDM **a load of crap, garbage, etc.** (*informal*) nonsense

**get a load of sb/sth** (*informal*) (used to tell sb to look at sb/sth that is funny, surprising, etc.): *Hey guys, get a load of that dude's hat!*

★**load**[2] /loʊd/ *verb* **1** [I,T] to put or have a LOAD[1] or large quantity of sth in or on sb/sth: *Are you finished loading yet?* ◇ *Uncle Tim arrived loaded down with presents.* ◇ *They loaded the plane with supplies for the refugees.* **2** [I] to receive a LOAD[1]: *The ship is still loading.* **3** [I,T] (*computing*) to put a program or disk into a computer, or to move onto another computer or disk: *The graphics may take a while to load.* **4** [T] to put sth into a machine, a weapon, etc. so that it can be used: *to load film into a camera* ◇ *He loaded the gun.*

**load·ed** /ˈloʊdəd/ *adj.* **1** carrying a load, or filled with sth: *a loaded gun* **2** giving an unfair advantage: *That's a loaded question – I can't give you an accurate answer.*

IDM **loaded with sth** (*informal*) containing a lot of sth: *a cereal loaded with vitamins*

**loaf** /loʊf/ *noun* [C] (*pl.* **loaves** /loʊvz/) bread shaped and baked in one piece: *a loaf of bread* ➲ picture at **bread**.

**Loaf·er**™ *noun* [C] a flat shoe that you can slide your foot into, without fastening it

★**loan**[1] /loʊn/ *noun* [C] money, etc. that sb/sth lends you: *to take out a bank loan* ◇ *to make a loan to sb* ◇ *to pay off a loan* ➲ Look also at **savings and loan**.

IDM **on loan (from sb/sth)** borrowed from sb/sth: *This painting is on loan from a museum in Italy.*

**loan**[2] /loʊn/ *verb* [T] **loan sth (to sb)** to lend sth; to let sb borrow sth: *I loaned him $15 to buy gas.* ◇ *Can you loan me your pen for a minute?* ➲ picture at **borrow**.

**loathe** /loʊð/ *verb* [T] (not used in the progressive) to dislike sb/sth very much: *They loathe each other.* ◇ *I loathe spinach.*

**loaves** *plural of* LOAF

**lob·by**[1] /ˈlɑbi/ *noun* [C] (*pl.* **lob·bies**) **1** the area that is inside the entrance to a large building. A lobby often has a reception desk and doors, stairs, elevators, etc. that lead to other parts of the building: *a hotel lobby* **2** a group of people who try to persuade the government to do or not to do sth: *the anti-abortion lobby*

**lob·by**[2] /ˈlɑbi/ *verb* [I,T] (*pres. part.* **lob·by·ing**; *3rd person sing. pres.* **lob·bies**; *pt, pp* **lob·bied**) to try to persuade the government that sth should or should not be done: *A group of victims lobbied Congress to vote for tighter gun control.*

**lob·by·ist** /ˈlɑbiɪst/ *noun* [C] a person who works for a LOBBY[1] (2): *environmental lobbyists*

**lobe** /loʊb/ *noun* [C] = EARLOBE

**lob·ster** /ˈlɑbstər/ *noun* **1** [C] a large shellfish that has eight legs. A lobster is bluish-black, but it turns red when it is cooked. ➲ picture at **shellfish**. **2** [U] a LOBSTER (1) when it is cooked and eaten as food

★**lo·cal**[1] /ˈloʊkl/ *adj.* of or in a particular place (near you): *local newspapers* ◇ *The local high school is the center of the community.* ◇ *a local phone call* ▸ **lo·cal·ly** *adv.*: *These potatoes were grown locally.*

**lo·cal**[2] /ˈloʊkl/ *noun* [C, usually pl.] a person who lives in a particular place: *One of the locals showed us around the town.*

ˌ**local anesˈthetic** *noun* [C,U] medicine that is put into one part of your body so that you do not feel pain there ➲ Look at **general anesthetic**.

**lo·cal·i·ty** /loʊˈkæləṭi/ *noun* [C] (*pl.* **lo·cal·i·ties**) (*formal*) a small geographical area including a city, town, etc.: *The state school board works closely with locality officials.*

**lo·cal·ized** /ˈloʊkəlaɪzd/ *adj.* (*formal*) limited to a particular place or area: *localized flooding*

ˈ**local time** *noun* [U] the time at a particular place in the world: *We arrive in Los Angeles at 2 o'clock in the afternoon, local time.*

★**lo·cate** /ˈloʊkeɪt/ *verb* **1** [T] to find the exact position of sb/sth: *The missing ship has been located.* **2 be located** to be in a particular place: *The new mall is located to the west of the city.* **3** [I,T] to put or build sth, especially a business, in a particular place: *The bank is planning to locate its new headquarters in Springfield.* ➲ Look at **relocate**.

★**lo·ca·tion** /loʊˈkeɪʃn/ *noun* **1** [C] a place or position: *Several locations have been suggested for the new stadium.* **2** [U] finding where sb/sth is: *The police investigation led to the location of the smuggled drugs.*

IDM **on location** (used about a movie, television program, etc.) made in a suitable place (= not in a studio): *The series was filmed on location in Baltimore.*

★**lock**[1] /lɑk/ *noun* [C] **1** something that is used to fasten a door, lid, etc. so that you need a key or a group of numbers to open it again: *to turn the key in the lock* ◇ *a combination lock* (= a lock that you can only open using a particular set of numbers) ➲ Look also at **padlock**. ➲ picture at **key**. **2** a part of a river or a canal where the level of water changes. Locks have gates at each end and are used to allow boats to move to a higher or lower part of the canal or river.

★**lock**[2] /lɑk/ *verb* **1** [I,T] to close or fasten with a lock: *Did you lock the car?* ◇ *The door won't lock.* ➲ Look at **unlock**. **2** [T] to put sb/sth inside sth that is locked: *Lock your passport in a safe place.* **3** [I,T] to stick sth or be stuck in one position: *The wheels locked and the car crashed into the wall.*

PHR V **lock sth away** to keep sth in a safe or secret place (that is locked)

**lock sb in/out** to lock a door so that a person cannot get in/out: *All the prisoners are locked in for the night.* ◇ *to lock yourself out of your house*

**lock (sth) up** to lock all the doors, windows, etc. of a building: *Make sure that you lock up before you leave.*

**lock sb up** to put sb in prison

**lock·er** /ˈlɑkər/ ***noun*** [C] a small cupboard or closet with a lock where personal things can be kept or left. Lockers are found in schools, sports centers, etc.

**ˈlocker room** ***noun*** [C] a room where people can change their clothes and leave them in lockers, especially before and after playing sports

**lock·et** /ˈlɑkət/ ***noun*** [C] a piece of jewelry that is worn around the neck on a chain. A locket is a small case that often contains a photograph.

**lock·smith** /ˈlɑksmɪθ/ ***noun*** [C] a person who makes and repairs LOCKS[1] (1)

**lo·co·mo·tive** /ˌloʊkəˈmoʊt̬ɪv/ ***noun*** [C] = ENGINE (2)

**lodge**[1] /lɑdʒ/ ***noun*** [C] **1** the main building at a hotel in the country, where people stay, especially to do sports or outdoor activities: *a ski lodge* **2** the members of a branch of a society such as the Freemasons; the building where they meet: *a masonic lodge* **3** the home of a beaver **4** a Native American's tent or home built of LOGS[1] (1)

**lodge**[2] /lɑdʒ/ ***verb*** **1** [I,T] to become firmly attached or stuck, or to make sth do this: *The bullet lodged in her shoulder.* ➲ Look at **dislodge**. **2** [T] (*formal*) to make an official statement complaining about sth: *to lodge a complaint*

**lodg·ing** /ˈlɑdʒɪŋ/ ***noun*** [U] a place where you can stay, especially when you are on vacation: *The tour package includes all meals and lodging.*

**loft** /lɔft/ ***noun*** [C] **1** a raised platform over part of a room or building, that is used for storing things, for sleeping, etc. **2** a large apartment that does not have many walls inside it, usually in a bulding that was a factory, etc. in the past

**log**[1] /lɔg; lɑg/ ***noun*** [C] **1** the trunk or large branch of a tree that has been cut or has fallen down: *a log cabin* ➲ picture at **tree**. **2** a small piece of wood for a fire **3** (*also* **logbook**) an official written record of sth, written over a period of time: *to keep a log of visitors to a building*

**log**[2] /lɔg; lɑg/ ***verb*** [T] (**log·ging**; **logged**) to write sth in a LOG[1] (3)

PHR V **log in/on** to start using a computer that is part of a larger system

**log off/out** to finish using a computer that is part of a larger system

**log·ging** /ˈlɔgɪŋ; ˈlɑg-/ ***noun*** [U] the industry of cutting down trees to be used for buildings, paper, etc.

**log·ic** /ˈlɑdʒɪk/ ***noun*** [U] **1** the science of using reason **2** the use of reason or good sense: *There is no logic in your argument.*

★**log·i·cal** /ˈlɑdʒɪkl/ ***adj.*** **1** according to the rules of logic; reasonable: *As I see it, there is only one logical conclusion.* **2** able to use logic: *a logical mind* OPP **illogical** ▸ **log·i·cal·ly** /-kli/ ***adv.***

**lo·go** /ˈloʊgoʊ/ ***noun*** [C] (*pl.* **lo·gos**) a symbol or design that is used as an advertisement by a company or organization. A logo appears on the things the company owns and produces.

**lol·li·pop** /ˈlɑlipɑp/ (*also* **sucker**) ***noun*** [C] a piece of hard candy on a stick

**lone** /loʊn/ ***adj.*** (only *before* a noun) without any other people; alone: *a lone swimmer*

★**lone·ly** /ˈloʊnli/ ***adj.*** (**lone·li·er**; **lone·li·est**) **1** unhappy because you are not with other people: *to feel sad and lonely* **2** (only *before* a noun) far from other people and places where people live: *a lonely house in the hills* ➲ Look at the note at **alone**. ▸ **lone·li·ness** ***noun*** [U]

**lon·er** /ˈloʊnər/ ***noun*** [C] a person who likes to be alone or who has no friends

**lone·some** /ˈloʊnsəm/ ***adj.*** lonely or making you feel lonely ➲ Look at the note at **alone**.

★**long**[1] /lɔŋ/ ***adj.*** (**long·er** /ˈlɔŋgər/, **long·est** /ˈlɔŋgəst/) **1** measuring a great amount in distance or time: *She has beautiful long hair.* ◇ *We had to wait a long time.* ◇ *a long dress* (= down to the floor) ➲ noun **length**

> NOTE **Long** is also used when you are asking for or giving information about how much something measures in length, distance or time: *How long is the movie?* ◇ *The insect was only 2 millimeters long.* ◇ *a five-mile-long traffic jam*

**2** having or seeming to have a greater length than usual: *It was a long day at work today.* ◇ *long, cold winter nights* ◇ *We're going to spend a long weekend in New York* (= Saturday and Sunday, plus one or two more days).

IDM **go a long way** (used about money, food, etc.) to be used for buying a lot of things, feeding a lot of people, etc.: *to make a little money go a long way*

**in the long run** after a long time; in the end: *We ought to buy a new car – it'll be cheaper in the long run.*

**the long haul** (*informal*) the entire time of an event, a process, etc.: *I don't plan to quit this project – I'm in it for the long haul.*

**in the long/short term** → TERM[1]

**long**[2] /lɔŋ/ ***noun*** [U] a long time: *They won't be gone for long.* ◇ *It shouldn't take long.*

★**long**[3] /lɔŋ/ ***adv.*** **1** for a LONG[1] time: *She didn't stay long.* ◇ *You shouldn't have to wait long.* ◇ *I hope we don't have to wait much longer.*

> NOTE **Long** and **a long time** are both used as expressions of time. In positive sentences **a long time** is usually used: *They stood there for a long time.* **Long** is only used in positive sentences with another adverb, e.g. "too," "enough," "ago," etc.: *We lived here long ago.* ◇ *I've put up with this noise long enough. I'm going to complain.* Both **long** and **a long time** can be used in questions: *Were you away long/a long time?* In negative sentences there is sometimes a difference in meaning between **long** and **a long time**: *I haven't been here long* (= I arrived only a short time ago). ◇ *I haven't been*

L

*here for a long time* (= it has been a long time since I was last here).

**2** at a time that is distant from a particular point in time: *All that happened long ago.* ◇ *We got married long before we moved here.* **3** for the whole of the time that is mentioned: *The baby cried all night long.*

IDM **as/so long as** on condition that: *As long as there are no problems, we should get the job done by Friday.*

**no/not any longer** not anymore: *They no longer live here.* ◇ *They don't live here any longer.*

**so long** (*informal*) goodbye

**long**[4] /lɔŋ/ ***verb*** [I] **long for sth**; **long (for sb) to do sth** to want sth very much: *He longed to hold her in his arms.*

**ˈlong-ˌdistance** ***adj.*** (only *before* a noun) (used about travel or communication) between places that are far from each other: *a long-distance truck driver* ▸ **ˌlong ˈdistance** ***adv.***: *to call long distance*

**ˌlong ˈhaul** ***adj.*** (only *before* a noun) connected with the transportation of people or goods over long distances: *a long-haul flight*

**long·ing** /ˈlɔŋɪŋ/ ***noun*** [C,U] a great desire (for sb/sth) ▸ **long·ing·ly** ***adv.***: *She gazed longingly at the cakes in the bakery window.*

**lon·gi·tude** /ˈlɑndʒətud/ ***noun*** [U] the distance of a place east or west of a line from the North Pole to the South Pole that passes through Greenwich, England. Longitude is measured in degrees. ➲ Look at **latitude**. ➲ picture at **earth**.

**long johns** /ˈlɔŋ dʒɑnz/ ***noun*** [pl.] (*informal*) = LONG UNDERWEAR

**the ˈlong jump** ***noun*** [sing.] the sport in which people try to jump as far as possible ➲ Look at **high jump**.

**long-lived** /ˌlɔŋ ˈlɪvd/ ***adj.*** living or lasting for a long time: *a long-lived dispute*

**ˈlong-range** ***adj.*** (only *before* a noun) **1** that can go or be sent over long distances: *long-range nuclear missiles* **2** of or for a long period of time starting from the present: *the long-range weather forecast* ➲ Look at **short-range**.

**ˈlong shot** ***noun*** [usually sing.] an event which is not likely to occur: *"Can he pass the exam?" "I don't know – it's a long shot."*

**ˌlong-ˈstanding** ***adj.*** that has lasted for a long time: *a long-standing arrangement*

**ˌlong-ˈsuffering** ***adj.*** (used about a person) having a lot of troubles but not complaining

**ˈlong-term** ***adj.*** (usually *before* a noun) of or for a long period of time: *long-term planning*

**ˈlong-time** (*also* **longtime**) ***adj.*** (only *before* a noun) having existed or done sth for a long period of time: *a long-time resident*

**ˌlong ˈunderwear** ***noun*** [U] (*also informal* **long johns** [pl.]) a piece of warm underwear that covers your legs from your waist to your ankles

**long-wind·ed** /ˌlɔŋˈwɪndəd/ ***adj.*** (used about sth that is written or spoken) boring because it is too long

★**look**[1] /lʊk/ ***verb***

➤ USE EYES **1** [I,T] to turn your eyes in a particular direction (in order to pay attention to sb/sth): *Look carefully at these pictures.* ◇ *She blushed and looked away.* ◇ *to look out of the window* ◇ *Look who's here!* ◇ *Look where you are going!*

NOTE You can **see** something without paying attention to it: *I saw a girl riding past on a horse.* If you **look** at something, you pay attention to it with your eyes: *Look carefully. Can you see anything strange?*

➤ SEEM/APPEAR **2** [I] **look (like sb/sth) (to sb)**; **look (to sb) as if.../as though.../like...** to seem or appear: *You look very nice in that shirt.* ◇ *to look tired/sick/sad/well/happy* ◇ *The boy looks like his father.* ◇ *The room looks (to me) like it needs a coat of paint.* ◇ *It looks like rain* (= as if it is going to rain).

➤ SEARCH **3** [I] **look (for sb/sth)** to try to find (sb/sth): *We looked for you everywhere. Where were you?* ◇ *"Did you find your watch?" "No, I'm still looking."* ◇ *to look for work*

➤ FACE **4** [I] to face a particular direction: *Our hotel room looks out onto the beach.*

IDM **look good** to seem to be encouraging: *This year's sales figures are looking good.*

**look on the bright side (of sth)** to think only about the good side of a bad situation and be happy and hopeful

PHR V **look after sb/sth/yourself** to be responsible for or take care of sb/sth/yourself: *The old lady's son looked after all her financial affairs.*

**look ahead** to think about or plan for the future: *Looking ahead a few years, there's going to be a shortage of skilled workers.*

**look around 1** to turn your head in order to see sb/sth **2** to look at many things (before buying sth): *She looked around but couldn't find anything she liked.*

**look around sth** to visit a place of interest, etc.: *to look around the museum*

**look at sth 1** to examine sth (closely): *My tooth aches. I think a dentist should look at it.* **2** to think about or study sth: *Management is looking at ways of cutting costs.* **3** to read sth: *Could I look at the newspaper when you're finished with it?* **4** to consider sth: *People from different cultures look at life differently.*

**look back (on sth)** to think about sth in your past

**look down on sb/sth** to think that you are better than sb/sth: *Don't look down on them just because they aren't as successful as you.*

**look forward to sth/doing sth** to wait with pleasure for sth to happen (because you expect to enjoy it): *The kids are really looking forward to going on vacation.*

**look into sth** to study or investigate sth: *A committee was set up to look into the causes of the accident.*

**look on** to watch sth happening: *All we could do was look on as the house burned.*

**look out** to be careful or to pay attention to sth dangerous, etc.: *Look out! There's a bike coming.*

**look through sth** to read sth quickly

**look to sb for sth**; **look to sb to do sth** to expect sb to do or to provide sth: *He always looked to his father for advice.*

**look up 1** to raise your eyes: *She looked up and*

smiled. **2** (*informal*) to improve: *Business is looking up.*

**look sth up** to search for information in a book: *to look up a word in a dictionary*

**look up to sb** to respect or admire sb

★**look²** /lʊk/ ***noun*** **1** [C] the act of looking: *Take a look at this article.* ◇ *I knew something was wrong – everybody was giving me funny looks* (= looking at me strangely). **2** [C, usually sing.] a search: *I had a good look, but I couldn't find it.* **3** [C] the expression or appearance of sb/sth: *He had a worried look on his face.* **4** [C] a fashion or style: *The store has a new look to appeal to younger customers.* **5 looks** [pl.] a person's appearance: *He's lucky – he's got good looks and intelligence.*

IDM **like the look/looks/sound of sb/sth** → LIKE¹

**look³** /lʊk/ ***interjection*** (used for asking sb to listen to what you are saying, especially when you are annoyed): *Look, I don't want to explain this again – so pay attention!*

**-look·ing** /ˈlʊkɪŋ/ ***combining form*** (used in compounds to form adjectives) having the type of appearance mentioned: *an odd-looking building* ◇ *He's very good-looking.*

**look·out** /ˈlʊkaʊt/ ***noun*** [C] a person who watches out for danger

IDM **be on the lookout for sb/sth** to pay attention in order to see, find or be careful of sb/sth

**loom¹** /lum/ ***noun*** [C] a machine that is used for making (weaving) cloth by passing pieces of thread across and under other pieces

**loom²** /lum/ ***verb*** [I] to appear as a shape that is not clear and in a way that seems frightening: *The mountain loomed in the distance.* ◇ (*figurative*) *The threat of war loomed over the country.*

**loon** /lun/ ***noun*** [C] (*Cdn*) a water bird with a sharp BILL¹ (5), which dives to catch fish and has a strange loud call

**loon·ie** (*also* **loon·y**) /ˈluni/ ***noun*** [C] (*Cdn*) **1** the Canadian one-dollar coin ➲ Look also at **toonie**. **2** (*informal*) the Canadian dollar

**loon·y** /ˈluni/ ***noun*** [C], ***adj.*** (*pl.* **loon·ies**) (*slang*) (a person who is) crazy

**loop¹** /lup/ ***noun*** [C] a curved or circular shape, e.g. in a piece of rope or string

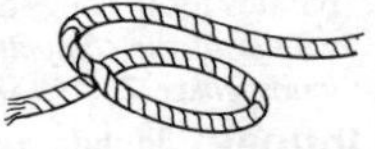

**loop²** /lup/ ***verb*** [T] **1** to make sth into a loop **2** to fasten or connect sth with a loop

IDM **be in/out of the loop** (*informal*) to feel connected to/left out of important information, news, events, etc.: *Keep me in the loop* (= pass any new information on to me). ◇ *I don't know what's happening with that project – I'm out of the loop on that one.*

**loop·hole** /ˈluphoʊl/ ***noun*** [C] a way of avoiding sth because the words of a rule or law are badly chosen: *a loophole in the tax law*

★**loose** /lus/ ***adj.*** **1** not tied up or shut in sth: *The dog broke loose and ran away.* ◇ *She wore her long hair loose.* **2** not firmly attached: *a loose tooth* **3** not contained in sth or connected together: *loose change* ◇ *some loose sheets of paper* **4** not fitting closely; not tight: *These pants are way too loose around the waist.*

IDM **loose ends** small parts of a project, etc. that are not finished yet: *We just have a few loose ends to tie up on that report.*

▸ **loose·ly** ***adv.***

**ˌloose ˈcannon** ***noun*** [C] a person, usually a public figure, who often behaves in a way that nobody can predict: *Recognizing that he was a loose cannon, party officials tried to limit the Senator's public speaking events.*

**ˈloose-leaf** ***adj.*** (used about a book, notebook, etc.) with pages that can be removed or added separately

**loos·en** /ˈlusn/ ***verb*** [I,T] to become or make sth loose or looser: *to loosen your tie*

PHR V **loosen (sb/sth) up** to relax or make sb move more easily: *These exercises will help you to loosen up.*

**loot¹** /lut/ ***noun*** [U] (*informal*) goods or money that have been stolen

**loot²** /lut/ ***verb*** [I,T] to steal things during a war or period of fighting: *Many stores were looted during yesterday's riots.* ▸ **loot·er** /ˈlut̬ər/ ***noun*** [C]

**lop·sid·ed** /ˈlɑpˌsaɪdəd/ ***adj.*** with one side lower or smaller, etc. than the other: *a lopsided smile*

**lord** /lɔrd/ ***noun*** **1 Lord** (*also* **the Lord**) [sing.] God; Christ **2** [C] (in some countries) a man who has been given the title "Lord," e.g. by a king or queen

IDM **(Good) Lord** (used for expressing surprise, worry, etc.)

**the ˌLord's ˈPrayer** ***noun*** [sing.] a very important Christian prayer that was first taught by Christ to his followers

★**lose** /luz/ ***verb*** (*pt, pp* **lost** /lɑst; lɔst/)

▸ NOT FIND **1** [T] to be unable to find sth: *I lost my purse. I can't find it anywhere.*

▸ HAVE STH TAKEN AWAY **2** [T] to no longer have sb/sth: *She lost a leg in the accident.* ◇ *He lost his wife last year* (= she died). ◇ *to lose your job*

▸ HAVE LESS **3** [T] to have less of sth: *to lose weight/interest/patience* ◇ *Downtown stores are losing business to the large malls.*

▸ NOT WIN **4** [I,T] not to win; to be defeated: *to lose a court case* ◇ *Michigan lost to Ohio State in their last football game.* ◇ *to lose an argument*

▸ TIME/CHANCE **5** [T] to waste time, a chance, etc.: *Hurry up! There's no time to lose.*

▸ CLOCK/WATCH **6** [T] (used about a clock, watch, etc.) to go too slowly: *My watch loses two minutes a day.* OPP **gain**

▸ MONEY **7** [I,T] to become poorer (as a result of sth): *The company lost on the deal.*

▸ NOT UNDERSTAND/HEAR **8** [T] (*informal*) to cause sb not to understand sth: *You totally lost me! Try to explain it again.*

IDM **keep/lose your balance** → BALANCE²

**lose your bearings** to become confused about where you are

**keep/lose your cool** → COOL²

**keep/lose count** → COUNT²

**lose/save face** → FACE¹

**lose heart** to believe that you will be unsuccessful
**lose it** (*informal*) to suddenly be unable to control your emotions because sth is very funny, shocking, etc.: *I just about lost it when that guy's pants fell down!*
**lose your life** to be killed
**lose your marbles** (*informal*) to go crazy
**lose your place** to be unable to find the place in a book, etc. where you stopped reading
**lose sight of sb/sth 1** to no longer be able to see sb/sth **2** to forget sb/sth: *Don't lose sight of your original aim.*
**keep/lose your temper** → TEMPER
**lose your touch** to lose a special skill or ability to do sth
**lose touch (with sb/sth)** to no longer have contact (with sb/sth): *I've lost touch with a lot of my old friends from high school.*
**keep/lose track of sb/sth** → TRACK[1]
**a losing battle** a competition, struggle, etc. in which it seems that you will be unsuccessful
PHRV **lose out (on sth)** (*informal*) to be at a disadvantage: *If a teacher pays too much attention to the bright students, the others lose out.*

**los·er** /ˈluzər/ ***noun*** [C] **1** a person who is defeated: *He is a bad loser. He always gets upset if I beat him.* **2** (*slang*) a person who is not successful or popular: *What a total loser!*

★**loss** /lɔs/ ***noun*** **1** [U] no longer having sth or not having as much as before; the act of losing sth: *loss of blood/money* ◇ *The loss* (= death) *of his wife was very sad for him.* ◇ *The plane crashed with heavy loss of life.* **2** [C, usually pl.] people who are killed or things that are destroyed, usually in a war: *The government troops suffered heavy losses in the fighting.* **3** [C] a disadvantage: *If she leaves, it will be a big loss to the department.* **4** [C] the amount of money which is lost by a business: *The company announced a loss of $5 million.*
IDM **at a loss (for sth/to do sth)** not knowing what to do or say: *She was at a loss for words.* ◇ *The police were at a loss to explain how the accident happened.*

**lost**[1] /lɔst/ *past tense, past participle of* LOSE

★**lost**[2] /lɔst/ ***adj.*** **1** (used about a person or an animal) unable to find the way: *This isn't the right road – we're completely lost!* ◇ *Don't get lost!* **2** difficult or impossible to find; missing: *The kids were looking for their lost dog.* **3 lost (without sb/sth)** not able to work in an efficient way or to live happily: *I'm lost without my watch!* ◇ *He would be lost without his pets for company.* **4 lost on sb** not noticed or understood by sb: *The humor of the situation was completely lost on Joe and he got really upset.*
IDM **get lost** (*informal*) go away: *"Get lost!" she shouted and walked off.*
**a lost cause** an ambition or aim that cannot be achieved

**ˌlost and ˈfound** ***noun*** [sing.] a special office where things that people have lost or left in a public place are kept for the owners to collect

★**lot**[1] /lɑt/ ***pronoun*** **a lot**; **lots** (*informal*) a large amount or number: *"How many people are coming to the party?" "I'm not sure, but a lot!"* ◇ *Have another piece of cake. There's lots left.*
IDM **a lot of sb/sth**; **lots of sb/sth** a large amount or number of (sb/sth): *There's been a lot of rain this year.* ◇ *We ate lots of cake at the birthday party.*

★**lot**[2] /lɑt/ ***adv.*** (*informal*) **1 a lot**; **lots** (before adjectives and adverbs in the comparative form) very much: *It's a lot faster now that there's a freeway.* ◇ *He plays tennis lots better than his brother does.* **2 a lot** very much or often: *Thanks a lot – that's very nice of you.* ◇ *It generally rains a lot at this time of year.*

★**lot**[3] /lɑt/ ***noun*** **1** [C] an area of land used for a particular purpose: *a parking lot* ◇ *We're going to build a house on this lot.* **2** [sing.] the quality or state of a person's life; your fate: *Women's lot in life has not always been easy.* **3** [C] a group of objects that were produced at the same time: *The defective packages all had the same lot number on their labels.* **4** [C] an object or group of objects that are for sale at an auction (= a sale at which the object goes to the person who offers the highest price): *Lot 27: 6 chairs*

**lo·tion** /ˈloʊʃn/ ***noun*** [C,U] liquid or cream that you use on your skin: *suntan lotion*

**lot·ter·y** /ˈlɑt̬əri/ ***noun*** [C] (*pl.* **lot·ter·ies**) a way of raising money by selling tickets with numbers on them and giving prizes to the people who have bought certain numbers which are chosen by chance

★**loud**[1] /laʊd/ ***adj.*** **1** making a lot of noise; not quiet: *He has a very loud laugh.* ◇ *Can you turn the TV down? It's too loud.*

> NOTE **Loud** is usually used to describe the sound itself or the thing producing the sound: *a loud noise/bang* ◇ *loud music.* **Noisy** is used to describe a person, an animal, a place, an event, etc. that is very or too loud: *a noisy street/party* ◇ *noisy neighbors/children*

**2** (used about clothes, colors, behavior, etc.) too bright or noticeable: *Isn't that shirt a little loud for a formal dinner?* ► **loud·ly** ***adv.*** ► **loud·ness** ***noun*** [U]

★**loud**[2] /laʊd/ ***adv.*** making a lot of noise: *Could you speak a little louder? The people at the back can't hear.*
IDM **out loud** → OUT[1]

**loud·speak·er** /ˈlaʊdˌspikər/ ***noun*** [C] **1** an apparatus for making sounds, voices, etc. louder: *The winner of the competition was announced over the loudspeaker.* **2** = SPEAKER (2)

**lounge**[1] /laʊndʒ/ ***noun*** [C] **1** a room in a hotel, office building, etc. where you can sit comfortably: *Let's go and have coffee in the lounge.* **2** a room at an airport where passengers wait: *the departure lounge*

**lounge**[2] /laʊndʒ/ ***verb*** [I] **lounge (around)** to sit or stand in a lazy way; to relax: *We spent the afternoon lounging in the sun.*

**louse** /laʊs/ ***noun*** [C] (*pl.* **lice** /laɪs/) a small insect that lives on the bodies of animals and people

**lous·y** /ˈlaʊzi/ ***adj.*** (**lous·i·er**; **lous·i·est**) (*informal*) very bad: *We had lousy weather on vacation.* ◇ *You'll feel lousy tomorrow if you drink too much.*

**lov·a·ble** /ˈlʌvəbl/ ***adj.*** easy to love because attractive and pleasant

★**love**[1] /lʌv/ ***noun***
➤AFFECTION **1** [U] a very strong feeling of affection for sb/sth: *It was love at first sight.* ◇ *I don't think she's marrying him for love!* ◇ *his love for his country* OPP **hate** or **hatred**
➤ENJOYMENT **2** [U, sing.] a strong feeling of interest in or enjoyment of sth: *a love of adventure*
➤SB/STH YOU LIKE **3** [C] a thing in which you are very interested: *Computers are the love of his life these days.*
➤PERSON **4** [C] a person who is loved: *Of course, my love.* SYN **darling**
➤IN TENNIS **5** [U] (used in tennis) a score of zero: *"15-love," called the umpire.*
➤FOR ENDING LETTER **6** [U] (*informal*) (a way of ending a letter to a friend or a member of your family): *Lots of love from us all, Denise.*
IDM **be in love (with sb)** to have a strong feeling of affection and sexual attraction (for sb): *They're very much in love (with each other).*
**fall in love (with sb)** to start to feel a strong affection and attraction for sb: *They fell in love and were married within two months.*
**make love (to sb)** to have sex

★**love**[2] /lʌv/ ***verb*** [T] **1** to have a strong feeling of affection for sb/sth: *"Do you love him?" "Yes, very much."* ◇ *It's wonderful to be loved.* **2** to like very much or to enjoy: *I love summertime!* ◇ *My father loves to listen/listening to music.* ◇ *"Would you like to come?" "I'd love to."* ◇ *The cat just loves it when you pet her right here.*

ˈ**love afˌfair** ***noun*** [C] a (usually sexual) relationship between two people who love each other but are not married

★**love·ly** /ˈlʌvli/ ***adj.*** (**love·li·er**; **love·li·est**) **1** beautiful or attractive: *a lovely room* ◇ *You look lovely with your hair short.* **2** very nice, enjoyable or pleasant: *What a lovely day!* ◇ *It's lovely to see you again.* ▶ **love·li·ness** ***noun*** [U]

★**lov·er** /ˈlʌvər/ ***noun*** [C] **1** a person who is having a sexual relationship outside marriage ➲ Look at **mistress**. **2 lovers** [pl.] (*old-fashioned*) two people who are in love or are having a sexual relationship without being married: *In the evening the park was full of young lovers walking hand in hand.* **3** a person who likes or enjoys the thing mentioned: *a music lover* ◇ *an animal lover*

ˈ**love ˌstory** ***noun*** [C] (*pl.* **love stories**) a story or novel that is mainly about love

**lov·ing** /ˈlʌvɪŋ/ ***adj.*** feeling or showing love or care ▶ **lov·ing·ly** ***adv.***

★**low**[1] /loʊ/ ***adj.***
➤NOT HIGH **1** not high: *The dog will be able to jump over that fence – it's way too low.*
➤NEAR BOTTOM **2** close to the ground or to the bottom of sth: *Hang that picture a little higher – it's still too low!*
➤LEVEL/VALUE **3** below the usual or normal level or amount: *Temperatures were very low last winter.* ◇ *The price of fruit is lower in the summer.* ◇ *low wages* **4** below what is normal in quality, importance or development: *a low standard of living* ◇ *low status*
➤SOUND **5** (used about a sound or voice) deep or soft and quiet: *I need some practice in order to sing those low notes.* ◇ *She spoke in a low voice so her boss couldn't hear her.*
➤DEPRESSED **6** not cheerful or bright: *He's been feeling awfully low since his wife died.*
IDM **keep a low profile** to act in a way that does not attract attention from other people

★**low**[2] /loʊ/ ***adv.*** **1** in or to a low position, level, etc.; near the ground or bottom; not high: *The helicopter flew low over the buildings.* ◇ *"Where is the pain? Here?" "A little lower down," she replied.* **2** (in music) with deep notes: *Jim can sing a lot lower than I can.*
IDM **high and low** → HIGH[2]
**run low** (used about supplies, etc.) to be or become almost finished: *Food and medical supplies were running low.*
**run low on sth** to have used almost all of sth: *We're running low on milk – could you buy some more today?*

**low**[3] /loʊ/ ***noun*** [C] a low point, level, figure, etc.: *The peso has fallen to a new low against the dollar.*

ˈ**low-down** ***adj.*** (*informal*) (used about behavior, etc.) not respectable or honest: *a low-down trick*

**low·er**[1] /ˈloʊər/ ***adj.*** at the bottom of sth; being the bottom part of sth: *She bit her lower lip.* ◇ *in the lower left-hand corner of the page* OPP **upper**

**low·er**[2] /ˈloʊər/ ***verb*** [T] **1** to move sb/sth down: *They lowered the boat into the water.* **2** to make sth less in amount or quality: *The virus lowers resistance to other diseases.* OPP The opposite for both senses is **raise**.

**low·er·case** /ˌloʊərˈkeɪs/ ***adj.***, ***noun*** [U] (in) small letters, not capitals: *A lowercase R looks like this: r.* OPP **uppercase**

ˌ**lower-ˈclass** ***adj.*** belonging to a low social and economic class ➲ Look at **middle-class**, **upper-class** and **working-class**.

ˌ**low-ˈkey** ***adj.*** (used about the style of sth) quiet, without a lot of preparation or fuss: *The wedding will be very low-key. We're only inviting ten people.*

ˌ**low-ˈlying** ***adj.*** (used about land) near to sea level; not high

ˌ**low-ˈpaid** ***adj.*** not paying or earning much money: *low-paid workers*

ˌ**low ˈtide** ***noun*** [U] the time when the ocean is at its lowest level: *At low tide, you can walk out to the island.* OPP **high tide**

★**loy·al** /ˈlɔɪəl/ ***adj.*** (used about a person) not changing in your friendship or beliefs; faithful: *a loyal friend* ◇ *Will you remain loyal to the party in the next election?* OPP **disloyal** ▶ **loy·al·ly** ***adv.***

**loy·al·ty** /ˈlɔɪəlti/ ***noun*** (*pl.* **loy·al·ties**) **1** [U] the quality of being loyal: *a dog's loyalty to its owner* **2** [C, usually pl.] a feeling of friendship that makes you faithful toward sth/sb: *I know where my loyalties lie.*

**loz·enge** /ˈlɑzndʒ/ ***noun*** [C] a candy that you suck if you have a cough or sore throat

**Ltd.** ***abbr.*** (*especially Cdn*) (used about companies) Limited ➲ Look at **Inc**. The word **incorporated** is usually used by U.S. businesses.

**lu·bri·cant** /ˈlubrɪkənt/ ***noun*** [C,U] a substance like oil used for making a machine, etc. work smoothly

**lu·bri·cate** /ˈlubrɪkeɪt/ ***verb*** [T] to put oil, etc.

L

onto or into sth so that it works smoothly ▶ **lu·bri·ca·tion** /ˌlubrɪˈkeɪʃn/ ***noun*** [U]

**lu·cid** /ˈlusəd/ ***adj.*** (*formal*) **1** (used about sth that is said or written) clear and easy to understand **2** (used about a person's mind) not confused; clear and normal ▶ **lu·cid·ly** ***adv.*** ▶ **lu·cid·i·ty** /luˈsɪdət̬i/ ***noun*** [U]

★**luck** /lʌk/ ***noun*** [U] **1** the fact of something happening by chance: *There's no skill in this game – it's all luck.* ◇ *to have good/bad luck* **2** success or good things that happen by chance: *We'd like to wish you lots of luck in your new career.*

IDM **be in luck/out of luck** to be lucky/unlucky: *I was in luck – the store had the book I wanted.*

**good luck (to sb)** (used to wish that sb is successful): *Good luck! I'm sure you'll get the job.*

**tough (luck)!** → TOUGH

**luck·i·ly** /ˈlʌkəli/ ***adv.*** fortunately: *Luckily, I remembered to bring my umbrella.*

★**luck·y** /ˈlʌki/ ***adj.*** (**luck·i·er**; **luck·i·est**) **1** (used about a person) having good luck: *We were very lucky with the weather on vacation* (= it was nice). ◇ *I'm very lucky to have such good friends.* **2** (used about a situation, an event, etc.) having a good result: *It's lucky you reminded me* (= or I would have forgotten). ◇ *a lucky escape* **3** (used about a thing) bringing success or good luck: *a lucky number* ◇ *It was not my lucky day.* OPP The opposite for all senses is **unlucky**.

**lu·cra·tive** /ˈlukrət̬ɪv/ ***adj.*** (*formal*) producing a lot of money

**lu·di·crous** /ˈludɪkrəs/ ***adj.*** very silly; ridiculous: *What a ludicrous idea!* ▶ **lu·di·crous·ly** ***adv.***

**lug** /lʌg/ ***verb*** [T] (**lug·ging**; **lugged**) (*informal*) to carry or pull sth with great difficulty

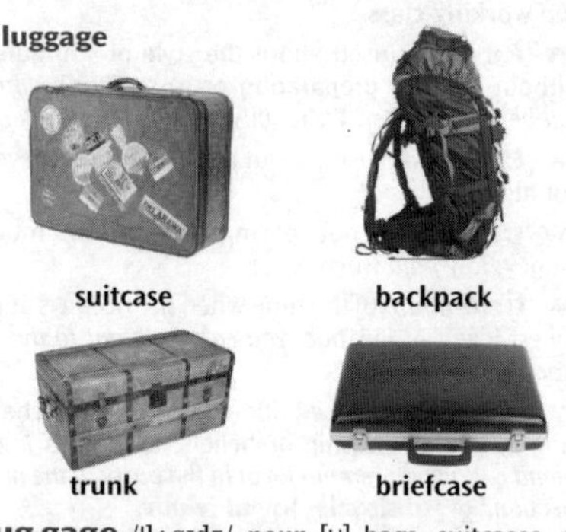


**lug·gage** /ˈlʌgɪdʒ/ ***noun*** [U] bags, suitcases, etc. used for carrying a person's things on a trip: *We can fit one more piece of luggage in the trunk!*

**ˈluggage rack** ***noun*** [C] a structure that you fasten to the roof of a car and use for carrying luggage or other large objects ➲ picture at **rack**.

**luke·warm** /ˌlukˈwɔrm/ ***adj.*** **1** (used about liquids) only slightly warm **2 lukewarm (about sb/sth)** not showing much interest; not eager: *John's fairly lukewarm about going to Iowa on vacation.*

**lull**[1] /lʌl/ ***verb*** [T] **1** to make sb/sth quiet or sleepy: *She sang a song to lull the children to sleep.* **2** to make sb/sth feel safe, especially by deceiving them: *Our first success lulled us into a false sense of security.*

**lull**[2] /lʌl/ ***noun*** [C, usually sing.] a short period of quiet; a pause in activity: *When she entered the room, there was a lull in the conversation.*

**lull·a·by** /ˈlʌləbaɪ/ ***noun*** [C] (*pl.* **lull·a·bies**) a gentle song that you sing to help a child to go to sleep

**lum·ber**[1] /ˈlʌmbər/ ***noun*** [U] wood that is going to be used for building

**lum·ber**[2] /ˈlʌmbər/ ***verb*** [I] to move in a slow, heavy way: *He heaved himself out of bed and lumbered into the bathroom.*

**lum·ber·jack** /ˈlʌmbərdʒæk/ ***noun*** [C] a person whose job is to cut down trees

**lum·ber·yard** /ˈlʌmbəryɑrd/ ***noun*** [C] a store that sells wood, etc. for building. The wood is usually kept outdoors or under a roof.

**lu·mi·nous** /ˈlumənəs/ ***adj.*** shining, especially in the dark: *a watch with luminous hands*

★**lump**[1] /lʌmp/ ***noun*** [C] **1** a piece of sth solid of any size or shape: *a lump of coal* ◇ *The sauce was full of lumps.* **2** a hard swelling on or in the body: *You'll have a little lump on your head where you hit it.*

**lump**[2] /lʌmp/ ***verb*** [T] **lump sb/sth together**; **lump sb/sth into sth** to put people or things together; to consider or treat them as being all alike: *Don't just lump everybody into one category.*

**ˌlump ˈsum** ***noun*** [C] an amount of money that is paid all at once, rather than in several smaller amounts

**lump·y** /ˈlʌmpi/ ***adj.*** (**lump·i·er**; **lump·i·est**) full of or covered with lumps

**lu·na·cy** /ˈlunəsi/ ***noun*** [U] very foolish behavior: *It was lunacy to swim so far from the shore.*

**lu·nar** /ˈlunər/ ***adj.*** connected with the moon: *lunar dust* ◇ *a lunar spacecraft*

**lu·na·tic** /ˈlunətɪk/ ***noun*** [C] **1** (*informal*) a person who behaves in a crazy or dangerous way **2** (*old-fashioned*) a person who is crazy ➲ Look at the note at **crazy**.

★**lunch**[1] /lʌntʃ/ ***noun*** [C,U] a meal that you have in the middle of the day: *What would you like for lunch?*

> NOTE You might take a **bag lunch** or a **picnic lunch** if you are out for the day. If you are working, you might have a **business lunch** (= working at the same time as having lunch). ➲ Look at the note at **dinner**.

**lunch**[2] /lʌntʃ/ ***verb*** [I] (*formal*) to eat lunch: *We will lunch with the ambassador next week.*

**lunch·box** /ˈlʌntʃbɑks/ ***noun*** [C] a metal or plastic box with a handle that you use to carry your lunch to school or to work

**lunch·eon** /ˈlʌntʃən/ ***noun*** [C] a formal meal eaten in the middle of the day: *The Ladies' Association will hold its annual luncheon next Wednesday.*

**ˈlunch hour** ***noun*** [C, usually sing.] the time around the middle of the day when you stop work or school to have lunch: *I went shopping on my lunch hour.*

**lunch·time** /ˈlʌntʃtaɪm/ ***noun*** [C,U] the time around the middle of the day when lunch is eaten: *I'll meet you at lunchtime.*

★**lung** /lʌŋ/ ***noun*** [C] one of the two parts of the body that are inside your chest and are used for breathing: *lung cancer*

**lunge** /lʌndʒ/ ***noun*** [C, usually sing.] a sudden forward movement of the body, especially when trying to attack sb ▶ **lunge** ***verb*** [I]: *The man lunged toward me with a knife in his hand.*

**lurch**[1] /lərtʃ/ ***noun*** [C] a sudden movement: *a sudden lurch forward*
IDM **leave sb in the lurch** → LEAVE[1]

**lurch**[2] /lərtʃ/ ***verb*** [I] to move suddenly, especially when out of control: *The truck lurched forward and hit a tree.*

**lure**[1] /lʊr/ ***noun*** [C] **1** a thing that is used to attract people or animals: *a fishing lure* **2** the power of attracting sb: *the lure of money/fame/adventure*

**lure**[2] /lʊr/ ***verb*** [T] to attract or tempt sb/sth: *It's such a nice day – can I lure you away from your work?*

**lu·rid** /ˈlʊrəd/ ***adj.*** **1** shocking, especially because violent or unpleasant: *The newspaper was criticized for its lurid description of the murder.* **2** having colors that are very or too bright: *a lurid dress in purple and orange* ▶ **lu·rid·ly** ***adv.***

**lurk** /lərk/ ***verb*** [I] to wait where you cannot be seen, especially when intending to do sth bad: *I thought I saw somebody lurking among the trees.*

**lush**[1] /lʌʃ/ ***adj.*** (used about plants) growing very thickly and well

**lush**[2] /lʌʃ/ ***noun*** [C] (*informal*) a person who often gets drunk

**lust**[1] /lʌst/ ***noun*** **1** [U] strong sexual desire **2** [C,U] (a) very strong desire to possess or get sth: *a lust for power*

**lust**[2] /lʌst/ ***verb*** [I] **lust after/for sb/sth** to have a very strong desire for sb/sth: *to lust for power/success/fame*

**Lu·ther·an** /ˈluθərən/ ***noun*** [C], ***adj.*** (a member) of a Protestant church that is based on the ideas of Martin Luther

**lux·u·ri·ous** /lʌgˈʒʊriəs/ ***adj.*** very comfortable; full of luxury: *a luxurious seaside hotel* ▶ **lux·u·ri·ous·ly** ***adv.***

**lux·u·ry** /ˈlʌkʃəri; ˈlʌgʒəri/ ***noun*** (*pl.* **lux·u·ries**) **1** [U] great comfort and pleasure, often including the use and enjoyment of expensive and beautiful things: *Somebody said she was living in luxury in Barbados.* ◇ *to lead a life of luxury* ◇ *a luxury hotel/car/yacht* **2** [C] something that is enjoyable and expensive that you do not really need: *A vacation is a luxury we just can't afford this year.* **3** [U, sing.] a pleasure which you do not often have: *It was a real luxury to do nothing all weekend.*

**lynch** /lɪntʃ/ ***verb*** [T] (used about a crowd of people) to kill sb (usually by hanging) who is thought to be guilty of a crime, without a legal trial

**lyr·ic** /ˈlɪrɪk/ ***adj.*** (used about poetry) expressing personal feelings

**lyr·i·cal** /ˈlɪrɪkl/ ***adj.*** like a song or a poem, expressing strong personal feelings

**lyr·ics** /ˈlɪrɪks/ ***noun*** [pl.] the words of a song: *Who wrote the lyrics?*

# M m

**M, m** /ɛm/ ***noun*** [C,U] (*pl.* **M's**; **m's**) the thirteenth letter of the English alphabet: *"Montana" begins with (an) "M."*

**M** (*also* **med.**) ***abbr.*** medium (size)

**m** /ɛm/ ***abbr.*** **1** = METER[1] (1) **2** (*also* **mi.**) = MILE

**M.A.** /ˌɛm ˈeɪ/ ***abbr.*** Master of Arts ➲ Look at **master's degree.**

**ma'am** /mæm/ ***noun*** [sing.] (used when speaking to a woman, as a short form for "madam")

**ma·ca·bre** /məˈkɑbrə/ ***adj.*** horrible and frightening because connected with death

**ma·ca·ro·ni** /ˌmækəˈroʊni/ ***noun*** [U] a type of Italian food made from dried flour and water (pasta) in the shape of curved hollow tubes: *When I was a child, my favorite dinner was macaroni and cheese.*

**ma·chet·e** /məˈʃɛt̬i/ ***noun*** [C] a large knife with a heavy curved blade, used as a weapon and for cutting down plants

★**ma·chine** /məˈʃin/ ***noun*** [C] **1** (often in compounds) a piece of equipment with several moving parts, made to perform a particular task: *a washing machine* ◇ *Can you operate/work this machine?* ◇ *One of the machines broke down.* ➲ Look at the note at **tool. 2** a system or organization carefully controlled and organized by a group of people: *It's hard to understand the workings of the party machine* (= a political party).

**ma'chine gun** ***noun*** [C] a gun that fires bullets very quickly and continuously

★**ma·chin·er·y** /məˈʃinəri/ ***noun*** [U] machines in general or the moving parts of a machine: *farm machinery* ◇ *the delicate machinery of a watch*

**ma·cho** /ˈmɑtʃoʊ/ ***adj.*** (*informal*) (used about a man or his behavior) very masculine in an aggressive way

**mac·ro** /ˈmækroʊ/ ***noun*** [C] (*pl.* **mac·ros**) an instruction that can tell a computer to perform a series of tasks

★**mad** /mæd/ ***adj.*** (**mad·der**; **mad·dest**) **1 mad (at sb)** very angry: *His laziness really makes me mad!* ◇ *Don't get mad at him. He didn't mean to do it.* **2** not controlled; wild or very excited: *We're always in a mad rush to get ready in the morning.* ◇ *The audience was cheering and clapping like mad* (= very hard). **3 mad about sb/sth** (*informal*) extremely interested in sb/sth: *He's mad about basketball.* ◇ *Steve's mad about Jane* (= he likes her very much). **4** with a sick mind; crazy: *a mad scientist*

**Mad·am** /ˈmædəm/ *noun* [sing.] **1** used for beginning a formal letter to a woman when you do not know her name: *Dear Madam, I am writing in reply...* **2** (*formal*) a polite way of speaking to a woman, especially to a leader of an organization or a politician: *Good morning, Madam President.* ➲ Look at **ma'am** and **sir**.

**ˌmad ˈcow disˌease** *noun* [U] a disease of cows which affects their brains and usually kills them

**mad·den** /ˈmædn/ *verb* [T] to make sb very angry or annoyed ▸ **mad·den·ing** /ˈmædn·ɪŋ/ *adj.*: *She has some really maddening habits.* ▸ **mad·den·ing·ly** *adv.*

**made**[1] *past tense, past participle of* MAKE[1]

**made**[2] /meɪd/ *adj.*

IDM **be made for sb/sth/each other** to be very suitable for sb/sth/each other: *Jim and Alice are just made for each other.*

**be made of sth** to have been built from sth, or to consist of sth (a particular material, etc.): *The desk is made of solid wood.*

**have (got) it made** (*informal*) (often used about sb whom you envy) to have an easy life with everything you need or want: *Bob has a new sports car, and he just won a trip to Hawaii – he's got it made!*

**mad·ly** /ˈmædli/ *adv.* **1** extremely: *They're madly in love.* **2** in a wild or crazy way: *She rushed around madly looking for her keys.*

**mad·man** /ˈmædmæn; -mən/ *noun* [C] (*pl.* **madmen**) a person who is MAD (4) or who behaves in a crazy, dangerous way: *He was running around like a madman!*

**mad·ness** /ˈmædnəs/ *noun* [U] **1** the state of being MAD (4) **2** a situation that is wild or not controlled: *It was sheer madness at the mall today – there were crowds everywhere.* **3** crazy, dangerous behavior: *It would be madness to take a boat out in such stormy weather.*

**ma·fi·a** /ˈmɑfiə/ (usually **the Mafia**) *noun* [sing.] a secret criminal organization that influences some business activities

★**mag·a·zine** /ˈmægəzin; ˌmægəˈzin/ *noun* [C] a type of book with a paper cover which is published every week or month and contains articles, advertisements, photographs and stories by various writers: *a women's/computer/fashion magazine* ◇ *a magazine article*

**ma·gen·ta** /məˈdʒɛntə/ *adj.* red-purple in color ▸ **ma·gen·ta** *noun* [U]

**mag·got** /ˈmægət/ *noun* [C] an insect that looks like a small worm. Maggots grow from the eggs of flies, which have been laid in meat, cheese, etc.

★**mag·ic**[1] /ˈmædʒɪk/ *noun* [U] **1** (in stories) a power that can make extraordinary or impossible things happen: *The witch had used her magic to turn the children into frogs.* ➲ Look at **black magic**. **2** the art of performing tricks to entertain people **3** a special or fascinating quality, or sth that has this quality: *I'll never forget the magic of that moment.* ◇ *The whole trip was magic from beginning to end.*

★**mag·ic**[2] /ˈmædʒɪk/ *adj.* **1** used in or using MAGIC[1] (1): *a magic spell* **2** wonderful; excellent: *The way she sings is absolutely magic.*

**mag·i·cal** /ˈmædʒɪkl/ *adj.* **1** that seems to use magic or to produce it: *a magical box that makes things disappear* **2** mysterious and exciting: *Santa Claus has a magical fascination for many children.* ▸ **mag·i·cal·ly** /ˈmædʒɪkli/ *adv.*

**ma·gi·cian** /məˈdʒɪʃn/ *noun* [C] **1** a person who performs magic tricks to entertain people **2** (in stories) a man who has magic power ➲ Look at **wizard**.

**mag·is·trate** /ˈmædʒəstreɪt; -strət/ *noun* [C] a judge in the lowest rank of court that deals especially with less serious crimes

**mag·na cum lau·de** /ˌmægnə kʊm ˈlaʊdə; -di; -kʌm ˈlɔdə/ *adv.*, *adj.* (*U.S.*) at the second of the three highest levels of achievement that students can reach when they finish high school or college: *Did you really graduate magna cum laude from Ohio State?* ➲ Look also at **cum laude** and **summa cum laude**.

**mag·nan·i·mous** /mægˈnænəməs/ *adj.* (*formal*) kind, generous and forgiving (especially toward an enemy or a competitor that you have beaten)

**mag·ne·si·um** /mægˈniziəm/ *noun* (*symbol* **Mg**) a silver-colored metal that burns with a bright white light

**mag·net** /ˈmægnət/ *noun* [C] a piece of iron that can attract and pick up iron and steel

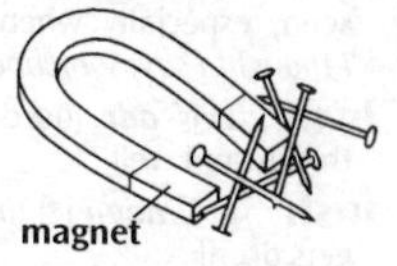


**mag·net·ic** /mægˈnɛt̬ɪk/ *adj.* **1** having the ability of a magnet to attract iron and steel: *Is this metal magnetic?* ◇ *a magnetic field* (= an area around a magnet where there is a magnetic force) **2** having a quality that strongly attracts people: *a magnetic personality*

**magˌnetic ˈtape** *noun* [C,U] plastic tape covered with a magnetic substance and used for recording computer data

**mag·net·ism** /ˈmægnətɪzəm/ *noun* [U] **1** the power of magnets to attract **2** strong personal attraction: *His personal magnetism made him a powerful and dangerous political figure.*

**mag·net·ize** /ˈmægnətaɪz/ *verb* [T] to make sth become magnetic: *a magnetized identification card*

**mag·nif·i·cent** /mægˈnɪfəsənt/ *adj.* extremely good or beautiful: *What a magnificent castle!* ▸ **mag·nif·i·cent·ly** *adv.* ▸ **mag·nif·i·cence** /-səns/ *noun* [U]

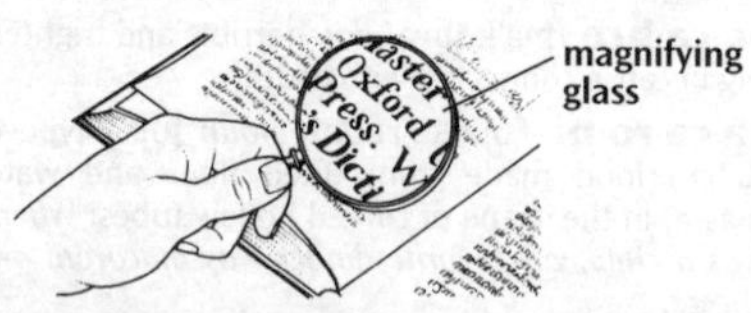


**mag·ni·fy** /ˈmægnəfaɪ/ *verb* [T] (*pres. part.* **mag·ni·fy·ing**; *3rd person sing. pres.* **mag·ni·fies**; *pt, pp* **mag·ni·fied**) **1** to make sth look bigger than it is: *to magnify sth under a microscope* **2** to make sth seem more important than it really is: *to magnify a problem* ▸ **mag·ni·fi·ca·tion** /ˌmægnəfəˈkeɪʃn/ *noun* [U]

**ˈmagnifying glass** *noun* [C] a lens that is held in

your hand, and used for making things look bigger than they are ➲ picture at **magnify**.

**mag·ni·tude** /ˈmægnətud/ ***noun*** [U] the great size or importance of sth: *the magnitude of the problem*

**mag·no·lia** /mægˈnoʊlyə/ ***noun*** [C] a tree that has large, sweet-smelling, usually pink or white flowers. The flowers are also called magnolias.

**mag·pie** /ˈmægpaɪ/ ***noun*** [C] a black and white bird with a long tail and a noisy cry. There is a popular belief that magpies like to steal small bright objects.

**ma·hog·a·ny** /məˈhɑgəni/ ***noun*** [U] hard reddish-brown wood (from a tropical tree) that is used for making expensive furniture

**maid** /meɪd/ ***noun*** [C] a woman whose job is to clean, etc. in a hotel or in sb else's house: *a luxury apartment with maid service*

**maiden** /ˈmeɪdn/ ***noun*** [C] (in literature) a young girl or woman who is not married: *stories of knights and fair maidens*

**ˌmaiden ˈname** ***noun*** [C] the family name that a woman had before she got married

**ˌmaiden ˈvoyage** ***noun*** [C] the first trip made by a new ship or spacecraft

**ˌmaid of ˈhonor** ***noun*** [C] (*pl.* **maids of honor**) in a wedding ceremony, the woman who helps the bride (usually her best friend or else a close family member) ➲ Look at the note at **wedding**.

⋆**mail**[1] /meɪl/ ***noun*** **1** [U] the system for collecting and delivering letters and packages: *to send a package by airmail/first-class mail* ◇ *The check is in the mail.* **2** [U] letters, packages, e-mails, etc. that are sent or received: *Is there any mail for me?* ◇ *to open the mail* ◇ *junk mail* (= letters, usually advertising sth, that are sent to people although they have not asked for them) ◇ *I turned on the computer to see if I had any mail.* **3** [C] an e-mail message: *Did I mention the invitation in my last mail?*

⋆**mail**[2] /meɪl/ **1** [T] ***verb*** to send a letter, package, etc. to sb by putting it in a mailbox or taking it to a post office: *to mail a letter* ◇ *I'll mail it to you tomorrow.* ◇ *I'll mail you a copy of my report.* **2** to send an e-mail message to sb: *Mail me when you're in town and we'll have lunch.* ◇ *The virus mails itself forward to everyone in your address book*

PHR V **mail sth in** to send sth by mail to a place where it will be officially dealt with: *Don't forget to mail in your entry form for the contest!*

**mail sth out** to send sth by mail, usually from a central place to various other places: *We've mailed out 10,000 copies of our new brochure to our customers.*

**mail·box** /ˈmeɪlbɑks/ ***noun*** [C] **1** a private box outside a house or building or a hole in a door which letters can be put into when they are delivered ➲ picture on study page **A31**. **2** a container in a public place where you put letters, etc. that you want to send

**ˈmail·ing list** ***noun*** [C] a list of the names and addresses of people to whom advertising material or information is sent

**mail·man** /ˈmeɪlmæn; -mən/ ***noun*** [C] (*pl.* **mailmen**) a man whose job is to collect and deliver letters, packages, etc. ➲ Look at **letter carrier**.

**ˈmail ˌor·der** ***noun*** [U] a method of shopping. You choose what you want from a special book (a catalog) and the products are then sent to you by mail.

**maim** /meɪm/ ***verb*** [T] to hurt sb so badly that part of the body can no longer be used

⋆**main**[1] /meɪn/ ***adj.*** (only *before* a noun) most important; chief: *My main reason for wanting to learn English is to get a better job.* ◇ *the main road into town* ◇ *the main course (of a meal)* ◇ *He doesn't earn very much, but he's happy. That's the main thing.*

**main**[2] /meɪn/ ***noun*** [C] a large pipe that carries water or natural gas to a building or that takes waste water away from it: *The water main burst.* ◇ *There's a crack in the sewer main.*

**ˌmain ˈdrag** ***noun*** [sing.] (*informal*) the main street of a city or town: *restaurants on Springfield's main drag*

**main·land** /ˈmeɪnlænd; -lənd/ ***noun*** [sing.] the main part of a country or continent, not including the islands around it: *Taiwan and mainland China* ◇ *the ferry between the island and the mainland*

⋆**main·ly** /ˈmeɪnli/ ***adv.*** mostly: *The students here are mainly from Japan.*

**main·stay** /ˈmeɪnsteɪ/ ***noun*** [C] a thing or person that helps sb/sth to work well or to continue: *Rice production is the mainstay of the country's economy.*

**main·stream** /ˈmeɪnstrim/ ***noun*** [sing.] the way that most people think or behave: *The Green Party is not in the mainstream of North American politics.* ▸ **main·stream** ***adj.***: *That politician is completely out of touch with mainstream views.*

⋆**main·tain** /meɪnˈteɪn/ ***verb*** [T] **1** to continue to have sth; to keep sth at the same level or standard: *We need to maintain the quality of our goods but not increase the price.* ◇ *to maintain law and order* **2** to support sb/sth by paying for the things he/she/it needs: *She works hard to maintain her family.* ◇ *Our company also maintains an office in Moscow.* **3** to keep sth in good condition: *to maintain a road/building/machine* **4** to say that sth is true: *In the Middle Ages, people maintained that the sun went around the Earth.* ◇ *The defendant maintained his innocence* (= that he was innocent) *during the trial.*

**main·te·nance** /ˈmeɪntn·əns/ ***noun*** [U] keeping sth in good condition: *This house needs a lot of maintenance.* ◇ *car maintenance*

**ˈmaintenance man** ***noun*** [C] (*pl.* **maintenance men**) a man whose job is to repair and maintain buildings, machines, etc.

**ma·jes·tic** /məˈdʒɛstɪk/ ***adj.*** making a strong impression because it is dignified or beautiful: *a majestic mountain landscape* ▸ **ma·jes·ti·cal·ly** /-kli/ ***adv.***

**maj·es·ty** /ˈmædʒəsti/ ***noun*** (*pl.* **maj·es·ties**) **1** [U] the quality of being grand or dignified like a king or queen: *the splendor and majesty of the Grand Canyon* **2** **Majesty** [C] (used when speaking to or about a royal person): *Her Majesty Queen Elizabeth II*

⋆**ma·jor**[1] /ˈmeɪdʒər/ ***adj.*** (only *before* a noun) great in size, importance, seriousness, etc.: *The patient*



M

*needs major heart surgery.* ◇ *a major road* ◇ *There haven't been any major problems.* OPP **minor**

**ma·jor²** /ˈmeɪdʒər/ ***noun*** [C] **1** the main subject that you study at a college or university: *Her major is chemistry.* **2** a person who studies sth as his/her main subject at a college or university: *She's a chemistry major.* **3** an officer of middle rank in the army

**major³** /ˈmeɪdʒər/ ***verb***

PHR V **major in sth** to study sth as your main subject at a college or university: *She's majoring in chemistry.* ➲ For more information on the U.S. educational system, look at study page **A8**. ➲ Look at **minor³**.

★**ma·jor·i·ty** /məˈdʒɔrət̬i; -ˈdʒɑr-/ ***noun*** (*pl.* **ma·jor·i·ties**) **1** [sing.] more than half of sth: *The majority of students in the class come from Japan.*

NOTE **Majority** can be used in the singular with either a singular or a plural verb. If we are thinking of the members of the group individually, we use a plural verb: *The majority has the power to create new laws.* ◇ *A majority of the residents are in favor of building the new road.* ➲ Look also at **minority**.

**2** [C] **majority (over sb)** the difference in the number of votes in an election between the person/party who came first and the person/party who came second: *He was elected by a majority of only 50 votes.*

IDM **be in the/a majority** to form more than half of sth: *Will the Republicans still be in the majority in Congress after the next election?*

ˌ**major ˈleague** ***noun*** [C] (*also* **Major League**) in baseball, the groups made up of the best teams and players ➲ Look at **minor league**.

**ma·jor·ly** /ˈmeɪdʒərli/ ***adv.*** (*slang*) very; extremely: *We were, like, majorly disappointed when we found out.*

★**make¹** /meɪk/ ***verb*** [T] (*pt, pp* **made** /meɪd/)

➤PRODUCE **1** to produce sth or to cause sth to appear: *I'll make some coffee.* ◇ *They make VW cars in Wolfsburg.* ◇ *made in Japan* (= on a label) ◇ *What's that shirt made of?* (= what material) ◇ *The blood made a stain on the carpet.*

➤PERFORM ACTION **2** (used with nouns) to perform a certain action: *to make a mistake/a noise/a statement/a suggestion* ◇ *to make progress*

NOTE Often there is a verb with a similar form, e.g. **decide/make a decision**. If you use "make" + noun, you can use an adjective with it: *He made the right decision.* ◇ *They made a generous offer.*

➤CAUSE TO HAPPEN **3** to cause a particular action, feeling or situation: *The movie made me cry.* ◇ *That dress makes you look thin.* ◇ *Flying makes him nervous.*

➤FORCE **4** to force sb/sth to do sth: *They made him wait at the police station all day.*

NOTE In the passive we must use **to**: *He was made to wait at the police station.*

➤MAKE CLEAR/SURE **5** (used with *clear, certain, plain* and *sure*): *She made it clear that she didn't agree.* ◇ *Make sure you lock the car.* ◇ *I made certain I had enough money.*

➤MONEY/NUMBERS **6** (used with money and numbers): *He makes* (= earns) *$40,000 a year.* ◇ *to make a lot of money* ◇ *5 and 7 make 12.*

➤BE SUITABLE **7** to have the right qualities to be sth; to make sth perfect: *She'll make a good teacher.* ◇ *The beautiful weather really made our trip.*

➤GIVE SB A JOB **8** to give sb a job or elect sb to a position: *She was made assistant manager.*

➤REACH **9** to reach a place; to be able to go somewhere: *We should make Seattle by about 10.* ◇ *I'm afraid I can't make the meeting next week.* **10** to reach a certain level; to become sth; to achieve sth: *I'm hoping to make head of the division by the time I'm 30.*

IDM **make do with sth** to use sth that is not good enough because nothing better is available: *If we can't get limes, we'll have to make do with lemons.*

**make it 1** to get to a place (in time); to go to a place you have been invited to: *The train leaves in five minutes. We'll never make it!* ◇ *I'm afraid I can't make it to your party.* **2** to be successful: *She'll never make it as an actress.*

**make the most of sth** to get as much pleasure, profit, etc. as possible from sth: *You won't get another chance – make the most of it!* ➲ For other expressions with **make**, look at the noun and adjective entries, e.g. for **make love** look at **love**.

PHR V **make for sb/sth** to move toward sb/sth: *As soon as the lecture was finished, they made for the door.*

**make for sth** to help or allow sth to happen: *Arguing all the time doesn't make for a happy marriage.*

**make sb/sth into sb/sth** to change sb/sth into sb/sth: *She made her other bedroom into an office.*

**make sth of sb/sth** to understand sb/sth: *I don't know what to make of my boss* (= I can't understand him).

**make off** (*informal*) to leave or escape in a hurry

**make off with sth** (*informal*) to steal sth and leave quickly with it: *The thieves made off with $5 million in cash.*

**make sb/sth out 1** to understand sb/sth: *I just can't make him out.* ◇ *Can you make this form out?* **2** to be able to see or hear sb/sth; to manage to read sth: *I could just make out her signature.*

**make sth out** to write or complete sth: *She made out a check for $100.* ◇ *He made out a will shortly before he died.*

**make sb/sth out to be sth** to say that sth is true and try to make people believe it: *The crime problem may not be as bad as it's been made out to be.* ◇ *She's not as smart as she makes herself out to be.*

**make (sb) up** to put powder, lipstick, etc. on the face

**make sth up 1** to form: *the different groups that make up our society* **2** to invent sth, often sth that is not true: *to make up an excuse* **3** to make a number or an amount complete: *We need one more person to make up our team.*

**make up for sth** to do sth that corrects a bad situation: *Her enthusiasm makes up for her lack of experience.* ◇ *You'll have to work longer today to make up for the hours you missed yesterday.*

**make it up to sb** (*informal*) to do sth that shows that you are sorry for what you have done to sb or that you are grateful for what he/she has done for you: *You've done me a big favor. How can I make it up to you?*

**make up (with sb)** to become friends again after an argument: *Has she made up with him yet?*

★**make²** /meɪk/ ***noun*** [C] the name of the company that produced sth: *"What make is your new car?" "It's a Toyota."*

**'make-be,lieve** ***noun*** [U] pretending or imagining sth; the things that are imagined: *I don't believe his stories – they're all make-believe.*

**mak·er** /'meɪkər/ ***noun*** [C] (in compounds) a person or company that makes sth: *a dressmaker*

**make·shift** /'meɪkʃɪft/ ***adj.*** used for a short time until there is sth better: *The refugees built makeshift shelters out of old cardboard boxes.*

**make·up** /'meɪkʌp/ ***noun*** **1** [U] powder, cream, etc. that you put on your face to make yourself more attractive. Actors use makeup to change their appearance when they are acting: *to put on/take off makeup* ◇ *She wears a lot of makeup.* ➲ Look at **cosmetics.** The verb is **make up/make yourself up**. **2** [sing.] the things or people that form sth: *the makeup of the board of directors* **3** [sing.] a person's character: *He can't help his temper. It's part of his makeup.* **4** [C] a special test, piece of work, etc. given to students who failed or missed an earlier one: *Students who were absent yesterday should write a book report as a makeup.* ◇ *There will be a makeup quiz on Thursday.*

**mak·ing** /'meɪkɪŋ/ ***noun*** [sing.] the act of doing or producing sth: *breadmaking*

IDM **have the makings of sth** to have the necessary qualities for sth: *The book has the makings of a good movie.*

**in the making** in the process of developing or being made: *What we're seeing is history in the making.* ◇ *Tonight's celebration has been three years in the making.*

**ma·lar·i·a** /mə'lɛriə/ ***noun*** [U] a serious disease that you may get when you have been bitten by a small flying insect (a **mosquito**) that lives in hot countries

★**male** /meɪl/ ***adj.*** belonging to the sex that does not give birth to babies or lay eggs: *A male deer is called a buck.* ➲ Look at the note at **female**. ▶ **male *noun*** [C]: *a white male in his 40s* ◇ *What a cute puppy! Is it a male or a female?*

**male 'chau·vin·ism** ***noun*** [U] the belief that men are better than women ▶ **male 'chau·vin·ist *noun*** [C]

**mal·func·tion** /,mæl'fʌŋkʃn/ ***verb*** [I] (used about machines, etc.) not to work normally or correctly: *The explosion was caused by a malfunctioning fuel valve.* ▶ **mal·func·tion *noun*** [C,U]: *a malfunction in the computer system* ◇ *to suffer from kidney malfunction*

**mal·ice** /'mæləs/ ***noun*** [U] a wish to hurt other people ▶ **ma·li·cious** /mə'lɪʃəs/ ***adj.*** ▶ **ma·li·cious·ly *adv.***

**ma·lig·nant** /mə'lɪgnənt/ ***adj.*** (used to describe tumors in the body) likely to cause death if not controlled ➲ Compare **benign**.

★**mall** /mɔl/ (*also* **shopping mall**) ***noun*** [C] a large building that has many stores, restaurants, etc. inside it: *teenagers hanging out at the mall*

**mal·let** /'mælət/ ***noun*** [C] a heavy wooden hammer ➲ picture at **tool**.

**mal·nour·ished** /,mæl'nərɪʃt/ ***adj.*** in bad health because of a lack of food or a lack of the right type of food

**mal·nu·tri·tion** /,mælnu'trɪʃn/ ***noun*** [U] bad health that is the result of not having enough food or enough of the right kind of food

**mal·prac·tice** /,mæl'præktəs/ ***noun*** [U] wrong or bad treatment or service, especially by a doctor or a lawyer: *He sued his doctor for malpractice.*

**malt** /mɔlt/ ***noun*** [U] **1** grain that has been left in water for a long time and then dried. Malt is used for making beer and whiskey. **2** (*also* **,malt·ed 'milk**) [C] a thick drink made of milk, ice cream, flavoring and usually MALT (1) powder: *a strawberry malt* ➲ Look at **milkshake**.

**mal·treat** /,mæl'trit/ ***verb*** [T] (*formal*) to treat a person or animal in a cruel or unkind way ▶ **mal·treat·ment *noun*** [U]

**ma·ma** /'mɑmə/ ***noun*** [C] (*informal*) mother

**mam·mal** /'mæml/ ***noun*** [C] an animal of the type that gives birth to live animals and does not lay eggs. Mammals feed their babies with milk from their bodies: *Birds and fish are not mammals, but whales and dolphins are.*

**mam·moth** /'mæməθ/ ***adj.*** very big; huge: *a mammoth construction project* ◇ *a mammoth tax increase*

★**man¹** /mæn/ ***noun*** (*pl.* **men** /mɛn/)

➤MALE PERSON **1** [C] an adult male person: *a handsome man in his mid-twenties* ◇ *men, women and children*

➤HUMAN BEING **2** [C] a person of either sex, male or female: *All men are equal.* ◇ *No man could survive long in such conditions.* **3** [sing.] the human race; human beings: *Early man lived by hunting and gathering.* ◇ *Why is man so destructive?*

> NOTE Some people do not like the way **man** is used in senses 2 and 3 (or the use of **mankind** to mean "all men and women") because it seems that women are not included. They prefer to use **humanity, the human race**, or **people**.

➤MALE PARTNER **4** [C] a husband, boyfriend or male lover: *There's a new man in her life.*

➤SOLDIER/WORKER **5** [C, usually pl.] a man of low rank in the army, etc. who takes orders from an officer: *officers and men*

➤FORM OF ADDRESS **6** (*slang*) (used when you are talking to sb): *Hey, man, can you lend me a quarter?*

IDM **man to man** (used about speaking) honestly and directly, between two men: *Let's talk man to man.* ◇ *to have a man-to-man talk*

**man²** /mæn/ ***interjection*** (*informal*) (used when you are annoyed or surprised): *Oh, man! Why does this always happen to me?* ◇ *Man! That's a great car!*

**man³** /mæn/ ***verb*** [T] (**man<u>n</u>ing**; **man<u>n</u>ed**) to operate sth or to provide people to operate sth: *to man a boat/gun/telephone* ◇ *When was the first manned space flight?*

★**man·age** /'mænɪdʒ/ ***verb*** **1** [T] to be in charge or

M

control of sth: *She manages a small advertising business.* **2** [I,T] (often with *can* or *could*) to be able to do sth or to deal with sth: *I'm sorry I didn't manage to write that report last week.* ◇ *I can't manage this suitcase. It's too heavy.* ◇ *How in the world did you manage to find us here?* **3** [I] **manage (on sth)**; **manage (without sb/sth)** to have a reasonable way of life: *They live in the country and couldn't manage without a car.* ◇ *It's hard for a family to manage on just one income.*

**man·age·a·ble** /ˈmænɪdʒəbl/ ***adj.*** not too big or too difficult to control or take care of: *a yard of manageable size* ◇ *This shampoo makes your hair shiny and more manageable.*

★**man·age·ment** /ˈmænɪdʒmənt/ ***noun*** **1** [U] the control or organization of sth: *Good management is the key to success in business.* ◇ *financial/risk management* **2** [C,U] the people who control a business or company: *The hotel is now* ***under new management.*** ◇ *The management is considering laying off some workers.*

★**man·ag·er** /ˈmænɪdʒər/ ***noun*** [C] **1** a man or woman who controls an organization or part of an organization: *Martha is the new manager of the bookstore.* ◇ *a sales manager* **2** a person who takes care of the business affairs of a singer, an actor, etc. **3** a person who is in charge of training a baseball team: *the Yankees' manager* ➲ Look at **coach**. ▸ **man·a·ge·ri·al** /ˌmænəˈdʒɪriəl/ ***adj.***: *Do you have any managerial experience?*

M

**Man·da·rin** /ˈmændərɪn/ (*also* ˌ**Mandarin Chiˈnese**) ***noun*** [U] the official spoken language of mainland China

**man·da·rin** /ˈmændərɪn/ (*also* ˌ**mandarin ˈorange**) ***noun*** [C] a type of small orange whose skin comes off easily

**man·date** /ˈmændeɪt/ ***noun*** [usually sing.] the power that a group of people has to do sth as a result of winning an election: *The members of Congress had a clear mandate from the voters to reduce taxes.*

**man·da·to·ry** /ˈmændəˌtɔri/ ***adj.*** that must be done by laws, rules, etc.: *mandatory drug testing for Olympic athletes*

**mane** /meɪn/ ***noun*** [C] the long hair on the neck of a horse or male lion ➲ picture at **horse**.

**ma·neu·ver**[1] /məˈnuvər/ ***noun*** **1** [C] a movement that needs care or skill: *In the driving test you will have to perform several maneuvers such as parallel parking.* **2** [C] something clever that you do in order to win sth, trick sb, etc. **3** [usually pl.] a way of training soldiers when large numbers of them practice fighting in battles: *large-scale military maneuvers*

**ma·neu·ver**[2] /məˈnuvər/ ***verb*** [I,T] to move to a different position using skill: *to maneuver into a parking space*

**man·gle** /ˈmæŋgl/ ***verb*** [T] **1** to damage sth greatly so that it is difficult to see what it used to look like: *Oh, no! The VCR mangled my new tape!* ◇ *The highway was covered with the mangled wreckage of cars and trucks.* **2** to ruin sth such as a song, speech, etc. by performing it badly: *a mangled translation/speech*

**man·go** /ˈmæŋgoʊ/ ***noun*** [C] (*pl.* **man·goes** or **man·gos**) a tropical fruit that has yellowish-red skin and is orange inside ➲ picture on study page **A28**.

**man·hole** /ˈmænhoʊl/ ***noun*** [C] a hole in the street with a lid over it through which sb can go to look at the pipes, wires, etc. that are underground

**man·hood** /ˈmænhʊd/ ***noun*** [U] the state of being a man rather than a boy: *to reach manhood*

**ma·ni·a** /ˈmeɪniə/ ***noun*** **1** [U] a serious mental illness that may cause a person to be very excited or violent **2** [C] (*informal*) a very great love (for sth) or interest (in sth): *My mom remembers the rock 'n' roll mania of the sixties.* ▸ **man·ic** /ˈmænɪk/ ***adj.***

**ma·ni·ac** /ˈmeɪniæk/ ***noun*** [C] **1** a person who is crazy and dangerous: (*figurative*) *to drive like a maniac* **2** a person who has a great love for sth: *a golf maniac*

**man·i·cure** /ˈmænəkyʊr/ ***noun*** [C,U] treatment to make your hands and fingernails look nice: *to have/get a manicure*

**man·i·fest** /ˈmænəfɛst/ ***verb*** [T] (*formal*) **1** to show sth clearly **2 manifest itself/themselves** to appear: *Mental illness can manifest itself in many forms.*

**man·i·fes·ta·tion** /ˌmænəfəˈsteɪʃn/ ***noun*** [C,U] (*formal*) a sign that sth is happening

**man·i·fes·to** /ˌmænəˈfɛstoʊ/ ***noun*** [C] (*pl.* **man·i·fes·tos** or **man·i·fes·toes**) a written statement by a political party or group that explains its beliefs or what it hopes to do

**ma·nil·a en·ve·lope** /məˌnɪlə ˈɛnvəloʊp; ˈɑn-/ ***noun*** [C] an envelope, usually large enough to hold a piece of paper that has not been folded, made from a strong, dark yellow paper

**ma·nip·u·late** /məˈnɪpyəleɪt/ ***verb*** [T] **1** to use or control sth with skill **2** to influence sb so that he/she does or thinks what you want: *Clever politicians know how to manipulate public opinion.* ▸ **ma·nip·u·la·tion** /məˌnɪpyəˈleɪʃn/ ***noun*** [C,U]

**man·kind** /ˌmænˈkaɪnd/ ***noun*** [U] all the people in the world: *A nuclear war would be a threat to all mankind.* ➲ Look at the note at **man**.

**man·ly** /ˈmænli/ ***adj.*** typical of or suitable for a man: *He had a deep manly voice.* ▸ **man·li·ness** ***noun*** [U]

ˌ**man-ˈmade** ***adj.*** made by people, not formed in a natural way; artificial: *man-made fabrics such as nylon and polyester* OPP **natural**

★**man·ner** /ˈmænər/ ***noun*** **1** [sing.] (*formal*) the way that you do sth or that sth happens: *They hoped to resolve the crisis in a peaceful manner.* **2** [sing.] (*formal*) the way that sb behaves toward other people: *He charmed the voters with his easy-going manner.* ➲ A less formal word is **way**. **3 manners** [pl.] the way of behaving that is thought to be polite in your society or culture: *In some countries it is bad manners to show the soles of your feet.* ◇ *Their kids have excellent table manners.*

IDM **all manner of...** (*formal*) every kind of...

**man·ner·ism** /ˈmænərɪzəm/ ***noun*** [C] a way of speaking or a movement of part of the body that is typical for a particular person

**mann·e·quin** /ˈmænəkən/ ***noun*** [C] a figure

shaped like a person's body, used to show clothes in a store

**man·pow·er** /ˈmænpaʊər/ ***noun*** [U] the people that you need to do a particular job: *There is a shortage of skilled manpower in the computer industry.*

**man·sion** /ˈmænʃn/ ***noun*** [C] a very large, expensive house

**man·slaugh·ter** /ˈmænslɔt̬ər/ ***noun*** [U] the crime of killing sb without intending to do so ➲ Look at **murder**.

**man·tel** /ˈmæntl/ (*also* **mantelpiece** /ˈmæntlpis/) ***noun*** [C] a shelf that is above a fireplace ➲ picture at **fireplace**.

**man·u·al**[1] /ˈmænyuəl/ ***adj.*** using your hands; operated by hand: *manual work* ◇ *a car with manual transmission* ◇ *a skilled manual worker*

**man·u·al**[2] /ˈmænyuəl/ ***noun*** [C] a book that explains how to do or operate sth: *a training manual* ◇ *Full instructions are given in the owner's manual.*

**man·u·al·ly** /ˈmænyuəli/ ***adv.*** by hand, not automatically

★**man·u·fac·ture** /ˌmænyəˈfæktʃər/ ***verb*** [T] to make sth in large quantities using machines: *a local factory that manufactures high-quality furniture* ◇ *manufacturing industries* ▸ **man·u·fac·ture *noun*** [U]: *The manufacture of chemical weapons should be illegal.* ▸ **man·u·fac·tur·er *noun*** [C]: *Faulty goods should be returned to the manufacturer.*

**ma·nure** /məˈnʊr/ ***noun*** [U] the waste matter from animals that is put on the ground in order to make plants grow better ➲ Look at **fertilizer**.

**man·u·script** /ˈmænyəskrɪpt/ ***noun*** [C] **1** a very old book or document that was written by hand **2** a typed or hand-written copy of a book that has not yet been printed

★**man·y** /ˈmɛni/ ***det., pronoun*** (used with plural nouns or verbs) **1** a large number of people or things: *Many people do not get enough to eat.* ◇ *There are too many mistakes in this essay.* ◇ *Many of the people at the meeting left early.* **2** (used with "how" to ask about the number of people or things): *How many kids do you have?* ◇ *How many mistakes did you make?* ◇ *How many came to the meeting?* **3** (used to form compound adjectives) having a lot of the thing mentioned: *a many-sided shape*

IDM **a good/great many** very many

**as many (as)** an equal number: *There aren't as many new Internet cafes as there were ten years ago.*

NOTE **As many as** can sometimes be used to show surprise at how big a number is: *Are there really as many as 45 students in your class?*

**Mao·ri** /ˈmaʊri/ ***noun*** [C] a member of the race of people who were the original inhabitants of New Zealand ▸ **Mao·ri *adj.***

★**map**[1] /mæp/ ***noun*** [C] a drawing or plan of (part of) the surface of the earth that shows countries, rivers, mountains, roads, etc.: *a map of the world* ◇ *a road map* ◇ *a street map of Yellowknife* ◇ *I can't find Portland on the map.* ◇ *to read a map* ➲ A book of maps is called an **atlas**.

**map**[2] /mæp/ ***verb*** [T] (**map·ping**; **mapped**) to make a map of a place

PHR V **map sth out** to plan sth in detail: *We need to map out our strategy for winning the election.*

**ma·ple** /ˈmeɪpl/ ***noun*** [C] a tree that has leaves with five points and that produces a very sweet liquid: *pancakes with maple syrup*

ˈ**maple leaf *noun*** [C] **1** the leaf of the maple tree, used as a symbol of Canada **2 the Maple Leaf** the Canadian flag

ˈ**Maple Leaf ˌCard *noun*** [C] (*Cdn*) = PERMANENT RESIDENT CARD

ˌ**maple ˈsyrup *noun*** [U] a sweet sticky sauce made with liquid (sap) obtained from some types of maple tree, often eaten with pancakes

**Mar.** ***abbr.*** = MARCH

**mar·a·thon** /ˈmærəθɑn/ ***noun*** [C] a long-distance running race in which people run about 26 miles: *Have you ever run a marathon?* ◇ *the New York City Marathon* ◇ (*figurative*) *a marathon meeting* (= one that lasts a very long time)

**mar·ble** /ˈmɑrbl/ ***noun*** **1** [U] a hard attractive stone that is used to make statues and parts of buildings: *a marble statue* ◇ *This staircase is made of marble.* **2** [C] a small ball of colored glass that children play with **3 marbles** [pl.] the children's game that you play by rolling marbles along the ground trying to hit other marbles

IDM **lose your marbles** → LOSE

**March** /mɑrtʃ/ ***noun*** [C,U] (*abbr.* **Mar.**) the third month of the year, coming before April ➲ For examples of the use of the months in sentences, look at **January**.

★**march**[1] /mɑrtʃ/ ***verb*** **1** [I] to walk with regular steps (like a soldier): *The President saluted as the troops marched past.* ◇ *He marched in and demanded an explanation.* **2** [I] to walk in a large group to protest about sth: *The demonstrators marched through the center of town.* **3** [T] to cause sb to walk or MARCH (1) somewhere: *The prisoner was marched away.* **4** [I] to walk in a determined way: *She marched right up to the teacher and demanded a higher grade!*

**march**[2] /mɑrtʃ/ ***noun*** [C] **1** an act of marching: *The soldiers were tired after their long march.* **2** an organized walk by a large group of people who are protesting about sth: *a peace march* ➲ Look at **demonstration**.

**Mardi Gras** /ˈmɑrdi grɑ/ ***noun*** [U] a festival before the beginning of a period called Lent

NOTE **Mardi Gras** is celebrated mainly in the southern U.S., especially in and around New Orleans, Louisiana. People go to parties and march in parades wearing fancy costumes.

**mare** /mɛr/ ***noun*** [C] a female horse or donkey ➲ Look at the note at **horse**.

**mar·ga·rine** /ˈmɑrdʒərən/ ***noun*** [U] a food that looks like butter, made of vegetable fats. Margarine is used for spreading on bread and in cooking.

**mar·gin** /ˈmɑrdʒən/ ***noun*** [C] **1** the empty space at the side of a page in a book, etc.: *notes in the margin* ◇ *a wide/narrow margin* **2** the amount of space, time, votes, etc. by which you win sth: *He won the race by a comfortable margin.* **3** an amount of space, time, etc. that is more than you need: *a*

M

*safety margin* **4** (*also* **profit margin**) the amount of profit that a company makes on sth

**mar·gin·al** /ˈmɑrdʒənl/ ***adj.*** small in size or importance: *The differences are marginal.*

**mar·gin·al·ly** /ˈmɑrdʒənəli/ ***adv.*** a little; slightly: *In most cases costs will increase only marginally.*

**ˌmargin of ˈerror** ***noun*** [C, usually sing.] an amount allowed for the possibility that numbers, calculations, etc. are not entirely correct: *The poll has a margin of error of plus or minus 4%.*

**mar·i·jua·na** /ˌmærəˈwɑnə/ ***noun*** [U] an illegal drug that is often smoked in cigarettes (**joints**) ➲ Look at **cannabis.**

**ma·ri·na** /məˈrinə/ ***noun*** [C] an area of water where people can leave their boats

**mar·i·nade** /ˌmærəˈneɪd; ˈmærəneɪd/ ***noun*** [C,U] a mixture of oil, wine, spices, etc., in which meat or fish is left before it is cooked in order to make it softer or to give it a particular flavor

**mar·i·nate** /ˈmærəneɪt/ (*also* **mar·i·nade**) ***verb*** [I,T] (used about food) to soak or be soaked in a marinade before cooking: *You should marinate the shrimp for an hour before grilling them.* ◇ *The shrimp should marinate for an hour.*

**Ma·rine** /məˈrin/ ***noun*** [C] a soldier who has been trained to fight on land or at sea

**ma·rine** /məˈrin/ ***adj.*** **1** connected with the sea: *a marine biologist* ◇ *the study of marine life* **2** connected with ships or sailing: *marine insurance*

**the Maˈrine Corps** ***noun*** [sing.] (*also* **the Marines** [pl.]) the branch of the U.S. military forces whose soldiers have been trained to fight on land or at sea: *My son's in the Marines.* ➲ Look at the note at **White House**.

**mar·i·tal** /ˈmærət̬l/ ***adj.*** (only *before* a noun) connected with marriage: *marital problems*

**ˈmarital ˌstatus** ***noun*** [U] (*formal*) whether you are married, single, widowed or divorced

**mar·i·time** /ˈmærətaɪm/ ***adj.*** connected with the ocean or ships

**the Mar·i·times** /ˈmærətaɪmz/ ***noun*** [pl.] (*Cdn*) the Canadian provinces of New Brunswick, Nova Scotia and PEI (Prince Edward Island) ➲ Look also at **Atlantic Canada.**

★**mark**[1] /mɑrk/ ***noun*** [C]

➤SPOT/DIRT **1** a spot or line that spoils the appearance of sth: *There's a dirty mark on the front of your shirt.* ◇ *If you press your nose against the window, it will leave a mark.* ➲ Look at **birthmark**.

➤IDENTIFYING CHARACTERISTIC **2** something that shows who or what sb/sth is or that gives information about sb/sth: *Did the bank robber have any identifying marks on his face?*

➤SYMBOL **3** a written or printed symbol that is a sign of sth: *a question/punctuation/check mark* ◇ *quotation marks*

➤SIGN **4** a sign of a quality or feeling: *They stood in silence for two minutes as a mark of respect.*

➤STANDARD/GRADE **5** a judgment of sb/sth's work or performance: *Voters gave the mayor high marks for his ability to improve the city's economy.* ◇ *to earn top marks for honesty*

➤LEVEL **6** the level of sth: *The company's sales have now reached the million-dollar mark.*

➤MACHINE/VEHICLE **7 Mark** (followed by a number) a particular type or model of a machine or vehicle: *the new SL 53 Mark III*

IDM **leave your/its/a mark (on sb/sth)** to have an effect on sb/sth, especially a bad one, that lasts for a long time: *Such a traumatic experience was bound to leave its mark on the children.*

**make your/a mark on sth** to be famous or successful or to leave a strong impression: *an actor who made his mark in action movies*

**on your mark(s), get set, go!** (used at the start of a sports race)

★**mark**[2] /mɑrk/ ***verb*** [T] **1** to put a sign on sth: *We marked the price on all items in the sale.* ◇ *The route is marked with a red line.* ◇ *Why did you mark that answer wrong?* **2** to show where sth is or where sth happened: *Flowers mark the spot where he died.* **3** to celebrate sth: *The ceremony marked the fiftieth anniversary of the opening of the school.* **4** to spoil the appearance of sth by making a mark on it: *The white walls were dirty and marked.* **5** (in sport) to stay close to a player of the opposite team so that he/she cannot play easily

**mark·down** /ˈmɑrkdaʊn/ ***noun*** [C] a reduction in the price of sth in a store

**marked** /mɑrkt/ ***adj.*** clear; noticeable: *There has been a marked increase in vandalism in recent years.*

**mark·er** /ˈmɑrkər/ ***noun*** [C] **1** something that shows the position of sth: *A historical marker shows where the battle took place.* **2** (*also* **Magic Marker™**) a type of pen that draws thick lines

★**mar·ket**[1] /ˈmɑrkət/ ***noun*** **1** [C] a place where people go to buy and sell things: *The farmers are taking their cattle to the livestock market today.* ◇ *an open-air/covered market* ◇ *a market square* ➲ Look at **flea market**, **farmers' market** and **supermarket. 2** [U, sing.] the people who want to buy a particular thing: *There's no market for lawnmowers in the middle of winter.* **3** [C] the business of buying and selling a particular thing: *High interest rates can have a significant effect on the automobile market.* **4** [C] a country, an area or a group of people that may want to buy sth: *The company is hoping to expand into the European market.* ◇ *the domestic/international market* ➲ Look at **black market. 5** [C] = STOCK MARKET

IDM **be in the market for sth** to be interested in buying sth: *I'm in the market for a used car.*

**on the market** for sale: *This is one of the best automatic cameras on the market.*

**mar·ket**[2] /ˈmɑrkət/ ***verb*** [T] to sell sth with the help of advertising

**mar·ket·a·ble** /ˈmɑrkət̬əbl/ ***adj.*** able to be sold easily, because people want it

★**mar·ket·ing** /ˈmɑrkət̬ɪŋ/ ***noun*** [U] deciding how sth can be sold most easily, e.g. what price it should be or how it should be advertised: *Effective marketing will lead to increased sales.* ◇ *the marketing department*

**ˌmarket ˈresearch** ***noun*** [U] the study of what people want to buy and why

**ˈmarket share** ***noun*** [C,U, usually sing.] the amount that a company sells of its products or services compared to other companies selling the same things:

# The environment

## Global warming

Scientists say the temperature of the earth could rise 4–5° Fahrenheit in the future. This is called **global warming** and may cause droughts in some parts of the world and floods in others as ice at the North and South Poles begins to melt and sea levels rise. Global warming is caused by the **greenhouse effect**. Normally, heat from the sun warms the earth and then escapes back into space. However, **carbon dioxide** and other gases trap the sun's heat and this is making the earth warmer.

## The ozone layer

The **ozone layer** is a layer of gas high above the surface of the earth that helps to protect the earth from the sun's **ultraviolet radiation**, which can cause **skin cancer**. Scientists have discovered holes in the ozone layer, caused by substances called **CFCs** (chlorofluorocarbons). CFCs are used in air conditioners, refrigerators, and aerosol cans. Today many countries are trying to reduce the amount of CFCs they use.

## Deforestation

**Rainforests** help to control global warming because they absorb carbon dioxide. However, large areas have been destroyed as trees are cut down for wood or burned to clear land for farming.

## Pollution

Factories, power stations, and motor vehicles are a major source of air pollution which increases the greenhouse effect. To reduce air pollution, factories and power stations are continually checked. City governments are also encouraging people to use **public transportation** or to **car-pool** (=have two or more people ride to work in one car).

## Recycling

**Recycling** is the processing of used objects and materials so that they can be used again. Glass, paper, and aluminum cans can be recycled very easily. Most cities have recycling centers and services.

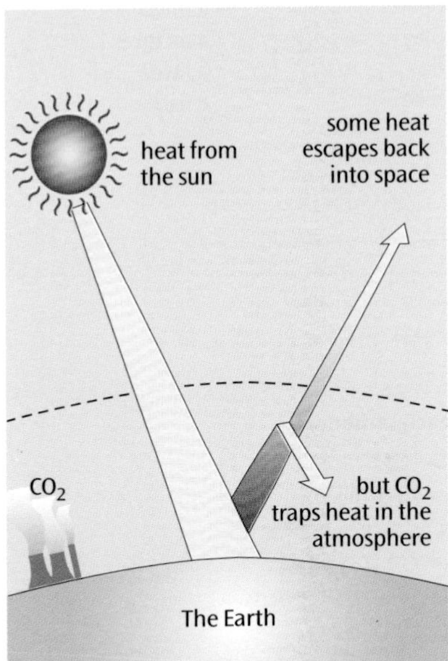


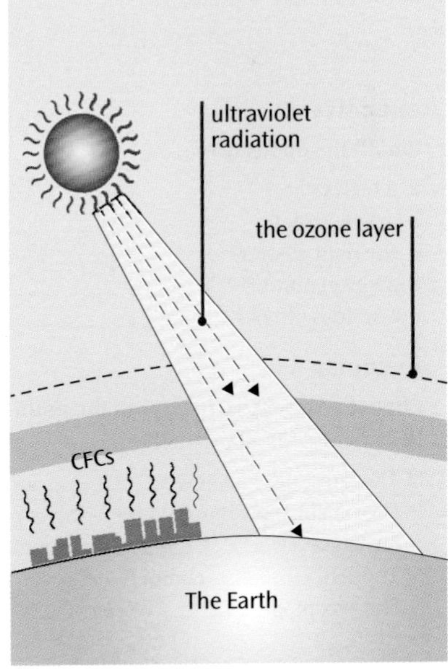

# Words that go together

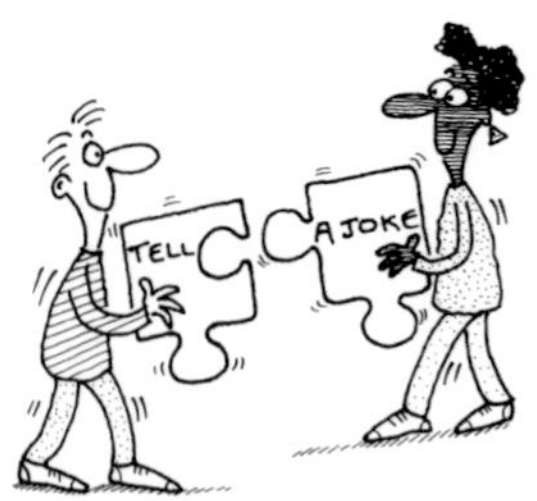


In addition to explaining the meaning of a word, the *Oxford ESL Dictionary* shows you how to use it correctly in a phrase or sentence.

## The example sentences

Do we talk about **stale** bread or **rotten** bread? Do you **say** a joke or **tell** a joke? (It's **stale** and **tell**.) If you look up a word in the dictionary, the example sentences show you which other words are often used with it:

★**mon·ey** /ˈmʌni/ ***noun*** [U] the means of paying for sth or buying sth, especially in the form of coins or bills: *How much money do you earn a year?* ◇ *Teenagers spend a lot of money on clothes.* ◇ *Our trip cost an awful lot of money.* ◇ *to borrow/lend money* ◇ *My father invested his money in stocks and bonds.* ◇ *Is this picture worth a lot of money?*

**Earn**, **spend**, **cost** and **save** are verbs that are often used with the word **money**.

★**wind**[1] /wmd/ ***noun*** **1** [C,U] (*also* **the wind**) air that is moving across the surface of the earth: *There was a strong wind blowing.* ◇ *A gust of wind blew his hat off.* ◇ *high winds* ◇ *a cold north wind* **2** [U] the breath that you need for doing exercise or playing a musical instrument: *She stopped running to get her wind back.*

**Strong**, **high**, **cold** and **north** are adjectives that are often used with the word **wind**.

**EXERCISE 1**

**Match a word in group A with a word in group B. Find the words in group B in the dictionary and look at the example sentences.**

| A | B |
|---|---|
| make | a contest |
| enter | an account |
| open | a mistake |
| play | a picture |
| do | a favor |
| take | a trick |

**EXERCISE 2**

**What's the opposite of ...?**

a a high salary? *a low salary*
b a wide street? ____________
c the right answer? ____________
d an even number? ____________
e a serious offense? ____________

**EXERCISE 3**

**Choose an adjective to go with the noun in each sentence:**

wild heavy full ~~sharp~~ fierce

1 The latest figures show a *sharp* increase in crime.
2 I've no idea how much it costs – this is just a ________ guess.
3 He'll face a ________ fine if he's found guilty of speeding.
4 There is ________ competition to get a place in that university.
5 She accepted ________ responsibility for the mistake.

## Prepositions and verb patterns

The dictionary also shows you which preposition to use after a noun, verb or adjective and which construction to use after a verb:

★**mar·ried** /'mærid/ *adj.* **1 married (to sb)** having a husband or wife: *a married man/woman/couple* ◇ *They've been married for almost 50 years.* ◇ *Jenny's married to Mark.* ◇ *They're getting married in June.* ➲ Look also at **divorced**, **unmarried**, **single** and **widowed**. **2** (only *before* a noun) of marriage(1): *How do you like married life?*

This shows that the preposition which goes with **married** is **to**.

★**en·joy** /ɪn'dʒɔɪ/ *verb* [T] **1 enjoy sth/enjoy doing sth** to get pleasure from: *I really enjoyed that meal.* ◇ *Do you enjoy your work?* ◇ *He enjoys listening to music while he's driving.* **2 enjoy yourself** to be happy; to have a good time: *I enjoyed myself at Sue's party last night – did you?*

You can say that you **enjoy something** or that you **enjoy doing something**.

### EXERCISE 4

**Use the dictionary to complete these sentences with the right preposition.**

a Everybody laughed ________ the joke.
b I don't agree ________ him at all.
c She has found a solution ________ the problem.
d It took her a long time to recover ________ the accident.
e Do you believe ________ life after death?
f I apologized ________ Sam ________ breaking the chair.
g She's very proud ________ her new car.
h The house is fairly close ________ Kari's school.

### EXERCISE 5

**Choose a verb to go with the noun in each sentence:**

catch form ~~break~~ draw tell drive commit achieve

1 He promised me he would come, but he *broke* his promise.
2 The sun was so hot the grass ________ fire.
3 People who arrived early ________ a line at the door.
4 She ________ her ambition of becoming a world champion.
5 How do you ________ the difference between the male bird and the female?
6 He ________ suicide at the age of 35.
7 His singing in the shower ________ me crazy!
8 ________ the curtains if there's too much sunlight.

### EXERCISE 6

**Fill in the blanks with the correct form of the verb in parentheses.**

a I want you to finish ________ (clean) your room.
b He keeps ________ (call) me late at night.
c I persuaded Jan ________ (come) to the party.
d Try to avoid ________ (make) mistakes.
e You're not allowed ________ (smoke) in here.
f The bank agreed ________ (loan) me the money.

# Phrasal verbs

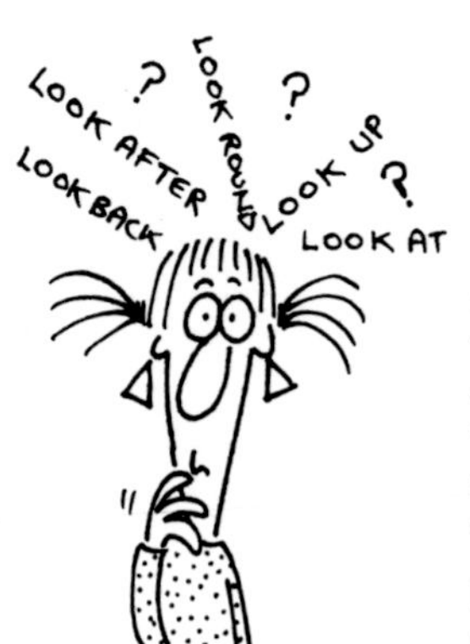


Phrasal verbs are verbs that consist of two (or three) parts – an ordinary verb and another word (or words) like, **for**, or **off**. They are very common in English. Here are some examples:

**lie down**  **give up**  **look for**  **get along with**

Some of them are easy to understand (you can guess the meaning of **lie down** if you know the words **lie** and **down**), but many phrasal verbs are more difficult because they have special meanings (you cannot guess that "**give up** smoking" means "stop smoking" even if you know the words **give** and **up**).

If you want to find a phrasal verb in the dictionary, look under the first word (to find **give up**, look under **give**). The "phrasal verbs" section comes after the ordinary meanings of the verb.

**EXERCISE 1**

**Use the dictionary to fill in the blanks with the correct word.**

a Business is pretty bad these days. A lot of workers have been laid ______ .
*(over, off, down)*

b "U.S." stands ______ United States.
*(out, to, for)*

c I can't figure ______ how to use this gadget.
*(up, out, for)*

d Sue came ______ the letter while she was cleaning her room.
*(to, across, for)*

e I'm sure that story wasn't true. I think Pete made it ______ .
*(up, for, in)*

f She was offered a job in Dallas, but she decided to turn it ______ .
*(over, up, down)*

g Alex dropped out ______ school when he was 16 years old.
*(for, of, from)*

h Please write ______ your address and phone number.
*(down, over, away)*

## The four types

There are four main types of phrasal verbs:

### Type 1 Phrasal verbs *without* an object

— *The fire* ***went out****.*
— *My car* ***broke down*** *on the highway.*

In the dictionary, these verbs are written like this:
— ***go out***
— ***break down***

## Type 2 Phrasal verbs that can be separated by an object

**a** If the object is a noun, it can go either *after* both parts of the phrasal verb or *between* them:
—*She* ***tried*** *on the red sweater.*
—*She* ***tried*** *the red sweater* ***on****.*

**b** If the object is a pronoun, it must go between the two parts of the phrasal verb:
—*She* ***tried*** *it* ***on.*** (NOT ~~*She tried on it.*~~)

In the dictionary, this verb is written like this: **try sth on**. When you see **sth** or **sb** between the two parts of the phrasal verb, you know that they can be separated by an object.

## Type 3 Phrasal verbs that cannot be separated by an object

The two parts of the phrasal verb must go together:
—*The teacher* ***called on*** *Doug.*
(NOT ~~*The teacher called Doug on.*~~)
—*The teacher* ***called on*** *him.*
(NOT ~~*The teacher called him on.*~~)

In the dictionary, this verb is written like this: **call on sb**. When you see **sb** or **sth** *after* the two parts of the phrasal verb, you know that they *cannot* be separated by an object.

## Type 4 Phrasal verbs with three parts

The three parts of the phrasal verb must go together:
—*I can't* ***put up with*** *this noise anymore.*

In the dictionary, this verb is written like this: **put up with sb/sth**. Again, when you see **sb** or **sth** after the three parts of the phrasal verb, you know that they *cannot* be separated by an object.

**EXERCISE 2**

**Fill in the blanks by putting the word "it" in the correct place. In each sentence you will have to leave one blank empty.**

a You must be hot with your coat on. Why don't you take ___ off ___?
b If you don't understand this word, look ___ up ___ in your dictionary.
c He had a very bad illness, and it will take him a long time to get ___ over ___.
d I was going to do my homework last night, but I didn't get around ___ to ___.
e I thought you were finished reading the newspaper, so I threw ___ away ___.
f Jill can't come to the meeting tomorrow, so we'll have to put ___ off ___ until next week.

# Word formation

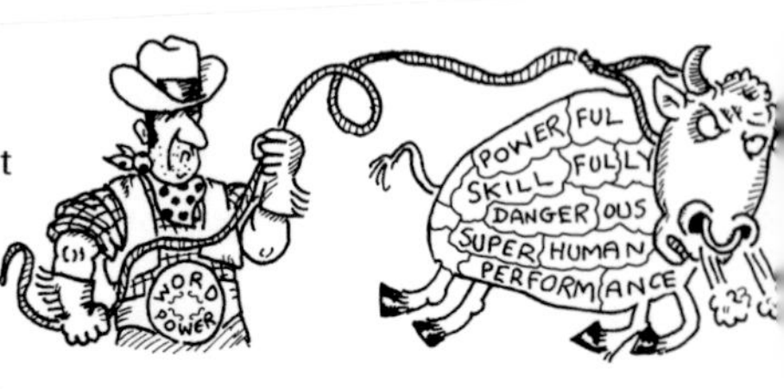


When you find a new word in English, what do you do? Look it up in a **mono**lingual or a **bi**lingual dictionary? Ask a teach**er** or another stud**ent**? Try to **pre**dict the meaning from the rest of the sentence or paragraph – the **con**text? There is another way to try to simpl**ify** difficult words. Often, long words are made from shorter words that you know, combined with a few letters added to the beginning (a **prefix**) or to the end (a **suffix**). Look at the prefixes and suffixes (in **dark** type) in this paragraph. They can all be used with many other words, so when you know their meaning, you have the key to a large number of new words. These pages show you some important groups of prefixes and suffixes. There is a longer alphabetical list on pages 814–815 at the back of this dictionary which will help you with the quiz questions.

## Prefixes

### Numbers

Many common words have prefixes that tell us about numbers. A word that begins with ***bi-*** shows that there are two of something. A *bicycle* has two wheels (but a *tricycle* has three). Words for metric measurements are often made with the prefixes **cent-**, **kilo-**, etc. 100 *centimeters* = 1 meter, 1 *kilogram* = 1,000 grams, and so on.

1 How many sides does an **octagon** have?
2 If 1976 was the **bicentennial** of Mozart's death, in which year did he die?
3 Which word is a **monosyllable,** "but," "although," or "however?"
4 Does a **multinational** company exist in only one country?

### Time

A number of prefixes are connected with time, for example **pre-** (before) and **ex-** (former). A *prearranged* meeting was arranged beforehand. A divorced man might talk about his *ex-wife*. The *ex-president* is no longer president.

5 If a house was built in the **postwar** period, was it built before or after the war?
6 Would a woman go to **prenatal** classes before or after her baby was born?
7 If your teacher told you to **rewrite** your essay, why would you be angry?

### Size and degree

Some common prefixes tell us "how big" or "how much." A word that begins with **maxi-** is large or the greatest; **mini-** refers to something small (*miniskirt*). **extra-** means "more" - *extra-strong glue* is stronger than usual.

8 Which flies faster than the speed of sound, a **subsonic** plane or a **supersonic** plane?
9 If something is **microscopic**, is it very large or very small?
10 How do you feel if you have **overeaten** – very full or still hungry?

### Negative

Many prefixes change the meaning of a word to its opposite or make it negative. A *nonsmoker* does not smoke; the opposite of happy is *unhappy*. Besides **non-** and **un-** we also use **in-** (or before certain letters **im-**, **il-**, or **ir-**) in this way. It is important to learn which is the correct prefix to make the opposite of a word.

11 Which of the prefixes **un-**, **in-**, **im-**, **il-**, **ir-** would you use to make the opposites of these words?

| | | | |
|---|---|---|---|
| **correct** | **certain** | **possible** | **regular** |
| **sure** | **legal** | **valid** | **relevant** |
| **patient** | **legible** | | |

If you are not sure, use the list to help you.

**Position**

These prefixes tell us where something is or happens. For example, **sub-** gives the idea of "under": a *subway* goes under the road; we read the *subtitles* under the pictures of a foreign movie.

12 Is an activity that is **extracurricular** part of the curriculum of a school?
13 Is a flight from New York to London **transatlantic**?
14 Is an **interstate** a road within one state or a road that links two or more states?

## Suffixes

A **suffix** is added to the end of a word, and it often changes the function of the word. There is one suffix that you probably use very often: **-ly** to make an adjective into an adverb. (*He sings beautifully. The car was badly damaged.*) A suffix can also be added to a noun to make it into an adjective: you can change the noun *Japan* into an adjective describing the nationality of the people who live there by adding **-ese**: *Japanese*.

**To make nouns** that describe a **state**, an **action** or a **quality** you can add a suffix such as **-ation**. e.g. *inform + ation = information*; *examine + ation = examination*. There may be small changes in the spelling, e.g. the second "e" is dropped in *examination*.

15 Use one of the suffixes **-ation**, **-ment**, **-ness** to make nouns from these verbs and adjectives:

**develop** **kind** **arrange**
**imagine** **happy** **organize**

What happens to the spelling of "happy?"

Other suffixes are used **to make nouns** that describe **people**, for example, **-er**, **-or**, **-ist**, **-ian**, **-ee**, **-ant**, **-ent**. They may be added to a verb to describe the person who does the action, e.g. *rider, sailor, cyclist,* or we can add them to nouns to describe someone who works on a particular subject (*artist, historian*).

16 Fill the gaps to make words that describe people and their jobs:

a __ or (works in a theater)
t ____ er (works in a school)
c ______ or (stands in front of an orchestra)
e ____ er (goes out to discover new countries)

We can also make a noun or an adjective into a **verb** by adding a suffix such as **-en**, **-ify** or **-ize**. If we make something wider, simpler or more modern, we *widen, simplify* or *modernize* it.

17 Which verbs can you make from these words, using one of the suffixes **-ize**, **-en** and **-ify**?

**magnet** **beauty** **sharp**
**general** **loose** **pure**

(You may need to change the spelling a little.)

**Adjectives** can be made with many different suffixes. Some very common ones are **-able** (or sometimes **-ible** or just **-ble**), which often means "possible to" (*acceptable, avoidable*), **-y** and **-ful**, which often describe qualities: *cloudy, helpful, beautiful*. To show that something is missing, we can add **-less**: a situation where there is no hope is *hopeless*.

18 Solve the clues to find these adjectives: (They all end in one of the suffixes mentioned)
a practical, that can be used a lot
b having no friends
c easy to see or notice
d needing something to drink.

# U.S. education system



## Schools

Most American children go to **public schools** which are free. There are also **private schools** where students have to pay. Parochial schools are supported by religious organizations.

## Assessment

Generally examination is by continuous assessment, which means that teachers **grade** (assess) students throughout the year on how well they do in tests, classroom discussions, homework, and written and oral work. At the end of a semester students must have achieved at least 70% **GPA** (grade point average) or they have to repeat the class. If students choose to go on to higher education, most colleges and universities require them to take the **SAT™** (**Scholastic Assessment Test**).

## Graduation

Students must collect units in the core courses – math, English, science, history, and government – in their first years of high school. They can then move on to **electives** (specialized subjects) in the last two years. Students can **graduate** from high school if they have collected enough **credits** in the core and elective subjects.

## Higher Education

To receive a **degree** most students study for four years. Students have to pay to go to a private or a state university. There are examinations at the end of each course; students graduate if they have collected enough credits in their **major**.

If students wish to continue their education after receiving a **Bachelor's degree**, they can do a **Master's degree**, which usually takes two years. Then they can go on to do a **Ph.D.** (a doctorate), which can take any number of years to complete.

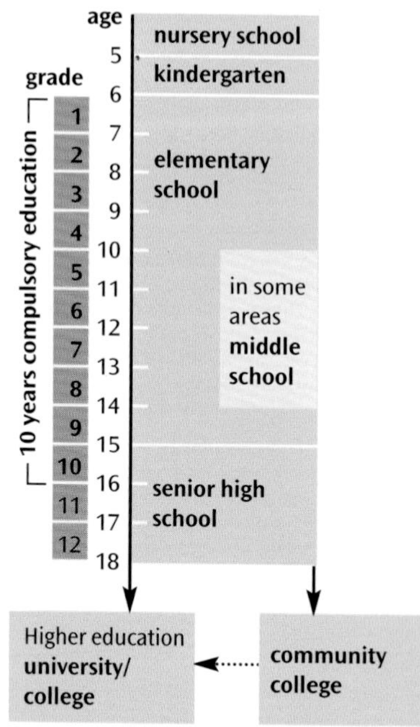


This chart shows how education is generally organized in the U.S., although in some states the system may be different.

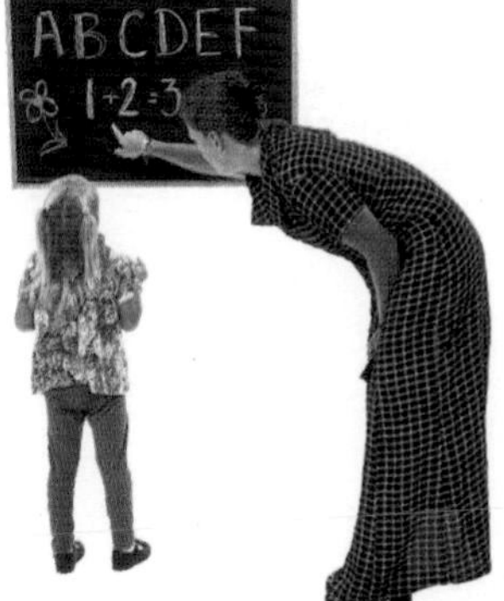


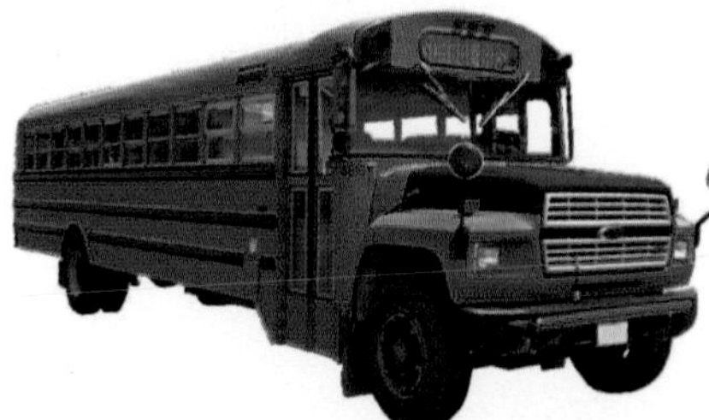

# Canadian education system



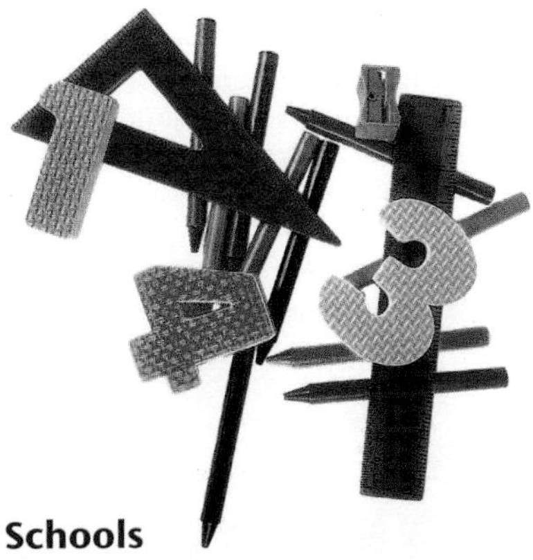

## Schools

Students in Canada attend either **public schools**, which are free, or **private schools**, which charge fees. In some provinces, some students may attend publicly-funded **separate schools** that offer religious education (usually Catholic) in addition to the regular school curriculum.

Most Canadian children attend **kindergarten** for one or two years at the age of four or five. All children begin **elementary school** in Grade 1 at about six years of age. **Secondary schools**, **high schools**, or **collegiate institutes** usually begin at Grade 8 or 9 and go up to Grade 11 or 12 , depending on the province. Students in some school systems may also attend **middle school** or **junior high school** for Grades 6–9.

## Assessment

Some schools use a percentage system, where **50%** is usually the minimum required to pass a subject. Other schools use a letter **grade** system, with A,B,C and D representing passes, and F for failure. In some provinces, students take exams set by the provincial government and in others, progress is measured by the work the students do throughout the year. Admission to Canadian universities and colleges is based solely on achievement in secondary school.

## Higher Education

After **graduation** from high school, students may attend **university**, **college** or, in the province of Quebec, **Cégep studies**. Cégep is a French abbreviation for **College of General and Professional Education**, and consists of two years of general, or three years of technical, education. After Cégep, students may go on to university, or find a job.

Canadian **universities** are large institutions offering three- and four-year degree programs, at the end of which students earn a **Bachelor's degree**. They can then go on to study for a **Master's degree**, and later a **Ph.D.** (**a doctorate**). **Colleges** are often smaller institutions that offer more specialized or technical education, in either two-, three- or four-year programs. Students **graduate** from college with either a **diploma** or a **degree**, depending on the program they complete.

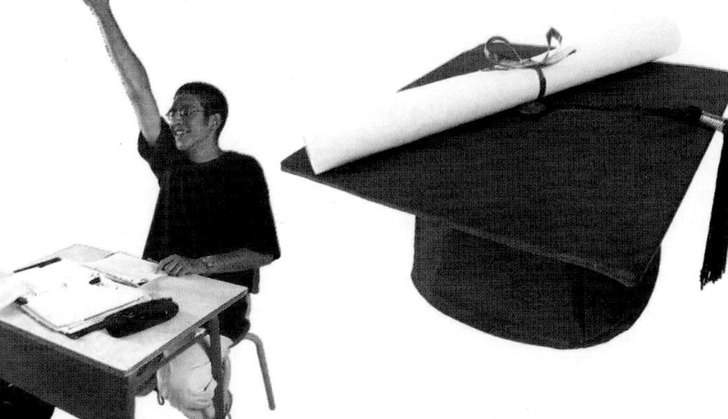

# U.S. government

## The federal government

The **United States Constitution** divides power between the **federal government** and the governments of the individual states. The federal government, which is based in Washington, DC, deals with national issues such as economic and foreign policy. There are three branches of the federal government: the Legislative, Executive and Judicial.

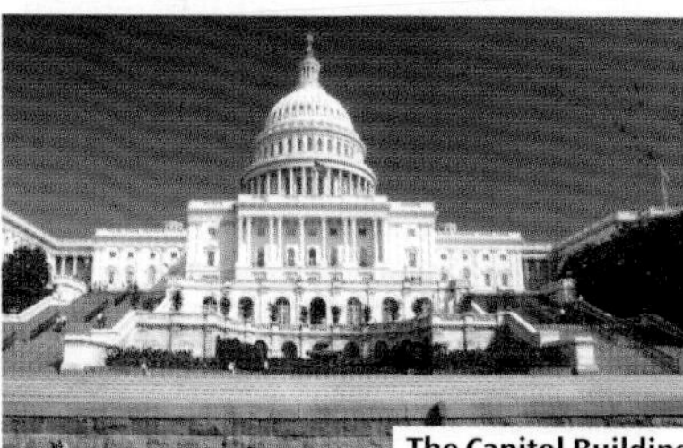

The Capitol Building

The Legislative branch is the **Congress** which meets in the **Capitol** and is made up of the **Senate** and the **House of Representatives**. The Senate has 100 **senators**, two from each state. The House of Representatives has 435 **representatives**; the number of representatives from each state depends on its population. Members of Congress introduce new laws.

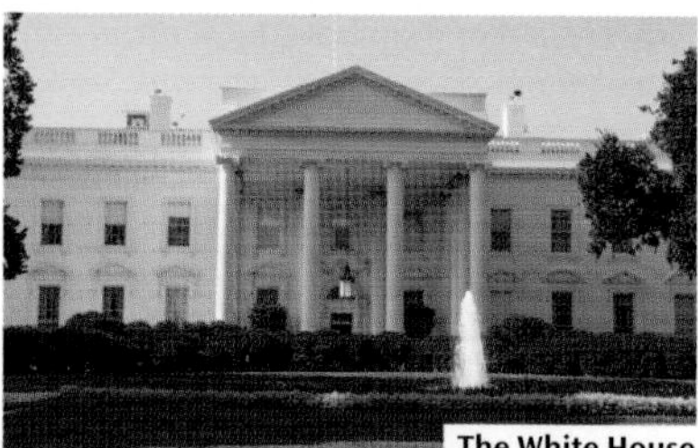

The White House

The Executive branch is led by the **President**, who lives and works in the **White House**. The President is assisted by a **Cabinet**, which consists of the heads of the departments of the federal government. The President signs laws passed by Congress. The President can also **veto** a law, but Congress can **override** the veto with the votes of more than two thirds of its members.

The Judicial branch consists of the **Supreme Court** and other federal courts. The Supreme Court is made up of nine **justices**, led by a **chief justice**, who are appointed by the President. The Supreme Court decides whether laws passed by Congress or decisions made by other courts are **constitutional**.

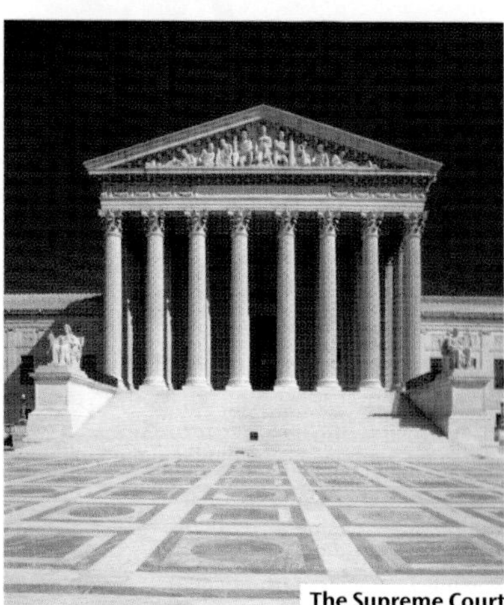

The Supreme Court

## Elections

The members of the House of Representatives are elected every two years. One third of senators are elected every two years for a six-year term. **Presidential elections** are held every four years. In each state, the candidates for President and Vice President who get the most votes win the state's **electoral votes**. The candidates who get the most electoral votes win the election. Most candidates in elections belong to one of two **political parties**, the **Democrats** and the **Republicans**.

## State government

Each state has its own laws and system of government. The head of every state government is the **governor** who is elected by the state's voters. The officials in state governments are chosen every two or four years.

# Canadian government

## Constitutional monarchy

Like the United States, Canada is a **democracy** with power divided between the **federal government** and the governments of the individual provinces and territories. However, Canada is also a **constitutional monarchy**, which means its official head of state is a King or Queen. The Queen of England is also the Queen of Canada. The Queen is represented in Canada by the **Governor General**, and by the **Lieutenant Governors** of all the provinces and **Commissioners** of the territories.

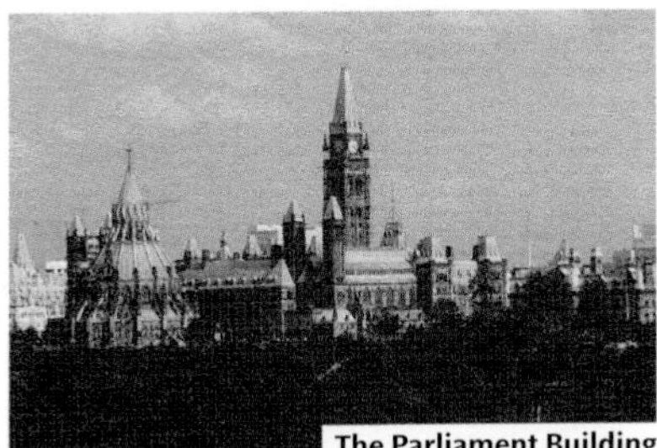
The Parliament Building

## The federal government

The laws that govern the country are made by the **federal government** (**Parliament**), under the leadership of the **Prime Minister** and his/her **Cabinet**. The **Cabinet** is made up of **Ministers** that control government departments, such as Foreign Affairs and Defence. The federal government is based in Ottawa, Ontario and is made up of a lower house, the **House of Commons** and an upper house, **the Senate**. The House of Commons is made up of 301 representatives, called **Members of Parliament** (**MPs**), who are elected by the Canadian people. It is the responsibility of the House of Commons to introduce and pass new laws. The Senate is made up of 105 representatives, called **Senators**, who are appointed by the Governor General and the Prime Minister. The main role of the Senate is to check all bills that are passed in the House of Commons before they become law.

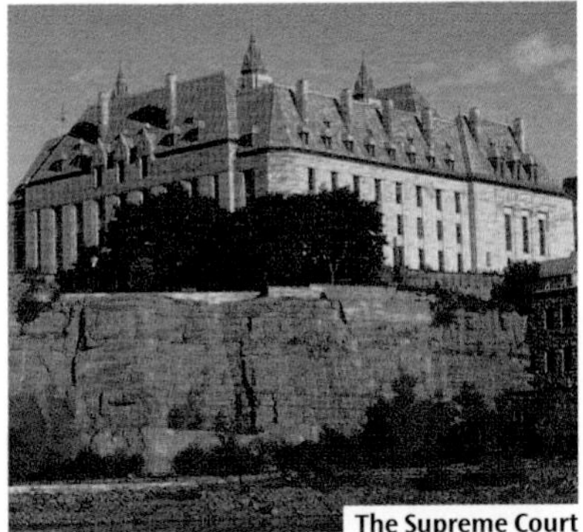
The Supreme Court

## Provincial and territorial governments

Canada has governments for each of its ten provinces and three territories. Each province or territory has its own **legislative assembly**, also called a **legislature** (or a provincial parliament in Ontario), headed by a **Premier** and composed of elected members. Provincial governments do not have a Senate.

## Political parties

Most representatives in the House of Commons, the Senate and the provincial legislatures belong to one of the major political parties in Canada – the **Conservative Party**, the **Liberal Party**, and the **New Democratic Party**. The party with the most candidates elected at the end of each election forms the government, and the leader of the majority party becomes head of government (the **Prime Minister** or the **Premier**).

## Elections

Federal and provincial elections are held every three to five years. However, if the government loses the support of the majority of members in the House of Commons or legislature, an election may be called at any time to form a new government.

# Writing an essay

## Using links and markers

When you are writing an essay that asks you to discuss a topic or give your opinion on a question, it is important to organize your thoughts and present your arguments clearly and to plan the structure of your essay before you start to write.

1 *Introduce the topic (say why it is important now)*
2 *Give one point of view, in support of the argument, with reasons*
3 *Give more information or arguments*
4 *Give a contrasting or different view*
5 *Conclude (give your own opinion or interpretation of the facts)*

**EXERCISE 1**

**In the list below are phrases that you can use to guide your readers through your essay. Which phrases could be used for each type of paragraph? Put a number 1–5 next to each of the expressions.**

| | |
|---|---|
| in conclusion (5) | nevertheless |
| furthermore | to sum up |
| recently | however |
| moreover | in addition |
| consequently | finally |
| as a result | while |
| therefore | nowadays (1) |
| on the other hand | |

**EXERCISE 2**

**Don't repeat yourself – say it another way.**

**In the lists on the right, you will find expressions that can be used to link your ideas together and give your paper a structure. Using these phrases will improve the style of your writing, and your language will be more varied as a result. Match up an expression on the left with one on the right, so that you have pairs of phrases with similar meanings. The first one has been done for you as an example.**

| | |
|---|---|
| compared with | serious problems |
| affect sth drastically | in comparison with |
| obviously | furthermore |
| in particular | plays an important role |
| appreciate | especially |
| moreover | have a devastating impact on sth |
| whereas | consequently |
| is a significant factor | while |
| in contrast | clearly |
| a cross section | on the other hand |
| as a result | a representative group |
| grave difficulties | value |

## Planning and writing an essay

- **Read the question or title carefully** to make sure that you understand what exactly is required.
- For many longer essays, you are given a topic to **discuss**. For these you should present more than one point of view on the subject, and support each point with arguments or examples.

  Now look at the following assignment:
  —*"Genetic engineering brings with it more dangers than benefits and should be banned worldwide."* Discuss.

**Brainstorming**

Quickly note down some ideas on the topic as you think of them. Then write down some vocabulary that you know you will need to write about this subject. If you are allowed to use a dictionary, check the spelling and grammar patterns now so that you can refer to your list quickly when you have begun to write your essay. Look at the next page for an example of brainstorming.

**IDEAS**

- — recent advances in science – new possibilities
- — unknown dangers
- —"designer babies"
- — new cures for diseases
- — cloning humans – political purposes
- — religious concerns
- — interfering with nature
- — banning impractical – impossible to regulate
- — can't go back

**VOCABULARY**

| | |
|---|---|
| genes | genetics |
| clone | scientific |
| modify | scientists |
| incurable | conduct research |
| therapy | possibility of doing sth |
| hereditary diseases | interfere with sth |

**EXERCISE 3**

**Now think about the structure of your essay. Look at the structure suggested in Exercise 1 and put the paragraph number against each of the arguments in the example above, according to where you think it fits into the plan suggested:**

— *recent advances in science – new possibilities*
*paragraph 1*

— *unknown dangers*
*paragraph 2*

**EXERCISE 4**

**Look at the final version of the essay. Using the expressions from Exercises 1 and 2, fill in the blanks with appropriate links.**

**"Genetic engineering brings with it more dangers than benefits and should be banned worldwide." Discuss.**

__________, advances in science have demonstrated to us that things that once seemed possible only in science fiction could become a reality. The cloning of a sheep brought the possibility of using genetic engineering to create new organs, or even whole human beings, one step closer.

Some people consider this to be a dangerous development, and believe that all such research should be banned. Interfering with nature in this way could bring with it dangers that none of us can imagine. We have no idea how an artificially-created person might behave, or indeed how he or she might suffer. __________, we may find ourselves in a position which we do not like, but which we are unable to reverse.

__________, many people would say it is not for human beings to decide what other human beings should be like. It is not only people with deep religious beliefs who feel that it is wrong, for example, for parents to choose whether their baby will be a boy or a girl, or have blue eyes or musical talent. The idea of a political regime cloning its citizens until it has the right sort of population for its purposes is even more horrific.

__________, the latest research in genetics has also opened up the possibility of new treatment for many diseases which up to now have been incurable. If it were possible to prevent a baby from developing a hereditary disease by modifying genes, should we stop the scientists? If doctors could replace a diseased organ with a new one grown from cells, should it not be allowed?

__________, I believe that genetic engineering has the potential to be both a huge benefit and a terrible curse for humankind. To make sure we benefit from it, it will be necessary to control it very strictly. The real challenge will be to find ways of monitoring the research that is conducted in laboratories all over the world and to make sure that it is only used for the good of everyone.

## Writing a report

If you are asked to write a report, for example, analyzing the results of some research, summarizing articles, or interpreting statistics, your aim should be to present facts clearly so that the reader will understand the main points quickly.

- Look at the report below and notice how the information is divided up using headings.
- The style of a report is impersonal: it is not important who the writer is or what his or her opinion is.
- Notice whether you are told who the reader is. This will help you decide how much you need to explain.
- In many reports, the important information involves numbers. Read the report again and find out what these expression refer to:

| | | |
|---|---|---|
| 50+50 | two thirds | eight out of ten |
| four | 75% | the majority |
| 5% | a half | a large majority |
| twice | three | |

Your style of writing will not be personal, but it need not be boring. Vary your language so that you do not overuse the same expressions. Think of other ways of saying the words and phrases that are written in **dark type** in the report below. Look at "Don't repeat yourself" in Exercise 2 if you need help.

**Aim**

The objective of the survey was to find out whether shopping habits have changed since the building of the new suburban mall at Lakewater, and to identify trends for the future.

**Method**

The survey targeted four groups of people: (A) downtown residents, (B) suburban residents up to three miles from the center of town, (C) business owners in the central area of town, and (D) merchants in the new mall.

Shoppers received one questionnaire, while merchants received another. Researchers visited 50 homes in the center of town and 50 in the suburbs as well as **a cross section** of stores in both locations.

**Results**

SHOPPERS

75% of all residents said that they had been to the new mall at least twice during the last month. Of these, the majority were from group B. Among the most popular reasons cited for shopping at Lakewater instead of downtown were the ample free parking there **compared with** the difficulties of parking in the center of town and the convenience of having a large number of stores in one location in the mall. Families **in particular** mentioned the Lakewater children's play area as an important advantage.

**In contrast**, two thirds of those questioned in group A reported that they **valued** the convenience of being able to walk to the stores. Eight out of ten of the older shoppers surveyed said that their daily shopping trip was their only contact with other people. **Moreover**, they preferred the personal attention of the smaller stores compared with the anonymous atmosphere of the larger outlets. They were, **however**, concerned that prices were increasing.

MERCHANTS

The merchants in town have seen business drop off by up to a half, **whereas** Lakewater businesses have recorded a steady increase in sales over the year. When asked whether they viewed the future with optimism, a large majority of group D replied positively, while only 5% of group C said that they expected to see a growth in their business in the coming year.

**Conclusions**

The opening of Lakewater mall has **clearly had a devastating effect** on downtown shopping, and this trend seems set to continue. Parking problems downtown **have been a significant factor** in changing people's habits. Mobile, better-off consumers are deserting the main street for the new mall, leaving downtown merchants to rely on the business of local residents, particularly the elderly and those without cars. **As a result**, many long-established businesses now face **grave difficulties**.

# Interpreting graphs

## Line graphs

The verbs in the box on the right can all be used to describe changes commonly represented on line graphs. Use your dictionary to look up the meanings of the verbs and then answer the following questions:

| | |
|---|---|
| plummet | increase |
| peak | soar |
| rocket | fluctuate |
| level out | drop |
| decrease | decline |
| rise | fall |

1 Which 5 verbs mean go up?
2 Of these, which 3 mean go up suddenly/a lot?
3 Which 5 verbs mean go down?
4 Which verb means reach its highest level?
5 Which verb means stay the same?
6 Which verb means go up and down?

Now decide which parts of the graphs below, showing the sales of a book between 1994 and 2003, can be described using the verbs given.

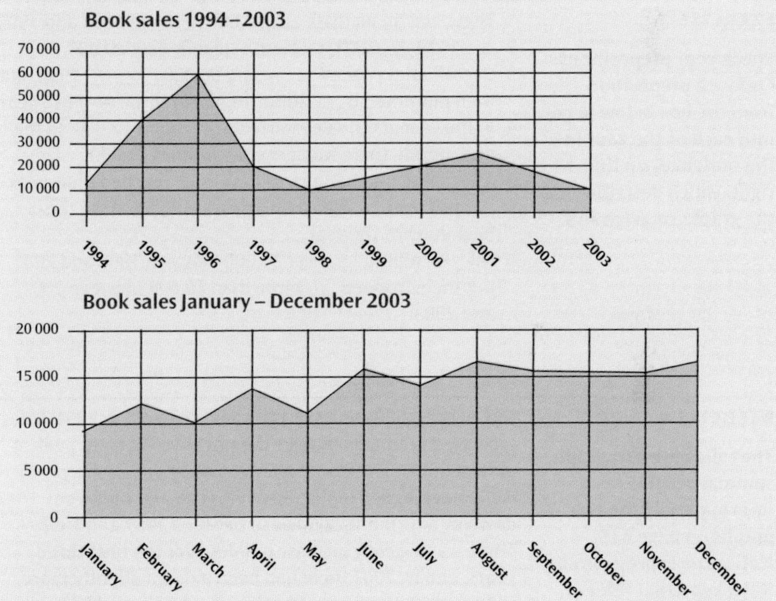


**EXERCISE 1**

**Now, using the verbs above, complete these sentences using the information shown on the graphs:**

1 In the year 2003, sales ___ at the beginning of August.
2 Sales rocketed between 19___ and 19___.
3 From 1996 to 1997, sales of the book ___.
4 Book sales fluctuated between ___ and ___ 2003.
5 Sales ___ between September and November 2003.
6 Sales started to fall for the first time in 19___.
7 Book sales ___ from 1998 to 2001.
8 However, from 2001 to 2003, sales ___.

**EXERCISE 2**

**Changes can also be described in more detail by modifying a verb with an adverb. Using a verb from the box on the left, and an adverb from the box on the right, make sentences describing the changes represented on the line graphs on page A15 for the years or months shown. The first one has been done for you as an example.**

| | |
|---|---|
| increase | fall |
| decrease | rise |
| decline | drop |

| | | |
|---|---|---|
| slightly | slowly | sharply |
| rapidly | steadily | gradually |
| moderately | dramatically | |

1 1994–1996
*Sales increased/rose dramatically/sharply.*
2 1996–1998
3 1998–2001
4 2001–2003
5 May–June 2003
6 November–December 2003

Look at the following two ways of expressing the same idea:

- *Sales **increased dramatically** from 1994 to 1996.*
  Subj + verb + adverb
- *There was **a dramatic increase** in sales from 1994 to 1996.*
  There was/were + adjective + noun + in + sth

Now turn the rest of the sentences you made in **exercise 2** into similar sentences with an adjective + a noun.

---

**EXERCISE 3**

**Check your prepositions. Choose a preposition from the box below to go into each of the gaps in the sentences on the right, which describe the graphs on page A15.**

| | | |
|---|---|---|
| at | in | to |
| of | by | from |

1 There was an increase ___ 50,000 between 1994 and 1996.
2 ___ 1998 ___ 2001, sales rose steadily over 20,000.
3 Overall sales peaked ___ nearly 60,000________1996, but then plummeted ___ about 10,000 over the next two years.
4 In the year 2003, sales started ___ around 10,000. In the first month, there was a rise ___ around 21,000.
5 After some fluctuations, sales in 2003 reached their peak ___ just over 15,000, an increase ___ 5,000 since the beginning of the year.
6 Sales increased ___ over 10,000 between 1998 and 2001, but then dropped ___ more than 10,000 between 2001 and 2003.

---

**EXERCISE 4**

**The following paragraph summarizes the information in the two graphs on page A15. Notice the expressions in dark type that refer to time and amount.**

**Just over** 10,000 copies of the book were sold in 1994. Sales increased dramatically **over the next two years**, to peak at **almost** 60,000 in 1996. However, sales then fell sharply to well under 30,000 in the following year, and they went down by a further 12,000 **or so** between 1997 and 1998. There was a steady increase in sales **over the next three years**, and by 2001 there had been a rise of **slightly more than** 10,000. However, after this sales began to drop once more and declined to **approximately** 10,000 in 2003.

**In the first six months** of the year 2003, sales fluctuated, although there was a moderate increase in July-August, reaching a peak at **well over** 15,000. A sharp decrease followed, with sales falling to around 12,000 in September. They remained steady until November, when there was a slight increase.

**Now put the expressions from the box on the left into the table on the right, from the greatest amount to the smallest. The first one has been done for you as an example.**

**Look at the two tables below for other ways to express amounts:**

| | | |
|---|---|---|
| ~~well over~~ | *well over* | |
| just under | ______ | |
| almost/nearly | ______ | 10,000 |
| well under | ______ | half |
| exactly | ______ | |
| just over | ______ | |

**APROXIMATIONS**

| | |
|---|---|
| approximately | |
| around | 10,000 |
| about | half |
| roughly | 3 times |
| more or less | |

**COMPARISONS**

| | |
|---|---|
| a little/slightly<br>far<br>a lot<br>much<br>considerably<br>significantly | more than<br>less than [+ uncountable noun]<br>fewer than [+ countable noun] |

**EXERCISE 5**

**The two pie charts below illustrate two families' average monthly expenditure. In the summary there are ten factual errors. Using the information in the pie charts, underline the mistakes and then rewrite the text, making the necessary corrections. The first one has been done for you as an example.**

**Family A's monthly income**

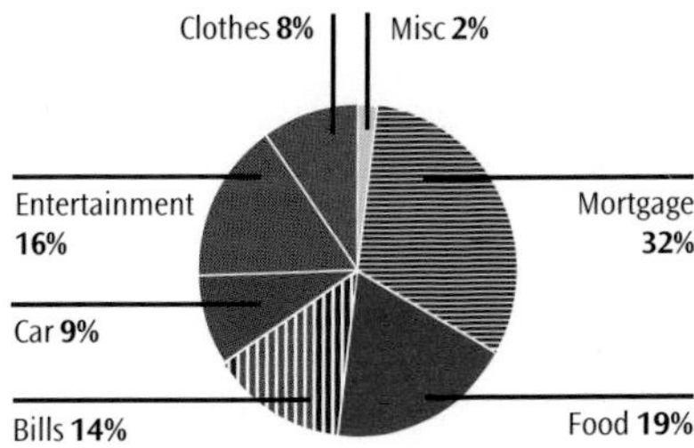


**Family B's monthly income**

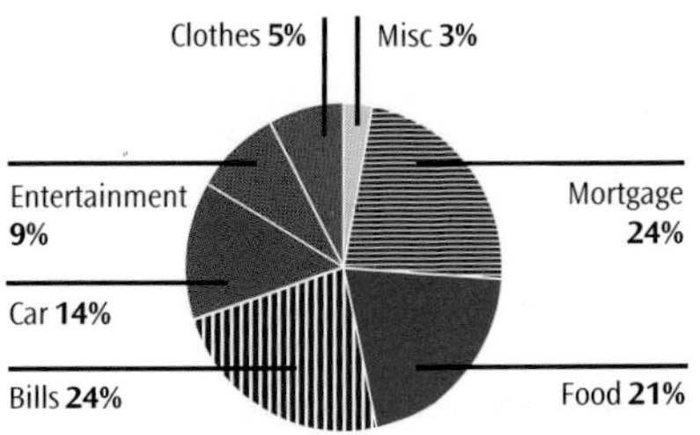


<u>Both families</u>' biggest expenditure each month is the mortgage. Family A spends far more on their mortgage than they do on anything else (32%). This is exactly half of what they spend on entertainment each month. Their food budget (19%) is significantly higher than their entertainment budget, while they spend well under 10% each month on clothes. Family B's clothes budget is far less (5%). Family B's entertainment budget is similar to Family A's, at just 9%. In contrast, family B spends much more on bills each month, over a quarter of the whole monthly budget. They compensate for this by spending less on their mortgage, which is slightly less than Family A's, at only 24%. Just over 15% of their month budget goes on the car, significantly more than the 9% that family A spends each month. In general, Family B spends more on necessary items such as bills, food and their car, while Family A allows slightly more money for entertainment and clothes.

—*<u>Family A's</u> biggest expenditure each month is the mortgage ..*

# Letter Writing

## Formal Letters

A cover letter to enclose with a job application

Do not write your name at the top of the letter.

3 Brook Road
St. Louis, Missouri
63130

Write your own address here. This lines up with your closing and signature at the bottom of the letter. You can also choose to line up every paragraph on the left side of the page.

Write the name, position and address of the person you are writing to here.

Chris Summit
Director of Human Resources
BLC Computers
15 Laclede Street
St. Louis, Missouri 63157

Write the date in full here.

April 20, 2003

Dear Mr. Summit,

Use the person's title (Mr., Ms., etc.) and his or her family name. Use "Dear **Sir** or **Madam**," only if you can not find out the name.

Avoid contractions.

I am writing to apply for the position of software technician advertised in *The Echo* on April 16. I have enclosed a copy of my résumé. ❶

Use formal linking words and phrases.

Since graduating from the University of Michigan, I have been working in software design and have gained considerable experience in developing personalized packages. I am proficient at programming in five different languages, including C++ and Java. My job has also given me some insight into systems analysis. ❷

I am now seeking employment with a company where I can gain more experience and where there are more opportunities for promotion. I am sure I could make a significant contribution and would be happy to demonstrate some of my programs to you. ❸

I am available for an interview at your convenience and look forward to hearing from you soon. ❹

Sincerely yours,
*Andrew Mason*
Andrew Mason

End your letter with "Sincerely" or "Sincerely yours."

Sign your name in full above where you key it in.

**paragraph ❶**
Explain which job you are applying for and how/where you heard about it.

**paragraph ❷**
Briefly describe your most relevant qualifications and/or experience.

**paragraph ❸**
Explain why you want the job and why you think you would be good at it.

**paragraph ❹**
Say how you can be contacted and/or when you are available for an interview.

Here are some useful expressions that you might include in a cover letter of this type:

**paragraph ❶**

— I noted with interest your advertisement for a... in today's edition of...
— I am writing in response to your advertisement in... for the position of...
— I am writing to apply for the post of ... advertised in...
— With reference to your advertisement in... I am interested in applying for the position of...

— As you will see from my résumé...
— I have enclosed a copy of my résumé, from which you will see...
— Please find enclosed a copy of my résumé.

**paragraph ❷**

— After graduating from ... I...
— Since leaving college, I have...
— Having gained a degree in... I...
— While I was working at...
— During my employment at ...

**paragraph ❸**

— I would welcome the chance to...
— I would appreciate for the opportunity to...

**paragraph ❹**

— I am available for an interview any afternoon and would be pleased to discuss the position in person.
— I can arrange to attend an interview at your convenience.

**EXERCISE 1**

**Choosing the correct register**

**Knowing how formal or informal to be is very important when communicating in writing. To practice identifying formal and informal phrases, match the formal phrase on the left with its informal equivalent on the right. The first one has been done for you as an example.**

| **Formal letter** | **Informal letter** |
|---|---|
| a I regret to inform you that... | 1 Let us know when you get... |
| b I would like to inform you that... | 2 I'm happy to tell you... |
| c It appears that... | 3 I'm sorry... |
| d Please accept our apologies for... | 4 I'm writing to let you know that |
| e I would be grateful if you could... | 5 We're waiting for... |
| f We would appreciate it if... | 6 I'm sorry to tell you that... |
| g I can assure you that... | 7 I'm writing to ask... |
| h We are pleased to confirm... | 8 We'd be really happy if... |
| i We have the pleasure of enclosing... | 9 I want to tell you that... |
| j We look forward to receiving... | 10 I'm writing back to you... |
| k We are writing to advise you that... | 11 I'm sending it with this letter. |
| l In reply to your query... | 12 Could you please... |
| m Please confirm receipt of... | 13 I promise... |
| n I am writing to inquire... | 14 It seems... |

## A letter of complaint

Most letters of complaint use formal language and have a standard organization.

**paragraph 1** explain why you are writing
**paragraph 2** explain what the problem is
**paragraph 3** say what inconvenience it has caused you
**paragraph 4** state what you want done about the problem

**EXERCISE 2**

**Below is a memo written in an informal style because it is from one colleague to another. Read the memo and the formal letter of complaint underneath. Change the underlined expression in the memo into formal language using the expressions listed a–f and then fill in the blanks 1–6 in the formal letter.**

a We will be obliged to…
b We must insist that…
c Please confirm…
d We are writing to express our dissatisfaction…
e We are unable…
f We would like to remind you…

MEMO

To: Alice Porter
From: Yolanda Stevens
Date: January 16, 2004
Re: faulty DVD players

---

Please write to Lassiters and tell them we are really unhappy with their last order. Say we simply can't accept the goods in their current condition. Remind them how long we've been customers of theirs! Say we want the goods replaced now or we'll have to cancel the order. Ask them to let us know what they're going to do about it.

Yolanda

Dear Mr. Waldron,

**Order 5600: 20 DVD players**

**1** ______ with the last order you sent us on December 22, 2003.

Most of the DVD players have faulty wiring and are unusable. **2** ______ to accept these goods in their current condition. **3** ______ that we have been good customers of yours for several years and expect better service than this.

**4** ______ these goods are replaced immediately or **5** ______ cancel our order. **6** ______ when you will be able to replace the goods.

Sincerely,

*Alice Porter*

Alice Porter
Administrative Assistant to Ms. Adams

## Writing e-mails and faxes

**Business e-mails** between colleagues can be very informal, but e-mails to clients, etc. may be either semi-formal or formal depending on the individual relationship and what the e-mail contains. However, all e-mails should follow certain basic rules:

- Be consistent in style. Don't vary between formal and informal.
- Appearance is still important – remember to use paragraphs and proper sentences.
- Keep it short and to the point.
- Use the subject line to summarize the point of the message so the reader is clear about the content.
  — *Question about delivery dates*
- Refer to any original message in your e-mail.
- Paraphrase relevant parts of the original e-mail rather than quoting whole chunks.
- In a more formal e-mail it is better to write *Dear*…, but you do not have to use a particular formula at the end; you can just write your name.

**EXERCISE 3**

**E-mail requests**

**Here are three different e-mails requesting something. The relationship between the sender and receiver is different and what is being asked for varies in difficulty. Use appropriate phrases from the list below to fill in the blanks in the three e-mails.**

a I am writing to ask you
b I need to know
c Should we also
d We need to know
e We would like you to
f Could you please
g I would be grateful if you
h Can you arrange this
i Can you also let me know

**Informal request to a colleague:**

Andrew
**1** ______ re-order 20 packs of the high-grade photocopy paper. **2** ______ and let me know the delivery date? **3** ______ get some packs of staples at the same time?
Sarah

**Semi-formal request to a known business contact:**

Dear Alan,
**4** ______ send details of this year's April conference? **5** ______ by next week to arrange numbers. **6** ______ if accommodation is available?
Thanks,
David

**Formal request to someone in business if you have not met him/her before:**

Dear Mr. Webb,
**7** ______ if you would be able to give a presentation at our board meeting on Thursday, February 7.
**8** ______ talk about your current projects and how your consultants could help our company.
**9** ______ could let me know as soon as possible.
Regards,
Elaine Jackson

## Faxes

People often fax forms, maps, etc. Normal business letters can also be sent as faxes. You can send a fax which is a note, but if it is to business clients, etc., you should use the language of a formal letter.

Bute Electronics
Fax #: (617) 541-3432

February 23, 2004

From: Sandra Cohen
Production Department

Attn: Alan Wheeler
Operations Manager
Tuckerman Chevrolet

Re: Car components: Order no. 6133

Our suppliers have only just delivered the parts we need to complete the above order. We will therefore not be able to deliver until Friday. I apologize for any inconvenience this may cause.

Sandra Cohen

# TOEIC® and TOEFL® practice tests

**Items 1–12 are incomplete sentences. They are similar to questions you might find on the TOEFL® or TOEIC® exams. Choose the best answer to complete the sentence. Use the dictionary to look up any words that you do not understand.**

**1** Many farmers ____________ four-year college programs to prepare for the complex scientific, business, and financial decisions involved in modern farming.
**A** achieve **B** complete **C** conclude **D** succeed

**2** When the first typewriters were introduced to the public ____________ the nineteenth century, businesses did not understand their potential impact.
**A** along **B** since **C** during **D** toward

**3** Laws to ____________ consumers often conflict with the interests of big corporations.
**A** produce **B** provide **C** progress **D** protect

**4** Because crows are difficult to trap, there is ____________ less scientific study of their behavior than there is of blackbirds, pigeons and gulls.
**A** such **B** very **C** more **D** much

**5** Rising production and falling unemployment are ____________ signs of economic recovery from a recession.
**A** encouraging **B** encourage **C** encouraged **D** encourages

**6** Before clocks, calendars, or compasses were invented, constellations helped people tell time and ____________ in the dark.
**A** their way is **B** find their way **C** what their way **D** of their way

**7** Using machines for bonding and gluing clothes ____________ sewing them is a practice that is expected to become more and more widespread in the clothing industry.
**A** instead of **B** in spite of **C** because of **D** in view of

**8** Employers cannot always afford to hire the job applicant ____________ the most experience.
**A** who is **B** whose **C** who has **D** who was

**9** Structural damage of small bridges is often caused ____________ heavy rainstorms and flooding.
**A** for **B** with **C** of **D** by

**10** During the seventeenth century, Galileo Galilei ____________ pendulums as measurement devices in many of his experiments.
**A** used to **B** used **C** using **D** is used

**11** The ability of snakes to see at night is due to a structure in the lining of their lips that ____________ them see heat patterns of mammals.
**A** lets **B** permits **C** allows **D** supports

**12** A company's business plan should ____________ how it expects to succeed and how it will measure success.
**A** to describe **B** describes **C** describing **D** describe

**Sentences 1–14 each contain an error. They are similar to questions you might find on the TOEFL® or TOEIC® exams. Identify one underlined word or phrase that must be changed in order for the sentence to be correct. Use the dictionary to look up any words that you do not understand.**

**1** According to (A) a government report, mortgage rates have never (B) fluctuated as much than (C) they have this past (D) year.

**2** The spelling system of present-day English is based (A) on the pronunciation what (B) was used when (C) Chaucer and Shakespeare were alive (D).

**3** The newspaper and broadcasting industries are sensible (A) to economic ups and downs (B) because (C) of their dependence on advertising revenue (D).

**4** Despite (A) water was distributed (B) to homes in ancient Rome through (C) lead pipes, plumbing became (D) almost non-existent during the Middle Ages.

**5** Librarians are increasingly (A) applying their (B) information management and research skills to (C) developing database (D) and training database users.

**6** Most factory assembly lines have (A) conveyor belts which move (B) components to a point where (C) they can be process (D).

**7** Resistance to (A) antibiotics develop (B) when bacteria change in a way that reduces or (C) eliminates the effectiveness (D) of antibiotic treatment.

**8** Customers should disrespect (A) any (B) bill or renewal (C) notice received soon after (D) mailing a payment or order.

**9** Ringing (A) cell phones have replaced (B) talking as most annoying (C) disruption during movies, concerts, and (D) public lectures.

**10** All (A) participants and their guests have notified (B) that in the event of (C) bad weather, the graduation ceremony will be moved indoors (D).

**11** A well-written résumé should focus (A) not only on previous (B) responsibilities at work (C) if (D) also on accomplishments.

**12** Theories about when the life (A) could have evolved (B) and when planets formed are (C) changing as (D) more planets are discovered outside of the solar system.

**13** In many cities around the world, (A) there (B) takes the average worker more than (C) forty minutes to (D) get to work each morning

**14** If average globally (A) temperatures rise even (B) moderately, melting ice will (C) cause rising (D) sea levels and coastal flooding.

# Taking notes

When you are studying you will often want to write notes to help you remember what you have heard or read. These pages will show you how to take notes efficiently by using symbols and abbreviations and how to organize your notes.

## Symbols

Using symbols can save you a lot of time. The symbols in this section are widely used and understood.

**EXERCISE 1**

**Look at the symbols and match them to their meanings below:**

\+ = < > ♂ ≠
♀ @ & * ≈ "

1 this is an important point
2 is approximately equal to
3 is not, does not equal
4 plus, and
5 equals, is
6 at
7 is more than
8 is less than
9 male
10 female
11 and
12 the same as the word above

You can use these symbols in place of a range of words. For example, + can mean *also, in addition* or *as well as*. Try to think of some other words or phrases that the other symbols could stand for.

**Arrows** are also useful symbols:

↗ or ↑ an increase/a rise/an improvement in something

↘ or ↓ a decrease/a fall/a reduction/a deterioration in something

→ causes/results in/becomes/makes
— *Certain chemicals used in industry have caused a hole to develop in the ozone layer.*
This could be written in note form as:
— *Chemicals used in industry → hole in ozone layer.*

← is caused by/is the result of/is made from
— *We can help reduce pollution by using environmentally-friendly forms of transportation.*
This could be written in note form as:
— *Reduce pollution ← using environmentally-friendly transportation.*

## Abbreviations

You have probably come across some abbreviations in your textbook or dictionary:

**esp.** = especially
**p.** = page
**sb** = somebody
**ch.** = chapter
**etc.** = and so on

**NOTE** A period is often used at the end of an abbreviation to show that this is not the full form of the word.

**EXERCISE 2**

**The following abbreviations are very common. Try to guess what the full forms are.**

vol. usu. sing. incl.
ex. diffs. approx.

**EXERCISE 3**

**Do you know what these common abbreviations mean? If not, look them up in the dictionary.**

i.e e.g. c. pp.

You should try to develop your own system of abbreviations, especially for words that you use frequently. These are some widely used methods:

- Write only the first few letters of the word:
  **pop.** = population
  **prog.** = program
  **elec.** = electricity

- Write the first few letters of the word, and the last letter:
  **govt** = government
  **dept** = department
  **assn** = association
  **appt** = appointment
- Write only the consonants, omitting the vowels:
  **mrkt** = market
  **mngr** = manager
  **pls** = please

**EXERCISE 4**

**Now suggest some abbreviations of your own for the following words:**

| | |
|---|---|
| industry | industrialization |
| chemicals | technology |
| global warming | underdevelopment |
| temperature | international |

However you abbreviate the words, remember that you will need to understand your abbreviations when you look at your notes later.

## Omitting words

Another way of keeping your notes short is by omitting words. Many words in a sentence just show the grammar and do not carry much meaning. Look at this sentence. The underlined words are the **content words** that give the meaning; the others are the **grammar words**:
—*It is useful to be able to take notes from lectures and textbooks quickly and efficiently.*
You could write this in note form as: *Useful: take notes – lectures, textbooks quickly, efficiently*. Notice how the colon (:), the dash (–) and the comma (,) are used instead of words here.

You can omit:

- **articles** (a, an, the):
  —*The Internet is an enormous network that covers the world.*
  —*Internet = enormous network that covers world.*
- **most forms of the verb "be"**:
  —*The President was assassinated on November 22, 1963.*
  —*Pres. assassinated 11/22/63.*
- **pronouns** (I, me, my, he, his, we, us, our, etc.):
  —*We pollute our water by dumping waste.*
  —*Pollute water ← dumping waste.*
- that, which, who:
  —*We are producing too much carbon dioxide, which is causing temperatures to rise.*
  —*Producing too much carbon dioxide → temperatures ↑.*

Always try to look for the shortest, simplest way to write things. For example, *The government of the United States* could be written: *U.S. govt.*

## Organizing notes

Your notes will be much easier to understand later if you use headings and underlining for the main points, and numbers, letters, etc. for the subordinate points. Start new points on a new line. Underline important points or anything else you especially wish to remember. Think carefully about the layout of your notes. It should be clear and reflect the structure of the lecture or text.

**EXERCISE 5**

**Now read the sample text below and take notes, using the abbreviations, symbols and headings suggested on this page. When you have finished, compare your notes with the sample notes in the key on pages 826–7.**

ENERGY
Most of the energy we use to heat and light buildings, run machines, etc. is made by burning fossil fuels. These will eventually run out, so we need to use more alternative sources of energy, such as wind and solar power, that are renewable and do not pollute the air. We should also avoid wasting energy by using less electricity and water and insulating our houses.

## Further practice

You can continue to practice taking notes by reading newspaper articles or passages from a textbook, or by asking a friend to read a text to you.

# Writing a résumé

- Many people choose to include a job objective. This is a clearly stated goal that shows you have a sense of direction.
- Most people do not include birth date, marital status, children, etc. You do NOT have to include ethnic or religious affiliation.
- Include your work experience first if you have any. If you are a student or have just graduated, include your education first.
- Include references if the employer asks for them specifically. Otherwise write "References furnished upon request" or "References available upon request" at the end of your résumé.
- You may choose to include hobbies or interests.

## Some useful phrases

- Near-native command of English
- Working knowledge of Dutch and German
- Native French speaker
- Bachillerato (equivalent of high school diploma)

## Example of a résumé

Jenny Woo

1450 Diamond Street
San Francisco, California 65952
tel: (650) 498 7851
e-mail: jenny_woo@usaemail.com

**Objective**

To obtain an entry level financial analyst position with a major bank.

**Education**

| | |
|---|---|
| 1999–2003 | University of California, Berkeley<br>Bachelor of Arts in Business Studies, 2003.<br>Major: Economics,<br>Minor: Political Science |

**Work Experience**

| | |
|---|---|
| Summer 2002 | Research intern, Golden Gate Bank, San Francisco.<br>Analyzed financial data and collaborated on detailed daily reports to investors. |
| Summer 2001 | Administrative Assistant, Suntech Consulting, Berkeley.<br>Managed calendar, files and correspondence for a senior partner. |

**Skills**

Proficiency in several software packages, including MS Word, Excel, Access and Powerpoint.
Working knowledge of Spanish.

**Interests**

Travel, hiking, politics.

References available upon request.

# Computers

Computers are no longer used just in the office; more and more people are using them at home for study, for communication or for entertainment. This page presents some of the language you might need if you were explaining to someone how to use a computer.

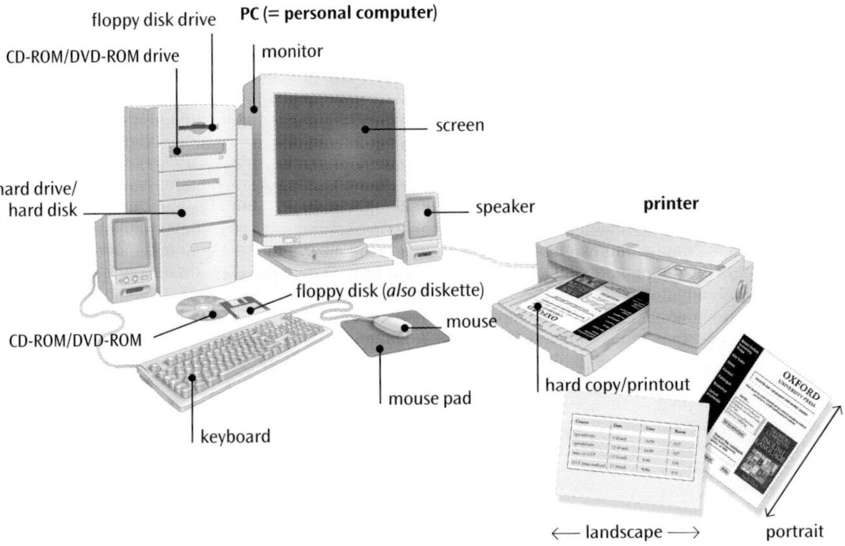


- A computer can **store** and **process** information. This information is called **data** and can be words, numbers or **graphics** (= pictures/images). To process data the computer uses a **program**, which is a set of instructions stored on the computer's **hard drive**.
- To **input** data, you can **enter** it using the keyboard. If you want to store this data, you **save** it in the computer's **memory** or onto a **floppy disk**. Large amounts of information such as books, can be stored on a **CD-ROM** or a **DVD**.
- On the screen, **icons** (= special symbols) and **menus** show you what programs and data are stored on the computer and what jobs the computer can do. You use the **mouse** to tell the computer what you want it to do and which part of the screen you want to work on. A small symbol called a **cursor** shows your position on the screen.
- Computers can be connected to other computers to form a **network**. This allows different people to have access to the same information and to communicate with each other using **e-mail** (= electronic mail). To communicate with someone using e-mail, you send your message to their **e-mail address**. For example, John_Jones@aol.com is a typical e-mail address. To say this address, you say "John underscore Jones at A O L dot com."
- **The Internet** or **the Net** is an enormous network that covers the world. People who want to make information available to the whole world can pay for their own space on the Internet. This is called a **website**. **The Web** or **the World Wide Web** is the system which lets you **download** (= look at) information on the Internet. You can also enter a subject and find all the websites that have information about it. This is called **surfing the Net**.

# Fruit and vegetables

## citrus fruit

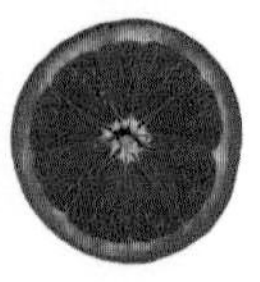
orange

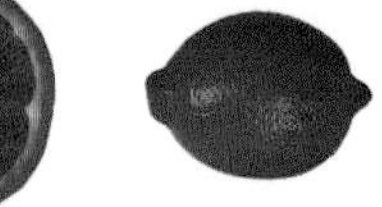
lemon

lime

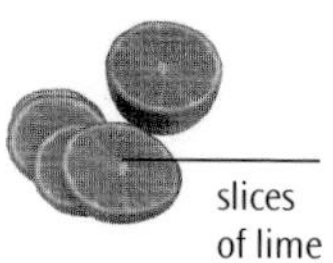


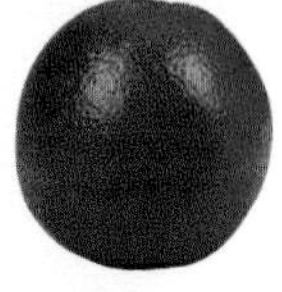
grapefruit

## tropical fruit

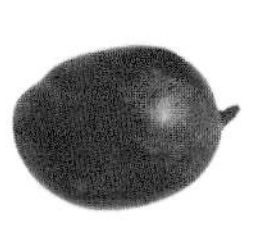
mango

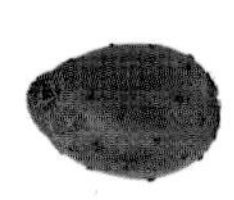
prickly pear

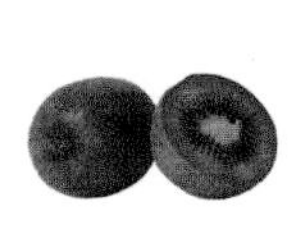
kiwi

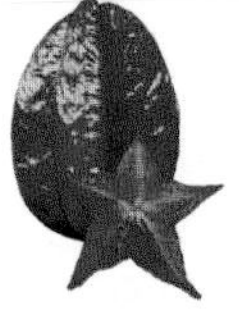
star fruit

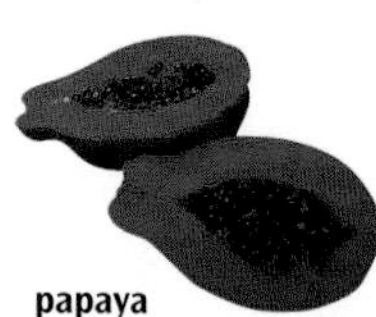
papaya

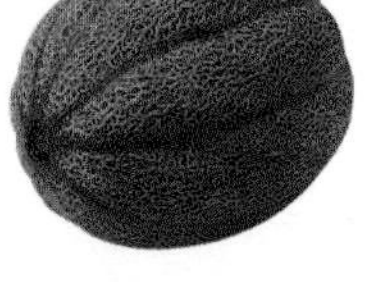
cantaloupe (melon)

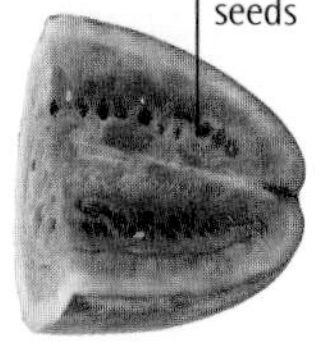

watermelon

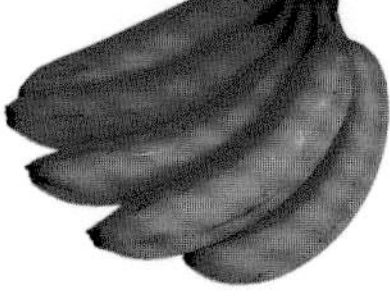
a bunch of bananas

## berries

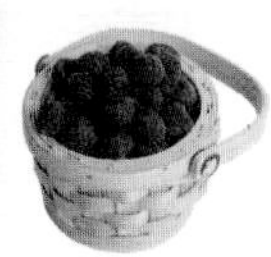
raspberries

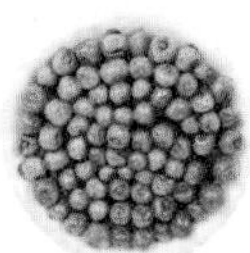
blueberries

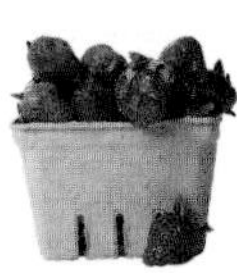
strawberries

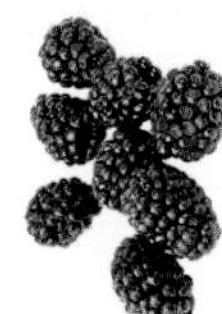
blackberries

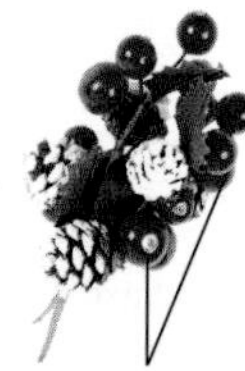
cranberries

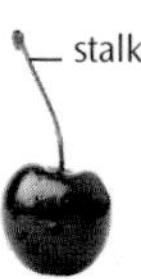

cherry

## herbs and spices

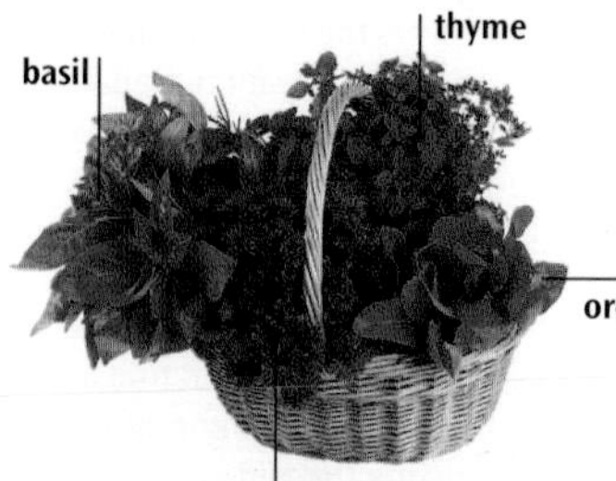


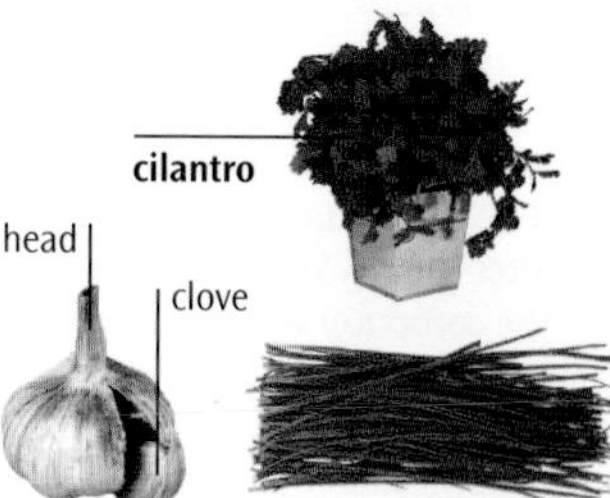


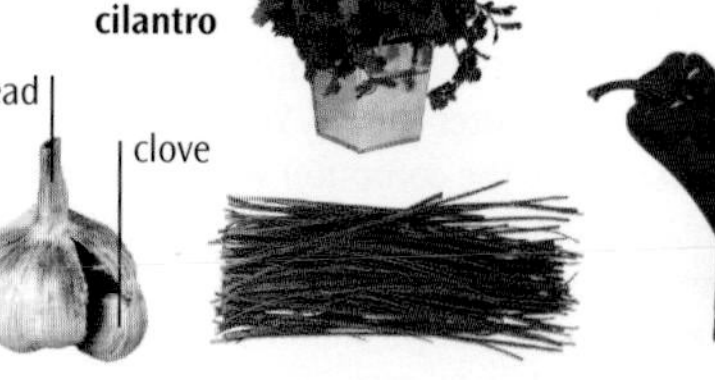
garlic

chives

chili pepper

## salad vegetables

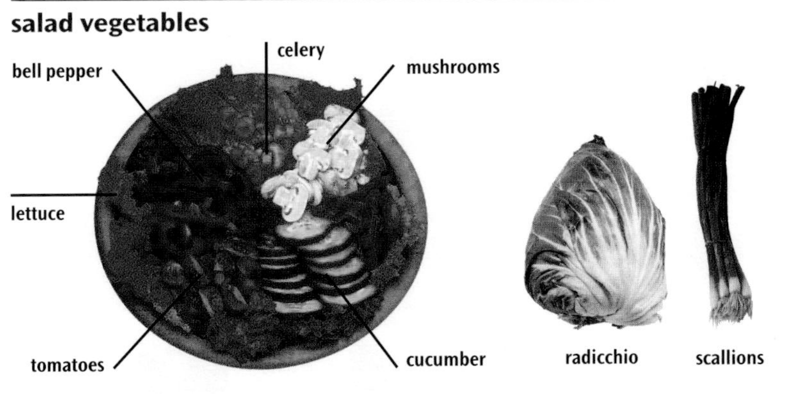


## other vegetables

cauliflower

bok choy
broccoli
cabbage
artichoke
carrots

asparagus
peas
pod
Brussels sprouts
onion
potatoes

beet
eggplant
turnip
rutabaga
jalapeño pepper
sweet potatoes

## squash

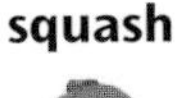

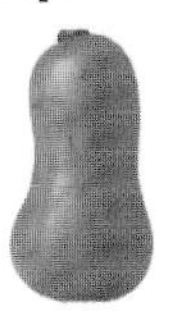

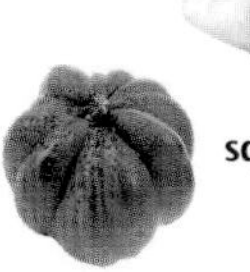

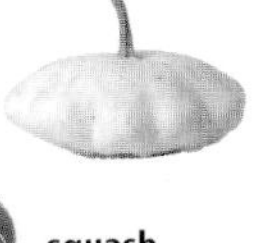

squash

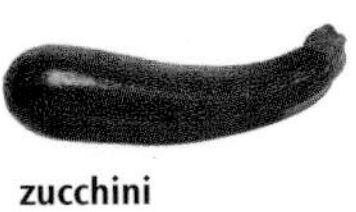

zucchini

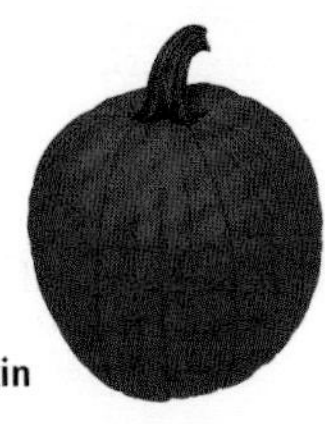

pumpkin

# Clothes

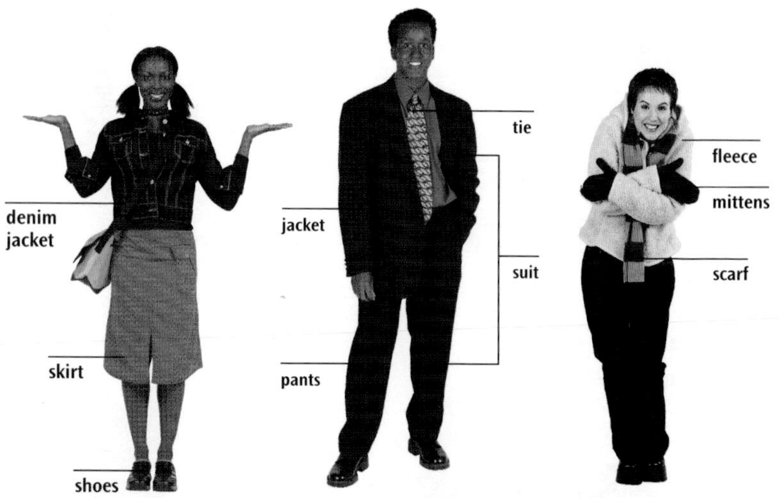


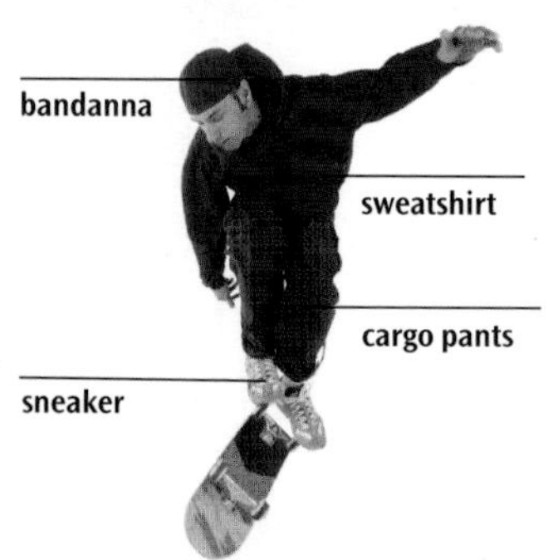


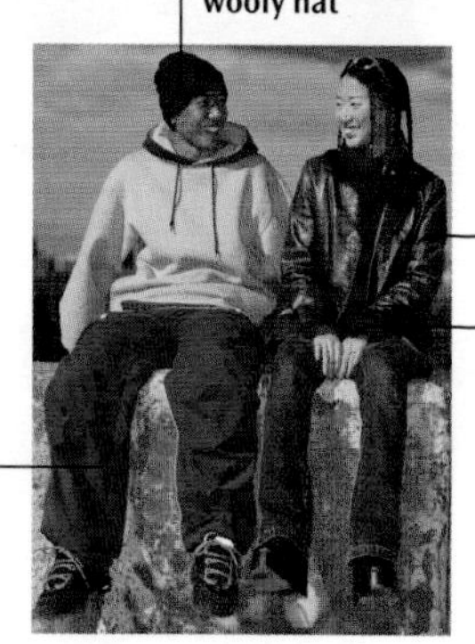


## Patterns

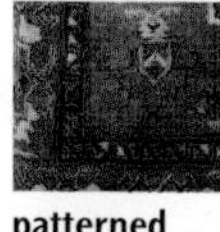
patterned

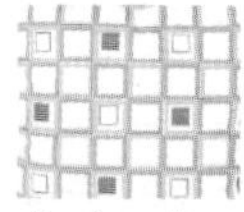
checkered

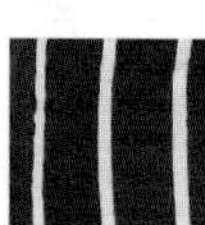
striped

solid

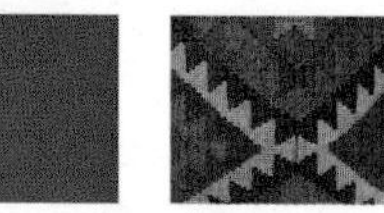
zigzag

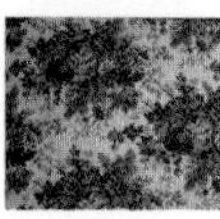
flowered

bow ties

plaid

polka dot

## Useful expressions

**to be wearing sth**
**to have sth on**
**to be dressed in sth**

**to get dressed/undressed**
**to dress/undress**
**to put sth on**
**to take sth off**
**to change your clothes**
**to change into sth**
**to try sth on**
**to dress well/badly/casually**
**to dress up**

Clothes can **fit** you or **look good on** you

*For more information about how to use these expressions, look them up in the main part of the dictionary.*

# Houses

## a house

## an apartment

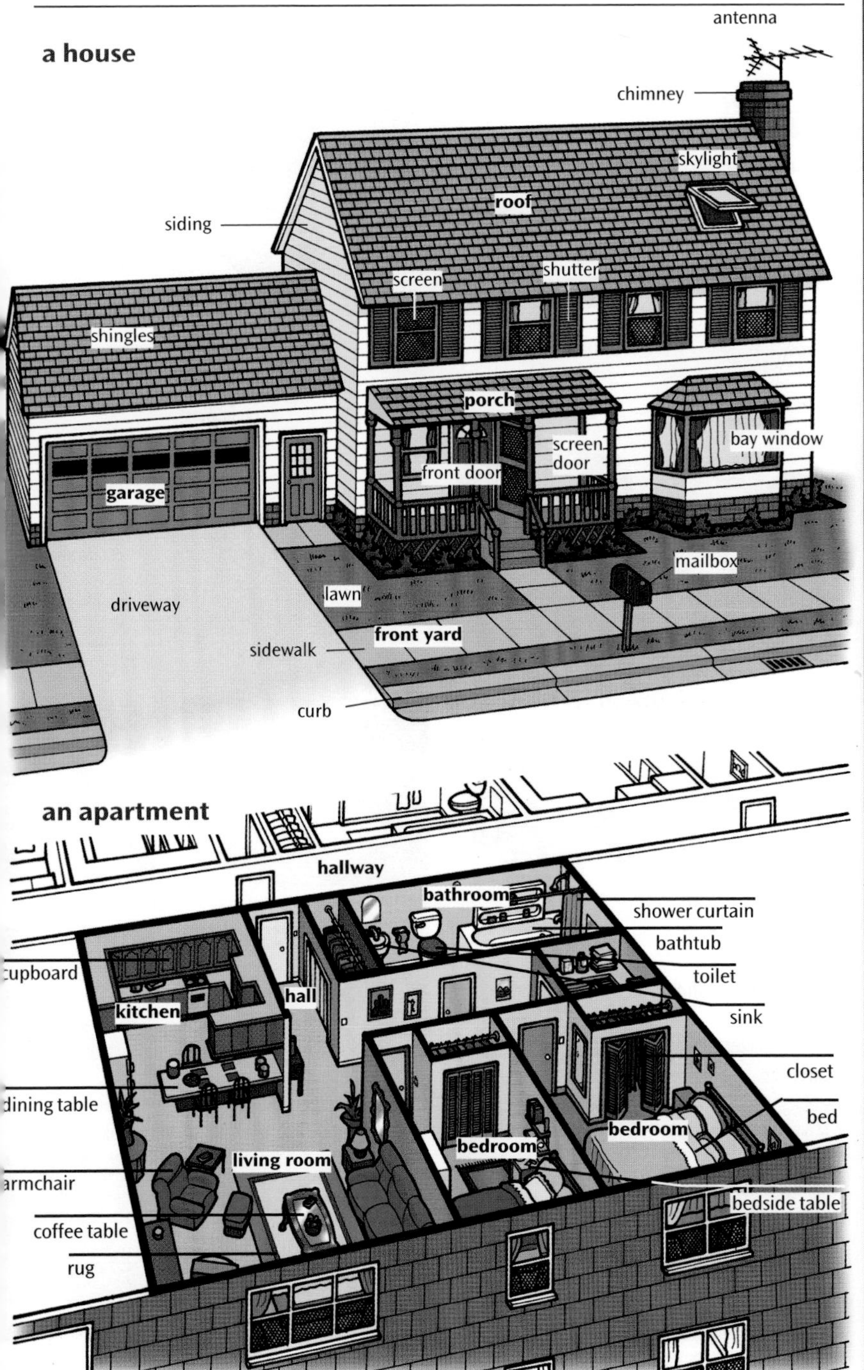

# Health and fitness

## working out

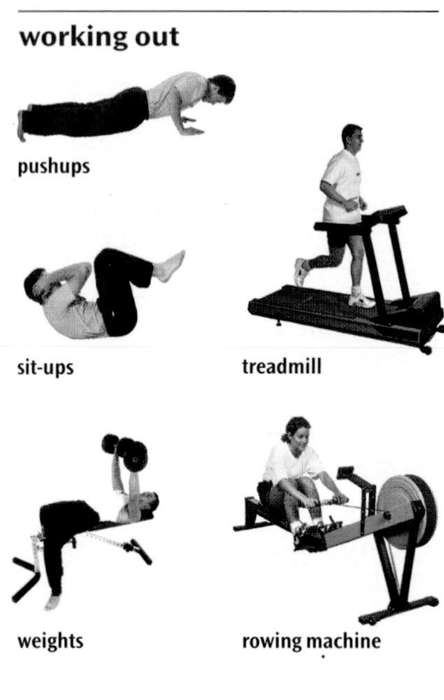
pushups
sit-ups
treadmill
weights
rowing machine

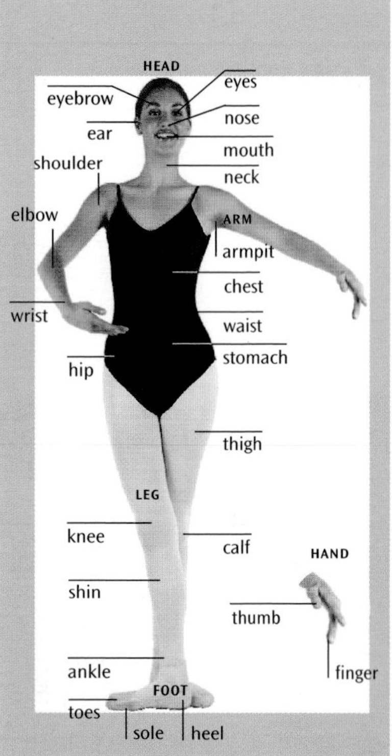


## sports and leisure activities

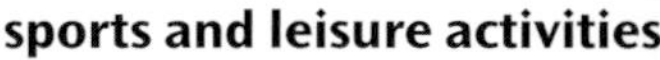

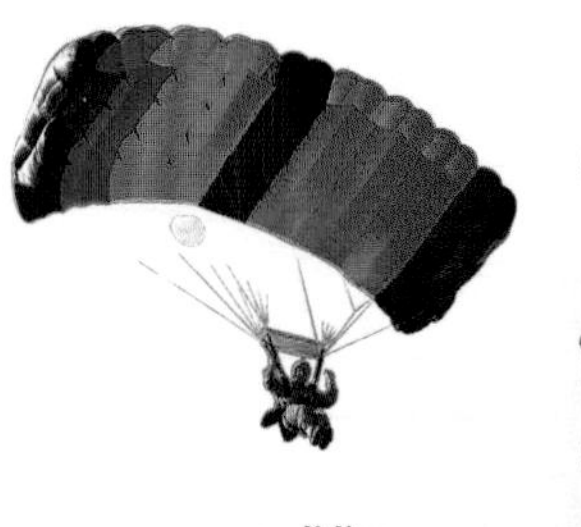
paragliding

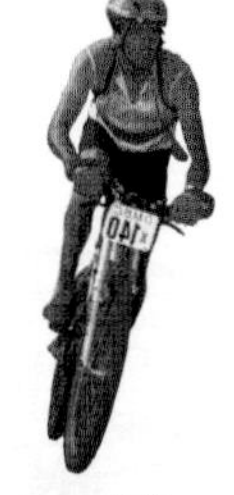
mountain biking

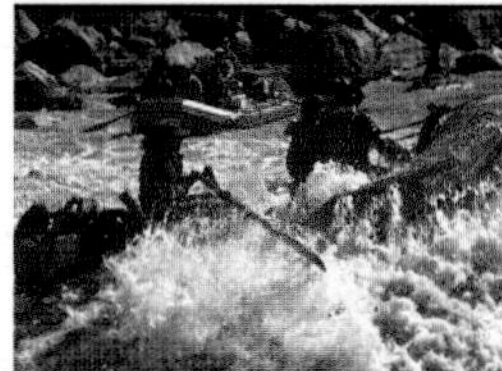
whitewater rafting

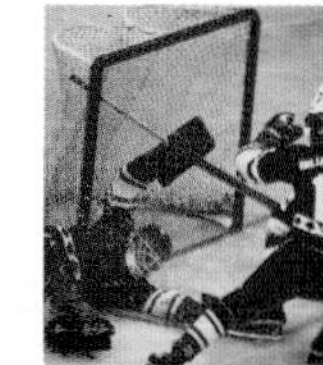
hockey

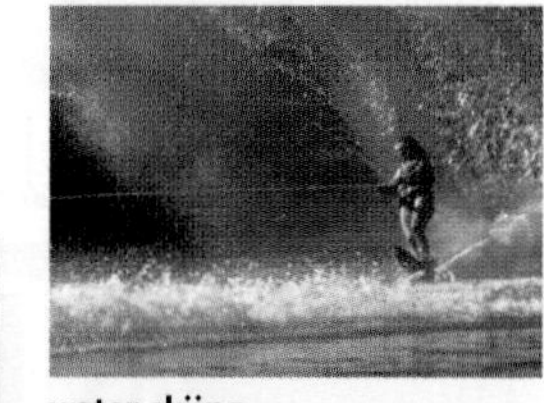
water-skiing

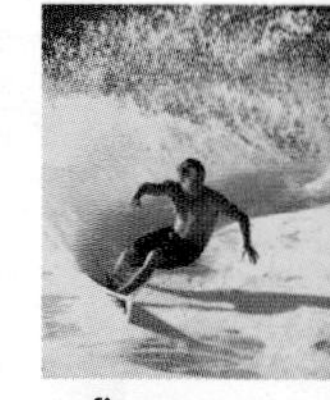
surfing

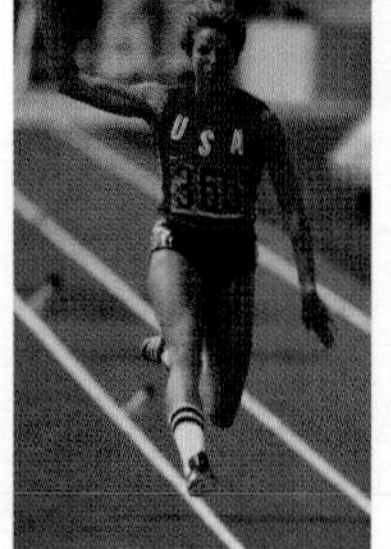

athletics

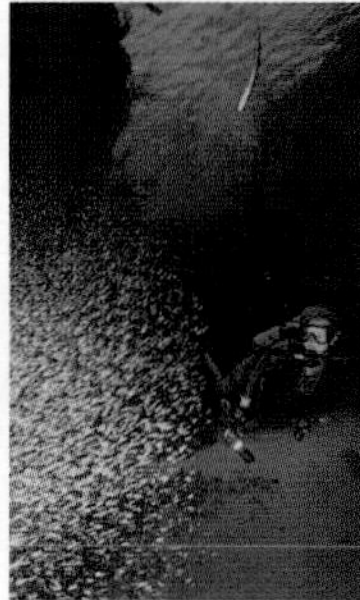
scuba diving

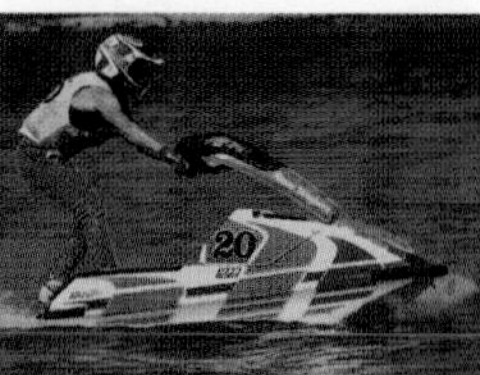
jet-skiing

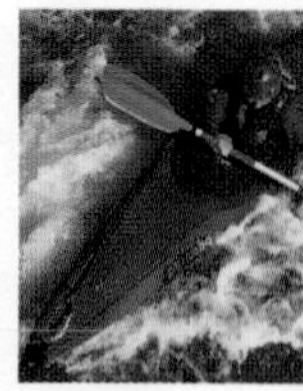
kayaking

*They claim to have a 40% worldwide market share.* ◇ *The merger will give them a larger market share.*

**mark·ing** /ˈmɑrkɪŋ/ ***noun*** [C, usually pl.] a pattern of color on an animal or a bird

**marks·man** /ˈmɑrksmən/ ***noun*** [C] (*pl.* **marks-men**) a man who can shoot very well with a gun

**mar·ma·lade** /ˈmɑrməleɪd/ ***noun*** [U] a type of jam that is made from oranges: *toast and marmalade for breakfast*

**ma·roon** /məˈrun/ ***adj.*** dark brownish-red in color ➲ Look at **crimson** and **scarlet**.

**ma·rooned** /məˈrund/ ***adj.*** in a place that you cannot leave: *The sailors were marooned on a desert island.*

**mar·quee** /mɑrˈki/ ***noun*** [C] a sign over the entrance to a theater that shows the names of the movies being shown or the play being performed

★**mar·riage** /ˈmærɪdʒ/ ***noun*** **1** [C,U] the state of being husband and wife: *They are getting divorced after five years of marriage.* ◇ *a happy/an unhappy marriage* ◇ *an arranged marriage* (= one where your partner is chosen for you by your parents) ◇ *a mixed marriage* (= one between people of different races or religions) **2** [C] a wedding ceremony: *The marriage took place in the bride's parents' home.* ➲ verb marry ➲ Look at the note at **wedding**.

★**mar·ried** /ˈmærid/ ***adj.*** **1 married (to sb)** having a husband or wife: *a married man/woman/couple* ◇ *They've been married for almost 50 years.* ◇ *Jenny's married to Mark.* ◇ *They're getting married in June.* ➲ Look also at **divorced**, **unmarried**, **single** and **widowed**. **2** (only *before* a noun) of marriage (1): *How do you like married life?*

**mar·row** /ˈmæroʊ/ ***noun*** [U] = BONE MARROW

★**mar·ry** /ˈmæri/ ***verb*** (*pres. part.* **mar·ry·ing**; *3rd person sing. pres.* **mar·ries**; *pt, pp* **mar·ried**) **1** [I,T] to take sb as your husband or wife: *They married when they were very young.* ◇ *When did Roger ask you to marry him?* ➲ **Get married** is more commonly used than **marry**: *When are Sue and Jack getting married?* ◇ *They got married in 1999.* ◇ *Many people live together without getting married.* **2** [T] to join two people together as husband and wife: *We asked John's priest to marry us.* ➲ noun marriage

**Mars** /mɑrz/ ***noun*** [sing.] the planet that is fourth in order from the sun and second nearest to the Earth ➲ adjective and noun Martian

**marsh** /mɑrʃ/ ***noun*** [C,U] an area of soft wet land ▸ **marsh·y** ***adj.***

**mar·shal** /ˈmɑrʃl/ ***noun*** [C] **1** (*U.S.*) an officer whose job is to carry out court orders: *Federal marshals brought the defendant into the courtroom.* **2** an officer of high rank in some police or fire departments: *a deputy fire marshal* **3** a military officer of high rank in some countries: *Field Marshal Montgomery of the British army*

**marsh·mal·low** /ˈmɑrʃmɛloʊ/ ***noun*** [C,U] a soft, sweet, white food that comes in small round pieces and is often used to decorate other foods

**mar·tial** /ˈmɑrʃl/ ***adj.*** (*formal*) connected with war

**ˌmartial ˈart** ***noun*** [usually pl.] a type of fighting sport, originally from Asia, in which you use your hands and feet as weapons

**ˌmartial ˈlaw** ***noun*** [U] military government of a country, especially during a war or other emergency: *The country has been under martial law for three years.* ◇ *to declare martial law*

**Mar·tian** /ˈmɑrʃn/ ***noun*** [C] (in stories) a creature that comes from the planet Mars

**ˌMartin ˌLuther ˌKing ˈJr. Day** ***noun*** [C,U] (*U.S.*) a legal holiday on the third Monday in January to celebrate the birthday of Dr. Martin Luther King, Jr., who was active in the fight to win more rights for Black Americans (**the civil rights movement**)

**mar·tyr** /ˈmɑrt̬ər/ ***noun*** [C] **1** a person who is killed because of what he/she believes **2** a person who does not do or have what he/she wants in order to help other people or to be admired by them: *Don't be such a martyr! You don't have to do all the housework.* ▸ **mar·tyr·dom** /-dəm/ ***noun*** [U]

**mar·vel¹** /ˈmɑrvl/ ***noun*** [C] a person or thing that surprises you because it is wonderful: *the marvels of modern technology*

**mar·vel²** /ˈmɑrvl/ ***verb*** [I] (*formal*) to be very surprised at how good, beautiful, etc. sb/sth is: *We marveled at how much they had been able to do in a short time.*

**mar·vel·ous** /ˈmɑrvl·əs/ ***adj.*** very good; wonderful: *Studying abroad is a marvelous opportunity to learn about another culture.* ◇ *It was marvelous to come home again after being in the hospital.* ▸ **mar·vel·ous·ly** ***adv.***

**Marx·ism** /ˈmɑrksɪzəm/ ***noun*** [U] the political and economic thought of Karl Marx, who said that important changes in history were caused by the struggle between social classes ➲ Look at **communism** and **socialism**. ▸ **Marx·ist** /ˈmɑrksɪst/ ***noun*** [C], ***adj.***: *Their president was a Marxist.* ◇ *Marxist ideology*

**mas·car·a** /mæˈskærə/ ***noun*** [U] a type of make-up that is used to make your eyelashes look darker and thicker

**mas·cot** /ˈmæskɑt/ ***noun*** [C] a person, animal or thing that is thought to bring good luck, especially as a symbol of a sports team or other organization

**mas·cu·line** /ˈmæskyələn/ ***adj.*** with the qualities that people think are typical of men

> **NOTE** In English grammar, **masculine** words refer to male people or animals: *"He" is a masculine pronoun.* In some other languages all nouns are given a gender, either **masculine**, **feminine** or **neuter**. Look also at **male** and **manly**, and at **feminine** and the note at **female**.

▸ **mas·cu·lin·i·ty** /ˌmæskyəˈlɪnət̬i/ ***noun*** [U]

**mash** /mæʃ/ ***verb*** [T] to mix or crush sth until is it soft: *mashed potatoes*

**mask¹** /mæsk/ ***noun*** [C] something that you wear that covers your face or part of your face. People wear masks in order to hide or protect their faces or to make themselves look different: *The bank robbers wore stocking masks.* ◇ *The kids wore animal masks to the party.* ➲ Look at **gas mask** and **goggles**.

**mask²** /mæsk/ ***verb*** [T] **1** to cover or hide your

M

masks

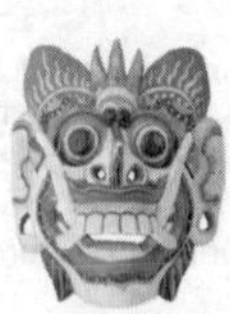

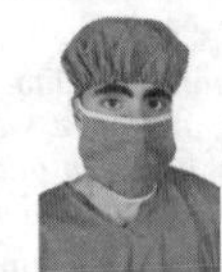

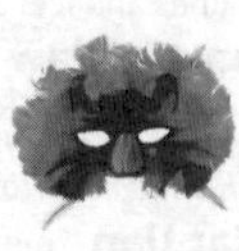

surgeon's mask

Halloween mask masquerade mask

face with a mask: *a masked gunman* **2** to hide your feelings: *He masked his anger with a smile.*

**mas·och·ism** /'mæsəkɪzəm/ **noun** [U] getting (sexual) pleasure from feeling pain ➲ Look at **sadism**. ▸ **mas·o·chist** /'mæsəkɪst/ **noun** [C] ▸ **mas·och·is·tic** /ˌmæsə'kɪstɪk/ **adj.**

**ma·son** /'meɪsn/ **noun** [C] **1** a person who makes things from stone or brick **2 Mason** (*also* **Freemason**) a man who belongs to an international secret society whose members help each other and who recognize each other by secret signs

**ma·son·ry** /'meɪsənri/ **noun** [U] the parts of a building that are made of stone or brick: *The building is old and the masonry is crumbling.*

**mas·quer·ade¹** /ˌmæskə'reɪd/ **noun** [C] a party at which people dress up to look like a different person (e.g. from history or a story): *I'm going to the masquerade ball dressed as Napoleon.* ➲ picture at **mask**.

M

**mas·quer·ade²** /ˌmæskə'reɪd/ **verb** [I] to pretend to be sb/sth: *Two people, masquerading as doctors, knocked on the door and asked to see the child.*

**Mass** (*also* **mass**) /mæs/ **noun** [C,U] the ceremony in some Christian churches, especially Roman Catholic churches, when people eat bread and drink wine in order to remember the last meal that Christ had before he died: *to go to Mass* ◇ *Fifty people attended Mass.*

★ **mass¹** /mæs/ **noun** **1** [C] a large amount or number of sth: *The garden was a mass of flowers.* ◇ *a dense mass of smoke* **2** [U] (in physics) the amount of material that sth contains; weight **3 the masses** [pl.] ordinary people when considered as a political group

★ **mass²** /mæs/ **adj.** (only *before* a noun) involving a large number of people: *a mass murderer* ◇ *a mass meeting*

**mass³** /mæs/ **verb** [I,T] to gather together in a MASS¹ (1): *The students massed in the center of campus.*

**mas·sa·cre** /'mæsəkər/ **noun** [C] the killing of a large number of people or animals ▸ **mas·sa·cre verb** [T] ➲ Look at the note at **kill**.

**mas·sage** /mə'sɑʒ/ **noun** [C,U] rubbing or pressing sb's body in order to reduce pain or to help the person move more easily: *to give sb a massage* ▸ **massage verb** [T]

★ **mas·sive** /'mæsɪv/ **adj.** very big: *a massive increase in prices*

**ˌmass 'media noun** [pl.] the means of communicating with large numbers of people, i.e. newspapers, television and radio

**ˌmass-pro'duce verb** [T] to make large numbers of similar things by machine in a factory ▸ **ˌmass pro'duction noun** [U]

**mast** /mæst/ **noun** [C] a tall wooden or metal pole for a flag, ship's sails, etc. ➲ picture at **boat**.

★ **mas·ter¹** /'mæstər/ **noun** [C] **1** a man who has people or animals in his control: *The dog ran to its master.* ➲ Look at **mistress**. **2** a person who has great skill at doing sth: *a master carpenter* ◇ *a master of disguise* ◇ *He's a master at manipulating the news media.* **3** a tape, document, etc. from which copies can be made

**mas·ter²** /'mæstər/ **verb** [T] **1** to learn how to do sth well: *It takes a long time to master a foreign language.* **2** to control sth: *to master a situation*

**ˌmaster 'key noun** [C] a key that can open many different locks, each of which can be opened by its own separate key

**mas·ter·mind** /'mæstərmaɪnd/ **noun** [C] a very clever person (who planned or organized sth) ▸ **mas·ter·mind verb** [T]: *The police failed to catch the man who masterminded the whole operation.*

**mas·ter·piece** /'mæstərpis/ **noun** [C] a work of art, music, literature, etc. that is of the highest quality

**ˌmaster 'plan noun** [C, usually sing.] a detailed plan for success in a complex operation: *It was all part of my master plan for taking over the company.*

**'master's deˌgree** (*also* **master's**) **noun** [C] a second or higher university degree. You usually get a master's degree by studying for one or two years after your first degree: *Master of Arts (M.A.)* ◇ *Master of Science (M.S.)* ◇ *She has a master's in chemistry.* ➲ For more information on the North American eductional systems, look at study pages **A8-A9**. ➲ Look at **bachelor's degree**.

**mas·ter·y** /'mæstəri/ **noun** [U] **1 mastery (of sth)** great skill at doing sth: *His mastery of the violin was exceptional for a child of his age.* **2 mastery (of/over sb/sth)** control over sb/sth: *The battle was fought for mastery of the territory near the border.*

**mas·tur·bate** /'mæstərbeɪt/ **verb** [I] to make yourself feel sexually excited by touching and rubbing your sex organs ▸ **mas·tur·ba·tion** /ˌmæstər'beɪʃn/ **noun** [U]

**mat** /mæt/ **noun** [C] a piece of thick material that you put on the floor: *a welcome mat* (= a mat in front of the door to a house, usually with the word "welcome" on it) ◇ *an exercise mat for gymnasts* ◇ *a straw mat* ➲ Look at **rug**.

★ **match¹** /mætʃ/ **noun** **1** [C] a short piece of wood or cardboard with a tip that catches fire when it is rubbed against another surface: *to light/strike a match* ◇ *a box/book of matches* **2** [C] an organized game or sports event: *a tennis/boxing match* **3** [sing.] a person or thing that is as good as or better than sb/sth else: *Carol is no match for her mother when it comes to cooking* (= she doesn't cook as well as her mother). ◇ *Jason had thought he was the best chess player in the school, but he finally met his match in Valerie* (= she could beat him). **4** [sing.] **a match (for/with sb/sth)** something that looks good with sth else, e.g. because it has the same color or pattern: *Those shoes aren't a very good* *match with your dress.* ◇ (*figurative*) *Bill and Sue are a good match. They should be very happy together.*

★**match**[2] /mætʃ/ ***verb*** **1** [I,T] to have the same color or pattern as sth else, or to look nice with sth else: *That blouse doesn't match your skirt.* ◇ *We've chosen the curtains, but now we need a carpet to match.* **2** [T] to find sb/sth that is like or suitable for sb/sth else: *The agency tries to match single people with suitable partners.* **3** [T] to be as good as or better than sb/sth else: *The two teams are very evenly matched.* ◇ *Taiwan produces the goods at a price that the U.S. cannot match.*

PHR V **match up** to be the same: *The statements of the two witnesses don't match up.*

**match sth up (with sth)** to fit or put sth together (with sth else): *What you have to do is match up each celebrity with his or her pet.*

**match·book** /ˈmætʃbʊk/ ***noun*** [C] a small container made of folded paper, with matches attached inside

**match·box** /ˈmætʃbɑks/ ***noun*** [C] a small box for matches

**match·stick** /ˈmætʃstɪk/ ***noun*** [C] the thin wooden part of a match

★**mate**[1] /meɪt/ ***noun*** **1** [C] (especially in compounds) a friend or sb you live or work with: *a roommate* (= sb with whom you share a house an apartment, or a room) ◇ *a classmate* ➲ Look at **running mate**. **2** [C] one of a male and female pair of animals, birds, etc.: *The female sits on the eggs while her mate hunts for food.* **3** [C] an officer on a ship: *the captain and his first mate* **4** [U] = CHECKMATE

★**mate**[2] /meɪt/ ***verb*** **1** [I] (used about animals and birds) to have sex and produce young: *Pandas rarely mate in zoos.* **2** [T] to bring two animals together so that they can have sex and produce young

★**ma·te·ri·al**[1] /məˈtɪriəl/ ***noun*** **1** [C,U] a substance that can be used for making or doing sth: *Many African countries export raw materials* (= natural substances that are used to make things in factories, etc.). ◇ *writing materials* (= pens, paper, etc.) **2** [C,U] cloth (for making clothes, etc.): *Is there enough material for a dress?* **3** [U] facts or information that you collect before you write a book, article, etc.

**ma·te·ri·al**[2] /məˈtɪriəl/ ***adj.*** **1** connected with real or physical things rather than the spirit or emotions: *We should not value material comforts too highly.* ➲ Look at **spiritual**. **2** important: *material evidence* ➲ Compare **immaterial**.

**ma·te·ri·al·ism** /məˈtɪriəlɪzəm/ ***noun*** [U] the belief that money and possessions are the most important things in life ▸ **ma·te·ri·al·ist** /məˈtɪriəlɪst/ ***noun*** [C] ▸ **ma·te·ri·al·is·tic** /məˌtɪriəˈlɪstɪk/ ***adj.***

**ma·te·ri·al·ize** /məˈtɪriəlaɪz/ ***verb*** [I] to become real; to happen: *The pay raise that they had promised never materialized.*

**ma·ter·nal** /məˈtərnl/ ***adj.*** **1** of or like a mother: *maternal love* **2** related through your mother's side of the family: *your maternal grandfather* ➲ Look at **paternal**.

**ma·ter·ni·ty** /məˈtərnət̮i/ ***adj.*** connected with women who are going to have or have just had a baby: *maternity clothes* ◇ *Our manager had her baby at the end of June, so she's on maternity leave until September.*

**math** /mæθ/ (*also formal* **mathematics**) ***noun*** [U] the science or study of numbers, quantities or shapes: *Math is my favorite subject.* ◇ *math teachers*

**math·e·ma·ti·cian** /ˌmæθməˈtɪʃn/ ***noun*** [C] a person who studies or is an expert in mathematics

**math·e·mat·ics** /ˌmæθˈmæt̮ɪks/ ***noun*** [U] (*formal*) = MATH ▸ **math·e·mat·i·cal** /ˌmæθˈmæt̮ɪkl/ ***adj.*** ▸ **math·e·mat·i·cal·ly** /-kli/ ***adv.***: *It is now mathematically impossible for him to win.*

**mat·i·nee** /ˌmætn̩ˈeɪ/ ***noun*** [C] an afternoon performance of a play, movie, etc.

**mat·ri·mo·ny** /ˈmætrəmoʊni/ ***noun*** [U] (*formal*) the state of being married ▸ **mat·ri·mo·ni·al** /ˌmætrəˈmoʊniəl/ ***adj.***

**ma·tron** /ˈmeɪtrən/ ***noun*** [C] an older married woman or widow, usually from a high social class: *wealthy society matrons*

**ma·tron·ly** /ˈmeɪtrənli/ ***adj.*** (a polite word used about an older woman) fat: *a matronly figure*

ˌ**matron of ˈhonor** ***noun*** [C] (*pl.* **matrons of honor**) in a wedding ceremony, the married woman who helps the bride (usually her best friend or a close family member) ➲ Look at the note at **wedding**.

**matte** /mæt/ ***adj.*** not shiny: *This paint gives a matte finish.* ➲ Look at **glossy**.

**mat·ted** /ˈmæt̮əd/ ***adj.*** (used especially about hair or fur) forming a thick mass, especially because it is wet and/or dirty

★**mat·ter**[1] /ˈmæt̮ər/ ***noun*** **1** [C] a subject or situation that you must think about and give your attention to: *It's a personal matter and I don't want to discuss it with you.* ◇ *They should try to settle matters between themselves before going to court.* ◇ *to simplify/complicate matters* **2** [U] all physical substances; a substance of a particular kind: *waste matter* **3** [sing.] **the matter (with sb/sth)** the reason for unhappiness, pain, problems, etc.: *She looks sad. **What's the matter** with her?* ◇ *Eat your dinner! There's **nothing the matter** with it.* **4** [U] the contents of a book, film, etc.: *I don't think the subject matter of this program is appropriate for children.* ◇ *reading matter*

IDM **as a matter of fact** to tell the truth; in reality: *I like him very much, as a matter of fact.*

**for that matter** in addition; as well: *Mick is fed up with his classes. I am too, for that matter.*

**make matters/things worse** → WORSE[1]

**a matter of opinion** a subject on which people do not agree: *"I think the principle is doing a good job." "That's a matter of opinion."*

**a matter of sth/doing sth** something that needs or requires sth: *Learning a language is largely a matter of practice.*

**no matter who, what, where, etc.** whoever, whatever, wherever, etc.: *They never listen no matter what you say.*

★**mat·ter**[2] /ˈmæt̮ər/ ***verb*** [I] to be important: *It doesn't really matter how much it costs.* ◇ *Does it matter if we're a little late?* ◇ *What matters most is giving the kids a good start in life.*



M

NOTE **Matter** is often used in negative sentences, questions and sentences containing *what, who, when, if,* etc. It is not used in the *-ing* forms.

ˌ**matter-of-ˈfact** *adj.* said or done without showing any emotion, especially when it would seem more normal to express your feelings: *He was very matter-of-fact about his illness.*

**mat·tress** /ˈmætrəs/ *noun* [C] a large soft thing that you lie on to sleep, usually on a bed ➲ picture at **bed**[1].

**ma·ture**[1] /məˈtʃʊr; -ˈtʊr/ *adj.* **1** fully grown or fully developed: *a mature tree/bird/animal* **2** behaving in a sensible adult way: *Is she mature enough to stay home alone this weekend?* OPP **immature** ▸ **ma·tur·i·ty** /məˈtʃʊrət̬i; -ˈtʊr-/ *noun* [U]

**ma·ture**[2] /məˈtʃʊr; -ˈtʊr/ *verb* [I] to become mature: *He matured a lot during his four years at university.*

**mat·zo** (*also* **mat·zoh, mat·zah**) /ˈmɑtsə/ (*pl.* **mat·zos**) *noun* [C,U] a type of flat bread eaten especially by Jewish people: *There are only a few matzos left in the box.* ◇ *Can you put the matzoh on the table?*

**maul** /mɔl/ *verb* [T] (usually used about a wild animal) to attack and injure sb

**mauve** /moʊv/ *adj., noun* [U] pinkish purple

M

**mav·er·ick** /ˈmævərɪk/ *noun* [C] **1** a person with independent or unusual views: *a political maverick* **2** a young animal, especially a cow, that has become separated from its mother and does not have its owner's mark (a **brand**) on it

**max** /mæks/ *noun* [sing.] (*informal*) = MAXIMUM: *I can fit six people in my car – that's the absolute max.* ▸ **max** *adv.*: *I can afford to pay $600 a month max.*

**max·im** /ˈmæksəm/ *noun* [C] a few words that express a rule for good or sensible behavior: *Their maxim is: "If a job's worth doing, it's worth doing well."*

**max·i·mize** /ˈmæksəmaɪz/ *verb* [T] to increase sth as much as possible: *to maximize profits* ◇ *Maximize the window to full screen.* OPP **minimize**

★**max·i·mum** /ˈmæksəməm/ *noun* [sing.] (*abbr.* **max**) the greatest amount or level of sth that is possible, allowed, recorded, etc.: *The bus can carry a maximum of 40 people.* ◇ *$500 is the maximum we can afford.* OPP **minimum** ▸ **max·i·mum** *adj.* (only *before* a noun): *a maximum speed of 120 miles per hour* ◇ *a maximum security prison*

★**May** /meɪ/ *noun* [C,U] the fifth month of the year, coming before June ➲ For examples of the use of the months in sentences, look at **January**.

★**may** /meɪ/ *modal verb* (*negative* **may not**) **1** (*formal*) (used for saying that sth is possible): *You may be right.* ◇ *They may have forgotten the meeting.* ◇ *He may have been driving too fast.* ➲ Look at **might**[1](2). **2** (*formal*) (used as a polite way of asking for and giving permission): *May I use your phone?* ◇ *You may only borrow books for two weeks.* ➲ It is more common to say **can**. **3** (used in the negative as a way of forbidding sb to do sth): *You may not take photographs in the museum.* **4** (used for contrasting two facts): *He may be smart, but he can't do anything practical.* **5** (*formal*) (used for expressing wishes and hopes): *May God be with you.*

IDM **may/might as well (do sth)** → WELL[1]

★**may·be** /ˈmeɪbi/ *adv.* perhaps; possibly: *"Are you going to come?" "Maybe."* ◇ *There were three, maybe four armed men.* ◇ *Maybe I'll go to the party and maybe I won't.* ➲ Look at the note at **perhaps**.

ˈ**May Day** *noun* [C] May 1st

NOTE **May Day** is traditionally celebrated as a spring festival and in some countries it is also a day for socialist groups to hold meetings and demonstrations.

**may·on·naise** /ˌmeɪəˈneɪz; ˈmeɪəneɪz/ (*also informal* **mayo** /ˈmeɪoʊ/) *noun* [U] a thick white sauce made with eggs and oil, often eaten in sandwiches

**may·or** /ˈmeɪər/ *noun* [C] a person who is elected to be the leader of the group of people (a **council**) who manage the affairs of a town or city

**maze** /meɪz/ *noun* [C] **1** a complicated pattern of paths, in which it is difficult to find your way: *a maze of winding streets* **2** a puzzle in which you draw a line through a complex group of lines without touching any of them

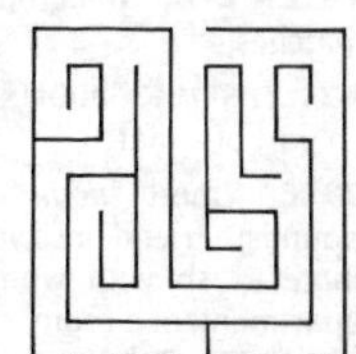

**MB** (*also* **Mb**) = MEGABYTE

**M.B.A.** /ˌɛm bi ˈeɪ/ *abbr.* Master of Business Administration; an advanced degree for people who study how to run a business

**M.D.** /ˌɛm ˈdi/ *abbr.* Doctor of Medicine

★**me** /mi/ *pronoun* (used as an object or after the verb *be*) the person who is speaking or writing: *He called me yesterday.* ◇ *She wrote to me last week.* ◇ *"Somebody spilled the wine." "Sorry, it was me."* ◇ *"Who's this picture of?" "Me."*

NOTE **It is/was me** is much more common than **it is/was I**, although this can be used in formal speech or writing.

**mead·ow** /ˈmɛdoʊ/ *noun* [C] a field of grass: *sheep grazing in a meadow*

**mea·ger** /ˈmigər/ *adj.* too small in amount: *a meager income* ◇ *The refugees carried their meager belongings across the border.*

★**meal** /mil/ *noun* [C] a certain time when you eat or the food that is eaten at that time: *Do you have your main meal at lunchtime or in the evening?* ◇ *a heavy/light meal*

NOTE The main meals of the day are **breakfast**, **lunch** and **dinner**. **Brunch** is a meal that people often eat late in the morning on weekends, instead of breakfast and lunch. **Supper** is usually a smaller meal (but look at the note at **dinner**). A very small meal is called a **snack**.

**meal·time** /ˈmiltaɪm/ *noun* [C] a time at which a meal is usually eaten

★**mean**[1] /min/ *verb* [T] (*pt, pp* **meant** /mɛnt/) ➤ HAVE AS MEANING **1** (not used in the *-ing* forms) to express, show or have as a meaning: *What does this* *word mean?* ◇ *The bell means that class is over.* ◇ *"What does that symbol mean?"* ◇ *Does the name "Charles Bell" mean anything to you?*

➤INTEND AS MEANING **2** to want or intend to say sth; to refer to sb/sth: *I don't understand what you mean.* ◇ *She said "yes," but I think she really meant "no."* ◇ *What do you mean by "a lot of money?"*

> NOTE Note that **mean** cannot be used with the meaning "to have the opinion that." We say: *I think (that)...* or *In my opinion...*: *I think she'd be silly to buy that car.* **I mean** is often used in conversation when you want to explain something you have just said or to add more information: *I think I'm falling in love with Rick – I mean, he's so cute!* ◇ *I could hear their conversation – I mean, they were standing right next to me.* **I mean** is also used to correct something you have just said: *We went there on Tuesday, I mean Thursday.*

➤BE IMPORTANT **3** (not used in the *-ing* forms) to be important to sb: *This job means a lot to me.*

➤HAVE AS RESULT **4** (not used in the *-ing* forms) to make sth likely; to cause: *The shortage of teachers means that classes are larger.* ◇ *The new law means higher taxes for businesses.*

➤PURPOSE/INTENTION **5** (not used in the *-ing* forms) to be serious or sincere about sth: *He said he loved me, but I don't think he meant it!* **6** to want or plan to do sth; to intend sth: *I'm sure she didn't mean to upset you.* ◇ *They didn't mean any harm.* ◇ *I didn't mean you to cook the whole meal!* **7** (usually passive) to intend or expect sth to be or do sth: *It was only meant as a joke.* ◇ *What's this picture meant to be?* ◇ *This dessert is meant to be served chilled.*

IDM **mean well** to want to be kind and helpful but usually without success: *My mother means well, but I wish she'd stop treating me like a child.*

**mean²** /min/ ***adj.*** **1 mean (to sb)** (used about people or their behavior) unkind; not nice: *It was mean of him not to invite you, too.* ◇ *Don't be mean to your little sister!* **2** (only *before* a noun) average: *What is the mean annual temperature in California?*

**mean³** /min/ ***noun*** [C] (*technical*) average

**me·an·der** /mi'ændər/ ***verb*** [I] **1** (used about a river, road, etc.) to have a lot of curves and bends **2** (used about a person or animal) to walk or travel slowly or without any definite direction

★**mean·ing** /'minɪŋ/ ***noun*** **1** [C,U] what sth means or expresses; its sense or intention: *This word has two different meanings in English.* ◇ *What do you think is the meaning of the last line of the poem?* **2** [U] purpose or importance: *With his daughter dead, there seemed to be no meaning in life.*

**mean·ing·ful** /'minɪŋfl/ ***adj.*** **1** useful, important or interesting: *Most people need a meaningful relationship with another person.* **2** (used about a look, expression, etc.) trying to express a certain feeling or idea: *They kept giving each other meaningful glances across the table.* ▶ **mean·ing·ful·ly** ***adv.***

**mean·ing·less** /'minɪŋləs/ ***adj.*** without meaning, reason or sense: *The figures are meaningless if we have nothing to compare them with.*

★**means** /minz/ ***noun*** (*pl.* **means**) **1** [C, with sing. or pl. verb] a method of doing sth: *buses, cars, and other means of transportation* ◇ *Is there any means of contacting your husband?* **2** [pl.] (*formal*) money or wealth: *a family of modest means*

IDM **a means to an end** an action or thing that is not important in itself but is a way of achieving sth else: *I don't like my job very much, but it's a means to an end.*

**by means of** by using: *We got out of the hotel by means of the fire escape.*

**by no means; not by any means** (*formal*) (used for emphasis) not at all: *I'm by no means sure that this is the right thing to do.*

**meant** /mɛnt/ *past tense, past participle of* MEAN¹

**mean·time** /'mintaɪm/ ***noun***

IDM **in the meantime** in the time between two things happening: *Our new house isn't finished yet, so in the meantime we're living with my mother.*

★**mean·while** /'minwaɪl/ ***adv.*** during the same time or during the time between two things happening: *Peter was at home studying. Tony, meanwhile, was out with his friends.* ◇ *The new computer will arrive next week. Meanwhile you'll have to manage without one.*

**mea·sles** /'mizlz/ ***noun*** [U] (*also* **the measles**) a common infectious disease, especially among children. You have a fever and your skin is covered in small red spots.

> NOTE **Measles** looks like a plural noun, but it is used with a singular verb: *In many countries, measles is a very dangerous disease.*

**mea·sly** /'mizli/ ***adj.*** (*informal*) much too small in size, amount or value: *He paid me a measly three bucks to mow his lawn.*

★**meas·ure¹** /'mɛʒər/ ***verb*** **1** [I,T] to find the size, weight, etc. of sb/sth often by using an instrument such as a ruler: *Could you measure the table to see if it will fit into our dining room?* ◇ *Height is measured in feet and inches.* ◇ *Most countries use the metric system for measuring.* **2** [T] to be a certain height, width, length, etc.: *The pool measures 25 meters by 5 meters.* **3** [T] to show or judge the size, amount, etc. of sth: *A speedometer measures speed.* ◇ (*figurative*) *How do you measure a person's success?*

PHR V **measure up (to sth)** to be as good as you need to be or as sb expects you to be: *Did the trip measure up to your expectations?*

★**meas·ure²** /'mɛʒər/ ***noun*** **1** [C] a way of describing the size, amount, etc. of sth: *A yard is a measure of length.* **2** [sing.] (*formal*) a certain amount or quantity; some but not much: *The play achieved a measure of success.* **3** [sing.] a way of understanding or judging sth: *The school's popularity is a measure of the teachers' success.* **4** [C, usually pl.] an action that is done for a special reason: *The government is taking new measures to reduce inflation.* ◇ *As a temporary measure, the road will have to be closed.* ◇ *emergency measures* ◇ *safety measures*

★**meas·ure·ment** /'mɛʒərmənt/ ***noun*** **1** [C] a size, amount, etc. that is found by measuring: *What are the exact measurements of the room?* (= how wide/long is it?) ◇ *What's your waist measurement?* ◇ *Let's start by taking your measurements* (= measuring the size of your chest, waist and other parts of the body). **2** [U] the act of measuring: *I'm not sure how accurate his measurement of the area was.*

M

**'measuring cup** *noun* [C] a glass, plastic or metal container with marks on it used for measuring food

★**meat** /mit/ *noun* [U] the flesh of animals or birds that people eat: *She doesn't eat meat – she's a vegetarian.*

NOTE Some types of meat have different names from the animals they come from. We get **pork**, **ham** or **bacon** from a pig, **beef** from a cow, **veal** from a calf and **venison** from a deer. **Mutton** comes from a sheep, but we get **lamb** from a lamb. For specific types of birds and fish there is not a different word, but the meat from birds in general is called **poultry**. We often call beef, mutton and lamb **red meat**. We can **fry**, **grill**, **broil**, **roast** or **stew** meat. We **carve** a turkey, for example, or **slice** a ham or a **roast**. Meat can be described as **tough** or **tender**, **lean** or **fatty**. Uncooked meat is **raw**.

**meat·ball** /'mitbɔl/ *noun* [C] a thick ball made of meat that has been cut (**ground**) into very small pieces: *spaghetti and meatballs*

**meat·loaf** /'mitloʊf/ *noun* a mixture of meat that has been cut into very small pieces (**ground**) and bread, eggs, salt and other things to give it flavor, formed into a rectangular shape and baked

M

**Mec·ca** /'mɛkə/ *noun* **1** the city in Saudi Arabia where Muhammad was born, which is the center of Islam **2** [C, usually sing.] **mecca** a place that many people wish to visit because of a particular interest: *Italy is a mecca for art lovers.*

**me·chan·ic** /mə'kænɪk/ *noun* [C] a person whose job is to repair and work with machines and tools: *a car mechanic*

**me·chan·i·cal** /mə'kænɪkl/ *adj.* **1** connected with, worked by or produced by machines: *a mechanical pump* ◇ *mechanical engineering* ◇ *a mechanical mind* (= a mind that understands machines) **2** (used about a person's behavior) done like a machine as if you are not thinking about what you are doing: *He played the piano in a dull and mechanical way.* ▸ **me·chan·i·cal·ly** /-kli/ *adv.*

**me·chan·ics** /mə'kænɪks/ *noun* **1 the mechanics** [pl.] the way in which sth works or is done: *Don't ask me – I don't understand the mechanics of the legal system.* **2** [U] the science of how machines work

**mech·a·nism** /'mɛkənɪzəm/ *noun* [C] **1** a part of a piece of equipment or a machine that does a certain task: *Our car has an automatic locking mechanism.* **2** the way in which sth works or the process by which sth is done: *the mechanism of the heart* ◇ *The new committee will provide a mechanism for investigating complaints.*

**mech·a·nize** /'mɛkənaɪz/ *verb* [I,T] to use machines instead of people to do work: *We have mechanized the entire production process.* ▸ **mech·a·ni·za·tion** /ˌmɛkənə'zeɪʃn/ *noun* [U]: *Increased mechanization has led to unemployment.*

**med** /mɛd/ (*informal*) = MEDICAL: *She's in med school.* ◇ *a med student*

**med·al** /'mɛdl/ *noun* [C] a flat piece of metal, usually with a design and words on it, which is given to sb for bravery or as a prize in a sports event: *He was awarded a medal for bravery.* ◇ *to win a gold/silver/bronze medal in the Olympics*

**med·al·ist** /'mɛdəlɪst/ *noun* [C] a person who has won a medal, especially in a sport: *an Olympic gold medalist*

**me·dal·lion** /mə'dælyən/ *noun* [C] a small round piece of metal on a chain which is worn as jewelry around the neck

**med·dle** /'mɛdl/ *verb* [I] **meddle (in/with sth)** to take too much interest in sth that you should not: *She criticized her mother for meddling in her personal life.*

★**me·di·a** /'midiə/ *noun* [pl.] **the media** television, radio and newspapers used as a means of communication: *The reports in the media have been greatly exaggerated.*

NOTE Sometimes **media** is used with a singular verb, although it is a plural noun: *The media always take/takes a great interest in Hollywood stars' lives.* ➲ Look also at **mass media** and **the press**.

**me·di·an** /'midiən/ (*also* **ˌmedian 'strip**) *noun* [C] a narrow strip of land that separates the traffic moving in different directions on a large road or highway

**me·di·ate** /'midieɪt/ *verb* [I,T] to try to settle a disagreement between two or more people or groups: *As a supervisor, she had to mediate between her colleagues and the management.* ▸ **me·di·a·tion** /ˌmidi'eɪʃn/ *noun* [U] ▸ **me·di·a·tor** *noun* [C]

**Med·i·caid** (*also* **medicaid**) /'mɛdɪkeɪd/ *noun* [U] the system that provides medical care for poor people in the U.S. and that is paid for by taxes

★**med·i·cal** /'mɛdɪkl/ *adj.* connected with medicine and the treatment or prevention of illness: *a medical school/student* ◇ *Have you had any medical treatment during the last three years?* ◇ *medical research*

**'medical exˌaminer** *noun* [C] an official person, usually a doctor, whose job is to examine a dead body in order to find out how the person died

**Med·i·care** (*also* **medicare**) /'mɛdɪkɛr/ *noun* [U] **1 Medicare** (in the U.S.) the system that provides medical care for old people and that is paid for by taxes **2 medicare** (in Canada) a national health care program for all people that is paid for by taxes

**med·i·cat·ed** /'mɛdɪkeɪṭəd/ *adj.* containing a substance like a medicine: *medicated shampoo*

**med·i·ca·tion** /ˌmɛdɪ'keɪʃn/ *noun* [C,U] pills, liquids, etc. that you take in order to treat an illness: *Are you currently taking any medication?* ◇ *Many flu medications are available without a prescription.*

**me·dic·i·nal** /mə'dɪsənl/ *adj.* **1** useful for curing illness or infection: *medicinal plants* **2** like medicine: *a medicinal taste*

★**med·i·cine** /'mɛdɪsn/ *noun* **1** [U] the science of preventing and treating illness: *to study/practice medicine* **2** [C,U] pills, liquids, etc. that you take in order to treat an illness: *Medicines should be kept out of the reach of children.* ◇ *to take medicine* ◇ *Did the doctor prescribe any medicine?* ◇ *cough medicine*

**me·di·e·val** /ˌmɛd'ivl; ˌmɪd-; ˌmid-/ *adj.* of the Middle Ages in European history; i.e. between about 1100 and 1500 AD: *medieval art*

**me·di·o·cre** /ˌmidiˈoʊkər/ ***adj.*** of not very high quality: *a mediocre performance* ▶ **me·di·oc·ri·ty** /ˌmidiˈɑkrət̬i/ ***noun*** [U]

**med·i·tate** /ˈmɛdəteɪt/ ***verb*** [I] **1** to think carefully and deeply (about sth): *I've been meditating on what you said last week.* **2** to spend time thinking deeply in a special way so that you become calm and peaceful, often as part of religious training ▶ **med·i·ta·tion** /ˌmɛdəˈteɪʃn/ ***noun*** [U]: *Meditation is practiced by certain Eastern religions.*

**the Med·i·ter·ra·ne·an** /ˌmɛdətəˈreɪmiən/ ***noun*** [sing.] the Mediterranean Sea or the countries around it ➲ Look at the note at **White House**. ▶ **Med·i·ter·ra·ne·an** ***adj.***: *Mediterranean cuisine*

★**me·di·um**[1] /ˈmidiəm/ ***noun*** [C] **1** (*pl.* usually **me·di·a**) a means you can use to express or communicate sth: *Many actors feel that the theater is a more rewarding medium than television.* ◇ *He tried to keep the story out of the media* (= television, radio and newspapers). ➲ Look at **media** and **mass media**. **2** (*pl.* **me·di·ums**) a person who says that he/she can speak to and take messages from the spirits of dead people

★**me·di·um**[2] /ˈmidiəm/ ***adj.*** of a size or amount that is neither very large nor very small; average: *She was of medium height and weight.* ◇ *Would you like a small, medium or large drink?* ◇ *a medium-sized dog*

**med·ley** /ˈmɛdli/ ***noun*** [C] **1** a piece of music consisting of several tunes or songs played one after the other without a break **2** a mixture of different things: *a medley of styles/flavors*

**meek** /mik/ ***adj.*** (used about people) quiet, and doing what other people say without asking questions or arguing: *a meek and humble servant* ▶ **meek·ly** ***adv.*** ▶ **meek·ness** ***noun*** [U]

★**meet** /mit/ ***verb*** (*pt, pp* **met** /mɛt/)
➤BY CHANCE/BY ARRANGEMENT **1** [I,T] to come together by chance or because you have arranged it: *You'll never guess who I met today!* ◇ *What time should we meet for lunch?*
➤FOR THE FIRST TIME **2** [I,T] to see and know sb for the first time: *Have you two met before?* ◇ *Where did you first meet your husband?*
➤WAIT FOR SB **3** [T] to go to a place and wait for sb/sth to arrive: *I'll come and meet you at the bus station.* ◇ *A limousine will meet your plane and take you to your hotel.*
➤HAVE A MEETING **4** [I] (used about a group of people) to come together for a special purpose: *Representatives from both countries will meet for talks in New York.* ◇ *How often does the city council meet?*
➤SATISFY **5** [T] to be enough for sth; to be able to deal with sth: *The money that I earn is enough to meet our basic needs.* ◇ *I'm afraid this piece of work doesn't meet our requirements* (= it's not good enough). ◇ *This year is going to be difficult, but I'm sure that we can meet the challenge.*
➤TOUCH/JOIN **6** [I,T] to touch, join or make contact with: *The rivers meet in St. Louis.* ◇ *Can you see where the road meets the freeway on the map?* ◇ *His eyes met hers.*
IDM **make ends meet** → END[1]
**there is more to sb/sth than meets the eye** sb/sth is more interesting or complex than you might think at first: *Do you think there's more to their relationship than meets the eye?*
PHRV **meet up (with sb)** to meet sb, especially after first going in different directions or doing different things: *Let's both do our own shopping and meet up with each other for coffee.*
**meet with sb** to meet sb, especially for discussion: *I met with my financial advisor.*
**meet with sth** to get a certain answer, reaction or result: *The mayor's proposal met with a great deal of resistance.*

★**meet·ing** /ˈmit̬ɪŋ/ ***noun*** [C] an organized occasion when a number of people come together in order to discuss or decide sth: *The next committee meeting will be held on August 19.* ◇ *What's on the agenda for the department meeting?* ◇ *to attend a meeting*

NOTE We **call**, **set up**, **arrange** or **organize** a meeting. We can also **cancel** or **postpone** a meeting.

**mega-** /ˈmɛgə/ ***prefix*** (in compounds) **1** a million: *a power plant with a capacity of 600 megawatts* **2** (*informal*) very large or great: *I bet she's making megabucks in her new job.*

**meg·a·byte** /ˈmɛgəbaɪt/ (*also informal* **meg**) ***noun*** [C] (*abbr.* **MB**) (*computing*) a unit of computer memory, equal to $2^{20}$ (= or about 1 million) bytes: *a 250-megabyte hard drive*

**meg·a·phone** /ˈmɛgəfoʊn/ ***noun*** [C] a piece of equipment that you speak through to make your voice sound louder, especially outside

**mel·an·chol·y** /ˈmɛlənkɑli/ ***noun*** [U] (*formal*) a feeling of sadness that lasts for a long time ▶ **mel·an·chol·y** ***adj.***

**mel·low** /ˈmɛloʊ/ ***adj.*** **1** (used about colors, flavors or sounds) soft and pleasant **2** (*informal*) (used about people) calm and relaxed, especially because of age ▶ **mel·low** ***verb*** [I,T]: *Experience had mellowed her views about many things.*

**mel·o·dra·ma** /ˈmɛlədrɑmə/ ***noun*** [C,U] a type of play or novel in which a lot of exciting things happen and in which people's emotions are stronger than in real life

**mel·o·dra·mat·ic** /ˌmɛlədrəˈmæt̬ɪk/ ***adj.*** (used about a person's behavior) making things seem more exciting and serious than they really are

**mel·o·dy** /ˈmɛlədi/ ***noun*** [C] (*pl.* **mel·o·dies**) **1** a song or tune: *to play a melody* **2** the main tune in a piece of music that is played by several instruments or sung by several voices: *The tenors have the melody here.*

**mel·on** /ˈmɛlən/ ***noun*** [C,U] a large round fruit with a thick yellow or green skin and many seeds: *a slice of melon* ➲ Look at **watermelon** and **cantaloupe**.

★**melt** /mɛlt/ ***verb*** **1** [I,T] to change from solid to liquid by means of heat: *When we got up in the morning the snow had melted.* ◇ *First melt the butter in a saucepan.* **2** [I] (used about sb's feelings, etc.) to become softer or less strong: *My heart melted when I saw the tiny puppy.*
PHRV **melt away** to disappear: *The crowd melted away when the speaker had finished.*
**melt sth down** to heat a metal or glass object until it becomes soft

**melt·down** /ˈmɛltdaʊn/ ***noun*** [C,U] a serious accident in which the central part of a nuclear power

M

plant (a reactor) becomes much too hot, causing the release of a dangerous form of energy (radiation)

ˈ**melting pot** *noun* [C] a place where large numbers of people from different countries live together: *New York is a melting pot of different nationalities.*

★**mem·ber** /ˈmɛmbər/ *noun* [C] a person, animal or thing that belongs to a group, club, organization, etc.: *All the members of the family were there.* ◇ *a staff member* ◇ *a member of Parliament*

ˌ**Member of ˈParliament** *noun* [C] = MP

★**mem·ber·ship** /ˈmɛmbərʃɪp/ *noun* **1** [U] the state of being a member of a group, organization, etc.: *To apply for membership, please complete the enclosed form.* ◇ *Annual membership costs $200.* **2** [C,U] the people who belong to a group, organization, etc.: *Membership* (= the number of members) *has fallen in the past year.*

**mem·brane** /ˈmɛmbreɪn/ *noun* [C] (*formal*) a thin skin which covers or connects parts inside a person's or an animal's body

**me·men·to** /məˈmɛntoʊ/ *noun* [C] (*pl.* **me·men·tos** or **me·men·toes**) something that you keep to remind you of a person, a place or of sth that has happened

**mem·o** /ˈmɛmoʊ/ *noun* [C] (*pl.* **mem·os**) (*also formal* **memorandum**) a note sent from one person or office to another within an organization

**mem·oirs** /ˈmɛmwɑrz/ *noun* [pl.] a person's written account of his/her own life and experiences

**mem·o·ra·bil·i·a** /ˌmɛmərəˈbɪliə; -biliə/ *noun* [U] things that people buy because they are connected with a famous person, event, etc.: *Beatles/Titanic/war memorabilia*

**mem·o·ra·ble** /ˈmɛmrəbl/ *adj.* worth remembering or easy to remember because it is special in some way: *The concert was a memorable experience.* ▸ **mem·o·ra·bly** /-bli/ *adv.*

**mem·o·ran·dum** /ˌmɛməˈrændəm/ *noun* [C] (*pl.* **mem·o·ran·da** /-də/ or **mem·o·ran·dums**) (*formal*) = MEMO

**me·mo·ri·al** /məˈmɔriəl/ *noun* [C] **memorial (to sb/sth)** something that is built or done to remind people of an event or a person: *a war memorial* (= a statue or cross) ◇ *a memorial service*

**Meˈmorial Day** *noun* [C] a holiday in the U.S. on the last Monday in May, for remembering soldiers who died in war

**mem·o·rize** /ˈmɛməraɪz/ *verb* [T] to learn sth so that you can remember it exactly: *Actors have to memorize their lines.*

★**mem·o·ry** /ˈmɛməri/ *noun* (*pl.* **mem·o·ries**) **1** [C] a person's ability to remember things: *a good/bad memory* ◇ *A teacher needs to have a good memory for names.* **2** [C,U] the part of your mind in which you store things that you remember: *That day remained firmly in my memory for the rest of my life.* ◇ *The appointment completely slipped my memory* (= I forgot it). ◇ *He recited the whole poem from memory.* **3** [C] something that you remember: *That is one of my happiest memories.* ◇ *I have no memories of that time at all.* ◇ *childhood memories* **4** [U] the part of a computer where information is stored so that it can be changed or removed: *This computer has 512 MB of memory.* ➲ Look at **RAM**.

IDM **in memory of sb/to the memory of sb** in order to remind people of sb who has died: *A service was held in memory of the dead.*

**refresh your/sb's memory** → REFRESH

**men** *plural of* MAN[1]

**men·ace**[1] /ˈmɛnəs/ *noun* **1** [C] a danger or threat: *The escaped prisoner is a menace to public safety.* **2** [U] a quality, feeling, etc. that is threatening or frightening: *He spoke with menace in his voice.*

**men·ace**[2] /ˈmɛnəs/ *verb* [T] to be likely to hurt sb/sth; to threaten

**men·ac·ing** /ˈmɛnəsɪŋ/ *adj.* threatening or frightening

**mend**[1] /mɛnd/ *verb* [T] to repair a hole in a piece of clothing: *to mend a sock* ◇ (*figurative*) *The management tried to mend relations with the unions.*

IDM **mend fences (with sb)** (especially in politics) to improve relations with sb after an argument: *The governor hopes to mend fences with the opposing party.*

**mend**[2] /mɛnd/ *noun*

IDM **on the mend** to be getting better after an illness or injury; to be recovering: *She's been in bed for a week, but she's on the mend now.*

**me·ni·al** /ˈminiəl/ *adj.* (used about work) not skilled or important: *a menial job*

**men·in·gi·tis** /ˌmɛnənˈdʒaɪt̬əs/ *noun* [U] a serious illness which affects the brain and the spine

**men·o·pause** /ˈmɛnəpɔz/ *noun* [U] the time when a woman stops losing blood once a month (menstruating). This usually happens around the age of 50.

**me·no·rah** /məˈnɔrə/ *noun* [C] a traditional Jewish object to hold seven or nine candles

ˈ**men's room** *noun* [C, usually sing.] a room with toilets in it for men in a public building: *go to the men's room* ➲ Look at **ladies' room**, **restroom** and at the note at **toilet**.

**men·stru·ate** /ˈmɛnstrueɪt; -streɪt/ *verb* [I] (*formal*) to lose blood from the uterus about once a month SYN (*informal*) **have your period** ▸ **men·stru·al** /ˈmɛnstruəl; -strəl/ *adj.* ▸ **men·stru·a·tion** /ˌmɛnstruˈeɪʃn; -ˈstreɪʃn/ *noun* [U]

★**men·tal** /ˈmɛntl/ *adj.* (only *before* a noun) **1** of or in the mind: *He has the mental capacity of a 7-year-old.* ◇ *I'm not very good at mental arithmetic.* ◇ *mental health* **2** connected with illness of the mind: *a mental hospital* ▸ **men·tal·ly** /ˈmɛntəli/ *adv.*: *a home for mentally ill people*

**men·tal·i·ty** /mɛnˈtælət̬i/ *noun* [C] (*pl.* **men·tal·i·ties**) a type of mind or way of thinking: *Grandma says that kids today have a herd mentality – nobody wants to be independent.* ◇ *the criminal mentality*

★**men·tion**[1] /ˈmɛnʃn/ *verb* [T] to say or write sth about sb/sth; to talk about sb/sth: *I wouldn't mention her exams to her – she's feeling nervous.* ◇ *Did she mention what time the movie starts?* ◇ *Whenever I mention going out together, she makes an excuse.* ◇ *She mentioned Freeport as a good place for shopping.*

IDM **don't mention it** (used as an informal polite reply when sb thanks you for sth) I'm pleased to help; not at all: *"Thanks for all your help." "Don't mention it."*

**not to mention** (used for emphasis) and also; as well as: *She's a mother and a doctor, not to mention being a board member.*

**men·tion²** /ˈmɛnʃn/ ***noun*** [C,U] a brief remark about sb/sth: *There wasn't even a mention of the riots in the newspaper.* ◇ *The candidate made no mention of her opponent in her speech.*

**men·tor** /ˈmɛntɔr; -tər/ ***noun*** [C] a person who gives advice to a younger or less experienced person

★**men·u** /ˈmɛnyu/ ***noun*** [C] **1** a list of the food that you can choose in a restaurant: *Could we have/see the dessert menu, please?* ◇ *I hope there's some pizza* ***on the menu***. **2** a list of choices in a computer program which is shown on the screen ➲ Look at **drop-down menu**.

**me·ow** /miˈaʊ/ ***noun*** [C] one of the sounds that a cat makes ▶ **me·ow** ***verb*** [I] ➲ Look at **purr**.

**mer·ce·nar·y** /ˈmərsəˌnɛri/ ***noun*** [C] (*pl.* **mer·ce·nar·ies**) a person who fights for any group or country that will pay him/her

**mer·chan·dise¹** /ˈmərtʃəndaɪz; -daɪs/ ***noun*** [U] goods that are for sale

**mer·chan·dise²** /ˈmərtʃəndaɪz/ ***verb*** [T] to sell sth using advertising, etc.

**mer·chant** /ˈmərtʃənt/ ***noun*** [C] a person whose job is to buy and sell goods, usually of one particular type: *a wine merchant*

**mer·ci·ful** /ˈmərsəfl/ ***adj.*** feeling or showing kindness to sb: *His death was a merciful release from pain.*

**mer·ci·ful·ly** /ˈmərsəfəli/ ***adv.*** luckily: *It was bitterly cold, but mercifully it was not snowing.*

**mer·ci·less** /ˈmərsələs/ ***adj.*** showing no kindness or pity; cruel ▶ **mer·ci·less·ly** ***adv.***

**Mer·cu·ry** /ˈmərkyəri/ ***noun*** [sing.] the planet that is nearest to the sun

**mer·cu·ry** /ˈmərkyəri/ ***noun*** [U] (*symbol* **Hg**) a heavy silver-colored metal that is usually in liquid form. Mercury is used in thermometers.

**mer·cy** /ˈmərsi/ ***noun*** [U] kindness or forgiveness (that is shown to sb who has done sth wrong): *The prisoners begged for mercy from the king.* ◇ *The rebels were shown no mercy.*

**IDM** **at the mercy of sb/sth** having no power against sb/sth strong: *We spent the night on the mountain at the mercy of the wind and rain.*

**ˈmercy ˌkilling** ***noun*** [C,U] = EUTHANASIA

**mere** /mɪr/ ***adj.*** (only *before* a noun) **1** (used for emphasizing how small or unimportant sth is) nothing more than: *Our market share has been reduced to a mere 10 %.* **2** used to say that just the fact that sb/sth is present in a situation is enough to have an influence: *The mere thought of giving a speech makes me nervous.*

★**mere·ly** /ˈmɪrli/ ***adv.*** (*formal*) only; just: *The President can stop a bill from becoming law merely by refusing to sign it.*

**merge** /mərdʒ/ ***verb*** [I,T] **merge (sth) (with/into sth)** to join together or to join things together so that they become one: *Three small companies merged into one large one.* ◇ *This creek merges with the Fraser River a few miles downstream.* ◇ *Those colors seem to merge into each other.* ◇ *The story merges fact and fantasy.* ◇ *We have merged the two classes into one.*

**merg·er** /ˈmərdʒər/ ***noun*** [C,U] the act of joining two or more companies together

**me·ringue** /məˈræŋ/ ***noun*** [C,U] a mixture of sugar and egg whites that is beaten together and cooked in the oven

**mer·it¹** /ˈmɛrət/ ***noun*** **1** [U] high quality; excellence: *There is a lot of merit in her ideas.* ◇ *a certificate of merit* ◇ *a novel of great artistic merit* **2** [C, usually pl.] an advantage or a good quality of sb/sth: *What are the merits of this new proposal?* ◇ *Each case must be judged separately on its own merits* (= not according to general principles).

**mer·it²** /ˈmɛrət/ ***verb*** [T] (*formal*) to be good enough for sth; to deserve: *This suggestion certainly merits further discussion.*

**mer·maid** /ˈmərmeɪd/ ***noun*** [C] (in stories) a woman who has the tail of a fish instead of legs and who lives in the ocean

**mer·ri·ment** /ˈmɛrəmənt/ ***noun*** [U] (*formal*) laughter and enjoyment

**mer·ry** /ˈmɛri/ ***adj.*** (**mer·ri·er**; **mer·ri·est**) happy and cheerful: *merry laughter* ◇ *Merry Christmas!* ▶ **mer·ri·ly** /ˈmɛrəli/ ***adv.***

**ˈmerry-go-round** ***noun*** [C] (*also* **carousel**) a big round platform at a fair, etc. that turns around and around by the use of a motor. It has model horses, etc. on it for children to ride on: *to have a ride on a merry-go-round*

**mesh** /mɛʃ/ ***noun*** [C,U] material that is like a net (= made of plastic, wire or rope threads with holes in between): *a wire mesh fence*

**mes·mer·ize** /ˈmɛzməraɪz/ ***verb*** [T] to hold sb's attention completely: *The audience seemed to be mesmerized by the speaker's voice.*

★**mess¹** /mɛs/ ***noun*** **1** [sing.] a thing or place that is dirty or not organized: *Who spilled flour on the kitchen floor? Come here and clean up your mess!* ◇ *My hair is a mess.* **2** [C, usually sing.] the state of being dirty or not organized: *The kitchen's in a real mess!* ➲ adjective **messy** **3** [sing.] the state of having problems or troubles: *The company is in a financial mess.* ◇ *to make a mess of your life* **4** [C] (*also* **ˈmess hall**) the room or building where soldiers eat together: *the officers' mess*

**mess²** /mɛs/ ***verb***

**PHR V** **mess around** to behave in a foolish way: *We were just messing around when Greg broke the lamp.*

**mess around with sth** to touch or use sth in a careless or foolish way: *Stop messing around with those tools before somebody gets hurt!*

**mess sth up** **1** to make sth dirty or not organized **2** to do sth badly or spoil sth: *I really messed up the last question on the test.*

**mess with sb** (*informal*) to treat sb in a way that is not fair or reasonable: *Don't mess with Big John – he's got a pretty bad temper!*

★**mes·sage** /ˈmɛsɪdʒ/ ***noun*** **1** [C] a written or spoken piece of information that is passed from one person to another: *Mr. Thomas is not here right*

M

now. *Can I take a message?* ◇ *to get/receive a message from sb* ◇ *Please leave a message after the beep.* **2** [sing.] the main idea of a book, speech, etc.: *It was a funny movie, but it also had a serious message.*

IDM **get the message** (*informal*) to understand what sb means even if it is not said directly: *He finally got the message and left Dick and Sarah alone together.*

**mes·sen·ger** /ˈmɛsəndʒər/ ***noun*** [C] a person who carries a message

**Mes·si·ah** (*also* **messiah**) /məˈsaɪə/ ***noun*** [C] a person, e.g. Jesus Christ, who is expected to come and save the world

**mess·y** /ˈmɛsi/ ***adj.*** (**mess·i·er**; **mess·i·est**) **1** dirty or not neat: *a messy room* **2** needing a lot of cleaning up: *Painting the ceiling is a messy job.* **3** having or causing problems or trouble: *a messy divorce*

**met** *past tense, past participle of* MEET

**me·tab·o·lism** /məˈtæbəlɪzəm/ ***noun*** [U, sing.] the chemical processes in living things that change food, etc. into energy and materials for growth: *The body's metabolism is slowed down by extreme cold.* ▸ **met·a·bol·ic** /ˌmɛt̬əˈbɑlɪk/ ***adj.*** (usually before noun): *a low/high metabolic rate* ◇ *a metabolic disorder/process*

M

★**met·al** /ˈmɛt̬l/ ***noun*** [C,U] a type of solid mineral substance, e.g. tin, iron, gold, steel, etc.: *Aluminum is a non-magnetic metal.* ◇ *to recycle scrap metal* ◇ *a metal bar*

**me·tal·lic** /məˈtælɪk/ ***adj.*** looking like metal or making a noise like one piece of metal hitting another: *a metallic blue car* ◇ *harsh metallic sounds*

**met·a·mor·pho·sis** /ˌmɛt̬əˈmɔrfəsəs/ ***noun*** [C] (*pl.* **met·a·mor·pho·ses** /-fəsiz/) (*formal*) a complete change of form (as part of natural development): *the metamorphosis of a tadpole into a frog*

**met·a·phor** /ˈmɛt̬əfɔr/ ***noun*** [C,U] a way of describing sth by comparing it to sth else which has the same qualities (but without using the words "as" or "like"). For example, if you say sb is a "parrot," you are using a metaphor to express the fact that the person just repeats things without thinking. ➲ Look also at **simile.** ▸ **met·a·phor·i·cal** /ˌmɛt̬əˈfɔrɪkl/ ***adj.***: *a metaphorical expression* ▸ **met·a·phor·i·cal·ly** /-kli/ ***adv.***

**me·te·or** /ˈmit̬iər/ ***noun*** [C] a small piece of rock, etc. in space. When a meteor enters the earth's atmosphere, it makes a bright line in the night sky.

**me·te·or·ic** /ˌmit̬iˈɔrɪk; -ˈɑr-/ ***adj.*** very fast or successful: *a meteoric rise to fame*

**me·te·or·ol·o·gist** /ˌmit̬iəˈrɑlədʒɪst/ ***noun*** [C] a person who studies the weather in order to produce a report on what will happen (a **forecast**)

**me·te·or·ol·o·gy** /ˌmit̬iəˈrɑlədʒi/ ***noun*** [U] the study of the weather and climate ▸ **me·te·or·o·log·i·cal** /ˌmit̬iərəˈlɑdʒɪkl/ ***adj.***: *meteorological data*

**me·ter**[1] /ˈmit̬ər/ ***noun*** [C] **1** (*abbr.* **m**) a measure of length; 100 centimeters: *A meter is about 39 inches.* ◇ *Who holds the record in the 100 meters?* (= the race). **2** a piece of equipment that measures the amount of gas, water, electricity, time, etc. that you have used: *to read the gas meter* ◇ *a parking meter*

**me·ter**[2] /ˈmit̬ər/ ***verb*** [T] to measure sth with a METER[1] (2)

★**meth·od** /ˈmɛθəd/ ***noun*** [C] a way of doing sth: *modern methods of teaching languages* ◇ *a simple method for calculating loan payments*

**me·thod·i·cal** /məˈθɑdɪkl/ ***adj.*** having or using a well-organized and careful way of doing sth: *Paul is a very methodical worker.* ▸ **me·thod·i·cal·ly** /-kli/ ***adv.***

**Meth·od·ist** /ˈmɛθədɪst/ ***noun*** [C], ***adj.*** (a member) of a Protestant Church that was started by John Wesley in the 18th century

**meth·od·o·log·y** /ˌmɛθəˈdɑlədʒi/ (*pl.* **meth·od·o·log·ies**) ***noun*** [C,U] a way of doing sth based on particular principles and methods: *language teaching methodologies* ▸ **meth·od·o·log·i·cal** /ˌmɛθədəˈlɑdʒɪkl/ ***adj.***

**me·tic·u·lous** /məˈtɪkyələs/ ***adj.*** giving or showing great attention to detail; very careful ▸ **me·tic·u·lous·ly** ***adv.***

**Me·tis** /meɪˈti/ ***noun*** [C] (*pl.* **Me·tis** /meɪˈti; -ˈtis; -ˈtiz/) (*Cdn*) (especially in Canada) a person with one Aboriginal parent and one European parent, or a person whose family comes from both Aboriginal and European backgrounds

**met·ric** /ˈmɛtrɪk/ ***adj.*** using the system of measurement that is based on meters, grams, liters, etc. (the **metric system**)

**met·ro** /ˈmɛtroʊ/ ***adj.*** = METROPOLITAN

**me·trop·o·lis** /məˈtrɑpələs/ ***noun*** [C] a very large city

**met·ro·pol·i·tan** /ˌmɛtrəˈpɑlətn/ (*also* **metro**) ***adj.*** connected with a large city: *the population of metropolitan Detroit* (= the city and its suburbs) ◇ *the six-county metro area*

**mg** ***abbr.*** = MILLIGRAM

**MHA** /ˌɛm eɪtʃ ˈeɪ/ ***noun*** [C] (*Cdn*) a Member of the House of Assembly, the governing body (**legislature**) in Newfoundland and Labrador

**mi.** ***abbr.*** = MILE

**mice** *plural of* MOUSE

**mi·cro·chip** /ˈmaɪkroʊtʃɪp/ = CHIP[1]

**mi·cro·cosm** /ˈmaɪkrəkɑzəm/ ***noun*** [C] something that is a small example of sth larger: *Some people say a company is a microcosm of society as a whole.*

**mi·cro·film** /ˈmaɪkroʊfɪlm/ ***noun*** [C,U] a piece of film on which information is stored in very small print

**mi·cro·phone** /ˈmaɪkrəfoʊn/ (*also informal* **mike**) ***noun*** [C] a piece of electrical equipment that is used for making sounds louder or for recording them: *Speak into the microphone so that everyone can hear you.*

**mi·cro·scope** /ˈmaɪkrəskoʊp/ ***noun*** [C] a piece of equipment that makes very small objects look large enough for you to be able to see them: *to examine sth under a microscope*

**mi·cro·scop·ic** /ˌmaɪkrəˈskɑpɪk/ ***adj.*** too small to be seen without a microscope

**mi·cro·wave** /ˈmaɪkrəweɪv/ ***noun*** [C] **1** a short electric wave that is used for sending radio messages and for cooking food **2** (*also* **microwave oven**) a type of oven that cooks or heats food very quickly using microwaves

**mid-** /mɪd/ ***prefix*** (in compounds) in the middle of: *a mid-air collision* ◇ *the mid- 1990s* ◇ *in mid-June*

★**mid·day** /ˌmɪdˈdeɪ/ ***noun*** [U] the middle of the day: *the midday temperature* ◇ *The stock market had fallen three points by midday.* ➲ Look at **midnight**.

★**mid·dle**[1] /ˈmɪdl/ ***noun*** **the middle** [sing.] the part, point or position that is at about the same distance from the two ends of sth: *There was a broken bottle lying in the middle of the road.* ◇ *Here's a picture of me with my two brothers. I'm the one in the middle.*

> NOTE **Center** and **middle** are often very similar in meaning, but **center** is used when you mean the exact middle of something: *How do you find the center of a circle?* ◇ *There was a large table in the middle of the room.* When you are talking about a period of time, only **middle** may be used: *the middle of July* ◇ *The baby woke up in the middle of the night.*

IDM **be in the middle of sth/of doing sth** to be busy doing sth: *We were right in the middle of supper when the phone rang.*
**the middle of nowhere** (*informal*) a place that is far away from big cities

★**mid·dle**[2] /ˈmɪdl/ ***adj.*** (only *before* a noun) in the MIDDLE[1]: *I wear my mother's ring on my middle finger.* ◇ *Unfortunately, I had a middle seat on the plane.*

**ˌmiddle ˈage** ***noun*** [U] the time when you are about 40 to 60 years old: *in late middle age* ▸ **ˌmiddle-ˈaged** ***adj.***: *middle-aged people*

**the ˌMiddle ˈAges** ***noun*** [pl.] the period of European history from about AD 1100 to AD 1500

**ˌMiddle Aˈmerica** ***noun*** [U] the middle class people in the U.S. who represent the most common social and political values, especially in small towns in the Midwest

**the ˌmiddle ˈclass** ***noun*** [sing.] the people in society who are in the middle income group. Middle-class people include business people, managers, teachers, etc.: *taxpayers who belong to the middle class* ◇ *students from middle-class families*

**the ˌMiddle ˈEast** ***noun*** [sing.] the group of countries that are situated at the point where Europe, Africa and Asia meet ➲ Look at the note at **White House**.

**mid·dle·man** /ˈmɪdlmæn/ ***noun*** [C] (*pl.* **mid·dle·men**) a person who buys sth in order to sell it to sb else for more money

**ˌmiddle ˈname** ***noun*** [C] the second of two given names

**ˈmiddle school** ***noun*** [C] a school for children in grades 5 or 6 through 8 ➲ For more information on the North American educational systems, look at study pages **A8-A9**.

**midg·et** /ˈmɪdʒət/ ***noun*** [C] an offensive word for a very small person

★**mid·night** /ˈmɪdnaɪt/ ***noun*** [U] twelve o'clock at night: *They left the party at midnight.* ◇ *The clock struck midnight.* ➲ Look at **noon**.

**mid·riff** /ˈmɪdrɪf/ ***noun*** [C] the part of your body between your chest and your waist

**midst** /mɪdst/ ***noun*** [U] **in the midst of** in the middle of sth: *The police department is in the midst of a murder investigation.*

**mid·sum·mer** /ˌmɪdˈsʌmər/ ***noun*** [U] the time around the middle of summer

**mid·term** /ˈmɪdtərm/ ***noun*** [C] an examination that you take in the middle of a course: *a biology midterm* ▸ **mid·term** ***adj.***: *a midterm exam*

**mid·way** /ˌmɪdˈweɪ/ ***adj.***, ***adv.*** **midway (between sth and sth)** in the middle or halfway (between sth and sth): *Our farm is midway between Lincoln and Omaha.*

**mid·week** /ˌmɪdˈwik/ ***noun*** [U] the middle of the week (= Tuesday, Wednesday and Thursday) ▸ **midweek** ***adv.***: *If you travel midweek, it will be less crowded.*

**the Mid·west** /ˌmɪdˈwɛst/ ***noun*** [sing.] the northern central part of the U.S.. The Midwest includes the states of Minnesota, Wisconsin, Illinois, Michigan, Indiana, Nebraska, Iowa, Kansas and Missouri. ▸ **Mid·west·ern** /ˌmɪdˈwɛstərn/ ***adj.***

**mid·wife** /ˈmɪdwaɪf/ ***noun*** [C] (*pl.* **mid·wives** /-waɪvz/) a person who has been trained to help women give birth to babies

**mid·win·ter** /ˌmɪdˈwɪntər/ ***noun*** [U] the time around the middle of winter

★**might**[1] /maɪt/ ***modal verb*** (*negative* **might not**) **1** (used for saying that sth is possible): *"Where's William?" "He might be upstairs."* ◇ *We might be going to Spain on vacation this year.* ◇ *She might not come if she's very busy.* ◇ *If I had known the movie was about dinosaurs, I might have gone to see it* (= but I didn't know, so I didn't go). **2** (used as the past form of *may* when you report what sb has said): *He said he might be late* (= his words were, "I may be late"). **3** (used to suggest sth politely): *If you need more information, you might try the library.*

IDM **may/might as well (do sth)** → WELL[1]
**I might have known** (used for saying that you are not surprised that sth has happened): *I might have known he wouldn't help.*

**might**[2] /maɪt/ ***noun*** [U] (*formal*) great strength or power: *We pushed with all our might, but the rock did not move.*

**might·y**[1] /ˈmaɪt̬i/ ***adj.*** (**might·i·er**; **might·i·est**) very strong or powerful

**mi·graine** /ˈmaɪgreɪn/ ***noun*** [C,U] a very bad headache that makes you feel sick

**mi·grant** /ˈmaɪgrənt/ ***noun*** [C] a person who goes from place to place in search of work: *migrant farm workers*

**mi·grate** /ˈmaɪgreɪt/ ***verb*** [I] **1** (used about animals and birds) to travel from one part of the world to another at the same time every year **2** to move from one place to go and live and work in another: *Many of the poorer people were forced to migrate to the cities to look for work.* ➲ Look at **emigrate**. ▸ **mi·gra·tion** /maɪˈgreɪʃn/ ***noun*** [C,U]: *the annual migration south*

M

**mike** /maɪk/ *noun* [C] (*informal*) = MICROPHONE

★**mild** /maɪld/ *adj.* **1** gentle, not strong or severe: *a mild soap that is gentle to your skin* ◇ *a mild winter* ◇ *a mild punishment* **2** (used about food) not having a strong taste: *mild cheese* ◇ *mild, medium or hot chili sauce* ▶ **mild·ness** *noun* [U]

**mil·dew** /ˈmɪldu/ *noun* [U] a substance (a fungus) that grows in warm, damp places

**mild·ly** /ˈmaɪldli/ *adv.* **1** in a mild way **2** not very; slightly: *The audience was only mildly enthusiastic.*

**mile** /maɪl/ *noun* [C] **1** a measure of length; 1.6 kilometers. There are 1,760 yards in a mile: *The nearest beach is seven miles away.* ◇ *It's a seven-mile drive to the lake.* ◇ *My car gets 35 miles to the gallon.* **2** (*also informal* **miles**) a lot: *to miss a target by a mile* **3 miles** a long way: *How much farther is it? We've walked miles already.*

**mile·age** /ˈmaɪlɪdʒ/ *noun* **1** [C,U] the distance that has been traveled (measured in miles): *The car is five years old, but it has very low mileage.* **2** [C,U] the distance that a car, etc. can travel using a certain amount of fuel: *Our car gets good gas mileage* (= it can go a long way on each gallon of gasoline). **3** [U] (*informal*) the amount of use or benefit you get from sth: *You've gotten a lot of mileage out of that coat – it's five years old and still looks good.*

M

**mile·stone** /ˈmaɪlstoʊn/ *noun* [C] **1** (*old-fashioned*) a stone at the side of the road that shows how far it is to the next town **2** a very important event: *Jenny's first day of kindergarten was a real milestone.*

**mil·i·tant¹** /ˈmɪlətənt/ *adj.* using or willing to use force or strong pressure to get what you want: *Members of a militant group placed a bomb near police headquarters.* ▶ **mil·i·tan·cy** /-tənsi/ *noun* [U]

**mil·i·tant²** /ˈmɪlətənt/ *noun* [C] a militant person

★**mil·i·tar·y¹** /ˈmɪləˌtɛri/ *adj.* (only *before* a noun) of or for soldiers, the army, navy, etc.: *Do you have military service in your country?* ◇ *to take military action*

**mil·i·tar·y²** /ˈmɪləˌtɛri/ **the military** *noun* the army, navy, etc.: *Our son's in the military.* ◇ *to join the military*

**mi·li·tia** /məˈlɪʃə/ *noun* [C] a group of people who are not regular soldiers but who have had some military training

★**milk¹** /mɪlk/ *noun* [U] **1** a white liquid that is produced by women and animals to feed their babies. People drink cows', goats', etc. milk and use it to make butter and cheese: *whole/skim/powdered/condensed/lowfat milk* ◇ *2% milk* (= milk which contains two percent fat) ◇ *Don't use that milk – it's sour.* ◇ *coffee with milk and sugar* ◇ *a carton of milk* ◇ *a milk carton* **2** the juice of some plants or trees that looks like milk: *coconut milk*

**milk²** /mɪlk/ *verb* **1** [I,T] to take milk from a cow, goat, etc. **2** [T] to get as much money, information, etc. as you can from sb/sth: *The colonists milked the country of its natural resources.*

ˌ**milk ˈchocolate** *noun* [U] chocolate that is made with milk

**milk·man** /ˈmɪlkmæn/ *noun* [C] (*pl.* **milk·men**) a person who delivers milk to your house

**milk·shake** /ˈmɪlkʃeɪk/ (*also* **shake**) *noun* [C] a drink made of milk, ice cream and flavoring ➲ Look at **malt**.

**milk·y** /ˈmɪlki/ *adj.* (**milk·i·er**; **milk·i·est**) **1** made with milk: *a hot milky drink* **2** of a pale white color

**the ˌMilky ˈWay** *noun* [sing.] the system of stars that contains our sun and its planets

**mill¹** /mɪl/ *noun* [C] **1** a building that contains a large machine that is used for grinding grain into flour: *a water mill* ➲ Look also at **windmill**. **2** a factory that is used for making certain kinds of material: *a paper mill* ◇ *a steel mill* **3** a kitchen tool that is used for making sth into powder or into smaller pieces: *a pepper/coffee mill*

**mill²** /mɪl/ *verb* [T] to grind sth in a MILL¹ (1)

PHR V **mill around** (*informal*) (used about a large number of people or animals) to move around in one place with no real purpose

**mil·len·ni·um** /məˈlɛniəm/ *noun* [C] (*pl.* **mil·len·ni·a** /məˈlɛniə/ or **mil·len·ni·ums**) a period of 1,000 years

**mil·li·gram** /ˈmɪləgræm/ *noun* [C] (*abbr.* **mg**) a measure of weight. There are 1,000 milligrams in a gram.

**mil·li·li·ter** /ˈmɪləliṭər/ *noun* [C] (*abbr.* **ml**) a measure of liquid. There are 1,000 milliliters in a liter.

**mil·li·me·ter** /ˈmɪləmiṭər/ *noun* [C] (*abbr.* **mm**) a measure of length. There are 1,000 millimeters in a meter.

**mil·lion** /ˈmɪlyən/ *number* 1,000,000: *Almost 250 million people live in the United States.* ◇ *Millions are at risk from the disease.*

NOTE Notice that when you are counting, you use million without **s**: *six million dollars.*

**mil·lion·aire** /ˌmɪlyəˈnɛr; ˈmɪlyənɛr/ *noun* [C] a person who has a million dollars, etc.; a very rich person

**mil·lionth¹** /ˈmɪlyənθ/ *det.* 1,000,000th: *the store's millionth customer*

**mil·lionth²** /ˈmɪlyənθ/ *noun* [C] one of a million equal parts of sth: *a millionth of a second*

**mime¹** /maɪm/ *noun* **1** [C,U] (*also* **pantomime**) acting or telling a story without speaking, by using your hands, body and the expressions on your face **2** [C] an actor who performs using mime

**mime²** /maɪm/ *verb* [I,T] to act or express sth using MIME¹ (1)

**mim·ic¹** /ˈmɪmɪk/ *verb* [T] (*pres. part.* **mim·ick·ing**; *pt, pp* **mim·icked**) to copy sb's behavior in an amusing way

**mim·ic²** /ˈmɪmɪk/ *noun* [C] a person who can mimic other people

**min.** *abbr.* = MINIMUM, MINUTE

**mince** /mɪns/ *verb* [T] to cut sth into very small pieces: *half a cup of minced onion*

★**mind¹** /maɪnd/ *noun* [C,U] the part of your brain that thinks and remembers; your thoughts and intelligence: *He has a very sharp mind.*

IDM **be out of your mind** (*informal*) to be crazy: *He must be out of his mind to give up a job like that.*

**bear in mind (that)** → BEAR[2]
**blow your mind** → BLOW[1]
**change your mind** → CHANGE[1]
**cross your mind** → CROSS[2]
**frame of mind** → FRAME[1]
**give sb a piece of your mind** → PIECE[1]
**have/keep an open mind** → OPEN[1]
**in mind** in your/sb's thoughts: *I understand your concern and I'll keep it in mind for the future.*
**in the back of your mind** → BACK[1]
**keep your mind on sth** to continue to pay attention to sth: *Stop talking and try to keep your mind on your work!*
**make up your mind** to decide: *I can't make up my mind which sweater to buy.*
**on your mind** worrying you: *Don't bother her with that. She's got enough on her mind already.*
**slip your mind** → SLIP[1]
**state of mind** → STATE[1]
**take your/sb's mind off sth** to help you/sb not to think or worry about sth

★**mind**[2] /maɪnd/ ***verb*** **1** [I,T] (especially in questions, answers and negative sentences) to feel annoyed, unhappy or uncomfortable: *"Do you mind if I smoke?" "No, not at all."* ◇ *I'm sure Frank won't mind if you don't invite him.* ◇ *We have four kids so I hope you won't mind about the mess!* ◇ *Do you mind having to travel so far to work every day?* ◇ *I wouldn't mind a vacation in the Caribbean this year!* (= I would like it.) **2** [T] (used in a question as a polite way of asking sb to do sth) could you...?: *Would you mind closing the window for me?* ◇ *Do you mind driving? I'm feeling pretty tired.*
IDM **mind your own business** (*informal*) to pay attention to your own affairs, not other people's: *Mom, tell Todd to mind his own business and stop listening to my private calls!*
**never mind** don't worry; it doesn't matter: *"I forgot to mail your letter." "Never mind, I'll do it later."*

**mind-bog·gling** /ˈmaɪnd ˌbɑɡəlɪŋ; -ˌbɑɡlɪŋ/ ***adj.*** (*informal*) difficult to imagine, understand or believe: *Mind-boggling amounts of money were being discussed.*

**-mind·ed** /ˈmaɪndəd/ ***adj.*** **1** (in compounds) having the type of mind mentioned: *a independent-minded person* ➲ Look at **open-minded**. **2** (in compounds) interested in the thing mentioned: *career-minded*

**mind·less** /ˈmaɪndləs/ ***adj.*** not having or not needing thought or intelligence: *mindless violence* ◇ *mindless factory work*

★**mine**[1] /maɪn/ ***pronoun*** of or belonging to me: *"Whose jacket is this?" "It's mine."* ◇ *Don't take your car – you can come in mine.* ◇ *May I introduce a friend of mine?* (= one of my friends) ➲ Look at **my**.

★**mine**[2] /maɪn/ ***noun*** [C] **1** a hole, or system of holes and passages, that people dig under the ground in order to obtain coal, tin, gold, etc.: *a coal mine* **2** a bomb that is hidden under the ground or under water: *to step on a land mine*

**mine**[3] /maɪn/ ***verb*** **1** [I,T] to dig in the ground for coal, gold, etc.; to get coal, etc. by digging: *Diamonds are mined in South Africa.* ➲ Look at **mining**. **2** [T] to put hidden MINES[2] (2) in an area of land or ocean

**mine·field** /ˈmaɪnfild/ ***noun*** [C] **1** an area of land or ocean where MINES[2] (2) have been hidden **2** a situation that is full of hidden dangers or difficulties: *The question of raising taxes was a political minefield.*

**min·er** /ˈmaɪnər/ ***noun*** [C] a person whose job is to work in a MINE[2] (1) to get coal, etc.

★**min·er·al** /ˈmɪnərəl/ ***noun*** [C] a natural substance such as coal, salt, iron, etc., especially one that is dug out of the ground for people to use: *a country rich in minerals* ◇ *Vegetables are excellent sources of vitamins and minerals.*

ˈ**mineral** ˌ**water** ***noun*** [U] water that comes directly from the ground, contains minerals and is thought to be good for your health: *a bottle of mineral water*

**min·gle** /ˈmɪŋɡl/ ***verb*** [I,T] to mix with another thing or with other people: *His excitement was mingled with fear.* ◇ *She was too shy to mingle with the other party guests.*

**min·i-** /ˈmɪni/ ***prefix*** (in compounds) very small: *a miniskirt* (= a very short skirt)

**min·i·a·ture** /ˈmɪnətʃʊr; -tʃər/ ***adj.*** very small; much smaller than usual: *a collection of miniature cars*

**min·i·mal** /ˈmɪnəməl/ ***adj.*** very small in amount or level: *The project has had minimal support.*

**min·i·mize** /ˈmɪnəmaɪz/ ***verb*** [T] to make sth as small as possible (in amount or level): *We will try to minimize the risks to the public.* OPP **maximize**

★**min·i·mum**[1] /ˈmɪnəməm/ ***noun*** [sing.] the smallest amount or level that is possible or allowed: *I need a minimum of seven hours' sleep.* ◇ *The minimum he will accept is $20,000 a year.* ◇ *We will try and keep the cost of the tickets to a minimum.* OPP **maximum**

★**min·i·mum**[2] /ˈmɪnəməm/ ***adj.*** (only *before* a noun) the smallest possible or allowed: *What's the minimum age for leaving school in your country?* OPP **maximum**

ˌ**minimum** ˈ**wage** ***noun*** [sing.] the lowest amount of money that an employer is allowed to pay workers

**min·ing** /ˈmaɪnɪŋ/ ***noun*** [U] (often in compounds) the process or industry of getting coal, metals, salt, etc. out of the ground by digging: *tin mining* ◇ *a mining town*

**min·i·se·ries** /ˈmɪniˌsɪriz/ ***noun*** [C] (*pl.* **min·i·se·ries**) a television play that is divided into a number of parts and shown on different days

★**min·is·ter** /ˈmɪnəstər/ ***noun*** [C] **1** a religious leader, especially in a Protestant church ➲ Look at **pastor** and at the note at **priest**. **2** (in some countries) a senior member of the government who is often the head of a department ➲ Look at **Prime Minister** and **Secretary**.

**min·is·te·ri·al** /ˌmɪnəˈstɪriəl/ ***adj.*** connected with a government minister or department, in countries in which the government is organized into MINISTRIES (2)

★**min·is·try** /ˈmɪnəstri/ ***noun*** (*pl.* **min·is·tries**) **1 the ministry** [sing.] the profession of being a priest (in Protestant churches): *to enter the ministry*

M

(= to become a minister) **2** (in some countries) a division of the government responsible for a particular subject ➲ Look at **department**.

**min·i·van** /'mɪnivæn/ ***noun*** a large car that can carry five to seven people

**mink** /mɪŋk/ ***noun*** [C] a small wild animal whose fur is used for expensive coats: *a mink coat*

★**mi·nor¹** /'maɪnər/ ***adj.*** **1** not very big, serious or important (when compared with others): *It's only a minor problem. Don't worry.* ◇ *She's in the hospital for a minor operation.* **2** of one of the two types of KEY¹(2) in which music is usually written: *a symphony in F minor* OPP The opposite for both senses is **major**.

**mi·nor²** /'maɪnər/ ***noun*** [C] **1** a person who is not old enough to do sth legally: *The purchase of cigarettes by minors is strictly prohibited.* ◇ *He was arrested for providing alcohol to minors.*

NOTE In the U.S., you must be at least 16 years old in order to buy tobacco products and at least 21 in order to buy and drink alcohol. In Canada, you must be at least 18 to buy tobacco products and at least 18 or 19 to buy or drink alcohol, depending on which province you live in. Your parents are legally responsible for taking care of you until you are 18.

**2** a subject that you study at a college or university and that is less important than your main subject: *He's studying French with a minor in art history.* **3** a person who is studying sth as a less important subject: *He's an art history minor.* ➲ Look at **major²**.

**mi·nor³** /'maɪnər/ ***verb***

PHRV **minor in sth** to study sth as a less important subject at a college or university: *He's minoring in art history.* ➲ Look at **major³**.

**mi·nor·i·ty** /mə'nɔrət̬i; maɪ-; -'nɑr-/ ***noun*** [C] (*pl.* **mi·nor·i·ties**) **1** [usually sing., with sing. or pl. verb] the smaller number or part of a group; less than half: *Most women continue to work when they are married. Only a minority stays/stay at home.* ◇ *to hold a minority interest in a company* (= to own less than half of a company) ◇ *the Senate minority leader* OPP **majority 2** a group of people who are of a different race or religion from most of the people in the country where they live: *children from racial and ethnic minorities* ◇ *minority neighborhoods* ◇ *minority-owned businesses*

IDM **be in a/the minority** to be the smaller of two groups: *Smokers are in the minority in our company.* ➲ Look at **be in a/the majority**.

**ˌminor 'league** ***noun*** [C] (in baseball) groups of small teams made up of players with relatively low skill levels ➲ Look at **major league**.

**mint** /mɪnt/ ***noun*** **1** [U] a small plant (an **herb**) whose leaves are used for giving a fresh flavor to food, drinks, toothpaste, etc.: *mint-flavored mouthwash* ◇ *a candy bar with mint filling* **2** [C] a candy with a strong fresh flavor ➲ Look also at **peppermint**. **3** [sing.] a place where paper money and coins are made by the government

**mint·y** /'mɪnti/ ***adj.*** tasting like mint

**mi·nus¹** /'maɪnəs/ ***prep.*** **1** less; subtract; take away: *Six minus two is four.* OPP **plus 2** (used about a number) below zero: *The temperature will fall to minus 10.* **3** (*informal*) without: *The police found my car – minus the radio – shortly after it had been stolen.*

**mi·nus²** /'maɪnəs/ ***adj.*** (only *after* a noun) (used with grades given for school work) slightly lower than: *I got an A minus (A–) on the test.* ➲ Look at **plus**.

**mi·nus³** /'maɪnəs/ (*also* **'minus sign**) ***noun*** [C] the sign (–) which is used in mathematics to show that a number is below zero or that you should subtract the second number from the first

**min·us·cule** /'mɪnəskyul/ ***adj.*** very small; tiny

★**min·ute¹** /'mɪnət/ ***noun*** **1** [C] (*abbr.* **min.**) one of the 60 parts that make up one hour; 60 seconds: *It's five minutes to/after nine.* ◇ *He called ten minutes ago.* ◇ *Hurry up! The plane leaves in twenty minutes!* ◇ *The show lasts for about 50 minutes.* **2** [sing.] a very short time; a moment: *Wait a minute! You forgot your notes.* ◇ *Do you have a minute to spare? I want to talk to you.* **3 the minutes** [pl.] a written record of what is said and decided at a meeting: *to take (the) minutes* (= to write them down)

IDM **(at) any minute/moment (now)** very soon: *The aircraft will be landing any minute now.*

**in a minute** very soon: *I'll be with you in a minute – I'm almost finished.*

**just a minute** (*informal*) (used for stopping a person, pausing to think, etc.) to wait for a short time: *Just a minute. Is that your book or mine?*

**the last minute/moment** → LAST¹

**the minute/moment (that)** as soon as: *I'll tell him you called the minute (that) he gets here.*

**wait a minute/second** → WAIT¹

**mi·nute²** /maɪ'nut/ ***adj.*** (**mi·nu·ter**; **mi·nu·test**) **1** very small; tiny: *I just have one minute criticism.* **2** very exact or accurate: *She was able to describe the man in minute detail.*

**mir·a·cle** /'mɪrəkl/ ***noun*** [C] a wonderful and very unusual event that is impossible to explain and that is thought to be caused by God or a god: *Christ performed many miracles, even bringing dead people back to life.* ◇ *She's doing her best, but nobody can work miracles!* ◇ *It will be a miracle if he passes his driving test.*

**mi·rac·u·lous** /mə'rækyələs/ ***adj.*** extremely lucky, but impossible to explain or understand: *She made a miraculous recovery from her illness.* ▶ **mi·rac·u·lous·ly** ***adv.***

**mi·rage** /mə'rɑʒ/ ***noun*** [C] something that you think you see in very hot weather but that does not really exist, especially water in a desert

**Mi·ran·da rights** /mə'rændə raɪts/ ***noun*** [pl.] the rights that people have when they are questioned by the police, and which the police must tell people that they have; these include the right to say nothing and the right to speak to a lawyer

**mi·ran·dize** /mə'rændaɪz/ ***verb*** [T] to tell a person who has been arrested what rights he/she has

★**mir·ror¹** /'mɪrər/ ***noun*** [C] a piece of special glass that you can look into in order to see yourself or what is behind you: *That dress looks great on you. Take a look in the mirror.* ◇ *Check your rear view mirror before you change lanes.*

NOTE A mirror **reflects** images. What you see in a mirror is a **reflection**.

**mir·ror²** /'mɪrər/ ***verb*** [T] to reflect sth as if in a mirror: *The trees were mirrored in the lake.*

**mirth** /mərθ/ ***noun*** [U] (*formal*) amusement or laughter

**mis·ap·pre·hen·sion** /ˌmɪsæprɪ'hɛnʃn/ ***noun*** [C,U] (*formal*) to have the wrong idea about sth or to believe sth is true when it is not: *I was under the misapprehension that this course was for beginners.*

**mis·be·have** /ˌmɪsbɪ'heɪv/ ***verb*** [I] to behave badly ▸ **mis·be·hav·ior** /ˌmɪsbɪ'heɪvyər/ ***noun*** [U]

**misc.** ***abbr.*** = MISCELLANEOUS

**mis·cal·cu·late** /ˌmɪs'kælkyəleɪt/ ***verb*** [I,T] to make a mistake in calculating or estimating (a situation or an amount, a distance, etc.): *The driver miscalculated the speed at which the other car was traveling.* ▸ **mis·cal·cu·la·tion** /mɪsˌkælkyə'leɪʃn/ ***noun*** [C,U]

**mis·car·riage** /'mɪskærɪdʒ; mɪs'kærɪdʒ/ ***noun*** [C,U] giving birth to a baby before it is ready to be born, with the result that it cannot live: *She's had several miscarriages.* ➲ Look at **abortion**.

**misˌcarriage of 'justice** ***noun*** [C] a situation in which a court of law treats a person unfairly

**mis·car·ry** /'mɪsˌkæri; ˌmɪs'kæri/ ***verb*** [I] (*pres. part.* **mis·car·ry·ing**; *3rd person sing. pres.* **mis·car·ries**; *pt, pp* **mis·car·ried**) to give birth to a baby before it is ready to be born, with the result that it cannot live

**mis·cel·la·ne·ous** /ˌmɪsə'leɪniəs/ ***adj.*** (*abbr.* **misc.**) of various, different types; mixed: *a box of miscellaneous items for sale*

**mis·chief** /'mɪstʃəf/ ***noun*** [U] (*old-fashioned*) bad behavior (usually of children) that is not very serious: *You can go and see your friends, but keep out of mischief this time.*

**mis·chie·vous** /'mɪstʃəvəs/ ***adj.*** (*old-fashioned*) (usually used about children) liking to have fun by doing things that are not allowed ▸ **mis·chie·vous·ly** ***adv.***

**mis·con·cep·tion** /ˌmɪskən'sɛpʃn/ ***noun*** [C] a wrong idea or understanding of sth: *It is a popular misconception* (= many people wrongly believe) *that snakes have slimy skin.*

**mis·con·duct** /ˌmɪs'kɑndʌkt/ ***noun*** [U] (*formal*) bad behavior, especially by a professional person

**mis·con·strue** /ˌmɪskən'stru/ ***verb*** [T] (*formal*) **misconstrue sth (as sth)** to understand sb's words or actions wrongly

**mis·de·mean·or** /ˌmɪsdɪ'minər/ ***noun*** [C] something slightly bad or wrong that a person does; a minor crime: *to be charged with a misdemeanor*

**mi·ser** /'maɪzər/ ***noun*** [C] a person who loves having a lot of money but hates spending any

**mis·er·a·ble** /'mɪzərəbl; 'mɪzrəbl/ ***adj.*** **1** very unhappy; sad: *You look miserable. What's wrong?* **2** unpleasant (because difficult or uncomfortable): *It's miserable working in such an unfriendly atmosphere.* ▸ **mis·er·a·bly** /-bli/ ***adv.***: *I stared miserably out of the window.* ◇ *Our first business venture failed miserably* (= in a disappointing way).

**mis·er·y** /'mɪzəri/ ***noun*** [C,U] (*pl.* **mis·er·ies**) great unhappiness or lack of comfort; suffering: *There was an expression of pain and misery on his face.* ◇ *The period after the war was a time of economic misery.* ◇ *the miseries of poverty*

**mis·fit** /'mɪsfɪt/ ***noun*** [C] a person who is or feels different from other people: *a couple of social misfits with no friends or hobbies*

**mis·for·tune** /ˌmɪs'fɔrtʃən/ ***noun*** [C,U] (an event, accident, etc. that brings) bad luck or disaster: *Various misfortunes had made her sad and bitter.* ◇ *I hope I don't ever have the misfortune of meeting him again.*

**mis·giv·ing** /ˌmɪs'gɪvɪŋ/ ***noun*** [U, usually pl.] a feeling of doubt, worry or suspicion: *I had serious misgivings about leaving him on his own in that condition.*

**mis·guid·ed** /ˌmɪs'gaɪdəd/ ***adj.*** **1** (used about a person) acting in a way that is not sensible **2** (used about behavior or opinions) based on wrong ideas or information

**mis·hap** /'mɪshæp/ ***noun*** [C,U] an unlucky accident or bad luck that does not have serious results: *to have a slight mishap*

**mis·in·form** /ˌmɪsən'fɔrm/ ***verb*** [T] to give sb the wrong information: *It seems that the public has been misinformed about the cause of the disease.*

**mis·in·ter·pret** /ˌmɪsən'tərprət/ ***verb*** [T] to understand sth wrongly ▸ **mis·in·ter·pre·ta·tion** /ˌmɪsənˌtərprə'teɪʃn/ ***noun*** [C,U]: *Parts of the speech were open to misinterpretation* (= easy to misunderstand).

**mis·judge** /ˌmɪs'dʒʌdʒ/ ***verb*** [T] to form a wrong opinion of sb/sth or to estimate sth wrongly ▸ **mis·judg·ment** ***noun*** [C,U]

**mis·lead** /ˌmɪs'lid/ ***verb*** [T] (*pt, pp* **mis·led** /ˌmɪs'lɛd/) to make sb have the wrong idea or opinion: *Don't be misled by his smile – he's not really very friendly.*

**mis·lead·ing** /ˌmɪs'lidɪŋ/ ***adj.*** giving a wrong idea or impression: *a misleading advertisement*

**mis·man·age** /ˌmɪs'mænɪdʒ/ ***verb*** [T] to manage or organize sth badly or without skill ▸ **mis·man·age·ment** ***noun*** [U]

**mis·place** /ˌmɪs'pleɪs/ ***verb*** [T] to lose sth, usually for a short time because you cannot remember where you left it: *I seem to have misplaced my purse – have you seen it anywhere?*

**mis·placed** /ˌmɪs'pleɪst/ ***adj.*** given to sb/sth that does not deserve to have it: *misplaced loyalty*

**mis·print** /'mɪsprɪnt/ ***noun*** [C] a mistake in printing

**mis·pro·nounce** /ˌmɪsprə'naʊns/ ***verb*** [T] to pronounce a word or letter wrongly: *Be careful not to mispronounce "live" as "leave."* ▸ **mis·pro·nun·ci·a·tion** /ˌmɪsprəˌnʌnsi'eɪʃn/ ***noun*** [C,U]

**mis·read** /ˌmɪs'rid/ ***verb*** [T] (*pt, pp* **mis·read** /ˌmɪs'rɛd/) to read or understand sth wrongly: *I misread the bus schedule and missed the last bus home.* ◇ *He misread my silence as a refusal.*

**mis·rep·re·sent** /mɪsˌrɛprɪ'zɛnt/ ***verb*** [T] (usually passive) to give a wrong description of sb/sth ▸ **mis·rep·re·sen·ta·tion** /mɪsˌrɛprɪzɛn'teɪʃn/

M

***noun*** [C,U]: *That's a misrepresentation of what was actually said.*

**Miss** /mɪs/ **1** (used as a title before the name of a girl or unmarried woman): *Our math teacher is Miss Lopez.* ◇ *"Dear Miss Harris," the letter began.* **2** (*also* **miss**) (used as a polite way of speaking to a woman, especially a young one, whose name you do not know): *Miss, could I please have some more coffee?* ◇ *Can I help you, miss?* **3** the title given to the winner of a beauty contest in a particular country, town, etc.: *Miss America/Bangor* ◇ *The Miss World contest*

★**miss**[1] /mɪs/ ***verb*** **1** [T] to not see, hear, understand, etc. sb/sth: *The house is on the corner, so you can't miss it.* ◇ *There was so much noise that I missed a lot of what the speaker said.* ◇ *They completely missed the point of what I was saying.* **2** [I,T] to not hit, catch, etc. sth: *She tried hard to hit the ball but missed.* ◇ *Drive more carefully. You just barely missed that car.* **3** [T] to feel sad because sb is not with you anymore, or because you do not have or cannot do sth that you once had or did: *I'll really miss you when you go away.* ◇ *I don't miss teaching at all. I prefer my new job.* **4** [T] to arrive too late for sth or to fail to be at sth: *Hurry up or you'll miss the bus!* ◇ *She'll be really upset if you miss her birthday party.* **5** [T] to avoid sth unpleasant: *If we leave now, we'll miss the rush-hour traffic.*

PHR V **miss out (on sth)** to lose a chance to gain sth/enjoy yourself, etc.: *You'll miss out on all the fun if you stay home.*

M

★**miss**[2] /mɪs/ ***noun*** [C] a failure to hit, catch, etc. sth that you are aiming at: *After several misses, he finally managed to hit the target.*

IDM **a near miss** → NEAR[1]

**mis·sile** /ˈmɪsl/ ***noun*** [C] a powerful exploding weapon that can be sent long distances through the air: *nuclear missiles*

★**mis·sing** /ˈmɪsɪŋ/ ***adj.*** lost, or not in the right or usual place: *Some of my books are missing – have you seen them?* ◇ *The roof has some shingles missing.* ◇ *The little girl has been missing from home for two days.* ◇ *a missing person*

**mis·sion** /ˈmɪʃn/ ***noun*** [C]

➤OFFICIAL JOB/GROUP **1** an important task or purpose that a person or group of people are sent somewhere to do: *Your mission is to send back information about the enemy.* **2** a group of people who are sent to another country to perform a special task: *a trade mission to China*

➤SPACE FLIGHT **3** a special trip made by a space rocket or military airplane: *a mission to the moon*

➤YOUR DUTY **4** a particular task or duty which you feel that you should do: *Her work with the poor was more than just a job – it was her mission in life.*

➤TEACHING CHRISTIANITY **5** a place where the local people are taught about religion, given medical help, etc. by people who are sent to do this (**missionaries**).

**mis·sion·ar·y** /ˈmɪʃəˌnɛri/ ***noun*** [C] (*pl.* **missionaries**) a person who is sent abroad to teach about religion

**mis·spell** /ˌmɪsˈspɛl/ ***verb*** [T] to spell sth wrongly

**mis·spent** /ˌmɪsˈspɛnt/ ***adj.*** (used about time or money) used in a foolish way; wasted

**mist**[1] /mɪst/ ***noun*** [C,U] clouds made of small drops of water, close to the ground, which make it difficult to see very far; a thin fog: *The fields were covered in mist.* ➲ Look at the notes at **fog** and **weather**.

**mist**[2] /mɪst/ ***verb***

PHR V **mist (sth) up** to cover or be covered with mist: *The bathroom mirror always mists up when I take a hot shower.*

★**mis·take**[1] /mɪˈsteɪk/ ***noun*** [C,U] something that you think or do that is wrong: *The teacher corrected my mistakes.* ◇ *a spelling mistake* ◇ *I must have made a mistake in adding these numbers together.* ◇ *I think there must be some mistake. My name is Sedgley, not Selley.* ◇ *It was a big mistake not to reserve our seats earlier.* ◇ *We made the mistake of asking Paul to take care of our plants while we were away.*

IDM **by mistake** as a result of a mistake or carelessness: *The terrorists shot the wrong man by mistake.*

> NOTE **Error** is more formal than **mistake**: (*formal*) *Please accept my apologies. I opened your letter* ***in error***. ◇ (*informal*) *I'm sorry. I opened your letter* ***by mistake***. There are some expressions, e.g. *error of judgment, human error, computer error* where only **error** can be used. **Fault** indicates who is to blame: *The accident wasn't my fault. The other driver pulled out in front of me.* **Fault** is also used to describe something that is wrong with, or not good about, a person or a thing: *a technical fault* ◇ *Laziness is not one of her faults.*

**mis·take**[2] /mɪˈsteɪk/ ***verb*** [T] (*pt* **mis·took** /mɪˈstʊk/; *pp* **mis·tak·en** /mɪˈsteɪkən/) **mistake sb/sth for sb/sth** to think (wrongly) that sb/sth is sb/sth else: *Police mistook my car for one that had been used in a bank robbery.*

**mis·tak·en** /mɪˈsteɪkən/ ***adj.*** wrong; not correct: *I thought I saw Jackie sitting over there, but I must have been mistaken.* ◇ *a case of mistaken identity* ▶ **mis·tak·en·ly** ***adv.***

**mis·ter** /ˈmɪstər/ → MR.

**mis·tle·toe** /ˈmɪsl·toʊ/ ***noun*** [U] a plant with white berries and leaves that are green at all times of the year. Mistletoe grows on trees.

> NOTE **Mistletoe** is used as a decoration inside houses in Canada and the United States at Christmas time. There is a tradition of kissing people **under the mistletoe**.

**mis·took** /mɪˈstʊk/ *past tense of* MISTAKE[2]

**mis·treat** /ˌmɪsˈtrit/ ***verb*** [T] to behave badly or cruelly toward a person or animal ▶ **mis·treat·ment** /ˌmɪsˈtritmənt/ ***noun*** [U]

**mis·tress** /ˈmɪstrəs/ ***noun*** [C] a man's mistress is a woman who is having a (secret) sexual relationship with him ➲ Look at **lover**.

**mis·trust** /ˌmɪsˈtrʌst/ ***noun*** [U, sing.] a lack of belief or confidence in sb/sth; a lack of trust: *She has a deep mistrust of strangers.* ▶ **mis·trust** ***verb*** [T]

**mist·y** /ˈmɪsti/ ***adj.*** (**mist·i·er**; **mist·i·est**) full of or covered with mist: *a misty day* ➲ Look at **foggy**.

**mis·un·der·stand** /ˌmɪsʌndərˈstænd/ ***verb*** [T] (*pt, pp* **mis·un·der·stood** /ˌmɪsʌndərˈstʊd/) to understand sb/sth wrongly: *Don't misunderstand me. I'm only trying to help.* ◇ *I misunderstood the* *instructions and answered three questions instead of four.*

**mis·un·der·stand·ing** /ˌmɪsʌndərˈstændɪŋ/ ***noun*** [C,U] not understanding sb/sth correctly; an example of this: *There must have been some misunderstanding. I ordered spaghetti, not pizza.* ◇ *It was all a misunderstanding, but we've got it straightened out now.*

**mis·use**[1] /ˌmɪsˈyuz/ ***verb*** [T] to use sth in the wrong way or for the wrong purpose: *These chemicals can be dangerous if misused.*

**mis·use**[2] /ˌmɪsˈyus/ ***noun*** [C,U] using sth in the wrong way or for the wrong purpose: *The former mayor was on trial for misuse of public funds.*

**mit·i·gate** /ˈmɪt̬əgeɪt/ ***verb*** [T] (*formal*) to make sth less serious, painful, unpleasant, etc. ▶ **mit·i·gat·ing** /-geɪt̬ɪŋ/ ***adj.***: *Because of the mitigating circumstances* (= that made the crime seem less bad), *the judge gave her a lighter sentence.*

**mitt** /mɪt/ ***noun*** [C] **1** a type of large, thick glove that you wear to protect your hand: *oven mitts* **2** (in baseball) a thick leather glove that is worn for catching the ball ➲ picture at **baseball**. **3** = MITTEN

**mit·ten** /ˈmɪtn/ (*also* **mitt**) ***noun*** [C] a type of glove that has one part for the thumb and another part for the other four fingers: *a pair of mittens* ➲ picture on study page **A30**.

★**mix**[1] /mɪks/ ***verb***

➤COMBINE **1** [T] to put two or more substances together and shake or stir them until they form a new substance: *to mix oil and vinegar together to make a salad dressing* ◇ *Mix yellow and blue together to make green.* **2** [I] to join together to form a separate substance: *Oil and water don't mix.* **3** [T] to make sth (by mixing two or more substances together): *to mix cement* **4** [T] to do or have two or more things at the same time: *to mix business and pleasure*

➤MEET PEOPLE **5** [I] to be with and talk to other people: *He mixes with all types of people at work.* ◇ *She is very shy and doesn't mix well.*

IDM **be/get mixed up in sth** (*informal*) to be/become involved in sth bad or unpleasant

PHR V **mix sb up** (*informal*) to confuse sb: *Don't mix me up when I'm trying to count all these pennies.*

**mix sth up** to get something in the wrong order: *He dropped his folder and got the papers all mixed up.*

**mix sb/sth up (with sb/sth)** to confuse sb/sth with sb/sth else: *I think you've got us mixed up. I'm Jane and she's Sally.*

★**mix**[2] /mɪks/ ***noun*** **1** [C, usually sing.] a group of different types of people or things: *We need a good ethnic mix in the police force.* **2** [C,U] a special powder that contains most of the substances needed to make a cake, bread, etc. You add water or another liquid, eggs, etc. to this powder: *Did you make these muffins from a mix?* ◇ *a box of cake mix*

**mixed** /mɪkst/ ***adj.*** made or consisting of different types of sth: *mixed vegetables* ◇ *The reaction to our suggestion has been very mixed.*

IDM **have mixed feelings (about sb/sth)** to have some good and some bad feelings about sb/sth; not to be sure about what you think: *I have very mixed feelings about graduating.*

ˌ**mixed-ˈup** ***adj.*** (*informal*) confused or unsure about sth/yourself: *He has been very mixed-up since his parents' divorce.*

**mix·er** /ˈmɪksər/ ***noun*** [C] a machine that is used for mixing sth: *a cement mixer*

**mixer**

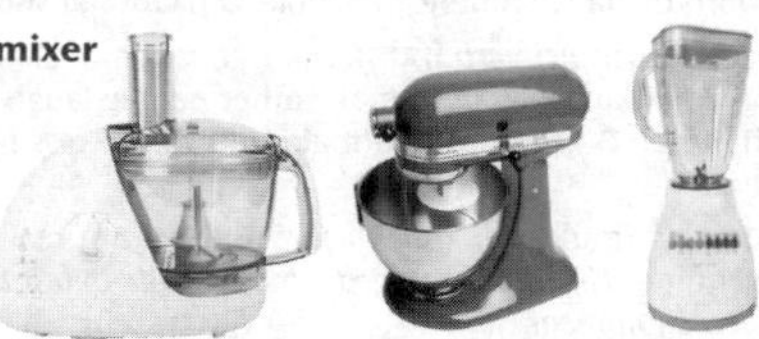

**food processor** **mixer** **blender**

★**mix·ture** /ˈmɪkstʃər/ ***noun*** **1** [C] something that is made by mixing together two or more substances: *Put the mixture into a baking pan and bake for half an hour.* **2** [sing.] something that consists of several things that are different from one another: *I stood and stared with a mixture of amazement and horror.*

ˈ**mix-up** (*also* **mix·up**) ***noun*** [C] (*informal*) a mistake in the planning or organization of sth: *Because of a mix-up at the travel agency, we didn't get our tickets on time.*

**ml** ***abbr.*** = MILLILITER

**MLA** /ˌɛm ɛl ˈeɪ/ ***noun*** [C] (*Cdn*) a Member of the Legislative Assembly, the governing body in a particular province

**mm** ***abbr.*** = MILLIMETER

**MNA** /ˌɛm ɛn ˈeɪ/ ***noun*** [C] (*Cdn*) a Member of the National Assembly, the governing body (**legislature**) in Quebec

**mo.** ***abbr.*** (*pl.* **mos.**) = MONTH

**moan**[1] /moʊn/ ***noun*** [C] a low sound that you make if you are in pain or very sad

**moan**[2] /moʊn/ ***verb*** [I] **1** to make the sound of a MOAN[1]: *to moan with pain* **2** (*informal*) to keep saying what is wrong about sth; to complain: *People always moan about the weather, even though they can't change it.*

**moat** /moʊt/ ***noun*** [C] a deep ditch that was dug around a castle and filled with water in order to protect the castle

**mob**[1] /mɑb/ ***noun*** [C] **1** a large crowd of people that may become violent or cause trouble: *The police used tear gas to disperse the angry mob.* **2** [sing.] **the mob** = MAFIA

**mob**[2] /mɑb/ ***verb*** [T] (**mob·bing**; **mobbed**) to gather around sb, with a large crowd of people, because you are angry or are very interested in him/her: *The rock singer was mobbed as he left the hotel.*

**mo·bile** /ˈmoʊbl/ ***adj.*** able to move or be moved easily ➲ Look at **immobile**. ▶ **mo·bil·i·ty** /moʊˈbɪlət̬i/ ***noun*** [U]

ˌ**mobile ˈhome** (*also* **trailer**) ***noun*** [C] a long, narrow house that is built in a factory and can be moved with a truck

ˌ**mobile ˈphone** ***noun*** [C] (*also* **mobile**) = CELLULAR PHONE



M

**mo·bi·lize** /ˈmoʊbəlaɪz/ ***verb*** [I,T] to get ready or to organize sb/sth for a particular purpose: *Police officers mobilized in anticipation of further riots.* ◇ *They mobilized the local residents to oppose the new development.*

**moc·ca·sin** /ˈmɑkəsn/ ***noun*** [C] a type of soft leather shoe, especially one that is traditionally worn by Native American people ➲ picture at **shoe**.

**mock**[1] /mɑk/ ***verb*** [I,T] (*formal*) to laugh at sb/sth in an unkind way or to make other people laugh at him/her ➲ **Laugh at** and **make fun of** are less formal.

**mock**[2] /mɑk/ ***adj.*** (only *before* a noun) not real or genuine: *The soldiers staged a mock battle to test the new equipment.*

**ˈmock-up** ***noun*** [C] a model of sth that shows what it will look like or how it will work

**mo·dal** /ˈmoʊdl/ (*also* **modal ˈverb, modal auxˈiliary**) ***noun*** [C] a verb, e.g. "might," "can" or "must" that is used with another verb for expressing possibility, permission, necessity, etc.

**mode** /moʊd/ ***noun*** [C] **1** (*formal*) a type of sth or way of doing sth: *a mode of transportation* **2** (used about machines, etc.) a way of operating: *I put the generator in standby mode, so it will be ready in case we need it.*

★**mod·el**[1] /ˈmɑdl/ ***noun*** [C]
➤SMALL COPY **1** a copy of sth that is usually smaller than the real thing: *a scale model of an antique car* ◇ *a model airplane*
➤DESIGN **2** one of the machines, vehicles, etc. that is made by a particular company: *This has been a very popular model of car.*
➤EXAMPLE TO COPY **3** a person or thing that is a good example to copy: *Our city's school system could serve as a model for other communities.* ◇ *a role model*
➤FASHION **4** a person who is employed to wear clothes at a fashion show or for magazine photographs: *a male fashion model*
➤FOR ARTISTS **5** a person who is painted, drawn or photographed by an artist ➲ Look also at **model home**.

**mod·el**[2] /ˈmɑdl/ ***verb*** **1** [T] to try to copy or be like sb/sth: *He modeled himself after his favorite teacher.* ◇ *The house is modeled on the Palace of Versailles.* **2** [I,T] to wear and show clothes as a MODEL[1] (4): *to model swimsuits* **3** [I,T] to make a MODEL[1] (1) of sth

**ˌmodel ˈhome** ***noun*** [C] a house in a group of new houses that has been painted and filled with furniture, so that people who might want to buy one of the houses can see what they will be like

**mod·el·ing** /ˈmɑdl·ɪŋ/ ***noun*** [U] working as a MODEL[1] (4): *a career in modeling*

**mo·dem** /ˈmoʊdəm/ ***noun*** [C] a piece of equipment that connects two or more computers together (e.g. by means of a telephone line) so that information can go from one to the other

**mod·er·ate**[1] /ˈmɑdərət/ ***adj.*** **1** average or not very great in size, amount or degree: *a moderate speed* ◇ *The change will affect thousands of people on moderate incomes.* **2** (used about a person's political opinions) not very different from those of most other people; not extreme: *a moderate position on an issue* ◇ *disagreement between conservative and moderate Republicans* ➲ Look at **extreme** and **radical**.

**mod·er·ate**[2] /ˈmɑdərət/ ***noun*** [C] a person who has moderate political, etc. opinions ➲ Look at **extremist**.

**mod·er·ate**[3] /ˈmɑdəreɪt/ ***verb*** [I,T] (*formal*) to become or to make sth less strong or extreme

**mod·er·ate·ly** /ˈmɑdərətli/ ***adv.*** not very; a little: *His career has been moderately successful.*

**mod·er·a·tion** /ˌmɑdəˈreɪʃn/ ***noun*** [U] the quality of being able to control your feelings or actions: *The people reacted violently, but their leaders called for moderation.*

IDM **in moderation** within limits that are sensible: *Alcohol can harm fetuses even if it's drunk in moderation.*

★**mod·ern** /ˈmɑdərn/ ***adj.*** **1** of the present or recent times: *Pollution is one of the major problems in the modern world.* ◇ *to study modern history* ➲ Look at **ancient** and **traditional**. **2** with all the newest methods, equipment, buildings, etc.: *It is one of the most modern hospitals in the country.* ➲ Look at **old-fashioned**.

**mod·ern·ize** /ˈmɑdərnaɪz/ ***verb*** [I,T] to become or to make sth suitable for what is needed today: *We need to modernize our production line in order to manufacture the new model.* ▸ **mod·ern·i·za·tion** /ˌmɑdərnəˈzeɪʃn/ ***noun*** [U]: *The factory equipment requires extensive modernization.*

**ˌmodern ˈlanguage** ***noun*** [C] a language that is spoken now

**mod·est** /ˈmɑdəst/ ***adj.*** **1** not having or expressing a high opinion of your own qualities or abilities: *She got the best grade on the test, but she was too modest to tell anybody.* ➲ Look at **humble** and **proud**. **2** shy and easily embarrassed by anything that is connected with sex **3** not very large: *a modest salary* ◇ *a modest increase in price* **4** ordinary and plain; not expensive: *They live in a modest suburb north of the city.* ▸ **mod·est·ly *adv.***

**mod·es·ty** /ˈmɑdəsti/ ***noun*** [U] the quality of being MODEST (1,2)

**mod·i·fi·ca·tion** /ˌmɑdəfəˈkeɪʃn/ ***noun*** [C,U] a small change: *There have been some minor modifications to our original design.*

**mod·i·fy** /ˈmɑdəfaɪ/ ***verb*** [T] (*pres. part.* **mod·i·fy·ing**; *3rd person sing. pres.* **mod·i·fies**; *pt, pp* **mod·i·fied**) to change sth slightly: *We will need to modify the existing plan.*

**mod·ule** /ˈmɑdʒul/ ***noun*** [C] a unit that forms part of sth bigger: *The lunar module separated from the spacecraft.*

**mo·hair** /ˈmoʊhɛr/ ***noun*** [U] very soft wool that comes from a type of goat

**moist** /mɔɪst/ ***adj.*** slightly wet; damp: *Her eyes were moist with tears.* ◇ *Keep the soil moist, but be careful not to water the plant too much.* ➲ Look at the note at **wet**.

**mois·ten** /ˈmɔɪsn/ ***verb*** [I,T] to become or to make sth moist

**mois·ture** /ˈmɔɪstʃər/ ***noun*** [U] water in small drops on a surface, in the air, etc.

**mo·lar** /ˈmoʊlər/ ***noun*** [C] one of the large teeth in the back of your mouth

**mo·las·ses** /məˈlæsəz/ ***noun*** [U] a thick, dark, sticky liquid that is made from sugar ➲ Look at **syrup**.

**mold[1]** /moʊld/ ***noun*** **1** [C] a hollow container that you use to make sth into a particular shape. You put a liquid substance into a mold and wait for it to become solid (**set**) in the shape of the mold. **2** [sing.] a particular type of person: *You can't force every student to fit the same mold.* **3** [U] a soft green substance (a type of fungus) that grows in warm, damp places or on food that has been kept too long ▸ **mold·y** /ˈmoʊldi/ ***adj.***: *moldy cheese/bread* ➲ Look also at **rotten**, **sour** and **stale**.

**mold[2]** /moʊld/ ***verb*** [T] to make sth into a particular shape or form

**mole** /moʊl/ ***noun*** [C] **1** a small dark spot on a person's skin that never goes away ➲ Look at **freckle**. **2** a small animal with dark fur that lives underground and is almost blind **3** (*informal*) a person who works in one organization and gives secret information to another organization or country ➲ Look at **spy**.

**mol·e·cule** /ˈmɑləkyul/ ***noun*** [C] the smallest unit into which a substance can be divided without changing its chemical nature. A molecule consists of one or more atoms. ▸ **mo·lec·u·lar** /məˈlɛkyələr/ ***adj.***

**mo·lest** /məˈlɛst/ ***verb*** [T] to attack sb (especially a child) in a sexual way ➲ Look at **rape**. ▸ **mo·lest·er** /məˈlɛstər/ ***noun*** [C]

**mol·ten** /ˈmoʊltn/ ***adj.*** (used about metal or rock) made liquid by very great heat: *molten lava*

**mom** /mɑm/ ***noun*** [C] (*informal*) mother: *My mom works in a bank.* ◇ *Hi Mom, I'm home!* ➲ Look also at **mommy**.

★**mo·ment** /ˈmoʊmənt/ ***noun*** **1** [C] a very short period of time: *Would you mind waiting for a moment?* ◇ *He hesitated for a few moments and then knocked on the door.* **2** [sing.] a particular point in time: *Just at that moment my mother arrived.* ◇ *the moment of birth/death*

IDM **(at) any minute/moment (now)** → MINUTE[1]

**at the moment** now: *She's busy at the moment. Can I take a message?*

**for the moment/present** for a short time; for now: *I'm not very happy at work but I'll stay there for the moment.*

**in a moment** very soon: *Just wait here. I'll be back in a moment.*

**the last minute/moment** → LAST[1]

**the minute/moment (that)** → MINUTE[1]

**on the spur of the moment** → SPUR[1]

**mo·men·tar·i·ly** /ˌmoʊmənˈtɛrəli/ ***adv.*** **1** for a very short time **2** in a very short time; very soon: *We will be landing in Dallas momentarily.*

**mo·men·tar·y** /ˈmoʊmənˌtɛri/ ***adj.*** lasting for a very short time: *a momentary lack of concentration*

**mo·men·tous** /moʊˈmɛntəs; mə-/ ***adj.*** very important: *The birth of our daughter was a momentous occasion for us.*

**mo·men·tum** /moʊˈmɛntəm; mə-/ ***noun*** [U] strength or speed: *The ball gained momentum as it rolled downhill.* ◇ *The environmental movement is gathering momentum.*

**mom·my** /ˈmɑmi/ ***noun*** [C] (*pl.* **mom·mies**) (*informal*) (used by or to children) mother: *I want my mommy!*

**Mon.** ***abbr.*** = MONDAY

**mon·arch** /ˈmɑnərk; -ɑrk/ ***noun*** [C] a king or queen

**mon·ar·chy** /ˈmɑnərki/ ***noun*** (*pl.* **mon·ar·chies**) **1** [sing., U] the system of government or rule by a monarch: *Should Britain abolish its monarchy?* **2** [C] a country that is governed by a monarch ➲ Look at **republic**.

**mon·as·ter·y** /ˈmɑnəˌstɛri/ ***noun*** [C] (*pl.* **mon·as·ter·ies**) a place where men (**monks**) live in a religious community ➲ Look at **convent**.

**Mon·day** /ˈmʌndeɪ; -di/ ***noun*** [C,U] (*abbr.* **Mon.**) the day of the week after Sunday and before Tuesday: *I'm going to see her (on) Monday.* ◇ *We usually play tennis on Mondays.* ◇ *They have piano lessons every Monday.* ◇ *Monday morning/afternoon/evening/night* ◇ *last/next Monday* ◇ *this coming Monday* ◇ *a week from Monday* (= not next Monday, but the Monday after that) ◇ *The museum is open Monday through Friday, 10 to 4:30.* ◇ *Did you see that article about Italy in Monday's paper?*

**mon·e·tar·y** /ˈmɑnəˌtɛri/ ***adj.*** connected with money: *the government's monetary policy*

★**mon·ey** /ˈmʌni/ ***noun*** [U] the means of paying for sth or buying sth, especially in the form of coins or bills: *How much money do you earn a year?* ◇ *Teenagers spend a lot of money on clothes.* ◇ *Our trip cost an awful lot of money.* ◇ *to borrow/lend money* ◇ *My father invested his money in stocks and bonds.* ◇ *Is this picture worth a lot of money?* ➲ Look also at **allowance**.

**money**

coins bills
cash

IDM **get your money's worth** to get full value for the money you have spent: *The meal was expensive, but we got our money's worth because there were five courses.*

**make money** to earn money or to make a profit on a business

**ˈmoney ˌor·der** ***noun*** [C] an official piece of paper, similar to a check, that you can use to send money to sb, e.g. through the mail

★**mon·i·tor[1]** /ˈmɑnət̬ər/ ***noun*** [C] **1** a machine, often a part of a computer, that shows information or pictures on a screen like a television **2** a machine that records or checks sth: *A monitor checks the baby's heartbeat.* **3** a person who checks, records, or watches sth and reports the information to sb in authority: *human rights monitors in a war zone* ◇ *a playground monitor*

★**mon·i·tor[2]** /ˈmɑnət̬ər/ ***verb*** [T] to check, record or watch sth regularly for a period of time: *Pollution levels in the lake are being monitored closely.* ◇ *to monitor foreign radio broadcasts*

**monk** /mʌŋk/ ***noun*** [C] a man who has decided to

leave the ordinary world and live a religious life in a community (monastery) ➲ Look at **nun**.

★**mon·key** /ˈmʌŋki/ ***noun*** [C] (*pl.* **mon·keys**) a small, usually brown, animal with a long tail that lives in hot countries and can climb trees ➲ Look at **ape**. **Chimpanzees** and **gorillas** are apes, although people often call them monkeys.

**ˈmonkey ˌwrench** ***noun*** [C] a tool that can be adjusted to hold and turn things of different widths ➲ picture at **tool**.

**mo·nog·a·my** /məˈnɑgəmi/ ***noun*** [U] being married to, or having a sexual relationship with only one person at a time ▸ **mo·nog·a·mous** /məˈnɑgəməs/ ***adj.***

**mon·o·lin·gual** /ˌmɑnəˈlɪŋgwəl/ ***adj.*** using only one language: *This is a monolingual dictionary.* ➲ Look at **bilingual**.

**mon·o·logue** (*also* **mon·o·log**) /ˈmɑnəlɔg; -lɑg/ ***noun*** [C] a long speech by one person, e.g. in a play

**mo·nop·o·lize** /məˈnɑpəlaɪz/ ***verb*** [T] to control sth so that other people cannot have or use it: *She completely monopolized the conversation. I couldn't get a word in.*

**mo·nop·o·ly** /məˈnɑpəli/ ***noun*** [C] (*pl.* **mo·nop·o·lies**) **1** the control of an industry or service by one company: *Standard Oil had a monopoly on supplying kerosene for lamps in the 19th century.* **2** a company or organization that controls an industry: *The government passed a law to prohibit monopolies in the telephone industry.*

**mon·o·rail** /ˈmɑnəreɪl/ ***noun*** [C] a train that runs on a single track

**mon·o·syl·la·ble** /ˈmɑnəsɪləbl/ ***noun*** [C] a short word, such as "leg," that has only one syllable

**mo·not·o·nous** /məˈnɑtn·əs/ ***adj.*** boring and uninteresting because it does not change: *monotonous work* ◇ *a monotonous voice* ▸ **mo·not·o·nous·ly** ***adv.*** ▸ **mo·not·o·ny** /məˈnɑtn·i/ ***noun*** [U]: *The monotony of the speaker's voice made us all feel sleepy.*

**mon·soon** /ˌmɑnˈsun/ ***noun*** [C] the season of heavy rain in Southern Asia, or the wind which brings the rain

★**mon·ster** /ˈmɑnstər/ ***noun*** [C] (in stories) a type of animal that is large, ugly and frightening: *a story about dragons, goblins and other monsters* ◇ (*figurative*) *The murderer was described as a dangerous monster.*

★**month** /mʌnθ/ ***noun*** [C] (*abbr.* **mo.**) **1** one of the twelve periods of time into which the year is divided, e.g. January: *They are starting work next month.* ◇ *The rent is $500 a month.* ◇ *"When are the final exams?" "Later in the month."* ◇ *at the beginning/end of the month* ◇ *on the 15th of every month* **2** a period of about four weeks: *"How long will you be gone?" "For about a month."* ◇ *"When will Sue be back?" "About a month from now."* ◇ *a three-month course* ◇ *The window cleaner will come again in a month.* ◇ *Little Eric will be eighteen months old on Sunday.*

**month·ly** /ˈmʌnθli/ ***adj., adv.*** (happening or produced) once a month or every month: *a monthly meeting* ◇ *a monthly magazine* ◇ *Are you paid weekly or monthly?*

**mon·u·ment** /ˈmɑnyəmənt/ ***noun*** [C] **1** a building or statue that is built to remind people of a famous person or event: *the Washington Monument* **2** an old building or other place that is of historical importance: *The pyramids in Eygpt are famous monuments from ancient times.*

**mon·u·men·tal** /ˌmɑnyəˈmɛntl/ ***adj.*** **1** (used about a building) very large and impressive **2** very great: *a monumental success*

**moo** /mu/ ***noun*** [C] the sound that a cow makes ▸ **moo** ***verb*** [I]

★**mood** /mud/ ***noun*** **1** [C] the way that you feel at a particular time, i.e. if you are happy, sad, etc.: *Leave Dad alone for a while. He's in a really bad mood.* ◇ *You're in a good mood today!* ◇ *a sudden change of mood* ◇ *Turn that music down – I'm not in the mood for it.* **2** [C] a time when you are angry or bad-tempered: *Debby's in one of her moods again.* **3** [sing.] the way that a group of people feel about sth: *After a year of record-breaking sales, the mood at company headquarters is very optimistic.*

**mood·y** /ˈmudi/ ***adj.*** (**mood·i·er**; **mood·i·est**) **1** having MOODS (1) that change often **2** bad-tempered or unhappy ▸ **mood·i·ly** /ˈmudəli/ ***adv.*** **mood·i·ness** ***noun*** [U]

★**moon** /mun/ ***noun*** **1 the moon** [sing.] the object that shines in the sky at night and that moves around the earth once every 28 days: *The moon's very bright tonight.* ◇ *When was the first landing on the moon?*

> NOTE You may see a **new moon**, a **full moon** or a **crescent moon**.

**2** [C] an object like the moon that moves around another planet: *How many moons does Neptune have?*

IDM **once in a blue moon** → ONCE[1]

**moon·light[1]** /ˈmunlaɪt/ ***noun*** [U] light that comes from the moon: *The lake looked beautiful in the moonlight.*

**moon·light[2]** /ˈmunlaɪt/ ***verb*** [I] (*informal*) to work at a second job in addition to your main job: *police officers who moonlight as private security guards* ▸ **moon·light·ing** /-laɪṭɪŋ/ ***noun*** [U]

**moon·lit** /ˈmunlɪt/ ***adj.*** having light from the moon: *a moonlit evening*

**moor[1]** /mʊr/ ***noun*** [C,U] a wild open area of high land that is covered with grass and other low plants

**moor[2]** /mʊr/ ***verb*** [I,T] to fasten a boat to the land or to an object in the water, with a rope or chain

**moor·ing** /ˈmʊrɪŋ/ ***noun*** [C] a place where a boat is moored

**moose** /mus/ ***noun*** [C] (*pl.* **moose**) a type of very large deer with broad flat horns (**antlers**) that comes from North America ➲ In northern Europe the same animal is called an **elk**. ➲ picture at **elk**.

**mop[1]** /mɑp/ ***noun*** [C] a tool that is used for washing floors. A mop has a long handle and a bunch of thick strings or a sponge at the end.

**mop[2]** /mɑp/ ***verb*** [T] (**mop·ping**; **mopped**) **1** to clean sth with a MOP[1] **2** to remove liquid from sth using a dry cloth: *to mop your forehead with a handkerchief*

PHRV **mop sth up** to clean unwanted liquid with a mop or dry cloth: *Mop up that grape juice you spilled or it'll leave a stain!*

**mope** /moʊp/ ***verb*** [I] to feel unhappy and not try to do anything to make yourself feel better: *Why don't you quit moping around the house and go out for a walk?*

**mo·ped** /ˈmoʊpɛd/ ***noun*** [C] a type of small, not very powerful, motorcycle with pedals ➲ Look also at **motorbike** and **scooter**.

★**mor·al**[1] /ˈmɔrəl; ˈmɑrəl/ ***adj.*** **1** concerned with what you believe is the right way to behave: *Some people refuse to eat meat on moral grounds* (= because they believe that it is wrong). ◇ *the moral dilemma of whether or not animals should be used in laboratory tests* **2** having high standards of behavior: *She has always led a very moral life.* OPP **immoral**

★**mor·al**[2] /ˈmɔrəl; ˈmɑrəl/ ***noun*** **1** [C] a lesson in the right way to behave that can be learned from a story or from sth that happens: *The moral of the play is that friendship is more important than money.* **2 morals** [pl.] standards or principles of good behavior

**mo·rale** /məˈræl/ ***noun*** [U] the way that a group of people feel at a particular time: *The team's morale was high before the game* (= they were confident that they would win). ◇ *Low pay in recent years has led to low morale among blue-collar workers.*

**mo·ral·i·ty** /məˈræləṭi/ ***noun*** [U] principles and standards relating to whether sth is right or wrong: *There was a lively debate about the morality of the death penalty.* OPP **immorality**

**mor·al·ly** /ˈmɔrəli; ˈmɑr-/ ***adv.*** **1** in a way that is good or right: *to behave morally* **2** connected with standards of what is right or wrong: *to be morally responsible for sb* (e.g. because it is your duty to take care of him/her) ◇ *What he did wasn't illegal, but it was morally wrong.*

**ˌmoral supˈport** ***noun*** [U] help or encouragement that you give to sb (by being with him/her or saying that you agree with him/her): *I went to the dentist with him just to give him some moral support.*

**mor·bid** /ˈmɔrbəd/ ***adj.*** having or showing great interest in unpleasant things, e.g. disease and death

★**more**[1] /mɔr/ ***det., pronoun*** a larger number of people/things or larger amount of sth; sth in addition to what you already have: *There were more people than I expected.* ◇ *I bought some more plants for the garden.* ◇ *There's enough room for three more people.* ◇ *Tell me more about your job.* ◇ *There's no more milk in the refrigerator.* ◇ *I couldn't eat any more cake.* ➲ Look also at **anymore**.

IDM **more and more** an increasing amount or number: *There are more and more cars on the road.*

★**more**[2] /mɔr/ ***adv.*** **1** (used to form the comparative of adjectives and adverbs with two or more syllables): *He was more frightened than I was.* ◇ *Please write more carefully.* **2** to a greater extent: *I like him more than I like his wife.* ◇ *This one costs more.*

IDM **more or less** approximately; almost: *We are more or less the same age.*

**no more** (*formal*) not any longer: *The last remaining barrier to peace in the region exists no more.*

**what's more** (used for adding another fact): *Joanna and her mother look very much alike. What's more, they even sound alike.*

★**more·o·ver** /mɔrˈoʊvər/ ***adv.*** (*formal*) (used, especially in writing, when you are giving some extra information that supports what you are saying) in addition; also: *The value of this stock rose 17% last year. Moreover, analysts say it should continue to increase this year.*

**morgue** /mɔrg/ ***noun*** [C] a building or a place in a hospital, etc. where dead bodies are kept until they are buried or burned ➲ Look at **mortuary**.

**Mor·mon** /ˈmɔrmən/ ***adj.***, ***noun*** [C], ***adj.*** (a member of) a religious group founded in the U.S. in 1830, officially called "The Church of Jesus Christ of Latter-day Saints"

★**morn·ing** /ˈmɔrnɪŋ/ ***noun*** [C,U] **1** the early part of the day between the time when the sun rises and noon: *Pat's going to Chicago tomorrow morning.* ◇ *Pat stayed with us on Sunday night and went to Chicago the next/the following morning.* ◇ *I've been studying hard all morning.* ◇ *Dave makes breakfast every morning.* ◇ *She only works in the mornings.* ◇ *the morning paper* **2** the part of the night that is after midnight: *I was woken by a strange noise in the early hours of the morning.*

IDM **good morning** (used when you see sb for the first time in the morning)

> NOTE Often we just say **Morning**: *"Good morning, Mrs. Stevenson." "Morning, Mr. Chang."*

**in the morning 1** during the morning of the next day; tomorrow morning: *I'll try to talk to her about it in the morning.* **2** not in the afternoon or evening: *The time of death was about 10:30 in the morning.*

> NOTE When you use the adjectives *early* or *late* before 'morning' or 'afternoon,' you must use the preposition **in**: *The accident happened in the early morning.* ◇ *We arrived in the late afternoon.* With other adjectives, use **on**: *School starts on Monday morning.* ◇ *They set out on a cold, windy afternoon.* No preposition is used before *this, tomorrow or yesterday*: *Let's go swimming this morning.* ◇ *We went to the zoo yesterday afternoon.* ➲ Look also at the notes at **evening** and **night**.

**mo·ron** /ˈmɔrɑn/ ***noun*** [C] (*informal*) a very foolish or stupid person ▶ **mo·ron·ic** /məˈrɑnɪk/ ***adj.***

**mor·phine** /ˈmɔrfin/ ***noun*** [U] a very strong drug that is used for reducing pain

**Morse code** /ˌmɔrs ˈkoʊd/ ***noun*** [U] a system for sending messages, using combinations of long and short sounds or flashes of light to represent letters of the alphabet and numbers

**mor·sel** /ˈmɔrsl/ ***noun*** [C] a very small piece of food

**mor·tal**[1] /ˈmɔrṭl/ ***adj.*** **1** not living forever: *We are all mortal.* OPP **immortal** **2** that will result in death: *a mortal wound* ➲ Look at **fatal**, which is more common. **3** very great or extreme: *They were in mortal fear of the enemy.*

**mor·tal**[2] /ˈmɔrṭl/ ***noun*** [C] a human being



M

**mor·tal·i·ty** /mɔrˈtæləṭi/ ***noun*** [U] **1** the fact that nobody can live forever **2** the number of deaths in a certain period of time or in a certain place: *Infant mortality is high in the region.*

**mor·tal·ly** /ˈmɔrṭəli/ ***adv.*** **1** in a way that will result in death: *to be mortally wounded* **2** very; extremely: *to be mortally offended*

**mor·tar** /ˈmɔrṭər/ ***noun*** **1** [U] a mixture of cement, sand and water that you put between bricks when you are building sth **2** [C] a type of heavy gun

**mort·gage** /ˈmɔrgɪdʒ/ (*also* **home loan**) ***noun*** [C] money that you borrow in order to buy a house: *We took out a $60,000 mortgage.* ◇ *mortgage payments*

NOTE You usually borrow money from a **bank** or a **credit union**, which decides what **rate of interest** you must pay on the **loan**. In the United States, you can also borrow money from a **savings and loan association**.

**mor·ti·cian** /mɔrˈtɪʃn/ ***noun*** [C] = FUNERAL DIRECTOR

**mor·tu·ar·y** /ˈmɔrtʃuˌɛri/ ***noun*** [C] (*pl.* **mor·tu·ar·ies**) a building or a place in a hospital, etc. where dead bodies are kept before they are buried or burned ➲ Look at **morgue**.

**mo·sa·ic** /moʊˈzeɪɪk/ ***noun*** [C,U] a picture or pattern that is made by placing together small colored stones, pieces of glass, etc.

**Mos·lem** /ˈmɑzləm/ ***noun*** [C], ***adj.*** = MUSLIM

**mosque** /mɑsk/ ***noun*** [C] a building where Muslims worship

**mos·qui·to** /məˈskiṭoʊ/ ***noun*** [C] (*pl.* **mos·qui·toes** or **mos·qui·tos**) a small flying insect. Mosquitoes bite people and animals in order to suck their blood, and some types of mosquito spread a very serious disease (**malaria**).

**moss** /mɔs/ ***noun*** [C,U] a small green plant, with no flowers, that grows in a flat mass in damp places, especially on rocks or trees

★**most**[1] /moʊst/ ***det.***, ***pronoun*** (used as the superlative of *many, much*) **1** greatest in number or amount: *Who picked the most apples?* ◇ *The kids had the most fun.* ◇ *We all worked hard, but I did the most.* **2** nearly all of a group of people or things: *Most families in this country have a TV set.* ◇ *I like most Italian food.*

NOTE When **most** is followed by a noun which has **the**, **this**, **my**, etc. before it, we must use **most of**: *Most of our friends were able to come to the party.* ◇ *It rained most of the time we were in Ireland.*

IDM **at (the) most** not more than a certain number, and probably less: *There were 20 people there, at the most.*

**make the most of sth** → MAKE[1]

★**most**[2] /moʊst/ ***adv.*** **1** (used to form the superlative of adjectives and adverbs that have two or more syllables): *It's the most beautiful house I've ever seen.* ◇ *I think this machine works the most efficiently.* **2** more than anybody/anything else: *What do you miss most when you're away from home?* **3** (*formal*) very: *We heard a most interesting talk about Japan.* **4** (*informal*) = ALMOST: *most everyone*

★**most·ly** /ˈmoʊstli/ ***adv.*** **1** almost all: *The people at work are mostly very nice.* **2** usually: *We mostly go shopping in Vancouver, not Seattle.*

**mo·tel** /moʊˈtɛl/ ***noun*** [C] a hotel for people who are traveling by car. At a motel you can usually park your car near your room.

**moth** /mɔθ/ ***noun*** [C] an insect like a butterfly that usually flies at night. Moths do not have such bright colors as butterflies. ➲ picture at **insect**.

**moth·ball** /ˈmɔθbɔl/ ***noun*** [C] a small white ball made of a chemical substance with a strong smell that protects clothes in closets from moths

★**moth·er**[1] /ˈmʌðər/ ***noun*** [C] the female parent of a person or an animal: *an expectant mother* ◇ *a single mother* ◇ *a foster mother* ◇ *Working mothers need good daycare facilities.* ◇ *a mother cow and her calf* ➲ Look at **mom**, **mommy** and **stepmother**.

**moth·er**[2] /ˈmʌðər/ ***verb*** [T] to care for sb as a mother does: *Tim complained that his girlfriend tried to mother him too much.*

**moth·er·hood** /ˈmʌðərhʊd/ ***noun*** [U] the state of being a mother

**ˈmother-in-law** ***noun*** [C] (*pl.* **mothers-in-law**) the mother of your husband or wife

**moth·er·ly** /ˈmʌðərli/ ***adj.*** of a mother or like a mother: *She's a motherly type of person.*

**ˈMother's Day** ***noun*** [C,U] a day on which mothers traditionally receive cards and gifts from their children, celebrated in North America on the 2nd Sunday in May

**ˌmother ˈtongue** ***noun*** [C] the first language that you learned to speak as a child

**mo·tif** /moʊˈtif/ ***noun*** [C] a picture or pattern on sth: *The blouse has a butterfly motif on each sleeve.*

★**mo·tion**[1] /ˈmoʊʃn/ ***noun*** **1** [U] movement or a way of moving: *The swaying motion of the ship made us all feel sick.* ◇ *Pull the lever to set the machine in motion.* ➲ Look at **slow motion**. **2** [C] a suggestion that you discuss and vote on at a meeting: *The motion was carried/rejected by a majority of eight votes.*

**mo·tion**[2] /ˈmoʊʃn/ ***verb*** [I,T] to make a movement that shows sth or tells sb what to do: *She was motioning to us that she couldn't breathe.*

**mo·tion·less** /ˈmoʊʃnləs/ ***adj.*** not moving

**ˌmotion ˈpicture** ***noun*** [C] (*formal*) a movie

**mo·ti·vate** /ˈmoʊṭəveɪt/ ***verb*** [T] **1** to cause sb to act in a particular way: *Her reaction was motivated by fear.* ◇ *The attack was politically motivated.* **2** to make sb want to do sth (by making it interesting): *Our new teacher certainly knows how to motivate his classes.* ▶ **mo·ti·vat·ed** /-veɪṭəd/ ***adj.***: *highly motivated students*

**mo·ti·va·tion** /ˌmoʊṭəˈveɪʃn/ ***noun*** [C,U] the need or reason for doing sth; a feeling of interest in doing sth: *I'm suffering from a lack of motivation. My new job is really boring.*

**mo·tive** /ˈmoʊṭɪv/ ***noun*** [C,U] a reason for doing sth: *Nobody seemed to have a motive for the murder.*

IDM **an ulterior motive** → ULTERIOR

★**mo·tor**[1] /ˈmoʊṭər/ ***noun*** [C] a machine that changes power into movement: *The washing machine doesn't work. I think something is wrong with the motor.* ◇ *to start/turn off a motor*

**NOTE** **Engine**, not **motor**, is usually used in connection with cars and motorcycles, but sometimes **motor** is also used. In fact, cars used to be called **motor cars**. **Engines** generally use gasoline and **motors** use electricity.

**mo·tor²** /ˈmoʊt̬ər/ ***adj.*** (only *before* a noun) connected with vehicles that have an engine or a motor: *motor vehicles* (= cars/trucks/vans) ◇ *motor oil*

**motorbike**

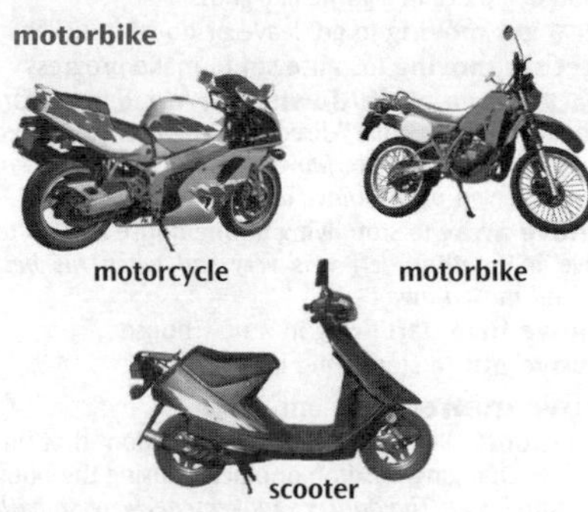


**mo·tor·bike** /ˈmoʊt̬ərbaɪk/ ***noun*** [C] a light, two-wheeled vehicle with a small engine

**mo·tor·boat** /ˈmoʊt̬ərboʊt/ ***noun*** [C] a small fast boat that has an engine ➲ picture at **boat**.

★**mo·tor·cy·cle** /ˈmoʊt̬ərˌsaɪkl/ ***noun*** [C] a two-wheeled vehicle with a powerful engine ➲ picture at **motorbike**.

**mo·tor·cy·clist** /ˈmoʊt̬ərˌsaɪklɪst/ ***noun*** [C] a person who rides a motorcycle

ˈ**motor home** ***noun*** [C] a large vehicle that you can sleep, cook, etc. in when you are traveling or on vacation SYN **RV**

**mo·tor·ist** /ˈmoʊt̬ərɪst/ ***noun*** [C] a person who drives a car ➲ Look at **pedestrian**.

**mo·tor·ized** /ˈmoʊt̬əraɪzd/ ***adj.*** having an engine or a motor: *a motorized wheelchair*

**mot·to** /ˈmɑt̬oʊ/ ***noun*** [C] (*pl.* **mot·toes**) a short sentence that expresses a rule for a person's or an organization's behavior: *Our company has adopted the motto, "The customer is always right."*

**mound** /maʊnd/ ***noun*** [C] **1** a large pile of soil; a small hill **2** a pile or heap of things: *Look at this mound of dirty clothes on the floor!* **3** (*sports*) (in baseball) the small hill where the player who throws the ball (the pitcher) stands ➲ picture at **baseball**.

**mount¹** /maʊnt/ ***noun*** [C] (*abbr.* **Mt.**) (used in names) a mountain: *Mt. Everest*

**mount²** /maʊnt/ ***verb***

- ›GO UP STH **1** [T] (*formal*) to go to the top of sth: *The conductor mounted the podium.*
- ›INCREASE **2** [I] to increase in level or amount: *The tension mounted as the end of the game approached.*
- ›PICTURE/JEWEL, ETC. **3** [T] to attach sth on or in sth else: *A video camera was mounted above the cash register in the store.*
- ›ORGANIZE **4** [T] to organize sth: *to mount an exhibition* ◇ *to mount an attack*
- ›HORSE **5** [I,T] to get on a horse OPP **dismount**

★**moun·tain** /ˈmaʊntn/ ***noun*** [C] **1** a very high hill: *What's the name of the highest mountain in the world?* ◇ *Have you ever climbed a mountain?* ◇ *a steep mountain road* ◇ *a range of mountains* **2** a large amount of sth: *There is a mountain of unanswered letters on her desk.*

ˈ**mountain bike** ***noun*** [C] a bicycle with a strong frame and wide tires that you can ride over rough ground ▸ ˈ**mountain ˌbiking** ***noun*** [U] ➲ picture on study page **A32**.

ˌ**Mountain ˈDaylight Time** ***noun*** [U] (*abbr.* **MDT**) the time system used in the central-western part of the U.S. and Canada from April to October, when the clocks are set one hour ahead of Mountain Standard time ➲ Look at **daylight-saving time**.

**moun·tain·eer** /ˌmaʊntn·ˈɪr/ ***noun*** [C] a person who climbs mountains

**moun·tain·eer·ing** /ˌmaʊntn·ˈɪrɪŋ/ ***noun*** [U] the sport of climbing mountains

ˈ**mountain ˌlion** (*also* **cougar**, **puma**) ***noun*** [C] a large wild cat that lives in western North America

**moun·tain·ous** /ˈmaʊntn·əs/ ***adj.*** **1** having many mountains: *mountainous terrain* **2** very large: *The mountainous waves made sailing impossible.*

**moun·tain·side** /ˈmaʊntnsaid/ ***noun*** [C] one of the steep sides of a mountain

ˌ**Mountain ˈStandard Time** ***noun*** [U] (*abbr.* **MST**) the time system used in the central-western part of the U.S. and Canada from October to April when clocks are set one hour behind standard time ➲ Look at **Standard Time**.

ˈ**Mountain Time** ***noun*** [U] (*abbr.* **MT**) the time system used in the central-western part of the U.S. and Canada ➲ Compare **Central Time**, **Eastern Time** and **Pacific Time**.

**mount·ed** /ˈmaʊntəd/ ***adj.*** riding a horse: *mounted police*

**Mount·ie** /ˈmaʊnti/ ***noun*** [C] (*informal*) (*Cdn*) a member of the Royal Canadian Mounted Police

**mount·ing** /ˈmaʊntɪŋ/ ***adj.*** increasing: *mounting unemployment*

**mourn** /mɔrn/ ***verb*** [I,T] **mourn (for/over sb/sth)** to feel great sadness, especially because sb has died: *She is still mourning for her child.* ◇ *They are mourning the death of her father.*

**mourn·er** /ˈmɔrnər/ ***noun*** [C] a person who goes to a funeral as a friend or relative of the person who has died

**mourn·ful** /ˈmɔrnfl/ ***adj.*** sad: *a mournful song* ▸ **mourn·ful·ly** ***adv.***

**mourn·ing** /ˈmɔrnɪŋ/ ***noun*** [U] a time when people feel or show great sadness because sb has died: *He wore a black armband to show he was **in mourning**.*

★**mouse** /maʊs/ ***noun*** [C] (*pl.* **mice** /maɪs/) **1** a small furry animal with a long tail: *a field mouse* ➲ **Mice**, like **rats**, **hamsters**, etc. are members of the **rodent** family. **2** (*pl.* also **mous·es**) a piece of equipment, connected to a computer, for entering commands without using the keyboard

**NOTE** The mouse controls the **cursor** when you **click** its **buttons**.

M

**mousse** /mus/ ***noun*** **1** [C,U] a type of food that is made by beating together cream and eggs with sth else: *a chocolate mousse* ◇ *salmon mousse* **2** [U] a white substance with a lot of air in it that you put in your hair to shape it and hold it in place: *a can of styling mousse*

**mous·tache** = MUSTACHE

★**mouth**[1] /maʊθ/ ***noun*** [C] (*pl.* **mouths** /maʊðz/) **1** the part of your face that you use for eating and speaking: *Don't talk with your mouth full.* ◇ *Open your mouth, please!* ◇ *You can close your mouth now.* ◇ *Keep your mouth closed when you're eating.* ◇ (*figurative*) *They have a low income and five mouths to feed.* ◇ (*figurative, informal*) *Don't tell him any secrets – he's got a big mouth* (=he says things he should not say). ➲ picture on study page A32. **2** the place where a river enters the ocean

**mouth**[2] /maʊð/ ***verb*** [I,T] to move your mouth as if you were speaking but without making any sound: *Don't worry if you can't sing – you can just mouth the words.*

**-mouthed** /maʊðd/ ***combining form*** **1** having a particular type of mouth: *We stared open-mouthed in surprise.* **2** having a particular way of speaking: *He's loud-mouthed and obnoxious.*

**mouth·ful** /ˈmaʊθfʊl/ ***noun*** **1** [C] the amount of food or drink that you can put in your mouth at one time **2** [sing.] a word or phrase that is long or difficult to say

M

**mouth·piece** /ˈmaʊθpis/ ***noun*** [C] **1** the part of a telephone, musical instrument, etc. that you put in or near your mouth **2** a person, newspaper, etc. that a particular group uses to express its opinions: *The paper was the mouthpiece of the Soviet government.*

**mouth·wash** /ˈmaʊθwɑʃ; -wɔʃ/ ***noun*** [U] liquid that you use for cleaning your mouth and making it smell nice

**mouth·wa·ter·ing** /ˈmaʊθˌwɑt̬ərɪŋ/ ***adj.*** (used about food) that looks or smells very good

**mov·a·ble** /ˈmuvəbl/ ***adj.*** that can be moved ➲ Look at **portable**.

★**move**[1] /muv/ ***noun*** [C]

➤CHANGE OF POSITION **1** a change of place or position: *She sat and watched every move I made.* ◇ *One false move and I'll shoot!*

➤CHANGE OF HOUSE/JOB **2** a change in the place where you live or work: *a move to a bigger house* ◇ *I've been in the same job for six years and think it's time for a move.*

➤ACTION **3** action that you take because you want to achieve a particular result: *Moves are being made to secure the release of the hostages.* ◇ *Both sides want to negotiate, but neither is prepared to make the first move.* ◇ *Asking him to help me was a good move.*

➤IN BOARD GAMES **4** a change in the position of a piece in a game like chess: *It's Lori's move.*

IDM **get a move on** (*informal*) to hurry: *I'm late. I'll have to get a move on.*

★**move**[2] /muv/ ***verb*** **1** [I,T] to change position or to put sth in a different position: *Don't move – there's a bee on your arm.* ◇ *Move your car. It's blocking the driveway.* ◇ *I thought I heard something moving in the bushes over there.* ◇ *They are moving the patient to another hospital.* **2** [I] to go and live in another house, etc.: *Our neighbors have sold their house and are moving next week.* **3** [I] to change or make progress: *When the new team of construction workers arrived things started moving very quickly.* **4** [T] to cause sb to have strong feelings (often of sadness): *The reports about the starving children moved many people to tears.* **5** [I] to take action: *Unless we move quickly, lives will be lost.* **6** [I,T] to change the position of a piece in a game like chess

IDM **get moving** to go, leave or do sth quickly

**get sth moving** to cause sth to make progress

PHR V **move aside/down/over/up** to move farther in a particular direction in order to make space for sb/sth else: *Move over so I can sit down!* ◇ *Could you please move down a seat?*

**move away** to stop living in one house and go to live in another: *Jeff was very sad when his best friend moved away.*

**move in** to start living in a new house

**move out** to stop living in a house

★**move·ment** /ˈmuvmənt/ ***noun***

➤CHANGING POSITION **1** [C,U] an action that involves changing position or place or using the body in some way: *The dancer's movements were smooth and beautifully controlled.* ◇ *The man lay still in the long grass, knowing that any movement would be seen by the police.* ◇ *the slow movement of the clouds across the sky*

➤CHANGE OF IDEAS/BEHAVIOR **2** [C, usually sing.] **a movement (away from/toward sth)** a general change in the way people think or behave: *There's been a slight movement away from the materialism of the 1990s.*

➤PERSON'S ACTIVITIES **3** **movements** [pl.] a person's actions or plans during a period of time: *Investigators have been watching the man's movements for several days.*

➤GROUP OF PEOPLE **4** [C] a group of people who have the same aims or ideas (and who want to persuade other people that they are right): *I support the animal rights movement.*

➤MUSIC **5** [C] one of the main parts of a long piece of music: *a symphony in four movements*

**mov·er** /ˈmuvər/ ***noun*** [C] a person or business that moves sb's furniture, etc. to a new house

★**mov·ie** /ˈmuvi/ ***noun*** **1** [C] a story, play, etc. shown in moving pictures in a theater or on television: *Would you like to go and see a movie?* ◇ *We stayed home last night and watched a movie on TV.* ◇ *a science fiction movie* ◇ *a movie director* ➲ Look at the note at **film**[1](2). **2** **the movies** [pl.] a building where movies are shown: *Let's go to the movies.*

★ˈ**movie ˌtheater** ***noun*** [C] = THEATER (2)

**mov·ing** /ˈmuvɪŋ/ ***adj.*** **1** (only *before* a noun) that moves: *It's an electronic system with few moving parts.* **2** causing strong feelings: *a moving story about a young boy's fight against cancer*

ˈ**moving van** ***noun*** [C] a truck that is used for transporting furniture, etc. from one house to another

**mow** /moʊ/ ***verb*** [I,T] (*pt* **mowed**; *pp* **mown** /moʊn/ or **mowed**) to cut grass using a machine or an instrument: *You need to mow the lawn at least once a week.*

**mow·er** /ˈmoʊər/ ***noun*** [C] a machine for cutting grass or crops: *a lawnmower*

**MP** /ˌɛm ˈpi/ ***noun*** [C] (in Canada) the abbreviation for"Member of Parliament"; an elected member of the House of Commons

**mpg** (*also* **m.p.g.**) /ˌɛm pi ˈdʒi/ ***abbr.*** miles per gallon (of fuel)

**mph** (*also* **m.p.h.**) /ˌɛm pi ˈeɪtʃ/ ***abbr.*** miles per hour

**MPP** /ˌɛm pi ˈpi/ ***noun*** [C] (*Cdn*) a Member of the Provincial Parliament in Ontario, Canada

**MPV** /ˌɛm pi ˈvi/ ***noun*** [C] abbreviation for *multi-purpose vehicle*; a type of car with large tires, which can drive on rough ground and places where there are no roads

★**Mr.** /ˈmɪstər/ ***abbr.*** (used as a title before the name of a man): *Mr. (John) Brown*

★**Mrs.** /ˈmɪsəz/ ***abbr.*** (used as a title before the name of a married woman): *Mrs. (Jane) Brown*

**M.S.** /ˌɛm ˈɛs/ ***abbr.*** Master of Science; a degree that you receive when you complete a program of study at a college or university ➲ Compare **M.A.** and **master's degree**.

**MS** /ˌɛm ˈɛs/ ***abbr.*** multiple sclerosis

★**Ms.** /mɪz/ ***abbr.*** (used as a title before the name of a woman, either married or unmarried): *Ms. (Joan) Smith*

NOTE We can use the title **Ms.** when we do not know whether or not a woman is married. Some women also prefer it to **Mrs.** or **Miss**.

**MT** ***abbr.*** (*written*) = MOUNTAIN TIME

**mt.** (*also* **Mt.**) ***abbr.*** = MOUNT, MOUNTAIN

**mu** /mu; myu/ ***noun*** [C] (*symbol* M, μ) the twelfth letter of the Greek alphabet ➲ Look at the note at **fraternity**.

★**much**[1] /mʌtʃ/ ***det.***, ***pronoun*** (used with uncountable nouns, mainly in negative sentences and questions, or after *as, how, so, too*) a large amount of sth: *I don't have much money.* ◇ *Did you have much difficulty finding the house?* ◇ *You've given me too much food.* ◇ *How much time do you have?* ◇ *I didn't write much.* ◇ *Did she say much?* ◇ *How much do you want?* ◇ *Eat as much as you can.* ◇ *"Is there any mail?" "Not much."*

NOTE In statements we usually use **a lot of**, not **much** (which is extremely formal): *I have a lot of experience.*

IDM **not much of a...** not very good: *Bob's not much of a cook.*

★**much**[2] /mʌtʃ/ ***adv.*** **1** to a great extent or degree: *I don't like her very much.* ◇ *Thank you very much for a wonderful weekend.* ◇ *We are very much looking forward to meeting you.* ◇ *Do you go to the opera much?* (= very often) ◇ *Their house is much nicer than ours.* ◇ *You ate much more than I did.* **2** (with past participles used as adjectives) to a great extent or degree: *a much-needed rest* ◇ *Katie was much loved by all her friends.* ➲ Compare: *Katie was very popular.*

IDM **much the same** very similar: *Polish food is much the same as German food.*

**not much good (at sth)** not very good: *I'm not much good at singing.*

**muck** /mʌk/ ***noun*** [U] (*informal*) a thick, wet, dirty substance, such as mud

**mu·cus** /ˈmyukəs/ ***noun*** [U] (*formal*) a sticky substance that is produced in some parts of the body, especially the nose ➲ Look at **phlegm** and **snot**.

★**mud** /mʌd/ ***noun*** [U] soft, wet earth: *He came home from the football game covered in mud.* ▶ **mud·dy** /ˈmʌdi/ ***adj.***: *Take those muddy boots off by the door!* ◇ *It's very muddy down by the river.*

**mud·dle**[1] /ˈmʌdl/ ***verb***

PHRV **muddle through (sth)** to achieve a goal even though you do not act efficiently, have the right equipment, etc.: *I don't speak Spanish very well, but I managed to muddle through during my vacation in Mexico.*

**mud·dle**[2] /ˈmʌdl/ ***noun*** [C,U] a state of disorder or confusion, in a place or in the mind: *We need to organize this information – it's all in a muddle right now.*

**mud·dled** /ˈmʌdld/ ***adj.*** not clear; confused: *His thoughts were all muddled because he was very sleepy.*

**mud·slide** /ˈmʌdslaɪd/ ***noun*** [C] the sudden fall of wet earth down the side of a hill or mountain

**muf·fin** /ˈmʌfən/ ***noun*** [C] a small sweet cake, often with fruit in it: *fresh blueberry muffins*

**muf·fle** /ˈmʌfl/ ***verb*** [T] to make a sound quieter and more difficult to hear: *He put his hand over her mouth to muffle her cries.*

**muf·fled** /ˈmʌfld/ ***adj.*** (used about sounds) difficult to hear; quiet or not clear: *I could hear muffled voices outside, but I couldn't tell what they were saying.*

**muf·fler** /ˈmʌflər/ ***noun*** [C] **1** the part of a car which reduces the engine noise coming from the back of a car **2** = SCARF (1)

**mug**[1] /mʌg/ ***noun*** [C] a deep cup with straight sides, used without a saucer; the contents of a mug: *Would you rather have a cup or a mug?* ◇ *a mug of coffee* ➲ picture at **cup**.

**mug**[2] /mʌg/ ***verb*** [T] (**mug·ging**; **mugged**) to attack and rob sb in a public place ▶ **mug·ging** ***noun*** [C,U]: *an increase in the number of muggings and other violent crimes*

**mug·ger** /ˈmʌgər/ ***noun*** [C] a person who attacks and robs sb in a public place

**mug·gy** /ˈmʌgi/ ***adj.*** (used about the weather) too warm and damp

**muk·luk** /ˈmʌklʌk/ ***noun*** [C] (*Cdn*) a tall winter boot with a heavy rubber base (sole) which is usually tied with laces

**mule** /myul/ ***noun*** [C] an animal that has a horse and a donkey as its parents: *to be as stubborn as a mule*

NOTE We say that a mule is a **cross** between a horse and a donkey.

**mull** /mʌl/ ***verb***

PHRV **mull sth over** to think about sth carefully and for a long time: *Don't ask me for a decision right now. I'll have to mull it over.*

M

**multi-** /ˈmʌlti/ ***prefix*** (in compounds) having several or many of sth: *a multinational corporation* ◇ *a multi-billion-dollar deal* (= one that costs several billion dollars)

**mul·ti·cul·tur·al** /ˌmʌltiˈkʌltʃərəl/ ***adj.*** for or including people from several different races, religions, languages or traditions: *a multicultural society* ◇ *the college's Office of Multicultural Affairs*

**mul·ti·lat·er·al** /ˌmʌltiˈlæt̬ərəl/ ***adj.*** in which three or more groups, nations, etc. take part: *a multilateral agreement* ➲ Compare **unilateral**.

**mul·ti·me·di·a** /ˌmʌltiˈmidiə/ ***adj.*** (only *before* a noun) using sound, pictures and film in addition to text on a screen: *multimedia systems/products*

**mul·ti·mil·lion·aire** /ˌmʌltiˌmɪlyəˈnɛr; -ˈmɪlyənɛr/ ***noun*** [C] a person who has several million dollars, etc.; an extremely rich person

**mul·ti·ple¹** /ˈmʌltəpl/ ***adj.*** involving many people or having many parts, types, etc.: *a multiple crash on the highway* ◇ *to receive multiple injuries*

**mul·ti·ple²** /ˈmʌltəpl/ ***noun*** [C] a number that contains another number an exact number of times: *12, 18 and 24 are multiples of 6.*

**ˌmultiple-ˈchoice** ***adj.*** (used about test questions) showing several different answers from which you have to choose the right one

**mul·ti·ple scle·ro·sis** /ˌmʌltəpl skləˈroʊsəs/ ***noun*** [U] (*abbr.* **MS**) a serious disease which slowly causes you to lose control of your body and of the ability to move

**mul·ti·plex** /ˈmʌltɪplɛks/ (*also* **Cin·e·plex™**) ***noun*** [C] a large movie theater with several separate screens

**mul·ti·pli·ca·tion** /ˌmʌltəpləˈkeɪʃn/ ***noun*** [U] the process of multiplying a number: *The students will be tested on addition, subtraction, multiplication and division.*

★**mul·ti·ply** /ˈmʌltəplaɪ/ ***verb*** (*pres. part.* **mul·ti·ply·ing**; *3rd person sing. pres.* **mul·ti·plies**; *pt, pp* **mul·ti·plied**) **1** [I,T] **multiply A by B**; **multiply A and B (together)** to increase a number by the number of times mentioned: *to learn to multiply and divide* ◇ *2 multiplied by 4 makes 8 (2 x 4 = 8)* ◇ *What do you get if you multiply 13 and 11?* ◇ *Multiply the two numbers together and you should get the answer.* **2** [I,T] to become bigger or greater; to make sth bigger or greater; to increase: *Our profits have multiplied over the last two years.* ◇ *Using this method, you can multiply your profit in a very short time.* **3** [I] (used especially about animals) to increase in number by producing large numbers of young

**mul·ti·pur·pose** /ˌmʌltiˈpərpəs/ ***adj.*** (*also* **multi-purpose**) that can be used for several different purposes: *a multi-purpose tool/machine*

**mul·ti·tude** /ˈmʌltətud/ ***noun*** [C] (*formal*) a very large number of people or things: *a multitude of difficulties*

**mum** /mʌm/ ***noun*** [C] (*Cdn informal*) = MOM

**mum·ble** /ˈmʌmbl/ ***verb*** [I,T] to speak quietly without opening your mouth enough so that people cannot really hear the words: *I can't hear if you mumble – speak up!* ◇ *Last night you kept mumbling something about a car crash in your sleep.* ➲ Look at **mutter**.

**mum·my** /ˈmʌmi/ ***noun*** [C] (*pl.* **mum·mies**) a dead body of a person or an animal which has been preserved by rubbing it with special oils and wrapping it in cloth: *an Egyptian mummy*

**mumps** /mʌmps/ ***noun*** [U] an infectious disease, especially of children. Mumps causes the neck and lower face to swell: *to have/catch the mumps*

**munch** /mʌntʃ/ ***verb*** [I,T] **munch (sth)**; **munch (on) sth** to eat steadily, especially with pleasure: *He sat there munching (on) his sandwich and didn't say a word.*

**mun·dane** /mʌnˈdeɪn/ ***adj.*** ordinary; not interesting or exciting: *a mundane life/job/conversation*

**mu·nic·i·pal** /myuˈnɪsəpl/ ***adj.*** connected with a town or city that has its own local government: *municipal employees*

**mu·ni·tions** /myuˈnɪʃnz/ ***noun*** [pl.] military supplies, especially bombs and guns

**mu·ral** /ˈmyʊrəl/ ***noun*** [C] a large picture which is painted on a wall

★**mur·der¹** /ˈmərdər/ ***noun*** **1** [C,U] the crime of killing a person illegally and on purpose: *Police believe that both murders were committed by the same person.* ◇ *He was sentenced to life imprisonment for murder.* ◇ *the murder victim* ◇ *the murder weapon* **2** [U] (*informal*) a very difficult or bad experience: *It's murder trying to work when it's as hot as this.*

★**mur·der²** /ˈmərdər/ ***verb*** [T] to kill a person illegally and on purpose: *It seems that she was murdered with a knife.* ➲ Look at the note at **kill**.

**mur·der·er** /ˈmərdərər/ ***noun*** [C] a person who has murdered sb

**mur·der·ous** /ˈmərdərəs/ ***adj.*** likely to murder, or capable of murder

**murk·y** /ˈmərki/ ***adj.*** (**murk·i·er**; **murk·i·est**) dark and unpleasant or dirty: *They couldn't see anything in the murky water of the lake.*

**mur·mur¹** /ˈmərmər/ ***noun*** **1** [C] the sound of words that are spoken quietly: *A murmur of disagreement ran through the room.* **2** [sing.] a low, gentle, continuous sound that is often not very clear: *the murmur of the wind in the trees*

**mur·mur²** /ˈmərmər/ ***verb*** [I,T] to say sth in a low quiet voice: *"Thank you," he murmured.* ◇ *Samantha murmured an answer.*

★**mus·cle** /ˈmʌsl/ ***noun*** **1** [C,U] a piece of flesh inside the body which you can tighten or relax to produce movement: *Do some stretching before you run or you'll pull a muscle.* ◇ *Riding a bicycle is good for developing the leg muscles.* ◇ *The heart is made of muscle.* **2** [U] strength or power: *political muscle*

**mus·cu·lar** /ˈmʌskyələr/ ***adj.*** **1** connected with muscles: *muscular pain* **2** having large strong muscles: *a muscular body*

★**mu·se·um** /myuˈziəm/ ***noun*** [C] a building where collections of valuable and interesting objects are kept and shown to the public: *Have you been to the Science Museum in St. Paul?*

**mush·room** /ˈmʌʃrum/ ***noun*** [C] a type of plant (a fungus) which grows very quickly, has a flat rounded top on a short stem and can be eaten as a vegetable: *mushrooms with garlic* ◇ *mushroom soup*

NOTE A mushroom is a type of **fungus**. Some, but not all, **fungi** can be eaten. **Toadstool** is another name for some types of poisonous fungi. ➲ picture on study page **A28-29**.

★**mu·sic** /ˈmyuzɪk/ ***noun*** [U] **1** an arrangement of sounds in patterns to be sung or played on instruments: *What sort of music do you like?* ◇ *classical/folk/pop/rock music* ◇ *Who composed this piece of music?* ◇ *That poem has been set to music.* ◇ *a music lover* ◇ *a music lesson* **2** the written signs that represent the sounds of music; the sheet or book where these signs are printed: *Can you read music?* ◇ *I forgot my music – can I share yours?*

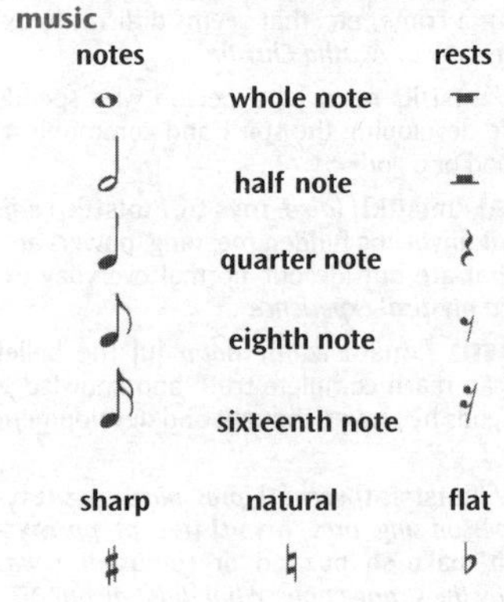


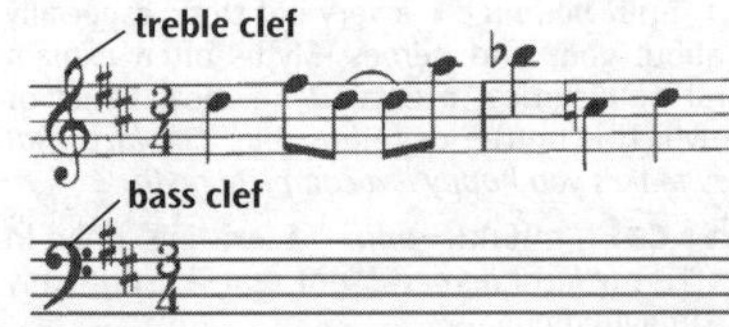


★**mu·si·cal¹** /ˈmyuzɪkl/ ***adj.*** **1** connected with music: *musical instruments* (= the piano/the violin/the trumpet) ◇ *Would you like our program of this month's musical events?* **2** interested in or good at music: *He's very musical.* ◇ *a musical child* **3** pleasant to listen to because it is like music: *a musical voice*

**mu·si·cal²** /ˈmyuzɪkl/ ***noun*** [C] a play or movie which has singing and dancing in it: *a Broadway musical*

★**mu·si·cian** /myuˈzɪʃn/ ***noun*** [C] **1** a person whose job is to play a musical instrument: *The band consists of ten musicians.* **2** a person who is good at writing or playing music: *At the age of ten, he was already a fine musician.*

**Mus·lim** /ˈmʌzləm; ˈmʊz-; ˈmʊs-/ (*also* **Moslem** /ˈmɑzləm/) ***noun*** [C] a person whose religion is Islam ▸ **Mus·lim** (*also* **Moslem**) ***adj.***: *Muslim traditions/beliefs*

**mus·sel** /ˈmʌsl/ ***noun*** [C] a type of sea animal that lives inside a black shell and can be eaten ➲ picture at **shellfish**.

★**must¹** /məst; *strong form* mʌst/ ***modal verb*** (*negative* **must not**; *short form* **must·n't** /ˈmʌsnt/) **1** (*formal*) (used for saying that it is necessary for sth to happen): *All visitors must report to the security desk.* ◇ *Cars must not park in front of the entrance.*

NOTE In more informal English, it is more common to use **have (got) to** to express this meaning. To tell people not to do sth, we usually use **can't** or **cannot**: *You can't park in front of the entrance – it's prohibited.*

**2** (used for giving sb advice): *You really must come and see us sometime.*

NOTE It is more common to use **should** or **ought to** when giving advice: *You really ought to come and see us sometime.*

**3** (used for saying that you are sure that sth is true): *Have something to eat. You must be hungry.* ◇ *I can't find my checkbook. I must have left it at home.* ◇ *It must have been a great shock when your mother died.* ◇ *That car that passed us must have been going 100 miles an hour.*

**must²** /məst; *strong form* mʌst/ ***noun*** [C] a thing that is absolutely necessary, or that must be seen, done, etc.: *This book is a must for all science fiction fans.*

**mus·tache** (*also* **mous·tache**) /ˈmʌstæʃ; məˈstæʃ/ ***noun*** [C] hair that grows on the top lip, between the mouth and the nose: *My dad has a mustache.* ➲ picture at **beard**.

**mus·tard** /ˈmʌstərd/ ***noun*** [U] a yellow or brown sauce which is made from the seeds of the mustard plant. The sauce has a strong taste and is eaten in small amounts, usually with meat: *a hot dog with ketchup and mustard*

**must·y** /ˈmʌsti/ ***adj.*** having an unpleasant stale or damp smell: *The rooms in the old house were dark and musty.*

**mu·tant** /ˈmyutnt/ ***noun*** [C] a living thing that is different from other living things of the same type because of a change in its basic (genetic) structure

**mu·ta·tion** /myuˈteɪʃn/ ***noun*** [C,U] a change in the basic structure of a living or developing thing; an example of such a change: *genetic mutations caused by radiation*

**mute** /myut/ ***adj.*** **1** unable to speak **2** (*formal*) silent; not speaking: *a look of mute terror*

**mut·ed** /ˈmyut̬əd/ ***adj.*** **1** (used about colors or sounds) not bright or loud; soft **2** (used about a feeling or reaction) not strong or not openly expressed: *muted criticism* ◇ *a muted response*

**mu·ti·late** /ˈmyut̬əleɪt/ ***verb*** [T] (usually passive) to damage sb's body very badly, often by cutting off parts: *The body was too badly mutilated to be identified.* ▸ **mu·ti·la·tion** /ˌmyut̬əˈleɪʃn/ ***noun*** [C,U]

**mu·ti·ny¹** /ˈmyutn·i/ ***noun*** [C,U] (*pl.* **mu·ti·nies**) an act that involves a group of people, especially sailors or soldiers, refusing to obey the person who is in command: *There'll be a mutiny if conditions don't improve.*

**mu·ti·ny²** /ˈmyutn·i/ ***verb*** [I] (*pres. part.* **mu·ti·ny·ing**; *3rd person sing. pres.* **mu·ti·nies**; *pt, pp* **mu·ti·nied**) **mutiny (against sb/sth)** to refuse to obey your leader or to accept sth



M

**mutt** /mʌt/ ***noun*** [C] a dog which has parents of different types (**breeds**)

**mut·ter** /ˈmʌt̬ər/ ***verb*** [I,T] to speak in a low, quiet and sometimes rather angry voice that is difficult to hear: *He muttered something about being late for an appointment and left the room.*

**mut·ton** /ˈmʌtn/ ***noun*** [U] the meat from an adult sheep: *a leg of mutton* ◇ *a mutton chop* ➲ Look at the note at **meat**.

**mu·tu·al** /ˈmyutʃuəl/ ***adj.*** **1** (used about a feeling or an action) felt or done by both or all the people involved: *Harry left the company by mutual agreement* (= both Harry and the company agreed). ◇ *I just can't stand her and I'm sure the feeling is mutual* (= she doesn't like me either). **2** shared by two or more people: *We get along very well together because we have so many mutual interests.* ◇ *It seems that Jane is a mutual friend of ours.* ▶ **mu·tu·al·ly** /ˈmyutʃuəli; -tʃəli/ ***adv.***: *The statements of the two witnesses were mutually exclusive* (= they could not both be true).

ˈ**mutual fund** ***noun*** [C] a way to use money so that you can earn more money (**invest**) by buying shares in a number of different companies, together with other people (**investors**)

**muz·zle** /ˈmʌzl/ ***noun*** [C] **1** the nose and mouth of an animal (e.g. a dog or fox) **2** a cover made of leather or wire that is put over an animal's nose and mouth so that it cannot bite **3** the open end of a gun where the bullets come out

★**my** /maɪ/ ***det.*** **1** of or belonging to me: *This is my husband, Jim.* ◇ *It's my turn, not yours!* ◇ *My favorite color is blue.* **2** (used before a noun or an adjective as a way of talking to sb): *My dear Anne, ...* ◇ *Goodbye, my darling.* **3** (used in exclamations): *My goodness! Look at the time.*

★**my·self** /maɪˈsɛlf/ ***pronoun*** **1** (used as the object of a verb or preposition when the person who does an action is also affected by it): *I saw myself in the mirror.* ◇ *I felt pretty pleased with myself.* **2** (used for emphasis): *I'll speak to her myself.* ◇ *I myself don't agree.* ◇ *I'll do it myself* (= if you don't want to do it for me).

IDM **(all) by myself 1** alone: *I live by myself.* ➲ Look at the note at **alone**. **2** without help: *I painted the house all by myself.*

★**mys·te·ri·ous** /mɪˈstɪriəs/ ***adj.*** **1** that you do not know about or cannot explain; strange: *Several people reported seeing mysterious lights in the sky.* **2** (used about a person) keeping sth secret or refusing to explain sth: *They're being very mysterious about where they're going this evening.* ▶ **mys·te·ri·ous·ly** ***adv.***

**mys·ter·y** /ˈmɪstəri/ ***noun*** (*pl.* **mys·ter·ies**) **1** [C] a thing that you cannot understand or explain: *The police are still trying to solve the mystery of his disappearance.* ◇ *It's a mystery to me what my daughter sees in her boyfriend.* ◇ *It's one of the great mysteries of the natural world.* ◇ *a mystery guest/ person* (= one that you don't know anything about) **2** [U] the quality of being strange and secret and full of things that are difficult to explain: *novels full of mystery and suspense* ◇ *a mystery story* **3** [C] a book or story about a crime, etc. that seems difficult to explain: *a mystery by Agatha Christie*

**mys·tic** /ˈmɪstɪk/ ***noun*** [C] a person who spends his/her life developing the spirit and communicating with God or a god

**mys·ti·cal** /ˈmɪstɪkl/ (*also* **mys·tic** /ˈmɪstɪk/) ***adj.*** of the spirit; involving hidden meaning, powers and feelings that are outside our normal everyday experience: *a mystical experience*

**mys·ti·cism** /ˈmɪstəsɪzəm/ ***noun*** [U] the belief that you can reach complete truth and knowledge of God or gods by prayer, thought and development of the spirit

**mys·ti·fy** /ˈmɪstəfaɪ/ ***verb*** [T] (*pres. part.* **mys·ti·fy·ing**; *3rd person sing. pres.* **mys·ti·fies**; *pt, pp* **mys·ti·fied**) to make sb puzzled or confused: *I was mystified by the strange note. What did it mean?*

**myth** /mɪθ/ ***noun*** [C] **1** a very old story, especially one about gods and heroes. Myths often explain natural or historical events. **2** an idea, belief or story which is untrue or impossible: *The idea that money makes you happy is a complete myth.*

**myth·i·cal** /ˈmɪθɪkl/ ***adj.*** **1** existing only in MYTHS (1): *mythical heroes* **2** not real; existing only in the imagination

**my·thol·o·gy** /mɪˈθɑlədʒi/ ***noun*** [U] very old stories and the beliefs contained in them: *Greek and Roman mythology*

# Nn

**N, n** /ɛn/ ***noun*** [C,U] (*pl.* **N's** or **n's**) the fourteenth letter of the English alphabet: *"Nicholas" begins with (an) "N."*

**N** (*also* **N.**) ***abbr.*** north: *N. American*

**na·chos** /ˈnɑtʃoʊz/ ***noun*** [pl.] a dish made with thin pieces of fried corn (**tortilla chips**), served with cheese, beans, meat, sauces, etc.

**nag** /næg/ ***verb*** (**nag·ging**; **nagged**) **1** [I,T] **nag (at) sb** to talk to sb continuously in a complaining or critical way: *Quit nagging! I'll do it as soon as I can.* ◇ *My parents are always nagging me to clean my room.* **2** [T] to worry or hurt sb continuously: *a nagging doubt in my mind* ◇ *a nagging backache*

**nails**

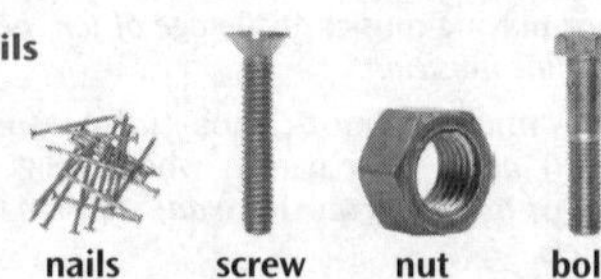


★**nail**[1] /neɪl/ ***noun*** [C] **1** a small thin piece of metal with a point at one end. It is used for holding pieces of wood together, hanging pictures on, etc.: *to hammer a nail into a wall* **2** the thin hard layer that covers the ends of your fingers and toes: *fingernails ◇ toenails ◇ I still bite my nails sometimes when I'm nervous.*

IDM **hit the nail on the head** → HIT[1]

**nail**[2] /neɪl/ ***verb*** [T] to fasten sth with a NAIL[1] (1) or nails: *Do you think we should nail these pieces together or use glue?*

PHRV **nail sb down (to sth)** to make a person say clearly what he/she wants or intends to do: *She says she'll visit us in the summer, but I can't nail her down to a definite date.*

**ˈnail brush** ***noun*** [C] a small brush for cleaning your fingernails ➲ picture at **brush**[1].

**ˈnail file** ***noun*** [C] a small tool with a rough surface that you use for shaping your nails

**ˈnail ˌpolish** ***noun*** [U] a liquid that people paint on their nails to give them color or to make them shine

**na·ive** (*also* **naïve**) /nɑˈiv; naɪ-/ ***adj.*** without enough experience of the world and too ready to believe what other people say: *I was too naive to really understand what was going on. ◇ a naive remark* ▶ **na·ive·ly** (*also* **naïvely**) ***adv.***: *She naively accepted the first price he offered.* ▶ **na·ive·te** (*also* **naïveté** /nɑˌivˈteɪ; nɑˈivəteɪ; naɪ-/) ***noun*** [U]: *He showed complete naivete in financial matters.*

★**na·ked** /ˈneɪkəd/ ***adj.*** **1** without any clothes on: *He came to the door naked except for a towel.* ➲ Look at **bare** (1) and **nude**. **2** (only *before* a noun) not covered (used about sth that is usually covered): *a naked flame* **3** (only *before* a noun) openly shown or expressed; easy to see and often shocking: *naked aggression*

IDM **the naked eye** the eye without the help of a microscope or telescope: *Bacteria are too small to be seen with the naked eye.*

**stark naked** → STARK[2]

★**name**[1] /neɪm/ ***noun*** **1** [C] a word or words by which a person, an animal, a place or a thing is known: *What's your name? ◇ Do you know the name of this flower? ◇ Does this kind of sauce have a name?*

> NOTE Your **first name** (also **given name**) is the name your parents choose for you when you are born. Most people in the United States and Canada also have a **middle name** which is also chosen by their parents, but they may not use it very often. Some people use their **middle initial** on forms, documents, etc. (such as "Steven N. Palmer"). **Last name** is the expression usually used for your family name which you are born with. When a woman gets married, she may change her last name to be the same as her husband's. Her last name before marriage is then called her **maiden name** and many women choose to use their maiden name in place of their middle name.

**2** [sing.] an opinion that people have of a person or thing; reputation: *That area of Miami has a pretty bad name. ◇ The company needs to build up a good name for itself.* **3** [C] a famous person: *All the big names in show business were invited to the party.*

IDM **by name** using the name of sb/sth: *It's a big school, but the principal knows all the students by name.*

**in the name of sth** because you believe in sth; for the sake of: *They acted in the name of democracy.*

**in the name of sb** representing a certain group of people: *Could you write a letter in the name of our class at school?*

**make a name for yourself; make your name** to become well known and respected: *an actor who made his name in comedies*

**the name of the game** the most important thing in a particular activity, business, etc.: *Staying ahead of our competitors is the name of the game here.*

★**name**[2] /neɪm/ ***verb*** [T] **1 name sb/sth (after/for sb)** to give sb/sth a name: *What are you going to name your baby? ◇ The boy was named for his grandfather Harold. ◇ Washington, D.C., was named after George Washington.*

> NOTE Be careful. When you are talking about being known by a particular name, **be named** or **be called** is used: *The baby is named Dan and his brother is Joe.*

**2** to say what the name of sb/sth is: *The journalist refused to name the person who had given her the information. ◇ Can you name all the planets in order?* **3** to state a date, price, etc.: *Have Alex and Julie named a date for their wedding?*

**ˈname-ˌcalling** ***noun*** [U] the act of using rude or insulting words about sb: *Children have to learn that name-calling is not appropriate behavior.*

**ˈname-ˌdrop** ***verb*** [I] to mention the names of famous or important people you know or have met in order to impress other people: *She's fun to be with except when she starts to name-drop.* ▶ **ˈname-ˌdropping** ***noun*** [U]

**name·less** /ˈneɪmləs/ ***adj.*** **1** without a name or with a name that you do not know or want to say: *the nameless slaves who built the pyramids* **2** not easily described or explained, e.g. because it is so terrible: *the nameless horrors of war*

**name·ly** /ˈneɪmli/ ***adv.*** (used for giving more detail about what you are saying) that is to say: *We both reached the same conclusion – namely, that it was time to sell the business.*

**name·sake** /ˈneɪmseɪk/ ***noun*** [C] a person who has the same name as another

**nan·ny** /ˈnæni/ ***noun*** [C] (*pl.* **nan·nies**) a woman whose job is taking care of young children. A nanny usually works at or lives in the child's home.

**nap**[1] /næp/ ***noun*** [C] a short sleep that you have during the day

**nap**[2] /næp/ ***verb*** [I] (**nap·ping; napped**) to have a short sleep

**nape** /neɪp/ ***noun*** [sing.] the back part of the neck

**nap·kin** /ˈnæpkən/ ***noun*** [C] **1** a piece of cloth or paper that you use when you are eating to protect your clothes or for wiping your hands and mouth: *a paper/cloth napkin* **2** = SANITARY NAPKIN

**nar·cot·ic** /nɑrˈkɑṭɪk/ ***noun*** [C] a drug that makes you feel sleepy or stops you from feeling pain. Many types of narcotics are illegal. Some people take narcotics for pleasure and then cannot stop taking them (= they become addicted). ▶ **nar·cot·ic** ***adj.***

**nar·rate** /ˈnæreɪt; næˈreɪt/ ***verb*** [T] (*formal*) to tell a story

**nar·ra·tion** /næ'reɪʃn/ ***noun*** [C,U] telling a story; the story that you tell

**nar·ra·tive** /'nærət̬ɪv/ ***noun*** [C] *(formal)* a story or an account

**nar·ra·tor** /'næreɪt̬ər/ ***noun*** [C] the person who tells a story or explains what is happening in a play, movie, etc.

★ **nar·row¹** /'næroʊ/ ***adj.*** **1** having only a short distance from side to side: *The bridge is too narrow for two cars to pass.* OPP **wide** or **broad** **2** not large: *a narrow circle of friends* **3** by a small amount: *That was a very narrow escape. You were lucky.* ◇ *a narrow defeat/victory* ▸ **nar·row·ness** ***noun*** [U]

**nar·row²** /'næroʊ/ ***verb*** [I,T] to become narrow or to make sth narrow: *The road narrows ahead.*

PHR V **narrow sth down** to make a list of things smaller: *We had a huge list of places we wanted to visit on vacation, but we managed to narrow it down to three.*

**nar·row·ly** /'næroʊli/ ***adv.*** only by a small amount: *The driver swerved and narrowly missed hitting the boy.*

**ˌnarrow-'minded** ***adj.*** not willing to accept new ideas or the opinions of other people if they are not the same as your own

**NASA** /'næsə/ ***abbr.*** National Aeronautics and Space Administration; the department of the government that is responsible for space exploration

**na·sal** /'neɪzl/ ***adj.*** connected with the nose

**nas·ty** /'næsti/ ***adj.*** (**nas·ti·er**; **nas·ti·est**) **1** angry or aggressive: *When she was asked to leave, she got really nasty.* **2** very unkind: *Nick said some pretty nasty things about his ex-wife.* **3** very bad: *nasty weather* ◇ *That sounds like a nasty cough.* **4** *(informal)* bad or ugly: *Yuck! This stuff tastes nasty!* ▸ **nas·ti·ly** /'næstəli/ ***adv.*** ▸ **nas·ti·ness** ***noun*** [U]

★ **na·tion** /'neɪʃn/ ***noun*** [C] a country or all the people in a country: *The President is going to speak to the nation on television.* ◇ *a summit of the leaders of seven nations*

★ **na·tion·al¹** /'næʃənl/ ***adj.*** concerning all of a nation or country; typical of a particular nation: *Here is today's national and international news.* ◇ *a national newspaper* ◇ *a young Swede dressed in his national costume* ◇ *a national holiday* ➲ Look at **international** and **local**. ▸ **na·tion·al·ly** ***adv.***: *to advertise sth nationally*

**na·tion·al²** /'næʃənl/ ***noun*** [C] *(formal)* a person who comes from a particular country: *There are many Algerian nationals working in France.*

**ˌnational 'anthem** ***noun*** [C] the official song of a country that is played at public events

**ˌNational As'sembly** ***noun*** [sing.] *(Cdn)* the provincial governing body (**legislature**) in Quebec

**ˌnational 'debt** ***noun*** [usually sing.] the total amount of money that the government of a country owes

**the ˌNational 'Guard** ***noun*** [sing.] a type of army in each state of the U.S. Most members of the National Guard are only part-time soldiers: *The governor called in the National Guard to prevent further riots.*

**na·tion·al·ism** /'næʃənl·ɪzəm/ ***noun*** [U] **1** the strong feeling of love or pride that you feel for your own country. Nationalism often makes people think that their own country is better than others. ➲ Look at **patriotism**. **2** the desire of a group of people to form an independent country

**na·tion·al·ist** /'næʃənl·ɪst/ ***noun*** [C] a person who wants a particular group of people to be able to form an independent country: *an Irish nationalist*

**na·tion·al·is·tic** /ˌnæʃənə'lɪstɪk/ ***adj.*** having or showing strong feelings of love for or pride in your own country

NOTE **Nationalistic** is usually used in a critical way, meaning that a person's feelings of pride are too strong. ➲ Look also at **patriotic**.

**na·tion·al·i·ty** /ˌnæʃə'næləṯi/ ***noun*** [C,U] (*pl.* **na·tion·al·i·ties**) being a member of a particular nation or country: *students of many nationalities* ◇ *to have **dual nationality*** (= of two countries) ➲ Look at **citizenship**.

**na·tion·al·ize** /'næʃnəlaɪz/ ***verb*** [T] to put a company or an organization under the control of the government: *The new prime minister wanted to nationalize the country's oil industry.* ➲ Look at **privatize**. ▸ **na·tion·al·i·za·tion** /ˌnæʃənələ'zeɪʃn/ ***noun*** [U]

**ˌnational 'park** ***noun*** [C] a large area of beautiful land that is protected by the federal government so that the public can enjoy it

**na·tion·wide** /ˌneɪʃnwaɪd/ ***adj.***, ***adv.*** over the whole of a country: *The police launched a nationwide hunt for the killer.*

**na·tive¹** /'neɪt̬ɪv/ ***noun*** [C] **1** a person who was born in a particular place: *She lives in Arizona but she's a native of New York.* **2** (usually used by white people about non-white people) a person who lives in a particular place: *When explorers first arrived in South America, they were given a warm welcome by the natives.*

NOTE This sense of **native** is used by people who feel that they are better than the local people and it is becoming rare.

**3** an animal or a plant that lives or grows naturally in a particular place: *The koala is a native of Australia.*

**na·tive²** /'neɪt̬ɪv/ ***adj.*** **1** (only *before* a noun) connected with the place where you were born: *Tadeusz's native land is Poland, but he left in 1938.* **2** (used about an animal or a plant) living or growing naturally in a particular place: *The koala is native to Australia.* **3** **Native** = NATIVE AMERICAN

**ˌNative A'merican** (*also* **Aˌmerican 'Indian**, **Indian**, **Native**) ***adj.***, ***noun*** [C] (of) a member of the race of people who were the original inhabitants of North America; especially the area that is now the U.S. (but not Alaska or Hawaii)

NOTE Some people do not like the names **American Indian** and **Indian**.

**ˌNative Ca'nadian** ***noun*** [C] *(Cdn)* an Aboriginal Canadian; a Canadian Indian, Inuit or Metis

**ˌnative 'speaker** ***noun*** [C] a person who learned a particular language as a very young child: *Are you a native speaker of Dutch?*

**NATO** /ˈneɪt̬oʊ/ ***abbr.*** North Atlantic Treaty Organization; a group of European countries, Canada and the U.S., who agree to give each other military help if necessary

★**nat·u·ral** /ˈnætʃərəl/ ***adj.*** **1** connected with things that were not made by people: *natural disasters such as earthquakes and floods* ◇ *We use only natural flavorings in our products.* ◇ *I prefer to see animals in their natural surroundings rather than in zoos.*

> NOTE If somebody dies of **natural causes**, he/she dies because he/she was sick or old, not because he/she was killed in an accident.

**2** usual or normal; what you would expect: *It's natural to feel nervous before an interview.* ◇ *It's only natural for people to be nervous.* OPP **unnatural** **3** that you had from birth or that was easy for you to learn: *a natural gift for languages* ◇ *natural charm*

ˌ**natural ˈgas** ***noun*** [U] a mixture of gases taken from the earth that is used for heating, cooking, etc.: *We heat our home with natural gas.* ◇ *a natural gas pipeline*

ˌ**natural ˈhistory** ***noun*** [U] the study of plants and animals

**nat·u·ral·ist** /ˈnætʃrəlɪst/ ***noun*** [C] a person who studies plants and animals

**nat·u·ral·ize** /ˈnætʃrəlaɪz/ ***verb*** [T] (usually passive) to make sb a citizen of a country where he/she was not born: *a naturalized American citizen* ▶ **nat·u·ral·i·za·tion** /ˌnætʃrələˈzeɪʃn/ ***noun*** [U]

★**nat·u·ral·ly** /ˈnætʃrəli/ ***adv.*** **1** in a NATURAL (3) way: *Vera is naturally a very cheerful person.* ◇ *Working with computers comes naturally to Nick.* **2** of course; as you would expect: *Naturally, the team was upset about its defeat.* **3** in a way that is normal: *You look very stiff and tense. Try to stand naturally.* ◇ *Don't try and impress people. Just act naturally.* **4** in a way that is not made or done by people: *naturally wavy hair*

★**na·ture** /ˈneɪtʃər/ ***noun*** **1** [U] all the things in the world that were not made or caused by people: *the forces of nature* (e.g. volcanoes/hurricanes) ◇ *If we destroy too many forests, we may upset the balance of nature.* ◇ *the wonders of nature* **2** [C,U] the qualities or features of a person or thing: *He's basically honest by nature.* ◇ *It's not in Shelley's nature to tell lies.* ◇ *The nature of my work is secret and I cannot discuss it.* ◇ *human nature* **3** [sing.] the type or sort of sth: *I'm not very interested in things of that nature.*
IDM **second nature** → SECOND[1]

**-natured** /ˈneɪtʃərd/ ***combining form*** having a particular quality or feature: *good-natured*

**naugh·ty** /ˈnɔt̬i/ ***adj.*** (**naugh·ti·er**; **naugh·ti·est**) (used when you are talking to or about a child) not doing what an adult says; badly-behaved; causing trouble: *one of the naughtiest children in the class* ▶ **naugh·ti·ly** /ˈnɔt̬əli/ ***adv.*** **naugh·ti·ness** ***noun*** [U]

**nau·se·a** /ˈnɔziə; ˈnɔʒə/ ***noun*** [U] the feeling that you are going to vomit (= bring up food from your stomach): *A wave of nausea came over him at the sight of all the blood.* ➲ Look at **sick** (2).

**nau·se·ate** /ˈnɔzieɪt/ ***verb*** [T] to cause sb to feel nausea or strong dislike ▶ **nau·se·at·ing** /-eɪt̬ɪŋ/ ***adj.***

**nau·ti·cal** /ˈnɔt̬ɪkl/ ***adj.*** connected with ships, sailors or sailing

**na·val** /ˈneɪvl/ ***adj.*** connected with the navy: *a naval battle*

**na·vel** /ˈneɪvl/ ***noun*** [C] (*formal*) the small hollow in the middle of your stomach ➲ Look at **belly button** and **umbilical cord**.

**nav·i·ga·ble** /ˈnævɪgəbl/ ***adj.*** that boats can sail along: *a navigable river*

**nav·i·gate** /ˈnævəgeɪt/ ***verb*** **1** [I] to use a map, etc. to find out which way a car, ship, plane, etc. should go: *Early explorers used the stars to navigate.* ◇ *If you drive, I'll navigate.* **2** [T] to move or guide a ship, etc. in a particular direction; to find a way through a difficult place: *We managed to navigate the yacht through the rocks.* ◇ *Nobody had navigated the Amazon until then.* ▶ **nav·i·ga·tion** /ˌnævəˈgeɪʃn/ ***noun*** [U]

**nav·i·ga·tor** /ˈnævəgeɪt̬ər/ ***noun*** [C] a person who navigates

★**na·vy** /ˈneɪvi/ ***noun*** [C] (*pl.* **na·vies**) **1 the Navy** the organization that controls the warships of a country and the people that work on them: *to join the Navy* ➲ Look at **army**, **air force**, **Marine Corps** and **merchant marine**. **2** a group of warships belonging to a country: *Does Switzerland have a navy?*

ˈ**navy bean** (*especially Cdn* **haricot**) ***noun*** [C] a type of small white bean that is usually sold dried or in cans

ˌ**navy ˈblue** (*also* **navy**) ***adj.***, ***noun*** [U] dark blue

**NBA** /ˌɛn bi ˈeɪ/ ***abbr.*** National Basketball Association; the organization of professional basketball teams in North America

**NC-17** /ˌɛn si ˌsɛvənˈtin/ ***adj.*** (used about movies that children under age 17 are not allowed to see)

**NDP** /ˌɛn di ˈpi/ ***abbr.*** (*Cdn*) = THE NEW DEMOCRATIC PARTY

**NDT** /ˌɛn di ˈti/ ***abbr.*** (*Cdn*) = NEWFOUNDLAND DAYLIGHT TIME

**NE** ***abbr.*** northeast; northeastern ➲ Look also at the abbreviations for U.S. states on page **820-821**.

★**near**[1] /nɪr/ ***adj.*** **1** not far in time or distance (from sb/sth): *We're hoping to move to Victoria in the near future.* ◇ *Our new house is very near to Kara's school.* ◇ *Where's the nearest post office?*

> NOTE **Close** and **near** are often the same in meaning, but in some phrases only one of them may be used: *a close friend* ◇ *the near future* ◇ *a close contest.* Look at the note at **next**.

**2** closely related to you: *My nearest relative who's still alive is my cousin.*
IDM **a near miss** a situation where sth nearly hits sth else or where sth bad nearly happens: *Two military planes were involved in a near miss over the desert yesterday.*

★**near**[2] /nɪr/ ***adv.***, ***prep.*** not far in time or distance; close to: *It's a little town near the Oklahoma border.* ◇ *I don't want to sit near the window.* ◇ *Her birthday is near mine.* ◇ *I wasn't sitting near enough to see.* ◇ *They live very near.*

N

IDM **nowhere near** far from: *We've sold nowhere near enough tickets to make a profit.*

**near³** /nɪr/ *verb* [I,T] to get closer to sth in time or distance: *The day was nearing when we would have to decide.* ◇ *The job is nearing completion.*

★ **near·by¹** /ˈnɪrbaɪ/ *adj.* (only *before* a noun) not far away in distance: *We went out to a nearby restaurant.*

NOTE Notice that **nearby** is only used before the noun. **Near** cannot be used before a noun in this way: *We went out to a restaurant near our house.* ◇ *The restaurant is pretty near there.*

★ **near·by²** /ˌnɪrˈbaɪ/ *adv.* not far away in distance: *A new restaurant has opened nearby.*

★ **near·ly** /ˈnɪrli/ *adv.* almost; not completely or exactly: *It's been nearly five years since the last time I saw him.* ◇ *Linda was so badly hurt she nearly died.* ◇ *It's not far now. We're nearly there.* ◇ *He earns nearly $50,000 a year.*

IDM **not nearly** far from: *It's not nearly as warm as it was yesterday.*

**near-sighted** /ˈnɪrˌsaɪt̬əd/ *adj.* only able to see things clearly when they are close OPP **far-sighted**

★ **neat** /nit/ *adj.* **1** with everything arranged in its place or done carefully: *Please keep your room neat and clean.* ◇ *neat handwriting* (= with all the letters carefully formed) **2** (used about a person) liking things to be done or arranged carefully **3** (*informal*) good; nice; interesting: *We saw a lot of neat stuff at the Science Museum.* ▸ **neat·ly** *adv.* **neat·ness** *noun* [U]

★ **nec·es·sar·i·ly** /ˌnɛsəˈsɛrəli/ *adv.* in all cases; always: *Shouting is not necessarily the best way to make yourself understood.*

★ **nec·es·sar·y** /ˈnɛsəˌsɛri/ *adj.* needed in order to get sth or to do sth: *A good diet is necessary for a healthy life.* ◇ *Don't spend more than $20 unless it's absolutely necessary.* ◇ *It's not necessary for you all to come.*

**ne·ces·si·tate** /nəˈsɛsəteɪt/ *verb* [T] (*formal*) to make sth necessary

**ne·ces·si·ty** /nəˈsɛsət̬i/ *noun* (*pl.* **ne·ces·si·ties**) **1** [U] (*formal*) **necessity (for sth/to do sth)** being necessary; need: *Is there any necessity for change?* ◇ *There's no necessity to write every single name down.* **2** [C] something that you must have: *Clean water is an absolute necessity.* ◇ *Food, clothing and shelter are all necessities of life.*

★ **neck** /nɛk/ *noun* [C] **1** the part of the body that joins your head to your shoulders: *She wrapped a scarf around her neck.* ◇ *Giraffes have long necks.* **2** the part of a piece of clothing that goes around your neck: *The neck on this sweater is too tight.* ◇ *a V-neck sweater* **3** the narrow part of sth that looks like a neck: *the neck of a bottle*

IDM **neck and neck (with sb/sth)** equal or level: *At the halfway point, the two cars were neck and neck.*

**pain in the neck** → PAIN¹

**be up to your ears/eyes/neck in sth** → UP¹

**neck·lace** /ˈnɛkləs/ *noun* [C] a piece of jewelry that you wear around your neck ➲ picture at **jewelry**.

**neck·tie** /ˈnɛktaɪ/ (*also* **tie**) *noun* [C] a long thin piece of cloth that you wear around your neck with a shirt ➲ Look at **bow tie**.

**nec·tar·ine** /ˌnɛktəˈrin/ *noun* [C] a soft round red and yellow fruit with a smooth skin

★ **need¹** /nid/ *verb* [T] (not usually used in the continuous forms) **1** to require sth; to think that sth is necessary: *All living things need water.* ◇ *I need a new roll of film for my camera.* ◇ *Does Bob need any help?* ◇ *Can I borrow your dictionary or do you need it?* ◇ *She needs three volunteers to bring the food.* ◇ *This sweater needs washing/to be washed.* ◇ *He needed his eyes tested.* **2** to have to; to be obliged to: *Do we need to buy the tickets in advance?* ◇ *I need to ask some advice.* ◇ *You didn't need to bring any food, but it was very kind of you.*

NOTE Note that the question form of the main verb **need** is **do I need**?, etc. and the past tense is **needed** (question form **did you need**?, etc.; negative **didn't need**).

★ **need²** /nid/ *noun* **1** [U, sing.] a situation in which sth is wanted or required: *We are all in need of a rest.* ◇ *There is a growing need for low-cost housing in this area.* ◇ *There's no need for you to come if you don't want to.* ◇ *Is there any need for all that noise?* ◇ *Please call me if you feel the need to talk.* **2 needs** [pl.] the things that you must have: *He doesn't earn enough to pay for his basic needs.* ◇ *Parents must consider their children's emotional as well as their physical needs.* **3** [U] the state of not having enough money: *a campaign to help families in need*

★ **nee·dle** /ˈnidl/ *noun* [C] **1** a small thin piece of metal with a point at one end and a hole (an eye) at the other that is used for sewing: *to thread a needle* **2** (*also* **knitting needle**) a long thin piece of metal, plastic or wood with a point at one end that is used for knitting ➲ picture at **knit**. **3** the thin hollow part of a syringe that is used for injecting liquids into your body **4** something that looks like a needle: *the needle of a compass* ◇ *a pine needle* ➲ picture at **tree**. ➲ Look also at **pins and needles**.

**need·less** /ˈnidləs/ *adj.* that is not necessary: *We had gone through a lot of needless worry. He was safe at home.* SYN **unnecessary** ▸ **need·less·ly** *adv.*

**need·le·work** /ˈnidlwərk/ *noun* [U] work that you do by hand using a NEEDLE (1). Needlework includes sewing and embroidery.

**need·y** /ˈnidi/ *adj.* (**need·i·er**; **need·i·est**) not having enough money, etc.; poor

**ne·gate** /nɪˈgeɪt/ *verb* [T] (*formal*) **1** to stop sth from having any effect: *Alcohol negates the effects of the drug.* **2** to state that sth does not exist

★ **ne·ga·tive¹** /ˈnɛgət̬ɪv/ (*abbr.* **neg.**) *adj.* **1** (used about a word, phrase or sentence) saying or meaning "no" or "not": *a negative sentence* ◇ *"Don't you like Maryland?" is a negative question.* ➲ Look at **affirmative**. **2** only thinking about the bad qualities of sb/sth: *I wish you wouldn't be so negative about everything – try to look on the bright side.* OPP **positive** **3** (used about a medical or scientific test) showing that sth has not happened or has not been found: *The results of the pregnancy test were negative.* OPP **positive** **4** (used about a number) less than zero OPP **positive** **5** bad or harmful: *The* *effects of the new rule have been negative.* OPP **positive**

**ne·ga·tive²** /ˈnɛgət̬ɪv/ ***noun*** [C] **1** a word, phrase or sentence that says or means "no" or "not": *Carol answered in the negative* (= she said no). ◇ *"Never," "neither" and "nobody" are all negatives.* **2** a piece of film from which we can make a photograph. The light areas of a negative are dark on the final photograph and the dark areas are light: *If you give me the negative, I can have another print made.*

**ne·glect¹** /nɪˈglɛkt/ ***verb*** [T] to give too little or no attention or care to sb/sth: *to neglect your studies*

**ne·glect²** /nɪˈglɛkt/ ***noun*** [U] giving too little care to sb/sth; the state of being neglected: *The house was empty and in a state of total neglect.* ◇ *The parents were arrested and charged with child neglect.*

**ne·glect·ed** /nɪˈglɛktəd/ ***adj.*** having or showing a lack of care and attention: *Neglected children often have trouble in school.*

**neg·li·gee** (*also* **neg·li·gée**) /ˌnɛglɪˈʒeɪ; ˈnɛglɪʒeɪ/ ***noun*** [C] a sort of loose coat (**dressing gown**) made of very light fabric and worn by women

**neg·li·gence** /ˈnɛglɪdʒəns/ ***noun*** [U] not being careful enough; lack of care: *The accident was a result of human negligence.*

**neg·li·gent** /ˈnɛglɪdʒənt/ ***adj.*** not giving enough care or attention to sth (that you are responsible for) ▸ **neg·li·gent·ly *adv.***

**neg·li·gi·ble** /ˈnɛglɪdʒəbl/ ***adj.*** not important because it is too small

**ne·go·tia·ble** /nəˈgoʊʃəbl/ ***adj.*** that can be decided or changed by discussion: *The price is not negotiable* (= it can't be changed).

**ne·go·ti·ate** /nəˈgoʊʃieɪt/ ***verb*** **1** [I] to talk to sb in order to decide or agree about sth: *Union leaders are still negotiating with the management about this year's pay increase.* **2** [T] **negotiate sth (with sb)** to decide or agree sth by talking about it: *to negotiate an agreement* **3** [T] to get over, past or along sth difficult: *The bike racers had to negotiate several difficult turns along the route.*

**ne·go·ti·a·tion** /nəˌgoʊʃiˈeɪʃn/ ***noun*** [C,U] discussions at which people try to decide or agree on sth: *The salary is open to negotiation.* ◇ *The negotiations were extremely difficult.* ◇ *to enter/break off negotiations*

**ne·go·ti·a·tor** /nəˈgoʊʃieɪt̬ər/ ***noun*** [C] a person who NEGOTIATES (1,2)

**Ne·gro** /ˈnigroʊ/ ***noun*** [C] (*pl.* **Ne·groes**) (*old-fashioned*) a black person

> NOTE This word is now considered offensive. Look at **African-American**.

**neigh** /neɪ/ ***noun*** [C] the long high sound that a horse makes ▸ **neigh *verb*** [I]

★**neigh·bor** /ˈneɪbər/ ***noun*** [C] **1** a person who lives near you: *Don't make too much noise, or you'll wake the neighbors.* ◇ *our next-door neighbors* **2** a person or thing that is near or next to another: *The United States is Canada's neighbor.* ◇ *Try not to look at what your neighbor is writing.*

★**neigh·bor·hood** /ˈneɪbərhʊd/ ***noun*** [C] a particular part of a town or city and the people who live there: *We just moved into the neighborhood and don't know our way around yet.* ◇ *a friendly neighborhood*

**neigh·bor·ing** /ˈneɪbərɪŋ/ ***adj.*** (only *before* a noun) near or next to: *Kids from all the neighboring towns will attend the new school.*

**neigh·bor·ly** /ˈneɪbərli/ ***adj.*** friendly and helpful

★**nei·ther¹** /ˈniðər; ˈnaɪ-/ ***det.***, ***pronoun*** (used about two people or things) not one and not the other: *Neither team played very well.* ◇ *Neither of the teams played very well.* ◇ *"Would you like a sandwich? Or a piece of cake?" "Neither, thank you. I'm not hungry."* ◇ *I asked both Jamal and Terry, but neither one wanted to come along.*

> NOTE Notice that **neither** is followed by a singular noun and verb: *Neither day was suitable.* The noun or pronoun that follows **neither of** is in the plural, but the verb may be singular or plural: *(formal) Neither of the days is suitable.* ◇ *(informal) Neither of the days are suitable.*

★**nei·ther²** /ˈniðər; ˈnaɪ-/ ***adv.***, ***conj.*** **1** also not; not either: *I don't eat meat and neither does Tom.* ◇ *Stella didn't attend the meeting and neither did Jane.* ◇ *"I haven't seen that play." "Neither have I."*

> NOTE In this sense **nor** can be used in the same way in formal English: *"I haven't seen that play." "Nor have I."* Notice that when you use **not ... either** the order of words is different: *I don't eat meat and Tom doesn't either.* ◇ *"I haven't seen that play." "I haven't either."*

**2 neither... nor** not... and not: *Neither Tom nor I eat meat.*

> NOTE **Neither ... nor** can be used with a singular or a plural verb: *(formal) Neither Stella nor Jane was at the meeting.* ◇ *(informal) Neither Stella nor Jane were at the meeting.*

**ne·on** /ˈniɑn/ ***noun*** [U] (*symbol* **Ne**) a type of gas that is used for making bright lights and signs: *the neon lights of the city*

**neph·ew** /ˈnɛfyu/ ***noun*** [C] the son of your brother or sister, or the son of your husband's or wife's brother or sister ➲ Look at **niece**.

**Nep·tune** /ˈnɛptun/ ***noun*** [sing.] the planet that is eighth in order from the sun

**nerd** /nərd/ ***noun*** [C] (*slang*) a person who is boring and unfashionable and who is often very interested in science and computers: *a computer nerd* ➲ This word is used in a critical way. ▸ **nerd·y *adj.***

★**nerve** /nərv/ ***noun*** **1** [C] one of the long thin threads in your body that carry feelings or other messages to and from your brain **2 nerves** [pl.] the ability to stay calm and not get worried: *You need strong nerves for this job.* **3 nerves** [pl.] the state of being very nervous or worried: *Breathing deeply should help to calm your nerves.* **4** [U] the courage that you need to do sth difficult or dangerous: *Race car drivers need a lot of nerve.* ◇ *He didn't have the nerve to ask Mandy to go out with him.* ◇ *She climbed to the highest diving board but lost her nerve and couldn't jump.* **5** [U] the rudeness that is needed to do sth: *He had the nerve to ask me to loan him some money, and he still owes me $20.*

IDM **get on sb's nerves** (*informal*) to annoy sb or

N

make sb angry: *Turn that music down – it's getting on my nerves.*

**nerve-racking** (*also* **nerve-wracking**) /ˈnərv-ˌrækɪŋ/ ***adj.*** making you very nervous or worried: *Waiting for test scores can be very nerve-racking.*

★**nerv·ous** /ˈnərvəs/ ***adj.*** **1** connected with the nerves of the body: *a nervous disorder* **2** worried or afraid: *I'm a little nervous about traveling on my own.* ◇ *I always get nervous just before a game.* ◇ *nervous laughter* ▸ **nerv·ous·ly** ***adv.***: *He sat there, biting his fingernails nervously.* ▸ **nerv·ous·ness** ***noun*** [U]

ˌ**nervous ˈbreakdown** (*also* **break·down**) ***noun*** [C] a time when sb is so depressed that he/she cannot continue living and working normally: *to have a nervous breakdown*

ˈ**nervous ˌsystem** ***noun*** [C] your brain and all the nerves in your body

**nest¹** /nɛst/ ***noun*** [C] **1** a round hollow structure that a bird builds to lay its eggs in **2** the home of certain animals or insects: *a wasps' nest*

**nest²** /nɛst/ ***verb*** [I] to use or build a NEST¹

ˈ**nest egg** ***noun*** [C] (*informal*) a sum of money that you save to use in the future

**nes·tle** /ˈnɛsl/ ***verb*** [I,T] to move yourself or a part of your body into a comfortable position, against a person or sth soft: *The child nestled up against his mother.* ◇ *The baby nestled her head on her mother's shoulder.* ◇ (*figurative*) *a beautiful town nestled in a river valley*

★**net¹** /nɛt/ ***noun*** **1** [U] material that is made of long pieces of string, thread, etc. that are tied together, with spaces between them: *a piece of nylon net* ➲ Look also at **netting**. **2** [C] a piece of net that is used for a particular purpose: *a tennis net* (= in the center of the court) ◇ *a fishing net* ◇ *a hairnet* ➲ picture at **tennis**. ➲ Look at **safety net**. **3 the Net** [sing.] (*informal*) = INTERNET

**net²** /nɛt/ ***adj.*** (only *before* a noun) from which nothing more needs to be taken away: *What is your net income?* (= after taxes, etc. have been paid) ◇ *The net weight of the jam is 12 ounces* (= not including the jar). ◇ *net profit* OPP **gross**

**net³** /nɛt/ ***verb*** [T] (**net<u>t</u>ing**; **net<u>t</u>ed**) **1** to gain sth as a profit: *The sale of the land netted the county $2 million.* **2** to catch sth using a NET¹ (2)

**net·ting** /ˈnɛt̬ɪŋ/ ***noun*** [U] material that is made of long pieces of string, thread, wire, etc. that are tied together with spaces between them: *a bridal veil made of white netting*

★**net·work** /ˈnɛtwərk/ ***noun*** [C] **1** a group of people or companies, etc. that work together closely: *We have a network of agents who sell our products all over the country.* **2** a group of television or radio companies that broadcasts the same programs in different parts of a country **3** a complicated system of roads, train tracks, etc.: *The subway network covers all areas of the capital.* **4** a system of computers that are connected by cables or telephone lines

**neu·ro·sis** /nʊˈroʊsəs/ ***noun*** [C] (*pl.* **neu·ro·ses** /-siz/) a mental illness that causes strong feelings of fear and worry

**neu·rot·ic** /nʊˈrɑt̬ɪk/ ***adj.*** **1** suffering from neurosis **2** worried about things in a way that is not normal

**neu·ter¹** /ˈnut̬ər/ ***adj.*** (used about a word) not masculine or feminine according to the rules of grammar

**neu·ter²** /ˈnut̬ər/ ***verb*** [T] to remove the sexual parts of an animal

**neu·tral¹** /ˈnutrəl/ ***adj.*** **1** not supporting or belonging to either side in an argument, war, etc.: *Switzerland remained neutral during the war.* ◇ *The two sides agreed to meet on neutral ground.* **2** having or showing no strong qualities, feelings or color: *a blouse in a neutral color that will go with anything*

**neu·tral²** /ˈnutrəl/ ***noun*** [U] the position that the gears of a car, etc. are in when no power is sent from the engine to the wheels, but the wheels can still turn: *Make sure the car is in neutral before you turn on the engine.* ➲ Look also at **drive²**(4), **park¹**(4) and **reverse²**(2).

**neu·tral·i·ty** /nuˈtræləṭi/ ***noun*** [U] the state of being NEUTRAL¹ (1) in an argument, war, etc.

**neu·tral·ize** /ˈnutrəlaɪz/ ***verb*** [T] to take away the effect of sth

**neu·tron** /ˈnutrɑn/ ***noun*** [C] a very small piece of matter with no electric charge, found in all atoms ➲ Look also at **electron** and **proton**.

★**nev·er** /ˈnɛvər/ ***adv.*** at no time; not ever: *I never start work before 9 o'clock.* ◇ *I've never been to Portugal.* ◇ *We'll never go back to that hotel.* ◇ *You should never leave valuables in your car.* ◇ *He never ever eats meat.* ◇ (*formal*) *Never before has such a high standard been achieved.*

IDM **never mind** → MIND²

★**nev·er·the·less** /ˌnɛvərðəˈlɛs/ ***adv.*** (*formal*) in spite of that: *It was a cold, rainy day. Nevertheless, more people came than we had expected.* ◇ *She knew that the accident wasn't her fault. She still felt guilty, nevertheless.*

★**new** /nu/ ***adj.*** **1** that has recently been built, made, invented, etc.: *We went shopping at the new mall yesterday.* ◇ *There have been record sales of new cars this month.* ◇ *Have you seen Tom Cruise's new movie?* ◇ *a new method of treating mental illness* ◇ *Paula came to show us her new baby.* **2** different; other; changed from what was before: *Our new house is a lot bigger than the old one.* ◇ *I've just started reading a new book.* ◇ *to make new friends* **3 new (to sb)** that has not been seen, learned, etc. before: *This type of machine is new to me.* ◇ *to learn a new language* ◇ *We just moved here, so the area is still new to us.* **4 new (to sth)** having just started being or doing sth: *We are new to the area.* ◇ *a new parent* ◇ *She's new to the job and needs a lot of help.* ◇ *a new member of the club*

IDM **break fresh/new ground** → GROUND¹

▸ **new·ness** ***noun*** [U]

**new-** /nu/ ***combining form*** recently: *a newborn baby*

ˌ**New ˈAge** ***noun*** [U] a set of beliefs connected with religion, health and the environment that are not part of any traditional Western religion ▸ **New ˈAge** ***adj.***: *New Age philosophy*

**new·born** /ˈnubɔrn/ ***adj.*** (used about a baby)

that has been born very recently ▶ **new·born** ***noun*** [C]: *There's nothing as cute as a newborn.*

**new·com·er** /ˈnukʌmər/ ***noun*** [C] a person who has just arrived in a place

**ˌNew ˈDemocrat** ***noun*** [C] (in Canada) a member or supporter of the New Democratic Party

**the ˌNew Demoˌcratic ˈParty** ***noun*** [sing.] (*abbr.* **NDP**) (in Canada) one of the three main political parties, in favor of social reform ➲ Look also at the **Liberal Party** and the **Conservative Party**. For more information about the political system in Canada, look at study page **A11**.

**new·fan·gled** /ˈnufæŋgld/ ***adj.*** new or modern in a way that the speaker dislikes or refuses to accept: *I don't need all these newfangled gadgets in the kitchen.*

**ˌNewfoundland ˈDaylight Time** ***noun*** [U] (*abbr.* **NDT**) (*Cdn*) the time system used in Newfoundland from April to October when clocks are set two and a half hours behind Greenwich Mean Time

**ˌNewfoundland ˈStandard Time** ***noun*** [U] (*abbr.* **NST**) (*Cdn*) the time system used in Newfoundland from October to April when clocks are set three and a half hours behind Greenwich Mean Time

**ˈNewfoundland Time** ***noun*** [U] (*Cdn*) the standard time system that is used in a zone which includes the island of Newfoundland

★**new·ly** /ˈnuli/ ***adv.*** (usually before a past participle) recently: *the newly appointed Secretary of Defense*

**new·ly·wed** /ˈnuliwɛd/ ***noun*** [C, usually pl.] a person who has recently gotten married

**ˌnew ˈmoon** ***noun*** [sing.] the moon when it appears as a thin line ➲ Look at **full moon**.

★**news** /nuz/ ***noun*** **1** [U] information about sth that has happened recently: *Have you heard the latest news? Mary and Joe are getting married!* ◇ *That's news to me* (= I didn't know that). ◇ *News is coming in of a plane crash in Thailand.* ◇ *There will be another news bulletin at 1 o'clock.* ◇ *Our town has been in the news a lot recently* (= a lot has been written in newspapers, etc.).

NOTE **News** is an uncountable noun. If we are talking about an individual item, we must say "a piece of news": *We had a piece of good news yesterday.*

**2 the news** [sing.] a regular broadcast of the latest NEWS (1) on the radio and TV: *We always watch the six o'clock news on TV.* ◇ *I heard on the news that there was a plane crash in Thailand.* ◇ *the local/national news*

IDM **break the news (to sb)** to be the first to tell sb about sth important that has happened

**news·cast** /ˈnuzkæst/ ***noun*** [C] a news program on TV or radio

**news·cast·er** /ˈnuzkæstər/ ***noun*** [C] a person who reads the news on TV or radio

**news·let·ter** /ˈnuzlɛt̬ər/ ***noun*** [C] a printed report about a club or an organization that is sent regularly to members and other people who may be interested

★**news·pa·per** /ˈnuzˌpeɪpər/ ***noun*** **1** (*also* **paper**) [C] large folded pieces of paper printed with news, advertisements and articles on various subjects. Newspapers are usually printed and sold either daily or weekly: *a national/local newspaper* ◇ *a morning/an evening paper* ◇ *a newspaper article/headline* **2** (*also* **paper**) [C] an organization that produces a newspaper: *Which paper is he from?* **3** [U] the paper on which newspapers are printed: *Wrap those glasses in some newspaper so they won't break.*

NOTE **Journalists** and **reporters** collect news for newspapers. The **editor** decides what is printed.

**news·stand** /ˈnuzstænd/ ***noun*** [C] a type of small store which is open at the front and sells newspapers, magazines, and sometimes books

**the ˌNew ˈTestament** ***noun*** [sing.] the second part of the Christian Bible, that tells the story of the life of Jesus Christ and later events ➲ Look at **Old Testament** and at the note at **White House**.

**ˈnew year** ***noun*** [U,sing.] the first few days of January: *Happy New Year!* ◇ *We will get in touch in the new year.*

**ˌNew Year's ˈDay** ***noun*** [U] January 1

**ˌNew Year's ˈEve** ***noun*** [U] December 31

★**next**[1] /nɛkst/ ***adj.*** **1** (usually with *the*) coming immediately after sth in order, space or time; closest: *The next bus leaves in 20 minutes.* ◇ *She went into the hospital on a Sunday and the next day she died.* ◇ *the next name on the list* ◇ *I will be on vacation for the next two weeks.* ◇ *How far is it to the next gas station?* ◇ *Go past the post office and take the next left.*

NOTE Compare **nearest** and **next**. **The next** means "the following" in a series of events or places: *When is your next appointment?* ◇ *Turn left at the next intersection.*(**The**) **nearest** means "the closest" in time or place: *Where's the nearest grocery store?*

**2** (used without *the* before days of the week, months, seasons, years, etc.) the one immediately following the present one: *See you again next Monday.* ◇ *Let's go camping next weekend.* ◇ *We are going to Florida next spring.* ◇ *Rachel hopes to get a job as a teacher next year.* **3 the next *noun*** [sing.] the person or thing that is NEXT (1): *If we miss this train, we'll have to wait two hours for the next.*

IDM **next/second/third to last** → LAST[1]

★**next**[2] /nɛkst/ ***adv.*** **1** after this or that; then: *I wonder what will happen next.* ◇ *I know Joe finished first, but who came next?* ◇ *First brown half a pound of ground beef. Next add one chopped onion.* **2 next to sb/sth** at the side of sb/sth; beside: *He sat down next to Pam.* ◇ *There's a mailbox next to the phone booth over there.* **3 next to sb/sth** in a position after sb/sth: *Next to San Francisco, I think my favorite city is Santa Fe.*

IDM **next to nothing** almost nothing: *We took $50, but we've got next to nothing left.*

**ˌnext ˈbest** ***adj.*** not the best, but good enough if you cannot have the best

★**ˌnext ˈdoor** ***adj., adv.*** in or into the next house or building: *our next-door neighbors* ◇ *Who lives next door?* ◇ *The school is next door to a nursing home.*



N

**ˌnext of ˈkin** *noun* [pl., U] your closest living family member or members

NOTE **Next of kin** is used to mean both a single relative and a group of relatives: *My husband is my next of kin.* ◇ *Her next of kin have been informed of her death.*

**NFL** /ˌɛn ɛf ˈɛl/ ***abbr.*** National Football League; the organization of professional football teams in the U.S.

**NHL** /ˌɛn eɪtʃ ˈɛl/ ***abbr.*** National Hockey League; the organization of professional hockey teams in North America

**nib·ble** /ˈnɪbl/ ***verb*** [I,T] to eat sth by taking small bites ▸ **nib·ble** ***noun*** [C]

★**nice** /naɪs/ ***adj.*** **1** pleasant; good: *The weather was really nice yesterday.* ◇ *Have a nice day!* ◇ *You look very nice today.* ◇ *Go and pick out some nice bananas.* **2** kind; friendly: *What a nice girl!* ◇ *Try and be nice to Julie. She's not feeling well.*
IDM **nice and ...** (*informal*) (used for saying that you like sth): *It's nice and warm by the fire.*

**nice·ly** /ˈnaɪsli/ ***adv.*** **1** in a pleasant way: *You can have a cookie if you ask nicely.* **2** (*informal*) very well: *Things are coming along very nicely on our project.*

**niche** /nɪtʃ; niʃ/ ***noun*** [C] **1** a hollow place in a wall, often with a shelf **2** a job, position, etc. that is suitable for you: *to find your niche in life*

N

**nick¹** /nɪk/ ***noun*** [C] a small cut in sth
IDM **in the nick of time** just barely in time: *The ambulance arrived in the nick of time.*

**nick²** /nɪk/ ***verb*** [T] to make a small cut in sb/sth

**nick·el** /ˈnɪkl/ ***noun*** **1** [C] an American or a Canadian coin that is worth five cents **2** [U] (*symbol* **Ni**) a hard silver-white metal that is often mixed with other metals

**nick·name** /ˈnɪkneɪm/ ***noun*** [C] an informal name that is used instead of your own name, usually by your family or friends

**nic·o·tine** /ˈnɪkətin/ ***noun*** [U] the poisonous chemical substance in tobacco

**niece** /nis/ ***noun*** [C] the daughter of your brother or sister; the daughter of your husband's or wife's brother or sister ➲ Look at **nephew**.

**nig·ger** /ˈnɪgər/ ***noun*** [C] a black person

NOTE This word is extremely offensive.

★**night** /naɪt/ ***noun*** [C,U] **1** the part of the day when it is dark and when most people sleep: *a dark night* ◇ *We will be away for a few nights.* ◇ *Did you sleep well last night?* ◇ *a sleepless night* ◇ *The baby cried all night long.* ◇ *It's a long way home. Why don't you stay the night?* ◇ *Owls come out at night.* **2** the time between late afternoon and when you go to bed: *Let's go out on Saturday night.* ◇ *He doesn't get home until 8 o'clock at night.* ◇ *I tried to call Walter last night, but he was out.*

NOTE Note the use of different prepositions with **night**. **At** is most common: *I'm not allowed out after 11 o'clock at night.* **By** is used about something that you usually do in the daytime: *They slept by day and traveled by night.* **In/during** the night is used for the night that has just passed, but it is also common to use **last night** to talk about that night: *I woke up twice in the night.* ◇ *I woke up twice last night.* **On** is used when we are talking about one particular night: *On the night of Saturday, June 30.* **Tonight** means the night or evening that will come next: *Where are you staying tonight?*

IDM **an early/a late night** to go to bed earlier/later than usual: *Let's make it an early night tonight.* ◇ *I've been spending a lot of late nights in front of the computer.*
**a night on the town/out** an evening that you spend away from home enjoying yourself
**in the dead of night** → DEAD²
**good night** (said late in the evening, before you go home or before you go to sleep)

**night·club** /ˈnaɪtklʌb/ ***noun*** [C] a place where you can go to eat, drink, dance, listen to sb singing, etc. until late at night

**night·gown** /ˈnaɪtgaʊn/ (*also informal* **nightie** /ˈnaɪt̬i/) ***noun*** [C] a loose dress that a girl or woman wears in bed

**night·in·gale** /ˈnaɪtn·geɪl; ˈnaɪtɪŋgeɪl/ ***noun*** [C] a small brown European bird that sings very beautifully

**night·life** /ˈnaɪtlaɪf/ ***noun*** [U] the entertainment that is available at night in a particular place: *It's a small town with very little nightlife.*

★**night·ly** /ˈnaɪtli/ ***adj., adv.*** (done or happening) every night: *The band will be appearing nightly at the Cavern Club.*

**night·mare** /ˈnaɪtmɛr/ ***noun*** [C] **1** a dream that is frightening: *I had a terrible nightmare last night.* **2** something that is very unpleasant or frightening: *Driving in rush-hour traffic can be a real nightmare.*

**ˈnight school** ***noun*** [C] a place where adults can go to classes in the evening

**night·time** /ˈnaɪttaɪm/ ***noun*** [U] the time when it is dark: *Many old people are afraid to go out at nighttime.*

**nil** /nɪl/ ***noun*** [U] nothing: *Our chances of success are virtually nil.*

**nim·ble** /ˈnɪmbl/ ***adj.*** able to move quickly and lightly: *For a large person she's very nimble on her feet.* ▸ **nim·bly** /-bli/ ***adv.***

**nine** /naɪn/ ***number*** 9; one more than eight ➲ For examples of how to use numbers in sentences, look at **six**.
IDM **nine to five** the hours that you work in most offices: *a nine-to-five job*

**nine·teen** /ˌnaɪnˈtin/ ***number*** 19; one more than eighteen ➲ For examples of how to use numbers in sentences, look at **six**. ▸ **nine·teenth** /ˌnaɪnˈtinθ/ ***pronoun, det., adv.*** ➲ Look at the examples at **sixth**.

**nine·ty** /ˈnaɪnt̬i/ ***number*** 90; one more than 89 ➲ For examples of how to use numbers in sentences, look at **sixty**. ▸ **nine·ti·eth** /ˈnaɪnt̬iəθ/ ***pronoun, det., adv.*** ➲ Look at the examples at **sixth**.

**ninth¹** /naɪnθ/ ***pronoun, det., adv.*** 9th; next after eighth ➲ Look at the examples at **sixth**.

**ninth²** /naɪnθ/ ***noun*** [C] the fraction ⅑; one of nine equal parts of sth ➲ Look at the examples at **sixth**.

**nip** /nɪp/ ***verb*** (**nip·ping**; **nipped**) [I,T] to bite or pinch sb/sth lightly: *The dog nipped him on the ankle.*

IDM **nip sth in the bud** to stop or destroy sth at an early stage in its development: *Federal agents managed to nip the consipiracy in the bud.*

PHR V **nip sth off (sth)** to remove a part of sth, usually with your fingers: *to nip off some dead leaves*

**nip·ple** /ˈnɪpl/ ***noun*** [C] **1** the dark hard part in the center of a woman's breast from which a baby drinks milk **2** one of the similar parts on a man's chest **3** a rubber part with a small hole in it through which a baby can drink milk, etc. from a bottle

**ni·tro·gen** /ˈnaɪtrədʒən/ ***noun*** [U] (*symbol* **N**) a gas that has no color, taste or smell. Nitrogen forms about 80% of the air around the earth.

**nitty-gritty** /ˌnɪt̬iˈgrɪt̬i/ ***noun*** [U] **the nitty-gritty** (*informal*) the most important facts, not the small or unimportant details

**No.** ***abbr.*** north

★**no**[1] /noʊ/ ***det.*** **1** not any; not a: *I have no time to talk now.* ◇ *No visitors may enter without a ticket.* ◇ *He's no friend of mine.* ◇ *There are no jobs for high school drop-outs in this town.* **2** (used for saying that sth is not allowed): *No smoking.* ◇ *No children under 16.* ◇ *No parking.*

★**no**[2] /noʊ/ ***interjection*** **1** (used for giving a negative reply or statement): *"Are you ready?" "No, I'm not."* ◇ *"Would you like something to eat?" "No, thank you. I'm not hungry."* ◇ *"Can I borrow the car?" "No, you can't."* ◇ *It's about 70 – no, I'm wrong – 80 miles from Topeka.* ◇ *No! Don't touch it. It's very hot.*

> NOTE You can also use **no** when you want to agree with a negative statement: *"This program's not very good." "No, you're right. It isn't."*

**2** (used for expressing surprise or shock): *"Mike's been in an accident." "Oh, no!"*

**no**[3] /noʊ/ ***adv.*** not any: *There will be no more talking during the test.* ◇ *Applications must be returned no later than July 31.*

**no·bil·i·ty** /noʊˈbɪlət̬i/ ***noun*** **1** [U] the quality of being noble **2** **the nobility** [sing.] the group of people who belong to the highest social class, with titles: *Members of the nobility and other wealthy people were invited to the duke's wedding.*

**no·ble** /ˈnoʊbl/ ***adj.*** **1** belonging to the highest social class, with a title: *a noble family* **2** honest; brave; that other people should admire: *They made a noble effort in the face of many difficulties.*

**no·bly** /ˈnoʊbli/ ***adv.*** in a way that is honest, brave, or that other people should admire: *He nobly sacrificed his own happiness for that of his family.*

★**no·bod·y**[1] /ˈnoʊbʌdi; -bɑdi/ (*also* **no one** /ˈnoʊ wʌn/) ***pronoun*** no person; not anybody: *He screamed, but nobody came to help him.* ◇ *No one else was around.* ◇ *There was nobody home.*

> NOTE **None of**, not **nobody**, must be used before words like *the, his, her, those*, etc. or before a pronoun: *Nobody remembered my birthday.* ◇ *None of my friends remembered my birthday.* ◇ *I asked all my classmates, but nobody is free.* ◇ *None of them are free.*

**no·bod·y**[2] /ˈnoʊbʌdi; -bɑdi/ ***noun*** [C] (*pl.* **no·bod·ies**) a person who is not very important: *Do you want to be a nobody all your life?*

**no-brain·er** /ˌnoʊˈbreɪnər/ ***noun*** [C, usually sing.] (*slang*) a project, problem, question, etc. that is very easy to finish or solve: *The issue of whether to build a new stadium is a real no-brainer for most fans.*

**noc·tur·nal** /nɑkˈtərnl/ ***adj.*** **1** happening in the night: *a nocturnal adventure* **2** (used about animals and birds) awake and active at night: *Owls are nocturnal birds.*

**nod** /nɑd/ ***verb*** (**nod·ding**; **nod·ded**) [I,T] to move your head down and then up again quickly as a way of saying "yes" or as a greeting or a sign: *"Would you like to come too?" he asked. She nodded and got up.* ◇ *Everybody at the meeting nodded in agreement.* ◇ *Nod your head if you understand what I'm saying.* ◇ *We nodded to each other across the room.* ▸ **nod** ***noun*** [C]: *She gave him a quick nod.*

ˌ**no-ˈfault** ***adj.*** (only *before* a noun) not involving a decision as to who is to blame for sth: *no-fault insurance* (in which the insurance company pays for damage no matter who caused it) ◇ *a no-fault divorce*

★**noise** /nɔɪz/ ***noun*** [C,U] something that you hear; a sound, especially one that is loud, unpleasant or unwanted: *Did you hear a noise downstairs?* ◇ *Why is the engine making so much noise?*

**noise·less** /nɔɪzləs/ ***adj.*** making no sound ▸ **noise·less·ly** ***adv.***

★**nois·y** /ˈnɔɪzi/ ***adj.*** (**nois·i·er**; **nois·i·est**) making a lot of or too much noise; full of noise: *Are small boys noisier than girls?* ◇ *We live on a very noisy street.* ➲ Look at the note at **loud**. ▸ **nois·i·ly** /ˈnɔɪzəli/ ***adv.***

**no·mad** /ˈnoʊmæd/ ***noun*** [C] a member of a tribe that travels around to find grass for its animals instead of living in one place ▸ **no·mad·ic** /noʊˈmædɪk/ ***adj.***

ˈ**no man's land** ***noun*** [U] land between two armies in a war, between two borders, etc.

**nom·i·nal** /ˈnɑmənl/ ***adj.*** **1** being sth in name only but not in reality: *the nominal leader of the country* (= sb else is really in control) **2** (used about a price, sum of money, etc.) very small; less than is normal: *Because we were friends, he only charged me a nominal fee.*

**nom·i·nate** /ˈnɑməneɪt/ ***verb*** [T] **1 nominate sb/sth (for/as sth)** to suggest that sb/sth should be considered for an official position, prize, etc.: *I would like to nominate Don Jones as chairman.* ◇ *The movie was nominated for an Oscar for best soundtrack.* **2 nominate sb (to/as sth) (to do sth)** to choose sb/sth for a position: *You may nominate a representative to speak for you.*

**nom·i·na·tion** /ˌnɑməˈneɪʃn/ ***noun*** [C,U] a formal suggestion that sb/sth should be considered for an official position, prize, etc.; the appointment of sb/sth to such a position: *The closing date for nominations is September 8th.* ◇ *The movie received 10 Oscar nominations.* ◇ *His nomination as the party's candidate was announced at the convention.*

**nom·i·nee** /ˌnɑməˈni/ ***noun*** [C] a person who is suggested or chosen for a position



N

**non·al·co·hol·ic** /ˌnɑnælkəˈhɔlɪk; -ˈhɑlɪk/ ***adj.*** (used about drinks) not containing any alcohol: *nonalcoholic beer*

**non·cha·lant** /ˌnɑnʃəˈlɑnt/ ***adj.*** not feeling or showing interest or excitement; seeming calm ▸ **non·cha·lance** /-ˈlɑns/ ***noun*** [U] ▸ **non·cha·lant·ly** ***adv.***

**non·com·mit·tal** /ˌnɑnkəˈmɪt̬l/ ***adj.*** not saying or showing exactly what you think, or what you are going to do

**non·con·form·ist** /ˌnɑnkənˈfɔrmɪst/ ***noun*** [C] a person who behaves or thinks differently from most other people in society ▸ **non·con·form·ist *adj.***

**non·count noun** /ˌnɑnkaʊnt ˈnaʊn/ ***noun*** [C] (*grammar*) = UNCOUNTABLE NOUN

**non·de·script** /ˈnɑndəskrɪpt/ ***adj.*** not very interesting; dull

★**none¹** /nʌn/ ***pronoun*** not any, not one (of a group of three or more): *"Could you pour me some more juice?" "Sorry, there's none left."* ◇ *They gave me a lot of information, but none of it was very helpful.* ◇ *I went to several stores, but none had what I was looking for.* ◇ *I have four brothers, but none of them live/lives nearby.*

> NOTE When we use **none of** with a plural noun, the verb can be singular, which is formal, or plural, which is informal: *None of the buses is/are going downtown.* When we are talking about two people or things we use **neither**, not **none**: *Neither of my brothers lives nearby.* ➲ Note the difference between **none** and **no**: *I told him that I had no money left.* ◇ *When he asked me how much money I had left, I told him that I had none.*

**none²** /nʌn/ ***adv.*** (with *the* and a comparative adjective) not at all: *We talked for a long time, but I'm still none the wiser* (= I don't know any more than before).

**none·the·less** /ˌnʌnðəˈlɛs/ ***adv.*** anyway; in spite of what has just been said: *It won't be easy, but they're going to try nonetheless.* SYN **Nevertheless** has the same meaning.

**non·ex·ist·ent** /ˌnɑnɪgˈzɪstənt/ ***adj.*** not existing or not available: *In some areas public transportation is completely nonexistent.*

**non·fat** /ˌnɑnˈfæt/ ***adj.*** (about a food or drink) having no fat or almost no fat: *I only drink nonfat milk.*

**non·fic·tion** /ˌnɑnˈfɪkʃn/ ***noun*** [U] writing that is about real people, events and facts

**no-no** /ˈnoʊ noʊ/ (*pl.* **no-nos**) ***noun*** [C] (*informal*) a thing or way of behaving that is not acceptable in a particular situation: *Calling other people names in a chat room is a no-no.*

**non·plussed** /ˌnɑnˈplʌst/ ***adj.*** very surprised or confused

**non·prof·it** /ˌnɑnˈprɑfət/ (*also* ˌ**not-for-ˈprofit**) ***adj.*** (used about a company, organization, etc.) that does not aim to make a profit. Nonprofit organizations usually offer services to help people.

★**non·sense** /ˈnɑnsɛns; -səns/ ***noun*** [U] **1** something that sb says or writes that is not true or is just silly: *What you're saying is nonsense.* ◇ *Any rumors about my resignation are a lot of nonsense.* ◇ *"I'm no good at sports," said Tim. "Nonsense!" said his mother, "You're very good."* **2** foolish or bad behavior: *Mr. Davidson doesn't allow any nonsense in his classroom.*

**non·sen·si·cal** /nɑnˈsɛnsɪkl/ ***adj.*** not intelligent or sensible; stupid: *That was a completely nonsensical thing to say.*

**non·smok·er** /ˌnɑnˈsmoʊkər/ ***noun*** [C] a person who does not smoke ▸ **non·smok·ing** /ˌnɑnˈsmoʊkɪŋ/ ***adj.***: *Would you like a table in the smoking or the nonsmoking section?*

**non·stick** /ˌnɑnˈstɪk/ ***adj.*** (used about a pan, etc.) covered with a substance that prevents food from sticking to it

**non·stop** /ˌnɑnˈstɑp/ ***adj., adv.*** without a stop or a break: *a nonstop flight to London* ◇ *He talked nonstop for two hours about his trip.*

**non·vi·o·lence** /ˌnɑnˈvaɪələns/ ***noun*** [U] the refusal to use violence against the government, police, etc. in order to bring about political or social change ▸ **non·vi·o·lent** /-lənt/ ***adj.***

**noo·dle** /nudl/ ***noun*** [C, usually pl.] food made of flour, water and usually egg that is cut into long thin pieces and cooked in boiling water or used in soups

**nook** /nʊk/ ***noun*** [C] a small quiet place or corner (in a house, garden, etc.)

IDM **every nook and cranny** every part of a place

**noon** /nun/ ***noun*** [U] 12 o'clock in the middle of the day: *At noon the sun is at its highest point in the sky.* ◇ *They arrived around noon and stayed all afternoon.* ➲ Look at **midnight**.

ˈ**no one *pronoun*** = NOBODY

**noose** /nus/ ***noun*** [C] a circle that is tied in the end of a rope and that can be made tighter or looser. A noose is used for killing people by hanging.

**nope** /noʊp/ ***interjection*** (*informal*) no: *"Hey, Mike! Are you coming with us?" "Nope."*

★**nor** /nɔr/ ***conj., adv.*** **1** (used after *neither* or *not*) and not: *I received neither a telephone call nor a letter during the whole six months.* ◇ (*formal*) *Not a building nor a tree was left standing.* **2** (used after a negative statement to add some further information) also not: *The sun hardly shone at all during the first week. Nor during the second, for that matter.*

**norm** /nɔrm/ ***noun*** [C] (often with *the*) a pattern of behavior that is normal or expected: *Is it the norm in your country for young people to leave home before they get married?*

★**nor·mal¹** /ˈnɔrml/ ***adj.*** **1** usual, ordinary or what you expect: *I'll pick you up at the normal time.* ◇ *I just want to lead a normal life again.* ◇ *We're just a normal middle-class family.* ◇ *It's quite normal to feel angry in a situation like this.* ◇ *Under normal circumstances, the meeting would only have lasted an hour.* **2** (used about a person or animal) formed or developed in the usual way: *The child was completely normal at birth.* ➲ Look at **abnormal**.

**nor·mal²** /ˈnɔrml/ ***noun*** [U] the usual or average state, level, standard, etc.: *Your temperature is slightly above normal.* ◇ *I hope the situation will soon return to normal.* ◇ *Things are back to normal at work now.*

**nor·mal·cy** /ˈnɔrmlsi/ (*also* **normality** /nɔrˈmæləṭi/) *noun* [U] the state of being normal

**nor·mal·ize** /ˈnɔrml·aɪz/ *verb* [I,T] (*formal*) to become or make sth normal, good or friendly again

★**nor·mal·ly** /ˈnɔrməli/ *adv.* **1** usually: *I normally leave the house at 8 o'clock.* ◇ *We don't normally have people over for dinner.* ◇ *Normally, he takes the bus.* **2** in a usual or an ordinary way: *The man wasn't behaving normally.*

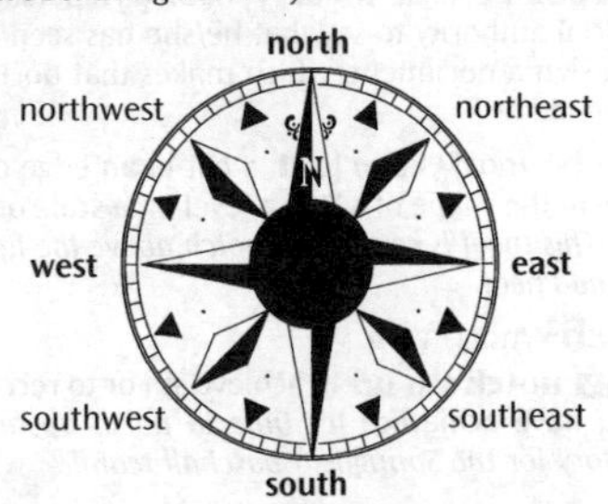


★**north¹** /nɔrθ/ *noun* [sing.] (*abbr.* **N.**; **No.**) **1** (*also* **the north**) one of the four main points of the compass; the direction that is on your left when you face the sunrise: *cold winds from the north* ◇ *Which way is north?* **2 the north** the part of any country, city, etc. that lies farther toward the north than other parts: *Rebels have taken control of several towns in the north.*

★**north²** /nɔrθ/ *adj.* in or toward the north, or from the NORTH¹: *The new offices will be in North Minneapolis.* ◇ *The north wing of the school was destroyed by a tornado.* ◇ *a cold north wind*

★**north³** /nɔrθ/ *adv.* to or toward the NORTH¹: *We got onto the expressway going north instead of south.* ◇ *The house faces north.* ◇ *Is Phoenix north of Tucson?*

IDM **up north** in or to the north: *We're going up north on vacation.*

**north·bound** /ˈnɔrθbaʊnd/ *adj.* traveling or leading toward the north: *the northbound lanes of the expressway*

**north·east¹** /ˌnɔrθˈist/ *noun* [sing.] (*abbr.* **NE**) **1** (*also* **the northeast**) the direction or point of the compass that is between north and east **2 the northeast**; **the Northeast** a region that is toward the northeast: *the Northeast of France* ➲ picture at **north**.

**north·east²** /ˌnɔrθˈist/ *adj.*, *adv.* in, from or to the northeast of a place or country: *the northeast coast of Florida* ◇ *If you look northeast, you can see the ocean.*

**north·east·er·ly** /ˌnɔrθˈistərli/ *adj.* **1** toward the northeast: *in a northeasterly direction* **2** (used about a wind) coming from the northeast

**north·east·ern** /ˌnɔrθˈistərn/ *adj.* in or from the northeast of a place or country: *northeastern Africa*

**north·east·ward** /ˌnɔrθˈistwərd/ *adv.* toward the northeast: *Follow the road northeastward.*

**north·er·ly** /ˈnɔrðərli/ *adj.* **1** to, toward or in the north: *Keep going in a northerly direction.* **2** (used about a wind) coming from the north

★**north·ern** /ˈnɔrðərn/ *adj.* of, in or from the north of a place: *in northern Australia* ◇ *the northern hemisphere* ➲ picture at **earth**.

**north·ern·er** (*also* **Northerner**) /ˈnɔrðərnər/ *noun* [C] a person who was born in or who lives in the northern part of a country

**the ˌNorthern ˈLights** (*also* **aurora borealis**) *noun* [pl.] bands of colored light, mainly green and red, that are sometimes seen in the sky at night in the most northern parts of the world

**north·ern·most** /ˈnɔrðərnmoʊst/ *adj.* farthest north

**the ˌNorth ˈPole** *noun* [sing.] the point on the Earth's surface which is farthest north ➲ picture at **earth**.

**north·ward** /ˈnɔrθwərd/ *adj.*, *adv.* toward the north: *in a northward direction* ◇ *Continue northward out of the city for about five miles.*

**north·west¹** /ˌnɔrθˈwɛst/ *noun* [sing.] (*abbr.* **NW**) **1** (*also* **the northwest**) the direction or point of the compass that is between north and west **2 the northwest**; **the Northwest** a region that is toward the northwest: *the Northwest of France* ➲ picture at **north**.

**north·west²** /ˌnɔrθˈwɛst/ *adj.*, *adv.* in, from or to the northwest of a place or country: *the northwest coast of Canada* ◇ *If you look northwest you can see the ocean.*

**north·west·er·ly** /ˌnɔrθˈwɛstərli/ *adj.* **1** toward the northwest: *in a northwesterly direction* **2** (used about a wind) coming from the northwest

**north·west·ern** /ˌnɔrθˈwɛstərn/ *adj.* in or from the northwest of a place or country: *northwestern Australia*

**north·west·ward** /ˌnɔrθˈwɛstwərd/ *adv.* toward the northwest: *Follow Interstate 94 northwestward.*

★**nose¹** /noʊz/ *noun* [C] **1** the part of the face, above the mouth, that is used for breathing and smelling: *a broken nose* ◇ *The baseball hit him on the nose.* ◇ *This medicine should help your runny nose.* ◇ *Breathe in through your nose and out through your mouth.* ➲ picture on study page A32. ➲ adjective **nasal** **2** the front part of sth, especially an airplane: *The nose of the plane was badly damaged.*

IDM **blow your nose** → BLOW¹

**look down your nose at sb/sth** to think that you are better than sb; to think that sth is of poor quality

**poke/stick your nose into sth** to interfere in sth when you should not: *He's always poking his nose into other people's business!*

**turn your nose up at sth** to refuse sth because you do not think it is good or do not like it

**nose²** /noʊz/ *verb* [I] to go forward slowly and carefully: *The bus nosed out into the line of traffic.*

PHR V **nose around** (*informal*) to look around a private place trying to find sth interesting

**nose·bleed** /ˈnoʊzblid/ *noun* [C] a time when a lot of blood comes from your nose: *to have a nosebleed*

**-nosed** /noʊzd/ *combining form* having a nose of the type mentioned: *red-nosed* ◇ *runny-nosed*

**nose·dive** /ˈnoʊzdaɪv/ *noun* [C] **1** the sudden fall

N

of an aircraft toward the ground with its front part pointing down **2** a sudden fall or drop; a situation where sth suddenly becomes worse or begins to fail: *These policies have sent the construction industry into an abrupt nosedive.*

IDM **take a nosedive** (*informal*) to fall suddenly or become worse: *The team started the season well but then took a nosedive.*

**'nose job** *noun* [C] (*informal*) an operation to improve the appearance of sb's nose: *Do you think she's had a nose job?*

**'no-show** *noun* [C] (*informal*) a person who is expected to be somewhere and does not come; a situation in which this happens: *No-shows are a big problem in the hotel business.* ◇ *Fans were disappointed by his no-show at the fair.*

**nos·tal·gi·a** /nə'stældʒə; nɑ-/ *noun* [U] a feeling of affection, mixed with sadness, for things that are in the past ▶ **nos·tal·gic** /-dʒɪk/ *adj.* ▶ **nos·tal·gi·cal·ly** /-kli/ *adv.*

**nos·tril** /'nɑstrəl/ *noun* [C] one of the two openings at the end of the nose

**nos·y** (*also* **nosey**) /'noʊzi/ *adj.* (**nos·i·er**; **nos·i·est**) too interested in other people's affairs

★**not** /nɑt/ *adv.* **1** (used to form the negative with verbs like *be, can, do, have, must, will*, etc. and often shortened to *n't* in speech and informal writing): *It's not/it isn't raining now.* ◇ *He's not coming/He isn't coming.* ◇ *I cannot/can't see from here.* ◇ *You shouldn't have said that.* ◇ *He didn't invite me.* ◇ *Don't you like spaghetti?* ◇ *I hope she will not/won't be late.* ◇ *You're German, aren't you?* **2** (used to give the following word or phrase a negative meaning or to reply in the negative): *He told me not to call after 10:00.* ◇ *I remember her but not her sister.* ◇ *Not everybody was able to come.* ◇ *"Whose turn is it to do the dishes?" "Not mine."* ◇ *"Do you see each other a lot?" "No, not often."* **3** (used after *be afraid, believe, expect, guess, hope, suppose*, etc., to give a negative reply): *"Do you think they'll get married?" "I hope not."* (= I hope that they will not.) ◇ *"You can't drive all that way alone." "I suppose not."* ◇ *"Did you see her?" "I'm afraid not."* **4** (used with *or* to give a negative possibility): *Should we tell her or not?* ◇ *I don't know if he's telling the truth or not.* **5** (used for saying that sth is not possible or that you do not want to do sth): *"Can I borrow $20?" "Absolutely not!"* ◇ *"Are you coming to the movie with us?" "I'd rather not, if you don't mind."* **6** (used for showing that you mean the opposite of the word or phrase that follows): *It's not easy* (= it's difficult).

IDM **not at all 1** (a way of saying *no* or *not*): *"Do you mind if I come too?" "Not at all."* ◇ *The instructions are not at all clear.* **2** (*formal*) (a way of replying when sb has thanked you): *"Thanks for the present." "Not at all – it was my pleasure."*

**not only... (but) also** (used for emphasizing the fact that there is something more): *They not only have two houses in the U.S., they also have one in France.*

**no·ta·ble** /'noʊt̬əbl/ *adj.* deserving to be noticed; interesting or important: *The area is notable for its scenery and wildlife.*

**no·ta·bly** /'noʊt̬əbli/ *adv.* (used for giving an especially important example of what you are talking about): *Many countries, notably Denmark, have refused to sign the agreement.*

**no·ta·rize** /'noʊt̬əraɪz/ *verb* [T] to mark a document to show that an official has seen sb sign it, so that the signature is valid in law

**no·ta·ry pub·lic** /ˌnoʊt̬əri 'pʌblɪk/ (*pl.* **no·ta·ries pub·lic**) (*also* **no·ta·ry**) *noun* [C] a person with official authority to say that he/she has seen a person sign a document, which makes that document valid in law

**notch**[1] /nɑtʃ/ *noun* [C] **1** a cut in an edge or surface in the shape of a V **2** a level on a scale of quality: *This meal is certainly a notch above the last one we had here.*

**notch**[2] /nɑtʃ/ *verb*

PHR V **notch sth up** to achieve sth or to record sth you have achieved: *It's time to notch up another victory for the Springfield baseball team!*

★**note**[1] /noʊt/ *noun*

➤SHORT LETTER **1** [C] a short letter: *This is just a note to thank you for letting us stay at your house.*

➤TO REMIND YOU **2** [C] some words that you write down quickly to help you remember sth: *I'd better make a note of your name and address.* ◇ *Keep a note of who has paid and who hasn't.* ◇ *The professor advised the students to take* (= write down) *notes while he was speaking.*

➤IN BOOK **3** [C] a short explanation or extra piece of information that is given at the back of a book, etc. or at the bottom or side of a page: *See note 5, page 340.* ➲ Look at **footnote**.

➤IN MUSIC **4** [C] a single musical sound made by a voice or an instrument: *I can only remember the first few notes of the song.* ◇ *high/low notes* ➲ picture at **music**. **5** [C] a written sign that represents a musical sound

➤QUALITY **6** [sing.] (something that suggests) a certain quality or feeling: *There was a note of embarrassment in her voice.* ◇ *The meeting ended on a fairly negative note.*

★**note**[2] /noʊt/ *verb* [T] **1** to notice or be aware of sth: *He noted a slight change in her attitude toward him.* **2** to mention sth: *I'd like to note that the project has been extremely successful so far.*

PHR V **note sth down** to write sth down so that you remember it: *The police officer noted down the girl's description of the man.*

**note·book** /'noʊtbʊk/ *noun* [C] **1** a book with plain paper in which you write things **2** (*also* **ˌnote·book com'puter**) a small computer that is easy to carry around and that can use batteries for power ➲ Look at **laptop**.

**not·ed** /'noʊt̬əd/ *adj.* **noted (for/as sth)** (*formal*) well-known; famous: *The hotel is noted for its gourmet cuisine.*

**note·pad** /'noʊtpæd/ *noun* [C] **1** some sheets of paper in a block that are used for writing things on **2** a computer small enough that it can be held in a hand

**note·pa·per** /'noʊtˌpeɪpər/ *noun* [U] paper that you write letters on

**note·wor·thy** /ˈnoʊtˌwərði/ ***adj.*** deserving to be noticed; interesting or important: *a noteworthy development*

**ˌnot-for-ˈprofit** ***adj.*** = NONPROFIT

**ˈnoth·er** /ˈnʌðər/ ***adj.*** = ANOTHER: *Now that's a whole'nother question.*

> NOTE **'Nother** is an incorrect form which some people use instead of **another**.

★**noth·ing** /ˈnʌθɪŋ/ ***pronoun*** not anything; no thing: *There's nothing in this suitcase.* ◇ *Nothing exciting ever happens to me.* ◇ *There was nothing else to say.* ◇ *"What's the matter?" "Oh, nothing."* ◇ *"Thank you so much for all your help." "It was nothing."* (= nothing of any importance) ➲ Look at the note at **zero**.
IDM **have nothing to do with sb/sth** to have no connection with sb/sth: *That question has nothing to do with what we're discussing.*
**for nothing** **1** for no good reason or with no good result: *His hard work was all for nothing.* **2** for no payment; free: *Children under four are allowed in for nothing.*
**nothing but** only: *He was wearing nothing but a pair of swimming trunks.*
**(there's) nothing to it** (it's) very easy: *You just need to practice – there's nothing to it really.*

★**no·tice¹** /ˈnoʊt̬əs/ ***noun*** **1** [C] a written statement giving information or news that is put where everybody can read it: *There's a notice on the board saying that the meeting has been canceled.* **2** [U] a warning that sth is going to happen: *I can't produce a big dinner on such short notice!* ◇ *I wish you had given me more notice that you were going on vacation.* ◇ *The swimming pool is closed until further notice* (= until we are told that it will open again). ◇ *We've been given a month's notice to move out* (= we have been told we must leave in a month).
IDM **on notice** having been told or warned that sth is going to happen: *The police have put the public on notice that drugs will not be tolerated.*
**take notice (of sth)** to act in a way that shows that you know sth is important: *The protests are finally making the government take notice.*
**not take any notice (of sb/sth)** to pay no attention (to sb/sth): *Some people don't take any notice of speed limits.*

> NOTE If you **don't notice** something, e.g. a speed limit, it means that you don't see it at all. However if you **don't take any notice** of it, it means that you see it but you choose to ignore it.

★**no·tice²** /ˈnoʊt̬əs/ ***verb*** [I,T] to see and be aware of sth: *"What kind of car was the man driving?" "I didn't notice."* ◇ *Did you notice her eyes?* ◇ *I noticed (that) he was carrying a black briefcase.* ◇ *Did you notice which direction she went in?* ◇ *We didn't notice him leave/leaving.*

★**no·tice·a·ble** /ˈnoʊt̬əsəbl/ ***adj.*** easy to see or notice: *The scar from the accident was hardly noticeable.* ◇ *a noticeable difference* ▶ **no·tice·a·bly** /-bli/ ***adv.***: *The crowds at this year's event were noticeably smaller than at last year's.*

**no·ti·fy** /ˈnoʊt̬əfaɪ/ ***verb*** [T] (*pres. part.* **no·ti·fy·ing**; *3rd person sing. pres.* **no·ti·fies**; *pt, pp* **no·ti·fied**) **notify sb (of sth)** to inform sb (about sth) officially: *The police should be notified of the theft.* ◇ *You must notify your landlady that you intend to move out.* ▶ **no·ti·fi·ca·tion** /ˌnoʊt̬əfəˈkeɪʃn/ ***noun*** [C,U]

★**no·tion** /ˈnoʊʃn/ ***noun*** [C] something that you have in your mind; an idea: *I had a vague notion that I had seen her before.* ◇ *You seem to have no notion of how difficult it is going to be.*

**no·to·ri·e·ty** /ˌnoʊt̬əˈraɪət̬i/ ***noun*** [U] the state of being famous for sth bad

**no·to·ri·ous** /noʊˈtɔriəs/ ***adj.*** **notorious (for/as sth)** well-known for sth bad: *a notorious drug dealer* ◇ *This road is notorious for the number of accidents on it.* ▶ **no·to·ri·ous·ly** ***adv.***: *English cuisine is notoriously bad.*

**not·with·stand·ing¹** /ˌnɑtwɪθˈstændɪŋ/ ***prep.*** (*formal*) without being affected by; in spite of: *The plane landed on time, notwithstanding the terrible weather conditions.*

**not·with·standing²** /ˌnɑtwɪθˈstændɪŋ/ ***adv.*** (*formal*) anyway; in spite of this: *He was advised against the deal, but went ahead notwithstanding.*

**noun** /naʊn/ ***noun*** [C] (*grammar*) a word that is the name of a person, place, thing or idea: *"Jane," "London," "table" and "happiness" are all nouns.* ➲ Look at **proper noun**, **countable** and **uncountable**.

**ˈnoun phrase** ***noun*** [C] (*grammar*) a group of words in a sentence that behaves in the same way as a noun

**nour·ish** /ˈnərɪʃ/ ***verb*** [T] **1** to give a person or animal the right kind of food so that he/she/it can grow and be healthy **2** (*formal*) to allow a feeling or belief to grow stronger

**nour·ish·ment** /ˈnərɪʃmənt/ ***noun*** [U] food that you need to stay healthy

**Nov.** ***abbr.*** = NOVEMBER

★**nov·el¹** /ˈnɑvl/ ***noun*** [C] a book that tells a story about people and events that are not real: *the novels of Charles Dickens* ◇ *a romantic novel*

**nov·el²** /ˈnɑvl/ ***adj.*** new and different: *That's a novel idea! Let's try it.*

**nov·el·ist** /ˈnɑvəlɪst/ ***noun*** [C] a person who writes novels

**nov·el·ty** /ˈnɑvlti/ ***noun*** (*pl.* **nov·el·ties**) **1** [U] the quality of being new and different: *The novelty of her new job soon wore off.* **2** [C] something new and unusual: *It was quite a novelty not to have to get up at 7 o'clock.* **3** [C] a small, cheap object that is sold as a toy or souvenir

**No·vem·ber** /noʊˈvɛmbər/ ***noun*** [C,U] (*abbr.* **Nov.**) the eleventh month of the year, coming before December ➲ For examples of the use of the months in sentences, look at **January**.

**nov·ice** /ˈnɑvəs/ ***noun*** [C] a person who is new and without experience in a certain job, situation, etc.; a beginner

★**now¹** /naʊ/ ***adv.*** **1** (at) the present time: *Where are you living now?* ◇ *It's too late now to do anything about it.* ◇ *From now on, the nights will be getting longer.* ◇ *I've been living with my parents until now.* ◇ *Up to now, we haven't been able to afford a house of our own.* ◇ *He should be on his way home by now.* **2** because of what has happened: *I lost my pen.*



N

*Now I'll have to buy a new one.* **3** (used to introduce a new subject or to emphasize a request, command, etc., or while pausing to think): *Now, this is how it all began.* ◇ *Now listen to what he's saying.* ◇ *Now, let me think.* ➲ **Now then** is also used: *Now then, are there any questions?* ◇ *Now then, what was I saying?*
IDM **now and again/then**; **(every) now and then** occasionally: *We see each other now and then, but not very often.*
**just now** → JUST[1]
**right now** → RIGHT[2]

**now**[2] /naʊ/ ***conj.*** **now (that)...** because of the fact that: *Now (that) the kids have left home, we can move to a smaller house.*

**now·a·days** /ˈnaʊədeɪz/ ***adv.*** at the present time (when compared with the past): *Kids don't get much exercise nowadays* (= but they did in the past).

★**no·where** /ˈnoʊwɛr/ ***adv.*** not anywhere; (in or to) no place: *There's nowhere to stay in this town.* ◇ *There's nowhere interesting to go around here.* ◇ *It's so hot I'm getting nowhere with this work* (= making no progress). ◇ *"Don't leave the car there!" "There's nowhere else to park it."*
IDM **in the middle of nowhere** → MIDDLE[1]
**nowhere near** → NEAR[2]

**nox·ious** /ˈnɑkʃəs/ ***adj.*** (*formal*) harmful or poisonous: *noxious gases*

**noz·zle** /ˈnɑzl/ ***noun*** [C] a narrow tube that is put on the end of a pipe, etc. to control the liquid or gas coming out

**NPR** /ˌɛn pi ˈɑr/ ***abbr.*** (in the U.S.) National Public Radio; a group of radio stations that do not have COMMERCIALS[2]

**NST** /ˌɛn ɛs ˈti/ ***abbr.*** (*Cdn*) = NEWFOUNDLAND STANDARD TIME

**nu** /nu/ ***noun*** [C] (*symbol* N, ν) the thirteenth letter of the Greek alphabet ➲ Look at the note at **fraternity**.

**nu·ance** /ˈnuɑns/ ***noun*** [C] a very small difference in meaning, feeling, sound, etc.

★**nu·cle·ar** /ˈnukliər/ ***adj.*** **1** connected with the nucleus of an atom: *nuclear physics* **2** connected with the energy that is produced when the nucleus of an atom is split: *nuclear energy/weapons* ◇ *nuclear disarmament* (= stopping the use and development of nuclear weapons) OPP **non-nuclear** ➲ Look also at **atomic**.

ˌ**nuclear ˈfamily** ***noun*** [C] a family that consists of father, mother and children, when it is thought of as a unit in society: *Not everyone today lives in a traditional nuclear family.* ➲ Look at **extended family**.

ˌ**nuclear reˈactor** (*also* **reactor**) ***noun*** [C] a very large machine that produces nuclear energy

**nu·cle·us** /ˈnukliəs/ ***noun*** [C] (*pl.* **nu·cle·i** /ˈnukliaɪ/) **1** the central part of an atom **2** the central or most important part of sth

**nude**[1] /nud/ ***adj.*** not wearing any clothes SYN **bare, naked**

**nude**[2] /nud/ ***noun*** [C] a picture or photograph of a person who is not wearing clothes
IDM **in the nude** not wearing any clothes

**nudge** /nʌdʒ/ ***verb*** [T] to touch or push sb/sth with your elbow ▶ **nudge** ***noun*** [C]: *to give sb a nudge*

**nu·dist** /ˈnudɪst/ ***noun*** [C] a person who likes to be nude, often in groups with other people: *a nudist beach*

**nu·di·ty** /ˈnudəti/ ***noun*** [U] the state of being nude

**nug·get** /ˈnʌgət/ ***noun*** [C] a lump of a valuable metal that is found in the earth: *a gold nugget*

**nui·sance** /ˈnusns/ ***noun*** [C] a person, thing or situation that annoys you or causes you trouble: *The neighbors' dog has been causing a real nuisance.*

**nuke**[1] /nuk/ ***noun*** [C] (*slang*) a weapon that uses nuclear energy

**nuke**[2] /nuk/ ***verb*** [T] (*slang*) **1** to attack a place using nuclear weapons **2** to cook sth in a microwave oven

**numb**[1] /nʌm/ ***adj.*** not able to feel anything; not able to move: *My fingers were numb with cold.* ◇ *I'll give you an anesthetic and the tooth will go completely numb.* ◇ *He was numb with fear.* ▶ **numb·ness** ***noun*** [U]: *The numbness should wear off after a few hours.*

**numb**[2] /nʌm/ ***verb*** [T] to make sb/sth numb: *The whole family was numbed and shocked by the news.*

★**num·ber**[1] /ˈnʌmbər/ ***noun***

➤WORD/SYMBOL **1** [C] a word or symbol that indicates a quantity: *Pick a number between ten and twenty.* ◇ *2 is an even number and 3 is an odd number.* ◇ *a three-digit number* (= more than 99 and less than 1,000) ◇ *high/low numbers* ◇ *cardinal/ordinal numbers*

➤TELEPHONE, ETC. **2** [C] a group of numbers that is used to identify sb/sth: *What's your car's license plate number?* ◇ *a telephone number* ◇ *"Hello, could I talk to Julie?" "Sorry, you've got the wrong number."*

➤QUANTITY **3** [C,U] a quantity or amount: *a large number of visitors* ◇ *Part-time students have doubled in number in recent years.* ◇ *a number of* (= several) *questions* ◇ *We're trying to reduce the number of accidents in the home.*

> NOTE When **number** has an adjective before it, it is always followed by a plural verb: *A small number of students study Latin.*

➤POSITION IN SERIES **4** [C] (*abbr.* **No.**; **no.**) (*symbol* #) (used before a number to show the position of sth in a series): *I live in apartment number 5C.* ◇ *room no. 347* ◇ *Example #3*

➤MUSIC **5** [C] (*informal*) a song or dance: *Our next number will be a classic love song.*
IDM **any number of** very many: *We've given the workers any number of offers, but they still voted to strike.*

**num·ber**[2] /ˈnʌmbər/ ***verb*** **1** [T] to give a number to sth: *We keep our photos in numbered boxes.* **2** [I] (used for expressing how many people or things there are): *Our forces number 40,000.*

**nu·mer·al** /ˈnumərəl/ ***noun*** [C] a sign or symbol that represents a quantity: *Roman numerals*

**nu·mer·ate** /ˈnumərət/ ***adj.*** having a basic knowledge of mathematics ➲ Look at **literate**

**nu·mer·a·tor** /ˈnuməreɪt̬ər/ ***noun*** [C] the number above the line in a FRACTION (2), for example 3 in the fraction ¾ ➲ Compare **denominator**.

**nu·mer·i·cal** /nuˈmɛrɪkl/ ***adj.*** of or shown by numbers: *to put sth in numerical order*

**nu·mer·ous** /ˈnumərəs/ ***adj.*** (*formal*) very many; existing in large quantities

**nun** /nʌn/ ***noun*** [C] a woman who has gone to live in a religious community (convent) and who is not allowed to get married or own property ➲ Look at **monk**.

★**nurse¹** /nərs/ ***noun*** [C] a person whose job is to take care of sick or injured people: *a trained nurse* ◇ *a male nurse* ◇ *Nurse Mills*

**nurse²** /nərs/ ***verb*** **1** [T] to take care of sb who is sick or injured: *She nursed her mother until she died in 1979.* ◇ *The boys found a sick puppy and nursed it back to health.* **2** [I,T] to feed a baby with milk from the breast: *nursing mothers* SYN **breastfeed** **3** [I] (used about a baby) to suck milk from a woman's breast

**nurs·e·ry** /ˈnərsəri/ ***noun*** [C] (*pl.* **nurs·e·ries**) **1** a baby's bedroom in a house **2** a room in a hospital for babies **3** a place where parents can leave their children for a short time while the parents do sth else **4** a place where young trees and plants are grown and sold ➲ Look at **greenhouse**.

ˈ**nursery rhyme** ***noun*** [C] a traditional poem or song for children

ˈ**nursery school** ***noun*** [C] = PRESCHOOL

**nurs·ing** /ˈnərsɪŋ/ ***noun*** [U] the job of being a nurse: *She has decided to go into nursing.*

ˈ**nursing home** ***noun*** [C] a small private hospital, usually for old people

★**nut** /nʌt/ ***noun*** [C] **1** a dry fruit that consists of a hard shell with a seed (**kernel**) inside. Many types of nut may be eaten: *chopped hazelnuts and almonds* **2** a six-sided piece of metal with a round hole in the middle through which you screw a long round piece of metal (**bolt**). Nuts and bolts are used for fastening things together: *Tighten the nut with a wrench.* ➲ picture at **nail**. **3** (*informal*) a crazy or foolish person ➲ Look at **nuts** and **nutty**.

**nut·crack·er** /ˈnʌtkrækər/ ***noun*** [C] a tool that you use to break open the shell of a nut

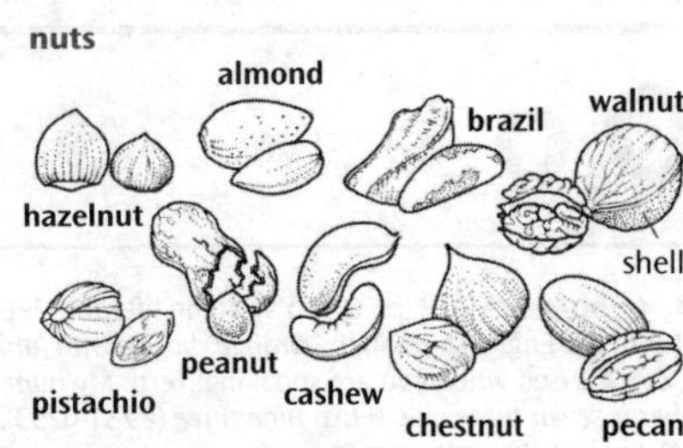


**nut·meg** /ˈnʌtmɛg/ ***noun*** [C,U] a type of spice, used for giving flavor to food

**nu·tri·ent** /ˈnutriənt/ ***noun*** [C] (*technical*) a substance that is needed to keep a living thing alive and to help it to grow: *a lack/supply of essential nutrients* ◇ *Plants draw minerals and other nutrients from the soil.*

**nu·tri·tion** /nuˈtrɪʃn/ ***noun*** [U] the food that you eat and the way that it affects your health: *Good nutrition is essential for children's growth.* ▶ **nu·tri·tion·al** ***adj.***

**nu·tri·tious** /nuˈtrɪʃəs/ ***adj.*** (used about a food) very good for you

**nuts** /nʌts/ ***adj.*** (not before a noun) (*informal*) **1** crazy or foolish: *You're completely nuts!* **2** very interested in and excited about sth: *She's nuts about ice skating.*

**nut·shell** /ˈnʌtʃɛl/ ***noun***

IDM **in a nutshell** using few words: *That, in a nutshell, is the answer to your question.*

**nut·ty** /ˈnʌt̬i/ ***adj.*** (**nut·ti·er**; **nut·ti·est**) **1** containing or tasting like nuts **2** (*informal*) crazy or foolish: *a nutty idea*

**nuz·zle** /ˈnʌzl/ ***verb*** [T] to press or rub sb/sth gently with the nose

**NW** ***abbr.*** northwest; northwestern

**ny·lon** /ˈnaɪlɑn/ ***noun*** **1** [U] a very strong artificial material that is used for making clothes, rope, brushes, etc.: *a nylon raincoat* **2 nylons** [pl.] = PANTYHOSE

N

# Oo

**O, o** /oʊ/ ***noun*** [C,U] (*pl.* **O's; o's**) **1** the fifteenth letter of the English alphabet: *"Orange" begins with (an) "O."* **2** (used when you are speaking) zero: *My number is seven three one, 0 two nine three* (=731-0293). ➲ Look at the note at **zero**.

**oak** /oʊk/ ***noun*** **1** (*also* **ˈoak tree**) [C] a type of large tree with hard wood that is common in many northern parts of the world **2** [U] the wood from the oak tree: *a solid oak table*

NOTE The fruit of the oak is an **acorn**.

**oar** /ɔr/ ***noun*** [C] a long pole that is flat at one end and that is used for moving a small boat through water (**rowing**) ➲ Look at **paddle**.

**OAS** /ˌoʊ eɪ ˈɛs/ ***abbr.*** (*Cdn*) = OLD AGE SECURITY

**o·a·sis** /oʊˈeɪsəs/ ***noun*** [C] (*pl.* **o·a·ses** /-siz/) a place in the desert where there is water and where plants grow

**oat** /oʊt/ ***noun*** [usually pl.] a type of grain that is used as food for people and animals: *oat bran* ◇ *The horses were eating oats and hay.*

**oath** /oʊθ/ ***noun*** [C] a formal promise: *They have to swear an oath of loyalty.* ◇ *She took the oath of office as the country's new president.*

IDM **under oath** having made a formal promise to tell the truth in a court of law: *He was accused of lying under oath.*

**oat·meal** /ˈoʊtmil/ ***noun*** [U] **1** oats which have been prepared in a special way so that they can be cooked: *instant oatmeal* **2** a food that is made from oats mixed with hot milk or water and usually eaten for breakfast: *a steaming bowl of oatmeal*

**o·be·di·ent** /oʊˈbidiənt/ ***adj.*** doing what you are told to do: *He was an obedient child and never caused any problems.* OPP **disobedient** ▸ **o·be·di·ence** /-əns/ ***noun*** [U]: *They acted out of obedience to their leader.* ▸ **o·be·di·ent·ly** ***adv.***

**o·bese** /oʊˈbis/ ***adj.*** (used about people) extremely fat ▸ **o·be·si·ty** /oʊˈbisət̬i/ ***noun*** [U]: *Obesity among children is on the increase in the U.S.*

★**o·bey** /oʊˈbeɪ/ ***verb*** [I,T] to do what you are told to do: *Soldiers are trained to obey orders.* OPP **disobey**

**o·bit·u·ar·y** /oʊˈbɪtʃuˌɛri/ ***noun*** [C] (*pl.* **o·bit·u·ar·ies**) an article about a person's life that is printed in a newspaper soon after he/she has died

★**ob·ject**[1] /ˈɑbdʒɛkt; -dʒɪkt/ ***noun*** [C] **1** a thing that can be seen and touched: *The shelves were filled with objects of all shapes and sizes.* **2 the object of sth** a person or thing that causes a feeling, interest, thought, etc. **3** an aim or a purpose: *Making money is his sole object in life.* **4** (*grammar*) the noun or phrase describing the person or thing that is affected by the action of a verb

NOTE In the sentences: *I sent a letter to Melanie* and: *I sent Melanie a letter,* **a letter** is the **direct** object of the verb and **Melanie** is the **indirect** object.

IDM **money, etc. is no object** money, etc. is not important or is no problem: *She only buys the best clothes – money is no object for her.*

★**ob·ject**[2] /əbˈdʒɛkt/ ***verb*** **1** [I] **object (to sb/sth)** to not like or to be against sb/sth: *Many people object to the new tax.* **2** [T] to say that you do not like sth or to say that sth is wrong: *"I think that's unfair," he objected.*

**ob·jec·tion** /əbˈdʒɛkʃn/ ***noun*** [C,U] a statement or feeling that you do not like or are against sb/sth: *We listed our objections to the proposed new road and sent them to the city council.* ◇ *My parents have no objection to our marriage.*

**ob·jec·tion·a·ble** /əbˈdʒɛkʃənəbl/ ***adj.*** very unpleasant

★**ob·jec·tive**[1] /əbˈdʒɛktɪv/ ***adj.*** not influenced by your own personal feelings or opinions; considering only facts: *Please try and give an objective report of what happened.* ◇ *It's hard to be objective about your own strengths and weaknesses.* OPP **subjective** ▸ **ob·jec·tive·ly** ***adv.***: *He is too upset to see things objectively.* ▸ **ob·jec·tiv·i·ty** /ˌɑbdʒɛkˈtɪvət̬i/ ***noun*** [U]

★**ob·jec·tive**[2] /əbˈdʒɛktɪv/ ***noun*** [C] your aim or purpose: *Our objective is to finish by the end of the year.* ◇ *to achieve your objective*

**ob·jec·tor** /əbˈdʒɛktər/ ***noun*** [C] a person who objects to sth ➲ Look also at **conscientious objector**.

**ob·li·gate** /ˈɑbləgeɪt/ ***verb*** [T] **obligate sb (to do sth)** (often passive) to force sb to do sth

**ob·li·ga·tion** /ˌɑbləˈgeɪʃn/ ***noun*** **1** [C] something that you must do because it is your duty or because you promised to do it: *We have a moral obligation to help people who are in need.* **2** [U] having to do sth because it is is your duty: *The company is under no obligation to give out that information* (= they do not have to give the information).

**o·blig·a·to·ry** /əˈblɪgəˌtɔri/ ***adj.*** (*formal*) that you must do: *obligatory military service*

**o·blige** /əˈblaɪdʒ/ ***verb*** **1** [T] (usually passive) to force sb to do sth: *You are not obliged to answer these questions, but it would be a great help if you did.* **2** [I,T] (*formal*) to do what sb asks; to be helpful: *The service there is excellent. They are always happy to oblige.*

**o·bliged** /əˈblaɪdʒd/ ***adj.*** grateful: *Thank you, ma'am. I'm much obliged to you.*

**o·blig·ing** /əˈblaɪdʒɪŋ/ ***adj.*** friendly and helpful

**o·blit·er·ate** /əˈblɪt̬əreɪt/ ***verb*** [T] (*formal*) to destroy or ruin sth completely

**o·bliv·i·on** /əˈblɪviən/ ***noun*** [U] **1** the state of having forgotten sth or of not being aware of sth: *I was in a state of complete oblivion.* **2** the state of being forgotten: *His work faded into oblivion after his death.*

**o·bliv·i·ous** /ə'blɪviəs/ ***adj.*** not noticing or being aware of sth: *The baby slept, oblivious to everything that was going on around him.*

**ob·long** /'ɑblɔŋ/ ***adj.***, ***noun*** [C] (of) a shape with two long sides and two short sides ➲ Look at **rectangle**.

**ob·nox·ious** /əb'nɑkʃəs/ ***adj.*** very unpleasant

**o·boe** /'oʊboʊ/ ***noun*** [C] a musical instrument that is made of wood. You play an oboe by blowing through a very narrow piece (reed) at the top.

**ob·scene** /əb'sin/ ***adj.*** (used about words, thoughts, books, pictures, etc.) shocking or disgusting (usually because of the way they talk about or show sex): *an obscene book* ◇ (*figurative*) *It's obscene to spend so much on food when millions are starving.*

**ob·scen·i·ty** /əb'sɛnəṭi/ ***noun*** (*pl.* **ob·scen·i·ties**) **1** [U] the state of being obscene **2** [C] an obscene word or act

**ob·scure**[1] /əb'skyʊr/ ***adj.*** **1** not easy to see or understand: *The reasoning behind his comments was somewhat obscure.* **2** not well-known: *an obscure Spanish poet* ▸ **ob·scu·ri·ty** /əb'skyʊrəṭi/ ***noun*** [U]: *The artist died penniless and in obscurity.*

**ob·scure**[2] /əb'skyʊr/ ***verb*** [T] to make sth difficult to see or understand: *Our view was obscured by a high fence.*

**ob·ser·vance** /əb'zərvəns/ ***noun*** [U] (*formal*) the practice of obeying or following a law, custom, ceremony, etc.

**ob·ser·vant** /əb'zərvənt/ ***adj.*** quick at noticing things: *An observant witness gave the police a description of the men.* OPP **unobservant**

★**ob·ser·va·tion** /ˌɑbzər'veɪʃn; -sər-/ ***noun*** **1** [U] the act of watching sb/sth carefully or the state of being watched carefully: *the observation of animals in their natural surroundings* **2** [U] the ability to notice things: *Scientists need good powers of observation.* **3** [C] something that you say or write; a remark: *to make an observation about the weather* ➲ Look at **remark** and **comment**. These words are more common.

IDM **under observation** being watched carefully: *After his car accident, Mick was kept under observation in the hospital overnight.* ➲ Look at **surveillance**.

**ob·ser·va·to·ry** /əb'zərvəˌtɔri/ ***noun*** [C] (*pl.* **ob·ser·va·to·ries**) a building from which scientists can look at the stars, the moon, etc. with telescopes

★**ob·serve** /əb'zərv/ ***verb*** [T] **1** to notice sb/sth or watch sb/sth carefully: *A man and a woman were observed leaving by the back door.* ◇ *We observed the birds throughout the breeding season.* **2** (*formal*) to say or remark: *"The bus is running late," she observed.* **3** (*formal*) to obey a law, rule, etc.: *to observe the speed limit*

**ob·serv·er** /əb'zərvər/ ***noun*** [C] **1** a person who watches sb/sth: *Political observers have been predicting trouble for quite a while.* **2** a person who attends a meeting, lesson, etc. to watch and listen but who does not say anything

**ob·sess** /əb'sɛs/ ***verb*** [T] (usually passive) to fill sb's mind all the time: *He became obsessed with getting good grades in college.* ◇ *Alison is obsessed with an older man.*

**ob·ses·sion** /əb'sɛʃn/ ***noun*** **1** [U] the state of being obsessed **2** [C] a person or thing that obsesses you: *Football is an obsession to some people.*

**ob·ses·sive** /əb'sɛsɪv/ ***adj.*** having or showing a way of thinking or behaving that you cannot stop: *He's obsessive about not being late.* ◇ *obsessive cleanliness*

**ob·so·lete** /ˌɑbsə'lit/ ***adj.*** no longer used because it is out of date

**ob·sta·cle** /'ɑbstəkl/ ***noun*** [C] something that makes it difficult for you to go somewhere or do sth: *Not speaking a foreign language was a major obstacle to her career.*

**ob·ste·tri·cian** /ˌɑbstə'trɪʃn/ ***noun*** [C] a doctor who treats women who are pregnant and helps them while their babies are being born

**ob·sti·nate** /'ɑbstənət/ ***adj.*** not willing to change your mind if you have decided sth: *an obstinate refusal to apologize* ➲ This word is usually used in a critical way. Look at **stubborn**, which has the same meaning. ▸ **ob·sti·na·cy** /'ɑbstɪnəsi/ ***noun*** [U] ▸ **ob·sti·nate·ly** ***adv.***

**ob·struct** /əb'strʌkt/ ***verb*** [T] to stop sb/sth from happening or moving: *You're obstructing traffic if you park there.*

**ob·struc·tion** /əb'strʌkʃn/ ***noun*** **1** [U] stopping sth from happening or making progress: *obstruction of justice* **2** [C] a thing that stops sb/sth from moving: *This car is causing an obstruction.*

**ob·struc·tive** /əb'strʌktɪv/ ***adj.*** trying to stop sth from happening

★**ob·tain** /əb'teɪn/ ***verb*** [T] (*formal*) to get sth: *This book can now be obtained in paperback.*

**ob·tain·a·ble** /əb'teɪnəbl/ ***adj.*** that can be obtained: *That brand of vacuum cleaner is no longer obtainable.* OPP **unobtainable**

★**ob·vi·ous** /'ɑbviəs/ ***adj.*** easily seen or understood; clear: *It was obvious that he was not well.* ◇ *His disappointment was obvious to everyone.* ◇ *an obvious lie*

★**ob·vi·ous·ly** /'ɑbviəsli/ ***adv.*** as can easily be seen or understood; clearly: *There has obviously been a mistake.* ◇ *Obviously we don't want to spend too much money if we can avoid it.*

★**oc·ca·sion** /ə'keɪʒn/ ***noun*** **1** [C] a particular time when sth happens: *I have met Bill on two occasions.* **2** [sing.] **occasion (for sth)** the suitable or right time (for sth): *I'll tell her what I think if the occasion arises.*

> NOTE You use **occasion** when you mean the time is right or suitable for something: *I saw them at the funeral, but it was not a suitable occasion for discussing vacation plans.* You use **opportunity** or **chance** when you mean that it is possible to do something: *I was only in Paris for one day, and I didn't get the opportunity/chance to visit the Louvre.*

**3** [C] a special event, ceremony, etc.: *Their wedding was a memorable occasion.* ◇ *an official/special/great occasion*

IDM **on occasion** sometimes



O

**oc·ca·sion·al** /əˈkeɪʒənl/ ***adj.*** done or happening from time to time but not very often: *I rarely drink alcohol – just an occasional glass of wine.* ▶ **oc·ca·sion·al·ly** ***adv.***: *We see each other occasionally.*

**oc·cult** /əˈkʌlt/ ***adj.*** connected with magic or supernatural powers ▶ **the oc·cult** ***noun*** [sing.]: *He's interested in witchcraft and the occult.*

**oc·cu·pant** /ˈɑkyəpənt/ ***noun*** [C] (*formal*) a person who lives in or uses a room, house, etc.

**oc·cu·pa·tion** /ˌɑkyəˈpeɪʃn/ ***noun*** **1** [C] a job: *Please state your occupation on the form.* ➲ Look at the note at **work**[1]. **2** [U] the control of a country by the army of another country

**oc·cu·pa·tion·al** /ˌɑkyəˈpeɪʃənl/ ***adj.*** connected with your work: *Accidents are an occupational hazard on construction sites.*

**oc·cu·pied** /ˈɑkyəpaɪd/ ***adj.*** **1** being used: *Is this seat occupied?* **2** busy: *Taking care of the kids keeps me fully occupied.* **3** (used about a country or a piece of land) under the control of another country: *occupied territory*

★**oc·cu·py** /ˈɑkyəpaɪ/ ***verb*** [T] (*pres. part.* **oc·cu·py·ing**; *3rd person sing. pres.* **oc·cu·pies**; *pt, pp* **oc·cu·pied**) **1** to live in or use a house, piece of land, etc.: *The house next door has not been occupied for some months.* **2** to take control of a building, country, etc. by force: *The rebel forces have occupied the parliament building.* **3** to fill a space or period of time: *The large table occupied most of the room.* **4 occupy sb/yourself (in doing sth/with sth)** to keep sb/yourself busy: *How does he occupy himself now that he's retired?*

★**oc·cur** /əˈkər/ ***verb*** [I] (**oc·cur̲·ring**; **oc·cur̲red**) **1** (*formal*) to happen: *The accident occurred late last night.* ➲ Look at the note at **happen**. **2** to be or exist: *Child abuse occurs in all classes of society.* **3 occur to sb** to come into sb's mind: *It never occurred to John that his wife might be unhappy.*

**oc·cur·rence** /əˈkərəns/ ***noun*** [C] something that happens: *Car theft is now a very common occurrence.*

**o·cean** /ˈoʊʃn/ ***noun*** **1** [sing.] the mass of salt water that covers most of the surface of the earth: *Did you ever go swimming in the ocean?* ◇ *the ocean floor* **2** [C] **Ocean** one of the five main areas into which the sea is divided: *the Atlantic Ocean*

★**o'clock** /əˈklɑk/ ***adv.*** (used after the numbers one to twelve for saying what the time is): *Lunch is at twelve o'clock.*

> NOTE Be careful. **O'clock** can only be used with full hours: *We arranged to meet at 5 o'clock. It's 5:30 already and he's still not here.*

**Oct.** ***abbr.*** = OCTOBER

**oc·ta·gon** /ˈɑktəgɑn/ ***noun*** [C] a shape that has eight straight sides ▶ **oc·tag·o·nal** /ɑkˈtægənl/ ***adj.***

**oc·tave** /ˈɑktɪv/ ***noun*** [C] the set of eight musical notes that western music is based on

**Oc·to·ber** /ɑkˈtoʊbər/ ***noun*** [C,U] (*abbr.* **Oct.**) the tenth month of the year, coming before November ➲ For examples of the use of the months in sentences, look at **January**.

**oc·to·pus** /ˈɑktəpəs/ ***noun*** [C] (*pl.* **oc·to·pus·es** or **oc·to·pi** /ˈɑktəpaɪ/) a sea animal with a soft body and eight long arms (tentacles)

**OD** /ˌoʊˈdi/ ***verb*** [I] (*pres. part.* **OD'ing**; *3rd person sing. pres.* **OD's**; *pt, pp* **OD'd**) (*informal*) **OD (on sth)** = OVERDOSE[2] (*figurative*) *Ugh! I think I OD'd on Halloween candy.*

★**odd** /ɑd/ ***adj.***
- ➤STRANGE **1** strange; unusual: *There's something odd about him.* ◇ *It's kind of odd that she didn't call to say she couldn't come.*
- ➤NUMBERS **2** (used about a number) that cannot be divided by two: *One, three, five and seven are all odd numbers.* OPP **even**
- ➤VARIOUS **3** (only *before* a noun) that remains after other similar things have been used: *He made the bookshelves out of a few odd pieces of wood.*
- ➤-ODD **4** (usually used after a number) a little more than: *There must have been 30-odd people at the meeting.*
- ➤NOT REGULAR **5** not regular or fixed: *My neighbor seems to work odd hours.*

▶ **odd·ness** ***noun*** [U]

**odd·i·ty** /ˈɑdət̬i/ ***noun*** (*pl.* **odd·i·ties**) **1** [U] the quality of being strange or unusual **2** [C] a person or thing that is unusual

**ˌodd ˈjobs** ***noun*** [pl.] small jobs of various kinds: *Our son does a few odd jobs for the neighbors like raking leaves and shoveling snow.*

**odd·ly** /ˈɑdli/ ***adv.*** in a strange way: *He's behaving very oddly.*

**odds** /ɑdz/ ***noun*** [pl.] the chance or probability that sth will or will not happen: *The odds that he'll survive are very slim.* ◇ *The odds are against you.* ◇ *The odds against winning the lottery are fourteen million to one* (= there are fourteen million combinations of numbers which are possible).

IDM **against all the odds; against the odds** happening although it seemed impossible; in spite of problems or disadvantages: *Dave passed his exam against all the odds.*

**odds and ends** (*informal*) small things of little value or importance

**o·dom·e·ter** /oʊˈdɑmət̬ər/ ***noun*** [C] a piece of equipment that measures the distance you have traveled: *My car only has 12,000 miles on the odometer.*

**o·dor** /ˈoʊdər/ ***noun*** [C] (*formal*) a smell (often a bad one)

★**of** /əv; *strong form* ʌv; *informal* ə/ ***prep.*** **1** belonging to, relating to, or part of sth: *the result of the survey* ◇ *the back of the book* ◇ *the leader of the party* **2** relating to a person: *a friend of mine* (= one of my friends) ◇ *the poems of Milton* ◇ *That was nice of her* (= she was nice to do that). **3** (used for saying what sb/sth is or what a thing contains or consists of): *a woman of intelligence* ◇ *the city of Paris* ◇ *a glass of milk* ◇ *a crowd of people* ◇ *It's made of silver.* ◇ *a feeling of anger* **4** showing sth: *a map of New York* **5** (showing that sb/sth is part of a larger group): *some of the people* ◇ *three of the houses* **6** (with measurements and expressions of time): *five miles north of Bismarck* ◇ *a gallon of milk* ◇ *the fourth of August* **7** (with some adjectives): *I'm proud of you.* ◇ *She's jealous of her.* **8** (with some verbs): *They accused him of espionage.* ◇ *Think of a*



O

*number.* ◇ *It reminds me of you.* **9** (used after a noun which is connected with a verb. The noun after "of" can be either the subject or the object): *the arrival of the President* (= he arrives) ◇ *the murder of the President* (= he is murdered) **10** (used about time) before: *It's five minutes of two.* ◇ *The movie starts at a quarter of eight.* ➲ Look at **to**[1](5).

★**off**[1] /ɔf; ɑf/ ***adv., prep.*** ➲ For special uses with many verbs and nouns, e.g. **turn off, off the record**, look at the verb and noun entries. **1** down or away from a place: *He fell off the ladder.* ◇ *We got off the bus.* ◇ *I shouted to him, but he just walked off.* ◇ *When are you off to Brazil?* ◇ *(figurative) We've gotten off the subject.* **2** (used with verbs that mean "remove"): *She took her coat off.* ◇ *He shook the rain off his umbrella.* ◇ *Don't leave the cap off the toothpaste.* **3** at a distance from sth: *Key West is just off the southern tip of Florida.* ◇ *Summer is still a long way off* (= it is a long time until then). **4** joined to and leading from: *My office is off the central corridor.* **5** (used about a machine, a light, etc.) not working or being used: *Please make sure the lights are off.* **6** when you do not work: *I'm taking a day off next week.* **7** no longer happening: *The meeting next Monday is off.* **8** cheaper; costing a certain amount less: *Today only: 20% off all red-tagged items* ◇ *This jacket was on sale for $10 off.*

NOTE Some people say **off of** before a noun in conversation, but it is not considered correct in written English: *Hey! You kids stay off of my lawn!*

IDM **(be) better off** → BETTER[2]

**off and on**; **on and off** sometimes, but not all the time

**well/badly off** having/not having a lot of money

★**off**[2] /ɔf; ɑf/ ***adj.*** (not before a noun) **1** not as good as usual or normal: *The team's playing seems a little off today.* **2** not correct: *Their estimate for the job was off by about $500.*

**off**[3] /ɔf; ɑf/ ***verb*** [T] **off sb** (*slang*) to kill sb

★**of·fend** /ə'fɛnd/ ***verb*** **1** [T] (often passive) to hurt sb's feelings; to upset sb: *I hope they won't be offended if I don't come.* ◇ *He felt offended that she hadn't written for so long.* **2** [I,T] to be wrong or act wrongly according to law, usual behavior, certain beliefs, etc.: *Wilson offended* (= committed a crime) *again within days of his release from prison.* ◇ *Parts of the book offended their religious beliefs.*

**of·fend·er** /ə'fɛndər/ ***noun*** [C] **1** (*formal*) a person who commits a crime: *juvenile offenders who are sent to adult prisons* ◇ *a first-time/repeat offender* **2** a person or thing that causes harm or trouble: *When it comes to polluting the environment, heavy industry is by far the worst offender.*

★**of·fense**[1] (*Cdn* **of·fence**) /ə'fɛns/ ***noun*** **1** [C] **offense (against sth)** (*formal*) a crime; breaking the law: *to commit an offense* ◇ *The new law makes it a criminal offense to drink alcohol in public places.* ◇ *a minor/serious offense* ◇ *She pleaded guilty to five traffic offenses.* **2** [U] **offense (to sb/sth)** annoyance, anger or sadness or sth that causes these feelings: *I didn't mean to cause you any offense.*

IDM **take offense (at sth)** to feel upset or hurt: *Be careful what you say – she takes offense very easily.*

**of·fense**[2] (*Cdn* **of·fence**) /'ɔfɛns; 'ɑf-/ ***noun*** [C,U, usually sing.] the part of a sports team that is responsible for scoring points: *The Bears' offense is the best in the league this year.* OPP **defense**

**of·fen·sive**[1] /ə'fɛnsɪv/ ***adj.*** **1** unpleasant; insulting: *an offensive remark* ◇ *offensive behavior* ➲ Look at **inoffensive**. **2** (*formal*) used for or connected with attacking: *offensive weapons* OPP **defensive**

★**of·fen·sive**[2] /ə'fɛnsɪv/ ***noun*** [C] an attack

IDM **take the offensive** to be the first to attack

★**of·fer**[1] /'ɔfər; 'ɑf-/ ***verb*** **1** [T] **offer sth (to sb)** to ask if sb would like sth or to give sb the opportunity to have sth: *He offered his seat on the bus to an old lady.* ◇ *I've been offered a job in Toronto.* ◇ *She offered me a cigarette.* **2** [I,T] to say or show that you are willing to do sth: *I don't want to do it, but I suppose I'll have to offer.* ◇ *My brother offered to help me paint the house.* **3** [T] to give or provide sth: *The brochure offers very little information about the surrounding area.* ◇ *The job offers plenty of opportunity for travel.* **4** [T] to say that you will pay a certain amount: *He offered (me) $6,000 for the car and I took it.*

★**of·fer**[2] /'ɔfər; 'ɑf-/ ***noun*** [C] **1** a statement offering to do sth or give sth to sb: *She accepted my offer of help.*

NOTE We can **make, accept, refuse** or **withdraw** an offer.

**2** a low price for sth in a store, or sth extra that you get when buying sth: *"Fantastic offers," the advertisement said. "Buy now!"* ◇ *See below for details of our special offer.* **3** an amount of money that you say you will give for sth: *They made an offer on the house.* ◇ *We turned down* (= refused) *an offer of $90,000.*

**of·fer·ing** /'ɔfərɪŋ; 'ɑf-/ ***noun*** [C] something that is given or produced: *He gave me a bouquet of flowers as a peace offering.* ◇ *to give an offering in church*

**off·hand**[1] /ˌɔf'hænd; ˌɑf-/ ***adj.*** (used about statements, comments, etc.) without thought or preparation: *an offhand remark*

**off·hand**[2] /ˌɔf'hænd; ˌɑf-/ ***adv.*** without having time to think; immediately: *I can't tell you what it's worth offhand.*

★**of·fice** /'ɔfəs; 'ɑf-/ ***noun*** **1** [C] a room or building where written work is done, especially work connected with a business: *The company's main office is in Philadelphia.* ◇ *office furniture/equipment* ◇ *Please call again during office hours.* ◇ *a doctor's/dentist's office* ➲ Look also at **box office** and **post office**. **2 Office** [sing.] (often in compounds) a government department, including the people who work there and the work they do: *the Office of Management and Budget* **3** [U] an official position, often as part of a government or other organization: *to run for office* ◇ *to be voted into/out of office*

★**of·fi·cer** /'ɔfəsər; 'ɑf-/ ***noun*** [C] **1** a person who gives the orders to others in the army, navy, etc.: *an army officer* **2** (often in compounds) a person with a position of authority or responsibility in the government or other organization: *a loan officer at a bank* **3** = POLICE OFFICER: *Excuse me, officer, is this the way to the stadium?* ➲ Look at the note at **official**.

★**of·fi·cial**[1] /ə'fɪʃl/ ***adj.*** **1** accepted and approved by the government or some other authority: *official*

O

*documents* ◇ *The project has not yet received official approval.* **2** connected with a position of authority: *official duties* ◇ *Her official title is now "Vice President for Finance."* **3** known publicly: *Their engagement is not yet official.* ◇ *The official reason for his resignation* (= but maybe not the real reason) *was that he wanted to spend more time with his family.* OPP **unofficial**

★**of·fi·cial²** /əˈfɪʃl/ ***noun*** [C] a person who has a position of authority: *The reception was attended by the ambassador and other high-ranking officials.* ◇ *a council official*

> NOTE An **office worker** is a person who works in an office, at a desk. An **official** is a person who has a position of responsibility in an organization, often the government: *senior government officials.* An **officer** is either a person who gives orders to others in the army, navy, etc. or a policeman or woman. However the word is sometimes used like **official**: *She's an executive officer on the board of directors.*

**of·fi·cial·dom** /əˈfɪʃldəm/ ***noun*** [U] groups of people in positions of authority in large organizations who seem more interested in following the rules than in being helpful

★**of·fi·cial·ly** /əˈfɪʃəli/ ***adv.*** **1** as announced publicly but perhaps not strictly true: *Officially we don't accept children under six, but we'll make an exception in this case.* **2** in an official way: *The new school was officially opened last week.*

**of·fi·cious** /əˈfɪʃəs/ ***adj.*** too ready to tell other people what to do and use the power you have to give orders

**off·ing** /ˈɔfɪŋ; ˈɑf-/ ***noun***
IDM **in the offing** likely to appear or happen soon

ˌ**off-ˈkey** ***adj., adv.*** (used about music) slightly too high or too low: *to sing off-key*

ˌ**off-ˈlimits** ***adj.*** forbidden; not to be entered by sb: *The teachers' lounge is off-limits to students.*

**off·line** /ˌɔfˈlaɪn; ˌɑf-/ (*also* ˌ**off-ˈline**) ***adj.*** (*computing*) not directly controlled by or connected to a computer or the Internet ➲ Look at **on·line**. ▸ **off·line** (*also* ˌ**off-ˈline**) ***adv.***: *How do I write an e-mail offline?*

**off·load** (*also* **off-load**) /ˈɔfloʊd; ˈɑf-; ˌɔfˈloʊd; ˌɑf-/ ***verb*** [T] **offload sth/sb (onto sb)** to get rid of sth or sb that you do not need or want by passing it to sb else: *She's always trying to offload her work onto her colleagues.*

ˌ**off-ˈpeak** ***adj.*** available or used at a less popular or busy time: *Off-peak plane fares have been reduced.*

ˈ**off-ramp** ***noun*** [C] = EXIT RAMP

**off·set** /ˌɔfˈsɛt; ˌɑf-; ˈɔfsɛt; ˈɑf-/ ***verb*** [T] (**off·set·ting**; *pt, pp* **off·set**) to make the effect of sth less strong or noticeable; to balance: *The disadvantages of the project are more than offset by the advantages.*

**off·shoot** /ˈɔfʃut; ˈɑf-/ ***noun*** [C] a thing that develops from sth else, especially a small organization that develops from a larger one

**off·shore** /ˌɔfˈʃɔr; ˌɑf-/ ***adj., adv.*** in the ocean, away from the land: *offshore oil drilling*

**off·spring** /ˈɔfsprɪŋ; ˈɑf-/ ***noun*** [C] (*pl.* **off·spring**) (*formal*) a child or children; the young of an animal: *Parents can pass many diseases on to their offspring.*

ˌ**off-ˈstage** (*also* **offstage**) ***adj., adv.*** away from or not on the stage: *to walk off-stage* ◇ *off-stage laughter*

ˌ**off-ˈwhite** ***adj.*** not pure white

★**of·ten** /ˈɔfn; ˈɔftn; ˈɑf-/ ***adv.*** **1** many times; frequently: *We often go swimming on weekends.* ◇ *I'm sorry I didn't write very often.* ◇ *How often should you go to the dentist?* ◇ *Write as often as you can.* **2** in many cases: *Women often go back to work after they have had a baby.*
IDM **more often than not** usually: *More often than not, the buses are late in the morning.*
**every so often** occasionally; from time to time

**o·gre** /ˈoʊgər/ ***noun*** [C] **1** (in children's stories) a cruel and frightening giant **2** a person who is unkind and frightening

★**oh** /oʊ/ ***interjection*** **1** (used for introducing a reply or remark, for attracting sb's attention or when pausing to think): *"What time should we leave?" "Oh, early, I think."* ◇ *"I'm a teacher." "Oh really? Where?"* ◇ *Oh, Jill, could you mail this letter for me?* **2** (used for expressing surprise, fear, etc.): *Oh, no! Look what happened!*

★**oil¹** /ɔɪl/ ***noun*** [U] **1** a thick liquid that comes from under the ground and is used as a fuel or to make machines work smoothly: *The United States relies heavily on imported oil.* ◇ *Your bicycle chain needs a little oil.* ◇ *Crude oil* (= the raw material) *is transported by tanker to the refinery.* **2** a thick liquid that comes from plants and is used in cooking: *cooking/vegetable/olive oil*

**oil²** /ɔɪl/ ***verb*** [T] to put oil on or into sth, to make it work smoothly

**oil·field** /ˈɔɪlfild/ ***noun*** [C] an area where oil is found under the ground or the ocean

ˈ**oil** ˌ**painting** ***noun*** [C] a painting that has been done using paint made with oil

ˈ**oil rig** ***noun*** [C] a large platform, with special equipment for bringing oil out of the ground

ˈ**oil slick** ***noun*** [C] an area of oil that floats on the ocean, usually when a ship carrying oil has leaked

ˈ**oil well** (*also* **well**) ***noun*** [C] a hole that is made deep in the ground or under the ocean in order to obtain oil

**oil·y** /ˈɔɪli/ ***adj.*** (**oil·i·er**; **oil·i·est**) covered with oil or like oil

**oint·ment** /ˈɔɪntmənt/ ***noun*** [C,U] a smooth substance that you put on sore skin or on an injury to help it to heal: *The doctor gave me an ointment to rub in twice a day.*

★**OK¹** (*also* **o·kay**) /ˌoʊˈkeɪ/ ***adj., adv.*** (*informal*) all right; good or well enough: *"How's your mom doing?" "OK."* ◇ *If it's okay with you, I'll come around 7.*

★**OK²** (*also* **o·kay**) /ˌoʊˈkeɪ/ ***interjection*** yes; all right: *"Do you want to go to the movies?" "OK."*

**OK³** (*also* **o·kay**) /ˌoʊˈkeɪ/ ***noun*** [sing.] agreement or permission: *My parents have given me the OK to stay out late.* ▸ **OK** (*also* **o·kay**) ***verb*** [T] (*pp* **O·K'ing** or **o·kay·ing**; *3rd person sing. pres.* **O·K's** or **o·kays**;

*pt, pp* **O·K'd** or **o·kayed**): *The boss okayed my request to take some time off.*

**o·kra** /'oʊkrə/ ***noun*** a vegetable with long green seed containers (**pods**) that are cooked and eaten

★**old** /oʊld/ ***adj.***

➤AGE **1** (used about people, animals, etc.) having lived a long time; not young: *My mother wasn't very old when she died.* ◇ *He's only 50, but he looks older.* ◇ *to get, grow, become old* **2** (used with a period of time or with *how*) of a particular age: *Our car is only a year old.* ◇ *They have a two-year-old* (= a child who is two years old). ◇ *How old are you?* ◇ *Are you older or younger than your sister?* ◇ *my older sister* ➲ Look at the note at **age**[1].

➤NOT NEW **3** having existed for a long time; not modern: *a beautiful old stone house* ◇ *old ideas/traditions* **4** having been used a lot; not new: *My younger brother gets all my old clothes.* ◇ *I'm going to trade in my old car for a new one.* **5** (only *before* a noun) former; previous: *I earn more now than I did in my old job.* **6** (only *before* a noun) known for a long time (but maybe not old in years): *She's a very old friend of mine.*

➤GOOD OLD/POOR OLD **7** (only *before* a noun) (*informal*) (used for expressing friendship and affection): *Good old Tom solved the problem!*

➤ANY OLD **8** (only *before* a noun) (*informal*) (used for emphasizing that sth is not important): *"What time should I come?" "Oh, any old time – it doesn't matter."*

➤OLD PEOPLE **9** **the old** ***noun*** [pl.] old people

NOTE Nowadays it is more acceptable to use the expression **senior citizens** to talk about old people.

IDM **be an old hand (at sth)** to be good at sth because you have done it often before

**old hat** (*informal*) no longer interesting or exciting because it has been done, seen, etc. too many times: *Staying in fancy hotels soon becomes old hat when you travel a lot on business.*

**plain old** → PLAIN[1]

ˌ**old 'age** ***noun*** [U] the part of your life when you are old: *He's enjoying life in his old age.* ➲ Look at **youth**.

ˌ**old ˌage se'curity** ***noun*** [U] (*abbr.* **OAS**) (*Cdn*) a regular income paid by the government to people above the age of 65

★**old-fash·ioned** /ˌoʊld 'fæʃənd/ ***adj.*** **1** not modern; not commonly worn, used, etc. now: *an old-fashioned record player* **2** (used about people) believing in old ideas, customs, etc.: *My parents are pretty old-fashioned about some things.*

**the ˌOld 'Testament** ***noun*** [sing.] the first part of the Bible, that tells the history of the Jewish people ➲ Look at **New Testament** and at the note at **White House**.

**ol·ive**[1] /'ɑlɪv/ ***noun*** [C] a small green or black fruit with a bitter taste, used for food and oil

**ol·ive**[2] /'ɑlɪv/ (*also* ˌ**olive 'green**) ***adj.*** of a dark color between yellow and green

'**olive oil** ***noun*** [U] oil obtained from olives and used in cooking or on salads

**O·lym·pic** /ə'lɪmpɪk/ ***adj.*** connected with the Olympic Games: *Who holds the Olympic record for the 1,500 meters?*

**the Oˌlympic 'Games** (*also* **the Olympics**) ***noun*** [pl.] the international sports competitions which are organized every four years in a different country: *to win a medal at/in the Olympics* ◇ *the 1994 Winter Olympics*

**om·buds·man** /'ɑmbʌdzmən; -mæn/ ***noun*** [C] (*pl.* **om·buds·men** /-mən/) an official who reports on complaints made by ordinary people against public authorities, newspapers, etc.

**o·me·ga** /oʊ'meɪgə; -'mi-/ ***noun*** [C] (*symbol* **Ω, ω**) the last letter of the Greek alphabet ➲ Look at the note at **fraternity**.

**om·e·let** (*also* **omelette**) /'ɑmlət/ ***noun*** [C] a mixture of eggs and milk which is beaten, fried, and usually folded over other foods. In the U.S. and Canada, omelets are usually eaten at breakfast: *a mushroom and cheese omelet*

**o·men** /'oʊmən/ ***noun*** [C] a sign of sth that will happen in the future: *a good/bad omen*

**om·i·cron** /'ɑmɪkrɑn; 'oʊ-/ ***noun*** [C] (*symbol* **O, o**) the fifteenth letter of the Greek alphabet ➲ Look at the note at **fraternity**.

**om·i·nous** /'ɑmənəs/ ***adj.*** suggesting that sth bad is going to happen: *Those black clouds look ominous.*

**o·mis·sion** /oʊ'mɪʃn; ə-/ ***noun*** **1** [C] something that has not been included: *There were several omissions from the list of names.* **2** [U] the act of not including sb/sth: *The program was criticized for its omission of certain important details.*

**o·mit** /oʊ'mɪt; ə-/ ***verb*** [T] (**omit<u>t</u>ing**; **omit<u>t</u>ed**) **1** to not include sth: *Several verses of the song can be omitted.* **2** (*formal*) to not do sth: *He omitted to mention the man's name.*

★**on** /ɑn; ɔn/ ***adv., prep.*** ➲ For special uses with many verbs and nouns, e.g. **get on**, **on vacation**, look at the verb and noun entries. **1** supported by a surface: *The plates are on the table.* ◇ *We sat on the floor.* ◇ *Make sure you put the lid on.* **2** touching or forming part of sth: *There's a mark on your skirt.* ◇ *paintings on the wall* ◇ *Write it down on a piece of paper.* **3** at a place: *on the farm* ◇ *I live on Walnut Street.* ◇ *a house on the banks of the river* **4** (showing direction): *on the right/left* **5** (used with means of transportation): *on the bus, train, plane* ◇ *"I took the bus." "Where did you get on?"* ◇ *We came on foot* (= walking). ◇ *on a bicycle* ➲ Note that we say **in** a car, truck, van, or taxi. **6** (with expressions of time): *on August 19th* ◇ *on Monday* ◇ *on Thanksgiving* ◇ *What are you doing on your birthday?* **7** immediately or soon after: *He called her on his return from New York.* ◇ *She began to sob on hearing the news.* **8** (showing that sth continues): *The man shouted at us, but we walked on.* ◇ *The war went on for five years.* **9** about sth: *We have a test on irregular verbs tomorrow.* ◇ *a lecture on Japan* **10** working; being used: *All the lights were on.* ◇ *Turn the TV on.* **11** happening: *There's a great play on in town next week.* ◇ *Is the party still on for tonight?* **12** using sth; by means of sth: *I spoke to her on the phone.* ◇ *There's a good movie on TV tonight.* ◇ *I heard it on the radio.* **13** wearing sth: *What did she have on?* **14** having sth with you: *I don't have any money on me.* **15** using drugs or medicine: *I've been on antibiotics for two weeks.* **16** receiving a certain amount of money: *I can't support a family on the salary I earn.*

O

**17** (showing the way sth is spent): *He spends a lot on clothes.* ◇ *Don't waste your time on that.* **18** paid for by sb: *The drinks are on me!*

IDM **from now/then on** starting from this/that time and continuing: *From then on he never smoked another cigarette.*

**off and on; on and off** → OFF[1]

**on and on** without stopping: *He just went on and on about his work.*

★**once**[1] /wʌns/ ***adv.*** **1** one time only; on one occasion: *I've only been to Mexico once.* ◇ *once a week/month/year* ◇ *I have the car serviced once every six months.* **2** at some time in the past; formerly: *This house was once the general store.*

IDM **all at once** all at the same time or suddenly: *People began talking all at once.* ◇ *All at once she got up and left the room.*

**at once 1** (*formal*) immediately; now: *The treaty requires all fighting to cease at once.* **2** at the same time: *I can't understand anything if you all talk at once.*

**just this once** on this occasion only: *"Have a glass of wine." "Oh, all right. Just this once."*

**once again** again, as before: *Spring will soon be here once again.*

**once and for all** now and for the last time: *You've got to make a decision once and for all.*

**once in a blue moon** (*informal*) very rarely; almost never: *We live in Amarillo, so I only go to Dallas once in a blue moon.*

**(every) once in a while** occasionally, but not often: *We like to order Chinese food every once in a while.*

**once more 1** one more time: *All right. We'll read the story once more, but then it's time for bed.* **2** again, as before: *The valuable painting is once more in the hands of its rightful owner.*

**once upon a time** (used at the beginning of a children's story) a long time ago; in the past: *Once upon a time, there was a beautiful princess...*

★**once**[2] /wʌns/ ***conj.*** as soon as; when: *Once you've practiced a little, you'll find that it's fairly easy.* ◇ *Once the meal was finished, the discussions began.*

**on·com·ing** /ˈɑnkʌmɪŋ; ˈɔn-/ ***adj.*** (only *before* a noun) coming toward you: *oncoming traffic*

★**one**[1] /wʌn/ ***pronoun, det., noun*** [C] **1** the number 1: *There's only one cookie left.* ◇ *The trip takes one hour.* ◇ *If you take one from ten, it leaves nine.* ➲ Look at **first**. **2** (used for emphasizing sth) only: *She's the one person I trust.* **3** (used when you are talking about a time in the past or future without actually saying which one) a certain: *He came to see me one evening last week.* ◇ *We ought to go and visit them one day.* **4** (*formal*) (used in front of sb's name to show that you do not know the person) a certain: *I believe that one Wanda Smith is the person you need to see.* **5** (used with *the other, another* or *other(s)* to make a contrast): *The twins are so much alike that it's hard to tell one from the other.* **6** the same: *We can't all get in this one car.*

IDM **(all) in one** all together or combined: *It's a shampoo and a conditioner all in one.*

**one after another/the other** first one, then the next, etc.: *One after another, the winners went up to get their prizes.*

**one by one** individually or separately: *One by one, the boys were called in to the principal's office.*

**one of a kind** not similar to anything or anyone else: *I miss my grandpa – he was really one of a kind.*

**one or two** a few: *I borrowed one or two new books from the library.* ◇ *Just take one or two – not too many.*

★**one**[2] /wʌn/ ***pronoun*** **1** (used instead of repeating a noun): *I think I'll have an apple. Would you like one?* **2 one of** one member (of a certain group): *One of the plates is broken.* ◇ *He's staying with one of his friends.* ◇ *One of the kids is crying.*

> NOTE **One of** is always followed by a plural noun. The verb is singular because the subject is **one**: *One of our assistants is sick.* ◇ *One of the buses was late.*

**3** (*formal*) (used for referring to people in general, including the speaker or writer): *One should try not to get annoyed.* ◇ *Plenty of exercise makes one physically fit.*

> NOTE It is very formal to use **one** in this way. In everyday English it is more common to use **you**. Note that the possessive form is **one's**: *One must be sure of one's facts before criticizing other people.* **One's** is also the short form of "one is" or "one has."

IDM **one another** each other: *We exchanged news with one another.* ◇ *You should listen to one another more often.*

★**one**[3] /wʌn/ ***noun*** [C] **1** (used after *this, that, which* or after an adjective which cannot stand alone): *"Which dress do you like?" "This one."* ◇ *"Can I borrow some books of yours?" "Yes. Which ones?"* ◇ *This coat's a little too small. You need a bigger one.* ◇ *That idea is a very good one.* **2** (used before a group of words that show which person or thing you are talking about): *My house is the one after the post office.* ◇ *The girl he's going out with is the one with red hair.* ◇ *If you find some questions difficult, leave out the ones you don't understand.* **3** someone: *She's not one to get upset easily.*

**ˌone-on-ˈone** (*also* **ˌone-to-ˈone**) ***adj., adv.*** between only two people: *one-on-one English lessons* (= one teacher with one student)

**one·self** /wʌnˈsɛlf/ ***pronoun*** (*formal*) **1** (used for referring to people in general when *one* is the subject of the sentence): *One can teach oneself to play the piano, but it is easier to have lessons.* **2** (used for emphasizing *one*): *One could easily arrange it all oneself.*

IDM **(all) by oneself 1** alone **2** without help

> NOTE **Oneself** is very formal. It is much more common to say **yourself** when talking about people in general.

**ˌone-ˈsided** ***adj.*** **1** involving one person more than the other: *Her feelings for him seem to be kind of one-sided* (= he doesn't feel the same). **2** unfair; seeing only one side (of an argument, etc.): *I think you're being very one-sided. Think of my point of view.*

**ˌone-ˈway** ***adv., adj.*** **1** (used about roads) that you can only drive along in one direction: *a one-way* *street* **2** (used about a ticket) that you can use to travel somewhere but not back again: *I'd like to buy a one-way ticket to the Caribbean!* ➲ Look at **round-trip**.

**on·go·ing** /ˈɑngoʊɪŋ; ˈɔn-/ ***adj.*** (only *before* a noun) continuing to exist now: *It's an ongoing problem.* ◇ *an ongoing relationship*

**on·ion** /ˈʌnyən/ ***noun*** [C,U] a small white vegetable with many layers and a brown skin. Onions have a strong smell and taste, and are often used in cooking: *onion soup* ➲ picture on study page **A28-29**.

**on·line** /ˌɑnˈlaɪn; ˌɔn-/ ***adj.*** (*technical*) connected to and controlled by a computer: *an online ticket reservation system* ➲ Look at **offline**. ▶ **online** ***adv.***: *Do you like to shop online?*

**on·look·er** /ˈɑnlʊkər; ˈɔn-/ ***noun*** [C] a person who watches sth happening without taking part in it: *The police were questioning several onlookers about the incident.*

★**on·ly¹** /ˈoʊnli/ ***adj.*** (only *before* a noun) **1** with no others existing or present: *I was the only woman in the bar.* ◇ *This is the only dress we have in your size.* **2** the most suitable or the best: *It's so cold that the only thing to do is to sit by the fire.*

★**on·ly²** /ˈoʊnli/ ***adv.*** and no one or nothing else; no more than: *She only likes rock music.* ◇ *I only asked a few friends to the party.* ◇ *It was only a little spider.* ◇ *It's only one o'clock. There's plenty of time.*

NOTE In written English **only** is usually placed before the word it refers to. In spoken English we can use stress to show which word it refers to and so **only** can have different positions: *I only kissed 'Jane* (= I kissed Jane and no one else). ◇ *I only 'kissed Jane* (= I kissed Jane, but I didn't do anything else).

IDM **if only** → IF

**not only...but also** both...and: *He not only did the shopping but he also cooked the meal.*

★**on·ly³** /ˈoʊnli/ ***conj.*** (*informal*) except that; but: *The movie was really good, only it was a little too long.*

**ˌonly ˈchild** ***noun*** [C] a child who has no brothers or sisters

**ˈon-ramp** ***noun*** [C] = ENTRANCE RAMP

**on·set** /ˈɑnsɛt; ˈɔn-/ ***noun*** [sing.] the beginning (often of sth bad): *the onset of winter*

**on·slaught** /ˈɑnslɔt; ˈɔn-/ ***noun*** [C] **onslaught (on sb/sth)** a fierce attack: *an onslaught on government policy*

★**on·to** (*also* **on to**) /ˈɑntə; ˈɔn-; *before vowels* ˈɑntu; ˈɔn-/ ***prep.*** to a position on sth: *The cat jumped onto the sofa.* ◇ *The bottle fell onto the floor.*

IDM **be onto sb/sth** (*informal*) to have some information about sb/sth that could lead to an important discovery, etc.: *The police were onto the car thieves.* ◇ *I think you may be onto something big here.*

**on·ward** /ˈɑnwərd; ˈɔn-/ (*also* **onwards** /ˈɑnwərdz; ˈɔn-/) ***adv.*** **1** and after: *From September onward it usually begins to get colder.* **2** forward or toward progress: *The road stretched onward into the distance.* ◇ *The President said the economy would soon be moving onward and upward.*

**oops** /ʊps; ups/ (*also* **whoops** /wʊps/) ***interjection*** (*informal*) (used when you have, or almost have, a small accident): *Oops! I almost spilled my juice.*

**ooze** /uz/ ***verb*** [I,T] to flow slowly out or to allow sth to flow slowly out: *Blood was oozing from a cut on his head.* ◇ *The container started to ooze a strange green liquid.* ◇ (*figurative*) *She was oozing confidence* (= she was very confident).

**o·paque** /oʊˈpeɪk/ ***adj.*** **1** that you cannot see through; not transparent: *opaque glass in the door* **2** (*formal*) difficult to understand; not clear

★**o·pen¹** /ˈoʊpən/ ***adj.***

➤NOT CLOSED **1** not closed: *Don't leave the door open.* ◇ *an open window* ◇ *I can't get this carton of milk open.* ◇ *She stared at me with her eyes wide open.* ◇ *The diary was lying open on her desk.* ◇ *The curtains were open so that we could see into the room.*

➤PERSON'S CHARACTER **2** honest and willing to talk: *Jane will tell you exactly what happened at the meeting – she's a very open person.*

➤NOT HIDDEN **3** not hidden or secret: *He looked at him with open dislike.*

➤FOR CUSTOMERS/VISITORS **4** with its doors unlocked so that customers can enter: *The bank isn't open until 9:30.*

➤OF BUILDING **5** (used about a new building, public area, etc.) ready to be used for the first time: *The new shopping mall will soon be open.*

➤AVAILABLE **6 open (to sb/sth)** (used about a road, a course of action, etc.) possible to use, do, etc.: *After the heavy snow many minor roads were not open to traffic.* **7 open (to sb/sth)** that anyone can enter, visit, etc.: *The competition is open to everyone.* ◇ *The building is open to the public in the summer.*

➤CLOTHES **8** (used about clothes) with the buttons not fastened: *His shirt was open at the neck.*

➤NOT ENCLOSED **9** (only *before* a noun) with few buildings, towns, etc. near (used about an area of land): *open country* **10** (only *before* a noun) at a distance from the land (used about an area of ocean): *Once we were out in the open sea, the wind got stronger.*

➤NOT COVERED **11** (only *before* a noun) not covered: *an open fire*

➤NOT YET DECIDED **12** not finally decided; still being considered: *Let's leave the details open.*

IDM **have/keep an open mind (about/on sth)** to be willing to listen to or consider new ideas and suggestions

**in the open air** outside: *Somehow, food eaten in the open air tastes much better.*

**open to sth** willing to receive sth: *I'm always open to suggestions.*

**with open arms** in a friendly way that shows that you are pleased to see sb or have sth

★**o·pen²** /ˈoʊpən/ **the open** ***noun*** [sing.] outside: *After working in an office I like to be out in the open on weekends.*

IDM **bring sth out into the open; come out into the open** to make sth known publicly; to be known publicly: *I'm glad our secret has come out into the open at last.*

★**o·pen³** /ˈoʊpən/ ***verb***

➤DOOR/WINDOW/CONTAINER **1** [I,T] to become

open or to make sth open: *This window won't open – it's stuck.* ◇ *Do you mind if I open this window?* ◇ *When I opened my eyes, she was gone.* ◇ *Can I open my presents now?*

➤ TO FOLD/SPREAD OUT **2** [I,T] to fold out, back, etc.: *The book opened at the very page I needed.* ◇ *Open your hand – what have you got inside?* ◇ *She opened the curtains and looked out.* **3** [I,T] **open (sth) (out)** (used about a map, etc.) to fold out: *Open the map out and let's all take a look.*

➤ OF BUSINESS/STORE, ETC. **4** [I,T] (used about a store, an office, etc.) to be unlocked so that business, work, etc. can start; to unlock sth: *The store hasn't opened yet.* ◇ *They open the museum an hour later on Sundays.*

➤ WITH CEREMONY **5** [T] to say officially that a new building, etc. is ready for use: *The mayor will open the stadium next week.*

➤ START **6** [I,T] to start: *The play opens on Broadway next month.* ◇ *The chairman opened the meeting by welcoming everybody.* ◇ *I'd like to open a bank account.*

➤ BORDER/ROAD **7** [T] to make a road, etc. available for use again: *Snowplows have opened many major roads.*

IDM **open fire (at/on sb/sth)** to start shooting: *He ordered his men to open fire on the advancing enemy troops.*

PHRV **open into/onto sth** to lead straight to sth: *This door opens onto the lawn.*

**open (sth) up 1** to become available or to make sth available: *After I graduated from college, all sorts of opportunities opened up for me.* ◇ *Parts of the desert may soon be opened up for farming.* **2** to open a door: *"Open up!" shouted the police to the man inside.*

O

**ˌopen-ˈair** *adj.* outside; not indoor: *an open-air concert*

**o·pen·er** /ˈoʊpənər/ *noun* [C] (in compounds) a thing that takes the lid, etc. off sth: *a can opener*

**ˌopen ˈhouse** *noun* [C, usually sing.] a day when the public can visit a place that is usually closed to them: *to have/hold an open house*

★**o·pen·ing¹** /ˈoʊpənɪŋ/ *noun* **1** [sing.] beginning: *The book is famous for its dramatic opening.* **2** [C] a hole; a way in or out: *We were able to get through an opening in the hedge.* **3** [C] an opportunity: *There are many new openings for trade with Eastern Europe.* **4** [C] a job which is available: *We currently have an opening for a sales manager.* **5** [C] the occasion when a public building, etc. is officially opened or ready for use: *the opening of the new theater*

**o·pen·ing²** /ˈoʊpənɪŋ/ *adj.* (only *before* a noun) first: *the opening chapter of a book* ◇ *His opening remarks were very witty.*

**o·pen·ly** /ˈoʊpənli/ *adv.* not secretly; honestly: *I think you should discuss your feelings openly with each other.*

**ˌopen-ˈminded** *adj.* willing to consider new ideas and opinions

**o·pen·ness** /ˈoʊpənəs/ *noun* [U] the quality of being honest and willing to talk: *I was surprised by her openness about her relationship with Jerry.*

**ˌopen-ˈplan** *adj.* (used about a large area indoors) not divided into separate rooms: *an open-plan office*

**o·pe·ra** /ˈɑprə; ˈɑpərə/ *noun* **1** [C] a play in which the actors (opera singers) sing the words to music: *an opera by Wagner* ◇ *a comic opera* **2** [U] works of this kind: *Do you like opera?* ◇ *grand* (= serious) *opera* ◇ *light* (= not serious) *opera* ➲ Look at **soap opera**. ► **op·er·at·ic** /ˌɑpəˈrætɪk/ *adj.*: *operatic music*

**ˈopera house** *noun* [C] a theater where operas are performed

★**op·er·ate** /ˈɑpəreɪt/ *verb* **1** [I,T] to work, or to make sth work: *I don't understand how this machine operates.* ◇ *These controls here operate the air conditioning.* **2** [I] to act or to have an effect: *Several factors were operating to our advantage.* **3** [I,T] to do business; to manage or direct sth: *The corporation operates from its headquarters in Atlanta.* ◇ *Many companies operate mail order services now.* **4** [I] **operate (on sb) (for sth)**; **operate (on sth)** to cut open a patient's body in order to deal with a part that is damaged, diseased, etc.: *The surgeon is going to operate on her in the morning.* ◇ *He was operated on for appendicitis.*

**ˈoperating room** *noun* [C] a room in a hospital where OPERATIONS (3) are performed

**ˈoperating ˌsystem** *noun* [C] a computer program that organizes a number of other programs at the same time

★**op·er·a·tion** /ˌɑpəˈreɪʃn/ *noun* **1** [C] an activity, often highly organized, that involves many people, actions, days, etc.: *A rescue operation was launched to find the missing children.* ◇ *military operations* ◇ *Putting up the new wallpaper was a very tricky operation.* **2** [C] a business company: *a huge international operation* **3** [C] **operation (on sb/sth) (for sth)** cutting open a patient's body in order to deal with a part inside: *The surgeon performed an operation on her for a kidney problem.* ◇ *He had an operation to remove some damaged lung tissue.* **4** [U] the way in which sth works; working: *The operation of these machines is quite simple.*

IDM **in operation** working or having an effect: *The water heater should be back in operation in the next few hours.*

**op·er·a·tion·al** /ˌɑpəˈreɪʃənl/ *adj.* **1** connected with an OPERATION (1,4) **2** ready for use: *The new factory is now fully operational.*

**op·er·a·tor** /ˈɑpəreɪt̬ər/ *noun* [C] **1** a person whose job is to connect telephone calls, for the public or in a particular building: *Dial 0 for the operator.* ◇ *a switchboard operator* **2** a person whose job is to work a particular machine or piece of equipment: *a computer operator* **3** a person or company that does certain types of business: *a tour operator*

★**o·pin·ion** /əˈpɪnyən/ *noun* **1** [C] **opinion (of sb/sth)**; **opinion (on/about sth)** what you think about sb/sth: *She asked me for my opinion of her new hairstyle and I told her.* ◇ *He has very strong opinions on almost everything.* **2** [U] what people in general think about sth: *Public opinion is in favor of a change in the law.*

IDM **be of the opinion that...** (*formal*) to think or believe that...: *In this case we are of the opinion that you made the right decision.*

**have a high, low, etc. opinion of sb/sth** to think that sb/sth is good, bad, etc.

**in my, your, etc. opinion** I, you, etc. think that...: *In my opinion, you're making a terrible mistake.*
**a matter of opinion** → MATTER[1]

**o'pinion poll** ***noun*** [C] = POLL[1] (1)

**o·pi·um** /'oʊpiəm/ ***noun*** [U] a drug that is made from the seeds of the poppy flower

**o·pos·sum** /ə'pɑsəm/ (*also* **possum**) ***noun*** [C] a type of small furry animal that lives in trees and carries its young in a pocket of skin (a **pouch**) on its stomach. When they are afraid, opossums act as if they are dead.

★**op·po·nent** /ə'poʊnənt/ ***noun*** [C] **1** (in sport or games) a person who plays against sb **2 an opponent (of sth)** a person who disagrees with sb's actions, plans or beliefs and tries to stop or change them

★**op·por·tu·ni·ty** /ˌɑpər'tunət̬i/ ***noun*** [C,U] (*pl.* **op·por·tu·ni·ties**) a chance to do sth that you would like to do; a situation or a time in which it is possible to do sth that you would like to do: *There will be plenty of opportunity for asking questions later.* ◇ *The trip gave me a great opportunity to use my Spanish.* ◇ *I'd like to take this opportunity to thank you for all your help.* ◇ *an equal opportunity employer* (= an employer who employs people regardless of sex/race) ➲ Look at the note at **occasion**.

★**op·pose** /ə'poʊz/ ***verb*** [T] to disagree with sb's beliefs, actions or plans and to try to change or stop them: *They opposed the plan to widen the main road through their town.*

★**op·posed** /ə'poʊzd/ ***adj.*** **opposed to sth** disagreeing with a plan, action, etc.; believing that sth is morally wrong: *I'm not opposed to the idea, but I need more details.* ◇ *She has always been opposed to experiments on animals.*
IDM **as opposed to** (used to emphasize the difference between two things) in contrast with: *Your work will be judged on the basis of quality, as opposed to quantity.*

★**op·po·site[1]** /'ɑpəzət/ ***adj.***, ***adv.*** **1** as different as possible: *I can't walk with you because I'm going in the opposite direction.* ◇ *the opposite sex* (= men for women, women for men) **2** in a position directly on the other side of sb/sth; facing: *The two farms are on opposite sides of the river.* ◇ *The two families sat at opposite ends of the room to each other.*

NOTE Sometimes **opposite** is used after the noun: *Write your answer in the space opposite.*

★**op·po·site[2]** /'ɑpəzət/ ***noun*** [C] the word, thing or person that is as different as possible from sb/sth: *"Hot" is the opposite of "cold."* ◇ *She's very friendly, whereas her brother is the complete opposite.*

**op·po·site[3]** /'ɑpəzət/ ***prep.*** directly on the other side of a space between sth and sth else; facing sb/sth: *I always buy my paper from the store opposite our house.*

★**op·po·si·tion** /ˌɑpə'zɪʃn/ ***noun*** **1** [U] **opposition (to sb/sth)** the feeling of disagreeing with sth and the action of trying to change it: *Despite strong opposition from local people, the new prison was built on the edge of town.* ◇ *to express your opposition to sth* **2 the opposition** [sing.] the person or team who plays against sb in sports or games: *Their coach told them not to underestimate the opposition.* **3 the opposition** [sing.] (used about the political system of some countries) the politicians or the political parties that are in Parliament, but do not control the country's government

**op·press** /ə'prɛs/ ***verb*** [T] (usually passive) to rule sb (especially a nation or a part of society) in a way that allows the people no freedom; to control sb in an unjust way, using force

**op·pressed** /ə'prɛst/ ***adj.*** unfairly ruled or treated; not free: *an oppressed minority*

**op·pres·sion** /ə'prɛʃn/ ***noun*** [U] the system or act of oppressing; the state of being oppressed: *a struggle against oppression*

**op·pres·sive** /ə'prɛsɪv/ ***adj.*** **1** allowing no freedom; controlling by force; unjust: *The military government announced oppressive new laws.* **2** (used especially about heat or the atmosphere) causing you to feel very uncomfortable

**op·pres·sor** /ə'prɛsər/ ***noun*** [C] a person who oppresses sb

**opt** /ɑpt/ ***verb*** [T] **opt to do sth** to choose or decide to do sth after thinking about it
PHR V **opt for sb/sth** to choose sth after you have decided that you do not want the other possibilities
**opt out (of sth)** to choose not to take part in sth; to decide to stop being involved in sth: *Several employees have opted out of the strike which was called by the union last week.*

**op·ti·cal** /'ɑptɪkl/ ***adj.*** connected with the sense of sight: *optical instruments*

ˌ**optical il'lusion** ***noun*** [C] something that tricks the eye and makes you believe sth is there or is true when it is not

**op·ti·cian** /ɑp'tɪʃn/ ***noun*** [C] a person who is qualified to make and sell eyeglasses ➲ Look at **optometrist**.

**op·ti·mism** /'ɑptəmɪzəm/ ***noun*** [U] the feeling that the future or sth in the future will be good or successful: *There is considerable optimism that the economy will improve.* OPP **pessimism**

**op·ti·mist** /'ɑptəmɪst/ ***noun*** [C] a person who is always hopeful that things will be good or successful in the future OPP **pessimist**

**op·ti·mis·tic** /ˌɑptə'mɪstɪk/ ***adj.*** hoping or believing that what happens in the future will be good or successful: *I applied for the job, but I'm not very optimistic about my chances of getting it.* OPP **pessimistic** ▶ **op·ti·mis·ti·cal·ly** /-kli/ ***adv.***

★**op·tion** /'ɑpʃn/ ***noun*** **1** [U, sing.] the freedom to choose; choice: *If you're late again, you will give us no option but to fire you.* **2** [C] a thing that you choose or can choose; choice: *She looked carefully at all her options before deciding on a college.* **3** [C] something, especially a piece of equipment, that you can choose to have in a new car, truck, etc. but must pay for: *Options like a CD player and leather seat covers can add quite a bit to the price of a car.*

**op·tion·al** /'ɑpʃənl/ ***adj.*** that you can choose or not choose: *an optional subject at school* ◇ *an optional extra* (= sth that you can have as an extra thing but must pay for) OPP **compulsory** or **mandatory**

**op·tom·e·trist** /ɑp'tɑmətrɪst/ ***noun*** [C] a person

O

who is qualified to test your eyes and tell you which glasses, etc. you need ➲ Look at **optician**.

★**or** /ər; *strong form* ɔr/ ***conj.*** **1** (used before another possibility or the last of a series of possibilities): *Would you like to sit here or next to the window?* ◇ *Are you interested or not?* ◇ *You can have chicken, beef or fish.* ➲ Look at **either...or**. **2** if not; otherwise: *Don't drive so fast or you'll have an accident!* ◇ *She must have loved him, or she wouldn't have married him.* SYN **Or else** and **otherwise** can be used with this meaning. **3** (after a negative) and neither; and not: *She hasn't called or written to me for weeks.* ◇ *I've never been to Chile or Peru.* ➲ Look at **neither...nor**. **4** (used before a word or phrase that explains or comments on what has been said before): *20% of the population, or one out of every five* ◇ *Minneapolis and St. Paul, or the "Twin Cities" as they are sometimes known*

IDM **or else** → ELSE

**or so** about: *I would think the repairs will cost you $100 or so.*

**or sb/sth/someplace/somewhere** (*informal*) (used for showing that you are not sure, cannot remember or do not know which person, thing or place): *She's a computer programmer or something.* ◇ *The movie was set in Sweden or somewhere.* ➲ Another phrase that shows that you are not sure is **...or other**: *He muttered something or other about not having any time and disappeared.*

**o·ral¹** /ˈɔrəl/ ***adj.*** **1** spoken, not written: *an oral exercise* **2** concerning or using the mouth: *oral hygiene*

O

**o·ral²** /ˈɔrəl/ ***noun*** [C] a spoken examination: *I have my German oral next week.*

**o·ral·ly** /ˈɔrəli/ ***adv.*** **1** using speech, not writing: *Orally her English is good.* **2** through the mouth and swallowed

★**or·ange¹** /ˈɔrɪndʒ; ˈɑr-/ ***noun*** **1** [C] a round fruit with a thick skin, that is divided into sections (segments) inside, and is a color between red and yellow: *orange juice* ➲ picture on study page **A28-29**. **2** [U] the color of this fruit, between red and yellow

★**or·ange²** /ˈɔrɪndʒ; ˈɑr-/ ***adj.*** having the color ORANGE¹ (2): *orange paint*

**or·a·tor** /ˈɔrət̬ər; ˈɑr-/ ***noun*** [C] (*formal*) a person who is good at making public speeches

**or·bit¹** /ˈɔrbət/ ***noun*** [C,U] the path taken by sth (a planet, moon, spacecraft, etc.) going around sth else in space: *to put a satellite into orbit*

**or·bit²** /ˈɔrbət/ ***verb*** [I,T] to move around sth (the moon, the sun, a planet etc.) in orbit ▶ **or·bit·al** /ˈɔrbət̬l/ ***adj.***

**or·chard** /ˈɔrtʃərd/ ***noun*** [C] a piece of land in which fruit trees are grown: *a cherry orchard*

★**or·ches·tra** /ˈɔrkəstrə/ ***noun*** [C] a large group of musicians who play different musical instruments together: *a symphony orchestra*

NOTE An orchestra usually plays classical music. Rock music, jazz, etc. are played by a **group** or **band**.

**or·ches·tral** /ɔrˈkɛstrəl/ ***adj.*** played by or written for an orchestra

**or·chid** /ˈɔrkəd/ ***noun*** [C] a plant that has flowers of unusual shapes and bright colors

**or·dain** /ɔrˈdeɪn/ ***verb*** [T] **ordain sb (as) (sth)** to make sb a priest or minister in a religion

**or·deal** /ɔrˈdil/ ***noun*** [C] a very bad experience: *The woman who was attacked last night is in the hospital recovering from her ordeal.*

★**or·der¹** /ˈɔrdər/ ***noun***

➤ARRANGEMENT **1** [U] the way in which people or things are arranged in relation to each other: *a list of names in alphabetical order* ◇ *a list of dates in chronological order*

➤ORGANIZED STATE **2** [U] an organized state, when everything is in its right place: *Make sure your notes are in order before you start your speech.* **3** [U] the situation in which laws, rules, authority, etc. are obeyed: *Police have restored order on the streets following last week's violence.* ➲ Look at **disorder**.

➤INSTRUCTION **4** [C] an instruction or demand that sb must do sth, given by sb who has power over that person: *In the army, you have to obey orders at all times.* ◇ *Frank's ex-wife obtained a court order allowing her to keep their children.*

➤GOODS **5** [C] a request asking for sth to be made, supplied or delivered: *The company has just received a major export order.*

➤FOOD/DRINKS **6** [C] a request for food, drink, etc. in a hotel, restaurant, etc.: *Can I take your order now, sir?*

IDM **in order to do sth** with the purpose or intention of doing sth; so that sth can be done: *In order to obtain a passport, you need a birth certificate and two photographs.* ◇ *We left early in order to avoid the traffic.*

**in working order** (used about machines, etc.) working correctly, not broken: *It's an old stove, but it's still in good working order.*

**law and order** → LAW

**out of order** → OUT²

★**or·der²** /ˈɔrdər/ ***verb*** **1** [T] **order sb (to do sth)** to tell sb to do sth in a strong way which does not permit him/her to refuse, and without saying "please": *I'm not asking you to do your homework – I'm ordering you!* ◇ *The police ordered the demonstrators to stop.* **2** [T] to ask for sth to be made, supplied or delivered: *The store didn't have the book I wanted, so I ordered it.* ◇ *We ordered some new chairs for the living room.* **3** [I,T] to ask for food, drink, etc. in a restaurant, hotel, etc.: *Are you ready to order yet, ma'am?*

PHR V **order sb around** to keep telling sb what to do and how to do it: *Quit ordering me around! You're not my boss.*

**or·der·ly¹** /ˈɔrdərli/ ***adj.*** **1** well-arranged; well-organized; neat and clean: *an orderly office* **2** well-behaved; peaceful: *The teacher told the class to form an orderly line.*

**or·der·ly²** /ˈɔrdərli/ ***noun*** [C] (*pl.* **or·der·lies**) a hospital assistant who has not had special training

**or·di·nal** /ˈɔrdənl; ˈɔrdn·l/ (*also* ˌ**ordinal ˈnumber**) ***noun*** [C] a number that shows the order or position in a series: *"First," "second," and "third" are ordinals.* ➲ Look at **cardinal¹**(4).

**or·di·nar·i·ly** /ˌɔrdn·ˈɛrəli/ ***adv.*** usually; generally: *I don't ordinarily work as late as this.*

★**or·di·nar·y** /ˈɔrdn̩ˌɛri/ ***adj.*** normal; not special or unusual or different from others: *It's interesting to see how ordinary people live in other countries.* ◇ *For my next magic trick, I'll need an ordinary handkerchief.*
IDM **out of the ordinary** unusual; different from normal

**ore** /ɔr/ ***noun*** [C,U] rock or earth from which metal can be obtained: *iron ore*

**o·reg·a·no** /əˈrɛgənoʊ/ ***noun*** [U] a plant with leaves that have a sweet smell and are used in cooking as an herb ➲ picture on study page **A28-29**.

★**or·gan** /ˈɔrgən/ ***noun*** [C] **1** a part of the body that has a particular function: *vital organs* (= those such as the heart which help to keep you alive) ◇ *sexual organs* **2** a large musical instrument of the piano family which you play with your hands and feet. Many organs have pipes through which air is forced in order to make sounds, and they are often found in churches: *a church organ* ◇ *a pipe organ* ◇ *organ music* ➲ Note that you play **the** organ: *When did you learn to play the organ?*

**or·gan·ic** /ɔrˈgænɪk/ ***adj.*** **1** produced by or existing in living things: *You need to add a lot of organic matter to the soil.* OPP **inorganic** **2** (used about food or agricultural methods) produced by or using natural materials, not chemicals: *organic vegetables* ◇ *organic farming* **3** connected with substances which contain carbon: *organic chemistry* ▸ **or·gan·i·cal·ly** /-kli/ ***adv.***: *organically grown vegetables*

**or·gan·ism** /ˈɔrgənɪzəm/ ***noun*** [C] an animal or plant, especially one that is so small that you can only see it with a special instrument (**microscope**)

**or·gan·ist** /ˈɔrgənɪst/ ***noun*** [C] a person who plays the organ

★**or·gan·i·za·tion** /ˌɔrgənəˈzeɪʃn/ ***noun*** **1** [C] an organized group of people who do sth together: *She works for a volunteer organization helping homeless people.* **2** [U] the activity of organizing or arranging: *An enormous amount of organization went into the festival.* **3** [U] the way in which sth is organized: *The students all complained about the poor organization of the course.* ▸ **or·gan·i·za·tion·al** /-ʃənl/ ***adj.***: *The job requires a high level of organizational ability.*

★**or·gan·ize** /ˈɔrgənaɪz/ ***verb*** **1** [T] to plan or arrange an event, an activity, etc.: *The school organizes trips to various historic sites.* **2** [I,T] to put things into order; to arrange into a system or logical order: *Can you decide what needs to be done? I'm terrible at organizing.*

**or·gan·ized** /ˈɔrgənaɪzd/ ***adj.*** **1** planned or arranged: *My department is badly organized.* **2** having a good system; working well: *Jenny's always very organized.*

**or·gan·iz·er** /ˈɔrgənaɪzər/ ***noun*** [C] a person who organizes an event, etc.: *The organizers of the concert said that it had been a great success.*

**or·gasm** /ˈɔrgæzəm/ ***noun*** [C,U] the point of greatest sexual pleasure: *to have an orgasm*

**or·gy** /ˈɔrdʒi/ ***noun*** [C] (*pl.* **or·gies**) **1** a wild party, involving a lot of sex and/or alcohol or drugs **2 an orgy (of sth)** a period of doing sth in an uncontrolled way: *an orgy of violence*

**the O·ri·ent** /ˈɔriənt; -ɛnt/ ***noun*** [sing.] (*old-fashioned*) the countries of the Far East (China, Japan, etc.)

NOTE Nowadays most people prefer to say **Asia** or **the Far East**.

**o·ri·ent** /ˈɔriɛnt/ ***verb*** [T] **1** to put sth in the correct place or position: *A computer sensor is used to orient the spacecraft in orbit.* **2 orient yourself** to find out where you are; to become familiar with a place: *When I came out of the airport, I couldn't orient myself at first.*

**O·ri·en·tal** /ˌɔriˈɛntl/ ***adj.*** (*old-fashioned*) coming from or belonging to the Far East: *Oriental languages*

NOTE This word is sometimes considered offensive. Nowadays most people prefer to say **Asian**.

**o·ri·en·ta·tion** /ˌɔriənˈteɪʃn/ ***noun*** [U] **1** the direction in which sth is pointing: *the orientation of the radar* **2** the process of becoming familiar with sth new: *a two-week orientation course for new employees* **3** the kind of interests or aims that a person or organization has: *sexual orientation* (= whether sb is attracted to people of the opposite sex, the same sex, or both sexes) ◇ *the theme park's family orientation*

**o·ri·ent·ed** /ˈɔriɛntəd/ ***adj.*** aimed or directed at a particular type of person or thing: *Our products are male-oriented.* ◇ *She's very career-oriented.*

**o·ri·ga·mi** /ˌɔrəˈgɑmi/ ***noun*** [U] the Japanese art of folding paper into attractive shapes

★**or·i·gin** /ˈɔrədʒɪn; ˈɑr-/ ***noun*** [C,U] **1** the time when or place where sth first comes into existence; the reason why sth starts: *Could you explain to me the origins of this tradition to me?* ◇ *Many English words are of Latin origin.* **2** the family, race, class, etc. that a person comes from: *people of African origin* ◇ *middle-class origins*

O

★**o·rig·i·nal**[1] /əˈrɪdʒənl/ ***adj.*** **1** first; earliest (before changes or developments): *The original meaning of this word is different from the meaning it has nowadays.* **2** new and interesting; different from others of its type: *There are no original ideas in his work.* **3** made or created first, before copies: *"Is that an original painting?" "No, it's a copy."*

★**o·rig·i·nal**[2] /əˈrɪdʒənl/ ***noun*** [C] the first one made or created; not a copy: *Could you make a copy and give the original back to me?*

**o·rig·i·nal·i·ty** /əˌrɪdʒəˈnæləṭi/ ***noun*** [U] the quality of being new and interesting

★**o·rig·i·nal·ly** /əˈrɪdʒənəli/ ***adv.*** **1** in the beginning; in the first form (before changes or developments): *I'm originally from Ohio, but we moved to Ontario when I was very young.* **2** in a way or style that is unlike others: *She has a talent for expressing simple ideas originally.*

**o·rig·i·nate** /əˈrɪdʒəneɪt/ ***verb*** (*formal*) **1** [I] to start or be caused to start: *This game originated in the nineteenth century.* **2** [T] to start or create first: *I wonder who originated the custom of sending birthday cards.*

**o·ri·ole** /ˈɔrioʊl; ˈɔriəl/ ***noun*** [C] a small bird with black and yellow or orange feathers

**or·na·ment** /ˈɔrnəmənt/ ***noun*** [C] an object that you have because it is attractive, not because it is useful. Ornaments are used to decorate rooms, etc.: *Christmas tree ornaments*

**or·na·men·tal** /ˌɔrnəˈmɛntl/ ***adj.*** made or put somewhere in order to look attractive, not for any practical use

**or·nate** /ɔrˈneɪt/ ***adj.*** having a lot of decoration: *an ornate building*

**or·ni·thol·o·gist** /ˌɔrnəˈθɑlədʒɪst/ ***noun*** [C] a person whose job is to study birds

**or·ni·thol·o·gy** /ˌɔrnəˈθɑlədʒi/ ***noun*** [U] the study of birds

**or·phan**[1] /ˈɔrfən/ ***noun*** [C] a child whose parents are dead

**or·phan**[2] /ˈɔrfən/ ***verb*** [T] (usually passive) to cause a child to become an ORPHAN[1]: *She was orphaned when she was three and went to live with her grandparents.*

**or·phan·age** /ˈɔrfənɪdʒ/ ***noun*** [C] an institution where orphans live and are taken care of

**or·tho·don·tist** /ˌɔrθəˈdɑntɪst/ ***noun*** [C] a dentist who treats problems concerning the position of the teeth and jaws

**or·tho·dox** /ˈɔrθədɑks/ ***adj.*** **1** generally believed, done or accepted: *orthodox opinions* ◇ *orthodox methods* OPP **unorthodox** **2** practicing the old, traditional beliefs, ceremonies, etc. of certain religions: *an orthodox Jew* ◇ *the Greek Orthodox Church*

**Os·car** /ˈɑskər/ ***noun*** [C] = ACADEMY AWARD™: *How many Oscars has Woody Allen won?*

O

**os·cil·late** /ˈɑsəleɪt/ ***verb*** **1** [I] **oscillate (between A and B)** (*formal*) to keep changing from one extreme of feeling or behavior to another, and back again: *Her moods oscillated between depression and elation.* **2** (*technical*) to keep moving from one position to another and back again: *The needle on the dial oscillated.* ▸ **os·cill·a·tion** ***noun*** [C,U] (*formal*)

**os·ten·ta·tious** /ˌɑstənˈteɪʃəs/ ***adj.*** showing wealth, importance, etc. very openly in order to attract attention and impress other people ▸ **os·ten·ta·tious·ly** ***adv.***

**os·trich** /ˈɑstrɪtʃ; ˈɔ-/ ***noun*** [C] a very large African bird with a long neck and long legs, which can run very fast but which cannot fly

★**oth·er** /ˈʌðər/ ***det., pronoun*** **1** in addition to or different from the one or ones that have already been mentioned or understood: *I didn't have any other plans that evening, so I accepted their invitation.* ◇ *How many other students are there in your class?* ◇ *If you're busy now, I'll come back some other time.* ◇ *Some of my friends went to college, others didn't.* ◇ *She doesn't care what other people think.*

NOTE **Other** cannot be used after "an." Look at **another**.

**2** (after *the* or a possessive with a singular noun) second of two: *I can only find one sock. Have you seen the other one?* ◇ *My glasses broke, but fortunately I had my other pair with me.* **3** (after *the* or a possessive with a plural noun) the rest of a group or number of people or things: *Their youngest son still lives with them, but their other kids have left home.* ◇ *I'll have to wear this shirt because all my others are dirty.*

IDM **in other words** saying sth in a different way
**(on the one hand...) on the other hand** (used for showing opposite points of view): *It's cheaper to travel by bus. On the other hand, flying is so much faster.*
**one after another/the other** → ONE[1]
**other than** **1** (usually after a negative) apart from; except (for): *The plane was a little bit late, but other than that the trip was fine.* **2** different(ly) from; not: *Justin is never anything other than a perfect gentleman.*
**the other day, morning, week, etc.** recently, not long ago: *An old friend called me the other day.*
**sb/sth/someplace/somewhere or other** → OR

★**oth·er·wise** /ˈʌðərwaɪz/ ***adv.*** **1** in all other ways; apart from that: *I'm a little tired, but otherwise I feel fine.* **2** in a different or another way: *Follow these instructions exactly unless the boss tells you otherwise.* **3** (used for stating what would happen if you do not do sth or if sth does not happen) if not: *You have to press the red button; otherwise it won't work.*

IDM **or otherwise** (indicating another possibility or a contrast to what has just been mentioned): *I have no opinion, good or otherwise, on this subject.*

**ot·ter** /ˈɑt̬ər/ ***noun*** [C] an animal with brown fur that lives in water and eats fish

**ouch** /aʊtʃ/ ***interjection*** (used when reacting to a sudden feeling of pain): *Ouch! You're hurting me.* ➲ Look also at **ow**.

★**ought to** /ˈɔt̬ə; *before vowels and in final position* ˈɔt tu/ ***modal verb*** (*negative* **ought not to**; *short form* **ought·n't to** /ˈɔtnt tə/ before vowels and in final position /ˈɔtnt tu/) **1** (used for asking for and giving advice about what to do): *You ought to read this book. It's really interesting.* ◇ *Do you think I ought to call her before we go?* ◇ *"Should I tell her what happened?" "Yes, I think you ought to."* **2** (used for telling sb what his/her duty is): *You ought to visit your parents more often.* ◇ *She oughtn't to make private phone calls in work time.* ◇ *I ought to have helped. I'm sorry.* **3** (used for saying that you expect sth is true, or that you expect sth to happen/to have happened): *She ought to pass her test.* ◇ *They ought to be here by now. They left at six.* ◇ *I bought six loaves of bread. That ought to have been enough.*

NOTE We usually use **should** instead of **ought to** in questions. Many people leave out **to** after **oughtn't**: *You oughtn't do that.* However, some people consider this use incorrect.

**ounce** /aʊns/ ***noun*** **1** [C] (*abbr.* **oz.**) a measure of weight; 28.35 grams. There are 16 ounces in a pound: *Our daughter weighed seven pounds, four ounces when she was born.* **2** [C] = FLUID OUNCE: *a 12-ounce can of pop* **3** [sing.] **an ounce of sth** a very small amount of sth: *He doesn't have an ounce of imagination.*

★**our** /ɑr; ˈaʊər/ ***det.*** **1** belonging to or connected with us: *Our house is on the corner.* ◇ *Our teacher is excellent.* ◇ *This is our first visit to Britain.* **2 Our** used to refer to, or address, God or a holy person: *Our Father* (= God) ◇ *Our Lady* (= the Virgin Mary)

★**ours** /ɑrz; ˈaʊərz/ ***pronoun*** the one or ones belonging to, connected with or done by us: *Your stereo* *system is exactly the same as ours.* ◇ *Their new car is nice, but I like ours better.* ◇ *That clock was a gift from a friend of ours.*

★**our·selves** /ɑr'sɛlvz; aʊər'sɛlvz/ ***pronoun*** **1** (used as the object of a verb or preposition when "we" do an action and are also affected by it): *We should be angry with ourselves for making such a stupid mistake.* ◇ *They asked us to wait, so we sat down and made ourselves comfortable.* **2** (used for emphasis): *We don't have any kids ourselves, but many of our friends do.* ◇ *Do you think we should paint the house ourselves?* (= or should we ask sb else to do it for us?)

IDM **(all) by ourselves** **1** without help from anyone else: *We managed to move the piano by ourselves.* **2** not with anyone else; alone: *Now that we're by ourselves, can I ask you a personal question?* ➲ Look at the note at **alone**.

★**out**[1] /aʊt/ ***adj., adv.*** ➲ For special uses with many verbs, e.g. **try sb/sth out**, look at the verb entries. **1** (used for showing movement away from a place): *He opened the case and took a gun out.* ◇ *I threw out that old shirt of yours.* ◇ *He opened the window and put his head out.* **2** not at home or in your place of work: *I was out when she called.* ◇ *We usually eat out on Saturdays.* ◇ *They took me out for dinner when I was in New Orleans.* **3** outside a house, building, etc.: *You should be out in the fresh air.* **4** (used for showing that sth is no longer hidden): *Oh look! The sun's out.* **5** not in fashion: *Short skirts are completely out.* **6** (used about electric power, a light or a fire) not on; not burning: *The lights are out. They must be in bed.* **7** not possible or acceptable: *I'm afraid Friday is out. I have a meeting that day.* **8** in a loud voice; clearly: *She cried out in pain.* **9** (used about the tide) away from the shore: *Don't swim when the tide is going out.* **10** (in sports, especially baseball) no longer allowed to play in a game or a part of a game: *Strike three – you're out!*

IDM **be out for sth**; **be out to do sth** to try hard to get or do sth

**out-and-out** complete: *It was out-and-out war between us.*

**ˌout 'loud** in a normal speaking voice that other people can hear, not silently

★**out**[2] /aʊt/ **out of** /'aʊt̬əv/ ***prep.*** **1** (used with verbs expressing movement away from the inside of sth): *She took her wallet out of her purse.* ◇ *to get out of bed* **2** away from, or no longer in, a place or situation: *He's out of the country on business.* ◇ *The doctors say she's out of danger.* **3** at a distance from a place: *We live a long way out of Boise.* **4** (used for saying what you use to make sth): *You could make a table out of this wood.* **5** from among a number: *Nine out of ten people prefer this model.* **6** (used for saying that you no longer have sth): *We're out of milk.* ◇ *I'm out of breath.* ◇ *out of work* **7** (used for saying which feeling causes you to do sth): *I only helped them out of pity.* **8** from: *I copied the recipe out of a book.* ◇ *I'd rather drink coffee out of a cup, not a mug.*

IDM **be/feel out of it** (*informal*) to be/feel unable to think clearly because you are tired, not feeling well, etc.: *I felt really out of it at the meeting and decided to go home early.*

**out of order** (used about a machine, etc.) not working correctly or not working at all

**out there** (*informal*) strange; far from what most people consider normal: *Her art's kind of out there; maybe that's why it doesn't sell very well.*

**out·age** /'aʊt̬ɪdʒ/ ***noun*** [C] a period of time when sth (especially electricity) is cut off temporarily: *widespread power outages due to a severe storm*

**out·back** /'aʊtbæk/ ***noun*** [sing.] the part of a country (especially Australia) which is a long way from where most people live

**out·board mo·tor** /ˌaʊtbɔrd 'moʊt̬ər/ ***noun*** [C] an engine that can be attached to a boat

**out·break** /'aʊtbreɪk/ ***noun*** [C] the sudden beginning or appearance of sth bad (especially disease or violence): *an outbreak of cholera* ◇ *outbreaks of fighting*

**out·burst** /'aʊtbərst/ ***noun*** [C] a sudden expression of a strong feeling, especially anger: *an angry outburst*

**out·cast** /'aʊtkæst/ ***noun*** [C] a person who is no longer accepted by society or by a group of people: *a social outcast*

**out·come** /'aʊtkʌm/ ***noun*** [C, usually sing.] how an event, an action or a situation ends; the result of sth: *We will inform you of the outcome of the interview within a week.*

**out·cry** /'aʊtkraɪ/ ***noun*** [C, usually sing.] (*pl.* **outcries**) a strong protest by a large number of people because they disagree with sth: *The public outcry forced the government to change its mind.*

**out·dat·ed** /ˌaʊt'deɪt̬əd/ ***adj.*** not useful or common anymore; old-fashioned: *A lot of the computer equipment is getting outdated.*

**out·do** /ˌaʊt'du/ ***verb*** [T] (*pres. part.* **out·do·ing**; *3rd person sing. pres.* **out·does** /-'dʌz/; *pt* **out·did** /-'dɪd/; *pp* **out·done** /-'dʌn/) to do sth better than another person; to be more successful than sb else: *He doesn't want to be outdone by his brother.*

★**out·door** /'aʊtdɔr/ ***adj.*** (only *before* a noun) happening, done or used in the open air (not in a building): *an outdoor concert* ◇ *outdoor furniture* OPP **indoor**

★**out·doors** /ˌaʊt'dɔrz/ ***adv.*** in the open air; outside a building: *It's such a nice evening – why don't we sit outdoors?* OPP **indoors**

★**out·er** /'aʊt̬ər/ ***adj.*** **1** on the outside: *the outer layer of skin* **2** far from the inside or the center: *the outer suburbs of a city* OPP **inner**

**out·er·belt** /'aʊt̬ərbɛlt/ ***noun*** [C] a road that is built around a city to connect the main roads that go into the city

**out·er·most** /'aʊt̬ərmoʊst/ ***adj.*** farthest from the inside or center; most distant: *the outermost planet in the solar system* OPP **innermost**

**ˌouter 'space** ***noun*** [U] = SPACE[1] (2)

**out·fit** /'aʊtfɪt/ ***noun*** [C] **1** a set of clothes that are worn together **2** (*informal*) an organization, a company, etc.: *He works for a computer outfit I've never heard of.*

**out·go·ing** ***adj.*** **1** /ˌaʊt'goʊɪŋ/ friendly and interested in other people and new experiences **2** /'aʊtgoʊɪŋ/ (only *before* a noun) leaving a job or a place: *The outgoing mayor gave a short speech.* ◇ *Put all the outgoing mail in a pile there.* OPP **incoming**

O

**out·grow** /ˌaʊtˈgroʊ/ *verb* [T] (*pt* **out·grew** /-ˈgru/; *pp* **out·grown** /-ˈgroʊn/) to become too old or too big for sth (especially clothes): *Kids outgrow their shoes so quickly.*

**out·house** /ˈaʊthaʊs/ *noun* [C] (*pl.* **out·houses** /ˈaʊthaʊzɪz/) (especially in former times) a very small building, separate from a house, with a type of toilet inside

**out·ing** /ˈaʊṭɪŋ/ *noun* [C] a short trip for pleasure: *to go on an outing to the zoo*

**out·land·ish** /aʊtˈlændɪʃ/ *adj.* very strange or unusual: *outlandish clothes*

**out·last** /ˌaʊtˈlæst/ *verb* [T] to last or live longer than sb/sth

**out·law**[1] /ˈaʊtlɔ/ *noun* [C] (especially in former times) a criminal who is living outside society and trying to avoid being captured: *The movie is about a band of outlaws in the Wild West.*

**out·law**[2] /ˈaʊtlɔ/ *verb* [T] to make sth illegal

**out·lay** /ˈaʊtleɪ/ *noun* [C, usually sing.] (*formal*) money that is spent, especially in order to start a business or a project

**out·let** /ˈaʊtlɛt; -lət/ *noun* [C] **1** a place in a wall where an electrical appliance can be connected to the electricity supply **2** a hole or a place through which a gas or liquid can escape: (*figurative*) *Gary found an outlet for his energy in playing football.* **3** a store or a branch of a large company: *We found some real bargains at the factory outlet* (= a store that sells products directly from a factory at cheaper prices).

★**out·line**[1] /ˈaʊtlaɪn/ *noun* [C] **1** a line that shows the shape or outside edge of sb/sth: *She could see the outline of a person through the mist.* **2** the most important facts or ideas about sth: *a brief outline of Mexican history* **3** a list or diagram that shows how sth is to be organized: *Before you start writing an essay, it's a good idea to make a brief outline.*

**out·line**[2] /ˈaʊtlaɪn/ *verb* [T] to give the most important facts or ideas about sth

**out·live** /ˌaʊtˈlɪv/ *verb* [T] to live or exist longer than sb/sth: *This bridge has outlived its usefulness and should be replaced.* ➲ Look at **outlast**.

★**out·look** /ˈaʊtlʊk/ *noun* [C] **1** your attitude to or feeling about life: *an optimistic outlook on life* **2 outlook (for sth)** what will probably happen: *The outlook for the economy is not good.*

**out·ly·ing** /ˈaʊtlaɪɪŋ/ *adj.* (only *before* a noun) far from the center of a town or city

**out·mod·ed** /ˌaʊtˈmoʊdəd/ *adj.* no longer common or fashionable

**out·num·ber** /ˌaʊtˈnʌmbər/ *verb* [T] (often passive) to be greater in number than sb/sth: *The enemy troops outnumbered us by three to one.* ◇ *We were completely outnumbered.*

**out·pa·tient** /ˈaʊtpeɪʃənt/ *noun* [C] a person who goes to see a doctor for treatment but who does not stay in the hospital overnight ➲ Look at **inpatient**.

**out·put** /ˈaʊtpʊt/ *noun* [U] **1** the amount that a person or machine produces: *Output has increased in the past year.* **2** the information that is given by a computer ➲ Look at **input**.

**out·rage**[1] /ˈaʊtreɪdʒ/ *noun* **1** [C] something that is very bad or wrong and that causes you to feel great anger: *It's an outrage that they show things like that on TV.* **2** [U] great anger: *a feeling of outrage*

**out·rage**[2] /ˈaʊtreɪdʒ/ *verb* [T] (often passive) to make sb feel very angry or upset: *His parents were outraged when he dyed his hair green.*

**out·ra·geous** /aʊtˈreɪdʒəs/ *adj.* **1** making you very angry: *I refuse to pay such outrageous prices.* **2** very strange or unusual; shocking ▶ **out·ra·geous·ly** *adv.*

**out·reach** /ˈaʊtritʃ/ *noun* [U] the activity of providing help or a service to particular people in a community, usually not in regular offices, schools, health centers, etc.: *educational outreach programs for families in rural areas*

**out·right**[1] /aʊtˈraɪt/ *adv.* **1** without hiding anything; openly: *She told them outright what she thought about it.* **2** immediately or completely: *to be killed outright* ◇ *They were able to buy the house outright.*

**out·right**[2] /ˈaʊtraɪt/ *adj.* (only *before* a noun) complete and clear, without any doubt: *an outright lie*

**out·set** /ˈaʊtsɛt/ *noun*

IDM **at/from the outset (of sth)** at/from the beginning (of sth): *There have been difficulties with this supplier right from the outset.*

★**out·side**[1] /ˈaʊtsaɪd; ˌaʊtˈsaɪd/ *noun* **1** [C, usually sing.] the outer side or surface of sth: *There is a list of all the ingredients on the outside of the package.* ◇ *to paint the outside of a house* **2** [sing.] **the outside** the area that is near or around a building, etc.: *We've only seen the church from the outside.*

★**out·side**[2] /ˈaʊtsaɪd/ *adj.* **1** of or on the outer side or surface of sth: *the outside walls of a building* **2** not connected with or belonging to a particular group or organization: *We can't do all the work by ourselves. We'll need outside help.* ◇ *She spends so much time studying that she has no time for outside interests.* **3** (used about a chance, possibility, etc.) very small

IDM **the outside world** → WORLD

★**out·side**[3] /ˌaʊtˈsaɪd; ˈaʊtsaɪd/ *prep.* **1** in, at or to a place that is not in but close to a building, etc.: *Leave your muddy boots outside the door.* **2** (*also* **outside of**) not in: *You can do whatever you want outside of office hours.* ◇ *a suburb just outside Miami* **3 outside of** (*informal*) except; other than: *I don't know what else we can do, outside of starting all over again.*

★**out·side**[4] /ˌaʊtˈsaɪd/ *adv.* **1** in or to a place that is not in a room: *Please wait outside for a few minutes.* **2** in or to a place that is not in a building: *Let's eat outside. The weather is just perfect.* ◇ *Go outside and see if it's raining.* ➲ Look at **outdoors** and **out of doors** (at the entry for **door**).

**out·sid·er** /ˌaʊtˈsaɪdər/ *noun* [C] **1** a person who is not accepted as a member of a particular group **2** a person or animal in a race or competition that is not expected to win

**out·skirts** /ˈaʊtskərts/ *noun* [pl.] **the outskirts** the parts of a town or city that are farthest from the center

**out·source** /ˈaʊtsɔrs/ *verb* [I,T] to arrange for sb

outside a company to do work or provide goods for that company: *We outsource all our computing work* ▶ **out·sourc·ing** ***noun*** [U]

**out·spo·ken** /ˌaʊtˈspoʊkən/ ***adj.*** saying exactly what you think or feel: *Linda is very outspoken in her criticism.* ▶ **out·spo·ken·ness** ***noun*** [U]

★**out·stand·ing** /ˌaʊtˈstændɪŋ/ ***adj.*** **1** very good; excellent: *Your work in this course has been outstanding.* **2** not yet paid or done: *outstanding debts*

**out·stand·ing·ly** /ˌaʊtˈstændɪŋli/ ***adv.*** very well: *Jeff played outstandingly.*

**out·stretched** /ˌaʊtˈstrɛtʃt/ ***adj.*** spread out as far as possible: *outstretched arms*

**out·ward**[1] /ˈaʊtwərd/ ***adj.*** (only *before* a noun) of or on the outside: *She showed no outward signs of emotion when she heard the bad news.*

**out·ward**[2] /ˈaʊtwərd/ (*also* **outwards** /ˈaʊtwərdz/) ***adv.*** toward the outside or away from the place where you are: *This door opens outward.*

**out·ward·ly** /ˈaʊtwərdli/ ***adv.*** on the outside or surface: *He remained outwardly calm so as not to frighten the children.*

**out·weigh** /ˌaʊtˈweɪ/ ***verb*** [T] to be more important than sth: *The advantages outweigh the disadvantages.*

**o·val** /ˈoʊvl/ ***adj., noun*** [C] shaped like an egg; a shape like that of an egg: *an oval mirror* ➲ picture at **shape**.

**o·va·ry** /ˈoʊvəri/ ***noun*** [C] (*pl.* **o·va·ries**) one of the two parts of the female body that produce eggs

**o·va·tion** /oʊˈveɪʃn/ ***noun*** [C] a long period of enthusiastic clapping by an audience as a sign of their approval: *to give sb a huge/rapturous/rousing ovation* ➲ Look at **standing ovation**.

★**ov·en** /ˈʌvən/ ***noun*** [C] a piece of equipment with a door that you use to cook food: *Bake in a 375° oven for 50 minutes.* ◇ *a microwave oven* ➲ picture at **stove**. ➲ Note that you **roast** or **bake** food in an oven.

**over/above**

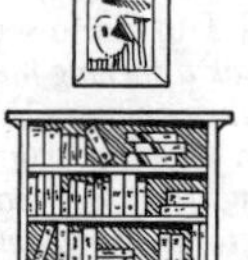

a painting **over/above** a bookcase

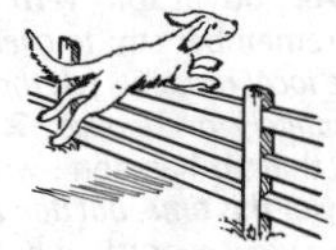

a dog jumping **over** a fence

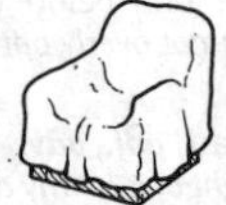

a cover **over** an armchair

★**o·ver**[1] /ˈoʊvər/ ***adv., prep.*** ➲ For special uses with many verbs, e.g. **get over sth**, look at the verb entries. **1** directly above sth, but not touching: *There's a painting over the bookcase.* ◇ *We watched the plane fly over.* **2** on, and partly or completely covering or touching: *There's a cover over the chair.* ◇ *She hung her coat over the back of the chair.* **3** down or sideways from an upright position: *He leaned over to speak to the woman next to him.* ◇ *I knocked my glass over during supper.* **4** across to the other side of sth: *The dog is jumping over the fence.* ◇ *a bridge over the river* **5** on or to the other side: *a town just over the border* ◇ *Turn the record over.* **6** (used for expressing distance): *He's over in Japan right now.* ◇ *Sit down over there.* **7** above or more than a number, price, etc.: *She lived in Juno for over ten years.* ◇ *suitable for children ages 10 and over* **8** (used with *all*) in every part or place: *There was blood all over the place.* ◇ *I can't find my glasses. I've looked all over for them.* **9** (used for saying that sth is repeated): *You'll have to start all over again* (= from the beginning). ◇ *She kept saying the same thing over and over again.* **10** about; on the subject of: *We had an argument over money.* **11** during: *What did you do over the weekend?*

IDM **left over** → LEFT[4]

**over the counter** → COUNTER[1]

★**o·ver**[2] /ˈoʊvər/ ***adj.*** (not before a noun) finished: *Summer vacation will be over soon.*

IDM **over (and done) with** (*informal*) (used about a bad situation, etc.) finished: *"Are you ready to start the test?" "OK, let's get it over with."* ◇ *I'm glad that's over and done with!*

**over easy/medium/hard** (used about eggs) fried on both sides for a short time/for a moderate length of time/for a longer time: *I'll have two eggs over easy and a cup of coffee, please.*

★**o·ver·all**[1] /ˈoʊvərɔl/ ***adj.*** (only *before* a noun) including everything: *The overall cost of the work will be about $200.*

★**o·ver·all**[2] /ˌoʊvərˈɔl/ ***adv.*** **1** speaking generally about sth: *Overall, I can say that we are pleased with your work.* **2** including everything or everybody: *Denise finished third overall in the 100-meter dash.*

**overalls**

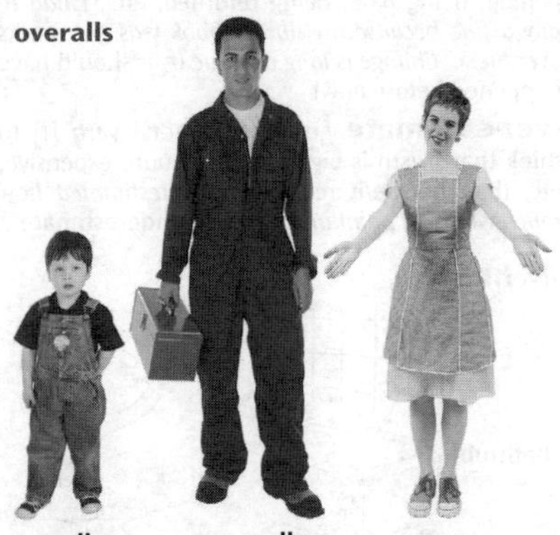

overalls coveralls apron

**o·ver·alls** /ˈoʊvərɔlz/ (*also* **bib overalls**) ***noun*** [pl.] a piece of clothing, similar to jeans, but also covering your chest and with straps that go over your shoulders: *a pair of overalls*

**o·ver·board** /ˈoʊvərbɔrd/ ***adv.*** over the side of a boat or ship into the water: *Man overboard!* ◇ *She fell overboard and drowned.*

IDM **go overboard (about sb/sth)** to react in a way that is extreme, often when you are too excited about sb/sth

O

**o·ver·cast** /ˈoʊvərkæst/ ***adj.*** (used about the sky) covered with clouds

**o·ver·charge** /ˌoʊvərˈtʃɑrdʒ/ ***verb*** [I,T] to ask sb to pay too much money: *The man in the post office overcharged me by 50¢.*

**o·ver·coat** /ˈoʊvərkoʊt/ ***noun*** [C] a long thick coat that you wear in cold weather

★**o·ver·come** /ˌoʊvərˈkʌm/ ***verb*** [T] (*pt* **o·ver·came** /-ˈkeɪm/; *pp* **o·ver·come**) **1** to control or succeed in defeating sb/sth: *She tried hard to overcome her fear of flying.* **2** (usually passive) to cause sb to become weak or sick or to lose control: *He was overcome with emotion and had to leave the room.* ◇ *to be overcome by smoke*

**o·ver·crowd·ed** /ˌoʊvərˈkraʊdəd/ ***adj.*** (used about a place) with too many people: *The subway is always overcrowded during rush hour.*

**o·ver·do** /ˌoʊvərˈdu/ ***verb*** [T] (*pt* **o·ver·did** /-ˈdɪd/; *pp* **o·ver·done** /-ˈdʌn/) **1** to use or show too much of sth: *You look nice, but you overdid the makeup a little.* **2** to cook sth too long: *The meat was overdone.*

IDM **overdo it** to work, etc. too hard: *Exercise is fine, but don't overdo it.*

**o·ver·dose¹** /ˈoʊvərdoʊs/ ***noun*** [C] an amount of a drug or medicine that is too large and so is not safe: *Jake killed himself by taking an overdose.*

**o·ver·dose²** /ˈoʊvərdoʊs/ (*also informal* **OD**) ***verb*** [I] **overdose (on sth)** to become very sick or die from taking too much of a drug or medicine

O

**o·ver·drawn** /ˌoʊvərˈdrɔn/ ***adj.*** having spent more money than you have in your bank account: *Darren is $50 overdrawn.*

**o·ver·due** /ˌoʊvərˈdu/ ***adj.*** late in arriving, happening, being paid, being returned, etc.: *I had to pay a fine because my library book was two weeks overdue.* ◇ *Change is long overdue* (= it should have happened before now).

**o·ver·es·ti·mate** /ˌoʊvərˈɛstəmeɪt/ ***verb*** [T] to think that sb/sth is bigger, better, more expensive, etc. than he/she/it really is: *I overestimated how much we could paint in a day.* OPP **underestimate**

**overflow**

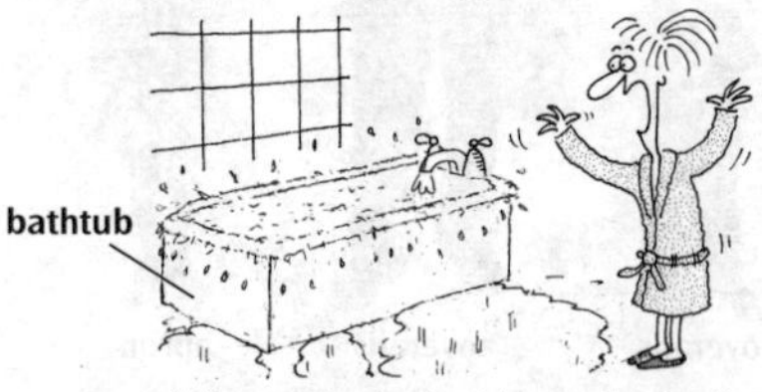


"Oh, no! The bathtub's overflowing!"

**o·ver·flow** /ˌoʊvərˈfloʊ/ ***verb*** [I,T] to be so full that the contents go over the sides or beyond the limits; to go over the sides or beyond the limits of sth: *The water was left on and the bathtub overflowed.* ◇ *shopping bags overflowing with clothes and gifts* ◇ *After the heavy rains, the river overflowed its banks.*

**o·ver·grown** /ˌoʊvərˈgroʊn/ ***adj.*** covered with plants that have not been taken care of and that have grown too big: *The vegetable garden is neglected and overgrown with weeds.*

**o·ver·haul** /ˌoʊvərˈhɔl; ˈoʊvərhɔl/ ***verb*** [T] to look at sth carefully and change or repair it if necessary: *to overhaul an engine* ▸ **o·ver·haul** /ˈoʊvərhɔl/ ***noun*** [C]: *a complete overhaul of the welfare system*

**o·ver·head¹** /ˈoʊvərhɛd/ ***adj.*** above your head: *an overhead luggage compartment in an airplane* ▸ **o·ver·head** /ˌoʊvərˈhɛd/ ***adv.***: *A helicopter flew overhead.*

**o·ver·head²** /ˈoʊvərhɛd/ ***noun*** [C,U] money that a company must spend on things like salaries, heat, light, rent, etc.

**ˌoverhead proˈjector** ***noun*** [C] a piece of equipment that uses an electric light to show words, pictures, etc. in a larger size on a wall or screen

**o·ver·hear** /ˌoʊvərˈhɪr/ ***verb*** [T] (*pt, pp* **o·ver·heard** /-ˈhərd/) to hear what sb is saying when he/she is speaking to sb else and not to you

**o·ver·joyed** /ˌoʊvərˈdʒɔɪd/ ***adj.*** (not before a noun) **overjoyed (at sth/to do sth)** very happy: *We were overjoyed at the news.*

**overlap**

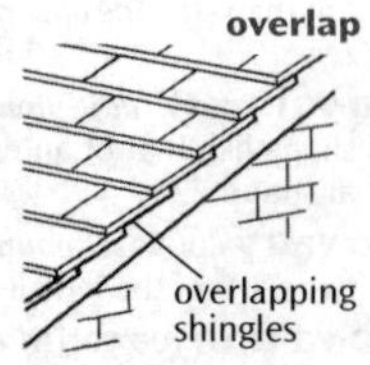


**o·ver·lap** /ˌoʊvərˈlæp/ ***verb*** [I,T] (**o·ver·lap·ping**; **o·ver·lapped**) **1** when two things overlap, part of one covers part of the other: *Make sure that the two pieces of material overlap.* **2** to be partly the same as sth: *Our jobs overlap to some extent.* ▸ **o·ver·lap** ***noun*** [C,U]: *There will be some overlap between my duties in my old job and in my new one.*

**o·ver·load** /ˌoʊvərˈloʊd/ ***verb*** [T] **1** (often passive) to put too many people or things into or onto sth: *an overloaded vehicle* ◇ (*figurative*) *to be overloaded with work* **2** to put too much electricity through sth: *If you use too many electrical appliances at one time, you could overload the circuit.*

★**o·ver·look** /ˌoʊvərˈlʊk/ ***verb*** [T] **1** to fail to see, notice or remember sth: *to overlook a spelling mistake* ◇ *The local residents felt that their opinions had been completely overlooked.* **2** to take no action about sth that sb has done wrong: *I will overlook your behavior this time, but don't let it happen again.* **3** to have a view over sth: *a hotel room overlooking the river*

**o·ver·ly** /ˈoʊvərli/ ***adv.*** (only before an adjective) too; too much; very: *I'm not overly optimistic about our chances of success.*

★**o·ver·night** /ˌoʊvərˈnaɪt/ ***adj.***, ***adv.*** **1** for or during the night: *an overnight bag* ◇ *Why don't you stay overnight?* **2** (happening) very suddenly: *an overnight success* ◇ *She became a star overnight.*

**o·ver·pass** /ˈoʊvərpæs/ ***noun*** [C] a type of bridge that carries a road over another road ➲ Look at **underpass**.

**o·ver·pow·er** /ˌoʊvərˈpaʊər/ ***verb*** [T] to be too strong for sb; to defeat sb because you are stronger than he/she is: *The police overpowered the gunman.*

◇ *The firefighter was overpowered by the heat and smoke.*

**o·ver·pow·er·ing** /ˌoʊvərˈpaʊərɪŋ/ ***adj.*** very strong: *an overpowering smell*

**o·ver·rate** /ˌoʊvərˈreɪt/ ***verb*** [T] (often passive) to have too high an opinion of sb/sth: *I think this movie is greatly overrated* (= people think that it is better than it really is). OPP **underrate**

**o·ver·ride** /ˌoʊvərˈraɪd/ ***verb*** [T] (*pt* **o·ver·rode** /-ˈroʊd/; *pp* **o·ver·rid·den** /-ˈrɪdn/) **1** (used about sb/sth with authority) to pay no attention to a person's decisions or actions: *Congress can vote to override the President's veto.* **2** to be more important than sth: *Corporate profits should not override environmental concerns.* **3** to interrupt an automatic machine, process, etc. and control it yourself: *Press this key to override the "print" command.*

**o·ver·rid·ing** /ˌoʊvərˈraɪdɪŋ/ ***adj.*** (only *before* a noun) more important than anything else

**o·ver·rule** /ˌoʊvərˈrul/ ***verb*** [T] (used about sb/sth with authority) to decide that another person's decisions or actions are not valid: *The judge overruled the defense attorney's objection.*

**o·ver·run** /ˌoʊvərˈrʌn/ ***verb*** (*pt* **o·ver·ran** /-ˈræn/; *pp* **o·ver·run** /-ˈrʌn/) [T] to spread all over an area in great numbers: *The city was overrun by rats.* ◇ *Army troops overran the rebel camp.*

★**o·ver·seas**[1] /ˌoʊvərˈsiz/ ***adj.*** (only *before* a noun) in, to or from another country (especially one that you have to cross the ocean to get to): *We have lost some important clients to our overseas competitors.*

**o·ver·seas**[2] /ˌoʊvərˈsiz/ ***adv.*** in or to another country (especially one that you have to cross the ocean to get to): *It's cheaper to produce these goods overseas.* ◇ *People overseas will be able to vote in the election.*

**o·ver·see** /ˌoʊvərˈsi/ ***verb*** [T] (*pt* **o·ver·saw** /-ˈsɔ/; *pp* **o·ver·seen** /-ˈsin/) to watch sth to make sure that it is done correctly

**o·ver·shad·ow** /ˌoʊvərˈʃædoʊ/ ***verb*** [T] **1** to cause sth to be less happy: *The holiday celebrations were overshadowed by her illness.* **2** to cause sb/sth to seem less important or successful: *Doug always seemed to be overshadowed by his sister.*

★**o·ver·sight** /ˈoʊvərsaɪt/ ***noun*** **1** [C,U] something that you do not notice or do (that you should have noticed or done): *Through an oversight Leroy's name did not appear on the list.* **2** (*formal*) the state of being in charge of something: *The committee has responsibility for oversight of academic regulations.*

**o·ver·sim·pli·fy** /ˌoʊvərˈsɪmpləfaɪ/ ***verb*** [I,T] (*pres. part.* **o·ver·sim·pli·fy·ing**; *3rd person sing. pres.* **o·ver·sim·pli·fies**; *pt, pp* **o·ver·sim·pli·fied**) to explain sth in such a simple way that its real meaning is lost

**o·ver·sized** /ˈoʊvərsaɪzd/ ***adj.*** (often used about clothes) larger than usual

**o·ver·sleep** /ˌoʊvərˈslip/ ***verb*** [I] (*pt, pp* **o·ver·slept** /-ˈslɛpt/) to sleep longer than you should have

**o·ver·step** /ˌoʊvərˈstɛp/ ***verb*** [T] (*pres. part.* **o·ver·step·ping**; *pt, pp* **o·ver·stepped**) to go beyond what is normal or allowed: *He has **overstepped the limits** of his authority.*

NOTE we often use **overstep** with words like **boundary**, **line**, or **limit** or others that have a similar meaning.

**o·vert** /oʊˈvərt; ˈoʊvərt/ ***adj.*** (usually *before* a noun) (*formal*) done in an open way and not secretly ▸ **o·vert·ly** ***adv.***

**o·ver·take** /ˌoʊvərˈteɪk/ ***verb*** (*pt* **o·ver·took** /-ˈtʊk/; *pp* **o·ver·tak·en** /-ˈteɪkən/) [T] to increase or develop and become bigger, better, etc. than sb/sth else: *Our company has now overtaken all its competitors.*

ˌ**over-the-ˈcounter** ***adj.*** (only *before* a noun) (of drugs and medicines) that you can buy without a written order from a doctor (**a prescription**)

**o·ver·throw** /ˌoʊvərˈθroʊ/ ***verb*** [T] (*pt* **o·ver·threw** /-ˈθru/; *pp* **o·ver·thrown** /-ˈθroʊn/) to remove a leader or government from power, by using force: *The dictator was overthrown in a military coup.* ▸ **o·ver·throw** /ˈoʊvərθroʊ/ ***noun*** [sing.]: *the overthrow of the French monarchy in 1789*

★**o·ver·time** /ˈoʊvərtaɪm/ ***noun*** [U] **1** time that you spend at work after your usual working hours: *Betty did ten hours of overtime last week.* ◇ *Do you get paid extra for overtime?* **2** (*sports*) an extra period of play at the end of a football, basketball, etc. game when the scores are equal at the end of the normal period: *The game went into overtime.* ▸ **o·ver·time** ***adv.***: *I have been working overtime for weeks.*

**o·ver·tone** /ˈoʊvərtoʊn/ ***noun*** [C, usually pl.] something that is suggested but not expressed openly: *It's a funny play, but it has serious overtones.*

**o·ver·ture** /ˈoʊvərtʃər; -tʃʊr/ ***noun*** **1** [C, usually pl.] (*formal*) an act of being friendly toward sb (perhaps because you want sth): *The government's peace overtures to the rebels were rejected.* **2** [C] a piece of music that is the introduction to an opera, a ballet, etc.

**o·ver·turn** /ˌoʊvərˈtərn/ ***verb*** [I,T] to turn over so that the top is at the bottom: *The car overturned, but the driver escaped unhurt.* ◇ (*figurative*) *to overturn a decision* (= to change it)

**o·ver·type** /ˈoʊvərtaɪp/ = OVERWRITE

**o·ver·weight** /ˌoʊvərˈweɪt/ ***adj.*** too heavy or fat: *You're a little overweight. Maybe you should go on a diet.* ➲ Look at the note at **fat**.

**o·ver·whelm** /ˌoʊvərˈwɛlm/ ***verb*** [T] (usually passive) **1** to cause sb to feel a very strong emotion: *The new world champion was overwhelmed by all the publicity.* **2** to defeat sb/sth because you have more people

**o·ver·whelm·ing** /ˌoʊvərˈwɛlmɪŋ/ ***adj.*** very great or strong: *Anna had an overwhelming desire to return home.* ▸ **o·ver·whelm·ing·ly** ***adv.***: *The city council voted overwhelmingly against the plan.*

**o·ver·work** /ˌoʊvərˈwərk/ ***verb*** [I,T] to work too hard or to make sb work too hard: *They are overworked and underpaid.* ▸ **o·ver·work** /ˌoʊvərˈwərk/ ***noun*** [U]

**o·ver·write** /ˌoʊvərˈraɪt/ (*also* **overtype**) ***verb*** [T] (*pt* **o·ver·wrote** /-ˈroʊt/; *pp* **o·ver·writ·ten** /-ˈrɪtn/) (*computing*) to replace information on the screen or in a file by putting new information over it

O

**ow** /aʊ/ ***interjection*** (used when reacting to a sudden feeling of pain): *Ow! That hurts!* ➲ Look also at **ouch**.

★**owe** /oʊ/ ***verb*** [T] **1 owe sth (to sb) (for sth); owe sb for sth** to have to pay money to sb for sth that he/she has done or given: *We owe the bank $5,000.* ◇ *We owe $5,000 to the bank.* ◇ *I still owe you for that coffee you bought me yesterday.* ◇ (*figurative*) *Claudia owes me an explanation.* **2** to feel grateful to sb for sth: *I owe you a lot for all you did for me when I was young.* **3 owe sth (to sb/sth)** to have sth (for the reason given): *I owe my life to the firefighters who rescued me.*

IDM **owe it to yourself/sb (to do sth)** to feel that you should do sth for yourself/sb because it is your duty or because you want to: *We owe it to our children to protect the environment.* ◇ *Let's eat out tonight – we owe it to ourselves after a week of hard work!*

ˈ**owing to** /ˈoʊɪŋ tə; *strong form* ˈoʊɪŋ tu/ ***prep.*** because of: *The game was canceled owing to the severe weather.*

**owl** /aʊl/ ***noun*** [C] a bird that flies at night and that catches and eats small animals. Owls are used as a symbol of wisdom.

owl

★**own¹** /oʊn/ ***det., pronoun*** **1** (used to emphasize that sth belongs to a particular person): *I saw him do it with my own eyes.* ◇ *Use your own pen. I need mine.* ◇ *This is his own house.* ◇ *This house is his own.* ◇ *Rachel would like her own room* (= she doesn't want to share one).

NOTE **Own** cannot be used after **an** or **the**. You CANNOT say: *I would like an own car.* You CAN say: *I would like my own car* or: *I would like a car of my own.*

**2** (used to show that sth is done or made without help from another person): *The kids are old enough to get their own breakfast.* ◇ *They grow all their own vegetables.*

IDM **hold your own (against sb/sth)** to be as strong, good, etc. as sb/sth else

**of your, etc. own** belonging to you and not to anyone else: *Kate has always wanted a pony of her own.*

**(all) on your, etc. own 1** alone: *John lives on his own.* ➲ Look at the note at **alone**. **2** without help: *I managed to fix the car all on my own.*

★**own²** /oʊn/ ***verb*** [T] to have sth belonging to you; possess: *We don't own the house. We just rent it.* ◇ *Who is this land owned by?*

PHR V **own up (to sth)** (*informal*) to tell sb that you have done sth wrong: *None of the kids owned up to breaking the window.* SYN A more formal word is **confess**.

★**own·er** /ˈoʊnər/ ***noun*** [C] a person who owns sth: *a dog owner*

**own·er·ship** /ˈoʊnərʃɪp/ ***noun*** [U] the state of owning sth

**ox** /ɑks/ ***noun*** [C] (*pl.* **ox·en** /ˈɑksn/) a male cow that has been castrated. Oxen are sometimes used for pulling or carrying heavy loads. ➲ Look at **bull**.

★**ox·y·gen** /ˈɑksɪdʒən/ ***noun*** [U] (*symbol* **O**) a gas that you cannot see, taste or smell. Plants and animals cannot live and fire cannot burn without oxygen.

**oys·ter** /ˈɔɪstər/ ***noun*** [C] a shellfish that is eaten as food. Some oysters produce pearls.

**oz.** ***abbr.*** = OUNCE: *net weight 12 oz.*

**o·zone** /ˈoʊzoʊn/ ***noun*** [U] (*symbol* $O_3$) a poisonous gas with a strong smell that is a form of oxygen

ˌ**ozone-ˈfriendly** ***adj.*** (used about cleaning products, etc.) not containing chemicals that could harm the ozone layer

ˈ**ozone ˌlayer** ***noun*** [sing.] the layer of ozone high above the surface of the earth that helps to protect it from the dangerous rays of the sun: *a hole in the ozone layer*

# Pp

**P** ***abbr.*** (on a sign) parking

**P, p** /pi/ ***noun*** [C,U] (*pl.* **P's; p's**) the sixteenth letter of the English alphabet: *"Pencil" begins with (a) "P."*

**p** ***abbr.*** (*also* **p.**) (*pl.* **pp.**) = PAGE¹: *See p. 94.* ◇ *pp. 63–96*

**PA** /ˌpi ˈeɪ/ ***abbr.*** = PUBLIC ADDRESS SYSTEM

★**pace¹** /peɪs/ ***noun*** **1** [C] the distance that you move when you take one step: *Take two paces forward and then stop.* **2** [sing.] the speed at which you do sth or at which sth happens: *Run at a steady pace and you won't get tired so quickly.* ◇ *I can't stand the pace of life in New York.*

IDM **keep pace (with sb/sth)** to move or do sth at the same speed as sb/sth else; to change as quickly as sth else is changing: *Incomes are not keeping pace with inflation.*

**set the pace** to move or do sth at the speed that others must follow

**pace²** /peɪs/ ***verb*** [I,T] to walk with slow regular steps: *Fran paced nervously up and down the room, waiting for news.*

**pace·mak·er** /ˈpeɪsmeɪkər/ ***noun*** [C] a small machine that helps to make a person's heart beat regularly or more strongly

**Paˌcific ˈDaylight Time** ***noun*** [U] (*abbr.* **PDT**) the time system used in the western part of the U.S. and Canada from April to October, when the clocks are set one hour ahead of Pacific Standard time ➲ Look at **daylight-saving time**.

**Paˌcific 'Standard Time** *noun* [U] (*abbr.* **PST**) the time system used in the western part of the U.S. and Canada from October to April when clocks are set one hour behind standard time ➲ Look at **Standard Time**.

**'Pacific Time** *noun* [U] (*abbr.* **PT**) the standard time system that is used in the western part of the U.S. and Canada ➲ Compare **Central Time**, **Eastern Time** and **Mountain Time**.

**pac·i·fi·er** /'pæsəfaɪər/ *noun* [C] a plastic or rubber object that you put in a baby's mouth to keep him/her quiet and happy

**pac·i·fism** /'pæsəfɪzəm/ *noun* [U] the belief that all wars are wrong and that you should not fight in them

**pac·i·fist** /'pæsəfɪst/ *noun* [C] a person who believes in pacifism

**pac·i·fy** /'pæsəfaɪ/ *verb* [T] (*pres. part.* **pac·i·fy·ing**; *3rd person sing. pres.* **pac·i·fies**; *pt, pp* **pac·i·fied**) to cause sb who is angry or upset to be calm or quiet SYN **placate**

★**pack¹** /pæk/ *noun* [C] **1** a number of things that are wrapped or tied together: *The donkey had a heavy pack on its back.* ◇ *She put an ice pack on her forehead to ease the pain.* ◇ (*figurative*) *Everything she told me was a pack of lies.* ➲ Look at **backpack**. **2** a package or group of things that are sold together: *a pack of cigarettes* ◇ *a pack of chewing gum* ◇ *a six-pack of beer* ➲ Look at **package¹** and **packet**. **3** a group of animals that hunt together: *a pack of wolves*

★**pack²** /pæk/ *verb*

➤PUT INTO CONTAINER **1** [I,T] to put your things into a suitcase, etc. before you go away or go on a trip: *I'll pack my suitcase in the morning.* ◇ *Have you packed yet?* ◇ *Did you pack your toothbrush?* **2** [I,T] to put things into boxes, containers, etc. so that they can be stored, transported, etc.: *The moving van is already here, but I'm not finished packing!* ◇ *Be sure to pack those glasses in plenty of newspaper.* OPP for **1** and **2** is **unpack**.

➤FILL **3** [T] **pack sth (with sth)** to fill sth that is going to be stored, transported, etc.: *to pack a box* ◇ *Pack the carton with tissue paper first.* **4** [T] (often passive) to fill or crowd: *The bus was totally packed. We couldn't get a seat.* ◇ *an action-packed movie*

➤PRESS **5** [T] to press sth so that it forms a hard, thick mass: *Pack the dirt firmly around the roots of the plant.* ◇ *Add one cup of packed brown sugar.*

PHR V **pack it in** (*informal*) to stop doing sth: *I'm getting too old for this kind of work – it's time to pack it in.*

**pack sth in**; **pack sth in/into sth** to do a lot in a short time: *They packed an awful lot into their three days in Boston.*

**pack up** (*informal*) to finish working or doing sth: *There was nothing else to do, so we packed up and went home.*

★**pack·age¹** /'pækɪdʒ/ *noun* [C] **1** (*abbr.* **pkg.**) something, or a number of things, in a box or wrapped up in paper and sent by mail, or carried: *to send/mail a package* **2** something, or a number of things, wrapped up, or in a bag, etc., to be sold in a store: *a package of hamburger buns* ➲ Look at **pack¹** and **packet**. **3** a box, bag, etc. in which things are wrapped or packed: *Check the list of ingredients on the side of the package.* ◇ *Don't throw the package away after you open your present!* **4** a number of things that must be bought or accepted together: *a software package* ◇ *The Council voted to approve the tax reform package.* ◇ *a financial aid package*

★**pack·age²** /'pækɪdʒ/ *verb* [T] to wrap sth or put sth into a box, etc. before it is sold or sent somewhere: *Products that are attractively packaged sell more quickly.*

**'package tour** *noun* [C] a vacation that is organized by a company that arranges your transportation and hotel room, etc. for you

**pack·ag·ing** /'pækɪdʒɪŋ/ *noun* [U] all the materials that are used to wrap sth before it is sold or sent somewhere: *Cookies and crackers often have two or three layers of packaging.*

**pack·et** /'pækət/ *noun* [C] a small flat bag that is closed on all four sides, in which things are packed to be sold in a store: *a packet of instant cocoa mix* ◇ *to tear open a foil packet*

**pack·ing** /'pækɪŋ/ *noun* [U] putting things into a suitcase, box, package, etc.: *I haven't done any packing yet and we're going away this evening.* ◇ *the meat packing industry*

**'pack rat** *noun* [C] (*informal*) a person who collects and stores a lot of things that he/she does not really need

**pact** /pækt/ *noun* [C] a formal agreement between two people, groups or countries

**pad¹** /pæd/ *noun* [C]

➤OF SOFT MATERIAL **1** a thick piece of soft material, used for protecting sth or giving sth a full, round shape: *Soccer players wear shin pads to protect their legs.* ◇ *a jacket with shoulder pads* ◇ *Press the gauze pad onto the wound to stop the bleeding.* **2** (*also* **ˌsanitary 'pad**) a piece of material, like thick soft paper, that women use to absorb blood during their monthly PERIOD (3)

➤OF PAPER **3** a number of pieces of paper that are fastened together at one end: *a notepad*

➤FOR SPACECRAFT/HELICOPTER **4** the place from which helicopters and space rockets take off: *a launch pad*

➤OF ANIMAL'S FOOT **5** the soft part on the bottom of the foot of some animals, e.g. dogs, cats, etc.

**pad²** /pæd/ *verb* (**pad·ding**; **pad·ded**) **1** [T] (usually passive) to fill or cover sth with soft material in order to protect it, make it larger or more comfortable, etc.: *a padded bra* ◇ *Violent patients in mental hospitals are put in padded cells.* **2** [T] **pad sth (out)** to make a book, speech, etc. longer by adding things that are not necessary **3** [I] **pad along, around, etc.** to walk quickly and quietly

**pad·ding** /'pædɪŋ/ *noun* [U] material that you use to PAD² sth

**pad·dle¹** /'pædl/ *noun* [C] **1** a short pole that is wide at one or both ends and that you use for moving a small boat through water ➲ Look at **oar**. **2** a round flat piece of wood with a handle that is used for hitting the ball in table tennis **3** a flat piece of wood with a handle that is used for hitting sb's buttocks as a punishment

**pad·dle²** /'pædl/ *verb* **1** to move a small boat

P

through water using a PADDLE[1] (1): *to paddle a canoe* ➲ Look at **row**. **2** [I] **paddle along, around, etc.** to swim with short quick movements of the arms and legs **3** [T] to hit sb's buttocks with a PADDLE[1] (3) as a punishment

**ˈpaddle ˌsteamer** ***noun*** [C] an old-fashioned type of boat driven by steam and moved forward by a large wheel or wheels at the side

**pad·dy** /ˈpædi/ ***noun*** [C] (*pl.* **pad·dies**) a field in which rice is grown: *a rice paddy*

**pad·lock**[1] /ˈpædlɑk/ ***noun*** [C] a type of lock that is used for fastening gates, bicycles, etc. ➲ picture at **chain**[1].

**pad·lock**[2] /ˈpædlɑk/ ***verb*** [T] to fasten sth with a PADLOCK[1]

**pa·gan** /ˈpeɪgən/ ***adj.*** having religious beliefs that do not belong to any of the main religions: *Halloween is an ancient pagan festival.*

★**page**[1] /peɪdʒ/ ***noun*** [C] (*abbr.* **p.**, **pg.**) **1** one side of a piece of paper: *The letter was three pages long.* ◇ *Full details are given on page 63.* ◇ *the front page of a newspaper* ◇ *the sports page* **2** one piece of paper in a book, etc.: *One page had been torn from her address book.* ◇ *to turn the page*

**page**[2] /peɪdʒ/ ***verb*** [T] to call sb's name over a loudspeaker in a place where there are a lot of people so that you can give him/her a message

**pag·eant** /ˈpædʒənt/ ***noun*** [C] **1** a competition in which girls or young women are judged according to their beauty, and sometimes also according to other qualities: *a beauty pageant* **2** a type of outdoor public entertainment at which there is a procession of people, often dressed up in historical costume

**pag·eant·ry** /ˈpædʒəntri/ ***noun*** [U] the feeling and appearance of a grand ceremony when people are dressed in colorful costumes: *The Olympic Games began in a blaze of pageantry.*

**pag·er** /ˈpeɪdʒər/ (*also* **beeper**) ***noun*** [C] a small piece of equipment that makes noises to let a person know when sb is trying to contact him/her

**pa·go·da** /pəˈgoʊdə/ ***noun*** [C] a religious building in Asia in the form of a tall tower with several levels

**paid** *past tense, past participle of* PAY[2]

**pail** /peɪl/ ***noun*** [C] = BUCKET

★**pain**[1] /peɪn/ ***noun*** **1** [C,U] the unpleasant feeling that you have when a part of your body has been hurt or when you are sick: *to be in pain* ◇ *I have a terrible pain in my back.* ◇ *to scream with pain* ◇ *chest pains* ◇ *After I took the pills the pain wore off.* ◇ *The pills relieved the pain.*

NOTE Look at **ache**. Notice that we usually say: *I have a headache, etc.* instead of using an expression with "pain."

**2** [U] unhappiness that you feel because sth bad has happened or because sb has been unkind: *It took me years to get over the pain of my mother's death.*

IDM **a pain (in the neck)** (*informal*) a person, thing or situation that causes you to be angry or annoyed: *Having to scrape the ice off the windshield every morning is a real pain in the neck.*

**be at/go to (great) pains to do sth** to make a special effort to do sth: *He went to great pains to hide his true feelings.*

**take great pains (with/to do sth)** to take great care with sth or to make a special effort to do sth: *She always takes great pains with her writing.*

**pain**[2] /peɪn/ ***verb*** [T] to cause sb to feel unhappy or upset

**pained** /peɪnd/ ***adj.*** showing that you are unhappy or upset: *a pained expression*

★**pain·ful** /ˈpeɪnfl/ ***adj.*** that causes pain: *A wasp sting can be very painful.* ◇ *The breakup of their marriage was very painful for the kids.* ▶ **pain·ful·ly** ***adv.***: *Progress is still painfully slow.*

**pain·kill·er** /ˈpeɪnkɪlər/ ***noun*** [C] a medicine that is used for reducing or removing pain

**pain·less** /ˈpeɪnləs/ ***adj.*** that does not cause pain: *The animals' death is quick and painless.* ▶ **pain·less·ly** ***adv.***

**pains·tak·ing** /ˈpeɪnzteɪkɪŋ/ ***adj.*** very careful: *The painstaking search of the wreckage gave us clues as to the cause of the crash.* ▶ **pains·tak·ing·ly** ***adv.***

★**paint**[1] /peɪnt/ ***noun*** **1** [C,U] a liquid that you put onto a surface with a brush in order to give it color or to protect it: *The door will need two more coats of paint.* ◇ *Wet paint!* ◇ *The paint was peeling off the walls.* ◇ *chemicals used in paints* **2** [C,U] colored liquid that you can use to make a picture: *red paint* ◇ *oil paints* **3** **paints** [pl.] a collection of tubes, blocks, etc. of PAINT (2) that an artist uses

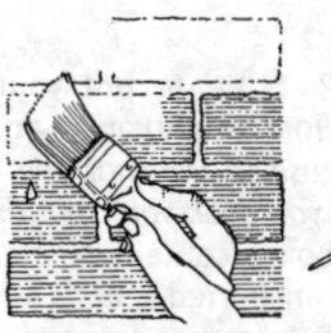

painting a wall

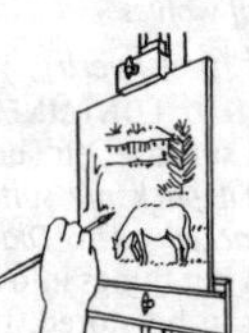

painting a picture

★**paint**[2] /peɪnt/ ***verb*** [I,T] **1** to put PAINT[1] (1) onto sth: *The bathroom needs to be painted.* ◇ *Wear old clothes when you're painting.* ◇ *The walls were painted pink.* **2** to make a picture of sb/sth using paints: *Vicky paints well.* ◇ *to paint a self-portrait*

**paint·brush** /ˈpeɪntbrʌʃ/ ***noun*** [C] a brush that you use to paint ➲ picture at **brush**[1].

★**paint·er** /ˈpeɪntər/ ***noun*** [C] **1** a person whose job is to paint buildings, walls, etc. **2** a person who paints pictures ➲ Look at **artist**.

★**paint·ing** /ˈpeɪntɪŋ/ ***noun*** **1** [U] the act of painting pictures or buildings **2** [C] a picture that sb has painted: *a famous painting by Van Gogh* ➲ Look at **drawing**.

**ˈpaint ˌthinner** ***noun*** [U] a liquid that is used to make paint more liquid or to remove paint from brushes or surfaces

**paint·work** /ˈpeɪntwərk/ ***noun*** [U] the layer of paint on the surface of a car, wall, door, etc.

★**pair**[1] /pɛr/ ***noun*** **1** [C] two things that are the same or almost the same and that are used together: *a pair of shoes* ◇ *a pair of gloves* ◇ *a pair of earrings* **2** [C] a thing that consists of two parts that are joined together: *a pair of scissors* ◇ *a pair of glasses* ◇ *two pairs of pants*

NOTE In informal speech, some people also use **pair** as a plural form: *three pair of socks*. However, this is not considered correct in written English.

**3** [C, with sing. or pl. verb] two people or animals that are closely connected with each other: *Tony and his wife make a wonderful pair.* ◇ *A pair of blackbirds are nesting in the apple tree.* ➲ Look at **couple**.
IDM **in pairs** two at a time: *These earrings are only sold in pairs.*

**pair²** /pɛr/ ***verb***
PHRV **pair (sb/sth) off (with sb)** to form a pair or pairs: *Stop trying to pair me off with your brother – I'm not interested.*
**pair up (with sb)** to join together with another person or group

**pa·ja·mas** /pəˈdʒæməz/ ***noun*** [pl.] loose pants and a loose jacket or shirt that you wear in bed: *a pair of pajamas*

NOTE Notice that you use **pajama** (without an "s") before another noun: *pajama pants.* ➲ Look also at the note at **pants**.

**pal** /pæl/ ***noun*** [C] (*informal*) a friend

**pal·ace** /ˈpæləs/ ***noun*** [C] a large house that is or was the home of a king or queen

**pal·at·a·ble** /ˈpælət̬əbl/ ***adj.*** (*formal*) **1** (used about food or drinks) having a good taste **2 palatable (to sb)** acceptable to sb: *Some of the lyrics were changed to make the songs more palatable to modern listeners.*

**pal·ate** /ˈpælət/ ***noun*** [C] the top part of the inside of your mouth

★**pale** /peɪl/ ***adj.*** **1** (used about a person or his/her face, etc.) having less color than usual; very light in color: *Are you OK? You look a little pale.* ◇ *She has a very pale complexion.* **2** not bright or strong in color: *pale yellow*

**pal·ette** /ˈpælət/ ***noun*** [C] a board or flat object on which an artist mixes different colors of paint together

**pal·in·drome** /ˈpæləndroʊm/ ***noun*** [C] a word or phrase that is the same when it is read backward, such as "level" or "nurses run"

**pall** /pɔl/ ***noun*** [usually sing.] something that ruins an event or a situation that should have been enjoyable: *News of his death **cast a pall over** (= spoiled the happiness of) the event.*

**pall·bear·er** /ˈpɔlˌbɛrər/ ***noun*** [C] a person who helps to carry the box containing a dead person's body (casket) at a funeral

**pal·let** /ˈpælət/ ***noun*** [C] a square object made of flat narrow pieces of wood, used as a base for storing or moving goods

**palm¹** /pɑm/ ***noun*** [C] **1** the flat part of the front of your hand: *Laura held the bird in the palm of her hand.* **2** (*also* ˈ**palm tree**) a type of tree that grows in hot regions. Palms have no branches and a mass of large leaves at the top: *a date/coconut palm*

**palm²** /pɑm/ ***verb***
PHRV **palm sth off as sth** (*informal*) to pretend that sth is what it is not, especially in order to sell it: *He was trying to palm cheap copies off as original works of art.*

**palm·top** /ˈpɑmtɑp/ ***noun*** [C] a small computer that can be held in the PALM¹ (1) of one hand

**pal·pa·ble** /ˈpælpəbl/ ***adj.*** (*formal*) easily noticed or strongly felt: *a palpable sense of relief*

**pal·sy** /ˈpɔlzi/ → CEREBRAL PALSY

**pal·try** /ˈpɔltri/ ***adj.*** very small and so not worth very much

**pam·per** /ˈpæmpər/ ***verb*** [T] to treat sb very or too kindly

**pam·phlet** /ˈpæmflət/ ***noun*** [C] a thin book with a paper cover that gives you information about sth

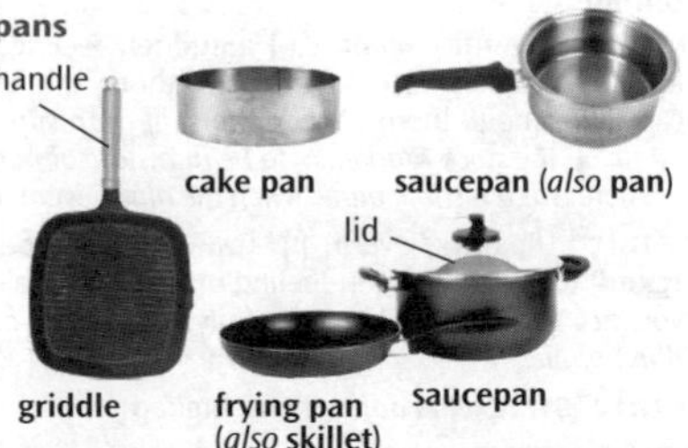


★**pan¹** /pæn/ ***noun*** [C] a metal container that is used for cooking or baking: *a frying pan* ◇ *Pour the batter into a greased cake pan.*

**pan²** /pæn/ ***verb*** (**pan·ning**; **panned**) **1** [T] (*informal*) (usually passive) to severely criticize sth such as a movie or play, especially in a newspaper or magazine **2** [I,T] (used about a film or video camera) to turn slowly to the left or right in order to follow a person or object
PHRV **pan out** (*informal*) to develop or happen in a particular way, or the way you expected: *How did your interview pan out?*

**pan·a·ce·a** /ˌpænəˈsiə/ ***noun*** [usually sing.] something that will solve all the problems in a situation

**pan·cake** /ˈpænkeɪk/ ***noun*** [C] a type of very thin round cake that is made by frying a mixture of flour, milk and eggs (batter). Pancakes are usually eaten for breakfast: *pancakes with maple syrup*

**pan·da** /ˈpændə/ ***noun*** [C] a large black and white animal that looks like a bear and that comes from China. Pandas are very rare nowadays.

**pan·de·mo·ni·um** /ˌpændəˈmoʊniəm/ ***noun*** [U] a state of great noise and confusion

**pan·der** /ˈpændər/ ***verb***
PHRV **pander to sb/sth** to do or say what sb wants even if it is wrong or unpleasant: *The government cannot go on pandering to the rich and powerful.*

**pane** /peɪn/ ***noun*** [C] a piece of glass in a window, etc.: *a pane of glass* ◇ *a window pane*

★**pan·el** /ˈpænl/ ***noun*** [C] **1** a group of people who are chosen to discuss sth, decide sth, answer questions, etc.: *All the candidates were interviewed by a panel of four judges.* ◇ *a panel of experts* ◇ *an advisory panel* **2** a piece of wood, metal or glass that forms part of a door, wall, etc. or that is attached to it: *They smashed the glass panel in the front door.* **3** a surface that contains the equipment for

P

controlling a car, machine, etc.: *the instrument panel* ◇ *a control panel*

**pan·el·ing** /ˈpænl·ɪŋ/ ***noun*** [U] flat pieces of wood used to cover and decorate walls

**pan·el·ist** /ˈpænl·ɪst/ ***noun*** [C] a member of a PANEL (1)

**pang** /pæŋ/ ***noun*** [C, usually pl.] a sudden strong feeling (of pain, hunger, guilt, etc.)

**pan·han·dle¹** /ˈpænhændl/ ***noun*** [C] a narrow part of a state extending from the wider part of the state: *the Oklahoma panhandle*

**pan·han·dle²** /ˈpænhændl/ ***verb*** [I] (*informal*) to beg for money from strangers on the street ▸ **pan·han·dler** ***noun*** [C]

**pan·ic¹** /ˈpænɪk/ ***noun*** [C,U] a sudden feeling of fear that makes you do things without thinking carefully about them: *The rumors of war spread panic on the stock market.* ◇ *to be in a state of panic* ◇ *There was a terrible panic when the alarm went off.*

**pan·ic²** /ˈpænɪk/ ***verb*** [I] (**pan·ick·ing**; **pan·icked**) to have a sudden feeling of fear that makes you act without thinking carefully: *Stay calm and don't panic.*

ˈ**panic-ˌstricken** ***adj.*** very frightened

**pan·o·ram·a** /ˌpænəˈræmə; -ˈrɑmə/ ***noun*** [C] a view over a wide area of land ▸ **pan·o·ram·ic** /ˌpænəˈræmɪk/ ***adj.***: *a panoramic view from the top of the hill*

**pant** /pænt/ ***verb*** [I] to take short quick breaths, e.g. after running or because the weather is very hot ➲ Look also at the note at **pants**.

**pan·ther** /ˈpænθər/ ***noun*** [C] a large wild cat (usually black)

**pant·ies** /ˈpæntiz/ ***noun*** [pl.] a small piece of clothing that women and girls wear under their other clothes (from their waists to the top of their legs) ➲ Look at **underpants**.

**pan·to·mime** /ˈpæntəmaɪm/ ***noun*** [C,U] = MIME¹ (1)

**pan·try** /ˈpæntri/ ***noun*** [C] (*pl.* **pan·tries**) a small room where food is kept

**pants** /pænts/ ***noun*** [pl.] (*also formal* **trousers**) a piece of clothing that covers both legs and reaches from your waist to your ankles ➲ picture on study page **A30**.

> **NOTE** Note that, because **pants** is a plural word, we cannot say, for example, "a new pants." The following are possible: *I need some new pants.* ◇ *I need a new pair of pants.* Before another noun, the form **pant** is usually used: *a pant leg.*

**pant·suit** /ˈpæntsut/ ***noun*** [C] a suit for women, consisting of a jacket and pants

**pant·y·hose** /ˈpæntihoʊz/ (*also* **nylons**) ***noun*** [pl.] a piece of thin clothing worn by women, that fits tightly from the waist over the legs and feet: *a pair of pantyhose* ➲ Look at **tights**.

**pa·pa** /ˈpɑpə/ ***noun*** [C] (*old-fashioned*) father

**pa·pa·cy** /ˈpeɪpəsi/ ***noun*** [sing.] **the papacy** the position or authority of the Pope

**pa·pal** /ˈpeɪpl/ ***adj.*** connected with the Pope

**pa·pa·ya** /pəˈpaɪə/ ***noun*** [C,U] a tropical fruit with yellow and green skin and round black seeds ➲ picture on study page **A28-29**.

★**pa·per** /ˈpeɪpər/ ***noun*** **1** [U] a material that consists of thin sheets that you wrap things in, write or draw on, etc.: *a blank piece/sheet of paper* ◇ *Waste paper can be recycled.* ◇ *a brown paper bag* ◇ *a paper napkin* ◇ *paper money* (= money that is made of paper, i.e. not coins)

> **NOTE** Types of paper include **tissue**, **toilet**, **typing**, **wrapping** and **writing** paper.

**2** [C] = NEWSPAPER: *Where's today's paper?* ◇ *a daily paper* ◇ *I read it in the local paper.* **3 papers** [pl.] pieces of paper that have information written on them. Papers are usually important: *If you don't have all your papers with you, you won't be allowed to cross the border.* ◇ *The file you want is somewhere in the pile of papers on her desk.* **4** [C] a piece of writing on a particular subject: *We have to write a ten-page paper for history.*

**IDM** **on paper** **1** in writing: *I won't make any commitment until I see something on paper.* **2** from what appearances show; in theory: *The project sounds fine on paper, but would it work in practice?*

**pa·per·back** /ˈpeɪpərbæk/ ***noun*** [C,U] a book that has a paper cover: *The novel is available in paperback.* ◇ *a cheap paperback*

**pa·per·boy** /ˈpeɪpərbɔɪ/ (*feminine* **pa·per·girl**) ***noun*** [C] a boy or girl who delivers newspapers to people's houses

ˈ**paper clip** ***noun*** [C] a piece of wire or plastic that is used for holding pieces of paper together

**paper clip**

**pa·per·weight** /ˈpeɪpərweɪt/ ***noun*** [C] a small heavy object that you put on top of loose papers to keep them in place

**pa·per·work** /ˈpeɪpərwərk/ ***noun*** [U] the written work that you do in an office, including writing letters and reports, filling out forms, etc.

**pa·pier mâ·ché** /ˌpeɪpər məˈʃeɪ/ ***noun*** [U] paper mixed with wet glue, that becomes hard when it dries and is used to make decorations, etc.

**pa·pri·ka** /pæˈprikə; pə-/ ***noun*** [U] red powder that is made from a type of sweet PEPPER¹ (2) and is used to flavor and sometimes also to decorate food

**Pap smear** /ˈpæp smɪr/ ***noun*** [C] a medical test in which a few cells are removed from inside a woman's sexual organs in order to examine them for signs of disease

**par** /pɑr/ ***noun***

**IDM** **below par** (*informal*) not as good or as well as usual

**on a par with sb/sth** of an equal level, standard, etc. to sb/sth else

**par·a·ble** /ˈpærəbl/ ***noun*** [C] a short story (especially in the Bible) that teaches a lesson

**par·a·chute** /ˈpærəʃut/ ***noun*** [C] a large piece of strong cloth that is folded and fastened with thin ropes to a person's body. A parachute lets the person fall to the ground slowly when he/she jumps from an airplane: *a parachute jump* ➲ picture on study page **A32**. ▸ **par·a·chute** ***verb*** [I]

**pa·rade¹** /pəˈreɪd/ ***noun*** [C] an occasion when people, bands, vehicles, etc. go down the street so that people can watch them: *our town's Fourth of July parade* ◇ *to march in a parade*

**pa·rade²** /pəˈreɪd/ ***verb*** [I,T] **parade (sth) around, through, etc.** to walk around or show sth proudly so that people notice you: *Ben was parading around in his underwear.*

**par·a·digm** /ˈpærədaɪm/ ***noun*** [C] a typical example or way of doing sth

**par·a·dise** /ˈpærədaɪs/ ***noun*** **1 Paradise** [sing.] (without *a* or *the*) the place where some people think good people go after they die; heaven **2** [C] a perfect place: *This beach is a paradise for surfers.*

**par·a·dox** /ˈpærədɑks/ ***noun*** [C] **1** a statement that seems to be impossible but that is or may be true: *"A deafening silence" is a paradox.* **2** a situation that has two or more qualities that you would not expect to find together: *It's a paradox that some countries produce too much food while in other countries people are starving.* ▸ **par·a·dox·i·cal** /ˌpærəˈdɑksɪkl/ ***adj.***

**par·af·fin** /ˈpærəfɪn/ ***noun*** [U] a type of white wax that is used for making candles

**par·a·glid·ing** /ˈpærəˌglaɪdɪŋ/ ***noun*** [U] a sport in which you wear sth similar to a parachute and jump from an airplane or a high place and are carried along by the wind before coming down to earth: *to go paragliding*

★**par·a·graph** /ˈpærəgræf/ ***noun*** [C] a part of a piece of writing that consists of one or more sentences. A paragraph always starts on a new line.

**par·a·keet** /ˈpærəkit/ ***noun*** [C] a small, brightly colored bird that people often keep as a pet in a cage

**par·a·le·gal** /ˌpærəˈligl/ ***noun*** [C] a person who is trained to help a lawyer

★**par·al·lel¹** /ˈpærəlɛl/ ***adj., adv.*** **1** (used about two lines, etc.) with the same distance between them for all their length: *parallel lines* ◇ *The train tracks run parallel to the road.* **2** similar: *The two brothers followed parallel careers in different companies.*

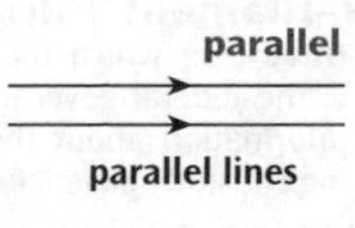


**par·al·lel²** /ˈpærəlɛl/ ***noun*** **1** [C] (*also* ˌ**parallel ˈline**) a line, etc. that is parallel to another **2** [C,U] a person, thing or situation that is similar to sb/sth else: *Japan's economic success is without parallel in the postwar period.* **3** [C] an act of comparing sb/sth with sb/sth else: *He drew a parallel between George Washington and Simon Bolivar.*

**pa·ral·y·sis** /pəˈræləsəs/ ***noun*** **1** [U] the state of being unable to move your body or a part of it **2** [C,U] being unable to work in a normal way: *There has been a complete paralysis of the subway system.*

**par·a·lyze** /ˈpærəlaɪz/ ***verb*** [T] **1** to make a person unable to move his/her body or a part of it: *Mary Ann is paralyzed from the waist down.* **2** to make sb/sth unable to work in a normal way: *The automobile plant was completely paralyzed by the strike.*

**par·a·med·ic** /ˌpærəˈmɛdɪk/ ***noun*** [C] a person who has had special training in caring for sick or injured people, but who is not a doctor or nurse

**pa·ram·e·ter** /pəˈræmət̬ər/ ***noun*** [usually pl.] a rule or limit: *How can we achieve our goals within the parameters of this year's budget?*

**par·a·mil·i·tar·y** /ˌpærəˈmɪləˌtɛri/ ***adj.*** organized in the same way as, but not belonging to, an official army

**par·a·mount** /ˈpærəmaʊnt/ ***adj.*** (*formal*) most important

**par·a·noi·a** /ˌpærəˈnɔɪə/ ***noun*** [U] a type of mental illness in which sb wrongly believes that other people are trying to hurt him/her

**par·a·noid** /ˈpærənɔɪd/ ***adj.*** wrongly believing that other people are trying to hurt you

**par·a·pher·na·lia** /ˌpærəfəˈneɪliə; -fər-/ ***noun*** [U] a large number of different objects that you need for a particular purpose

**par·a·phrase** /ˈpærəfreɪz/ ***verb*** [T] to express sth again using different words so that it is easier to understand ▸ **par·a·phrase *noun*** [C]

**par·a·ple·gic** /ˌpærəˈplidʒɪk/ ***noun*** [C] a person who has no feelings or control in the legs and lower body ▸ **par·a·ple·gic *adj.***

**par·a·sail·ing** /ˈpærəˌseɪlɪŋ/ ***noun*** [U] a sport in which you wear a parachute and are pulled along behind a boat so that you rise up into the air: *to go parasailing*

**par·a·site** /ˈpærəsaɪt/ ***noun*** [C] a plant or an animal that lives in or on another plant or animal and gets its food from it

**par·a·sol** /ˈpærəsɔl; -sɑl/ ***noun*** [C] a type of umbrella used to give shade from the sun

**par·a·troop·er** /ˈpærətrupər/ ***noun*** [C] a soldier who is trained to drop from an airplane by parachute

**par·cel** /ˈpɑrsl/ ***noun*** [C] **1** a piece of land: *a 20-acre parcel of land* **2** = PACKAGE¹ (1)

ˌ**parcel ˈpost** ***noun*** [U] one of the post office's systems for sending packages in North America. It is cheaper and slower than first-class mail.

**parched** /pɑrtʃt/ ***adj.*** very hot, dry or thirsty: *Can I have a drink? I'm parched!* ◇ *parched fields during a drought*

**parch·ment** /ˈpɑrtʃmənt/ ***noun*** [U] **1** a type of thick yellowish paper **2** material made from the skin of a sheep or goat, used in the past for writing on

**par·don¹** /ˈpɑrdn/ ***noun*** [C,U] an act of forgiving sb. If a prisoner receives a pardon, he/she is released from prison. ➲ **I beg your pardon** is a formal way of saying "sorry": *Oh, I beg your pardon. I had no idea this was your seat.* It can also be used when you want to ask somebody to repeat what they said because you did not understand.

**par·don²** /ˈpɑrdn/ ***verb*** [T] **pardon sb (for sth/for doing sth)** to forgive sb or to say that sb will not be punished

**par·don³** /ˈpɑrdn/ (*also* ˌ**pardon ˈme**) ***interjection*** (a very polite way of asking sb to repeat what he/she has just said because you did not hear or understand it, or of saying that you are sorry for sth that you have done) ➲ Look at **excuse me** and **sorry**.



P

**par·don·a·ble** /ˈpɑrdn·əbl/ ***adj.*** (*formal*) that can be forgiven or excused

**pare** /pɛr/ ***verb*** [T] **1** to cut the thin outer layer off sth: *She pared the apples and cut them into slices.* ◇ *First, pare the rind from the lemon.* **2 pare sth (back/down)** to gradually reduce the size or number of sth: *The company's workforce was pared down to 25.*

★**par·ent** /ˈpɛrənt/ ***noun*** [C] a mother or father: *Most parents try to bring up their kids to be good citizens.*

NOTE A **single parent** is a mother or father who is bringing up his/her child or children alone, without the other parent. A **foster parent** is a person who takes care of a child who is not legally his/her own.

**pa·ren·tal** /pəˈrɛntl/ ***adj.*** (only *before* a noun) of a parent or parents: *parental support*

**pa·ren·the·ses** /pəˈrɛnθəsiz/ ***noun*** [pl.] a pair of marks, (), that you put around extra information in a piece of writing or around part of a math problem: *Add the numbers in parentheses first.* ➲ Look at **bracket**.

**par·ent·hood** /ˈpɛrənthʊd/ ***noun*** [U] the state of being a parent: *the joys and sorrows of parenthood*

**par·ish** /ˈpærɪʃ/ ***noun*** [C] **1** an area or district which has its own church and priest **2** (in Louisiana) a county

**par·i·ty** /ˈpærət̬i/ ***noun*** [U] (*formal*) the state of being equal: *Female employees are demanding pay parity with their male coworkers.*

★**park**[1] /pɑrk/ ***noun*** **1** [C] a piece of beautiful land with grass and trees, where anybody can go to walk, play, etc.: *a walk in the park* ◇ *a park ranger* ◇ *Central Park* ➲ Look also at **national park**. **2** [C] (in compounds) a large area of land that is open to the public and is used for special purposes: *an amusement park* ◇ *a business park* ◇ *an industrial park* **3** [C] a field or stadium where people play baseball **4** [U] the position of the gears of a car, etc. with automatic transmission in which the engine is not sending power to the wheels and the brakes are on, so that the car cannot move: *Put the car in park before you turn off the ignition.* ➲ Look at **drive**[2](4), **neutral**[2] and **reverse**[2](2).

★**park**[2] /pɑrk/ ***verb*** **1** [I,T] to stop and leave a car, truck, etc. somewhere for a time: *You can't park in front of the exit.* ◇ *Somebody parked their car in front of my driveway.* **2** [T] to put or leave sth/sb in a suitable place until you need it/him/her; to put sth aside until later: *Investors are parking money elsewhere until they know where the market is going.*

**par·ka** /ˈpɑrkə/ ***noun*** [C] a warm jacket or coat with a hood that has fur around its edge

**park·ade** /pɑrˈkeɪd/ ***noun*** [C] (*Cdn*) a parking garage for many cars

**park·ing** /ˈpɑrkɪŋ/ ***noun*** [U] **1** leaving a car, truck, etc. somewhere for a time: *The sign said, "No Parking."* **2** an area where you can leave a car, truck, etc. for a time: *There is parking for employees behind the office buildings.* ◇ *These parking spaces are reserved for customers.*

ˈ**parking ga,rage** ***noun*** [C] a building, usually with more than one level, where people can park their cars, trucks, etc.

ˈ**parking lot** ***noun*** [C] an area for parking cars

ˈ**parking ,meter** ***noun*** [C] a metal post that you put coins into to pay for parking a car in the space beside it

ˈ**parking ,ticket** ***noun*** [C] a piece of paper that orders you to pay money (a fine) for parking your car where it is not allowed

**park·way** /ˈpɑrkweɪ/ ***noun*** [C] **1** a wide street in a town or city with trees along the sides and often with an area of grass in the middle **2 Parkway** [sing.] (*abbr.* **Pkwy.**) (used in the names of some streets): *1200 Bay State Parkway*

**par·lay** /ˈpɑrleɪ; -li/ ***verb***

PHR V **parlay sth into sth** to use or develop sth such as money or a skill to make it more successful or worth more: *She hopes to parlay her success as a model into an acting career.*

★**par·lia·ment** /ˈpɑrləmənt/ ***noun*** **1** [C] the group of people who are elected to make and change the laws of a country: *The German parliament is called the 'Bundestag.'* **2** [C,U] **Parliament** the national parliament of countries such as Canada and the United Kingdom. In Canada the federal parliament consists of the House of Commons and the Senate: *a Member of Parliament* ◇ *The issue was debated in* ***Parliament***. ➲ For more information about the Canadian political system, look at study page **A11**.

**par·lia·men·ta·ry** /ˌpɑrləˈmɛntəri/ ***adj.*** (only *before* a noun) connected with parliament: *parliamentary debates*

ˈ**Parliament ,Buildings** ***noun*** [pl.] (*Cdn*) the group of buildings where the Canadian Parliament meets in Ottawa ➲ For more information about the Canadian political system, look at study page **A11**.

ˌ**Parliament ˈHill** ***noun*** [sing.] (*Cdn*) **1** the hill in Ottawa on which the Parliament Buildings stand **2** the federal government of Canada ➲ For more information about the Canadian political system, look at study page **A11**.

**par·lor** /ˈpɑrlər/ ***noun*** [C] **1** (in compounds) a store that provides a particular type of goods or services: *an ice cream parlor* ◇ *a beauty parlor* **2** (*old-fashioned*) a living room in a house

**Par·me·san** /ˈpɑrməzɑn; -ʒɑn; -zən/ (*also* ˌ**Parmesan ˈcheese**) ***noun*** [U] a type of hard Italian cheese that is usually eaten on Italian food

**pa·ro·chi·al school** /pəˈroʊkiəl skul/ ***noun*** [C] a school that is connected with or run by a church

**par·o·dy**[1] /ˈpærədi/ ***noun*** [C,U] (*pl.* **par·o·dies**) (a piece of) writing, speech or music that copies a writer's or musician's style, often as a joke: *His first novel,* Snow White, *is a parody of a traditional fairy tale.*

**par·o·dy**[2] /ˈpærədi/ ***verb*** [T] (*pres. part.* **par·o·dy·ing**; *3rd person sing. pres.* **par·o·dies**; *pt, pp* **par·o·died**) to make a parody of sb/sth

**pa·role** /pəˈroʊl/ ***noun*** [U] allowing a prisoner to go free before the official end of his/her time (sentence) in prison on condition that he/she continue to behave well: *She's hoping to get parole.* ◇ *He's going to be released on parole.*

**par·rot** /ˈpærət/ ***noun*** [C] a type of tropical bird with a curved beak and usually with very bright feathers. Parrots that are kept as pets often copy what people say.

**pars·ley** /ˈpɑrsli/ ***noun*** [U] a plant (an herb) with small curly leaves that are used for flavoring or decorating food ➲ picture on study page **A28-29**.

★**part**[1] /pɑrt/ ***noun***

➤PIECE/AREA, ETC. **1** [C] (often without *a/an*) **part (of sth)** one of the pieces, areas, periods, divisions, etc. of sth; some, but not all: *Which part of Chile do you come from?* ◇ *I enjoyed some parts of the movie.* ◇ *A large part of my job involves dealing with the public.* ◇ *Part of the problem is lack of information.* ◇ *a part of the body* ◇ *Getting up in the morning is always the hardest part of the day.*

➤IN MACHINE **2** [C] one of the essential pieces that make up a machine: *They couldn't find the right spare parts for my car at the repair shop.*

➤EQUAL PORTION **3** [C] an amount or quantity (of a liquid or substance): *Use one part (of) juice concentrate to three parts (of) water.*

➤FOR ACTOR **4** [C] a role or character in a play, movie, etc.: *He played the part of Macbeth.* ◇ *a small part in the school play*

➤IN ACTIVITY **5** [C,U] **part (in sth)** a person's share in an activity, event, etc.: *Did you have any part in the decision?*

➤IN HAIR **6** [C] the line on your head where you divide your hair and comb it in different directions: *a center/side part*

IDM **the better part of sth** most of sth; more than half of sth, often a period of time: *They've lived here for the better part of forty years.*

**for the most part** usually or mostly: *The countryside is, for the most part, flat and uninteresting.*

**for my, your, etc. part** as far as it concerns me, you, etc.: *I, for my part, am willing to go.*

**in part** not completely; to some extent: *The accident was, at least in part, the fault of the driver.*

**on the part of sb/on sb's part** made, done or felt by sb: *I'm sorry. It was a mistake on my part.* ◇ *There is concern on the part of the teachers that class size will increase.*

**play a part (in sth)** to have a share in sth or to have an effect on sth

**take part (in sth)** to join with other people in an activity: *He was unable to take part in the race because of his recent accident.* ◇ *Everybody took part in the discussion.*

★**part**[2] /pɑrt/ ***adv.*** not completely one thing and not completely another: *A mule is part donkey and part horse.*

**part**[3] /pɑrt/ ***verb*** **1** [I,T] **part (from sb); part sb (from sb)** to leave or go away from sb; to separate people or things: *We exchanged telephone numbers when we parted.* ◇ *She parted from her husband several years ago.* ◇ *He hates being parted from his kids.* **2** [I,T] to divide or separate: *The curtains parted and a face looked out.* **3** [T] to separate the hair on the head with a comb so as to make a clear line: *Don't part your hair in the middle. It looks awful.*

IDM **part company (with sb/sth)** to go different ways or to separate after being together

PHR V **part with sth** to give or sell sth to sb else: *When we went to live in Japan, we had to part with our horses and dogs.*

**par·tial** /ˈpɑrʃl/ ***adj.*** **1** not complete: *The outing was only a partial success.* **2 partial to sb/sth** (*old-fashioned*) liking sth very much: *He's very partial to a glass of wine.*

**par·ti·al·i·ty** /ˌpɑrʃiˈæləti/ ***noun*** [U] acting unfairly toward one person or side: *The judge was accused of partiality toward the defendent.* ➲ Look at **impartial**.

**par·tial·ly** /ˈpɑrʃəli/ ***adv.*** partly; not completely: *The road was partially blocked by a fallen tree.*

**par·tic·i·pant** /pɑrˈtɪsəpənt/ ***noun*** [C] a person who takes part in an activity, etc.

**par·tic·i·pate** /pɑrˈtɪsəpeɪt/ ***verb*** [I] **participate (in sth)** to share or join (in an activity); to take part: *Students are encouraged to participate in extracurricular activities.* ► **par·tic·i·pa·tion** /pɑrˌtɪsəˈpeɪʃn/ ***noun*** [U]

**par·ti·ci·ple** /ˈpɑrtəsɪpl/ ***noun*** [C] (*grammar*) a word that is formed from a verb and that ends in *–ing* (*present participle*) or *– ed, – en*, etc. (*past participle*). Participles are used to form tenses of the verb, or as adjectives: *"Hurrying" and "hurried" are the present and past participles of "hurry."*

**par·ti·cle** /ˈpɑrtɪkl/ ***noun*** [C] **1** a very small piece; a bit: *Particles of the substance were examined under a microscope.* **2** (*grammar*) a minor word that is not as important as a noun, a verb or an adjective: *In the phrasal verb "break down" "down" is an adverbial particle.*

★**par·tic·u·lar** /pərˈtɪkyələr/ ***adj.*** **1** (only *before* a noun) (used to make it clear that you are talking about one person, thing, time, etc. and not about others): *At that particular time I was working in Washington.* ◇ *One particular school, which I won't name, is having a lot of problems.* **2** (only *before* a noun) special or extra; more than usual: *Are you going to Pittsburgh for any particular reason?* ◇ *This article is of particular interest to you.* **3** connected with one person or thing and not with others: *Everybody has their own particular problems.* **4** (not before a noun) **particular (about sth)** difficult to please: *Some people are extremely particular about the food they eat.* ➲ Look at **fussy**.

IDM **in particular 1** especially: *Is there anything in particular you'd like to do this weekend?* **2** (used for giving more detail about sth that you have said): *You have to be careful about what you eat. In particular, avoid anything fatty.*

★**par·tic·u·lar·ly** /pərˈtɪkyələrli/ ***adv.*** especially: *I'm particularly interested in European history.* ◇ *The meal was excellent, particularly the dessert.*

**par·tic·u·lars** /pərˈtɪkyələrz/ ***noun*** [pl.] (*formal*) details; facts: *The police took down all the particulars about the missing child.*

**part·ing** /ˈpɑrt̬ɪŋ/ ***noun*** [C,U] saying goodbye to, or being separated from, another person (usually for quite a long time): *the sadness of parting*

**par·ti·san** /ˈpɑrt̬əzən; -sən/ ***adj.*** showing too much support for one person, group, or idea, especially unfairly

**par·ti·tion** /pɑrˈtɪʃn/ ***noun*** **1** [C] something that divides a room, etc. into two parts, especially a thin

P

or temporary wall in a house **2** [U] the division of a country into two or more countries: *the partition of Germany after World War II* ▸ **par·ti·tion** *verb* [T]

★**part·ly** /ˈpɑrtli/ *adv.* to some extent; not completely: *She was only partly responsible for the mistake.* ◇ *I love Italy — partly because of the food, but mostly because of the people.*

★**part·ner** /ˈpɑrtnər/ *noun* [C] **1** a person that you are dancing with or playing a game with **2** one of the people who own a business: *a partner in a law firm* ◇ *business partners* ◇ *a junior/senior partner* **3** the person that you are married to or have a sexual relationship with **4** a country or organization that has an agreement with another: *the United States' trading partners*

★**part·ner·ship** /ˈpɑrtnərʃɪp/ *noun* **1** [U] the state of being a partner or partners, especially in business: *Mary went into partnership with her sister and opened a toy store in Springfield.* **2** [C] an arrangement or a business with two or more partners: *"Does your husband own the company?" "Well, it's a partnership."*

ˌ**part of ˈspeech** *noun* [C] (*pl.* **parts of speech**) (*grammar*) one of the groups that words are divided into, e.g. noun, verb, adjective, etc.

ˌ**part-ˈtime** *adj.*, *adv.* for only a part of the working day or week: *She has a part-time job.* ◇ *I work part-time, about 20 hours a week.* ➲ Look at **full-time**.

**part·way** /ˌpɑrtˈweɪ; ˈpɑrtweɪ/ *adv.* some of the way: *Ann was already* ***partway through*** *her speech when Ed came in.*

P

★**par·ty**[1] /ˈpɑrt̬i/ *noun* [C] (*pl.* **par·ties**) **1** a social occasion to which people are invited in order to eat, drink and enjoy themselves: *to have a party* ◇ *to go to a party* ◇ *When they moved into the new house, they had a housewarming party.* ◇ *a birthday/dinner party* **2** (*also* **Party**) a group of people who have the same political aims and ideas and who are trying to win elections to Congress, Parliament, etc.: *the Republican Party platform* ◇ *a member of the Conservative Party* ◇ *the party's national convention* ◇ *the party chairman*

NOTE The two main political parties in the United States are the **Democrats** and the **Republicans**. The symbol of the Democratic Party is a donkey, and the symbol of the Republican Party is an elephant. In Canada there are three main political parties, the **Conservative Party**, the **Liberal Party** and the **New Democratic Party**. ➲ For more information about the political systems of the United States and Canada, look at study pages **A10-11**.

**3** (often in compounds) a group of people who are working, traveling, etc. together: *A search party has set out to try and find the missing child.* ◇ *a party of tourists* ◇ *I'd like to reserve a table for a party of five.* **4** (*formal*) a person or group of people forming one side of a legal agreement or argument: *the guilty party* ➲ Look at **third party**.

**par·ty**[2] /ˈpɑrt̬i/ *verb* [I] (*pres. part.* **par·ty·ing**; *3rd person sing. pres.* **par·ties**; *pt, pp* **par·tied**) (*informal*) to have or attend a PARTY[1] (1): *Hey, dudes – let's party!* ◇ *We partied all night long at Dave's house.*

ˈ**par·ty ˌan·i·mal** *noun* [C] (*slang*) a person who goes to a lot of parties and often drinks a lot of alcohol and behaves in a loud, excited way

ˈ**party ˌfavor** (*also* **favor**) *noun* [C] a small gift that is given to guests at a party

**par·ty poop·er** /ˈpɑrt̬i ˌpupər/ *noun* [C] (*informal*) a person who spoils the fun for other people

**pass**[1] /pæs/ *noun* [C] **1** the act of kicking, hitting or throwing the ball to sb on your own team in various sports **2** an official card or piece of paper that gives you permission to enter or leave a building, travel on a bus or train, etc.: *Visitors must obtain a pass from the reception desk.* ◇ *a bus pass* **3** a road or way over or through mountains: *The pass was blocked by snow.* **4** a successful result on an examination, etc.: *There are no letter grades in this course. Students will receive a "pass" or a "fail."*

★**pass**[2] /pæs/ *verb*

➤MOVE **1** [I,T] to move forward or to the other side of sb/sth; to leave sth behind or on one side as you go past: *The kids waved to the clowns as they passed in the parade* ◇ *They passed a police checkpoint.* ◇ *Do we pass a mailbox on the way to the store?* ◇ (*figurative*) *The number of students at the school has passed 500.*

NOTE The past tense of **pass** is **passed**. It sounds like **past**, which is an adjective or a preposition: *The summer months passed slowly.* ◇ *The past week was very hot.* ◇ *Our house is just past the church.*

**2** [I,T] to go past another person, car, etc. because you are moving faster: *DO NOT PASS* (= on a sign) ◇ *The car that passed us must have been going 80 miles an hour.* **3** [I] **pass along, down, etc. (sth)** to go or move in the direction mentioned: *Which towns do we pass through on the way to Boston?* ◇ *You pass over a bridge, and then the restaurant is on the right.* **4** [T] **pass sth across, around, through, etc. sth** to put or move sth in the direction mentioned: *We'll have to pass the cord behind the couch.*

➤GIVE **5** [T] **pass sth (to sb)** to pick sth up and give it to sb; to hand sth: *Could you pass (me) the salt, please?* ◇ *He passed the bottle to his father.*

➤BALL **6** [I,T] **pass (sth) (to sb)** to kick, hit or throw the ball to sb on your own team in various sports

➤TIME **7** [I] (used about time) to go by: *At least a year has passed since I last saw them.* ◇ *The time passed very quickly.* **8** [T] to spend time: *I'll have to think of something to do to pass the time in the hospital.*

➤TEST/EXAM **9** [I,T] to achieve the necessary standard on an examination, test, etc.: *Good luck on the exam! I'm sure you'll pass.* **10** [T] to test sb/sth and say that he/she/it is good enough: *The professor passed most of the people in her course.*

➤LAW/PROPOSAL **11** [T] to officially approve a law, proposal, etc.: *One of the functions of Congress is to pass new laws.*

➤SAY/STATE STH **12** [T] **pass sth (on sb/sth)** to give an opinion, judgment, etc.: *The judge passed sentence on the young man* (= said what his punishment would be).

➤BE ACCEPTED **13** [I] to be allowed or accepted: *I didn't like what they were saying, but I let it pass without comment.*

IDM **pass the buck (to sb)** to give the responsibility or the blame for sth to sb else

**pass water** (*old-fashioned, formal*) to urinate
PHR V **pass sth along/on (to sb)** to give sth (to sb else) especially after you have been given it or used it yourself: *Could you pass along the message to Eli, please?*
**pass away** a polite way of saying "die": *The old man passed away in his sleep.*
**pass by (sb/sth)** to go past: *I pass by your house on the way to work.*
**pass sth down** to give sth (to people who live after you have died): *The family home has been passed down from one generation to the next.*
**pass for sb/sth** to be accepted as sb/sth, but without really being that person or thing: *You'll never pass for a real cowboy in that ridiculous hat.*
**pass sb/sth off (as sb/sth)** to say that a person or a thing is sth that he/she/it is not: *He managed to pass the work off as his own.*
**pass out** to become unconscious; to faint
**pass sth up** to choose not to take or make use of sth, especially an opportunity: *The offer was too good to pass up.*

**pass·a·ble** /ˈpæsəbl/ *adj.* **1** (not before a noun) (used about roads, rivers, etc.) possible to use or cross; not completely blocked OPP **impassable** **2** good enough but not very good: *My French is not great, but it's passable.*

★**pas·sage** /ˈpæsɪdʒ/ *noun*
›LONG NARROW WAY **1** [C] (*also* **pas·sage·way** /ˈpæsɪdʒweɪ/) a long, narrow way through sth, especially one in a building that leads to other rooms; a corridor: *We had to go down a dark passage to reach the bathroom.*
›IN THE BODY **2** [C] a tube in your body which air, liquid, etc. can pass through: *the nasal passages*
›SECTION FROM BOOK **3** [C] a short part of a book, speech or piece of music: *The students were given a passage from the novel to study in detail.*
›JOURNEY **4** [U] the movement or progress of sb/sth from one place or stage to another: *We watched the ants' slow passage across the road.*
›OF TIME **5** [U] (used about time) the passing: *With the passage of time, these seeds will grow into beautiful flowers.* ➲ Look at **rite of passage**.

★**pas·sen·ger** /ˈpæsəndʒər/ *noun* [C] a person who is traveling in a car, bus, train, plane, etc. but who is not driving it or working on it: *Passengers are asked to remain seated until the plane has come to a complete standstill.* ◇ *the passenger seat of a car*

**pas·ser·by** /ˌpæsərˈbaɪ/ *noun* [C] (*pl.* **pas·sers·by** /ˌpæsərzˈbaɪ/) a person who is walking past sb/sth (by chance): *None of the passersby had seen how the accident happened.*

**pass·ing¹** /ˈpæsɪŋ/ *adj.* lasting for only a short time; brief: *No, I wasn't serious about going to Hawaii. It was only a passing thought.*

**pass·ing²** /ˈpæsɪŋ/ *noun* [U] the process of going by: *the passing of time*
IDM **in passing** done or said quickly, while you are thinking or talking about sth else: *He mentioned the house in passing, but he didn't give any details.*

**pas·sion** /ˈpæʃn/ *noun* **1** [U] very strong sexual love or attraction: *They loved each other, but there was no passion in their relationship.* **2** [C,U] (a) very strong feeling, especially of love, hate or anger: *He was a violent man, controlled by his passions.* ◇ *She argued her case with passion.* **3** [sing.] **a passion for sth** a very strong liking for or interest in sth: *He has a passion for chocolate.*

**pas·sion·ate** /ˈpæʃn·ət/ *adj.* showing or caused by very strong, sometimes sexual feelings: *a passionate believer in democracy* ◇ *a passionate relationship/kiss* ▸ **pas·sion·ate·ly** *adv.*

**pas·sive** /ˈpæsɪv/ *adj.* **1** showing no reaction, feeling or interest; not active: *Television encourages people to be passive.* **2** (used about the form of a verb or a sentence when the subject of the sentence is affected by the action of the verb): *In the sentence "He was bitten by a dog," the verb is passive.* ➲ You can also say: "The verb is in the passive." Look at **active**. ▸ **pas·sive·ly** *adv.*

ˌ**passive ˈsmoking** (*also* ˌ**secondary ˈsmoking**) *noun* [U] the act of breathing in smoke from other people's cigarettes

**Pass·o·ver** /ˈpæsoʊvər/ *noun* [U] the Jewish religious festival which celebrates the freeing of the Jews from being slaves in Egypt

**pass·port** /ˈpæspɔrt/ *noun* [C] **1** an official document that identifies you and that you have to show when you enter or leave a country: *Do you have to show your passport at the check-in counter?* **2 a passport to sth** a thing that makes it possible to achieve sth: *a passport to success*

**pass·word** /ˈpæswərd/ *noun* [C] **1** a secret word or phrase that you need to know in order to be allowed into a place **2** a secret word that you must type in order to use a computer system: *Please enter your password.*

★**past¹** /pæst/ *adj.* **1** already gone; belonging to a time before the present: *in past years/centuries* ◇ *I'd rather forget some of my past mistakes.* ◇ *Mr. Garcia is a past president of the city council.* **2** (only before a noun) just finished; last: *He had to work very hard during the past year.* ◇ *The past few weeks have been very difficult.* **3** (not before a noun) over; finished; no longer existing: *Suddenly his childhood was past and he was a young man.*

★**past²** /pæst/ *noun* **1 the past** [sing.] the time before the present; the things that happened in that time: *The story was set in the distant past.* ◇ *We spent the evening talking about the past.* **2** [C] a person's life before now: *May I ask you a few questions about your past?* **3 the past** [sing.] = PAST TENSE

★**past³** /pæst/ *prep.* **1** from one side to the other of sb/sth; further than or on the other side of sb/sth: *He walked straight past me.* ◇ *Go past the school and our house is the second on the right.* ◇ *The telephone booth is just past the gas station.* **2** beyond the limits or age when you can do sth: *She was past the age when she could have children.* **3** older than: *She's past 40.* **4** (used when telling the time) after; later than: *It's ten (minutes) past three.* ◇ *It's a quarter past seven.*
IDM **not put it past sb (to do sth)** → PUT

★**past⁴** /pæst/ *adv.* by; from one side of sb/sth to another: *The bus went right past without stopping.* ◇ *He waved as he drove past.*

**pas·ta** /ˈpɑstə/ *noun* [U] a type of food made from a mixture of flour, water and sometimes eggs which is cut into various shapes and cooked: *Macaroni is a type of pasta.*

P

**paste¹** /peɪst/ *noun* **1** [C,U] a soft, wet mixture, usually made of a powder and a liquid and sometimes used for sticking things together: *wallpaper paste* ◇ *Mix the flour and milk into a paste.* **2** [U] (usually in compounds) a soft mixture of food that has been cut into very small pieces to make it smooth: *tomato paste*

**paste²** /peɪst/ *verb* **1** [T] to stick sth to sth else using glue or paste: *He pasted the picture into his book.* **2** [I,T] to copy or move text, etc. into a computer document from another place or document: *This function allows you to* ***cut and paste*** *text.*

**pas·tel** /pæˈstɛl/ *adj.* (used about colors) pale; not strong

**pas·teur·ized** /ˈpæstʃəraɪzd/ *adj.* (used about milk or milk products) free from bacteria because it has been heated

**pas·time** /ˈpæstaɪm/ *noun* [C] something that you enjoy doing when you are not working: *What are your favorite pastimes?* ➲ Look at **hobby**.

**pas·tor** /ˈpæstər/ *noun* [C] a religious leader in some Protestant churches ➲ Look at **minister** and at the note at **priest**.

**pas·tor·al** /ˈpæstərəl/ *adj.* **1** connected with the work of a pastor **2** (*formal*) connected with the countryside and country life: *a pastoral scene*

**the ˌpast ˈperfect** (*also* **the pluperfect**) *noun* [sing.] (*grammar*) the tense of a verb that describes an action that was finished before another event happened: *In the sentence "After they had finished the meal, they went for a walk," "had finished" is in the past perfect.*

**pas·tra·mi** /pəˈstrɑmi/ *noun* [U] spicy smoked beef that is usually eaten cold in thin slices

**pas·try** /ˈpeɪstri/ *noun* (*pl.* **pas·tries**) **1** [U] a mixture of flour, fat and water that is used for making pies, etc. and is baked in an oven ➲ picture at **pie**. **2** [C] a small cake made with pastry: *Danish pastries*

**the ˌpast ˈtense** (*also* **the past**, **the simple past**) *noun* [sing.] (*grammar*) a form of a verb used to describe actions in the PAST² (1): *The past tense of the verb "come" is "came."*

**pas·ture** /ˈpæstʃər/ *noun* [C,U] a field or land covered with grass, where farm animals can eat

**ˌP'A ˌsystem** (*also formal* **public-address system**) *noun* [C, usually sing.] an electronic system that makes sb's voice louder or carries it into many rooms of a large building, such as an airport, a school, etc.

**pat¹** /pæt/ *verb* [T] (**pat·ting**; **pat·ted**) to tap sb/sth very gently with a flat hand or with sth flat: *"Good dog," she said, patting him.*

**pat²** /pæt/ *noun* [C] a gentle tap with a flat hand or with sth flat: *Jerry gave his friend a pat on the shoulder to congratulate him.*

IDM **a pat on the back** congratulations for sth good that a person has done

**pat³** /pæt/ *adj.* (only *before* a noun) too quick (used about an answer, comment, etc.)

**pat⁴** /pæt/ *adv.*

IDM **have sth down pat** to know sth perfectly so that you can say or do it without having to think about it

**patch¹** /pætʃ/ *noun* [C] **1** a piece of material that you use to cover a hole in clothes, etc.: *an old pair of jeans with patches on both knees* ◇ *to sew a patch on* **2** a small piece of material that you wear over one eye: *an eye patch* **3 a patch (of sth)** a part of a surface that is different in some way from the area around it: *Drive carefully. There are patches of ice on the roads.* ◇ *a damp patch on the ceiling* **4** a small piece of land: *a vegetable patch*

**patch²** /pætʃ/ *verb* [T] to put a piece of material over a hole in clothes, etc. or to repair sth by doing this: *to patch a hole in sth* ◇ *to patch an old pair of pants*

PHRV **patch sth up 1** to repair sth quickly or not very carefully: *The car had been patched up after an accident.* **2** to settle an argument: *It's time the boys patched up their differences and made friends.*

**patch·work** /ˈpætʃwərk/ *noun* **1** [U] a type of sewing in which small pieces of cloth of different colors and patterns are sewn together: *a patchwork quilt* **2** [sing.] a thing that is made of many different pieces or parts

**patch·y** /ˈpætʃi/ *adj.* (**patch·i·er**; **patch·i·est**) **1** not all the same or not complete: *His work is patchy* (= some, but not all, of it is good). ◇ *We have only patchy* (= not complete) *information on the accident.* **2** in small quantities, not everywhere: *patchy fog*

**pat·ent¹** /ˈpætnt/ *noun* [C] an official license from the government that gives one person or company the right to make or sell a certain product and prevents others from copying it: *a patent on a new invention*

**pat·ent²** /ˈpætnt/ *verb* [T] to obtain a PATENT¹ for sth

**pat·ent³** /ˈpætnt/ *adj.* (*formal*) clear; obvious: *a patent lie*

**patent leather** /ˈpætnt ˈlɛðər; ˈpeɪ-/ *noun* [U] a type of leather with a hard, shiny surface

**pat·ent·ly** /ˈpætntli/ *adv.* clearly: *She was patently very upset.* ◇ *He was patently honest.*

**pa·ter·nal** /pəˈtərnl/ *adj.* (only *before* a noun) **1** of a father: *the importance of paternal interest and support* **2** related through the father's side of the family: *my paternal grandparents* ➲ Look at **maternal**.

**pa·ter·ni·ty** /pəˈtərnət̬i/ *noun* [U] the state of being a father

★**path** /pæθ/ *noun* [C] (*pl.* **paths** /pɑðz; pæðz/) **1** a way across a piece of land that is made by or used by people walking: *a path through the woods* ◇ *Stay on the path or you could get lost.* ◇ *Where does this path lead to?* SYN **pathway** ➲ Look also at **trail**. **2** the line along which sb/sth moves: *He threw himself* ***into the path of*** *an oncoming vehicle.* ◇ *The grasshoppers moved across the country eating everything* ***in their path***. ➲ Look also at **flight path**. **3** a plan of action or a way of achieving sth: *the path to freedom/success/victory*

IDM **off the beaten path/track** → BEAT¹

**pa·thet·ic** /pəˈθɛt̬ɪk/ *adj.* **1** causing you to feel pity or sadness: *the pathetic cries of the hungry children* **2** (*informal*) very bad, weak or useless: *What a* *pathetic performance! The team deserved to lose.* ▸ **pa·thet·i·cal·ly** /-kli/ ***adv.***

**path·o·log·i·cal** /ˌpæθəˈlɑdʒɪkl/ ***adj.*** **1** connected with pathology **2** (*informal*) caused by feelings that you cannot control; not reasonable: *He's a pathological liar.* ◇ *a pathological fear of water* ▸ **path·o·log·i·cal·ly** /-kli/ ***adv.***

**pa·thol·o·gist** /pəˈθɑlədʒɪst/ ***noun*** [C] a person who is an expert in pathology, especially one who tries to find out why a person has died

**pa·thol·o·gy** /pəˈθɑlədʒi/ ***noun*** [U] the scientific study of the diseases of the body

**path·way** /ˈpæθweɪ/ ***noun*** [C] = PATH (1): *There was a narrow pathway leading down the cliff.*

★**pa·tience** /ˈpeɪʃns/ ***noun*** [U] **patience (with sb/sth)** the quality of being able to remain calm and not get angry, especially when there is a difficulty or you have to wait a long time: *I have no patience with people who don't even try.* ◇ *to lose your patience with sb* ◇ *After three hours of waiting, our patience was wearing thin.* OPP **impatience**

★**pa·tient**[1] /ˈpeɪʃnt/ ***adj.*** able to remain calm and not get angry, especially when there is a difficulty or you are waiting for sth: *It's hard to be patient with a screaming child.* ◇ *It won't be long now. Just sit there and be patient.* OPP **impatient** ▸ **pa·tient·ly** ***adv.***: *to wait patiently*

★**pa·tient**[2] /ˈpeɪʃnt/ ***noun*** [C] a person who is receiving medical treatment: *a hospital patient* ◇ *a specialist who treats patients with heart problems*

**pat·i·o** /ˈpæt̬ioʊ/ ***noun*** [C] (*pl.* **pat·i·os** /-oʊz/) an area with a hard surface next to a house where people can sit, eat, etc. outdoors ➲ Look at **deck**, **porch** and **veranda**.

**pa·tri·arch** /ˈpeɪtriɑrk/ ***noun*** [C] an older man who is the respected leader of a family or tribe

**pa·tri·ar·chal** /ˌpeɪtriˈɑrkl/ ***adj.*** ruled or controlled by men: *a patriarchal society*

**pa·tri·ot** /ˈpeɪtriət/ ***noun*** [C] a person who loves his/her country: *the patriots who fought for American independence*

**pa·tri·ot·ic** /ˌpeɪtriˈɑt̬ɪk/ ***adj.*** having or showing a love for your country ▸ **pa·tri·ot·i·cal·ly** /-kli/ ***adv.***

**pa·tri·ot·ism** /peɪtriətɪzəm/ ***noun*** [U] love of your country ➲ Look at **nationalism**.

**pa·trol**[1] /pəˈtroʊl/ ***verb*** [I,T] (**pa·trol_l_ing**; **pa·trol_l_ed**) to go around a town, building, etc. to make sure that there is no trouble and that nothing is wrong: *Guards patrol the grounds at regular intervals.*

**pa·trol**[2] /pəˈtroʊl/ ***noun*** [C] **1** the act of patrolling: *The army makes hourly patrols of the area.* **2** a person or group of people that patrols sth: *a police patrol* ◇ *a patrol car*

IDM **on patrol** patrolling sth

**pa·trol·man** /pəˈtroʊlmən/ (*feminine* **pa·trol·wom·an** /-wʊmən/) ***noun*** [C] a police officer who goes around a particular part of a town to make sure that there is no trouble and to prevent crime

**pa·tron** /ˈpeɪtrən/ ***noun*** [C] **1** a person who gives money to artists, musicians, etc. or who supports a good cause: *a patron of the arts* ◇ *She is a patron of the Metropolitan Opera.* **2** a person who goes to a store, theater, restaurant, etc.: *This parking lot is reserved for store patrons.*

**pa·tron·age** /ˈpeɪtrənɪdʒ; ˈpæ-/ ***noun*** [U] support or money that is given to a person, organization, or business

**pa·tron·ize** /ˈpeɪtrənaɪz; ˈpæ-/ ***verb*** [T] **1** to go regularly to a store, theater, restaurant, etc. **2** to treat sb in a friendly way but as if you were better than him/her

**pa·tron·iz·ing** /ˈpeɪtrənaɪzɪŋ; ˈpæ-/ ***adj.*** treating sb in a friendly way but as if you were better than him/her: *I really hate that patronizing smile of hers.* ▸ **pa·tron·iz·ing·ly** ***adv.***

**ˌpatron ˈsaint** ***noun*** [C] a saint who is believed to give help and protection to a particular place or to people doing a particular activity: *St. Patrick is the patron saint of Ireland.*

**pat·ter** /ˈpæt̬ər/ ***noun*** **1** [U, sing.] fast continuous talk by sb who is trying to entertain you or sell you sth: *sales patter* **2** [sing.] the sound made by sth repeatedly hitting a surface quickly and lightly: *the patter of rain on the tin roof*

★**pat·tern** /ˈpæt̬ərn/ ***noun*** [C] **1** an arrangement of lines, shapes, colors, etc. Patterns are often used to decorate clothes, wallpapers, carpets, etc.: *Our new china has a flower pattern on it.* ◇ *a geometrical pattern* ➲ Picture on study page **A30**. **2** the way in which sth happens, develops, is arranged, etc.: *Her periods of mental illness all followed the same pattern.* ◇ *patterns of behavior* **3** something that helps you to make sth, e.g. a piece of clothing, by showing the shape it should be: *a paper pattern*

**pat·terned** /ˈpæt̬ərnd/ ***adj.*** having a PATTERN (1): *patterned curtains* ➲ Picture on study page **A30**.

**pat·ty** /ˈpæt̬i/ ***noun*** [C] (*pl.* **pat·ties**) food, especially meat, that has been cut into very small pieces and then formed into a round flat shape: *a hamburger patty*

★**pause**[1] /pɔz/ ***noun*** [C] a short stop in sth: *He continued playing for twenty minutes without a pause.* ◇ *a pause in the conversation*

> NOTE **Pause**, **break**, **recess** and **intermission** have similar meanings. A **pause** is a short period of time when you stop speaking or doing sth: *After a brief pause, she answered.* A **break** is especially used in connection with periods of work or study, e.g. **a lunch/coffee break** in an office, a factory or a school: *We've been working pretty hard – let's take a break.* ◇ *students spending their spring break in Florida.* A break during the school day, especially after lunch, is called **recess**. A **recess** is also a longer period of time when work in Congress, Parliament or in a court of law stops: *senators returning from the Memorial Day recess.* We use **intermission** for a break in a concert or performance.

★**pause**[2] /pɔz/ ***verb*** [I] **pause (for sth)** to stop for a short time: *to pause for breath*

**pave** /peɪv/ ***verb*** [T] (often passive) to cover an area of ground with a hard surface: *There were no paved roads through the jungle.*

IDM **pave the way (for sb/sth)** to create a situation in which sb will be able to do sth or sth will be possible: *The ambassador's visit helped to*

P

*pave the way for better relations between the two countries.*

**pave·ment** /ˈpeɪvmənt/ ***noun*** [U] the hard surface of a street, sidewalk, etc.

**pa·vil·ion** /pəˈvɪlyən/ ***noun*** [C] a building, often in a park, which has a roof but usually no walls, where people can rest or look at things: *a demonstration about making quilts in the craft pavilion*

**paw¹** /pɔ/ ***noun*** [C] the foot of animals such as dogs, cats, bears, etc. ➲ Paws have sharp **claws** and soft **pads** underneath. Look at **hoof**. ➲ picture at **cat**. ➲

**paw²** /pɔ/ ***verb*** [I,T] **paw (at) sth** (used about an animal) to touch sb/sth with a paw or foot

**pawn¹** /pɔn/ ***noun*** [C] **1** one of the eight pieces in the game of chess that are of least value and importance ➲ picture at **chess**. **2** a person who is used or controlled by another person

**pawn²** /pɔn/ ***verb*** [T] to give sth of value to a person who lends you money (a **pawnbroker**). If you cannot pay back the money after a certain period, the pawnbroker can keep or sell the thing that you gave him/her.

**pawn·bro·ker** /ˈpɔnbroʊkər/ ***noun*** [C] a person who lends money to people when they leave sth of value with him/her

★**pay¹** /peɪ/ ***noun*** [U] money that you get regularly for work that you have done: *It's a tough job, but the pay is good.* ◇ *a pay increase*

> NOTE **Pay** is the general word for money that you get regularly for work that you have done. **Wages** are paid every week or every two weeks, based on how many hours you have worked. A **salary** is a fixed amount that is paid every week, every two weeks or every month, depending on a company's system. You pay a **fee** for professional services, e.g. to a doctor, lawyer, etc. **Payment** is money that you get for work that you do once or not regularly.

★**pay²** /peɪ/ ***verb*** (*pt, pp* **paid**) **1** [I,T] **pay (sb) (for sth); pay sth (to sb) (for sth)** to give sb money for sth: *She is very well paid.* ◇ *Do you want to pay by check or by credit card?* ◇ *The work's finished, but we haven't paid the plumber yet.* ◇ *to be paid by the hour* ◇ *We paid the dealer $5,000 for the car.* **2** [T] **pay sth (to sb)** to give the money that you owe for sth: *Did you pay the gas bill?* **3** [I,T] to make a profit; to be worth doing: *The factory closed down because the owners couldn't make it pay.* ◇ *I've learned that it pays to be prepared.* **4** **pay (for sth)** to suffer or be punished for sth you believe or have done: *I'll make him pay for embarrassing me like that!*

IDM **cost/pay an arm and a leg** → ARM¹

**pay attention (to sb/sth)** to listen carefully to or to take notice of sb/sth

**pay sb a compliment; pay a compliment to sb** to say that you like sth about sb; to praise sb

**pay your respects (to sb)** (*formal*) to visit sb, especially sb who is dead or very sick, as a sign of respect

**pay tribute to sb/sth** to praise and show your respect for sb/sth, especially sb who is dead

PHRV **pay sb back (sth); pay sth back** to give money back to sb that you borrowed from him/her: *Can you lend me $10? I'll pay you back/I'll pay it back to you on Friday.*

**pay sb back (for sth)** to do sth unkind to sb who did sth unkind to you: *What a mean trick! I'll pay you back one day.*

**pay sth down** to pay back money that you owe: *to pay down a debt*

**pay off** (*informal*) to be successful: *All their hard work has paid off! The house is finished at last.*

**pay sth off** to pay all the money that you owe for sth: *to pay off a debt*

**pay up** (*informal*) to pay the money that you owe: *If you don't pay up, we'll take you to court.*

**pay·a·ble** /ˈpeɪəbl/ ***adj.*** that should or must be paid: *This bill is payable immediately.* ◇ *Make the check payable to Diane Weller.*

**pay·back** /ˈpeɪbæk/ ***noun*** **1** [U] (*informal*) something that you do to punish sb who has hurt you, made you suffer, etc. SYN **revenge** **2** [C,U] the profit or an advantage that you receive later from money you have put into sth or sth you have done; the time it takes to receive this: *Now is a good time to invest because the long-term paybacks can be large.* ◇ *a 10-year payback period*

IDM **it's payback time** (*informal*) (used to say that you are now going to make sb suffer because of sth bad he/she did to you)

**pay·check** /ˈpeɪtʃɛk/ ***noun*** [C] a special printed form that an employee receives regularly as payment for work that he/she has done: *I need to go to the bank to cash my paycheck.*

**pay·day** /ˈpeɪdeɪ/ ***noun*** [C,U] the day on which you get paid for work you have done: *Can I wait until payday to give you the money for my ticket?*

**pay·er** /ˈpeɪər/ ***noun*** [C] a person who pays for sth: *to be a good/prompt/slow/late payer*

**pay·load** /ˈpeɪloʊd/ ***noun*** [C] the goods, passengers, etc. that a ship, spacecraft, truck, etc. is paid to carry

★**pay·ment** /ˈpeɪmənt/ ***noun*** **payment (for sth)** **1** [U] paying or being paid: *You get a 5% discount for prompt payment.* ◇ *payment of a bill* ◇ *I did the work last month, but I haven't had any payment yet.* ➲ Look at the note at **pay¹**. **2** [C] an amount of money that you must pay: *They asked for a payment of $100 as a deposit.*

**pay·off** /ˈpeɪɔf; -ɑf/ ***noun*** [C] **1** (*informal*) a payment of money that is made to someone, often illegally **2** an advantage or a reward from sth you have done

**pay·out** /ˈpeɪaʊt/ ***noun*** [C] a large amount of money that is given to sb

**pay-per-view** /ˌpeɪ pər ˈvyu/ ***noun*** [U] a television channel that makes you pay for each program you watch: *We watched the fight on pay-per-view.*

ˈ**pay phone** ***noun*** [C] a telephone in a public place, which you can use by putting in money or using a special card

**pay·roll** /ˈpeɪroʊl/ ***noun*** [C] a list of people who work for a company and the amount of money to be paid to each person: *Our company has over 250 people on the payroll.*

**PC¹** /ˌpiˈsi/ (*pl.* **PCs**) ***noun*** [C] personal computer; a small computer that is designed for home or business use

NOTE The term **PC** is usually used to refer to a specific type of computer manufactured by IBM, or to other computers that work in a similar way: *The software is available in both PC and Macintosh versions.*

**PC**[2] /ˌpiˈsi/ ***adj.*** (*informal*) = POLITICALLY CORRECT

**PD day** /ˌpi ˈdi deɪ/ ***noun*** [C] (*especially Cdn*) = PROFESSIONAL DEVELOPMENT DAY

**P.E.** /ˌpi ˈi/ ***noun*** [U] = PHYSICAL EDUCATION

**pea** /pi/ ***noun*** [C] a small round green seed that is eaten as a vegetable

NOTE A number of peas grow together in a **pod**. ➲ picture on study page **A28-29**.

★**peace** /pis/ ***noun*** [U] **1** the state of not being at war or of not having fighting, disorder, etc.: *fifty years of peace in Europe* ◇ *a peace treaty* **2** the state of being calm or quiet: *He longed to escape from the city to the peace of the countryside.* ◇ *I'm tired – can't you just leave me in peace?* ◇ *The noise of lawnmowers disturbed the peace of the afternoon.*

**the ˈPeace Corps** ***noun*** [sing.] a U.S. government organization that sends young people to other countries to work on projects to help local people: *to join the Peace Corps* ◇ *a Peace Corps volunteer* ➲ Look at the note at **White House**.

★**peace·ful** /ˈpisfl/ ***adj.*** **1** not wanting or involving war, fighting or disorder: *a peaceful demonstration* ◇ *Nuclear power can be used for peaceful or military purposes.* ◇ *a peaceful solution to the conflict* **2** calm and quiet: *a peaceful spot near the river* ▸ **peace·ful·ly** ***adv.*** ▸ **peace·ful·ness** ***noun*** [U]

**peace·keep·ing** /ˈpisˌkipɪŋ/ ***noun*** [U] work that is done by soldiers to prevent other people or groups from fighting each other: *peacekeeping troops/forces* ▸ **peace·keep·er** ***noun*** [C]

**ˈpeace pipe** ***noun*** [C] a holy pipe which some Native Americans use to smoke tobacco during ceremonies. It is passed from one person to another as a sign of peace.

**peace·time** /ˈpistaɪm/ ***noun*** [U] a period when a country is not at war

**peach** /pitʃ/ ***noun*** [C] a soft round fruit with orange-red skin. A peach is soft inside and has a large hard part (**pit**) in its center: *canned peaches*

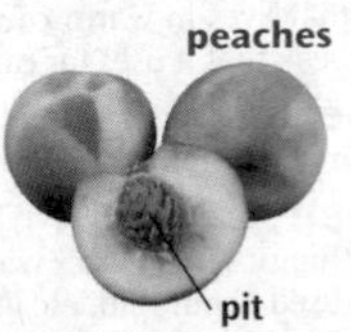


**peach·y** /ˈpitʃi/ ***adj.*** (**peach·i·er**; **peach·i·est**) (*informal, old-fashioned*) very good or nice: *Everything's just peachy here.*

**pea·cock** /ˈpikɑk/ ***noun*** [C] a large bird with beautiful long blue and green tail feathers that it can lift up and spread out like a fan

★**peak**[1] /pik/ ***noun*** [C] **1** the pointed top of a mountain: *snow-covered peaks in the distance* **2** the highest level, value, rate, etc.: *In the early evening demand for electricity is at its peak.* ◇ *a man at the peak of his career* ➲ Look at **off-peak**.

**peak**[2] /pik/ ***verb*** [I] to reach the highest level, value, rate, etc.: *Sales usually peak just before the holidays.*

**peal** /pil/ ***noun*** [C] the loud ringing of a bell or of a set of bells that all have different notes: (*figurative*) *peals of laughter*

**pea·nut** /ˈpinʌt/ ***noun*** [C] a nut that grows in a shell under the ground: *roasted and salted peanuts* ➲ picture at **nut**.

**ˈpeanut ˌbutter** ***noun*** [U] a thick soft food made from crushed peanuts. It is usually eaten on bread: *a peanut butter and jelly sandwich*

**pear** /pɛr/ ***noun*** [C] a fruit that has yellow or green skin and is white inside. Pears are thinner at the top than at the bottom.

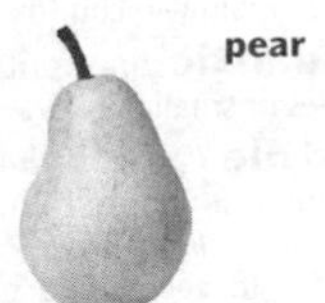


**pearl** /pərl/ ***noun*** [C] a small, hard, round, white object that grows inside the shell of an oyster (a type of shellfish). Pearls are used to make jewelry: *a pearl necklace*

**peas·ant** /ˈpɛznt/ ***noun*** [C] (especially in former times or in poorer countries) a poor person who owns or rents a small piece of land on which he/she grows food and keeps animals in order to feed his/her family

**peat** /pit/ ***noun*** [U] a natural substance that is made of decayed plants. Peat is formed underground in cool, wet places. It can be burned as a fuel or put on the garden to make plants grow better.

**peb·ble** /ˈpɛbl/ ***noun*** [C] a smooth round stone that is usually found in or near water

**pe·can** /pəˈkɑn; -ˈkæn/ ***noun*** [C] a nut that you can eat, with a smooth reddish-brown shell. It grows on trees in the southern U.S: *pecan pie* ➲ picture at **nut**.

**peck** /pɛk/ ***verb*** [I,T] **peck (at sth)** (used about a bird) to eat or bite sth with the beak: *The sparrows were pecking around for food.* ◇ *Don't touch the bird – it might peck you.* ▸ **peck** ***noun*** [C] (*figurative*): *She gave him a quick peck* (= kiss) *on the cheek and then left.*

**pec·to·rals** /ˈpɛktərəlz/ (*also informal* **pecs** /pɛks/) ***noun*** [pl.] the muscles of the chest

**pe·cu·liar** /pɪˈkyulyər/ ***adj.*** **1** odd or strange: *Warren has some very peculiar habits.* ◇ *Our new neighbor seems a little peculiar.* **2** only belonging to a particular person or thing or found in a particular place: *a problem peculiar to this type of car*

**pe·cu·li·ar·i·ty** /pɪˌkyuliˈærət̮i/ ***noun*** (*pl.* **pe·cu·li·ar·i·ties**) **1** [U] the quality of being strange or odd **2** [C] something that is strange or odd: *One of his peculiarities is that he never wears socks.* **3** [C] sth that only belongs to or is only found in sb/sth

**pe·cu·liar·ly** /pɪˈkyulyərli/ ***adv.*** **1** in a PECULIAR (1) way: *Luke is behaving very peculiarly.* **2** in a way that is especially typical of sb/sth: *Is talking about the weather a peculiarly Canadian habit?*

**ped·al**[1] /ˈpɛdl/ ***noun*** [C] **1** a flat bar on a machine such as a bicycle, car, etc. that you push down with your foot in order to make parts of the machine move or work ➲ picture at **bicycle**. ➲ Look also at **accelerator**. **2** a bar on a musical instrument such as a piano or an organ that you push with your foot in order to control the sound ➲ picture at **keyboard**.

P

**ped·al²** /ˈpɛdl/ ***verb*** [I,T] to push the pedals of a bicycle: *She had to pedal hard to get up the hill.*

**ˌpedal ˌsteel guiˈtar** (*also* **ˈpedal steel, ˌsteel guiˈtar**) ***noun*** [C] a type of electric guitar on a flat stand, which has a metal bar that you slide up and down the steel strings with one hand, while you pull (pluck) them with the other. You also control the sound it makes by pressing PEDALS¹ (2) with your feet and sometimes your knees. Pedal steel guitars are used mainly in country music.

**pe·dan·tic** /pəˈdæntɪk/ ***adj.*** too worried about rules or small details ▸ **pe·dan·ti·cal·ly** /-kli/ ***adv.***

**ped·dle** /ˈpɛdl/ ***verb*** [T] **1** to try to sell things by going from house to house or from place to place: *to peddle illegal drugs* **2** to spread an idea or story in order to get people to accept it, even though it might not be true ▸ **ped·dler** ***noun*** [C]

**ped·es·tal** /ˈpɛdəstl/ ***noun*** [C] the base on which a column, statue, etc. stands

IDM **to put sb on a pedestal** to admire sb so much that you do not see his/her faults

**pe·des·tri·an¹** /pəˈdɛstriən/ ***noun*** [C] a person who is walking on or near the street (not traveling in a vehicle): *Motorists must yield to pedestrians in crosswalks.*

**pe·des·tri·an²** /pəˈdɛstriən/ ***adj.*** **1** of or for pedestrians: *a pedestrian bridge* **2** (*formal*) ordinary; not interesting; dull

**pe·di·a·tri·cian** /ˌpidiəˈtrɪʃn/ ***noun*** [C] a doctor who specializes in treating sick babies and children ▸ **pe·di·at·ric** /ˌpidiˈætrɪk/ ***adj.***

**ped·i·cure** /ˈpɛdɪkyʊr/ ***noun*** [C] a treatment to make your feet and toenails look nice: *to have a pedicure* ➲ Look also at **manicure**.

**ped·i·gree** /ˈpɛdəgri/ ***noun*** [C] **1** the parents, grandparents and other previous family members of an animal. The names of the ancestors are recorded on a document which is also called a "pedigree." **2** a person's background

**ped·i·greed** /ˈpɛdəgrid/ ***adj.*** (used about an animal) of high quality because the parents, grandparents, etc. are all of the same breed and specially chosen

**pe·do·phile** /ˈpɛdəfaɪl; ˈpi-/ ***noun*** [C] a person who is sexually attracted to children

**pee** /pi/ ***verb*** [I] (*informal*) to send out waste water from your body; to urinate

NOTE It is more polite to say **go to the bathroom**.

▸ **pee** ***noun*** [sing.] (*informal*): *I have to take a pee.*

**peek** /pik/ ***verb*** [I] (*informal*) **peek (at sth)** to look at sth quickly or secretly: *No peeking at the presents before Christmas.* ▸ **peek** ***noun*** [sing.]: *to take a quick peek at the answers*

**peel¹** /pil/ ***verb*** **1** [T] to take the skin off a fruit or vegetable: *Could you peel the potatoes for me?* **2** [I] to come off in one piece or in small pieces: *Soak the envelope in water and the stamp will peel off easily.* ◇ *My nose got sunburned and now it is peeling* (= the skin is coming off). ◇ *The paint is starting to peel.*

**peel²** /pil/ ***noun*** [C,U] the skin of a fruit or vegetable: *apple peel* ➲ Look at **rind**.

**peel·er** /ˈpilər/ ***noun*** [C] (usually in compounds) a special type of knife for taking the skin off fruit and vegetables: *a potato peeler* ➲ picture at **kitchen**.

**peep¹** /pip/ ***verb*** [I] **1 peep (at sth)** to look at sth quickly and secretly: *to peep through a keyhole* **2** (used about part of sth) to appear: *The moon is peeping out from behind the clouds.* **3** to make a weak high sound, like a young bird makes

**peep²** /pip/ ***noun*** [sing.] **1** a quick or secret look: *Take a peep in the bedroom and see if the baby is asleep.* **2** the weak high sound that is made, for example, by a young bird: *There hasn't been a peep out of the kids for hours.*

**peer¹** /pɪr/ ***noun*** [C] a person who is of the same age or rank: *A lot of teenagers worry about being accepted by their peers.* ◇ *peer pressure* (= the feeling that young people have that they must do what others of their age do)

**peer²** /pɪr/ ***verb*** [I] **peer (at sb/sth)** to look closely or carefully at sb/sth, e.g. because you cannot see very well: *I peered outside, but it was too dark to see much.* ◇ *I had to peer very hard at the handwriting to make out what it said.*

**peeve** /piv/ ***noun*** → PET PEEVE

**peg¹** /pɛg/ ***noun*** [C] a round piece of wood, metal, etc. that you can hang things on or use to fasten things together: *Most of the tools were hanging on pegs on the wall.* ◇ *To assemble the bookcase, insert a wooden peg into each hole as shown in the diagram.* ◇ *a tent peg*

**peg²** /pɛg/ ***verb*** [T] (**peg·ging; pegged**) **1** to fasten sth with a peg **2** to fix or keep sth at a certain level; often in relation to sth else: *Inflation was pegged at 7% last year.* ◇ *Some countries' currencies are pegged to the dollar.*

IDM **peg sb/sth as sth; have sb/sth pegged as sth** (*informal*) to regard sb/sth in a particular way: *I had him pegged as a real jerk, but he's actually a nice guy.*

**pe·jo·ra·tive** /pɪˈdʒɔrət̬ɪv; -ˈdʒɑr-/ ***adj.*** (*formal*) expressing criticism or disapproval: *a pejorative expression*

**pel·i·can** /ˈpɛlɪkən/ ***noun*** [C] a large water bird that lives in warm countries. A pelican has a large beak that it uses for catching and holding fish.

**pel·let** /ˈpɛlət/ ***noun*** [C] a small hard ball that is made from mud, metal, etc.: *shotgun pellets*

**pelt¹** /pɛlt/ ***verb*** **1** [T] to attack sb/sth by throwing things: *The speaker was pelted with tomatoes.* **2** [T] (used about rain, etc.) to hit sth or to fall very heavily: *Much of Nebraska was pelted by hail yesterday.*

**pelt²** /pɛlt/ ***noun*** [C] the skin of an animal, especially with the fur or hair still on it: *beaver pelts*

**pel·vis** /ˈpɛlvəs/ ***noun*** [C] (*pl.* **pel·vis·es**) the set of wide bones at the bottom of your back, to which your leg bones are joined ▸ **pel·vic** /ˈpɛlvɪk/ ***adj.***

★ **pen** /pɛn/ ***noun*** [C] **1** an instrument that you use for writing in ink: *a fountain pen* ◇ *a ballpoint pen* ◇ *a felt-tip pen* **2** a small piece of ground with a fence around it that is used for keeping animals in ➲ Look also at **playpen**.

**pe·nal** /ˈpinl/ ***adj.*** (only *before* a noun) connected with punishment by law

ˈ**pe·nal code** ***noun*** [C, usually sing.] a system of laws connected with crime and punishment

**pe·nal·ize** /ˈpinl·aɪz; ˈpɛn-/ ***verb*** [T] **1** to punish sb for breaking a law or rule: *Players must be penalized if they touch the ball with their hands.* ◇ *Motorists who drink and drive should be heavily penalized.* **2** to cause sb to suffer a disadvantage: *The new tax unfairly penalizes single parents.*

**pen·al·ty** /ˈpɛnlti/ ***noun*** [C] (*pl.* **pen·al·ties**) **1** a punishment for breaking a law or rule: *We need stiffer penalties for people who litter.* ◇ *the death penalty* ◇ *The judge ordered him to pay a penalty of $50.* **2** a disadvantage or sth bad that happens as the result of sth: *I didn't work hard enough and I paid the penalty. I failed all my final exams.* **3** (in sports) a punishment for one team and an advantage for the other team because a rule has been broken: *The goalie was fouled and the referee awarded a penalty.*

NOTE In soccer and hockey, a penalty is a free shot at the goal. ➲ picture at **soccer**.

ˈ**penalty box** ***noun*** [C] (in hockey) a small area off the ice where a player who has broken a rule must sit for a certain length of time

**pen·ance** /ˈpɛnəns/ ***noun*** [C,U] a punishment that you give yourself to show you are sorry for doing sth wrong

**pen·chant** /ˈpɛntʃənt/ ***noun*** [usually sing.] **a penchant for sth** a special liking for sth: *She has a real penchant for large jewelry.*

⋆**pen·cil**[1] /ˈpɛnsl/ ***noun*** [C,U] an object that you use for writing or drawing. Pencils are usually made of wood and contain a thin stick of a black or colored substance: *colored pencils for children* ◇ *Write in pen, not pencil.*

**pen·cil**[2] /ˈpɛnsl/ ***verb*** [T] to write or draw with a pencil

PHRV **pencil sb/sth in** to plan a meeting, event, etc., which you know might have to be changed later: *I'll pencil you in for Friday, okay?*

ˈ**pencil case** ***noun*** [C] a small bag or box that you keep pens, pencils, etc. in

ˈ**pencil ˌcrayon** ***noun*** [C] (*Cdn*) a pencil with a colored center, used for art, coloring, etc.

ˈ**pencil ˌsharpener** ***noun*** [C] an instrument that you use for making pencils sharp

**pen·dant** /ˈpɛndənt/ ***noun*** [C] an ornament that you wear on a chain around your neck

**pend·ing**[1] /ˈpɛndɪŋ/ ***adj.*** (*formal*) waiting to be done or decided: *The judge's decision is still pending.*

**pend·ing**[2] /ˈpɛndɪŋ/ ***prep.*** (*formal*) until: *Roberts was set free pending an appeal in the Supreme Court.*

**pen·du·lum** /ˈpɛndʒələm; -dələm/ ***noun*** [C] a string or stick with a heavy weight at the bottom. Some large clocks are worked by a swinging pendulum.

**pen·e·trate** /ˈpɛnətreɪt/ ***verb*** [I,T] to make or force a way into or through sth: *The bullet hadn't penetrated his lung.* ◇ *The car's headlights could not penetrate the thick fog.* ◇ *The troops managed to penetrate into enemy territory.* ▸ **pen·e·tra·tion** /ˌpɛnəˈtreɪʃn/ ***noun*** [U]

**pen·e·trat·ing** /ˌpɛnəˈtreɪt̬ɪŋ/ ***adj.*** **1** showing the ability to think and understand quickly and well: *a penetrating question* **2** (used about a voice or sound) loud and carrying for a long way: *a penetrating scream* **3** (used about sb's eyes or the way sb looks at sth) very powerful and direct, making you feel uncomfortable: *a penetrating stare*

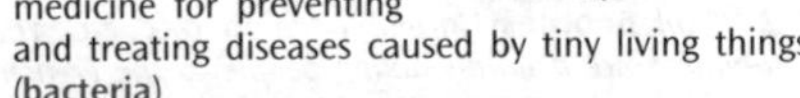

**penguin**

**pen·guin** /ˈpɛŋgwən/ ***noun*** [C] a black and white sea bird that lives in the Antarctic. Penguins cannot fly.

**pen·i·cil·lin** /ˌpɛnəˈsɪlən/ ***noun*** [U] a substance that is used as a medicine for preventing and treating diseases caused by tiny living things (bacteria)

**pen·in·su·la** /pəˈnɪnsələ/ ***noun*** [C] an area of land that is almost surrounded by water

**pe·nis** /ˈpinəs/ ***noun*** [C] the male sex organ that is used for passing waste water and having sex

**pen·i·ten·tia·ry** /pɛnəˈtɛnʃəri/ ***noun*** [C] (*pl.* **pen·i·ten·tia·ries**) a prison

**pen·knife** /ˈpɛnnaɪf/ ***noun*** [C] (*pl.* **pen·knives**) = POCKET KNIFE

ˈ**pen name** ***noun*** [C] = PSEUDONYM

**pen·nant** /ˈpɛnənt/ ***noun*** [C] **1** a long narrow pointed flag, for example one used on a ship to give signals **2** a flag given to the winning team in a sports league, especially in baseball: *The Dodgers defeated the Mets 6–0 to win the pennant.*

**pen·ni·less** /ˈpɛnɪləs/ ***adj.*** having no money; poor

⋆**pen·ny** /ˈpɛni/ ***noun*** [C] (*pl.* **pen·nies**) a small brown American or Canadian coin that is worth one cent

IDM **every penny** all of the money: *She earns a high salary, but I'm sure she deserves every penny.*

**not a penny** no money at all: *It didn't cost a penny.* ◇ *He has never paid me a penny.*

ˈ**pen pal** ***noun*** [C] a person that you become friendly with by sending and receiving letters

**pen·sion** /ˈpɛnʃn/ ***noun*** [C] money that sb who has stopped working (retired) because of old age receives regularly from the company or organization where he/she used to work: *to pay money into a pension fund* ➲ Look also at **Social Security**.

**pen·ta·gon** /ˈpɛntəgɑn/ ***noun*** **1** [C] a shape that has five straight sides **2 the Pentagon** [sing.] a large government building near Washington, D.C., that contains the main offices of the U.S. military forces; the military officials who work here

**Pen·te·cos·tal** /ˌpɛntɪˈkɑstl; -ˈkɔs-/ ***adj.*** connected with a group of Christian Churches that emphasize the gifts of the Holy Spirit, such as the power to heal the sick

**pent·house** /ˈpɛnthaʊs/ ***noun*** [C] an expensive apartment at the top of a tall building

**pent up** /ˌpɛnt ˈʌp/ ***adj.*** (used about feelings) that you do not express: *pent-up anger and frustration*

**pe·on** /ˈpiɑn; -ən/ ***noun*** [C] **1** a worker on a farm in Latin America **2** a person with a hard or boring job that is not well paid and not considered important

⋆**peo·ple** /ˈpipl/ ***noun*** **1** [pl.] more than one person:



P

*How many people are coming to the party?* ◇ *Young people often rebel against their parents.* ◇ *What will people say if you go out looking like that?* ◇ *He meets a lot of famous people in his job.*

NOTE Be careful. **People** is almost always used instead of the plural form **persons. Persons** is very formal and is usually used in legal language, etc.: *Persons under the age of twenty-one are not permitted to buy alcohol.* **Folk(s)** is an informal word for people. It is often used when you are talking about older people or people who live in the country: *The old folks have seen many changes in the town over the years.*

**2** [C] (*pl.* **peoples**) (*formal*) a nation, race, etc.: *The Japanese are a hard-working people.* ◇ *the French-speaking peoples of the world* **3 the peo·ple** [pl.] the ordinary citizens of a country: *a man of the people*

**pep**[1] /pɛp/ ***noun*** [U] (*informal*) energy and positive attitude

**pep**[2] /pɛp/ ***verb*** (**pep·ping; pepped**)

PHR V **pep sb/sth up** (*informal*) to make sb/sth more lively, interesting, etc.: *A spoonful of curry powder should pep up the sauce.*

★**pep·per**[1] /ˈpɛpər/ ***noun*** **1** [U] a powder with a hot taste that is used for flavoring food: *salt and pepper* **2** (*also* ˌ**bell** ˈ**pepper**) [C] a hollow green, red or yellow vegetable: *stuffed green peppers*

**pep·per**[2] /ˈpɛpər/ ***verb*** [T] **1** to put PEPPER (1) on sth **2 pepper sb/sth with sth** to hit sb/sth many times with sth: *The wall had been peppered with bullets.*

**pep·per·mint** /ˈpɛpərmɪnt/ ***noun*** [U] a natural substance with a strong flavor that is used in candy

**pep·per·o·ni** /ˌpɛpəˈroʊni/ ***noun*** [U] a type of spicy sausage: *a pepperoni pizza*

**pep·py** /ˈpɛpi/ ***adj.*** (**pep·pi·er; pep·pi·est**) (*informal*) lively and full of energy or enthusiasm: *a peppy advertising jingle*

ˈ**pep** ˌ**rally** ***noun*** [C] (*pl.* ˈ**pep** ˌ**rallies**) a meeting for all the students in a school before a sports game in which the students shout, sing songs, etc. in order to encourage their team to win

ˈ**pep talk** ***noun*** [C] a speech that is given to encourage people or to make them work harder

★**per** /pər/ ***prep.*** for each: *The speed limit is 30 miles per hour.* ◇ *It costs $10 per hour to rent a boat.*

**per cap·i·ta** /pər ˈkæpət̬ə/ ***adj.*** for each person: *Per capita income rose sharply last year.* ▶ **per cap·i·ta** ***adv.***: *average earnings per capita*

**per·ceive** /pərˈsiv/ ***verb*** [T] (*formal*) **1** to notice or realize sth: *Scientists failed to perceive how dangerous the levels of pollutants had become.* **2** to see or think of sth in a particular way: *I perceived his comments as a criticism.* ➲ noun perception

★**per·cent**[1] /pərˈsɛnt/ ***adj.***, ***adv.*** (*symbol* %) in or of each hundred: *There is a ten percent service charge.* ◇ *a two percent fall in the price of oil*

★**per·cent**[2] /pərˈsɛnt/ ***noun*** [C, with sing. or pl. verb] (*pl.* **per·cent**) (*symbol* %) one part in every hundred: *Nearly ten percent of all children attend private schools.* ◇ *95% of the population owns a television.* ◇ *The price of bread has gone up by 50 percent in two years.*

NOTE We usually use **percent** and **percentage** with a singular verb when we are talking about a singular or an uncountable noun: *About 75 percent of the population owns a VCR.* But we use a plural verb when we are talking about a plural noun: *About 75 percent of all households own a VCR.*

**per·cent·age** /pərˈsɛntɪdʒ/ ***noun*** [C, with sing. or pl. verb] a part of an amount, expressed as a number of parts in every hundred of that amount: *"What percentage of the voters chose George Bush?" "About 43 percent."* ◇ *Please express your answer as a percentage.*

NOTE If we say **the percentage of sth**, we must use a singular verb: *The percentage of people with university degrees is increasing.* ➲ Look also at the note at **percent**[2].

**per·cen·tile** /pərˈsɛntaɪl/ ***noun*** [C, usually sing.] (*technical*) a number that expresses how well sb did on an exam, etc., in comparison to the other people who took the same exam: *I scored in the 85th percentile on the TOEFL* (= I did better than 85% of the other people).

**per·cep·ti·ble** /pərˈsɛptəbl/ ***adj.*** (*formal*) that can be seen or felt: *a barely perceptible change in color* OPP **imperceptible** ▶ **per·cep·ti·bly** /-əbli/ ***adv.***

**per·cep·tion** /pərˈsɛpʃn/ ***noun*** **1** [U] the ability to notice or understand sth **2** [C] a particular way of looking at or understanding sth; an opinion: *What is your perception of the situation?* ➲ verb perceive

**per·cep·tive** /pərˈsɛptɪv/ ***adj.*** (*formal*) quick to notice or understand things ▶ **per·cep·tive·ly** ***adv.***

**perch**[1] /pərtʃ/ ***noun*** [C] **1** a branch (or a bar in a cage) where a bird sits **2** a high position where sb can sit: *From our perch on the hill, we had a good view of the parade.* **3** (*pl.* **perch**) a fish that lives in rivers and lakes and is sometimes used for food

**perch**[2] /pərtʃ/ ***verb*** **1** [I] (used about a bird) to rest on a branch, etc. **2** [I,T] to sit, or be put, on a high place or on the edge of sth: *The house was perched on the edge of a cliff.* ◇ *He perched on a stool at the end of the bar.*

**per·co·la·tor** /ˈpərkəleɪt̬ər/ ***noun*** [C] a pot for making coffee, in which boiling water is forced up a central tube and then comes down again through the coffee ➲ picture at **coffee**.

**per·cus·sion** /pərˈkʌʃn/ ***noun*** [U, sing.] the section of an orchestra that consists of the drums and other instruments that you play by hitting them

**per·en·ni·al** /pəˈrɛniəl/ ***adj.*** that happens often or that lasts for a long time: *the perennial problem of poverty in the inner cities*

**the per·fect** /ˈpərfɪkt/ ***noun*** [sing.] the PERFECT[1] (3) tense: *the present/past perfect*

★**per·fect**[1] /ˈpərfɪkt/ ***adj.*** **1** as good as can be; without fault: *The car is two years old, but it is still in perfect condition.* ◇ *Nobody is perfect!* ◇ *These shoes are a perfect fit.* ◇ *What perfect weather!* ◇ *a perfect score on a quiz* **2 perfect (for sb/sth)** very suitable or right: *Ken would be perfect for the job.*

◇ *Orlando is the perfect place for a family vacation.* ◇ *the perfect solution to a problem* **3** (used to describe the tense of a verb that is formed with *has/have/had* and the past participle) **4** (only *before* a noun) complete; total: *What he was saying made perfect sense to me.* ◇ *a perfect stranger*

**per·fect**[2] /pərˈfɛkt/ ***verb*** [T] to make sth PERFECT[1]: *Derek is spending a year in France to perfect his French.*

**per·fec·tion** /pərˈfɛkʃn/ ***noun*** [U] the state of being PERFECT[1] or without fault: *Perfection is impossible to achieve.* ◇ *The steak was cooked to perfection.*

**per·fec·tion·ist** /pərˈfɛkʃn·ɪst/ ***noun*** [C] a person who always does things as well as he/she possibly can and who expects others to do the same

★**per·fect·ly** /ˈpərfɪktli/ ***adv.*** **1** in a PERFECT[1] (1) way: *He played the piece of music perfectly.* **2** very; completely: *Laura understood perfectly well what I meant.*

**per·fo·rate** /ˈpərfəreɪt/ ***verb*** [T] to make a hole or holes in sth: *Tear along the perforated line.* ▶ **per·fo·ra·tion** ***noun*** [C, usually pl.]: *Tear the sheet of stamps along the perforations.*

★**per·form** /pərˈfɔrm/ ***verb*** **1** [T] to do a piece of work or sth that you have been ordered to do: *Doctors performed an emergency operation.* ◇ *to perform a task* **2** [I,T] to take part in a play, or to sing, dance, etc. in front of an audience: *She is currently performing on Broadway.* ◇ *Children performed square dances for the visiting president.* ◇ *This play has never been performed previously.* **3** [I] (used about a machine, etc.) to work: *The car performs badly in cold weather.*

★**per·form·ance** /pərˈfɔrməns/ ***noun*** **1** [sing.] (*formal*) doing sth: *the performance of your duties* **2** [C] sth that you PERFORM (2) in front of an audience: *a live performance by Celine Dion* ◇ *a performance of one of Shakespeare's plays* **3** [C] the way in which you do sth, especially how successful you are: *The company's performance was disappointing last year.* ◇ *The Yankees' fine performance in the World Series* **4** [U] (used about a machine, etc.) the ability to work well: *This car has a high-performance engine.*

★**per·form·er** /pərˈfɔrmər/ ***noun*** [C] a person who PERFORMS (2) in front of an audience

**per·fume** /pərˈfyum/ ***noun*** [C,U] **1** a liquid with a sweet smell that women put on their bodies to make themselves smell nice: *You're wearing too much perfume.* **2** a pleasant smell

★**per·haps** /pərˈhæps/ ***adv.*** (*formal*) (used when you are not sure about sth) maybe; possibly: *She was, perhaps, one of the most famous writers of the time.* ◇ *This is an excellent restaurant, though perhaps not the best in the city.*

> NOTE **Perhaps** and **maybe** are similar in meaning. They are often used to make what you are saying sound more polite. **Perhaps** is more formal than **maybe**: *Perhaps you would like to join us for dinner sometime?* ◇ *Maybe I ought to go.*

**per·il** /ˈpɛrəl/ ***noun*** (*formal*) **1** [U] great danger **2** [C] sth that is very dangerous: *the perils of drug use* SYN **Danger** is more common.

**per·il·ous** /ˈpɛrələs/ ***adj.*** (*formal*) dangerous SYN **Dangerous** is more common.

**pe·rim·e·ter** /pəˈrɪmət̬ər/ ***noun*** [C] the outside edge or boundary of an area of land: *the perimeter fence of the army camp*

★**pe·ri·od** /ˈpɪriəd/ ***noun*** [C] **1** a length of time: *The plan will be in effect for a six-month trial period.* ◇ *Her son is going through a difficult period right now.* ◇ *The play is set in the colonial period in New England.* ◇ *Camels can go for long periods without water.* **2** one of the equal lengths of time that the school day is divided into: *I have English during second period.* **3** the monthly loss of blood from a woman's body: *My period started this morning.* **4** a mark (.) that is used when you are writing to show the end of a sentence, etc.

IDM **... period.** (used when you are speaking to emphasize a fact or an opinion that you are not willing to discuss anymore): *No late papers will be accepted, period.*

**pe·ri·od·ic** /ˌpɪriˈɑdɪk/ ***adj.*** happening fairly regularly ▶ **pe·ri·od·i·cal·ly** /-kli/ ***adv.***: *All machines need to be checked periodically.*

**pe·ri·od·i·cal** /ˌpɪriˈɑdɪkl/ ***noun*** [C] (*formal*) a magazine that is produced at regular intervals

**the ˌperiodic ˈtable** ***noun*** [sing.] a list of all the chemical elements, arranged according to the number of parts with a positive electric charge (**protons**) that they each have in their center (**nucleus**)

**pe·riph·er·al**[1] /pəˈrɪfərəl/ ***adj.*** **peripheral (to sth)** **1** (*formal*) not as important as the main aim or part of sth: *Fundraising is peripheral to their main activities.* **2** (*technical*) connected with the outer edge of a particular area: *peripheral vision* **3** (*computing*) (used about equipment) connected to a computer: *a peripheral device*

**pe·riph·er·al**[2] /pəˈrɪfərəl/ ***noun*** [C] (*computing*) a piece of equipment that is connected to a computer: *monitors, printers and other peripherals*

**pe·riph·er·y** /pəˈrɪfəri/ ***noun*** [C, usually sing.] (*pl.* **pe·riph·er·ies**) (*formal*) **1** the outer edge of a particular area: *industrial development **on the periphery of** the town* ◇ *The condition makes it difficult for patients to see objects at the periphery of their vision.* **2** the less important part of sth, for example of a particular activity or of a social or political group: *minor parties **on the periphery of** American politics*

**per·ish** /ˈpɛrɪʃ/ ***verb*** [I] (*formal*) to die or be destroyed: *Thousands perished in the war.*

**per·ish·a·ble** /ˈpɛrɪʃəbl/ ***adj.*** (used about food) that will go bad quickly

**per·ju·ry** /ˈpərdʒəri/ ***noun*** [U] the crime of telling a lie (in a court of law)

**perk**[1] /pərk/ ***verb***

PHR V **perk up** to become more cheerful or lively **perk sb/sth up** to make sb/sth more cheerful or lively

**perk**[2] /pərk/ ***noun*** [C] something extra that you get from your employer in addition to your salary: *International travel is one of the perks of the job.*

**perk·y** /ˈpərki/ ***adj.*** (**perk·i·er**; **perk·i·est**) lively and cheerful: *a perky TV show host*

**perm** /pərm/ (*also old-fashioned* **permanent**) ***noun*** [C] a treatment of the hair with special chemicals in order to give it curls or waves ▸ **perm** *verb* [T]: *She had her hair permed.*

**per·ma·frost** /'pərməfrɔst/ *noun* [U] (*technical*) a layer of soil that is permanently frozen, in very cold regions of the world

★**per·ma·nent**[1] /'pərmənənt/ *adj.* lasting for a long time or forever; that will not change: *The accident left him with a permanent scar.* ◇ *Are you looking for a permanent or a temporary job?* ▸ **per·ma·nence** /-nəns/ *noun* [U] ▸ **per·ma·nent·ly** *adv.*: *Is she gone permanently?*

**per·ma·nent**[2] /'pərmənənt/ *noun* [C] (*old-fashioned*) = PERM

ˌ**Permanent** ˈ**Resident** ˌ**Card** (*also* ˈ**Maple Leaf** ˌ**Card**) *noun* [C] (*Cdn*) an official card that shows that sb from another country is allowed to live and work in Canada

**per·mis·si·ble** /pər'mɪsəbl/ *adj.* (*formal*) that is allowed (by the rules): *They have been exposed to radiation above the permissible level.*

★**per·mis·sion** /pər'mɪʃn/ *noun* [U] the act of allowing sb to do sth: *You can't leave without permission.* ◇ *Children under 18 need their parents' permission to attend.* ◇ *to ask permission for sth* ◇ *to give permission for sth* ◇ *The refugees have been refused permission to stay in this country.*

NOTE Be careful. **Permission** is uncountable. A piece of paper that says that you are allowed to do something is a **permit**.

**per·mis·sive** /pər'mɪsɪv/ *adj.* having, allowing or showing a lot of freedom, especially in sexual matters: *the permissive society of the 1960s*

P

★**per·mit**[1] /pər'mɪt/ *verb* (*formal*) (**per·mit·ting**; **per·mit·ted**) **1** [T] to allow sth: *Food and drink are not permitted in this building.* ◇ *You are not permitted to smoke in the hospital.* ◇ *His visa does not permit him to work.* ➲ Look at the note at **allow**. **2** [I,T] to make possible: *The game will start at 2:00, weather permitting.*

**per·mit**[2] /'pərmɪt/ *noun* [C] an official piece of paper that says you are allowed to do sth: *a work permit* ◇ *a parking permit*

**per·ox·ide** /pə'rɑksaɪd/ (*also* **hy·dro·gen per·oxi·de**) *noun* [U] a clear liquid used to kill bacteria and to make hair lighter in color (**bleach it**): *a woman with peroxide blonde hair*

**per·pen·dic·u·lar** /ˌpərpən'dɪkyələr/ *adj.* **1 perpendicular (to sth)** at an angle of 90° to sth ➲ Look at **horizontal**, **vertical** and **parallel**. **2** pointing straight up; not leaning to either side

**per·pe·trate** /'pərpətreɪt/ *verb* [T] (*formal*) to do sth that is wrong or illegal ▸ **per·pe·tra·tor** /-treɪt̬ər/ *noun* [C]: *The police have arrested the perpetrators.*

**per·pet·u·al** /pər'pɛtʃuəl/ *adj.* (*formal*) not stopping or changing: *They lived in perpetual fear of losing their jobs.* ◇ *the perpetual roar of traffic*

**per·pet·u·al·ly** /pər'pɛtʃuəli; -tʃəli/ *adv.* always: *a company that is perpetually in debt*

**per·pet·u·ate** /pər'pɛtʃueɪt/ *verb* [T] (*formal*) to cause sth to continue

**per·plexed** /pər'plɛkst/ *adj.* not understanding sth; confused

**per se** /pər 'seɪ/ *adv.* (used to show that you are referring to sth on its own, rather than in connection with other things): *The drug is not harmful per se, but is dangerous when taken with alcohol.*

**per·se·cute** /'pərsəkyut/ *verb* [T] to cause sb to suffer, especially because of what he/she believes ▸ **per·se·cu·tion** /ˌpərsə'kyuʃn/ *noun* [C,U]: *the persecution of minorities* ▸ **per·se·cu·tor** /'pərsəkyut̬ər/ *noun* [C]

**per·se·vere** /ˌpərsə'vɪr/ *verb* [I] **persevere (in/with sth)** to continue trying or having sth that is difficult: *The treatment is painful, but I'm going to persevere with it.* ▸ **per·se·ver·ance** /ˌpərsə'vɪrəns/ *noun* [U]: *It takes a lot of perseverance to become a champion at any sport.*

**per·sist** /pər'sɪst/ *verb* [I] **1** to continue to exist: *If your symptoms persist, you should consult your doctor.* **2 persist (in sth/in doing sth)** (*formal*) to continue doing sth even though other people say that you are wrong or that you cannot do it: *We will persist in our efforts to get rid of gangs in our neighborhood.*

**per·sist·ent** /pər'sɪstənt/ *adj.* **1** continuing to do sth even though people say that you are wrong or that you cannot do it: *Some salespeople can be very persistent.* **2** lasting for a long time or happening often: *a persistent cough* ◇ *persistent rain* ▸ **per·sist·ence** /-əns/ *noun* [U]: *Thanks to her persistence, she finally got what she wanted.* ◇ *the persistence of unemployment* ▸ **per·sist·ent·ly** *adv.*

★**per·son** /'pərsn/ *noun* (*pl.* **peo·ple** or **per·sons**) ➲ Look at the note at **people**. **1** [C] a man, woman or child: *I would like to speak to the person in charge.* **2** [C] (*informal*) (usually *after* another noun) somebody who likes or is interested in the thing mentioned: *I'm not really much of a sports person.* ◇ *a computer person* **3** [sing.] one of the three types of pronoun in grammar. *I/we* are the first person, *you* is the second person and *he/she/it/they* are the third person.

IDM **in person** seeing or speaking to sb face to face (not speaking on the telephone or writing a letter): *I went to apologize to her in person.*

**-per·son** /'pərsn/ *combining form* someone who has a particular job or role, especially when it could be either a man or a woman: *a salesperson* ◇ *the chairperson of a committee* ◇ *a pizza delivery person*

**per·so·na** /pər'soʊnə/ *noun* [C] (*pl.* **per·so·nae** /-ni/ or **per·so·nas**) (*formal*) the aspects of a person's character that he/she shows to other people, especially when his/her real character is different: *His public persona is very different from the family man described in the book.*

**per·son·a·ble** /'pərsənəbl/ *adj.* (used about a person) attractive to other people because of having a pleasant appearance and character: *The salesclerk was a very personable young man.*

★**per·son·al**[1] /'pərsənl/ *adj.*

➤ YOUR OWN **1** (only *before* a noun) of or belonging to a particular person: *Judges should not let their personal feelings influence their decisions.* ◇ *a personal savings account*

➤ FEELINGS/HEALTH/RELATIONS **2** connected with your feelings, health, relations with other people, etc.: *I would like to speak to you in private. I have*

*something personal to discuss.* ◇ *The letter was marked "personal," so I did not open it.*
➤NOT OFFICIAL **3** (only *before* a noun) connected with your private life and not with your work: *Employees are not allowed to make personal calls during office hours.* ◇ *Maybe Julie can arrange a meeting with the senator – she's a personal friend of his.* ◇ *Do you have a good personal relationship with your boss?*
➤DONE BY PERSON **4** (only *before* a noun) done or made by a particular person: *The president made a personal visit to the victims in the hospital.*
➤OFFENSIVE **5** speaking about sb's appearance or character in an unkind or unfriendly way: *It started as a general discussion, but then people started making personal remarks and an argument began.*
➤CONNECTED WITH BODY **6** (only *before* a noun) connected with the body: *personal hygiene*

**per·son·al²** /ˈpərsn·l/ ***noun*** [C] = PERSONAL AD

**ˌpersonal ˈad** (*also* **per·son·al**) ***noun*** [C] (*informal*) a private advertisement or message that is placed in a newspaper, especially by sb who is looking for a romantic partner

**ˌpersonal comˈputer** ***noun*** [C] = PC[1]

★**per·son·al·i·ty** /ˌpərsəˈnælət̬i/ ***noun*** (*pl.* **per·son·al·i·ties**) **1** [C] the qualities and features of a person: *Joe has a very forceful personality.* **2** [C] a famous person (especially in sports, on television, etc.): *a television personality* **3** [U] the quality of having a strong, interesting and attractive character: *A good entertainer needs a lot of personality.*

**per·son·al·ize** /ˈpərsənəlaɪz/ ***verb*** [T] (often passive) **1** to mark sth with your name, etc. to show that it belongs to you: *a car with personalized license plates* **2** to make sth suitable for a particular person: *a computer service that offers personalized vacation planning*

★**per·son·al·ly** /ˈpərsənəli/ ***adv.*** **1** in person, not with sb else acting for you: *I would like to deal with this matter personally.* **2** (used for expressing your own opinions): *Personally, I think that nurses deserve more money.* **3** as a person: *I wasn't talking about you personally – I meant all teachers.* ◇ *The ship's captain was held personally responsible for the accident.*

**ˌpersonal ˈpronoun** ***noun*** [C] (*grammar*) any of the pronouns *I, me, she, her, he, him, we, us, you, they, them.*

**ˈpersonals ˌcolumn** ***noun*** [C, usually pl.] a section of newspaper in which personal ads and private messages are published

**ˌpersonal ˈstereo** ***noun*** [C] a small CD or cassette player with headphones that you carry with you and use while you are moving around

**ˌpersonal ˈtrainer** ***noun*** [C] a person whose job is to help sb exercise, especially by deciding what types of exercise are best for him/her

**per·son·i·fi·ca·tion** /pərˌsɑnəfəˈkeɪʃn/ ***noun*** [C, usually sing.] **the personification of sth** a person who has a lot of a particular quality or characteristic: *She was the personification of evil.*

**per·son·i·fy** /pərˈsɑnəfaɪ/ ***verb*** [T] (*pres. part.* **per·son·i·fy·ing**; *3rd person sing. pres.* **per·son·i·fies**; *pt, pp* **per·son·i·fied**) **1** to be an example in human form of a particular quality **2** to describe sth as if it were a person, e.g. in a poem

**per·son·nel** /ˌpərsəˈnɛl/ ***noun*** **1** [pl.] the people who work for a large company or organization: *The army cannot afford to lose qualified personnel.* **2** [U] (*also* **personˈnel department**) = HUMAN RESOURCES

**per·spec·tive** /pərˈspɛktɪv/ ***noun*** **1** [U] the art of drawing on a flat surface so that some objects appear to be farther away than others: *the laws of perspective* **2** [C,U] the way that you think about sth; your point of view: *If you go away for a few days, you will see everything from a new perspective.*
IDM **keep/put sth in perspective** to recognize what is really important and what is not important in a particular situation: *Let's try to keep things in perspective here – it's not a complete disaster.*

**per·spi·ra·tion** /ˌpərspəˈreɪʃn/ ***noun*** [U] (*formal*) **1** the act of perspiring **2** the liquid that you lose through your skin: *a drop of perspiration* SYN **Sweat** is more common. ➲ Look also at **antiperspirant**.

**per·spire** /pərˈspaɪər/ ***verb*** [I] (*formal*) to lose liquid through your skin SYN **Sweat** is more common.

★**per·suade** /pərˈsweɪd/ ***verb*** [T] **1 persuade sb (to do sth)** to cause sb to do sth by giving him/her good reasons: *It was difficult to persuade Louise to change her mind.* OPP **dissuade** **2 persuade sb (of sth); persuade sb (that...)** to cause sb to believe sth: *The jury was persuaded of her innocence.* ◇ *The attorney persuaded the jury that she was innocent.* ➲ Look at **convince**.

**per·sua·sion** /pərˈsweɪʒn/ ***noun*** **1** [U] persuading or being persuaded: *It took a lot of persuasion to get Alan to agree.* **2** [C] (*formal*) a religious or political belief: *There were people of every political persuasion at the meeting.*

**per·sua·sive** /pərˈsweɪsɪv/ ***adj.*** able to make sb do or believe sth: *The arguments were very persuasive.* ▸ **per·sua·sive·ly** ***adv.*** ▸ **per·sua·sive·ness** ***noun*** [U]

**per·tain** /pərˈteɪn/ ***verb*** [I] **pertain to sth** (*formal*) to be directly connected with sth: *documents pertaining to a court case*

**per·ti·nent** /ˈpərtn·ənt/ ***adj.*** **pertinent (to sth)** directly connected with sth: *to ask a pertinent question*

**per·turb** /pərˈtərb/ ***verb*** [T] (*formal*) to make sb worried or anxious: *Her sudden appearance did not seem to perturb him in the least.* ◇ *I was perturbed by his lack of interest.* SYN **alarm** ▸ **per·turbed** ***adj.*** **perturbed (at/about sth)**: *She didn't seem perturbed at the change of plan.* OPP **unperturbed**

**pe·ruse** /pəˈruz/ ***verb*** [T] (*formal*) to read sth, especially in a careful way: *A copy of the report is available for you to peruse at your leisure.* ▸ **pe·ru·sal** ***noun*** [U, sing.]: *a brief/casual perusal of a document*

**per·vade** /pərˈveɪd/ ***verb*** [T] (*formal*) to spread through and be noticeable in every part of sth: *a pervading mood of fear* ◇ *the sadness that pervades most of her novels*

**per·va·sive** /pərˈveɪsɪv/ ***adj.*** that is present in all parts of sth: *a pervasive mood of pessimism and gloom*

**per·verse** /pərˈvərs/ ***adj.*** (*formal*) having or

P

showing behavior that is not reasonable or that upsets other people: *Derek gets perverse pleasure from shocking his parents.* ▶ **per·verse·ly** *adv.* ▶ **per·ver·si·ty** *noun* [U]

**per·ver·sion** /pər'vərʒn/ *noun* [C,U] **1** the changing of sth from right to wrong or good to bad: *That statement is a perversion of the truth.* **2** sexual behavior that is unnatural or not acceptable

**per·vert¹** /'pərvərt/ *noun* [C] a person whose sexual behavior is not natural or normal

**per·vert²** /pər'vərt/ *verb* [T] to change sth so that it becomes bad or is used wrongly: *to pervert the original meaning of a document*

**per·vert·ed** /pər'vərṭəd/ *adj.* not thought to be normal or acceptable by most people: *sexual acts, both normal and perverted* ◇ *They clearly take a perverted delight in watching others suffer.*

**pes·ky** /'pɛski/ *adj.* (**pes·ki·er**; **pes·ki·est**) (*informal*) annoying and not going away: *These pesky mosquitoes won't leave me alone!*

**pe·so** /'peɪsoʊ/ *noun* [C] (*pl.* **pe·sos**) the unit of money in many Latin American countries and the Philippines

**pes·si·mism** /'pɛsəmɪzəm/ *noun* [U] the state of expecting or believing that bad things will happen OPP **optimism**

**pes·si·mist** /'pɛsəmɪst/ *noun* [C] a person who always thinks that what is going to happen will be bad OPP **optimist** ▶ **pes·si·mis·tic** /ˌpɛsə'mɪstɪk/ *adj.* OPP **optimistic** ▶ **pes·si·mis·ti·cal·ly** /-kli/ *adv.*

**pest** /pɛst/ *noun* [C] **1** an insect or animal that destroys plants, food, etc.: *pest control* **2** (*informal*) a person or thing that annoys you

P

**pes·ter** /'pɛstər/ *verb* [T] to annoy or bother sb, e.g. by asking him/her sth many times: *to pester sb for money*

**pes·ti·cide** /'pɛstəsaɪd/ *noun* [C,U] a chemical substance that is used for killing animals or insects that eat food crops ➲ Look at **insecticide**.

**pes·to** /'pɛstoʊ/ *noun* [U] an Italian sauce made with the leaves of an herb (**basil**) and olive oil

★ **pet¹** /pɛt/ *noun* [C] an animal that you keep in your home for company or for pleasure: *a pet guinea pig* ◇ *to have/own a pet* ➲ Look also at **teacher's pet**.

**pet²** /pɛt/ *verb* (**pet·ting**; **pet·ted**) [T] to rub an animal in a loving way: *Can I pet your dog?*

**pet³** /pɛt/ *adj.* (only *before* a noun) that you are very interested in: *his pet subject/theory/project*

IDM **sb's pet peeve** something that you particularly dislike

**pet·al** /'pɛṭl/ *noun* [C] one of the thin soft colored parts of a flower

**pe·ter** /'piṭər/ *verb*

PHR V **peter out** to finish or come to an end gradually: *The flow of water slowed down and finally petered out.*

**pe·tite** /pə'tit/ *adj.* (used about a girl, woman or her figure) small and thin: *a petite blonde*

**pe·ti·tion¹** /pə'tɪʃn/ *noun* [C] a written document, signed by many people, that asks a government, etc. to do sth: *More than 50,000 area residents signed the petition protesting against the new waste dump.*

**pe·ti·tion²** /pə'tɪʃn/ *verb* [I,T] **1 petition sb (for sth)** to make a formal request to sb in authority, especially by sending him/her a petition: *Local residents have successfully petitioned against the building of a prison in their area.* ◇ *The group intends to petition Congress for reform of the law.* ◇ *Residents petitioned the City to rename the street.* **2 petition (sb) (for sth)** to formally ask for sth in a court of law: *to petition for divorce*

**pe·tri·fied** /'pɛtrəfaɪd/ *adj.* **1** very frightened: *I'm petrified of snakes.* SYN **terrified** **2** (only *before* a noun) petrified trees, insects, etc. have died and been changed into stone over a very long period of time: *a petrified forest*

**pe·tro·le·um** /pə'troʊliəm/ *noun* [U] oil that is found under the surface of the earth and that is used for making gasoline and other types of chemical substances

**peˌtroleum 'jelly** (*also* **pet·ro·la·tum** /ˌpɛtrə'leɪṭəm/) *noun* [U] a soft clear substance obtained from petroleum, used to heal injuries on the skin or to make machine parts move together more smoothly

**pet·ti·coat** /'pɛṭikoʊt/ *noun* [C] (*old-fashioned*) a piece of women's underwear like a thin dress or skirt, worn under a dress or skirt SYN **slip**

**'petting zoo** *noun* [C] a park containing many kinds of animals that children can touch

**pet·ty** /'pɛṭi/ *adj.* **1** small or not important: *He didn't want to get involved with the petty details.* ◇ *petty crime* **2** unkind or unpleasant (for a reason that does not seem very important): *He tried so hard that it would be petty to criticize him now.*

**ˌpetty 'cash** *noun* [U] a small amount of money kept in an office for small payments

**pew** /pyu/ *noun* [C] one of the long seats in a church

**pew·ter** /'pyuṭər/ *noun* [U] a gray metal made by mixing the metals tin and lead together, used especially in the past for making cups, dishes, etc.; objects made from pewter: *a pewter tankard*

**PG** /ˌpi 'dʒi/ *abbr.* parental guidance (used about movies that may not be suitable for young children to see)

**pg.** *abbr.* (*written*) = PAGE¹ (1)

**PG-13** /ˌpi dʒi ˌθər'tin/ *abbr.* (used about movies that may not be suitable for children under age 13 to see): *a PG-13 movie*

**pH** /ˌpi 'eɪtʃ/ *noun* [sing.] (in chemistry) a measurement of the level of acid or alkali in a solution or substance: *a pH of 7.5* ◇ *to test the pH level of the soil*

NOTE In the pH range of 0 to 14, a value below 7 shows an **acid** and above 7 shows an **alkali**.

**phan·tom** /'fæntəm/ *noun* [C] **1** something with the shape of a dead person that seems to appear on earth and behave as if it were alive SYN **Ghost** is a more common word. **2** something that you think exists, but that is not real: *phantom aircraft on a radar screen*

**Phar·aoh** /'fɛroʊ; 'feɪroʊ/ (*also* **phar·aoh**) *noun* a ruler of ancient Egypt

**Phar·ma·care** /'fɑrməkɛr/ *noun* [U] (*Cdn*) (in some provinces) a system in which the government pays sth toward the price of medicinal drugs, in order to keep prices low

**phar·ma·ceu·ti·cal**[1] /ˌfɑrməˈsuṭɪkl/ ***adj.*** connected with the production of medicines: *the pharmaceutical industry*

**phar·ma·ceu·ti·cal**[2] /ˌfɑrməˈsuṭɪkl/ ***noun*** [usually pl.] (*technical*) a drug or medicine: *the development of new pharmaceuticals*

**phar·ma·cist** /ˈfɑrməsɪst/ ***noun*** [C] a person whose job is to prepare and sell medicines

**phar·ma·cy** /ˈfɑrməsi/ ***noun*** [C] (*pl.* **phar·ma·cies**) a place where medicines are prepared and sold

★**phase**[1] /feɪz/ ***noun*** [C] a period in the development of sth: *the final phase of construction* ◇ *to enter a new phase*

**phase**[2] /feɪz/ ***verb***

PHR V **phase sth in** to introduce sth slowly or over a period of time: *The wage increases were phased in over three years.*

**phase sth out** to take away or remove sth slowly or over a period of time: *The older machines are gradually being phased out and replaced by new ones.*

**phat** /fæt/ ***adj.*** (**phat·ter**; **phat·test**) (*slang*) excellent

**Ph.D.** /ˌpi eɪtʃ ˈdi/ ***abbr.*** Doctor of Philosophy; the highest university degree that you can earn: *She has a Ph.D. in history.* ◇ *Richard Cruz, Ph.D.* ➲ For more information on the North American eductional systems, look at study pages **A8-A9**.

**pheas·ant** /ˈfɛznt/ ***noun*** [C,U] (*pl.* **pheas·ants** or **pheas·ant**) a type of bird with a long tail. The males have brightly colored feathers. Pheasants are often hunted and eaten as food. The meat of this bird is also called pheasant.

**phe·nom·e·nal** /fəˈnɑmənl/ ***adj.*** unusual because it is so good or so great: *phenomenal success* ▸ **phe·nom·e·nal·ly** /-nəli/ ***adv.***

**phe·nom·e·non** /fəˈnɑmənən; -nɑn/ ***noun*** [C] **1** (*pl.* **phe·nom·e·na** /-ənə/) something that happens or exists (often sth unusual): *Acid rain is not a natural phenomenon. It is caused by pollution.* **2** (*pl.* **phe·nom·e·nons**) (*informal*) a person or thing that has a lot of ability or is very successful: *golfing phenomenon Tiger Woods*

**phi** /faɪ/ ***noun*** [C] (*symbol* Φ, ϕ) the twenty-first letter of the Greek alphabet ➲ Look at the note at **fraternity**.

**phi·lan·thro·pist** /fəˈlænθrəpɪst/ ***noun*** [C] a rich person who helps the poor and those in need, especially by giving money: *The money was given by businessman and philanthropist, George Soros.*

**phi·lan·thro·py** /fəˈlænθrəpi/ ***noun*** [U] the practice of helping the poor and those in need, especially by giving money: *Hospitals were built as a result of private philanthropy and government intervention.* ▸ **phi·lan·thro·pic** /ˌfɪlənˈθrɑpɪk/ ***adj.***: *philanthropic work*

**phil·is·tine** /ˈfɪləstin; fəˈlɪstin/ ***noun*** [C] a person who does not like or understand art, literature, music, etc.: *She dismissed critics of her work as philistines.* ▸ **phil·is·tine** ***adj.***: *philistine attitudes* ▸ **phil·is·tin·ism** /ˈfɪləstɪnɪzəm; fəˈlɪstɪnɪzəm/: *the philistinism of the vast majority of the population*

**phi·los·o·pher** /fəˈlɑsəfər/ ***noun*** [C] a person who has developed a set of ideas and beliefs about the meaning of life

**phil·o·soph·i·cal** /ˌfɪləˈsɑfɪkl/ ***adj.*** **1** of or concerning philosophy: *a philosophical debate* **2 philosophical (about sth)** having or showing a calm, quiet attitude when you are in danger or are suffering or disappointed: *The team captain was philosophical about their loss and praised the other team's skill.* ▸ **phil·o·soph·i·cal·ly** /-kli/ ***adv.***

★**phi·los·o·phy** /fəˈlɑsəfi/ ***noun*** (*pl.* **phi·los·o·phies**) **1** [U] the study of ideas and beliefs about the meaning of life **2** [C] a belief or set of beliefs that tries to explain the meaning of life or give rules about how to behave: *the philosophy of Nietzsche* ◇ *Her philosophy is "If a job's worth doing, it's worth doing well."*

**phlegm** /flɛm/ ***noun*** [U] the thick yellowish substance that is produced in your throat when you have a cough

**pho·bi·a** /ˈfoʊbiə/ ***noun*** [C] a very strong fear or dislike that you cannot explain

**phone**[1] /foʊn/ ***noun*** (*informal*) **1** [U] = TELEPHONE[1] (1): *to make a phone call* ◇ *What's your phone number?* ◇ *You can buy the tickets by phone.* **2** [C] = TELEPHONE[1] (2): *to answer the phone* ◇ *The phone is ringing – can you get* (= answer) *it?* ➲ Look also at **cellular phone**.

IDM **on the phone/telephone** using the telephone: *"Where's Rob?" "He's on the phone."*

**phone**[2] /foʊn/ ***verb*** [I,T] = TELEPHONE[2] [T]: *Could you phone the restaurant and make a reservation?* ➲ **Call** is more common than **phone**.

ˈ**phone book** ***noun*** [C] = TELEPHONE BOOK

ˈ**phone booth** (*also* ˈ**telephone booth**) ***noun*** [C] a small place that is partly enclosed, containing a public telephone, in a hotel, restaurant, in the street, etc.

ˈ**phone card** ***noun*** [C] a card that you pay for in advance which allows you to make a call from any telephone

**pho·net·ic** /fəˈnɛṭɪk/ ***adj.*** **1** connected with the sounds of human speech **2** using a system for writing a language that has a different sign for each sound: *the phonetic alphabet* ▸ **pho·net·i·cal·ly** /-kli/ ***adv.***

**pho·net·ics** /fəˈnɛṭɪks/ ***noun*** [U] the study of the sounds of human speech

**pho·nics** /ˈfɑnɪks/ ***noun*** [U] a method of teaching people to read based on the sounds that letters represent

**pho·no·graph** /ˈfoʊnəgræf/ ***noun*** [C] (*old-fashioned*) = RECORD PLAYER

**pho·ny**[1] /ˈfoʊni/ ***adj.*** not real; false

**pho·ny**[2] /ˈfoʊni/ ***noun*** [C] (*pl.* **pho·nies**) a person who is not what he/she pretends to be

★**pho·to** /ˈfoʊṭoʊ/ ***noun*** [C] (*pl.* **pho·tos** /-ṭoʊz/) (*informal*) = PHOTOGRAPH[1]

**pho·to·cop·i·er** /ˈfoʊṭəkɑpiər/ ***noun*** [C] (*formal*) = COPIER

**pho·to·cop·y** /ˈfoʊṭəkɑpi/ ***noun*** [C] (*pl.*

P

pho·to·cop·ies) (*formal*) = COPY¹ (2) ▶ **pho·to·cop·y** *verb* [I,T] (*pres. part.* **pho·to·cop·y·ing**; *3rd person sing. pres.* **pho·to·cop·ies**; *pt, pp* **pho·to·cop·ied**)

**ˌphoto ˈfinish** *noun* [C, usually sing.] the end of a race in which the leading runners or horses are so close together that only a photograph of them passing the finishing line can show which is the winner

**pho·to·gen·ic** /ˌfoʊt̬əˈdʒɛnɪk/ *adj.* (used especially about a person) looking attractive in photographs: *I'm not very photogenic.*

★**pho·to·graph¹** /ˈfoʊt̬əgræf/ (*also* **photo**) *noun* [C] a picture that is taken with a camera: *to take a photo* ◇ *a color photograph* ◇ *to have a photo enlarged*

> NOTE We use **photograph** and **photo** especially when it is necessary to show a difference between pictures that were made with a camera and other types of pictures: *an exhibit of the artist's paintings and photographs.*

**pho·to·graph²** /ˈfoʊt̬əgræf/ *verb* [T] (*formal*) (often passive) to take a photograph of sb/sth: *Suzanne was never photographed with her glasses on.*

★**pho·tog·ra·pher** /fəˈtɑgrəfər/ *noun* [C] a person who takes photographs ➲ Look at **cameraman**.

**pho·to·graph·ic** /ˌfoʊt̬əˈgræfɪk/ *adj.* connected with photographs or photography: *photographic equipment*

★**pho·tog·ra·phy** /fəˈtɑgrəfi/ *noun* [U] the skill or process of taking photographs: *wildlife photography*

**pho·to·jour·nal·ism** /ˌfoʊt̬oʊˈdʒərnl·ɪzəm/ *noun* [U] the work of reporting news using mainly photographs, especially in a magazine

**ˈphoto opporˌtunity** *noun* [C] (*pl.* **ˈphoto opporˌtunities**) (*also informal* **ˈphoto op**) an event at which a politician or some other famous person appears, with the main purpose of allowing journalists to take photographs which show that person in a favorable or attractive way

**phras·al verb** /ˌfreɪzl ˈvərb/ *noun* [C] a verb that is combined with an adverb or a preposition to give a new meaning, such as "take over" or "call sb up"

★**phrase¹** /freɪz/ *noun* [C] a group of words that are used together. A phrase does not contain a full verb: *"First of all" and "a cup of coffee" are phrases.*

**phrase²** /freɪz/ *verb* [T] to express sth in a particular way: *The statement was phrased so that it would not offend anyone.*

**ˈphrase book** *noun* [C] a book containing lists of common expressions translated into another language, especially for people visiting a foreign country

**phys. ed.** (*also* **phys ed**) /ˌfɪz ˈɛd/ *noun* [U] = PHYSICAL EDUCATION

★**phys·i·cal¹** /ˈfɪzɪkl/ *adj.* **1** of or for your body: *physical exercise* ◇ *Parents must consider their children's physical and emotional needs.* **2** connected with real things that you can touch, or with the laws of nature: *physical geography* ◇ *It is a physical impossibility to be in two places at once.* **3** connected with physics ▶ **phys·i·cal·ly** /-kli/ *adv.*: *to be physically fit* ◇ *It will be physically impossible to fit all this stuff into the car.*

**phys·i·cal²** /ˈfɪzɪkl/ *noun* [C] an examination of your body by a doctor to check the condition of your general health: *to go for a physical*

**ˌphysical eduˈcation** *noun* [U] (*formal*) (*also* **P.E., phys. ed.**) a class in school in which you do physical exercises and play sports

**ˌphysical ˈtherapy** *noun* [U] the treatment of disease or injury by exercise, heat, etc. ▶ **ˌphysical ˈtherapist** *noun* [C]

**phy·si·cian** /fəˈzɪʃn/ *noun* [C] (*formal*) a medical doctor

**phys·i·cist** /ˈfɪzəsɪst/ *noun* [C] a person who is an expert in physics

**phys·ics** /ˈfɪzɪks/ *noun* [U] the scientific study of natural forces such as light, sound, heat, electricity, pressure, etc.

**phy·sique** /fəˈzik/ *noun* [C] the size and shape of a person's body: *a strong muscular physique*

**pi** /paɪ/ *noun* **1** [C] (*symbol* Π , π) the sixteenth letter of the Greek alphabet ➲ Look at the note at **fraternity**. **2** [sing.] (*technical*) (*symbol* π) (in geometry) the symbol used to show the ratio of the distance around a circle (its **circumference**) to the distance across (its **diameter**), that is about 3.14159

**pi·an·ist** /piˈænɪst; ˈpiənɪst/ *noun* [C] a person who plays the piano

★**pi·an·o** /piˈænoʊ/ *noun* [C] (*pl.* **pi·an·os** /-noʊz/) a large musical instrument that you play by pressing down black and white bars (keys). This causes small hammers to hit strings inside the instrument: *an upright piano* ◇ *a grand piano* ➲ picture at **keyboard**.

**pi·can·te** /pɪˈkɑnteɪ/ *adj.* (used about food) hot and spicy: *tortilla chips dipped in a picante sauce*

**pic·co·lo** /ˈpɪkəloʊ/ *noun* [C] (**pic·co·los**) a musical instrument like a small flute that plays high notes when you blow into it

★**pick¹** /pɪk/ *verb* [T] **1** to choose sb/sth from a group of people or things: *She picked her words carefully so she wouldn't upset anybody.* ◇ *to be picked to play for the team* ◇ *We picked a good day to go to the beach.* **2** to take a flower, fruit or vegetable from the place where it is growing: *I picked a bunch of flowers for you.* ◇ *Don't pick wild flowers.* ◇ *a freshly picked apple* **3** to remove a small piece or pieces from sth with your fingers: *Don't pick your nose!* ◇ *Don't pick all the nuts off the top of the cake.* ◇ *She picked a hair off her jacket.* **4** to open a lock without a key, e.g. with a piece of wire

IDM **pick a fight (with sb)** to start a fight with sb deliberately

**pick sb's pocket** to steal money, etc. from sb's pocket or bag

PHR V **pick on sb** to behave unfairly or unkindly toward sb

**pick sb/sth out** to choose or recognize sb/sth from a number of people or things: *You can go to the video store and pick out a movie to watch.* ◇ *I immediately picked Jean out in the picture.*

**pick up** to become better; to improve

**pick sb up 1** (*informal*) to start talking to sb you do not know and try to start a sexual relationship with him/her **2** (used about the police) to stop sb and question him/her: *The drug dealers were picked up downtown.*

**pick sb/sth up 1** to take hold of and lift sb/sth: *The phone stopped ringing just as I picked up the receiver.* ◇ *Lucy picked up the child and gave him a hug.* **2** to go and get sb/sth in a car, etc.: *My sister is coming to pick me up at 10:00.* ◇ *Can you pick up some stuff for supper on your way home?* **3** to hear or see sb/sth by means of a radio, television, etc.: *You can't pick up many stations on this cheap radio.*

**pick sth up 1** to put sth in its correct place, or to make a place clean and neat by doing this: *to pick up your toys* ◇ *Pick up your room before Grandma comes!* **2** to learn sth without formal lessons: *Joe picked up a lot of Spanish by playing with the neighborhood kids.*

**pick up on sth** to notice and understand sth and change your behavior based on this: *TV comedians were quick to pick up on the President's mistake and make jokes about him.*

**pick²** /pɪk/ ***noun* 1** [sing.] the one that you choose: *You can have whichever piece you want. Take your pick.* **2** [C, usually sing.] an act of choosing sth: *Jill got the first pick of the seats in the classroom.* **3** [C] a small piece of plastic that you use for playing a guitar **4** [C] (*also* **pickax** /ˈpɪkæks/) a tool that consists of a curved iron bar with sharp points at both ends, attached to a wooden handle. Picks are used for breaking rocks or hard ground.

**pick·er** /ˈpɪkər/ ***noun*** [C] a person whose job is to pick fruits or vegetables from trees, in fields, etc.: *tomato pickers*

**pick·et** /ˈpɪkət/ (*also* ˈ**picket line**) ***noun*** [C] a group of workers who stand or walk around, holding signs, in front of a factory, etc. during a protest (a strike) and try to persuade other people not to go in ▸ **pick·et** ***verb*** [I,T]

ˌ**picket** ˈ**fence** ***noun*** [C] a fence made from vertical sticks of wood that are pointed at the top

**pick·ings** /ˈpɪkɪŋz/ ***noun*** [pl.] something that can be gained from a particular situation, especially in an easy or a dishonest way: *Bring plenty to eat. It's* ***slim pickings*** *here.* ◇ *The strike affecting the country's largest airline is producing* ***easy pickings*** *for smaller companies.*

**pick·le** /ˈpɪkl/ ***noun*** [C,U] a cucumber that is put in vinegar or salt water to give it a sour taste: *a jar of pickles* ▸ **pick·le** ***verb*** [T]: *pickled onions*

**pick·pock·et** /ˈpɪkpɑkət/ ***noun*** [C] a person who steals things from other people's pockets or bags in public places

**pick·up** /ˈpɪkʌp/ ***noun* 1** (*also* ˈ**pickup truck**) [C] a type of light truck that has a large open part with low sides in the back ➲ picture at **truck**. **2** [C,U] an act of taking sth from a place in order to transport it to another place: *The mayor promised to increase garbage pickups and improve street maintenance.* ◇ *We offer free pickup and delivery in the local area.* **3** [C] an increase or improvement in sth: *a pickup in exports*

**pick·y** /ˈpɪki/ ***adj.*** (**pick·i·er**; **pick·i·est**) (*informal*) difficult to please: *a picky eater* ➲ Look at **fussy**.

★**pic·nic** /ˈpɪknɪk/ ***noun*** [C] a meal that you eat outdoors (in the country or on a beach, etc.): *a picnic lunch* ◇ *We had a picnic on the beach.*

IDM **be no picnic** (*informal*) to be difficult or unpleasant: *Being in the army is definitely no picnic!*

▸ **pic·nic** ***verb*** [I] (*pres. part.* **pic·nick·ing**; *pt, pp* **pic·nicked**)

**pic·to·ri·al** /pɪkˈtɔriəl/ ***adj.*** expressed in pictures

★**pic·ture¹** /ˈpɪktʃər/ ***noun* 1** [C] a painting, drawing or photograph: *Here's a picture of my brother.* ◇ *to draw/paint a picture* ◇ *Look at the picture on page 96 and describe what you see.* ◇ *Come and have your picture* (= photograph) *taken.* **2** [C] an idea or memory of sth in your mind: *Jack London's novels give a good picture of what life was like in the Alaskan wilderness.* **3** [C] the quality of what you see on a television: *I can't get a good picture on this TV.* ➲ Look also at **motion picture**.

IDM **get the picture** (*informal*) to understand a situation: *He just doesn't seem to get the picture.*

**in the picture/out of the picture** (*informal*) involved in a situation/no longer involved in a situation: *Now that Jenkins is out of the picture, Yamada will probably be chosen as the next manager.*

**pic·ture²** /ˈpɪktʃər/ ***verb*** [T] **1** to imagine sth in your mind: *Kevin used to be so wild. I can't picture him as a father.* **2** to make a picture of sb/sth: *The happy couple, pictured above, left for a honeymoon in Bali.*

**pic·tur·esque** /ˌpɪktʃəˈrɛsk/ ***adj.*** (usually used about a place) attractive and interesting: *a picturesque town on the coast*

**pie** /paɪ/ ***noun*** [C,U] a type of food made of a pastry case or shell which is filled with fruit and then baked: *apple pie* ◇ *a piece of pie*

**pie**

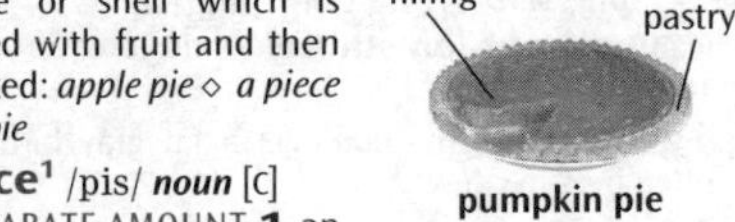


**pumpkin pie**

★**piece¹** /pis/ ***noun*** [C]

➤SEPARATE AMOUNT **1** an amount or example of sth: *a piece of paper* ◇ *a nice piece of furniture* ◇ *Would you like another piece of cake?* ◇ *a piece of advice* ◇ *a very interesting piece of information*

➤PART **2** one of the parts that sth is made of: *a 500-piece jigsaw puzzle* **3** one of the parts into which sth breaks: *The plate fell to the floor and smashed to pieces.*

➤IN CHESS, ETC. **4** one of the small objects that you use when you are playing indoor board games: *chess pieces*

➤NEWS ARTICLE **5** an article in a newspaper or magazine

➤SINGLE ITEM **6** a single work of art, music, etc.: *He played a piece by Chopin.*

IDM **give sb a piece of your mind** (*informal*) to criticize sb in an angry way

**go to pieces** to be unable to control yourself: *When his wife died, he seemed to go to pieces.*

**in one piece** not injured or broken: *He was in a car accident, but he came out of it in one piece.*

**a piece of cake** (*informal*) something that is very easy

**piece²** /pis/ ***verb***

PHR V **piece sth together 1** to put sth together from several pieces **2** to discover the truth about sth from different pieces of information

ˈ**pie chart** ***noun*** [C] a diagram consisting of a circle that is divided into sections to show the size of



P

particular amounts in relation to the whole ➲ picture at **graph**.

**pier** /pɪr/ ***noun*** [C] a large wooden, metal or concrete structure that is built out into the ocean. Boats can stop at piers so that people can get on or off and goods can be loaded or unloaded.

**pierce** /pɪrs/ ***verb*** [T] **1** to make a hole in sth with a sharp point: *Paul has had one ear pierced.* ◇ *The sharp thorns pierced the ball.* **2** (used about light or a sound) to be seen or heard suddenly: *A scream pierced the air.*

**pierc·ing¹** /ˈpɪrsɪŋ/ ***adj.*** **1** (used about the wind, pain, a loud noise, etc.) strong and unpleasant **2** (used about eyes or a look) seeming to know what you are thinking

**pierc·ing²** /ˈpɪrsɪŋ/ ***noun*** **1** [C] the hole that is made in your ear, nose or some other part of your body so that you can wear jewelry there: *She has a tongue piercing.* ➲ picture at **jewelry**. **2** [U] = BODY PIERCING

★**pig¹** /pɪg/ ***noun*** [C] **1** a fat animal with short legs and a curly tail that is kept on farms for its meat (pork)

> NOTE A male pig is called a **hog** or a **boar**, a female pig is a **sow** and a young pig is a **piglet**. When they make a noise, pigs **grunt**. ➲ Look at the note at **meat**.

**2** (*informal*) a dirty person, or a person who eats too much ➲ Look also at **guinea pig**.

**pig²** /pɪg/ ***verb*** [T] (**pig·ging; pigged**)
PHR V **pig out (on sth)** (*informal*) to eat or drink too much

**pi·geon** /ˈpɪdʒən/ ***noun*** [C] a fat gray bird that often lives in cities

**pi·geon·hole¹** /ˈpɪdʒənhoʊl/ ***noun*** [C] one of a set of small boxes that are fixed on a wall and open at the front, used for putting letters, messages, etc. in; one of a similar set of boxes that are part of a desk, used for keeping papers, documents, etc. in: *If you can't come, leave a note in my pigeonhole.*

**pi·geon·hole²** /ˈpɪdʒənhoʊl/ ***verb*** [T] **1 pigeonhole sb (as sth)** to decide that sb belongs to a particular group or type without thinking deeply enough about it and considering what other qualities he/she might have: *People try to pigeonhole him as a rapper, but this CD shows another side.* SYN **categorize**, **label**²(2) **2** to decide to deal with sth later or to forget it: *Plans for a new school have been pigeonholed.*

**pig·gy·back** /ˈpɪgibæk/ ***adj., adv.*** (used about a way of carrying sb) on sb's back: *to give sb a piggyback ride*

**pig·gy bank** /ˈpɪgi bæŋk/ ***noun*** [C] a small box, often shaped like a pig, that children use for saving money

**pig·let** /ˈpɪglət/ ***noun*** [C] a young pig

**pig·ment** /ˈpɪgmənt/ ***noun*** [C,U] a substance that gives color to things: *The color of your skin depends on the amount of pigment in it.*

**pig·pen** /ˈpɪgpɛn/ ***noun*** [C] (*also* **pig·sty**) **1** [C] a small building or an enclosed area where pigs are kept **2** [sing.] (*informal*) a very dirty or messy house or room

**pig·skin** /ˈpɪgskɪn/ ***noun*** [sing.] (*informal*) the ball used in football

**pig·sty** /ˈpɪgstaɪ/ ***noun*** (*pl.* **pig·sties**) = PIGPEN

**pig·swill** /ˈpɪgswɪl/ ***noun*** [U] = SWILL (1)

**pig·tail** /ˈpɪgteɪl/ ***noun*** [C] one of two pieces of hair that is tied together at the sides of sb's head

★**pile¹** /paɪl/ ***noun*** [C] **1** a number of things lying on top of one another, or an amount of sth that is in a large mass: *He always left his books in a neat pile.* ◇ *The truck dumped a large pile of sand in the road.*

> NOTE A **pile** may be neat or messy. A **heap** is not neat.

**2** (*informal*) a lot of sth: *I have piles of work to do this evening.* ◇ *She won a pile of money in the lottery.*

★**pile²** /paɪl/ ***verb*** [T] **1 pile sth (up)** to put things one on top of the other to form a PILE¹: *Pile them on top of each other.* **2 pile A on(to) B; pile B with A** to put a lot of sth on sth: *She piled the papers on the desk.* ◇ *The desk was piled with papers.*
PHR V **pile into sth/out of sth** (*informal*) to go in or out of sth in a disorganized way: *All the students tried to pile into the bus at the same time.*
**pile up 1** to increase in quantity: *The problems really piled up while I was away.* **2** (used about several cars, etc.) to crash into each other

**pile·up** /ˈpaɪlʌp/ ***noun*** [C] a crash that involves several cars, etc.

**pil·grim** /ˈpɪlgrəm/ ***noun*** [C] **1 Pilgrim** one of the group of people who came from England to the area that is now Massachusetts in 1620 **2** a person who travels to a holy place for religious reasons: *Many pilgrims visit Mecca every year.*

**pil·grim·age** /ˈpɪlgrəmɪdʒ/ ***noun*** [C,U] a trip that is made by a PILGRIM (2): *to make a pilgrimage to Lourdes*

**pill** /pɪl/ ***noun*** **1** [C] a small round piece of medicine that you swallow: *Take one pill, three times a day after meals.* ◇ *a sleeping pill* SYN **tablet** **2 the pill** [sing.] a pill that some women take regularly so that they do not become pregnant: *She is on the pill.*

**pil·lar** /ˈpɪlər/ ***noun*** [C] **1** a column of stone, wood or metal that is used for supporting part of a building **2** an important and active member of sth, who usually has strong moral values: *He is a real pillar of the community.*

**pil·low** /ˈpɪloʊ/ ***noun*** [C] a large cushion that you put under your head when you are in bed ➲ picture at **bed¹**.

**pil·low·case** /ˈpɪloʊkeɪs/ ***noun*** [C] a cover for a pillow, that can be removed

★**pi·lot¹** /ˈpaɪlət/ ***noun*** [C] a person who flies an aircraft: *Philip is an airline pilot.*

**pi·lot²** /ˈpaɪlət/ ***adj.*** (only *before* a noun) done as an experiment or to test sth: *The pilot program will run for six months, and then we will judge how successful it was.*

**pi·lot³** /ˈpaɪlət/ ***verb*** [T] **1** to act as the PILOT¹ of a vehicle **2** to guide or help sb/sth (through sth)

**pimp** /pɪmp/ ***noun*** [C] a man who controls prostitutes, finds customers for them and takes part of the money they earn

**pim·ple** /ˈpɪmpl/ (*also slang* **zit**) ***noun*** [C] a small red spot on your skin

**PIN** /pɪn/ (*also* ˈ**PIN number**) ***noun*** [C] personal identification number; a secret number that you use with a special card to get money from a cash machine (an ATM)

**pins**

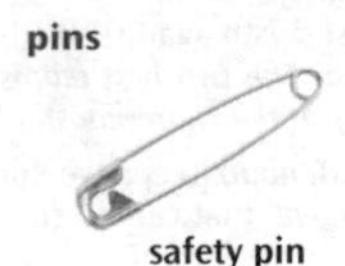

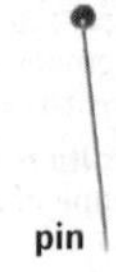

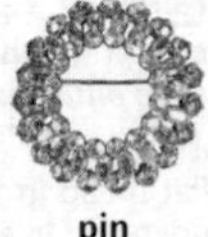

safety pin pin pin

★**pin**[1] /pɪn/ ***noun*** [C] **1** a short thin piece of metal with a round head at one end and a sharp point at the other. Pins are used for fastening together pieces of cloth, paper, etc. ➲ Look also at **clothespin**, **rolling pin** and **safety pin**. **2** a small piece of wood or metal that is used to fasten things together **3** a small piece of jewelry with a PIN (1) on the back that you wear on your shirt, jacket, etc. as a decoration **4** a wooden object, shaped like a bottle, that you try to knock over in the sport of bowling

★**pin**[2] /pɪn/ ***verb*** [T] (**pin·ning**; **pinned**) **pin sth to/on sth**; **pin sth together** to fasten sth with a PIN[1] or pins: *to pin a notice on the bulletin board* ◇ *The dress is just pinned together. I haven't sewn it yet.* ◇ (*figurative*) *The police officer held him with his arms pinned to his sides.* ◇ (*figurative*) *All our hopes are pinned on her.*

PHRV **pin sb/sth against/under sth** to keep sb/sth in one position so that it is impossible to move: *He was pinned under the fallen tree.* ◇ *to be pinned against a wall*

**pin sb down 1** to cause sb to be unable to move **2** to make sb decide sth or say exactly what he/she is going to do: *Can you pin her down and find out what time she will be coming?*

**pin sth down** to describe or explain exactly what sth is

**pi·ña·ta** (*also* **pi·na·ta**) /pɪnˈyɑt̬ə; pin-/ ***noun*** [C] a brightly decorated figure, filled with toys and candy, which children try to hit with a stick with their eyes covered (**blindfolded**) in order to break it open as a party game

**pin·ball** /ˈpɪnbɔl/ ***noun*** [U] a game played on a machine, in which the player sends a small metal ball up a sloping board and scores points as it bounces off objects. The player tries to prevent the ball from reaching the bottom of the machine by pressing two buttons at the side.

**pincer** /ˈpɪnsər; ˈpɪntʃər/ ***noun*** **1** [C] one of a pair of curved claws of some types of animal, e.g. crabs and lobsters: *Crabs normally catch food with their pincers.* **2 pincers** [pl.] a tool made of two crossed pieces of metal, used for holding things firmly and pulling things, for example nails out of wood: *a pair of pincers*

**pinch**[1] /pɪntʃ/ ***verb*** [T] to squeeze a piece of sb's skin tightly between your thumb and finger, or between two hard surfaces: *The lecture was so boring I had to pinch myself to stay awake.* ◇ *Paul pinched his finger in the car door.*

**pinch**[2] /pɪntʃ/ ***noun*** [C] **1** an act of PINCHING[1]: *She gave him a little pinch on the arm.* **2** the amount of sth that you can pick up with your thumb and finger: *a pinch of salt*

IDM **in a pinch** if necessary but with some difficulty: *We really need three, but we could manage with two in a pinch.*

ˌ**pinch-ˈhit** ***verb*** [I] **1** (in baseball) to hit the ball for another player **2 pinch-hit (for sb)** (*informal*) to do sth for sb else who is suddenly unable to do it

**pine** /paɪn/ ***noun*** **1** [C] (*also* ˈ**pine tree**) a tall tree that has thin sharp leaves (**needles**) and woody fruit (**pine cones**): *a northern pine forest*

> NOTE Trees, like the pine, that do not lose their leaves in winter are called **evergreen**.

**2** [U] the wood from pine trees (which is often used for making furniture): *a pine table*

**pine·ap·ple** /ˈpaɪnæpl/ ***noun*** [C,U] a large juicy fruit that is yellow inside and has a thick brown skin with sharp points. Pineapples grow in hot regions: *pineapple juice*

**pineapple**

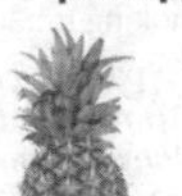

**Ping-Pong™** /ˈpɪŋpɔŋ; -pɑŋ/ ***noun*** [U] = TABLE TENNIS

★**pink** /pɪŋk/ ***adj.*** pale red in color: *Baby girls are often dressed in pink clothes.* ▶ **pink *noun*** [U]: *The bedroom was decorated in pink.*

**pink·ie** (*also* **pinky**) /ˈpɪŋki/ ***noun*** [C] (*pl.* **pinkies**) the smallest finger on your hand

ˈ**pink slip** ***noun*** [C] (*informal*) a letter given to sb to say that he/she must leave his/her job: *About 40% of the department's 78 engineers received pink slips.*

ˈ**pink-slip** ***verb*** [T] (**pink-slip·ping**; **pink-slipped**) to fire sb from his/her job

**pin·na·cle** /ˈpɪnəkl/ ***noun*** [C] **1** [usually sing.] the highest point of sth: *Mary is at the pinnacle of her career.* **2** a high rock on a mountain **3** a pointed stone ornament on the top of a church or castle

**pin·point** /ˈpɪnpɔɪnt/ ***verb*** [T] **1** to find the exact position of sth: *to pinpoint a place on the map* **2** to describe or explain exactly what sth is: *Once the cause of the failure has been pinpointed, we can decide what to do about it.*

ˌ**pins and ˈneedles** ***noun*** [pl.] (*informal*) the little pains that you get in a part of your body after it has been in one position for too long and when the blood is returning to it: *I've got pins and needles in my hand.*

IDM **on pins and needles** (*informal*) very nervous, worried or anxious: *Everybody was on pins and needles waiting for the results.*

**pin·stripe** /ˈpɪnstraɪp/ ***noun*** [C,U] a thin, usually light-colored line on cloth; a type of cloth with a pattern of these lines on it: *a pinstripe suit*

**pint** /paɪnt/ ***noun*** [C] (*abbr.* **pt.**) **1** (in the U.S.) a measure of liquid equal to 0.47 of a liter. There are eight pints in a gallon: *a pint of whipping cream* **2** (in Canada) a measure of liquid equal to 0.57 of a liter

ˈ**pint-sized** (*also* ˈ**pint-size**) ***adj.*** (*informal*) very small



P

**pi·o·neer**[1] /ˌpaɪəˈnɪr/ ***noun*** [C] **1** a person who is one of the first to go and live in a particular area: *the pioneers of the American West* **2** a person who is one of the first to go somewhere or do sth: *Yuri Gagarin was one of the pioneers of space exploration.*

**pi·o·neer**[2] /ˌpaɪəˈnɪr/ ***verb*** [I,T] to be one of the first people or organizations to go somewhere, do sth or develop sth: *We've pioneered new breakthroughs in Artificial Intelligence.*

**pi·o·neer·ing** /ˌpaɪəˈnɪrɪŋ/ ***adj.*** introducing ideas and methods that have never been used before: *pioneering work on infant mortality*

**pi·ous** /ˈpaɪəs/ ***adj.*** having or showing a deep belief in and love of religion ▸ **pi·ous·ly** ***adv.***

★**pipe**[1] /paɪp/ ***noun*** [C] **1** a hollow tube that carries gas or liquid: *a gas pipe* ◇ *The hot water pipe burst.* **2** a small tube with a bowl at one end that is used for smoking tobacco: *Does Don smoke a pipe?*

**pipe**[2] /paɪp/ ***verb*** [T] to carry liquid or gas in PIPES (1): *Water is being piped into the city.* ◇ (*figurative*) *Many supermarkets have piped music playing all the time.*

PHR V **pipe up** (*informal*) to start speaking suddenly: *Just then Alex piped up, "No way!"*

**pipe down** (*informal*) (used especially in orders to tell sb to stop talking or to be less noisy)

**pipe·line** /ˈpaɪplaɪn/ ***noun*** [C] a line of PIPES[1] (1) that are used for carrying liquid or gas: *The oil pipeline stretches across Alaska.*

IDM **in the pipeline** something that is in the pipeline is being discussed, planned or prepared and will happen or exist soon: *Important new laws are already in the pipeline.*

P

ˌ**piping ˈhot** ***adj.*** (used about liquids or food) very hot

**pi·ra·cy** /ˈpaɪrəsi/ ***noun*** [U] **1** robbery by pirates **2** illegal copying of books, videos, etc.

**pi·ra·nha** /pəˈrɑnə; -ˈrɑnyə; -ˈrænə/ ***noun*** [C] a small South American freshwater fish that attacks and eats live animals

**pi·rate**[1] /ˈpaɪrət/ ***noun*** [C] **1** a sailor who attacks and robs ships on the oceans **2** a person who copies books, videos, computer programs, etc. in order to sell them illegally

**pi·rate**[2] /ˈpaɪrət/ ***verb*** [T] to copy a book, video, etc. in order to sell it illegally: *pirated software*

**Pi·sces** /ˈpaɪsiz/ ***noun*** [C,U] the twelfth sign of the zodiac, the Fish; a person who was born under this sign

**pis·tach·i·o** /pəˈstæʃioʊ/ ***noun*** [C,U] (*pl.* **pis·tach·i·os**) **1** (*also* **pisˈtachio nut**) the small green nut of an Asian tree ➲ picture at **nut**. **2** a pale green color

**pis·tol** /ˈpɪstl/ ***noun*** [C] a small gun that you hold in one hand: *She aimed the pistol and fired.* ◇ *a water pistol* (= a children's toy that shoots water) ➲ Look at the note at **gun**.

**pis·ton** /ˈpɪstən/ ***noun*** [C] a piece of metal in an engine, etc. that fits tightly inside a tube. The piston is moved up and down inside the tube and itself causes other parts of the engine to move.

**pit**[1] /pɪt/ ***noun*** [C] **1** a large hole that is made in the ground: *a gravel pit* **2** the large hard seed in some fruits: *a peach/cherry/plum pit* ➲ picture at **peach**. **3** (*also* **the pits** [pl.]) the place near a race track where cars stop for fuel, new tires, etc. during a race

IDM **be the pits** (*informal*) to be very bad: *The food in that restaurant is the pits!*

**pit**[2] /pɪt/ ***verb*** [T] (**pit·ting**; **pit·ted**) to make shallow holes in the surface of sth: *The front of the building was pitted with bullet marks.*

PHR V **pit A against B** to test sb/sth against sb/sth else in a fight or competition: *The two best teams were pitted against each other in the championship.*

**pi·ta** /ˈpit̬ə/ (*also* ˈ**pita bread**) ***noun*** [U,C] a type of flat bread in the shape of an oval that can be split open and filled

ˈ**pit bull** (*also* ˌ**pit bull ˈterrier**) ***noun*** [C] a small strong aggressive dog, sometimes used in dog fights where people bet on which dog will win

**pitch**[1] /pɪtʃ/ ***verb***

➤THROW **1** [T] to throw sth, especially with force and/or careful aim: *Doug pitched his empty can into the bushes.*

➤IN SPORTS **2** [I,T] (in baseball) to throw the ball to a person from the other team who tries to hit it: *Clemens pitched a near-perfect game against the Dodgers on Friday.*

➤SET LEVEL **3** [T] to set sth at a particular level: *The talk was pitched at people with far more experience than I have.* ◇ *a high-pitched voice*

➤TRY TO SELL **4** [T] to try and persuade sb to buy or use sth, such as a product or an idea: *companies that hire movie stars to pitch their products on TV*

➤FALL **5** [I,T] (to cause sb/sth) to fall in a particular direction: *His bike hit a rock and he was pitched forward over the handlebars.*

➤OF SHIP/AIRCRAFT **6** [I] (used about a ship or an airplane) to move up and down or from side to side

➤TENT **7** [T] to put up a tent or tents: *They pitched their tents in the valley.*

PHR V **pitch in** (*informal*) to join in and work together with other people: *Everybody has to pitch in at home when Mom's sick.*

**pitch**[2] /pɪtʃ/ ***noun*** **1** [C] (in baseball) an act of throwing the ball to the player who tries to hit it, or a particular way of throwing: *Ripken hit the first pitch of the game deep into center field.* ◇ *a wild pitch* **2** [C] a speech or statement, etc., that you make in order to persuade sb to buy, use, or do sth: *a sales pitch for a new soft drink* ◇ *The politician made a pitch for his proposed tax cut.* **3** [U] the degree of how high or low a musical note or a voice is **4** [sing.] the level of sth: *The crowd's excitement reached fever pitch* (= they were very excited).

ˌ**pitch-ˈblack** ***adj.*** completely dark; with no light at all

**pitch·er** /ˈpɪtʃər/ ***noun*** [C] **1** a container with a handle, used for holding and pouring liquids **2** (in baseball) the player who throws the ball to players from the other team, who try to hit it ➲ picture at **baseball**.

**pitcher**

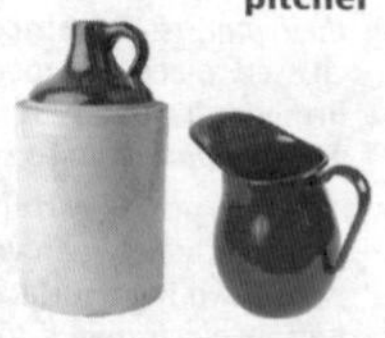

jug pitcher

**pitch·fork** /ˈpɪtʃfɔrk/ ***noun*** [C] a tool that looks like a large fork, that is used on farms for lifting and moving cut grass, etc. ➲ picture at **garden**.

**pit·fall** /ˈpɪtfɔl/ ***noun*** [C, usually pl.] an unexpected danger; a mistake that you might easily make

**pit·i·ful** /ˈpɪt̬ɪfl/ ***adj.*** causing you to feel pity or sadness: *the pitiful groans of the wounded soldiers* ➲ Look at **pathetic**. ▶ **pit·i·ful·ly** ***adv.***: *The children were pitifully thin.*

**pit·i·less** /ˈpɪt̬ɪləs/ ***adj.*** having or showing no pity for other people's suffering

ˈ**pit stop** ***noun*** [C] **1** (in motor racing) an occasion when a car stops during a race for more fuel, etc. **2** (*informal*) a short stop during a long trip for a rest, a meal, etc.

**pit·y**[1] /ˈpɪt̬i/ ***noun*** **1** [U] a feeling of sadness that you have for sb/sth that is suffering or in trouble: *He showed no pity at the way they had been treated.* ◇ *All I feel for her now is pity – I'm not mad anymore.* **2** [sing.] something that makes you feel sad or disappointed: *It's a pity that he never took good care of her.*

IDM **take pity on sb** to help sb who is suffering or in trouble because you feel sorry for him/her

**pit·y**[2] /ˈpɪt̬i/ ***verb*** [T] (*pres. part.* **pit·y·ing**; *3rd person sing. pres.* **pit·ies**; *pt, pp* **pit·ied**) to feel PITY[1] or sadness for sb who is suffering or in trouble: *It is not enough to pity these people; we should try to help them.* ◇ *I pity the person who has to clean his room!*

**piv·ot**[1] /ˈpɪvət/ ***verb*** [I] to balance or turn on a central point

**piv·ot**[2] /ˈpɪvət/ ***noun*** [C] the central point on which sth balances or turns

**piv·ot·al** /ˈpɪvət̬l/ ***adj.*** (*written*) of great importance because other things depend on it: *He played a pivotal role in the revolution.*

**pix·el** /ˈpɪksl/ ***noun*** [C] (*computing*) any of the small individual areas on a computer screen, which together form the whole display

**piz·za** /ˈpitsə/ ***noun*** [C,U] a round flat piece of bread that is covered with tomatoes, cheese, onions, etc. and cooked in an oven

**piz·zazz** (*also* **piz·azz**) /pəˈzæz/ ***noun*** [U] (*informal*) a lively and exciting quality or style: *We need someone with youth, glamor and pizzazz.*

**piz·ze·ri·a** /ˌpitsəˈriə/ (*also* ˈ**pizza** ˌ**parlor**) ***noun*** [C] a restaurant that serves mostly pizzas

**pkg.** ***abbr.*** (*pl.* **pkgs.**) = PACKAGE

**Pkwy.** ***abbr.*** = PARKWAY (2)

**Pl.** ***abbr.*** = PLACE[1] (10)

**pl.** ***abbr.*** = PLURAL

**plac·ard** /ˈplækərd; -kɑrd/ ***noun*** [C] a large notice that is hung on a wall or carried (in a demonstration, etc.)

**pla·cate** /ˈpleɪkeɪt; ˈplæ-/ ***verb*** [T] to make sb feel less angry about sth: *The concessions did little to placate the students.* SYN **pacify**

★**place**[1] /pleɪs/ ***noun*** [C]

➤ POSITION/AREA **1** a particular position or area: *No one can be in two places at once.* ◇ *This is a good place for a picnic.* ◇ *The wall was damaged in several places.* ◇ *I lost my place in my book* (= where I was reading) *when the phone rang.* ◇ *Do you think that lamp is in the right place?*

➤ BUILDING/TOWN/COUNTRY **2** a building, town, country, etc.: *Monterey is a very beautiful place.* ◇ *Do you know of a good place to eat* (= a restaurant) *around here?*

➤ SEAT **3** a seat or position for sb/sth: *If you get there early, save me a place in line.*

> NOTE A **place** [C] is a seat or position for sb/sth: *If you get there first, can you save a place for me?* A place where you can park your car is also called a **space** [C]. You use **space** [U] and **room** [U] when you are talking about area in general: *This piano takes up a lot of space/room.* ◇ *There is enough space/room for three people in the back of the car.*

➤ ROLE/IMPORTANCE **4** your rank or position in society; your role: *I feel it is not my place to criticize my boss.*

➤ AT COLLEGE/ON TEAM **5** an opportunity to study at a college, play for a team, etc.: *There were many applicants for places in the freshman class.* ◇ *Lucy is now sure of a place on the Olympic team.*

➤ CORRECT POSITION **6** the usual or proper position or occasion for sth: *The room was neat. Everything had been put away in its place.* ◇ *I saw him at the funeral, but it was not the place to discuss business.*

➤ MATH **7** the position of a number after the decimal point: *Your answer should be correct to three decimal places.*

➤ IN RACE/COMPETITION **8** the position that you have at the end of a race, competition, etc.: *Claire finished in second place.*

➤ HOME **9** (*informal*) the house, etc. where you live: *Why not spend the night at our place?*

➤ STREET/SQUARE **10 Place** (*abbr.* **Pl.**) (used in the names of some streets): *We live at 220 Jefferson Place.*

IDM **all over the place** → ALL[2]

**change/trade places (with sb)** to take sb's seat, position, etc. and let him/her have yours: *Let's change places so that you can look out of the window.*

**come, fall, fit, etc. into place** (used about sth that is complicated or difficult to understand) to become organized or clear in your mind: *Pete spent two hours working on the schedule before it all fell into place.*

**in the first, second, etc. place** (used when you are explaining or giving reasons for sth) first, second, etc.

**in place** in the correct position; ready for sth: *Everything is in place for the governor's visit tomorrow.*

**in place of sb/sth**; **in sb/sth's place** instead of sb/sth: *You can use milk in place of the cream in the recipe.* ◇ *Prof. Brown was too sick to travel, but she sent one of her colleagues in her place.*

**put yourself in sb else's/sb's place** to imagine that you are sb else: *Put yourself in Steve's place and you will realize how worried he must be.*

**out of place 1** not in the correct or usual place **2** not suitable for a particular situation: *I felt totally out of place around all those smart people.*

**take place** to happen: *The ceremony took place outdoors.*

**take sb's/sth's place**; **take the place of sb/sth** to replace sb/sth: *The President died and the*



P

*vice-president took his place.* ◇ *Computers have taken the place of typewriters in most offices.*

★**place²** /pleɪs/ ***verb*** [T] **1** to put sth in a particular position or in its usual or correct position: *Dominic placed the cup on the table.* ◇ *The chairs had all been placed in neat rows.* ◇ *to place an ad in a newspaper* ◇ *(figurative) We placed our trust in you, and you failed us.* ◇ *(figurative) The blame for the disaster was placed firmly on the company.* **2** to put sb in a particular position or situation: *His behavior placed me in a difficult situation.* ◇ *to place sb in charge* **3** to remember who sb is or where you have seen him/her before **4** to give an order for sth to a person or company: *We placed an order for 150 T-shirts with a company in New York.*

ˈ**place mat** (*also* **placemat**) ***noun*** [C] a piece of cloth, plastic, paper, etc. that you put on a table under one person's plate, bowl, etc.

**plac·id** /ˈplæsəd/ ***adj.*** calm or not easily excited ▶ **plac·id·ly** ***adv.***

**pla·gia·rize** /ˈpleɪdʒəraɪz/ ***verb*** [T] **plagiarize sth (from sb/sth)** to take sb else's ideas or words and use them as if they were your own: *Most of his essay was plagiarized from articles in other journals.* ➲ This word shows disapproval. ▶ **pla·gia·rism** /ˈpleɪdʒərɪzəm/ ***noun*** [U]: *to be accused of plagiarism*

**plague¹** /pleɪg/ ***noun*** **1** [C,U] a disease that spreads quickly and kills many people **2** [C] a large number of unpleasant animals or insects that come into an area at one time: *a plague of ants*

**plague²** /pleɪg/ ***verb*** [T] to cause sb/sth trouble or discomfort: *The project was plagued by a series of disasters.*

**plaid** /plæd/ ***adj.*** a pattern on material with colored squares and stripes that cross each other: *a plaid flannel shirt* ➲ Picture on study page **A30**.

★**plain¹** /pleɪn/ ***adj.*** **1** ordinary; not special or unusual: *plain country folks* ◇ *You can use plain soap and water to remove that stain.* **2** simple in style; without any decoration, etc.: *a plain black dress* ◇ *My father likes plain, hearty food.* ◇ *The documents will be delivered in a plain brown envelope.* **3** without any extra flavors, etc.: *plain yogurt* ◇ *Which kind of chocolate bar do you want: plain or with nuts?* **4** easy to see, hear or understand; clear: *It was plain that he didn't want to talk about it.* ◇ *She made it plain that she didn't want to see me again.* ◇ *The mugging took place in plain view of the police station.* **5** (used about people, thoughts, actions, etc.) saying what you think; direct and honest: *The senator has a reputation for plain speaking.* **6** (used especially about the appearance of a woman or girl) not beautiful: *She has very plain features.*

IDM **plain old** (*informal*) (only *before* a noun) ordinary; basic: *What that boy needs is some plain old common sense.*

**plain²** /pleɪn/ ***adv.*** (*informal*) completely: *That is just plain wrong.*

**plain³** /pleɪn/ ***noun*** [C] a large area of flat land with few trees: *a coastal plain* ◇ *snowstorms moving across the central plains* ◇ *the Great Plains of the central United States*

ˌ**plain ˈclothes** ***noun*** [pl.] (used in connection with the police) ordinary clothes; not uniform: *The detectives were in plain clothes.* ▶ ˈ**plain·clothes** ***adj.***: *a plainclothes detective*

**plain·ly** /ˈpleɪnli/ ***adv.*** clearly: *Smoke was plainly visible nearly 20 miles away.* ◇ *He was plainly very upset.*

**plain·tiff** /ˈpleɪntəf/ ***noun*** [C] a person who starts a legal action against sb in a court of law ➲ Look at **defendant**.

**plait** /plæt/ ***noun*** [C] (*Cdn*) = BRAID²(1) ▶ **plait** ***verb*** [T]

★**plan¹** /plæn/ ***noun*** [C] **1** an idea or arrangement for doing or achieving sth in the future: *Do you have any plans for the weekend?* ◇ *We usually make our vacation plans in January.* ◇ *The company has no plans to hire more people.* ◇ *The best plan is to ask him to meet us on Monday.* ◇ *I wrote down my plan for the project – take a look.* **2** a drawing, diagram, etc. that shows how sth such as a building, part of a building, machine, etc. is arranged: *This brochure contains a floor plan of the museum.* ◇ *We're having an architect draw up some plans for an addition to the house.*

IDM **go according to plan** to happen as planned

★**plan²** /plæn/ ***verb*** (**plan<u>n</u>ing**; **plan<u>n</u>ed**) **1** [I,T] to decide, organize or prepare for sth: *to plan for the future* ◇ *You need to plan your work more carefully.* **2** [I,T] **plan (on sth/to do sth)** to intend to do sth: *I'm planning on taking a vacation in July.* ◇ *We're planning to arrive at about 4 o'clock.* **3** [T] to make a plan of or for sth; to design sth: *You need an expert to help you plan your financial investments.* ◇ *The new shopping center seems to be very poorly planned.*

★**plane¹** /pleɪn/ ***noun*** [C] **1** = AIRPLANE: *We boarded the plane in Atlanta.* ◇ *a plane ticket* ◇ *Has her plane landed yet?* ◇ *a Lufthansa plane* ◇ *a plane crash* **2** (*technical*) a flat surface **3** a tool used for making the surface of wood smooth by taking very thin pieces off it

**plane²** /pleɪn/ ***verb*** [T] to make a piece of wood smoother or flatter with a PLANE¹(3): *Plane the surface down first.*

**plane·load** /ˈpleɪnloʊd/ ***noun*** [C] the number of people or the amount of goods that can be carried in an airplane: *two planeloads of refugees*

★**plan·et** /ˈplænət/ ***noun*** [C] a large body in space that moves around the sun or another star: *The planets of our solar system are Mercury, Venus, Earth, Mars, Jupiter, Saturn, Uranus, Neptune and Pluto.* ◇ *the natural resources of our planet* (= of the Earth)

**plan·e·tar·i·um** /ˌplænəˈtɛriəm/ ***noun*** [C] (*pl.* **plan·e·tar·i·ums** or **plan·e·tar·i·a** /-ˈtɛriə/) a building that contains equipment for showing the positions and movements of the planets and stars

**plank** /plæŋk/ ***noun*** [C] **1** a long flat piece of wood (that is used for making floors, etc.) **2** an idea that is one of a set of political plans

**plan·ner** /ˈplænər/ ***noun*** [C] **1** a person whose job is to plan the growth and development of a town or city: *A meeting was held with the architects and planners to finalize plans for the new mall.* **2** a person who makes plans for a particular area of activity: *financial/economic/media planners* **3** a book, computer program, etc. that contains dates and is used for recording information, arranging meetings, etc.: *a trip planner ◇ a daily planner*

★**plan·ning** /ˈplænɪŋ/ ***noun*** [U] making plans or arrangements: *The project requires careful planning.* ◇ ***Family planning*** (= using contraception) *enables people to control the number of children they have.*

★**plant**[1] /plænt/ ***noun*** **1** [C] a living thing that grows in soil and has a stem, leaves and roots: *a tomato plant ◇ a house plant* (= one that grows in a pot inside a house) ◇ *to water the plants* **2** [C] a building where an industrial process takes place; a large factory: *a power plant* (= where electricity is produced)

★**plant**[2] /plænt/ ***verb*** [T] **1** to put plants, seeds, etc. in the ground to grow: *Bulbs should be planted in the fall.* **2 plant sth (with sth)** to cover or supply a garden, area of land, etc. with plants: *It takes a lot of hard work to plant a vegetable garden.* ◇ *The field was planted with wheat this year.* **3** to put sb/sth firmly in a certain position: *He planted himself in the best seat.* **4 plant sth (on sb)** to hide sth somewhere for a secret and usually criminal purpose (sometimes in order to make sb seem guilty of a crime): *The police think that terrorists may have planted the bomb.* ◇ *The women claimed that the drugs had been planted on them.*

**plan·tain** /ˈplæntən/ ***noun*** [C,U] **1** a fruit like a large banana, but less sweet, that is cooked and eaten as a vegetable **2** [C] a wild plant with small green flowers and broad flat leaves that spread out close to the ground

**plan·tar wart** /ˈplæntər wɔrt; ˈplæntɑr-/ ***noun*** [C] a small hard infectious growth (a wart) on the bottom of the foot

**plan·ta·tion** /plænˈteɪʃn/ ***noun*** [C] a large farm, especially in a tropical country or formerly in the southern U.S., where tea, cotton, tobacco, etc. are grown: *Some slaves managed to escape from plantations before the Civil War.*

**plant·er** /ˈplæntər/ ***noun*** [C] **1** an attractive container to grow a plant in **2** a person who owns or manages a plantation in a tropical country: *sugar planters*

**plaque** /plæk/ ***noun*** **1** [C] a flat piece of stone or metal with writing on it that is attached to a wall as a way of remembering a famous person or past event: *a memorial plaque* **2** [U] a harmful substance that forms on teeth

**plas·ma** /ˈplæzmə/ ***noun*** [U] the liquid part of blood, in which the blood cells are carried

**plas·ter**[1] /ˈplæstər/ ***noun*** **1** [U] a soft mixture of sand, water, etc. that becomes hard when it is dry. Plaster is put on walls and ceilings to form a smooth surface. **2** [U] a white substance that becomes hard when dry and is used to make figures, decorations, etc. and for putting around broken bones, etc. until they heal: *We'll have to put a plaster cast on your arm.*

**plas·ter**[2] /ˈplæstər/ ***verb*** [T] **1** to cover a wall, etc. with PLASTER[1] (1) **2** to cover sth thickly with sth; to put things onto a surface: *The car was plastered with mud.* ◇ *She had plastered her room with posters.* ◇ *She plastered pictures of the singer all over her room.*

**plas·tered** /ˈplæstərd/ ***adj.*** (*not* before a noun) (*informal*) very drunk: *to be/get plastered*

★**plas·tic** /ˈplæstɪk/ ***noun*** **1** [C,U] a light, artificial material which does not break easily and is used for making many different sorts of objects: *A lot of kitchen utensils are made of plastic.* ◇ *plastics and other synthetic materials* **2** [U] (*informal*) (a way of talking about) credit cards: *Do they take plastic?* ◇ *He paid with plastic.* ▶ **plas·tic *adj.***: *plastic cups and spoons* ◇ *a plastic bag*

ˌ**plastic ˈsurgeon** ***noun*** [C] a doctor who is qualified to perform plastic surgery

ˌ**plastic ˈsurgery** ***noun*** [U] surgical operations to repair or replace damaged skin or to improve the appearance of a person's face or body: *facelifts and other types of plastic surgery*

ˌ**plastic ˈwrap** ***noun*** [U] a thin transparent plastic material that sticks to a surface and to itself, used especially for wrapping food

**plate**

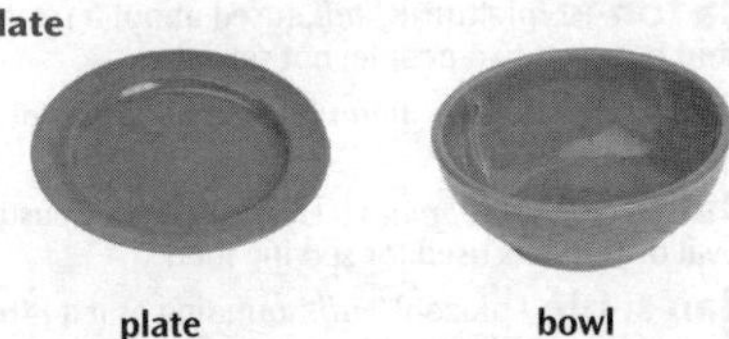

plate bowl

★**plate**[1] /pleɪt/ ***noun***

➤ FOR FOOD **1** [C] a flat, usually round, dish that you eat or serve food from: *Put the cake on a plate.* ◇ *a china plate* ◇ *a paper plate*

> NOTE You eat your main course from a **dinner plate.** You may put your cup on a **saucer.** You usually eat cereal, soup or pudding from a **bowl** or a **dish.**

➤ THIN FLAT PIECE OF METAL **2** [C] a thin flat piece of metal, used especially to join or make sth stronger: *The tanks were mainly constructed of steel plates.*

➤ FOR INFORMATION **3** [C] a flat piece of metal with sth written on it: *I couldn't read the car's license plate.*

➤ SILVER/GOLD **4** [U] a thin covering of gold, silver, etc. on another metal: *gold plate*

➤ PRINTING/PHOTOGRAPHY **5** [C] a picture or photograph in a book that takes up a whole page: *color plates*

➤ IN MOUTH **6** [C] a piece of plastic with artificial teeth attached to it that fits inside a person's mouth: *an upper/a lower plate*

**plate**[2] /pleɪt/ ***verb*** [T] (usually passive) to cover a metal with a thin layer of another metal, especially gold or silver: *a silver ring plated with gold*

**pla·teau** /plæˈtoʊ/ ***noun*** [C] **1** a large area of high, flat land **2** a state where there is little development or change: *House prices seem to have reached a plateau.*

**plate·ful** /ˈpleɪtfʊl/ ***noun*** [C] the amount of food that a PLATE (1) can hold: *a plateful of spaghetti*

ˌ**plate ˈglass** ***noun*** [U] very clear glass of good quality, made in thick sheets, used for doors, windows of stores, etc.: *plate-glass windows*

★**plat·form** /ˈplætfɔrm/ ***noun*** [C]

P

➤FOR PERFORMERS **1** a raised floor in a public place, where people stand to make speeches or to perform: (*figurative*) *The newspaper's editor uses his column as a platform for his conservative views.*
➤AT TRAIN STATION **2** a flat raised surface, especially the area beside the track at a train station where passengers get on and off trains: *a subway platform*
➤FOR EQUIPMENT **3** a flat raised surface on which equipment stands: *an offshore oil platform* (= for drilling oil)
➤COMPUTING **4** a particular type of computer system and the way it operates: *This software operates on a UNIX platform.*
➤POLITICS/OPINIONS **5** the ideas and aims of a political party, especially as expressed before an election: *The Democratic party platform*

**plat·i·num** /ˈplætn·əm/ ***noun*** [U] (*symbol* **Pt**) a valuable grayish-white metal that is often used for making jewelry: *a platinum ring*

**pla·ton·ic** /pləˈtɑnɪk/ ***adj.*** (used about a relationship between two people) not sexual

**pla·toon** /pləˈtun/ ***noun*** [C] a small group of soldiers

**plat·ter** /ˈplæt̮ər/ ***noun*** [C] a large, shallow, usually oval dish that is used for serving food

**plau·si·ble** /ˈplɔzəbl/ ***adj.*** sounding as if it is true; reasonable: *a plausible excuse* OPP **implausible**

★**play**[1] /pleɪ/ ***verb***
➤OF CHILDREN **1** [I] to do sth to enjoy yourself; to have fun: *They've been playing on the beach all day.* ◇ *He's playing with his new toy.* ◇ *Jane found a new friend to play with.*
➤SPORTS/GAMES **2** [I,T] to take part in a sport or game: *"How about a game of chess?" "Sorry, but I don't know how to play."* ◇ *Who's playing in the game tonight?* ◇ *I play football on Saturdays.* **3** [I,T] **play (sth) (with/against sb)**; **play sb (at sth)** to compete against sb in a game or sport: *I usually play against Bob.* ◇ *Our team plays baseball against other schools nearby.* ◇ *She played him at cards and won!*
➤TRICK **4** [T] **play sth (on sb)** to do sth which may surprise or annoy sb for your own amusement: *The kids decided to play a trick on their teacher.*
➤ACT/PERFORM **5** [I,T] to act a part in a PLAY[2] (1): *Steve is going to play Romeo.*

NOTE **Play a part**, **role**, etc. is often used in a figurative way: *The United Nations has played an active part in the recent discussions.* ◇ *Sarah played a key role in organizing the protest.*

➤MUSIC **6** [I,T] to make music with a musical instrument: *My son's learning the piano. He plays very well.* ◇ *She played a few notes on the violin.* ◇ *Could you play that piece of music again?*

NOTE We usually use the definite article **the** before the names of musical instruments: *to play the piano* ◇ *to learn the trumpet, etc.*

**7** [T] to turn on a record, tape, etc. so that it produces sound: *Should I play the tape for you again?*
➤OF LIGHT/A SMILE **8** [I] (*formal*) to move quickly and lightly: *A smile played on her lips.*

IDM **play ball 1** to play a ball game, especially baseball **2** to agree to do what sb wants you to do
**play possum** → POSSUM

PHR V **play along (with sb/sth) 1** to pretend to agree or work together with sb/sth: *I decided to play along with her idea for a while.* **2** to play a game that sb else is also playing, without competing against him/her: *This game show has a lot of viewers who like to play along at home.*
**play sth back (to sb)** to turn on a tape or a movie after recording the material on it: *We made a video of the party and played it back to all the guests before they left.*
**play sth down/up** to make sth seem less/more important than it really is: *to play down a crisis*

★**play**[2] /pleɪ/ ***noun*** **1** [C] a story which is written to be performed by actors in the theater, on television or on the radio: *Would you like to go to a Broadway play while you're in New York?* ◇ *a radio play* ◇ *to have a part in the school play* ◇ *the opening night of the play*

NOTE Actors and actresses **rehearse** a play. A director **directs**. A play is usually performed on a **stage**.

**2** [U] activities that are done for enjoyment only, especially by children: *Young children learn through play.* ◇ *Everybody needs a balance of work and play.* **3** [U] the playing of a game or sport; the way it is played: *Bad weather stopped play yesterday.* ◇ *rough play*

NOTE We **play** tennis, football, etc. but we CANNOT say **a play** of tennis. We play **a game** of tennis.

IDM **fair play** → FAIR[1]

**play·boy** /ˈpleɪbɔɪ/ ***noun*** [C] a rich man who spends his time enjoying himself and spending money

**ˌplay-by-ˈplay** ***noun*** [usually sing.] a report on what is happening in a sports game, given as the game is being played: *The game was broadcast live but we couldn't hear the play-by-play.* ► **pˌlay-by-ˈplay** ***adj.***: *a play-by-play announcer*

★**play·er** /ˈpleɪər/ ***noun*** [C] **1** a person who plays a game: *a game for four players* ◇ *She's an excellent tennis player.* **2** a person who plays a musical instrument: *a piano player* **3** (*old-fashioned*) an actor

**ˈplayer piˌano** ***noun*** [C] a piano that can play automatically

**play·ful** /ˈpleɪfl/ ***adj.*** **1** done or said in fun; not serious: *a playful remark* **2** full of fun; lively: *a playful puppy*

**play·ground** /ˈpleɪgraʊnd/ ***noun*** [C] a public area of land where children can play: *the school playground*

**ˈplaying card** ***noun*** [C] = CARD[1] (3)

**ˈplaying field** ***noun*** [C] a large field used for sports such as football and soccer

**play·off** /ˈpleɪɔf/ ***noun*** [C] a series of sports games that are played by the best teams or players in a particular sport, in order to find the overall winner

**play·pen** /ˈpleɪpɛn/ ***noun*** [C] a small movable platform with wooden bars or a net around its sides in which a baby or small child can play safely

**play·thing** /ˈpleɪθɪŋ/ ***noun*** [C] **1** (*old-fashioned*) a toy: *The teddy bear was his favorite plaything.* **2** a person or thing that you treat like a toy: *She was an intelligent woman who refused to be a rich man's plaything.*

**play·wright** /ˈpleɪraɪt/ ***noun*** [C] a person who writes plays for the theater, TV or radio

**pla·za** /ˈplɑzə; ˈplæzə/ ***noun*** [C] **1** an open space in a town or city that has buildings around it: *The demonstrators gathered on the plaza in front of the company's offices.* **2** (*also* **shopping plaza**) a row of stores with an open area for parking in front

**plea** /pli/ ***noun*** [C] **1** a strong request; an appeal: *a last plea for mercy* **2** a statement made by sb in a court of law in which he/she claims to be guilty or not guilty of a certain crime: *to enter a plea of guilty/not guilty*

**ˈplea-ˌbargain** ***verb*** [I] to say, in a court of law, that you are guilty of a less serious crime in order to get a lighter punishment and avoid a trial for a more serious crime ▶ **ˈplea ˌbargain** ***noun*** [C]: *He agreed to a plea bargain to avoid a trial.*

**plead** /plid/ ***verb*** (*pt, pp* **plead·ed** or **pled** /plɛd/) **1** [I] **plead (with sb) (for sth)** to ask sb for sth in a very strong and emotional or serious way: *She pleaded with him not to leave her.* ◇ *The hostages' families pleaded for their release.* **2** [T] (*formal*) to give sth as an excuse or explanation for sth: *He pleaded family problems as the reason for his lack of concentration.* **3** [T] (*formal*) (used about sb accused of a crime in a court of law) to say that you are guilty or not guilty: *The defendant pleaded not guilty to the charge of theft.*

★**pleas·ant** /ˈplɛznt/ ***adj.*** nice, enjoyable or friendly: *The weather was very pleasant.* ◇ *What a pleasant surprise!* ◇ *It must be pleasant to live in such a peaceful place.* ◇ *He's not a very pleasant young man.* ◇ *Mr. Lee is always very pleasant to me when I'm in his store.* OPP **unpleasant** ▶ **pleas·ant·ly** ***adv.***

**pleas·ant·ry** /ˈplɛzəntri/ ***noun*** [usually pl.] (*pl.* **pleas·an·tries**) (*formal*) a friendly remark made in order to be polite: *After exchanging the usual pleasantries, they got down to serious discussion.*

★**please**[1] /pliz/ ***verb*** **1** [I,T] to make sb happy; to satisfy: *Our customer service department always aims to please.* ◇ *I'll put on my best clothes to please my mother.* ◇ *That teacher's very hard to please.* ◇ *We were very pleased by the judge's decision.* **2** [I] (not used as the main verb in a sentence; used after words like *as, what, whatever, anything,* etc.) to want; to choose: *You can't always do exactly as you please.* ◇ *She has so much money she can buy anything she pleases.*

★**please**[2] /pliz/ ***interjection*** (used as a polite way of making a request, an inquiry or giving an order): *Come in, please.* ◇ *Could you help me, please?* ◇ *Please don't touch the paintings.* ◇ *Sit down, please.* ◇ *Two cups of coffee, please.* ◇ *"Would you like something to drink?" "Yes, please."*

NOTE We do not use **please** in English when we are giving something to somebody.

★**pleased** /plizd/ ***adj.*** (not before a noun) **pleased (at sth)**; **pleased (with sb/sth)**; **pleased to do sth** happy or satisfied: *We were quite pleased at the outcome of the investigation.* ◇ *John seems very pleased with his new car.* ◇ *My parents weren't at all pleased with me when I came home late.* ◇ *We were very pleased to hear your wonderful news.* ◇ *I'm pleased that you've decided to stay another week.* ➲ Look at the note at **glad**. OPP **displeased**

**pleas·ing** /ˈplizɪŋ/ ***adj.*** giving pleasure: *The results of our research are very pleasing.* OPP **displeasing**

★**pleas·ure** /ˈplɛʒər/ ***noun*** **1** [U] the feeling of being happy or satisfied: *Parents get a lot of pleasure out of watching their children grow up.* ◇ *She expressed pleasure at the judge's decision.* ◇ *It gives me great pleasure to introduce our next speaker.* **2** [U] enjoyment (rather than work): *Are you in Paris on business, or is it for pleasure?* **3** [C] an event or activity that you enjoy or that makes you happy: *It's been a pleasure to work with you.* ◇ *This car is a pleasure to drive.* ◇ *"Thanks for your help." "It's a pleasure."*

IDM **take (no) pleasure in sth/doing sth** to enjoy/not enjoy (doing) sth: *Billy seems to take great pleasure in teasing his little sister.*

**pleat** /plit/ ***noun*** [C] a fold that is sewn or pressed into a piece of cloth: *a skirt with pleats at the front*

**pled** *past tense, past participle of* PLEAD

**pledge**[1] /plɛdʒ/ ***noun*** [C] a promise or agreement, especially a promise to give money: *The government made a pledge to reduce unemployment.*

**pledge**[2] /plɛdʒ/ ***verb*** **1** [T] **pledge sth (to sb/sth)** to promise to give or do sth: *They pledged their support to us.* ◇ *The organization has pledged $250,000 to help the victims of the crash.* ◇ *We all had to* **pledge allegiance** *to the flag* (= state that we are loyal to our country). **2** [I,T] (*U.S.*) to promise to become a junior member of a fraternity or a sorority: *Do you think you'll pledge this semester?* ◇ *My brother pledged Sigma Nu.* ➲ For more information about the U.S. education system, look at study page A8.

**the ˌPledge of Alˈlegiance** ***noun*** [sing.] (*U.S.*) an official statement made by citizens of the U.S., in which they promise to be loyal to their country

**plen·ti·ful** /ˈplɛntɪfl/ ***adj.*** available in large amounts or numbers: *Strawberries are plentiful at this time of year.* ➲ Look at **scarce**.

★**plen·ty**[1] /ˈplɛnti/ ***pronoun*** as much or as many as you need; a lot: *"Should I get some more coffee?" "No, we've still got plenty."* ◇ *Make sure you take plenty of warm clothes with you.* ◇ *There's still plenty of time to get there.* ◇ *You and your friends will have plenty to talk about tonight.*

★**plen·ty**[2] /ˈplɛnti/ ***adv.*** **1** (before *more*) a lot: *There's plenty more ice cream.* **2** (*informal*) (with *big, long, tall,* etc. followed by *enough*): *"This shirt's too small." "Well, it looks plenty big enough to me."*

**Plex·i·glas™** /ˈplɛksɪglæs/ (*also* **plex·i·glas, plex·i·glass**) ***noun*** [U] a strong transparent plastic material that is often used instead of glass

**pli·a·ble** /ˈplaɪəbl/ ***adj.*** **1** easy to bend or shape: *Plastic is more pliable than wood.* **2** (used about a person or a person's mind) easy to influence

**pli·ers** /ˈplaɪərz/ ***noun*** [pl.] a tool that is used for holding things tightly, pulling nails out of wood, bending things, etc.: *Do you have the/any pliers?* ◇ *a pair of pliers* ➲ picture at **tool**.

P

**plight** /plaɪt/ ***noun*** [sing.] (*formal*) a bad or difficult state or situation: *the plight of the city's homeless people*

**plod** /plɑd/ ***verb*** [I] (**plod·ding**; **plod·ded**) **plod (along, through, etc.)** **1** to walk slowly and in a heavy or tired way: *We plodded along in the rain for nearly an hour.* **2** to do sth or to work slowly and with difficulty: *I spent the whole day plodding through the pile of paperwork on my desk.*

**plop** /plɑp/ ***noun*** [usually sing.] a sound like that of a small, smooth object dropping into water: *With a tiny plop the ring disappeared into the water.* ▶ **plop** ***verb*** [I] (**plop·ping**; **plopped**): *The fish plopped back into the water.*

★**plot¹** /plɑt/ ***noun*** [C] **1** a secret plan made by several people, to do sth that is wrong: *a plot to kill the Pope* **2** the events in a story, movie, etc. and how they develop: *The play had a very strong plot, but the acting was terrible.* ◇ *I can't follow the plot of this novel.* **3** a piece of land (usually small), used for a special purpose: *a garden plot* ◇ *a burial plot in a cemetery* ◇ *a 20-acre plot of land*

**plot²** /plɑt/ ***verb*** [I,T] (**plot·ting**; **plot·ted**) **1** to make a secret plan to do sth: *They were accused of* ***plotting against*** *the government.* ◇ *The terrorists had been plotting this campaign for years.* **2** to mark sth on a map, diagram, graph, etc.: *to plot the ship's course on the map* ◇ *to plot the figures on a graph*

**plough** /plaʊ/ ***noun*** [C] (*Cdn*) = PLOW¹ ▶ **plough** ***verb*** [I,T]

**plow¹** /plaʊ/ ***noun*** [C] a large tool which is used on a farm and is pulled by a tractor or by an animal. A plow turns the soil over and is used especially before seeds are planted. ➲ Look also at **snowplow**.

**plow²** /plaʊ/ ***verb*** [I,T] to break up or move soil, snow, etc. using a PLOW¹: *to plow the fields*

PHRV **plow into sb/sth** (*informal*) (used about a car, truck, etc.) to hit sb/sth with great force: *His car went out of control and plowed into a tree.*

**plow through sth** (*informal*) to finish reading something or doing some work, even though it is long and boring

**ploy** /plɔɪ/ ***noun*** [C] something that you say or do in order to get what you want or to persuade sb to do sth: *He realized that her kindness had been a ploy to get him to stay.*

**pluck** /plʌk/ ***verb*** [T] **1** to pull sth in order to pick or remove it: *He plucked the letter from my hands.* ◇ *to pluck your eyebrows* (= to pull out the hairs you do not want) **2** to pull the feathers out of a chicken, etc. in order to prepare it for cooking **3** to pull the strings of a musical instrument and let them go again, in order to make music

**pluck·y** /ˈplʌki/ ***adj.*** (**pluck·i·er**; **pluck·i·est**) brave; having a lot of courage

**plug¹** /plʌg/ ***noun*** [C] **1** a plastic or rubber object with two or three metal pins, which connects the wire on a piece of electrical equipment to a point in the wall where there is electricity (an outlet): *If the plug is damaged, do not attempt to use the appliance.* **2** a piece of rubber, metal or plastic that fits tightly into a hole (e.g. in a bathtub, sink, etc.) **3** a favorable reference to a book, record, etc. made in public in order to make people buy the thing mentioned

IDM **pull the plug (on sb/sth)** → PULL¹

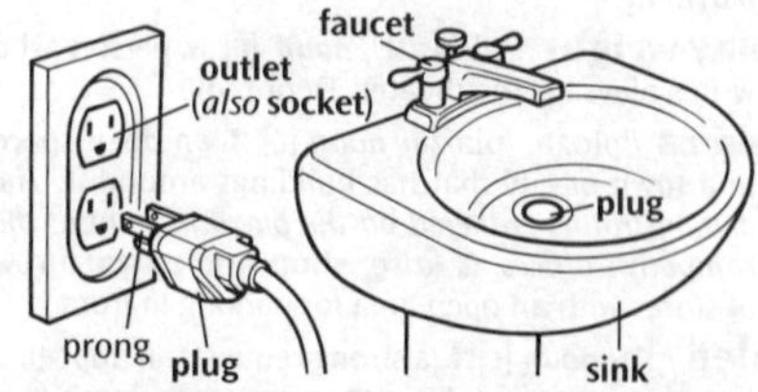


**plug²** /plʌg/ ***verb*** [T] (**plug·ging**; **plugged**) **1** to fill or block a hole with sth: *He managed to plug the leak in the pipe with a piece of plastic.* **2** (*informal*) to praise a book, record, etc. in public in order to make people buy the thing mentioned: *He went on the talk show in order to plug his new book.*

PHRV **plug sth in** to connect sth to the supply of electricity with a PLUG¹ (1): *The VCR isn't plugged in.* OPP **unplug**

ˈ**plug-in¹** ***adj.*** **1** able to be connected using a PLUG¹ (1): *a plug-in telephone* **2** (*computing*) able to be added to a computer system so that it can do more things: *a plug-in graphics card* ◇ *Some of the smaller notebooks use plug-in drives which saves power and makes them even more portable.*

ˈ**plug-in²** ***noun*** [C] **1** (*computing*) a piece of computer software that can be added to a system so that it can do more things: *Plug-ins for palmtops are a booming industry.* **2** (*Cdn*) a connection to an electricity supply (outlet) in a garage, near a parking space, etc. for plugging in an electric heater that is used to warm the engine of a car, etc. so that it starts more easily

**plum¹** /plʌm/ ***noun*** [C] a soft, round fruit with red or purple skin and a large hard part (pit) in the middle

**plum²** /plʌm/ ***adj.*** (used about a job, etc.) considered very good and worth having: *She's landed a plum job as the producer's assistant.*

**plumb¹** /plʌm/ ***verb*** [T] **1** (*written*) to try to understand or succeed in understanding sth mysterious: *She spent her life plumbing the mysteries of the human psyche.* **2** **plumb sth (in)** to connect a washing machine, a toilet, etc. to the water supply in a building

IDM **plumb the depths of sth** to be or to experience an extreme example of sth unpleasant: *His latest novel plumbs the depths of horror and violence.* ◇ *The team's poor performances* ***plumbed new depths*** *last night when they lost 10-2.*

**plumb²** /plʌm/ ***adv.*** **1** (used before a preposition) exactly: *He was standing plumb in the middle of the street.* **2** completely: (*informal*) *He's plumb crazy.*

**plumb·er** /ˈplʌmər/ ***noun*** [C] a person whose job is to put in and repair water pipes, bathtubs, sinks, etc.

**plumb·ing** /ˈplʌmɪŋ/ ***noun*** [U] **1** all the pipes, water tanks, etc. in a building: *The plumbing in this house is very old.* **2** the work of a person who puts in and repairs the water pipes, tanks, etc.

**plume** /plum/ ***noun*** [C] a quantity of smoke, gas, etc. that rises in the air

**plum·met** /ˈplʌmət/ ***verb*** [I] to fall suddenly and quickly from a high level or position: *Share prices plummeted to an all-time low.* ◇ *Her spirits plummeted at the thought of meeting him again.*

**plump¹** /plʌmp/ ***adj.*** (used about a person or an animal) a little bit fat, but looking nice: *the baby's plump cheeks* ◇ *a nice, plump chicken*

**plump²** /plʌmp/ ***verb*** **1** [T] **plump sth (up)** to make sth larger, softer and rounder: *He leaned forward while the nurse plumped up his pillows.* **2** [I] **plump (up)** to become rounder and fatter: *Stew the fruits gently until they plump up.*

PHR V **plump for sb/sth** (*informal*) to choose sb/sth from a number of people or things, especially after thinking carefully

**plun·der** /ˈplʌndər/ ***verb*** [I,T] to steal things from a place, especially during war or fighting: *They captured the city, killing and plundering as they advanced.*

**plunge¹** /plʌndʒ/ ***verb*** **1** [I] **plunge (into sth)** to go, jump, dive, fall, etc. suddenly and with force into sth: *He turned and plunged into the crowd.* ◇ *A woman plunged to her death from a downtown skyscraper yesterday.* **2** [T] **plunge sth in/into sth** to push sth suddenly and with force into sth: *He plunged the knife into the woman's arm and ran off.* **3** [T] to cause sb/sth to be in the state mentioned: *The state has been plunged into chaos by the hurricane.* **4** [I] **plunge into sth** to suddenly start or become involved in sth: *She plunged into her new job with enthusiasm.* **5** [I] to move suddenly downward; to decrease: *The value of the dollar plunged overnight.*

**plunge²** /plʌndʒ/ ***noun*** [C] a sudden forward or downward movement; a dive, fall or decrease: *a quick plunge into cold water* ◇ *the plunge in house prices*

IDM **take the plunge** to decide to do sth difficult after thinking about it for a long time

**plung·er** /ˈplʌndʒər/ ***noun*** [C] **1** a piece of equipment used for clearing kitchen and bathroom pipes, which consists of a rubber cup fixed to a handle **2** a part of a piece of equipment that works by being pushed downward: *Brew the coffee for two minutes before pushing down the plunger.* ➲ picture at **coffee**.

**plunk** /plʌŋk/ ***verb***

PHR V **plunk sth down** (*informal*) **1** to put sth down or drop sth heavily: *He plunked his suitcase down on my foot.* **2** to spend (a lot of) money on sth: *Some people plunk down $20 every week for lottery tickets.*

**plu·per·fect** /ˌpluˈpərfɪkt/ ***noun*** [sing.] (*grammar*) = PAST PERFECT

**plu·ral** /ˈplʊrəl/ ***noun*** [C] (*abbr.* **pl.**) (*grammar*) the form of a noun, verb, etc. which refers to more than one person or thing: *The plural of "man" is "men."* ◇ *The verb should be in the plural.* ▶ **plu·ral** ***adj.*** (*grammar*) : *A plural noun must be followed by a plural verb.* ➲ Look at **singular**.

**plu·ral·i·ty** /plʊˈræləṭi/ ***noun*** [C] (*U.S.*) (in an election with more than two candidates) the number of votes received by the winner, if this number is less than 50% of all the votes ➲ Look also at **majority**.

★**plus¹** /plʌs/ ***prep.*** **1** and; added to: *Two plus two is four (2 + 2 = 4).* ➲ Look at **minus**. **2** and; in addition to: *I have a paper to write tonight, plus some reading.*

**plus²** /plʌs/ ***conj.*** (*informal*) and; in addition: *Ron has to take a test tomorrow, plus his science project is due Friday.*

**plus³** /plʌs/ ***adj.*** **1** (used after a number) or more: *He must earn $100,000 plus.* **2** (used before a number) higher than zero: *Low temperatures could go down to plus 5 degrees tonight.* **3** (used after a letter grade on students' work) slightly above: *I got a B plus (written "B+") on my homework.* ➲ Look at **minus**.

**plus⁴** /plʌs/ ***noun*** [C] **1** (*also* ˈ**plus sign**) the sign (+): *He mistook a plus for a minus.* **2** an advantage: *The job involves a lot of travel, which is a big plus.* ➲ Look at **minus**.

**plush** /plʌʃ/ ***adj.*** fashionable and expensive: *a plush hotel*

**Plu·to** /ˈpluṭoʊ/ ***noun*** [sing.] the planet that is farthest from the sun

**plu·to·ni·um** /pluˈtoʊniəm/ ***noun*** [U] a dangerous substance that is used especially as a fuel in nuclear power plants

**ply¹** /plaɪ/ ***verb*** (*pres. part.* **ply·ing**; *3rd person sing. pres.* **plies**; *pt, pp* **plied** /plaɪd/) [I,T] (*formal*) (used about ships, boats, etc.) to travel regularly on a certain route: *ships that ply the Atlantic*

**ply²** /plaɪ/ ***noun*** [U] (used especially in compounds) a measurement of wool, rope, wood, etc. that tells you how thick it is: *four-ply knitting yarn*

**ply·wood** /ˈplaɪwʊd/ ***noun*** [U] a type of board that is made by sticking thin layers of wood on top of each other

**P.M.** (*also* **p.m.**) /ˌpi ˈɛm/ ***abbr.*** after noon: *2 p.m.* (= 2 o'clock in the afternoon) ◇ *10:30 p.m.* (= 10:30 in the evening)

**PMO** /ˌpi ɛm ˈoʊ/ ***abbr.*** (*Cdn*) = THE PRIME MINISTER'S OFFICE

**PMS** /ˌpi ɛm ˈɛs/ ***abbr.*** premenstrual syndrome; physical and emotional problems such as pain and feeling depressed that many women experience before their period (= flow of blood) each month

**pneu·mo·nia** /nuˈmoʊnyə/ ***noun*** [U] a serious illness of the lungs which makes breathing difficult

**poach** /poʊtʃ/ ***verb*** **1** [T] to cook an egg without its shell in boiling water: *poached eggs* **2** [T] to cook food (especially fish) in water or liquid that is boiling gently **3** [I,T] to catch or kill birds, animals or fish illegally, especially on sb else's land **4** [T] to take an idea from sb else and use it in an unfair way

**poach·er** /ˈpoʊtʃər/ ***noun*** [C] a person who catches or kills birds, animals or fish illegally

**PO Box** (*also* **P.O. Box**) /ˌpi ˈoʊ bɑks/ ***noun*** [C] = POST OFFICE BOX

★**pock·et¹** /ˈpɑkət/ ***noun*** [C] **1** a small bag that is sewn inside or on sth you wear and that you can carry things in: *He always walks with his hands in his pants pockets.* ◇ *a pocket dictionary/calculator* (= one small enough to fit in your pocket) ➲ picture

P

at **shirt**. **2** a bag or flap that is fastened to the inside of a car door, suitcase, etc. and that you can put things in: *There are safety instructions in the pocket of the seat in front of you.* **3** a small area or group of sth: *pockets of unemployment* ◇ *a pocket of warm air*

IDM **pick sb's pocket** → PICK[1]

**pock·et**[2] /ˈpɑkət/ ***verb*** [T] **1** to put sth in your POCKET[1] (1): *He took the letter and pocketed it quickly.* **2** to steal sth or to keep money for yourself

**pock·et·book** /ˈpɑkətbʊk/ ***noun*** [C] (*old-fashioned*) = PURSE[1] (*figurative*) *Most people worry about how government policies will affect their pocketbooks* (= how much money they have).

**pock·et·ful** /ˈpɑkətfʊl/ ***noun*** [C] the amount that a POCKET[1] (1) holds

ˈ**pocket knife** ***noun*** [C] (*pl.* **pocket knives**) (*also* **penknife, jackknife**) a small knife with one or more blades that fold down into the handle

**pocket knife**

blade

**pod** /pɑd/ ***noun*** [C] the long, green part of some plants, such as peas and beans, that holds the seeds ➲ picture on study page **A28-29**.

**po·di·a·trist** /pəˈdaɪətrɪst/ ***noun*** [C] a person whose job is the care and treatment of people's feet ▶ **po·di·a·try** /pəˈdaɪətri/ ***noun*** [U]

**po·di·um** /ˈpoʊdiəm/ ***noun*** [C] a tall, narrow desk that sb stands behind when speaking formally to a large group of people

P

★**po·em** /ˈpoʊəm/ ***noun*** [C] a piece of writing, often arranged in short lines with similar sounds at the ends of lines. Poems try to express thoughts and feelings with the help of sound and rhythm: *a Robert Frost poem* (= written by him) ◇ *to write a poem*

**po·et** /ˈpoʊət/ ***noun*** [C] a person who writes poems

**po·et·ic** /poʊˈɛt̬ɪk/ ***adj.*** **1** beautiful and full of imagination **2** of or like poets and poetry: *poetic language* ▶ **po·et·i·cal·ly** /-kli/ ***adv.***

**poˌetic ˈlicense** ***noun*** [U] the freedom to change facts, the normal rules of language, etc. in a special piece of writing or speech in order to achieve a particular effect: *He used a little poetic license to embroider a good story.*

★**po·et·ry** /ˈpoʊətri/ ***noun*** [U] poems, thought of as a group or a form of literature: *Shakespeare's poetry and plays* ◇ *poetry and prose*

**poign·ant** /ˈpɔmyənt/ ***adj.*** causing sadness or pity: *a poignant memory* ▶ **poign·an·cy** /-yənsi/ ***noun*** [U] (*formal*) ▶ **poign·ant·ly** ***adv.***

**poin·set·tia** /pɔmˈsɛt̬ə; -ˈsɛt̬iə/ ***noun*** [C] a tropical plant with large red or pink leaves that grow to look like flowers, often grown indoors in pots

★**point**[1] /pɔɪnt/ ***noun*** [C, sing.]

➤OPINION/FACT **1** [C] something that you say as part of a discussion; a particular fact, idea or opinion: *During the meeting, she made some interesting points.* ◇ *I see your point, but I don't agree with you.* ◇ *"How are we going to pay for everything?" "That's a good point."*

NOTE We **bring up, raise, make, emphasize** and **illustrate** a point.

➤MAIN IDEA **2 the point** [sing.] the most important part of what is being said; the main piece of information: *The point is that we can't go on vacation until the car is fixed.* ◇ *She always talks and talks and takes forever to get to the point.* ◇ *You're still missing* (= not understanding) *the point here.*

➤QUALITY **3** [C] a detail, single item, quality of sb/sth: *What would you say are your strong and weak points?* (= good and bad qualities)

➤PURPOSE **4** [sing.] the meaning, reason, purpose, etc. of sth: *What's the point of calling her again?* ◇ *There's no point in telling my parents all my problems.*

➤PLACE **5** [C] (often in compounds) a particular place or position: *We should be reaching the point where the road joins the freeway.* ◇ *The library is a good starting point for that sort of information.* ◇ *He aimed the gun at a point just above the man's head.*

➤SHARP END **6** [C] the thin, sharp end of sth: *the point of a pin/needle/pencil*

➤IN NUMBERS **7** [C] a small round dot used when writing parts of numbers

➤TIME **8** [C] a particular time or moment; a stage of progress, development, etc.: *At one point I thought I was going to laugh.* ◇ *He has reached the high point of his career.* ◇ *the boiling/freezing point of water*

➤MEASUREMENT **9** [C] a single unit in some games, sports, etc. that you add to others to get the score: *to score a point* ◇ *Kari won the game by one point over Mark.* **10** [C] a unit of measurement for certain things: *The stock market gained 27 points today.*

IDM **beside the point** not connected with the subject you are discussing

**make a point of doing sth** to be especially careful to do sth: *I'll make a point of inviting them to our next party.*

**point of view** a way of looking at a situation; an opinion: *You should try to understand other people's points of view.* ◇ *From my point of view it would be better to wait a little longer.*

NOTE Do not confuse **from my point of view** with **in my opinion**. The first means "from my position in life" i.e. as a woman, child, teacher, etc. The second means "I think": *From an advertiser's point of view, television is a wonderful medium.* ◇ *In my opinion, people watch too much television.*

**a sore point** → SORE[1]

**to the point** connected with what is being discussed: *His speech was short and to the point.*

**up to a point** partly: *I agree with you up to a point.*

★**point**[2] /pɔɪnt/ ***verb*** **1** [I] **point (at/to sb/sth)** to show where sth is or to draw attention to sth using your finger, a stick, etc.: *"I'll take that one," she said, pointing to a big chocolate cake.* **2** [T] **point sth (at/toward sb/sth)** to aim sth in the direction of sb/sth: *The farmer pointed his gun at the rabbit and fired.* **3** [I] to face in a particular direction or to show that sth is in a particular direction: *Go down this road and you'll see the sign pointing toward the highway.* **4** [I] **point to sth** to show that sth is likely to exist, happen, be true, etc.: *Research points to a connection between smoking and cancer.*

IDM **point a/the finger at sb/sth** to blame sb/sth for sth; to accuse sb/sth: *It's too easy to point the finger at somebody else when things go wrong.*

PHR V **point sth out (to sb)** to direct attention to sth; to make sth clear to sb: *The guide pointed out all the places of interest to us on the way.* ◇ *I'd like to point out that we don't have much time left to make a decision.*

**ˌpoint-ˈblank** ***adj., adv.*** **1** (used about sth that is said) in a way that is very direct and often not polite; not allowing any discussion: *He told her point-blank to get out of the house.* **2** (used about a shot) from a very close position: *The shot was fired at point-blank range.*

★**point·ed** /ˈpɔɪntəd/ ***adj.*** **1** (*also informal* **point·y**) having a POINT[1] (6) at one end: *She has a pointed nose.* **2** done or spoken in a way that makes it clear that you are being critical: *She made a pointed comment about people who are always late.* ▸ **point·ed·ly** ***adv.***

**point·er** /ˈpɔɪntər/ ***noun*** [C] **1** a piece of helpful advice or information: *Could you give me some pointers on the best way to tackle the problem?* **2** a stick or rod which is used to point to things on a map, etc.

**point·less** /ˈpɔɪntləs/ ***adj.*** without any use or purpose: *It's pointless to try and make him agree.* ◇ *My whole life seemed pointless after my husband died.* ▸ **point·less·ly** ***adv.*** ▸ **point·less·ness** ***noun*** [U]

**point·y** /ˈpɔɪnti/ ***adj.*** (*informal*) = POINTED (1)

**poise** /pɔɪz/ ***noun*** [U] a calm, confident way of behaving: *The job requires poise and an ability to deal with people.*

**poised** /pɔɪzd/ ***adj.*** **1 poised (to do sth)** ready to act; about to do sth: *The Red Cross is poised to take action if the crisis continues.* **2** not moving but ready to move: *"Should I call the doctor or not?" he asked, his hand poised above the telephone.* **3** calm and confident

★**poi·son**[1] /ˈpɔɪzn/ ***noun*** [C,U] a substance that kills or harms you if you eat or drink it: *The label on the bottle said, "Poison. Do not take internally."* ◇ *rat poison* ◇ *poison gas*

★**poi·son**[2] /ˈpɔɪzn/ ***verb*** [T] **1** to give poison to sb/sth; to kill, harm or damage sb/sth with poison: *The police confirmed that the murder victim had been poisoned.* **2** to put poison in sth: *The cup of coffee had been poisoned.* ◇ *a poisoned drink* **3** to spoil or ruin sth: *The fight had poisoned their relationship.*

**poi·son·ing** /ˈpɔɪzn·ɪŋ/ ***noun*** [U] the giving or taking of poison or a dangerous substance: *His death was the result of poisoning.* ◇ *food poisoning* (= illness as a result of eating bad food)

**ˌpoison ˈivy** ***noun*** [U] a wild plant with a substance on its leaves that makes your skin red and painful if you touch it

★**poi·son·ous** /ˈpɔɪzn·əs/ ***adj.*** **1** causing death or illness if you eat or drink it: *a poisonous plant* **2** (used about animals, etc.) producing and using poison to attack its enemies: *poisonous snakes/insects*

**poke** /poʊk/ ***verb*** [T] **1** to push sb/sth with a finger, stick or other long, thin object: *He poked the insect with his finger to see if it was alive.* **2 poke sth into, through, out of, down, etc.** to push sth quickly into sth or in a certain direction: *"Hi Jane," she said, poking her head through the doorway.* ◇ *He poked the stick into the hole to see how deep it was.*

IDM **poke fun at sb/sth** to make jokes about sb/sth, often in an unkind way

**poke/stick your nose into sth** → NOSE[1]

PHR V **poke around** (*informal*) to try to find sth by looking behind, under, etc. things: *I noticed that somebody had been poking around in my desk.*

**poke out of/through sth; poke out/through/up** to be visible coming through a hole, an open space, etc.: *A pen was poking out of her bag.*

▸ **poke** ***noun*** [C]: *I gave him a poke in the side to wake him up.*

**pok·er** /ˈpoʊkər/ ***noun*** **1** [U] a type of card game usually played to win money: *to play poker* ◇ *a game of poker* **2** [C] a metal stick for moving the coal or wood in a fire ➲ picture at **fireplace**.

**pok·y** /ˈpoʊki/ (*US also* **pok·ey**) ***adj.*** (**pok·i·er; pok·i·est**) **1** slow and therefore annoying **2** (used about a room, etc.) small

**po·lar** /ˈpoʊlər/ ***adj.*** (only *before* a noun) of or near the North or South Pole: *the polar regions*

**ˈpolar bear** ***noun*** [C] a large white bear that lives in the area near the North Pole

**po·lar·ize** /ˈpoʊləraɪz/ ***verb*** [I,T] to separate or make people separate into two groups with completely opposite opinions: *Public opinion has polarized on this issue.* ◇ *The issue has polarized public opinion.*

**Po·lar·oid™** /ˈpoʊlərɔɪd/ ***noun*** [C] a special type of photograph that comes directly out of the camera and develops by itself in just a few minutes, or a camera that takes these photographs

★**pole** /poʊl/ ***noun*** [C] **1** a long, thin piece of wood or metal: *a fishing pole* ◇ *a tent pole* ➲ picture at **ski**. **2** either of the two points at the exact top and bottom of the earth: *the North/South Pole* ➲ picture at **earth**.

**the ˈpole vault** ***noun*** [sing.] the sport of jumping over a high bar with the help of a long pole

★**po·lice**[1] /pəˈlis/ ***noun*** [pl.] the official organization whose job is to make sure that people obey the law, and to prevent and solve crime, etc.: *Did you call the police when your car was stolen?* ◇ *a police car* ◇ *a police report*

> NOTE **Police** is a plural noun, always used with a plural verb. You cannot say "a police" meaning one man or woman. When we are talking about the organization, we always use **the**: *The police are investigating the murder.*

**po·lice**[2] /pəˈlis/ ***verb*** [T] to keep control in a place by using the police or by making people follow the rules: *The cost of policing the neighborhood is extremely high.* ◇ *One of the teachers' jobs is policing the student cafeteria.*

**poˈlice deˌpartment** ***noun*** [C] the official organization of the police in a town or city

**poˈlice force** ***noun*** [C] all the police officers in a town or an area: *the campus police force*

**po·lice·man** /pəˈlismən/ ***noun*** [C] (*pl.* **po·lice·men** /-mən/) a man who is a member of the police

**po'lice ˌofficer** (*also* 'officer) **noun** [C] a person who is a member of the police: *a plainclothes police officer* (= one who is not wearing a uniform) ➲ Look at **detective**.

**po'lice ˌstation** **noun** [C] an office of a local police department

**po·lice·wo·man** /pə'lisæsstress:wʊmən/ **noun** [C] (*pl.* **-wo·men**) (*old-fashioned*) a woman who is a member of the police

NOTE **Police officer** is more common nowadays.

★**pol·i·cy** /'pɑləsi/ **noun** [C,U] (*pl.* **pol·i·cies**) **1** **policy (on sth)** a plan of action or statement of aims and ideas, especially that of a government, company or other organization: *the administration's new policy on women in the military* ◇ *Company policy does not allow smoking in the building.* ➲ Look at the note at **politics**. **2** a document that shows an agreement that you have made with an insurance company: *an insurance policy*

**po·li·o** /'poʊlioʊ/ **noun** [U] a serious disease which can cause you to lose the power in certain muscles

**poli sci** /ˌpɑli 'saɪ/ **noun** [U] (*informal*) = POLITICAL SCIENCE

★**pol·ish¹** /'pɑlɪʃ/ **verb** [T] **1** to make sth shine by rubbing it and often by putting a special cream or liquid on it: *Don't forget to polish your shoes!* **2** to spend time in order to improve sth: *She spent the whole weekend polishing her big speech.*

PHRV **polish sth off** (*informal*) to finish sth, especially food, quickly: *The kids polished off a whole carton of ice cream.*

P

★**pol·ish²** /'pɑlɪʃ/ **noun** [U] a cream, liquid, wax, etc. that you put on sth to clean it and make it shine: *a can of shoe polish* ➲ Look also at **nail polish**.

**pol·ished** /'pɑlɪʃt/ **adj.** **1** shiny because of polishing: *polished wood floors* **2** (used about a performance, etc.) of a high standard: *a polished performance on television* **3** (used a person) confident and skillful: *a polished political speaker*

★**po·lite** /pə'laɪt/ **adj.** having or showing good manners, e.g. that you are helpful and thoughtful toward other people and do not say or do things that might upset them; not rude: *The clerks in that store are always very helpful and polite.* ◇ *It's polite to say thank you.* ◇ *He gave me a polite smile.* OPP **impolite** or **rude** ▸ **po·lite·ly** **adv.** ▸ **po·lite·ness** **noun** [U]

★**po·lit·i·cal** /pə'lɪt̬ɪkl/ **adj.** **1** connected with politics and government: *She has very strong political opinions.* ◇ *a political prisoner* (= one who has been put in prison for criticizing the government) ◇ *an important local political figure* **2** (used about people) interested or active in politics: *I'm not really very political.* ▸ **po·lit·i·cal·ly** /-kli/ **adv.**: *Politically, he's pretty right wing.*

**poˌlitically cor'rect** (*also* **PC**) **adj.** (used about words, behavior, etc.) that many people consider polite and acceptable and not likely to offend women, people of other races, etc.: *It is no longer politically correct to call young women "girls."*

NOTE **Politically correct** terms are sometimes used in a critical way by people who believe it is not necessary to find new words for ones that may be unacceptable to some people.

▸ **poˌlitical cor'rectness** **noun** [U]

**poˌlitical 'science** (*also informal* **poli sci**) **noun** [U] the study of politics and systems of government

★**pol·i·ti·cian** /ˌpɑlə'tɪʃn/ **noun** **1** [C] a person who works in an official government job to which he/she has been elected, or who is trying to be elected: *Politicians from all parties supported the war.* **2** a person who is good at dealing with people and at using different situations in an organization to try to get power or advantage for himself/herself

★**pol·i·tics** /'pɑlətɪks/ **noun** **1** [U] the work and ideas that are connected with governing a country, a town, etc.: *Are you interested in politics?* ◇ *My son wants to go into politics* (= become a politician). ◇ *local politics* ◇ *Politics has never been a big interest of mine.* **2** [pl.] a person's political opinions and beliefs: *She is well-known for her liberal politics.* ➲ A government's **policy** (= plan of action or aim) will depend on its **politics** (= its ideas and beliefs). **3** [pl.] actions within a group that are done in order to gain power or control: *office politics*

**pol·ka dot** /'poʊkə dɑt/ **noun** [C] one of a pattern of round spots on fabric, etc.: *a blue scarf with white polka dots* ➲ picture on study page **A30**. ▸ **pol·ka-dot·ted** /'poʊkə dɑt̬əd/ **adj.**

**poll¹** /poʊl/ **noun** **1** [C] (*also* **opinion poll**) a way of finding out public opinion by asking a number of people what they think about sth: *The Democratic candidate had a five point lead over the Republican in the latest poll.* ➲ Look also at **exit poll**. **2** **the polls** [pl.] voting in a political election: *The state will go to the polls to choose a new governor tomorrow.* ◇ *The polls close at 8:00.*

**poll²** /poʊl/ **verb** [T] to ask sb his/her opinion on a subject: *Of those polled, only 20 percent were in favor of changing the law.*

**pol·len** /'pɑlən/ **noun** [U] a fine, usually yellow, powder which is formed in flowers. It makes other flowers of the same type produce seeds when it is carried to them by the wind, insects, etc.

**'pollen count** **noun** [usually sing.] a number that shows the amount of pollen in the air, used to warn people whose health is affected by it: *Hay fever sufferers should check the pollen count every day.*

**pol·li·nate** /'pɑləneɪt/ **verb** [T] to put pollen into a flower or plant so that it produces seeds: *flowers pollinated by bees/the wind* ▸ **pol·li·na·tion** /ˌpɑlə'neɪʃn/

**'polling ˌplace** (*also* **'polling ˌstation**) **noun** [C] a place where people go to vote in an election

**poll·ster** /'poʊlstər/ **noun** [C] a person who makes or asks the questions in a POLL¹ (1)

**pol·lut·ant** /pə'lutnt/ **noun** [C] a substance that pollutes air, water, etc.

**pol·lute** /pə'lut/ **verb** [T] to make air, rivers, etc. dirty and dangerous: *Many East Coast beaches are polluted.*

**pol·lu·tion** /pə'luʃn/ **noun** [U] **1** the act of polluting: *Major steps are being taken to control the pollution of beaches.* **2** substances that pollute: *Five years after the disaster, the pollution on the coast of Alaska had still not been cleaned up.*

**po·lo** /'poʊloʊ/ **noun** [U] a game for two teams of

horses and riders. The players try to score points by hitting a ball with long wooden hammers.

ˈ**polo shirt** ***noun*** [C] a shirt made of a light, knit fabric, with short sleeves, a collar and two or three buttons in the front

**pol·ter·geist** /ˈpoʊltərgaɪst/ ***noun*** [C] a ghost that makes loud noises and throws objects

**pol·y·es·ter** /ˌpɑliˈɛstər; ˈpɑliɛstər/ ***noun*** [U] a type of artificial material that is used for making clothes, etc.: *The sheets are 50% cotton and 50% polyester.*

**po·lyg·a·my** /pəˈlɪgəmi/ ***noun*** [U] the custom of having more than one wife or husband at the same time ▶ **po·lyg·a·mist** /pəˈlɪgəmɪst/ ***noun*** [C]

**pol·y·gon** /ˈpɑligɑn/ ***noun*** [C] a flat shape with at least three straight sides and angles, and usually five or more ▶ **po·lyg·o·nal** /pəˈlɪgənl/ ***adj.***

**pol·y·graph** /ˌpɑligræf/ (*also* **lie detector**) ***noun*** [C] a piece of equipment that can show whether a person is lying or not

**pol·y·mer** /ˈpɑləmər/ ***noun*** [C] (in chemistry) a natural or artificial compound consisting of large groups of atoms (**molecules**) that are made from combinations of small simple molecules

**pol·yp** /ˈpɑləp/ ***noun*** [C] **1** (*medical*) a small lump that grows inside the body, especially in the nose, that is caused by disease but is usually harmless **2** a small and very simple sea creature with a body shaped like a tube

**pol·y·un·sat·u·rat·ed** /ˌpɑliʌnˈsætʃəreɪt̬əd/ ***adj.*** (used about many vegetable fats and some animal fats) having a chemical structure which does not encourage the harmful development of cholesterol. Polyunsaturated fats are considered healthier in the diet than other fats. ➲ Compare **saturated** and **unsaturated** fats.

**pomp** /pɑmp/ ***noun*** [U] the impressive clothes, decorations, music, etc. and traditional customs that are part of an official occasion or ceremony: *all the pomp and ceremony of a royal wedding*

IDM **pomp and circumstance** formal and impressive ceremony

**pom·pom** /ˈpɑmpɑm/ (*also* **pompon** /ˈpɑmpɑn/) ***noun*** [C] a large ball made of thin strips of paper, fabric or plastic tied together, that people wave around in the air to show enthusiasm at football games, etc.

**pom·pous** /ˈpɑmpəs/ ***adj.*** feeling or showing that you think you are more important than other people, e.g. by using long and important-sounding words.

NOTE This word is used in a critical way.

**pon·cho** /ˈpɑntʃoʊ/ ***noun*** [C] (*pl.* **pon·chos**) a type of coat without sleeves, made from one large piece of cloth with a hole in the middle for your head to go through

**pond** /pɑnd/ ***noun*** [C] an area of water that is smaller than a lake

**pon·der** /ˈpɑndər/ ***verb*** [I,T] **ponder (on/over sth)** to think about sth carefully or for a long time

**pon·der·ous** /ˈpɑndərəs/ ***adj.*** (*written*) **1** (used about speech and writing) too slow and careful; serious and boring: *He spoke in a slow ponderous voice.* **2** moving slowly and heavily; able to move only slowly: *She watched the cow's ponderous progress.* ▶ **pon·der·ous·ly** ***adv.***

**pon·tiff** /ˈpɑntəf/ ***noun*** (*formal*) the leader of the Roman Catholic Church (**the Pope**)

**pon·tif·i·cate** /pɑnˈtɪfəkeɪt/ ***verb*** [I] **pontificate (about/on sth)** to give your opinions about sth in a way that shows that you think you are right

**po·ny** /ˈpoʊni/ ***noun*** [C] (*pl.* **po·nies**) a type of small horse

**po·ny·tail** /ˈpoʊniteɪl/ ***noun*** [C] long hair that is tied at the back of the head and that hangs down like the tail of a horse: *She wore her hair in a ponytail.* ➲ picture at **braid**.

**pooch** /putʃ/ ***noun*** [C] (*informal*) a dog

**poo·dle** /ˈpudl/ ***noun*** [C] a type of dog with thick curly hair which is often cut into a special pattern

★**pool**[1] /pul/ ***noun*** **1** [C] = SWIMMING POOL: *a heated indoor pool* ◇ *He swam ten lengths of the pool.* **2** [C] a small area of water or another liquid, or of light: *They found her lying in a pool of blood.* ◇ *a pool of light* **3** [C] a quantity of money, goods, workers, etc. that is shared between a group of people: *a great pool of talent* ◇ *a pool of potential jurors* ➲ Look also at **car pool**. **4** [U] an indoor game that is played on a table with 16 colored and numbered balls. Two players try to hit these balls into holes in the table (**pockets**) with long thin sticks (**cues**): *to play/shoot pool* ◇ *a pool table* ◇ *a pool hall* (= a building where people can go to play pool)

**pool**[2] /pul/ ***verb*** [T] to collect money, ideas, etc. from a number of people and share them: *If we pool our ideas we should come up with a good plan.*

**poop**[1] /pup/ ***noun*** [U] (*informal*) solid waste material that is passed out of the body through the bowels: *Careful – don't step in that dog poop!* ➲ **Excrement** and **feces** are formal words with the same meaning.

**poop**[2] /pup/ ***verb*** [I] (*informal*) to push solid waste material out of the body through the bowels ➲ **Defecate** is a more formal word with the same meaning. A polite expression is **go to the bathroom**.

**pooped** /pupt/ (*also* ˌ**pooped** ˈ**out**) ***adj.*** (*informal*) (not before a noun) very tired

**poop·er scoop·er** /ˈpupər ˌskupər/ ***noun*** [C] (*informal*) a tool used by dog owners for removing their dogs' solid waste from the streets

★**poor** /pʊr; pɔr/ ***adj.*** **1** having very little money and a very low standard of living: *The family was too poor to buy good food.* ◇ *We ought to help poorer countries.* OPP **rich** **2** of low quality or in a bad condition: *Paul is in very poor health.* ◇ *The airline has a poor safety record.* ◇ *Attendance at the meeting was poor* (= not as many people came as had been expected). **3** (used when you are showing that you feel sorry for somebody): *That poor child lost both her parents.* ◇ *Poor Don! His car got stolen yesterday.* **4 the poor** ***noun*** [pl.] people who have little money

NOTE Note that we use **the poor** in the plural. It always means "poor people" and CANNOT mean "the poor person."

P

**poor·ly** /ˈpʊrli; ˈpɔrli/ *adv.* not well; badly: *a poorly paid job* ◇ *The science lab is very poorly equipped.*

★**pop**[1] /pɑp/ *noun* **1** [C] a short sharp sound like a small explosion: *There was a loud pop as the champagne cork came out of the bottle.* **2** [U] = SODA **3** (*also* ˈ**pop music**) [U] a type of modern music that is most popular among young people: *I like to listen to rock, pop and jazz.* **4** [C] (*old-fashioned*) father

**pop**[2] /pɑp/ *verb* (**pop·ping**; **popped**) [I,T] (to cause sth) to make a short sharp sound like a small explosion: *The balloon popped.* ◇ *He popped the balloon.*
PHR V **pop out** to come out (of sth) suddenly or quickly: (*figurative*) *Her eyes almost popped out of her head in surprise.*
**pop up** (*informal*) to appear or happen suddenly: *There are new fast-food restaurants popping up everywhere.* ◇ *If you click here, another window will pop up on the screen.*

**pop**[3] /pɑp/ *adj.* (*informal*) (only *before* a noun) connected with the culture of ordinary people; not for experts: *You shouldn't rely on advice from those pop psychology books.*

**pop·corn** /ˈpɑpkɔrn/ *noun* [U] a type of corn that is heated until it bursts and becomes light and full of air

ˌ**pop** ˈ**culture** *noun* [U] commercial art, music, literature, etc. which is enjoyed by a lot of ordinary people

**pope** /poʊp/ *noun* [C] the head of the Roman Catholic Church: *Pope John Paul II*

**pop·lar** /ˈpɑplər/ *noun* [C] a tall straight tree with soft wood

P

**pop·o·ver** /ˈpɑpoʊvər/ *noun* [C] a type of food made from a mixture of eggs, milk and flour which rises to form a hollow shell when it is baked

**pop·py** /ˈpɑpi/ *noun* [C] (*pl.* **pop·pies**) a bright red wild flower that has small black seeds: *a roll with poppy seeds on top*

ˌ**pop** ˈ**quiz** *noun* [C] (*pl.* ˌ**pop** ˈ**quiz·zes**) a short test that a teacher gives in class without warning, in order to check whether students have been studying

**Pop·si·cle**™ /ˈpɑpsɪkl/ *noun* [C] a piece of flavored ice on a stick

**pop·u·lace** /ˈpɑpyələs/ *noun* [sing.] (*formal*) (usually **the populace**) all the ordinary people of a particular country or area: *He had the support of large sections of the local populace.* ◇ *The populace at large is/are opposed to sudden change.*

★**pop·u·lar** /ˈpɑpyələr/ *adj.* **1** liked by many people or by most people in a group: *Computer games are popular with kids.* ◇ *Niagara Falls is a popular place to go for a honeymoon.* ◇ *He's very popular with his students.* OPP **unpopular 2** for ordinary people (= not for specialists or people with a high level of education): *People were surprised that such a respected scientist had written a popular book on astronomy.* **3** (only *before* a noun) of or for a lot of people: *The program is being repeated by popular demand.*

**pop·u·lar·i·ty** /ˌpɑpyəˈlærət̬i/ *noun* [U] the quality or state of being liked by many people: *A presidential campaign should be more than a popularity contest.* ◇ *to lose popularity*

**pop·u·lar·ize** /ˈpɑpyələraɪz/ *verb* [T] to make sth popular with, or known to, a lot of people: *The movie did a lot to popularize her novels.*

**pop·u·lar·ly** /ˈpɑpyələrli/ *adv.* by many people; generally: *The Republican Party is popularly known as the GOP.*

**pop·u·late** /ˈpɑpyəleɪt/ *verb* [T] (usually passive) to fill a particular area with people: *the North is very thinly populated.* ◇ *Most of New England is very densely populated.*

★**pop·u·la·tion** /ˌpɑpyəˈleɪʃn/ *noun* **1** [C,U] a number of people who live in a particular place: *What is the population of Canada?* ◇ *a town with a population of over 10,000* ◇ *an increase/a fall in population* **2** [C] all the people who live in a particular area: *The report examines the effects of the changes on the local population.* **3** [C] all the people or animals of a particular type that live in an area: *The prison population has increased a lot in recent years.* ◇ *the civilian population* (= the people who are not soldiers) ◇ *the penguin population of the island*

**pop·u·list** /ˈpɑpyəlɪst/ *noun* [C] a person who believes in or supports a type of politics that claims to represent the opinions and wishes of ordinary people: *a party of populists* ▸ **pop·u·list** *adj.*: *a populist leader*

**pop·u·lous** /ˈpɑpyələs/ *adj.* (*formal*) where a large number of people live: *one of America's most populous states*

ˈ**pop-up** *adj.* (only *before* a noun) (used about a computer menu, etc.) that can be brought to the screen quickly while you are working on another document: *a pop-up ad/menu/window*

**por·ce·lain** /ˈpɔrsələn/ *noun* [U] a hard white substance that is made by baking clay in an oven. Porcelain is used for making expensive cups, plates, etc.

**porch** /pɔrtʃ/ *noun* [C] an area attached to a house, usually at the front, with a roof and a floor but no outside walls: *On warm summer evenings, we sit out on the porch and talk.* ➲ Picture on study page **A31**. ➲ Look at **deck**, **patio** and **veranda**.

**por·cu·pine** /ˈpɔrkyəpaɪn/ *noun* [C] a small brown or black animal that is covered with stiff, sharp needles which point out from its body when it is angry or afraid

**pore**[1] /pɔr/ *noun* [C] one of the small holes in your skin through which sweat can pass

**pore**[2] /pɔr/ *verb*
PHR V **pore over sth** to study or read sth very carefully

**pork** /pɔrk/ *noun* [U] meat from a pig: *roast pork* ◇ *pork sausages* ➲ Look at **bacon** and **ham** and at the note at **meat**.

ˈ**pork-**ˌ**barrel** *noun* [U] (*slang*) local projects that are given a lot of government money in order to win votes; the money that is used: *pork-barrel spending/politics*

**pork·y** /ˈpɔrki/ *adj.* (**pork·i·er**; **pork·i·est**) (*informal*) (used about people) fat

**por·nog·ra·phy** /pɔrˈnɑgrəfi/ (*also informal* **porn** /pɔrn/) *noun* [U] books, magazines, movies, etc. that describe or show sexual acts in order to cause sexual excitement ▶ **por·no·graph·ic** /ˌpɔrnə'græfɪk/ ***adj.***: *pornographic movies*

**po·rous** /'pɔrəs/ ***adj.*** allowing liquid or air to pass through slowly: *Sand is a porous material.*

**por·poise** /'pɔrpəs/ ***noun*** [C] a sea animal that looks like a large fish. It is very similar to a dolphin and also lives in groups.

★**port** /pɔrt/ ***noun*** **1** [C,U] an area where ships load and unload goods and passengers: *a fishing port* ◇ *The ship spent two days in port.* **2** [C] a town or city that has a harbor: *Baltimore is a major port.* **3** [U] the side of a ship or aircraft that is on the left when you are facing forward ➲ Compare **starboard**. **4** [U,C] a strong sweet wine, usually dark red, that is made in Portugal. It is usually drunk at the end of a meal.

**port·a·ble** /'pɔrt̬əbl/ ***adj.*** that can be moved or carried easily: *a portable TV set*

**por·tal** /'pɔrt̬l/ ***noun*** [C] (*computing*) a website that is used as a point of entry to the Internet, where information has been collected that will be useful to a person interested in particular kinds of things: *a business/news/shopping portal*

**por·ter** /'pɔrt̬ər/ ***noun*** [C] a person whose job is to carry suitcases, etc. at a train station

**port·fo·li·o** /pɔrt'foʊlioʊ/ ***noun*** [C] (*pl.* **port·fo·li·os**) **1** a collection of pieces of work by an artist, a student, etc.: *50% of your final grade will be based on your homework portfolio.* **2** a collection of shares in companies that are owned by a person or another company: *a stock portfolio*

**port·hole** /'pɔrthoʊl/ ***noun*** [C] a small round window in a ship: *Anna spent the entire voyage staring out of a porthole at the sea.*

**por·ti·co** /'pɔrt̬ɪkoʊ/ ***noun*** [C] (*pl.* **por·ti·coes** or **-os**) (*formal*) a roof that is supported by columns, especially one that forms the entrance to a large building: *They stood under the classical portico of the White House.*

**por·tion** /'pɔrʃn/ ***noun*** [C] **1** a part or share of sth: *What portion of your salary is deducted for taxes?* ◇ *We both have to accept a portion of the blame.* **2** an amount of food for one person (especially in a restaurant): *They don't serve very large portions here.* ➲ Look at **helping** and **serving**.

**por·trait**[1] /'pɔrtrət/ ***noun*** [C] **1** a picture, painting or photograph of a person: *to paint sb's portrait* **2** a description of sb/sth in words

**por·trait**[2] /'pɔrtrət/ ***adj.*** (*computing*) (used about a page of a document) printed so that the top of the page is one of the shorter sides ➲ Look at **landscape**[2]

**por·tray** /pɔr'treɪ/ ***verb*** [T] **1** to describe sb/sth in words; to show sb/sth in a particular way: *The attorney portrayed her client as an honest family man.* **2** to act the part of sb in a play or movie: *It's hard for a young actress to portray a very old woman.* ▶ **por·tray·al** /pɔr'treɪəl/ ***noun*** [C]: *He won an award for his portrayal of Abraham Lincoln.*

★**pose**[1] /poʊz/ ***verb*** **1** [I] to sit or stand in a particular position for a painting, photograph, etc.: *After the wedding, we all posed for pictures.* **2** [I] **pose as sb/sth** to pretend to be sb/sth: *The thieves got into the house by posing as salesmen.* **3** [T] to set, cause or create sth: *The rise in the cost of living is posing problems for many families.* ◇ *to pose a question*

**pose**[2] /poʊz/ ***noun*** [C] a position in which you pose, e.g. for a painting or photograph: *The kids struck a silly pose for the camera.*

**posh** /pɑʃ/ ***adj.*** fashionable and expensive: *a posh neighborhood*

**po·si·tion**[1] /pə'zɪʃn/ ***noun***

➤ PLACE **1** [C,U] the place where sb/sth is or should be: *The enemy's position was marked on the map.* ◇ *That plant's in the wrong position. It's getting too much sun.* ◇ *All the dancers were in position waiting for the music to begin.*

➤ WAY OF SITTING/STANDING **2** [C,U] the way in which sb/sth sits, stands or is placed: *I have a stiff neck. I must have been sitting in an awkward position.* ◇ *Turn the switch to the "off" position.* ◇ *He woke up in pain every time he changed position.*

➤ OPINION **3** [C] **a position (on sth)** what you think about sth; your opinion: *What is the government's position on the refugee crisis?*

➤ SITUATION **4** [C, usually sing.] a state or situation: *What would you do if you were in my position?* ◇ *I'm sorry, I'm not in a position to help you financially.*

➤ LEVEL OF IMPORTANCE **5** [C,U] your place or rank in society, in a group, or in a race or competition: *He's always been in a respected position in the community.*

➤ JOB **6** [C] (*formal*) a job: *I am writing to apply for the position which was advertised in yesterday's newspaper.*

➤ IN SPORTS **7** [C] the part you play in a team game: *"What position do you play?" "Catcher."*

★**po·si·tion**[2] /pə'zɪʃn/ ***verb*** [T] to put sb/sth in a particular place or POSITION[1] (1): *Mary positioned herself near the door so she could get out quickly.*

★**pos·i·tive** /'pɑzət̬ɪv/ ***adj.***

➤ SURE/DEFINITE **1 positive (about sth/that...)** certain; sure: *Are you positive that this is the woman you saw?* **2** clear; definite: *There is no positive evidence that he is guilty.* ◇ *We have to take positive action to keep the situation from getting worse.*

➤ EFFECTIVE/USEFUL **3** helpful or encouraging: *The teacher tried to make positive suggestions.* ◇ *Their reaction to my idea was pretty positive.*

➤ FEELING HOPEFUL **4** hopeful or confident: *I feel very positive about our team's chances this season.* ◇ *Positive thinking will help you succeed.*

➤ SCIENTIFIC TEST **5** (used about a medical or scientific test) showing that sth has happened or is present: *The result of the pregnancy test was positive.*

➤ NUMBER **6** (used about a number) more than zero OPP The opposite for senses **3 – 6** is **negative**.

**pos·i·tive·ly** /'pɑzət̬ɪvli; ˌpɑzə'tɪvli/ ***adv.*** **1** in a helpful or encouraging way: *Our customers have reacted positively to the changes.* **2** (used for emphasizing sth) really; extremely: *A lot of the people in the audience looked positively ancient!* **3** certainly or firmly: *I was positively convinced that I was doing the right thing.*

**pos·se** /'pɑsi/ ***noun*** [C] **1** (in the past) a group of people who were brought together by a law officer (a **sheriff**) to find a criminal, etc. **2** (*slang*) a group

P

of friends who spend a lot of time together and do things together

★**pos·sess** /pəˈzɛs/ ***verb*** [T] **1** (*formal*) to have or own: *They lost everything they possessed in the fire.* ◇ *It is illegal to possess a gun without a license.* **2** to influence sb or to make sb do sth: *What in the world possessed you to say a thing like that?*

★**pos·ses·sion** /pəˈzɛʃn/ ***noun*** **1** [U] the state of having or owning sth: *Enemy forces took possession of the hill.* ◇ *He was arrested for possession of an illegal weapon.* **2** [C, usually pl.] something that you have or own: *Bob packed all his possessions into a suitcase and left.*

IDM **in possession (of sth)** having or owning sth: *Two teenagers were caught in possession of stolen property.*

**pos·ses·sive** /pəˈzɛsɪv/ ***adj.*** **1** not wanting to share sb/sth: *Dan is so possessive with his toys – he won't let anyone else play with them.* **2** (used in grammar to describe words that show who or what a person or thing belongs to): *"My," "your" and "his" are possessive adjectives.* ◇ *"Mine," "yours" and "his" are possessive pronouns.*

★**pos·si·bil·i·ty** /ˌpɑsəˈbɪləṭi/ ***noun*** (*pl.* **pos·si·bil·i·ties**) **1** [U] **possibility (of sth/of doing sth)**; **possibility (that...)** the situation when sth might happen or be true; the state of being possible: *There's not much possibility of the letter reaching you before Saturday.* ◇ *Is there any possibility that I can see you this weekend?*

> NOTE Be careful. We CANNOT say "a/the possibility to do sth" in English. To say that something is possible, we can use the verb **can**: *You can learn about North American culture by staying with a host family.* We can use **opportunity** to talk about something that is possible in a certain situation: *The exchange trip gave us a unique opportunity to learn about North American culture.*

**2** [C] something that might happen or be true; sth that is possible: *There is a strong possibility that the fire was started deliberately.* ◇ *One possibility would be for you to take the bus and for me to come later by car.*

★**pos·si·ble** /ˈpɑsəbl/ ***adj.*** **1** that can happen or be done: *I'll call you back as soon as possible.* ◇ *It is now possible to use the Internet for shopping.* ◇ *The doctors did everything possible to save his life.* ◇ *You were warned of all the possible dangers.* OPP **impossible** **2** that may be true or suitable: *There are several possible explanations for her strange behavior.* ◇ *There are four possible candidates for the job.* ➲ Look at **probable**.

★**pos·si·bly** /ˈpɑsəbli/ ***adv.*** **1** perhaps; maybe: *Tomorrow's weather will be cloudy with showers or possibly heavy rain.* ◇ *We will have to postpone the meeting until Thursday or possibly even Friday.* **2** (used for emphasizing sth) according to what is possible: *I will leave as soon as I possibly can.*

**pos·sum** /ˈpɑsəm/ ***noun*** [C] = OPOSSUM

IDM **play possum** (*informal*) to pretend you are asleep or dead: *Neil was just playing possum when his mom knocked on his door.*

★**post**¹ /poʊst/ ***noun*** **1** [C] an upright piece of metal or wood that is put in the ground to mark a position or to support sth: *a goal post* ◇ *a fence post* **2** [C] an important job, especially with the government or in the military forces: *She was given a diplomatic post in Paris.* **3** [C] a place where sb is on duty or is guarding sth: *The soldiers had to remain at their posts all night.*

★**post**² /poʊst/ ***verb*** [T] **1** to put a sign, notice, etc. on a wall or in a public place so that everyone can see it: *The notice was posted on every bulletin board on campus.* **2** to send sb to go and work somewhere, especially in an official government job or in the military forces: *After two years in Germany, Rosa was posted to an Air Force base in Texas.* **3** to put sb on guard or on duty in a particular place: *Police officers were posted at the front door of the building.*

**post·age** /ˈpoʊstɪdʒ/ ***noun*** [U] the amount that it costs to send a letter, package, etc.: *The cost of postage and handling is $2.*

ˈ**postage stamp** ***noun*** [C] = STAMP¹

**post·al** /ˈpoʊstl/ ***adj.*** connected with the collecting and delivering of letters, packages, etc.: *postal workers* ◇ *the Postal Service*

ˈ**postal code** ***noun*** [C] (*Cdn*) a group of six letters and numbers that you put at the end of an address. The postal code helps the post office to sort letters by machine.

**post·card** /ˈpoʊstkɑrd/ ***noun*** [C] a card that you write a message on and send to sb. Postcards often have a picture on one side and are usually sent without an envelope.

**post·doc·tor·al** /ˌpoʊstˈdɑktərəl/ (*also informal* **postdoc** /ˈpoʊstdɑk/) ***adj.*** connected with work or studying that sb does after he/she has received the highest university degree (a **Ph.D.**): *postdoctoral research*

**post·er** /ˈpoʊstər/ ***noun*** [C] **1** a large printed picture or a notice that is used to advertise sth or to decorate a room **2** a person who POSTS² (1) a message to a place on a website where people can read or write messages (**message board**)

**pos·te·ri·or** /pɑˈstɪriər; poʊ-/ ***noun*** [C] the part of your body that you sit on; the buttocks

**pos·ter·i·ty** /pɑˈstɛrəṭi/ ***noun*** [U] the future and the people who will be alive then: *We should protect our environment for the sake of posterity.*

**post·grad·u·ate** /ˌpoʊstˈgrædʒuət/ ***adj.*** (*formal*) connected with further studies that sb does at a university after he/she has received his/her first (**bachelor's**) degree ➲ Look at **graduate**³, **undergraduate** and **postdoctoral**.

**post·hu·mous** /ˈpɑstʃəməs/ ***adj.*** given or happening after sb has died: *a posthumous medal for bravery* ▶ **post·hu·mous·ly** ***adv.***: *Her last novel was published posthumously.*

**post·ing** /ˈpoʊstɪŋ/ ***noun*** [C] **1** an act of sending sb to a place to do his/her job, especially for a limited period of time: *overseas postings* **2** (*computing*) a message sent to a discussion group on the Internet: *The newsgroup gathers postings on a particular topic and distributes them to the newsgroup's subscribers.*

**post·mark** /ˈpoʊstmɑrk/ ***noun*** [C] an official mark over a stamp on a letter, package, etc. that says when and where it was mailed

**post·mas·ter** /ˈpoʊstmæstər/ *noun* [C] a person who is in charge of a post office

**post·mod·ern·ism** /ˌpoʊstˈmɑdərnɪzəm/ *noun* [U] a style and movement in art, architecture, literature, etc. in the late 20th century that reacts against modern styles, e.g. by mixing features from traditional and modern styles ▸ **post·mod·ern·ist** /ˌpoʊstˈmɑdərnɪst/ *noun* [C], *adj.* (*also* **post·mod·ern**): *postmodernist culture/writing/cinema*

★ **ˈpost ˌoffice** *noun* [C] a building where you can buy stamps, send packages, etc.

**ˈpost office ˌbox** (*also* **PO box**) *noun* [C] a place in a post office where letters, packages, etc. are kept until they are picked up by the person they were sent to

**post·pone** /poʊstˈpoʊn; poʊsˈpoʊn/ *verb* [T] to arrange that sth will happen at a later time than the time you had planned; to delay: *The wedding was postponed until August because the bride's mother was in the hospital.* ◇ *Because of illness, the concert is postponed until further notice* (= no date for it can be given now). ➲ Look at **cancel.** ▸ **post·pone·ment** *noun* [C,U]

**post·script** /ˈpoʊstskrɪpt; ˈpoʊsskrɪpt/ *noun* [C] (*figurative*) extra facts or information about a story, an event, etc. that are added after it has finished: *News of the award comes as a fitting postscript to a long and successful career.*

**pos·ture** /ˈpɑstʃər/ *noun* [U] the way that a person sits, stands, walks, etc.: *Poor posture can lead to backache.*

**post·war** /ˌpoʊstˈwɔr/ *adj.* existing or happening in the period after the end of a war, especially after World War II: *postwar reconstruction*

★ **pot[1]** /pɑt/ *noun* **1** [C] a round container that is used for cooking food: *pots and pans* **2** [C] a container that you use for a particular purpose: *That plant needs a larger pot.* ◇ *a flowerpot* ◇ *a coffee pot* ➲ picture at **coffee**. **3** [C] the amount that a POT (2) contains: *We drank two pots of coffee.* **4** [U] (*informal*) the illegal drug marijuana: *to smoke pot*

**pot[2]** /pɑt/ *verb* [T] (**pot__t__ing**; **pot__t__ed**) to put a plant into a container

**po·tas·si·um** /pəˈtæsiəm/ *noun* [U] (*symbol* **K**) a chemical element. Potassium is a soft silver-white metal that exists mainly in compounds which are used in industry and farming.

★ **po·ta·to** /pəˈteɪt̬oʊ; -t̬ə/ *noun* [C,U] (*pl.* **po·ta·toes**) a round vegetable with a brown, yellow or red skin. Potatoes are white or yellow inside. They grow under the ground on the roots of the potato plant ➲ picture on study page **A28-29**. [C]: *mashed potatoes with gravy* ◇ *baked potatoes* (= baked in the oven inside their skins) ◇ *potato salad* ◇ *Linda peeled the potatoes for supper.* ➲ Look also at **couch potato.**

**poˈtato chip** *noun* [C] a very thin piece of potato that is fried in oil, dried and then sold in bags. Potato chips usually have salt on them.

**po·tent** /ˈpoʊtnt/ *adj.* strong or powerful: *a potent force* ▸ **po·ten·cy** /-nsi/ *noun* [U]

★ **po·ten·tial[1]** /pəˈtɛnʃl/ *adj.* (only *before* a noun) that may possibly become sth, happen, be used, etc.: *Wind power is a potential source of energy.* ◇ *potential customers* ▸ **po·ten·tial·ly** /-ʃəli/ *adv.*: *That machine is very rusty and is potentially very dangerous.*

★ **po·ten·tial[2]** /pəˈtɛnʃl/ *noun* [U] the qualities or abilities that sb/sth has but that may not be fully developed yet: *That boy has great potential as a pianist.* ◇ *to realize your full potential*

**pot·hole** /ˈpɑthoʊl/ *noun* [C] a hole in the surface of a road, etc.

**po·tion** /ˈpoʊʃn/ *noun* [C] (used especially in stories) a drink of medicine or poison; a liquid with magic powers: *a magic/love potion*

**pot·luck** /ˌpɑtˈlʌk; ˈpɑtlʌk/ *noun* [C] a meal to which each guest brings some food, which is then shared out among the guests

IDM **take potluck 1** to have to choose sth from what is available and hope that it will be good or acceptable: *He'd have to take potluck in a town not noted for its hotels.* **2** to have a meal at sb's home in which you eat whatever he/she has available ▸ **pot·luck** *adj.*: *a potluck meal/supper*

**pot·pour·ri** /ˌpoʊpʊˈri/ *noun* **1** [C,U] a mixture of dried flowers and leaves used for making a room smell pleasant **2** [sing.] a mixture of various things that were not originally intended to form a group: *a potpourri of tunes*

**ˈpot roast** *noun* [C] a piece of meat cooked with vegetables in a pot ▸ **ˈpot-roast** *verb* [T]

**pot·shot** /ˈpɑtʃɑt/ *noun* [C] (*informal*) a shot that sb fires without aiming carefully: *Somebody* **took a potshot** *at him as he drove past.* ◇ (*figurative*) *The newspapers took constant potshots at* (= criticized) *the President.*

**pot·ter** /ˈpɑt̬ər/ *noun* [C] a person who makes pots, dishes, etc. (**pottery**) from baked clay

**pot·ter·y** /ˈpɑt̬əri/ *noun* [U] pots, dishes, etc. that are made from baked clay

**pot·ty** /ˈpɑt̬i/ *noun* [C] (*pl.* **pot·ties**) (*informal*) (used especially by and to small children) a toilet: *Do you need to go potty* (= use the toilet) *before we leave?*

**pouch** /paʊtʃ/ *noun* [C] **1** a small bag, usually with one main part inside for carrying things in **2** a pocket of skin in which some animals, e.g. kangaroos, carry their babies ➲ picture at **kangaroo**.

**poul·try** /ˈpoʊltri/ *noun* **1** [pl.] birds, e.g. chickens, ducks, turkeys, etc. that are kept on farms for their eggs or their meat: *to raise poultry* **2** [U] the meat from these birds ➲ Look at the note at **meat**.

**pounce** /paʊns/ *verb* [I] **pounce (on sb/sth)** to jump or land on sb/sth suddenly in order to attack: *The cat sat motionless, waiting to pounce on the mouse.* ◇ (*figurative*) *He was quick to pounce on any mistakes I made.*

★ **pound[1]** /paʊnd/ *noun* **1** [C] (*abbr.* **lb.**) a measure of weight; 0.454 of a kilogram. There are 16 ounces in a pound: *The carrots cost 49¢ a pound.* ◇ *The baby weighed six pounds at birth.* ◇ *I lost 15 pounds on my diet.* ◇ *Get a pound of coffee if you're going to the grocery store.* ◇ *a five-pound bag of flour* **2** [C] (*symbol* **£**) the unit of money in Britain

**pound[2]** /paʊnd/ *verb* **1** [T] to beat sth with a heavy tool to make it soft or like powder **2** [I] **pound (away) (at/against/on sth)** to hit or beat



P

sth many times: *Giant waves pounded against the rocks. ◇ to pound on a door ◇ (figurative) My heart was pounding with excitement.* **3** [T] (*informal*) to attack sb fiercely, or to defeat sb: *The Panthers pounded the Sharks in their game Friday, beating them 8-1.*

**'pound sign** (*Cdn* **hash mark**) ***noun*** [C] the symbol (#), especially one on a telephone

★**pour** /pɔr/ ***verb*** **1** [I] (used about a liquid) to flow out of or into sth, quickly and steadily, and in large quantities: *Water poured through the hole in the ceiling. ◇ Tears were pouring down her cheeks. ◇ There was blood pouring out of the wound. ◇ (figurative) People were pouring out of the stadium.* **2** [T] to make sth flow steadily out of or into a container: *I spilled some of the oil when I tried to pour it back into the bottle. ◇ Pour the sugar into a bowl.* **3** [T] **pour sth (for sb)** to serve drinks to sb: *Pour me another glass of wine.* **4** [I] to rain heavily: *I'm not going out. It's pouring.*

PHRV **pour sth out** to speak freely about what you think or feel about sth that has happened to you: *to pour out all your troubles*

**pout** /paʊt/ ***verb*** [I] to push your lips, or your bottom lip, forward to show that you are unhappy about sth

**pou·tine** /pu'tin/ ***noun*** [U] (*Cdn*) a dish of French fries with pieces of cheese on top that is usually served with sauce (gravy)

**pov·er·ty** /'pɑvərt̬i/ ***noun*** [U] the state of having very little money; the state of being poor: *to live in poverty*

**the 'poverty ˌline** ***noun*** [sing.] a minimum level of income, below which the government says it is impossible to buy the things that sb needs to live: *families living above/below the poverty line*

**'poverty-ˌstricken** ***adj.*** very poor

**POW** /ˌpi oʊ 'dʌblyu; -'dʌbəyu/ ***abbr.*** (*pl.* **POW's** or **POWs**) = PRISONER OF WAR

★**pow·der¹** /'paʊdər/ ***noun*** **1** [C,U] a dry substance that is in the form of very small grains: *This new scouring powder doesn't get the bathtub very clean. ◇ baking powder* ➲ Look also at **gunpowder**. **2** [U] POWDER (1) that you use on your skin: *face powder ◇ baby powder*

**pow·der²** /'paʊdər/ ***verb*** [T] to put powder on sth: *She powdered her face and put on her lipstick.*

IDM **powder your nose** (*old-fashioned*) (used as a polite way of referring to the fact that a woman is going to the bathroom): *I'm just going to powder my nose.*

**pow·dered** /'paʊdərd/ ***adj.*** (used about a substance that is usually a liquid) dried in the form of a powder: *powdered milk*

**ˌpowdered 'sugar** ***noun*** [U] (*U.S.*) = CONFECTIONER'S SUGAR

**'powder room** ***noun*** [C] a polite word for a women's bathroom in a public building

★**pow·er¹** /'paʊər/ ***noun***

➤ABILITY **1** [C,U] the ability to do sth: *The ambassador promised to do everything in her power to make sure the hostages were not harmed. ◇ He has great powers of observation.*

➤ENERGY **2** [U] force or strength: *The ship was helpless against the power of the storm.* **3** [U] energy that is used for making machines work, giving light, heat, etc.: *nuclear power ◇ the power supply*

➤INFLUENCE **4** [U] control or influence over other people: *The military government came to power after a long struggle. ◇ the power of the unions ◇ He sacrificed everything for power and money. ◇ to have sb in your power*

➤AUTHORITY **5** [C] the right or authority to do sth: *Do the police have the power to stop cars without a good reason?*

➤PERSON/THING THAT CONTROLS **6** [C] a person, an organization or a country that controls or influences others: *a meeting of the world's major economic powers*

**pow·er²** /'paʊər/ ***verb*** [T] to supply energy to sth so that it can work: *a portable generator that can power several pieces of equipment ◇ vehicles powered by electricity or natural gas*

★**pow·er·ful** /'paʊərfl/ ***adj.*** **1** very strong in a physical way: *That car has a very powerful engine. ◇ Sue is a powerful swimmer.* **2** having a strong effect: *The chairman made a powerful speech.* **3** having a lot of influence over other people: *There was a meeting of some of the most powerful people in the country.* ▶ **pow·er·ful·ly** ***adv.***

**pow·er·less** /'paʊərləs/ ***adj.*** **1** without strength or influence **2** not able to do sth: *I stood and watched him struggle, powerless to help.*

**'power ˌoutage** (*also* **'power ˌfailure**) ***noun*** [C] a time when the supply of electricity is cut off, especially by accident, such as during a storm

**'power plant** ***noun*** [C] a place where electricity is made (generated)

**pow·wow** /'paʊwaʊ/ ***noun*** [C] a traditional Native American ceremony or meeting, often with dancing

**pp.** ***abbr.*** pages: *See pp. 10-12.*

**PR** /ˌpi 'ɑr/ ***abbr.*** public relations

**prac·ti·ca·ble** /'præktɪkəbl/ ***adj.*** (*formal*) (used about an idea, a plan or a suggestion) able to be done; likely to be successful: *at the earliest practicable date/opportunity ◇ as soon as (is) practicable* SYN **feasible**

★**prac·ti·cal** /'præktɪkl/ ***adj.*** **1** concerned with actually doing sth rather than ideas or theory: *A degree in agriculture is not very useful without practical experience working on a farm.* ➲ Look at **theoretical**. **2** very suitable for a particular purpose; useful: *Plastic tablecloths are practical but they're not very elegant.* **3** (used about people) making sensible decisions and good at dealing with problems: *We have to be practical. There's no point in looking at a house we can't afford to buy.* **4** that is likely to succeed: *Your plan just isn't practical.* OPP The opposite in senses **2**, **3**, **4** is **impractical**. ▶ **prac·ti·cal·i·ty** /ˌpræktɪ'kælət̬i/ ***noun*** [U]: *Price and practicality are more important factors for us than style.*

**ˌpractical 'joke** ***noun*** [C] a trick that you play on sb (that involves doing sth that will make him/her look silly)

**prac·ti·cal·ly** /-kli/ ***adv.*** **1** almost; nearly: *The streets downtown are practically deserted on Sundays.*

◇ *He practically begged me not to go.* **2** in a practical way

★**prac·tice¹** /ˈpræktəs/ ***noun*** **1** [U] the actual doing of sth rather than ideas or theory: *Your suggestion sounds fine in theory, but would it work in practice?* ◇ *I can't wait to put what I've learned into practice.* **2** [C,U] (a period of) doing sth many times so that you become good at it: *You need plenty of practice when you're learning how to drive.* ◇ *His accent should improve with practice.* ◇ *Our team's first practice is tomorrow.* **3** [C,U] (*formal*) the usual way of doing sth; sth that is done regularly: *It is standard practice to check the accuracy of our data.* ◇ *Working more than 40 hours a week is a common practice in many North American companies.* **4** [C] the business of a doctor or lawyer: *Sarah wants to leave her father's law firm and set up her own practice.*

**IDM** **out of practice** not having spent a lot of time practicing sth recently: *I'm not playing very well right now. I'm really out of practice.*

★**prac·tice²** (*Cdn. also* **practise**) /ˈpræktəs/ ***verb*** **1** [I,T] to do sth many times so that you become very good at it: *to practice the piano every day* ◇ *The team is practicing for their big game on Friday.* ◇ *They practiced the dance until it was perfect.* ◇ *You need to practice saying "th" in front of a mirror.* **2** [T] to do sth or take part in sth regularly or openly: *For many years people were not allowed to practice their religion.* **3** [I,T] to work as a doctor or lawyer: *She's practicing medicine in Philadelphia.*

**IDM** **practice what you preach** to follow the advice that you give to other people: *Dr. Rosen always tells me to get plenty of exercise, but he doesn't always practice what he preaches* (= he is often lazy).

**prac·tic·ing** (*Cdn* **practising**) /ˈpræktəsɪŋ/ ***adj.*** (only *before* a noun) taking an active part in a particular religion/profession etc.: *a practicing Christian/teacher*

**prac·ti·tion·er** /prækˈtɪʃənər/ ***noun*** [C] (*formal*) a person who works in a particular profession, especially as a doctor or a lawyer

**prag·mat·ic** /prægˈmæt̬ɪk/ ***adj.*** dealing with problems in a practical way rather than by following theory or principles

**prai·rie** /ˈprɛri/ ***noun*** [C] **1** a very large area of flat land covered in grass with few trees (especially in the middle of North America) **2 the Prairies** (*Cdn*) the Canadian provinces of Manitoba, Saskatchewan and Alberta

ˈ**prairie dog** ***noun*** [C] a small brown North American animal of the squirrel family that lives in holes on the prairies

★**praise¹** /preɪz/ ***verb*** [T] **1 praise sb/sth (for sth)** to say that sb/sth is good and should be admired: *Her new novel has been highly praised.* ◇ *The mayor praised the efforts of the firefighters.* ◇ *The police officer was praised for his courage.* **2** to express thanks or honor to God: *Praise the Lord!*

★**praise²** /preɪz/ ***noun*** [U] what you say when you are expressing admiration for sb/sth: *His new play has received a lot of praise.* ◇ *Children respond better to praise than to criticism.*

**prance** /præns/ ***verb*** [I] to walk as if you were jumping or dancing, often because you feel proud of yourself or happy

**prank** /præŋk/ ***noun*** [C] a trick that is played on sb as a joke: *a childish/silly prank* ▸ **prank·ster** /ˈpræŋkstər/ ***noun*** [C]: *Student pranksters have done considerable damage to the school buildings.*

**pray** /preɪ/ ***verb*** [I,T] **1 pray (to sb) (for sb/sth)** to speak to God or a god in order to give thanks or to ask for sth: *Let us pray.* ◇ *They knelt down and prayed for peace.* ◇ *to pray to Allah* ◇ *They prayed that the war would end soon.* **2 pray (for sth)** to hope for sth very strongly: *Cubs fans are praying for a big win against the Mets tonight.*

★**prayer** /prɛr/ ***noun*** **1** [C] the words that you use when you speak to God or a god: *The priest said a prayer for all the people who were sick.* **2** [U] the act of praying: *to kneel in prayer*

**preach** /pritʃ/ ***verb*** **1** [I,T] to give a talk (a sermon) on a religious subject: *The minister preached a sermon on the meaning of love.* ◇ *Jesus preached that we should love our neighbors as ourselves.* **2** [I] to tell sb in an annoying way what he/she should do: *Quit preaching at me!* **3** [T] to say that sth is good and to persuade others to accept it: *I always preach caution in situations like this.*

**IDM** **practice what you preach** → PRACTICE²

**preach·er** /ˈpritʃər/ ***noun*** [C] a person who gives religious talks (**sermons**) and often performs religious ceremonies, e.g. in a church ➲ Look at the note at **priest**.

**pre·ar·ranged** /ˌpriəˈreɪndʒd/ ***adj.*** planned or arranged in advance: *a prearranged signal*

**pre·car·i·ous** /prɪˈkɛriəs/ ***adj.*** not safe or certain; dangerous: *The construction workers were in a very precarious position on the roof of the building.* ▸ **pre·car·i·ous·ly** ***adv.***: *They lived precariously on his small income.*

**pre·cau·tion** /prɪˈkɔʃn/ ***noun*** [C] something that you do in order to avoid danger or problems: *We took the precaution of locking our valuables in the hotel safe.* ◇ *precautions against fire* ▸ **pre·cau·tion·ar·y** /prɪˈkɔʃəˌnɛri/ ***adj.***: *I'm going to copy all these documents as a* ***precautionary measure****.*

**pre·cede** /prɪˈsid/ ***verb*** [I,T] (*formal*) to come or go before sb/sth: *The program was preceded by a warning about the strong language and violence in it.* ◇ *Look at the diagram on the preceding page.*

**prec·e·dence** /ˈprɛsədəns/ ***noun*** [U] **precedence (over sb/sth)** the right that sb/sth has to come before sb/sth else because of greater importance: *In business, making a profit seems to take precedence over everything else.*

**prec·e·dent** /ˈprɛsədənt/ ***noun*** [C,U] something that is considered as an example or rule for what happens later: *We don't want to set a precedent by allowing one person to come in late, or else they'll all want to do it.* ◇ *an event without precedent anywhere in the world* ➲ Look at **unprecedented**.

**pre·ced·ing** /prɪˈsidɪŋ/ ***adj.*** coming before sth/sb: *the years preceding the war*

**pre·cinct** /ˈprisɪŋkt/ ***noun*** [C] **1** a part of a city that has its own police station **2** one of the parts into which a city or town is divided in order to organize voting in an election

P

**pre·cious** /ˈprɛʃəs/ ***adj.*** **1** of great value (usually because there is not very much of it available): *Gold and silver are precious metals.* ◇ *our precious natural resources* **2** loved very much: *My mother's old ring is one of my most precious possessions.* ◇ *my precious little daughter*

ˌ**precious ˈstone** ***noun*** [C] a stone which is very rare and valuable and often used in jewelry: *diamonds, rubies and other precious stones*

**prec·i·pice** /ˈprɛsəpəs/ ***noun*** [C] a very steep side of a high cliff, mountain or rock: (*figurative*) *The country was now **on the edge of a precipice*** (= very close to disaster). ➲ Look also at **precipitous**.

**pre·cip·i·ta·tion** /prɪˌsɪpəˈteɪʃn/ ***noun*** [U] (*formal*) rain, snow, etc. that falls to the ground

**pre·cip·i·tous** /prɪˈsɪpət̮əs/ ***adj.*** (*formal*) **1** very steep, high and often dangerous: *a precipitous drop at the side of the road* ➲ Look at **precipice. 2** sudden and great: *a precipitous decline in exports* **3** done very quickly, without enough thought or care: *a precipitous action* ▸ **pre·cip·i·tous·ly** ***adv.***: *The land dropped precipitously down to the rocky shore.*

★**pre·cise** /prɪˈsaɪs/ ***adj.*** **1** clear and accurate; giving a lot of details: *Try to be precise in your measurements.* ◇ *I gave them precise instructions on how to get here.* ◇ *The answer was 10, or 9.98 to be precise.* ◇ *She couldn't be very precise about what her attacker was wearing.* **2** (only *before* a noun) exact; particular: *It is difficult to determine the precise moment when the crime occurred.* **3** (used about a person) taking care to get small details right: *He's very precise.* OPP In senses **1** and **3** the opposite is **imprecise**.

★**pre·cise·ly** /prɪˈsaɪsli/ ***adv.*** (*formal*) **1** clearly or exactly: *That's precisely what I mean.* ◇ *I mean precisely what I say.* **2** (used for agreeing with a statement) yes, that is right: *"So, if we don't make a reservation now, we probably won't get seats?" "Precisely."* ➲ A less formal word with the same meaning as senses **1** and **2** is **exactly**. **3** (used before "because" to emphasize that the reason you are giving is different from the reason that people might expect): *"But he was so friendly." "I didn't trust him precisely because he was so friendly."*

**pre·ci·sion** /prɪˈsɪʒn/ ***noun*** [U] the quality of being clear or exact: *The plans were drawn with great precision.*

**pre·clude** /prɪˈklud/ ***verb*** [T] (*formal*) **preclude sth; preclude sb from doing sth** to prevent sth from happening or sb from doing sth; to make sth impossible: *Lack of time precludes any further discussion.* ◇ *Your failure to become a member this year does not preclude the possibility of you/your applying next year.*

**pre·co·cious** /prɪˈkoʊʃəs/ ***adj.*** (used about children) acting in a way that makes them seem older or more intelligent than they really are

NOTE This word is often used in a critical way.

**pre·con·ceived** /ˌprikənˈsivd/ ***adj.*** (used about an idea or opinion) formed before you have knowledge or experience: *When I visited Russia last year I soon forgot all my preconceived ideas about the country.*

**pre·con·cep·tion** /ˌprikənˈsɛpʃn/ ***noun*** [C, usually pl., U] an idea or opinion that is formed before you have enough information or experience: *a book that will challenge your preconceptions about rural life*

**pre·cooked** /ˌpriˈkʊkt/ ***adj.*** (used about food) prepared and partly cooked in advance so that it can be quickly heated and eaten later

**pre·cur·sor** /prɪˈkərsər; ˈprikərsər/ ***noun*** [C] (*formal*) **precursor (of/to sth)** a person or thing that comes before sb/sth similar and that leads to or influences its development: *a stringed instrument that was the precursor of the guitar* SYN **forerunner**

**pred·a·tor** /ˈprɛdət̮ər/ ***noun*** [C] an animal that kills and eats other animals

**pred·a·to·ry** /ˈprɛdəˌtɔri/ ***adj.*** **1** (*technical*) (used about animals) living by killing and eating other animals: *predatory birds/insects* **2** (*written*) (used about people) using weaker people for their own financial or sexual advantage: *a predatory look/smile*

**pred·e·ces·sor** /ˈprɛdəsɛsər/ ***noun*** [C] **1** the person who was formerly in the job or position that sb else is in now: *The new principal is much better than her predecessor.* **2** something that is no longer used and has been replaced by sth else: *Our new car is more reliable than most of its predecessors.* ➲ Look at **successor**.

**pre·de·ter·mine** /ˌpridɪˈtərmən/ ***verb*** [T] (*formal*) to decide sth in advance so that it does not happen by chance: *The sex of the embryo is predetermined at fertilization.* ◇ *The way in which surveys are run often predetermines the results that are obtained.* ▸ **predetermined *adj.***

**pre·dic·a·ment** /prɪˈdɪkəmənt/ ***noun*** [C] a difficult situation

**pred·i·cate** /ˈprɛdɪkət/ ***noun*** [C] (*grammar*) the part of a sentence that contains the main verb and often describes the subject: *In the sentence "The cat sat on the mat," "sat on the mat" is the predicate.*

★**pre·dict** /prɪˈdɪkt/ ***verb*** [T] to say that sth will happen (often because you have special knowledge): *to predict the results of the election* ◇ *Scientists still cannot predict when earthquakes will happen.* ◇ *Mrs. Jones predicted that all the students would pass the test, and they did.*

**pre·dict·a·ble** /prɪˈdɪktəbl/ ***adj.*** **1** that was or could be expected **2** (used about a person) always behaving in the way that is expected: *I knew you were going to say that – you're so predictable.* OPP **unpredictable** ▸ **pre·dict·a·bly** ***adv.***: *Predictably, all the applause came from his own supporters.*

**pre·dic·tion** /prɪˈdɪkʃn/ ***noun*** [C,U] saying what will happen; what sb thinks will happen: *new technology to improve the prediction of earthquakes* ◇ *to make a prediction about the future*

**pre·di·gest·ed** /ˌpridɪˈdʒɛstəd; -daɪ-/ ***adj.*** (used about information) put in a simple form that is easy to understand: *predigested news*

**pre·dis·pose** /ˌpridɪˈspoʊz/ ***verb*** [T] (*formal*) **1 predispose sb to sth/to do sth** to influence sb so that he/she is likely to think or behave in a particular way: *He believes that some people are predisposed to criminal behavior.* ◇ *Her good mood* *predisposed her to enjoy the play.* **2 predispose sb to sth** to make it likely that you will suffer from a particular illness: *Stress can predispose people to heart attacks.*

**pre·dom·i·nance** /prɪ'dɑmənəns/ ***noun*** **1** [sing.] the situation of being greater in number or amount than other things or people: *a predominance of female teachers in elementary schools* **2** [U] the state of having more power or influence than others: *the ongoing struggle for global predominance*

**pre·dom·i·nant** /prɪ'dɑmənənt/ ***adj.*** most noticeable, powerful or important: *The predominant color was yellow.*

**pre·dom·i·nant·ly** /prɪ'dɑmənəntli/ ***adv.*** mostly; mainly: *The population of this neighborhood is predominantly Hispanic.*

**pre·dom·i·nate** /prɪ'dɑməneɪt/ ***verb*** [I] **predominate (over sb/sth)** (*formal*) to be most important or greatest in number: *Pine trees predominate in the north of the state.*

**pree·mie** /'primi/ ***noun*** [C] (*informal*) a baby that is born before the expected time (**premature**)

**pre·em·i·nent** /pri'ɛmənənt/ ***adj.*** (*formal*) more important, more successful or of a higher standard than others: *a preeminent example of the artist's work* ▶ **pre·em·i·nence** ***noun*** [U]

**pre·empt** /pri'ɛmpt/ ***verb*** [T] **1** to prevent sth from happening by taking action to stop it: *Her departure preempted any further questions.* **2** to do or say sth before sb else does: *She was just about to apologize when he preempted her.* **3** to replace a planned program on television: *"Roseanne" will be preempted by a special news bulletin.*

**pre·ex·ist·ing** (*also* **pre-existing**) /ˌpriɪg'zɪstɪŋ/ ***adj.*** existing before sth else, or existing already: *My health insurance does not cover any preexisting medical conditions* (= that I had before I took out the insurance).

**pref·ace** /'prɛfəs/ ***noun*** [C] a written introduction to a book that explains what it is about or why it was written

**pre·fec·ture** /'prifɛktʃər/ ***noun*** [C] an area of local government in some countries, e.g. Japan

★**pre·fer** /prɪ'fər/ ***verb*** [T] (**pre·fer·ring**; **pre·ferred**) **prefer sth (to sth)** (*formal*) to choose sth rather than sth else; to like sth better: *Would you prefer tea or coffee?* ◇ *I prefer skating to skiing.* ◇ *Marianne prefers not to walk home on her own at night.*

> **NOTE** Notice the different ways that **prefer** can be used: *Helen prefers going by bus to flying.* ◇ *Helen prefers to go by bus rather than to fly.* ◇ *My parents would prefer it if I went to law school.* The last sentence is more formal. Note that **prefer** is generally used in formal English. Instead of: *Would you prefer coffee or tea?* we can say: *Would you rather have coffee or tea?* Instead of: *I prefer skating to skiing* we can say: *I like skating better than skiing.*

**pref·er·a·ble** /'prɛfərəbl/ ***adj.*** **preferable (to sth/to doing sth)** better or more suitable: *Going anywhere is preferable to staying home all weekend.* ◇ *Cold drinks are preferable in hot weather.* ▶ **pref·er·a·bly** /'prɛfərəbli/ ***adv.***: *Give me a call Sunday morning but preferably not before 10:00!*

**pref·er·ence** /'prɛfərəns; -frəns/ ***noun*** **1** [sing., U] **preference (for sth)** a liking for sth rather than for sth else: *What you wear is a matter of personal preference.* ◇ *We have both red and white wine. Do you have a preference for one or the other?* **2** [U] **preference (to sb)** special, better treatment that you give to one person or group but not to others: *When assigning seats, we will give preference to families with young children.* ◇ *Please list your choices in order of preference* (= put the thing you want most at the top of the list, and so on).

**pref·er·en·tial** /ˌprɛfə'rɛnʃl/ ***adj.*** giving or showing better treatment to one person or group than to others: *I don't see why he should get preferential treatment – I've worked here just as long!*

**pre·fix** /'prifɪks/ ***noun*** [C] a word or group of letters that you put at the beginning of a word to change its meaning: *The prefix "im-" means "not," e.g. "impossible."* ➲ Look at **suffix**.

**preg·nan·cy** /'prɛgnənsi/ ***noun*** (*pl.* **preg·nan·cies**) **1** [U] the state of being pregnant: *You should be sure to get plenty of exercise during pregnancy.* ◇ *a pregnancy test* **2** [C] the period of time when a woman or female animal is pregnant: *to have a difficult pregnancy*

★**preg·nant** /'prɛgnənt/ ***adj.*** (used about a woman or female animal) having a baby developing in her body: *Elizabeth is five months pregnant.*

> **NOTE** It is also common to say: *She's expecting a baby* or: *She's going to have a baby.*

**pre·heat** /ˌpri'hit/ ***verb*** [T] to heat an oven to a particular temperature before you put food in it to cook

**pre·his·tor·ic** /ˌprihɪ'stɔrɪk; -'stɑrɪk/ ***adj.*** of the time before history was written down: *prehistoric cave paintings*

**prej·u·dice**[1] /'prɛdʒədɪs/ ***noun*** [C,U] a strong feeling of like or dislike toward sb/sth that is not based on reason: *racial prejudice* ◇ *He has a prejudice against female doctors.*

**prej·u·dice**[2] /'prɛdʒədɪs/ ***verb*** [T] **1 prejudice sb (against/in favor of sb/sth)** to influence sb; to cause sb to have a PREJUDICE[1]: *The media coverage had prejudiced the jury against him.* **2** (*formal*) to have an influence on sth that will cause it to be unfair: *Discussing these matters could prejudice the outcome of the trial.*

**prej·u·diced** /'prɛdʒədɪst/ ***adj.*** having or showing PREJUDICE[1]: *Why is he so prejudiced against women?*

**pre·lim·i·nar·y** /prɪ'lɪməˌnɛri/ ***adj.*** coming before sth else that is more important: *After a few preliminary remarks, the discussions began.*

**prel·ude** /'preɪlud; 'prɛlyud/ ***noun*** [C] **1** something that comes before sth else or that forms an introduction to sth: *The buildup of troops seemed to be a prelude to war.* **2** a piece of music that forms the first part of a longer piece of serious music

**pre·mar·i·tal** /ˌpri'mærət̮l/ ***adj.*** (only *before* a noun) existing or happening before marriage: *premarital sex*

**pre·ma·ture** /ˌprimə'tʃʊr; -'tʊr/ ***adj.*** **1** coming or happening before the right or expected time:

P

*Premature babies* (= babies who are born before the expected time) *need special care.* **2** acting or happening too soon: *I think our decision was premature. We should have thought about it for longer.* ▸ **pre·ma·ture·ly** *adv.*: *The shock caused her hair to go prematurely gray.*

**pre·med** /ˌpriˈmɛd/ (*also* **ˌpre-ˈmed**) *adj.* (*informal*) connected with the classes that students take in preparation for medical school, or with the students who are taking those classes: *She's a premed student at Harvard.*

**pre·med·i·tat·ed** /ˌpriˈmɛdəteɪt̬əd/ *adj.* planned in advance: *Was the attack premeditated?*

**pre·men·stru·al** /priˈmɛnstruəl; -strəl/ *adj.* happening or experienced before a woman loses blood each month (**menstruation**): *Many women suffer from* ***premenstrual syndrome****, causing headaches and depression.* ➲ Look at **PMS**.

**pre·mier[1]** /prɪˈmɪr; -ˈmyɪr/ *noun* [C] **1** / (*Cdn*) ˈprimyər/ (in Canada) the first minister of a province or territory ➲ For more information on the Canadian political system, look at study page **A11**. **2** the Prime Minister or head of government in several other countries

**pre·mier[2]** /prɪˈmɪr; -ˈmyɪr/ / (*Cdn*) ˈprimyər/ *adj.* (only *before* a noun) most important; best: *He's the premier performer of his time.*

**pre·miere** (*also* **première**) /prɪˈmɪr; -ˈmyɪr; -ˈmyɛr/ *noun* [C] the first performance of a play, movie, etc.

★**pre·mis·es** /ˈprɛməsəz/ *noun* [pl.] (*formal*) a building and the land that surrounds it: *Smoking is not allowed on the premises.*

**pre·mi·um[1]** /ˈprimiəm/ *noun* [C] **1** an amount of money that you pay regularly to a company for insurance: *monthly premiums of $150* **2** an extra amount of money: *You pay a premium for the convenience of shopping close to home.*

**pre·mi·um[2]** /ˈprimiəm/ *adj.* (only *before* a noun) very high (and higher than usual); of high quality: *premium prices/products.*

**pre·na·tal** /ˌpriˈneɪt̬l/ *adj.* happening or existing before a baby is born: *a prenatal checkup*

**pre·nup·tial a·gree·ment** /priˌnʌpʃl əˈgrimənt; -ˌnʌptʃl-/ *noun* [C] (*also informal* **prenup** /ˈprinʌp; ˌpriˈnʌp/) an agreement made by a couple before they get married in which they say how their money and property should be divided if they get divorced

**pre·oc·cu·pa·tion** /priˌɑkyəˈpeɪʃn/ *noun* **1** [U] **preoccupation (with sth)** the state of thinking or being worried about sth all the time **2** [C] a thing that you think or worry about all the time: *The family's main preoccupation at that time was finding somewhere to live.*

**pre·oc·cu·pied** /priˈɑkyəpaɪd/ *adj.* (not before a noun) **preoccupied (with sb/sth)** not paying attention because you are thinking or worrying about sb/sth else

**pre-owned** /ˌpriˈoʊnd/ *adj.* not new; owned by sb else before: *pre-owned automobiles*

**prep** /prɛp/ *verb* [I,T] (**prep·ping; prepped**) (*informal*) to prepare (sth): *Prep the vegetables in advance.* ◇ *They're* ***prepping for*** *college.*

★**prep·a·ra·tion** /ˌprɛpəˈreɪʃn/ *noun* **1** [U] the act of getting sb/sth ready: *Hygiene is essential during the preparation of food.* **2** [C, usually pl.] **preparation (for sth/to do sth)** something that you do to get ready for sth: *The wedding preparations are almost complete.*

IDM **in preparation (for sth)** in order to get ready for sth: *Get a good night's sleep in preparation for the trip.*

**pre·par·a·to·ry** /prɪˈpærəˌtɔri; -ˈpɛr-; ˈprɛprəˌtɔri/ *adj.* (*formal*) done in order to get ready for sth: *preparatory discussions before an important meeting*

**ˈpreparatory ˌschool** *noun* [C] (*formal*) = PREP SCHOOL

★**pre·pare** /prɪˈpɛr/ *verb* [I,T] **prepare (sb/sth) (for sb/sth)** to get ready or to make sb/sth ready: *Bob helped me prepare for the party.* ◇ *I didn't leave myself enough time to prepare for the test.* ◇ *to prepare a meal* ◇ *The spokesman read out a prepared statement but refused to answer any questions.* ◇ *You'd better prepare yourself for a shock.*

IDM **be prepared for sth** to be ready for sth difficult or unpleasant

**be prepared to do sth** (*formal*) to be willing to do sth: *I am not prepared to answer that question at this time.*

**prep·o·si·tion** /ˌprɛpəˈzɪʃn/ *noun* [C] a word or phrase that is used before a noun or pronoun to show place, time, direction, etc.: *"In," "for," "to," "out of" and "from" are all prepositions.*

**prep·py** (*also* **preppie**) /ˈprɛpi/ *adj.* (*informal*) connected with or typical of people who go to expensive private schools: *preppy clothes*

**ˈprep school** (*also formal* **preˈparatory ˌschool**) *noun* [C] a private school that prepares students for college

**pre·quel** /ˈprikwəl/ *noun* [C] a book or a movie about events that happened before those in a popular book or movie: *Fans waited for years for* ***a prequel to*** *Star Wars.* ➲ Compare **sequel**.

**pre·re·cord·ed** /ˌpririˈkɔrdəd/ *adj.* (used about a piece of music, a film, radio or TV program) that has been recorded in advance so that it can be played later: *a prerecorded interview*

**pre·req·ui·site** /ˌpriˈrɛkwəzɪt/ *noun* [C] **prerequisite (for/to sth)** something that is necessary before sth else can happen, exist, or be done: *English 101 is a prerequisite for all higher-level courses.*

**pre·rog·a·tive** /prɪˈrɑgət̬ɪv/ *noun* [C] (*formal*) a right or privilege belonging to a particular person or group because of his/her/its importance or social position: *In many countries education is still the prerogative of the rich.*

**Pres·by·te·ri·an** /ˌprɛsbəˈtɪriən; ˌprɛz-/ *noun* [C], *adj.* (a member) of a Protestant church that was started by John Knox in Scotland in the 16th century

**pre·school** /ˈpriskul/ (*also* **nursery school**) *noun* [C] a school for children who are about three to five years old ➲ Look also at **kindergarten**. ▸ **pre·school** *adj.* ▸ **pre·school·er** /ˈpriskulər/ *noun* [C] ➲ For more information on the U.S. educational system, look at study page **A8**.

**pre·scribe** /prɪˈskraɪb/ *verb* [T] **1** to say what

medicine or treatment you should have; to order medicine on a special form (**prescription**): *The doctor prescribed some medication for the pain.* **2** (*formal*) (used about a person or an organization with authority) to say that sth must be done: *a procedure prescribed by the company's handbook*

**pre·scrip·tion** /prɪˈskrɪpʃn/ ***noun*** **1** [C,U] a form on which a doctor has written the name of the medicine that you need. You take your prescription to a drugstore and get the medicine there: *a prescription for sleeping pills* ◇ *Some medicines are only available by prescription* (= with a prescription from a doctor). **2** [U] the act of prescribing sth

**pre·sea·son** /ˌpriˈsizn/ (*also* ˌ**pre-ˈseason**) ***adj.*** (used about a sports event) happening before the regular SEASON[1] (2) for a particular sport begins: *a preseason game*

★**pres·ence** /ˈprɛzns/ ***noun*** **1** [U] being in a place or with sb: *He apologized to her in the presence of the whole family.* ◇ *to request sb's presence at a meeting* OPP **absence** **2** [sing.] a number of soldiers or police officers who are in a place for a special reason: *There was a huge police presence at the demonstration.*

★**pres·ent**[1] /ˈprɛznt/ ***adj.*** **1** (not before a noun) being in a particular place: *There were 200 people present at the meeting.* OPP **absent** **2** (only *before* a noun) existing or happening now: *We hope to solve our present problems very soon.*

IDM **the present day** modern times: *In some countries, traditional methods of farming have survived to the present day.* ◇ *present-day attitudes toward women*

★**pres·ent**[2] /ˈprɛznt/ ***noun*** **1** [C] something that you give to sb or receive from sb; a gift: *The tie was a present from my sister.* ◇ *a birthday/wedding/Christmas present* ◇ *I have to buy a present for my friend.* ➲ **Gift** has the same meaning and is often used in stores, catalogs, etc. **2 the present** [sing.] the time now: *We live in the present, but we must learn from the past.* **3 the present** [sing.] = PRESENT TENSE

IDM **for the moment/present** → MOMENT

★**pre·sent**[3] /prɪˈzɛnt/ ***verb*** [T]

➤GIVE **1 present sb with sth; present sth (to sb)** to give sth to sb, e.g. at a formal ceremony: *All the dancers were presented with flowers.* ◇ *Flowers were presented to all the dancers.* ◇ *The principal presented a trophy to the winner.*

➤STH TO BE CONSIDERED **2** to give or show sth: *Good teachers try to present their material in an interesting way.* ◇ *to present a report to the board of directors*

➤PROVIDE **3** to cause or provide sth: *Learning English presented no problem to him.* ◇ *The course aims to present each participant with new challenges.*

➤PLAY/BROADCAST **4** to show a play, etc. to the public: *The local theater company is presenting a musical this summer.*

➤INTRODUCE SB **5** (*formal*) **present sb (to sb)** to introduce sb in a formal situation, especially to a person of higher social rank: *Ladies and gentlemen, allow me to present my associate, Mr. Steve Jackson.*

**pre·sent·a·ble** /prɪˈzɛntəbl/ ***adj.*** good enough, and suitable to be seen in public: *This dress is a few years old – do I still look presentable?*

★**pres·en·ta·tion** /ˌprɛznˈteɪʃn; ˌprizn-/ ***noun*** **1** [U] presenting sth or being presented: *the presentation of new material in a textbook* **2** [U] the appearance of sth or the impression that it makes on other people: *Contest entries will be judged on content and artistic presentation.* **3** [C] a formal ceremony at which a prize, etc. is given to sb **4** [C] a talk that gives information on a particular subject: *to give a presentation on sth*

**pres·ent·ly** /ˈprɛzntli/ ***adv.*** (*formal*) now: *She is presently employed as the manager of our downtown branch.*

ˌ**present ˈparticiple** ***noun*** [C] (*grammar*) the form of the verb that ends in *– ing*: *"Going," "walking" and "trying" are all present participles.*

**the** ˌ**present ˈperfect** ***noun*** [sing.] (*grammar*) the tense of a verb that describes an action that happened from a time in the past up to now: *In the sentence "We have lived in Colorado for three years," "have lived" is in the present perfect.*

**the** ˌ**present ˈtense** (*also* **the present, the simple present**) ***noun*** [sing.] (*grammar*) the tense of the verb that you use when you are talking about what is true or what exists now

**pres·er·va·tion** /ˌprɛzərˈveɪʃn/ ***noun*** [U] keeping sth in the same or in good condition: *the preservation of law and order* ◇ *The society is working for the preservation of wildlife.*

**pre·ser·va·tive** /prɪˈzərvət̬ɪv/ ***noun*** [C,U] a substance that is used for keeping food, etc. in good condition

★**pre·serve** /prɪˈzərv/ ***verb*** [T] to keep sth safe or in good condition: *They have managed to preserve most of the wall paintings in the caves.* ◇ *Before people had refrigerators, they used salt to preserve meat.* ◇ *Efforts to preserve peace have failed.*

**pre·set** /ˌpriˈsɛt/ (*also* **pre-set**) ***verb*** [T] (*pres. part.* **pre·set·ting**; *pt, pp* **pre·set**) to set the controls of a piece of electrical equipment so that it will start to work at a particular time: *to preset TV channels/radio stations* (= to set the controls so that particular channels are selected when you press particular buttons) ◇ *The water is heated to a preset temperature.* ▶ **pre·set** ***noun*** [C]

**pre·side** /prɪˈzaɪd/ ***verb*** [I] to be in charge of a discussion, meeting, etc.: *District Judge Gerhard Gesell presided at some of the Watergate trials.*

PHRV **preside over sth** to be in control of or responsible for sth: *Mr. Wender has presided over a period of expansion at the company.*

**pres·i·den·cy** /ˈprɛzədənsi/ ***noun*** (*pl.* **pres·i·den·cies**) **1 the presidency** [sing.] the position of being president: *to be nominated for the presidency* **2** [C] the period of time that sb is president

★**pres·i·dent** /ˈprɛzədənt/ ***noun*** [C] **1** (*also* **President**) the leader of the country and head of the government in many countries. A president is usually chosen in an election: *May I ask you a question, Mr. President?* ◇ *President Chirac of France* ➲ For more information on the U.S. political system, look at study page **A10**. ➲ Look also at **vice president**. **2** the person with the highest position in some

P

companies and organizations ▶ **pres·i·den·tial** /ˌprɛzəˈdɛnʃl/ ***adj.***

**ˈPresidents' Day** ***noun*** [C] a holiday that is held on the third Monday in February to celebrate the birthdays of George Washington and Abraham Lincoln

★**press**[1] /prɛs/ ***verb***

➤ PUSH/SQUEEZE **1** [I,T] to push firmly: *Just press that button, and the door will open.* ◇ *Don't press too hard on the brakes.* ◇ *The girl pressed her nose against the window.* **2** [T] to hold sb/sth firmly as a sign of love, etc.: *She pressed his hand to her heart.*

➤ MAKE FLAT/SMOOTH **3** [T] to make a piece of clothing smooth by using an iron

➤ FRUIT/VEGETABLES **4** [T] to put weight onto sth, e.g. in order to get juice out of it: *to press grapes*

➤ TRY TO PERSUADE **5** [I,T] **press (sb) (for sth/to do sth)** to try to get sth or to make sb do sth: *to press sb for an answer* ◇ *Their lobbyists are pressing Congress to take action quickly.*

IDM **be pressed for sth** to not have enough of sth, especially time or money: *I have to hurry. I'm really pressed for time.*

**press charges (against sb)** to make an official statement that sb has done sth illegal, so that he/she must go to court

PHRV **press against, around, etc. (sth)** (used about people) to move in a particular direction by pushing: *The crowd pressed up against the fence.*

**press ahead/forward/on (with sth)** to continue doing sth even though it is difficult or hard work: *They pressed on with their efforts to find the killer.*

★**press**[2] /prɛs/ ***noun*** **1 the press** [sing.] newspapers, and the journalists who work for them. The news departments of television and radio are also part of the press: *The candidate refused to speak to the press.* ◇ *members of the local press* ◇ *The law ensures the freedom of the press in this country.* **2** [C] a company that publishes books: *Oxford University Press* **3** = PRINTING PRESS

IDM **good/bad press** favorable/unfavorable attention in newspapers, on television or the radio, etc.: *The governor's tax proposals have gotten a lot of bad press recently.*

**ˈpress ˌconference** ***noun*** [C] a meeting in which a famous or important person answers questions from newspaper and television journalists: *to hold a press conference*

**press·ing** /ˈprɛsɪŋ/ ***adj.*** that you must do or deal with immediately: *the nation's most pressing economic problem*

**ˈpress reˌlease** ***noun*** [C] an official statement made to journalists by a large organization, a political party or a government department: *The company issued a press release to end speculation about its future.*

**ˈpress ˌsecretary** ***noun*** [C] person who works for a politician or a political organization and gives information about them to journalists, the newspapers, etc.

★**pres·sure**[1] /ˈprɛʃər/ ***noun*** **1** [U] the force that is produced when you press on or against sth: *Apply pressure to the cut and it will stop bleeding.* **2** [C,U] the force that a gas or liquid has when it presses against sth: *high/low blood pressure* ◇ *You should check your tire pressure regularly.* ◇ *Low air pressure often brings rain.* **3** [C,U] a situation that causes you to be worried or unhappy: *financial pressures* ◇ *They moved to the suburbs to escape the pressure of city life.*

IDM **put pressure on sb (to do sth)** to persuade or force sb to do sth: *The press is putting pressure on the mayor to resign.*

**under pressure 1** (used about liquid or gas) having great force: *Water is forced out through the hose under pressure.* **2** being forced to do sth: *The workers were under a lot of pressure to get the job finished as quickly as possible.*

**pres·sure**[2] /ˈprɛʃər/ ***verb*** [T] **pressure sb into sth/into doing sth** to use force or influence to make sb do sth: *Her parents pressured her into going to a college near home.*

**ˈpressure ˌcooker** ***noun*** [C] a large pan with a lid in which you can cook things quickly using steam under high pressure: (*figurative*) *The atmosphere on campus is like a pressure cooker during finals week.*

**pres·sur·ized** /ˈprɛʃəraɪzd/ ***adj.*** (used about air in an airplane, or air or another gas in a tank) kept under pressure

**pres·tige** /prɛˈstiʒ; -ˈstidʒ/ ***noun*** [U] the respect and admiration that people feel for sb/sth, especially because of success, wealth, etc.: *He had always wanted a job with a lot of power and prestige.*

**pres·ti·gious** /prɛˈstidʒəs; -ˈstɪdʒ-/ ***adj.*** respected or admired because of success, wealth, high quality, etc.: *a prestigious private school*

**pres·to** /ˈprɛstoʊ/ ***interjection*** something that people say when they have just done sth so quickly and easily that it seems to have been done by magic: *You just press the button and, presto, a perfect cup of coffee!*

**pre·sum·a·bly** /prɪˈzuməbli/ ***adv.*** I imagine; I suppose: *Presumably, this rain means the parade will be canceled.*

**pre·sume** /prɪˈzum/ ***verb*** [T] (*formal*) to think that sth is true even if you do not know for sure; to suppose: *The soldiers were missing, presumed dead.*

**pre·tax** /ˌpriˈtæks/ ***adj.*** (only *before* a noun) before the TAX[1] has been taken away: *pretax profits/losses/income*

**pre·teen** /ˌpriˈtin/ ***adj.*** (used about a boy or girl just under the age of thirteen): *preteen girls* ▶ **preteen** ***noun*** [C]

★**pre·tend**[1] /prɪˈtɛnd/ ***verb*** [I,T] to appear to do or be sth, in order to trick or deceive sb: *Frances walked past, pretending (that) she didn't see me.* ◇ *Paul's not really asleep. He's just pretending.* ◇ *The kids are pretending to be astronauts.*

**pre·tend**[2] /prɪˈtɛnd/ ***adj.*** (*informal*) (often used by children) not real; imaginary: *pretend cakes/toys*

**pre·tense** (*Cdn. also* **pre·tence**) /ˈpritɛns; prɪˈtɛns/ ***noun*** [C, sing.] an action that makes people believe sth that is not true: *He kept up the pretense that he was sick.*

IDM **under false pretenses** → FALSE

**pre·ten·tious** /prɪˈtɛnʃəs/ ***adj.*** trying to appear important, intelligent, etc. in order to impress other people; trying to be sth that you are not, in order to impress: *That's a pretentious name for a dog!* ◇ *It was just an ordinary house—nothing pretentious.* OPP **unpretentious** ▶ **pre·ten·tious·ly** *adv.* ▶ **pre·ten·tious·ness** *noun* [U]: *There was no hint of pretentiousness in her manner.*

**pre·test** /ˈpritɛst/ *noun* [C] a test that you take to find out how much you already know or can do before learning or doing sth ▶ **pre·test** *verb* [T]

**pre·text** /ˈpritɛkst/ *noun* [C] a reason that you give for doing sth that is not the real reason: *Tom left on the pretext of having a doctor's appointment.*

**pre·tri·al** /ˌpriˈtraɪəl/ *adj.* happening before an official TRIAL (1) in a court of law: *a pretrial hearing*

★**pret·ty¹** /ˈprɪt̬i/ *adj.* (**pret·ti·er**; **pret·ti·est**) pleasant to look at; attractive: *Rachel looks really pretty in that dress, doesn't she?* ◇ *very pretty material with yellow and blue flowers on it*

> NOTE When we are talking about people, we use **pretty** to describe girls and women. To describe men we use **good-looking** or **handsome**. We can use **cute** in informal English to describe children and young women and men. ➲ Look also at **beautiful**.

▶ **pret·ti·ly** *adv.*

★**pret·ty²** /ˈprɪt̬i/ *adv.* (*informal*) **1** very, but not completely: *You should wear a heavier coat – it's pretty cold outside.* ◇ *I'm pretty sure that Alex will agree.* **2** a little; fairly: *It was a pretty good concert, but not the best I've ever seen.*

> NOTE In spoken English, we use different stress and intonation for these two meanings of **pretty**. For example, if someone asks,: *"How was the movie?"* we can say: *"ˌPretty ˈgood!"* (= really good) or: *"ˈPretty good."* (= not really good).

IDM **pretty much/near/well** almost: *I won't be long. I'm pretty much finished.*

**pret·zel** /ˈprɛtsl/ *noun* [C] a type of bread which is rolled thin and twisted into a special shape, then baked and covered with salt. Some pretzels are thin and hard like crackers.

**pre·vail** /prɪˈveɪl/ *verb* [I] (*formal*) **1** to win or gain control: *Justice prevailed and the killer was sent to prison for life.* **2** to exist or be common in a particular area: *Dry, sunny weather usually prevails in the eastern region.*

**pre·vail·ing** /prɪˈveɪlɪŋ/ *adj.* (only *before* a noun) most common or general in a particular area: *the prevailing opinion among residents*

**prev·a·lent** /ˈprɛvl·ənt/ *adj.* (*formal*) common in a particular place at a particular time: *The prevalent atmosphere was one of fear.*

★**pre·vent** /prɪˈvɛnt/ *verb* [T] **prevent sb/sth (from doing sth)** to stop sth from happening or to stop sb from doing sth: *Everyone hopes the negotiations will prevent a war.* ◇ *Her parents tried to prevent her from going to live with her boyfriend.* ➲ **Prevent** is more formal than **stop**. ▶ **pre·vent·a·ble** *adj.*: *Many accidents are preventable.*

**pre·ven·tion** /prɪˈvɛnʃn/ *noun* [U] the act of preventing sth: *fire prevention tips*

**pre·ven·tive** /prɪˈvɛntɪv/ (*also* **preventative** /prɪˈvɛntət̬ɪv/) *adj.* intended to stop or prevent sth (especially crime or disease) from happening: *preventive measures to reduce crime* ◇ *preventative medicine*

**pre·view¹** /ˈprivyu/ *noun* [C] **1** a chance to see a play, movie, etc. before it is shown to the general public ➲ Look at **sneak preview**. **2** a series of short scenes from a movie, shown in advance to advertise it

**pre·view²** /ˈprivyu/ *verb* [T] **1** see a movie, a television program, etc. before it is shown to the general public and write an account of it for a newspaper or magazine: *The exhibition was previewed in last week's issue.* **2** give sb a short account of sth that is going to happen, be studied, etc.: *The professor previewed the course for us.*

★**pre·vi·ous** /ˈpriviəs/ *adj.* coming or happening before or earlier: *Do you have previous experience in this type of work?* ◇ *Frank has one daughter from his previous marriage.* ◇ *The previous owners of our house moved to Ohio.* ▶ **pre·vi·ous·ly** *adv.*: *Before I got this job, I had previously worked in a department store.*

**prey¹** /preɪ/ *noun* [U] an animal or bird that is killed and eaten by another animal or bird: *The lion silently watched its prey.* ◇ *The eagle is **a bird of prey*** (= it kills and eats other birds or small animals).

**prey²** /preɪ/ *verb*

PHRV **prey on sb/sth** to watch sb/sth carefully and then attack him/her/it: *Cats prey on rats and mice.* ◇ *a killer who preys on young women*

**prez** /prɛz/ *noun* [C] (*slang*) = PRESIDENT

★**price¹** /praɪs/ *noun* [C] the amount of money that you must pay in order to buy sth: *What's the price of gas now?* ◇ *to charge high/low prices* ◇ *We can't afford to buy the car at that price.* ◇ *There's no price tag on this jacket.* ◇ *This shirt was on sale for half price.* ◇ (*figurative*) *Is pollution the price we have to pay for progress?*

> NOTE A **charge** is the amount of money that you must pay for using something: *Is there a charge for parking here?* ◇ *service charges*. You use **cost** when you are talking about paying for services or about prices in general without mentioning an actual sum of money: *The cost of electricity is going up.* ◇ *the cost of living*. The **price** of something is the amount of money that you must pay in order to buy it. A store may **raise/increase** or **reduce/lower** its prices. The prices **rise/go up** or **fall/go down**.

IDM **at any price** even if the cost is very high or if it will have bad results: *Richard was determined to succeed at any price.*

**price²** /praɪs/ *verb* [T] **1** to set the PRICE¹ of sth: *The books were priced between $15 and $20.* **2** to mark the price on goods in a store

**price·less** /ˈpraɪsləs/ *adj.* of very great value: *priceless jewels and antiques* ➲ Look at **worthless**, **valuable** and **invaluable**.

ˈ**price tag** *noun* [C] a label on sth that shows how much you must pay: (*figurative*) *The new quarterback comes with a price tag of $2 million.*

**pric·ey** /ˈpraɪsi/ *adj.* (**pric·i·er**; **pric·i·est**) (*informal*) expensive

**prick¹** /prɪk/ *verb* [T] to make a small hole in sth or to cause sb pain with a sharp point: *You should prick*

P

*the pie crust before you bake it.* ◇ *Ouch! I pricked myself on that needle.*

**prick²** /prɪk/ ***noun*** [C] the sharp pain that you feel when sth pricks you: *the sharp prick of a needle*

**prick·ly** /ˈprɪkli/ ***adj.*** covered with sharp points: *a prickly bush*

**ˈprickly pear** ***noun*** [C] **1** a type of cactus with sharp parts like needles (**prickles**), and yellow flowers **2** the fruit of the prickly pear that is shaped like a pear and can be eaten ➲ picture on study page **A28-29**.

★**pride¹** /praɪd/ ***noun*** **1** [U] **pride (in sb/sth)** the feeling of pleasure that you have when you (or people who are close to you) do sth good or own sth good: *Her parents watched with pride as Mary went up to get her diploma.* ◇ *her pride in her achievement* ➲ adjective **proud 2** [sing.] **the pride of sth** a person or thing that is very important or of great value to sb: *The new stadium was the pride of the whole town.* **3** [U] the feeling that you are better than other people: *the sin of pride* **4** [U] the sense of your own worth or value; self-respect: *You'll hurt his pride if you don't accept the gift.*

IDM **take pride in sb/sth** to feel pleased and proud about sth good that sb has done: *The coach took great pride in his team's success.*

**take pride in sth/in doing sth** to do sth very well or carefully: *I wish you took more pride in your work.*

**pride²** /praɪd/ ***verb***

PHRV **pride yourself on sth/on doing sth** to feel pleased about sth that you can do well: *Henry prides himself on his ability to cook.*

P

★**priest** /prist/ ***noun*** [C] a person who performs religious ceremonies in a Christian church: *a parish priest* ◇ *the ordination of women priests*

> NOTE **Priest** is a general word and is used in many churches but especially in the Roman Catholic Church. A priest in a Protestant church is usually called a **minister**, a **pastor** or a **preacher**. A general term which can also be used for other religions is **clergyman** or (for a man or a woman) **a member of the clergy**.

**priest·ess** /ˈpristəs/ ***noun*** [C] a female priest in some religions that are not Christian

**priest·hood** /ˈpristhʊd/ ***noun*** [sing.] **the priesthood** the job or position of being a priest: *to enter the priesthood* (= to become a priest)

**prim** /prɪm/ ***adj.*** (used about a person) always behaving very correctly and easily shocked by swearing, talking about sex, etc. ▸ **prim·ly** ***adv.***

★**pri·mar·i·ly** /praɪˈmɛrəli/ ***adv.*** more than anything else; mainly: *The course will be aimed primarily at people who have no previous experience.*

★**pri·mar·y¹** /ˈpraɪˌmɛri/ ***adj.*** most important; main: *Smoking is one of the primary causes of lung cancer.* ◇ *A high standard of quality should be of primary importance.*

**pri·mar·y²** /ˈpraɪˌmɛri/ (*also* ˌ**primary eˈlection**) ***noun*** [C] (*pl.* **pri·mar·ies**) (*U.S.*) an election in which people vote for the person who will be a political party's candidate in a later important election, e.g. for President ➲ Look at **caucus** (2)

ˌ**primary ˈcare** ***noun*** [U] the general medical care that you get from your family doctor (not from a doctor with special skills in a specific area)

ˌ**primary ˈcolor** ***noun*** [C] any of the colors red, yellow or blue. You can make any other color by mixing primary colors in different ways.

**pri·mate** /ˈpraɪmeɪt/ ***noun*** [C] any animal that belongs to the group of mammals that includes humans, apes and monkeys

**prime¹** /praɪm/ ***adj.*** (only *before* a noun) **1** most important; main: *The prime cause of the company's bankruptcy was high interest rates.* **2** of very good quality; best: *prime pieces of beef* **3** having all the typical qualities: *That's a prime example of what I was talking about.*

**prime²** /praɪm/ ***noun*** [sing.] the time when sb is strongest, most beautiful, most successful, etc.: *Agassi is past his prime as a tennis player.* ◇ *to be in the prime of life*

**prime³** /praɪm/ ***verb*** [T] **prime sb/sth for sth/to do sth** to prepare sb/sth for a situation or to do sth: *The candidate had been primed for the interview with all the facts.*

ˌ**prime ˈminister** (*also* **premier**) ***noun*** [C] the leader of the government in countries that have a parliament, e.g. Canada ➲ For more information on the Canadian political system, look at study page **A11**.

**the ˌPrime ˈMinister's ˌOffice** ***noun*** [sing.] (*abbr.* **PMO**) (*Cdn*) the political staff of the prime minister, responsible for arranging his/her appointments and advising the prime minister on who to employ for various positions, etc.

ˌ**prime ˈnumber** ***noun*** [C] a number that can be divided exactly only by itself and 1, for example 7, 17 and 41

**prim·er** ***noun*** **1** /ˈpraɪmər/ [C,U] a type of paint that is put on wood, metal, etc. before it is painted to help the paint to stay on the surface **2** /ˈprɪmər/ [C] a book that contains basic instructions, explanations, etc.: *The President doesn't need a primer on national security.*

ˌ**prime ˈrate** ***noun*** [C] the lowest amount of interest that a bank charges its best customers at a particular time for borrowing money

ˌ**prime ˈrib** ***noun*** [C,U] a piece of good quality beef from the chest of the cow

ˌ**prime ˈtime** ***noun*** [U] the time in the evening, usually from 7:00 to 10:00 or from 8:00 to 11:00, when the largest number of people watch television

**prim·i·tive** /ˈprɪməṭɪv/ ***adj.*** **1** (only *before* a noun) connected with a very early stage of development (particularly of human life): *Primitive humans lived in caves and hunted wild animals.* **2** very simple; not developed: *The bathroom facilities at the campground were very primitive.* ◇ *a primitive shelter made out of pieces of wood and cloth*

★**prince** /prɪns/ ***noun*** [C] **1** a son or other close male relative of a king or queen: *Prince Charles* **2** the male ruler of a small country

★**prin·cess** /ˈprɪnsəs; -sɛs/ ***noun*** [C] **1** a daughter or other close female relative of a king or queen: *Princess Anne* **2** the wife of a prince

★**prin·ci·pal¹** /ˈprɪnsəpl/ ***adj.*** (only *before* a noun) most important; main: *The principal aim of the talks is to reduce the numbers of weapons.* ◇ *the principal characters in a play*

**prin·ci·pal²** /ˈprɪnsəpl/ ***noun*** [C] the person who is in charge of a school

**prin·ci·pal·ly** /ˈprɪnsəpli/ ***adv.*** mainly; mostly: *Our products are designed principally for the North American market.*

★**prin·ci·ple** /ˈprɪnsəpl/ ***noun*** **1** [C] a basic general rule or truth about sth: *We believe in the principle of equal opportunity for everyone.* ◇ *The class teaches the basic principles of car maintenance.* **2** [C,U] a rule for good behavior, based on what each person believes is right: *She refuses to wear fur. It's a matter of principle.* ◇ *a person of high moral principles* **3** [sing.] a law of science: *The system works on the principle that heat rises.*

IDM **in principle** in general, but possibly not in detail: *His proposal sounds fine in principle, but there are a few points I'm not happy about.*

**on principle** because of your moral beliefs or PRINCIPLES (2): *Helen refuses to wear leather on principle.*

**prin·ci·pled** /ˈprɪnsəpld/ ***adj.*** **1** having strong beliefs about what is right and wrong; based on strong beliefs: *a principled woman* ◇ *to take a principled stand against abortion* OPP **unprincipled** **2** based on rules or truths: *a principled approach to language teaching*

★**print¹** /prɪnt/ ***noun***

➤ LETTERS/NUMBERS **1** [U] the letters, words, etc. in a book, newspaper, etc.: *The print is too small for me to read without my glasses.* ➲ Look also at **fine print**.

➤ MARK **2** [C] a mark that is made by sth pressing onto sth else: *The neighbors' dog left paw prints in our fresh cement!* ➲ Look also at **fingerprint** and **footprint**.

➤ PICTURE **3** [C] a picture that was made by printing

➤ PHOTOGRAPH **4** [C] a photograph (when it has been printed from a negative): *I'd like an extra set of prints from this film.*

➤ FABRIC **5** [C,U] cloth with a colored pattern on it, or the pattern itself: *a floral print blouse*

IDM **out of print** (used about a book, etc.) that is not available from the publisher; not being printed anymore: *I'm sorry, the book you ordered is out of print.*

★**print²** /prɪnt/ ***verb***

➤ LETTERS/PICTURES **1** [T] to put words, pictures, etc. onto paper by using a metal or wood surface covered with ink: *How much did it cost to print the posters?* **2** [I,T] **print (sth) (off/out)** (*computing*) to put information from a computer onto paper: *Can you print that file for me?* ◇ *I can't get this document to print out.*

➤ BOOKS/NEWSPAPERS **3** [I,T] to produce a book, newspaper, etc.: *50,000 copies of the textbook were printed.*

➤ PUBLISH **4** [T] to include sth in a book, newspaper, etc.: *The newspaper printed a photograph of the killer.*

➤ WRITE **5** [I,T] to write with letters that are not joined together: *Please print your name and address on this form.*

➤ MAKE DESIGN **6** [T] to put a pattern onto cloth/paper: *printed cotton, wallpaper, etc.*

➤ PHOTOGRAPH **7** [T] to make a photograph from a piece of film

▸ **print·ing** ***noun*** [U]: *the invention of printing by Gutenberg*

★**print·er** /ˈprɪntər/ ***noun*** [C] **1** a machine that prints out information from a computer onto paper: *a laser printer* **2** a person or company that prints books, newspapers, etc.

ˈ**print·ing press** ***noun*** [C] a machine that is used for printing books, newspapers, etc.

**print·out** /ˈprɪntaʊt/ ***noun*** [C,U] information from a computer that is printed onto paper

★**pri·or** /ˈpraɪər/ ***adj.*** (only *before* a noun) coming before or earlier: *Ms. Parker was unable to attend the ceremony because of a prior commitment.*

IDM **prior to sth** (*formal*) before: *Passengers are asked to report to the check-in desk prior to departure.*

**pri·or·i·tize** /praɪˈɔrətaɪz; -ˈɑr-/ ***verb*** [I,T] **1** to put tasks, problems, etc. in order of importance, so that you can deal with the most important first: *You should make a list of all the tasks you have to do and prioritize them.* **2** (*formal*) to treat sth as being more important than other things: *The organization was formed to prioritize the needs of older people.*

▸ **pri·or·i·ti·za·tion** /praɪˌɔrət̬əˈzeɪʃn; -ˌɑrə-/ ***noun*** [U]

★**pri·or·i·ty** /praɪˈɔrət̬i; -ˈɑr-/ ***noun*** (*pl.* **pri·or·i·ties**) **1** [U] **priority (over sb/sth)** the state of being more important than sb/sth or of coming before sb/sth else: *Families with small children will be given priority.* ◇ *Emergency cases take priority over other patients in the hospital.* **2** [C] something that is most important or that you must do before anything else: *Our top priority is to get food and water to the refugee camps.* ◇ *You have to decide what your priorities are.*

**prism** /ˈprɪzəm/ ***noun*** [C] **1** a solid figure with ends that are parallel and of the same size and shape, and with sides whose opposite edges are equal and parallel **2** a transparent glass or plastic object, often with ends in the shape of a triangle, which separates light that passes through it into the colors of the rainbow

★**pris·on** /ˈprɪzn/ ***noun*** [C,U] a building where criminals are kept as a punishment: *She was sent to a maximum-security federal prison.* ◇ *The terrorists were sent to prison for twenty-five years.* ◇ *to escape from prison* ◇ *He will be released from prison next month.* ◇ *a prison guard*

> NOTE You talk about **prison** (without "**the**") when you are talking about somebody going or being there as a prisoner: *He's in prison.* You talk about **the prison** if you are talking about people going there for a different reason: *The governor will visit the prison tomorrow.* You also use **a** or **the** when more information is given: *a high-security prison.* ➲ Look also at **imprison** and **jail**.

★**pris·on·er** /ˈprɪzn·ər/ ***noun*** [C] a person who is being kept in a prison: *In many prisons, there are three prisoners in a cell.* ◇ *a political prisoner*

ˌ**prisoner of** ˈ**war** ***noun*** [C] (*pl.* **prisoners of**

P

war) (*abbr.* **POW**) a soldier, etc. who is caught by the enemy during a war and who is kept in a prison until the end of the war

**pri·va·cy** /ˈpraɪvəsi/ ***noun*** [U] the state of being alone or away from other people who may disturb you: *He locked the bathroom door so he could have some privacy.*

★**pri·vate¹** /ˈpraɪvət/ ***adj.***
➤NOT PUBLIC **1** belonging to one particular person or group and not to be used by others: *This is private property. You can't park here.* **2** secret; not to be shared by other people: *a private letter*
➤CONVERSATION/MEETING **3** with no one else present: *I'd like to have a private talk with you.*
➤NOT WORK **4** not connected with work or business: *He never discusses his private life with his coworkers.*
➤NOT OWNED/RUN BY THE GOVERNMENT **5** owned, done or organized by a person or company, and not by the government: *investment in the private sector of the economy* ◇ *a private school* ◇ *a private detective* (= one who is not in the police) ◇ *an attorney in private practice* ➲ Look at **public**.
▶ **pri·vate·ly** ***adv.***: *She said she agreed, but privately she had her doubts.* ◇ *privately-owned businesses*

**pri·vate²** /ˈpraɪvət/ ***noun*** [C] a person of the lowest rank in some branches of the military forces
IDM **in private** with no one else present: *Can I talk to you in private?*

ˌ**private inˈvestigator** ***noun*** [C] (*also* ˌ**private deˈtective**, (*informal* ˌ**private ˈeye**) a person who can be employed to find out information, look for a missing person, follow sb, etc.

**pri·va·tize** /ˈpraɪvətaɪz/ ***verb*** [T] to change the ownership of an organization from the government to a private company: *a proposal to privatize the Social Security system* ▶ **pri·va·ti·za·tion** /ˌpraɪvəṭəˈzeɪʃn/ ***noun*** [U]

★**priv·i·lege** /ˈprɪvlɪdʒ; -vəlɪdʒ/ ***noun*** **1** [C,U] a special right or advantage that only one person or group has: *Prisoners who behave well have special privileges.* ◇ *the wealth and privilege of certain families* **2** [C] a special advantage or opportunity that gives you great pleasure: *It was a great privilege to hear her sing in person.*

**priv·i·leged** /ˈprɪvlɪdʒd; -vəlɪdʒd/ ***adj.*** having an advantage or opportunity that most people do not have: *I feel very privileged to be attending this university.* ➲ Look at **underprivileged**.

★**prize¹** /praɪz/ ***noun*** [C] something of value that is given to sb who is successful in a race, competition, game, etc.: *He won first prize in the competition.* ◇ *Her pickles were awarded second prize in the state fair.* ◇ *a prize-winning novel*

**prize²** /praɪz/ ***adj.*** (only *before* a noun) winning, or good enough to win, a prize: *a prize flower display*

**prize³** /praɪz/ ***verb*** [T] to consider sth to be very valuable: *This picture is one of my most prized possessions.*

**pro¹** /proʊ/ ***adj.*** (*informal*) = PROFESSIONAL¹ (3,4): *a pro basketball player*

**pro²** /proʊ/ ***noun*** [C] (*pl.* **pros**) (*informal*) = PROFESSIONAL² (2,3): *a golf pro*
IDM **the pros and cons** the reasons for and against doing sth: *We should consider all the pros and cons before making a final decision.*

**pro·ac·tive** /proʊˈæktɪv/ ***adj.*** (used about a person or policy) controlling a situation by making things happen rather than waiting for things to happen and then reacting to them: *a proactive approach/role* ◇ *Managers must be proactive in identifying and preventing potential problems.* ➲ Compare **reactive.** ▶ **pro·ac·tive·ly** ***adv.***

**prob·a·bil·i·ty** /ˌprɑbəˈbɪləṭi/ ***noun*** (*pl.* **prob·a·bil·i·ties**) **1** [U, sing.] the state of being probable or likely: *At that time, there seemed to be little probability of success.* **2** [C] something that is probable or likely: *It might happen, but it's not a real probability.*

★**prob·a·ble** /ˈprɑbəbl/ ***adj.*** that you expect to happen or to be true; likely: *It's possible that they might still come, but it doesn't seem very probable.*

> NOTE Notice that **probable** and **likely** mean the same but are used differently: *It's probable that he will be late.* ◇ *He is likely to be late.*

OPP **improbable**

★**prob·a·bly** /ˈprɑbəbli/ ***adv.*** almost certainly: *I'll call you next week, probably on Wednesday.* ◇ *"Are you going to the mall with us?" "Probably not."*

**pro·ba·tion** /proʊˈbeɪʃn/ ***noun*** [U] **1** the system of keeping an official check on a person who has broken the law instead of sending him/her to prison or after he/she has left prison: *The prisoner was released on probation.* ◇ *He was sentenced to two years' probation.* **2** a period of time at the start of a new job when you are tested to see if you are really suitable: *a three-month probation period* **3** a period of time when a student who has behaved badly or has received bad grades must try to improve his/her performance: *Daryl's on academic probation this quarter – if he doesn't pass all his classes, he'll get kicked out.*

**proˈbation ˌofficer** ***noun*** [C] a person who keeps an official check on people who are on PROBATION (1)

**probe¹** /proʊb/ ***noun*** [C] **1** a long thin tool that you use for examining sth that is difficult to reach, especially a part of the body **2** asking questions, collecting facts, etc. in order to find out all the information about sth: *a police probe into illegal gambling*

**probe²** /proʊb/ ***verb*** **1** [T] to examine sth carefully with a PROBE¹ (1) or sth similar **2** [I,T] **probe (into sth)** to try to find out all the facts about sth ▶ **probing** ***adj.***: *to ask probing questions*

★**prob·lem** /ˈprɑbləm/ ***noun*** [C] **1** a difficult situation that you must deal with: *Unemployment causes a lot of social problems.* ◇ *The problem of racial discrimination is very difficult to solve.* ◇ *I'm facing a lot of big problems at work these days.* ◇ *to have financial problems* ◇ *There's a problem with the washing machine. It won't work.* ◇ *He has a drinking problem* (= he drinks too much alcohol). ◇ *Finding a good plumber is a real problem these days.* ◇ *Bruce had a lot of stomach problems when we were on vacation.* **2** a question that you have to solve by thinking about it: *Vicky had ten physics problems to do for homework.*
IDM **no problem** (*informal*) **1** (used to say that

sth is very easy to do and you are willing to do it): *"Can you fix this for me?" "Sure, no problem."* **2** (used as a friendly, very informal response after sb has said "thank you" or "sorry," to say that sth was not important): *"Thanks a lot for helping us out." "Hey, no problem."* ◇ *"Oops! Sorry I stepped on your toe." "No problem."*

**prob·lem·at·ic** /ˌprɑbləˈmæt̬ɪk/ ***adj.*** causing a lot of problems, or full of problems

**pro bo·no** /ˌproʊ ˈboʊnoʊ/ ***adj., adv.*** (only *before* a noun) (used especially about legal work) done without asking for payment: *pro bono legal services*

★**pro·ce·dure** /prəˈsidʒər/ ***noun*** [C,U] the action or series of actions that you must take in order to do sth in the usual or correct way: *If you want to make a complaint, please follow the correct procedure.*

★**pro·ceed** /prəˈsid; proʊ-/ ***verb*** [I] (*formal*) **1** to go on to do sth else: *After getting an estimate, we can decide whether or not to proceed with the work.* ◇ *Once he had calmed down, he proceeded to tell us what had happened.* **2** to continue or go on in a particular way or direction: *The construction work was proceeding according to schedule.* ◇ *The marchers proceeded over the bridge toward City Hall.*

**pro·ceed·ings** /prəˈsidɪŋz; proʊ-/ ***noun*** [pl.] **1 proceedings (against sb/for sth)** legal action in court: *to start divorce proceedings* **2** events that happen, especially at a formal meeting, ceremony, etc.: *The proceedings of the city council were interrupted by the demonstrators.*

**pro·ceeds** /ˈproʊsidz/ ***noun*** [pl.] **proceeds (from/of sth)** money that you get when you sell sth, or for sth that you have organized: *The proceeds from the sale will benefit the Red Cross.*

★**proc·ess**[1] /ˈprɑsɛs; ˈproʊ-/ ***noun*** [C] **1** a series of actions that you do for a particular purpose: *the process of producing steel* ◇ *Foreign residents who want to work in the U.S. have to go through the complicated process of getting a work permit.* **2** a series of changes that happen naturally: *Trees go though the process of growing and losing leaves every year.*

IDM **in the process** while you are doing sth else: *We washed the dog yesterday – and we all got very wet in the process.*

**in the process of sth/doing sth** in the middle of doing sth: *They are in the process of selling their house.*

★**proc·ess**[2] /ˈprɑsɛs; ˈproʊ-/ ***verb*** [T] **1** to change a raw material, e.g. with chemicals, before it is sold or used: *Cheese is processed so that it lasts longer.* ◇ *to process a film* (= to develop it so that you can print photographs from it) **2** to deal with information, e.g. on a computer: *When we have collected all the data, it will be processed by computer.* ◇ *It will take about ten days to process your application.*

**pro·ces·sion** /prəˈsɛʃn/ ***noun*** [C,U] a number of people, vehicles, etc. that move slowly in a line, e.g. as part of a ceremony: *a funeral procession*

**proc·es·sor** /ˈprɑsɛsər/ ***noun*** [C] (used in compounds) a machine that processes food or information: *a food processor* ◇ *a word processor*

**ˌpro-ˈchoice** ***adj.*** believing that a pregnant woman should be able to choose to have an ABORTION (1) if she wants: *pro-choice activists* ➲ Look at **pro-life**.

**pro·claim** /prəˈkleɪm; proʊ-/ ***verb*** [T] (*formal*) to make sth known officially or publicly: *Environmentalists have proclaimed the oil spill the worst disaster in recent times.* ◇ *to proclaim a state of emergency* ▸ **proc·la·ma·tion** /ˌprɑkləˈmeɪʃn/ ***noun*** [C,U]

**pro·cras·ti·nate** /prəˈkræstəneɪt/ ***verb*** [I] (*formal*) to delay doing sth that you should do, usually because you do not want to do it ▸ **pro·cras·ti·na·tion** /-ˌkræstəˈneɪʃn/

**proc·tor** /ˈprɑktər/ ***verb*** [I,T] to watch students while they are taking a test to make sure that they keep to the rules, etc.: *to proctor an exam* ▸ **proc·tor *noun*** [C]

**pro·cure** /prəˈkyʊr; proʊ-/ ***verb*** [I,T] **procure sth (for sb/sth)** (*formal*) to obtain sth, especially with difficulty: *She managed to procure a ticket for the concert.*

**pro·cure·ment** /prəˈkyʊrmənt; proʊ-/ ***noun*** [U] (*formal*) the process of obtaining supplies of sth, especially for a government or an organization: *arms procurement* ◇ *She has responsibility for the procurement of equipment in the company.*

**prod** /prɑd/ ***verb*** [I,T] (**prod·ding**; **prod·ded**) to push or press sb/sth with your finger or some other pointed object: (*figurative*) *I had to prod him to give me some information about the project.* ▸ **prod·ding *noun*** [U] (*figurative*): *Harold needs a lot of prodding before he will go and see a doctor.*

**prod·i·gal** /ˈprɑdɪgl/ ***adj.*** (*formal*) too willing to spend money or waste time, energy or materials: *a prodigal administration* SYN **extravagant**

IDM **the/a prodigal (son)** a person who leaves home and wastes his/her money and time on a life of pleasure, but who later is sorry about this and returns home

**prod·i·gy** /ˈprɑdədʒi/ ***noun*** [C] (*pl.* **prod·i·gies**) a person (especially a child) who is unusually good at sth: *a 14-year-old tennis prodigy* ➲ Look at **genius**.

★**pro·duce**[1] /prəˈdus/ ***verb*** [T] **1** to make or grow sth: *Some VW cars are produced in the U.S.* ◇ *The Prairies produce most of the country's wheat.* ◇ *The students have produced some beautiful pictures for the exhibit.* ◇ *Burning coal produces carbon dioxide.* **2** to cause sth to happen: *Her remarks produced roars of laughter.* **3** (*formal*) to show sth so that sb else can look at or examine it: *to produce evidence in court* **4** to organize a play, movie, etc. so that it can be shown to the public: *She is producing a Shakespeare play at the local theater.*

**pro·duce**[2] /ˈprɑdus; ˈproʊ-/ ***noun*** [U] food that comes from a farm, especially fresh fruit and vegetables ➲ Look at the note at **production**.

★**pro·duc·er** /prəˈdusər/ ***noun*** [C] **1** a person, company or country that makes or grows sth: *Brazil is a major producer of coffee.* **2** a person who deals with the business side of organizing a play, movie, etc.

★**prod·uct** /ˈprɑdʌkt/ ***noun*** [C] **1** something that is made in a factory or that is formed naturally: *Coal is an important product of West Virginia.* ◇ *waste products* ◇ *We have to find the right product for the market.* ◇ *The finished product should look a lot like this design.* ➲ Look at the note at **production**. **2 a/the product of sth** the result of sth: *The industry's problems are the product of a lack of investment.*

P

**3** the amount that you get if you multiply one number by another: *The product of three and five is fifteen.*

★**pro·duc·tion** /prəˈdʌkʃn/ ***noun*** **1** [U] the act of making or growing sth: *This farm specializes in the production of organic vegetables.* ◇ *mass production* ◇ *The price increases were the result of rising production costs.* **2** [U] the amount of sth that is made or grown: *Saudi Arabia is increasing its oil production.* **3** [C] a play, movie, etc.

NOTE Notice that **produce** means food, etc. that comes from a farm and a **product** is something that was made in a factory. A **production** is a play, movie, etc.: *fresh organic produce* ◇ *The company's main products are plastic toys.* ◇ *the local theater's production of a Broadway comedy*

IDM **in production** being made: *That model is no longer in production.*

**pro·duc·tive** /prəˈdʌktɪv/ ***adj.*** **1** that can make or grow sth well or in large quantities: *productive workers* ◇ *productive farmland* **2** useful (because results come from it): *a productive discussion* OPP **unproductive**

**pro·duc·tiv·i·ty** /ˌprɑdʌkˈtɪvət̬i; ˌproʊ-/ ***noun*** [U] the state of being PRODUCTIVE (1) or the amount that sb/sth PRODUCES (1): *More efficient methods will lead to greater productivity.*

**Prof.** ***abbr.*** = PROFESSOR

**prof** /prɑf/ ***noun*** [C] (*informal*) = PROFESSOR

**pro·fane** /proʊˈfeɪn; prə-/ ***adj.*** (*formal*) having or showing a lack of respect for God or holy things: *profane language*

P

**pro·fan·i·ty** /proʊˈfænət̬i; prə-/ ***noun*** (*formal*) **1** (*pl.* **pro·fan·i·ties**) [C, usually pl.] offensive words, or religious words used in a way that shows a lack of respect for God or holy things: *He uttered a stream of profanities.* **2** [U] behavior that shows a lack of respect for God or holy things

**pro·fess** /prəˈfɛs/ ***verb*** [T] (*formal*) **1** to say that sth is true (even if it is not): *The government professes concern about homelessness, but does little to help homeless people.* **2** to say openly that you think or believe sth: *He professed his hatred of war.*

★**pro·fes·sion** /prəˈfɛʃn/ ***noun*** **1** [C] a job that requires a lot of training and that is respected by other people: *the medical/legal/teaching profession* ➲ Look at the note at **work**[1]. **2 the profession** [sing.] all the people who work in a particular profession: *The legal profession is trying to resist the reforms.*

★**pro·fes·sion·al**[1] /prəˈfɛʃənl/ ***adj.*** **1** (only *before* a noun) of or concerning sb who has a profession: *The apartment would be ideal for a professional couple.* ◇ *Get professional advice from your lawyer before you take any action.* **2** doing sth in a way that shows skill, training or care: *The police are trained to deal with every situation in a calm and professional manner.* ◇ *Her application was neatly typed and looked very professional.* OPP **unprofessional** **3** (*also informal* **pro**) doing a sport, etc. as a job or for money: *After his success at the Olympic Games, he turned professional.* **4** (*also informal* **pro**) (used about a sport, etc.) done by people who are paid: *professional football* OPP The opposite for **3** and **4** is **amateur**.

★**pro·fes·sion·al**[2] /prəˈfɛʃənl/ ***noun*** [C] **1** a person who works in a PROFESSION (1): *medical professionals* **2** (*also informal* **pro**) a person who plays or teaches a sport, etc. for money **3** (*also informal* **pro**) a person who does his/her work with skill and care

**proˌfessional deˈvelopment day** ***noun*** [C] (*also* ˌ**P'D Day**) (*especially Cdn*) a day on which classes are canceled so that teachers can go to seminars etc. for their professional development

**pro·fes·sion·al·ism** /prəˈfɛʃənl·ɪzəm/ ***noun*** [U] the quality of showing great skill or care when you are doing a job: *Although they were students, they performed with great professionalism.*

**pro·fes·sion·al·ly** /prəˈfɛʃənl·i/ ***adv.*** **1** in a PROFESSIONAL[1] (1,2) way **2** for money, by a professional person: *Rob plays the saxophone professionally.* ◇ *to have your photograph taken professionally*

★**pro·fes·sor** /prəˈfɛsər/ (*also informal* **prof**) ***noun*** [C] (*abbr.* **Prof.**) a teacher at a college or university: *Professor Rosen* ◇ *Professor Alison Waters* ◇ *My French professor says that my accent needs work.* ➲ Look also at **assistant professor** and **associate professor**.

**pro·fi·cien·cy** /prəˈfɪʃnsi/ ***noun*** [U] **proficiency (in sth/doing sth)** the ability to do sth well; skill: *students with limited English proficiency*

**pro·fi·cient** /prəˈfɪʃnt/ ***adj.*** **proficient (in/at sth/doing sth)** able to do a particular thing well; skilled: *We are looking for someone who is proficient in French.*

★**pro·file** /ˈproʊfaɪl/ ***noun*** [C] **1** a person's face or head seen from the side, not the front **2** a short description of the characteristics of sb/sth that gives useful information: *a job/employee profile* ◇ *We first build up a detailed profile of our customers and their requirements.*

IDM **keep a low profile** → LOW[1] ➲ Look also at **high-profile**.

**pro·fil·ing** /ˈproʊfaɪlɪŋ/ ***noun*** [U] **1** the act of stopping and searching people who belong to a particular race or group, for example by the police or at an airport, because they are believed to be more likely to commit crimes: *racial profiling* **2** the process of collecting and analyzing information about sb/sth in order to build up a picture of what he/she/it is like: *customer profiling*

★**prof·it**[1] /ˈprɑfət/ ***noun*** [C,U] the money that you make when you sell sth for more than it cost you: *Did you make a profit on your house when you sold it?* ◇ *an annual profit of $25,000* ◇ *We fixed up an old car and sold it at a profit.* ◇ *We won't make much profit in the first year.* ➲ Look at **loss**.

**prof·it**[2] /ˈprɑfət/ ***verb***

PHR V **profit from sth** (*formal*) to get some advantage from sth: *We hope to profit from our competitors' mistakes.*

**prof·it·a·ble** /ˈprɑfət̬əbl/ ***adj.*** **1** that makes a profit: *a profitable business* **2** helpful or useful: *We had a very profitable discussion yesterday.* ▶ **prof·it·a·bil·i·ty** /ˌprɑfət̬əˈbɪlət̬i/ ***noun*** [U] ▶ **prof·it·a·bly**

/-əbli/ ***adv.***: *to invest money profitably ◇ to spend your time profitably*

**pro·found** /prə'faʊnd/ ***adj.*** **1** great; that you feel very strongly: *The experience had a profound influence on her.* **2** serious; showing knowledge or thought: *profound statements about the meaning of life*

**pro·found·ly** /prə'faʊndli/ ***adv.*** (*formal*) very; extremely: *an invention that profoundly changed people's lives*

**pro·fuse** /prə'fyus; proʊ-/ ***adj.*** produced in large amounts: *profuse apologies/thanks* ▸ **pro·fuse·ly** ***adv.***: *to sweat profusely*

**prog·no·sis** /prɑg'noʊsəs/ ***noun*** [C] (*pl.* **prog·no·ses** /-siz/) a judgment that predicts how sth, especially a disease, will develop in the future

★**pro·gram¹** /'proʊgræm/ ***noun*** [C] **1** an official plan or system of services or activities for doing sth: *the state's proposed welfare-to-work program ◇ an intense training program ◇ plans to expand the university's graduate programs* **2** a show or other item that is broadcast on the radio or on television: *a TV program ◇ an interesting program about the Gold Rush* **3** a set of instructions that you give to a computer so that it will carry out a particular task: *to write a program* **4** a little book or piece of paper which you get at a play, concert, etc. that gives you information about what you are going to see

IDM **get with the program** (*informal*) (used to tell sb to take notice of what is happening around him/her and to do what needs to be done)

★**pro·gram²** /'proʊgræm; -grəm/ ***verb*** [T] (**pro·gram·ming; pro·grammed**) **1** to give a set of instructions to a computer **2** to make a piece of equipment work or act automatically in a particular way: *The lights are programmed to come on as soon as it gets dark.*

**pro·gram·mer** /'proʊgræmər/ ***noun*** [C] a person whose job is to write PROGRAMS¹ (3) for a computer: *a computer programmer*

★**pro·gress¹** /'prɑgrɛs; -grəs/ ***noun*** [U] **1** movement forward or toward achieving sth: *The heavy traffic meant that we made very slow progress. ◇ Anna's making steady progress in school. ◇ The talks made very little progress toward solving the problem. ◇ a progress report* **2** change or improvement in society: *scientific progress ◇ People who oppose new technologies are accused of holding back progress.*

IDM **in progress** happening now: *Quiet! Examination in progress.*

★**prog·ress²** /prə'grɛs/ ***verb*** [I] **1** to become better; to develop (well): *Medical knowledge has progressed rapidly in the last twenty years.* **2** to move forward; to continue: *I got more and more tired as the evening progressed.*

**pro·gres·sion** /prə'grɛʃn/ ***noun*** [C,U] **progression (from sth) (to sth)** movement forward or a development from one stage to another: *I can't see any logical progression in your thoughts in this paper.*

**pro·gres·sive** /prə'grɛsɪv/ ***adj.*** **1** using or agreeing with modern methods and ideas: *a progressive school* **2** happening or developing steadily: *a progressive reduction in the number of workers*

**pro·gres·sive·ly** /prə'grɛsɪvli/ ***adv.*** steadily; a little at a time: *The situation got progressively worse.*

**the pro'gressive tense** ***noun*** [sing.] = CONTINUOUS TENSE

**pro·hib·it** /proʊ'hɪbət; prə-/ ***verb*** [T] (*formal*) **prohibit sb/sth (from doing sth)** to say that sth is not allowed by law; to forbid: *Federal law prohibits smoking on all domestic airline flights. ◇ That sign means that parking is prohibited here.*

**pro·hi·bi·tion** /ˌproʊə'bɪʃn/ ***noun*** **1** [C,U] (*formal*) a law or rule that forbids sth, or the act of forbidding sth **2 Prohibition** [U] the period between 1920 and 1933, when it was illegal to produce and sell alcoholic drinks in the U.S.

**pro·hib·i·tive** /proʊ'hɪbət̬ɪv; prə-/ ***adj.*** **1** (used about a price or a cost) so high that it prevents people from buying sth or doing sth: *prohibitive costs ◇ a prohibitive tax on imported cars* **2** preventing people from doing sth by law: *prohibitive legislation* ▸ **pro·hib·i·tive·ly** ***adv.***

★**proj·ect¹** /'prɑdʒɛkt; -dʒɪkt/ ***noun*** [C] **1** a piece of work, often involving many people, that is planned and organized carefully; a plan for some work: *a major project to reduce pollution in our rivers ◇ His latest project is fixing up an old car.* **2** a piece of school work in which a student has to collect information about a certain subject and then write about it: *The whole class is doing a project on rainforests.* **3** (*informal*) = HOUSING PROJECT

**pro·ject²** /prə'dʒɛkt/ ***verb***

➤ PLAN **1** [T] (usually passive) to plan: *the President's projected tour of Europe*

➤ ESTIMATE **2** [T] (usually passive) to estimate or calculate: *a projected increase of 10%*

➤ LIGHT/IMAGE **3** [T] **project sth (on/onto sth)** to make sth (light, a shadow, a picture from a movie, etc.) fall on a surface: *Colored lights were projected onto the dance floor.*

➤ PRESENT YOURSELF **4** [T] to show or represent sb/sth/yourself in a certain way: *The candidate's advisers told him to project a more conservative image.*

➤ STICK OUT **5** [I] (*formal*) to stick out: *The porch projects three yards from the front of the house.*

**pro·jec·tile** /prə'dʒɛktəl; -taɪl/ ***noun*** [C] (*formal*) or (*technical*) **1** an object, such as a bullet, that is fired from a gun or other weapon **2** any object that is thrown as a weapon

**pro·jec·tion** /prə'dʒɛkʃn/ ***noun*** **1** [C] a guess about a future amount, situation, etc. based on the information you have now: *sales projections for the next five years* **2** [U] the act of making light, a picture from a movie, etc. fall on a surface: *film projection*

**pro·jec·tor** /prə'dʒɛktər/ ***noun*** [C] an apparatus that projects pictures or movies onto a screen or wall: *a movie projector ◇ a slide projector ◇ an overhead projector*

ˌ**pro-'life** ***adj.*** opposed to the belief that a pregnant woman should be able to choose to have an ABORTION (1) if she wants: *a pro-life campaigner* ➲ Look at **pro-choice**.

**pro·lif·er·ate** /prə'lɪfəreɪt/ ***verb*** [I] (*formal*) to increase quickly in number ▸ **pro·lif·er·a·tion** /prəˌlɪfə'reɪʃn/ ***noun*** [U]

**pro·lif·ic** /prə'lɪfɪk/ ***adj.*** (used especially about a writer, an artist, etc.) producing a lot: *a prolific writer of short stories*

**pro·logue** /'proʊlɔg; -lɑg/ ***noun*** [C] a speech, etc. at the beginning of a play, book, or movie that introduces it: *the Prologue to Chaucer's "Canterbury Tales"*

**pro·long** /prə'lɔŋ; -'lɑŋ/ ***verb*** [T] to make sth last longer: *Careful treatment will prolong the life of the furniture.*

**pro·longed** /prə'lɔŋd; -'lɑŋd/ ***adj.*** (only *before* a noun) continuing for a long time: *There was a prolonged silence before anybody spoke.*

**prom** /prɑm/ ***noun*** [C] a formal dance that is held for high school students near the end of a school year

**prom·e·nade** /ˌprɑmə'neɪd; -'nɑd/ ***noun*** [C] a public place for walking, usually a wide path beside a waterfront

**prom·i·nent** /'prɑmənənt/ ***adj.*** (usually *before* a noun) **1** important or famous: *a prominent political figure* ◇ *The First Lady often plays a prominent role in charity work.* **2** noticeable; easy to see: *The Space Needle is the most prominent feature of Seattle's skyline.* ▶ **prom·i·nence** /-əns/ ***noun*** [U]: *She gained national prominence after appearing in a popular commercial.* ▶ **prom·i·nent·ly** ***adv.***: *The Chinese leader's visit was prominently featured on the TV news.*

**pro·mis·cu·ous** /prə'mɪskyuəs/ ***adj.*** (*formal*) having sexual relations with many people ▶ **prom·is·cu·i·ty** /ˌprɑmə'skyuət̬i/ ***noun*** [U]

★**prom·ise¹** /'prɑməs/ ***noun*** **1** [C] a written or spoken statement or agreement that you will or will not do sth: *He made a promise not to tell anyone what he had seen.* ◇ *Her parents kept their promise to buy her a dog for her birthday.* ◇ *He said he would help us, but he broke his promise.* ◇ *They both gave me a promise of their complete support.* **2** [U] signs that you will be able to do sth well or be successful: *He showed great promise as a musician.*

★**prom·ise²** /'prɑməs/ ***verb*** **1** [I,T] to say definitely that you will or will not do sth: *I'll try to be back at 6 o'clock, but I can't promise.* ◇ *"I'll pay you back tomorrow," his friend promised.* ◇ *She promised that she would write every week.* ◇ *Tom promised me that he'd never be late again.* ◇ *The mayor has promised to clean up local government.* **2** [T] **promise sth (to sb)** to say definitely that you will give sth to sb: *My father has promised me a new bike.* ◇ *Can you promise your support?* **3** [T] to show signs of sth, so that you expect it to happen: *The picnic promises to be a lot of fun.*

**prom·is·ing** /'prɑməsɪŋ/ ***adj.*** showing signs of being very good or successful: *a promising young writer*

**pro·mo** /'proʊmoʊ/ ***noun*** [C] (*pl.* **pro·mos**) an advertisement to PROMOTE (3) sth, especially in the form of a short movie or video: *to make a new promo for the game show* ▶ **pro·mo** ***adj.*** (*informal*): *a promo video*

★**pro·mote** /prə'moʊt/ ***verb*** [T] **1** (often passive) to give sb a higher position, more important job, etc.: *He's been promoted from assistant manager to manager.* OPP **demote** **2** to encourage sth; to help sth to happen or develop: *The meetings of the leaders have helped to promote good relations between the two countries.* **3** to advertise sth (in order to increase its sales or popularity): *In order to sell a new product, you need to promote it in the right way.*

**pro·mo·ter** /prə'moʊt̬ər/ ***noun*** [C] a person who organizes or provides the money for an event

★**pro·mo·tion** /prə'moʊʃn/ ***noun*** **1** [C,U] (the giving or receiving of) a higher position or more important job: *She's hoping to receive a promotion this year.* ◇ *The job offers a good salary and excellent chances of promotion.* OPP **demotion** **2** [U] making sth successful or popular: *We need to work on the promotion of health, not the treatment of disease.* **3** [C,U] things that you do in order to advertise a product: *It's all part of a special promotion of the new book.* ◇ *Millions of dollars were spent on advertising and promotion.*

**pro·mo·tion·al** /prə'moʊʃənl/ ***adj.*** connected with advertising: *a promotional tour* ◇ *promotional material*

★**prompt¹** /prɑmpt/ ***adj.*** **1** quick; done without delay: *I received a prompt reply from my lawyer.* ◇ *We need a prompt decision on this matter.* **2 prompt (in doing sth/to do sth)** (used about a person) quick; acting without delay: *We are always prompt in paying our bills.* ◇ *She was prompt to point out my mistake.*

★**prompt²** /prɑmpt/ ***verb*** **1** [T] to cause sth; to make sb decide to do sth: *What prompted that remark?* ◇ *What prompted you to give up your job?* **2** [I,T] to help sb to continue speaking or to remind an actor of his/her words: *"And can you tell the court what happened next?" the lawyer prompted.* ◇ *The speaker had to be prompted several times.* ▶ **prompt·ing** ***noun*** [C,U]: *He apologized without any prompting.*

**prompt³** /prɑmpt/ ***noun*** [C] (*computing*) a special symbol that appears on a computer screen when the computer is ready to receive an instruction

**prompt·ly** /'prɑmptli/ ***adv.*** **1** immediately; without delay: *I invited her to dinner and she promptly accepted.* **2** punctually; at the time that you have arranged: *We arrived promptly at 12 o'clock.*

**prone** /proʊn/ ***adj.*** (not before a noun) **prone to sth** likely to suffer from sth or to do sth: *Young people are especially prone to this disease.* ◇ *to be accident-prone* (= to have a lot of accidents)

**prong** /prɔŋ; prɑŋ/ ***noun*** [C] **1** each of the two or more long pointed parts of a fork ➲ picture at **garden**. **2** each of the separate parts of an attack, argument, etc., that move toward a place, subject, etc. from different positions

**-pronged** ***combining form*** (used in adjectives) having the number or types of prongs mentioned: *a two-pronged fork* ◇ *a three-pronged attack*

**pro·noun** /'proʊnaʊn/ ***noun*** [C] (*grammar*) a word that is used in place of a noun or a phrase that contains a noun: *"He," "it," "hers," "me" and "them" are all pronouns.*

★**pro·nounce** /prə'naʊns/ ***verb*** **1** [T] to make the sound of a word or letter: *You don't pronounce the "b" at the end of "comb."* ◇ *How do you pronounce* *your last name?* **2** [T] (*formal*) to say in a formal or official way that sb/sth is in a particular condition: *The doctors pronounced him dead on arrival at the hospital.* ▸ **pro·nounce·ment** ***noun*** [C]

**pro·nounced** /prəˈnaʊnst/ ***adj.*** very noticeable: *to walk with a pronounced limp*

**pron·to** /ˈprɑntoʊ/ ***adv.*** (*informal*) quickly; immediately: *Get back here, pronto!*

★**pro·nun·ci·a·tion** /prəˌnʌnsiˈeɪʃn/ ***noun*** **1** [C,U] the way in which a language or a word is pronounced: *The dictionary gives two different pronunciations for this word.* ◇ *standard pronunciation* **2** [U] a person's way of speaking a language: *His grammar is good but his pronunciation is awful!*

★**proof**[1] /pruf/ ***noun*** [U] a fact or piece of information which shows that sth is true: *Keep your receipt as proof of purchase.* ◇ *What proof do we have that what he is saying is true?* ➲ verb **prove**

**proof**[2] /pruf/ ***adj.*** (in compounds) able to protect from or to be protected against the thing mentioned: *a soundproof room* ◇ *bulletproof glass*

**prop**[1] /prɑp/ ***verb*** [T] (**prop·ping; propped**) **1** to support sth or keep sth in the correct position: *I'll use this book to prop the window open.* **2** to lean sth against sth else: *He propped his bicycle against the wall.*

PHR V **prop sb/sth up** to put an object under or behind sb/sth in order to give support

**prop sth up** to support sth that would otherwise fail: *to prop up a corrupt administration*

**prop**[2] /prɑp/ ***noun*** [C, usually pl.] a piece of furniture or another object that is used in a play, movie, etc.

**prop·a·gan·da** /ˌprɑpəˈgændə/ ***noun*** [U] information and ideas, especially ones that are not true, that are made public by a government or large organization, in order to influence people or persuade them about sth: *political propaganda* ◇ *anti-immigrant propaganda*

**prop·a·gate** /ˈprɑpəgeɪt/ ***verb*** [I,T] **1** (*formal*) to spread an idea, a belief or a piece of information among many people: *Television advertising propagates a false image of the ideal family.* **2** (*technical*) to produce new plants from a parent plant: *The plant can be propagated from seed.* ▸ **prop·a·ga·tion** /ˌprɑpəˈgeɪʃn/

**pro·pane** /ˈproʊpeɪn/ ***noun*** [U] a gas found in natural gas and oil and used as a fuel for cooking and heating: *a propane gas cylinder*

**pro·pel** /prəˈpɛl/ ***verb*** [T] (**pro·pel·ling; pro·pelled**) to move, drive or push sb/sth forward ➲ noun **propulsion**

**pro·pel·lant** /prəˈpɛlənt/ ***noun*** [C,U] **1** a gas that forces out the contents of an aerosol **2** a thing or substance that propels sth, e.g. the fuel that fires a rocket

**pro·pel·ler** /prəˈpɛlər/ ***noun*** [C] a piece of equipment with several blades, which turns around very fast in order to make a ship or an aircraft move

**pro·pen·si·ty** /prəˈpɛnsəṭi/ ***noun*** [C] (*pl.* **pro·pen·si·ties**) **propensity (for doing sth); propensity (to do sth)** (*formal*) a tendency to a particular kind of behavior: *He showed a propensity for violence.*

★**prop·er** /ˈprɑpər/ ***adj.*** **1** (only *before* a noun) right or correct: *information on the proper use of chemicals* ◇ *It is important to use the proper tool for the job.* **2** (*formal*) accepted as socially correct or appropriate: *Is it considered proper to wear a hat indoors?* OPP **improper** **3** (only *after* a noun) real or main: *We traveled through miles of suburbs before we got to the city proper.*

★**prop·er·ly** /ˈprɑpərli/ ***adv.*** **1** correctly: *a lock that was not properly installed* **2** in a way that is socially correct; politely OPP **improperly**

ˌ**proper ˈnoun** (*also* ˌ**proper ˈname**) ***noun*** [C] (*grammar*) a word which is the name of a particular person or place and begins with a capital letter: *"Mary," "Rome" and "the White House" are all proper nouns.*

★**prop·er·ty** /ˈprɑpərṭi/ ***noun*** (*pl.* **prop·er·ties**) **1** [U] something that belongs to sb; all the things that belong to sb: *"Is this your property?" the police officer asked, pointing to a small suitcase.* ◇ *The bag contained stolen property.* **2** [C,U] land and/or a building or buildings on it: *property tax* ◇ *private/public property* ◇ *to invest your money in property* ◇ *They own several commercial properties in Florida.* **3** [C] a special quality that a substance, etc. has: *Some plants have healing properties.*

**proph·e·cy** /ˈprɑfəsi/ ***noun*** [C] (*pl.* **proph·e·cies**) a statement about what is going to happen in the future: *His prophecy that there would be a disaster came true.*

**proph·e·sy** /ˈprɑfəsaɪ/ ***verb*** [T] (**proph·e·sies; proph·e·sy·ing; proph·e·sied**) to say what will happen in the future (done in the past using religious or magic powers): *to prophesy war* ◇ *The event was prophesied in the Old Testament.*

**proph·et** /ˈprɑfət/ ***noun*** [C] **1** (*also* **Prophet**) a person who is chosen by God to give his message to people: *the Prophet Muhammed* ◇ *the prophets of the Old Testament* **2** a person who tells or claims to tell what will happen in the future ▸ **pro·phet·ic** /prəˈfɛṭɪk/ ***adj.***

**pro·phy·lac·tic** /ˌproʊfəˈlæktɪk/ ***noun*** [C] = CONDOM

**pro·po·nent** /prəˈpoʊnənt/ ***noun*** [C] (*formal*) **proponent (of sth)** a person who supports an idea or course of action SYN **advocate**[2]

★**pro·por·tion** /prəˈpɔrʃn/ ***noun*** **1** [C] a part or share of a whole: *A large proportion of the earth's surface is covered by oceans.* **2** [C] **proportion (of sth to sth)** the relationship between the size or amount of two things: *The proportion of teachers to students was too low* (= there were not enough teachers for the number of students). **3 proportions** [pl.] the size and shape of sth: *He stood and gazed at the magnificent proportions of the cathedral.* ◇ *Violent crime is reaching alarming proportions.*

IDM **in proportion** in the correct relation to other things: *to draw sth in proportion* (= so that the parts are balanced as they are in reality) ◇ *She's so upset that she can't see the problem in proportion anymore* (= it seems more important than it really is).

**in proportion to sth** **1** by the same amount or number as sth else: *Salaries have not risen in proportion to inflation.* **2** compared with: *In*



P

*proportion to the number of students as a whole, there are very few women.*

**out of proportion (to sth) 1** too big, small, etc. in relation to other things **2** too great, serious, important, etc. in relation to sth: *His reaction was completely out of proportion to the situation.* ◇ *Aren't you getting this thing completely out of proportion* (= you think it's more important than it really is)?

**pro·por·tion·al** /prəˈpɔrʃənl/ ***adj.*** directly linked in size, amount, etc. to sth else: *The cost will be **proportional to** the amount used.* ▶ **pro·por·tion·al·ly** ***adv.***

**pro·por·tion·ate** /prəˈpɔrʃənət/ ***adj.*** (*formal*) = PROPORTIONAL ▶ **pro·por·tion·ate·ly** ***adv.***

★**pro·pos·al** /prəˈpoʊzl/ ***noun*** [C] **1** a plan that is suggested: *to submit a new proposal for raising money* ◇ *The recent proposal was rejected.* **2** an act of asking sb to marry you

★**pro·pose** /prəˈpoʊz/ ***verb* 1** [T] to suggest sth officially as a possible plan or action: *The idea will be proposed at the next committee meeting.* ◇ *I propose that we wait until next week to discuss it.* **2** [T] to intend; to have sth as a plan: *And just how do they propose to pay for all this?* **3** [I] **propose (to sb)** to ask sb to marry you: *We've been going out for a long time, but he still hasn't proposed.*

**prop·o·si·tion** /ˌprɑpəˈzɪʃn/ ***noun*** [C] **1** an idea or opinion that sb expresses about sth: *That's a very interesting proposition. But can you prove it?* **2** an arrangement or offer, especially in business; a suggestion: *He made me a proposition to buy my share of the company.* **3** (*also* **Proposition**) (in the U.S.) a plan for a new law that people vote on in order to decide whether it becomes a law or not: *California voters approved Proposition 187 in 1994.*

**pro·pri·e·tar·y** /prəˈpraɪəˌtɛri/ ***adj.*** **1** (used about goods) made and sold by a particular company and protected by a registered trade name: *proprietary software* ◇ *proprietary brands* **2** relating to an owner or to the fact of owning sth: *The company has a proprietary right to the property.*

**pro·pri·e·tor** /prəˈpraɪəṭər/ ***noun*** [C] (*formal*) the owner of a business

**pro·pul·sion** /prəˈpʌlʃn/ ***noun*** [U] (*technical*) the force that drives sth forward: *wind/steam/jet propulsion* ➲ verb **propel**

**prose** /proʊz/ ***noun*** [U] written or spoken language that is not poetry: *to write in prose* ◇ *a prose writer*

**pros·e·cute** /ˈprɑsəkyut/ ***verb*** [I,T] **prosecute (sb) (for sth)** to officially charge sb with a crime in a court of law: *the prosecuting attorney in the murder trial* ◇ *He was prosecuted for theft.* ➲ Look at **defend**.

**pros·e·cu·tion** /ˌprɑsəˈkyuʃn/ ***noun* 1** [sing.] a person or group of people who try to prove in a court of law that sb is guilty of a crime: *a witness for the prosecution* ◇ *The prosecution claims that Thompson was driving at 100 miles per hour.* ➲ Look at **defense**. **2** [C,U] (an example of) accusing sb of a crime and trying to prove it in a court of law: *Failure to pay your parking ticket will result in prosecution.*

**pros·e·cu·tor** /ˈprɑsəˌkyuṭər/ ***noun*** [C] **1** a public official who charges sb officially with a crime and prosecutes him/her in a court of law: *the public/state prosecutor* **2** a lawyer who leads the case against the accused person (**defendant**) in a court of law

**pros·e·ly·tize** /ˈprɑsələtaɪz/ ***verb*** [I] (*formal*) to try to persuade other people to accept your beliefs, especially about religion or politics

★**pros·pect¹** /ˈprɑspɛkt/ ***noun* 1** [C,U] **prospect (of sth/of doing sth)** the chance or hope that sth will happen: *There's not much prospect of better weather before next week.* ◇ *Prospects for peace do not look good.* **2** [C,U] an idea of what may or will happen: *the awful prospect of the air conditioning breaking in July* **3 prospects** [pl.] chances of being successful: *A degree will improve your job prospects.*

**pros·pect²** /ˈprɑspɛkt/ ***verb*** [I] **prospect (for sth)** to search an area for gold, minerals, oil, etc.: *Thousands moved to the area to prospect for gold.* ◇ (*figurative*) *to prospect for new clients* ▶ **pros·pec·tor** ***noun*** [C]: *gold prospectors*

**pro·spec·tive** /prəˈspɛktɪv/ ***adj.*** likely to be or to happen; possible: *prospective changes to the law* ◇ *a prospective car buyer*

**pro·spec·tus** /prəˈspɛktəs/ ***noun*** [C] **1** a book or printed document that gives information about a school, college, etc. in order to advertise it **2** (in business) a document that gives information about a company's SHARES¹ (2) before they are offered for sale

**pros·per** /ˈprɑspər/ ***verb*** [I] to be successful, especially financially

**pros·per·i·ty** /prɑˈspɛrəṭi/ ***noun*** [U] the state of being financially successful: *Tourism has brought prosperity to central B.C.* ◇ *economic prosperity*

**pros·per·ous** /ˈprɑspərəs/ ***adj.*** rich and successful: *the prosperous counties of northern California*

**pros·tate** /ˈprɑsteɪt/ (*also* **ˈprostate gland**) ***noun*** [C] a small organ in men that produces a liquid in which sperm is carried (**semen**)

**pros·the·sis** /prɑsˈθisəs/ ***noun*** [C] (*pl.* **pros·the·ses** /-siz/) (*medical*) an artificial part of the body, for example a leg, an eye or a tooth ▶ **pros·the·tic** /-ˈθɛṭɪk/ ***adj.***: *a prosthetic arm*

**pros·ti·tute** /ˈprɑstətut/ (*also informal* **hooker**, *old-fashioned* **whore**) ***noun*** [C] a person, especially a woman, who earns money by having sex with people ▶ **pros·ti·tu·tion** /ˌprɑstəˈtuʃn/ ***noun*** [U]

**pro·tag·o·nist** /proʊˈtægənɪst/ ***noun*** [C] (*formal*) the main character in a play, movie or book

★**pro·tect** /prəˈtɛkt/ ***verb*** [T] **protect sb/sth (against/from sth)** to keep sb/sth safe; to defend sb/sth: *It was interesting to watch the bird trying to protect its young.* ◇ *basic rights that are protected by the Constitution* ◇ *Politicians always try to protect themselves against criticism.* ◇ *Parents try to protect their children from danger.* ◇ *Alligators are a protected species in Florida* (= they must not be killed). ▶ **pro·tec·tor** /prəˈtɛktər/ ***noun*** [C]

★**pro·tec·tion** /prəˈtɛkʃn/ ***noun*** [U] **protection (against/from sth)** (a way of) keeping sb/sth safe so that he/she/it is not harmed or damaged: *the protection of the environment* ◇ *Vaccination against measles gives you protection against the disease.* ◇ *A* *good sunblock provides protection from the sun's harmful rays.*

**pro·tec·tion·ism** /prəˈtɛkʃənɪzəm/ ***noun*** [U] (in economics) the principle or practice of protecting a country's own industry by taxing foreign goods ▸ **pro·tec·tion·ist** /prəˈtɛkʃənɪst/ ***adj.***: *protectionist measures/policies*

**pro·tec·tive** /prəˈtɛktɪv/ ***adj.*** **1** that prevents sb/sth from being damaged or harmed: *All employees must wear protective clothing in this area.* **2 protective (of sb)** wanting to protect sb and keep him/her safe: *parents who are overly protective of their children*

**pro·té·gé** (*also* **pro·te·ge**) (*feminine* **pro·té·gée/ pro·te·gee**) /ˈproʊt̬əʒeɪ; ˌproʊt̬əˈʒeɪ/ ***noun*** [C] a young person who is helped in his/her career and personal development by a more experienced person: *a protégé of the great violinist Yehudi Menuhin*

**pro·tein** /ˈproʊtin/ ***noun*** [C,U] a substance found in food such as meat, fish and beans. It is important for helping people and animals to grow and be healthy.

★**pro·test**[1] /ˈproʊtɛst/ ***noun*** [C,U] the showing of disagreement; a statement or action that shows that you do not like or agree with sth: *The union organized a protest against the layoffs.* ◇ *The planned site for the prison was moved after protests from local residents.* ◇ *We received thousands of letters of protest.* ◇ *He resigned in protest against the decision.* ◇ *a protest march*

IDM **under protest** not happily or willingly: *Carol finally agreed to pay, but only under protest.*

★**pro·test**[2] /ˈproʊtɛst; prəˈtɛst/ ***verb*** **1** [I,T] **protest (about/against/at sth)**; **protest sth** to say or show that you do not like or agree with sth: *Thousands gathered to protest against the new tax.* ◇ *The kids protested loudly at being taken home early.* ◇ *Several customers protested about the poor service in the restaurant.* ◇ *They protested the government's handling of the situation.* **2** [T] to say sth firmly: *He protested a total lack of knowledge of the affair.* ◇ *He protested that he hadn't been in the area when the robbery took place.* ◇ *"That's just not true," she protested.*

NOTE **Protest** is stronger and usually used about more serious things than **complain**. You **protest** about something that you feel is not right or fair; you **complain** about the quality of something or about a less serious action: *to protest about the tax increase* ◇ *to complain about the weather.*

▸ **pro·test·er** ***noun*** [C]: *Protesters lined the sidewalks as the President's car drove up.*

**Prot·es·tant** /ˈprɑt̬əstənt/ ***noun*** [C] a member of the Christian church that separated from the Catholic church in the 16th century ▸ **Prot·es·tant** ***adj.***: *a Protestant church* ➲ Look at **Catholic**.

**pro·to·col** /ˈproʊtəkɔl; -kɑl/ ***noun*** **1** [U] the system of rules for correct behavior in formal, official situations **2** [C] (*technical*) the first or original version of an official written agreement **3** [C] (*computing*) a set of signals and rules that control how information is sent from one computer to another

**pro·ton** /ˈproʊtɑn/ ***noun*** [C] a very small piece of matter with a positive electric charge that forms part of the central part (**nucleus**) of an atom ➲ Look also at **neutron** and **electron**.

**pro·to·type** /ˈproʊtətaɪp/ ***noun*** [C] the first model or design of sth from which other forms are copied or developed

**pro·tract·ed** /proʊˈtræktəd; prə-/ ***adj.*** (*written*) lasting longer than expected or longer than usual: *protracted delays/disputes/negotiations*

**pro·trac·tor** /proʊˈtræktər; prə-/ ***noun*** [C] an instrument for measuring and drawing angles, usually made from a half circle of clear plastic with degrees (0° to 180°) marked on it

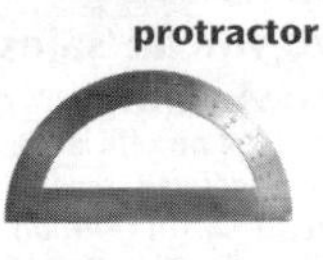
**protractor**

**pro·trude** /proʊˈtrud; prə-/ ***verb*** [I] to stick out from a surface: *protruding teeth* ▸ **pro·tru·sion** /proʊˈtruʒn; prə-/ ***noun*** [C,U]

★**proud** /praʊd/ ***adj.*** **1 proud (of sb/sth)**; **proud (to do sth/that...)** feeling pleased and satisfied about sth that you own or have done, or are connected with: *a proud father of twins* ◇ *They are very proud of their new house.* ◇ *I feel extremely proud to be part of such a successful organization.* ◇ *You should feel proud that you were chosen.* **2** not wanting help from other people: *He was too proud to ask for help.* **3** feeling that you are better than other people: *a proud, impatient man* ➲ noun **pride** ▸ **proud·ly** ***adv.***: *"I did all the work myself," he said proudly.*

★**prove** /pruv/ ***verb*** (*pp* **prov·en** or **proved**) **1** [T] **prove sth (to sb)** to show that sth is true: *It will be difficult to prove that she was lying.* ◇ *to prove sb's innocence to the court* ➲ noun **proof** **2** [I,T] (*formal*) to be found to be sth: *The job proved more difficult than we'd expected.* ◇ *He was proven innocent.* ◇ *Lisa proved herself to be just as strong as the men.*

**prov·en** /ˈpruvn/ ***adj.*** that has been shown to be true: *a proven fact*

**prov·erb** /ˈprɑvərb/ ***noun*** [C] a short well-known sentence or phrase that gives advice or a general truth about life: *Benjamin Franklin's proverb, "a penny saved is a penny earned"*

★**pro·vide** /prəˈvaɪd/ ***verb*** [T] **provide sb (with sth)**; **provide sth (for sb)** to give or supply sth to sb: *This book will provide you with all the information you need.* ◇ *The university cannot provide housing for all students.* ◇ *The seminar lasts all day and lunch will be provided.*

PHR V **provide for sb** to give sb all that he/she needs to live: *Robin has four children to provide for.* **provide for sth** to make arrangements to deal with sth that might happen in the future: *We did not provide for such a large increase in prices.*

★**pro·vid·ed** /prəˈvaɪdəd/ (*also* **provided that**, **providing**, **providing that**) ***conj.*** only if: *She agreed to go and work abroad provided that her family could go with her.*

**pro·vid·er** /prəˈvaɪdər/ ***noun*** [C] a person or an organization that supplies sb with sth he/she needs or wants: *We are one of the largest providers of employment in the area.* ◇ *The eldest son is the family's sole provider* (= the only person in the family who



P

earns money). ➲ Look at **ISP** (Internet Service Provider).

**prov·ince** /ˈprɑvəns/ ***noun*** [C] one of the main parts into which some countries are divided: *Canada has ten provinces.* ➲ Look at **county** and **state**. ▸ **pro·vin·cial** /prəˈvɪnʃl/ ***adj.*** (only *before* a noun): *the Ontario provincial government*

ˈ**Province House** ***noun*** [sing.] (*Cdn*) the name of the government building in Nova Scotia and Prince Edward Island

**proˌvincial ˈsales tax** ***noun*** [U] (*Cdn*) = PST

**pro·vi·sion** /prəˈvɪʒn/ ***noun*** **1** [C] one of the parts of an official agreement or document: *The rebels violated several key provisions of the peace treaty.* **2** [U] (*formal*) the act of giving or supplying sth to sb: *The state is responsible for the provision of education.* **3 provisions** [pl.] (*formal*) supplies of food and drink **4** [C,U] **provision(s) for/against sth** arrangements that you make to deal with sth that might happen in the future: *The budget makes no provision for the effects of inflation.*

**pro·vi·sion·al** /prəˈvɪʒn·l/ ***adj.*** only for the present time, that may be changed: *UN troops helped to set up a provisional government in the region.*

**prov·o·ca·tion** /ˌprɑvəˈkeɪʃn/ ***noun*** **1** [U] the act of trying to make sb angry: *The guards fired their weapons without provocation.* **2** [C] something that sb does to make you angry: *The attack was a response to deliberate provocations.*

**pro·voc·a·tive** /prəˈvɑkət̬ɪv/ ***adj.*** **1** intending to cause anger or argument: *a provocative question* **2** intending to cause sexual excitement

**pro·voke** /prəˈvoʊk/ ***verb*** [T] **1** to make a person or an animal angry by annoying him/her/it: *The cat will scratch if you provoke it.* ◊ *Stop trying to provoke me!* **2** to cause a feeling or reaction: *The judge's remarks provoked a storm of controversy.*

**pro·vost** /ˈproʊvoʊst/ ***noun*** [C] an important official at some colleges and universities

**prow·ess** /ˈpraʊəs/ ***noun*** [U] (*formal*) skill at doing sth

**prowl** /praʊl/ ***verb*** [I] **prowl (around)** (used about an animal that is hunting or a person who is waiting for a chance to steal sth, etc.) to move quietly so that you are not seen or heard: *I could hear someone prowling around outside, so I called the police.* ➲ A person or animal that is prowling is **on the prowl**. ▸ **prowl·er** ***noun*** [C]: *The police arrested a prowler outside the hospital.*

**prox·im·i·ty** /prɑkˈsɪmət̬i/ ***noun*** [U] (*formal*) the state of being near to sth: *One advantage is the town's proximity to the beach.*

**prox·y** /ˈprɑksi/ ***noun*** [U] the right that you give to sb to act for you: *to vote by proxy*

**Pro·zac™** /ˈproʊzæk/ ***noun*** [U] a drug used to treat the illness of depression (an **antidepressant**): *She's been* ***on Prozac*** *for two years.*

**prude** /prud/ ***noun*** [C] a person who does not like to see or hear anything connected with sex ▸ **prud·ish** /ˈprudɪʃ/ ***adj.***

**pru·dent** /ˈprudnt/ ***adj.*** (*formal*) having or showing careful thought; wise and sensible: *It would be prudent to find out more before you decide.* OPP **imprudent** ▸ **pru·dence** ***noun*** [U] ▸ **pru·dent·ly** ***adv.***

**prune**[1] /prun/ ***noun*** [C] a dried plum

**prune**[2] /prun/ ***verb*** [T] to cut branches or parts of branches off a tree or bush in order to make it a better shape or improve its growth

**pry** /praɪ/ ***verb*** (*pres. part.* **pry·ing**; *3rd person sing. pres.* **pries**; *pt, pp* **pried**) **1** [T] to use force to open sth, remove a lid, etc.: *He pried the door open with a steel bar.* **2** [I] **pry (into sth)** to try to find out about other people's private affairs: *I don't want to pry – but is everything all right?*

**P.S.** /ˌpi ˈɛs/ ***abbr.*** (used at the end of a letter to add extra information): *...Love, Deanna. P.S. I'll meet you Thursday at 7:00.*

**psalm** (*also* **Psalm**) /sɑm; sɑlm/ ***noun*** [C] a song, poem or prayer that praises God, especially one in the Bible: *the Book of Psalms*

**pseu·do·nym** /ˈsudənɪm/ (*also* ˈ**pen name**) ***noun*** [C] a name used by an author, etc. that is not his/her real name: *to write under a pseudonym*

**psi** /saɪ; psaɪ/ ***noun*** [C] (*symbol* Ψ , ψ) the twenty-third letter of the Greek alphabet ➲ Look at the note at **fraternity**.

**PST** /ˌpi ɛs ˈti/ ***noun*** [U] (*Cdn*) a tax that is added to the price of goods in some Canadian provinces ➲ Look also at **GST** and **HST**.

**psych**[1] /saɪk/ ***verb***

PHR V **psych sb out** (*informal*) to convince sb that you will defeat him/her by acting in a very confident way

**psych yourself up (for sth)** (*informal*) to prepare yourself in your mind for sth difficult, e.g. by telling yourself that you will be successful

**psych**[2] /saɪk/ ***noun*** [U] (*informal*) = PSYCHOLOGY (1): *Cindy's majoring in psych and art history.*

**psy·che** /ˈsaɪki/ ***noun*** [C] (*formal*) the mind; your deepest feelings and attitudes: *the human/feminine/national psyche* ◊ *She knew, at some deep level of her psyche, that what she was doing was wrong.*

**psyched** /saɪkt/ ***adj.*** (*slang*) (not before a noun) **be/get psyched** to be prepared or to prepare yourself mentally for sth and to be or become excited: *Wow! You must be totally psyched about getting into college!* ◊ *Let's get psyched for tonight's game!*

**psy·che·del·ic** /ˌsaɪkəˈdɛlɪk/ ***adj.*** **1** (used about drugs) causing the user to see and hear things that are not there or that do not exist (to **hallucinate**) **2** (used about art, music, clothes, etc.) having bright colors, strange sounds, etc. like those that are experienced when taking psychedelic drugs

**psy·chi·at·ric** /ˌsaɪkiˈætrɪk/ ***adj.*** connected with psychiatry: *a psychiatric hospital*

**psy·chi·a·trist** /saɪˈkaɪətrɪst; sə-/ ***noun*** [C] a medical doctor who is trained to treat people with mental illness

**psy·chi·a·try** /saɪˈkaɪətri; sə-/ ***noun*** [U] the study and treatment of mental illness ➲ Look at **psychology**.

**psy·chic**[1] /ˈsaɪkɪk/ ***adj.*** (used about a person or his/her mind) seeming to have unusual powers, e.g. knowing what sb else is thinking or being able to predict the future

**psy·chic²** /ˈsaɪkɪk/ ***noun*** [C] a person who claims to have strange mental powers so that he/she can do things that are not possible according to natural laws, such as predicting the future and speaking to dead people

**psy·cho** /ˈsaɪkoʊ/ ***noun*** [C] (*pl.* **psy·chos**) (*slang*) a person who is crazy or dangerous ▸ **psy·cho** ***adj.***

**psy·cho·a·nal·y·sis** /ˌsaɪkoʊəˈnæləsəs/ ***noun*** [U] a way of treating sb with a mental illness by asking about his/her past life and dreams in order to find out what is causing his/her illness

**psy·cho·an·a·lyst** /ˌsaɪkoʊˈænl·ɪst/ ***noun*** [C] a person who uses psychoanalysis to treat people

**psy·cho·an·a·lyze** /ˌsaɪkoʊˈænl·aɪz/ ***verb*** [T] to treat sb who has a mental illness using psychoanalysis

**psy·cho·log·i·cal** /ˌsaɪkəˈlɑdʒɪkl/ ***adj.*** **1** connected with the mind or the way that it works: *Did her ordeal cause her long-term psychological damage?* **2** connected with psychology: *psychological tests* ▸ **psy·cho·log·i·cal·ly** /-kli/ ***adv.***: *Psychologically, it was a bad time to be starting a new job.*

**psy·chol·o·gist** /saɪˈkɑlədʒɪst/ ***noun*** [C] a person who is trained in psychology

**psy·chol·o·gy** /saɪˈkɑlədʒi/ ***noun*** **1** (*also informal* **psych**) [U] the study of the mind and the way that people behave: *child psychology* ➲ Look at **psychiatry**. **2** [sing.] the type of mind that a person or group of people has: *If we understood the psychology of the killer, we would have a better chance of catching him.*

**psy·cho·path** /ˈsaɪkəpæθ/ ***noun*** [C] a person who has a serious mental illness and who may hurt or kill other people ▸ **psy·cho·path·ic** /ˌsaɪkəˈpæθɪk/ ***adj.***

**psy·cho·sis** /saɪˈkoʊsəs/ ***noun*** [C,U] (*pl.* **psy·cho·ses** /-siz/) a serious mental illness that affects the whole personality ➲ Look at **psychotic**.

**psy·cho·ther·a·py** /ˌsaɪkoʊˈθɛrəpi/ (*also* **therapy**) ***noun*** [U] the treatment of mental illness by discussing sb's problems with him/her rather than by giving him/her drugs ▸ **psy·cho·ther·a·pist** /ˌsaɪkoʊˈθɛrəpɪst/ (*also* **therapist**) ***noun*** [C]

**psy·chot·ic** /saɪˈkɑṭɪk/ ***noun*** [C] (*medical*) a person suffering from severe mental illness ▸ **psy·cho·tic** ***adj.***: *a psychotic disorder* ◇ *a psychotic patient* ➲ Look at **psychosis**.

**PT** ***abbr.*** (*written*) = PACIFIC TIME

**pt.** (*also* **pt**) ***abbr.*** **1** (*also* **Pt**) part: *Shakespeare's Henry IV Pt 2* **2** pint **3** point: *The winner scored 10 pts.* **4** **Pt.** (especially on a map) port

**PTA** /ˌpi ti ˈeɪ/ ***noun*** [C] the abbreviation for "parent-teacher association" (a group run by parents and teachers in a school that organizes social events and helps the school in different ways)

**pu·ber·ty** /ˈpyubərṭi/ ***noun*** [U] the time when a child's body is changing and becoming physically like that of an adult: *to reach puberty*

**pu·bic** /ˈpyubɪk/ ***adj.*** of the area around the sexual organs: *pubic hair*

★**pub·lic¹** /ˈpʌblɪk/ ***adj.*** **1** of or concerning all the people in a country or area: *The town's old sewage system is a danger to public health.* ◇ *How much public support is there for the administration's policy?* ◇ *to increase public awareness* **2** connected with the government and not with private companies: *public employees* ◇ *budget cuts in the public sector* ◇ *public spending* (= money that the government spends on education/roads) **3** provided for the use of people in general; not private: *a public library* ◇ *a public park* **4** known by many people: *We're going to make the news public soon.* ➲ Compare **keep sth secret**. ▸ **pub·lic·ly** /-kli/ ***adv.***: *The company refused to admit publicly that it had made a mistake.*

★**pub·lic²** /ˈpʌblɪk/ ***noun*** [sing.] **the public** people in general: *Is the church open to the public?* ◇ *The police have asked for information from members of the public.* ◇ *The public is mostly in favor of the new law.*

IDM **in public** when other people are present: *This is the first time that Jane has spoken about her experience in public.*

**ˌpublic-adˈdress ˌsystem** ***noun*** [C, usually sing.] (*formal*) = PA SYSTEM

**ˌpublic asˈsistance** ***noun*** [U] money, food, etc. that the government gives to poor people: *families living on public assistance*

★**pub·li·ca·tion** /ˌpʌbləˈkeɪʃn/ ***noun*** **1** [U] the act of printing a book, magazine, etc. and making it available to the public: *His latest book has just been accepted for publication.* **2** [C] a book, magazine, etc. **3** [U] the act of making sth known to the public: *the publication of the company's annual report*

**ˌpublic deˈfender** ***noun*** [C] a lawyer who works for the government of a city, county, etc. and who defends people who cannot pay for a lawyer themselves in court cases

**ˌpublic ˈholiday** ***noun*** [C] (*Cdn*) a yearly holiday from work or school that usually celebrates a historical, religious, etc. occasion

**ˌpublic ˈhousing** ***noun*** [U] houses and apartments that are built by the government for people who do not have enough money to pay for housing

**ˌpublic ˈhousing ˌproject** ***noun*** [C] = HOUSING PROJECT

**pub·li·cist** /ˈpʌbləsɪst/ ***noun*** [C] a person whose job is to make sth known to the public, for example a new product, an actor, etc.

**pub·lic·i·ty** /pʌbˈlɪsəṭi/ ***noun*** [U] **1** notice or attention from the newspapers, television, etc.: *to seek/avoid publicity* **2** giving information about sth in order to attract people's attention; advertising: *There has been a lot of publicity for Brad Pitt's latest movie.* ◇ *a publicity campaign*

**pub·li·cize** /ˈpʌbləsaɪz/ ***verb*** [T] to attract people's attention to sth or to give people information about sth: *The event has been well publicized and should attract a lot of people.*

**ˌpublic oˈpinion** ***noun*** [U] what people in general think about sth: *Public opinion was in favor of the new law.*

**ˌpublic reˈlations** ***noun*** (*abbr.* **PR**) **1** [pl.] the state of the relationship between an organization and the public: *Giving money to local charities is*

P

*good for public relations.* **2** [U] the job of making a company, an organization, etc. popular with the public

**ˌpublic ˈschool** ***noun*** [C] a local school that any child can go to, that provides free education ➲ For more information on the North American educational systems, look at study pages **A8 – A9**.

**ˌpublic ˈtelevision** (*also* **ˌpublic ˌTˈV**) ***noun*** [U] a television service that shows mainly educational programs and is paid for by the government, the public and some companies

**ˌpublic ˌtransporˈtation** ***noun*** [U] (the system of) buses, trains, etc. that run according to a schedule and that anybody can use: *to use public transportation*

**ˌpublic uˈtility** ***noun*** [C] (*pl.* **ˌpublic uˈtilities**) a company that is controlled by the government, that provides sth important such as water or electricity to the public

★**pub·lish** /ˈpʌblɪʃ/ ***verb*** **1** [I,T] to prepare and print a book, magazine, etc. and make it available to the public: *This dictionary was published by Oxford University Press.* **2** [T] (used about a writer, etc.) to have your work put in a book, magazine, etc.: *Dr. Fraser has published several articles on the subject.* **3** [T] to make sth known to the public: *Large companies must publish a report every year.*

**pub·lish·er** /ˈpʌblɪʃər/ ***noun*** [C] a person or company that publishes books, magazines, etc.

**pub·lish·ing** /ˈpʌblɪʃɪŋ/ ***noun*** [U] the business of preparing books, magazines, etc. to be printed and sold

**puck** /pʌk/ ***noun*** [C] a hard round flat rubber object that players hit with sticks in the sport of hockey

**puck·er** /ˈpʌkər/ ***verb*** [I,T] **pucker (sth) (up)** to form or to make sth form small folds or lines: *His face puckered, and he was ready to cry.* ◇ *She puckered her lips.*

**pud·ding** /ˈpʊdɪŋ/ ***noun*** [U] a soft, sweet food that is made from a special powder mixed with milk, or from milk, eggs, sugar, flavoring, etc. and baked or cooked at a low temperature until it becomes firmer: *chocolate pudding*

**pud·dle** /ˈpʌdl/ ***noun*** [C] a small amount of water (especially rain) that has gathered on the ground ➲ Look at **pool**.

**pudg·y** /ˈpʌdʒi/ ***adj.*** (**pudg·i·er**; **pudg·i·est**) (*informal*) slightly fat: *pudgy arms/hands*

**puff**[1] /pʌf/ ***noun*** [C] **1** a small amount of air, smoke, wind, etc. that is blown or sent out: *a puff of smoke* **2** one breath that you take when you are smoking a cigarette or pipe: *to take a puff on a cigarette* **3** a type of light food with a lot of air in it: *a cream puff*

**puff**[2] /pʌf/ ***verb*** **1** [I,T] (to cause air, smoke, wind, etc.) to blow or come out in puffs: *Smoke was puffing out of the chimney.* ◇ *Stop puffing smoke in my face.* **2** [I,T] to smoke a cigarette, pipe etc.: *to puff away at a cigarette* ◇ *He sat puffing his pipe.* **3** [I] to breathe loudly or quickly, e.g. when you are running: *He was puffing hard as he ran up the hill.*

**PHRV** **puff sth out/up** to cause sth to become larger by filling it with air

**puf·fin** /ˈpʌfn/ ***noun*** [C] a black and white bird with a large, brightly colored beak that lives near the ocean, common in the North Atlantic

**puff·y** /ˈpʌfi/ ***adj.*** looking soft and round: *Your eyes look a little puffy. Have you been crying?* ◇ *puffy clouds*

**puke** /pyuk/ ***verb*** [I,T] (*slang*) to bring food up from the stomach and out of the mouth; to vomit **SYN** A more polite word is **throw up**. ▶ **puke** ***noun*** [U]

**pull/drag/push**

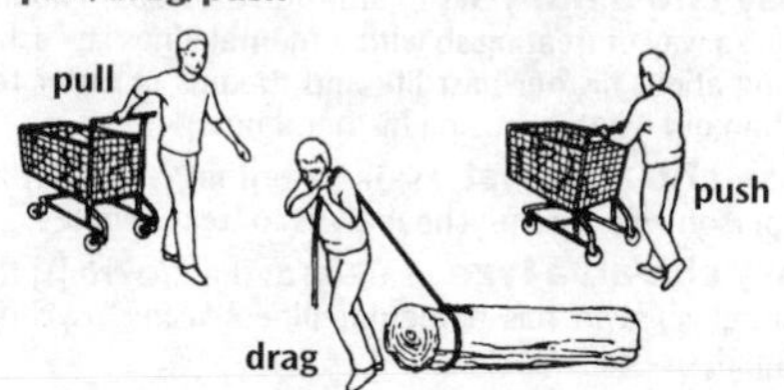


★**pull**[1] /pʊl/ ***verb*** **1** [I,T] to use force to move or try to move sb/sth toward yourself: *Wendy pulled at the rope to make sure that it was secure.* ◇ *to pull sb's hair* ◇ *to pull a door open* ◇ *You push and I'll pull.* ◇ *to pull the trigger of a gun* ◇ *They managed to pull the child out of the water just in time.* **2** [T] to move sth in the direction that is described: *She pulled her sweater on/She pulled on her sweater.* ◇ *He pulled up his pants/He pulled his pants up.* ◇ *Pull your chair a little bit closer to the table.* ◇ *Pull the sheets off the bed.* **3** [T] to move sth behind you in the direction that you are moving: *The little boy pulled his wagon behind him.* ◇ *That cart is too heavy for one horse to pull.* **4** [T] to damage a muscle, etc. by using too much force

**IDM** **pull sb's leg** (*informal*) to make fun of sb by trying to make him/her believe sth that is not true

**pull strings/wires** to use your influence to gain an advantage

**pull the plug (on sb/sth)** (*informal*) to force a plan, project, etc. to end: *The network pulled the plug on the series after only three episodes.*

**pull your weight** to do your fair share of the work

**PHRV** **pull (sth) away** to move your body or part of it away with force: *She pulled away as he tried to kiss her.*

**pull in (to sth)**; **pull into sth** (used about a car, etc.) to leave the road and enter another place in order to stop there: *He pulled into a gas station.*

**pull sth off** (*informal*) to succeed in sth: *to pull off a business deal*

**pull out** (used about a car, etc.) to move away from the side of the road: *I braked as a car suddenly pulled out in front of me.*

**pull (sb/sth) out (of sth)** (to cause sb/sth) to leave sth: *The President has decided to pull all U.S. troops out of the region.* ◇ *We pulled out of the deal.*

**pull sth out** to take sth out of a place suddenly or with force: *She walked into the bank and pulled out a gun.*

**pull (sb/sth) over** (used about a car, etc.) to move to the side of the road in order to stop, or to order sb in a car to do this: *Paul was pulled over by the police for speeding.*

**pull yourself together** to control your feelings and behave in a calm way: *Pull yourself together and stop crying.*

**pull up** (used about a car, etc.) to stop: *to pull up to the traffic lights*

★**pull²** /pʊl/ ***noun*** [C] **a pull (at/on sth)** an act of pulling: *Give the handle a good pull.*

**ˈpull-down ˌmenu** ***noun*** [C] (*computing*) a list of possible choices that appears on a computer screen below a MENU (2) title, when you select it ➲ Compare **drop-down menu**.

**pul·ley** /ˈpʊli/ ***noun*** [C] (*pl.* **pul·leys**) a piece of equipment, consisting of a wheel and a rope, that is used for lifting heavy things

**pull·o·ver** /ˈpʊloʊvər/ (*also* **ˌpullover ˈsweater**) ***noun*** [C] a piece of clothing that is usually made of wool and that covers the top part of your body and your arms. You put a pullover on by pulling it over your head. SYN **sweater**

**pul·mo·nar·y** /ˈpʊlməˌnɛri; ˈpʌl-/ ***adj.*** (only *before* a noun) (*medical*) connected with the lungs: *pulmonary disease* ◇ *the pulmonary artery*

**pulp** /pʌlp/ ***noun*** **1** [U] the soft inner part of some fruits or vegetables **2** [U] a soft substance made from wood that is used for making paper **3** [sing., U] a soft substance that you make by pressing and mixing sth for a long time: *Crush the strawberries to a pulp.*

**pul·pit** /ˈpʊlpɪt; ˈpʌl-/ ***noun*** [C] a raised platform in a church where the priest stands when he/she is speaking to the people there

**pul·sate** /ˈpʌlseɪt/ ***verb*** [I] to move or shake with strong regular movements: *a pulsating rhythm*

**pulse¹** /pʌls/ ***noun*** [C, usually sing.] the regular beating in your body as blood is pumped through it by your heart. You can feel your pulse in your wrist, neck, etc.: *Your pulse rate increases after exercise.* ◇ *to have a strong/weak pulse* ◇ *to feel/take sb's pulse* (= to count how many times it beats in one minute)

**pulse²** /pʌls/ ***verb*** [I] **pulse (through sth)** to move with strong regular movements

**pul·ver·ize** /ˈpʌlvəraɪz/ ***verb*** [T] **1** (*formal*) to crush sth into a fine powder **2** (*informal*) to defeat or destroy sb/sth completely: *We pulverized them in the second half of the game.*

**pu·ma** /ˈpumə/ ***noun*** [C] = MOUNTAIN LION

**pum·ice** /ˈpʌməs/ (*also* **ˈpumice stone**) ***noun*** [U] a type of gray stone that comes from volcanoes and is very light in weight. It is used in powder form for cleaning and polishing, and in pieces for rubbing on the skin to make it softer.

**pum·mel** /ˈpʌml/ ***verb*** [I,T] to keep hitting sb/sth hard, especially with your tightly closed hands (fists): *He pummeled the pillow with his fists.* ◇ *Her fists pummeled at his chest.*

**pump¹** /pʌmp/ ***noun*** [C] **1** a machine that is used for forcing a gas or liquid in a particular direction: *Do you have a bicycle pump? My tire's flat.* ◇ *a gasoline pump* ➲ picture at **bicycle**. **2** a type of formal shoe for women, usually with a high heel ➲ picture at **shoe**.

**pump²** /pʌmp/ ***verb*** [I,T] to force a gas or liquid to go in a particular direction: *Your heart pumps blood around your body.*

IDM **pump iron** (*informal*) to do exercises in which you lift heavy weights in order to make your muscles stronger

PHR V **pump sth up 1** to fill sth with air, e.g. by using a PUMP¹ (1): *to pump up a car tire* **2** to increase the amount, value or volume of sth: *to pump up the loudspeakers*

**pum·per·nick·el** /ˈpʌmpərˌnɪkl/ ***noun*** [U] a type of heavy dark brown bread made from rye, originally from Germany

**pump·kin** /ˈpʌmpkɪn/ ***noun*** [C,U] a very large round fruit with thick orange-colored skin that is cooked and eaten like a vegetable: *pumpkin pie* ➲ picture on study page **A28-29**. ➲ Look also at **jack-o'-lantern** and at the note at **Halloween**.

**pun** /pʌn/ ***noun*** [C] **pun (on sth)** an amusing use of a word that can have two meanings or of different words that sound the same: *Mr. Stevens, who likes making puns, said after a very long meeting that he was "the chairman of the bored* (= board)."

★**punch¹** /pʌntʃ/ ***verb*** [T] **1** to hit sb/sth hard with your closed hand (fist): *Annie punched him hard in the stomach and ran away.* **2** to make a hole in sth with a special tool: *He punched a hole in the ticket.* ◇ *He punched the ticket.*

PHR V **punch in** to put a card into a special machine that records the time you arrive at work

**punch out** to put a card into a special machine that records the time you leave work

**punch²** /pʌntʃ/ ***noun*** **1** [C] a hard hit with your closed hand (fist) **2** [C] a machine or tool that you use to make holes in sth: *a paper punch* **3** [U] a drink, often served at parties, made from fruit juice, sugar and, sometimes, alcohol

**ˈpunching bag** ***noun*** [U] a heavy leather bag, hung on a rope, which is PUNCHED¹ (1), especially by boxers as part of training, or as a form of exercise

**ˈpunch line** ***noun*** [C] the last and most important words of a joke or story

**punc·tu·al** /ˈpʌŋktʃuəl/ ***adj.*** (*formal*) doing sth or happening at the right time; not late ➲ The phrase **on time** is more common than **punctual**. ▶ **punc·tu·al·i·ty** /ˌpʌŋktʃuˈæləṭi/ ***noun*** [U]

**punc·tu·ate** /ˈpʌŋktʃueɪt/ ***verb*** **1** [I,T] to divide writing into sentences and phrases by using punctuation marks **2** [T] **punctuate sth (with sth)** (often passive) to interrupt sth many times: *Her speech was punctuated with bursts of applause.*

**punc·tu·a·tion** /ˌpʌŋktʃuˈeɪʃn/ ***noun*** [U] the use of punctuation marks when you are writing

**ˌpunctuˈation mark** ***noun*** [C] one of the signs that you use when you are writing in order to divide the words into sentences, show that sb is speaking, etc.: *Punctuation marks include periods, commas, question marks and quotation marks.*

**punc·ture** /ˈpʌŋktʃər/ ***verb*** [T] to make a small hole in sth with sth sharp: *That nail must have punctured the tire.*

**pun·dit** /ˈpʌndət/ ***noun*** [C] a person who knows a lot about a particular subject and who often talks about it in public; an expert: *a political pundit*

**pun·gent** /ˈpʌndʒənt/ ***adj.*** having a very strong smell

★**pun·ish** /ˈpʌnɪʃ/ ***verb*** [T] **punish sb (for sth) (by/with sth)** to cause sb to suffer because he/she



P

has done sth wrong: *They broke the law and they deserve to be punished.* ◇ *The boys were severely punished for shoplifting.* ◇ *Petty criminals should be punished by having to do community service.* ◇ *Drunk driving should be punished with imprisonment.*

**pun·ish·a·ble** /ˈpʌnɪʃəbl/ ***adj.*** **punishable (by sth)** (used about a crime, etc.) that you can be punished for doing: *In some countries, drug smuggling is punishable by death.*

**pun·ish·ing** /ˈpʌnɪʃɪŋ/ ***adj.*** that makes you very tired or weak: *The band had a punishing schedule of nine concerts in one week.*

★**pun·ish·ment** /ˈpʌnɪʃmənt/ ***noun*** **1** [U] the act of punishing or the state of being punished: *Most Southern states have capital punishment* (= punishment by death). **2** [C] a way in which sb is punished: *Ideally, the punishment should fit the crime.*

**pu·ni·tive** /ˈpyunət̬ɪv/ ***adj.*** intended as a punishment: *The jury awarded the victim $2 million in punitive damages against the company.*

**punk** /pʌŋk/ ***noun*** **1** (*also* **punk music**) [U] a type of rock music that was popular in the late 1970s and early 1980s. Punk music often protests strongly about the way that society is organized. **2** [C] a person who likes punk music and often has brightly-colored hair and unusual clothes: *punks wearing torn jeans and safety pins in their ears* **3** [C] (*informal*) a boy or a young man who you think is unimportant, especially one who is often involved in fights, illegal activities, etc.: *What do you think you're looking at, punk?*

**punt**[1] /pʌnt/ ***noun*** [C] **1** a long kick made after dropping the ball from your hands, especially in football **2** a long shallow boat with a flat bottom and square ends which is moved by pushing the end of a long pole against the bottom of a river

**punt**[2] /pʌnt/ ***verb*** [I,T] **1** to kick a ball hard so that it goes a long way, sometimes after it has dropped from your hands and before it reaches the ground **2** to travel in a PUNT (2), especially for pleasure: *We spent the day punting on the river.*

**pu·ny** /ˈpyuni/ ***adj.*** (**pu·ni·er**; **pu·ni·est**) small and weak

**pup** /pʌp/ ***noun*** [C] **1** = PUPPY **2** the young of some animals, e.g. seals

★**pu·pil** /ˈpyupl/ ***noun*** [C] **1** (*formal* or *old-fashioned*) a child in school: *There are 28 pupils in the class.* ➲ **Student** is more common than **pupil**. **2** the round black hole in the middle of the eye

**pup·pet** /ˈpʌpət/ ***noun*** [C] **1** a model of a person or animal that you can move by pulling the strings which are attached to it or by putting your hand inside it and moving your fingers **2** a person or organization that is controlled by sb else: *a puppet government*

**pup·pet·eer** /ˌpʌpəˈtɪr/ ***noun*** [C] a person who performs with PUPPETS (1)

**pup·py** /ˈpʌpi/ ***noun*** [C] (*pl.* **pup·pies**) (*also* **pup**) a young dog

ˈ**pup tent** ***noun*** [C] a small triangular shelter made of cloth (a tent) for two people

★**pur·chase**[1] /ˈpərtʃəs/ ***noun*** (*formal*) **1** [U,C] the act of buying sth: *Please state the date and place of purchase.* ◇ *to make a purchase* (= to buy sth) **2** [C] something that you buy: *Employees will help you carry your purchases to your car.*

★**pur·chase**[2] /ˈpərtʃəs/ ***verb*** [T] (*formal*) to buy sth: *advice for people planning to purchase a new home*

**pur·chas·er** /ˈpərtʃəsər/ ***noun*** [C] (*formal*) a person who buys sth: *a law requiring security checks on handgun purchasers*

★**pure** /pyʊr/ ***adj.***

➤NOT MIXED **1** not mixed with anything else: *a pure silk blouse* ◇ *She was dressed in pure white.* ◇ *pure Florida orange juice*

➤CLEAN **2** not containing any harmful substances: *the pure mountain air*

➤MORALLY GOOD **3** (*old-fashioned*) not doing or knowing anything evil or anything that is connected with sex: *to remain spiritually pure* OPP for **2** and **3** is **impure**.

➤COMPLETE **4** (only *before* a noun) complete: *We met by pure chance.* ◇ *a pure waste of time*

➤COLOR/SOUND **5** very clear; perfect: *pure white sand* ◇ *a pure voice*

➤SUBJECT YOU STUDY **6** (only *before* a noun) (used about an area of learning) concerned only with theory rather than practical uses: *pure math* ➲ Compare **applied**.

**pu·rée** /pyʊˈreɪ/ ***noun*** [C,U] food that you make by cooking a fruit or vegetable and then pressing and mixing it until it is a smooth liquid: *apple purée*

★**pure·ly** /ˈpyʊrli/ ***adv.*** only or completely: *It's not purely a question of money.*

**pur·ga·to·ry** /ˈpərgəˌtɔri/ ***noun*** [U] (usually **Purgatory**) (in Roman Catholic teaching) a place or state in which the souls of dead people suffer for the bad things they did when they were living, so that they can become pure enough to go to heaven

**purge** /pərdʒ/ ***verb*** [T] to remove people that you do not want from a political party or other organization ▶ **purge *noun*** [C]

**pu·ri·fi·er** /ˈpyʊrəfaɪər/ ***noun*** [C] a machine that makes air or water clean

**pu·ri·fy** /ˈpyʊrəfaɪ/ ***verb*** [T] (*pres. part.* **pu·ri·fy·ing**; *3rd person sing. pres.* **pu·ri·fies**; *pt, pp* **pu·ri·fied**) to remove dirty or harmful substances from sth: *purified water* ▶ **pu·ri·fi·ca·tion** /ˌpyʊrəfəˈkeɪʃn/ ***noun*** [U]: *a water purification plant*

**Pu·rim** /ˈpʊrɪm; pʊˈrim/ ***noun*** [sing.] a Jewish festival that is celebrated in the spring

**pu·ri·tan** /ˈpyʊrɪtn/ ***noun*** [C] **1 Puritan** a member of a Christian religious group in England and North America in the 1600s and 1700s who had very strict moral beliefs **2** a person who has strong religious beliefs and strict, traditional attitudes toward moral behavior, sex, etc.

**pu·ri·tan·i·cal** /ˌpyʊrəˈtænɪkl/ ***adj.*** having strict, traditional attitudes toward moral behavior, sex, etc. ➲ This word is often used in a critical way.

**pu·ri·ty** /ˈpyʊrət̬i/ ***noun*** [U] the state of being pure: *to test the purity of the air* OPP **impurity**

★**pur·ple** /ˈpərpl/ ***adj.*** of a reddish-blue color: *a purple plum* ▶ **pur·ple *noun*** [U]

ˌ**Purple ˈHeart *noun*** [C] (*U.S.*) a special award (a medal) given to a member of the armed forces of the U.S. who has been wounded in battle

**pur·port**[1] /pər'pɔrt/ ***verb*** [T] (*formal*) to give the impression of being sth or of having done sth, when this may not be true: *The book does not purport to be a complete history of the period.*

**pur·port**[2] /'pərpɔrt/ ***noun*** [sing.] **the purport of sth** (*formal*) the general meaning of sth: *The purport of his remarks was all too clear.*

★**pur·pose** /'pərpəs/ ***noun*** **1** [C] the reason for doing or making sth: *The main purpose of this meeting is to decide on a name for our new product.* ◇ *You may only use the telephone for business purposes.* ◇ *These complicated rules serve no useful purpose.* **2** [U] (*formal*) having an aim or plan and acting according to it: *A good leader inspires people with a sense of purpose.*

IDM **on purpose** not by accident; with a particular intention: *"You tore a page out of my book!" "Sorry, I didn't do it on purpose."* ◇ *I came a little early on purpose, to see if I could help you.*

**pur·pose·ful** /'pərpəsfl/ ***adj.*** having a definite aim or plan: *Greg strode off down the street looking purposeful.* ▶ **pur·pose·ful·ly** /-fəli/ ***adv.***

**pur·pose·ly** /'pərpəsli/ ***adv.*** with a particular intention: *I purposely waited until everyone was gone so that I could talk to you in private.*

**purr** /pər/ ***verb*** [I] (used about a cat) to make a continuous low sound that shows pleasure

**purse**[1] /pərs/ (*also* **handbag**, *old-fashioned* **pocketbook**) ***noun*** [C] a small bag in which a woman carries money, keys, etc.

**purse**[2] /pərs/ ***verb***

IDM **purse your lips** to press your lips together to show that you do not like sth

★**pur·sue** /pər'su/ ***verb*** [T] (*formal*) **1** to follow sb/sth in order to catch him/her/it: *The robber ran off, pursued by two police officers.* ◇ (*figurative*) *He is pursuing a completely unrealistic goal.* ➲ **Pursue** is more formal than **chase**. **2** to continue with sth; to find out more about sth: *to pursue a career in banking* ◇ *She didn't seem to want to pursue the discussion, so I changed the subject.*

**pur·suit** /pər'sut/ ***noun*** **1** [U] the act of pursuing sb/sth: *the pursuit of pleasure* **2** [C] something that you spend your time doing, either for work or for pleasure: *outdoor pursuits* ◇ *leisure pursuits*

IDM **in pursuit (of sb/sth)** trying to catch or get sb/sth: *a dog in pursuit of a cat* ◇ *He neglected his family in pursuit of his own personal ambitions.*

**pur·vey·or** /pər'veɪər/ ***noun*** [C] (*formal*) a person or company that supplies sth: *Brown and Son, purveyors of fine wines*

**pus** /pʌs/ ***noun*** [U] a thick yellowish liquid that may form in a part of your body that has been hurt

★**push**[1] /pʊʃ/ ***verb***

➤USING HANDS/ARMS/BODY **1** [I,T] to use force to move or try to move sb/sth forward or away from you: *You push and I'll pull.* ◇ *You can pull a rope but you can't push it!* ◇ *Christine pushed him into the water.* ◇ *to push sb in a wheelchair* ◇ *to push a baby carriage* ◇ *She pushed the door shut with her foot.* **2** [I,T] to move forward by pushing sb/sth: *John pushed his way through the crowd.* ◇ *to push past sb*

➤SWITCH/BUTTON **3** [I,T] to press or use force, e.g. with your finger, to move sth: *Push this button to call the nurse.*

➤PERSUADE **4** [T] (*informal*) to try to make sb do sth, e.g. by asking or telling him/her many times: *Kim will not work hard unless you push her.* ◇ *to push sb for an answer*

➤NEW IDEA/PRODUCT **5** [T] (*informal*) to try to make sth seem attractive, e.g. so that people will buy it: *They are launching a major advertising campaign to push their new product.* ◇ *dealers pushing drugs on street corners*

IDM **push your luck; push it** (*informal*) to take a risk because you have successfully avoided problems in the past: *You didn't get caught last time, but don't push your luck!*

PHR V **push ahead (with sth)** to continue with sth

**push sb around** (*informal*) to give sb orders in a rude way: *You shouldn't let your husband push you around like that.*

**push for sth** to try hard to get sth: *Journalists are always pushing for greater freedom of information.*

★**push**[2] /pʊʃ/ ***noun*** **1** [C] an act of pushing: *Paul gave the door a push and it opened.* ◇ *The car windows opened at the push of a button.* ➲ picture at **drag**. **2** [usually sing.] a strong effort to do or finish sth: *the company's big push to improve customer service* ◇ *a push for increased government spending on education*

IDM **when push comes to shove** (*informal*) when there is no other choice; when everything else has failed

'**push-,button** (*also* **pushbutton**) ***adj.*** (only *before* a noun) (used about a machine, etc.) that you work by pushing a button: *a push-button phone*

**push·er** /'pʊʃər/ ***noun*** [C] (*informal*) a person who sells illegal drugs

**push·o·ver** /'pʊʃoʊvər/ ***noun*** [C] (*informal*) a person who is easy to persuade, convince, or defeat

**push·up** /'pʊʃʌp/ ***noun*** [C] a type of exercise in which you lie on your front on the floor and push your body up with your arms ➲ picture on study page A32.

**push·y** /'pʊʃi/ ***adj.*** (**push·i·er**; **push·i·est**) (*informal*) (used about a person) behaving in a rude, forceful way in order to get an advantage or to make people notice you: *a pushy salesclerk*

**puss·y·cat** /'pʊsikæt/ ***noun*** [C] (*informal*) (used by and to small children) a cat

**pus·sy·foot** /'pʊsifʊt/ ***verb*** [I] **pussyfoot (around)** (*informal*) to be careful or anxious about what you say or do in case you upset sb: *There was no point in pussyfooting around. I had to say what I really thought.*

★**put** /pʊt/ ***verb*** [T] (*pres. part.* **put·ting**; *pt, pp* **put**)

➤IN PLACE/POSITION **1** to move sb/sth so that it is in a particular place or position: *She put the book on the table.* ◇ *I put the knife back in the drawer.* ◇ *Did you put sugar in my coffee?* ◇ *When do you put your kids to bed?*

➤ATTACH **2** to fasten sth to or in sth else: *Can you put (= sew) a button on this shirt?* ◇ *We're going to put new carpeting in this room.*

➤AFFECT SB/STH **3** to make sb feel or experience sth: *This kind of weather always puts me in a bad*

P

*mood.* ◇ *Your decision puts me in a difficult position.*
➤EXPRESS **4** to say or express sth: *I don't know exactly how to put this, but...*
➤WRITE **5** to write sth: *12:30 on Friday? I'll put it on my calendar.* ◇ *What did you put for question 2?*
IDM **be put off (by sb/sth)** to feel uncomfortable or uncertain because of sb/sth: *Don't be put off by the restaurant's ugly exterior – they serve excellent food.*
**I wouldn't put it past sb (to do sth)** (used to say that you think sb is capable of doing sth wrong, illegal, etc.): *I wouldn't put it past him to do a thing like that.*
**put together** (used after a noun or nouns referring to a group of people or things) combined: *You got more presents than the rest of the family put together.*

NOTE For other idioms containing **put**, look at the entries for the nouns, adjectives, etc., e.g. **put an end to sth** is at **end**.

PHR V **put sth across** to say sth clearly, so that people can understand it: *He didn't put his ideas across very well at the meeting.*
**put sth aside** to save sth, especially money, to use later
**put sb away** (*informal*) to send sb to prison
**put sth away 1** to put sth where you usually keep it, e.g. in a cupboard: *Put your toys away – our guests are coming soon.* **2** to save money to use later: *Her grandparents had put some money away for her education.* **3** (*informal*) to eat or drink a lot of sth: *I saw him put away an entire ham once!*
**put sth back** to return sth to its correct place: *to put books back on the shelf*
**put sb down** (*informal*) to say things to make sb seem stupid or foolish: *He's always putting his wife down.*
**put sth down 1** to place sth, e.g. on the floor, a table, etc.: *The police officer persuaded him to put the gun down.* **2** to write sth: *I can tell you exactly what she said – I put it all down in my notebook.* **3** (used about a government, an army or the police) to stop sth by force: *to put down a rebellion*
**put sth forward** to suggest sth: *a proposal put forward by one of the school board members*
**put sth in; put sth into sth/into doing sth** to spend time, etc. on sth: *I put in 10 hours at work yesterday.* ◇ *She puts all her time and energy into her business.*
**put in for sth** to make an official request for sth: *She put in for a transfer to the company's California office.*
**put sth off; put off doing sth** to delay doing sth: *"I've got to go to the store." "Can't you put it off?"* ◇ *She put off writing her paper until the last minute.*
**put sth on 1** to place clothes on your body: *Put on your coat!* ◇ *I'll have to put my glasses on.* **2** to make a piece of electrical equipment, etc. start working, usually by pressing a switch: *It's not hot enough to put the air conditioning on yet.* **3** to begin cooking food in a pan: *I'll put the carrots on while you set the table.* **4** to make sth (e.g. a CD, a tape, etc.) begin to play: *Let's put some music on.* **5** to become fatter or heavier (especially by the amount mentioned): *I put on weight very easily.* ◇ *She's put on several pounds since the last time I saw her.*
**put sb out** to give sb trouble or extra work: *I really don't want to put you out – I'll take a taxi home.*
**put sth out 1** to make sth stop burning: *to put out a fire* **2** to give or tell the public sth, often by using the television, radio or newspapers: *The police put out a warning about the escaped prisoner.* **3** to move your hand, foot, etc. away from the rest of your body: *If you want a piece of candy, put your hand out and I'll give you one.*
**put sb through sth** to make sb experience sth bad
**put sb/sth through** to make a telephone connection that allows sb to speak to sb: *Hold on while I put you through to Mr. Weber's voice mail.*
**put sth to sb** (*formal*) to suggest sth to sb; to ask sb sth: *She put a proposal to the chairman of the board.*
**put sth together** to build or repair sth by joining its parts together: *The furniture comes with instructions on how to put it together.*
**put up sth** to offer or give resistance in a fight, etc.: *The old lady put up a struggle against her attacker.*
**put sb up** to give sb food and a place to stay: *Her car wouldn't start, so I offered to put her up for the night.*
**put sth up 1** to build sth: *to put up a fence* **2** to fasten sth to a wall, etc. so that everyone can see it: *to put up a notice*
**put up with sb/sth** to suffer sb/sth bad and not complain about it: *I don't know how they put up with this noise.*

**pu·trid** /ˈpyutrəd/ ***adj.*** **1** (used about dead animals or plants) decaying and therefore smelling very bad: *the putrid smell of rotten meat* **2** (*informal*) very bad or unpleasant: *a putrid pink color*

**putt** /pʌt/ ***verb*** [I,T] (used in golf) to hit the ball gently when it is near the hole ► **putt** ***noun*** [C]

**put·ter** /ˈpʌt̬ər/ ***verb*** [I] **putter (around)** to spend your time doing small jobs in a relaxed way: *Grandpa spends most of the day puttering around in the back yard.*

**put·ty** /ˈpʌt̬i/ ***noun*** [U] a substance that is used especially for fastening glass into wooden window frames. Putty is soft when you use it, but it turns hard later.

**putz** /pʌts/ ***verb***
PHR V **putz around** (*informal*) to waste time not doing anything useful or important: *You need to stop putzing around and do some real work.*

**puz·zle¹** /ˈpʌzl/ ***noun*** [C] **1** a game or toy that tests your knowledge, skill, intelligence, etc.: *to do a crossword puzzle* ◇ *The solution to the puzzle is on page 27.* **2** = JIGSAW PUZZLE **3** [usually sing.] something that is difficult to understand or explain; a mystery: *The reasons for his action have remained a puzzle to historians.*

**puz·zle²** /ˈpʌzl/ ***verb*** **1** [T] to cause sb to think hard about sth he/she cannot understand or explain: *Scientists are puzzled by the recent changes in weather patterns.* **2** [I] **puzzle over sth** to think hard about sth in order to understand or explain it: *to puzzle over a mathematical problem*

**puz·zled** /ˈpʌzld/ ***adj.*** not able to understand or explain sth: *a puzzled expression*

**puz·zling** /ˈpʌzlɪŋ/ ***adj.*** difficult to understand; confusing: *one of the most puzzling aspects of the crime*

**Pyg·my** /ˈpɪgmi/ (*also* **Pig·my**) ***noun*** [c] (*pl.* **Pyg·mies**) a member of a race of very short people living in parts of Africa and SE Asia

**pyg·my** /ˈpɪgmi/ ***adj.*** (only *before* a noun) used to describe a plant or type (**species**) of animal that is much smaller than other similar kinds: *a pygmy shrew*

**py·ja·mas** /pəˈdʒæməz/ ***noun*** [pl.] (*Cdn*) = PAJAMAS

**pyr·a·mid** /ˈpɪrəmɪd/ ***noun*** [c] a shape with a flat base and three or four triangular sides ➲ picture at **cube**.

**pyre** /ˈpaɪər/ ***noun*** [c] a pile of wood on which a dead body is placed and burned in a funeral ceremony

**py·ro·ma·ni·a** /ˌpaɪroʊˈmeɪniə/ ***noun*** [U] (*technical*) a mental illness that causes a strong desire to set fire to things

**py·ro·ma·ni·ac** /ˌpaɪroʊˈmeɪniæk/ ***noun*** [c] **1** (*technical*) a person who suffers from pyromania **2** (*informal*) a person who enjoys making or watching fires

**py·ro·tech·nics** /ˌpaɪrəˈtɛknɪks/ ***noun*** [pl.] a display of fireworks

**py·thon** /ˈpaɪθɑn/ ***noun*** [c] a large snake that kills animals by squeezing them very hard

# Q q

**Q, q** /kyu/ ***noun*** [C,U] (*pl.* **Q's**; **q's** /kyuz/) the seventeenth letter of the English alphabet: *"Queen" begins with (a) "Q."*

**Q** ***abbr.*** question: *a Q & A* (= question and answer) *column in the newspaper*

**QPP** /ˌkyu pi ˈpi/ ***noun*** [sing.] (*Cdn*) Quebec Pension Plan ➲ Look at **Canada Pension Plan**.

**qt.** ***abbr.*** quart(s)

**Q-Tip™** /ˈkyu tɪp/ ***noun*** [c] a small thin stick with soft material such as cotton at each end, that is used for cleaning small places such as your ears

**quack¹** /kwæk/ ***noun*** [c] **1** the sound that a duck makes **2** (*informal*) a person who dishonestly claims to have medical knowledge or skills: *quack doctors*

**quack²** /kwæk/ ***verb*** [I] to make the sound that a duck makes

**quad** /kwɑd/ ***noun*** [c] **1** (*also formal* **quad·ran·gle** /ˈkwɑdræŋgl/) a square open area with buildings around it, in a school, college, etc. **2** = QUADRUPLET

**quad·ri·ple·gic** /ˌkwɑdrəˈplidʒɪk/ ***noun*** [c] a person who is permanently unable to use his/her arms and legs ▸ **quad·ri·ple·gic** ***adj.***

**quad·ru·ple** /kwɑˈdrupl/ ***verb*** [I,T] to multiply or be multiplied by four: *Profits have quadrupled in the past ten years.*

**quad·ru·plet** /kwɑˈdruplət/ (*also* **quad**) ***noun*** [c] one of four children born at the same time to the same mother

**quag·mire** /ˈkwægmaɪər; ˈkwɑg-/ ***noun*** [c] **1** an area of soft wet ground: *The heavy rain soon turned the field into a quagmire.* **2** a difficult or dangerous situation

**quail** /kweɪl/ ***noun*** [C,U] (*pl.* **quails** or **quail**) a small brown bird, whose meat and eggs are used for food; the meat of this bird

**quaint** /kweɪnt/ ***adj.*** attractive or unusual because it seems to belong to the past: *New England has many quaint old towns.*

**quake¹** /kweɪk/ ***verb*** [I] to shake: *to quake with fear/cold*

**quake²** /kweɪk/ ***noun*** [c] (*informal*) = EARTHQUAKE

**Quak·er** /ˈkweɪkər/ ***noun*** [c] a member of the Society of Friends, a Christian religious group that meets without any formal ceremony and is strongly opposed to violence and war ▸ **Quak·er** ***adj.***: *a Quaker school*

★**qual·i·fi·ca·tion** /ˌkwɑləfəˈkeɪʃn/ ***noun*** **1** [c] a skill or quality that makes you suitable to do sth, such as a job: *She has all the right qualifications for the manager's job.* ◇ *He does not meet the qualifications for citizenship.* **2** [C,U] success in one part of a competition so that you can go on to the next part: *the team's qualification for the state tournament* ◇ *the world championship qualification match* **3** [C,U] (*formal*) something that limits or weakens the meaning of a general statement: *These attacks must be condemned without qualification.*

**qual·i·fied** /ˈkwɑləfaɪd/ ***adj.*** **1** having the skill, knowledge or quality that you need to do sth: *I don't feel qualified to comment – I know nothing about the subject.* ◇ *Since he passed the bar exam, he's a fully qualified lawyer.* **2** (*formal*) not complete; limited: *My boss gave only qualified approval to the plan.* OPP **unqualified**

★**qual·i·fy** /ˈkwɑləfaɪ/ ***verb*** (*pres. part.* **qual·i·fy·ing**; *3rd person sing. pres.* **qual·i·fies**; *pt, pp* **qual·i·fied**)

➤ FOR JOB **1** [T] to give sb the right to do a particular job: *This certificate will qualify me to teach music.*

➤ HAVE/GIVE RIGHT **2** [I,T] to have or give sb the right to have or do sth: *How many years do you have to work to qualify for a company pension?* ◇ *To qualify for the scholarship, you have to be a resident of the state of Texas.* ◇ *Residence in this country does not qualify you to vote.*

➤ IN COMPETITION **3** [I] to be successful in one part

of a competition and to go on to the next part: *Our team has qualified for the final round.*

➤FIT DESCRIPTION **4** [I] to have the right qualities to be described as sth: *A cup of coffee and a muffin doesn't really qualify as a meal.*

➤STATEMENT **5** [T] to limit or weaken the meaning of a general statement: *I should qualify what I said earlier – it wasn't quite true.*

**qual·i·ta·tive** /ˈkwɑləˌteɪt̬ɪv/ ***adj.*** connected with how good sth is, rather than with how much of it there is: *qualitative analysis/research* ➲ Compare **quantitative**.

★**qual·i·ty**[1] /ˈkwɑləti/ ***noun*** (*pl.* **qual·i·ties**) **1** [U] how good or bad sth is: *This paper isn't very good quality.* ◇ *These photos are of poor quality.* ◇ *a high-quality magazine* ◇ *the quality of life in our cities* **2** [U] a high standard or level: *We aim to provide quality at a reasonable price.* **3** [C] something that is typical of a person or thing: *Vicky has all the qualities of a good manager.* ◇ *One quality of oil is that it floats on water.*

**qual·i·ty**[2] /ˈkwɑləti/ ***adj.*** (only *before* a noun) of a high standard or level: *We want employees who can produce quality work.* ◇ *I ought to spend more quality time with my kids* (= paying attention to them, doing special activities together, etc.).

**qualm** /kwɑm; kwɔm/ ***noun*** [C, usually pl.] a feeling of doubt or worry about whether what you are doing is right: *I don't have any qualms about asking them to loan us some money.*

**quan·da·ry** /ˈkwɑndəri; -dri/ ***noun*** [C] (*pl.* **quan·da·ries**) a state of not being able to decide what to do; a difficult situation: *to be in a quandary*

**quan·ti·fy** /ˈkwɑntəfaɪ/ ***verb*** [T] (*3rd person sing. pres.* **quan·ti·fies**; *pres. part.* **quan·ti·fy·ing**; *pt, pp* **quan·ti·fied**) to describe or express sth as an amount or a number: *The risks to health are impossible to quantify.* ▶ **quan·ti·fi·a·ble** /ˌkwɑntəˈfaɪəbl/ ***adj.***: *quantifiable data*

**quan·ti·ta·tive** /ˈkwɑntəˌteɪt̬ɪv/ ***adj.*** connected with the amount or number of sth rather than with how good it is: *quantitative analysis/research* ◇ *There is no difference between the two in quantitative terms.* ➲ Compare **qualitative**.

★**quan·ti·ty** /ˈkwɑnt̬əti/ ***noun*** (*pl.* **quan·ti·ties**) **1** [U] the measurement of sth by stating how much of it there is: *Don't write too much in your essay – quality is more important than quantity.* **2** [C,U] a number or an amount: *Add a small quantity of salt.* ◇ *It's cheaper to buy goods in quantity* (= in large amounts). ◇ *It's cheaper to buy goods in large quantities.*

**quar·an·tine**[1] /ˈkwɔrəntin; ˈkwɑr-/ ***noun*** [U] a period of time when a person or animal that has or may have a disease must be kept away from other people or animals: *to keep a dog in quarantine*

**quar·an·tine**[2] /ˈkwɔrəntin; ˈkwɑr-/ ***verb*** [T] to put an animal or a person into quarantine

**quar·rel**[1] /ˈkwɔrəl; ˈkwɑrəl/ ***noun*** [C] (*formal*) an angry argument or disagreement: *Several people pulled out knives during a quarrel on Elm Street last night.* ➲ Look at **argument** and **fight**.

IDM **have no quarrel with sb/sth** to have no reason for complaining about or disagreeing with sb/sth: *I have no quarrel with what has just been said.*

**quar·rel**[2] /ˈkwɔrəl; ˈkwɑrəl/ ***verb*** [I] (*formal*) **1 quarrel (with sb) (about/over sth)** to have an angry argument or disagreement: *Politicians quarreled bitterly over whether to send troops to the area.* ➲ Look at **argue** and **fight**. **2 quarrel with sth** to disagree with sth: *I wouldn't quarrel with Mary's description of what happened.*

**quar·ry** /ˈkwɔri; ˈkwɑri/ ***noun*** [C] (*pl.* **quar·ries**) a place where sand, stone, etc. is dug out of the ground ➲ Look at **mine**[2](1).

**quart** /kwɔrt/ ***noun*** [C] (*abbr.* **qt.**) a measure of liquid equal to 0.94 liters in the U.S. and 1.14 liters in Canada: *a quart of milk* ➲ There are two **pints** in a quart and four quarts in a **gallon**.

★**quar·ter** /ˈkwɔrt̬ər/ ***noun***

➤1 OF 4 PARTS **1** [C] one of four equal parts into which sth is divided: *The program lasts for three quarters of an hour.* ◇ *a mile and a quarter* ◇ *to cut an apple into quarters*

➤15 MINUTES **2** [sing.] fifteen minutes before or after every hour: *I'll meet you at a quarter after six.* ◇ *It's a quarter to three.*

➤25 CENTS **3** [C] a coin that is worth 25 cents (¼ dollar)

➤3 MONTHS **4** [C] a period of three months: *The company had record profits for the last quarter.*

➤SCHOOLS/UNIVERSITIES **5** [C] (at some schools, colleges and universities) one of the four equal parts that the academic year is divided into: *I'm going to take chemistry next quarter.*

➤ROOMS TO LIVE IN **6 quarters** [pl.] a place that is provided for a person to live in, usually not in a private house: *The White House living quarters are not open to the public.*

IDM **in some quarters** among people who have certain opinions: *Racist attitudes still exist in some quarters.*

**quar·ter·back**[1] /ˈkwɔrt̬ərbæk/ ***noun*** [C] the player on a football team who tells the other players what to do and throws the ball to them ➲ Look at the note at **football**.

**quar·ter·back**[2] /ˈkwɔrt̬ərbæk/ ***verb*** **1** [I] (in football) to play in the position of quarterback **2** [T] to direct or organize a project, an event, etc.

**quar·ter·fi·nal** /ˌkwɔrt̬ərˈfaɪnl/ ***noun*** [C] one of the four games between the eight remaining players or teams in a competition. The players that win in the quarterfinals go on to the semifinals.

**quar·ter·ly** /ˈkwɔrt̬ərli/ ***adj., adv.*** (produced or happening) once every three months: *a quarterly magazine* ◇ *The committee meets quarterly.*

ˈ**quarter note** ***noun*** [C] (*symbol* ♩) (in music) a NOTE[1](5) that lasts for a quarter of the length of a whole note ➲ picture at **music**.

**quar·tet** /kwɔrˈtɛt/ ***noun*** [C] **1** four people who sing or play music together **2** a piece of music for four people to sing or play together

**quartz** /kwɔrts/ ***noun*** [U] a type of hard rock that is used in making very accurate clocks or watches

**quash** /kwɑʃ/ ***verb*** [T] (*formal*) **1** to stop or defeat sth by force: *to quash a rebellion* **2** to declare that an official decision, judgment, etc. is no longer true or legal: *The Supreme Court quashed the verdict of the lower court.*

**quea·sy** /ˈkwizi/ ***adj.*** (**quea·si·er**; **quea·si·est**) **1** feeling sick in your stomach; wanting to vomit **2** slightly nervous or worried about sth ▶ **quea·si·ly** ***adv.*** ▶ **quea·si·ness** ***noun*** [U]

★**queen** /kwin/ ***noun*** [C] **1** (*also* **Queen**) the female ruler of a country that has a royal family, or the wife of a king: *Queen Elizabeth II*

NOTE Queen Elizabeth **II** is pronounced "Queen Elizabeth **the Second**." ➲ Look also at **king** and **princess**.

**2** the largest and most important female in a group of insects: *the queen bee* **3** one of the four playing cards in a deck with a picture of a QUEEN (1) on it: *the queen of hearts* ➲ Look at the note at **card**. **4** one of the pieces used in the game of chess ➲ picture at **chess**.

ˈ**queen-size** ***adj.*** larger than usual: *queen-size pantyhose* ◇ *a queen-size bed* ➲ Look at the note at **bed**.

ˌ**Queen's ˈPark** ***noun*** [sing.] (*Cdn*) the government (legislature) of Ontario, located in Toronto

**queer¹** /kwɪr/ ***adj.*** **1** (*old-fashioned*) strange; odd **2** (*slang*) homosexual

NOTE **Queer** is often used in an offensive way, but some homosexual people use it about themselves. ➲ Compare **gay**.

**queer²** /kwɪr/ ***noun*** [C] (*slang*) a homosexual man ➲ Look at the note at **queer¹**.

**quell** /kwɛl/ ***verb*** [T] to put an end to sth: *to quell a rebellion*

**quench** /kwɛntʃ/ ***verb*** [T] to satisfy your feeling of thirst by drinking: *to quench your thirst*

**que·ry¹** /ˈkwɪri/ ***noun*** [C] (*pl.* **que·ries**) a question: *The company spokesperson answered reporters' queries about the policy.*

**que·ry²** /ˈkwɪri/ ***verb*** [T] (*pres. part.* **que·ry·ing**; *3rd person sing. pres.* **que·ries**; *pt, pp* **que·ried**) to ask sb a question about sth: *1,000 people were queried about their eating habits for the survey.*

**que·sa·dil·la** /ˌkeɪsəˈdiə/ ***noun*** [C] a piece of thin flat Mexican bread (a **tortilla**) filled with cheese and heated

**quest** /kwɛst/ ***noun*** [C] (*formal*) a long search for sth that is difficult to find: *the quest for eternal youth*

★**ques·tion¹** /ˈkwɛstʃən/ ***noun*** **1** [C] a sentence or phrase that asks for an answer: *Are there any questions about what I just said?* ◇ *Raise your hand if you want to ask a question.* ◇ *On the test, you have to answer five questions in one hour.* ◇ *What's the answer to question 5?* ➲ Look at the note at **doubt¹**. Look also at **tag question**. **2** [C] a problem or difficulty that needs to be discussed or dealt with: *His resignation raises the question of who will take over from him.* ◇ *It's not difficult. It's just a question of finding the time to do it.* ◇ *We all agree that more money should be spent on education. The question is where that money is going to come from.* **3** [U] doubt or uncertainty: *There is no question about Brenda's enthusiasm for the job.* ◇ *Robert's honesty is beyond question.*

IDM **in question** (*formal*) that is being considered or talked about: *The lawyer asked where she was on the night in question.*

**no question of sth/doing sth** no possibility of sth/doing sth: *There was no question of any illegal activity in the company.*

**out of the question** impossible: *A new car is out of the question. It's just too expensive.*

★**ques·tion²** /ˈkwɛstʃən/ ***verb*** [T] **1** to ask sb a question or questions, especially in a formal situation or in an aggressive way: *The police questioned him for several hours.* ◇ *The interviewers questioned me about my previous experience.* **2** to express or feel doubt about sth: *She told me she was an employee, so I didn't question her right to be there.* ◇ *to question sb's sincerity*

**ques·tion·a·ble** /ˈkwɛstʃənəbl/ ***adj.*** **1** that is not certain: *It's questionable whether we'll be able to finish in time.* **2** that may not be true, suitable or honest: *A lot of money has been spent on very questionable projects.* ◇ *questionable motives*

ˈ**question mark** ***noun*** [C] the sign (?) that you use when you write a question

**ques·tion·naire** /ˌkwɛstʃəˈnɛr/ ***noun*** [C] a list of questions that are answered by many people. A questionnaire is used to collect information about a particular subject: *to complete/fill out a questionnaire*

**queue** /kyu/ ***noun*** [C] (*Cdn*) = LINE¹ (5)

**quib·ble¹** /ˈkwɪbl/ ***verb*** [I] **quibble (about/over sth)** to argue or complain about a small matter or an unimportant detail: *It isn't worth quibbling over such a small amount.*

**quib·ble²** /ˈkwɪbl/ ***noun*** [C] a small complaint or criticism, especially one that is not important: *minor quibbles*

**quiche** /kiʃ/ ***noun*** [C,U] a pie without a top that is filled with a mixture of eggs and milk with cheese, ham, etc. and cooked in the oven.

★**quick¹** /kwɪk/ ***adj.*** **1** doing sth at a high speed or in a short time: *It's quicker to travel by plane.* ◇ *Nick is a quick worker.* ◇ *She was quick to point out all the mistakes I had made.* **2** done in a short time: *Could I make a quick phone call?*

NOTE **Fast** is more often used for describing a person or thing that moves or can move at great speed: *a fast horse/car/runner.* **Quick** is more often used for describing sth that is done in a short time: *a quick decision/breakfast/visit*

**quick²** /kwɪk/ ***adv.*** (*informal*) quickly: *to get rich quick* ◇ *The stove's on fire – do something quick!*

**quick·en** /ˈkwɪkən/ ***verb*** [I,T] (*written*) **1** to become quicker or make sth quicker: *She felt her heartbeat quicken as he approached.* ◇ *He quickened his pace to catch up with them.* **2** to become more active; to make sth more active: *His interest quickened as he heard more about the plan.*

**quick·ie** /ˈkwɪki/ ***noun*** (*informal*) a thing that only takes a short time: *I have a question—it's just a quickie.* ◇ *a quickie divorce*

★**quick·ly** /ˈkwɪkli/ ***adv.*** at a high speed or in a short time: *Tom undressed quickly and got into bed.* ◇ *I'd like you to get here as quickly as possible.*



Q

**quick·sand** /ˈkwɪksænd/ *noun* [U] (*also* **quick·sands** [pl.]) deep wet sand that you sink into if you walk on it

**ˌquick-ˈwitted** *adj.* able to think quickly; intelligent: *a quick-witted student/response* OPP **slow-witted**

**quid pro quo** /ˌkwɪd proʊ ˈkwoʊ/ *noun* [sing.] a thing given in return for sth else

★**qui·et**[1] /ˈkwaɪət/ *adj.* **1** with very little or no noise: *Be quiet!* ◇ *His voice was quiet but firm.* ◇ *Please keep the kids quiet when I'm on the phone.* ◇ *Go into the library if you want to work. It's a lot quieter in there.* OPP **loud 2** without many people or much activity; without anything very exciting happening: *It's very quiet downtown on Sundays.* ◇ *"Have you been busy?" "No, it was a very quiet day today."* ◇ *a quiet suburb* ◇ *a quiet life* **3** (used about a person) not saying very much; not attracting other people's attention: *You're very quiet today. Is anything wrong?*

IDM **keep quiet about sth**; **keep sth quiet** to say nothing about sth: *Can you keep quiet about my new job until I tell the boss?*

▸ **qui·et·ly** *adv.*: *Try and close the door quietly!* ◇ *"She was my best friend," Rose said quietly.* ◇ *He quietly got up and left the room.* ▸ **qui·et·ness** *noun* [U]

**qui·et**[2] /ˈkwaɪət/ *noun* [U] the state of being QUIET[1] (1,2): *the peace and quiet of the countryside*

**qui·et**[3] /ˈkwaɪət/ *verb* [T] to make sb/sth QUIET[1] (1): *to quiet a crowd*

PHRV **quiet (sb/sth) down** to become quiet or to make sb/sth quiet: *Quiet down! I want to listen to the radio.*

**quill** /kwɪl/ *noun* [C] **1** (*also* ˈ**quill ˌfeather**) a large feather from the wing or tail of a bird **2** (*also* ˌ**quill ˈpen**) a pen made from a quill feather **3** one of the long sharp stiff spines a porcupine has on its back

**quilt** /kwɪlt/ *noun* [C] a cover for a bed that has a thick warm material, e.g. cotton or feathers, inside it. Some quilts are made with pieces of colored cloth that have been sewn together to make a design: *a patchwork quilt*

**quilt·ed** /ˈkwɪltəd/ *adj.* (used about clothes, bed coverings etc.) made of two layers of cloth with soft material between them, held in place by lines of stitches: *a quilted jacket/bedcover*

**quin·tes·sen·tial** /ˌkwɪntəˈsɛnʃl/ *adj.* being the most typical or perfect example of a quality or a type of person or thing: *He was the quintessential tough guy.*

**quin·tet** /kwɪnˈtɛt/ *noun* [C] **1** a group of five people who sing or play music together **2** a piece of music for five people to sing or play together

**quip** /kwɪp/ *verb* [I] (**quip·ping**; **quipped**) to make a quick and clever remark ▸ **quip** *noun* [C]

**quirk** /kwərk/ *noun* [C] **1** a strange habit or type of behavior **2** a strange happening: *By a quirk of fate, they met again several years later.*

**quirk·y** /ˈkwərki/ *adj.* (used about a person's behavior) unusual

★**quit** /kwɪt/ *verb* (*pres. part.* **quit·ting**; *pt, pp* **quit**) **1** [I,T] to leave a job, etc.: *I've had enough of this stupid company – I quit!* ◇ *Joe quit his job to go back to college.* **2** [T] (*informal*) to stop doing sth: *to quit smoking* **3** [I,T] (*computing*) to close a computer program

★**quite** /kwaɪt/ *adv.* (used before an adjective or adverb) (*formal*) very, but not completely or extremely: *We are quite pleased with the results of our experiments.* ◇ *She shouldn't be so modest – she really speaks English quite well.*

IDM **not quite** (used for showing that sth is nearly suitable or almost happens): *There's not quite enough bread for breakfast.* ◇ *I can't quite reach it – can you give it to me?* ◇ *These shoes don't quite fit.*

**quite a** (used for emphasizing that sth is unusual, or larger, longer, etc. than usual): *That's quite a hairstyle, Ben!* ◇ *That's quite a big problem.* ◇ *We'll have to wait quite a while.*

**quite a bit (of sth)**; **quite a few**; **quite a lot (of sth)** a lot, but not an extremely large amount or number of sth: *I learned quite a bit during the tour of the museum.* ◇ *We received quite a few responses to our ad.* ◇ *They've worked hard, but there's still quite a lot left to do.*

**quits** /kwɪts/ *adj.*

IDM **call it quits** → CALL[2]

**quit·ter** /ˈkwɪt̬ər/ *noun* [C] (*informal*) a person who becomes discouraged too easily when a job, etc. becomes difficult and is likely to stop doing it

**quiv·er** /ˈkwɪvər/ *verb* [I] to tremble or shake: *to quiver with rage/excitement/fear*

**quiz**[1] /kwɪz/ *noun* [C] (*pl.* **quiz·zes**) a short, informal test: *We have a quiz in math class today.* ➲ Look also at **pop quiz**.

**quiz**[2] /kwɪz/ *verb* [T] (**quiz·zing**; **quizzed**) **1** to ask sb a lot of questions about sth in order to get information from them: *We were quizzed on our views about education.* **2** to give students a short test: *You will be quizzed on chapter 6 tomorrow.*

**quo·ta** /ˈkwoʊt̬ə/ *noun* [C] the number or amount of sth that is allowed or that you must do: *There is a quota on the number of cars that can be imported each year.* ◇ *We have a fixed quota of work to get through each day.*

**quo·ta·tion** /kwoʊˈteɪʃn/ (*also informal* **quote**) *noun* [C] **1** a group of words from a book, speech, play, etc., that you repeat exactly: *That's a quotation from a poem by Longfellow.* ◇ *Please include quotations from the text to support your argument.* **2** the amount that sb thinks a piece of work will probably cost: *You should get a quotation from three mechanics.* ➲ Look at **estimate**.

**quoˈtation marks** (*also informal* **quotes**) *noun* [pl.] the signs ("...") that you use at the beginning and end of words that were spoken or that are being quoted, or that you are using in an unusual way

★**quote**[1] /kwoʊt/ *verb* **1** [I,T] **quote (sth) (from sb/sth)** to repeat exactly sth that sb else has said or written before: *The journalist quoted a statement that the senator had made several years earlier.* ◇ *to quote from the Bible* ◇ *She was quoted as saying that she disagreed with the decision.* ◇ *The mayor asked the newspaper not to quote him.* **2** [T] to give sth as an example to support what you are saying: *She quoted several reasons why she was unhappy about* *the decision.* **3** [T] to say what the cost of a piece of work, etc. will probably be: *The insurance company quoted us a rate for insuring our car.*

IDM **quote (...unquote)** (*informal*) (used to show the beginning (and end) of a word, phrase, etc. that has been said or written by sb else): *It was quote, "the hardest decision of my life", unquote, and one that he lived to regret.*

**quote²** /kwoʊt/ ***noun*** (*informal*) **1** = QUOTATION (1): *Her history paper was full of quotes.* **2** = QUOTATION (2): *Their quote for the job was way too high.* **3 quotes** [pl.] = QUOTATION MARKS: *If you take text from other sources, place it* ***in quotes.***

**quo·tient** /ˈkwoʊʃnt/ ***noun*** [C] (in math) a number which is the result when one number is divided by another ➲ Look at **IQ**.

# R r

**R, r** /ɑr/ ***noun*** [C,U] (*pl.* **R's; r's**) the eighteenth letter of the English alphabet: *"Rabbit" begins with an "R."*

**R** ***abbr.*** **1** restricted (used about movies that children under age 17 are not allowed to see without a parent) **2** (*also* **R.**) = REPUBLICAN

**rab·bi** /ˈræbaɪ/ ***noun*** [C] (*pl.* **rab·bis**) a Jewish religious leader and teacher of Jewish law

**rab·bit** /ˈræbət/ ***noun*** [C] a small animal with long ears: *a wild rabbit* ◇ *a pet rabbit* ➲ The children's word for rabbit is **bunny**.

rabbit

**rab·id** /ræbəd/ ***adj.*** **1** (used about a type of person) having very strong feelings about sth and acting in an unacceptable way: *rabid right-wing fanatics* **2** (used about feelings or opinions) violent or extreme: *rabid speculation* **3** suffering from rabies: *a rabid dog*

**ra·bies** /ˈreɪbiz/ ***noun*** [U] a serious, usually fatal, disease that can be given to humans by the bite of an animal that has the disease

**rac·coon** /ræˈkun/ ***noun*** [C] a small wild animal with brownish-gray fur on its body, black fur around its eyes and a thick tail with rings of black and white fur on it

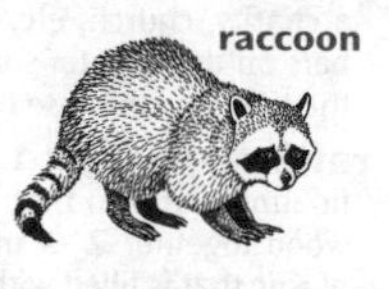

raccoon

★**race¹** /reɪs/ ***noun*** **1** [C] **race (against/with sb/sth)** a competition between people, animals, cars, etc. to see which is the fastest: *to run/win/lose a race* ◇ *to come first/second/last in a race* ◇ *a five-mile race* ◇ *a horse race* ◇ *Let's have a race to the end of the road.* ◇ (*figurative*) *the race to find a cure for AIDS* ◇ (*figurative*) *the nuclear arms race* ➲ Look also at **rat race**. **2** [C] an election and the speeches, meetings, etc. that come before it: *Officials have now announced the winner in the race for governor.* ◇ *the 2004 presidential race* **3** [C,U] one of the groups into which people can be divided according to the color of their skin, their hair type, the shape of their face, etc.: *the different races of South Africa* ◇ *a child of mixed race* ◇ *People should not be discriminated against on grounds of race, religion or gender.* ➲ Look at **human race**.

★**race²** /reɪs/ ***verb*** **1** [I,T] **race (against/with/sb/sth)** to have a competition with sb/sth to find out who is the fastest: *I'll race you home.* ◇ *In the 5,000 meters he'll be racing against some of the finest runners in the country.* **2** [I,T] to go very fast or to move sb/sth very fast: *We raced to catch the bus.* ◇ *The child had to be raced to the hospital.*

**race·track** /ˈreɪstræk/ (*also* **race·course** /ˈreɪskɔrs/) ***noun*** [C] **1** a ground or track for horse racing or dog racing **2** a track for races between runners, cars, bicycles, etc.: *You can't cross the street – it's like a racetrack.*

**ra·cial** /ˈreɪʃl/ ***adj.*** connected with people's RACE¹ (3); happening between people of different races: *racial tension* ◇ *racial discrimination* ▶ **ra·cial·ly** ***adv.***: *a racially integrated neighborhood*

★**rac·ing** /ˈreɪsɪŋ/ ***noun*** [U] the sport of taking part in races: *car racing* ◇ *horse racing* ◇ *bike racing*

**ra·cism** /ˈreɪsɪzəm/ ***noun*** [U] the belief that some races are better than others and people of other races are not as good as people of your own race; ways of treating people that show this belief: *to take measures to combat racism* ▶ **rac·ist** /ˈreɪsɪst/ ***noun*** [C], ***adj.***: *He's a racist.* ◇ *a racist remark*

racks

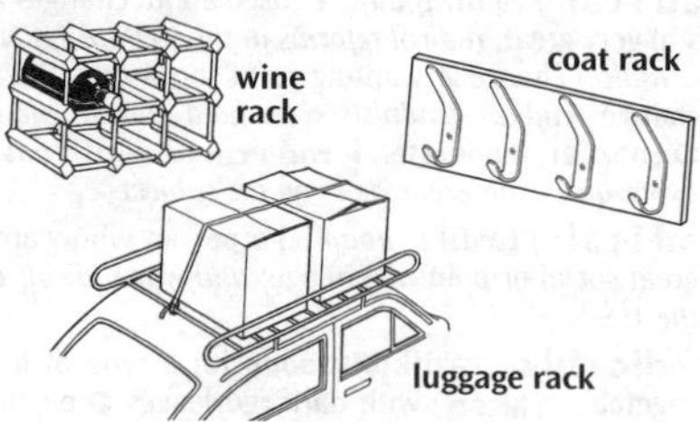


**rack¹** /ræk/ ***noun*** [C] (often in compounds) a type of shelf, made of bars, that you can put things in or on: *a towel rack* ◇ *racks of clothing in a department store*

**rack²** (*also* **wrack**) /ræk/ ***verb*** [T] (usually passive) to make sb suffer great physical or mental pain: *to be racked with/by guilt* ◇ *Her face was racked with pain.*

IDM **rack your brains** to try hard to think of sth or remember sth: *Steve racked his brains trying to remember where they'd met before.*

**rack·et** /ˈrækət/ ***noun*** **1** [C] (*also* **racquet**) a piece of sports equipment that you use to hit the ball in games such as tennis

NOTE Rackets are different from **bats** because they have **strings**. ➲ Look also at **club**[1](4) and **stick**[1](2).

**2** [sing.] (*informal*) a loud noise: *Quit making that racket!* **3** [C] an illegal way of making money: *a drug racket*

**rack·et·eer·ing** /ˌrækəˈtɪrɪŋ/ ***noun*** [U] making money through dishonest or illegal activities: *He was charged with fraud and racketeering.* ▸ **rack·et·eer** ***noun*** [C]: *drug traffickers and racketeers*

**rac·y** /ˈreɪsi/ ***adj.*** (**rac·i·er**; **rac·i·est**) having a style that is exciting and amusing, sometimes in a way that is connected with sex: *a racy novel*

**ra·dar** /ˈreɪdɑr/ ***noun*** [U] a system that uses radio waves to find the position and movement of objects, for example airplanes and ships, when they cannot be seen ➲ Look at **sonar**.

**ra·di·ant** /ˈreɪdiənt/ ***adj.*** **1** sending out light or heat: *radiant energy* **2** showing great happiness: *a radiant smile*

**ra·di·ate** /ˈreɪdieɪt/ ***verb*** **1** [T] to send out heat or light: (*figurative*) *to radiate health* **2** [I] **radiate (out) from sth** to go out in all directions from a central point: *several corridors which radiate out from the lobby*

**ra·di·a·tion** /ˌreɪdiˈeɪʃn/ ***noun*** [U] powerful and very dangerous rays of energy that are sent out from certain substances. You cannot see or feel radiation, but it can cause serious illness or death: *High levels of radiation have been recorded near the power plant.* ◇ *to be exposed to radiation* ➲ Look at **radioactivity**.

**ra·di·a·tor** /ˈreɪdiˌeɪṭər/ ***noun*** [C] **1** a piece of equipment that is used for heating a room. Radiators are made of metal and filled with hot water: *Turn the radiator down a little!* **2** a piece of equipment that is used for keeping an engine cool

**rad·i·cal**[1] /ˈrædɪkl/ ***adj.*** **1** (used about changes in sth) very great: *radical reforms in the welfare system* ◇ *radical change* **2** wanting great social or political change: *radical feminists* ◇ *to hold radical views* ➲ Look at **moderate**. ▸ **rad·i·cal·ly** /-kli/ ***adv.***: *two radically different views on the subject*

**rad·i·cal**[2] /ˈrædɪkl/ ***noun*** [C] a person who wants great social or political change: *anti-war radicals of the 1990s*

**ra·dic·chi·o** /rəˈdikioʊ/ ***noun*** [U] a type of leaf vegetable (chicory) with dark red leaves ➲ picture on study page **A28-29**.

**ra·di·i** *plural of* RADIUS

★**ra·di·o**[1] /ˈreɪdioʊ/ ***noun*** (*pl.* **ra·di·os**) **1** [C] a piece of equipment that is used for receiving and/or sending messages or broadcasts that you listen to (on a ship, airplane, etc. or in the house): *a portable radio* ◇ *A radio cassette player was stolen from the car.*

NOTE You may **turn** or **switch** a radio **on** or **off**. You may also **turn it up** or **down** to make it louder or quieter.

**2** (often **the radio**) [U, sing.] the broadcasting of programs for people to listen to on their RADIOS (1): *I always listen to the radio in the car.* ◇ *I heard an interesting report on the radio this morning.* ◇ *a radio station/show* **3** [U] the process of sending or receiving messages through the air by electrical signals: *The yachtsman was in contact with the coast by radio.* ◇ *a radio signal*

**ra·di·o**[2] /ˈreɪdioʊ/ ***verb*** [I,T] (*pt, pp* **ra·di·oed**) to send a message by RADIO[1]: *to radio for help*

**ra·di·o·ac·tive** /ˌreɪdioʊˈæktɪv/ ***adj.*** sending out powerful and very dangerous rays of energy that are produced when atoms are broken up. These rays cannot be seen or felt but can cause serious illness or death: *the problem of the disposal of radioactive waste from power plants*

**ra·di·o·ac·tiv·i·ty** /ˌreɪdioʊækˈtɪvəṭi/ ***noun*** [U] **1** the state of being radioactive **2** the energy that is produced by radioactive substances ➲ Look at **radiation**.

**ra·di·ol·o·gist** /ˌreɪdiˈɑlədʒɪst/ ***noun*** [C] a doctor who is trained in radiology

**ra·di·ol·o·gy** /ˌreɪdiˈɑlədʒi/ ***noun*** [U] the study and use of X-rays and different types of radiation in medicine, for example to treat disease

**ra·di·o·ther·a·py** /ˌreɪdioʊˈθerəpi/ ***noun*** [U] the treatment of disease by radiation: *radiotherapy treatments* ➲ Look at **chemotherapy**. ▸ **ra·di·o·ther·a·pist** ***noun*** [C]

**rad·ish** /ˈrædɪʃ/ ***noun*** [C] a small red vegetable with a strong taste that you eat raw, especially in salads. A radish is the root of a radish plant.

**ra·di·us** /ˈreɪdiəs/ ***noun*** [C] (*pl.* **ra·di·i** /-diaɪ/) **1** the distance from the center of a circle to the outside edge ➲ Look at **diameter**. **2** a circular area that is measured from a point in its center: *The wreckage of the plane was scattered over a radius of several miles.*

**ra·don** /ˈreɪdɑn/ ***noun*** [U] (*symbol* **Rn**) a radioactive gas that is used in the treatment of diseases such as cancer

**raf·fle** /ˈræfl/ ***noun*** [C] a way of making money for a charity, church, etc. by selling tickets with numbers on them. Later some numbers are chosen and the tickets with these numbers on them win prizes.

**raft** /ræft/ ***noun*** [C] **1** a type of simple flat boat or floating platform that you make by tying pieces of wood together **2** a small boat made of rubber or plastic that is filled with air: *an inflatable raft* ➲ picture at **boat**.

**raft·er** /ˈræftər/ ***noun*** [C] one of the long pieces of wood that support a roof

**raft·ing** /ˈræftɪŋ/ ***noun*** [U] the sport or activity of traveling down a river on a RAFT (2): *We went white-water rafting on the Colorado River.* ➲ picture on study page **A32**.

**rag**[1] /ræg/ ***noun*** **1** [C,U] a small piece of old cloth that you use for cleaning **2 rags** [pl.] clothes that are very old and torn: *to be dressed in rags*

**rag**[2] /ræg/ ***verb*** (**rag·ging**; **ragged**)

PHR V **rag on sb** (*slang*) to criticize sb in order to make him/her feel embarrassed or because you are angry at him/her: *Everybody was totally ragging on me at school today.*

**rage**[1] /reɪdʒ/ ***noun*** [C,U] great anger: *He was trembling with rage.* ◇ *to fly into a rage* (= to suddenly become very angry)

**rage**[2] /reɪdʒ/ ***verb*** [I] (used about a battle, disease,

R

storm, etc.) to continue with great force: *The fire raged out of control.*

**rag·ged** /'rægəd/ ***adj.*** (used about clothes, etc.) old and torn

**rag·ing** /'reɪdʒɪŋ/ ***adj.*** **1** (used about feelings or emotions) very strong: *a raging appetite/thirst* ◇ *raging lust/jealousy* **2** (used about natural forces) very powerful: *a raging storm* ◇ *The building was now a raging inferno.* **3** (used about a pain or an illness) very strong or painful: *a raging headache*

**rag·time** /'rægtaɪm/ ***noun*** [U] an early form of jazz, especially for the piano, first played by African American musicians in the early 1900s

**rag·weed** /'rægwid/ ***noun*** [U] a North American plant with small green flowers that contain a lot of a fine, yellow powder (**pollen**), which causes an allergic reaction in some people (**hay fever**)

**raid**[1] /reɪd/ ***noun*** [C] **raid (on sth) 1** a surprise attack on an enemy: *an air raid* **2** an attack in order to steal sth: *a bank raid* **3** a surprise visit by the police: *Police found large supplies of cocaine during a raid on a hotel last night.*

**raid**[2] /reɪd/ ***verb*** [T] to make a RAID[1] on a place: *Police raided the bar looking for drugs.*

★**rail** /reɪl/ ***noun*** **1** (*also* **railing**) [C] a bar, usually of metal or wood, which protects people from falling (on stairs, from a building, etc.): *Hold on to the handrail – these steps are very slippery.* ➲ picture at **balcony 2** [C, usually pl.] the tracks that trains run on **3** [U] the railroad system; trains as a means of transportation: *commuter rail lines* ◇ *The goods were shipped by rail.*

**rail·ing** /'reɪlɪŋ/ ***noun*** [C] = RAIL (1)

★**rail·road** /'reɪlroʊd/ ***noun*** [C] the system of trains, the metal lines (**tracks**) that they run on, and the companies that own them: *railroad tracks* ◇ *This town got a lot bigger after the railroad came in the 1860s.*

**'railroad ˌcrossing** ***noun*** [C] a place where a railroad track crosses the surface of a road

**rail·way** /'reɪlweɪ/ ***noun*** [C] (*Cdn*) = RAILROAD

★**rain**[1] /reɪn/ ***noun*** **1** [U] the water that falls from the sky: *Seattle gets a lot of rain.* ◇ *Take your umbrella – it looks like rain.* ◇ *Half an inch of rain fell on the city yesterday.* ➲ Look at **shower**[1](3) and **acid rain** and at the note at **weather**. **2** [C] an occasion when RAIN (1) falls: *Everything smells fresh after a good rain.* ◇ *recent heavy rains* **3 the rains** [pl.] (in tropical countries) the time of the year when there is a lot of RAIN (1): *When the rains come in July, the people move their houses to higher ground.*

★**rain**[2] /reɪn/ ***verb*** [I] (used with *it*) to fall as RAIN[1] (1): *Oh no! It's raining again!* ◇ *Is it raining hard?* ◇ *We'll go out when it stops raining.*

PHR V **rain (sth) out** (usually passive) to stop sth from happening because it is raining: *I'm sorry, but the picnic has been rained out.*

**rain·bow** /'reɪnboʊ/ ***noun*** [C] an arch of many colors that sometimes appears in the sky when the sun shines through rain: *all the colors of the rainbow*

**'rain check** ***noun***

IDM **take a rain check (on sth)** (*informal*) to refuse an invitation or offer, but say that you might accept it later

**rain·coat** /'reɪnkoʊt/ ***noun*** [C] a special coat that you wear when it is raining

**rain·drop** /'reɪndrɑp/ ***noun*** [C] a single drop of rain

**rain·fall** /'reɪnfɔl/ ***noun*** [U] the total amount of rain that falls in a particular place during a month, year, etc.: *The annual rainfall in Cairo is less than 2 inches.*

**'rain ˌforest** ***noun*** [C] a forest in a tropical part of the world

**rain·storm** /'reɪnstɔrm/ ***noun*** a heavy fall of rain

**rain·wa·ter** /'reɪnˌwɔt̬ər; -ˌwɑ-/ ***noun*** [U] water that has fallen as rain: *a barrel for collecting rainwater*

**rain·y** /'reɪni/ (**rain·i·er**; **rain·i·est**) ***adj.*** having a lot of rain: *the rainy season*

IDM **keep/save sth for a rainy day** to save money or sth valuable or useful so that you can use it at a later time when you really need to

★**raise**[1] /reɪz/ ***verb*** [T]

➤MOVE UPWARD **1** to lift sth: *If you want to leave the room, raise your hand.* ◇ *The captain of the winning team raised the trophy in the air.*

➤INCREASE **2** to increase sth or to make sth better or stronger: *They've raised their prices a lot since last year.* ◇ *The hotel needs to raise its standards.* ◇ *There's no need to raise your voice* (= speak angrily).

➤COLLECT MONEY **3** to get sth; obtain: *We managed to raise nearly $100 for the school at the bake sale.*

➤CHILD **4** to take care of a child until he/she is an adult: *You can't raise a family on what I earn.*

➤FARM ANIMALS/CROPS **5** to make a plant or animal grow so that you can use it: *In New Zealand, sheep are raised for meat and wool.*

➤MENTION SUBJECT **6** to introduce a subject that needs to be talked about: *I would like to raise the subject of money.* ◇ *This raises the question of why nothing was done before.*

IDM **raise your eyebrows** to show that you are surprised or that you do not approve of sth

**raise/sound the alarm** → ALARM[1]

**raise**[2] /reɪz/ ***noun*** [C] an increase in pay: *I'm going to ask the boss for a raise.*

**rai·sin** /'reɪzn/ ***noun*** [C] a dried grape

**rake**[1] /reɪk/ ***noun*** [C] a garden tool with a long handle, used for collecting leaves or making the earth smooth ➲ picture at **garden**.

**rake**[2] /reɪk/ ***verb*** [T] to use a RAKE[1] on sth: *to rake the leaves*

PHR V **rake sth in** (*informal*) to earn a lot of money, especially without working hard: *Spielberg's new movie raked in $10 million during its first week.*

**ral·ly**[1] /'ræli/ ***noun*** [C] (*pl.* **ral·lies**) a meeting of people to express support for a person, a political idea, etc.: *20,000 people attended the rally for the new candidate.* ➲ Look also at **pep rally**.

**ral·ly**[2] /'ræli/ ***verb*** (*pres. part.* **ral·ly·ing**; *3rd person sing. pres.* **ral·lies**; *pt, pp* **ral·lied**) **1** [I] to get stronger: *The dollar rallied against the yen late yesterday.* ◇ *The Sharks rallied in the third period to win the game 2-1.* **2** [I,T] to come together or to bring people together: *Gore has rallied the party behind him.*

R

PHRV **rally around (sb/sth)** to come together to help or support sb/sth: *When I was in trouble, my family rallied around me.*

**RAM** /ræm/ ***noun*** [U] (*computing*) random-access memory; the part of a computer where information is used or changed: *a computer with 32 megabytes of RAM* ➲ Look at **ROM**.

**ram**[1] /ræm/ ***noun*** [C] a male sheep ➲ picture at **sheep**.

**ram**[2] /ræm/ ***verb*** [I,T] (**ram·ming**; **rammed**) **ram (into) sth** to crash into sth or push sth with great force: *The stolen car rammed into the side of a bus.*

**Ram·a·dan** /ˈrɑmədɑn/ ***noun*** [U] the ninth month of the Muslim year, when Muslims do not eat or drink anything between the time when the sun rises and the time when it sets

**ram·ble** /ˈræmbl/ ***verb*** [I] to talk for a long time in a confused way: *Grandpa has a tendency to ramble.*

**ram·bler** /ˈræmblər/ ***noun*** [C] a plant, especially a rose, that grows up walls, fences, etc.

**ram·bling** /ˈræmblɪŋ/ ***adj.*** (usually *before* a noun) **1** (used about writing or speech) not saying things in a clear way; confused: *a long, rambling speech* **2** (used about a building) spreading in many directions

**ram·bunc·tious** /ræmˈbʌŋkʃəs/ ***adj.*** (*informal*) full of energy in a cheerful and noisy way

**ram·i·fi·ca·tion** /ˌræməfəˈkeɪʃn/ ***noun*** [usually pl.] one of the large number of complicated and unexpected results that follow an action or a decision: *These changes are bound to have widespread social ramifications.*

**ramp** /ræmp/ ***noun*** [C] a sloping path which people can use instead of steps to get from one place to another higher or lower place: *a wheelchair ramp at the side of a building* ➲ Look also at **entrance ramp** and **exit ramp**.

**ram·page**[1] /ˈræmpeɪdʒ/ ***noun*** [C, usually sing.] a period of wild, violent behavior: *Five people were injured in a shooting rampage at the Glenville Mall yesterday.*

IDM **be/go on the rampage** to rush around breaking things and attacking people

**ram·page**[2] /ˈræmpeɪdʒ; ræmˈpeɪdʒ/ ***verb*** [I] to rush from one place to another, breaking things and attacking people: *The elephant escaped and rampaged through the zoo.*

**ram·pant** /ˈræmpənt/ ***adj.*** very common and very difficult to control: *rampant crime and drug abuse*

**ram·part** /ˈræmpɑrt/ ***noun*** [C, usually pl.] a high wide wall of stone or earth with a path on top, built around a castle, town, etc. to defend it

**ram·rod** /ˈræmrɑd/ ***noun*** [C]

IDM **ramrod straight/stiff** (used about a person) with a very straight back and looking serious and formal

**ram·shack·le** /ˈræmʃækl/ ***adj.*** (used about a building or a car, etc.) old and needing repair

**ran** *past tense of* RUN[1]

**ranch** /ræntʃ/ ***noun*** [C] a large farm in the western U.S. or Canada, usually where cows, horses or sheep are raised

**ˌranch ˈdressing** ***noun*** [U] a mixture of yoghurt, herbs, spices, etc. that is used to add flavor to salads

**ranch·er** /ˈræntʃər/ ***noun*** [C] a person who owns or manages a ranch: *a cattle/sheep rancher*

**ˈranch house** ***noun*** [C] a type of house for one family, that usually has only one level above the ground and a low roof

**ran·cid** /ˈrænsəd/ ***adj.*** if food containing fat is rancid, it tastes or smells unpleasant because it is no longer fresh: *rancid butter*

**R & B** /ˌɑr ən ˈbi/ ***abbr.*** = RHYTHM AND BLUES

**R & D** /ˌɑr ən ˈdi/ ***abbr.*** = RESEARCH AND DEVELOPMENT

**ran·dom** /ˈrændəm/ ***adj.*** happening or chosen by chance: *random drug testing* ◇ *a random number, selected by a computer*

IDM **at random** not in any special order or for any special reason: *He ran through the town shooting people at random.* ◇ *The competitors were chosen at random from the audience.*

▶ **ran·dom·ly** ***adv.***

**ˌrandom-ˌaccess ˈmemory** ***noun*** [U] = RAM

**R & R** (*also* **R and R**) /ˌɑr ən ˈɑr/ ***abbr.*** (*informal*) **1** rest and recreation (= time spent doing things for enjoyment rather than working): *She took time out from her schedule to go to a spa for some R & R.* **2** (*medical*) rescue and resuscitation

**rang** *past tense of* RING[2]

★**range**[1] /reɪndʒ/ ***noun***

➤ VARIETY **1** [C] different things that belong to the same group: *The course will cover a whole range of topics.* ◇ *We offer a full range of services to meet all your needs.*

➤ LIMITS **2** [C] the amount between certain limits: *There's a very wide range of ability in the class.* ◇ *That car is outside my price range.* ◇ *I'm looking for a bike in the $200-250 range.*

➤ OF MOUNTAINS **3** [C] a line of mountains or hills

➤ DISTANCE **4** [C,U] the distance that it is possible for sb or sth to travel, see or hear, etc.: *The gunman shot the police officer at close range.* ◇ *They can pick up signals at a range of 400 yards.*

➤ STOVE **5** [C] = STOVE

**range**[2] /reɪndʒ/ ***verb*** [I] **range from A to B** to stretch from one thing to another, within certain limits: *The students range in age from 18 to 24.*

**rang·er** /ˈreɪndʒər/ ***noun*** [C] a person who works in a public park or forest and takes care of the land and animals in it

★**rank**[1] /ræŋk/ ***noun*** **1** [C,U] the level of importance that sb has in an organization, especially the military forces: *General is one of the highest ranks in the army.* ◇ *She's much higher in rank than I am.* **2 ranks** [pl.] the ordinary members of a large group or organization: *the ranks of the unemployed*

IDM **the rank and file** the ordinary members of an organization

★**rank**[2] /ræŋk/ ***verb*** [I,T] to have or to give a place in an order of importance: *She's ranked first among U. S. tennis players.* ◇ *I think Tokyo ranks as one the world's most expensive cities.* ◇ *a high-ranking police officer*

**ran·sack** /ˈrænsæk/ ***verb*** [T] to cause damage to a place when you are looking for sth: *Her home had been ransacked by burglars.*

R

**ran·som** /'rænsəm/ ***noun*** [C,U] the money that you must pay to free sb who has been captured by criminals: *The kidnappers demanded a ransom of $500,000 for the boy's release.*
IDM **hold sb for ransom** to capture sb and say that you will not free him/her until you have received some money ➲ Look at **hostage**.

**rant** /rænt/ ***verb*** [I] **rant (on) (about sth)** to speak or complain about sth in a loud and/or angry way: *He was still ranting on about the unfairness of it all.*
IDM **rant and rave** to show that you are angry by shouting or complaining loudly for a long time
▸ **rant** ***noun*** [C]

**rap¹** /ræp/ ***noun*** **1** [C] a knock, on a door or window, etc., which is quick and fairly loud **2** [C,U] a style or piece of music with a strong beat, in which the words of a song are spoken, not sung: *a rap artist* ➲ Look also at **hip-hop**.

**rap²** /ræp/ ***verb*** (**rap·ping**; **rapped**) **1** [I,T] to hit sth quickly and lightly, making a noise **2** [I] to speak the words of a song (a rap) that has music with a very strong beat

**ra·pa·cious** /rə'peɪʃəs/ ***adj.*** (*formal*) wanting more money or goods than you need or have a right to; greedy: *rapacious landlords* ▸ **ra·pa·cious·ly** ***adv.***

**rape¹** /reɪp/ ***verb*** [T] to force a person to have sex when he/she does not want to

**rape²** /reɪp/ ***noun*** [C,U] **1** the act of forcing sb to have sex: *to commit rape* ◇ *a rape victim* **2** the destruction of sth beautiful: *Industry has been responsible for the rape of the countryside.*

★**rap·id** /'ræpəd/ ***adj.*** happening very quickly or moving with great speed: *She made rapid progress and was soon the best in the class.* ◇ *After leaving the hospital, he made a rapid recovery and was soon back at work.* ▸ **ra·pid·i·ty** /rə'pɪdət̬i/ ***noun*** [U] (*formal*) ▸ **rap·id·ly** ***adv.***

ˌ**rapid-'fire** ***adj.*** (only *before* a noun) (used about questions, comments, etc.) spoken very quickly, one after the other

**rap·ids** /'ræpədz/ ***noun*** [pl.] the part of a river where the water flows very fast over rocks

ˌ**rapid 'transit** ***noun*** [U] a system of public transportation in a city that uses trains which run above or under the ground

**rap·ist** /'reɪpɪst/ ***noun*** [C] a person who has forced sb to have sex

**rap·per** /'ræpər/ ***noun*** [C] a person who speaks the words of a RAP¹ (2)

**rap·port** /rə'pɔr; ræ-/ ***noun*** [U, sing.] a friendly situation in which people understand each other very well: *to establish a good rapport with your coworkers*

**rap·ture** /'ræptʃər/ ***noun*** [U] (*formal*) a feeling of extreme pleasure and happiness: *The children gazed at her in rapture.*
IDM **be in, go into, etc. raptures (about/over sb/sth)** to feel or express extreme pleasure or enthusiasm for sb/sth: *The critics went into raptures about her new CD.*

★**rare** /rɛr/ ***adj.*** **1** not found or seen very often: *a rare bird/flower* ◇ *It's very rare to have hot weather like this in April.* **2** (used about meat) not cooked for very long: *a rare steak* ➲ Look at the note at **meat**.

★**rare·ly** /'rɛrli/ ***adv.*** not often: *We rarely eat out because it's too expensive.*

**rar·i·ty** /'rɛrət̬i/ ***noun*** (*pl.* **rar·i·ties**) **1** [C] a thing or a person that is not found very often: *Women truck drivers are still quite a rarity.* **2** [U] being unusual or difficult to find: *The rarity of this stamp increases its value a lot.*

**ras·cal** /'ræskl/ ***noun*** [C] a person, especially a child or man, who shows a lack of respect for other people and enjoys playing tricks on them: *Come here, you little rascal!*

**rash¹** /ræʃ/ ***noun*** [C, usually sing.] an area of small red spots that appear on your skin when you are sick or have been stung by an insect, plant, etc.: *He broke out in a rash where the plant had touched him.*
IDM **a rash of sth** a series of bad events of the same kind happening close together: *There has been a rash of attacks on senior citizens this month.*

**rash²** /ræʃ/ ***adj.*** **1** done without much thought: *a rash decision* ◇ *a rash promise* (= one which you cannot keep easily) **2** doing things that might be dangerous without thinking about it: *There's no need to be rash or irresponsible.*

**rasp·ber·ry** /'ræzˌbɛri/ ***noun*** [C] (*pl.* **rasp·berries**) a small, soft, red fruit which grows on bushes: *raspberry jam* ➲ picture on study page **A28-29**.

**Ras·ta·far·i·an** /ˌræstə'fɛriən; ˌrɑstə'fɑr-/ (*also informal* **Ras·ta** /'ræstə/) ***noun*** [C] a member of a Jamaican religious group which worships the former Emperor of Ethiopia, Haile Selassie, and which believes that Blacks will one day return to Africa. Rastafarians often wear their hair in dreadlocks and have other distinguishing patterns of behavior and dress. ▸ **Ras·ta·far·i·an** ***adj.*** ▸ **Ras·ta·far·i·an·ism** /ˌræstə'fɛriənɪzəm; ˌrɑstə'fɑr-/ ***noun*** [U]

**rat** /ræt/ ***noun*** [C] **1** an animal like a large mouse ➲ Rats belong to the family of animals that are called **rodents**. **2** (*informal*) a person who is not honest or loyal: *You dirty rat!* ➲ Look also at **rat race** and **rats**.

**ratch·et¹** /'rætʃət/ ***noun*** [C] a wheel or bar with teeth along the edge and a metal piece that fits between the teeth, allowing movement in one direction only

**ratch·et²** /'rætʃət/ ***verb***
PHRV **ratchet (sth) up** to increase (sth) repeatedly and by small amounts: *Overuse of credit cards has ratcheted up consumer debt.*

★**rate¹** /reɪt/ ***noun*** [C] **1** a measurement of one amount or of how fast or how often sth is happening in relation to another amount: *The birth rate is falling.* ◇ *a rise in the annual rate of inflation from 6 to 7%* ◇ *The population increased at a rate of less than 0.5% a year.* ◇ *an exchange rate of 112 yen to the dollar* **2** the amount that sth costs or that sb is paid: *The bank raised the interest rate on our loan to 6.25%.* ◇ *We offer reliable service at affordable rates.* ➲ Look at **first-rate** and **second-rate**.
IDM **at any rate 1** (used when you are giving more exact information about sth): *He said that they would be here by ten. At any rate, I think that's what he said.* **2** regardless of anything else that

R

might happen: *Well, that's one good piece of news at any rate.*
**at this/that rate** if this/that situation continues in the same way: *At this rate, we won't be finished before next summer!*
**the going rate (for sth)** → GOING[2]

**rate**[2] /reɪt/ ***verb*** [T] **1** to say how good you think sb/sth is: *She's rated among the best tennis players of all time.* **2** (often passive) to put sth into an official group or class, for example in order to show that it is suitable for a certain group of people: *This movie is rated PG-13.* **3** to deserve or to get sth: *The accident wasn't very serious – it didn't rate a mention in the local newspaper.*

★**rath·er** /ˈræðər/ ***adv.*** **1** (*formal*) to some extent; very but not extremely: *The paintings seemed rather traditional and unoriginal.* ➲ **Fairly** and **pretty** are less formal words with the same meaning. **2** (*formal*) (used to show that sth contrasts with sth that was mentioned earlier): *The damage was not caused by vandals, but rather by some curious wild animals.*
IDM **or rather** (a way of correcting sth you have said, or making it more exact): *She lives in Los Angeles, or rather a suburb of Los Angeles.*
**rather than** in the place of; instead of: *I think I'll just have a sandwich rather than a full meal.*
**would rather... (than)** would prefer to: *"How old are you?" "I'd rather not say."* ◇ *Would you rather eat at home tonight or go out?*

**rat·i·fy** /ˈræṭəfaɪ/ ***verb*** [T] (*pres. part.* **rat·i·fy·ing**; *3rd person sing. pres.* **rat·i·fies**; *pt, pp* **rat·i·fied**) to make a document, a decision, etc. official and legal, especially by signing it: *to ratify an amendment to the Constitution*

**rat·ing** /ˈreɪṭɪŋ/ ***noun*** [C] a measurement of how popular, good, difficult, etc. sth is: *The principle's popularity rating has fallen sharply.* ◇ *a movie with an "R" rating* ◇ *The network's ratings soared during the broadcasts of the Olympics.*

**ra·tio** /ˈreɪʃioʊ; ˈreɪʃoʊ/ ***noun*** [C] the relation between two numbers which shows how much bigger one quantity is than another: *The ratio of students to books in this class is two to one* (= there are two times as many students as books).

**ra·tion**[1] /ˈræʃn; ˈreɪʃn/ ***noun*** [C] the amount of food, gasoline, etc. that you get when there is not enough for everybody to get as much as they want: *emergency food rations*

**ra·tion**[2] /ˈræʃn/ ***verb*** [T] to give people only a small amount of sth, not as much as they want, because there is not enough or because it is too expensive: *Will we have to start rationing health care?* ▶ **ra·tion·ing** ***noun*** [U]: *gasoline rationing*

**ra·tion·al** /ˈræʃənl/ ***adj.*** **1** (used about a person) able to use thought to make decisions, not just feelings: *We're both rational human beings – let's sit down and talk about the problem.* OPP **irrational** **2** based on reason; sensible or logical: *There must be a rational explanation for his behavior.* ▶ **ra·tion·al·ly** ***adv.***

**ra·tion·al·ize** /ˈræʃənl·aɪz/ ***verb*** [I,T] to find reasons that explain why you have done sth (perhaps because you do not like the real reason): *She rationalized her theft from the office by saying that the company had plenty of money and wouldn't miss a few things.* ▶ **ra·tion·al·i·za·tion** /ˌræʃənl·əˈzeɪʃn/ ***noun*** [C,U]

**the ˈrat race** ***noun*** [sing.] (*informal*) the situation in which everybody is competing with each other in order to be better, more successful, etc.

**rats** /ræts/ ***interjection*** (used to show that you are annoyed when you do sth stupid or when sth goes wrong): *Oh rats! I forgot my keys.*

**rat·tle**[1] /ˈræṭl/ ***verb*** **1** [I,T] to make a noise like things hitting each other, or to shake sth so that it makes this noise: *The windows were rattling all night in the wind.* ◇ *He rattled the ice cubes in his glass.* **2** [T] (*informal*) to make sb unsure and afraid: *The news of his arrival really rattled her.*
PHRV **rattle sth off** to say a list of things very quickly: *She rattled off the names of every player on the team.*

**rat·tle**[2] /ˈræṭl/ ***noun*** **1** [C, sing.] a noise made by things hitting each other: *There's a funny rattle coming from the back of the car.* **2** [C] a toy that a baby can shake to make a noise

**rat·tle·snake** /ˈræṭlsneɪk/ ***noun*** [C] a poisonous snake that makes a noise with its tail when it is angry or afraid

**rat·ty** /ˈræṭi/ ***adj.*** (**rat·ti·er**; **rat·ti·est**) **1** (*informal*) in bad condition: *long ratty hair* ◇ *a ratty old pair of jeans* **2** looking like a rat

**rau·cous** /ˈrɔkəs/ ***adj.*** (used about people's voices) loud and rough: *The raucous laughter in the bar could be heard across the road.*

**raun·chy** /ˈrɔntʃi; ˈrɑn-/ ***adj.*** (**raun·chi·er**; **raun·chi·est**) (*informal*) **1** intended to be sexually exciting or to make you think about sex: *a raunchy magazine/movie* ◇ *Their stage act is a little too raunchy for television.* **2** looking dirty and unpleasant: *The bed was broken and raunchy-looking.*

**rav·age** /ˈrævɪdʒ/ ***verb*** [T] to damage sth very badly: *The forests were ravaged by the winter storms.*

**rave**[1] /reɪv/ ***verb*** [I] **1 rave (about sb/sth)** to praise sb/sth very much: *Critics raved about the new restaurant.* **2** to speak angrily or wildly ➲ Look at **rant and rave**.

**rave**[2] /reɪv/ ***noun*** [C] **1** (*slang*) a large party or event at which people dance to fast electronic music and sometimes take illegal drugs: *rave culture/bands* **2** → RAVE REVIEW

**ra·ven** /ˈreɪvən/ ***noun*** [C] a large black bird that has a loud voice

**rav·en·ous** /ˈrævənəs/ ***adj.*** (used about a person or an animal) extremely hungry: *What's for lunch? I'm absolutely ravenous.* ▶ **rav·en·ous·ly** ***adv.***

**ˌrave reˈview** (*also informal* **rave**) ***noun*** [C] an article in a newspaper, etc. that praises a book, movie, record, etc. very much

**ra·vine** /rəˈvin/ ***noun*** [C] a narrow deep valley with steep sides

**rav·ing** /ˈreɪvɪŋ/ ***adj.*** (*informal*) (only *before* a noun) acting in a wild, uncontrolled way: *He's a raving lunatic!*

**ra·vi·o·li** /ˌræviˈoʊli/ ***noun*** [U] pasta in the shape of small squares filled with meat, cheese, etc., usually served with a sauce

R

**rav·ish·ing** /ˈrævɪʃɪŋ/ ***adj.*** extremely beautiful: *a ravishing blonde/dress/smile* SYN **gorgeous**

★**raw** /rɔ/ ***adj.*** **1** not cooked: *Have you ever eaten raw fish?* ◇ *Raw vegetables are good for your teeth.* **2** (used about an injury where the skin has been rubbed away): *I scratched this mosquito bite until my skin was red and raw.* **3** in the natural state: *raw sugar* ◇ *raw materials* (= that are used to make things, in factories etc.)

★**ray** /reɪ/ ***noun*** [C] a line of light, heat or energy: *A single ray of light came through a hole in the roof.* ◇ *the rays of the sun* ➲ Look at **X-ray**.

IDM **a ray of hope** a small chance that things will get better

**ray·on** /ˈreɪɑn/ ***noun*** [U] a smooth fabric like silk that is used for making clothes

**raze** /reɪz/ ***verb*** [T] (usually passive) to completely destroy a building, town, etc. so that nothing is left: *The village was **razed to the ground**.*

**ra·zor** /ˈreɪzər/ ***noun*** [C] a sharp instrument which people use to cut off the hair from their skin (= to shave): *an electric razor*

ˈ**razor blade** (*also* ˈ**razorblade**) ***noun*** [C] the thin sharp piece of metal that you put in a razor

ˌ**razor-ˈsharp** ***adj.*** **1** extremely sharp: *razor-sharp teeth* **2** showing that sb is extremely intelligent: *a razor-sharp mind*

**raz·zle-daz·zle** /ˌræzl ˈdæzl/ (*also* **razz·ma·tazz** /ˈræzmətæz; ˌræzməˈtæz/) ***noun*** [U] (*informal*) a lot of exciting activity, images, sounds, etc. that are intended to make people want to watch sth

**RCMP** /ˌɑr si ɛm ˈpi/ ***abbr.*** Royal Canadian Mounted Police; the national police force of Canada ➲ Look also **Mountie**.

**Rd.** ***abbr.*** = ROAD (2)

**RDA** /ˌɑr di ˈeɪ/ ***abbr.*** the abbreviation for "recommended daily allowance"; the amount of a chemical, e.g. a vitamin or a mineral, which you should have every day

**re** /ri/ ***prep.*** (*formal*) (used in formal letters or messages to introduce the topic) connected with; about: *Re: your memo dated May 3*

★**reach**[1] /ritʃ/ ***verb*** **1** [T] to arrive at a place or condition: *The letter should reach you on Wednesday.* ◇ *We won't reach the airport in time.* ◇ *Tell me when you have reached the end of the book.* ◇ *Anyone who has reached the age of 60 knows something about the world.* ◇ *Sometimes the temperature reaches 100°F.* ◇ *We finally reached an agreement after hours of discussion.* ◇ *to reach a decision* **2** [I,T] **reach (out) (for sb/sth)** to stretch out your arm to try and touch sth or get sth: *The child reached for her mother.* ◇ *The monkey reached out its hand for the banana.* ◇ *She reached into her bag for her wallet.* **3** [I,T] to be able to touch sth: *Can you get me that book off the top shelf? I can't reach that high.* ◇ *He couldn't reach the light switch.* ◇ *I need a longer ladder. This one won't reach.* **4** [T] to contact sb: *You can reach me at this number.* ◇ *She can't be reached until Monday morning.*

PHR V **reach out (to sb)** to make an effort to help or communicate with sb: *We need to reach out to elderly people in our community.*

**reach**[2] /ritʃ/ ***noun*** [U] the distance that you can stretch your hand: *Keep this medication out of the reach of children.*

IDM **beyond/out of (sb's) reach** not able to be gotten or done by sb: *A job like that is completely beyond his reach.*

**within (sb's) reach 1** inside the distance that you can stretch your arm: *Always keep a glass of water within reach.* **2** able to be gotten or done by sb: *Hewitt led by five games to two – victory was almost within reach!*

★**re·act** /riˈækt/ ***verb*** [I] **1 react (to sb/sth)** to do or say sth because of sth that has happened or been said: *I haven't told her about the problem yet – I don't know how she'll react.* ◇ *He wasn't sure how to react to the news.* **2 react (against sb/sth)** to behave or talk in a way that shows that you do not like the influence of sb/sth (e.g. authority, your family, etc.): *She reacted against the strict way she had been brought up.*

★**re·ac·tion** /riˈækʃn/ ***noun*** **1** [C,U] **(a) reaction (to sb/sth)** sth that you do or say because of sth that has happened or been said: *What is your reaction to the news?* ◇ *a hostile reaction* ◇ *I shook him to try and wake him up, but there was no reaction.* **2** [C,U] **(a) reaction (against sb/sth)** behavior that shows that you do not like the influence of sb/sth (e.g. authority, your family, etc.): *Her strange clothes are a reaction against the conservative way she was brought up.* **3** [C, usually pl.] the physical ability to act quickly when sth happens: *If the other driver's reactions hadn't been so good, there would have been an accident.*

**re·ac·tion·ar·y** /riˈækʃəˌnɛri/ ***noun*** [C] (*pl.* **re·ac·tion·ar·ies**) a person who tries to prevent (political) progress or change: *The reactionaries in the party oppose any form of gun control.* ▶ **re·ac·tion·ar·y** ***adj.***

**re·ac·ti·vate** /ˌriˈæktəveɪt/ ***verb*** [T] (*written*) to make sth start working or happening again after a period of time

**re·ac·tive** /riˈæktɪv/ ***adj.*** **1** (*formal*) showing a reaction or response: *The police presented a reactive rather than preventive strategy against crime.* ➲ Compare **proactive**. **2** (in chemistry) tending to show chemical change when mixed with another substance: *highly reactive substances*

**re·ac·tor** /riˈæktər/ ***noun*** [C] = NUCLEAR REACTOR

★**read** /rid/ ***verb*** (*pt, pp* **read** /rɛd/) **1** [I,T] to look at words and understand them: *In their first years in school, children learn to read and write.* ◇ *Don't bother me – I'm reading.* ◇ *Have you read any good books lately?* ◇ *I read an interesting article about Japan recently.* ◇ *I read in the paper that they found a cure for migraines.* **2** [I,T] **read (sb) (sth); read sth (to sb)** to say written words to sb: *My father used to read me stories when I was little.* ◇ *Read that sentence to me again – I didn't understand it.* ◇ *I hate reading out loud.* **3** [T] to be able to see and understand sth: *Can you read music?* ◇ (*figurative*) *She doesn't know what you're thinking. She can't read your mind.* **4** [T] to show sth; to have sth written on it: *The sign read "Keep Right."* ◇ *What does the thermometer read?*

PHR V **read sth into sth** to think that there is meaning in sth that it may not really have: *Don't*



R

*read too much into the letter. They're only asking you for an interview, not offering you the job.*
**read sth out** to read sth to other people

**read·a·ble** /'ridəbl/ ***adj.*** easy or pleasant to read: *a highly readable overview of the Civil War*

★**read·er** /'ridər/ ***noun*** [C] **1** a person who reads sth (a particular newspaper, magazine, type of book, etc.) **2** (with an adjective) a person who reads (in a particular way): *a fast/slow reader*

**read·er·ship** /'ridərʃɪp/ ***noun*** [sing.] the number of people who regularly read a particular newspaper, magazine, etc.

**read·i·ly** /'rɛdl·i/ ***adv.*** **1** easily, without difficulty: *Most vegetables are readily available at this time of year.* **2** without hesitating: *He readily admitted that he was wrong.*

**read·i·ness** /'rɛdinəs/ ***noun*** [U] **1** the state of being ready or prepared **2** willingness: *The bank has indicated its readiness to loan him the money.*

★**read·ing** /'ridɪŋ/ ***noun*** [U] **1** what you do when you read sth: *I haven't had time to do much reading lately.* ◇ *On the form she described her interests as reading and tennis.* ◇ *This report makes for interesting reading* (= reading it is an interesting thing to do). **2** the figure or measurement that is shown on a piece of equipment: *a reading of 20°*

'**reading week** ***noun*** [C] (*Cdn*) a week, usually halfway through a university semester, during which there are no classes, so that students can concentrate on their reading, research, etc.

**re·ad·just** /ˌriə'dʒʌst/ ***verb*** **1** [I,T] **readjust (to sth)** to get used to being in a situation again that you have been in before: *After her divorce, it took her a long time to readjust to being alone again.* **2** [T] to change the position or organization of sth again in order to make it correct ▸ **re·ad·just·ment** ***noun*** [C,U]

★**read·y**[1] /'rɛdi/ ***adj.*** **1 ready (for sb/sth); ready (to do sth)** prepared and able to be used or to do sth: *Dinner will be ready in ten minutes.* ◇ *The car will be ready for you to pick up Friday.* ◇ *He isn't ready for his driving test – he hasn't had enough practice.* ◇ *I can't talk now – I'm getting ready to go out.* **2 ready to do sth** willing to do sth: *You know me – I'm always ready to help.* **3** in a place which makes it possible for you to use or reach it easily and quickly: *Have your ticket ready before you get on the bus.*

**read·y**[2] /'rɛdi/ ***verb*** [T] (*pres. part.* **read·y·ing**; *3rd person sing. pres.* **read·ies**; *pt, pp* **read·ied**) (*formal*) **ready sb/yourself/sth (for sth)** to prepare sb/yourself/sth for sth: *Western companies were readying themselves for a new challenge from Eastern markets.*

**read·y**[3] /'rɛdi/ ***adv.*** (before a past participle) already; previously: *ready-mixed concrete*

ˌ**ready-'made** ***adj.*** already prepared and ready for use, not made especially for you: *You can buy ready-made reading glasses now.* ◇ (*figurative*) *He always has a ready-made answer to every question.*

**re·af·firm** /ˌriə'fərm/ ***verb*** [T] (*written*) to state sth again in order to emphasize that it is still true

**real**[1] /ril/ ***adj.*** **1** actually existing, not imagined: *The program contained interviews with real people* (= not actors). ◇ *This isn't a real word – I made it up.* **2** actually true, not what may appear to be true: *The name he gave to the police wasn't his real name.* ◇ *She said she had missed the bus, but that's not the real reason why she was late.* **3** natural, not artificial: *This shirt is real silk.* **4** (used when you are making what you say stronger, usually when you are saying how bad sth is) big; complete: *The meal I cooked was a real disaster.* ◇ *Money is a real problem for us right now.*

IDM **be for real** (*informal*) to be genuine and not imagined or pretended: *OK, that was just for practice – but this time it's for real!* ◇ *How could Darren say a thing like that – is he for real?* (= I am shocked and surprised by what he said.)

**real life; the real world** the way that things in general actually are, not the way sb imagines they are: *He looks shorter in real life than he does on TV.* ◇ *That's not how things work in the real world.*

**the real thing 1** something genuine, not artificial: *This painting is just a copy. The real thing is in a museum.* **2** the best example of sth: *She's had boyfriends before, but this time she says it's the real thing* (= real love).

**real**[2] /ril/ ***adv.*** (*informal*) very; really: *It was real nice of you to help me.*

★'**real eˌstate** (*also* **realty**) ***noun*** [U] property that cannot be moved, such as land and buildings

'**real eˌstate ˌagent** (*also* **Realtor™**) ***noun*** [C] a person who buys and sells houses and land for other people

**re·a·lign** /ˌriə'laɪn/ ***verb*** [T] (*written*) **1** to change the position or direction of sth in relation to sth else **2** to make changes to sth in order to adapt it to a new situation: *The company has been forced to realign its operations in the area.* **3 realign yourself (with sb/sth)** to change your opinions, policies, etc. so that they are the same as those of another person, group, etc. ▸ **re·a·lign·ment** ***noun*** [U,C]: *the realignment of personal goals*

**re·al·ism** /'riəlɪzəm/ ***noun*** [U] **1** behavior that shows that you accept the facts of a situation and are not too influenced by your feelings **2** (in art, literature, etc.) showing things as they really are

**re·al·ist** /'riəlɪst/ ***noun*** [C] a person who accepts the facts of life and situations, and who thinks and behaves according to them: *I'm a realist – I don't expect the impossible.*

★**re·al·is·tic** /ˌriə'lɪstɪk/ ***adj.*** **1** accepting the facts of a situation (not believing or making yourself believe that they are different): *Be realistic! You're not going to get a job like that without any experience.* ◇ *a realistic price* **2** showing things as they really are: *a realistic description of the lives of ordinary people in rural Alaska* **3** not real but appearing to be real: *The monsters in the movie were very realistic.* OPP The opposite for **1**, **2** and **3** is **unrealistic**. ▸ **re·al·is·ti·cal·ly** /-kli/ ***adv.***: *Think about your future realistically.*

★**re·al·i·ty** /ri'æləṭi/ ***noun*** (*pl.* **re·al·i·ties**) **1** [U] the way life really is, not the way it may appear to be or what you would like it to be: *It was a great vacation, but now it's back to reality.* **2** [C] the way sth really is when you experience it: *We had hoped that things would get easier, but the reality was very different.*

◇ *The realities of living in a foreign country were too much for Susan and she went home.* **3** [C] something that really exists, not sth that is imagined: *Death is a reality that everyone has to face eventually.*

IDM **in reality** in fact, really (not the way sth appears or has been described): *People say this is an exciting city, but in reality it's pretty boring.*

**re'ality check** *noun* [C, usually sing.] (*informal*) a time when you stop working, talking, etc. in order to consider what is really important in a situation, and not what you think is important: *I think those politicians are in need of a reality check.*

★**re·al·ize** /'riəlaɪz/ *verb* [T] **1** to know and understand that sth is true or that sth has happened: *I'm sorry I mentioned the subject – I didn't realize how much it upset you.* ◇ *Do you realize how much work I did today?* **2** to become aware of sth or that sth has happened, usually some time later: *When I got home, I realized that I had left my keys at the office.* ◇ *I'm starting to realize that this job isn't as easy as I thought it was.* **3** to make sth (an ambition, hope, etc.) become reality: *She finally realized her ambition to see the Taj Mahal.* ▶ **re·al·i·za·tion** /ˌriələ'zeɪʃn/ *noun* [U]: *He was suddenly hit by the realization that he might die.* ◇ *Becoming Chief Executive Officer was the realization of all her dreams.*

★**re·al·ly** /'rili; 'rɪli/ *adv.* **1** actually; in fact; truly: *I couldn't believe it was really happening.* ◇ *He said that he was sorry, but I don't think he really meant it.* ◇ *She wasn't really mad – she was only pretending.* ◇ *Is it really true?* **2** very; very much: *I'm really tired.* ◇ *He really enjoys his job.* ◇ *Are you really sure?* ◇ *I really tried, but I couldn't do it.* **3** (used as a question for expressing surprise, interest, doubt, etc.): *"She left her husband." "Really? When did that happen?"* ◇ *"He's a very happy person." "Really? I've never seen him smile."* **4** (used in questions when you are expecting sb to answer "No"): *You don't really expect me to believe that, do you?* **5** (*informal*) (used to agree with sth that sb has just said): *"Kevin's such a jerk." "Yeah, really."*

IDM **not really** not completely: *I'm not really sure this is the right way.* ◇ *"Did you have to wait a long time?" "No, not really."*

**realm** /rɛlm/ *noun* [C, usually sing.] an area of activity, interest or knowledge: *These beliefs are completely outside the realm of science.*

**'real-time** *adj.* (only *before* a noun) (used about computer systems and information) able to respond immediately so that the user is not aware of a delay: *real-time Internet video games* ▶ **'real time** *noun* [U]: *The Web site shows images taken from the space shuttle in real time.*

**Re·al·tor™** /'riltər/ *noun* [C] = REAL ESTATE AGENT

**re·al·ty** /'rilti/ *noun* [U] = REAL ESTATE

**ream** /rim/ *noun* **1** [C] (*technical*) 500 sheets of paper **2 reams** [pl.] (*informal*) a large quantity of writing or paper: *The book contains reams of information.*

**reap** /rip/ *verb* [T] to cut and pick up a crop (corn, wheat, etc.): (*figurative*) *Work hard now and you'll reap the benefits later on.*

**re·ap·pear** /ˌriə'pɪr/ *verb* [I] to appear again or be seen again: *If any symptoms reappear, see your doctor immediately.* ▶ **re·ap·pear·ance** /-rəns/ *noun* [C,U]

★**rear¹** /rɪr/ *noun* [sing.] **1 the rear** the back part: *There are some empty seats in the rear of the bus.* ◇ *I only saw him from the rear* (= from behind). **2** (*also informal* ˌ**rear 'end**) the part of your body that you sit on; buttocks

IDM **bring up the rear** to be the last one in a race, a line of people, etc.: *The fastest runners are nearing the finish line now, with Ben Smith bringing up the rear.*

★**rear²** /rɪr/ *adj.* (only *before* a noun) (used especially about parts of a car) placed at the back: *the rear window* ◇ *rear lights*

**rear³** /rɪr/ *verb* **1** [T] to care for and educate a child until it is an adult: *She was born and reared in Kentucky.* **2** [I] **rear (up)** (used about horses) to stand on the back legs

ˌ**rear 'end** *noun* [sing.] = REAR¹ (2)

ˌ**rear-'end** *verb* [T] (*informal*) to hit the back of another car while you are driving: *We got rear-ended on Lake Street today.*

**re·ar·range** /ˌriə'reɪndʒ/ *verb* [T] to change the way that sth is organized or arranged: *We rearranged the living room to make more space.* ◇ *I'll have to rearrange my schedule for next week.*

**rear·view mir·ror** /ˌrɪrvyu 'mɪrər/ (*also* **rear-view 'mirror**) *noun* [C] a mirror fixed inside a car, in which a driver can see the vehicle or road behind

★**rea·son¹** /'rizn/ *noun* **1** [C,U] **reason (for sth/for doing sth); reason (why.../that...)** the cause of sth; sth that explains why sth happens or exists: *What's your reason for being so late?* ◇ *Is there any reason why you couldn't tell me this before?* ◇ *The main reason that I'm calling you is to ask for a favor.* ◇ *For some reason or other, they can't give us an answer until next week* (= I don't know what the reason is). ◇ *She quit her job for personal reasons.* **2** [C,U] **reason (for sth); reason (to do sth)** something that shows that it is right or logical to do sth: *There is a reason for doing things this way – it's cheaper.* ◇ *I chose this color for a reason* (= the reason was important). ◇ *He had no reason to be mean to me – I never did anything to him.* ◇ *You have every reason* (= you are completely right) *to be upset, considering what happened to you.* ◇ *I have reason to believe that you lied to me.* **3** [U] the ability to think and to make sensible decisions: *Any new law must be based on reason, not emotion.*

IDM **(do anything) within reason** if it is not too extreme or completely unacceptable: *I'll pay anything within reason for a ticket.*

**rea·son²** /'rizn/ *verb* [I,T] to form a judgment or opinion, after thinking about sth in a logical way

PHR V **reason with sb** to talk to sb in order to persuade him/her to behave or think in a more reasonable or less extreme way: *The police tried to reason with the gunman, but he refused to put down his rifle.*

★**rea·son·a·ble** /'rizn·əbl/ *adj.* **1** (used about people) willing to listen to other people's opinions; not asking too much; fair: *I tried to be reasonable even though I was really mad.* **2** (used about actions, decisions, etc.) resulting from good reasons;

R

logical: *That seems like a reasonable decision under the circumstances.* **3** (used about opinions or about what you expect people to do) not expecting too much; fair: *I think it's reasonable to expect people to keep their promises.* **4** (used about a price) not too high; not higher than it should be: *It was great food and the prices were very reasonable!* OPP The opposite for **1**, **2**, **3** and **4** is **unreasonable**. **5** fairly good; not bad: *His work is of a reasonable standard.* **6** (used about amounts or numbers) not very large: *They have a reasonable amount of money, but they certainly aren't rich.*

**rea·son·a·bly** /ˈrizn·əbli/ ***adv.*** **1** fairly or quite (but not very): *The weather was reasonably good but not terrific.* **2** in a reasonable way: *If you think about my suggestion reasonably, you'll see that I'm right.*

**rea·son·ing** /ˈrizn·ɪŋ/ ***noun*** [U] **reasoning (behind sth)** the process of thinking and making a judgment or decision: *What's the reasoning behind his sudden decision to quit?*

**re·as·sur·ance** /ˌriəˈʃʊrəns/ ***noun*** [C,U] an act of reassuring or being reassured: *I need some reassurance that I'm doing things the right way.* ◇ *The government issued reassurances that the area is safe.*

**re·as·sure** /ˌriəˈʃʊr/ ***verb*** [T] to say or do sth in order to make sb feel less frightened, worried or nervous: *I keep trying to reassure my parents that my friends don't take drugs, but they just don't believe me.*

**re·as·sur·ing** /ˌriəˈʃʊrɪŋ/ ***adj.*** causing sb to feel less worried, frightened or nervous ▸ **re·as·sur·ing·ly *adv.***

**re·bate** /ˈribeɪt/ ***noun*** [C] a sum of money that is given back to you because of a special offer or because you have paid too much: *a $500 rebate on a new car*

**re·bel¹** /ˈrɛbl/ ***noun*** [C] **1** a person who fights against his/her country's government because he/she wants things to change: *Rebels have taken control of the capital.* **2** a person who fights against or refuses to cooperate with authority, society, an order, a law, etc.: *He had a reputation as a rebel in high school.*

R

**re·bel²** /rɪˈbɛl/ (**re·bel̲ling**; **re·bel̲led**) ***verb*** [I] **rebel (against sb/sth)** **1** to fight against authority, society, an order, a law, etc.: *She rebelled against her parents by dropping out of high school.* **2** to fight against the government in order to bring change

**re·bel·lion** /rɪˈbɛlyən/ ***noun*** [C,U] fighting against authority or the government: *The rebellion ended in failure when all the leaders were shot.* ◇ *Burning the flag was an act of open rebellion.*

**re·bel·lious** /rɪˈbɛlyəs/ ***adj.*** not doing what authority, society, etc. wants you to do: *rebellious teenagers*

**re·birth** /ˌriˈbərθ; ˈribərθ/ ***noun*** [U, sing.] **1** a period of new life, growth or activity: *the seasonal cycle of death and rebirth* **2** a spiritual change when a person's faith becomes stronger or they change to another religion (**convert**)

**re·boot** /ˌriˈbut/ ***verb*** [I,T] (*computing*) if you reboot a computer or it reboots, you switch it off and then start it again immediately

**re·born** /ˌriˈbɔrn/ ***adj.*** **1** having become active again: *a reborn version of social democracy* **2** having experienced a complete spiritual change: *reborn evangelical Christians* ➲ Look at **born-again**.

**re·bound¹** /ˈribaʊnd; rɪˈbaʊnd/ ***verb*** **1** [I] to hit sth and then go in a different direction: *The puck rebounded off a defender and went into the goal.* **2** [I,T] (in basketball) to catch and control the ball after sb has tried unsuccessfully to throw it through the basket: *Rodman quickly rebounded and scored the winning basket.*

**re·bound²** /ˈribaʊnd/ ***noun*** [C] **1** a sudden increase or improvement after a period of decreasing or getting worse: *last month's rebound in home prices* **2** (in sports) a ball or puck that hits sth and then goes in a different direction **3** (in basketball) an act of catching the ball after sb has tried unsuccessfully to throw it through the basket

IDM **on the rebound** **1** increasing or improving again, after a period of getting worse: *California's economy is on the rebound.* **2** (*informal*) upset, sad and confused because of the end of a romantic relationship: *I'd never go out with a guy who's on the rebound!*

**re·buff** /rɪˈbʌf/ ***noun*** [C] (*formal*) an unkind refusal of a friendly offer, request or suggestion: *Any attempt to win her friendship was met with rebuffs.* ▸ **re·buff *verb*** [T]: *They rebuffed her request for help.*

**re·build** /ˌriˈbɪld/ ***verb*** [T] (*pt, pp* **re·built** /ˌriˈbɪlt/) to build again: *Following the storm, dozens of houses will have to be rebuilt.* ◇ (*figurative*) *She's trying to rebuild her life now that her husband is dead.*

**re·buke** /rɪˈbyuk/ ***verb*** [T] (often passive) **rebuke sb (for sth/for doing sth)** (*formal*) to speak severely to sb because he/she has done sth wrong: *The company was publicly rebuked for having neglected safety procedures.* SYN **reprimand** ▸ **re·buke *noun*** [C, U]: *They were silenced by her stinging rebuke.*

**re·bus** /ˈribʌs/ ***noun*** [C] (*pl.* **re·bus·es**) a combination of pictures and single letters which represent a word that must be guessed as a game

**re·but** /rɪˈbʌt/ ***verb*** [T] (**re·but̲ting**; **re·but̲ted**) (*formal*) to say or prove that a statement or criticism is false SYN **refute** ▸ **re·but·tal** /rɪˈbʌt̬l/ ***noun*** [C, U]

★**re·call¹** /rɪˈkɔl/ ***verb*** [T] **1** to remember sth (a fact, event, action, etc.) from the past: *I don't recall exactly when I first met her.* ◇ *She couldn't recall meeting him before.* **2** to ask people to bring a product back to the store where they bought it because of a possible problem: *The manufacturer is recalling all washing machines made in 2001.*

**re·call²** /ˈrikɔl/ ***noun*** [C] a request or an order from a company for people to return a particular type of product to the store where they bought it because of a possible problem: *a voluntary recall of all 2002 station wagons*

**re·cap** /ˈrikæp; riˈkæp/ (*informal*) ***noun*** [C, usually sing.] a short summary which repeats the main points of sth: *Here is a brief recap of the events leading up to the trial:...*

**re·cap·ture** /ˌriˈkæptʃər/ ***verb*** [I,T] **1** to capture again a person or an animal that has escaped **2** to create or experience again a feeling or period from the past: *The movie magnificently recaptures the lives of ordinary people in the 1930s.*

**re·cede** /rɪˈsid/ ***verb*** [I] to move away or seem to move away and begin to disappear: *Flood waters have now begun to recede in most areas.* ➲ If a person's **hairline is receding**, he is losing his hair from the front of his head.

**re·ceipt** /rɪˈsit/ ***noun*** **1** [C] (*also* **ˈsales slip**) a piece of paper that is given to show that you have paid for sth: *Keep the receipt in case you want to exchange the sweater.* ◇ *Can I get a receipt for that?* **2** [U] **receipt (of sth)** (*formal*) the act of receiving: *Payment must be made within seven days of receipt of the shipment.*

**re·ceiv·a·ble** /rɪˈsivəbl/ ***adj.*** (usually after a noun) (used about bills, accounts, etc.) for which money has not yet been received: *accounts receivable*

★**re·ceive** /rɪˈsiv/ ***verb*** [T] **1 receive sth (from sb/sth)** (*formal*) to get or take sth that sb sends or gives to you: *The independent candidate received only 210 votes in the election.* ◇ *We received hundreds of cards and letters from our supporters.* ◇ *Mrs. DeAngelis received her master's degree in 1989.* ➲ **Get** is less formal than **receive** in this sense. **2** (*formal*) to have medical treatment: *Stan received a liver transplant last year.* ➲ **Have** is less formal than **receive** in this sense. **3** (often passive) to react to sth (news, ideas, work, etc.) in a particular way: *My suggestions at the committee meeting were received in silence.*

**re·ceiv·er** /rɪˈsivər/ ***noun*** [C] **1** the part of a telephone that is used for listening and speaking

> NOTE To answer or make a telephone call you **pick up** or **lift** the receiver. To end a telephone call you **put down** the receiver or you **hang up**. ➲ picture at **telephone**.

**2** (in football) a player who plays in a position in which the ball can be caught when it is being passed forward

★**re·cent** /ˈrisənt/ ***adj.*** (usually *before* a noun) having happened, been done or produced a short time ago: *There have been many changes in recent years.* ◇ *In a recent interview, the mayor promised to hire more police.* ◇ *This is a recent picture of my son.*

★**re·cent·ly** /ˈrisəntli/ ***adv.*** **1** a short time ago: *I don't know her very well – I only met her recently.* ◇ *She worked here until fairly recently.* **2** during a period between not long ago and now: *Have you seen Paul recently?* ◇ *She hasn't been feeling well recently.*

> NOTE **Recently** can refer to both a point in time and a period of time. If it refers to a point in time, use the past simple tense: *He died recently.* If it refers to a period of time, use the present perfect or present perfect continuous tense: *I haven't done anything interesting recently.* ◇ *She's been working hard recently.* **Lately** can only refer to a period of time. Use only the present perfect or present perfect continuous tense: *I've seen a lot of movies lately.* ◇ *I've been spending too much money lately.*

**re·cep·ta·cle** /rɪˈsɛptəkl/ ***noun*** [C] (*formal*) a container: *a trash receptacle*

**re·cep·tion** /rɪˈsɛpʃn/ ***noun*** **1** [C] a formal party to celebrate sth (especially a wedding) or to welcome an important person: *Their wedding reception was held at a local hotel.* ◇ *There will be an official reception at the embassy for the visiting ambassadors.* **2** [sing.] the way people react to sth: *The play got a mixed reception* (= some people liked it, some people didn't). ◇ *The President received a warm reception during his visit to the state* (= people showed that they liked him). **3** [U] the quality of radio or television signals: *We can't get good TV reception here in the valley.*

**re·cep·tion·ist** /rɪˈsɛpʃn·ɪst/ ***noun*** [C] a person who works in a hotel, an office, etc. answering the telephone, dealing with guests, customers, visitors, etc.

**re·cep·tive** /rɪˈsɛptɪv/ ***adj.*** **receptive (to sth)** willing to listen to new ideas, suggestions, etc.

**re·cess** /ˈrisɛs; rɪˈsɛs/ ***noun*** **1** [U] a period of free time during the day at school, especially after lunch: *We'll finish the story after recess.* ➲ Look at the note at **pause**. **2** [C,U] a period of time when a government, a court of law, etc. stops its work: *The judge will take a short recess to consider his decision.*

**re·cessed** /ˈrisɛst; rɪˈsɛst/ ***adj.*** built or fitted into a wall or a surface and not sticking out: *recessed ceiling lights* ◇ *a recessed alcove/doorway*

**re·ces·sion** /rɪˈsɛʃn/ ***noun*** [C] a period of time when the businesses and industries of a country are not successful: *The country is now in a recession.* ➲ Look also at **depression**.

**re·charge** /ˌriˈtʃɑrdʒ/ ***verb*** [I,T] **1** to fill a battery with electrical power; to be filled with electrical power: *He plugged his cell phone in to recharge it.* ◇ *The drill takes about three hours to recharge.* **2** [I] (*informal*) to get back your strength and energy by resting for a time: *We needed the break in order to recharge.*

IDM **recharge your batteries** to get back your strength and energy by resting for a while

▸ **re·charge·a·ble** /ˌriˈtʃɑrdʒəbl/ ***adj.***: *rechargeable batteries*

**rec·i·pe** /ˈrɛsəpi/ ***noun*** [C] **1 a recipe (for sth)** the instructions for cooking or preparing sth to eat. A recipe tells you what to use (**the ingredients**) and what to do. **2 a recipe for sth** the way to get or produce sth: *What's the recipe for a happy marriage?*

**re·cip·i·ent** /rɪˈsɪpiənt/ ***noun*** [C] (*formal*) a person who receives sth

**re·cip·ro·cal** /rɪˈsɪprəkl/ ***adj.*** both given and received: *The arrangement is reciprocal. They help us and we help them.*

**re·cip·ro·cate** /rɪˈsɪprəkeɪt/ ***verb*** [I,T] to behave or feel toward sb in the same way as he/she behaves or feels toward you: *The favor was reciprocated.* ◇ *Perhaps I was expected to reciprocate with some remark of my own.* ▸ **re·cip·ro·ca·tion** ***noun*** [U]

**re·cit·al** /rɪˈsaɪţl/ ***noun*** [C] a public performance of music or poetry, by one person or a small group: *a piano recital* ➲ Look at **concert**.

**re·cite** /rɪˈsaɪt/ ***verb*** [I,T] to say a piece of writing (especially a poem) or a list from memory: *He can recite the names and dates of all the Presidents of the United States.*

**reck·less** /ˈrɛkləs/ ***adj.*** not thinking about whether what you are doing is dangerous or might have bad results: *reckless driving* ▸ **reck·less·ly** ***adv.***



R

**reck·on** /ˈrɛkən/ ***verb*** [T] **1** (*informal*) (used especially in the southern U.S.) to think, suppose or believe: *Billy Joe reckons we'd better start heading home.* **2** to calculate approximately or guess: *The plant's annual production is reckoned to be around 50 million units.*

PHR V **reckon with sb/sth** to expect sth; to think about sth as a possible problem: *When they decided to buy a bigger house, they didn't reckon with the enormous cost involved.*

**re·claim** /rɪˈkleɪm/ ***verb*** [T] **1 reclaim sth (from sb/sth)** to get back sth that you have lost, or to get back control of sth that you controlled in the past: *We hope to reclaim our position as the nation's number one auto manufacturer.* **2** to make land suitable for use: *farmland that has been reclaimed from the spreading desert*

**re·cline** /rɪˈklaɪn/ ***verb*** [I] to lie back or down in order to be more comfortable: *If you want to recline, press the button on the side of your seat.*

**re·clin·er** /rɪˈklaɪnər/ (*also* **reˈcliner chair**) ***noun*** [C] a soft comfortable chair with a back that can be pushed back at an angle so that you can lean back in it

**re·clin·ing** /rɪˈklaɪnɪŋ/ ***adj.*** lying back; able to be adjusted so that you can lie back: *The car has reclining front seats.*

**rec·luse** /ˈrɛklus; rɪˈklus/ ***noun*** [C] a person who lives alone and likes to avoid other people: *to lead the life of a recluse* ▸ **re·clu·sive** ***adj.***: *a reclusive millionaire/lifestyle*

★**rec·og·ni·tion** /ˌrɛkəgˈnɪʃn/ ***noun*** [U] the act of recognizing sth or of showing or receiving respect: *He showed no sign of recognition when he passed me in the street.* ◇ *She has received public recognition for her services to the community.*

**re·cog·ni·zance** /rɪˈkɑgnəzəns; -ˈkɑnə-/ ***noun*** [U] (in law) a promise by sb who is accused of a crime to appear in a court of law on a particular date; a sum of money paid as a guarantee of this promise: *He was released **on his own recognizance**.*

R

★**rec·og·nize** /ˈrɛkəgnaɪz/ ***verb*** [T] **1 recognize sb/sth (by/from sth)** to know again sb/sth that you have seen or heard before: *I recognized him, but I couldn't remember his name.* ◇ *This neighborhood has changed so much since the last time I was here that I hardly recognize it now.* **2** to accept or admit that sth is true: *I recognize that some of my ideas are unrealistic.* **3** to accept sth officially (usually done by institutions or governments): *My degree is not recognized in other countries.* **4** to show that you think sth that sb has done is good: *The company gave her a special gift to recognize her long years of service.* ▸ **rec·og·niz·a·ble** /ˈrɛkəgnaɪzəbl; ˌrɛkəgˈnaɪzəbl/ ***adj.*** ▸ **rec·og·niz·a·bly** /-əbli/ ***adv.***

**re·coil** /rɪˈkɔɪl/ ***verb*** [I] (*written*) to move your body quickly away from sb/sth because you find him/her/it frightening or unpleasant: *She recoiled from his touch.* ◇ *He **recoiled in horror** at the sight of the corpse.*

**rec·ol·lect** /ˌrɛkəˈlɛkt/ ***verb*** [T] (*formal*) (not used in the progressive tenses) to remember sth, especially by making an effort to remember it: *She could no longer recollect the details of the letter.* ◇ *I don't recollect what he said.*

**rec·ol·lec·tion** /ˌrɛkəˈlɛkʃn/ ***noun*** **1** [U] **recollection (of sb/sth)** the ability to remember: *I have no recollection of promising to loan you any money.* **2** [C, usually pl.] something that you remember: *I have only vague recollections of my grandfather.*

★**rec·om·mend** /ˌrɛkəˈmɛnd/ ***verb*** [T] **1** to say that sb/sth is good and that it would be liked or useful: *Which movie would you recommend?* ◇ *We hope that you'll recommend this restaurant to all your friends.* ◇ *The manager of her department recommended her for a promotion.* ◇ *Doctors don't always recommend medication as the best treatment for every illness.*

> NOTE Notice that we cannot use **recommend** with an indirect object immediately after it. So we CANNOT say e.g: *Can you recommend me a good hotel?* or: *I can recommend you a very nice restaurant.* We must say instead: *Can you recommend a good hotel?* or: *I can recommend a very nice restaurant.*

**2** to strongly suggest sth; to tell sb what you strongly believe he/she should do: *My doctor recommended a long period of rest.* ◇ *I recommend that you get some legal advice.* ◇ *I wouldn't recommend traveling on your own. It could be dangerous.*

> NOTE Note the form of the verb which must be used after **recommend/recommendation that...**, **suggest/suggestion that...**, etc.: *We recommend that Susan's proposal* be *approved.* ◇ *I suggest that he* see *a doctor.* ◇ *They requested that the newspaper* not print *their real names.* ◇ *The salesclerk ignored our demand that she* give *us our money back.*

**rec·om·men·da·tion** /ˌrɛkəmənˈdeɪʃn/ ***noun*** [C] **1** a statement about what should be done in a particular situation: *After the train crash, an independent commission made several recommendations on how safety could be improved.* **2** an official letter from an employer, a teacher, etc. that says that sb is suitable for a job, etc.: *I asked my former boss to write a recommendation for me.*

**rec·om·pense** /ˈrɛkəmpɛns/ ***noun*** [U] **recompense (for sth/sb)** (*formal*) something, usually money, that you are given because you have suffered in some way, or as a payment for sth: *There must be adequate recompense for workers who lose their jobs.* ◇ *I received $15,000 **in recompense** for loss of earnings.*

**rec·on·cile** /ˈrɛkənsaɪl/ ***verb*** **1** [I,T] (often passive) **reconcile (with sb)** (to cause people) to become friendly with or close to each other again: *After years of not speaking to each other, she and her parents were eventually reconciled.* **2** [T] **reconcile sth (with sth)** to find a way to make two things (ideas, situations, statements, etc.) be possible together, when in fact they seem to oppose each other: *She finds it difficult to reconcile her career ambitions with her responsibilities to her children.*

**rec·on·cil·i·a·tion** /ˌrɛkənˌsɪliˈeɪʃn/ ***noun*** [C,U] becoming friendly or close again (after an argument, etc.): *to bring about a reconciliation between the two sides*

**re·con·di·tion** /ˌrikənˈdɪʃn/ ***verb*** [T] (usually passive) to repair a machine or a piece of equipment so that it is in good condition and works well

**re·con·nais·sance** /rɪˈkɑnəsəns; -zəns/ ***noun*** [C,U] the study of a place or area for military reasons

**re·con·sid·er** /ˌrikənˈsɪdər/ ***verb*** [I,T] to think again about sth (a decision, situation, etc.): *Public protests have forced the government to reconsider its policy.*

**re·con·sti·tute** /ˌriˈkɑnstətut/ ***verb*** [T] **1 reconstitute sth/itself (as sth)** (*formal*) to form an organization or a group again in a different way: *The group reconstituted itself as a political party.* **2** (usually passive) to bring dried food, etc. back to its original form by adding water: *reconstituted orange juice*

**re·con·struct** /ˌrikənˈstrʌkt/ ***verb*** [T] **1** to build again sth that has been destroyed or damaged: *The cathedral was reconstructed after the fire.* **2** to get a full description or picture of sth using the facts that are known: *The police are trying to reconstruct the victim's movements on the day of the murder.* ▸ **re·con·struc·tion** /-ˈstrʌkʃn/ ***noun*** [C,U]: *the reconstruction of the city after the earthquake* ◇ *a reconstruction of the crime using actors*

★**re·cord[1]** /ˈrɛkərd/ ***noun*** [C] **1 record (of sth)** a written account of what has happened, been done, etc.: *The teachers keep records of the students' progress.* ◇ *medical records* **2** (*also* **album**) a large, thin, round, usually black piece of plastic which can store music and other sound so that you can play it when you want: *to listen to/play some records* ◇ *a record collection* **3** the best performance or the highest or lowest level, etc. ever reached in sth, especially in sports: *Who holds the **world record** for the high jump?* ◇ *to set a new record* ◇ *to break a record* ◇ *We've had so little rain this year – I'm sure it must be a record* (= the lowest amount ever). ◇ *He did it **in record time*** (= very fast). **4** [sing.] the facts, events, etc. that are known (and sometimes written down) about sb/sth: *The police said that the man had **a criminal record*** (= he had been found guilty of crimes in the past). ◇ *This airline has a poor safety record.*

IDM **off the record** (used about sth that sb says) not officially; not intended to be published: *She told me off the record that the school was going to close.*

**on the record** (used about sth that sb says) officially; intended to be published: *The senator was not willing to speak to us on the record.*

**set the record straight** to correct a misunderstanding by telling sb the true facts

★**re·cord[2]** /rɪˈkɔrd/ ***verb*** **1** [T] to write sth down, put it into a computer, film it, etc. so that it can be used later and will not be forgotten: *All property sales are recorded in the county courthouse.* **2** [I,T] to put music, a movie, a program, etc. onto a cassette or record so that it can be listened to or watched again later: *Quiet, everybody! We're recording.* ◇ *The band recently recorded a new album.* ◇ *I forgot to record my favorite TV show last night.*

**ˈrecord-ˌbreaking** ***adj.*** (only *before* a noun) the best, fastest, highest, etc. ever: *She finished the race in record-breaking time.*

**re·cord·er** /rɪˈkɔrdər/ ***noun*** [C] **1** a machine for recording sound and/or pictures: *a tape recorder* ◇ *a video recorder* **2** a type of musical instrument that is often played by children. You play it by blowing through it and covering the holes in it with your fingers. ➲ picture at **flute**.

★**re·cord·ing** /rɪˈkɔrdɪŋ/ ***noun*** **1** [C] sound or pictures that have been put onto a cassette, record or movie: *I taped the concert last week, but it's not a very good recording.* **2** [U] the process of making cassettes, records or movies: *a recording studio*

**ˈrecord ˌplayer** ***noun*** [C] a machine for playing RECORDS[1] (2) in order to listen to the music, etc. on them

**re·count[1]** /rɪˈkaʊnt/ ***verb*** [T] (*formal*) **recount sth (to sb)** to tell sb about sth, especially sth that you have experienced: *She was asked to recount the details of the conversation to the court.*

**re·count[2]** /ˈrikaʊnt/ ***noun*** [usually sing.] an act of counting sth again, especially votes in an election: *The defeated candidate demanded a recount.*

**re·coup** /rɪˈkup/ ***verb*** [T] to get back an amount of money that you have spent or lost: *We hope to recoup our initial investment in the first year.*

**re·course** /ˈrikɔrs; rɪˈkɔrs/ ***noun*** [U] (*formal*) the fact of having to, or being able to, use sth that can provide help in a difficult situation: *Your only recourse is legal action.* ◇ *She made a complete recovery **without recourse to** surgery.* ◇ *The administration, when necessary, **has recourse to** the armed forces.*

★**re·cov·er** /rɪˈkʌvər/ ***verb*** **1** [I] **recover (from sth)** to become well again after you have been sick: *It took him two months to recover from the operation.* **2** [I] **recover (from sth)** to get back to normal again after a bad experience, etc.: *It took her a long time to recover from her father's death.* **3** [T] **recover sth (from sb/sth)** to find or get back sth that has been lost or stolen: *Police recovered the stolen goods from a warehouse in South Chicago.* **4** [T] to get back a state of health, an ability to do sth, etc.: *He needs daily exercise if he's going to recover the use of his legs.* ◇ *She recovered consciousness in the ambulance.*

★**re·cov·er·y** /rɪˈkʌvəri/ ***noun*** **1** [sing., U] **recovery (from sth)** a return to good health after an illness or to a normal condition after a difficult period of time: *to make a good/quick/slow recovery* ◇ *Nobody is optimistic about the prospects of economic recovery this year.* **2** [U] **recovery (of sth/sb)** getting sth back: *He offered a reward for the recovery of the paintings.*

**rec·re·a·tion** /ˌrɛkriˈeɪʃn/ ***noun*** [U] doing activities that you enjoy when you are not working: *What do you do for recreation?* ◇ *The Recreation and Parks Department offers swimming lessons in the summer.* ➲ Look at **rec room**. ▸ **rec·re·a·tion·al** /ˌrɛkriˈeɪʃənl/ ***adj.***

**ˌrecreˌational ˈvehicle** ***noun*** [C] = RV

**re·crim·i·na·tion** /rɪˌkrɪməˈneɪʃn/ ***noun*** [C,U, usually pl.] an angry statement that sb makes accusing sb else of sth, especially in response to a similar statement from him/her: *bitter recriminations* ◇ *We spent the rest of the evening in mutual recrimination.* ▸ **re·crim·i·na·to·ry** /-ˈkrɪmənəˌtɔri/ ***adj.***

R

**rec room** /ˈrɛk rum; -rʊm/ (*also formal* **recreˈation room**) ***noun*** [C] (*informal*) **1** a room in a private house, usually in the basement, for watching TV, listening to music, playing games, etc. **2** a public room in a place of work, in a hospital, etc. that is used for social activities or games

**re·cruit[1]** /rɪˈkrut/ ***noun*** [C] a person who has just joined the army or another organization; a new member

**re·cruit[2]** /rɪˈkrut/ ***verb*** [I,T] to get sb to work as sth, to help with sth or to join sth, such as the military forces or a sports team: *to recruit young people into the army* ▸ **re·cruit·er** /rɪˈkrut̬ər/ ***noun*** [C] ▸ **re·cruit·ment** ***noun*** [U]

**rec·tal** /ˈrɛktl/ ***adj.*** (*medical*) relating to the end of the tube which solid waste passes through before leaving the body (**rectum**): *a rectal thermometer*

**rec·tan·gle** /ˈrɛktæŋgl/ ***noun*** [C] a shape with four straight sides and four angles of 90 degrees (**right angles**). Two of the sides are usually longer than the other two. ➲ picture at **shape**. ▸ **rec·tan·gu·lar** /rɛkˈtæŋgyələr/ ***adj.***

**rec·ti·fy** /ˈrɛktəfaɪ/ ***verb*** [T] (*pres. part.* **rec·ti·fy·ing**; *3rd person sing. pres.* **rec·ti·fies**; *pt, pp* **rec·ti·fied**) (*formal*) to change sth so that it is right: *All these errors will need to be rectified.*

**rec·tum** /ˈrɛktəm/ ***noun*** [C] (*pl.* **rec·tums** or **rec·ta** /-tə/) the end section of the tube through which solid waste leaves the body at the anus

**re·cu·per·ate** /rɪˈkupəreɪt/ ***verb*** [I] to get well again after an illness or injury ▸ **re·cu·per·a·tion** /rɪˌkupəˈreɪʃn/ ***noun*** [U]

**re·cur** /rɪˈkər/ ***verb*** [I] (**re·cur̲r̲ing**; **re·cur̲r̲ed**) to happen again or many times: *a recurring problem* ◇ *It was a theme that recurred in many of her books.* ▸ **re·cur·rence** /rɪˈkərəns/ ***noun*** [C,U] ▸ **re·cur·rent** /-ənt/ ***adj.***

**re·cy·cle** /riˈsaɪkl/ ***verb*** [T] **1** to process used objects and materials so that they can be used again: *recycled paper* ◇ *Aluminum cans can be recycled.* ◇ *We return our empty bottles to the store for recycling.* **2** to keep used objects and materials and use them again: (*figurative*) *She just keeps recycling the same old jokes.* ▸ **re·cy·cla·ble** /riˈsaɪkləbl/ ***adj.***: *Most plastics are recyclable.*

★**red[1]** /rɛd/ ***adj.*** (**red·der**; **red·dest**) **1** of the color of blood: *red wine* ◇ *The berries on that bush turn bright red in October.*

NOTE We use **crimson**, **maroon** and **scarlet** to describe different shades of red.

**2** (used about a person's face) a darker color than usual because of anger, sadness, shame, etc.: *He turned bright red when she talked to him.* **3** (used about a person's hair or an animal's fur) of a color between red, orange and brown: *She has red hair and freckles.*

IDM **a red herring** an idea or subject which takes people's attention away from what is really important

★**red[2]** /rɛd/ ***noun*** [C,U] the color of blood: *She was dressed in red* (= in red clothes).

IDM **(be) in the red** to have spent more money than you have in the bank, etc.: *The airline ended the year $40 million in the red.* ➲ Look at **in the black** at **black[2]**.

**ˌred-ˈblood·ed** ***adj.*** (*informal*) full of strength and energy, often sexual energy: *red-blooded young males*

**ˌred ˈcarpet** ***noun*** [sing.] a piece of red carpet that is put out for an important visitor; a special welcome for an important visitor

**the ˌRed ˈCross** ***noun*** [sing.] an international organization that takes care of people suffering because of war or natural disasters

**red·dish** /ˈrɛdɪʃ/ ***adj.*** slightly red

**re·deem** /rɪˈdim/ ***verb*** [T] **1** to exchange sth for money, products, etc. with an equal value: *This gift certificate can be redeemed in any one of our stores.* **2** to prevent sth from being completely bad: *The only redeeming feature of the job is the good salary.* **3 redeem yourself** to say or do sth in order to remove the bad effect of sth you did: *It was all his fault. There's nothing he can say to redeem himself.*

**re·demp·tion** /rɪˈdɛmpʃn/ ***noun*** [U] (*formal*) being saved or redeemed

**re·de·vel·op** /ˌridəˈvɛləp/ ***verb*** [I,T] to change an area by building new roads, houses, factories, etc.: *The city has plans to redevelop the site.* ▸ **re·de·vel·op·ment** ***noun*** [U]: *inner-city redevelopment*

**re·de·vel·op·ment** /ˌridəˈvɛləpmənt/ ***noun*** [U] new building work, especially more modern buildings which will replace older ones: *There's a lot of redevelopment going on downtown.*

**ˈred-eye** ***noun*** **1** (*also* **ˈred-eye flight**) [C] (*informal*) a flight in a plane at night, on which you cannot get enough sleep: *We took the red-eye to Boston.* **2** [U] the appearance of having red eyes that people sometimes have in photographs taken using a FLASH[1] (3): *a flash mode that is designed to reduce the red-eye effect*

**ˌred-ˈhand·ed** ***adj.***

IDM **catch sb red-handed** → CATCH[1]

**red·head** /ˈrɛdhɛd/ ***noun*** [C] a person, especially a woman, who has red hair

**ˌred-ˈhot** ***adj.*** **1** (used about a metal) so hot that it turns red **2** (*informal*) new, exciting and of great interest to people: *a red-hot issue*

**re·di·al** /ˈridaɪəl; ˌriˈdaɪəl/ ***verb*** [I,T] **1** to call a telephone number again by pressing all of the individual numbers again **2** to call a telephone number again, using the device that automatically calls the last number that was called (last number redial) ▸ **re·di·al** ***noun*** [U,C]

**re·dis·trib·ute** /ˌridɪˈstrɪbyut/ ***verb*** [T] to share sth among people, groups, etc. in a different way ▸ **re·dis·tri·bu·tion** /ˌridɪstrəˈbyuʃn/ ***noun*** [U]

**ˌred-ˈlight ˌdistrict** ***noun*** [C] a part of a town where there are many prostitutes

**ˌred ˈmeat** ***noun*** [U] meat that is dark brown in color when it has been cooked, such as beef and lamb

**red·neck** /ˈrɛdnɛk/ ***noun*** [C] (*informal*) a person from a small town or the countryside, especially in the southern U.S., who comes from a low social class, is not well educated and often does not like people of other races

**re·do** /ˌri'du/ ***verb*** [T] (*3rd person sing. pres.* **re·does**; *pt* **re·did**; *pp* **re·done**) to do sth again or in a different way: *A whole day's work had to be redone.* ◇ *We've just redone the bathroom* (= painted it again).

**re·dress¹** /rɪ'drɛs/ ***verb*** [T] (*formal*) to correct sth that is unfair or wrong: *to redress an injustice/a grievance*

IDM **redress the balance** to make a situation equal or fair again

**re·dress²** /'ridrɛs; rɪ'drɛs/ ***noun*** [U] **redress (for/against sth)** (*formal*) payment, etc. that you should get for sth wrong that has happened to you or harm that you have suffered: *to seek legal redress for unfair dismissal* SYN **compensation**

**red·skin** /'rɛdskɪn/ ***noun*** [C] (*old-fashioned*) a Native American

NOTE This word is considered offensive nowadays.

**ˌred 'tape** ***noun*** [U] official rules that seem unnecessary and often cause delay and difficulty in achieving sth

★**re·duce** /rɪ'dus/ ***verb*** [T] **1** to make sth less: *Doctors have advised us to reduce the amount of fat in our diets.* OPP **increase** **2 reduce sb/sth (from sth) to sth** (often passive) to make sb/sth be in the (usually bad) state mentioned: *One of the older boys reduced the little child to tears.* ◇ *They were reduced from wealth to poverty almost overnight.*

★**re·duc·tion** /rɪ'dʌkʃn/ ***noun*** [C,U] an act of making sth less or smaller; the state of being made less or smaller: *a reduction in the numbers of unemployed people* ◇ *a reduction in the rate of inflation*

**re·dun·dant** /rɪ'dʌndənt/ ***adj.*** more than is wanted; not needed, especially because sth else has the same function: *"Revert back" is a redundant expression.* ▸ **re·dun·dan·cy** /-ənsi/ ***noun*** [U]

**ˌred 'wine** ***noun*** [U] wine that is made from purple grapes ➲ Look at **white wine** and **rosé**.

**red·wood** /'rɛdwʊd/ (*also* **sequoia**) ***noun*** [C] an extremely large, tall tree that grows near the west coast of the U.S.

**reed** /rid/ ***noun*** [C] **1** a tall plant, like grass, that grows in or near water **2** a very small, thin piece of wood in some types of musical instruments (woodwinds) that you blow over or through in order to make a sound

**reef** /rif/ ***noun*** [C] a long line of rocks, sand, etc. just below or above the surface of the ocean: *a coral reef*

**reek** /rik/ ***verb*** [I] to have a very strong, bad smell: *His breath reeked of alcohol.*

**reel¹** /ril/ ***noun*** [C] a round object that film for movies, a fishing line, etc. is wound around: *a fishing rod and reel*

**reel²** /ril/ ***verb*** [T] **reel sth in/out** to wind sth on or off a reel or to pull it toward you using a reel: *to reel out the hose* ◇ *to reel in a fish*

IDM **be reeling (from sth)** to be shocked and confused because of sth that has happened: *The Florida coast is still reeling from the effects of the hurricane.*

PHR V **reel sth off** to say or repeat sth from memory quickly and without effort: *She reeled off a list of all the people she invited to the party.*

**re·e·lect** /ˌriə'lɛkt/ (*also* **re-elect**) ***verb*** [T] to elect sb again: *The committee voted to reelect him (as) chairman.* ▸ **re·e·lec·tion** (*also* **re-e·lec·tion**) /ˌriə'lɛkʃn/ ***noun*** [U]: *to run for reelection*

**re·en·act** /ˌriə'nækt/ (*also* **re-enact**) ***verb*** [T] to repeat the actions of a past event: *Bombers gathered together to reenact the historic first air attack.* ▸ **re·en·act·ment** (*also* **re-enactment**) ***noun*** [C]

**re·en·ter** /ˌri'ɛntər/ ***verb*** [I,T] to return to a place or to an area of activity that you used to be in ▸ **re·en·try** /ˌri'ɛntri/ ***noun*** [C] (*pl.* **re·en·tries**)

**ref** /rɛf/ ***noun*** [C] (*informal*) = REFEREE

**re·fec·to·ry** /rɪ'fɛktəri/ ***noun*** [C] (*pl.* **re·fec·to·ries**) a large room in which meals are served, especially in religious institutions and some colleges

★**re·fer** /rɪ'fər/ ***verb*** (**re·fer·ring**; **re·ferred**) **1** [I] **refer to sb/sth** to mention or talk about sb/sth: *When he said "some students," do you think he was referring to us?* ◇ *Many people still refer to Russia as the Soviet Union.* **2** [I] **refer to sb/sth** to be used to describe sb/sth: *The term "adolescent" refers to young people between the ages of 12 and 17.* **3** [I] to be connected with or important for: *The numbers in parentheses refer to diagrams at the end of the chapter.* **4** [I] **refer to sb/sth** to go to sb/sth or to look at sth for information: *If you don't understand a particular word, you can refer to your dictionaries.* **5** [T] **refer sb/sth to sb/sth** to send or direct sb/sth to sb/sth for help or to be dealt with: *My doctor referred me to a specialist.* ◇ *The dispute was referred to the United Nations.*

**ref·e·ree** /ˌrɛfə'ri/ ***noun*** [C] (*also informal* **ref**) the person in football, basketball, etc. who controls the game and prevents the rules from being broken ➲ Look at **umpire**. ➲ picture at **soccer**. ▸ **ref·e·ree** ***verb*** [I,T]: *Who refereed the boxing match?*

★**ref·er·ence** /'rɛfrəns/ ***noun*** **1** [C,U] **reference (to sb/sth)** a statement that mentions sb/sth; the act of mentioning sb/sth: *The article made a direct reference to a certain member of the White House staff.* ◇ *Don't make any reference to his behavior last night.* **2** [C] a note, especially in a book, etc., that tells you where certain information has been or can be found **3** [C] a person who gives a statement or writes a letter describing a person's character and ability to do a job, etc.: *Would you be willing to be a reference for me?*

IDM **in/with reference to sb/sth** (*formal*) about or concerning sb/sth: *I am writing in reference to your letter dated April 10th...*

**'reference book** ***noun*** [C] a book that is used for obtaining information, not for reading straight through

**ref·er·en·dum** /ˌrɛfə'rɛndəm/ ***noun*** [C] (*pl.* **ref·er·en·dums** or (*formal*)**ref·er·en·da** /-də/) an occasion when all the people of a state, county, etc. are able to vote on a particular political question

**re·fer·ral** /rɪ'fərəl/ ***noun*** [C,U] **referral (to sb/sth)** the act of sending sb who needs professional help to a person or place that can provide it: *patients requiring referral to hospitals* ◇ *to make a referral*

R

**re·fill** /ˌriˈfɪl; ˈrifɪl/ *verb* [T] to fill sth again: *I need to go to the drugstore to refill my prescription.* ▶ **re·fill** /ˈrifɪl/ *noun* [C]: *They charge $1.50 for a cup of coffee, but refills are free.*

**re·fine** /rɪˈfaɪn/ *verb* [T] **1** to make a substance pure and free from other substances: *to refine sugar/oil* **2** to improve sth by changing little details: *to refine a theory* ▶ **re·fine·ment** *noun* [C,U]

**re·fined** /rɪˈfaɪnd/ *adj.* **1** (used about a person) having extremely good manners and knowing a lot about art, literature, etc. **2** that has been improved or made pure: *refined sugar* OPP **unrefined**

**re·fin·er·y** /rɪˈfaɪnəri/ *noun* [C] (*pl.* **re·fin·er·ies**) a factory where a certain substance is refined: *an oil refinery*

★**re·flect** /rɪˈflɛkt/ *verb* **1** [T] to show or express sth: *The increase in the cost of paper will be reflected in higher prices for books and newspapers.* **2** [I,T] to send back light, heat, sound or an image, or to be sent back off a surface: *She saw herself reflected in the store window.* ◇ *The fireworks lit up the sky and reflected off the skyscrapers downtown.* **3** [I,T] **reflect (on/upon sth)** to think, especially deeply: *I really need some time to reflect on what you've said.*
PHR V **reflect (well, badly, etc.) on sb/sth** to give a particular impression of sb/sth: *It reflects badly on the whole school if some of the students get involved in crime.*

**re·flec·tion** /rɪˈflɛkʃn/ *noun* **1** [C] a thing that shows or expresses sth: *His success is a reflection of all the hard work he puts into his job.* **2** [C] an image that you see in a mirror or in water **3** [U] (*technical*) the process of sending light, heat or sound back from a surface **4** [C,U] **reflection (on sth)** thinking deeply about sth, or a deep thought or thoughts that you express: *She wrote about her reflections on being an immigrant in a small town.* **5** [sing.] **a reflection on/upon sb/sth** a thing that causes a bad impression of sb/sth: *Parents often feel that their children's behavior is a reflection on themselves.*

**re·flec·tive** /rɪˈflɛktɪv/ *adj.* **1 reflective of sth** showing a good example of sth; typical of sth: *His insulting remarks are not reflective of the whole group's opinions.* **2** (used about a surface) reflecting light: *Wear reflective clothing when you're riding your bike at night.* **3** (used about a person, mood, etc.) thoughtful: *a reflective expression*

**re·flec·tor** /rɪˈflɛktər/ *noun* [C] a thing, usually made of plastic, that reflects light

**re·flex** /ˈriflɛks/ *noun* **1** [C] a sudden movement or action that you make automatically: *"I'm going to tap your knee to test your reflexes," said the doctor.* **2 reflexes** [pl.] the ability to act quickly when necessary: *A good tennis player needs to have excellent reflexes.*

**re·flex·ive** /rɪˈflɛksɪv/ *adj.*, *noun* [C] (*grammar*) (a word or verb form) showing that the action of a sentence is done to the subject of the sentence: *In the sentence "He cut himself," "himself" is a reflexive pronoun.*

★**re·form¹** /rɪˈfɔrm/ *verb* **1** [T] to change sth in order to make it better: *to reform the welfare system* **2** [I,T] to behave better or fit into society better; to make sb do this: *He's done wrong in the past, but he has made serious efforts to reform.* ◇ *a reformed criminal*

★**re·form²** /rɪˈfɔrm/ *noun* [C,U] (a) change in sth in order to make it better: *major economic reforms* ◇ *political reform in Mexico*

**re·for·ma·tion** /ˌrɛfərˈmeɪʃn/ *noun* **1** [U] (*formal*) the act of improving or changing sb/sth **2 the Reformation** [sing.] new ideas in religion in 16th century Europe that led to attempts to REFORM¹ (1) the Roman Catholic Church and to the forming of the Protestant Churches; the period of time when these changes were taking place

**re·form·a·to·ry** /rɪˈfɔrməˌtɔri/ (*pl.* **re·form·a·to·ries**) (*also* **reˈform school**) *noun* [C] a place that young criminals are sent to as an alternative to prison

**re·form·er** /rɪˈfɔrmər/ *noun* [C] a person who tries to change society and make it better

**reˈform school** *noun* [C] = REFORMATORY

**re·frain¹** /rɪˈfreɪn/ *verb* [I] **refrain (from sth/doing sth)** (*formal*) to stop yourself from doing sth; not do sth: *Please refrain from smoking in the hospital.*

**re·frain²** /rɪˈfreɪn/ *noun* [C] = CHORUS (2)

**re·fresh** /rɪˈfrɛʃ/ *verb* [T] to make sb/sth feel fresh, strong or full of energy again: *A good night's sleep will refresh you.*
IDM **refresh your/sb's memory (about sb/sth)** to remind yourself/sb about sth: *Could you refresh my memory about what we said on this point last week?*

**re·fresh·ing** /rɪˈfrɛʃɪŋ/ *adj.* **1** interesting, different and enjoyable: *It's refreshing to meet somebody who is so enthusiastic.* **2** making you feel fresh and strong again: *a refreshing swim*

**re·fresh·ment** /rɪˈfrɛʃmənt/ *noun* **1 refreshments** [pl.] light food and drinks that are available at a concert, theater or other public event: *Refreshments will be sold during the intermission.* **2** [U] (*formal*) being refreshed, or the food and drink that makes you feel refreshed: *There will be two stops for refreshment on the trip.*

**re·fried beans** /ˌrifraɪd ˈbinz/ *noun* [pl.] beans that have been boiled and fried in advance and are heated again when needed, used especially in Mexican cooking

**re·frig·er·ate** /rɪˈfrɪdʒəreɪt/ *verb* [T] to put food, etc. in a refrigerator in order to keep it fresh and cool

**re·frig·er·a·tor** /rɪˈfrɪdʒəreɪt̬ər/ (*also informal* **fridge**, *old-fashioned* **icebox**) *noun* [C] a piece of electrical equipment in which food, etc. is kept cold so that it stays fresh ➲ Look at **freezer**.

**ref·uge** /ˈrɛfyudʒ/ *noun* [C,U] **refuge (from sb/sth)** a place that is safe; the protection that this place gives you against sth bad: *a wildlife refuge* (= where wild animals cannot be hunted) ◇ *They took refuge in foreign embassies.*

**ref·u·gee** /ˌrɛfyuˈdʒi/ *noun* [C] a person who has been forced to leave his/her country for political or religious reasons or because there is a war, not enough food, etc.: *political refugees* ◇ *a refugee camp*

R

**re·fund¹** /rɪˈfʌnd; ˈrifʌnd/ ***verb*** [T] to pay back money: *Your travel expenses will be refunded.* ▸ **re·fund·a·ble** ***adj.***: *The deposit is not refundable.*

**re·fund²** /ˈrifʌnd/ ***noun*** [C] a sum of money that is returned to you, for example if you take sth back to the store where you bought it

**re·fur·bish** /riˈfərbɪʃ/ ***verb*** [T] to clean, paint, and often change the furnishings and other things in a room or building in order to make it more attractive, more useful, etc. ▸ **re·fur·bish·ment** ***noun*** [C,U]: *The hotel is closed for refurbishment.*

★**re·fus·al** /rɪˈfyuzl/ ***noun*** [C,U] **refusal (to do sth)** an act of saying or showing that you will not do or accept sth: *Did they give a reason for their refusal to offer you the job?* ◇ *So far we've had ten replies to the invitation: eight acceptances and two refusals.*

★**re·fuse¹** /rɪˈfyuz/ ***verb*** [I,T] to say or show that you do not want to do, give, accept, etc. sth: *I asked her to come but she refused.* ◇ *He refused to listen to what I was saying.* ◇ *My application for a loan has been refused.* ◇ *We offered her a ride home, but she refused it.*

**ref·use²** /ˈrɛfyus/ ***noun*** [U] (*formal*) things that you throw away; garbage: *a refuse dump*

**re·fute** /rɪˈfyut/ ***verb*** [T] (*formal*) **1** to prove that sth is wrong: *to refute an argument/a theory* SYN **rebut** **2** to say that sth is not true or fair: *She refutes any suggestion that she behaved unprofessionally.* SYN **deny**

**re·gain** /rɪˈgeɪn/ ***verb*** [T] to get sth back that you have lost: *to regain your freedom* ◇ *to regain consciousness*

**re·gal** /ˈrigl/ ***adj.*** very grand; like or suitable for a king or queen

**re·gale** /rɪˈgeɪl/ ***verb***

PHR V **regale sb with sth** to amuse or entertain sb with stories, jokes, etc.: *He regaled us with tales of his days as a jazz pianist.*

**re·ga·li·a** /rɪˈgeɪlyə/ ***noun*** [U] the special clothes that are worn or objects that are carried at official ceremonies

★**re·gard¹** /rɪˈgɑrd/ ***verb*** [T] **regard sb/sth (as sth)**; **regard sb/sth (with sth)** to think of sb/sth (in the way mentioned): *I regard him as my best friend.* ◇ *Do you regard this issue as important?* ◇ *Her work is highly regarded* (= people have a very good opinion of it). ◇ *In some neighborhoods, newcomers are regarded with suspicion.*

★**re·gard²** /rɪˈgɑrd/ ***noun*** **1** [U] **regard (for sb/sth)** a feeling of admiration for sb/sth: respect: *She obviously has great regard for your ability.* **2** [U] **regard to/for sb/sth** care or consideration for sb/sth: *He shows little regard for other people's feelings.* **3 regards** [pl.] (used especially at the end of a letter) kind thoughts and greetings: *Please give my regards to your parents.*

IDM **in/with regard to sb/sth**; **in this/that/one regard** (*formal*) about sb/sth; concerning this or that: *With regard to the details – these will be finalized later.* ◇ *It has been a successful year financially, so in this regard we have been fortunate.*

**re·gard·ing** /rɪˈgɑrdɪŋ/ ***prep.*** (*formal*) about or concerning: *Please write if you require further information regarding this matter.*

**re·gard·less** /rɪˈgɑrdləs/ ***adv.*** **regardless of sb/sth** paying no attention to sb/sth: *Everyone wil receive the same bonus, regardless of how long they have been working here.*

**re·gat·ta** /rɪˈgɑt̬ə; -ˈgæt̬ə/ ***noun*** [C] a sporting event in which races between boats or yachts are held

**re·gen·er·ate** /rɪˈdʒɛnəreɪt/ ***verb*** **1** [T] to make an area, institution, etc. develop and grow strong again: *The money will be used to regenerate the commercial heart of the city.* **2** [I] to grow again; to make sth grow again: *Once destroyed, brain cells do not regenerate.* ◇ *If the forest is left alone, it will regenerate itself in a few years.* ▸ **re·gen·er·a·tion** /rɪˌdʒɛnəˈreɪʃn; ˌri-/ ***noun*** [U]: *the regeneration of cells in the body*

**reg·gae** /ˈrɛgeɪ/ ***noun*** [U] a type of Caribbean popular music with a strong rhythm

**re·gime** /reɪˈʒim/ ***noun*** [C] a method or system of government: *a military regime* ➲ This word is used to show disapproval.

**reg·i·men** /ˈrɛdʒəmən/ (*also* **re·gime**) ***noun*** [C] (*medical*) a set of rules about food and exercise or medical treatment that you follow in order to stay healthy or to improve your health

**reg·i·ment** /ˈrɛdʒəmənt/ [C] a large group of soldiers in the military forces ▸ **reg·i·men·tal** /ˌrɛdʒəˈmɛntl/ ***adj.***

**reg·i·ment·ed** /ˈrɛdʒəˌmɛntəd/ ***adj.*** involving strict discipline and/or organization: *The school imposes a very regimented lifestyle on its students.*

★**re·gion** /ˈridʒən/ ***noun*** [C] **1** a part of the country or the world; a large area of land: *desert/tropical/polar regions* ◇ *This region of the country is very flat.* ◇ *She is responsible for sales in the West Coast region.* ➲ Look at the note at **district**. **2** an area of your body: *He's been having pains in his abdominal region.*

IDM **in the region of sth** about or approximately: *It must have cost somewhere in the region of $1,000.*

★**re·gion·al** /ˈridʒənl/ ***adj.*** connected with a particular REGION (1): *regional accents*

★**reg·is·ter¹** /ˈrɛdʒəstər/ ***noun*** [C] **1** = CASH REGISTER **2** an official list of names, etc. or a book that contains such a list: *Be sure to record each check that you write in your checkbook register.*

★**reg·is·ter²** /ˈrɛdʒəstər/ ***verb*** **1** [I,T] to put a name or other information on an official list: *I'd like to register for the course in June.* ◇ *to register to vote* ◇ *All births, deaths and marriages must be registered.* **2** [I,T] to show on a measuring instrument: *The thermometer registered 32°F.* **3** [T] (*formal*) to show feelings, opinions, etc.: *Her face registered intense dislike.*

**ˌregistered ˈmail** ***noun*** [U] a postal service that you pay extra for, in which the post office records when you sent the letter or package and each point that it passes until it arrives at the correct place

**ˌregistered ˈnurse** ***noun*** [C] (*abbr.* **RN**) a person who has passed a special state examination and has received official permission to work as a nurse

**ˌRegistered ReˌtirementˈSavings Plan** ***noun*** [sing.] (*Cdn*) → RRSP

**reg·is·trar** /ˈrɛdʒəstrɑr/ ***noun*** [C] **1** a person who is responsible for official records, etc. at a college or university **2** a person whose job is to keep official lists, especially in a government office

**reg·is·tra·tion** /ˌrɛdʒəˈstreɪʃn/ ***noun*** **1** [U] the act of putting sth or sb's name on an official list: *Registration for evening classes will take place on September 8th.* **2** [C] an official piece of paper with information about a car, truck, etc. and the name of its owner: *Can I see your license and registration, please?*

**reg·is·try** /ˈrɛdʒəstri/ ***noun*** [C] (*pl.* **reg·is·tries**) a place where official lists are kept: *the Registry of Motor Vehicles*

**re·gress** /rɪˈgrɛs/ ***verb*** [I] (*formal*) **regress (to sth)** to return to an earlier or less advanced form or way of behaving ▸ **re·gres·sion** /rɪˈgrɛʃn/ ***noun*** [C,U]: *He began to show signs of regression to his childhood.*

**re·gret**[1] /rɪˈgrɛt/ ***noun*** [C,U] a feeling of sadness about sth that cannot now be changed: *Do you have any regrets that you didn't go to college?* ◇ *I accepted his decision to leave with great regret.*

**re·gret**[2] /rɪˈgrɛt/ ***verb*** [T] (**re·gret·ting**; **re·gret·ted**) **1** to feel sorry or sad about sth; to wish that you had not done sth: *I hope you won't regret your decision later.* ◇ *I really regretted not saying goodbye to her.* ◇ *Do you regret what you said to him?* **2** (*formal*) (used as a way of saying that you are sorry for sth): *I regret to inform you that your application has not been approved.*

**re·gret·ful** /rɪˈgrɛtfl/ ***adj.*** feeling or expressing sadness ▸ **re·gret·ful·ly** ***adv.***

**re·gret·ta·ble** /rɪˈgrɛt̬əbl/ ***adj.*** that you should feel sorry or sad about

**re·gret·ta·bly** /rɪˈgrɛt̬əbli/ ***adv.*** (*formal*) **1** in a way that makes you feel sad or sorry **2** it is to be regretted that: *Regrettably, some hotels are not well-equipped for disabled people.*

**re·group** /ˌriˈgrup/ ***verb*** **1** [I,T] **regroup (sth) (for sth)** to arrange the way people or soldiers work together in a new way, especially in order to continue fighting or attacking sb: *They regrouped their forces and renewed the attack.* ◇ *After its election defeat, the party needs to regroup.* **2** [I] (used about a person) to return to a normal state after an unpleasant experience or a period of difficulty, and become ready to make an effort again with new enthusiasm or strength: *Summer is a time to relax, regroup and catch up on all those things you've been putting off all year.*

★**reg·u·lar**[1] /ˈrɛgyələr/ ***adj.***

➤FOLLOWING PATTERN **1** having the same amount of space or time between each thing or part: *regular breathing* ◇ *Nurses checked her blood pressure at regular intervals.*

➤FREQUENT **2** happening at the same time each day, week, etc. (as a result of an arrangement or a plan): *We have regular meetings every Thursday.* **3** going somewhere or doing sth often: *a regular customer* ◇ *We're regular passengers of the airline.*

➤USUAL **4** normal or usual: *Who is your regular dentist?*

➤EVENLY SHAPED **5** evenly shaped: *regular teeth* ◇ *a regular geometric pattern*

➤MEDIUM SIZE **6** of a medium size: *I'll have a cheeseburger and a regular Coke.*

➤ORDINARY **7** ordinary; without any special or extra features: *Do you want regular or diet cola?* ◇ *I just want to buy a regular white shirt – nothing fancy.*

➤GRAMMAR **8** (*grammar*) (used about a noun, verb, etc.) having the usual or expected plural, verb form, etc.: *"Walk" is a regular verb.* ➲ Look at **irregular**.

▸ **reg·u·lar·i·ty** /ˌrɛgyəˈlærət̬i/ ***noun*** [U]

**reg·u·lar**[2] /ˈrɛgyələr/ ***noun*** [C] (*informal*) a person who goes to a particular store, bar, etc. very often

★**reg·u·lar·ly** /ˈrɛgyələrli/ ***adv.*** **1** at regular times or in a regular way: *to have a car serviced regularly* **2** often: *Mr. Davis regularly takes part in contests, but this is the first one that he has won.*

**reg·u·late** /ˈrɛgyəleɪt/ ***verb*** [T] **1** to control sth by using laws: *a strict law to regulate pollution from factories* **2** to control a machine, piece of equipment, etc.: *Individual controls allow you to regulate the temperature in each room.*

★**reg·u·la·tion** /ˌrɛgyəˈleɪʃn/ ***noun*** **1** [U] control of sth: *government regulation of agriculture* **2** [C, usually pl.] a law or rule that controls how sth is done: *to observe/obey the safety regulations* ◇ *It is against fire regulations to smoke at a gas station.* ◇ *The plans must comply with the new federal regulations.* ◇ *to enforce a regulation*

**re·gur·gi·tate** /rɪˈgərdʒəteɪt/ ***verb*** [T] **1** (*formal*) to bring food that has been swallowed back up into the mouth again **2** to repeat sth you have heard or read without really thinking about it or understanding it

**re·hab** /ˈrihæb/ ***noun*** [U] (*informal*) the process of helping sb to stop using drugs or alcohol: *Brett is in drug rehab.*

**re·ha·bil·i·tate** /ˌriəˈbɪləteɪt; ˌrihə-/ ***verb*** [T] to help sb to live a normal life again after an illness, being in prison, etc. ▸ **re·ha·bil·i·ta·tion** /ˌriəˌbɪləˈteɪʃn; ˌrihə-/ ***noun*** [U]

**re·hash** /ˌriˈhæʃ/ ***verb*** [T] to arrange ideas, pieces of writing or pieces of film into a new form but without any great change or improvement: *He just rehashes songs from the 60s.* ▸ **re·hash** /ˈrihæʃ/ ***noun*** [sing.]: *The movie is just a rehash of the best TV episodes.*

**re·hears·al** /rɪˈhərsl/ ***noun*** [C,U] the time when you practice a play, dance, piece of music, etc. before you perform it for other people: ***a dress rehearsal*** (= when all the actors wear their stage clothes) SYN **run-through**

**re·hearse** /rɪˈhərs/ ***verb*** [I,T] to practice a play, dance, piece of music, etc. before you perform it for other people

**re·heat** /ˌriˈhit/ ***verb*** [T] to heat cooked food again after it has been left to go cold

**reign**[1] /reɪn/ ***noun*** [C] the period of time that a king or queen rules a country: *the long reign of Queen Victoria*

**reign**[2] /reɪn/ ***verb*** [I] **1** **reign (over sb/sth)** (used about a king or queen) to rule a country: (*figurative*) *the reigning world champion* **2** to be present as the most important feature of a particular situation: *Chaos reigned after the first snow of the winter.*

**re·im·burse** /ˌriɪmˈbərs/ ***verb*** [T] (*formal*) to pay money back to sb: *The company will reimburse you in full for your traveling expenses.* ◇ *Your expenses will be reimbursed in full.* ▶ **re·im·burse·ment** ***noun*** [U]: *You will receive reimbursement for any additional costs incurred.*

**rein¹** /reɪn/ ***noun*** [C, usually pl.] a long thin piece of leather that you use to control a horse ➲ picture at **horse**.

IDM **give/allow sb/sth free/full rein** to give sb complete freedom of action; to allow a feeling to be expressed freely: *The designer was given free rein.*

**rein²** /reɪn/ ***verb*** [T]

PHR V **rein sth in 1** to start to control sb/sth more strictly: *She kept her emotions tightly reined in.* **2** to stop a horse or make it go more slowly by pulling back the REINS¹

**rein·deer** /ˈreɪndɪr/ ***noun*** [C] (*pl.* **rein·deer**) a type of large deer that lives in Arctic regions

NOTE According to tradition, reindeer pull Santa Claus's sleigh on the night before Christmas when he brings presents to children.

**re·in·force** /ˌriɪnˈfɔrs/ ***verb*** [T] to make sth stronger: *Concrete can be reinforced by putting steel bars inside it.* ◇ *evidence to reinforce her argument*

**re·in·force·ment** /ˌriɪnˈfɔrsmənt/ ***noun*** **1** [U] the act of supporting or strengthening sth: *The roof is weak in places and needs reinforcement.* **2 reinforcements** [pl.] extra people who are sent to make an army, navy, etc. stronger

**re·in·state** /ˌriɪnˈsteɪt/ ***verb*** [T] to bring sb/sth back into his/her/its previous job, position or condition: *The Supreme Court reinstated the lower court's original decision.* ▶ **re·in·state·ment** ***noun*** [U]

**re·in·vent** /ˌriɪnˈvɛnt/ ***verb*** [T]

IDM **reinvent the wheel** to waste time creating sth that already exists and works well

**re·it·er·ate** /riˈɪt̬əreɪt/ ***verb*** [T] (*formal*) to repeat sth that you have already said, especially to emphasize it: *to reiterate an argument/offer* ▶ **re·it·er·a·tion** /-ˌɪt̬əˈreɪʃn/ ***noun*** [sing.]: *a reiteration of her previous statement*

★**re·ject¹** /rɪˈdʒɛkt/ ***verb*** [T] to refuse to accept sb/sth: *The plan was rejected as being impractical.* ◇ *I rejected all the applicants for the job except one.* ▶ **re·jec·tion** ***noun*** [C,U]: *Penny got a rejection letter from Harvard.* ◇ *There has been total rejection of the new policy.*

**re·ject²** /ˈridʒɛkt/ ***noun*** [C] a person or thing that is not accepted because he/she/it is not good enough: *Rejects are sold at half price.*

**re·jig·ger** /ˌriˈdʒɪgər/ (*Cdn* **re·jig** /ˌriˈdʒɪg/) ***verb*** [T] (*informal*) to make changes to sth; to arrange sth in a different way

**re·joice** /rɪˈdʒɔɪs/ ***verb*** [I] **rejoice (at/in/over sth)** (*formal*) to feel or show great happiness: *The people rejoiced at the news of the victory.* ▶ **re·joic·ing** ***noun*** [U]

**re·ju·ve·nate** /rɪˈdʒuvəneɪt/ ***verb*** [T] to cause sb/sth to feel or look younger ▶ **re·ju·ve·na·tion** /rɪˌdʒuvəˈneɪʃn/ ***noun*** [U]

**re·kin·dle** /ˌriˈkɪndl/ ***verb*** [T] (*written*) to make sth become active again: *to rekindle feelings/hopes/interest/memories*

**re·lapse** /rɪˈlæps; ˈrilæps/ ***noun*** [C] a time when sb/sth becomes worse again after an improvement: *The patient suffered a relapse and then died.*

★**re·late** /rɪˈleɪt/ ***verb*** **1** [T] **relate sth to/with sth** to show a connection between two or more things: *The report relates heart disease to high levels of stress.* **2** [T] **relate sth (to sb)** (*formal*) to tell a story to sb

PHR V **relate to sb/sth 1** to be concerned with; to have sth to do with: *That question is very interesting, but it doesn't really relate to the subject that we're discussing.* **2** to be able to understand how sb feels: *Some teenagers find it hard to relate to their parents.*

★**re·lat·ed** /rɪˈleɪt̬əd/ ***adj.*** **related (to sb/sth) 1** connected with sb/sth: *The rise in the cost of living is directly related to the price of oil.* **2** of the same family: *We are related by marriage.* ◇ *Are you related to Joe Garcia?* ◇ *to be closely/distantly related*

★**re·la·tion** /rɪˈleɪʃn/ ***noun*** **1** [U] **relation (between sth and sth)**; **relation (to sth)** the connection between two or more things: *There seems to be no relation between the cost of the houses and their size.* ◇ *The movie bears no relation to the book* (= it is very different). **2** [C] a member of your family: *a close/distant relation* **3 relations** [pl.] the way that people, groups, countries, etc. feel about or behave toward each other: *The police officer stressed that good relations with the community were essential.* ◇ *to break off diplomatic relations*

IDM **in/with relation to sb/sth 1** concerning sb/sth: *Many questions were asked, particularly in relation to the cost of the new buildings.* **2** compared with: *Prices are low in relation to those in other parts of the country.*

★**re·la·tion·ship** /rɪˈleɪʃnʃɪp/ ***noun*** [C] **1** the way that people, groups, countries, etc. feel about or behave toward each other: *The police have a poor relationship with the local people.* ◇ *The relationship between the parents and the school has improved greatly.* **2** a friendship or love affair: *to have a relationship with sb* ◇ *Are you currently in a relationship?* ◇ *The movie describes the relationship between a young man and an older woman.* ◇ *a close relationship* **3** a family connection: *"What is your relationship to Bruce?" "He is married to my cousin."* **4** the connection between two or more things: *Is there a relationship between violence on TV and the increase in crime?*

★**rel·a·tive¹** /ˈrɛlət̬ɪv/ ***noun*** [C] a member of your family: *a close/distant relative*

★**rel·a·tive²** /ˈrɛlət̬ɪv/ ***adj.*** **1** when compared to sb/sth else: *They live in relative luxury.* ◇ *We're in a period of relative calm after the winds of the past few days.* ◇ *It's hard to assess the relative importance of the two jobs.* **2** (*grammar*) referring to an earlier noun, phrase or sentence: *In the phrase "the woman who lives next door," "who" is a relative pronoun.*

★**rel·a·tive·ly** /ˈrɛlət̬ɪvli/ ***adv.*** to a certain degree; fairly: *Spanish is a relatively easy language to learn.* ◇ *It's a small house, but the back yard is relatively large.*

★**re·lax** /rɪˈlæks/ ***verb*** **1** [I,T] to make or become

R

less worried or tense; to spend time not doing very much: *This vacation will give you a chance to relax.* ◇ *A hot bath will relax you after a hard day's work.* ◇ *They spent the evening relaxing in front of the TV.* **2** [I,T] to make or become less stiff or tight: *You should be able to feel all your muscles relaxing.* **3** [T] to make rules or laws less strict: *The regulations on importing animals have been relaxed.*

**re·lax·a·tion** /ˌrilækˈseɪʃn/ ***noun*** [U] **1** the act of RELAXING (1,2,3): *the relaxation of a rule* **2** sth that you do in order to rest or RELAX (1): *Everyone needs time for rest and relaxation.*

★**re·laxed** /rɪˈlækst/ ***adj.*** not worried or anxious: *The relaxed atmosphere made everyone feel at ease.*

**re·lax·ing** /rɪˈlæksɪŋ/ ***adj.*** pleasant, helping you to rest and become less worried: *a quiet, relaxing vacation*

**re·lay**[1] /ˈrileɪ/ (*also* **ˈrelay race**) ***noun*** [C] a race in which each member of a team runs, swims, etc. one part of the race: *the 4 x 100-meter relay*

**re·lay**[2] /ˈrileɪ; rɪˈleɪ/ ***verb*** [T] (*pt, pp* **re·layed**) to receive and send on a signal or message

★**re·lease**[1] /rɪˈlis/ ***verb*** [T]
➤SET SB/STH FREE **1** to allow sb/sth to be free: *The hostages will be released before Christmas.* ◇ *He was released from prison.* ◇ *The driver of the wrecked car had to be released by firefighters.*
➤MOVE STH **2** to move sth from a fixed position: *Pull this lever to release the hood latch.*
➤STOP HOLDING STH **3** to stop holding sth: *She released his hand and walked off.*
➤MAKE AVAILABLE **4** to allow sth to be known by the public: *The identity of the victim has not been released.* **5** to make a movie, record, etc. available so the public can see or hear it: *Their new compact disc is due to be released next week.*
➤GAS/CHEMICAL **6** to let substances escape into the air, ocean, etc.: *The new power plant would release 230,000 tons of carbon dioxide into the atmosphere every year.*

★**re·lease**[2] /rɪˈlis/ ***noun*** **1** [C,U] **release (from sth)** the act of freeing or the state of being freed: *The release of the hostages took place this morning.* ◇ *I had a great feeling of release when my final exams were over.* **2** [C] a book, movie, record, piece of news, etc. that has been made available to the public: *a press release* ◇ *The band played their latest release.*

**rel·e·gate** /ˈrɛləgeɪt/ ***verb*** [T] **relegate sb/sth (to sth)** to give sb a lower or less important position, rank, etc. than before: *She was then relegated to the role of assistant.* ◇ *He relegated the incident to the back of his mind.*

**re·lent** /rɪˈlɛnt/ ***verb*** [I] (*formal*) to become less strict or hard, e.g. by allowing sth that you had previously forbidden: *Her parents finally relented and let her go to the party.* SYN A less formal expression is **give in**.

**re·lent·less** /rɪˈlɛntləs/ ***adj.*** not stopping or changing: *the relentless fight against crime* SYN **remorseless** ▸ **re·lent·less·ly** ***adv.***: *The sun beat down relentlessly.*

★**rel·e·vant** /ˈrɛləvənt/ ***adj.*** **relevant (to sb/sth)** **1** connected with what is happening or being talked about: *Please enclose all the relevant documents with your visa application.* ◇ *Much of what they said was not directly relevant to my case.* **2** important and useful: *Many people feel that poetry is no longer relevant in today's world.* OPP **irrelevant** ▸ **rel·e·vance** /-əns/ ***noun*** [U]: *I honestly can't see the relevance of what he said.* ◇ *Does the Bible have any relevance to life today?*

**re·li·a·ble** /rɪˈlaɪəbl/ ***adj.*** that you can trust: *Japanese cars are usually very reliable.* ◇ *I'm surprised she didn't call back – she's usually very reliable.* ◇ *reliable information* ◇ *Is he a reliable witness?* OPP **unreliable** ➲ verb **rely** ▸ **re·li·a·bil·i·ty** /rɪˌlaɪəˈbɪləṭi/ ***noun*** [U]: *These cars have a good reputation for reliability.* ▸ **re·li·a·bly** /-əbli/ ***adv.***

**re·li·ance** /rɪˈlaɪəns/ ***noun*** [U] **1** **reliance on sb/sth** being able to trust sb/sth: *Don't place too much reliance on her promises.* **2** not being able to live or work without sb/sth; being dependent on sb/sth: *the nation's reliance on fossil fuels*

**re·li·ant** /rɪˈlaɪənt/ ***adj.*** **reliant on sb/sth** (not before a noun) not being able to live or work without sb/sth: *She is totally reliant on her parents for financial support.* ➲ verb **rely**. Look also at **self-reliant**.

**rel·ic** /ˈrɛlɪk/ ***noun*** [C] something from the past that still exists today

★**re·lief** /rɪˈlif/ ***noun*** **1** [U, sing.] **relief (from sth)** the feeling that you have when sth unpleasant stops or becomes less strong: *The medication brought him some relief from the pain.* ◇ *What a relief! That terrible noise finally stopped.* ◇ *It was a great relief to know they were safe.* ◇ *to breathe a sigh of relief* ◇ *To my relief, he didn't argue with my suggestion at all.* **2** [U] money or food that is given to help people who are in trouble: *disaster relief for the flood victims*

**re·lieve** /rɪˈliv/ ***verb*** [T] **1** to make a bad feeling or situation better: *These pills should relieve the pain.* ◇ *Four new prisons are being built to relieve overcrowding.* **2** **relieve yourself** (used as a polite way of saying "to go to the bathroom"): *I had to relieve myself behind a bush.*

PHR V **relieve sb of sth** to take sth away from sb: *If you feel you have too much money, I'd be happy to relieve you of some of it!*

**re·lieved** /rɪˈlivd/ ***adj.*** pleased because your fear or worry has been taken away: *I was very relieved to hear that you weren't seriously hurt.*

★**re·lig·ion** /rɪˈlɪdʒən/ ***noun*** **1** [U] the belief in a god or gods who made the world and who can control what happens in it: *I never discuss politics or religion with them.* **2** [C] one of the systems of worship that is based on this belief: *the Christian/Hindu/Muslim religion*

★**re·lig·ious** /rɪˈlɪdʒəs/ ***adj.*** **1** connected with religion: *religious faith* **2** having a strong belief in a religion: *I'm not very religious, but I do go to church at Easter.*

**re·lig·ious·ly** /rɪˈlɪdʒəsli/ ***adv.*** **1** in a religious way **2** regularly: *They brush their teeth religiously, every night and every morning.*

**re·lin·quish** /rɪˈlɪŋkwɪʃ/ ***verb*** [T] (*formal*) to stop having or doing sth ➲ **Give up** is more common.

**rel·ish¹** /ˈrɛlɪʃ/ *verb* [T] to enjoy sth or to look forward to sth very much

**rel·ish²** /ˈrɛlɪʃ/ *noun* [U] **1** a cold sauce, usually made with chopped pickles, that is eaten with meat: *a hot dog with mustard and relish* **2** great enjoyment: *They all sang with great relish.*

**re·live** /ˌriˈlɪv/ *verb* [T] to remember sth and imagine that it is happening again

**re·load** /ˌriˈloʊd/ *verb* [T] **1** to put more bullets into a gun, more film into a camera, etc. **2** to put data or a program into the memory of a computer again

**re·lo·cate** /ˌriˈloʊkeɪt/ *verb* [I,T] to move (sb/sth) to a new place: *The company plans to relocate to Mexico.* ▸ **re·lo·ca·tion** /ˌriloʊˈkeɪʃn/ *noun* [U]

**re·luc·tant** /rɪˈlʌktənt/ *adj.* **reluctant (to do sth)** slow to agree to do sth, because you are unwilling: *I was reluctant to loan him my car because he's such a fast driver.* ▸ **re·luc·tance** /-əns/ *noun* [U] **reluctance (to do sth)**: *the government's reluctance to raise taxes* ▸ **re·luc·tant·ly** *adv.*

★**re·ly** /rɪˈlaɪ/ *verb* [I] (*pres. part.* **re·ly·ing**; *3rd person sing. pres.* **re·lies**; *pt, pp* **re·lied**) **rely on/upon sb/sth (to do sth) 1** to need sb/sth and not be able to live or work well without him/her/it: *The old lady had to rely on other people to go shopping for her.* ◇ *Many students have to rely on their parents for money.* **2** to trust sb/sth to work or behave well: *You can't rely on the weather in the springtime.* ◇ *Can I rely on you to keep a secret?* ➲ noun **reliance**. Look at the adjectives **reliable** and **reliant**.

★**re·main** /rɪˈmeɪn/ *verb* [I] **1** to be left after other people or things have gone: *Today only a few veterans of the First World War remain.* ◇ *They spent the two remaining days of their vacation buying presents to take home.* ◇ *The Giants scored a touchdown with five minutes of the game remaining.* **2** to stay or continue in the same place or condition: *They remained silent throughout the trial.* ◇ *They're divorced but they remain friends.* ◇ *Officials refused to allow him to remain in the United States.* ◇ (*figurative*) *Although he seems very pleasant, the fact remains that I don't trust him.*

**re·main·der** /rɪˈmeɪndər/ *noun* [sing., with sing. or pl. verb] (*formal*) **the remainder (of sth)** the people, things, etc. that are left after the others have gone away or been dealt with; the rest: *Fifty percent of local residents are in favor of the proposal, 45% are against it and the remainder are undecided.* ◇ *The remainder of the week is expected to be warm and sunny.* SYN **Rest** is less formal then **remainder**.

**re·mains** /rɪˈmeɪnz/ *noun* [pl.] **1** what is left behind after other parts have been used or taken away: *The construction workers found the remains of a Native American burial ground.* **2** (*formal*) a dead body (sometimes one that has been found somewhere a long time after death): *Human remains were discovered in the woods.*

**re·make¹** /ˌriˈmeɪk/ *verb* [T] (*pt, pp* **re·made**) to make a new or different version of sth such as an old movie or song; to make sth again: *"The Seven Samurai" was remade in Hollywood as "The Magnificent Seven."*

**re·make²** /ˈrimeɪk/ *noun* [C] a new or different version of an old movie or song

★**re·mark¹** /rɪˈmɑrk/ *verb* [I,T] **remark (on/upon sb/sth)** to say or write sth; to comment: *"What a strange movie," he remarked.* ◇ *Millie remarked that she had found the movie very interesting.* ◇ *A lot of people have remarked on the similarity between them.*

★**re·mark²** /rɪˈmɑrk/ *noun* [C] something that you say or write; a comment: *a few personal remarks at the end of the letter* ◇ *to make a nasty remark*

★**re·mark·a·ble** /rɪˈmɑrkəbl/ *adj.* unusual or noticeable: *She certainly is a remarkable woman.* ◇ *That is a remarkable achievement for someone so young.* ▸ **re·mark·a·bly** /-əbli/ *adv.*

**re·mar·ry** /riˈmæri/ *verb* [I,T] (*pres. part.* **re·mar·ry·ing**; *3rd person sing. pres.* **re·mar·ries**; *pt, pp* **re·mar·ried**) to marry again after being divorced or after your husband or wife has died

**re·match** /ˈrimætʃ/ *noun* [C, usually sing.] a match or game played again between the same people or teams, especially because neither side won the first match or game

**re·me·di·al** /rɪˈmidiəl/ *adj.* **1** helping people who are slow at learning sth: *remedial English classes* **2** used to improve sth (e.g. a difficult situation)

**rem·e·dy¹** /ˈrɛmədi/ *noun* [C] (*pl.* **rem·e·dies**) **remedy (for sth) 1** something that makes you better when you are sick or in pain: *Hot tea with honey is a good remedy for colds.* **2** a way of solving a problem: *There is no easy remedy for unemployment.*

**rem·e·dy²** /ˈrɛmədi/ *verb* [T] (*pres. part.* **rem·e·dy·ing**; *3rd person sing. pres.* **rem·e·dies**; *pt, pp* **rem·e·died**) to change or improve sth that is wrong or bad: *to remedy an injustice*

★**re·mem·ber** /rɪˈmɛmbər/ *verb* **1** [I,T] to have sth in your mind or to bring sth back into your mind: *"When did they move to Texas?" "I just don't remember."* ◇ *I'm sorry. I don't remember your name.* ◇ *Do you remember the night we first met?* ◇ *Remember that we're having company tonight.* ◇ *I know her face, but I can't remember what her name is.* ◇ *Can you remember when we bought the stereo?*

> NOTE If you remember **to do** something, you don't forget to do it: *I remembered to buy the coffee.* ◇ *Remember to turn the lights off before you leave.* If you remember **doing** something, you have a picture or memory in your mind of doing it: *Polly remembers seeing her keys on the table yesterday.*

**2** [T] to give money, etc. to sb/sth: *to remember sb in your will* ➲ Look at the note at **remind**.

**re·mem·brance** /rɪˈmɛmbrəns/ *noun* [U] (*formal*) the act of remembering and showing respect for sb who is dead: *a service in remembrance of those killed in the war*

**Re'membrance Day** *noun* [C] a holiday in Canada on 11 November, in honor of members of the armed forces and others who have died in war

> NOTE On 11 November in the U.S., Americans celebrate **Veterans Day**.

★**re·mind** /rɪˈmaɪnd/ *verb* [T] **1** to say sth to help sb

R

remember sth: *"Christmas is in two weeks!" "Don't remind me – I haven't bought any presents yet."* ◇ *She reminded him of his appointment at two o'clock.* ◇ *He reminded the kids to wash their hands.* ◇ *The doctor reminded me that I should see her again in two months.* **2 remind sb of sb/sth** to cause sb to remember sb/sth: *This song reminds me of Paris.* ◇ *You remind me of your father.*

NOTE You **remember** something by yourself. If somebody or something **reminds** you of something, he/she/it causes you to remember it: *Kristi remembered to say thank you after the party.* ◇ *Mom reminded Kristi to say thank you after the party.*

**re·mind·er** /rɪˈmaɪndər/ ***noun*** [C] something that makes you remember sth: *We received a reminder that we hadn't paid the electric bill.* ◇ *Eddie kept the ring as a reminder of happier days.*

**rem·i·nisce** /ˌrɛməˈnɪs/ ***verb*** [I] **reminisce (about sb/sth)** to talk about (pleasant) things that happened in the past

**rem·i·nis·cent** /ˌrɛməˈnɪsnt/ ***adj.*** **reminiscent of sb/sth** that makes you remember sb/sth; similar: *I think that painting is very reminiscent of one by Monet.*

**re·mis·sion** /rɪˈmɪʃn/ ***noun*** [C,U] a period of time when a serious disease improves or seems to go away: *Rebecca's cancer has been in remission for two years.*

**rem·nant** /ˈrɛmnənt/ ***noun*** [C] a piece of sth that remains after the rest is gone

**re·mod·el** /ˌriˈmɑdl/ ***verb*** [I,T] to change the structure or appearance of sth, especially a building: *Our neighbors are remodeling their house.* ◇ *We're thinking of remodeling, but we're not sure we can afford it.*

**re·morse** /rɪˈmɔrs/ ***noun*** [U] a feeling of sadness because you have done sth wrong: *She was filled with remorse for what she had done.* SYN **guilt** ▸ **re·morse·ful** /-fl/ ***adj.***

**re·morse·less** /rɪˈmɔrsləs/ ***adj.*** (*written*) **1** cruel and having or showing no pity for other people: *a remorseless killer* **2** (used especially about an unpleasant situation) seeming to continue or become worse in a way that cannot be stopped: *the remorseless increase in crime* SYN **relentless** ▸ **re·morse·less·ly** ***adv.***

**re·mort·gage** /ˌriˈmɔrgɪdʒ/ ***verb*** [T] to arrange a second mortgage on your house or apartment, or to increase or change your first one

**re·mote** /rɪˈmoʊt/ ***adj.*** **1** far away from where other people live: *a cabin in a remote area of the country* **2** far away in time: *the remote past/future* **3** not very great: *a remote possibility* ▸ **re·mote·ness** ***noun*** [U]

**reˌmote conˈtrol** ***noun*** **1** [C] (*also informal* **remote, zapper**) a piece of equipment for controlling sth, such as a television, toy, etc. from a distance **2** [U] a system for controlling sth from a distance: *You can open the garage door by remote control.*

**re·mote·ly** /rɪˈmoʊtli/ ***adv.*** (used in negative sentences) to a very small degree; at all: *I'm not remotely interested in your problems.*

★**re·mov·al** /rɪˈmuvl/ ***noun*** [U] taking sb/sth away: *I demanded the removal of my name from the list.* ◇ *the city's budget for snow removal*

★**re·move** /rɪˈmuv/ ***verb*** [T] (*formal*) **1 remove sb/sth (from sth)** to take sb/sth off or away: *Please remove your shoes before entering the temple.* ◇ *This detergent will remove most stains.* ◇ *to remove doubts/fears/problems* ◇ *I would like you to remove my name from your mailing list.* ➲ **Take off, take out**, etc. are less formal. **2 remove sb (from sth)** to make sb leave his/her job, especially an official position: *Citizens voted to remove the senator from office.*

**re·moved** /rɪˈmuvd/ ***adj.*** (not before a noun) **removed (from sth)** far or different from sth: *Hospitals today are far removed from what they were fifty years ago.*

**re·mov·er** /rɪˈmuvər/ ***noun*** [C,U] a substance that cleans off paint, stains, etc.: *a stain remover*

**ren·ais·sance** /ˈrɛnəsɑns; -zɑns; ˌrɛnəˈsɑns/ ***noun*** [sing.] **1 the Renaissance** the period in Europe during the 14th, 15th and 16th centuries when people became interested in the ideas and culture of ancient Greece and Rome and used these influences in their own art, literature, etc.: *Renaissance art* **2** a situation when there is new interest in a particular subject, form of art, etc. after a period when it was not very popular: *to experience/enjoy a renaissance*

**re·name** /ˌriˈneɪm/ ***verb*** [T] to give sb/sth a new name: *to rename a street*

**ren·der** /ˈrɛndər/ ***verb*** [T] (*formal*) to cause sb/sth to be in a certain condition: *She was rendered speechless by the attack.*

**rend·er·ing** /ˈrɛndərɪŋ/ ***noun*** [C] **1** a performance of a piece of music, drama, etc.: *her dramatic rendering of Lady Macbeth* **2** [C] a piece of writing that has been translated into a different language: *a faithful rendering of the original text*

**ren·dez·vous**[1] /ˈrɑndeɪvu; -dɪ-/ ***noun*** (*pl.* **ren·dez·vous** /ren·dez·vous; -vuz/) **1 rendezvous (with sb)** an arrangement to meet sb at an agreed time and place **2** a place where people have arranged to meet **3** a bar, etc. that is a popular place for people to meet ▸ **ren·dez·vous** ***verb*** [I]

**ren·dez·vous**[2] /ˈrɑndeɪvu/ ***noun*** [C] (*pl.* **ren·dez·vous** /-z/) **1 rendezvous (with sb)** a meeting that you have arranged with sb **2** a place where people often meet

**ren·di·tion** /rɛnˈdɪʃn/ ***noun*** [C] a performance of sth, especially a song or piece of music; the particular way in which it is performed: *a wonderful rendition of "Nessum Dorma"*

**ren·e·gade** /ˈrɛnɪgeɪd/ ***noun*** [C] a person who leaves one political, military, religious, etc. group to join another that has very different views ▸ **ren·e·gade** ***adj.***: *renegade soldiers*

**re·nege** /rɪˈnɛg; -ˈnɪg; -ˈneɪg/ ***verb*** [I] **renege (on sth)** (*formal*) to break a promise, an agreement, etc.: *to renege on a deal/debt/contract*

**re·new** /rɪˈnu/ ***verb*** [T] **1** to give new strength or energy: *After a break, he went to work with renewed enthusiasm.* **2** to start sth again: *renewed outbreaks of violence* ◇ *to renew a friendship* **3** to make sth valid for a further period of time: *to renew your driver's license* ▶ **re·new·al** /-'nuəl/ *noun* [C,U]

**re·new·a·ble** /rɪ'nuəbl/ *adj.* that can be continued or replaced so that it is never finished or used completely: *renewable energy sources such as solar power and wind*

**re·nounce** /rɪ'naʊns/ *verb* [T] (*formal*) **1** to state officially that you are no longer going to keep a title, position, etc.: *to renounce a claim/title/privilege/right* **2** to state publicly that you no longer have a particular belief or that you will no longer behave in a particular way: *to renounce ideals/principles/beliefs* ◇ *to renounce terrorism/war* **3** to state publicly that you no longer wish to have a connection with sb/sth because you disapprove of him/her/it: *He had renounced his former associates.*

**ren·o·vate** /'rɛnəveɪt/ *verb* [T] to repair an old building and put it back into good condition ▶ **ren·o·va·tion** /ˌrɛnə'veɪʃn/ *noun* [C,U]: *The house is in need of complete renovation.*

**re·nown** /rɪ'naʊn/ *noun* [U] (*formal*) fame and respect because of sth you have done that people admire: *He **won renown as** a fair judge.* ◇ *a pianist **of some/international/great** renown*

**re·nowned** /rɪ'naʊnd/ *adj.* **renowned (as/for sth)** famous and talked about by a lot of people: *It is renowned as one of the province's best restaurants.* ◇ *She is renowned for her patience.*

★**rent**[1] /rɛnt/ *noun* [C,U] money that you pay regularly for the use of land, a house or a building: *a high/low rent* ◇ *How much rent do you pay?*

IDM **for rent** offered for sb to rent: *apartment for rent* (= on a sign)

★**rent**[2] /rɛnt/ *verb* **1** [I,T] to pay money for the use of sth, usually for a fixed period of time: *Let's rent a movie tonight.* ◇ *We rented a car to go on vacation.* ◇ *"Do you own your home?" "No, we're just renting."* **2** [T] **rent sth (out) (to sb)** to allow sb to use sth for money, usually for a fixed period of time: *We could rent out the basement apartment to somebody.* ◇ *Does the video store also rent VCRs?*

**rent·al**[1] /'rɛntl/ *noun* **1** [C,U] the system of renting sth: *The travel agency can arrange your car rental before you go on your trip.* **2** [U] money that you pay when you rent sth: *Video rental is $2.75 for 24 hours.*

**rent·al**[2] /'rɛntl/ *adj.* that is being rented or available to rent: *a rental car*

**'rent conˌtrol** *noun* [U] a situation in a city, state or province in which the cost of renting an apartment is controlled by law ▶ **'rent-conˌtrolled** *adj.*: *rent-controlled apartments*

**re·o·pen** /ˌri'oʊpən/ *verb* [T] **1** to open a store, theater, etc. again, or to be opened again, after being closed for a period of time: *The school was reopened just two weeks after the fire.* ◇ *The store will reopen at 9 a.m. on January 2.* **2** to deal with or begin sth again after a period of time; to start again after a period of time: *to reopen an argument/a discussion/a debate* ◇ *The police have decided to reopen the case.*

IDM **reopen old wounds** to remind sb of sth unpleasant that happened or existed in the past ▶ **re·op·en·ing** *noun* [U, sing.]

**re·or·der** /ˌri'ɔrdər/ *verb* [T] **1** to ask sb to supply you with more of a product: *Please quote this reference number when reordering stock.* **2** to change the order in which sth is arranged

**re·or·gan·ize** /ˌri'ɔrgənaɪz/ *verb* [I,T] to organize sth again or in a new way so that it works better ▶ **re·or·gan·i·za·tion** /riˌɔrgənə'zeɪʃn/ *noun* [C,U]

**Rep.** *abbr.* (in U.S. politics) **1** = REPRESENTATIVE[1] (1): *Rep. James T. Walsh of New York* **2** = REPUBLICAN

**rep** /rɛp/ *noun* (*informal*) **1** [C] (*also formal* **representative**) a person whose job is to travel around a particular area and visit companies, etc., to sell the products of the company for which he/she works: *a sales rep* **2** [U] = REPERTORY: *I played the part when I was a young actor **in rep.*** **3** [C] = REPUTATION: *I don't know why caffeine's suddenly got such a bad rep.* **4** [usually pl.] (in bodybuilding) a set of exercises which are repeated

**re·pack·age** /ˌri'pækɪdʒ/ *verb* [T] **1** to present sth/sb to the public in a new way, so that people will think of it/him/her in a different way **2** to change the way that a product is packaged or presented to its buyers: *The product was repackaged for the teenage market.*

★**re·pair**[1] /rɪ'pɛr/ *verb* [T] to put sth old or damaged back into good condition: *How much will it cost to repair the car?* ◇ (*figurative*) *It's difficult to see how their marriage can be repaired.* ➲ Look at **irreparable**.

★**re·pair**[2] /rɪ'pɛr/ *noun* [C,U] something that you do to fix sth that is damaged: *The bridge is under repair.* ◇ *The swimming pool is closed for repairs to the roof.* ◇ *to be damaged beyond repair*

IDM **in good, bad, etc. repair** (*formal*) in a good, bad, etc. condition

**rep·a·ra·tion** /ˌrɛpə'reɪʃn/ *noun* (*formal*) **1** [U] the act of giving sth to sb or doing sth for him/her in order to show that you are sorry for suffering that you have caused: *Offenders should be forced to **make reparation to** the community.* **2** **reparations** [pl.] money that is paid by a country that has lost a war, for the damage, injuries, etc. that it has caused

**rep·ar·tee** /ˌrɛpɑr'ti; -'teɪ; ˌrɛpər-/ *noun* [U] clever and amusing comments and replies that are made quickly

**re·pa·tri·ate** /ri'peɪtrieɪt/ *verb* [T] **1** to send or bring sb back to his/her own country: *The refugees were forcibly repatriated.* **2** to send money or profits back to your own country ▶ **re·pa·tri·a·tion** *noun* [C,U]: *a voluntary repatriation program*

**re·pay** /ri'peɪ/ *verb* [T] (*pt, pp* **re·paid** /ri'peɪd/) **1 repay sth (to sb)** to pay back money that you owe to sb: *to repay a debt* **2 repay sb (for sth)** to give sth to sb in return for help, kindness, etc.: *How can I ever repay you for all you have done for me?* ▶ **re·pay·ment** *noun* [C,U]: *the repayment of a loan*

**re·peal** /rɪ'pil/ *verb* [T] (e.g. in Congress or Parliament) to make a law no longer valid

★**re·peat**[1] /rɪ'pit/ *verb* **1** [I,T] to say, write or do sth more than once: *Can you repeat what you said? I didn't catch it.* ◇ *"I really don't want to do it," he repeated.* ◇ *Your essay is pretty good, but you repeat yourself several times* (= you say the same thing more than once). ◇ *Billy may have to repeat third grade.* ◇ *History often seems to repeat itself.* **2** [T] to



R

say or write sth that sb else has said or written or that you have learned: *Repeat each sentence after me.* ◇ *Please don't repeat what you've heard here.* ➲ noun repetition

**re·peat²** /rɪˈpit; ˈripit/ ***noun*** [C] something that is done, shown, given, etc. again, especially a program on television

**re·peat·ed** /rɪˈpit̬əd/ ***adj.*** (only *before* a noun) done or happening many times: *There have been repeated accidents on this stretch of road.*

★**re·peat·ed·ly** /rɪˈpit̬ədli/ ***adv.*** many times; often

**re·pel** /rɪˈpɛl/ ***verb*** [T] (**re·pel̲l̲ing**; **re·pel̲l̲ed**) **1** to send or push sb/sth back or away: *The army repelled the enemy attack.* **2** to cause sb to feel strong dislike or disgust: *The dirt and smell repelled her.* ➲ noun **repulsion**

**re·pel·lent** /rɪˈpɛlənt/ ***noun*** [U] a chemical substance that is used to keep insects, etc. away: *mosquito repellent*

**re·pent** /rɪˈpɛnt/ ***verb*** [I,T] (*formal*) to be very sorry about sth bad that you have done: *to repent your sins* ▸ **re·pen·tance** /-əns/ ***noun*** [U] ▸ **re·pen·tant** /-ənt/ ***adj.***

**re·per·cus·sion** /ˌripərˈkʌʃn/ ***noun*** [C, usually pl.] the bad effect or result of sth that you do: *His resignation will have serious repercussions.* ➲ Look at **reverberation** (2).

**rep·er·toire** /ˈrɛpərtwɑr/ ***noun*** [C] all the plays or music that an actor or a musician knows and can perform

**rep·er·to·ry** /ˈrɛpərˌtɔri/ ***noun*** **1** [U] (*also informal* **rep**) the type of work of a theater company in which different plays are performed for short periods of time: *an actor in repertory* ◇ *a repertory actor/theater /company* **2** [C] (*formal*) = REPERTOIRE

**rep·e·ti·tion** /ˌrɛpəˈtɪʃn/ ***noun*** [C,U] doing sth again; sth that you do or that happens again: *We don't want any repetition of what happened on Friday.* ◇ *We're trying to avoid a repetition of what happened on Friday.* ➲ verb **repeat**

**rep·e·ti·tious** /ˌrɛpəˈtɪʃəs/ ***adj.*** involving sth that is often repeated: *a long and repetitious speech* ▸ **rep·e·ti·tious·ly** ***adv.***

**re·pet·i·tive** /rɪˈpɛt̬ət̬ɪv/ ***adj.*** not interesting because the same thing is repeated many times: *repetitive factory work*

**re·phrase** /ˌrɛpəˈtɪʃəs/ ***verb*** [T] to say or write sth using different words in order to make the meaning clearer

★**re·place** /rɪˈpleɪs/ ***verb*** [T] **1** to put sth back in the right place: *Please replace the books on the shelves when you are finished with them.* ➲ **Put back** is more common and less formal. **2** to take the place of sb/sth: *Credit cards have replaced cash in many situations.* **3 replace sb/sth (with sb/sth)** to exchange sb/sth for sb/sth that is better or newer: *We will replace any goods that are damaged.* ▸ **re·place·a·ble** /-əbl/ ***adj.*** OPP **irreplaceable**

**re·place·ment** /rɪˈpleɪsmənt/ ***noun*** **1** [U] exchanging sb/sth for sb/sth that is better or newer: *The carpets are in need of replacement.* **2** [C] a person or thing that will take the place of sb/sth: *Mary is leaving next month, so we need to advertise for a replacement for her.*

**re·play¹** /ˌriˈpleɪ/ ***verb*** [T] to play again sth that you have recorded

**re·play²** /ˈripleɪ/ ***noun*** [C] something on television, on a video or a cassette that you watch or listen to again: *Now let's see a replay of that incredible home run!* ➲ Look also at **instant replay**.

**re·plen·ish** /rɪˈplɛnɪʃ/ ***verb*** [T] (*formal*) **replenish sth (with sth)** to make sth full again by replacing what has been used: *to replenish food and water supplies*

**re·plete** /rɪˈplit/ ***adj.*** (*formal*) **1** (not before a noun) **replete (with sth)** filled with sth; with a full supply of sth: *literature replete with drama and excitement* **2** very full of food

**rep·li·ca** /ˈrɛplɪkə/ ***noun*** [C] an exact copy of sth

**rep·li·cate** /ˈrɛpləkeɪt/ ***verb*** [T] (*formal*) to copy sth exactly: *Subsequent experiments failed to replicate these findings.* ➲ Compare **duplicate³**. ▸ **rep·li·ca·tion** /ˌrɛpləˈkeɪʃn/ ***noun*** [U,C]

★**re·ply¹** /rɪˈplaɪ/ ***verb*** [I,T] (*pres. part.* **re·ply· ing**; *3rd person sing. pres.* **re·plies**; *pt, pp* **re·plied**) to give an answer: *I wrote to Sue, but she hasn't replied.* ◇ *"Yes, I will," she replied.* ◇ *I asked Matthew if he was sorry, and he replied that he was.* ◇ *to reply to a question* ➲ Look at the note at **answer**.

★**re·ply²** /rɪˈplaɪ/ ***noun*** [C,U] (*pl.* **re·plies**) (an) answer: *Alison nodded in reply to my question.* ◇ *How many replies did you get to your ad?*

★**re·port¹** /rɪˈpɔrt/ ***verb*** **1** [I,T] **report (on sb/sth) (to sb/sth)**; **report sth (to sb)** to say or write what you have seen, heard, done, etc.: *All accidents must be reported to the police.* ◇ *Several people reported having seen the boy.* ◇ *Several people reported that they had seen the boy.* **2** [I,T] (in a newspaper or on the television or radio) to write or speak about sth that has happened: *Kate reported on the events in China for the network news.* ◇ *The strike was not reported in the newspapers.* **3** [T] **report sb (to sb) (for sth)** to tell a person in authority about sth wrong that sb has done: *She was reported to the principal for smoking.* **4** [I] **report (to sb/sth) (for sth)** to tell sb in authority that you have arrived in a place: *All visitors must report to the school office.* ◇ *Team members reported for their first practice session today.*

★**re·port²** /rɪˈpɔrt/ ***noun*** [C] a written or spoken description of what you have seen, heard, done, studied, etc.: *a report of an earthquake in California* ◇ *newspaper reports* ◇ *Your assignment is to write a report on the state's economy.* ◇ *a book report* (= about a book that you have read) ◇ *an eyewitness report* (= from the person who saw what happened)

**reˈport card** ***noun*** [C] a written statement about the work of a student: *He had four A's and two B's on his report card.*

**re·port·ed·ly** /rɪˈpɔrt̬ədli/ ***adv.*** according to what people say or what has been reported: *The mayor was taken to the hospital after reportedly suffering chest pains.*

**reˌported ˈspeech** (*also* **indirect speech**) ***noun*** [U] (*grammar*) reporting what sb said earlier, not using the actual words

NOTE For example, Tim's words were, *"I'll call*

*back later."* In reported speech this becomes *"Tim said that he would call back later."*

**re·port·er** /rɪˈpɔrt̬ər/ ***noun*** [C] a person who writes about the news in a newspaper or speaks about it on television or on the radio ➲ Look at **journalist**.

**re·pos·i·to·ry** /rɪˈpɑzəˌtɔri/ ***noun*** [C] (*pl.* **re·pos·i·to·ries**) (*formal*) **1** a place where sth is stored in large quantities **2** a person or book that is full of information: *My father is a repository of family history.*

**re·pos·sess** /ˌripəˈzɛs/ ***verb*** [T] (usually passive) to take back property or goods from sb who has arranged to buy them but who still owes money for them or cannot pay ▸ **re·pos·ses·sion** ***noun*** [C]

**rep·re·hen·si·ble** /ˌrɛprɪˈhɛnsəbl/ ***adj.*** (*formal*) morally wrong and deserving criticism

★**rep·re·sent** /ˌrɛprɪˈzɛnt/ ***verb*** [T] **1** to be a picture, sign, example, etc. of sb/sth: *The yellow lines on the map represent gravel roads.* ◇ *an abstract painting that represents pain* ◇ *Which sound does this phonetic symbol represent?* **2** to describe sb/sth in a particular way: *Susan is represented as a very ordinary person in the book.* **3** to be equal to: *A 3% raise represents a drop in real income if you take inflation into account.* **4** to act or speak in the place of sb else; to be the representative of a group or country: *You will need an attorney to represent you in court.* ◇ *The ambassador represented the President at the funeral.*

**rep·re·sen·ta·tion** /ˌrɛprɪzɛnˈteɪʃn; -zən-/ ***noun*** **1** [U] representing or being represented: *Minority groups are demanding better representation in Congress.* **2** [C] (*formal*) a picture, sign, etc. of sb/sth

**rep·re·sen·ta·tion·al** /ˌrɛprɪzɛnˈteɪʃənl; -zən-/ ***adj.*** **1** (*technical*) (used especially about a style of art or painting) trying to show things as they really are ➲ Compare **abstract**[1](2). **2** involving the act of representing sb/sth: *local representational democracy*

★**rep·re·sen·ta·tive**[1] /ˌrɛprɪˈzɛntət̬ɪv/ ***noun*** [C] **1 Representative** (*abbr.* **Rep.**) a member of the House of Representatives in the U.S. Congress, or of a similar group in the government of a particular state ➲ For more information on the U.S. political system, look at study page **A10**. **2** a person who has been chosen to act or speak for sb else or for a group **3** (*formal*) = REP

★**rep·re·sen·ta·tive**[2] /ˌrɛprɪˈzɛntət̬ɪv/ ***adj.*** **representative (of sb/sth)** typical of a larger group to which it belongs: *Tonight's audience is not representative of the entire nation.* ◇ *a representative sample of the student population* OPP **unrepresentative**

**re·press** /rɪˈprɛs/ ***verb*** [T] **1** to prevent an action or a protest **2** to control an emotion or to try to prevent it from being shown or felt ▸ **re·pres·sion** /rɪˈprɛʃn/ ***noun*** [U]: *memories of political repression in Eastern Europe*

**re·pressed** /rɪˈprɛst/ ***adj.*** **1** (used about a person) not able to show feelings, especially about sex **2** (used about an emotion) that you do not show

**re·pres·sive** /rɪˈprɛsɪv/ ***adj.*** allowing very little freedom: *a repressive government*

**re·prieve** /rɪˈpriv/ ***noun*** [C] an act of stopping or delaying the punishment of a prisoner who has been condemned to death: *to grant sb a last-minute reprieve*

**rep·ri·mand** /ˈrɛprəmænd/ ***verb*** [T] **reprimand sb (for sth)** to tell sb officially that he/she has done sth wrong ▸ **rep·ri·mand** ***noun*** [C]: *a severe reprimand*

**re·print** /ˈriprɪnt/ ***noun*** [C] a copy of sth, especially a photograph or a magazine article: *I'd like to get two reprints of this picture.*

**re·pri·sal** /rɪˈpraɪzl/ ***noun*** [C,U] punishment, especially by military force, for harm that one group of people did to another: *The army carried out reprisals on the village that had sheltered the rebels.* ◇ *Civilian targets were bombed in reprisal.*

**re·prise** /rɪˈpriz/ ***noun*** [usually sing.] a repeated part of sth, especially a piece of music

**re·proach** /rɪˈproʊtʃ/ ***noun*** [U] (*formal*) blame or criticism: *His behavior is* ***beyond reproach*** (= cannot be criticized).

**re·proach·ful** /rɪˈproʊtʃfl/ ***adj.*** expressing blame or criticism: *a reproachful look* ▸ **re·proach·ful·ly** ***adv.***

**rep·ro·bate** /ˈrɛprəbeɪt/ ***noun*** [C] (*formal*) a person who behaves in a way that society thinks is immoral ▸ **rep·ro·bate** ***adj.***

★**re·pro·duce** /ˌriprəˈdus/ ***verb*** **1** [T] to produce a copy of sth: *It is very hard to reproduce a natural environment in the laboratory.* **2** [I,T] (used about people, animals and plants) to produce young: *Fish reproduce by laying eggs.*

**re·pro·duc·tion** /ˌriprəˈdʌkʃn/ ***noun*** **1** [U] the act or process of reproducing or being reproduced: *The sound reproduction on a CD is better than on a cassette.* ◇ *sexual reproduction* **2** [C] a copy of a painting, etc.: *That painting is a reproduction, not an original.*

**re·pro·duc·tive** /ˌriprəˈdʌktɪv/ ***adj.*** connected with the production of young animals, plants, etc.: *the male reproductive organs*

★**rep·tile** /ˈrɛptaɪl; -tl/ ***noun*** [C] an animal, such as a snake or a crocodile, that has rough skin, lays eggs, and whose body temperature changes with the temperature around it ▸ **rep·til·i·an** /rɛpˈtɪliən; -ˈtɪlyən/ ***adj.*** (*figurative*): *He licked his lips in an unpleasantly reptilian way.*

**re·pub·lic** /rɪˈpʌblɪk/ ***noun*** [C] a country that has an elected government and is not ruled by a king or queen: *the Republic of Ireland*

**Re·pub·li·can** /rɪˈpʌblɪkən/ ***noun*** [C] (*abbr.* **R**; **Rep.**) a member or supporter of the Republican Party of the U.S.

**re·pub·li·can** /rɪˈpʌblɪkən/ ***adj.*** **1 Republican** connected with the Republican Party of the U.S: *Republican Congressmen* **2** connected with or supporting a republic ➲ For more information on the U.S. political system, look at study page **A10**.

**the Reˌpublican ˈParty** ***noun*** [sing.] one of the two main political parties in the U.S. ➲ For more information about the political system in the U.S., look at study page **A10**.

**re·pu·di·ate** /rɪˈpyudieɪt/ ***verb*** [T] (*formal*) **1** to



R

refuse to accept sth: *to repudiate a proposal/suggestion* **2** to say officially and/or publicly that sth is not true: *to repudiate an article/a report/a claim* ▸ **re·pu·di·a·tion** /-ˌpyudiˈeɪʃn/ ***noun*** [U]

**re·pug·nant** /rɪˈpʌgnənt/ ***adj.*** (*formal*) making you feel strong dislike or disgust: *The idea of eating meat was repugnant to her.*

**re·pulse** /rɪˈpʌls/ ***verb*** [T] (*formal*) **1** to fight sb who is attacking you and drive him/her away: *to repulse an attack/invasion/offensive* **2** to refuse to accept sb's help, attempts to be friendly, etc.: *She repulsed his advances.* **3** (usually passive) to make sb feel disgust or strong dislike: *I was repulsed by the horrible smell.*

**re·pul·sion** /rɪˈpʌlʃn/ ***noun*** [U] a feeling of very strong dislike of sth that you find extremely unpleasant

**re·pul·sive** /rɪˈpʌlsɪv/ ***adj.*** that causes a strong feeling of dislike; disgusting

**rep·u·ta·ble** /ˈrɛpyəṭəbl/ ***adj.*** that is known to be good: *Make sure you take your car to a reputable mechanic.* ➲ Look at **disreputable**.

★**rep·u·ta·tion** /ˌrɛpyəˈteɪʃn/ ***noun*** [C] (*also informal* **rep**) **reputation (for sth)** the opinion that people in general have about what sb/sth is like: *to have a good/bad reputation* ◇ *The restaurant has a reputation for serving some of the finest food in the city.* ◇ *an international reputation* ◇ *She began to make her reputation as a novelist in the 1990s.*

**re·put·ed** /rɪˈpyuṭəd/ ***adj.*** generally said to be sth, although it is not certain: *He's reputed to earn more than $1 million a year.* ◇ *a reputed gang leader* ▸ **re·put·ed·ly** ***adv.***

★**re·quest**[1] /rɪˈkwɛst/ ***noun*** [C] **request (for sth/that...)** an act of asking for sth: *a request for help* ◇ *to make an official request* ◇ *to grant/turn down a request* ◇ *The judge denied the attorney's request that Nelson be released from jail.* ➲ Look at the grammar note at **recommend**.

**IDM at sb's request/at the request of sb** because sb asked for it: *This report was prepared at the request of the Millville School Board.*

**on/upon request** if you ask: *Nonsmoking rooms are available on request.*

★**re·quest**[2] /rɪˈkwɛst/ ***verb*** [T] **request sth (from/of sb); request that...** (*formal*) to ask for sth: *to request a brochure from a resort* ◇ *We request that all passengers remain seated.* ➲ **Request** is more formal than **ask**.Look at the grammar note at **recommend**.

**req·ui·em** /ˈrɛkwiəm/ (*also* ˌ**requiem** ˈ**mass**) ***noun*** [C] **1** a Christian ceremony for a person who has recently died, at which people say prayers for his or her soul **2** a piece of music for this ceremony

★**re·quire** /rɪˈkwaɪər/ ***verb*** [T] **1** to need: *Please contact us if you require further information.* ◇ *a situation that requires tact and diplomacy* ➲ **Require** is more formal than **need**. **2 require sth; require that...** (often passive) to demand or order sth: *Passengers are required by law to wear seat belts.* ◇ *Province law requires that all drivers have adequate auto insurance.* ➲ Look at the grammar note at **recommend**.

★**re·quire·ment** /rɪˈkwaɪərmənt/ ***noun*** [C] something that you need or that is demanded: *I'm sorry, but you do not meet the requirements for the job that was advertised.* ◇ *college entrance requirements*

**req·ui·site** /ˈrɛkwəzət/ ***adj.*** (*formal*) (only *before* a noun) necessary for a particular purpose: *She lacks the requisite experience for the job.*

**req·ui·si·tion** /ˌrɛkwəˈzɪʃn/ ***verb*** [T] to officially demand the use of a building, vehicle, etc., especially during a war or an emergency: *The school was requisitioned as a military hospital.*

**re·re·lease** /ˌririˈlis/ (*also* **re-release**) ***verb*** [T] to make a movie or a piece of music available to the public again: *The singer plans to rerelease his classic album in April.* ▸ **re·re·lease** /ˈririlis; ˌririˈlis/ ***noun*** [C]: *the rerelease of Disney's 1937 classic*

**re·route** /ˌriˈrut; -ˈraʊt/ ***verb*** [T] to change the route that a road, vehicle, etc. normally follows: *to reroute a phone call* ◇ *to reroute traffic*

**re·run** /ˈrirʌn/ ***noun*** [C] (*informal*) a television program that is being shown again: *"Is there anything good on TV tonight?" "No, just reruns."*

**re·sale** /ˈriseɪl; ˌriˈseɪl/ ***noun*** [U] the sale to another person of sth that you have bought: ***the resale value** of a property*

**re·sched·ule** /ˌriˈskɛdʒəl; -dʒul/ ***verb*** [T] to change the time at which sth has been arranged to happen, especially so that it takes place later: *The meeting has been rescheduled for next week.*

**re·scind** /rɪˈsɪnd/ ***verb*** [T] (*formal*) to officially state that a law, contract, decision, etc. is no longer valid

★**res·cue**[1] /ˈrɛskyu/ ***verb*** [T] **rescue sb/sth (from sb/sth)** to save sb/sth from a situation that is dangerous or unpleasant: *to rescue sb from drowning* ◇ *You rescued me from an embarrassing situation.* ▸ **res·cu·er** ***noun*** [C]

★**res·cue**[2] /ˈrɛskyu/ ***noun*** [C,U] an act of rescuing or the state of being rescued: *The attempted rescue of the mountain climber failed when snow began to fall.*

**IDM come to the/sb's rescue** to try to help or rescue sb: *She was attacked on the street and no one came to her rescue.*

★**re·search**[1] /ˈrisərtʃ; rɪˈsərtʃ/ ***noun*** [U] **research (into/on sth)** a detailed and careful study of sth to find out more information about it: *Bob is doing research into the practical applications of solar power.* ◇ *scientific/medical/historical research* ◇ *Market research has shown that many people now prefer low-fat foods.*

**re·search**[2] /rɪˈsərtʃ; ˈrisərtʃ/ ***verb*** [I,T] to study sth carefully and in detail: *Scientists are still researching the possible causes of so many cases of childhood cancer in the area.* ▸ **re·search·er** ***noun*** [C]

ˌ**research and de**ˈ**velopment** ***noun*** [U] (*abbr.* **R & D**) (in industry, etc.) work that tries to find new products and processes or to improve existing ones

**re·sell** /ˌriˈsɛl/ ***verb*** [T] (*pt, pp* **re·sold**) to sell sth that you have bought to sb else: *He resells the goods at a profit.* ▸ **re·sel·ler** ***noun*** [C]

**re·sem·ble** /rɪˈzɛmbl/ ***verb*** [T] to be or look like sb/sth else: *Laura closely resembles her brother.* ▸ **re·sem·blance** /rɪˈzɛmbləns/ ***noun*** [C,U] **resemblance (between A and B); resemblance**

R

**(to sth)** [C]: *a family resemblance* ◇ *The movie bears no resemblance to the novel* (= it is very different).

**re·sent** /rɪˈzɛnt/ *verb* [T] to feel angry about sth because you think it is unfair: *Louise bitterly resented being treated differently from the men.* ▶ **re·sent·ful** /-fl/ *adj.*: *William felt very resentful at being criticized unfairly.* ▶ **re·sent·ment** *noun* [sing., U]: *Do you feel any resentment toward her new husband?*

**res·er·va·tion** /ˌrɛzərˈveɪʃn/ *noun* **1** [C] an arrangement in which a seat, table, room, etc. is kept available for you to use: *I made a reservation for a table for two in the name of Morgan.* ◇ *Do you have a reservation?* **2** [C,U] a feeling of doubt about sth (such as a plan or an idea): *I still have some reservations about Jerry's proposal.* **3** [C] an area of land where the U.S. government forced Native Americans to live in the past, and where some Native Americans still live

★**re·serve¹** /rɪˈzərv/ *verb* [T] **reserve sth (for sb/sth)** **1** to arrange for a seat, table, room, etc. to be kept available for you to use: *I reserved a table in the nonsmoking section.* **2** to keep sth for a special reason or to use at a later time: *The parking lot is reserved for hotel guests only.*

★**re·serve²** /rɪˈzərv/ *noun*
➤SUPPLY **1** [C, usually pl.] a supply of sth that you keep for a special reason or to use at a later date: *The Middle East still has huge oil reserves.*
➤PROTECTED LAND **2** [C] an area of land where the plants, animals, etc. are protected by law: *a nature/game reserve* **3** [C] (especially in Canada) an area of land which is protected by law and kept especially for the use of a particular group of Aboriginal people
➤SHYNESS **4** [U] the quality of being shy or keeping your feelings hidden: *It took a long time to break down her reserve and get her to relax.*
➤MILITARY FORCE **5 the reserve** [sing.] (*also* **the reserves** [pl.]) extra military forces that a country can use in addition to the regular army, etc. in an emergency
IDM **in reserve** that you keep and do not use unless you need to: *Keep some money in reserve for emergencies.*

**re·served** /rɪˈzərvd/ *adj.* shy and keeping your feelings hidden: *Fred is very reserved until you get to know him well.*

**re·serv·ist** /rɪˈzərvɪst/ *noun* [C] a soldier, etc. who is a member of the RESERVES² (4)(= a military force that can be used in an emergency)

**res·er·voir** /ˈrɛzərvwɑr; -vwɔr/ *noun* [C] a large lake where water to be used in a town or city is stored

**re·set** /ˌriˈsɛt/ *verb* [T] (*pres. part.* **re·set·ting**; *pt, pp* **re·set**) **1** to change a machine, an instrument or a control so that it gives a different time or number or is ready to use again: *You need to reset your watch to local time.* **2** to place sth in the correct position again: *to reset a broken bone*

**re·set·tle** /ˌriˈsɛtl/ *verb* [I,T] **1** to help people go and live in a new country or area; to go and live in a new country or area: *Many of the refugees were resettled in Britain and Canada.* **2** to start to use an area again as a place to live: *The region was only resettled 200 years later.*

**re·side** /rɪˈzaɪd/ *verb* [I] (*formal*) **reside (in/at...)** to have your home in or at a particular place

**res·i·dence** /ˈrɛzədəns/ *noun* **1** [C] (*formal*) the place where sb lives: *The President's official residence is the White House.* **2** [U] the state of having your home in a particular place: *The family applied for permanent residence in Canada.* SYN **residency**

ˈ**residence hall** *noun* [C] (*formal*) = DORMITORY

**res·i·den·cy** /ˈrɛzədənsi/ *noun* (*pl.* **res·i·den·cies**) (*formal*) **1** [C,U] the state of having your home in a particular place: *She has been granted permanent residency in the USA.* SYN **residence** **2** [C,U] the period of time that an artist, a writer or a musician spends working for a particular institution **3** [C,U] the period of time when a doctor working in a hospital receives special advanced training; the position of RESIDENT (2) **4** (*also* **residence**) [C] the official house of sb such as an ambassador

★**res·i·dent¹** /ˈrɛzədənt/ *noun* [C] **1** a person who lives in a place: *Local residents have complained about the smell from the factory.* **2** a doctor who has finished medical school and is continuing his/her training in a hospital

**res·i·dent²** /ˈrɛzədənt/ *adj.* living in a particular place: *the town's* ***resident population*** (= not tourists or visitors) ◇ *to be resident abroad/in the U.S.* ◇ *Tom's our* ***resident expert*** (= our own expert) *on foreign movies.*

ˌ**resident ˈalien** *noun* [C] (*U.S.*) a person from another country who has permission to stay in the U.S.

**res·i·den·tial** /ˌrɛzəˈdɛnʃl/ *adj.* **1** (used about a place or an area) that has houses rather than offices, large stores or factories: *residential suburbs* **2** where you live or stay: *This home provides residential care for the elderly.*

**re·sid·u·al** /rɪˈzɪdʒuəl/ *adj.* (*formal*) (only *before* a noun) remaining at the end of a process: *There are still a few residual problems with the computer program.*

**res·i·due** /ˈrɛzədu/ *noun* [C,U, usually sing.] what remains of sth after the main part is taken or used

**re·sign** /rɪˈzaɪn/ *verb* **1** [I,T] **resign (from sth)** to leave your job or position: *She's threatening to resign if she doesn't get a raise.* ◇ *He resigned as chairman of the committee.* ◇ *I wonder why she resigned from her job.* **2** [T] **resign yourself to sth/doing sth** to accept sth that is bad but that cannot be changed: *Larry resigned himself to the fact that she was not coming back to him.*

**res·ig·na·tion** /ˌrɛzɪɡˈneɪʃn/ *noun* **1** [C,U] **resignation (from sth)** a letter or statement that says you want to leave your job or position: *to hand in your resignation* ◇ *a letter of resignation* **2** [U] the state of accepting sth bad that you cannot change

**re·signed** /rɪˈzaɪnd/ *adj.* accepting sth that is bad but that cannot be changed: *a resigned sigh*
IDM **be resigned to sth/doing sth** to accept sth that is bad but that cannot be changed: *Ben was resigned to the fact that he would never be a pro basketball player.*

**re·sil·ient** /rɪˈzɪlyənt/ *adj.* strong enough to recover quickly from damage, illness, a shock, change, etc. ▶ **re·sil·ience** /-əns/ *noun* [U]

R

**res·in** /ˈrɛzn/ ***noun*** [C,U] **1** a sticky substance that is produced by some trees and is used in making varnish, medicine, etc. **2** an artificial substance similar to resin, used in making plastics

★**re·sist** /rɪˈzɪst/ ***verb*** [I,T] **1** to try to stop sth from happening or to stop sb from doing sth; to fight against sb/sth: *The unions are resisting the proposal to move the factory to Mexico.* ◇ *If the enemy attacks, we will not resist.* ◇ *to resist arrest* **2** to stop yourself from having or doing sth that you want to have or do: *The cake looked so delicious that I couldn't resist it.* ◇ *I couldn't resist opening my present.* ◇ *"Are you coming to the party?" "How could I resist?"*

★**re·sis·tance** /rɪˈzɪstəns/ ***noun*** [U] **1 resistance (to sb/sth)** trying to stop sth from happening or to stop sb from doing sth; fighting against sb/sth: *The government troops overcame the resistance of the rebel army.* ◇ *There is strong resistance to the plan for a new shopping mall in the area.* **2 resistance (to sth)** the power in a person's body not to be affected by disease: *People with AIDS have very little resistance to infection.*

**re·sis·tant** /rɪˈzɪstənt/ ***adj.*** **resistant (to sth) 1** not wanting sth and trying to prevent it from happening: *resistant to change* **2** not harmed by sth: *This watch is water-resistant.*

**res·o·lute** /ˈrɛzəlut; ˌrɛzəˈlut/ ***adj.*** having or showing great determination: *resolute action/leadership* ◇ *He became even more resolute in his opposition to the plan.* ▶ **res·o·lute·ly** ***adv.***: *They remain resolutely opposed to the idea.*

**res·o·lu·tion** /ˌrɛzəˈluʃn/ ***noun*** **1** [U] the quality of being firm and determined ➲ Look at **resolve²**. **2** [C] a firm decision to do or not to do sth: *Rose made a New Year's resolution to quit smoking.* **3** [C] a formal decision that is made after a vote by a group of people: *The UN resolution condemned the invasion.*

★**re·solve¹** /rɪˈzɑlv/ ***verb*** (*formal*) **1** [T] to find a solution to a problem: *Most of the difficulties have been resolved.* **2** [I,T] to decide sth and be determined not to change your mind: *Ray resolved never to let the same thing happen again.* **3** [I,T] **resolve (to do sth)**; **resolve (that...)** to make a formal decision after a vote by a group of people

**re·solve²** /rɪˈzɑlv/ ***noun*** [U] (*formal*) strong determination to achieve sth: *The difficulties in her way merely* ***strengthened her resolve.*** ➲ Look at **resolution.**

**res·o·nance** /ˈrɛzənəns/ ***noun*** **1** [U] (used about sound) the quality of being RESONANT (1): *Her voice had a strange and thrilling resonance.* **2** [C,U] (*technical*) the sound or other vibration produced in an object by sound or vibrations of a similar frequency from another object **3** [C,U] (*written*) (in a piece of writing, music, etc.) the power to bring images, feelings, etc. into the mind of the person reading or listening; the images, etc. produced in this way

**res·o·nant** /ˈrɛzənənt/ ***adj.*** **1** (*formal*) (used about sound) deep, clear and continuing for a long time: *a deep resonant voice* **2** (*technical*) causing sounds to continue for a long time: *resonant frequencies* **3** having the power to bring images, feelings, memories, etc. into your mind: *a poem filled with resonant imagery*

**res·o·nate** /ˈrɛzəneɪt/ ***verb*** (*formal*) [I] **1** (used about a voice, an instrument, etc.) to make a deep, clear sound that continues for a long time: *Her voice resonated around the theater.* **2 resonate (with sth)** of a place to be filled with sound; to make a sound continue longer: *The room resonated with the chatter of 100 people.* **3 resonate (with sb/sth)** to remind sb of sth; to be similar to what sb thinks or believes: *These issues resonated with the voters.*

PHRV **resonate with sth** (*written*) to be full of a particular quality or feeling: *She makes a simple story resonate with complex themes and emotions.*

★**re·sort¹** /rɪˈzɔrt/ ***verb*** [I] **resort to sth** to do or use sth bad or unpleasant because you feel you have no choice: *People who owe huge amounts of money have had to resort to selling their houses.*

★**re·sort²** /rɪˈzɔrt/ ***noun*** [C] a place in the country, in the mountains, near the ocean, etc. where people can stay when they are on vacation and do activities such as swimming and golf: *a ski resort*

IDM **(as) a last resort** → LAST¹

**re·sound** /rɪˈzaʊnd/ ***verb*** [I] (*written*) **1 resound (through sth)** (used about a sound, voice, etc.) to fill a place with sound: *Laughter resounded through the house.* ◇ (*figurative*) *The tragedy resounded around the world.* **2 resound (with sth)** (used about a place) to be filled with sound: *The street resounded with the thud of marching feet.*

**re·sound·ing** /rɪˈzaʊndɪŋ/ ***adj.*** (only *before* a noun) **1** very loud: *resounding cheers* **2** (used about a success, etc.) very great: *a resounding victory*

★**re·source¹** /ˈrisɔrs; rɪˈsɔrs/ ***noun*** [C, usually pl.] something that a person, country, etc. has or can use: *Russia is rich in natural resources such as oil and minerals.* ◇ *The video is an excellent resource for teachers.* ➲ Look also at **human resources.**

**re·source²** /ˈrisɔrs; -zɔrs; rɪˈsɔrs; -ˈzɔrs/ ***verb*** [T] (usually passive) to give a person or an organization the materials, money, staff, etc. that he/she/it needs in order to be able to do sth or achieve sth successfully: *We need to ensure that primary health care workers are adequately resourced.*

**re·source·ful** /rɪˈsɔrsfl/ ***adj.*** good at finding ways of doing things

★**re·spect¹** /rɪˈspɛkt/ ***noun*** **1** [U] **respect (for sb/sth)** the feeling that you have when you admire or have a very high opinion of sb/sth: *I don't have much respect for politicians.* ◇ *to win/lose sb's respect* ➲ Look at **self-respect**. **2** [U] **respect (for sb/sth)** the quality of being polite to sb: *We should all treat older people with more respect.* OPP **disrespect 3** [U] **respect (for sb/sth)** care for or attention to sb/sth: *The military regime shows little respect for human rights.* **4** [C] a detail or point: *In what respects do you think things have changed in the last ten years?* ◇ *Her performance was outstanding in every respect.*

IDM **with respect to sth** (*formal*) about or concerning: *I am writing with respect to your recent letter.*

**pay your respects** → PAY²

★**re·spect²** /rɪˈspɛkt/ ***verb*** [T] **1 respect sb/sth**

**(for sth)** to admire or have a high opinion of sb/sth: *I respect him for his honesty.* **2** to show care for or pay attention to sb/sth: *We should respect other people's cultures and values.* ◇ *to respect sb's wishes* (= do what they want)

**re·spect·a·ble** /rɪ'spɛktəbl/ ***adj.*** **1** considered by society to be good, proper or correct: *a respectable, hard-working family* ◇ *Wear something respectable to the party!* **2** fairly good or large: *a respectable salary* ▸ **re·spect·a·bil·i·ty** /rɪˌspɛktə'bɪləṭi/ ***noun*** [U]

**re·spect·ful** /rɪ'spɛktfl/ ***adj.*** **respectful (to/toward sb)** showing RESPECT[1] (2) or politeness toward sb/sth: *The crowd listened in respectful silence.* OPP **disrespectful** ▸ **re·spect·ful·ly** ***adv.***

**re·spec·tive** /rɪ'spɛktɪv/ ***adj.*** (only *before* a noun) belonging separately to each of the people who have been mentioned: *After lunch, we all went back to our respective offices.*

**re·spec·tive·ly** /rɪ'spɛktɪvli/ ***adv.*** in the same order that sb/sth was mentioned: *German and Italian courses are offered in Munich and Rome respectively.*

**res·pi·ra·tion** /ˌrɛspə'reɪʃn/ ***noun*** [U] (*formal*) the act of breathing ▸ **res·pi·ra·to·ry** /'rɛsprəˌtɔri/ ***adj.***

**res·pi·ra·tor** /'rɛspəˌreɪṭər/ ***noun*** [C] **1** a piece of equipment that makes it possible for sb to breathe over a long period when he/she is unable to do so naturally: *She was* ***put on a respirator.*** **2** a device worn over the nose and mouth to allow sb to breathe in a place where there is a lot of smoke, gas, etc.

**res·pite** /'rɛspət/ ***noun*** [sing., U] **respite (from sth)** a short period of rest from sth that is difficult or unpleasant: *There was a brief respite from the fighting.*

**re·splen·dent** /rɪ'splɛndənt/ ***adj.*** (*written*) **resplendent (in sth)** brightly colored and attractive in an impressive way: *He glimpsed Sonia, resplendent in a red silk dress.*

★**re·spond** /rɪ'spɑnd/ ***verb*** [I] **1 respond (to sb/sth) (with/by sth)** (*formal*) to say or do sth as an answer or reaction to sth: *I wrote to them last week, but they haven't responded yet.* ◇ *He responded to my question with a nod.* ◇ *The administration has responded to criticism by promising to spend more on education.* ➲ **Respond** is more formal than **answer** or **reply**. **2 respond (to sb/sth)** to have or show a good or quick reaction to sb/sth: *The patient did not respond well to the new treatment.*

★**re·sponse** /rɪ'spɑns/ ***noun*** [C,U] **response (to sb/sth)** an answer or reaction to sb/sth: *I've sent my resume to 20 companies, but I haven't received any responses yet.* ◇ *The company acted in response to economic pressure.* ◇ *He knocked on the door, but there was no response.* ◇ *Julia Roberts' new movie has received a positive response.*

★**re·spon·si·bil·i·ty** /rɪˌspɑnsə'bɪləṭi/ ***noun*** (*pl.* **re·spon·si·bil·i·ties**) **1** [U] **responsibility (for sb/sth)** the state of being responsible; having to make decisions about sth so that you are blamed if sth goes wrong: *The new job means taking on more responsibility.* ◇ *I refuse to take responsibility if anything goes wrong.* ◇ *A terrorist group claimed responsibility for planting the bomb.* **2** [U] the quality of being sensible: *I wish you would show a little more responsibility.* **3** [C] a job or duty that you must do: *It is John's responsibility to make sure the orders are sent out on time.* ◇ *I feel that I have a responsibility to help them – after all, they did help me.* ◇ *the responsibilities of parenthood* ◇ *The kids are my responsibility* (= I am responsible for them).

★**re·spon·si·ble** /rɪ'spɑnsəbl/ ***adj.*** **1** (not before a noun) **responsible (for sb/sth)**; **responsible (for doing sth)** having the job or duty of doing or taking care of sb/sth (so that you are blamed if sth goes wrong): *The school is responsible for the safety of the children between 9 a.m. and 3 p.m.* ◇ *The manager is responsible for making sure the store is run according to company policy.* **2** (not before a noun) **responsible (for sth)** being the cause of or to blame for sth: *Who was responsible for the accident?* ◇ *If anything goes wrong, the boss will hold me responsible!* **3** (not before a noun) **responsible (to sb/sth)** having to report to sb/sth with authority or in a higher position about what you have been doing: *Members of Congress are responsible to their voters.* **4** (used about a person) that you can trust to behave well and sensibly: *All children must be accompanied by a responsible adult.* OPP **irresponsible**

**re·spon·si·bly** /rɪ'spɑnsəbli/ ***adv.*** in a sensible and RESPONSIBLE (4) way: *I hope you will behave responsibly while I am out.*

**re·spon·sive** /rɪ'spɑnsɪv/ ***adj.*** paying attention to sb/sth and reacting in a suitable or positive way: *The company has achieved success by being responsive to sudden changes in the market.*

★**rest**[1] /rɛst/ ***verb***

➤ RELAX **1** [I] to relax, sleep or do nothing after a period of activity or because of illness: *We've been walking for hours. Let's rest here for a while.* ◇ *The nurse said we couldn't visit him because he was resting.* **2** [T] to allow sb/sth to REST (1): *Your knee will get better if you rest it as much as you can.*

➤ BE SUPPORTED **3** [I,T] **rest (sth) on/against sth** to place sth in a position where it is supported by sth else; to be in such a position: *She rested her head on his shoulder and went to sleep.*

➤ IN COURT OF LAW **4** [I] in a court of law, if one side rests that lawyer stops asking questions because he/she thinks that enough has been said to prove the accused person's guilt or innocence: *Your Honor, the prosecution rests.*

➤ BE BURIED **5** [T] to be buried. People say "rest" to avoid saying "be buried": *She rests beside her husband in the local cemetery.* ◇ *May he* ***rest in peace.*** ➲ Look at **RIP**.

IDM **rest assured (that...)** (*formal*) (used to emphasize that what you say is true or will definitely happen): *You may rest assured that we will do all we can to find him.*

**I rest my case** (used to say that you do not need to say any more about sth because you think that you have proved your point)

PHR V **rest on/upon sb/sth** to depend or be based on sth: *The whole theory rests on a very simple idea.*

**rest with sb** to be sb's responsibility: *We can*

R

*make some recommendations, but the final decision rests with the manager.*

★**rest²** /rɛst/ ***noun*** **1 the rest (of sth)** [sing.] the part that is left: *We ate lunch and spent the rest of the day at the beach.* ◇ *If you don't want the rest, I'll eat it.* ◇ *She takes no interest in what happens in the rest of the world.* **2 the rest** [pl.] the ones that are left; the others: *One of the questions was tough, but the rest were pretty easy.* ◇ *They were the first people to arrive. The rest came later.* **3** [C,U] a period or the action of relaxing, sleeping or doing nothing: *I can't walk any farther! I need a rest.* ◇ *Try not to worry now. Get some rest and think about it again tomorrow.* **4** [C,U] (in music) a period of silence between notes; a sign that shows a rest between notes ➲ picture at **music**.

IDM **at rest** (*formal*) not moving: *Do not open the door until the vehicle is at rest.*

**come to (a) rest** to stop moving: *The car crashed through a fence and came to rest in a field.*

**put sth to rest** to show that a belief, an idea, etc. is not true: *We want to put to rest people's fears about the new power plant.*

**re·start** /ˌriˈstɑrt/ ***verb*** [I,T] to start again, or to make sth start again, after it has stopped: *to restart a game/car/meeting* ◇ *The doctors struggled to restart his heart.*

★**res·tau·rant** /ˈrɛstrɑnt; -tərɑnt; -tərənt/ ***noun*** [C] a place where you can buy and eat a meal: *a fast-food restaurant* ◇ *Andy took me out to lunch at a Chinese restaurant.* ◇ *She works as a waitress in a local restaurant.* ➲ Look at **cafe** and **cafeteria**.

**rest·ful** /ˈrɛstfl/ ***adj.*** that makes you feel relaxed and peaceful: *a hotel with a restful atmosphere*

**ˈrest home** ***noun*** [C] a place where old or sick people are cared for

**rest·less** /ˈrɛstləs/ ***adj.*** unable to relax or sit still because you are bored, nervous or impatient: *The kids always get restless on long car trips.* ▸ **rest·less·ly** ***adv.***

★**re·store** /rɪˈstɔr/ ***verb*** [T] **restore sb/sth (to sb/sth) 1** to bring sth back into existence or use, or to put sb/sth back into a previous condition or position: *The police have restored law and order following the riots.* ◇ *Winning their last two games has restored the team's confidence.* ◇ *The former leader has been restored to power.* **2** to put sth (a building, a painting, a piece of furniture, etc.) back into a condition that is as close as possible to its original condition: *I'm restoring my grandmother's antique dresser.* ▸ **res·to·ra·tion** /ˌrɛstəˈreɪʃn/ ***noun*** [U]: *a campaign for the restoration of democracy*

**re·strain** /rɪˈstreɪn/ ***verb*** [T] **restrain sb/sth (from sth/from doing sth)** to keep sb or sth under control; to prevent sb or sth from doing sth: *Can't you restrain your dog?* ◇ *I had to restrain myself from saying something nasty.*

**re·strained** /rɪˈstreɪnd/ ***adj.*** not showing strong feelings; calm

**reˈstraining ˌorder** ***noun*** [C] **restraining order (against sb)** an official order given by a judge which demands that sth must or must not be done. A restraining order does not require a trial in court but only lasts for a limited period of time. ➲ Look at **injunction**.

**re·straint** /rɪˈstreɪnt/ ***noun*** **1** [U] the quality of behaving in a calm or moderate way: *It took a lot of restraint on my part not to hit him.* **2** [C] **restraint (on sb/sth)** a limit or control on sth: *Are there any restraints on what newspapers are allowed to publish?* **3** [C] a piece of equipment in a car, plane, etc. that helps to hold sb/sth in place: *The use of child safety restraints is required in automobiles.*

★**re·strict** /rɪˈstrɪkt/ ***verb*** [T] to limit the number, amount, size, freedom, etc. of sb/sth: *I'm trying to restrict myself to two cups of coffee a day.* ◇ *Having small children tends to restrict your freedom.* ◇ *There is a plan to restrict the use of cars on the college campus.*

**re·strict·ed** /rɪˈstrɪktəd/ ***adj.*** controlled or limited in some way: *The junior tournament is restricted to players under age 16.* ◇ *The land around the military base is a restricted area.*

★**re·stric·tion** /rɪˈstrɪkʃn/ ***noun*** **restriction (on sth) 1** [U] the act of limiting the freedom of sb/sth: *He is opposed to any restriction on people's right to free speech.* **2** [C] something (sometimes a rule or law) that limits the number, amount, size, freedom, etc. of sb/sth: *parking restrictions in the downtown area* ◇ *The government has imposed restrictions on the number of immigrants permitted to enter this country.*

**re·stric·tive** /rɪˈstrɪktɪv/ ***adj.*** limiting; preventing people from doing what they want

★**rest·room** /ˈrɛstrum/ ***noun*** [C] a room with toilets in it in a public building ➲ Look also at **men's room**, **ladies' room** and at the note at **toilet**.

**re·struc·ture** /ˌriˈstrʌktʃər/ ***verb*** [T] to organize sth such as a system or a company in a new and different way ▸ **re·struc·tur·ing** ***noun*** [U,C, usually sing.]: *The corporation is undergoing a major restructuring.*

★**re·sult¹** /rɪˈzʌlt/ ***noun*** **1** [C,U] **result (of sth)** something that happens because of sth else; the final situation at the end of a series of actions: *The result of our argument was that we never spoke to each other again.* ◇ *The traffic was very heavy, and as a result, I arrived late.* ◇ *This wasn't really the result that I was expecting.* **2** [C,U] a good effect of an action: *He has tried very hard to find a job, but with no result.* ◇ *The treatment is beginning to show results.* **3** [C] the score or final position at the end of a game, competition or election: *Stay tuned for today's playoff results.* ◇ *The results of the contest will be published next week.* ◇ *The result of the election was a gain for the Democrats in the House.* **4** [C] something that is discovered by a medical test: *I'm still waiting for the result of my X-ray.*

★**re·sult²** /rɪˈzʌlt/ ***verb*** [I] **result (from sth)** to happen or exist because of sth: *Ninety percent of the deaths resulted from injuries to the head.*

PHRV **result in sth** to cause sth to happen or exist; to produce as an effect: *There has been an accident on the freeway, resulting in long delays.*

**re·sume** /rɪˈzum/ ***verb*** [I,T] to begin again or continue after a pause or interruption: *The meeting resumed after a short break.* ◇ *After the birth of the baby, she resumed her career.* ▸ **re·sump·tion** /rɪˈzʌmpʃn/ ***noun*** [sing., U] (*formal*): *a resumption of diplomatic relations between the two countries*

**ré·su·mé** (*also* **re·su·mé, re·su·me**) /ˈrɛzəmeɪ; ˌrɛzəˈmeɪ/ (*also* **cur·ric·u·lum vi·tae**) ***noun*** [C] a written account of your education and work experience, often used when you are applying for a new job: *Applicants should send a résumé and cover letter to the following address:...*

**res·ur·rect** /ˌrɛzəˈrɛkt/ ***verb*** [T] to bring sth that has not been used or has not existed for a long time back into use or existence: *From time to time, they resurrect classic TV programs and show them again on cable.*

**res·ur·rec·tion** /ˌrɛzəˈrɛkʃn/ ***noun*** **1 the Resurrection** [sing.] (in the Christian religion) the return to life of Jesus Christ **2** [U] the act of resurrecting sth: *the resurrection of the nation's auto industry*

**re·sus·ci·tate** /rɪˈsʌsəteɪt/ ***verb*** [T] to bring sb who has stopped breathing back to life: *All efforts to resuscitate the patient failed.* ► **re·sus·ci·ta·tion** /rɪˌsʌsəˈteɪʃn/ ***noun*** [U]

**re·tail¹** /ˈriteɪl/ ***noun*** [U] the selling of goods to the public in stores, etc. (for personal use, not to be sold again): *the recommended retail price* ➲ Look at **wholesale.**

**re·tail²** /ˈriteɪl/ ***verb*** [I] **retail at/for sth** to be for sale in a store at a particular price: *This camera retails for $99.95.*

**re·tail·er** /ˈriteɪlər/ ***noun*** [C] a person or company that sells products in a store

★**re·tain** /rɪˈteɪn/ ***verb*** [T] (*formal*) to keep or continue to have; not to lose: *Despite all her problems, she has managed to retain a sense of humor.* ◇ *The Democrats retained control of the Senate after the election.* ◇ *The house has retained much of its original character.* ◇ *These cups retain the heat.* ➲ noun **retention**

**re·tain·er** /rɪˈteɪnər/ ***noun*** [C] **1** a sum of money that is paid to sb, especially a lawyer, for work he/she is going to do: *The agency will pay you a monthly retainer.* **2** a plastic and wire device that you wear inside your mouth to keep your teeth straight

**re·take¹** /ˌriˈteɪk/ ***verb*** [T] (*pt* **re·took**; *pp* **re·taken**) **1** (used especially about an army) to take control of sth such as a town again: *Forces moved in to retake the city.* ◇ (*figurative*) *Moore fought back to retake the lead later in the race.* **2** to film or photograph sth again **3** to take an exam or a test again, usually after failing it the first time

**re·take²** /ˈriteɪk/ ***noun*** [C] the act of filming a scene in a movie again, because it was not right before: *We had to do several retakes before we got it right.*

**re·tal·i·ate** /rɪˈtælieɪt/ ***verb*** [I] **retaliate (against sb/sth)** to react to sth bad that sb does to you by doing sth bad in return: *They have announced that they will retaliate against anyone who attacks their country.* ► **re·tal·i·a·tion** /rɪˌtæliˈeɪʃn/ ***noun*** [U] **retaliation (against sb/sth)**; **retaliation (for sth)**: *He was shot in retaliation for his attack on a gang member.*

**re·tard·ed** /rɪˈtɑrdəd/ ***adj.*** (*old-fashioned*) (used about people) less advanced mentally than other people of the same age

**NOTE** This word is often considered offensive nowadays. If a person has difficulties in learning things, we can say that he/she has **special needs**, has a **learning disability** or is **mentally disabled**.

**retch** /rɛtʃ/ ***verb*** [I] to make sounds and movements as if you are vomiting: *The smell made her retch.*

**re·tell** /ˌriˈtɛl/ ***verb*** [T] (*pt, pp* **re·told**) to tell a story again, often in a different way

**re·ten·tion** /rɪˈtɛnʃn/ ***noun*** [U] the act of keeping sth or of being kept: *Many experts are against the retention of this law.*

**re·think** /ˌriˈθɪŋk/ ***verb*** [I,T] (*pt, pp* **re·thought** /-ˈθɔt/) to think about sth again because you probably need to change it: *The administration has been forced to rethink its economic policy.*

**ret·i·cent** /ˈrɛt̬əsənt/ ***adj.*** **reticent (about sth)** unwilling to tell people about things: *He was extremely reticent about his personal life.* ► **ret·i·cence** ***noun*** [U] (*formal*): *That night she had overcome her natural reticence and talked about their married life.*

**ret·i·na** /ˈrɛtn·ə/ ***noun*** [C] (*pl.* **ret·i·nas** or **ret·i·nae** /ˈrɛtn·i/) a layer of tissue at the back of the eye that is sensitive to light and sends signals to the brain about what is seen

★**re·tire** /rɪˈtaɪər/ ***verb*** [I] **retire (from sth)** to leave your job and stop working, usually because you have reached a certain age: *She's worried that she won't have enough money to live on when she retires.* ◇ *Michael Stich retired from professional tennis when he was still a young man.* ◇ *He retired as the team's coach in 2003.*

**re·tired** /rɪˈtaɪərd/ ***adj.*** having stopped work permanently, usually because of having reached a certain age: *a retired teacher* ◇ *He's retired, but his wife is still working.*

**re·tir·ee** /rɪˌtaɪəˈri/ ***noun*** [C] a person who is retired

★**re·tire·ment** /rɪˈtaɪərmənt/ ***noun*** **1** [C,U] the act of stopping or being forced to stop working permanently, usually because of reaching a certain age: *Is there a mandatory retirement age at your company?* ◇ *There have been a number of retirements in our department this year.* ◇ *She decided to take early retirement.* ◇ *The former world champion has announced his retirement* (= that he is not going to play, etc. again). **2** [sing., U] the situation or period after retiring from work: *We all wish you a long and happy retirement.*

**re·tort** /rɪˈtɔrt/ ***verb*** [T] to reply quickly to what sb says, in an angry or amusing way: *"Who asked you for your opinion?" she retorted.* ◇ *He retorted that there was no such thing as an honest politician.* ► **retort** ***noun*** [C]: *an angry retort*

**re·touch** /ˌriˈtʌtʃ/ ***verb*** [T] to make small changes to a picture or photograph so that it looks better

**re·trace** /riˈtreɪs/ ***verb*** [T] to repeat a past trip, series of events, etc.: *I retraced my steps* (= I went back the way I had come) *in an attempt to find my wallet.*

**re·tract** /rɪˈtrækt/ ***verb*** **1** [T] (*formal*) to say that sth you have said earlier is not true or correct or that you did not mean it: *He made a false confession which he later retracted.* **2** [I,T] to move back into the main part of sth; to pull sth back into the

R

main part of sth: *The animal retracted into its shell.* ◇ *The undercarriage failed to retract.* ◇ *The undercarriage was fully retracted.* ▶ **re·trac·tion** /-ˈtrækʃn/ ***noun*** [C]

**re·train** /ˌriˈtreɪn/ ***verb*** [I,T] **retrain (sb) (as sth)** to learn, or to teach sb, a new type of work, a new skill, etc.: *She retrained as a teacher.* ◇ *Staff have been retrained to use the new technology.*

**re·treat[1]** /rɪˈtrit/ ***verb*** [I] **1** (of an army, etc.) to move backward in order to leave a battle or in order not to become involved in a battle: *The general gave an order to retreat from the area.* OPP **advance 2** to move backward; to go to a safe or private place: *Firefighters were forced to retreat by the intense heat.* ◇ *(figurative) She seems to retreat into a world of her own sometimes.*

**re·treat[2]** /rɪˈtrit/ ***noun*** **1** [C,U] the act of retreating: *The invading forces are now in retreat.* ◇ *the candidate's retreat from his original position* **2** [C] a private place where you can go when you want to be quiet or to rest

**re·tri·al** /ˈritraɪl; ˌriˈtraɪl/ ***noun*** [C] a process in which a case is presented again in a court of law, usually because there was a problem the first time

**ret·ri·bu·tion** /ˌrɛtrəˈbyuʃn/ ***noun*** [U] **retribution (against sb) (for sth)** (*formal*) punishment for a crime or sth that you have done: *The witnesses did not want their real names to be used for fear of retribution.*

**re·trieve** /rɪˈtriv/ ***verb*** [T] **1 retrieve sth (from sb/sth)** to get sth back from the place where it was left or lost: *The police retrieved the body from the river.* **2** (*computing*) to find information that has been stored: *The computer can retrieve all the data about a particular customer.* ▶ **re·triev·al** /-vl/ ***noun*** [U]: *Retrieval of the bodies from the wreckage of the plane took several hours.*

**re·triev·er** /rɪˈtrivər/ ***noun*** [C] a large dog used in hunting to bring back birds that have been shot

**ret·ro** /ˈrɛtroʊ/ ***adj.*** using styles or fashions from the recent past: *the current Seventies retro trend*

**ret·ro·ac·tive** /ˌrɛtroʊˈæktɪv/ ***adj.*** (used about laws, decisions, payments, etc.) applying to the past, as well as to the present and the future: *a tax increase that is retroactive to January 1* ▶ **ret·ro·ac·tive·ly** ***adv.***

**ret·ro·spect** /ˈrɛtrəspɛkt/ ***noun***

IDM **in retrospect** thinking about sth that happened in the past (and often seeing it differently from the way you saw it at the time): *In retrospect, I can see what a stupid mistake it was.*

★**re·turn[1]** /rɪˈtərn/ ***verb***

➤COME/GO BACK **1** [I] **return (to...)**; **return (from...)** to come or go back to a place: *I will be returning to this country in six months.* ◇ *When did you return from Japan?* ◇ *He left his hometown when he was 18 and never returned.*

NOTE **Return** is more formal than **come/go back**.

➤TO PREVIOUS STATE **2** [I] **return (to sth)** to start doing a previous activity or talking about a previous subject again: *The strike is over and they will be returning to work on Monday.* ◇ *We'll return to this subject in next week's lecture.* **3** [I] **return (to sth/to doing sth)** to come or go back to a previous situation or condition: *Telephone services should return to normal soon.*

➤OF FEELING/QUALITY **4** [I] to come back; to happen again: *If the pain returns, make another appointment to see me.*

➤BRING/GIVE BACK **5** [T] **return sth (to sb/sth)** to give, send, put or take sth back: *I stopped loaning him things because he never returns them.* ◇ *If that shirt doesn't fit your husband, you can always return it* (= take it back to the store where you bought it).

➤DO/GIVE THE SAME **6** [T] to react to sth that somebody does, says or feels by doing, saying, or feeling sth similar: *I called them several times and left messages, but they haven't returned any of my calls.* ◇ *Thanks a lot for helping me – I hope I can return the favor sometime.*

★**re·turn[2]** /rɪˈtərn/ ***noun***

➤COMING BACK **1** [sing.] **a return (to/from...)** the act of coming or going back to a place, a previous activity, a previous situation or a previous condition: *the return of warm summer weather* ◇ *a former leader's return to power* ◇ *Our return flight is at 3 o'clock in the morning.*

➤GIVING/SENDING BACK **2** [U] the act of giving, sending, putting or taking sth back: *I demand the return of my passport immediately.*

➤OFFICIAL FORM **3** [C] an official form that you send to the government with information about how much money you have earned and how much tax you must pay: *Federal income tax returns must be filed in April.*

➤PROFIT **4** [C,U] (*also* **returns** [pl.]) the profit from a business or an investment: *They're not expecting any return on their new restaurant for at least a year.* ◇ *This account offers high returns on your savings.*

➤ON COMPUTER **5** [U] (*also* **enter**) (*computing*) the key on a computer that you press in order to begin writing on a new line or to tell the computer to do sth: *Type in your password and press return.*

IDM **in return (for sth)** as payment or in exchange (for sth); as a reaction to sth: *Please accept this gift in return for all your help.*

**reˌturn adˈdress** ***noun*** [C] the address written on a letter or package of the person who sent it

**re·un·ion** /riˈyunyən/ ***noun*** **1** [C] a party or occasion when friends or colleagues meet again after they have not seen each other for a long time: *The college holds an annual reunion for alumni.* ◇ *a family reunion* **2** [C,U] the act of coming together again after a separation: *The released hostages had an emotional reunion with their families at the airport.*

**re·u·nite** /ˌriyuˈnaɪt/ ***verb*** [I,T] **reunite (sb/sth) (with sb/sth)** to come together again; to cause sb/sth to come together again: *The original band members have reunited for a national tour.* ◇ *The missing child was reunited with his parents.*

**re·use** /ˌriˈyuz/ ***verb*** [T] to use sth again or more than once: *Please reuse your envelopes.* ▶ **re·use** /ˌriˈyus/ ***noun*** [C]: *the reuse of materials* ▶ **re·us·a·ble** /ˌriˈyuzəbl/ ***adj.***

**Rev.** ***abbr.*** = REVEREND

**rev** /rɛv/ ***verb*** [T] (**rev·ving**; **revved**) **rev sth (up)** to increase the speed of an engine (usually before driving the car): *Rev the engine for a while to warm it up.*

**re·vamp** /ˌri'væmp/ ***verb*** [T] to make changes to the form of sth, usually to improve its appearance ▸ **re·vamp** /'rivæmp/ ***noun*** [sing.]: *a revamp of the company's offices*

⋆**re·veal** /rɪ'vil/ ***verb*** [T] **1 reveal sth (to sb)** to make sth known that was previously secret or unknown: *She revealed that she had serious financial problems.* ◇ *He refused to reveal any names to the police.* **2** to allow sth to be seen that was previously hidden: *Close inspection of the photograph revealed the identity of the gunman.* ◇ *In a moment, the curtains will open to reveal tonight's grand prize.*

**re·veal·ing** /rɪ'vilɪŋ/ ***adj.*** **1** allowing sth (facts previously unknown, secrets, etc.) to be known: *This book provides a revealing insight into the world of politics.* **2** allowing sth to be seen that is usually hidden: *a very revealing swimsuit*

**rev·el** /'rɛvl/ ***verb***

PHRV **revel in sth/in doing sth** to enjoy sth very much: *He likes being famous and revels in the attention he gets.*

**rev·e·la·tion** /ˌrɛvə'leɪʃn/ ***noun*** [C] something that is made known, that was previously secret or unknown (especially sth surprising): *This magazine is full of revelations about the private lives of famous people.*

**rev·el·er** /'rɛvələr/ (*also* **rev·el·ler**) ***noun*** [C] a person who is having fun in a noisy way, usually with a group of other people and often after drinking alcohol

**rev·el·ry** /'rɛvlri/ ***noun*** [U] (*also* **rev·el·ries** [pl.]) noisy fun, usually involving a lot of eating and drinking: *We could hear sounds of revelry from the house opposite.*

**re·venge** /rɪ'vɛndʒ/ ***noun*** [U] something that you do to punish sb who has hurt you, made you suffer, etc.: *He made a fool of me and now I want revenge.* ◇ *The attack was an act of revenge.*

IDM **take/get revenge (on sb) (for sth)** to punish sb in return for sth bad that he/she has done to you: *He wants to take revenge on the judge who sent him to prison.*

**out of revenge (for sth)**; **in revenge (for sth)** as a way of punishing sb in return for sth bad he/she has done to you: *The shooting was in revenge for an attack on the drug dealer's family.*

**rev·e·nue** /'rɛvənu/ ***noun*** [U, pl.] income received by a government, company, etc.: *Revenue from income tax rose last year.* ◇ *Oil revenues are a vital part of the country's economy.* ➲ Look also at **IRS** and **CCRA**.

**ˌRevenue 'Canada** ***noun*** [sing.] (*Cdn*) = CCRA

**re·ver·ber·ate** /rɪ'vərbəreɪt/ ***verb*** [I] **1** (used about a sound) to be repeated several times as it is reflected off different surfaces: *Her voice reverberated around the hall.* SYN **echo 2 reverberate (with/to sth)** (used about a place) to seem to shake because of a loud noise: *The hall reverberated with the sound of music and dancing.* **3** (*formal*) to have a strong effect on people for a long time or over a large area: *Repercussions of the case continue to reverberate through the financial world.*

**re·ver·ber·a·tion** /rɪˌvərbə'reɪʃn/ ***noun*** **1** [C,U, usually pl.] a loud noise that continues for some time after it has been produced because of the surfaces around it: *The house shook with the reverberation of the bomb.* SYN **echo 2 reverberations** [pl.] the effects of sth that happens, especially unpleasant ones that spread among a large number of people: *the political reverberations of the scandal* ➲ Look at **repercussion**.

**re·vere** /rɪ'vɪr/ ***verb*** [T] (*formal*) (usually passive) **revere sb (as sth)** to feel great respect or admiration for sb/sth: *He is now revered as a national hero.*

**rev·er·ence** /'rɛvərəns/ ***noun*** [U] a feeling of great respect: *She has great reverence for classical literature.*

**Rev·er·end** /'rɛvərənd; 'rɛvrənd/ ***adj.*** (*also formal* **the Reverend**) (*abbr.* **Rev.**) the title of a Christian minister: *(the) Reverend Charles Gray*

**re·ver·sal** /rɪ'vərsl/ ***noun*** [C,U] the act of changing sth to the opposite; an occasion when sth changes to the opposite of what is usual or expected: *The administration insists that there will be no reversal of policy.* ◇ *The decision announced yesterday was a complete reversal of last week's decision.* ◇ *a reversal of roles* (= when each person does what the other person was doing)

**re·verse**[1] /rɪ'vərs/ ***adj.*** opposite to what is expected or has just been described: *In Brazil, the reverse situation is true.*

⋆**re·verse**[2] /rɪ'vərs/ ***noun*** **1** [sing.] **the reverse (of sth)** the complete opposite of the previous statement or of what is expected: *This should have been a relaxing trip, but it was just the reverse.* **2** [U] the position of the gears in a car, etc. that makes it move backward: *Put the car in reverse and back into that parking space.* ➲ Look also at **drive**[2](4), **neutral**[2] and **park**[1](4).

IDM **in reverse** in the opposite order, starting at the end and going backward to the beginning; in the opposite way of the previous direction

⋆**re·verse**[3] /rɪ'vərs/ ***verb*** [T] **1** to change a decision, a process, etc. to the opposite: *It's too late to reverse your decision now; you've already signed the contract.* ◇ *Some experts say that exercise and good nutrition can reverse the early signs of aging.* ◇ *to reverse a trend* **2 reverse yourself** to change your opinion to the opposite: *The city council reversed itself and approved the proposal to build a new fire station.* **3** to put sth in the opposite position: *Writing is reversed in a mirror.* ◇ *My husband and I have reversed roles – he stays home now and I go to work.*

**re·vers·i·ble** /rɪ'vərsəbl/ ***adj.*** **1** (used about clothes) that can be worn with either side on the outside: *a reversible coat* **2** that can be undone: *Some of the harmful effects of smoking may be reversible if you quit early enough.* OPP **irreversible**

**re·vert** /rɪ'vərt/ ***verb*** [I] **revert (to sth)** to return to a previous state or to sth that you did previously: *The land will soon revert to jungle if it is not farmed.*

⋆**re·view**[1] /rɪ'vyu/ ***noun*** **1** [C,U] the act of examining or considering sth again in order to decide whether changes are necessary: *There will be a review of your performance after the first six months.* ◇ *The system is in need of review.* **2** [C] the act of looking back at sth in order to check, remember, or be clear about sth: *a review of the major events of the year* **3** [C] a newspaper or magazine article, or an item on television or radio, in which sb gives

R

an opinion on a new book, movie, play, etc.: *The show got bad reviews.* ◇ *a book review*

★**re·view²** /rɪˈvyu/ ***verb*** **1** [T] to examine or consider again in order to decide whether changes are necessary: *Your progress will be reviewed after one year.* **2** [I,T] to look at or think about sth again to make sure that you understand it, especially when preparing for a test: *Let's review what we've covered in this chapter so far.* **3** [T] to write an article or to talk on television or radio, giving an opinion on a new book, movie, play, etc.: *A movie critic reviews the latest releases.*

**re·view·er** /rɪˈvyuər/ ***noun*** [C] a person who writes REVIEWS¹ (3) of books, movies, etc.

**re·vise** /rɪˈvaɪz/ ***verb*** [T] to make changes to sth in order to correct or improve it: *The book has been revised for this new edition.* ◇ *a revised estimate of the cost of the project* ▸ **re·vi·sion** /rɪˈvɪʒn/ ***noun*** [C,U]: *The whole system is in need of revision.*

**re·vi·tal·ize** /riˈvaɪţl·aɪz/ ***verb*** [T] to make sth stronger or more active: *plans to revitalize inner-city neighborhoods*

**re·viv·al** /rɪˈvaɪvl/ ***noun*** **1** [C,U] the act of becoming or making sth strong or popular again: *economic revival* ◇ *a revival of interest in traditional farming methods* **2** [C] a new performance of a play that has not been performed for some time: *a revival of a popular musical on Broadway*

**re·vive** /rɪˈvaɪv/ ***verb*** [I,T] **1** to become or make sb/sth strong or healthy again; to come or to bring sb back to life or consciousness: *Hopes have revived for an early end to the fighting.* ◇ *I'm awfully tired, but I'm sure a cup of coffee will revive me.* ◇ *Attempts were made to revive him, but he was already dead.* **2** to become or make sth popular again; to begin to do or use sth again: *Attendance at games has revived since the team started winning.* ◇ *to revive an old custom*

**re·voke** /rɪˈvoʊk/ ***verb*** [T] (*formal*) to officially cancel sth so that it is no longer valid: *After the appeal, his sentence was revoked.*

**re·volt** /rɪˈvoʊlt/ ***verb*** **1** [I] **revolt (against sb/sth)** to protest in a group (often violently) against the person or people in power: *A group of generals revolted against the government.* **2** [T] to make sb feel disgusted or sick: *The sight and the smell revolted him.* ➲ noun revulsion ▸ **re·volt *noun*** [C,U]: *The revolt was quickly put down by the army.* ◇ *What started as a small protest has turned into widespread revolt.*

**re·volt·ing** /rɪˈvoʊltɪŋ/ ***adj.*** extremely bad; disgusting: *a revolting smell of fish*

★**rev·o·lu·tion** /ˌrɛvəˈluʃn/ ***noun*** **1** [C,U] changing or trying to change the political system by violent action, etc.: *the French Revolution of 1789* ◇ *Student leaders are calling for revolution.* **2** [C] **a revolution (in sth)** a complete change in methods, opinions, etc., often as a result of progress: *a revolution in the treatment of diseases such as cancer* ◇ *the Industrial Revolution* **3** [C,U] a movement around sth; one complete turn around a central point (e.g. in a car engine): *400 revolutions per minute*

**rev·o·lu·tion·ar·y¹** /ˌrɛvəˈluʃn·ˌɛri/ ***adj.*** **1** connected with or supporting political revolution: *Revolutionary forces have attacked the country's capital.* ◇ *the revolutionary leaders* **2** producing great changes; very new and different: *a revolutionary new method of treating cancer*

**rev·o·lu·tion·ar·y²** /ˌrɛvəˈluʃn·ˌɛri/ ***noun*** [C] (*pl.* **rev·o·lu·tion·ar·ies**) a person who takes part in and supports a revolution

**the ˌRevoˌlutionary ˈWar** ***noun*** [sing.] the war (1775-1783) in which the United States won its independence from Britain ➲ Look at the note at **White House**.

**rev·o·lu·tion·ize** /ˌrɛvəˈluʃn·aɪz/ ***verb*** [T] to change sth completely: *a discovery that could revolutionize the treatment of mental illness*

**re·volve** /rɪˈvɑlv/ ***verb*** [I] to move in a circle around a central point; to go around: *The earth revolves around the sun.*

PHRV **revolve around sb/sth** to have sth as the most important part: *Her life revolves around her career.*

**re·volv·er** /rɪˈvɑlvər/ ***noun*** [C] a type of small gun with a container for bullets that goes around ➲ Look at the note at **gun**.

**reˌvolving ˈdoor** ***noun*** **1** [C] a type of door in an entrance to a large building that turns around in a circle as people go through it **2** [sing.] (used to talk about a place or an organization that people enter and then leave again very quickly): *The newsroom became a revolving-door workplace.* **3** [sing.] (used to talk about a situation in which the same events or problems keep happening): *The lack of juvenile detention facilities creates a "revolving door" for young criminal suspects* (= they keep being arrested by the police and then released again very quickly).

**re·vul·sion** /rɪˈvʌlʃn/ ***noun*** [U] a feeling of disgust (because sth is extremely bad)

★**re·ward¹** /rɪˈwɔrd/ ***noun*** **1** [C,U] something that is given in return for work, effort, etc.: *She feels that she has done a lot of work for little or no reward.* ◇ *Being a parent is often hard work but it has its rewards.* **2** [C] an amount of money that is given in exchange for helping the police, returning sth that was lost, etc.: *The police are offering a $5,000 reward for information leading to a conviction.*

★**re·ward²** /rɪˈwɔrd/ ***verb*** [T] **reward sb (for sth/for doing sth)** to give a REWARD¹ (1,2) to sb: *Eventually her efforts were rewarded and she got a job.* ◇ *His parents bought him a bicycle to reward him for getting straight A's on his report card.*

**re·ward·ing** /rɪˈwɔrdɪŋ/ ***adj.*** giving satisfaction: *She finds her work with disabled children very rewarding.*

**re·wind** /ˌriˈwaɪnd/ ***verb*** [T] (*pt, pp* **re·wound**) to make a tape go backward: *Please rewind the tape before you return it.*

**re·word** /ˌriˈwərd/ ***verb*** [T] (*written*) to write sth again using different words in order to make it clearer or more acceptable

**re·work** /ˌriˈwərk/ ***verb*** [T] to make changes to sth in order to improve it or make it more suitable: *We're constantly reworking our old songs.* ▸ **re·work·ing *noun*** [C,U]: *The movie is a reworking of the Frankenstein story.*

**re·write** /ˌriˈraɪt/ ***verb*** [T] (*pt* **re·wrote** /-roʊt/; *pp*

R

**re·writ·ten** /-ˈrɪtn/) to write sth again in a different or better way

**rhap·so·dy** /ˈræpsədi/ ***noun*** [C] (*pl.* **rhap·so·dies**) **1** (often in titles) a piece of music that is full of feeling and is not regular in form: *Liszt's Hungarian Rhapsodies* **2** (*written*) the expression of great enthusiasm or happiness in speech or writing

**rhet·o·ric** /ˈrɛt̬ərɪk/ ***noun*** [U] speech or writing that is intended to impress or influence people ▸ **rhe·tor·i·cal** /rɪˈtɔrɪkl; -ˈtɑr-/ ***adj.*** ▸ **rhe·tor·i·cal·ly** /-kli/ ***adv.***

**rheˌtorical ˈquestion** ***noun*** [C] a question that is not really a question because it does not expect an answer

**rheu·ma·tism** /ˈrumətɪzəm/ ***noun*** [U] a disease that makes the muscles and joints painful, stiff and swollen ▸ **rheu·ma·tic** /rʊˈmæt̬ɪk/ ***adj.***: *rheumatic complaints/pains*

**rhine·stone** /ˈraɪnstoʊn/ ***noun*** [C] a cheap artificial jewel that is made to look like a diamond

**rhi·no** /ˈraɪnoʊ/ ***noun*** [C] (*pl.* **rhi·nos**) (*informal*) = RHINOCEROS

**rhi·noc·er·os** /raɪˈnɑsərəs/ ***noun*** [C] (*pl.* **rhi·noc·er·os** or **rhi·noc·er·os·es**) a large animal from Africa or Asia, with thick skin and either one or two horns on its nose

**rho** /roʊ/ ***noun*** [C] (*symbol* Ρ , ρ) the seventeenth letter of the Greek alphabet ➲ Look at the note at **fraternity**.

**rhu·barb** /ˈrubɑrb/ ***noun*** [U] a plant with long red stems and very large leaves. The stems can be cooked and eaten as fruit.

**rhyme¹** /raɪm/ ***noun*** **1** [U] the technique of using words that have the same sound as each other, especially at the ends of lines: *All of his poetry was written in rhyme.* **2** [C] a word that has the same sound as another: *Can you think of a rhyme for "peace?"* **3** [C] a short piece of writing, or something spoken, in which the words at the end of each line sound the same as the words at the end of previous lines ➲ Look at **nursery rhyme**.

**rhyme²** /raɪm/ ***verb*** **1** [I] to have the same sound as another word; to consist of lines that end with words that sound the same: *"Tough" rhymes with "stuff."* ◇ *"Book" and "look" rhyme.* ◇ *He thinks that all poetry should rhyme.* **2** [T] to put together words that have the same sound: *You can't rhyme "face" with "stays."*

★**rhythm** /ˈrɪðəm/ ***noun*** [C,U] a regular repeated pattern of sound or movement: *the rhythms of jazz* ◇ *I don't care for the tune, but I love the rhythm.* ◇ *He's a terrible dancer because he has no sense of rhythm.*

**rhythm and blues** /ˌrɪðəm ən ˈbluz/ ***noun*** [U] (*abbr.* **R & B**) a type of music that is a mixture of blues and jazz and has a strong rhythm

**rhyth·mic** /ˈrɪðmɪk/ ***adj.*** having rhythm: *the rhythmic qualities of African music* ▸ **rhyth·mi·cal·ly** /-kli/ ***adv.***

**rib¹** /rɪb/ ***noun*** [C] **1** one of the curved bones that go around the chest: *He's so thin that you can see his ribs.* **2** [usually pl.] meat, especially from a cow or pig, that contains an animal's RIB (1): *barbecued ribs*

**rib²** /rɪb/ ***verb*** [T] (**rib·bing**; **ribbed**) (*informal*) to laugh at sb and make jokes about him/her, but in a friendly way: *He always ribbed her about her accent.* ▸ **rib·bing** ***noun*** [U]: *Joe's taken a lot of ribbing from friends who support the Yankees.*

**ribbed** /rɪbd/ ***adj.*** (used especially about fabrics for clothes) having raised lines: *a ribbed sweater*

**rib·bon** /ˈrɪbən/ ***noun*** **1** [C,U] a long, thin piece of material that is used for tying or decorating sth ➲ picture at **knot**. **2** [C] a piece of RIBBON (1), often folded into the shape of a flower, that is given as a prize in a competition: *Carol's apple pie won a blue ribbon* (= the first prize) *at the county fair.* **3** [C] a long, thin piece of material that contains ink: *a typewriter ribbon*

**ˈrib cage** ***noun*** [C] the structure of curved bones, (ribs), that surrounds and protects the chest

★**rice** /raɪs/ ***noun*** [U] the grain from a plant grown in hot, wet countries, that we cook and eat: *a bowl of rice* ◇ *brown rice* ◇ *boiled rice*

**ˈrice ˌpaddy** ***noun*** [C] (*pl.* **rice pad·dies**) = PADDY

★**rich** /rɪtʃ/ ***adj.***

▸WITH A LOT OF MONEY **1** having a lot of money or property; not poor: *a rich family* ➲ Look at **wealthy**. **2 the rich** ***noun*** [pl.] rich people: *The rich are getting richer and the poor are getting poorer.*

▸CONTAINING/PROVIDING STH **3** (not before a noun) **rich in sth** containing a lot of sth: *Oranges are very rich in vitamin C.*

▸SOIL **4** able to produce sth in large amounts: *rich soil*

▸FOOD **5** (used about food) containing a lot of fat, oil, sugar, cream, etc.: *a rich sauce* ◇ *a rich chocolate cake*

▸COLORS/SOUNDS **6** (used about colors, sounds or smells) strong and deep: *a rich purple*

▸ **rich·ness** ***noun*** [U]

**rich·es** /ˈrɪtʃəz/ ***noun*** [pl.] (*formal*) a lot of money or property; wealth: *Despite all his riches, he was a deeply unhappy man.*

**rich·ly** /ˈrɪtʃli/ ***adv.*** **1** extremely well: *She was richly rewarded for her hard work.* **2** fully: *His promotion was richly deserved.* **3** in a beautiful way that looks very expensive: *a richly decorated palace*

**rick·et·y** /ˈrɪkət̬i/ ***adj.*** likely to fall or break; not strongly made: *a rickety old fence*

**rick·sha** /ˈrɪkʃɔ; -ʃɑ/ (*also* **rick·shaw**) ***noun*** [C] a small light vehicle with two wheels used in some Asian countries to carry passengers. The ricksha is pulled by sb walking or riding a bicycle.

**ricksha**

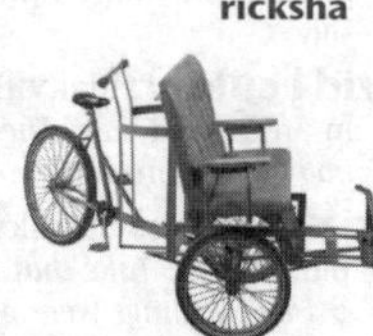

**ric·o·chet** /ˈrɪkəʃeɪ; ˌrɪkəˈʃeɪ/ ***verb*** [I] **ricochet (off sth)** (used about a bullet, etc.) to fly away from a surface after hitting it

★**rid** /rɪd/ ***verb*** [T] (*pres. part.* **rid·ding**; *pt, pp* **rid**) **rid sb/sth of sb/sth** (*formal*) to make sb/sth free from sb/sth that is bad or unwanted: *They have managed to rid the world of smallpox.* ◇ *He was unable to rid himself of his fears and suspicions.*

R

IDM **get rid of sb/sth** to become free of sb/sth or to remove sb/sth: *I didn't enjoy having my family stay at my place. In fact, I was glad to get rid of them.* ◇ *I can't get rid of this stain on the carpet.* ◇ *Let's get rid of that old chair and buy a new one.*

**rid·dance** /ˈrɪdns/ ***noun***
IDM **good riddance** (*informal*) (used for expressing pleasure or relief that sb/sth that you do not like has gone)

**rid·den**[1] *past participle of* RIDE[2]

**rid·den**[2] /ˈrɪdn/ ***adj.*** (usually in compounds) full of sth (usually sth bad): *She was ridden with guilt.* ◇ *She was guilt-ridden.*

**rid·dle** /ˈrɪdl/ ***noun*** [C] **1** a type of question that you ask people for fun that has a clever or amusing answer **2** a person, a thing or an event that you cannot understand

**rid·dled** /ˈrɪdld/ ***adj.*** **riddled with sth** full of: *The car was was riddled with bullet holes.* ◇ *This essay is riddled with mistakes.*

★**ride**[1] /raɪd/ ***noun*** [C] **1** a trip on a horse or bicycle, or in a car, bus, etc.: *They went for a bike ride through the park.* ◇ *She gave me a ride home after the party.* **2** a large machine with small trains or moving seats that people ride for fun: *We went on every single ride at the amusement park!*
IDM **take sb for a ride** (*informal*) to cheat or deceive sb

★**ride**[2] /raɪd/ ***verb*** [I,T] (*pt* **rode** /roʊd/; *pp* **rid·den** /ˈrɪdn/) **1** to sit on a bicycle, horse, etc. and be carried along, controlling its movements: *I've never ridden on a horse.* ◇ *She jumped onto her motorcycle and rode away.* ◇ *I usually ride my bike to school.* **2** to travel as a passenger in a bus, car, etc.: *He's been riding the city bus to work for years.*
IDM **ride roughshod over sb** to treat sb badly and not worry about his/her feelings
PHRV **ride sth out** to manage to survive a difficult situation or time without being harmed by it: *Some residents refused evacuation and chose to stay home and* ***ride out the storm****.*

★**rid·er** /ˈraɪdər/ ***noun*** [C] a person who rides a horse, bicycle, etc.

**ridge** /rɪdʒ/ ***noun*** [C] **1** a long, narrow piece of high land along the top of hills or mountains **2** a line where two sloping surfaces meet

**rid·i·cule**[1] /ˈrɪdəkyul/ ***noun*** [U] unkind laughter or behavior that is meant to make sb/sth appear silly

**rid·i·cule**[2] /ˈrɪdəkyul/ ***verb*** [T] to laugh at sb/sth in an unkind way: *The idea was ridiculed by everybody at the meeting.*

★**ri·dic·u·lous** /rɪˈdɪkyələs/ ***adj.*** very silly or stupid; foolish: *Take that hat off – you look ridiculous!* ◇ *I knew things were going to be bad, but this is ridiculous* (= much worse than I expected). ◇ *They're asking a ridiculous* (= very high) *price for that house.*
▸ **ri·dic·u·lous·ly** ***adv.***: *She gets paid a ridiculously low salary for the work she does.*

**rife** /raɪf/ ***adj.*** (not before a noun) (*formal*) **1 rife with sth** full of sth unpleasant or bad: *a department rife with corruption* **2** (used especially about bad things) very common: *The drug use was rife among certain groups of students.*

**ri·fle**[1] /ˈraɪfl/ ***noun*** [C] a long gun that you hold against your shoulder to shoot with

> NOTE We **load**, **aim** and **fire** a rifle. ➲ Look at the note at **gun**.

**ri·fle**[2] /ˈraɪfl/ ***verb***
PHRV **rifle (through) sth** to search quickly through sth in order to find or steal sth: *She rifled through her clothes for something suitable to wear.*

**rift** /rɪft/ ***noun*** [C] **1** a serious disagreement between friends, groups, etc.: *a growing rift between the brothers* **2** a crack or split in sth

**rig**[1] /rɪg/ ***verb*** [T] (**rig·ging**; **rigged**) **1** to arrange or control an event, etc. in an unfair way, in order to get the result you want: *They claimed that the election had been rigged.* **2 rig sth (up)** to make sth simple or change the way sth works, using any materials you can find: *They found the car was rigged with explosives.*

**rig**[2] /rɪg/ ***noun*** [C] **1** (usually in compounds) a large platform, with special equipment for bringing oil and natural gas out of the ground: *an oil rig* **2** (*informal*) a large truck

★**right**[1] /raɪt/ ***adj.***
➤ NOT LEFT **1** on or of the side of the body that faces east when a person is facing north; not left: *Do you write with your right hand or your left?* ◇ *Your seats are on the right side of the plane.*
➤ CORRECT/TRUE **2** correct; true: *Sorry, that's not the right answer.* ◇ *Do you have the right time?* ◇ *You're absolutely right – the movie does start at 7 o'clock.* ◇ *You were right about the weather – it did rain.*
➤ APPROPRIATE **3** best; most suitable: *I don't think this is the right color for the walls.* ◇ *I hope I made the right decision.* ◇ *We wouldn't have missed the flight if we'd left at the right time.* ◇ *You have to know the right people if you want to join that golf club.*
➤ NORMAL **4** normal; satisfactory: *Her voice didn't sound quite right on the phone.*
➤ MORALLY GOOD **5** (used about behavior/actions) good; fair or what the law allows: *It's not right to pay people so little.* ◇ *It was right of her to give you the news at once.* ◇ *It's never right to steal.*
➤ USED AS QUESTION **6** (*informal*) (used as a question at the end of a sentence to check whether sb agrees with you or whether what you said is correct): *We want to be the best company in the business, right?* ◇ *Let's see – you ordered a cheeseburger and fries, right?*
➤ SHOWING UNDERSTANDING **7** (*informal*) (used to tell sb that you agree with or understand what he/she has just said, or that you will do what he/she has asked you to do): *"...And then we went to that new restaurant on Sunset Drive." "Right."* ◇ *"Take this package down to the post office." "Right."*
IDM **all right** → ALL[2]
**right side up** with the top part turned to the top; in the correct, normal position: *Fortunately my toast landed right side up when I dropped it on the floor.* OPP **upside down**
**on the right/wrong track** → TRACK[1]
▸ **right·ness** ***noun*** [U]

★**right**[2] /raɪt/ ***adv.***
➤ NOT LEFT **1** to the RIGHT[1](1) side; not left: *Turn right at the traffic light.*



R

➤SATISFACTORILY **2** correctly; in a satisfactory way: *Did I spell your name right?* ◇ *Nothing seems to be going right for me these days.* ◇ *These shoes don't fit right.*
➤EXACTLY **3** exactly: *The bus was right on time.* ◇ *The accident happened right here.*
➤COMPLETELY **4** all the way: *He kicked his foot right through the door!*
➤IMMEDIATELY **5** immediately: *He left right after dinner.* ◇ *Wait here a minute – I'll be right back.*
IDM **right away** immediately; without any delay: *I'll take care of that right away.* ◇ *I understood right away what she wanted me to do.*
**right now 1** at this moment; exactly now: *We can't discuss this right now.* **2** at the present time (when compared with the past or the future): *Interest rates are relatively low right now.*
**right off the bat** (*informal*) without delay; at the beginning: *We both liked each other right off the bat.*
**serve sb right** → SERVE

★**right**[3] /raɪt/ ***noun***
➤NOT LEFT SIDE **1** [U] the RIGHT[1] (1) side or direction; not left: *We live in the first house on the right.* ◇ *If you look slightly to your right, you will see the Rocky Mountains in the distance.* **2** [C] a turn to the right, or a street or road on the right: *Make a right at the next intersection.* ◇ *Take the first right after the gas station.*
➤STH MORALLY GOOD **3** [U] what is morally good and fair: *Children learn about right and wrong from a very early age.*
➤MORAL/LEGAL CLAIM **4** [C] a thing that you are allowed to do according to the law: *In the U.S., citizens have the right to vote at 18.* ◇ *Freedom of speech is one of the basic human rights.* ◇ *civil rights* (= the rights each person has to political and religious freedom, etc.) **5** [U] **right to sth/to do sth** a moral authority to do sth: *You have no right to tell me what to do.*
➤POLITICS **6 the right** (*also* **the Right**) [sing.] the people or political parties who support low taxes, very little government control over businesses and strict, traditional moral behavior
IDM **in your own right** because of what you are yourself and not because of other people: *She's a very wealthy woman in her own right* (= not only because she married somebody who is rich).
**within your rights (to do sth)** acting in a reasonable or legal way: *You are perfectly within your rights to demand to see your lawyer.*

**right**[4] /raɪt/ ***verb*** [T] **1** to return to a normal position: *The boat tipped over and then righted itself again.* **2** to correct sth

> NOTE This verb is almost always used in this sense with the noun **wrong**: *There are many wrongs that need to be righted.* You do not "right" a mistake; you **correct** it.

ˌ**right ˈangle** ***noun*** [C] an angle of 90°: *A square has four right angles.* ➲ picture at **angle**.

ˌ**right-angled ˈtriangle** ***noun*** [C] = RIGHT TRIANGLE

**right·eous** /ˈraɪtʃəs/ ***adj.*** (*formal*) morally good or fair ➲ Look at **self-righteous**.

**right·ful** /ˈraɪtfl/ ***adj.*** (only *before* a noun) (*formal*) fair, proper or legal: *You have a rightful claim to your father's property.* ▶ **right·ful·ly** ***adv.***

ˈ**right-hand** ***adj.*** (only *before* a noun) of or on the right of sb/sth: *The mailbox is on the right-hand side of the road.* ◇ *a sharp right-hand turn*

ˌ**right-ˈhand·ed** ***adj.*** using the right hand more than the left for writing, etc.

ˌ**right-hand ˈman** ***noun*** [C] (*pl.* **right-hand men**) the person you rely on most to help and support you in your work

**right·ly** /ˈraɪtli/ ***adv.*** correctly or fairly: *As you rightly said, it's time to decide what we want.*

ˌ**right of ˈway** ***noun*** [U, sing.] (used in road traffic) the RIGHT[3] (4) to continue while other traffic must stop: *Pedestrians always have the right of way at intersections.*

ˌ**right ˈtriangle** (*also* ˌ**right-angled ˈtriangle**) ***noun*** [C] a triangle with one angle of 90° (a right angle)

ˌ**right ˈwing** ***noun*** [sing.] the people in a political party who support ideas such as low taxes, very little government control over businesses and strict, traditional moral behavior: *the right wing of the Republican party* ▶ ˌ**right-ˈwing** ***adj.***: *a right-wing talk show host* OPP **left-wing**

**rig·id** /ˈrɪdʒɪd/ ***adj.*** **1** not able or willing to change or be changed; strict: *rigid rules and regulations* **2** stiff; not easy to bend: *For air travel, a rigid suitcase is better than a soft bag.* ◇ *She was rigid with fear.* ▶ **ri·gid·i·ty** /rɪˈdʒɪdət̬i/ ***noun*** [U] ▶ **rig·id·ly** ***adv.***: *regulations that are rigidly enforced*

**rig·or** /ˈrɪgər/ ***noun*** (*formal*) **1** [C, usually pl.] severe conditions; difficulties: *the rigors of a harsh climate* **2** [U] care and attention to detail

**rig·or·ous** /ˈrɪgərəs/ ***adj.*** thorough and careful: *Rigorous tests have been carried out on the drinking water.* ▶ **rig·or·ous·ly** ***adv.***

**rile** /raɪl/ ***verb*** [T] (usually passive) to annoy sb or make him/her angry: *Nothing ever seemed to rile him.*
IDM **be/get (all) riled up** (*informal*) to be or get very annoyed: *What are you getting all riled up about?*

**rim** /rɪm/ ***noun*** [C] an edge at the top or outside of sth that is round: *the rim of a cup* ◇ *glasses with silver rims* ➲ picture at **cup**.

**rind** /raɪnd/ ***noun*** [C,U] the thick hard skin on the outside of some fruits and some types of cheese, etc.

> NOTE **Rind** is hard and is not usually removed with the fingers. We say the **rind** or **peel** of a lemon or an orange, but only the **rind** of a watermelon. A fruit with a thinner or softer covering has a **skin**. So apples, pears, etc. all have **skins**. We usually say that a banana has a **peel**.

★**ring**[1] /rɪŋ/ ***noun*** [C]
➤JEWELRY **1** a piece of jewelry, a round piece of metal, often of silver or gold, that you wear on your finger: *a wedding ring* ◇ *an engagement ring* ◇ *a gold/diamond ring* ➲ picture at **jewelry**.
➤CIRCLE **2** (usually in compounds) a round object of any material with a hole in the middle: *a key ring* (= for holding keys) **3** a circle: *His coffee cup left an*

R

*ugly ring on the table.* ◇ *The house was surrounded by a ring of police officers.*
➤SOUND **4** the sound made by a bell: *I thought I heard a ring at the door.*
➤FOR PERFORMANCE/COMPETITION **5** the space with seats all around it where a performance, sports match, etc. takes place: *a circus ring* ◇ *a boxing ring*
➤GROUP OF PEOPLE **6** a number of people who are involved together in sth that is secret or not legal: *a smuggling ring*

★**ring²** /rɪŋ/ ***verb*** (*pt* **rang** /ræŋ/; *pp* **rung** /rʌŋ/) **1** [I,T] to make a sound like a bell or to cause sth to make this sound: *Is that the phone ringing?* ◇ *We rang the doorbell again and again, but nobody answered.* **2** [I] **ring (for sb/sth)** to ring a bell in order to call sb, ask for sth, etc.: *"Did you ring?" asked the nurse.* **3** [I] to be filled with loud sounds: *My ears were still ringing an hour after the concert.*
IDM **ring a bell** to sound familiar or to remind you, not very clearly, of sth: *"Do you know Jane Sykes?" "Well, the name rings a bell."*
**ring off the hook** (used about a telephone) to ring all the time because many people are calling: *I haven't had a break yet – the phone's been ringing off the hook all morning!*
**ring true/hollow** to sound as if you should/should not believe it: *Her words just didn't ring true.*
PHR V **ring out** to sound loudly and clearly: *A pistol shot rang out.*
**ring sth up** to add together the costs of things, e.g. prices of things that sb is buying in a store: *When the cashier rang up my total, I was shocked.*

**ring³** /rɪŋ/ ***verb*** (*pt, pp* **ringed** /rɪŋd/) [T] to surround sb/sth: *The whole area was ringed by police.*

ˈ**ring** ˌ**finger** ***noun*** [C] the finger next to the smallest one, especially on the left hand, on which a wedding ring is traditionally worn

**ring·lead·er** /ˈrɪŋlidər/ ***noun*** [C] a person who leads a group of people who are doing sth wrong or causing trouble: *Who is the ringleader of the group?*

**rink** /rɪŋk/ ***noun*** [C] **1** (*also* ˈ**ice rink**) a large area of ice, or a building containing a large area of ice, that people can skate or play hockey on **2** an area or a building where you can roller skate

**rinse** /rɪns/ ***verb*** [T] to wash sth in water in order to remove soap or dirt, etc.: *Rinse your hair thoroughly after each shampoo.* ◇ *You should rinse the apples before you eat them.* ▶ **rinse** ***noun*** [C]: *Give the paint brush a good rinse after using it.*

**ri·ot** /ˈraɪət/ ***noun*** [C] fighting and noisy violent behavior by a crowd of people: *Further riots have broken out in the downtown area.* ◇ *Police have been brought in to deal with the riots.* ▶ **ri·ot** ***verb*** [I]: *There is a danger that the prisoners will riot if conditions don't improve.* ▶ **ri·ot·er** ***noun*** [C]

**ri·ot·ous** /ˈraɪət̬əs/ ***adj.*** (*formal*) wild or violent; lacking in control: *The crowd was becoming increasingly riotous.*

**RIP** /ˌɑr aɪ ˈpi/ ***abbr.*** rest in peace (often written on graves)

**rip¹** /rɪp/ ***verb*** (**rip·ping**; **ripped**) **1** [I,T] to tear quickly and sharply: *My jeans ripped when I was climbing over the fence.* ◇ *He ripped the letter in two and threw it in the trash.* ◇ *The blast of the bomb ripped the house apart.* **2** [T] to pull sth quickly and violently: *He ripped the poster from the wall.* ◇ *The roof was ripped off by the tornado.* **3** [I] to move very quickly: *The house was badly damaged when fire ripped through the roof and second floor.*
PHR V **rip sb off** (*informal*) to steal from sb, or to cheat sb by asking too much money for sth
**rip sth up** to tear sth into small pieces

**rip²** /rɪp/ ***noun*** [C] a long tear or cut (in material, etc.)

**ripe** /raɪp/ ***adj.*** (used about fruit, grain, etc.) ready to be picked and eaten
IDM **be ripe for sth** to be ready for sth or in a suitable state for sth: *Conditions in the area are ripe for hurricane formation.*

**rip·en** /ˈraɪpən/ ***verb*** [I,T] to make sth ripe or to become ripe

ˈ**rip-off** ***noun*** [C] (*informal*) something that costs too much money: *$5 for a cup of coffee is a total rip-off!*

**rip·ple¹** /ˈrɪpl/ ***noun*** [C] **1** a very small wave or movement on the surface of water: *The breeze sent tiny ripples across the lake.* **2** a gentle sound: *A ripple of laughter ran around the room.*

**rip·ple²** /ˈrɪpl/ ***verb*** [I,T] to move gently: *The branches of the trees rippled in the wind.* ◇ *The wind rippled the surface of the ocean.*

★**rise¹** /raɪz/ ***noun*** **1** [C] an increase: *There has been a rise in the number of people out of work.* ◇ *a sharp price rise* ➲ Look at **drop²**(4) and **fall¹**(1). **2** [sing.] the process of becoming more powerful or important: *His rise in the world of politics was remarkable.*
IDM **be on the rise** to be increasing: *Violent crime is on the rise in several major cities.*
**give rise to sth** to cause sth: *The news gave rise to considerable anxiety among many people.*

★**rise²** /raɪz/ ***verb*** [I] (*pt* **rose** /roʊz/; *pp* **ris·en** /ˈrɪzn/)
➤MOVE UPWARD **1** to move upward, to become higher or to increase: *Smoke was rising from the chimney.* ◇ *Her voice rose in anger* (= became louder). ◇ *Do you think inflation will continue to rise?* ◇ *The temperature has risen to nearly ninety degrees.* ◇ *Let the dough rise for an hour.* ➲ Look at **fall**.
➤GET UP **2** to stand up: *The audience rose and applauded the singers.* **3** (*formal*) to get out of bed: *They rose at dawn in order to be in Washington by eight.* ➲ In this sense **get up** is more common.
➤OF SUN/MOON **4** (used about the sun, moon, etc.) to appear above the horizon: *The sun rises in the east and sets in the west.*
➤BECOME VISIBLE **5** to show (as sth tall above the surroundings): *A range of mountains rose in the distance.*
➤OF SOUND **6** to come from: *Shouts of protest rose from the crowd.*
➤FIGHT **7 rise (up) (against sb/sth)** to start opposing or fighting people in authority: *The people were afraid to rise up against the dictator.*
➤BECOME POWERFUL/IMPORTANT **8** to move to a higher position (in rank, society, career, etc.): *He rose rapidly within the company.*
IDM **rise to the occasion, challenge, task, etc.** to be successful in dealing with sth by working

harder or doing things better than you normally do: *Do you think she will rise to the demands of the job?*

★**risk**[1] /rɪsk/ ***noun*** **1** [C,U] **risk (of sth/that...)** a possibility (that sth dangerous or bad could happen): *There's always a risk that the price will go up if you wait too long.* ◇ *Do you think there's any risk of fire?* **2** [C] a dangerous or stupid thing to do: *It was an unnecessary risk to pass that truck on the hill.* **3** [C] a person or thing that might cause danger: *That open window is a real security risk.*

IDM **at your own risk** having the responsibility for whatever may happen: *This building is in a dangerous condition – enter at your own risk.*

**at risk** in danger: *Small children are most at risk from the disease.*

**at the risk of sth/doing sth** with the possibility of sth bad: *At the risk of sounding pushy, can I give you some advice?*

**run the risk of (doing sth)** to do sth knowing that the result might be bad or unpleasant; to risk: *If we don't leave early, we run the risk of missing the plane.*

**take a risk**; **take risks** to do sth that you know might fail or be dangerous, etc.: *You shouldn't take risks when driving.* ◇ *He's very young, but I'm prepared to take a risk and give him a job.*

★**risk**[2] /rɪsk/ ***verb*** [T] **1** to take the chance that sth bad could happen: *If you don't study hard now, you risk failing your final exams.* **2** to put sth or yourself in a dangerous position: *The man risked his life to save the little boy.*

**risk·y** /ˈrɪski/ ***adj.*** (**risk·i·er**; **risk·i·est**) dangerous; involving a chance that sth bad could happen: *risky business investments*

**ris·qué** /rɪˈskeɪ/ ***adj.*** a risqué performance, comment, joke, etc. is a little shocking, usually because it is about sex

**rite** /raɪt/ ***noun*** [C] a ceremony performed by a particular group of people, often for religious purposes: *fertility/funeral rites* ◇ *initiation rites* (= performed when a new member joins a secret society) ➲ Look at **last rites**.

**ˌrite of ˈpassage** ***noun*** [C, usually pl.] (*pl.* **ˌrites of ˈpassage**) a ceremony or an event that marks an important stage in sb's life

**rit·u·al**[1] /ˈrɪtʃuəl/ ***noun*** [C,U] an action, ceremony or process which is usually repeated in the same pattern: *priests performing a ritual in a temple*

**rit·u·al**[2] /ˈrɪtʃuəl/ ***adj.*** (only *before* a noun) done according to a particular pattern or tradition ▸ ***rit·u·al·ly adv.***

**ritz·y** /ˈrɪtsi/ ***adj.*** (**ritz·i·er**; **ritz·i·est**) (*informal*) fashionable and expensive: *a ritzy hotel*

★**ri·val**[1] /ˈraɪvl/ ***noun*** [C] a person or thing that is competing with another: *They're business rivals.* ◇ *The top candidate has a 3% lead over her closest rival.* ◇ *a gun battle between rival gangs*

★**ri·val**[2] /ˈraɪvl/ ***verb*** [T] **rival sb/sth (for sth)** to be as good as sb/sth: *This novel doesn't rival his earlier writing.* ◇ *Nothing rivals skiing for sheer excitement.*

**ri·val·ry** /ˈraɪvl·ri/ ***noun*** [C,U] (*pl.* **ri·val·ries**) competition between people, groups, etc.: *There was a lot of rivalry between the sisters.*

★**riv·er** /ˈrɪvər/ ***noun*** [C] a large natural stream of water that flows across the land: *the Mississippi River* ◇ *a picnic on the bank of the river*

> NOTE A river **flows** into a lake or an ocean. The **mouth** of the river is the place where it joins the lake or ocean. A boat travels **on** the river. We walk, sail, etc. **up** or **down** the river. A small river is a **creek** or **stream**.

**riv·er·front** /ˈrɪvərfrʌnt/ ***noun*** [sing.] the land or property by the side of a river: *People were strolling along the riverfront.* ◇ *a riverfront restaurant*

**riv·er·side** /ˈrɪvərsaɪd/ ***noun*** [sing.] the ground along either side of a river: *a riverside path/restaurant* ◇ *They've built a new house on the riverside.*

**riv·et**[1] /ˈrɪvət/ ***noun*** [C] a metal pin for fastening two pieces of metal together

**riv·et**[2] /ˈrɪvət/ ***verb*** [T] (usually passive) to interest sb very much: *I was riveted by her story.*

**riv·et·ing** /ˈrɪvət̬ɪŋ/ ***adj.*** extremely interesting: *His speech was absolutely riveting.*

**roach** /roʊtʃ/ ***noun*** [C] = COCKROACH

★**road** /roʊd/ ***noun*** **1** [C] a way between places, with a hard surface which cars, buses, etc. can drive on: *Route 27 is the main road into town.* ◇ *The traffic was terrible because of all the road construction.* ◇ *a few miles up/down the road* (= farther along the road) ◇ *a dirt/gravel road* ◇ *back roads* (= small, minor roads) ◇ *road signs*

> NOTE **Highways** are roads that connect cities and towns. A road in a town or city that has buildings at the side is usually called a **street**. **Street** is not used for roads outside towns: *a street map of San Francisco.* However, streets in cities or towns may have the word **Road** as part of their names. ➲ Look also at the note at **freeway**.

**2 Road** (*abbr.* **Rd.**) [sing.] (used in names of roads): *60 Stone Road*

IDM **hit the road** → HIT[1]

**on the road 1** traveling: *We were on the road for 14 hours.* **2** (used about a sports team) playing in another team's city: *The Cubs have lost all their games on the road so far this season.*

**on the road to sth** on the way to achieving sth: *The nation's economy is on the road to recovery.*

**road·block** /ˈroʊdblɑk/ ***noun*** [C] a barrier put across the road by the police or army to stop traffic

**road·ie** /ˈroʊdi/ ***noun*** [C] (*informal*) a person who works with musicians, especially pop bands, when they are on tour, and helps move and set up their equipment

**road·kill** /ˈroʊdkɪl/ ***noun*** [U] (*informal*) animals that have been killed by cars on a road

**ˈroad map** ***noun*** [C] **1** a map that shows the roads of an area, especially one that is designed for a person who is driving a car **2** a set of instructions or suggestions about how to do sth or find out about sth: *a road map to peace*

**road·run·ner** /ˈroʊdˌrʌnər/ ***noun*** [C] a N American bird of the cuckoo family, that lives in desert areas and can run very fast

**road·side** /ˈroʊdsaɪd/ ***noun*** [C, usually sing.] the

R

edge of a road: *cars parked along the roadside ◇ a roadside vegetable stand*

**ˈroad trip** *noun* [C] (*informal*) a trip made in a car over a long distance

**road·way** /ˈroʊdweɪ/ *noun* [C] the part of the road used by cars, etc.; not the side of the road

**roam** /roʊm/ *verb* [I,T] to walk or travel with no particular plan or aim: *There were several dogs roaming the neighborhood last night.*

**roam·ing** /ˈroʊmɪŋ/ *noun* [U] the use of or the ability to use a cellular phone outside its normal area

**roar¹** /rɔr/ *noun* [C] a loud, deep sound like that made by a lion: *the roar of a jet plane overhead ◇ roars of laughter*

**roar²** /rɔr/ *verb* **1** [I] to make a loud, deep sound: *We watched as a jet roared overhead. ◇ She roared with laughter at the joke. ◇ 50,000 fans roared as the Cowboys won the Super Bowl.* **2** [I] to make the sound that is typical of a lion: *The lion opened its huge mouth and roared.* **3** [T] **roar sth (out)** to express sth very loudly: *The audience roared its approval.*

PHRV **roar along, down, past, etc.** to move in the direction mentioned, making a loud, deep sound: *A motorcycle roared past us.*

**roar·ing** /ˈrɔrɪŋ/ *adj.* **1** making a very loud noise: *the roaring waves* **2** (used about a fire) burning very well **3** very great: *a roaring success*

**roast¹** /roʊst/ *verb* **1** [I,T] to cook or be cooked in an oven or over a fire: *a smell of roasting meat ◇ to roast a chicken* ➲ Look at the note at **cook**. **2** [T] to heat and dry sth: *roasted peanuts* **3** [I] (*informal*) to be very hot: *Turn on the air conditioner – I'm roasting in here!*

**roast²** /roʊst/ *adj.* (only *before* a noun) cooked by roasting: *roast beef*

**roast³** /roʊst/ *noun* **1** [C,U] a piece of meat that has been roasted **2** [C] an outdoor meal at which food is roasted: *a hot dog roast* ➲ Look at **barbecue** and **cookout**.

**rob** /rɑb/ *verb* [T] (**rob·bing**; **robbed**) **rob sb/sth (of sth)** **1** to take sth (money, property, etc.) from a person or place illegally: *to rob a bank ◇ Several people on the bus were robbed of their money and jewelry.* ➲ Look at the note at **steal**. **2** to take sth away from sb/sth that he/she/it should have: *His injury robbed him of the chance to play in the Super Bowl.*

**rob·ber** /ˈrɑbər/ *noun* [C] a person who steals from a bank, etc. ➲ Look at the note at **thief**.

**rob·ber·y** /ˈrɑbəri/ *noun* [C,U] (*pl.* **rob·ber·ies**) the crime of stealing from a bank, etc.: *They were accused of armed robbery. ◇ There's been a robbery. They took half a million dollars.*

**robe** /roʊb/ *noun* [C] **1** a long, loose piece of clothing: *a judge's black robe* **2** = BATHROBE

**rob·in** /ˈrɑbən/ *noun* [C] a small brown bird with a bright red breast. Robins are thought to be a sign of spring.

**ro·bot** /ˈroʊbɑt/ *noun* [C] a machine that can move and that can be made to do some of the work that a person does. Some robots are made to look like people.

**ro·bust** /roʊˈbʌst/ *adj.* strong and healthy: (*figurative*) *a robust economy*

★**rock¹** /rɑk/ *noun* **1** [U] the very hard substance that forms part of the earth's surface: *layers of rock formed over millions of years* **2** [C] a piece or an area of stone: *The ship hit the rocks and started to sink. ◇ to go rock climbing ◇ The boy threw a rock at the dog.* **3** [U] (*also* ˈ**rock** ˌ**music**) a type of popular music with a very strong beat, played on electric guitars, etc.: *I like jazz better than rock. ◇ a rock singer ◇ a rock band*

**rock²** /rɑk/ *verb* **1** [I,T] to move backward and forward or from side to side; to make sb/sth do this: *sailboats rocking gently on the waves ◇ The baby won't go to sleep unless you rock her for a while.* **2** [T] to shake sth violently: *San Francisco was rocked by an earthquake.* **3** [T] to cause shock to sb/sth: *Riots rocked downtown Los Angeles.*

ˌ**rock and** ˈ**roll** *noun* [U] = ROCK 'N' ROLL

ˌ**rock** ˈ**bottom** *noun* [U] the lowest or worst point: *Jerry hit rock bottom when he went to jail.*

**rock·er** /ˈrɑkər/ *noun* [C] **1** a person who performs, dances to or enjoys rock music: *punk rockers* **2** = ROCKING CHAIR **3** one of the two curved pieces of wood on the bottom of a rocking chair

**rock·et¹** /ˈrɑkət/ *noun* [C] **1** a vehicle shaped like a tube, that is used for travel into space: *to launch a rocket ◇ a rocket engine* **2** an object shaped like a tube that is used as a weapon and that carries a bomb

**rock·et²** /ˈrɑkət/ *verb* [I] **1** to increase very quickly and suddenly: *rocketing crime/prices ◇ Sales have rocketed by 213 percent.* **2** to achieve or to make sb/sth achieve a successful position very quickly: *The band* ***rocketed to stardom*** *with their first single.*

ˈ**rocket** ˌ**scientist** *noun* [usually sing.]

IDM **it doesn't take a rocket scientist (to do sth)** (used to emphasize that sth is easy to do or understand): *It doesn't take a rocket scientist to figure out what's going to happen next.*

ˈ**rocking chair** *noun* [C] a type of chair with two curved pieces of wood attached to the bottom of the legs

**rock 'n' roll** /ˌrɑknˈroʊl/ (*also* ˌ**rock and** ˈ**roll**) *noun* [U] a type of music with a strong beat that was most popular in the 1950s: *Elvis Presley was the king of rock 'n' roll.*

**rock·y** /ˈrɑki/ *adj.* (**rock·i·er**; **rock·i·est**) **1** full of rocks or not level and smooth: *a rocky beach ◇ rocky hills* **2** (*informal*) difficult and full of problems: *a rocky marriage*

**rod** /rɑd/ *noun* [C] (often in compounds) a thin straight piece of wood or metal: *a fishing rod*

**rode** *past tense of* RIDE²

**ro·dent** /ˈroʊdnt/ *noun* [C] a type of small animal (such as a rat, a rabbit, a mouse, etc.) that has strong sharp front teeth

**ro·de·o** /ˈroʊdioʊ; roʊˈdeɪoʊ/ *noun* [C] (*pl.* **ro·de·os**) a contest or performance in which people show their skill in riding wild horses, catching cows, etc.

**rog·er** /ˈrɑdʒər/ *interjection* people say "Roger!" in

communication by radio to show that they have received and understood a message

**rogue** /roʊg/ *adj.* (only *before* a noun) causing trouble by not following official rules: *an attack by a rogue nation*

★**role** /roʊl/ *noun* [C] **1** a person's part in a play, movie, etc.: *Many actresses have played the role of Cleopatra.* ◇ *a leading role in the next James Bond movie* **2** the position or importance of sb/sth: *Parents play a vital role in their children's education.*

**ˈrole ˌmodel** *noun* [C] a person that you admire and try to copy: *We need positive role models for young women to aspire to.* ◇ *Parents are a child's primary role models.*

**ˈrole-play** *noun* [C,U] (*also* **role-playing** [U]) an activity, used especially in teaching, in which a person acts a part

★**roll**[1] /roʊl/ *noun* [C] **1** something made into the shape of a tube by winding it around itself: *a roll of toilet paper* ◇ *a roll of film* **2** bread that has been baked in a round shape, small enough for one person: *a basket of warm rolls* ◇ *I'll have a cinnamon roll and a cup of coffee.* ➲ picture at **bread**. **3** an official list of names: *The teacher called the roll* (= read the names of the students in the class). **4** a long, low sound: *a roll of drums*

★**roll**[2] /roʊl/ *verb*

➤TURN OVER **1** [I,T] to move by turning over and over; to make sth move in this way: *The apples fell out of the bag and rolled everywhere.* ◇ *We couldn't stop the ball from rolling into the river.* ◇ *It was Michael's turn to roll the dice.* ◇ *Tears were rolling down her cheeks.* **2** [I,T] to turn over or upward; to make sb/sth do this: *We taught the dog to roll over and play dead.* ◇ *The medical team rolled the patient onto her back.*

➤MOVE **3** [I,T] to move smoothly (on wheels or as if on wheels); to make sth move in this way: *The car began to roll back down the hill.* ◇ *Workers rolled the airplane out of the hangar.*

➤MAKE BALL/TUBE **4** [I,T] **roll (sth) (up)** to make sth into the shape of a ball or tube; to be made into this shape: *He rolls his own cigarettes.* ◇ *Beth rolled up her sleeves.* ◇ *The insect rolled up when I touched it.* OPP **unroll**

➤MAKE STH FLAT **5** [T] to make sth become flat by moving sth heavy over it: *Roll the pastry on a floured surface.*

➤MOVE FROM SIDE TO SIDE **6** [I] to rock or swing from side to side: *The ship was beginning to roll in the storm.* ◇ *She was rolling with laughter.*

PHRV **roll in** (*informal*) to arrive in large numbers or quantities: *Offers of help have been rolling in.*

**roll sth out 1** to make sth become flat by pushing sth heavy over it: *Roll out the dough* (= using a rolling pin). **2** to officially make a new product available or start a new political campaign: *The new model is to be rolled out in July.* SYN **launch**

**roll·er** /ˈroʊlər/ *noun* [C] **1** a long object in the shape of a tube, which can be rolled over a surface or which can turn over and over as part of a machine: *He used a roller to paint the wall.* **2** = CURLER

**Roll·er·blade™** /ˈroʊlərbleɪd/ (*also* **ˌin-line ˈskate**) *noun* [C] a kind of boot with one row of narrow wheels on the bottom. It allows you to move quickly over a smooth surface: *a pair of Rollerblades* ➲ picture at **skate**. ▶ **Roll·er·blade** *verb* [I]

**ˈroller ˌcoaster** *noun* [C] a type of train track with small open trains, sharp bends and very steep slopes. People go on roller coasters for fun at fairs, etc.

**ˈroller skate** (*also* **skate**) *noun* [C] a type of shoe with two pairs of small wheels on the bottom. It allows you to move quickly over a smooth surface: *a pair of roller skates* ➲ picture at **skate**. ▶ **ˈroller skate** *verb* [I]

**ˈrolling pin** *noun* [C] a piece of wood, etc. in the shape of a tube, that you use for making cookies, etc. flat and thin before baking ➲ picture at **kitchen**.

**ro·ly-po·ly** /ˌroʊli ˈpoʊli/ *adj.* (*informal*) (used about people) short, round and fat

**ROM** /rɑm/ *noun* [U] (*computing*) read-only memory; the part of a computer where information is stored but cannot be changed ➲ Look at **RAM** and **CD-ROM**.

**Ro·man** /ˈroʊmən/ *adj.* connected with ancient Rome: *the remains of a Roman villa* ◇ *a Roman soldier*

**the ˌRoman ˈalphabet** *noun* [sing.] the letters A to Z, used especially in West European languages

**ˌRoman ˈCatholic** *noun* [C], *adj.* = CATHOLIC

**ˌRoman ˈCatholicism** *noun* [U] = CATHOLICISM

**ro·mance** /ˈroʊmæns; roʊˈmæns/ *noun* **1** [C] a love affair: *The movie was about a teenage romance.* **2** [U] a feeling or atmosphere of love or of sth new, special and exciting: *The stars were out, the night was warm and romance was in the air.* **3** [C] a novel about a love affair: *She writes historical romances.*

**ˌRoman ˈnumeral** *noun* [C] one of the letters that were used by the ancient Romans as numbers

> NOTE Roman numerals, e.g. IV=4 and X=10, are still used sometimes. For example, they may be found numbering the pages and chapters of books or on some clocks.

★**ro·man·tic**[1] /roʊˈmæntɪk/ *adj.* **1** having a quality that strongly affects your emotions or makes you think about love; showing feelings of love: *a romantic dinner by candlelight* ◇ *He isn't very romantic – he never says he loves me.* **2** involving a love affair; describing situations involving love: *Reports of a romantic involvement between the two movie stars have been strongly denied.* ◇ *a romantic comedy* **3** having or showing ideas about life and love that are emotional rather than real or practical: *Now that I've been here for a while, I have a much less romantic view of life in the city.* ▶ **ro·man·ti·cal·ly** /-kli/ *adv.*

**ro·man·tic**[2] /roʊˈmæntɪk/ *noun* [C] a person who is emotional and has a lot of imagination, and who has ideas and hopes that may not be realistic: *an incurable romantic* ◇ *He was a romantic at heart and longed for adventure.*

**ro·man·ti·cize** /roʊˈmæntəsaɪz/ *verb* [I,T] to make sth seem more interesting, exciting, etc. than it really is

**romp**[1] /rɑmp/ *verb* [I] **1** to play in a happy and noisy way: *kids romping around in the snow* ◇ *Two*



R

*fox cubs romped playfully on the river bank.* **2** to easily win a race or game: *The Vikings romped to victory.*

**romp²** /rɑmp/ ***noun*** (*informal*) (often used in newspapers) **1** [C] an enjoyable sexual experience that is not serious: *politicians involved in sex romps with prostitutes* **2** [C] an amusing book, play or movie that is full of action or adventure: *His latest film is an enjoyable romp.* **3** [sing.] (*informal*) an easy victory in a sports competition: *They won in a 5–1 romp.*

★**roof** /ruf; rʊf/ ***noun*** [C] (*pl.* **roofs**) **1** the part of a building, vehicle, etc. which covers the top of it: *the roof of the school* ◇ *a hole in the roof* ◇ *The library and the gymnasium are under one roof* (= in the same building). ◇ *A couple of shingles have fallen off the roof.* ➲ Picture on study page **A31**. **2** the highest part inside sth: *The roof of the cave collapsed.* ◇ *the roof of your mouth*

IDM **go through the roof 1** (used about prices, etc.) to rise or increase very fast **2** (*also* **hit the roof**) (*informal*) to suddenly become very angry

**roof·top** /ˈruftɑp; ˈrʊf-/ ***noun*** [C] the outside of the roof of a building: *From the plane we could see the rooftops of our town.*

**rook** /rʊk/ (*also* **castle**) ***noun*** [C] one of the pieces used in the game of chess ➲ picture at **chess**.

**rook·ie** /ˈrʊki/ ***noun*** [C] a person who has just started doing a job or playing a professional sport: *a rookie cop/quarterback/pitcher*

★**room** /rum; rʊm/ ***noun*** **1** [C] a part of a house or building that is separated from the rest by its own walls, floor and ceiling: *The house has three rooms downstairs and four bedrooms upstairs.* ◇ *a dining room* ◇ *a hotel room* ◇ *a conference room* **2** [U] **room (for sb/sth)**; **room (to do sth)** space; enough space: *There isn't room for any more furniture in here.* ◇ *The table takes up too much room.* ◇ *They're tearing down those old factories to make room for a new development.* ◇ *There were so many people that there wasn't any room to move.* **3** [U] **room (for sth)** the opportunity or need for sth: *There's room for improvement in your work* (= it could be much better). ➲ Look at the note at **place¹**.

**room·ful** /ˈrumfʊl/ ***noun*** [C, usually sing.] **a roomful of sb/sth** the amount or number that a room can contain: *There was a roomful of reporters waiting to interview him.*

**room·ie** /ˈrumi/ ***noun*** [C] (*informal*) = ROOMMATE

**room·mate** /ˈrumeɪt/ (*also informal* **room·ie**) ***noun*** [C] a person that you share a room or an apartment, a house, etc. with

**ˈroom ˌservice** ***noun*** [U] a service in some hotels in which food or drinks are brought to guests in their rooms

**ˌroom ˈtemperature** ***noun*** [U] the normal temperature inside a building: *Serve the wine **at room temperature**.*

**room·y** /ˈrumi/ ***adj.*** (**room·i·er**; **room·i·est**) having plenty of space: *a roomy house/car*

**roost¹** /rust/ ***noun*** [C] a place where birds sleep

IDM **rule the roost** → RULE²

**roost²** /rust/ ***verb*** [I] (used about birds) to rest or go to sleep somewhere

IDM **the chickens come home to roost**; **sth comes home to roost** (used to say that if sb says or does sth bad or wrong, it will affect him/her badly in the future)

**roost·er** /ˈrustər/ ***noun*** [C] an adult male chicken: *The rooster crowed at dawn.*

★**root¹** /rut; rʊt/ ***noun*** **1** [C] the part of a plant that grows under the ground and takes in water and food from the soil ➲ picture at **tree**. **2** [C] the part of a hair or tooth that is under the skin and that attaches it to the rest of the body **3 roots** [pl.] the place where you feel that you belong, because you grew up there, live there or your relatives once lived there: *Sam is proud of his African roots.* **4** [C] the cause, source or main part of sth: *Let's try and get to the root of the problem.* ➲ Look also at **grass roots** and **square root**.

**root²** /rut; rʊt/ ***verb***

IDM **be rooted in sth** to have origins in sth and so be influenced by it: *These attitudes are deeply rooted in the nation's history.*

PHR V **root for sb/sth** to give support to sb who is in a game, contest, etc.: *The crowd was rooting for the home team.*

**root sb/sth out** to find and destroy sth bad completely: *to root out corruption in the city government*

**ˈroot beer** ***noun*** [U] a type of sweet brown drink with a lot of small bubbles in it, but no alcohol

**ˈroot caˌnal** ***noun*** [C] a treatment in which the dentist removes a diseased area in the ROOT¹ (2) of your tooth

**root·less** /ˈrutləs; ˈrʊt-/ ***adj.*** having nowhere that you really think of as home, or as the place where you belong: *She had had a rootless childhood moving from town to town.*

★**rope¹** /roʊp/ ***noun*** [C,U] very thick, strong cord, that is used for tying or lifting heavy things, climbing up, etc.: *We need some rope to tie up the boat.* ◇ *The victim was found with a rope tied around her neck.* ➲ Look also at **jump rope**.

IDM **at the end of your rope** → END¹

**rope²** /roʊp/ ***verb*** [T]

PHR V **rope sb in**; **rope sb into sth** (usually passive) (*informal*) to persuade sb to join in an activity or to help to do sth, even when he/she does not want to: *Everyone was roped in to help with the show.* ◇ *Ben was roped into making the coffee for the whole team.*

**rope sth off** to put ropes around or across an area in order to keep people out of it

**ro·sa·ry** /ˈroʊzəri/ ***noun*** [C] (*pl.* **ro·sa·ries**) a string of beads used by Roman Catholics for counting prayers

**rose¹** *past tense of* RISE²

**rose²** /roʊz/ ***noun*** [C] a flower with a sweet smell, that grows on a bush and usually has sharp points (thorns) on its stem

**ro·sé** /roʊˈzeɪ/ ***noun*** [U] pink wine

**rose·bud** /ˈroʊzbʌd/ ***noun*** [C] the flower of a rose before it is open: (*figurative*) *a rosebud mouth* (= one that is small and round)

**ˈrose-ˌcolored** ***adj.*** **1** pink in color **2** (*also* **ˈrose-ˌtinted**) (used to describe an idea or a way of looking at a situation as being better or more positive than it really is): *a rose-tinted vision of married life* ◇ *He tends to view the world* ***through rose-colored glasses.***

**Rosh Ha·sha·nah** (*also* **Rosh Ha·sha·na**) /ˌrɑʃ həˈʃɑnə/ ***noun*** [U] the Jewish New Year, which is celebrated in September or early October

**ros·in** /ˈrɑzn/ ***noun*** [U] a substance that is used on the BOW³ (3) of a musical instrument such as a violin so that it moves across the strings more easily

**ros·ter** /ˈrɑstər/ ***noun*** [C] a list of people's names, often showing the jobs that they must do and when they must do those jobs: *a flight/duty roster* ◇ *There are ten new players on the team's roster.*

**ros·y** /ˈroʊzi/ ***adj.*** (**ros·i·er**; **ros·i·est**) **1** deep pink in color and (used about a person) healthy-looking: *rosy cheeks* **2** (used about a situation) full of good possibilities: *The future was looking rosy.* ◇ *The speech painted a rosy picture of the economy* (= described it in a very positive way).

**rot** /rɑt/ ***verb*** (**rot·ting**; **rot·ted**) **1** [I] to go bad (as part of a natural process); to decay: *Wood will rot in damp conditions.* **2** [T] to make sth go bad or decay: *Too much candy will rot your teeth!*

**ro·ta·ry¹** /ˈroʊt̬əri/ ***adj.*** (only *before* a noun) **1** (used about a movement) moving in a circle around a central fixed point: *rotary motion* **2** (used about a machine or piece of equipment) having parts that move in this way: *a rotary mower*

**ro·ta·ry²** /ˈroʊt̬əri/ ***noun*** [C] (*pl.* **ro·ta·ries**) a place where two or more roads meet, forming a circle that all traffic must go around in the same direction: *At the rotary, take the second exit.*

**ro·tate** /ˈroʊteɪt/ ***verb*** [I,T] **1** to turn in circles around a central point; to make sth do this: *The earth rotates around the sun.* ◇ *You can see the parts that rotate the hands of the clock.* **2** to happen in a particular order; to make sth do this: *We rotate the night shift so no one has to do it all the time.*

**ro·ta·tion** /roʊˈteɪʃn/ ***noun*** **1** [U] movement in circles: *the earth's rotation* **2** [C] one complete turn around sth: *one rotation every 24 hours* **3** [C,U] the regular changing around of people or things, or of the order of events: *a planned rotation of troops in the area* ◇ *crop rotation*

**rote** /roʊt/ ***noun*** [U] a way of learning sth in which you remember information after repeating it many times, but do not understand it: *to learn sth by rote* ◇ *This class focuses on critical thinking skills rather than rote learning.*

**ro·tor** /ˈroʊt̬ər/ ***noun*** [C] a part of a machine that turns around a central point: *rotor blades on a helicopter*

**rot·ten** /ˈrɑtn/ ***adj.*** **1** (used about food and other substances) old and not fresh enough or good enough to use: *rotten vegetables* ◇ *Some of the stairs were rotten and unsafe.* **2** (*informal*) very bad: *We had rotten weather all week.* **3** (*informal*) unfair, unkind or bad: *What a rotten thing to say!*

**ro·tun·da** /roʊˈtʌndə/ ***noun*** [C] a round building or hall, especially one with a curved roof (a **dome**)

**rouge** /ruʒ/ ***noun*** [U] (*old-fashioned*) a red powder or cream used by women for giving color to their cheeks

★**rough¹** /rʌf/ ***adj.*** **1** not smooth or level: *It's not easy to walk over such rough terrain.* ◇ *Her hands were rough from too much work.* **2** moving or behaving with too much force and not enough care; not gentle or calm: *Football is a rough game.* ◇ *The ferry was canceled because the ocean was too rough* (= because of a storm). ◇ *He grew up in a rough neighborhood* (= where there is a lot of crime or violence). **3** made or done quickly or without much care; approximately correct: *a rough draft of an essay* ◇ *a rough estimate of what the work would cost* ◇ *Can you give me a rough idea of what time you'll be arriving?* **4** not easy; full of difficulty: *She's had a rough life.*

IDM **a hard/rough time** → TIME¹

▸ **rough·ness** ***noun*** [U]

**rough²** /rʌf/ ***adv.*** (*informal*) in a ROUGH¹ (2) way: *One of the boys was told to leave because he was playing too rough.*

**rough³** /rʌf/ ***verb***

IDM **rough it** to live without the usual comforts of life: *The girls love roughing it when they go camping in the summer.*

PHRV **rough sb up** (*informal*) to attack sb by hitting him/her: *He claimed he had been roughed up by a police officer.*

**rough·age** /ˈrʌfɪdʒ/ ***noun*** [U] the part of food that helps to keep a person healthy by keeping the bowels working and moving other food quickly through the body: *Fruit and vegetables are important sources of roughage.* SYN **fiber**

**rough·en** /ˈrʌfn/ ***verb*** [I,T] to become ROUGH¹; to make sth ROUGH¹: *His voice roughened with every word.* ◇ *Cold weather roughens your skin.*

**rough·house** /ˈrʌfhaʊz/ ***verb*** [I,T] (*informal*) to fight sb or play with sb roughly: *Quit roughhousing, you two!*

★**rough·ly** /ˈrʌfli/ ***adv.*** **1** in a violent way; not gently: *He grabbed her roughly by the arm.* **2** not exactly; approximately: *It took roughly three hours, I think.*

**rough·shod** /ˈrʌfʃɑd/ ***adv.***

IDM **ride roughshod over sb** → RIDE²

**rou·lette** /ruˈlɛt/ ***noun*** [U] a gambling game in which a ball is dropped onto a moving wheel that has holes with numbers on them. Players bet on which hole the ball will be in when the wheel stops. ➲ Look also at **Russian roulette**.

★**round¹** /raʊnd/ ***adj.*** **1** having the shape of a circle or a ball: *a round table* ◇ *People used to think the earth was flat, not round.* ◇ *He had a round face and white hair.* **2** (used about a number) given to the nearest 10, 100, 1,000, etc.; not exact: *In round numbers, we've sold a quarter of a million of these gadgets so far.*

★**round²** /raʊnd/ ***noun*** [C]

➤ STAGE IN PROCESS **1** a number or set of events, etc.: *a further round of talks between the company and the union*

➤ REGULAR ACTIVITIES/ROUTE **2** a regular series of visits, etc., often as part of a job: *The mail carrier's round takes him about three hours.*

➤ IN COMPETITION/SPORTS **3** one part of a game or competition: *the third round of the boxing match* ◇ *The winners of the first round will go on to the*

R

*second stage of the tournament.* **4** (in golf) one game: *to play a round of golf*
➤SHOT **5** a bullet or a number of bullets, fired from a gun: *He fired several rounds at us.*
IDM **a round of applause** a time when people clap after a performance, etc.: *to give sb a round of applause*

**round³** /raʊnd/ *verb* [T] to go around sth: *The police car rounded the corner at high speed.*
PHRV **round sth down** to decrease a number to the nearest whole number
**round sth off** to increase or decrease a number, price, etc. to the nearest whole number or to the nearest 10, 100, 1,000, etc.: *The price has been rounded off to the nearest dollar.*
**round sb/sth up** to gather sb/sth in one place: *The teacher rounded up the kids.*
**round sth up** to increase a number to the nearest whole number

★**round⁴** /raʊnd/ *adv.*
IDM **all year round** → YEAR

**round·a·bout** /ˈraʊndəbaʊt/ *adj.* not direct: *He answered in a roundabout way.*

**round·ed** /ˈraʊndəd/ *adj.* (usually before a noun) **1** having a round shape: *a surface with rounded edges* ◇ *rounded shoulders* **2** well developed; complete and balanced: *a fully rounded education* ◇ *She is a more rounded performer than her sister.*

ˌ**round ˈrobin** *noun* [C] **1** (*sports*) a competition (tournament) in which every player or team plays every other player or team **2** something that is made, written, etc. by several people who each add a part one after another: *a round robin story* **3** a letter intended to be read by many people that is copied and sent to each one

ˈ**round-the-ˌclock** *adj.* (only *before* a noun) happening continuously, 24 hours a day: *round-the-clock news*

ˌ**round ˈtrip** *noun* [C] a trip that you take from one place to another and back again

ˈ**round-trip** (*also* ˈ**roundtrip**) *adj.* (only *before* a noun) for traveling to a place and back again: *a round-trip ticket* ◇ *a round-trip fare of $50* ➲ Look at **one-way** (2).

ˈ**round-up** *noun* [C, usually sing.] **1** a summary of the most important points of a particular subject, especially the news: *We'll be back after the break with a round-up of today's other stories.* ◇ *a news/sports round-up* **2** an act of bringing people or animals together in one place for a particular purpose: *the round-up of sheep for shearing*

**rouse** /raʊz/ *verb* [T] **1** to make sb/sth very angry, excited, interested, etc.: *a fiery speech that roused voters* **2** (*formal*) to make sb wake up: *She was sleeping so soundly that I couldn't rouse her.*

**rous·ing** /ˈraʊzɪŋ/ *adj.* exciting and powerful: *a rousing speech*

**rout** /raʊt/ *noun* [C] a complete defeat ▸ **rout** *verb* [T]

★**route** /rut; raʊt/ *noun* **1** [C] a way from one place to another: *We took the fastest and most direct route to New York.* ◇ *My apartment is close to a major bus route.* ◇ *Thousands of people were waiting along the parade route.* ➲ Look also at **en route**. **2** a way of achieving sth: *Hard work is the best route to success.* **3 Route** (*abbr.* **Rte.**) [sing.] (*U.S.*) (used in the names of some roads, especially major roads in the country): *Route 66*

★**rou·tine¹** /ruˈtin/ *noun* [C,U] the fixed and usual way of doing things: *If you work out a routine, you will get things done more quickly.* ◇ *Children like routine.*

**rou·tine²** /ruˈtin/ *adj.* normal and regular; not unusual or special: *My doctor discovered the cancer after a routine medical test.*

**rou·tine·ly** /ruˈtinli/ *adv.* very often; regularly; as part of a routine: *The machines are routinely checked for signs of wear and tear.*

**rove** /roʊv/ *verb* [I,T] (*written*) to travel from one place to another, often with no particular purpose: *A quarter of a million refugees roved around the country.* ◇ *bands of thieves who roved the countryside*

**rov·ing** /ˈroʊvɪŋ/ *adj.* traveling from one place to another and not staying anywhere permanently: *a roving reporter for ABC news*
IDM **have a roving eye** (*old-fashioned*) to always be looking for the chance to have a new sexual relationship

★**row¹** /roʊ/ *noun* [C] **1** a line of people or things: *a row of books* ◇ *The kids were standing in a row at the front of the classroom.* **2** a line of seats in a theater, etc.: *Our seats were in the back row.* ◇ *a front-row seat*
IDM **in a row** one after another; without a break: *It rained steadily for four days in a row.*

**row²** /roʊ/ *verb* [I,T] to move a boat through the water using long wooden poles with wide, flat ends (oars): *Jill and I took turns rowing.* ◇ *He rowed the boat slowly down the river.*

**row³** /raʊ/ *noun* [C] (*Cdn*) = FIGHT² (2) ▸ **row** *verb* [I]

**row·boat** /ˈroʊboʊt/ *noun* [C] a small boat that you move through the water using long wooden poles with wide, flat ends (oars)

**row·dy** /ˈraʊdi/ *adj.* (**row·di·er**; **row·di·est**) noisy and uncontrolled: *The crowd were getting rowdy.* ▸ **row·di·ness** *noun* [U]

ˈ**rowing maˌchine** *noun* [C] a piece of sports equipment on which you make the same movements as sb who is ROWING² a boat ➲ picture on study page **A32**.

★**roy·al** /ˈrɔɪəl/ *adj.* connected with a king, queen or a member of his/her family: *the British royal family*

ˌ**royal ˈblue** *adj.* deep bright blue in color

ˌ**Royal CaˌnadianˌMounted Poˈlice** *noun* [pl.] (*Cdn*) → RCMP

ˌ**Royal Comˈmission** *noun* [sing.] (*Cdn*) an important investigation into a serious matter that the government can ask to be carried out

**roy·al·ty** /ˈrɔɪəlti/ *noun* (*pl.* **roy·al·ties**) **1** [U] members of a royal family **2** [C, usually pl.] an amount of money that is paid to the person who wrote a book, piece of music, etc. every time his/her work is sold or performed

**rpm** /ˌɑr pi ˈɛm/ *abbr.* revolutions per minute (a measurement of the speed of an engine or a record when it is playing)

**RRSP** /ˌɑr ɑr ɛs ˈpi/ ***abbr.*** (*Cdn*) registered retirement savings plan; a special type of savings plan in which you can save money without paying taxes on it until you stop working (retire) when you are older

**RSVP** (*also* **R.S.V.P.**) /ˌɑr ɛs vi ˈpi/ ***abbr.*** (written on invitations) please reply (from the French "répondez s'il vous plaît")

**Rte.** ***abbr.*** = ROUTE (3)

★**rub**[1] /rʌb/ ***verb*** (**rub·bing**; **rubbed**) **1** [I,T] to move your hand, a cloth, etc. backward and forward on the surface of sth while pressing firmly: *Ralph rubbed his hands together to keep them warm.* ◇ *If you rub hard, the mark should come out.* ◇ *The cat rubbed against my leg.* ◇ *The cat rubbed its head against my leg.* ◇ *He rubbed his face with his hand.* ◇ *He rubbed his hand across his face.* ◇ *He rubbed the sweat off his face with his hand.* **2** [T] to put a cream, liquid, etc. onto a surface by RUBBING (1): *Apply a little of the lotion and rub it into the skin.* **3** [I,T] **rub (on/against sth)** to press on/against sth (often causing pain or damage): *These new shoes are rubbing my heels.*

IDM **rub elbows/shoulders with sb** to spend time at parties and social events with sb, especially famous people

**rub it in** (*informal*) to remind sb of sth bad, in order to make him/her feel stupid or embarrassed: *I know I'm the one who screwed up – don't rub it in.*

PHR V **rub off (on/onto sb)** (used about a good quality) to be transferred from one person to another: *Let's hope some of her enthusiasm rubs off onto her brother.*

**rub**[2] /rʌb/ ***noun*** [C] an act of RUBBING (1): *to give sb a back rub*

★**rub·ber** /ˈrʌbər/ ***noun*** **1** [U] a strong substance that is made chemically or from the juice of a tropical tree. Rubber is elastic (= it can stretch and then return to its original shape) and water cannot pass through it: *Car tires are made of rubber.* ◇ *foam rubber* ◇ *The surgeon put on a pair of rubber gloves.* **2** [C] (*slang*) = CONDOM

**ˌrubber ˈband** ***noun*** [C] a thin circular piece of rubber that is used for holding things together: *Her hair was tied back with a rubber band.*

**ˌrubber ˈstamp** ***noun*** [C] a piece of equipment with rubber letters and numbers on it that you use for printing a name, date, etc. on a document

**ˌrubber-ˈstamp** ***verb*** [T] (usually used about sb with authority) to agree to sth without thinking about it carefully

**rub·ber·y** /ˈrʌbəri/ ***adj.*** like rubber

**ˈrubbing ˌalcohol** ***noun*** [U] a clear liquid, consisting mainly of alcohol, used for cleaning wounds, etc.

★**rub·bish** /ˈrʌbɪʃ/ ***noun*** [U] (*formal*) = GARBAGE

**rub·ble** /ˈrʌbl/ ***noun*** [U] pieces of broken brick, stone, etc., especially from a damaged building

**ru·bel·la** /ruˈbɛlə/ ***noun*** [U] = GERMAN MEASLES

**rub·ric** /ˈrubrɪk/ ***noun*** [C] (*formal*) a title or set of instructions written in a book, an exam paper, etc.

**ru·by** /ˈrubi/ ***noun*** [C] (*pl.* **ru·bies**) a type of precious stone that is red

**ruck·sack** /ˈrʌksæk; ˈrʊk-/ (*also* **back·pack**) ***noun*** [C] a bag that you use for carrying things on your back. You often use a backpack when you are walking, camping, etc. ➲ picture at **luggage**.

**ruck·us** /ˈrʌkəs/ ***noun*** [sing.] (*informal*) a noisy argument or disturbance

**rud·der** /ˈrʌdər/ ***noun*** [C] a piece of wood or metal that is used for controlling the direction of a boat or an airplane

**rud·dy** /ˈrʌdi/ ***adj.*** (**rud·di·er**; **rud·di·est**) **1** (used about a person's face) looking red and healthy: *ruddy cheeks* ◇ *a ruddy complexion* **2** (*written*) red in color: *a ruddy sky*

★**rude** /rud/ ***adj.*** **1** not polite: *It's rude to interrupt when other people are speaking.* ◇ *You shouldn't be so rude to your parents.* SYN **impolite** **2** sudden and unpleasant: *If you're expecting any help from him, you're in for a rude surprise.* ▸ **rude·ly** ***adv.*** ▸ **rude·ness** ***noun*** [U]

**ru·di·men·ta·ry** /ˌrudəˈmɛntəri/ ***adj.*** (*formal*) basic or very simple

**ru·di·ments** /ˈrudəmənts/ ***noun*** [pl.] **the rudiments (of sth)** (*formal*) the most basic or essential facts of a particular subject, skill, etc.: *You'll only have time to learn the rudiments of windsurfing in a week.*

**rue** /ru/ ***verb*** [T] (**rue·ing** or **ru·ing**; **rued**)*old-fashioned* or *formal*) to feel bad about sth that happened or sth that you did because it had bad results: *He* ***rued the day*** *he first met Monica.* SYN **regret**

**rue·ful** /ˈrufl/ ***adj.*** (*written*) feeling or showing that you are sad or sorry: *a rueful expression/laugh* ▸ **rue·ful·ly** /-fəli/ ***adv.***: *He ruefully admitted that he envied her.*

**ruf·fi·an** /ˈrʌfiən/ ***noun*** [C] (*old-fashioned*) a violent man, especially one who commits crimes: *a gang of young ruffians*

**ruf·fle**[1] /ˈrʌfl/ ***verb*** [T] **1** to make sth messy or no longer smooth: *to ruffle sb's hair* **2** (often passive) to make sb annoyed or confused

IDM **ruffle sb's feathers** to annoy or upset sb: *He certainly ruffled a few feathers at the meeting with that comment.*

**ruf·fle**[2] /ˈrʌfl/ ***noun*** [C] a narrow piece of cloth with many folds in it which is used to decorate the edge of a curtain, a cover for a bed, etc.

★**rug** /rʌg/ ***noun*** [C] **1** a piece of thick material that covers a small part of a floor ➲ Look at **carpet**. **2** (*slang*) = TOUPEE: *That's quite a rug he's got on!*

**Rug·by** /ˈrʌgbi/ ***noun*** [U] a game similar to football that is played by two teams of 13 or 15 players with an oval ball that can be carried or kicked

**rug·ged** /ˈrʌgəd/ ***adj.*** **1** (used about the landscape) not level or smooth and having rocks rather than plants or trees: *They admired the rugged beauty of the coastline.* ◇ *He loves the rugged outdoor life* (= the lack of comfort connected with being outside). **2** (used about a man's face) having strong, attractive features: *She was attracted by his rugged good looks.* **3** (used about a person) determined to succeed in a difficult situation, even if this means using force or upsetting other people **4** (used about equipment, clothing, etc.) strong and designed to be used in difficult conditions: *A less rugged vehicle*

R

*would never have made the trip.* ▸ **rug·ged·ly** *adv.*: *ruggedly handsome*

**rug·rat** /ˈrʌɡræt/ (*also* ˈ**rug rat**) *noun* [C] (*slang*) a child

★**ru·in**[1] /ˈruɪn/ *verb* [T] **1** to damage sth badly, to destroy: *the ruined city* ◇ *The crops were ruined by the late frost.* **2** to change sth so that it is no longer good: *My dress was ruined when I spilled wine over it.* ◇ *The scandal ruined his chances for re-election.* **3** to cause sb to lose all his/her money, hope of being successful, etc.: *The cost of the court case nearly ruined them.*

★**ru·in**[2] /ˈruɪn/ *noun* **1** [U] a state of destruction, when sth is very badly damaged: *The city was in a state of ruin.* **2** [U] the cause or state of having lost all your money, hope of being successful, etc.: *Many small companies are facing financial ruin.* **3** [C] a building, town, etc. that has been badly damaged or destroyed; the parts of a building, town, etc. that are left when it has been almost completely destroyed: *The old house is now a ruin.* ◇ *We went to look at the ruins of the old fort.* ◇ *the ruins of the ancient city of Pompeii*

IDM **in ruins** badly damaged or destroyed: *After the accident, her life seemed to be in ruins.* ◇ *The city of Berlin was in ruins at the end of World War II.*

★**rule**[1] /rul/ *noun* **1** [C] an official statement that tells you what you can or cannot do, say, etc.: *to obey/break a rule* ◇ *If you want to be on the team, you'll have to follow the rules.* ◇ *Do you know the rules of chess?* ◇ *It's against the rules to touch the ball with your hands.* ◇ *rules and regulations*

NOTE A **law** is stronger. You can be officially punished if you break it.

**2** [C] (in a language) a description of what is usual or correct: *What is the rule for forming the past tense?* **3** [sing.] what is usual: *Large families are the exception rather than the rule nowadays.* **4** [U] government; control: *the collapse of Communist rule* ◇ *the rule of law*

IDM **as a (general) rule** (*formal*) usually: *Women, as a rule, live longer than men.*

**bend the rules** → BEND[1]

★**rule**[2] /rul/ *verb* **1** [I,T] **rule (over sb/sth)** to have the power over a country, etc.: *Great Britain once ruled over a vast empire.* ◇ *A military government ruled the country for over a decade.* ◇ (*figurative*) *His whole life was ruled by his ambition to become a millionaire.* **2** [I,T] **rule (on) sth** to make an official decision: *The Supreme Court ruled that the law was unconstitutional.* **3** [I] (*slang*) to be excellent and much better than anything or anybody else: *The Dallas Cowboys rule!* OPP For this slang sense the opposite is **suck**.

IDM **rule the roost** (*informal*) to be the most powerful member of a group

PHR V **rule sb/sth out** to say that sb/sth is not thought to be possible: *The President has not ruled out sending troops to the area.* ◇ *She has been ruled out as a suspect in the murder investigation.*

**rule·book** /ˈrulbʊk/ (*also* ˈ**rule book**) *noun* [C] the set of rules that must be followed in a particular job, organization or game

★**rul·er** /ˈrulər/ *noun* [C] **1** a person who rules a country, etc. **2** a straight piece of wood, plastic, etc. marked with inches or centimeters, that you use for measuring sth or for drawing straight lines

**rul·ing**[1] /ˈrulɪŋ/ *adj.* (only *before* a noun) with the most power in an organization, a country, etc.: *the nation's ruling party*

**rul·ing**[2] /ˈrulɪŋ/ *noun* [C] an official decision: *the first major Supreme Court ruling on* (= about) *the Internet*

**rum** /rʌm/ *noun* [U] a strong alcoholic drink that is made from sugar

**rum·ble** /ˈrʌmbl/ *verb* [I] to make a deep heavy sound: *Thunder was rumbling in the distance.* ◇ *The truck rumbled past us.* ▸ **rum·ble** *noun* [sing.]: *the distant rumble of thunder*

**ru·mi·nate** /ˈrumənert/ *verb* [I] (*formal*) **ruminate (on/over/about sth)** to think deeply about sth ▸ **ru·mi·na·tion** /ˌruməˈneɪʃn/ *noun* [C,U]

**rum·mage** /ˈrʌmɪdʒ/ *verb* [I] to move things and make them messy while you are looking for sth: *Nina rummaged through the drawer, looking for a spoon.*

ˈ**rummage sale** *noun* [C] a sale of old things that people do not want anymore. Clubs, churches, schools and other organizations hold rummage sales in order to get money. ➲ Look also at **garage sale** and **yard sale**.

**ru·mor** /ˈrumər/ *noun* [C,U] (a piece of) news or information that many people are talking about but that is possibly not true: *There's a rumor going around that the plant is going to close.* ◇ *Rumor has it* (= people are saying) *that Len has resigned.* ◇ *to confirm/deny a rumor* (= to say that it is true/not true)

**ru·mored** /ˈrumərd/ *adj.* said in an unofficial way (and perhaps not true): *It is rumored that they are getting divorced.* ◇ *They are rumored to be getting divorced.*

**rump** /rʌmp/ *noun* [C] **1** the back end of an animal **2** (*informal*) the part of the body that you sit on

**rum·ple** /ˈrʌmpl/ *verb* [T] (usually passive) to make sth messy or not smooth and neat: *The bed was rumpled where he had slept.* ◇ *a rumpled linen suit*

**rum·pus** /ˈrʌmpəs/ *noun* [C, usually sing.] (*informal*) a lot of noise that is made especially by people who are complaining about sth: *Fans* ***kicked up a rumpus*** *when the concert was canceled.* SYN **commotion**

ˈ**rumpus room** *noun* [C] (*old-fashioned*) a room, usually in the basement of a private house, used for playing games, having parties, etc.

★**run**[1] /rʌn/ *verb* [I,T] (*pres. part.* **run·ning**; *pt* **ran** /ræn/; *pp* **run**)

➤ MOVE FAST ON FOOT **1** [I,T] to move using your legs, going faster than when you walk: *I had to run to catch the bus.* ◇ *The children came running to meet us.* ◇ *She's running in the relay race.* ◇ *I ran almost five miles this morning.* **2** [I] **run (across, down, out, over, etc.)** (*informal*) to go somewhere quickly: *Can you run to the store and get a quart of milk?* ◇ *I'm just going to run across to the neighbors' house for a while.*

➤ MOVE SOMEWHERE **3** [I,T] to move, or move sth, quickly in a particular direction: *The car ran* *downhill and crashed into a wall.* ◇ *She ran her finger down the list of passengers.* **4** [I] to go in a particular direction: *The road runs along the side of a lake.*

➤LIQUID **5** [I] (used about water, a liquid, or a river, etc.) to flow: *When it's really cold, my nose runs.* ◇ *I can hear a faucet running somewhere* (= the water from a faucet). **6** [T] to start water flowing, e.g. for a bath: *Run some more hot water into the tub.*

➤OF COLOR **7** [I] (used about the color in material, etc.) to spread (e.g. when the material is washed): *Don't put that red shirt in the washing machine. It might run.*

➤BUSES/TRAINS **8** [I] (used about buses, trains, etc.) to travel at regular times: *The school bus is running late this morning.*

➤MACHINE/ORGANIZATION/SYSTEM, ETC. **9** [I] (used about a machine, an organization, a system, etc.) to work or function: *The engine is running very smoothly now.* **10** [T] to start a machine, etc. and make it work: *Run the engine for a few minutes before you start off.* ◇ *We're running a new computer program today.* **11** [T] to organize or be in charge of sth: *They run a restaurant in Buffalo.*

➤IN ELECTION **12** [I] to be one of the people to be chosen (a **candidate**) in an election: *He's running for President.*

➤CONTINUE **13** [I] to continue for a time: *The play ran for almost two years on Broadway.*

➤OF NEWSPAPER/MAGAZINE **14** [T] to publish sth in a newspaper or magazine: *The local paper is running a series of articles on pollution.*

IDM **be running at** to be at a certain level: *The interest rate is now running at 10%.*

**up and running** → UP[2]

NOTE For other idioms containing **run**, look at the entries for the nouns, adjectives, etc., e.g. **run in the family** is at **family**.

PHR V **run across sb/sth** to meet or find sb/sth by chance

**run away** to escape from somewhere: *The dog jumped over the fence and ran away.* ◇ *This is the second time Angie has run away from home.* ➲ Look also at **runaway**[1].

**run sb/sth down** to hit sb/sth with a car, etc.: *Somebody ran him down in the parking lot.*

**run into sb** to meet sb by chance

**run into sth** to have difficulties or a problem: *If you run into any problems, just let me know.*

**run into sb/sth** to hit sb/sth with a car, etc.: *He ran his car into a brick wall.*

**run sth off** to copy sth, using a machine: *Can you run off ten copies of this, please?*

**run off with sth** to take or steal sth: *They ran off with his jacket.*

**run out (of sth)** to finish your supply of sth; to come to an end: *We've run out of coffee.* ◇ *Time is running out.*

**run sb/sth over** to hit sb or drive over sb/sth with a car, etc.: *The boy was run over as he was crossing the street.*

**run through sth** to discuss or read sth quickly: *She ran through the names on the list.*

**run sth up** to make a bill, cost, etc. greater: *She ran up a huge phone bill when her boyfriend was away at college.*

★**run**[2] /rʌn/ ***noun***

➤ON FOOT **1** [C] an act of running on foot: *Kate goes for a three-mile run every morning.* ◇ *a cross-country run*

➤TRIP **2** [C] a regular trip that a bus, truck, train, etc. makes: *The school bus was on its last morning run when the accident occurred.*

➤IN SPORTS **3** [C] a point in the game of baseball ➲ Look also at **home run** and at the note at **baseball**.

➤IN ELECTION **4** [C] an attempt to win a political position in an election: *his unsuccessful run for the city council*

➤OF PLAY/MOVIE **5** [C] a continuous series of performances of a play, movie, etc.: *The play had a successful run off Broadway.*

➤OF SUCCESS/FAILURE **6** [sing.] a series of similar events or sth that continues for a very long time: *We've had a run of bad luck recently.*

➤SUDDEN DEMAND **7** [sing.] **a run on sth** a sudden great demand for sth: *There's always a run on ice cream in the hot weather.*

➤IN PANTYHOSE **8** a long hole that forms from a small tear in a pair of pantyhose

➤ILLNESS **9 the runs** [pl.] (*informal*) = DIARRHEA

IDM **in the long run** → LONG[1] (2)

**on the run** hiding or trying to escape from sb/sth: *The escaped prisoner is still on the run.*

**run·a·round** /ˈrʌnəraʊnd/ ***noun***

IDM **give sb the runaround** (*informal*) to treat sb badly by not telling him/her the truth, or by not giving the help or the information he/she needs: *You know where she is, don't you, but you're just giving me the runaround.*

**run·a·way**[1] /ˈrʌnəweɪ/ ***noun*** [C] a child or young person who has left his/her home without permission, especially in order to avoid problems there: *teenage runaways*

**run·a·way**[2] /ˈrʌnəweɪ/ ***adj.*** (only *before* a noun) **1** out of control: *a runaway train* **2** happening very easily: *His first novel was a runaway success.*

**run·down**[1] /ˌrʌnˈdaʊn/ (*also* ˌ**run-ˈdown**) ***adj.*** **1** in bad condition: *a rundown section of town* **2** tired and not healthy: *You look very rundown.*

**run·down**[2] /ˈrʌndaʊn/ ***noun*** [C, usually sing.] **a rundown (of sth)** a short list or explanation of the way sth is happening or organized: *Here's a rundown of the events at the county fair this weekend...*

**rung**[1] /rʌŋ/ ***noun*** [C] one of the bars that form the steps of a ladder ➲ picture at **ladder**.

**rung**[2] *past participle of* RING[2]

★**run·ner** /ˈrʌnər/ ***noun*** [C] **1** a person who runs, especially in a race: *a long-distance runner* **2** a person who takes guns, drugs, etc. illegally from one country to another **3** (*Cdn*) → RUNNING SHOE

ˌ**runner-ˈup** ***noun*** [C] (*pl.* **runners-up**) the person or team that finished second in a race or competition

**run·ning**[1] /ˈrʌnɪŋ/ ***noun*** [U] **1** the act or sport of running: *Scott goes running every morning.* ◇ *running shoes* **2** the management of a business or other organization: *Jackie's in charge of the day-to-day running of the project.*

IDM **in the running/out of the running (for**

sth) (*informal*) having/not having a good chance of getting or winning sth

**run·ning²** /ˈrʌnɪŋ/ ***adj.*** (only *before* a noun) **1** not stopping; continuous: *a running battle between two rival gangs* **2** flowing or available from a faucet (used about water): *Her grandparents lived in a one-room shack with no running water.*

**run·ning³** /ˈrʌnɪŋ/ ***adv.*** (used after a number and a noun) one after another, without a break: *Our school has won the championship for four years running.*

**ˈrunning back** ***noun*** [C] (in football) a player whose main job is to run forward carrying the ball

**ˈrunning mate** ***noun*** [C] (*U.S.*) a person who is chosen to be the candidate for the second-highest position in the government of the U.S. or of a particular state. In an election, people give one vote to a candidate and his/her running mate together.

**ˈrunning shoe** (*also* ˈ**runner**) ***noun*** [C] (*Cdn*) a type of comfortable shoe that you wear to play sports or with informal clothes

**run·ny** /ˈrʌni/ ***adj.*** (**run·ni·er**; **run·ni·est**) (*informal*) **1** containing more liquid than is usual or than you expected: *The cake batter is very runny.* **2** (used about your eyes or nose) producing too much liquid: *Their kids always seem to have runny noses.*

**ˌrun-of-the-ˈmill** ***adj.*** ordinary, with no special or interesting features: *a run-of-the-mill suburban house*

**ˌrun-on ˈsen·tence** ***noun*** [C] (*grammar*) a sentence that contains two or more parts (**clauses**) which could stand alone as sentences, and which have not been joined together correctly. For example, *"Barry is a good student, he always does his homework."* is a run-on sentence.

**runt** /rʌnt/ ***noun*** [C] **1** the smallest, weakest animal of the young that are born from the same mother at the same time: *the runt of the litter* **2** (*informal*) a rude way of referring to a small, weak or unimportant person

**ˈrun-through** ***noun*** [C] a practice for a performance of a play, show, etc. SYN **rehearsal**

**run·way** /ˈrʌnweɪ/ ***noun*** [C] a long piece of ground with a hard surface where aircraft take off and land

**rup·ture¹** /ˈrʌptʃər/ ***noun*** [C,U] **1** a sudden breaking or tearing **2** = HERNIA

**rup·ture²** /ˈrʌptʃər/ ***verb*** [I,T] to break or tear

★**ru·ral** /ˈrʊrəl/ ***adj.*** connected with the country, not large towns or cities: *He comes from rural Georgia.* ◇ *a lack of adequate health care in rural areas* OPP **urban**

**ruse** /ruz/ ***noun*** [C] (*written*) a way of doing sth or of getting sth by deceiving sb: *She tried to think of a ruse to get him out of the house.*

★**rush¹** /rʌʃ/ ***verb*** **1** [I] to go or come very quickly: *Don't rush – take your time.* ◇ *The doctor rushed down the hallway.* ◇ *I rushed back home when I got the news.* ◇ *Don't rush off – I want to talk to you.* **2** [I] **rush to do sth** to do sth without delay: *People rushed to buy stock in the new software company.* **3** [T] to take sb/sth to a place very quickly: *He suffered a heart attack and was rushed to the hospital.* **4** [I,T] **rush (sb) (into sth/into doing sth)** to do sth in a hurry or without enough thought; to make sb act in this way: *We rushed into buying the house – it turned out to be a mistake.* ◇ *Don't rush your project – there's plenty of time.* ◇ *Don't let yourself be rushed into marriage.*

★**rush²** /rʌʃ/ ***noun*** **1** [sing.] a sudden quick movement: *At the end of the game there was a mad rush for the exits.* **2** [sing., U] (a need for) hurry: *I can't stop now. I'm in a big rush.* ◇ *You can give it to me when you finish. There's no rush.* **3** [sing.] a time when many people try to get or do sth in a hurry: *There's been a rush to buy gas before the price goes up.* ◇ *You should do your shopping now to avoid the holiday rush.* ➲ Look also at **gold rush**. **4** [C, usually sing.] (*slang*) a sudden, strong feeling that you get especially from taking a drug or doing sth exciting: *Wow, what a rush – let's go on the roller coaster again!*

**ˈrush hour** ***noun*** [C,U] the time each day when the traffic is busy because people are traveling to or from work: *rush-hour traffic*

**rus·set** /ˈrʌsət/ ***adj.*** reddish-brown in color ▸ **russet** ***noun*** [U]: *leaves of russet and gold*

**Rus·sian rou·lette** /ˌrʌʃn ruˈlɛt/ ***noun*** [U] a dangerous game in which a person shoots at his/her own head with a gun that contains a bullet in only one of its chambers, so that the person does not know if the gun will fire or not: (*figurative*) *The airline was accused of playing Russian roulette with passenger safety.*

**rust¹** /rʌst/ ***noun*** [U] a reddish-brown substance that forms on the surface of iron, etc., caused by the action of air and water

**rust²** /rʌst/ ***verb*** [I,T] to (cause sth to) be attacked by RUST¹: *Some parts of the machine had rusted pretty badly.* ◇ *Road salt had rusted the car pretty badly.*

**the ˈRust Belt** ***noun*** [U] (*informal*) a region that used to have a lot of industry, but that has now decreased in importance and wealth

**rus·tic** /ˈrʌstɪk/ ***adj.*** typical of the country (and therefore simple and old-fashioned): *The rooms are decorated in a rustic style.* ➲ Look at **rural** and **urban**.

**rus·tle** /ˈrʌsl/ ***verb*** [I,T] to make a sound like dry leaves moving together; to cause sth to make this sound: *There was a rustling noise in the bushes.* ◇ *Somebody behind me was rustling his newspaper all through the concert.*

PHR V **rustle sb/sth up** (*informal*) to find sb or prepare sth in a short time: *to rustle up a quick snack*

▸ **rus·tle** ***noun*** [sing.]: *the rustle of leaves in the woods*

**rus·tler** /ˈrʌslər/ ***noun*** [C] a person who steals farm animals

**rust·y** /ˈrʌsti/ ***adj.*** (**rust·i·er**; **rust·i·est**) **1** covered with RUST¹: *rusty cans* **2** (used about a skill) of poor quality because you have not used it for a long time: *I can speak French well, but my Spanish is pretty rusty.*

**rut** /rʌt/ ***noun*** [C] a deep track that a wheel makes in soft ground

IDM **be (stuck) in a rut** to have a boring way of life that is difficult to change

**ru·ta·ba·ga** /ˈruṭəˌbeɪgə; ˌruṭəˈbeɪgə/ ***noun*** [C,U] a large round yellow root vegetable ➲ picture on study page **A28-29**.

**ruth·less** /ˈruθləs/ ***adj.*** showing no pity or sympathy toward other people; thinking first about yourself and what you want: *You have to be ruthless to succeed in politics.* ▶ **ruth·less·ly** ***adv.*** ▶ **ruth·less·ness** ***noun*** [U]

**RV** /ˌɑr ˈvi/ ***noun*** [C] the abbreviation for "recreational vehicle"; a large vehicle that you can sleep, cook, etc. in when you are traveling or on vacation SYN **motor home**

**Rx** /ˌɑr ˈɛks/ ***noun*** [C] **1** the written abbreviation for a doctor's prescription **2** a solution to a problem: *There's no Rx for unemployment.*

**rye** /raɪ/ ***noun*** [U] a plant that is grown for its grain, which is used to make flour and also whiskey

# S s

**S, s** /ɛs/ ***noun*** [C,U] (*pl.* **S's**; **s's**) the nineteenth letter of the English alphabet: *"School" begins with (an) "S."*

**S** (*also* **S.**) ***abbr.*** south

**the Sab·bath** /ˈsæbəθ/ ***noun*** [sing.] the day of the week for rest and worship in certain religions (Sunday for most Christians, Saturday for Jews) ➲ Look at **Shabbat**.

**sab·bat·i·cal** /səˈbæṭɪkl/ ***noun*** [C,U] a long paid break that teachers, especially at colleges and universities, take in order to study, write books, etc.: *Prof. Ramos is on sabbatical this quarter.*

**sa·ber** (*Cdn* **sabre**) /ˈseɪbər/ ***noun*** [C] **1** a heavy sword with a curved blade **2** a light sword with a thin blade used in the sport of fencing

**sa·ble** /ˈseɪbl/ ***noun*** **1** [C] a small animal from northern Asia with dark yellowish-brown fur **2** [U] the skin and fur of the sable, used for making expensive coats and artists' brushes

**sab·o·tage¹** /ˈsæbətɑʒ/ ***noun*** [U] the act of damaging or destroying machinery, roads, bridges, etc. or of ruining plans on purpose and secretly, in order to prevent an enemy or a competitor from being successful: *The explosion at the oil refinery was caused by sabotage.*

**sab·o·tage²** /ˈsæbətɑʒ/ ***verb*** [T] to destroy or damage sth by using SABOTAGE¹: *There are rumors that the plane which crashed had been sabotaged.*

**sab·o·teur** /ˌsæbəˈtər; -ˈtʊr/ ***noun*** [C] a person who does deliberate damage to sth to prevent an enemy from using it, or to protest about sth: *Saboteurs blew up a small section of the track.*

**sac** /sæk/ ***noun*** [C] a part inside the body of a person, an animal or a plant, that is shaped like a bag, has thin skin around it, and contains liquid or air

**sac·cha·rin** /ˈsækərɪn/ ***noun*** [U] a very sweet artificial substance that can be used instead of sugar

**sac·cha·rine** /ˈsækərən; -rin/ ***adj.*** (used about people or things) too emotional in a way that seems exaggerated: *a saccharine smile* ◇ *saccharine songs*

**sa·chet** /sæˈʃeɪ/ ***noun*** [C] a small bag containing dried herbs or flowers that you put with your clothes to make them smell pleasant: *Her nightdresses were neatly folded, with a lavender sachet between each.*

**sack¹** /sæk/ ***noun*** [C] a large bag made from paper, plastic or rough, heavy material, used for carrying or storing things (e.g. vegetables, coal, etc.): *a paper sack* ◇ *sacks of onions* ◇ *They carried several sacks of groceries in from the car.*

**sack²** /sæk/ ***verb*** [T] (*Cdn*) = FIRE² (2)

**sac·ra·ment** /ˈsækrəmənt/ ***noun*** (in Christianity) **1** [C] an important religious ceremony such as marriage, baptism or Communion **2 the sacrament** [sing.] the bread and wine that are eaten and drunk during the service of Communion: *to receive the sacrament*

**sa·cred** /ˈseɪkrəd/ ***adj.*** **1** connected with God, a god or religion; having a special religious meaning: *sacred music* (= music played in religious services) ◇ *The Koran is the sacred book of Islam.* **2** too important and special to be changed or harmed: *a sacred tradition*

**sac·ri·fice¹** /ˈsækrəfaɪs/ ***noun*** **1** [U] the act of offering sth, e.g. an animal that has been killed, to a god **2** [C] a thing, e.g. an animal that has been killed, that is offered to a god **3** [C,U] the act of giving up sth that is important or valuable in order to achieve sth; the thing that you give up in this way: *If we're going to take a trip this year, we'll have to make some sacrifices.* ◇ *He was willing to make any sacrifice in order to succeed.*

**sac·ri·fice²** /ˈsækrəfaɪs/ ***verb*** **1** [I,T] to offer sth to a god, often by killing it **2** [T] to give up sth important or valuable in order to achieve sth: *to sacrifice your life for your country* ◇ *She is not willing to sacrifice her career in order to have children.*

**sac·ri·fi·cial** /ˌsækrəˈfɪʃl/ ***adj.*** (usually before a noun) offered as a SACRIFICE¹ (2): *a sacrificial lamb* ◇ (*figurative*) *Our department became the sacrificial lamb when the company decided to downsize* (= we lost our jobs so that other departments could stay in business).

**sac·ri·lege** /ˈsækrəlɪdʒ/ ***noun*** [U, sing.] an act of treating a holy thing or place without respect: (*figurative*) *It would be sacrilege to alter the composer's original markings.*

**sac·ri·le·gious** /ˌsækrəˈlɪdʒəs/ ***adj.*** treating sth that is considered holy or very special without the respect that it deserves: *Leading clerics condemned the book as a sacrilegious attack on their faith.*

★**sad** /sæd/ ***adj.*** (**sad·der**; **sad·dest**) **1** unhappy or causing unhappiness: *I was sad to hear of the death of your father.* ◇ *She felt terribly sad when her friend moved away.* ◇ *That's one of the saddest stories I've ever heard!* **2** bad or unsatisfactory: *It's a sad state* *of affairs when your best friend doesn't trust you.* ▸ **sad·ness** *noun* [C,U]

**sad·den** /'sædn/ *verb* [T] (often passive) to cause sb to feel sad: *We were deeply saddened by the news of your mother's death.*

**sad·dle¹** /'sædl/ *noun* [C] **1** a seat, usually made of leather, that you put on a horse so that you can ride it ➲ picture at **horse**. **2** a seat on a bicycle or motorcycle ➲ picture at **bicycle**.

**sad·dle²** /'sædl/ *verb* [I,T] to put a SADDLE¹ (1) on a horse, etc.

PHR V **saddle sb with sth** to give sb a responsibility or task that he/she does not want: *I've been saddled with organizing the office party.*

**sad·dle·bag** /'sædlbæg/ *noun* [C] a bag for carrying things that is attached to the saddle on a horse, bicycle or motorcycle

**'saddle shoe** *noun* [C] a white shoe with a piece of leather in a contrasting color (usually black or brown) stitched across the front

**sa·dism** /'seɪdɪzəm/ *noun* [U] getting enjoyment or sexual pleasure from being cruel or causing pain ▸ **sa·dist** /'seɪdɪst/ *noun* [C] ▸ **sa·dis·tic** /sə'dɪstɪk/ *adj.* ▸ **sa·dis·ti·cal·ly** /-kli/ *adv.*

★**sad·ly** /'sædli/ *adv.* **1** in a way that shows unhappiness: *He spoke sadly about the death of his father.* **2** unfortunately, in a way that makes you feel sad or sorry: *Sadly, Morgan died before his book was published.* **3** in a way that is wrong: *If you think that I've forgotten what you did, you're sadly mistaken.*

**sa·fa·ri** /sə'fɑri/ *noun* [C,U] (*pl.* **sa·fa·ris**) a trip, especially in Africa, for hunting or looking at wild animals

★**safe¹** /seɪf/ *adj.* **1 safe (from sb/sth)** free from danger; not able to be hurt: *You shouldn't walk home alone at night. You won't be safe.* ◇ *Do you think my car will be safe on this street?* ◇ *Keep the papers where they will be safe from fire.* **2** not causing danger, harm or risk: *Don't sit on that chair – it isn't safe.* ◇ *I left my suitcase in a safe place and went for a cup of coffee.* ◇ *Is this drug safe for children?* ◇ *He hid from the police until it was safe to come out.* ◇ *She's a very safe driver.* ◇ *I thought it would be a safe investment, but I lost everything.* ◇ *Is it safe to drink the water here?* ◇ *I think it's safe to say that the situation is unlikely to change for quite a while.* **3** not hurt or damaged: *After the accident, he made sure that all the passengers were safe.*

IDM **be on the safe side** to avoid taking risks; to be very careful: *I think this is enough money to pay for the meal, but I'll take a little more just to be on the safe side.*

**safe and sound** not hurt or damaged: *The missing child was found safe and sound by the police.*

▸ **safe·ly** *adv.*: *I called my parents to tell them I had arrived safely.*

**safe²** /seɪf/ *noun* [C] a strong metal box or cabinet with a special lock where you can keep money, jewelry, documents, etc.

**,safe-de'posit ,box** *noun* [C] a box or drawer in a special room in a bank where you can keep valuable things such as documents, jewelry, etc.

**safe·guard¹** /'seɪfgɑrd/ *noun* [C] **a safeguard (against sb/sth)** something that protects against possible dangers: *Make a copy of all your computer disks as a safeguard against accidents.*

**safe·guard²** /'seɪfgɑrd/ *verb* [T] **safeguard sb/sth (against sb/sth)** to keep sth safe; to protect: *When parents get divorced, the children's rights must be safeguarded.*

**safe·keep·ing** /,seɪf'kipɪŋ/ *noun* [U] the fact of sth being in a safe place where it will not be lost or damaged: *She had put her watch in her pocket for safekeeping.*

**,safe 'sex** (*also* **,safer 'sex**) *noun* [U] ways of having sex that can reduce the chance of passing a sexual disease such as AIDS from one person to another, e.g. using a condom

★**safe·ty** /'seɪfti/ *noun* [U] the state of being safe; not being dangerous or in danger: *In the interests of safety, all employees must wear hard hats.* ◇ *safety regulations* ◇ *She has been missing for several days, and the police are very concerned about her safety.* ◇ *The new law will improve the quality and safety of these products.*

**'safety belt** *noun* [C] = SEAT BELT

**'safety net** *noun* [C] **1** a net that is placed to catch sb who is performing high above the ground if he/she falls **2** something that will help you (usually with money) in a difficult situation

**'safety pin** *noun* [C] a metal pin that is used for fastening things together. The pin is bent around and the point goes under a cover so that it cannot be dangerous. ➲ picture at **pin**.

**'safety valve** *noun* [C] **1** a device that lets out steam or pressure in a machine when it becomes too great **2** a harmless way of letting out feelings of anger, excitement, etc.: *Exercise is a good safety valve for the tension that builds up at work.*

**saf·flow·er** /'sæflaʊər/ *noun* [C,U] a plant with orange flowers, whose seeds produce an oil which is used in cooking

**saf·fron** /'sæfrən; -frɑn/ *noun* [U] **1** bright orange threads that come from certain flowers, used in cooking to give color and flavor to food **2** a bright orange-yellow color ▸ **saf·fron** *adj.*: *Buddhist monks in saffron robes*

**sag** /sæg/ *verb* [I] (**sag·ging; sagged**) to hang loosely or to sink down, especially in the middle: *The skin on your face starts to sag as you get older.*

**sa·ga** /'sɑgə/ *noun* [C] a very long story; a long series of events

**sage¹** /seɪdʒ/ *noun* **1** [U] a plant with flat, light green leaves that have a strong smell and are used in cooking as an herb: *duck with sage and onion stuffing* **2** [C] (*formal*) a very wise person

**sage²** /seɪdʒ/ *adj.* wise, especially because you have a lot of experience: *sage comments/remarks* ▸ **sage·ly** *adv.*: *She nodded sagely.*

**sage·brush** /'seɪdʒbrʌʃ/ *noun* [U] a small bush that grows in dry areas of western North America

**sag·gy** /'sægi/ *adj.* (**sag·gi·er; sag·gi·est**) (*informal*) no longer firm; hanging or sinking down in way that is not attractive: *a saggy mattress*

**Sag·it·tar·i·us** /,sædʒə'tɛriəs/ *noun* [C,U] the ninth sign of the zodiac, the Hunter; a person who was born under this sign

**sa·gua·ro** /sə'gwɑroʊ; sə'wɑroʊ/ ***noun*** [C] (*pl.* **sa·gua·ros**) a type of plant with a thick stem and sharp points (cactus), which grows in hot desert areas. Saguaros are common in Mexico and the south-western U.S.

**said** *past tense, past participle of* SAY[1]

★**sail[1]** /seɪl/ ***noun*** [C] a large piece of strong material that is fastened onto a ship or boat. The wind blows against the sail and drives the ship along. ➲ picture at **boat**.

IDM **set sail** to begin a trip by sea: *Columbus set sail for India.*

★**sail[2]** /seɪl/ ***verb*** **1** [I] to travel on water in a ship or boat of any type; to move on water: *On the cruise, we sailed into the Caribbean.* ◇ *I stood at the window and watched the ships sailing by.* **2** [I,T] to travel in and control a boat with sails, especially as a sport: *I've never sailed this kind of boat before.*

> NOTE When you are talking about spending time sailing a boat, the form **go sailing** is very common: *We often go sailing on weekends.*

**3** [I] to begin a trip on water: *When does the ship sail?* ◇ *We sail for the Bahamas at six o'clock tomorrow morning.* **4** [I] to move somewhere quickly in a smooth or confident way: *The ball sailed over the fence and into the neighbor's yard.* ◇ *Mary sailed into the room and sat down at the head of the table.*

IDM **sail through (sth)** to get through a test or a difficult process easily: *He studied hard and sailed through all his exams.*

**sail·board** /'seɪlbɔrd/ ***noun*** [C] a board with a sail that you hold while standing, as the wind moves it across the surface of the water

**sail·boat** /'seɪlboʊt/ ***noun*** [C] a boat that uses a sail or sails ➲ picture at **boat**.

**sail·ing** /'seɪlɪŋ/ ***noun*** [U] the sport of being in, and controlling, small boats with sails: *They do a lot of sailing.*

★**sail·or** /'seɪlər/ ***noun*** [C] a member of the crew of a ship (usually not an officer)

★**saint** /seɪnt/ ***noun*** [C] **1** a very good or holy person who is given special respect after death by the Christian Church

> NOTE When it is used as a title, **saint** is written with a capital letter: *Saint Patrick.* In the names of places, churches, etc., the short form **St.** is usually used: *St. Louis, Missouri.* ➲ Look at **patron saint**.

**2** a very good, kind person

**saint·ly** /'seɪntli/ ***adj.*** (**saint·li·er**; **saint·li·est**) like a saint; very holy and good: *to lead a saintly life*

**St Patrick's Day** /seɪnt 'pætrɪks deɪ/ ***noun*** [C] March 17, the day on which people celebrate Saint Patrick, the patron saint of Ireland

**sake** /seɪk/ ***noun*** [C]

IDM **for Christ's, God's, goodness', Heaven's, Pete's sake** (used as part of a question or order, to make it stronger or to show that you are angry): *What took you so long, for God's sake?* ◇ *For Christ's sake, don't be so stupid!* ◇ *For goodness' sake, hurry up!*

> NOTE **For Christ's sake** and **for God's sake** are stronger and may offend some people.

**for the sake of sb/sth; for sb's/sth's sake** in order to help sb/sth: *Don't go to any trouble for my sake.* ◇ *They only stayed together for the sake of their children/for their children's sake.*

**for the sake of sth/of doing sth** in order to get or keep sth; for the purpose of sth: *It's not worth complaining for the sake of a few pennies.* ◇ *You're just arguing for the sake of arguing* (= because you like arguing).

**sa·la·cious** /sə'leɪʃəs/ ***adj.*** (*formal*) (used about stories, pictures, etc.) encouraging sexual desire or containing too much sexual detail: *The papers concentrated on the more salacious aspects of the case.*

★**sal·ad** /'sæləd/ ***noun*** [C,U] a mixture of vegetables, usually uncooked, often with spices and sometimes small pieces of meat: *potato salad* ◇ *I don't feel like a big meal – I think I'll just have a salad.*

**'salad bar** ***noun*** [C] a place in a restaurant where you can choose several kinds of salads and put them on your plate yourself

**'salad ˌdressing** (*also* **'dressing**) ***noun*** [C] a sauce used to add flavor to salads, usually made from oil, vinegar, yogurt, etc.: *a low-calorie dressing*

**sal·a·man·der** /'sæləˌmændər/ ***noun*** [C] an animal like a lizard, with short legs and a long tail, that lives both on land and in water (**an amphibian**)

**sa·la·mi** /sə'lɑmi/ ***noun*** [C,U] a type of large sausage with a strong flavor, usually eaten in thin slices ➲ picture at **sausage**.

**sal·a·ried** /'sælərid/ ***adj.*** **1** of a person receiving a salary: *a salaried employee* **2** of a job for which a salary is paid: *a salaried position* ◇ *salaried employment*

★**sal·a·ry** /'sæləri/ ***noun*** [C,U] (*pl.* **sal·a·ries**) the money that a person receives regularly for the work he/she has done: *My salary is deposited directly into my bank account.* ◇ *a high/low salary* ➲ Look at the note at **pay[1]**.

**sal·a·ry·man** /'sælərimæn/ ***noun*** [C] (*pl.* **sal·a·ry·men** /-mɛn/) (especially in Japan) a man who works in an office

★**sale** /seɪl/ ***noun*** **1** [C,U] the act of selling or being sold; the exchange of an item for money; the occasion when sth is sold: *The sale of alcohol to children is against the law.* ◇ *Business is bad. I haven't made a sale all week.* ◇ *a sale of used toys* ➲ Look also at **garage sale**, **rummage sale** and **yard sale**. **2** **sales** [pl.] the amount sold: *Sales of personal computers have increased rapidly.* **3** **sales** [U] (*also* **'sales deˌpartment**) the part of a company that deals with selling its products: *a sales and marketing director* ◇ *She works in sales/the sales department.* ◇ *The company has a 6,000 strong* ***sales force****.* **4** [C] a time when stores sell things at prices that are lower than usual: *Sale! All week! Everything half price!* ◇ *I'm not going to buy a coat now – I'll wait until there's a sale.*

IDM **for sale** offered for sb to buy: *This painting is not for sale.*

**on sale 1** offered at a lower price than usual: *I bought this jacket on sale at the mall.* **2** available for sb to buy, especially in stores: *Tickets for the concert go on sale Saturday morning at 10:00.*

**sales·clerk** /ˈseɪlzklərk/ (*also* **clerk**) ***noun*** [C] a person whose job is to sell things to people in a store

**sales·man** /ˈseɪlzmən/ (*also* **sales·wom·an**, **sales·per·son**) ***noun*** [C] a person whose job is to sell things to people: *an insurance salesman*

**sales·man·ship** /ˈseɪlzmənʃɪp/ ***noun*** [U] skill in persuading people to buy things

**ˈsales repreˌsentative** (*also informal* **ˈsales rep**) ***noun*** [C] an employee of a company who travels around a particular area selling the company's goods to stores, etc.

**ˈsales slip** ***noun*** [C] = RECEIPT (1)

**ˈsales tax** ***noun*** [C,U] a tax that is added to the price of sth that you buy

**sa·li·ent** /ˈseɪliənt/ ***adj.*** (only *before* a noun) most important or noticeable: *She pointed out the* ***salient features*** *of the new design.* ◇ *He summarized the* ***salient points.***

**sa·line¹** /ˈseɪlin; -laɪn/ ***adj.*** (*technical*) containing salt: *Wash the lenses in* ***saline solution.***

**sa·line²** /ˈseɪlin; -laɪn/ ***noun*** [U] (*technical*) a mixture of salt in water

**sa·li·va** /səˈlaɪvə/ ***noun*** [U] the liquid that is produced in the mouth

**sal·low** /ˈsæloʊ/ ***adj.*** (used about a person's skin or face) having a slightly yellow color that does not look healthy: *He was a small man with a thin sallow face.*

**Sal·ly Ann** /ˌsæli ˈæn/ ***noun*** [sing.] = THE SALVATION ARMY

**salm·on** /ˈsæmən/ ***noun*** [C,U] (*pl.* **sal·mon**) a large fish with silver skin and pink flesh: *smoked salmon*

**sal·mo·nel·la** /ˌsælməˈnɛlə/ ***noun*** [U] a type of very small living thing (**bacteria**) that causes food poisoning

**sa·lon** /səˈlɑn/ ***noun*** [C] a store where you can have your hair cut or have beauty treatments: *a hair salon* ◇ *a beauty salon*

**sa·loon** /səˈlun/ ***noun*** [C] a bar where alcoholic drinks were sold in the western U.S. and Canada in the 1800s

**sal·sa** /ˈsɔlsə/ ***noun*** [U] **1** a type of Mexican sauce with a hot taste, made from tomatoes, onions, red or green peppers, and sometimes other vegetables or fruit **2** a type of Latin American dance music with a strong beat

★**salt¹** /sɔlt/ ***noun*** [U] a common white substance that is found in ocean water and the earth, that is used especially for flavoring and preserving food: *Season with salt and pepper.* ◇ *Could you please pass the salt?* ◇ *Add a pinch* (= a small amount) *of salt.*
IDM **take sth with a grain of salt** → GRAIN

**salt²** /sɔlt/ ***verb*** [T] to put salt on or in sth: *salted peanuts*

**salt³** /sɔlt/ ***adj.*** having the taste of or containing salt: *salt water*

**sal·tine** /sɔlˈtin/ ***noun*** [C] a type of thin flat dry bread (a cracker) with salt on top of it

**salt·wa·ter** /ˈsɔltwɔt̬ər; -wɑ-/ ***adj.*** living in the ocean: *a saltwater fish* ➲ Fish in rivers and lakes are **freshwater** fish.

★**salt·y** /ˈsɔlti/ ***adj.*** (**salt·i·er**; **salt·i·est**) having the taste of, or containing, salt: *I didn't like the meat – it was too salty.*

**sal·u·bri·ous** /səˈlubriəs/ ***adj.*** (*formal*) healthy, clean and pleasant

**sal·u·tar·y** /ˈsælyəˌtɛri/ ***adj.*** (used about an experience) having a good effect on sb/sth, though often seeming unpleasant: *a salutary lesson/experience/warning* ◇ *The accident was a* ***salutary reminder*** *of the dangers of climbing.*

**sal·u·ta·tion** /ˌsælyəˈteɪʃn/ ***noun*** **1** [C,U] (*formal*) something that you say to welcome or say hello to sb; the action of welcoming or saying hello to sb: *They greeted the newcomers with friendly salutations.* ◇ *He raised his hand in salutation.* **2** [C] (*technical*) the words that are used in a letter to address the person you are writing to, for example "Dear Sir"

**sa·lu·ta·to·ri·an** /səˌlut̬əˈtɔriən/ ***noun*** [C] the student who received the second-highest grades in his/her class in high school or college, and who gives a speech at the graduation ceremony ➲ Look also at **valedictorian**.

**sa·lute¹** /səˈlut/ ***noun*** [C] **1** a sign that a soldier, etc. makes to show respect, by raising his/her hand to the forehead: *to give a salute* **2** an action that shows respect for sb: *The next program is a salute to one of Hollywood's greatest stars.*

**sa·lute²** /səˈlut/ ***verb*** [I,T] to show respect with a SALUTE¹ (1,2): *The soldiers saluted as they marched past the general.* ◇ *The soldiers saluted the general.* ◇ *This is the day on which we salute those who died in the war.*

**sal·vage** /ˈsælvɪdʒ/ ***verb*** [T] to rescue sth from a damaged building or ship; to rescue sth from a disaster: *They salvaged as much as they could from the house after the fire.* ◇ (*figurative*) *The team has only 5 minutes left to salvage something from the game.*
▶ **sal·vage** ***noun*** [U]: *a salvage operation*

**sal·va·tion** /sælˈveɪʃn/ ***noun*** **1** [U, sing.] a thing or a person that saves sb/sth from danger or a difficult situation **2** [U] (in the Christian religion) the state of being saved from evil

**the Salˌvation ˈArmy** (*also informal* **ˌSally ˈAnn**) ***noun*** [sing.] a Christian organization whose members work to help poor people, run second-hand stores, etc.

**salve¹** /sæv/ ***noun*** [C,U] a substance that you put on a wound or sore skin to help it heal or to protect it: *lip salve*

**salve²** /sæv/ ***verb*** [T] (*formal*) **salve your conscience** to do sth that makes you feel less guilty: *He took them presents to salve his conscience.*

**sal·vo** /ˈsælvoʊ/ ***noun*** [C] (*pl.* **sal·vos** or **sal·voes**) the act of firing several guns or dropping several bombs, etc. at the same time; a sudden attack: *The first salvo exploded a short distance away.* ◇ (*figurative*) *This statement provoked* ***a salvo of*** *accusations.*

**Sa·mar·i·tan** /səˈmærətn/ ***noun*** [C]
IDM **a good Samaritan** a person who gives help and sympathy to people who need it

★**same¹** /seɪm/ ***adj.*** **1 the same ... (as sb/sth...)**; **the same ... (that...)** not different, not another or other; exactly the one or ones that you have mentioned before: *My brother and I had the same teacher in school.* ◇ *She comes from the same town as I do.*

◇ *I'm going to wear the same clothes as I wore yesterday.* ◇ *Are you the same person (that) I talked to on the phone yesterday?* **2 the same ... (as sb/sth...); the same ... (that...)** exactly like the one already mentioned: *I wouldn't buy the same car again* (= the same model of car). ◇ *We both came to the party wearing the same outfit.* ◇ *I had the same experience as you some time ago.* ◇ *I've had the same experience (that) you had.*

NOTE We cannot say **a** same ...To express this idea we use **the same kind/sort/type of**: *I'd like the same type of job my dad has.*

IDM **at the same time 1** together; at one time: *I can't concentrate on two things at the same time.* ◇ *Can he really watch TV and study at the same time?* **2** on the other hand; however: *It's a really good idea, but at the same time it's pretty risky.*
**be in the same boat** to be in the same difficult situation as sb else: *Nobody's happy about the boss's decision – we're all in the same boat here.*
**by the same token** in a similar way; using the same reasons: *I agree that Dad shouldn't have gotten so mad at you. But, by the same token, you should try not to aggravate him so much.*
**on the same wavelength** able to understand sb because you have similar ideas and opinions
**the same old sth** (used for sth that has existed or has been used for a long time): *He always gives the same old excuses.*

★**same²** /seɪm/ ***pronoun*** **the same (as sb/sth/...)** the same thing, person, situation, etc.: *Is there another word that means the same as this?* ◇ *Look at what I'm doing and then do the same.* ◇ *Things will never be the same again now that my mom has passed away.*
IDM **all/just the same** even though sth is true; in spite of this/that: *I understand your point of view. All the same, it doesn't change my opinion.* ◇ *They tried to act naturally, but I knew just the same that something was wrong.*
**much the same** → MUCH²
**same here** (*informal*) the same thing is also true for me: *"I'm bored." "Same here."*
**(the) same to you** (*informal*) (used as an answer when sb says sth rude to you or wishes you sth): *"You jerk!" "Same to you!"* ◇ *"Have a nice weekend." "The same to you."*

**same³** ***adv.*** **the same** in the same way; not differently: *We treat everyone in the class the same.*

ˌ**same-ˈsex** ***adj.*** (only *before* a noun) **1** of the same sex: *The child's same-sex parent acts as a role model.* **2** involving people of the same sex: *a same-sex friendship*

★**sam·ple¹** /ˈsæmpl/ ***noun*** [C] **1** a small quantity of sth that is typical of the rest of it: *She sent a sample of her work in an attempt to get a job.* ◇ *a blood sample* **2** a small number of people who are asked questions in order to find out information about a larger group **3** a small amount of a product, that is given free to the public in order to show what it is like: *They were giving out free samples of candy at the store.* **4** a piece of recorded music or sound that is reused in a new piece of music

**sam·ple²** /ˈsæmpl/ ***verb*** [T] **1** to taste or use a small amount of sth (in order to find out what it is like or to decide whether you like it or not): *Let me sample a little of your cake.* **2** (*technical*) to record part of a piece of music, or a sound, in order to use it in a new piece of music

**samp·ling** /ˈsæmplɪŋ/ ***noun*** [U] the process of copying and recording parts of a piece of music in an electronic form so that they can be used in a different piece of music

**sam·u·rai** /ˈsæməraɪ/ ***noun*** [C] (*pl.* **sam·u·rai**) (in the past) a member of a powerful military class in Japan: *a samurai sword/warrior*

**san·a·to·ri·um** /ˌsænəˈtɔriəm/ (*also* **san·i·ta·ri·um** /ˌsænəˈtɛriəm/) ***noun*** [C] a place like a hospital where patients who have a lasting illness or who are getting better after an illness are treated

**sanc·ti·fy** /ˈsæŋktəfaɪ/ ***verb*** [T] (*pres. part.* **sanc·ti·fy·ing**; *3rd person sing. pres.* **sanc·ti·fies**; *pt, pp* **sanc·ti·fied**) (usually passive) (*formal*) **1** to make sth holy **2** to make sth seem right or legal; to give official approval to sth: *This was a practice sanctified by tradition.* ▸ **sanc·ti·fi·ca·tion** /ˌsæŋktəfəˈkeɪʃn/ ***noun*** [U]

**sanc·ti·mon·i·ous** /ˌsæŋktəˈmoʊniəs/ ***adj.*** giving the impression that you feel you are better and more moral than other people: *a sanctimonious voice* ◇ *I wish she'd stop being so sanctimonious.*

**sanc·tion¹** /ˈsæŋkʃn/ ***noun*** **1** [C, usually pl.] an action, especially the stopping of trade, that is taken by other countries against a country that has broken an international law: *The United Nations imposed economic sanctions against South Africa during the 1980s.* **2** [U] (*formal*) official permission to do sth

**sanc·tion²** /ˈsæŋkʃn/ ***verb*** [T] (*formal*) to give official permission for sth: *an officially sanctioned protest march*

**sanc·ti·ty** /ˈsæŋktət̬i/ ***noun*** [U] **1 sanctity (of sth)** the state of being very important and worth protecting: *the sanctity of marriage* ◇ *I believe in the sanctity of human life.* **2** the state of being holy: *a life of sanctity, like that of St Francis* ◇ *the sanctity of the Church*

**sanc·tu·ar·y** /ˈsæŋktʃuˌɛri/ ***noun*** (*pl.* **sanc·tu·ar·ies**) **1** [C] a place where birds or animals are protected from hunters and other dangers: *a wildlife sanctuary* **2** [C,U] a place where sb can be safe from enemies, the police, etc.

**sanc·tum** /ˈsæŋktəm/ ***noun*** [C, usually sing.] (*formal*) **1** a private room where sb can go and not be disturbed: *She once allowed me into her **inner sanctum**.* **2** a holy place

★**sand¹** /sænd/ ***noun*** [U] a powder consisting of very small grains of rock, found in deserts and on beaches: *You need sand to make concrete.* ◇ *Wait a minute – I have some sand in my shoe.* ◇ *When we go on vacation, all we want is sun, sea and sand.*

**sand²** /sænd/ ***verb*** [T] **1** to make sth, especially wood, smooth by rubbing it with sandpaper **2** to put SAND¹ onto a road, sidewalk, etc. which is covered in ice and snow in the winter in order to make it safer to walk or drive on

**san·dal** /ˈsændl/ ***noun*** [C] a type of light, open shoe with straps that people wear when the weather is warm ➲ picture at **shoe**.

**san·dal·wood** /ˈsændlwʊd/ ***noun*** [U] a type of

S

oil with a sweet smell that is obtained from a hard tropical wood, also called sandalwood, and is used to make perfume

**sand·bag**[1] /'sændbæg/ ***noun*** [C] a bag filled with sand used to build a wall as a protection against floods or explosions

**sand·bag**[2] /'sændbæg/ ***verb*** [T] (*pres. part.* **sand·bag·ging**; *pt, pp* **sand·bagged**) **1** to put sandbags in or around sth as protection against floods or explosions **2** (*informal*) to attack sb by criticizing him/her strongly; to treat sb badly

**sand·bank** /'sændbæŋk/ ***noun*** [C] a raised area of sand in a river or the sea: *Our boat got caught on a sandbank as we returned home.*

**sand·blast** /'sændblæst/ ***verb*** [T] (often passive) to clean, polish, decorate, etc. a surface by firing sand at it from a special machine: *The building would have to be sandblasted to remove the black soot.*

**sand·box** /'sændbɑks/ ***noun*** [C] an area in the ground or a shallow container, filled with sand for children to play in

**sand·cas·tle** /'sændkæsl/ ***noun*** [C] a pile of sand that looks like a castle, made by children playing on a beach

**'sand dune** ***noun*** [C] = DUNE

**sand·er** /'sændər/ ***noun*** [C] an electric tool with a rough surface used for making wood smooth

**S & L** /ˌɛs ən 'ɛl/ ***noun*** [C] (*U.S. informal*) = SAVINGS AND LOAN

**sand·lot** /'sændlɑt/ ***adj.*** (used about a sport) played for enjoyment rather than as a job for money: *sandlot football/baseball*

**sand·pa·per**[1] /'sændpeɪpər/ ***noun*** [U] strong paper with sand on it that is used for rubbing surfaces in order to make them smoother

**sand·pa·per**[2] /'sændpeɪpər/ ***verb*** [T] **sandpaper sth (down)** to make sth smooth by rubbing it with sandpaper

S

**sand·stone** /'sændstoʊn/ ***noun*** [U] a type of stone that is formed of grains of sand tightly pressed together, used in building

**sand·storm** /'sændstɔrm/ ***noun*** [C] a storm in a desert in which sand is blown into the air by strong winds

**'sand trap** ***noun*** [C] an area of sand on a golf course, where it is difficult to hit the ball

**sand·wich**[1] /'sænwɪtʃ/ ***noun*** [C] two slices of bread with food between them: *a ham and cheese sandwich* ◇ *It's going to be a long trip, so let's take some sandwiches.* ◇ *What's in that sandwich?*

**sand·wich**[2] /'sænwɪtʃ/ ***verb*** [T] **sandwich sb/sth (between sb/sth)** to place sb/sth in a very narrow space between two other things or people: *I wasn't very comfortable during the flight, sandwiched between two very large people.*

**sand·y** /'sændi/ ***adj.*** (**sand·i·er**; **sand·i·est**) covered with sand or with a lot of sand in it: *miles of sandy beach* ◇ *sandy soil*

**sane** /seɪn/ ***adj.*** **1** (used about a person) mentally normal; not crazy: *With a job like mine, it's incredible that I'm still sane!* **2** (used about a person or an idea, a decision, etc.) sensible; showing good judgment: *I had to accept the offer. It was the only sane thing to do.* OPP **insane** ➲ noun sanity

**sang** *past tense of* SING

**san·gri·a** /sæŋ'griə/ ***noun*** [U] a Spanish drink made of red wine mixed with fruit, and sometimes with water, fruit juice, lemonade or brandy added

**san·guine** /'sæŋgwən/ ***adj.*** (*formal*) cheerful and confident about the future: *He tends to* ***take a sanguine view*** *of the problems involved.*

**san·i·ta·ri·um** /ˌsænə'tɛriəm/ ***noun*** [C] = SANATORIUM

**san·i·tar·y** /'sænəˌtɛri/ ***adj.*** **1** for or connected with the protection of health, e.g. how human waste is removed: *a refugee camp with no sanitary facilities or clean drinking water* **2** clean; without any tiny living things (germs) that can cause disease: *Don't let the dog lick your face – it's not sanitary!*

**ˌsanitary 'landfill** ***noun*** [C] a place where large amounts of garbage or other waste materials are put into the ground and covered with earth

**ˌsanitary 'napkin** (*also* **ˌsanitary 'pad**) ***noun*** [C] a thick piece of soft material that women wear in their underwear to absorb the blood during their PERIOD (3)

**san·i·ta·tion** /ˌsænə'teɪʃn/ ***noun*** [U] a system for protecting public health, especially by removing waste and garbage

**san·i·tize** /'sænətaɪz/ ***verb*** [T] (*formal*) **1** to clean sth thoroughly using chemicals to remove bacteria **2** to remove the parts of sth that could be considered unpleasant: *This sanitized account of his life does not mention his time in prison.*

**san·i·ty** /'sænət̬i/ ***noun*** [U] **1** the ability to think and behave in a normal way **2** sensible or normal thought or behavior OPP **insanity**

**sank** *past tense of* SINK[1]

**San·ta Claus** /'sæntə klɔz/ (*also* **Santa**) ***noun*** [sing.] an old man with a red coat and a long white beard who, some children believe, brings presents in the night before Christmas

> NOTE Children believe that Santa Claus lives at the North Pole. He rides in a **sleigh** which is pulled by **reindeer** that can fly through the air.

**sap**[1] /sæp/ ***noun*** [U] the liquid in a plant or tree

**sap**[2] /sæp/ ***verb*** [T] (**sap·ping**; **sapped**) to make sth weak or to destroy it

**sap·ling** /'sæplɪŋ/ ***noun*** [C] a young tree ➲ picture at **tree**.

**sap·phire** /'sæfaɪər/ ***noun*** [C,U] a bright blue precious stone

**sap·py** /'sæpi/ ***adj.*** (**sap·pi·er**; **sap·pi·est**) (*informal*) silly and sentimental; full of unnecessary emotion: *sappy love songs* ◇ *I get all sappy about my cats.*

**Sa·ran Wrap**™ /sə'ræn ræp/ ***noun*** [U] a thin transparent plastic material that sticks to a surface and to itself, used especially for wrapping food SYN **plastic wrap**

**sar·casm** /'sɑrkæzəm/ ***noun*** [U] the use of words or expressions to mean the opposite of what they actually say. People use sarcasm in order to criticize other people or to make them look stupid: *"No, you didn't take long to get ready. Only two hours," she* *said with heavy sarcasm.* ▶ **sar·cas·tic** /sɑrˈkæstɪk/ ***adj.***: *a sarcastic comment* ▶ **sar·cas·ti·cal·ly** /-kli/ ***adv.***

**sar·dine** /sɑrˈdin/ ***noun*** [C] a type of very small fish, usually sold packed very tightly in cans

IDM **(packed, crammed, etc.) like sardines** (*informal*) pressed tightly together in a way that is uncomfortable or unpleasant

**sarge** /sɑrdʒ/ ***noun*** [C] (*informal*) (used to talk to or about a sergeant)

**sa·ri** (*also* **sa·ree**) /ˈsɑri/ ***noun*** [C] a long piece of cloth that is wrapped around the body and worn as the main piece of clothing, traditionally by women in the Indian Subcontinent

**sa·rong** /səˈrɔŋ; -ˈrɑŋ/ ***noun*** [C] a long piece of cloth wrapped around the body from the waist or the chest, worn by Malaysian and Indonesian men and women

**SARS** /sɑrz/ ***noun*** [U] the abbreviation for "severe acute respiratory syndrome"; a serious illness which causes a high fever and affects the lungs

**SASE** ***abbr.*** = SELF-ADDRESSED STAMPED ENVELOPE

**sash** /sæʃ/ ***noun*** [C] a long piece of material that is worn around the waist or over the shoulder, often as part of a uniform, etc.

**sa·shay** /sæˈʃeɪ/ ***verb*** [I] to walk in a very confident but relaxed way, especially in order to be noticed: *I watched her as she sashayed across the room.*

**sass**[1] /sæs/ ***noun*** [U] (*informal*) behavior or talk that is rude and lacking respect: *Don't give me any of your sass!*

**sass**[2] /sæs/ ***verb*** [T] (*informal*) to speak to sb in a rude way, without respect: *Don't sass your mother!*

**sas·sy** /ˈsæsi/ ***adj.*** (**sas·si·er**; **sas·si·est**) (*informal*) **1** rude; showing a lack of respect **2** fashionable and confident: *his sassy, streetwise daughter* ◇ *a sassy black linen dress*

**SAT™** /ˌɛs eɪ ˈti/ ***noun*** [C] Scholastic Assessment Test; an exam that students in high school in the U.S. take before they go to college: *to take the SAT* ◇ *SAT scores* ➲ For more information on the U.S. educational system, look at study page **A8**.

**Sat.** ***abbr.*** = SATURDAY

**sat** *past tense, past participle of* SIT

**Sa·tan** /ˈseɪtn/ ***noun*** [C] the Devil ▶ **sa·tan·ic** /səˈtænɪk/ ***adj.***

**sa·tan·ism** (*also* **Sa·tan·ism**) /ˈseɪtn-ɪzəm/ ***noun*** [U] the worship of Satan (the Devil) ▶ **sa·tan·ist** ***noun*** [C]

**sa·tay** /sɑˈteɪ; ˈsɑteɪ/ ***noun*** [U] an Indonesian and Malaysian dish consisting of small pieces of meat or fish cooked on sticks and served with a sauce made with peanuts

**sat·el·lite** /ˈsæt̬l-aɪt/ ***noun*** [C] **1** a natural object in space that goes around a bigger object, usually a planet **2** an artificial object that has been sent into space and that moves around a planet for a particular purpose: *satellite pictures of today's weather*

ˌ**satellite ˈtelevision** (*also* ˌ**satellite** ˌ**TˈV**) ***noun*** [U] a system of broadcasting television programs by satellite

NOTE In order to receive satellite TV, you need a **satellite dish**. ➲ Look also at **cable television**.

**sat·in** /ˈsætn/ ***noun*** [U] a type of cloth that is smooth and shiny

**sat·ire** /ˈsætaɪər/ ***noun*** **1** [U] the use of humor to attack a person, an idea or behavior that you think is bad or foolish **2** [C] **satire (on sb/sth)** a piece of writing or a play, movie, etc. that uses SATIRE (1): *a political satire* ▶ **sa·tir·i·cal** /səˈtɪrɪkl/ ***adj.***: *a satirical magazine* ▶ **sa·tir·i·cal·ly** /-kli/ ***adv.***

★**sat·is·fac·tion** /ˌsæt̬əsˈfækʃn/ ***noun*** **1** [U] the feeling of pleasure that you have when you have done, gotten or achieved what you wanted: *Gwen stood back and looked at her work with a sense of satisfaction.* ◇ *We finally made a decision that was to everyone's satisfaction* (= that everyone was pleased with). OPP **dissatisfaction** **2** [C] something that gives you a feeling of pleasure: *It was a great satisfaction to me to know that I had done the job well.*

**sat·is·fac·to·ry** /ˌsæt̬əsˈfæktəri/ ***adj.*** good enough for a particular purpose: *a satisfactory solution to a conflict* ◇ *This piece of work is not satisfactory. Please do it again.* ◇ *She is in the hospital in a satisfactory condition.* OPP **unsatisfactory** ▶ **sat·is·fac·to·ri·ly** /-tərəli/ ***adv.***: *Work is progressing satisfactorily.*

★**sat·is·fied** /ˈsæt̬əsfaɪd/ ***adj.*** **satisfied (with sb/sth)** pleased because you have had or done what you wanted: *a satisfied smile* ◇ *a satisfied customer* ◇ *I hope you're satisfied with what you did!* OPP **dissatisfied**

★**sat·is·fy** /ˈsæt̬əsfaɪ/ ***verb*** [T] (*pres. part.* **sat·is·fy·ing**; *3rd person sing. pres.* **sat·is·fies**; *pt, pp* **sat·is·fied**) **1** to make sb pleased by doing or giving him/her what he/she wants: *Nothing satisfies him – he's always complaining.* **2** to have or do what is necessary for sth: *She satisfied all the requirements for her bachelor's degree.* ◇ *I had a quick look inside the package just to satisfy my curiosity.* **3 satisfy sb (that...)** to show or prove to sb that sth is true or has been done: *The jury were not satisfied that she was telling the truth.* ◇ *She checked the room once again to satisfy herself that everything was ready.*

**sat·is·fy·ing** /ˈsæt̬əsfaɪɪŋ/ ***adj.*** pleasing; giving satisfaction: *It was a very satisfying feeling, knowing that we'd finished the job on time.*

**sat·u·rate** /ˈsætʃəreɪt/ ***verb*** [T] **1** to make sth very wet: *Her clothes were completely saturated.* **2** to fill sth completely: *The market is saturated with cheap imports.* ▶ **sat·u·ra·tion** /ˌsætʃəˈreɪʃn/ ***noun*** [U]: *The market for VCRs has reached saturation point* (= there can be no more increases in sales).

ˌ**saturated ˈfat** ***noun*** [C, usually pl.] saturated fats come from meat and milk products and are not easily processed by the body when eaten because of the way their chemical structure is arranged. Saturated fats are considered less healthy than other kinds of fat because they can cause heart disease. ➲ Look at **polyunsaturated** and **unsaturated**.

**Sat·ur·day** /ˈsæt̬ərdeɪ; -di/ ***noun*** [C,U] (*abbr.* **Sat.**) the day of the week after Friday and before Sunday ➲ For examples of the use of the days of the week in sentences, look at **Monday**.

S

**Sat·urn** /ˈsæt̬ərn/ ***noun*** [sing.] the planet that is sixth in order from the sun and that has rings around it

★**sauce** /sɔs/ ***noun*** [C,U] a thick liquid (that can be hot or cold) that you eat on or with other food: *The chicken was served in a delicious sauce.* ◇ *tomato sauce* ◇ *I opened a jar of spaghetti sauce.*

➲ **Gravy** is a type of thin sauce that is made from meat juices and eaten hot with meat. **Dressing** is a type of sauce that is eaten cold on salads.

**sauce·pan** /ˈsɔspæn/ ***noun*** [C] a round metal pot that is used for cooking things on top of a stove. A saucepan usually has a lid and one or more handles. ➲ picture at **pan**.

**sau·cer** /ˈsɔsər/ ***noun*** [C] a small round plate that you put under a cup: *a cup and saucer*

**sau·cy** /ˈsɔsi/ ***adj.*** (**sau·ci·er**; **sau·ci·est**) (*old-fashioned*) rude or referring to sex in a way that is amusing but not offensive: *saucy comments/jokes*

**sau·er·kraut** /ˈsaʊərkraʊt/ ***noun*** [U] cabbage (= a type of green vegetable) that is preserved in salt water and then cooked

**sau·na** /ˈsɔnə/ ***noun*** [C] a room or small building that is very hot and full of steam, where you can sit to relax: *The health club has a swimming pool and sauna.*

**saun·ter** /ˈsɔntər; ˈsɑn-/ ***verb*** [I] to walk in a slow relaxed way: *He sauntered by, looking as if he had all the time in the world.*

**sausages**

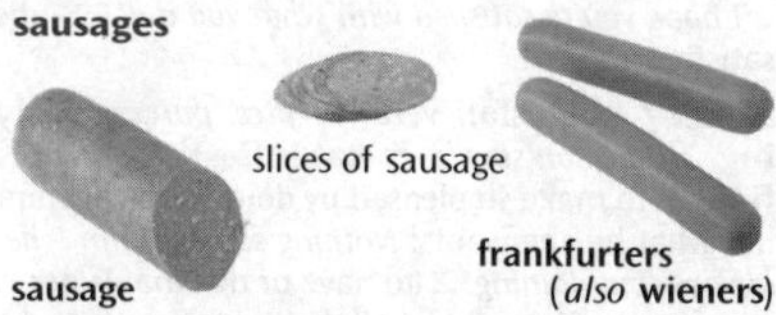


★**sau·sage** /ˈsɔsɪdʒ/ ***noun*** [C,U] a mixture of chopped meat, spices, etc. that is made into a long thin shape. Some sausage is eaten cold in slices; other types are cooked and then served whole: *Italian sausage* ◇ *sausage and eggs*

**sau·té** /sɔˈteɪ; soʊ-/ ***verb*** [T] (*pres. part.* **sau·té·ing**; *pt, pp* **sau·téed** or **sau·téd**) to fry food quickly in a little hot fat ▸ **sau·té** ***adj.***: *sauté potatoes*

**sav·age**[1] /ˈsævɪdʒ/ ***adj.*** very cruel or fierce: *a savage attack by a big dog* ◇ *The book has received some savage criticism.* ▸ **sav·age·ly** ***adv.***

**sav·age**[2] /ˈsævɪdʒ/ ***verb*** [T] to attack sb/sth fiercely

**sav·age·ry** /ˈsævɪdʒri/ ***noun*** [U] very cruel or violent behavior

**sa·van·na** /səˈvænə/ ***noun*** [C,U] a wide flat open area of land, especially in Africa, that is covered with grass but has few trees

★**save**[1] /seɪv/ ***verb***

▸KEEP SAFE **1** [T] **save sb/sth (from sth/from doing sth)** to make or keep sb/sth safe from death, loss, changes, etc.: *to save sb's life* ◇ *to save sb from drowning* ◇ *a campaign to save the whales* ◇ *We are trying to save the school from closing.*

▸MONEY **2** [I,T] **save (sth) (up) (for sth)** to keep or not spend money, etc. so that you can use it later: *Carol is saving up for a new car.* ◇ *We try and save $100 a month.*

▸KEEP FOR FUTURE **3** [T] to keep sth for future use: *I'll be home late, so save me some dinner.* ◇ *Save that box. It might come in handy.* ◇ *If you get there first, save me a seat.*

▸COMPUTING **4** [T] to store information in a computer by giving it a special instruction: *Don't forget to save the file before you close it.*

▸NOT WASTE **5** [I,T] to prevent the spending or waste of time or money: *You can save on gas by getting a smaller car.* ◇ *This car will save you a lot on gas.* ◇ *I saved over $5 on groceries by using coupons today.*

▸AVOID STH **6** [T] to make sth unnecessary; to make it unnecessary for sb to use sth, spend sth, etc.: *You could save yourself a lot of time and effort if you organized your work better.* ◇ *Can you give me a ride? It'll save me having to walk.*

▸IN SPORTS **7** [T] to stop a goal from being scored in soccer, hockey, etc.

IDM **keep/save sth for a rainy day** → RAINY
**lose/save face** → FACE[1]

**save**[2] /seɪv/ ***noun*** [C] (in soccer, hockey, etc.) an act of preventing a goal from being scored: *The goalie made a great save.*

**save**[3] /seɪv/ (*also* **save for**) ***prep.*** (*written*) except sth: *They knew nothing about her save her name.*

**sav·er** /ˈseɪvər/ ***noun*** [C] a person who saves money in a bank: *The increase in interest rates is good news for savers.*

★**sav·ing** /ˈseɪvɪŋ/ ***noun*** **1** [C] an amount of time, money, etc. that you do not have to use or spend: *The sale price represents a saving of 25%.* **2 savings** [pl.] money that you have saved for future use: *He used his life savings to buy the business.*

ˈ**savings acˌcount** ***noun*** [C] a type of bank account where your money earns interest ➲ Look at **checking account**.

ˌ**savings and ˈloan** (*also informal* **S & L**) ***noun*** [C] (*U.S.*) a business like a bank where people can save money in order to earn interest and borrow money in order to buy houses, etc.

**sav·ior** /ˈseɪvyər/ ***noun*** **1** [C] a person who rescues or saves sb/sth from danger, loss, death, etc. **2** (often **Savior**) [sing.] (in the Christian religion) Jesus Christ

**sa·vor·y** /ˈseɪvəri/ ***adj.*** **1** (used about food) having a very good taste or smell **2** having a taste that is salty not sweet: *savory snacks*

**sav·vy**[1] /ˈsævi/ ***noun*** [U] (*informal*) practical knowledge or understanding of sth: *business/political savvy*

**sav·vy**[2] /ˈsævi/ ***adj.*** (*informal*) (often in compounds) having practical knowledge and understanding of sth; having common sense: *savvy shoppers/travelers* ◇ *More people are cholesterol savvy today than five years ago.* ◇ *He's very Web-savvy.*

**saw**[1] *past tense of* SEE

**saw**[2] /sɔ/ ***noun*** [C] a tool that is used for cutting wood, etc. A saw has a long metal blade with sharp teeth on it: *a power saw* ➲ picture at **tool**.

**saw**[3] /sɔ/ ***verb*** [I,T] (*pt* **sawed**; *pp* **sawed** or **sawn**

/sɔn/) to cut sth with a SAW[2]: *to saw through the trunk of a tree* ◇ *Paula sawed the branch off the tree.* ◇ *He sawed the log up into firewood.*

**saw·dust** /ˈsɔdʌst/ ***noun*** [U] very small pieces of wood that fall like powder when you are sawing

**saw·horse** /ˈsɔhɔrs/ ***noun*** [C] a wooden frame that supports wood that is being cut with a SAW[2]

**saw·mill** /ˈsɔmɪl/ ***noun*** [C] a factory in which wood is cut into boards using machinery

**sax** /sæks/ ***noun*** [C] (*informal*) = SAXOPHONE

**sax·o·phone** /ˈsæksəfoʊn/ (*also informal* **sax**) ***noun*** [C] a metal musical instrument that you play by blowing into it. Saxophones are usually used for playing jazz. ➲ picture at **clarinet**.

★**say[1]** /seɪ/ ***verb*** (*3rd person sing. pres.* **says** /sɛz/; *pt, pp* **said** /sɛd/) **1** [T] **say sth (to sb)** to speak words: *"Please come back," she said.* ◇ *The teacher said we should hand in our papers by Friday.* ◇ *to say goodbye* ◇ *to say your prayers* ◇ *He said to his mother that he would call back later.* ◇ *They just sat there without saying anything.* ◇ *"This isn't going to be easy," she said to herself* (= she thought).

NOTE **Say** or **tell**? **Say** is often used with the actual words that were spoken or before **that** in indirect speech: *"I'll catch the 9 o'clock flight," he said.* ◇ *He said that he would catch the 9 o'clock flight.* Notice that you say sth **to** sb: *He said to me that he would catch the 9 o'clock flight.* **Tell** is always followed by a noun or pronoun, showing who you were speaking to: *He told me that he would catch the 9 o'clock flight.* **Tell**, not **say**, can also be used when you are talking about giving orders or advice: *I told them to hurry up.* ◇ *She's always telling me what I ought to do.*

**2** [T] (used about a book, notice, etc.) to give information: *What time does it say on that clock?* ◇ *The map says the hotel is just a couple of blocks away.* **3** [I,T] to express a thought, feeling, answer, opinion, etc.: *"What time is she coming?" "I don't know – she didn't say."* ◇ *I would like to say how happy I am to be here today.* ◇ *He is said to be very rich* (= people say that he is very rich). ◇ *What is the artist trying to say in this painting?* ◇ *Don't get mad at me – all I'm saying is that we should wait a little longer.* ◇ *Well, what do you say? Do you think it's a good idea?* **4** [T] to suppose sth: *We will need, say, $10,000 for a new car.* ◇ *Say you don't get into college – what will you do then?*

IDM **go without saying** to be clear, so that you do not need to say it: *It goes without saying that the children will be taken care of at all times.*

**that is to say...** (*formal*) which means...: *A car which cost $15,000 two years ago now costs $16,500. That is to say, the price has gone up by 10%.*

**to say the least** (used to say that you are describing a situation in a very mild way): *Mom was pretty upset, to say the least* (= she was really very angry).

**say[2]** /seɪ/ ***noun*** [sing., U] **say (in sth)** the power or right to decide sth: *I'd like to have some say in the arrangements for the party.*

IDM **have your say** to express your opinion: *Thank you for your comments. Now let somebody else have their say.*

**say[3]** /seɪ/ ***interjection*** (*informal*) (used in order to get sb's attention or to introduce a new topic in a conversation): *Say, Kelly – how about going to see a movie tomorrow night?*

**say·ing** /ˈseɪɪŋ/ ***noun*** [C] a well-known phrase that gives advice about sth: *"A stitch in time saves nine" is an old saying.* ➲ Look at **proverb**.

ˈ**say-so** ***noun*** [sing.] (*informal*) the power or authority to make decisions and give permission for things to be done: *The measure gives state government more say-so in these types of legal matters.* ◇ *ordinary employees with little say-so against the management.*

IDM **without sb's say-so** without permission that sb gives to do sth: *Nothing could be done without her say-so.* ◇ *She took some of his money without his say-so.*

**scab** /skæb/ ***noun*** [C] a mass of dried blood that forms over a part of the body where the skin has been cut or broken ➲ Look at **scar**.

**sca·bies** /ˈskeɪbiz/ ***noun*** [U] a skin disease that causes itching and small red raised spots

**scads** /skædz/ ***noun*** [pl.] (*informal*) **scads (of sth)** large numbers or amounts of sth: *scads of $20 bills*

**scaf·fold** /ˈskæfəld; -foʊld/ ***noun*** [C] = SCAFFOLDING

**scaf·fold·ing** /ˈskæfəldɪŋ/ ***noun*** [U] (*also* **scaffold** [C]) a structure made of long metal poles and wooden boards, that is put next to a building, high wall, etc. for people to stand on while they repair, clean or paint the building or wall

**scaffolding**

**scal·a·wag** /ˈskæləwæg/ (*also* **scal·ly·wag**) ***noun*** [C] (*informal*) a person, especially a child, who shows a lack of respect for other people and enjoys playing tricks on them SYN **rascal**

**scald** /skɔld/ ***verb*** [T] to burn sb/sth with very hot liquid ▸ **scald·ing** ***adj.***, ***adv.***: *scalding hot water*

★**scale[1]** /skeɪl/ ***noun***

➤RANGE OF LEVELS **1** [C] a series of numbers, amounts, etc. that are used for measuring or setting the level of sth: *The earthquake measured 6.5 on the Richter scale.* ◇ *the new pay scale for city employees* ◇ *The test is graded on a scale of 1 to 100.*

➤SIZE **2** [C,U] the size or extent of sth when compared to other things: *We will be making the product on a large scale next year.* ◇ *I think we have just begun to realize the scale of the problem* (= how serious it is).

➤WEIGHING INSTRUMENT **3** [C] a piece of equipment that is used for weighing sb/sth: *I put the box on the bathroom scale.*

**scale**

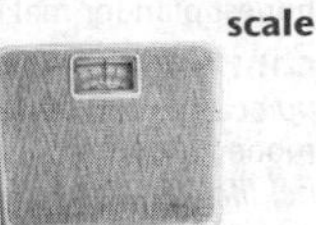

**bathroom scale**

➤MARKS FOR MEASURING **4** [C] a series of marks on a tool or piece of

S

equipment that you use for measuring sth: *The ruler has one scale in centimeters and one scale in inches.*
➤ OF MAP/DIAGRAM/MODEL **5** [C] the relationship between the actual size of sth and its size on a map or plan: *The map has a scale of one inch to one mile.* ◇ *a scale of 1:50,000* ◇ *The plan of the building is not **drawn to scale*** (= the parts of the drawing do not have the same relationship to each other as the parts of the actual building do).
➤ IN MUSIC **6** [C] a series of musical notes which go up or down in a fixed order. People play or sing scales to practice their musical technique.
➤ OF FISH/REPTILE **7** [C] one of the small flat pieces of hard material that cover the bodies of some fish and animals: *the scales of a snake*

**scale²** /skeɪl/ ***verb*** [T] to climb up a high wall, steep cliff, etc.
PHR V **scale sth back/down** to reduce the size or amount of sth: *The company plans to scale back its workforce by 10%.*

**scal·lion** /ˈskælyən/ ***noun*** [C] a type of small onion with a long green stem and leaves. Scallions are eaten raw in salads. ➲ picture on study page **A28-29**.

**scallop**

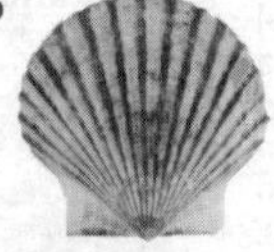

scallop

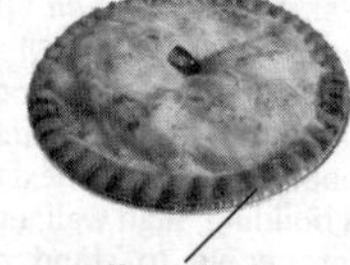

scalloped edge

**scal·lop** /ˈskæləp; ˈskɑ-/ ***noun*** [C] **1** a shellfish that can be eaten, with two flat round shells that fit together: *a scallop shell* **2** any one of a series of small curves cut on the edge of fabric, pastry, etc. for decoration

**scal·loped** /ˈskæləpt; ˈskɑ-/ ***adj.*** decorated round the edge with SCALLOPS (2): *a dress with a scalloped neckline*

**scal·ly·wag** /ˈskæliwæg/ ***noun*** [C] = SCALAWAG

**scalp¹** /skælp/ ***noun*** [C] the skin on the top of your head that is under your hair

**scalp²** /skælp/ ***verb*** [T] (*informal*) to sell a ticket for a sports game, a concert, etc. at a price that is much higher than the original price ▶ **scalp·er *noun*** [C]

**scal·pel** /ˈskælpəl/ ***noun*** [C] a small knife that is used by doctors (surgeons) when they are doing operations

**sca·ly** /ˈskeɪli/ ***adj.*** (**sca·li·er**; **sca·li·est**) (used about skin) covered with SCALES¹ (7): *scaly skin/monsters*

**scam¹** /skæm/ ***noun*** [C] (*informal*) a clever and dishonest plan for making money: *an insurance scam*

**scam²** /skæm/ ***verb*** [T] (*pres. part.* **scam<u>m</u>ing**; *pt, pp* **scam<u>m</u>ed**) (*informal*) to trick sb in order to get money dishonestly: *He scammed the old lady out of her life's savings.*

**scam·per** /ˈskæmpər/ ***verb*** [I] (often used about a child or small animal) to run quickly

**scam·pi** /ˈskæmpi; ˈskɑm-/ (*also* ˌ**shrimp ˈscampi**) ***noun*** [U] a dish of large shrimp cooked in butter and garlic

**scan** /skæn/ ***verb*** [T] (**scan<u>n</u>ing**; **scan<u>n</u>ed**) **1** to examine sth carefully because you are looking for sth: *The sailors scanned the horizon for signs of land.* **2** to look at or read sth quickly: *Matt scanned the list until he found his own name.* **3** (used about a machine) to use beams of light or energy to examine what is inside a person's body or inside an object such as a suitcase, or to examine the surface of an object: *All luggage will be scanned before it is loaded onto the plane.* ◇ *to scan groceries at the supermarket checkout* **4** (*computing*) to copy a picture, etc. from a piece of paper into a computer ▶ **scan *noun*** [C]: *Doctors performed a brain scan on the accident victim.*

**scan·dal** /ˈskændl/ ***noun*** [C,U] an action or a situation or behavior that shocks people; the public feeling that is caused by such behavior: *another government scandal involving illegal campaign contributions* ◇ *There was no suggestion of scandal in his private life.* ◇ *If this information is published, it will cause a huge scandal!*

**scan·dal·ize** /ˈskændl·aɪz/ ***verb*** [T] to do sth that people find very shocking: *She scandalized her family with her wild lifestyle.*

**scan·dal·ous** /ˈskændələs/ ***adj.*** very shocking or wrong: *It is scandalous that murderers are allowed to go free.*

**Scan·di·na·vi·a** /ˌskændɪˈneɪviə/ ***noun*** [U] the group of countries in northern Europe that consists of Denmark, Norway and Sweden. Finland and Iceland are also usually considered to be part of Scandinavia. ▶ **Scan·di·na·vi·an *adj.***

**scan·ner** /ˈskænər/ ***noun*** [C] a machine that SCANS (3,4)

**scant** /skænt/ ***adj.*** (*formal*) (only *before* a noun) not very much; not as much as necessary: *They paid scant attention to my advice.*

**scape·goat** /ˈskeɪpgoʊt/ ***noun*** [C] a person who is blamed for sth that sb else has done

**scar¹** /skɑr/ ***noun*** [C] a mark on the skin that is caused by a cut or wound that has now healed: *The operation didn't leave a very big scar.* ◇ (*figurative*) *Parts of the city still bear the scars of the riots.* ➲ Look at **scab**.

**scar²** /skɑr/ ***verb*** [I,T] (**scar<u>r</u>ing**; **scar<u>r</u>ed**) to leave a scar on sb/sth: *Will's face was scarred for life in the accident.*

**scarce** /skɛrs/ ***adj.*** not existing in large quantities; hard to find: *Food for birds and animals is scarce in the winter.* OPP **plentiful** ▶ **scar·ci·ty** /ˈskɛrsət̬i/ ***noun*** [C,U] (*pl.* **scar·ci·ties**): *There will be food scarcities in most regions.* ◇ *The scarcity of qualified workers is a serious problem for business.*

**scarce·ly** /ˈskɛrsli/ ***adv.*** almost not; just: *There was scarcely a car in sight.* ◇ *She's not a friend of mine. I scarcely know her.* ➲ Look at **hardly**.

**scare¹** /skɛr/ ***verb*** [T] to make a person or an animal frightened: *The sudden noise scared us all.*
PHR V **scare sb/sth away/off** to make a person or animal leave or stay away by frightening him/her/it: *Don't make any noise or you'll scare the birds away.*



S

**scare sth up** (*informal*) to find or make sth by using whatever is available: *I'll see if I can scare up enough chairs for us all.*

**scare²** /skɛr/ ***noun*** [C] **1** a feeling of being frightened: *It wasn't a serious heart attack, but it gave him a scare.* **2** a situation where many people are afraid or worried about sth: *Last night there was a bomb scare at Union Station.*

**scare·crow** /'skɛrkroʊ/ ***noun*** [C] a model of a person that is dressed in old clothes and put in a field to frighten away the birds

**scared** /skɛrd/ ***adj.*** **scared (of sb/sth); scared (of doing sth/to do sth)** frightened: *Are you scared of the dark?* ◇ *She's scared of walking home alone.* ◇ *Everyone was too scared to move.*

**scarf¹** /skɑrf/ ***noun*** [C] (*pl.* **scarfs** /skɑrfs/ or **scarves** /skɑrvz/) **1** a long thin piece of cloth, usually made of wool, that you wear around your neck to keep warm: *He wrapped a scarf around his neck.* ➲ picture on study page **A30**. **2** a square piece of cloth that (usually) women wear around their neck or shoulders or over their heads to keep warm or for decoration: *She tied a scarf around her neck and went out.*

**scarf²** /skɑrf/ ***verb*** [T] (*informal*) eat a lot of sth quickly: *Who **scarfed down** all the nachos?*

**scar·let** /'skɑrlət/ ***adj.***, ***noun*** [U] (of) a bright red color ➲ Look at **crimson** and **maroon**.

**ˌscarlet 'fever** ***noun*** [U] a serious infectious disease that causes fever and red marks on the skin

**scar·y** /'skɛri/ ***adj.*** (**scar·i·er**; **scar·i·est**) (*informal*) frightening: *a scary ghost story* ◇ *It was pretty scary driving in the mountains at night.*

**scat¹** /skæt/ ***noun*** [U] **1** a style of jazz singing in which the voice is made to sound like a musical instrument **2** solid waste from the bodies of wild animals: *bear scat* SYN **droppings**

**scat²** /skæt/ ***interjection*** (*informal*) (used to tell sb to leave or go away): *Scat! Leave me alone.*

**scath·ing** /'skeɪðɪŋ/ ***adj.*** expressing a very strong negative opinion about sb/sth; very critical: *a scathing attack on the candidate* ◇ *scathing criticism*

**scat·o·log·i·cal** /ˌskæṭl'ɑdʒɪkl/ ***adj.*** (*formal*) connected with human waste from the body in an unpleasant way: *scatological humor*

**scat·ter** /'skæṭər/ ***verb*** **1** [I] (used about a group of people or animals) to move away quickly in different directions: *The deer scattered when they heard us approaching.* **2** [T] to drop or throw things in different directions over a wide area: *The wind scattered the papers all over the room.*

**scat·ter·brain** /'skæṭərbreɪn/ ***noun*** [C] (*informal*) a person who is always losing or forgetting things and cannot think in an organized way ▶ **scat·ter·brained** ***adj.***

**scat·tered** /'skæṭərd/ ***adj.*** spread over a large area or over a period of time: *The weather will be partly cloudy with scattered showers today.*

**scav·enge** /'skævɪndʒ/ ***verb*** [I,T] to look for food, etc. among waste and garbage ▶ **scav·en·ger** ***noun*** [C]

**'scavenger hunt** ***noun*** [C] a game or competition in which people are given a list of things that they must find and bring to a particular place

**sce·nar·i·o** /sə'nɛrioʊ; -'nær-/ ***noun*** [C] (*pl.* **sce·nar·i·os**) **1** one way that things may happen in the future: *The doctor described a scenario in which the disease spread rapidly across the whole country.* **2** a description of what happens in a play or movie

★**scene** /sin/ ***noun***

➤PLACE **1** [C] the place where sth happened: *the scene of a crime/an accident*

➤STRONG EMOTION **2** [C] an occasion when sb expresses great anger or another strong emotion in public: *She made a real scene when the waiter brought the wrong drinks.* ◇ *There were emotional scenes at the airport as the students boarded the plane.*

➤IN MOVIE/PLAY, ETC. **3** [C] one part of a book, play, movie, etc. in which the events happen in one place: *His character appears in Act IV, Scene 2.* ◇ *There are too many sex scenes in that movie.*

➤VIEW **4** [C,U] what you see around you in a particular place: *Remington painted many scenes of life in the West.* ◇ *Her new job was no better, but at least it would be a change of scene.*

➤AREA OF ACTIVITY **5 the scene** [sing.] the way of life or present situation in a particular area of activity: *The political scene in the region is very confused.* ◇ *the fashion scene*

IDM **behind the scenes** in secret; without the knowledge of most people: *Several people have been working behind the scenes to destroy the mayor's reputation.*

★**scen·er·y** /'sinəri/ ***noun*** [U] **1** the natural features that you see around you in the country: *The scenery is fantastic in the mountains.*

> NOTE We say that an area of the country has beautiful **scenery** when it is attractive to look at. The **landscape** of a particular area is the way the natural features of it are arranged: *Rugged mountains are a typical feature of the landscape in Colorado.* You have a **view** of something when you look out of a window or down from a tower: *There was a terrific view of the ocean from our hotel room.*

**2** the furniture, painted cloth, boards, etc. that are used on the stage in a theater: *The scenery is changed during intermission.*

**sce·nic** /'sinɪk/ ***adj.*** having beautiful scenery: *a scenic route along the coast*

**scent¹** /sɛnt/ ***noun*** [C,U] **1** a pleasant smell: *This flower has no scent.* **2** the smell that an animal leaves behind and that some other animals can follow

IDM **put/throw sb off the scent** to do sth to stop sb from finding you or discovering sth: *She changed taxis to throw her pursuers off the scent.*

**scent²** /sɛnt/ ***verb*** [T] **1** to find sth by using the sense of smell: *The dog scented a rabbit.* **2** (*written*) to begin to feel that sth exists or is about to happen: *The press could scent a scandal.* **3 scent sth (with sth)** (often passive) to give sth a particular, pleasant smell: *Roses scented the night air.* ◇ *Scent the room with your favorite aromas.* ▶ **scent·ed** /'sɛntəd/ ***adj.***: *scented candles*

★**sched·ule¹** /'skɛdʒəl; -dʒul/ ***noun*** **1** [C,U] a plan of things that will happen or of work that must be

S

done: *Max has a busy schedule for the next few days.* ◇ *to be ahead of/behind schedule* (= to have done more/less than was planned) ◇ *to be on schedule* (= to have done the amount that was planned) **2** a list that shows when planes, buses, etc. arrive at and leave a particular place

★**sched·ule²** /ˈskɛdʒəl; -dʒul/ ***verb*** [T] **schedule sth (for sth/to do sth)** (often passive) to arrange for sth to happen or be done at a particular time: *The hearing has been scheduled for Monday morning.* ◇ *The train was scheduled to arrive at 10:07.* ◇ *This concludes our special news bulletin – we now return to our regularly scheduled program.*

**sche·mat·ic** /skiˈmæṭɪk; skɪ-/ ***adj.*** **1** in the form of a diagram that shows the main features or relationships but not the details: *a schematic diagram* **2** arranged according to a fixed plan or pattern: *The play has a very schematic plot.*

★**scheme¹** /skim/ ***noun*** [C] a plan to do sth, especially sth that is morally wrong or illegal: *an elaborate scheme to influence the outcome of the election* ➲ Look at **color scheme**.

IDM **the/sb's scheme of things** the way things seem to be organized; the way sb wants everything to be organized: *My personal problems are not really important in the* ***grand scheme of things.*** ◇ *I don't think marriage figures in his scheme of things.*

**scheme²** /skim/ ***verb*** [I] to make a secret or dishonest plan

**schism** /ˈskɪzəm; ˈsɪzəm/ ***noun*** [C,U] (*formal*) strong disagreement within an organization, especially a religious one, that makes its members divide into separate groups: *the threat of a schism within the Church*

**schiz·o** /ˈskɪtsoʊ/ ***adj.***, ***noun*** [C] (*slang*) *short for* SCHIZOPHRENIC

**schiz·o·phre·ni·a** /ˌskɪtsəˈfriniə/ ***noun*** [U] a serious mental illness in which a person confuses the real world and the world of the imagination and often behaves in strange and unexpected ways ▸ **schiz·o·phren·ic** /ˌskɪtsəˈfrɛnɪk/ ***adj.***, ***noun*** [C]

S

**schlep** /ʃlɛp/ ***verb*** [I,T] (**schlep·ping; schlepped**) **schlep (sth) (across, around, down, up, etc.)** (*informal*) to carry sth or go somewhere, using a lot of effort: *I don't want to schlep your suitcase all the way upstairs!*

**schlock** /ʃlɑk/ ***noun*** [U] (*informal*) something that is of low quality ▸ **schlock·y** ***adj.***: *a schlocky horror movie*

**schmaltz** /ʃmɑlts; ʃmɔlts/ ***noun*** [U] (*informal*) the quality of being too SENTIMENTAL (2): *At the end of the movie we drown in a sea of schmaltz.* ▸ **schmaltz·y** /ˈʃmɑltsi; ˈʃmɔl-/ ***adj.***

**schmooze** /ʃmuz/ ***verb*** [I] (*informal*) to talk about unimportant things at a social event, e.g. a party

**schmuck** /ʃmʌk/ ***noun*** [C] (*informal*) a stupid and often clumsy person: *He's such a schmuck!*

**schnau·zer** /ˈʃnaʊzər; ˈʃnaʊtsər/ ***noun*** [C] a dog with short rough hair which forms curls

**schol·ar** /ˈskɑlər/ ***noun*** [C] **1** a person who studies and has a deep knowledge of a particular subject: *a leading Shakespeare scholar* **2** a person who has received an amount of money (a **scholarship**) to help pay for his/her studies or for travel or research connected with his/her studies: *a Fulbright scholar*

**schol·ar·ship** /ˈskɑlərʃɪp/ ***noun*** **1** [C] an amount of money that is given to a person by an organization or a school or college, in order to help pay for his/her studies or for travel or research connected with his/her studies: *to win a full scholarship to Yale* **2** [U] serious study; the work of scholars

**scho·las·tic** /skəˈlæstɪk/ ***adj.*** (*formal*) (only *before* a noun) connected with schools and education: *scholastic achievements*

★**school** /skul/ ***noun***

➤WHERE CHILDREN LEARN **1** [C] the place where children go to be educated: *They're building a new school in our area.* ◇ *Paula goes to Kennedy High School.* ◇ *Do you have to wear a school uniform?* ◇ *We go on the school bus.* ◇ *a public/private/parochial school* ➲ Look also at **elementary school**, **middle school** and **high school**. **2** [U] the time you spend at a school; the process of being educated in a school: *Children start school at age 5 in Canada and the U.S. and can quit school when they are 16.* ◇ *School starts at 8:30 and finishes at about 3 o'clock.* ◇ *After school we usually have homework to do.* ◇ *Because of the snow, there will be no school today.*

> NOTE You talk about **school** (without "**the**") when you are talking about going there for the usual reason (that is, as a student or teacher): *Where do your kids go to school?* ◇ *I enjoyed being in school.* ◇ *Do you walk to school?* You talk about **the school** if you are talking about going there for a different reason (for example, as a parent): *I have to go to the school on Thursday to talk to John's teacher.* You must also use **a** or **the** when more information about the school is given: *Pat goes to the neighborhood school.* ◇ *She teaches at a school in Atlanta.*

➤STUDENTS AND TEACHERS **3** [sing.] all the students and teachers in a school: *The whole school cheered the winner.*

➤FOR PARTICULAR SKILL **4** [C] a place where you go to learn a particular subject: *a driving school* ◇ *a language school*

➤COLLEGE/UNIVERSITY **5** [C,U] a college or university: *Jack had to pay his own way through school.* **6** [C,U] a department of some colleges or universities that teaches a particular subject or group of subjects: *the School of Arts and Sciences* ◇ *She's in law school.*

➤OF WRITERS/ARTISTS **7** [C] a group of writers, painters, etc. who have the same ideas or style

IDM **a school of thought** the ideas or opinions that one group of people share: *There are various schools of thought on this matter.*

**at school** in the school building: *Kristy stayed at school until 4:30 to finish her science project.*

**in school** being a student; attending a school, college, or university: *I wasn't happy in school, so I got a job.*

ˈ**school board** ***noun*** [C] a group of people who have been elected to be in charge of the public schools in a city or an area

**school·boy** /ˈskulbɔɪ/ (*also* **school·girl** /ˈskulgərl/ **school·child** /ˈskultʃaɪld/) ***noun*** [C] (*formal*) a boy/girl/child who goes to school ➲ **Student** is more common.

**ˈschool ˌdistrict** ***noun*** [C] an area in which all the public schools are governed by one group of people (the school board)

**school·house** /ˈskulhaʊs/ ***noun*** [C] a school building, especially one in a small town in the past

**school·ing** /ˈskulɪŋ/ ***noun*** [U] the time that you spend in school; your education: *Her grandfather had only six years of schooling.*

**school·marm** /ˈskulmɑrm/ ***noun*** [C] a woman who teaches in a school, especially one who is old-fashioned and strict ▸ **ˈschool-ˌmarmish** ***adj.***: *a school-marmish tone of voice*

**ˈschool night** ***noun*** [C] a night before you have to go to school the following morning: *I have to be home by 10 on a school night.*

**school·teach·er** /ˈskultitʃər/ ***noun*** [C] (*old-fashioned*) a person who teaches in a school

**school·work** /ˈskulwərk/ ***noun*** [U] work that teachers give their students to do

**schwa** /ʃwɑ/ ***noun*** [C] (*technical*) a vowel sound in parts of words that are not stressed, for example the "a" in *about* or the "e" in *moment*; the phonetic symbol for this ( /ə/)

★**sci·ence** /ˈsaɪəns/ ***noun*** **1** [U] the study of and knowledge about the physical world and natural laws: *science and technology* ◇ *Modern science has discovered a lot about the origin of life.* ◇ *Fewer young people are studying science in school.* ◇ *a science teacher* (= one who teaches biology, chemistry or physics) **2** [C,U] one of the subjects into which science can be divided: *Biology, chemistry and physics are all sciences.* ◇ *Is mathematics a science?* ➲ Subjects connected with the study of people and society are called **social sciences**. Look also at **political science**.

**ˌscience ˈfiction** (*also informal* **sci-fi** , **SF**) ***noun*** [U] books, movies, etc. about events that take place in the future, especially connected with travel in space

★**sci·en·tif·ic** /ˌsaɪənˈtɪfɪk/ ***adj.*** **1** connected with science: *We need more funding for scientific research.* **2** using the methods that are used in SCIENCE (1) (= observing facts and testing ideas with experiments): *a scientific study of the way people use language* ▸ **sci·en·tif·i·cal·ly** /-kli/ ***adv.***: *It will be hard to prove the idea scientifically* (= using the methods of science).

★**sci·en·tist** /ˈsaɪəntɪst/ ***noun*** [C] a person who studies or teaches science, especially biology, chemistry or physics

**sci-fi** /ˌsaɪˈfaɪ/ ***noun*** [U] (*informal*) = SCIENCE FICTION

**scin·til·la** /sɪnˈtɪlə/ ***noun*** [sing.] **scintilla (of sth)** (*formal*) (usually in negative sentences) a very small amount of sth: *There is not a scintilla of truth in what she says.* ◇ *They had not found a scintilla of evidence against him.*

**scin·til·lat·ing** /ˈsɪntlˌeɪt̬ɪŋ/ ***adj.*** very interesting and showing humor and intelligence: *a scintillating conversation* ◇ *Statistics on unemployment levels hardly make for scintillating reading.*

★**scis·sors** /ˈsɪzərz/ ***noun*** [pl.] a tool for cutting things that consists of two flat sharp blades that are joined together

> NOTE **Scissors** is a plural noun: *These scissors are blunt.* We CANNOT say "a scissors"; we must use the word **pair**: *I need a new pair of scissors.*

**scissors**

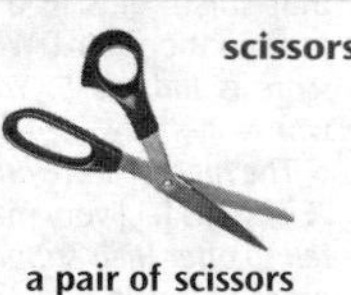

**a pair of scissors**

**scle·ro·sis** /skləˈroʊsəs/ ***noun*** [U] (*medical*) a condition in which soft tissue in the body becomes hard, in a way that is not normal ➲ Look at **multiple sclerosis**

**scoff** /skɔf; skɑf/ ***verb*** [I] **scoff (at sb/sth)** to speak about sb/sth without respect

**scoff·law** /ˈskɑflɔ; ˈskɔf-/ ***noun*** [C] (*informal*) a person who often breaks the law but in a way that is not serious: *The city hopes that this program will encourage scofflaws to pay their parking fines.*

**scold** /skoʊld/ ***verb*** [I,T] **scold sb (for sth/for doing sth)** to speak angrily to sb because he/she has done something bad or wrong: *The teacher scolded her for being late.*

**sco·li·o·sis** /ˌskoʊliˈoʊsəs/ ***noun*** [U] (*medical*) a condition in which the spine is curved in a way that is not normal

**scone** /skoʊn; skɑn/ ***noun*** [C] a small round cake, sometimes with dried fruit in it

**scoop**[1] /skup/ ***noun*** [C] **1** a tool like a spoon used for picking up ice cream, sugar, etc. **2** the amount that one SCOOP (1) contains: *apple pie served with a scoop of ice cream* **3** an exciting piece of news that is reported by one newspaper, television or radio station before it is reported anywhere else

**scoop**[2] /skup/ ***verb*** [T] **scoop sth (out/up)** to make a hole in sth or to take sth out by using a SCOOP (1) or sth similar: *Scoop out the middle of the pineapple.* ◇ *He scooped up a handful of change for the parking meter.*

**scoot**[1] /skut/ ***verb*** [I] (*informal*) to go or leave somewhere in a hurry: *I'd better scoot or I'll be late.*

**scoot**[2] /skut/ ***interjection*** (*informal*) (used to tell sb to leave or go away)

**scoot·er** /ˈskut̬ər/ ***noun*** [C] **1** (*also* **ˈmotor ˌscooter**) a light motorcycle, usually with small wheels and a curved metal cover at the front to protect the rider's legs ➲ picture at **motorbike**. **2** a light vehicle with two small wheels attached to a narrow board with a vertical handle. The rider holds the handle, puts one foot on the board and pushes against the ground with the other.

**scope**[1] /skoʊp/ ***noun*** **1** [sing.] the range of subjects that are being discussed or considered: *The government was unwilling to extend the scope of the investigation.* **2** [U] **scope (for sth/to do sth)** the chance or opportunity to do sth: *The job offers plenty of scope for creativity.*

**scope**[2] /skoʊp/ ***verb***

PHR V **scope sth out** to look at sth carefully in order to see what it is like

**scorch** /skɔrtʃ/ ***verb*** [T] to burn sth slightly so that its color changes but it is not destroyed: *I scorched*

S

*my blouse when I was ironing it.* ◇ (*figurative*) *the scorched landscape of the Arizona desert*

**scorch·ing** /ˈskɔrtʃɪŋ/ ***adj.*** very hot: *scorching temperatures*

★**score¹** /skɔr/ ***noun*** **1** [C] the number of points that sb/sth gets in a game, a competition, on an examination, etc.: *What was the final score?* ◇ *The score is Indians 5, Yankees 2.* ◇ *I don't know who won – nobody kept score* (= recorded the scores). ◇ *The highest score on the test was 80%.* ◇ *SAT scores* **2 scores** [pl.] very many: *Scores of people have written to offer their support.* **3** [C] the written form of a piece of music

IDM **on that score** about that: *I have no concerns on that score.*

★**score²** /skɔr/ ***verb*** **1** [I,T] to get points in a game, a competition, on an examination, etc.: *The team still hadn't scored by halftime.* ◇ *The Blue Jays scored two runs in the third inning.* **2** [T] to give a number that shows how well sb does on an examination, in a competition, etc.: *The written driving test is scored by computer.* **3** [I,T] (*slang*) to succeed in getting sth, especially sex or illegal drugs

**score·board** /ˈskɔrbɔrd/ ***noun*** [C] a large board that shows the SCORE¹ (1) during a game, competition, etc. ➲ picture at **football**.

**score·card** /ˈskɔrkɑrd/ ***noun*** [C] a card or piece of paper that people watching or playing a game can use to write the score on, or on which the score can be officially recorded

**score·keep·er** /ˈskɔrˌkipər/ ***noun*** [C] a person who keeps a record of the points, goals, etc. scored in a game or competition

**scorn¹** /skɔrn/ ***noun*** [U] the strong feeling that you have when you do not respect sb/sth: *She looked at him with scorn.* ▸ **scorn·ful** /-fl/ ***adj.***: *a scornful look/smile* ▸ **scorn·ful·ly** /-fəli/ ***adv.***

**scorn²** /skɔrn/ ***verb*** [T] to show that you do not respect sb/sth by making unkind comments, etc.: *The candidate scorned his rival.*

**Scor·pi·o** /ˈskɔrpioʊ/ ***noun*** [C,U] (*pl.* **Scor·pi·os**) the eighth sign of the zodiac, the Scorpion; a person who was born under this sign

**scor·pi·on** /ˈskɔrpiən/ ***noun*** [C] a creature that looks like a large insect and lives in warm climates. A scorpion has a long tail with a poisonous sting in it.

**Scotch** /skɑtʃ/ ***noun*** [C,U] a strong alcoholic drink (whiskey) that is made in Scotland, or a glass of this drink ➲ Look at the note at **Scottish**.

**ˌScotch ˈtape™** ***noun*** [U] a type of clear tape that is sticky on one side. It is sold in rolls and is used for sticking things together.

**Scot·tish** /ˈskɑt̬ɪʃ/ ***adj.*** of or connected with Scotland, its people, culture, etc. ➲ **Scottish** is used about Scotland and about both people and things that come from Scotland: *She speaks with a strong Scottish accent.* ◇ *the Scottish Highlands.* **Scotch** is used for a type of whiskey that comes from Scotland and for some kinds of food. You should not use it for Scottish people.

**scoun·drel** /ˈskaʊndrəl/ ***noun*** [C] (*old-fashioned*) a man who behaves very badly toward other people, especially by being dishonest

**scour** /ˈskaʊər/ ***verb*** [T] **1** to search a place very carefully because you are looking for sb/sth: *A search party scoured the area, looking for the missing boy.* **2** to clean sth by rubbing it hard with sth rough: *to scour dirty pots and pans*

**scourge** /skərdʒ; skɔrdʒ/ ***noun*** [C] **1** [usually sing.] **scourge (of sb/sth)** (*written*) a person or thing that causes trouble or suffering: *the scourge of war/disease/poverty* **2** a whip used to punish people in the past

**ˈscouring pad** ***noun*** [C] a small ball of wire or stiff plastic used for cleaning pans

**scout¹** /skaʊt/ ***noun*** [C] **1 Scout** (*US usually* **Boy Scout, Girl Scout**) a member of an organization which teaches boys and girls to be responsible and help other people. Scouts also learn useful skills, go camping, etc. **2** a soldier who is sent on in front of the rest of the group to find out where the enemy is or which is the best route to take **3** a person whose job is to find people who are good at sports, music, etc. in order to give them jobs: *a football scout*

**scout²** /skaʊt/ ***verb*** [I] **scout around (for sth)**; **scout for sth** to search for sth in a particular place: *Go scout around for some firewood.*

**Scout·ing** /ˈskaʊt̬ɪŋ/ ***noun*** [U] the activities that Boy and Girl Scouts take part in; the Scout organization

**scowl** /skaʊl/ ***noun*** [C] a look on your face that shows you are angry or in a bad mood SYN **frown** ▸ **scowl** ***verb*** [I]

**scrag·gly** /ˈskræɡli/ ***adj.*** (**scrag·gli·er**; **scrag·gli·est**) (*informal*) thin and growing in a way that is not even: *a scraggly beard*

**scram** /skræm/ ***interjection*** (*old-fashioned, informal*) (used to tell sb to go away quickly): *Scram! I don't want you here.*

**scram·ble¹** /ˈskræmbl/ ***verb*** **1** [I] to move or do something quickly because you are in a hurry: *Rescue workers scrambled to find survivors in the wreckage.* **2** [I] **scramble (for sth)** to struggle to get sth which a lot of people want: *Everyone was scrambling to get the best bargains.* **3** [T] to change a television, radio, etc. signal so that it cannot be understood without a special machine

**scram·ble²** /ˈskræmbl/ ***noun*** [sing.] a situation in which a lot of people are in a hurry and struggling to get or do sth: *There was a mad scramble as everyone rushed for the best seats.*

**ˌscrambled ˈeggs** ***noun*** [pl.] eggs that are mixed together and then cooked in a pan

**scrap¹** /skræp/ ***noun*** **1** [C] a small piece or amount of sth: *a scrap of paper* ◇ *scraps of food* **2** [U] something that you do not want anymore but that is made of material that can be used again: *scrap metal*

**scrap²** /skræp/ ***verb*** [T] (**scrap·ping**; **scrapped**) (*informal*) to get rid of sth that you do not want anymore: *I think we should scrap that idea.*

**scrap·book** /ˈskræpbʊk/ ***noun*** [C] a large book with blank pages that you can stick pictures, newspaper articles, etc. in

**scrape¹** /skreɪp/ ***verb*** **1** [T] **scrape sth (off)** to make sth clean or smooth by moving a sharp edge across it firmly: *Scrape your plate into the garbage* *can.* **2** [T] to remove sth by moving a sharp edge across a surface: *Scrape all the mud off your boots before you come in.* **3** [T] **scrape sth (against/along/on sth)** to damage or hurt sth by rubbing it against sth rough or hard: *Mark fell and scraped his knee.* ◇ *Jenny scraped the car against a tree.* **4** [I,T] **scrape (sth) against/along/on sth** to rub (sth) against sth and make a sharp unpleasant noise: *The branch scraped against the window.*

PHRV **scrape by** to have just enough money to buy the things that you need: *We're just able to scrape by on my welfare checks.*

**scrape sth together/up** to get enough money together with difficulty: *We barely managed to scrape together enough money for a week's vacation.*

**scrape²** /skreɪp/ ***noun*** [C] **1** a mark or small wound on your skin from scraping it against sth: *Tom only suffered minor scrapes and bruises in the accident.* **2** (*informal*) a difficult situation or problem, often that was caused by your own behavior: *She had several scrapes with the law, but managed to stay out of prison.*

**scrap·py** /ˈskræpi/ ***adj.*** (**scrap·pi·er**; **scrap·pi·est**) (*informal*) **1** (used about a person) very determined and willing to fight or argue with people in order to achieve sth **2** consisting of individual sections, events, etc. that are not organized into a whole: *a scrappy report*

★**scratch¹** /skrætʃ/ ***verb*** **1** [I,T] to rub a part of the body with your fingernails: *Your mosquito bites will become infected if you don't stop scratching.* ◇ *to scratch an itch* ◇ *Could you scratch my back for me?* **2** [I,T] to make a mark on a surface or a small wound on a person's skin with sth sharp: *The cat will scratch if you make her mad.* ◇ *The paint is badly scratched on the car door.* **3** [T] to put sth somewhere or to take it away by SCRATCHING (2): *He scratched his name on the top of his desk.*

★**scratch²** /skrætʃ/ ***noun*** [C] a cut, mark or sound that was made by sb/sth scratching sb/sth else: *There's a scratch on the car door.* ◇ *They survived the accident without even a scratch.*

IDM **from scratch** from the very beginning: *to start from scratch* ◇ *to make a cake from scratch*

**ˌscratch-and-ˈsniff** ***adj.*** (only *before* a noun) a scratch-and-sniff book, magazine, card, etc. has a special surface which gives out a smell when it is scratched

**scratch·pad** /ˈskrætʃpæd/ (*also* ˈ**scratch pad**) ***noun*** [C] a small book of cheap paper for writing notes on

**scratch·y** /ˈskrætʃi/ ***adj.*** (**scratch·i·er**; **scratch·i·est**) **1** (used about clothes or fabric) rough and unpleasant to the touch: *This sweater is too scratchy.* ◇ *a scratchy blanket* **2** (used about a record, voice, etc.) making a rough, unpleasant sound like sth being scratched across a surface: *a scratchy recording of Mario Lanza* ◇ *a scratchy pen* **3** (used about writing or drawings) done without care: *She had scrawled me a note in her familiar scratchy handwriting.*

**scrawl** /skrɔl/ ***verb*** [I,T] to write in a messy and careless way ▸ **scrawl *noun*** [sing.]: *Her signature was just a scrawl.* ➲ Look at **scribble**.

**scrawn·y** /ˈskrɔni/ ***adj.*** (**scrawn·i·er**; **scrawn·i·est**) of people or animals very thin in a way that is not attractive: *He had long scrawny fingers.* ◇ *There were a few scrawny chickens in the yard.*

★**scream¹** /skrim/ ***verb*** [I,T] **scream (sth) (out) (at sb)** to cry out loudly in a high voice because you are afraid, excited, angry, in pain, etc.: *She saw a rat hiding in the corner of the room and screamed.* ◇ *"Don't touch that!" he screamed.* ◇ *She screamed at the girls to stop fighting.* ◇ *When the car hit him, he screamed with pain.* ◇ *He clung to the edge of the cliff, screaming for help.* ➲ Look at **shout**.

**scream²** /skrim/ ***noun*** **1** [C] a loud high cry made by sb who is hurt, frightened, excited, etc.; a loud high noise: *We heard a scream from the apartment next door.* **2** [sing.] (*old-fashioned, informal*) a person or thing that causes you to laugh: *He's a scream.*

**screech** /skritʃ/ ***verb*** [I,T] to make an unpleasant loud high sound: *The car's brakes screeched as it came to a halt.* ➲ Compare **shriek**. ▸ **screech *noun*** [C]

★**screen¹** /skrin/ ***noun***

➤OF TV/COMPUTER **1** [C] the glass surface of a television or computer where the picture or information appears

➤MOVIES **2** [C] the white surface on which movies are shown **3** [sing., U] movies: *a star of stage and screen* (= a famous actor who appears in both plays and movies)

➤FOR HIDING/PROTECTING STH/SB **4** [C] something that prevents sb from seeing or being aware of sth, or that protects sb/sth: *We planted a screen of tall trees.* ◇ *A screen of bodyguards protected the President.*

➤ON WINDOW/DOOR **5** [C] a wire or plastic net that is held in a frame and fastened on a door or an open window to let in air but keep out insects: *Do you have screens on all your windows?* ➲ Look at **screen door**.

➤PIECE OF FURNITURE **6** [C] a flat vertical surface that is used for dividing a room or keeping sb/sth out of sight

**screen²** /skrin/ ***verb*** [T] **1 screen sb (for sth)** to examine or test sb to find out if he/she has a particular disease or if he/she is suitable for a particular job: *All children are screened for vision problems in school.* ◇ *The Department of Defense carefully screens all job applicants.* **2 screen sb/sth (off) (from sb/sth)** to hide or protect sb/sth from sb/sth: *The bed was screened off while the doctor examined him.* ◇ *to screen your eyes from the sun* **3** to show sth on TV or in a movie theater: *The program was too violent to be screened before 9 o'clock.* **4** to check sth to see if it is suitable or if you want it: *I use my answering machine to screen my phone calls.*

ˈ**screen door *noun*** [C] an outside door, usually on a house, that is like a frame of wire net, so that fresh air can come into the house in summer but insects cannot ➲ Picture on study page **A31**.

**screen·ing** /ˈskrinɪŋ/ ***noun*** **1** [C] the act of showing a movie or television program: *This will be the movie's first screening in this country.* **2** [C,U] the testing or examining of a large number of people or things for disease, faults, etc.: *breast cancer screening*

**screen·play** /ˈskrinpleɪ/ ***noun*** [C] the words that

S

are written for a movie (a script), together with instructions for how it is to be acted and filmed

**ˈscreen ˌsaver** *noun* [C] (*computing*) a computer program that replaces a screen display on a computer with another, moving, display after a particular length of time, to stop the screen from being damaged

**ˈscreen test** *noun* [C] a filmed test to see if sb is suitable to appear in a movie

**screen·writ·er** /ˈskrinˌraɪt̬ər/ *noun* [C] a person who writes screenplays ➲ Look also at **scriptwriter**.

★**screw**[1] /skru/ *noun* [C] a small piece of metal with a sharp end and a round head used for fastening two things, e.g. pieces of wood, together. A screw is like a nail, but you fasten it into sth by turning it around with a special tool (a **screwdriver**). ➲ picture at **nail**.

IDM **have a screw loose** (*informal*) to be slightly strange in your behavior

★**screw**[2] /skru/ *verb* **1** [T] to fasten sth with a SCREW[1] or screws: *The bookcase is screwed to the wall.* **2** [I,T] to fasten sth, or to be fastened, by turning: *The legs screw into holes on the underside of the table.* ◇ *to screw in a lightbulb* **3** [I,T] (*taboo, slang*) to have sex with sb

IDM **be screwed** (*slang*) to be in trouble; to be in a very difficult situation with no hope: *If my dad finds out we took his car, we're screwed!*

PHR V **screw around** (*taboo, slang*) to have sex with a lot of different people

**screw up** (*slang*) to make a mistake: *You really screwed up this time, Jeff!*

**screw sth up** (*slang*) to ruin sth or cause sth to fail: *You'd better not screw up this deal.*

**screw·ball** /ˈskrubɔl/ *noun* [C] (*informal*) a strange or crazy person: *That guy's a complete screwball.*

**screw·dri·ver** /ˈskrudraɪvər/ *noun* [C] a tool that you use for turning SCREWS[1] (1) ➲ picture at **tool**.

**ˌscrewed-ˈup** *adj.* (*informal*) upset and anxious, especially because of sth bad that has happened to you in the past: *an extremely screwed-up kid*

**screw·y** /ˈskrui/ *adj.* (**screw·i·er**; **screw·i·est**) (*informal*) strange or crazy: *What a screwy idea!*

**scrib·ble** /ˈskrɪbl/ *verb* [I,T] to write sth quickly and carelessly: *to scribble down a note on a pad* ➲ Look at **scrawl**. ▶ **scrib·ble** *noun* [C,U]

**scrib·bler** /ˈskrɪblər/ *noun* [C] (*Cdn*) a book with plain paper for writing in, especially for schoolchildren

**scribe** /skraɪb/ *noun* [C] (in the past) a person who made copies of written documents before printing was invented

**scrim·mage** /ˈskrɪmɪdʒ/ *noun* [C] **1** a confused struggle or fight **2** (in football) a period of play that begins with the ball being placed on the ground **3** (used especially about football) a practice game

**scrimp** /skrɪmp/ *verb* [I] to spend very little money on the things that you need to live, especially so that you can save it to spend on sth else: *They* ***scrimped and saved*** *to give the children a good education.*

PHR V **scrimp on sth** to spend too little money on sth or buy sth that is of poor quality: *If you're going to do a good job of renovating an old house, don't scrimp on materials.*

**script** /skrɪpt/ *noun* **1** [C] the written form of a play/movie/speech **2** [C,U] a system of writing: *Arabic, Roman, etc. script* **3** [U] a style of writing with letters that are joined together

**script·ed** /ˈskrɪptəd/ *adj.* read from a SCRIPT (1): *a scripted discussion* OPP **unscripted**

**scrip·tur·al** /ˈskrɪptʃərəl/ *adj.* relating to or based on the Scriptures

**Scrip·ture** /ˈskrɪptʃər/ *noun* [U] (*also* **the Scriptures** [pl.]) the holy books of a religion, such as the Bible

**script·writ·er** /ˈskrɪptˌraɪt̬ər/ *noun* [C] a person who writes the SCRIPT (1) for movies, television and radio plays ➲ Look also at **screenwriter**.

**scroll**[1] /skroʊl/ *noun* [C] a long roll of paper with writing on it

**scroll**[2] /skroʊl/ *verb* [I,T] to move text up or down on a computer screen until you find the part you want

**scro·tum** /ˈskroʊt̬əm/ *noun* [C] (*pl.* **scro·tums** or **scro·ta** /-t̬ə/) the bag of skin that contains the testicles in men and most male animals

**scrounge** /skraʊndʒ/ *verb* [I,T] (*informal*) **scrounge (sth) (off/from sb)**; **scrounge (for sth)** to get sth from sb by asking him/her for it rather than by paying for it: *He's always scrounging free meals off us.* ◇ *What is she scrounging for this time?* SYN **sponge**[2](3)

**scrub**[1] /skrʌb/ *noun* **1** [U] small trees and bushes that grow in an area that has poor soil or low rainfall **2 scrubs** [pl.] (*technical*) the special clothes worn by surgeons when they are doing medical operations

**scrub**[2] /skrʌb/ *verb* (**scrub·bing**; **scrubbed**) **1** [I,T] to clean sth with soap and water by rubbing it hard, often with a brush: *to scrub the floor/walls* **2** [T] **scrub sth (off)** to remove sth by scrubbing: *to scrub the dirt off the walls* **3** [T] (*informal*) to cancel a plan, project, etc.: *They were forced to scrub their vacation plans.* ▶ **scrub** *noun* [sing.]

**scruff** /skrʌf/ *noun* [C]

IDM **by the scruff of the/sb's neck** roughly holding the back of an animal's or person's neck: *She grabbed him by the scruff of the neck and threw him out.*

**scruff·y** /ˈskrʌfi/ *adj.* (**scruff·i·er**; **scruff·i·est**) dirty and messy: *a group of scruffy teenagers*

**scrump·tious** /ˈskrʌmpʃəs/ *adj.* (*informal*) tasting very good SYN **delicious**

**scrunch** /skrʌntʃ/ *verb* **1** [I] to make a loud sound like the one that is made when you walk on small stones (gravel): *The snow scrunched underfoot.* **2** [T] **scrunch sth (up)** to squeeze sth into a small round shape in your hands: *He scrunched up the note and threw it on the fire.* **3** [T] **scrunch sth (up)** to make sth become smaller: *The hedgehog scrunched itself up into a ball.* **4** [T] to create a style of hair with loose curls by squeezing the hair with the hands

**scrunch·ie** /ˈskrʌntʃi/ *noun* [C] a circular band of

elastic that is covered with fabric and is used for fastening the hair

**scru·ples** /'skruplz/ ***noun*** [pl.] moral beliefs that stop you from doing sth that you think is wrong: *If you had any scruples, you'd return the money.*

**scru·pu·lous** /'skrupyələs/ ***adj.*** **1** very careful or paying great attention to detail: *a scrupulous investigation into the causes of the disaster* **2** careful to do what is right or honest: *Even the most scrupulous businessman might have been tempted.* OPP **unscrupulous** ▸ **scru·pu·lous·ly** ***adv.***: *scrupulously honest*

**scru·ti·nize** /'skrutn·aɪz/ ***verb*** [T] to look at or examine sth carefully

**scru·ti·ny** /'skrutn·i/ ***noun*** [U] careful examination or study of sb/sth: *The police kept all the suspects under close scrutiny.*

**SCSI** /'skʌzi/ ***abbr.*** (*computing*) the abbreviation for "small computer systems interface"; a standard way of connecting a PERIPHERAL², such as an external CD-ROM or disk drive, to a small or medium-sized computer

**scu·ba div·ing** /'skubə ˌdaɪvɪŋ/ ***noun*** [U] swimming under water, using special equipment for breathing ➲ picture on study page **A32**.

**Scud** /skʌd/ (*also* **'Scud ˌmissile**) ***noun*** [C] a powerful exploding weapon that can be sent long distances through the air

**scuff** /skʌf/ ***verb*** [T] **scuff sth (on sth)** to make a mark on the smooth surface of sth when you rub it against sth rough: *I scuffed the heel of my shoe on the bricks.* ▸ **scuff** (*also* **'scuff mark**) ***noun*** [C] ▸ **scuffed** ***adj.***: *After only one day, his shoes were already scuffed and dirty.*

**scuf·fle** /'skʌfl/ ***noun*** [C] a fight in which people try to push each other roughly: *There were scuffles between police and demonstrators.*

**sculpt** /skʌlpt/ ***verb*** [T] (usually passive) **1 sculpt sth (in/from/out of sth)** to make figures or objects by carving or shaping wood, stone, clay, metal, etc.: *a display of animals sculpted in ice* ◇ *The figures were sculpted from single blocks of marble.* **2** (*written*) to give sth a particular shape: *a coastline sculpted by the wind and sea*

**sculpt·ed** /'skʌlptəd/ ***adj.*** having a clear, smooth shape as though sculpted by an artist: *models with high, sculpted cheekbones*

**sculp·tor** /'skʌlptər/ ***noun*** [C] a person who makes figures or objects from stone, wood, clay, etc.

**sculp·tur·al** /'skʌlptʃərəl/ ***adj.*** of or relating to sculpture or appearing to have been sculpted by an artist: *sculptural works/decoration*

**sculp·ture** /'skʌlptʃər/ ***noun*** **1** [U] the art of making figures or objects from stone, wood, clay, etc. **2** [C,U] a work or works of art that were made from stone, wood, clay, etc.: *a modern sculpture in bronze*

**scum** /skʌm/ ***noun*** [U] **1** a covering of a dirty or unpleasant substance on the surface of a liquid **2** (*informal*) a person or people who you think should not be respected

**scur·ril·ous** /'skərələs/ ***adj.*** (*formal*) very rude and insulting, and intended to damage sb's reputation: *scurrilous gossip/rumors/attacks* ◇ *He wrote a scurrilous piece about me in the local press.*

**scur·ry** /'skəri/ ***verb*** [I] (*pres. part.* **scur·ry·ing**; *3rd person sing. pres.* **scur·ries**; *pt, pp* **scur·ried**) to run quickly with short steps; to hurry: *The mice scurried across the floor.*

**scur·vy** /'skərvi/ ***noun*** [U] a disease caused by a lack of vitamin C from not eating enough fruit and vegetables

**scuzz·y** /'skʌzi/ ***adj.*** (*informal*) dirty and unpleasant

**scythe** /saɪð/ ***noun*** [C] a tool with a long handle and a slightly curved blade, used for cutting long grass, etc. ➲ picture at **garden**.

**SE** ***abbr.*** southeast; southeastern

★**sea** /si/ ***noun*** **1** [C] (often **Sea**) a particular large area of salt water. A sea is smaller than an ocean and may be surrounded by land: *the Mediterranean Sea* ◇ *the Black Sea* **2** [C,U] (used especially in stories) the ocean: *a stormy sea* ◇ *The pieces of wood floated out to sea.*

IDM **a sea of sth** a large amount or number of sth: *The stadium was just a sea of people.* ◇ *a sea of green at the St. Patrick's Day parade*

**at sea** sailing in a ship: *They spent about three weeks at sea.*

**sea·board** /'sibɔrd/ ***noun*** [C] the part of a country that is along its coast: *Canada's eastern seaboard*

**'sea breeze** ***noun*** [C] a wind blowing from the ocean toward the land

**sea·food** /'sifud/ ***noun*** [U] fish and other animals from the ocean that can be eaten as food

**sea·gull** /'sigʌl/ (*also* **gull**) ***noun*** [C] a bird with long wings and usually white and gray or black feathers that lives near the ocean. There are several types of seagull.

seahorse

**sea·horse** /'sihɔrs/ ***noun*** [C] a small ocean fish that swims in a vertical position and has a head that looks like the head of a horse

**seal¹** /sil/ ***noun*** [C] **1** a gray animal with short fur that lives in and near the ocean and that eats fish. Seals have no legs and swim with the help of short flat limbs (**flippers**). **2** a special mark that you put on an important piece of paper or letter to show that it is genuine or that it has not been opened: *the Presidential seal* **3** something that stops air or liquid from getting in or out of something: *The plane lost pressure because of a faulty seal.* **4** a small piece of paper, metal, plastic, etc. on a package, bottle, etc. that you must break before you can open it

★**seal²** /sil/ ***verb*** [T] **1** to close or fasten an envelope, a package, etc.: *Courtney sealed the package with tape.* ◇ *a sealed envelope* **2 seal sth (up)** to fill a hole or cover sth so that air or liquid does not get in or out **3** (*formal*) to make sth definite: *to seal an agreement* ◇ *Another goal at the end of the game sealed their victory.*

PHRV **seal sth off** to stop any person or thing

from entering or leaving an area or building: *The building was sealed off by the police.*

**seal·ant** /ˈsilənt/ (*also* **seal·er**) **noun** [C,U] a substance that is put onto a surface to stop air, water, etc. from entering or escaping from it

★ **ˈsea ˌlevel** **noun** [U] the level of the ocean when it is halfway between high tide and low tide (used for measuring the height of things on land): *200 feet above/below sea level*

**ˈsea ˌlion** **noun** [C] a type of gray animal with short fur and no legs, that lives in and near the ocean and eats fish ➲ A sea lion is a type of **seal**[1](1).

**seam** /sim/ **noun** [C] the line where two pieces of cloth are sewn together

**sea·man** /ˈsimən/ **noun** [C] (*pl.* **-men** /-mən/) a member of the navy or a sailor on a ship below the rank of an officer: *a merchant seaman*

**seam·less** /ˈsimləs/ **adj.** **1** (used about a fabric) without a seam: *a seamless garment* **2** with no spaces or pauses between one part and the next: *a seamless flow of talk* ▸ **seam·less·ly** **adv.**

**seam·stress** /ˈsimstrəs/ **noun** [C] (*old-fashioned*) a woman who can sew or whose job is sewing and making clothes

**seam·y** /ˈsimi/ **adj.** (**seam·i·er**; **seam·i·est**) unpleasant and immoral: *a seamy sex scandal* ◇ *the seamier side of life* SYN **sordid**

**sé·ance** /ˈseɪɑns/ **noun** [C] a meeting at which people try to make contact with and talk to the spirits of dead people

**sea·plane** /ˈsipleɪn/ **noun** [C] an airplane that can take off from and land on water

**sea·port** /ˈsipɔrt/ **noun** [C] a town with a harbor used by large ships: *the Baltic seaports*

**sear** /sɪr/ **verb** **1** [T] to burn the surface of sth in a way that is sudden and powerful: *The heat of the sun seared their faces.* ◇ *Sear the meat first* (= cook the outside of it quickly at a high temperature) *to retain its juices.* **2** [I,T] (*written*) to cause sb to feel sudden and great pain: *The pain seared along her arm.* ➲ Look at **searing**.

S

★ **search**[1] /sərtʃ/ **verb** [I,T] **search (sb/sth) (for sb/sth)**; **search (through sth)(for sth)** to examine sb/sth carefully because you are looking for something; to look for sth that is missing: *to search sb for drugs* ◇ *The police searched the area for clues.* ◇ *They are still searching for the missing child.* ◇ *She searched through the papers on the desk, looking for the letter.*

★ **search**[2] /sərtʃ/ **noun** [C] an act of searching: *the search for the missing boy*

IDM **in search of sb/sth** looking for sb/sth: *The early explorers went in search of gold.*

**ˈsearch ˌengine** **noun** [C] (*computing*) a computer program that searches the Internet for information, especially by looking for documents containing a particular word or group of words

**search·ing** /ˈsərtʃɪŋ/ **adj.** (used about a look, question, etc.) trying to find out the truth: *The customs officers asked a lot of searching questions about our trip.*

**search·light** /ˈsərtʃlaɪt/ **noun** [C] a powerful outdoor electric light that can be turned in any direction, used, for example, for finding people or vehicles at night

**ˈsearch ˌparty** **noun** [C] (*pl.* **search parties**) a group of people who look for sb who is lost or missing: *to send out a search party*

**ˈsearch ˌwarrant** **noun** [C] an official piece of paper that gives the police the right to search a building, etc.

**sear·ing** /ˈsɪrɪŋ/ **adj.** (*written*) **1** so strong that it seems to burn you: *the searing heat of a tropical summer* ◇ *searing pain* **2** (used about words or a speech) powerful and critical: *a searing indictment of the government's performance*

**sea·shell** /ˈsiʃɛl/ **noun** [C] the empty shell of a small animal that lives in the ocean

**sea·shore** /ˈsiʃɔr/ **noun** [U] the part of the land that is next to the ocean

**sea·sick** /ˈsisɪk/ **adj.** feeling sick because of the movement of a boat or ship: *to feel/get seasick* ▸ **sea·sick·ness** **noun** [U]

**sea·side** /ˈsisaɪd/ **adj.** (only *before* a noun) on the coast: *a seaside resort/community/hotel*

★ **sea·son**[1] /ˈsizn/ **noun** [C] **1** one of the four periods into which the year is divided (spring, summer, fall and winter) **2** the period of the year when sth is common or popular or when sth usually happens or is done: *The football season is from September to January.* ◇ *the dry/rainy season* ◇ *the holiday season* (= late December and early January)

IDM **in season** (used about fresh foods) available in large quantities: *Tomatoes are cheapest when they are in season.*

**out of season** (used about wild animals or fish) not able to be hunted or caught legally because it is the wrong time of year: *He was arrested for shooting ducks out of season.*

**season's greetings** (used to wish sb a nice Christmas, Hanukkah, New Year, etc.)

**sea·son**[2] /ˈsizn/ **verb** [T] to add salt, pepper, spices, etc. to food in order to make it taste better

**sea·son·al** /ˈsizənl/ **adj.** happening or existing at a particular time of the year: *We hire several seasonal employees each summer.*

**sea·soned** /ˈsiznd/ **adj.** (only *before* a noun) having a lot of experience of sth: *a seasoned traveler*

**sea·son·ing** /ˈsizn·ɪŋ/ **noun** [C,U] salt, pepper, spices, etc. that you add to food to make it taste better

**ˌseason ˈticket** **noun** [C] a ticket that allows you to go to sports games, concerts, etc. as often as you want during a particular period of time

★ **seat**[1] /sit/ **noun** [C]

➤ PLACE TO SIT **1** something that you sit on: *Please take a seat* (= please sit down). ◇ *the back seat of a car* ◇ *We're in row 26, seats A and B.* ◇ *I'd like a window seat* (= next to a window).

➤ PART OF CHAIR, ETC. **2** the part of a chair, bicycle, etc. that you sit on

➤ PART OF BODY **3** (*old-fashioned*) the part of the body that you sit on

➤ PART OF PANTS **4** the part of a piece of clothing that covers your SEAT (3)

➤ OFFICIAL POSITION **5** a position in the government of a country, state, city, etc. that you win in an election: *to win/lose a seat* ◇ *She's running for a seat on the school board.*

IDM **(fly) by the seat of your pants** (*informal*) to act without careful thought and without a plan that you have made in advance, hoping that you will be lucky and be successful

**seat²** /sit/ ***verb*** [T] **1** (often passive) (*formal*) to sit down: *Please be seated.* **2** to find a place for sb to sit, e.g. in a restaurant: *Please wait here – the hostess will seat you.* **3** to have seats or chairs for a particular number of people: *The hall can seat about 500 people.*

**ˈseat belt** (*also* **ˈsafety belt**) ***noun*** [C] a belt that you wear in a car or an airplane to protect you from injury if there is an accident: *Please fasten your seat belts during takeoff and landing.*

**seat·ing** /ˈsit̬ɪŋ/ ***noun*** [U] the seats or chairs in a place, or the way that they are arranged: *The seating will need to be changed.* ◇ *a seating plan*

**ˈseat sale** ***noun*** [C] (*Cdn*) a sale of tickets, especially airline tickets, at a reduced price

**ˈsea ˌurchin** (*also* **ur·chin**) ***noun*** [C] a small ocean creature with a round shell which is covered with SPINES (2)

**sea·wa·ter** /ˈsiˌwɔt̬ər; -ˌwɑ-/ ***noun*** [U] water from the ocean, which is salty

**sea·way** /ˈsiweɪ/ ***noun*** [C] a passage from the ocean through the land, along which large ships can travel: *In 1959 the St. Lawrence Seaway opened to shipping.*

**sea·weed** /ˈsiwid/ ***noun*** [U] a plant that grows in the ocean

**sea·wor·thy** /ˈsiˌwərði/ ***adj.*** (used about a ship) in a suitable condition to sail

**se·ba·ceous** /sɪˈbeɪʃəs/ ***adj.*** (*technical*) producing a substance like oil in the body: *the **sebaceous** glands in the skin*

**se·bum** /ˈsibəm/ ***noun*** [U] (*technical*) an oil-like substance produced by the sebaceous glands

**Sec.** ***abbr.*** (*U.S.*) = SECRETARY (3)

**sec** /sɛk/ ***noun*** [C] (*informal*) = SECOND³ (2)

**se·cede** /səˈsid/ ***verb*** [I] **secede (from sth)** (used about a state, a region, etc.) to officially stop being part of a country: *South Carolina was the first state to secede from the Union in 1860.* ▸ **se·ces·sion** /səˈsɛʃn/ ***noun*** [U]

**se·clud·ed** /səˈkludəd/ ***adj.*** far away from other people, roads, etc.; very quiet: *secluded sandy beaches* ◇ *a secluded area* ▸ **se·clu·sion** /səˈkluʒn/ ***noun*** [U]

★**sec·ond¹** /ˈsɛkənd/ ***pronoun, det., adv.*** 2nd; next after first: *We are going on vacation the second week in July.* ◇ *She poured herself a second glass of wine.* ◇ *students who speak English as a second language* ◇ *Our team finished second in the contest.* ◇ *New York is the second most populous state, after California.*

IDM **have second thoughts (about sb/sth)** to have doubts or not to be sure if you have made the right decision about sb/sth: *I'm having second thoughts about accepting their offer.*

**next/second/third to last** → LAST¹

**on second thought** (used to say that you have changed your opinion about sth): *Let's do it tomorrow. Wait – on second thought, let's do it today.*

★**sec·ond²** /ˈsɛkənd/ ***noun, pronoun*** (*also* **the second**) [sing.] a person or thing that comes next after the first: *January second* (= the 2nd day in January) ◇ *the second of January* ◇ *Terry was the second to arrive.*

★**sec·ond³** /ˈsɛkənd/ ***noun*** **1** [C] one of the 60 parts into which a minute is divided: *the second hand on a watch* **2** [C] (*also informal* **sec**) a short time: *Just a second – I'm coming!* **3** [C, usually pl.] a product that has a small fault and that is sold cheaply: *The clothes are all seconds.* **4 seconds** [pl.] another amount of food that you take after you have eaten your first amount of that food: *There's plenty of spaghetti left – who wants seconds?*

IDM **wait a minute/second** → WAIT¹

**sec·ond⁴** /ˈsɛkənd/ ***verb*** [T] to support sb's proposal or idea at a meeting so that it can then be discussed and voted on

**sec·ond-** /ˈsɛkənd/ ***combining form*** (used with a superlative) next in rank after the one that is best, largest, fastest, etc.: *the city's second-largest bank* ◇ *the second-highest mountain in the world*

**sec·ond·ar·y** /ˈsɛkənˌdɛri/ ***adj.*** **1** of less importance than sth else: *These are secondary issues which can be discussed later.* **2** caused by or developing from sth else: *She developed a secondary infection following a bad cold.*

**ˈsecondary school** ***noun*** [C] (*formal*) a school for children who are about twelve to eighteen years old ➲ Look at **elementary school**, **middle school** and **high school**. ➲ For more information on the Canadian educational system, look at study page A9.

**ˌsecond-ˈclass** ***adj.*** of little importance: *Old people should not be treated as second-class citizens.*

**ˌsecond-ˈguess** ***verb*** [T] **1** to guess what sb will do before he/she does it: *It was impossible to second-guess the decision of the jury.* **2** to criticize sb after a decision has been made; to criticize sth after it has happened: *There's no point in second-guessing the issue now.*

**sec·ond·hand** /ˌsɛkəndˈhænd/ ***adj., adv.*** **1** already used or owned by sb else: *a secondhand car* ◇ *I bought this camera secondhand.* **2** (used about news or information) that you heard from sb else and did not see or experience yourself

**ˌsecondhand ˈsmoke** ***noun*** [U] smoke in the air that you breathe in from a cigarette, etc. that sb else is smoking ➲ Look at **passive smoking**.

**sec·ond·ly** /ˈsɛkəndli/ ***adv.*** (used when you are giving your second reason or opinion) also: *Anyway, I think it's too expensive, and secondly, we don't really need it.*

**ˌsecond ˈnature** ***noun*** [U] something that has become a habit or that you can do easily because you have done it so many times: *With practice, typing becomes second nature.*

**ˌsecond-ˈrate** ***adj.*** of poor quality: *a second-rate poet*

**se·cre·cy** /ˈsikrəsi/ ***noun*** [U] the state of being or keeping sth secret: *The negotiations took place in*

S

*total secrecy.* ◇ *To ensure secrecy, no visitors are allowed in the research center.*

★**se·cret¹** /ˈsikrət/ ***adj.*** **1 secret (from sb)** that is not or must not be known by other people: *The file was marked "Top Secret."* ◇ *a secret address* ◇ *secret talks between the two governments* ◇ *a secret love affair* **2** doing sth that you do not tell anyone else about: *a secret drinker* ◇ *She has a secret admirer.* ▶ **se·cret·ly** ***adv.***: *They had been secretly engaged for several years.*

★**se·cret²** /ˈsikrət/ ***noun*** **1** [C] something that is not or must not be known by other people: *to keep a secret* ◇ *to tell sb a secret* ◇ *I can't tell you where we're going – it's a secret.* ◇ *It's no secret that they don't like each other* (= everybody knows). **2** [sing.] the only way or the best way of doing or achieving sth: *What is the secret of your success* (= how did you become so successful)?

IDM **in secret** without other people knowing: *to meet in secret*

ˌ**secret ˈagent** ***noun*** [C] = AGENT (3)

**sec·re·tar·i·al** /ˌsɛkrəˈtɛriəl/ ***adj.*** connected with the work that a SECRETARY (1) does: *secretarial skills*

**sec·re·tar·i·at** /ˌsɛkrəˈtɛriət/ ***noun*** [C] the department of a large international or political organization which deals with administration

★**sec·re·tar·y** /ˈsɛkrəˌtɛri/ ***noun*** [C] (*pl.* **sec·re·tar·ies**) **1** a person who works in an office. A secretary types letters, answers the telephone, makes appointments, etc. **2** a person in a club or other organization whose duty is to write down records of meetings, etc. **3** (often **Secretary**) (*abbr.* **Sec.**) (*U.S.*) a person who is the head of a large department in the U.S. government: *the Secretary of Agriculture/the Agriculture Secretary*

ˌ**Secretary of ˈState** ***noun*** [C] (*pl.* **Secretaries of State**) **1** the official in the U.S. government who is responsible for dealing with foreign countries **2 secretary of state** (*Cdn*) a government minister who is responsible for a particular area within a department

S

**se·crete** /sɪˈkrit/ ***verb*** [T] (used about a part of a plant, animal or person) to produce a liquid: *a hormone secreted by the female of the species* ▶ **se·cre·tion** /sɪˈkriʃn/ ***noun*** [C,U] (*formal*)

**se·cre·tive** /ˈsikrət̬ɪv/ ***adj.*** liking to keep things secret from other people: *Wendy is very secretive about her private life.* ▶ **se·cre·tive·ly** ***adv.***

**the** ˌ**secret ˈservice** ***noun*** [sing.] **1** a government department that is responsible for protecting its government's military and political secrets and for finding out the secrets of other governments **2 the Secret Service** (*U.S.*) a U.S. government department that deals with protecting the President and other special police work

**sect** /sɛkt/ ***noun*** [C] a group of people who have a particular set of religious or political beliefs. A sect has often broken away from a larger group.

**sec·tar·i·an** /sɛkˈtɛriən/ ***adj.*** connected with the differences that exist between groups of people who have different religious views: *sectarian attacks/violence*

★**sec·tion** /ˈsɛkʃn/ ***noun*** [C] **1** one of the parts into which something can be or has been divided: *I'd like to sit in the nonsmoking section.* ◇ *the string section of an orchestra* ◇ *the financial section of a newspaper* ◇ *The library has an excellent reference section.* **2** a view or drawing of sth as if it were cut from the top to the bottom and seen from the side

**sec·tion·al** /ˈsɛkʃənl/ ***adj.*** **1** made of separate sections: *a sectional sofa* **2** connected with one particular group within a community or an organization: *the sectional interests of managers and workers*

★**sec·tor** /ˈsɛktər/ ***noun*** [C] **1** a part of the business activity of a country: *The manufacturing sector has declined in recent years.* ◇ *the public/private sector* **2** a part of an area that has been divided for military or government purposes: *Shots were fired near the central sector of the border.*

**sec·u·lar** /ˈsɛkyələr/ ***adj.*** not concerned with religion

★**se·cure¹** /səˈkyʊr/ ***adj.*** **1** free from worry or doubt; confident: *to feel secure about the future* ◇ *Children need to feel secure.* ◇ *to be financially secure* OPP **insecure** **2** not likely to be lost; safe: *Business is good, so his job is secure.* ◇ *a secure investment* **3** not likely to fall or be broken; firmly fastened: *That ladder doesn't look very secure.* **4 secure (against/from sth)** well locked or protected: *This hospital is not secure enough to hold violent patients.* ◇ *a country with secure borders* ▶ **se·cure·ly** ***adv.***: *All doors and windows must be securely fastened.*

★**se·cure²** /səˈkyʊr/ ***verb*** [T] **1** to fasten or lock sth firmly: *The load was secured with ropes.* ◇ *Secure the rope to a tree or a rock.* **2** to get sth, especially after using a lot of effort: *to secure a victory in the election*

★**se·cu·ri·ty** /səˈkyʊrət̬i/ ***noun*** [U] **1** the state of feeling safe and being free from worry: *Children need the security of a stable home environment.* ◇ *financial security* (= having enough money for your present and future needs) OPP **insecurity** ➲ Look also at **Social Security**. **2** things that you do to protect sb/sth from thieves, attack, war, etc.: *Security was tightened at the airport before the President arrived.* ◇ *a maximum-security prison* (= for dangerous criminals) ◇ *a security guard* **3** the department of a company, a college, etc. that is responsible for protecting its buildings and people: *If you see something suspicious, call security immediately.*

**seˈcurity** ˌ**blanket** ***noun*** [C] a blanket or other familiar object that makes sb feel safe and comfortable, especially a child

**seˈcurity** ˌ**clearance** ***noun*** [C,U] official permission that is given to sb before he/she can work somewhere, have particular information, etc.: *All employees at the submarine base require security clearance.*

**seˈcurity deˌposit** ***noun*** [C] a sum of money that you pay when you rent sth and that you get back when you return it or finish using it without damage

**seˈcurity guard** ***noun*** [C] a person whose job is to guard money, valuables, a building, etc.

**seˈcurity** ˌ**service** ***noun*** [C] a government organization that protects a country and its secrets from enemies

**se·dan** /səˈdæn/ ***noun*** [C] a car with a hard roof,

usually four doors and a separate area (**trunk**) for luggage ➲ picture at **car**.

**se·date¹** /sə'deɪt/ ***adj.*** quiet, calm or formal

**se·date²** /sə'deɪt/ ***verb*** [T] to give sb a drug or medicine to make him/her calm or sleepy ▶ **se·da·tion** /sə'deɪʃn/ ***noun*** [U]: *The doctor put her under sedation.*

**sed·a·tive** /'sɛdət̬ɪv/ ***noun*** [C] a drug or medicine that makes you calm or sleepy ➲ Look at **tranquilizer**.

**sed·en·tar·y** /'sɛdn̩ˌtɛri/ ***adj.*** that involves a lot of time sitting down: *a sedentary lifestyle*

**Se·der** /'seɪdər/ ***noun*** [sing.] (in the Jewish religion) a special dinner that takes place at the beginning of the festival which celebrates the time when the Jews left Egypt (Passover)

**sed·i·ment** /'sɛdəmənt/ ***noun*** [C,U] a solid substance that forms at the bottom of a liquid

**sed·i·men·ta·ry** /ˌsɛdə'mɛntri; -'mɛntəri/ ***adj.*** (*technical*) connected with or formed from the sand, stones, mud, etc. that settle at the bottom of lakes, etc.: *sedimentary rocks*

**se·di·tion** /sə'dɪʃn/ ***noun*** [U] (*formal*) the use of words or actions that are intended to encourage people to oppose the authority of a state or government: *sedition laws* ◇ *to commit sedition* ▶ **se·di·tious** /-ʃəs/ ***adj.***: *The letter was declared seditious.*

**se·duce** /sə'dus/ ***verb*** [T] **1** to persuade sb to have sex with you, especially sb young and without much experience **2** to persuade sb to do sth that he/she would not usually agree to do: *stores attempting to seduce customers into parting with their money* ▶ **se·duc·tion** /sə'dʌkʃn/ ***noun*** [C,U]

**se·duc·tive** /sə'dʌktɪv/ ***adj.*** **1** sexually attractive, especially referring to a woman: *a seductive smile* **2** very attractive or appealing: *the seductive climate of the islands* ◇ *a seductive argument/opinion* (= one which you are tempted to agree with)

★**see** /si/ ***verb*** (*pt* **saw** /sɔ/; *pp* **seen** /sin/)

➤USE EYES **1** [I,T] to become aware of sth, using your eyes: *It was so dark that we couldn't see.* ◇ *I can't see that car's license number without my glasses.* ◇ *I just saw a rat!* ◇ *He looked for her but couldn't see her in the crowd.* ➲ Look at the note at **look¹**.

➤WATCH **2** [T] to look at or watch a movie, play, television program, etc.: *Did you see that program on alligators on TV last night?* ◇ *Have you seen Spielberg's new movie yet?*

➤GET INFORMATION **3** [T] to get information: *Go and see if the mailman has come yet.* ◇ *I saw in the paper that they're going to build a new stadium.*

➤MEET/VISIT **4** [T] to meet or visit sb: *I saw Marie this weekend; we had dinner together.* ◇ *You should see a doctor about that cough.* ◇ *I've been seeing a lot of Paul these days* (= meeting him often).

➤UNDERSTAND **5** [I,T] to understand sth; to realize sth: *Do you see what I mean?* ◇ *"You have to press the return key first." "Oh, I see."* ◇ *She doesn't see the point in spending so much money on a car.* ◇ *I thought he was a nice guy, but now I see I was wrong.* ◇ *I always saw my dad as a good role model.*

➤IMAGINE **6** [T] to imagine: *I can't see her changing her mind now.*

➤MAKE SURE **7** [T] to do what is necessary in a situation; to make sure that sb does sth: *I'll see that he gets the letter.* ◇ *Please see that the kids brush their teeth.*

➤GO WITH SB **8** [T] (*formal*) to go with or accompany sb: *He asked me if he could see me home, but I said no.*

IDM **as far as I can see/tell** → FAR²

**I'll see; We'll see** I'll think about what you have asked me and give you my decision later: *"Can we go swimming today, Dad?" "I'll see."*

**let me see; let's see** → LET

**see if...** to try: *I'll see if I can find time to do it.*

**see you (around/later)** (*informal*) (used for saying goodbye to sb)

**wait and see** → WAIT¹

**you see** (used for giving a reason): *She's very unhappy. You see, he was her first real boyfriend.*

PHR V **see about sth/doing sth** to deal with sth: *I've got to go to the bank to see about my loan.*

**see sb off** to say goodbye to sb who is leaving a place, especially at an airport, a bus station, etc.

**see through sb/sth** to be able to see that sb/sth is not what he/she/it appears: *The police immediately saw through his story.*

**see to it that...** to make sure that sth happens: *Please see to it that there are enough chairs for everyone.*

★**seed** /sid/ ***noun*** [C,U] the small hard part of a plant from which a new plant of the same kind can grow: *a packet of sunflower seeds* ◇ *Grass seed should be sown in the spring.* ➲ picture on study page **A28-29**.

**seed·less** /'sidləs/ ***adj.*** having no seeds: *seedless grapes*

**seed·ling** /'sidlɪŋ/ ***noun*** [C] a very young plant that has grown from a seed

**seed·y** /'sidi/ ***adj.*** (**seed·i·er**; **seed·i·est**) looking messy, dirty, or in bad condition; not respectable: *a seedy nightclub/hotel*

**See·ing Eye dog™** /ˌsiɪŋ 'aɪ dɔg/ ***noun*** [C] a dog that has been trained to guide a person who is unable to see

★**seek** /sik/ ***verb*** [T] (*pt, pp* **sought** /sɔt/) (*formal*) **1** to try to find or get sth: *Politicians are still seeking a peaceful solution.* ◇ *The mayor plans to seek a second term in office.* **2 seek sth (from sb)** to ask sb for sth: *You should seek advice from a lawyer about what to do next.* ◇ *to seek help* **3 seek (to do sth)** to try to do sth: *The new law seeks to protect the rights of single parents.*

★**seem** /sim/ ***verb*** [I] **seem (to sb) (to be) sth; seem like sth** (not in the continuous tenses) to give the impression of being or doing sth; to appear: *Shelly seems like a very nice girl.* ◇ *Shelly seems to be a very nice girl.* ◇ *It seems to me that we have no choice.* ◇ *Keith seems very interested in a career in medicine.* ◇ *It doesn't seem as if/though they will find a solution to the problem.* ◇ *It seems like we've been waiting for hours.* ▶ **seem·ing·ly** ***adv.***: *a seemingly endless list of complaints*

**seem·ing** /'simɪŋ/ ***adj.*** (*formal*) (only *before* a noun) appearing to be sth: *Despite her seeming enthusiasm, Sandra didn't really help much.*

**seen** *past participle of* SEE

**seep** /sip/ ***verb*** [I] (used about a liquid) to flow very slowly through sth: *Water started seeping in through small cracks.*

S

**seer·suck·er** /ˈsɪrˌsʌkər/ ***noun*** [U] a light cotton fabric with a pattern of raised lines and squares on its surface

**see·saw¹** (*also* **see-saw**) /ˈsisɔ/ (*also* **ˈteeter-ˌtotter**) ***noun*** [C] an outdoor toy for children that consists of a long flat piece of wood that is supported in the middle. A child sits at each end and makes the seesaw move up and down.

**see·saw²** (*also* **see-saw**) /ˈsisɔ/ ***verb*** [I] to keep changing from one situation, opinion, emotion, etc. to another and back again: *Her emotions seesawed from anger to fear.* ◇ *Stock prices seesawed all day.*

**seethe** /sið/ ***verb*** [I] **1** to be very angry: *I was just seething at what he had said.* **2** to be very crowded: *The streets were seething with people.* ◇ *a seething mass of people* (= a lot of people crowded together)

**ˈsee-through** ***adj.*** (used about fabric) very thin so that you can see through it: *a see-through blouse* ◇ *This material goes see-through when it's wet.*

**seg·ment** /ˈsɛgmənt/ ***noun*** [C] **1** a section or part of sth: *a segment of a circle* ◇ *a segment of the population* **2** one of the parts into which an orange can be divided

**seg·re·gate** /ˈsɛgrəgeɪt/ ***verb*** [T] **segregate sb/sth (from sb/sth)** to separate one group of people from the rest, especially because of race or religion, or to separate people in a particular place: *the effects of segregating African-American children in schools* ➲ Look at **desegregate** and **integrate**. ▶ **seg·re·ga·tion** /ˌsɛgrəˈgeɪʃn/ ***noun*** [U]: *racial segregation* (= separating people of different races)

**se·gue** /ˈsɛgweɪ; ˈseɪ-/ ***verb*** [I] to move smoothly from one song, subject, place, etc. to another: *a spiritual that segued into a singalong chorus* ◇ *He then segued into a discussion of atheism.* ▶ **se·gue** ***noun*** [C]

**seis·mic** /ˈsaɪzmɪk/ ***adj.*** (only *before* a noun) **1** connected with or caused by earthquakes: *seismic data/waves* **2** having a very great effect; of very great size: *a* ***seismic shift*** *in the political process*

**seize** /siz/ ***verb*** [T] **1** to take hold of sth suddenly and firmly: *The thief seized her purse and ran off with it.* ◇ *to seize sb by the arm* ◇ (*figurative*) *Mark was seized by a strong desire to laugh.* **2** to take control or possession of sb/sth: *The police seized 50 pounds of illegal drugs.* ◇ *to seize power* ◇ *Rebel forces seized the capital early this morning.*

IDM **seize/take the initiative** → INITIATIVE

PHR V **seize (on/upon) sth** to recognize an opportunity and to use it eagerly: *The President's opponents seized upon any opportunity to embarrass him.*

**sei·zure** /ˈsiʒər/ ***noun*** **1** [U] seizing or being seized: *the seizure of 30 pounds of heroin by the Coast Guard* **2** [C] a sudden loss of consciousness with movements that are not controlled and sometimes violent: *an epileptic seizure*

**sel·dom** /ˈsɛldəm/ ***adv.*** not often: *It seldom snows here in March.* ◇ *We very seldom go to the theater.*

★**se·lect¹** /səˈlɛkt/ ***verb*** [T] to choose sb/sth from a number of similar things: *You can select whatever you want from the prizes on display.* ◇ *The best candidates will be selected for interview.*

NOTE **Select** is more formal than **choose** and suggests that a great deal of care is taken when making the decision.

**se·lect²** /səˈlɛkt/ ***adj.*** consisting of or available to only a small group of special people: *a select audience of business executives*

★**se·lec·tion** /səˈlɛkʃn/ ***noun*** **1** [U] the act of choosing or being chosen: *All candidates must go through a rigorous selection procedure.* ◇ *the selection of athletes for the Olympics* **2** [C] a number of people or things that have been chosen: *a selection of hits from the fifties and sixties* **3** [C,U] a collection of products in a store that are for sale: *They have a wide selection of toys at the mall.* ◇ *Selection is as important as price to shoppers.*

**se·lec·tive** /səˈlɛktɪv/ ***adj.*** **1** careful when choosing: *She's very selective about who she invites to her parties.* ◇ *a college with a highly selective admissions policy* **2** of or concerning only some people or things; not general: *selective enforcement of a law* ▶ **se·lec·tive·ly** ***adv.***

**se·lec·tor** /səˈlɛktər/ ***noun*** [C] a device in an engine, a piece of machinery, etc. that allows you to choose a particular function: *a gear selector* ◇ *a selector lever/switch*

★**self** /sɛlf/ ***noun*** [C] (*pl.* **selves** /sɛlvz/) a person's own nature or qualities: *It's good to see you* ***back to your old self*** *again* (= said to sb who has been sick/sad/worried). ◇ *Her mean remark revealed her* ***true self.***

**ˌself-abˈsorbed** ***adj.*** only concerned about or interested in yourself

**ˌself-adˌdressed ˌstamped ˈenvelope** ***noun*** [C] (*abbr.* **SASE**) an empty envelope with your own address and a stamp on it, that you send to a company in order to receive sth back from them

**ˌself-apˈpointed** ***adj.*** giving yourself a particular title, job, etc., especially without the agreement of other people

**ˌself-asˈsured** ***adj.*** believing that you can do sth or succeed at sth ▶ **ˌself-asˈsurance** /-əˈʃʊrəns/ ***noun*** [U]

**ˌself-ˈcentered** ***adj.*** thinking only about yourself and not about other people ➲ Look at **selfish**.

**ˌself-conˈfessed** ***adj.*** (only *before* a noun) admitting that you are a particular type of person or have a particular problem, especially a bad one: *a self-confessed criminal/cynic*

**ˌself-ˈconfident** ***adj.*** feeling sure about your own value and abilities ▶ **ˌself-ˈconfidence** ***noun*** [U]: *Some women still lack the self-confidence to apply for executive jobs.*

**self-con·grat·u·la·to·ry** /ˌsɛlf kənˈgrætʃələˌtɔri; -ˈgrædʒə-/ ***adj.*** showing that you think you have done sth very well and are pleased with yourself: *The winners gave themselves a self-congratulatory round of applause.*

**ˌself-ˈconscious** ***adj.*** too worried about what other people think about you: *Men are often very self-conscious about losing their hair.* ▶ **ˌself-ˈconsciously** ***adv.*** ▶ **ˌself-ˈconsciousness** ***noun*** [U]

**ˌself-conˈtrol** ***noun*** [U] the ability to control your emotions and appear calm even when you are angry, afraid, excited, etc.: *to lose/keep your self-control*

**ˌself-deˈfense** (*Cdn* ˌ**self-deˈfence**) ***noun*** [U] the use of force to protect yourself or your property: *Lee is learning karate for self-defense.* ◇ *to shoot sb in self-defense* (= because he/she is about to attack you)

**ˌself-deˈnial** ***noun*** [U] the fact of not having or doing the things you like, either because you do not have enough money, or for moral or religious reasons: *a life of self-denial and sacrifice*

**self-dep·re·cat·ing** /ˌsɛlf ˈdɛprɪkeɪt̮ɪŋ/ ***adj.*** (*written*) done in a way that makes your own achievements or abilities seem unimportant: *He gave a self-deprecating shrug.*

**self-de·struct** /ˌsɛlf dɪˈstrʌkt/ ***verb*** [I] (used especially about an explosive device, a machine, etc.) to destroy itself, usually by exploding: *This tape will self-destruct in 30 seconds.* ◇ (*figurative*) *In the last half-hour of the movie the plot rapidly self-destructs.*

**ˌself-deˈstructive** ***adj.*** self-destructive actions, feelings, etc. are likely to harm or kill the person who does or has them: *a self-destructive lifestyle/relationship*

**ˌself-ˈdiscipline** ***noun*** [U] the ability to control yourself and do the things that you must do, especially in order to improve your life

**ˌself-ˈdoubt** ***noun*** [C,U] the feeling that you are not good enough: ◇ *His life was plagued by fear and self-doubt.*

**self-ef·fac·ing** /ˌsɛlf ɪˈfeɪsɪŋ/ ***adj.*** not wanting to attract attention to yourself or your abilities: *In spite of her success, she remains self-effacing and reserved.* ◇ *a shy, self-effacing man* SYN **modest**

**ˌself-emˈployed** ***adj.*** working for yourself and earning money from your own business

**ˌself-esˈteem** ***noun*** [U] the feeling of pride that you have about yourself: *Many teenagers suffer from low self-esteem.*

**ˌself-ˈevident** ***adj.*** obvious and needing no further proof or explanation: *The dangers of such action are self-evident.* ◇ *a self-evident truth*

**ˌself-exˈplanatory** ***adj.*** easy to understand and not needing any more explanation: *I think the title is self-explanatory.*

**ˌself-ˈhelp** ***noun*** [U] using your own efforts to do sth or deal with your problems, instead of relying on other people: *a self-help book*

**ˌself-ˈimage** ***noun*** [C] the opinion or idea you have of yourself, especially of your appearance or abilities: *to have a positive/poor self-image*

**ˌself-imˈprovement** ***noun*** [U] the activity of trying to improve your knowledge, social position or character by your own efforts

**ˌself-inˈdulgent** ***adj.*** allowing yourself to have or do things you enjoy (sometimes when it would be better to control yourself): *a self-indulgent morning spent relaxing in the bathtub* ▶ ˌ**self-inˈdulgence** ***noun*** [C,U]

**ˌself-inˈflicted** ***adj.*** (used about an injury) that you have done to yourself: *He died of a self-inflicted gunshot wound to the head.*

**ˌself-ˈinterest** ***noun*** [U] concern for what is best for yourself rather than for other people

**self·ish** /ˈsɛlfɪʃ/ ***adj.*** thinking only about your own needs or wishes and not about other people's needs or wishes: *a selfish attitude* ◇ *I'm sick of your selfish behavior!* OPP **unselfish** ▶ **self·ish·ly** ***adv.*** ▶ **self·ish·ness** ***noun*** [U]

**self·less** /ˈsɛlfləs/ ***adj.*** (*formal*) thinking about other people's needs or wishes rather than your own: *his years of selfless devotion to his sick wife*

**ˌself-ˈmade** ***adj.*** having become rich or successful by your own efforts: *a self-made multimillionaire*

**ˌself-ˈpity** ***noun*** [U] the state of thinking too much about your own problems or troubles and feeling how unlucky you are

**ˌself-ˈportrait** ***noun*** [C] a picture that you drew or painted of yourself

**ˌself-posˈsessed** ***adj.*** able to remain calm and confident in a difficult situation: *She always seems so calm and self-possessed.*

**ˌself-preserˈvation** ***noun*** [U] the fact of protecting yourself in a dangerous or difficult situation: *She was held back by some sense of self-preservation.*

**ˌself-reˈliant** ***adj.*** not depending on help from sb/sth else ▶ ˌ**self-reˈliance** ***noun*** [U]

**ˌself-reˈspect** ***noun*** [U] the feeling of pride in yourself: *Old people need to keep their dignity and self-respect.* ▶ ˌ**self-reˈspecting** ***adj.*** (in negative sentences): *No self-respecting Elvis Presley fan* (= nobody who is proud to be a fan of Elvis Presley) *should be without this book.*

**ˌself-ˈrighteous** ***adj.*** believing that you are always right and other people are wrong; thinking that you are better than other people ▶ ˌ**self-ˈrighteousness** ***noun*** [U]

**ˌself-ˌrising ˈflour** (*Cdn* ˌ**self-ˌraising ˈflour**) ***noun*** [U] flour that contains baking powder, which makes cakes rise and become light as they are baked

**ˌself-ˈservice** (*also* ˌ**self-ˈserve**) ***adj.*** (only *before* a noun) (used about a store, a gas station, etc.) where you serve yourself and then pay a person who works there (cashier)

**ˌself-ˈstarter** ***noun*** [C] a person who is able to work alone and make decisions without needing anyone to tell him/her what to do

**ˌself-ˈstyled** ***adj.*** (only *before* a noun) using a name or title that you have given yourself, especially when you do not have the right to do it: *the self-styled king of fashion*

**ˌself-sufˈficient** ***adj.*** able to produce or provide everything that you need without help from or having to buy from others

**ˌself-ˈtaught** ***adj.*** having learned sth by reading books, etc., rather than by sb teaching you: *a self-taught artist*

**ˌself-ˈworth** ***noun*** [U] a feeling of confidence in yourself that you are a good and useful person: *Praise your child to increase her sense of self-worth.*

★**sell**[1] /sɛl/ ***verb*** (*pt, pp* **sold** /soʊld/)
➤ EXCHANGE FOR MONEY **1** [I,T] **sell (sb) (sth)**; **sell (sth) (to sb)** to give sth to sb who pays for it and is then the owner of it: *We are going to sell our car.*

S

◇ *I sold my guitar for $200.* ◇ *Would you sell me your ticket?* ◇ *I was too late – the car had already been sold.* ◇ *I offered them a lot of money, but they wouldn't sell.* ◇ *He sold his business at an enormous profit.*
➤OFFER FOR SALE **2** [T] to offer for sale: *Excuse me, do you sell greeting cards?*
➤BE SOLD **3** [I] **sell (for/at sth)** to be sold or available for sale at a particular price: *These watches sell for $1,000 each in the retail stores, but you can have this one for $500.* **4** [I] to be sold to or bought by many people; to attract buyers: *Her books sell well in Europe.* **5** [T] to be sold in a particular quantity: *This newspaper sells over a million copies a day.*
➤PERSUADE **6** [T] to cause people to want to buy sth; to help sth to attract buyers: *They rely on advertising to sell their products.* ➲ The noun for senses 1 – 6 is sale. **7** [T] **sell sth to sb** to persuade sb to accept sth: *to sell an idea to sb*
IDM **be sold on (doing) sth** (*informal*) to be very enthusiastic about sth: *She's completely sold on the idea of moving to Florida* (= she thinks it's a very good idea and wants to do it).
**be sold out (of sth)** (used about a concert, an event, a store, etc.) to have had all the tickets or goods bought so that no more are available: *The concert was sold out weeks ago.* ◇ *We're sold out of the book, but we could order a copy for you.*
PHRV **sell sth off** to sell a number of things, often at a low price, in order to get rid of them or to get money quickly: *They had to sell off several antiques in order to pay their tax bill.*
**sell out** to be sold completely, so that no more are available for sale: *By the time I got to the store, all the newspapers had sold out.*

**sell²** /sɛl/ ***noun*** [C]
IDM **a hard/tough sell** something that is difficult to persuade people to buy or accept

**sell·er** /ˈsɛlər/ ***noun*** [C] **1** a person or business that sells sth: *a flower seller* ◇ *The real estate market has many sellers but few buyers right now.* **2** something that is sold (especially in the amount described): *This magazine is a big seller in the 25-40 age group.* ➲ Look at **bestseller**.

**sell·out** /ˈsɛlaʊt/ ***noun*** [C] a concert, sports event, etc. for which all the tickets are sold: *The concert was a sellout.* ◇ *The Orioles won 5–2 before a sellout crowd of 46,444.*

**selt·zer** /ˈsɛltsər/ (*also* **ˈseltzer ˌwater**) ***noun*** [C,U] a naturally bubbly water with minerals in it, used as a drink

**selves** *plural of* SELF

**se·man·tics** /səˈmæntɪks/ ***noun*** [U] **1** the study of the meanings of words and phrases **2** the meaning of words, phrases or systems: *the semantics of the language*

**sem·blance** /ˈsɛmbləns/ ***noun*** [sing., U] (*formal*) **(a) semblance of sth** the appearance of being sth or of having a certain quality: *After the earthquake, life slowly returned to some semblance of normality.*

**se·men** /ˈsimən/ ***noun*** [U] the liquid containing sperm that is produced by the male sex organs

**se·mes·ter** /səˈmɛstər/ ***noun*** [C] one of two periods of time into which a school, college or university year is divided: *I'm taking an art history course second semester.*

**sem·i** /ˈsɛmi; ˈsɛmaɪ/ ***noun*** [C] (*pl.* **sem·is**) (*informal*) **1** a very large truck that consists of two connected parts, which can carry a large quantity of things over a long distance **2** = SEMIFINAL

**semi-** /ˈsɛmaɪ; ˈsɛmi/ ***prefix*** (in adjectives and nouns) half; partly: *a semivowel* (= w, y) ◇ *semiconscious*

**sem·i·cir·cle** /ˈsɛmiˌsərkl/ ***noun*** [C] one half of a circle; something that is arranged in this shape: *I want you all to sit in a semicircle.*

**sem·i·co·lon** /ˈsɛmiˌkoʊlən/ ***noun*** [C] a mark (;) used in writing or printing for separating parts of a sentence or items in a list

**sem·i·con·duc·tor** /ˈsɛmikənˌdʌktər; ˈsɛmaɪ-/ ***noun*** [C] (*technical*) a solid substance (e.g. silicon) that allows some electric currents to pass through it in particular conditions

**sem·i·fi·nal** /ˈsɛmifaɪnl; ˈsɛmaɪ-; ˌsɛmiˈfaɪnl/ (*also* **semi**) ***noun*** [C] one of the two games in a sports competition whose winners play in the final

**sem·i·fi·nal·ist** /ˌsɛmiˈfaɪnl·ɪst; ˌsɛmaɪ-/ ***noun*** [C] a player or team that plays in a semifinal; a person who has reached the last stage of a competition before the final

**sem·i·nal** /ˈsɛmənl/ ***adj.*** (*formal*) very important and having a strong influence on later developments: *a seminal work/article/study* ◇ *His book on social policy proved to be seminal.*

**sem·i·nar** /ˈsɛmənɑr/ ***noun*** [C] **1** a short course or meeting in which a certain subject is taught or discussed: *a seminar on health and nutrition* **2** a class at a college etc. in which a small group of students discuss or study a subject with a teacher

**sem·i·nar·y** /ˈsɛməˌnɛri/ ***noun*** [C] (*pl.* **sem·i·nar·ies**) a college that prepares students to be priests, ministers or rabbis

**se·mi·ot·ics** /ˌsimiˈɑt̬ɪks; ˌsɛmi-/ ***noun*** [U] the study of signs and symbols and of their meaning and use ▸ **se·mi·ot·ic** ***adj.***: *semiotic analysis*

**sem·i·pre·cious** /ˌsɛmiˈprɛʃəs; ˌsɛmaɪ-/ ***adj.*** (usually before a noun) (used about a jewel) less valuable than the most valuable types of jewels: *semiprecious stones*

**sem·i·pri·vate** /ˌsɛmiˈpraɪvət; ˌsɛmaɪ-/ ***adj.*** (used about a hospital room) shared by two patients

**sem·i·pro·fes·sion·al** /ˌsɛmiprəˈfɛʃənl; ˌsɛmaɪ-/ ***adj.*** semi-professional musicians or sports players are paid for what they do, but do not do it as their main job ▸ **sem·i·pro·fes·sion·al** ***noun*** [C]

**sem·i·re·tired** (*also* **semi-retired**) /ˌsɛmirɪˈtaɪərd; ˌsɛmaɪ-/ ***adj.*** having officially retired from a full-time job, but continuing to work part-time or occasionally

**sem·i·sweet** (*also* **semi-sweet**) /ˌsɛmiˈswit; ˌsɛmaɪ-/ ***adj.*** (used especially about chocolate for cooking with) slightly sweetened, but less so than normal

**Sen.** ***abbr.*** (*written*) = SENATOR: *Sen. John K Nordqvist*

★**Sen·ate** /ˈsɛnət/ ***noun*** [C] (often **the Senate**) the upper body of government in the U.S., Canada and some other countries or in many U.S. states: *the Senate Foreign Affairs Committee*

NOTE Look at **Congress**, **House of Representatives**, **House of Commons** and **Parliament**. ➲ For more information about the political systems in the U.S. and Canada, look at study pages **A10-11**.

★**sen·a·tor** /ˈsɛnət̬ər/ ***noun*** [C] (*abbr.* **Sen.**) a member of a Senate: *She's a former senator from Maryland.* ◇ *Senator Kennedy* ➲ For more information on the North American political systems, look at study pages **A10-A11**. ▸ **sen·a·to·ri·al** /ˌsɛnəˈtɔriəl/ ***adj.***: *a senatorial committee*

★**send** /sɛnd/ ***verb*** [T] (*pt, pp* **sent** /sɛnt/) **1 send sth/sb (to sb/sth)**; **send (sb) sth** to cause sth/sb to go or be taken somewhere without going there yourself: *to send a letter/an e-mail* ◇ *to send a message to sb* ◇ *Don't forget to send me a postcard.* ◇ *We sent out the invitations two months before the wedding.* ◇ *She sent the children to bed early.* ◇ *My company is sending me on a business trip next month.* ◇ *to send sb to prison* **2** to cause sb/sth to move in a particular direction, often quickly or as a reaction that cannot be prevented: *The news sent stock prices soaring yesterday.*

PHR V **send sth in** to send sth to a place where it will be officially dealt with: *I sent my application in three weeks ago, but I still haven't had a reply.*

**send sth off** to mail sth: *I'll send the information off today.*

**se·nile** /ˈsinaɪl/ ***adj.*** confused, unable to remember things or to take care of yourself (because of old age) ▸ **se·nil·i·ty** /səˈnɪlət̬i/ ***noun*** [U]

★**sen·ior**[1] /ˈsinyər/ ***adj.*** **1 senior (to sb)** having a high or higher rank in a company, an organization, etc.: *a senior managerial position* ◇ *He's senior to me.* ◇ *a meeting of senior government officials* **2 Senior** (*abbr.* **Sr.**) (used to show that a man is the father of sb with the same name): *John Brown Sr.* ➲ Look at **junior**. **3** connected with the final year of high school or college: *the senior class*

**sen·ior**[2] /ˈsinyər/ ***noun*** [C] **1** a student in the final year of high school or college: *He's a senior at Yale.* ➲ Look at **freshman**, **sophomore** and **junior**. **2** = SENIOR CITIZEN: *Tickets are $7 for adults and $5 for seniors and students.* **3** somebody who is older or of higher rank (than one or more other people): *My oldest sister is ten years my senior.*

**ˌsenior ˈcitizen** (*also* **senior**) ***noun*** [C] a person who is 65 years old or older

**ˌsenior ˈhigh school** ***noun*** [C] a school that is usually for students in grades 10, 11 and 12 ➲ Look at **high school** and **junior high school.** ➲ For more information on the North American educational systems, look at study pages **A8-A9**.

**sen·ior·i·ty** /ˌsinˈyɔrət̬i; -ˈyɑr-/ ***noun*** [U] the rank or importance that a person has in a company, organization, etc. in relation to others, often related to how long he/she has worked there: *Decisions about employee layoffs are based on seniority.*

**sen·sa·tion** /sɛnˈseɪʃn/ ***noun*** **1** [C] a feeling that is caused by sth affecting the body or part of the body: *a pleasant/an unpleasant sensation* ◇ *I felt a burning sensation on my skin.* **2** [U] the ability to feel when touching or being touched: *For some time after the accident, he had no sensation in his legs.* **3** [C] a feeling or impression in the mind or body that is not caused by anything definite and may be false: *I had the peculiar sensation that I was floating in the air.* **4** [C] a feeling of great excitement, surprise or interest among a group of people or people in general; sb/sth that causes this: *The young Canadian caused a sensation by beating the top seed.* ◇ *The band was an overnight sensation* (= became famous and popular immediately).

**sen·sa·tion·al** /sɛnˈseɪʃn·l/ ***adj.*** **1** causing, or trying to cause, a feeling of great excitement or shock among people, especially in a way that you do not approve of: *sensational events* ◇ *the most sensational murder trial this century* ◇ *This magazine specializes in sensational stories about the rich and famous.* **2** extremely good; beautiful; very exciting: *You look sensational!* ▸ **sen·sa·tion·al·ly** ***adv.***

**sen·sa·tion·al·ize** /sɛnˈseɪʃənl·aɪz/ ***verb*** [T] (used especially about newspapers) to exaggerate a story so that it seems more exciting or shocking than it really is

★**sense**[1] /sɛns/ ***noun***

➤ SIGHT/HEARING, ETC. **1** [C] one of the five natural physical powers that make it possible for a person or animal to get information about the world around: *I have a cold and I've lost my sense of smell.*

➤ UNDERSTANDING/JUDGMENT **2** [U, sing.] the ability to understand or appreciate sth; the ability to recognize what sth is: *She seems to have lost all sense of reality.* ◇ *I like him – he's got a great sense of humor.* ◇ *I'm always getting lost. I have absolutely no sense of direction.* **3** [U] the ability to think or act in a reasonable or sensible way; practical intelligence: *At least he had enough sense to stop when he realized he was making a mistake.* ◇ *I think there's a lot of sense in what you're saying.* ➲ Look at **common sense**. **4** [U] good reason; use or point: *There's no sense in going any further – we're obviously lost.* ◇ *What's the sense in making things more difficult for yourself?*

➤ NATURAL ABILITY **5** [U, sing.] a natural ability to do or produce sth well: *Good business sense made her a millionaire.*

➤ FEELING **6** [U, sing.] a feeling or consciousness of sth: *I felt a tremendous sense of relief when all of my final exams were over.* ◇ *She only visits her family out of a sense of duty.*

➤ MEANING **7** [C] (used about a word, phrase, etc.) a meaning or possible meaning: *This word has two senses.* ◇ *It was awesome in the traditional sense of the word.*

IDM **in a sense** in one particular way but not in other ways; partly: *In a sense you're right, but there's more to the matter than that.*

**make sense 1** to be possible to understand; to have a clear meaning: *What does this sentence mean? It doesn't make sense to me.* **2** (used about an action) to be sensible or logical: *I think it would make sense to wait for a while before making a decision.*

**make sense of sth** to manage to understand sth that is not clear or is difficult to understand: *I can't make sense of these instructions.*

**sense**[2] /sɛns/ ***verb*** [T] to realize or become aware

S

of sth; to get the feeling that sth is the case: *I sensed that something was wrong.*

**sense·less** /'sɛnsləs/ ***adj.*** **1** having no meaning or purpose: *The police described the murder as "a senseless act of violence."* **2** unconscious

**sen·si·bil·i·ty** /ˌsɛnsə'bɪləṭi/ ***noun*** (*pl.* **sen·si·bil·i·ties**) **1** [U,C] the ability to experience and understand deep feelings, especially in art and literature: *musical/artistic sensibility* **2 sensibilities** [pl.] a person's feelings, especially when the person is easily offended or influenced by sth: *The article offended her religious sensibilities.*

★**sen·si·ble** /'sɛnsəbl/ ***adj.*** having or showing the ability to think or act in a reasonable way; having or showing good judgment: *a sensible man* ◇ *It was a realistic and sensible plan.* ▸ **sen·si·bly** /-əbli/ ***adv.***: *Melissa tries to eat sensibly and exercise every day.*

NOTE Compare **sensible** and **sensitive**. **Sensible** is connected with common sense, reasonable action and good judgment. **Sensitive** is connected with feelings and emotions and with the five senses.

★**sen·si·tive** /'sɛnsəṭɪv/ ***adj.***
➤TO PEOPLE'S FEELINGS **1 sensitive (to sth)** showing that you are aware of and understand people's feelings, problems, etc.: *to be sensitive to sb's feelings/wishes* OPP **insensitive**
➤EASILY UPSET **2 sensitive (about/to sth)** easily upset, offended or annoyed, perhaps because of having strong feelings about a particular matter: *Don't be so sensitive! I was only joking.* ◇ *She's still sensitive about her divorce.* ◇ *He's very sensitive to criticism.*
➤EASILY HURT/DAMAGED **3** easily hurt or damaged; painful, especially if touched: *a new soap for sensitive skin*
➤TO SMALL CHANGES **4** (used about a scientific instrument, a piece of equipment, etc.) able to measure very small changes
➤INFORMATION/SUBJECT **5** (used about a subject, a situation, etc.) needing to be dealt with carefully because it is likely to cause anger or trouble: *Religion is often a sensitive subject.* ◇ *sensitive files/documents* ◇ *This is a sensitive period in the negotiations between the two countries.*
▸ **sen·si·tive·ly** ***adv.*** ▸ **sen·si·tiv·i·ty** /ˌsɛnsə'tɪvəṭi/ ***noun*** [U]: *I think your comments showed a complete lack of sensitivity.*

**sen·si·tize** /'sɛnsətaɪz/ ***verb*** [T] (usually passive) **sensitize sb/sth (to sth)** to make sb/sth more aware of sth, especially a problem or sth bad: *People are becoming more sensitized to the dangers threatening the environment.*

**sen·sor** /'ʃɛnsər/ ***noun*** [C] a piece of equipment that can find certain sounds, movements, etc.

**sen·so·ry** /'sɛnsəri/ ***adj.*** (*technical*) connected with your physical senses of sight, hearing, smell, taste and touch: *sensory organs* ◇ *sensory deprivation*

**sen·su·al** /'sɛnʃuəl/ ***adj.*** connected with physical or sexual pleasure: *the sensual rhythms of Latin music* ◇ *a life devoted to sensual pleasure and luxury* ▸ **sen·su·al·i·ty** /ˌsɛnʃu'æləṭi/ ***noun*** [U]

**sen·su·ous** /'sɛnʃuəs/ ***adj.*** giving pleasure to or affecting the mind or body through the senses: *a soft and sensuous voice*

**sent** *past tense, past participle of* SEND

★**sen·tence**[1] /'sɛntns/ ***noun*** **1** [C] (*grammar*) a group of words containing a subject and a verb, that expresses a statement, a question, etc. When a sentence is written, it begins with a capital letter and ends with a period: *a grammatically correct sentence* ◇ *You don't need to write a long letter. A couple of sentences will be enough.* ➲ Look also at **run-on sentence**. **2** [C,U] the punishment given by a judge to sb who has been found guilty of a crime: *a 25-year prison sentence* ◇ *He is serving a life sentence in a maximum security prison.* ◇ *the death sentence*

**sen·tence**[2] /'sɛntns/ ***verb*** [T] **sentence sb (to sth)** (used about a judge) to tell sb who has been found guilty of a crime what the punishment will be: *The judge sentenced her to three months in prison for shoplifting.* ◇ *He was sentenced to life imprisonment for murder.*

**sen·ti·ment** /'sɛntəmənt/ ***noun*** **1** [C,U] an attitude or opinion that is often caused or influenced by emotion: *His comments expressed my sentiments exactly.* ◇ *a strong anti-war sentiment* **2** [U] gentle feelings such as sympathy, love, happy memories, etc. that influence action or behavior (sometimes in situations where this is not suitable): *There's no room for sentiment in business.*

**sen·ti·men·tal** /ˌsɛntə'mɛntl/ ***adj.*** **1** caused by or connected with gentle feelings such as sympathy, love, happy memories, etc.: *The jewelry had great sentimental value to me.* **2** having or showing these gentle emotions, sometimes in a silly way: *How can you be sentimental about that old car?* ◇ *a sentimental love song* ▸ **sen·ti·men·tal·i·ty** /ˌsɛntəmɛn'tæləṭi/ ***noun*** [U]

**sen·try** /'sɛntri/ ***noun*** [C] (*pl.* **sen·tries**) a soldier who stands outside a building and guards it

**sep·a·ra·ble** /'sɛpərəbl/ ***adj.*** able to be separated OPP **inseparable**

★**sep·a·rate**[1] /'sɛprət/ ***adj.*** **1 separate (from sth/sb)** apart; not joined or together: *You should always keep your cash and credit cards separate.* **2** different; not connected: *A lot of married couples have separate bank accounts.* ◇ *In a separate incident, a man was shot in a night club last night.* ▸ **sep·a·rate·ly** ***adv.***: *Accessories are sold separately.*

★**sep·a·rate**[2] /'sɛpəreɪt/ ***verb*** **1** [I,T] **separate (sb/sth) (from sb/sth)** to stop being together; to cause people or things to stop being together; to divide people or things: *I think we should separate into two groups.* ◇ *I got separated from my friends in the crowd.* ◇ *Separate the egg white from the yolk.* **2** [T] **separate sb/sth (from sb/sth)** to keep people or things apart, or to be between people or things with the result that they are apart: *I always try to separate business from pleasure.* ◇ *When the players started fighting, the referee moved in to separate them.* ◇ *The two sides of the city are separated by the river.* **3** [I] (used about a married couple, etc.) to stop living together: *His parents separated when he was still a baby.*

**sep·a·rat·ed** /'sɛpəreɪṭəd/ ***adj.*** (used about a

S

married couple) not living together anymore but not divorced: *My wife and I are separated.*

**'separate school** *noun* [C] (*Cdn*) a public school for especially Catholic children in some Canadian provinces ➲ For more information on the Canadian educational system, look at study page **A9**.

★**sep·a·ra·tion** /ˌsɛpəˈreɪʃn/ *noun* [C,U] **1** the act of separating or being separated; a situation or period of being apart: *The soldiers are returning home after a long separation from their families.* **2** a legal agreement where a married couple lives apart (but does not get a divorce): *a trial separation*

**se·pi·a** /ˈsipiə/ *noun* [U] **1** a brown substance used in inks and paints and used in the past for printing photographs **2** a reddish-brown color ▶ **se·pi·a** *adj.*: *sepia ink/prints/photographs*

**Sep·tem·ber** /sɛpˈtɛmbər/ *noun* [C,U] (*abbr.* **Sept.**) the ninth month of the year; coming before October ➲ For examples of the use of the months in sentences, look at **January**.

**septic tank** /ˈsɛptɪk tæŋk/ *noun* [C] a large container, usually underground, that holds human waste from toilets until the action of bacteria makes it liquid enough to be absorbed by the ground

**se·quel** /ˈsikwəl/ *noun* [C] **1** a book, movie, etc. that continues the story of the previous one ➲ Compare **prequel**. **2** something that happens after, or is the result of, a previous event

★**se·quence** /ˈsikwəns/ *noun* **1** [C] a number of related actions, events, etc. that happen or come one after another: *Investigators are trying to determine the sequence of events that led to the accident.* **2** [U] the order in which a number of things happen or are arranged: *The photographs are arranged in sequence.*

**se·ques·ter** /sɪˈkwɛstər/ *verb* [T] to keep all the members of a jury together in a place, in order to prevent them from talking to other people about a court case, or learning about it in the newspapers, on television, etc.

**se·quin** /ˈsikwən/ *noun* [C] a small round shiny disk sewn onto clothing as decoration: *a dress covered in gold sequins* ▶ **se·quinned** *adj.*: *a sequinned evening bag*

**se·quoi·a** /sɪˈkwɔɪə/ *noun* [C] = REDWOOD

**ser·e·nade¹** /ˌsɛrəˈneɪd/ *noun* [C] a song or tune played or sung at night by a lover outside the window of the woman he loves

**ser·e·nade²** /ˌsɛrəˈneɪd/ *verb* [T] to sing or play music to sb (as done in the past by a man singing under her window to the woman he loved): *We were serenaded by a string quartet.*

**ser·en·dip·i·ty** /ˌsɛrənˈdɪpət̬i/ *noun* [U] (*written*) the fact of sth interesting or pleasant happening by chance: *Meeting her like that, and there of all places, was true serendipity!* ▶ **ser·en·dip·i·tous** /-ət̬əs/ *adj.*: *serendipitous discoveries*

**se·rene** /səˈrin/ *adj.* calm and peaceful: *a serene smile* ▶ **se·rene·ly** *adv.* ▶ **se·ren·i·ty** /səˈrɛnət̬i/ *noun* [U]

**serf** /sərf/ *noun* [C] (in the past) a person who was forced to live and work on land that belonged to a landowner whom he/she had to obey

**ser·geant** /ˈsɑrdʒənt/ *noun* [C] (*abbr.* **Sgt.**) an officer of low rank in the military forces or police

**se·ri·al** /ˈsɪriəl/ *noun* [C] a single story in a magazine or on television that is told in a number of parts over a period of time: *the first part of a six-part drama serial* ➲ Look at the note at **series**.

**se·ri·al·ize** /ˈsɪriəlaɪz/ *verb* [T] to publish or broadcast sth in parts as a serial: *The novel was serialized on TV in six parts.* ▶ **se·ri·al·i·za·tion** /ˌsɪriələˈzeɪʃn/ *noun* [C,U]: *a newspaper serialization of the book*

**'serial ˌkiller** *noun* [C] a person who has killed several people, one after another, using the same method

**'serial ˌnumber** *noun* [C] the number marked on sth to identify it and to distinguish it from other things of the same type: *the serial numbers of computer equipment*

★**se·ries** /ˈsɪriz/ *noun* [C] (*pl.* **se·ries**) **1** a number of things that come one after another and are of the same type or connected: *a series of events* ◇ *a concert series* ◇ *There has been a series of burglaries in the area recently.* **2** a number of programs on television or on the radio which have the same main characters and each tell a complete story

> NOTE Compare **series** and **serial**. In a **series**, each part is a different, complete story involving the same main characters. In a **serial**, the same story continues in each part.

**3** (in sports) a number of games that are played one after another by the same two teams: *the NBA championship series between the Chicago Bulls and the Los Angeles Lakers*

★**se·ri·ous** /ˈsɪriəs/ *adj.* **1** (used about problems, situations, etc.) bad; important; causing worry: *a serious injury* ◇ *serious consequences* ◇ *Pollution is a very serious problem.* ◇ *serious crime* **2** needing to be treated as important, not just for fun: *Don't laugh – it's a serious matter.* ◇ *a serious discussion* ◇ *She's had quite a few boyfriends, but only one serious relationship.* **3** (used about a person) not joking; thoughtful: *Are you serious about starting your own business* (= are you really going to do it)? ◇ *He's extremely serious. I don't think I've ever seen him laugh.* ◇ *You're looking very serious. Was it bad news?* ▶ **se·ri·ous·ness** *noun* [U]: *We must make people aware of the seriousness of the situation.*

★**se·ri·ous·ly** /ˈsɪriəsli/ *adv.* **1** in a serious way: *Three people were seriously injured in the accident.* ◇ *My sister is seriously considering buying a house in Maine.* ◇ *It's time you started to think seriously about the future.* **2** (used for indicating that you are not joking or that you really mean what you are saying): *Seriously, I do appreciate all your help.* ◇ *Seriously, you have nothing to worry about.*

IDM **take sb/sth seriously** to treat sb or sth as important: *Nobody takes him seriously.* ◇ *You take everything too seriously! Relax and enjoy yourself.*

**ser·mon** /ˈsərmən/ *noun* [C] a speech on a religious or moral matter that is given as part of a service in a church or temple

**ser·pent** /ˈsərpənt/ *noun* [C] (*written*) (in literature) a snake, especially a large one

**ser·ra·ted** /səˈreɪt̬əd; ˈsɛreɪt̬əd/ *adj.* having a row

S

of points in V-shapes along the edge: *a knife with a serrated edge*

**se·rum** /ˈsɪrəm/ *noun* (*pl.* **se·ra** /ˈsɪrə/ or **se·rums**) **1** [U] the thin liquid that remains from blood when the rest has become thick (**clotted**) **2** [C,U] (*medical*) serum taken from the blood of an animal and given to people to protect them from disease, poison, etc.: *snakebite serum*

★**ser·vant** /ˈsərvənt/ *noun* [C] a person who is paid to work in sb's house, doing work such as cooking, cleaning, etc. ➲ Look at **maid** and **civil servant**.

★**serve** /sərv/ *verb*

➤WORK **1** [I,T] to work for a country, a company, an organization, the army, etc.; to be useful to sb: *The role of the police is to serve the community.* ◇ *She has served on a number of committees.* ◇ *He served in the army during the Korean War.* ◇ *During his long political career he served under six different Presidents.*

➤FOOD/DRINK **2** [T] to give food or drinks to sb during a meal; to take an order and then bring food or drinks to sb (in a restaurant, bar, etc.): *Breakfast is served from 7:30 to 9:00 a.m.* ◇ *We waited for half an hour until a waiter finally served us.*

➤PROVIDE STH **3** [T] to provide sb (especially the public) with sth necessary or useful in daily life: *The area is served by two major airports.*

➤BE SUITABLE **4** [I,T] **serve (sb) (as sth)** to be good enough for or suitable for a particular purpose; to perform a particular function: *The smallest bedroom serves as my office.* ◇ *His bad attitude only served to make him even less popular.* ◇ *The program no longer serves any useful purpose.* **5** [T] (used about an amount of food) to be enough for a certain number of people: *According to the recipe, this dish serves four.*

➤TIME IN PRISON **6** [T] to spend a period of time in prison as a punishment: *He is currently serving a ten-year sentence for fraud.*

➤IN SPORTS **7** [I,T] (in tennis and similar sports) to start play by hitting the ball

IDM **serve sb right** (used when sth bad happens to sb and you have no sympathy) to be deserved by sb: *"I feel sick." "It serves you right for eating so much."*

**serv·er** /ˈsərvər/ *noun* [C] **1** a computer that controls information which can be shared by a group of connected computers **2** a person whose job is to take orders and bring people food and drinks in a restaurant

★**serv·ice**[1] /ˈsərvəs/ *noun*

➤WORK FOR ORGANIZATION **1** [U] working for a country, a company, an organization, the army, etc.: *The congressman was thanked for his years of service to the party.* ◇ *He was accused of trying to avoid military service during the Vietnam War.* ◇ *He left the police force after thirty years' service.*

➤PROVIDING STH **2** [C] a system or an organization that provides the public with sth necessary or useful in daily life; the job that an organization does: *a personal shopping service* ◇ *an Internet service provider* ◇ *The delivery company is starting a new overnight service.* ◇ *We offer a number of financial services.* **3** [C, usually sing.] one of certain government departments or public institutions: *the foreign service*

➤ARMY/NAVY/AIR FORCE **4 the service** [sing.] the military forces: *Our daughter was in the service for five years.*

➤IN HOTEL/STORE/RESTAURANT **5** [U] the work or the quality of work done by sb when serving a customer: *I enjoyed the food, but the service was terrible.* ◇ *If you have any problem with the computer, call our customer service department.*

➤RELIGIOUS CEREMONY **6** [C] a religious ceremony, usually including prayers, singing, etc.: *a funeral service*

➤IN TENNIS **7** [C] (in tennis and similar sports) the act of hitting the ball at the start of play; a player's turn to serve ➲ picture at **tennis**.

**serv·ice**[2] /ˈsərvəs/ *verb* [T] to examine and, if necessary, repair a car, machine, etc.: *My car hasn't been serviced since last year.*

**serv·ice·a·ble** /ˈsərvəsəbl/ *adj.* suitable to be used: *The carpet is worn but still serviceable.*

**ˈservice charge** *noun* [C] the amount of money that is added to the cost of sth for special extra services: *There is a $2 service charge for each ticket ordered by phone.*

**ˈservice ˌstation** *noun* [C] = GAS STATION

**ser·vi·ette** /ˌsərviˈɛt/ *noun* [C] (*Cdn*) a piece of paper or cloth used at meals for protecting your clothes and cleaning your lips and fingers SYN **napkin** (1)

**ser·vile** /ˈsərvl; -vaɪl/ *adj.* wanting too much to please sb and obey him/her: *Parents have no right to demand servile obedience from their children.*

**serv·ing** /ˈsərvɪŋ/ *noun* [C] an amount of food for one person: *This cake has 450 calories per serving!*

**ses·a·me** /ˈsɛsəmi/ *noun* [U] a tropical plant grown for its seeds and their oil that are used in cooking: *sesame seeds*

★**ses·sion** /ˈsɛʃn/ *noun* [C] **1** a meeting or series of meetings of an official body (a court, Congress, Parliament, etc.) **2** a period of doing a particular activity: *The whole tape was recorded in one session.* ◇ *a weekly session with a therapist*

IDM **in session** (used about an official committee, a court, etc.) holding a meeting; doing its official work; not closed for vacation: *This court is now in session.*

★**set**[1] /sɛt/ *noun* [C] **1 set (of sth)** a number of things that belong together: *a set of dishes* ◇ *a 4-piece towel set* ◇ *a set of rules* **2** a piece of equipment for receiving television signals: *a TV set* **3** the scenery for a play or movie: *a musical with spectacular sets* **4** (in tennis) a group of games forming part of a match: *She won the match in three straight sets.*

★**set**[2] /sɛt/ *verb* (*pres. part.* **set·ting**; *pt, pp* **set**)

➤PUT/START **1** [T] to put sb/sth in a particular position; to place sth somewhere: *He set a large bowl of soup in front of me.* ◇ *The hotel is set in a beautiful area.* **2** [T] to cause a particular state or event; to start sth happening: *The new governor set the prisoners free.* ◇ *The rioters set a number of cars on fire.* ◇ *Her comment set him thinking.*

➤PLAY/BOOK/MOVIE **3** [T] (often passive) to place the action of a book, play, movie, etc. in a

particular time, situation, etc.: *The movie is set in 16th-century Spain.*
➤ARRANGE **4** [T] to prepare or arrange sth for a particular purpose: *I set my alarm for 6:30.* ◇ *to set the table* (= put the plates/knives/forks on it) ◇ *Did you set the VCR to record that movie?*
➤EXAMPLE/STANDARD, ETC. **5** [T] to establish sth or make sth definite: *Try to set a good example for the younger kids.* ◇ *Can we set a limit of $100 on the cost of materials?* ◇ *They haven't set a date for their wedding yet.* ◇ *He has set a new world record.*
➤BECOME FIRM **6** [I] to become firm or hard: *Put the dessert in the refrigerator for two hours to set.*
➤JEWELRY **7** [T] to fasten a precious stone, etc. in a piece of jewelry: *The pin had three diamonds set in gold.*
➤SUN **8** [I] (used about the sun, etc.) to go down below the horizon OPP **rise**
➤BONE **9** [T] to put a broken bone in its correct position and often to put it in a special hard case (cast) so that it can heal: *The doctor set her broken leg.*
➤HAIR **10** [T] (*old-fashioned*) to arrange sb's hair while it is wet so that it becomes curly, wavy, etc.: *She went to the salon to have her hair set.*

PHR V **set sb/sth apart (from sb/sth)** to make sb/sth different from or better than others: *Her terrific sense of humor really sets her apart from the other candidates.*

**set sth aside 1** to leave or save sth for a particular purpose: *Roll out the pie crust, then set it aside while you prepare the filling.* ◇ *Part of the hall has been set aside for an exhibit of students' artwork.* **2** to agree to pay no attention to sth for a period of time because other things are more important: *We decided to set aside our differences for the sake of the kids.*

**set sb/sth back** to delay sb/sth: *The bad weather has set our plans back by six weeks.*

**set in** to arrive and remain for a period of time: *It looks like some dark clouds are beginning to set in.*

**set off** to leave on a trip: *We set off at 3 o'clock this morning.*

**set sth off** to do sth which starts a reaction: *When this door is opened, it sets off an alarm.*

**set out** to leave on a trip: *They set out at dawn.*

**set out to do sth** to decide to achieve sth: *She set out to become America's first woman President.*

**set (sth) up** to start; to establish a business, etc.: *The company has set up a new branch in Atlanta.* ◇ *After she finished law school, she set up in a practice in her hometown.*

**set**[3] /sɛt/ ***adj.*** **1** definite and not changing; firm: *There are no set hours in my job.* ◇ *He's getting more and more set in his ways* (= with fixed habits and routines which he is unwilling to change) *as he gets older.* **2 set (for sth)**; **set (to do sth)** ready, prepared or likely to do sth: *Okay, I'm all set – let's go!* ◇ *I was all set to leave when the phone rang.* ◇ *The Chicago Bulls look set for another victory.*

IDM **be set against sth/against doing sth** to be opposed to sth: *She's dead* (= extremely) *set against moving to the country.*

**be set on sth/on doing sth** to be determined to do sth: *She's set on a career in acting.* ◇ *My heart was set on that house* (= I really wanted it).

**set·back** /ˈsɛtbæk/ ***noun*** [C] a difficulty or problem that stops you from making progress as fast as you want to

**set·ter** /ˈsɛt̬ər/ ***noun*** [C] a large dog with long hair, sometimes used in hunting. There are several types of setter: *an Irish setter* ◇ *a red setter*

★**set·ting** /ˈsɛt̬ɪŋ/ ***noun*** [C] **1** surroundings; the place where sth happens: *The resort is in a beautiful setting in the woods.* ◇ *They decided that a rural church would be the perfect setting for their wedding.* **2** one of the positions of the controls of a machine: *Use the iron's lowest setting for this delicate fabric.* **3** a piece of metal in which a precious stone is fixed to form a piece of jewelry: *a ruby in a heavy gold setting*

★**set·tle** /ˈsɛt̬l/ ***verb***
➤CHOOSE PERMANENT HOME **1** [I,T] to go and live permanently in a new country, an area, a town, etc.: *the pioneers who settled the Wild West* ◇ *He served in the Army for eight years before settling in New Haven.*
➤END ARGUMENT **2** [I,T] to reach an agreement about sth; to end an argument; to find a solution to a disagreement: *They settled the lawsuit without going to court.* ◇ *They were willing to settle out of court.*
➤DECIDE/ARRANGE **3** [T] to decide or arrange sth finally (e.g. a plan, an action, etc.): *Everything's settled. We leave on the nine o'clock flight on Friday.*
➤INTO COMFORTABLE POSITION/STATE **4** [I] to get into or put sb into a comfortable position: *I settled back in front of the TV for the evening.* **5** [I,T] to become or to make sth (e.g. your stomach or nerves) calm or relaxed: *Have a drink. It might settle your nerves.*
➤PAY MONEY **6** [T] to pay sth (a bill, a debt, etc.): *to settle a bill* ◇ *The insurance company settled the claim very quickly.*
➤COME TO REST **7** [I] to come to rest in a certain position; to land: *Snow settled on some parts of the Midwest for the first time this season.*
➤OF A LIQUID **8** [I] (used about a liquid) to become clear or still

PHR V **settle down 1** to become calm and quiet: *Settle down! It's time to start class.* **2** to get into a comfortable position, sitting or lying: *I made a cup of tea and settled down with a good book.* **3** to start having a quieter way of life, especially by staying in the same place or getting married, etc.: *She had a number of part-time jobs before she eventually settled down.*

**settle for sth** to accept sth that is not as good as you hoped it would be: *You'll have to settle for something cheaper.*

**settle in**; **settle into sth** to get used to or start feeling comfortable in a new home, job, etc.: *How are the kids settling in at their new school?* ◇ *to settle into a routine*

**settle on sth** to choose sth after considering many different things; to decide on sth

**set·tled** /ˈsɛt̬ld/ ***adj.*** feeling comfortable, calm and not likely to change (in a home, a job, a way of life, etc.): *We feel very settled here.*

**set·tle·ment** /ˈsɛt̬lmənt/ ***noun*** **1** [C,U] an agreement, usually official, that ends an argument; the act of reaching this kind of agreement: *The strike lasted for several weeks until a settlement was*

S

*reached.* ◇ *the settlement of a dispute* **2** [C] an amount of money that is officially given to sb to end an argument: *The judge awarded a $4 million settlement to the accident victim.* **3** [C] a place that a group of people have built and live in, where few or no people lived before: *a settlement in the jungle*

**set·tler** /ˈsɛtlər; ˈsɛt̬l·ər/ ***noun*** [C] a person who goes to live permanently in a new country, particularly an undeveloped one or one with a small population: *early settlers in Virginia*

**set·up** /ˈsɛt̬ʌp/ ***noun*** [C, usually sing.] (*informal*) **1** a way of organizing sth; a system: *I've only been here a couple of weeks and I don't really know the setup.* ◇ *What's the setup in your family—who does the cooking?* **2** a situation in which sb tricks you or makes it seem as if you have done sth wrong: *He didn't steal the goods. It was a setup.*

**sev·en** /ˈsɛvən/ ***number*** 7; one more than 6 ➲ For examples of how to use numbers in sentences, look at **six**.

**sev·en-** /ˈsɛvən/ ***combining form*** having seven of the thing mentioned: *a seven-headed monster*

**sev·en·teen** /ˌsɛvənˈtin/ ***number*** 17; one more than sixteen ➲ For examples of how to use numbers in sentences, look at **six**. ▸ **sev·en·teenth** /ˌsɛvən-ˈtinθ/ ***pronoun, det., adv.*** ➲ Look at the examples at **sixth**.

**sev·enth**[1] /ˈsɛvənθ/ ***pronoun, det., adv.*** 7th, next after sixth ➲ Look at the examples at **sixth**.

**sev·enth**[2] /ˈsɛvənθ/ ***noun*** [C] the fraction $\frac{1}{7}$; one of seven equal parts of sth ➲ Look at the examples at **sixth**.

**Seventh-Day Adventist** /ˌsɛvənθ deɪ ˈædvɛntɪst; -ədˈvɛntɪst/ ***noun*** [C] a member of a Christian group who go to church on Saturdays and who believe that Jesus Christ will come again to Earth very soon

**sev·en·ty** /ˈsɛvənt̬i/ ***number*** 70; one more than sixty-nine ➲ For examples of how to use numbers in sentences, look at **sixty**. ▸ **sev·en·ti·eth** /ˈsɛvən-t̬iəθ/ ***pronoun, det., adv.*** ➲ Look at the examples at **sixth**.

**sev·er** /ˈsɛvər/ ***verb*** [T] **1** to break, separate or divide by cutting: *The construction workers accidentally severed a power line.* **2** to end sth (a relationship, etc.): *He has severed all ties with his former friends.*

★**sev·er·al** /ˈsɛvrəl/ ***pronoun, det.*** more than two but not very many; some: *It took her several days to recover from the shock.* ◇ *There were lots of applications for the job – several of them from very well-qualified people.* ◇ *I've asked him several times for the money.*

**sev·er·ance** /ˈsɛvrəns; ˈsɛvərəns/ ***noun*** [sing., U] (*formal*) **1** the act of ending a connection or relationship: *the severance of diplomatic relations* **2** the act of ending sb's work contract: *employees given notice of severance*

**ˈseverance pay** ***noun*** [U] money that you are paid when you leave a company because there is no longer any work for you there

★**se·vere** /səˈvɪr/ ***adj.*** **1** very bad; causing bad results or feelings: *The company is in severe financial difficulty.* ◇ *a severe cold/headache/illness/pain* ◇ *a severe winter* (= a very cold one) **2** not kind or gentle: *I think your criticism of her work was too severe.* ◇ *a very severe punishment* ▸ **se·vere·ly** ***adj.***: *The roof was severely damaged in the storm.* ◇ *The report severely criticizes the mayor.* ▸ **se·ver·i·ty** /səˈvɛrət̬i/ ***noun*** [U]: *I don't think you realize the severity of the problem.*

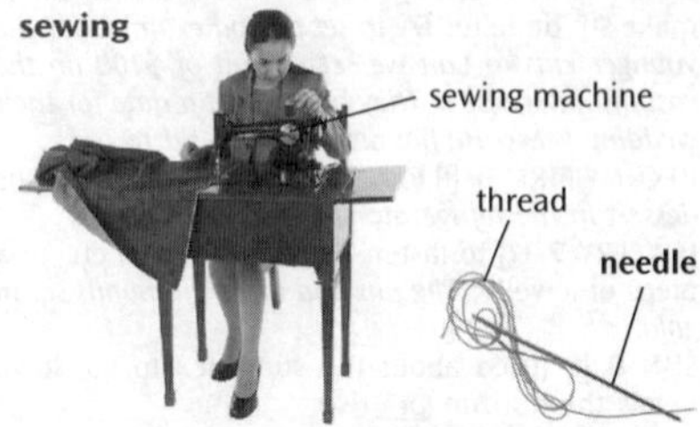


★**sew** /soʊ/ ***verb*** (*pt* **sewed**; *pp* **sewn** /soʊn/ or **sewed**) [I,T] to join pieces of cloth, or to join sth to cloth, using a needle and thread or a machine and forming stitches: *I can't sew.* ◇ *to sew a new button onto a shirt* ◇ *I'll have to sew the pocket by hand.*

PHR V **sew sth up 1** to join two things by sewing; to repair sth by sewing two things together: *to sew up a hole* ◇ *The surgeon sewed up the wound.* **2** (usually passive) to arrange or organize sth so that it is certain to happen or be successful: *I think we have the deal all sewn up.*

▸ **sew·ing** ***noun*** [U]

**sew·age** /ˈsuɪdʒ/ ***noun*** [U] the waste material from people's bodies and dirty water that is carried away from people's homes in large underground pipes (sewers)

**sew·er** /ˈsuər/ ***noun*** [C] an underground pipe that carries used water and waste to a place where it can be cleaned and made safe with special chemicals

**ˈsew·ing maˌchine** ***noun*** [C] a machine that is used for sewing

**sewn** *past participle of* SEW

★**sex** /sɛks/ ***noun*** **1** (*also formal* **intercourse**, **ˌsex-ual ˈintercourse**) [U] the physical act in which the sexual organs of two people touch and which can result in a woman having a baby: *to have sex with somebody* ◇ *It's against their religion to have sex before marriage.* ➲ Look also at **safe sex**. **2** [U] activities or matters connected with the act of SEX (1): *There's too much sex and violence on TV.* **3** [U] the state of being either male or female: *We do not discriminate on the basis of race, sex, religion or disability.* ◇ *Do you mind what sex your baby is?* SYN **Gender** has the same meaning. **4** [C] one of the two groups consisting of all male people or all female people: *the male/female sex* ◇ *He's always found it difficult to get along with members of **the opposite sex*** (= women).

**ˈsex apˌpeal** ***noun*** [U] the quality of being attractive in a sexual way: *He exudes sex appeal.*

**ˈsex drive** ***noun*** [U] a person's interest in sex or ability to have sex

**sex·ism** /ˈsɛksɪzəm/ ***noun*** [U] treating a person unfairly, or thinking that he/she is inferior because of his/her sex, e.g. thinking that only men can do certain jobs, such as being a firefighter

S

**sex·ist** /'sɛksɪst/ ***adj.*** connected with or showing sexism: *a sexist attitude toward women* ◇ *sexist jokes* ▶ **sex·ist** ***noun*** [C]

**'sex life** ***noun*** [C] a person's sexual activities: *ways to improve your sex life*

**'sex ˌsymbol** ***noun*** [C] a famous person who is thought by many people to be sexually attractive

**sex·tet** ***noun*** [C] **1** a group of six musicians or singers who play or sing together **2** a piece of music for six musicians or singers

**'sex ˌtherapy** ***noun*** [U] treatment to help people with sexual problems ▶ **'sex ˌtherapist** ***noun*** [C]

★**sex·u·al** /'sɛkʃuəl/ ***adj.*** connected with sex: *sexual problems* ◇ *the sexual organs* ◇ *sexual harassment* ▶ **sex·u·al·ly** /-əli/ ***adv.***: *to be sexually attracted to somebody* ◇ *a sexually transmitted disease*

**ˌsexual ha'rassment** ***noun*** [U] comments about sex, physical contact, etc. usually happening at work, that a person finds annoying and offensive

**ˌsexual 'intercourse** ***noun*** [U] (*formal*) = SEX (1)

**sex·u·al·i·ty** /ˌsɛkʃu'æləṭi/ ***noun*** [U] the nature of sb's sexual activities or desires: *He found it difficult to come to terms with his sexuality.*

**'sex ˌworker** ***noun*** [C] (a polite way of referring to a prostitute)

**sex·y** /'sɛksi/ ***adj.*** (**sex·i·er**; **sex·i·est**) (*informal*) sexually attractive: *a sexy man* ◇ *a sexy dress* ➲ Look at **sexual**.

**SF** /ˌɛs 'ɛf/ ***abbr.*** = SCIENCE FICTION

**SGML** /ˌɛs dʒi ɛm 'ɛl/ ***abbr.*** (*computing*) the abbreviation for "Standard Generalized Mark-up Language"; a system used for marking text on a computer so that the text can be read on a different computer system or displayed in different forms

**Sgt.** ***abbr.*** = SERGEANT

**sh** /ʃ/ ***interjection*** be quiet!: *Sh! People are trying to sleep in here.*

**Shab·bat** /ʃə'bɑt; 'ʃɑbəs/ ***noun*** [sing.] Saturday; the day of rest and prayer in the Jewish religion ➲ Look at **Sabbath**.

**shab·by** /'ʃæbi/ ***adj.*** (**shab·bi·er**; **shab·bi·est**) **1** in bad condition because of having been used or worn too much: *a shabby suit* **2** (used about the way that sb is treated) unfair; not generous ▶ **shab·bi·ly** /'ʃæbəli/ ***adv.***: *shabbily dressed*

**shack¹** /ʃæk/ ***noun*** [C] a small, roughly built house or building

**shack²** /ʃæk/ ***verb***

PHR V **shack up with sb; be shacked up with sb** (*slang*) to start/be living with sb that you have a sexual relationship with, but that you are not married to: *I hear he's shacked up with his secretary.*

★**shade¹** /ʃeɪd/ ***noun***

➤OUT OF SUN **1** [U] an area that is out of direct sunlight and is darker and cooler than areas in the sun: *It was so hot that I had to go and sit in the shade.*

NOTE **Shade** [U] is an area or part of a place that is protected from the heat of the sun. **A shadow** [C] is a dark shape made by light shining on a person or object. **Shadow** [U] is an area of darkness in which it is difficult to distinguish things easily.

➤ON WINDOW/LAMP, ETC. **2** [C] something that keeps out light or makes it less bright, especially a covering that you can pull down in front of a window: *Pull* (= close) *the shades – the sun is too bright.* ◇ *to open/close a shade* ➲ Look at **lampshade.** ➲ picture at **curtain**.

➤FOR THE EYES **3 shades** [pl.] (*informal*) = SUNGLASSES

➤OF COLOR **4** [C] **a shade (of sth)** a type of a particular color: *a shade of green* ◇ *I'd rather have a darker shade if you have one.* ◇ *a pale shade of gray*

➤OF OPINION/MEANING **5** [C] a small difference or variation in the form or quality of sth: *a word with various shades of meaning*

➤SLIGHTLY **6** [sing.] a little bit: *Current prices are just a shade higher than last year.*

**shade/shadow**

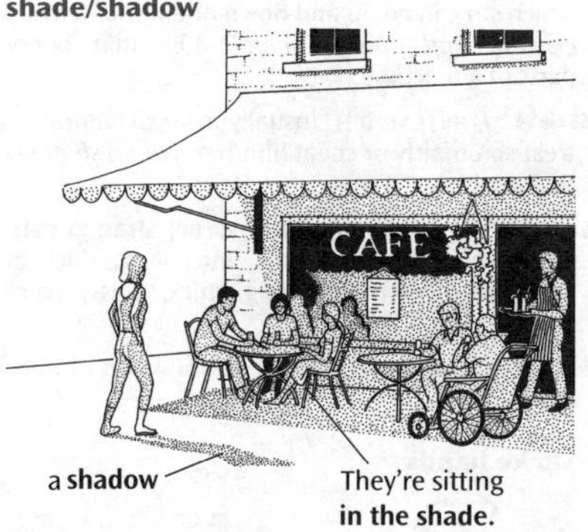


**shade²** /ʃeɪd/ ***verb*** [T] to protect sth from direct light; to give SHADE¹ (1) to sth: *The sun was so bright that I had to shade my eyes.*

**shad·ing** /'ʃeɪdɪŋ/ ***noun*** **1** [U] the use of color, pencil lines, etc. to give an impression of light and shade in a picture or to emphasize areas of a map, diagram, etc. **2 shadings** [pl.] slight differences that exist between different aspects of the same thing: *the shadings of opinion found among church leaders*

★**shad·ow¹** /'ʃædoʊ/ ***noun*** **1** [C] a dark shape on a surface that is caused by sth being between light and that surface: *The dog was chasing its own shadow.* ◇ *The shadows lengthened as the sun went down.* ◇ (*figurative*) *News of the tragedy* ***cast a shadow over*** (= spoiled) *the day.* ➲ Look also at **eye shadow. 2** [U] an area that is dark because sth prevents direct light from reaching it: *His face was* ***in shadow***. ➲ Look at the note and the picture at **shade**.

IDM **be frightened/nervous/scared of your own shadow** to be very easily frightened; to be very nervous

**beyond/without a shadow of doubt** with no doubt at all: *His guilt has been proven beyond a shadow of doubt.*

**in/under the shadow of 1** very close to: *The new market is in the shadow of the City Hall.* **2** when you say that sb is in or under the shadow of another person, you mean that he/she does not receive as much attention as that person: *I lived the*

S

*first half of my childhood in the shadow of my elder brother.*

**shad·ow²** /ˈʃædoʊ/ ***verb*** [T] to follow and watch the actions of sb, often secretly: *The police shadowed the suspect for three days.*

**shad·ow·y** /ˈʃædoʊi/ ***adj.*** **1** having many shadows; dark: *a shadowy forest* **2** difficult to see or identify clearly: *a shadowy figure coming toward me* **3** mysterious; difficult to know much about: *the shadowy world of organized crime*

**shad·y** /ˈʃeɪdi/ ***adj.*** (**shad·i·er**; **shad·i·est**) **1** giving shade; giving shelter from the sun: *We ate our picnic in a shady spot.* **2** (*informal*) not completely honest or legal: *She's made a lot of money from some pretty shady deals.*

**shaft¹** /ʃæft/ ***noun*** [C] **1** a long, narrow hole in which sth can go up and down or enter or leave: *an elevator shaft* ◇ *a mine shaft* **2** a bar that connects parts of a machine

**shaft²** /ʃæft/ ***verb*** [T] (usually passive) (*informal*) to treat sb unfairly or cheat him/her: *We got shafted on that deal.*

**shag·gy** /ˈʃægi/ ***adj.*** (**shag·gi·er**; **shag·gi·est**) **1** (used about hair, material, etc.) long, thick and messy **2** covered with long, thick, messy hair: *a shaggy dog*

**shah** /ʃɑ/ ***noun*** [C] the title of the kings of Iran in the past

**shake hands**

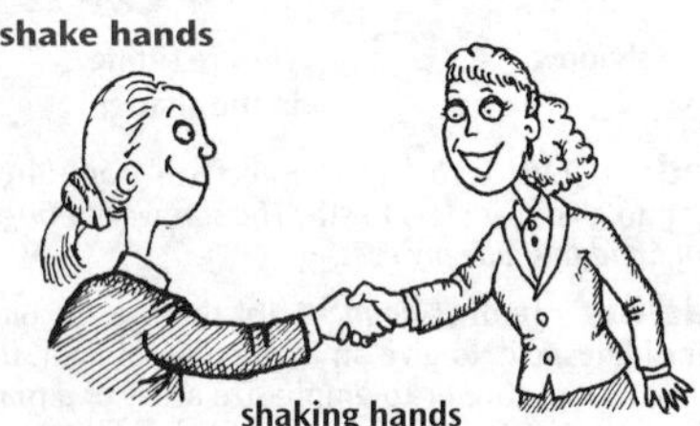

**shaking hands**

★**shake¹** /ʃeɪk/ ***verb*** (*pt* **shook** /ʃʊk/; *pp* **shak·en** /ˈʃeɪkən/) **1** [I,T] to move from side to side or up and down with short, quick movements: *I was so nervous that I was shaking.* ◇ *The whole building shakes when big trucks go past.* ◇ (*figurative*) *His voice shook with emotion as he described the tragedy.* ◇ *Shake the bottle before you pour the medicine out.* ◇ *She shook him to wake him up.* **2** [T] to disturb or upset sb/sth: *The scandal has shaken the whole country.* **3** [T] to cause sth to be less certain; to cause doubt about sth: *Nothing seems to shake her belief that she was right.*

IDM **shake sb's hand/shake hands (with sb)** to take sb's hand and move it up and down (as a greeting, to show that you have agreed on sth, etc.) **shake your head** to move your head from side to side, as a way of expressing that you mean "No"

PHR V **shake sb/sth off** to escape from sb/sth; to remove by shaking: *I don't seem to be able to shake off this cold.* ◇ *Shake the crumbs off the tablecloth.*

**shake²** /ʃeɪk/ ***noun*** [C] **1** the act of shaking or being shaken physically: *a shake of the head* ◇ *You'll have to give the bottle a few shakes.* **2** = MILKSHAKE

**shak·en** /ˈʃeɪkən/ (*also* ˌ**shaken** ˈ**up**) ***adj.*** shocked, upset or frightened by sth: *She was visibly shaken by the incidents.* ◇ *He was too shaken up to drive.*

**Shak·er¹** /ˈʃeɪkər/ ***noun*** [C] a member of a religious group in the U.S. who live simply in a community and do not marry or have partners

**Shak·er²** /ˈʃeɪkər/ ***adj.*** (used to describe a style of plain attractive furniture that was traditionally made by Shaker communities): *a Shaker dresser*

**shak·er** /ˈʃeɪkər/ ***noun*** [C] (often in compounds) a container that is used for shaking things: *a salt shaker* ◇ *a cocktail shaker*

**shake·up** /ˈʃeɪkʌp/ ***noun*** [C] a complete change in the structure or organization of sth: *a dramatic government shake-up*

**shak·y** /ˈʃeɪki/ ***adj.*** (**shak·i·er**; **shak·i·est**) **1** shaking or feeling weak because you are frightened or ill **2** not firm; weak or not very good: *The table's a little shaky, so don't put anything heavy on it.* ◇ *They had a shaky start to the season, losing their first two games.* ▶ **shak·i·ly** /-əli/ ***adv.***

**shale** /ˈʃeɪl/ ***noun*** [U] a type of soft stone that splits easily into thin flat layers

★**shall** /ʃəl; *strong form* ʃæl/ ***modal verb*** (*negative* **shall not**) **1 shall I/we...** (used in questions in order to offer to do sth or to make a suggestion): *Shall I give you a ride home?* ◇ *Shall we go out to eat tonight?*

> NOTE **Should** is also used with this meaning, especially in informal speech.

**2** (*formal*) (used for saying that sth must or will happen or that sb must/must not do sth): *These arrangements shall remain in effect until further notice.*

> NOTE This sense of **shall** is very formal and is used mainly in official situations, e.g. in a court of law. **Will** is more common and less formal.

**shal·lot** /ˈʃælət; ʃəˈlɑt/ ***noun*** [C] a vegetable like a small onion with a very strong taste

★**shal·low** /ˈʃæloʊ/ ***adj.*** **1** not deep; with not much distance between top and bottom: *The lake is very shallow here.* ◇ *Put in a shallow dish and bake for 20 minutes.* **2** not having or showing serious or deep thought: *rather a shallow young man* ▶ **shal·low·ness** ***noun*** [U]

**sha·lom** /ʃɑˈloʊm; ʃə-/ ***interjection*** a Hebrew word for "hello" or "goodbye" that means "peace"

**sham** /ʃæm/ ***noun*** [C] a thing or a plan that is not really what sb pretends that it is: *Detectives quickly realized that the business was a sham.*

**sha·man** /ˈʃeɪmən; ˈʃɑ-/ ***noun*** [C] a person in some religions and societies who is believed to be able to contact good and evil spirits and cure people of illnesses

**sham·bles** /ˈʃæmblz/ ***noun*** [sing.] (*informal*) **1** a situation in which there is a lot of confusion: *The press conference was a complete shambles.* ◇ *The funding cuts left the military* ***in a shambles.*** **2** a place which is dirty or messy: *The house was a shambles.* SYN **mess**

★**shame¹** /ʃeɪm/ ***noun*** **1** [U] the guilty feeling that you have when you think that you have done sth morally wrong, sth that causes other people to have a bad opinion of you, or sth extremely embarrassing: *She was filled with shame at the thought of how she had lied to her mother.* ➲ adjective **ashamed** **2** [U] the ability to have SHAME (1): *He doesn't care how he behaves in public. He has no shame!* **3** [U] loss of respect from others; loss of honor: *There's no shame in finishing second.* ◇ *His actions have brought shame on his whole family.* **4 a shame** [sing.] a fact or situation that makes you feel disappointed: *It's a shame you can't come. I was looking forward to seeing you.* ◇ *"I failed my test." "Oh, that's such a shame."* ◇ *What a shame you have to leave so soon!*

IDM **Shame on you!** (*informal*) (used to tell sb that he/she should feel ashamed): *Shame on you for behaving like that in front of our guests!*

**shame**[2] /ʃeɪm/ ***verb*** [T] to make sb feel ashamed

**shame·faced** /ˈʃeɪmfeɪst/ ***adj.*** feeling or looking ashamed or embarrassed because you have done sth bad or stupid: *a shamefaced smile* ◇ *She looked shamefaced.* ▸ **shame·fac·ed·ly** /ˈʃeɪmˌfeɪsədli/ ***adv.***: *He smiled rather shamefacedly.*

**shame·ful** /ˈʃeɪmfl/ ***adj.*** that sb should be ashamed of: *a shameful waste of taxpayers' money* ▸ **shame·ful·ly** /-fəli/ ***adv.***: *I think you behaved shamefully.*

**shame·less** /ˈʃeɪmləs/ ***adj.*** not having or showing the feeling of shame that people would expect you to have in a particular situation: *a shameless display of greed and bad manners* ▸ **shame·less·ly** ***adv.***

**sham·poo**[1] /ʃæmˈpu/ ***noun*** (*pl.* **sham·poos**) **1** [C,U] a liquid that you use to wash your hair: *a shampoo for oily hair* **2** [C] the act of washing sth with shampoo

**sham·poo**[2] /ʃæmˈpu/ ***verb*** [T] (*pres. part.* **sham·poo·ing**; *3rd person sing. pres.* **sham·poos**; *pt, pp* **sham·pooed**) to wash sth with shampoo

**sham·rock** /ˈʃæmrɑk/ ***noun*** [C,U] a plant with three leaves on each stem, which is the national symbol of Ireland

**shank** /ʃæŋk/ ***noun*** **1** [C] the straight narrow part between the two ends of a tool or an object **2** [C,U] a piece of meat cut from the leg of an animal **3** [C, usually pl.] (often **shanks**) the part of an animal's or a person's leg between the knee and ankle

**shan·ty·town** /ˈʃæntitaʊn/ ***noun*** [C] a small town or part of a city where poor people live in bad conditions in small badly built houses, etc.

★**shape**[1] /ʃeɪp/ ***noun*** **1** [C,U] the physical outline or outer form of sb/sth: *a round/square/oblong shape* ◇ *a card in the shape of a heart* ◇ *clothes to fit women of all shapes and sizes* **2** [C] something that has a particular outline or outer form: *Squares, circles and triangles are all different shapes.* **3** [U] the condition of sb or sth; the good or bad state of sb or sth: *The house is old, but it's still in pretty good shape.* ◇ *She was in such bad shape* (= so sick) *that she had to be taken to the hospital.* **4** [sing.] **the shape of sth** the organization, form or structure of sth: *Recent developments have changed the shape of the company.*

IDM **be/get bent out of shape** → BENT[2]

**in shape** healthy and physically fit: *Regular exercise will keep your body in shape.*

**out of shape** not physically fit: *You're out of shape. You should get more exercise.*

**take shape** to start to develop well: *Plans to expand the company are beginning to take shape.*

**shapes**

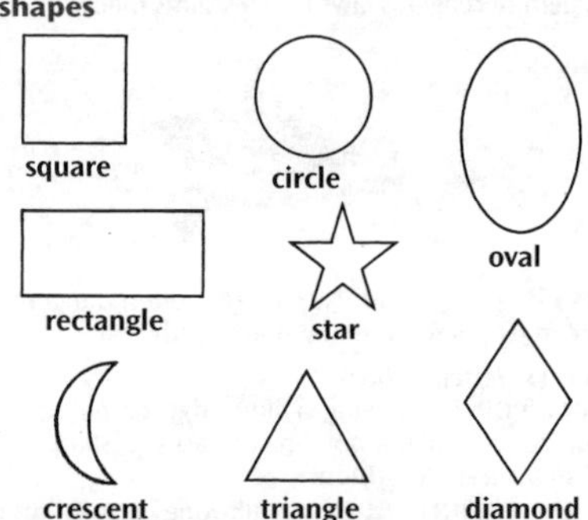


**shape**[2] /ʃeɪp/ ***verb*** [T] **1 shape sth (into sth)** to make sth into a particular form: *Shape the dough into small balls.* **2** to influence the way in which sth develops; to cause sth to have a particular form or nature: *His political ideas were shaped by his upbringing.*

**-shaped** /ʃeɪpt/ ***combining form*** having a certain shape; having the shape of the thing mentioned: *an L-shaped room*

**shape·ly** /ˈʃeɪpli/ ***adj.*** (**shape·li·er**; **shape·li·est**) (used especially about a woman's body) having an attractive curved shape: *a shapely young woman* ◇ *a shapely figure/leg*

**shard** /ʃɑrd/ ***noun*** [C] (*written*) a piece of broken glass, metal, etc.: *shards of glass/pottery*

★**share**[1] /ʃɛr/ ***noun*** **1** [sing.] **share (of sth)** a part or an amount of sth that has been divided between several people: *We each pay a share of the household bills.* ◇ *I'm willing to take my share of the blame.* **2** [C] **share (in/of sth)** one of the equal parts into which the ownership of a company is divided. Shares in a company can be bought and sold: *She holds 100 shares of Kellogg stock.*

IDM **have (more than) your (fair) share of sth** to have (more than) the usual or expected amount of sth: *We've had more than our fair share of trouble today.*

**share**[2] /ʃɛr/ ***verb*** **1** [I,T] **share (sth) (with sb)** to have, use, do or pay sth together with another person or other people; to have sth that sb else also has: *I share an apartment with four other people.* ◇ *There's only one room available, so we'll have to share.* ◇ *We share the same interests.* **2** [I,T] **share (sth) (with sb)** to let sb else have or use sth that you have: *I shared my sandwich with Kim at lunch.* **3** [T] **share sth (with sb)** to tell sb about sth; to allow sb to know sth: *Sometimes it helps to share your problems.*

**share·crop·per** /ˈʃɛrˌkrɑpər/ ***noun*** [C] a farmer who gives part of his/her crop as rent to the owner of the land

**share·hold·er** /ˈʃɛrhoʊldər/ ***noun*** [C] an owner of SHARES[1] (2) in a company



S

**share·ware** /ˈʃɛrwɛr/ ***noun*** [U] (*computing*) computer programs, etc. (software) that is available free for a user to test, after which he/she must pay if he/she wants to continue using it ➲ Compare **freeware**.

**sha·ri·a** (*also* **sha·ri·ah**) /ʃəˈriə; ʃɑ-/ ***noun*** [U] the system of religious laws that Muslims follow

**shark**

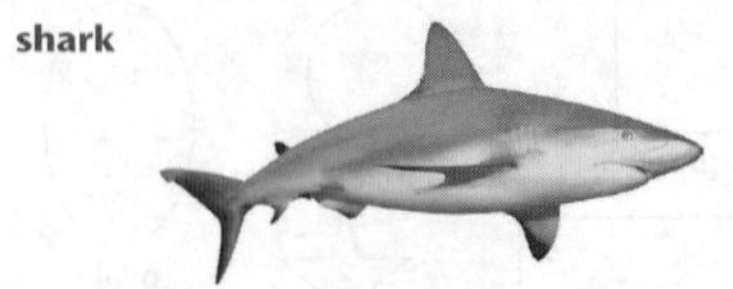

**shark** /ʃɑrk/ ***noun*** [C,U] a large, often dangerous, ocean fish that has many sharp teeth

★**sharp¹** /ʃɑrp/ ***adj.***
➤ EDGE/POINT **1** having a fine edge or point; that can cut or make a hole in sth easily: *a sharp knife* ◇ *sharp teeth* OPP **blunt**
➤ CLEAR/DEFINITE **2** clear; allowing details to be seen clearly: *the sharp outline of the hills* ◇ *a sharp contrast between the lives of the rich and the poor*
➤ MIND/EYES **3** able to think, act, understand, see or hear quickly: *a sharp mind* ◇ *sharp eyesight*
➤ RISE/DROP/CHANGE **4** (used about a change of direction) very great and sudden: *a sharp rise/fall in inflation* ◇ *Take a sharp right at the next intersection.*
➤ MOVEMENTS **5** (used about actions or movements) quick and sudden: *One sharp blow was enough to end the fight.*
➤ CRITICAL **6** (used about words, remarks, etc.) angry or severe; intended to upset or be critical: *During the debate there was a sharp exchange of views between the two candidates.*
➤ FEELING **7** (used about pain) very strong and sudden: *a sharp pain in the chest* OPP **dull**
➤ FLAVOR/SMELL **8** (used about sth that affects the senses) not mild or gentle, often causing a bad feeling: *sharp cheese*
➤ CLOTHES **9** (*informal*) fashionable and attractive: *a sharp suit*
➤ IN MUSIC **10** (*symbol* ♯) (in music) half a tone higher than the stated note: *in the key of C sharp minor* ➲ Look at **flat¹**(5). ➲ picture at **music**. **11** (in music) higher than the correct note: *That last note was sharp. Can you sing it again?* ➲ Look at **flat¹**(6).
▸ **sharp·ly** ***adv.***: *The road bends sharply to the left.* ◇ *"Mind your own business!" she said sharply.* ◇ *Stock prices fell sharply this morning.* ▸ **sharpness** ***noun*** [U]

**sharp²** /ʃɑrp/ ***adv.*** **1** (used about a time) exactly: *Be here at three o'clock sharp.* **2** (in music) slightly higher than the correct note ➲ Look at **flat²**(2).

**sharp³** /ʃɑrp/ ***noun*** [C] (*symbol* ♯) (in music) a note that is half a tone higher than the note with the same letter ➲ Look at **flat³**.

**sharp·en** /ˈʃɑrpən/ ***verb*** [I,T] to become, or to make sth, sharp or sharper: *to sharpen a knife* ◇ *The campaign sharpened public awareness of the problem.*

**sharp·en·er** /ˈʃɑrpənər/ ***noun*** [C] an object or tool that is used for making sth sharp

**sharp·shoot·er** /ˈʃɑrpˌʃuṭər/ ***noun*** [C] a person who is skilled at shooting a gun

**shat·ter** /ˈʃæṭər/ ***verb*** **1** [I,T] (of glass, etc.) to break into very small pieces: *I dropped the glass and it shattered on the floor.* ◇ *The force of the explosion shattered the windows.* **2** [T] to destroy completely: *Her hopes were shattered by the news.*

**shat·ter·proof** /ˈʃæṭərpruf/ ***adj.*** designed not to SHATTER (1): *shatterproof glass*

★**shave¹** /ʃeɪv/ ***verb*** [I,T] **shave (sth) (off)** to remove hair from the face or another part of the body with a razor: *He's too young to shave.* ◇ *I was shaving when the doorbell rang.* ◇ *to shave your legs* ◇ *When did you shave off your mustache?* ➲ Look also at **clean-shaven**.

PHRV **shave sth off (sth)** to cut very thin pieces from a surface (in order to make it smooth or to make it fit sth): *We'll have to shave a little off the door to make it close.*

**shave²** /ʃeɪv/ ***noun*** [C, usually sing.] the act of shaving: *He hadn't had a shave yet.*

IDM **a close call/shave** → CLOSE¹

**shav·er** /ˈʃeɪvər/ (*also* **eˌlectric ˈrazor**) ***noun*** [C] an electric tool that is used for shaving hair

ˈ**shaving cream** ***noun*** [U] special cream or foam for spreading over the face before shaving

**shav·ings** /ˈʃeɪvɪŋz/ ***noun*** [pl.] thin pieces cut from a piece of wood, etc. using a sharp tool, especially a PLANE (3): *wood shavings*

**shawl** /ʃɔl/ ***noun*** [C] a large piece of cloth, made of wool, etc. that is worn by a woman around the shoulders or that is wrapped around a baby

★**she** /ʃi/ ***pronoun*** (the subject of a verb) the female person or animal who has already been mentioned: *"What does your sister do?" "She's a dentist."* ◇ *I asked her a question, but she didn't answer.*

**s/he** /ˌʃi ər ˈhi; ˌʃi ˈhi/ ***pronoun*** (used in writing when the subject of the verb could be either female (she) or male (he): *If a person is not actively seeking work, s/he is not a member of the labor force.*

**sheaf** /ʃif/ ***noun*** [C] (*pl.* **sheaves**) **1** a number of pieces of paper tied or held together: *He waved a sheaf of documents at me.* **2** a bunch of wheat tied together after being cut

**shear** /ʃɪr/ ***verb*** [T] (*pt* **sheared**; *pp* **sheared** or **shorn**) to cut the wool off a sheep

**shears** /ʃɪrz/ ***noun*** [pl.] a tool that is like a very large pair of scissors and that is used for cutting things, often outdoors ➲ picture at **garden**.

**sheath** /ʃiθ/ ***noun*** [C] (*pl.* **sheaths** /ʃiðz; ʃiθs/) **1** a cover that fits closely over the blade of a knife or other sharp weapon or tool: *He put the dagger back in its sheath.* **2** a woman's dress that fits the body closely: *a simple black silk sheath* **3** any covering that fits closely over sth for protection: *the sheath around an electric cable*

**sheathe** /ʃið/ ***verb*** [T] (usually passive) **1** to put a knife or sword into a SHEATH (1) **2** **sheathe sth (in/with sth)** to cover sth in a material, especially in order to protect it

**she·bang** /ʃɪˈbæŋ/ ***noun*** [sing.]

IDM **the whole shebang** (*informal*) the whole thing; everything



S

**shed¹** /ʃɛd/ ***noun*** [C] a small building where things are stored: *Put the lawnmower back in the shed.* ◇ *a tool shed*

**shed²** /ʃɛd/ ***verb*** (*pres. part.* **shed·ding**; *pt, pp* **shed**) **1** [I,T] to lose sth, such as hair or skin, because it falls off: *This snake sheds its skin every year.* ◇ *The cat shed all over my new jacket!* ◇ *Fall is coming and the trees are beginning to shed their leaves.* **2** [T] to get rid of or remove sth that is not wanted: *The town hopes to shed its image as a dull place.* ◇ *Companies in the area have shed thousands of jobs in the past year.*

IDM **shed blood** (*formal*) (usually passive) to kill or injure people: *A great deal of blood was shed during the war.*

**shed light on sth** to make sth clear and easy to understand

**shed tears** (*formal*) to cry: *It was a sad occasion and many tears were shed.*

**she'd** /ʃid/ *short for* SHE HAD, SHE WOULD

**sheen** /ʃin/ ***noun*** [sing., U] a soft smooth shiny quality: *hair with a healthy sheen*

**sheep**

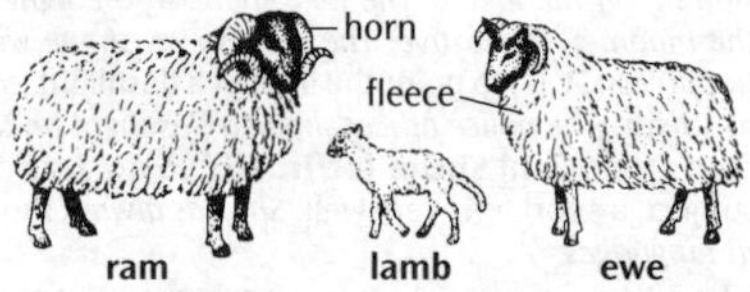


★**sheep** /ʃip/ ***noun*** [C] (*pl.* **sheep**) an animal with a coat of wool that is kept on farms and used for its wool or meat

NOTE A male sheep is a **ram**, a female sheep is a **ewe** and a young sheep is a **lamb**. The noise that sheep make is written as **baa**. The meat from sheep is called **mutton**. Look at the note at **meat**.

**sheep·dog** /ˈʃipdɔg/ ***noun*** [C] a dog that is trained to help control sheep on a farm

**sheep·ish** /ˈʃipɪʃ/ ***adj.*** feeling ashamed or embarrassed because you have done sth silly: *a sheepish grin* ▸ **sheep·ish·ly** ***adv.***

**sheer** /ʃɪr/ ***adj.*** **1** (only *before* a noun) complete, absolute; involving nothing else except: *It's sheer stupidity to drink and drive.* ◇ *Her success is due to sheer hard work.* ◇ *The first thing you notice is the sheer size of the building.* **2** very steep; almost vertical: *Don't walk near the edge. It's a sheer drop to the ocean.*

★**sheet** /ʃit/ ***noun*** [C] **1** a large piece of material used on a bed. Sheets are used in pairs and you sleep between the top and bottom sheet. ➲ picture at **bed¹**. **2** a piece of paper: *a sheet of notebook paper* ◇ *Write each answer on a separate sheet.* ➲ Look at **balance sheet** and **spreadsheet**. **3** a flat, thin piece of any material, especially glass or metal

**Sheet·rock™** /ˈʃitrɑk/ ***noun*** [U] a building material made of sheets of cardboard with plaster between them, used for inside walls and ceilings

**sheik** /ʃik; ʃeɪk/ ***noun*** [C] an Arab ruler

★**shelf** /ʃɛlf/ ***noun*** [C] (*pl.* **shelves** /ʃɛlvz/) a long flat piece of wood, glass, etc. that is fastened to a wall or in a cupboard, that you can stand things on: *I put up a shelf in the kitchen.* ◇ *a bookshelf*

★**shell¹** /ʃɛl/ ***noun*** **1** [C,U] a hard covering that protects eggs, nuts and some animals: *a collection of seashells* ◇ *an empty shell* ◇ *a turtle's shell* ➲ pictures at **egg** and **snail**. **2** [C] a metal container filled with explosives that is fired by a large gun

**shell²** /ʃɛl/ ***verb*** [T] **1** to take the SHELL¹ (1) off sth that can be eaten: *to shell peanuts* ➲ picture at **nut**. **2** to fire SHELLS¹ (2) at a place: *They shelled the city all night.*

PHR V **shell (sth) out (for sth)** (*informal*) to pay a lot of money for sth, especially when it is more than you want to spend: *The bus didn't come, so I had to shell out $20 for a cab ride home.*

**she'll** /ʃil/ *short for* SHE WILL

**shel·lac¹** /ʃəˈlæk/ ***noun*** [U] a natural substance used in making varnish to protect surfaces and make them hard

**shel·lac²** /ʃəˈlæk/ ***verb*** [T] (*pres. part.* **shel·lack·ing**; *pt, pp* **shel·lacked**) **1** to paint sth with shellac **2** (usually passive) (*informal*) to defeat sb very easily: *The Republicans got shellacked in the elections.*

**shellfish**

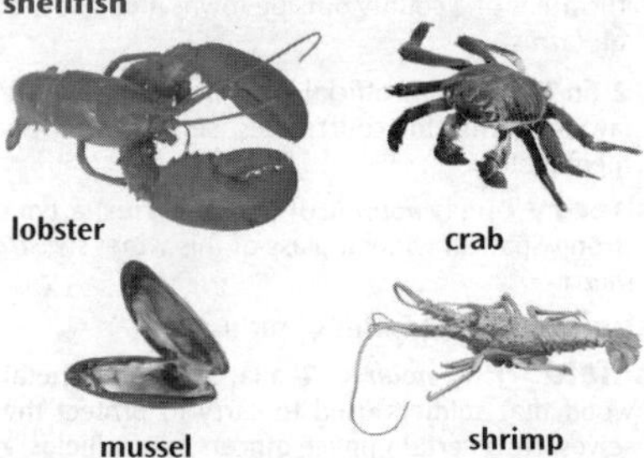


**shell·fish** /ˈʃɛlfɪʃ/ ***noun*** [C,U] (*pl.* **shell·fish**) a creature with a shell, that lives in water, especially one of the types that can be eaten: *Oysters, clams and crabs are all shellfish.* ➲ Compare **crustacean**.

**ˈshell shock** ***noun*** [U] a mental illness that can affect soldiers who have been in battle for a long time

**ˈshell-shocked** ***adj.*** **1** shocked, confused or anxious because of a difficult situation, and unable to think or act normally: *I felt completely shell-shocked after I heard the news.* **2** suffering from shell shock

★**shel·ter¹** /ˈʃɛltər/ ***noun*** **1** [U] **shelter (from sth)** protection from danger or bad weather: *to give somebody food and shelter* ◇ *I took shelter under his umbrella.* **2** [C] a building or a structure that gives protection or cover, e.g. from danger, bad weather or attack: *a shelter for the homeless* ◇ *a picnic shelter* ◇ *a bomb shelter*

★**shel·ter²** /ˈʃɛltər/ ***verb*** **1** [I] **shelter (from sth)** to find protection or SHELTER¹ (1): *They sheltered from the rain under a tree.* ◇ *There are 100 refugees sheltering in foreign embassies.* **2** [T] **shelter sb/sth (from sb/sth)** to protect sb/sth; to give sb/sth SHELTER¹ (1): *The trees shelter the house from the wind.* ◇ *The embassy is now sheltering nearly 100 refugees.*

**shel·tered** /ˈʃɛltərd/ ***adj.*** **1** (used about a place)

S

protected from bad weather: *The campers found a sheltered spot for their tent.* **2** protected from bad things in your life: *a sheltered childhood in the country*

**shelve** /ʃɛlv/ ***verb*** [T] to decide not to continue with a plan, etc.: *Plans for a new stadium have been shelved.*

**shelves** /ʃɛlvz/ *plural of* SHELF

**shelv·ing** /ˈʃɛlvɪŋ/ ***noun*** [U] a set of shelves

**she·nan·i·gans** /ʃəˈnænɪgənz/ ***noun*** [pl.] (*informal*) secret or dishonest activities that people find interesting or amusing: *political/financial/sexual shenanigans*

**shep·herd** /ˈʃɛpərd/ ***noun*** [C] (especially in the past) a person who takes care of sheep ➲ Look also at **German shepherd**.

**sher·bet** /ʃərbət/ ***noun*** [U] a frozen sweet food, similar to ice cream, made from water, sugar, fruit juice and sometimes milk

**sher·iff** /ˈʃɛrəf/ ***noun*** [C] **1** (in the U.S.) the law officer who is elected to the highest position in the police force of a county

NOTE The **police** work in towns and cities; the **sheriff** and the sheriff's **deputies** are in charge of the areas of a county outside towns and cities, e.g. on farms.

**2** (in Canada) an official who works in a court of law preparing for court cases, serving legal documents, etc.

**sher·ry** /ˈʃɛri/ ***noun*** [C,U] (*pl.* **sher·ries**) a type of strong Spanish wine; a glass of this wine: *sweet/dry sherry*

**she's** /ʃiz/ *short for* SHE IS, SHE HAS

**shield¹** /ʃild/ ***noun*** [C] **1** a large piece of metal or wood that soldiers used to carry to protect themselves. Now certain police officers carry shields: *riot shields* **2** a person or thing that is used for protection: *The metal door acted as a shield against the explosion.*

S

**shield²** /ʃild/ ***verb*** [T] **shield sb/sth (against/from sb/sth)** to protect sb/sth from danger or damage: *I shielded my eyes from the bright light with my hand.*

★**shift¹** /ʃɪft/ ***verb*** **1** [T] to move sb/sth from one position to another: *This plan will shift more responsibility onto individual citizens.* **2** [I] to change position or direction: *The media's attention has shifted to the possible cause of the accident.* **3** [I,T] to change the position of the gears in a car: *She shifted into first and quickly drove off.*

★**shift²** /ʃɪft/ ***noun*** **1** [C] **a shift (in sth)** a change in the position or nature of sth: *There has been a shift in public opinion away from war.* ◇ *a shift in policy/a policy shift* **2** [C] (in a factory, etc.) a division of the working day; the people who work during this period: *an eight-hour shift* ◇ *to work the day/night shift* **3** [U] (*also* ˈ**shift key** [C]) the key on a computer keyboard, etc. that you press in order to type capital letters

**shift·less** /ˈʃɪftləs/ ***adj.*** lazy and having no ambition to succeed in life: *She worked hard but she had to support a shiftless husband.*

**shift·y** /ˈʃɪfti/ ***adj.*** (**shift·i·er**; **shift·i·est**) (*informal*) seeming to be dishonest; looking guilty about sth: *shifty eyes* ◇ *to look shifty*

**shi·i·ta·ke** (*also* **shi·ta·ke**) /ʃɪˈtɑki; ʃi-/ ***noun*** [C] a type of Japanese or Chinese mushroom

**shim** /ʃɪm/ ***noun*** [C] a thin piece of wood, rubber, metal, etc. which is thicker at one end than the other, that you use to fill a space between two things that do not fit together well

**shim·mer** /ˈʃɪmər/ ***verb*** [I] to shine with a soft light that seems to be moving: *The tears shimmered in her eyes.* ◇ *moonlight shimmering on the lake*

**shim·my** /ˈʃɪmi/ ***verb*** [I] (*3rd person sing. pres.* **shim·mies**; *pres. part.* **shim·my·ing**; *pt, pp* **shim·mied**) to dance or move in a way that involves shaking your hips and shoulders: *She shimmied onto the dance floor.*

**shin** /ʃɪn/ ***noun*** [C] the front part of your leg above your ankle and below your knee ➲ picture on study page **A32**.

**shin·dig** /ˈʃɪndɪg/ ***noun*** [C] (*informal*) a big noisy party

★**shine¹** /ʃaɪn/ ***verb*** (*pt, pp* **shone** /ʃoʊn; (*Cdn*) ʃɑn/) **1** [I] to give out or to reflect light: *moonlight shining on the lake* ◇ *The lake shone in the light of the moon.* ◇ (*figurative*) *The child's eyes shone with happiness.* **2** [T] to point the light of a flashlight, etc. at sb/sth: *The police officer shone a flashlight on the man's face.* **3** [I] **shine (at/in sth)** to do a school subject, a sport, etc. very well: *She has always shone at languages.*

**shine²** /ʃaɪn/ ***verb*** [T] (*pt, pp* **shined**) to polish sth so that it reflects light: *to shine your shoes*

**shine³** /ʃaɪn/ ***noun*** [sing., U] brightness, caused by light reflecting, because sth has been polished: *There's a beautiful shine on that table.*

**shin·er** /ˈʃaɪnər/ ***noun*** [C] an area of dark skin (a bruise), that forms around sb's eye when he/she has been hit there

**shin·gle** /ˈʃɪŋgl/ ***noun*** [C] one of many flat pieces of wood or other material which are put one on top of another to make the roof of a house ➲ picture on study page **A31**.

**shin·ny** /ˈʃɪni/ ***verb*** [I] (*3rd person sing. pres.* **shin·nies**; *pres. part.* **shin·ny·ing**; *pt, pp* **shin·nied**)

PHR V **shinny up/down sth** (*informal*) to climb up or down sth quickly, using your hands and legs: *He shinnied down the rope and disappeared.*

ˈ**shin splints** ***noun*** [pl.] sharp pain in the front parts of the lower legs caused by too much exercise, especially on a hard surface

★**shin·y** /ˈʃaɪni/ ***adj.*** (**shin·i·er**; **shin·i·est**) bright; reflecting light: *The shampoo leaves your hair soft and shiny.* ◇ *a shiny new car*

★**ship¹** /ʃɪp/ ***noun*** [C] a large boat used for carrying passengers or cargo by sea: *to travel by ship* ◇ *a cruise ship* ◇ *The captain went on board ship.* ◇ *The ship sails at noon.* ◇ *The ship sank.*

NOTE A **boat** is smaller than a ship. We use **vessel** in formal English for ship. ➲ picture at **boat**.

**ship²** /ʃɪp/ ***verb*** [T] (**ship·ping**; **shipped**) to send or carry sth from one place to another, especially in large quantities: *The pineapples are shipped by air* (= in airplanes) *to ensure freshness.*

**ship·load** /ˈʃɪploʊd/ ***noun*** [C] as many goods or passengers as a ship can carry: *a shipload of food and medical supplies*

**ship·ment** /ˈʃɪpmənt/ ***noun*** **1** [C] a quantity of goods sent from one place to another: *a shipment of grain* **2** [U] the transportation of goods from one place to another: *cargo ready for shipment*

**ship·per** /ˈʃɪpər/ ***noun*** [C] a company that arranges for goods to be sent from one place to another, especially by ship but also by land and air

**ship·ping** /ˈʃɪpɪŋ/ ***noun*** [U] the transportation of goods from one place to another: *The price of the book is $17.95, plus $2.00 for shipping and handling.*

**ship·shape** /ˌʃɪpˈʃeɪp; ˈʃɪpʃeɪp/ ***adj.*** clean and neat; in good order and ready to use: *They had to rush to get everything shipshape before the official opening.*

**ship·wreck** /ˈʃɪprɛk/ ***noun*** [C] **1** an accident at sea in which a ship is destroyed by a storm, rocks, etc. ➲ A person or a ship that has suffered such an accident has been **shipwrecked**. **2** a ship that has been damaged or destroyed in an accident or by a storm, etc.

**ship·yard** /ˈʃɪpyɑrd/ ***noun*** [C] a place where ships are built or repaired: *shipyard workers*

**shirk** /ʃərk/ ***verb*** [I,T] (*formal*) to avoid doing sth that is difficult or unpleasant: *to shirk your responsibilities*

**shirred** /ʃərd/ ***adj.*** (used about an area of fabric or clothing) pulled into very small folds by lines of stitches that are sewn with a special elastic thread: *a swimsuit with a shirred front*

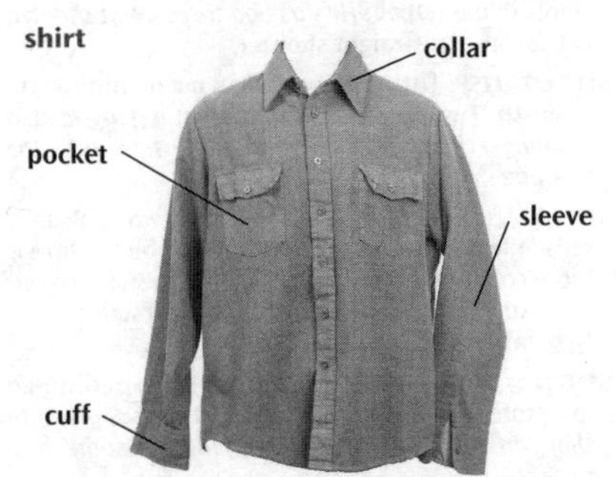


★**shirt** /ʃərt/ ***noun*** [C] a piece of clothing made of cotton, etc., worn (especially by men) on the upper part of the body: *He wears a shirt and tie for work.*

> NOTE A shirt usually has a **collar** at the neck, long or short **sleeves**, and **buttons** on the front.

**shirt·sleeve** /ˈʃərtsliv/ ***noun*** [C, usually pl.] a sleeve of a shirt: *He rolled up his shirtsleeves.*

IDM **in (your) shirtsleeves** wearing a shirt without a jacket, etc. on top of it: *It was a hot day and most of the men were in shirtsleeves.*

**shirt·tail** /ˈʃərtteɪl/ ***noun*** [C] the part of a shirt that is below the waist and is usually inside your pants: *He ran out of the house, his tie in his hand and his shirttail hanging out.*

**shish ke·bab** /ˈʃɪʃ kəˌbɑb/ ***noun*** [C] small pieces of meat and vegetables cooked on a wooden or metal stick

**shiv·er** /ˈʃɪvər/ ***verb*** [I] to shake slightly, especially because you are cold or frightened: *shivering with cold/fright* ▸ **shiv·er** ***noun*** [C]: *The thought sent a shiver down my spine.*

★**shock**[1] /ʃɑk/ ***noun*** **1** [C,U] the feeling that is caused by sth unpleasant happening suddenly; the situation that causes this feeling: *The sudden noise gave him a real shock.* ◇ *The bad news came as a huge shock to her.* ◇ *I'm still suffering from shock at the news.* **2** [C] = ELECTRIC SHOCK: *Don't touch that wire – you'll get a shock.* **3** [C] a violent hit or shaking (from a crash, an explosion, etc.): *the shock of the earthquake* ➲ Look also at **aftershock**. **4** [U] (in medicine) a condition of extreme weakness caused by damage to the body: *He was in/went into shock after the accident.*

★**shock**[2] /ʃɑk/ ***verb*** [T] **1** to cause an unpleasant feeling of surprise in sb: *We were shocked by his death.* ◇ *The employees were shocked at the news that the store was going to close.* **2** to make sb feel disgust and anger: *The pictures of the starving children shocked the world.*

**ˈshock abˌsorber** ***noun*** [C] a device that is fitted to each wheel of a vehicle in order to reduce the effects of traveling over rough ground, so that passengers can be more comfortable

★**shock·ing** /ˈʃɑkɪŋ/ ***adj.*** making you feel worried, upset or angry: *a shocking act of violence*

**ˈshock jock** ***noun*** [C] (*informal*) a person who presents a radio show (a **DJ**), who deliberately expresses opinions or uses language that many people find offensive

**ˈshock wave** ***noun*** **1** [C] a movement of very high air pressure that is caused by an explosion, earthquake, etc. **2 shock waves** [pl.] feelings of shock that people experience when sth bad happens suddenly: *The murder sent shock waves through the whole community.*

**shod·dy** /ˈʃɑdi/ ***adj.*** (**shod·di·er**; **shod·di·est**) made carelessly or with poor quality materials: *shoddy goods* ▸ **shod·di·ly** /-əli/ ***adv.***

★**shoe** /ʃu/ ***noun*** [C] a type of covering for the foot, usually made of leather or plastic: *a pair of shoes* ◇ *running shoes* ◇ *What size shoes do you wear?* ◇ *I tried on a nice pair of shoes, but they didn't fit.* ◇ *Wait for me – I just have to tie my shoes.* ➲ Look also at **horseshoe**. ➲ picture on **next page**.

IDM **in sb's shoes** in the situation that sb else is in: *Put yourself in my shoes – how would you feel?* ◇ *I would hate to be in his shoes right now.*

**shoe·box** /ˈʃubɑks/ ***noun*** [C] the box in which a new pair of shoes is sold

**shoe·horn**[1] /ˈʃuhɔrn/ ***noun*** [C] a curved piece of plastic or metal, used to help your heel slide into a shoe

**shoe·horn**[2] /ˈʃuhɔrn/ ***verb*** [T] to force sb/sth into a small space or a place where it does not fit very easily: *They managed to shoehorn the material onto just one CD.*

**shoe·lace** /ˈʃuleɪs/ ***noun*** [C] = SHOESTRING

**shoe·mak·er** /ˈʃuˌmeɪkər/ ***noun*** [C] a person whose job is making shoes and boots

S

**shoes**

moccasins | slippers | sandals | cowboy boot | boot

lace | sole | heel

slingback | pump | sneakers (*also* tennis shoe) | shoes

**shoe·string** /ˈʃustrɪŋ/ (*also* **shoelace**) ***noun*** [C] a long piece of string or leather that is used to fasten a shoe: *to tie/untie your shoestrings*

IDM **on a shoestring** using very little money: *My mother brought up five children on a shoestring.*

**shone** *past tense, past participle of* SHINE[1]

**shoo**[1] /ʃu/ ***interjection*** (usually said to animals or small children) Go away!

**shoo**[2] /ʃu/ ***verb*** (*pt, pp* **shooed**)

PHRV **shoo sb/sth away, off, out, etc.** to make sb/sth go away by saying "shoo" and waving your hands: *I shooed the birds away from the garden.*

**ˈshoo-in** ***noun*** [C] (*informal*) a person or team that will win easily: *He's a **shoo-in for** re-election.*

**shook** *past tense of* SHAKE[1]

**ˌshook ˈup** ***adj.*** (*informal*) (not before a noun) feeling upset or shocked

★**shoot**[1] /ʃut/ ***verb*** (*pt, pp* **shot** /ʃɑt/)

➤ WEAPON **1** [I,T] **shoot (sth) (at sb/sth)** to fire a gun, etc.: *Don't shoot!* ◇ *She shot an arrow at the target but missed it.* **2** [T] to injure or kill sb/sth with a gun: *The police officer was shot in the arm.* ◇ *The soldier was shot dead.*

➤ MOVE QUICKLY **3** [I,T] to move quickly and suddenly in one direction; to make sth move in this way: *The car shot past me at 100 miles per hour.* ◇ *She shot her boyfriend an angry look* (= looked at him very quickly and angrily).

➤ OF PAIN **4** [I] **shoot down, up, etc. sth** (of pain) to go very suddenly along part of your body: *The pain shot up my leg.*

➤ IN SPORTS **5** [I,T] to try to kick or hit the ball into the net: *Let's go out and shoot some baskets* (= throw the ball through the basket).

➤ MOVIE/PHOTOGRAPH **6** [I,T] to make a movie or photograph of sth: *They shot the scene ten times.*

PHRV **shoot sb down** to kill sb with a gun

**shoot sth down** to make an airplane, etc. crash to the ground by shooting it: *The helicopter was shot down by a missile.*

**shoot up 1** to increase very quickly: *Prices have shot up in the past year.* **2** (*slang*) to put illegal drugs into your body, using a special type of needle

**shoot**[2] /ʃut/ ***noun*** [C] **1** an occasion when a professional photographer or director takes photographs or makes a movie: *a video shoot* **2** a new part of a plant or tree

**shoot**[3] /ʃut/ ***interjection*** (*informal*) (used to show that you are annoyed, disappointed, or surprised): *Oh, shoot – I just missed the bus.*

**shoot·er** /ˈʃut̬ər/ ***noun*** [C] **1** (especially in compounds) a person or weapon that shoots **2** (*informal*) a gun **3** (*sports*) a player who is good at throwing the ball through the basket and scoring points in basketball: *He's a good three-point shooter.* ➲ Look also at **straight shooter**.

**shoot·ing** /ˈʃut̬ɪŋ/ ***noun*** [C,U] an act of firing a gun at sb/sth: *Two people were injured in a gang-related shooting Friday night.* ◇ *They hid inside until the shooting stopped.*

★**shop**[1] /ʃɑp/ ***noun*** **1** [C] a small store which usually sells only one type of product: *a gift shop* ➲ **Store** is more common than **shop**. **2** [C] = WORKSHOP (1): *Our car is still in the shop.* **3** [U] = INDUSTRIAL ARTS

IDM **talk shop** → TALK[1]

★**shop**[2] /ʃɑp/ ***verb*** [I] (**shop·ping**; **shopped**) to go to a store or stores in order to buy things: *I prefer to shop on my own.* ◇ *He's shopping for some new clothes.*

NOTE **Go shopping** is more common than **shop**: *We go shopping every Saturday.* ◇ *to go Christmas shopping*

PHRV **shop around (for sth)** to look at the price and quality of an item in different stores before you decide where to buy it: *We shopped around for the best deal on a new car.*

▸ **shop·ping** ***noun*** [U]: *She did the grocery shopping.*

**shop·a·hol·ic** /ˌʃɑpəˈhɔlɪk; -ˈhɑlɪk/ ***noun*** [C] (*informal*) a person who spends a lot of time shopping

**shop·keep·er** /ˈʃɑpkipər/ (*also* **ˈstorekeeper**) ***noun*** [C] a person who owns or manages a small store

**shop·lift** /ˈʃɑplɪft/ ***verb*** [I,T] to steal sth from a store while pretending to be a customer

▸ **shop·lift·er** ***noun*** [C]: *Shoplifters will be prosecuted.* ➲ Look at the note at **thief**. ▸ **shop·lift·ing** ***noun*** [U]: *He was arrested for shoplifting.*

**shop·per** /ˈʃɑpər/ ***noun*** a person who buys goods from stores: *The streets were full of Christmas shoppers.* ◇ *Competition between stores can result in big savings for the shopper.*

ˈ**shopping bag** ***noun*** [C] a large bag, usually made of heavy paper with a flat bottom and two handles, that you can put things into after you have bought them

ˈ**shopping cart** ***noun*** [C] a large basket on wheels that you push around in a store and put things in when you are shopping ➲ picture at **cart**[1].

ˈ**shopping** ˌ**center** ***noun*** [C] a place where there are many stores, either outside or in a covered building

ˈ**shopping list** ***noun*** [C] a list that you make of all the things that you need to buy when you go shopping

ˈ**shopping mall** ***noun*** [C] = MALL

**shop·worn** /ˈʃɑpwɔrn/ ***adj.*** (used about goods for sale) dirty or not in perfect condition because they have been on display in a store for a long time: (*figurative*) *a shopworn argument* (= that is no longer new or useful)

**shore**[1] /ʃɔr/ ***noun*** **1** [C,U] the land along the edge of an ocean, a lake or a sea: *The swimmer kept close to the shore.* ◇ *The sailors went **on shore*** (= on land). SYN **Ashore** has the same meaning as "on shore." **2** [pl.] **shores** (in literature) a country, especially one with a coast: *foreign/distant shores* ◇ *What brings you to these shores?*

**shore**[2] /ʃɔr/ ***verb*** [T]

PHRV **shore sth up 1** to support part of a building or other large structure by placing large pieces of wood or metal against or under it so that it does not fall down: *Timbers were used to shore up the tunnel.* **2** to help to support sth that is weak or going to fail: *The measures were aimed at shoring up the economy.*

**shore·line** /ˈʃɔrlaɪn/ ***noun*** [C, usually sing.] the edge of the ocean, a lake or a sea: *a rocky shoreline* ◇ *The road follows the shoreline for a few miles.*

**shorn** *past participle of* SHEAR

★**short**[1] /ʃɔrt/ ***adj.*** **1** not measuring much from one end to the other: *a short line* ◇ *a short distance* ◇ *This essay is pretty short.* ◇ *short hair* OPP **long** **2** less than the average height: *a short, fat man* OPP **tall** **3** not lasting a long time: *a short visit* ◇ *She left a short time ago.* ◇ *to have a short memory* (= to only remember things that happened recently) **4 short (of/on sth)** not having enough of what is needed: *Because of illness, the team is two players short.* ◇ *Good secretaries are in short supply* (= there are not enough of them). ◇ *We're a little short of money right now.*

IDM **be short for sth** to be used as a shorter way of saying sth: *"Bill" is short for "William."*

**for short** as a short form: *Her name is Diana, but we call her "Di" for short.*

**get the short end of the stick** (*informal*) to be treated unfairly, or to be forced to do sth that nobody else wants to do

**in the long/short term** → TERM[1]

**short**[2] /ʃɔrt/ ***adv.*** suddenly: *She stopped short when she saw the accident.*

IDM **fall short (of sth)** not to be enough; not to reach sth: *The raise fell short of the union's demands.*

**run short (of sth)** to have used up most of sth so there is not much left: *We're running short of coffee.*

**short of sth** except for: *He's tried to make money by every means, short of stealing it.*

**stop short of sth/doing sth** → STOP[1]

**short**[3] /ʃɔrt/ ***noun*** [C] (*informal*) = SHORT CIRCUIT ➲ Look also at **shorts**.

IDM **in short** in a few words; briefly: *Einstein had one of the greatest minds the world has ever known: in short, he was a genius.*

**short·age** /ˈʃɔrtɪdʒ/ ***noun*** [C] a situation where there is not enough of sth: *a food/housing/water shortage* ◇ *a shortage of science teachers*

**short·cake** /ˈʃɔrtkeɪk/ ***noun*** [U] a cake with a pastry base and cream and fruit on top: *strawberry shortcake*

ˌ**short** ˈ**circuit** (*also informal* **short**) ***noun*** [C] a bad electrical connection that causes a machine to stop working

ˌ**short-**ˈ**circuit** ***verb*** [I,T] to have a short circuit or to cause a machine to have one: *The lights short-circuited.*

**short·com·ing** /ˈʃɔrtkʌmɪŋ/ ***noun*** [C, usually pl.] a fault or weakness: *As a leader, she had many shortcomings.*

**short·cut** /ˈʃɔrtkʌt/ ***noun*** [C] a quicker, easier or more direct way to get somewhere or to do sth: *He took a shortcut to school through the park.*

**short·en** /ˈʃɔrtn/ ***verb*** [I,T] to become shorter or to make sth shorter: *I'll have to shorten these pants – they're way too long.*

**short·en·ing** /ˈʃɔrtn·ɪŋ/ ***noun*** [U] a type of white fat made from vegetable oil that is used in making cookies, etc.

**short·fall** /ˈʃɔrtfɔl/ ***noun*** [C] **shortfall (in sth)** if there is a shortfall in sth, there is less of it than you need or expect: *a shortfall of over 500,000 tons in the grain supply* ◇ *Several staff were fired to meet a shortfall of funds.*

**short·hand** /ˈʃɔrthænd/ ***noun*** [U] a method of writing quickly that uses signs or short forms of words

**short·ie** /ˈʃɔrt̬i/ ***noun*** [C] = SHORTY

**short-lived** /ˌʃɔrtˈlɪvd; -ˈlaɪvd/ ***adj.*** lasting only for a short time

★**short·ly** /ˈʃɔrtli/ ***adv.*** soon; in a short time: *The manager will see you shortly.*

ˌ**short-**ˌ**order** ˈ**cook** ***noun*** [C] a person who works in a restaurant cooking food that can be prepared quickly

ˌ**short-**ˈ**range** ***adj.*** **1** (used about weapons) designed to travel only over short distances: *short-range missiles* **2** (used about plans, etc.) connected with a short period of time in the future: *a short-range weather forecast* ➲ Look at **long-range**.

ˈ**short ribs** ***noun*** [pl.] a narrow cut of meat from a

S

cow (**beef**) that includes part of the bones that go around its chest (**ribs**)

**shorts** /ʃɔrts/ ***noun*** [pl.] **1** a type of short pants ending above the knee that you wear in hot weather, while playing sports, etc. ➲ picture on study page **A30**. **2** men's underpants: *boxer shorts*

NOTE Notice that, because **shorts** is a plural word, we cannot say, for example, "a new short." The following are possible: *I need to get some new shorts.* ◇ *I need to get a new pair of shorts.*

**short·sight·ed** /ˌʃɔrt'saɪt̬əd/ ***adj.*** not considering what will probably happen in the future: *a short-sighted attitude* ➲ Look also at **nearsighted**.

**short·stop** /'ʃɔrtstɑp/ ***noun*** [C] (in baseball) a player whose job is to catch the ball (a **fielder**), who plays in the inner part of a sports field between second and third base

**ˌshort 'story** ***noun*** [C] (*pl.* **ˌshort 'stories**) a piece of writing that is shorter than a novel: *a collection of short stories by O. Henry*

**'short-term** ***adj.*** (only *before* a noun) lasting for a short period of time from the present: *short-term plans*

**short·y** (*also* **short·ie**) /'ʃɔrt̬i/ ***noun*** [C] (*pl.* **shorties**) (*slang*) a person who is not very tall

★**shot**[1] /ʃɑt/ ***noun*** [C]
➤WITH GUN **1** an act of firing a gun, etc., or the noise that this makes: *to take a shot at the target* ◇ *The police officer fired a warning shot into the air.*
➤ATTEMPT **2** **a shot (at sth/at doing sth)** (*informal*) an attempt to do sth: *Let me have a shot at it* (= let me try to do it).
➤IN SPORTS **3** an act of kicking or throwing a ball: *He took a shot from near the foul line.*
➤PHOTOGRAPH **4** a photograph or a picture in a movie: *I got some good shots of the runners as they crossed the line.*
➤DRUG **5** an injection of a drug, especially in order to prevent a disease: *a shot of penicillin* ◇ *a flu shot*
➤DRINK **6** a small drink of strong alcohol

**shot**[2] *past tense, past participle of* SHOOT[1]

**shot·gun** /'ʃɑtgʌn/ ***noun*** [C] a gun used for shooting small animals and birds that fires small metal balls ➲ Look at the note at **gun**.
IDM **ride shotgun** (*informal*) to ride in the front passenger seat of a car or truck

**ˌshotgun 'wedding** (*also* **ˌshotgun 'marriage**) ***noun*** [C] (*old-fashioned, informal*) a wedding that has to take place quickly, e.g. because the woman is pregnant

**the 'shot put** ***noun*** [sing.] a sport in which people try to throw a heavy metal ball as far as possible

★**should** /ʃəd; *strong form* ʃʊd/ ***modal verb*** (*negative* **should not**; *short form* **should·n't** /'ʃʊdnt/) **1** (used for giving your opinon or asking for advice): *You should try that new restaurant.* ◇ *The police should do something about it.* ◇ *He really shouldn't work so hard.* ◇ *Should I try again?* **2** (used with "have" to say that sb did the wrong thing): *I'm tired. I shouldn't have gone to bed so late/I should have gone to bed earlier.* **3** (used for saying that you expect sth is true or will happen): *It's 4:30. They should be in New York by now.* ◇ *The party should be a lot of fun.* **4** (*formal*) (used after "if" or with the same meaning as "if," when you think that sth is not likely to happen): *If you should decide to accept, please phone us.* ◇ *Should you decide to accept...* **5** (used after certain adjectives, in phrases beginning with "that"): *It's not right that something like this should happen.* ◇ *It's funny that you should mention that...*

★**shoul·der**[1] /'ʃoʊldər/ ***noun*** [C] **1** the part of the body between the neck and the top of the arm: *He hurt his shoulder.* ◇ *He carried his little girl on his shoulders.* ◇ *to shrug your shoulders* (= to raise your shoulders, especially as a way of showing that you do not know an answer or that you are not interested) ➲ picture on study page **A32**. **2** a part of a dress, coat, etc. that covers this part of the body **3** a narrow part along the side of a road where cars can stop in an emergency
IDM **have a chip on your shoulder** → CHIP[1]
**rub elbows/shoulders with sb** → RUB

**shoul·der**[2] /'ʃoʊldər/ ***verb*** [T] **1** to accept the responsibility for sth: *She shouldered all the blame for the accident.* **2** to push sb/sth with your SHOULDER[1] (1): *He shouldered everybody aside and disappeared through the door.*

**'shoulder bag** ***noun*** [C] a type of bag that you carry over one shoulder with a long strap

**'shoulder blade** ***noun*** [C] one of the two large flat bones on each side of your back, below your SHOULDERS[1] (1)

**'shoulder-length** ***adj.*** (used especially about hair) long enough to reach your shoulders

**should·n't** /'ʃʊdnt/ *short for* SHOULD NOT

**should·'ve** /'ʃʊdəv/ *short for* SHOULD HAVE

★**shout**[1] /ʃaʊt/ ***verb*** **1** [I] **shout (at/to sb); shout (out)** to speak or cry out in a very loud voice: *There's no need to shout – I can hear you.* ◇ *The teacher shouted angrily at the boys.* ◇ *to shout out in pain/excitement* **2** [T] **shout sth (at/to sb); shout sth out** to say sth in a loud voice: *"Look out!" she shouted.* ◇ *The captain shouted out instructions to his team.*
PHRV **shout sb down** to prevent sb from being heard by shouting at him/her (often in a public meeting): *to shout down a speaker*

★**shout**[2] /ʃaʊt/ ***noun*** [C] a loud cry of anger, fear, excitement, etc.: *a shout of anger/pain/joy*
IDM **give sb a shout** (*informal*) to tell sb something: *Give me a shout when you're ready.*

**shove**[1] /ʃʌv/ ***verb*** [I,T] to push with a sudden, rough movement: *They pushed and shoved to the front of the line.* ◇ *The police officer shoved the suspect into a cell.* ◇ (*informal*) *"What should I do with this box?" "Oh, just shove it in the closet."*

**shove**[2] /ʃʌv/ ***noun*** [C, usually sing.] a strong push: *She gave the door a shove with her elbow.*
IDM **when push comes to shove** → PUSH[2]

**shov·el**[1] /'ʃʌvl/ ***noun*** [C] a tool with a long handle that is used for moving dirt, snow, sand, etc.: *a snow shovel* ➲ picture at **garden**.

**shov·el**[2] /'ʃʌvl/ ***verb*** [I,T] to move sth or clean sth with a shovel: *to shovel dirt into a hole* ◇ *to shovel the sidewalk* (= to clear snow off it)

★**show**[1] /ʃoʊ/ ***noun***
➤ENTERTAINMENT **1** [C] a program on television or on the radio: *There's a show I want to see tonight.*

◇ *my favorite TV show* **2** [C] a play in a theater: *a Broadway show*
➤ COLLECTION OF THINGS **3** [C] a collection of things for people to look at, often in a special large building: *a dog show* ◇ *the Detroit auto show* (= where new types of cars are displayed)
➤ INSINCERE ACT **4** [C,U] the outward expression of an emotion that is not what you really feel or that does not have much meaning: *Although she hated him, she put on a show of politeness.* ◇ *His bravery is all show* (= he is not as brave as he pretends to be).
➤ SIGN **5** [sing.] a sign of sth: *The military conducted exercises as a show of strength in the region.*
IDM **for show** intended to impress people; not to be used: *Those dishes are only for show – nobody ever uses them.*
**be on show** to be located in a place where people can see it: *The collection is on show at the Museum of Modern Art.*

★**show**[2] /ʃoʊ/ ***verb*** (*pt* **showed**; *pp* **shown** /ʃoʊn/ or **showed**)
➤ LET SB SEE STH **1** [T] **show sb/sth (to sb)** to make it possible for other people to see sb/sth: *I showed the letter to him.* ◇ *I showed him the letter.* ◇ *She showed me what she had bought.* ◇ *They're showing his latest movie at the theater at the mall.*
➤ GUIDE **2** [T] to lead or guide sb to a place: *Let me show you to your room.* ◇ *A guide showed us around the museum.*
➤ TEACH **3** [T] to help sb to do sth by doing it yourself; to explain sth: *Can you show me how to put the disk in the computer?*
➤ MAKE CLEAR **4** [T] to make sth clear; to give information about sth: *Research shows that most people get too little exercise.* ◇ *The picture showed the effects of the storm.*
➤ BE VISIBLE **5** [I] to be able to be seen; to appear: *Her anger showed in her eyes.* ◇ *There's a hole in my sock, but it doesn't show.* **6** [T] to allow sth to be seen: *This gray carpet doesn't show the dirt.*
➤ QUALITY/BEHAVIOR/FEELING **7** [T] to cause people to notice a particular quality: *She was the only one who ever showed him any kindness.* ◇ *He didn't want to show what he was really thinking.* ◇ *She was showing signs of stress.*
PHR V **show (sth) off** (*informal*) to try to impress people by showing them how good you are at sth or by showing them sth that you are proud of: *He's always showing off in front of his friends.* ◇ *She wanted to show off her new bike.*
**show up 1** (*informal*) to arrive, especially when sb is expecting you: *I thought you'd never show up.* **2** to be able to be seen: *The fracture showed up clearly on the X-ray.*

ˌ**show-and-ˈtell** (*also* ˌ**show and ˈtell**) ***noun*** [U] a teaching method in which young children are asked to bring sth to show their class and describe it to the other children

ˈ**show ˌbusiness** (*also informal* **show·biz** /ˈʃoʊbɪz/) ***noun*** [U] the business of entertaining people, in the theater, in movies, on television, etc.

**show·case** /ˈʃoʊkeɪs/ ***noun*** [C] **1** a box with a glass top or sides that is used for showing objects in a store, museum, etc. **2** [usually sing.] an event that presents sb's abilities or the good qualities of sth in an attractive way: *The festival was **a showcase for** young musicians.* ▶ **show·case *verb*** [T]: *Jack found a film role that showcased all his talents.*

**show·down** /ˈʃoʊdaʊn/ ***noun*** [C] a final argument at the end of a long disagreement

★**show·er**[1] /ˈʃaʊər/ ***noun*** [C] **1** a way of washing your body by standing under running water: *He took a shower after the football practice.* **2** a place in a bathroom where you can stand under running water to wash your whole body: *She's in the shower.* **3** a short period of rain **4** a lot of very small objects that fall together: *a shower of debris* **5** a party at which people give presents to a woman who is about to get married or have a baby: *a bridal shower*

**show·er**[2] /ˈʃaʊər/ ***verb*** **1** [T] **shower sb/sth with sth** to cause a great number of very small objects to fall on sb/sth: *to be showered with debris/broken glass/confetti* ◇ (*figurative*) *He was showered with praise for his excellent work.* **2** [I] to take a SHOWER[1] (1)

ˈ**shower cap *noun*** [C] a plastic hat that you wear to keep your hair dry when you take a shower

**show·girl** /ˈʃoʊgərl/ ***noun*** [C] a female performer who sings and dances in a musical SHOW[1] (2)

**show·ing** /ˈʃoʊɪŋ/ ***noun*** **1** [C] an act of showing a movie, etc.: *The second showing of the movie begins at 8 o'clock.* **2** [sing.] how sb/sth behaves; how successful sb/sth is in a competition, etc.: *After a strong showing throughout the campaign, he should win the party's nomination.*

**shown** *past participle of* SHOW[2]

**show·off** /ˈʃoʊɔf; -ɑf/ ***noun*** [C] a person who tries to impress others by showing them how good he/she is at sth: *She's such a showoff.* ➲ This word is used when we are criticizing somebody.

**show·room** /ˈʃoʊrum/ ***noun*** [C] a type of store where products such as cars or furniture are displayed

ˈ**show-ˌstopper *noun*** [C] (*informal*) a performance that is very impressive and receives a lot of applause from the audience ▶ ˈ**show-ˌstopping *adj.***: *a show-stopping performance*

**show·time** /ˈʃoʊtaɪm/ ***noun*** [U] the time that a theater performance or movie will begin: *It's five minutes to showtime and the theater is packed.* ◇ (*figurative*) *Everybody ready? It's showtime!*

**show·y** /ˈʃoʊi/ ***adj.*** (**show·i·er**; **show·i·est**) so brightly colored, large or exaggerated that it attracts a lot of attention: *showy flowers*

**shrank** *past tense of* SHRINK

**shrap·nel** /ˈʃræpnəl/ ***noun*** [U] small pieces of metal that are thrown in various directions from an exploding bomb or bullet

**shred**[1] /ʃrɛd/ ***noun*** **1** [C, usually pl.] a small thin piece that has been cut or torn from sth: *He tore the letter to shreds.* ◇ *After the storm, the boat's sails were in shreds.* **2 a shred of sth** [sing.] (in negative sentences) a very small amount of sth: *There wasn't a shred of evidence against her.*

**shred**[2] /ʃrɛd/ ***verb*** [T] (**shred·ding**; **shred·ded**) to tear or cut sth into SHREDS[1] (1)

**shred·der** /ˈʃrɛdər/ ***noun*** [C] a machine that tears

S

sth into small pieces, especially paper, so that nobody can read what was printed on it

**shrew** /ʃru/ ***noun*** [C] **1** a small animal like a mouse with a long pointed nose and very small eyes **2** (*old-fashioned*) a bad-tempered unpleasant woman

**shrewd** /ʃrud/ ***adj.*** using or showing good judgment, especially in order to achieve success: *a shrewd politician* ◇ *a shrewd investment* ▶ **shrewd·ly** ***adv.***

**shriek** /ʃrik/ ***verb*** **1** [I] to give a sudden scream in a high voice: *He shrieked in fright.* ◇ *The girls were shrieking with laughter.* **2** [T] to scream sth in a high voice: *"Stop it!" he shrieked.* ▶ **shriek *noun*** [C]: *She gave a loud shriek of pain.*

**shrift** /ʃrɪft/ ***noun*** [U]
IDM **give sb/sth/get short shrift** to give sb/sth/get little attention or sympathy

**shrill** /ʃrɪl/ ***adj.*** (used about a sound) high and unpleasant: *a shrill whistle*

**shrimp** /ʃrɪmp/ ***noun*** [C] (*pl.* **shrimp** or **shrimps**) **1** a small sea creature with a shell that turns pink when you cook it ➲ picture at **shellfish**. **2** (*informal*) a small, physically weak person

**ˌshrimp ˈcocktail** ***noun*** [C,U] a dish eaten before the main course, consisting of shrimp served with a pink sauce

**shrine** /ʃraɪn/ ***noun*** [C] a place that is holy for members of a religion, or that people want to visit because it is associated with a special person or thing

**shrink**

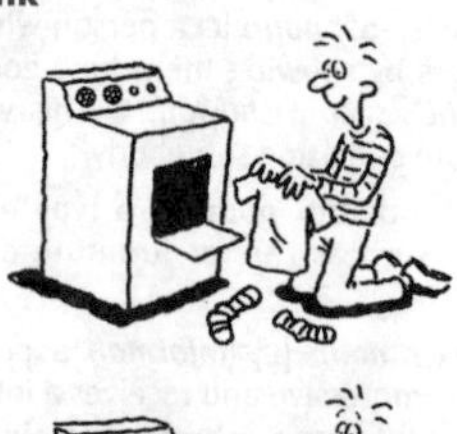

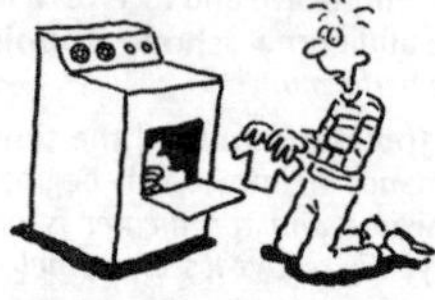

"Oh, no! My T-shirt **shrank** in the dryer!"

**shrink¹** /ʃrɪŋk/ ***verb*** [I,T] (*pt* **shrank** /ʃræŋk/ or **shrunk** /ʃrʌŋk/; *pp* **shrunk** or **shrunk·en**) to become smaller, often after being washed; to make sth smaller: *Oh no! My T-shirt shrank!* ◇ *I shrank my T-shirt. The water must have been too hot.* ◇ *The rate of inflation has shrunk to 4%.*
PHRV **shrink from sth/doing sth** to be unwilling to do sth because you find it unpleasant

**shrink²** /ʃrɪŋk/ ***noun*** [C] (*slang*) a psychiatrist or psychologist: *She sees her shrink once a week.*

**ˈshrink-wrapped** ***adj.*** wrapped tightly in a thin plastic covering: *cheese in a shrink-wrapped pack* ◇ *shrink-wrapped software*

**shriv·el** /ˈʃrɪvl/ ***verb*** [I,T] **shrivel (sth) (up)** to dry up and become smaller and full of lines, usually in hot or dry conditions; to make sth do this: *The drought is killing animals and shriveling crops.* ◇ (*figurative*) *Profits shriveled up during the recession.*

**shroud¹** /ʃraʊd/ ***noun*** [C] **1** a cloth or sheet that is used in some countries to wrap a dead body before it is buried **2** something that covers or hides sth: *a shroud of secrecy*

**shroud²** /ʃraʊd/ ***verb*** [T] (usually passive) to cover or hide sth with sth: *The tops of the mountains were shrouded in mist.* ◇ *His past is shrouded in mystery.*

**shrub** /ʃrʌb/ ***noun*** [C] a small bush

**shrub·ber·y** /ˈʃrʌbəri/ ***noun*** [C,U] (*pl.* **shrub·ber·ies**) an area planted with shrubs

**shrug** /ʃrʌg/ ***verb*** [I,T] (**shrug·ging**; **shrugged**) to raise your shoulders as a way of showing that you do not know or do not care about sth: *"Who knows?" he said and shrugged.* ◇ *"It doesn't matter to me," he said, shrugging his shoulders.*
PHRV **shrug sth off** to treat sth as if it is not important to you
▶ **shrug** ***noun*** [C, usually sing.]: *He answered his mother with a shrug.*

**shrunk, shrunken** → SHRINK

**shtick** (*also* **schtick**) /ʃtɪk/ ***noun*** [U, sing.] (*informal*) **1** a style of humor that is typical of a particular performer **2** a particular ability that sb has: *That's not my shtick.*

**shucks** /ʃʌks/ ***interjection*** (*old-fashioned, informal*) (used to express embarrassment or disappointment): *"You're real cute." "Aw shucks, do you think so?"*

**shud·der** /ˈʃʌdər/ ***verb*** [I] to shake with fear, etc.: *Just thinking about the accident makes me shudder.* ◇ *I shudder to think how much this dinner is going to cost.* ▶ **shud·der *noun*** [C]

**shuf·fle¹** /ˈʃʌfl/ ***verb*** **1** [I] to walk by sliding your feet along instead of lifting them off the ground: *A little girl shuffled past, wearing her mother's shoes.* **2** [T] **shuffle sb/sth (around)** to move things or people around so that they are in a different order or position: *My job is so boring – all I do is shuffle papers.* **3** [I,T] to mix a deck of playing cards before a game: *It's your turn to shuffle.* ◇ *He shuffled the cards carefully.*

**shuf·fle²** /ˈʃʌfl/ ***noun*** [C, usually sing.] **1** a SHUFFLING¹ (1) way of walking **2** an act of moving things or people around so that they are in a different order or position: *a major shuffle of senior management* **3** an act of SHUFFLING¹ (3) cards

**shuf·fle·board** /ˈʃʌflbɔrd/ ***noun*** [U] a game in which players use long sticks to push disks toward spaces with numbers on a board

**shun** /ʃʌn/ ***verb*** [T] (**shun·ning**; **shunned**) to avoid sb/sth; to keep away from sb/sth: *The aging actress shunned publicity.*

**shush¹** /ʃʌʃ; ʃʊʃ/ ***interjection*** (used to tell sb to be quiet): *Shush! Do you want to wake everyone up?*

**shush²** /ʃʌʃ; ʃʊʃ/ ***verb*** [T] to tell sb to be quiet, especially by saying "shush", or by putting your finger against your lips: *Lyn shushed the children.*

★**shut¹** /ʃʌt/ ***verb*** [I,T] (*pres. part.* **shut·ting**; *pt, pp* **shut**) **1** [T] to change the position of sth so that it covers a hole, etc.; to fold sth together; to close: *Could you shut the door?* ◇ *I can't shut my suitcase.* ◇ *He shut his eyes and tried to go to sleep.* **2** [I] to move or be moved into a closed position: *This window won't shut all the way.* **3** [T] to prevent sb/sth from leaving or moving; to trap sth: *She shut herself in her room and refused to come out.* ◇ *Tony shut his fingers in the door of the car.*

PHR V **shut (sth) down** (used about a factory, etc.) to be closed for a long time or forever; to close sth (a factory, etc.) for a long time or forever: *Financial problems forced the business to shut down.* ◇ *They shut down the factory for safety reasons.*

**shut sb/sth off (from sth)** to keep sb/sth apart from sth: *He shuts himself off from the rest of the world.*

**shut sth off** to turn off a supply of electricity, water, gas, etc.: *The utility company shut off gas to the building after the fire was reported.*

**shut sb/sth out 1** to keep sb/sth out: *Anna was shut out of the decision-making process.* ◇ *He tried to shut out all thoughts of the accident.* **2** to win a game without letting the other team score any points: *Pittsburgh shut out Atlanta 5-0.*

**shut up** (*informal*) to stop talking; to be quiet: *Tell her to shut up and get back to work.* ◇ *Shut up! I'm trying to work.*

NOTE It is not polite to tell somebody to shut up.

**shut sb up** (*informal*) to make sb stop talking: *Nothing can shut him up once he gets started.*

★**shut²** /ʃʌt/ *adj.* (not before a noun) in a closed position: *Make sure the door is shut before you leave.*

NOTE Remember that we can use **closed** before a noun: *a closed door*, but not **shut**.

**shut·down** /ˈʃʌtdaʊn/ *noun* [C] the closing of a company or the stopping of a machine: *Even a temporary shutdown could cost the airline millions of dollars.*

ˈ**shut-eye** *noun* [U] (*informal*) sleep

ˈ**shut-in** *noun* [C, usually pl.] a person who cannot leave his/her home very easily because he/she is sick or disabled: *He worked as a volunteer, delivering hot meals to shut-ins.*

**shut·off** /ˈʃʌt̬ɔf/ (*also* ˈ**shut-off**) *noun* **1** [C] a device for cutting off the supply of water, gas, electricity, etc.: *a shutoff valve* **2** [U] the act of stopping the flow of water, gas, electricity, etc. into sth

**shut·out** /ˈʃʌt̬aʊt/ *noun* [C] a sports game in which one side or team prevents the other from getting any points

**shut·ter** /ˈʃʌt̬ər/ *noun* [C] **1** one of a pair of wooden or metal covers that is attached to a window and that can be opened or closed ➲ picture on study page **A31**. **2** the part at the front of a camera that opens for a very short time to let light in so that a photograph can be taken

**shut·ter·bug** /ˈʃʌt̬ərbʌg/ *noun* [C] (*informal*) a person who likes to take a lot of photographs

**shut·tle¹** /ˈʃʌt̬l/ *noun* [C] **1** an airplane, a bus or a train that travels regularly between two places: *I'm catching the seven o'clock shuttle to Washington.* **2** = SPACE SHUTTLE

**shut·tle²** /ˈʃʌt̬l/ *verb* **1** [T] to carry people between two places that are close, making regular trips between the two places: *A bus shuttles passengers back and forth from the station to the terminal.* **2** [I] **shuttle (between A and B)** to travel between two places frequently: *Her childhood was spent shuttling between her mother and father.*

★**shy¹** /ʃaɪ/ *adj.* (**shy·er**; **shy·est**) nervous and uncomfortable with other people. Shy people do not usually say very much to people they do not know: *She's very shy around strangers.* ◇ *a shy smile* ◇ *He isn't shy about expressing his opinions.* ▶ **shy·ly** *adv.*: *Meg smiled shyly at the camera.* ▶ **shy·ness** *noun* [U]: *He didn't overcome his shyness until he was in his twenties.*

**shy²** /ʃaɪ/ *verb* [I] (*pres. part.* **shy·ing**; *3rd person sing. pres.* **shies**; *pt, pp* **shied**)

PHR V **shy (away) from sth/from doing sth** to avoid doing sth because you are afraid: *He shied away from telling her the truth.*

**shy·ster** /ˈʃaɪstər/ *noun* [C] (*informal*) a dishonest person, especially a lawyer or businessman

**sib·ling** /ˈsɪblɪŋ/ *noun* [C] (*formal*) a brother or a sister: *Jealousy between siblings is very common.*

NOTE In ordinary language we use **brother(s) and sister(s)**: *Do you have any brothers and sisters?*

**sic** /sɪk/ *verb* [T] (*pres. part.* **sic·cing**; *pt, pp* **sicced**) (*also* **sick**) (*informal*) to attack sb: *Sic him, Duke!* (= said to a dog)

PHR V **sic sth on sb** (*informal*) to tell a dog to attack sb

★**sick** /sɪk/ *adj.* **1** not in good health; not well; ill: *a sick child* ◇ *You're more likely to get sick when you haven't had enough sleep.* ◇ *I was sick last week and missed three days of school.* ➲ Look at the note at **ill**. **2** (not before a noun) (*also* **sick to your stomach**) having a bad feeling in your stomach so that any food in it may be thrown up through your mouth: *I feel sick – I think it was that fish I ate.* **3** (*informal*) cruel or in bad taste: *a sick joke about blind people* **4 the sick** *noun* [pl.] people who are not in good health: *The sick and injured were carried away from the battlefield.*

IDM **be sick** to bring food up from the stomach through your mouth: *I think I'm going to be sick.*

**be sick (and tired) of sb/sth**; **be sick to death of sb/sth** to feel tired of or annoyed by sb/sth: *I'm sick and tired of his attitude.*

**make sb sick** to make sb very angry: *Oh, quit complaining. You make me sick!*

•**sick·bay** /ˈsɪkbeɪ/ (*also* ˈ**sick bay**) *noun* [C] a room or rooms, for example on a ship or in a school, with beds for people who are sick

**sick·bed** /ˈsɪkbɛd/ *noun* [sing.] the bed on which a person who is sick is lying: *The President left his sickbed to attend the ceremony.*

ˌ**sick ˈbuilding ˌsyndrome** *noun* [U] a condition that affects people who work in large offices, making them feel tired and causing headaches, sore eyes and breathing problems, thought to be caused by, for example, the lack of fresh air or by chemicals in the air that people breathe

ˈ**sick day** *noun* [C] a day when you are unable to go to work because of illness

S

**sick·en** /'sɪkən/ ***verb*** [T] to make sb feel disgusted: *Even the smell of the place sickens me.*

**sick·en·ing** /'sɪkənɪŋ/ ***adj.*** disgusting; very unpleasant: *It was a sickening sight.*

**sick·le** /'sɪkl/ ***noun*** [C] a tool with a curved blade and a short handle, used for cutting grass, etc.

**'sick leave** ***noun*** [U] a period of time spent away from work, etc. because of illness: *Joe has been on sick leave for two weeks.*

**ˌsickle ˌcell a'nemia** ***noun*** [U] a serious form of anemia that is found mostly in people of African family origins, which is passed down from parents to children

**sick·ly** /'sɪkli/ ***adj.*** **1** often sick: *He was a sickly child.* **2** not looking healthy and strong: *She looked pale and sickly.* ◇ *sickly plants* **3** that makes you feel sick, especially because it is too sweet or full of false emotion: *a sickly sweet smell* ◇ *She gave me a sickly smile.* **4** (used about colors) unpleasant to look at: *a sickly green color*

**sick·ness** /'sɪknəs/ ***noun*** **1** [U] the state of being sick: *A lot of workers are absent because of sickness.* **2** [C,U] a particular type of illness: *motion sickness*

**sick·o** /'sɪkoʊ/ ***noun*** [C] (*pl.* **sick·os**) (*informal*) a person who gets enjoyment from doing strange and cruel things: *child molesters and other sickos*

**'sick pay** ***noun*** [U] pay given to an employee who is away from work because of illness

★**side[1]** /saɪd/ ***noun*** [C]
➤SURFACE **1** any of the flat outer surfaces of an object: *A cube has six sides.* ◇ *this side up* (= an instruction on a box, etc. that tells you which way to store it)
➤NOT TOP OR BOTTOM **2** any of the flat outer surfaces of an object except the top or the bottom: *A box has a top, a bottom and four sides.*
➤LEFT/RIGHT **3** any of the surfaces of sth except the top, bottom, front or back: *I went around to the side of the building.* ◇ *The side of the car was damaged.* **4** the right or the left part of your body, especially from under your arm to the top of your leg: *She lay on her side.* **5** either of the two parts of a place or an object, separated by a real or an imaginary line: *She was arrested for driving on the wrong side of the road.* ◇ *He moved to the other side of the room.* ◇ *on the other side of the wall* ◇ (*figurative*) *We don't often see her generous side.*
➤EDGE **6** the edge of sth; the area near this: *A triangle has three sides.* ◇ *He waited at the side of the road.*
➤OF STH FLAT AND THIN **7** either of the two flat surfaces of sth thin: *Write on both sides of the paper.*
➤OF FOOD **8** = SIDE ORDER
➤IN GAME/WAR/ARGUMENT **9** either of two teams or groups of people who play or fight against each other: *Whose side are you on?* (= Who do you support?) ◇ *The two sides agreed to stop fighting.* **10** the position, opinion or attitude of a person or group of people that is different from that held by another person or group of people: *Do you believe his side of the story?*
➤OF FAMILY **11** your mother's or your father's family: *There is no history of cancer on his mother's side.*

IDM **from side to side** moving continuously from right to left and back again: *The boat rocked from side to side.*
**get on the right/wrong side of sb** to please/annoy sb: *He tried to get on the right side of his new boss.*
**on/from all sides** in/from all directions; generally: *There was agreement on all sides.*
**on the big, small, high, etc. side** (*informal*) slightly too big, small, high, etc.
**on the safe side** → SAFE[1]
**on the side 1** in addition to your main job: *He's a waiter on the side.* **2** served separately: *a salad with dressing on the side*
**right side up** → RIGHT[1]
**side by side** next to each other; close together: *They walked side by side along the road.*
**take sides (with sb)** to show that you support one person rather than another: *Parents should never take sides when their children are fighting.*

**side[2]** /saɪd/ ***verb*** [I]
PHRV **side with sb (against sb)** to support sb in an argument: *She always sides with her son against her husband.*

**side[3]** /saɪd/ ***adj.*** (only *before* a noun) at the SIDE[1] (3) of a building: *The thief entered the house by breaking a side window.*

**side·bar** /'saɪdbɑr/ ***noun*** [C] **1** a short article in a newspaper or magazine, usually with a box drawn around it, that is placed next to another article and gives extra information relating to it **2** (in a court of law) a discussion between the lawyers and the judge during a court case, which the jury are not able to hear

**side·burns** /'saɪdbərnz/ ***noun*** [pl.] hair that grows down a man's face in front of and below his ears

**side·car** /'saɪdkɑr/ ***noun*** [C] a small vehicle attached to the side of a motorcycle in which a passenger can ride

**-sided** /'saɪdəd/ ***combining form*** having a certain number or type of sides: *A cube is a six-sided figure.*

**'side dish** ***noun*** [C] = SIDE ORDER

**'side efˌfect** ***noun*** [C] an unpleasant effect that sth may have in addition to the effects it is supposed to have: *Side effects of the drug may include headaches or diarrhea.*

**side·kick** /'saɪdkɪk/ ***noun*** [C] (*informal*) a person who helps and spends a lot of time with sb who is more important: *the Lone Ranger and his sidekick, Tonto*

**side·line** /'saɪdlaɪn/ ***noun*** **1 the sidelines** [pl.] the lines that mark the two long sides of a sports field or tennis court; the area behind this outside the playing area: *The team's coach was giving orders from the sidelines.* ◇ (*figurative*) *It was a controversial issue, so she decided to remain on the sidelines.* ➲ picture at **tennis**. **2** [C] something that you do in addition to your regular job, usually to earn extra money: *He's an engineer, but he makes furniture as a sideline.*

**side·long** /'saɪdlɔŋ/ ***adj.*** (only *before* a noun) (used about a look) out of the corner of your eye, especially in a way that is secret or disapproving: *She cast* ***a sidelong glance*** *at Eric to see if he had noticed her blunder.*

**ˈside ˌorder** (*also* **ˈside dish**, *informal* **side**) ***noun*** [C] an item of food that you order in a restaurant to have with your main meal: *I'll have a steak with a side (order) of fries.*

**side·show** /ˈsaɪdʃoʊ/ ***noun*** [C] **1** a separate small show or attraction at a fair or circus where you pay to see a performance or take part in a game **2** an activity or event that is much less important than the main activity or event

**side·step** /ˈsaɪdstɛp/ ***verb*** [T] (*pres. part.* **side·step·ping**; *pt, pp* **side·stepped**) **1** to avoid answering a question or dealing with a problem: *Did you notice how she neatly sidestepped the question?* ◇ *He sidestepped the issue by saying it was not his responsibility.* **2** to avoid sth, for example being hit, by stepping to one side: *He cleverly sidestepped the tackle.*

**ˈside street** ***noun*** [C] a narrow or less important street that usually joins a main street

**side·swipe** /ˈsaɪdswaɪp/ ***noun*** [C] **1** a hit from the side: *a sideswipe by a truck* **2 sideswipe (at sb/sth)** (*informal*) a critical comment made about sb/sth while you are talking about sb/sth completely different: *It was a good speech, but he couldn't resist taking a sideswipe at his opponent.* ▶ **side·swipe** ***verb*** [T]: *The bus sideswiped two parked cars.*

**side·track** /ˈsaɪdtræk/ ***verb*** [T] (often passive) to make sb forget what he/she is supposed to be doing or talking about and start doing or talking about sth less important

**side·walk** /ˈsaɪdwɔk/ ***noun*** [C] a slightly raised narrow surface at the side of a street, for people to walk on: *The kids rode their bikes on the sidewalk.* ➲ Picture on study page **A31**.

★**side·ways** /ˈsaɪdweɪz/ ***adj., adv.*** **1** to, toward or from one side: *The truck slid sideways and hit a barrier.* ◇ *a sideways glance* **2** with one of the sides at the top: *We'll have to turn the table sideways to get it through the door.*

**side·wind·er** /ˈsaɪdˌwaɪndər/ ***noun*** [C] a poisonous North American snake, found in the desert, which moves sideways by throwing its body in an S shape

**sid·ing** /ˈsaɪdɪŋ/ ***noun*** [C] horizontal boards that cover the outside walls of a house ➲ Picture on study page **A31**.

**si·dle** /ˈsaɪdl/ ***verb*** [I] **sidle up/over (to sb/sth)** to move toward sb/sth in a nervous way, as if you do not want anybody to notice you

**SIDS** /sɪdz/ (*also* **ˈcrib death**) ***noun*** [U] the abbreviation for "sudden infant death syndrome"; the sudden death while sleeping of a baby which appears to be healthy

**siege** /sidʒ/ ***noun*** [C,U] **1** the situation in which an army surrounds a town in order to capture it. When there is a siege nobody is allowed into or out of the town: *the siege of Sarajevo* **2** a situation in which a building containing a criminal is surrounded by police for a long period of time: *The house was under siege for several hours, until the man released the hostages.*

**si·es·ta** /siˈɛstə/ ***noun*** [C] a short rest that people take after lunch, especially in hot countries: *to have/take a siesta*

**sieve** /sɪv/ ***noun*** [C] a type of kitchen tool that has a metal or plastic net, used for separating solids from liquids or very small pieces of food from large pieces ➲ picture at **kitchen.** ▶ **sieve** ***verb*** [T]

**sift** /sɪft/ ***verb*** **1** [T] to pass flour, sugar, etc. through a sieve **2** [I,T] **sift (through) sth** to examine sth very carefully: *It took weeks to sift through all the evidence.*

**sigh** /saɪ/ ***verb*** **1** [I] to let out a long, deep breath that shows you are tired, sad, relieved, etc.: *She sighed with disappointment at the news.* **2** [T] to say sth with a SIGH (1): *"I'm so tired," he sighed.* ▶ **sigh** ***noun*** [C]: *"Well, that's over," she said, with a sigh of relief.*

★**sight**[1] /saɪt/ ***noun***

➤ABILITY TO SEE **1** [U] the ability to see: *He lost his sight in the war* (= he became blind).

➤ACT OF SEEING **2** [sing.] **sight of sb/sth** the act of seeing sb/sth: *We flew over Paris and had our first sight of the Eiffel Tower.* ◇ *Throw that dress away. I can't stand the sight of it anymore.*

➤WHERE SB/STH CAN BE SEEN **3** [U] a position where sb/sth can be seen: *When the finish line was within sight, the Kenyan runner accelerated.* ◇ *She didn't let her nephew out of her sight.*

➤WHAT YOU CAN SEE **4** [C] something that you see: *the familiar sights and sounds of home*

➤INTERESTING PLACES **5 sights** [pl.] places of interest that are often visited by tourists: *When you come to New York, I'll show you the sights.*

IDM **at first glance/sight** → FIRST[1]

**catch sight/a glimpse of sb/sth** → CATCH[1]

**in sight** likely to happen or come soon: *A peace settlement is in sight.*

**lose sight of sb/sth** → LOSE

**on sight** as soon as sb/sth is seen: *The soldiers were ordered to shoot the enemy on sight.*

**set your sights on sth** to decide that sth is your goal and try hard to achieve it: *Josh set his sights on an acting career.*

**sight unseen** if you buy sth sight unseen, you do not have an opportunity to see it before you buy it

**sight**[2] /saɪt/ ***verb*** [T] to see sb/sth, especially after looking out for him/her/it: *The wanted man has been sighted in Miami.*

**sight·ed** /ˈsaɪt̬əd/ ***adj.*** **1** able to see; not blind: *the blind parents of sighted children* **2 -sighted** (in compounds) able to see in the way mentioned: *partially sighted* ◇ *shortsighted* ◇ *nearsighted*

**sight·ing** /ˈsaɪt̬ɪŋ/ ***noun*** [C] an occasion when sb/sth is seen: *the first sighting of a new star*

**ˈsight-read** ***verb*** [I,T] to play or sing written music when you see it for the first time, without practicing it first

**sight·see·ing** /ˈsaɪtsiɪŋ/ ***noun*** [U] visiting the sights of a city, etc. as a tourist: *We did some sightseeing in Rome.*

**sight·se·er** /ˈsaɪtsiər/ ***noun*** [C] a person who visits the sights of a city ➲ Look at **tourist**.

**sig·ma** /ˈsɪgmə/ ***noun*** [C] (*symbol* Σ, σ) the eighteenth letter of the Greek alphabet ➲ Look at the note at **fraternity**.

★**sign**[1] /saɪn/ ***noun*** [C]

➤FOR INFORMATION/WARNING **1** a board, notice, etc. that gives you a piece of information, an

S

instruction or a warning: *What does that sign say?* ◇ *a road sign* ◇ *Follow the signs to Route 66.*

➤SHOWING STH **2 sign (of sth)** something that shows that sb/sth is present or exists or may happen: *The patient was showing some signs of improvement.* ◇ *The first sign of trouble was last week.* ◇ *As we drove down Main Street, there was no sign of life anywhere* (= we couldn't see anyone).

➤MOVEMENT **3** a movement that you make with your head, hands or arms that has a particular meaning: *I made a sign for him to follow me.* ◇ *He gave the thumbs-up sign to his crew.*

➤SYMBOL **4** a type of shape, mark or symbol that has a particular meaning: *a plus sign* ◇ *the dollar sign*

➤STAR SIGN **5** (*also* ˌ**sign of the ˈzodiac**) one of the twelve divisions or symbols of the zodiac: *I'm a Leo. What's your sign?*

★**sign²** /saɪn/ ***verb*** **1** [I,T] to write your name on a letter, document, etc. to show that you have written it or that you agree with what it says. When you sign your name you always write it in the same way: *"Could you sign here, please?"* ◇ *I forgot to sign the check.* ◇ *The two presidents signed the treaty.* **2** [T] (in sports, entertainment, etc.) to employ sb by having him/her SIGN² (1) an official statement: *The Baltimore Orioles signed Fernandez to a one-year contract.* **3** [I,T] to communicate by using sign language

PHR V **sign in/out** to write your name to show you have arrived at or left a building, etc.

**sign up (for sth)** to agree formally to do sth: *I signed up for driving lessons.*

★**sig·nal¹** /ˈsɪgnəl/ ***noun*** [C] **1** a sign, an action or a sound that sends a particular message: *The army waited for the signal to attack.* ◇ *The flag went down as a signal for the race to begin.* **2** a set of lights used to tell drivers when they should stop or go: *a traffic signal* ➲ Look also at **turn signal**. **3** a series of radio waves, etc. that are sent out or received: *a signal from a satellite*

★**sig·nal²** /ˈsɪgnəl/ ***verb*** [I,T] to make a signal; to send a particular message using a signal: *She was signaling wildly that something was wrong.* ◇ *He signaled his disapproval by leaving the room.* ◇ *The police officer signaled to the driver to stop.*

**sig·na·to·ry** /ˈsɪgnəˌtɔri/ ***noun*** [C] (*pl.* **sig·na·to·ries**) (*formal*) a person, a country or an organization that has signed an official agreement: *a signatory of the Declaration of Independence*

★**sig·na·ture** /ˈsɪgnətʃər/ ***noun*** [C] a person's name, written by himself/herself and always written in the same way: *I couldn't read his signature.*

**sig·nif·i·cance** /sɪgˈnɪfəkəns/ ***noun*** [U] the importance or meaning of sth: *Few people realized the significance of the discovery.*

★**sig·nif·i·cant** /sɪgˈnɪfəkənt/ ***adj.*** **1** important: *Police said that the time of the murder was extremely significant.* **2** so large that you notice it: *There has been a significant increase in the number of crimes reported this year.* **3** having a particular meaning: *She gave me a significant smile.*

**sig·nif·i·cant·ly** /sɪgˈnɪfəkəntli/ ***adv.*** **1** in a noticeable way: *Attitudes have changed significantly since the 1970s.* **2** in a way that shows a particular meaning: *He thanked almost everybody but, significantly, he did not mention Terry.*

**sigˌnificant ˈother** ***noun*** [C] your husband, wife, partner or sb that you have a special relationship with

**sig·ni·fy** /ˈsɪgnəfaɪ/ ***verb*** [T] (*pres. part.* **sig·ni·fy·ing**; *3rd person sing. pres.* **sig·ni·fies**; *pt, pp* **sig·ni·fied**) (*formal*) to be a sign of sth; to mean: *What do those lights signify?*

ˈ**sign ˌlanguage** ***noun*** [U] a language, used especially by people who cannot hear or speak, using hand movements instead of spoken words

**Sikh** /sik/ ***noun*** [C] a member of one of the religions of India (Sikhism) that developed from Hinduism but teaches that there is only one god ▶ **Sikh·ism** /ˈsikɪsm/ ***noun*** [U]

**si·lage** /ˈsaɪlɪdʒ/ ***noun*** [U] grass or other green crops that are stored without being dried and are used to feed farm animals in winter

★**si·lence¹** /ˈsaɪləns/ ***noun*** **1** [U] complete quiet; no sound: *A loud crash broke the silence.* ◇ *There must be absolute silence during the exam.* **2** [C] a period when nobody speaks or makes a noise: *His response was a stony silence.* **3** [U] not making any comments on sth: *I can't understand his silence on the matter.*

IDM **in silence** without talking or making a noise

**si·lence²** /ˈsaɪləns/ ***verb*** [T] to make sb/sth be silent or quiet: *She silenced the crowd by raising her hand.* ◇ *He was determined to silence his critics* (= to make them stop criticizing him).

**si·lenc·er** /ˈsaɪlənsər/ ***noun*** [C] a part that can be attached to the end of a gun to reduce the noise when it is fired

**si·lent** /ˈsaɪlənt/ ***adj.*** **1** making no noise; very quiet: *The house was empty and silent.* **2** not speaking; not using spoken words: *The police officer told her she had the right to remain silent.* ◇ *a silent prayer* (= one that is not said out loud) ◇ *So far, she has remained silent about her future plans.* **3** (of a letter) not pronounced: *The "b" in "comb" is silent.* ▶ **si·lent·ly** ***adv.***

**sil·hou·ette** /ˌsɪluˈɛt/ ***noun*** [C] the dark outline or black shape of sth seen against a light background

**sil·i·con** /ˈsɪlɪkɑn; -kən/ ***noun*** [U] (*symbol* **Si**) a chemical substance that is used for making computer parts (**chips**), glass, etc.

**sil·i·cone** /ˈsɪləkoʊn/ ***noun*** [U] a chemical compound of silicon. There are several different types of silicone, used to make paint, artificial rubber, varnish, etc.: *a silicone breast implant*

★**silk** /sɪlk/ ***noun*** [U] the soft smooth cloth that is made from threads produced by an insect: *a silk blouse*

**silk·screen** /ˈsɪlkskrin/ (*also* ˈ**silk screen**) ***noun*** **1** [U] a method of printing in which ink is forced through a design cut in a piece of fine cloth: *silkscreen prints* **2** [C] a picture, etc. produced by this method: *Warhol's silkscreen of Marilyn Monroe* ▶ **silk·screen** ***verb*** [T] (usually passive)

**silk·y** /ˈsɪlki/ ***adj.*** (**silk·i·er**; **silk·i·est**) smooth, soft and shiny; like silk: *silky hair*

**sill** /sɪl/ ***noun*** [C] a long thin piece of wood that is at the bottom of a window

★**sil·ly** /ˈsɪli/ ***adj.*** (**sil·li·er**; **sil·li·est**) **1** not showing thought or understanding; foolish: *a silly question* ◇ *Stop being so silly!* **2** appearing ridiculous so that people will laugh: *I'm not wearing that costume – I'd look too silly in it.* ▶ **sil·li·ness** ***noun*** [U]

**si·lo** /ˈsaɪloʊ/ ***noun*** [C] (*pl.* **si·los**) a tall round building on a farm, used for storing grain ➲ picture at **barn**

**silt** /sɪlt/ ***noun*** [U] sand, soil or mud that is carried along by a river and then left somewhere when the river flows more slowly

★**sil·ver**[1] /ˈsɪlvər/ ***noun*** [U] **1** a valuable gray-white metal that is used for making jewelry, ornaments, coins, etc.: *That's a nice ring. Is it silver?* **2** objects that are made of silver, e.g. cups, dishes, etc.: *The thieves stole some jewelry and some valuable silver.*

★**sil·ver**[2] /ˈsɪlvər/ ***adj.*** made of SILVER[1] (1) or having the color of silver: *a silver spoon* ◇ *a silver sports car*

**ˌsilver ˌanniˈversary** ***noun*** [C] the 25th anniversary of a wedding ➲ Look at **golden anniversary**.

**sil·ver·fish** /ˈsɪlvərfɪʃ/ ***noun*** [C] (*pl.* **sil·ver·fish**) a small silver insect without wings that lives in houses and that can cause damage to materials such as cloth and paper

**ˌsilver ˈmedal** ***noun*** [C] a small flat round piece of silver that is given to the person or team that comes second in a sports competition: *to win a silver medal at the Olympic Games* ➲ Look at **gold medal** and **bronze medal**.

**ˌsilver ˈmedalist** ***noun*** [C] a person who wins a silver medal

**the ˌsilver ˈscreen** ***noun*** [sing.] (*old-fashioned*) the movie industry: *stars of the silver screen*

**sil·ver·smith** /ˈsɪlvərsmɪθ/ ***noun*** [C] a person who makes, repairs or sells articles made of silver

**sil·ver·ware** /ˈsɪlvərwɛr/ ***noun*** [U] knives, forks, spoons, etc. that are made of silver or some other metal

**sim** /sɪm/ ***noun*** [C] (*informal*) a computer or video game that artificially creates the feeling of experiencing (**simulates**) an activity such as flying an aircraft or playing a sport

**SIM card** /ˈsɪm kɑrd/ ***noun*** [C] a plastic card inside a cellular phone that stores personal information about the person using the phone

★**sim·i·lar** /ˈsɪmələr/ ***adj.*** **similar (to sb/sth)** the same in a way or in some ways but not completely the same: *All the books he writes are very similar.* ◇ *Your handwriting is very similar to mine.*

**sim·i·lar·i·ty** /ˌsɪməˈlærət̬i/ ***noun*** (*pl.* **sim·i·lar·i·ties**) **1** [U] the quality of being similar: *I noticed the similarity in the way the two sisters thought and spoke.* **2** [C] a way in which people or things are similar: *Although there are some similarities between the two towns, there are a lot of differences too.*

★**sim·i·lar·ly** /ˈsɪmələrli/ ***adv.*** (*formal*) also; in a similar way: *The plural of "shelf" is "shelves." Similarly, the plural of "wolf" is "wolves."*

**sim·il·e** /ˈsɪməli/ ***noun*** [C,U] a way of describing sth by comparing it to sth else which has the same qualities, using the words "like" or "as." For example, if you say that sb has hair like gold, it means that he/she has very shiny blond hair. ➲ Look also at **metaphor**.

**sim·mer** /ˈsɪmər/ ***verb*** [I,T] to cook gently in a liquid that is just below the boiling point: *Let the vegetables simmer for a few more minutes.*

PHR V **simmer down** (*informal*) to become more calm and less angry, excited, etc.

**sim·pa·ti·co** /sɪmˈpɑt̬ɪkoʊ; -ˈpæ-/ ***adj.*** (*informal*) **1** (used about a person) pleasant; easy to like **2** (used about a person) with similar interests and ideas to yours SYN **compatible**

**sim·per** /ˈsɪmpər/ ***verb*** [I] (*written*) to smile in a silly and annoying way: *a silly simpering girl* ◇ *He just simpered at me.*

★**sim·ple** /ˈsɪmpl/ ***adj.***

➤ EASY **1** easy to understand, do or use; not difficult or complicated: *This dictionary is written in simple English.* ◇ *a simple task* ◇ *I can't just quit my job. It's not as simple as that.*

➤ BASIC/PLAIN **2** without decoration or unnecessary extra things; plain: *a simple black dress* ◇ *The food is simple but perfectly cooked.*

➤ ORDINARY **3** (used about a person or a way of life) natural and uncomplicated: *a simple life in the country*

➤ FOR EMPHASIS **4** (used for saying that the thing you are talking about is the only thing that is important or true): *I'm not going to buy it for the simple reason that I don't have enough money.*

➤ NOT INTELLIGENT **5** (*old-fashioned*) unintelligent; slow to understand

**ˌsimple-ˈminded** ***adj.*** not intelligent; not able to understand how complicated things are: *a simple-minded person* ◇ *a simple-minded view/approach*

**the ˌsimple ˈpast** ***noun*** [sing.] = PAST TENSE

**the ˌsimple ˈpresent** ***noun*** [sing.] = PRESENT TENSE

**sim·ple·ton** /ˈsɪmpltən/ ***noun*** [C] (*old-fashioned*) a person who is not very intelligent and can be tricked easily

**sim·plic·i·ty** /sɪmˈplɪsət̬i/ ***noun*** [U] **1** the quality of being uncomplicated and easy to understand, do or use: *We all admired the simplicity of the plan.* **2** the quality of having no decoration or unnecessary extra things: *I like the simplicity of her paintings.*

**sim·pli·fy** /ˈsɪmpləfaɪ/ ***verb*** [T] (*pres. part.* **sim·pli·fy·ing**; *3rd person sing. pres.* **sim·pli·fies**; *pt, pp* **sim·pli·fied**) to make sth easier to do or understand; to make sth less complicated: *The process of registering to vote has been simplified.* ▶ **sim·pli·fi·ca·tion** /ˌsɪmpləfəˈkeɪʃn/ ***noun*** [C,U]

**sim·plis·tic** /sɪmˈplɪstɪk/ ***adj.*** making sth that is complicated seem simpler than it really is

★**sim·ply** /ˈsɪmpli/ ***adv.*** **1** in a way that makes sth easy to understand: *Could you explain it more simply?* **2** in a plain way; without decoration or unnecessary extra things: *They live simply, with very few luxuries.* **3** (used for emphasis) absolutely; completely: *This is simply the best book ever written on the subject.* **4** only; just: *Don't get mad. The whole problem is simply a misunderstanding.*

**sim·u·late** /ˈsɪmyəleɪt/ ***verb*** [T] to create the effect or appearance of sth else: *The astronauts*

S

*trained in a machine that simulates conditions in space.*

**sim·u·la·tion** /ˌsɪmyəˈleɪʃn/ ***noun*** [C,U] the act of simulating or a simulated form of a real situation, event, etc.: *a computer simulation of a trip in the space shuttle*

**si·mul·cast** /ˈsaɪmlkæst/ ***verb*** [T] (*pt, pp* **sim·ul·cast**) to broadcast sth on radio and television at the same time or on two or more channels: *It will be simulcast live to 201 countries.* ▶ **sim·ul·cast *noun*** [C]

**si·mul·ta·ne·ous** /ˌsaɪmlˈteɪniəs/ ***adj.*** happening at exactly the same time: *simultaneous broadcasts of the President's speech on all major TV networks* ▶ **si·mul·ta·ne·ous·ly *adv.***

**SIN** /sɪn/ ***noun*** [C] (*Cdn*) = SOCIAL INSURANCE NUMBER

**sin¹** /sɪn/ ***noun*** [C,U] an act or way of behaving that breaks a religious law: *He believes it is a sin for two people to live together without being married.* ◇ *They confess their sins to the priest every week.*

**sin²** /sɪn/ ***verb*** [I] (**sin<u>n</u>ing**; **sin<u>n</u>ed**) to do sth that breaks a religious law ➲ Look at **sinner**.

★**since¹** /sɪns/ ***prep.*** from a particular time in the past until a later time in the past or until now: *It was the first time they'd won since 1984.* ◇ *I haven't seen him since last Tuesday.* ◇ *Where have you been? I've been waiting for you since 5:30.* ◇ *She has had a number of jobs since college.*

> NOTE We use both **since** and **for** to talk about how long something has been happening. We use **since** when we are talking about the *beginning* of the period of time, and **for** when we are talking about the *length* of the period of time: *I've known her since 2001.* ◇ *I've known her for four years.*

★**since²** /sɪns/ ***conj.*** **1** from the time when sth happened until a later time in the past or until now: *He hasn't written to us since he moved to Britain.* ◇ *I've been working in a bank ever since I finished high school.* ◇ *It was strange to see my old house again because I hadn't been there since I was a child.* **2** because; as: *Since they obviously forgot to call me, I'll have to call them.*

**since³** /sɪns/ ***adv.*** **1** from a particular time in the past until a later time in the past or until now: *He had come to see us a few weeks earlier, but he hadn't been back since.* ◇ *We went out for dinner together about six months ago, but I haven't seen her since.* ◇ *My parents bought this house in 1985, and we've lived here ever since.* **2** at a time after a particular time in the past: *We got divorced two years ago and she has since married someone else.* ◇ *He had dropped out of school at the age of 16 and had since found a job in a restaurant.*

★**sin·cere** /sɪnˈsɪr/ ***adj.*** **1** (used about a person) really meaning or believing what you say; honest; not pretending: *Do you think she was being sincere when she said she admired me?* **2** (used about sth that a person says or feels) true; that is really meant: *Please accept our sincere apologies.* OPP **insincere** ▶ **sin·cere·ly *adv.***: *I am sincerely grateful to you for all your help.* ◇ *Sincerely, ...* (at the end of a formal letter)

**sin·cer·i·ty** /sɪnˈsɛrəţi/ ***noun*** [U] the quality of being sincere; honesty: *Nobody doubts the sincerity of her political views.* OPP **insincerity**

**sin·ew** /ˈsɪnyu/ ***noun*** [C,U] a strong band of tissue in the body that joins a muscle to a bone

**sin·ful** /ˈsɪnfl/ ***adj.*** morally wrong or evil: *sinful acts/thoughts* ◇ *It is sinful to lie.* ◇ (*informal*) *It's sinful to waste good food!* ▶ **sin·ful·ly *adv.*** /-fəli/

★**sing** /sɪŋ/ ***verb*** [I,T] (*pt* **sang** /sæŋ/; *pp* **sung** /sʌŋ/) to make musical sounds with the voice: *He always sings when he's in the shower.* ◇ *The birds were singing outside my window.* ◇ *She sang all her most popular songs at the concert.* ▶ **sing·ing *noun*** [U]: *singing lessons*

**sing·a·long** /ˈsɪŋəlɔŋ/ ***noun*** [C] an informal occasion at which people sing songs together: *a singalong in the local bar*

**singe** /sɪndʒ/ ***verb*** [I,T] (*pres. part.* **singe·ing**) to burn or to make sth burn slightly on the edge or tip: *The bear's fur was singed in the forest fire.*

★**sing·er** /ˈsɪŋər/ ***noun*** [C] a person who sings, especially in public

★**sin·gle¹** /ˈsɪŋgl/ ***adj.*** **1** (only *before* a noun) only one: *He gave her a single red rose.* ◇ *I managed to finish the whole job in a single afternoon.* **2** (only *before* a noun) (used for emphasis when you are thinking about an individual thing, especially when it forms part of a group): *You answered every single question right. Good job!* ◇ *the single most important issue facing the country today* **3** not married: *Are you married, single or divorced?* ◇ *a single mother* **4** (only *before* a noun) for the use of only one person: *a single bed* ➲ Look at **double**.

IDM **(in) single file** in a line, one behind the other: *You'll have to walk (in) single file – the path is very narrow.*

**sin·gle²** /ˈsɪŋgl/ ***noun*** **1** [C] a CD or small record that has only one song on each side: *the new single from S Club 7* ➲ Look at **LP** and **album**. **2 singles** [pl.] people who are not married: *Thursday is singles night at Bill's Bar.* **3 singles** [pl.] a game of tennis, etc. in which one player plays against one other player: *the final of the women's singles* ➲ Look at **doubles**.

**sin·gle³** /ˈsɪŋgl/ ***verb*** [T]

PHR V **single sb/sth out (for sth)** to give special attention or treatment to one person or thing from a group: *He singled Sue Taylor out for praise.*

**ˌsingle-ˈbreasted** ***adj.*** (used about a jacket or coat) having only one row of buttons that fasten in the middle ➲ Compare **double-breasted**.

**ˌsingle-ˈdigit** ***adj.*** (only *before* a noun) connected with a number from 1 to 9: *single-digit inflation*

**ˌsingle-ˈfamily** ***adj.*** (only *before* a noun) (used about a house) built to be used by one family: *sales of single-family homes*

**ˌsingle-ˈhandedly** ***adv.*** done by one person; done without help from anybody else

**ˌsingle-ˈminded** ***adj.*** having one clear aim or purpose: *I admired her single-minded determination to win.*

**ˌsingle ˈparent** ***noun*** [C] a parent who takes care of his/her child or children alone: *a single-parent family*

ˌ**single-ˈsex** ***adj.*** (used about a school, education, etc.) only for boys or only for girls ➲ Look at **coeducational**.

**sin·gly** /ˈsɪŋgli/ ***adv.*** one by one; individually: *You can buy the tapes either singly or in packages of three.*

ˈ**sing-song** ***adj.*** (only *before* a noun) a sing-song voice keeps rising and falling

**sin·gu·lar**[1] /ˈsɪŋgyələr/ ***adj.*** (*grammar*) in the form that is used for talking about one person or thing only: *"Table" is a singular noun; "tables" is a plural noun.*

**sin·gu·lar**[2] /ˈsɪŋgyələr/ ***noun*** [sing.] (*grammar*) the form that is used for talking about one person or thing only: *The word "clothes" has no singular.* ◇ *What's the singular of "people?"*

**sin·gu·lar·i·ty** /ˌsɪŋgyəˈlærət̬i/ ***noun*** [U] (*formal*) the quality of sth that makes it unusual or strange: *the singularity of his sculptures*

**sin·gu·lar·ly** /ˈsɪŋgyələrli/ ***adv.*** (*formal*) very; in an unusual way: *singularly beautiful/foolish* ◇ *He chose a singularly inappropriate moment to make his request.*

**sin·is·ter** /ˈsɪnəstər/ ***adj.*** making you feel that sth bad will happen; frightening: *a sinister atmosphere* ◇ *There's something sinister about him. He frightens me.*

★**sink**[1] /sɪŋk/ ***verb*** (*pt* **sank** /sæŋk/ or **sunk** /sʌŋk/; *pp* **sunk**) **1** [I,T] to go down or make sth go down under the surface or to the bottom of water, etc.: *If you throw a stone into water, it sinks.* ◇ *The boat sank to the bottom of the ocean.* ◇ *Three ships were sunk by enemy planes.* ◇ *My feet sank into the mud.* ➲ picture at **float**. **2** [I] to get lower; to fall to a lower position or level: *After a few days, the flood water began to sink.* ◇ *We watched the sun sink slowly below the horizon.* **3** [I] (used about a person) to move or fall to a lower position, usually because you are tired or weak: *I came home very tired and sank into a chair.* **4** [I] to decrease in value, number, amount, strength, etc.: *The price of the stock has sunk from over $2 to 65¢ per share.*

IDM **your heart sinks** → HEART

PHR V **sink in** (used about information, an event, an experience, etc.) to be completely understood; to become clear in the mind: *It took a long time for the shocking news to sink in.*

**sink**[2] /sɪŋk/ ***noun*** [C] a large bowl in a kitchen or bathroom that is connected to the water supply with pipes and faucets. You wash things such as dishes, vegetables, etc. or your hands or face in a sink.

**sink·er** /ˈsɪŋkər/ ***noun*** [C] a weight that is attached to a fishing line or net to keep it under the water

IDM **hook, line and sinker** → HOOK[1]

**sink·hole** /ˈsɪŋkhoʊl/ ***noun*** [C] **1** a large circular hole that forms naturally in the ground **2** (*informal*) something that uses up a lot of money or time over a long period

**sin·ner** /ˈsɪnər/ ***noun*** [C] a person who breaks a religious law or behaves in a way that is morally wrong

**si·nus** /ˈsaɪnəs/ ***noun*** [C] (often plural) one of the spaces in the bones of the face that are connected to the nose: *I have a terrible cold and all my sinuses are blocked.*

**sip** /sɪp/ ***verb*** [I,T] (**sip·ping**; **sipped**) to drink, taking only a very small amount of liquid into your mouth at a time: *We sat in the sun, sipping lemonade.* ▶ **sip** ***noun*** [C]: *to take a sip of water*

**si·phon** /ˈsaɪfn/ ***verb*** [T] **siphon sth into/out of sth; siphon sth off/out** to remove a liquid from a container (or to transfer it from one container to another) through a tube

**sir** /sər/ ***noun*** (used as a polite way of speaking to a man, especially one of higher social or military rank than you, or one whose name you do not know): *Good morning, sir.* ◇ *Excuse me, sir – is this your briefcase?* ◇ *Dear Sir/Dear Madam:...* (= used at the beginning of a formal letter to a person that you do not know) ➲ Look also at **ma'am**.

**sire**[1] /ˈsaɪər/ ***noun*** [C] **1** (*technical*) the male parent of an animal, especially a horse ➲ Compare **dam**. **2** (*old-fashioned*) (a word that people used in the past when they addressed a king)

**sire**[2] /ˈsaɪər/ ***verb*** [T] to be the male parent of an animal, especially a horse

**si·ren** /ˈsaɪrən/ ***noun*** [C] a machine that makes a long, loud sound in order to warn people about sth, e.g. on an ambulance, a fire engine or a police car: *a police siren*

**sir·loin** /ˈsərlɔɪn/ ***noun*** [C,U] (a piece of) good quality beef that comes from the back of a cow: *a sirloin steak*

**sis** /sɪs/ ***noun*** [C] (*informal*) sister (used when you are speaking to her)

**sis·sy** /ˈsɪsi/ ***noun*** [C] (*pl.* **sis·sies**) (*informal*) a boy that other men or boys laugh at because they think he is weak or frightened, or only interested in the sort of things girls like: *The other boys kept calling him a sissy and a wimp.* ▶ **sis·sy** ***adj.***

★**sis·ter** /ˈsɪstər/ ***noun*** [C] **1** a girl or woman who has the same parents as another person: *I have one brother and two sisters.* ◇ *We're sisters.* ◇ *Keisha is my sister.* ➲ Look at **half-sister** and **stepsister**. In English there is no common word that means "both brothers and sisters": *Do you have any brothers or sisters?* The word **sibling** is very formal. **2 Sister** a member of certain female religious groups; a nun: *Sister Mary Louise* **3** (*informal*) a girl or woman who is your friend or who is from the same social class, race, etc. as you **4** a company, an organization or a ship, etc. that belongs to the same group: *We have a sister company in France.*

ˌ**sister ˈcity** ***noun*** [C] (*pl.* **sister cities**) one of two towns or cities in different countries that have a special relationship: *Okayama is San José's sister city in Japan.*

**sis·ter·hood** /ˈsɪstərhʊd/ ***noun*** **1** [U] the close loyal relationship between women who share ideas and aims **2** [C] a group of women who live in a community together, especially a religious one

ˈ**sister-in-law** ***noun*** [C] (*pl.* **sisters-in-law**) **1** the sister of your husband or wife **2** the wife of your brother

★**sit** /sɪt/ ***verb*** (*pres. part.* **sit·ting**; *pt, pp* **sat** /sæt/)
➤ ON CHAIR, ETC. **1** [I] to be in a position on a chair, etc. in which the upper part of your body is upright

S

and your weight is supported at the bottom of your back: *We sat in the back yard all afternoon.* ◇ *She was sitting on the sofa, talking to her mother.* ◇ *Just sit still and behave yourself!* **2** [I] **sit (down)** to lower the body into the position of sitting: *Come and sit next to me. I want to talk to you.* **3** [T] **sit sb (down)** to put sb into a sitting position; to make sb sit down: *He picked up his daughter and sat her down on a chair.* ◇ *She sat me down and offered me a cup of coffee.*

➤OF THINGS **4** [I] to be in a particular place or position: *The letter sat on the table for several days before anybody opened it.*

➤OF OFFICIAL GROUP **5** [I] (*formal*) (used about an official group of people) to have a meeting or series of meetings: *The Supreme Court is sitting this week.*

PHR V **sit around** (*informal*) to sit and do nothing active for a period of time: *people sitting around, visiting about the weather*

**sit back** to relax and not take an active part in what other people are doing: *Sit back and relax for a while – Bobby will mow the lawn.*

**sit in on sth** to go to a meeting, class, etc. as a visitor, but without taking part in it actively: *We sat in on a history seminar at the college.*

**sit sth out** to not take part in an activity, e.g. a game, a dance etc.: *I've played enough cards tonight; I think I'll sit this one out.*

**sit through sth** to stay in your seat until sth has finished (especially if it is boring): *I don't think I can sit through another hour of this movie.*

**sit up 1** to move into a sitting position when you have been lying down or leaning back: *Sit up straight or you'll hurt your back!* **2** to not go to bed although it is very late: *We sat up all night talking.*

**sit·com** /ˈsɪtkɑm/ ***noun*** [C] a funny program on television that shows the same characters in a different situation each week

★**site** /saɪt/ ***noun*** [C] **1** a piece of land that is used or will be used for building on or for another special purpose: *a construction site* (= a place where a building is being constructed) ◇ *The company is looking for a site for its new offices.* **2** a place where sth happened or existed in the past: *the site of a Civil War battle* **3** = WEBSITE

**sit·ter** /ˈsɪt̬ər/ ***noun*** [C] = BABYSITTER

**sit·ting** /ˈsɪt̬ɪŋ/ ***noun*** [C] **1** a period of time that a person spends sitting and doing an activity: *I read the book **in one sitting**.* **2** a period of time when sb sits or stands to have his/her picture painted or to be photographed: *It took three sittings to complete the portrait.*

**ˌsitting ˈduck** ***noun*** [C] a person or thing that is easy to attack

**ˈsitting room** ***noun*** [C] (*old-fashioned*) = LIVING ROOM

**sit·u·at·ed** /ˈsɪtʃueɪt̬əd/ ***adj.***

IDM **be situated (at, in, on, etc.)** (*formal*) to be in a particular place or position: *The hotel is conveniently situated close to the beach.*

NOTE **Be located** is more common than **be situated**.

★**sit·u·a·tion** /ˌsɪtʃuˈeɪʃn/ ***noun*** [C] the things that are happening in a particular place or at a particular time: *The situation in the Middle East is extremely serious.* ◇ *Tim is in a difficult situation right now.* ◇ *the economic situation*

**ˈsit-up** ***noun*** [C] a physical exercise in which you lie on your back and use the muscles in your stomach to raise the upper part of your body to a sitting position: *Kristi does 25 sit-ups every morning.* ➲ picture on study page **A32**.

**six** /sɪks/ ***number*** 6; one more than five: *The answers are on page six.* ◇ *She invited twenty people, but only six came.* ◇ *Six (of the students) are absent today.* ◇ *They have six cats.* ◇ *My son is six (years old) next month.* ◇ *The class is in room 6.* ◇ *a birthday card with a big six on it* ◇ *We're having dinner at six (o'clock).*

**six-** /sɪks/ ***combining form*** having 6 of the thing mentioned: *a six-day week*

**ˈsix-pack** ***noun*** [C] **1** a group of six cans or bottles that are sold together: *a six-pack of soda* **2** (*informal*) stomach muscles that are very strong and that you can see clearly across sb's stomach

**ˈsix-shooter** ***noun*** [C] a small gun that holds six bullets

**six·teen** /sɪkˈstin/ ***number*** 16; one more than fifteen ➲ For examples of how to use numbers in sentences, look at **six**. ▶ **six·teenth** /sɪkˈstinθ/ ***pronoun, det., adv.*** ➲ Look at the examples at **sixth**.

**sixˈteenth note** ***noun*** [C] (*symbol* 𝅘𝅥𝅯) (in music) a note that lasts half as long as an eighth note ➲ picture at **music**.

**sixth**[1] /sɪksθ/ ***pronoun, det., adv.*** 6th; next after fifth: *I've had five cups of coffee already, so this is my sixth.* ◇ *This is the sixth time I've tried to call him.* ◇ *Mahler's Sixth Symphony* ◇ *King George VI* (= King George the Sixth) *of England*

**sixth**[2] /sɪksθ/ ***noun*** [C] the fraction ⅙; one of six equal parts of sth

**ˌsixth ˈsense** ***noun*** [sing.] a special ability to know sth without using any of the five senses that include sight, touch, etc.: *My sixth sense told me to stay here and wait.* ◇ *Often our intuition or sixth sense warns us of impending danger.*

**six·ty** /ˈsɪksti/ ***number*** **1** 60; one more than fifty-nine: *Sixty people went to the meeting.* ◇ *There are sixty pages in the book.* ◇ *He retired at age sixty/when he was sixty.* **2 the sixties** [pl.] the numbers, years or temperatures between 60 and 69: *I don't know the exact number of members, but it's in the sixties.* ◇ *The Beatles were the most famous band of the sixties.* ◇ *The temperature tomorrow will be in the high sixties.*

IDM **in your sixties** between the age of 60 and 69: *I'm not sure how old she is, but I should think she's in her sixties.* ◇ *in your early/mid/late sixties*

▶ **six·ti·eth** /ˈsɪkstiəθ/ ***pronoun, det., adv.*** ➲ Look at the examples at **sixth**.

**siz·a·ble** (*also* **size·a·ble**) /ˈsaɪzəbl/ ***adj.*** fairly large: *a sizable chunk of our income*

★**size**[1] /saɪz/ ***noun*** **1** [U] the amount by which sth is big or small: *I was surprised at the size of the hotel. It was enormous!* ◇ *Canadian quarters are about the same size as American ones.* ◇ *The planet Uranus is about four times the size of Earth.*

NOTE When we ask about the size of something, we usually say, "How big...?": *How big is your house?* We say, "What size...?" when we ask about the size of something that is produced in a number of fixed measurements: *What size shoes do you wear?*

**2** [C] one of a number of fixed measurements in which sth is made: *Do you have this dress in a larger size?* ◇ *What size pizza do you want: medium or large?* ◇ *I wear size 9 shoes.*

**size²** /saɪz/ ***verb*** [T]

PHR V **size sb/sth up** to think carefully about sb/sth in order to form an opinion: *The team members sized up their opponents as they went out onto the field.*

**-sized** /saɪzd/ (*also* **-size**) ***combining form*** of the size that is mentioned: *a medium-sized apartment*

**siz·zle** /ˈsɪzl/ ***verb*** [I] to make the sound of food frying in hot fat: *I could hear the bacon sizzling in the kitchen.*

**skank·y** /ˈskæŋki/ ***adj.*** (*informal*) very unpleasant

**skates**

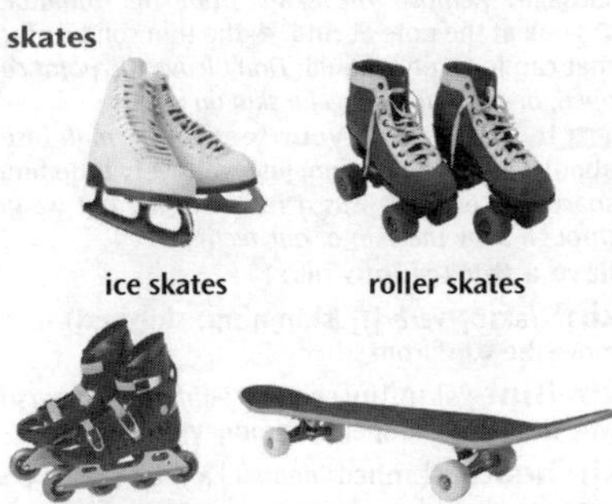

ice skates roller skates

Rollerblades™ (*also* in-line skates) skateboard

**skate¹** /skeɪt/ ***noun*** [C] **1** = ICE SKATE¹ **2** = ROLLER SKATE ➲ Look also at **in-line skate**.

**skate²** /skeɪt/ ***verb*** [I] **1** = ICE SKATE²: *They skated across the frozen lake.* **2** = ROLLER SKATE

**skate·board** /ˈskeɪtbɔrd/ ***noun*** [C] a narrow board with wheels attached to it that you can stand on and ride ➲ picture at **skate**. ▶ **skate·board *verb*** [I] ▶ **skate·board·er *noun*** [C] ▶ **skate·board·ing *noun*** [U]

**skat·er** /ˈskeɪt̬ər/ ***noun*** [C] **1** a person who skates for pleasure or as a sport: *a figure/speed skater* ◇ *ice/roller skaters* **2** a person who skateboards

**ske·dad·dle** /skɪˈdædl/ ***verb*** [I] (*informal*) to move away or leave a place quickly, especially in order to avoid sb

**skeet** /skit/ (*also* **ˈskeet ˌshooting**) ***noun*** [U] a sport in which a clay disk is thrown into the air for people to shoot at

**skee·ter** /ˈskit̬ər/ ***noun*** [C] (*slang*) = MOSQUITO

**skel·e·ton¹** /ˈskɛlətn/ ***noun*** [C] the structure formed by all the bones in a human or animal body: *a dinosaur skeleton in the Science Museum* ◇ *the human skeleton*

**skel·e·ton²** /ˈskɛlətn/ ***adj.*** (only *before* a noun) (used about an organization, a service, etc.) having the smallest number of people that is necessary for it to operate: *On Sundays, the office is kept open by a skeleton staff.*

**ˈskeleton key *noun*** [C] a key that will open several different locks

**skep·tic** /ˈskɛptɪk/ ***noun*** [C] a person who doubts that sth is true, right, etc.

**skep·ti·cal** /ˈskɛptɪkl/ ***adj.*** **skeptical (about/of sth)** having doubts that a claim or statement is true or that sth will happen: *I am skeptical about his chances of winning.* ◇ *The public remain skeptical of these claims.* ▶ **skep·ti·cal·ly** /-kli/ ***adv.***: *The announcement was greeted skeptically by the press.*

**skep·ti·cism** /ˈskɛptəsɪzəm/ ***noun*** [U, sing.] an attitude of doubting that claims or statements are true or that sth will happen: *Such claims should be regarded with a certain amount of skepticism.* ◇ *Other scientists have expressed skepticism about these results.*

**sketch¹** /skɛtʃ/ ***noun*** [C] **1** a simple, quick drawing without many details: *He drew a rough sketch of the new building on the back of an envelope.* **2** a short comedy scene, usually part of a television program **3** a short description without any details: *a sketch of life in Paris in the 1920s*

**sketch²** /skɛtʃ/ ***verb*** [I,T] to draw a SKETCH¹ (1): *I sat on the grass and sketched the lake.*

**sketch·book** /ˈskɛtʃbʊk/ (*also* **sketch·pad** /ˈskɛtʃpæd/) ***noun*** [C] a book of sheets of paper for drawing on

**sketch·y** /ˈskɛtʃi/ ***adj.*** (**sketch·i·er**; **sketch·i·est**) not having many or enough details: *He only gave me a sketchy account of the accident.*

**skew** /skyu/ ***verb*** [T] to change or influence sth with the result that it is not accurate, fair, normal, etc.: *to skew the statistics*

**skewed** /skyud/ ***adj.*** **1** (used about information) not accurate or correct: *skewed statistics* **2 skewed (toward sb/sth)** directed toward a particular group, place, etc. in a way that may not be accurate or fair: *The tax breaks are skewed toward the rich.* **3** not straight or level: *The car had ended up skewed across the road.*

**skew·er** /ˈskyuər/ ***noun*** [C] a long thin pointed piece of metal or wood that is pushed through pieces of meat, vegetables, etc. to hold them together while they are cooking, or used to test whether sth is completely cooked ➲ picture at **kitchen**.

★**ski¹** /ski/ ***noun*** [C] one of a pair of long, flat, narrow pieces of wood, metal or plastic that are fastened to boots and used for moving over snow: *a pair of skis*

★**ski²** /ski/ ***verb*** [I] (*pres. part.* **ski·ing**; *pt, pp* **skied**) to move over snow on skis: *When did you learn to ski?*

NOTE **Go skiing** is a common way of talking about skiing for pleasure: *They go skiing in the Rockies every year.*

▶ **ski·er** /ˈskiər/ ***noun*** [C]: *a good skier* ▶ **ski·ing *noun*** [U]: *downhill/cross-country skiing* ➲ picture on **page 640**.

**skid** /skɪd/ ***verb*** [I] (**skid·ding**; **skid·ded**) (used about a vehicle) to be out of control and move or slide sideways on the road: *I skidded on a patch of ice.* ▶ **skid *noun*** [C]

S

skiing

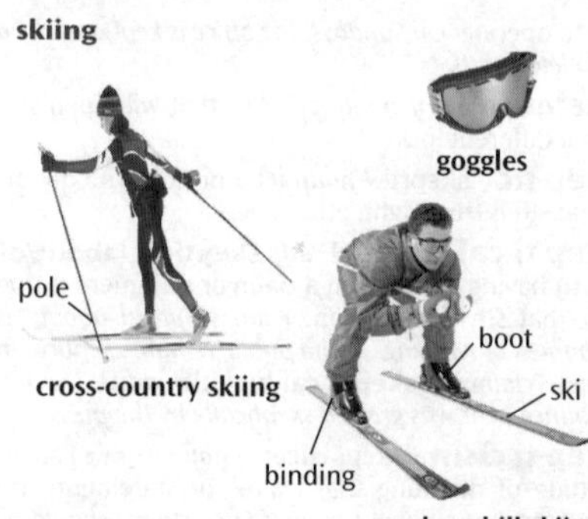


**ˌskid ˈrow** ***noun*** [U] (*informal*) (used to describe the poorest part of a town, often where homeless people, alcoholics and drug users live): *to be **on skid row***

**skies** /skaɪz/ *plural of* SKY

**ˈski jump** ***noun*** [C] a very steep artificial slope that ends suddenly and that is covered with snow. People ski down the slope, jump off the end and see how far they can travel through the air before landing. ▶ **ˈski-ˌjumper** ***noun*** [C] ▶ **ˈski-ˌjumping** ***noun*** [U]: *Is ski-jumping an Olympic sport?* ◇ *the Canadian ski-jumping team*

**ˈski lift** ***noun*** [C] a machine for taking skiers up a slope so that they can then ski down

★**skill** /skɪl/ ***noun*** **1** [U] the ability to do sth well, especially because of training, practice, etc.: *It takes great skill to make such beautiful jewelry.* ◇ *This is an easy game to play. No skill is required.* **2** [C] an ability that is required in order to do a job, an activity, etc. well: *The course will help you to develop your reading and listening skills.* ◇ *management skills* ◇ *Typing is a skill I have never mastered.*

S

★**skilled** /skɪld/ ***adj.*** **1** (used about a person) having skill; skillful: *a skilled worker* **2** (used about work, a job etc.) requiring skill or skills; done by people who have been trained: *a highly skilled job* ◇ *Skilled work is difficult to find in this area.* OPP **unskilled**

**skil·let** /ˈskɪlət/ ***noun*** [C] = FRYING PAN ➲ picture at **pan**.

★**skill·ful** /ˈskɪlfl/ ***adj.*** **1** (used about a person) very good at doing sth: *a skillful painter/politician* ◇ *He's very skillful with his hands.* **2** done very well: *skillful guitar playing* ▶ **skill·ful·ly** /-fəli/ ***adv.***: *The play was skillfully directed by a young student.*

**skim** /skɪm/ ***verb*** (**skim·ming**; **skimmed**) **1** [T] to remove sth from the surface of a liquid: *to skim the fat off the gravy* **2** [I,T] **skim (through/over) sth** to read sth quickly in order to get the main idea, without paying attention to the details and without reading every word: *I usually just skim through the newspaper in the morning.* **3** [I,T] to move quickly over a surface, near it but without touching it, or without touching it very often: *The plane flew very low, skimming the tops of the buildings.* ◇ *I watched a big bird skim across the water.*

**ˈski mask** ***noun*** [C] a type of hat made of wool that covers most of the head, neck and face: *The two attackers were wearing ski masks.*

**ˌskim ˈmilk** ***noun*** [U] milk from which all the cream has been removed ➲ Compare **whole milk**.

**skimp** /skɪmp/ ***verb*** [I] **skimp (on sth)** to try to spend less time, money, etc. on sth than is really needed: *Older people should not skimp on food or heating.*

**skimp·y** /ˈskɪmpi/ ***adj.*** (**skimp·i·er**; **skimp·i·est**) using or having less than is necessary: *a skimpy meal* ◇ *a skimpy swimsuit* (= not covering much of the body)

★**skin¹** /skɪn/ ***noun*** [C,U] **1** the natural outer covering of a human or animal body: *to have light/dark/sensitive skin* ◇ *skin cancer* **2** (often in compounds) the skin of an animal that has been removed from its body and that is often used for making things: *a sheepskin jacket* **3** the natural outer covering of some fruits or vegetables; the outer covering of a sausage: *Remove the skins from the tomatoes.* ➲ Look at the note at **rind**. **4** the thin solid surface that can form on a liquid: *Don't leave the paint can open, or the paint will get a skin on it.*

IDM **by the skin of your teeth** (*informal*) (used about a successful action) just; with very little time, space etc. extra: *It was a real struggle, but we got through it by the skin of our teeth.*

**have a thick skin** → THICK¹

**skin²** /skɪn/ ***verb*** [T] (**skin·ning**; **skinned**) to remove the SKIN¹ from sth

**skin·flint** /ˈskɪnflɪnt/ ***noun*** [C] (*informal*) a person who does not like spending money SYN **miser**

**skin·head** /ˈskɪnhɛd/ ***noun*** [C] a young white person with shaved or extremely short hair. Skinheads are often associated with violent behavior against people of other races.

**skin·ny** /ˈskɪni/ ***adj.*** (**skin·ni·er**; **skin·ni·est**) (*informal*) **1** (used about a person) too thin ➲ Look at the note at **thin**. **2** low in fat: *a skinny caffè latte*

**ˈskinny-ˌdipping** ***noun*** [U] (*informal*) swimming without any clothes on

**skin·tight** /ˌskɪnˈtaɪt/ ***adj.*** (used about a piece of clothing) fitting very tightly and showing the shape of the body

**skip** /skɪp/ ***verb*** (**skip·ping**; **skipped**) **1** [I] to move along quickly and lightly in a way that is similar to dancing, with little jumps and steps, from one foot to the other: *A little girl came skipping along the street.* **2** [T] to not go to sth that you should go to; to not have sth that you should have: *I got up late, so I skipped breakfast.* **3** [I,T] **skip (over) sth** (used about part of a book, story, etc.) to leave sth out; to not read or talk about sth and move to the next part: *I think I'll skip the next chapter. It looks really boring.*

IDM **cut/skip class** → CLASS

**skip·per** /ˈskɪpər/ ***noun*** [C] the captain of a boat or ship

**ˈskipping rope** ***noun*** [C] (*Cdn*) = JUMP ROPE

**skir·mish** /ˈskərmɪʃ/ ***noun*** [C] a small fight or battle

★**skirt¹** /skərt/ ***noun*** [C] a piece of clothing that is worn by women and girls and that hangs down from the waist: *a short skirt* ➲ picture on study page **A30**.

**skirt²** /skərt/ ***verb*** [T] **1** to go around the edge of sth: *a road that skirts the western edge of the metro area* **2** to avoid talking about sth directly: *The boss has been skirting the issue of our raise.*

**skit** /skɪt/ ***noun*** [C] a short, funny play or scene

**skit·tish** /ˈskɪt̬ɪʃ/ ***adj.*** **1** (used about horses) easily excited or frightened and therefore difficult to control **2** (used about people) not very serious and with ideas and feelings that keep changing **3** likely to change suddenly: *skittish financial markets* ◇ *skittish investors/traders*

**skiv·vies™** /ˈskɪviz/ ***noun*** [pl.] (*old-fashioned*) men's underwear

**skull** /skʌl/ ***noun*** [C] the bone structure of a human or animal head: *a fractured skull*

**skull·cap** /ˈskʌlkæp/ ***noun*** [C] a small round cap without a BILL¹ (6) worn on top of the head, especially by male Jews and Catholic bishops ➲ picture at **yarmulke**.

**skunk**

**skunk** /skʌŋk/ ***noun*** [C] a small wild animal with black and white fur and a thick tail. Skunks spray a liquid with a very strong, bad smell from their bodies when they are in danger.

★**sky** /skaɪ/ ***noun*** [C,U] (*pl.* **skies**) the space that you can see when you look up from the earth, and where you can see the sun, moon and stars: *a clear blue sky* ◇ *I saw a little bit of blue sky between the clouds.*

NOTE We usually talk about **the sky**: *I saw a plane high up in the sky.* ◇ *The sky looks very dark. I think it's going to rain.* However, when **sky** follows an adjective, we usually use **a/an**: *a cloudless sky* or sometimes the plural form **skies**: *cloudless skies.*

**ˌsky ˈblue** ***adj.*** bright blue in color, like the sky on a clear day ▸ **ˌsky ˈblue** ***noun*** [U]

**sky·cap** /ˈskaɪkæp/ ***noun*** [C] a person whose job is to carry people's bags at an airport

**sky·div·ing** /ˈskaɪˌdaɪvɪŋ/ ***noun*** [U] a sport in which you jump from a plane and fall for as long as you safely can before opening your parachute: *to go skydiving* ▸ **sky·div·er** ***noun*** [C]

**ˌsky-ˈhigh** ***adj.***, ***adv.*** very high

**sky·jack** /ˈskaɪdʒæk/ ***verb*** [T] to use violence or threats to take control of an aircraft, in order to force it to travel to a different place or to demand sth from a government SYN **hijack** ▸ **sky·jack·er** ***noun*** [C] ▸ **sky·jack·ing** ***noun*** [U]

**sky·light** /ˈskaɪlaɪt/ ***noun*** [C] a window in the roof of a house or other building ➲ Picture on study page **A31**.

**sky·line** /ˈskaɪlaɪn/ ***noun*** [C] the shape that is made by tall buildings, etc. against the sky: *the Manhattan skyline*

**sky·rock·et** /ˈskaɪrɑkət/ ***verb*** [I] to increase or rise very quickly: *skyrocketing prices*

**sky·scrap·er** /ˈskaɪskreɪpər/ ***noun*** [C] a very tall building

**sky·ward** /ˈskaɪwərd/ ***adv.***, ***adj.*** toward the sky: *We all turned our gazes skyward.*

**slab** /slæb/ ***noun*** [C] a thick, flat piece of sth: *huge concrete slabs*

**slack¹** /slæk/ ***adj.*** **1** loose; not tightly stretched: *Leave the rope slack.* **2** (used about a period of business) not busy; not having many customers or much activity: *Prices remained low because of slack demand for the products.*

**slack²** /slæk/ ***noun*** [U] a part of a rope, etc. that is loose or not tightly stretched ➲ Look also at **slacks**.
IDM **cut/give sb some slack** (*informal*) to be less critical of sb and not get angry if he/she makes mistakes

**pick/take up the slack** to do some extra work because the person, group, etc. who usually does it is not there: *If those government benefits are cut, charities and volunteer organizations will have to take up the slack.*

**slack·en** /ˈslækən/ ***verb*** [I,T] **1** to become or make sth slower or less active: *Industrial production has slackened in recent months.* ◇ *His pace slackened toward the end of the race.* **2** to become or make sth less tight: *The rope slackened and he pulled his hand free.* ◇ *After a while she slackened her grip on my arm.*

**slack·er** /ˈslækər/ ***noun*** [C] (*informal*) a person who does not work hard and wastes a lot of time

**slacks** /slæks/ ***noun*** [pl.] (*old-fashioned*) pants: *a pair of slacks*

**slain** *past participle of* SLAY

**sla·lom** /ˈslɑləm/ ***noun*** [C] a race for people on skis or in canoes along a course on which they have to move from side to side between poles

**slam** /slæm/ ***verb*** (**slam·ming**; **slammed**) **1** [I,T] to close or make sth close very loudly and with great force: *I heard the front door slam.* ◇ *She slammed her book shut and rushed out of the room.* **2** [T] to put sth somewhere very quickly and with great force: *He slammed my letter on the table and stormed out.* ➲ Look at **grand slam**. **3** [T] to criticize sb/sth very strongly: *Citizens' groups slammed the proposal to increase the sales tax.*

**ˌslam-ˈdunk** (*also* **ˌslam ˈdunk**) ***noun*** [C] (in basketball) an act of jumping very high and pushing the ball through the basket with great force from above ▸ **ˌslam-ˈdunk** ***verb*** [I,T]

**slam·mer** /ˈslæmər/ ***noun*** **1 the slammer** [sing.] (*slang*) prison: *He'll end up in the slammer one day.* **2** [C] (*also* **teˌquila ˈslammer**) an alcoholic drink made by mixing tequila and a particular kind of soda, which is drunk quickly after covering the glass and hitting it on the table to make the drink fill with bubbles

**slan·der** /ˈslændər/ ***noun*** [C,U] an untrue spoken statement about sb that is intended to damage the good opinion that other people have of him/her; the crime of making this kind of statement ➲ Look at **libel**. ▸ **slan·der** ***verb*** [T] ▸ **slan·der·ous** /ˈslændərəs/ ***adj.***

**slang** /slæŋ/ ***noun*** [U] very informal words and expressions that are more common in spoken

S

language. Slang is sometimes used only by a particular group of people (e.g. children, soldiers) and often stays in fashion for a short time. Some slang is not polite: *"Barf" is slang for "vomit."*

**slant**[1] /slænt/ ***verb*** **1** [I,T] to lean or make sth lean in a particular direction; to be not straight: *My handwriting slants backward.* **2** [T] (usually passive) to describe information, events, etc. in a way that supports a particular group or opinion: *All the political articles in that newspaper are slanted toward the administration.*

**slant**[2] /slænt/ ***noun*** **1** [sing.] a position that leans or slopes in a particular direction **2** [C] an attitude or a way of thinking about sth, especially one that supports a particular group or opinion: *This new information puts a completely different slant on the discussion.*

**slant·ed** /ˈslæntəd/ ***adj.*** **1** sloping in one direction: *She had slanted brown eyes.* **2 slanted (toward sb/sth)** tending to be in favor of one person or thing in a way that may be unfair to others: *a biased and slanted view of events*

**slap**[1] /slæp/ ***verb*** [T] (**slap·ping**; **slapped**) **1** to hit sb/sth with the inside of your hand: *She slapped him across the face.* ◇ *to slap sb on the back* (= to congratulate him/her) **2** to put sth onto a surface quickly and carelessly: *to slap some paint onto a wall*

**slap**[2] /slæp/ ***noun*** [C] an act of hitting sb/sth with the inside of your hand: *I gave him a slap across the face.*
IDM **a slap on the wrist** a punishment that is not severe, or that sb thinks is not severe enough: *a drug dealer who only got a slap on the wrist from the judge*

**slap·dash** /ˈslæpdæʃ/ ***adj.*** done, or doing sth, too quickly and carelessly: *She has a very slapdash approach to keeping accounts.* ◇ *a slapdash piece of writing*

**slap·hap·py** /ˈslæpˌhæpi/ (*also* **ˈslap-ˌhappy**) ***adj.*** (*informal*) **1** cheerful, but careless about things that should be taken seriously: *a slaphappy approach to life* **2** unable to think clearly; in a confused state

**slap·shot** /ˈslæpʃɑt/ (*also* **ˈslap shot**) ***noun*** [C] (*sports*) (in hockey) a way of hitting the puck or ball by raising the stick up high, and then hitting it hard

**slap·stick** /ˈslæpstɪk/ ***noun*** [U] a type of comedy that is based on simple jokes, e.g. people falling over or hitting each other

**slash**[1] /slæʃ/ ***verb*** **1** [I,T] to make a long cut in sth with a violent action: *Several cars have had their tires slashed in that parking lot.* **2** [T] to reduce an amount of money, etc. very much: *The price of coffee has been slashed by about 20%.*

**slash**[2] /slæʃ/ ***noun*** [C] the symbol (/) used to show alternatives, as in lunch and/or dinner and 4/5 people and to write fractions, as in ¾ ➲ Look also at **backslash** and **forward slash**.

**ˌslash-and-ˈburn** ***adj.*** **1** relating to a method of farming in which existing plants, crops etc. are cut down and burned before new seeds are sown: *slash-and-burn agriculture* **2** aggressive and causing a lot of harm or damage: *a slash-and-burn takeover*

**slat** /slæt/ ***noun*** [C] one of the long narrow pieces of wood, metal or plastic in a cupboard door, a fence, a covering for a window, etc.

**slate**[1] /sleɪt/ ***noun*** [U] a type of dark gray rock that can easily be split into thin flat pieces

**slate**[2] /sleɪt/ ***verb*** [T]
IDM **be slated to do sth**; **be slated for sth** to be planned to do sth or to happen at a particular time: *The new store is slated to open in April.* ◇ *an empty lot that has been slated for development*

**slath·er** /ˈslæðər/ ***verb*** [T] to cover sth/sb with a thick layer of a substance: *hot dogs slathered with mustard* ◇ *She slathered on plenty of sunblock.*

**slat·ted** /ˈslæt̬əd/ ***adj.*** (usually before a noun) made of slats: *slatted blinds/chairs/shelves*

**slaugh·ter** /ˈslɔt̬ər/ ***verb*** [T] **1** to kill an animal, usually for food **2** to kill a large number of people at one time, especially in a cruel way or when they cannot defend themselves: *Men, women and children were slaughtered and whole villages destroyed.* ➲ Look at the note at **kill**. ▸ **slaugh·ter** ***noun*** [U]: *the slaughter of innocent people during the war*

**slaugh·ter·house** /ˈslɔt̬ərhaʊs/ ***noun*** [C] a place where animals are killed for food

**slave**[1] /sleɪv/ ***noun*** [C] a person who is owned by another person and has to work for that person

**slave**[2] /sleɪv/ ***verb*** [I] **slave (away)** to work very hard: *I slaved over a hot stove for hours to cook this meal!*

**ˈslave ˌdriver** ***noun*** [C] a person who makes people work extremely hard: *My boss is a real slave driver.*

**ˌslave ˈlabor** ***noun*** [U] **1** work that is done by slaves; the slaves who do the work: *Huge palaces were built by slave labor.* **2** (*informal*) work that is very hard and very badly paid: *I left because the job was just slave labor.*

**slav·er·y** /ˈsleɪvəri/ ***noun*** [U] **1** the system of having slaves: *the abolition of slavery after the Civil War* **2** the situation of being a slave: *The two boys were captured and sold into slavery.*

**slav·ish** /ˈsleɪvɪʃ/ ***adj.*** following or copying sb/sth exactly without having any original thought at all: *slavish devotion/obedience* ◇ *a slavish imitation of Hitchcock's films*

**slay** /sleɪ/ ***verb*** [T] (*pt* **slew** /slu/; *pp* **slain** /sleɪn/) to kill violently; to murder: *Many young soldiers were slain in the battle.* ▸ **slay·ing** /ˈsleɪɪŋ/ ***noun*** [C,U]

**sleaze** /sliz/ ***noun*** [U] behavior or conditions that are unpleasant and not socially acceptable, especially because sex is involved: *the sleaze of a town that was once a naval base*

**sleaze·ball** /ˈslizbɔl/ (*also* **sleaze·bag** /ˈslizbæg/) ***noun*** [C] (*slang*) a dishonest or immoral person

**slea·zy** /ˈslizi/ ***adj.*** (**slea·zi·er**; **slea·zi·est**) (often used about a place) dirty, in bad condition and having an immoral or criminal atmosphere: *a sleazy nightclub*

**sled** /slɛd/ ***noun*** [C] a vehicle without wheels that is used for traveling on snow. You can slide down a hill on a small sled. Large sleds are often pulled by dogs. ➲ Look at **toboggan**. ➲ picture at **sleigh**.

**sled·ding** /ˈslɛdɪŋ/ ***noun*** [U] the sport or activity of traveling on snow on a sled: *When we were kids we used to go sledding in the park.*

**sledge·ham·mer** /ˈslɛdʒˌhæmər/ ***noun*** [C] a large heavy hammer with a long handle

**sleek** /slik/ ***adj.*** **1** (used about a vehicle) having an elegant, smooth shape: *a sleek new sports car* **2** (used about hair, fur or skin) smooth and shiny

★**sleep¹** /slip/ ***noun*** **1** [U] the natural condition of rest when your eyes are closed and your mind and body are not active or conscious: *Most people need about eight hours' sleep every night.* ◇ *I didn't get much sleep last night.* ◇ *Do you ever talk in your sleep?* **2** [sing.] a period of SLEEP (1): *I haven't had a decent night's sleep in months.*

IDM **get to sleep** to succeed in sleeping: *I couldn't get to sleep last night.*

**go to sleep 1** to start sleeping; to enter the state of sleep: *He got into bed and went to sleep quickly.* ◇ *Go to sleep. Everything will seem better in the morning.* **2** (used about an arm, a leg, etc.) to lose the sense of feeling in it

**put (an animal) to sleep** to kill an animal that is sick or injured because you want to stop it from suffering

★**sleep²** /slip/ ***verb*** (*pt, pp* **slept** /slɛpt/) **1** [I] to be in a state of SLEEP¹ (1) for a period of time: *Did you sleep well last night?* ◇ *I only slept for a couple of hours last night.*

NOTE We use **to sleep** for talking about sleeping in general, but we use **to be asleep** to talk about being in the state of sleep when something else happens: *I was asleep when the telephone rang.* We use **to go to sleep** to talk about starting to sleep. (NOT: *I slept at ten o'clock last night* but: *I went to sleep at ten o'clock last night.*)

**2** [T] (used about a place) to have enough beds for a particular number of people: *a camper that sleeps four people*

PHR V **sleep in** to sleep until later than usual in the morning because you do not have to get up

**sleep over** to sleep at sb else's house

**sleep together**; **sleep with sb** to have sex with sb (usually when you are not married to or living with that person): *Do you think she's slept with him?*

**sleep·er** /ˈslipər/ ***noun*** [C] (with an adjective) a person who sleeps in a particular way. If you are a light sleeper you wake up easily: *a light/heavy sleeper*

ˈ**sleeping bag** ***noun*** [C] a large soft bag that you sleep in when you go camping, etc.

ˈ**sleeping pill** ***noun*** [C] a pill that helps you to sleep

ˈ**sleeping ˌsickness** ***noun*** [U] a tropical disease carried by an insect (the tsetse fly) that causes a feeling of wanting to go to sleep and usually causes death

**sleep·less** /ˈslipləs/ ***adj.*** (used about a period, usually the night) without sleep ▸ **sleep·less·ness** ***noun*** [U] ➲ Look at **insomnia**.

**sleep·o·ver** /ˈslipˌoʊvər/ ***noun*** [C] = SLUMBER PARTY

**sleep·walk** /ˈslipwɔk/ ***verb*** [I] to walk around while you are asleep

**sleep·wear** /ˈslipwɛr/ ***noun*** [U] clothing such as pajamas that you wear in bed

**sleep·y** /ˈslipi/ ***adj.*** (**sleep·i·er** **sleep·i·est**) **1** tired and ready to go to sleep: *These pills might make you feel a little sleepy.* **2** (used about a place) very quiet and not having much activity: *a sleepy rural town* ▸ **sleep·i·ly** /-əli/ ***adv.***

**sleep·y·head** /ˈslipihɛd/ ***noun*** [C] (*informal*) (used to speak to sb, especially a child, who looks as if he/she is falling asleep): *Come on, sleepyhead. It's time for bed.*

**sleet** /slit/ ***noun*** [U] a mixture of rain and snow ➲ Look at the note at **weather**. ▸ **sleet** ***verb*** [I]

★**sleeve** /sliv/ ***noun*** [C] one of the two parts of a piece of clothing that cover the arms or part of the arms: *a blouse with long sleeves* ➲ picture at **shirt**.

**-sleeved** /slivd/ (*also* **-sleeve**) ***combining form*** with sleeves of a particular kind: *a short-sleeved shirt* ◇ *a long-sleeved dress*

**sleeve·less** /ˈslivləs/ ***adj.*** without sleeves

**sleigh**

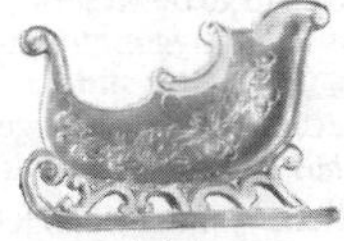

**sled** **sleigh**

**sleigh** /sleɪ/ ***noun*** [C] a vehicle that is used for traveling on snow and that is usually pulled by horses ➲ Look at **sled** and at the note at **Santa Claus**.

**sleight of hand** /ˌslaɪt̬ əv ˈhænd/ ***noun*** [U] **1** skillful movements of your hand that other people cannot see: *The trick is done simply by sleight of hand.* **2** an act of deceiving people in a clever way: *Last year's profits were more the result of financial sleight of hand than genuine growth.*

**slen·der** /ˈslɛndər/ ***adj.*** **1** (used about a person or part of sb's body) thin in an attractive way: *long slender fingers* **2** smaller in amount or size than you would like: *a slender margin of victory*

**slept** *past tense, past participle of* SLEEP²

**sleuth** /sluθ/ ***noun*** [C] (*old-fashioned*) a person who investigates crimes: *an amateur sleuth* ◇ *Agatha Christie's super sleuth, Hercule Poirot* SYN **detective**

**sleuth·ing** /ˈsluθɪŋ/ ***noun*** [U] the act of investigating a crime or mysterious event: *to do some private sleuthing*

**slew¹** /slu/ ***noun*** [sing.] (*informal*) **a slew of sth** a large number or amount of sth

**slew²** *past tense of* SLAY

★**slice¹** /slaɪs/ ***noun*** [C] **1** a flat piece of food that is cut from a larger piece: *a thick/thin slice of bread* ◇ *a slice of pizza* ➲ picture at **bread**. **2** a part of sth: *The owners had taken a large slice of the profits.*

**slice²** /slaɪs/ ***verb*** **1** [T] to cut into SLICES¹ (1): *Peel and slice the apples.* ◇ *thinly sliced ham* **2** [I,T] to cut through or into sth: *He sliced through the rope with a knife.*

IDM **any way you slice it** (*informal*) however you choose to look at a situation

**slick¹** /slɪk/ ***adj.*** **1** done smoothly and well, and seeming to be done without any effort: *The actors gave a slick, highly professional performance.* **2** skillful at persuading people but perhaps not completely honest: *slick advertising* **3** (used about a surface) smooth and slippery: *The truck's wheels were spinning on the slick, icy road.*

S

**slick²** /slɪk/ ***noun*** [C] = OIL SLICK

**slick³** /slɪk/ ***verb*** [T] (usually passive) to make hair very flat and smooth by putting oil, water, etc. on it: *His hair was **slicked back/down** with gel.*

**slick·er** /ˈslɪkər/ ***noun*** [C] a long loose coat that keeps you dry in the rain ➲ Look at **city slicker**.

**slide¹** /slaɪd/ ***verb*** (*pt, pp* **slid** /slɪd/) **1** [I,T] to move or make sth move smoothly along a surface: *She slid on the ice and fell down.* ◇ *A large drop of rain slid down the window.* ◇ *"Here you are," he said, sliding the keys across the table.* ◇ *a sliding door* (= one that you open by sliding it to one side) **2** [I,T] to move or make sth move quietly without being noticed: *I slid out of the room when nobody was looking.* ◇ *She slid her hand into her bag and took out a gun.* **3** [I] (used about prices, values, etc.) to go down slowly and continuously: *The pound is sliding against the dollar.*

IDM **let sth slide** to ignore sth or not take any action to stop sth getting worse: *He just let the business slide after his wife's death.*

★**slide²** /slaɪd/ ***noun*** [C]

➤ PHOTOGRAPH **1** a small piece of photographic film in a plastic or cardboard frame

NOTE If you shine light through a slide using a **projector,** you can make the photograph appear on a **screen**.

➤ FOR MICROSCOPE **2** a small piece of glass that you put sth on when you want to examine it under a microscope

➤ FOR CHILDREN **3** a long piece of metal, etc. that children can slide down (e.g. in a playground)

➤ BECOMING LOWER/WORSE **4** a continuous slow movement down (e.g. of prices, values, levels, etc.): *a slide in the value of the dollar*

➤ FALL OF ROCKS, ETC. **5** (usually in compounds) a sudden fall of rocks, earth, etc. down a slope: *a mudslide*

★**slight¹** /slaɪt/ ***adj.*** **1** very small; not important or serious: *I've got a slight problem, but it's nothing to get worried about.* ◇ *a slight change/difference/increase/improvement* ◇ *I don't have the slightest idea* (= no idea at all) *what you're talking about.* **2** (used about a person's body) thin and delicate: *his slight figure*

S

**slight²** /slaɪt/ ***noun*** [C] **a slight (on sb/sth)** an act or a remark that criticizes sth or offends sb: *Nick took her comment as a slight on his abilities as a manager.*

**slight³** /slaɪt/ ***verb*** [T] (usually passive) to treat sb rudely or without respect; to insult sb: *She **felt slighted** because she hadn't been invited.*

★**slight·ly** /ˈslaɪtli/ ***adv.*** a little: *I'm slightly older than she is.*

**slim** /slɪm/ ***adj.*** (**slim·mer**; **slim·mest**) **1** thin in an attractive way: *a tall, slim woman* ➲ Look at the note at **thin**. **2** not as big as you would like: *Her chances of success are very slim.*

**slime** /slaɪm/ ***noun*** [U] a thick unpleasant sticky liquid: *The pond was covered with green slime and smelled terrible.*

**slime·ball** /ˈslaɪmbɔl/ ***noun*** [C] (*slang*) a dishonest or immoral person that you do not like or trust at all

**slim·y** /ˈslaɪmi/ ***adj.*** (**slim·i·er**; **slim·i·est**) **1** covered with slime **2** (*informal*) (used about a person) very friendly, but in a way that you do not trust or like

**sling¹** /slɪŋ/ ***noun*** [C] a piece of cloth that you put under your arm and tie around your neck to support a broken arm, wrist, etc. ➲ picture at **bandage**.

**sling²** /slɪŋ/ ***verb*** [T] (*pt, pp* **slung**) **1** to put or throw sth somewhere in a rough or careless way: *He slung his bat to the side of the field in anger.* **2** to put sth into a position where it hangs loosely: *She was carrying her bag slung over her shoulder.*

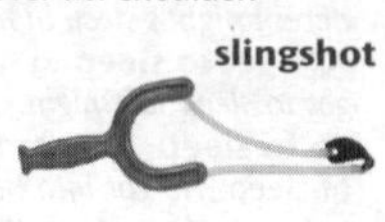
**slingshot**

**sling·back** /ˈslɪŋbæk/ ***noun*** [C] a woman's shoe that is open at the back with a narrow piece of leather, etc. around the heel ➲ picture at **shoe**.

**sling·shot** /ˈslɪŋʃɑt/ ***noun*** [C] a Y-shaped stick with a band of rubber attached to each side, that is used by children for shooting stones

**slink** /slɪŋk/ ***verb*** [I] (*pt, pp* **slunk**) to move somewhere very quietly and slowly, especially because you are ashamed or do not want to be seen: *John was trying to slink into the house by the back door.* ◇ *The dog howled and slunk away.*

**slink·y** /ˈslɪŋki/ ***adj.*** (**slink·i·er**; **slink·i·est**) **1** (used about a woman's clothes) fitting closely to the body in a sexually attractive way: *a slinky black dress* **2** (used about movement or sound) smooth and slow, often in a way that is sexually attractive: *a slinky voice*

★**slip¹** /slɪp/ ***verb*** (**slip·ping**; **slipped**)

➤ SLIDE/FALL **1** [I] **slip (on sth)** to slide accidentally, lose your balance and fall or nearly fall: *Don't slip on that floor. I just mopped it.* ◇ *His foot slipped on the step and he fell down.*

➤ OUT OF POSITION **2** [I] to slide accidentally out of the correct position or out of sb's hand: *This hat's too big. It keeps slipping down over my eyes.* ◇ *The glass slipped out of my hand and smashed on the floor.* ◇ (*figurative*) *I didn't intend to tell them. It just slipped out.*

➤ GO/PUT QUICKLY **3** [I] to move or go somewhere quietly, quickly, and often without being noticed: *While everyone was dancing, we slipped away and went home.* **4** [T] **slip sth (to sb)**; **slip (sb) sth** to put sth somewhere or give sth quietly and often without being noticed: *She picked up the money and slipped it into her pocket.*

➤ CLOTHES ON/OFF **5** [I,T] **slip into/out of sth; slip sth on/off** to put on or take off a piece of clothing quickly and easily: *I'm just going to slip into something cooler.* ◇ *I slipped off my shoes.*

➤ BECOME WORSE **6** [I] to fall a little (in value, level, etc.): *Sales have been slipping slightly over the last few months.*

IDM **fall/slip through the cracks** → CRACK¹

**let sth slip** to tell a secret, some information, etc. without intending to: *He let slip that he had been in prison.*

**slip your mind** to be forgotten: *I'm sorry – the meeting completely slipped my mind.*

PHR V **slip up** (*informal*) to make a mistake: *It looks like somebody slipped up. Your name isn't on the list.*

**slip²** /slɪp/ ***noun*** [C]
▸ACT OF SLIPPING **1** an act of SLIPPING¹ (1): *Be careful when you go up onto the roof. One slip and you could fall off.*
▸BECOMING WORSE **2** a slight fall in value, level, etc.: *a slip in the governor's popularity*
▸SMALL MISTAKE **3** a small mistake: *to make a slip of the tongue* (= to say sth wrong, without intending to)
▸PIECE OF PAPER **4** a small piece of paper: *I made a note of her name on a slip of paper.* ◇ *a bank deposit slip*
▸CLOTHING **5** a piece of clothing that is worn by a woman under a dress or skirt
IDM **give sb the slip** (*informal*) to escape from sb who is following or chasing you

**slip·cov·er** /ˈslɪpˌkʌvər/ ***noun*** [C, usually pl.] a cover for a chair, etc. that you can take off, for example to wash it

**ˈslip knot** (*also* **ˈslip-knot**) ***noun*** [C] a KNOT¹ that can slide easily along the rope, etc. on which it is tied, in order to make the loop or rope tighter or looser

**ˈslip-on** ***adj.*** (used about a shoe) that you can slide your feet into without having to tie laces: *slip-on shoes* ▸ **ˈslip-on** ***noun*** [C]: *a pair of slip-ons*

**slip·page** /ˈslɪpɪdʒ/ ***noun*** [C, usually sing., U] (*written*) **1** failure to achieve an aim or complete a task by a particular date: *The smallest slippage could delay completion of the project.* **2** a slight or gradual fall in the amount, value, etc. of sth: *There has been some slippage of support for the government's policies.*

**ˌslipped ˈdisk** ***noun*** [C] an injury that happens when one of the soft parts between the bones in sb's back has moved out of its correct position, causing pain

**slip·per** /ˈslɪpər/ ***noun*** [C] a light soft shoe that is worn in the house: *a pair of slippers* ➲ picture at **shoe**.

**slip·per·y** /ˈslɪpəri/ ***adj.*** (used about a surface or an object) difficult to move over or hold because it is smooth, wet, greasy, etc.: *a slippery floor* ◇ *The fish was cold and slippery.*

**slip·shod** /ˈslɪpʃɑd/ ***adj.*** done without care; doing things without care: *The work was done in a slipshod manner.* SYN **careless**

**ˈslip-up** ***noun*** [C] (*informal*) a careless mistake: *We cannot afford another slip-up like this one.*

**slit¹** /slɪt/ ***noun*** [C] a long narrow cut or opening: *We could see into the room through a slit in the curtains.*

**slit²** /slɪt/ ***verb*** [T] (**slit·ting**; *pt, pp* **slit**) to make a long narrow cut in sth: *She slit the envelope open with a knife.* ◇ *He slit his wrists in a suicide attempt.*

**slith·er** /ˈslɪðər/ ***verb*** [I] to slide along in an unsteady or twisting way: *I saw a snake slithering down a rock.*

**sliv·er** /ˈslɪvər/ ***noun*** [C] a small or thin piece of sth that is cut or broken off from a larger piece: *slivers of glass/wood* ◇ (*figurative*) *A sliver of light showed under the door.*

**slob** /slɑb/ ***noun*** [C] (*informal*) (used as an insult) a very lazy or messy person

**slob·ber** /ˈslɑbər/ ***verb*** [I] to let saliva come out of your mouth: *The dog was slobbering all over me.*
PHR V **slobber over sb/sth** (*informal*) to show, without any pride or control, how much you like or want sb/sth: *I know he's in love with you but does he have to slobber over you in public?*

**slog** /slɑg/ ***verb*** [I] (*pres. part.* **slog·ging**; *pt, pp* **slog·ged**) (*informal*) **1 slog (through sth); slog (away) (at sth)** to work hard and steadily at sth, especially sth that takes a long time and is boring or difficult: *The teacher made us slog through long lists of vocabulary.* ◇ *My mother slogged all her life for us.* **2** to walk or travel somewhere steadily, with great effort or difficulty: *He started to* ***slog his way*** *through the undergrowth.*

**slo·gan** /ˈsloʊgən/ ***noun*** [C] a short phrase that is easy to remember and that is used in politics or advertising: *Anti-war slogans had been painted all over the walls.* ◇ *"Faster than light" is the advertising slogan for the new car.*

**slop¹** /slɑp/ ***verb*** [I,T] (**slop·ping**; **slopped**) (*informal*) (used about a liquid) to spill over the edge of its container, or to cause a liquid to do this: *He filled his glass too full, and some of the beer slopped onto the table.*

**slop²** /slɑp/ ***noun*** [U] (*also* **slops** [pl.]) **1** waste food, sometimes fed to animals **2** liquid or partly liquid waste, for example urine or dirty water from baths: *a slop bucket* ◇ *She emptied the slops into the gutter.* **3** food in the form of liquid, or part liquid, which looks and tastes unpleasant: *I'm not eating that slop!*

★**slope¹** /sloʊp/ ***noun*** **1** [C] a piece of land that goes up or down: *We walked down a slope and came to the river.* ◇ *a steep/gentle slope* ◇ *ski slopes* **2** [sing.] the amount that a surface is not level; the fact of not being level: *a slope of 20 degrees* ◇ *The slope of the field makes it really difficult to play on.*

**slope²** /sloʊp/ ***verb*** [I] to not be level or upright; to have a SLOPE (2): *The road slopes down to the river.* ◇ *a sloping roof*

**slop·py** /ˈslɑpi/ ***adj.*** (**slop·pi·er**; **slop·pi·est**) **1** (used about a piece of work, etc.) not done carefully, neatly or thoroughly **2** (used about a person) careless or messy: *a sloppy worker*

**slop·py joe** /ˌslɑpi ˈdʒoʊ/ ***noun*** [C] (*informal*) a type of sandwich filled with finely chopped meat (beef) in a spicy tomato sauce

**slosh** /slɑʃ/ ***verb*** (*informal*) **1** [I] (used about a liquid) to move around noisily inside a container: *The water sloshed around in the bucket.* **2** [T] to put liquid somewhere in a careless and messy way: *Careful! You're sloshing water all over the floor!*

**sloshed** /slɑʃt/ ***adj.*** (*informal*) drunk

**slot¹** /slɑt/ ***noun*** [C] **1** a long straight narrow opening in a machine, etc.: *Put your money into the slot and take the ticket.* **2** a place in a schedule, a system, etc.: *The network has moved the program to a later time slot.*

**slot²** /slɑt/ ***verb*** [I,T] (**slot·ting**; **slot·ted**) to fit into a particular space: *These two metal pieces slot into the frame here.*

**sloth** /slɔθ; slɑθ; sloʊθ/ ***noun*** **1** [C] a South American animal that lives in trees and moves very

S

slowly **2** [U] (*formal*) the bad habit of being lazy and unwilling to work

**'slot ma,chine** ***noun*** [C] a machine on which you can play games and win money. You work it by putting money into a slot and then pushing a button or pulling a handle.

**slouch¹** /slaʊtʃ/ ***verb*** [I] to sit, stand or walk in a lazy way, with your head and shoulders hanging down

**slouch²** /slaʊtʃ/ ***noun*** [C]

IDM **be no slouch (at sth/at doing sth)** (*informal*) to be very good at doing sth: *Ashley's a very good tennis player, and she's no slouch at golf, either.*

**slough** /slʌf/ ***verb*** [T]

PHRV **slough sth off** (*formal*) to get rid of sth that you no longer want: *Responsibilities are not sloughed off so easily.*

**slov·en·ly** /'slʌvnli/ ***adj.*** careless, dirty, or not neat in appearance or habits: *He grew lazy and slovenly in his habits.* ◇ *a slovenly attitude/appearance*

★**slow¹** /sloʊ/ ***adj.***

➤NOT FAST **1** moving, doing sth or happening without much speed; not fast: *The traffic is always very slow downtown.* ◇ *Aren't you finished with your homework yet? You're always so slow!* ◇ *a slow improvement in his condition*

➤WITH DELAY **2** **slow to do sth**; **slow (in/about) doing sth** not doing sth immediately: *Jane was slow to react to the news.* ◇ *They've been very slow in answering my letter.*

➤NOT BUSY **3** not busy, lively or exciting: *Business is pretty slow these days.*

➤NOT CLEVER **4** not quick to learn or understand: *I'm sorry, but I don't understand what you mean. I must be a little slow.* ◇ *a slow learner*

➤WATCH/CLOCK **5** showing a time that is earlier than the real time: *That clock is five minutes slow* (= e.g. it says it is 8:55 when the correct time is 9:00).

▶ **slow·ness** ***noun*** [U]

**slow²** /sloʊ/ ***adv.*** at a slow speed; slowly

> NOTE It is possible to use **slow** as an adverb, but **slowly** is much more common, especially in more formal writing. However, **slow** is often used in compounds: *slow-moving traffic.* The comparative forms **slower** and **more slowly** are both common: *Could you speak a little slower/more slowly, please?*

★**slow³** /sloʊ/ ***verb*** [I,T] to start to move, do sth or happen at a slower speed; to cause sth to do this: *Jane ran along the path for a few minutes and then slowed to a walk.*

PHRV **slow (sb/sth) down/up** to start to move, do sth or happen at a slower speed; to cause sth to do this: *Can't you slow down a little bit? You're driving way too fast.* ◇ *These problems have slowed up the whole process.*

**slow·down** /'sloʊdaʊn/ ***noun*** [C] **1** a reduction in speed or activity: *a slowdown in economic growth* **2** a protest that workers make by doing their work more slowly than usual

★**slow·ly** /'sloʊli/ ***adv.*** at a slow speed; not quickly: *He walked slowly along the street.* ◇ *The economy is slowly improving.* ➲ Look at the note at **slow²**.

**,slow 'motion** ***noun*** [U] (in a movie or on television) a method of making action appear much slower than in real life: *They showed the winning touchdown again, this time in slow motion.*

**slow·poke** /'sloʊpoʊk/ ***noun*** [C] (*informal*) a person who moves, acts or works too slowly

**,slow-'witted** ***adj.*** not able to think quickly; slow to learn or understand things OPP **quick-witted**

**sludge** /slʌdʒ/ ***noun*** [U] thick, soft mud or waste

**slug¹** /slʌg/ ***noun*** [C] a small animal with a long wet body, that moves slowly along the ground and eats plants ➲ picture at **snail**.

**slug²** /slʌg/ ***verb*** [T] (*pres. part.* **slug·ging**; *pt, pp* **slugged**) **1** (*informal*) to hit sb hard, especially with your closed hand **2** (in baseball) to hit the ball hard

IDM **slug it out** to fight or compete until it is clear who has won

**slug·ger** /'slʌgər/ ***noun*** [C] (in baseball) a player who hits the ball very hard

**slug·gish** /'slʌgɪʃ/ ***adj.*** slow-moving; not lively: *This hot weather is making me feel very sluggish.* ◇ *sluggish economic growth*

**slum¹** /slʌm/ ***noun*** [C] (*also* **the slums** [pl.]) an area of a city where living conditions are extremely bad, and where the buildings are dirty and have not been repaired for a long time

**slum²** /slʌm/ ***verb*** [I] (*pres. part.* **slum·ming**; *pt, pp* **slum·med**) **be slumming** (*informal*) to spend time in places or conditions that are much worse than those you are used to: *There are plenty of ways you can cut costs on your trip without slumming.*

IDM **slum it** (*informal*) to accept conditions that are worse than those you are used to: *Several businessmen had to slum it in economy class.*

**slum·ber** /'slʌmbər/ ***noun*** [C] (*old-fashioned*) sleep: *The princess fell into a deep slumber.* ▶ **slumber** ***verb*** [I]

**'slumber ,party** (*also* **sleep·o·ver**) ***noun*** [C] a party for children or young people when a group of them spend the night at one house

**slum·lord** /'slʌmlɔrd/ ***noun*** [C] (*slang*) a person who owns houses or apartments in a poor area and who charges very high rent for them even though they are in bad condition

**slump¹** /slʌmp/ ***verb*** [I] **1** to fall or sit down suddenly when your body feels heavy and weak, usually because you are tired or sick: *Her face turned very white, and then suddenly she slumped over the table.* **2** (used about trade, prices, the value of sth, etc.) to fall suddenly and by a large amount: *Shares in the company slumped 33¢ to $1.81 yesterday.*

**slump²** /slʌmp/ ***noun*** [C] **1** a sudden large fall in business, the value of sth, etc.: *a slump in house prices* **2** a period when a country's economy is doing very badly and there is a lot of unemployment

**slung** *past tense, past participle of* SLING²

**slur¹** /slər/ ***noun*** [C] **a slur (against/on sb/sth)** a false statement or an insult that is unfair and is intended to harm sb/sth: *Two white students were banned from campus for making racial slurs against a black student.*

**slur²** /slər/ ***verb*** [T] (**slur·ring**; **slurred**) to speak words in a way that is not clear, often because you are drunk

**slurp** /slərp/ ***verb*** [I,T] (*informal*) to drink noisily: *I hate the way he slurps when he drinks coffee.* ▶ **slurp** ***noun*** [C]

**slush** /slʌʃ/ ***noun*** **1** [U] snow that has partly melted and that is often very wet and dirty **2** [C,U] a drink that is made from crushed ice with a fruit flavor ▶ **slush·y** ***adj.***

ˈ**slush fund** ***noun*** [C] a sum of money kept for illegal purposes, especially in politics

**slut** /slʌt/ ***noun*** [C] a sexually immoral woman

NOTE This word is used as a very strong insult.

▶ **slut·ty** (*also* **slut·tish**) ***adj.***

**sly**[1] /slaɪ/ ***adj.*** **1** (used about a person) good at deceiving people or doing things in secret **2** (used about an action) suggesting that you know sth secret: *a sly smile* ▶ **sly·ly** ***adv.***

**sly**[2] /slaɪ/ ***noun*** [U]

IDM **on the sly** secretly; not wanting other people to discover what you are doing: *He has to visit them on the sly.*

**smack**[1] /smæk/ ***verb*** [T] to hit sb/sth with the inside flat part of your hand: *She smacked him right on the head.*

PHRV **smack of sth** to make you think that sb/sth has an unpleasant attitude or quality: *This change in the admissions policy smacks of racism.*

**smack**[2] /smæk/ ***noun*** **1** [C] a sharp hit given with your open hand, usually on the face: *She gave him a smack and ran out of the room.* **2** [U] (*slang*) the drug heroin: *smack addicts/dealers*

**smack**[3] /smæk/ (*also* ˌ**smack-ˈdab**) ***adv.*** (*informal*) exactly; right; directly: *He ran right smack into the wall.*

★**small** /smɔl/ ***adj.*** **1** not large in size, number, amount, etc.: *a small car/apartment/town* ◇ *a small group of people* ◇ *a small amount of money* **2** young: *He has a wife and three small children.* **3** not important or serious; slight: *Don't worry. It's only a small problem.*

NOTE **Small** is the most usual opposite of **big** or **large**. **Little** is often used with another adjective to express an emotion, as well as the idea of smallness: *a sweet little girl* ◇ *a nice little house.* The comparative and superlative forms **smaller** and **smallest** are common, and small is often used with words like "fairly," "pretty" and "very": *My room is smaller than yours.* ◇ *The town is pretty small.* ◇ *a very small car.* **Little** does not usually have a comparative or superlative form in more formal written English.

IDM **in a big/small way** → WAY[1]

▶ **small** ***adv.***: *She painted the picture way too small.*

ˌ**small ˈchange** ***noun*** [U] coins that have a low value

ˌ**small ˈclaims court** ***noun*** [C,U] a court that deals with cases involving small amounts of money, where people do not need lawyers to speak for them

ˌ**small-ˈminded** ***adj.*** having fixed opinions and ways of doing things and not willing to change them or consider other people's opinions or feelings; interested in small problems and details and not in things which are really important

**small·pox** /ˈsmɔlpɑks/ ***noun*** [U] a serious infectious disease that causes a high fever and leaves marks on the skin. In the past, many people died from smallpox.

ˌ**small-ˈscale** ***adj.*** (usually *before* a noun) (used about an organization or activity) not large; limited in what it does: *a small-scale business*

ˈ**small talk** ***noun*** [U] polite conversation, e.g. at a party, about unimportant things

ˈ**small-town** ***adj.*** (only *before* a noun) **1** not showing much interest in new ideas or what is happening outside your own environment: *small-town values/views* SYN **narrow-minded** **2** connected with a small town: *small-town America* (= people who live in small towns in America)

**smarm·y** /ˈsmɑrmi/ ***adj.*** (**smarm·i·er**; **smarm·i·est**) (*informal*) too polite in a way that is not sincere: *a smarmy salesman/comment*

★**smart**[1] /smɑrt/ ***adj.*** **1** intelligent; able to learn and think quickly: *He's not smart enough to be a politician.* ◇ *a very smart little girl* **2** showing good judgment or resulting from quick thinking: *smart investments* ◇ *a smart decision* OPP The opposite for senses **1** and **2** is **stupid**. **3** (*informal*) being impolite by saying things or making jokes in a way that shows a lack of respect: *Don't get smart with me, kid.*

**smart**[2] /smɑrt/ ***verb*** [I] to feel a stinging pain in your body: *The smoke made her eyes smart.* ◇ (*figurative*) *He was still smarting from her insult.*

**smart al·eck** /ˈsmɑrṭ ˌælɪk/ (*also* **smart·ass**, **smart-ass** /ˈsmɑrṭæs/, ˈ**smarty-pants**) ***noun*** [C] (*informal*) a person who thinks he/she is very clever and likes to show people this in an annoying way

ˈ**smart bomb** ***noun*** [C] a bomb controlled by a computer, which helps to guide it to its target

ˈ**smart card** ***noun*** [C] a small plastic card on which information is stored in electronic form

**smarts** /smɑrts/ ***noun*** [U] (*informal*) intelligence; the ability to think quickly and in a practical way: *He doesn't have enough smarts to run his own business.*

**smart·y-pants** /ˈsmɑrṭi pænts/ ***noun*** [C] (*informal*) = SMART ALECK

**smash**[1] /smæʃ/ ***verb*** **1** [I,T] to break violently into many pieces: *The glass smashed into a thousand pieces.* ◇ *The police had to smash the door open.* **2** [I,T] **smash (sth) against, into, through, etc.** to move with great force in a particular direction: *The car smashed into a tree.* ◇ *He smashed his hand through the window.* **3** [T] to destroy, defeat or put an end to sth/sb: *Police say they have smashed a major drug ring.* ◇ *She has smashed the world record* (= broken it by a large amount).

PHRV **smash sth up** to destroy sth deliberately: *The phone booth had been completely smashed up.*

**smash**[2] /smæʃ/ ***noun*** [C] (*also* ˌ**smash ˈhit**) (*informal*) a song, play, movie, etc. that is very successful

**smashed** /smæʃt/ ***adj.*** (not before a noun) (*slang*) very drunk or high on drugs

**smash·ing** /ˈsmæʃɪŋ/ ***adj.*** (*old-fashioned*,

S

*informal*) very good or enjoyable: *We had a smashing time.*

**smat·ter·ing** /ˈsmæt̬ərɪŋ/ ***noun*** [sing.] **a smattering (of sth)** a small amount of sth, especially knowledge of a language: *I only speak a smattering of Spanish.*

**smear**[1] /smɪr/ ***verb*** [T] **1 smear sth on/over sth/sb; smear sth/sb with sth** to spread a sticky substance across sth/sb: *The little boy had smeared chocolate all over his clothes.* ◇ *Her face was smeared with grease.* **2** to say unfavorable and untrue things about an important person in order to damage his/her reputation

**smear**[2] /smɪr/ ***noun*** [C] **1** a mark made by smearing: *a smear of paint on her dress* ➲ Look also at **Pap smear**. **2** something unfavorable and untrue that is said in a newspaper, etc. about an important person

★**smell**[1] /smɛl/ ***verb*** **1** [T] to notice, identify or examine sb/sth by using your nose: *He could smell something burning.* ◇ *Can you smell gas?* **2** [I] to be able to SMELL (1): *I can't smell very well because I have a cold.* **3** [I] **smell (like sth)** to have a particular smell: *Dinner smells good!* ◇ *This perfume smells like roses.* **4** [I] to have a bad smell: *Your feet smell.*

NOTE We do not use **smell** or other verbs of the senses (e.g. **taste**, **see**, **hear**) in the continuous tense. Instead we often use **can**, e.g: *I can smell smoke.* ◇ *Do you hear somebody outside?*

★**smell**[2] /smɛl/ ***noun*** **1** [U] the ability to SMELL[1] (1): *Dogs have a very good sense of smell.* **2** [C,U] the impression that you get of sth by using your nose; the thing that is smelled: *the great smell of steaks cooking on the grill* ◇ *a strong smell* **3** [C] an unpleasant SMELL (2): *What's that smell?*

**ˈsmelling ˌsalts** ***noun*** [pl.] a chemical with a very strong smell, kept in a small bottle, used especially in the past for putting under the nose of a person who has become unconscious (**fainted**)

**smell·y** /ˈsmɛli/ ***adj.*** (**smell·i·er**; **smell·i·est**) (*informal*) having a bad smell: *smelly feet*

**smelt** /smɛlt/ ***verb*** [T] to heat and melt rock that contains metal (**ore**) in order to obtain the metal it contains: *a method of smelting iron*

**smelt·er** /ˈsmɛltər/ ***noun*** [C] a piece of equipment for smelting metal

**smid·gen** (*also* **smid·geon**, **smid·gin**) /ˈsmɪdʒən/ ***noun*** [sing.] (*informal*) **a smidgen (of sth)** a small piece or amount of sth: *"Sugar?" "Just a smidgen."*

★**smile** /smaɪl/ ***noun*** [C] an expression on your face in which the corners of your mouth turn up, showing happiness, pleasure, etc.: *to have a smile on your face* ◇ *"It's nice to see you," he said with a smile.* ▸ **smile *verb*** [I]: *She smiled at the camera.* ◇ *He was smiling with happiness.*

**smil·ey** /ˈsmaɪli/ ***noun*** [C] **1** (*computing*) a series of keyboard symbols,:-), that represents a smiling face when you look at it sideways, used in e-mail, etc. to show that the person sending the message is pleased or joking **2** = SMILEY FACE

**ˈsmiley face** (*also* **ˈsmiley**) ***noun*** [C] a simple picture of a smiling face that is drawn as a circle with two eyes and a curved mouth

**smirk** /smərk/ ***noun*** [C] a silly or unpleasant smile which you have when you are pleased with yourself or think sb/sth is stupid ▸ **smirk *verb*** [I]

**smith·er·eens** /ˌsmɪðəˈrinz/ ***noun*** [pl.]

IDM **smash, blow, etc. sth to smithereens** (*informal*) to destroy sth completely by breaking it into small pieces: *The bomb blew the car to smithereens.*

**smit·ten** /ˈsmɪtn/ ***adj.*** (only *before* noun) **smitten (with/by sb/sth)** suddenly feeling that you are in love with sb: *From the moment they met, he was completely smitten by her.*

**smock** /smɑk/ ***noun*** [C] a type of long loose shirt that you wear over your clothes to protect them while you are working, painting, etc.

**smog** /smɑg; smɔg/ ***noun*** [U] a mixture of fog and smoke, caused by pollution, that is in the air over some cities ▸ **smog·gy *adj.*** (**smog·gi·er**; **smog·gi·est**)

★**smoke**[1] /smoʊk/ ***noun*** **1** [U] the gas that you can see in the air when something is burning: *Thick smoke poured from the chimney.* ◇ *a room full of cigarette smoke* **2** [C, usually sing.] (*informal*) an act of smoking a cigarette, etc.: *He went outside for a quick smoke.*

★**smoke**[2] /smoʊk/ ***verb*** **1** [I,T] to breathe in smoke through a cigarette, etc. and let it out again; to have the habit of doing this regularly: *Is it all right if I smoke?* ◇ *I used to smoke a pack of cigarettes a day.* **2** [I] to give out smoke: *The factory chimneys were smoking.* ▸ **smok·ing** /ˈsmoʊkɪŋ/ ***noun*** [U]: *She's trying to quit smoking.* ▸ **smok·ing *adj.***: *I'd like a table in the smoking section.*

**ˈsmoke aˌlarm** ***noun*** [C] = SMOKE DETECTOR

**smoked** /smoʊkt/ ***adj.*** (used of certain types of food) preserved and given a special taste by being hung in smoke: *smoked salmon*

**ˈsmoke deˌtector** (*also* **ˈsmoke aˌlarm**) ***noun*** [C] a device that makes a loud noise if smoke is in the air to warn you of a fire

**ˌsmoke-ˈfree** ***adj.*** (used about a place) where people are not allowed to smoke cigarettes, etc.: *smoke-free offices*

**smok·er** /ˈsmoʊkər/ ***noun*** [C] a person who smokes cigarettes, etc.: *She's a chain smoker* (= she finishes one cigarette and then immediately lights another). OPP **nonsmoker**

**smoke·screen** /ˈsmoʊkskrin/ ***noun*** [C] **1** something that you do or say in order to hide what you are really doing or intending **2** a cloud of smoke used to hide soldiers, ships, etc. during a battle

**ˈsmoke ˌsignal** ***noun*** [C] smoke from a fire, which is used as a way of sending a message to sb who is far away

**smoke·stack** /ˈsmoʊkstæk/ ***noun*** [C] **1** a tall chimney that takes away smoke from factories **2** a metal chimney, for example on a ship or an engine, through which smoke comes out

**ˌsmoking ˈgun** ***noun*** [sing.] (*informal*) something that seems to prove that sb has done sth wrong or illegal: *This memo could be the smoking gun that investigators have been looking for.*

**smok·y** /ˈsmoʊki/ ***adj.*** (**smok·i·er**; **smok·i·est**)

**1** full of smoke; producing a lot of smoke: *a smoky hallway* ◇ *a smoky fire* **2** with the smell, taste or appearance of smoke: *This bacon has a smoky flavor.*

**smol·der** /ˈsmoʊldər/ *verb* [I] to burn slowly without a flame: *a cigarette smoldering in the ashtray* ◇ (*figurative*) *Her eyes were smoldering with rage.*

**smooch** /smutʃ/ *verb* [I] (*informal*) to kiss and hold sb closely

★**smooth¹** /smuð/ *adj.*
➤FLAT/EVEN **1** having a flat surface with no lumps or holes: *smooth skin* ◇ *a smooth piece of wood*
➤WITHOUT LUMPS **2** (of a liquid mixture) without lumps: *Stir the sauce until it is smooth.*
➤MOVEMENT **3** (of a trip in a car, etc.) with an even, comfortable movement: *The flight was very smooth.*
➤WITHOUT PROBLEMS **4** without difficulties: *The transition from the old method to the new one has been very smooth.*
➤MAN **5** too pleasant or polite to be trusted ➲ We use this word in a critical way, usually about a man or his actions. ▸ **smooth·ness** *noun* [U]

**smooth²** /smuð/ *verb* [T] **smooth sth (back, down, out, etc.)** to move your hands in the direction mentioned over the surface of sth to make it smooth: *I smoothed the tablecloth out.* ◇ (*figurative*) *They are trying to smooth out the problems in the manufacturing process.*
PHR V **smooth sth over** to make problems or difficulties seem less important or serious, especially by talking to people: *She spoke to both sides in the dispute in an attempt to smooth things over.*

**smooth·ie** /ˈsmuði/ *noun* [C] **1** a thick drink made of fruit or fruit juice mixed with milk, yoghurt or ice cream: *a banana smoothie* **2** (*informal*) a man who talks very politely and confidently but who is often not honest or sincere: *I wouldn't trust that smoothie if I were you.* ◇ *He's a real smoothie.*

★**smooth·ly** /ˈsmuðli/ *adv.* without any difficulty: *My work has been going really smoothly.*

**smor·gas·bord** /ˈsmɔrgəsbɔrd/ *noun* [U, sing.] **1** a meal at which you serve yourself from a large range of hot and cold dishes **2 a smorgasbord (of sth)** a large variety of sth

**smoth·er** /ˈsmʌðər/ *verb* [T] **1** to kill sb by not allowing him/her to breathe: *She was smothered with a pillow.* **2** to cover sth (with too much of a substance): *He smothered his toast with jelly.* **3** to stop sth from burning by covering it: *to smother the flames with a blanket*

**smudge¹** /smʌdʒ/ *noun* [C] a dirty or messy mark: *His homework was covered in ink smudges.*

**smudge²** /smʌdʒ/ *verb* **1** [T] to make sth dirty or messy by touching it: *Leave your painting to dry or you'll smudge it.* **2** [I] to become messy, without a clean line around it: *Her lipstick smudged when she kissed him.*

**smug** /smʌg/ *adj.* (**smug·ger**; **smug·gest**) too pleased with yourself: *Don't look so smug.* ➲ We use this word in a critical way. ▸ **smug·ly** *adv.* ▸ **smug·ness** *noun* [U]

**smug·gle** /ˈsmʌgl/ *verb* [T] to take things into or out of a country in a way which is against the law; to take a person into or out of a place in secret: *The drugs had been smuggled through customs.* ◇ *The illegal immigrants were smuggled across the border.* ▸ **smug·gler** /ˈsmʌglər/ *noun* [C]: *a drug smuggler* ▸ **smug·gling** /ˈsmʌglɪŋ/ *noun* [U]

**smut** /smʌt/ *noun* **1** [U] (*informal*) stories, pictures or comments about sex that deal with it in a way that some people find offensive: *He can entertain audiences without resorting to smut.* **2** [C,U] dirt, ash, etc. that causes a black mark on sth; a black mark made by this: *His face was covered with smuts from the engine.* ▸ **smut·ty** *adj.* (**smut·ti·er**; **smut·ti·est**): *smutty jokes*

**snack¹** /snæk/ *noun* [C] a small amount of food, e.g. cookies or candy, that you eat quickly between main meals: *I had a snack at the mall.*

**snack²** /snæk/ *verb* [I] to eat a snack instead of a meal or between meals: *Encourage your children to snack on healthy things instead of junk food.*

**ˈsnack bar** *noun* [C] a type of small restaurant where you can buy a snack

**sna·fu** /snæˈfu/ *noun* [sing.] (*informal*) a situation in which nothing happens as planned: *It was another bureaucratic snafu.*

**snag¹** /snæg/ *noun* [C] **1** a small difficulty or disadvantage that is often unexpected or hidden: *Plans to build the prison hit a snag when local residents started to protest.* **2** a thread in a piece of clothing that has been pulled by accident because it got caught on sth sharp

**snag²** /snæg/ *verb* [T] (**snag·ging**; **snagged**) **1** to catch a piece of clothing, etc. on sth sharp and tear it **2** (*informal*) to succeed in getting sth before other people have a chance to get it: *Quick – let's snag those seats in the front row!*

**snail**

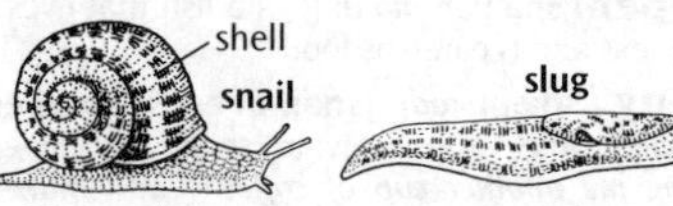


**snail** /sneɪl/ *noun* [C] a type of animal with a soft body without legs that is covered by a shell. Snails move very slowly.

**ˈsnail mail** *noun* [U] (*slang*) letters, messages, etc. that are written and sent on paper and not from one computer to another ➲ Look at **e-mail**.

★**snake¹** /sneɪk/ *noun* [C] a type of long thin animal without legs that slides along the ground by moving its body from side to side: *a poisonous snake* ◇ *Todd got bitten by a snake.* ➲ Look also at **rattlesnake**.

**snake²** /sneɪk/ *verb* [I] (*also* **snake its way**) to move like a snake: *The road snakes its way through the mountains.*

**snake·bite** /ˈsneɪkbaɪt/ *noun* [C,U] a wound that you get when a poisonous snake bites you: *Three people have recently died from snakebites.* ◇ *remedies for snakebite*

**snake charm·er** /ˈsneɪk ˌtʃɑrmər/ *noun* [C] an entertainer who seems to be able to control snakes and make them move by playing music to them

**ˈsnake oil** *noun* [U] (*informal*) something, for example medicine, that sb tries to sell you, but that is not effective or useful: *a snake-oil salesman*

**snake·skin** /ˈsneɪkskɪn/ ***noun*** [U] the skin of a snake, used for making expensive shoes, bags, etc.

**snap¹** /snæp/ ***verb*** (**snap·ping**; **snapped**)
▸ BREAK **1** [I,T] to break suddenly with a sharp noise: *The branch snapped.* ◇ *The weight of the snow snapped the branch in two.* ◇ *(figurative) Suddenly, something just snapped and I lost my temper with him.*
▸ OPEN/CLOSE/MOVE INTO POSITION **2** [I,T] to close quickly with a sharp noise: *The lid of the box snapped shut.*
▸ SPEAK IMPATIENTLY **3** [I,T] to speak or say sth in a quick angry way: *"Do it now!" she snapped.*
▸ OF ANIMAL **4** [I] to try to bite sb/sth: *The dog snapped at the child's hand.*
▸ TAKE PHOTOGRAPH **5** [T] (*informal*) to take a quick photograph of sb/sth
IDM **snap your fingers** to make a sharp noise by moving your middle finger quickly against your thumb
PHR V **snap sth up** to buy or take sth quickly, especially because it is very cheap

**snap²** /snæp/ ***noun*** [C] **1** an act or the sound of snapping: *The piece of wood broke with a snap.* **2** a small round metal object with two parts that you press together in order to fasten a piece of clothing

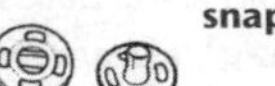
snaps

**snap³** /snæp/ ***adj.*** (*informal*) (only *before* a noun) done quickly and suddenly, often without much careful thought: *a snap decision*

**snap·drag·on** /ˈsnæpˌdrægən/ ***noun*** [C] a small garden plant with red, white, yellow or pink flowers that open and shut like a mouth when squeezed

**snap·per** /ˈsnæpər/ ***noun*** [C,U] a fish that lives in warm seas and is eaten as food

**snap·py** /ˈsnæpi/ ***adj.*** (**snap·pi·er**; **snap·pi·est**) (*informal*) quick and lively: *a snappy ad slogan* ◇ *Bring me another cup of coffee – and make it snappy* (= do it quickly)*!*

**snap·shot** /ˈsnæpʃɑt/ ***noun*** [C] a photograph that is taken quickly and informally

**snare** /snɛr/ ***noun*** [C] a trap used to catch birds or small animals ▸ **snare *verb*** [T] (*figurative*): *The killer was snared by undercover police.*

**ˈsnare drum** ***noun*** [C] a small drum with metal strings across one side that make a continuous sound when the drum is hit

**snarf** /snɑrf/ ***verb*** [T] (*informal*) to eat or drink sth very quickly or in a way that people think is greedy: *The kids snarfed up all the cookies.*

**snarl¹** /snɑrl/ ***verb*** [I,T] (used about an animal) to make an angry sound while showing the teeth: *The dog snarled at the stranger.* ◇ *(figurative) "Get out of here!" he snarled.*
PHR V **snarl (sth) up** to involve sb/sth in a situation that stops his/her/its movement or progress; to become involved in a situation like this: *The accident snarled up the traffic all day.*

**snarl²** /snɑrl/ ***noun*** [C] **1** an angry sound or remark **2** a mass of hair, threads, etc. that are twisted together and messy: *Her hair was full of snarls.* ◇ *(figurative) traffic snarls*

**snatch¹** /snætʃ/ ***verb*** [T] **1** to (try to) take or pull sth/sb away quickly: *He snatched the gun from her hand.* SYN **grab** **2** to take sb/sth away from a person or place, especially by force; to steal sth: *Kidnappers snatched the newborn baby from the hospital's maternity ward.* ◇ *My bag was snatched* (= stolen). **3** to take or get sth quickly when you have just enough time to do so

**snatch²** /snætʃ/ ***noun*** **1** [sing.] an act of snatching sth: *I made a snatch at the ball.* **2** [C, usually pl.] a short part or period of something: *I heard snatches of conversation from the next room.*

**snaz·zy** /ˈsnæzi/ ***adj.*** (**snaz·zi·er**; **snaz·zi·est**) (*informal*) (used about clothes, cars, etc.) fashionable, bright and modern, and attracting your attention: *a snazzy suit/car* ◇ *snazzy graphics for the new computer game*

**sneak** /snik/ ***verb*** (*pt, pp* **sneaked** or **snuck** /snʌk/) **1** [I] **sneak into, out of, past, etc. sth; sneak in, out, away, etc.** to go very quietly in the direction mentioned, so that no one can see or hear you: *Instead of working, he sneaked out to go shopping.* ◇ *The prisoner sneaked past the guards.* **2** [T] (*informal*) to take sth secretly or without permission: *She snuck a piece of candy when no one was looking.*

> NOTE Many people do not like the use of **snuck**, especially in formal writing. However, it is very common in informal speech.

PHR V **sneak up (on sb/sth)** to approach sb very quietly, especially so that you can surprise him/her

**sneak·er** /ˈsnikər/ (*also* **ˈtennis shoe**) ***noun*** [C] a type of comfortable shoe that you wear to play sports or with informal clothes: *a pair of sneakers* ➲ picture at **shoe**.

**sneak·ing** /ˈsnikɪŋ/ ***adj.*** (only *before* a noun) (of feelings, etc.) not expressed; secret: *I have a sneaking suspicion that he's lying.*

**ˌsneak ˈpreview** ***noun*** [C] an opportunity to see sth before it is officially shown to the public

**sneak·y** /ˈsniki/ ***adj.*** (**sneak·i·er**; **sneak·i·est**) (*informal*) behaving in a secret and sometimes dishonest or unpleasant way: *That was a sneaky trick!* ▸ **sneak·i·ly *adv.***

**sneer** /snɪr/ ***verb*** [I] **sneer (at sb/sth)** to behave or speak as if sth is not good enough for you: *She sneered at his attempts to speak French.* ▸ **sneer *noun*** [C]

**cough/sneeze**

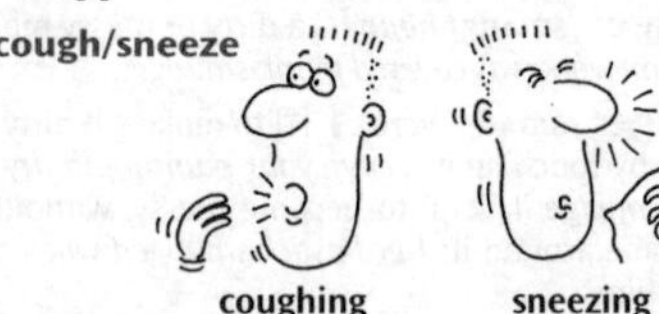


**sneeze** /sniz/ ***noun*** [C] a sudden burst of air coming out through your nose and mouth that happens, for example, when you have a cold ▸ **sneeze *verb*** [I]: *Dust makes me sneeze.*

**snick·er** /ˈsnɪkər/ ***verb*** [I] **snicker (at sb/sth)** to laugh quietly to yourself in an unkind way: *They snickered at his old clothes.* ▸ **snick·er *noun*** [C]

**snide** /snaɪd/ ***adj.*** (*informal*) criticizing sb/sth in an unkind and indirect way: *snide comments/remarks*

**sniff** /snɪf/ ***verb*** **1** [I] to breathe air in through the nose in a way that makes a sound, especially because you have a cold or you are crying: *Quit sniffing and blow your nose.* **2** [I,T] **sniff (at) sth** to smell sth by sniffing: *"I smell gas," he said, sniffing the air.* ◇ *The dog sniffed at the bone.* ▶ **sniff** ***noun*** [C]

**snif·fle¹** /snɪfl/ ***verb*** [I] to sniff continuously, especially because you have a cold or you are crying

**snif·fle²** /ˈsnɪfl/ ***noun*** [C] an act or the sound of sniffling: *After a while, her sniffles died away.*

IDM **get, have, etc. the sniffles** (*informal*) to get, have, etc. a slight cold

**snip** /snɪp/ ***verb*** [I,T] (**snip·ping**; **snipped**) to cut using scissors, with a short quick action ▶ **snip** ***noun*** [C]

**snip·er** /ˈsnaɪpər/ ***noun*** [C] a person who shoots at sb from a hidden position: *Two soldiers were shot by snipers.* ◇ *sniper fire*

**snip·pet** /ˈsnɪpət/ ***noun*** [C] **1** a small piece of information or news: *a snippet of information/gossip* **2** a short piece of a conversation, piece of music, etc.

**snip·py** /ˈsnɪpi/ ***adj.*** (**snip·pi·er**; **snip·pi·est**) (*informal*) rude; not showing respect

**snit** /snɪt/ ***noun*** [C]

IDM **be in a snit** to be bad-tempered and refuse to speak to anyone for a time because you are angry about sth

**snitch¹** /snɪtʃ/ ***verb*** **1** [I] **snitch (on sb) (to sb)** to tell a parent, teacher, etc. about sth wrong that another child has done: *Johnnie snitched on me to his mom.* **2** [T] to take sth without the owner's permission, usually sth small and not important or valuable: *I snitched some of my son's Halloween candy.*

**snitch²** /snɪtʃ/ ***noun*** [C] a person who tells sb in authority about sth wrong that another person has done: *You little snitch! I'll never tell you anything again!*

**snob** /snɑb/ ***noun*** [C] a person who thinks he/she is better than sb of a lower social class and who admires people who have a high social position: *Don't be such a snob!* ▶ **snob·bish** /ˈsnɑbɪʃ/ (*also* **snob·by** /ˈsnɑbi/) ***adj.***: *She had a snobbish attitude toward her husband's family.*

**snob·ber·y** /ˈsnɑbəri/ ***noun*** [U] behavior or attitudes that are typical of a snob

**snoop** /snup/ ***verb*** [I] to look around secretly and without permission in order to find out information, etc.: *If I catch you snooping around here again, I'll call the police!* ▶ **snoop·er** ***noun*** [C]

**snoop·y** /ˈsnupi/ ***adj.*** (**snoop·i·er**; **snoop·i·est**) (*informal*) always trying to find out private information about people or things

**snooze** /snuz/ ***verb*** [I] (*informal*) to sleep for a short period of time, especially during the day ▶ **snooze** ***noun*** [C, usually sing.]: *I had a little snooze on the couch.* ➲ Look at **nap**.

**snore** /snɔr/ ***verb*** [I] to breathe noisily through your nose and mouth while you are asleep: *She heard her father snoring in the next room.* ▶ **snore** ***noun*** [C]

**snor·kel** /ˈsnɔrkl/ ***noun*** [C] a short tube that a swimmer who is just below the surface of the water can use to breathe through

**snor·kel·ing** /ˈsnɔrkəlɪŋ/ ***noun*** [U] the sport or activity of swimming underwater with a snorkel: *to go snorkeling*

**snort** /snɔrt/ ***verb*** [I] **1** (used about animals) to make a noise by blowing air through the nose: *The horse snorted in fear.* **2** (used about people) to make a noise through your nose as a way of showing that you do not like sth, or that you are impatient ▶ **snort** ***noun*** [C]

**snot** /snɑt/ ***noun*** [U] (*informal*) the liquid produced by the nose

**snot·ty** /ˈsnɑṭi/ (*also* **ˈsnotty-nosed**) ***adj.*** (*informal*) **1** treating people as if they are not as good or as important as you **2** full of or covered in snot: *a snotty nose* ◇ *snotty kids*

**snout** /snaʊt/ ***noun*** [C] the long nose of certain animals: *a pig's snout*

★**snow¹** /snoʊ/ ***noun*** [U] **1** small, soft, white pieces of frozen water that fall from the sky in cold weather: *Three inches of snow fell during the night.* ◇ *Most of the snow had melted by early March.* ◇ *Greg shoveled the snow off the front steps.* ➲ Look at the note at **weather**. **2** white spots on a television screen caused by a poor signal, etc.

★**snow²** /snoʊ/ ***verb*** [I] (used with the subject *it*) (used of snow) to fall from the sky: *It snowed all night.*

IDM **be snowed in** to be unable to leave home or travel because the snow is too deep

**be snowed under** to have more work, etc. than you can deal with

**snow·ball¹** /ˈsnoʊbɔl/ ***noun*** [C] a lump of snow that is pressed into the shape of a ball and that children play with and throw

**snow·ball²** /ˈsnoʊbɔl/ ***verb*** [I] to quickly grow bigger and bigger or more and more serious, etc.: *After Ted lost his job, our debts just seemed to snowball until we went bankrupt.*

**snow·bird** /ˈsnoʊbərd/ ***noun*** [C] (*informal*) a person from Canada or the northern U.S. who moves to a southern state, where it is warm, for the winter

**snow·blow·er** /ˈsnoʊˌbloʊər/ ***noun*** [C] a machine that removes snow from roads or paths by blowing it to one side

**snow·board** /ˈsnoʊbɔrd/ ***noun*** [C] a type of wide board that you fasten to both your feet and use for moving down hills or mountains that are covered with snow ▶ **snow·board·er** ***noun*** [C] ▶ **snow·board·ing** ***noun*** [U]

**snowboarding**

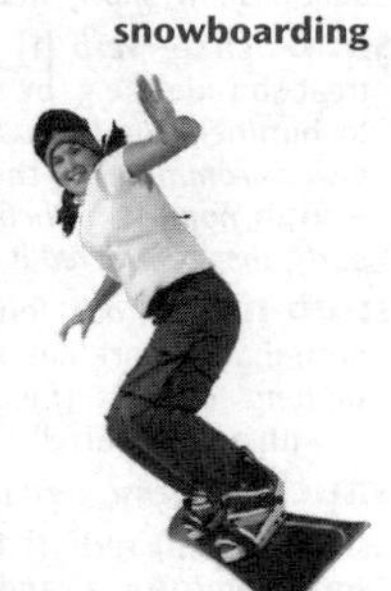

**ˈsnow cone** ***noun*** [C] a sweet dish (dessert) of flavored crushed ice, served in a paper cone

**ˈsnow day** ***noun*** [C] a



S

day when schools and businesses are closed because it has snowed, or is snowing, heavily

**snow·drift** /ˈsnoʊdrɪft/ (*also* **drift**) ***noun*** [C] a deep pile of snow that has been made by the wind

**snow·fall** /ˈsnoʊfɔl/ ***noun*** **1** [C] the snow that falls on one occasion: *heavy snowfalls* **2** [U] the amount of snow that falls in a particular place: *What is the average annual snowfall in Manitoba?*

**snow·flake** /ˈsnoʊfleɪk/ ***noun*** [C] one of the small, soft, white pieces of frozen water that fall together as snow

ˈ**snow job** ***noun*** [C] (*informal*) an attempt to deceive sb or to persuade sb to support sth by telling him/her things that are not true, or by praising him/her too much

**snow·man** /ˈsnoʊmæn/ ***noun*** [C] (*pl.* **snow·men** /-mɛn/) the figure of a person made out of snow, usually by children

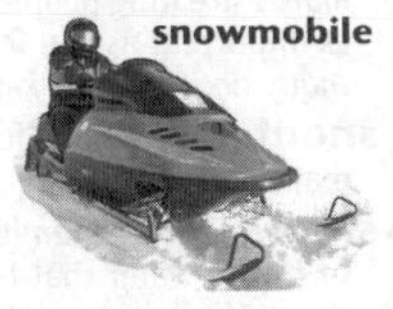
**snowmobile**

**snow·mo·bile** /ˈsnoʊmoʊbil/ ***noun*** [C] a small vehicle with two parts like skis in the front and special wheels in the back for moving over snow and ice

**snow·plow** /ˈsnoʊplaʊ/ ***noun*** [C] a type of vehicle that is used to clear snow away from roads

ˈ**snow route** ***noun*** [C] an important road in a city which is one of the first to be cleared when heavy snow falls so that people can get in and out of the city

**snow·shoe** /ˈsnoʊʃu/ ***noun*** [C] one of a pair of flat frames that you attach to the bottom of your shoes so that you can walk on deep snow without sinking in

**snow·storm** /ˈsnoʊstɔrm/ ***noun*** [C] a winter storm in which a lot of snow falls, often with strong winds SYN **blizzard**

**snow·suit** /ˈsnoʊsut/ ***noun*** [C] a warm waterproof jacket and a pair of pants, sometimes combined in a single piece of clothing, that children wear to play in the snow

ˈ**snow tire** ***noun*** [C] a tire with deep TREADS² that makes it easier to travel on roads that are slippery from snow and ice

ˌ**snow-ˈwhite** ***adj.*** (*written*) pure white in color: *snow-white sheets*

**snow·y** /ˈsnoʊi/ ***adj.*** (**snow·i·er**; **snow·i·est**) with a lot of snow: *snowy weather* ◇ *a snowy scene*

**snub** /snʌb/ ***verb*** [T] (**snub·bing**; **snubbed**) to treat sb rudely, e.g. by refusing to look at or speak to him/her: *His latest movie was snubbed by the awards committee* (= they did not give it an award). ▸ **snub** ***noun*** [C]: *When they weren't invited to the party, they considered it a snub.*

ˈ**snub-nosed** ***adj.*** (only *before* a noun) having a nose that is short, flat and turned up at the end: *a snub-nosed child* ◇ (*figurative*) *a snub-nosed revolver* (= with a short barrel)

**snuck** *past tense, past participle of* SNEAK

**snuff¹** /snʌf/ ***verb*** [T] **1 snuff sth (out)** to stop a small flame (e.g. a candle) from burning, especially by pressing it between your fingers or covering it with sth **2** (used about an animal) to smell sth by breathing in noisily through the nose: *The dogs were snuffing gently at my feet.*

PHR V **snuff sth out** (*written*) to stop or destroy sth completely: *An innocent child's life has been snuffed out by this senseless shooting.*

**snuff²** /snʌf/ ***noun*** [U] tobacco in the form of a powder that people take by breathing it into their noses

IDM **(not) be up to snuff** (*informal*) to (not) be as good as sth/sb should be: *I want to make sure everything's up to snuff before the inspector arrives.*

ˈ**snuff film** (*also* ˈ**snuff** ˌ**movie**) ***noun*** [C] (*informal*) a pornographic movie that shows the real murder of one of the actors in it, intended as entertainment

**snug** /snʌg/ ***adj.*** **1** warm and comfortable: *The children were snug in bed.* **2** fairly tight: *Make sure your seat belt is snug across your lap.* ▸ **snug·ly** ***adv.***

**snug·gle** /ˈsnʌgl/ ***verb*** [I] **snuggle (up to sb)**; **snuggle (up)** to get into a position that makes you feel safe, warm and comfortable, usually next to another person: *She snuggled up to her mother.* ◇ *I snuggled under the blanket to get warm.*

**So.** ***abbr.*** south

★**so¹** /soʊ/ ***adv.*** **1** (used to emphasize an adjective or adverb, especially when there is a particular result) to the extent (that); to a great degree: *She's so sick (that) she can't get out of bed.* ◇ *He was driving so fast that he couldn't stop.* ◇ *I haven't enjoyed myself so much in years.* ◇ *So many people came to the concert that some couldn't get in.* ➲ Look at the note at **such**. **2** (*informal*) very: *You've been so nice. How can I thank you?* ◇ *Rob is so cute!* ◇ *That is so disgusting!* ◇ *Thanks so much!* **3** (used in place of something that has been said already, to avoid repeating it): *Are you flying in? If so* (= if you are flying), *I can meet you at the airport.* ◇ *"I failed, didn't I?" "I'm afraid so, Susan."*

NOTE In formal language, you can refer to actions that somebody has mentioned using **do** with **so**: *If you have not yet paid your bill, please do so* (= pay your bill) *immediately.*

**4** (not with verbs in the negative) also, too: *He's a teacher and so is his wife.* ◇ *"I've been to New York." "So have I."* ◇ *I like singing and so does Helen.*

NOTE For negative sentences, look at **neither**.

**5** (used to show that you agree that sth is true, especially when you are surprised): *"It's getting late." "So it is. We'd better go."*

IDM **and so on (and so forth)** (used at the end of a list to show that it continues in the same way): *They sell pens, pencils, paper and so on.*

**I told you so** (used to tell sb that he/she should have listened to your advice): *"I missed the bus." "I told you so. I said you needed to leave earlier."*

**it (just) so happens** (used to introduce a surprising fact) by chance: *It just so happened that we were going the same way, so he gave me a ride.*

**or so** (used to show that a number, time, etc. is not exact): *A hundred or so people came to the meeting.*

**so as to do sth** (*formal*) with the intention of doing sth; in order to do sth: *We must change the*

*law so as to improve its effectiveness.* ◇ *They moved silently so as not to scare the animals.*
**so long** (*informal*) goodbye: *So long! See you next week!*
**so much for sth** (used for expressing that sth is finished or not helpful): *So much for that diet! I didn't lose any weight at all.*

★**so²** /soʊ/ ***conj.*** **1** with the result that; therefore: *She felt very tired, so she went to bed early.* **2 so (that)** with the purpose that; in order that: *She wore dark glasses so that nobody would recognize her.* **3** (used to introduce a new topic into a conversation): *So, Jason, how's it going in school?* **4** (used to show how one part of a story follows another): *So that's how I first met your mother.*
IDM **so what?; so?** (*informal*) (showing that you think sth is not important) Why should I care?: *"It's late." "So what? We don't have to go to school tomorrow."*

**so³** /soʊ/ ***adj.*** (not before a noun)
IDM **be so** to be true: *"Ms. Smith, you claim you were at home on June 14. Is that so?" "Yes, that is so."* ◇ *Oh, no! Say it isn't so!*
**just so** → JUST²

**soak** /soʊk/ ***verb*** **1** [I,T] to become or make sth completely wet: *Leave the dishes to soak for a while.* ◇ *I'm going to soak these pants in hot water to get the stain out.* **2** [I] **soak into/through sth; soak in** (used about a liquid) to pass into or through sth: *Blood had soaked through the bandage.*
PHR V **soak sth up** to draw sth in (especially a liquid): *I soaked the water up with a cloth.* ◇ (*figurative*) *She loves to lie on a beach, soaking up the sunshine.*

**soaked** /soʊkt/ ***adj.*** (not before a noun) extremely wet: *I got soaked waiting for my bus in the rain.*

**soak·ing** /ˈsoʊkɪŋ/ (*also* ˌ**soaking ˈwet**) ***adj.*** extremely wet

ˈ**so-and-so** ***noun*** [C] (*pl.* **so-and-sos**) (*informal*) **1** a person who is not named: *If somebody calls and says, "This is so-and-so and I'm selling storm windows," just hang up.* **2** a person that you do not like (used to avoid saying a swear word): *He's a mean old so-and-so.*

★**soap** /soʊp/ ***noun*** **1** [U] a substance that you use for washing and cleaning: *He washed his hands with soap.* ◇ *a bar of soap* **2** [C] (*informal*) = SOAP OPERA

**soap·box** /ˈsoʊpbɑks/ ***noun*** [C] a small temporary platform that sb stands on to make a speech in a public place, usually outdoors
IDM **get/be on your soapbox** (*informal*) to express the strong opinions that you have about a particular subject: *She's on her soapbox about animal rights again!*

ˈ**soap** ˌ**opera** (*also informal* **soap**) ***noun*** [C] a story about the lives and problems of a group of people which continues every day or several times a week on television or radio

**soap·suds** /ˈsoʊpsʌdz/ ***noun*** [pl.] = SUDS

**soap·y** /ˈsoʊpi/ ***adj.*** full of soap: *Wash in plenty of warm soapy water.*

**soar** /sɔr/ ***verb*** [I] **1** to fly high in the air: *There were eagles soaring overhead.* **2** to rise very fast: *The plane soared into the air.* ◇ *Prices are soaring because of inflation.* **3** to be very high or tall: *The ceiling soars 65 feet above the main hall.*

**sob** /sɑb/ ***verb*** [I,T] (**sob·bing; sobbed**) to cry loudly while taking in sudden, sharp breaths; to speak while you are crying: *"He doesn't love me anymore!" she sobbed.* ▶ **sob noun** [C]

**so·ber¹** /ˈsoʊbər/ ***adj.*** **1** (of a person) not under the influence of alcohol **2** (of a person or an attitude) serious or thoughtful: *a sober expression* ◇ *a sober reminder of just how dangerous drugs can be* **3** (of a color) not bright or likely to be noticed: *a sober gray suit*

**so·ber²** /ˈsoʊbər/ ***verb*** [I,T]
PHR V **sober (sb) up** to become, or to make sb, SOBER¹ (1): *I need a cup of black coffee to sober me up.*

**so·ber·ing** /ˈsoʊbərɪŋ/ ***adj.*** making you feel serious: *sobering news*

**so·bri·e·ty** /səˈbraɪət̬i/ ***noun*** [U] (*formal*) **1** the state of being sober (= not being drunk) **2** the fact of being sensible and serious: *She was a model of sobriety and honesty.*

ˈ**sob** ˌ**story** ***noun*** [C] (*pl.* **sob stories**) (*informal*) a story that sb tells you just to make you feel sorry for him/her, especially one that does not have that effect or is not true

ˈ**so-called** ***adj.*** (only *before* a noun) (used to show that the words you use to describe sb/sth are not correct): *Her so-called friends only wanted her money* (= they are not really her friends).

**soc·cer** /ˈsɑkər/ ***noun*** [U] a game that is played by two teams of eleven players who try to kick a round ball into a goal: *a soccer game*

ˈ**soccer mom** ***noun*** [C] a mother who spends a lot of time taking her children to activities such as playing sports and having music lessons (used as a way of referring to a typical mother from the middle classes)

**so·cia·ble** /ˈsoʊʃəbl/ ***adj.*** enjoying the company of other people; friendly

★**so·cial** /ˈsoʊʃl/ ***adj.*** **1** concerning the relations between people or groups of people; relating to the organization of society: *a period of rapid social change* ◇ *social problems* **2** concerning the rank of people in society: *We share the same social background.* **3** connected with meeting people and enjoying yourself: *a social club* ◇ *She has a busy social life.* **4** (used about animals) living and looking for food together: *Lions are social animals.* ▶ **so·cial·ly** /-ʃəli/ ***adv.***: *We work together, but I don't know him socially.*

ˌ**social asˈsistance** // ***noun*** [U] (*Cdn*) = SOCIAL SECURITY

ˌ**social ˈhousing** ***noun*** [U] (*Cdn*) = PUBLIC HOUSING

ˌ**Social Inˈsurance** ˌ**Number** ***noun*** [C] (*abbr.* **SIN**) (*Cdn*) a number that the Canadian government uses to identify you, and that you use when you fill out official forms, apply for a job, etc.

**so·cial·ism** /ˈsoʊʃl·ɪzəm/ ***noun*** [C] the political theory and practice that is based on the belief that all people are equal, that wealth should be equally divided and that most large businesses and industries should be owned by the government ➲ Look at

S

capitalism and **communism.** ▸ **so·cial·ist** /ˈsoʊʃ-l·ɪst/ ***noun*** [C], ***adj.***

**so·cial·ite** /ˈsoʊʃəlaɪt/ ***noun*** [C] a person who goes to a lot of fashionable parties and is often written about in the newspapers, etc.

**so·cial·ize** /ˈsoʊʃl·aɪz/ ***verb*** **1** [I] **socialize (with sb)** to spend time with people in a friendly way, e.g. at parties, etc. **2** [T] (usually passive) to take control of a business, an industry, etc. away from its private owners and give control to the government: *a socialized economy*

**ˌsocialized ˈmedicine** ***noun*** [U] (*especially US*) medical and hospital care provided by the government for everyone by paying for it with public money

**ˌsocial ˈscience** (*also* **ˌsocial ˈstudies** [pl.]) ***noun*** **1** [U] the study of people in society **2** [C] a particular subject connected with the study of people in society, e.g. economics or sociology

**ˌSocial Seˈcurity** ***noun*** [U] (*abbr.* **SS**) a type of insurance system that is run by the government, which pays money regularly to people who are old or unable to work: *old people living on Social Security* ◇ *to receive your Social Security check*

**ˌSocial Seˈcurity ˌnumber** ***noun*** [C] (*abbr.* **SSN**) (*U.S.*) a number that the U.S. government uses to identify you, and that you use when you fill out official forms, apply for a job, etc.

**ˈsocial ˌstudies** ***noun*** [pl.] = SOCIAL SCIENCE

**ˈsocial work** ***noun*** [U] work that involves giving help to people with problems because they are poor, unable to work, etc. ▸ **ˈsocial ˌworker** ***noun*** [C]

**so·ci·e·tal** /səˈsaɪət̬l/ ***adj.*** (only *before* a noun) (*technical*) connected with society and the way it is organized: *societal values/structure*

★**so·ci·e·ty** /səˈsaɪət̬i/ ***noun*** (*pl.* **so·ci·e·ties**) **1** [C,U] the people in a country or an area, thought of as a group, who have shared customs and laws: *a civilized society* ◇ *in Western society* ◇ *The aim is to create a less violent society.* ◇ *Society's attitude toward women has changed considerably during the last century.* **2** [C] (used especially in names) an organization of people who share a particular interest or purpose: *the Oregon Historical Society*

**so·ci·o·ec·o·nom·ic** /ˌsoʊsioʊˌɛkəˈnɑmɪk; -ˌikə-/ ***adj.*** (only *before* a noun) connected with both social and economic conditions

**so·ci·ol·o·gist** /ˌsoʊsiˈɑlədʒɪst/ ***noun*** [C] an expert in sociology

**so·ci·ol·o·gy** /ˌsoʊsiˈɑlədʒi/ ***noun*** [U] the study of human societies and social behavior ▸ **so·ci·o·log·i·cal** /ˌsoʊsiəˈlɑdʒɪkl/ ***adj.***

**so·ci·o·path** /ˈsoʊsiəpæθ; ˈsoʊʃiə-/ ***noun*** [C] a person who has a mental illness and who behaves in an aggressive or dangerous way toward other people

★**sock**[1] /sɑk/ ***noun*** [C] a piece of clothing that you wear on your foot and lower leg, inside your shoe: *a pair of socks*

IDM **knock your socks off** → KNOCK[2]

**sock**[2] /sɑk/ ***verb*** [T] (*informal*) to hit sb hard: *She got angry and socked him in the mouth.* ◇ (*figurative*) *The banks are socking customers with higher charges.*

IDM **be socked in** (used about an airport) to be closed because of snow, fog, etc.

**sock it to sb** (*informal*) to do sth or tell sb sth in a strong and effective way: *Go in there and sock it to 'em!*

PHR V **sock sth away** (usually passive) to save money: *She already has $500 socked away for college.*

**sock·et** /ˈsɑkət/ ***noun*** [C] **1** = OUTLET (1) ➲ picture at **plug**. **2** a hollow place where sth fits: *your eye socket*

**sod** /sɑd/ ***noun*** [U,C] a layer of earth with grass growing on it; a piece of this that has been cut from the ground and is used especially for making lawns (= the area of grass in the yard)

★**so·da** /ˈsoʊdə/ ***noun*** **1** [C,U] (*also* **pop**, **ˈsoda pop**) a sweet drink with bubbles in it that does not contain alcohol **2** [U] (*also* **ˈsoda ˌwater**) water that has bubbles in it and is often mixed with

S

**soccer**

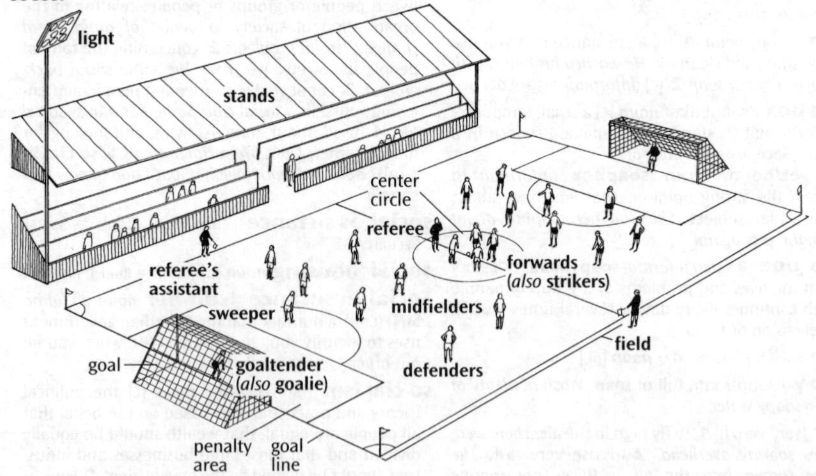

alcohol: *a scotch and soda* **3** [U] a chemical substance in common use that is a compound of sodium: *baking/washing soda*

**'soda ˌfountain** *noun* [C] (*old-fashioned*) a type of bar where you can buy sodas to drink, ice cream, etc.

**so·di·um** /'soʊdiəm/ *noun* [U] (*symbol* **Na**) a soft silver-white metal that is found naturally only in compounds, such as salt

**so·fa** /'soʊfə/ *noun* [C] = COUCH: *a sofa bed* (= a sofa that you can pull out to make a bed) ➲ picture at **chair**[1].

★**soft** /sɔft/ *adj.*

➤NOT HARD **1** not hard or firm: *a soft bed* ◇ *The ground is very soft after all that rain.*

➤NOT ROUGH **2** smooth and nice to touch; not rough: *soft skin/hands* ◇ *a soft towel*

➤SOUNDS **3** (used about sounds, voices, words, etc.) quiet or gentle; not loud or angry: *She spoke in a soft whisper.* ◇ *soft music in the background*

➤LIGHT/COLORS **4** (used about light, colors etc.) gentle and pleasant; not bright: *The room was decorated in soft pinks and greens.*

➤SYMPATHETIC **5** (used about people and animals) (too) kind and gentle; not hard or strict: *They criticized the mayor for being soft on crime.*

IDM **have a soft spot for sb/sth** (*informal*) to be especially fond of sb/sth: *I've got a soft spot for my old Math teacher.*

▶ **soft·ness** *noun* [U]

**soft·ball** /'sɔfbɔl/ *noun* **1** [U] a team game that is similar to baseball, but played with a slightly larger ball on a slightly smaller field **2** [C] the ball that is used in this game

**ˌsoft-'boiled** *adj.* (used about an egg) boiled inside its shell for a short time so that the yellow part (the yolk) is still soft

**'soft drink** *noun* [C] a cold drink that contains no alcohol

**ˌsoft 'drug** *noun* [C] an illegal drug, e.g. cannabis, that some people take for pleasure and which is not considered very harmful or likely to make them dependent (**addicted**) ➲ Look at **hard drug**.

**soft·en** /'sɔfn/ *verb* **1** [I,T] to become softer or gentler; to make sb/sth softer or gentler: *Add one cup softened butter or margarine.* ◇ *The teacher's expression softened as I explained why I was late.* **2** [T] to make sth seem less severe: *to try to soften the effect of bad news*

PHR V **soften sb up** (*informal*) **1** to try to persuade sb to do sth for you by being very nice to him/her before you ask for anything: *Potential customers are softened up with free gifts before the sales talk.* **2** to make an enemy weaker and easier to attack

**soft·en·er** /'sɔfənər/ *noun* [C,U] a substance that you add when washing clothes to make them feel soft

**soft·ie** (*also* **soft·y**) /'sɔfti/ *noun* [C] (*pl.* **soft·ies**) a kind, sympathetic or emotional person: *There's no need to be afraid of him – he's a big softie.*

**soft·ly** /'sɔfli/ *adv.* gently or quietly: *"Don't wake the kids up," she whispered softly.*

**ˌsoft-'spoken** *adj.* having a gentle, quiet voice: *He was a kind, soft-spoken man.*

**soft·ware** /'sɔftwɛr/ *noun* [U] programs that you use to operate a computer: *There's a lot of educational software available now.* ➲ Look at **hardware**.

**sog·gy** /'sɑgi/ *adj.* (**sog·gi·er**; **sog·gi·est**) wet and soft; having too much liquid in it

★**soil**[1] /sɔɪl/ *noun* **1** [C,U] the substance that plants, trees, etc. grow in; earth: *poor soil* ➲ Look at the note at **ground**[1]. **2** [U] the land that is part of a country: *to set foot on American soil* (= to arrive in the U.S.)

**soil**[2] /sɔɪl/ *verb* [T] (*formal*) to make sth dirty

**so·journ** /'soʊdʒərn/ *noun* [C] (*formal*) a temporary stay in a place away from your home

**sol·ace** /'sɑləs/ *noun* [U, sing.] (*formal*) a feeling of emotional comfort when you are sad or disappointed; a person or thing that makes you feel better or happier when you are sad or disappointed: *He sought solace in the whiskey bottle.* ◇ *She turned to Johnny for solace.*

**so·lar** /'soʊlər/ *adj.* **1** of or relating to the sun: *solar energy* **2** using the sun's energy: *solar heating*

**ˌsolar 'cell** *noun* [C] a device that converts light and heat energy from the sun into electricity

**so·lar·i·um** /sə'lɛriəm/ *noun* [C] a room enclosed mainly by glass or having special lamps, where people go to make their skin become brown (get a suntan) using light from the sun or artificial light

**so·lar plex·us** /ˌsoʊlər 'plɛksəs/ *noun* [sing.] (*informal*) the front part of the body at the top of the stomach, below the chest: *a painful punch in the solar plexus*

**the 'solar ˌsystem** *noun* [sing.] the sun and the planets that move around it

**sold** *past tense, past participle of* SELL

**sol·der**[1] /'sɑdər/ *noun* [U] a mixture of metals that is heated and melted and then used to join metals, wires, etc. together

**sol·der**[2] /'sɑdər/ *verb* [T] **solder sth (to/onto sth)**; **solder (A and B together)** to join pieces of metal or wire with solder: *These wires must be soldered to the pins.* ◇ *Solder the two pieces together.*

★**sol·dier**[1] /'soʊldʒər/ *noun* [C] a member of an army: *The soldiers marched past.*

**sol·dier**[2] /'soʊldʒər/ *verb*

PHR V **soldier on** to continue with what you are doing or trying to achieve, especially when this is difficult or unpleasant: *His partner left and he had to soldier on alone.*

**ˌsoldier of 'fortune** *noun* [C] a person who fights for any country or person who will pay him/her SYN **mercenary**

**'sold-out** *adj.* (only *before* a noun) (used about a concert, performance, game, etc.) for which all the available tickets have been sold

**sole**[1] /soʊl/ *adj.* (only *before* a noun) **1** only; single: *His sole interest is football.* **2** belonging to one person only; not shared: *My ex-wife has sole custody of our kids.* ▶ **sole·ly** /'soʊlli/ *adv.* (*formal*): *I agreed to come solely on account of your mother.*

**sole**[2] /soʊl/ *noun* **1** [C] the flat part of your foot that you walk on **2** [C] the part of a shoe or sock that covers the bottom surface of your foot: *These shoes have leather uppers and synthetic soles.* ➲ picture at **shoe**. **3** [C,U] (*pl.* **sole**) a small flat sea fish that can be eaten as food

**-soled** /soʊld/ ***combining form*** (used about shoes) having the type of SOLE² (2) mentioned: *rubber-soled shoes*

**sol·emn** /ˈsɑləm/ ***adj.*** **1** very serious: *Her solemn face told them that the news was bad.* **2** sincere; done or said in a formal way: *to make a solemn promise* ◇ *a solemn warning* ▸ **so·lem·ni·ty** /səˈlɛmnət̬i/ ***noun*** [U] ▸ **sol·emn·ly** ***adv.***: *"I have something very important to tell you," she began solemnly.*

**so·lic·it** /səˈlɪsət/ ***verb*** (*formal*) **1** [T] to ask sb for money, help, support, etc.: *They tried to solicit support for the proposal.* **2** [I,T] to approach sb, especially in a public place, and offer sex in return for money **3** [I,T] to try to sell sth to sb

**so·lic·i·tor** /səˈlɪsət̬ər/ ***noun*** [C] **1** a person who tries to sell things to people: *telephone solicitors* (= who call people and try to sell them sth over the telephone) **2** (*Cdn*) a lawyer

**so·lic·i·tous** /səˈlɪsət̬əs/ ***adj.*** (*formal*) being very concerned for sb and wanting to make sure that he/she is comfortable, well or happy: *She was very solicitous of our welfare.* ◇ *a solicitous host* ▸ **so·lic·i·tous·ly** ***adv.*** (*formal*): *"Are you cold?" he asked solicitously.*

★**sol·id¹** /ˈsɑləd/ ***adj.***

➤NOT LIQUID/GAS **1** hard and firm; not in the form of liquid or gas: *It was so cold that the pond was frozen solid.* ◇ *Is the baby eating solid food yet?*

➤WITHOUT HOLES OR SPACES **2** having no holes or spaces inside; not hollow: *a solid mass of rock* ◇ *The briefcase was packed solid with $50 bills.*

➤COLOR **3** of the color mentioned, with no other color and no pattern: *One cat is black and white, the other solid black.* ➲ Picture on study page **A30**.

➤MATERIAL **4** (only *before* a noun) made of the same substance inside and outside: *a solid gold necklace*

➤STRONG **5** strong and well made: *a solid little car*

➤RELIABLE **6** reliable; of sufficient quality and amount: *He was arrested by the police with no solid evidence against him.*

➤PERIOD OF TIME **7** without a break or pause: *I slept for twelve solid hours/twelve hours solid.* ▸ **so·lid·i·ty** /səˈlɪdət̬i/ ***noun*** [U]

**sol·id²** /ˈsɑləd/ ***noun*** [C] **1** a substance or object that is hard; not a liquid or gas: *Liquids become solids when frozen.* **2** an object that has length, width and height, not a flat object: *A cube is a solid.*

**sol·i·dar·i·ty** /ˌsɑləˈdærət̬i/ ***noun*** [U] the support of one group of people for another, because they agree with their aims: *Many local people expressed solidarity with the strikers.*

**so·lid·i·fy** /səˈlɪdəfaɪ/ ***verb*** [I,T] (*pres. part.* **so·lid·i·fy·ing**; *3rd person sing. pres.* **so·lid·i·fies**; *pt, pp* **so·lid·i·fied**) to become or make sth hard or solid

**sol·id·ly** /ˈsɑlɪdli/ ***adv.*** **1** strongly: *a solidly built house* **2** continuously: *It rained solidly all day.*

**so·lil·o·quy** /səˈlɪləkwi/ ***noun*** [C,U] (*pl.* **so·lil·o·quies**) a speech in a play in which a character, who is alone on the stage, speaks his or her thoughts; the act of speaking thoughts in this way: *Hamlet's famous soliloquy, "To be or not to be"*

**sol·i·taire** /ˌsɑləˈtɛr/ ***noun*** **1** [U] a card game for one player **2** [C] a single precious stone; a piece of jewelry with a single precious stone in it: *a solitaire ring*

**sol·i·tar·y** /ˈsɑləˌtɛri/ ***adj.*** **1** alone; without other people: *She lives a solitary life in a remote part of Montana.* **2** (only *before* a noun) one on its own with no others around: *a solitary figure walking up the hillside* **3** (only *before* a noun) only one; single: *I can't think of a solitary example* (= not even one).

**ˌsolitary conˈfinement** (*also informal* **solitary**) ***noun*** [U] a punishment in which a person in prison is kept completely alone: *to be kept in solitary confinement*

**sol·i·tude** /ˈsɑlətud/ ***noun*** [U] the state of being alone: *to live in solitude*

**so·lo¹** /ˈsoʊloʊ/ ***noun*** [C] (*pl.* **so·los**) a piece of music for only one person to play or sing: *a piano solo* ◇ *to sing/play a solo* ➲ Look at **duet**.

**so·lo²** /ˈsoʊloʊ/ ***adj., adv.*** (done) alone; by yourself: *a solo flight* ◇ *to fly solo*

**so·lo·ist** /ˈsoʊloʊɪst/ ***noun*** [C] a person who plays or sings a piece of music alone

**sol·stice** /ˈsɑlstəs; ˈsoʊl-; ˈsɔl-/ ***noun*** [C] either of the two times of the year at which the sun reaches its highest or lowest point in the sky at midday, marked by the longest and shortest days: *the summer/winter solstice*

**sol·u·ble** /ˈsɑlyəbl/ ***adj.*** that will dissolve in liquid: *These tablets are soluble in water.* OPP **insoluble**

★**so·lu·tion** /səˈluʃn/ ***noun*** **1** [C] **a solution (to sth)** a way of solving a problem, dealing with a difficult situation, etc.: *a solution to the conflict in the Middle East* **2** [C] **a solution (to sth)** the answer (to a puzzle, etc.): *The solution to the crossword will be published next week.* **3** [C,U] (a) liquid in which sth solid has been dissolved

★**solve** /sɑlv/ ***verb*** [T] to find an answer to or a way of dealing with a problem, question, difficulty, etc.: *The government is trying to solve the problem of inflation.* ◇ *The police have not managed to solve the crime.* ◇ *to solve a puzzle/mystery* ➲ noun **solution**

**sol·vent¹** /ˈsɑlvənt/ ***noun*** [C,U] a liquid that can dissolve another substance

**sol·vent²** /ˈsɑlvənt/ ***adj.*** **1** having enough money to pay your debts; not in debt: *The company managed to remain solvent during the recession.* OPP **insolvent** **2** (*technical*) able to dissolve another substance, or be dissolved in another substance: *Lead is more solvent in acidic water.*

**som·ber** /ˈsɑmbər/ ***adj.*** sad and serious: *a somber mood* ▸ **som·ber·ly** ***adv.***

**som·bre·ro** /sɑmˈbrɛroʊ; səm-/ ***noun*** [C] (*pl.* **som·bre·ros**) a Mexican hat for men that is tall with a very wide edge (**brim**), turned up at the edges

★**some** /səm; *strong form* sʌm/ ***det., pronoun*** **1** a certain amount or number: *We need some butter and some potatoes.* ◇ *I don't need any more money – I've still got some.*

S

NOTE In negative sentences and in questions we use **any** instead of **some**: *Do we need any butter?* ◇ *I need some more money. I don't have any.* But look at **2** for examples of questions where **some** is used.

**2** (used in questions when you expect or want the answer "yes"): *Would you like some more cake?* ◇ *Can I take some of this paper?* **3** (used when you are referring to certain members of a group or certain types of a thing and not all of them): *Some students enjoy this kind of work; some don't.* ◇ *Some of his books are very exciting.* **4** (*also* **some...or other**) (used for talking about a person or thing whose name you do not know): *There's some woman at the door.* ◇ *I read about it in some newspaper or other.*

★**some·bod·y** /ˈsʌmbʌdi; -bɑdi/ (*also* **some·one** /ˈsʌmwʌn/) ***pronoun*** a person (not known or not mentioned by name): *How are you? Somebody said that you were sick.* ◇ *She's getting married to someone she met at work.* ◇ *There's somebody at the door.* ◇ *I think you should talk to someone else* (= another person) *about this problem.*

NOTE **Somebody**, **anybody** and **everybody** are used with a singular verb but are sometimes followed by a plural pronoun (except in formal language): *Somebody is coming.* ◇ *Somebody left their coat behind.* ◇ *Does everybody have something to eat?* ◇ *I'll see everybody at work and tell them the news.* The difference between **somebody** and **anybody** is the same as the difference between **some** and **any**. ➲ Look at the note at **some**.

**some·day** /ˈsʌmdeɪ/ (*also* ˈ**some day**) ***adv.*** at some time in the future: *I hope you'll come and visit me someday.*

★**some·how** /ˈsʌmhaʊ/ ***adv.*** **1** in a way that is not known or certain: *The car's in the shop, but I'll get to work somehow.* ◇ *Somehow we had gotten completely lost.* **2** for a reason you do not know or understand: *I somehow get the feeling that I've been here before.*

★**some·one** /ˈsʌmwʌn/ ***pronoun*** = SOMEBODY

**some·place** /ˈsʌmpleɪs/ ***adv.*** = SOMEWHERE

**som·er·sault** /ˈsʌmərsɔlt/ ***noun*** [C] a movement in which you roll all the way over with your feet going over your head: *to do a forward/backward somersault*

★**some·thing** /ˈsʌmθɪŋ/ ***pronoun*** **1** a thing that is not known or not named: *I've got something in my eye.* ◇ *Wait a minute – I forgot something.* ◇ *Would you like something else* (= another thing) *to drink?* ◇ *Let's get something to eat.* ◇ *I have something important to tell you.*

NOTE The difference between **something** and **anything** is the same as the difference between **some** and **any**. Look at the note at **some**.

**2** a thing that is helpful, useful or worth considering: *There's something in what your mother says.*

IDM **have something to do with** to be connected or concerned with: *The program has something to do with the environment.*

**or something** (*informal*) (used for showing that you are not sure about what you have just said): *"What's his job?" "I think he's a plumber or something."*

**something like** similar to: *A blackberry is something like a raspberry.*

**some·time** /ˈsʌmtaɪm/ ***adv.*** at a time that you do not know exactly or have not yet decided: *I'll call you sometime this evening.* ◇ *I should go and see her sometime.*

★**some·times** /ˈsʌmtaɪmz/ ***adv.*** on some occasions; now and then: *Sometimes I drive to work and sometimes I take the bus.* ◇ *I sometimes watch TV in the evenings.*

★**some·what** /ˈsʌmwʌt/ ***adv.*** a little: *Somewhat to my surprise, he apologized.* ◇ *The newspaper got somewhat wet in the rain, but we could still read it.*

★**some·where** /ˈsʌmwɛr/ (*also* **some·place**) ***adv.*** **1** at, in, or to a place that you do not know or name exactly: *I saw your glasses somewhere downstairs.* ◇ *"Did they go to the lake?" "No, I think they went somewhere else* (= to another place) *this year."*

NOTE The difference between **somewhere** and **anywhere** is the same as the difference between **some** and **any**. ➲ Look at the note at **some**.

**2** (used when you do not know the exact time, number, etc.): *Your ideal weight should probably be somewhere around 140 pounds.*

★**son** /sʌn/ ***noun*** [C] a male child ➲ Look at **daughter**.

**so·nar** /ˈsoʊnɑr/ ***noun*** [U] equipment or a system for finding objects underwater using sound waves ➲ Look at **radar**.

**so·na·ta** /səˈnɑt̬ə/ ***noun*** [C] a piece of music for one instrument or for one instrument and piano, usually divided into three or four parts: *Beethoven's piano sonatas* ◇ *a violin sonata*

★**song** /sɔŋ/ ***noun*** **1** [C] a piece of music with words that you sing: *a folk song* **2** [U] the act of singing: *to burst into song* **3** [C,U] the musical sounds that a bird makes

**song·bird** /ˈsɔŋbərd/ ***noun*** [C] a bird that has a musical call, for example a blackbird or thrush

**song·book** /ˈsɔŋbʊk/ ***noun*** [C] a book containing the music and words of different songs

**song·writ·er** /ˈsɔŋraɪt̬ər/ ***noun*** [C] a person whose job is to write songs

**son·ic** /ˈsɑnɪk/ ***adj.*** connected with sound waves

ˌ**sonic** ˈ**boom** ***noun*** [C] the explosive sound that is made when an aircraft travels faster than the speed of sound

ˈ**son-in-law** ***noun*** [C] (*pl.* **sons-in-law**) your daughter's husband

**son·ny** /ˈsʌni/ ***noun*** [sing.] (*informal*) (a word used by an older person to address a young man or boy): *Don't try and teach me my job, sonny.*

ˌ**son of a** ˈ**gun** ***noun*** [sing.] (*informal*) **1** a person or thing that you are annoyed with: *My car's at the shop – the son of a gun broke down again.* **2** (used to express the the fact that you are surprised or annoyed): *Well, son of a gun—and I thought the old guy couldn't dance!*

★**soon** /sun/ ***adv.*** **1** not long after the present time or the time mentioned: *It will soon be dark.* ◇ *He left soon after me.* ◇ *We should arrive at your house soon*

S

*after twelve.* **2** early; quickly: *Don't leave so soon. Stay for dinner.* ◇ *How soon can you get here?*

IDM **as soon as** at the moment (that); when: *Call me as soon as you hear some news.* ◇ *I'd like your reply as soon as possible* (= at the earliest possible moment).

**no sooner did/had ... than ...** immediately when or after: *No sooner had I shut the door than I realized I'd left my keys inside.*

**sooner or later** at some time in the future; one day: *I suppose I'll hear from her sooner or later.*

**would just as soon as do sth** → JUST[1]

**soot** /sʊt/ ***noun*** [U] black powder that comes from burning things and collects in chimneys ▸ **soot·y** ***adj.***

**soothe** /suð/ ***verb*** [T] **1** to make sb calmer or less upset; to comfort sb: *to soothe a crying child* **2** to make aches or pains less severe: *The doctor gave me some skin cream to soothe the irritation.* ▸ **sooth·ing** ***adj.***: *soothing music* ◇ *a soothing massage* ▸ **sooth·ing·ly** ***adv.***

**sooth·er** /ˈsuðər/ ***noun*** [C] (*Cdn*) = PACIFIER

**sop** /sɑp/ ***noun*** [C] **sop (to sb/sth)** a small, not very important, thing that is offered to sb who is angry or disappointed in order to make him/her feel better

**so·phis·ti·cat·ed** /səˈfɪstəkeɪt̬əd/ ***adj.*** **1** having or showing a lot of experience of the world and social situations; knowing about things such as fashion, new ideas, etc.: *She's a very sophisticated young woman.* **2** able to understand difficult or complicated things: *Voters are much more sophisticated these days.* **3** (used about machines, systems, etc.) advanced and complicated: *sophisticated computer equipment* OPP **unsophisticated** ▸ **so·phis·ti·ca·tion** /səˌfɪstəˈkeɪʃn/ ***noun*** [U]

**soph·o·more** /ˈsɑfmɔr/ ***noun*** [C] (*U.S.*) a student who is in the tenth grade in high school or the second year of college ➲ Look at **freshman**, **junior** and **senior**.

**soph·o·mor·ic** /ˌsɑfəˈmɔrɪk; sɑfˈmɔr-/ ***adj.*** childish and silly: *sophomoric wit/humor/jokes*

**sop·o·rif·ic** /ˌsɑpəˈrɪfɪk/ ***adj.*** (*formal*) making you want to go to sleep: *the soporific effect of the sun*

**sop·ping** /ˈsɑpɪŋ/ (*also* ˌ**sopping** ˈ**wet**) ***adj.*** (*informal*) very wet: *Your clothes are sopping wet!*

**so·pran·o** /səˈprænoʊ/ ***noun*** [C] (*pl.* **so·pran·os**) the highest singing voice; a woman, girl, or boy with this voice

**sor·bet** /sɔrˈbeɪ/ ***noun*** [C,U] a sweet frozen food made from sugar, water and fruit juice, often eaten as a dessert

**sor·cer·er** /ˈsɔrsərər/ ***noun*** [C] (in stories) a man with magic powers, who is helped by evil spirits

**sor·cer·ess** /ˈsɔrsərəs/ ***noun*** [C] (in stories) a woman with magic powers, who is helped by evil spirits

**sor·cer·y** /ˈsɔrsəri/ ***noun*** [U] magic that uses evil spirits: *sorcery and witchcraft*

**sor·did** /ˈsɔrdəd/ ***adj.*** unpleasant; not honest or moral: *We discovered the truth about his sordid past.*

★**sore[1]** /sɔr/ ***adj.*** painful: *to have a sore throat* ◇ *I feel all right after the operation, but my stomach is still very sore.*

IDM **a sore point** a subject that is likely to make sb upset or angry when mentioned

▸ **sore·ness** ***noun*** [U]: *You might get some soreness of the skin.*

**sore[2]** /sɔr/ ***noun*** [C] a painful place on the body where the skin is infected

**sore·ly** /ˈsɔrli/ ***adv.*** (*formal*) very greatly; very much: *You'll be sorely missed when you leave.*

**sor·ghum** /ˈsɔrgəm/ ***noun*** [U] very small grain grown as food in tropical countries; the plant that produces this grain

**so·ror·i·ty** /səˈrɔrət̬i; -ˈrɑr-/ ***noun*** [C] (*pl.* **so·ror·i·ties**) a social organization for female students at some colleges and universities ➲ Look also at **fraternity** (1).

**sor·row** /ˈsɑroʊ; ˈsɔ-/ ***noun*** (*formal*) **1** [U] great sadness: *I'd like to express my sorrow at the death of your father.* **2** [C] an event, etc. that causes great sadness: *the joys and sorrows of our relationship* ▸ **sor·row·ful** /-fl/ ***adj.*** ▸ **sor·row·ful·ly** /-fəli/ ***adv.***

★**sor·ry[1]** /ˈsɑri; ˈsɔri/ ***adj.*** (**sor·ri·er**; **sor·ri·est**) **1** (not before a noun) **sorry (for/about sth)**; **sorry (to do sth/that...)** (used for apologizing for sth that you have done): *I'm sorry I kept you all waiting.* ◇ *I'm really sorry for spilling that wine.* ◇ *I'm sorry about not telling you the news earlier.* ◇ *I'm sorry to be so late.* ◇ *I'm so sorry that I interrupted your meal. I'll call you back later.* ➲ Look at the note at **excuse[2]**. **2** (not before a noun) **sorry (to do sth/that)**; **sorry (for/about sth)** sad or disappointed: *I was sorry to miss you on Saturday.* ◇ *I was sorry not to get the job.* ◇ *"Simon's mother died last week." "Oh, I'm sorry."* **3** (used for politely saying "no" to sth, disagreeing with sth or introducing bad news): *"Would you like to come to supper on Friday?" "I'm sorry, I'm busy that evening."* ◇ *I'm sorry, I don't agree with you. I think we should accept the offer.* ◇ *We are sorry to inform you that your application has been unsuccessful.* **4** (only *before* a noun) very bad: *the sorry state of education in this school district*

IDM **be/feel sorry for sb** to feel sympathy or pity for sb: *I feel very sorry for the families of the victims.* ◇ *Stop feeling sorry for yourself!*

**sor·ry[2]** /ˈsɑri; ˈsɔri/ ***interjection*** **1** (used for apologizing, making excuses, etc.): *Sorry, I didn't see you standing behind me.* ◇ *Sorry I'm late – the bus didn't come on time.* ➲ Look at the note at **excuse[2]**. **2** (used for asking sb to repeat sth you did not hear correctly): *"My name's Maggie Wiseman." "Sorry? Maggie who?"*

★**sort[1]** /sɔrt/ ***noun*** [C] a type or kind: *What sort of music do you like?* SYN **kind**

IDM **out of sorts** sick or upset: *She was tired and out of sorts by the time she arrived home.*

**a sort of sth**; **sort of a sth** (*informal*) a type of sth; sth similar to sth: *Can you hear a sort of ticking noise?*

**sort of** (*informal*) fairly; in a way: *I feel sort of sick.* ◇ *I'd sort of like to go, but I'm not sure.*

★**sort[2]** /sɔrt/ ***verb*** [T] to put things into different groups or places so that they are organized correctly: *I'm just sorting these papers into the right files.* ◇ *The computer will sort the words into alphabetical order.*

PHRV **sort sth out 1** to organize sth or make sth clean and neat: *It will take time to sort out all this information.* **2** to find an answer to a problem: *I haven't found an apartment yet, but I hope to sort something out soon.*

**sort through sth** to go through a number of things, in order to organize them or find sth that you are looking for

**sort·a** /'sɔrt̬ə/ (*informal*) *short for* SORT OF

**sort·ie** /'sɔrti; sɔr'ti/ ***noun*** [C] **1** a flight that is made by an aircraft during military operations; an attack made by soldiers: *a bombing sortie* ◇ *They had made several sorties against enemy troops.* SYN **raid 2 sortie into sth** an effort that you make to do or join sth new: *His first sortie into politics was unsuccessful.*

**SOS** /ˌɛs oʊ 'ɛs/ ***noun*** [sing.] a call or signal from sb/sth that needs help, especially a ship or plane

**'so-ˌso** ***adj., adv.*** (*informal*) all right, but not really good/well: *"How are you?" "So-so."*

**souf·flé** /su'fleɪ/ ***noun*** [C,U] a dish made from egg whites, milk and flour mixed together to make it light, flavored with cheese, fruit, etc. and baked until it rises: *a chocolate/cheese soufflé*

**sought** *past tense, past participle of* SEEK

**'sought-ˌafter** ***adj.*** (usually *before* a noun) that people want very much, because it is of high quality or rare

★**soul** /soʊl/ ***noun***

➤ SPIRIT OF PERSON **1** [C] the part of a person that is believed to continue to exist after the body is dead: *Christians believe that their souls go to heaven when they die.*

➤ INNER CHARACTER **2** [C,U] deep feeling and thought: *The music was performed perfectly, but it lacked soul.*

➤ PERSON **3** [C] (used with adjectives expressing affection or pity) a person of a particular type: *She's a kind old soul.* **4** [C] (used especially in negative statements) a person: *There wasn't a soul in sight* (= there was nobody).

➤ MUSIC **5** [U] (*also* **'soul music**) a type of popular African-American music which expresses deep feelings: *a soul singer*

**'soul food** ***noun*** [U] the type of food that was traditionally eaten by African-Americans in the southern U.S.

**soul·ful** /'soʊlfl/ ***adj.*** having or showing deep feeling: *a soulful expression*

**soul·less** /'soʊl·ləs/ ***adj.*** **1** (used about things and places) lacking any attractive or interesting qualities that make people feel happy: *They live in soulless concrete blocks.* SYN **depressing 2** (used about a person) lacking the ability to feel emotions

**'soul mate** ***noun*** [C] a person that you have a special friendship with because you understand each other's feelings and interests

★**sound**[1] /saʊnd/ ***verb*** **1** [I] to give a particular impression when heard or heard about; to seem: *That sounds like a child crying.* ◇ *She sounded upset and angry on the phone.* ◇ *The rain sounds heavy.* ◇ *You sound like my mother!* ◇ *He sounds like a very nice person from his letter.* ◇ *It doesn't sound as if he's very reliable.* ◇ *Your idea sounds pretty good – let's give it a try.* **2** [T] to cause sth to make a sound: *to sound the horn of your car*

IDM **raise/sound the alarm** → ALARM[1]

PHRV **sound sb out** to ask sb questions in order to find out what he/she thinks or intends: *I'm going to sound out the boss about my proposal.*

★**sound**[2] /saʊnd/ ***noun*** **1** [C] something that you hear or that can be heard: *the sound of voices* ◇ *She opened the door without a sound.* **2** [U] what you hear; impressions received by hearing: *Light travels faster than sound.* ◇ *sound waves* **3 the sound** [sing.] the loudness on a television, radio, etc.: *Can you turn the sound up/down?* **4** [C] a long, fairly wide area of water that connects two large bodies of water

IDM **the sound of sth** the impression that you have of sth when you hear or read about it: *She must be an interesting person, by the sound of it.* ◇ *I don't like the sound of these new regulations.*

★**sound**[3] /saʊnd/ ***adj.*** **1** healthy and strong; in good condition: *a sound state of health* ◇ *The structure of the bridge is basically sound.* **2** sensible; that you can rely on: *sound advice*

IDM **safe and sound** → SAFE[1]

▶ **sound·ness** ***noun*** [U]

**sound**[4] /saʊnd/ ***adv.***

IDM **be sound asleep** to be deeply asleep

**'sound ˌbarrier** ***noun*** [sing.] the point at which an aircraft's speed is the same as the speed of sound, causing reduced control, a very loud noise (**sonic boom**) and various other effects: *to break the sound barrier* (= to travel faster than the speed of sound)

**'sound bite** ***noun*** [C] a part of a speech by a politician, etc. which is broadcast on television and radio and is short enough for people to remember

**'sound card** ***noun*** [C] (*computing*) a device that can be put into a computer to allow the use of sound with multimedia software

**'sound check** ***noun*** [C] a process of checking that the equipment used for recording music, or for playing music at a concert, is working correctly and producing sound of a good quality

**'sound efˌfects** ***noun*** [pl.] sounds other than speech or music that are used in a play, movie, computer game, etc. to create the required effect

**sound·less** /'saʊndləs/ ***adj.*** (*written*) without making any sound; silent: *Her lips parted in a soundless scream.* ▶ **sound·less·ly** ***adv.***: *He slipped soundlessly into the house.*

**sound·ly** /'saʊndli/ ***adv.*** thoroughly or deeply: *Our team was soundly beaten this afternoon.* ◇ *The children were sleeping soundly.*

**sound·proof** /'saʊndpruf/ ***adj.*** made so that sound cannot pass through it or into it: *a soundproof room* ▶ **sound·proof** ***verb*** [T] ▶ **soundproof·ing** ***noun*** [U]

**sound·track** /'saʊndtræk/ ***noun*** [C] the recorded sound and music from a movie or computer game

★**soup**[1] /sup/ ***noun*** [U] liquid food made by cooking meat, vegetables, etc. in water: *chicken soup* ◇ *a can of soup*

**soup**[2] /sup/ ***verb*** [T]

PHRV **soup sth up** (*informal*) to make changes to



S

sth such as a car or computer, so that it is more powerful or exciting than before

**ˈsoup kitchen** *noun* [C] a place where very poor people can go to get meals for free or for a very low cost

**ˈsoup spoon** *noun* [C] a large round spoon that is used for eating soup

★**sour** /ˈsaʊər/ *adj.* **1** having a sharp taste like that of a lemon: *sour pickles* **2** (used especially about milk) tasting or smelling bad because it is no longer fresh **3** having or showing a bad temper; unpleasant: *a sour expression*

IDM **go/turn sour** to become unpleasant or unsatisfactory: *Their relationship turned sour after a few months.*

**sour grapes** pretending to dislike or not to want sth when you secretly want it but cannot have it: *She said she didn't want to come to the party anyway, but I think that was just sour grapes.*

▶ **sour·ly** *adv.* ▶ **sour·ness** *noun* [U]

★**source** /sɔrs/ *noun* [C] **1** a place, person or thing where sth comes or starts from or where sth is obtained: *Sales tax is an important source of income for the government.* ◇ *the source of the Nile* (= the place where the river starts) **2** a person, book, etc. that supplies information: *Police have refused to reveal the source of their information.*

**ˌsour ˈcream** *noun* [U] a type of thick cream with a sour taste, used in cooking and as a sauce on foods

**sour·dough** /ˈsaʊərdoʊ/ *noun* [U] a mixture of flour, fat and water (**dough**) that is left to ferment so that it has a sour taste, used for making bread; bread made with this dough

**sour·puss** /ˈsaʊərpʊs/ *noun* [C] (*informal*) a person who is not cheerful or pleasant

★**south**[1] /saʊθ/ *noun* [sing.] (*abbr.* **S.**; **So.**) **1** (*also* **the south**) one of the four main points of the compass; the direction that is on your right when you face the sunrise: *warm winds from the south* ◇ *Which way is south?* ➲ picture at **north**. **2 the south** the part of any country, city, etc. that lies farther toward the south than other parts: *Temperatures will be lower across the whole state, with some snow in the south.* **3 the South** the southeastern states of the U.S., especially the states that fought against the northern states in the Civil War ➲ Look also at **Deep South**.

★**south**[2] /saʊθ/ *adj.* in or toward the south, or from the south: *the south coast of the island* ◇ *The new offices will be on the city's south side.* ◇ *a south wind*

★**south**[3] /saʊθ/ *adv.* to or toward the south: *If you keep going south, you will soon reach the freeway.* ◇ *We live just south of Chicago.* ◇ *The house faces south.*

IDM **down south** in or to the south of a state, province or country: *We all headed down south for our spring vacation.* ➲ picture at **north**.

**ˌSouth ˈAsian** *noun* [C] (*Cdn*) **1** a person who lives or was born in the Indian subcontinent **2** a person whose family originally came from the Indian subcontinent ➲ Look also at **East Indian**.

**south·bound** /ˈsaʊθbaʊnd/ *adj.* traveling or leading toward the south: *the southbound lanes of I-95*

**south·east**[1] /ˌsaʊθˈist/ (*also* **the southeast**) *noun* [sing.] (*abbr.* **SE**) **1** the direction or point of the compass that is between south and east **2** a region that is toward the southeast: *the southeast of the country*

**south·east**[2] /ˌsaʊθˈist/ *adj., adv.* in, from or to the southeast of a place or country: *the coast of southeast Florida* ◇ *Continue southeast for about ten miles.* ➲ picture at **north**.

**south·east·er·ly** /ˌsaʊθˈistərli/ *adj.* **1** toward the southeast: *in a southeasterly direction* **2** (used about a wind) coming from the southeast

**south·east·ern** /ˌsaʊθˈistərn/ *adj.* in or from the southeast of a place or country

**south·east·ward** /ˌsaʊθˈistwərd/ *adv.* toward the southeast: *Follow the highway southeastward.*

**south·er·ly** /ˈsʌðərli/ *adj.* **1** to, toward or in the south: *Keep going in a southerly direction.* **2** (used about winds) coming from the south: *a southerly wind*

★**south·ern** (*also* **South·ern**) /ˈsʌðərn/ *adj.* of, in or from the south of a place: *Los Angeles is in southern California.* ◇ *She speaks with a southern accent.*

**south·ern·er** (*also* **South·ern·er**) /ˈsʌðərnər/ *noun* [C] a person who was born in or lives in the southern part of a country

**south·paw** /ˈsaʊθpɔ/ *noun* [C] (*informal*) a person who prefers to use his/her left hand rather than the right, especially in sports such as boxing or baseball

**the ˌSouth ˈPole** *noun* [sing.] the point on the surface of the Earth which is farthest south ➲ picture at **earth**.

**south·ward** /ˈsaʊθwərd/ *adj., adv.* toward the south: *in a southward direction*

**south·west**[1] /ˌsaʊθˈwɛst/ *noun* [sing.] (*abbr.* **SW**) **1** (*also* **the southwest**) the direction or point of the compass that is between south and west ➲ picture at **north**. **2** (*also* **the southwest**, **the Southwest**) a region that is toward the southwest of a place or country. In the U.S., this includes Arizona, New Mexico and southern California: *paintings that show scenes of the old Southwest*

**south·west**[2] /ˌsaʊθˈwɛst/ *adj., adv.* in, from or to the southwest of a place or country: *the southwest coast of France* ◇ *If you look southwest, you can see the ocean.*

**south·west·er·ly** /ˌsaʊθˈwɛstərli/ *adj.* **1** toward the southwest: *in a southwesterly direction* **2** (used about a wind) coming from the southwest

**south·west·ern** /ˌsaʊθˈwɛstərn/ *adj.* in or from the southwest of a place or country: *southwestern Italy*

**south·west·ward** /ˌsaʊθˈwɛstwərd/ *adv.* toward the southwest: *Follow the road southwestward.*

**sou·ve·nir** /ˌsuvəˈnɪr; ˈsuvənɪr/ *noun* [C] something that you buy and keep to remind you of a place where you have been on vacation or of a special event

**sov·er·eign**[1] /ˈsɑvərən; ˈsɑvrən/ *adj.* (usually *before* a noun) (used about a country) not controlled by any other country; independent

**sov·er·eign**[2] /ˈsɑvərən; ˈsɑvrən/ *noun* [C] a king or queen

**sov·er·eign·ty** /ˈsɑvrənti/ ***noun*** [U] the power that a country has to control its own government

**the Soviet Union** /ˌsoʊviət ˈyunyən; -viɛt-/ ***noun*** [sing.] a large country that formerly existed in eastern Europe and northern Asia, including what is now Russia, Ukraine, Kazakhstan and several other countries. The Soviet Union had a Communist government. ▶ **Sov·i·et** ***noun*** [C], ***adj.***

**sow**[1] /saʊ/ ***noun*** [C] an adult female pig ➲ Look at the note at **pig**.

**sow**[2] /soʊ/ ***verb*** [T] (*pt* **sowed**; *pp* **sown** /soʊn/ or **sowed**) **sow A (in B)**; **sow B (with A)** to plant seeds in the ground: *to sow seeds in the garden* ◇ *to sow a field with wheat*

**sox** /sɑks/ ***noun*** [pl.] a nonstandard plural spelling of SOCKS[1], used especially in advertising

**soy·bean** /ˈsɔɪbin/ ***noun*** [C] a type of bean that can be used to make food products such as artificial meat and milk

ˈ**soy sauce** ***noun*** [U] a dark brown sauce that is made from soybeans and that you add to food, especially Chinese or Japanese food

**spa** /spɑ/ ***noun*** [C] (*pl.* **spas**) **1** (*also* ˈ**health spa**) a place where people go to relax, exercise, eat healthy foods and have health and beauty treatments, especially as a vacation **2** a bathtub or pool with a pump that moves the hot water around, giving a pleasant feeling to your body SYN **Jacuzzi**™

★**space**[1] /speɪs/ ***noun*** **1** [C,U] an area that is empty or not used: *Is there enough space for me to park the car there?* ◇ *a parking space* ◇ *We're a little short of space.* ◇ *There's a space here for you to write your name.* ◇ *wide open spaces* (= empty areas of countryside) ➲ Look at **room** and the note at **place**[1]. **2** [U] (*also* ˌ**outer** ˈ**space**) the area which surrounds the Earth and all the other planets and stars: *Sally Ride was the first American woman to go into space.* ◇ *space travel* **3** [C, usually sing.] a period of time: *Mandy has been sick three times in the space of four months.*

**space**[2] /speɪs/ ***verb*** **1** [T] **space sth (apart/out)** to arrange things so that there are spaces between them **2** [I] **space (out)** (*slang*) to stop paying close attention and start thinking about nothing in particular

ˈ**space-age** ***adj.*** (*informal*) (used especially about design or technology) very modern and advanced: *a space-age kitchen*

ˈ**space bar** ***noun*** [C] a bar on the keyboard of a computer or typewriter that you press to make spaces between words

ˈ**space caˌdet** ***noun*** [C] (*slang*) a person who behaves strangely and often forgets things, as though he/she were on drugs

**space·craft** /ˈspeɪskræft/ ***noun*** [C] (*pl.* **spacecraft**) a vehicle that travels in space

**spaced** /speɪst/ (*also* ˌ**spaced** ˈ**out**) ***adj.*** (*informal*) not completely conscious of what is happening around you, often because of taking drugs: *He sat in the corner looking completely spaced out.*

**space·man** /ˈspeɪsmæn; -mən/ ***noun*** [C] (*pl.* **space·men** /-mən; -mɛn/) **1** (*informal*) a man who travels into space; an astronaut **2** (in stories) a creature that visits the earth from another planet SYN **alien**[1](2)

**space·ship** /ˈspeɪsʃɪp/ ***noun*** [C] a vehicle in which people can travel into space

ˈ**space ˌshuttle** (*also* **shuttle**) ***noun*** [C] a vehicle in which people can travel into space, that can be used more than once

ˈ**space ˌstation** ***noun*** [C] a large structure that is sent into space and remains above the Earth as a base for people working and traveling in space

**space·suit** /ˈspeɪs·sut/ ***noun*** [C] a special suit that covers the whole body and has a supply of air, allowing sb to survive and move around in space

**space·walk** /ˈspeɪswɔk/ ***noun*** [C] a period of physical activity by an astronaut in space outside a spacecraft

**spac·ey** (*also* **spac·y**) /ˈspeɪsi/ ***adj.*** (**spac·i·er**; **spac·i·est**) (*informal*) behaving as though you are not completely conscious of what is happening around you

**spac·ing** /ˈspeɪsɪŋ/ ***noun*** [U] **1** the amount of space that is left between things, especially between the words or lines printed on a page: *single/double spacing* (= with one or two lines left between lines of type) **2** the amount of time that is left between things happening: *In music, the spacing of intervals is vital.*

**spa·cious** /ˈspeɪʃəs/ ***adj.*** having a lot of space or room; large in size ▶ **spa·cious·ness** ***noun*** [U]

**spade** /speɪd/ ***noun*** **1** [C] a tool that you use for digging. A spade has a long wooden handle and a flat, often pointed, piece of metal (a **blade**) at one end. ➲ picture at **garden**. **2 spades** [pl.] the group (suit) of playing cards with pointed black leaves on them: *the king of spades* ➲ picture at **card**[1]. **3** [C] one of the cards from this suit: *Do you have a spade?*

**spa·ghet·ti** /spəˈgɛt̬i/ ***noun*** [U] a type of Italian food (pasta) made from flour and water, that looks like long strings: *I'll cook some spaghetti.* ◇ *spaghetti sauce*

**spa·ghet·ti bo·lo·gnese** /spəˌgɛt̬i boʊləˈneɪz; -ˈnyeɪz; -ˈniz/ ***noun*** [C,U] a dish of spaghetti with a sauce made with meat, tomatoes, etc.

**spam** /spæm/ ***verb*** [T] (**spam·ming**; **spammed**) to send the same e-mail message to a large number of people, usually in order to advertise sth ▶ **spammer** ***noun*** [C]

**spam**[1] /spæm/ ***noun*** [U] **1 Spam**™ finely chopped cooked meat that has been pressed together in a container, usually sold in cans and served cold in slices **2** (*informal*) advertising material sent by e-mail to people who have not asked for it

**span**[1] /spæn/ ***noun*** [C] **1** the length of sth from one end to the other: *the span of a bridge* **2** the length of time that sth lasts or continues: *Young children have a short attention span.*

**span**[2] /spæn/ ***verb*** [T] (**span·ning**; **spanned**) **1** to form a bridge over sth: *The river is spanned by a concrete bridge.* **2** to last or continue for a particular period of time: *Her career in politics spanned more than fifty years.*

**span·dex** /ˈspændɛks/ ***noun*** [U] an artificial



S

material that stretches, used for making clothes that fit close to the body: *spandex exercise pants*

**span·gle¹** /ˈspæŋgl/ ***noun*** [C] a small piece of shiny metal or plastic used to decorate clothes: *a dress covered with red spangles* SYN **sequin**

**span·gle²** /ˈspæŋgl/ ***verb*** [T] **spangle sth (with sth)** (usually passive) to cover or to decorate sth with small pieces of shiny material ▸ **span·gled** ***adj.***: *white spangled jumpsuits*

**span·iel** /ˈspænyəl/ ***noun*** [C] a dog with large soft ears that hang down. There are several types of spaniel: *a cocker spaniel* ◇ *a springer spaniel*

**spank** /spæŋk/ ***verb*** [T] to hit a child on his/her buttocks with an open hand as a punishment

**spank·ing¹** /ˈspæŋkɪŋ/ ***noun*** [C,U] a series of hits on the buttocks, given to sb, especially a child, as a punishment: *to give sb a spanking* ◇ *I don't agree with spanking.*

**spank·ing²** /ˈspæŋkɪŋ/ ***adv.*** (*informal*) when you say that sth is spanking new, etc., you are emphasizing that it is very new, etc.

**spar** /spɑr/ ***verb*** [I] (**spar̲r̲ing**; **spar̲r̲ed**) **1** to make the movements used in boxing, either in training or to test the speed of your opponent's reaction **2** to argue with sb, usually in a friendly way

**spare¹** /spɛr/ ***adj.*** (only *before* a noun) **1** extra; kept available for use in case it is needed: *The spare tire is kept in the trunk.* ◇ *a spare room* **2** not used for work: *What do you do in your spare time?*

**spare²** /spɛr/ ***noun*** [C] an extra thing of the same kind that you can use: *I blew a fuse. Where do you keep your spares?*

**spare³** /spɛr/ ***verb*** [T] **1** to be able to give sb/sth to sb: *Can you spare any change?* ◇ *I am very grateful that you could spare the time to see me.* **2** to not hurt or damage sb/sth: *to spare sb's life* **3** to use as little as possible of sth: *No expense was spared at the wedding.* **4** to stop sb from having a bad experience: *I told him what happened, but spared him all the details.*

IDM **to spare** more than is needed: *There's no time to spare. We need to leave right away.*

**ˌspare ˈpart** ***noun*** [C] a part for a machine, engine, etc. that you can use to replace an old part which is damaged or broken

**spare·ribs** /ˈspɛr·rɪbz/ ***noun*** [pl.] meat from the bones in the chest (**ribs**) of a pig, served on the bones as a meal: *barbecued spareribs*

**spar·ing·ly** /ˈspɛrɪŋli/ ***adv.*** (*formal*) using only a little of sth; carefully: *to use sth sparingly*

**spark¹** /spɑrk/ ***noun*** [C] **1** a small bright piece of burning material **2** a flash of light that is caused by electricity: (*figurative*) *a spark of anger*

**spark²** /spɑrk/ ***verb*** [T] to cause sth: *Eric's comments sparked a tremendous argument.*

**spar·kle** /ˈspɑrkl/ ***verb*** [I] to shine with many small points of light: *The river sparkled in the sunlight.* ◇ (*figurative*) *Patty's eyes sparkled with excitement.* ▸ **spar·kle** ***noun*** [C,U]

**spark·ler** /ˈspɑrklər/ ***noun*** [C] a type of small firework that you hold in your hand and light. It burns with many bright SPARKS¹ (1).

**spar·kling** /ˈspɑrklɪŋ/ ***adj.*** **1** that sparkles: *sparkling blue eyes* **2** (used about wine or water) with bubbles in it: *sparkling white wine* **3** very clean: *sparkling floors and counters*

**spark·plug** /ˈspɑrkplʌg/ ***noun*** [C] the small piece of equipment that produces sparks in an engine

**ˈsparring ˌpartner** ***noun*** [C] **1** a person that you regularly have friendly arguments or discussions with **2** (in boxing) a person that a boxer regularly practices with during training

**spar·row** /ˈspæroʊ/ ***noun*** [C] a small brown bird that is very common

**sparse** /spɑrs/ ***adj.*** small in quantity or amount: *a sparse crowd* ▸ **sparse·ly** ***adv.***: *a sparsely populated area* ▸ **sparse·ness** ***noun*** [U]

**Spar·tan** (*also* **spar·tan**) /ˈspɑrtn/ ***adj.*** (*formal*) very simple and not comfortable: *Spartan living conditions*

**spasm** /ˈspæzəm/ ***noun*** [C,U] a sudden tightening of a muscle that you cannot control: *painful muscular spasms in the leg*

**spas·mod·ic** /spæzˈmɑdɪk/ ***adj.*** **1** happening suddenly for short periods of time; not regular or continuous: *There was spasmodic fighting in the area yesterday.* **2** (*technical*) caused by your muscles becoming tight in a way that you cannot control: *spasmodic movements* ▸ **spas·mod·i·cal·ly** /-kli/ ***adv.***

**spat** *past tense, past participle of* SPIT¹

**spate** /speɪt/ ***noun*** [sing.] a sudden large number or amount of sth: *a spate of robberies in town*

**spa·tial** /ˈspeɪʃl/ ***adj.*** (*formal*) connected with the size or position of sth

**spat·ter** /ˈspæt̬ər/ ***verb*** **1** [T] **spatter sb/sth (with sth)**; **spatter sth (on/over sb/sth)** to cover sb/sth with drops of liquid, dirt, etc., especially by accident: *blood-spattered walls* ◇ *As the bus passed, it spattered us with mud.* ◇ *Oil was spattered on the floor.* **2** [I] (used about liquid) to fall on a surface in drops, often noisily: *We heard the rain spattering on the roof.* ▸ **spat·ter** ***noun*** [sing.]: *a spatter of rain against the window*

**spat·u·la** /ˈspætʃələ/ ***noun*** [C] (*pl.* **spat·u·las**) a kitchen tool with a wide flat blade and a long handle, that is used for turning or lifting food ➲ picture at **kitchen**.

**spawn** /spɔn/ ***verb*** **1** [I] (used about fish, frogs, etc.) to lay eggs **2** [T] to cause sth to develop or be produced: *The band's album spawned a string of hit singles.*

**spay** /speɪ/ ***verb*** [T] (*technical*) to remove part of the sex organs of a female animal, to prevent it from having babies: *Have you had your cat spayed?* ➲ Look at **neuter²**.

**spaz** /spæz/ ***noun*** [C] (*pl.* **spaz·zes**) (*slang*) an offensive word, used especially by children to refer to sb who often falls over or drops things or becomes too excited or upset

★**speak** /spik/ ***verb*** (*pt* **spoke** /spoʊk/; *pp* **spok·en** /ˈspoʊkən/) **1** [I] **speak (to sb) (about sb/sth)** to talk or say things: *I'd like to speak to the manager, please.* ◇ *Could you speak more slowly?* ◇ *I was so angry I could hardly speak.*

S

NOTE **Speak** and **talk** have almost the same meaning, although **speak** is slightly more formal. In addition, **talk** is more likely to be used about a conversation, while **speak** is often used when only one person is saying something: *Speaking personally, I'm all in favor of the idea.* ◇ *We talked all night.* ◇ *I ought to speak to Ben's parents about his bad behavior.*

**2** [T] to know and be able to use a language: *Does anyone here speak German?* ◇ *a French-speaking guide* **3** [I] **speak (on/about sth)** to make a speech to a group of people: *Professor Hurst has been invited to speak on British foreign policy.* **4** [I] **speak (to sb)** (*informal*) (usually in negative sentences) to be friendly with sb: *They had an argument and now they're not speaking to each other.*

IDM **be on speaking terms (with sb)** to be friendly with sb (after an argument): *Thankfully, they are back on speaking terms again.*

**so to speak** (used when you are describing sth in an unusual way or in a way which is not strictly true): *She lost her head, so to speak, when the fire alarm rang.*

**speak for itself** to be very clear so that no other explanation is needed: *The statistics speak for themselves.*

**speak your mind** to say exactly what you think, even though you might offend sb

PHR V **speak for sb** to express the thoughts or opinions of sb else: *I cannot speak for my colleagues.*

**speak out (against sth)** to say clearly and publicly that you think sth is bad or wrong

**speak up** to speak louder

**speak·eas·y** /ˈspikˌizi/ ***noun*** [C] (*pl.* **speak·eas·ies**) a bar or nightclub where people could buy alcohol illegally, at the time in the 1920s and 1930s when it was illegal to make or sell alcohol

★**speak·er** /ˈspikər/ ***noun*** [C] **1** a person who makes a speech to a group of people: *Tonight's speaker is a well-known writer.* **2** (*also formal* **loudspeaker**) the part of a radio, stereo system, etc. from which the sound comes out **3** a person who speaks a particular language: *a native Russian speaker*

**spear¹** /spɪr/ ***noun*** [C] a long pole with a sharp point at one end, used for hunting or fighting

**spear²** /spɪr/ ***verb*** [T] to throw or push a spear or other pointed object through sth/sb: *They were standing in the river spearing fish.* ◇ *She speared an olive with her fork.*

**spear·head** /ˈspɪrhɛd/ ***verb*** [T] to lead an attack, etc.: *The Environmental Agency is spearheading the campaign.*

**spear·mint** /ˈspɪrmɪnt/ ***noun*** [U] a type of leaf with a fresh taste that is used in candy, etc.: *spearmint chewing gum* ➲ Look at **peppermint**.

**spec** /spɛk/ ***noun*** [C] a detailed description of sth, especially the design and materials needed to produce sth: *We want the machine manufactured to our own spec.* ➲ Look at **specification**.

★**spe·cial¹** /ˈspɛʃl/ ***adj.*** **1** not usual or ordinary; important for some particular reason: *He shouldn't get special treatment just because he's famous.* ◇ *a special occasion* ◇ *Are you doing anything special tonight?* **2** (only *before* a noun) for a particular purpose: *special education for children with learning difficulties* ◇ *There's a special tool for doing that.*

**spe·cial²** /ˈspɛʃl/ ***noun*** [C] **1** something, such as a television program, that is not usual or ordinary but is made or done for a particular occasion: *a prime-time news special on TV* **2** something, such as a meal in a restaurant, or a product in a store, that is available for only a short time or at a lower price than usual: *Today's special is roast beef and mashed potatoes.*

**ˌspecial ˈagent** ***noun*** [C] (*U.S.*) a detective who works for the federal government in the U.S., for example for the FBI

**ˌspecial eduˈcation** (*also informal* ˌ**special ˈed** /ˌspɛʃl ˈɛd/) ***noun*** [U] the education of children who have physical or learning problems

**ˌspecial efˈfects** ***noun*** [pl.] unusual or exciting pieces of action in movies or television shows, that are created by computers or special photographic techniques to show things that do not normally exist or happen

★**spe·cial·ist** /ˈspɛʃl·ɪst/ ***noun*** [C] a person with special or deep knowledge of a particular subject: *My doctor sent me to see a heart specialist.*

**spe·cial·ize** /ˈspɛʃl·aɪz/ ***verb*** [I] **specialize (in sth)** to give most of your attention to one subject, type of product, etc.: *This store specializes in clothes for big and tall men.* ◇ *a lawyer who specializes in divorce cases* ▶ **spe·cial·i·za·tion** /ˌspɛʃl·əˈzeɪʃn/ ***noun*** [U]

**spe·cial·ized** /ˈspɛʃl·aɪzd/ ***adj.*** to be used for a particular purpose: *a specialized system* ◇ *specialized training*

★**spe·cial·ly** /ˈspɛʃl·i/ ***adv.*** (usually before a past participle) for a particular purpose or reason: *These dogs have been specially trained to find smuggled drugs.* ◇ *a specially designed chair for people with back problems*

**ˌspecial ˈneeds** ***noun*** [pl.] needs that a person has because of mental or physical problems: *She teaches children with special needs.*

**spe·cial·ty** /ˈspɛʃl·ti/ ***noun*** [C] (*pl.* **spe·cial·ties**) **1** an area of study or a subject that you know a lot about **2** something made by a person, place, business, etc. that is very good and that he/she/it is famous for: *The chef's specialty is baked salmon in a cream sauce.*

**spe·cies** /ˈspiʃiz; -siz/ ***noun*** [C] (*pl.* **spe·cies**) a group of plants or animals that are very similar to each other and that can breed together: *an endangered species*

★**spe·cif·ic** /spəˈsɪfɪk/ ***adj.*** **1** detailed or exact: *You need to give the class specific instructions on what they should do.* **2** particular; not general: *Everyone was given a specific job to do.* ▶ **spe·cif·i·cal·ly** /-kli/ ***adv.***: *paper manufactured specifically for laser printers* ◇ *I specifically told you not to do that.*

**spec·i·fi·ca·tion** /ˌspɛsəfəˈkeɪʃn/ ***noun*** [C, usually pl.] detailed information about how sth has been or must be built or made: *The parts that were supplied do not meet our technical specifications.*

**spe·cif·ics** /spəˈsɪfɪks/ ***noun*** [pl.] the details of a

S

subject that you need to think about or discuss: *Okay, that's the broad plan—let's get down to the specifics.*

**spec·i·fy** /ˈspɛsəfaɪ/ ***verb*** [T] (*pres. part.* **spec·i·fy·ing**; *3rd person sing. pres.* **spec·i·fies**; *pt, pp* **spec·i·fied**) to say or name sth clearly or in detail: *Please specify any dates when you are not available.* ◇ *The regulations specify the maximum number of people the building can hold.*

**spec·i·men** /ˈspɛsəmən/ ***noun*** [C] **1** an example of a particular type of thing, often studied by experts or scientists: *There is a fine specimen of that type of tree in Yosemite National Park.* **2** a small amount of sth that is tested for medical or scientific purposes: *Specimens of the patient's blood were tested in the hospital laboratory.*

**speck** /spɛk/ ***noun*** [C] a very small spot or mark: *a speck of dust* ◇ *The car was just a tiny speck on the horizon.*

**speck·led** /ˈspɛkld/ ***adj.*** covered with small marks or spots

**spec·ta·cle** /ˈspɛktəkl/ ***noun*** [C,U] something that is impressive, interesting or unusual to look at: *the thrilling spectacle of the New Year's Day parade*

**spec·ta·cles** /ˈspɛktəklz/ ***noun*** [pl.] (*old-fashioned, formal*) = GLASSES

**spec·tac·u·lar**[1] /spɛkˈtækyələr/ ***adj.*** very impressive, interesting or attractive: *The view from the top of the hill is really spectacular.* ◇ *a spectacular display of fireworks* ▸ **spec·tac·u·lar·ly *adv.***

**spec·tac·u·lar**[2] /spɛkˈtækyələr/ ***noun*** [C] an impressive show or performance: *a Christmas TV spectacular*

**spec·tate** /ˈspɛkteɪt/ ***verb*** [I] to watch sth, especially a sports event

★**spec·ta·tor** /ˈspɛkteɪt̬ər/ ***noun*** [C] a person who watches a show, sports game, etc.

**spec·ter** /ˈspɛktər/ ***noun*** [C, usually sing.] **the specter (of sth)** an idea that frightens you because of sth bad that might happen in the future: *the specter of unemployment*

**spec·trum** /ˈspɛktrəm/ ***noun*** [C, usually sing.] (*pl.* **spec·tra** /ˈspɛktrə/ or **spec·trums**) **1** the set of seven colors into which white light can be separated: *You can see the colors of the spectrum in a rainbow.* **2** a full or wide range of sth: *speakers representing the whole spectrum of political opinions*

**spec·u·late** /ˈspɛkyəleɪt/ ***verb*** **1** [I,T] **speculate (about/on sth)** to think about sth without having all the facts or information: *to speculate about the outcome of the next election* **2** [I] to buy and sell with the aim of making money but with the risk of losing it: *to speculate on the stock market* ▸ **spec·u·la·tor** /-leɪt̬ər/ ***noun*** [C] ▸ **spec·u·la·tion** /ˌspɛkyəˈleɪʃn/ ***noun*** [C,U]: *The report prompted speculation that the company would have to close one of its factories.* ◇ *stock market speculation*

**spec·u·la·tive** /ˈspɛkyələt̬ɪv; -ˌleɪt̬ɪv/ ***adj.*** (*written*) **1** based on guessing or on opinions that have been formed without knowing all the facts: *The report is highly speculative and should be ignored.* **2** showing that you are trying to guess sth: *She cast a speculative look at Kate.* **3** (used about business activity) done in the hope of making a profit but involving the risk of losing money: *speculative investment*

**sped** *past tense, past participle of* SPEED[2]

**speech** /spitʃ/ ***noun*** **1** [U] the act of speaking or the state of being able to speak: *to lose the power of speech* ◇ *freedom of speech* (= to say your opinions openly) **2** [U] the particular way of speaking of a person or group of people: *She's writing a paper on children's speech patterns.* **3** [C] a formal talk that you give to a group of people: *The mayor is going to make a speech to city businesspeople.* ◇ *to give a speech*

**speech·less** /ˈspitʃləs/ ***adj.*** not able to speak, e.g. because you are shocked, very angry, etc.: *His remark left the group totally speechless.*

**ˈspeech ˌtherapy** ***noun*** [U] special treatment to help people who have problems in speaking clearly, for example in pronouncing particular sounds ▸ **ˈspeech ˌtherapist *noun*** [C]

**speech·writ·er** /ˈspitʃˌraɪt̬ər/ ***noun*** [C] a person whose job is to write speeches for a politician or public figure

★**speed**[1] /spid/ ***noun*** **1** [U] fast movement: *to gather/pick up speed* ◇ *With a final burst of speed, Jackson won the race.* **2** [C,U] the rate at which sb/sth moves or travels: *The car was traveling at a speed of 40 miles an hour.* ◇ *to travel at high speed*

IDM **bring/get sb up to speed (on sth)** to give sb the most recent and accurate information about a situation: *I'll bring you up to speed on the latest developments.*

**speed**[2] /spid/ ***verb*** [I] (*pt, pp* **sped** /spɛd/ or **speed·ed**) **1** to go or move very quickly: *He sped around the corner on his bicycle.* ◇ *The fire engine sped past us.* **2** (only used in the continuous tenses) to drive a car, etc. faster than the legal speed limit: *The police said she had been speeding.*

PHR V **speed (sth) up** (to cause sth) to go faster: *plans to speed up mail delivery* ◇ *The traffic sped up once it reached the expressway.*

**speed·boat** /ˈspidboʊt/ ***noun*** [C] a small fast boat with an engine

**ˈspeed bump** ***noun*** [C] a narrow raised area across a road that is put there to make traffic go slower

**ˈspeed ˌdial** ***noun*** [U] a feature on a telephone that allows you to dial a phone number very quickly by just pressing one or two buttons

**speed·ing** /ˈspidɪŋ/ ***noun*** [U] the act of driving a car, etc. faster than the legal speed limit: *Maria got a speeding ticket on the interstate yesterday.*

**ˈspeed ˌlimit** ***noun*** [C, usually sing.] the highest speed that you may drive without breaking the law on a particular piece of road

**speed·om·e·ter** /spɪˈdɑmət̬ər/ ***noun*** [C] a piece of equipment in a car, etc. that tells you how fast you are traveling

**ˈspeed-read** ***verb*** [I,T] to read very quickly, paying attention to sentences and phrases rather than to every word ▸ **ˈspeed-ˌreading *noun*** [U]

**ˈspeed trap** ***noun*** [C] a place on a road where police use special equipment to catch drivers who are going too fast

**speed·way** /ˈspidweɪ/ ***noun*** [C] a type of track that is specially built for car or motorcycle racing

**speed·y** /ˈspidi/ ***adj.*** (**speed·i·er**; **speed·i·est**) fast; quick: *to make a speedy recovery from an illness* ▸ **speed·i·ly** ***adv.***

★**spell**[1] /spɛl/ ***verb*** (*pt, pp* **spelled** /spɛld/ or **spelt** /spɛlt/) **1** [I,T] to write or say the letters of a word in the correct order: *I never learned to spell very well in school.* ◇ *How do you spell your last name?* ◇ *His name is spelled P-H-I-L-I-P.* **2** [T] (used about a set of letters) to form a particular word: *A-I-S-L-E spells "aisle."* **3** [T] to mean; to have sth as a result: *Another poor harvest would spell disaster for the region.*
PHRV **spell sth out 1** to write or say the letters of a word or name in the correct order **2** to explain sth in detail or in a very clear way

**spell**[2] /spɛl/ ***noun*** [C] **1** a short period of time: *the recent cold spell* **2** [usually sing.] (in stories, etc.) a state or condition that was caused by magic, or the special words that sb says in order to use magic: *The evil witch* ***cast a spell on*** *the prince.* ◇ (*figurative*) *He's completely* ***under her spell.***

**spell·bind·ing** /ˈspɛlˌbaɪndɪŋ/ ***adj.*** holding your attention completely: *a spellbinding performance*

**spell·bound** /ˈspɛlbaʊnd/ ***adj.*** with your attention completely held by what you are listening to or watching: *a storyteller who can hold audiences spellbound* ◇ *The kids watched and listened spellbound to the performance.*

**spell·check·er** /ˈspɛlˌtʃɛkər/ ***noun*** [C] a computer program that checks your writing to see if your spelling is correct

**spel·ler** /ˈspɛlər/ ***noun*** [C] if sb is a good/bad speller, he/she finds it easy/difficult to spell words correctly

★**spell·ing** /ˈspɛlɪŋ/ ***noun*** **1** [C,U] the way that a word is spelled: *My grandfather changed the spelling of his name when he came to North America.* **2** [U] the act of using letters to form words, or the ability to spell words correctly: *Roger is very good at spelling.*

ˈ**spelling bee** ***noun*** [C] a competition in which children take turns spelling words out loud. The child who can spell the most words correctly is the winner.

**spe·lunk·ing** /spɪˈlʌŋkɪŋ/ ***noun*** [U] the sport or activity of going into caves under the ground: *He had always wanted to* ***go spelunking.*** ▸ **spe·lunk·er** ***noun*** [C]

★**spend** /spɛnd/ ***verb*** (*pt, pp* **spent** /spɛnt/) **1** [I,T] **spend (sth) (for/on sth)** to give or pay money for sth: *How much do you spend on food each week?* ◇ *You can't keep on spending like that if you want to retire early.* **2** [T] to pass time: *I spent a whole evening writing letters.* ◇ *I'm spending the weekend at my parents' house.* ◇ *He spent two years in Rome.*

**spend·er** /ˈspɛndər/ ***noun*** [C] a person who spends money in the particular way mentioned: *a big spender* (= who spends a lot of money)

**spend·ing** /ˈspɛndɪŋ/ ***noun*** [U] the giving of large amounts of money by an organization to pay for services such as education: *The government wants to increase spending on health care.*

**spend·thrift** /ˈspɛndθrɪft/ ***noun*** [C] a person who spends too much money or who wastes money ▸ **spend·thrift** ***adj.***: *spendthrift governments/institutions*

**spent** /spɛnt/ ***adj.*** **1** that has been used, so that it cannot be used again: *spent bullets/matches* **2** (*written*) very tired: *After the grueling test, he felt totally spent.*
IDM **a spent force** a person or group that no longer has any power or influence: *The opposition party is now a spent political force.*

**sperm** /spərm/ ***noun*** **1** [C] (*pl.* **sperm** or **sperms**) a very small cell that is produced by a male animal and that can join with a female egg to create a new life **2** [U] the liquid that contains sperm

ˈ**sperm bank** ***noun*** [C] a place where sperm is kept and then used to help women become pregnant artificially

**sper·mi·cide** /ˈspərməsaɪd/ ***noun*** [C,U] a substance that kills sperm, used during sex to prevent the woman from becoming pregnant ▸ **sper·mi·cid·al** /ˌspərməˈsaɪdl/ ***adj.*** (only *before* a noun): *spermicidal cream*

ˈ**sperm whale** ***noun*** [C] a large whale that is hunted for its oil and fat

**spew** /spyu/ ***verb*** [I,T] **1 spew (sth) (out)** to flow out quickly, or to make sth flow out quickly, in large amounts: *Massive chimneys were spewing out smoke.* ◇ *Flames spewed from the aircraft's engine.* **2 spew (sth) (up)** (*informal*) to vomit

**SPF** /ˌɛs pi ˈɛf/ ***abbr.*** the abbreviation for "sun protection factor"; a number that shows how much protection from the sun a particular cream (a sunblock) will give you

**sphere** /sfɪr/ ***noun*** [C] **1** any round object shaped like a ball ➲ picture at **cube**. **2** an area of interest or activity: *Many countries are having difficulties in the economic sphere.* ▸ **spher·i·cal** /ˈsfɪrɪkl; ˈsfɛr-/ ***adj.***

**sphinx** /sfɪŋks/ ***noun*** [sing.] **the Sphinx** an ancient Egyptian stone statue of a creature with a human head and the body of a lion lying down

S

**spic** /spɪk/ ***noun*** [C] (*taboo, slang*) a very offensive word for a person from a country where Spanish is spoken, for example a Mexican or Puerto Rican

★**spice**[1] /spaɪs/ ***noun*** **1** [C,U] a substance (especially a powder) that is made from part of a plant and used to give flavor to food: *I use a lot of herbs and spices in my cooking.* ◇ *Pepper and paprika are two common spices.* **2** [U] excitement and interest: *to add spice to a drama*

**spice**[2] /spaɪs/ ***verb*** [T] **1 spice sth (with sth)** to add SPICE[1] (1) to food **2 spice sth (up) (with sth)** to add excitement to sth

**spick** /spɪk/ ***adj.***
IDM **spick and span** neat and clean: *Their house is always spick and span.*

★**spic·y** /ˈspaɪsi/ ***adj.*** (**spic·i·er**; **spic·i·est**) containing spice: *Mexican food is very spicy.*

**spi·der** /ˈspaɪdər/ ***noun*** [C] a type of small animal

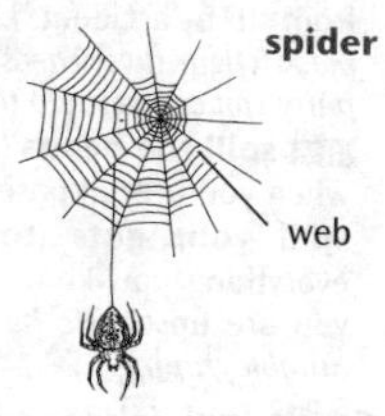

(like an insect) with eight legs. Spiders make (**spin**) special nets (**webs**) to catch insects for food.

**spi·der·web** /ˈspaɪdərwɛb/ ***noun*** [C] a fine net of threads made by a spider to catch insects: (*figurative*) *to be caught in a spiderweb of confusion*

**spi·der·y** /ˈspaɪdəri/ ***adj.*** long and thin, like the legs of a spider: *spidery fingers* ◇ *spidery handwriting* (= consisting of thin lines that are not very clear)

**spiel** /ʃpil; spil/ ***noun*** [C] (*informal*) a long fast speech that sb has used many times, that is intended to persuade you to believe sth or buy sth: *The salesman went into a long spiel about the merits of the new design.*

**spif·fy** /ˈspɪfi/ ***adj.*** (*informal*) (**spif·fi·er**; **spif·fi·est**) attractive and fashionable: *a spiffy outfit/haircut*

**spig·ot** /ˈspɪgət/ ***noun*** [C] **1** (*U.S.*) a faucet, especially one outdoors **2** (*technical*) a device that controls the flow of liquid from a container

**spike¹** /spaɪk/ ***noun*** [C] a piece of metal, wood, etc. that has a sharp point at one end: *an iron fence with spikes on the top*

**spike²** /spaɪk/ ***verb*** [T] **1** to push a sharp piece of metal, wood, etc. into sb/sth; to injure sth on a sharp point **2 spike sth (with sth)** to add alcohol, poison or a drug to sb's drink or food without him/her knowing: *He gave her a drink spiked with tranquillizers.* ◇ (*figurative*) *Her words were spiked with malice.* **3** to reject sth that a person has written or said; to prevent sth from happening or being made public: *The article was spiked for fear of legal action against the newspaper.* **4** to rise quickly and reach a high value: *The U.S. dollar spiked to a three-month high.*

IDM **spike the ball** (in football) to throw the ball to the ground with great force, in order to celebrate scoring points (a **touchdown**)

**ˌspike ˈheel** ***noun*** [C] a very thin high heel on a woman's shoe; a shoe with such a heel SYN **stiletto**

**spik·y** /ˈspaɪki/ ***adj.*** **1** having sharp points: *spiky leaves/plants* **2** (used about hair) sticking straight up from the head

**spill**

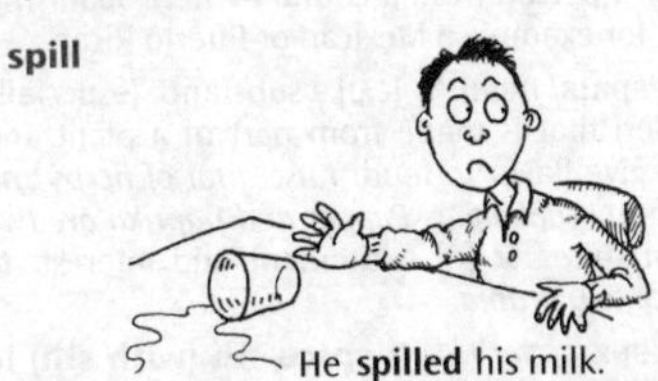

He **spilled** his milk.

**spill¹** /spɪl/ ***verb*** [I,T] (to cause a liquid) to pour out from sth by accident: *I spilled some wine on the carpet.* ◇ (*figurative*) *There were so many people that the party spilled over into the neighbors' yard.*

IDM **spill the beans** (*informal*) to tell a person sth when you are supposed to be keeping it secret

**spill your guts (to sb)** (*informal*) to tell sb everything you know or feel about sth, because you are upset: *He has spilled his guts in his new autobiography.*

**spill²** /spɪl/ (*also formal* **spill·age**) ***noun*** [C,U] an act of spilling (a large amount of) sth; the amount that is spilled: *an oil spill* ◇ *Clean up any spills immediately.*

**spill·age** /ˈspɪlɪdʒ/ ***noun*** [C,U] (*formal*) = SPILL²: *Put the bottle in a plastic bag in case of spillage.*

★**spin¹** /spɪn/ ***verb*** [I,T] (**spin·ning**; *pt, pp* **spun** /spʌn/) **1 spin (sth) (around)** (to cause sth) to turn around quickly: *Mary spun around when she heard someone call her name.* ◇ (*figurative*) *After three glasses of whiskey, my head was spinning.* **2** to make thread from a mass of wool, cotton, etc.

**spin²** /spɪn/ ***noun*** **1** [C] an act of SPINNING (1): *The car skidded on the ice and went into a spin.* **2** [U] fast turning motion: *to put some spin on a ball* (= in sports like pool/tennis) **3** [sing., U] a way of reporting about a person or an event that is intended to influence the public's opinion of him/her/it: *Government aides attempted to put* ***a positive spin on*** *the reports of budget cuts.* ➲ Look also at **spin doctor**.

**spin·ach** /ˈspɪnɪtʃ/ ***noun*** [U] a plant with large green leaves that can be cooked and eaten as a vegetable

**spi·nal** /ˈspaɪnl/ ***adj.*** connected with the bones of the back (the **spine**)

**ˈspinal cord** ***noun*** [C] the mass of nerves inside the backbone (**spine**) that connects all parts of the body to the brain

**ˈspin ˌdoctor** ***noun*** [C] a person who works for sb else, e.g. for a politician, and tries to give the public a favorable impression of that person and his/her actions

**spine** /spaɪn/ ***noun*** [C] **1** the bones of the back of a person or animal **2** one of the sharp points on some plants and animals **3** the narrow part of a book that you can see when it is on a shelf

**ˈspine-ˌchilling** ***adj.*** (used about a book, movie, etc.) frightening in an exciting way

**spine·less** /ˈspaɪnləs/ ***adj.*** **1** (used about people) weak and easily frightened **2** (used about animals) having no backbone (**spine**)

**spin·et** /ˈspɪnət/ ***noun*** [C] **1** (*U.S.*) a small upright piano **2** a kind of harpsichord (= an early type of musical instrument), played like a piano

**ˈspinning wheel** ***noun*** [C] a simple machine that people used in their homes in the past for twisting wool, etc. It has a large wheel operated with the foot.

**spin·off** /ˈspɪnɔf; -ɑf/ (*also* **ˈspin-off**) ***noun*** [C] **1** a useful result that you did not expect **2** a book, a movie, a TV program, or an object that is based on a book, movie or television series that has been very successful: *The TV comedy series is a spinoff of the original movie.* ◇ *spinoff merchandise from the latest Disney movie*

**spin·ster** /ˈspɪnstər/ ***noun*** [C] (*old-fashioned*) a woman who has never been married

> NOTE **Bachelor** can be used about a man of any age, but you usually use **spinster** when you are talking about an older woman.

**spi·ral¹** /ˈspaɪrəl/ ***noun*** [C] a long curve that goes around and around a central point ▶ **spi·ral** ***adj.***: *a spiral staircase*

**spi·ral²** /ˈspaɪrəl/ ***verb*** [I] to move upward or

downward in a spiral, especially very quickly: *Food prices are spiraling out of control.*

**spire** /ˈspaɪər/ ***noun*** [C] a tall pointed tower on the top of a church, etc.

★**spir·it** /ˈspɪrɪt/ ***noun***
➤SOUL **1** [C] the part of a person that many people believe still exists after his/her body is dead: *the spirits of the dead* **2** [C] a ghost or being that exists but that does not have a body: *the Holy Spirit*
➤MIND/FEELINGS/CHARACTER **3** [U] energy, strength of mind or courage: *The constant setbacks finally broke his spirit.*
➤ATTITUDE **4** [C,U] the mood or attitude of mind of sb/sth: *the spirit of goodwill in the holiday season* ◇ *to be in high/low spirits* (= in a happy/sad mood) ◇ *Everyone got into the spirit of the party* (= joined in with enthusiasm). ◇ *the modern spirit of enterprise and innovation*
➤LOYAL FEELING **5** [U] a strong feeling of loyalty toward a group, an organization, etc. and of wanting to help it: *fun activities to build school spirit* ◇ *community spirit*
➤REAL MEANING **6** [U] the real and intended meaning of a rule, agreement, etc.: *Judges should consider the spirit as well as the letter of the law.*
➤LIQUOR **7 spirits** [pl.] = LIQUOR

**spir·it·ed** /ˈspɪrɪt̬əd/ ***adj.*** lively and full of energy: *The president gave a spirited defense of his policies.* ◇ *a spirited debate*

★**spir·i·tu·al¹** /ˈspɪrɪtʃuəl; -tʃəl/ ***adj.*** **1** concerning your deep thoughts, feelings or emotions: *to fulfill your spiritual needs* ➲ Look at **material**. **2** concerning a church or religion: *Tibet's exiled spiritual leader, the Dalai Lama* ▶ **spir·i·tu·al·ly** ***adv.***

**spir·i·tu·al²** /ˈspɪrɪtʃuəl; -tʃəl/ ***noun*** [C] a religious song, often expressing deep feelings, that was first sung by African-Americans when they were slaves in the southern U.S.

**spir·it·u·al·ism** /ˈspɪrɪtʃuəlɪzəm; -tʃəlɪzəm/ ***noun*** [U] the belief that people who have died can send messages to living people, usually through a person who has special powers (a **medium**)

**spir·it·u·al·i·ty** /ˌspɪrɪtʃuˈæləti/ ***noun*** [U] the quality of being concerned with religion or the human spirit

**spit¹** /spɪt/ ***verb*** [I,T] (**spit·ting**; *pt, pp* **spat** /spæt/ or **spit**) **spit (sth) (out)** to send liquid, food, etc. out from your mouth: *No spitting allowed!* ◇ *You're not allowed to chew gum in class – spit it out.*
IDM **be the spitting image of sb** (*informal*) to be very similar to, or almost exactly like sb/sth else: *He's the spitting image of his father.*

**spit²** /spɪt/ ***noun*** [U] (*informal*) the liquid in your mouth SYN **saliva, spittle**.

**spit·ball** /ˈspɪtbɔl/ ***noun*** [C] a piece of paper that has been inside sb's mouth and then made into a ball to throw at sb

**spite¹** /spaɪt/ ***noun*** [U] the desire to hurt or annoy sb: *He stole her letters out of* (= because of) *spite.*
IDM **in spite of sth** (used to show that sth did not have the result or effect that you would have expected): *The game was played in spite of the bad weather.* ◇ *In spite of all her hard work, Sue failed the test.*

**spite²** /spaɪt/ ***verb*** [T] (only used in the infinitive with *to*) to deliberately annoy or upset sb: *They're playing the music loud just to spite us.*

**spite·ful** /ˈspaɪtfl/ ***adj.*** behaving in an unkind way in order to hurt or upset sb: *a spiteful child* ◇ *He made some very spiteful remarks to me.* SYN **malicious** ▶ **spite·ful·ly** /-fəli/ ***adv.***: *"I don't need you," she said spitefully.*

**spit·tle** /ˈspɪt̬l/ ***noun*** [U] (*old-fashioned*) the liquid that forms in the mouth SYN **saliva, spit**.

**spit·toon** /spɪˈtun/ ***noun*** [C] a container, used especially in the past, for people to spit into

**splash¹** /splæʃ/ ***verb*** [I,T] (to cause a liquid) to fly in drops and make sb/sth wet: *The girls were splashing each other with water.* ◇ *They were splashing around in the pool.* ◇ *Be careful not to splash paint onto the floor.*

**splash²** /splæʃ/ ***noun*** [C] **1** an act or sound of splashing: *Paul jumped into the pool with a big splash.* **2** a mark or spot that was made by sth splashing: *splashes of oil on the stove* **3** a bright area of color: *Flowers add a splash of color to a room.*

**splash·y** /ˈsplæʃi/ ***adj.*** (**splash·i·er**; **splash·i·est**) (*informal*) bright and very easy to notice: *a splashy advertising campaign* ◇ *a dress in a splashy print*

**splat** /splæt/ ***noun*** [sing.] (*informal*) the sound made by sth wet hitting a surface with force: *The tomato hit the wall with a splat.* ▶ **splat** ***adv.***: *The omelet fell splat onto the floor.*

**splat·ter** /ˈsplæt̬ər/ ***verb*** [I,T] (used about a liquid) to splash and make sb/sth wet or dirty; to make a liquid do this: *The paint was splattered all over the floor.*

**splay** /spleɪ/ ***verb*** [I,T] **splay (sth) (out)** to make fingers, legs, etc. become further apart from each other or spread out; to be spread out wide apart: *She lay on the bed, her arms and legs splayed out.* ◇ *His long fingers splayed across her back.*

**spleen** /splin/ ***noun*** **1** [C] a small organ near the stomach that controls the quality of the blood: *a ruptured spleen* **2** [U] (*formal*) anger: *He **vented his spleen*** (= shouted in an angry way) *on the assembled crowd.*

**splen·did** /ˈsplɛndəd/ ***adj.*** **1** very good; excellent: *a splendid example of early American art* **2** of impressive or grand appearance: *a splendid Gothic cathedral* ▶ **splen·did·ly** ***adv.***

**splen·dor** /ˈsplɛndər/ ***noun*** [U] beauty that is grand and that impresses people: *They spent $10 million to restore the hotel to its former splendor.*

**splice** /splaɪs/ ***verb*** [T] **splice sth (together)** **1** to join the ends of two pieces of rope by weaving them together **2** to join the ends of two pieces of film, tape, etc. by sticking them together

**splint** /splɪnt/ ***noun*** [C] a piece of wood or metal that is used to keep a broken bone in the right position

**splin·ter¹** /ˈsplɪntər/ ***noun*** [C] a small thin sharp piece of wood, metal or glass that has broken off a larger piece: *I have a splinter in my finger.* ◇ (*figurative*) *a radical splinter group* (= that has separated from the main group)

S

**splin·ter²** /ˈsplɪntər/ ***verb*** [I,T] to break into small thin sharp pieces

★**split¹** /splɪt/ ***verb*** (*pres. part.* **split·ting**; *pt, pp* **split**) **1** [I,T] **split (sb) (up) (into sth)** (to cause people) to divide into different groups: *Let's split into two groups.* ◇ *The students have been split into five groups according to their ability.* ◇ *Voters are split over the issue of gun control.* **2** [T] to divide or share sth: *We split the cost of the meal between us.* **3** [I,T] **split (sth) (into sth)** to break into two or more parts, usually from end to end, making a long line: *My grocery bag split open.*

IDM **split hairs** to pay too much attention in an argument to differences that are very small and not important

PHR V **split up (with sb)** to end a marriage or relationship: *He split up with his girlfriend.*

★**split²** /splɪt/ ***noun*** [C] **1** a division in a group: *Disagreement about foreign policy led to a split within the party.* **2** a long cut or hole in sth

ˌ**split ˈends** ***noun*** [pl.] if you have split ends some of the hairs on your head have divided into parts at the ends because they are dry or in poor condition: *shampoo for split ends*

ˌ**split inˈfinitive** ***noun*** [C] (*grammar*) the form of the verb with *to*, with an adverb placed between *to* and the verb, as in *She seems to really like it.*

NOTE Some people consider this to be bad English style.

ˌ**split-ˈlevel** ***adj.*** (used about a room, floor, etc.) having parts at different levels

ˌ**split ˈsecond** ***noun*** [C] a very short period of time: *It only took me a split second to decide.*

**split·ting** /ˈsplɪt̬ɪŋ/ ***adj.*** (only *before* a noun) if you have a splitting headache, you have a very bad pain in your head

**splotch** /splɑtʃ/ ***noun*** [C] (*informal*) a large mark or spot of ink, paint, mud, etc.; a small area of color or light ▶ **splotch·y** ***adj.***

**splurge** /splərdʒ/ ***verb*** [I] **splurge (on sth)** (*informal*) to spend a lot of money on sth that you do not really need: *We splurged on lunch at the Ritz.*

**splut·ter¹** /ˈsplʌt̬ər/ ***verb*** [I,T] **1** to speak quickly and with difficulty, making soft spitting sounds, because you are angry or embarrassed: *"But, but...you can't!" she spluttered.* ◇ *Her father spluttered with indignation.* SYN **sputter** (2) **2** to make a series of short explosive sounds: *The firework spluttered and went out.* ◇ *She fled from the blaze, **coughing and spluttering**.* SYN **sputter** (1)

**splut·ter²** /ˈsplʌt̬ər/ ***noun*** [C] a short explosive sound: *The car started with a splutter.*

★**spoil** /spɔɪl/ ***verb*** **1** [T] to make sth useless or unsuccessful, or not as good as before: *The new apartment building will spoil the view.* ◇ *Our vacation was spoiled by bad weather.* ◇ *Eating between meals will spoil your appetite.* **2** [T] to do too much for sb, especially a child, so that you have a bad effect on his/her character: *His grandmother spoils him by buying him all the candy he wants.* **3** [I] (used about food) to begin to decay and therefore not be good to eat or drink: *These vegetables have spoiled.* **4** [T] to treat sb/yourself very well for a certain period of time in order to make this person/yourself happy: *Sometimes I spoil my wife and take her breakfast in bed.*

**spoiled** /spɔɪld/ ***adj.*** (used about a child) rude and badly behaved because he/she is given everything he/she asks for and not enough discipline: *Her son's a **spoiled brat**.* ◇ *He's **spoiled rotten*** (= very spoiled).

**spoils** /spɔɪlz/ ***noun*** [pl.] things that have been stolen, or taken in a war or battle

**spoil·sport** /ˈspɔɪlspɔrt/ ***noun*** [C] (*informal*) a person who spoils other people's enjoyment, for example by not taking part in an activity or by trying to stop other people from doing it: *Don't be such a spoilsport!*

**spoke¹** /spoʊk/ ***noun*** [C] one of the thin pieces of metal that connect the center of a wheel to the outside edge ➲ picture at **bicycle**.

**spoke²** *past tense of* SPEAK

**spo·ken** *past participle of* SPEAK

★**spokes·man** /ˈspoʊksmən/ ***noun*** [C] (*pl.* **spokes·men** /-mən/) a person who is chosen to speak for a group or an organization

NOTE A woman is called a **spokeswoman**. **Spokesperson** is now often preferred because it can be used for a man or a woman.

**sponge¹** /spʌndʒ/ ***noun*** [C,U] a piece of rubber or plastic (or of a natural substance also called "sponge"). Sponges have many small holes, soak up water and are used for cleaning things or for washing yourself.

**sponge²** /spʌndʒ/ ***verb*** **1** [T] **sponge sb/yourself/sth (down)** to wash sb/yourself/sth with a wet cloth or sponge: *She sponged his hot face.* ◇ *Take your jacket off and I'll sponge it down with water.* **2** [T] to remove sth using a wet cloth or sponge: *We tried to sponge the blood off my shirt.* **3** [I] **sponge (off/on sb)** (*informal*) to get money, food, etc. regularly from other people without doing anything for them or offering to pay: *He spent his whole life sponging off his relatives.*

ˈ**sponge cake** ***noun*** [C,U] a light cake made from eggs, sugar and flour, with or without fat

**spong·er** /ˈspʌndʒər/ ***noun*** [C] (*informal*) a person who gets money, food, etc. from other people without doing anything for them or offering to pay

**spong·y** /ˈspʌndʒi/ ***adj.*** (**spong·i·er**; **spong·i·est**) soft and able to absorb water easily like a sponge: *spongy moss* ◇ *The ground was soft and spongy.* ◇ *The bread had a spongy texture.*

**spon·sor¹** /ˈspɑnsər/ ***noun*** [C] **1** a person or an organization that helps to pay for a special sports event, etc. or pays for an event or program to be broadcast on television (usually so that it can advertise its products) **2** a person who agrees to pay money to a charity if sb else completes a particular activity: *I need sponsors for a marathon in aid of cancer research.* **3** a person who suggests or supports a proposal for a new law: *She is a chief sponsor of the new anti-drug legislation.*

**spon·sor²** /ˈspɑnsər/ ***verb*** [T] **1** (used about a company, etc.) to pay some of the costs of a particular event, program, etc. as a way of advertising: *sports events sponsored by the tobacco industry* **2** to arrange for sth official to take place: *The U.S. is* *sponsoring negotiations between the two sides.* **3** to agree to give sb money for a charity if he/she completes a particular task: *Will you sponsor me for a charity walk I'm doing?* ◇ *a sponsored walk/swim* **4** to support sb by paying for his/her training or education: *She found a company to sponsor her through college.* **5** to introduce a proposal for a new law, etc.: *The bill was sponsored by a Republican Senator.* ▸ **spon·sor·ship** ***noun*** [U]: *Corporate sponsorship has brought millions of dollars into tennis.*

**spon·ta·ne·ous** /spɑn'temiəs/ ***adj.*** done or happening naturally; not planned: *a spontaneous burst of applause* ▸ **spon·ta·ne·ous·ly** ***adv.*** **spon·ta·ne·i·ty** /ˌspɑntə'neɪəṭi; ˌspɑntn·eɪ-/ ***noun*** [U]

**spoof** /spuf/ ***noun*** [C] (*informal*) a humorous copy of a movie, television program, etc. that exaggerates its main features: *It's a spoof on horror movies.* ◇ *a spoof game show/a game show spoof* ▸ **spoof** ***verb*** [T]

**spook¹** /spuk/ ***noun*** [C] (*informal*) **1** a ghost: *a castle haunted by spooks* **2** a spy: *a CIA spook*

**spook²** /spuk/ ***verb*** [I,T] (*informal*) (usually passive) to frighten a person or an animal; to become frightened: *We were spooked by the strange noises and lights.* ◇ *The horse spooked at the siren.*

**spook·y** /'spuki/ ***adj.*** (**spook·i·er**; **spook·i·est**) (*informal*) frightening: *The house is dark and spooky.*

**spool** /spul/ ***noun*** [C] a round object that thread, film, wire, etc. are wound around when you buy them ➲ Look at **reel**.

★**spoon¹** /spun/ ***noun*** [C] an object with a round end and a long handle that you use for eating, stirring or serving food: *Give each person a knife, fork and spoon.* ◇ *a wooden spoon for cooking* ➲ picture at **kitchen**.

**spoon²** /spun/ ***verb*** [T] to lift or serve sth with a spoon: *Spoon the mixture into a pan.*

'**spoon-feed** ***verb*** [T] (*pt, pp* **spoon-fed**) **1** to teach people sth in a way that gives them too much help and does not make them think for themselves: *The students here do not expect to be spoon-fed.* ◇ *They had information spoon-fed to them.* **2** to feed sb, especially a baby, with a spoon

**spoon·ful** /'spunfʊl/ ***noun*** [C] the amount that one spoon can hold: *a spoonful of sugar*

**spo·rad·ic** /spə'rædɪk/ ***adj.*** not done or happening regularly: *There have been sporadic outbursts of gunfire during the night.* ▸ **spo·rad·i·cal·ly** /-kli/ ***adv.***

**spore** /spɔr/ ***noun*** [C] one of the very small cells like seeds that are produced by some plants and that develop into new plants: *Ferns, mosses and fungi produce spores.*

★**sport¹** /spɔrt/ ***noun*** [C,U] a physical game or activity that you do for exercise or because you enjoy it: *Soccer is my favorite sport.* ◇ *John played a lot of sports when he was in high school.* ◇ *an Olympic sport* ◇ *amateur/professional sports* ◇ *the sports section of the newspaper*

IDM **a good sport** a person who reacts in a good way when things do not go well for him/her

**sport²** /spɔrt/ ***verb*** [T] to wear or have sth in order to impress other people: *She showed up sporting her new baseball cap.*

**sport·ing** /'spɔrṭɪŋ/ ***adj.*** (only *before* a noun) connected with sports: *a sporting event* ◇ *sporting goods*

IDM **a sporting chance** a reasonable chance of success

'**sports car** ***noun*** [C] a low, fast car, often with a roof that you can open

**sports·cast** /'spɔrtskæst/ ***noun*** [C] a television or radio broadcast of sports news or a sports event ▸ **sports·cast·er** ***noun*** [C]

'**sports day** ***noun*** [C] (*Cdn*) a day once a year on which schoolchildren take part in games, run races and do other sports activities

**sports·man** /'spɔrtsmən/ ***noun*** [C] (*pl.* **sports·men** /-mən/) a man who plays several different sports, especially outdoor sports

**sports·man·ship** /'spɔrtsmənʃɪp/ ***noun*** [U] good behavior and fair play in sports

**sports·wear** /'spɔrtswɛr/ ***noun*** [U] clothes that are worn in informal situations

**sports·wom·an** /'spɔrtswʊmən/ ***noun*** [C] (*pl.* **sports·wom·en** /-wɪmən/) a woman who plays several different sports, especially outdoor sports

ˌ**sport-u'tility** ˌ**vehicle** ***noun*** [C] → SUV

**sport·y** /'spɔrṭi/ ***adj.*** (**sport·i·er**; **sport·i·est**) (*informal*) (used about cars) fast and attractive in design: *a sporty Mercedes*

★**spot¹** /spɑt/ ***noun*** [C] **1** a particular place or area: *The Grand Canyon is a popular vacation spot.* **2** a small round mark of a different color on sth: *Leopards have dark spots.* **3** a small dirty mark on sth: *You have a spot of gravy on your shirt.* **4** a short item of entertainment or an advertisement on television or the radio: *a thirty-second TV spot*

IDM **have a soft spot for sb/sth** → SOFT

**on the spot** at the same time and place as sth else that is happening or that just happened: *Paul was caught stealing money and was fired on the spot.*

**put sb on the spot** to make sb answer a difficult question or make a difficult decision without having much time to think

**spot²** /spɑt/ ***verb*** [T] (**spot̲·ting**; **spot̲·ted**) to see or notice sb/sth: *The suspect was spotted at Miami International Airport.*

'**spot check** ***noun*** [C] a test on one of a group of people or things which is not planned or expected

**spot·less** /'spɑtləs/ ***adj.*** having no SPOTS¹ (3) or marks; very clean: *Her house is always spotless.* ◇ (*figurative*) *She has a spotless record of public service.*

**spot·light** /'spɑtlaɪt/ ***noun*** **1** [C] a lamp that can send a strong beam of light onto a small area. Spotlights are often used in theaters. ➲ picture at **light**. **2** **the spotlight** [sing.] the center of public attention or interest: *to be in the spotlight*

**spot·ter** /'spɑṭər/ ***noun*** [C] (especially in compounds) **1** a person who looks for a particular type of thing or person, as a hobby or job: *a trend/celebrity spotter* **2** a person who watches and helps a gymnast to make sure he/she does not get injured

**spot·ty** /'spɑṭi/ ***adj.*** (**spot·ti·er**; **spot·ti·est**) not complete; good in some parts, but not in others: *a spotty knowledge of Spanish* ◇ *It was a spotty performance.*

S

**spouse** /spaʊs/ ***noun*** [C] (*formal*) your husband or wife

NOTE **Spouse** is a formal or official word, used on forms, documents, etc.

▸ **spous·al** /ˈspaʊzl; -sl/ ***adj.*** (only *before* a noun) (*formal*): *spousal consent/support* ◇ *spousal abuse*

**spout¹** /spaʊt/ ***noun*** [C] a tube or pipe through which liquid comes out

**spout²** /spaʊt/ ***verb*** [I,T] **1** (used about a liquid) to come out from sth with force; to make a liquid do this: *The broken pipe spouted several gallons of water per minute.* **2** (*informal*) to say sth, using a lot of words, in a way that is not interesting: *He spouted racist remarks all through dinner.*

**sprain** /spreɪn/ ***verb*** [T] to injure part of your body by bending or turning it suddenly: *to sprain your ankle* ▸ **sprain** ***noun*** [C]: *Your wrist isn't broken. It's just a bad sprain.*

**sprang** *past tense of* SPRING²

**sprawl** /sprɔl/ ***verb*** [I] **1** to sit or lie with your arms and legs spread out: *kids sprawling on the couch, watching TV* **2** to cover a large area of land (in a way that is not planned): *The city sprawls across 40 square miles.* ▸ **sprawl** ***noun*** [U]: *suburban sprawl* ▸ **sprawled** /sprɔld/ ***adj.*** (not before a noun): *They were all sprawled on the floor when I came in.* ▸ **sprawl·ing** ***adj.***: *the sprawling suburbs*

★**spray¹** /spreɪ/ ***noun*** **1** [U] liquid in very small drops that is blown through the air: *the spray of a fountain* **2** [C,U] liquid in a special can that is forced out under pressure when you push a button: *hair spray* ◇ *spray paint*

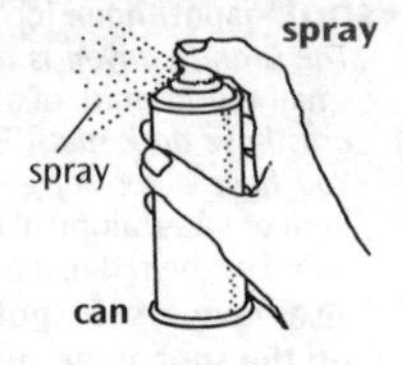


★**spray²** /spreɪ/ ***verb*** [I,T] (used about a liquid) to be sent out in very small drops with great force; to send a liquid out in this way: *The water sprayed out from the hole in the pipe.* ◇ *Somebody sprayed paint on my door!* ◇ *Somebody sprayed my door with paint.*

★**spread¹** /sprɛd/ ***verb*** (*pt, pp* **spread**)
- ▸OPEN/ARRANGE **1** [T] **spread sth (out) (on/over sth)** to open or arrange sth so that you can see all of it: *Jenny's homework was spread out on the kitchen table.*
- ▸SOFT LAYER **2** [T] **spread A on B**; **spread B with A** to cover a surface with a soft substance: *to spread butter on bread* ◇ *to spread bread with butter*
- ▸AMONG PEOPLE **3** [I,T] to affect a larger area or a bigger group of people; to make sth do this: *Violence has spread throughout the region.* ◇ *Rats and flies spread disease.*
- ▸COVER LARGE AREA **4** [I] to continue for a great distance: *The swamp spreads for several miles along the coast.*
- ▸DIVIDE **5** [T] **spread sth (over sth)** to divide sth so that it continues for a longer period of time: *You can spread your payments over a period of three years.*

PHRV **spread (yourself) out** to move away from the others in a group of people: *The police spread out to search the whole area.*

**spread²** /sprɛd/ ***noun*** **1** [U] the act of spreading sth or being spread: *Dirty drinking water encourages the spread of disease.* **2** [C,U] soft food that you eat on bread: *Don't eat butter. Use a low-fat spread.* **3** [C] a newspaper or magazine article that covers one or more pages: *a four-page spread* **4** [C] a large farm or open area of land: *My grandfather owns a 1500-acre spread in New Mexico.*

**spread·sheet** /ˈsprɛdʃit/ ***noun*** [C] a computer program that is used, for example, when doing financial or project planning. You enter data in rows and columns and the program calculates costs, etc. from it.

**spree** /spri/ ***noun*** [C] (*informal*) a time when you go out and do a lot of sth that you enjoy: *a shopping spree*

**sprig** /sprɪg/ ***noun*** [C] a small piece of a plant with leaves on it

**spright·ly** /ˈspraɪtli/ (*also* **spry**) ***adj.*** (**spright·li·er**; **spright·li·est**) (used especially about older people) full of life and energy: *a sprightly 80-year-old* ◇ *She's very sprightly for her age.*

★**spring¹** /sprɪŋ/ ***noun*** **1** [C,U] the season of the year which follows winter and comes before summer. In spring the weather gets warmer and plants begin to grow: *a cold, wet spring* ◇ *in the spring of 2004* ◇ *There's a feeling of spring in the air.* **2** [C] a place where water comes up naturally from under the ground: *a hot spring* **3** [C] a long piece of thin metal or wire that is bent around and around. After you push or pull a spring it goes back to its original shape and size: *bed springs* **4** [C] an act of jumping up or moving quickly: *With one spring the cat landed on the table.*

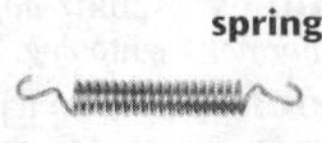


IDM **be no spring chicken** to be no longer young: *Take it easy. You're no spring chicken yourself, you know.*

**spring²** /sprɪŋ/ ***verb*** [I] (*pt* **sprang** /spræŋ/; *pp* **sprung** /sprʌŋ/) to jump or move quickly: *When the alarm went off, Ray sprang out of bed.* ◇ *to spring to your feet* ◇ (*figurative*) *Everyone* ***sprang to her defense*** *when the boss started criticizing her.*

PHRV **spring for sth** (*informal*) to pay for sth, especially as a treat for sb else: *He's never offered to spring for dinner.*

**spring from sth** (*written*) to be caused by sth; to start from sth: *The idea for the novel sprang from a trip to India.*

**spring sth on sb** (*informal*) to tell sb sth that is a surprise or not expected: *I hate to spring this on you, but can you get me that data by tomorrow?*

**spring up** to appear or develop quickly or suddenly: *Internet cafes are springing up everywhere.*

**spring·board** /ˈsprɪŋbɔrd/ ***noun*** [C] a low board that you jump on before jumping into water, over sth, etc. It helps you jump higher.

ˌ**spring ˈbreak** ***noun*** [C,U] a vacation for high school or college students in the spring: *We went to Florida for spring break.*

ˌ**spring ˈfever** ***noun*** [U] a feeling of wanting to do sth new and exciting that you sometimes get in the spring

**ˈspring roll** *noun* [C] a type of Chinese food consisting of a tube of thin pastry, filled with vegetables and/or meat and fried until it is crisp

**spring·time** /ˈsprɪŋtaɪm/ *noun* [U] the period of spring

**spring·y** /ˈsprɪŋi/ *adj.* (**spring·i·er**; **spring·i·est**) **1** returning quickly to the original shape after being pushed, pulled, stretched, etc.: *We walked across the springy turf.* **2** full of energy and confidence: *She's 73, but hasn't lost that youthful, springy step.*

**sprin·kle** /ˈsprɪŋkl/ *verb* **1** [T] **sprinkle A (on/onto/over B)**; **sprinkle B (with A)** to throw drops of water or small pieces of sth over a surface: *to sprinkle sugar on cereal* ◇ *to sprinkle cereal with sugar* **2** [I] to rain lightly

**sprin·kler** /ˈsprɪŋklər/ *noun* [C] a piece of equipment that sends out water in small drops. Sprinklers are used on grass and for putting out fires in buildings: *a sprinkler system*

**sprint¹** /sprɪnt/ *verb* [I,T] to run a short distance as fast as you can ▶ **sprint·er** *noun* [C]

**sprint²** /sprɪnt/ *noun* [C] a short run or a short fast race

**sprite** /spraɪt/ *noun* [C] (in stories) a small creature with magic powers, especially one that is graceful or likes playing tricks

**spritz** /sprɪts; ʃprɪts/ *verb* [T] to spray very small drops of liquid on sth quickly: *Lightly spritz your hair with water.*

**spritz·er** /ˈsprɪtsər; ˈʃprɪt-/ *noun* [C] a drink made with wine (usually white) mixed with soda water: *a white wine spritzer*

**sprock·et** /ˈsprɑkət/ *noun* [C] **1** (*also* **ˈsprocket wheel**) a wheel with a row of teeth around the edge that connect with the holes of a bicycle chain or with holes in a film, etc. in order to turn it **2** one of the teeth on such a wheel

**sprout¹** /spraʊt/ *verb* [I,T] (used about a plant) to begin to grow or to produce new leaves: *The seeds are sprouting.*

**sprout²** /spraʊt/ *noun* [C] **1** a new part that has grown on a plant **2** a young plant that is used as a vegetable: *bean sprout* ➲ Look also at **Brussels sprouts**.

**spruce¹** /sprus/ *noun* [C,U] a type of tree with thin sharp leaves

**spruce²** /sprus/ *verb*

PHR V **spruce (sb/sth/yourself) up** to make sb/sth/yourself clean, attractive or impressive

**sprung** *past participle of* SPRING²

**spry** /spraɪ/ *adj.* = SPRIGHTLY

**spud** /spʌd/ *noun* [C] (*informal*) a potato

**spun** *past participle of* SPIN¹

**spunk** /spʌŋk/ *noun* [U] (*informal*) courage; determination: *She's got a lot of spunk.*

**spunk·y** /ˈspʌŋki/ *adj.* (*informal*) having a lot of energy or courage: *a spunky cheerleader*

**spur¹** /spər/ *noun* [C] **1** a sharp piece of metal that a rider wears on the back of his/her boots to help control a horse and to make it go faster **2** something that encourages you or that makes sth happen more quickly

IDM **on the spur of the moment** without planning; suddenly: *I decided to go on the spur of the moment.*

**spur²** /spər/ *verb* [T] (**spur·ring**; **spurred**) to encourage sb to do sth; to make sth increase more quickly: *new policies designed to spur economic growth*

**spu·ri·ous** /ˈspyʊriəs/ *adj.* **1** false, although seeming to be genuine: *He had managed to create the entirely spurious impression that the company was thriving.* **2** based on false ideas or ways of thinking: *a spurious argument*

**spurn** /spərn/ *verb* [T] (*formal*) to refuse sth that sb has offered to you: *to spurn an offer of friendship*

**spurt¹** /spərt/ *verb* [I,T] (used about a liquid) to come out with great force; to make a liquid do this: *Blood spurted from the wound.*

**spurt²** /spərt/ *noun* [C] **1** a stream of liquid that comes out suddenly and with great force **2** a sudden increase in speed or effort: *a growth spurt*

**sput·ter** /ˈspʌt̬ər/ *verb* **1** [I] to make a series of sounds like a person spitting or coughing: *He fell into the pool and came up coughing and sputtering.* ◇ *The engine suddenly sputtered and stopped.* **2** [I,T] to speak with difficulty e.g. because you are very angry or excited: *"How dare you!" she sputtered.*

**spy¹** /spaɪ/ *noun* [C] (*pl.* **spies**) a person who tries to get secret information about another country, person or organization

**spy²** /spaɪ/ *verb* (*pres. part.* **spy·ing**; *3rd person sing. pres.* **spies**; *pt, pp* **spied**) **1** [I] **spy (on sb/sth)** to try to get (secret) information about sb/sth ➲ Look at **espionage**. **2** [T] (*formal*) to see: *They spied a campfire in the distance.*

**sq.** *abbr.* square

**squab·ble** /ˈskwɑbl/ *verb* [I] to argue in a noisy way about sth that is not very important ▶ **squabble** *noun* [C]

**squad** /skwɑd/ *noun* [C] a group of people who work as a team: *the rescue squad*

**ˈsquad car** *noun* [C] a police car

**squad·ron** /ˈskwɑdrən/ *noun* [C] a group of soldiers, military ships or airplanes, etc.

**squal·id** /ˈskwɑləd/ *adj.* very dirty, messy and unpleasant: *squalid housing conditions*

**squall** /skwɔl/ *noun* [C] a sudden storm with strong winds

**squal·or** /ˈskwɑlər/ *noun* [U] the state of being very dirty, messy or unpleasant: *to live in squalor*

**squan·der** /ˈskwɑndər/ *verb* [T] to waste time, money, etc.: *Karen squandered everything she earned on clothes and music.*

★**square¹** /skwɛr/ *adj.*

▸SHAPE **1** having four straight sides of the same length: *a square table* ➲ picture at **shape**. **2** shaped like a square: *a square face* ◇ *a dress with a square neck*

▸MEASUREMENT **3** (*abbr.* **sq.**) (used for talking about the area of sth): *If a room is 12 feet long and 10 feet wide, its area is 120 square feet.* **4** (used

S

about sth that is SQUARE (1) in shape) having sides of a particular length: *The picture is eight inches square* (= each side is eight inches long).

➤WITH MONEY **5** not owing any money: *Here is the $10 I owe you. Now we're square.*

➤BORING **6** (*informal*) (used about a person) unfashionable and uncomfortable in social situations

IDM **a square meal** a good meal that makes you feel full

★**square²** /skwɛr/ ***noun*** [C] **1** a shape that has four sides of the same length and four angles of 90 degrees (**right angles**): *There are 64 squares on a chess board.* **2** (*also* **Square**) (*abbr.* **sq.**; **Sq.**) an open space in a town or city that has buildings all around it: *Times Square in New York City ◇ the market square* **3** the number that you get when you multiply another number by itself: *Sixteen is the square of four.* ➲ Look at **square root**.

**square³** /skwɛr/ ***verb*** **1** [I,T] **square (sth) with sth** to agree, or make sth agree, with sth else: *Your conclusion doesn't really square with the facts.* **2** [T] to multiply a number by itself

**square⁴** /skwɛr/ ***adv.*** (*informal*) directly: *to look sb square in the eye*

IDM **fair and square** → FAIR²

ˈ**square dance** ***noun*** [C] a traditional North American country dance for four couples who face each other, forming a square

**square·ly** /ˈskwɛrli/ ***adv.*** directly: *I think the blame falls squarely on her.*

ˌ**square ˈroot** ***noun*** [C] a number that produces another particular number when it is multiplied by itself: *The square root of sixteen is four.* ➲ Look at **square²**(3).

**squash¹** /skwɑʃ; skwɔʃ/ ***verb*** **1** [T] to damage or crush sth by pressing it hard so that it becomes flat: *Carlos squashed a cockroach with his shoe.* **2** [I,T] to go into a place, or move sb/sth to a place, where there is not much space: *We all squashed into the back of the car.*

S

**squash²** /skwɑʃ; skwɔʃ/ ***noun*** [C,U] a type of large heavy fruit with thick skin that is cooked and eaten as a vegetable ➲ picture on study page **A28-29**.

**squat¹** /skwɑt/ ***verb*** [I] (**squat<u>t</u>ing**; **squat<u>t</u>ed**) **1** to sit down with your feet on the ground and your knees bent and your buttocks just above the ground **2** to go and live in an empty building without permission from the owner

**squat²** /skwɑt/ ***adj.*** (**squat·ter**; **squat·test**) short and fat or thick: *an ugly, squat building*

**squat³** /skwɑt/ (*informal*) *short for* DIDDLY-SQUAT

**squat·ter** /ˈskwɑt̬ər/ ***noun*** [C] a person who SQUATS¹ (2) in a building

**squaw** /skwɔ/ ***noun*** [C] (*old-fashioned*) a word for a Native American woman that is now often considered offensive: *an Indian squaw*

**squawk** /skwɔk/ ***verb*** [I] (used especially about a bird) to make a loud unpleasant noise ▸ **squawk** ***noun*** [C]

**squeak** /skwik/ ***verb*** [I,T] to make a short high noise that is not very loud: *Dave's new shoes squeaked as he walked. ◇ I heard a mouse squeaking.* ▸ **squeak** ***noun*** [C]

**squeak·y** /ˈskwiki/ ***adj.*** (**squeak·i·er**; **squeak·i·est**) making a short, high sound; squeaking: *squeaky floorboards ◇ a high squeaky voice*

ˌ**squeaky ˈclean** ***adj.*** (*informal*) **1** completely clean, and therefore attractive: *squeaky clean hair* **2** morally correct in every way; that cannot be criticized: *an all-American boy with a squeaky clean image*

**squeal** /skwil/ ***verb*** [I,T] to make a loud high noise that is a sign of pain, fear or enjoyment: *The baby squealed with delight at the new toy.* ▸ **squeal** ***noun*** [C]: *The car stopped with a squeal of tires.*

NOTE A **squeal** is louder and longer than a **squeak**, but it is not as loud as a **scream**.

**squea·mish** /ˈskwimɪʃ/ ***adj.*** (used about a person) easily upset by sth unpleasant, e.g. the sight of blood

**squee·gee** /ˈskwidʒi/ ***noun*** [C] a tool with a rubber edge and a handle, used for removing water from smooth surfaces such as windows

★**squeeze¹** /skwiz/ ***verb*** **1** [T] **squeeze sth (out)**; **squeeze sth (from/out of sth)** to press sth hard for a particular purpose: *She squeezed his hand and wished him luck. ◇ to squeeze a tube of toothpaste ◇ to squeeze an orange/a lemon* (= to get the juice) *◇ to squeeze juice from an orange* **2** [I,T] **squeeze (sb/sth) into, through, etc. sth**; **squeeze (sb/sth) through, in, past, etc.** to go or move sb/sth into, through, etc. a place where there is not much space: *Excuse me. Can I squeeze past? ◇ We can squeeze another person into the back of the car.* [T] (*figurative*) *Do you think you can squeeze in another appointment this afternoon?*

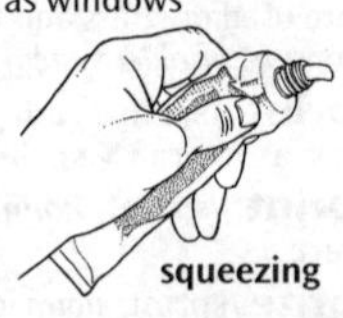
squeezing

**squeeze²** /skwiz/ ***noun*** **1** [C] an act of SQUEEZING (1) sb/sth, e.g. as a sign of love or affection: *Doug gave my shoulder a squeeze.* ➲ Look at **hug**. **2** [sing.] a situation where there is not much space: *It was a tight squeeze to get everybody in the car.* **3** [C] the amount of liquid that you get from squeezing an orange, a lemon, etc.: *a squeeze of lemon* **4** [C, usually sing.] a difficult situation in which there is not enough money, time, etc.: *A budget squeeze forced the administration to reduce spending.*

**squelch** /skwɛltʃ/ ***verb*** [T] to stop sth, e.g. an idea, from continuing: *to squelch a rumor*

**squid** /skwɪd/ ***noun*** [C] (*pl.* **squids** or **squid**) a sea animal with a long, soft body and ten long arms (**tentacles**)

**squig·gle** /ˈskwɪgl/ ***noun*** [C] a line, for example in sb's handwriting that is drawn or written in a careless way with twists and curls in it: *Are these dots and squiggles supposed to be your signature?* ▸ **squig·gly** /-gli/ ***adj.***

**squint** /skwɪnt/ ***verb*** [I] to look at sth with your eyes almost closed: *to squint in bright sunlight*

**squirm** /skwərm/ ***verb*** [I] to move your body in a way which shows you are uncomfortable, bored or embarrassed

**squir·rel¹** /ˈskwərəl/ ***noun*** [C] a small

brownish-gray animal with a long thick tail that lives in trees and eats nuts

**squir·rel²** /ˈskwərəl/ ***verb***
PHRV **squirrel sth away** to hide or store sth so that it can be used later: *She had money squirreled away in various bank accounts.*

**squir·rel·ly** /ˈskwərəli/ ***adj.*** (*informal*) **1** unable to keep still or be quiet: *squirrelly kids* **2** crazy

**squirt¹** /skwərt/ ***verb*** [I,T] (used about a liquid) to be forced out from sth in a thin fast stream; to make a liquid move in this way; to hit sb/sth with a liquid in this way: *I squeezed the bottle and mustard squirted out.* ◇ *He squirted water at me from a hose.* ◇ *He squirted me with water.*

**squirt²** /skwərt/ ***noun*** [C] **1** a thin, fast stream of a liquid that comes out of a small opening: *a squirt of perfume* ◇ *a squirt of ketchup on the french fries* **2** (*informal*) a word used to refer to a short, young or unimportant person that you do not like or that you find annoying; a kid

**ˈsquirt gun** ***noun*** [C] a toy gun that shoots water

**squish** /skwɪʃ/ ***verb*** [I,T] (*informal*) **1** if sth soft squishes or is squished, it is crushed out of shape when it is pressed **2** to make a soft wet sucking sound

**squish·y** /ˈskwɪʃi/ ***adj.*** (**squish·i·er**; **squish·i·est**) (*informal*) soft and wet

**Sr.** ***abbr.*** (*written*) = SENIOR

**SS** ***abbr.*** (*written*) **1** = SOCIAL SECURITY **2** = STREAMSHIP: *the SS Canberra*

**SSN** ***noun*** [C], ***abbr.*** (*U.S.*) = SOCIAL SECURITY NUMBER

**ST** ***abbr.*** (*written*) = STANDARD TIME

**St.** ***abbr.*** **1** Saint: *St. Peter* **2** Street: *220 Jefferson St.*

**stab¹** /stæb/ ***verb*** [T] (**stab·bing**; **stabbed**) to push a knife or other pointed object into sb/sth: *The man was stabbed fourteen times.*

**stab²** /stæb/ ***noun*** [C] **1** an injury that was caused by a knife, etc.: *a stab wound* **2** a sudden sharp pain: *a stab of pain* ◇ (*figurative*) *a stab of guilt*
IDM **take a stab at sth/doing sth** (*informal*) to try to do sth: *I'll take a stab at painting your portrait.*

**stab·bing** /ˈstæbɪŋ/ ***noun*** [C] an occasion when sb stabs sb else: *There have been two stabbings in the neighborhood this week.*

**sta·bi·lize** /ˈsteɪbl·aɪz/ ***verb*** [I,T] to become or to make sth unlikely to move, change or end: *The patient's condition has stabilized.* ◇ *The government has tried to stabilize prices.* OPP **destabilize**

**sta·ble¹** /ˈsteɪbl/ ***adj.*** not likely to move, change or end: *This ladder doesn't seem very stable.* ◇ *The patient is in stable condition.* ◇ *a stable relationship* OPP **unstable** ▸ **sta·bil·i·ty** /stəˈbɪləṭi/ ***noun*** [U]: *After so much change, we now need a period of stability.*

**sta·ble²** /ˈsteɪbl/ ***noun*** [C] a building where horses are kept

**stac·ca·to** /stəˈkɑṭoʊ/ ***adj.*** **1** (in music) with each note played separately in order to produce short, sharp sounds: *staccato sounds* **2** with short, sharp sounds: *a peculiar staccato voice* ◇ *staccato bursts of gunfire* ▸ **stac·ca·to** ***adv.***

**stack¹** /stæk/ ***noun*** [C] **1** a neat pile of sth: *a stack of plates/books* **2 the stacks** [pl.] the area of a library with many shelves where most of the books are kept

**stack²** /stæk/ ***verb*** [T] **stack sth (up)** to put sth into a pile: *Could you stack those chairs for me?*
PHRV **stack up (against sb/sth)** (used especially in questions or in negatives) to compare with sb/sth else; to be as good as sb/sth else: *Let's try him in the job and see how he stacks up.* ◇ *A mobile home simply doesn't stack up against a traditional house.*
SYN **measure up**

**sta·di·um** /ˈsteɪdiəm/ ***noun*** [C] (*pl.* **sta·di·ums** or (*formal*) **sta·di·a** /-diə/) a large sports ground with rows of seats around it: *a football stadium*

★**staff** /stæf/ ***noun*** [C, usually sing.] **1** the group of people who work for a particular organization: *the hospital's administrative staff*

> NOTE **Staff** is usually used in the singular. We say **a staff member** (NOT **a staff**) to talk about one person who works for an organization.

**2** the people who work at a school, college, or university, but do not teach students (e.g. secretaries, library employees, etc.): *faculty, staff and administrators* ▸ **staff** ***verb*** [T] (usually passive): *The service department is staffed by trained professionals.*

**staff·er** /ˈstæfər/ ***noun*** [C] a member of staff in a big organization: *Whitehouse staffers*

**ˈstaff room** ***noun*** [C] (*Cdn*) a room in a school, where students are not allowed, and teachers can have their lunch, meetings, etc.

**stag** /stæg/ ***noun*** [C] = BUCK¹ (2)

★**stage¹** /steɪdʒ/ ***noun*** **1** [C] one part of the progress or development of sth: *The first stage of the project lasts for three weeks.* ◇ *the early stages of the game* ◇ *At this stage, it's too early to say what will happen.* **2** [C] a raised floor in a theater or concert hall, etc. on which actors, musicians, etc. perform: *to go on stage* **3** [sing., U] the world of theater; the profession of acting in front of people in a theater: *a star of stage and screen*

★**stage²** /steɪdʒ/ ***verb*** [T] **1** to organize a performance of a play, concert, etc. for the public **2** to organize an event: *to stage a protest march*

**stage·coach** /ˈsteɪdʒkoʊtʃ/ ***noun*** [C] a type of vehicle, pulled by horses, that was used in past times to carry passengers over a fixed route, often over long distances

**ˈstage fright** ***noun*** [U] nervous feelings felt by performers before they appear in front of an audience

**stage·hand** /ˈsteɪdʒhænd/ ***noun*** [C] a person whose job is to help move scenery, etc. in a theater, to prepare the stage for the next play or the next part of a play

**ˈstage name** ***noun*** [C] a name that an actor uses instead of his/her real name

**stag·fla·tion** /stægˈfleɪʃn/ ***noun*** [U] an economic situation where there is high inflation (= prices rising continuously) but no increase in the jobs that are available or in business activity

**stag·ger** /ˈstægər/ ***verb*** **1** [I] to walk in an unsteady way, as if you are going to fall down, e.g.

S

because you are sick, drunk or carrying sth heavy **2** [T] to arrange a number of events so that they do not all happen at the same time

**stag·ger·ing** /ˈstægərɪŋ/ ***adj.*** that you find difficult to believe: *a staggering $2 billion profit* ▸ **stag·ger·ing·ly** ***adv.***

**stag·ing** /ˈsteɪdʒɪŋ/ ***noun*** **1** [C,U] the way in which a play is produced and presented on stage: *a modern staging of "King Lear"* **2** [U] a temporary platform used for standing or working on

**stag·nant** /ˈstægnənt/ ***adj.*** **1** (used about water) not flowing and therefore dirty and having a bad smell **2** (used about business, etc.) not active; not developing: *a stagnant economy*

**stag·nate** /ˈstægneɪt/ ***verb*** [I] to not be active; not to develop or change: *a stagnating economy* ▸ **stag·na·tion** /stægˈneɪʃn/ ***noun*** [U]

**staid** /steɪd/ ***adj.*** (**staid·er; staid·est**) not amusing or interesting; boring and old-fashioned: *The museum is trying to get rid of its staid image.*

**stain** /steɪn/ ***verb*** [I,T] to leave a colored mark that is difficult to remove: *Don't spill any of that red wine. It'll stain the carpet.* ▸ **stain** ***noun*** [C]: *The blood left a stain on his shirt.*

ˌ**stained ˈglass** ***noun*** [U] pieces of colored glass that are used in church windows, etc.: *a stained-glass window*

**stain·less steel** /ˌsteɪnləs ˈstil/ ***noun*** [U] steel that does not stain or rust: *a stainless steel pan*

★**stair** /stɛr/ ***noun*** **1 stairs** [pl.] a series of steps that lead from one level of a building to another: *The elevator wasn't working, so I had to use the stairs.* ◇ *at the bottom/top of the stairs* ◇ *two **flights** (= sets) **of stairs*** ◇ *I heard somebody coming down the stairs.* ◇ *She ran up the stairs.* ➲ Look at **downstairs** and **upstairs**. **2** [C] one of the steps in a series of STAIRS (1): *She sat down on the bottom stair to read the letter.*

**stair·case** /ˈstɛrkeɪs/ ***noun*** [C] a set of stairs, usually with bars (rails) on each side that you can hold onto ➲ Look at **escalator**.

**stair·way** /ˈstɛrweɪ/ ***noun*** [C] a set of stairs inside or outside a building

**stair·well** /ˈstɛrwɛl/ ***noun*** [usually sing.] the space in a building in which the stairs are built

★**stake**[1] /steɪk/ ***noun*** **1** [C] a wooden or metal pole with a point at one end that you push into the ground, e.g. to support a tent **2 stakes** [pl.] the things that you might win or lose in a game or in a particular situation: *We play cards for money, but never for very high stakes.* **3** [C] a part of a company, etc. that you own, usually because you have invested money in it: *Foreign investors now have a 20% stake in the company.*

IDM **at stake** in danger of being lost; at risk: *He thought very carefully about the decision because he knew his future was at stake.*

**stake**[2] /steɪk/ ***verb*** [T] **stake sth (on sth)** to put your future, etc. in danger by doing sth, because you hope that it will bring you a good result: *She is staking her political reputation on this issue.*

IDM **stake a/your claim (to/on sth)** to say that you have a right to have sth: *Both towns have staked their claim to the title of "The Hot Dog Capital of America."*

PHR V **stake sth out 1** (used especially about the police, etc.) to watch a place secretly, over a period of time: *Police staked out the airport after a bomb threat was made.* **2** to say publicly that sth belongs to you or that you have a right to it: *The Police Chief has staked out a tough position on crime.*

**stake·hold·er** /ˈsteɪkˌhoʊldər/ ***noun*** [C] **1** a person or company that is involved in a particular organization, project, system, etc., especially because they have invested money in it: *All our employees are stakeholders in the company.* ◇ *A **stakeholder economy** is one in which all members of society feel that they have an interest in its success.* **2** a person who holds all the bets placed on a game or race and who pays the money to the winner

**stake·out** /ˈsteɪkaʊt/ ***noun*** [C] a situation in which police watch a building secretly to find evidence of illegal activities

**stale** /steɪl/ ***adj.*** **1** (used about food or air) old and not fresh anymore: *The bread is stale.* ◇ *stale cigarette smoke* **2** not interesting or exciting anymore: *She says her marriage has gone stale.*

**stale·mate** /ˈsteɪlmeɪt/ ***noun*** [sing., U] a situation in an argument in which neither side can win or make any progress

**stalk**[1] /stɔk/ ***noun*** [C] one of the long thin parts of a plant which the flowers, leaves or fruit grow on ➲ picture on study page **A28-29**.

**stalk**[2] /stɔk/ ***verb*** **1** [T] to follow an animal or a person quietly and secretly in order to get close and possibly hurt or kill him/her/it: *a lion stalking its prey* ◇ *He was arrested for stalking a Hollywood actress.* **2** [I] to walk stiffly in an angry or arrogant way: *He got up and stalked out of the room.* ▸ **stalk·er** ***noun*** [C] ▸ **stalk·ing** ***noun*** [U]

**stall**[1] /stɔl/ ***noun*** [C] **1** a small area with walls around it and a toilet or a shower in it: *There were only two stalls in the women's restroom.* ◇ *a shower stall* **2** a small enclosed area inside a building (a barn) for one animal, especially a horse

**stall**[2] /stɔl/ ***verb*** [I,T] **1** (used about a vehicle) to stop suddenly because the engine fails; to make a vehicle do this accidentally: *The bus stalled in the middle of the street.* **2** to avoid doing sth or to try to stop sth from happening until a later time: *I've asked them several times for the money, but they keep stalling.*

**stal·lion** /ˈstælyən/ ***noun*** [C] an adult male horse ➲ Look at the note at **horse**.

**stal·wart** /ˈstɔlwərt/ ***adj.*** loyal and hard-working: *a stalwart member of the volunteer committee* ▸ **stal·wart** ***noun*** [C]: *a committee of party stalwarts*

**stam·i·na** /ˈstæmənə/ ***noun*** [U] the ability to do sth that requires a lot of physical or mental effort for a long time: *It takes a lot of stamina to run a marathon.*

**stam·mer** /ˈstæmər/ ***verb*** [I,T] to speak with difficulty when sb is feeling nervous, repeating sounds or words and often stopping, before saying things correctly: *"W-w-what?" he stammered.* ◇ *She was barely able to **stammer out** a description of her attacker.*

★**stamp**[1] /stæmp/ ***noun*** [C] **1** (*also* **postage stamp**) a small piece of paper that you stick onto a letter or package to show that you have paid for it to be mailed: *I need three 32-cent stamps.* ➲ Look also at **food stamp**. **2** a small object that prints some words, a design, the date, etc. when you press it onto a surface: *a rubber stamp* **3** the mark made by a STAMP (2): *a stamp in my passport*

★**stamp**[2] /stæmp/ ***verb*** [T] **stamp A (on B); stamp B (with A)** to print some words, a design, the date, etc. by pressing a small object (a stamp) onto a surface: *to stamp a passport* ◇ *The date is stamped on the receipt.* ➲ Look also at **self-addressed stamped envelope**.

IDM **stamp your feet** to put your feet down very heavily on the ground, one at a time, again and again

PHR V **stamp sth out** to put an end to sth completely: *The police are trying to stamp out this kind of crime.*

**stam·pede** /stæm'pid/ ***verb*** [T] (used about a group of animals or people) to rush in a particular direction in a wild and uncontrolled way ▸ **stampede *noun*** [C]: *a stampede toward the exits*

**stance** /stæns/ ***noun*** [C, usually sing.] **1 stance (on sth)** an attitude (especially moral or political) toward sth: *the President's stance on foreign affairs* **2** the position in which sb stands (especially in sports when you are preparing to hit the ball)

★**stand**[1] /stænd/ ***verb*** [I,T] (*pt, pp* **stood** /stʊd/)

➤ON FEET/UPRIGHT **1** [I] to be on your feet; to be upright: *He was standing near the window.* **2** [I] **stand (up)** to rise to your feet from another position: *He stood up when I entered the room.*

➤PUT UPRIGHT **3** [T] to put sb/sth in a particular place or in an upright position: *She stood the vacuum cleaner in the closet.*

➤BE IN PLACE/SITUATION **4** [I] to be or to remain in a particular position or situation: *The lighthouse stands on a hill.* ◇ *The house has stood empty for ten years.* ◇ *He is very critical of the law as it stands* (= as it is now).

➤OFFER/DECISION **5** [I] (used about an offer, a decision, etc.) to be or to remain unchanged: *Does your decision still stand?*

➤BE AT HEIGHT/LEVEL **6** [I] to be of a particular height, level, amount, etc.: *The world record stands at 6 feet, 10 inches.*

➤HAVE OPINION **7** [I] to have an opinion or view (about sth): *I don't know where I stand on immigration.*

➤BE LIKELY TO DO STH **8** [I] **stand to do sth** to be in a situation where you are likely to do sth: *If he has to sell the company, he stands to lose a lot of money.*

➤DISLIKE **9** [T] (in negative sentences and questions, with *can/could*) to be able to bear or tolerate sb/sth: *I can't stand that obnoxious guy on the local radio.* ◇ *How can you stand it when she practices her trumpet?*

IDM **stand in line** to wait in a line of people: *We stood in line for two hours to buy tickets.*

PHR V **stand aside** to move to one side: *People stood aside to let the police past.*

**stand back** to move back: *The police officer told everybody to stand back.*

**stand by 1** to be present, but do nothing in a situation: *How can you stand by and let them treat their animals like that?* **2** to be ready to act: *The ambulance is standing by in case anyone gets injured.*

**stand by sb** to continue to support sb in a difficult situation: *Phil stood by his wife when she was suffering from depression.*

**stand by sth** to not change a decision, a belief, an idea, etc.: *School officials stood by their plan despite heavy criticism from parents.*

**stand for sth 1** to be a short form of sth: *What does NAACP stand for?* **2** to support sth (e.g. an idea or opinion): *I hate everything that the party stands for.*

**stand out** to be easily seen or noticed

**stand sb up** (*informal*) not keep an appointment with sb: *Ed's date stood him up, so he went to the movie alone.*

**stand up for sb/sth** to say or do sth which shows that you support sb/sth: *I admire her. She really stands up for what she believes in.*

**stand up to sb/sth** to defend yourself against sb who is stronger or more powerful

★**stand**[2] /stænd/ ***noun*** **1** [C] a table or small store on the sidewalk or in a large public building from which you can buy things or get information: *a popcorn stand* ◇ *a company stand at a trade show* **2** [C] a piece of furniture that you can put things on or in: *a music stand* **3 stands** [pl.] a large area with rows of seats at the side of a sports field where people sit to watch the sports game ➲ picture at **football**. **4** [C, usually sing.] = WITNESS STAND

IDM **make a stand (against sb/sth)** to defend yourself, your opinion, etc. strongly against sb/sth

**take a stand (on sth)** to say publicly what you think and intend to do about sth

**stand·a·lone** /'stændəloʊn/ ***adj.*** (used especially about a computer) able to be operated on its own without being connected to a larger system

★**stan·dard**[1] /'stændərd/ ***noun*** [C] **1** a level of quality: *a high standard of teaching* ◇ *We need to improve educational standards in this state.* ◇ *This work is not up to your usual standard.* ➲ Look also at **standard of living**. **2** a level of quality that you compare sth else with: *By my mother's standards, this house is extremely messy.* ◇ *He is an excellent player by any standard.* **3** [usually pl.] a level of behavior that is morally acceptable: *Many people are worried about falling standards in modern society.*

★**stan·dard**[2] /'stændərd/ ***adj.*** **1** of the normal type; without anything special or extra: *This is the standard model. The deluxe version costs more.* **2** part of the normal situation; not unusual in any way: *It is standard practice to ask students to fill out this form when they arrive.* **3** (used about language) that people generally accept as normal and correct: *standard English*

**stan·dard·ize** /'stændərdaɪz/ ***verb*** [T] (often passive) to make things of a certain type the same as each other: *students' scores on standardized tests* ▸ **stan·dard·i·za·tion** /stændərdə'zeɪʃn/ ***noun*** [U]

**ˌstandard of 'living** ***noun*** [C] (*pl.* **standards of living**) the level of wealth and comfort that a person, group or country has in everyday life: *Most people enjoy a high standard of living in this country.*

**ˈstandard time** *noun* [sing.] the time to which all the clocks in a particular part of the world are set

**stand·by** /ˈstændbaɪ/ *noun* [C] (*pl.* **stand·bys**) a person or thing that is ready to be used if necessary: *I have a computer now, but I still keep my old typewriter as a standby.* ◇ *a standby ticket* (= a cheap ticket, e.g. for a flight, that you can get at the last moment if a seat is available)

IDM **on standby** ready; waiting to do sth: *When the fighting began, all local hospitals were put on standby.*

**ˈstand-in** *noun* [C] **1** a person who does sb's job for a short time when he/she is not available: *I acted as Amanda's stand-in when she was away.* ◇ *the stand-in captain* **2** a person who replaces an actor in some scenes in a movie, especially dangerous ones: *Most of the stunts are performed by stand-ins.*

**stand·ing¹** /ˈstændɪŋ/ *noun* [C,U] the opinion that other people have of sb: *The consequences for the team's international standing could be extremely serious.*

**stand·ing²** /ˈstændɪŋ/ *adj.* (only *before* a noun) continuing to exist; permanent: *I have a* ***standing invitation*** *to go and stay with them whenever I want to.*

**ˌstanding oˈvation** *noun* [C] an occasion when an audience stands up from their seats and claps their hands enthusiastically to show their approval: *The soloist got a ten-minute standing ovation.*

**ˈstanding room** *noun* [U] space for people to stand in, especially in a theater, sports stadium, etc.: *standing room for 12,000 fans* ◇ *It was* ***standing room only*** *at the concert* (= all the seats were sold).

**stand·off** /ˈstændɔf; -ɑf/ *noun* [C] a situation in an argument, a battle, etc. in which no one can gain an advantage or no progress can be made

**stand·point** /ˈstænpɔɪnt/ *noun* [C] a particular way of thinking about sth: *The program looked at the problems of education from the standpoint of the teacher.*

**stand·still** /ˈstænstɪl/ *noun* [sing.] a situation of no movement, progress or activity: *The traffic came to a complete standstill.*

**ˈstand-up¹** *adj.* (only *before* a noun) stand-up comedy consists of one person standing in front of an audience and telling jokes: *a stand-up act* ◇ *a stand-up comedian*

**ˈstand-up²** *noun* **1** [C] a person who performs STAND-UP¹ comedy **2** [U] STAND-UP¹ comedy: *When did you start doing stand-up?*

**stank** *past tense of* STINK

**stan·za** /ˈstænzə/ *noun* [C] (*technical*) a group of lines in a repeated pattern that form a unit in some types of poem SYN **verse** (2)

**sta·ple¹** /ˈsteɪpl/ *noun* [C] **1** a small thin piece of bent wire that you push through pieces of paper in order to fasten them together using a special tool (stapler) **2** a basic or main part of sth: *Rice is a staple of the Japanese diet.* ◇ *game shows and soap operas, the traditional daytime TV staples*

**sta·ple²** /ˈsteɪpl/ *verb* [T] to fasten sth to sth else using a STAPLE¹ (1): *Staple the letter to the application form.* ▸ **sta·pler** /ˈsteɪplər/ *noun* [C]

**sta·ple³** /ˈsteɪpl/ *adj.* (only *before* a noun) forming a basic, large or important part of sth: *The staple crop is rice.* ◇ *Jeans are a staple part of everyone's wardrobe.*

★**star¹** /stɑr/ *noun* [C]

➤ IN SKY **1** a large ball of burning gas in outer space that you see as a small point of light in the sky at night: *It was a clear night and the stars were shining brightly.*

➤ SHAPE **2** a shape with a number of points sticking out in a regular pattern: *The children decorated the classroom with paper stars.* ➲ picture at **shape**.

➤ MARK OF QUALITY **3** a printed shape like a STAR (2) that is used for indicating a level of quality: *a five-star hotel*

➤ PERFORMER **4** a famous person in acting, music or sports: *a movie star*

➤ BEST OF GROUP **5** a person who does sth extremely well: *She's one of the star players on the team.*

**star²** /stɑr/ *verb* (**star<u>r</u>ing**; **star<u>r</u>ed**) **1** [I] **star (in sth)** to be one of the main actors in a play, movie, etc.: *Michelle Pfeiffer is set to star in an exciting new adventure movie.* **2** [T] to have sb as a main actor: *The movie stars Sandra Bullock as a computer programmer.*

**star·board** /ˈstɑrbərd/ *noun* [U] the side of a ship or an aircraft that is on the right when you are facing forward ➲ Compare **port** (3).

**starch¹** /stɑrtʃ/ *noun* [C,U] **1** a white substance with no taste in foods such as potatoes, rice and bread **2** a substance that is used for making cloth stiff

**starch²** /stɑrtʃ/ *verb* [T] (usually passive) to make clothes, sheets, etc. stiff using STARCH¹ (2): *a starched white shirt*

**starch·y** /ˈstɑrtʃi/ *adj.* **1** (used about food) containing a lot of STARCH¹ (1): *starchy foods like rice and bread* **2** (*informal*) used about a person or his/her behavior) very formal; not friendly or relaxed: *The organization is trying to shake off its starchy image.*

**ˈstar-crossed** *adj.* (in literature) not able to be happy because of bad luck or fate: *Shakespeare's* ***star-crossed lovers****, Romeo and Juliet*

**star·dom** /ˈstɑrdəm/ *noun* [U] the position of being a famous person in acting, music or sports

**star·dust** /ˈstɑrdʌst/ *noun* [U] stars that are very far from the earth and appear like bright dust in the sky at night

★**stare** /stɛr/ *verb* [I] **stare (at sb/sth)** to look at sb or sth continuously for a long time because you are interested, surprised, etc.: *Everybody stared at his hat.* ◇ *I stared at her in disbelief.* ◇ *He didn't reply; he just stared into the distance.*

**star·fish** /ˈstɑrfɪʃ/ *noun* [C] (*pl.* **star·fish**) a flat ocean creature in the shape of a star with five arms

**star·fruit** /ˈstɑrfrut/ *noun* [C] (*pl.* **star·fruit**) a green or yellow tropical fruit with a shape like a star ➲ picture on study page **A28-29**.

**stark¹** /stɑrk/ *adj.* **1** very bare and plain and therefore not attractive: *a stark landscape* **2** clearly unpleasant: *the stark realities of a life of poverty* **3** very clear: *a stark contrast between the inner city and the suburbs*

**stark²** /stɑrk/ *adv.*

IDM **stark naked** completely naked

**star·let** /ˈstɑrlət/ ***noun*** [C] a young woman actor who plays small parts and hopes to become famous

**star·light** /ˈstɑrlaɪt/ ***noun*** [U] light from the stars: *We walked home by starlight.*

**star·lit** /ˈstɑrlɪt/ ***adj.*** (*written*) with light from the stars: *a starlit night*

**the ˌStars and ˈStripes** ***noun*** [sing.] the national flag of the U.S.

**star·ship** /ˈstɑrʃɪp/ ***noun*** [C] (in science fiction) a large spacecraft in which people or other beings travel around space

**ˈstar-ˌstudded** ***adj.*** (*written*) including many famous performers: *a star-studded cast*

★**start**[1] /stɑrt/ ***verb***

➤DOING STH **1** [I,T] **start (sth/to do sth/doing sth)** to begin doing sth: *Turn over your test papers and start now.* ◇ *We'll have to start* (= leave) *early if we want to be in Toronto by 10.* ◇ *Prices start at $5.* ◇ *What time do you have to start work in the morning?* ◇ *After waiting for an hour, the customers started to complain.* ◇ *She started playing the piano when she was six.*

➤HAPPENING **2** [I,T] to begin to happen or to make sth begin to happen: *What time does the concert start?* ◇ *I'd like to start the meeting now.* ◇ *The fight started when the boys were leaving the club.* ◇ *The police think a young woman may have started the fire.* ➲ Look at the note at **begin**.

➤BEGINNING **3** [I] to have a beginning or a first part: *Her last name starts with "W," not "V."* ◇ *Our property starts by the fence over there.*

➤EXISTING **4** [I,T] **start (sth) (up)** to create a company, an organization, etc.; to be created: *They've decided to start their own business.* ◇ *There are a lot of new companies starting up in that area now.*

➤MACHINE/VEHICLE **5** [I,T] **start (sth) (up)** (used about a machine, a car, etc.) to begin to work; to make a machine, a car, etc. begin to work: *The car won't start.* ◇ *We heard an engine starting up in the street.* ◇ *Start up the computer and enter your password.* ◇ *He got onto his motorcycle, started the engine and rode away.*

IDM **to start (off) with 1** in the beginning; at first: *Everything was fine to start with, but then there were problems.* **2** (used for giving your first reason for sth): *"Why are you so mad?" "Well, to start off with, you're late, and secondly you lied to me."*

**get/start the ball rolling** → BALL

PHRV **start (sth) off** to begin (sth) in a particular way: *I'd like to start off the conference by welcoming you all to New York.*

**start on sth** to begin doing sth that needs to be done: *I suppose we should get started on those dirty dishes.*

**start out** to begin your life, career, etc. in a particular way: *She started out as a teacher in Canada.*

**start over** to begin again: *I've made a lot of mistakes – I'd better start over.*

★**start**[2] /stɑrt/ ***noun*** **1** [C, usually sing.] the beginning or first part of sth: *The chairman made a short speech at the start of the meeting.* ◇ *I told you it was a bad idea from the start.* **2** [C, usually sing.] an act of starting: *We've got a long way to drive today, so let's get an early start.* ◇ *to make a fresh start in life* ➲ Look also at **head start**. **3** [C, usually sing.] a sudden quick movement that your body makes because you are surprised or afraid

IDM **get off to a good, bad, etc. start** to start well, badly, etc.: *My day got off to a good start – I got money in the mail this morning.*

**start·er** /ˈstɑrt̬ər/ ***noun*** [C] a player on a sports team who plays when the game begins

IDM **for starters** (*informal*) (used for givng your first reason for sth): *"Why can't we go on vacation?" "Well, for starters, we can't afford it..."*

**ˈstarter home** ***noun*** [C] a small home for sb who is buying property for the first time

**star·tle** /ˈstɑrt̬l/ ***verb*** [T] to make sb/sth suddenly surprised or frightened ▶ **star·tled** ***adj.***: *He had a startled look on his face.* ▶ **star·tling** ***adj.***: *I have some startling news for you!*

**ˈstart-up** ***noun*** [C] a company that is just beginning to operate, especially an Internet company: *dot-com start-ups* ◇ *the fast-moving world of Internet start-ups* ▶ **ˈstart-up** ***adj.***: *start-up costs/problems*

**star·va·tion** /stɑrˈveɪʃn/ ***noun*** [U] suffering or death because there is not enough food: *to die of starvation*

**starve** /stɑrv/ ***verb*** [I,T] to suffer very badly or die from hunger; to make sb/sth suffer or die in this way: *Millions of people are starving in the poorer countries of the world.* ◇ *That winter many animals starved to death.* ◇ *You need to eat more – you're starving yourself.*

IDM **be starved for/of sth** to suffer because you are not getting enough of sth that you need: *The children had been starved of love for years.*

**be starving**; **be starved** (*informal*) to be extremely hungry: *When will dinner be ready? I'm starving!*

**stash**[1] /stæʃ/ ***verb*** [T] (*informal*) to store sth in a safe or secret place: *She has a fortune* ***stashed away*** *in various bank accounts.* ◇ *The gun was stashed under the bed.*

**stash**[2] /stæʃ/ ***noun*** [C, usually sing.] (*informal*) an amount of sth that is kept secretly: *a stash of money*

**stat**[1] /stæt/ ***noun*** [C, usually pl.] = STATISTIC

**stat**[2] /stæt/ ***adv.*** (*medical*) immediately

★**state**[1] /steɪt/ ***noun***

➤CONDITION OF SB/STH **1** [C] the condition that sb/sth is in at a particular time: *the state of the economy* ◇ *a state of shock*

➤PART OF COUNTRY **2** [C] a part of a country that has its own government and can make some of its own laws: *state and federal laws* ◇ *the former governor of the state of Ohio* ◇ *Fill in your city, state and Zip code on the last line.* ◇ *Iowa State University* (= the public university that is supported by money from the state of Iowa)

➤COUNTRY **3** [C] (*formal*) a country, especially outside the U.S: *Pakistan has been an independent state since 1947.*

NOTE **State** is usually used for one of the 50 parts of the United States: *the state of Oklahoma* ◇ *state and federal income taxes*. However, **state** can also be used in more formal situations for talking

S

about a whole country as an organized political unit with one government, or for talking about the government itself. It is not used to talk about the U.S. as a whole: *the member states of the European Union* ◇ *state censorship of the news media.*

▸ GOVERNMENT **4** [U, sing.] the government of a country: *the relationship between church and state* ◇ *heads of state* (= government leaders) ➲ Look also at **Secretary of State**.

▸ OFFICIAL CEREMONY **5** [U] very formal events and behavior connected with governments and the leaders of countries: *President Nixon's state visit to China*

**IDM state of affairs** a situation: *This state of affairs cannot be allowed to continue.*

**state of mind** mental condition: *How would you describe her state of mind at that time?*

★**state²** /steɪt/ *verb* [T] to say or write sth, often formally: *Your letter states that you sent the package on March 31, but we never received it.* ◇ *As I stated earlier, I do not believe that this information is accurate.*

**the 'State De,partment** *noun* [sing.] the U.S. government department that is in charge of dealing with foreign countries ➲ Look at **Secretary of State**.

**state·hood** /'steɪthʊd/ *noun* [U] (*written*) **1** the fact of being an independent country and of having the rights and powers of a country: *Slovakia's path to independent statehood* **2** the condition of being one of the states within a country such as the U.S: *West Virginia was granted statehood in 1863.*

**state·ly** /'steɪtli/ *adj.* (**state·li·er**; **state·li·est**) formal and dignified: *a stately old building*

★**state·ment** /'steɪtmənt/ *noun* [C] **1** something that you say or write, often formally: *The Vice President will make a statement about the defense cuts today.* ◇ *After the accident I had to go to the police station to give a statement.* **2** a printed record of money paid, received, etc. during a certain period of time ➲ Look at **bank statement**.

**,state-of-the-'art** *adj.* (usually *before* a noun) using the most modern knowledge or technology that is available: *a state-of-the-art sound system*

**states·man** /'steɪtsmən/ *noun* [C] (*pl.* **states·men** /-mən/) an important and experienced politician who has earned public respect

**state·wide** /,steɪt'waɪd/ *adj.*, *adv.* across a whole state: *a statewide poll*

**stat hol·i·day** /,stæt 'hɑlədeɪ/ *noun* [C] (*Cdn*) = STATUTORY HOLIDAY

**stat·ic¹** /'stæṭɪk/ *adj.* not moving or changing: *House prices are static.*

**stat·ic²** /'stæṭɪk/ *noun* [U] **1** (*also* **,static elec'tricity**) electricity that collects on a surface **2** sudden loud noises on a radio or television, caused by electricity in the atmosphere

**,static 'cling** *noun* [U] the fact of your clothes sticking tightly to your body because of static electricity

★**sta·tion¹** /'steɪʃn/ *noun* [C] **1** a building or structure along a road, railroad track, etc. where buses, trains, etc. stop so that passengers can get on and off: *a railroad/train station* ◇ *a bus station* ◇ *a subway station* **2** a building where a particular service or activity is based: *a fire station* (= where the fire department is based) ◇ *a gas station* ◇ *a police station* **3** a company that broadcasts programs on the radio or on television: *a local radio station* ➲ Look at **channel**.

**sta·tion²** /'steɪʃn/ *verb* [T] (often passive) to send soldiers, etc. to a particular place: *During his time in the army, he was stationed in South Korea.*

**sta·tion·ar·y** /'steɪʃn·,ɛri/ *adj.* not moving: *He crashed into the back of a stationary vehicle.*

**sta·tion·er·y** /'steɪʃn·,ɛri/ *noun* [U] paper and envelopes for writing letters

**'station ,wagon** (*also informal* **wagon**) *noun* [C] a car with a door at the back and a large area for luggage inside, behind the back seat ➲ picture at **car**.

**sta·tis·tic** /stə'tɪstɪk/ *noun* **1** [C] (*also informal* **stat**) a number that shows a fact or provides information about sth: *the grim statistic that crime increased by 12% last year* **2** **statistics** [pl.] numbers that have been collected in order to provide information about sth: *Statistics indicate that more than 95% of North American homes have a television.* ◇ *crime statistics* **3** **statistics** [U] the science of collecting and analyzing numbers that provide information about sth ▸ **sta·tis·ti·cal** /stə'tɪstɪkl/ *adj.*: *statistical information/evidence* ▸ **sta·tis·ti·cal·ly** /-kli/ *adv.*

★**stat·ue** /'stætʃu/ *noun* [C] a figure of a person or animal, that is made of stone or metal and usually put in a public place: *Michelangelo's statue of David*

**stat·u·esque** /,stætʃu'ɛsk/ *adj.* (*written*) (usually used about a woman) tall and beautiful in an impressive way; like a statue

**stat·ure** /'stætʃər/ *noun* [U] (*formal*) **1** the height of a person: *He's fairly small in stature.* **2** the importance that sb has because people have a high opinion of his/her skill or achievement: *Her research has given her considerable stature in the scientific world.*

★**sta·tus** /'stæṭəs; 'steɪṭəs/ *noun* **1** [sing.] your social or professional position in relation to other people: *Teachers don't have a very high status in this country.* **2** [U] a high social position: *The new job gave him much more status.* **3** [U] your legal position: *Please indicate your name, age and marital status* (= whether you are married, single, or divorced).

**the status quo** /,stæṭəs 'kwoʊ; ,steɪṭəs-/ *noun* [sing.] the situation that exists at a particular time

**'status ,symbol** *noun* [C] something that a person owns that shows that he/she is rich or has a high position in society

**stat·ute** /'stætʃut/ *noun* [C] a rule or law

**stat·u·to·ry** /'stætʃə,tɔri/ *adj.* decided or controlled by law: *a statutory right*

**,statutory 'holiday** (*also* **,stat 'holiday**) *noun* [C] (*Cdn*) a public holiday that is fixed by law

**staunch** /stɔntʃ/ *adj.* believing in sth or supporting sb/sth very strongly; loyal: *a staunch supporter of the Democratic Party*

**stave** /steɪv/ *verb*

**PHR V stave sth off** to stop sth bad from

happening now, although it may happen at a later time: *to stave off a financial crisis*

★**stay**[1] /steɪ/ ***verb*** [I] **1** to continue to be somewhere and not go away: *Sara stayed in bed until 11 o'clock.* ◇ *I can't stay long.* ◇ *Stay on this road until you get to Wells Street.* **2** to continue to be in a particular state or situation without change: *I can't stay awake any longer.*

NOTE **Remain** and **stay** are similar in meaning but **remain** is more formal.

**3** to be somewhere as a visitor or guest: *We stayed with friends in Boston.* ◇ *to stay at a hotel* ◇ *Can you stay for lunch?*

IDM **stay put** (*informal*) to remain in one place: *We like this apartment, so we'll probably stay put for a few years.*

PHR V **stay behind** to remain in a place after other people have gone

**stay in** to remain at home: *I'm going to stay in and watch TV.*

**stay on** to remain at a place or in a position longer than necessary or normal, or after other people have left: *He decided to stay on as the financial manager after the business had been sold.*

**stay out** to remain out, especially late at night

**stay up** to not go to bed: *I'm going to stay up to watch the late movie.*

**stay**[2] /steɪ/ ***noun*** [C] a period of time that you stay somewhere: *Did you enjoy your stay in Texas?*

**STD** /ˌɛs ti ˈdi/ ***noun*** [C] the abbreviation for "sexually transmitted disease"; a disease that is passed from one person to another during sexual activity

**std.** ***abbr.*** (*written*) standard

**stead** /stɛd/ ***noun*** [U]

IDM **in sb's/sth's stead** (*formal*) instead of sb/sth: *Foxton was dismissed and John Smith was appointed in his stead.*

**stand sb in good stead** to be useful or helpful to sb when needed: *Your languages will stand you in good stead when it comes to finding a job.*

**stead·fast** /ˈstɛdfæst/ ***adj.*** not changing in your attitudes or aims: *steadfast loyalty* ◇ *He remained steadfast in his determination to bring the killers to justice.* ▸ **stead·fast·ly** ***adv.***: *She steadfastly refused to speak.*

★**stead·y**[1] /ˈstɛdi/ ***adj.*** (**stead·i·er**; **stead·i·est**) **1** not moving or shaking: *You need a steady hand to take good pictures.* OPP **unsteady** **2** developing or happening at a regular rate: *a steady increase in exports* **3** staying the same; not changing over a period of time: *If you drive at a steady 55 miles an hour, you will use less gas.* ◇ *He hasn't been able to find a steady job.* ▸ **stead·i·ly** /ˈstɛdəli/ ***adv.***: *Unemployment has fallen steadily since 1995.*

**stead·y**[2] /ˈstɛdi/ ***verb*** [I,T] (*pres. part.* **stead·y·ing**; *3rd person sing. pres.* **stead·ies**; *pt, pp* **stead·ied**) to make sth steady or to become steady: *She thought she was going to fall, so she put out a hand to steady herself.*

**steak** /steɪk/ ***noun*** [C,U] a thick, flat piece of meat (especially from a cow) or fish: *a piece of steak* ◇ *a salmon steak* ➲ Look at **chop**[2].

**steak·house** /ˈsteɪkhaʊs/ ***noun*** [C] a restaurant that serves mainly steak

★**steal** /stil/ ***verb*** (*pt* **stole** /stoʊl/; *pp* **stolen** /ˈstoʊlən/) **1** [I,T] **steal (sth) (from sb/sth)** to take sth that belongs to another person secretly and without permission: *The terrorists were driving a stolen car.*

NOTE You **steal** things, but you **rob** people (of things): *My camera was stolen!* ◇ *I've been robbed!* ◇ *They robbed me of all my money!* ◇ *He was arrested for robbing a bank.* ➲ Look also at **burglarize** and at the note at **thief**.

**2** [I] **steal away, in, out, etc.** (*formal*) to move somewhere secretly and quietly

**stealth** /stɛlθ/ ***noun*** [U] (*formal*) behavior that is secret or quiet: *The terrorists operate by stealth.* ▸ **stealth·y** ***adj.*** ▸ **stealth·i·ly** ***adv.***

★**steam**[1] /stim/ ***noun*** [U] **1** the hot gas that water changes into when it boils: *Steam was rising from the coffee.* **2** the power that can be produced from STEAM (1): *a steam engine*

IDM **blow/let off steam** (*informal*) to release energy or express strong feeling by behaving in a noisy or uncontrolled way

**get, etc. somewhere under your own steam** (*informal*) to go somewhere without help from other people: *I'll get to the party under my own steam.*

**run out of steam** (*informal*) to have no more energy

**steam**[2] /stim/ ***verb*** **1** [I] to send out steam: *steaming hot soup* **2** [T] to cook sth in steam: *steamed vegetables*

IDM **be/get steamed (up)** (*informal*) to be/become very angry or worried about sth

PHR V **steam (sth) up** to cover sth or become covered with steam: *My glasses steam up when I come in from the cold.*

**steam·boat** /ˈstimboʊt/ ***noun*** [C] a large boat that is driven by steam, especially on rivers

**steam·er** /ˈstimər/ ***noun*** [C] **1** a boat or ship driven by steam ➲ Look at **paddle steamer**. **2** a metal container with small holes in it, that is placed over a pan of boiling water in order to cook food in the steam

**steam·rol·ler** /ˈstimroʊlər/ ***noun*** [C] a big heavy vehicle with wide wheels that is used for making the surface of a road flat

**steam·ship** /ˈstimʃɪp/ ***noun*** [C] (*abbr.* **SS**) a ship driven by steam

**steam·y** /ˈstimi/ ***adj.*** **1** full of steam; covered with steam: *a steamy bathroom* ◇ *steamy windows* ◇ *the steamy heat of Tokyo* **2** (*informal*) sexually exciting: *a steamy love scene* SYN **erotic**

★**steel**[1] /stil/ ***noun*** [U] a very strong metal that is made from iron mixed with carbon. Steel is used for making knives, tools, machines, etc. ➲ Look also at **stainless steel**.

**steel**[2] /stil/ ***verb*** [T] **steel yourself** to prepare yourself for sth difficult or unpleasant: *Steel yourself for a shock.*

**ˌsteel ˈdrum** (*also* **ˌsteel ˈpan**) ***noun*** [C] a type of drum made from oil barrels, which you hit in different places with two sticks to produce different notes, used in West Indian music

**ˌsteel guiˈtar** ***noun*** [C] *short for* PEDAL STEEL GUITAR

S

ˌ**steel ˈwool** ***noun*** [U] a mass of fine steel threads that you use for cleaning pots and pans, making surfaces smooth, etc.

**steel·work·er** /ˈstilˌwərkər/ ***noun*** [C] a person who works in a factory where steel is made (a steelworks)

**steel·y** /ˈstili/ ***adj.*** **1** (used about a person's character or behavior) strong, hard and unfriendly: *a cold, steely voice* ◇ *a look of steely determination* **2** like steel in color: *steely blue eyes* ◇ *The sky was cold and steely.*

★**steep** /stip/ ***adj.*** **1** (used about a hill, mountain, street, etc.) rising or falling quickly: *I don't think I can ride my bike up that hill. It's too steep.* **2** (used about an increase in sth) very big and sudden **3** (*informal*) very expensive ▸ **steep·ly** ***adv.***: *House prices have risen steeply this year.* ▸ **steep·ness** ***noun*** [U]

**steeped** /stipt/ ***adj.*** **be steeped in sth** having a lot of sth; full of sth: *The city of Boston is steeped in history.*

**stee·ple** /ˈstipl/ ***noun*** [C] a church tower that has a pointed top

★**steer**[1] /stɪr/ ***verb*** [I,T] to control the direction that a vehicle is going in, by using a wheel, etc.: *Can you push the car while I steer?* ◇ *to steer a boat/ship/bicycle/motorcycle* ◇ (*figurative*) *She tried to steer the conversation away from the subject of money.*

> NOTE **Steer** means to control the direction of a vehicle. If you **drive** a car or truck, **ride** a bicycle/motorcycle or **sail** a boat, you steer it and you are also in control of everything else.

**steer**[2] /stɪr/ ***noun*** [C] a young male cow that has had part of its sexual organs removed and is usually raised for its meat

**steer·ing** /ˈstɪrɪŋ/ ***noun*** [U] the mechanical parts that control the direction that a vehicle is going in

ˈ**steering wheel** (*also* **wheel**) ***noun*** [C] the wheel in a car, etc. that you use to steer it

**stein** /staɪn/ ***noun*** [C] a large decorated ceramic cup for drinking beer, often with a lid

**stel·lar** /ˈstɛlər/ ***adj.*** **1** (*technical*) connected with the stars **2** (*informal*) excellent: *a stellar performance/career*

★**stem**[1] /stɛm/ ***noun*** [C] **1** one of the long thin parts of a plant which the leaves or flowers grow on **2** the main part of a word onto which other parts are added: *"Writ-" is the stem of the words "write," "writing," "written" and "writer."*

**stem**[2] /stɛm/ ***verb*** (**stem·ming**; **stemmed**) [T] to stop sth that is flowing from spreading or increasing: *The cut was bandaged to stem the bleeding.* ◇ *They discussed ways of* ***stemming the flow*** *of smuggled drugs.* ◇ *The administration had failed to* ***stem the tide*** *of factory closures.*

PHR V **stem from sth** to be the result of sth: *Most people's insecurities stem from something that happened in their childhood.*

**stench** /stɛntʃ/ ***noun*** [C, usually sing.] a very bad smell

**sten·cil** /ˈstɛnsl/ ***noun*** [C] a thin piece of metal, plastic or cardboard with a design cut out of it, that you put onto a surface and paint over so that the design is left on the surface; the pattern or design that is produced in this way

**ste·nog·ra·pher** /stəˈnɑgrəfər/ (*also informal* **sten·o** /ˈstɛnoʊ/) ***noun*** [C] a person whose job is to write down what sb else says, using a quick system of signs or abbreviations

**ste·nog·ra·phy** /stəˈnɑgrəfi/ ***noun*** [U] the action or process of writing very quickly by using special signs or abbreviations (**shorthand**), especially to record what sb is saying

★**step**[1] /stɛp/ ***verb*** [I] (**step·ping**; **stepped**) to lift one foot and put it down in a different place when you are walking: *Be careful! Don't step in the mud.* ◇ *to step forward/back* ◇ *Ouch! You stepped on my foot!*

PHR V **step down** to give up a position of authority: *Anne is stepping down as chairperson at the end of the year.*

**step in** to become involved in a difficult situation, usually in order to help

**step out** to leave a place for a short period of time: *Sorry, Mrs. Brown just stepped out. Can I take a message?*

**step sth up** to increase sth: *The army has decided to step up its recruiting efforts.*

★**step**[2] /stɛp/ ***noun*** [C] **1** the act of lifting one foot and putting it down in a different place: *Nick took two steps forward and then stopped.* ◇ *I heard steps outside the window.* **2** one action in a series of actions that you take in order to achieve sth: *the first step toward peace* **3** one of the surfaces on which you put your foot when you are going up or down stairs, a ladder, etc.: *the top/bottom step* ◇ *a flight* (= a set) *of steps* ➲ Look at the note at **stair**.

IDM **in step (with sb/sth)**; **out of step (with sb/sth)** moving/not moving your feet at the same time as other people when you are marching, dancing, etc.: (*figurative*) *politicians who are totally out of step with young people today*

**take steps to do sth** to take action in order to achieve sth: *to take steps to reduce unemployment*

**watch your step** → WATCH[2]

**step·brother** /ˈstɛpbrʌðər/ ***noun*** [C] the son of your stepmother or stepfather from an earlier marriage or relationship

ˌ**step-by-ˈstep** ***adj.*** (only *before* a noun) moving slowly and gradually from one action or stage to the next: *clear step-by-step instructions*

**step·child** /ˈstɛptʃaɪld/ ***noun*** [C] (*pl.* **step·children** /-tʃɪldrən/) the child of your husband or wife from an earlier marriage or relationship

**step·daughter** /ˈstɛpdɔt̮ər/ ***noun*** [C] the daughter of your husband or wife from an earlier marriage or relationship

**step·father** /ˈstɛpfɑðər/ ***noun*** [C] the man who has married your mother after the death or divorce of your father

**step·lad·der** /ˈstɛplædər/ ***noun*** [C] a short ladder with two parts that can stand on its own. You can fold it up when you are not using it. ➲ picture at **ladder**.

**step·mother** /ˈstɛpmʌðər/ ***noun*** [C] the woman who has married your father after the death or divorce of your mother

**steppe** /stɛp/ ***noun*** [C, usually pl., U] a large area of land with grass but few trees, especially in southeast Europe and Siberia: *the vast Russian steppes*

**'stepping stone** ***noun*** [C] **1** one of a line of flat stones that you step on in order to cross a stream or river **2** something that allows you to make progress or begin to achieve sth: *a stepping stone to a more lucrative career*

**step·son** /'stɛpsʌn/ ***noun*** [C] the son of your husband or wife from an earlier marriage or relationship

**ster·e·o** /'stɛrioʊ/ ***noun*** **1** [U] the system for playing recorded music, speech, etc. in which the sound is directed through two channels: *This program is in stereo.* **2** [C] (*also* **'stereo system**) a piece of equipment for playing recorded music, etc. that has two speakers: *a car stereo* ▶ **ster·e·o** ***adj.***: *a stereo broadcast*

**ster·e·o·type¹** /'stɛriətaɪp/ ***noun*** [C] a common idea about a type of person or thing, which is often not true in reality: *the stereotype of the loud, obnoxious New Yorker* ▶ **ster·e·o·typ·i·cal** /ˌstɛriə'tɪpɪkl/ ***adj.***

**ster·e·o·type²** /'stɛriətaɪp/ ***verb*** [T] to have or show a common, fixed idea about a type of person or thing, which is often not true in reality: *Women are often stereotyped as housewives in TV commercials.*

**ster·ile** /'stɛrəl/ ***adj.*** **1** not able to produce young animals or babies **2** completely clean and free from tiny living things that can cause disease (**bacteria**): *sterile medical instruments* **3** with no interest or creative ideas: *a sterile discussion* ▶ **ste·ril·i·ty** /stə'rɪləṭi/ ***noun*** [U]

**ster·il·ize** /'stɛrəlaɪz/ ***verb*** [T] **1** to make sb/sth completely clean and free from tiny living things that can cause disease (**bacteria**) **2** (usually passive) to perform an operation on a person or an animal so that he/she/it cannot have babies ▶ **ster·il·i·za·tion** /ˌstɛrələ'zeɪʃn/ ***noun*** [U]

**ster·ling** /'stərlɪŋ/ ***adj.*** of very high quality: *a sterling performance* ◇ *sterling silver* (= that is 92.5% pure silver)

**stern¹** /stərn/ ***adj.*** very serious and severe; not smiling: *a stern expression* ◇ *a stern warning* ▶ **stern·ly** ***adv.***

**stern²** /stərn/ ***noun*** [C] the back end of a ship or boat ➲ Look at **bow²**(2).

**ster·oid** /'stɛrɔɪd; 'stɪr-/ ***noun*** [C, usually pl.] a type of drug that can be used to treat illnesses or injuries, but that some people take illegally in order to make their muscles bigger or to improve their performance in sports

**steth·o·scope** /'stɛθəskoʊp/ ***noun*** [C] a piece of equipment that a doctor uses in order to listen to your heart and breathing

**stew¹** /stu/ ***noun*** [C,U] a type of food that you make by cooking meat and vegetables in liquid for a long time

**stew²** /stu/ ***verb*** **1** [I,T] to cook sth slowly, or allow sth to cook slowly, in liquid in a closed dish: *stewed apples* ◇ *The meat needs to stew for two hours.* **2** [I] to think or worry about sth: *I've been stewing over the problem for a while.* ◇ *Leave him to stew.*

IDM **let sb stew in his/her own juice** (*informal*) to leave sb to worry and suffer the unpleasant effects of his/her own actions

**stew·ard** /'stuərd/ ***noun*** [C] (*old-fashioned*) a man who serves the passengers on an airplane

> NOTE **Flight attendant** is more common nowadays.

**stew·ard·ess** /'stuərdəs/ ***noun*** [C] (*old-fashioned*) a woman who serves the passengers on an airplane

> NOTE **Flight attendant** is more common nowadays.

★**stick¹** /stɪk/ ***noun*** **1** [C] a small thin piece of wood from a tree **2** [C] a long thin piece of wood that you use in some sports: *a hockey stick* ➲ Look at **bat¹**(2), **club¹**(4) and **racket** (1). **3** [C] a long thin piece of sth: *a stick of dynamite* **4** **the sticks** [U] (*informal*) an area that is far away from big cities and does not have interesting cultural activities

IDM **the short end of the stick** → SHORT¹

★**stick²** /stɪk/ ***verb*** (*pt, pp* **stuck** /stʌk/) **1** [I,T] **stick (sth) in/into (sth)** to push a pointed object into sth; to be pushed into sth: *Stick a fork into the meat to see if it's done.* ◇ *I can't move. There's a piece of wire sticking in my leg.* **2** [I,T] to attach sth to sth else or to become attached to sth else by using glue, etc.: *to stick a stamp on an envelope* ◇ *Jelly sticks to your fingers.* **3** [I] **stick (in sth)** (used about sth that can usually be moved) to become firmly attached in one position so that it cannot be moved: *The car was stuck in the mud.* **4** [T] (*informal*) to put sth somewhere: *Just stick your umbrella in the closet.*

IDM **poke/stick your nose into sth** → NOSE¹

PHR V **stick around** (*informal*) to stay or wait somewhere

**stick by sb** (*informal*) to continue to give sb help and support even in difficult times

**stick by sth** to refuse to change a decision, belief, etc.: *Despite this news, analysts are sticking by their earlier economic forecasts.*

**stick out** (*informal*) to be very noticeable: *The new apartment building really sticks out from the older buildings around it.*

**stick (sth) out** to be further out than sth else or to push sth further out than sth else: *The boy's head was sticking out of the window.* ◇ *Don't stick your tongue out.*

**stick it/sth out** (*informal*) to stay in a difficult or unpleasant situation until the end

**stick to sth** to continue with sth and not change to anything else: *You need to plan a sensible budget and then stick to it.*

**stick together** (*informal*) (used about two or more people) to stay friendly and loyal to each other

**stick up** to point upward: *You look funny. Your hair's sticking up!*

**stick up for sb/yourself/sth** to support or defend sb/yourself/sth: *Don't worry. I'll stick up for you if there's any trouble.*

**stick·er** /'stɪkər/ ***noun*** [C] a sticky label with a picture or message on it, that you stick on to sth: *window/car/bumper stickers*

**'sticker price** ***noun*** [C] the price that is marked on sth, especially a car

S

**ˈstick ˌfigure** *noun* [C] a picture of a person drawn only with thin lines for the arms and legs, a circle for the head, etc.

**stick·ler** /ˈstɪklər/ *noun* [C] a person who thinks that a particular quality or type of behavior is very important and expects other people to think and behave in the same way: *She's **a stickler for** punctuality.*

**stick·pin** /ˈstɪkpɪn/ *noun* [C] a decorative pin that is worn on a tie to keep it in place, or as a piece of jewelry

**ˈstick shift** *noun* [C] a system of gears in a car that the driver must move (**shift**) by hand, or a car with this system of gears

**stick-to-it-iveness** /stɪk ˈtu ɪṭ ɪvnəs/ *noun* [U] (*informal*) the quality of continuing to try to achieve a particular aim despite difficulties SYN **perseverance**

**ˈstick-up** *noun* [C] (*informal*) an act of stealing from a bank, etc. using a gun: *a stick-up at the local bank* ◇ *This is a stick-up!*

★**stick·y** /ˈstɪki/ *adj.* (**stick·i·er**; **stick·i·est**) **1** (used for describing a substance that can stick to sth else, or sth that is covered with this kind of substance): *This candy is very sticky.* ◇ *I have sticky fingers after eating that ice cream.* **2** (*informal*) (used about a situation) difficult or unpleasant

★**stiff¹** /stɪf/ *adj.*

➤ DIFFICULT TO BEND/MOVE **1** (used about material, paper, etc.) fairly hard and not easy to bend: *My new shoes feel a little stiff.*

➤ MUSCLES **2** (used about parts of the body) not easy to move: *My arm feels really stiff after playing tennis yesterday.*

➤ MIXTURE **3** (used about a liquid) very thick; almost solid: *Beat the egg whites until they are stiff.*

➤ DIFFICULT/SEVERE **4** difficult or strong: *We face some stiff competition from the Bloomington High team.* ◇ *stiff opposition to the plan*

➤ NOT FRIENDLY **5** (used about sb's behavior) not relaxed or friendly; formal: *She's often a little stiff around strangers.*

➤ WIND **6** (used about a wind) fairly strong and steady: *a stiff breeze*

➤ ALCOHOLIC DRINK **7** (used about an alcoholic drink) strong: *a stiff whiskey*

▶ **stiff·ly** *adv.*: *He smiled stiffly.* ▶ **stiff·ness** *noun* [U]

**stiff²** /stɪf/ *adv.* (used *after* a past participle) extremely: *to be bored/frozen/scared stiff*

**stiff³** /stɪf/ *verb* [T] (*informal*) to cheat sb or not pay what you owe him/her, especially by not leaving any money as a TIP¹ (3)

**stiff·en** /ˈstɪfn/ *verb* **1** [I] (used about a person) to suddenly become very still, usually because you are afraid or angry: *Alison stiffened as she heard a noise outside the door.* **2** [I,T] to make sth stronger or more severe: *Congress voted to stiffen penalties for convicted drug dealers.*

**sti·fle** /ˈstaɪfl/ *verb* **1** [T] to stop sth from happening, developing or continuing: *Her strict education had stifled her natural creativity.* ◇ *to stifle a yawn* **2** [I,T] to be or to make sb unable to breathe easily: *Richard was almost stifled by the smoke.* ▶ **sti·fling** *adj.*: *The heat was stifling.*

**stig·ma** /ˈstɪgmə/ *noun* [C,U] a bad reputation that sth has because a lot of people have a set idea that it is wrong, often unfairly: *There is still a lot of stigma attached to being unemployed.* ▶ **stig·ma·tize** /ˈstɪgmətaɪz/ *verb* [T]

**sti·let·to** /stɪˈlɛṭoʊ/ *noun* [C] (*pl.* **sti·let·tos** or **sti·let·toes**) **1** a woman's shoe with a very high narrow heel; the heel on such a shoe SYN **spike heel** **2** a small knife with a narrow pointed blade

★**still¹** /stɪl/ *adv.* **1** (used for talking about sth that started at an earlier time) continuing until now or until the time you are talking about: *Do you still live in Miami?* ◇ *It's still raining.* ◇ *In 1994, Rob was still a student.* **2** in addition; more: *There are still ten days to go until my vacation.* **3** (used before or after a comparative adjective or adverb, to make it stronger): *It was very cold yesterday, but today it's colder still.* ◇ *The country's biggest shopping mall will soon be surrounded by still more stores and restaurants.* **4** (used for talking about an action or opinion that you do not expect, because sth else makes it surprising) even so: *He had a bad headache, but he still went to the party.*

★**still²** /stɪl/ *adj., adv.* **1** without moving: *Stand still! I want to take your picture!* **2** quiet or calm: *The water was perfectly still.* ▶ **still·ness** *noun* [U]: *the stillness of the air on a cold winter night*

**still³** /stɪl/ *noun* [C] a single photograph that is taken from a scene in a movie

**still·born** /ˈstɪlbɔrn/ *adj.* (used about a baby) dead when it is born

**ˈstill life** *noun* [C,U] (*pl.* **still lifes**) the art of painting or drawing arrangements of objects such as flowers, fruit, etc.; a painting, etc. like this: *She prefers still life to landscape painting.* ◇ *a still life in oils*

**stilt** /stɪlt/ *noun* [C, usually pl.] **1** one of two long pieces of wood, with places to rest your feet on, on which you can walk above the ground: *a pair of stilts* **2** one of a set of poles that support a building above the ground or water

**stilt·ed** /ˈstɪltəd/ *adj.* (used about a way of speaking or writing) unnatural and very formal

**stim·u·lant** /ˈstɪmyələnt/ *noun* [C] a drug or medicine that makes you feel more active: *Caffeine is a mild stimulant.*

**stim·u·late** /ˈstɪmyəleɪt/ *verb* [T] **1** to make sth active or more active: *Exercise stimulates the blood circulation.* ◇ *The President has decided to cut taxes in order to stimulate the economy.* **2** to make sb feel interested and excited about sth: *School doesn't really stimulate him.* ▶ **stim·u·la·tion** /ˌstɪmyəˈleɪʃn/ *noun* [U]

**stim·u·lat·ing** /ˈstɪmyəleɪṭɪŋ/ *adj.* interesting and exciting: *a stimulating discussion*

**stim·u·lus** /ˈstɪmyələs/ *noun* [C,U] (*pl.* **stim·u·li** /-laɪ/) something that causes activity, development or interest: *The President recommended using tax cuts as an economic stimulus.*

★**sting¹** /stɪŋ/ *verb* [I,T] (*pt, pp* **stung** /stʌŋ/) **1** (used about an insect, a plant, etc.) to make sb/sth feel a sudden pain by pushing sth sharp into the skin and injecting poison into him/her/it: *Ow! I just got stung by a wasp!* ◇ *Be careful. Those plants sting.* **2** to make sb/sth feel a sudden, sharp pain: *Soap stings*

S

*if it gets in your eyes.* **3** to make sb feel very hurt and upset because of sth you say: *Kate was stung by her father's criticism.*

★**sting²** /stɪŋ/ ***noun*** [C] **1** an injury that is caused by an insect pushing a sharp pointed part of its body into you: *a bee sting on the leg* **2** (*also* **sting·er**) the sharp pointed part of an insect or creature that can go into the skin leaving a small, painful, and sometimes poisonous, wound **3** a sharp pain that feels like a STING² (1): *the sting of soap in your eyes* **4** a complicated investigation in which the police use a trick in order to catch sb while he/she is doing sth illegal

**sting·er** /ˈstɪŋər/ ***noun*** [C] = STING² (2)

**sting·ray** /ˈstɪŋreɪ/ ***noun*** [C] a large wide flat ocean fish that has a long tail with a sharp STING² (2) in it that can cause serious wounds

**stin·gy** /ˈstɪndʒi/ ***adj.*** (**stin·gi·er**; **stin·gi·est**) not willing to give or share sth (especially money); not generous: *Don't be so stingy with the gravy!*

**stink¹** /stɪŋk/ ***verb*** [I] (*pt* **stank** /stæŋk/ or **stunk** /stʌŋk/; *pp* **stunk**) **1** to have a very strong and unpleasant smell: *Yuck! Something stinks in here!* **2** (*informal*) to seem to be very bad or unpleasant: *This job really stinks!*

**stink²** /stɪŋk/ ***noun*** (*informal*) **1** [C, usually sing.] a very unpleasant smell: *the stink of sweat and urine* **2** [sing.] a lot of trouble and anger about sth: *The whole business caused quite a stink.*

**stink·er** /ˈstɪŋkər/ ***noun*** [C] (*informal*) a person, particularly a child, or thing that is very unpleasant or difficult: *It's been a real stinker of a day.* ◇ *That movie was a stinker.*

**stink·y** /ˈstɪŋki/ ***adj.*** (**stink·i·er**; **stink·i·est**) (*informal*) having a strong or bad smell

**stint** /stɪnt/ ***noun*** [C] a fixed period of time that you spend doing sth: *Her employment experience includes a two-year stint in the navy.*

**sti·pend** /ˈstaɪpɛnd; -pənd/ ***noun*** [C] (*formal*) an amount of money that is paid regularly to sb, such as a priest or a student as a salary or money to live on: *an annual/monthly stipend* ◇ *a summer internship with a small stipend*

**stip·u·late** /ˈstɪpyəleɪt/ ***verb*** [T] (*formal*) to say exactly and officially what must be done: *The law stipulates that all schools provide special education for children who require it.* ▸ **stip·u·la·tion** /ˌstɪpyəˈleɪʃn/ ***noun*** [C,U] (*formal*): *One of the stipulations in his will prohibits the sale of the paintings to private collectors.*

★**stir¹** /stər/ ***verb*** (**stir·ring**; **stirred**) **1** [T] to move a liquid, etc. around and around, using a spoon, etc.: *She stirred her coffee with a teaspoon.* **2** [I,T] to move or make sb/sth move gently: *The boy stirred in his sleep.* ◇ *A sudden wind stirred the leaves.* **3** [T] to make sb feel a strong emotion: *The story stirred Carol's imagination.* ◇ *a stirring speech*

PHRV **stir sth up** to cause a strong feeling in other people: *The manager accused him of stirring up trouble.*

**stir²** /stər/ ***noun*** **1** [C] the action of stirring: *Give the soup a stir.* **2** [sing.] general excitement or shock: *Short skirts caused quite a stir when they first appeared in the 1960s.*

ˈ**stir-ˌcrazy** ***adj.*** (*informal*) showing signs of mental illness because of being kept in prison

ˈ**stir-fry** ***verb*** [T] (*pres. part.* **stir-fry·ing**; *3rd person sing. pres.* ˈ**stir-fries**; *pt, pp* ˈ**stir-fried**) to cook vegetables, meat, etc. by frying them for a short time in very hot oil while stirring them ▸ ˈ**stir-fry** ***noun*** [C,U] (*pl.* ˈ**stir-fries**)

**stir·rup** /ˈstərəp/ ***noun*** [C] one of the two metal objects that you put your feet in when you are riding a horse ➲ picture at **horse**.

★**stitch¹** /stɪtʃ/ ***noun*** [C] **1** one of the small lines of thread that you can see on a piece of material after it has been sewn ➲ picture at **knit**. **2** [usually pl.] one of the small pieces of thread that a doctor uses to sew your skin together if you cut yourself very badly, or after an operation **3** one of the small circles of yarn that you put around a needle when you are knitting **4** [usually sing.] a sudden pain that you get in the side of your body, e.g. after you have been running

IDM **in stitches** (*informal*) laughing so much that you cannot stop

**stitch²** /stɪtʃ/ ***verb*** [I,T] to sew or fasten sth together using STITCHES¹: *Can you stitch my bag back together?* ➲ picture at **knit**.

**stoat** /stoʊt/ ***noun*** [C] a small wild animal with a long body and brown fur that, in northern areas, turns white in winter

★**stock¹** /stɑk/ ***noun*** **1** [C,U] a supply of things that are available to be sold or used: *The new store has a large stock of CDs.* ◇ *We'll have to order extra stock if we sell a lot more this week.* ◇ *farmers' stocks of grain and hay for the winter* **2** [C,U] a share in a company that people can buy and sell; the value of the shares in a company that have been sold to people (**investors**): *to invest in stocks and bonds* ◇ *They own over $1 million worth of stock in a major oil company.* **3** [C,U] a liquid that you use to make soups, sauces, etc. It is made by boiling meat, bones, vegetables, etc. in water.

IDM **in stock/out of stock** in/not in the supply of things that a store, etc. has available for sale

**take stock (of sth)** to think about sth very carefully before deciding what to do next: *Let's see how things go for a week or so and then take stock of the situation.*

**stock²** /stɑk/ ***verb*** [T] **1** (usually used about a store) to have a supply of sth: *They stock foods from all over the world.* **2** to provide sth with a supply of sth: *a well-stocked bookstore*

PHRV **stock up** to collect a large supply of sth for future use: *to stock up with food for the winter*

**stock³** /stɑk/ ***adj.*** (only *before* a noun) (used for describing sth that sb says) used so often that it does not have much meaning: *She just uses the same stock phrases over and over.*

**stock·ade** /stɑˈkeɪd/ ***noun*** [C] a line or wall of strong wooden posts built to defend a place

**stock·bro·ker** /ˈstɑkbroʊkər/ (*also* **broker**) ***noun*** [C] a person whose job is to buy and sell STOCKS¹ (2) for other people

ˈ**stock car** ***noun*** [C] an ordinary car that has been made stronger for use in stock-car racing

ˈ**stock car ˌracing** ***noun*** [U] a type of race in

S

which the competing cars are allowed to hit and crash into each other

**'stock ex,change** *noun* [C] **1** a place where STOCKS[1] (2) are bought and sold: *the New York Stock Exchange* **2** (*also* **'stock market**) the business or activity of buying and selling STOCKS[1] (2)

**stock·hold·er** /'stɑk,hoʊldər/ *noun* [C] a person who owns STOCKS[1] (2) in a business

**stock·ing** /'stɑkɪŋ/ *noun* [C] one of a pair of thin pieces of clothing that fit tightly over a woman's foot and leg: *a pair of stockings* ➲ Look at **pantyhose** and **tights**.

**'stocking cap** *noun* [C] a type of warm, soft knitted hat

stocking cap

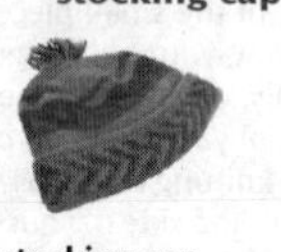

stocking cap

**stock·man** /'stɑkmən/ *noun* [C] (*pl.* **stock·men** /-mən/) **1** a man whose job is to take care of farm animals **2** a man who owns farm animals **3** a man who is in charge of the goods in a warehouse, etc.

**'stock ,market** *noun* [C] **1** = STOCK EXCHANGE (2) **2** the prices of stocks that are bought and sold in general: *Low interest rates and a rising stock market could lead to more takeovers of companies.*

**stock·pile** /'stɑkpaɪl/ *noun* [C] a large amount or number of sth that is kept available for use in the future: *the nation's stockpile of nuclear weapons* ▸ **stock·pile** *verb* [T]

**stock·room** /'stɑkrum/ *noun* [C] a room for storing things in a store, an office, etc.

**stock·y** /'stɑki/ *adj.* (used about a person's body) short but strong and heavy

**stock·yard** /'stɑkyɑrd/ *noun* [C] a place where farm animals are kept for a short time before they are sold at a market

**stodg·y** /'stɑdʒi/ *adj.* (**stodg·i·er**; **stodg·i·est**) (*informal*) **1** serious and boring; not exciting: *The article was very stodgy – too many facts.* **2** (*Cdn*) (used about food) heavy and making you feel very full

**sto·gie** (*also* **stog·y**) /'stoʊgi/ *noun* [C] (*pl.* **stogies**) (*informal*) a cigar, especially a thin, cheap one

**sto·ic** /'stoʊɪk/ *noun* [C] (*formal*) a person who is able to suffer pain or trouble without complaining or showing what he/she is feeling ▸ **sto·ic** (*also* **sto·ic·al** /'stoʊɪkl/) *adj.*: *her stoic endurance* ◇ *his stoical acceptance of death* ▸ **sto·ic·al·ly** /-kli/ *adv.*: *They reacted stoically to the news.*

**stoke** /stoʊk/ *verb* [T] **1 stoke sth (up) (with sth)** to add fuel to a fire, etc.: *to stoke up a fire with more coal* ◇ *to stoke a furnace* **2 stoke sth (up)** to make people feel sth more strongly: *to stoke up anger/envy* ◇ *The publicity was intended to stoke up interest in her music.*

PHR V **stoke up (on/with sth)** to eat or drink a lot of sth, especially so that you do not feel hungry later: *Stoke up for the day on a good breakfast.*

**stoked** /stoʊkt/ *adj.* (*informal*) excited and pleased about sth: *I'm really stoked that they chose me for the team.*

**stole** *past tense of* STEAL

**sto·len** *past participle of* STEAL

★**stom·ach**[1] /'stʌmək/ *noun* [C] **1** the part of your body where food is digested after you have eaten it **2** the front part of your body below your chest and above your legs: *a fat stomach* ◇ *She turned over onto her stomach.* ➲ picture on study page **A32**. ➲ Look at **belly** and **tummy**.

**stom·ach**[2] /'stʌmək/ *verb* [T] (usually in negative sentences and questions) to be able to watch, listen to, accept, etc. sth that you think is unpleasant: *I can't stomach too much violence in movies.*

**stom·ach·ache** /'stʌməkeɪk/ *noun* [C] a pain in your stomach: *I have a terrible stomachache.* ➲ Look at the note at **ache**.

**stomp** /stɑmp/ *verb* [I] **1 stomp (on sth)** to put your foot down very heavily on the ground or on sth else: *She stomped on the spider and squashed it.* **2** to walk with heavy steps, especially because you are angry: *He stomped up the stairs to his room and slammed the door.*

**'stomping ground** *noun* [C] (*informal*) a place that sb likes and often goes to: *This bar used to be one of my brother's old stomping grounds.*

★**stone**[1] /stoʊn/ *noun* **1** [U] a hard solid substance that is found in the ground: *The house was made of gray stone.* ◇ *a stone wall* **2** [C] a small piece of rock: *The boy picked up a stone and threw it into the river.* **3** [C] = PRECIOUS STONE **4** [C] (often in compounds) a small piece of hard material that can form in certain parts of the body, such as the gall bladder or kidney, and cause pain: *kidney stones*

IDM **a stone's throw** a very short distance away: *We live just a stone's throw from here.*

**stone**[2] /stoʊn/ *verb* [T] to throw STONES[1] (2) at sb/sth, e.g. as a punishment: *The two women were stoned to death.*

**the 'Stone Age** *noun* [sing.] the very early period of human history when tools and weapons were made of stone: (*figurative*) *My dad's taste in music is from the Stone Age* (= very old-fashioned).

**,stone-'cold** *adj.* completely cold, when it should be warm or hot: *The soup was stone cold.*

**stoned** /stoʊnd/ *adj.* (*slang*) under the influence of illegal drugs, especially marijuana

**ston·er** /'stoʊnər/ *noun* [C] (*slang*) a person who regularly uses drugs such as marijuana

**stone·washed** /'stoʊnwɑʃt; -wɔʃt/ *adj.* (used about jeans, etc.) washed in a special way so that the cloth loses some color and looks older

**ston·y** /'stoʊni/ *adj.* (**ston·i·er**; **ston·i·est**) **1** (used about the ground) having a lot of stones in it, or covered with stones **2** not friendly: *There was a stony silence as he walked into the room.*

**stood** *past tense, past participle of* STAND[1]

**stooge** /studʒ/ *noun* [C] **1** (*informal*) a person who is used by sb to do things that are unpleasant or dishonest **2** a performer in a show whose role is to appear silly so that the other performers can make jokes about him/her

**stool** /stul/ *noun* **1** [C] a seat that does not have a back or arms: *a bar stool* ➲ picture at **chair**. **2** [C,U] (*formal*) a piece of solid waste from the body

**'stool ,pigeon** *noun* [C] (*informal*) a person,

S

especially a criminal, who helps the police to catch another criminal, for example by spending time with him/her and getting secret information SYN **informer**

**stoop**[1] /stup/ ***verb*** [I] to bend your head and shoulders forward and downward: *Cathy had to stoop to get through the low doorway.*

PHRV **stoop to sth/to doing sth** to do sth bad or wrong (that you would normally not do): *I would never stoop to cheating.*

**stoop**[2] /stup/ ***noun*** **1** [C] a small set of steps that lead to the door of a house, with a flat area at the top: *neighbors sitting on the front stoop* **2** [sing.] a way of holding your body, bending your head and shoulders forward and downward: *to walk with a stoop*

★**stop**[1] /stɑp/ ***verb*** (**stop·ping**; **stopped**)

➤FINISH MOVING **1** [I] to finish moving, happening or operating: *He walked along the road for a while, and then stopped.* ◇ *I need to stop at the store to get some milk.* ◇ *I think the rain's stopped.* ◇ *Oh no! My watch stopped.* **2** [T] to make sb/sth finish moving, happening or operating: *I stopped someone on the street to ask the way to the post office.* ◇ *Stop the car – I need to get out!*

➤END **3** [T] to end or finish an activity: *Stop making that noise!* ◇ *We stopped work for half an hour to have a cup of coffee.* ◇ *It's stopped raining now.*

NOTE If you **stop to do** something, you stop in order to do it: *On the way into the office, I stopped to smoke a cigarette.* If you **stop doing** something, you do not do it anymore: *I'm trying to stop smoking.*

**4** [T] **stop sb/sth from doing sth** to make sb/sth end or finish an activity; to prevent sb/sth from doing sth: *Can't you stop the car from making that noise?* ◇ *Nothing will stop me from loving you.*

➤PREVENT **5** [T] to prevent money, especially a check, from being paid: *The bank stopped the payment because there was no money in his account.*

IDM **stop at nothing** to do anything in order to get what you want, even if it is wrong or dangerous

**stop short of sth/doing sth** to almost do sth, but then decide not to do it at the last minute: *They made several indirect comments, but they stopped short of calling her a thief.*

PHRV **stop by (sth)** to visit sb/sth for a short time, especially before going to another place: *You'll have to stop by our house if you're ever in Washington.*

**stop off (at/in…)** to stop during a trip to do sth: *We stopped off in Oakland to see some friends before coming home.*

★**stop**[2] /stɑp/ ***noun*** [C] **1** an act of stopping or a state of being stopped: *Be sure your seat belt is fastened in case we have to make a sudden stop.* ◇ *The elevator came to a stop on the third floor.* **2** the place where a bus, train, etc. stops so that people can get on and off: *a bus stop* **3** a place where sb stops during a trip, or the time he/she spends there: *Our first stop on the tour will be the Museum of Modern Art.*

IDM **to put a stop to sth** to prevent sth bad or unpleasant from continuing

**stop·gap** /ˈstɑpgæp/ ***noun*** [C] something that you use or do for a short time while you are looking for sth better: *The arrangement was only intended as a stopgap.* ◇ *stopgap measures*

**stop·light** /ˈstɑplaɪt/ ***noun*** [C] = TRAFFIC LIGHT

**stop·o·ver** /ˈstɑpoʊvər/ ***noun*** [C] a short stop in a long trip, especially by plane: *a stopover in Chicago on the way to Montreal*

**stop·page** /ˈstɑpɪdʒ/ ***noun*** [C] **1** a situation in which people stop working as part of a protest or strike: *400 workers were involved in the stoppage.* **2** a situation in which sth does not move forward or is blocked: *a stoppage of blood to the heart* **3** (*sports*) an interruption in the game for a particular reason

**stop·per** /ˈstɑpər/ ***noun*** [C] an object that you put into the top of a bottle in order to close it. A stopper can be made of glass, plastic or cork.

**stop·watch** /ˈstɑpwɑtʃ/ ***noun*** [C] a watch which can be started and stopped by pressing a button so that you can measure exactly how long sth takes

**stor·age** /ˈstɔrɪdʒ/ ***noun*** [U] the keeping of things until they are needed; the place where they are kept: *storage space* ◇ *I'm going to keep my stuff in storage on campus this summer.*

★**store**[1] /stɔr/ ***noun*** [C] **1** a building or part of a building where things are bought and sold: *a furniture store* ◇ *Can you go to the store and pick up some bread and milk?* ➲ Look at **convenience store**, **department store** and **grocery store**. **2** a supply of sth that you keep for future use

IDM **in store (for sb/sth)** going to happen in the future: *There's a surprise in store for you when you get home!*

★**store**[2] /stɔr/ ***verb*** [T] to keep sth or a supply of sth for future use: *to store information in a computer* ◇ *All the documents are stored in a safe.*

**store·front** /ˈstɔrfrʌnt/ ***noun*** [C] **1** the outside of a store that faces the street: *The old drugstore still has its original storefront.* **2** a room at the front of a store: *They run their business from a small storefront.* ◇ *a storefront office*

**store·house** /ˈstɔrhaʊs/ ***noun*** [C] **1** a building where things are stored SYN **warehouse** **2** (used about information, knowledge, etc.) a place or thing that has or contains a lot of information: *This book is a storehouse of useful information.*

**store·keep·er** /ˈstɔrkipər/ ***noun*** [C] = SHOPKEEPER

**store·room** /ˈstɔrrum/ ***noun*** [C] a room where things are kept until they are needed

**stork** /stɔrk/ ***noun*** [C] a large white bird with a long beak, neck and legs. Storks often live near water.

★**storm**[1] /stɔrm/ ***noun*** [C] very bad weather, with heavy rain, strong winds, etc.: *Look at those black clouds. I think there's going to be a storm.* ◇ *a thunderstorm/snowstorm* ◇ (*figurative*) *The proposed tax increase caused a storm of protest.*

NOTE **Storm** is the general word for very bad weather. A very strong wind is a **gale**. A very bad snowstorm is a **blizzard**. A storm with a very strong circular wind is called a **cyclone**, **hurricane** or **tornado**.

IDM **take sth by storm 1** to be extremely

S

successful very quickly in a particular place or among particular people: *The show took Broadway by storm.* **2** to attack a place suddenly and capture it

**storm**[2] /stɔrm/ ***verb*** **1** [I] to enter or leave somewhere in a very angry and noisy way: *She grabbed her books and stormed out of the room.* **2** [T] to attack a building, town, etc. suddenly and violently in order to take control of it: *Heavily armed police stormed the building and freed the hostages inside.*

**ˈstorm door** ***noun*** [C] an extra door that is fitted to the outside door of a house, etc. to give protection from bad weather

**storm·troop·er** /ˈstɔrmˌtrupər/ ***noun*** [C] a soldier who is specially trained for violent attacks, especially one in Nazi Germany in the 1930s and 1940s

**ˈstorm ˌwindow** ***noun*** [C] an extra window that is fitted to a window of a house to give protection from bad weather

**storm·y** /ˈstɔrmi/ ***adj.*** (**storm·i·er**; **storm·i·est**) **1** (used for talking about very bad weather, with strong winds, heavy rain, etc.): *a stormy night* **2** involving a lot of angry arguments and strong feeling: *a stormy debate in Congress* ◇ *a stormy relationship*

★**sto·ry** /ˈstɔri/ ***noun*** [C] (*pl.* **sto·ries**) **1** a description of people and events that are not real: *He always reads the children a bedtime story.* ◇ *a detective/ghost/love story* ◇ *She told us a story about an old woman who lived in a shoe.* **2** a description of true events that happened in the past: *the story of the American Revolution* ◇ *his life story* **3** an article or report in a newspaper or magazine: *The plane crash was the front-page story in most newspapers.* **4** one floor or level of a building: *The building will be ten stories high.* ◇ *a two-story house*

**sto·ry·book** /ˈstɔribʊk/ ***noun*** [C] (used in compounds) a book of stories for children: *a picture in a storybook* ◇ *storybook adventures* (= like the ones in stories for children) ◇ *storybook wedding/romance*

**sto·ry·tell·er** /ˈstɔriˌtɛlər/ ***noun*** [C] a person who tells or writes stories ▶ **sto·ry·tell·ing** ***noun*** [U]: *She has a gift for storytelling.* ◇ *storytelling sessions*

**stout**[1] /staʊt/ ***adj.*** (**stout·er**; **stout·est**) **1** (used about a person) rather fat **2** (usually before a noun) strong and thick: *a stout pair of shoes* ◇ *a stout rope/stick* **3** (usually before a noun) (*formal*) brave and determined: *He put up a stout defense in court.*

**stout**[2] /staʊt/ ***noun*** [C,U] a strong dark beer made with malt or barley

**stoves**

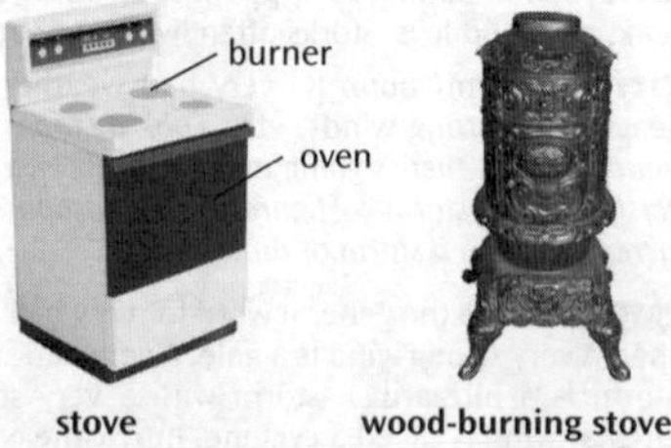


**stove** **wood-burning stove**

★**stove** /stoʊv/ ***noun*** [C] **1** (*also* **range**) a piece of equipment in a kitchen that uses electricity or natural gas to heat and cook food. A stove has an oven for baking things and a flat top for cooking food in pots and pans. **2** a type of heater. A stove is a closed metal box in which you burn wood, coal, etc.: *a wood-burning stove*

**stove·top** /ˈstoʊvtɑp/ ***noun*** [C] the top part of a stove where food is cooked in pans on burners: *an electric/a gas stovetop*

**stow** /stoʊ/ ***verb*** [T] **stow sth (away)** to put sth away in a particular place until it is needed

**stow·a·way** /ˈstoʊəweɪ/ ***noun*** [C] a person who hides in a ship or an airplane so that he/she can travel without paying

**strad·dle** /ˈstrædl/ ***verb*** [T] **1** (used about a person) to sit or stand with one leg on each side of sth: *to straddle a chair* **2** (used about a building, bridge, etc.) to be on both sides of sth: *The park straddles the border between the two states.*

**strag·gle** /ˈstrægl/ ***verb*** [I] to walk, etc. slowly and in a disorganized way, not together with the rest of a group: *By 5:00, most of the tour group had straggled back to the bus.*

**strag·gly** /ˈstrægli/ ***adj.*** growing or hanging in a way that does not look neat or attractive: *a thin woman with grey, straggly hair*

★**straight**[1] /streɪt/ ***adj.*** **1** not bent or curved: *a straight line* ◇ *straight hair* (= not curly) ◇ *straight teeth* (= in even rows) ◇ *Keep your back straight!* ➲ pictures at **hair** and **line**. **2** (not before a noun) in a level or upright position: *That picture isn't straight.* **3** honest, truthful and direct: *Politicians never give straight answers.* ◇ *Are you being straight with me?* **4** (*also formal* **heterosexual**) sexually attracted to people of the other sex (= a man to a woman or a woman to a man) ➲ Look also at **gay**. **5** (used between a number and a noun) happening or coming one after another; in a row: *The Sharks celebrated four straight wins on the road last night.* ◇ *Inflation has fallen for the fifth straight month.* **6** (used about an alcoholic drink) on its own, without ice, water or any other liquid: *a straight Scotch*

IDM **earn/get straight A's** to receive the grade "A" (= the best grade) in all of your classes

**get sth straight** to make sure that you understand sth completely: *Let's get this straight. You're sure that you've never seen this man before?*

**keep a straight face** to stop yourself from smiling or laughing

**set the record straight** → RECORD[1]

★**straight**[2] /streɪt/ ***adv.*** **1** in a straight line: *Go straight for about two miles until you come to some traffic lights.* ◇ *He was looking straight ahead.* ◇ *to sit up straight* (= with a straight back) **2** without any delay; directly: *I want you to come straight home after school.* ◇ *to walk straight past sb/sth* **3** happening or coming one after another, without stopping: *Jody slept for twelve hours straight last night.* **4** (*informal*) in an honest and direct way: *Tell me straight, Doctor – how bad is the cancer?*

**straight·en** /ˈstreɪtn/ ***verb*** **1** [I,T] **straighten (sth) (up/out)** to become straight or to make sth straight: *The road straightens at the bottom of the hill.* ◇ *to straighten your tie* **2** [T] **straighten sth**

(**up**) to make sth, e.g. a room or a desk, clean and neat: *to straighten up the living room*
PHR V **straighten sth out** to remove the confusion or difficulties from a situation
**straighten up** to stand up straight and tall

**straight·for·ward** /ˌstreɪt'fɔrwərd/ ***adj.*** **1** easy to do or understand; simple: *straightforward instructions* **2** honest and open: *a straightforward person*

**ˌstraight 'shooter** ***noun*** [C] (*informal*) a person who is very direct and always says what he/she thinks ▸ **ˌstraight-'shooting *adj.***

★**strain¹** /streɪn/ ***noun*** **1** [C,U] the condition of being pulled or stretched too tightly: *The rope finally broke under the strain.* ◇ (*figurative*) *The war has put a great strain on the country's economy.* **2** [C,U] a state of worry and tension, or something that causes this: *to be under a lot of strain at work* ◇ *Mom's illness put a strain on the whole family.* ◇ *the strain of being a manager* **3** [C,U] an injury to part of your body that is caused by using it too much: *a back strain* **4** [C] one type of plant, animal etc. which has particular characteristics: *a new strain of the bacteria which is resistant to medication*

**strain²** /streɪn/ ***verb*** **1** [I,T] to make a great effort to do sth: *I had to strain to hear what they were saying.* **2** [T] to injure a part of your body by using it too much: *Don't read in the dark. You'll strain your eyes.* ◇ *to strain a muscle* **3** [T] to put a lot of pressure on sth: *Money problems have strained their relationship.* **4** [T] to separate a solid and a liquid by pouring them into a special container with small holes in it

**strained** /streɪnd/ ***adj.*** not natural or friendly: *Relations between the two countries are strained.*

**strait** /streɪt/ ***noun*** [C] a narrow area of water that joins two larger seas or oceans: *the Bering Strait*

**strait·jack·et** /'streɪtdʒækət/ ***noun*** [C] a type of strong jacket that is used to stop mental patients, etc. from moving their arms so that they cannot hurt themselves or other people

**strait·laced** /ˌstreɪt'leɪst/ ***adj.*** having very strict or old-fashioned ideas about people's moral behavior

**strand** /strænd/ ***noun*** [C] a single piece of cotton, wool, hair, etc.

**strand·ed** /'strændəd/ ***adj.*** left in a place that you cannot get away from, e.g. because you have no money or transportation

★**strange** /streɪndʒ/ ***adj.*** **1** unusual or unexpected: *A very strange thing happened to me on the way home.* ◇ *a strange noise* ◇ *She usually wears jeans. It's really strange to see her in a skirt.* **2** that you have not seen, visited, met, etc. before: *a strange town* ◇ *My mother told me not to talk to strange men.*

NOTE We do not use **strange** to talk about a person or thing that comes from a different country. ➲ Look at **foreign**.

▸ **strange·ly *adv.***: *The streets were strangely quiet.* ◇ *Tim's been acting strangely these days.* ▸ **strange·ness *noun*** [U]

**strang·er** /'streɪndʒər/ ***noun*** [C] **1** a person that you do not know: *I had to ask a complete stranger to help me with my suitcase.*

NOTE We do not use **stranger** to talk about a person who comes from a different country. ➲ Look at **foreigner**.

**2** a person who is in a place that he/she does not know: *I'm a stranger to this part of the country.*

**stran·gle** /'stræŋgl/ ***verb*** [T] **1** to kill sb by squeezing his/her neck or throat with your hands, a rope, etc. **2** to prevent sth from developing

**stran·gle·hold** /'stræŋglhoʊld/ ***noun*** [sing.] **1** a strong hold around sb's neck that makes it difficult for him/her to breathe: *Both arms were around his neck in a stranglehold.* **2** complete control over sth that makes it impossible for it to grow or develop well: *The company now had **a stranglehold on** the market.*

**stran·gu·la·tion** /ˌstræŋgyə'leɪʃn/ ***noun*** [U] **1** the act of killing sb by squeezing the throat tightly; the state of being killed in this way: *to die of slow strangulation* **2** the act of preventing sth from growing or developing: *the strangulation of the human spirit*

**strap¹** /stræp/ ***noun*** [C] a long narrow piece of leather, cloth, plastic, etc. that you use for carrying sth or for keeping sth in position: *a dress with thin shoulder straps*

**strap²** /stræp/ ***verb*** [T] (**strapped**; **strap·ping**) to keep sb/sth in position by using a strap or straps: *The fighter pilot was securely strapped into the cockpit.*

**strap·less** /'stræpləs/ ***adj.*** (used especially about a dress or bra) without STRAPS¹

**strapped** /stræpt/ ***adj.*** having very little money: *The local school system is strapped for cash.* ◇ *financially strapped state governments*

**strap·ping** /'stræpɪŋ/ ***adj.*** (only *before* a noun) (*informal*) (used about people) big, tall and strong: *a strapping young man*

**stra·ta** /'streɪt̬ə; 'stræ-/ *plural of* STRATUM

**stra·te·gic** /strə'tidʒɪk/ ***adj.*** **1** helping you to achieve a plan; giving you an advantage **2** connected with a country's plans to achieve success in a war or in its defense system: *strategic planning* **3** (used about bombs and other weapons) intended to hit places of military or economic importance in an enemy country ▸ **stra·te·gi·cal·ly** /-kli/ ***adv.***: *The island is strategically important.*

**strat·e·gist** /'stræt̬ədʒɪst/ ***noun*** [C] a person who is skilled at planning things, especially military activities: *a military strategist* ◇ *a brilliant political strategist*

★**strat·e·gy** /'stræt̬ədʒi/ ***noun*** (*pl.* **strat·e·gies**) **1** [C] a plan that you use in order to achieve sth: *a strategy to reduce inflation* **2** [U] the act of planning how to do or achieve sth: *military strategy*

**strat·i·fied** /'stræt̬əfaɪd/ ***adj.*** **1** arranged in layers (strata): *stratified rock* **2** arranged in different levels or classes: *a highly stratified society*

**strat·o·sphere** /'stræt̬əsfɪr/ ***noun*** **the stratosphere** [sing.] the layer of the earth's atmosphere between about 10 and 50 kilometers above the surface of the earth
IDM **in/into the stratosphere** at or to an

S

extremely high level: *The technology boom sent share prices into the stratosphere.*

**stra·tum** /'streɪṭəm; 'stræ-/ ***noun*** [C] (*pl.* **stra·ta** /'streɪṭə; 'stræ-/) **1** a layer or set of layers of rock, soil, etc.: *a thick stratum of flint/gravel* ◇ *geological/limestone strata* **2** (*written*) a class in a society: *people from all social strata*

**straw** /strɔ/ ***noun*** **1** [U] the long stems of plants (e.g. wheat) that are dried and then used for animals to sleep on or for making baskets, mats, etc.: *a straw hat* **2** [C] one piece of STRAW (1) **3** [C] a long plastic or paper tube that you can drink through

IDM **draw straws** → DRAW[1]

**the last/final straw** an extra problem that is added to a difficult or unpleasant situation, and which makes you think you cannot tolerate the situation any longer

**straw·ber·ry** /'strɔˌbɛri/ ***noun*** [C] (*pl.* **straw·ber·ries**) a small soft red fruit with small yellow seeds on the outside: *fresh strawberries* ◇ *strawberry jam* ➲ picture on study page **A28-29**.

**ˌstrawberry 'blond** (*also* **ˌstrawberry 'blonde**) ***adj.*** (used about a person's hair) of a reddish yellow color ▸ **ˌstrawberry 'blond** ***noun*** [C]

**'straw poll** (*also* **'straw vote**) ***noun*** [C] an occasion when a number of people are asked in an informal way to give their opinion about sth or to say how they are likely to vote in an election

**stray[1]** /streɪ/ ***verb*** [I] **1** to go away from the place where you should be for no particular reason: *The children had strayed from their mother in the grocery store.* **2** not keeping to the subject you should be thinking about or discussing: *The discussion strayed from the official agenda.*

**stray[2]** /streɪ/ ***adj.*** (only *before* a noun) accidentally lost or separated, or going in the wrong direction: *a stray dog* ◇ *She was killed by a stray bullet.*

**stray[3]** /streɪ/ ***noun*** [C] (*pl.* **strays**) an animal that is lost from home

S

**streak[1]** /strik/ ***noun*** [C] **1 streak (of sth)** a thin line or mark: *The cat had brown fur with streaks of white in it.* **2** a part of a person's character that sometimes shows in the way he/she behaves: *a selfish streak* **3** a continuous period of good or bad luck in a sports game: *a winning/losing streak*

**streak[2]** /strik/ ***verb*** [I] to run or move very fast

**streak·er** ***noun*** [C] a person who runs through a public place with no clothes on as a way of getting attention

★**stream[1]** /strim/ ***noun*** [C] **1** a small river **2** the constant movement of a liquid or gas: *a stream of cool air coming from the vent* **3** a constant movement of people or things: *a stream of traffic* **4** a large number of things which happen one after another: *a stream of letters/telephone calls/questions*

**stream[2]** /strim/ ***verb*** [I] **1** (used about a liquid, gas or light) to flow in large amounts: *Blood was streaming from the cut on his forehead.* ◇ *Sunlight was streaming in through the windows.* **2** (used about people or things) to move somewhere in a continuous flow: *People were streaming out of the stadium.*

**stream·er** /'strimər/ ***noun*** [C] a long piece of colored paper that you use for decorating a room before a party, etc.

**stream·line** /'strimlaɪn/ ***verb*** [T] **1** to give a vehicle, etc. a long smooth shape so that it will move easily through air or water **2** to make an organization, process, etc. work better by making it simpler and more efficient: *The company has decided to streamline its production processes.*

**ˌstream of 'consciousness** ***noun*** [U] a continuous flow of ideas, thoughts, and feelings, as they are experienced by a person; a style of writing that expresses this without using the usual methods of description and conversation: *Woolf's use of stream of consciousness in her novel "Mrs Dalloway"*

★**street** /strit/ ***noun*** [C] **1** a road in a town or city that has stores, houses, etc. on one or both sides: *to walk along/down the street* ◇ *to cross the street* ◇ *Don't stand in the street – you'll get hit by a car!* ◇ *a narrow/wide street* ◇ *a street map* ➲ Look at the notes at **avenue** and **road**. **2 Street** (*abbr.* **St.**) [sing.] (used in names of streets): *to go shopping on Main Street* ◇ *264 Chestnut St.*

IDM **on the street(s) 1** in public; among most people: *additional government funding to put more police on the streets* ◇ *the most common opinion on the street* **2** without a home or job: *teenagers living on the streets*

**street·car** /'stritkɑr/ (*also* **trolley**) ***noun*** [C] a type of city bus that uses electricity and runs on metal tracks in the street

**street·light** /'stritlaɪt/ ***noun*** [C] a light at the top of a tall post in the street

**street·wise** /'stritwaɪz/ (*also* **street·smart** /'stritsmɑrt/) ***adj.*** (*informal*) having the knowledge and experience that is needed to deal with the difficulties and dangers of life in a big city: ◇ *Kids seem much more streetwise these days.*

★**strength** /strɛŋkθ/ ***noun*** **1** [U] the quality of being physically strong; the amount of this quality that you have: *a woman of great physical strength* ◇ *He pulled with all his strength, but the rock would not move.* **2** [U] the ability of an object to hold heavy weights or not to break or be damaged easily: *All our suitcases are tested for strength before they leave the factory.* **3** [U] the quality of being powerful: *America's economic strength* ◇ *extra-strength pain relief capsules* **4** [U] how strong a feeling or opinion is: *I didn't realize the strength of her hatred of politics.* **5** [C,U] the good qualities and abilities of a person or thing: *His greatest strength is his ability to communicate with people.* ◇ *the strengths and weaknesses of a plan*

IDM **on the strength of sth** as a result of information, advice, etc.: *Many people voted for him on the strength of his performance in the debates.*

**streng·then** /'strɛŋkθən/ ***verb*** [I,T] to become stronger or to make sth stronger: *exercises to strengthen your muscles* ◇ *Support for the campaign seems to be strengthening.*

**stren·u·ous** /'strɛnyuəs/ ***adj.*** needing or using a lot of effort or energy: *You should avoid strenuous physical exercise for a while.* ▸ **stren·u·ous·ly** ***adv.***

**strep throat** /ˌstrɛp 'θroʊt/ ***noun*** [U] (*informal*) an infection of the throat

★**stress**[1] /strɛs/ ***noun*** **1** [C,U] a state of worry and tension that is caused by difficulties in your life, having too much work, etc.: *He's been under a lot of stress since his wife went into the hospital.* ◇ *The doctor told her that she was suffering from stress.* ◇ *the stresses and strains of life in a big city* **2** [U] **stress (on sth)** the special force or emphasis that you give to sth because you think it is important: *There should be more stress on learning foreign languages in schools.* **3** [U] the force or emphasis that you put on a word or part of a word when you say it: *In the word "dictionary," the main stress is on the first syllable.* **4** [C,U] **stress (on sth)** a physical force that may cause sth to bend or break

★**stress**[2] /strɛs/ ***verb*** **1** [T] to give sth special force or emphasis because you think it is important: *The diplomat stressed the need for a peaceful solution.* **2** [I,T] **stress (sb) (out)** (*informal*) to feel or cause sb to feel worried and unable to relax: *Ben's really stressing over his biology exam.*

**stressed** /strɛst/ (*also* ˌ**stressed** ˈ**out**) ***adj.*** (*informal*) feeling worried and unable to relax: *I'm totally stressed about my final exam.*

★**stress·ful** /ˈstrɛsfl/ ***adj.*** causing STRESS[1] (1): *a stressful job*

★**stretch**[1] /strɛtʃ/ ***verb*** **1** [I,T] to pull sth so that it becomes longer or wider; to become longer or wider in this way: *The artist stretched the canvas tightly over the frame.* ◇ *My T-shirt stretched out of shape when I washed it.* **2** [I,T] to push out your arms, legs, etc. as far as possible: *He got out of bed and stretched before going into the bathroom.* ◇ *She stretched out her arm to take the book.* **3** [I] (used about a piece of land or water, etc.) to cover a large area: *The long white beaches stretch for miles along the coast.* **4** [I,T] to last or make sth last a long time: *The heat wave stretched into early September.* ◇ *We'll have to think of a way to stretch our food budget.*

IDM **stretch your legs** to go for a walk after sitting down for a long time

PHR V **stretch out** to relax by lying down with all your body flat: *to stretch out in front of the fire*

**stretch**[2] /strɛtʃ/ ***noun*** **1** [C] **stretch (of sth)** an area of land or water: *a beautiful stretch of coastline* **2** [C, usually sing.] the act of STRETCHING[1] (2)

IDM **at a stretch** without stopping: *six hours at a stretch*

**not by any stretch of the imagination** (used to say strongly that sth is not true, even if you try to imagine or believe it): *She could not, by any stretch of the imagination, be called beautiful.*

**the home stretch** → HOME[2]

**stretch·er** /ˈstrɛtʃər/ ***noun*** [C] a piece of cloth supported by two poles that is used for carrying a person who has been injured in an accident, etc.

ˌ**stretch** ˈ**limo** ***noun*** [C] (*pl.* ˌ**stretch** ˈ**limos**) (*also formal* ˌ**stretch** ˈ**limousine**) a very large comfortable car that has been made longer so that it can have extra seats

ˈ**stretch mark** ***noun*** [C] the marks that are left on a person's skin after it has been stretched, particularly after a woman has been pregnant

**stretch·y** /ˈstrɛtʃi/ ***adj.*** (used especially about clothing or fabric) that can easily be made longer or wider without tearing or breaking: *a stretchy skirt*

**strew** /stru/ ***verb*** [T] (*pt* **strewed**, *pp* **strewed** or **strewn**) **1** (usually passive) to cover a surface with things: *Clothes were strewn across the floor.* ◇ *The streets were strewn with corpses.* ◇ (*figurative*) *The way ahead is strewn with difficulties.* **2** to be spread or lying over a surface: *Leaves strewed the path.*

**strick·en** /ˈstrɪkən/ ***adj.*** (*formal*) **1 stricken (with/by sth)** seriously affected by an unpleasant feeling or disease or by a difficult situation: *She raised her stricken face and begged for help.* ◇ *Whole villages were stricken with the disease.* ◇ *He was stricken by a heart attack on his fiftieth birthday.* ◇ *We went to the aid of the stricken boat.* **2** (in compounds) seriously affected by the thing mentioned: *grief-stricken relatives* ➲ Look also at **panic-stricken** and **poverty-stricken**.

★**strict** /strɪkt/ ***adj.*** **1** not allowing people to break rules or behave badly: *Tom's always very strict with his children.* ◇ *a strict teacher* ◇ *I went to a very strict school.* **2** that must be obeyed completely: *I gave her strict instructions to be home before 9:00.* **3** exactly correct; precise: *a strict interpretation of the law*

★**strict·ly** /ˈstrɪkli/ ***adv.*** **1** in a strict way: *Speed limits are strictly enforced in this county.* **2 strictly for sb/sth** only for sb/sth, and nobody/nothing else: *Mom's cell phone is strictly for business calls.*

IDM **strictly speaking** to be exactly correct or precise: *Strictly speaking, the tomato is not a vegetable. It's a fruit.*

**stride**[1] /straɪd/ ***verb*** [I] (*pt* **strode** /stroʊd/; *pp* **strid·den** /ˈstrɪdn/) to walk with long steps, often because you are feeling very confident or determined: *He strode up to the house and knocked on the door.*

**stride**[2] /straɪd/ ***noun*** [C] a long step

IDM **make great strides** to make very quick progress

**take sth in stride** to deal with a new or difficult situation easily and without worrying

**strife** /straɪf/ ***noun*** [U] (*formal*) angry or violent disagreement between two people or groups of people: *civil/industrial/political strife* ◇ *The country was torn apart by strife.* SYN **conflict**

★**strike**[1] /straɪk/ ***noun*** [C] **1** a period of time when people refuse to go to work, usually because they want more money or better working conditions: *a one-day strike* ◇ *to go on strike for better working conditions* ◇ *The workers have been on strike for two weeks now.* **2** a sudden military attack, especially by aircraft **3** (in baseball) an act of trying but failing to hit a ball that was thrown, or a ball that was thrown correctly but not hit ➲ Look at the note at **baseball**. **4 a strike against sb/sth** an unfavorable quality or a disadvantage that sb/sth has: *These kids already have two strikes against them: they live in a dangerous neighborhood, and their parents aren't home enough.*

★**strike**[2] /straɪk/ ***verb*** (*pt, pp* **struck** /strʌk/)

➤ HIT SB/STH **1** [T] (*formal*) to hit: *The stone struck me on my face.* ◇ *to strike sb with your hand* ◇ *The boat struck a rock and began to sink.*

NOTE In these three examples it is more common to use the word **hit**: *The stone hit me on my face,*

S

but if you are talking about lightning you must use **strike**: *The building had been struck by lightning.*

**2** [I,T] to attack sb/sth suddenly: *The enemy aircraft struck just after 2 a.m.* ◇ *The earthquake struck Northridge in 1994.*
➤ THOUGHT/IDEA/IMPRESSION **3** [T] **strike sb (as sth)** to give sb a particular impression, often a strong one: *Does anything here strike you as unusual?* **4** [T] (used about a thought or an idea) to come suddenly into sb's mind: *It suddenly struck me that she would be the ideal person for the job.*
➤ OF CLOCK **5** [I,T] (used about a clock) to ring a bell so that people know what time it is: *The church clock struck three.*
➤ GOLD/OIL, ETC. **6** [T] to discover gold, oil, etc.
➤ WORKERS **7** [I] to go on STRIKE[1] (1): *The workers voted to strike for more money.*
IDM **strike a balance (between A and B)** to find a middle way between two extremes
**strike a deal (with sb)** to make an agreement with sb
**strike a chord (with sb)** to say or do sth that makes other people feel sympathy, excitement, etc.
PHR V **strike back** to attack sb/sth that has attacked you: *The president threatened to strike back if the rebels attacked the military base.*
**strike out** (*informal*) to be unsuccessful at sth that you are trying to do: *The company struck out with its first attempt to produce a laptop computer, but its latest product looks like a winner.*
**strike (sb) out** (in baseball) to try to hit the ball unsuccessfully three times, so that you are not allowed to try any longer, or to cause sb to do this
**strike up sth (with sb)** to start a conversation or friendship with sb

**strike·out** /ˈstraɪkaʊt/ **noun** [C] (*sports*) (in baseball) a situation in which the player who is supposed to be hitting the ball has to stop because he/she has tried to hit the ball three times and missed, or has failed to try to hit good PITCHES[2] (1) three times

S

**strik·er** /ˈstraɪkər/ **noun** [C] **1** a person who is on STRIKE[1] (1) **2** = FORWARD[4]

**strik·ing** /ˈstraɪkɪŋ/ **adj.** very noticeable; making a strong impression: *There was a striking similarity between the two men.* ▸ **strik·ing·ly adv.**: *strikingly attractive*

★**string[1]** /strɪŋ/ **noun**
➤ FOR TYING **1** [C,U] the thin cord that you use for tying things, etc.; a piece of this: *I need some string to tie around this box.* ◇ *a ball of string* ◇ *a balloon on the end of a string* ➲ picture at **knot**.
➤ MUSICAL INSTRUMENTS **2** [C] a piece of thin wire, etc. on a musical instrument: *A guitar has six strings.* ➲ picture at **guitar**. **3 the strings** [pl.] the musical instruments in an orchestra, etc. that have strings ➲ picture at **violin**.
➤ THINGS JOINED **4** [C] **a string of sth** a line of things that are joined together on the same piece of thread: *a string of pearls*
➤ SERIES **5** [C] **a string of sth** a series of people, things or events that follow one after another: *a string of visitors* ◇ *a string of complaints*
IDM **(with) no strings attached** with no special conditions: *We will send you a free copy of the magazine, with no strings attached.*
**pull strings** → PULL[1]

**string[2]** /strɪŋ/ **verb** [T] (*pt, pp* **strung** /strʌŋ/) **string sth (up)** to hang up a line of things with a piece of string, etc.: *Colored lights were strung up along the front of the hotel.*
PHR V **string sb along** (*informal*) to allow sb to believe sth that is not true, for example that you love him/her, intend to help him/her, etc.: *She has no intention of giving you a divorce; she's just stringing you along.*
**string sb/sth out** to make people or things form a line with spaces between each person or thing
**string sth together** to put words or phrases together to make a sentence, speech, etc.
**string sb up** (*informal*) to kill sb by hanging him/her, especially illegally: *If I ever find out who did this, I'll string them up.*

ˈ**string bean** (*also* ˈ**green bean**) **noun** [C] a long, thin green vegetable that is cooked and eaten when the seeds inside are still small

**strin·gent** /ˈstrɪndʒənt/ **adj.** (used about a law, rule, etc.) very severe and strict

**string·er** /ˈstrɪŋər/ **noun** [C] (*informal*) a journalist who is not on the regular staff of a newspaper, but who often supplies stories for it

**string·y** /ˈstrɪŋi/ **adj.** **1** (used about a person's hair) long and thin and looking as if it has not been washed **2** (used about food) containing long thin pieces like string and difficult to chew: *tough, stringy meat* **3** (used about a person or part of the body) thin so that you can see the muscles: *a stringy neck*

★**strip[1]** /strɪp/ **noun** [C] a long narrow piece of sth: *a strip of paper* ◇ *a strip of sandy beach*

★**strip[2]** /strɪp/ **verb** (**strip·ping**; **stripped**) **1** [I,T] to take off your clothes; to take off sb else's clothes: *The doctor asked him to strip to the waist* (= above his waist). ◇ *I was stripped and searched at the airport by two customs officers.* **2** [T] **strip sb/sth (of sth)** to take sth away from sb/sth: *They stripped the house of all its furniture.* ◇ *The judge had been stripped of most of his power.* **3** [T] **strip sth (off)** to remove sth that is covering a surface: *to strip the paint off a door*

**stripe** /straɪp/ **noun** [C] a long narrow band of color: *Zebras have black and white stripes.* ➲ Picture on study page **A30**. ➲ Look at **Stars and Stripes**.

**striped** /straɪpt; ˈstraɪpəd/ **adj.** having stripes: *a red-and-white striped dress* ➲ Picture on study page **A30**.

**strip·per** /ˈstrɪpər/ **noun** [C] a person whose job is to take off his/her clothes in order to entertain people

ˌ**strip ˈpoker** **noun** [U] a form of poker in which a player with losing cards has to take off a layer of clothing

ˈ**strip search** **noun** [C] an act of searching a person for illegal drugs, weapons, etc., e.g. at an airport or in a prison, after he/she has been made to take off all his/her clothes ▸ ˈ**strip-search** **verb** [T]

**strip·tease** /ˈstrɪptiz/ **noun** [C,U] entertainment in which sb takes off his/her clothes, usually to music

**strive** /straɪv/ **verb** [I] (*pt* **strove** /stroʊv/; *pp* **striv·en** /ˈstrɪvn/) (*formal*) **strive (for sth)** to try very hard to do or get sth: *The company always strives to satisfy its customers.*

**strobe** /stroʊb/ (*also* ˈ**strobe light**) ***noun*** [C] a bright light that flashes rapidly on and off, used especially at discos and nightclubs

**strode** *past tense of* STRIDE[1]

★**stroke[1]** /stroʊk/ ***verb*** [T] to move your hand gently over sb/sth, in a loving way: *She stroked his hair affectionately.*

★**stroke[2]** /stroʊk/ ***noun*** **1** [C] one of the movements that you make when you are writing or painting: *a brush stroke* **2** [C] a sudden illness which attacks the brain and can leave a person unable to move part of his/her body, speak clearly, etc.: *to have/suffer a stroke* **3** [C] one of the movements that you make when you are swimming, rowing, playing tennis, etc.: *a forehand stroke* (= in tennis, etc.) **4** [C,U] one of the styles of swimming: *backstroke* ➲ Look at **crawl**.

IDM **a stroke of luck** something lucky that happens unexpectedly

**stroll** /stroʊl/ ***verb*** [I] to take a slow walk for pleasure: *to stroll along the beach* ▶ **stroll** ***noun*** [C]: *to take a stroll through the park*

**stroller**

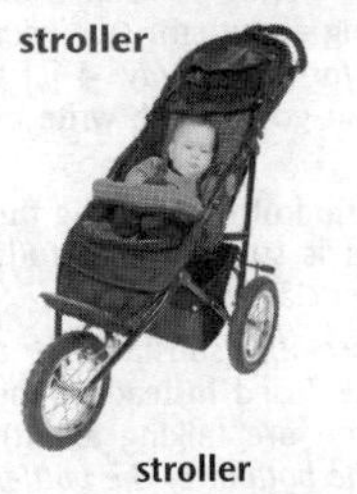

stroller

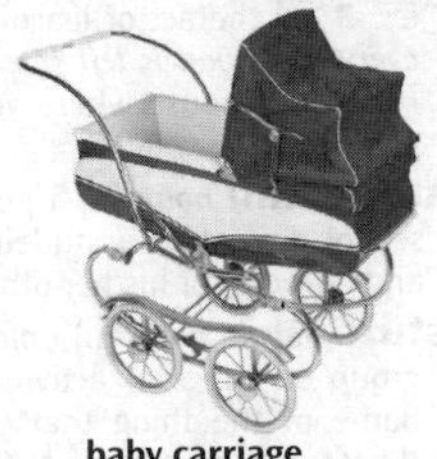

baby carriage

**stroll·er** /ˈstroʊlər/ ***noun*** [C] a type of chair with three or four wheels that you can push a small child in as you walk along

★**strong[1]** /strɔŋ/ ***adj.***

➤ HAVING PHYSICAL POWER **1** (used about a person) physically powerful; able to lift or carry heavy things: *I need someone strong to help me move this bookcase.* ◇ *to have strong arms/muscles* ➲ noun **strength** **2** (used about an object) able to hold heavy weights; not easily broken or damaged: *That chair isn't strong enough for you to stand on.* ◇ *a strong piece of rope* **3** powerful and moving quickly: *strong winds*

➤ OPINION/BELIEF/FEELING **4** intense; felt deeply: *There was strong opposition to the idea.* ◇ *strong support for the new plan* ◇ *He has strong views on the subject* (= he will not change them easily). ◇ *strong feelings*

➤ LIKELY TO SUCCEED **5** powerful and likely to succeed: *She's a strong candidate for the job.*

➤ EASY TO SEE/HEAR/FEEL/SMELL **6** (used about a smell, taste, etc.) powerful and intense: *a strong smell of garlic* ◇ *strong coffee* ◇ *a strong drink* (= with a lot of alcohol in it)

➤ NUMBER **7** (used after a noun) having a particular number of people: *The army was 50,000 strong.*

**strong[2]** /strɔŋ/ ***adv.***

IDM **be going strong** (*informal*) to be continuing, even after a long time: *The company was formed in 1851 and is still going strong.*

**strong·hold** /ˈstrɔŋhoʊld/ ***noun*** [C] **1** an area in which there is a lot of support for a particular belief or group of people, especially a political party: *a Republican stronghold/a stronghold of Republicanism* ◇ *The college is a stronghold of the child-centered approach to teaching.* **2** a castle or a place that is strongly built and difficult to attack: *Troops surrounded the mountain stronghold of the guerrillas.*

★**strong·ly** /ˈstrɔŋli/ ***adv.*** very much; to a great degree: *The directors are strongly opposed to the idea.* ◇ *to feel very strongly about sth*

ˌ**strong-ˈminded** ***adj.*** having strong opinions that are not easily influenced by what other people think or say: *My mother was a very strong-minded woman who always got her own way.* SYN **determined**

ˌ**strong-ˈwilled** ***adj.*** determined to do what you want to do, even if other people advise you not to

**strove** *past tense of* STRIVE

**struck** *past tense, past participle of* STRIKE[2]

**struc·tur·al·ism** /ˈstrʊktʃərəlɪzəm/ ***noun*** [U] (in literature, language and social science) a theory that considers any text as a structure whose various parts only have meaning when they are considered in relation to each other ▶ **struc·tur·al·ist** ***noun*** [C], ***adj.***: *a structuralist critic/approach*

★**struc·ture[1]** /ˈstrʌktʃər/ ***noun*** **1** [C,U] the way that the parts of sth are put together or organized: *the structure of the brain* ◇ *the political and social structure of a country* **2** [C] a building or sth that has been built or made from a number of parts: *a two-story wooden structure* ▶ **struc·tur·al** /ˈstrʌktʃərəl/ ***adj.***: *Several windows were broken in the explosion but there was no structural damage* (= no damage to the walls/floors).

**struc·ture[2]** /ˈstrʌktʃər/ ***verb*** [T] to arrange sth in an organized way: *a carefully structured English course*

**stru·del** /ˈstrudl; ˈʃtru-/ ***noun*** [C,U] a sweet dish made from pieces of fruit, especially apple, rolled in thin pastry and baked

★**strug·gle[1]** /ˈstrʌgl/ ***verb*** [I] **1** to try very hard to do sth although it is difficult: *Maria was struggling with her English homework.* ◇ *We struggled up the hill with our heavy suitcases.* **2** to make violent movements when you are trying to escape from sb/sth: *He shouted and struggled, but he couldn't get free.*

★**strug·gle[2]** /ˈstrʌgl/ ***noun*** [C] **1** a fight: *All countries should join together in the struggle against terrorism.* **2** [usually sing.] a great effort: *After a long struggle, she finally managed to graduate.*

**strum** /strʌm/ ***verb*** [I,T] (**strum<u>m</u>ing**; **strum<u>m</u>ed**) to play a guitar by moving your hand up and down over the strings

**strung** *past tense, past participle of* STRING[2]

ˌ**strung ˈout** ***adj.*** (*slang*) **1 strung out (on sth)** strongly affected by an illegal drug such as heroin **2** extremely anxious and tired

**strut** /strʌt/ ***verb*** [I] (**strut<u>t</u>ing**; **strut<u>t</u>ed**) to walk in a proud way

IDM **strut your stuff** (*informal*) to proudly show your ability, especially at dancing or performing: *strutting your stuff to the latest sounds*

**strych·nine** /ˈstrɪknaɪn; -nən; -nin/ **noun** [U] a poisonous substance used in very small amounts as a medicine

**stub**[1] /stʌb/ **noun** [C] **1** a short piece of sth, such as a pencil, that remains after the rest of it has been used **2** the part of a ticket, check, etc. that you can keep as a record of payment

**stub**[2] /stʌb/ **verb** [T] (**stub·bing; stubbed**)
IDM **stub your toe (against/on sth)** to hurt your toe by accident by hitting it against sth hard: *She stubbed her toe on the step.*
PHRV **stub sth out** to stop a cigarette, etc. from burning by pressing the end against sth hard: *He stubbed out his cigarette in the ashtray.*

**stub·ble** /ˈstʌbl/ **noun** [U] **1** the lower short stiff part of the stems of crops such as wheat that are left in the ground after the top part has been cut and collected **2** the short stiff hairs that grow on a man's face when he has not shaved recently ➲ picture at **beard**

**stub·born** /ˈstʌbərn/ **adj.** not wanting to do what other people want you to do; refusing to change your plans or decisions: *She's too stubborn to apologize.* ◇ *a stubborn refusal* ▸ **stub·born·ly** **adv.** ▸ **stub·born·ness** **noun** [U]

**stub·by** /ˈstʌbi/ **adj.** (**stub·bi·er**; **stub·bi·est**) (usually before a noun) short and thick: *stubby fingers*

**stuc·co** /ˈstʌkoʊ/ **noun** [U] a type of plaster that is used for covering ceilings and the outside walls of buildings ▸ **stuc·coed** **adj.**: *a stuccoed house/wall*

**stuck**[1] *past tense, past participle of* STICK[2]

**stuck**[2] /stʌk/ **adj.** (not before a noun) **1** not able to move: *This drawer's stuck. I can't open it at all.* **2** not able to continue with an exercise, etc. because it is too difficult: *If you get stuck, ask your teacher for help.*

**ˌstuck-ˈup** **adj.** (*informal*) thinking that you are more important than other people and behaving in an unfriendly way toward them SYN **snobbish**

**stud** /stʌd/ **noun** [C] **1** [C] a small round piece of metal on the surface of sth: *a black leather jacket with studs all over it* **2** [C] (*slang*) a man who is thought to be sexually attractive and who has many relationships **3** a small round earring that you wear through a hole in your ear **4** [C,U] a horse or a number of horses or other animals that are kept for breeding young animals (of high quality): *a stud farm*

**stud·ded** /ˈstʌdəd/ **adj.** **studded with sth** covered or decorated with STUDS (1) or other small objects: *The crown is studded with diamonds.*

★**stu·dent** /ˈstudnt/ **noun** [C] a person who is studying at a school, college or university: *Julia is a medical student at Harvard.* ◇ *a part-time college student* ◇ *Ashley wasn't a very good student in high school.* ➲ Look at **graduate** and **undergraduate**.

**ˌstudent ˈbody** **noun** [C] (*pl.* **student bodies**) all the students at a school, college or university

**ˌstudent ˈteaching** **noun** [U] the part of a course for people who are training to become teachers which involves teaching classes of students ▸ **ˌstudent ˈteacher** **noun** [C]

**ˌstudent ˈunion** **noun** [C] a building where students at a university or college can go to meet socially

★**stu·di·o** /ˈstudioʊ/ **noun** [C] (*pl.* **stu·di·os**) **1** a room where an artist or photographer works **2** a room or building where television or radio programs, movies, or records are made **3** (*also* **ˌstudio aˈpartment**) an apartment with only one main room which is used as a living room and bedroom

**stu·di·ous** /ˈstudiəs/ **adj.** (*formal*) (used about a person) spending a lot of time studying

★**stud·y**[1] /ˈstʌdi/ **verb** (*pres. part.* **stud·y·ing**; *3rd person sing. pres.* **stud·ies**; *pt, pp* **stud·ied**) **1** [I,T] to spend time learning about sth: *Lawrence has been studying hard for his final exams.* ◇ *to study French in school* **2** [T] to look at sth very carefully: *to study a map*

★**stud·y**[2] /ˈstʌdi/ **noun** (*pl.* **stud·ies**) **1** [C] scientific research into a particular subject and a book or article that a person writes after studying it: *a scientific study of the causes of heart disease* **2** **studies** [pl.] a group of several related subjects that sb studies at a college or university: *She's majoring in media studies.* **3** [U] the act of learning about sth: *One hour every afternoon is left free for quiet study.* **4** [C] a room in a house where you go to read, write or study

**ˈstudy hall** **noun** [U] a period of time during the school day when a student is supposed to study and do work for his/her other classes

★**stuff**[1] /stʌf/ **noun** [U] (*informal*) a substance or a group of things or activities (used instead of the name of the thing that you are talking about): *What's that green stuff at the bottom of the bottle?* ◇ *You can just put your stuff on the chair over there.* ◇ *The hotel was great – there was a swimming pool and a game room and stuff.* ◇ *I have a whole bunch of stuff to do this weekend.*

**stuff**[2] /stʌf/ **verb** **1** [T] **stuff sth (with sth)** to fill sth with sth: *The pillow was stuffed with feathers.* **2** [T] **stuff sth into sth** to put sth into sth quickly or carelessly: *He quickly stuffed a few clothes into a suitcase.* **3** [T] **stuff yourself (with sth)** to eat a lot: *The kids have been stuffing themselves with candy and ice cream all afternoon.* **4** [T] **stuff sth (with sth)** to put a mixture of small pieces of food (stuffing) into a chicken, vegetable, etc. before you cook it: *stuffed green peppers* **5** [T] to fill the body of a dead bird or animal with special material so that it continues to look as if it is alive
IDM **be stuffed** (*informal*) to have eaten so much food that you cannot eat any more: *I can't eat another bite – I'm stuffed!*

**ˌstuffed ˈanimal** **noun** [C] a toy in the shape of an animal, that is made of soft fabric and is filled with soft material

**stuff·ing** /ˈstʌfɪŋ/ **noun** [U] **1** (*also* **dressing**) a mixture of small pieces of food that you put inside a chicken, vegetable, etc. before you cook it **2** the material that you put inside pillows, etc.: *Oh, no! My teddy bear's stuffing is coming out!*

**stuff·y** /ˈstʌfi/ **adj.** (**stuff·i·er**; **stuff·i·est**) **1** (used about a room, etc.) having air that is not fresh

**2** (*informal*) (used of a person, of behavior, etc.) formal and old-fashioned **3** if you have a stuffy nose, your nose is blocked and you are not able to breathe easily

**stum·ble** /'stʌmbl/ ***verb*** [I] **1** to hit your foot against sth when you are walking or running and almost fall down: *I stumbled as I was getting out of the boat.* **2 stumble (over sth)** to make a mistake when you are speaking, playing music, etc.: *The news anchor stumbled over the name of the Russian tennis player.*

PHR V **stumble across/on/upon sb/sth** to meet or find sb/sth by chance

**'stum·bling block** ***noun*** [C] something that causes trouble or a difficulty, so that you cannot get what you want

**stump**[1] /stʌmp/ ***noun*** [C] the part that is left after sth has been cut down, broken off, etc.: *a tree stump*

**stump**[2] /stʌmp/ ***verb*** **1** [T] (*informal*) to cause sb to be unable to answer a question or find a solution for a problem: *I was completely stumped by question 14.* **2** [I] **stump (for sb)** to give speeches in order to persuade people to vote for a particular person in an election

**'stump speech** ***noun*** [C] the speech a politician makes before an election while traveling to different places trying to get people's support: *The senator gave his standard stump speech.*

**stun** /stʌn/ ***verb*** [T] (**stun<u>n</u>ing**; **stun<u>n</u>ed**) **1** to make a person or animal unconscious or confused by hitting him/her/it on the head **2** to make a person very surprised by giving him/her some unexpected news: *His sudden death stunned his friends and colleagues.* ▶ **stunned** ***adj.***: *There was a stunned silence after Margaret announced her resignation.*

**stung** *past tense, past participle of* STING[1]

**'stun gun** ***noun*** [C] a weapon that makes a person or an animal unconscious or unable to move for a short time, usually by giving him/her/it a small electric shock

**stunk** *past participle of* STINK

**stun·ning** /'stʌnɪŋ/ ***adj.*** (*informal*) very attractive or impressive: *a stunning woman* ◇ *a stunning success*

**stunt**[1] /stʌnt/ ***noun*** [C] **1** something that you do to get people's attention: *a publicity stunt* **2** a very difficult or dangerous thing that sb does to entertain people: *His latest stunt was jumping over ten cars on his motorcycle.*

**stunt**[2] /stʌnt/ ***verb*** [T] to stop sb/sth from growing or developing properly: *A bad diet can stunt a child's growth.*

**stunt·man** /'stʌntmæn/ (*also* **stunt·wom·an** /'stʌntwʊmən/) ***noun*** [C] (*pl.* **stunt·men**; **stunt·wom·en**) a person who does a STUNT[1] (2) in a movie in the place of an actor

**stu·pe·fy** /'stupəfaɪ/ ***verb*** [T] (*pres. part.* **stu·pe·fy·ing**; *3rd person sing. pres.* **stu·pe·fies**; *pt, pp* **stu·pe·fied**) (usually passive) to surprise or shock sb; to make sb unable to think clearly: *He was stupefied by the amount they had spent.* ◇ *She was stupefied with cold.*

**stu·pen·dous** /stu'pɛndəs/ ***adj.*** very large, grand or impressive: *a stupendous achievement*

★**stu·pid** /'stupəd/ ***adj.*** **1** not intelligent; foolish: *Don't be so stupid – of course I'll help you!* ◇ *It was stupid of him to trust her.* ◇ *He was stupid to trust her.* **2** (only *before* a noun) (*informal*) (a word that shows that you do not like sb/sth): *I'm tired of hearing about his stupid car.* ▶ **stu·pid·i·ty** /stu'pɪdəṭi/ ***noun*** [U] ▶ **stu·pid·ly** ***adv.***

**stur·dy** /'stərdi/ ***adj.*** (**stur·di·er**; **stur·di·est**) strong; that will not break easily: *a sturdy chair* ▶ **stur·di·ness** ***noun*** [U]

**stut·ter** /'stʌṭər/ ***verb*** [I,T] to have difficulty when you speak, so that you keep repeating the first sound of a word ▶ **stut·ter** ***noun*** [C]: *to speak with a stutter*

**sty** /'staɪ/ ***noun*** [C] **1** (*pl.* **sties**) a place where pigs are kept SYN **pigsty** **2** (*also* **stye**) (*pl.* **sties** or **styes**) an infection of the skin above or below the eye (the eyelid) which makes it red and sore

★**style**[1] /staɪl/ ***noun*** **1** [C,U] the way that sth is done, built, etc.: *a new style of architecture* ◇ *a Japanese-style noodle restaurant* **2** [C,U] the way that sb usually writes, behaves, etc.: *Hemingway's style is very clear and simple.* ◇ *Going to nightclubs just isn't my style.* **3** [U] the state of being of very good quality in appearance or behavior: *a dress with real style* ◇ *They don't have many parties but when they do, they do it in style.* **4** [C,U] the fashion, shape or design of sth: *We stock all the newest styles.* ◇ *a hairstyle*

IDM **in style/out of style** fashionable/unfashionable: *This simple gray jacket will never go out of style.*

**style**[2] /staɪl/ ***verb*** [T] to arrange sb's hair in an attractive way

**styl·ing** /'staɪlɪŋ/ (*also* **stylin**) /-lɪn/ ***adj.*** (*slang*) fashionable and attractive SYN **cool**[1](5)

**styl·ish** /'staɪlɪʃ/ ***adj.*** fashionable and attractive

**sty·lis·tic** /staɪ'lɪstɪk/ ***adj.*** (only *before* a noun) connected with the style an artist uses in a particular piece of art, writing or music: *stylistic analysis/features/devices*

**sty·lis·tics** /staɪ'lɪstɪks/ ***noun*** [U] the study of style and the methods used in written language

**styl·ized** /'staɪəlaɪzd; 'staɪlaɪzd/ ***adj.*** drawn, written, etc. in a way that is not natural or realistic: *a stylized drawing of a house* ◇ *the highly stylized form of acting in Japanese theater*

**sty·mie** /'staɪmi/ ***verb*** [T] (*pres. part.* **sty·mie·ing** or **sty·my·ing**; *pt, pp* **sty·mied**) (usually passive) (*informal*) to prevent sb from doing sth that he/she has planned or wants to do; to prevent sth from happening: *He found himself stymied by an old opponent.* ◇ *Financial difficulties have stymied the company's growth.* SYN **foil**[2]

**Sty·ro·foam™** /'staɪrəfoʊm/ ***noun*** [U] a light, firm plastic substance that is used to stop heat from escaping or to pack things so that they do not get broken: *a Styrofoam coffee cup*

**suave** /swɑv/ ***adj.*** (usually used about a man) very polite, charming, and well behaved (sometimes too much so)

S

**sub¹** /sʌb/ ***noun*** [C] (*informal*) **1** = SUBMARINE **2** = SUBSTITUTE¹ (2)

**sub²** /sʌb/ ***verb*** [I] (**sub<u>b</u>ing**; **sub<u>b</u>ed**) (*informal*) = SUBSTITUTE² (2)

**sub·a·tom·ic** /ˌsʌbəˈtɑmɪk/ ***adj.*** (*technical*) smaller than, or found in, an atom: *subatomic particles*

**sub·com·mit·tee** /ˈsʌbkəˌmɪṭi/ ***noun*** [C, with sing. or pl. verb] a smaller committee formed from a main committee in order to study a particular subject in more detail: *the House of Representatives subcommittee on taxation*

**sub·com·pact** /ˌsʌbˈkɑmpækt/ ***noun*** [C] a small car, smaller than a COMPACT² (1)

**sub·con·scious** /ˌsʌbˈkɑnʃəs/ ***noun*** [sing.] the hidden part of your mind that can affect the way that you behave, even though you do not know it exists ▶ **sub·con·scious *adj.***: *the subconscious mind* ▶ **sub·con·scious·ly *adv.***

**sub·con·ti·nent** /ˌsʌbˈkɑntənənt; -ˈkɑntn·ənt/ ***noun*** [usually sing.] a large land mass that forms part of a continent, especially the part of Asia that includes India, Pakistan and Bangladesh: *the Indian subcontinent*

**sub·con·tract** /ˌsʌbˈkɑntrækt/ ***verb*** [T] **subcontract sth (to sb)** to pay a person or company to do some of the work that you have been given a contract to do: *We subcontracted the work to a small engineering firm.* ◇ *We subcontracted a small engineering firm to do the work.* ▶ **sub·con·tract *noun*** [C]

**sub·con·trac·tor** /ˌsʌbˈkɑntræktər/ ***noun*** [C] a person or company that does part of the work given to another person or company

**sub·cul·ture** /ˈsʌbˌkʌltʃər/ ***noun*** [C] the behavior and beliefs of a particular group of people in society that are different from those of most people: *the criminal/drug/youth subculture*

**sub·di·vide** /ˈsʌbdəvaɪd; ˌsʌbdəˈvaɪd/ ***verb*** [I,T] to divide or be divided into smaller parts

**sub·di·vi·sion** /ˈsʌbdəvɪʒn/ ***noun*** [C] an area with a lot of houses that were built at the same time, often in a similar style

**sub·due** /səbˈdu/ ***verb*** [T] to defeat or bring sb/sth under control: *to subdue a rebel army* ◇ *She tried hard to subdue her emotions.*

**sub·dued** /səbˈdud/ ***adj.*** **1** not very loud or bright: *subdued lighting* **2** (used about a person) sad or quiet

**subj.** ***abbr.*** (*written*) = SUBJECT

★**sub·ject¹** /ˈsʌbdʒɛkt; -dʒɪkt/ ***noun*** [C] **1** a person or thing that is being considered, shown or talked about: *the subject of a paper* ◇ *What are your views on this subject?* ◇ *to change the subject* (= start talking about sth else) ◇ *I tried several times to bring up the subject of money.* ◇ *the novel's controversial subject matter* **2** an area of knowledge that you study in school, college, etc.: *She's taking four subjects this semester: French, English, psychology and history.* **3** (*grammar*) the person or thing that performs the action described by the verb in a sentence: *In the sentence "The cat sat on the mat," "the cat" is the subject.*

**sub·ject²** /səbˈdʒɛkt/ ***verb***

PHR V **subject sb/sth to sth** to cause sb/sth to experience sth bad

**sub·ject³** /ˈsʌbdʒɛkt; -dʒɪkt/ ***adj.*** **subject to sth** **1** controlled or affected by sth: *Restaurants are subject to strict health regulations.* ◇ *All times listed are approximate and subject to change.* **2** depending on sth as a condition: *Construction will begin in May, subject to approval by the city council.*

**sub·jec·tive** /səbˈdʒɛktɪv/ ***adj.*** influenced by your own feelings and opinions instead of by facts alone: *a subjective interpretation of events* OPP **objective** ▶ **sub·jec·tive·ly *adv.***

**the sub·junc·tive** /səbˈdʒʌŋktɪv/ ***noun*** [sing.] (*grammar*) the form of a verb that expresses doubt, possibility, a wish, etc. in certain languages. For example, in the sentence, "I recommend that she see a doctor," "see" is in the subjunctive. ▶ **sub·junc·tive *adj.***

**sub·let** /ˈsʌblɛt/ ***verb*** [T] to rent to sb else a room, an apartment, etc. that you are renting from sb else, usually for a short period of time ▶ **sub·let *noun*** [C]: *a list of summer sublets available near campus*

**sub·lime** /səˈblaɪm/ ***adj.*** wonderful; having a quality that makes you admire it very much

**sub·lim·i·nal** /səˈblɪmənl/ ***adj.*** affecting your mind even though you are not aware of it: *subliminal advertising* ◇ *music containing subliminal messages*

**sub·ma·chine gun** /ˌsʌbməˈʃin ɡʌn/ ***noun*** [C] a light machine gun that you can hold in your hands to fire

**sub·ma·rine** /ˈsʌbmərin; ˌsʌbməˈrin/ ***noun*** [C] **1** a type of boat that can travel under the water as well as on the surface **2** (*also* **ˌsubmarine ˈsandwich**) a type of sandwich in a large, long bread roll, filled with different kinds of meats and cheese, lettuce, tomatoes, etc.

**sub·merged** /səbˈmərdʒd/ ***adj.*** under water: *submerged rocks just below the surface*

**sub·mis·sion** /səbˈmɪʃn/ ***noun*** **1** [C,U] the act of sending a plan or statement to an official organization so that it can be discussed or considered; the plan or statement that you send: *Send us your submission of no more than 300 words by noon Friday.* **2** [U] the state of accepting sb else's power or control

**sub·mis·sive** /səbˈmɪsɪv/ ***adj.*** too willing to accept sb else's authority and willing to obey him/her without questioning anything he/she wants you to do: *He expected his daughters to be meek and submissive.* ◇ *She followed him like a submissive child.* OPP **assertive**

★**sub·mit** /səbˈmɪt/ ***verb*** (**sub·mit<u>t</u>ing**; **sub·mit<u>t</u>ed**) **1** [T] **submit sth (to sb/sth)** to give or propose sth to sb/sth so that it can be discussed or considered: *Applications must be submitted by March 31.* **2** [I] **submit (to sb/sth)** to accept sb/sth's power or control: *After a bitter struggle, the rebels were forced to submit.*

**sub·or·di·nate¹** /səˈbɔrdn·ət/ ***adj.*** (*formal*) **subordinate (to sth)** less important than sth else

**sub·or·di·nate²** /səˈbɔrdn·ət/ ***noun*** [C] a person who is of lower rank or position

**subˌordinate ˈclause** ***noun*** [C] (*grammar*) a group of words that is not a sentence but adds information to the main part of a sentence, for example *when it rang* in *She answered the phone when it rang.*

**sub·orn** /sə'bɔrn/ ***verb*** [T] to pay or persuade sb to do sth illegal, especially to tell lies in court: *to suborn a witness*

**sub·poe·na** /sə'pinə/ ***noun*** [C] an official legal document that orders sb to go and give evidence (testify) in a court of law ▶ **sub·poe·na** ***verb*** [T]: *She was subpoenaed to testify for the defense.*

**sub·scribe** /səb'skraɪb/ ***verb*** [I] **1 subscribe (to sth)** to pay for a newspaper or magazine to be sent to you regularly, or for a special computer or television service: *Do you subscribe to a daily paper?* **2 subscribe to sth** (*formal*) to agree with an idea, belief, etc.: *I don't subscribe to the view that all war is wrong.*

**sub·scrib·er** /səb'skraɪbər/ ***noun*** [C] a person who pays to receive a newspaper or magazine regularly, or to use a special computer or television service: *cable TV subscribers*

**sub·script** /'sʌbskrɪpt/ ***adj.*** (*technical*) written or printed below the normal line of writing or printing ➲ Compare **superscript**. ▶ **sub·script** ***noun*** [C]

★**sub·scrip·tion** /səb'skrɪpʃn/ ***noun*** [C] an amount of money that you pay to receive a newspaper or magazine regularly or to use a special computer or television service

**sub·se·quent** /'sʌbsəkwənt/ ***adj.*** (only *before* a noun) (*formal*) coming after or later: *Many homes were damaged by the heavy rains and subsequent flooding.* ▶ **sub·se·quent·ly** ***adv.***: *The suspect was arrested and subsequently charged with first-degree murder.*

**sub·ser·vi·ent** /səb'sərviənt/ ***adj.*** **1 subservient (to sb/sth)** too willing to obey other people: *She could not accept her subservient role.* **2 subservient (to sth)** (*formal*) less important than sth else: *The needs of individuals were subservient to those of the group as a whole.* ▶ **sub·ser·vi·ence** ***noun*** [U]: *his subservience to his brother*

**sub·side** /səb'saɪd/ ***verb*** [I] to become less strong: *The storm seems to be subsiding.*

**sub·sid·i·ar·y** /səb'sɪdiˌɛri/ ***noun*** [C] (*pl.* **sub·sid·i·ar·ies**) a business that belongs to a larger company

**sub·si·dize** /'sʌbsədaɪz/ ***verb*** [T] (used about a government, etc.) to pay money in order to keep prices or the cost of a service low: *The government subsidizes school lunch programs.*

**sub·si·dized** /'sʌbsədaɪzd/ ***adj.*** that is partly paid for by the government: *subsidized housing for low-income families*

**sub·si·dy** /'sʌbsədi/ ***noun*** [C] (*pl.* **sub·si·dies**) money that the government, etc. pays to help an organization or a group of people or to help keep the cost of sth low: *agricultural subsidies*

**sub·sist** /səb'sɪst/ ***verb*** [I] (*formal*) to manage to live with very little food or money ▶ **sub·sis·tence** /-təns/ ***noun*** [U]: *The soil is only good enough for subsistence farming.*

★**sub·stance** /'sʌbstəns/ ***noun*** **1** [C] a solid or liquid material: *poisonous substances* ◇ *The cloth is coated in a new waterproof substance.* **2** [U] the most important points or ideas of sth: *Don't repeat everything. Just tell me the substance of what they said.* **3** [U] importance, value or truth: *The novel has little substance, but it's very entertaining.*

**'substance aˌbuse** ***noun*** [U] the habit of taking too many illegal drugs and/or drinking too much alcohol

**sub·stan·dard** /ˌsʌb'stændərd/ ***adj.*** of poor quality; not as good as usual or as it should be

★**sub·stan·tial** /səb'stænʃl/ ***adj.*** **1** large in amount: *The storms caused substantial damage.* ◇ *a substantial sum of money* **2** large or strong: *The furniture was cheap and not very substantial.*

**sub·stan·tial·ly** /səb'stænʃl·i/ ***adv.*** **1** by a large amount: *Real estate prices have risen substantially.* **2** (*formal*) generally; in most points: *Our policy has remained substantially unchanged.*

**sub·stan·ti·ate** /səb'stænʃieɪt/ ***verb*** [T] (*formal*) to provide information or evidence to prove that sth is true: *The results of the tests substantiated his claims.* ◇ *They made accusations which could not be substantiated.*

**sub·stan·tive** /'sʌbstəntɪv/ ***adj.*** (*formal*) dealing with real, important or serious matters: *substantive issues/matters* ◇ *The report concluded that no substantive changes were necessary.*

**sub·sta·tion** /'sʌbsteɪʃn/ ***noun*** [C] a place where the strength of electric power from a power plant is reduced before it is passed on to homes and businesses

**sub·sti·tute**[1] /'sʌbstətut/ ***noun*** [C] **1 substitute (for sb/sth)** something that is used or done in place of sth else: *Margarine is an inexpensive substitute for butter.* **2** (*also informal* **sub**) a person who takes the place of sb/sth else, e.g. at work: *a substitute teacher*

**sub·sti·tute**[2] /'sʌbstətut/ ***verb*** **1** [T] **substitute sb/sth (for sb/sth)** to put a person or thing in the place of sb/sth else: *You can substitute milk for the cream in the recipe.* **2** [I] (*also informal* **sub**) **substitute (for sb/sth)** to do sth or be used instead of sb/sth: *I'm too sick to work tonight – can you sub for me?* ▶ **sub·sti·tu·tion** /ˌsʌbstə'tuʃn/ ***noun*** [C,U]

**sub·sume** /səb'sum/ ***verb*** [T] (*formal*) (usually passive) to include sth in a particular group and not consider it separately: *All these different ideas can be subsumed under just two broad categories.*

**sub·ter·ra·ne·an** /ˌsʌbtə'reɪmiən/ ***adj.*** (*formal*) under the ground: *a subterranean cave/tunnel*

**sub·text** /'sʌbtɛkst/ ***noun*** [C] a hidden meaning or reason for doing sth

**sub·ti·tle** /'sʌbtaɪt̬l/ ***noun*** [C] **1** [usually pl.] the words at the bottom of the picture on television or in a movie. The subtitles translate the words of a foreign movie or program. **2** a second title of a book that appears after the main title and gives more information

**sub·tle** /'sʌt̬l/ ***adj.*** **1** not very noticeable; not very strong or bright: *subtle colors* ◇ *I noticed a subtle difference in her.* **2** very skillful, e.g. at deceiving or persuading people: *Advertisements persuade us to buy things in very subtle ways.* ▶ **sub·tle·ty** /'sʌt̬lti/ ***noun*** [C,U] (*pl.* **sub·tle·ties**) ▶ **sub·tly** /'sʌt̬li/ ***adv.***

**sub·to·tal** /'sʌbtoʊt̬l/ ***noun*** [C] the total of a set of

S

numbers which is then added to other totals to give a final number

**sub·tract** /səb'trækt/ ***verb*** [T] **subtract sth (from sth)** to take one number or quantity away from another: *If you subtract five from nine, you get four.* ▶ **sub·trac·tion** /səb'trækʃn/ ***noun*** [C,U]

**sub·urb** /'sʌbərb/ ***noun*** [C] an area where people live that is outside the central part of a city: *people who commute from the suburbs to their jobs downtown* ◇ *a residential suburb of St. Louis* ▶ **sub·ur·ban** /sə'bərbən/ ***adj.***: *suburban school districts* ◇ *suburban Calgary* (= the suburbs around Calgary)

**sub·ur·ban·ite** /sə'bərbənaɪt/ ***noun*** [C] a person who lives in the suburbs of a city: *middle-class suburbanites*

**sub·ur·bi·a** /sə'bərbiə/ ***noun*** [U] the suburbs of cities, considered as a whole

**sub·ver·sive** /səb'vərsɪv/ ***adj.*** trying to weaken or destroy a government, religion, etc. or to challenge accepted ideas ▶ **sub·ver·sive** ***noun*** [C]

**sub·vert** /səb'vərt/ ***verb*** [T] (*formal*) **1** to try to destroy the authority of a political, religious, etc. system by attacking it secretly or indirectly SYN **undermine** **2** to try to destroy a person's beliefs or loyalties

**sub·way** /'sʌbweɪ/ ***noun*** [C] an underground train system in a city: *Kristi rides the subway to work every day.*

**ˌsub-'zero** ***adj.*** (used about temperatures) below zero; freezing

★**suc·ceed** /sək'sid/ ***verb*** **1** [I] **succeed (in sth/in doing sth)** to manage to achieve what you want; to do well: *Our plan succeeded.* ◇ *If you keep on trying, you will eventually succeed.* ◇ *A good education will help you succeed in life.* ◇ *to succeed in gaining admission to college* OPP **fail** **2** [I,T] to have a job or important position after sb else: *Who succeeded Kennedy as President?*

S

★**suc·cess** /sək'sɛs/ ***noun*** **1** [U] achieving what you want; doing well: *Hard work is the key to success.* ◇ *Her first novel achieved great commercial success.* **2** [C] something or somebody that achieves what he/she/it wants to, or becomes very popular: *You should try to make a success of your marriage.* ◇ *The school carnival was a huge success.* ◇ *I'm sure she'll be a success, no matter what career she chooses.* OPP **failure**

★**suc·cess·ful** /sək'sɛsfl/ ***adj.*** having achieved what was wanted; having become popular: *a successful attempt to climb Mount Everest* ◇ *a successful actor* ▶ **suc·cess·ful·ly** ***adv.***

**suc·ces·sion** /sək'sɛʃn/ ***noun*** [C] a number of people or things that follow one after another: *We've had a succession of hot, dry summers recently.*

IDM **in succession** following one after another: *There have been three deaths in the family in rapid succession.*

**suc·ces·sive** /sək'sɛsɪv/ ***adj.*** (only *before* a noun) following one after another: *He came to work late on three successive days.* ▶ **suc·ces·sive·ly** ***adv.***

**suc·ces·sor** /sək'sɛsər/ ***noun*** [C] a person who has a job or an important position after sb else ➲ Look at **predecessor.**

**suc·cinct** /sək'sɪŋkt/ ***adj.*** said clearly, in a few words ▶ **suc·cinct·ly** ***adv.***

**suc·cu·lent** /'sʌkyələnt/ ***adj.*** (used about food) very good to eat because it is not dry

**suc·cumb** /sə'kʌm/ ***verb*** [I] **succumb (to sth)** (*formal*) to stop fighting against sth: *He succumbed to temptation and started taking drugs again.* ◇ *to succumb to an illness* (= to die)

★**such**[1] /sʌtʃ/ ***det.*** **1** (used for referring to sb/sth that you are talking about or that you mentioned earlier) of this or that type: *"Can I talk to Mr. Wallis?" "Sorry, there's no such person here."* ◇ *I don't believe in ghosts. There's no such thing.* **2** (used for emphasizing the degree of sth): *It was such a boring movie that I fell asleep.* ◇ *Let's have lunch outdoors. It's such a nice day.* ◇ *It seems like such a long time since the last time we met.*

> NOTE You use **such** before a noun or before a noun that has an adjective in front of it: *Tommy is such a jerk!* ◇ *Susan is such a good athlete.* You use **so** before an adjective that is used without a noun: *Don't be so dumb.* ◇ *It was so cold we stayed at home.* Compare: *It was such a cold night that we stayed at home.*

**3** (used for talking about the result of sth): *The statement was worded in such a way that it did not upset anyone.*

★**such**[2] /sʌtʃ/ ***pronoun*** (*formal*) (used for referring to sb/sth that you are talking about or that you mentioned earlier) this or that type of person or thing: *The economic situation is such that we all have less money to spend.*

IDM **as such** (*formal*) **1** in the exact meaning of the word: *I don't believe in capital punishment as such, but I do believe that the punishment should fit the crime.* **2** without anything else; alone: *Poverty as such does not mean unhappiness, but it can make life very uncomfortable.*

**such as** for example: *Fatty foods such as French fries are bad for you.*

**such·like** /'sʌtʃlaɪk/ ***pronoun*** things of the type mentioned: *You can buy brushes, paint, varnish and suchlike there.* ▶ **such·like det.**: *food, drink, clothing and suchlike provisions*

★**suck** /sʌk/ ***verb*** **1** [I,T] to pull a liquid into your mouth, by making your lips into a round shape and pulling your cheeks in: *to suck milk through a straw* ➲ picture at **blow**[1] **2** [T] to pull sth in a particular direction, using force: *This vacuum cleaner really sucks up the dirt.* **3** [I,T] to have sth in your mouth and keep touching it with your lips and tongue: *All my kids sucked their thumbs.* **4** [I] (*slang*) to be very bad or unpleasant: *"How was school today?" "It sucked."* ◇ *It totally sucks having to work on a Friday night.*

PHR V **suck up (to sb)** (*informal*) to try to please sb in authority by praising him/her too much, helping him/her, etc., in order to gain some advantage for yourself

▶ **suck** ***noun*** [usually sing.]: *The lamb staggered to its feet and took its first suck of milk.*

**suck·er** /'sʌkər/ ***noun*** [C] **1** (*informal*) a person who believes everything that you tell him/her and who is easy to cheat **2** = LOLLIPOP

**su·crose** /ˈsukroʊs/ ***noun*** [U] the form of sugar that is obtained from sugar beet and sugar cane

**suc·tion** /ˈsʌkʃn/ ***noun*** [U] **1** the act of removing air from a space so that another substance is pulled in: *A vacuum cleaner works by suction.* **2** the act of making two surfaces stick together by removing the air between them: *The hook is attached to the wall by a suction cup.*

★**sud·den** /ˈsʌdn/ ***adj.*** done or happening quickly, or when you do not expect it: *a sudden decision* ◇ *a sudden loud noise*

IDM **all of a sudden** suddenly; unexpectedly: *All of a sudden, a rabbit ran in front of the car.*

▸ **sud·den·ness** ***noun*** [U]

ˌ**sudden ˈdeath** ***noun*** [U] (in sports) a way of deciding the winner of a game when the scores are equal at the end. The players or teams continue playing and the game ends as soon as one of them gains the lead: *a sudden-death playoff*

ˌ**Sudden ˌInfant ˈDeath ˌSyndrome** ***noun*** [U] (*abbr.* **SIDS**) the sudden death while sleeping of a baby which appears to be healthy

★**sud·den·ly** /ˈsʌdnli/ ***adv.*** quickly and unexpectedly: *"Listen!" said Doyle suddenly.* ◇ *I suddenly realized what I had to do.* ◇ *It all happened so suddenly.*

**suds** /sʌdz/ (*also* **soap·suds**) ***noun*** [pl.] the bubbles that you get when you mix soap and water

**sue** /su/ ***verb*** [I,T] **sue (sb) (for sth)** to go to a court of law and ask for money from sb because he/she has done sth bad to you, or said sth bad about you: *She sued the business's owners for $5 million.* ◇ *to sue sb for* (= because of) *racial discrimination*

**suede** /sweɪd/ ***noun*** [U] a type of soft leather which does not have a smooth surface and feels somewhat like cloth

★**suf·fer** /ˈsʌfər/ ***verb*** **1** [I,T] to experience sth bad, e.g. pain, sadness, difficulty, etc.: *Mary often suffers from severe headaches.* ◇ *Our troops suffered heavy losses.* ◇ *In a recession, it's the poor who suffer most.* **2** [I] to become worse in quality: *If you have problems at home, your work will suffer.* ▸ **suf·fer·er** /ˈsʌfərər/ ***noun*** [C]: *cancer sufferers* ▸ **suf·fer·ing** /ˈsʌfərɪŋ/ ***noun*** [C,U]: *The famine caused great hardship and suffering.*

**suf·fice** /səˈfaɪs/ ***verb*** [I] (*formal*)

IDM **suffice (it) to say (that)** (used to suggest that although you could say more, what you do say will be enough to explain what you mean): *I won't go into all the details. Suffice it to say that the whole event was a complete disaster.*

★**suf·fi·cient** /səˈfɪʃnt/ ***adj.*** (*formal*) as much as is necessary; enough: *We have sufficient oil reserves to last for three months.* OPP **insufficient** ▸ **suf·fi·cient·ly** ***adv.***

**suf·fix** /ˈsʌfɪks/ ***noun*** [C] a letter or group of letters that you add at the end of a word, and that change its meaning or the way it is used: *To form the noun from the adjective "sad," add the suffix "-ness."* ➲ Look at **prefix**.

**suf·fo·cate** /ˈsʌfəkeɪt/ ***verb*** [I,T] to die because there is no air to breathe; to kill sb in this way ▸ **suf·fo·cat·ing** /-keɪt̬ɪŋ/ ***adj.***: *the suffocating summer heat* ▸ **suf·fo·ca·tion** /ˌsʌfəˈkeɪʃn/ ***noun*** [U]

**suf·fuse** /səˈfyuz/ ***verb*** [T] (*written*) (often passive) **suffuse sb/sth (with sth)** (used especially about a color, light or feeling) to spread all over or through sb/sth: *Her face was suffused with color.* ◇ *Color suffused her face.* ◇ *The room was suffused with a soft golden light.*

★**sug·ar** /ˈʃʊgər/ ***noun*** a sweet substance that you get from certain plants: *coffee with cream and sugar* ▸ **sug·ar·y** /ˈʃʊgəri/ ***adj.***

ˈ**sugar beet** ***noun*** [U] a plant with a large round root, from which sugar is made

★**sug·gest** /səgˈdʒɛst; səˈdʒ-/ ***verb*** [T] **1 suggest sth (to sb)** to propose a plan or idea for sb to discuss or consider: *Can anybody suggest ways of raising more money?* ◇ *Tony suggested going out for a walk.* ◇ *Tony suggested that we go out for a walk.* ◇ *Tony suggested a walk.* ◇ *How do you suggest we get out of this mess?*

> NOTE Note that we cannot use an indirect object immediately after **suggest**. So we CANNOT say e.g: *Can you suggest me a good hotel?* We must say instead: *Can you suggest a good hotel?* ➲ Look also at the note at **recommend** (2).

**2** to say that a person or thing is suitable, especially a person or thing that you know about from your own experience: *Can you suggest someone for the job?* **3** to say or show sth in an indirect way: *Are you suggesting the accident was my fault?* ◇ *Forecasts suggest that inflation will fall by the end of next year.*

★**sug·ges·tion** /səgˈdʒɛstʃən; səˈdʒ-/ ***noun*** **1** [C] a plan or idea that sb proposes or suggests: *Can I make a suggestion?* ◇ *The board rejected the suggestion that they give themselves smaller bonuses.* ➲ Look at the note at **recommend** (2). **2** [U] putting an idea into a person's mind; giving advice about what to do: *the power of suggestion in advertising* **3** [sing.] a small amount or sign of sth: *Investigations found no suggestion of illegal activities.*

**sug·ges·tive** /səgˈdʒɛstɪv; səˈdʒ-/ ***adj.*** **1** making you think of sth: *music that was suggestive of Asia* **2** making you think about sex: *a suggestive dance* ▸ **sug·ges·tive·ly** ***adv.***

**su·i·cid·al** /ˌsuəˈsaɪdl/ ***adj.*** **1** (used about a person) wanting to kill himself/herself: *to feel suicidal* **2** that will probably result in your being killed: *a suicidal risk*

**su·i·cide** /ˈsuəsaɪd/ ***noun*** [C,U] the act of killing yourself: *Ben has tried to commit suicide several times.* ◇ *an increase in the number of suicides*

★**suit**[1] /sut/ ***noun*** [C] **1** a set of clothes that are made of the same material and that are fairly formal. A man's suit usually consists of a jacket and pants, and a woman's suit of a jacket and a skirt or pants. ➲ picture on study page **A30**. **2** a piece of clothing or set of clothes that you wear for a particular activity: *a spacesuit* ◇ *a swimsuit* ◇ *a suit of armor* **3** one of the four sets of thirteen playing cards (= hearts, clubs, diamonds and spades) ➲ Look at the note at **card**. **4** = LAWSUIT

IDM **file suit (against sb)** → FILE[2]

**follow suit** → FOLLOW

★**suit**[2] /sut/ ***verb*** [T] to be convenient or suitable for sb/sth: *How would Thursday at 9:30 suit you?* ◇ *It was hard to find a house that would suit our needs.*

S

IDM **be suited for/to sb/sth** to be suitable or right for sb/sth: *She and her husband are very well suited to each other.*

★**suit·a·ble** /ˈsut̬əbl/ ***adj.*** **suitable (for sb/sth)** right or convenient for sb/sth: *The movie isn't suitable for children.* ◇ *Is this a suitable time to have a meeting?* OPP **unsuitable** ▸ **suit·a·bil·i·ty** /ˌsut̬əˈbɪləti/ ***noun*** [U] ▸ **suit·a·bly** /-əbli/ ***adv.***: *to be suitably dressed for the party*

★**suit·case** /ˈsutkeɪs/ ***noun*** [C] a flat box with a handle that you use to carry your clothes, etc. in when you are traveling ➲ picture at **luggage**.

**suite** /swit/ ***noun*** [C] a set of connected rooms in a hotel

**suit·or** /ˈsut̬ər/ ***noun*** [C] (*old-fashioned*) a man who wants to marry a particular woman

**sul·fur** /ˈsʌlfər/ ***noun*** [U] (*symbol* **S**) a yellow substance with a strong, bad smell

**sulk** /sʌlk/ ***verb*** [I] to be very quiet or to look unhappy because you are angry with sb about sth ▸ **sulk·y** ***adj.***

**sul·len** /ˈsʌlən/ ***adj.*** looking bad-tempered and not speaking to people: *a sullen teenager* ▸ **sul·len·ly** ***adv.***

**sul·ly** /ˈsʌli/ ***verb*** [T] (*3rd person sing. pres.* **sul·lies**; *pres. part.* **sul·ly·ing**; *pt, pp* **sul·lied**) (*formal*) to spoil or reduce the value of sth that was good: *By cheating they have sullied the good name of their country.*

**sul·tan** /ˈsʌltn/ ***noun*** [C] the ruler in some Muslim countries: *the Sultan of Brunei*

**sul·try** /ˈsʌltri/ ***adj.*** **1** (used about the weather) hot and damp **2** (used about a woman) very sexually attractive

★**sum**[1] /sʌm/ ***noun*** [C] **1** an amount of money: *The industry has spent huge sums of money to update its equipment.* ➲ Look at **lump sum**. **2** [usually sing.] the amount that you get when you add two or more numbers together: *The sum of two and five is seven.*

IDM **in sum** (*formal*) (used to introduce a short statement of the main points of a discussion, speech, etc.): *In sum, we have no chance of winning the case.*

**sum**[2] /sʌm/ ***verb*** (**sum<u>m</u>ing**; **sum<u>m</u>ed**)

PHRV **sum (sth) up** to describe in a few words the main ideas of what sb has said or written: *to sum up the main points of an argument*

**sum·ma cum lau·de** /ˌsʊmə kʊm ˈlaʊdə; ˌsʌmə kʌm ˈlɔdi/ ***adv., adj.*** (*U.S.*) at the highest level of achievement that students can reach when they finish high school or college: *She graduated summa cum laude from Harvard.* ➲ Look also at **cum laude** and **magna cum laude**.

★**sum·ma·ry**[1] /ˈsʌməri/ ***noun*** [C] (*pl.* **sum·ma·ries**) a short description of the main ideas or events of sth: *A brief summary of the experiment is given at the beginning of the report.* ◇ *a news summary* ▸ **sum·ma·rize** /ˈsʌməraɪz/ ***verb*** [T]: *Could you summarize the story so far?*

**sum·ma·ry**[2] /ˈsʌməri/ ***adj.*** (only *before* a noun) **1** (*formal*) giving only the main points of sth, not the details: *a summary financial statement* ◇ *I made a summary report for the records.* **2** done immediately, without paying attention to the normal process that should be followed: *summary justice/executions* ◇ *a summary judgment*

★**sum·mer** /ˈsʌmər/ ***noun*** [C,U] the hottest season of the year, after spring and before fall: *Are you going away this summer?* ◇ *a summer job* ◇ *summer vacation* ▸ **sum·mer·y** /ˈsʌməri/ ***adj.***: *summery weather* ◇ *a summery dress*

ˈ**summer camp** ***noun*** [C,U] a place where children go during the summer and take part in sports and other activities

ˈ**summer school** ***noun*** [C,U] classes held during the summer at a high school or college, especially for students who need extra help

ˈ**summer ˌstudent** ***noun*** [C] (*Cdn*) a student, especially a university student, who is working at a job for the summer

**sum·mer·time** /ˈsʌmərtaɪm/ ***noun*** [U] the season of summer: *It's busy here in the summertime.*

**sum·mit** /ˈsʌmət/ ***noun*** [C] **1** the top of a mountain **2** an important meeting between the leaders of two or more countries: *an economic summit in China*

**sum·mon** /ˈsʌmən/ ***verb*** [T] **1** (*formal*) to order a person to come to a place: *Several employees were summoned to the manager's office.* ◇ *to summon help* **2 summon sth (up)** to find strength, courage or some other quality that you need, even though it is difficult for you to do so: *She couldn't summon up the courage to leave him.*

**sum·mons** /ˈsʌmənz/ ***noun*** [C] (*pl.* **sum·mons·es**) an official order to go somewhere, especially to a court of law

**su·mo** /ˈsumoʊ/ (*also* ˌ**sumo ˈwrestling**) ***noun*** [U] a Japanese style of wrestling, in which the people taking part are extremely large: *a sumo wrestler*

**sump** /sʌmp/ ***noun*** [C] a hole or hollow area in which liquid waste collects

**sump·tu·ous** /ˈsʌmptʃuəs/ ***adj.*** (*written*) very expensive and looking very impressive: *a sumptuous dinner/room* ◇ *We dined in sumptuous surroundings.* ◇ *The interior is painted in sumptuous reds and golds.*

**Sun.** ***abbr.*** Sunday

★**sun**[1] /sʌn/ ***noun*** **1 the sun** [sing.] the star that shines in the sky during the day and that gives the earth heat and light: *The sun rises in the east and sets in the west.* ◇ *the sun's rays* **2** [sing., U] light and heat from the SUN (1): *Don't sit in the sun too long.* ◇ *Too much sun can be harmful.*

**sun**[2] /sʌn/ ***verb*** [T] (**sun<u>n</u>ing**; **sun<u>n</u>ed**) **sun yourself** sit or lie in the sun in order to enjoy the heat: *a snake sunning itself on a rock*

**sun·bathe** /ˈsʌnbeɪð/ ***verb*** [I] to sit or lie in the sun in order to make your skin turn brown

**sun·beam** /ˈsʌnbim/ ***noun*** [C] a ray of light from the sun

**Sun·belt** /ˈsʌnbɛlt/ (*also* ˈ**Sun Belt**) ***noun*** [sing.] **the Sunbelt** the southern and western parts of the U.S. that are warm for most of the year

**sun·block** /ˈsʌnblɑk/ (*also* **sun·screen**) ***noun*** [U] a cream that you put on your skin to protect it from the sun

**sun·burn** /ˈsʌnbərn/ ***noun*** [U] red painful skin

S

that you get after being in strong sunlight for too long ▸ **sun·burned** /ˈsʌnbərnd/ (*also* **sunburnt** /ˈsʌnbərnt/) ***adj.***

**sun·burst** /ˈsʌnbərst/ ***noun*** [C] a design or an ornament that represents the sun and its rays: *a pair of sunburst gold earrings*

**sun·dae** /ˈsʌndeɪ; -di/ ***noun*** [C] a type of food that consists of ice cream with fruit, nuts, sweet sauce, etc. on the top

**Sun·day** /ˈsʌndeɪ; -di/ ***noun*** [C,U] (*abbr.* **Sun.**) the first day of the week, coming before Monday ➲ For examples of the use of the days of the week in sentences, look at **Monday**.

ˈ**Sunday school** ***noun*** [C,U] a class held in a church on Sundays to teach children about their religion

**sun·di·al** /ˈsʌndaɪəl/ ***noun*** [C] a device used outdoors, especially in the past, for telling the time when the sun is shining. A pointed piece of metal throws a shadow on a flat surface that is marked with the hours like a clock, and the shadow moves around as the sun moves across the sky.

**sun·down** /ˈsʌndaʊn/ ***noun*** [U] = SUNSET

ˈ**sun-drenched** ***adj.*** (only *before* a noun) having a lot of hot sun: *sun-drenched Mediterranean beaches*

**sun·dress** /ˈsʌndrɛs/ ***noun*** [C] a dress that does not cover the arms, neck or shoulders, worn in hot weather

ˈ**sun-dried** ***adj.*** (only *before* a noun) (used especially about food) dried naturally by the heat of the sun: *sun-dried tomatoes*

**sun·dries** /ˈsʌndriz/ ***noun*** [pl.] (*written*) various items, especially small ones, that are not important enough to be named separately: *You can claim up to $10 a day for sundries.*

**sun·dry** /ˈsʌndri/ ***adj.*** (*formal*) (only *before* a noun) various; not important enough to be named separately: *a watch, a diary and sundry other items* IDM **all and sundry** (*informal*) everyone, not just a few special people: *She was known to all and sundry as Bella.* ◇ *The club is open to all and sundry.*

**sun·flow·er** /ˈsʌnflaʊər/ ***noun*** [C] a tall plant that has a very large yellow flower with a black center. The seeds of the plant can be eaten or used to make cooking oil.

**sung** *past participle of* SING

**sun·glass·es** /ˈsʌnglæsəz/ (*also informal* **shades**) ***noun*** [pl.] dark glasses that protect your eyes from bright sunlight ➲ picture at **glasses**.

**sunk** *past participle of* SINK[1]

**sunk·en** /ˈsʌŋkən/ ***adj.*** **1** below the water: *a sunken ship* **2** (used about cheeks or eyes) curving in and making you look sick **3** at a lower level than the surrounding area: *a luxury bathroom with a sunken bathtub*

**sun·light** /ˈsʌnlaɪt/ ***noun*** [U] the light from the sun

**sun·ny** /ˈsʌni/ ***adj.*** (**sun·ni·er**; **sun·ni·est**) having a lot of light from the sun: *a sunny day* ◇ *Tomorrow will be mostly sunny, hot and humid.*

ˌ**sunny-side** ˈ**up** ***adj.*** (used about eggs) fried on one side only

**sun·rise** /ˈsʌnraɪz/ (*also* **sun·up**) ***noun*** [U] the time when the sun comes up and the day begins: *to get up at sunrise* ➲ Look at **dawn**.

**sun·roof** /ˈsʌnruf; -rʊf/ ***noun*** [C] (*pl.* **sun·roofs**) a part of the roof of a car that you can open to let air and light in

**sun·screen** /ˈsʌnskrin/ ***noun*** [U] = SUNBLOCK

**sun·set** /ˈsʌnsɛt/ ***noun*** [C,U] (*also informal* **sun·down**) [U] the time when the sun goes down and night begins; the appearance of the sky when this happens: *The park closes at sunset.* ◇ *a beautiful sunset*

**sun·shine** /ˈsʌnʃaɪn/ ***noun*** [U] heat and light from the sun: *warm spring sunshine*

**sun·stroke** /ˈsʌnstroʊk/ ***noun*** [U] an illness with fever, weakness, headache, etc. caused by too much direct sun, especially on the head

**sun·tan** /ˈsʌntæn/ ***noun*** [C] = TAN[1] (1): *suntan lotion*

**sun·up** /ˈsʌnʌp/ ***noun*** [U] the time when the sun rises and day begins SYN **sunrise**

**su·per**[1] /ˈsupər/ ***adj.*** (*informal*) very good; wonderful: *You did a super job.*

**su·per**[2] /ˈsupər/ ***adv.*** (*informal*) extremely: *We're super busy this week.* ◇ *a super hot day*

**su·per**[3] /ˈsupər/ ***noun*** [C] (*informal*) = SUPERINTENDENT (2)

**su·perb** /suˈpərb/ ***adj.*** very good, excellent ▸ **su·perb·ly** ***adv.***

ˈ**Super Bowl** ***noun*** [C] (*U.S.*) (in the U.S.) a football game played every year to decide the winner of the National Football League

**su·per·charged** /ˈsupərtʃɑrdʒd/ ***adj.*** **1** (used about an engine) powerful because it is supplied with air or fuel at a pressure that is higher than normal **2** (*informal*) stronger, more powerful or more effective than usual: *supercharged words, like "terrorism" or "fascism"*

**su·per·com·put·er** /ˈsupərkəmˌpyut̬ər/ ***noun*** [C] a powerful computer with a large amount of memory and a very fast central processing unit

**su·per-du·per** /ˌsupər ˈdupər/ ***adj.*** (*informal*) excellent

**su·per·fi·cial** /ˌsupərˈfɪʃl/ ***adj.*** **1** (used about people) not caring about serious or important things **2** only on the surface; not deep: *Don't worry. It's only a superficial wound.* **3** not deep, complete or thorough: *a superficial knowledge of the subject* ▸ **su·per·fi·cial·ly** /-ʃəli/ ***adv.***

**su·per·flu·ous** /suˈpərfluəs/ ***adj.*** (*formal*) more than is wanted; not needed: *Any further explanation is superfluous.*

**su·per·glue** /ˈsupərglu/ ***noun*** [U] a very strong glue that sticks very quickly and is used in small quantities for repairing things

**su·per·he·ro** /ˈsupərˌhɪroʊ/ ***noun*** [C] (*pl.* **su·per·he·roes**) a character in a story, movie, etc. who has unusual strength or power and uses it to help people; a real person who has done sth unusually brave to help sb

**su·per·high·way** /ˌsupərˈhaɪweɪ/ ***noun*** **1** [C] a

S

very wide road on which you can travel very fast **2** [sing.] (*computing*) = INFORMATION SUPERHIGHWAY

**su·per·hu·man** /ˌsupərˈhyumən/ ***adj.*** greater than is usual for human beings: *superhuman strength*

**su·per·im·pose** /ˌsupərɪmˈpoʊz/ ***verb*** [T] **superimpose sth (on/onto sth) 1** to put one image on top of another so that the two can be seen combined: *A diagram of the new road layout was superimposed on a map of the city.* **2** to add some of the qualities of one system or pattern to another one in order to produce sth that combines the qualities of both: *She has tried to superimpose her own attitudes onto this ancient story.*

**su·per·in·ten·dent** /ˌsupərɪnˈtɛndənt/ ***noun*** [C] **1** (*abbr.* **Supt.**) a person in a position of high rank and with a lot of authority, especially sb who is in charge of all the schools in a particular area **2** (*also informal* **super**) a person who is in charge of a building and makes small repairs, etc. to it

**su·pe·ri·or**[1] /səˈpɪriər/ ***adj.*** **1** better than usual or than sb/sth else: *He is clearly superior to all the other candidates.* OPP **inferior 2** higher in rank: *a superior officer* **3** thinking that you are better than other people: *I don't like that superior attitude of hers.* ▸ **su·pe·ri·or·i·ty** /səˌpɪriˈɔrət̬i; -ˈɑr-/ ***noun*** [U]: *the superiority of the new method*

**su·pe·ri·or**[2] /səˈpɪriər/ ***noun*** [C] a person of higher rank or position

**su·per·la·tive** /səˈpərlət̬ɪv/ ***noun*** [C] (*grammar*) the form of an adjective or adverb that expresses its highest degree: *"Most beautiful," "best" and "fastest" are all superlatives.*

★**su·per·mar·ket** /ˈsupərmɑrkət/ ***noun*** [C] a large store that sells food, drinks, things for cleaning your house, etc. You choose what you want from the shelves in a supermarket and pay for everything when you leave. ➲ **Grocery store** is more common, especially in informal speech.

**su·per·mod·el** /ˈsupərˌmɑdl/ ***noun*** [C] a very famous and highly paid fashion model

**the su·per·nat·u·ral** /ˌsupərˈnætʃərəl/ ***noun*** [sing.] things that cannot be explained by the laws of science: *I don't believe in the supernatural.* ▸ **su·per·nat·u·ral** ***adj.***: *a creature with supernatural powers*

**su·per·pow·er** /ˈsupərpaʊər/ ***noun*** [C] a country that has a very large amount of military, political and economic power

**su·per·script** /ˈsupərskrɪpt/ ***adj.*** (*technical*) written or printed above the normal line of writing or printing ➲ Compare **subscript**. ▸ **su·per·script** ***noun*** [U]

**su·per·sede** /ˌsupərˈsid/ ***verb*** [T] (often passive) to take the place of sth/sb that is considered to be old-fashioned or no longer the best available: *The theory has been superseded by more recent research.*

**su·per·son·ic** /ˌsupərˈsɑnɪk/ ***adj.*** faster than the speed of sound

**su·per·star** /ˈsupərstɑr/ ***noun*** [C] (*informal*) a singer, sports player, etc. who is very famous and popular

**su·per·sti·tion** /ˌsupərˈstɪʃn/ ***noun*** [C,U] a belief that cannot be explained by reason or science: *the superstition that black cats are unlucky* ▸ **su·per·sti·tious** /-ˈstɪʃəs/ ***adj.***: *I never do anything important on Friday the 13th – I'm superstitious.*

**ˌSuper ˈTuesday** ***noun*** [sing.] (*informal*) (in the U.S.) a day on which several U.S. states hold primary elections

**su·per·vise** /ˈsupərvaɪz/ ***verb*** [I,T] to watch sb/sth to make sure that work, etc. is being done correctly or that behavior is appropriate: *Her job is to supervise the construction work.* ▸ **su·per·vi·sion** /ˌsupərˈvɪʒn/ ***noun*** [U]: *Children should not play here without supervision.* ▸ **su·per·vi·sor** /-vaɪzər/ ***noun*** [C]: *He reported the incident to his supervisor.*

**sup·per** /ˈsʌpər/ ***noun*** [C,U] a meal that people eat in the evening ➲ Look at the note at **dinner**.

**ˈsupper club** ***noun*** [C] a restaurant or small nightclub where you can eat dinner, dance, listen to music, etc.

**sup·per·time** /ˈsʌpərtaɪm/ ***noun*** [C] the time of day when the evening meal is eaten

**sup·ple** /ˈsʌpl/ ***adj.*** that bends or moves easily; not stiff

**sup·ple·ment**[1] /ˈsʌpləmənt/ ***noun*** [C] **a supplement (to sth)** something that is added to sth else: *a nutritional supplement*

**sup·ple·ment**[2] /ˈsʌpləmənt/ ***verb*** [T] **supplement sth (with sth)** to improve sth by adding sth else to it: *to supplement your diet with vitamins*

**sup·ple·men·tal** /ˌsʌpləˈmɛntl/ (*also* **supplementary** /ˌsʌpləˈmɛntəri; -tri/) ***adj.*** added to sth else; extra: *supplemental income*

★**sup·ply**[1] /səˈplaɪ/ ***verb*** [T] (*pres. part.* **sup·ply·ing**; *3rd person sing. pres.* **sup·plies**; *pt, pp* **sup·plied**) **supply sth (to sb)**; **supply sb (with sth)** to give or provide sth: *The lake supplies water to the surrounding towns.* ◇ *The lake supplies the surrounding towns with water.* ◇ *The car matched the description supplied by the witness.* ▸ **sup·pli·er** /səˈplaɪər/ ***noun*** [C]: *The computer company is one of our biggest suppliers.*

★**sup·ply**[2] /səˈplaɪ/ ***noun*** (*pl.* **sup·plies**) **1** [C] something that is given or provided: *The water supply was contaminated.* **2** [C,U] the amount of sth that is available: *They only had a week's supply of medicine left.* ◇ *In many parts of the country, water is* ***in short supply*** (= there is not much of it). **3 sup·plies** [pl.] things that people need to use in their daily lives: *Food and medical supplies were dropped by helicopter.*

**supˌply and deˈmand** ***noun*** [U] (in economics) the relationship between the amount of goods or services that are available and the amount that people want to buy, especially when this controls prices: *the law of supply and demand*

★**sup·port**[1] /səˈpɔrt/ ***verb*** [T] **1** to carry the weight of sb/sth: *Large columns support the roof.* **2** to agree with the aims of sb/sth or with an idea, a plan, etc., and to give him/her/it help, money, etc.: *I'll support you as much as I can.* ◇ *a candidate who supports tougher drug laws* **3** to show that sth is true or correct: *What evidence do you have to support what you say?* **4** to give or provide sb with the money he/she needs for food, clothes, etc.: *Jim has to support two children from his previous marriage.*

S

★**sup·port²** /sə'pɔrt/ ***noun*** **1** [U] **support (for sth)** help that you give to a person or thing (often sth that is encouraging in a difficult situation): *public support for the campaign* ◇ *The software manual includes a free number to call for technical support.* ◇ *Thank you for your support at this difficult time.* **2** [C,U] something that carries the weight of sb/sth: *bridge supports* **3** [U] money to buy food, clothes, etc.: *She has no job, no home and no means of support.* ➲ Look at **child support**.
IDM **in support of sb/sth** supporting or agreeing with sb/sth: *Steve spoke in support of the proposal.*

★**sup·port·er** /sə'pɔrt̬ər/ ***noun*** [C] a person who supports a political candidate, a plan, etc.: *The candidate's supporters gave thousands of dollars to his campaign.*

**sup·por·tive** /sə'pɔrt̬ɪv/ ***adj.*** giving help or sympathy

★**sup·pose** /sə'poʊz/ ***verb*** [T] **1** to think, believe or consider that sth is probable: *I suppose he seems unfriendly because he is shy.* ◇ *What effect do you suppose the drought is having?* **2** to pretend that sth will happen or is true: *Suppose you won a million dollars. What would you do?*
IDM **be supposed to be sth** to be considered or thought to be sth: *I haven't seen it, but it's supposed to be a good play.* ◇ *This is supposed to be the best Mexican restaurant in town.*
**be supposed to do sth** to be expected to do sth or to have to do sth: *The plane was supposed to arrive 45 minutes ago.* ◇ *I'm not supposed to talk about what happened at the meeting.*
**I suppose 1** (used to show that you are not certain about sth): *It's about ten years old, I suppose.* **2** (used when you agree with sth, but are not very happy about it): *"Can I have another cookie?" "I suppose so, but only one."*

**sup·pos·ed·ly** /sə'poʊzədli/ ***adv.*** as people believe or suppose: *George Washington supposedly spent the night here once.*

**sup·pos·ing** /sə'poʊzɪŋ/ ***conj.*** (*informal*) if sth happens or is true: *Supposing the plan goes wrong – what are we going to do then?*

**sup·pos·i·to·ry** /sə'pɑzə,tɔri/ ***noun*** [C] (*pl.* **sup·pos·i·to·ries**) a small piece of solid medicine that is placed in the rectum or vagina and left to dissolve gradually

**sup·press** /sə'prɛs/ ***verb*** [T] **1** to stop sth by using force: *The army suppressed the rebellion.* **2** to stop sth from being seen or known: *to suppress the truth* **3** to stop yourself from expressing your feelings, etc.: *to suppress a yawn* ◇ *suppressed anger* ▶ **sup·pres·sion** /sə'prɛʃn/ ***noun*** [U]

**sup·pres·sant** /sə'prɛsnt/ ***noun*** [C] a drug that is used to prevent one of the body's functions from working normally: *an appetite suppressant*

**su·prem·a·cist** /sə'prɛməsɪst/ ***noun*** [C] a person who believes that his/her own race is better than others and should be in power: *a white supremacist*

**su·prem·a·cy** /sə'prɛməsi/ ***noun*** [U] **supremacy (over sb/sth)** the state of being most powerful: *the military supremacy of the United States*

**su·preme** /sə'prim/ ***adj.*** **1** highest in rank or position: *a supreme commander* **2** greatest or most important: *a matter of supreme importance*

**the Su,preme 'Court** ***noun*** [sing.] the court of law with the highest authority in a country, state, province, etc.: *the Chief Justice of the Supreme Court*

**su·preme·ly** /sə'primli/ ***adv.*** (*formal*) very: *to be supremely confident*

**Supt.** ***abbr.*** (*written*) = SUPERINTENDENT

**sur·charge** /'sərtʃɑrdʒ/ ***noun*** [C] an extra amount of money that you have to pay for sth: *Most banks impose a surcharge on customers who use other banks' cash machines.*

★**sure¹** /ʃʊr/ ***adj.*** **1** (not before a noun) having no doubt about sth; certain: *I'm not sure what to do next.* ◇ *Craig was sure that he'd made the right decision.* ◇ *I think I had my bag when I got off the bus, but I'm not sure.*

> NOTE **Sure** and **certain** are very similar in meaning. **Sure**, however, cannot be used in the phrase "It is ...that ..." **Certain** can be used in this phrase: *It is certain that there will be a strike soon.* With **sure** we must say: *There is sure to be a strike soon.* **Sure** is less formal and more common than **certain**.

**2** (not before a noun) **sure of sth** certain to get sth: *If you go and see them, you can be sure of a warm welcome.* **3 sure to do sth** (not before a noun) certain to happen or do sth: *If you study hard, you are sure to get a good grade.* **4** that you can trust: *A noise like that is a sure sign of engine trouble.*
IDM **Be sure and/to do sth** Don't forget to do sth: *Be sure to write and tell me what happens.* ◇ *Be sure and take your keys.*
**make sure 1** to find out whether sth is in a certain state or has been done: *I'll go back and make sure I closed the window.* **2** to take the action that is necessary to make sth happen: *Make sure you are back home by 11 o'clock.*
**sure of yourself** confident about your opinions, or about what you can do

★**sure²** /ʃʊr/ ***adv.*** (*informal*) **1** (used as an answer to a question) yes; of course: *"Can I borrow this book?" "Sure."* **2** without doubt; definitely: *It sure is hot today.* ◇ *"Do you like ice cream?" "I sure do!"*
IDM **sure enough** as you/sb had expected: *I expected him to be early, and sure enough, he arrived five minutes before the others.*

**'sure-fire** ***adj.*** (*informal*) (only before a noun) certain to be successful or to happen as you expect: *a sure-fire success* ◇ *Bad behavior is a sure-fire way of getting people's attention.*

★**sure·ly** /'ʃʊrli/ ***adv.*** **1** without doubt: *This will surely cause problems.* **2** (used for expressing surprise at sb else's opinions, plans, actions, etc.): *Surely you're not going to walk home in the dark?*

**sur·e·ty** ***noun*** [C,U] (*pl.* **sur·e·ties**) **1** money given as a promise that you will pay a debt, appear in court, etc.: *She was granted bail with a surety of $500.* ◇ *They have offered a large amount of money as surety.* **2** a person who accepts responsibility if sb else does not pay a debt, appear in court, etc.: *to act as surety for sb* ◇ *She has promised to **stand surety** for $5,000.*

**surf¹** /sərf/ ***verb*** **1** [I] to stand or lie on a special board (a **surfboard**) in the ocean and ride on a wave toward the shore ➲ picture on study page **A32**.

S

**NOTE** **go surfing** is a common way of talking about surfing for pleasure.

**2** [I,T] (*informal*) to search for information on the Internet: *I spent two hours last night surfing the Net.* ▸ **surf·er** *noun* [C]

**surf²** /sərf/ *noun* [U] the white part on the top of waves in the ocean

★**sur·face¹** /ˈsərfəs/ *noun* **1** [C] the outside part of sth: *the earth's surface* ◇ *a special paint for metal surfaces* **2** [C, usually sing.] the top part of an area of water: *The submarine slowly rose to the surface.* **3** [sing.] the qualities of sb/sth that you see or notice, that are not hidden: *Everybody seems very friendly, but there is a lot of tension beneath the surface.*

**sur·face²** /ˈsərfəs/ *verb* **1** [T] to cover the SURFACE¹ (1) of sth: *to surface a road with asphalt* **2** [I] to come to the surface of a liquid: *The submarine surfaced quickly.* **3** [I] (*informal*) to appear or become known: *New evidence surfaced last night.*

**surf·board** /ˈsərfbɔrd/ (*also* **board**) *noun* [C] a long narrow board used for SURFING¹ (1)

**surge¹** /sərdʒ/ *verb* [I] **1** to move forward with great strength: *The crowd surged toward the stage.* **2** to increase quickly: *Stock prices surged late yesterday.*

**surge²** /sərdʒ/ *noun* [C, usually sing.] **a surge (of/in sth) 1** a sudden increase in sth: *a surge in health care costs* **2** a sudden strong feeling: *a surge of pity*

**sur·geon** /ˈsərdʒən/ *noun* [C] a doctor who performs medical operations (surgery): *a brain surgeon*

**sur·ger·y** /ˈsərdʒəri/ *noun* [C,U] (*pl.* **sur·ger·ies**) medical treatment in which your body is cut open so that part of it can be removed or repaired: *to undergo emergency surgery* ◇ *I've already had three surgeries on my elbow.* ➲ Look at **plastic surgery**.

**sur·gi·cal** /ˈsərdʒɪkl/ *adj.* used in surgery or connected with surgery: *surgical instruments* ◇ *surgical procedures* ▸ **sur·gi·cal·ly** /-kli/ *adv.*: *Her tooth had to be surgically removed.*

S

**sur·ly** /ˈsərli/ *adj.* (**sur·li·er**; **sur·li·est**) unfriendly and rude: *a surly expression*

**sur·mise** /sərˈmaɪz/ *verb* [I,T] (*formal*) to guess or suppose sth using the evidence you have, without definitely knowing: *From the looks on their faces, I surmised that they had had an argument.*

**sur·mount** /sərˈmaʊnt/ *verb* [T] (*formal*) to deal successfully with a difficulty: *She was well aware of the difficulties that had to be surmounted.* SYN **overcome**

**sur·name** /ˈsərneɪm/ *noun* [C] (*formal*) a name shared by all the members of a family SYN **family name, last name**

**sur·pass** /sərˈpæs/ *verb* [T] (*formal*) do sth better than sb/sth else or better than expected

**sur·plus** /ˈsərpləs/ *noun* [C,U] an amount that is extra or more than you need: *a trade surplus of $10 billion* ▸ **sur·plus** *adj.* (only *before* a noun): *surplus food*

★**sur·prise¹** /sərˈpraɪz; səˈpraɪz/ *noun* **1** [U] the feeling that you have when sth happens that you do not expect: *They looked up in surprise when she walked in.* ◇ *To my surprise, the boss agreed.* **2** [C] something that you did not expect: *What a nice surprise to see you again!* ◇ *a surprise visit/attack* ◇ *"What's my present?" "It's a surprise."*

**IDM** **take sb by surprise** to happen or do sth when sb is not expecting it: *His remarks took me by surprise.*

★**sur·prise²** /sərˈpraɪz; səˈpraɪz-/ *verb* [T] **1** to cause sb to feel SURPRISE¹ (1): *It wouldn't surprise me if you got the job.* **2** to attack or find sb suddenly and unexpectedly: *We surprised the burglars just as they were leaving our house.*

★**sur·prised** /sərˈpraɪzd; səˈpraɪzd/ *adj.* feeling or showing SURPRISE¹ (1): *I was very surprised to see Cynthia there. I thought she was still on vacation.*

★**sur·pris·ing** /sərˈpraɪzɪŋ; səˈpraɪzɪŋ/ *adj.* that causes SURPRISE¹ (1): *It's surprising how many adults can't read or write.* ▸ **sur·pris·ing·ly** *adv.*

**sur·re·al** /səˈril/ (*also* **sur·re·al·is·tic** /səˌriəˈlɪstɪk/) *adj.* very strange, like a dream

**sur·re·al·ism** /səˈriəlɪzəm/ *noun* [U] a 20th century style and movement in art and literature in which images and events that are not connected are put together in a strange or impossible way, like a dream, to try to express what is happening deep in the mind ▸ **sur·re·al·ist** *adj.*, *noun* [C]: *a surrealist painter/painting*

**sur·ren·der** /səˈrɛndər/ *verb* **1** [I,T] **surrender (to sb)** to stop fighting and admit that you have lost **2** [T] **surrender sb/sth (to sb)** (*formal*) to give sb/sth to sb else: *The police ordered them to surrender their weapons.* ▸ **sur·ren·der** *noun* [C,U]

**sur·rep·ti·tious** /ˌsərəpˈtɪʃəs/ *adj.* (*written*) done secretly or quickly, in the hope that other people will not notice: *She sneaked a surreptitious glance at her watch.* ▸ **sur·rep·ti·tious·ly** *adv.*

**sur·ro·gate** /ˈsərəgət; -geɪt/ *noun* [C], *adj.* (a person or thing) that takes the place of sb/sth else: *a surrogate mother* (= a woman who has a baby for another woman who cannot have children)

★**sur·round** /səˈraʊnd/ *verb* [T] **surround sb/sth (by/with sth)** to be or go all around sb/sth: *The yard is surrounded by a fence.* ◇ *The police have surrounded his house.* ◇ (*figurative*) *He is surrounded by friends.*

**sur·round·ing** /səˈraʊndɪŋ/ *adj.* (only *before* a noun) that is near or around sth: *Boston and the surrounding area*

★**sur·round·ings** /səˈraʊndɪŋz/ *noun* [pl.] everything that is near or around you; the place where you live: *to live in pleasant surroundings* ◇ *animals living in their natural surroundings* (= not in zoos) ➲ Compare **environment**.

**sur·veil·lance** /sərˈveɪləns/ *noun* [U] a careful watch on sb who may have done sth wrong: *The suspect was under police surveillance.*

★**sur·vey¹** /sərˈveɪ/ *verb* [T] **1** to ask people questions about their habits, opinions, etc. for a study of sth: *Seventy percent of those surveyed said they liked cheese.* **2** to look at the whole of sth; to examine or study sth as a whole: *They surveyed the damage after the earthquake.* ◇ *Her new book surveys the problems of developing countries in today's world.* **3** to measure an area of land in order to make a map of it

★**sur·vey²** /ˈsərveɪ/ *noun* [C] **1** a set of questions

about people's habits, opinions, etc., for a study of sth: *Surveys have shown that more and more people are getting into debt.* ◇ *According to a recent survey, 75% of smokers would like to quit.* **2** an act of examining an area of land and making a map of it

**'survey course** ***noun*** [C] a college course that gives an introduction to a subject for people who are thinking about studying it further

**sur·vey·or** /sər'veɪər/ ***noun*** [C] a person whose job is to examine and record the details of a piece of land

**sur·viv·al** /sər'vaɪvl/ ***noun*** [U] the state of continuing to live or exist: *Small companies have to struggle for survival in today's economy.* ◇ *The survival rate for this type of cancer is very low.*

**sur·viv·al·ist** /sər'vaɪvəlɪst/ ***noun*** [C] a person who prepares for a dangerous or unpleasant situation such as a war by learning how to survive outdoors, practicing how to use weapons, storing food, etc. ▸ **sur·viv·al·ism** ***noun*** [U]

**sur'vival kit** ***noun*** [C] a set of emergency equipment, including food, medical supplies and tools

★**sur·vive** /sər'vaɪv/ ***verb*** [I,T] to continue to live or exist, in or after a difficult or dangerous situation: *More than a hundred people were killed in the crash and only five passengers survived.* ◇ *to survive a plane crash* ◇ *The old man survived all his children* (= lived longer than them). ◇ (*figurative*) *She has managed to survive two divorces* (= to deal with them well and to continue with her life). ▸ **sur·vi·vor** ***noun*** [C]: *There were five survivors of the crash.*

**sus·cep·ti·bil·i·ty** /sə,sɛptə'bɪləṭi/ ***noun*** (*pl.* **sus·cep·ti·bil·i·ties**) (*written*) **1** [U] **susceptibility (to sth)** the state of being very likely to be influenced, harmed or affected by sth: *susceptibility to disease/infection* **2 susceptibilities** [pl.] a person's feelings which are likely to be easily hurt: *It was all carried out without any consideration for the susceptibilities of the bereaved family.* SYN **sensibilities**

**sus·cep·ti·ble** /sə'sɛptəbl/ ***adj.*** (not before a noun) **susceptible to sth** easily damaged, affected or influenced by sb/sth: *Officials worry that that air base could be susceptible to an attack.* ◇ *Small babies are highy susceptible to infection.*

**su·shi** /'suʃi/ ***noun*** [U] a Japanese dish of small cakes of cold cooked rice, flavored with vinegar and served with raw fish, etc. on top: *a sushi bar*

★**sus·pect¹** /sə'spɛkt/ ***verb*** [T] **1** to believe that sth may happen or be true: *The situation is worse than we first suspected.* ◇ *She strongly suspected that he was lying.* **2** to have doubts about whether you can trust sb or believe sth: *I suspect his motives for offering to help.* **3 suspect sb (of sth)** to believe that sb is guilty of sth: *I suspected Laura of taking the money.* ➲ Look at **suspicion**. ▸ **sus·pect·ed** ***adj.***: *suspected terrorists* ◇ *a suspected fracture*

★**sus·pect²** /'sʌspɛkt/ ***noun*** [C] a person who is thought to be guilty of a crime

**sus·pect³** /'sʌspɛkt/ ***adj.*** possibly not true or to be trusted: *to have suspect motives* ◇ *His methods are suspect.*

**sus·pend** /sə'spɛnd/ ***verb*** [T] **1 suspend sth (from sth)** to hang sth: *to suspend a decoration from the ceiling* **2** to stop or delay sth for a time: *The woman was given a suspended sentence* (= she will not go to prison unless she commits another crime). **3 suspend sb (from sth)** to send sb away from his/her school, job, position, etc. for a period of time, usually as a punishment for doing sth bad: *Gary was suspended for fighting in school.* ➲ noun **suspension**

**sus·pend·ers** /sə'spɛndərz/ ***noun*** [pl.] a pair of straps that hold your pants up. You put the suspenders over your shoulders and attach them to the top of your pants at the front and back.

**sus·pense** /sə'spɛns/ ***noun*** [U] the feeling that you have when you are waiting for news or for sth exciting or important to happen: *We wanted to know where we were going, but he kept us in suspense.* ◇ *a movie full of action and suspense*

**sus·pen·sion** /sə'spɛnʃn/ ***noun*** **1** [C,U] delaying sth for a period of time: *The judge announced a suspension of the trial.* **2** [C,U] not being allowed to do your job or go to school for a period of time, as a punishment: *Possession of a weapon on school property will result in immediate suspension.* **3** [U] the parts that are attached to the wheels of a car, etc. that make it more comfortable to ride in

★**sus·pi·cion** /sə'spɪʃn/ ***noun*** **1** [C,U] a feeling or belief that sth is wrong or that sb has done sth wrong: *He always treats new situations with suspicion.* ◇ *She was arrested on suspicion of murder.* **2** [C] a feeling that sth may happen or be true: *We had a suspicion that they would show up late.*

IDM **under suspicion** (used about a person) believed to have done sth wrong

★**sus·pi·cious** /sə'spɪʃəs/ ***adj.*** **1** that makes you feel or believe that sth is wrong or that sb has done sth wrong: *The old man died under suspicious circumstances.* ◇ *It's very suspicious that she was not at home on the night of the murder.* ◇ *a suspicious-looking person* **2 suspicious (of/about sb/sth)** not trusting sb/sth: *His strange behavior made the police suspicious.* ▸ **sus·pi·cious·ly** ***adv.***: *The house was suspiciously quiet* (= as if something were wrong). ◇ *to behave suspiciously*

**sus·tain** /sə'steɪn/ ***verb*** [T] **1** to cause sth to continue for a long period of time: *to sustain economic growth* **2** to keep sb/sth alive or healthy: *His faith in God sustained him after the death of his son.* **3** (*formal*) to suffer an injury, etc.: *The victim sustained minor injuries.* ◇ *The buildings sustained heavy damage in the earthquake.*

**sus·tain·a·ble** /sə'steɪnəbl/ ***adj.*** **1** involving the use of natural products and energy in a way that does not harm the environment: *sustainable forest management* ◇ *an environmentally sustainable society* **2** that can continue or be continued for a long time: *sustainable economic growth/recovery* ◇ *Unfortunately, this level of output is not sustainable.* ▸ **sus·tain·a·bil·i·ty** ***noun*** [U]

**sus·te·nance** /'sʌstənəns/ ***noun*** [U] (*formal*) the food and drink that people, animals and plants need to live and stay healthy: *There's not much sustenance in a bowl of soup.* ◇ (*figurative*) *Arguing would only give further sustenance to his allegations.*

**su·ture** /'sutʃər/ ***noun*** [C] (*medical*) a stitch or stitches made when sewing up a wound, especially after an operation ▸ **su·ture** ***verb*** [T]

S

**SUV** /ˌɛs yu ˈvi/ ***noun*** [C] the abbreviation for "sport-utility vehicle"; a type of large car, often with four-wheel drive and made originally for traveling over rough ground ➲ picture at **car**.

**svelte** /svɛlt/ ***adj.*** (used about a person, especially a woman) thin in a graceful and attractive way

**SW** ***abbr.*** southwest; southwestern

**swab¹** /swɑb/ ***noun*** [C] **1** a piece of soft material used by a doctor, nurse, etc. for cleaning wounds or taking a sample from sb's body for testing **2** an act of taking a sample from sb's body, with a SWAB (1): *to take a throat swab*

**swab²** /swɑb/ ***verb*** [T] (**swab·bing**; **swabbed**) **1** to clean or remove liquid from a wound, etc., using a SWAB¹ (1) **2 swab sth (down)** to clean or wash a floor, surface, etc. using water and a cloth, etc.

**swag·ger** /ˈswægər/ ***verb*** [I] to walk with a swinging movement that shows that you are too confident or proud of yourself ▸ **swag·ger** ***noun*** [sing.]

★**swal·low¹** /ˈswɑloʊ/ ***verb*** **1** [T] to make food, drink, etc. pass from your mouth down your throat: *It's easier to swallow pills if you take them with water.* ◇ (*figurative*) *The rent swallows up most of our monthly income.* ➲ picture at **lick**. **2** [I] to make a movement in your throat, often because you are afraid or surprised, etc.: *She swallowed hard and tried to speak, but nothing came out.* **3** [T] to accept or believe sth, often too easily: *You shouldn't swallow everything they tell you!* **4** [T] to accept an insult, etc. without protest: *I find her criticisms very hard to swallow.*

**swal·low²** /ˈswɑloʊ/ ***noun*** [C] **1** an act of SWALLOWING¹ (1,2) **2** a common small bird

**swam** *past tense of* SWIM

**swamp¹** /swɑmp/ ***noun*** [C,U] (an area of) soft wet land

**swamp²** /swɑmp/ ***verb*** [T] **1** to cover or fill sth with water: *The boat was swamped by enormous waves.* **2** (usually passive) **swamp sb/sth (with sth)** to give sb so much of sth that he/she cannot deal with it: *We've been swamped with applications for the job.*

**swan** /swɑn/ ***noun*** [C] a large, usually white, bird with a very long neck that lives on lakes and rivers

swan

**swank·y** /ˈswæŋki/ (**swank·i·er**; **swank·i·est**) (*also* **swank** /swæŋk/) ***adj.*** (*informal*) fashionable and expensive in a way that is intended to impress people: *a swanky hotel/car*

**swap** /swɑp/ ***verb*** [T] (**swap·ping**; **swapped**) (*informal*) to give sth for sth else; to exchange: *They sat by the fire, swapping stories from their days in school.* ▸ **swap** ***noun*** [C]

**swarm¹** /swɔrm/ ***noun*** [C] **1** a large group of insects, especially bees, moving around together **2** a large number of people together

**swarm²** /swɔrm/ ***verb*** [I] to fly or move in large numbers: *When the gates opened, the fans swarmed into the stadium.*

PHRV **swarm with sb/sth** to be too crowded or full: *The beaches are swarming with tourists at this time of year.*

**swarth·y** /ˈswɔrði/ ***adj.*** (*old-fashioned*) (used especially about a person or his/her face) having dark skin: *a swarthy complexion/face/man*

**swash·buck·ling** /ˈswɑʃbʌklɪŋ; ˈswɔʃ-/ ***adj.*** (only *before* a noun) (used especially about movies) set in the past and full of action, adventure, fighting with swords, etc.: *a swashbuckling tale of adventure on the high seas* ◇ *the swashbuckling hero of Hollywood epics*

**swas·ti·ka** /ˈswɑstɪkə/ ***noun*** [C] an ancient symbol in the form of a cross with its ends bent at an angle of 90°, used in the 20th century as the symbol of the German Nazi party

**SWAT** /swɑt/ (*also* **ˈSWAT team**) ***noun*** [C] (in the U.S.) a group of police officers who are especially trained to deal with violent situations. SWAT stands for "Special Weapons and Tactics".

**swat** /swɑt/ ***verb*** [T] (**swat·ting**; **swat·ted**) to hit sth, especially an insect, with sth flat

**swatch** /swɑtʃ/ ***noun*** [C] a small piece of fabric used to show people what a larger piece would look or feel like

**swathe¹** /sweɪð/ (*also* **swath**) /swɑð/ ***noun*** [C] (*written*) **1** a long strip of land, especially one on which the plants or crops have been cut: *Development has affected vast* ***swathes of*** *our countryside.* **2** a large strip or area of sth: *a swathe of hair/fabric/sunlight* ◇ *The mountains rose above a swathe of thick cloud.*

IDM **cut a swathe through sth** (used about a person, fire, etc.) to pass through a particular area destroying a large part of it: *Building the tunnel would involve cutting a huge swathe through the forest.*

**swathe²** /sweɪð; swɑð/ ***verb*** [T] (usually passive) **swathe sb/sth (in sth)** (*written*) to wrap or cover sb/sth in sth: *He was lying on the hospital bed, swathed in bandages.* ◇ *The village was swathed in early morning mist.*

**sway¹** /sweɪ/ ***verb*** **1** [I,T] to move or swing slowly from side to side **2** [T] to influence: *Many people were swayed by his convincing arguments.*

**sway²** /sweɪ/ ***noun*** [U] **1** a movement from side to side: *The sway of the yacht was making her feel sick.* **2** power or influence over sb: *Rebel forces* ***hold sway*** *over much of the island.* ◇ *He was quick to exploit those who fell* ***under his sway***.

★**swear** /swɛr/ ***verb*** (*pt* **swore** /swɔr/; *pp* **sworn** /swɔn/) **1** [I] **swear (at sb/sth)** to use bad or offensive language: *He hit his thumb with the hammer and swore loudly.* ◇ *There's no point in swearing at the car just because it won't start!* **2** [I,T] to make a serious promise: *When you testify in court, you have to swear to tell the truth.* ◇ *Will you swear not to tell anyone?* ◇ *I could have sworn* (= I was sure) *I heard a knock at the door.*

PHRV **swear by sb/sth** to believe completely in the value of sth

**swear sb in** (usually passive) to make sb declare that he/she will accept the responsibility of a new position: *The judge will be sworn in next week.*

**ˈswear word** ***noun*** [C] a word that is considered bad and that may offend people

★**sweat**[1] /swɛt/ ***noun*** **1** [U] the liquid that comes out of your skin when you are hot, ill or afraid: *He stopped digging and wiped the sweat from his forehead.* ➲ Look at **perspiration**. **2** **sweats** [pl.] (*also* **sweat suit**) a two-piece set of clothes made of thick soft cotton fabric, usually worn for exercising or relaxing

IDM **no sweat** (*informal*) (used to say that sth is very easy to do): *"Can you reach that shelf up there?" "Sure, no sweat."*

★**sweat**[2] /swɛt/ ***verb*** [I] **1** to produce sweat through your skin **2** **sweat (over sth)** to work hard: *I've been sweating over that problem all day.*

IDM **don't sweat it** (*slang*) (used to tell sb not to worry about sth): *Hey, don't sweat it. Everything's going to be OK.*

★**sweat·er** /ˈswɛt̬ər/ ***noun*** [C] a warm piece of clothing with long sleeves, often made of wool or cotton yarn: *a pullover sweater* ◇ *a cardigan sweater* (= with buttons down the front) ➲ picture on study page **A30**.

**sweat·pants** /ˈswɛtpænts/ ***noun*** [pl.] a type of comfortable pants made from thick cotton cloth, often worn for exercising or relaxing

**sweat·shirt** /ˈswɛtʃərt/ ***noun*** [C] a piece of clothing like a sweater made from thick cotton cloth, often with a part (**hood**) to cover your head ➲ picture on study page **A30**.

**sweat·shop** /ˈswɛtʃɑp/ ***noun*** [C] a factory where people are forced to work very hard in poor conditions for very little money, often illegally

**ˈsweat suit** ***noun*** [C] = SWEAT[1] (2)

**sweat·y** /ˈswɛt̬i/ ***adj.*** (**sweat·i·er**; **sweat·i·est**) **1** wet with sweat: *I was hot and sweaty after the game and needed a shower.* **2** causing you to sweat: *a hot, sweaty day*

★**sweep**[1] /swip/ ***verb*** (*pt, pp* **swept** /swɛpt/) **1** [I,T] to clean by moving dust, dirt, etc. away with a broom: *Could you sweep under the table too?* ◇ *Take your shoes off! I just swept the floor.* ◇ *I'm going to sweep the leaves off the sidewalk.* ➲ Look at the note at **clean**[2]. **2** [T] to push, move or remove sb/sth quickly and smoothly: *He swept the money into his pocket and went out.* ◇ *The huge waves swept her overboard.* **3** [I,T] to move quickly and smoothly over the area or in the direction mentioned: *Fire swept through the building.* ◇ *The epidemic swept the country within weeks.* **4** [I] to move in a proud or impressive way: *Five black limousines swept past us.* ◇ *She swept angrily out of the room.*

PHR V **sweep (sth) up** to remove dirt, dust, leaves, etc. using a broom

**sweep**[2] /swip/ ***noun*** [C] a long, curving shape or movement: *a bay with a broad sweep of golden sand* ◇ *"Some day, all this will be yours," she said with a sweep of her hand.*

IDM **a clean sweep** → CLEAN[1]

**sweep·er** /ˈswipər/ ***noun*** [C] **1** a person or thing that SWEEPS[1] (1): *street sweepers* **2** (in soccer) a player who stays near the goalkeeper and whose job is to defend the goal ➲ picture at **soccer**.

**sweep·ing** /ˈswipɪŋ/ ***adj.*** **1** (used about statements, etc.) too general and possibly not accurate: *a sweeping generalization* **2** having a great and important effect: *sweeping reforms*

**sweep·stakes** /ˈswipsteɪks/ (*also* **sweepstake**) ***noun*** [C] **1** a type of betting in which the winner gets all the money bet by everyone else **2** a prize or prizes won in a sweepstakes

★**sweet**[1] /swit/ ***adj.*** **1** tasting like sugar; not sour or salty: *This frosting's too sweet.* **2** (used about a person) kind and thoughtful: *It's very sweet of you to remember my birthday!* **3** (used about a smell or a sound) pleasant: *The garden was full of the sweet smells of summer.* ◇ *the sweet sound of children singing* **4** making you feel happy and satisfied: *an especially sweet victory*

IDM **have a sweet tooth** to like eating sweet things

▶ **sweet·ness** ***noun*** [U]

★**sweet**[2] /swit/ ***noun*** **sweets** [pl.] foods that are sweet, such as candy, cookies, cake, etc.: *His dentist told him to avoid sweets between meals.*

**sweet·en** /ˈswitn/ ***verb*** [T] to make sth sweet by adding sugar, honey, etc.

**sweet·en·er** /ˈswitn·ər/ ***noun*** [C,U] a substance used instead of sugar for sweetening food or drink: *artificial sweeteners*

**sweet·heart** /ˈswithɑrt/ ***noun*** [C] (*old-fashioned*) a boyfriend or girlfriend: *They were childhood sweethearts.*

**sweet·ie** /ˈswit̬i/ ***noun*** [C] (*informal*) a person who is loved

**sweet·ly** /ˈswitli/ ***adv.*** in an attractive, kind or pleasant way: *She smiled sweetly.* ◇ *sweetly-scented flowers*

**ˈsweet poˌtato** ***noun*** [C,U] (*pl.* **sweet potatoes**) a yellowish-orange root that looks like a potato with pointed ends, that is cooked and eaten as a vegetable ➲ picture on study page **A28-29**. ➲ Look also at **yam**.

**ˈsweet-talk** ***verb*** [T] **sweet-talk sb (into sth/into doing sth)** to try to persuade sb to do sth by praising him/her and saying things he/she likes to hear: *I can't believe you let him sweet-talk you into working for him!* ▶ **ˈsweet talk** ***noun*** [U]

★**swell**[1] /swɛl/ ***verb*** (*pt* **swelled** /swɛld/; *pp* **swol·len** /ˈswoʊlən/ or **swelled**) **1** [I,T] **swell (up)** to become or to make sth bigger, fuller or thicker: *After she fell down, her ankle began to swell up.* ◇ *His eyes swelled with tears.* ◇ *Heavy rain had swollen the rivers.* **2** [I,T] to increase: *The crowd swelled to 600 by the end of the evening.* **3** [I] (*formal*) (used about feelings or sound) to become stronger or louder suddenly: *Hatred swelled inside him.*

**swell**[2] /swɛl/ ***noun*** **1** [C, usually sing.] the movement of the ocean when it rises and falls without the waves breaking: *The boat was caught in a heavy* (= strong) *swell.* **2** [sing.] a situation in which sth increases in size, number, strength, etc.: *a swell of panic/pride* ◇ *swells of protest*

**swell**[3] /swɛl/ ***adj.*** (*old-fashioned*) very good; wonderful

★**swell·ing** /ˈswɛlɪŋ/ ***noun*** **1** [C] a place on the body that is bigger or fatter than usual because of an injury or illness: *a swelling on my knee* **2** [U] the

S

condition of being swollen: *Try to rest your ankle until the swelling goes down.*

**swel·ter·ing** /ˈswɛltərɪŋ/ ***adj.*** (*informal*) much too hot: *It was sweltering downtown today.*

**swept** *past tense, past participle of* SWEEP[1]

**swerve** /swərv/ ***verb*** [I] to change direction suddenly: *The car swerved to avoid the child.*

**swift** /swɪft/ ***adj.*** quick or fast; happening without delay: *a swift runner* ◇ *a swift reaction* ▸ **swift·ly** ***adv.***

**swig** /swɪg/ ***verb*** [T] (**swig·ging**; **swigged**) (*informal*) to take a quick drink of sth, especially alcohol: *They sat around swigging beer from bottles.* ▸ **swig** ***noun*** [C]: *She took a swig of wine.*

**swill** /swɪl/ ***noun*** [U] **1** (*also* **pig·swill**) a mixture of waste food and water that is given to pigs to eat **2** (*informal*) food or drink that is unpleasant or of a poor quality

★**swim** /swɪm/ ***verb*** (*pres. part.* **swim·ming**; *pt* **swam** /swæm/; *pp* **swum** /swʌm/) **1** [I] to move your body through water: *How far can you swim?* ◇ *Hundreds of tiny fish swam past.*

> **NOTE** **Go swimming** is a common way of talking about swimming for pleasure: *We go swimming every Saturday.* ◇ *They went swimming before breakfast.* We can also say **go for a swim** when we are talking about one particular occasion: *I went for a swim this morning.*

**2** [T] to cover or cross a distance, etc. by swimming: *I swam 25 lengths of the pool.* **3** [I] to seem to be moving or turning: *The floor began to swim before my eyes and I fainted.* **4** [I] (used about your head) to feel unclear or confused: *My head was swimming with so much new information.* ▸ **swim** ***noun*** [sing.]: *Would you like to take a swim in the lake?* ▸ **swim·mer** ***noun*** [C]: *a strong swimmer*

ˈ**swimming hole** ***noun*** [C] a place where it is deep enough to swim in a river or stream

**swim·ming·ly** /ˈswɪmɪŋli/ ***adv.*** (*informal*) without any problems or difficulties: *We hope everything will go swimmingly.*

★ˈ**swimming pool** (*also* **pool**) ***noun*** [C] a pool that is built especially for people to swim in: *an indoor/outdoor swimming pool*

ˈ**swimming trunks** (*also* **trunks**) ***noun*** [pl.] a piece of clothing like shorts that a man or boy wears to go swimming: *a pair of swimming trunks*

**swim·suit** /ˈswɪmsut/ (*also* **bathing suit**) ***noun*** [C] a piece of clothing that a woman or girl wears to go swimming ➲ Look at **bikini**.

**swim·wear** /ˈswɪmwɛr/ ***noun*** [U] (*written*) clothing that you wear for swimming in: *a new swimwear collection*

**swin·dle** /ˈswɪndl/ ***verb*** [T] **swindle sb/sth (out of sth)** (*formal*) to cheat sb (in order to get money, etc.): *He swindled his sister out of her inheritance.* ▸ **swin·dle** ***noun*** [C]: *a tax swindle* ▸ **swin·dler** /ˈswɪndlər/ ***noun*** [C]

**swine** /swaɪn/ ***noun*** **1** [pl.] pigs **2** [C] (*informal*) a very unpleasant person: *Her husband's a complete swine.*

★**swing**[1] /swɪŋ/ ***verb*** (*pt, pp* **swung** /swʌŋ/) **1** [I,T] to move backward and forward or from side to side, while hanging from sth; to make sb/sth move in this way: *The rope was swinging from a branch.* ◇ *She sat on the wall, swinging her legs.* **2** [I,T] to move in a curve or to make sb/sth move in this way: *The door swung open and the whole class rushed out.* ◇ *He swung the child up onto his shoulders.* **3** [I] to turn quickly: *She swung around when she heard the door open.* ◇ (*figurative*) *His moods swing from one extreme to the other.* **4** [I,T] **swing (at sb/sth)** to try to hit sb/sth: *He swung violently at the other man but missed.*

★**swing**[2] /swɪŋ/ ***noun*** **1** [sing.] a swinging movement or action: *He took a swing at the ball.* **2** [C] a seat that you can swing backward and forward on, e.g. in a children's playground **3** [C] a change (in public opinion, etc.): *Opinion polls indicate a significant swing toward the right.*

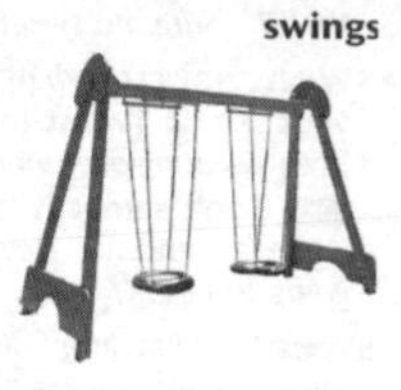
swings

**IDM** **in full swing** → FULL[1]

**swing·ing** /ˈswɪŋɪŋ/ ***adj.*** (*informal*) lively, exciting and fashionable: *swinging singles* ◇ *the* ***Swinging Sixties*** (= the period during the 1960s when people began to have more sexual freedom)

ˈ**swing set** ***noun*** [C] a frame for children to play on including one or more SWINGS[2] (2) and often a SLIDE[2] (3)

**swipe**[1] /swaɪp/ ***verb*** [T] **1** (*informal*) to steal sth **2** to pass a special plastic card through a piece of equipment that can read the information that the card contains

**PHRV** **swipe at sth** (*informal*) to (try to) hit sb/sth in an uncontrolled way: *He swiped at the wasp with a newspaper but missed.*

**swipe**[2] /swaɪp/ ***noun*** [C] **1** an act of hitting sb/sth or trying to hit sb/sth in an uncontrolled way **2 a swipe (at sb/sth)** an act of criticizing or making an unfair comment about sb/sth: *During the debate, she took several swipes at her opponent's record.*

**swirl** /swərl/ ***verb*** [I,T] to move around and around quickly; to make sth do this: *Her long skirt swirled around her legs as she danced.* ▸ **swirl** ***noun*** [C]

**swish** /swɪʃ/ ***verb*** [I,T] to move quickly through the air in a way that makes a soft sound; to make sth do this: *A large car swished past them and turned into the embassy gates.* ◇ *The pony swished its tail.*

**Swiss cheese** /ˌswɪs ˈtʃiz/ ***noun*** [C,U] any hard cheese with holes in it

★**switch**[1] /swɪtʃ/ ***noun*** [C] **1** a small button or sth similar that you press up or down in order to turn on electricity: *a light switch* **2** a sudden change: *a switch in policy*

★**switch**[2] /swɪtʃ/ ***verb*** **1** [I,T] **switch (sth) (over) (to sth)** to change or be changed from one thing to another: *We've switched from eating fried foods to more fresh fruit and vegetables.* ◇ *The game has been switched from Saturday to Sunday.* **2** [I,T] **switch (sth) (with sb/sth); switch (sth) (around/over)** to exchange positions, activities, etc.: *This week you can have the car and I'll drive the pickup, and next* *week we'll switch.* ◇ *Someone switched the signs around and everyone went the wrong way.*

PHR V **switch (sth) off/on** to press a switch in order to connect/disconnect electric power: *Don't forget to switch off the lights downstairs.*

**switch·blade** /ˈswɪtʃbleɪd/ ***noun*** [C] a knife with the sharp edge (the **blade**) inside the handle and which jumps out quickly when a button is pressed

**switch·board** /ˈswɪtʃbɔrd/ ***noun*** [C] the place in a large office, etc. where all the telephone calls are connected

**ˌswitch-ˈhitter** ***noun*** [C] (in baseball) a player who can hit with the BAT[1] (2) on either side of his/her body

**swiv·el** /ˈswɪvl/ ***verb*** [I,T] **swivel (sth) (around)** to turn around a central point; to make sth do this: *She swiveled around to face me.* ◇ *He swiveled his chair toward the door.*

**swol·len¹** *past participle of* SWELL[1]

**swol·len²** /ˈswoʊlən/ ***adj.*** thicker or wider than usual: *Her leg was badly swollen after the accident.*

**swoon** /swun/ ***verb*** [I] **1 swoon (over sb)** to feel very excited, emotional, etc. about sb that you think is sexually attractive, so that you almost become unconscious: *He's used to having women swooning over him.* **2** (*old-fashioned*) to become unconscious SYN **faint²**

**swoop** /swup/ ***verb*** [I] to fly or move down suddenly: *The bird swooped down on its prey.*

**swoosh** /swʊʃ; swuʃ/ ***verb*** [I] to move quickly through the air in a way that makes a sound: *Cars and trucks swooshed past.* ▸ **swoosh *noun*** [sing.]

★**sword** /sɔrd/ ***noun*** [C] a weapon with a handle and a long thin metal blade

**sword·fish** /ˈsɔrdfɪʃ/ ***noun*** [C,U] (*pl.* **sword·fish**) a large ocean fish with a very long thin pointed upper jaw: *swordfish steaks*

**swore** *past tense of* SWEAR

**sworn** *past participle of* SWEAR

**swum** *past participle of* SWIM

**swung** *past tense, past participle of* SWING[1]

**syc·a·more** /ˈsɪkəmɔr/ ***noun*** [C] a type of large tree with broad leaves

**syc·o·phant** /ˈsɪkəfənt; -fænt; ˈsaɪ-/ ***noun*** [C] (*formal*) a person who praises important or powerful people too much and in a way that is not sincere, especially in order to get sth from them ▸ **syc·o·phan·tic** /ˌsɪkəˈfæntɪk; ˌsaɪ-/ ***adj.***

**syl·la·ble** /ˈsɪləbl/ ***noun*** [C] a word or part of a word which contains one vowel sound: *"Mat" has one syllable and "mattress" has two syllables.*

**syl·la·bus** /ˈsɪləbəs/ ***noun*** [C] (*pl.* **syl·la·bus·es** or **syl·la·bi** /ˈsɪləbaɪ/) a list of subjects, etc. that are included in a course: *Required texts are listed on the syllabus and available in the campus bookstore.*

★**sym·bol** /ˈsɪmbl/ ***noun*** [C] **1 a symbol (of sth)** a sign, object, etc. which represents an idea or an aspect of life: *The cross is the symbol of Christianity.* ◇ *Some people think a fast car is a symbol of power and strength.* **2 symbol (for sth)** a letter, number or sign that has a particular meaning: *O is the symbol for oxygen.*

**sym·bol·ic** /sɪmˈbɑlɪk/ ***adj.*** used or seen as a symbol: *The violent sea is symbolic of the character's emotions.* ▸ **sym·bol·i·cal·ly** /-kli/ ***adv.***

**sym·bol·ism** /ˈsɪmbəlɪzəm/ ***noun*** [U] the use of symbols to represent things, especially in art and literature

**sym·bol·ize** /ˈsɪmbəlaɪz/ ***verb*** [T] to be a symbol of sth: *The deepest notes in music often symbolize danger or despair.*

**sym·met·rical** /sɪˈmɛtrɪk/ ***adj.*** having two halves that are exactly the same in size and shape ▸ **sym·met·ri·cal·ly** /-kli/ ***adv.***

**sym·me·try** /ˈsɪmətri/ ***noun*** [U] the state of having two halves that match each other exactly in size, shape, etc.

★**sym·pa·thet·ic** /ˌsɪmpəˈθɛt̬ɪk/ ***adj.*** **1** showing that you understand other people's feelings, especially their problems: *When Sandra's father died, everyone was very sympathetic.* ◇ *I felt very sympathetic toward him.* ◇ *He gave me a sympathetic smile.*

NOTE In English, **sympathetic** does not mean "friendly and pleasant." If you want to express this meaning, you say a person is **nice**: *I met Alex's sister yesterday. She's very nice.*

**2 sympathetic (to sb/sth)** being in agreement with or willing to support sb/sth: *I explained our ideas, but she wasn't sympathetic to them.* OPP **unsympathetic** ▸ **sym·pa·thet·i·cal·ly** /-kli/ ***adv.***

**sym·pa·thize** /ˈsɪmpəθaɪz/ ***verb*** [I] **sympathize (with sb/sth) 1** to understand and share sb's feelings: *I sympathize with her, but I don't know what I can do to help.* **2** to be in agreement with sb/sth: *I find it difficult to sympathize with his opinions.*

**sym·pa·thiz·er** /ˈsɪmpəθaɪzər/ ***noun*** [C] a person who agrees with and supports an idea or aim: *a Communist sympathizer* ➲ This word shows disapproval.

★**sym·pa·thy** /ˈsɪmpəθi/ ***noun*** (*pl.* **sym·pa·thies**) **1** [U] **sympathy (for/toward sb)** an understanding of other people's feelings, especially their problems: *Everyone feels great sympathy for the victims of the bombing.* ◇ *I don't expect any sympathy from you.* ◇ *When his wife died, he received dozens of letters of sympathy.* **2 sympathies** [pl.] feelings of support or agreement: *Some members of the party have sympathies with terrorist groups.*

IDM **in sympathy (with sb/sth)** in agreement, showing that you support or approve of sb/sth: *Several union members demonstrated sympathy with the striking auto workers.*

**sym·pho·ny** /ˈsɪmfəni/ ***noun*** [C] (*pl.* **sym·pho·nies**) a long piece of music written for a large orchestra

**sym·po·si·um** /sɪmˈpoʊziəm/ ***noun*** [C] (*pl.* **sym·po·si·a** or **sym·po·si·ums**) **a symposium (on sth)** a meeting at which experts have discussions about a particular subject; a small conference

★**symp·tom** /ˈsɪmptəm/ ***noun*** [C] **1** a change in your body that is a sign of illness: *What are the symptoms of the flu?* **2** a sign (that sth bad is happening or exists): *The riots are a symptom of a deeper problem.*

**symp·to·mat·ic** /ˌsɪmptəˈmæt̬ɪk/ ***adj.*** (*written*)

S

**symptomatic (of sth)** being a sign of an illness or a problem: *a symptomatic infection* ◇ *These disagreements are symptomatic of the tensions within the party.*

**syn·a·gogue** /'sɪnəgɑg/ (*also* **temple**) ***noun*** [C] a building where Jewish people go to pray or to study their religion

> **NOTE** Notice that when you are talking about going to a ceremony (a service) in a synagogue, you say "at synagogue/temple" or "to synagogue/temple" without " **a**" or " **the**": *I saw Mrs. Brown at temple today.*

**sync** /sɪŋk/ ***noun***
**IDM** **be in sync/out of sync (with sb/sth)** (*informal*) **1** to be happening/not to be happening at the same time or speed: *The movie's soundtrack wasn't in sync with the picture.* **2** to be suitable/unsuitable for a particular situation, time etc.: *Are politicians out of sync with the concerns of young people?*

**syn·chro·nize** /'sɪŋkrənaɪz/ ***verb*** [T] to make sth happen or work at the same time or speed

**syn·di·cate** /'sɪndɪkət/ ***noun*** [C] a group of people or companies who work together and help each other in order to achieve a particular aim: *a crime syndicate*

**syn·di·cated** /'sɪndəkeɪt̬əd/ ***adj.*** (used about a television series, a regular newspaper column, etc.) sold to and appearing on, many television stations or in many newspapers: *a nationally syndicated comic strip*

**syn·drome** /'sɪndroʊm/ ***noun*** [C] **1** a group of signs or changes in the body that are typical of an illness: *Down's syndrome* ◇ *Acquired Immune Deficiency Syndrome (AIDS)* **2** a group of events, actions attitudes, etc. that are typical of a particular state or condition

**syn·er·gy** /'sɪnərdʒi/ ***noun*** [C,U] (*pl.* **syn·er·gies**) (*technical*) the extra energy, power, success, etc. that is achieved by two or more people or companies working together, instead of on their own: *Managing effective teams is a matter of achieving synergy between the individual members.* ◇ *attempts to re-establish synergy between mankind and nature*

**syn·od** /'sɪnəd/ ***noun*** [C] an official meeting of church leaders to discuss religious matters and make important decisions

**syn·o·nym** /'sɪnənɪm/ ***noun*** [C] a word or phrase that has the same meaning as another word or phrase in the same language: *"Big" and "large" are synonyms.* ▶ **syn·on·y·mous** /sə'nɑnəməs/ ***adj.*** **synonymous (with sth)** (*figurative*): *Wealth is not always synonymous with happiness.*

**syn·op·sis** /sɪ'nɑpsəs/ ***noun*** [C] (*pl.* **syn·op·ses** /-siz/) a summary of a piece of writing, a play, etc.: *The program gives a brief synopsis of the plot.*

**syn·tax** /'sɪntæks/ ***noun*** [U] the system of rules for the structure of a sentence

**syn·the·sis** /'sɪnθəsəs/ ***noun*** (*pl.* **syn·the·ses** /-siz/) **1** [C,U] **synthesis (of sth)** the act of combining separate ideas, beliefs, styles, etc.; a mixture or combination of ideas, beliefs, styles, etc.: *the synthesis of art with everyday life* ◇ *a synthesis between/of traditional and modern values* **2** [U] (*technical*) the natural chemical production of a substance in animals and plants: *protein synthesis* ◇ *the synthesis of nucleic acids* **3** [U] the production of sounds, music or speech by electronic means: *digital/sound/speech synthesis*

**syn·the·size** /'sɪnθəsaɪz/ ***verb*** [T] **1** (*technical*) to produce a substance by means of chemical or biological processes **2** to produce sounds, music or speech using electronic equipment **3** to combine separate ideas, beliefs, styles, etc.

**syn·the·siz·er** /'sɪnθəsaɪzər/ ***noun*** [C] an electronic musical instrument that can produce a wide range of different sounds

**syn·thet·ic** /sɪn'θɛt̬ɪk/ ***adj.*** made by a chemical process; not natural: *synthetic fabrics* ▶ **syn·thet·i·cal·ly** /-kli/ ***adv.***

**syph·i·lis** /'sɪfələs/ ***noun*** [U] a serious disease that passes from one person to another by sexual contact

**sy·ringe** /sə'rɪndʒ/ ***noun*** [C] an instrument that consists of a tube and a needle. It is used for taking a small amount of blood out of the body or for giving injections of drugs or medicine.

★**syr·up** /'sɪrəp/ ***noun*** [U] **1** a type of thick, sweet sauce that is made by boiling sugar with water or fruit juice: *pancakes with maple syrup* **2** liquid medicine that you swallow: *cough syrup*

★**sys·tem** /'sɪstəm/ ***noun*** **1** [C] a set of ideas or rules for organizing sth: *What kind of filing system do you have for your papers?* ◇ *the metric system* **2** [C] a group of things or parts that work together: *The whole computer system crashed.* ◇ *The mayor is planning to reform the school system.* **3** [C] the body of a person or animal; parts of the body that work together: *We have to get him to the hospital before the poison gets into his system.* ◇ *the central nervous system* **4 the system** [sing.] the traditional methods and rules of a society: *Bob claims that he knows how to beat the system and avoid paying income taxes.*
**IDM** **get sth out of your system** (*informal*) to free yourself of a strong feeling

**sys·tem·at·ic** /ˌsɪstə'mæt̬ɪk/ ***adj.*** done using a fixed plan or method: *a systematic search* ▶ **sys·tem·at·i·cal·ly** /-kli/ ***adv.***

S

# Tt

**T, t** /ti/ ***noun*** [C,U] (*pl.* **T's**; **t's**) the twentieth letter of the English alphabet: *"Table" begins with (a) "T."*

**T.** ***abbr.*** = TABLESPOON (2)

**t.** ***abbr.*** = TEASPOON (2)

**TA** /ˌti 'eɪ/ ***abbr.*** = TEACHING ASSISTANT

**tab** /tæb/ ***noun*** [C] **1** a small piece of cloth, metal or paper that is fastened to sth to help you open, hold or identify it: *You open the can by pulling the metal tab.* **2** [usually sing.] (*informal*) a bill, especially for meals or drinks in a bar or restaurant: *The office picks up the tab* (= pays the bill) *when I eat out on business trips.* ◇ *I don't have any cash right now – can you put it on my tab?*

IDM **keep tabs on sb/sth** (*informal*) to watch sb/sth carefully; to check sth

**tab·by** /'tæbi/ ***noun*** [C] (*pl.* **tab·bies**) (*also* **'tabby cat**) a cat with brown or gray fur marked with dark lines or spots

★**ta·ble**[1] /'teɪbl/ ***noun*** [C] **1** a piece of furniture with a flat top on one or more legs: *a kitchen table* ◇ *a coffee table* ◇ *Could you set the table for lunch?* (= put the knives/forks/plates on it) ◇ *Don't read the newspaper at the table* (= during the meal). ◇ *table manners* (the way that you behave when you are eating)

NOTE We put things **on the table,** but we sit **at the table** (= around the table).

**2** a list of facts or figures, usually arranged in rows down a page: *a table of contents* ◇ *Table 3 shows the results.*

IDM **wait tables** → WAIT[1]

**ta·ble**[2] /'teɪbl/ ***verb*** [T] to leave an idea, a proposal, etc. to be discussed at a later date: *They voted to table the proposal until the following meeting.*

**ta·ble·cloth** /'teɪblklɔθ; -klɑθ/ ***noun*** [C] a piece of cloth that you put over a table, especially when having a meal

**ta·ble·spoon** /'teɪblspun/ ***noun*** [C] **1** a large spoon used for serving or measuring food **2** (*also* **tablespoonful** /-fʊl/) (*abbr.* **T.**; **tbsp.**) the amount that a tablespoon holds: *Add two tablespoons of sugar.*

**tab·let** /'tæblət/ ***noun*** [C] a small amount of medicine in solid form, that you swallow: *Take two tablets every four hours.*

**'table ˌtennis** (*also* **Ping-Pong**) ***noun*** [U] a game with rules like tennis in which you hit a light plastic ball across a table with a small flat, round wooden object (**paddle**)

**tab·loid** /'tæblɔɪd/ ***noun*** [C] a newspaper with small pages, a lot of pictures and short simple articles

**ta·boo** /tə'bu; tæ-/ ***noun*** [C] (*pl.* **ta·boos**) a religious or social custom that forbids certain actions or words ▸ **ta·boo** ***adj.***: *a taboo subject*

**tac·it** /'tæsət/ ***adj.*** (*written*) that is suggested indirectly or understood, rather than said in words: *tacit approval/support/knowledge* ◇ *By* ***tacit agreement****, the subject was never mentioned again.*

**tack**[1] /tæk/ ***noun*** **1** [C] = THUMBTACK **2** [C] a small nail with a broad head **3** [sing.] a way of achieving sth: *If people won't listen, we'll have to try a different tack.*

**tack**[2] /tæk/ ***verb*** [T] to fasten sth with TACKS[1] (1,2)

PHR V **tack sth on (to sth)** to put sth extra on the end of sth: *Restaurants sometimes tack a service charge onto the bill.*

**tack·le**[1] /'tækl/ ***verb*** **1** [T] to deal boldly with sth difficult: *The government must tackle the problem of rising unemployment.* ◇ *Firefighters were brought in to tackle the blaze.* **2** [T] (in football) to stop another player by pulling him down **3** [I,T] (in soccer) to try to take the ball from sb on the other team

**tack·le**[2] /'tækl/ ***noun*** **1** [C] the act of TACKLING[1] (2,3) sb: *a powerful tackle by Walker* **2** [C] (in football) a player whose job is to stop opponents by knocking them to the ground **3** [U] the equipment you use for fishing: *bait and tackle*

**tack·y** /'tæki/ ***adj.*** (**tack·i·er**; **tack·i·est**) **1** (*informal*) cheap and of poor quality: *tacky souvenirs* **2** (used about paint, glue, etc.) not quite dry; sticky

**ta·co** /'tɑkoʊ/ ***noun*** [C] (*pl.* **ta·cos**) a Mexican food that consists of a thin, crisp shell made of ground corn, that is filled with meat or beans and cheese, tomatoes, etc.

**tact** /tækt/ ***noun*** [U] the ability to deal with people without offending or upsetting them: *a situation that reqires patience and tact*

**tact·ful** /'tæktfl/ ***adj.*** careful not to say or do things that could offend people: *Talking about his ex-wife like that wasn't very tactful!* ▸ **tact·ful·ly** /-fəli/ ***adv.***

**tac·tic** /'tæktɪk/ ***noun*** **1** [C, usually pl.] a way of achieving sth: *We need to decide what our tactics are going to be at the next meeting.* ◇ *I don't think this tactic will work.* **2 tactics** [pl.] the skillful arrangement and use of military forces in order to win a battle

**tac·ti·cal** /'tæktɪkl/ ***adj.*** **1** connected with TACTICS (2): *a tactical error* **2** designed to bring a future advantage: *a tactical decision* ▸ **tac·ti·cal·ly** /-kli/ ***adv.***

**tad** /tæd/ ***noun*** [sing.] (*informal*) **a tad** a small amount; a little: *The meat was just a tad overcooked.*

**tad·pole** /'tædpoʊl/ ***noun*** [C] a young form of a frog, when it has a large black head and a long tail

**taf·fy** /'tæfi/ ***noun*** (*pl.* **taf·fies**) [C] a type of soft candy made of brown sugar boiled until it is very thick and given different shapes and colors

**tag**[1] /tæg/ ***noun*** **1** [C] a small piece of card, material, etc. fastened to sth to give information about it;

a label: *a name tag* ◇ *How much is this dress? There's no price tag on it.* **2** [U] a children's game in which one child runs around after the other children and tries to touch them: *to play tag*

**tag²** /tæg/ ***verb*** [T] (**tag·ging**; **tagged**) to fasten a TAG¹ (1) to sth

PHRV **tag along** to follow or go with sb: *The little boy tagged along with the older kids when they went to the mall.*

**'tag ˌquestion** ***noun*** [C] (*grammar*) a short phrase at the end of a sentence that changes it into a question. For example, in the sentence "It's really expensive, isn't it?" the use of the tag question means that the speaker is asking the listener to agree.

**tail¹** /teɪl/ ***noun*** **1** [C] the long thin part at the end of the body of an animal, bird, fish, etc.: *The dog barked and wagged its tail.* ➲ picture at **cat**. **2** [C] a thing like an animal's tail in its shape or position: *the tail of an airplane* **3 tails** [pl.] the side of a coin that does not have the head of a person on it: *"We'll toss a coin to decide," said my father. "Heads or tails?"* ➲ Look at **heads**. **4 tails** [pl.] a man's coat, short at the front but with a long, divided piece at the back. It is worn on very formal occasions, such as weddings.

**tail²** /teɪl/ ***verb*** [T] to follow sb closely, especially to watch where he/she goes, etc.

PHRV **tail off** to become less, smaller, quieter, etc.: *His voice tailed off into a whisper.*

**tail·gate¹** /'teɪlgeɪt/ ***verb*** [I,T] to drive too closely behind another vehicle

**tail·gate²** /'teɪlgeɪt/ ***noun*** [C] **1** a door at the back of a truck that opens downward and that you can open or remove when you are loading or unloading the vehicle **2** = TAILGATE PARTY

**'tailgate ˌparty** ***noun*** [C] a party that a group of sports fans has before a sports event, usually a football game, in which food and alcohol are brought to the parking lot of the stadium where the game will be played, and eaten and drunk there

**tai·lor¹** /'teɪlər/ ***noun*** [C] a person whose job is to make clothes, especially for men

T

**tai·lor²** /'teɪlər/ ***verb*** [T] (usually passive) **1** to make clothes: *a well-tailored coat* **2** to make or design sth for a special purpose: *We specialize in bank accounts tailored to meet your individual needs.*

**ˌtailor-'made** ***adj.*** **tailor-made (for sb/sth)** very suitable; perfect

**tail·pipe** /'teɪlpaɪp/ ***noun*** [C] a pipe through which a vehicle's waste gases come out: *My car needs a new tailpipe.*

**taint** /teɪnt/ ***verb*** [T] (usually passive) to have a bad effect on sth; to spoil sth so that it is no longer pure, fresh, etc.: *Dozens of people became sick after eating the tainted meat.*

★**take¹** /teɪk/ ***verb*** [T] (*pt* **took** /tʊk/; *pp* **tak·en** /'teɪkən/)

➤CARRY/LEAD **1** to carry sb/sth or to go with sb from one place to another: *Take your coat with you – it's cold.* ◇ *Could you take this letter home to your parents?* ◇ *The ambulance took him to the hospital.* ◇ *I'm taking the kids swimming this afternoon.* ➲ Picture at **bring**.

➤REACH AND HOLD **2** to put your hand around sth and hold it (and move it toward you): *She held out the keys, and I took them.* ◇ *He took a sweater out of the drawer.* ◇ *She took my hand/me by the hand.*

➤REMOVE **3** to remove sth without permission: *Who took my pen?*

➤ACCEPT/RECEIVE **4** to accept or receive sth: *Will you take $2,000 for the car?* ◇ *Do you take traveler's checks?* ◇ *I'm not taking the blame for the accident.* ◇ *She's not going to take the job.*

➤CHOOSE/BUY **5** to choose sth to buy: *I'll take the blue one.*

➤NEED **6** to need or require sth: *It takes about an hour to drive to my office from here.* ◇ *I took two years to graduate from law school.* ◇ *It took a lot of courage to say that.*

➤HOLD/CONTAIN **7** to have enough space for sth: *How many passengers can this bus take?*

➤TRANSPORTATION/ROAD **8** to use a form of transportation; to go by a particular road: *I always take the train to work.* ◇ *Which road do you take to get to Madison?*

➤MEDICINE/DRUGS **9** to swallow or put a medicine or drug into your body: *Take two tablets four times a day.* ◇ *teenagers who take illegal drugs*

➤WRITE DOWN **10** to write or record sth: *She took notes during the lecture.*

➤EXAM **11** to write the answers to an examination: *to take a test*

➤STUDY **12** to have lessons or go to a course in a particular subject: *Liz is taking biology next semester.*

➤MEASUREMENT **13** to measure sth: *I took his temperature and it was almost 103°.*

➤ACTION **14** (used with nouns to say that sb is performing an action): *Take a look at this article* (= look at it). ◇ *She took a deep breath* (= breathed deeply).

➤PHOTOGRAPH **15** to photograph sth: *I took a lot of pictures at the wedding.*

➤HAVE FEELING/OPINION **16** to have a particular feeling or opinion: *He takes great pleasure in visiting his grandchildren.* ◇ *I wish you would take things more seriously.*

➤CONSIDER **17** to understand sth in a particular way: *She took what he said as a compliment.*

➤BEAR **18** to be able to bear sth: *I find his criticism a little hard to take.*

➤CAPTURE **19** to capture a place by force: *The allied forces took the enemy's capital last night.*

➤GRAMMAR **20** (not used in the continuous tenses) to have or need a word to go with it in a sentence or other structure: *The verb "depend" takes the preposition "on."*

IDM **be taken with sb/sth** to find sb/sth attractive or interesting

**I take it (that...)** I suppose: *I take it that you're not coming?*

**take it from me** believe me: *Take it from me – she's going to resign.*

**take a lot out of sb** to make sb very tired

**take some doing** to require a lot of work or effort

NOTE For other idioms containing **take**, look at the entries for the nouns, adjectives, etc., e.g. **take place** is at **place¹**.

PHRV **take after sb** to look or behave like an older member of your family

**take sth apart** to separate sth into the different parts it is made of

**take sth away** to cause a feeling, etc. to disappear: *This asprin will take the pain away.*

**take sb/sth away (from sb)** to remove sb/sth: *She took the scissors away from the child.*

**take sth back 1** to return sth to the place that you got it from **2** to admit that sth you said was wrong

**take sth down 1** to remove a structure by separating it into the pieces it is made of: *They took the fence down and put up a brick wall.* **2** to write down sth that is said

**take sb in** to deceive sb: *I was completely taken in by her story.*

**take sth in** to understand what you see, hear or read: *There was too much in the museum to take in at one time.*

**take off 1** (used about an airplane, etc.) to leave the ground and start flying **2** to become successful or popular

**take sth off 1** to remove sth, especially clothes: *Come in and take your coat off.* **2** to have the period of time mentioned as a vacation: *I'm going to take a week off.*

**take sth on** to accept or decide to do sth: *He's taken on a lot of extra work.*

**take sb out** to go somewhere with sb (for a social occasion): *I'm taking Sarah out to dinner tonight.*

**take sth out 1** to remove sth from inside sth else: *He took out a notebook and began to write.* **2** to arrange officially to have sth, especially from a bank or a court of law: *to take out insurance/a bank loan/a court order*

**take it out on sb** to behave badly toward sb because you are angry or upset about sth, even though it is not this person's fault: *I know you've been having problems, but don't take it out on me!*

**take (sth) over** to get control of sth or responsibility for sth: *The business is being taken over by a large corporation.* ◇ *Who's going to take over as assistant when Tim leaves?*

**take to sb/sth** to feel a liking for sb/sth: *I took to his parents immediately.*

**take to sth/doing sth** to begin doing sth regularly: *Many people have taken to eating healthier foods.*

**take up sth** to use or fill an amount of time or space: *All her time is taken up with the new baby.*

**take sth up** to start doing sth regularly (e.g. as a hobby): *I recently took up yoga.*

**take sb up on sth** to accept an offer, etc. that sb has made: *"Come and stay with us sometime." "We'll take you up on that!"*

**take sth up with sb** to ask or complain about sth: *I'll take the matter up with my lawyer.*

**take²** /teɪk/ ***noun*** [C] **1** a scene or part of a movie that is filmed at one time without stopping the camera: *They managed to shoot the scene in just two takes.* **2** [usually sing.] (*informal*) an amount of money that sb receives, especially the money that is earned by a business during a particular period of time: *How much is my share of the take?* **3 a take on sth** the particular opinion or idea that sb has about sth: *What's his take on the plan?* ◇ *a new take on the Romeo and Juliet story* (= a way of presenting it)

**take·off** /'teɪkɔf; -ɑf/ ***noun*** [C,U] the time when an airplane leaves the ground: *The plane crashed on takeoff.*

**take·out** (*also* **take-out**) /'teɪkaʊt/ ***adj.*** **1** (used about food) that you buy already cooked from a restaurant to eat somewhere else: *a takeout dinner* **2** (used about a restaurant) that sells cooked food that you can eat somewhere else ▸ **take-·out** (*also* **carryout**) ***noun*** [C,U]

**take·o·ver** /'teɪkoʊvər/ ***noun*** [C] the act of taking control of sth: *the takeover of a company* ◇ *a military takeover* (= in a country)

**tak·ings** /'teɪkɪŋz/ ***noun*** [pl.] the amount of money that a store, theater, etc. receives from selling goods or tickets over a particular period of time: *The box office takings are up on last week.*

**tal·cum pow·der** /'tælkəm ˌpaʊdər/ (*also informal* **talc** /tælk/) ***noun*** [U] a fine soft powder, usually with a pleasant smell, that you put on your skin to make it feel smooth and dry

**tale** /teɪl/ ***noun*** [C] **1** a story about events that are not real: *fairy tales* **2** a report or description of sb/sth that is not necessarily true: *I've heard a lot of tales about the people who live in that house.*

**tal·ent** /'tælənt/ ***noun*** [C,U] **talent (for sth)** a natural skill or ability: *She has a talent for painting.* ◇ *His work shows great talent.* ▸ **tal·ent·ed** ***adj.***: *a talented musician*

★**talk¹** /tɔk/ ***verb***

➤SPEAK TO SB **1** [I] **talk (to/with sb)**; **talk (about sb/sth)** to say things; to speak: *I could hear them talking downstairs.* ◇ *Their little boy is just learning to talk.* ◇ *Can I talk to you for a minute?* ◇ *Anne is not an easy person to talk to.* ◇ *We need to talk about the plans for the weekend.* ◇ *I didn't understand what she was talking about.* ➲ Look at the note at **speak**.

➤DISCUSS **2** [I] to discuss people's personal affairs: *His strange lifestyle started the local people talking.* **3** [T] to discuss sth: *Could we talk business after dinner?*

➤LECTURE/SPEECH **4** [I] **talk on/about sth** to give a lecture or speech to a group of people about a certain subject: *Mrs. Phipps will be talking about early American art.*

➤GIVE INFORMATION **5** [I] to give information: *"He hasn't talked yet," said the detective, "but he will."*

IDM **know what you are talking about** → KNOW

**talk shop** to talk about work with colleagues outside working hours

PHR V **talk back (to sb)** to speak rudely to sb who is older or who has a higher rank than you

**talk down to sb** to talk to sb as if he/she is less intelligent, important, etc. than you

**talk sb into/out of doing sth** to persuade sb to do/not to do sth: *I didn't really want to go with them, but they talked me into it.*

**talk sth over** to discuss sth thoroughly, especialy to reach an agreement or a decision

★**talk²** /tɔk/ ***noun*** **1** [C] a conversation or discussion: *Tim and I had a long talk about the problem.* **2 talks** [pl.] formal discussions: *The leaders of the two countries will meet for talks next week.* **3** [U] talking, especially without action, results or the right information: *You don't believe all that talk*

T

*about layoffs at work, do you?* ➲ Look also at **small talk**. **4** [C] a lecture or speech: *He's giving a talk on the importance of computers in education.*

**talk·a·tive** /ˈtɔkət̬ɪv/ ***adj.*** liking or tending to talk a lot

**ˈtalk show** ***noun*** [C] a television program on which people talk about their lives and answer questions, often from the audience

⋆**tall** /tɔl/ ***adj.*** **1** (used about people or things) of more than average height; not short: *a tall young man* ◇ *a tall tree/tower/chimney* ◇ *Nick is taller than his brother.* **2** (used about people) of a particular height: *Claire is only five feet tall.* ◇ *How tall are you?*

> NOTE **Tall** and **high** have similar meanings. We use **tall** to describe the height of people (*He is six feet three inches tall.*), of trees (*A tall oak tree stood in the front yard.*), and also sometimes to talk about narrow objects (*the tall skyscrapers of Manhattan*).

**the Tal·mud** /ˈtɑlmʊd; ˈtælməd/ ***noun*** [sing.] a collection of ancient writings on Jewish law and traditions

**talon** /ˈtælən/ ***noun*** [C] a long sharp curved nail on the feet of some birds, especially birds that kill other creatures for food (**birds of prey**) ➲ picture at **eagle**.

**tam·bou·rine** /ˌtæmbəˈrin/ ***noun*** [C] a small round musical instrument with metal discs around the edge. You can hit it or shake it.

**tambourine**

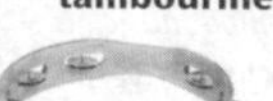

**tame¹** /teɪm/ ***adj.*** **1** (used about animals or birds) not wild or afraid of people: *The birds are so tame they will eat from your hand.* **2** boring; not interesting or exciting: *After the big city, you must find country life very tame.*

**tame²** /teɪm/ ***verb*** [T] to bring sth wild under your control

**tamp·er** /ˈtæmpər/ ***verb*** [I] **tamper with sth** to use, touch, change, etc. sth when you should not: *Don't eat the candy if the packaging has been tampered with.*

**tam·pon** /ˈtæmpɑn/ ***noun*** [C] a tightly-rolled piece of cotton that a woman puts inside her body to collect blood during her PERIOD (3)

**tan¹** /tæn/ ***noun*** **1** [C] (*also* **suntan**) a darker color that your skin has after you spend time in the sun: *to get a tan* **2** [U] a pale color between yellow and brown

**tan²** /tæn/ ***adj.*** **1** having a pale color between yellow and brown: *tan shoes* **2** having darker skin than usual because of spending time in the sun: *You look very tan – have you been on vacation?*

**tan³** /tæn/ ***verb*** [I,T] (**tan·ning**; **tanned**) to become or to let sth, especially your skin, become brown with the effect of the sun: *Do you tan easily?* ◇ *I'm trying to tan my legs.*

**tan·dem** /ˈtændəm/ ***noun*** [C] a bicycle for two riders, one behind the other

IDM **in tandem (with sb/sth)** a thing that works or happens in tandem with sth else works together with it or happens at the same time as it: *The two systems are designed to work in tandem.* ◇ *Stock prices pushed sharply higher this afternoon in tandem with a rise in the dollar.*

**tan·ger·ine** /ˌtændʒəˈrin/ ***noun*** [C] a fruit like a small sweet orange with a skin that is easy to take off

**tan·gi·ble** /ˈtændʒəbl/ ***adj.*** (*formal*) clear and definite: *There are tangible benefits in the new system.*

**tan·gle** /ˈtæŋgl/ ***noun*** [C] a confused mass, especially of threads, hair, branches, etc. that cannot easily be separated from each other: *My hair's full of tangles.* ▸ **tan·gled** ***adj.***: *The yarn was all tangled up.*

**tan·go¹** /ˈtæŋgoʊ/ ***noun*** [C] (*pl.* **tan·gos**) a fast South American dance with a strong beat, in which two people hold each other closely; a piece of music for this dance

**tan·go²** /ˈtæŋgoʊ/ ***verb*** [T] (*pres. part.* **tan·go·ing**; *pt, pp* **tan·goed**) to dance the tango

IDM **it takes two to tango** (*informal*) (used to say that two people or groups, and not just one, are responsible for sth bad that has happened

⋆**tank** /tæŋk/ ***noun*** [C] **1** a container for holding liquids or gas: *How many gallons does the gas tank hold?* ◇ *a water tank* **2** a large, heavy military vehicle covered with steel and armed with guns, that moves on special wheels: *Hundreds of tanks have crossed the border and are ready to attack.*

**tank·er** /ˈtæŋkər/ ***noun*** [C] a ship for carrying gasoline, etc. in large amounts: *an oil tanker*

**tan·ta·liz·ing** /ˈtæntl-aɪzɪŋ/ ***adj.*** (used about sth that you cannot have) attractive or tempting: *A tantalizing smell of cooking was coming from the kitchen.* ▸ **tan·ta·liz·ing·ly** ***adv.***: *tantalizingly close*

**tan·trum** /ˈtæntrəm/ ***noun*** [C] a sudden burst of anger, especially in a child

⋆**tap¹** /tæp/ ***verb*** (**tap·ping**; **tapped**) **1** [I,T] **tap (at/on sth)**; **tap sb/sth (on/with sth)** to touch or hit sb/sth quickly and gently: *Their feet were tapping in time to the music.* ◇ *They won't hear if you only tap on the door – knock harder!* ◇ *She tapped me on the shoulder and said, "Excuse me, I think you dropped this notebook."* **2** [I,T] **tap (into) sth** to make use of sth from a supply or reserve: *to tap the skills of young people* **3** [T] to attach a piece of equipment to sb's telephone wires so that you can listen to telephone conversations on that line

**tap²** /tæp/ ***noun*** [C] **1** a quick gentle hit or the sound it makes: *a tap on the shoulder* **2** = FAUCET ➲ Look also at **tap water**. **3** a device that is fitted to sb's telephone so that his/her telephone calls can be listened to secretly

IDM **on tap 1** (used especially about beer) served directly from a large container (**barrel**), not in a bottle or can **2** (*informal*) ready and available for use: *information on tap via the Internet*

**ˈtap dance** ***noun*** [C] a dance in which you tap the rhythm with your feet, wearing special shoes with metal pieces on the bottoms to make noise ▸ **ˈtap-dance** ***verb*** [I]

⋆**tape¹** /teɪp/ ***noun*** **1** [U] a long, narrow piece of plastic or paper that is sticky on one side and is used for wrapping packages, fastening pieces of paper together, etc.: *a roll of tape* ◇ *electrical tape* ➲ Look also at **Scotch tape**. **2** [U] magnetic material used for recording sound, pictures or information: *I have the whole concert on tape* (= recorded). **3** [C] a cassette with magnetic material wound around it, which is used for recording or playing music, videos, etc.: *a blank tape* ◇ *to rewind a tape* ➲ Look at **cassette**, **CD** and **record**[1](2). **4** [C] a long narrow strip of material that is stretched across the place where a race will finish: *the finishing tape*

**tape**[2] /teɪp/ ***verb*** [T] **1** to fasten sth with TAPE[1] (1): *to tape an envelope shut* **2** to record sound, music, television programs, etc. using a cassette: *There's a movie on TV tonight that I want to tape.*

**ˈtape deck** ***noun*** [C] the part of a stereo system on which you play TAPES[1] (3)

**ˈtape ˌmeasure** ***noun*** [C] a long thin piece of plastic or cloth with inches or centimeters marked on it. It is used for measuring things.

**ˈtape player** ***noun*** [C] a machine that is used for playing recordings of music or other sounds on TAPE[1] (2)

**ˈtape reˌcorder** ***noun*** [C] a machine that is used for recording or playing back music or other sounds on TAPE[1] (2)

**tap·es·try** /ˈtæpəstri/ ***noun*** [C,U] (*pl.* **tap·es·tries**) a piece of heavy cloth with pictures or designs sewn on it in colored thread

**ˈtap ˌwater** ***noun*** [U] water that comes out of taps, not water sold in bottles

**tar** /tɑr/ ***noun*** [U] **1** a thick black sticky liquid that becomes hard when it is cold. It is used for making roads, etc. **2** a harmful solid substance that is formed by burning tobacco: *low-tar cigarettes*

**ta·ran·tu·la** /təˈræntʃələ/ ***noun*** [C] a large spider covered with hair that lives in hot countries. Some types of tarantula have a poisonous bite.

tarantula

**tar·dy** /ˈtɑrdi/ ***adj.*** (*formal*) late ▸ **tar·di·ness** ***noun*** [U]

★**tar·get**[1] /ˈtɑrgət/ ***noun*** [C] **1** a person or thing that you aim at when shooting or attacking: *Attacks have been launched on military targets such as army bases.* ◇ *The bomb missed its target and fell into the ocean.* ◇ *The embassy was a likely target for terrorist attacks.* **2** an object, often a round board with circles on it, that you aim at in shooting practice: *I hit the target twice but missed it once.* **3** a person or thing that people blame, criticize, laugh at, etc.: *The educational system has been the target of heavy criticism.* **4** a result that you are aiming at: *Our target is to raise $10,000 for the Red Cross.* ◇ *So far, we're right on target* (= making the progress we expected).

**tar·get**[2] /ˈtɑrgət/ ***verb*** [T] **1** **target sth (at/to sb/sth)** to aim or direct sth at sb/sth: *He targeted most of his criticism at the secretaries.* **2** to try to have an effect on sb/sth: *an ad campaign that targets young professional women*

**tar·iff** /ˈtærɪf/ ***noun*** [C] a tax that has to be paid on goods brought into a country

**tar·mac** /ˈtɑrmæk/ ***noun*** [U] an area at an airport with a hard surface where planes can stand or drive across: *The plane waited for two hours on the tarmac.*

**tar·nish** /ˈtɑrnɪʃ/ ***verb*** **1** [I,T] (used about a mirror, metal, etc.) to become less bright; to make less bright **2** [T] (used about a reputation) to spoil: *His reputation was tarnished by the scandal.*

**tarp** /tɑrp/ (*also formal* **tar·pau·lin** /tɑrˈpɔlən/) ***noun*** [C] a large piece of strong, waterproof material that is used for covering things

**tart**[1] /tɑrt/ ***adj.*** having a sharp, sour taste: *a tart apple*

**tart**[2] /tɑrt/ ***noun*** [C,U] a small pie with a sweet filling, such as fruit or jam

**tar·tar sauce** /ˈtɑrt̬ər sɔs/ ***noun*** [U] a thick cold white sauce made from mayonnaise mixed with chopped onions, capers, etc., that is usually eaten with fish

★**task** /tæsk/ ***noun*** [C] a piece of work that has to be done, especially an unpleasant or difficult one: *Your first task will be to type these letters.* ◇ *I found learning Arabic an almost impossible task.* ◇ *They assigned me the task of organizing the class trip.*

**ˈtask force** ***noun*** [C] **1** a military force that is brought together and sent to a particular place **2** a group of people who are brought together to deal with a particular problem: *a drug task force*

★**taste**[1] /teɪst/ ***noun***

▸SENSE **1** [U] the ability to recognize the flavor of food or drink: *Taste is one of the five senses.*

▸FLAVOR **2** [sing.] the flavor of food or drink: *I don't like the taste of this coffee.*

▸SMALL QUANTITY **3** [C, usually sing.] **a taste (of sth)** a small amount of sth to eat or drink: *Have a taste of this cheese to see if you like it.*

▸ABILITY TO CHOOSE WELL **4** [U] the ability to make good choices about whether things are suitable, of good quality, etc.: *He has excellent taste in music.*

▸WHAT YOU LIKE **5** [sing.] **a taste (for sth)** a liking for sth: *She has developed a taste for modern art.*

▸SHORT EXPERIENCE **6** [sing.] a short experience of sth: *This was my **first taste** of live theater.* ◇ *Although we didn't know it, this incident was **a taste of things to come**.*

IDM **(be) in bad taste** (used about sb's behavior) (to be) unsuitable and unkind: *Some of his comments were in very bad taste.*

★**taste**[2] /teɪst/ ***verb*** (not in the *-ing* forms) **1** [T] to be aware of or recognize the flavor of food or drink: *Can you taste the garlic in this soup?* **2** [T] to try a small amount of food and drink; to test: *Can I taste a piece of that cheese to see what it's like?* **3** [I] **taste (like sth)** to have a particular flavor: *Some people say that frog legs taste like chicken.* ◇ *to taste sour/sweet/delicious*

**taste·ful** /ˈteɪstfl/ ***adj.*** attractive and well-chosen: *The furniture was very tasteful.* ▸ **taste·ful·ly** ***adv.***

**taste·less** /ˈteɪstləs/ ***adj.*** **1** likely to offend sb: *His joke about the funeral was very tasteless.* **2** having little or no flavor: *We had some tasteless cheese sandwiches for lunch.* **3** unattractive; not well-chosen: *She was wearing a lot of tasteless jewelry.*

**tast·y** /ˈteɪsti/ ***adj.*** (**tast·i·er**; **tast·i·est**) having a



T

good, strong flavor: *spaghetti with a tasty mushroom sauce*

**tat·tered** /ˈtæt̬ərd/ ***adj.*** old and torn: *a tattered coat*

**tat·ters** /ˈtæt̬ərz/ ***noun***
**IDM in tatters** badly torn or damaged: *Her dress was in tatters.* ◇ *(figurative) After the divorce, my life seemed to be in tatters.*

**tat·tle** /ˈtæt̬l/ ***verb*** [I] *(informal)* **tattle (on sb) (to sb)** to tell sb, especially sb in authority, about sth bad that sb else has done: *You should learn that you just don't* ***tattle on*** *classmates.*

**tat·tle·tale** /ˈtæt̬lteɪl/ ***noun*** [C] *(informal)* a child who tells an adult what another child has done wrong: *You told Mom? You're such a tattletale!*

**tat·too** /tæˈtu/ ***noun*** [C] (*pl.* **tat·toos**) a picture or pattern on sb's body that is made by sticking a needle into his/her skin and filling the holes with colored liquid ▶ **tat·too** ***verb*** [T]: *She had the word "love" tattooed on her left hand.*

**tattoo**

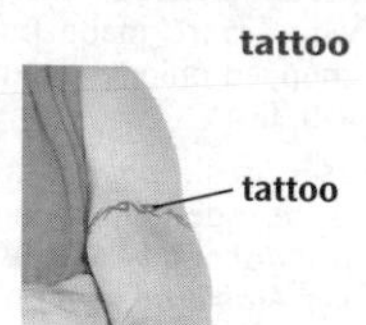


**tau** /taʊ/ ***noun*** [C] *(symbol* Τ, τ*)* the nineteenth letter of the Greek alphabet ➲ Look at the note at **fraternity**.

**taught** *past tense, past participle of* TEACH

**taunt** /tɔnt; tɑnt/ ***verb*** [T] to try to make sb angry or unhappy by saying unkind or cruel things: *They taunted him with cries of "Big nose!"* ▶ **taunt** ***noun*** [C]

**Tau·rus** /ˈtɔrəs/ ***noun*** [C,U] the second sign of the zodiac, the Bull; a person who was born under this sign

**taut** /tɔt/ ***adj.*** (used about rope, wire, etc.) stretched very tight; not loose

**tav·ern** /ˈtævərn/ ***noun*** [C] a bar that serves mainly beer and wine

T

★**tax¹** /tæks/ ***noun*** [C,U] the money that you have to pay to the government so that it can provide public services: *to pay your federal income taxes* ◇ *to file a tax return* ◇ *How much tax is there on a pack of cigarettes?* ◇ *tax cuts* ➲ Look also at **sales tax**.

★**tax²** /tæks/ ***verb*** [T] (often passive) **1** to take a tax from a sum of money, or to add it to the price of goods and services: *Lottery winnings are heavily taxed.* ◇ *Diesel fuel is taxed at 24.3 cents a gallon.* **2** to make a person or an organization pay tax: *A government should tax its citizens fairly.*

**tax·a·ble** /ˈtæksəbl/ ***adj.*** on which you have to pay tax: *taxable income*

**tax·a·tion** /tækˈseɪʃn/ ***noun*** [U] **1** the system by which a government takes money from people so that it can pay for public services: *direct/indirect taxation* **2** the amount of money that people have to pay in taxes: *to increase/reduce taxation* ◇ *high/low taxation*

ˌ**tax-deˈductible** ***adj.*** that can be taken off your total income before you calculate how much income tax you must pay

ˌ**tax-exˈempt** ***adj.*** (usually *before* a noun) free from having to pay taxes, or on which you do not have to pay taxes: *a tax-exempt organization* ◇ *tax-exempt savings bonds*

★**tax·i¹** /ˈtæksi/ (*pl.* **tax·is**) (*also* ˈ**tax·i·cab** /ˈtæksikæb/, **cab**) ***noun*** [C] a car with a driver, whose job is to take you somewhere in exchange for money: *Do you want to drive there or take a taxi?*

> **NOTE** The amount of money that you have to pay (your **fare**) is shown on a **meter**. People often give the taxi driver a **tip** (= a small extra amount of money that is not included in the fare).

**tax·i²** /ˈtæksi/ ***verb*** [I] (*pres. part.* **tax·i·ing**; *3rd person sing. pres.* **tax·is**; *pt, pp* **tax·ied**) (used about an aircraft) to move slowly along the ground before or after flying

**tax·ing** /ˈtæksɪŋ/ ***adj.*** difficult; needing a lot of effort: *a taxing problem*

**tax·pay·er** /ˈtækspeɪər/ ***noun*** [C] a person who pays taxes

ˈ**tax return** ***noun*** [C] an official document in which you give details of the amount of money that you have earned and calculate the amount of tax that you have to pay

**TB** /ˌti ˈbi/ ***abbr.*** = TUBERCULOSIS (2)

**T-bone steak** /ˌti boʊn ˈsteɪk/ ***noun*** [C] a thick slice of beef containing a bone in the shape of a T

**tbsp.** ***abbr.*** = TABLESPOON (2)

★**tea** /ti/ ***noun*** **1** [U] a hot brown drink that you make by pouring boiling water onto the dried leaves of a bush grown in hot countries such as India and China: *a cup/pot of tea* ◇ *I'll make some tea.* ◇ *weak/strong tea* **2** [C,U] the dried leaves that are used for making TEA (1), or a particular type of these leaves **3** [U] a drink that you make by pouring hot water onto the dried leaves of other plants: *herbal tea*
**IDM (not) sb's cup of tea** → CUP¹

ˈ**tea bag** ***noun*** [C] a small paper bag with tea leaves in it, that you use for making tea

★**teach** /titʃ/ ***verb*** (*pt, pp* **taught** /tɔt/) **1** [I,T] to give sb lessons or instructions so that he/she knows how to do sth: *Colin is teaching us how to use the computer.* ◇ *My mother taught me to play the piano.* ◇ *He teaches English to international students.* **2** [T] to make sb believe sth or behave in a certain way: *The story teaches us that history often repeats itself.* ◇ *My parents taught me always to tell the truth.* **3** [T] to persuade sb not to do sth again by making him/her suffer so much that he/she is afraid to do it: *Lost all your money?* ***That'll teach you*** *to gamble.* ◇ *I'll teach you to call* (= punish you for calling) *me a liar!* ◇ *The accident* ***taught me a lesson*** *I'll never forget.*

★**teach·er** /ˈtitʃər/ ***noun*** [C] a person whose job is to teach, especially in a school: *Mrs. Wilson was my science teacher in eighth grade.* ◇ *a piano teacher*

> **NOTE** In English-speaking countries, we do not use the word **teacher** when we speak to a teacher. The most common way to address a teacher is to use a title, e.g. **Mr.**, **Mrs.**, or **Ms.** with the teacher's last name: *Good morning, Mrs. Brown.* If the teacher is a professor at a college or university, we usually use the title **Professor** or **Doctor** with the person's last name: *Excuse me, Dr. Waters – I have*

*a question.* In language schools and informal lessons, most teachers allow students to call them by their first names: *Can you repeat that, Micky?*

ˌ**teacher's ˈpet** *noun* [C] (*informal*) a student who makes an effort to become a teacher's favorite student, and who is often disliked by other students because of this

⋆**teach·ing** /ˈtitʃɪŋ/ *noun* **1** [U] the work or profession of a teacher: *My son went into teaching and my daughter became a doctor.* ◇ *part-time teaching* ◇ *teaching methods* **2** [U, pl.] ideas and beliefs that are taught by sb/sth: *the teachings of Gandhi*

ˈ**teaching asˌsistant** *noun* [C] (*abbr.* **TA**) a more advanced student who teaches or helps to teach some classes for other students at a university, while he/she is studying for a more advanced degree

**tea·cup** /ˈtikʌp/ *noun* [C] a cup that you drink tea from

**tea·ket·tle** /ˈtikɛt̬l/ (*also* **kettle**) *noun* [C] a metal container with a lid, handle and a place to pour water out of (**a spout**). It is used for boiling water.

**tea·light** /ˈtilaɪt/ (*also* ˈ**tea light**) *noun* [C] a small candle that is used for decoration and which often gives off a pleasant smell: *scented tealights* ➲ picture at *candle*.

⋆**team**[1] /tim/ *noun* [C] **1** a group of people who play a sport or game together against another group: *a football team* ◇ *Are you on the team?* **2** a group of people who work together: *a team of medical workers*

**team**[2] /tim/ *verb*

PHR V **team up (with sb)** to join sb in order to do sth together

**team·work** /ˈtimwərk/ *noun* [U] the ability of people to work together: *Good teamwork between nurses and doctors is very important.*

**tea·pot** /ˈtipɑt/ *noun* [C] a container that you make tea in and use to pour tea into cups. It has a lid, a handle and a small thin tube (**a spout**) that the tea is poured out of.

⋆**tear**[1] /tɪr/ *noun* [C, usually pl.] a drop of water that comes from your eye when you are crying, etc.: *She wiped away his tears.* ◇ *I was in tears* (= crying) *at the end of the movie.* ◇ *The little girl burst into tears* (= suddenly started to cry).

**tear**

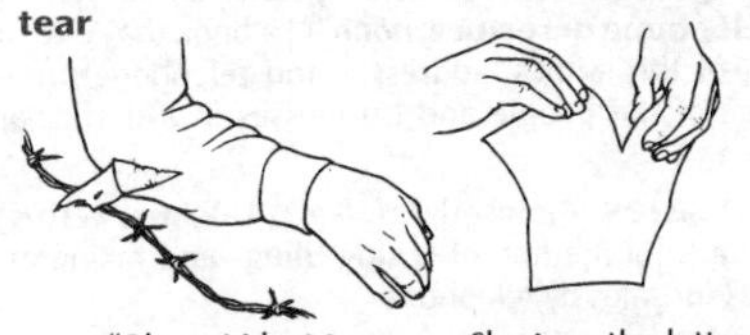

"Oh, no! I just **tore** my shirt!"

She **tore** the letter in half.

⋆**tear**[2] /tɛr/ *verb* (*pt* **tore** /tɔr/; *pp* **torn** /tɔrn/) **1** [T] to pull paper, cloth, etc. so that it comes apart or gets a hole in it: *I tore my shirt on that nail.* ◇ *He tore a hole in his favorite jacket.* ◇ *Tear the paper along the dotted line.* ◇ *She tore the letter in half.* ◇ *I tore a page out of my notebook.* **2** [I] to become damaged by pulling: *This material doesn't tear easily.* **3** [T] to remove sth by pulling it violently and quickly: *Paul tore the poster down from the wall.* **4** [I] to move very quickly in a particular direction, often in a careless way: *Katy went tearing through the kitchen and out the door.*

PHR V **tear sth apart 1** to pull sth violently into pieces: *The bird was torn apart by the two dogs.* **2** to cause serious problems in a place, an organization, etc.: *Drugs are tearing our communities apart.*

**tear yourself away (from sb/sth)** to make yourself leave sb/sth or stop doing sth: *Tim can't tear himself away from that computer game.*

**be torn between A and B** to find it difficult to choose between two things or people

**tear sth down** to destroy a building: *They tore down the old houses and built a shopping mall.*

**tear sth up** to pull sth (usually sth made of paper) into pieces: *"I hate this picture," she said, tearing it up.*

⋆**tear**[3] /tɛr/ *noun* [C] a hole in paper, cloth, etc. that is caused by tearing

IDM **wear and tear** → WEAR[2]

**tear·ful** /ˈtɪrfl/ *adj.* crying or very sad: *a tearful farewell*

**tear·gas** /ˈtɪrgæs/ *noun* [U] a type of gas that makes people's eyes fill with TEARS[1]. It is used by the police, etc. to control large groups of people.

**tease** /tiz/ *verb* **1** [I,T] to say unkind or personal things to sb because you think it is funny: *Don't pay any attention to those boys. They're only teasing.* ◇ *They teased her about being fat.* **2** [T] to comb your hair in the opposite direction to the way it grows so that it looks thicker

⋆**tea·spoon** /ˈtispun/ *noun* [C] **1** a small spoon that is used for stirring tea, eating, etc. **2** (*also* **teaspoonful** /-fʊl/) (*abbr.* **t.**; **tsp.**) the amount that a TEASPOON (1) can hold

ˈ**tea ˌtowel** *noun* [C] (*Cdn*) a small towel used for drying cups, plates, knives, etc. after they have been washed SYN **dishtowel**

⋆**tech·ni·cal** /ˈtɛknɪkl/ *adj.* **1** involving detailed knowledge of the machines, materials, systems, etc. that are used in industry or science: *They don't have the technical knowledge to develop nuclear weapons.* **2** (used about sb's practical ability in a particular activity): *The pianist performed with great technical skill but without much feeling.* **3** (only *before* a noun) relating to a particular subject: *the technical terms connected with computers*

**tech·ni·cal·i·ty** /ˌtɛknɪˈkæləṭi/ *noun* [C] (*pl.* **tech·ni·cal·i·ties**) one of the details of a particular subject or activity: *The jury's verdict was thrown out on a legal technicality.*

**tech·ni·cal·ly** /ˈtɛknɪkli/ *adv.* **1** following a very exact interpretation of facts or laws: *Technically, you should pay by May 1st, but it doesn't matter if it's a few days late.* **2** in a way that involves detailed knowledge of the machines, etc. that are used in industry or science: *The country is not very advanced technically.* **3** (used about sb's practical ability in a particular activity): *a technically outstanding performance*

**tech·ni·cian** /tɛkˈnɪʃn/ *noun* [C] a person whose work involves practical skills, especially in industry or science: *a laboratory technician*

⋆**tech·nique** /tɛkˈnik/ *noun* **1** [C] a particular

T

way of doing sth: *new techniques for teaching languages* **2** [U] your practical ability in sth

**tech·nol·o·gist** /tɛk'nɑlədʒɪst/ ***noun*** [C] a person who is an expert in technology

★**tech·nol·o·gy** /tɛk'nɑlədʒi/ ***noun*** (*pl.* **tech·nol·o·gies**) **1** [U] the study and use of science for practical purposes in industry, etc. **2** [C,U] the scientific knowledge that is needed for a particular industry, etc.: *developments in computer technology* ▸ **tech·no·log·i·cal** /ˌtɛknə'lɑdʒɪkl/ ***adj.***: *technological developments*

**ted·dy bear** /'tɛdi bɛr/ ***noun*** [C] a toy for children that looks like a bear

**teddy bear**

**te·di·ous** /'tidiəs/ ***adj.*** boring and lasting for a long time: *a tedious lecture*

**teem** /tim/ ***verb*** [I] **teem with sth** (usually in the *-ing* forms) (used about a place) having a lot of people or things moving around in it: *The streets were teeming with people.*

**teen** /tin/ ***adj., noun*** [C] teenage; teenager: *unmarried teen mothers*

**teen·age** (*also* **teen-age**) /'tineɪdʒ/ (*also* **teen-aged, teen-aged** /'tineɪdʒd/) ***adj.*** (only *before* a noun) **1** between 13 and 19 years old: *teenage children* **2** typical of or suitable for people between 13 and 19 years old: *teenage fashion*

**teen·ag·er** (*also* **teen-ager**) /'tineɪdʒər/ ***noun*** [C] a person who is between 13 and 19 years old: *Her music is very popular with teenagers.*

**teens** /tinz/ ***noun*** [pl.] the period of a person's life between the ages of 13 and 19: *to be in your late/early teens*

**tee·pee** = TEPEE

**tee·ter-tot·ter** /'tit̬ərˌtɑt̬ər/ ***noun*** [C] = SEESAW

**teeth** *plural of* TOOTH

**teethe** /tið/ ***verb*** [I] (usually used in the *-ing* forms) (used about a baby) to start growing its first teeth

**T**

**tee·to·ta·ler** /'titoʊt̬l·ər/ ***noun*** [C] a person who never drinks alcohol

**Tef·lon™** /'tɛflɑn/ ***noun*** [U] a special smooth substance that is often used on the inside surfaces or pans to prevent food from sticking

**tele-** /'tɛlə/ ***prefix*** (in nouns, verbs, adjectives and adverbs) **1** over a long distance; far: *telepathy* ◇ *telescopic* **2** connected with television: *teletext* **3** done using a telephone: *telesales*

**tel·e·com·mu·ni·ca·tions** /ˌtɛləkəˌmyunə'keɪʃnz/ ***noun*** [pl.] the process of communicating over long distances by using electronic equipment, e.g. by radio or telephone, or the business of providing equipment and services to communicate in this way

**tel·e·com·mut·ing** /'tɛləkəmyut̬ɪŋ/ ***noun*** [U] working at home, using a computer that is connected with the computers in your company's office through telephone lines ▸ **tel·e·com·mut·er** ***noun*** [C]

**tel·e·con·fer·ence** /'tɛləˌkɑnfrəns; -fərəns/ ***noun*** [C] a conference or discussion at which members are in different places and speak to each other using telephone and video connections ▸ **tel·e·con·fer·ence** ***verb*** [I]

**tel·e·gram** /'tɛləgræm/ ***noun*** [C] a type of short message that is sent through wires over a long distance using electrical signals and is delivered to sb on a printed form. Telegrams were more common in the past.

**tel·e·graph** /'tɛləgræf/ ***noun*** [C,U] a system or a piece of equipment for sending telegrams

**tel·e·mar·ket·ing** /ˌtɛlə'mɑrkət̬ɪŋ; 'tɛləˌmɑr-/ ***noun*** [U] = TELESALES

**te·le·pa·thy** /tə'lɛpəθi/ ***noun*** [U] the direct communication of thoughts or feelings from one person to another without using speech, writing, or any other normal method ▸ **te·le·pa·thic** /ˌtɛlə'pæθɪk/ ***adj.***

★**tel·e·phone[1]** /'tɛləfoʊn/ (*also* **phone**) ***noun*** **1** [U] an electrical system for talking to sb in another house, town, country, etc. by speaking into a special piece of equipment: *Can I contact you by telephone?* ◇ *to make a telephone call* ◇ *a telephone number*

**telephone**

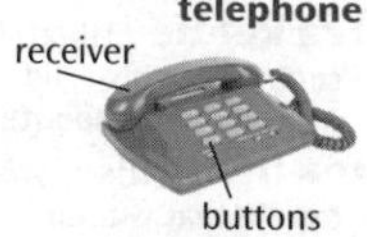


NOTE It is more common to use **phone** rather than **telephone**, especially when you are speaking. When you make a telephone call, you first **pick up the receiver** and **dial** the number. The telephone **rings** and the person at the other end **answers** it. If he/she is already using the telephone, it is **busy**. When you finish speaking, you **hang up**.

**2** [C] the piece of equipment that you use when you talk to sb by TELEPHONE (1): *Could I use your telephone?* ➲ Look also at **cellular phone** and **pay phone**.

IDM **on the phone/telephone** → PHONE[1]

**tel·e·phone[2]** /'tɛləfoʊn/ (*also* **phone**) ***verb*** [I,T] (*formal*) to use a telephone in order to speak to sb: *The president telephoned the astronauts to congratulate them on their success.* ➲ **Call** is more common than **telephone** or **phone**.

★'**telephone book** (*also* '**phone book**, *formal* '**telephone diˌrectory**) ***noun*** [C] a book that gives a list of the names, addresses and telephone numbers of the people and businesses in a particular area

**tel·e·sales** /'tɛləseɪlz/ (*also* ˌ**tele'marketing**) ***noun*** [U] a method of selling things and taking orders for sales by telephone

**tel·e·scope** /'tɛləskoʊp/ ***noun*** [C] an instrument in the shape of a tube with special glass inside it. You look through it to make distant things, especially in outer space, appear bigger and nearer. ➲ Compare **microscope**. ➲ picture at **binoculars**.

**tel·e·van·ge·list** /ˌtɛlə'vændʒəlɪst/ ***noun*** [C] a person who appears regularly on television to try to persuade people to become Christians and to give money ▸ **tel·e·van·ge·lism** ***noun*** [U]

**tel·e·vise** /'tɛləvaɪz/ ***verb*** [T] to show sth on television: *a televised concert*

★**tel·e·vi·sion** /ˈtɛləvɪʒn/ (*also* **TV**) ***noun*** **1** [C] (*also* ˈ**television set**, ˌ**TˈV set**) a piece of electrical equipment in the shape of a box. It has a glass screen which shows programs with moving pictures and sounds: *to turn the television on/off* **2** [U] the electrical system and business of sending out programs so that people can watch them on their television sets: *in the days before television* ◇ *cable/satellite television* ◇ *the major TV networks* ◇ *She works in television.* ➲ Look also at **public television**. **3** [U] the programs that are shown on a television set: *Paul's watching television.*
IDM **on television** being shown by television: *What's on television tonight?*

★**tell** /tɛl/ ***verb*** (*pt, pp* **told** /toʊld/)
➤GIVE INFORMATION **1** [T] **tell sb (sth); tell sth (to sb)** to give information to sb by speaking or writing: *She told me her address, but I forgot it.* ◇ *He wrote to tell me that his mother died.* ◇ *Tell us about your vacation.* ◇ *Tell me what you did yesterday.* ◇ *to tell the truth/a lie* ◇ *to tell a story* ◇ *Excuse me, can you tell me where the post office is?* ➲ Look at the note at **say**. **2** [T] (used about a thing) to give information to sb: *This book will tell you all you need to know.*
➤ORDER **3** [T] **tell sb (to do sth)** to order or advise sb to do sth: *The police officer told us to get out of the car.* ◇ *Dad told me not to worry about my final exams.* ◇ *Please tell me what to do.* ◇ *You'll be all right if you do as you're told.*
➤KNOW/JUDGE **4** [I,T] to know, see or judge (sth) correctly: *"What do you think Jenny will do next?" "It's hard to tell."* ◇ *I could tell that he enjoyed the evening.* ◇ *I can't tell which coat is mine. They look exactly the same.*
➤INFORM AUTHORITIES **5** [I] **tell (on sb)** (*informal*) to inform a person in authority that sb has done sth wrong: *If you do that again, I'm going to tell on you!*
IDM **as far as I can see/tell** = FAR²
**I told you (so)** (*informal*) I warned you that this would happen
**tell A and B apart** → APART
**tell time** to read the time from a clock or watch
**to tell (you) the truth** (used to emphasize that you are being honest about sth): *Well, to tell you the truth, I never even considered the cost.*
PHRV **tell sb off (for sth/for doing sth)** to speak to sb angrily because he/she has done sth wrong

**tell·er** /ˈtɛlər/ ***noun*** [C] a person who works in a bank and whose job is to receive and pay out money ➲ Look also at **ATM**.

**tell·ing** /ˈtɛlɪŋ/ ***adj.*** (usually *before* a noun) **1** showing your real feelings or thoughts: *a telling remark* **2** having a great effect: *the most telling evidence in the case*

**tell·tale** /ˈtɛlteɪl/ ***adj.*** giving information about sth secret or private: *the telltale signs of child abuse*

**temp** /tɛmp/ ***noun*** [C] a temporary employee, especially a secretary, who works somewhere for a short period of time when sb else is sick or on vacation, or when a business needs extra help for a short time ▶ **temp** ***verb*** [I]: *Julie's temping at an insurance company this summer.*

**tem·per** /ˈtɛmpər/ ***noun*** [C,U] a tendency to become angry and impatient easily, and to be unable to control your behavior: *Be careful of Paul. He has a violent temper.* ◇ *You need to learn to control your temper.*
IDM **keep/lose your temper** to stay calm/to become angry

**tem·per·a** /ˈtɛmpərə/ ***noun*** [U] a kind of paint in which the color is mixed with egg and water; a method of painting that uses this kind of paint

**tem·per·a·ment** /ˈtɛmprəmənt/ ***noun*** [C,U] a person's character, especially as it affects the way he/she behaves and feels: *to have a calm temperament*

**tem·per·a·men·tal** /ˌtɛmprəˈmɛntl/ ***adj.*** often and suddenly changing the way you behave

**tem·per·ate** /ˈtɛmpərət/ ***adj.*** (used about a climate) not very hot and not very cold

★**tem·per·a·ture** /ˈtɛmprətʃər/ ***noun*** **1** [C,U] how hot or cold sth is: *Heat the oven to a temperature of 450°F.* ◇ *Temperatures in some parts of Michigan will fall below freezing tomorrow.* ◇ *a high/low temperature* **2** [C] how hot or cold a person's body is
IDM **have a temperature** to have a temperature of the body that is higher than normal (when you are sick)
**take sb's temperature** to measure the temperature of sb's body with a special instrument (thermometer)

**tem·ple** /ˈtɛmpl/ ***noun*** [C] **1** a building where people pray and worship in some religions: *a Buddhist temple* **2** = SYNAGOGUE **3** one of the flat parts on each side of your forehead

**tem·po** /ˈtɛmpoʊ/ ***noun*** (*pl.* **tem·pos** /ˈtɛmpoʊz/) **1** [C,U] the speed of a piece of music **2** [sing., U] the speed of an activity or event

★**tem·po·rar·y** /ˈtɛmpəˌrɛri/ ***adj.*** lasting for a short time; not permanent: *a temporary job* ◇ *This arrangement is only temporary.* ▶ **tem·po·rar·i·ly** /ˌtɛmpəˈrɛrəli/ ***adv.***

**tempt** /tɛmpt/ ***verb*** [T] to try to persuade or attract sb to do sth, especially sth that is wrong or silly: *His dream of riches had tempted him into a life of crime.* ◇ *She was tempted to stay in bed all morning.* ◇ *I'm very tempted by the idea of working in another country.*

**temp·ta·tion** /tɛmpˈteɪʃn/ ***noun*** **1** [U] a feeling that you want to do sth, although you know that it is wrong or silly: *I resisted the temptation to have another glass of wine.* **2** [C] a thing that attracts you to do sth wrong or silly: *All that money is certainly a big temptation.*

**tempt·ing** /ˈtɛmptɪŋ/ ***adj.*** attractive and making you want to do sth: *a tempting offer* ◇ *That chocolate cake looks very tempting!*

**ten** /tɛn/ ***number*** 10; one more than nine ➲ For examples of how to use numbers in sentences, look at **six**.

**te·na·cious** /təˈneɪʃəs/ ***adj.*** very determined about sth; not likely to give up or accept defeat: *a tenacious defender of human rights* ▶ **te·nac·i·ty** /təˈnæsət̬i/ ***noun*** [U]

**ten·ant** /ˈtɛnənt/ ***noun*** [C] a person who pays money (rent) to the owner of an apartment,

T

building or a piece of land so that he/she can live in it or use it: *The previous tenants of the apartment were college students.* ➲ The owner is called a **landlord** or **landlady**.

★**tend** /tɛnd/ ***verb*** **1** [I] **tend to do sth** to often or normally do or be sth: *Women tend to live longer than men.* ◊ *There tends to be a lot of traffic on that road.* ◊ *My brother tends to talk a lot when he's nervous.* **2** [I,T] **tend (to) sb/sth** (*formal*) to take care of sb/sth: *He lovingly tended the roses in his garden.*

★**ten·den·cy** /ˈtɛndənsi/ ***noun*** [C] (*pl.* **ten·den·cies**) something that a person or thing does; a way of behaving: *He has a tendency to be late for appointments.* ◊ *a patient with suicidal tendencies* ◊ *There's a growing tendency for people to work at home.*

**ten·der**[1] /ˈtɛndər/ ***adj.*** **1** kind and loving: *She whispered a few tender words in his ear.* **2** (used about meat) soft and easy to cut or bite; not tough **3** (used about a part of the body) painful when you touch it **4** young and without much experience of life: *She went to live in London at the tender age of 15.* ▸ **ten·der·ly** ***adv.*** ▸ **ten·der·ness** ***noun*** [U]

**ten·der**[2] /ˈtɛndər/ ***verb*** [T] (*formal*) to offer or give sth formally: *After the scandal, the Senator was forced to tender her resignation.*

**ten·don** /ˈtɛndən/ ***noun*** [C] a strong cord in your body that connects a muscle to a bone

**ten·e·ment** /ˈtɛnəmənt/ ***noun*** [C] a large, old building that is divided into small apartments, especially in a poor area of a city

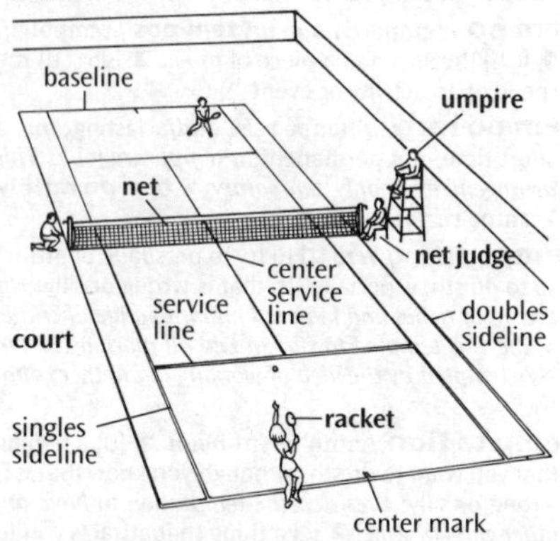


**ten·nis** /ˈtɛnəs/ ***noun*** [U] a game for two or four players who hit a ball to each other over nets with rackets: *Let's play tennis.* ◊ *a tennis match*

NOTE In tennis you can play **singles** (a game between two people) or **doubles** (a game between two teams of two people).

ˈ**tennis shoe** ***noun*** [C] (*especially US*) = SNEAKER ➲ picture at **shoe**.

**ten·or** /ˈtɛnər/ ***noun*** [C] **1** the highest normal singing voice for a man; a man with this voice: *a beautiful tenor voice* ◊ *Pavarotti is a famous Italian tenor.* **2** a musical instrument with the same range as a tenor voice: *a tenor saxophone*

**tense**[1] /tɛns/ ***adj.*** **1** (used about a person) not able to relax because you are worried or nervous: *She looked pale and tense.* **2** (used about a person's body) having stiff muscles because you are not relaxed **3** (used about a situation) making people feel worried and not relaxed: *Reporters described the atmosphere in the capital as "very tense."*

**tense**[2] /tɛns/ ***verb*** [I,T] to become TENSE[1] (2) or to make your body tense

**tense**[3] /tɛns/ ***noun*** [C,U] (*grammar*) a form of a verb that shows whether sth happens in the past, present or future

★**ten·sion** /ˈtɛnʃn/ ***noun*** **1** [C,U] the condition of not being able to relax that is caused by worry or nervousness: *I could hear the tension in her voice as she spoke.* **2** [C,U] a condition of bad feeling and lack of trust between people, countries, etc.: *There are signs of growing tensions between the two countries.* **3** [U] (used about a rope, wire, etc.) how tightly it is stretched

★**tent** /tɛnt/ ***noun*** [C] a shelter made of cloth that is held up by poles and ropes. You can sleep in a tent when you go camping.

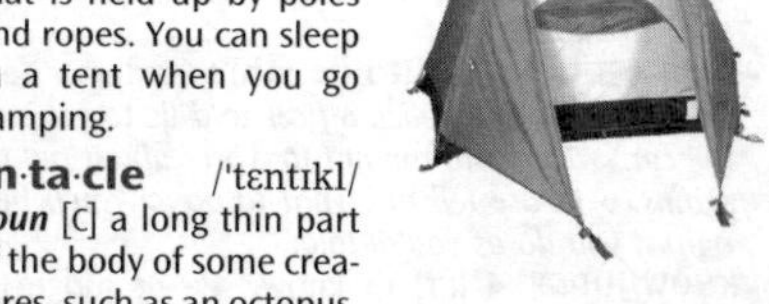


**ten·ta·cle** /ˈtɛntɪkl/ ***noun*** [C] a long thin part of the body of some creatures, such as an octopus, used for feeling or holding things, for moving or for getting food: (*figurative*) *Tentacles of fear closed around her body.*

**ten·ta·tive** /ˈtɛntət̬ɪv/ ***adj.*** **1** (used about plans, etc.) uncertain; not definite: *tentative arrangements for the meeting* **2** (used about a person or a person's behavior) not confident about what you are saying or doing: *a tentative smile* ▸ **ten·ta·tive·ly** ***adv.***

**ten·ter·hooks** /ˈtɛntərhʊks/ ***noun*** [pl.]

IDM **(be) on tenterhooks** (to be) very anxious or excited while you are waiting to find out sth or see what will happen: *I've been on tenterhooks all week waiting for the results.* SYN **(be) on pins and needles**

**tenth**[1] /tɛnθ/ ***pronoun, det., adv.*** 10th; next after ninth

**tenth**[2] /tɛnθ/ ***noun*** [C] the fraction ¹⁄₁₀; one of ten equal parts ➲ Look at the examples at **sixth**.

**ten·u·ous** /ˈtɛnyuəs/ ***adj.*** **1** so weak or uncertain that it hardly exists: *a tenuous hold on life* ◊ *His links with the organization turned out to be, at best, tenuous.* **2** extremely thin and easily broken: *the tenuous threads of a spider's web*

**ten·ure** /ˈtɛnyər/ ***noun*** [U] the right to stay in a teaching job permanently at a school, college or university

**te·pee** (*also* **teepee**, **tipi**) /ˈtipi/ ***noun*** [C] a type of tent made of animal skins or the outer covering (**bark**) of trees, with a round base and a pointed top, that some Native Americans traditionally lived in ➲ Look also at **wigwam**.

**tep·id** /ˈtɛpəd/ ***adj.*** (used about liquids) only slightly warm

**te·qui·la** /təˈkilə/ ***noun*** [U] a strong alcoholic drink that is made from a Mexican plant

★**term**[1] /tərm/ ***noun*** **1** [C] a word or group of words, especially one that is used in connection with a particular subject: *What exactly do you mean by the term "racist?"* ◇ *a technical term* **2 terms** [pl.] **in ...terms; in terms of ...** (used for indicating which particular way you are thinking about sth or from which point of view): *We ought to think about this in financial terms.* ◇ *The apartment would be ideal in terms of size, but it's very expensive.* **3 terms** [pl.] the conditions of an agreement: *Under the terms of the contract, you must finish the project by January 31.* ◇ *peace terms* **4** [C] one of the periods of time into which the academic year is divided at some colleges and universities ➲ Look at **semester**. **5** [C] a period of time for which sth lasts: *The President is now in his second term of office.*

IDM **be on good, friendly etc. terms (with sb)** to have a friendly relationship with sb

**come to terms with sth** to accept sth bad or difficult

**in the long/short term** over a long/short period of time in the future: *We're aiming at an increase of 20% in the long term.* ➲ Look also at **long-term** and **short-term**.

**on equal terms (with sb)** → EQUAL[1]

**term**[2] /tərm/ ***verb*** [T] to describe sb/sth by using a particular word or expression: *the period of history that is often termed the "Dark Ages"*

**ter·mi·nal**[1] /ˈtərmənl/ ***adj.*** (used about an illness) slowly causing death: *terminal cancer* ▶ **ter·mi·nal·ly** ***adv.***: *a terminally ill patient*

**ter·mi·nal**[2] /ˈtərmənl/ ***noun*** **1** [C] a large building where airplanes, buses, ships, or trains begin or end their trips: *the bus terminal* ◇ *United Airlines flights depart from Terminal 1 at O'Hare Airport.* **2** a piece of computer equipment (usually a keyboard and screen) that you use for getting information from a central computer or for putting information into it

**ter·mi·nate** /ˈtərməneɪt/ ***verb*** [I,T] (*formal*) to end or to make sth end: *to terminate a contract* ▶ **ter·mi·na·tion** /ˌtərməˈneɪʃn/ ***noun*** [U] (*formal*)

**ter·mi·na·tion** /ˌtərməˈneɪʃn/ ***noun*** **1** [C,U] (*formal*) the act of ending sth; the end of sth: *Failure to comply with these conditions will result in termination of the contract.* **2** [C] (*medical*) a medical operation to end a pregnancy at an early stage SYN **abortion**

**ter·mi·nol·o·gy** /ˌtərməˈnɑlədʒi/ ***noun*** [C,U] (*pl.* **ter·mi·nol·o·gies**) the special words and expressions that are used in a particular profession, subject or activity: *computer terminology*

**ter·mite** /ˈtərmaɪt/ ***noun*** [C] an insect that lives mainly in warm regions and eats wood, often causing damage to buildings

ˈ**term ˌpaper** ***noun*** [C] a long piece of writing that a student does as his/her most important work for a course, often including research from books in the library, etc.: *to write a term paper on the causes of global warming*

**ter·race** /ˈtɛrəs/ ***noun*** **1** [C] a flat area of stone next to a house, restaurant, etc. where people can eat, sit in the sun, etc.: *lunch on the terrace* ➲ Look at **patio**. **2** [usually pl.] one of a series of steps that are cut into the side of a hill so that crops can be grown there **3 Terrace** (*abbr.* **Terr.**) [sing.] (used in names of some streets in towns and cities, especially on hills): *133 Stanton Terrace*

**ter·rain** /təˈreɪn/ ***noun*** [U] a type of land: *rough terrain*

**ter·res·tri·al** /təˈrɛstriəl/ ***adj.*** **1** (*technical*) (used about animals and plants) living on the land or on the ground, rather than in water, in trees or in the air: *terrestrial species/animals/plants* ◇ *a terrestrial habitat* **2** connected with the planet Earth: *terrestrial life* ➲ Compare **extraterrestrial**. **3** (used about television and broadcasting systems) operating on earth rather than from a satellite

★**ter·ri·ble** /ˈtɛrəbl/ ***adj.*** **1** very bad or serious: *a terrible accident* ◇ *That was a terrible thing to do!* **2** sick or very upset: *I feel terrible. I think I'm going to throw up!* ◇ *You look terrible. Are you all right?* ◇ *He felt terrible when he realized what he had done.* **3** very bad; of low quality: *The hotel was terrible.* **4** (only *before* a noun) very big or great: *You are making a terrible mistake!*

**ter·ri·bly** /ˈtɛrəbli/ ***adv.*** **1** very: *I'm terribly sorry.* **2** very badly: *I played terribly.*

**ter·ri·er** /ˈtɛriər/ ***noun*** [C] a type of small dog

**ter·rif·ic** /təˈrɪfɪk/ ***adj.*** **1** (*informal*) extremely nice or good; excellent: *You're doing a terrific job!* **2** (only *before* a noun) very great or big: *We were under a terrific amount of pressure.*

**ter·ri·fied** /ˈtɛrəfaɪd/ ***adj.*** **terrified (of sb/sth)** very afraid: *to be terrified of spiders* ◇ *a terrified face*

**ter·ri·fy** /ˈtɛrəfaɪ/ ***verb*** [T] (*pres. part.* **ter·ri·fying**; *3rd person sing. pres.* **ter·ri·fies**; *pt, pp* **ter·ri·fied**) to frighten sb very much

**ter·ri·to·ri·al** /ˌtɛrəˈtɔriəl/ ***adj.*** (only *before* a noun) connected with the land or area of ocean that belongs to a country or ruler: *territorial waters*

★**ter·ri·to·ry** /ˈtɛrəˌtɔri/ ***noun*** (*pl.* **ter·ri·to·ries**) [C,U] **1** an area of land that belongs to one country or ruler: *U.S. territories in the Pacific* ◇ *to fly over enemy territory* **2** an area that sb is responsible for, e.g. in business: *Each sales rep's territory covers several counties.* **3** an area that an animal has as its own

**ter·ror** /ˈtɛrər/ ***noun*** **1** [U] very great fear: *He screamed in terror as the rats came toward him.* **2** [C] a person or thing that makes you feel afraid: *the terrors of the night* **3** [U] violent action (e.g. bombing, killing) for political purposes: *a terror campaign* **4** [C] (*informal*) a person (usually a child) or an animal that causes you trouble or is difficult to control: *Their kids are real little terrors.*

**ter·ror·ism** /ˈtɛrərɪzəm/ ***noun*** [U] the use of violent action (e.g. bombing, killing) for political purposes: *an act of terrorism*

**ter·ror·ist** /ˈtɛrərɪst/ ***noun*** [C] a person who is involved in the use of violent action (e.g. bombing, killing) for political purposes ▶ **ter·ror·ist** ***adj.***

**ter·ror·ize** /ˈtɛrəraɪz/ ***verb*** [T] to make sb feel frightened by using or threatening to use violence against him/her

**terse** /tərs/ ***adj.*** said in only a few words and in a not very friendly way: *a terse reply*



T

★**test**[1] /tɛst/ ***noun*** [C] **1** a group of questions, usually written, to measure sb's knowledge or skill in sth: *a spelling test*

**NOTE** When you **take** a test, you can either **pass** it (which is good) or **fail** it (which is bad).

**2** a short medical examination of a part of your body: *to have an eye test* ◇ *The doctor took a blood test.* **3** an experiment to find out whether sth works or to find out more information about it: *Tests show that the new drug is safe and effective.* **4** a situation or event that shows how good, strong, effective, etc. sb/sth is: *The congressional elections will be a good test of the President's popularity.*

★**test**[2] /tɛst/ ***verb*** [T] **1 test sb (on sth)** to examine sb's knowledge or skill in sth: *Are we going to be tested on this stuff?* **2** to examine a part of the body to find out if it is healthy: *to have your eyes tested* **3 test sb/sth (for sth)**; **test sth (on sb/sth)** to try, use or examine sth carefully to find out if it is working properly or what it is like: *These cars have all been tested for safety.* ◇ *Do you think medications should be tested on animals?*

**tes·ta·ment** /ˈtɛstəmənt/ ***noun*** [C] **1 Testament** one of the two main parts into which the Christian Bible is divided: *the Old Testament* (= that describes events before the birth of Jesus Christ) ◇ *the New Testament* (= that describes events since the birth of Jesus Christ) **2** [usually sing.] (*formal*) **a testament (to sth)** something that shows that sth else exists or is true: *Spielberg's new movie is a testament to his talent and experience.*

**tes·ti·cle** /ˈtɛstɪkl/ ***noun*** [C] one of the two male sex organs that produce sperm

**tes·ti·fy** /ˈtɛstəfaɪ/ ***verb*** (*pres. part.* **tes·ti·fy·ing**; *3rd person sing. pres.* **tes·ti·fies**; *pt, pp* **tes·ti·fied**) [I,T] to make a formal statement that sth is true, especially as a witness in a court of law

**tes·ti·mo·ny** /ˈtɛstəmoʊni/ ***noun*** (*pl.* **tes·ti·mo·nies**) **1** [U] a formal statement that sth is true, especially one that is made in a court of law **2** [U, sing.] (*formal*) something that shows that sth else exists or is true: *The design was testimony to her architectural skill.*

ˈ**test tube** ***noun*** [C] a thin glass tube that is used in chemical experiments

**tet·a·nus** /ˈtɛtn·əs/ ***noun*** [U] a serious disease that makes your muscles, especially the muscles of your face, become stiff. It is caused by bacteria that enter the body when a cut becomes infected.

**Tex-Mex** /ˌtɛks ˈmɛks/ ***adj.*** (only *before* a noun) connected with the variety of Mexican cooking, music, etc. that is found in Texas and the south western part of the U.S: *a Tex-Mex restaurant*

★**text**[1] /tɛkst/ ***noun*** **1** [U] the main written part of a book, newspaper, etc. (not the pictures, notes, index, etc.) **2** [C] the written form of a speech, interview, article, etc.: *The newspaper printed the complete text of the interview.* **3** = TEXT MESSAGE: *Send a text to this number to vote.* **4** = TEXTBOOK

**text**[2] /tɛkst/ ***verb*** [I,T] to write a message that you send using a cellular phone: *I texted him to say we were waiting in the restaurant.* ◇ *Too much texting can cause serious injury to the hands.*

**text·book** /ˈtɛksbʊk/ (*also* **text**) ***noun*** [C] a book that teaches a particular subject

**tex·tile** /ˈtɛkstaɪl/ ***noun*** [C] (in industry) a material that is made by weaving or knitting: *cotton textiles*

ˈ**text ˌmessage** (*also* **text**) ***noun*** [C] a written message that you send using a cellular phone: *Send a text message to this number to vote.* ▶ ˈ**text-ˌmessage** (*also* **text**) ***verb*** [I,T]

**tex·ture** /ˈtɛkstʃər/ ***noun*** [C,U] the way that sth feels when you touch it: *material with a silky texture*

**T4** /ˌti ˈfɔr/ ***noun*** [C] (*Cdn*) an official document, supplied by your employer, that shows how much money you have earned in one year so that the amount of tax you owe to the government can be calculated

★**than** /ðən; ðɛn; *strong form* ðæn/ ***conj., prep.*** **1** (used when you are comparing two things): *He's taller than you.* ◇ *He's taller than you are.* ◇ *New York is more expensive than most cities.* ◇ *You speak French a lot better than she does.* **2** (used with "more" and "less" before numbers, expressions of time, distance, etc.): *He earns more than $50,000 a year.* **3** (used after "would rather" to say that you prefer one thing to another): *I'd rather go to Florida than to Winnipeg.*

★**thank** /θæŋk/ ***verb*** [T] **thank sb (for sth/for doing sth)** to tell sb that you are grateful: *I'm writing to thank you for the present you sent me.* ◇ *I'll go and thank him for offering to help.*

**NOTE** **Thank you** and **thanks** are both used for telling somebody that you are grateful for something. **Thanks** is more informal: *Thank you very much for your letter.* ◇ *"How are you, Rachel?" "A lot better – thanks."* You can also use **thank you** and **thanks** to accept something that somebody has offered to you: *"Have a piece of cake." "Thank you. It looks delicious."* When you want to refuse something you can say **no, thank you** or **no, thanks**: *"Would you like another cup of coffee?" "No, thanks."*

**IDM** **thank God/goodness/heaven** (used for expressing relief): *Thank goodness it stopped raining!* ➲ Look at the note at **God** (2).

★**thank·ful** /ˈθæŋkfl/ ***adj.*** (not before a noun) pleased and grateful: *We were thankful that no one was was seriously hurt in the fire.* ◇ *They were thankful for all the help they received.*

**thank·ful·ly** /ˈθæŋkfəli/ ***adv.*** fortunately: *Thankfully, no one was injured.*

**thank·less** /ˈθæŋkləs/ ***adj.*** involving hard work that other people do not notice or thank you for: *Being a housewife can sometimes be a thankless task.*

★**thanks**[1] /θæŋks/ ***noun*** [pl.] words which show that you are grateful: *I'd like to express my thanks to all of you for coming here today.* ➲ Look at the note at **thank**.

**IDM** **thanks to sb/sth** because of sb/sth: *We missed the bus, thanks to you!*

★**thanks**[2] /θæŋks/ ***interjection*** (*informal*) thank you: *Thanks a lot!*

**Thanks·giv·ing** /ˌθæŋksˈgɪvɪŋ/ ***noun*** [U] a holiday that is celebrated in the U.S. on the fourth Thursday in November, and in Canada on the second Monday in October

NOTE **Thanksgiving** was first celebrated in 1621 by the **Pilgrims** who came from England to what is now Massachusetts in the United States. They wanted to thank God for their health and the harvest. Nowadays people celebrate Thanksgiving by getting together with their families for a big meal and by thinking about what they are thankful for, e.g. their families, homes and food. Some foods that are traditionally eaten at Thanksgiving are **turkey**, **cranberry sauce** and **pumpkin pie**.

**'thank-you** ***noun*** [C] an expression of thanks: *We sent them some flowers as a thank-you for their help.*

★**that**[1] /ðæt/ ***det.***, ***pronoun*** (*pl.* **those** /ðoʊz/) **1** (used for describing a person or thing, especially when it is not near the person speaking): *I like that house over there.* ◇ *What's that on the road?* ◇ *"Can you hand me the book?" "This one?" "No, that one over there."* **2** (used for talking about a person or thing already known or mentioned): *That was the year we went to Spain, wasn't it?* ◇ *Can you give me back that money I loaned you last week?*

IDM **that is, ...** (used when you are giving more information about sb/sth): *The meeting will be on the 26th – that is, two weeks from today.*

**that's that** there is nothing more to say or do: *I'm not going and that's that.*

★**that**[2] /ðət; *strong form* ðæt/ ***pronoun*** (used for introducing a relative clause) the person or thing already mentioned: *I'm reading the book that won the Pulitzer prize.* ◇ *The people that live next door are French.*

NOTE When **that** is the object of the verb in the relative clause, it is often left out: *I want to see the doctor (that) I saw last week.* ◇ *I wore the dress (that) I bought on sale.*

★**that**[3] /ðət; *strong form* ðæt/ ***conj.*** (used after certain verbs, nouns and adjectives to introduce a new part of the sentence): *She told me that she was leaving.* ◇ *I hope that you feel better soon.* ◇ *I'm sure that he will come.* ◇ *It's funny that you should say that.*

NOTE **That** is often left out in this type of sentence, especially in informal speech: *I thought (that) you would like it.*

★**that**[4] /ðæt/ ***adv.*** (used with adjectives, adverbs) to that degree or extent: *30 miles? I can't walk that far.* ◇ *She can't play the piano that well.*

**thaw** /θɔ/ ***verb*** [I,T] **thaw (sth) (out)** to become or to make sth become soft or liquid again after freezing: *Is the snow thawing?* ◇ *It's starting to thaw* (= the weather is getting warmer). ◇ *Always thaw chicken thoroughly before you cook it.* ➲ Look at **melt**. ▸ **thaw** ***noun*** [C, usually sing.]

★**the** /ðə; *before a vowel* ði; *strong form* ði/ ***definite article*** **1** (used for talking about a person or thing that is already known or that has already been mentioned): *I took the kids to the dentist.* ◇ *The Johnsons are on vacation.* ◇ *We met the man who bought your house.* ◇ *The milk is in the refrigerator.* **2** (used when there is only one or only one group): *The sun is very strong today.* ◇ *Who won the team championship?* **3** (used with numbers and dates): *This is the third piece of cake I've eaten.* ◇ *I grew up in the sixties.* **4** (used with adjectives to name a group of people): *the French* ◇ *the poor* **5** (used with a singular noun when you are talking generally about sth): *The dolphin is an intelligent animal.* **6** (with units of measurement, meaning "every"): *The car gets twenty miles to the gallon.* **7** (with musical instruments): *Do you play the piano?* **8** best known or most important: *You don't mean you met the Brad Pitt?*

NOTE "The" is pronounced /ði/ in this sense.

**9 the ... the ...** (used for saying that two things change to the same extent): *The more you eat, the fatter you get.*

★**the·a·ter** /ˈθiət̬ər/ ***noun*** **1** [C] a building where you go to see plays, etc.: *I'm going to the theater* (= to see a play). **2** [C] (*also* **movie theater**) a building where you go to see movies **3** [sing., U] the work of acting in or producing plays: *He's worked in the theater for thirty years.*

**the·at·ri·cal** /θiˈætrɪkl/ ***adj.*** **1** (only *before* a noun) connected with the THEATER (3) **2** (used about behavior) unnatural and dramatic because you want people to notice it: *a theatrical gesture*

**theft** /θɛft/ ***noun*** [C,U] the crime of taking sth that belongs to another person secretly and without permission: *There have been a lot of thefts in this area recently.* ◇ *She was arrested for theft.* ➲ Look at the note at **thief**.

★**their** /ðɛr/ ***det.*** belonging to them: *What color is their car?* ◇ *The students picked up their books and walked to the door.*

★**theirs** /ðɛrz/ ***pronoun*** of or belonging to them: *Our house isn't as big as theirs.*

★**them** /ðəm; *strong form* ðɛm/ ***pronoun*** (the object of a verb or preposition) **1** the people, animals or things mentioned earlier: *I'll call them now.* ◇ *"I have the keys here." "Oh, good. Give them to me."* ◇ *We have students from several countries, but most of them are Mexican.* ◇ *"Did you mail those letters?" "Oh no – I forgot about them."* **2** (*informal*) him or her: *If anybody calls, tell them I'm busy.*

**theme** /θim/ ***noun*** [C] **1** a subject of a talk, a piece of writing, etc.: *The theme of today's discussion will be "Our Changing Cities."* ◇ *their campaign theme* **2** an idea that is developed or repeated in the work of a writer or artist: *The themes of heaven and hell were very common in paintings of this period.* **3** (*also* **'theme song**, **'theme tune**) a song that is always played at the beginning of a television or radio program

**'theme park** ***noun*** [C] a place with a lot of things to do, see, ride on, etc., which are all based on a single idea

★**them·selves** /ðəmˈsɛlvz/ ***pronoun*** **1** (used as the object of a verb or preposition when the people or animals who do an action are affected by it): *Helen and Sarah seem to be enjoying themselves.* ◇ *People often talk to themselves when they are worried.* **2** (used for emphasis): *They themselves say that the situation cannot continue.* ◇ *Did they paint the house themselves?* (= or did sb else do it for them?)

IDM **(all) by themselves 1** alone: *The boys are too young to go shopping by themselves.* ➲ Look at

T

the note at **alone**. **2** without help: *The kids cooked dinner all by themselves.*

★**then** /ðen/ ***adv.*** **1** (at) that time: *In 1996? I was in college then.* ◇ *I'll be on vacation then.* ◇ *I haven't seen him since then.* ◇ *I'm going tomorrow. Can you wait until then?* **2** next; after that: *We're going hiking in the mountains for a week and then to the beach.* ◇ *There was silence for a minute. Then he replied.* **3** in that case; therefore: *"I don't feel very well." "Then why don't you go to the doctor?"* **4** (used for emphasis after words like *now, okay, well,* etc.): *Now then, are we all ready to go?* ◇ *Well then, I'll see you tomorrow.*

IDM **but then (again); then again** (used for introducing a new and different piece of information): *The weather forecast says it'll rain, but then again it's often wrong.*

**(right) then and there** immediately; at that time and place: *They agreed to buy the house right then and there, without even looking upstairs.*

**the·ol·o·gy** /θiˈɑlədʒi/ ***noun*** [U] the study of religion ▸ **the·o·log·i·cal** /ˌθiəˈlɑdʒɪkl/ ***adj.***: *a theological college*

**the·o·ret·i·cal** /ˌθiəˈrɛtɪkl/ ***adj.*** **1** based on ideas and principles, not on practical experience: *Your paper is too theoretical – you need to give more concrete examples.* **2** based on ideas about sth which may not be true in reality: *a theoretical possibility* (= which will probably never happen) ▸ **the·o·ret·i·cal·ly** /-kli/ ***adv.***: *Theoretically, we could still win, but I don't think we will.*

★**the·o·ry** /ˈθɪri; ˈθiəri/ ***noun*** (*pl.* **the·o·ries**) **1** [C] an idea or set of ideas that try to explain sth: *the theory about how life on earth began* **2** [U] the general idea or principles of a particular subject: *political theory*

IDM **in theory** as a general idea which may not be true in reality: *Your plan sounds fine in theory, but I don't know if it'll work in practice.*

**ther·a·peu·tic** /ˌθɛrəˈpyuṭɪk/ ***adj.*** **1** helping you to relax and feel better: *I find listening to music very therapeutic.* **2** helping you to recover from an illness: *therapeutic treatment*

**ther·a·py** /ˈθɛrəpi/ ***noun*** [U] **1** treatment to help or cure an illness, injury or a mental problem, usually without drugs or medical operations **2** = PSYCHOTHERAPY: *He was **in therapy** for years after his wife left him.* ➲ Look also at **physical therapy** and **speech therapy**. ▸ **ther·a·pist** /ˈθɛrəpɪst/ ***noun*** [C]: *I have an appointment with my therapist* (= psychotherapist) *today.*

★**there**[1] /ðɛr/ ***adv.*** **1** in, at or to that place: *Put the table right there in the corner.* ◇ *I like Boston. My husband and I met there.* ◇ *"Have you been to the new mall?" "We're going there next week."* ◇ *Did you look under there?* **2** at that point (in a conversation, story, etc.): *Can I interrupt you there for a minute?* **3** available: *Her parents are always there if she needs help.*

IDM **be there for sb** to be available if sb wants to talk to you or if he/she needs help: *You know I'll always be there for you.*

**(right) then and there** → THEN

**there (you are/go) 1** (used when you give sth to sb): *There you are. Would you like any ketchup with that?* **2** (used when you are explaining sth to sb): *There – just press the switch and it starts.* **3** (used for saying that you are not surprised): *"My new tape player is already broken." "Well, there you go – that's what happens when you buy cheap stuff."*

**there**[2] /ðər; *strong form* ðɛr/ ***pronoun*** **1** (used as the subject of "be," "seem," "appear," etc. to say that sth exists): *Is there a god?* ◇ *There's a man at the door.* ◇ *There wasn't much to eat.* ◇ *There's somebody singing outside.* ◇ *There seems to be a mistake here.* **2** (used for calling attention to sth): *Oh look, there's Kate!*

**there·af·ter** /ˌðɛrˈæftər/ ***adv.*** (*formal*) after that: *She suffered a heart attack and died shortly thereafter.*

**there·by** /ˌðɛrˈbaɪ/ ***adv.*** (*formal*) in that way: *We started our trip early, thereby avoiding most of the traffic.*

★**there·fore** /ˈðɛrfɔr/ ***adv.*** for that reason: *The new cars have more efficient engines and therefore consume less gas.*

**there·in** /ˌðɛrˈɪn/ ***adv.*** (*formal*) in the place, object, document, etc. mentioned: *The insurance policy covers the building and any fixtures contained therein.* ◇ *In court she denied any knowledge of the article and the allegations made therein.*

IDM **therein lies** (used to emphasize the result or consequence of a particular situation): *He works extremely hard and therein lies the key to his success.*

**there·up·on** /ˈðɛrəˌpɑn; ˌðɛrəˈpɑn/ ***adv.*** (*formal*) **1** immediately after the situation mentioned; as a direct result of the situation mentioned: *The audience thereupon rose cheering to their feet.* **2** on the thing mentioned: *a large notice with black letters printed thereupon*

**ther·mal** /ˈθərml/ ***adj.*** **1** connected with heat: *thermal energy* **2** (used about clothes) made to keep you warm in cold weather: *thermal underwear*

**ther·mom·e·ter** /θərˈmɑməṭər/ ***noun*** [C] an instrument for measuring the temperature of sb's body or of a room (= how hot or cold it is)

**Ther·mos™** /ˈθərməs/ ***noun*** [C] (*pl.* **Ther·mos·es**) (*also* **ˈThermos ˌbottle**) a type of container that is used for keeping a liquid or food hot or cold

**ther·mo·stat** /ˈθərməstæt/ ***noun*** [C] a device that controls the level of heat in a house or machine by switching it on and off as necessary

**the·sau·rus** /θɪˈsɔrəs/ ***noun*** [C] (*pl.* **the·sau·rus·es**) a book that contains lists of words and phrases with similar meanings

**these** *plural of* THIS[1]

**the·sis** /ˈθisəs/ ***noun*** [C] (*pl.* **the·ses** /ˈθisiz/) a long piece of writing on a particular subject that you do as part of a university degree

**the·ta** /ˈθeɪṭə/ ***noun*** [C] (*symbol* Θ, θ) the eighth letter of the Greek alphabet ➲ Look at the note at **fraternity**.

★**they** /ðeɪ/ ***pronoun*** (the subject of a verb) **1** the people, animals or things that have been mentioned: *We have two children. They're both boys.* ◇ *"Have you seen my keys?" "Yes, they're on the table."* **2** people in general, or people whose identity is not known or stated: *They say it's going to be a hard winter.* **3** (used informally instead of *he* or *she): Somebody called for you, but they didn't leave their name.*

**they'd** /ðeɪd/ *short for* THEY HAD, THEY WOULD

**they'll** /ðeɪl/ *short for* THEY WILL

**they're** /ðɛr/ *short for* THEY ARE

**they've** /ðeɪv/ *short for* THEY HAVE

★**thick**[1] /θɪk/ ***adj.***

➤DISTANCE BETWEEN SIDES **1** (used about sth solid) having a large distance between its opposite sides; not thin: *a thick black line* ◇ *These walls are very thick.* **2** (used for saying what the distance is between the two opposite sides of something): *The ice was six inches thick.*

➤HAIR/FUR/TREES **3** having a lot of things close together: *a thick forest* ◇ *thick hair*

➤LIQUID **4** (used about a liquid) stiff; that does not flow easily: *a thick sauce* ◇ *This paint is too thick.* OPP The opposite for senses **1** to 4 is **thin.**

➤FOG/SMOKE/AIR **5** (used about fog, smoke, etc.) difficult to see through

➤ACCENT **6** (used about sb's accent) very strong

IDM **have (a) thick skin** to be not easily upset or worried by what people say about you

▸ **thick** ***adv.***: *snow lying thick on the ground* ▸ **thick·ly** ***adv.***: *Spread the butter thickly.* ◇ *a thickly wooded area*

**thick**[2] /θɪk/ ***noun***

IDM **in the thick of sth** in the most active or crowded part of sth; very involved in sth: *She always likes to be in the thick of things.*

**through thick and thin** through difficult times and situations: *He promised to stay with her through thick and thin.*

**thick·en** /ˈθɪkən/ ***verb*** [I,T] to become thicker or to make sth thicker: *Tonight, the fog will thicken and then more rain will move in from the southwest.* ◇ *Add flour to thicken the sauce.*

★**thick·ness** /ˈθɪknəs/ ***noun*** [U, sing.] the quality of being thick, or how thick sth is: *Broil the steaks for 6-8 minutes, depending on the thickness of the meat.*

★**thief** /θif/ ***noun*** [C] (*pl.* **thieves** /θivz/) a person who steals things from another person

NOTE A **thief** is a general word for a person who steals things, usually secretly and without violence. The name of the crime is **theft**. A **robber** steals from a bank, store, etc. and often uses violence or threats. A **burglar** steals things by breaking into a house, store, etc., usually at night, and a **shoplifter** goes into a store when it is open and takes things without paying. ➲ Look also at the note at **steal**.

**thigh** /θaɪ/ ***noun*** [C] the top part of the leg, above the knee ➲ picture on study page **A32**.

**thim·ble** /ˈθɪmbl/ ***noun*** [C] a small object made of metal or plastic that you wear on the end of your finger to protect it when you are sewing

★**thin**[1] /θɪn/ ***adj.*** **(thin·ner; thin·nest)**

➤NOT THICK **1** (used about sth solid) having a small distance between the opposite sides; not thick: *a thin brown book* ◇ *a thin cotton shirt* ◇ *a thin slice of meat*

➤NOT FAT **2** having very little flesh on the body; not fat: *You need to eat more. You're too thin!*

NOTE **Thin, skinny, slim** and **underweight** all have a similar meaning. **Thin** is the most general word for describing people who have very little flesh on their bodies. **Slim** is used to describe people who are thin in an attractive way: *You're so slim! How do you do it?* If you say sb is **skinny**, you mean that he/she is too thin and not attractive. **Underweight** is a much more formal word, and is often used for describing people who are too thin in a medical sense: *The doctor says I'm underweight.*

➤LIQUID **3** (used about a liquid) that flows easily; not stiff or thick: *a thin sauce*

➤SMOKE **4** (used about mist, smoke, etc.) not difficult to see through

➤FEW IN NUMBER **5** having only a few people or things with a lot of space between them: *a thin covering of trees*

IDM **disappear, vanish, etc. into thin air** to disappear completely

**through thick and thin** → THICK[2]

**wear thin** → WEAR[1]

▸ **thin** ***adv.*** (*informal*): *Don't spread the frosting too thin.* ▸ **thin·ly** ***adv.***: *thinly sliced bread* ◇ *thinly populated areas*

**thin**[2] /θɪn/ ***verb*** [I,T] (**thin<u>n</u>ing; thin<u>n</u>ed**) **thin (sth) (out)** to become thinner or fewer in number; to make sth thinner: *The trees thin out toward the edge of the woods.* ◇ *Thin the sauce by adding milk.*

★**thing** /θɪŋ/ ***noun***

➤OBJECT **1** [C] an object that is not named: *What's that red thing on the table?* ◇ *A pen is a thing you write with.* ◇ *I need to get a few things at the grocery store.*

➤FACT/EVENT/SITUATION/ACTION **2** [C] a quality or state: *There's no such thing as evil* (= it doesn't exist). ◇ *The best thing about my job is the way it changes all the time.* **3** [C] an action, event or statement: *When I get home, the first thing I do is turn on the TV.* ◇ *A strange thing happened to me yesterday.* ◇ *What a nice thing to say!* **4** [C] a fact, subject, etc.: *He told me a few things that I didn't know before.* **5 things** [pl.] the circumstances or conditions of your life: *Things seem to be going very well for him right now.*

➤POSSESSIONS **6 things** [pl.] your clothes or personal possessions: *I'll go and pack my things.*

➤PERSON/ANIMAL **7** [C] (used for expressing your feelings about a person or animal): *Look how thin that cat is! Poor little thing!*

➤WHAT IS NEEDED/RIGHT **8** [C, usually sing.] what is needed or socially acceptable: *You need something to cheer you up—I know just the thing!* ◇ *to do/say **the right/wrong thing*** ◇ *The best thing to do is to apologize.*

IDM **be a good thing (that)** to be lucky that: *It's a good thing you remembered your umbrella.*

**do your own thing** (*informal*) to do what you want to do, without worrying about what other people think

**first thing** → FIRST[1]

**for one thing** (used for introducing a reason for something): *I think we should go by bus. For one thing, it's cheaper.*

**make matters/things worse** → WORSE[1]

**not a thing** nothing; not anything: *"Do you need*

*anything else?" "No, not a thing."* ◇ *There wasn't a thing we could do about it.*

**take it/things easy** → EASY²

**the thing is ...** (*informal*) (used for giving a reason for sth or explaining a problem, especially when you are trying not to hurt sb's feelings): *It sounds like a fun party, but the thing is, my parents are coming to visit then – so I can't go.*

★**think** /θɪŋk/ **verb** (*pt, pp* **thought** /θɔt/)
➤USE MIND **1** [I] **think (about sth)** to use your mind to consider sth or to form connected ideas: *Think before you speak.* ◇ *What are you thinking about?* ◇ *He had to think hard* (= a lot) *about the question.*
➤HAVE OPINION/BELIEF **2** [T] to consider or believe; to have as an opinion: *"Do you think it's going to snow?" "No, I don't think so."* ◇ *"Sue's coming tomorrow, isn't she?" "Yes, I think so."* ◇ *I think that they moved to New York, but I'm not sure.* ◇ *What did you think of the movie?* ◇ *I don't think they are very good musicians.*
➤IMAGINE **3** [I,T] to form an idea of sth; to imagine sth: *We couldn't think where you'd gone.* ◇ ***Just think** —we'll be lying on the beach this time tomorrow.* ◇ *If I'm late home, my mother always **thinks the worst**.*
➤INTEND **4** [I] **think of/about doing sth** to intend or plan to do sth: *We're thinking of buying a new house.*
➤CONSIDER SB'S FEELINGS **5** [I] **think about/of sb** to consider the feelings of sb else: *She never thinks about anyone but herself.*
➤EXPECT **6** [T] to expect sth: *The job took longer than we thought.*

IDM **think better of (doing) sth** to decide not to do sth; to change your mind
**think highly, a lot, not much, etc. of sb/sth** to have a good, bad, etc. opinion of sb/sth
**think the world of sb** to love and admire sb very much
**think twice (about sth/before doing sth)** to consider a plan very carefully, because it may not be a good idea

PHRV **think of sth** to create an idea in your imagination: *Who first thought of the plan?*
**think sth over** to consider sth carefully: *I'll think over your offer and let you know tomorrow.*
**think sth through** to consider carefully all the details of a plan, idea, etc.: *Let's think this thing through –it's a big decision.*
**think sth up** to create sth in your mind; to invent: *to think up a new advertising slogan*

**think·er** /ˈθɪŋkər/ **noun** [C] a person who thinks about serious and important subjects

**think·ing¹** /ˈθɪŋkɪŋ/ **adj.** intelligent and using your mind to think about important subjects: *a newspaper for thinking people*

**think·ing²** /ˈθɪŋkɪŋ/ **noun** [U] **1** the act of using your mind to think about sth: *clear thinking* **2** an opinion: *This accident will make them change their thinking on safety matters.*

IDM **wishful thinking** = WISHFUL

ˈ**think tank** **noun** [C] a group of experts who provide advice and ideas on political, social or economic issues: *a study published by a leading economic think tank*

**third¹** /θərd/ **pronoun, det., adv.** 3rd; next after second ➲ Look at the examples at **sixth**.

IDM **next/second/third to last** = LAST¹

**third²** /θərd/ **noun** [C] the fraction ⅓; one of three equal parts of sth ➲ Look at the examples at **sixth**.

ˌ**third ˈparty** **noun** [C] (*pl.* **third parties**) a person who is not one of the two main people or groups involved in sth

**the ˌThird ˈWorld** **noun** [sing.] the poorer countries of Asia, Africa and South America

> NOTE This expression is often considered offensive nowadays. Many people prefer to call these countries **the developing world**.

**thirst** /θərst/ **noun** **1** [U, sing.] the feeling that you have when you want or need to drink: *Iced tea really quenches your thirst.* ◇ *to die of thirst* **2** [sing.] **a thirst for sth** a strong desire for sth

★**thirst·y** /ˈθərsti/ **adj.** (**thirst·i·er**; **thirst·i·est**) wanting or needing a drink: *I'm thirsty. Can I have a drink of water?*

**thir·teen** /ˌθərˈtin/ **number** 13; one more than twelve ➲ For examples of how to use numbers in sentences, look at **six**. ▸ **thir·teenth** /ˌθərˈtinθ/ **pronoun, det., adv.** ➲ Look at the examples at **sixth**.

**thir·ty** /ˈθərṭi/ **number** 30; one more than twenty-nine ➲ For examples of how to use numbers in sentences, look at **sixty**. ▸ **thir·ti·eth** /ˈθərṭiəθ/ **pronoun, det., adv.** ➲ Look at the examples at **sixth**.

★**this¹** /ðɪs/ **det., pronoun** (*pl.* **these** /ðiz/) **1** (used for talking about sb/sth that is close to you in time or space): *Take a look at this picture.* ◇ *These boots are really comfortable. My old ones weren't.* ◇ *Is this the book you asked for?* ◇ *These are the letters to be filed, not those over there.* **2** (used for talking about sth that was mentioned or talked about before): *Where did you hear about this?* **3** (used for introducing sb or showing sb sth): *Chuck, this is my wife, Claudia, and these are our kids, David and Vicky.* ◇ *Hello, this is Maria Diaz* (= on the telephone). **4** (used with days of the week or periods of time) of today or the present week, year, etc.: *Are you busy this afternoon?* ◇ *this Friday* (= the Friday of this week) **5** (*informal*) (used when you are telling a story) a certain: *Then this woman said...*

IDM **this and that** various things: *We talked about this and that.*

★**this²** /ðɪs/ **adv.** (used when you are describing sth) so; as much as this: *The road is not usually this busy.*

**this·tle** /ˈθɪsl/ **noun** [C] a wild plant with purple flowers and sharp points (**thorns**) on its leaves

**thong** /θɔŋ; θɑŋ/ **noun** [C] **1** (*also* ˈ**flip-flop**) a type of open shoe (**sandal**) that has a narrow strip of rubber, leather, etc. which goes between the big toe and the toe next to it **2** a pair of underwear that has only a very narrow strip of cloth, like a string, at the back **3** a narrow strip of leather that is used to fasten sth or as a whip

**thorn** /θɔrn/ **noun** [C] one of the hard sharp points on the stem of some plants and bushes, e.g. on rose bushes

**thorn·y** /ˈθɔrni/ **adj.** (**thorn·i·er**; **thorn·i·est**) **1** (used about a problem, etc.) difficult **2** having thorns

★**thor·ough** /ˈθəroʊ/ ***adj.*** **1** careful and complete: *The police made a thorough search of the house.* **2** doing things in a very careful way, making sure that you look at every detail: *Pam is slow, but she is very thorough.* ▸ **thor·ough·ness** ***noun*** [U]

**thor·ough·bred** /ˈθərəbrɛd; ˈθəroʊ-/ ***noun*** [C] an animal, especially a horse, of high quality, that has parents that are both of the same breed ▸ **thor·ough·bred** ***adj.***: *a thoroughbred mare*

**thor·ough·ly** /ˈθərəli; -roʊ-/ ***adv.*** **1** in a thorough way: *to study a subject thoroughly* **2** completely; very; very much: *We thoroughly enjoyed our vacation.*

**those** *plural of* THAT[1]

★**though**[1] /ðoʊ/ ***conj.*** **1** in spite of the fact that; although: *Though he had very little money, Alex always managed to dress well.* ◇ *She still loved him even though he had treated her so badly.* **2** but: *I'll come as soon as I can, though I can't promise to be on time.*

IDM **as if/though** → AS

★**though**[2] /ðoʊ/ ***adv.*** (*informal*) however: *I really like Jonathan. I don't like his wife, though.* ➲ Look at the note at **although**.

**thought**[1] *past tense, past participle of* THINK

★**thought**[2] /θɔt/ ***noun*** **1** [C,U] the act of thinking: *Kim sat, lost in thought, looking at the old photographs.* **2** [U] particular ideas or a particular way of thinking: *a change in medical thought on the subject* **3** [sing., U] an act of being kind to or paying attention to sb/sth: *He didn't give any thought to the rest of his family.* **4** [C] an idea or opinion: *What are your thoughts on this subject?* ◇ *The thought of living alone filled her with fear.*

IDM **have second thoughts (about sb/sth)** → SECOND[1]

**on second thought** → SECOND[1]

**a school of thought** → SCHOOL

**thought·ful** /ˈθɔtfl/ ***adj.*** **1** thinking deeply: *a thoughtful expression* **2** thinking about what other people want or need: *It was very thoughtful of you to send Mrs. Brown some flowers.* ▸ **thought·ful·ly** ***adv.*** ▸ **thought·ful·ness** ***noun*** [U]

**thought·less** /ˈθɔtləs/ ***adj.*** not thinking about what other people want or need or what the result of your actions will be ▸ **thought·less·ly** ***adv.*** ▸ **thought·less·ness** ***noun*** [U]

**thou·sand** /ˈθaʊznd/ ***number*** 1,000; one more than nine hundred ninety-nine

NOTE Notice that you use **thousand** in the singular when you are talking about a number. You use **thousands** when you mean "a lot": *She earns twenty-five thousand dollars a year.* ◇ *Thousands of people attended the meeting.*

**thou·sandth**[1] /ˈθaʊznθ/ ***det.*** 1,000th; next after nine hundred ninety-ninth

**thou·sandth**[2] /ˈθaʊznθ/ ***noun*** [C] the fraction $^1/_{1000}$; one of a thousand equal parts of sth

**thrash** /θræʃ/ ***verb*** **1** [T] to hit sb/sth many times with a stick, whip, etc. **2** [I] **thrash (about/around)** to move your arms, legs, etc. in an uncontrolled way, e.g. because you are in pain

PHR V **thrash sth out** to talk about sth until you reach an agreement

**thread**[1] /θrɛd/ ***noun*** **1** [C,U] a long thin piece of cotton, etc. that you use for sewing, etc.: *a needle and thread* ➲ picture at **sew**. **2** [C] the connection between ideas, the parts of a story, etc.: *a common thread linking all the accidents*

**thread**[2] /θrɛd/ ***verb*** [T] **1** to put THREAD[1] (1) through the hole in a needle: *to thread a needle* **2** to link things together by putting them onto a string, etc. **3** to pass sth narrow through a space and into a particular position: *He threaded the belt through the loops on his pants.*

IDM **thread your way through sth** to pass through sth with difficulty, moving around things or people that are in your way

**thread·bare** /ˈθrɛdbɛr/ ***adj.*** (used about material or clothes) old and very thin

★**threat** /θrɛt/ ***noun*** **1** [C,U] a warning that sb may hurt, kill or punish you if you do not do what he/she wants: *Under threat of death, he did as they asked.* ◇ *to make a threat against sb* ◇ *to carry out a threat* **2** [C, usually sing.] a person or thing that may damage sth or hurt sb; something that indicates future danger: *a serious threat to national security*

★**threat·en** /ˈθrɛtn/ ***verb*** **1** [T] **threaten sb (with sth); threaten (to do sth)** to warn that you may hurt, kill or punish sb if he/she does not do what you want: *to threaten sb with a knife* ◇ *She was threatened with dismissal.* ◇ *The man threatened to kill her if she didn't tell him where the money was.* **2** [I,T] to seem likely to do sth bad: *The oil slick is threatening the coastline with pollution.* ▸ **threat·en·ing** ***adj.*** ▸ **threat·en·ing·ly** ***adv.***

**three** /θri/ ***number*** 3; one more than two ➲ Look at **third**. For examples of how to use numbers in sentences, look at **six**.

**three-** /θri/ ***combining form*** having three of the thing mentioned: *a three-bedroom apartment*

**three-di·men·sion·al** /ˌθri dəˈmɛnʃn·l/ (*also* **3-D** /ˌθri ˈdi/) ***adj.*** having length, width and height: *a three-dimensional model*

**thresh·old** /ˈθrɛʃhoʊld; -ʃoʊld/ ***noun*** [C] **1** the bottom part of the opening for a door; the entrance to a room or building: *She stood on the threshold* (= in the entrance). **2** the time when you are just about to start sth or find sth: *on the threshold of a scientific breakthrough* **3** [usually sing.] the point at which sth begins to have an effect: *people who have a low pain threshold*

**threw** *past tense of* THROW[1]

ˈ**thrift shop** /ˈθrɪft ʃɑp/ (*also* ˈ**thrift store**) ***noun*** [C] a store that sells clothes and other goods given by people to raise money for a charity

**thrift·y** /ˈθrɪfti/ ***adj.*** (**thrift·i·er**; **thrift·i·est**) (*old-fashioned*) careful not to spend too much money

**thrill**[1] /θrɪl/ ***noun*** [C] a sudden strong feeling of pleasure or excitement

**thrill**[2] /θrɪl/ ***verb*** [T] to make sb feel a THRILL[1]: *His singing thrilled the audience.*

**thrilled** /θrɪld/ ***adj.*** (usually not before a noun) very pleased or excited: *I was just thrilled with your present.*

T

**thrill·er** /ˈθrɪlər/ ***noun*** [C] a movie, book, etc. with a very exciting story, often about a crime

**thrill·ing** /ˈθrɪlɪŋ/ ***adj.*** very exciting: *a thrilling victory*

**thrive** /θraɪv/ ***verb*** [I] to grow or develop well ▶ **thriv·ing** ***adj.***: *a thriving industry*

★**throat** /θroʊt/ ***noun*** [C] **1** the front part of your neck: *The attacker grabbed the man by the throat.* **2** the back part of your mouth and the passage down your neck through which air and food pass: *She got a piece of candy stuck in her throat.* ◇ *I have a really sore throat.*

IDM **clear your throat** → CLEAR[3]

**throb** /θrɑb/ ***verb*** [I] (**throb·bing**; **throbbed**) to make strong regular movements or noises; to beat strongly: *His heart was throbbing.* ◇ *Her finger throbbed with pain.* ▶ **throb** ***noun*** [U]: *the throb of the ship's engines*

**throne** /θroʊn/ ***noun*** **1** [C] the special chair where a king or queen sits **2 the throne** [sing.] the position of being king or queen: *The prince is second in line to the British throne.*

**throng** /θrɔŋ; θrɑŋ/ ***noun*** [C] (*formal*) a large crowd of people

**throt·tle** /ˈθrɑt̬l/ ***verb*** [T] to hold sb tightly by the throat and stop him/her from breathing

★**through**[1] /θru/ ***prep.*** **1** from one end or side of sth to the other: *We drove through the center of town.* ◇ *She could see the outline of a tree through the mist.* ◇ *to look through a telescope* ◇ *James cut through the rope.* ◇ *to push through a crowd of people* **2** from the beginning to the end of sth: *Food supplies will not last through the winter.* ◇ *We're halfway through the book.* **3** until, and including: *The museum is open from Monday through Saturday.* **4** because of; with the help of: *Errors were made through bad organization.* ◇ *David got the job through his uncle.*

★**through**[2] /θru/ ***adv.*** **1** from one end or side to the other: *The gate was opened and they ran through.* **2** from the beginning to the end of sth: *He read the letter through and handed it back.*

PHR V **be through (with sb/sth)** to be finished with sb/sth

★**through·out** /θruˈaʊt/ ***prep., adv.*** **1** in every part of sth: *The game will be shown live on television throughout the world.* **2** from the beginning to the end of sth: *We didn't enjoy the vacation because it rained throughout.* ◇ *Food was scarce throughout the war.*

★**throw**[1] /θroʊ/ ***verb*** (*pt* **threw** /θru/; *pp* **thrown** /θroʊn/)

➤WITH HAND **1** [I,T] to send sth through the air by pushing it out of your hand: *How far can you throw?* ◇ *Throw the ball to Wayne.* ◇ *Throw Wayne the ball.* ◇ *Protesters threw rocks at the police.*

➤PUT CARELESSLY **2** [T] to put sth somewhere quickly or carelessly: *He threw his bag down in a corner.*

➤MOVE WITH FORCE **3** [T] to move your body or part of it quickly or suddenly: *Jenny threw herself onto the bed and sobbed.* ◇ *Lee threw back his head and roared with laughter.*

➤MAKE SB FALL **4** [T] to cause sb to fall down: *The bus braked and we were thrown to the floor.*

➤INTO PARTICULAR STATE **5** [T] (*informal*) to make sb feel upset, confused or surprised: *The question really threw me – I had no idea how to answer it.* **6** [T] to put sb in a particular (usually bad) situation: *Many people were thrown out of work during the recession.*

➤LIGHT/SHADE **7** [T] to send light or shade onto sth: *The house threw a shadow across the lawn.*

IDM **throw sb a curve** → CURVE[1]

PHR V **throw sth away 1** (*also* **throw sth out**) to get rid of sth that you do not want, e.g. by putting it in a garbage can: *That's garbage. You can throw it away.* **2** to waste or not use sth useful: *to throw away a good opportunity*

**throw sth in** (*informal*) to include sth else without increasing the price

**throw sb out** to force sb to leave

**throw sth out 1** to refuse to accept sb's idea or suggestion **2** = THROW STH AWAY

**throw up** to send out the food in your stomach through your mouth

**throw**[2] /θroʊ/ ***noun*** [C] **1** an act of throwing **2** the distance that sb throws sth: *a record throw of 75 meters*

**thru** /θru/ ***prep.*** (used especially on signs) through ➲ Look also at **drive-thru**.

**thrust**[1] /θrʌst/ ***verb*** [I,T] (*pt, pp* **thrust**) **1** to push sb/sth/yourself suddenly and with force: *The man thrust her out of the way and ran off.* **2** to make a sudden forward movement with a knife, etc.

PHR V **thrust sb/sth upon sb** to force sb to accept sb/sth

**thrust**[2] /θrʌst/ ***noun*** **1** [C] a strong push **2** [U] the main part or ideas of sth: *The main thrust of our research is to find ways of preventing cancer.*

**thud** /θʌd/ ***noun*** [C] the low sound that is made when sth heavy falls down ▶ **thud** ***verb*** [I] (**thud·ding**; **thud·ded**): *A snowball thudded against the window.*

**thug** /θʌg/ ***noun*** [C] a violent person who may hurt other people

★**thumb**[1] /θʌm/ ***noun*** [C] **1** the short thick finger at the side of each hand ➲ picture on study page **A32**. **2** the part of a glove, etc. that covers your THUMB (1)

IDM **have a green thumb** → GREEN[1]

**thumbs up/down** a sign or an expression that shows approval/disapproval: *This show got a big thumbs up from all the critics.*

**thumb**[2] /θʌm/ ***verb***

PHR V **thumb through sth** to turn the pages of a book, etc. quickly

**thumb·tack** /ˈθʌmtæk/ (*also* **tack**) ***noun*** [C] a short pin with a flat top, used for fastening paper, etc. to a board or wall

**thump** /θʌmp/ ***verb*** **1** [T] to hit sb/sth with sth heavy, usually your fist **2** [I] to make a loud sound by hitting or beating heavily: *His heart was thumping with excitement.* ▶ **thump** ***noun*** [C]

**thun·der**[1] /ˈθʌndər/ ***noun*** [U] the loud noise that comes after lightning when there is a storm

**thun·der**[2] /ˈθʌndər/ ***verb*** **1** [I] (used with *it*) to make the sound of THUNDER[1]: *The rain poured down and it started to thunder.* **2** [I,T] to make a loud noise like THUNDER[1]: *Traffic thundered across the bridge.* ◇ *"Get back to class!" the principal thundered.*

**thun·der·storm** /ˈθʌndərstɔrm/ ***noun*** [C] a storm with thunder and lightning

**Thurs·day** /ˈθərzdeɪ; -di/ ***noun*** [C,U] (*abbr.* **Thur.**; **Thurs.**) the day of the week after Wednesday and before Friday ➲ For examples of the use of the days of the week, look at **Monday**.

**thus** /ðʌs/ ***adv.*** (*formal*) **1** because of or as a result of this: *Documents can be sent electronically, thus saving paper.* **2** like this; in this way: *Thus began the series of incidents which changed her life.*

**thwart** /θwɔrt/ ***verb*** [T] to stop sb doing what he/she planned to do; to prevent sth from happening

**thyme** /taɪm/ ***noun*** [U] a plant with small leaves that have a sweet smell and are used in cooking as an herb ➲ picture on study page **A28-29**.

**thy·roid** /ˈθaɪrɔɪd/ (*also* ˈ**thyroid gland**) ***noun*** [C] a small organ at the front of the neck that produces hormones that control the way in which the body grows and functions: *an underactive/overactive thyroid*

**tic** /tɪk/ ***noun*** [C] a sudden quick movement of a muscle, especially in your face or head, that you cannot control: *a nervous tic*

**tick**[1] /tɪk/ ***verb*** [I] (used about a clock or watch) to make regular short sounds: *I could hear the clock ticking all night.*

PHR V **tick away/by** (used about time) to pass: *The minutes ticked by, but there was still no sign of Teri.*

**tick**[2] /tɪk/ ***noun*** [C] **1** the regular short sound that a watch or clock makes when it is working **2** a very small animal with eight legs, like an insect, that attaches itself to the skin of animals or people in order to suck their blood **3** (*Cdn*) = CHECK MARK

★**tick·et** /ˈtɪkət/ ***noun*** [C] **1** a piece of paper or card that shows you have paid to travel on public transportation, or to enter a place of entertainment, etc.: *a one way/round trip ticket* ◇ *two tickets for the concert* ➲ Look at **season ticket**. **2** an official piece of paper that you get when you have parked in the wrong place, driven too fast, etc.: *a parking ticket* **3** [usually sing.] a list of candidates in an election who are supported by a particular political party: *to join the Republican ticket*

**tick·le** /ˈtɪkl/ ***verb*** **1** [T] to touch sb lightly with your fingers or with sth soft so that he/she laughs: *She tickled the baby's toes.* **2** [I,T] to feel or to cause the sensation of sth touching you lightly: *My nose tickles/is tickling.* ◇ *The wool scarf tickled her neck.* **3** [T] (*informal*) to amuse or please sb: *We were just tickled when Steve Martin visited our store.* ▶ **tick·le** ***noun*** [C]: *I have a tickle in my throat.*

**tick·lish** /ˈtɪklɪʃ/ ***adj.*** (used about a person) sensitive and laughing a lot when sb tickles him/her

**tic-tac-toe** (*also* **tick-tack-toe**) /ˌtɪktækˈtoʊ/ ***noun*** [U] a game for two players that is played with a pencil and paper. Each person tries to win by writing three O's or three X's in a line in a frame of nine squares.

**tic-tac-toe**

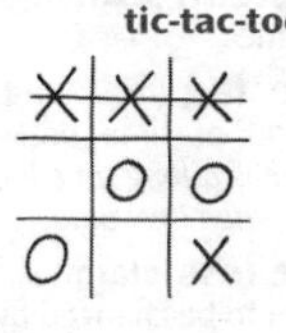

**tid·al** /ˈtaɪdl/ ***adj.*** connected with the tides in the ocean

ˈ**tidal wave** ***noun*** [C] a very large wave in the ocean, often caused by a storm

**tid·bit** /ˈtɪdbɪt/ ***noun*** [C] **1** a small but very good piece of food **2** an interesting piece of information

**tide**[1] /taɪd/ ***noun*** [C,U] the regular change in the level of the ocean. At high tide the ocean is closer to the shore; at low tide it is farther away: *The tide is coming in/going out.* ◇ (*figurative*) *The tide* (= of public opinion) *seems to have turned in the President's favor.*

**tide**[2] /taɪd/ ***verb***

PHR V **tide sb over** to help sb get through a difficult time

★**ti·dy** /ˈtaɪdi/ ***adj.*** (**ti·di·er**; **ti·di·est**) (*formal*) arranged in good order; neat: *If you keep your room tidy, it is easier to find things.* ➲ **Neat** is more common than **tidy**.

★**tie**[1] /taɪ/ ***noun*** [C] **1** (*also* **necktie**) a long thin piece of cloth that you wear around your neck with a shirt ➲ picture on study page **A30**. ➲ Look at **bow tie**. **2** [usually pl.] something that connects you with a particular group of people: *Police believe he has ties to the Mafia.* ◇ *family ties* **3** something that limits your freedom: *He never got married because he didn't want any ties.* **4** a game or competition in which two or more teams or players get the same score: *There was a tie for first place.*

★**tie**[2] /taɪ/ ***verb*** (*pres. part.* **ty·ing**; *3rd person sing. pres.* **ties**; *pt, pp* **tied**) **1** [T] to fasten sb/sth or fix sb/sth in position with rope, string, etc.: *The prisoner was tied to a chair.* ◇ *Kay tied her hair back with a ribbon.* ◇ *to tie sth in a knot* ◇ *to tie your shoelaces* **2** [I,T] **tie (sth) (with sb) (for sth)** to have the same score as another player or team in a game or competition: *Wallace's touchdown tied the score at 13 in the third quarter.* ◇ *Jenny tied with Sara for third place.*

PHR V **tie sb/yourself down** (often passive) to limit your freedom: *She felt too tied down at home with the kids.*

**tie in (with sth)** to agree with other facts or information that you have

**tie sb/sth up 1** to keep sb/sth in position with rope, string, etc.: *The dog was tied up in the back yard.* **2** (usually passive) to occupy or keep sb busy: *Mr. Jones is tied up in a meeting.*

**tier** /tɪr/ ***noun*** [C] one of a number of levels: *a stadium with two tiers of seats*

**ti·ger** /ˈtaɪgər/ ***noun*** [C] a large wild cat that has yellow fur with black stripes. Tigers live in Asia.

NOTE A baby tiger is called a **cub**.

★**tight**[1] /taɪt/ ***adj.***

➤FIXED FIRMLY **1** firm and difficult to move: *a tight knot* ◇ *Keep a tight hold on this rope.*

➤CLOTHES **2** fitting very closely: *These shoes hurt. They're too tight.* OPP **loose**

➤-TIGHT **3** (in compounds) not allowing sth to get in or out: *an airtight container*

➤MONEY/TIME **4** not having much spare time, space or money: *My schedule this week is very tight.*

➤STRETCHED **5** stretched or pulled hard: *A tennis net must be kept tight.*

T

➤CONTROL **6** controlled very strictly: *Security is very tight at the airport.*

▶ **tight·ness** *noun* [U]

**tight²** /taɪt/ ***adv.*** firmly; closely: *Hold tight – there's a bump in the road ahead.*

NOTE **Tightly**, not **tight**, is used before a past participle: *The van was packed tight with boxes.* ◇ *The van was tightly packed with boxes.*

**tight·en** /ˈtaɪtn/ *verb* [I,T] **1 tighten (sth) (up)** to become tighter; to make sth tighter: *His grip on her arm tightened.* ◇ *He tightened the screws as far as they would go.* **2 tighten sth (up)**; **tighten up (on sth)** to become more strict or to cause sth to become more strict: *to tighten up the law on the sale of alcohol to minors*

IDM **tighten your belt** (*informal*) to start making more careful choices about spending your money

★**tight·ly** /ˈtaɪtli/ ***adv.*** firmly; closely: *Screw the lid on tightly.* ◇ *She kept her eyes tightly closed.* ➲ Look at the note at **tight²**.

**tight·rope** /ˈtaɪtroʊp/ *noun* [C] a rope stretched high above the ground on which people walk, e.g. in a circus

**tights** /taɪts/ *noun* [pl.] a piece of thin clothing, usually worn by women and girls, that fits tightly from the waist over the legs and feet: *a pair of tights* ➲ **Pantyhose/nylons** are thinner than **tights**.

**'til** /tɪl/ ***prep.*** (*informal*) = UNTIL

**tile** /taɪl/ *noun* [C] one of the flat, square objects that are arranged in rows to cover floors, bathroom walls, etc. ▶ **tile** *verb* [T]: *to tile the bathroom*

**till** /tɪl/ ***prep.*** (*informal*) = UNTIL

**tilt** /tɪlt/ *verb* [I,T] to have one end or side higher than the other; to put sth in this position: *The front seats of the car tilt forward.* ◇ *She tilted her head to one side.* ▶ **tilt** *noun* [sing.]

**tim·ber** /ˈtɪmbər/ *noun* **1** [U] trees that are used as a source of wood for building houses, etc. **2** [C] a large piece of wood: *a ship's timbers*

T

★**time¹** /taɪm/ *noun*

➤MINUTES/HOURS/YEARS, ETC. **1** [C] a particular point in the day or night: *What time is it?* ◇ *Can you tell me the new time for the meeting?* ◇ *It's time to go home.* ◇ *By the time I get home, Alex will have dinner ready.* **2** [U] the passing of minutes, hours, days, etc.: *As time passed and there was still no news, we got more worried.* **3** [C,U] an amount of minutes, hours, days, etc.: *You're wasting time – get back to work!* ◇ *I'll fax this letter to save time.* ◇ *free time* ◇ *We don't have time to stop now.* ◇ *It takes a long time to learn a language.* ➲ Look also at **full-time** and **part-time**. **4** [sing.] a system for measuring time in a particular part of the world: *Eastern Standard Time* ◇ *We arrive in Atlanta at 11:00 local time.*

➤PERIOD **5** [C] a period in the past: *Did you enjoy your time in Spain?* ◇ *In Shakespeare's times, few people could read.*

➤OCCASION/EVENT **6** [C,U] an occasion when sb does sth or sth happens: *I called them three times.* ◇ *This is the first time I've ever done this.* ◇ *I'll do it better next time.* ◇ *The last time I saw him, he looked sick.* **7** [C,U] a period or an occasion when sth special happens or that is suitable for sth: *harvest time* ◇ *May is strawberry-picking time.*

➤FOR RACE **8** [C,U] the number of minutes, etc. taken to complete sth, especially a race: *What was his time in the hundred meters?*

➤FOR COMPARING **9 times** [pl.] (used with a number, for comparing things): *A decent apartment is three times as expensive in New York as it is in Toronto* (= e.g. if it cost $500 in Toronto, it costs $1500 in New York).

IDM **all the time** during the time that sb was doing sth or that sth was happening: *I looked everywhere for my keys and they were in my pocket all the time.*

**at the same time** → SAME¹

**at a time** on each occasion: *The elevator can hold six people at a time.*

**at one time** in the past; previously: *At one time, this land was covered with trees.*

**at the time** at a particular moment or period in the past: *I agreed at the time but later changed my mind.*

**at times** sometimes: *At times I wish we'd never had children.*

**beat time (to sth)** → BEAT¹

**before your time** before you were born

**behind the times** not modern or fashionable

**for the time being** just for now; not for long

**from time to time** sometimes; not often

**give sb a hard time** → HARD¹

**have a bad, rotten, etc. time** to not enjoy yourself: *I had a lousy time at summer camp.*

**have a good, great, etc. time** to enjoy yourself: *We had a wonderful time at the party.*

**have a hard/rough/tough time** to have problems or difficulties

**have no time for sb/sth** to not like sb/sth: *I have no time for people who aren't prepared to work.*

**in the nick of time** → NICK¹

**in time (for sth/to do sth)** not late; with enough time remaining for sth: *Don't worry. We'll get to the airport in time to catch your flight.*

**kill time** → KILL¹

**once upon a time** → ONCE¹

**on time** not late or early: *Our flight arrived right on time.*

**take your time** to do sth without hurrying

**tell time** → TELL

**time after time**; **time and (time) again** again and again; many times

**time²** /taɪm/ *verb* [T] **1** to choose or arrange the time that sth happens: *They timed their trip to avoid rush hour.* **2** to measure how long sb/sth takes

**ˈtime clock** *noun* [C] a special type of clock that prints out the time on a card that you put into it, e.g. to show when you start and finish work each day

**ˈtime-conˌsuming** *adj.* that takes or needs a lot of time

**ˈtime lag** (*also* **lag**, **ˈtime lapse**) *noun* [C] the period of time between two connected events: *There is a long time lag between when I do the work and when I get paid.*

**time·less** /ˈtaɪmləs/ ***adj.*** (*formal*) that does not seem to be changed by time

**'time ˌlimit** ***noun*** [C] a time during which sth must be done

**time·ly** /ˈtaɪmli/ ***adj.*** happening at just the right time: *The accident was a timely reminder of the dangers of driving on icy roads.*

**tim·er** /ˈtaɪmər/ ***noun*** [C] a machine or part of a machine that measures time

**times** /taɪmz/ ***prep.*** (used when you are multiplying one number by another): *Three times four is twelve.* ➲ Look also at **time**[1](9).

**time·ta·ble** /ˈtaɪmteɪbl/ ***noun*** [C] a plan that shows the times when a series of events are supposed to happen: *a timetable for the removal of the troops from the region*

**'time zone** ***noun*** [C] one of the areas that the world is divided into, each with its own time: *Chicago is in the Central time zone.*

**tim·id** /ˈtɪməd/ ***adj.*** easily frightened; shy ▸ **ti·mid·i·ty** /tɪˈmɪdəṭi/ ***noun*** [U] ▸ **tim·id·ly** ***adv.***

**tim·ing** /ˈtaɪmɪŋ/ ***noun*** [U] **1** the act of choosing or arranging when sth will happen: *Good timing is important when you introduce a new product.* **2** your skill at choosing or arranging the best time for sth

**tin** /tɪn/ ***noun*** (*symbol* **Sn**) [U] a soft white-colored metal that is often mixed with other metals

**tinge** /tɪndʒ/ ***noun*** [usually sing.] a small amount of a color or a feeling: *a tinge of anxiety* ▸ **tinged** ***adj.*** **tinged with sth**: *Her joy at leaving was tinged with regret.*

**tin·gle** /ˈtɪŋgl/ ***verb*** [I] to have a slight stinging or prickling feeling in the skin: *His cheeks tingled as he came in from the cold.* ▸ **tin·gle** ***noun*** [usually sing.]: *a tingle of excitement*

**tin·ker** /ˈtɪŋkər/ ***verb*** [I] **tinker (with sth)** to try to repair or improve sth without having enough skill or knowledge: *So many people have tinkered with the copier that it doesn't work at all anymore.*

**tin·kle** /ˈtɪŋkl/ ***verb*** [I] to make a light, ringing sound, like that of a small bell ▸ **tin·kle** ***noun*** [C, usually sing.]

**tin·sel** /ˈtɪnsl/ ***noun*** [U] strings covered with little pieces of shiny paper, used as a Christmas decoration

**tint**[1] /tɪnt/ ***noun*** [C] a type or shade of a color: *white paint with a pinkish tint*

**tint**[2] /tɪnt/ ***verb*** [T] to add a little color to sth: *tinted glass*

★**ti·ny** /ˈtaɪni/ ***adj.*** (**ti·ni·er**; **ti·ni·est**) very small: *the baby's tiny fingers*

★**tip**[1] /tɪp/ ***noun*** [C] **1** the thin or pointed end of sth: *the tips of your toes/fingers* ◇ *the southern tip of South America* **2** a piece of useful advice: *Thanks for the tip!* **3** an extra amount of money that you give to a waiter/waitress, taxi driver, etc. to thank him/her for good service

IDM **(have sth) on the tip of your tongue** to be about to remember or say sth that you have forgotten for a short time: *Their name is on the tip of my tongue. It'll come back to me in a minute.*

**the tip of the iceberg** a small part of a problem that is much larger

★**tip**[2] /tɪp/ ***verb*** [I,T] (**tip·ping**; **tipped**) **1** to move so that one side is higher than the other; to make sth move in this way: *Tip the table so you can fit it through the doorway.* **2 tip (sth) (over)** to fall or turn over; to make sth turn over: *The tractor turned the corner too fast and the trailer tipped over.* ◇ *The baby leaned out of his stroller and tipped it over.* **3** to give a waiter/waitress, taxi driver, etc. an extra amount of money (a **tip**) to thank him/her for good service: *You should tip the waitress about 15% of the bill.*

PHR V **tip sb off** to give sb secret information: *The police had been tipped off and were waiting when the burglars broke in.*

**ti·pi** /ˈtipi/ ***noun*** [C] = TEPEE

**'tip-off** ***noun*** [C] secret information that sb gives, for example to the police, to warn them about an illegal activity that is going to happen: *Acting on a tip-off, the police searched the house for drugs.*

**tip·toe**[1] /ˈtɪptoʊ/ ***noun***

IDM **on tiptoe** standing or walking on the ends of your toes with your heels off the ground

**tip·toe**[2] /ˈtɪptoʊ/ ***verb*** [I] (*pres. part.* **tip·toe·ing**; *3rd person sing. pres.* **tip·toes**; *pt, pp* **tip·toed**) to walk quietly and carefully on TIPTOE[1]

**tire**[1] /ˈtaɪər/ ***noun*** [C] the thick rubber ring that fits around the outside of a wheel: *a flat tire* ◇ *Remember to check your tire pressure.* ➲ Picture at **bicycle**.

★**tire**[2] /ˈtaɪər/ ***verb*** **1** [I,T] **tire (sb) (out)** to feel that you need to rest or sleep; to make sb feel like this: *However hard he works, he never seems to tire.* ◇ *The long walk tired us all out.* **2** [I] **tire of sth/of doing sth** (*formal*) to become bored or not interested in sth/doing sth: *I never tire of this view.* ➲ **Get tired of sth/of doing sth** is less formal and more common.

★**tired** /ˈtaɪərd/ ***adj.*** feeling that you need to rest or sleep: *She was tired after a hard day's work.* ◇ *Older people get tired easily.*

IDM **be sick and tired of sb/sth** → SICK

**be tired of sb/sth/doing sth** to be impatient with or annoyed by sb/sth/doing sth: *I'm tired of this game. Let's play something else.* ◇ *I'm tired of listening to the same thing over and over.*

**tired out** very tired

▸ **tired·ness** ***noun*** [U]

**tire·less** /ˈtaɪərləs/ ***adj.*** (*formal*) not getting tired: *a tireless campaigner for human rights*

**tire·some** /ˈtaɪərsəm/ ***adj.*** (*formal*) that makes you bored or annoyed

**tir·ing** /ˈtaɪərɪŋ/ ***adj.*** making you tired: *a long and tiring trip*

**tis·sue** /ˈtɪʃu/ ***noun*** **1** [C,U] the material that the bodies of animals and plants are made of: *brain tissue* ◇ *Radiation can destroy the body's tissues.* **2** [C] = KLEENEX

**'tissue ˌpaper** ***noun*** [U] thin, soft paper that you use for wrapping things that may break

★**ti·tle** /ˈtaɪṭl/ ***noun*** **1** [C] the name of a book, play, movie, picture, etc. ➲ Look also at **subtitle**. **2** [C] a word that shows a person's rank or profession: *"Doctor," "Reverend," "Mrs." and "General" are all titles.* **3** [C] the position of champion in a sport: *Sue is playing this match to defend her title* (= to stay champion). **4** [C,U] **title (to sth)** a legal right to

T

own sth, e.g. a car or a house, or an official piece of paper that says that sb owns sth

**ˌtitle ˈrole** ***noun*** [C] the part in a play or movie that is used as the title of it

★**to**[1] /tə; *before vowels* tʊ; *strong form* tu/ ***prep.*** **1** in the direction of; as far as: *She's going to Canada.* ◇ *This road goes to Denver.* ◇ *Evanston is to the north of Chicago.* ◇ *He went to school.* **2** (used before the person or thing that receives, sees, etc. sth): *Give that to me.* ◇ *We should be kind to animals.* **3** (almost) touching sth: *He put his hands to his ears.* ◇ *They sat back to back.* **4** (used to show that sth is part of sth else or fits together with sth else): *the key to the back door* ◇ *Where's the lid to this pan?* ◇ *the answer to my question* **5** (used about time) before: *It's two minutes to three.* **6** (used before the upper limit of a range): *a game suitable for children who are 8 to 12 years old* ◇ *from beginning to end* ◇ *They sell everything from matches to washing machines there.* **7** (used for expressing a reaction to sth): *To my surprise, I saw two strangers coming out of my house.* **8** (used when comparing things): *I prefer coffee to tea.* ◇ *The final score was 13 to 10.* **9** (used for expressing quantity) for each unit of money, measurement, etc.: *There are 2.54 centimeters to the inch.* **10** reaching a particular state: *The vegetables were cooked to perfection.* ◇ *He tore the letter to pieces.* ◇ *She sang the baby to sleep.* ◇ *The letter reduced her to tears* (= made her cry). ◇ *His expression changed from amazement to joy.* **11** (used to show what sb's opinion or feeling about sth is): *It sounded like crying to me.*

★**to**[2] /tə; *before vowels* tʊ; *strong form* tu/ (used with verbs to form the infinitive): *I want to go home now.* ◇ *Don't forget to write.* ◇ *She's learning English in order to get a better job.* ◇ *Do you know which button to press?* ◇ *I didn't know what to do.* ◇ *He asked me to go, but I didn't want to.*

**to**[3] /tu/ ***adv.***

IDM **to and fro** backward and forward

**toad** /toʊd/ ***noun*** [C] a small cold-blooded animal that looks similar to a frog but that is bigger, has rough skin and lives mainly on land

**toad·stool** /ˈtoʊdstul/ ***noun*** [C] a type of poisonous fungus that looks like a mushroom

**toast**[1] /toʊst/ **1** ***noun*** [U] a thin piece of bread that is heated to make it brown: *a piece/slice of toast* ◇ *buttered toast* **2** [C] an occasion at a party or a formal meal when you hold up your glass and wish sb success, happiness, etc. before you drink: *I'd like to propose a toast to the bride and groom.*

IDM **be toast** (*slang*) to be in very serious trouble: *If Dad finds out about this, we're toast!*

**toast**[2] /toʊst/ ***verb*** [T] **1** to heat bread in order to make it brown **2** to hold up your glass and wish sb success, happiness, etc. before you drink at a party or a formal meal: *Everyone stood up and toasted the bride and groom.*

**toast·er** /ˈtoʊstər/ ***noun*** [C] an electrical machine that makes bread into toast

**to·bac·co** /təˈbækoʊ/ ***noun*** [U] the dried leaves of a plant that people smoke in cigarettes and pipes, or the plant that produces these leaves

**to·bog·gan** /təˈbɑgən/ ***noun*** [C] a type of flat board that curves up at the front and that you can sit on and ride down hills covered in snow for fun

★**to·day** /təˈdeɪ/ ***noun*** [U], ***adv.*** **1** (on) this day: *Today is Monday.* ◇ *What should we do today?* ◇ *School ends a week from today* (= on this day next week). ◇ *Where is today's paper?* **2** (in) the present age: *Young people have more spending money today than in the past.* ◇ *Today's computers are much smaller than the early models.*

**tod·dler** /ˈtɑdlər/ ***noun*** [C] a child who has just learned to walk

★**toe**[1] /toʊ/ ***noun*** [C] **1** one of the five small parts like fingers at the end of each foot ➲ picture on study page A32. **2** the part of a sock, shoe, etc. that covers your TOES (1)

IDM **stub your toe (on/against sth)** → STUB[2]

**toe**[2] /toʊ/ ***verb***

IDM **toe the line** to say or do what sb in authority tells you to say or do, even if you do not share the same opinions, etc.: *One or two of them refused to toe the line.*

**TOEFL™** /ˈtoʊfl/ ***noun*** [sing.] Test of English as a Foreign Language; a test that measures your ability to read and understand English if it is not your first language. Most North American colleges and universities require foreign students to take the TOEFL exam before they can study there: *to take the TOEFL* ◇ *What was your TOEFL score?*

**TOEIC™** /ˈtoʊɪk/ ***noun*** [sing.] Test of English for International Communication; a test that measures your ability to read and understand English if it is not your first language

**toe·nail** /ˈtoʊneɪl/ ***noun*** [C] one of the hard pieces that cover the end of your toes

**to·fu** /ˈtoʊfu/ ***noun*** [U] a white food made from a type of bean (soybeans), that is eaten in salads or in cooked foods, often instead of meat

★**to·geth·er**[1] /təˈgɛðər/ ***adv.*** **1** with each other; in or into the same place as or near to sb/sth else: *Can we have lunch together?* ◇ *They walked home together.* ◇ *I'll get all my stuff together tonight because I want to leave early.* ◇ *Stand with your feet together.* **2** so that two or more things are mixed with, joined to or added to each other: *Mix the butter and sugar together.* ◇ *Tie the two ends together.* ◇ *Add these numbers together to find the total.* **3** at the same time: *We'll sing the next song together.*

IDM **get your act together** → ACT[2]

**together with** in addition to; as well as: *I enclose my order together with a check for $15.*

**to·geth·er**[2] /təˈgɛðər/ ***adj.*** (*informal*) (usually not before a noun) (used about a person) organized, capable

**to·geth·er·ness** /təˈgɛðərnəs/ ***noun*** [U] a feeling of friendship

**tog·gle**[1] /ˈtɑgl/ ***noun*** [C] **1** a short piece of wood, plastic, etc. that is put through a loop of thread to fasten sth, such as a coat or bag, instead of a button **2** (*also* ˈ**toggle switch**) (*computing*) a key on a computer that

**toggle**

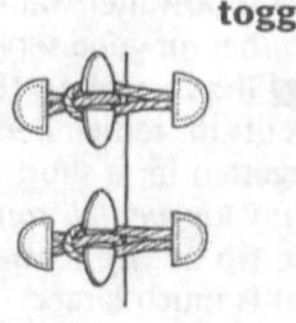

you press to change from one style or operation to another, and back again

**tog·gle²** /ˈtɑɡl/ ***verb*** [I,T] (*computing*) to press a key or set of keys on a computer keyboard in order to turn a feature on or off, or to move from one program, etc. to another: *He toggled between the two windows.* ◇ *This key toggles various views of the data.*

**toil** /tɔɪl/ ***verb*** [I] (*formal*) to work very hard or for a long time at sth ▸ **toil** ***noun*** [U] (*formal*)

★**toi·let** /ˈtɔɪlət/ ***noun*** [C] a large bowl with a seat, attached to a drain, that you use when you need to get rid of waste material or water from your body: *to flush the toilet* ◇ *Who left the toilet seat up?*

> NOTE We do not use **toilet** to talk about a room that has a toilet in it. A **bathroom** is any room that has a toilet, in a house or a public building: *Scott got caught smoking in the boys' bathroom at school.* We can also use **restroom**, **ladies' room**, **women's room** or **men's room** to talk about a room with toilets in a public building: *Can you tell me where the restrooms are?* In Canada, we can also use **washroom. Go to the bathroom/washroom** is a polite expression for what we do on the toilet.

**ˈtoilet ˌpaper** ***noun*** [U] paper that you use to clean your body after using the toilet

**toi·let·ries** /ˈtɔɪlətriz/ ***noun*** [pl.] things such as soap, toothpaste, etc. that you use when you are washing yourself, doing your hair, etc.

**to·ken¹** /ˈtoʊkən/ ***noun*** [C] **1** something that represents or is a sign of sth else: *Please accept this gift as a token of our gratitude.* **2** a piece of metal, plastic, etc. that you use for a particular purpose, often instead of a coin: *a subway token*
IDM **by the same token** → SAME¹

**to·ken²** /ˈtoʊkən/ ***adj.*** (only *before* a noun) **1** done, chosen, etc. to give the impression that you are interested in sth when you do not mean it sincerely: *There is a token woman on the board.* ◇ *They only made a token effort to fix the problem.* **2** small, but done or given as a sign that sth larger or more serious could follow: *a token payment*

**told** *past tense, past participle of* TELL

**tol·er·a·ble** /ˈtɑlərəbl/ ***adj.*** of a level that you can tolerate: *Medication can reduce the pain to a tolerable level.*

**tol·er·ance** /ˈtɑlərəns/ ***noun*** [U] the ability or willingness to allow or accept sth that is bad or that you do not like or agree with: *religious tolerance* OPP **intolerance** ▸ **tol·er·ant** /-rənt/ ***adj.*** **tolerant (of/toward sb/sth)** OPP **intolerant**

**tol·er·ate** /ˈtɑləreɪt/ ***verb*** [T] **1** to allow or accept sth that you do not like or agree with: *In a democracy, we have to be willing to tolerate opinions that are different from our own.* **2** to accept or stand sb/sth bad without complaining: *The noise was more than she could tolerate.*

**toll** /toʊl/ ***noun*** [C] **1** money that you pay to use a road, bridge, etc. **2** [usually sing.] the amount of damage done or the number of people who were killed or injured by sth: *At least 150 people died in the earthquake, though some reports say the toll was much higher.* ➲ Look also at **death toll**.
IDM **take a heavy toll/take its toll (on sth)** to cause loss, damage, suffering, etc.

**ˌtoll-ˈfree** ***adj.*** (used about a telephone number or call) that does not cost anything

> NOTE Toll-free telephone numbers in the U.S. and Canada have **800** or **888** as their area codes.

▸ **ˌtoll-ˈfree** ***adv.***

★**to·ma·to** /təˈmeɪţoʊ/ ***noun*** [C] (*pl.* **to·ma·toes**) a soft red fruit that is often eaten raw in salads or cooked as a vegetable: *tomato juice* ➲ picture on study page **A28-29**.

**tomb** /tum/ ***noun*** [C] a place where a body is buried, often one with a large decorated stone above it

**tom·boy** /ˈtɑmbɔɪ/ ***noun*** [C] a young girl who likes to play rough games

**tomb·stone** /ˈtumstoʊn/ ***noun*** [C] a stone over a grave that shows the name of the person who is buried there

**tom·cat** /ˈtɑmkæt/ ***noun*** [C] a male cat

★**to·mor·row** /təˈmɑroʊ; -ˈmɔr-/ ***noun*** [U], ***adv.*** **1** (on) the day after today: *Today is Friday, so tomorrow is Saturday.* ◇ *The ad will appear in tomorrow's paper.* ◇ *See you tomorrow.* ◇ *I'm going to bed. I have to get up early tomorrow morning.* ◇ *Tomorrow night's concert has been canceled.* ◇ *a week from tomorrow*

> NOTE Notice that we say **tomorrow morning**, **tomorrow afternoon**, etc. and NOT "tomorrow in the morning," etc. ➲ Look also at the note at **morning**.

**2** the future: *The children of today are tomorrow's leaders.*
IDM **the day after tomorrow** → DAY

**ton** /tʌn/ ***noun*** **1** [C] a measure of weight; 2,000 pounds **2 a ton (of sth)**; **tons (of sth)** (*informal*) a lot: *tons of homework* ◇ *What's in this box? It weighs a ton!*

★**tone¹** /toʊn/ ***noun***
➤ OF VOICE **1** [C,U] the quality of a sound, especially of the human voice: *"Do you know each other?" she asked in a casual tone of voice.* ◇ *His tone suddenly changed when Amy entered the room.*
➤ CHARACTER/ATMOSPHERE **2** [sing.] the general quality or style of sb/sth: *The tone of the meeting was optimistic.*
➤ COLOR **3** [C] one of the shades of a color: *warm tones of red and orange*
➤ ON TELEPHONE **4** [C] a sound that you hear on the telephone: *the dial tone*
➤ OF MUSCLES/SKIN **5** [U] how firm and strong your skin or muscles are: *exercises to improve your muscle tone*

**tone²** /toʊn/ ***verb***
PHR V **tone sth down** to change sth that you have said, written, etc., to make it seem less strong

**ˈtone-deaf** ***adj.*** not able to sing or hear the difference between notes in music

**tongs** /tɑŋz; tɔŋz/ ***noun*** [pl.] a tool that looks like a pair of scissors but that you use to hold or pick things up ➲ picture at **kitchen**.

★**tongue** /tʌŋ/ ***noun*** [C] **1** the soft part inside your mouth that you can move. You use your tongue for speaking, tasting things, etc. **2** (*formal*) a language: *your mother tongue* (= the language you learned as a child)
IDM **on the tip of your tongue** → TIP¹

T

**stick your tongue out** to put your tongue outside your mouth, for the doctor to examine or to be rude to sb

**tongue depressor** /ˈtʌŋ dɪˌprɛsər/ *noun* [C] (*medical*) a thin flat instrument that doctors use for pressing the tongue down when they are examining sb's throat

**ˌtongue-in-ˈcheek** *adj.* (usually *before* a noun) done or said as a joke; not meant seriously

**ˈtongue ˌtwister** *noun* [C] a phrase or sentence that is difficult to say correctly when you are speaking quickly

**ton·ic** /ˈtɑnɪk/ *noun* [C,U] something that makes you feel stronger, healthier, happier, etc.: *a vitamin tonic*

**ˈtonic ˌwater** (*also* **tonic**) *noun* [U] a type of water with bubbles in it and a bitter taste, that is often added to alcoholic drinks: *a gin and tonic*

★**to·night** /təˈnaɪt/ *noun* [U], *adv.* (in) the evening or night of today: *Tonight is the last night of our vacation.* ◇ *tonight's weather forecast* ◇ *What's on TV tonight?* ◇ *We are staying with friends tonight and traveling home tomorrow.*

**ton·sil** /ˈtɑnsl/ *noun* [C] one of the two soft lumps in your throat on each side of the back of your tongue

**ton·sil·li·tis** /ˌtɑnsəˈlaɪt̬əs/ *noun* [U] an illness in which the tonsils become very sore

**too/enough**

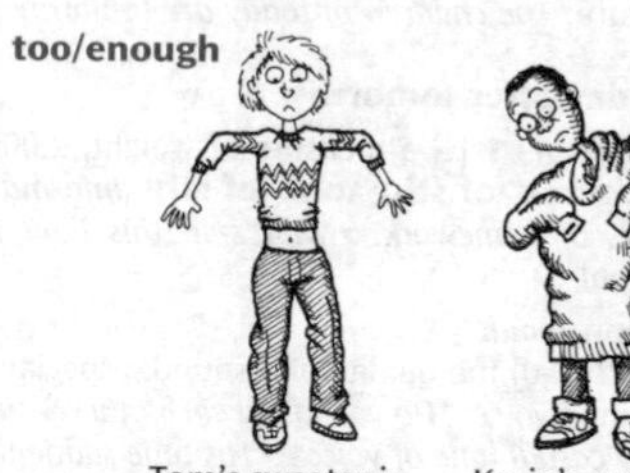

Tom's sweater is **not big enough**. Kevin's sweater is **too** big.

★**too** /tu/ *adv.* **1** in addition; also: *Red is my favorite color but I like blue, too.* ◇ *Phil thinks you're right and I do too.*

NOTE Notice that you say "There were lions and tigers at the zoo. There were elephants, **too**," but "There were no zebras and there were no giraffes, **either**." ➲ Look at the note at **also**.

**2** (used for expressing surprise or disappointment): *Her purse was stolen. And on her birthday, too.* **3** (used before adjectives and adverbs) more than is good, allowed, possible, etc.: *These boots are too small.* ◇ *It's too cold to go out without a coat.* ◇ *It's too long a trip for you to go alone.*

NOTE Notice that you cannot say "It's a too long trip."

**4** (used in negative sentences) very: *Darla didn't do too well on her test – she only got a C.*

IDM **too bad** (*informal*) **1** (used to express sympathy or to say that you are sorry about sth): *"My dog died yesterday." "Gee, that's too bad."* **2** (used to express a lack of sympathy): *"I don't like liver." "Well, too bad – that's all there is for supper."*

**took** *past tense of* TAKE

★**tool** /tul/ *noun* [C] a piece of equipment that you use to help you do a particular type of job: *garden tools* ◇ *A cellular phone is an indispensable tool for a journalist.*

NOTE A tool is usually something you can hold in your hand, e.g. a wrench or hammer. An **implement** is often used outside, e.g. for farming or gardening. A **machine** has moving parts and works with electricity, with an engine, etc. An **instrument** is often used for technical or delicate work: *a dentist's instruments* ◇ *precision instruments.* A **device** is a more general word for a piece of equipment that you consider to be useful: *The machine has a safety device which switches the power off if there is a problem.*

**tool·bar** /ˈtulbɑr/ *noun* [C] (*computing*) a row of symbols at the top of a computer screen that represent certain functions which the computer can perform

**too·nie** /ˈtuni/ *noun* [C] (*Cdn*) the Canadian two-dollar coin ➲ Look also at **loonie**.

**toot** /tut/ *noun* [C] the short sound that a whistle, horn, etc. makes ▸ **toot** *verb* [I,T]

★**tooth** /tuθ/ *noun* [C] (*pl.* **teeth** /tiθ/) **1** one of the hard white parts in your mouth that you use for biting and chewing: *to have a tooth pulled* ◇ *The old man took out his false teeth.* ◇ *wisdom teeth*

NOTE You **brush** your teeth to remove pieces of food. If a tooth is **decayed** or has a **cavity** in it, the dentist may **fill** it or **extract** it/ **pull** it **out**. If your teeth are **crooked**, you can have **braces** put on them to make them **straight**. If you have had

**tools**

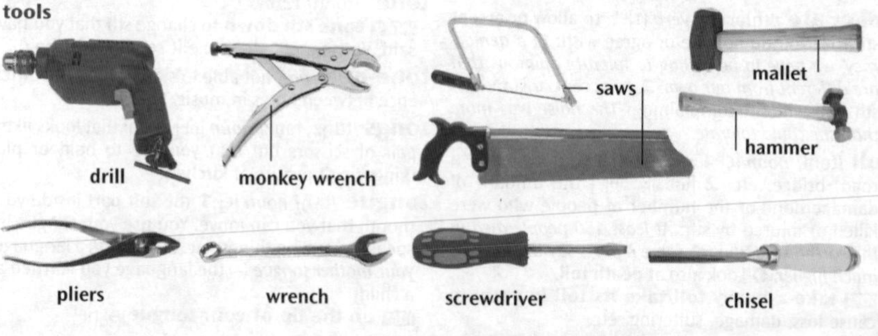

all your teeth out, you can have **false teeth** or **dentures**.

**2** one of the long pointed parts of a comb, saw, etc.

IDM **by the skin of your teeth** → SKIN[1]
**grit your teeth** → GRIT[2]
**have a sweet tooth** → SWEET[1]

**tooth·ache** /ˈtuθeɪk/ ***noun*** [C] a pain in your tooth or teeth ➲ Look at the note at **ache**.

**tooth·brush** /ˈtuθbrʌʃ/ ***noun*** [C] a small brush with a handle that you use for brushing your teeth ➲ picture at **brush**[1].

**tooth·paste** /ˈtuθpeɪst/ ***noun*** [U] a substance that you put on your toothbrush and use for cleaning your teeth

**tooth·pick** /ˈtuθpɪk/ ***noun*** [C] a short pointed piece of wood that you use for getting pieces of food out from between your teeth

★**top**[1] /tɑp/ ***noun***
➤HIGHEST POINT **1** [C] the highest part of sth: *The apartment is at the top of the building.* ◇ *the top of the stairs* ◇ *Start reading at the top of the page.*
➤UPPER SURFACE **2** [C] the upper surface of sth: *a desktop*
➤HIGHEST RANK **3** [sing.] **the top (of sth)** the highest or most important rank or position: *to be at the top of your profession*
➤OF PEN/BOTTLE, ETC. **4** [C] the cover that you put onto sth in order to close it: *Put the tops back on the felt-tip pens or they will dry out.*

NOTE A **top** or a **cap** is often small and round. You take it off by turning or screwing: *a bottle top* ◇ *Unscrew cap to open.* A **lid** may be larger. You can lift it off: *a garbage can lid* ◇ *Put the lid back on the box.*

➤CLOTHING **5** [C] a piece of clothing, especially for women or girls, that you wear on the top part of your body: *I need a top to match my new skirt.*
➤TOY **6** [C] a child's toy that spins around quickly, balancing on a point

IDM **at the top of your voice** as loudly as possible
**off the top of your head** (*informal*) without preparing or thinking about sth before you speak
**on top 1** on or onto the highest point: *There's a pile of books on the desk. Just put this one on top.* **2** stronger or better: *Throughout the game, the Bulls were on top.*
**on top of sb/sth 1** on or onto sb/sth else: *Several demonstrators stood on top of the tank, waving flags and shouting.* **2** in addition to sb/sth else: *On top of all our other problems, the car broke down.*

★**top**[2] /tɑp/ ***adj.*** (only *before* a noun) highest in position, rank or degree: *one of the country's top business executives* ◇ *at top speed* ◇ *the top floor of the building*

**top**[3] /tɑp/ ***verb*** [T] (**top·ping**; **topped**) **1** to be or form a top for sth: *cauliflower topped with cheese sauce* **2** to be higher or greater than sth: *Inflation has topped the 10% mark.*

IDM **to top it (all) off** as a final piece of bad luck: *What a rotten vacation! The flight was delayed, the airline lost our baggage and to top it all off, Rob broke his leg skiing.*

**ˈtop hat** ***noun*** [C] a tall black or gray hat that a man wears on formal occasions

**ˈtop-ˌheavy** ***adj.*** heavier at the top than the bottom and likely to fall over

★**top·ic** /ˈtɑpɪk/ ***noun*** [C] a subject that you talk, write or learn about

**top·i·cal** /ˈtɑpɪkl/ ***adj.*** connected with sth that is happening now; that people are interested in now

**ˌtopic ˈsentence** ***noun*** [C] a sentence, usually at the beginning of a paragraph, that gives the main idea of that paragraph

**top·less** /ˈtɑpləs/ ***adj., adv.*** with the breasts not covered: *a topless dancer* ◇ *to sunbathe topless*

**top·most** /ˈtɑpmoʊst/ ***adj.*** (only *before* a noun) (*written*) highest: *the topmost branches of the tree*

**ˌtop-of-the-ˈline** ***adj.*** (used to describe the best or most expensive of a group of similar products): *Let me show you our top-of-the-line model.*

**top·ping** /ˈtɑpɪŋ/ ***noun*** [C,U] something that is put on the top of food to decorate it or make it taste better: *What toppings do you want on the pizza?*

**top·ple** /ˈtɑpl/ ***verb*** **1** [I,T] **topple (sth) (over)** to become unsteady and fall down, or to cause sth to do this: *High winds toppled several trees in the area.* **2** [T] to cause a government or leader of a country to lose power: *The country's leader was toppled by a military coup.*

**ˌtop-ˈsecret** ***adj.*** that must be kept very secret

**toque** /tuk/ ***noun*** [C] (*Cdn*) a close-fitting knitted cap, often with a pompom on the top

**torch**[1] /tɔrtʃ/ ***noun*** [C] a long piece of wood with burning material at the end that you carry to give light

**torch**[2] /tɔrtʃ/ ***verb*** [T] (*informal*) to burn sth, especially a building, on purpose in order to destroy it

**tore** *past tense of* TEAR[2]

**tor·ment**[1] /tɔrˈmɛnt/ ***verb*** [T] to cause sb great pain or unhappiness: *She was tormented by nightmares.*

**tor·ment**[2] /ˈtɔrmɛnt/ ***noun*** [C,U] great pain in your mind or body; sth that causes this pain: *to be in torment*

**torn** *past participle of* TEAR[2]

**tor·na·do** /tɔrˈneɪdoʊ/ ***noun*** [C] (*pl.* **tor·na·does** or **tor·na·dos**) (*also informal* **twister**) a violent storm with a very strong wind that blows in a circle ➲ Look at the note at **storm**.

**tor·pe·do** /tɔrˈpidoʊ/ ***noun*** [C] (*pl.* **tor·pe·does**) a bomb, shaped like a tube, that is fired under water from one ship toward another

**tor·rent** /ˈtɔrənt; ˈtɑr-/ ***noun*** [C] a strong fast stream of sth, especially water: *The heavy rain turned the creek into a savage torrent.* ◇ (*figurative*) *She poured out a torrent of abuse at him.*

**tor·ren·tial** /təˈrɛnʃl/ ***adj.*** (used about rain) very heavy

**tor·so** /ˈtɔrsoʊ/ ***noun*** [C] (*pl.* **tor·sos**) the main part of the body, not the head, arms and legs

**tor·til·la** /tɔrˈtiyə/ ***noun*** [C] a type of very thin, round Mexican bread made of ground corn or wheat flour

T

**tor·toise** /ˈtɔrt̬əs/ *noun* [C] = TURTLE ➲ Look at the note and picture at **turtle**.

**tor·tu·ous** /ˈtɔrtʃuəs/ *adj.* **1** (used about a road, etc.) with many bends: *a tortuous route through the mountains* **2** complicated, not clear and simple: *a tortuous explanation*

**tor·ture** /ˈtɔrtʃər/ *noun* [C,U] the act of causing very great pain to a person, as a punishment or to make him/her give some information: *The rebel army has been accused of rape, torture and murder.* ▶ **tor·ture** *verb* [T]: *Most of the prisoners were tortured into making a confession.* ◇ (*figurative*): *She was tortured by the thought that the accident was her fault.* ▶ **tor·tur·er** /ˈtɔrtʃərər/ *noun* [C]

**To·ry** /ˈtɔri/ *noun* [C] (*Cdn*) a member or supporter of the Conservative Party

**toss** /tɔs/ *verb* **1** [T] to throw sth lightly, not using all your strength: *We tossed a ball around for an hour after school.* **2** [T] **toss sth (out)** to get rid of sth that you do not need anymore, especially by putting it into the garbage: *You can just toss those magazines – I'm finished with them.* **3** [T] to mix food, e.g. salad, together in a bowl **4** [I,T] to keep moving up and down or from side to side; to make sb/sth do this: *He lay tossing and turning in bed, unable to sleep.* ◇ *The rough seas tossed the ship for hours.* ▶ **toss** *noun* [C]

**toss·up** /ˈtɔsʌp/ *noun*

IDM **sth is a tossup** (*informal*) (used to say that two things have an equal chance of happening, or that you cannot choose between two things or people): *It's a tossup whether mortgage rates will increase next year.*

**tot** /tɑt/ *noun* [C] a small child

★**to·tal¹** /ˈtoʊt̬l/ *adj.* (usually *before* a noun) **1** counting everything; complete: *What was the total number of people killed?* ◇ *a total failure* ◇ *They ate in total silence.* **2** (*slang*) (used to emphasize how good or bad sb/sth is): *Brad is such a total jerk!*

★**to·tal²** /ˈtoʊt̬l/ *noun* [C] the number that you get when you add two or more numbers or amounts together

IDM **in total** when you add two or more numbers or amounts together: *The campaign raised $4 million in total.*

**to·tal³** /ˈtoʊt̬l/ *verb* [T] **1** to add up to a certain amount or number; to make a total of: *His debts totaled more than $10,000.* **2** (*informal*) to destroy a car completely so that it cannot be repaired

★**to·tal·ly** /ˈtoʊt̬l·i/ *adv.* **1** completely: *Their lives were totally changed.* ◇ *The situation is totally different now.* **2** (*slang*) (used to agree with sth that sb has just said): *"This class is so boring." "Yeah, totally!"*

**to·tem** /ˈtoʊt̬əm/ *noun* [C] an animal or other natural object that is chosen and respected as a special symbol of a community or family, especially among Native Americans; an image of this animal, etc.

ˈ**totem pole** *noun* [C] **1** a tall wooden pole that has symbols and pictures (totems) carved or painted on it, traditionally made by Native Americans and Canadians on the west coast **2** (*informal*) a range of different levels or ranks in an organization, etc.: *I didn't want to be* ***low man on the totem pole*** *for ever.*

**tot·ter** /ˈtɑt̬ər/ *verb* [I] to stand or move in an unsteady way as if you are going to fall ➲ Look also at **teeter-totter**.

★**touch¹** /tʌtʃ/ *verb*

➤ NO SPACE BETWEEN **1** [I,T] (used about two or more things, surfaces, etc.) to be or go so close together that there is no space between them: *They were sitting so close that their heads touched.* ◇ *This bicycle is too big. My feet don't touch the ground.*

➤ WITH HANDS/FINGERS **2** [T] to put a part of your body, usually your hand or fingers, onto sb/sth: *He touched her gently on the cheek.* ◇ *The police asked us not to touch anything.* ◇ (*figurative*) *June never touches alcohol* (= she never drinks it).

➤ AFFECT SB/STH **3** [T] to make sb feel sadness, sympathy, thanks, etc.: *a sad story that touched our hearts* ➲ Look at **touched**.

➤ BE INVOLVED WITH **4** [T] (usually in negative sentences) to deal with a problem or become involved in a situation: *There were rumors of illegal activities at the bank, but no newspaper would touch the story.*

➤ EQUAL SB **5** [T] (in negative sentences) to be as good as sb/sth: *He's a much better player than all the others. No one else can touch him.*

IDM **touch base (with sb)** (*informal*) to contact sb and speak with him/her for a short time in order to exchange information

PHR V **touch down** (used about an airplane) to land

**touch on/upon sth** to talk or write about sth for only a short time

**touch sth up** to improve sth by making small changes or repairs: *Use a small paintbrush to touch up any scratches.*

★**touch²** /tʌtʃ/ *noun*

➤ WITH HANDS/FINGERS **1** [C, usually sing.] an act of TOUCHING¹ (2) sb/sth: *I felt the touch of her hand on my arm.*

➤ SENSE **2** [U] one of the five senses: the ability to feel: *The sense of touch is very important to blind people.*

➤ WAY STH FEELS **3** [U] the way sth feels when you touch it: *Marble is cold to the touch.*

➤ SMALL DETAIL **4** [C] a small detail: *The flowers on our table were a nice touch.*

➤ SMALL AMOUNT **5** [sing.] **a touch (of sth)** a small amount of sth: *He's not very sick. It's just a touch of the flu.*

➤ WAY OF DOING STH **6** [sing.] a way or style of doing sth: *She prefers to answer any fan mail herself for a more personal touch.* ◇ *Computer graphics will give your presentation the professional touch.* ◇ *He couldn't find his* ***magic touch*** *with the ball today* (= he didn't play well). ◇ *This food is awful. I think I'm* ***losing my touch*** (= my ability to do sth).

IDM **in touch/out of touch (with sb)** being/not being in contact with sb by speaking or writing to him/her: *During the year she was in prison, they kept in touch by mail.*

**in touch/out of touch with sth** having/not having recent information about sth: *We're out of touch with what's going on in the rest of the world.*

**lose touch** → LOSE

**lose your touch** → LOSE

ˌ**touch and** ˈ**go** *adj.* (*informal*) (used to say that the result of a situation is uncertain and that there is a possibility that sth bad or unpleasant will happen): *She's fine now, but it was touch and go for a while* (= there was a possibility that she might die). ◇ *It was touch and go whether they'd allow him into the country or not.*

**touch·down** /ˈtʌtʃdaʊn/ ***noun*** [C] (in football) an act of carrying the ball into the area at the end of the field (end zone) or of catching the ball there. A touchdown is worth six points: *to score a touchdown* ➲ Look at the note at **football**.

**touched** /tʌtʃt/ ***adj.*** (not before a noun) made to feel sadness, sympathy, thanks, etc.: *We were very touched by your thoughtful gift.*

**touch·ing** /ˈtʌtʃɪŋ/ ***adj.*** that makes you feel sadness, sympathy, thanks, etc.: *The play is a touching story of young love.*

**ˈtouch screen** ***noun*** [C] a computer screen which allows you to give instructions to a computer by touching areas on the screen

**touch·y** /ˈtʌtʃi/ ***adj.*** **1** easily upset or made angry: *Don't ask about her first marriage. She's very touchy about it.* **2** (used about a subject, situation, etc.) that may easily upset people or make them angry

★**tough** /tʌf/ ***adj.***

➤STRONG **1** not easily broken or cut; very strong: *tough boots* ◇ *tough plastic*

➤NOT EASILY DAMAGED **2** not easily weakened by pain or difficulty; very strong: *You need to be tough to go camping in the winter.*

➤MEAT **3** difficult to cut and eat: *This meat is tough.*

➤STRICT/FIRM **4** strict; firm: *The government is introducing tough new laws against drinking and driving.*

➤DIFFICULT **5** difficult: *It will be a tough decision to make.* ◇ *He's been having a very tough time recently.*

IDM **tough (luck)!** (*informal*) (used to express a lack of sympathy): *"I left my wallet at home." "Well, tough – I'm not going to loan you any money."*

▶ **tough·ness** ***noun*** [U]

**tough·en** /ˈtʌfn/ ***verb*** [I,T] **toughen (sb/sth) (up)** to become tough; to make sb/sth tough

**tou·pee** /tuˈpeɪ/ (*also* **hairpiece**, *slang* **rug**) ***noun*** [C] a piece of artificial hair that some men wear because they do not want people to see that they have lost some of their own hair

★**tour¹** /tʊr/ ***noun*** **1** [C] a short visit around a city, building, etc., usually in a group with sb who explains the things in it: *to take a guided tour through the White House* ◇ *Sandy gave us a tour of their new house.* ➲ Look at the note at **travel**. **2** [C] a trip that you make for pleasure during which you visit many places: *to go on a tour of the Caribbean islands* **3** [C,U] a series of visits to different places to play sports, give concerts, etc.: *Jon Bon Jovi is on tour this summer.*

**tour²** /tʊr/ ***verb*** [I,T] to go on a TOUR¹ of a place: *We toured a candy factory and learned how chocolate is made.*

**tour·ism** /ˈtʊrɪzəm/ ***noun*** [U] the business of providing and arranging vacations and services for people who are visiting a place: *the country's tourism industry*

★**tour·ist** /ˈtʊrɪst/ ***noun*** [C] a person who visits a place for pleasure: *a foreign tourist*

**tour·na·ment** /ˈtərnəmənt; ˈtʊr-/ ***noun*** [C] a competition in which many players or teams play games against each other

**tou·sled** /ˈtaʊzld; ˈtaʊsld/ ***adj.*** (used about hair) messy: *a boy with blue eyes and tousled hair*

**tow¹** /toʊ/ ***verb*** [T] to pull a car, etc. along by a rope or chain: *Unauthorized vehicles will be towed away* (on a sign).

**tow²** /toʊ/ ***noun***

IDM **in tow** (*informal*) following behind: *He arrived with his wife and five children in tow.*

★**to·ward** /tɔrd; təˈwɔrd/ (*also* **towards** /tɔrdz; təˈwɔrdz/) ***prep.*** **1** in the direction of sb/sth: *I saw Ken walking toward the bus stop.* ◇ *She had her back toward me.* ◇ *a first step toward world peace* **2** (used when you are talking about your feelings about sb/sth) in relation to: *Pat felt very protective toward her younger brother.* ◇ *What is your attitude toward private education?* **3** as part of the payment for sth: *The money will go toward the cost of a new school bus.* **4** near a time, date or place: *It gets cool toward evening.* ◇ *The accident happened out toward the Hansons' farm.*

★**tow·el** /ˈtaʊəl/ ***noun*** [C] a piece of cloth or paper that you use for drying sb/sth/yourself: *a bath towel* ◇ *paper towels*

★**tow·er** /ˈtaʊər/ ***noun*** [C] a tall narrow building or part of a building: *the Eiffel Tower* ◇ *an observation tower*

★**town** /taʊn/ ***noun*** **1** [C] a place with many streets and buildings. A town is smaller than a city: *She grew up in a small town in Idaho.* ◇ *I have to go into town this afternoon.* ➲ Look also at **hometown**. **2** [sing.] all the people who live in a TOWN (1): *The whole town was on the streets, waving flags and shouting.*

IDM **go to town (on sth)** (*informal*) to do sth, especially eating, with a lot of energy and enthusiasm: *Boy, the kids sure went to town on those cookies* (= ate them eagerly)*!*

**in town** in the same town or city as the person who is speaking or writing: *The governor was in town yesterday to view the flood damage.*

**a night on the town** → NIGHT

**out of town** not in the same town or city as the person who is speaking or writing: *Mrs. Perez is out of town on business.* ◇ *Wendy's new boyfriend is from out of town.*

**ˌtown ˈhall** ***noun*** [C] a building that contains the offices of a town's local government

**town·ship** /ˈtaʊnʃɪp/ ***noun*** [C] a part of a county that has its own local government

**tox·ic** /ˈtɑksɪk/ ***adj.*** poisonous: *Toxic chemicals had leaked into the water.*

★**toy¹** /tɔɪ/ ***noun*** [C] an object for a child to play with: *Here are some toys to keep the kids occupied.* ◇ *toy cars* ◇ *a toy soldier* ◇ *a toy store*

**toy²** /tɔɪ/ ***verb***

PHRV **toy with sth** **1** to think about doing sth, perhaps not very seriously: *She's toying with the idea of taking a year off from college.* **2** to move sth around without thinking about what you are doing: *He toyed with his food but hardly ate any of it.*

★**trace**[1] /treɪs/ ***noun*** **1** [C,U] a mark or sign that shows that sb/sth existed or happened: *traces of a prehistoric village* ◇ *The man disappeared without trace.* **2** [C] a very small amount of sth: *Traces of blood were found under her fingernails.*

★**trace**[2] /treɪs/ ***verb*** [T] **1** to find out where sb/sth is by following marks, signs or other information: *The wanted man was traced to an address in Tacoma.* **2** to find out or describe the development of sth: *She traced her family tree back to the 19th century.* **3** to make a copy of sth by placing a piece of transparent paper over it and drawing over the lines

★**track**[1] /træk/ ***noun***
➤MARKS ON GROUND **1** [C, usually pl.] a line or series of marks that are left behind by a car, person, animal, etc.: *The hunter followed the tracks of a deer.* ◇ *tire tracks* ➲ Look at **footprint**.
➤FOR TRAIN **2** [C, usually pl.] the two metal rails on which a train runs: *It's dangerous to play on the railroad tracks.*
➤ROUGH PATH **3** [C] a special path, often in a round shape, where people, animals or cars race
➤FOR RACES **4** [U] = TRACK AND FIELD: *the track team*
➤ON TAPE/CD **5** [C] one song or piece of music on a cassette, CD or record
➤IN SCHOOL **6** [C] a group of school students who are in the same class because they have similar abilities
IDM **keep/lose track of sb/sth** to know/not know what is happening somewhere or to sb/sth: *I can't keep track of all my kids' activities and practice sessions.*
**off the beaten path/track** → BEAT[1]
**on the right/wrong track** having the right/wrong kind of ideas about sth: *That's not the answer, but you're on the right track.*
**on/off track** happening or developing in a way that will lead to success/failure: *She tried to get the discussion back on track.*

**track**[2] /træk/ ***verb*** [T] **1** **track sb/sth (to sth)** to follow tracks or signs in order to find sb/sth: *to track enemy planes on a radar screen* **2** to carry dirt, etc. on your shoes and leave it on the ground when you walk: *Don't track mud on the carpet!*
PHR V **track sb/sth down** to find sb/sth after searching for him/her/it

ˌ**track and ˈfield** (*also* **track**) ***noun*** [U] sports events such as running, jumping and throwing

ˈ**track meet** ***noun*** [C] a sports competition that includes running, jumping and throwing events

ˈ**track ˌrecord** ***noun*** [C] what a person or organization has achieved that other people know about

**trac·tor** /ˈtræktər/ ***noun*** [C] a large vehicle that is used on farms for pulling heavy pieces of machinery, especially in fields

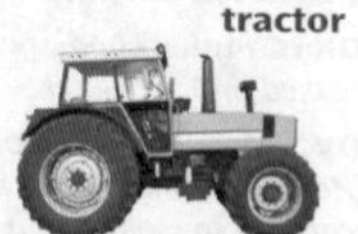
tractor

ˌ**tractor-ˈtrailer** ***noun*** [C] a very large truck that consists of two connected parts, which can carry a large quantity of things over a long distance ➲ picture at **truck**.

★**trade**[1] /treɪd/ ***noun*** **1** [U] the buying or selling of goods or services; business: *an international trade agreement* ◇ *the nation's trade deficit* ◇ *Many resort towns depend on the tourist trade.* **2** [C] an act of exchanging sth for sth else: *to make a trade* **3** [C,U] a job for which you need special skill, especially with your hands: *to learn a trade* ➲ Look at the note at **work**.

★**trade**[2] /treɪd/ ***verb*** **1** [I] **trade (in sth) (with sb)** to buy or sell goods or services: *More and more countries are trading with China.* ◇ *to trade in arms* **2** [T] **trade (sb) sth (for sth)** to exchange sth for sth else: *I'll trade you my sandwich for yours.*
IDM **change/trade places (with sb)** → PLACE[1]
PHR V **trade sth in (for sth)** to give sth old in part payment for sth new or newer: *Jeff traded in his station wagon for a flashy sports car.*

**trade·mark** /ˈtreɪdmɑrk/ ***noun*** [C] (*abbr.* **TM**) a special mark or name that a company can put on its products and that cannot be used by any other company

**trad·er** /ˈtreɪdər/ ***noun*** [C] a person who buys and sells things: *Wall Street bond traders*

★**tra·di·tion** /trəˈdɪʃn/ ***noun*** [C,U] a custom or belief that has continued from the past to the present: *It's a tradition to play tricks on people on April 1st.* ◇ *New Orleans has a great musical tradition.* ◇ *By tradition, the bride's family pays the costs of the wedding.*

★**tra·di·tion·al** /trəˈdɪʃn·l/ ***adj.*** **1** connected with customs or beliefs that have continued from the past to the present: *It is traditional to eat turkey on Thanksgiving.* ◇ *traditional holiday decorations* **2** following or using ideas or ways of doing things that have existed for a long time; old-fashioned: *women's traditional roles as housewives and mothers* ▸ **tra·di·tion·al·ly** ***adv.***

★**traf·fic**[1] /ˈtræfɪk/ ***noun*** [U] **1** the cars, etc. that are on a road: *heavy/light traffic* ◇ *The traffic is at a standstill.* **2** the movement of ships, airplanes, etc.: *air traffic controllers* **3** **traffic (in sth)** the illegal buying and selling of sth: *the traffic in arms*

**traf·fic**[2] /ˈtræfɪk/ ***verb*** [I] (*pres. part.* **traf·fick·ing**; *pt, pp* **traf·ficked**) **traffic (in sth)** to buy and sell sth illegally: *drug trafficking* ▸ **traf·fick·er** ***noun*** [C]

ˈ**traffic jam** ***noun*** [C] a long line of cars, etc. that cannot move or that can only move very slowly

ˈ**traffic light** (*also* **stoplight**, ˈ**traffic signal**) ***noun*** [C] a sign with three colored lights (red, yellow and green) that is used for controlling the traffic where two or more streets meet

**trag·e·dy** /ˈtrædʒədi/ ***noun*** (*pl.* **trag·e·dies**) **1** [C,U] an event or situation that causes great sadness: *A class trip to the coast ended in tragedy when the school bus was involved in a serious accident.* ◇ *It's a tragedy that there are so many homeless people on the streets.* **2** [C] a serious play that has a sad ending ➲ Look at **comedy**.

**trag·ic** /ˈtrædʒɪk/ ***adj.*** **1** that causes great sadness: *It's tragic that he died so young.* ◇ *a tragic accident* **2** (only *before* a noun) with a sad ending or in the style of TRAGEDY (2): *a tragic novel* ▸ **trag·i·cal·ly** /-kli/ ***adv.***

**trail**[1] /treɪl/ ***noun*** [C] **1** a series of marks in a long line that a person or thing leaves behind: *a trail of muddy footprints ◇ The storm left behind a trail of destruction.* **2** a path through the countryside: *a nature trail in the woods* **3** the tracks or smell that you follow when you are hunting sb/sth: (*figurative*) *The thieves took off in a stolen car with the police on their trail.*

**trail²** /treɪl/ ***verb*** **1** [I,T] to be pulled or dragged along behind you; to make sth do this: *The bride's long dress trailed behind her as she walked down the aisle.* **2** [I] **trail behind (sb/sth)** to move or walk slowly behind sb/sth else, usually because you are tired **3** [I,T] **trail (behind) (sb)** to have a lower score than the other player or team during a game or competition: *At halftime, Cleveland was trailing seven to ten.*

**trail·er** /ˈtreɪlər/ ***noun*** [C] **1** a vehicle with no engine that is pulled by a car, truck, etc. **2** a large vehicle in which you can sleep, cook, etc. when traveling on vacation. It can be pulled by a car or small truck. ➲ picture at **truck**. ➲ Look at **camper** (2). **3** = MOBILE HOME

**ˈtrailer park** ***noun*** [C] an area of land where there are many houses that are built in factories (**mobile homes**)

★**train¹** /treɪn/ ***noun*** [C] **1** a number of wagons that are pulled by an engine along railroad tracks: *a commuter/passenger/freight train ◇ to catch/take a train ◇ to get on/off a train ◇ Hurry up or we'll miss the train. ◇ The train pulled into/out of the station.* ➲ Note that we travel **by** train. We can also say **on the** train. **2** [usually sing.] a series of thoughts or events that are connected: *A knock at the door interrupted my train of thought.*

★**train²** /treɪn/ ***verb*** **1** [T] **train sb/sth (as sth/to do sth)** to teach a person or an animal to do sth which is difficult or which needs practice: *The organization trains guide dogs for the blind. ◇ There is a shortage of trained teachers.* **2** [I] **train (as sth/to do sth)** to learn how to do a job: *She's training as a chef.* **3** [I,T] to prepare for a race or an event by exercising; to help a person or an animal to do this: *I'm training for the Boston Marathon. ◇ to train racehorses*

**train·ee** /treɪˈni/ ***noun*** [C] a person who is being TRAINED² (1,2): *management trainees*

**train·er** /ˈtreɪnər/ ***noun*** [C] a person who TRAINS² (1,3) animals or members of sports teams

★**train·ing** /ˈtreɪnɪŋ/ ***noun*** [U] preparation for a sport or job, or learning new skills: *computer training ◇ to be in training for the Olympics*

**trait** /treɪt/ ***noun*** [C] a quality; part of sb's character

**trai·tor** /ˈtreɪt̬ər/ ***noun*** [C] a person who is not loyal to his/her country, friends, etc. and harms them ➲ Look at **betray** and at **treason**.

**tramp** /træmp/ ***noun*** [C] (*old-fashioned*) a person who has no home or job and who moves from place to place

**tram·ple** /ˈtræmpl/ ***verb*** [I,T] **trample (on) sb/sth** to walk on sb/sth and damage or hurt him/her/it: *The cows trampled the corn. ◇ The child was trampled to death by the crowd.*

**tram·po·line** /ˌtræmpəˈlin/ ***noun*** [C] a piece of equipment that you can jump up and down on, made of a piece of strong material attached to a metal frame with springs

**trance** /træns/ ***noun*** [C] a condition of the mind in which you do not notice what is going on around you or in which you move and speak as if you were being controlled by another person or force: *to be in a trance*

**tran·quil** /ˈtræŋkwəl/ ***adj.*** (*formal*) calm and quiet

**tran·qui·li·zer** /ˈtræŋkwəlaɪzər/ ***noun*** [C] a drug that is used to make people sleepy or more calm

**trans·ac·tion** /trænˈzækʃn/ ***noun*** [C] a piece of business: *financial transactions*

**trans·at·lan·tic** /ˌtrænzətˈlæntɪk/ ***adj.*** to or from the other side of the Atlantic Ocean; across the Atlantic Ocean: *a transatlantic flight*

**tran·scend** /trænˈsɛnd/ ***verb*** [T] (*formal*) to be greater or more important than sb/sth; to go beyond the limits of sth: *Environmental issues transcend national boundaries.*

**trans·con·ti·nen·tal** /ˌtrænzkɑntnˈɛntl; ˌtræns-/ ***adj.*** going across a continent

**tran·script** /ˈtrænskrɪpt/ ***noun*** [C] **1** a written copy of what sb said **2** an official list of all the classes that sb took in high school or college and the grades that he/she received

★**trans·fer¹** /ˈtrænsfər; trænsˈfər/ ***verb*** (**trans·fer-ring; trans·ferred**) **1** [I,T] **transfer (sb/sth) (from...) (to...)** to move, or to make sb/sth move, from one place to another: *He has been transferred to our Tokyo branch. ◇ I want to transfer $1,000 from my savings to my checking account. ◇ Transfer the data onto a floppy disk. ◇ I transferred to this school after my freshman year.* **2** [T] (*formal*) to change the ownership of sth from one person to another ▸ **trans·fer·a·ble** /-fərəbl/ ***adj.***: *This ticket is not transferable.*

★**trans·fer²** /ˈtrænsfər/ ***noun*** **1** [C,U] moving or being moved from one place, job, school or condition to another: *Paul is not happy here and has asked for a transfer. ◇ the transfer of power from a military to a civilian government ◇ a transfer student* **2** [C] a ticket that allows you to travel on two or more buses, etc. during one trip

**trans·form** /trænsˈfɔrm/ ***verb*** [T] **transform sb/sth (from sth) (into sth)** to change sb/sth completely: *The arrival of electricity transformed people's lives.* ▸ **trans·for·ma·tion** /ˌtrænsfərˈmeɪʃn/ ***noun*** [C,U]

**trans·fu·sion** /trænsˈfyuʒn/ ***noun*** [C] the act of putting one person's blood into another person's body: *a blood transfusion*

**tran·sis·tor** /trænˈzɪstər/ ***noun*** [C] a small piece of electrical equipment that is used in radios and televisions

**tran·sit** /ˈtrænzət; -sət/ ***noun*** [U] the act of moving or being taken from one place to another: *The cartons had been damaged in transit.* ➲ Look also at **rapid transit**.

**tran·si·tion** /trænˈzɪʃn/ ***noun*** [C,U] **transition (from sth) (to sth)** a change from one condition or form to another: *the transition from childhood to*

T

adolescence ▸ **tran·si·tion·al** /-ʃn·l/ ***adj.***: *We're still in a transitional stage.*

**tran·si·tive** /'trænsət̬ɪv; -zə-/ ***adj.*** (*grammar*) (used about a verb) that has a direct object: *In this dictionary, transitive verbs are marked* "[T]." OPP **intransitive**

★**trans·late** /'trænsleɪt; 'trænz-; træns'leɪt; trænz-/ ***verb*** [I,T] **translate (sth) (from sth) (into sth)** to change sth from one language to another: *This book has been translated from Czech into English.* ➲ Look at **interpret**. ▸ **trans·la·tion** /-'leɪʃn/ ***noun*** [C,U]: *a word-for-word translation* ◇ *to read foreign literature in translation*

**trans·la·tor** /'trænsleɪt̬ər; 'trænz-/ ***noun*** [C] a person who translates sth that has been written ➲ Look at **interpreter**.

**trans·mis·sion** /træns'mɪʃn; trænz-/ ***noun*** **1** [U] sending sth out or passing sth on: *the transmission of television pictures by satellite* ◇ *the transmission of disease* **2** [C,U] the set of parts of a car, etc. that take power from the engine to the wheels: *automatic transmission* ◇ *5-speed manual transmission* **3** [C] (*formal*) a TV or radio program

**trans·mit** /træns'mɪt; trænz-/ ***verb*** [T] (**trans·mit·ting**; **trans·mit·ted**) **1** to send out television or radio programs, electronic signals, etc.: *The concert was transmitted live all over the world.* **2** to send or pass sth from one person or place to another: *a sexually transmitted disease*

**trans·mit·ter** /træns'mɪt̬ər; trænz-/ ***noun*** [C] a piece of equipment that sends out television or radio programs, electronic signals, etc.

**trans·par·en·cy** /træns'pærənsi/ ***noun*** [C] (*pl.* **trans·par·en·cies**) a type of photograph that is printed on transparent plastic, or a piece of plastic on which you can write or draw. You look at a transparency by putting it in a special machine (**projector**) and shining light through it: *a transparency for the overhead projector* ➲ Look at **slide**.

★**trans·par·ent** /træns'pærənt/ ***adj.*** that you can see through: *Glass is transparent.*

**trans·plant**[1] /træns'plænt; 'trænsplænt/ ***verb*** [T] **1** to take a plant out of the soil and plant it in another place **2** to take out an organ or other part of sb's body and put it into another person's body

**trans·plant**[2] /'trænsplænt/ ***noun*** [C] an operation in which an organ, etc. is transplanted: *a heart transplant*

★**trans·port** /træn'spɔrt; 'trænspɔrt/ ***verb*** [T] to move sb/sth from one place to another in a vehicle

★**trans·portation** /'trænspɔrt/ ***noun*** [U] **1** (*also* **transport**) moving sb/sth from one place to another by vehicle **2** vehicles that you travel in: *The city is providing free transportation to the stadium from downtown.* ➲ Look also at **public transportation**.

**trans·ves·tite** /træns'vɛstaɪt; trænz-/ ***noun*** [C] a person who likes to wear the clothes of sb of the opposite sex

★**trap**[1] /træp/ ***noun*** [C] **1** a piece of equipment that you use for catching animals: *a mousetrap* ◇ *The rabbit's leg was caught in the trap.* **2** [usually sing.] an unpleasant situation that is difficult to escape from: *the trap of credit card debt* **3** something that tricks or deceives you: *He thought he was going to meet a dealer, but it was a trap – the police were waiting for him.*

★**trap**[2] /træp/ ***verb*** [T] (**trap·ping**; **trapped**) **1** to catch an animal, etc. in a trap **2** to keep sb in a place from which he/she cannot move or escape: *They were trapped in the room by the flames in the hallway.* **3** to catch and keep or store sth: *Special glass panels trap heat from the sun.* **4** **trap sb (into sth/into doing sth)** to make sb do sth by tricking or deceiving him/her

IDM **be trapped (in sth)** to be unable to escape from an unpleasant situation: *Many people are trapped in low-paying jobs.*

**trap·door** /ˌtræp'dɔr/ (*also* ˌ**trap 'door**) ***noun*** [C] a door in a floor or ceiling

**tra·peze** /træ'piz/ ***noun*** [C] a bar hanging from two ropes high above the ground, used as a swing especially by people who perform in a circus

**trap·pings** /'træpɪŋz/ ***noun*** [pl.] **the trappings (of sth)** clothes, possessions, etc. which are signs of a particular rank or position: *a big car, expensive clothes and all the other trappings of success*

**trash**[1] /træʃ/ ***noun*** [U] **1** = GARBAGE (1,2,3) **2** (*slang*) people that you do not respect because they are poor, not well educated, and often do not behave morally ➲ Look also at **white trash**.

**trash**[2] /træʃ/ ***verb*** [T] (*informal*) **1** to damage or destroy sth, especially because you are angry: *Somebody broke into our house, stole our TV and trashed the living room.* **2** to criticize sb/sth very strongly: *My history professor trashed my paper and gave me a "D."*

**'trash can** ***noun*** [C] = GARBAGE CAN ➲ picture at **garbage can**.

**trash·y** /'træʃi/ ***adj.*** of poor quality, and often having low moral values: *trashy novels*

**trau·ma** /'trɔmə; 'traʊmə/ ***noun*** [C,U] (an event that causes) a state of great unhappiness or shock ➲ Look at **stress**[1](1). ▸ **trau·mat·ic** /trə'mæt̬ɪk; trɔ-/ ***adj.***: *Getting divorced can be a traumatic experience.*

★**trav·el**[1] /'trævl/ ***verb*** **1** [I] to make a trip: *John travels a lot on business.* ◇ *to travel by bus/air* ◇ *They traveled through New England last fall.* ◇ (*figurative*) *News travels fast in our office.* **2** [T] to make a trip of a particular distance or at a particular speed: *They traveled 200 miles to come and see us.* ◇ *Their car was traveling at 70 miles an hour when it hit a tree.*

★**trav·el**[2] /'trævl/ ***noun*** **1** [U] the act of traveling: *Air travel has made the world seem a lot smaller.* ◇ *a travel book*

NOTE This sense of **travel** is uncountable and you can only use it to talk about the general activity of moving from place to place: *Foreign travel is very popular these days.* When you talk about going from one particular place to another, you use **trip**. A **trip** may be short: *a day trip*, or longer: *a trip around the world*, and can be for business or pleasure: *He's on a trip to New York to meet a client.* ◇ *How about a trip to the lake this weekend?* A **tour** is a trip or walk during which you visit several places. You may go on a **tour** of a country, city, place of interest, etc.: *a guided tour of the campus.* A **journey** is a long, often difficult trip. **Journey** is often used in stories: *the pioneers' journey across America.*

**2 travels** [pl.] trips, especially to places that are far away: *You must have seen lots of interesting places on your travels.*

**'travel ˌagency** *noun* [C] (*pl.* **travel agencies**) a company that makes travel arrangements for people (reserving plane tickets and hotel rooms, etc.)

**'travel ˌagent** *noun* [C] a person who works in a travel agency

★**trav·el·er** (*especially Cdn* **trav·el·ler**) /'trævl·ər/ *noun* [C] a person who is traveling or who travels often

**'traveler's check** (*Cdn* **'traveller's cheque**) *noun* [C] a CHECK[2] (2) that you can change into foreign money when you are traveling in other countries, or that you can use instead of cash to pay for things in the U.S. or Canada: *to cash a traveler's check*

**tray** /treɪ/ *noun* [C] a flat piece of wood, plastic, metal, etc. with raised edges that you can carry food, drinks, etc. on: *When she was sick in bed, he took her meals to her on a tray.*

**treach·er·ous** /'trɛtʃərəs/ *adj.* **1** that you cannot trust **2** full of hidden danger: *The roads are treacherous after yesterday's blizzard.*

**treach·er·y** /'trɛtʃəri/ *noun* [U] the act of causing harm to sb/sth that trusts you

**tread[1]** /trɛd/ *verb* (*pt* **trod** /trɑd/; *pp* **trod·den** /'trɑdn/) [I] **tread (in/on sth)** (*old-fashioned, formal*) to step or put your foot down in or on sth

IDM **tread carefully/cautiously/lightly/softly** to act very carefully in a difficult situation: *Most of the candidates are treading very carefully on the issue of capital punishment.*

**tread[2]** /trɛd/ *noun* [C,U] the raised pattern on the outside surface of a tire

**tread·mill** /'trɛdæsstress:ævthinsp:mɪl/ *noun* [C] an exercise machine that has a moving surface that you can walk or run on while remaining in the same place ➲ picture on study page **A32**.

**trea·son** /'trizn/ *noun* [U] the act of causing harm to your country, e.g. by helping its enemies ➲ Look at **traitor**.

**treas·ure[1]** /'trɛʒər/ *noun* **1** [C,U] a collection of very valuable objects, e.g. made of gold, silver, etc.: *to find buried treasure* **2** [C] something that is very valuable: *the museum's art treasures*

**treas·ure[2]** /'trɛʒər/ *verb* [T] to consider sb/sth to be very special or valuable: *I will treasure those memories forever.*

**treas·ur·er** /'trɛʒərər/ *noun* [C] the person who is in charge of the money that belongs to a government, a club, an organization, etc.: *the church treasurer*

**treas·ur·y** /'trɛʒəri/ *noun* [C, usually sing.] **1** the money that belongs to a club, an organization, etc. **2** (often **Treasury**) the government department that controls public money

★**treat[1]** /trit/ *verb* [T]

➤BEHAVE TOWARD SB/STH **1** to act or behave toward sb/sth in a particular way: *Teenagers hate being treated like children.* ◇ *You should treat older people with respect.* ◇ *to treat sb badly/fairly*

➤CONSIDER **2 treat sth as sth** to consider sth in a particular way: *The bomb threat was not taken seriously. It was treated as a hoax.* **3** to deal with or discuss: *This book treats the subject in great detail.*

➤ILLNESS/INJURY **4** to use medicine or medical care to try to make a sick or injured person well again: *a new drug to treat cancer* ◇ *The boy was treated for burns at the hospital.*

➤USE CHEMICAL **5 treat sth (with sth)** to put a substance onto sth or to put sth throught a special process in order to protect it from damage, or to make it safe to use: *Most vegetables are treated with insecticide.* ◇ *to treat waste water*

➤PAY FOR STH ENJOYABLE **6 treat sb/yourself (to sth)** to give sb/yourself sth that is very special or enjoyable: *Claire treated the kids to ice cream cones* (= she paid for them).

**treat[2]** /trit/ *noun* [C] something that is very special or enjoyable: *I brought some donuts as a treat for dessert.* ◇ *It's a real treat for me to stay in bed late.*

IDM **trick or treat** → TRICK[1]

★**treat·ment** /'tritmənt/ *noun* **1** [U] the way that you behave toward sb or deal with sth: *I don't see why girls should get any special treatment.* **2** [C,U] the use of medicine or medical care to try to make a sick or injured person well again: *a new treatment for HIV infection* ◇ *emergency medical treatment* **3** [U] the use of special substances or processes in order to protect sth or make sth safe to use: *a sewage treatment plant* (= that takes sewage out of water)

**trea·ty** /'triṭi/ *noun* [C] (*pl.* **trea·ties**) **1** a written agreement between two or more countries: *to sign a peace treaty* **2** (*especially Cdn*) a formal agreement between a government and a group of Aboriginal people in Canada that determines the right to own or use a particular area of land

**'treaty band** *noun* [C] (*Cdn*) an officially-recognized Indian community (a **band**) that has signed an agreement with the federal government (a **treaty**)

**treb·le** /'trɛbl/ *noun* [C] (in music) the highest voice, instrument, or range

★**tree** /tri/ *noun* [C] a tall plant with a thick wooden stem from which branches grow: *an oak tree* ◇ *short/tall trees* ◇ *to climb a tree* ◇ *to plant/cut down a tree* ➲ picture on page *740*.

NOTE The stem of a tree is called a **trunk**. The outer surface of this is **bark**. The **branches** grow out from the trunk. A tree may have **leaves** or **needles**. ➲ Look at **Christmas tree** and **family tree**.

**trek** /trɛk/ *noun* [C] a long hard journey, often on foot ▶ **trek** *verb* [I] (**trek·king**; **trekked**)

**trem·ble** /'trɛmbl/ *verb* [I] to shake, e.g. because you are cold, frightened, weak, etc.: *She was pale and trembling with shock.* ◇ *His hand was trembling as he picked up his pen to sign.* ◇ *Sue's voice trembled with excitement.* ▶ **trem·ble** *noun* [C]: *There was a tremble in his voice as he told them the sad news.*

**tre·men·dous** /trɪ'mɛndəs/ *adj.* **1** very large or

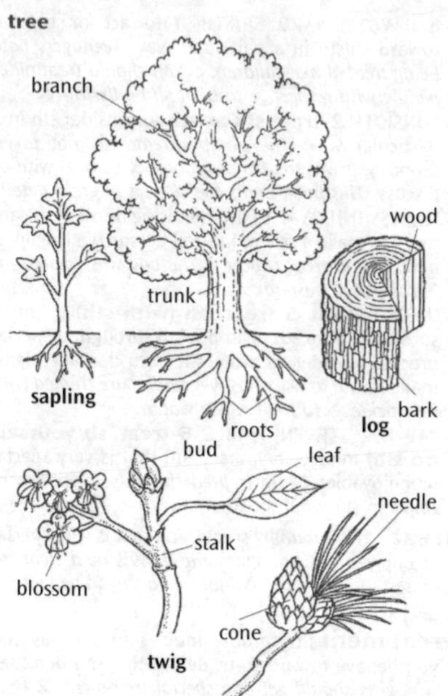


great: *a tremendous amount of work* ◇ *a tremendous difference* ◇ *a tremendous explosion* **2** (*informal*) very good: *You were tremendous!*

**tre·men·dous·ly** /trɪˈmɛndəsli/ ***adv.*** very; very much: *tremendously exciting* ◇ *Prices vary tremendously from one store to another.*

**trem·or** /ˈtrɛmər/ ***noun*** [C] a slight shaking or trembling: *a tremor in his voice* ◇ *Some residents felt a few tremors several hours before the earthquake struck.*

**trench** /trɛntʃ/ ***noun*** [C] a long narrow hole in the ground: *to dig a trench for a pipeline*

★**trend** /trɛnd/ ***noun*** [C] a general movement or change in society or in a situation: *The current trend is toward smaller families.* ◇ *a general trend for women to get married later* ◇ *to follow the latest fashion trends*

IDM **set a/the trend** to start a new style or fashion

**trend·y** /ˈtrɛndi/ ***adj.*** (**trend·i·er**; **trend·i·est**) (*informal*) fashionable

**tres·pass** /ˈtrɛspæs/ ***verb*** [I] to go onto sb's land without permission ▸ **tres·pass·er** ***noun*** [C]: *Trespassers will be prosecuted.*

★**tri·al** /ˈtraɪəl/ ***noun*** **1** [C,U] the process in a court of law where lawyers present evidence in order for the court to decide whether sb is guilty of a crime or not: *a fair trial* ◇ *He was on trial for murder.* ◇ *trial by jury* **2** [C,U] an act of testing sb/sth: *New drugs must go through extensive trials.* ◇ *a trial period of three months*

IDM **trial and error** trying different ways of doing sth until you find the best one

**ˌtrial ˈrun** (*also informal* **dry run**) ***noun*** [C] an occasion when you practice doing sth in order to make sure you can do it correctly later on

★**tri·an·gle** /ˈtraɪæŋgl/ ***noun*** [C] **1** a shape that has three straight sides and three angles: *a right triangle* (= with one angle of 90°) ➲ picture at **shape**. **2** a metal musical instrument in the shape of a TRIANGLE (1) that you play by hitting it with a metal stick

**tri·an·gu·lar** /traɪˈæŋgyələr/ ***adj.*** shaped like a TRIANGLE (1)

**tribe** /traɪb/ ***noun*** [C] a group of people that have the same language and customs and that are ruled by a chief or chiefs: *Native American tribes* ▸ **trib·al** /ˈtraɪbl/ ***adj.***: *tribal dances*

**tri·bu·nal** /traɪˈbyunl; trɪ-/ ***noun*** [C] a court or group of officials who have the authority to decide who is right in particular types of disagreements, especially in cases involving international law: *a military tribunal*

**trib·u·tar·y** /ˈtrɪbyəˌtɛri/ ***noun*** [C] (*pl.* **trib·u·tar·ies**) a river or stream that flows into a larger river

**trib·ute** /ˈtrɪbyut/ ***noun*** **1** [C,U] something that you say or do to show that you respect or admire sb/sth: *A special concert was held as a tribute to the composer on his 80th birthday.* **2** [sing.] **a tribute (to sth)** a sign of how good sb/sth is: *The success of the festival is a tribute to the organizers.*

IDM **pay tribute to sb/sth** → PAY[2]

★**trick**[1] /trɪk/ ***noun*** [C] **1** something that you do to deceive sb, in order to make him/her look stupid or to cheat him/her: *The children played a trick on the teacher.* **2** a clever or the best way of doing sth: *I can't get the top off this jar. Is there a trick to it?* **3** an act that uses special skills to make people believe sth which is not true: *The magician performed a trick in which he made a rabbit disappear.*

IDM **do the job/trick** → JOB

**trick or treat** (said by children on Halloween to ask people to give them candy. If sb does not give a child any candy, then the child might do sth bad to him/her.)

> NOTE We use the phrase **go trick-or-treating** to talk about what children do on Halloween. ➲ Look at the note at **Halloween**.

★**trick**[2] /trɪk/ ***verb*** [T] to deceive sb in order to make him/her do or believe sth: *He tricked me into lending him money.* ◇ *Stella was tricked out of her share of the money.*

**trick**[3] /trɪk/ ***adj.*** (only before a noun) intended to trick sb: *It was a* ***trick question*** (= one to which the answer seems easy but actually is not). ◇ *It's all done using* ***trick photography*** (= photography that uses clever techniques to show things that do not actually exist or are impossible).

**trick·er·y** /ˈtrɪkəri/ ***noun*** [U] the use of a TRICK[1] (1) in order to deceive sb

**trick·le** /ˈtrɪkl/ ***verb*** [I] (used about a liquid) to flow in a thin stream: *Tears trickled down his cheek.* ◇ (*figurative*) *At first no one came, but then people began to trickle in.* ▸ **trick·le** ***noun*** [C, usually sing.]: *The stream was only a trickle.* ◇ (*figurative*): *The flood of refugees had been reduced to a trickle.*

**trick·y** /ˈtrɪki/ ***adj.*** (**trick·i·er**; **trick·i·est**) difficult to do or deal with: *a tricky situation*

**tri·cy·cle** /ˈtraɪsɪkl/ (*also informal* **trike**) ***noun*** [C] a small vehicle, like a bicycle, that has one wheel at the front and two at the back

**tri·fle** /ˈtraɪfl/ ***noun*** (*formal*) [C] something that is of little value or importance

IDM **a trifle** a little: *It's a trifle odd that they didn't call.*

**trig·ger¹** /ˈtrɪgər/ ***noun*** [C] the piece of metal that you press to fire a gun: *to pull the trigger*

**trig·ger²** /ˈtrɪgər/ ***verb*** [T] to cause sth to start or happen: *The smoke from her cigarette triggered the fire alarm.*

**trike** /traɪk/ ***noun*** [C] (*informal*) = TRICYCLE

**tril·lion** /ˈtrɪlyən/ ***number*** the number 1,000,000,000,000

**tril·o·gy** /ˈtrɪlədʒi/ ***noun*** [C] (*pl.* **tril·o·gies**) a group of three books, plays, etc. that form one set

**trim¹** /trɪm/ ***verb*** [T] (**trim·ming**; **trimmed**) **1** to cut a little bit off sth so that it is neat and attractive: *to trim a beard* **2 trim sth (off sth/off)** to cut sth off because you do not need it: *Trim the fat off the meat.* **3 trim sth (with sth)** to decorate the edge of sth with sth: *a skirt trimmed with lace*

**trim²** /trɪm/ ***adj.*** not fat: *She still looks slim and trim.*

**trim³** /trɪm/ ***noun*** **1** [C, usually sing.] an act of cutting a little bit off sth in order to make it neat and attractive: *My hair needs a trim.* **2** [U] material that you use for decorating sth

**trim·mings** /ˈtrɪmɪŋz/ ***noun*** [pl.] extra things which you add to sth to improve its appearance, taste, etc.: *turkey with all the trimmings*

**trin·i·ty** /ˈtrɪnət̬i/ ***noun*** [sing.] **the Trinity** (in the Christian religion) the three forms of God: the Father, Jesus the Son and the Holy Spirit

**tri·o** /ˈtrioʊ/ ***noun*** (*pl.* **tri·os**) [C] **1** a group of three people who play music or sing together **2** a piece of music for three people to play or sing

★**trip¹** /trɪp/ ***verb*** (**trip·ping**; **tripped**) **1** [I] to knock your foot against sth when you are walking and fall or nearly fall down: *Don't leave your bag on the floor. Someone might trip over it.* ◇ *She caught her foot in the root of a tree and tripped.* **2** [T] to cause sb to fall or nearly fall down: *Lee stuck out his foot and tripped John.*

PHR V **trip (sb) up** to make a mistake; to make sb say sth that he/she did not want to say: *The journalist asked a difficult question to try to trip the candidate up.*

★**trip²** /trɪp/ ***noun*** [C] **1** an occasion during which you visit a place and return: *to take a trip to the mountains* ◇ *to go on a business trip to Europe* ◇ *We had to make three trips to the car to bring all the groceries in.* ➲ Look at the note at **travel**. **2** (*slang*) an experience that sb has after he/she takes a powerful drug that affects the mind and makes him/her imagine things

**tri·ple¹** /ˈtrɪpl/ ***adj.*** **1** made up of three parts: *the triple jump* **2** happening three times or containing three times as much as usual: *a triple world champion* (= one who has won three times) ◇ *a triple whiskey*

**tri·ple²** /ˈtrɪpl/ ***verb*** [I,T] to make sth, or to become, three times greater

**trip·let** /ˈtrɪplət/ ***noun*** [C] one of three children or animals that are born to one mother at the same time ➲ Look at **twin**.

**tri·pod** /ˈtraɪpɑd/ ***noun*** [C] a piece of equipment with three legs that you can put a camera, etc. on

**tri·umph¹** /ˈtraɪʌmf/ ***noun*** [C,U] success, especially in a competition or battle; the feeling of joy that you have because of this: *The soldiers returned home in triumph.* ◇ *The fans gave a shout of triumph.* ◇ *Putting people on the moon was one of the triumphs of the twentieth century.*

**tri·umph²** /ˈtraɪʌmf/ ***verb*** [I] **triumph (over sb/sth)** to achieve success; to defeat sb/sth: *Chicago triumphed over Utah in the championships.* ◇ *Although he was blind, he triumphed over his disability to become a college professor.*

**tri·um·phant** /traɪˈʌmfənt/ ***adj.*** feeling or showing great happiness because you have won or succeeded at sth: *a triumphant cheer* ▶ **tri·um·phant·ly** ***adv.***

**triv·i·a** /ˈtrɪviə/ ***noun*** [pl.] detailed pieces of information that are often considered unimportant: *a trivia quiz*

**triv·i·al** /ˈtrɪviəl/ ***adj.*** of little importance

**triv·i·al·ize** /ˈtrɪviəlaɪz/ ***verb*** [T] to make sth seem less important than it is

**trod** *past tense of* TREAD¹

**trod·den** *past participle of* TREAD¹

**trol·ley** /ˈtrɑli/ ***noun*** [C] (*pl.* **trol·leys**) = STREETCAR

**trom·bone** /trɑmˈboʊn/ ***noun*** [C] a large brass musical instrument that you play by blowing into it and moving a long tube backward and forward ➲ picture at **trumpet**.

**troop¹** /trup/ ***noun*** **1** [C] a large group of people or animals **2 troops** [pl.] soldiers

**troop²** /trup/ ***verb*** [I] **troop in, out, over, etc.** to move in a large group: *All the students trooped into the auditorium.*

**troop·er** /ˈtrupər/ ***noun*** [C] (in the U.S.) a member of a state police force, whose duties include making sure that people obey traffic laws

**tro·phy** /ˈtroʊfi/ ***noun*** [C] (*pl.* **tro·phies**) a silver cup, etc. that you get for winning a competition or race

**trop·ic** /ˈtrɑpɪk/ ***noun*** **1** [C, usually sing.] one of the two lines of latitude that are 23° 27´ north and south of the equator: *the tropic of Cancer* ◇ *the tropic of Capricorn* ➲ picture at **earth**. **2 the tropics** [pl.] the part of the world that is between these two lines, where the climate is hot

★**trop·i·cal** /ˈtrɑpɪkl/ ***adj.*** coming from or connected with the hottest, wettest parts of the world: *tropical fruit* ◇ *tropical rain forests*

**trot** /trɑt/ ***verb*** (**trot·ting**; **trot·ted**) [I] (used about a horse) to move fairly quickly, lifting the feet high off the ground: (*figurative*) *The boy trotted along behind his father.*

PHR V **trot sb/sth out** (*informal*) to show sb/sth to other people, even though they find him/her/it boring: *Phil always trots out his high school yearbooks when he has dinner guests.*

▶ **trot** ***noun*** [sing.]

★**trou·ble¹** /ˈtrʌbl/ ***noun*** **1** [C,U] (a situation that causes) problems, difficulty, worry, etc.: *If I don't*



T

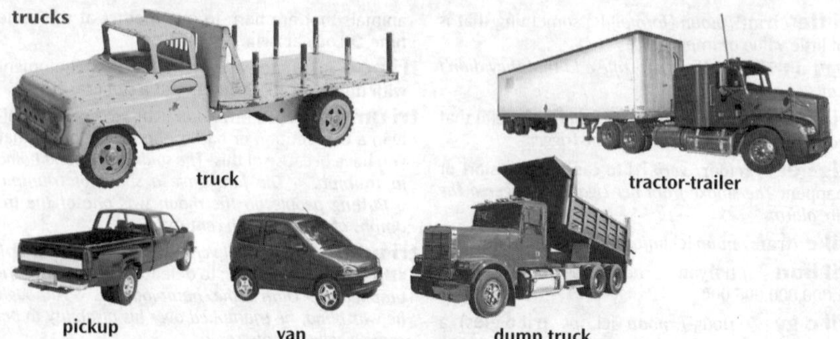


*get home by 11 o'clock, I'll be in trouble.* ◇ *I'm having trouble getting the car started.* ◇ *financial troubles* ◇ *It's a very good school. The only trouble is, it's a little too far away.* **2** [sing., U] extra work or effort: *Let's eat out tonight. It will save you the trouble of cooking.* ◇ *Why don't you stay overnight with us? It's no trouble.* ◇ *I'm sorry to cause you so much trouble.* **3** [C,U] a situation where people are fighting or arguing with each other: *There's usually trouble in town on Saturday night after the bars close.* **4** [U] illness or pain: *I have back trouble again.*

IDM **ask for trouble** → ASK

**get into trouble** to get into a situation which is dangerous or in which you may be punished

**go to a lot of trouble (to do sth)** to put a lot of work or effort into sth: *They went to a lot of trouble to make us feel welcome.*

**take the trouble to do sth** to do sth even though it means extra work or effort: *He took the trouble to write and thank everyone for his presents.*

**trou·ble²** /ˈtrʌbl/ ***verb*** [T] **1** to cause sb worry, problems, etc. **2 trouble sb (for sth)** (*formal*) (used when you are asking sb extremely politely for sth or to do sth): *I hate to trouble you, but could I use your phone?* ◇ *Could I trouble you for some change?*

**trou·ble·mak·er** /ˈtrʌblmeɪkər/ ***noun*** [C] a person who often causes TROUBLE¹ (1,3)

**trou·ble·shoot·er** /ˈtrʌblʃuṭər/ ***noun*** [C] a person whose job is to find and fix problems in machines, etc. ▸ **trou·ble·shoot·ing** ***noun*** [U]

**trou·ble·some** /ˈtrʌblsəm/ ***adj.*** that causes TROUBLE¹ (1)

**trough** /trɔf/ ***noun*** [C] a long narrow container from which farm animals eat or drink

**trou·sers** /ˈtraʊzərz/ ***noun*** (*formal*) = PANTS

**trout** /traʊt/ ***noun*** [C,U] (*pl.* **trout**) a type of fish that lives in rivers and that is eaten as food

**trow·el** /ˈtraʊəl/ ***noun*** [C] **1** a small garden tool with a curved blade for lifting plants and digging holes **2** a small tool with a flat blade, used in building for spreading cement or plaster ➲ picture at **garden**.

**tru·ant** /ˈtruənt/ ***noun*** [C] a student who stays away from school without permission ▸ **tru·ant** ***adj.*** ▸ **tru·an·cy** /-ənsi/ ***noun*** [U]

**truce** /trus/ ***noun*** [C] an agreement to stop fighting for a period of time SYN **ceasefire**

★**truck¹** /trʌk/ ***noun*** [C] a large strong motor vehicle that is used for carrying things by road ➲ Look also at **pickup** (1).

**truck²** /trʌk/ ***verb*** [T] to transport sth by TRUCK¹: *The city's garbage is trucked to a landfill west of town.*

**truck·er** /ˈtrʌkər/ ***noun*** [C] a person whose job is driving a truck, especially over long distances

**truck·ing** /ˈtrʌkɪŋ/ ***noun*** [U] the business of transporting things by truck

**truck·load** /ˈtrʌkloʊd/ ***noun*** [C] an amount of sth that a truck can carry at one time: *a truckload of fruit* ◇ *They were selling furniture by the truckload.*

ˈ**truck stop** ***noun*** [C] a place near a main road where you can buy gasoline, and with a cheap restaurant especially for truckers

**trudge** /trʌdʒ/ ***verb*** [I] to walk with slow, heavy steps, e.g. because you are very tired

★**true** /tru/ ***adj.*** **1** that really happened: *The novel was based on a true story.* **2** right or correct; agreeing with fact: *Is it true that Adam is leaving?* ◇ *Read the statements and decide if they are true or false.* ◇ *I didn't think the movie was very true to life* (= it didn't show life as it really is). **3** real or genuine: *How do you know when you have found true love?* ◇ *the true value of the house* **4 true (to sth)** behaving as expected or as promised: *to be true to your word* (= to do what you promised) ➲ noun truth

IDM **come true** to happen in the way you hoped or dreamed: *My dream finally came true!*

**ring true** → RING²

**tru·ly** /ˈtruli/ ***adv.*** **1** really: *We are truly grateful to you for your help.* **2** completely: *Now that she was a U.S. citizen, she felt truly American.* **3** expressing the truth: *I cannot truly say that I was surprised at the news.* ➲ **Yours truly** is often used at the end of a letter.

**trump** /trʌmp/ ***noun*** [C] (in some card games) a card of the suit that has a higher value than the other three suits during a particular game: *Spades are trumps.*

**trum·pet** /ˈtrʌmpət/ ***noun*** [C] a brass musical instrument that you play by blowing into it. There are three buttons on it which you can press to make different notes. ➲ picture on page **743**.

**trun·dle** /ˈtrʌndl/ ***verb*** **1** [I] to move slowly: *The army trundled down the hill.* **2** [T] to push or pull sth along slowly on wheels

**trunk** /trʌŋk/ ***noun*** **1** [C] the thick main stem of a tree ➲ picture at **tree**. **2** [C] the main part of your

trumpet

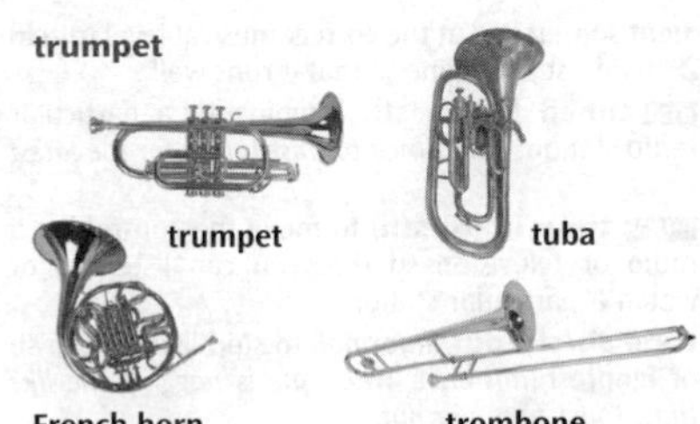


body (not including your head, arms and legs) **3** [C] the part at the back of a car where you put luggage, etc. **4** [C] a large box, like a large suitcase, that you use for storing or transporting things ➲ picture at **luggage**. **5** [C] an elephant's long nose ➲ picture at **elephant**. **6** **trunks** [pl.] = SWIMMING TRUNKS

★**trust¹** /trʌst/ ***noun*** **1** [U] **trust (in sb/sth)** the feeling that you have when you know that you can rely on sb/sth to do what he/she/it is supposed to do: *Our marriage is based on love and trust.* ◇ *I put my trust in him, but he failed me.* **2** [U] responsibility: *As a teacher, you are in a position of trust.* **3** [C,U] an arrangement by which a person or an organization manages money and property for sb else: *The money was put into a trust fund for the children.*

IDM **on trust** without having proof; without checking: *I can't prove it. You must take it on trust.*

★**trust²** /trʌst/ ***verb*** **1** [T] to believe that you can rely on sb/sth to do what he/she/it is supposed to do; to believe that sb/sth will not harm you: *He said the car was safe, but I just don't trust him.* ◇ *Can I trust you to behave while I am out?* ◇ *You can't trust her with money.* ◇ *She is not to be trusted with money.* ◇ *I don't trust that dog. It looks dangerous.* **2** [I,T] **trust (in) sb/sth** to depend on sb/sth or have faith in sb/sth: *to trust in God* ◇ *I'll trust your judgment.*

**trus·tee** /trʌˈsti/ ***noun*** [C] a person who manages money or property for sb else

**trust·ing** /ˈtrʌstɪŋ/ ***adj.*** having or showing trust, often in situations where it is not wise to do this

**trust·wor·thy** /ˈtrʌstwərði/ ***adj.*** that you can trust

★**truth** /truθ/ ***noun*** (*pl.* **truths** /truðz/) **1** [U] the state or quality of being true: *There's a lot of truth in what she says.* **2** [sing.] what is true: *Please tell me the truth.* ◇ *the whole truth* **3** [C] a fact or idea that is true: *scientific truths*

**truth·ful** /ˈtruθfl/ ***adj.*** **1** true or correct: *a truthful account* **2** (used about a person) who tells the truth; honest ▸ **truth·ful·ly** ***adv.***

★**try¹** /traɪ/ ***verb*** (*pres. part.* **try·ing**; *3rd person sing. pres.* **tries**; *pt, pp* **tried**) **1** [I] to make an effort to do sth: *I tried to call you, but I couldn't get through.* ◇ *She was trying hard not to laugh.* ◇ *to try your best/hardest* ◇ *I'm sure you can do it if you try.*

> NOTE **Try and** is more informal than **try to**. **Try and** cannot be used in the past tense: *I'll try to get there on time.* ◇ (*informal*) *I'll try and get there on time.* ◇ *I tried to get there on time, but I was too late.*

**2** [T] to do, use or test sth in order to see how good or successful it is: *"I've tried everything but I can't get the baby to sleep." "Did you try taking her out in the stroller?"* ◇ *Have you ever tried raw fish?* ◇ *We tried the door, but it was locked.* ◇ *He tried several bookstores, but none of them had the books he wanted.* **3** [T] to examine sb in a court of law in order to decide if he/she is guilty of a crime or not: *He was tried for murder.*

PHR V **try sth on** to put on a piece of clothing to see if it fits you properly: *Can I try these jeans on?*

**try sb/sth out** to test sb/sth by using him/her/it

**try out for sth** to try to become a member of a sports team or an actor in a play by having your skills tested: *Dave tried out for the wrestling team.*

**try²** /traɪ/ ***noun*** [C] (*pl.* **tries**) an occasion when you make an effort to do sth; an attempt: *I don't know if I can move it by myself, but I'll give it a try.*

**try·ing** /ˈtraɪɪŋ/ ***adj.*** that makes you tired or angry: *a trying day at work*

**try·out** /ˈtraɪaʊt/ ***noun*** [C] a competition in which people's skills are tested in order to see whether they are suitable to be members of a team, actors in a play, etc.: *Tryouts for the cheerleading squad will be held next week.*

**tset·se fly** /ˈtsɛtsi ˌflaɪ; ˈtɛtsi-/ ***noun*** [C,U] an African fly that bites humans and animals and sucks their blood and can spread a disease called sleeping sickness

**T-shirt** /ˈtiʃərt/ ***noun*** [C] a shirt with short sleeves, a round opening for your head to go through and no buttons

**tsp.** ***abbr.*** = TEASPOON

**tub** /tʌb/ ***noun*** [C] **1** = BATHTUB: *Julie can't come to the phone – she's in the tub.* **2** a large round container with a flat bottom and no lid **3** a small plastic container with a lid, that is used for holding food: *a tub of margarine*

**tu·ba** /ˈtubə/ ***noun*** [C] a large brass musical instrument that makes a low sound ➲ picture at **trumpet**.

★**tube** /tub/ ***noun*** **1** [C] a long hollow pipe made of glass, metal, rubber, etc.: *Blood flowed along the tube into the bottle.* ◇ *the inner tube of a bicycle tire* ◇ *a laboratory test tube* **2** [C] a long thin soft container with a cap at one end made of plastic or metal. Tubes are used for holding soft substances, and you squeeze them to get the substance out: *a tube of toothpaste* ➲ picture at **container**. **3** **the tube** [sing.] (*informal*) television: *What's on the tube tonight?*

**tu·ber·cu·lo·sis** /tʊˌbərkyəˈloʊsəs/ ***noun*** [U] (*abbr.* **TB**) a serious disease that especially affects the lungs

**tub·ing** /ˈtubɪŋ/ ***noun*** [U] a long piece of metal, rubber, etc. in the shape of a TUBE (1), or a system of tubes

**tuck** /tʌk/ ***verb*** [T] **1** to put or fold the ends or edges of sth into or around sth else so that it looks neat: *Tuck your shirt in – it looks messy like that.* ◇ *He tucked the blanket around the old man's knees.* **2** to put sth away neatly or in a safe or hidden place: *He tucked his wallet away in his inside pocket.* ◇ *The letter was tucked behind a pile of books.*

PHR V **tuck sth away** (*informal*) **1** to store sth:



T

*They have a lot of money tucked away.* **2** to hide sth: *Their house is tucked away behind those trees.*
**tuck sb in** to put blankets, sheets, etc. tightly around sb, especially a child, in bed to make him/her feel comfortable and safe

**Tues·day** /ˈtuzdeɪ; -di/ ***noun*** [C,U] (*abbr.* **Tue.**; **Tues.**) the day of the week after Monday and before Wednesday ➲ For examples of the use of the days of the week in sentences, look at **Monday**.

**tuft** /tʌft/ ***noun*** [C] a small bunch of hair, grass, etc.

**tug¹** /tʌg/ ***verb*** [I,T] (**tug·ging; tugged**) to pull sth hard and quickly

**tug²** /tʌg/ ***noun*** [C] **1** a sudden hard pull: *She gave the rope a tug.* **2** (*also* **tug·boat** /ˈtʌgboʊt/) a small, strong boat that is used for pulling larger ships into a harbor

**ˌtug of ˈwar** (*also* **ˌtug-of-ˈwar**) ***noun*** [C] (*pl.* **tugs of war**) a game in which two people or teams pull on the ends of a rope in opposite directions. The winner is the person or team who pulls the other one over a line in the middle: (*figurative*) *Kara was caught in an emotional tug of war between her parents when they got divorced.*

**tu·i·tion** /tuˈɪʃn/ ***noun*** [U] the money that a student must pay in order to take classes at a college, university, or private school

**tu·lip** /ˈtuləp/ ***noun*** [C] a brightly-colored flower, shaped like a small cup, that grows from a large round root (**bulb**) in the spring

**tum·ble** /ˈtʌmbl/ ***verb*** [I] **1** to fall suddenly in a heavy way, without control: *He tripped, and tumbled all the way down the steps.* **2** (used about prices, etc.) to become lower: *The price of gas has tumbled.* **3** to move in a particular direction in a clumsy way: *I got undressed and tumbled into bed.* ◇ *She opened her suitcase and all her things tumbled out of it.*
PHR V **tumble down** to fall down; to collapse: *The walls of the old house were tumbling down.*
▸ **tum·ble** ***noun*** [C]

**tum·bler** /ˈtʌmblər/ ***noun*** [C] a drinking glass with straight sides that has no handle or stem

**tum·my** /ˈtʌmi/ ***noun*** [C] (*pl.* **tum·mies**) (*informal*) (used by and to small children) stomach

**tu·mor** /ˈtumər/ ***noun*** [C] a group of diseased cells that are growing abnormally in the body: *a brain tumor*

**tu·mul·tu·ous** /tʊˈmʌltʃuəs/ ***adj.*** very noisy or confused, because people are excited: *a tumultuous welcome*

**tu·na** /ˈtunə/ ***noun*** (*pl.* **tu·na**) **1** [C] a large fish that lives in the ocean **2** [U] (*also* **ˈtuna fish**) the flesh of the fish, which is often sold in cans

★**tune¹** /tun/ ***noun*** [C,U] a series of musical notes that are arranged in a pleasant pattern: *Tina played a tune on the piano.* ◇ *I can't remember the tune to that song.*
IDM **change your tune** → CHANGE¹
**in tune/out of tune 1** at/not at the correct musical level (**pitch**): *You're singing out of tune.* **2** in/not in agreement with sb/sth: *The legislation doesn't seem to be in tune with what ordinary people are thinking.*

**tune²** /tun/ ***verb*** [T] **1** to adjust a musical instrument so that it is at the correct musical level (**pitch**) **2** to adjust an engine so that it runs well
IDM **tuned (in) to sth** listening to a particular radio station: *Stay tuned to this station for the latest news.*
PHR V **tune in (to sth)** to move the controls of a radio or television so that you can listen to or watch a particular station
**tune sb/sth out** (*informal*) to stop listening to sb or ignore him/her/it: *When she is nagging me like that, I just tune her out.*

**tu·nic** /ˈtunɪk/ ***noun*** [C] a piece of loose clothing that is like a long shirt

★**tun·nel¹** /ˈtʌnl/ ***noun*** [C] a passage under the ground or a river, etc. for cars, trucks and/or trains to drive through: *The train disappeared into a tunnel.* ◇ *the Lincoln Tunnel*

**tun·nel²** /ˈtʌnl/ ***verb*** [I,T] to dig a TUNNEL¹

**tur·ban** /ˈtərbən/ ***noun*** [C] a covering for the head that is made by wrapping a long piece of cloth around the head

**tur·bu·lent** /ˈtərbyələnt/ ***adj.*** **1** in a state of disorder and confusion when things are changing fast **2** (used about water or air) moving in a violent way
▸ **tur·bu·lence** /-ləns/ ***noun*** [U]

**turf** /tərf/ ***noun*** [U] **1** short thick grass and the layer of soil underneath it: *a stadium with artificial turf* **2** (*informal*) (an area that sb considers as his/her own and does not want to share with other people): *Two people were shot when they entered a rival gang's turf.*

**tur·key** /ˈtərki/ ***noun*** (*pl.* **tur·keys**) **1** [C,U] a large bird, somewhat like a very large chicken, or its meat. Turkey is a traditional part of Thanksgiving dinner. **2** [C] (*informal*) something, especially a movie, that is unsuccessful and of very bad quality
IDM **cold turkey** → COLD¹

**tur·moil** /ˈtərmɔɪl/ ***noun*** [U, sing.] a state of great excitement, noise or confusion: *to be in emotional/mental/political turmoil*

★**turn¹** /tərn/ ***verb***
▸MOVE ROUND **1** [I] to move or go around a fixed point: *The wheels turned faster and faster.* **2** [T] to hold and move sth around a central point; to make sth go around: *She turned the doorknob.* ◇ *Turn the steering wheel to the right.*
▸CHANGE POSITION/DIRECTION **3** [I] to change your position so that you are facing in a different direction: *He turned around when he heard my voice.* **4** [T] to change the position of sth: *I turned the box upside down.* ◇ *She turned the page and started the next chapter.* **5** [I,T] to change direction when you are moving: *Go straight ahead and turn left by the church.* ◇ *The car turned the corner.* ◇ *He turned the van into the driveway.*
▸BECOME **6** [I,T] **turn (sb/sth) (into/to sth)** (to cause) to become: *He turned very red when I asked him about the money.* ◇ *How did you feel when you turned 30?* ◇ *Everything the king touched turned into gold.*

NOTE For expressions with **turn**, look at the noun and adjective entries, e.g. for **turn a blind eye**, look at **blind**.



T

PHR V **turn away** to stop looking at sb/sth: *She turned away in horror at the sight of the blood.*
**turn sb away** to refuse to allow a person to go into a place
**turn back** to go back in the same direction as you came
**turn sb/sth down** to refuse an offer, etc. or the person who makes it: *Why did you turn that job down?* ◇ *He asked her to marry him, but she turned him down.*
**turn sth down** to reduce the sound or heat that sth produces: *Turn the TV down!*
**turn sb in** to inform the police where a criminal is
**turn sth in** to give sth to a person in authority: *All essays must be turned in by Friday at 5:00.* ◇ *I was relieved to hear that somebody had turned my keys in to the security guard.*
**turn off (sth)** to leave one road and go on another: *We turn off the highway at exit 10.*
**turn sth off** to move the switch, etc. on a machine, etc. to stop it from working: *He turned the TV off.*
**turn sth on** to move the switch, etc. on of machine, etc. to start it working: *Turn the lights on!*
**turn out (for sth)** to be present or appear for sth: *Thousands of people turned out to welcome the team home.*
**turn out (to be sth)** to be sth in the end: *The weather turned out fine.* ◇ *The house that they had promised us turned out to be a tiny apartment.*
**turn sth out** to move the switch, etc. on a light so that it is no longer shining: *Turn the lights out before you go to bed.*
**turn to sb** to go to sb to get help
**turn to sth** to find a page in a book: *Turn to page 45.*
**turn up 1** to arrive: *What time did they finally turn up?* **2** to be found: *I lost my glasses a week ago and they still haven't turned up.*
**turn sth up** to increase the sound or heat that sth produces: *Turn the heat up – it's freezing!*

★**turn²** /tərn/ *noun* [C]
➤MOVEMENT **1** an act of turning sb/sth around: *Give the screw another couple of turns to make sure it is really tight.*
➤CHANGE OF DIRECTION **2** a change of direction: *to make a left/right turn* ◇ *a U-turn* (= when you turn around and go back in the opposite direction)
➤OF ROAD **3** a bend or corner in a road, river, etc.: *Take the next turn on the left.*
➤TIME **4** [usually sing.] the time when you must or may do sth: *Please wait in line until it is your turn.*
➤ILLNESS **5** a change: *The patient's condition has taken a turn for the worse.*
IDM **in turn** one after the other: *I spoke to each of the children in turn.*
**take turns (doing sth)** to do sth one after the other: *You can't both play on the computer at the same time. You'll have to take turns.*
**wait your turn** → WAIT¹

ˈ**turning point** *noun* [C] a time when an important change happens

**tur·nip** /ˈtərnəp/ *noun* [C,U] a round white vegetable that grows under the ground ➲ picture on study page **A28-29**.

**turn·out** /ˈtərnaʊt/ *noun* [C, usually sing.] the number of people who attend a sports or entertainment event, vote in an election, etc.

**turn·o·ver** /ˈtərnoʊvər/ *noun* **1** [sing.] the rate at which workers leave a company and are replaced by new ones: *a high turnover of personnel* **2** a small pie made of pastry that is folded over and filled with fruit

**turn·pike** /ˈtərnpaɪk/ *noun* [C] (in the U.S.) a type of road that you have to pay money (a **toll**) to drive on

ˈ**turn** ˌ**signal** *noun* [C] the flashing light on a car, etc. that shows that it is going to turn right or left

**turn·stile** /ˈtərnstaɪl/ *noun* [C] a gate that goes around and allows one person at a time to enter a place

**tur·pen·tine** /ˈtərpəntaɪn/ *noun* [U] a clear liquid with a strong smell that you use for removing paint or for making paint thinner

**tur·quoise** /ˈtərkwɔɪz/ *adj., noun* [U] (of) a greenish-blue color

**turtles**

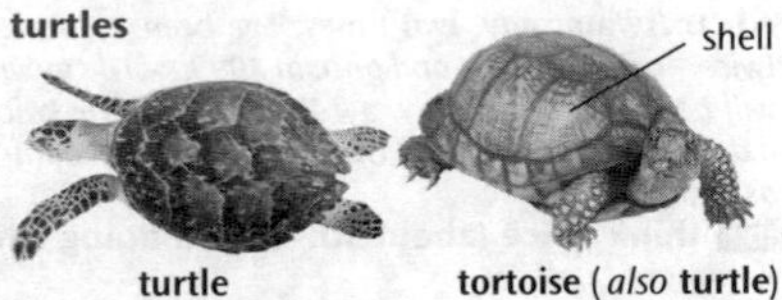


**tur·tle** /ˈtərṭl/ (*also* **tortoise**) *noun* [C] an animal that has a hard shell and moves very slowly. A turtle can pull its head and legs into its shell to protect them

> NOTE In scientific language, **tortoise** is used for the animals that live on land, and **turtle** is used only for the animals that live mainly in water. However, most people usually use **turtle** for both types of animals.

**tur·tle·neck** /ˈtərṭlnɛk/ *noun* [C] a sweater or shirt with a high collar that covers most of your neck

**tusk** /tʌsk/ *noun* [C] one of the two very long pointed teeth of an elephant, etc. ➲ Elephants' tusks are made of **ivory**. ➲ picture at **elephant**.

**tus·sle** /ˈtʌsl/ *noun* [C] (*informal*) a rough fight, e.g. between two or more people who want to have the same thing

**tu·tor¹** /ˈtuṭər/ *noun* [C] a private teacher who teaches one person or a very small group, especially to give extra help in a particular subject

**tu·tor²** /ˈtuṭər/ *verb* [T] to give one person or a group extra help in a particular subject ▶ **tu·tor·ing** *noun* [U]

**tux·e·do** /tʌkˈsidoʊ/ *noun* [C] (*pl.* **tux·e·dos** /-doʊz/) (*also informal* **tux** /tʌks/) a black or white jacket and pants that a man wears on formal occasions. A tuxedo is normally worn with a bow tie.

★**TV** /ˌtiˈvi/ *noun* [C,U] (*pl.* **TVs** or **TV's**) television: *Turn the TV on.* ◇ *What's* **on TV** *tonight?*

ˌ**TV** ˈ**dinner** *noun* [C] a meal that has been prepared and frozen in a factory, and that you can buy in a store and heat up in the oven at home

**twang** /twæŋ/ *noun* [C] a tone that sb's voice

makes when the sound comes from his/her nose and mouth together, especially if he/she speaks with a southern U.S. accent

**tweed** /twid/ ***noun*** [U] thick wool cloth with a rough surface

**tweez·ers** /ˈtwizərz/ ***noun*** [pl.] a small tool consisting of two pieces of metal that are joined at one end. You use tweezers for picking up or pulling out very small things: *a pair of tweezers*

**twelve** /twɛlv/ ***number*** 12; one more than eleven ➲ Look at **dozen**. For examples of how to use numbers in sentences, look at **six**. ▸ **twelfth** /twɛlfθ/ ***pronoun, det., adv.*** ➲ Look at the examples at **sixth**.

**twen·ty** /ˈtwɛnti/ ***number*** 20; one more than nineteen ➲ For examples of how to use numbers in sentences, look at **sixty**. ▸ **twen·ti·eth** /ˈtwɛntiəθ/ ***pronoun, det., adv.*** ➲ Look at the examples at **sixth**.

**24 Sussex Drive** /ˌtwɛnti ˌfɔr ˌsʌsɪks ˈdraɪv/ ***noun*** [sing.] (*Cdn*) the official home of the Canadian prime minister in Ottawa ➲ For more information about the Canadian political system, look at study page **A11**.

★**twice** /twaɪs/ ***adv.*** two times: *I've been to Mexico twice – once last year and once in 1999.* ◇ *The movie will be shown twice daily.* ◇ *Take the medicine twice a day.* ◇ *Prices have risen twice as fast in this country as in Japan.*

IDM **think twice (about sth/before doing sth)** → THINK

**twig** /twɪg/ ***noun*** [C] a small thin branch on a tree or bush ➲ picture at **tree**.

**twi·light** /ˈtwaɪlaɪt/ ***noun*** [U] the time after the sun has set and before it gets completely dark

★**twin**[1] /twɪn/ ***noun*** [C] one of two children or animals that are born to the same mother at the same time: *They look very much alike. Are they twins?* ◇ *a twin brother/sister* ◇ *identical twins*

**twin**[2] /twɪn/ ***adj.*** (only *before* a noun) **1** that is the same as, or very similar to, another thing: *a ship with twin propellers* **2** (*also* ˈ**twin-size**) (used about a bed or a blanket, etc. for a bed) big enough for one person ➲ Look at the note and the picture at **bed**[1].

**twinge** /twɪndʒ/ ***noun*** [C] **a twinge (of sth) 1** a sudden thought or feeling: *a twinge of fear* **2** a sudden short pain

**twin·kle** /ˈtwɪŋkl/ ***verb*** [I] **1** to shine with a light that seems to be moving: *Stars twinkled in the night sky.* **2** (used about your eyes) to look bright because you are happy ▸ **twin·kle** ***noun*** [sing.]: *From the twinkle in her eyes, we knew she was joking.*

**twirl** /twərl/ ***verb*** **1** [I] to spin or turn around, e.g. when you are dancing **2** [T] to twist or turn sth

★**twist**[1] /twɪst/ ***verb***

▸TURN BODY **1** [I,T] to turn yourself or a part of your body: *She twisted around to reach the switch behind her.* ◇ *He kept twisting his head from side to side.*

▸BEND INTO SHAPE **2** [I,T] to turn or make sth turn into a shape or position that is not normal: *The metal twisted into strange shapes.* ◇ *He twisted his knee while he was playing basketball.*

▸TURN WITH HAND **3** [T] to turn sth in a particular direction: *Twist the knob as far as it will go.*

▸OF ROADS/RIVERS **4** [I] (used about a road, etc.) to change direction often: *a narrow, twisting driveway*

▸WIND AROUND **5** [T] to wind sth around and around an object: *I twisted the bandage around her knee.*

▸FACTS **6** [T] to change the meaning of what sb said: *She claimed that the reporter had twisted her words.*

IDM **twist sb's arm** (*informal*) to force or persuade sb to do sth

★**twist**[2] /twɪst/ ***noun*** [C] **1** an act of twisting sth: *She killed the chicken with one twist of its neck.* **2** a place where sth has become twisted: *Straighten out the cord so that there are no twists in it.* **3** a place where a road, river, etc. bends or changes direction: *the twists and turns of the river* **4** a change or development (especially one that you do not expect): *an unexpected twist at the end of the book*

**twist·er** /ˈtwɪstər/ ***noun*** [C] (*informal*) = TORNADO

**twitch** /twɪtʃ/ ***verb*** [I,T] to make a sudden movement; to cause sth to make a sudden movement: *The rabbit twitched and then lay still.* ▸ **twitch** ***noun*** [C]

**two** /tu/ ***number*** 2; one more than one ➲ Look at **second**[1]. For examples of how to use numbers in sentences, look at **six**.

IDM **in two** in or into two pieces: *The plate fell on the floor and broke in two.*

**two-** /tu/ ***combining form*** having two of the thing mentioned: *a two-week vacation*

**ty·coon** /taɪˈkun/ ***noun*** [C] a person who is very successful in business and who is rich and powerful

**Ty·le·nol**™ /ˈtaɪlənɑl/ ***noun*** [U] a common type of medicine, similar to aspirin, that reduces pain and fever

★**type**[1] /taɪp/ ***noun*** **1** [C] **a type (of sth)** a group of people or things that share certain qualities and that are part of a larger group; a kind or sort: *Which type of paint should you use on metal?* ◇ *There are several different types of apartments to choose from.* ◇ *That's just the type of situation that you should avoid.* ◇ *You meet all types of people in this job.* ◇ *the first building of its type in the world* **2** [C] a person of a particular kind: *He's the careful type.*

> NOTE If you say somebody is not **your type**, you mean that they are not the sort of person that you would be friendly with. ➲ Look at **typical**.

**3** [U] the letters that you use when you are typing or printing: *The type is too small to read.*

★**type**[2] /taɪp/ ***verb*** [I,T] to write sth using a computer, typewriter, etc.: *Can you type?* ◇ *to type a letter* ▸ **typ·ing** ***noun*** [U]

**type·writ·er** /ˈtaɪpraɪt̬ər/ ***noun*** [C] a machine that you use for writing in print

**type·writ·ten** /ˈtaɪprɪtn/ ***adj.*** written using a typewriter

**ty·phoid** /ˈtaɪfɔɪd/ ***noun*** [U] a serious disease that can cause death. People get typhoid from bad food or water.

**ty·phoon** /taɪˈfun/ ***noun*** [C] a violent tropical storm in the Pacific or Indian Ocean with very strong winds ➲ Look at the note at **storm**.

★**typ·i·cal** /ˈtɪpɪkl/ ***adj.*** **typical (of sb/sth)** having or showing the usual qualities of a particular person, thing or type: *a typical small town* ◇ *There's no such thing as a typical North American* (= they are all different). ◇ *Such detailed descriptions are typical of her writing.*

**NOTE** Compare **common**, **traditional** and **typical**. Something that is **common** is found often or in many places: *The robin is a common bird in America.* Something that is **traditional** has strong links with the past: *At the festival, we saw some Native Americans dressed in traditional* (NOT "typical") *costumes.* Something or someone that is **typical** is a good example of a category of people or things: *How much would a typical house cost in this neighborhood?*

**typ·i·cal·ly** /ˈtɪpɪkli/ ***adv.*** **1** in a usual or normal case: *New employees typically earn around $6 an hour.* **2** in the normal or usual way: *Her comments were typically direct.*

**typ·i·fy** /ˈtɪpəfaɪ/ ***verb*** [T] (*pres. part.* **typ·i·fy·ing**; *3rd person sing. pres.* **typ·i·fies**; *pt, pp* **typ·i·fied**) to be a typical example of sb/sth: *Larry's answer typified the attitudes of most students.*

**ty·po** /ˈtaɪpoʊ/ ***noun*** [C] (*pl.* **ty·pos**) a small mistake in sth that has been typed on a computer or typewriter

**tyr·an·ny** /ˈtɪrəni/ ***noun*** [U] the cruel and unfair use of power by a person or small group to govern a country or state ▸ **ty·ran·ni·cal** /tɪˈrænɪkl/ ***adj.***: *a tyrannical ruler*

**ty·rant** /ˈtaɪrənt/ ***noun*** [C] a cruel ruler who has complete power over the people in his/her country ➲ Look at **dictator**.

# Uu

**U,u** /yu/ ***noun*** [C,U] (*pl.* **U's**; **u's** /yuz/) the twenty-first letter of the English alphabet: *"Ulcer" begins with (a) "U."*

**U.** (*also* **U**) ***abbr.*** (*written*) (in names) university

**u·ber-** (*also* **über-**) /ˈubər/ ***prefix*** (*informal*) (in nouns and adjectives) of the greatest or best kind; to a very large degree: *His girlfriend was a real uberbabe, with long blonde hair and a big smile.* ◇ *The movie stars the uber-cool Jean Reno.*

**u·biq·ui·tous** /yuˈbɪkwət̬əs/ ***adj.*** (*formal*) seeming to be everywhere or in several places at the same time; very common: *the ubiquitous floral shirts sold in tourist shops* ◇ *the ubiquitous movie star, Tom Hanks*

**ud·der** /ˈʌdər/ ***noun*** [C] the part of a female cow, goat, etc. that hangs like a bag between its back legs and produces milk ➲ picture at **cow**

**UFO** /ˌyu ɛf ˈoʊ/ ***noun*** [C] (*pl.* **UFO's** or **UFOs**) unidentified flying object; a mysterious object that some people say they have seen in the sky, and that they believe may be a spacecraft from another planet: *Have you ever seen a UFO?*

**ugh** /ʌg; ʌh/ ***interjection*** (used in writing to express the sound that you make when you think sth is very unpleasant)

★**ug·ly** /ˈʌgli/ ***adj.*** (**ug·li·er**; **ug·li·est**) **1** unpleasant to look at or listen to; unattractive: *an ugly scar on her face* ◇ *an ugly modern office building* **2** (used about a situation) dangerous or threatening: *The situation turned ugly when people started throwing stones.* ▸ **ug·li·ness** ***noun*** [U]

**uh** /ʌ/ (*also* **um**) ***interjection*** (used in writing to show that sb cannot decide what to say next): *Well, uh, I guess it's, uh, about five miles away.*

**uh-huh** /ʌˈhʌ/ ***interjection*** (used in informal speech to say "yes" or to show that you understand or agree with sth): *"Do you see what I mean?" "Uh-huh."* ➲ Look at the note at **yes**.

**uh-oh** /ˈʌ oʊ/ ***interjection*** (used when you make a mistake or when you notice that there has been a small accident): *Uh-oh. I don't think this ink stain is going to come out.*

**uh-uh** /ˈʌ ʌ; ˈm m/ ***interjection*** (used in informal speech to say "no" or to show that you disagree with sth): *"Do you want any more chicken?" "Uh-uh. I'm full."*

**u·ku·le·le** /ˌyukəˈleɪli/ ***noun*** [C] a musical instrument with four strings that is like a small guitar

**ul·cer** /ˈʌlsər/ ***noun*** [C] a painful area on your skin or inside your body. Ulcers may produce a poisonous substance and sometimes bleed: *a stomach ulcer*

**ul·te·ri·or** /ʌlˈtɪriər/ ***adj.***

**IDM** **an ulterior motive** a hidden or secret reason for doing sth: *Why is he suddenly being so nice to me? He must have an ulterior motive.*

**ul·ti·mate¹** /ˈʌltəmət/ ***adj.*** (only *before* a noun) **1** being or happening at the end; last or final: *Our ultimate goal is complete independence.* **2** **the ultimate** the greatest, best or worst: *For me, the ultimate luxury is to stay in bed until noon on a Sunday.*

★**ul·ti·mate²** /ˈʌltəmət/ ***noun*** [sing.] **the ultimate (in sth)** (*informal*) the greatest or best: *This new car is the ultimate in comfort.*

★**ul·ti·mate·ly** /ˈʌltəmətli/ ***adv.*** **1** in the end: *Whatever decision we ultimately make will be in the best interests of the school.* **2** at the most basic level: *Ultimately, this discussion is not about quality but about money.*

**ul·ti·ma·tum** /ˌʌltəˈmeɪt̬əm/ ***noun*** [C] (*pl.* **ul·ti·ma·tums**) a warning to a person or country that, if they do not do what you ask, you will use force or take action against them: *to issue an ultimatum to sb*

**ultra-** /ˈʌltrə/ ***prefix*** extremely: *ultraconservative*

**ul·tra·son·ic** /ˌʌltrəˈsɑnɪk/ ***adj.*** (used about sounds) higher than humans can hear: *ultrasonic frequencies/waves/signals*

**ul·tra·sound** /ˈʌltrəsaʊnd/ ***noun*** **1** [U] sound that is higher than humans can hear **2** [C,U] a medical process that produces an image of what is inside your body: *Ultrasound showed she was expecting twins.* ◇ *an ultrasound scan* ◇ *ultrasound scanning*

**ul·tra·vi·o·let** /ˌʌltrəˈvaɪələt/ ***adj.*** (*abbr.* **UV**) (used about a type of light) that causes your skin to turn darker and that can be dangerous in large amounts

**um** /ʌm; m/ ***interjection*** = UH

**um·bil·i·cal cord** /ʌm'bɪlɪkl kɔrd/ ***noun*** [C] (*medical*) the tube that connects a baby to its mother before it is born

**um·brage** /'ʌmbrɪdʒ/ ***noun***

IDM **take umbrage (at sth)** (*formal*) to feel offended, insulted or upset by sth, often without a good reason: *He took umbrage at her remarks.*

★ **um·brel·la** /ʌm'brɛlə/ ***noun*** [C] **1** an object that you carry to keep you dry when it is raining. An umbrella consists of a piece of cloth on a frame and a long handle. You can fold an umbrella up when you are not using it: *to open/close an umbrella* **2** a thing that contains or includes many different parts or elements: *Many previously separate groups are now operating* ***under the umbrella of*** *a single authority.* ◇ *an umbrella organization/group/fund*

**um·pire** /'ʌmpaɪər/ ***noun*** [C] (*also informal* **ump** /ʌmp/) a person who watches a game such as baseball or tennis to make sure that the players obey the rules ➲ Compare **referee**. ➲ picture at **baseball**. ▸ **um·pire** ***verb*** [I,T]

**ump·teen** /'ʌmptin/ ***pronoun***, ***det.*** (*informal*) very many; a lot: *I've told you umpteen times to call me if you're going to be late.* ▸ **ump·teenth** /'ʌmptinθ/ ***pronoun***, ***det.***: *For the umpteenth time – call if you're going to be late!*

**UN** /ˌyu 'ɛn/ ***abbr.*** = UNITED NATIONS

**un·a·bashed** /ˌʌnə'bæʃt/ ***adj.*** (*written*) not ashamed, embarrassed or affected by people's disapproval, when other people would be: *He was unabashed by the reaction he had caused.* ◇ *He appeared unabashed by all the media attention.*

**un·a·ble** /ʌn'eɪbl/ ***adj.*** (not before a noun) **unable to do sth** not having the time, knowledge, skill, etc. to do sth; not able to do sth: *Thank you for the invitation. Unfortunately, I will be unable to attend.* ➲ The noun is **inability**.

**un·a·bridged** /ˌʌnə'brɪdʒd/ ***adj.*** (used about a novel, play, speech, etc.) complete, without being made shorter in any way OPP **abridged**

**un·ac·cept·a·ble** /ˌʌnək'sɛptəbl/ ***adj.*** that you cannot accept or allow ▸ **un·ac·cept·a·bly** /-bli/ ***adv.***

**un·ac·com·pa·nied** /ˌʌnə'kʌmpənid/ ***adj.*** alone; without sb/sth else going too: *unaccompanied children*

**un·ac·cus·tomed** /ˌʌnə'kʌstəmd/ ***adj.*** (*formal*) **1 unaccustomed to sth/to doing sth** not in the habit of doing sth; not used to sth: *He was unaccustomed to hard work.* ◇ *I am unaccustomed to being told what to do.* **2** not usual, normal or familiar: *I was surprised by her unaccustomed silence.* OPP **accustomed**

**un·a·dul·ter·at·ed** /ˌʌnə'dʌltəreɪt̬əd/ ***adj.*** **1** used to emphasize that sth is complete or total: *For me, the vacation was sheer unadulterated pleasure.* **2** not mixed with other substances; pure: *unadulterated foods*

**un·af·fect·ed** /ˌʌnə'fɛktəd/ ***adj.*** **unaffected (by sth)** not changed by sth: *Our department will be unaffected by the decision.*

**un·aid·ed** /ˌʌn'eɪdəd/ ***adv.*** without any help

**un-A·mer·i·can** /ʌnə'mɛrɪkən/ ***adj.*** (used about behavior, ideas, etc.) not supporting beliefs or ways of doing things that are considered typically American, e.g. freedom, honesty, a free economic system, etc.: *He says it's just un-American to restrict gun ownership.*

**u·nan·i·mous** /yu'nænəməs/ ***adj.*** **1** (used about a group of people) all agreeing about sth: *The members of the jury were unanimous in their decision.* **2** (used about a decision, etc.) agreed on by everybody ▸ **u·nan·i·mous·ly** ***adv.***

**un·an·nounced** /ˌʌnə'naʊnst/ ***adj.*** happening without anyone being told or warned in advance: *She just turned up unannounced on my doorstep.*

**un·armed** /ˌʌn'ɑrmd/ ***adj.*** having no guns, knives, etc.; not armed

**un·as·sum·ing** /ˌʌnə'sumɪŋ/ ***adj.*** not wishing to be noticed by other people

**un·at·tached** /ˌʌnə'tætʃt/ ***adj.*** **1** not connected to sb/sth else: *This group is unattached to any political party.* **2** not married or in a serious romantic relationship

**un·at·tain·a·ble** /ˌʌnə'teɪnəbl/ ***adj.*** (*written*) impossible to achieve or reach: *an unattainable dream/goal* OPP **attainable**

**un·at·tend·ed** /ˌʌnə'tɛndəd/ ***adj.*** not watched; alone: *Baggage should not be left unattended at the airport.*

**un·at·trac·tive** /ˌʌnə'træktɪv/ ***adj.*** **1** ugly; not beautiful **2** not favorable; that does not interest you: *an unattractive business offer*

**un·au·thor·ized** /ˌʌn'ɔθəraɪzd/ ***adj.*** done without permission

**un·a·vail·a·ble** /ʌnə'veɪləbl/ ***adj.*** not available: *The replacement parts are unavailable until June.* ◇ *The Senator was unavailable for comment yesterday.*

**un·a·void·a·ble** /ˌʌnə'vɔɪdəbl/ ***adj.*** that cannot be avoided or prevented ▸ **un·a·void·a·bly** /-əbli/ ***adv.***: *We were unavoidably delayed.*

**un·a·ware** /ˌʌnə'wɛr/ ***adj.*** (not before a noun) **unaware (of sb/sth)** not knowing about or not noticing sb/sth: *She seemed unaware of all the trouble she had caused.*

**un·bal·anced** /ˌʌn'bælənst/ ***adj.*** **1** (used about a person) somewhat crazy **2** not fair to all ideas or sides of an argument: *an unbalanced newspaper report*

**un·bear·a·ble** /ˌʌn'bɛrəbl/ ***adj.*** too bad, painful, etc. for you to accept ▸ **un·bear·a·bly** /-əbli/ ***adv.***: *It was unbearably hot.*

**un·beat·a·ble** /ˌʌn'bit̬əbl/ ***adj.*** that cannot be defeated or improved on: *The Chicago Bulls seemed unbeatable in the championship tournament.* ◇ *We offer you top quality at unbeatable prices!*

**un·beat·en** /ˌʌn'bitn/ ***adj.*** that has not been beaten or improved on: *Her world record remains unbeaten.*

**un·be·known** /ˌʌnbɪ'noʊn/ (*also* **unbeknownst**

/ˌʌnbɪˈnoʊnst/) **adj.** (*written*) **unbeknown to sb** without the person mentioned knowing: *Unbeknown to her they had organized a surprise party.*

**un·be·liev·a·ble** /ˌʌnbɪˈlivəbl/ **adj.** very surprising; difficult to believe ➲ Look at **incredible.** ▸ **un·be·liev·a·bly** /-bli/ **adj.**: *unbelievably bad*

**un·bi·ased** /ˌʌnˈbaɪəst/ **adj.** fair and not influenced by your own or sb else's opinions, desires, etc.: *unbiased advice/reporting/information* ◇ *an unbiased judge/observer* OPP **biased** SYN **impartial**

**un·born** /ˌʌnˈbɔrn/ **adj.** not yet born: *Smoking can damage your unborn child.*

**un·break·a·ble** /ˌʌnˈbreɪkəbl/ **adj.** impossible to break: *This new material is virtually unbreakable.* ◇ *the unbreakable bond between parent and child*

**un·bri·dled** /ˌʌnˈbraɪdld/ **adj.** (*formal*) not controlled and therefore extreme: *unbridled enthusiasm/lust/passion*

**un·bro·ken** /ˌʌnˈbroʊkən/ **adj.** **1** continuous; not interrupted: *a period of unbroken silence* **2** that has not been beaten: *His record for the most home runs in a season remains unbroken.*

**un·bur·den** /ʌnˈbərdn/ **verb** [T] **1 unburden yourself/sth (of sth) (to sb)** (*formal*) to talk to sb about your problems or sth you have been worrying about, so that you feel less anxious: *She needed to unburden herself to somebody.* ◇ *She unburdened herself of her feelings of guilt.* **2 unburden sb/sth (of sth)** to take sth that causes a lot of work or worry away from sb/sth

**un·but·ton** /ˌʌnˈbʌtn/ **verb** [T] to open a piece of clothing that had been fastened with buttons

**un·called-for** /ʌnˈkɔld fɔr/ **adj.** not necessary or right: *That comment was totally uncalled-for.*

**un·can·ny** /ʌnˈkæni/ **adj.** strange and mysterious; that you cannot easily explain

★**un·cer·tain** /ʌnˈsərtn/ **adj.** **1 uncertain (about/of sth)** not sure; not able to decide: *She was still uncertain of his true feelings for her.* ◇ *Chris seemed uncertain about what to do next.* **2** not known exactly or not decided: *He lost his job and his future seems very uncertain.* ▸ **un·cer·tain·ly** **adv.**: *Kate stood uncertainly, waiting for someone to talk to her.* ▸ **un·cer·tain·ty** /ʌnˈsərtnti/ **noun** [C,U] (*pl.* **un·cer·tain·ties**): *Today's decision will put an end to all the uncertainty.*

**un·changed** /ʌnˈtʃeɪndʒd/ **adj.** staying the same; not changed: *The house has remained almost unchanged since the nineteenth century.*

**un·char·ac·ter·is·tic** /ʌnˌkærəktəˈrɪstɪk/ **adj.** not typical or usual ▸ **un·char·ac·ter·is·tic·al·ly** /-kli/ **adv.**

**un·chart·ed** /ˌʌnˈtʃɑrt̬əd/ **adj.** that has not been visited or investigated before; not familiar: *They set off into the country's uncharted interior.* ◇ (*figurative*) *The company is sailing in* ***uncharted waters*** (= a situation it has not been in before). ◇ (*figurative*) *I was moving into* ***uncharted territory*** (= a completely new experience) *with this relationship.*

**un·checked** /ˌʌnˈtʃɛkt/ **adj.** if sth harmful is unchecked, it is not controlled or stopped from getting worse: *The rise in violent crime must not* ***go unchecked.*** ◇ *The plant will soon choke ponds and waterways if* ***left unchecked.*** ◇ *Tears flowed unchecked down his cheeks.*

★**un·cle** /ˈʌŋkl/ **noun** [C] **1** the brother of your father or mother: *my Uncle Steven* **2** the husband of your aunt ➲ Look at **aunt.**

IDM **say uncle** (*informal*) (used by children to tell sb to admit that he/she has been beaten or defeated in a game, etc.)

**un·clean** /ˌʌnˈklin/ **adj.** **1** (*formal*) dirty and therefore likely to cause disease: *unclean water* ◇ *unclean premises/hands* **2** considered to be bad, immoral or not pure in a religious way, and therefore not to be touched, eaten, etc.: *unclean thoughts* ◇ *unclean food/animals*

**un·clear** /ˌʌnˈklɪr/ **adj.** not easy to see, hear, know or understand: *It is unclear how the local economy will be affected by this decision.*

**Uncle Sam** /ˌʌŋkl ˈsæm/ **noun** [sing.] (*informal*) the U.S. government, often represented by a picture of an old man who wears a tall hat and a red, white and blue suit: *Jessica owes Uncle Sam $50,000 in income taxes.*

**Uncle Tom** /ˌʌŋkl ˈtɑm/ **noun** [C] (*informal, taboo*) (an offensive word sometimes used in the past to refer to a black man who wants to please or serve white people)

★**un·com·fort·a·ble** /ʌnˈkʌmftəbl; ʌnˈkʌmfərt̬əbl/ **adj.** **1** not pleasant to wear, sit in, lie on, etc.: *The chairs are hard and very uncomfortable.* **2** not able to sit, lie, etc. in a position that is pleasant: *I was very uncomfortable for most of the trip.* **3** feeling or causing worry or embarrassment: *I felt very uncomfortable when they started arguing in front of me.* ▸ **un·com·fort·a·bly** /-əbli/ **adv.**

**un·com·mon** /ʌnˈkɑmən/ **adj.** unusual: *Snowstorms are not uncommon* (= they are fairly common) *in this part of the country.*

**un·com·mon·ly** /ʌnˈkɑmənli/ **adv.** (*formal*) to an unusual degree; extremely: *an uncommonly gifted child* ◇ *He looks uncommonly like a younger version of his father.*

**un·com·pro·mis·ing** /ʌnˈkɑmprəmaɪzɪŋ/ **adj.** not willing to discuss sth or change a decision

**un·con·cerned** /ˌʌnkənˈsərnd/ **adj.** not interested in sth or not worried about it

**un·con·di·tion·al** /ˌʌnkənˈdɪʃənl/ **adj.** without limits or conditions: *an unconditional surrender* ▸ **un·con·di·tion·al·ly** /-ʃənəli/ **adv.**

**un·con·firmed** /ˌʌnkənˈfərmd/ **adj.** not official; that may not be true or correct: *There have been unconfirmed reports of a tornado in Brown County.*

★**un·con·scious**[1] /ʌnˈkɑnʃəs/ **adj.** **1** in a state that is like sleep. You may be unconscious after an accident if you hit your head: *She was found lying unconscious on the kitchen floor.* **2 unconscious of sb/sth** not knowing or aware of sb/sth: *He seemed unconscious of everything that was going on around him.* ▸ **un·con·scious·ly** **adv.** ▸ **un·con·scious·ness** **noun** [U]

**un·con·scious**[2] /ʌnˈkɑnʃəs/ **noun** [sing.] **the/sb's unconscious** the part of a person's mind with thoughts, feelings, etc. that he/she is not aware of and cannot control but which can sometimes be



U

understood by studying his/her behavior or dreams ➲ Compare **subconscious.**

**un·con·sti·tu·tion·al** /ˌʌnkɑnstəˈtuʃnl/ ***adj.*** not in agreement with or allowed by the basic laws (Constitution) of a country or state: *The Supreme Court declared the law unconstitutional.*

**un·con·trol·la·ble** /ˌʌnkənˈtroʊləbl/ ***adj.*** that you cannot control: *an uncontrollable urge to giggle* ▶ **un·con·trol·la·bly** /-əbli/ ***adv.***

**un·co·op·er·a·tive** /ˌʌnkoʊˈɑprət̬ɪv/ ***adj.*** not willing to be helpful to other people or do what they ask: *The witness was extremely uncooperative.* ◇ *She was an aggressive and uncooperative child.* OPP **cooperative**

**un·count·a·ble noun** /ʌnˌkaʊntəbl ˈnaʊn/ (*also* ˌ**noncount** ˈ**noun**) ***noun*** [C] (*grammar*) a noun that cannot be counted and so does not have a plural form in English, e.g. "air," "water," or "information." Uncountable nouns are marked "[U]" in this dictionary.

**un·cov·er** /ʌnˈkʌvər/ ***verb*** [T] **1** to remove the cover from sth **2** to find out or discover sth

**un·cut** /ˌʌnˈkʌt/ ***adj.*** **1** left to grow; not cut short: *The uncut grass came up to her waist.* **2** (used about a book, movie, etc.) left in its complete form; without any parts removed; not censored: *the original uncut version* **3** (used about a precious stone) not shaped by cutting: *uncut diamonds*

**un·daunt·ed** /ˌʌnˈdɔntəd/ ***adj.*** (*written*) still enthusiastic and determined, despite difficulties or disappointment: *He seemed undaunted by all the opposition to his idea.* SYN **undeterred**

**un·de·cid·ed** /ˌʌndɪˈsaɪdəd/ ***adj.*** **1** not having made a decision: *10% of voters were still undecided about the candidates.* **2** without any result or decision; not decided: *The future of our jobs is still undecided.*

**un·de·ni·a·ble** /ˌʌndɪˈnaɪəbl/ ***adj.*** clear, true or certain: *an undeniable link between smoking and cancer* ▶ **un·de·ni·a·bly** /-əbli/ ***adv.***

**under/below**

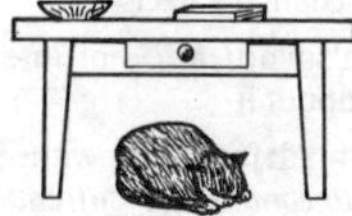

a cat asleep **under** a table

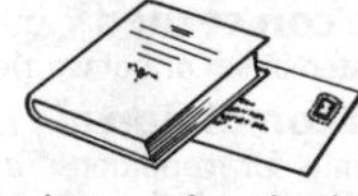

a letter **under** a book

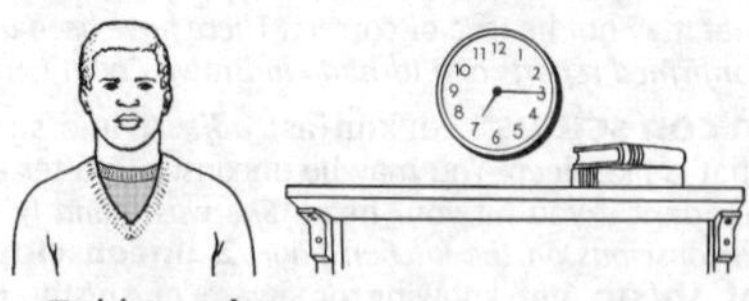

a T-shirt **under** his sweater

a shelf **below** a clock

★**un·der**[1] /ˈʌndər/ ***prep.*** **1** in or to a position that is below or beneath sth: *Put the suitcase under the bed.* ◇ *to hide under the table* ◇ *The dog crawled under the fence and ran into the street.*

NOTE Compare **under**, **below**, **beneath** and **underneath**. You use **under** to say that one thing is directly under another thing. There may be a space between the two things: *The cat is asleep under the table.* or one thing may be touching or covered by the other thing: *I think your letter is under that book.* You can use **below** to say that one thing is in a lower position than another thing when they are both in the same building, on the same part of the body, etc.: *They live on the floor below us.* ◇ *It hurts here – just below my knee.* ◇ *The phone book is on the shelf below the cookbooks.* You use **under** (not **below**) to talk about movement from one side of something to the other side: *We swam under the bridge.* You can use **beneath** to say that one thing is directly under another thing, but **under** is more common. **Beneath** is a more formal word. You can use **underneath** in place of **under** when you want to emphasize that something is being covered or hidden by another thing: *Did you look underneath the sofa as well as behind it?*

**2** below the surface of sth; covered by sth: *Most of an iceberg is under the water.* ◇ *Are you wearing a T-shirt under your sweater?* **3** younger than: *Nobody under twenty-one is allowed to buy alcohol.* **4** less than: *People earning under $4,000 a year are eligible for financial assistance.* **5** working for or in the control of sb: *This hotel is under new management.* **6** ruled or governed by sb/sth: *The country is now under martial law.* **7** according to a law, agreement, system, etc.: *Under our judicial system, you are considered innocent until you are proven guilty.* **8** in a particular state or condition: *under the influence of alcohol* ◇ *a building under construction* ◇ *I was under the impression that Bill was not very happy here.* **9** found in a particular part of a book, list, etc.: *You'll find some information on Budapest under "Hungary."*

★**un·der**[2] /ˈʌndər/ ***adv.*** **1** below the surface of water: *I saw him struggling for a while before his head went under.* **2** less; younger: *The prices quoted are for children age 12 and under.*

**un·der·a·chieve** /ˌʌndərəˈtʃiv/ ***verb*** [I] to do less well than you could do, especially in school work: *Too many boys are underachieving in school.* ▶ **un·der·a·chiev·er** ***noun*** [C]

**un·der·age** /ˌʌndərˈeɪdʒ/ ***adj.*** not legally old enough to do a particular thing: *It is illegal to sell cigarettes to children who are underage.* ◇ *underage driving/drinking/sex*

**un·der·arm** /ˈʌndərɑrm/ ***noun*** [C, usually pl.] the part of the body under the arm where it joins the shoulder SYN **armpit**

**un·der·bel·ly** /ˈʌndərˌbɛli/ ***noun*** [sing.] **1** the weakest part of sth that is most easily attacked: *The trade deficit remains the **soft underbelly** of the U.S. economy.* **2** the underneath part of an animal: (*figurative*) *He became familiar with the dark underbelly of life in the city* (= the parts that are usually hidden).

**un·der·brush** /ˈʌndərbrʌʃ/ ***noun*** [U] a mass of bushes and plants that grow close together under trees in woods and forests: *They used their knives to clear a path through the dense underbrush.* ◇ *The murder weapon was found concealed in underbrush.*

**un·der·charge** /ˌʌndərˈtʃɑrdʒ/ *verb* [I,T] **undercharge (sb) (for sth)** to charge too little for sth, usually by mistake OPP **overcharge**

**un·der·class** /ˈʌndərklæs/ *noun* [sing.] a social class that is very poor and has no status: *The long-term unemployed are becoming a new underclass.*

**un·der·class·man** /ˌʌndərˈklæsmən/ *noun* [C] (*pl.* **un·der·class·men** /-mən/) (*U.S.*) a student who is in his/her first or second year in high school or college ➲ Look at **upperclassman**.

**un·der·cov·er** /ˌʌndərˈkʌvər/ *adj.* working or happening secretly: *an undercover agent* (= a spy)

**un·der·cur·rent** /ˈʌndərˌkərənt/ *noun* [C] **undercurrent (of sth)** a feeling, especially a negative one, that is hidden but whose effects are felt: *I detect an undercurrent of resentment toward the new proposals.*

**un·der·cut** /ˌʌndərˈkʌt/ *verb* [T] (*pres. part.* **un·der·cut·ting**; *pt, pp* **un·der·cut**) **1** to sell at a lower price than other stores, etc.: *Big discounts chains can undercut smaller stores.* **2** to weaken sb's authority or make sth less effective: *efforts to undercut the new welfare reform plan* ➲ Look at **undermine**. It has a similar meaning.

**un·der·de·ve·loped** /ˌʌndərdɪˈvɛləpt/ *adj.* (used about a country, society, etc.) having few industries and a low standard of living

NOTE **Developing** country is now the usual expression used.

**un·der·dog** /ˈʌndərdɔg/ *noun* [C] a person who is in a weak position and is expected to lose a competition

**un·der·done** /ˌʌndərˈdʌn/ *adj.* not completely cooked ➲ Compare **well-done**.

**un·der·em·ployed** /ˌʌndərɪmˈplɔɪd/ *adj.* not having enough work to do; not having work that makes full use of your skills and abilities

**un·der·es·ti·mate** /ˌʌndərˈɛstəmeɪt/ *verb* [T] **1** to guess that the amount, etc. of sth will be less than it really is: *We underestimated the amount of food we would need.* **2** to think that sb/sth is not as strong, etc. as he/she/it really is: *Don't underestimate your opponent. She's a really good player.* OPP **overestimate**

**un·der·foot** /ˌʌndərˈfʊt/ *adv.* under your feet; on the ground where you are walking: *The ground was dry and firm underfoot.* ◇ *I was almost* ***trampled underfoot*** *by the crowd of people rushing for the door.*

**un·der·go** /ˌʌndərˈgoʊ/ *verb* [T] (*pt* **un·der·went** /-ˈwɛnt/; *pp* **un·der·gone** /-ˈgɔn; -ˈgɑn/) to have a difficult or bad experience: *She underwent a five-hour operation.*

**un·der·grad·u·ate** /ˌʌndərˈgrædʒuət/ (*also informal* **un·der·grad** /ˈʌndərgræd/) *noun* [C] a college or university student who has not yet earned his/her first (**bachelor's**) degree ➲ Look at **graduate**.

★**un·der·ground**[1] /ˈʌndərgraʊnd/ *adj.* **1** under the surface of the ground: *an underground parking garage* **2** secret or illegal: *an underground radio station that supports the militia movement*

★**un·der·ground**[2] /ˌʌndərˈgraʊnd/ *adv.* **1** under the surface of the ground: *The cables all run underground.* **2** into a secret place: *She went underground to escape from the police.*

**un·der·growth** /ˈʌndərgroʊθ/ *noun* [U] bushes and plants that grow around and under trees

**un·der·handed** /ˈʌndərhændəd/ *adj.* secret or not honest

**un·der·line** /ˈʌndərlaɪn/ *verb* [T] **1** (*also* **underscore**) to draw a line under a word, etc.: *Underline the subject of each sentence.* **2** to show clearly or to emphasize sth: *This accident underlines the need for more safety inspections.*

**un·der·ling** /ˈʌndərlɪŋ/ *noun* [C] a person with a lower rank or status: *He dishes out orders to his underlings.*

**un·der·ly·ing** /ˈʌndərlaɪɪŋ/ *adj.* (only *before* a noun) important but hidden: *the underlying causes of the disaster*

**un·der·mine** /ˈʌndərmaɪn; ˌʌndərˈmaɪn/ *verb* [T] to make sth weaker: *The public's trust in the police has been undermined.*

★**un·der·neath** /ˌʌndərˈniθ/ *prep., adv.* under or below: *The coin rolled underneath the chair.* ◇ *This sweater's not very warm, but I have a T-shirt on underneath.* ➲ Look at the note at **under**.

**un·der·paid** /ˌʌndərˈpeɪd/ *adj.* paid too little

★**un·der·pants** /ˈʌndərpænts/ *noun* [pl.] a piece of clothing that you wear under your pants or skirt ➲ Look at **panties** and **shorts** (2).

**un·der·pass** /ˈʌndərpæs/ *noun* [C] a road or path that goes under another road, etc.

**un·der·priv·i·leged** /ˌʌndərˈprɪvəlɪdʒd/ *adj.* having less money and fewer rights, opportunities, etc. than other people in society

**un·der·rated** /ˌʌndərˈreɪt̬əd/ *adj.* that people think is less intelligent, important, good, etc. than he/she/it really is

**un·der·score**[1] /ˈʌndərskɔr/ *verb* [T] = UNDERLINE

**un·der·score**[2] /ˈʌndərskɔr/ *noun* [C] (*computing*) the symbol (_) that is used to draw a line under a letter or word and used in computer commands and in Internet addresses

**un·der·sec·re·tar·y** /ˈʌndərˌsɛkrətɛri/ *noun* [C] (*pl.* **un·der·sec·re·tar·ies**) **1** (*U.S.*) an official of high rank in a government department, directly below a member of a cabinet **2** (*Cdn*) a junior minister or a senior civil servant

**un·der·shirt** /ˈʌndərʃərt/ *noun* [C] a piece of clothing that you wear on the top part of your body, under your other clothes

**un·der·shorts** /ˈʌndərʃɔrts/ *noun* [pl.] light short pants that men wear as underwear

**un·der·side** /ˈʌndərsaɪd/ *noun* [C] the side or surface of sth that is underneath SYN **bottom**

**un·der·staffed** /ˌʌndərˈstæft/ *adj.* not having enough people working and therefore not able to function well: *We're very understaffed at the moment.*

★**un·der·stand** /ˌʌndərˈstænd/ *verb* (*pt, pp* **un·der·stood** /-ˈstʊd/)

▸MEANING **1** [I,T] to get the meaning of sb/sth: *I'm not sure that I really understand.* ◇ *I didn't understand the instructions.* ◇ *Please speak more slowly. I*

U

*can't understand you. ◇ He can understand Italian, but he can't speak it.*
➤HOW STH WORKS/HAPPENS **2** [T] to know how or why sth happens: *I can't understand why the engine won't start.*
➤KNOW SB **3** [T] to know why sb behaves in a particular way and to feel sympathy: *It's easy to understand why she felt so mad. ◇ His parents don't understand him.*
➤THINK/BELIEVE **4** [T] (*formal*) to have heard or been told sth: *I understand that you have decided to leave.* **5** [T] to judge a situation, etc.: *As far as I understand it, the changes won't affect us.*
IDM **make yourself understood** to make your meaning clear: *I can just about make myself understood in Russian.*

**un·der·stand·a·ble** /ˌʌndərˈstændəbl/ ***adj.*** that you can understand ▸ **un·der·stand·a·bly** /-əbli/ ***adv.***: *She was understandably angry about the decision.*

★**un·der·stand·ing**[1] /ˌʌndərˈstændɪŋ/ ***noun*** **1** [U] the ability to think or learn about sth: *The book is beyond the understanding of most ten-year-olds.* **2** [U, sing.] knowledge of a subject, how sth works, etc.: *A basic understanding of physics is necessary for this course.* **3** [U, sing.] the ability to feel sympathy and trust for sb: *understanding between nations* **4** [U] the way in which you think sth is meant: *My understanding of the arrangement is that he will only call if there is a problem.* **5** [C, usually sing.] an informal agreement: *We came to an understanding about the money I owed him.*

**un·der·stand·ing**[2] /ˌʌndərˈstændɪŋ/ ***adj.*** kind; showing sympathy toward sb

**un·der·state** /ˌʌndərˈsteɪt/ ***verb*** [T] to say that sth is smaller or less important than it really is

**un·der·stat·ed** /ˌʌndərˈsteɪt̬əd/ ***adj.*** done in a very controlled way that seems appropriate and shows good taste: *the understated elegance of the furniture in their home*

**un·der·state·ment** /ˈʌndərsteɪtmənt/ ***noun*** [C] a statement that does not show how big, important, etc. sth really is: *"Is she pleased?" "That's an understatement. She's delighted."*

U

**un·der·stood** *past tense, past participle of* UNDERSTAND

**un·der·stud·y** /ˈʌndərstʌdi/ ***noun*** [C] (*pl.* **un·der·stud·ies**) an actor who learns the role of another actor and replaces him/her if he/she is sick

**un·der·take** /ˌʌndərˈteɪk/ ***verb*** [T] (*pt* **un·der·took** /-ˈtʊk/; *pp* **un·der·tak·en** /-ˈteɪkən/) to carry out: *The government is undertaking a major welfare reform plan.*

**un·der·tak·er** /ˈʌndərteɪkər/ ***noun*** [C] = FUNERAL DIRECTOR

**un·der·tak·ing** /ˈʌndərteɪkɪŋ/ ***noun*** [C, usually sing.] a piece of work or business: *a risky undertaking*

**un·der·tone** /ˈʌndərtoʊn/ ***noun*** [C] a feeling or attitude that is not directly expressed

**un·der·tow** /ˈʌndərtoʊ/ ***noun*** [C, usually sing.] **1** a current in the ocean that moves in the opposite direction to the water near the surface: *The children were carried along by the strong undertow.* **2 undertow (of sth)** a feeling or quality that influences people in a particular situation even though they are not really aware of it

**un·der·used** /ˌʌndərˈyuzd/ (*also formal* **un·der·u·ti·lized**) ***adj.*** not used as much as it could or should be: *The airport is currently grossly underused.*

**un·der·u·ti·lized** /ˌʌndərˈyut̬l·aɪzd/ ***adj.*** (*formal*) = UNDERUSED

**un·der·val·ue** /ˌʌndərˈvælyu/ ***verb*** [T] (usually passive) to not recognize how good, valuable or important sb/sth really is: *Education is currently undervalued in this country. ◇ He believes his house has been undervalued.*

★**un·der·wa·ter** /ˌʌndərˈwɔt̬ər; -ˈwɑ-/ ***adj.***, ***adv.*** existing, happening or used below the surface of water: *underwater exploration ◇ an underwater camera ◇ Can you swim underwater?*

**un·der·way** /ˌʌndərˈweɪ/ ***adj.***
IDM **be underway** having started: *Preparations are well under way for a week of special events in May.*

★**un·der·wear** /ˈʌndərwɛr/ ***noun*** [U] (*also informal* **un·dies**) clothing that is worn next to the skin under other clothes

**un·der·weight** /ˌʌndərˈweɪt/ ***adj.*** weighing less than is normal or correct ➲ Look at the note at **thin**.

**un·der·went** /ˌʌndərˈwɛnt/ *past tense of* UNDERGO

**un·der·whelmed** /ˌʌndərˈwɛlmd/ ***adj.*** (*informal*) not impressed with or excited about sth at all: *We were distinctly underwhelmed by the director's speech.* ▸ **un·der·whelm·ing** ***adj.***

**un·der·wired** /ˌʌndərˈwaɪərd/ ***adj.*** (used about a bra) having a thin metal strip sewn into the bottom to strengthen the shape

**un·der·world** /ˈʌndərwərld/ ***noun*** [sing.] (usually **the underworld**) people who are involved in crime

**un·der·write** /ˈʌndərˌraɪt; ˌʌndərˈraɪt/ ***verb*** [T] (*pt* **un·der·wrote**; *pp* **un·der·writ·ten**) (*technical*) **1** to accept financial responsibility for an activity so that you will pay for special costs or for losses it may make: *The record company may underwrite the costs of a band's first tour.* **2** to accept responsibility for an insurance policy so that you will pay money in case loss or damage happens

**un·de·sir·a·ble** /ˌʌndɪˈzaɪrəbl/ ***adj.*** unwanted or unpleasant; likely to cause problems

**un·de·vel·oped** /ˌʌndɪˈvɛləpt/ ***adj.*** **1** (used about land) not used for farming, industry, building, etc.: *The coastline is still largely undeveloped. ◇ undeveloped countryside/villages* **2** (used about a country) not having modern industries, and with a low standard of living ➲ Look at **underdeveloped**.

**un·did** *past tense of* UNDO

**un·dies** /ˈʌndiz/ ***noun*** [pl.] (*informal*) = UNDERWEAR

**un·dis·closed** /ˌʌndɪsˈkloʊzd/ ***adj.*** (only *before* a noun) that is not known by the public: *Negotiations are taking place at an undisclosed location.*

**un·div·id·ed** /ˌʌndɪˈvaɪdəd/ ***adj.***
IDM **get/have sb's undivided attention** to receive sb's full attention

★**un·do** /ʌnˈdu/ ***verb*** [T] (*3rd person sing. pres.* **un·does**; *pt* **un·did**; *pp* **un·done**) **1** to open sth that was tied or fastened: *to undo a knot* **2** to destroy the effect of sth that has already happened: *The damage cannot be undone.*

**un·doc·u·ment·ed** /ʌn'dɑkyəmɛntəd/ ***adj.*** not having the proper legal document or license: *undocumented aliens/immigrants/workers*

**un·do·ing** /ʌn'duɪŋ/ ***noun*** [sing.] the reason why sb fails at sth or is unsuccessful in life: *That one mistake was his undoing.* SYN **downfall** (2)

**un·done** /ʌn'dʌn/ ***adj.*** **1** open; not fastened or tied: *His necktie was partially undone.* **2** not done: *I left the housework undone.*

**un·doubt·edly** /ʌn'daʊt̬ədli/ ***adv.*** definitely; without doubt: *It was undoubtedly one of her finest performances.*

**un·dress** /ˌʌn'drɛs/ ***verb*** **1** [I] (*formal*) to take off your clothes: *I undressed and the doctor examined me.*

NOTE **Get undressed** is more commonly used than **undress**: *He got undressed and took a shower.*

**2** [T] to take off sb's clothes: *She undressed the child and put her into bed.* ▸ **un·dressed** ***adj.***: *He came to the door partially undressed.*

**un·due** /ˌʌn'du/ ***adj.*** (*formal*) (only *before* a noun) more than is necessary or reasonable: *regulations that place an undue burden on small businesses*

**un·du·ly** /ˌʌn'duli/ ***adv.*** (*formal*) more than you think is reasonable or necessary: *She didn't seem **unduly worried** by their unexpected arrival.*

**un·dy·ing** /ˌʌn'daɪɪŋ/ ***adj.*** (only *before* a noun) (used especially about an emotion) lasting for ever: *undying love/support/gratitude*

**un·earned** /ˌʌn'ərnd/ ***adj.*** (usually before a noun) (used to describe money that you receive but do not earn by working): *Declare all **unearned income**.*

**un·earth** /ʌn'ərθ/ ***verb*** [T] to dig sth up out of the ground; to discover sth that was hidden: *Archaeologists have unearthed a Native American burial site.* ◇ (*figurative*) *A journalist unearthed the real story behind the case.*

**un·eas·y** /ʌn'izi/ ***adj.*** **1** worried; not feeling relaxed or comfortable **2** not settled; unlikely to last: *an uneasy compromise* ▸ **un·eas·i·ness** (*also* **unease** /ʌn'iz/) ***noun*** [U] ▸ **un·eas·i·ly** /ʌn'izəli/ ***adv.***

**un·ed·u·cat·ed** /ʌn'ɛdʒəkeɪt̬əd/ ***adj.*** having had little or no formal education at a school; showing a lack of education: *an uneducated workforce* ◇ *an uneducated point of view*

★**un·em·ployed** /ˌʌnɪm'plɔɪd/ ***adj.*** **1** not having a job; out of work: *She lost her job six months ago and has been unemployed ever since.* **2 the unemployed** ***noun*** [pl.] the people who do not have a job: *a new training program for the unemployed*

**un·em·ploy·ment** /ˌʌnɪm'plɔɪmənt/ ***noun*** [U] **1** the situation of being unemployed: *If the plant closes, many local people will face unemployment.* **2** the number of people who are unemployed: *The unemployment rate rose 0.2% last month.* ◇ *cities with high unemployment* **3** (*also formal* **unemˌployment compen'sation**) money that the government pays to unemployed people for a certain length of time after they lose their jobs: *people living on unemployment*

**un·end·ing** /ʌn'ɛndɪŋ/ ***adj.*** having or seeming to have no end

**un·en·vi·a·ble** /ʌn'ɛnviəbl/ ***adj.*** difficult or unpleasant; that you would not want to have: *She was given the **unenviable task** of informing the losers.*

**un·e·qual** /ˌʌn'ikwəl/ ***adj.*** **1** different in size, amount, level, etc. **2** not fair or balanced: *It was an unequal contest because he's a much better player than I am.* ▸ **un·e·qual·ly** ***adv.***

**un·e·qualed** /ˌʌn'ɪkwəld/ ***adj.*** better than all others: *an unequaled record of success*

**un·e·quiv·o·cal** /ˌʌnɪ'kwɪvəkl/ ***adj.*** (*formal*) expressing your opinion or intention very clearly and firmly: *an unequivocal answer/rejection/warning* ◇ *The answer was an unequivocal "no."* ▸ **un·e·quiv·o·cal·ly** ***adv.***: *We are unequivocally in favor of the changes.*

**un·eth·i·cal** /ʌn'ɛθɪkl/ ***adj.*** not morally acceptable: *unethical behavior/conduct* ◇ *It would be unethical to carry out such experiments on animals.* OPP **ethical**

**un·e·ven** /ˌʌn'ivən/ ***adj.*** **1** not completely smooth, level or regular: *The sign was painted in uneven letters.* **2** not always of the same level or quality ▸ **un·e·ven·ly** ***adv.***: *The country's wealth is unevenly distributed.*

**un·e·vent·ful** /ˌʌnɪ'vɛntfl/ ***adj.*** in which nothing interesting, unusual or exciting happens: *an uneventful career/life/weekend* ◇ *The pregnancy itself was relatively uneventful.* OPP **eventful**

★**un·ex·pect·ed** /ˌʌnɪk'spɛktəd/ ***adj.*** not expected and therefore causing surprise: *an unexpected development in the case* ▸ **un·ex·pect·ed·ly** ***adv.***: *an unexpectedly large increase in the number of people with the disease*

**un·ex·plained** /ˌʌnɪk'spleɪnd/ ***adj.*** for which the reason or cause is not known; that has not been explained: *an unexplained mystery* ◇ *The reason for her strange behavior remained unexplained.*

**un·fail·ing** /ʌn'feɪlɪŋ/ ***adj.*** that you can rely on to always be there and always be the same: *unfailing devotion/support* ◇ *She fought the disease with unfailing good humor.*

★**un·fair** /ˌʌn'fɛr/ ***adj.*** **unfair (to sb)** not dealing with people as they deserve; not treating each person equally: *This law is unfair to women.* ◇ *It was unfair to blame her for something that was not her fault.* ▸ **un·fair·ly** ***adv.*** ▸ **un·fair·ness** ***noun*** [U]

**un·faith·ful** /ˌʌn'feɪθfl/ ***adj.*** **unfaithful (to sb/sth)** having a sexual relationship with sb who is not your husband, wife or partner: *Have you ever been unfaithful to your husband?*

**un·fa·mil·iar** /ˌʌnfə'mɪlyər/ ***adj.*** **1 unfamiliar (to sb)** not well-known to sb: *This part of town is unfamiliar to me.* **2 unfamiliar (with sth)** not having knowledge or experience of sth

**un·fash·ion·a·ble** /ˌʌn'fæʃn·əbl/ ***adj.*** not popular: *unfashionable ideas* ➲ Compare **old-fashioned**.

**un·fas·ten** /ˌʌn'fæsn/ ***verb*** [T] to undo sth that is fastened: *to unfasten a belt/button/chain/lock* OPP **fasten**

**un·fin·ished** /ˌʌn'fɪnɪʃt/ ***adj.*** not complete; not

U

finished: *We have some* ***unfinished business*** *to settle.* ◇ *an unfinished drink/game/book*

**un·fit** /ʌn'fɪt/ ***adj.*** **unfit (for sth/to do sth)** unsuitable or not good enough for sth: *Inspectors said the meat was unfit for human consumption.* ◇ *Newspaper reports called her an unfit mother.*

**un·flap·pa·ble** /ʌn'flæpəbl/ ***adj.*** (*informal*) able to stay calm in a difficult situation

**un·fo·cused** (*also* **un·fo·cussed**) /ˌʌn'foʊkəst/ ***adj.*** **1** (used especially about eyes) not looking at a particular thing or person; not having been focused: *an unfocused glance/look* ◇ *Her eyes were blank and unfocused.* **2** (used about plans, work, etc.) not having a clear aim or purpose; not well organized or clear: *The research is too unfocused to have any significant impact.*

**un·fold** /ʌn'foʊld/ ***verb*** [I,T] **1** to open out and become flat; to open out sth that was folded: *I unfolded the letter and read it.* **2** to become known, or to allow sth to become known a little at a time: *As the story unfolded, more and more surprising things were revealed.*

**un·fore·seen** /ˌʌnfər'sin; -fɔr-/ ***adj.*** (usually *before* a noun) not expected: *an unforeseen problem*

**un·for·get·ta·ble** /ˌʌnfər'gɛt̬əbl/ ***adj.*** making such a strong impression that you cannot forget it

**un·for·giv·a·ble** /ˌʌnfər'gɪvəbl/ ***adj.*** if sb's behavior is unforgivable, it is so bad or unacceptable that you cannot forgive the person: *It was an unforgivable thing to say.* ◇ *an unforgivable act of violence* SYN **inexcusable** OPP **forgivable**

★**un·for·tu·nate** /ʌn'fɔrtʃənət/ ***adj.*** **1** having bad luck: *The unfortunate people who lived near the river lost their homes in the flood.* **2** causing or caused by bad luck: *an unfortunate accident* **3** that you are sorry or embarrassed about: *I would like to apologize for this unfortunate mistake.*

★**un·for·tu·nate·ly** /ʌn'fɔrtʃənətli/ ***adv.*** unluckily; it is too bad that...: *Unfortunately, there was nothing we could do to help.*

**un·found·ed** /ˌʌn'faʊndəd/ ***adj.*** not based on or supported by facts: *He said that the rumor was completely unfounded.*

★**un·friend·ly** /ˌʌn'frɛndli/ ***adj.*** unkind or not polite to sb; not friendly

**un·furl** /ʌn'fərl/ ***verb*** [I,T] to open, or to make sth open, that is curled or rolled tightly: *The leaves slowly unfurled.* ◇ *to unfurl a flag/sail/banner*

**un·fur·nished** /ˌʌn'fərnɪʃt/ ***adj.*** without furniture: *We rented an unfurnished apartment.* OPP **furnished**

**un·gain·ly** /ʌn'geɪnli/ ***adj.*** moving in a way that is not graceful: *He was a tall, ungainly boy of 18.* SYN **awkward**

**un·grate·ful** /ʌn'greɪtfl/ ***adj.*** not feeling or showing thanks (to sb) ▶ **un·grate·ful·ly** ***adv.***

**un·guard·ed** /ˌʌn'gɑrdəd/ ***adj.*** **1** not protected or watched: *The museum was unguarded at night.* ◇ *an unguarded fire* (= that has nothing to stop people from burning themselves on it) **2** (used about a remark, look, etc.) said or done carelessly, at a time when you are not thinking about the effects of your words or are not paying attention: *an unguarded response/remark* ◇ *It was something I'd let out* ***in an unguarded moment***.

★**un·hap·py** /ʌn'hæpi/ ***adj.*** (**un·hap·pi·er**; **un·hap·pi·est**) **1 unhappy (about sth)** sad or miserable; not happy: *She's very unhappy about losing her job.* ◇ *an unhappy childhood* **2 unhappy (about/with sth)** not satisfied or pleased; worried: *I'm still unhappy about the way this dress looks.* ▶ **un·hap·pi·ly** /-əli/ ***adv.*** ▶ **un·hap·pi·ness** ***noun*** [U]

**un·harmed** /ʌn'hɑrmd/ ***adj.*** not injured or damaged; not harmed: *All eight climbers were rescued unharmed.* SYN **unhurt**

**un·health·y** /ʌn'hɛlθi/ ***adj.*** (**un·health·i·er**; **un·health·i·est**) **1** not having or showing good health: *He looks pale and unhealthy.* **2** likely to cause illness or poor health: *unhealthy conditions* **3** not natural: *an unhealthy interest in torture*

**un·heard-of** /ʌn'hərdəv/ ***adj.*** not known; never having happened before: *Years ago, it was unheard-of for women to do jobs like that.*

**un·help·ful** /ʌn'hɛlpfl/ ***adj.*** not helpful or useful; not willing to help sb: *an unhelpful response/reply* ◇ *The taxi driver was being very unhelpful.* OPP **helpful**

**un·ho·ly** /ʌn'hoʊli/ ***adj.*** **1** dangerous; likely to be harmful: *an* ***unholy alliance*** *between the medical profession and the pharmaceutical industry* **2** not respecting the laws of a religion OPP **holy** **3** (only *before* a noun) (*informal*) (used to emphasize how bad sth is): *She wondered how she had got into this unholy mess.* ◇ *There was an unholy racket being made next door.*

**un·hook** /ʌn'hʊk/ ***verb*** [T] **unhook sth (from sth)** to remove sth from a hook; to undo the hooks on clothes, etc.: *She unhooked her bra.*

**un·hurt** /ʌn'hərt/ ***adj.*** not injured or harmed: *He escaped from the crash unhurt.* SYN **unharmed**

**u·ni·cam·er·al** /ˌyunɪ'kæmərəl; -'kæmrəl/ ***adj.*** (*technical*) (used about a parliament) that has only one main governing body: *a unicameral legislature*

**u·ni·corn** /'yunəkɔrn/ ***noun*** [C] an imaginary animal that looks like a white horse and has one horn growing out of its forehead

**u·ni·cy·cle** /'yunəˌsaɪkl/ ***noun*** [C] a vehicle that is similar to a bicycle but that has only one wheel and is used by acrobats

**un·i·den·ti·fied** /ˌʌnaɪ'dɛntəfaɪd/ ***adj.*** whose identity is not known: *An unidentified body has been found in the river.* ➲ Look also at **UFO**.

**u·ni·form¹** /'yunəfɔrm/ ***adj.*** not changing; the same in all cases or at all times: *uniform safety standards across the country* ▶ **u·ni·for·mi·ty** /ˌyunə'fɔrməṭi/ ***noun*** [U]

★**u·ni·form²** /'yunəfɔrm/ ***noun*** [C,U] the set of clothes worn at work by the members of certain organizations or groups and by some students and sports teams: *Did you have to wear a school uniform?* ◇ *I didn't know he was a police officer because he wasn't in uniform.* ➲ picture at **baseball** ▶ **u·ni·formed** ***adj.***: *uniformed police officers*

**u·ni·fy** /'yunəfaɪ/ ***verb*** [T] (*pres. part.* **u·ni·fy·ing**; *3rd person sing. pres.* **u·ni·fies**; *pt, pp* **u·ni·fied**) to join or link separate parts together to make one unit, or to make them similar to each other ▶ **u·ni·fi·ca·tion** /ˌyunəfəˈkeɪʃn/ ***noun*** [U]

**u·ni·lat·er·al** /ˌyunəˈlæt̬ərəl/ ***adj.*** done by one member of a group or an organization without the agreement of the other members: *a unilateral decision* ◇ *a unilateral declaration of independence* ➲ Compare **multilateral**.

**un·im·ped·ed** /ˌʌnɪmˈpidəd/ ***adj.*** (*written*) with nothing blocking or stopping sb/sth: *an unimpeded view of the bay* ◇ *free and unimpeded trade*

**un·im·por·tant** /ˌʌnɪmˈpɔrtnt/ ***adj.*** not important: *They dismissed the problem as unimportant.* ◇ *This consideration was not unimportant.* ◇ *I was just a young girl from a small town and I felt very unimportant.*

**un·in·hab·it·a·ble** /ˌʌnɪnˈhæbət̬əbl/ ***adj.*** not possible to live in

**un·in·hab·it·ed** /ˌʌnɪnˈhæbət̬əd/ ***adj.*** with no people living there; not inhabited: *an uninhabited island*

**un·in·hib·it·ed** /ˌʌnɪnˈhɪbət̬əd/ ***adj.*** behaving in a free and natural way, showing what you feel without worrying what other people think of you

**un·in·sured** /ˌʌnɪnˈʃʊrd/ ***adj.*** not having or covered by insurance: *the cost of medical treatment for uninsured patients*

**un·in·tel·li·gi·ble** /ˌʌnɪnˈtɛlədʒəbl/ ***adj.*** impossible to understand

**un·in·ten·tion·al** /ˌʌnɪnˈtɛnʃənl/ ***adj.*** not done deliberately, but happening by accident: *Perhaps I misled you, but it was quite unintentional* (= I did not mean to). OPP **intentional**

**un·in·ter·est·ed** /ʌnˈɪntrəstəd; ʌnˈɪntərɛstəd/ ***adj.*** **uninterested (in sb/sth)** having or showing no interest in sb/sth: *She seemed uninterested in anything I had to say.* ➲ Look at **disinterested**. It has a different meaning.

**un·in·ter·rupt·ed** /ˌʌnɪntəˈrʌptəd/ ***adj.*** not stopped or blocked by anything; continuous and not interrupted: *We had an uninterrupted view of the stage.* ◇ *eight hours of uninterrupted sleep*

**un·in·vit·ed** /ˌʌnɪnˈvaɪt̬əd/ ***adj.*** doing sth or going somewhere when you have not been asked or invited to, especially when sb does not want you to: *uninvited guests at a party* ◇ *He turned up uninvited.*

★**un·ion** /ˈyunyən/ ***noun*** **1** [U, sing.] the act of joining or the situation of being joined: *the union of the separate groups into one organization* **2** [C] a group of people, organizations, countries, etc. that have been joined together to form one larger organization: *the European Union* **3** [C] (*also* **labor union**) an organization for people who do the same type of work. Unions try to get better pay and working conditions for their members.

★**u·nique** /yuˈnik/ ***adj.*** **1** unlike anything else; being the only one of its type: *Shakespeare made a unique contribution to the world of literature.* **2 unique to sb/sth** connected with only one place, person or thing: *This dance is unique to this region.* **3** very unusual: *There's nothing unique about that type of crime.*

**u·ni·sex** /ˈyunəsɛks/ ***adj.*** designed for and used by both men and women: *unisex fashions*

**u·ni·son** /ˈyunəsn/ ***noun***
IDM **in unison** saying, singing or doing the same thing at the same time as sb else: *"No, thank you," they said in unison.*

**u·nit** /ˈyunɪt/ ***noun*** [C]
➤SINGLE THING **1** a single thing which is complete in itself and is also part of sth larger: *The book is divided into ten units.*
➤MEASUREMENT **2** a fixed amount or number that is used as a standard of measurement: *a unit of currency*
➤GROUP OF PEOPLE **3** a group of people who perform a certain special function in a larger organization: *the intensive care unit of a hospital*
➤SMALL MACHINE **4** a small machine that performs a particular task or that is part of a larger machine: *The heart of a computer is the central processing unit.*
➤APARTMENT **5** an apartment in a large building: *There are four two-bedroom units on each floor.*
➤FURNITURE **6** a piece of furniture that can be connected to other pieces of furniture and has a particular use: *metal shelving units*

**U·ni·tar·i·an** /ˌyunəˈtɛriən/ ***noun*** [C] a member of a Christian church that does not believe in the Trinity (= the three forms of God: the Father, Jesus the Son and the Holy Spirit) ▶ **U·ni·tar·i·an** ***adj.***

★**u·nite** /yuˈnaɪt/ ***verb*** **1** [I,T] to join together and act in agreement; to make this happen: *Unless we unite, our enemies will defeat us.* ◇ *The President united his party behind him.* **2** [I] **unite (in sth/in doing sth)** to join together for a particular purpose: *We should all unite in seeking a solution to this terrible problem.*

★**u·nit·ed** /yuˈnaɪt̬əd/ ***adj.*** joined together by a common feeling or aim: *Throughout the crisis, the whole country remained united.*

**the Uˌnited ˈKingdom** ***noun*** (*abbr.* **U.K.**) England, Scotland, Wales and Northern Ireland

> NOTE **The UK** includes England, Scotland, Wales and Northern Ireland, but *not* the Republic of Ireland, which is a separate country. **Great Britain** is England, Scotland and Wales only. **The British Isles** include England, Scotland, Wales, Northern Ireland and the Republic of Ireland.

**the Uˌnited ˈNations** ***noun*** [sing.] (*abbr.* **UN**) the organization formed to encourage peace in the world and to deal with problems between nations

★**the Uˌnited ˈStates** (*also formal* **the Uˌnited ˌStates of Aˈmerica**) ***noun*** [sing.] (*abbr.* **U.S.**; **US**; **USA**) a large country in North America made up of 50 states and the District of Columbia

**u·ni·ty** /ˈyunət̬i/ ***noun*** [U] the situation in which people are united or in agreement

**Univ.** ***abbr.*** (*written*) University

**u·ni·ver·sal** /ˌyunəˈvərsl/ ***adj.*** connected with, done by or affecting everybody in the world or everybody in a particular group: *The environment is a universal concern.* ◇ *There was universal agreement that the festival was a success.* ▶ **u·ni·ver·sal·ly** ***adv.***

**ˌUniversal ˈProduct Code** ***noun*** [C] (*abbr.* **UPC**) Universal Product Code; a pattern of thick and thin parallel lines printed on products for sale



U

and which contains information that a computer can read SYN **bar code**

★**u·ni·verse** /'yunəvərs/ ***noun*** [sing.] **the universe** everything that exists, including the planets, stars, space, etc.

★**u·ni·ver·si·ty** /ˌyunə'vərsət̬i/ ***noun*** [C] (*pl.* **u·ni·ver·si·ties**) the highest level of educational institution, where students study for degrees and where people do academic research

NOTE Compare **college** and **university**. Both colleges and universities usually offer courses for students who are studying for their first degree (a **bachelor's degree**), while universities also offer courses for people who are studying for more advanced degrees. Note that in U.S. English, we use **college**, not **university**, in many expressions even when the place we are talking about has the word "University" in its name: *a college student* ◇ *"Where did you go to college?" "At Ohio State University."* In Canada, **colleges** offer courses for students in higher education, but in order to complete a **bachelor's degree**, students must usually go to a **university**. ➲ For more information about the education systems in both the U.S. and Canada, look at study pages **A8-9**.

**un·just** /ˌʌn'dʒʌst/ ***adj.*** not fair, right or reasonable: *an unjust legal system* ➲ noun **injustice**

**un·jus·ti·fied** /ˌʌn'dʒʌstəfaɪd/ ***adj.*** not fair or necessary: *The criticism was wholly unjustified.*

**un·kempt** /ˌʌn'kɛmpt/ ***adj.*** (used especially about sb's hair or general appearance) not well cared for; not neat or tidy: *greasy, unkempt hair* ◇ *The children were unwashed and unkempt.*

★**un·kind** /ˌʌn'kaɪnd/ ***adj.*** not friendly or thoughtful; cruel: *That was an unkind thing to say.* ▸ **un·kind·ly** ***adv.*** ▸ **un·kind·ness** ***noun*** [C,U]

**un·know·ing** /ˌʌn'noʊɪŋ/ ***adj.*** (*formal*) not aware of what you are doing or what is happening: *He was the unknowing cause of all the misunderstanding.* ▸ **un·know·ing·ly** ***adv.***: *She had unknowingly broken the rules.*

★**un·known**[1] /ˌʌn'noʊn/ ***adj.*** **1 unknown (to sb)** not known (by sb): *She left the job for unknown reasons.* **2** not famous or familiar to other people: *an unknown actress*

**un·known**[2] /ˌʌn'noʊn/ ***noun*** **1** (usually **the unknown**) [sing.] a place or thing that you know nothing about: *a fear of the unknown* **2** [C] a person who is not well-known by the public: *A complete unknown won the tournament.*

**un·law·ful** /ˌʌn'lɔfl/ ***adj.*** (*formal*) against the law; illegal: *He was charged with unlawful possession of a handgun.*

**un·lead·ed** /ˌʌn'lɛdəd/ ***adj.*** (used about gasoline) not containing the harmful substance, lead

**un·leash** /ʌn'liʃ/ ***verb*** [T] **unleash sth (on/upon sb/sth)** to suddenly let a strong force, emotion, etc. be felt or have an effect: *The governor's proposals unleashed a storm of protest in the press.*

**un·leav·ened** /ˌʌn'lɛvənd/ ***adj.*** (used about bread) made without any yeast and therefore flat and heavy

★**un·less** /ən'lɛs/ ***conj.*** if ... not; except if: *Unless something unexpected happens, I'll see you next week.* ◇ *I was told that unless my work improved, I would lose the job.* ◇ *Unless anyone has anything else to say, the meeting is finished.* ◇ *Don't use the oven unless I'm here.* ◇ *That's what I've decided to do – unless there are any objections.*

★**un·like** /ʌn'laɪk/ ***prep.*** **1** in contrast to; being different from: *Unlike all the others, I wasn't very interested in the idea.* ◇ *He's extremely ambitious, unlike me.* ◇ *She's unlike anyone else I've ever met.* **2** not typical of; unusual for: *It's unlike him to be late – he's usually right on time.*

★**un·like·ly** /ʌn'laɪkli/ ***adj.*** (**un·like·li·er**; **un·like·li·est**) **1** not likely to happen; not expected; not probable: *He is seriously ill and unlikely to recover.* ◇ *In the unlikely event of a fire, use the emergency exits.* ◇ *It's unlikely that I'll have any free time next week.* **2** difficult to believe: *an unlikely excuse*

**un·lim·it·ed** /ˌʌn'lɪmət̬əd/ ***adj.*** without limit; as much or as great as you want

**un·list·ed** /ˌʌn'lɪstəd/ ***adj.*** (used about a telephone number) not included in the list of telephone numbers in the telephone book so that it is not known by the public

★**un·load** /ˌʌn'loʊd/ ***verb*** **1** [I,T] **unload (sth) (from/off sth)** to take things that have been transported off or out of a vehicle: *to unload freight off a truck* ◇ *I unloaded the car when I got home from the mall.* **2** [I,T] (used about a vehicle) to have the things removed that have been transported: *Parking here is restricted to vehicles that are loading or unloading.* **3** [T] **unload sb/sth (on/onto sb)** (*informal*) to get rid of sth you do not want or to pass it to sb else

**un·lock** /ˌʌn'lɑk/ ***verb*** [T] to open the lock on sth using a key

**un·luck·y** /ʌn'lʌki/ ***adj.*** (**un·luck·i·er**; **un·luck·i·est**) having or causing bad luck; not lucky: *They were unlucky to lose because they played so well.* ◇ *Thirteen is often thought to be an unlucky number.*

**un·manned** /ˌʌn'mænd/ ***adj.*** if a machine, vehicle or place is unmanned, it does not have or need a person to control or operate it: *an unmanned spacecraft/station*

**un·mar·ried** /ˌʌn'mærid/ ***adj.*** not married; single: *unmarried mothers*

**un·men·tion·a·ble** /ʌn'mɛnʃənəbl/ ***adj.*** too shocking or embarrassing to be mentioned or spoken about: *an unmentionable disease/subject*

**un·mis·tak·a·ble** /ˌʌnmɪ'steɪkəbl/ ***adj.*** clear and obvious; easy to recognize ▸ **un·mis·tak·a·bly** /-əbli/ ***adv.***

**un·mit·i·gat·ed** /ʌn'mɪt̬əgeɪt̬əd/ ***adj.*** (only *before* a noun) (used to mean "complete," usually when describing sth bad): *The evening was an unmitigated disaster.*

**un·moved** /ˌʌn'muvd/ ***adj.*** not affected emotionally; feeling no sympathy, pity, sadness, etc.

**un·named** /ˌʌn'neɪmd/ ***adj.*** whose name is not given or not known: *information from an unnamed source*

**un·nat·u·ral** /ʌn'nætʃərəl/ ***adj.*** different from what is normal or expected; not natural, often in a

U

way that seems morally wrong ▸ **un·nat·u·ral·ly** ***adv.***: *unnaturally quiet*

★**un·nec·es·sar·y** /ʌnˈnɛsəˌsɛri/ ***adj.*** not necessary; more than is needed or acceptable: *It was unnecessary to ask because I already knew the answer.* ◇ *unnecessary expense* ▸ **un·nec·es·sar·i·ly** /ʌnˌnɛsəˈsɛrəli/ ***adv.***: *unnecessarily expensive*

**un·nerve** /ˌʌnˈnərv/ ***verb*** [T] to make sb feel nervous or frightened or lose confidence ▸ **un·nerv·ing** ***adj.***

**un·no·ticed** /ˌʌnˈnoʊt̬əst/ ***adj.*** not noticed or seen: *All my hard work went completely unnoticed.*

**un·ob·tru·sive** /ˌʌnəbˈtrusɪv/ ***adj.*** (*formal*) not attracting unnecessary attention: *The service at the hotel is efficient and unobtrusive.* ▸ **un·ob·tru·sive·ly** ***adv.***

**un·oc·cu·pied** /ˌʌnˈɑkyəpaɪd/ ***adj.*** **1** empty, with nobody living there or using it: *an unoccupied house* ◇ *I sat down at the nearest unoccupied table.* **2** of a region or country not controlled by foreign soldiers: *unoccupied territory*

**un·of·fi·cial** /ˌʌnəˈfɪʃl/ ***adj.*** **1** not accepted or approved by a person or people in authority: *an unofficial strike* **2** not known by the public: *The news of his resignation is still unofficial.* ▸ **un·of·fi·cial·ly** ***adv.***

**un·or·tho·dox** /ˌʌnˈɔrθədɑks/ ***adj.*** different from what is generally accepted, usual or traditional: *unorthodox medical treatments*

**un·pack** /ˌʌnˈpæk/ ***verb*** [I,T] to take out the things that were in a bag, suitcase, etc.: *When we got to the hotel, we unpacked and went straight to the beach.* ◇ *to unpack a suitcase*

**un·paid** /ˌʌnˈpeɪd/ ***adj.*** **1** not yet paid: *an unpaid bill* **2** not receiving money for work done: *an unpaid assistant* **3** (used about work) done without payment: *unpaid overtime*

**un·per·turbed** /ˌʌnpərˈtərbd/ ***adj.*** not worried or anxious: *She seemed unperturbed by the news.*

★**un·pleas·ant** /ʌnˈplɛznt/ ***adj.*** (*formal*) **1** causing you to have a bad feeling; not pleasant: *unpleasant memories* **2** not friendly; not polite: *unpleasant coworkers*

**un·plug** /ˌʌnˈplʌg/ ***verb*** [T] (**un·plug·ging**; **un·plugged**) to disconnect a piece of electrical equipment by removing the plug from the socket: *Be sure to unplug the iron when you're done with it.*

**un·plugged™** /ˌʌnˈplʌgd/ ***adj.*** (used about pop or rock music or musicians) performed or performing with acoustic rather than electric instruments: *Bob Dylan unplugged*

**un·pop·u·lar** /ˌʌnˈpɑpyələr/ ***adj.*** **unpopular (with sb)** not popular; not liked by many people: *an unpopular politician* ◇ *a product that was unpopular with consumers* ▸ **un·pop·u·lar·i·ty** /ˌʌnˌpɑpyəˈlærət̬i/ ***noun*** [U]

**un·prec·e·dent·ed** /ʌnˈprɛsədɛntəd/ ***adj.*** never having happened or existed before, or greater than anything that has happened or existed before: *an unprecedented number of visitors to the fair*

**un·pre·dict·a·ble** /ˌʌnprɪˈdɪktəbl/ ***adj.*** changing often so that you do not know what to expect: *unpredictable behavior*

**un·pre·ten·tious** /ˌʌnprɪˈtɛnʃəs/ ***adj.*** not trying to appear more special, intelligent, important, etc. than you really are OPP **pretentious**

**un·prin·ci·pled** /ʌnˈprɪnsəpld/ ***adj.*** without moral principles SYN **dishonest**

**un·pro·duc·tive** /ˌʌnprəˈdʌktɪv/ ***adj.*** not producing very much; not producing good results: *an unproductive discussion/meeting* ◇ *I've had a very unproductive day.*

**un·pro·fes·sion·al** /ˌʌnprəˈfɛʃənl/ ***adj.*** not reaching the standard expected in a particular profession: *She was found guilty of unprofessional conduct.*

**un·pro·tec·ted** /ˌʌnprəˈtɛktəd/ ***adj.*** not safe; that could be harmed or that could harm sb/sth IDM **unprotected sex** sex that could cause a sexual disease such as AIDS to be passed from one person to another, e.g. because of not using a condom

**un·pro·voked** /ˌʌnprəˈvoʊkt/ ***adj.*** not caused by an earlier action: *an unprovoked attack*

**un·qual·i·fied** /ʌnˈkwɑləfaɪd/ ***adj.*** **1** not having the qualifications or knowledge for sth: *unqualified job applicants* ◇ *Most applicants were unqualified for the job.* ◇ *I'm unqualified to offer an opinion on this matter.* **2** (only *before* a noun) (*formal*) complete; absolute: *an unqualified success*

**un·ques·tion·a·ble** /ʌnˈkwɛstʃənəbl/ ***adj.*** certain; that cannot be doubted ▸ **un·ques·tion·a·bly** /-əbli/ ***adv.***: *She is unquestionably the richest woman in the world.*

**un·quote** /ˈʌnkwoʊt/ ***verb***
IDM **quote ... unquote** → QUOTE[1]

**un·rav·el** /ʌnˈrævəl/ ***verb*** [I,T] **1** (used about threads or fabric) to start to come apart: *The sleeve of my sweater started to unravel.* **2** (used about a complicated story, etc.) to become or to make sth become clear: *detectives trying to unravel the mystery of her disappearance*

**un·real** /ˌʌnˈril/ ***adj.*** **1** (usually not before a noun) very strange and seeming to be imagined: *The whole situation was really weird – it just seemed so unreal.* **2** not real; imagined: *His theory only works under unreal conditions.*

**un·re·al·is·tic** /ˌʌnriəˈlɪstɪk/ ***adj.*** not based on facts or accepting a situation as it really is: *unrealistic expectations*

★**un·rea·son·a·ble** /ʌnˈrizn·əbl/ ***adj.*** **1** not willing to listen to other people; acting without good reasons: *I think she is being totally unreasonable.* **2** too great; expecting too much: *He makes unreasonable demands on his employees.* ▸ **un·rea·son·a·bly** /-əbli/ ***adv.***

**un·rec·og·niz·a·ble** /ˌʌnrɛkəgˈnaɪzəbl; -ˈrɛkəgnaɪ-/ ***adj.*** (used about a person or thing) so changed or damaged that you do not recognize them or it: *He was unrecognizable without his beard.*

**un·re·lat·ed** /ˌʌnrɪˈleɪt̬əd/ ***adj.*** not connected; not related to sth else: *The two events were totally unrelated.* ◇ *In my free time I like to do things that are unrelated to my work.*

**un·re·lent·ing** /ˌʌnrɪˈlɛntɪŋ/ ***adj.*** (*written*) **1** (used about an unpleasant situation) not stopping or becoming less severe: *unrelenting criticism/*

U

*pressure* ◇ *The heat was unrelenting.* SYN **relentless** **2** if a person is unrelenting, he/she continues with sth without considering the feelings of other people: *He was unrelenting in his search for the truth about his father.*

**un·re·li·a·ble** /ˌʌnrɪˈlaɪəbl/ *adj.* that you cannot trust or depend on: *an unreliable source of information*

**un·re·quit·ed** /ˌʌnrɪˈkwaɪţəd/ *adj.* (*formal*) (used about love) not returned by the person that you love

**un·re·solved** /ˌʌnrɪˈzɑlvd/ *adj.* (*formal*) (used about a problem or question) not yet solved or answered; not having been resolved

**un·res·pon·sive** /ˌʌnrɪˈspɑnsɪv/ *adj.* **unresponsive (to sth)** (*formal*) not reacting to sb/sth; not giving the response that you would expect or hope for: *a politician who is unresponsive to the mood of the country* ◇ *She is a cold, unfeeling and unresponsive woman.*

**un·rest** /ˌʌnˈrɛst/ ***noun*** [U] a situation in which people are angry or dissatisfied and likely to protest or fight: *social unrest*

**un·ri·valed** /ʌnˈraɪvld/ *adj.* better than any other of the same type; having no rival: *The hotel offers guests an unrivaled view of the coastline.*

**un·roll** /ˌʌnˈroʊl/ ***verb*** [I,T] to open from a rolled position: *He unrolled the poster and put it up on the wall.*

**un·ru·ly** /ʌnˈruli/ *adj.* difficult to control; without discipline: *an unruly crowd* ▶ **un·ru·li·ness** ***noun*** [U]

**un·safe** /ʌnˈseɪf/ *adj.* **1** dangerous; that could cause harm or damage: *That ladder looks very unsafe.* **2** in danger: *He felt very unsafe walking through the streets alone.*

**un·said** /ʌnˈsɛd/ *adj.* thought but not spoken: *Some things are better* ***left unsaid***.

**un·sat·is·fac·to·ry** /ˌʌnsæţəsˈfæktəri/ *adj.* not good enough: *Some students have been making unsatisfactory progress this semester.*

**un·sat·u·rat·ed** /ˌʌnˈsætʃəreɪţəd/ *adj.* unsaturated fats are easily dealt with by the body when eaten, because of the way their chemical structure is arranged: *soft spread with a high percentage of unsaturated fats* ➲ Look at **polyunsaturated** and **saturated fat**.

**un·sa·vor·y** /ˌʌnˈseɪvəri/ *adj.* unpleasant; that you do not trust: *an unsavory individual*

**un·scathed** /ˌʌnˈskeɪðd/ *adj.* not hurt; without injury: *He came out of the fight unscathed.*

**un·scram·ble** /ˌʌnˈskræmbl/ ***verb*** [T] to change a word, message, television signal, etc. that has been sent in a secret form (code) so that it can be read or understood

**un·screw** /ˌʌnˈskru/ ***verb*** [T] **1** to remove the screws from sth **2** to open sth by turning it: *Could you unscrew the top of this bottle for me?*

**un·scrip·ted** /ˌʌnˈskrɪptəd/ *adj.* (used about a speech, broadcast, etc.) not written or prepared in detail in advance

**un·scru·pu·lous** /ʌnˈskrupyələs/ *adj.* willing to be dishonest, cruel or unfair in order to get what you want

**un·seas·on·a·ble** /ʌnˈsizənəbl/ *adj.* (used about the weather) unusual for the time of year

**un·seen** /ˌʌnˈsin/ *adj.*
IDM **sight unseen** → SIGHT[1]

**un·set·tling** /ʌnˈsɛţl·ɪŋ/ *adj.* making you feel upset, nervous or worried: *Seeing Nicky again after so long was an unsettling experience.* ◇ *The country's economic crisis had an unsettling effect on world markets.*

**un·shav·en** /ˌʌnˈʃeɪvn/ *adj.* not having shaved or been shaved recently: *He looked pale and unshaven.* ◇ *his unshaven face*

**un·sight·ly** /ʌnˈsaɪtli/ *adj.* (*formal*) very unpleasant to look at; ugly: *an unsightly stain*

**un·skilled** /ˌʌnˈskɪld/ *adj.* not having or requiring special skill or training: *an unskilled job*

**un·so·lic·it·ed** /ˌʌnsəˈlɪsəţəd/ *adj.* not asked for: *unsolicited advice*

**un·solved** /ˌʌnˈsɑlvd/ *adj.* not having been solved: *an unsolved murder/mystery/problem*

**un·so·phis·ti·cat·ed** /ˌʌnsəˈfɪstəkeɪţəd/ *adj.* **1** not having or showing much experience of the world and social situations: *unsophisticated tastes/people* **2** simple and basic; not complicated: *unsophisticated equipment/methods* SYN **crude** (2)

**un·sound** /ˌʌnˈsaʊnd/ *adj.* **1** in poor condition; weak: *The building is structurally unsound.* **2** based on wrong ideas and therefore mistaken

**un·spec·i·fied** /ʌnˈspɛsəfaɪd/ *adj.* (only *before* a noun) that has not been mentioned specifically: *The man is being held under guard at an unspecified location.*

**un·spo·ken** /ʌnˈspoʊkən/ *adj.* that has not been said, but is understood by everyone involved: *the unspoken message behind the governor's comments*

**un·sta·ble** /ˌʌnˈsteɪbl/ *adj.* **1** likely to fall down or move; not firmly fastened **2** likely to change or fail: *a period of unstable government* **3** (used about a person's moods or behavior) likely to change suddenly or frequently: *an unstable personality*

**un·stead·y** /ʌnˈstɛdi/ *adj.* **1** not completely in control of your movements so that you might fall: *She is still a little* ***unsteady on her feet*** *after the operation.* **2** shaking or moving in a way that is not controlled: *an unsteady hand/voice/step*

**un·stop·pa·ble** /ʌnˈstɑpəbl/ *adj.* that cannot be stopped or prevented: *an unstoppable rise in prices* ◇ *When the team is playing well, they are unstoppable.*

★**un·suc·cess·ful** /ˌʌnsəkˈsɛsfl/ *adj.* not having or resulting in success: *an unsuccessful politician* ◇ *an unsuccessful attempt to climb the mountain* ▶ **un·suc·cess·ful·ly** *adv.*

**un·suit·a·ble** /ʌnˈsuţəbl/ *adj.* **unsuitable (for sb/sth)** not right or suitable: *material on the Internet that is unsuitable for children*

**un·sung** /ˌʌnˈsʌŋ/ *adj.* (*formal*) not praised or famous but deserving to be: *the* ***unsung heroes*** *of the war*

**un·sure** /ˌʌnˈʃʊr/ *adj.* **1 unsure (about/of sth)** not certain; having doubts: *I didn't argue because I was unsure of the facts.* **2 unsure (of**

**yourself)** not feeling confident about yourself: *He's young and still feels unsure of himself.*

**un·sus·pect·ing** /ˌʌnsəˈspɛktɪŋ/ ***adj.*** (only *before* a noun) not aware of danger: *He came up quietly behind his unsuspecting victim.*

**un·tamed** /ˌʌnˈteɪmd/ ***adj.*** (*written*) allowed to remain in a wild state; not changed, controlled or influenced by anyone; not tamed: *a wild and untamed landscape* ◇ *Her untamed curls fell around her face.*

**un·tan·gle** /ˌʌnˈtæŋgl/ ***verb*** [T] to separate threads, etc. which have become tied together in a confused way: *The wires got mixed up, and it took me a long time to untangle them.*

**un·think·a·ble** /ˌʌnˈθɪŋkəbl/ ***adj.*** (used of an event, etc.) impossible to imagine or consider, especially because it is too painful or difficult

**un·think·ing** /ˌʌnˈθɪŋkɪŋ/ ***adj.*** done, said, etc. without thinking carefully ▸ **un·think·ing·ly** ***adv.***

**un·tie** /ʌnˈtaɪ/ ***verb*** [T] (*pres. part.* **un·ty·ing**; *3rd person sing. pres.* **un·ties**; *pt, pp* **un·tied**) to undo a knot; to free sb by undoing a rope, etc.: *I can't get this knot untied.*

★**un·til¹** /ənˈtɪl/ (*also informal* **'til, till**) ***conj.*** up to the time when: *She waited until he was finished.* ◇ *You have to stay in school until you're 16.* ◇ *We won't leave until the police get here* (= we won't leave before they come). ➲ Look at the note at **until²**.

★**un·til²** /ənˈtɪl/ (*also informal* **'til, till**) ***prep.*** up to the time or the event mentioned: *The restaurant is open until midnight.* ◇ *Until that moment, she had been happy.* ◇ *We can't leave until 10 o'clock* (= we can leave at 10 but not before).

> NOTE We can use **until** in both formal and informal English. **Till/'til** are more common in informal English and are not usually used at the beginning of a sentence. Make sure that you only use **till/until** to talk about a time. We use **as far as** to talk about distance: *I walked as far as the river.* We use **up to** to talk about a number: *You can spend up to $20 on each person's present.*

**un·time·ly** /ʌnˈtaɪmli/ ***adj.*** (*formal*) happening too soon or sooner than is normal or expected: *She met a tragic and **untimely** death at 25.* ◇ *A cough from the doorway brought an untimely end to their embrace.* SYN **premature**

**un·told** /ˌʌnˈtoʊld/ ***adj.*** (*formal*) (only *before* a noun) very great; so big, etc. that you cannot count it: *untold suffering* ◇ *untold wealth*

**un·touch·a·ble** /ʌnˈtʌtʃəbl/ ***adj.*** **1** a person who is untouchable is in a position where he/she is unlikely to be punished or criticized: *Given his political connections, he thought he was untouchable.* **2** that cannot be touched or changed by other people: *The department's budget is untouchable.*

**un·true** /ˌʌnˈtru/ ***adj.*** **1** not true; not based on facts: *These accusations are totally untrue.* ◇ *an untrue claim/statement* ◇ *It would be untrue to say that something like this could never happen again.* **2 untrue (to sb/sth)** not loyal to sb/sth: *If he agreed to their demands, he would have to be untrue to his own principles.*

**un·trust·worth·y** /ʌnˈtrʌstwərði/ ***adj.*** that cannot be trusted or relied on

**un·truth·ful** /ʌnˈtruθfl/ ***adj.*** saying things that you know are not true: *an untruthful statement*

**un·used¹** /ˌʌnˈyuzd/ ***adj.*** that has not been used: *an unused stamp*

**un·used²** /ˌʌnˈyust/ ***adj.*** **unused to sth** not having any experience of sth; not accustomed to sth: *She was unused to so much attention.*

★**un·u·su·al** /ʌnˈyuʒuəl; -ˈyuʒl/ ***adj.*** **1** not expected or usual: *It's unusual for Joe to be late.* **2** interesting because it is different: *What an unusual hat!*

★**un·u·su·al·ly** /ʌnˈyuʒuəli; -ˈyuʒl·i/ ***adv.*** (usually before an adjective or adverb) **1** more than is common; extremely: *an unusually hot summer* **2** in a way that is not normal or typical of sb/sth: *She remained unusually quiet during the meeting.*

**un·veil** /ˌʌnˈveɪl/ ***verb*** [T] to remove a type of cloth or curtain in order to show a new painting, etc. to the public: *The governor unveiled a plaque and opened the new technology center.* ◇ (*figurative*) *The President unveiled his new plan today to create more jobs.*

**un·want·ed** /ˌʌnˈwɑntəd/ ***adj.*** not wanted: *an unwanted pregnancy* ◇ *a cream to remove unwanted hair*

**un·war·rant·ed** /ʌnˈwɔrəntəd; -ˈwɑr-/ ***adj.*** that is not deserved or for which there is no good reason

**un·wel·come** /ʌnˈwɛlkəm/ ***adj.*** not wanted or welcome, especially because it is unpleasant: *They received some unwelcome news yesterday.*

**un·well** /ʌnˈwɛl/ ***adj.*** (*formal*) (not before a noun) sick: *She said she was feeling unwell and went home.*

**un·wield·y** /ʌnˈwildi/ ***adj.*** difficult to move or carry because it is too big, heavy, etc.: *an unwieldy box*

**un·will·ing** /ʌnˈwɪlɪŋ/ ***adj.*** not wanting to do sth

**un·wind** /ˌʌnˈwaɪnd/ ***verb*** (*pt, pp* **un·wound** /-ˈwaʊnd/) **1** [I,T] (used of sth that is wound around sth else) to become undone or to be pulled out: *The cord had unwound.* **2** [I] to relax, especially after working hard: *After a hard day at the office, it takes me a couple of hours to unwind.*

**un·wise** /ˌʌnˈwaɪz/ ***adj.*** **unwise (to do sth)** showing a lack of good judgment: *an unwise decision/investment* SYN **foolish**

**un·wit·ting** /ʌnˈwɪṭɪŋ/ ***adj.*** not realizing sth; not intending to do sth: *experiments that were performed on unwitting subjects* ▸ **un·wit·ting·ly** ***adv.***: *The company may have unwittingly broken the law.*

**un·writ·ten** /ʌnˈrɪtn/ ***adj.*** not existing in written form, but known and accepted by the people involved: *an unwritten agreement*

**un·zip** /ˌʌnˈzɪp/ ***verb*** [T] (**un·zip·ping**; **un·zipped**) to open sth that had been closed or fastened with a zipper

★**up¹** /ʌp/ ***prep., adv.*** ➲ For special uses with many verbs e.g. **pick sth up**, look at the verb entries. **1** to a high or higher level or position: *The monkey climbed up the tree.* ◇ *I carried her suitcase up to the third floor.* ◇ *I walked up the hill.* **2** into an upright position: *Everybody stood up when the judge entered the courtroom.* ◇ *I had to get up early.* **3**



U

(used for showing that an action continues until it is completed): *Eat up – it's a long time until supper.* **4** (used with verbs of closing): *Zip up your coat. It's cold.* ◇ *She tied the package up with string.* **5** very close to a person or thing: *She ran up to her mother and kissed her.* **6** further along: *I live just up the street.* **7** in a particular direction, usually north: *We're going up to Minnesota tomorrow.* **8** into pieces: *We chopped the old boards up and used them for firewood.* **9** (used for showing that sth is increasing): *Prices have gone up.* ◇ *Turn the volume up.*

IDM **be up to sb** to be sb's responsibility: *I can't make the decision. It's not up to me.*

**be up to your ears/eyes/neck in sth** (*informal*) to have more of sth than you can easily do or manage: *I can't go out tonight – I'm up to my eyes in work.*

**up and down 1** rising and falling: *We knew she was still alive – her chest was moving up and down.* ◇ *The kids were jumping up and down with excitement.* **2** backward and forward: *He was running up and down the block, screaming with pain.*

**up to sth 1** as much/many as: *We're expecting up to 100 people at the meeting.* **2** until a particular point in time: *Up to now, things have been easy.* **3** capable of sth: *I don't feel up to cooking this evening. I'm too tired.* **4** doing sth secret and perhaps forbidden: *What are the kids up to? Go and see.*

★**up²** /ʌp/ ***adj.*** (not before a noun) **be up 1** at a higher level or position than before: *Sales are up for the third year in a row.* **2** awake and not in bed: *Aren't you up yet?* **3** (used about a period of time) finished: *Stop writing. Your time's up.* **4** (used about computers) working; in operation: *Are the computers back up yet?*

IDM **be up and running** (used about sth new) to be working well: *The new system is already up and running.*

**what's up?** (*informal*) what's happening?

**up³** /ʌp/ ***noun***

IDM **ups and downs** both good and bad luck: *Our marriage is happy, but we've had our ups and downs.*

**ˌup-and-ˈcoming** ***adj.*** (only *before* a noun) likely to be successful and popular in the future: *up-and-coming young actors*

**up·beat** /ˈʌpbit/ ***adj.*** (*informal*) positive and enthusiastic; making you feel that the future will be good: *The tone of the speech was upbeat.* ◇ *The presentation ended on an upbeat note.* OPP **downbeat**

**up·bring·ing** /ˈʌpbrɪŋɪŋ/ ***noun*** [sing.] the way a child is treated and taught how to behave by his/her parents: *a religious upbringing*

**UPC** /ˌyu pi ˈsi/ ***abbr.*** (*technical*) = UNIVERSAL PRODUCT CODE

**up·chuck** /ˈʌptʃʌk/ ***verb*** [I] (*informal*) to vomit

**up·com·ing** /ˈʌpkʌmɪŋ/ ***adj.*** (only *before* a noun) going to happen soon: *a schedule of upcoming events*

**up·date** /ˈʌpdeɪt; ˌʌpˈdeɪt/ ***verb*** [T] **1** to make sth more modern **2** to put the latest information into sth; to give sb the latest information: *Our database of addresses is updated regularly.* ◇ *Let me update you on what happened at the meeting.* ▶ **up·date** /ˈʌpdeɪt/ ***noun*** [C]: *an update on a news story* (= the latest information)

**up·grade** /ˈʌpgreɪd; ˌʌpˈgreɪd/ ***verb*** [T] to change sth so that it is of a higher standard ▶ **up·grade** /ˈʌpgreɪd/ ***noun*** [C]: *an upgrade of the computer system*

**up·heav·al** /ʌpˈhivl/ ***noun*** [C,U] a sudden big change, especially one that causes a lot of trouble

**up·hill** /ˌʌpˈhɪl/ ***adj.*** **1** going up a slope, toward the top of a hill OPP **downhill 2** (only *before* a noun) needing a lot of effort: *It was an uphill struggle to find a job.* ▶ **up·hill** ***adv.***: *a long walk uphill*

**up·hold** /ˌʌpˈhoʊld/ ***verb*** [T] (*pt, pp* **up·held** /-ˈhɛld/) to support sth (a decision, etc.) especially when other people are against it: *The Supreme Court upheld the lower court's decision.*

**up·hol·stered** /əˈpoʊlstərd/ ***adj.*** (used about a chair, etc.) covered with cloth, with a layer of soft material underneath

**up·hol·ster·y** /əˈpoʊlstəri/ ***noun*** [U] the thick soft materials used to cover chairs, car seats, etc.

**up·keep** /ˈʌpkip/ ***noun*** [U] the cost or process of keeping sth in a good condition: *The landlord pays for the upkeep of the building.*

**up·lift·ing** /ˌʌpˈlɪftɪŋ/ ***adj.*** producing a feeling of hope and happiness: *an uplifting speech*

**up·load¹** /ˈʌploʊd/ ***verb*** [T] (*computing*) to move data to a larger computer system from a smaller one OPP **download**

**up·load²** /ˈʌploʊd/ ***noun*** [C] (*computing*) data that has been moved to a larger computer system from a smaller one OPP **download**

★**up·on** /əˈpɑn/ ***prep.*** (*formal*) on: *a story based upon real events* ◇ *The singer was surrounded by reporters upon arrival at the airport.*

IDM **once upon a time** → ONCE¹

★**up·per** /ˈʌpər/ ***adj.*** in a higher position than sth else; situated above sth: *the upper floors of a building* ◇ *the upper lip* OPP **lower**

IDM **gain/get/have the upper hand** to get into a stronger position than another person; to gain or have control over sb

**up·per·case** /ˌʌpərˈkeɪs/ ***adj.***, ***noun*** [U] (in) letters that are written or printed in a large form; (in) capital letters: *"FBI" is always written in uppercase letters.* OPP **lowercase**

**ˌupper ˈclass** ***adj.***, ***noun*** [C] (of) the highest social and economic class; people with a lot of money which may have been passed down to them by older members of their family

**up·per·class·man** /ˌʌpərˈklæsmən/ ***noun*** [C] (*pl.* **up·per·class·men** /-mən/) (*U.S.*) a student who is in his/her third or fourth year in high school or college ➲ Look at **underclassman**.

**up·per·most** /ˈʌpərmoʊst/ ***adj.*** in the highest or most important position: *Concern for her family was uppermost in her mind.*

**up·pi·ty** /ˈʌpət̬i/ ***adj.*** (*informal*) behaving as if you are more important than you really are, especially when this means that you refuse to obey orders

**up·right¹** /ˈʌpraɪt/ ***adj.*** **1** with a straight back; standing vertically: *Please put the back of your seat* *in an upright position.* **2** honest and responsible: *an upright citizen*

**upright²** /ˌʌpˈraɪt/ ***adv.*** **1** with a straight back: *to stand upright* **2** in or into a vertical position: *to hold sth upright*

**up·ris·ing** /ˈʌpraɪzɪŋ/ ***noun*** [C] a situation in which a group of people start to fight against the people in power in their country: *an armed uprising*

**up·roar** /ˈʌprɔr/ ***noun*** [sing., U] a loud noise of excitement, confusion, anger, etc.; an angry discussion about sth: *The meeting ended in uproar.*

**up·root** /ˌʌpˈrut/ ***verb*** [T] **1** to tear up a plant by the roots: *Strong winds had uprooted the tree.* **2** to force sb to leave his/her home and move to a new place

**up·scale** /ˈʌpskeɪl/ ***adj.*** for or connected with people from a high social and economic class: *an upscale hotel*

★**up·set¹** /ˌʌpˈsɛt/ ***verb*** [T] (*pres. part.* **up·set·ting**; *pt, pp* **up·set**) **1** to make sb worry or feel unhappy: *The pictures of starving children upset her.* **2** to make sth go wrong: *to upset someone's plans* **3** to make sb sick in the stomach: *Rich food usually upsets my stomach.* **4** to defeat sb in a competition, sports game, etc. when you were expected to lose: *The Bears upset the Cowboys 17-10.*

★**up·set²** /ˌʌpˈsɛt/ ***adj.*** **1** worried and unhappy: *She looked very upset about something.* **2** slightly sick: *I've got an upset stomach.*

**NOTE** Note that the adjective is pronounced /ˈʌpsɛt/ when it comes before a noun and /ˌʌpˈsɛt/ in other positions in the sentence.

**up·set³** /ˈʌpsɛt/ ***noun*** **1** [C,U] the act of UPSETTING¹ (1,2) or being upset: *recent economic upsets* **2** [C] a slight illness in your stomach: *a stomach upset* **3** [C] an unexpected victory in a competition, sports game, etc.: *Williams' stunning upset of the world champion*

**up·shot** /ˈʌpʃɑt/ ***noun*** [C, sing.] **the upshot** the final result of a particular series of events: *The upshot of it all was that he left college and got a job.*

**upside down**

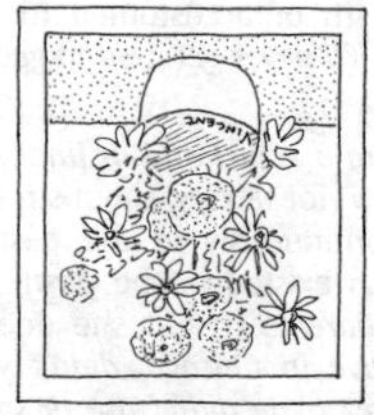
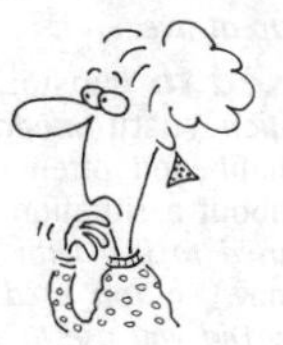

The painting is **upside down**.

★**up·side down** /ˌʌpsaɪd ˈdaʊn/ ***adj., adv.*** with the top part turned to the bottom: *You're holding the picture upside down.* ◇ *She was hanging upside down.* OPP **right side up**

**IDM** **turn sth upside down** (*informal*) to make sth very messy: *He turned the house upside down looking for his keys.*

**up·si·lon** /ˈʌpsəlɑn; ˈup-; ˈyup-/ ***noun*** [C] (*symbol* Υ, υ) the twentieth letter of the Greek alphabet ➲ Look at the note at **fraternity**.

**up·stage¹** /ˌʌpˈsteɪdʒ/ ***adv.*** at or toward the back of the stage in a theater

**up·stage²** /ˌʌpˈsteɪdʒ/ ***verb*** [T] (usually passive) to say or do sth that makes people notice you more than the person that they should be interested in: *She was furious at being upstaged by her younger sister.*

★**up·stairs¹** /ˌʌpˈstɛrz/ ***adv.*** to or on the upper floor of a building: *to go upstairs* ◇ *She's sleeping upstairs.*
▸ **up·stairs** /ˈʌpstɛrz/ ***adj.***: *an upstairs window*

**up·stairs²** /ˌʌpˈstɛrz/ ***noun*** [sing.] (*informal*) **the upstairs** the upper floor of a house: *We're going to paint the upstairs.*

**up·stand·ing** /ˌʌpˈstændɪŋ/ ***adj.*** (*formal*) behaving in a moral and honest way: *an upstanding member of the community* ➲ **upright¹**(2)

**up·state** /ˈʌpsteɪt/ ***adj.*** (only *before* a noun) in the northern part of a state: *a town in upstate New York*
▸ **up·state** /ʌpˈsteɪt/ ***adv.***

**up·stream** /ˌʌpˈstrim/ ***adv.*** moving against the direction that a river flows: *He swam slowly upstream.*

**up·surge** /ˈʌpsərdʒ/ ***noun*** [C, usually sing.] **an upsurge (in sth)** a sudden increase of sth: *an upsurge in violent crime*

**up·swing** /ˈʌpswɪŋ/ ***noun*** [usually sing.] (*written*) **an upswing (in sth)** a situation in which sth improves or increases over a period of time: *an upswing in economic activity* SYN **upturn**

**up·take** /ˈʌpteɪk/ ***noun*** [U, sing.] **1** the use that is made of sth that has become available: *There has been a high uptake of the free training.* **2** **uptake (of sth)** (*technical*) the process by which sth is taken into a body or system; the rate at which this happens: *the uptake of oxygen by muscles*

**IDM** **be quick/slow on the uptake** (*informal*) to be quick/slow to understand sth: *Is he always this slow on the uptake?*

**up·tight** /ˌʌpˈtaɪt/ ***adj.*** **1** nervous; unable to relax: *He always gets uptight before a test.* **2** angry: *Don't get so uptight – it's only a game.*

**up-to-date** /ˌʌptəˈdeɪt/ ***adj.*** (only *before* a noun) **1** modern: *up-to-date equipment* **2** having the most recent information: *an up-to-date dictionary* ➲ Look also at the expression *up to date* at **date¹**.

**up-to-the-minute** /ˌʌptəðəˈmɪnɪt/ (only *before* a noun) ***adj.*** having the most recent information possible: *an up-to-the-minute news report*

**up·town** /ˌʌpˈtaʊn/ ***adj., adv.*** in or to the northern part of a city, or the part where the streets have larger numbers in their names ➲ Look also at **downtown**.

**up·turn** /ˈʌptərn/ ***noun*** [C] **an upturn (in sth)** an improvement or gain in sth: *an upturn in support for the candidate* OPP **downturn**

★**up·ward¹** /ˈʌpwərd/ ***adj.*** moving or directed toward a higher place or level: *an upward glance* ◇ *an upward trend in exports* (= an increase)

★**up·ward²** /ˈʌpwərd/ (*also* **upwards** /-wərdz/)

U

*adv.* moving toward, or in the direction of, a higher place or level: *I looked upward.*

IDM **upwards of** more than (the number mentioned): *They invited upwards of a hundred guests.*

**up·ward·ly mo·bile** /ˌʌpwərdli ˈmoʊbl/ *adj.* moving toward a higher social position, usually in which you become richer: *upwardly mobile immigrant groups* ◇ *an upwardly mobile lifestyle*

**u·ra·ni·um** /yʊˈreɪniəm/ *noun* [U] (*symbol* **U**) a radioactive metal that can be used to produce nuclear energy

**U·ra·nus** /yʊˈreɪnəs; ˈyʊrənəs/ *noun* [sing.] the planet that is seventh in order from the sun

★**ur·ban** /ˈərbən/ *adj.* of a large city: *urban neighborhoods*

**ur·bane** /ərˈbeɪn/ *adj.* (*written*) (used especially about a man) good at knowing what to say and how to behave in social situations; appearing relaxed and confident: *He was charming and urbane, full of witty conversation.*

ˌ**urban ˈmyth** (*also* ˌ**urban ˈlegend**) *noun* [C] a story about an amusing or strange event that is supposed to have happened to sb, which is often repeated and which many people believe is true

**ur·chin** /ˈərtʃən/ *noun* [C] *short for* SEA URCHIN

**u·re·thra** /yʊˈriθrə/ *noun* [C] the tube that carries liquid waste out of the body. In men and male animals sperm also flows along this tube.

★**urge¹** /ərdʒ/ *verb* [T] **1** to try hard to persuade sb to do sth: *I urged him to fight the decision.* **2** to advise strongly, especially that sth is necessary: *Motorists are urged to drive carefully on icy roads.*

PHR V **urge sb on** to encourage sb: *The coach urged his team on.*

**urge²** /ərdʒ/ *noun* [C] a strong need or desire: *sexual urges* ◇ *She felt a strong urge to stand up and scream.*

★**ur·gent** /ˈərdʒənt/ *adj.* needing immediate attention: *an urgent message* ◇ *It's not urgent; I'll tell you about it later.* ▶ **ur·gen·cy** /-dʒənsi/ *noun* [U]: *a matter of the greatest urgency* ▶ **ur·gent·ly** *adv.*: *Mr. Wheeler needs to see you urgently.*

**u·ri·nal** /ˈyʊrənl; ˈyər-/ *noun* [C] a type of toilet for men that is attached to the wall; a room or building containing urinals

**u·ri·nar·y** /ˈyʊrəˌnɛri; ˈyər-/ *adj.* (*medical*) connected with urine or the parts of the body through which it passes: *a urinary infection* ◇ *the urinary tract*

**u·ri·nate** /ˈyʊrəneɪt/ *verb* [I] (*formal*) to pass waste water (urine) from the body ➲ **Go to the bathroom** is a polite, less formal expression with the same meaning.

**u·rine** /ˈyʊrɪn/ *noun* [U] the yellow liquid that is passed from your body when you use the toilet

**URL** *abbr.* (*computing*) the abbreviation for "uniform/universal resource locator"; the address of a World Wide Web page

**urn** /ərn/ *noun* [C] a type of vase, especially one in which the ashes of a dead person are kept

**u·rol·o·gy** /yʊˈrɑlədʒi/ *noun* [U] (*medical*) the scientific study of the urinary system ▶ **u·rol·o·gist** /-dʒɪst/ *noun* [C]

★**U.S.** (*also* **US**) /ˌyu ˈɛs/ (*also* **U.S.A., USA** /ˌyu ɛs ˈeɪ/) *abbr.* = THE UNITED STATES: *the smallest state in the U.S.*

★**us** /əs; *strong form* ʌs/ *pronoun* (used as the object of a verb, or after *be*) me and another person or other people; me and you: *Come with us.* ◇ *Leave us alone.* ◇ *Will you write to us?* ◇ *Hello, it's us again!*

**us·a·ble** /ˈyuzəbl/ *adj.* that can be used; in good enough condition to be used: *The bike is rusty but usable.* ◇ *How can we display this data in a usable form?*

**us·age** /ˈyusɪdʒ/ *noun* **1** [U] the way that sth is used; the amount that sth is used: *With normal usage, the machine should last for years.* **2** [C,U] the way that words are normally used in a language: *a guide to English grammar and usage*

★**use¹** /yuz/ *verb* [T] (*pres. part.* **us·ing**; *pt, pp* **used** /yuzd/) **1** when you use sth, you do sth with it for a purpose: *Could I use your phone?* ◇ *We used the money to buy a house.* ◇ *The building was used as a shelter for homeless people.* ◇ *This information cannot be used for commercial purposes* ◇ *Use your imagination!* ◇ *That's a word I never use.* **2** to need or to take sth: *Don't use all the milk.* **3** to treat sb/sth in a selfish or unkind way: *He just used me to get what he wanted and then forgot about me.*

PHR V **use sth up** to use sth until no more is left

★**use²** /yus/ *noun* **1** [U] using or being used: *The use of cellular phones is now widespread.* ◇ *She kept the money for use in an emergency.* ◇ *Turn off the coffee maker when it is not in use.* **2** [C,U] the purpose for which sth is used: *This gadget has many uses.* **3** [U] the ability or permission to use sth: *He lost the use of his hand after the accident.* ◇ *She offered them the use of her car.* **4** [U] the advantage of sth; how useful sth is: *It's no use studying for a test at the last minute.* ◇ *What's the use of trying?*

IDM **come into/go out of use** to start/stop being used

**make use of sth/sb** to use sth/sb in a way that will give you an advantage

★**used¹** /yuzd/ *adj.* that has had an owner before: *I bought a used car.* SYN **secondhand**

★**used²** /yust/ *adj.*

IDM **be/get used to sth/to doing sth** to be or become familiar with sth or accustomed to sth: *He's used to the heat.* ◇ *I'll never get used to getting up at five.*

★**used to** /ˈyustə; *before a vowel and in final position* ˈyustu/ *modal verb* (for talking about sth that happened often or continuously in the past or about a situation which existed in the past): *She used to live with her parents* (= but she doesn't now). ◇ *You used to live in Chicago, didn't you?* ◇ *Did you use to smoke?* ◇ *He didn't use to speak to me.*

NOTE **1** We usually use **did** to form negatives and questions with **used to**: *I didn't use to like jazz.* ◇ *Did she use to be in your class?* **2** Be careful not to confuse **used to** + infinitive, which only refers to the past, with **to be used to (doing) sth**, which can refer to the past, present or future. Compare: *I used to live on my own* (= but now I don't). ◇ *I'm used to living on my own* (= I am accustomed to it).

U

★**use·ful** /ˈyusfl/ ***adj.*** having some practical use; helpful: *a useful tool* ◇ *useful advice* ▶ **use·ful·ly** ***adv.***: *Make sure your time is spent usefully.* ▶ **use·ful·ness** ***noun*** [U]

★**use·less** /ˈyusləs/ ***adj.*** that does not work well, or is of no use: *This new machine is useless.* ◇ *It's useless to complain; you won't get your money back.* ▶ **use·less·ly** ***adv.*** ▶ **use·less·ness** ***noun*** [U]

★**us·er** /ˈyuzər/ ***noun*** [C] **1** (often in compounds) a person that uses a service, machine, place, etc.: *users of public transportation* **2** (*slang*) a person who takes illegal drugs

**user-friendly** /ˌyuzərˈfrɛndli/ ***adj.*** (used about computers, books, machines, etc.) easy or not too complicated to use

**ush·er**[1] /ˈʌʃər/ ***noun*** [C] a person who shows people to their seats in a theater, church, etc.

**ush·er**[2] /ˈʌʃər/ ***verb*** [T] to lead sb carefully in the direction mentioned: *I was ushered to my seat.*

PHR V **usher sth in** to mark the beginning of sth: *The agreement ushered in a new period of peace for the two countries.*

★**u·su·al** /ˈyuʒuəl; ˈyuʒəl/ ***adj.*** happening or used most often: *It's usual for her to work on weekends.* ◇ *He got home later than usual.* ◇ *I sat in my usual seat.*

IDM **as usual** in the way that has often happened before: *Here's Derek, late as usual!*

★**u·su·al·ly** /ˈyuʒuəli; ˈyuʒəli/ ***adv.*** in the way that is usual; most often: *She's usually home by six.* ◇ *Usually, we go out on Saturdays.*

**u·surp** /yuˈsərp/ ***verb*** [T] (*formal*) to take sb's position and/or power without having the right to do this

**u·ten·sil** /yuˈtɛnsl/ ***noun*** [C] a type of tool or object used in the home: *cooking utensils*

**u·ter·us** /ˈyut̬ərəs/ ***noun*** [C] (*pl.* **u·ter·us·es** or, in scientific use, **u·ter·i** /-raɪ/) (*also old-fashioned* **womb**) the part of a woman's body where a baby grows

**u·til·i·tar·i·an** /yuˌtɪləˈtɛriən/ ***adj.*** (*formal*) designed to be useful and practical rather than attractive: *a utilitarian building*

**u·til·i·ty** /yuˈtɪlət̬i/ ***noun*** (*pl.* **u·til·i·ties**) **1** [C] a useful public service such as the supplying of water or electricity: *Your share of the rent will be $250 a month, plus one third of the utility bills.* ➲ Look also at **public utility**. **2** [U] (*formal*) the usefulness (of a machine, etc.)

**u'tility room** ***noun*** [C] a small room in a house, often next to the kitchen, where people sometimes have a washing machine, etc.

**u·til·ize** /ˈyut̬l·aɪz/ ***verb*** [T] (*formal*) to use sth in an effective and practical way: *to utilize computer technology in the classroom*

**ut·most**[1] /ˈʌtmoʊst/ ***adj.*** (only *before* a noun) (*formal*) greatest: *a message of the utmost importance*

**ut·most**[2] /ˈʌtmoʊst/ ***noun*** [sing.] the greatest extent, amount, degree, etc. that is possible: *I did my utmost to help.*

**U·to·pi·a** /yuˈtoʊpiə/ ***noun*** [C,U] an imaginary society or place where everything is perfect ▶ **U·to·pi·an** /-piən/ ***adj.***

**ut·ter**[1] /ˈʌt̬ər/ ***adj.*** (only *before* a noun) complete; total: *That's utter nonsense!* ◇ *He felt like an utter fool.* ▶ **ut·ter·ly** ***adv.***: *It's utterly impossible.*

**ut·ter**[2] /ˈʌt̬ər/ ***verb*** [T] to speak or make a sound with your mouth: *She left without uttering a word.*

**ut·ter·ance** /ˈʌt̬ərəns/ ***noun*** [C] (*formal*) something that is said

**U-turn** /ˈyutərn/ ***noun*** [C] **1** a type of movement where a car, etc. turns around so that it goes back in the direction it came: *to make a U-turn* **2** a sudden change from one plan to a completely different one

**UV** /ˌyu ˈvi/ ***abbr.*** = ULTRAVIOLET: *UV radiation*

**UV In·dex** /ˌyu ˈvi ˌɪndɛks/ ***noun*** [sing.] (*Cdn*) a scale or a measure used to represent the strength of the sun's harmful rays (**ultraviolet rays**) in order to show how much they might burn human skin

**U·zi** /ˈuzi/ ***noun*** [C] a type of submachine gun

# V v

**V, v** /vi/ ***noun*** [C,U] (*pl.* **V's; v's**) **1** the twenty-second letter of the English alphabet: *"Van" begins with (a) "V."* **2** the shape of a V: *The birds were flying in a V.*

**V** ***abbr.*** (*written*) = VOLT, VOLTS

**va·can·cy** /ˈveɪkənsi/ ***noun*** [C] (*pl.* **va·can·cies**) **1** a room in a hotel, etc. that is not being used: *The sign outside the motel said "No Vacancies."* **2** a job that has not been filled: *There are two vacancies on the school board this year.*

**va·cant** /ˈveɪkənt/ ***adj.*** **1** (of a house, room, seat, etc.) not being used **2** (of a job, etc.) not filled: *The position of Marketing Director is currently vacant.* **3** showing no sign of intelligence or understanding: *a vacant expression* ▶ **va·cant·ly** ***adv.***: *She stared vacantly out of the window.*

**va·cate** /ˈveɪkeɪt/ ***verb*** [T] (*formal*) to leave a building, seat, etc., especially so that sb else can use it: *Guests are requested to vacate their rooms by noon on the day of departure.*

★**va·ca·tion** /veɪˈkeɪʃn; və-/ ***noun*** [C,U] a period of rest from work or school (often when you go and stay away from home): *The boss is on vacation.* ◇ *The job includes two weeks' paid vacation a year.* ◇ *Summer vacation starts next Friday!* ◇ *He took his vacation during the first week in July.*

**va·ca·tion·er** /veɪˈkeɪʃnər; və-/ ***noun*** [C] a person who is away from home on vacation

**vac·ci·nate** /ˈvæksn·eɪt/ ***verb*** [T] to give a person or animal a substance, often using a special needle, to prevent him/her/it from getting a particular disease: *Were you vaccinated against measles as a child?* ▸ **vac·ci·na·tion** /ˌvæksn·ˈeɪʃn/ ***noun*** [C,U]

**vac·cine** /vækˈsin/ ***noun*** [C] a substance that is given to people, often using a special needle, to protect them against a particular disease: *the search for an AIDS vaccine/a vaccine against AIDS*

**vac·il·late** /ˈvæsəleɪt/ ***verb*** [I] (*formal*) to keep changing your opinion or thoughts about sth, especially in a way that annoys other people: *The country's leaders are still vacillating between confrontation and compromise.* SYN **waver**

**vac·u·ous** /ˈvækyuəs/ ***adj.*** (*formal*) showing no sign of intelligence or sensitive feelings: *a vacuous look/expression/smile*

**vac·u·um¹** /ˈvækyum/ ***noun*** [C] **1** a space that contains no substance and no air or gas: (*figurative*) *a vacuum in her life* (= a feeling of emptiness) **2** = VACUUM CLEANER

**vac·u·um²** /ˈvækum/ ***verb*** [I,T] to clean sth using a vacuum cleaner

vacuum cleaner

**ˈvacuum ˌclean·er** (*also* **vacuum**) ***noun*** [C] an electric machine that cleans carpets, etc. by sucking up dirt

**vag·a·bond** /ˈvægəbɑnd/ ***noun*** [C] (*old-fashioned*) a person who has no home or job and who travels from place to place: *beggars, rogues and vagabonds*

**va·gi·na** /vəˈdʒaɪnə/ ***noun*** [C] the passage in the body of a woman or female animal that connects the outer sex organs to the part where a baby grows (uterus) ▸ **va·gi·nal** /ˈvædʒənl/ ***adj.***

**va·grant** /ˈveɪgrənt/ ***noun*** [C] (*formal*) a person who has no home or job, especially one who asks for money (**begs**) from people

**vague** /veɪg/ ***adj.*** **1** not clear or definite: *vague memories of my childhood home* **2** not clearly seen: *a vague shape in the distance*

**vague·ly** /ˈveɪgli/ ***adv.*** **1** in a way that is not clear; slightly: *Her name is vaguely familiar.* **2** without thinking about what is happening: *He smiled vaguely and walked away.* ▸ **vague·ness** ***noun*** [U]

**vain** /veɪn/ ***adj.*** **1** (*formal*) (used about a person) too proud of your appearance, of what you can do, etc. ➲ noun vanity **2** useless; without any hope of success: *a vain attempt*

IDM **in vain** without success: *The firefighters tried in vain to put out the fire.*

▸ **vain·ly** ***adv.***

**val·ance** /ˈvæləns; ˈveɪ-/ ***noun*** [C] **1** a narrow piece of cloth like a short curtain that hangs around the frame of a bed, under a shelf, etc. **2** a strip of wood or cloth above a window that hides the curtain rail

**val·e·dic·to·ri·an** /ˌvælədɪkˈtɔriən/ ***noun*** [C] the student who received higher grades than all the other students in his/her class in high school or college, and who gives a speech at the graduation ceremony ➲ Look also at **salutatorian**.

**val·en·tine** /ˈvæləntaɪn/ ***noun*** [C] **1** a card that you send, sometimes secretly, to someone you love or like in a romantic way ➲ It is traditional to send these cards on **Valentine's Day** (February 14). **2** the person you send a card to on Valentine's Day: *Be my valentine* (= written on a card).

**val·et** /væˈleɪ/ ***noun*** [C] a person whose job is to perform personal services for people, especially parking their cars at a hotel or restaurant

**val·iant** /ˈvæliənt/ ***adj.*** (*formal*) very brave ▸ **val·iant·ly** ***adv.***

★**val·id** /ˈvæləd/ ***adj.*** **1** that can be used or accepted legally at a certain time: *This ticket is valid for Sunday's game only.* **2** acceptable in a court of law: *a valid contract* **3** (used about a reason, etc.) strong enough to convince sb; acceptable: *I could think of no valid objections to the plan.* OPP **invalid** ▸ **va·lid·i·ty** /vəˈlɪdəṭi/ ***noun*** [U]: *the validity of an argument* ◇ *the validity of a law*

**val·i·date** /ˈvælədeɪt/ ***verb*** [T] (*formal*) **1** to prove that sth is true: *to validate a claim/theory* **2** to make sth legally valid: *to validate a contract* **3** to state officially that sth is useful and of an acceptable standard: *Check that their courses have been validated by a reputable organization.*

**Val·i·um™** /ˈvæliəm/ ***noun*** [U] a drug used to reduce anxiety: *The doctor prescribed Valium.*

★**val·ley** /ˈvæli/ ***noun*** [C] the flat land that lies between two lines of mountains or areas of higher ground, and which often has a river flowing through it

**val·or** /ˈvælər/ ***noun*** [U] great bravery, especially in war: *the soldiers' valor in battle*

NOTE This word is used in old, formal or poetic writing.

★**val·u·a·ble** /ˈvælyəbl; -yuəbl/ ***adj.*** **1** worth a lot of money: *Is this ring valuable?* **2** very useful: *a valuable piece of information* OPP **worthless** ➲ Look also at **invaluable**.

**val·u·a·bles** /ˈvælyəblz; -yuəblz/ ***noun*** [pl.] the small things that you own that are worth a lot of money, such as jewelry, etc.: *Please put your valuables in the hotel safe.*

**val·u·a·tion** /ˌvælyuˈeɪʃn/ ***noun*** [C,U] **1** a professional judgment about how much money sth is worth; its estimated value: *land valuation* ◇ *Surveyors carried out a valuation of the property.* ◇ *Experts set a high valuation on the painting.* **2** (*formal*) a judgment about how useful or important sth is; its estimated importance: *She puts a high valuation on trust between colleagues.*

★**val·ue¹** /ˈvælyu/ ***noun*** **1** [U] the usefulness or importance of sth: *the value of education* ◇ *of great/little value* **2** [C,U] the amount of money that sth is worth: *The thieves stole goods with a total value of $10,000.* ◇ *Shares of IBM have increased in value this month.* ◇ *to go up/down in value* ➲ Look at **face value**. **3** [C,U] the worth of sth compared with its price, or something that is worth a lot compared with its price: *The hotel offers good value at $25 a night.* ◇ *Some used equipment can be an excellent value.* **4 values** [pl.] a set of beliefs about the way people should behave; moral principles: *the* *traditional values of Western society* ➲ Look also at **family values**.

★**val·ue²** /ˈvælyu/ ***verb*** [T] (*pres. part.* **val·u·ing**) **1 value sth (at sth)** to decide the amount of money that sth is worth: *The house was valued at $70,000.* **2** to think sb/sth is very important and worth a lot: *Laura has always valued her independence.*

**valve** /vælv/ ***noun*** [C] a mechanical device which controls the flow of air, liquid or gas in a pipe or tube: *a radiator valve* ◇ *to open/close a valve*

**vam·pire** /ˈvæmpaɪər/ ***noun*** [C] (in horror stories) a dead person who comes out of his/her grave at night and sucks the blood of living people

★**van** /væn/ ***noun*** [C] a type of vehicle like a very large car or small covered truck, that is used for transporting people or things ➲ picture at **truck**.

**van·dal** /ˈvændl/ ***noun*** [C] a person who damages property (e.g. cars, store windows) on purpose ▸ **van·dal·ism** /-dl·ɪzəm/ ***noun*** [U]: *The police are worried about the recent increase in vandalism.*

**van·dal·ize** /ˈvændl·aɪz/ ***verb*** [T] (often passive) to damage property on purpose

**van·guard** /ˈvængɑrd/ ***noun*** [sing.] **the vanguard** the leaders of a movement in society, for example in politics, art, industry, etc.: *The company is proud to be* ***in the vanguard of*** *scientific progress.*

**va·nil·la¹** /vəˈnɪlə/ ***noun*** [U] a substance from a plant that is used for giving flavor to sweet food

**va·nil·la²** /vəˈnɪlə/ ***adj.*** **1** flavored with VANILLA¹: *vanilla ice cream* **2** (*informal*) ordinary; not special in any way: *The city is pretty much plain vanilla.* ◇ *This is only the vanilla version of the software.*

**van·ish** /ˈvænɪʃ/ ***verb*** [I] **1** to disappear suddenly and completely: *When he turned around, the two men had vanished.* ◇ *His fear vanished when he heard his sister's voice outside the door.* **2** (used about types of things) to disappear little by little over a period of time: *This species of plant is vanishing from North America.*

**van·i·ty** /ˈvænət̬i/ ***noun*** [U] the quality of being too proud of your appearance or abilities ➲ adjective vain

ˈ**vanity plate** ***noun*** [C, usually pl.] a metal sign (license plate) for a car with a special combination of letters and/or numbers that were chosen by the car's owner, e.g. to spell his/her name or an amusing word

**vant·age point** /ˈvæntɪdʒ pɔɪnt/ (*also formal* **vant·age** /ˈvæntɪdʒ/) ***noun*** [C] a position from which you watch sth; a point in time or a situation from which you consider sth, especially the past: *The cafe was a good vantage point for watching the world go by.* ◇ *From the vantage point of the present, the war seems to have achieved nothing.*

**va·por** /ˈveɪpər/ ***noun*** [C,U] a substance made of very small drops of liquid which hang together in the air like a cloud: *water vapor*

**va·por·ize** /ˈveɪpəraɪz/ ***verb*** [I,T] (*technical*) to turn into gas; to make sth turn into gas

**var·i·a·ble¹** /ˈvɛriəbl; ˈvær-/ ***adj.*** not staying the same; likely to change ▸ **var·i·a·bil·i·ty** /ˌvɛriəˈbɪlət̬i; ˈvær-/ ***noun*** [U]

**var·i·a·ble²** /ˈvɛriəbl; ˈvær-/ ***noun*** [C] something that is likely to change from one situation to another

**var·i·ance** /ˈvɛriəns; ˈvær-/ ***noun*** [C,U] (*formal*) the amount by which sth changes or is different from sth else: *variance in temperature/pay* ◇ *a note with subtle variances of pitch*

IDM **at variance (with sb/sth)** (*formal*) disagreeing with or opposing sb/sth: *These conclusions are totally at variance with the evidence.*

**var·i·ant** /ˈvɛriənt; ˈvær-/ ***noun*** [C] a different form of sth

★**var·i·a·tion** /ˌvɛriˈeɪʃn; ˈvær-/ ***noun*** **1** [C,U] **variation (in sth)** a difference in quality or quantity between a number of things: *There was a lot of variation in the test scores* (= the scores were very different from each other). ◇ *a slight variation in color from one piece to another* **2** [C] **variation (on/of sth)** something that is almost the same as another thing but has some small differences: *All their songs are just variations on a basic theme.*

**var·i·cose vein** /ˌværəkoʊs ˈveɪn/ ***noun*** [C] a vein, especially on the leg, which has become swollen and painful

**var·ied** /ˈvɛrid; ˈvær-/ ***adj.*** having many different kinds of things or activities: *a varied diet* ◇ *The work of an English teacher is interesting and varied.*

★**va·ri·e·ty** /vəˈraɪət̬i/ ***noun*** (*pl.* **va·ri·e·ties**) **1** [C] **a variety (of sth)** a number of different kinds of things: *You can take evening classes in a variety of subjects including photography, Spanish and computers.* **2** [U] the quality of not being the same: *There's so much variety in my new job. I do something different every day!* **3** [C] **a variety (of sth)** a type of sth: *a new variety of apple called "Perfection"*

**vaˈriety show** ***noun*** [C] a form of theater or television entertainment that consists of a series of short performances, such as singing, dancing and funny acts

★**var·i·ous** /ˈvɛriəs; ˈvær-/ ***adj.*** (used for describing things that are different from each other) more than one; several: *These chairs are available in various colors.* ◇ *I decided to leave school for various reasons.*

**var·i·ous·ly** /ˈvɛriəsli; ˈvær-/ ***adv.*** (*written*) in several different ways, usually by several different people: *He has been* ***variously described*** *as a hero, a genius and a bully.* ◇ *The cost has been variously estimated at between $10 million and $20 million.*

**var·nish** /ˈvɑrnɪʃ/ ***noun*** [U] a clear liquid that you paint onto wood or other hard surfaces to protect them and make them shine ▸ **var·nish** ***verb*** [T]

**var·si·ty** /ˈvɑrsət̬i/ ***adj.*** (only *before* a noun) (used about a sports team) that is the main team that represents a school, college or university in games against teams from other schools, colleges or universities: *the girls' varsity basketball team*

★**var·y** /ˈvɛri; ˈvær-/ ***verb*** (*pres. part.* **var·y·ing**; *3rd person sing. pres.* **var·ies**; *pt, pp* **var·ied**) **1** [I] (used about a number of things) to be different from each other: *The fruits vary greatly in size and quality – be careful when you choose.* **2** [I] to become different; to change: *The price of the vacation package varies from $1,500 to $3,200, depending on the time of*

V

*year.* **3** [T] to make sth different by changing it often in some way: *I try to vary my work as much as possible so I don't get bored.*

**vase** /veɪs; vɑz/ ***noun*** [C] a container used for holding cut flowers

**va·sec·to·my** /və'sɛktəmi/ ***noun*** [C] (*pl.* **va·sec·to·mies**) a small medical operation that prevents a man from having children, by cutting the tube that carries sperm

**Vas·e·line™** /'væsəlin; ˌvæsə'lin/ ***noun*** [U] a thick soft clear substance that is used on skin to heal or protect it, or as a lubricant to stop surfaces from sticking together SYN **petroleum jelly**

★**vast** /væst/ ***adj.*** extremely big: *a vast sum of money* ◇ *a vast country* ◇ *The vast majority of* (almost all) *local residents support the proposal.* ▸ **vast·ly** ***adv.***: *vastly different attitudes toward the problem*

**vat** /væt/ ***noun*** [C] a large container for holding liquids, especially in industrial processes: *distilling/fermenting vats* ◇ *a vat of whiskey*

**vaude·ville** /'vɔdvɪl; 'vɔdəvɪl/ ***noun*** [U] **1** a form of theater or television entertainment that consists of a series of short performances, such as singing, dancing and funny acts **2** a type of entertainment popular in the late 19th and early 20th centuries, including singing, dancing and comedy

**vault¹** /vɔlt/ ***noun*** [C] **1** a strong underground room in a bank, etc. used for keeping money and other valuable things safe **2** a room where dead people are buried

**vault²** /vɔlt/ ***verb*** [I,T] **vault (over sth)** to jump over or onto sth in one movement, using your hands or a pole to help you: *The boy vaulted over the wall.*

**V-chip** /'vi tʃɪp/ ***noun*** [C] (*computing*) a computer CHIP¹ (5) in a television receiver that can be programmed to block material that contains sex and violence

**VCR** /ˌvi si 'ɑr/ ***noun*** [C] (*pl.* **VCR's**) videocassette recorder; a machine that is connected to a television, on which you can record or play television programs or movies

**VD** /vi 'di/ ***abbr.*** = VENEREAL DISEASE

**veal** /vil/ ***noun*** [U] the meat from a young cow (calf) ➲ Look at the note at **meat**.

**vec·tor** /'vɛktər/ ***noun*** [C] (*technical*) **1** a quantity that has both size and direction: *Acceleration and velocity are both vectors.* **2** an insect, etc. that carries a particular disease from one living thing to another: *Mosquitoes are the vectors in malaria.* **3** a course taken by an aircraft

**veep** /vip/ ***noun*** [C] (*slang*) = VICE PRESIDENT

**veer** /vɪr/ ***verb*** [I] (used about vehicles) to change direction suddenly: *The car veered across the road and hit a tree.*

**veg** /vɛdʒ/ ***verb***

PHR V **veg out** (*informal*) to relax by doing sth that needs very little effort, for example watching TV

**veg·an** /'vigən/ ***noun*** [C] a person who does not eat or use any animal products at all ➲ Compare **vegetarian.**

★**veg·e·ta·ble** /'vɛdʒtəbl/ ***noun*** [C] **1** a plant which you eat as food, e.g. potatoes, carrots, onions: *fresh fruit and vegetables* ◇ *vegetable soup* ◇ *a vegetable garden* **2** a person who is physically alive but not capable of much mental or physical activity, for example because of an accident or illness: *Severe brain damage turned him into a vegetable.*

**veg·e·tar·i·an** /ˌvɛdʒə'tɛriən/ ***noun*** [C] a person who does not eat meat or fish ➲ Compare **vegan.** ▸ **veg·e·tari·an** ***adj.***: *a vegetarian diet*

**veg·e·tate** /'vɛdʒəteɪt/ ***verb*** [I] (used about a person) to spend time doing very little and feeling bored

**veg·e·ta·tion** /ˌvɛdʒə'teɪʃn/ ***noun*** [U] (*formal*) plant life in general; all the plants that are found in a particular place: *tropical vegetation*

**veg·gie** /'vɛdʒi/ ***noun*** [C, usually pl.] (*informal*) a vegetable

**ve·he·ment** /'viəmənt/ ***adj.*** (*written*) showing very strong feelings, especially anger: *a vehement denial/attack/protest* ◇ *He had been vehement in his opposition to the idea.* ▸ **ve·he·ment·ly** ***adv.***: *The charge was vehemently denied.*

★**ve·hi·cle** /'viɪkl/ ***noun*** [C] (*formal*) **1** something which transports people or things from place to place, especially on land, e.g. cars, bicycles, trucks and buses: *a motor vehicle* (a vehicle with an engine) **2 a vehicle (for sth)** something which is used for communicating particular ideas or opinions: *This magazine has become a vehicle for conservative opinion.*

**ve·hic·u·lar** /vi'hɪkyələr/ ***adj.*** (*formal*) intended for vehicles or consisting of vehicles: ***vehicular homicide*** (= causing death by driving dangerously) ◇ *The road is closed to vehicular traffic.*

**veil¹** /veɪl/ ***noun*** [C] **1** a piece of thin material for covering a woman's head and face **2** [sing.] (*written*) a thin layer that stops you from seeing sth: *The mountain tops were hidden beneath a veil of mist.*

**veil²** /veɪl/ ***verb*** [T] **1** to cover your face with a VEIL¹ (1) **2** to cover sth with sth that hides it partly or completely: *A fine drizzle began to veil the hills.*

**veiled** /veɪld/ ***adj.*** **1** not expressed directly or clearly because you do not want your meaning to be obvious: *a* ***thinly veiled*** *threat/attack/warning/criticism* ◇ *She made a* ***veiled reference to*** *his past mistakes.* **2** wearing a VEIL¹ (1): *a mysterious veiled woman*

**vein** /veɪn/ ***noun*** **1** [C] one of the tubes which carry blood from all parts of the body to the heart ➲ Look at **artery.** **2** [sing., U] a particular style or quality: *After a humorous beginning, the program continued in a more serious vein.*

**Vel·cro™** /'vɛlkroʊ/ ***noun*** a material that is used for fastening parts of clothes together. Velcro is used in small strips, one rough and one smooth, that stick together and make a noise when they are pulled apart.

**ve·loc·i·ty** /və'lɑsəṭi/ ***noun*** [U] (*technical*) the speed at which sth moves

**ve·lour** /və'lʊr/ ***noun*** [U] a silk or cotton fabric with a thick soft surface like velvet

**vel·vet** /'vɛlvət/ ***noun*** [U] a kind of material with a soft, thick surface on one side only

**vel·vet·een** /ˌvɛlvə'tin; 'vɛlvətin/ ***noun*** [U] a cotton fabric that looks like velvet but is less expensive

**vel·vet·y** /ˈvɛlvət̬i/ ***adj.*** pleasantly smooth and soft: *velvety skin* ◇ *a velvety red wine*

**vend** /vɛnd/ ***verb*** [T] (*formal*) to sell sth

**ven·det·ta** /vɛnˈdɛt̬ə/ ***noun*** [C] a serious argument that lasts for a long time (especially between an individual and an organization or between families)

**ˈvending maˌchine** ***noun*** [C] a machine in a public place into which you put money to buy candy, drinks in cans, etc.

**ven·dor** /ˈvɛndər/ ***noun*** [C] (*formal*) a person who sells sth: *a hot dog vendor at the stadium*

**ve·neer** /vəˈnɪr/ ***noun*** [C,U] **1** a thin layer of wood or plastic which you stick onto sth made of cheaper material to give it a better appearance **2 a veneer (of sth)** (*formal*) a part of sb's behavior or of a situation which hides what it is really like: *a thin veneer of politeness*

**ven·er·a·ble** /ˈvɛnərəbl/ ***adj.*** **1** (*formal*) venerable people or things deserve respect because they are old, important, wise, etc.: *a venerable institution/tradition* **2 the Venerable...** (only before a noun) (in the Anglican Church), a title of respect used when talking about an archdeacon: *the Venerable Martin Roberts* **3 the Venerable...** (only before a noun) (in the Roman Catholic Church), a title given to a dead person who is very holy but who has not yet been made a saint

**ve·ne·re·al dis·ease** /vəˈnɪriəl dɪˌziz/ ***noun*** [C,U] (*abbr.* **VD**) any disease caught by having sex with an infected person

**Ve·ne·tian blind** /vəˌniʃn ˈblaɪnd/ ***noun*** [C] a covering for a window that is made of horizontal strips of plastic or metal. You can change the position of the strips in order to let more or less light into the room.

**ven·geance** /ˈvɛndʒəns/ ***noun*** (*formal*) [U] the act of hurting sb because he/she has hurt you in some way that you think is wrong: *The man wanted vengeance for the death of his wife.* ➲ Look at **revenge**.

IDM **with a vengeance** with more force and determination than before or than you expected: *After a week of good weather, winter returned with a vengeance today.*

**venge·ful** /ˈvɛndʒfl/ ***adj.*** (*formal*) showing a desire to punish sb who has harmed you: *He was not a vengeful man.*

**ven·i·son** /ˈvɛnɪsn/ ***noun*** [U] the meat from a deer ➲ Look at the note at **meat**.

**ven·om** /ˈvɛnəm/ ***noun*** [U] **1** the poisonous liquid that snakes, etc. put into your body when they bite you **2** extreme anger or hatred that you show when you speak ▸ **ven·om·ous** /ˈvɛnəməs/ ***adj.***

**vent**[1] /vɛnt/ ***noun*** [C] a hole in the wall of a room or machine which allows air to come in, and allows smoke, steam or smells to go out: *an air vent*

**ven·ti·late** /ˈvɛntəleɪt/ ***verb*** [T] to allow air to move freely in and out of a room or building: *The office is poorly ventilated.* ▸ **ven·ti·la·tion** /ˌvɛntəˈleɪʃn/ ***noun*** [U]: *There was no ventilation in the room except for one tiny window.*

**ven·ti·la·tor** /ˈvɛntəˌleɪt̬ər/ ***noun*** [C] **1** a device or an opening for letting fresh air come into a room, etc. **2** a piece of equipment with a pump that helps sb to breathe by sending air in and out of the lungs: *He was put on a ventilator.*

**ven·tril·o·quist** /vɛnˈtrɪləkwɪst/ ***noun*** [C] a person who can speak without moving his/her lips and make it look as if his/her voice is coming from another person: *a ventriloquist's dummy* ◇ *Entertainment included a hypnotist and a ventriloquist.* ▸ **ven·tril·o·quism** ***noun*** [U]

★**ven·ture**[1] /ˈvɛntʃər/ ***noun*** [C] a project which is new and often involves a risk, because you cannot be sure that it will succeed: *I wish you luck in your new business venture.* ➲ Look also at **joint venture**.

**ven·ture**[2] /ˈvɛntʃər/ ***verb*** [I] to do sth or go somewhere new and perhaps dangerous, when you are not sure what will happen: *The company has decided to venture into Internet sales and marketing.* ◇ *He ventured out into the storm in a heavy coat, hat and scarf.*

IDM **nothing ventured, nothing gained** (used to say that you have to take risks if you want to achieve things and be successful)

**ˌventure ˈcapital** ***noun*** [U] money that is invested in a new company to help it develop, which may involve a lot of risk

**ven·ue** /ˈvɛnyu/ ***noun*** [C] the place where a concert, sports game, conference, etc. happens: *a change of venue*

**Ve·nus** /ˈvinəs/ ***noun*** [sing.] the planet that is second in order from the sun and nearest to the earth

**ve·ran·da** (*also* **verandah**) /vəˈrændə/ ***noun*** [C] a platform attached to the side of a house, with a roof and floor but no outside wall: *to sit on the veranda* ➲ Look at **deck**, **patio** and **porch**.

**verb** /vərb/ ***noun*** [C] a word or group of words that is used to indicate an action or state, e.g. *bring*, *happen*, or *be*

**ver·bal** /ˈvərbl/ ***adj.*** (*formal*) **1** spoken, not written: *a verbal warning* ➲ Look at **oral**. **2** connected with words, or the use of words: *verbal skill* ▸ **ver·bal·ly** ***adv.***

**ver·ba·lize** /ˈvərbəlaɪz/ ***verb*** [T] (*formal*) to express your feelings or ideas in words: *He's a real genius but he has difficulty verbalizing his ideas.*

**ver·bose** /vərˈboʊs/ ***adj.*** (*formal*) using or containing more words than are needed: *a verbose speaker/speech/style* SYN **wordy**

**ver·dict** /ˈvərdɪkt/ ***noun*** [C] **1** the decision in a court of law about whether a person is guilty or not guilty, or about the facts of a legal case: *The jury returned a verdict of "not guilty."* **2** your opinion or decision about sth, which you tell to other people: *The general verdict was that the restaurant was too expensive.*

**verge**[1] /vərdʒ/ ***noun*** [sing.]

IDM **on the verge of sth/doing sth** very near to doing sth, or to sth happening: *scientists on the verge of an exciting new discovery* ◇ *The company was on the verge of going bankrupt.*

**verge**[2] /vərdʒ/ ***verb***

PHR V **verge on sth** to be almost the same as sth; to be close to sth: *What they are doing verges on theft.*

**ver·i·fy** /ˈvɛrəfaɪ/ ***verb*** [T] (*pres. part.* **ver·i·fy·ing**;

V

3rd person sing. pres. **ver·i·fies**; pt, pp **ver·i·fied**) (formal) to check or state that sth is true: *to verify a statement* ▶ **ver·i·fi·ca·tion** /ˌvɛrəfəˈkeɪʃn/ ***noun*** [C,U]

**ver·i·ta·ble** /ˈvɛrət̬əbl/ ***adj.*** (only *before* a noun) (*formal*) (a word used to emphasize that sb/sth can be compared to sb/sth else that is more exciting, more impressive, etc.): *The meal that followed was a veritable banquet.*

**ver·min** /ˈvərmən/ ***noun*** [pl.] small wild animals (e.g. rats) that carry disease and destroy plants and food

**ver·mouth** /vərˈmuθ/ ***noun*** [U] a strong wine, flavored with herbs and spices, often mixed with other drinks as a cocktail

**ver·nac·u·lar** /vərˈnækyələr/ ***noun*** **the vernacular** [sing.] the language spoken in a particular area or by a particular group, especially one that is not the official or written language

**ver·sa·tile** /ˈvərsətl/ ***adj.*** **1** (used about a person) able to do many different things: *He's a versatile actor who has played a wide variety of parts.* **2** (used about food, a building, etc.) having many different uses: *Eggs are easy to cook and are an extremely versatile food.* ▶ **ver·sa·til·i·ty** /ˌvərsəˈtɪlət̬i/ ***noun*** [U]

★**verse** /vərs/ ***noun*** **1** [U] writing arranged in lines which have a definite beat and which often have the same sounds at the end: *He wrote his message of love to her in verse.* ➲ Look at **prose**. **2** [C] a group of lines which form one part of a song or poem: *This song has five verses.*

★**ver·sion** /ˈvərʒn/ ***noun*** [C] **1** a thing which is based on sth else but which has some details that are different: *The car is available in two- and four-door versions.* ◇ *the movie version of a classic novel* **2** a person's description of sth that has happened: *The two drivers gave very different versions of the accident.*

**ver·sus** /ˈvərsəs/ ***prep.*** **1** (*abbr.* **vs.**) (used in sports or in a court of law for showing that two teams or people are competing against each other): *the United States versus Canada* ◇ *the case of Brown vs. the Board of Education* **2** (used for showing that two ideas or things are in opposition to each other, especially when you are trying to choose one of them): *It's a question of quality versus price.*

**ver·te·bra** /ˈvərt̬əbrə/ ***noun*** [C] (*pl.* **ver·te·brae** /-breɪ; -bri/) any of the small bones that are connected together to form the spine

**ver·te·brate** /ˈvərt̬əbrət; -breɪt/ ***noun*** [C] (*technical*) any animal with a backbone, including all mammals, birds, fish, reptiles and amphibians ➲ Compare **invertebrate**.

★**ver·ti·cal** /ˈvərtɪkl/ ***adj.*** going straight up at an angle of 90° from the ground: *a vertical line* ◇ *The cliff was almost vertical.* ▶ **ver·ti·cal·ly** /-kli/ ***adv.***

**vertical**

vertical horizontal diagonal

**ver·ti·go** /ˈvərt̬ɪgoʊ/ ***noun*** [U] the feeling of dizziness and fear, and of losing your balance, that is caused in some people when they look down from a very high place

**verve** /vərv/ ***noun*** [U, sing.] (*written*) energy, excitement or enthusiasm: *It was a performance of verve and vitality.*

★**ver·y**[1] /ˈvɛri/ ***adv.*** (used with an adjective or adverb to make it stronger): *very small* ◇ *very slowly* ◇ *very much* ◇ *"Are you hungry?" "Not very."*

> **NOTE** We use **very** with superlative adjectives: *very best/youngest* but with comparative adjectives we use **much** or **very much** (or in informal English, **a lot**): *much/very much better; much/very much younger* ◇ *a lot better; a lot younger.*

**ver·y**[2] /ˈvɛri/ ***adj.*** (used with a noun for emphasis): *We climbed to the very top of the mountain* (= all the way to the top). ◇ *You're the very person I wanted to talk to* (= exactly the right person).

**ves·sel** /ˈvɛsl/ ***noun*** [C] (*formal*) a ship or large boat ➲ Look also at **blood vessel**.

**vest**[1] /vɛst/ ***noun*** [C] a piece of clothing with no sleeves, that is often worn over a shirt or blouse

**ves·ti·bule** /ˈvɛstəbyul/ ***noun*** [C] (*formal*) an entrance hall, for example where hats and coats can be left: *the vestibule of a church/theater/hotel*

**ves·tige** /ˈvɛstɪdʒ/ ***noun*** [C, usually pl.] **vestiges of sth** a small part of sth that remains after the rest of it is gone: *the vestiges of Communism in Eastern Europe*

**ves·try** /ˈvɛstri/ ***noun*** [C] (*pl.* **ves·tries**) a room in a church where a priest prepares for a service by putting on special clothes and where various objects used in worship are kept ➲ Look at **sacristy**.

**vet**[1] /vɛt/ ***noun*** [C] (*informal*) **1** = VETERAN (1): *Vietnam vets* (= who fought in the Vietnam War) **2** = VETERINARIAN

**vet**[2] /vɛt/ ***verb*** (**vet·ting**; **vet·ted**) [T] to check the contents, quality, etc. of sth carefully: *All reports are vetted before publication.* ◇ *She insists on vetting questions prior to an interview.*

**vet·er·an** /ˈvɛt̬ərən/ ***noun*** [C] **1** (*also informal* **vet**) a person who has served in the military forces, especially during a war **2** a person who has very long experience of a particular job or activity: *a veteran journalist*

ˈ**Veterans Day** ***noun*** [sing.] a holiday in the U.S. on 11 November, in honor of members of the armed forces and others who have died in war

> **NOTE** On 11 November in Canada, Canadians celebrate **Remembrance Day**.

**vet·er·i·nar·i·an** /ˌvɛt̬ərəˈnɛriən; ˌvɛt̬rə-; ˌvɛt̬n-ˈɛriən/ ***noun*** [C] (*also informal* **vet**) a person whose job is to give medical help to sick or injured animals; a doctor for animals ▶ **vet·er·i·nar·y** /ˈvɛt̬əˌrəˌnɛri; ˈvɛt̬rə-/ ***adj.***: *a veterinary hospital*

**ve·to**[1] /ˈvitoʊ/ ***verb*** [T] (*pres. part.* **ve·to·ing**; *3rd person sing. pres.* **ve·toes**; *pt, pp* **ve·toed**) to refuse to give official permission for an action or plan, when other people have agreed to it: *The director vetoed the renovation plans because they were too expensive.*

**ve·to²** /ˈvitoʊ/ ***noun*** (*pl.* **ve·toes**) [C,U] the official power to refuse permission for an action or plan, or an act of refusing permission: *Congress is likely to override the President's veto of the tax bill.*

**VHS™** /ˌvi eɪtʃ ˈɛs/ ***abbr.*** the abbreviation for "video home system"; the system used by video recorders and some camcorders: *The movie is now available on DVD and VHS.*

★**vi·a** /ˈviə; ˈvaɪə/ ***prep.*** **1** going through a place: *We flew from Los Angeles to Boston via Chicago.* **2** by means of; using: *These pictures come to you via our satellite link.*

**vi·a·ble** /ˈvaɪəbl/ ***adj.*** that will be successful: *Your idea is just not commercially viable.* ▶ **vi·a·bil·i·ty** /ˌvaɪəˈbɪləṭi/ ***noun*** [U]

**Vi·ag·ra™** /vaɪˈægrə/ ***noun*** [U] a drug used to treat men who are unable to have sex (**impotent**)

**vi·al** /ˈvaɪəl; vaɪl/ ***noun*** [C] a small glass container, for medicine or perfume

**vibe** /vaɪb/ ***noun*** [C, usually pl.] a mood or an atmosphere produced by a particular person, thing or place: *to get good/bad vibes from sb/sth* ◇ *The vibes weren't right.*

**vi·brant** /ˈvaɪbrənt/ ***adj.*** **1** full of life and energy; exciting: *a vibrant city/atmosphere/personality* **2** (used about colors) bright and strong

**vi·brate** /ˈvaɪbreɪt/ ***verb*** [I] to move continuously and very quickly from side to side: *When a guitar string vibrates, it makes a sound.* ▶ **vi·bra·tion** /vaɪˈbreɪʃn/ ***noun*** [C,U]: *Even at full speed, the engine causes very little vibration.*

**vi·car·i·ous** /vaɪˈkɛriəs/ ***adj.*** (only *before* a noun) felt or experienced by watching or reading about sb else doing sth, rather than by doing it yourself: *He got a vicarious thrill out of watching his son score the winning goal.* ▶ **vi·car·i·ous·ly** ***adv.***

**vice** /vaɪs/ ***noun*** **1** [U] illegal actions that are evil or immoral: *the police vice squad* (= the part of the police that deals with illegal drugs/prostitutes) **2** [C] a moral weakness or bad habit: *Greed and envy are terrible vices.* ◇ *My only vice is eating too much chocolate.* ➲ Look at **virtue**.

**vice-** /vaɪs/ ***prefix*** next in importance to the rank mentioned: *the vice-chairman*

**ˌvice ˈpresident** ***noun*** [C] (*abbr.* **VP**) (*also slang* **veep**) **1** the person with the second-highest rank in the government of some countries **2** a person in a large organization who controls a large department or group of departments: *the company's vice president of sales and marketing*

**vice ver·sa** /ˌvaɪs ˈvərsə; ˌvaɪsə-/ ***adv.*** in the opposite way to what has just been said: *All of the French documents were translated into English and vice versa* (= the English documents were translated into French).

**vi·cin·i·ty** /vəˈsɪnəṭi/ ***noun***

IDM **in the vicinity (of sth)** (*formal*) in the surrounding area: *There's no bank in the immediate vicinity.*

**vi·cious** /ˈvɪʃəs/ ***adj.*** **1** cruel; done in order to hurt sb/sth: *a vicious attack* **2** (used about an animal) dangerous

IDM **a vicious circle/cycle** a situation in which one problem leads to another and the new problem makes the first problem worse

▶ **vi·cious·ly** ***adv.***

★**vic·tim** /ˈvɪktəm/ ***noun*** [C] a person or animal that is injured, killed or hurt by sb/sth: *a murder victim* ◇ *The children are often the innocent victims of a divorce.*

**vic·tim·ize** /ˈvɪktəmaɪz/ ***verb*** [T] to punish or make sb suffer unfairly ▶ **vic·tim·i·za·tion** /ˌvɪktəməˈzeɪʃn/ ***noun*** [U]

**vic·tor** /ˈvɪktər/ ***noun*** [C] (*formal*) the person who wins a game, competition, battle, etc.

**Vic·to·ri·a Cross** /vɪkˌtɔriə ˈkrɔs/ ***noun*** [C] (*Cdn*) a medal for bravery that is given in the armed forces of Canada and other countries of the Commonwealth

**Vicˈtoria Day** (*Cdn. also* **ˌQueen's ˈBirthday**) ***noun*** [U,C] (*Cdn*) a public holiday that falls on the Monday before May 25

★**vic·to·ry** /ˈvɪktəri/ ***noun*** [C,U] (*pl.* **vic·to·ries**) success in winning a battle, game, competition, etc.: *the American colonists' victory over the British troops* ◇ *Sue Jenkins won a decisive victory in the school board election.* ◇ *Jordan led his team to victory in the championships.* ▶ **vic·to·ri·ous** /vɪkˈtɔriəs/ ***adj.***: *the victorious team* (= the one that won)

★**vid·e·o** /ˈvɪdioʊ/ ***noun*** (*pl.* **vid·e·os**) **1** [U] the system of recording moving pictures and sound by using a camera, and showing them by using a recorder and a television: *The movie is coming out on video in May.* ◇ *a video camera* **2** [C] a tape or cassette on which a movie or television program has been recorded: *We watched a video in English class today.* ◇ *a video rental store* **3** [C] a short movie that is made to be shown on television along with a popular song instead of speech: *the band's latest music video*

**vid·e·o·cas·sette** /ˌvɪdioʊkəˈsɛt/ ***noun*** [C] a cassette that contains tape on which you can record moving pictures and sound or television programs

**ˌvideocasˈsette reˌcorder** ***noun*** [C] = VCR

**ˈvideo game** ***noun*** [C] a game that you play on a special machine connected to a television, or on a special machine with a screen in a public place

**ˈvideo reˌcorder** ***noun*** [C] = VCR

**vid·e·o·tape¹** /ˈvɪdioʊteɪp/ ***noun*** [C,U] tape used for recording moving pictures and sound or television programs

**vid·e·o·tape²** /ˈvɪdioʊteɪp/ ***verb*** [T] to record moving pictures and sound or a movie or television program onto a VIDEOTAPE¹

**vie** /vaɪ/ ***verb*** (*pres. part.* **vy·ing**; *pt, pp* **vied**) [T] **vie (with sb) (for sth)** (*formal*) to compete strongly with sb in order to obtain or achieve sth: *She was surrounded by men all vying for her attention.* ◇ *a row of restaurants vying with each other for business* ◇ *Screaming fans vied to get closer to their idol.*

★**view¹** /vyu/ ***noun*** **1** [U] the ability to be seen from a particular place: *The garden was hidden from view behind a high wall.* ◇ *to come into/disappear from view* **2** [C] what you can see from a particular place. A view usually means sth pleasant to look at, e.g. a beautiful area of land: *There are breathtaking views*

V

*from the top of the mountain.* ◇ *a room with an ocean view* ➲ Look at the note at **scenery**. **3** [sing.] the ability to see sth from a particular place: *A large truck was blocking her view of the road.* **4** [C] **a view (about/on sth)** an opinion or idea about sth: *He expressed the view that standards were falling.* ◇ *In my view, she has done nothing wrong.* ◇ *strong views on the subject*

IDM **in full view (of sb/sth)** → FULL[1]

**in view of sth** because of sth; as a result of sth: *In view of her apology, we decided to take no further action.*

**point of view** → POINT[1]

**with a view to/toward sth/ doing sth** (*formal*) with the aim or intention of doing sth

★**view**[2] /vyu/ *verb* [T] (*formal*) **1 view sth (as sth)** to consider or think about sth: *She viewed vacations as a waste of time.* ◇ *He views these changes with suspicion.* **2** to watch or look at sth: *Viewed from this angle, the building looks much taller than it really is.*

**view·er** /ˈvyuər/ *noun* [C] a person who watches sth, especially television

**view·find·er** /ˈvyuˌfaɪndər/ *noun* [C] the part of a camera that you look through to see the area that you are photographing ➲ picture at **camera**.

**view·point** /ˈvyupɔɪnt/ *noun* [C] a way of looking at a situation; an opinion

**vig·il** /ˈvɪdʒəl/ *noun* [C,U] a period when you stay awake all night for a special purpose: *to hold a candlelight vigil for peace* ◇ *All night she kept vigil over the sick child.*

**vig·i·lant** /ˈvɪdʒələnt/ *adj.* (*formal*) careful and looking out for danger ▸ **vig·i·lance** /-əns/ *noun* [U]

**vig·i·lan·te** /ˌvɪdʒəˈlænti/ *noun* [C] a person (not a member of the police) who tries to prevent crime in a particular area, or to punish sb that he/she thinks has committed a crime

**vig·or** /ˈvɪgər/ *noun* [U] strength or energy: *After the break, we started work again with renewed vigor.* ▸ **vig·or·ous** /ˈvɪgərəs/ *adj.*: *vigorous exercise* ▸ **vig·or·ous·ly** *adv.*: *Citizens have protested vigorously against the plans to create a new waste dump.*

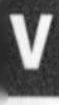

**Vi·king** /ˈvaɪkɪŋ/ *noun* [C] a member of a race of Scandinavian people who attacked and sometimes settled in parts of NW Europe, including Britain, in the 8th to the 11th centuries: *Viking invaders/ships*

**vile** /vaɪl/ *adj.* very bad or unpleasant: *She's in a vile mood.* ◇ *a vile smell*

**vil·la** /ˈvɪlə/ *noun* [C] a pleasant house in the country, usually in a warm region. A villa is often used as a vacation home.

★**vil·lage** /ˈvɪlɪdʒ/ *noun* **1** [C] a very small town: *a small fishing village*

NOTE We use **village** to talk about small towns in Canada, but not in the United States. **Village** is used for places that seem more old-fashioned than big North American cities: *a quaint English village.*

**2** [sing.] all the people who live in a VILLAGE (1): *The whole village is taking part in the festival.*

**vil·lain** /ˈvɪlən/ *noun* [C] an evil person, especially in a book or play: *In old westerns, the villains usually wear black hats.* ➲ Look at **hero**. ▸ **vil·lain·ous** /ˈvɪlənəs/ *adj.*

**vil·lain·y** /ˈvɪləni/ *noun* [U] (*formal*) immoral or cruel behavior

**vin·ai·grette** /ˌvɪnɪˈgrɛt/ *noun* [U] a mixture of oil, vinegar and various herbs, etc., used to add flavor to a salad

**vin·di·cate** /ˈvɪndəkeɪt/ *verb* [T] (*formal*) **1** to prove that sth is true or that you were right to do sth, especially when other people had a different opinion: *I'm sure that my decision will be vindicated.* **2** to prove that sb is not guilty when he/she has been accused of doing sth wrong or illegal: *New evidence emerged, vindicating him completely.* ▸ **vin·di·ca·tion** /ˌvɪndəˈkeɪʃn/ *noun* [U, sing.]

**vin·dic·tive** /vɪnˈdɪktɪv/ *adj.* trying to harm or upset sb, or showing that you want to, because you think that he/she has harmed you: *He accused her of being vindictive.* ◇ *a vindictive comment/person* ▸ **vin·dic·tive·ness** /vɪnˈdɪktɪvnəs/ *noun* [U]

**vine** /vaɪn/ *noun* [C] a plant that climbs up a surface, e.g. a wall, as it grows

**vin·e·gar** /ˈvɪnɪgər/ *noun* [U] a liquid with a strong sharp taste that is made from wine, etc. Vinegar is often mixed with oil and put onto salads.

**vine·yard** /ˈvɪnyərd/ *noun* [C] a piece of land where grapes are grown for making wine

**vin·tage** /ˈvɪntɪdʒ/ *adj.* (only *before* a noun) **1** (used about wine) that was produced in a particular year and district: *a bottle of vintage champagne* **2** of very high quality and showing typical characteristics of sb/sth: *a vintage performance by Dustin Hoffman* **3** very old, and often valuable: *vintage clothing*

**vi·nyl** /ˈvaɪnl/ *noun* [C,U] **1** a strong plastic that can bend easily, used for making wall, floor and furniture coverings, book covers, and, especially in the past, records **2** records made of vinyl, in contrast to CDs: *My dad had to buy CDs of all the albums he already owned* ***on vinyl***.

**vi·o·la** /viˈoʊlə/ *noun* [C] a musical instrument with strings that looks like a violin but is slightly larger ➲ Note that we play **the** viola.

**vi·o·late** /ˈvaɪəleɪt/ *verb* [T] **1** to break sth (e.g. a rule or agreement): *to violate a peace treaty* **2** to disturb sth; not to respect sth: *to violate sb's privacy/rights* ▸ **vi·o·la·tion** /ˌvaɪəˈleɪʃn/ *noun* [C,U]: *violation of human rights* ◇ *a ticket for a parking violation* ▸ **vi·o·la·tor** /ˈvaɪəleɪt̬ər/ *noun* [C]: *traffic violators*

★**vi·o·lence** /ˈvaɪələns/ *noun* [U] **1** violent behavior: *They threatened to use violence if we didn't give them the money.* ◇ *Is there too much violence on TV?* ◇ *an act of violence* **2** great force or energy: *the hurricane's violence*

★**vi·o·lent** /ˈvaɪələnt/ *adj.* **1** using physical strength, often in an uncontrolled way, to hurt or kill sb; caused by this behavior: *a violent man who abused his children* ◇ *The demonstration started peacefully but later turned violent.* ◇ *a violent death* **2** very strong; uncontrolled: *He has a violent temper.* ◇ *a violent storm* ▸ **vi·o·lent·ly** *adv.*

**vi·o·let** /ˈvaɪələt/ ***noun*** **1** [C] a small plant that grows wild or in gardens and has purple or white flowers and a pleasant smell **2** [U] a color similar to purple, between blue and red ▸ **vi·o·let** ***adj.***

**vi·o·lin** /ˌvaɪəˈlɪn/ ***noun*** [C] a musical instrument with strings, that you hold under your chin and play by moving a special stick (a **bow**) across the strings ➲ Note that we play **the** violin. Look also at **fiddle**[1].



**VIP** /ˌvi aɪ ˈpi/ ***noun*** [C] (*pl.* **VIPs**) (*informal*) very important person; a person who gets or deserves special treatment and attention: *the VIP lounge at the airport*

**vi·per** /ˈvaɪpər/ ***noun*** [C] a small poisonous snake

**vi·ral** /ˈvaɪrəl/ ***adj.*** like or caused by a virus: *a viral infection*

**vir·gin**[1] /ˈvərdʒən/ ***noun*** [C] a person who has never had sex ▸ **vir·gin·i·ty** /vərˈdʒɪnəṭi/ ***noun*** [U]: *to lose your virginity* (= to have sex for the first time)

**vir·gin**[2] /ˈvərdʒən/ ***adj.*** (only *before* a noun) that has not yet been used, touched, damaged, etc.: *virgin forest*

**Vir·go** /ˈvərgoʊ/ ***noun*** (*pl.* **Vir·gos**) [C,U] the sixth sign of the zodiac, the Virgin; a person who was born under this sign

**vir·ile** /ˈvɪrəl/ ***adj.*** (used about a man) strong and having great sexual energy ▸ **vi·ril·i·ty** /vəˈrɪləṭi/ ***noun*** [U]

**vir·tu·al** /ˈvərtʃuəl/ ***adj.*** (only *before* a noun) **1** being almost or nearly sth: *Traffic came to a virtual standstill on the highways during yesterday's storm.* **2** made to appear to exist by the use of computer software for example on the Internet: *New technology has enabled development of an online "virtual library."* ▸ **vir·tu·al·ly** /ˈvərtʃuəli; -tʃəli/ ***adv.***: *The building is virtually finished.*

ˌ**virtual reˈality** ***noun*** [U] pictures and often also sounds, that are produced by a computer and are intended to seem almost like a real place or situation

**vir·tue** /ˈvərtʃu/ ***noun*** **1** [U] behavior which shows high moral standards; goodness: *to lead a life of virtue* **2** [C] a good quality or habit: *Patience is a great virtue.* ➲ Look at **vice** (2). **3** [C,U] **the virtue (of sth/of doing sth)** an advantage or a useful quality of sth: *This new material has the virtue of being strong as well as very light.*

IDM **by virtue of** (*formal*) because of: *She got the job by virtue of her friendship with the company's owner.*

**vir·tu·o·so** /ˌvərtʃuˈoʊsoʊ/ ***noun*** [C] (*pl.* **vir·tu·o·sos** or **vir·tu·o·si** /-si/) a person who is extremely skillful at doing sth, especially playing a musical instrument: *a piano virtuoso*

**vir·tu·o·so** /ˌvərtʃuˈoʊsoʊ/ ***adj.*** (only *before* a noun) showing extremely great skill: *a virtuoso display/performance* ◇ *a virtuoso pianist*

**vir·tu·ous** /ˈvərtʃuəs/ ***adj.*** behaving in a moral or good way

**vir·u·lent** /ˈvɪrələnt; ˈvɪryə-/ ***adj.*** (*formal*) **1** (used about a poison or a disease) very strong and dangerous: *a particularly virulent form of the flu* **2** very strong and full of anger: *a virulent attack on the president*

**vi·rus** /ˈvaɪrəs/ ***noun*** [C] (*pl.* **vi·rus·es**) **1** a living thing, too small to be seen with the eye, that causes disease in people, animals and plants: *HIV, the virus that causes AIDS* ➲ Look at **bacteria** and **germ**. **2** (*computing*) instructions that are put into a computer program in order to cause errors and destroy information

**vi·sa** /ˈvizə/ ***noun*** [C] an official mark in your passport that shows you are allowed to enter, leave or travel through a country: *She applied for an extension when her visa expired.* ◇ *a tourist visa*

**vis-à-vis** /ˌvizəˈvi/ ***prep.*** **1** in relation to: *Britain's role vis-à-vis the United States* **2** in comparison with: *It was felt that the company had an unfair advantage vis-à-vis smaller companies elsewhere.*

**vis·cer·al** /ˈvɪsərəl/ ***adj.*** resulting from strong feelings rather than careful thought: *visceral fear/excitement* ◇ *She had a visceral dislike of all things foreign.*

**vis·cous** /ˈvɪskəs/ ***adj.*** (*technical*) (used about a liquid) thick and sticky; not flowing freely ▸ **vis·cos·i·ty** /vɪˈskɑsəṭi/ ***noun*** [U]

**vise** /vaɪs/ ***noun*** [C] a tool that you use to hold a piece of wood, metal, etc. firmly while you are working on it ▸ **vise·like** /ˈvaɪslaɪk/ ***adj.***: *He held my arm in a viselike* (= very firm) ***grip***.

**vis·i·bil·i·ty** /ˌvɪzəˈbɪləṭi/ ***noun*** [U] the distance that you can see in particular light or weather conditions: *In the fog, visibility was down to 100 feet.* ◇ *poor/good visibility*

★**vis·i·ble** /ˈvɪzəbl/ ***adj.*** that can be seen or noticed: *The stain was visible, even though he had washed his shirt twice.* ◇ *a visible improvement* OPP **invisible**

ˌ**visible miˈnority** ***noun*** [U] (*Cdn*) an ethnic group whose members are clearly racially different from those of the majority race in a society: *She encountered some prejudice because she was a visible minority.*

**vis·i·bly** /ˈvɪzəbli/ ***adv.*** clearly; in a way that is easy to notice: *Tom was visibly upset.*

★**vi·sion** /ˈvɪʒn/ ***noun*** **1** [U] the ability to see; sight: *to have good/poor/normal/perfect vision* **2** [U] the ability to make great plans for the future: *a statesman of great vision* **3** [C] a picture in your imagination: *They have a vision of a world without weapons.* ◇ *I had visions of being left behind, but in fact the others had waited for me.* **4** [C] a dreamlike state often connected with a religious experience: *God appeared to Paul in a vision.*

**vi·sion·ar·y** /ˈvɪʒəˌnɛri/ ***noun*** [C] (*pl.* **vi·sion·ar·ies**) a person who has the ability to think about or plan the future in a way that is intelligent or shows imagination: *She was a true visionary.* ◇ *The company needs visionaries to see opportunities.* ▸ **vi·sion·ar·y** ***adj.***: *a visionary leader*

★**vis·it**[1] /ˈvɪzət/ ***verb*** **1** [I,T] to come or go to see a person or place and to spend a short time there: *I don't live here. I'm just visiting.* ◇ *We often visit*

V

*relatives on weekends.* ◇ *She's going to visit her son in the hospital.* ◇ *When you go to New York City, you have to visit the Statue of Liberty.* **2** [I] **visit (with sb)** (*informal*) to talk in a friendly, informal way: *I was just visiting with Lynn in the backyard.*

★**vis·it²** /'vɪzət/ ***noun*** [C] a short stay with sb or in a particular place: *The President is on an official visit to Japan.* ◇ *We had a visit from Richard on Sunday.*

**vis·it·a·tion** /ˌvɪzə'teɪʃn/ ***noun*** **1** [U] the right of a parent who is divorced or separated from his or her partner to visit a child who is living with the partner: *visitation rights* **2** [C,U] **visitation (of/from sb/sth)** (*formal*) an official visit, especially to check that rules are being obeyed and everything is as it should be **3** [C] a meeting of family members before the funeral of sb who has died **4** [C] (*formal*) **visitation (of/from sb/sth)** an unexpected appearance of sb/sth, for example a ghost

★**vis·i·tor** /'vɪzət̬ər/ ***noun*** [C] a person who visits sb/sth: *We're not free on Sunday. We're having visitors.* ◇ *foreign visitors to California*

**vi·sor** /'vaɪzər/ ***noun*** [C] **1** the part of a hard hat (a helmet) that you can pull down to protect your eyes or face **2** a piece of plastic, cloth, etc. on a hat or in a car, which keeps the sun out of your eyes

**vis·ta** /'vɪstə/ ***noun*** [C] **1** a beautiful view, for example, of the countryside, a city, etc. **2** (*written*) a range of things that might happen in the future: *This new job could open up whole new vistas for her.*

★**vi·su·al** /'vɪʒuəl/ ***adj.*** connected with seeing: *the visual arts* (= painting/sculpture/movies) ▸ **vi·su·al·ly** ***adv.***: *to be visually impaired* (= to be partly or completely blind)

ˌ**visual 'aid** ***noun*** [C] a picture, movie, map, etc. that helps students to learn sth

**vi·su·al·ize** /'vɪʒuəlaɪz/ ***verb*** [T] to imagine or have a picture in your mind of sb/sth: *It's hard to visualize what this place looked like before the factory was built.* ◇ *I can't visualize Liz as a mother.*

★**vi·tal** /'vaɪt̬l/ ***adj.*** very important or necessary: *Practice is vital if you want to speak a language well.* ◇ *vital information* ▸ **vi·tal·ly** ***adv.***: *vitally important*

**vi·tal·i·ty** /vaɪ'tæləṭi/ ***noun*** [U] the state of being lively or full of energy

ˌ**vital 'signs** ***noun*** [usually pl.] (*medical*) a measurement that shows that sb is alive, such as the rate of his/her breathing, the body temperature or the heartbeat: *to check/monitor the patient's vital signs*

ˌ**vital sta'tistics** ***noun*** [pl.] **1** numbers that show how many births and deaths there have been in a country **2** (*informal*) the measurements of a woman's chest, waist and hips

**vi·ta·min** /'vaɪt̬əmən/ ***noun*** [C] one of several substances that are found in certain types of food and that are very important for growth and good health: *Oranges are rich in vitamin C.* ◇ *a vitamin deficiency*

**vit·ri·ol** /'vɪtriəl/ ***noun*** [U] (*formal*) very cruel and bitter comments or criticism ▸ **vit·ri·ol·ic** /ˌvɪtri'ɑlɪk/ ***adj.*** (*formal*): *The newspaper launched a vitriolic attack on the police force.*

**vi·va·cious** /vɪ'veɪʃəs; vaɪ-/ ***adj.*** (used about a person, usually a woman) full of energy; lively and cheerful

**viv·id** /'vɪvəd/ ***adj.*** **1** (used about light or a color) strong and bright: *the vivid reds and yellows of the flowers* **2** having or producing a strong, clear picture in your mind: *a vivid description of his time in the army* ◇ *a vivid dream* ▸ **viv·id·ly** ***adv.***

**viv·i·sec·tion** /ˌvɪvə'sɛkʃn; 'vɪvəˌsɛk-/ ***noun*** [U] the practice of doing experiments on live animals for medical or scientific research

**vix·en** /'vɪksən/ ***noun*** [C] **1** an attractive, sexy woman who is clever at getting what she wants, and does not show any respect **2** a female fox

'**V-neck** ***noun*** [C] an opening for the neck in a piece of clothing shaped like the letter V; a piece of clothing with a V-neck: *a V-neck sweater* ◇ *I went out and bought a navy V-neck.* ▸ '**V-necked** ***adj.***: *a V-necked sweater*

**vo·cab·u·lar·y** /voʊ'kæbyəˌlɛri; və-/ ***noun*** (*pl.* **vo·cab·u·lar·ies**) **1** [sing.] all the words in a language: *New words are always coming into the vocabulary.* **2** [C,U] all the words that sb knows or that are used in a particular book, subject, etc.: *He has a large vocabulary for such a small child.* ◇ *There are many ways to increase your English vocabulary.*

**vo·cal** /'voʊkl/ ***adj.*** **1** connected with the voice: *vocal music* **2** expressing your ideas or opinions loudly or freely: *a small but vocal group of protesters*

'**vocal ˌcords** ***noun*** [pl.] the thin strips of muscle in the throat that move to produce the voice

**vo·cal·ist** /'voʊkl·ɪst/ ***noun*** [C] a singer, especially one who sings popular or jazz music

**vo·cal·ize** /'voʊkəlaɪz/ ***verb*** (*formal*) **1** [T] to use words to express sth: *Showing children pictures sometimes helps them to vocalize their ideas.* **2** [I,T] to say or sing sounds or words: *Your baby will begin to vocalize long before she can talk.*

**vo·ca·tion** /voʊ'keɪʃn/ ***noun*** [C,U] (*formal*) the feeling that you are especially suited for a particular kind of work, often one which involves helping other people; the ability to do this kind of work: *Peter followed his vocation to become a priest.*

**vo·ca·tion·al** /voʊ'keɪʃn·l/ ***adj.*** connected with the skills or qualifications that you need to do a particular job, especially a job that involves working with tools: *vocational training* ◇ *a vocational school.* (= that teaches students to do jobs that involve working with tools)

**vo·cif·er·ous** /voʊ'sɪfərəs/ ***adj.*** (*formal*) expressing your opinions or feelings in a loud and confident way: *vociferous complaints/protests/demands* ▸ **vo·cif·er·ous·ly** ***adv.***: *to complain/protest vociferously*

**vod·ka** /'vɑdkə/ ***noun*** [U] a strong clear alcoholic drink originally from Russia

**vogue** /voʊg/ ***noun*** [C,U, usually sing.] **vogue (for sth)** a fashion for sth: *the current vogue for historical fiction* ◇ *Black is always* ***in vogue.*** ◇ *Sixties music has come back into vogue.*

★**voice¹** /vɔɪs/ ***noun*** **1** [C] the sounds that you make when you speak or sing; the ability to make these sounds: *I heard voices near the house and went out to see who it was.* ◇ *She has a beautiful voice* (= she can sing beautifully). ◇ *He had a bad cold and lost his voice.* ◇ *to speak in a loud/soft/low/hoarse voice* ◇ *Shh! Keep your voice down!* ◇ *to raise/lower your voice* (= to make it louder/quieter) ◇ *Alan is 13 and*

V

*his voice is beginning to break* (= to become deep and low like a man's). **2** [U, sing.] **voice (in sth)** (the right to express) your ideas or opinions: *The office employees have no voice in the running of the company.* **3** [sing.] (*grammar*) the form of a verb that shows the relationship between the subject and the verb in a sentence: *"Frost wrote this poem" is in the active voice.* ◇ *"This poem was written by Frost" is in the passive voice.*

IDM **at the top of your voice** → TOP[1]

**voice[2]** /vɔɪs/ ***verb*** [T] to express your opinions or feelings: *The employees voiced their objection to the proposed layoffs.*

**voice·box** /ˈvɔɪsbɑks/ (*also* ˈ**voice box**) ***noun*** [C] the area at the top of the throat that contains the vocal cords

ˈ**voice mail** ***noun*** [U] an electronic system that lets you record telephone messages for sb when he/she is not available to answer the telephone ➲ Look at **answering machine**.

ˈ**voice-ˌover** ***noun*** [C] information or comments in a movie, television program, etc. that are given by a person who is not seen on the screen

**void[1]** /vɔɪd/ ***noun*** [C, usually sing.] (*formal*) an empty space: (*figurative*) *Her death left a void in their lives.*

**void[2]** /vɔɪd/ ***adj.*** (*formal*) **void (of sth)** empty; without sth

**void[3]** /vɔɪd/ ***verb*** [T] **1** (in law) to state officially that sth is no longer valid **2** (*formal*) to empty waste matter from the bladder or bowels

**vol.** ***abbr.*** = VOLUME

**vol·a·tile** /ˈvɑlət̬l/ ***adj.*** **1** that can change suddenly: *The situation in the Middle East is still very volatile.* ◇ *a volatile personality* **2** (*technical*) (used about a liquid) that can easily change into a gas ▸ **vol·a·til·i·ty** /ˌvɑləˈtɪlət̬i/ ***noun*** [U]

**vol·ca·no** /vɑlˈkeɪnoʊ/ ***noun*** [C] (*pl.* **vol·ca·noes**) a mountain with a hole (crater) at the top through which steam, hot liquid rock (lava), fire, etc. sometimes come out: *an active/a dormant/an extinct volcano* ◇ *When did the volcano last erupt?* ▸ **vol·can·ic** /vɑlˈkænɪk/ ***adj.***

**vo·li·tion** /vəˈlɪʃn; voʊ-/ ***noun*** [U] (*formal*) the power to choose sth freely or to make your own decisions: *They left entirely* ***of their own volition*** (= because they wanted to).

**vol·ley[1]** /ˈvɑli/ ***noun*** [C] (*pl.* **vol·leys**) **1** a number of stones, bullets, etc. that are thrown, shot, etc. at the same time: *The soldiers fired a volley over the heads of the crowd.* ◇ (*figurative*) *a volley of abuse* **2** (in tennis, etc.) an act of hitting the ball before it touches the ground

**vol·ley[2]** /ˈvɑli/ ***verb*** [T] (in some sports, for example tennis or soccer) to hit or kick the ball before it touches the ground: *He volleyed the ball into the back of the net.*

**vol·ley·ball** /ˈvɑlibɔl/ ***noun*** [U] a game in which two teams try to hit a ball over a high net with their hands and not let it touch the ground

**volt** /voʊlt/ ***noun*** [C] (*abbr.* **V**) a unit for measuring electrical force

**volt·age** /ˈvoʊltɪdʒ/ ***noun*** [C,U] the electrical force that is measured in volts: *Danger! High voltage* (on a sign near electrical equipment)

★**vol·ume** /ˈvɑlyəm; -yum/ ***noun*** (*abbr.* **vol.**) **1** [C] a book, especially one of a set or series: *The library has over 100,000 volumes.* ◇ *The dictionary comes in three volumes.* **2** [C,U] the amount of space that sth contains or occupies: *What is the volume of this sphere?* ◇ *A pound of feathers is greater in volume than a pound of gold.* ➲ Look at **area**. **3** [U] the quantity or amount of sth: *the volume of traffic on the roads* **4** [U] the strength or degree of sound that sth makes: *to turn the volume on a radio up/down*

**vo·lu·mi·nous** /vəˈlumənəs/ ***adj.*** (*formal*) **1** (used about clothing) very large; having a lot of cloth: *a voluminous cloak/skirt* **2** (used about a piece of writing, a book, etc.) very long and detailed: *There is voluminous literature on modernism and post-modernism.* **3** (used about a container, piece of furniture, etc.) very large: *I sank down into a voluminous armchair.* ◇ *From one of his voluminous pockets he produced a bottle of whiskey.*

**vol·un·tar·y** /ˈvɑlənˌtɛri/ ***adj.*** done or given willingly, not because you have to do it: *voluntary guidelines to control advertising on the Internet* ➲ Something that you must do is **mandatory**. ▸ **vol·un·tar·i·ly** /ˌvɑlənˈtɛrəli/ ***adv.***: *She left the job voluntarily – she wasn't fired.*

★**vol·un·teer[1]** /ˌvɑlənˈtɪr/ ***noun*** [C] a person who offers or agrees to do sth without being forced or paid to do it: *He does a lot of volunteer work at the hospital.* ◇ *volunteer firefighters* ◇ *Are there any volunteers who want to write their answers on the board?*

**vol·un·teer[2]** /ˌvɑlənˈtɪr/ ***verb*** **1** [I,T] **volunteer (sth)**; **volunteer (for sth)**; **volunteer (to do sth)** to offer sth or to do sth which you do not have to do or for which you will not be paid: *They volunteered their services free of charge.* ◇ *She volunteered for the school's social committee.* ◇ *One of my friends volunteered to take us all in his car.* **2** [T] to give information, etc. or make a comment or suggestion without being asked to: *I volunteered a few helpful suggestions.*

**vo·lup·tu·ous** /vəˈlʌptʃuəs/ ***adj.*** **1** (*written*) (used about a woman) attractive in a sexual way with large breasts and hips: *a voluptuous woman* ◇ *a voluptuous body/mouth* **2** giving you physical pleasure: *voluptuous soft velvet*

**vom·it** /ˈvɑmət/ ***verb*** [I,T] (*formal*) to bring food, etc. up from the stomach and out of the mouth ➲ It is more common to say **throw up**: *I ate too much last night and threw up.* ▸ **vom·it** ***noun*** [U]: *the smell of vomit*

**voo·doo** /ˈvudu/ ***noun*** [U] a religion that is practiced especially in Haiti and involves magic and witchcraft

**vo·ra·cious** /vəˈreɪʃəs; vɔ-/ ***adj.*** (*written*) **1** eating or wanting large amounts of food: *to have a* ***voracious appetite*** **2** wanting a lot of new information and knowledge: *a voracious reader*

**vor·tex** /ˈvɔrtɛks/ ***noun*** [C] (*pl.* **vor·tex·es** or **vort·i·ces** /-t̬əsiz/) **1** (*technical*) a mass of air, water, etc. that spins around very fast and pulls things into its center **2** a very powerful feeling, force or situation

V

that you cannot avoid or escape from: *They were both caught up in a whirling vortex of emotion.*

★**vote**[1] /voʊt/ ***noun*** **1** [C] a method of deciding sth by asking people to express their choice and finding out what the majority want: *Let's take a vote. All those in favor, raise your hands.* **2** [C] **a vote (for/against sb/sth)** an expression of your choice in an election, etc., which you show by raising your hand or writing on a piece of paper: *The votes are still being counted.* ◇ *There were nearly 20,000 votes for Mr. Wells.* **3 the vote** [sing.] the votes given or received by a certain group in an election: *The Democratic candidate received 42% of the vote.*

★**vote**[2] /voʊt/ ***verb*** **1** [I,T] **vote (for/against sb/sth)**; **vote (on sth)** to show a choice of opinion with a vote: *Who did you vote for in the last election?* ◇ *Very few senators voted against the new law.* ◇ *Now that we've heard everybody's opinion, I think it's time to vote on it.* ◇ *They voted to ban smoking in the building.* ◇ *I voted Liberal.* **2** [T] to choose sb for a particular position or honor: *He was voted best actor.*

**vot·er** /ˈvoʊt̬ər/ ***noun*** [C] a person who votes or has the right to vote in a political election

**ˈvoting booth** ***noun*** [C] a small, partly enclosed place in a polling place where people vote by marking a card, etc.

**ˈvoting maˌchine** ***noun*** [C] a machine in which votes can be recorded automatically

**vouch** /vaʊtʃ/ ***verb***

PHR V **vouch for sb/sth** to state that a person is honest or good or that sth is true or genuine

**vouch·er** /ˈvaʊtʃər/ ***noun*** [C] an official piece of paper that you can exchange for certain goods or services, instead of using money

**vow**[1] /vaʊ/ ***noun*** [C] a formal promise (especially in a religious ceremony): *marriage vows* ◇ *a vow of silence*

**vow**[2] /vaʊ/ ***verb*** [T] to make a serious promise: *We vowed never to discuss the subject again.*

**vow·el** /ˈvaʊəl/ ***noun*** [C] a sound that you make with your lips and teeth open; one of the sounds represented in English by the letters "a," "e," "i," "o," or "u," and sometimes "y" ➲ Look at **consonant**.

**voy·age** /ˈvɔɪɪdʒ/ ***noun*** [C] a long trip by ship or in space: *Magellan's voyages of discovery* ◇ *a spacecraft on a voyage to Mars* ▸ **voy·ag·er** /ˈvɔɪɪdʒər/ ***noun*** [C]

**vo·yeur** /vɔɪˈər; vwɑˈyər/ ***noun*** [C] **1** a person who gets pleasure from secretly watching other people have sex **2** a person who enjoys watching the problems and private lives of others: *Most writers are voyeurs of a kind.* ▸ **vo·yeur·ism** /vɔɪˈərɪzəm; vwɑˈyər-; ˈvɔɪər-/ ***noun*** [U]

**VP** ***abbr.*** = VICE PRESIDENT

**vs.** ***abbr.*** = VERSUS

**vul·gar** /ˈvʌlgər/ ***adj.*** rude or likely to offend people, especially because it is about sex: *a vulgar joke* ◇ *a vulgar gesture* ▸ **vul·gar·i·ty** /vʌlˈgærət̬i; -ˈgɛr-/ ***noun*** [U,C] (*pl.* **vul·gar·i·ties**)

**vul·ner·a·ble** /ˈvʌlnərəbl/ ***adj.*** **vulnerable (to sth/sb)** easy to attack, hurt or defeat; open to danger: *Poor organization left the troops vulnerable to enemy attack.* ◇ *She felt lonely and vulnerable, living on her own in the city.* OPP **invulnerable** ▸ **vul·ner·a·bil·i·ty** /ˌvʌlnərəˈbɪlət̬i/ ***noun*** [U]

**vul·ture** /ˈvʌltʃər/ ***noun*** [C] a large bird that has no feathers on its head or neck and that eats the flesh of dead animals

**vy·ing** /ˈvaɪɪŋ/ → VIE

# Ww

**W, w** /ˈdʌblyu; ˈdʌbəyu; -yə/ ***noun*** [C,U] (*pl.* **W's; w's**) the twenty-third letter of the English alphabet: *"Water" begins with (a) "w."*

**W** ***abbr.*** **1** = WATT **2** (*also* **W.**) = WEST, WESTERN[1]

**w/** ***abbr.*** (*written*) with

**wack** /wæk/ ***adj.*** (*slang*) (*especially US*) **1** very bad; not of good quality: *That movie was really wack.* **2** very strange: *Man, that is just so wack.*

**wack·o** (*also* **whack·o**) /ˈwækoʊ/ ***noun*** [C] (**wack·os**) (*informal*) a crazy person: *He is a total wacko.* ▸ **wack·o** ***adj.*** (*informal*): *wacko opinions*

**wack·y** /ˈwæki/ ***adj.*** (**wack·i·er**; **wack·i·est**) (*informal*) exciting, new and crazy: *a wacky comedian*

**wad**[1] /wɑd/ ***noun*** [C] **1** a lump or ball of soft material that is used for blocking sth, keeping sth in place, etc.: *The nurse used a wad of cotton to stop the bleeding.* **2** a thick pile of pieces of paper, paper money, etc. folded or rolled together: *a wad of $100 bills*

**wad**[2] /wɑd/ ***verb*** [T] **wad sth (up)** to fold or press sth into a tight WAD[1] (2)

**wad·dle** /ˈwɑdl/ ***verb*** [I] to walk with short steps, leaning to one side and then to the other, like a duck: *A small, fat person waddled past.*

**wade** /weɪd/ ***verb*** [I] **1** to walk with bare feet in shallow water **2** to walk with difficulty through fairly deep mud, etc.

PHR V **wade through sth** (not passive) to deal with or read sth that is boring and takes a lot of time: *I spent the whole day wading through the paperwork on my desk.*

**ˈwading pool** ***noun*** [C] a shallow swimming pool for children to play in, especially a small plastic one that you fill with water

**wa·fer** /ˈweɪfər/ ***noun*** [C] **1** a thin, crisp light cookie, often eaten with ice cream: *vanilla wafers* **2** a very thin round piece of special bread given by the priest during a religious service (**Communion**)

**ˌwafer-ˈthin** ***adj.*** very thin: *wafer-thin mints* ◇ *Our profit margin is already wafer-thin.*

**waf·fle**[1] /ˈwɑfl/ ***noun*** **1** [C] a small, crisp cake, made of flour, eggs and milk, that has a pattern of squares on it and is usually eaten with a sweet sauce (syrup) **2** (*Cdn*) language that uses a lot of words but does not say anything important or interesting

**waf·fle²** /ˈwɑfl/ *verb* [I] (*informal*) **1 waffle (on/over sth)** to be unable to decide what to do about sth or what you think about sth: *The senator was accused of waffling on major issues.* **2** (*Cdn*) to talk or write using a lot of words but without saying anything interesting or important

ˈ**waffle ˌiron** *noun* [C] a kitchen tool, consisting of two shallow metal pans joined together, which is used for making waffles

**waft** /wɑft; wæft/ *verb* [I,T] to move lightly through the air; to make sth move in this way: *The smell of her perfume wafted through the room.*

**wag** /wæg/ *verb* [I,T] (**wag·ging; wagged**) to shake up and down or move from side to side: *The dog is wagging his tail.*

★**wage¹** /weɪdʒ/ *noun* **1** [sing.] the amount of money paid for a certain amount of work, usually one hour: *What's the average wage in this area?* **2 wages** [pl.] the pay that you receive, usually based on the number of hours that you have worked: *Any money missing from the cash register will be taken out of your wages.* ➲ Look at **salary** and at the note at **pay¹**.

**wage²** /weɪdʒ/ *verb* [T] **wage sth (against/on sb/sth)** to begin and continue sth, especially a war: *to wage war* ◇ *The police are waging a campaign against illegal drugs.*

**wag·on** /ˈwægən/ *noun* [C] **1** a vehicle with four wheels that is pulled by horses, etc. and used for transporting things **2** a children's toy like an open box on wheels, with a long handle for pulling it **3** (*informal*) = STATION WAGON

IDM **be/go on the wagon** (*informal*) to not drink alcohol, either for a short time or permanently

ˈ**wagon train** *noun* [C] a long line of wagons and horses, used by people traveling west in North America in the 19th century

**waif** /weɪf/ *noun* [C] a small thin person, usually a child, who looks as if he/she does not have enough to eat: *the* ***waifs and strays*** *of our society* (= people with no home)

**wail** /weɪl/ *verb* **1** [I,T] to cry or complain in a loud, high voice: *the sound of children wailing* ◇ *"Won't somebody help me?" she wailed.* **2** [I] to make a sound like this: *sirens wailing in the streets outside* ▶ **wail** *noun* [C]: *the wail of sirens*

★**waist** /weɪst/ *noun* [C, usually sing.] **1** the part around the middle of the body between the stomach and the hips (and often narrower than them): *What's your waist measurement?* ◇ *a 26-inch waist* ◇ *She put her arms around his waist.* ➲ picture on study page **A32**. **2** the part of a piece of clothing that goes around the waist

**waist·band** /ˈweɪstbænd/ *noun* [C] the strip of cloth that forms the waist of a piece of clothing, especially at the top of a skirt or pair of pants: *an elastic waistband*

**waist·line** /ˈweɪstlaɪn/ *noun* [C, usually sing.] **1** the measurement or size of the body around the waist: *a slim waistline* **2** the part of a piece of clothing that fits around or close to the waist: *a skirt with a high waistline*

★**wait¹** /weɪt/ *verb* [I] **1 wait (for sb/sth) (to do sth)** to remain in a particular place, and not do anything until sb/sth arrives or until sth happens: *Wait here. I'll be back in a few minutes.* ◇ *Have you been waiting long?* ◇ *If I'm a little late, can you wait for me?* ◇ *I wrote to them a few weeks ago and I'm still waiting for a reply.* ◇ *I'm waiting to see the doctor.* ◇ *He's waiting for them to tell him whether he got the job or not.* ◇ *I can't wait* (= I am very eager) *to find out what happens at the end.*

> NOTE Compare **wait** and **expect**: *I was expecting him to be there at 7:30, but at 8 I was still waiting.* ◇ *I'm waiting for my report card, but I'm not expecting to get any A's.* If you **wait**, you pass the time often doing little else, until sth happens: *I waited outside the theater until they arrived.* If you **expect** sth, you believe that sth will happen: *I'm expecting a reply from them soon, because it's been a month since I wrote.*

**2** to be left or delayed until a later time; not to be done or dealt with immediately: *Is this matter urgent or can it wait?*

IDM **keep sb waiting** to make sb wait: *I'm sorry if I kept you waiting.*

**wait a minute/second** (*informal*) **1** (used to tell sb to stop doing sth and wait for a short time): *Wait a minute – Jeff has to tie his shoes.* **2** (used to interrupt sb because you have just noticed sth): *Hey, wait a minute – this is sugar, not salt.*

**wait and see** to wait and find out what will happen (perhaps before deciding to do sth)

**wait tables** to work in a restaurant, taking people's orders and bringing them food and drinks

**wait your turn** to wait until the time when you are allowed to do sth

PHRV **wait around** to stay in a place doing nothing because sb or sth is late

**wait behind** to stay in a place after others have left it

**wait on sb** to bring food, drinks, etc. to sb, usually in a restaurant

**wait up (for sb)** to not go to bed because you are waiting for sb to come home: *I won't be back until very late, so don't wait up.*

**wait²** /weɪt/ *noun* [C, usually sing.] **a wait (for sth/sb)** a period of time when you wait: *a short/long wait*

**wait·er** /ˈweɪt̬ər/ *noun* [C] a man whose job is to take orders from customers and bring food and drinks to them in a restaurant ➲ **Server** is a word that can be used for a man or a woman who works in a restaurant.

ˈ**waiting list** *noun* [C] a list of people who are waiting for sth that will be available in the future: *to put sb's name on the waiting list*

ˈ**waiting room** *noun* [C] a room at a doctor's office, etc. where people can sit and wait

**wait·ress** /ˈweɪtrəs/ *noun* [C] a woman whose job is to take orders from customers and bring food and drinks to them in a restaurant

> NOTE **Server** is a word that can be used for a man or a woman who works in a restaurant.

V

**waive** /weɪv/ ***verb*** [T] (*formal*) to state that a rule, etc. does not have to be obeyed; to give up a right to sth: *The coach waived the age requirement so that Amy could play on the senior high team.* ◇ *He waived his right to a trial by jury.*

**waiv·er** /ˈweɪvər/ ***noun*** [C] an official document that says that a rule, etc. does not have to be obeyed

★**wake¹** /weɪk/ ***verb*** (*pt* **woke** /woʊk/; *pp* **wo·ken** /ˈwoʊkən/) **1** [I] **wake (up)** to stop being asleep: *I woke early in the morning and got right out of bed.* ◇ *Wake up! It's almost 8 o'clock!* ➲ **Wake** is more formal than **wake up**. **2** [T] **wake sb (up)** to make sb stop sleeping: *Could you wake me up at 7:30 tomorrow morning?* **3** [T] **wake sb/sth up** to make sb/sth become more lively or active: *She always has some coffee to wake her up when she gets to work.*

IDM **wake up and smell the coffee** (usually in orders) (used to tell sb to become aware of what is really happening in a situation, especially when this is sth unpleasant)

PHRV **wake up** (*informal*) to begin to pay attention: *Hey, wake up, Rob! It's your turn next.*

**wake up to sth** to become aware of sth: *By the time he had woken up to the danger, it was too late.*

**wake²** /weɪk/ ***noun*** [C] **1** the track that a moving ship or boat leaves behind on the surface of the water **2** an event before a funeral when friends and family members of the dead person meet to talk together and remember him/her

IDM **in the wake of sth; in sth's wake** following or happening after sth, often as a result of it: *The floods left a great deal of destruction in their wake.*

**wake·ful** /ˈweɪkfl/ ***adj.*** (*written*) **1** (used about a period at night) spent with little or no sleep: *She had spent many wakeful nights worrying about him.* **2** not sleeping; unable to sleep: *The baby was wakeful and fussy.*

**wak·en** /ˈweɪkən/ ***verb*** (*written*) **1** [I,T] **waken (sb) (up)** to wake, or make sb wake, from sleep: *The child had just wakened.* ◇ *I was wakened by a knock at the door.* **2** [T] to make sb remember sth or feel sth again: *The dream wakened a forgotten memory.*

ˈ**wake-up** ˌ**call** ***noun*** **1** a telephone call that you arrange to be made to you at a particular time, for example in a hotel, in order to wake you up: *I asked for a wake-up call at 6:30 a.m.* **2** [sing.] an event that makes people realize that there is a problem or other bad situation that they need to do sth about: *These riots should be a wake-up call for the administration.*

**wak·ing** /ˈweɪkɪŋ/ ***adj.*** (only *before* a noun) (*written*) (used to describe time when you are awake): *She spends all her waking hours caring for her mother.* ◇ *He thought of her every waking moment.*

★**walk¹** /wɔk/ ***verb*** **1** [I] to move along on foot at a fairly slow speed: *Our little girl is just learning to walk.* ◇ *"Did you drive here?" "No, I walked."* ◇ *He walked with a limp.* ◇ *Is the grocery store within walking distance?* (= is it close enough to walk to?) **2** [I] to move on foot for exercise or pleasure: *We walked through the park at sunset.* ➲ Look also at **hike**. **3** [T] to go on foot with sb/sth; to guide or help sb to walk: *I'll walk you home if you don't want to go on your own.* ◇ *people walking their dogs in the park* **4** [T] to go along or through sth on foot: *He walked the streets all night.*

IDM **walk all over sb** (*informal*) **1** to defeat sb completely: *Rachel played fantastically and walked all over her opponent.* **2** to deal with sb as if he/she is not important: *I don't know why she lets her husband walk all over her like that.*

**walk the walk** (*informal*) to act in a way that shows people you are really good at what you do, and not just good at talking about it: *You can talk the talk but can you walk the walk?*

PHRV **walk away (from sb/sth)** to leave a person or a situation, without caring about what will happen to him/her/it

**walk away with sth** to win sth easily: *She walked away with all the prizes.*

**walk off with sth** to steal sth; to take sth that does not belong to you by mistake: *When I got home, I realized that I had walked off with her pen.*

**walk out (of sth)** to leave suddenly and angrily: *She walked out of the meeting in disgust.*

**walk out (on sb)** (*informal*) to leave sb forever: *He walked out on his wife and children after 15 years of marriage.*

**walk up (to sb/sth)** to approach (sb/sth): *He walked up to her and asked her if she wanted to dance.*

★**walk²** /wɔk/ ***noun*** **1** [C] a trip on foot for pleasure, exercise, etc.: *We went for a walk in the park.* ◇ *I'm going to take the dog for a walk.* ➲ We use **go for a walk** when we are talking about a short walk that we take for pleasure. **2** [sing.] the time taken to go somewhere on foot; the distance to a place on foot: *The hotel is five minutes' walk from the beach.* **3** [sing.] a way or style of walking: *He has a funny walk.* **4** [sing.] the speed of walking: *She slowed to a walk.* **5** [C, usually sing.] a sidewalk that leads to a building, house, etc.: *She saw the mailman coming up the front walk.* **6** [C] a route that you can walk along for pleasure: *This map shows a scenic walk through the woods.*

IDM **a walk of life** position in society: *She has friends from many different walks of life.*

**walk·er** /ˈwɔkər/ ***noun*** [C] **1** a person who walks: *a fast walker* ◇ *This area is very popular with walkers.* **2** a metal frame that old or sick people push in front of themselves as they walk so that they do not fall down

**walk·ie-talk·ie** /ˌwɔki ˈtɔki/ ***noun*** [C] (*informal*) a small radio that you can carry with you and use to talk and listen to sb

ˈ**walk-in** ***adj.*** (only *before* a noun) **1** that is big enough for a person to walk into: *a walk-in closet* **2** (used about a business that offers services to the public) that you can go to without making an appointment earlier: *a walk-in health center*

**walk·ing** /ˈwɔkɪŋ/ ***adj.*** (only *before* a noun) (*informal*) (used to describe a human or living example of the thing mentioned): *She's a **walking dictionary*** (= she knows a lot of words). ◇ *That boy's a **walking disaster*** (= he is always having accidents).

ˈ**walking stick** ***noun*** [C] a stick that you use to lean on when you go for a walk in the country, mountains, etc.

W

**Walk·man™** /ˈwɔkmən/ ***noun*** [C] (*pl.* **Walkmans**) a small cassette player with headphones that you can carry around with you

**ˈwalk·out** (*also* **walk-out**) /ˈwɔkaʊt̬/ ***noun*** [C] an occasion when people leave a place or refuse to work, as a protest against sth: *Personnel staged a 24-hour walkout to protest against unsafe conditions.*

**ˈwalk-up** ***noun*** [C] a tall building with stairs but no elevator; an office or a apartment in such a building

**walk·way** /ˈwɔkweɪ/ ***noun*** [C] a passage or path for walking along, often outside and raised above the ground: *A covered walkway joins the two buildings.*

★**wall¹** /wɔl/ ***noun*** [C] **1** one of the sides of a room or building that join the ceiling and the floor: *You could hear people talking in the next room because the wall was so thin.* ◇ *He put the poster up on the wall.* **2** a solid, upright structure made of stone, brick, etc. that is built around an area of land to protect it or to show a boundary: *There is a high wall all around the prison.* ➲ picture at **hedge**.

IDM **off the wall** (*informal*) very unusual; crazy: *Some of her jokes are totally off the wall.*

**drive sb up the wall** → DRIVE¹

**wall²** /wɔl/ ***verb*** [T] (usually passive) to surround an area, a town, etc. with a wall or walls: *a walled city*

PHR V **wall sth/sb in** (usually passive) to surround sth/sb with a wall or barrier

**wall sth off** (usually passive) to separate one place or area from another with a wall

**wal·la·by** /ˈwɑləbi/ ***noun*** [C] (*pl.* **wal·la·bies**) an Australian animal like a small kangaroo, that moves by jumping on its strong back legs and keeps its young in a pocket of skin (**a pouch**) on the front of the mother's body

**wal·let** /ˈwɑlət; ˈwɔ-/ (*also* **billfold**) ***noun*** [C] a small, flat, folding case in which you keep paper money, credit cards, etc.

**wall·eye** /ˈwɔlaɪ/ ***noun*** [C] a common type of fish with big eyes that lives in rivers and lakes and is eaten as food

**wall·flow·er** /ˈwɔlˌflaʊər/ ***noun*** [C] **1** a garden plant with yellow, orange or red flowers with a sweet smell that appear in late spring **2** (*informal*) a person who does not dance at a party because he/she does not have sb to dance with or because he/she is too shy

**wal·lop** /ˈwɑləp/ ***verb*** [T] (*informal*) **1** to hit sb/sth very hard: *My father used to wallop me if I told lies.* **2** to defeat sb completely in a contest, match, etc.: *We walloped them 6–0.*

**wal·low** /ˈwɑloʊ/ ***verb*** [I] **wallow (in sth) 1** to lie and roll around in water, etc.: *I spent an hour wallowing in a hot bath.* **2** to take great pleasure in sth (a feeling, situation, etc.): *He seems to wallow in self-pity.*

**wall·pa·per** /ˈwɔlˌpeɪpər/ ***noun*** [U] paper with a pattern on it that you stick to the walls of a room ▸ **wall·pa·per** ***verb*** [T]: *We spent the weekend wallpapering the bedroom.*

**ˈWall Street** ***noun*** [sing.] **1** a street in New York City where many important banks and companies that exchange shares in other businesses (**stock exchanges**) are located **2** all the important companies and banks that control the financial situation in the U.S.

**ˈwall-to-ˌwall** ***adj.*** (only *before* a noun) (used especially about a carpet) covering the whole floor of a room

**wal·nut** /ˈwɔlnʌt/ ***noun*** **1** [C] a nut that you can eat, with a hard brown shell that is in two halves ➲ picture at **nut**. **2** [C] (*also* **ˈwalnut tree**) the tree on which WALNUTS (1) grow **3** [U] the wood from the walnut tree

**wal·rus** /ˈwɔlrəs; ˈwɑl-/ ***noun*** [C] a large sea animal that lives in Arctic regions. It has two long teeth (**tusks**) coming out of its face.

**waltz¹** /wɔlts; wɔls/ ***noun*** [C] a dance that you do with a partner, to music which has a rhythm of three beats; the music for this dance

**waltz²** /wɔlts; wɔls/ ***verb*** [I] **1** to dance a WALTZ¹: *They waltzed around the floor.* **2 waltz around, in, over, up, etc.** (*informal*) to move easily, carelessly or confidently: *You can't just waltz in and expect your meal to be ready for you.*

**wan** /wɑn/ ***adj.*** very pale and looking sick or tired

**wand** /wɑnd/ ***noun*** [C] a thin stick that magicians, etc. hold when they are doing magic: *I wish I could wave a magic wand and make everything better.*

**wan·der** /ˈwɑndər/ ***verb*** **1** [I,T] to move slowly around a place or to go from place to place with no particular purpose: *We spent the afternoon wandering around the town.* ◇ *He was found in a confused state, wandering the streets.* **2** [I] **wander (away/off)**; **wander (from/off sth)** to leave a place or the path that you were on: *This is a dangerous area, so I don't want anybody to wander off.* ◇ (*figurative*) *I seem to have wandered off the subject – what was I talking about?* **3** [I] (used about sb's mind, thoughts, etc.) to stop paying attention; to be unable to stay on one subject: *My attention started to wander during the lecture.* ◇ *The old man's mind is wandering. He doesn't know where he is anymore.*

**wane** /weɪn/ ***verb*** [I] **1** to become less powerful, less important, smaller or weaker: *Britain's influence on world events has been waning for years.* **2** (used about the moon) to appear to become smaller

**wan·gle** /ˈwæŋgl/ ***verb*** [T] **wangle sth (from/out of sb)** (*informal*) to get sth that you or another person wants by persuading sb or by a clever plan: *She had wangled an invitation to the opening night.* ◇ *We should be able to* ***wangle it*** *so that you can start tomorrow.* ◇ *He managed to* ***wangle his way*** *onto the course.*

**wan·na** /ˈwɑnə; ˈwɔnə; ˈwʌnə/ (*informal*) (a way of writing "want to" or "want a" to show that sb is speaking in an informal way): *I wanna go home now.*

NOTE Look at the note at **gonna**.

**wan·na·be** /ˈwɑnəbi; ˈwɔnə-; ˈwʌnə-/ ***noun*** [C] (*informal*) a person who behaves, dresses, etc. like sb famous because he/she wants to be like him/her: *a rock star wannabe*

★**want¹** /wɑnt; wɔnt/ ***verb*** [T] to desire; to wish for: *He wants a new bike.* ◇ *Do you want anything else?* ◇ *What do they want for breakfast?* ◇ *Is there anything you want to watch on TV?* ◇ *I don't want to discuss it now.* ◇ *I want you to call me when you get*



W

there. ◇ *The boss wants this letter typed.* ◇ *I don't want Katie going out on her own at night.*

NOTE **Want** and **would like** are similar in meaning, but "would like" is more polite and is used in formal situations: *"I want a drink!" screamed the child.* ◇ *"Would you like some more coffee, Mrs. Sternwood?"* ➲ Look also at **wanted**.

IDM **want in/out** (*informal*) **1** to want to enter/leave a place: *I think the dog wants out.* **2** to want to be involved/not involved in a plan or situation

**want²** /wɑnt; wɔnt/ ***noun*** [C] desire or need for sth; sth you desire or need: *All our wants were satisfied.*

IDM **for want of sth** (*formal*) because of a lack of sth: *I took the job for want of a better offer.*

**'want ad** ***noun*** [C] (*informal*) = CLASSIFIED ADVERTISEMENT

**want·ed** /'wɑntəd; 'wɔn-/ ***adj.*** (used about a person) that the police are trying to find, because they think that he/she committed a crime: *He is wanted for arson.*

**wan·ton** /'wɑntən; 'wɔn-/ ***adj.*** (usually *before* a noun) (used about an action) done in order to hurt sb or damage sth for no good reason

**wap·i·ti** /'wɑpəṭi/ ***noun*** [C] = ELK

★**war** /wɔr/ ***noun*** **1** [U] a state of fighting between different countries or groups within countries, using armies and weapons: *war and peace* ◇ *The two countries have been at war for six months.* ◇ *to declare war* (= announce that a war has started) ◇ *When war broke out, thousands of men were drafted into the army.* ➲ Look also at **civil war**. **2** [C] a period of military fighting: *the Second World War* (= from 1939 to 1945) ◇ *He was killed in the war.* ◇ *to fight a war* **3** [C,U] a struggle; very strong competition between groups of people: *a price war among gas stations* **4** [sing.] **a war (against/on sb/sth)** efforts to end sth: *the war against organized crime*

**war·ble** /'wɔrbl/ ***verb*** [I] (usually used about a bird) to sing gently, changing the notes up and down very quickly

**'war crime** ***noun*** [C] an extremely cruel act that is committed during a war and is against international law ▸ **'war criminal** ***noun*** [C]

★**ward¹** /wɔrd/ ***noun*** [C] **1** a separate part of a hospital, often for a particular group of patients: *the children's ward* **2** one of the sections into which a town is divided for elections **3** (*formal*) a child who is under the protection of a court of law or another adult (guardian), especially because his/her parents are dead

**ward²** /wɔrd/ ***verb***

PHR V **ward sb/sth off** to keep away sb/sth that is dangerous or bad: *They lit a fire to ward off wild animals.*

**war·den** /'wɔrdn/ ***noun*** [C] an official who is in charge of a prison

**ward·robe** /'wɔrdroʊb/ ***noun*** [C] a person's collection of clothes: *I need a whole new wardrobe.*

**ware** /wɛr/ ***noun*** **1** [U] (in compounds) made from a particular type of material or suitable for a particular use: *stainless steel cookware* ➲ Look also at **hardware**, **software** and **silverware**. **2 wares** [pl.] (*old-fashioned*) things that are for sale

**ware·house** /'wɛrhaʊs/ ***noun*** [C] a building where large quantities of products are kept before being sent to stores

**war·fare** /'wɔrfɛr/ ***noun*** [U] methods of fighting a war; types of war: *guerrilla warfare* ◇ *nuclear warfare*

**war·head** /'wɔrhɛd/ ***noun*** [C] the explosive part at the front of a bomb that can fly through the air (a missile)

**war·i·ly** → WARY

**war·lock** /'wɔrlɑk/ ***noun*** [C] a man who is believed to have magic powers, especially evil ones

**war·lord** /'wɔrlɔrd/ ***noun*** [C] the leader of a military group that is not official and that fights against other groups within a country or an area

★**warm¹** /wɔrm/ ***adj.*** **1** having a temperature that is fairly high, between cool and hot: *Are you warm enough, or should I turn the heat on?* ◇ *It's nice and warm in the sunshine.* ◇ *I jumped up and down to keep my feet warm.* ➲ Look at the note at **hot** (1). **2** (used about clothing) preventing you from getting cold: *Take plenty of warm clothes.* **3** friendly; kind and pleasant; sincere: *I was given a very warm welcome.* **4** creating a pleasant, comfortable feeling: *warm colors* ➲ noun **warmth** ▸ **warm·ly** ***adv.***: *warmly dressed* ◇ *She thanked him warmly for his help.*

★**warm²** /wɔrm/ ***verb*** [I,T] **warm (sb/sth) (up)** to become or to make sb/sth become warm or warmer: *It was cold earlier, but it's starting to warm up now.* ◇ *I sat in front of the fire to warm up.* ◇ *We'll just warm up some soup for lunch.*

PHR V **warm to/toward sb** to begin to like sb

**warm to sth** to become more interested in sth

**warm up** to prepare for sth by practicing gently: *The team warmed up before the match.*

**ˌwarm-'blooded** ***adj.*** having a blood temperature that does not change along with the temperature of the surroundings ➲ Look at **cold-blooded**.

**ˌwarm-'hearted** ***adj.*** kind and friendly

**war·mon·ger** /'wɔrˌmʌŋgər; -ˌmɑŋ-/ ***noun*** [C] (*formal*) a person, especially a politician or leader, who wants to start a war or encourages people to start a war ▸ **war·mon·ger·ing** ***noun*** [U]

★**warmth** /wɔrmθ/ ***noun*** [U] **1** a fairly high temperature or an effect created by this, especially when it is pleasant: *She felt the warmth of the sun on her face.* **2** friendliness or kindness: *I was touched by the warmth of their welcome.*

**'warm-up** (*also* **warm·up**) ***noun*** [C] a gentle exercise that you do to prepare yourself for some activity, e.g. a sports game

★**warn** /wɔrn/ ***verb*** **1** [I,T] **warn (sb) (of sth); warn (sb) about/against sb/sth; warn (sb) against doing sth** to tell sb to be careful or aware of sth, often bad or dangerous, that exists or might happen: *When I saw the car coming, I tried to warn him, but it was too late.* ◇ *She warned me that he was not an easy man to work for.* ◇ *The government is warning (the public) of possible terrorist attacks.* ◇ *The radio warned people about delays on the roads this morning.* ◇ *Most parents warn their kids against*

W

*experimenting with drugs.* **2** [T] to advise sb (not) to do sth: *I warned you not to trust him.*

★**warn·ing** /ˈwɔrnɪŋ/ ***noun*** [C,U] something that tells you to be careful or tells you about sth before it happens: *They ignored the warnings posted outside and entered the military base.* ◇ *The computer just shut down without warning.* ◇ *He gave me no warning of his arrival.*

**warp** /wɔrp/ ***verb*** [I,T] to become bent and out of shape (because of hot or damp conditions); to make sth become like this: (*figurative*) *His view of life had been warped by his unhappy experiences.* ▸ **warped** ***adj.***: *the killer's warped* (= abnormal) *mind*

**war·path** /ˈwɔrpæθ/ ***noun***

IDM **(be/go) on the warpath** (*informal*) to be very angry and ready to argue or fight

**war·plane** /ˈwɔrpleɪn/ ***noun*** [C] an airplane that is designed to be used in a war, to drop bombs, etc.

**war·rant**[1] /ˈwɔrənt; ˈwɑr-/ ***noun*** [C] a written statement that gives sb the authority to do sth: *a search warrant* (= a document that allows the police to search a house)

**war·rant**[2] /ˈwɔrənt; ˈwɑr-/ ***verb*** [T] (*formal*) to make sth seem right or necessary; to deserve: *I don't think her behavior warrants such criticism.*

**war·ran·ty** /ˈwɔrənti; ˈwɑr-/ ***noun*** [C,U] (*pl.* **war·ran·ties**) a written statement that you get when you buy sth, which promises to repair or replace it if it breaks or stops working within a certain period of time ➲ Look at **guarantee**.

**war·ring** /ˈwɔrɪŋ/ ***adj.*** (only *before* a noun) involved in a war: *A ceasefire has been agreed by the country's three **warring factions**.*

**war·ri·or** /ˈwɔriər; ˈwɑr-/ ***noun*** [C] (*old-fashioned, formal*) a person who fights in battle; a soldier

**war·ship** /ˈwɔrʃɪp/ ***noun*** [C] a ship for use in war

**wart** /wɔrt/ ***noun*** [C] a small hard dry lump that sometimes grows on the face or body

**wart·hog** /ˈwɔrthɔg; -hɑg/ ***noun*** [C] an African wild pig with two large outer teeth (tusks) and lumps like warts on its face

**war·time** /ˈwɔrtaɪm/ ***noun*** [U] a period of time during which there is a war

ˈ**war-torn** ***adj.*** (only *before* a noun) (*written*) a war-torn country or area is severely affected by the fighting that is taking place there

**war·y** /ˈwɛri/ ***adj.*** (**war·i·er**; **war·i·est**) **wary (of sb/sth)** careful because you are uncertain or afraid of sb/sth: *He was wary of accepting the suggestion in case it meant more work for him.* ▸ **war·i·ly** /-rəli/ ***adv.***

**was** /wʌz; wɑz/ → BE[1,2]

★**wash**[1] /wɑʃ; wɔʃ/ ***verb*** **1** [I,T] to clean sb/sth/yourself with water and often soap: *You'll have to wash this blouse by hand.* ◇ *Go wash your hands before dinner.* ◇ *I'll wash, you dry* (= the dishes). ➲ Look at the note at **clean**[2]. **2** [I] (used about water) to flow in the direction mentioned: *I let the waves wash over my feet.* **3** [T] to carry sth by the movement of water: *The tide washed the ball out to sea.* **4** [I] to be able to be washed without being damaged: *Does this material wash well, or does the color come out?*

IDM **wash your hands of sb/sth** to refuse to be responsible for sb/sth any longer

PHRV **wash sb/sth away** (used about water) to carry sb/sth away: *The floods had washed the path away.*

**wash (sth) off** to (make sth) disappear from sth by washing: *Go and wash that makeup off!*

**wash out** to be removed from a material by washing: *These grease marks won't wash out.*

**wash up** to wash your face and hands: *Go and wash up and put on some clean clothes.*

**wash sth up** (often passive) (used about water) to carry sth to land and leave it there: *Police found the girl's body washed up on the beach.*

**wash**[2] /wɑʃ; wɔʃ/ ***noun*** **1** [U] clothes that need to be washed or are being washed: *"Where's my red T-shirt?" "It's in the wash."* ◇ *He hung the wash out on the clothesline.* **2** [C, usually sing.] an act of cleaning or being cleaned with water: *The car needs a good wash this weekend.*

IDM **do the wash** to wash clothes: *You should learn to do your own wash before you go to university.*

**wash·a·ble** /ˈwɑʃəbl; ˈwɔʃ-/ ***adj.*** that can be washed without being damaged

**wash·board** /ˈwɑʃbɔrd; ˈwɔʃ-/ ***noun*** [C] a board with a surface with ridges on it, used in the past for rubbing clothes on when washing them; a similar board played as a musical instrument

**wash·cloth** /ˈwɑʃklɔθ; ˈwɔʃ-/ ***noun*** [C] a small square towel that is used for washing your face, hands, etc.

ˌ**washed ˈout** ***adj.*** **1** (used about fabric, clothes or colors) no longer brightly colored, often as a result of frequent washing: *She didn't like jeans that looked too washed out.* ◇ *a pair of washed-out old jeans* **2** (used about a person) pale and tired

ˌ**washed ˈup** ***adj.*** (*informal*) no longer successful and unlikely to succeed again in the future: *She was dating a washed-up football star.*

**wash·er** /ˈwɑʃər; ˈwɔʃ-/ ***noun*** [C] **1** = WASHING MACHINE: *a washer and dryer* **2** a small metal or rubber ring that is put between two parts of a machine to make them fit together better

ˈ**washing maˌchine** (*also* **washer**) ***noun*** [C] an electric machine that washes clothes

**wash·room** /ˈwɑʃrum; ˈwɔʃ-/ ***noun*** [C] (*especially Cdn*) a room in a public building with a toilet; a bathroom ➲ Look at the note at **toilet**.

**was·n't** /ˈwʌznt; ˈwɑznt/ *short for* WAS NOT

**Wasp** (*also* **WASP**) /wɑsp; wɔsp/ ***noun*** [C] the abbreviation for "White Anglo-Saxon Protestant"; a white North American whose family originally came from northern Europe and is therefore thought to be from the most powerful section of society

**wasp** /wɑsp; wɔsp/ ***noun*** [C] a black and yellow flying insect that can sting ➲ picture at **insect**.

**wast·age** /ˈweɪstɪdʒ/ ***noun*** **1** [U, sing.] **wastage (of sth)** the fact of losing or destroying sth, especially because it has been used or dealt with carelessly: *It was a new production technique aimed at minimizing wastage.* **2** [U] the amount of sth that is wasted: *There is little wastage from a lean cut of*

W

meat. ◇ *Always allow for some wastage when ordering building materials.*

★**waste**[1] /weɪst/ *verb* [T] **waste sth (on sb/sth)** to use or spend sth in a careless way or for sth that is not necessary: *She wastes a lot of money on cigarettes.* ◇ *Don't waste water – turn off the faucet while you brush your teeth.* ◇ *He wasted his time at university because he didn't work hard.*

IDM **be wasted on sb/sth** to be too good, intelligent, etc. for sb/sth: *Expensive wine is wasted on me. I don't know anything about it.*

**waste not, want not** if you never waste anything, especially food or money, you will always have it when you need it

PHR V **waste away** (used about a person) to become thin and weak, especially because of illness

★**waste**[2] /weɪst/ *noun* **1 a waste (of sth)** [sing., U] an action that involves not using sth carefully or using sth in an unnecessary way: *If he gives up acting, it will be a waste of great talent.* ◇ *The class was a waste of time – I'd heard it all before.* **2** [U] material, food, etc. that is not needed and is therefore thrown away: *nuclear waste* ◇ *A lot of household waste can be recycled and reused.* ➲ Look at **garbage** and **trash**.

IDM **go to waste** to not be used; to be thrown away and wasted: *I can't bear to see good food going to waste!*

**waste**[3] /weɪst/ *adj.* (only *before* a noun) no longer useful; to be thrown away: *waste material*

**waste·bas·ket** /ˈweɪstˌbæskət/ *noun* [C] a basket or other container in which you put paper, etc. which is to be thrown away ➲ picture at **garbage can**.

**wast·ed** /ˈweɪstəd/ *adj.* **1** not necessary or successful: *a wasted trip* **2** (*slang*) under the influence of a lot of alcohol or illegal drugs: *Doug got completely wasted at Tanya's party!*

**waste·ful** /ˈweɪstfl/ *adj.* using more of sth than necessary; causing waste: *a costly and wasteful advertising campaign*

**waste·land** /ˈweɪstlænd/ *noun* [C,U] an ugly area of land that is not used or not suitable for use

**wast·ing** /ˈweɪstɪŋ; / *adj.* a wasting disease or illness is one that causes sb to gradually become weaker and thinner

★**watch**[1] /wɑtʃ; wɔtʃ/ *noun* **1** [C] a small instrument that shows you what time it is. You wear it around your wrist: *a digital watch* ◇ *to wind/set your watch* ◇ *My watch is a little bit fast/slow* (= shows a time that is later/earlier than the correct time). ◇ *a watch band/strap* ➲ picture at **clock**. **2** [sing.] an act of guarding and protecting a place or a person, or the person or people who do this: *The police put a watch on the suspect's house.* ◇ *a neighborhood watch patrol*

IDM **keep a close eye/watch on sb/sth** → EYE[1]

**keep watch** to guard or to look out for danger

★**watch**[2] /wɑtʃ; wɔtʃ/ *verb* **1** [I,T] to look carefully at sb/sth: *"Do you want to play too?" "No thanks. I'll just watch."* ◇ *I watched in horror as the car swerved and crashed.* ◇ *I'm watching to see how you do it.* ◇ *We watch TV most evenings.* ◇ *Watch what she does next.* ◇ *I watched him open the door and walk away.* ◇ *Detectives are watching the suspect day and night.* **2** [I,T] **watch (for sth)** to pay very careful attention to a situation; to observe: *Doctors are watching for further signs of the disease.* **3** [T] to take care of sb/sth for a short time: *Could you watch the kids while I go to the store?* **4** [T] to be careful about sb/sth in order to do the right thing or keep control: *You'd better watch what you say to her. She gets upset very easily.* ◇ *No dessert for me – I'm watching my weight.*

IDM **watch it!** (*informal*) (used to warn sb to be more careful): *Hey, watch it, buddy! You almost hit my car!*

**watch your step 1** to be careful about where you are walking **2** to be careful about how you behave

PHR V **watch out** to be careful because of possible danger or trouble: *Watch out! There's a car coming.* ◇ *If you don't watch out, you'll lose your job.*

**watch out for sb/sth** to look carefully and be ready for sb/sth: *Watch out for snakes if you walk through the fields.*

**watch over sb/sth** to take care of or protect sb/sth: *For two weeks she watched over the sick child.*

**watch·dog** /ˈwɑtʃdɔg; ˈwɔtʃ-/ *noun* [C] **1** a dog that has been trained to guard people, buildings, or land **2** a person or group whose job is to protect people's rights, especially in relation to large companies: *an independent watchdog group*

**watch·er** /ˈwɑtʃər; wɔ-/ *noun* [C] (in compounds) a person who watches and studies sb/sth regularly: *an industry/a market watcher*

**watch·ful** /ˈwɑtʃfl; ˈwɔtʃ-/ *adj.* paying attention to what is happening in case of danger, accidents, etc.: *His mother* ***kept a watchful eye on him.*** ◇ *The children played* ***under the watchful eye of*** *their teacher.*

**watch·mak·er** /ˈwɑtʃˌmeɪkər; ˈwɔtʃ-/ *noun* [C] a person who makes and repairs watches and clocks as a job

★**wa·ter**[1] /ˈwɔt̬ər; ˈwɑ-/ *noun* **1** [U] the clear liquid that falls as rain and is in rivers, seas and lakes: *a glass of water* ◇ *They lived in a shack with no running water.* ◇ *After the heavy rain, several fields were under water.* ◇ *clean drinking water* ◇ *tap water* (= that comes out of a faucet) ◇ *mineral water* ◇ *Don't go too near the edge, or you'll fall in the water!*

> NOTE When water is **heated** to 212° Fahrenheit (100° C), it **boils** and becomes **steam**. When steam touches a cold surface, it **condenses** and becomes water again. When water is **cooled** below 32° Fahrenheit (0° C), it **freezes** and becomes ice. If the temperature increases, the ice **melts**. Frozen food **thaws** or **defrosts** when we take it out of the freezer.

**2** [pl.] the ocean near a particular country: *The ship was still in U.S. waters.* ◇ *international waters*

IDM **pass water** → PASS[2]

★**wa·ter**[2] /ˈwɔt̬ər; ˈwɑ-/ *verb* **1** [T] to give water to plants **2** [I] (used about the eyes or mouth) to fill with water: *The smoke in the room made my eyes water.* ◇ *The food smelled so good that it made my mouth water.*

PHR V **water sth down 1** to add water to a liquid

in order to make it weaker **2** to change a statement, report, etc. so that it is weaker

**wa·ter·bed** /ˈwɔt̬ərbɛd; ˈwɑ-/ ***noun*** [C] a bed with a rubber or plastic mattress that is filled with water

**wa·ter·borne** /ˈwɔt̬ərbɔrn; ˈwɑ-/ ***adj.*** spread or carried by water: *cholera and other waterborne diseases* ◇ *waterborne goods* ➲ Look at **airborne**.

**ˈwater ˌbuffalo** ***noun*** [C] a large Indian animal of the cow family, used for pulling vehicles and farm equipment in Asia

**ˈwater ˌchestnut** ***noun*** [C] the thick round white root of a tropical plant that grows in water, often used in Chinese cooking

**ˈwater ˌcloset** ***noun*** [C] (*abbr.* **WC**) (*old-fashioned*) = TOILET

**wa·ter·col·or** /ˈwɔt̬ərkʌlər; ˈwɑ-/ ***noun*** **1 watercolors** [pl.] paints that are mixed with water, not oil **2** [C] a picture that has been painted with watercolors

**ˈwater ˌcooler** ***noun*** [C] **1** a machine, for example in an office, that cools water and supplies it for drinking **2** (used when referring to a place where office workers talk in an informal way, for example near the water cooler): *It was a story they'd shared around the water cooler.*

**wa·ter·fall** /ˈwɔt̬ərfɔl; ˈwɑ-/ ***noun*** [C] a stream of water that falls down from a mountain, a high rock, etc.

**ˈwater ˌfountain** ***noun*** [C] = DRINKING FOUNTAIN

**wa·ter·fowl** /ˈwɔt̬ərfaʊl; ˈwɑ-/ ***noun*** [usually pl.] (*pl.* **wa·ter·fowl**) a bird that can swim and lives near water, especially a duck or goose

**wa·ter·front** /ˈwɔt̬ərfrʌnt; ˈwɑ-/ ***noun*** [C, usually sing.] a part of a town or an area that is next to water, for example in a harbor: *a waterfront apartment*

**ˈwatering can** ***noun*** [C] a metal or plastic container with a handle and a long spout, used for pouring water on plants ➲ picture at **garden**.

**ˈwatering hole** ***noun*** [C] **1** (*also* **wa·ter·hole** /ˈwɔt̬ərhoʊl/) a place in a hot country, where animals go to drink **2** (*informal*) a bar or place where people go to drink: *The Old Irish is one of Tony's favorite watering holes.*

**ˈwater ˌlily** ***noun*** [C] a plant that floats on the surface of water, with large round flat leaves and white, yellow or pink flowers

**wa·ter·line** /ˈwɔt̬ərlaɪn; ˈwɑ-/ ***noun*** [sing.] **the waterline** the level that the water reaches along the side of a ship

**wa·ter·logged** /ˈwɔt̬ərlɔgd; -lɑgd; ˈwɔt̬ər-/ ***adj.*** **1** very wet: *Our boots sank into the waterlogged ground.* **2** (used about a boat) full of water and likely to sink

**wa·ter·mel·on** /ˈwɔt̬ərˌmɛlən; ˈwɑ-/ ***noun*** [C] a large, round fruit with thick, green skin. It is pink or red inside with a lot of black seeds. ➲ picture on study page **A28-29**.

**ˈwater ˌmoccasin** ***noun*** [C] a poisonous North American snake which lives near water, especially in the south eastern U.S.

**ˈwater ˌpolo** ***noun*** [U] a game played by two teams of people swimming in a swimming pool. Players try to throw a ball into the other team's goal.

**wa·ter·proof** /ˈwɔt̬ərpruf; ˈwɑ-/ ***adj.*** that does not let water go through: *a waterproof jacket* ➲ picture on study page **A30**.

**wa·ter·shed** /ˈwɔt̬ərʃɛd; ˈwɑ-/ ***noun*** [C, usually sing.] an event or point which is important because it marks the beginning of sth new

**ˈwater-ski** ***verb*** [I] to move across the surface of water while standing on narrow boards (**water skis**) and being pulled by a boat ➲ picture on study page **A32**.

**ˈwater ˌsoftener** ***noun*** [C,U] a device or substance that removes particular minerals, especially chalk, from water

**ˈwater ˌtable** ***noun*** [usually sing.] (*technical*) the level at and below which water is found in the ground

**wa·ter·tight** /ˈwɔt̬ərtaɪt; ˈwɑ-/ ***adj.*** **1** that does not allow water to get in or out: *a watertight container/seal* ◇ *The roof has been made watertight.* **2** (used about an excuse, a plan, an argument, etc.) carefully prepared so that it contains no mistakes, faults or weaknesses: *a watertight alibi*

**ˈwater ˌtower** ***noun*** [C] a tall structure with a very large tank of water at the top which is used to keep the water supplied to a town, etc. at a steady pressure

**wa·ter·way** /ˈwɔt̬ərweɪ; ˈwɑ-/ ***noun*** [C] a canal, river, etc. along which boats or ships can travel

**wa·ter·works** /ˈwɔt̬ərwərks; ˈwɑ-/ ***noun*** (*pl.* **wa·ter·works**) **1** [C, with sing. or pl. verb] a building with machinery for supplying water to an area **2** [pl.] (*informal*) the organs of the body through which waste water (**urine**) is passed

IDM **turn on the waterworks** (*informal*) to start crying, especially in order to get sympathy or attention

**wa·ter·y** /ˈwɔt̬əri; ˈwɑ-/ ***adj.*** (used especially about food or drink) containing too much water; thin and weak

**watt** /wɑt/ ***noun*** [C] (*abbr.* **W**) a unit of electrical power: *a 60-watt light bulb*

**wat·tage** /ˈwɑt̬ɪdʒ/ ***noun*** [U] (*technical*) an amount of electrical power expressed in watts

★ **wave**[1] /weɪv/ ***verb*** **1** [I,T] **wave (your hand) (at/ to sb)** to move your hand from side to side in the air, usually to attract sb's attention or as you meet or leave sb: *She waved to me as the car drove off.* ◇ *Who are you waving at?* **2** [T] **wave sth (at sb)**; **wave sth (around)** to hold sth in the air and move it from side to side: *The crowd was waving flags as the President rode past.* ◇ *She was talking excitedly and waving her arms around.* **3** [T] **wave sth (to sb)** to give a greeting (to sb) by waving your hand: *Wave goodbye to Grandma, Tim.* **4** [I] to move gently up and down or from side to side: *The branches of the trees waved gently in the breeze.*

PHR V **wave sth aside** to decide not to pay attention to a comment, etc. because you think it is not important

**wave sb/sth away, on, etc.** to move your hand in a particular direction to show sb/sth which way to go: *There was a police officer in the middle of the road, waving us on.*

★ **wave**[2] /weɪv/ ***noun*** [C]

W

➤OF WATER **1** a raised line of water moving on the surface of water, especially the ocean: *boats bobbing up and down on the waves* ◇ *A huge wave swept me off my feet.* ◇ *We watched the waves roll in and break on the shore.* ◇ (*figurative*) *a wave of tourists*
➤OF ACTIVITY/FEELING **2** a sudden increase or spread of a feeling or type of behavior: *There has been a wave of public sympathy for the victims.* ◇ *the recent wave of burglaries* ➲ Look at **heat wave**.
➤OF HEAT/SOUND/LIGHT **3** a form in which some types of energy move, shaped like a wave in the ocean: *sound waves* ◇ *shock waves from the earthquake*
➤IN HAIR **4** a gentle curve in hair: *natural waves* ➲ Look at **perm**.
➤MOVEMENT OF ARM/HAND/BODY **5** a movement of sth, especially your hand, from side to side in the air: *With a wave of his hand, he said goodbye and left.*

**wave·length** /ˈweɪvlɛŋkθ; -lɛŋθ/ ***noun*** [C] the distance between two sound waves
IDM **on the same wavelength** → SAME[1]

**wav·er** /ˈweɪvər/ ***verb*** [I] **1** to become weak or uncertain: *He never wavered in his support for her.* **2 waver (between A and B)** to hesitate, especially when making a decision or choice

**wav·y** /ˈweɪvi/ ***adj.*** having curves: *wavy hair* ◇ *a wavy line* ➲ pictures at **hair** and **line**.

**wax[1]** /wæks/ ***noun*** [U] **1** a substance made from fat or oil that melts easily and is used for making candles, polish, etc. **2** (*also* **earwax**) a yellow substance like WAX (1) that is found in your ears

**wax[2]** /wæks/ ***verb*** **1** [T] (often passive) to polish or cover sth with WAX[1] (1): *a waxed jacket* **2** [T] (often passive) to remove hair from a part of the body using WAX[1] (1): *to wax your legs/to have your legs waxed* **3** [I] **wax lyrical, eloquent, sentimental, etc.** (*written*) to become lyrical, etc. when speaking or writing: *He waxed lyrical on the food at the new restaurant.*

**ˈwax bean** ***noun*** [C] a type of bean that is a long thin yellow pod, cooked and eaten whole as a vegetable

**ˈwaxed ˌpaper** (*also* **ˈwax ˌpaper**) ***noun*** [U] paper that does not let grease, oil, etc. pass through it, used in cooking and for wrapping food in

**wax·y** /ˈwæksi/ ***adj.*** (**wax·i·er**; **wax·i·est**) made of WAX[1] (1); looking or feeling like WAX[1] (1): *The cheese has a red waxy rind.* ◇ *potatoes with a waxy texture*

★**way[1]** /weɪ/ ***noun***
➤ROUTE/ROAD **1** [C, usually sing.] the route you take to reach somewhere: *Can you tell me the way to Elm Street?* ◇ *She lost her way and had to turn back.* ◇ *We stopped for a snack on the way home.* **2** [sing.] the route along which you move or would move if there were space: *There was a van parked in the alley, blocking our way.* ◇ *Get out of my way!*
➤DIRECTION **3** [sing.] a direction or position: *Look this way!* ◇ *Shouldn't you be wearing that hat the other way around?* (= facing in the other direction) ◇ *He thought I was older than my sister, but in fact it's the other way around* (= the opposite of what he thought).
➤DISTANCE/TIME **4** (*also informal* **ways**) [sing.] a distance in space or time: *It's a long way from Houston to Amarillo.* ◇ *Summer is still a long way off.*
➤METHOD/STYLE **5** [C] a method, style or manner of doing sth; a habit: *What is the best way to learn a language?* ◇ *I've discovered a terrific way of losing weight!* ◇ *There are various ways in which we can help.* ◇ *They'll have to find the money one way or another.* ◇ *He always does things his way.*
➤ASPECT **6** [C] a particular point or part of sth: *In some ways, the meeting was very useful.* ◇ *In a way, I sort of like him.* ◇ *Can I help you in any way?*
IDM **be set in your ways** to be unable to change your habits, attitudes, etc.
**by the way** → BY[2]
**get/have your own way** to get or do what you want, although others may want sth else
**give way** to break or fall down: *The tree branch suddenly gave way and came crashing down.*
**give way (to sb/sth) 1** to stop or to allow sb/sth else to happen, develop, etc. instead: *Old-fashioned methods have given way to new technology.* **2** to allow sb to have what he/she wants although you did not at first agree with it: *We will not give way to the terrorists' demands.*
**go out of your way (to do sth)** to make a special effort to do sth
**in a big/small way** (used for expressing the size or importance of an activity)
**in the way 1** blocking the road or path: *I can't get past. There's a big truck in the way.* **2** not needed or wanted: *I felt like I was in the way at my daughter's party.*
**no way 1** (*informal*) definitely not: *"Can we have a party here?" "No way! You'll wreck the house!"* **2** (*slang*) (used to show surprise, when you find sth difficult to believe): *"Vaughan got fired yesterday." "No way!"*
**under way** having started and making progress: *Discussions between the two sides are now under way.*
**a/sb's way of life** the behavior and customs that are typical of a person or group of people

**way[2]** /weɪ/ ***adv.*** **1** (*informal*) very far: *His name was way down at the bottom of the list.* **2** (*slang*) (used before a comparative) very much: *Paul ate way more than anybody else.* ◇ *This is way better than the old one.*

**way·lay** /ˈweɪleɪ/ ***verb*** [T] (*pt, pp* **way·laid**) to stop sb who is going somewhere, especially in order to talk to or attack him/her: *I **got waylaid** on my way here.*

**way·side** /ˈweɪsaɪd/ ***noun*** [sing.] the area at the side of a road or path: *a wayside hotel/inn/shrine*
IDM **fall by the wayside** to fail or be unable to make progress: *Many clubs fall by the wayside for financial reasons.* ◇ *Proposals for the new service fell by the wayside through lack of public support.*

**way·ward** /ˈweɪwərd/ ***adj.*** (*written*) difficult to control: *a wayward child/animal* ◇ *wayward emotions/thoughts*

**wa·zoo** /wɑˈzu/ ***noun*** [C]
IDM **out/up the wazoo** (*slang*) in large numbers or amounts: *We have Christmas ornaments out the wazoo, but no tree to hang them on.*

W

★**we** /wi/ ***pronoun*** (the subject of a verb; used for talking about the speaker and one or more other people): *We're going to the movies.* ◇ *We are both thrilled with the house.* ◇ *We all left together.*

★**weak** /wik/ ***adj.***
➤NOT PHYSICALLY STRONG **1** (used about the body) having little strength or energy; not strong: *The child was weak with hunger.* ◇ *Her legs felt weak.* ◇ *(figurative) a weak economy*
➤LIKELY TO BREAK **2** likely to break: *That bridge is too weak for trucks to drive on.*
➤OF PERSON'S CHARACTER **3** (used about a person's character) easy to influence; not firm: *He is too weak to be a good leader.*
➤NOT CONVINCING **4** (used about an argument, excuse, etc.) that does not convince you or seem right; not strong: *a weak argument against the proposal*
➤HARD TO SEE/HEAR **5** not easy to see or hear; not definite or strong: *I heard a weak voice whispering for help.* ◇ *She gave a weak smile.*
➤LIQUID **6** (used about liquids) containing a lot of water; not strong in taste: *weak tea*
➤NOT GOOD AT STH **7** **weak (at/in/on sth)** not able to achieve a high standard in sth: *He's weak at math.* ◇ *His math skills are weak.*
▶ **weak·ly** ***adv.***: *The little kitten struggled weakly to its feet.*

**weak·en** /ˈwikən/ ***verb*** [I,T] **1** to become less strong; to make sb/sth less strong: *The storm weakened as it approached the coast.* ◇ *The building had been weakened by the earthquake.* **2** to become less certain about sth: *Their mother was weakening. "Oh, all right," she said. "You can go."*

**weak·ling** /ˈwiklɪŋ/ ***noun*** [C] a person who is not physically strong

★**weak·ness** /ˈwiknəs/ ***noun*** **1** [U] the state of being weak: *They were relying on the enemy's weakness in the air.* **2** [C] a fault or lack of strength, especially in a person's character: *It's important to know your own strengths and weaknesses.* **3** [C, usually sing.] **a weakness for sth/sb** a special and often foolish liking for sth/sb: *I have a weakness for chocolate.*

★**wealth** /wɛlθ/ ***noun*** **1** [U] (owning) a lot of money, property, etc.: *They were a family of enormous wealth.* **2** [sing.] **a wealth of sth** a large number or amount of sth: *He has a wealth of experience in this area.*

**wealth·y** /ˈwɛlθi/ ***adj.*** (**wealth·i·er**; **wealth·i·est**) having a lot of money, etc.; rich

**wean** /win/ ***verb*** [T] **wean sb (from/off sth)** to start feeding a baby or young animal with other food as well as its mother's milk: *(figurative) to wean yourself off cigarettes*

**weap·on** /ˈwɛpən/ ***noun*** [C] an object which is used for fighting or for killing people, such as a gun, knife, bomb, etc.

**weap·on·ry** /ˈwɛpənri/ ***noun*** [U] *(written)* all the weapons of a particular type or belonging to a particular country or group: *high-tech weaponry*

★**wear**[1] /wɛr/ ***verb*** (*pt* **wore** /wɔr/; *pp* **worn** /wɔrn/)
➤CLOTHING/ORNAMENT **1** [T] to have clothes, jewelry, etc. on your body: *He was wearing a suit and tie.* ◇ *I wear glasses for reading.* ◇ *Would you like to wear my necklace?* ◇ *to wear your hair short*
➤EXPRESSION ON FACE **2** [T] to have a certain look on your face: *He was wearing an expression of delight.*
➤DAMAGE WITH USE **3** [I] to become thinner or damaged because of being used or rubbed a lot **4** [T] to make a hole, path, etc. in sth by rubbing, walking, etc.: *Cut your toenails or you'll wear a hole in your socks!*
➤STAY IN GOOD CONDITION **5** [I] to last for a long time without becoming thinner or damaged: *This material wears well.*
IDM **wear thin** to have less effect because of being used too much: *We've heard that story so often that it's beginning to wear thin.*
PHRV **wear (sth) away** to damage sth or to make it disappear over a period of time, by using, touching, etc. it a lot; to disappear or become damaged in this way: *The shiny finish on the floor had worn away over the years.* ◇ *The motion of the waves had worn a lot of the rocks away.*
**wear (sth) down** to become or to make sth smaller or shorter
**wear sb/sth down** to make sb/sth weaker by attacking, persuading, etc.: *They wore him down with constant arguments until he changed his mind.*
**wear off** to become less strong or to disappear completely: *The effects of the drug wore off after a few hours.*
**wear on** (used about time) to pass slowly: *They got to know each other better as the summer wore on.*
**wear (sth) out** to become too thin or damaged to use anymore; to cause sth to do this: *Children's shoes wear out very quickly.* ◇ *You've worn out two pairs of jeans in the last six months!*
**wear sb out** to make sb very tired: *She wore herself out walking home with the heavy bags.* ➲ Look at **worn out**.

**wear**[2] /wɛr/ ***noun*** [U] **1** wearing or being worn; use as clothing: *This sweater would be good for everyday wear.* **2** (usually in compounds) things that you wear; clothes: *sportswear* ◇ *underwear* **3** long use which damages the quality or appearance of sth
IDM **wear and tear** the damage caused by ordinary use
**the worse for wear** → WORSE[1]

**wear·er** /ˈwɛrər/ ***noun*** [C] the person who is wearing sth; a person who usually wears the thing mentioned: *The straps can be adjusted to fit the wearer.* ◇ *contact lens wearers*

**wea·ry** /ˈwɪri/ ***adj.*** (**wea·ri·er**; **wea·ri·est**) tired: *He gave a weary smile.* ▶ **wea·ri·ly** /-əli/ ***adv.*** ▶ **wea·ri·ness** ***noun*** [U]

**wea·sel**[1] /ˈwizl/ ***noun*** [C] a small wild animal with reddish-brown fur, a long thin body and short legs. Weasels eat smaller animals.

**wea·sel**[2] /ˈwizl/ ***verb*** [T]
PHRV **weasel out (of sth)** *(informal)* to avoid doing sth that you ought to do or have promised to do: *He's now trying to weasel out of our agreement.*

★**weath·er**[1] /ˈwɛðər/ ***noun*** [U] the climate at a certain place and time, how much wind, rain, sunshine, etc. there is and how hot or cold it is: *What was the weather like in Hawaii?* ◇ *We'll go to the beach if the weather stays nice.* ◇ *They say that the*

W

*weather won't change for the next few days.* ◇ *The weather forecast is on after the news.*

NOTE **Rain** is drops of water that fall from the clouds. **Snow** is frozen rain. It is soft and white and often settles on the ground. **Sleet** is rain that is not completely frozen. **Hail** is rain that is frozen so hard that it feels and sounds like small stones falling. When it is only raining very slightly, it is **drizzling**. When it is raining very hard, it is **pouring**. **Fog** is like a cloud at ground level. It makes it difficult to see very far ahead. **Mist** is a very thin type of fog. ➲ Look also at **storm**.

IDM **under the weather** (*informal*) not very healthy

**weath·er²** /ˈwɛðər/ ***verb*** **1** [T] (used about a ship or a person) to pass safely through a storm or a difficult time **2** [I,T] to change in appearance (because of the effect of the sun, air or wind)

**ˈweather-ˌbeaten** ***adj.*** (usually before a noun) (used especially about a person or his/her skin) rough and damaged because the person spends a lot of time outside: *the weather-beaten face of an old sailor*

**weath·er·strip·ping** /ˈwɛðərˌstrɪpɪŋ/ ***noun*** [U] material that helps to prevent cold air coming through a door, window, etc.

**weath·er vane** /ˈwɛðər veɪn/ ***noun*** [C] a metal object on the roof of a building that turns easily in the wind and shows which direction the wind is blowing from

**weave** /wiv/ ***verb*** [I,T] (*pt* **wove** /woʊv/ or in sense 2 **weaved**; *pp* **wo·ven** /ˈwoʊvən/ or in sense 2 **weaved**) **1** to make cloth, etc. by passing threads under and over a set of threads that is attached to a frame (**loom**): *woven cloth* **2** to change direction often when you are moving so that you are not stopped by anything: *He weaved in and out through the traffic.*

**weav·er** /ˈwivər/ ***noun*** [C] a person whose job is weaving cloth

**web** /wɛb/ ***noun*** **1** [C] a type of fine net that a spider makes in order to catch small insects: *A spider spins webs.* ➲ picture at **spider**. **2 the Web** [sing.] = WORLD WIDE WEB

**webbed** /wɛbd/ ***adj.*** (only *before* a noun) a bird or an animal (such as a duck or frog) that has webbed feet has pieces of skin between the toes

**web·bing** /ˈwɛbɪŋ/ ***noun*** [U] strong strips of woven material that are used to make belts, etc., and to support the seats of chairs, etc.

**Web·cam™** /ˈwɛbkæm/ ***noun*** [C] a video camera connected to a computer so that what it records can be seen on a website as it happens

**web·log** /ˈwɛblɑg; -lɔg/ ***noun*** [C] = BLOG

**Web·mas·ter** (*also* **web·mas·ter**) /ˈwɛbˌmæstər/ ***noun*** [C] (*computing*) a person who is responsible for particular pages of information on the World Wide Web

**web·site** (*also* **Web site**) /ˈwɛbsaɪt/ (*also* **site** /saɪt/) ***noun*** [C] (*computing*) a place connected to the Internet, where a company or an organization, or an individual person, puts information: *I found this information* ***on their website.*** ◇ *For current prices please* ***visit our website.***

**Wed.** ***abbr.*** = WEDNESDAY

**we'd** /wid/ *short for* WE HAD, WE WOULD

**wed** /wɛd/ ***verb*** [I,T] (**wed<u>d</u>ing**; **wed<u>d</u>ed**)(*formal* or *old-fashioned*) to get married

**wed·ding** /ˈwɛdɪŋ/ ***noun*** [C] a marriage ceremony and often the meal or party that follows it (the reception): *I've been invited to his sister's wedding.* ◇ *a wedding dress/guest/present* ◇ *a wedding ring* (= one that is placed on the third finger of the left hand during a marriage ceremony and worn to show that a person is married) ◇ *a wedding anniversary*

NOTE **Marriage** is the word for the state of being married to somebody. It can also be used for the ceremony, with the same meaning as **wedding**. The man who is getting married is the **groom**; the woman is the **bride**. Other important people at the ceremony are the **best man**, the **maid of honor** and the **bridesmaids**. A wedding can take place in a church or other religious building, or people may get married at home, in a park, a hotel, etc.

**wedge¹** /wɛdʒ/ ***noun*** [C] a piece of wood, etc. with one thick and one narrow end that you can push into a space, in order, for example, to keep things apart: *The door was propped open with a wedge.*

**wedge²** /wɛdʒ/ ***verb*** [T] **1** to force sth apart or to prevent sth from moving by using a WEDGE¹: *to wedge a door open* **2** to force sth/sb to fit into a space: *The chair was wedged between the table and the door.*

**wedg·ie** /ˈwɛdʒi/ ***noun*** [C] an act of lifting sb up by his/her underwear so that it hurts, usually done as a joke: *to give sb a wedgie*

**wed·lock** /ˈwɛdlɑk/ ***noun*** [U] (*formal*) marriage: *children born out of wedlock* (= to parents who are not married)

**Wednes·day** /ˈwɛnzdeɪ; -di/ ***noun*** [C,U] (*abbr.* **Wed.**) the day of the week after Tuesday and before Thursday ➲ For examples of the use of the days of the week in sentences, look at **Monday**.

**wee** /wi/ ***adj.***

IDM **the wee hours** the very early morning hours, soon after midnight

**weed¹** /wid/ ***noun*** **1** [C] a wild plant that is not wanted in a garden because it prevents other plants from growing well: *Our garden is full of weeds.* ➲ Look also at **seaweed**. **2** [U] (*slang*) the illegal drug marijuana

**weed²** /wid/ ***verb*** [I,T] to remove WEEDS¹ (1) from a piece of ground, etc.

PHR V **weed sth/sb out** to remove the things or people that you do not think are good enough: *He weeded out all the letters with spelling mistakes in them.*

**ˈweed ˌkiller** ***noun*** [U,C] a substance that is used to destroy WEEDS¹ (1): *a can of weed killer*

**weed·y** /ˈwidi/ ***adj.*** (**weed·i·er**; **weed·i·est**) **1** full of or covered with WEEDS¹ (1) **2** (*informal*) used about a person) having a thin weak body

★ **week** /wik/ ***noun*** [C] **1** a period of seven days (usually beginning on Sunday and ending on Saturday: *last week/this week/next week* ◇ *He left two weeks* *ago. ◇ I haven't seen her for a whole week. ◇ I play tennis twice a week. ◇ They'll be back in a week. ◇ I was on vacation the week before last. ◇ My course ends the week after next.* **2** the part of the WEEK (1) when people go to work, etc., usually from Monday through Friday: *She works hard during the week. ◇ I work a 40-hour week.*

IDM **week in, week out** every week without a rest or change

**week·day** /ˈwikdeɪ/ ***noun*** [C] any day except Saturday and Sunday: *I only work (on) weekdays.*

★**week·end** /ˈwikɛnd/ ***noun*** [C] Saturday and Sunday: *We're going camping this weekend* (= the weekend that is coming). *◇ What did you do over the weekend? ◇ The bank is closed on the weekends. ◇ a long weekend* (= Saturday and Sunday, plus Friday and/or Monday)

★**week·ly** /ˈwikli/ ***adj., adv.*** happening or appearing once a week or every week: *We are paid weekly. ◇ a weekly report*

**week·night** /ˈwiknaɪt/ ***noun*** [C] any night of the week except Saturday, Sunday and sometimes Friday night: *I have to stay in on weeknights.*

**wee·nie** /ˈwini/ ***noun*** [C] *(informal)* **1** a person who is not strong, brave or confident: *Don't be such a weenie!* **2** = FRANKFURTER **3** *(taboo, slang)* a penis

**weep** /wip/ ***verb*** [I,T] *(pt, pp* **wept** /wɛpt/) *(formal)* to let tears fall because of strong emotion; to cry: *She wept at the news of his death. ◇ to weep for joy ◇ to weep tears of pity*

ˌ**weeping ˈwillow** ***noun*** [C] a type of tree that has branches that hang downward

★**weigh** /weɪ/ ***verb*** **1** [T] to measure how heavy sth is, especially by using a machine (**scale**): *I weigh myself every day. ◇ Can you weigh this package for me?* **2** [T] to have or show a certain weight: *I weigh 156 pounds.* **3** [T] **weigh sth (against sb/sth)** to consider sth carefully, especially to see whether one thing is better, more important, etc. than sth else: *We need to weigh the advantages of the plan against the risks.*

PHR V **weigh against sb/sth** to be considered important when sb/sth is being judged: *She didn't get the job because her lack of experience weighed against her.*

**weigh sb down** to make sb feel worried and sad: *weighed down by responsibilities*

**weigh sb/sth down** to make it difficult for sb/sth to move (by being heavy): *I was weighed down by my heavy backpack.*

**weigh in** to join a discussion or an argument by saying sth important or expressing a strong opinion: *to weigh in with your opinion ◇ Mr. Goldman weighed in on the issue of teachers' salaries.*

**weigh on sb/sth** to make sb worry ➲ We also say **weigh on sb's mind**: *That problem has been weighing on my mind for a long time.*

**weigh sb up** to try and find out what a person is like so that you can form an opinion

★**weight**[1] /weɪt/ ***noun*** **1** [U] *(abbr.* **wt.**) the heaviness of sth or the amount that it weighs, especially as measured in pounds, etc.: *In two months, her weight has increased to 145 pounds. ◇ I need to* ***lose weight*** (= become thinner and less heavy) *before I go on vacation. ◇ He's* ***put on weight*** (= got fatter). *◇ The weight of the snow broke the branch.* **2** [C] a piece of metal with a certain heaviness that can be used to weigh an amount, especially using a scale. Weights are also used by athletes when they are practicing or in the sport of weightlifting: *a 50 pound weight* ➲ picture on study page **A32**. **3** [C] a heavy object: *My doctor told me not to lift heavy weights.* **4** [sing.] the worry that is caused by a problem: *Telling her the truth took a weight off his mind.*

IDM **carry weight** → CARRY

**pull your weight** → PULL[1]

**weight**[2] /weɪt/ ***verb*** [T] **1 weight sth (down) (with sth)** to hold sth down with a heavy object or objects: *to weight down a fishing net* **2** (usually passive) to organize sth so that a particular person or group has an advantage or a disadvantage: *The system is weighted in favor of people with a college degree.*

**weight·less** /ˈweɪtləs/ ***adj.*** having no weight, especially when traveling in space ▶ **weight·less·ness** ***noun*** [U]

**weight·lift·ing** /ˈweɪtˌlɪftɪŋ/ ***noun*** [U] a sport in which people lift heavy metal objects

**weight·y** /ˈweɪt̬i/ ***adj.*** (**weight·i·er**; **weight·i·est**) serious and important: *a weighty question*

**weird** /wɪrd/ ***adj.*** **1** strange and frightening: *a weird noise* **2** *(informal)* not normal: *weird clothes/ideas*

**weird·o** /ˈwɪrdoʊ/ ***noun*** [C] *(pl.* **weird·os**) *(informal)* a person who behaves in a way that is not normal and/or wears strange clothes

★**wel·come**[1] /ˈwɛlkəm/ ***adj.*** **1** received with pleasure; giving pleasure: *You're always welcome here. ◇ welcome news* **2 welcome to sth/to do sth** allowed to do sth: *You're welcome to use our swimming pool.*

IDM **sb is welcome to sth** (used to say that sb can have sth because you do not want it yourself): *Take the car if you want. You're welcome to it – it's always breaking down.*

**you're welcome** (used as a polite reply to sb who has just thanked you): *"Thank you for your help." "You're very welcome."*

★**wel·come**[2] /ˈwɛlkəm/ ***interjection*** (an expression used for greeting a person who is arriving at a place): *Welcome to America! ◇ Welcome home!*

★**wel·come**[3] /ˈwɛlkəm/ ***noun*** [C] a greeting to sb who has arrived: *Let's give a warm welcome to our next guest.*

★**wel·come**[4] /ˈwɛlkəm/ ***verb*** [T] **1** to greet sb when he/she arrives: *The kids rushed to the door to welcome their father home.* **2** to be pleased about sth and support it: *When I told my parents I wanted to work in the family business, they welcomed the idea.*

**wel·com·ing** /ˈwɛlkəmɪŋ/ ***adj.*** **1** (used about a person) friendly toward sb who is visiting or arriving: *The locals were extremely welcoming.* **2** of a place attractive and looking comfortable to be in: *His room was quiet, warm and welcoming.*

**weld** /wɛld/ ***verb*** [I,T] to join pieces of metal by heating them and pressing them together

**weld·er** /ˈwɛldər/ ***noun*** [C] a person whose job is welding metal

★**wel·fare** /ˈwɛlfɛr/ ***noun*** [U] **1** money that the

W

government pays regularly to people who are poor and have no job: *families on welfare* (= receiving welfare) ◇ *to cash your welfare check* **2** the good health and happiness of a person or group of people: *The doctor is concerned about the child's welfare.*

**we'll** /wil; wɪl/ *short for* WE SHALL, WE WILL

★**well**[1] /wɛl/ ***adv.*** (**bet·ter** /ˈbɛt̬ər/, **best** /bɛst/) **1** in a good or satisfactory way: *You speak English very well.* ◇ *I hope your work is going well.* ◇ *Did they treat you well?* ◇ *The car sounds a lot better since it was fixed.* **2** thoroughly, completely or carefully: *Shake the bottle well before opening.* **3** (used with *can, could, may* or *might* to show that sth is probably true): *He might well be right.* **4** very much: *They got home well past midnight.* ◇ *This book is well worth reading.*

IDM **as well (as sb/sth)** in addition (to sb/sth): *The book is available on CD-ROM as well.* ◇ *He has lived in Texas as well as in Washington.* ➲ Look at the note at **also**.

**bode well/ill (for sb/sth)** → BODE

**do well 1** to be successful: *Their daughter has done very well in college.* **2** to be getting better (after an illness): *Mr. Brown is doing well after his operation.*

**may/might (just) as well** (used for saying that sth can or should happen, especially when you have no choice): *I might as well tell you the truth – you'll find out anyway.*

**mean well** → MEAN[1]

**well/badly off** → OFF[1]

★**well**[2] /wɛl/ ***adj.*** (**bet·ter** /ˈbɛt̬ər/, **best** /bɛst/) (not before a noun) **1** (looking or feeling) healthy: *This medicine will make you feel better.* ◇ *Get well soon* (= written on a card that you send to somebody who is sick). **2** in a satisfactory state: *I hope all is well with you.*

IDM **be all very well (for sb)** (*informal*) (used for showing that you are not happy or do not agree with sth): *It's all very well for her to criticize* (= it's easy for her to criticize), *but it doesn't help the situation.*

**it is just as well (that)** → JUST[1]

★**well**[3] /wɛl/ ***interjection*** **1** (used when you begin the next part of a story or when you are thinking about what to say next): *Well, the next thing that happened was...* ◇ *Well now, let me see...* **2** (used for expressing doubt, hesitation, etc.): *"Do you like it?" "Well, I'm not really sure."* ◇ *Her new boyfriend seems, well, a little strange.* **3** (used for showing surprise): *Well, look who's here!* **4** (*also* **oh, well**) (used for showing that there is nothing you can do to change a situation): *Oh, well, there's nothing we can do about it.*

**well**[4] /wɛl/ ***noun*** [C] **1** a deep hole in the ground from which water is taken: *to dig a new well* **2** = OIL WELL

**well**[5] /wɛl/ ***verb*** [I] **well (up)** (used about a liquid) to come to the surface: *Tears welled up in her eyes.*

ˌ**well-adˈjusted** ***adj.*** (of a person) able to deal with people, problems and life in general in a normal, sensible way: *The school aims to produce well-adjusted members of society.*

ˌ**well-ˈbalanced** ***adj.*** **1** containing a sensible variety of the sort of things or people that are needed: *a well-balanced diet/meal* **2** (used about a person or his/her behavior) sensible and emotionally in control: *secure, well-balanced people*

ˌ**well-beˈhaved** ***adj.*** behaving in a way that most people think is correct

ˌ**well-ˈbeing** ***noun*** [U] a feeling of being healthy and happy

ˌ**well-ˈbuilt** ***adj.*** **1** (used about a person) with a solid, strong body **2** (used about a building or a machine) strongly made

ˌ**well-conˈnected** ***adj.*** (used about a person) having important or rich friends or relatives: *a well-connected family* ◇ *Her new husband is very well-connected.*

ˌ**well-ˈdone** ***adj.*** (used about meat, etc.) cooked for a long time ➲ Look at the note at **rare**.

ˌ**well-ˈdressed** ***adj.*** wearing attractive and fashionable clothes

ˌ**well-ˈearned** ***adj.*** much deserved: *a well-earned rest*

ˌ**well-enˈdowed** ***adj.*** **1** (*informal*) (used about a woman) having large breasts **2** (*informal*) (used about a man) having a large penis **3** (used about an organization) having a lot of money: *well-endowed colleges*

ˌ**well-ˈgroomed** ***adj.*** (used about a person) looking clean, neat and carefully dressed

ˌ**well-ˈgrounded** ***adj.*** **well-grounded in sth** having a good training in a subject or skill

ˌ**well-ˈheeled** ***adj.*** wealthy; having a lot of money

ˌ**well-inˈformed** ***adj.*** knowing a lot about one or several subjects

ˌ**well-ˈkept** ***adj.*** **1** kept neat and in good condition: *well-kept gardens* **2** (used about a secret) known only to a few people

ˌ**well-ˈknown** ***adj.*** known by a lot of people; famous

ˌ**well-ˈmeaning** ***adj.*** (used about a person) wanting to be kind or helpful, but often not having this effect

**well·ness** /ˈwɛlnəs/ ***noun*** [U] the state of being healthy

ˌ**well-ˈoff** ***adj.*** = WELL-TO-DO

ˌ**well-ˈpaid** ***adj.*** earning or providing a lot of money: *well-paid managers/jobs* ◇ *The job is very well paid.*

**well-read** /ˌwɛlˈrɛd/ ***adj.*** having read many books, and so knowing a lot about many subjects

ˌ**well-ˈrounded** ***adj.*** (usually *before* a noun) **1** (used about a person) with experiece and abilities in many different subjects **2** (used about an education, etc.) including many different subjects

ˌ**well-ˈspoken** ***adj.*** having a way of speaking that is considered correct or elegant

ˌ**well-ˈthumbed** ***adj.*** a well-thumbed book has been read many times: *a well-thumbed copy of "Catcher in the Rye"*

ˌ**well-to-ˈdo** (*also* ˌ**well-ˈoff**) ***adj.*** wealthy; with a lot of money

ˈ**well-ˌwisher** ***noun*** [C] a person who hopes that sb/sth will be successful

**ˌwell-ˈworn** *adj.* **1** worn or used a lot or for a long time: *a well-worn jacket* **2** (used about a phrase, story, etc.) heard so often that it does not sound interesting any more

**Welsh** /wɛlʃ/ *adj.* of Wales, its people or their language: *the Welsh coast* ◇ *He's Welsh. He was born in Cardiff.*

**welt** /wɛlt/ *noun* [C] a raised mark on the skin where sth has hit or rubbed you

**wel·ter** /ˈwɛltər/ *noun* [sing.] (*formal*) **a welter of sth** a large and confusing amount of sth: *a welter of criticism/enquiries/information*

**wench** /wɛntʃ/ *noun* [C] (*old-fashioned*) a young woman

**went** *past tense of* GO¹

**wept** *past tense, past participle of* WEEP

**we're** /wɪr/ *short for* WE ARE

**were** /wər/ → BE¹·²

**were·wolf** /ˈwɛrwʊlf; ˈwɪr-/ *noun* [C] (*pl.* **were-wolves**) (in stories) a person who sometimes changes into a wolf, especially at the time of the full moon

★**west¹** /wɛst/ *noun* [sing.] (*abbr.* **W**) **1** (*also* **the west**) one of the four main points of the compass; the direction you look toward in order to see the sun set: *Which way is west?* ◇ *Rain is spreading from the west.* ◇ *There's a gas station to the west of here.* ➲ picture at **north**. **2 the west**; **the West** the part of any country, city, etc. that lies further toward the west than other parts: *I live in the west of Montana.* ◇ *The climate in the west is generally drier than in the east.* **3 the West** the countries of North America and Western Europe

★**west²** (*also* **West**) /wɛst/ *adj.* in or toward the west, or from the west: *the West Coast* (= next to the Pacific Ocean) ◇ *West St. Paul* ◇ *a west wind*

★**west³** /wɛst/ *adv.* to or toward the west: *The island is five miles west of here.* ◇ *to travel west*

**west·bound** /ˈwɛstbaʊnd/ *adj.* traveling or leading toward the west: *The westbound lanes of the expressway are closed.*

**west·er·ly** /ˈwɛstərli/ *adj.* **1** to, toward or in the west: *in a westerly direction* **2** (used about winds) coming from the west

★**west·ern¹** /ˈwɛstərn/ *adj.* **1** in or of the west: *the western provinces* **2** (*also* **Western**) from or connected with countries of North America and western Europe: *Western literature*

**west·ern²** (*also* **Western**) /ˈwɛstərn/ *noun* [C] a movie or book about life in the past in the North American West

**west·ern·er** /ˈwɛstərnər/ *noun* [C] **1** a person who was born in or who lives in North America or western Europe **2** (*also* **Westerner**) a person who was born in or who lives in western Canada or the U.S.

**west·ern·ize** /ˈwɛstərnaɪz/ *verb* [T] to make a country or people more like North America or Western Europe, e.g. in the way people dress and behave: *The Japanese diet has become more westernized in recent years.*

**west·ward** /ˈwɛstwərd/ *adj.* toward the west: *in a westward direction* ▸ **west·ward** (*also* **westwards**) *adv.*: *to fly westward*

★**wet¹** /wɛt/ *adj.* (**wet·ter**; **wet·test**) **1** covered in a liquid, especially water: *wet clothes* ◇ *Don't get your feet wet.*

> NOTE **Moist** means slightly wet. **Damp** is used to describe things that are slightly wet and may feel unpleasant because of it: *Don't sit on the grass. It's damp.*

**2** (used about the weather, etc.) with a lot of rain: *a wet day* **3** (used about paint, etc.) not yet dry or hard: *The ink is still wet.*

IDM **wet behind the ears** (*informal*) young and without much experience SYN **naive**

**a wet blanket** (*informal*) a person who spoils other people's fun, especially because he/she will not join in

**wet²** /wɛt/ *verb* (*pres. part.* **wet·ting**; *pt, pp* **wet** or **wet·ted**) [T] **1** to make sth wet **2** (used especially about young children) to make yourself or your bed, clothes, etc. wet by passing waste water (**urine**) out of the body: *Joe wet his pants this morning.*

**wet·back** /ˈwɛtbæk/ *noun* [C] (*taboo, slang*) an offensive word for a Mexican person, especially one who enters the U.S. illegally

**wet·land** /ˈwɛtlænd; -lənd/ *noun* [U] (*also* **wetlands** [pl.]) an area of wet land: *The wetlands are home to a large variety of wildlife.* ▸ **wet·land** *adj.* (only *before* a noun): *wetland birds/plants/habitats*

**ˈwet suit** *noun* [C] a rubber suit that covers the whole body, used by people who swim under water or play sports in the water

**we've** /wiv/ *short for* WE HAVE

**whack¹** /wæk/ *verb* [T] (*informal*) to hit sb/sth hard

**whack²** /wæk/ *noun* [C] (*informal*) an act of hitting sb/sth hard

IDM **out of whack** (*informal*) not functioning correctly: *The whole system is completely out of whack.*

**whacked** /wækt/ *adj.* (*informal*) **1** (used about a person) very tired: *I'm whacked.* **2** = WHACKED OUT

**ˌwhacked ˈout** (*also* **whacked**) *adj.* (*informal*) crazy: *That guy is totally whacked out.*

whale

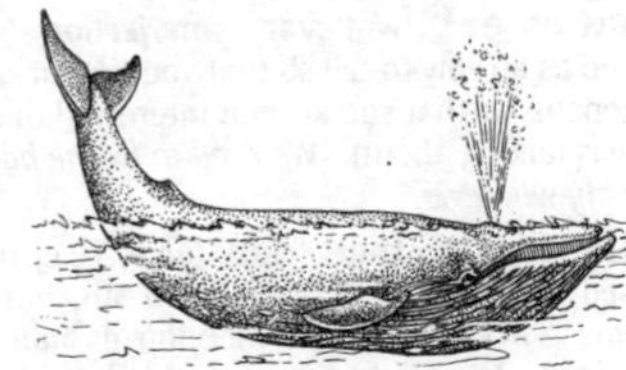

**whale** /weɪl/ *noun* [C] a very large animal that lives in the ocean and looks like a huge fish (but is, in fact, a mammal)

**whal·er** /ˈweɪlər/ *noun* [C] **1** a ship used for hunting whales **2** a person who hunts whales ▸ **whal·ing** *noun* [U]

**wham** /wæm/ *interjection* (*informal*) **1** (used to represent the sound of a sudden, loud hit): *The bombs went down – wham! – right on target.* **2** (used to show that sth that is unexpected has suddenly happened): *I saw him yesterday and – wham! – I realized I was still in love with him.*



W

**wharf** /wɔrf/ ***noun*** [C] (*pl.* **wharves** /wɔrvz/) a platform made of stone or wood at the edge of the ocean, etc. where ships and boats can be tied up

★**what** /wʌt; wɑt; *weak form* wət/ ***det., pronoun*** **1** (used for asking for information about sb/sth): *What time is it?* ◇ *What kind of music do you like?* ◇ *She asked him what he was doing.* ◇ *What's their phone number?* ➲ Look at the note at **which**. **2** the things (that); all the...: *What she says is true.* ◇ *I believe what she said.* ◇ *Is it true what she said?* ◇ *I don't have much, but you can borrow what money I have.* **3** (used for showing surprise, pleasure, etc.): *What a beautiful day!*

> NOTE **What** can also be used alone, to express surprise: *"I just spent a thousand dollars." "What?!"* It can also be used as a reply to sb who is trying to get your attention or when you did not hear sth correctly, though this usage is not very polite: *"Jerry?" "What?" "Come here a minute."*

IDM **how/what about...?** → ABOUT[2]

**how, what, where, who, etc. in the world** → WORLD

**... or what?** (*informal*) (used to ask about another possibility, especially when you are annoyed): *Are you guys coming along, or what?*

**what for** for what purpose; why: *What's this little switch for?* ◇ *What did you say that for?* ◇ *"Can you come here?" "What for?"*

**what if...?** what would happen if...?: *What if the car broke down?*

★**what·ev·er[1]** /wəṭˈɛvər; wɑṭ-/ ***adj., pronoun*** **1** any or every; anything or everything: *You can say whatever you want.* ◇ *He took whatever help he could get.* **2** no matter what: *I still love you, whatever you may think.* ◇ *Whatever she says, she doesn't really mean it.*

IDM **or whatever** (*informal*) or any other or others of a similar kind: *You don't need to wear anything fancy – jeans and a sweater or whatever.*

**what·ev·er[2]** /wəṭˈɛvər; wɑṭ-/ (*also* **what·so·ev·er** /ˌwʌtsoʊˈɛvər; ˌwɑt-/) ***adv.*** at all: *I have no reason whatever to doubt him.* ◇ *"Any questions?" "None whatsoever."*

**what·ev·er[3]** /wəṭˈɛvər/ ***interjection*** (*informal*) (used as a reply to tell sb that you do not care what happens, or that you are not interested in what he/she is talking about): *"We need to fix the back door." "Yeah, whatever."*

**what·not** /ˈwʌtnɑt; ˈwɑt-/ ***noun*** [U,C] (*informal*) (used when you are referring to sth, but are not being exact and do not mention its name): *It's a new firm. They make toys and whatnot.*

**whats·his·name** /ˈwʌtsɪzˌneɪm; ˈwɑt-/ (*feminine* **ˈwhats·her·ˌname** /ˈwʌtsərˌneɪm; ˈwɑt-/) ***noun*** [U, sing.] (used to refer to a person whose name you cannot remember): *She's just left with whatshisname.*

**what·so·ev·er** /ˌwʌtsoʊˈɛvər; ˌwɑt-/ ***adv.*** (used in negative sentences) not at all; not of any kind: *They received no help whatsoever.* ◇ *"Is there any doubt about it?" "None whatsoever."*

**wheat** /wit/ ***noun*** [U] **1** a type of grain which can be made into flour **2** the plant which produces this grain: *a field of wheat*

**wheat·germ** /ˈwitdʒərm/ ***noun*** [U] the center of the wheat grain, which is especially good for your health

**whee** /wi/ ***interjection*** used to express excitement

**whee·dle** /ˈwidl/ ***verb*** [T] to persuade sb to give you sth or do sth by saying nice things that you do not mean: *The kids can always wheedle money out of their father.* ◇ *She wheedled me into lending her my new coat.*

★**wheel[1]** /wil/ ***noun*** **1** [C] a round object that turns around a long stick (axle) that is attached to its center. Wheels are used to make a car, bicycle, etc. move or to make a machine work **2** [usually sing.] = STEERING WHEEL **3 wheels** [pl.] (*informal*) a car: *Dave's been without wheels ever since his accident in June.*

IDM **at/behind the wheel** driving a car: *Jon was behind the wheel when the accident happened.*

**wheel[2]** /wil/ ***verb*** **1** [T] to push along an object that has wheels; to move sb around in/on a vehicle with wheels: *He wheeled his bike up the hill.* ◇ *She was wheeled back to her bed after the operation.* **2** [I] to turn around suddenly: *The man wheeled around and fired several shots at the guards.*

**wheel·bar·row** /ˈwilˌbæroʊ/ ***noun*** [C] a type of small cart with one wheel, two legs and two handles used for carrying small loads, especially outdoors ➲ picture at **garden**.

**wheel·chair** /ˈwiltʃɛr/ ***noun*** [C] a chair with large wheels that a person who cannot walk can move around or be pushed in

**wheelchair**

**wheel·er-deal·er** /ˌwilər ˈdilər/ ***noun*** [C] (*informal*) a person who does a lot of complicated deals in business or politics, often in a dishonest way

**wheel·ie** /ˈwili/ ***noun*** [C] (*informal*) a trick that you can do on a bicycle or motorcycle by balancing on the back wheel, with the front wheel off the ground: *to do/pop a wheelie*

**wheeze** /wiz/ ***verb*** [I] to make noises when you breathe, especially if you have an illness in your chest

★**when[1]** /wɛn; *weak form* wən/ ***adv.*** **1** at what time: *When did she get here?* ◇ *I don't know when she got here.* **2** (used for talking about the time at which sth happens or happened): *Sunday is the day when I can relax.* ◇ *I saw her in May when she was in town.*

★**when[2]** /wɛn; *weak form* wən/ ***conj.*** **1** at or during the time that: *He jumped up when the phone rang.* ◇ *When we were walking home, we saw an accident.*

> NOTE Notice that we use the present tense after "when" if we are talking about a future time: *I'll call you when I'm ready.*

**2** since; as; considering that: *Why do you want more money when you've got enough already?*

> NOTE **When** is used for talking about something that you think will happen, but **if** is used for something you are not sure will happen. Compare: *I'll*

*ask her when she comes* (= you are sure that she will come). ◇ *I'll ask her if she comes* (= you are not sure whether she will come or not).

**whence** /wɛns/ ***adv.*** (*old-fashioned*) from where: *They returned whence they had come.*

★**when·ev·er** /wɛnˈɛvər; wən-/ ***conj.***, ***adv.*** at any time; no matter when: *You can borrow my car whenever you want.* ◇ *Don't worry. You can give it back the next time you see me, or whenever.*

★**where** /wɛr; *weak form* wər/ ***adv.***, ***conj.*** **1** at, in or to what place or position: *Where can I buy a paper?* ◇ *I asked him where he lived.* ◇ *Where are you going?* **2** at, in or to a place or a situation: *the town where you were born* ◇ *She ran to where they were standing.* ◇ *I know where we need to go.* ◇ *Where possible, you should travel by bus, not car.* **3** at which place: *We came to a town where we stopped for lunch.*

**where·a·bouts**[1] /ˈwɛrəbaʊts/ ***noun*** [U, with sing. or pl. verb] the place where sb/sth is: *The whereabouts of the stolen painting is/are unknown.*

**where·a·bouts**[2] /ˈwɛrəbaʊts/ ***adv.*** used to ask the general area where sb/sth is: *Whereabouts did you find it?*

★**where·as** /wɛrˈæz; ˈwɛrəz/ ***conj.*** (used for showing a fact that is different): *He eats meat, whereas she's a vegetarian.*

**where·by** /wɛrˈbaɪ; ˈwɛrbaɪ/ ***adv.*** (*formal*) by which: *The company has a system whereby employees can get regular training.*

**where·up·on** /ˌwɛrəˈpɑn; -ˈpɔn; ˈwɛrəpɑn/ ***conj.*** (*formal*) after which: *He fell asleep, whereupon she walked quietly from the room.*

★**wher·ev·er** /wɛrˈɛvər; wər-/ ***conj.*** **1** in or to any place: *You can sit wherever you want.* ◇ *She comes from Bahia, wherever that is* (= I don't know where it is). **2** everywhere, in all places that: *Wherever I go, he goes.*

**the where·with·al** /ˈwɛrwɪˌðɔl; -ˌθɔl/ ***noun*** [sing.] **the wherewithal (to do sth)** the money, things or skill that you need in order to be able to do sth: *They lacked the wherewithal to pay for the repairs.*

**whet** /wɛt/ ***verb*** (**whet·ting**; **whet·ted**)

IDM **whet sb's appetite** to make sb want more of sth: *The orchestra concert whetted my appetite for classical music.*

★**wheth·er** /ˈwɛðər/ ***conj.*** **1** (used after verbs like "ask", "doubt", "know", etc.) if: *He asked me whether we would be coming to the party.* **2** (used for expressing a choice or doubt between two or more possibilities): *I can't make up my mind whether to go or not.* ◇ *There was some doubt as to whether she should go.*

NOTE **Whether** and **if** can both be used in sense 1. Only **whether** can be used before "to" + verb: *Have you decided whether to accept the offer yet?* Only **whether** can be used after a preposition: *the problem of whether to accept the offer.*

IDM **whether or not** (used to say that sth will be true in either of the situations that are mentioned): *We will play on Saturday whether it rains or not.* ◇ *Whether or not it rains, we will play on Saturday.*

**whew** /hwyu; hwu; fyu/ ***interjection*** (used to show the sound which expresses tiredness, surprise, relief, shock, etc.): *Whew! It's hot in here!*

**whey** /weɪ/ ***noun*** [U] the thin liquid that is left from sour milk after the solid part (**the curds**) has been removed

★**which** /wɪtʃ/ ***det.***, ***pronoun*** **1** (used in questions when there are a number of people or things to choose from): *Which piece of cake do you want?* ◇ *Which hand do you write with?* ◇ *Which is your bag?* ◇ *She asked me which color I liked better.* ◇ *I can't remember which of the boys is older.*

NOTE **Which or what?** We use **which** when there is only a limited group to choose from: *Which car is yours? The Ford or the Buick?* We use **what** when the group is not limited: *What car would you choose, if you could have any one you wanted?*

**2** (used for saying what thing or things you are talking about): *This is an important book which contains some valuable information.* ◇ (*formal*) *The situation in which he found himself was very difficult.*

NOTE In less formal English we would write: *The situation which he found himself in was very difficult.* Often the "which" is left out: *The situation he found himself in...*

**3** (used for giving more information about a thing or animal): *His best film, which won several awards, was about the Nazi concentration camps.*

NOTE Note that there is a comma before "which" and at the end of the part of the sentence which it introduces.

**4** (used for making a comment on what has just been said): *We had to wait 16 hours for our plane, which was really annoying.*

NOTE Note that there is a comma before "which."

**which·ev·er** /wɪtʃˈɛvər/ ***det.***, ***pronoun*** any person or thing: *You can choose whichever book you want.*

**whiff** /wɪf/ ***noun***

IDM **catch/get a whiff of sth** to smell sth for just a short time: *I caught a whiff of his aftershave as he leaned toward me.*

★**while**[1] /waɪl/ ***conj.*** **1** during the time that; when: *He always calls while we're eating lunch.* **2** at the same time as: *She usually listens to the radio while she's driving to work.* **3** (*formal*) (used when you are contrasting two ideas): *Some countries are rich, while others are extremely poor.* ◇ *While I understand your point, I simply do not agree with you.*

★**while**[2] /waɪl/ ***noun*** [sing.] a period of time (usually short): *Let's sit down here for a while.*

IDM **once in a while** → ONCE[1]

**worth sb's while** → WORTH[1]

**while**[3] /waɪl/ ***verb***

PHR V **while sth away** to spend time in a pleasant lazy way: *We whiled away the time reading and playing cards.*

**whim** /wɪm/ ***noun*** [C] a sudden idea or desire to do sth (often sth that is not sensible)

**whim·per**[1] /ˈwɪmpər/ ***verb*** [I] to cry softly, especially with fear or pain

W

**whim·per²** /ˈwɪmpər/ ***noun*** [C] a soft cry, especially of fear or pain

IDM **without a whimper** if sth happens or is done without a whimper, it happens without anyone protesting or complaining about it

**whim·si·cal** /ˈwɪmzɪkl/ ***adj.*** (*written*) unusual and not serious in a way that is either amusing or annoying: *to have a whimsical sense of humor* ◇ *Much of his writing has a whimsical quality.*

**whine** /waɪn/ ***verb*** **1** [I] to make a long high unpleasant sound: *The dog is whining to go out.* **2** [I,T] to complain about sth in an annoying way: *Quit whining about the food and eat your vegetables!* ▸ **whine *noun*** [C]

**whip¹** /wɪp/ ***noun*** [C] **1** a long thin piece of leather, etc. with a handle, that is used for making animals go faster and for hitting people as a punishment **2** a member of a political party who encourages the other members of his/her political party to vote the same way on important decisions

**whip²** /wɪp/ ***verb*** (**whip·ping; whipped**) **1** [T] to hit a person or animal with a whip **2** [T] to mix the white part of an egg or cream, etc. until it is light and stiff: *whipped cream* **3** [T] (*informal*) to defeat sb easily in a sports game, competition, etc.: *We really whipped the Braves last night!* **4** [I,T] to move or hit sth quickly or violently: *The wind whipped through the trees.*

PHRV **whip sth out** (*informal*) to take sth out quickly or suddenly: *He whipped out a pen and made a note of the number.*

**whip sth up 1** to cause a strong emotion: *to whip up excitement* **2** (*informal*) to prepare food quickly: *to whip up a quick snack*

**whip·lash** /ˈwɪplæʃ/ ***noun*** **1** [C, usually sing.] a hit with a whip: *Her sharp voice cut the air like a whiplash.* **2** [U] a neck injury caused when your head moves forward and back suddenly, especially in a car accident: *He was bruised and suffering from whiplash.*

**ˈwhipped cream *noun*** [U] cream that has become thicker because it has been WHIPPED² (2)

**ˈwhipping ˌcream *noun*** [U] cream that becomes thicker when it is WHIPPED² (2)

**whir** /wər/ ***verb*** [I] (**whir·ring; whirred**) to make a continuous low sound: *The noise of the fan whirring kept me awake.* ▸ **whir *noun*** [C, usually sing.]

**whirl¹** /wərl/ ***verb*** [I,T] to move around very quickly; to make sb/sth move in this way: *The dancers whirled around the room.* ◇ *The wind whirled the leaves around and around.*

**whirl²** /wərl/ ***noun*** [sing.] the act or sound of whirling: *the whirl of the helicopter's blades*

IDM **be in a whirl** to be in a state of confusion: *My head's in a whirl – I'm so excited.*

**give sth a whirl** to try sth

**whirl·pool** /ˈwərlpul/ ***noun*** [C] **1** a place in a river or the ocean where the water moves around and around very quickly **2** (*also* ˌ**whirlpool ˈbath**) a special bath or swimming pool for relaxing in, in which the water moves in circles ➲ Look at **Jacuzzi**.

**whirl·wind¹** /ˈwərlwɪnd/ ***noun*** [C] a very strong wind that forms a tall column of air moving around and around in a circle as it travels across land or water

**whirl·wind²** /ˈwərlwɪnd/ ***adj.*** (only *before* a noun) happening very quickly, often in an exciting way: *a whirlwind tour of Europe* ◇ *a whirlwind romance*

**whisk¹** /wɪsk/ ***noun*** [C] a tool that you use for beating the white part of an egg, cream, etc. ➲ picture at **kitchen**.

**whisk²** /wɪsk/ ***verb*** [T] **1** to move sb/sth quickly: *The actress was whisked away in a black limousine.* **2** to beat eggs, cream, etc. very quickly with a WHISK¹

**whisk·er** /ˈwɪskər/ ***noun*** **1 whiskers** [pl.] the hair that is growing on a man's face **2** [C] one of the long hairs that grow near the mouth of a mouse, cat, etc. ➲ picture at **cat**.

IDM **by a whisker** by a very small amount

**whis·key** /ˈwɪski/ ***noun*** (*pl.* **whis·keys**) [C,U] a strong alcoholic drink that is made from grain, or a glass of this drink

**whis·per** /ˈwɪspər/ ***verb*** [I,T] to speak very quietly to sb, so that other people cannot hear what you are saying ▸ **whis·per *noun*** [C]: *to speak in a whisper*

★**whis·tle¹** /ˈwɪsl/ ***noun*** [C] **1** the long high sound that you make when you force air out between your lips **2** a simple musical instrument that produces a long high sound: *The referee blew his whistle to stop the game.*

IDM **blow the whistle on sb/sth** → BLOW¹

**whis·tle²** /ˈwɪsl/ ***verb*** **1** [I,T] to make sounds by forcing air out between your lips or through a WHISTLE¹ (2): *The girl was whistling as she walked down the street.* ◇ *He whistled a tune to himself.* ◇ *The referee whistled and the game was over.* **2** [I] to make a sound like a WHISTLE¹ (1): *A bullet whistled past his head* (= moved quickly, with the sound of a whistle).

**whis·tle·blow·er** (*also* **whistle-blower**) /ˈwɪslˌbloʊər/ ***noun*** [C] (used especially in newspapers) a person who informs people in authority or the public that the company he/she works for is doing sth wrong or illegal

**ˈwhistle-stop *adj.*** (only *before* a noun) visiting a lot of different places in a very short time: *to go on a whistle-stop tour of Europe*

★**white¹** /waɪt/ ***adj.*** **1** of the very light color of snow or milk: *an old lady with white hair* ◇ *white bread* **2** belonging to a race of people with pale skin, originally from Europe

IDM **black and white** → BLACK¹

★**white²** /waɪt/ ***noun*** **1** [U] white color, paint, etc.: *She was dressed in white.* **2** [C] a person who belongs to a race of people with pale skin, originally from Europe **3** [C,U] the part of an egg that turns white when it is cooked

> NOTE The yellow part of an egg is the **yolk**. ➲ picture at **egg**.

**4** [C] the white part of the eye

IDM **in black and white** → BLACK²

**white³** /waɪt/ ***verb***

PHRV **white sth out** to cover a mistake that you make when you are writing or typing, by covering it with a white fluid (correction fluid)

**ˌwhite-ˈcollar** ***adj.*** (only *before* a noun) connected with people who work in offices, not in factories: *white-collar workers* ◇ *white-collar jobs* ➲ Look at **blue-collar**.

**ˌwhite ˈelephant** ***noun*** [usually sing.] a thing that is useless and no longer needed, although it may have cost a lot of money: *The new office block has become an expensive white elephant.*

★**the ˈWhite House** ***noun*** [sing.] **1** the large house in Washington, D.C., where the U.S. President lives and works **2** the U.S. President and the branch of the U.S. government that includes the people who advise the President ➲ For more information on the U.S. political system, look at study page **A10**.

> NOTE Some nouns are always used with **the**: *the White House* ◇ *the FBI* ◇ *the Internet.* These nouns refer to things that are the only ones of their kind. However, we do not use **the** when we use these words in front of other words to describe them: *White House aides have denied the rumor.* ◇ *The house was surrounded by FBI agents.* ◇ *Visit our Internet site.*

**ˌwhite-ˈknuckle** ***adj.*** causing fear or excitement: *a white-knuckle flight*

**ˌwhite-ˌknuckle ˈride** ***noun*** [C] a ride at a fairground that makes you feel very excited and frightened at the same time

**ˌwhite ˈlie** ***noun*** [C] a lie that is not very harmful or serious

**ˈwhite meat** ***noun*** [U] **1** meat that is pale in color when it has been cooked, such as chicken ➲ Look at **red meat. 2** pale meat from the breast of a chicken or other bird that has been cooked

**whit·en** /ˈwaɪtn/ ***verb*** [T] to make sth white or paler in color ▸ **whit·en·er** ***noun*** [U]

**white·out** /ˈwaɪt̬aʊt/ ***noun*** [C] **1** weather conditions in which there is so much snow or cloud that it is impossible to see anything **2** [U] a white liquid that you use to cover mistakes that you make when you are writing or typing, and that you can write on top of; a type of correction fluid

**ˈwhite ˌpages** ***noun*** [pl.] a telephone book (on white paper), or a section of a book, that lists the names, addresses and telephone numbers of people living in a particular area ➲ Look at **Yellow Pages**.

**ˌwhite ˈtrash** ***noun*** [U] (*slang*) poor white people who are often not respected because they are not well educated and often do not behave morally

**white·wash¹** /ˈwaɪtwɑʃ; -wɔʃ/ ***noun*** [U] a white liquid that you use for painting houses or fences

**white·wash²** /ˈwaɪtwɑʃ; -wɔʃ/ ***verb*** [T] **1** to paint a wall or fence with WHITEWASH¹ **2** to try to hide sth bad or wrong that you have done

**white·wa·ter** (*also* **white water**) /ˈwaɪtˌwɔt̬ər; -ˌwɑt̬ər/ ***noun*** [U] water that moves very fast through a narrow or rocky part of a river: *to go whitewater rafting*

**ˌwhite ˈwine** ***noun*** [U] wine made from green grapes, that is clear or of a very pale yellow color ➲ Look at **red wine** and **rosé**.

**whit·ey** /ˈwaɪt̬i/ ***noun*** [C] (*informal*) an offensive word for a white person

**whith·er** /ˈwɪðər/ ***adv., conj.*** **1** (*old-fashioned*) where; to which: *Whither should they go?* ◇ *the place whither they were sent* **2** (*formal*) (used to ask what is likely to happen to sth in the future): *Whither modern architecture?*

**whit·tle** /ˈwɪt̬l/ ***verb***

PHR V **whittle sth away; whittle away at sth** to remove or decrease sth gradually: *Real estate development is whittling away at the birds' natural habitat.*

**whittle sth down** to reduce the size or number of sth gradually: *We have whittled down the list of candidates to two finalists.*

**whiz¹** (*also* **whizz**) /wɪz/ ***verb*** [I] (**whiz·zing; whizzed**) (*informal*) to move very quickly, often making a high continuous sound: *Somebody went whizzing past on a motorcycle.*

**whiz²** /wɪz/ ***noun*** [C] (*pl.* **whiz·zes**) (*informal*) a person who is very intelligent or is very skillful at a particular activity: *a math whiz*

**who** /hu/ ***pronoun*** **1** (used in questions to ask sb's name, etc.): *Who did this?* ◇ (*informal*) *Who did you meet at the party?* ◇ (*informal*) *Who did you go with?* **2** (used in reported questions and after certain verbs): *She wondered who he was.* ◇ *I can't remember who I asked to do this.* **3** (used for saying which person or what kind of person you are talking about): *I like people who say what they think.* ◇ *That's the man who I met at Ann's party.* ◇ *The woman who I work for is very nice.*

> NOTE In the last two examples (= when "who" is the object, or when it is used with a preposition) "who" can be left out: *That's the man I met at Ann's party.* ◇ *The woman I work for is very nice.*

**4** used for giving extra information about sb: *My mother, who's over 80, still drives a car.* ➲ Look at the note at **whom**.

IDM **how, why, where, who, etc. in the world** → WORLD

**whoa** /woʊ/ ***interjection*** (used as a command to a horse, etc. to make it stop or stand still)

**who'd** /hud/ *short for* WHO HAD, WHO WOULD

**who·dun·it** /huˈdʌnɪt/ ***noun*** [C] (*informal*) a story, play, etc. about a murder in which you do not know who did the murder until the end

★**who·ev·er** /huˈɛvər/ ***pronoun*** **1** the person who (used when you do not know that person's identity): *Whoever is responsible will have to pay for the damage.* ◇ *I want to speak to whoever is in charge.* **2** it does not matter who: *I don't want to see anybody – whoever it is.*

★**whole¹** /hoʊl/ ***adj.*** **1** complete; full: *He ate a whole chicken!* ◇ *Hooray! We have two whole weeks off from school!* ◇ *I'm just fed up with the whole thing* (= the entire situation). **2** not broken or cut: *Snakes swallow their prey whole* (= in one piece).

★**whole²** /hoʊl/ ***noun*** [sing.] **1 the whole of sth** all that there is of sth: *I spent the whole of the morning cooking.* **2** a thing that is complete or full: *Two halves make a whole.*

IDM **as a whole** as one complete thing or unit: *This is true not just in New York, but also in North America as a whole.*

W

**on the whole** generally, but not true in every case: *On the whole, I think it's a very good idea.*

**whole·heart·ed** /ˌhoʊlˈhɑrt̬əd/ ***adj.*** complete and without doubt: *to give sb your wholehearted support* ▸ **whole·heart·ed·ly** ***adv.***: *We wholeheartedly agree with you.*

**ˌwhole ˈmilk** ***noun*** [U] milk from which none of the cream has been removed ➲ Compare **skim milk**.

**ˈwhole note** ***noun*** [C] (*symbol* o) a note that lasts as long as four quarter notes ➲ picture at **music**.

**whole·sale** /ˈhoʊlseɪl/ ***adj.*** (only *before* a noun) **1** connected with buying and selling goods in large quantities: *The wholesale price was less than half the retail price in the store.* ➲ Look at **retail**. **2** (usually about sth bad) very great; on a very large scale: *the wholesale destruction of the rainforests* ▸ **wholesale** ***adv.***

**whole·sal·ing** /ˈhoʊlseɪlɪŋ/ ***noun*** [U] the business of buying and selling goods in large quantities, especially so they can be sold again to make a profit ▸ **whole·sal·er** ***noun*** [C]: *fruit and vegetable wholesalers*

**whole·some** /ˈhoʊlsəm/ ***adj.*** **1** good for your health: *simple wholesome food* **2** (used about a person) looking clean and attractive **3** having a moral effect that is good: *wholesome family entertainment*

**ˌwhole-ˈwheat** ***adj.*** containing flour made with whole grains of wheat, including the dry outer part: *whole-wheat bread/flour*

**who'll** /hul/ *short for* WHO WILL

**whol·ly** /ˈhoʊli/ ***adv.*** completely; fully: *The government is not wholly to blame for the situation.*

★**whom** /hum/ ***pronoun*** (*formal*) **1** (used in questions as the object form of "who" to ask sb's name, etc.): *Whom did you meet there?* ◇ *To whom did you give the money?* **2** (used as the object form of "who" in reported questions and after certain verbs): *He asked me whom I had met.* ◇ *I realized to whom I had been speaking.* **3** (used for saying which person or what kind of person the object of a verb or preposition is): *A man whom I had never met sat down beside me.* **4** (used for giving extra information about the object of a verb or preposition): *This is my wife, to whom I owe everything.*

NOTE The use of **whom** instead of **who** as the object pronoun or the pronoun after prepositions is used in more formal English and in writing. We usually express a sentence such as *"He asked me with whom I had discussed it."* as *"He asked me who I had discussed it with."* (Note the position of the preposition at the end.)

**whoop** /wup; hup/ ***verb*** [I] to shout loudly because you are happy or excited

IDM **whoop it up** (*informal*) **1** to enjoy yourself very much with a noisy group of people **2** to make people excited or enthusiastic about sth

▸ **whoop** ***noun*** [C]: *whoops of delight/laughter*

**whoop·ee** /ˈwʊpi; ˈwu-; wʊˈpi/ ***interjection*** (used to express happiness): *Whoopee, we've won!*

**ˈwhoopee ˌcushion** ***noun*** [C] a rubber cushion that makes a noise like a fart when sb sits on it, used as a joke

**whoop·ing cough** /ˈhupɪŋ kɔf/ ***noun*** [U] a serious disease, especially of children, in which they have a bad cough and make a loud noise when they breathe in after coughing

**whoops** /wʊps; wups/ ***interjection*** (*informal*) = OOPS

**whoosh** /wʊʃ; wuʃ/ ***verb*** [I] to move very fast, with the sound of air rushing ▸ **whoosh** ***noun*** [C,U]

**whop·per** /ˈwɑpər/ ***noun*** [C] (*informal*) **1** something that is very big for its type: *Pete has caught a whopper* (= a large fish). **2** a big lie: *She's told some whoppers about her past.*

**whop·ping** /ˈwɑpɪŋ/ (*also* **ˈwhopping great**) ***adj.*** (only *before* a noun) (*informal*) very big: *The company made a whopping 75 million dollar loss.*

**who're** /ˈhuər/ *short for* WHO ARE

**whore** /hɔr/ ***noun*** [C] (*old-fashioned*) = PROSTITUTE

**whore·house** /ˈhɔrhaʊs/ ***noun*** [C] (*old-fashioned*) a place where people pay to have sex SYN **brothel**

**who's** /huz/ *short for* WHO IS, WHO HAS

★**whose** /huz/ ***det.***, ***pronoun*** **1** (used in questions when you are asking who sth belongs to) of whom?: *Whose car is that?* ◇ *That's a nice coat – I wonder whose it is.* **2** of whom; of which: *That's the boy whose mother has just died.* ◇ *a company whose most famous product is chocolate*

**who've** /huv/ *short for* WHO HAVE

**whup** /wʊp; wʌp/ ***verb*** [T] (*pres. part.* **whup·ping**; *pt, pp* **whupped**) (*especially US informal*) to defeat sb easily in a game, a fight, an election, etc.

★**why** /waɪ/ ***adv.*** for what reason: *Why was she so late?* ◇ *I wonder why they went.* ◇ *"I'm not staying any longer." "Why not?"* ◇ *Can you tell me the reason why you are so unhappy?*

IDM **how, why, where, who, etc. in the world** → WORLD

**why not...** (used for making or agreeing to a suggestion): *Why not order a pizza tonight?*

**wick** /wɪk/ ***noun*** [C] the piece of string in the middle of a candle ➲ picture at **candle**.

**wick·ed¹** /ˈwɪkəd/ ***adj.*** **1** morally bad; evil: *The wicked witch turned the prince into a frog.* ➲ Look at the note at **evil**. **2** liking to annoy other people in a way that is not serious: *a wicked sense of humor* **3** (*slang*) very good: *Rob hit a wicked home run today.* ▸ **wick·ed·ly** ***adv.*** ▸ **wick·ed·ness** ***noun*** [U]

**wicked²** /ˈwɪkəd/ ***adv.*** (*slang*) (used for emphasizing an adjective): *Man, it's wicked hot out there!* ◇ *wicked good*

**wick·er** /ˈwɪkər/ ***noun*** [U] thin sticks of wood woven together to make baskets, furniture, etc.: *a wicker chair*

★**wide¹** /waɪd/ ***adj.*** **1** measuring a large amount from one side or edge to the other: *The bridge was not wide enough for two cars to go over.* ◇ *a wide river* ➲ noun **width** OPP **narrow** ➲ Look at the note at **broad**. **2** measuring a particular amount from one side or edge to the other: *The box was only 5 inches wide.* ◇ *How wide is the river?* **3** covering a large area or range, or a large number of people: *You're the nicest person in the whole wide world!* ◇ *This store carries a wide range of sizes.* ◇ *wide*



W

*support for the proposal* **4** fully open: *The children's eyes were wide with excitement.*

**wide²** /waɪd/ ***adv.*** as far or as much as possible; completely: *Open your mouth wide.* ◇ *wide awake* ◇ *a wide-open door*

★**wide·ly** /ˈwaɪdli/ ***adv.*** **1** to a large degree; a lot: *Their opinions differ widely.* **2** over a large area or range: *Steve traveled widely during his college years.*

**wid·en** /ˈwaɪdn/ ***verb*** [I,T] to become wider; to make sth wider: *The gap between rich and poor people is widening.*

**wide·out** /ˈwaɪdaʊt/ ***noun*** [C] = WIDE RECEIVER

**ˌwide-ˈranging** ***adj.*** covering a large area or many subjects: *a wide-ranging discussion*

**ˌwide reˈceiver** ***noun*** [C] (*also* ˈ**wideout**) (in football) an attacking player whose main job is to receive passes

**wide·spread** /ˌwaɪdˈsprɛd; ˈwaɪdsprɛd/ ***adj.*** found or happening over a large area; affecting a large number of people: *The storm caused widespread damage.*

**wid·ow** /ˈwɪdoʊ/ ***noun*** [C] a woman whose husband has died and who has not married again

**wid·owed** /ˈwɪdoʊd/ ***adj.*** being a widow or widower: *She's been widowed for ten years now.*

**wid·ow·er** /ˈwɪdoʊər/ ***noun*** [C] a man whose wife has died and who has not married again

★**width** /wɪdθ; wɪtθ/ ***noun*** [C,U] the amount that sth measures from one side or edge to the other: *The room is twelve feet in width.* ◇ *The carpet is available in two different widths.* ➲ picture at **length**.

**wield** /wild/ ***verb*** [T] to hold and use sth as a weapon: *Some of the men were wielding knives.* ◇ *to wield a great deal of power*

**wie·ner** /ˈwinər/ ***noun*** [C] = FRANKFURTER

ˈ**wiener dog** ***noun*** [C] = DACHSHUND

★**wife** /waɪf/ ***noun*** [C] (*pl.* **wives** /waɪvz/) the woman to whom a man is married

**wig¹** /wɪg/ ***noun*** [C] a covering made of real or artificial hair that you wear on your head, because you do not have any hair or because you want to cover up your own hair ➲ Look at **toupee**.

**wig²** /wɪg/ ***verb*** (*pres. part.* **wig·ging**; *pt, pp* **wigged**)

PHR V **wig out** (*informal*) to become very excited or very anxious about sth; to go crazy

**wig·gle** /ˈwɪgl/ ***verb*** [I,T] (*informal*) to move from side to side with small quick movements; to make sth do this: *Can you wiggle your ears?* ▸ **wig·gle** ***noun*** [C] (*informal*)

**wig·wam** /ˈwɪgwɑm/ ***noun*** [C] a type of tent that was used by some Native Americans in the past

★**wild¹** /waɪld/ ***adj.***

➤ANIMALS/PLANTS **1** living or growing in natural conditions, not controlled by people: *wild animals* ◇ *wild flowers*

➤SCENERY/LAND **2** (used about an area of land) not lived on, farmed, etc.: *the wild scenery of Alaska*

➤OUT OF CONTROL **3** (used about a person or his/her behavior or emotions) not controlled; somewhat crazy: *The crowd went wild with excitement.* ◇ *He had a wild look in his eyes.*

➤ENTHUSIASTIC **4** **wild (about sb/sth)** (*informal*) liking sb/sth very much: *I'm not wild about their new house.*

➤NOT SENSIBLE **5** not carefully done, planned or thought about: *Even if you don't know the answer, take a wild guess.*

➤EXCITING **6** (*informal*) exciting and interesting, especially because it is unusual: *a totally wild outfit*

IDM **a wild goose chase** a search for sth that is impossible for you to find or that does not exist, that makes you waste a lot of time: *The police had been sent on a wild goose chase.*

▸ **wild·ly** ***adv.***: *to wave your arms around wildly*

**wild²** /waɪld/ ***noun*** **the wild** [sing.] natural areas (= not on farms, in zoos, etc.): *the thrill of seeing elephants in the wild*

ˈ**wild card** ***noun*** [C] **1** (in card games) a card that has no value of its own and takes the value of any card that the player chooses **2** (*sports*) an opportunity for sb to play in a competition when he/she has not qualified in the usual way; a player who enters a competition in this way: *He was given a wild card for the tournament.* ◇ *She was beaten in the semi-finals by wild card Alison Waters.* ◇ *a wild-card entry/place* **3** (*computing*) a symbol that has no meaning of its own and can represent any letter or number: *An asterisk is commonly used as a wild card.* ◇ *a wild-card search* **4** a person or thing whose behavior or effect is difficult to predict: *The Nationalist party is the wild card in the election.*

**wild·cat¹** /ˈwaɪldkæt/ ***noun*** [C] a type of wild cat that lives in mountains and forests

**wild·cat²** /ˈwaɪldkæt/ ***adj.*** (only *before* a noun) **1** **a wildcat strike** a wildcat strike happens suddenly and without the official support of a trade union **2** (used about a business or project) that has not been carefully planned and that will probably not be successful; that does not follow normal standards and methods

**wild·cat³** /ˈwaɪldkæt/ ***verb*** [I] (**wild·cat·ting**; **wild·cat·ted**) to look for oil in a place where nobody has found any yet ▸ **wild·cat·ter** ***noun*** [C]

**wil·der·ness** /ˈwɪldərnəs/ ***noun*** [C, usually sing.] **1** an area of land with very few signs of human life: *The Antarctic is the last great wilderness.* **2** a place where plants are growing in an uncontrolled way

**wild·fire** /ˈwaɪldfaɪər/ ***noun*** [U]

IDM **spread like wildfire** (used about news, etc.) to become known by more and more people very quickly: *Rumors of his death spread like wildfire.*

**wild·fowl** /ˈwaɪldfaʊl/ ***noun*** [pl.] birds that people hunt for sport or food, especially birds that live near water such as ducks and geese

**wild·life** /ˈwaɪldlaɪf/ ***noun*** [U] wild birds, plants, animals, etc.

★**will¹** /wəl; əl; l; *strong form* wɪl/ ***modal verb*** (*short form* **'ll**; *negative* **will not**; *short form* **won't** /woʊnt/) **1** (used in forming the future tenses): *He will be here soon.* ◇ *I'm sure you'll pass your test.* ◇ *I'll be sitting on the beach this time next week.* ◇ *Next Sunday, she will have been in America for a year.* **2** (used for showing that sb is willing to do sth, or that sth is able to do sth): *"We need some more milk." "OK, I'll get some."* ◇ *Why won't you tell me where you were last night?* ◇ *I'll carry your bag for*



W

you. ◇ *My car won't start.* **3** (used for asking sb to do sth): *Will you please sit down?* ◇ *Just wait a minute, will you?* **4** (used for talking about sth that generally happens or is true): *People will stop and help if you ask politely.*

★**will**[2] /wɪl/ ***verb*** [T] to use the power of your mind to do sth or to make sth happen: *He willed himself to keep going to the end of the race.*

★**will**[3] /wɪl/ ***noun*** **1** [C,U] the power of the mind to choose what actions to take: *Both her children have very strong wills.* ◇ *My father seems to have lost the will to live.* **2** [sing.] what sb wants or desires: *She was put into a nursing home against her will.* **3** [C] a legal document in which you write down who should have your money and property after your death: *Have you made a will?* ◇ *Grandma left us some money in her will.*

IDM **at will** wherever and whenever you want: *The cat can go in and out of the house at will through the pet door.*

**of your own free will** → FREE[1]

**-willed** /wɪld/ ***combining form*** having a WILL[3] (1) of a particular type: *weak-willed*

**will·ful** /ˈwɪlfl/ ***adj.*** **1** done on purpose, e.g. to hurt or damage sb/sth: *willful damage* **2** doing exactly what you want, no matter what other people think or say ▸ **will·ful·ly** ***adv.***

**wil·lies** /ˈwɪliz/ ***noun*** [pl.] (*informal*) **the willies** if sth gives you the willies, you are frightened by it or find it unpleasant

★**will·ing** /ˈwɪlɪŋ/ ***adj.*** **1** (not before a noun) **be willing to do sth** prepared to do sth; having no objection to doing sth: *Are you willing to help us?* ◇ *I'm not willing to take any risks.* **2** ready or eager: *a willing helper* ▸ **will·ing·ly** ***adv.*** ▸ **will·ing·ness** ***noun*** [U, sing.]

**wil·low** /ˈwɪloʊ/ (*also* **ˈwillow tree**) ***noun*** [C] a tree with thin branches and long thin leaves, that grows near water

**wil·low·y** /ˈwɪloʊi/ ***adj.*** (used about a person, especially a woman) tall, thin and graceful

**will·pow·er** /ˈwɪlˌpaʊər/ ***noun*** [U] strength of mind; the ability to keep trying to succeed, even when sth is difficult: *It takes a lot of willpower to give up smoking.*

**wil·ly-nil·ly** /ˌwɪli ˈnɪli/ ***adv.*** (*informal*) **1** whether you want to or not: *She was forced willy-nilly to accept the company's proposals.* **2** in a careless way without planning: *Don't use your credit card willy-nilly.*

**wilt** /wɪlt/ ***verb*** [I] (used about a plant or flower) to bend and start to die, because of heat or lack of water

**wil·y** /ˈwaɪli/ ***adj.*** (**wil·i·er**; **wil·i·est**) clever at getting what you want, and willing to trick people: *The boss is a wily old fox.* ◇ *He was outwitted by his wily opponent.* SYN **cunning**

**wimp**[1] /wɪmp/ ***noun*** [C] (*informal*) a person who is weak or lacks courage ▸ **wimp·y** ***adj.***

**wimp**[2] /wɪmp/ ***verb***

PHRV **wimp out** (*slang*) to lose your courage to do sth: *"Did you both go on the roller coaster?" "No, Doug wimped out at the last minute."*

★**win**[1] /wɪn/ ***verb*** (*pres. part.* **win·ning**; *pt, pp* **won** /wʌn/) **1** [I,T] to be the best, first or strongest in a race/game/competition/battle/an election: *to win a game, race, etc.* ◇ *Murphy won and Lewis was second.* ◇ *I never win at card games.* ◇ *Who do you think will win the next election?* **2** [T] to get sth as a result of success in a competition, race, etc.: *How much did you win?* ◇ *Who won the gold medal?*

> NOTE Note that we **earn** (not **win**) money at our job: *I earn $25 000 a year.*

**3** [T] to get sth by hard work, great effort, etc.: *Her outstanding performance won her a great deal of praise.* ◇ *to win support for a plan*

PHRV **win sb over (to sth)** to persuade sb to support or agree with you

**win**[2] /wɪn/ ***noun*** [C] an act of winning a competition, game, race, etc.: *We have had two wins and three losses so far this season.*

**wince** /wɪns/ ***verb*** [I] to make a sudden quick movement (usually twisting the muscles of the face) because of a sharp pain or sth bad

**winch** /wɪntʃ/ ***noun*** [C] a machine that lifts or pulls heavy objects by using a thick chain, etc. that winds around and around a central part ▸ **winch** ***verb*** [T]: *The injured climber was winched up into a helicopter.*

★**wind**[1] /wɪnd/ ***noun*** **1** [C,U] (*also* **the wind**) air that is moving across the surface of the earth: *There was a strong wind blowing.* ◇ *A gust of wind blew his hat off.* ◇ *high winds* ◇ *a cold north wind* **2** [U] the breath that you need for doing exercise or playing a musical instrument: *She stopped running to get her wind back.*

IDM **get wind of sth** to hear about sth that is secret

★**wind**[2] /waɪnd/ ***verb*** (*pt, pp* **wound** /waʊnd/) **1** [T] to wrap sth long around sth else several times: *Wind the string around your finger or the balloon will fly away.* **2** [T] **wind sth (up)** to make sth work or move by turning a key, handle, etc.: *to wind a watch* ◇ *to wind up a mechanical toy* **3** [I] (used about a road, path, etc.) to have a lot of bends or curves in it: *The path winds through the woods.*

PHRV **wind down** to gradually come to an end: *The meeting started to wind down about 5:30.* ➲ Look at **unwind**.

**wind up** to be in a place at the end of a trip or in a particular situation after other things have happened: *We wound up in a bad part of town after taking a wrong turn.* ◇ *You'll wind up failing your math class if you go on like this.*

**wind·bag** /ˈwɪndbæg/ ***noun*** [C] (*informal*) a person who talks too much, and does not say anything important or interesting

**wind·break·er** /ˈwɪndˌbreɪkər/ ***noun*** [C] a jacket designed to protect you from the wind

**wind chill** ***noun*** [U] the amount by which wind can cool a person or thing, especially in cold weather: *It is cold outside today, but it feels even colder with the wind chill.*

**wind·chill** /ˈwɪndtʃɪl/ ***noun*** [U] the effect of low temperature combined with wind on sb/sth: *take the windchill factor into account*

**wind·ed** /ˈwɪndəd/ ***adj.*** having difficulty breathing, usually because you have been hit in the stomach

W

**wind·fall** /ˈwɪndfɔl/ ***noun*** [C] an unexpected gift or piece of good luck

**wind·ing** /ˈwaɪndɪŋ/ ***adj.*** with bends or curves in it: *a winding road through the hills*

**wind in·stru·ment** /ˈwɪnd ˌɪnstrəmənt/ ***noun*** [C] a musical instrument that you play by blowing through it

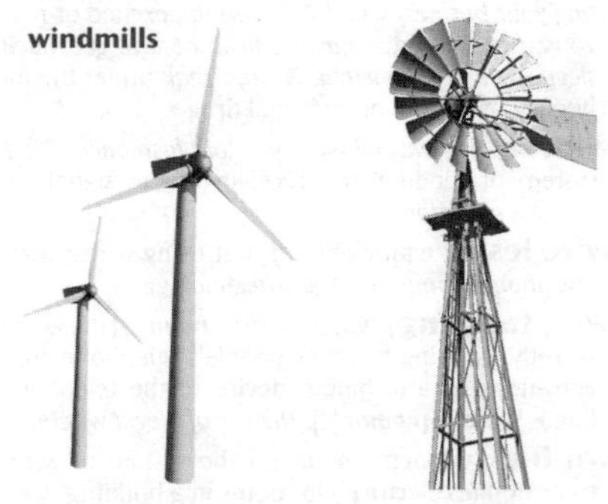
**windmills**

**wind·mill** /ˈwɪndmɪl/ ***noun*** [C] a tall building with long arms that stick out from it and turn in the wind. Windmills are used for pumping water, producing electricity, etc.

★**win·dow** /ˈwɪndoʊ/ ***noun*** [C] **1** the opening in a building, car, etc. that you can see through and that lets light in. A window usually has glass in it: *Open the window. It's hot in here.* ◇ *a store window* **2** the glass in a WINDOW (1): *to break a window* ◇ *to clean the windows* **3** an area on a computer screen that has a particular type of information in it

ˈ**window ˌdressing** ***noun*** [U] **1** the art of arranging goods in store windows in an attractive way **2** the fact of doing or saying sth in a way that creates a good impression but does not show the real facts: *The reforms have been interpreted as window dressing.*

**win·dow·pane** /ˈwɪndoʊpeɪn/ ***noun*** [C] one piece of glass in a window

ˈ**window ˌshopping** ***noun*** [U] looking at things in store windows without buying anything

**win·dow·sill** /ˈwɪndoʊsɪl/ ***noun*** [C] the shelf at the bottom of a window in a building, either inside or outside ➲ picture at **curtain**.

**wind·pipe** /ˈwɪndpaɪp/ ***noun*** [C] the tube that takes air from the throat to the lungs

**wind·shield** /ˈwɪndʃild/ ***noun*** [C] the window in the front of a car, truck, etc.

ˈ**windshield ˌwiper** (*also* **wiper**) ***noun*** [C] one of the two moving arms (**blades**) that remove water, snow, etc. from the windshield

**wind·storm** /ˈwɪndstɔrm/ ***noun*** [C] a storm where there is very strong wind but little rain or snow

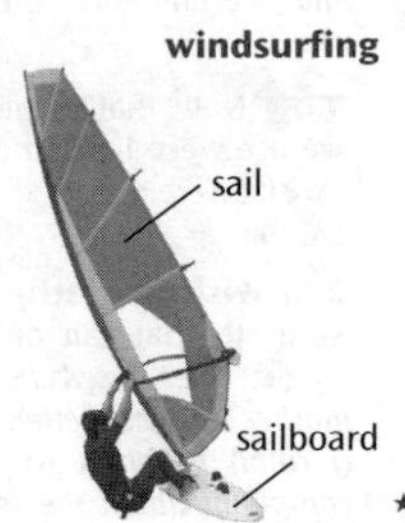

**windsurfing**

**wind·surf** /ˈwɪndsərf/ ***verb*** [I] to move through water standing on a special board with a sail ➲ We usually say **go windsurfing**: *Have you ever gone windsurfing?* ▸ **wind·surf·ing** ***noun*** [U]

**wind·swept** /ˈwɪndswɛpt/ ***adj.*** **1** (used about a place) that often has strong winds: *a windswept coastline* **2** looking messy because you have been in a strong wind: *windswept hair*

ˈ**wind ˌtunnel** ***noun*** [C] a large tunnel where aircraft, etc. are tested by forcing air past them

**wind·up** /ˈwaɪndʌp/ ***adj.*** (only *before* a noun) that you operate by turning a key or handle: *a windup toy*

**wind·y** /ˈwɪndi/ ***adj.*** (**wind·i·er**; **wind·i·est**) with a lot of wind: *a windy day*

★**wine**[1] /waɪn/ ***noun*** [C,U] an alcoholic drink that is made from grapes (or sometimes other fruit): *red/white/rosé wine* ◇ *sweet/dry wine* ◇ *French wines* ➲ picture at **rack**.

**wine**[2] /waɪn/ ***verb*** [I,T]

IDM **wine and dine (sb)** to entertain sb by buying him/her good food and drink; to go to restaurants, etc. and enjoy good food and drink: *The firm spent thousands of dollars wining and dining potential clients.* ◇ *The town offers many opportunities for wining and dining.*

ˈ**wine ˌcooler** ***noun*** [C] **1** a drink made with wine, fruit juice, ice and soda water **2** a container for putting a bottle of wine in to cool it

**wine·glass** /ˈwaɪnglæs/ ***noun*** [C] a glass for drinking wine from

**win·er·y** /ˈwaɪnəri/ ***noun*** (*pl.* **win·er·ies**) a place where wine is made ➲ Look at **vineyard**.

★**wing**[1] /wɪŋ/ ***noun***

▸OF BIRD/INSECT **1** [C] one of the body parts that a bird, an insect, etc. uses for flying

▸OF PLANE **2** [C] one of the two long parts that stick out from the side of an airplane and support it in the air

▸OF BUILDING **3** [C] a part of a building that sticks out from the main part or that was added on to the main part: *the maternity wing of the hospital*

▸OF POLITICAL PARTY **4** [C, usually sing.] a group of people in a political party that have particular beliefs or opinions: *the right wing of the Republican party* ➲ Look at **left-wing** and **right-wing**.

▸IN THEATER **5 the wings** [pl.] (in a theater) the area at the sides of the stage where you cannot be seen by the audience

**wing**[2] /wɪŋ/ ***verb***

IDM **wing it** (*slang*) to do sth, such as giving a speech, without planning or practicing

**wing·span** /ˈwɪŋspæn/ ***noun*** [C] the distance between the end of one wing and the end of the other when the wings are fully stretched: *a bird with a two-foot wingspan* ◇ *the wingspan of a glider*

**wing·tips** /ˈwɪŋtɪps/ ***noun*** [pl.] strong leather shoes that fasten with laces and have an extra piece of leather with small holes in it over the toe

**wink** /wɪŋk/ ***verb*** [I] **wink (at sb)** to close and open one eye very quickly, usually as a private signal to sb ➲ Look at **blink**. ▸ **wink** ***noun*** [C]: *to give sb a wink* ◇ *I didn't sleep a wink* (= not at all).

★**win·ner** /ˈwɪnər/ ***noun*** [C] **1** a person, team or an animal that wins a competition, game, race, etc. **2**

W

(*informal*) a person or thing that is successful or likely to be successful: *Their new design looks like a real winner!*

**win·ning** /ˈwɪnɪŋ/ ***adj.*** (only *before* a noun) **1** that is successful or wins a competition, game, race, etc.: *The winning ticket is number 65.* **2** attractive and showing confidence: *She flashed us her winning smile.*

**win·nings** /ˈwɪnɪŋz/ ***noun*** [pl.] something, especially money, that you have won in a game or competition

**win·o** /ˈwaɪnoʊ/ ***noun*** (*pl.* **win·os**) (*informal*) a person who drinks a lot of cheap alcohol and who has no home: *There were a couple of winos sleeping under the bridge.*

**win·some** /ˈwɪnsəm/ ***adj.*** (*formal*) (used about people or their manner) pleasant and attractive: *a winsome smile*

★**win·ter** /ˈwɪntər/ ***noun*** [C,U] the coldest season of the year between fall and spring: *It snows a lot here in the winter.* ◇ *a cold winter day* ◇ *We went skiing in Colorado last winter.* ▶ **win·try** /ˈwɪntri/ ***adj.***: *wintry weather* ◇ *a wintry wind*

**win·ter·green** /ˈwɪntərgrin/ ***noun*** [C,U] a North American plant with strong smelling leaves; the oil that is made from them

**win·ter·ize** /ˈwɪntəraɪz/ ***verb*** [T] (often passive) to prepare and adapt sth, especially a building or a car, for use in cold weather: *a waterfront cottage that John had winterized*

**win·ter·time** /ˈwɪntərtaɪm/ ***noun*** [U] the period or season of winter

ˌ**win-ˈwin** ***adj.*** (only *before* a noun) (used about a situation) in which there is a good result for each person involved: *We are aiming for a win-win situation.*

**wipe** /waɪp/ ***verb*** [T] **1 wipe sth (off)** to clean or dry sth by rubbing it with a cloth, piece of paper, etc.: *Wipe your hands on the towel.* ◇ *to wipe your nose on a handkerchief* ◇ *Could you wipe off the counter?* ➲ Look at the note at **clean**². **2 wipe sth from/off sth; wipe sth away/off/up** to remove sth by WIPING (1): *Wipe the dirt off your shoes.* ◇ *He wiped the sweat from his forehead.* ◇ *Wipe up the milk you spilled.*

PHR V **wipe sth out** to destroy sth completely: *Whole towns were wiped out in the bombing raids.*

ˌ**wiped ˈout** ***adj.*** (*informal*) (not before a noun) extremely tired: *You look wiped out.*

**wip·er** /ˈwaɪpər/ ***noun*** [C] = WINDSHIELD WIPER

★**wire**¹ /ˈwaɪər/ ***noun*** [C,U] **1** a long thin piece of metal like strong string that is used for fastening things or in fences, cages, etc.: *a piece of wire* ◇ *barbed wire* ◇ *a wire fence* **2** a piece of WIRE (1) that is used to carry electricity

IDM **get your wires crossed** (*informal*) to become confused about what sb has said to you so that you think he/she meant sth else: *I guess we got our wires crossed. I thought you were coming on Tuesday.*

**go, come, etc. (right) down to the wire** (*informal*) if you say that a situation goes, etc. down to the wire, you mean that the result will not be decided or known until the very end

**pull wires** → PULL¹

**wire**² /ˈwaɪər/ ***verb*** [T] **1** to fasten or connect two things together using WIRE¹ (1) **2 wire sth (up)** to connect sth to a supply of electricity by using WIRES¹ (2)

**wired** /ˈwaɪərd/ ***adj.*** (*informal*) **1** connected to a system of computers: *good economic reasons for getting your business wired* **2** (*informal*) excited or nervous; not relaxed: *I haven't been able to get much sleep so I'm a little wired.* **3** (*informal*) under the influence of alcohol or an illegal drug

**wire·less**¹ /ˈwaɪərləs/ ***noun*** (*old-fashioned*) [U] a system of sending and receiving radio signals: *a wireless operator*

**wire·less**² /ˈwaɪərləs/ ***adj.*** not using wires: *wireless phones/communications/technology*

**wire·tap·ping** /ˈwaɪərˌtæpɪŋ/ ***noun*** [U] the act of secretly listening to other people's telephone conversations by attaching a device to the telephone line ▶ **wire·tap** ***noun*** [C]: *the use of illegal wiretaps*

**wir·ing** /ˈwaɪərɪŋ/ ***noun*** [U] the system of wires that supplies electricity to rooms in a building

**wir·y** /ˈwaɪəri/ ***adj.*** (used about a person) small and thin but strong

**wis·dom** /ˈwɪzdəm/ ***noun*** [U] the quality of being wise; the ability to make sensible decisions and judgments because of your knowledge or experience

ˈ**wisdom tooth** ***noun*** [C] (*pl.* **wisdom teeth**) one of the four teeth at the back of your mouth that appear when you are about 20 years old

★**wise**¹ /waɪz/ ***adj.*** having or showing the knowledge or experience to make good or sensible decisions or judgments: *a wise choice* ◇ *It would be wiser to wait for a few days.* ◇ *a wise old man* ▶ **wise·ly** ***adv.***

**wise**² /waɪz/ ***verb***

PHR V **wise up (to sth)** (*informal*) to become aware of the unpleasant truth about a situation

**wise·crack** /ˈwaɪzkræk/ ***noun*** [C] (*informal*) a sarcastic remark or joke ▶ **wise·crack** ***verb*** [I]: *He plays a wisecracking detective.*

ˈ**wise guy** ***noun*** [C] **1** (*informal*) a person who speaks or behaves as if he/she knows more than other people: *OK, wise guy, what do we do now?* **2** (*U.S. slang*) a member of the Mafia

★**wish**¹ /wɪʃ/ ***verb*** **1** [T] **wish (that)** (often with a verb in the past tense) to want sth that cannot now happen or that probably will not happen: *I wish (that) I had listened more carefully.* ◇ *I wish (that) I knew what was going to happen.* ◇ *My father wishes (that) he had gone to college.* ◇ *I wish I could help you.*

> NOTE Note that in more formal, correct English we use **were** instead of **was** with "I" or "he/she": *I wish I were rich.* ◇ *She wishes she were in a different job.*

**2** [I] **wish (for sth)** to say to yourself that you want sth that can only happen by good luck or magic: *She closed her eyes and wished for her mother to get better.* **3** [T] **wish (to do sth)** (*formal*) to want to do sth: *I wish to make a complaint about the service here.* **4** [T] to say that you hope sb will have sth; to say sth as a greeting:

*I called him up to wish him a happy birthday.* ◊ *We wish you all the best for your future career.*

★**wish**[2] /wɪʃ/ ***noun*** **1** [C] a feeling that you want sth: *a wish for peace* ◊ *I have no wish to see her ever again.* ◊ *Doctors should respect the patient's wishes.* **2** [C] an act of saying to yourself secretly that you want to have sth or that you want sth to happen: *to make a wish* ◊ *My wish came true* (= I got what I asked for). **3 wishes** [pl.] a hope that sb will be happy or have good luck: *Best Wishes* (= at the end of a letter)

**wish·bone** /ˈwɪʃboʊn/ ***noun*** [C] a V-shaped bone between the neck and breast of a chicken, duck, etc. When the bird is eaten, this bone is sometimes pulled apart by two people, and the person who gets the larger part can make a wish.

**wish·ful** /ˈwɪʃfl/ ***adj.***
IDM **wishful thinking** ideas that are based on what you would like, not on facts

ˈ**wishing well** ***noun*** [C] a WELL[4] (1) or pool into which you can throw money and make a wish

ˈ**wish list** ***noun*** [C] (*informal*) all the things that you would like to have, or that you would like to happen

**wish·y-wash·y** /ˈwɪʃi ˌwɑʃi; -ˌwɔʃi/ ***adj.*** (*informal*) **1** not having clear or firm ideas or beliefs: *a wishy-washy liberal* **2** not strong or clear: *a wishy-washy blue*

**wisp** /wɪsp/ ***noun*** [C] **1** a small thin bunch of hair, grass, etc. **2** a small amount of smoke

**wist·ful** /ˈwɪstfl/ ***adj.*** feeling or showing sadness because you cannot have what you want: *a wistful sigh* ▸ **wist·ful·ly *adv.***

**wit** /wɪt/ ***noun*** **1** [U] the ability to use words in a clever and amusing way **2** (*also* **wits** [pl.]) intelligence; the ability to think quickly: *The game of chess is essentially a battle of wits.*
IDM **keep your wits about you** to be ready to act in a difficult situation

**witch** /wɪtʃ/ ***noun*** [C] (in former times and in stories) a woman who is thought to have magic powers that she uses to do bad things. Pictures of witches in stories show them wearing a long black coat and a tall pointed hat. ➲ Look at **wizard**.

**witch·craft** /ˈwɪtʃkræft/ ***noun*** [U] the use of magic powers to make things happen

ˈ**witch ˌdoctor** ***noun*** [C] (especially in Africa) a person who is believed to have special magic powers that can be used to heal sick people

ˈ**witch hunt** ***noun*** [C] an attempt to find and punish people who hold opinions that are thought to be unacceptable or dangerous to society

★**with** /wɪð; wɪθ/ ***prep.*** **1** in the company or presence of sb/sth: *I live with my parents.* ◊ *Are you coming with us?* ◊ *I talked about the problem with my teacher.* ◊ *Does this tie go with this shirt?* ◊ *Could you put this book with the other ones?* **2** in the care of sb: *We left the keys with the neighbors.* **3** having or carrying sth: *a girl with red hair* ◊ *a house with a two-car garage* ◊ *the man with a suitcase* **4** using sth: *Cut it with a knife.* ◊ *I did it with his help.* **5** (used for expressing what fills, covers, etc. sth): *Fill the bowl with water.* **6** against: *He's always fighting with his brother.* ◊ *I usually play tennis with my sister.* **7** agreeing with or supporting: *Is everyone with us on this issue?* **8** because of or as a result of sth: *We were shivering with cold.* **9** (used for expressing how sth happens or is done): *Open this package with care.* ◊ *to greet sb with a smile* **10** toward, concerning or compared with sb/sth: *Is he angry with us?* ◊ *There's a problem with my phone bill.* ◊ *Compared with New England, Virginia has mild winters.* **11** including: *With sales tax, the TV cost $275.* **12** at the same time as: *I can't concentrate with you watching me all the time.* **13** because of: *With all the problems we have, we're not going to finish on time.*
IDM **be with sb** to be able to follow what sb is saying: *I'm sorry, I'm not quite with you. Say it again.*
**with it** (*informal*) very fashionable or knowing a lot about fashionable clothes, music, etc. SYN **hip**[2]

★**with·draw** /wɪðˈdrɔ; wɪθ-/ ***verb*** (*pt* **with·drew** /-ˈdru/; *pp* **with·drawn** /-ˈdrɔn/) **1** [I,T] **withdraw (sb/sth) (from sth)** (to cause sb/sth) to move back or away: *The troops withdrew from the town.* **2** [T] to take money out of a bank account: *I'd like to withdraw a hundred dollars from my savings account.* ➲ Look at **deposit**. **3** [T] to remove sth or take sth away: *to withdraw an offer/a statement* **4** [I] to decide not to take part in sth: *Jackson withdrew from the race at the last minute.*

**with·draw·al** /wɪðˈdrɔəl; wɪθ-/ ***noun*** **1** [C,U] moving sth back or away: *the withdrawal of troops from the war zone* **2** [C] an act of taking an amount of money out of your bank account: *to make a withdrawal* **3** [U] the act of stopping doing sth, especially taking a drug: *When he quit drinking, he suffered severe withdrawal symptoms.*

**with·drawn** /wɪðˈdrɔn; wɪθ-/ ***adj.*** (used about a person) very quiet and not wanting to talk to other people

**with·er** /ˈwɪðər/ ***verb*** **wither (away) 1** [I,T] (used about plants) to become dry and die; to make a plant do this: *The plants withered in the hot sun.* **2** [I] to become weaker, until it disappears: *Our hopes gradually withered away.*

**with·er·ing** /ˈwɪðərɪŋ/ ***adj.*** (used about a look, remark, etc.) intended to make sb feel silly or ashamed: *She gave him **a withering look**.*

**with·hold** /wɪθˈhoʊld; wɪð-/ ***verb*** [T] (*pt, pp* **with·held** /-ˈhɛld/) (*formal*) **withhold sth (from sb/sth)** to refuse to give sth: *to withhold information from the police*

★**with·in** /wɪˈðɪn; wɪˈθɪn/ ***prep.*** **1** in a period not longer than a particular length of time: *I'll be back within an hour.* **2 within sth (of sth)** not further than a particular distance from sth: *The house is within three blocks of the high school.* **3** not outside the limits or range of sb/sth: *Each department must keep within its budget.* **4** (*formal*) inside sb/sth: *The anger was still there deep within him.*

★**with·out** /wɪˈðaʊt; wɪˈθaʊt/ ***prep.*** **1** not having, showing or being with sb/sth: *Don't go out without a coat on.* ◊ *Pam drinks her coffee without milk or cream.* ◊ *After three days without sleep, he was exhausted.* ◊ *He spoke without much enthusiasm.* ◊ *Don't leave without me.* **2** (used with a verb in the -*ing* form to mean "not"): *She left without saying goodbye.*

**with·stand** /wɪθ'stænd; wɪð-/ *verb* [T] (*pt, pp* **with·stood** /-'stʊd/) (*formal*) to be strong enough not to break, give up, be damaged, etc.: *The troops were too weak to withstand another attack.*

**wit·less** /'wɪtləs/ *adj.* silly or stupid
IDM **be scared/bored witless** (*informal*) to be extremely frightened or bored

★**wit·ness¹** /'wɪtnəs/ *noun* [C] **1** (*also* **eyewitness**) a person who sees sth happen and who can tell other people about it later: *There were two witnesses to the accident.* **2** a person who appears in a court of law to say what he/she has seen or what he/she knows about sb/sth: *Each witness was cross-examined.* ◇ *a witness for the defense/prosecution* **3** a person who sees sb sign an official document and who then signs it himself/herself

★**wit·ness²** /'wɪtnəs/ *verb* [T] **1** to see sth happen and to be able to tell other people about it later: *to witness a murder* **2** to see sb sign an official document and then sign it yourself: *to witness a will*

**'witness stand** (*also* **stand**) *noun* [C] the place in a court of law where a witness sits when he/she is giving evidence (**testifying**)

**-wit·ted** /'wɪţəd/ *combining form* having a particular type of intelligence: *quick-witted*

**wit·ti·cism** /'wɪţəsɪzəm/ *noun* [C] an intelligent and amusing remark

**wit·ty** /'wɪţi/ *adj.* (**wit·ti·er**; **wit·ti·est**) intelligent and amusing; using words in a clever way: *a very witty speech*

**wives** *plural of* WIFE

**wiz·ard** /'wɪzərd/ *noun* [C] (in stories) a man who is believed to have magic powers ➲ Look at **witch**.

**wk.** *abbr.* = WEEK

**w/o** *abbr.* (*written*) without

**wob·ble** /'wɑbl/ *verb* [T] to move from side to side in an unsteady way: *Put something under the leg of the table. It's wobbling.* ▸ **wob·bly** /'wɑbli/ *adj.* (*informal*): *a wobbly table*

**woe** /woʊ/ *noun* (*old-fashioned*) **1 woes** [pl.] the troubles and problems that sb has: *financial/economic woes* ◇ *Thanks for listening to my woes.* **2** [U] great unhappiness: *a tale of woe*
IDM **woe betide sb**; **woe to sb** (*formal*) (a phrase that is used humorously to warn sb that there will be trouble if he/she does sth or does not do sth): *Woe betide anyone who gets in her way!*
**woe is me!** (*old-fashioned*) (a phrase that is used humorously to say that you are very unhappy)

**woe·ful** /'woʊfl/ *adj.* **1** very bad or serious; that you disapprove of: *She displayed a woeful ignorance of the rules.* **2** (*formal*) very sad: *a woeful face* ◇ *woeful tales of broken romances* ▸ **woe·ful·ly** *adv.*: *His performance was woefully inadequate.* ◇ *"I'll never see him again," she sighed woefully.*

**wok** /wɑk/ *noun* [C] a large pan that is shaped like a bowl and used for cooking Chinese food

**woke** *past tense of* WAKE¹

**wok·en** *past participle of* WAKE¹

**wolf¹** /wʊlf/ *noun* [C] (*pl.* **wolves** /wʊlvz/) a wild animal that looks like a dog and that lives and hunts in a group (**pack**)

**wolf²** /wʊlf/ *verb* [T] **wolf sth (down)** (*informal*) to eat food very quickly, especially by putting a lot of it in your mouth at once SYN **gobble**

**'wolf ˌwhistle** *noun* [C] a whistle with a short rising note and a long falling note, used by sb, usually a man, to show that he finds sb else attractive, especially sb passing in the street: *She was sick of the construction workers' wolf whistles every time she walked by.* ▸ **'wolf-ˌwhistle** *verb* [I]

★**wom·an** /'wʊmən/ *noun* [C] (*pl.* **wom·en** /'wɪmən/) an adult female person: *men, women and children* ◇ *a single/married/divorced woman*

**-woman** /'wʊmən/ (*pl.* **-women** /'wɪmən/) ***combining form*** a woman who does a particular activity: *a businesswoman*

**wom·an·iz·er** /'wʊməˌnaɪzər/ *noun* [C] a man who has sexual relationships with many different women: *He has a reputation for being a womanizer.*

**wom·an·ly** /'wʊmənli/ *adj.* behaving, dressing, etc. in a way that people think is typical of or very suitable for a woman: *womanly qualities* ◇ *She has a soft womanly figure.* SYN **feminine**

**womb** /wum/ *noun* [C] (*old-fashioned*) = UTERUS

**'women's room** *noun* [C] a room with toilets in it for women in a public building ➲ Look at **restroom** and at the note at **toilet**.

**won** *past tense, past participle of* WIN¹

★**won·der¹** /'wʌndər/ *verb* **1** [I,T] to want to know sth; to ask yourself questions about sth: *I wonder what the new teacher will be like.* ◇ *He started to wonder if she was all right.* ◇ *I wonder who that woman over there is.* ◇ *It was something that she had been wondering about for a long time.* ◇ *Sometimes I wonder how they manage to live on the amount he earns.* **2** [T] **wonder (if...)** (used when you are asking sb politely to do sth): *I wonder if you could help me.* ◇ *I was wondering if you could help me.*

**won·der²** /'wʌndər/ *noun* **1** [U] a feeling of surprise and admiration: *They could do nothing but stand in wonder at the sight.* **2** [C] something that causes you to feel surprise or admiration: *the wonders of modern medicine*
IDM **it's a wonder (that)...** it's surprising that...: *It's a wonder we managed to get here on time, with all the traffic.*
**no wonder** it is not surprising: *You've been out every night this week. No wonder you're tired.*

★**won·der·ful** /'wʌndərfl/ *adj.* very good; giving great pleasure: *What wonderful weather!* ◇ *It's a wonderful opportunity.* ◇ *It's wonderful to see you again.* ▸ **won·der·ful·ly** /-fli/ *adv.*

**won·drous** /'wʌndrəs/ *adj.* strange, beautiful and impressive: *It was a wondrous thing to see the ocean for the first time.*

**wonk** /wɑŋk; wɔŋk/ *noun* [C] (*informal*) **1** a person who works too hard and is considered boring **2** (*especially US*) a person who takes too much interest in the less important details of political policy: *the President's chief economic* ***policy wonk***

**won't** /woʊnt/ *short for* WILL NOT

**woo** /wu/ *verb* [T] **1** to try to get the support of sb: *Voters are being wooed with promises of lower taxes.* ◇ *Selected items are being sold at half price to woo* *customers into the store.* **2** (*old-fashioned*) (used about a man) to try to persuade a woman to love him and marry him

★**wood** /wʊd/ ***noun*** **1** [U] the hard material that the trunk and branches of trees are made of: *He chopped some wood for the fire.* ◇ *Most furniture is made of wood.* **2** [C] a type of WOOD (1): *Pine is a soft wood.* **3 the woods** [pl.] an area of land that is covered with trees, smaller than a forest: *a walk in the woods*

IDM **knock on wood** → KNOCK[2]

**wood·chuck** /ˈwʊdtʃʌk/ (*also* **groundhog**) ***noun*** [C] a small animal with brown fur that lives in a hole in the ground

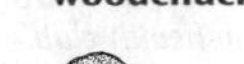
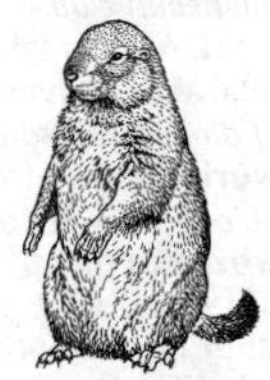
**woodchuck** (*also* **groundhog**)

**wood·ed** /ˈwʊdəd/ ***adj.*** (used about an area of land) having a lot of trees growing on it: *a heavily wooded valley*

★**wood·en** /ˈwʊdn/ ***adj.*** made of wood: *wooden toys*

**wood·land** /ˈwʊdlənd; -lænd/ ***noun*** [C,U] (*also* **wood·lands** [pl.]) an area of land that is covered with trees: *The house is fringed by fields and woodlands.* ◇ *woodland walks/scenery*

**wood·peck·er** /ˈwʊdˌpɛkər/ ***noun*** [C] a bird with a long beak that it uses to make holes in trees when it is looking for insects to eat

**wood·pile** /ˈwʊdpaɪl/ ***noun*** [C] a pile of wood that will be used for fuel

**woods·y** /ˈwʊdzi/ ***adj.*** (*informal*) covered with trees; connected with woods

**wood·wind** /ˈwʊdwɪnd/ ***noun*** [C, usually pl.] the set of musical instruments that are made of wood and that you play by blowing into them ▸ **wood·wind *adj.***: *woodwind instruments*

**wood·work** /ˈwʊdwərk/ ***noun*** [U] the parts of a building that are made of wood (e.g. the doors, stairs, etc.)

IDM **blend/fade into the woodwork** to behave in a way that does not attract any attention; to disappear or hide

**come/crawl out of the woodwork** (*informal*) if you say that sb comes/crawls out of the woodwork, you mean that he/she has suddenly appeared in order to express an opinion or to take advantage of a situation: *When he won all that money, all sorts of distant relatives came out of the woodwork.*

**wood·worm** /ˈwʊdwərm/ ***noun*** **1** [C] a small worm that eats wood, making a lot of small holes in it **2** [U] the damage caused by woodworms: *The beams are riddled with woodworm.*

**wood·y** /ˈwʊdi/ ***adj.*** (**wood·i·er**; **wood·i·est**) **1** (used about plants) having a thick, hard stem like wood **2** having a smell like wood: *This new fragrance has woody notes.* **3** covered with trees: *a woody valley*

**woof** /wʊf/ ***noun*** [C] (*informal*) (used for describing the sound (a **bark**) that a dog makes)

★**wool** /wʊl/ ***noun*** [U] **1** the soft thick hair of sheep, goats, etc. **2** thick cloth that is made from WOOL (1): *The sweater is 50% wool and 50% acrylic.* ▸ **wool *adj.***: *warm wool socks*

**wool·en** /ˈwʊlən/ ***adj.*** (*formal*) made of wool: *a warm woolen sweater*

**wool·y** /ˈwʊli/ ***adj.*** of or like wool: *The dog had a thick wooly coat.*

**wooz·y** /ˈwuzi/ ***adj.*** (**wooz·i·er**; **wooz·i·est**) (*informal*) **1** feeling unsteady, confused and unable to think clearly **2** feeling dizzy and weak

★**word[1]** /wərd/ ***noun*** **1** [C] a sound or letter or group of sounds or letters that expresses a particular meaning: *What's the Greek word for "computer?"* ◇ *Several words are spelled wrong.* ◇ *There are five letters in the word "apple."* **2** [C] a short statement or conversation: *Could I have a word with you in private?* ◇ *a few words of thanks* ◇ *Don't say a word about this to anyone.* **3** [sing.] a promise: *I give you my word that I won't let you down.*

IDM **a dirty word** → DIRTY[1]

**get a word in edgewise** to interrupt when sb else is talking so that you can say sth yourself

**have, etc. the last word** → LAST[1]

**in other words** → OTHER

**put in a (good) word for sb** to say sth good about sb to sb else: *If you could put in a good word for me, I might stand a better chance of getting the job.*

**take sb's word for it** to believe what sb says without any proof

**word for word 1** repeating sth exactly: *Sharon repeated word for word what he had told her.* **2** (in a translation) dealing with each word separately, not looking at the general meaning: *a word-for-word translation*

**word[2]** /wərd/ ***verb*** [T] (often passive) to choose carefully the words that you use to express sth: *The statement was carefully worded so that nobody would be offended by it.*

**word!** /wərd/ ***interjection*** (*slang*) (used to express agreement or acceptance of what sb has just said)

**word·ing** /ˈwərdɪŋ/ ***noun*** [sing.] the words that you use to express sth: *The wording of the contract was very vague.*

**word·play** /ˈwərdpleɪ/ ***noun*** [U] making jokes by using words in an intelligent or amusing way, especially by using a word that has two meanings, or different words that sound the same SYN **pun**

ˈ**word ˌprocessor** ***noun*** [C] a type of small computer or a computer program that you can use for writing letters, reports, etc. You can correct or change what you have written before you print it out. ▸ ˈ**word ˌprocessing *noun*** [U]

**word·smith** /ˈwərdsmɪθ/ ***noun*** [C] someone who is very skillful at using words

**word·y** /ˈwərdi/ ***adj.*** (**word·i·er**; **word·i·est**) using too many words, especially formal ones: *a wordy and repetitive essay* SYN **verbose**

**wore** *past tense of* WEAR[1]

★**work[1]** /wərk/ ***noun***

▸ JOB/TASK **1** [U] something that requires physical or mental effort. You usually do work because you feel you have to, not for pleasure: *Her success is due to sheer hard work.* ◇ *There is still a lot of work to be*

W

*done. ◇ Quit talking and get back to work!* **2** [U] what you do to earn money; the place where you go to earn money: *It is very difficult to find work in this city. ◇ out of work* (= without a job) *◇ When do you start work? ◇ I go to work at 8 o'clock. ◇ The people at work gave me some flowers for my birthday.*

NOTE **Work** is an uncountable noun. In some contexts we must use **job**: *I've found work at the hospital. ◇ I have a new job at the hospital.* **Employment** is the state of having a paid job and is more formal and official than **work** or **job**. It is an uncountable noun: *Many married women are in part-time employment.* **Occupation** is the word used on forms to ask what you are or what job you do: *Occupation: student. Occupation: bus driver.* A **profession** is a job that requires special training and higher education: *the medical profession.* A **trade** is a job that you do with your hands and that requires special skill: *He's a carpenter by trade.*

**3** [U] something that you are working on or have produced: *a piece of written work ◇ The teacher graded their work. ◇ Is this all your own work? ◇ an exhibit of the work of two young photographers*
➤ BOOK/PAINTING/MUSIC **4** [C] a book, painting, piece of music, etc.: *a work of art ◇ an early work by Picasso ◇ the complete works of Shakespeare*
➤ EVERYTHING **5 the works** [pl.] (*informal*) everything: *This car is equipped with air conditioning, a CD player, cruise control – the works!*
➤ BUILDING/REPAIRING **6 works** [pl.] the act of building or repairing sth: *The Department of Public Works*
➤ FACTORY **7 works** [C, with sing. or pl. verb] (often in compounds) a factory or similar building: *The city waterworks*
IDM **get/go to work (on sth)** to begin; to make a start (on sth)
**have your work cut out for you** to have a difficult task that you must do
**in the works** being prepared or developed: *A new movie about her life is currently in the works.*

★**work²** /wərk/ *verb*
➤ DO JOB/TASK **1** [I,T] to do sth which needs physical or mental effort; to do a job, especially in order to earn money: *I won't pass math class unless I work harder. ◇ I've been working in the yard all day. ◇ She works for a computer company in Washington. ◇ I'd like to work as a newspaper reporter. ◇ Doctors often work extremely long hours.*
➤ MACHINE/DEVICE **2** [I] (used about a machine, etc.) to do what it is meant to do, correctly; to function: *Our phone hasn't been working for several days. ◇ Can you show me how the copy machine works?*
➤ HAVE RESULT/EFFECT **3** [I] to have the result or effect that you want; to be successful: *Your idea sounds good, but I don't think it will really work.* **4** [I,T] to produce a particular effect; to help sth to happen: *His good reputation had obviously worked in his favor.*
➤ MAKE SB WORK **5** [T] to make yourself/sb work: *He works all his employees very hard.*
➤ OPERATE **6** [T] to use or operate sth: *Do you know how to work the fax machine?*
➤ MOVE GRADUALLY **7** [I,T] to move to a new position or condition: *The hinges on the door have worked loose. ◇ We worked our way from one end of the mall to the other.*
PHR V **work on sth** to make an effort to build, repair, finish, etc. sth: *I need to work on my history paper tonight. ◇ Dan works on old cars in his spare time. ◇ "Do you have that data for me?" "No, but I'm working on it!"*
**work out 1** to develop or progress, especially in a good way: *I hope things work out for you.* **2** to do physical exercises in order to keep your body healthy and strong: *Linda works out twice a week at the health club.*
**work out (to sth)** to come to a particular result or total after everything has been calculated: *The price of dinner worked out to around $30 each.*
**work sb out** to understand sb: *I've never been able to work her out.*
**work sth out 1** to find the answer to sth; to solve sth: *I can't work out how to do this.* **2** to calculate sth: *I worked out the total cost.* **3** to plan sth: *She asked her lawyer to work out the business deal.*
**work up to sth** to develop or progress to sth: *Start with 15 minutes' exercise and gradually work up to 30.*
**work sb/yourself up (into sth)** to make sb/yourself become angry, excited, upset, etc.: *He had worked himself up into a state of anxiety about his interview.* ➲ Look also at **worked up**.

**work·a·ble** /ˈwərkəbl/ ***adj.*** that can be used or that can operate in an efficient way OPP **unworkable**

**work·a·day** /ˈwərkədeɪ/ ***adj.*** (*written*) ordinary; not very interesting: *This was a far cry from her normal workaday world.* SYN **everyday**

**work·a·hol·ic** /ˌwərkəˈhɑlɪk/ ***noun*** [C] a person who works a lot and feels that he/she needs to work all the time

**work·bench** /ˈwərkbɛntʃ/ (*also* **bench**) ***noun*** [C] a long heavy table used for doing practical jobs, working with tools, etc.

**work·book** /ˈwərkbʊk/ ***noun*** [C] a book with questions and exercises in it that you use when you are studying sth

**work·day** /ˈwərkdeɪ/ ***noun*** [C] **1** the part of a day during which you work: *I spend most of my workday sitting at a desk. ◇ an 8-hour workday* **2** a day on which you usually work or on which most people usually work: *workday traffic*

**ˌworked ˈup** ***adj.*** (*informal*) (not before a noun) **worked up (about/over sth)** very nervous, excited or upset about sth: *There's no need to get all worked up about it!*

★**work·er** /ˈwərkər/ ***noun*** [C] **1** (often in compounds) a person who works, especially one who does a particular type of job or belongs to a certain group of people: *factory workers ◇ an office worker ◇ migrant workers* ➲ Look also at **coworker**. **2** a person who does physical work: *manual workers* **3** a person who works in a particular way: *a slow worker*

**ˌworkers' ˌcompenˈsation** (*also old-fashioned* **workmen's compensation**) ***noun*** [U] money that must be paid to a worker by his/her company if he/she is injured or becomes sick as a result of his/her work

**work·fare** /ˈwərkfɛr/ ***noun*** [U] a system in which poor people must do some work which is given to them by the government before they receive a regular payment from the government ➲ Look at **welfare**.

**work·force** /ˈwərkfɔrs/ ***noun*** [C] **1** the total number of people who work in a company, factory, etc. **2** the total number of people in a country who are able to work: *Ten percent of the workforce is unemployed.*

**work·ing** /ˈwərkɪŋ/ ***adj.*** (only *before* a noun) **1** employed; having a job: *the problems of childcare for working parents* **2** connected with your job: *He stayed with the same company for the whole of his working life.* ◇ *The company offers excellent working conditions.* **3** good enough to be used, although it could be improved: *I have a working knowledge of French.*

IDM **in working order** → ORDER[1]

**the ˈworking class** ***noun*** [sing.] the group of people in a society who usually do physical work, especially in industry: *unemployment among the working class* ◇ *a working-class area* ◇ *a working-class family*

**work·ings** /ˈwərkɪŋz/ ***noun*** [pl.] the way in which a machine, an organization, etc. operates: *It's very difficult to understand the workings of the legal system.*

**work·load** /ˈwərkloʊd/ ***noun*** [C] the amount of work that you have to do

**work·man** /ˈwərkmən/ ***noun*** [C] (*pl.* **work·men**) a man who works with his hands, especially building or making things

**work·man·ship** /ˈwərkmənʃɪp/ ***noun*** [U] the quality of sth that has been made or built

**ˌworkmen's compenˈsation** ***noun*** [U] (*old-fashioned*) = WORKERS' COMPENSATION

**work·out** /ˈwərkaʊt/ ***noun*** [C] a period of physical exercise, e.g. when you are practicing for a sport or staying healthy

**ˈwork ˌpermit** ***noun*** [C] an official document that sb needs in order to work in a particular foreign country

**work·place** /ˈwərkpleɪs/ ***noun*** [C] **the workplace** [sing.] the office, factory, etc. where people work: *the introduction of new technology into the workplace* ◇ *These safety standards apply to all workplaces.*

**work·sheet** /ˈwərkʃit/ ***noun*** [C] a piece of paper with questions or exercises on it that you use when you are studying sth

**work·shop** /ˈwərkʃɑp/ ***noun*** [C] **1** (*also* **shop**) a place where things are made or repaired **2** a time when a group of people meet and discuss or learn more about a particular subject

**work·sta·tion** /ˈwərkˌsteɪʃn/ ***noun*** [C] an area in an office for one person, with a desk and a computer that is connected to a large computer system

**ˌwork-ˈstudy** ***noun*** [U] work that a student does in order to gain experience and earn money to pay for his/her education: *a campus work-study program*

**work·up** /ˈwərkʌp/ ***noun*** [C] a series of medical tests carried out on sb in order to find out if he/she is completely healthy: *a full blood workup*

**work·week** /ˈwərkwik/ ***noun*** [C] the total amount of time that you spend at work during the week: *a 40-hour workweek*

★**world** /wərld/ ***noun***

➤THE EARTH/ITS PEOPLE **1 the world** [sing.] the Earth with all its countries and people: *an explorer who sailed around the world* ◇ *a map of the world* ◇ *changes in the world's climate* ◇ *the most beautiful place in the world* ◇ *English is a world language* (= used all over the world). **2** [sing.] a particular part of the earth: *the western world* ◇ *the English-speaking world*

➤TYPE OF LIFE **3** [sing.] the life and activities of people on earth; their experience: *It is hard to imagine what the world of our grandchildren will be like.* ◇ *It's time you learned something about the real world!* ◇ *the modern world* **4** [C] (often in compounds) a particular area of activity or group of people or things: *the world of sports* ◇ *the medical world* ◇ *the animal world*

➤ANOTHER PLANET **5** [C] a planet with life on it: *Do you believe there are other worlds out there?*

➤EVERYBODY **6** [sing.] everybody: *The whole world seemed to know the news before me!*

IDM **how, why, where, who, etc. in the world** (*informal*) (used for emphasizing sth or expressing surprise: *Where in the world have you been?*

**the outside world** people, places, activities, etc. that are beyond the area where you live and your everyday experience

**the real world** → REAL[1]

**think the world of sb/sth** → THINK

**do sb a world of good** (*informal*) to be very good or helpful for sb: *The vacation has done her a world of good.*

**ˌworld-ˈfamous** ***adj.*** known all over the world: *a world-famous writer*

**world·ly** /ˈwərldli/ ***adj.*** **1** connected with ordinary life, not with the spirit: *He left all his worldly possessions to his nephew.* **2** having a lot of experience and knowledge of life and people: *a sophisticated and worldly teenager*

**ˈworld ˌmusic** ***noun*** [U] a type of pop music that includes influences from different parts of the world, especially Africa and Asia

**the ˌWorld ˈSeries** ***noun*** [U] (*sports*) a series of baseball games played every year between the winners of the American League and the National League, which determines who is the best team in North America that year

**ˌworld ˈwar** ***noun*** [C] a war that involves a lot of important countries: *the Second World War* (= from 1939 to1945)

**world·wide** /ˌwərldˈwaɪd/ ***adj., adv.*** (happening) in the whole world: *The situation has caused worldwide concern.* ◇ *The product will be marketed worldwide.*

**the ˌWorld Wide ˈWeb** (*also informal* **the Web**) ***noun*** [sing.] (*abbr.* **WWW**) a multimedia system of sound, pictures and video for finding information on the Internet: *to browse a site on the World Wide Web*

**worm¹** /wərm/ ***noun*** [C] **1** a small animal with a long thin body and no bones or legs: *an earthworm* **2 worms** [pl.] worms (1) that live inside a person or an animal and may cause disease: *Our dog has worms.*

**worm²** /wərm/ ***verb***

PHRV **worm your way/yourself along, through, etc.** to move slowly or with difficulty in the direction mentioned, e.g. by moving in between a lot of people or things: *I managed to worm my way through the crowd.*

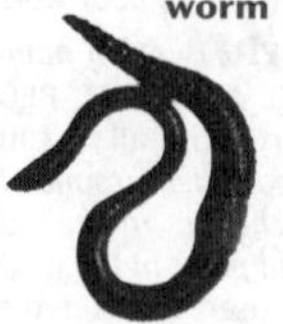
worm

**worm·wood** /ˈwərmwʊd/ ***noun*** [U] a plant with a bitter flavor, used in making alcoholic drinks and medicines

**worn** *past participle of* WEAR¹

**ˌworn-ˈout** (*also* ˌworn ˈout) ***adj.*** **1** too old or damaged to use any more: *a worn-out sweater* **2** extremely tired: *I'm all worn out. I think I'll go to bed early.*

★**wor·ried** /ˈwərid/ ***adj.*** **worried (about sb/sth)**; **worried (that...)** anxious or unhappy: *Don't look so worried. Everything will be all right.* ◇ *I'm worried about Jane.*

**wor·ri·some** /ˈwərisəm/ ***adj.*** making you worry and feel anxious

★**wor·ry¹** /ˈwəri/ ***verb*** (*pres. part.* **wor·rying**; *3rd person sing. pres.* **wor·ries**; *pt, pp* **wor·ried**) **1** [I] **worry (about sb/sth)** to be anxious (about sb, a problem, an event, etc.): *"Don't worry, Mom," said Peter, "I won't stay out late."* ◇ *There's nothing to worry about.* ◇ *He worries if I don't call every weekend.* **2** [T] **worry sb/yourself (about sb/sth)** to make sb/yourself anxious (about sb/sth): *You look depressed. What's worrying you?* ◇ *She worried herself sick when he was away.*

**wor·ry²** /ˈwəri/ ***noun*** (*pl.* **wor·ries**) **1** [U] an anxious state or feeling: *His son has caused him a lot of worry recently.* **2** [C] something that makes you worry; a problem: *financial worries*

**wor·ry·ing** /ˈwəriŋ/ ***adj.*** that makes you worry: *a worrying situation*

**wor·ry·wart** /ˈwəriwɔrt/ ***noun*** [C] (*informal*) a person who worries about unimportant things

★**worse¹** /wərs/ ***adj.*** (the comparative of *bad*) **1** not as good as sth else: *The weather in March was worse than in February.* ◇ *My English is getting worse and worse.* **2** (not before a noun) more sick; less well: *The doctors say that he's getting worse.*

IDM **make matters/things worse** to make a situation, problem, etc. even more difficult or dangerous than before

**the worse for wear** (*informal*) damaged; not in good condition: *This suitcase looks somewhat the worse for wear.*

★**worse²** /wərs/ ***adv.*** (the comparative of *badly*) **1** less well: *She speaks German even worse than I do.* **2** more severely or to a greater degree: *He was hurt worse than we had originally thought.*

★**worse³** /wərs/ ***noun*** [U] something that is WORSE¹ than sth else: *The situation was already bad, but there was worse to come.*

**wors·en** /ˈwərsn/ ***verb*** [I,T] to become worse or to make sth worse: *Relations between the two countries have worsened.*

★**wor·ship¹** /ˈwərʃəp/ ***noun*** [U] praying to and showing respect for God or a god: *Different religions have different forms of worship.*

★**wor·ship²** /ˈwərʃəp/ ***verb*** (**wor·ship·ing**; **wor·shiped** or **wor·ship·ping**; **wor·shipped**) **1** [I,T] to pray to and show respect for God or a god: *In primitive societies, people worshiped the sun.* **2** [T] to love or admire sb/sth very much: *She worshiped her husband.* ▶ **wor·ship·er** ***noun*** [C]

★**worst¹** /wərst/ ***adj.*** (the superlative of *bad*) the least pleasant or suitable: *It's been the worst winter that I can remember.*

★**worst²** /wərst/ ***adv.*** (the superlative of *badly*) **1** least well: *A lot of the kids were naughty, but my son behaved worst of all!* **2** the most severely or to the greatest degree: *All the rooms need to be painted, but the kitchen needs it worst of all.*

★**worst³** /wərst/ ***noun*** [sing.] **the worst** something that is the least satisfactory or desirable: *My parents always expect the worst if I'm late.*

IDM **at (the) worst** if the worst happens or if you consider sb/sth in the worst way: *The problem doesn't look too serious. At worst we'll have to make a few small changes.*

**if (the) worst comes to (the) worst** if the worst possible situation develops

**wor·sted** /ˈwʊstəd; ˈwərstəd/ ***noun*** [U] a type of tightly woven cloth made of wool with a smooth surface, used for making clothes: *worsted wool*

★**worth¹** /wərθ/ ***adj.*** **1** having a particular value (in money): *"How much is that house worth?" "It must be worth at least $200,000."* **2 worth doing, etc.** (used as a way of recommending or advising): *That museum's really worth visiting if you have time.* ◇ *It's already nine o'clock. It's not worth going shopping now.*

> NOTE We can say either: *It isn't worth repairing the car.* OR: *The car isn't worth repairing.*

IDM **for what it's worth** (used to emphasize that what you are saying is only your own opinion or suggestion and may not be very helpful): *I like this color better, for what it's worth.*

**get your money's worth** → MONEY

**worth it** enjoyable or useful to do or have, even if it means extra cost, effort, etc.: *Don't bother cooking a big meal. It isn't worth it – we're not hungry.*

**worth sb's while** helpful, useful or interesting to sb

**worth²** /wərθ/ ***noun*** [U] **1** value or usefulness: *She has proved her worth as a member of the team.* **2** the amount of sth that the money mentioned will buy: *ten dollars' worth of gasoline* **3** the amount of sth that will last for the time mentioned: *two days' worth of food*

**worth·less** /ˈwərθləs/ ***adj.*** **1** having no value or use: *It's worthless – it's only a piece of plastic!* **2** (used about a person) having bad qualities

**worth·while** /wərθˈwaɪl/ ***adj.*** enjoyable, useful

or satisfying enough to be worth the cost or effort: *Working for so little money just isn't worthwhile.* ◇ *Medicine is a very worthwhile career.*

**wor·thy** /ˈwərði/ ***adj.*** (**wor·thi·er**; **wor·thi·est**) **1 worthy of sth/to do sth** good enough for sth, or deserving sth: *The program is worthy of our support.* ◇ *He felt he was not worthy to accept such responsibility.* **2** (usually *before* a noun) deserving respect or consideration: *a worthy leader* ◇ *a worthy cause*

★**would** /wəd; əd; d/ strong form /wʊd/ ***modal verb*** (*short form* **'d**; *negative* **would not**; *short form* **would·n't** /ˈwʊdnt/) **1** (used when talking about the result of an event that you imagine): *He would be delighted if you went to see him.* ◇ *She'd be stupid not to accept.* ◇ *I would have done more if I'd had the time.* **2** (used as the past form of "will" when you report what sb says or thinks): *They said that they would help us.* ◇ *She didn't think he would do a thing like that.* **3** (used for asking sb politely to do sth): *Would you come this way, please?* **4** (used with "like" or "love" as a way of asking or saying what sb wants): *Would you like to come with us?* ◇ *I'd love a piece of cake.* **5** to be willing to do sth: *She just wouldn't do what I asked her.* **6** (used after "wish"): *I wish the sun would come out.* **7** (used for talking about things that often happened in the past): *When he was young, he would often walk in these woods.* **8** (used for commenting on behavior that is typical): *You would say that. You always support him.* **9** (used when you are giving your opinion): *I'd say she's about 40.*

★**wound¹** /wund/ ***noun*** [C] an injury to part of your body, especially a cut, often received in fighting: *Wash and bandage the wound.* ◇ *a bullet wound* ◇ *The wound is healing well.*

★**wound²** /wund/ ***verb*** [T] (usually passive) **1** to injure sb's body with a weapon: *He was wounded in the leg during the war.* ➲ Look at the note at **hurt**. **2** (*formal*) to hurt sb's feelings deeply: *I was wounded by his criticism.* ▶ **the ˈwounded *noun*** [pl.]: *the sick and the wounded*

**wound³** *past tense, past participle of* WIND³

**wove** *past tense of* WEAVE

**wov·en** *past participle of* WEAVE

**wow¹** /waʊ/ ***interjection*** (*informal*) (used for expressing how much you admire or are pleasantly surprised by sth): *Wow! What a great car!*

**wow²** /waʊ/ ***verb*** [T] **wow sb (with sth)** (*informal*) to impress sb very much, especially with a performance: *He wowed audiences around the country with his new show.*

**wpm** ***abbr.*** (*written*) words per minute: *to type at 60 wpm*

**wrack** /ræk/ = RACK²

**wran·gle¹** /ˈræŋgl/ ***noun*** [C] **wrangle (with sb) (over sth)**; **wrangle (between A and B)** an argument that is complicated and continues over a long period of time: *a legal wrangle between the company and their suppliers* ◇ *He is currently locked in a bitter wrangle with his wife over custody of the children.*

**wran·gle²** /ˈræŋgl/ ***verb*** [I] **wrangle (with sb) (over/about sth)** to argue angrily and usually for a long time about sth: *They're still wrangling over the financial details.*

**wran·gler** /ˈræŋglər/ ***noun*** [C] (*informal*) a cowboy or a cowgirl, especially one who takes care of horses

★**wrap¹** /ræp/ ***verb*** [T] (**wrap·ping**; **wrapped**) **1 wrap sth (up) (in sth)** to put paper or cloth around sb/sth as a cover: *to wrap up a present* ◇ *The baby was found wrapped in a blanket on the hospital doorstep.* **2 wrap sth around sb/sth** to tie sth such as paper or cloth around an object or a part of the body: *The man had a bandage wrapped around his head.*

IDM **be wrapped up in sth** to be deeply involved and interested in sb/sth: *They were completely wrapped up in each other. They didn't notice I was there.*

PHR V **wrap sth up** to bring sth to an end; to finish sth: *to wrap up a meeting*

**wrap (sb/yourself) up** to put warm clothes on (sb/yourself)

**wrap²** /ræp/ ***noun*** **1** [C] a piece of cloth that a woman wears around her shoulders for decoration or to keep warm: *a cotton/silk wrap* **2** [U] paper, plastic, etc. that is used for wrapping things in: *We stock a wide range of cards and* ***gift wrap****.* ◇ *Use* ***bubble wrap*** (= a sheet of plastic full of small bubbles of air) *to pack things which might get broken.* ➲ Look also at **plastic wrap**. **3** [sing.] (used when making a movie to say that filming has finished): *Cut! That's a wrap.* **4** [C] a type of sandwich made with a cold tortilla rolled around meat or vegetables

IDM **under wraps** (*informal*) being kept secret until some time in the future: *Next year's collection is still being kept under wraps.*

**wrap·a·round** /ˈræpəraʊnd/ ***adj.*** **1** curving or stretching around at the sides: *wraparound sunglasses* **2** (used about a piece of clothing) having one part that is pulled over to cover another part in the front and then loosely fastened

**wrap·per** /ˈræpər/ ***noun*** [C] a piece of paper or plastic which covers a piece of candy, a food package, etc.

**wrap·ping** /ˈræpɪŋ/ ***noun*** [C,U] paper or cloth that is used for covering or packing sth: *Remove the outer wrapping before heating the pie.*

**ˈwrapping ˌpaper** ***noun*** [U] paper which is used for wrapping presents: *a sheet of wrapping paper*

**ˈwrap-up** ***noun*** [C] a short summary of sth, especially of news or sporting events

**wrath** /ræθ/ ***noun*** [U] (*old-fashioned, formal*) very great anger

**wreak** /rik/ ***verb***

IDM **wreak havoc (on sth)** to cause great damage: *The earthquake wreaked havoc on the state.*

**wreath** /riθ/ ***noun*** [C] (*pl.* **wreaths** /riðz; riθz/) a circle of flowers or leaves, especially one that is used as a decoration at Christmas

**wreathe** /rið/ ***verb*** [T] (*written*) (usually passive) **wreathe sth (in/with sth)** to surround or cover sth: *The mountain tops were wreathed in mist.* ◇ (*figurative*) *Her face was* ***wreathed in smiles*** (= she was smiling a lot).

**wreck¹** /rɛk/ ***noun*** **1** [C] a car, plane, etc. which has been badly damaged, especially in an accident: *The car was a wreck, but the truck escaped almost without damage.* **2** [U] an accident that destroys or badly damages a car, truck, ship, etc.: *the wreck of the Titanic* **3** [C] a ship that has sunk or been badly damaged in the ocean: *Divers searched the wreck.* **4** [C, usually sing.] (*informal*) a person or thing that is in a very bad condition: *a nervous wreck*

**wreck²** /rɛk/ ***verb*** [T] to destroy, damage or spoil sth completely: *Vandals had wrecked the playground.* ◇ *A fishing boat was wrecked in the storms.* ◇ *The airline strike wrecked all our vacation plans.*

**wreck·age** /ˈrɛkɪdʒ/ ***noun*** [U] the broken pieces of sth that has been wrecked

**wreck·er** /ˈrɛkər/ ***noun*** [C] a vehicle used for moving other vehicles that have been damaged in an accident

**wren** /rɛn/ ***noun*** [C] a very small brown bird

**wrench¹** /rɛntʃ/ ***noun*** [C] **1** a metal tool with an end shaped so that it can be used for turning NUTS (2) ➲ picture at **tool**. **2** a sudden, violent pull or turn

**wrench²** /rɛntʃ/ ***verb*** [T] **wrench sb/sth (away, off, etc.)** to pull or turn sb/sth strongly and suddenly: *He wrenched the wheel to the left and stopped the car on the grass.* ◇ (*figurative*) *The movie was so exciting that I could hardly wrench myself away.*

**wrest** /rɛst/ ***verb***

PHRV **wrest sth from sb/sth** (*formal*) **1** to take sth such as power or control from sb/sth with great effort: *They attempted to **wrest control** of the town from government forces.* **2** to take sth from sb that he/she does not want to give, suddenly or violently: *He wrested the gun from my grasp.*

**wres·tle** /ˈrɛsl/ ***verb*** [I] to fight by trying to get hold of your opponent's body and throw him/her to the floor. People wrestle as a sport.

PHRV **wrestle with sth** to try hard to find an answer to sth; to struggle

**wres·tler** /ˈrɛslər/ ***noun*** [C] a person who wrestles as a sport

**wres·tling** /ˈrɛslɪŋ/ ***noun*** [U] a sport in which two people fight and try to throw each other to the floor: *a wrestling match*

**wretch·ed** /ˈrɛtʃəd/ ***adj.*** very unhappy; miserable

**wrig·gle** /ˈrɪgl/ ***verb*** [I,T] **1** to move about, or to move a part of your body, with short, quick movements, especially from side to side: *She wriggled her toes in the water.* **2** to move in the direction mentioned by making quick, turning movements: *The worm wriggled back into the soil.*

PHRV **wriggle out of sth/out of doing sth** (*informal*) to avoid sth by making clever excuses: *It's your turn to do the dishes – you can't wriggle out of it this time!*

**wring** /rɪŋ/ ***verb*** [T] (*pt, pp* **wrung** /rʌŋ/) **wring sth (out)** to press and squeeze sth in order to remove water from it

IDM **wring your hands** to hold your hands together, and twist and squeeze them in a way that shows you are anxious or upset, especially when you cannot change the situation

**wring sb's neck** (*informal*) when you say that you will wring sb's neck, you mean that you are very angry or annoyed with him/her

**wring·er** /ˈrɪŋər/ ***noun*** [C] a machine with two rolling parts, used especially in the past for squeezing the water out of clothes that had been washed

IDM **put sb through the wringer** (*informal*) to make sb have a difficult or unpleasant experience, or a series of them

**wrin·kle¹** /ˈrɪŋkl/ ***noun*** [C] a small line in sth, e.g. on the skin of your face which you get as you grow older, or in your clothes ▶ **wrin·kly** /-kli/ ***adj.*** (**wrin·kli·er**; **wrin·kli·est**) (*informal*)

**wrin·kle²** /ˈrɪŋkl/ ***verb*** [I,T] to form wrinkles (in sth): *She wrinkled her nose at the smell.* ◇ *This skirt wrinkles easily.* ▶ **wrin·kled** /ˈrɪŋkld/ ***adj.***: *an old lady with a wrinkled face*

★**wrist** /rɪst/ ***noun*** [C] the part of your body where your arm joins your hand ➲ picture on study page **A32**.

IDM **a slap on the wrist** → SLAP²

**wrist·watch** /ˈrɪstwɑtʃ; -wɔtʃ/ ***noun*** [C] a watch on a band which you wear around your wrist

**writ** /rɪt/ ***noun*** [C] a legal order to do or not to do sth, given by a court of law or a person in authority

★**write** /raɪt/ ***verb*** (*pt* **wrote** /roʊt/; *pp* **writ·ten** /ˈrɪtn/) **1** [I,T] to make words, letters, etc., especially on paper, using a pen, pencil, etc.: *Some children can read and write before they start school.* ◇ *I can't write with this pen.* ◇ *Write your account number on the bottom of your check.* **2** [T] to create a book, story, song, etc. and write it on paper: *He wrote his wife a poem.* ◇ *Who wrote the music for that movie?* **3** [I,T] to write and send a letter, etc. to sb: *Have you written to your mother recently?* ◇ *I'm writing to thank you for the birthday present you sent me.* ◇ *She wrote that they were all well and would be home soon.* ◇ *I wrote a letter to my son./I wrote my son a letter.* ◇ *I wrote her* (= wrote a letter to her) *yesterday.* **4** [T] **write sth (out) (for sb)** to fill or complete a form, check, document, etc. with the necessary information: *I wrote out a check for $10.* ◇ *The doctor quickly wrote a prescription for me.*

PHRV **write back (to sb)** to send a reply to sb

**write sth down** to write sth on paper, especially so that you can remember it

**write in (to sb/sth)** to write a letter to an organization, etc. to order sth, give an opinion, etc.

**write off/away (to sb/sth) (for sth)** to write a letter to an organization, etc. to order sth or ask for sth

**write sb/sth off** to accept or decide that sb/sth will not be successful or useful: *Don't write him off yet. He could still win.*

**write sth off** to accept that you will not get back an amount of money you have lost or spent: *to write off a debt*

**write sth out** to write the whole of sth on paper: *I want you to write out the exercise in your notebook.*

**write sth up** to write sth in a complete and final form, often using notes that you have made: *to write up your notes from a lecture*

**write-in** /ˈraɪt̬ɪn/ ***noun*** [C] (*U.S.*) a vote that you give to sb who is not an official candidate in an election, by writing his/her name on the piece of paper (**ballot**) used for voting

ˈ**write-off** /ˈraɪt̬ɔf/ ***noun*** [C] an amount of money

that you will not get back because it has been lost or because sb cannot pay a debt

★**writ·er** /ˈraɪt̬ər/ ***noun*** [C] a person who writes, especially one whose job is to write books, stories, etc.

ˈ**writer's ˌblock** ***noun*** [U] a problem that writers sometimes have when they cannot think of what to write and have no new ideas

ˈ**write-up** ***noun*** [C] an article in a newspaper or magazine in which sb writes what he/she thinks about a new book, play, product, etc.: *The performance got a good write-up in the local press.*

**writhe** /raɪð/ ***verb*** [I] to turn and roll your body around: *She lay writhing in pain.*

★**writ·ing** /ˈraɪt̬ɪŋ/ ***noun*** [U] **1** words that have been written or printed; the way a person writes: *This card has no writing inside. You can put your own message in it.* ◇ *I can't read your writing – it's too small.* **2** the books, etc. that sb has written or the style in which sb writes: *Love is a common theme in his early writing.* ◇ *Her writing lacks realism.* **3** the activity or job of writing books, etc.: *It's difficult to earn much money from writing.*

IDM **in writing** in written form: *I'll confirm the offer in writing next week.*

★**writ·ten** /ˈrɪtn/ ***adj.*** expressed on paper; not just spoken: *a written agreement* ◇ *a written test and an oral test*

★**wrong¹** /rɔŋ/ ***adj.*** **1** not true or not correct; not right: *the wrong answer* ◇ *What you said was totally wrong.* ◇ *You have the wrong number* (= on the telephone). **2** not the best; not suitable; not right: *That's the wrong way to hold the bat.* ◇ *I think she married the wrong man.* **3** (not before a noun) **wrong (with sb/sth)** not as it should be; not working correctly: *You look upset. Is something wrong?* ◇ *What's wrong with the car this time?* ◇ *She has something wrong with her leg.* **4** **wrong (to do sth)** bad or against the law; not good or right: *The man said that he had done nothing wrong.* ◇ *I think it was wrong of us not to invite him.*

IDM **get on the right/wrong side of sb** → SIDE¹
**on the right/wrong track** → TRACK¹

★**wrong²** /rɔŋ/ ***adv.*** in an incorrect way; not right: *I always pronounce that word wrong.* ➲ Look at the note at **wrongly**.

IDM **get sb wrong** (*informal*) to misunderstand sb: *Don't get me wrong! I don't dislike him.*
**go wrong (with sth)** to happen or develop in the wrong way: *I always get blamed for everything that goes wrong!* ◇ *Don't worry – nothing should go wrong with the equipment.*

★**wrong³** /rɔŋ/ ***noun*** **1** [U] what is bad or against the law: *Children quickly learn the difference between right and wrong.* **2** [C] an action or situation which is not fair: *A terrible wrong has been done. Those men should never have gone to prison.*

IDM **in the wrong** (*formal*) responsible for sth bad that has happened

**wrong⁴** /rɔŋ/ ***verb*** [T] (*formal*) to do sth to sb which is bad or unfair: *people who have been wronged by inaccurate reports in the media*

**wrong·do·er** /ˈrɔŋˌduər/ ***noun*** [C] (*formal*) a person who does sth dishonest or illegal

**wrong·ful** /ˈrɔŋfl/ ***adj.*** (*formal*) (only *before* a noun) not fair, not legal or not moral: *She sued her former employer for wrongful dismissal.* ▶ **wrong·ful·ly** ***adv.***

**wrong·ly** /ˈrɔŋli/ ***adv.*** in a wrong or mistaken way: *This letter was wrongly addressed.*

> NOTE The adverb **wrong** is used after a verb or the object of a verb, especially in conversation: *He spelled my name wrong.* The adverb **wrongly** is especially used before a past participle or a verb: *My name was wrongly spelled.*

**wrote** *past tense of* WRITE

**wrought iron** /ˌrɔt̬ ˈaɪərn/ ***noun*** [U] a form of iron used to make decorative fences, gates, etc.: *The gates were made of wrought iron.* ◇ *wrought-iron gates*

**wrung** *past tense, past participle of* WRING

**wry** /raɪ/ ***adj.*** expressing a mixture of disappointment and amusement: *"Never mind," she said with a wry grin. "At least we got one vote."* ▶ **wry·ly** ***adv.***

**wt.** ***abbr.*** = WEIGHT¹ (1)

**wuss** /wʊs/ ***noun*** [C] (*slang*) a person who is not strong or brave: *Don't be such a wuss!*

**WWW** /ˌdʌblyu ˌdʌblyu ˈdʌblyu/ ***abbr.*** = WORLD WIDE WEB

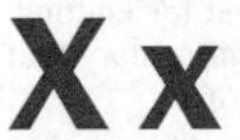

**X, x** /ɛks/ ***noun*** [C,U] (*pl.* **X's**; **x's**) the twenty-fourth letter of the English alphabet: *"Xylophone" begins with (an) "X."*

> NOTE X is used instead of the name of a person if you do not know or do not want to say the name: *Mr. and Mrs. X.*

**X** /ɛks/ ***adj.*** (used about movies that no one under age 17 is allowed to see, especially because they are about sex)

**xen·o·pho·bi·a** /ˌzɛnəˈfoʊbiə; ˌzinə-/ ***noun*** [U] fear or hatred of people from other countries ▶ **xen·o·pho·bic** /-ˈfoʊbɪk/ ***adj.***

**Xer·ox™** /ˈzɪrɑks/ ***noun*** [C] **1** a machine that produces copies of documents on paper **2** a copy produced by a Xerox machine: *a Xerox of the letter* ▶ **xer·ox** ***verb*** [T]

**xi** /zaɪ; ksaɪ/ ***noun*** [C] (*symbol* Ξ, ξ) the fourteenth letter of the Greek alphabet ➲ Look at the note at **fraternity**.

**XL** ***abbr.*** extra large

**X·mas** /ˈkrɪsməs; ˈɛksməs/ ***noun*** [U] (*informal*)

(used as a short form, especially in writing) Christmas: *Merry Xmas to all our customers.*

**X-rat·ed** /ˈɛksreɪt̬əd/ ***adj.*** (usually *before* a noun) not suitable for children because it is about sex or violence: *the album's X-rated lyrics*

**X-ray** /ˈɛksreɪ/ ***noun*** [C] **1** [usually pl.] a ray of energy that makes it possible to see inside solid objects (e.g. the human body) so that they can be examined and a photograph of them can be made **2** a photograph that is made with an X-ray machine: *The X-ray showed that the bone was not broken.* ▶ **X-ray** ***verb*** [T]: *She had her chest X-rayed.*

**xy·lo·phone** /ˈzaɪləfoʊn/ ***noun*** [C] a musical instrument that consists of a row of wooden bars of different lengths. You play it by hitting these bars with small hammers.

**xylophone**

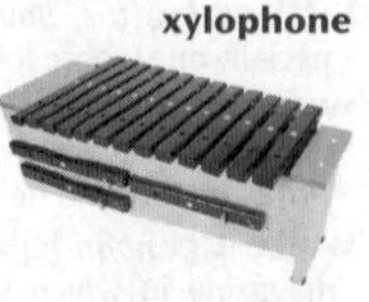

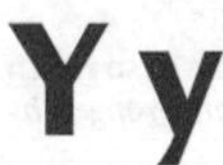

# Y y

**Y, y** /waɪ/ ***noun*** [C,U] (*pl.* **Y's**; **y's**) the twenty-fifth letter of the English alphabet: *"Yawn begins with (a) "Y."*

**yacht** /yɑt/ ***noun*** [C] a large boat with sails and/or a motor, used for pleasure: *a yacht race*

**yad·da yad·da yad·da** /ˌyɑdə ˌyɑdə ˈyɑdə/ ***noun*** [U] (*informal*) (used when you are talking about sth to show that some of the details are not worth saying because they are not important or are boring or obvious): *His new girlfriend is attractive, funny, smart, yadda yadda yadda.*

**ya·hoo[1]** /ˈyɑhu/ ***noun*** [C] (*informal*) a rude, noisy or violent person

**ya·hoo[2]** /yɑˈhu/ ***interjection*** (used to show excitement or happiness): *Yahoo – the plan worked!*

**yak[1]** /yæk/ ***noun*** [C] an animal of the cow family, with long horns and long hair, that lives in central Asia

**yak[2]** /yæk/ ***verb*** (**yak·king**; **yakked**) [I] (*informal*) to talk continuously about things that are not very serious or important: *My sister and I yakked for hours.*

**y'all** /yɔl/ ***pronoun*** (*informal*) (used in the southern U.S.) you; all of you: *Why don't y'all come in and have some iced tea?*

**yam** /yæm/ ***noun*** [C] an orange-colored root that looks like a potato with pointed ends, that is cooked and eaten as a vegetable ➲ Look also at **sweet potato**.

**Yank** /yæŋk/ ***noun*** (*informal*) = YANKEE (2,4)

**yank** /yæŋk/ ***verb*** [I,T] (*informal*) to pull with a sudden quick movement and with great force: *She yanked at the door handle and it came off in her hand.* ▶ **yank** ***noun*** [C]

**Yan·kee** /ˈyæŋki/ ***noun*** [C] **1** a person who comes from or lives in New England (= the northeastern states of the U.S.) **2** (*also informal* **Yank**) (used as an insult by people in the southern U.S.) a person who comes from or lives in the northern U.S. **3** a soldier who fought for the northern states in the U. S. Civil War (1861-1865) **4** (*also informal* **Yank**) (used as an insult by people outside the U.S.) an American

**yap** /yæp/ ***verb*** [I] (**yap·ping**; **yapped**) (used about dogs, especially small ones) to bark in an excited way, making short high noises

★**yard** /yɑrd/ ***noun*** [C] **1** a piece of land next to or around a house with grass, flowers, bushes, trees, etc. on it: *The kids were playing in the yard.* ◇ *the front/back yard* ➲ Picture on study page **A31**. ➲ Look at **garden** and **lawn**. **2** an area, usually without a roof, used for a particular type of work or purpose: *a shipyard* **3** (*abbr.* **yd.**) a measure of length; 0.914 of a meter. There are three feet (or 36 inches) in a yard: *This fabric costs $5.99 a yard.*

**yard·age** /ˈyɑrdɪdʒ/ ***noun*** [C,U] (*technical*) **1** size measured in yards or square yards: *a large yardage of canvas* **2** (in football) the number of yards that a team or player has moved forward

**ˈyard sale** ***noun*** [C] a sale, held outside sb's house, of used things that people do not want anymore ➲ Look also at **rummage sale**.

**yard·stick** /ˈyɑrdstɪk/ ***noun*** [C] a standard by which things can be compared: *Test scores should not be the only yardstick by which students are judged.*

**yar·mul·ke** (*also* **yar·mul·ka**) /ˈyɑməkə; ˈyɑrməlkə/ ***noun*** [C] a small round cap worn on top of the head by Jewish men; a type of skullcap

**yarmulke**

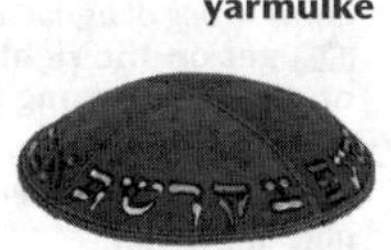

**yarn** /yɑrn/ ***noun*** **1** [U] thick thread (usually made of wool or cotton) that is used for knitting, etc. ➲ picture at **knit**. **2** [C] (*informal*) a story that sb tells, especially one that is exaggerated

**yawn** /yɔn/ ***verb*** [I] to open your mouth wide and breathe in deeply, especially when you are tired or bored: *"I just got up," she said, yawning.* ◇ *I kept yawning all through the lecture.* ▶ **yawn** ***noun*** [C]: *"How much longer will it take?" he said with a yawn.*

**yd.** ***abbr.*** = YARD (3)

**yeah** /yɛə/ ***interjection*** (*informal*) yes ➲ Look at the note at **yes**.

★**year** /yɪr/ ***noun*** (*abbr.* **yr.**) **1** [C] the time it takes the earth to go once around the sun, about 365 days **2** [C] (*also* ˈ**calendar year**) the period from January 1 to December 31; 365 or 366 days divided into 12 months or 52 weeks: *last year/this year/next year* ◇ *The population of the country will be 70 million by the year 2000.* ◇ *We go on vacation at this* *time every year.* ◇ *the year before last/the year after next* ◇ *a leap year* (= one that has 366 days) **3** [C] any period of 12 months, measured from any point: *It's been several years since the last time I saw him.* ◇ *She worked here for twenty years.* ◇ *He quit school just over a year ago.* ◇ *They've been living in New Jersey for the last few years.* **4** [C] a period of a year in connection with schools, the business world, etc.: *The school year runs from September through May.* ◇ *the fiscal year* **5** [C] (used in connection with the age of sb/sth) a period of 12 months: *He's ten years old today.* ◇ *a six-year-old daughter* ◇ *This car is almost five years old.* ◇ *The company is now in its fifth year.*

NOTE Note that you say: *He's ten* or: *He's ten years old* but NOT: *He's ten years.* ➲ Look at the note at **age**.

**6 years** [pl.] a long time: *It happened years ago.*
IDM **(all) year round** for the whole year: *Most of the resorts are open all year round.*
**year after year** every year for many years

**year·book** /ˈyɪrbʊk/ ***noun*** [C] a book that is produced each year by the students at a school or college, with pictures of students, teachers, sports teams, and events that happened during the year

**ˌyear-ˈend** (*also* **ˌyear ˈend**) ***noun*** [sing.] the end of the financial year: *year-end profits*

**year·ling** /ˈyɪrlɪŋ/ ***noun*** [C] an animal, especially a horse, between one and two years old

**year·long** /ˌyɪrˈlɔŋ/ ***noun*** continuing for a whole year: *a year-long dispute/investigation*

**year·ly** /ˈyɪrli/ ***adj., adv.*** (happening) every year or once a year: *a yearly pay raise* ◇ *The conference is held yearly in Santa Barbara.*

**yearn** /yərn/ ***verb*** [I] **yearn (for sb/sth)**; **yearn (to do sth)** to want sb/sth very much, especially sth that you cannot have ▸ **yearn·ing** ***noun*** [C,U]

**ˌyear-ˈround** ***adj., adv.*** all through the year: *an island with year-round sunshine*

**yeast** /yist/ ***noun*** [U] a substance used for making bread rise and for making beer, wine, etc.

**ˈyeast inˌfection** ***noun*** [C] an infectious disease, especially one that affects the vagina

**yell** /yɛl/ ***verb*** [I,T] to shout very loudly, often because you are angry, excited or in pain: *There's no need to yell at me – I can hear you perfectly well.* ▸ **yell** ***noun*** [C]

★**yel·low**[1] /ˈyɛloʊ/ ***adj.*** having the color of lemons or butter: *dark/light yellow* ◇ *a bright/pale yellow dress*

**yel·low**[2] /ˈyɛloʊ/ ***noun*** [C,U] the color of lemons or butter; something that is this color: *a bright shade of yellow* ◇ *the yellows and browns of the leaves in the fall*

**ˌyellow ˈfever** ***noun*** [U] an infectious tropical disease that makes the skin turn yellow and often causes death

**yel·low·ish** /ˈyɛloʊɪʃ/ ***adj.*** slightly yellow

**ˈYellow ˌPages™** ***noun*** [pl.] a telephone book (on yellow paper) that lists all the business companies, etc. in a certain area, in sections according to the products or services they provide ➲ Look at **white pages**.

**yelp** /yɛlp/ ***noun*** [C] a sudden short cry, especially of pain, fear or excitement ▸ **yelp** ***verb*** [I]

**yen** /yɛn/ ***noun*** **1** [C] (*pl.* **yen**) the unit of money in Japan **2 the yen** [sing.] the value of the yen compared with the value of the money of other countries **3** [C, usually sing.] **a yen for sth/to do sth** a strong desire: *I've always had a yen to travel around the world.*

**yep** /yɛp/ ***interjection*** (*informal*) yes

**yer** /yər/ ***det.*** (*informal*) (used in writing as a way of showing the way people sometimes pronounce the word "your"): *What's yer name?*

★**yes** /yɛs/ ***interjection*** **1** (used when answering a question to which another possible answer is "no"): *"Are you having a good time?" "Yes, I am!"* ◇ *I asked him if he wanted to come, and he said yes.* **2** (used for saying that a statement is correct or for agreeing with one): *"You spend way too much money." "Yes, you're right."* **3** (used when agreeing to a request): *"Is it all right if I sit here?" "Yes, of course."* **4** (used when accepting an offer): *"More coffee?" "Yes, please."* **5** (used for showing you have heard sb or will do what he/she asks): *"Waiter!" "Yes, ma'am."* **6** (used when saying that a negative statement that sb has made is not true): *"You don't care about anyone but yourself." "Yes, I do!"* **7** (*informal*) (used to express great pleasure or satisfaction): *Yes! Jordan scored the winning basket!*

NOTE **Yes** is used mainly in writing and more formal speech. In informal speech, we usually use other words such as **yeah** or **uh-huh**.

**ye·shi·va** /yəˈʃivə/ ***noun*** [C] a college or school for Orthodox Jews

**ˈyes-man** ***noun*** [C] (*pl.* **ˈyes-men**) a person who always agrees with people in authority in order to gain their approval

**ˌyes/ˈno ˌquestion** ***noun*** [C] (*grammar*) a question to which the answer is either "yes" or "no," e.g. "Do you like dogs?"

★**yes·ter·day** /ˈyɛstərdeɪ; -di/ ***adv., noun*** [C,U] (on) the day before today: *Did you watch that show on TV yesterday?* ◇ *yesterday morning/afternoon/evening* ◇ *I mailed the letter the day before yesterday* (= if I am speaking on Wednesday, I mailed it on Monday). ◇ *Did it really happen three weeks ago? It seems like only yesterday.* ◇ *Do you still have yesterday's newspaper?* ◇ *Yesterday was the best day I've had in a long time.*
IDM **not be born yesterday** used to say that you are not stupid enough to believe what sb is telling you: *Oh yeah? I wasn't born yesterday, you know.*

**yes·ter·year** /ˈyɛstəryɪr/ ***noun*** [U] (*old-fashioned*) the past, especially a time when attitudes and ideas were different

Y

★**yet**[1] /yɛt/ ***adv.*** **1** (used with negative verbs or in questions for talking about sth that has not happened but that you expect to happen): *We haven't had any serious problems yet.* ◇ *Has it stopped raining yet?* ◇ *There was a pile of work on my desk which I hadn't yet done.* ◇ *I haven't seen that movie yet.* ◇ *Did you do your homework yet?* **2** (used with negative verbs) now; as early as this: *You don't have to go yet – your flight doesn't leave until 5:00.* **3** (used especially with *may* or *might*) at some time in the future: *With a little bit of luck, they might win yet.* **4** (used with comparatives or "another" to emphasize the size or amount of sth): *This is yet another reason to cancel the project.* **5** (used with superlatives) until and including now/then; so far: *This is her best performance yet.* **6** but; in spite of that: *Their plan was simple yet successful.*

IDM **as yet** until now: *As yet, little is known about the disease.*

**yet again** (used for emphasizing how often sth happens) once more: *Yet again, Jim was late for class.*

**yet to do, etc.** (if you have yet to do sth, it means that you have not done it but may possibly do it in the future): *The final decision has yet to be made.*

**yet²** /yɛt/ ***conj.*** but (when sth is surprising after the first part of the statement): *He seems nice, yet there's something about him I don't like.*

**yet·i** /ˈyɛt̮i/ ***noun*** [sing.] a large creature covered with hair like a man or a bear, that some people believe lives in the Himalayan mountains

**yew** /yu/ ***noun*** **1** [C,U] (*also* ˈ**yew tree**) a small tree with dark green leaves and small red berries **2** [U] the wood of the yew tree

**Yid·dish** /ˈyɪdɪʃ/ ***noun*** [U] a Jewish language, originally used in central and eastern Europe, based on a form of German with words from Hebrew and several modern languages ▸ **Yid·dish** ***adj.***

**yield¹** /yild/ ***verb*** **1** [T] to produce crops, profits or results: *How much wheat does each field yield?* ◇ *Did the experiment yield any new information?* **2** [I] **yield (to sb/sth)** (*formal*) to stop resisting sb/sth (so that you do what sb has demanded): *The government refused to yield to the hostage takers' demands.* ➲ **Give in** is less formal. **3** [I] **yield (to sb/sth)** to allow other traffic to go first or to join the road in front of you: *You have to yield to traffic on the highway here.* **4** [T] to allow sb to have control of sth that you were controlling: *The army has yielded power to the rebels.* **5** [I] **yield to sth** (*formal*) to be replaced by sth, especially sth newer: *Old-fashioned methods have yielded to new technology.* ➲ **Give way** is more common. **6** [I] (*formal*) to bend or break: *The dam finally yielded under the weight of the water.* ➲ **Give way** is more common.

**yield²** /yild/ ***noun*** [C] the amount that is produced: *Wheat yields were down 5% this year.* ◇ *This investment has an annual yield of 12%.*

**yikes** /yaɪks/ ***interjection*** (*informal*) (used to show that you are surprised or suddenly afraid)

**yip·pee** /ˈyɪpi; yɪˈpi/ ***interjection*** (*old-fashioned, informal*) (used to show you are pleased or excited)

**yo** /yoʊ/ ***interjection*** (*slang*) (used in very informal situations to get sb's attention, as a greeting or as a response to sb who calls your name): *Yo, Mike! Over here!* ◇ *Yo, dudes – how's it going?* ◇ *"Rick?" "Yo!"*

**yo·del** /ˈyoʊdl/ ***verb*** [I] to sing or call in the traditional Swiss way, changing your voice frequently between its normal level and a very high level

**yo·ga** /ˈyoʊgə/ ***noun*** [U] a system of exercises that helps you control and relax both your mind and your body

**yo·gurt** /ˈyoʊgərt/ ***noun*** [C,U] a slightly sour, thick liquid food made from milk

**yoke** /yoʊk/ ***noun*** [C] a piece of wood fastened across the necks of two animals when they are pulling a cart, etc.: (*figurative*) *the yoke of slavery*

**yo·kel** /ˈyoʊkl/ ***noun*** [C] (if you call a person a yokel, you are saying that he/she does not have much education or understanding of modern life, because he/she lives far from any city)

**yolk** /yoʊk/ ***noun*** [C,U] the yellow part in the middle of an egg: *He ate the yolk and left the white.* ➲ picture at **egg**.

**Yom Kip·pur** /ˌyɑm kɪˈpʊr; ˌyɔm-/ ***noun*** [U] a Jewish religious holiday on which Jewish people do not eat, and pray that God will forgive them for the things they have done wrong

**yon·der** /ˈyɑndər/ ***adv.*** over there, at a place that is fairly far away: *I thought I saw a deer way over yonder.*

**yoo-hoo** /ˈyu hu/ ***interjection*** (*old-fashioned, informal*) (used to attract sb's attention, especially when he/she is some distance away)

★**you** /yu/ ***pronoun*** **1** the person or people being spoken or written to: *You can play the guitar, can't you?* ◇ *I've told you about this before.* ◇ *Bring your purse with you.* ◇ *Hey, you! Get off my lawn!*

> NOTE Notice that we do not write **you** with a capital "Y," even when we are writing a letter to someone.

**2** (used with a noun, adjective or phrase when calling sb sth): *You idiot! What do you think you're doing?* **3** a person (not a particular one); people in general: *You don't see many tourists here at this time of year.* ◇ *The more you earn, the more taxes you pay.*

> NOTE **One** has the same meaning, but is much more formal: *One tries to help as much as one can.*

IDM **you guys**; **you all** (*informal*) (used when speaking to two or more people): *Do you guys want to order a pizza?*

> NOTE **You guys** and **you all** can be used when speaking to both men and women.

**you'd** /yəd; *strong form* yud/ *short for* YOU HAD, YOU WOULD

**you'll** /yəl; *strong form* yul/ *short for* YOU WILL

★**young¹** /yʌŋ/ ***adj.*** (**young·er** /ˈyʌŋgər/, **young·est** /ˈyʌŋgəst/) not having lived or existed for very long: *They have two young children.* ◇ *young plants* ◇ *teenagers and young adults* ◇ *I'm a year younger than her.* ◇ *My father was the youngest of eight children.* ◇ *young fashions* (= for young people)

IDM **young at heart** behaving or thinking like a young person, even if you are not young

**young²** /yʌŋ/ ***noun*** [pl.] **1** young animals: *Swans will attack to protect their young.* **2 the young** young people when you are thinking about them as a group: *The young of today are the adults of tomorrow.*

**young·ster** /ˈyʌŋstər/ ***noun*** [C] (*old-fashioned*) a child or young person: *There is very little entertainment for youngsters in this town.*

★**your** /yər; *strong form* yɔr; yʊr/ ***det.*** **1** belonging to or connected with the person or people being spoken to: *What's your apartment like?* ◇ *Thanks* *for all your help.* ◇ *How old are your kids now?* ◇ *It would be helpful if you could all give me your addresses.* **2** belonging to or connected with people in general: *When your life is as busy as mine, you don't have much time to relax.* **3** (used for saying that sth is well-known to people in general): *So this is your typical Florida beach, is it?*

**you're** /yər; *strong form* yɔr; yʊr/ *short for* YOU ARE

★**yours** /yərz; *strong form* yɔrz; yʊrz/ ***pronoun*** **1** belonging to or connected with you: *Is this bag yours or mine?* ◇ *I was talking to a friend of yours the other day.* **2 Yours** (used at the end of a letter): *Yours truly...* ◇ *Yours...*

★**your·self** /yər'sɛlf/ ***pronoun*** (*pl.* **your·selves** /-'sɛlvz/) **1** (used as the object of a verb or preposition when you are speaking to sb and talking about this person/these people doing an action and also being affected by it): *Be careful or you'll hurt yourself.* ◇ *Here's some money. Buy yourselves a present.* ◇ *You're always talking about yourself!* **2** (used for emphasis): *You yourself told me there was a problem last week.* ◇ *Did you fix the car yourselves?* (= or did sb else do it for you?) **3** in your normal state; healthy: *You don't look yourself today.*

IDM **by yourself/yourselves 1** alone: *Do you live by yourself?* **2** without help: *You can't cook dinner for ten people by yourself. Let me help you.*

**youse** (*also* **yous**) /yuz/ ***pronoun*** (*slang*) (a word meaning "you" in dialect, used when talking to more than one person)

★**youth** /yuθ/ ***noun*** (*pl.* **youths** /yuðz/) **1** [U] the period of your life when you are young, especially the time between being a child and an adult: *He was a very good athlete in his youth.* **2** [U] the fact or state of being young: *I think that his youth will be a disadvantage in this job.* **3** [C] (*formal* or *old-fashioned*) a young person (usually a young man, and often one that you do not have a good opinion of): *There were groups of youths standing around on the street corners.* **4** (*also* **the youth**) [pl.] young people as a group: *What kind of future do the youth of this country have?*

**youth·ful** /'yuθfl/ ***adj.*** **1** having the qualities that are typical of young people: *She was almost fifty but still full of youthful enthusiasm.* **2** young or relatively young: *The movie stars a youthful Jimmy Stewart.*

**'youth ˌhostel** ***noun*** [C] a type of cheap and simple hotel where people (especially young people) can stay when they are traveling around on vacation

**you've** /yuv/ *short for* YOU HAVE

**yo-yo** /'yoʊyoʊ/ ***noun*** [C] (*pl.* **yo-yos**) a toy which is a round piece of wood or plastic with a string around the middle. You put the string around your finger and can make the yo-yo go up and down the string.

**yr.** ***abbr.*** (*pl.* **yrs.**) = YEAR

**yuck** /yʌk/ ***interjection*** (*informal*) (used for saying that you think sth is very bad or disgusting): *Oh, no – not cabbage! Yuck!*

**yuck·y** /'yʌki/ ***adj.*** (**yuck·i·er**; **yuck·i·est**) (*informal*) disgusting; very unpleasant: *What a yucky color!*

**yum** /yʌm/ ***interjection*** (*informal*) (used for saying that you think sth tastes very good): *Yum! Chocolate pudding!*

**yum·my** /'yʌmi/ ***adj.*** (**yum·mi·er**; **yum·mi·est**) (*informal*) tasting very good; delicious

**yup** /yʌp/ ***interjection*** (*informal*) yes

**yup·pie** /'yʌpi/ ***noun*** [C] a successful young professional person who earns a lot of money and spends it on expensive things ➲ This word is often used in a critical way.

# Zz

**Z, z** / (*U.S.*) zi (*Cdn*) zɛd/ ***noun*** [C,U] (*pl.* **Z's**; **z's**) the twenty-sixth letter of the English alphabet: *"Zero" begins with (a) "Z."*

**za·ny** /'zeɪni/ ***adj.*** (**za·ni·er**; **za·ni·est**) funny in an unusual and crazy way: *a zany comedian*

**zap** /zæp/ ***verb*** [T] (**zap·ping**; **zapped**) (*informal*) to kill sb with a weapon, especially one that uses electricity: *The object of the game is to zap the aliens with your laser cannon.*

**zap·per** /'zæpər/ ***noun*** [C] (*informal*) **1** = REMOTE CONTROL **2** a device or weapon that attacks or destroys sth quickly: *a bug zapper*

**zeal** /zil/ ***noun*** [U] (*formal*) great energy or enthusiasm: *religious zeal*

**zeal·ot** /'zɛlət/ ***noun*** [C] a person who is too enthusiastic about sth, especially religion or politics

**zeal·ous** /'zɛləs/ ***adj.*** using great energy and enthusiasm ▸ **zeal·ous·ly** ***adv.***

**ze·bra** /'zibrə/ ***noun*** [C] (*pl.* **ze·bra** or **ze·bras**) an African wild animal that looks like a horse, with black and white stripes all over its body

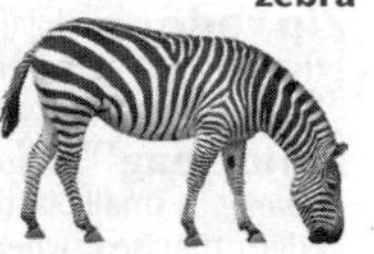
zebra

**zeit·geist** /'zaɪtgaɪst; 'tsaɪt-/ ***noun*** [sing.] (*formal*) the general mood or quality of a particular period of history, as shown by the ideas, beliefs, etc. common at the time

**ze·nith** /'zinəθ/ ***noun*** [C] **1** the highest point that the sun or moon reaches in the sky, directly above you: *The sun rose toward its zenith.* **2** (*formal*) the time when sth is strongest and most successful: *The band was* ***at the zenith*** *of its creative powers.* SYN **peak**[1](2)

★**ze·ro**[1] /'zɪroʊ/ ***number***, ***pronoun*** **1** 0; one less than one **2** nothing at all; none at all: *My chances of passing the test are zero.*

NOTE We often pronounce the number **0** as "oh" when we are saying long numbers, e.g. telephone numbers, out loud: *555-0390* (= "five five five, oh three nine oh") ◊ *My Zip code is 02134* (= "oh two one three four").

**ze·ro²** /ˈzɪroʊ/ *verb*
PHR V **zero in on sb/sth 1** to fix all your attention on the person or thing mentioned: *They zeroed in on the key issues.* **2** to aim guns, etc. at the person or thing mentioned

**ˌzero ˈtolerance** *noun* [U] the policy of applying laws very strictly so that people are punished even for offences that are not very serious

**zest** /zɛst/ *noun* [U, sing.] **zest (for sth)** a feeling of excitement, pleasure and interest: *She is a very active person, with a great zest for life.*

**zest·y** /ˈzɛsti/ *adj.* full of enthusiasm and energy; exciting

**ze·ta** /ˈzeɪt̬ə/ *noun* [C] (*symbol* Z , ζ) the sixth letter of the Greek alphabet ➲ Look at the note at **fraternity**.

**zig·zag** /ˈzɪgzæg/ *noun* [C] a line with left and right turns, one after the other at sharp angles: *curtains with a zigzag pattern* ➲ Picture on study page **A30**. ▸ **zig·zag** *verb* [I] (**zig·zag·ging**; **zig·zagged**): *We took a road that zigzagged through the mountains.*

**zilch** /zɪltʃ/ *noun* [U] (*informal*) nothing: *I arrived in this country with zilch.*

**zil·lion** /ˈzɪlyən/ *noun* [C] (*informal*) a very large number: *There was a bunch of kids waiting and zillions of reporters.* ◊ *This movie is a zillion times better than her last one.*

**zinc** /zɪŋk/ *noun* [U] (*symbol* **Zn**) a bluish-white metal that is mixed with copper to produce brass and is often used to cover other metals to prevent them from rusting

**zing** /zɪŋ/ *noun* [U] (*informal*) interest or excitement: *The juice adds zing to drinks.* ▸ **zing·y** *adj.*

**zing·er** /ˈzɪŋər/ *noun* [C] (*informal*) a short, witty remark or joke: *She opened the speech with a real zinger.*

**zip** /zɪp/ *verb* [T] (**zip·ping**; **zipped**) **zip sth (up)** to fasten sth with a zipper: *There was so much in the bag that it was difficult to zip it up.*

**ˈZip code** *noun* [C] (in the U.S.) a group of numbers that you put at the end of an address. The Zip code helps the post office to sort letters by machine.

**Ziploc bag™** (*also* **ziplock bag**) /ˌzɪplɑk ˈbæg/ *noun* [C] a small plastic bag for storing food, that has edges that seal when you press them together in order to keep the air out

**zip·per** /ˈzɪpər/ *noun* [C] a device for fastening clothes, bags, etc. which consists of two rows of metal or plastic teeth, one on each side of an opening. You can join these rows together to close the opening.

teeth zipper

**zit** /zɪt/ *noun* [C] (*slang*) = PIMPLE

**the zo·di·ac** /ˈzoʊdiæk/ *noun* [sing.] a diagram of the positions of the planets and stars, which is divided into twelve equal parts (signs)

NOTE The signs of the zodiac are used in **astrology** and **horoscopes** in newspapers and magazines. People often refer to the signs and to the influence that they think these have on a person's personality and future.

**zom·bie** /ˈzɑmbi/ *noun* [C] **1** (*informal*) a person who seems only partly alive, without any feeling or interest in what is happening **2** (in some African and Caribbean religions and in horror stories) a dead body that has been made alive again by magic

★**zone¹** /zoʊn/ *noun* [C] an area that is different from those around it e.g. because sth special happens there: *the war zone* ◊ *a no-passing zone* ➲ Look also at **time zone**.

**zone²** /zoʊn/ *verb*
PHR V **zone out** (*slang*) to be unable to pay attention to sb/sth or to think clearly, especially because you are tired or under the influence of drugs

★**zoo** /zu/ *noun* [C] (*pl.* **zoos**) a park where many kinds of living (especially wild) animals are kept so that people can look at them: *to go to the zoo* ◊ *She thinks that it's wrong to keep animals in zoos.*

**zoo·keep·er** /ˈzuˌkipər/ *noun* [C] a person who works in a zoo, taking care of the animals

**zo·ol·o·gy** /zoʊˈɑlədʒi/ *noun* [U] the scientific study of animals ➲ Look at **botany** and **biology**. ▸ **zo·o·log·i·cal** /ˌzoʊəˈlɑdʒɪkl/ *adj.* ▸ **zo·ol·o·gist** /zoʊˈɑlədʒɪst/ *noun* [C]

**zoom** /zum/ *verb* [I] to move very quickly and with a loud noise: *A motorcycle zoomed past.*
PHR V **zoom in (on sb/sth)** to make an object that you are filming appear bigger by using a special lens: *The camera zoomed in on a face in the crowd.*

**ˈzoom lens** *noun* [C] a camera lens that can make an object being photographed appear gradually bigger or smaller so that it seems to be getting closer or farther away

**zuc·chi·ni** /zuˈkini/ *noun* [C,U] (*pl.* **zuc·chi·ni** or **zuc·chi·nis**) a long vegetable with green skin, that is eaten cooked ➲ picture on study page **A28-29**.

**zy·de·co** /ˈzaɪdəˌkoʊ/ *noun* [U] a type of Cajun dance music, originally played by black Americans in southern Louisiana

# Irregular Verbs

In this list you will find the infinitive form of the verb followed by the past tense and the past participle. Where two forms are given, look up the verb in the main part of the dictionary to see whether there is a difference in meaning.

| Infinitive | Past Tense | Past Participle |
|---|---|---|
| **arise** | arose | arisen |
| **awake** | awoke | awoken |
| **be** | was/were | been |
| **bear** | bore | borne |
| **beat** | beat | beaten |
| **become** | became | become |
| **befall** | befell | befallen |
| **begin** | began | begun |
| **bend** | bent | bent |
| **bet** | bet | bet |
| **bid** | bid, bade | bid, bidden |
| **bind** | bound | bound |
| **bite** | bit | bitten |
| **bleed** | bled | bled |
| **blow** | blew | blown |
| **break** | broke | broken |
| **breed** | bred | bred |
| **bring** | brought | brought |
| **broadcast** | broadcast | broadcast |
| **build** | built | built |
| **burn** | burned, burnt | burned, burnt |
| **burst** | burst | burst |
| **buy** | bought | bought |
| **cast** | cast | cast |
| **catch** | caught | caught |
| **choose** | chose | chosen |
| **cling** | clung | clung |
| **come** | came | come |
| **cost** | cost | cost |
| **creep** | crept | crept |
| **cut** | cut | cut |
| **deal** | dealt | dealt |
| **dig** | dug | dug |
| **dive** | dived, dove | dived |
| **do** | did | done |
| **draw** | drew | drawn |
| **dream** | dreamed, dreamt | dreamed, dreamt |
| **drink** | drank | drunk |
| **drive** | drove | driven |
| **dwell** | dwelt, dwelled | dwelt, dwelled |
| **eat** | ate | eaten |
| **fall** | fell | fallen |
| **feed** | fed | fed |
| **feel** | felt | felt |
| **fight** | fought | fought |
| **find** | found | found |
| **flee** | fled | fled |
| **fling** | flung | flung |
| **fly** | flew | flown |
| **forbid** | forbade, forbad | forbidden |
| **forecast** | forecast, forecasted | forecast, forecasted |
| **foresee** | foresaw | foreseen |
| **foretell** | foretold | foretold |
| **forget** | forgot | forgotten |
| **forgive** | forgave | forgiven |
| **forgo** | forwent | forgone |
| **forsake** | forsook | forsaken |
| **freeze** | froze | frozen |
| **get** | got | gotten |
| **give** | gave | given |
| **go** | went | gone |
| **grind** | ground | ground |
| **grow** | grew | grown |
| **hang** | hung, hanged | hung, hanged |
| **have** | had | had |
| **hear** | heard | heard |
| **hide** | hid | hidden |
| **hit** | hit | hit |
| **hold** | held | held |
| **hurt** | hurt | hurt |
| **input** | input, inputted | input, inputted |
| **keep** | kept | kept |
| **kneel** | knelt, kneeled | knelt, kneeled |
| **know** | knew | known |
| **lay** | laid | laid |
| **lead** | led | led |
| **leap** | leaped, leapt | leaped, leapt |
| **leave** | left | left |
| **lend** | lent | lent |
| **let** | let | let |
| **lie**[3] | lay | lain |
| **light** | lit, lighted | lit, lighted |
| **lose** | lost | lost |
| **make** | made | made |
| **mean** | meant | meant |

| Infinitive | Past Tense | Past Participle |
|---|---|---|
| **meet** | met | met |
| **mislead** | misled | misled |
| **misread** | misread | misread |
| **mistake** | mistook | mistaken |
| **misunderstand** | misunderstood | misunderstood |
| **mow** | mowed | mown, mowed |
| **offset** | offset | offset |
| **outdo** | outdid | outdone |
| **outgrow** | outgrew | outgrown |
| **overcome** | overcame | overcome |
| **overdo** | overdid | overdone |
| **overhear** | overheard | overheard |
| **override** | overrode | overridden |
| **overrun** | overran | overrun |
| **oversee** | oversaw | overseen |
| **oversleep** | overslept | overslept |
| **overtake** | overtook | overtaken |
| **overthrow** | overthrew | overthrown |
| **pay** | paid | paid |
| **prove** | proved | proven, proved |
| **put** | put | put |
| **quit** | quit | quit |
| **read** | read | read |
| **rebuild** | rebuilt | rebuilt |
| **repay** | repaid | repaid |
| **rethink** | rethought | rethought |
| **rewind** | rewound | rewound |
| **rewrite** | rewrote | rewritten |
| **rid** | rid | rid |
| **ride** | rode | ridden |
| **ring** | rang | rung |
| **rise** | rose | risen |
| **run** | ran | run |
| **saw** | sawed | sawed, sawn |
| **say** | said | said |
| **see** | saw | seen |
| **seek** | sought | sought |
| **sell** | sold | sold |
| **send** | sent | sent |
| **set** | set | set |
| **sew** | sewed | sewn, sewed |
| **shake** | shook | shaken |
| **shear** | sheared | sheared, shorn |
| **shed** | shed | shed |
| **shine** | shone | shone |
| **shoot** | shot | shot |
| **show** | showed | shown, showed |
| **shrink** | shrank, shrunk | shrunk, shrunken |
| **shut** | shut | shut |
| **sing** | sang | sung |
| **sink** | sank | sunk |
| **sit** | sat | sat |
| **slay** | slew | slain |
| **sleep** | slept | slept |
| **slide** | slid | slid |
| **sling** | slung | slung |
| **slit** | slit | slit |
| **sneak** | sneaked, snuck | sneaked, snuck |
| **sow** | sowed | sown, sowed |
| **speak** | spoke | spoken |
| **speed** | sped | sped |
| **spell** | spelled, spelt | spelled, spelt |
| **spend** | spent | spent |
| **spin** | spun | spun |
| **spit** | spat, spit | spat, spit |
| **split** | split | split |
| **spread** | spread | spread |
| **spring** | sprang | sprung |
| **stand** | stood | stood |
| **steal** | stole | stolen |
| **stick** | stuck | stuck |
| **sting** | stung | stung |
| **stink** | stank, stunk | stunk |
| **stride** | strode | stridden |
| **strike** | struck | struck |
| **string** | strung | strung |
| **strive** | strove | striven |
| **swear** | swore | sworn |
| **sweep** | swept | swept |
| **swell** | swelled | swollen, swelled |
| **swim** | swam | swum |
| **swing** | swung | swung |
| **take** | took | taken |
| **teach** | taught | taught |
| **tear** | tore | torn |
| **tell** | told | told |
| **think** | thought | thought |
| **throw** | threw | thrown |
| **thrust** | thrust | thrust |
| **tread** | trod | trodden |
| **undercut** | undercut | undercut |
| **undergo** | underwent | undergone |
| **understand** | understood | understood |
| **undertake** | undertook | undertaken |
| **undo** | undid | undone |
| **unwind** | unwound | unwound |
| **uphold** | upheld | upheld |
| **upset** | upset | upset |
| **wake** | woke | woken |
| **wear** | wore | worn |
| **weave** | wove, weaved | woven, weaved |
| **weep** | wept | wept |
| **wet** | wet, wetted | wet, wetted |
| **win** | won | won |
| **wind**[2] | wound | wound |
| **withdraw** | withdrew | withdrawn |
| **withhold** | withheld | withheld |
| **withstand** | withstood | withstood |
| **wring** | wrung | wrung |
| **write** | wrote | written |

# List of prefixes and suffixes

## Prefixes

**a-** not: *atypical*
**anti-** against: *anti-American, antisocial*
**auto-** self: *autobiography* (= the story of the writer's own life)
**bi-** two: *bicycle, bilingual* (= using two languages), *bimonthly* (= twice a month or every two months)
**cent-**, **centi-** hundred: *centennial* (= the hundredth anniversary), *centimeter* (= one hundredth of a meter)
**circum-** around: circumnavigate (= sail around)
**co-** with; together: *copilot, coexist, cooperation*
**con-** with; together: context (= the words or sentences that come before and after a particular word or sentence)
**contra-** against; opposite: *contradict* (= say the opposite)
**counter-** against; opposite: *counter-revolution, counterproductive* (= producing the opposite of the desired effect)
**de-** taking sth away; the opposite: *defrost* (= removing the layers of ice from a fridge, etc.), *decentralize*
**deci-** one tenth: *deciliter*
**dis-** reverse or opposite: *displeasure, disembark, discomfort*
**ex-** former: *ex-wife, ex-president*
**extra-** **1** very; more than usual: *extra-thin, extra-special* **2** outside; beyond: *extraordinary, extraterrestrial* (= coming from somewhere beyond the earth)
**fore-** **1** before; in advance: *foretell* (= say what is going to happen), *foreword* (= at the beginning of a book) **2** front: *foreground* (= the front part of a picture), *forehead*
**in-** (**il-**, **im-**, **ir-**) not: *incorrect, invalid, illegal, illegible, immoral, impatient, impossible, irregular, irrelevant*
**inter-** between; from one to another: *international, interracial*
**kilo-** thousand: *kilogram, kilowatt*
**maxi-** most; very large: *maximum*
**mega-** million; very large: *megabyte, megabucks* (= a lot of money)
**micro-** millionth; very small: *microchip, microclimate* (= the climate of a small area)
**mid-** in the middle of: *mid-afternoon, midair*
**milli-** thousandth: *millisecond, millimeter*
**mini-** small: *miniskirt, miniseries*
**mis-** bad or wrong; not: *misbehave, miscalculate, misunderstand*
**mono-** one; single: *monolingual* (= using one language), *monorail*
**multi-** many: *multinational* (= involving many countries)
**non-** not: *nonalcoholic, nonsense, nonsmoker, nonstop*
**out-** more; to a greater degree: *outdo, outrun* (= run faster or better than sb)
**over-** more than normal; too much: *overeat, oversleep* (= sleep too long), *overestimate* (= guess too high)
**post-** after: *postwar*
**pre-** before: *prepay, preview*
**pro-** for; in favor of: *pro-democracy, pro-hunting*
**quad-** four: *quadruple* (= multiply by four), *quadruplet* (= one of four babies born at the same time)
**re-** again: *rewrite, rebuild*
**semi-** half: *semicircle, semiconscious*
**sub-** **1** below; less than: *subzero, subsonic* (= less than the speed of sound) **2** under: *subway, subtitles* (= translations under the pictures in a movie)
**super-** extremely; more than: *superhuman* (= having greater power than humans normally have), *supersonic* (= faster than the speed of sound)
**tele-** far; over a long distance: *telecommunications, telephoto lens*
**trans-** across; through: *transatlantic, transcontinental*
**tri-** three: *triangle, tricycle*
**ultra-** extremely; beyond a certain limit: *ultramodern, ultraviolet* (= light that is beyond what we can normally see)
**un-** not; opposite; taking sth away: *uncertain, uncomfortable, unsure, undo, undress*
**uni-** one; single: *uniform* (= having the same form)

## Suffixes

**-able**, **-ible**, **-ble** (to make adjectives); possible to ~: *acceptable, noticeable, convertible, divisible* (= possible to divide), *irresistible* (= that you cannot resist)

**-age** (to make nouns); a process or state: *storage, shortage*

**-al** (to make adjectives); connected with: *experimental, accidental, environmental*

**-ance**, **-ence**, (**-ancy**, **-ency**) (to make nouns); an action, process or state: *appearance, performance, importance, existence, intelligence, patience*

**-ant**, **-ent** (to make nouns); a person who does sth: *assistant, immigrant, student*

**-ation** (to make nouns); a state or action: *examination, imagination, organization*

**-ble** **-able**

**-ee** (to make nouns); a person to whom sth is done: *employee* (= sb who is employed), *trainee* (= sb who is being trained)

**-en** (to make verbs); to give sth a particular quality; to make sth more ~: *shorten, widen, blacken, sharpen, lossen,* (but note: *lengthen*)

**-ence** (**-ency**) **-ance**

**-ent** **-ant**

**-er** (to make nouns); a person who does sth: *rider, painter, baker, banker, driver, teacher*

**-ese** (to make adjectives); from a place: *Japanese, Chinese, Viennese*

**-ess** (to make nouns); a woman who does sth as a job: *waitress, actress*

**-ful** (to make adjectives); having a particular quality: *helpful, useful, thankful, beautiful*

**-hood** (to make nouns); **1** a state, often during a particular period of time: *childhood, motherhood* **2** a group with sth in common: *sisterhood, neighborhood*

**-ian** (to make nouns); a person who does sth as a job or hobby: *historian, comedian, politician*

**-ible** **-able**

**-ical** (to make adjectives from nouns ending in -y or -ics); connected with: *economical, mathematical, physical*

**-ify** (to make verbs); to produce a state or quality: *beautify, simplify, purify*

**-ish** (to make adjectives); **1** describing nationality or language: *English, Swedish, Polish* **2** like sth: *babyish, foolish* **3** fairly, sort of: *longish, youngish, brownish*

**-ist** (to make nouns); **1** a person who has studied sth or does sth as a job: *artist, scientist, economist* **2** a person who believes in sth or belongs to a particular group: *capitalist, pacifist, feminist*

**-ion** (to make nouns); a state or process: *action, connection, exhibition*

**-ive** (to make adjectives); able to ~, having a particular quality: *attractive, effective*

**-ize** (to make verbs); actions producing a particular state: *magnetize, standardize, modernize, generalize*

**-less** (to make adjectives); not having sth: *hopeless, friendless*

**-like** (to make adjectives); similar to: *childlike*

**-ly** (to make adverbs); in a particular way: *badly, beautifully, completely*

**-ment** (to make nouns); a state, action or quality: *development, arrangement, excitement, achievement*

**-ness** (to make nouns); a state or quality: *kindness, happiness, weakness*

**-ology** (to make nouns); the study of a subject: *biology, psychology, zoology*

**-or** (to make nouns); a person who does sth, often as a job: *actor, conductor, sailor*

**-ous** (to make adjectives); having a particular quality: *dangerous, religious, ambitious*

**-ship** (to make nouns); showing status: *friendship, membership, citizenship*

**-ward**, **-wards** (to make adverbs); in a particular direction: *backward, upward*

**-wise** (to make adverbs); in a particular way: *clockwise, edgewise*

**-y** (to make adjectives); having the quality of the thing mentioned: *cloudy, rainy, fatty, thirsty*

# Punctuation

## Period (.)

A **period** (.) is used at the end of a sentence, unless the sentence is a question or an exclamation:

*We went shopping.*
*He tried to go.*
*That's enough.*

It is also used after an abbreviation:

*Mr. Smith*  *Emerdale St.*  *etc.*  *a.m.*

## Question mark (?)

A **question mark** (?) is used at the end of a direct question:

*How old are you?*
*"When did they go?" Todd asked.*

It is not used after an indirect question:

*Todd asked when they went.*

## Exclamation point (!)

An **exclamation point** (!) is used with sentences that express strong emotion, such as surprise, enthusiasm, excitement, shock or horror:

*I can't believe it!*
*That man stole my purse!*
*Oh no!*
*That's wonderful!*

or after an interjection:

*Bye!*  *Ouch!*

## Comma (,)

A **comma** (,) separates items in a series. When and is used before the last item in a series, the comma that comes before and is optional:

*He liked to hunt, fish, hike, and climb.*
*I would like to visit France, Spain and Portugal.*

Commas are always used between three or more adjectives where and is not used:

*It was a warm, balmy, starlit night.*

Commas are also used to separate different parts of a sentence:

*He wanted to go, but didn't have time.*
*Although she is small, she is very strong.*

Commas appear before or around extra information in a relative clause or in a sentence:

*They don't like our dog, which barks constantly.*
*Shakespeare, the English playwright, is well-known throughout the world.*

A comma also usually comes before or after a quotation:

*David said, "I'll see you on Saturday."*
*"I'll see you on Saturday," David said, "at about 8 o'clock."*

and goes before or after a name when a person is being spoken to directly:

*Stuart, would you like to go?*
*I'm sorry, Mark.*

It also comes before tag questions:

*You don't have any, do you?*
*She's a doctor, isn't she?*

Commas also separate cities and towns from states:

*Des Moines, Iowa*  *Juneau, Alaska*
*San Francisco, California*

## Colon (:)

A **colon** (:) is used to introduce explanations, long quotations or a series:

*The girl had four pets: a dog, a cat, a horse, and a turtle.*
*The school offered several language courses: French, German, Spanish, and Russian.*

It is also used after the salutation in a formal letter:

*Dear Mr. Howard:*  *Dear Ms. Leigh:*
*Dear Sir/Madam:*

## Semicolon (;)

A **semicolon** (;) is used to separate two contrasting parts of a sentence:

*Humans use moral judgment; animals do not.*

It is also used in a series that already has commas within it:

*The menu featured hamburger, potato, and carrot casserole; and pecan pie.*

## Apostrophy (')

An **apostrophe** (') shows that one or more letters are missing in a short form:

*we've don't he's I'm they're*

It also shows that a person or thing belongs to someone:

*Janet's car Cynthia's keys John's sister*

With names that end in "s", you do can choose whether to add another "s" after the apostrophe to show possession:

*James' teacher or James's teacher*
(both are correct)

Note that with possessives, the apostrophe goes after the "s" if the noun is plural:

*the student's apartment*
(the apartment belonging to one student)
*the students' apartment*
(the apartment shared by several students)

## Quotation marks (" ")

**Quotation marks** (" ") are used to show what someone said:

*"Let's see a movie," Roger suggested.*
*Sylvia said, "I don't remember her name."*

or thoughts that are presented like speech:

*"Where did I put my keys?" I wondered.*
*"I should leave now," she thought.*

Quotation marks are also used around the titles of essays, songs, poems, etc. that are part of other works:

*They always play "The Star-Spangled Banner" before baseball games.*

They are also used to draw attention to a word or a phrase that is intended to be ironic:

*The "new" bride was recently married – to her seventh husband.*

## Hyphen (-)

A **hyphen** (-) connects two or more words that form one idea:

*a twelve-year-old boy*
*a well-known politician*

It sometimes, but not always, joins a prefix to a word:

*pro-Communist*
*anti-American*
*pre-packaged food*

A hyphen is also used with compound numbers:

*ninety-nine*
*twenty-seven*
*sixty-two*

You can also use a hyphen at the end of a line if you need to divide a word and write part of it on the next line:

*Though I had known her since we were children, I was hardly able to recognize her after ten years.*

## Dash (–)

A **dash** (–) separates a word or phrase from the rest of a sentence. It is often used near the end of a sentence to sum up or emphasize an idea:

*I lost my keys, forgot my homework, and missed a class – it was an awful day.*
*Art is about creativity, magic, dreams, illusion – and money.*

A dash can also be used before and after a phrase that gives extra information:

*I ran into her in – of all places – Denmark.*
*I got married – against my family's wishes – to Jim last June.*

It also shows that an idea has been interrupted mid-sentence or mid-thought:

*If only she would love me, I would – Oh, what's the use? It will never happen.*

## Parentheses ()

**Parentheses** () separate extra information from the rest of the sentence:

*The recipe calls for 1 pound (450 grams) of flour.*
*Howard ( the smallest boy in his class) was hurt playing football.*

Numbers and letters used in sentences, particularly with lists or choices, may have a parenthesis after them or parentheses around them:

*Airplanes have revolutionized travel by:*
*1) cutting travel time drastically,*
*2) providing a relatively cheap form of transportation, and 3) reducing the dangers of long-distance travel.*
*If you had a choice, would you rather live in (a) China, (b) Russia, (c) America or (d) France?*

# The United States and Canada

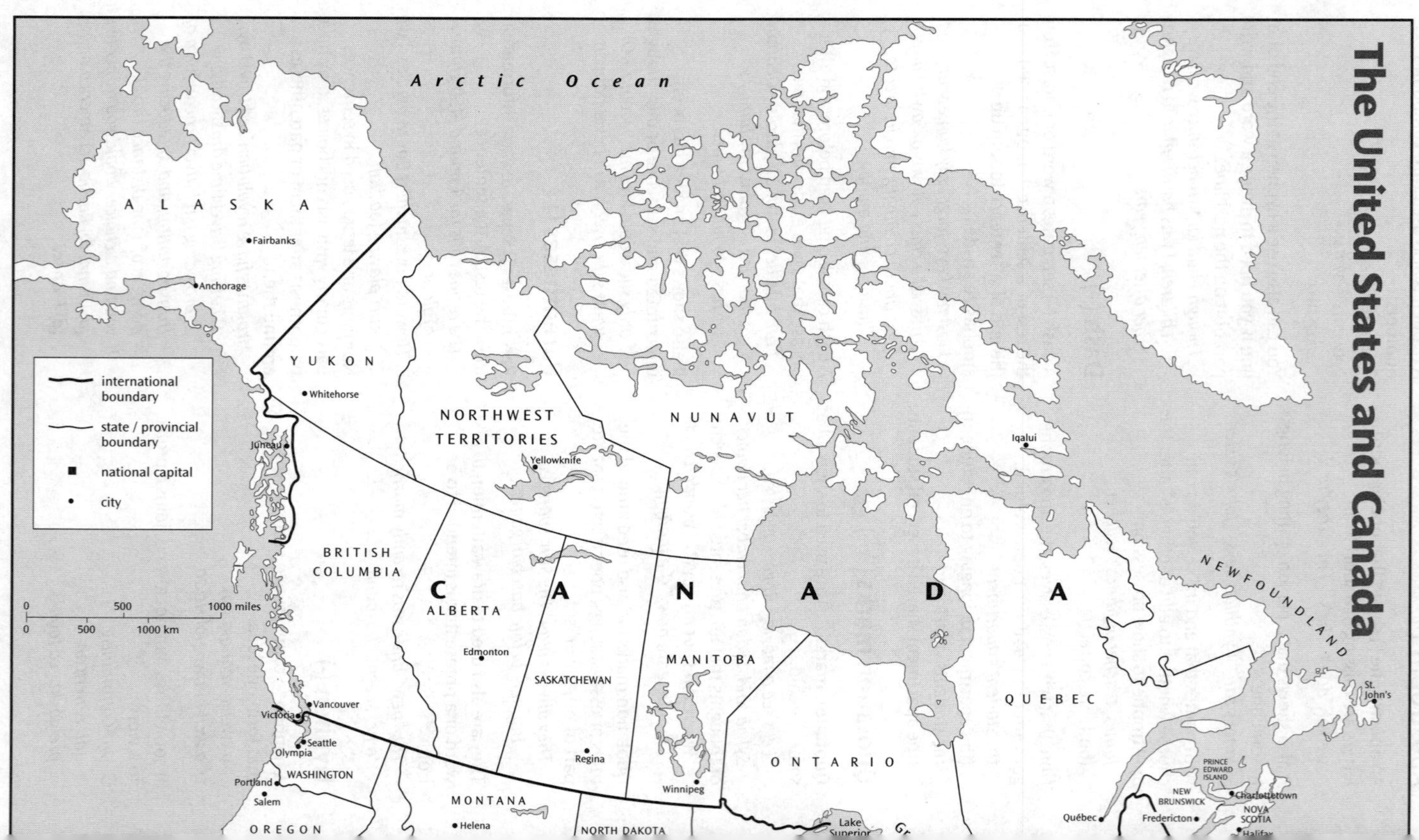

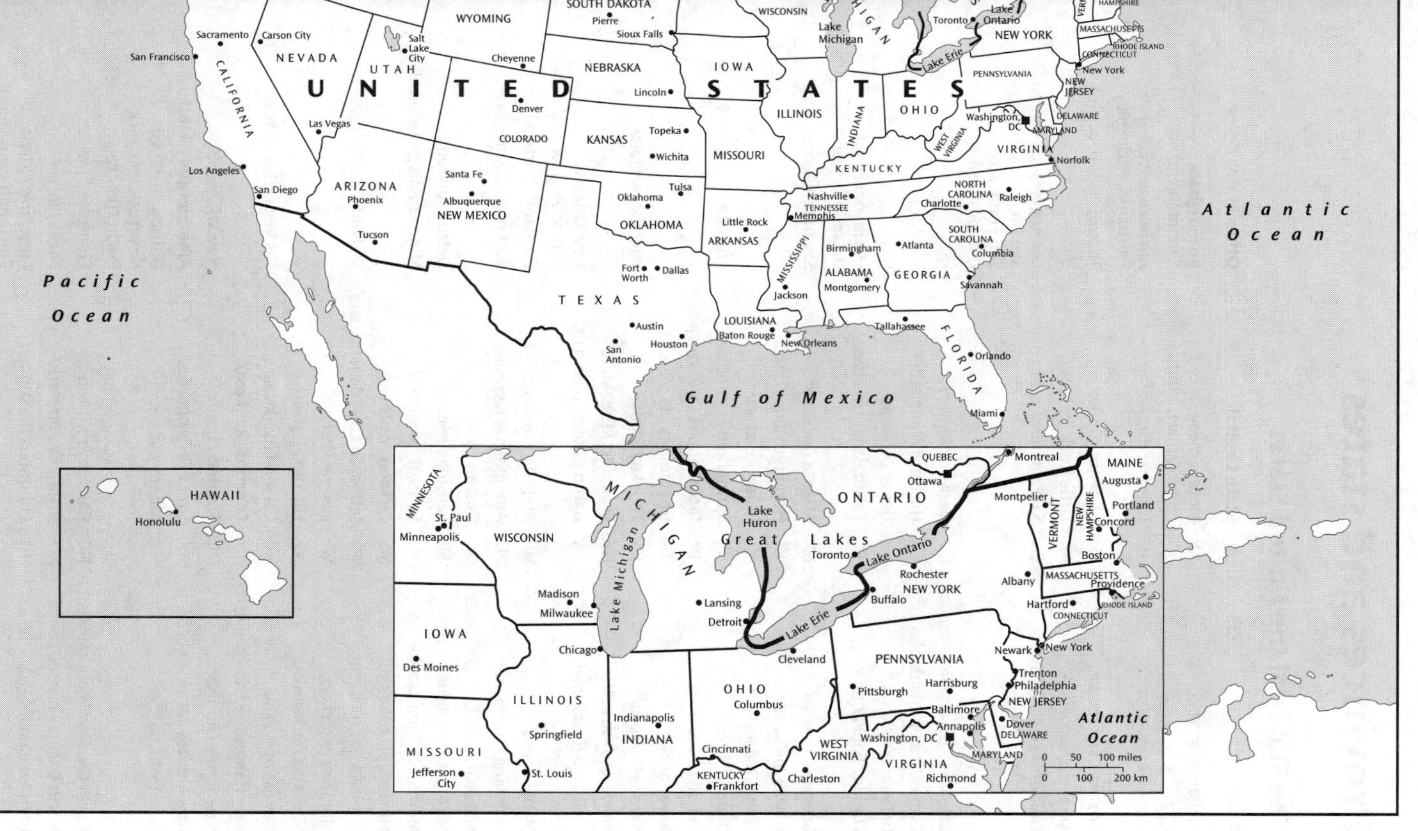

UNITED STATES
Pacific Ocean
Atlantic Ocean
Gulf of Mexico
CALIFORNIA
San Francisco
Sacramento
Los Angeles
San Diego
NEVADA
Carson City
Las Vegas
UTAH
Salt Lake City
ARIZONA
Phoenix
Tucson
WYOMING
Cheyenne
COLORADO
Denver
NEW MEXICO
Santa Fe
Albuquerque
SOUTH DAKOTA
Pierre
Sioux Falls
NEBRASKA
Lincoln
KANSAS
Topeka
Wichita
OKLAHOMA
Oklahoma
Tulsa
TEXAS
Fort Worth
Dallas
Austin
San Antonio
Houston
IOWA
MISSOURI
ARKANSAS
Little Rock
LOUISIANA
Baton Rouge
New Orleans
WISCONSIN
Lake Michigan
MICHIGAN
ILLINOIS
INDIANA
KENTUCKY
TENNESSEE
Nashville
Memphis
MISSISSIPPI
Jackson
ALABAMA
Birmingham
Montgomery
GEORGIA
Atlanta
Savannah
FLORIDA
Tallahassee
Orlando
Miami
SOUTH CAROLINA
Columbia
NORTH CAROLINA
Charlotte
Raleigh
VIRGINIA
Norfolk
WEST VIRGINIA
OHIO
Lake Erie
Toronto
Lake Ontario
NEW YORK
PENNSYLVANIA
Washington, DC
MARYLAND
DELAWARE
NEW JERSEY
New York
CONNECTICUT
RHODE ISLAND
MASSACHUSETTS
NEW HAMPSHIRE
HAWAII
Honolulu
QUEBEC
Montreal
Ottawa
ONTARIO
MAINE
Augusta
Portland
Concord
Montpelier
VERMONT
Boston
Albany
Providence
Hartford
Lake Huron
Great Lakes
Lake Ontario
Rochester
Buffalo
Lansing
Detroit
Cleveland
MINNESOTA
St. Paul
Minneapolis
Madison
Milwaukee
Chicago
Des Moines
Springfield
St. Louis
Jefferson City
Indianapolis
Columbus
Cincinnati
KENTUCKY
Frankfort
Charleston
Pittsburgh
Harrisburg
Baltimore
Annapolis
Richmond
Trenton
Philadelphia
Newark
Dover
Atlantic Ocean
0 50 100 miles
0 100 200 km

# Provinces and states

## The States of the United States

| State | abbreviation | State Capital | Other Major Cities |
|---|---|---|---|
| Alabama /ˌæləˈbæmə/ | AL | **Montgomery** /məntˈgʌməri, mɑnt-/ | **Birmingham** /ˈbərmɪŋhæm/ |
| Alaska /əˈlæskə/ | AK | **Juneau** /ˈdʒunoʊ/ | **Anchorage** /ˈæŋkərɪdʒ/<br>**Fairbanks** /ˈfɛrbæŋks/ |
| Arizona /ˌærəˈzoʊnə/ | AZ | **Phoenix** /ˈfinɪks/ | **Tucson** /ˈtusɑn, tuˈsɑn/ |
| Arkansas /ˈɑrkənsɔ/ | AR | **Little Rock** /ˈlɪt̬l rɑk/ | |
| California /ˌkæləˈfɔrnyə/ | CA | **Sacramento** /ˌsækrəˈmɛntoʊ/ | **Los Angeles** /lɔs ˈændʒələs/<br>**San Diego** /ˌsæn diˈeɪgoʊ/<br>**San Francisco** /ˌsæn frənˈsɪskoʊ/ |
| Colorado /ˌkɑləˈrædoʊ, -ˈrɑdoʊ/ | CO | **Denver** /ˈdɛnvər/ | |
| Connecticut /kəˈnɛt̬ɪkət/ | CT | **Hartford** /ˈhɑrtfərd/ | |
| Delaware /ˈdɛləwɛr/ | DE | **Dover** /ˈdoʊvər/ | |
| Florida /ˈflɔrədə, ˈflɑr-/ | FL | Tallahassee /ˌtæləˈhæsi/ | **Miami** /maɪˈæmi/<br>**Orlando** /ɔrˈlændoʊ/ |
| Georgia /ˈdʒɔrdʒə/ | GA | **Atlanta** /ətˈlæntə/ | **Savannah** /səˈvænə/ |
| Hawaii /həˈwaɪi/ | HI | **Honolulu** /ˌhɑnəˈlulu/ | |
| Idaho /ˈaɪdəhoʊ/ | ID | **Boise** /ˈbɔɪzi, -si/ | |
| Illinois /ˌɪləˈnɔɪ/ | IL | **Springfield** /ˈsprɪŋfild/ | **Chicago** /ʃɪˈkɑgoʊ, -ˈkɔgoʊ/ |
| Indiana /ˌɪndiˈænə/ | IN | **Indianapolis** /ˌɪndiəˈnæpələs/ | |
| Iowa /ˈaɪəwə/ | IA | **Des Moines** /də ˈmɔɪn/ | |
| Kansas /ˈkænzəs/ | KS | **Topeka** /təˈpikə/ | **Wichita** /ˈwɪtʃətɔ/ |
| Kentucky /kənˈtʌki/ | KY | **Frankfort** /ˈfræŋkfərt/ | |
| Louisiana /luˌiziˈænə/ | LA | **Baton Rouge** /ˌbætn ˈruʒ/ | **New Orleans** /ˌnu ˈɔrlənz, -ˈɔrlinz/ |
| Maine /meɪn/ | ME | **Augusta** /ɔˈgʌstə, ə-/ | **Portland** /ˈpɔrtlənd/ |
| Maryland /ˈmɛrələnd/ | MD | **Annapolis** /əˈnæpələs/ | **Baltimore** /ˈbɔltəmɔr/ |
| Massachusetts /ˌmæsəˈtʃusəts/ | MA | **Boston** /ˈbɔstən/ | |
| Michigan /ˈmɪʃɪgən/ | MI | **Lansing** /ˈlænsɪŋ/ | **Detroit** /dɪˈtrɔɪt/ |
| Minnesota /ˌmɪnəˈsoʊt̬ə/ | MN | **St. Paul** /ˌseɪnt ˈpɔl/ | **Minneapolis** /ˌmɪniˈæpələs/ |
| Mississippi /ˌmɪsəˈsɪpi/ | MS | **Jackson** /ˈdʒæksn/ | |
| Missouri /məˈzʊri, -ˈzʊrə/ | MO | **Jefferson City** /ˌdʒɛfərsn ˈsɪt̬i/ | **St. Louis** /ˌseɪnt ˈluəs/ |
| Montana /mɑnˈtænə/ | MT | **Helena** /ˈhɛlənə/ | |
| Nebraska /nəˈbræskə/ | NE | **Lincoln** /ˈlɪŋkən/ | |
| Nevada /nəˈvædə, -ˈvɑdə/ | NV | **Carson City** /ˌkɑrsn ˈsɪt̬i/ | **Las Vegas** /lɑs ˈveɪgəs/ |
| New Hampshire /ˌnu ˈhæmpʃər/ | NH | **Concord** /ˈkɑŋkərd/ | |
| New Jersey /ˌnu ˈdʒərzi/ | NJ | **Trenton** /ˈtrɛntn/ | **Newark** /ˈnuərk/ |
| New Mexico /ˌnu ˈmɛksɪkoʊ/ | NM | **Santa Fe** /ˌsæntə ˈfeɪ/ | **Albuquerque** /ˈælbəkərki/ |
| New York /ˌnu ˈyɔrk/ | NY | **Albany** /ˈɔlbəni/ | **Buffalo** /ˈbʌfəloʊ/<br>**New York** /ˌnu ˈyɔrk/<br>**Rochester** /ˈrɑtʃəstər, -tʃɛs-/ |
| North Carolina /ˌnɔrθ kærəˈlaɪnə/ | NC | **Raleigh** /ˈrɔli, ˈrɑli/ | **Charlotte** /ˈʃɑrlət/ |
| North Dakota /ˌnɔrθ dəˈkoʊt̬ə/ | ND | **Bismarck** /ˈbɪzmɑrk/ | **Fargo** /ˈfɑrgoʊ/ |
| Ohio /oʊˈhaɪoʊ/ | OH | **Columbus** /kəˈlʌmbəs/ | **Cleveland** /ˈklivlənd/<br>**Cincinnati** /ˌsɪnsəˈnæt̬i/ |

| State | abbreviation | State Capital | Other Major Cities |
|---|---|---|---|
| Oklahoma /ˌoʊkləˈhoʊmə/ | OK | Oklahoma City /ˌoʊkləhoʊmə ˈsɪţi/ | Tulsa /ˈtʌlsə/ |
| Oregon /ˈɔrəgən, ˈɑr-, -gɑn/ | OR | Salem /ˈseɪləm/ | Portland /ˈpɔrtlənd/ |
| Pennsylvania /ˌpɛnslˈveɪnyə/ | PA | Harrisburg /ˈhærəsbərg/ | Philadelphia /ˌfɪləˈdɛlfiə/<br>Pittsburgh /ˈpɪtsbərg/ |
| Rhode Island /ˌroʊd ˈaɪlənd/ | RI | Providence /ˈprɑvədəns/ | |
| South Carolina /ˌsaʊθ kærəˈlaɪnə/ | SC | Columbia /kəˈlʌmbiə/ | |
| South Dakota /ˌsaʊθ dəˈkoʊţə/ | SD | Pierre /pɪr/ | Sioux Falls /ˌsu ˈfɔlz/ |
| Tennessee /ˌtɛnəˈsi/ | TN | Nashville /ˈnæʃvɪl/ | Memphis /ˈmɛmfəs/ |
| Texas /ˈtɛksəs/ | TX | Austin /ˈɔstən/ | Dallas /ˈdæləs/<br>Fort Worth /ˌfɔrt ˈwərθ/<br>Houston /ˈhyustən/<br>San Antonio /ˌsæn ænˈtoʊnioʊ/ |
| Utah /ˈyutɔ, ˈyutɑ/ | UT | Salt Lake City /ˌsɔlt leɪk ˈsɪţi/ | |
| Vermont /vərˈmɑnt/ | VT | Montpelier /mɑntˈpilyər/ | |
| Virginia /vərˈdʒɪnyə/ | VA | Richmond /ˈrɪtʃmənd/ | Norfolk /ˈnɔrfək/ |
| Washington /ˈwɑʃɪŋtən, ˈwɔ-/ | WA | Olympia /əˈlɪmpiə/ | Seattle /siˈæţl/ |
| West Virginia /ˌwɛst vərˈdʒɪnyə/ | WV | Charleston /ˈtʃɑrlstən/ | |
| Wisconsin /wɪsˈkɑnsn/ | WI | Madison /ˈmædəsn/ | Milwaukee /mɪlˈwɔki/ |
| Wyoming /waɪˈoʊmɪŋ/ | WY | Cheyenne /ʃaɪˈæn/ | |

## The Great Lakes

Lake Erie /ˌleɪk ˈɪri/
Lake Huron /ˌleɪk ˈhyʊrɑn, -ən/
Lake Michigan /ˌleɪk ˈmɪʃɪgən/
Lake Ontario /ˌleɪk ɑnˈtɛrioʊ/
Lake Superior /ˌleɪk səˈpɪriər/

## The Provinces and territories of Canada

| Province/territory | Provincial/territorial Capital | Other Major Cities |
|---|---|---|
| Alberta /ælˈbərţə/ | Edmonton /ˈɛdməntən/ | |
| British Columbia /ˌbrɪţɪʃ kəˈlʌmbiə/ | Victoria /vɪkˈtɔriə/ | Vancouver /vænˈkuvər/ |
| Manitoba /ˌmænəˈtoʊbə/ | Winnipeg /ˈwɪnəpɛg/ | |
| New Brunswick /ˌnu ˈbrʌnzwɪk/ | Fredericton /ˈfrɛdrɪktən/ | |
| Newfoundland /ˈnufənlənd, -fənd-/ | St. John's /ˌseɪnt ˈdʒɑnz/ | |
| Northwest Territories /ˌnɔrθwɛst ˈtɛrətɔriz/ | Yellowknife /ˈyɛloʊnaɪf/ | |
| Nova Scotia /ˌnoʊvə ˈskoʊʃə/ | Halifax /ˈhæləfæks/ | |
| Ontario /ɑnˈtɛrioʊ/ | Toronto /təˈrɑntoʊ/ | Ottawa /ˈɑţəwə/ |
| Prince Edward Island /ˌprɪns ˌɛdwərd ˈaɪlənd/ | Charlottetown /ˈʃɑrləttaʊn/ | |
| Quebec /kwɪˈbɛk/ | Quebec /kwɪˈbɛk/ | Montreal /ˌmɑntriˈɔl, ˌmʌn/ |
| Saskatchewan /sæˈskætʃəwən, -wɑn/ | Regina /rɪˈdʒaɪnə/ | |
| Yukon Territory /ˌyukɑn ˈtɛrətɔri/ | Whitehorse /ˈwaɪthɔrs/ | |

# Geographical names



This list shows the English spelling and pronunciation of geographical names and the adjectives that go with them. If there are different words for the adjective and the person, both are given, e.g. **Denmark**: **Danish**; **Dane**.

To make the plural of a word for a person from a particular country, add **-s**, except for **Swiss** and words ending in **-ese** (such as **Japanese**), which stay the same, and for words that end in **-man** or **-woman**, which change to **-men** or **-women**, e.g. *three Frenchmen; two Englishwomen*.

If there is a different word for all the people as a group, this is given in parentheses: **France: French; Frenchman, Frenchwoman; (the French)**.

**Inclusion in this list does not imply status as a sovereign nation.**

| Noun | Adjective; Person |
|---|---|
| **Afghanistan** /æf'gænəstæn/ | **Afghan** /'æfgæn/; **Afghani** /æf'gæni/ |
| **Africa** /æfrɪkə/ | **African** /'æfrɪkən/ |
| **Albania** /æl'beɪniə/ | **Albanian** /æl'beɪniən/ |
| **Algeria** /æl'dʒɪriə/ | **Algerian** /æl'dʒɪriən/ |
| **America** /ə'mɛrɪkə/ → **(the) United States of America** | |
| **Andorra** /æn'dɔrə/ | **Andorran** /æn'dɔrən/ |
| **Angola** /æŋ'goʊlə/ | **Angolan** /æŋ'goʊlən/ |
| **Antarctica** /ænt'ɑrktɪkə; -'ɑrt̬ɪkə/ | **Antarctic** /ænt'ɑrktɪk; -'ɑrt̬ɪk/ |
| **Antigua and Barbuda** /ænˌtigə ən bɑr'budə; -ˌtigwə-/ | **Antiguan** /æn'tigən; -gwən/, **Barbudan** /bɑr'budn/ |
| (the) **Arctic** /'ɑrktɪk; 'ɑrt̬ɪk/ | **Arctic** /'ɑrktɪk; 'ɑrt̬ɪk/ |
| **Argentina** /ˌɑrdʒən'tinə/ | **Argentine** /'ɑrdʒəntin; - taɪn/<br>**Argentinian** /ˌɑrdʒən'tɪniən/ |
| **Armenia** /ɑr'miniə/ | **Armenian** /ɑr'miniən/ |
| **Asia** /'eɪʒə/ | **Asian** /'eɪʒn/ |
| **Australia** /ɔ'streɪlyə/ | **Australian** /ɔ'streɪlyən/ |
| **Austria** /'ɔstriə/ | **Austrian** /'ɔstriən/ |
| **Azerbaijan** /ˌæzərbaɪ'dʒɑn; ˌɑzər-/ | **Azerbaijani** /ˌæzərbaɪ'dʒɑni; ˌɑzər-/,<br>an **Azeri** /ə'zɛri/ |
| (the) **Bahamas** /bə'hɑməz/ | **Bahamian** /bə'heɪmiən/ |
| **Bahrain** /bɑ'reɪn/ | **Bahraini** /bɑ'reɪni/ |
| **Bangladesh** /ˌbɑŋglə'dɛʃ; ˌbæŋ-/ | **Bangladeshi** /ˌbɑŋglə'dɛʃi; ˌbæŋ-/ |
| **Barbados** /bɑr'beɪdoʊs/ | **Barbadian** /bɑr'beɪdiən/ |
| **Belarus** /ˌbyɛlə'rus; ˌbilə-/ | **Belorussian** /ˌbyɛlə'rʌʃn; ˌbilə-/ |
| **Belgium** /'bɛldʒəm/ | **Belgian** /'bɛldʒən/ |
| **Benin** /bə'nin/ | **Beninese** /bəˌni'niz; ˌbɛnə'niz/ |
| **Bhutan** /bu'tɑn/ | **Bhutanese** /ˌbutn'iz/ |
| **Bolivia** /bə'lɪviə/ | **Bolivian** /bə'lɪviən/ |
| **Bosnia-Herzegovina** /ˌbɑzniə ˌhɛrtsəgoʊ'vinə/ | **Bosnian** /'bɑzniən/ |
| **Botswana** /bɑt'swɑnə/ | **Botswanan** /bɑt'swɑnən/, person: **Motswana** /mɑt'swɑnə/, people: **Batswana** /bæt'swɑnə/ |
| **Brazil** /brə'zɪl/ | **Brazilian** /brə'zɪlyən/ |
| **Brunei Darussalam** /bruˌnaɪ ˌdɑrusə'lɑm/ | **Bruneian** /bru'naɪən/ |
| **Bulgaria** /bʌl'gɛriə/ | **Bulgarian** /bʌl'gɛriən/ |
| **Burkina** /bər'kinə/ | **Burkinese** /ˌbərkə'niz/ |
| **Burma** /'bərmə/ (now officially **Myanmar**) | **Burmese** /ˌbər'miz/ |
| **Burundi** /bʊ'rʊndi; -'run-/ | **Burundian** /bʊ'rʊndiən; -'run-/ |
| **Cambodia** /kæm'boʊdiə/ | **Cambodian** /kæm'boʊdiən/ |
| **Cameroon** /ˌkæmə'run / | **Cameroonian** /ˌkæmə'runiən/ |
| **Canada** /'kænədə/ | **Canadian** /kə'neɪdiən/ |
| **Cape Verde** /ˌkeɪp 'vərd/ | **Cape Verdean** /ˌkeɪp 'vərdiən/ |
| (the) **Central African Republic** /ˌsɛntrəl ˌæfrɪkən rɪ'pʌblɪk/ | **Central African** /ˌsɛntrəl 'æfrɪkən/ |
| **Chad** /tʃæd/ | **Chadian** /'tʃædiən/ |

| Noun | Adjective; Person |
|---|---|
| Chile /ˈtʃɪli/ | Chilean /ˈtʃɪliən; tʃɪˈleɪən/ |
| China /ˈtʃaɪnə/ | Chinese /ˌtʃaɪˈniz/ |
| Colombia /kəˈlʌmbiə/ | Colombian /kəˈlʌmbiən/ |
| Comoros /ˈkɑmərouz/ | Comoran /ˈkɑmərən; kəˈmɔrən/ |
| Congo /ˈkɑŋgoʊ/ | Congolese /ˌkɑŋgəˈliz/ |
| Costa Rica /ˌkoʊstə ˈrikə; ˌkɑstə-/ | Costa Rican /ˌkoʊstə ˈrikən; ˌkɑstə-/ |
| Côte d'Ivoire /ˌkoʊt diˈvwɑr/ | Ivorian /aɪˈvɔriən/ |
| Croatia /kroʊˈeɪʃə/ | Croatian /kroʊˈeɪʃn/ |
| Cuba /ˈkyubə/ | Cuban /ˈkyubən/ |
| Cyprus /ˈsaɪprəs/ | Cypriot /ˈsɪpriət/ |
| (the) Czech Republic /ˌtʃɛk rɪˈpʌblɪk/ | Czech /tʃɛk/ |
| (the) Democratic Republic of the Congo /dɛməˌkræt̬ɪk rɪˌpʌblɪk əv ðə ˈkɑŋgoʊ/ | Congolese /ˌkɑŋgəˈliz/ |
| Denmark /ˈdɛnmɑrk/ | Danish /ˈdeɪnɪʃ/, a Dane /deɪn/ |
| Djibouti /dʒɪˈbut̬i/ | Djiboutian /dʒɪˈbut̬iən/ |
| Dominica /ˌdɑməˈnikə/ | Dominican /dəˈmɪnɪkən/ |
| (the) Dominican Republic /dəˌmɪnɪkən rɪˈpʌblɪk/ | Dominican /dəˈmɪnɪkən/ |
| East Timor /ˌist ˈtimɔr; tiˈmɔr/ | East Timorese /ˌist tɪməˈriz/ |
| Ecuador /ˈɛkwədɔr/ | Ecuadorian /ˌɛkwəˈdɔriən/ |
| Egypt /ˈidʒɪpt/ | Egyptian /ɪˈdʒɪpʃn/ |
| El Salvador /ɛl ˈsælvədɔr/ | Salvadorean /ˌsælvəˈdɔriən/ |
| England /ˈɪŋglənd/ | English /ˈɪŋglɪʃ/, an Englishman /ˈɪŋglɪʃmən/, an Englishwoman /ˈɪŋglɪʃˌwʊmən/ |
| Equatorial Guinea /ˌikwəˌtɔriəl ˈgɪni; ˌɛkwə-/ | Equatorial Guinean /ˌikwəˌtɔriəl ˈgɪniən; ˌɛkwə-/ |
| Eritrea /ˌɛrəˈtriə/ | Eritrean /ˌɛrəˈtriən/ |
| Estonia /ɛˈstoʊniə/ | Estonian /ɛˈstoʊniən/ |
| Ethiopia /ˌiθiˈoʊpiə/ | Ethiopian /ˌiθiˈoʊpiən/ |
| Europe /ˈyʊrəp/ | European /ˌyʊrəˈpiən/ |
| Fiji /ˈfidʒi/ | Fijian /ˈfidʒiən/ |
| Finland /ˈfɪnlənd/ | Finnish /ˈfɪnɪʃ/, a Finn /fɪn/ |
| France /fræns/ | French /frɛntʃ/, a Frenchman /ˈfrɛntʃmən/, a Frenchwoman /ˈfrɛntʃˌwʊmən/ |
| (the) Former Yugoslav Republic of Macedonia /ˌfɔrmər ˌyugəslɑv rɪˈpʌblɪk əv ˌmæsəˈdoʊniə/ | Macedonian /ˌmæsəˈdoʊniən/ |
| Gabon /gæˈboʊn/ | Gabonese /ˌgæbəˈniz/ |
| (the) Gambia /ˈgæmbiə/ | Gambian /ˈgæmbiən/ |
| Georgia /ˈdʒɔrdʒə/ | Georgian /ˈdʒɔrdʒən/ |
| Germany /ˈdʒərməni/ | German /ˈdʒərmən/ |
| Ghana /ˈgɑnə/ | Ghanaian /gɑˈneɪən/ |
| Great Britain /ˌgreɪt ˈbrɪtn/ | British /ˈbrɪt̬ɪʃ/, a Briton /ˈbrɪtn/ |
| Greece /gris/ | Greek /grik/ |
| Grenada /grəˈneɪdə/ | Grenadian /grəˈneɪdiən/ |
| Guatemala /ˌgwɑt̬əˈmɑlə/ | Guatemalan /ˌgwɑt̬əˈmɑlən/ |
| Guinea /ˈgɪni/ | Guinean /ˈgɪniən/ |
| Guinea-Bissau /ˌgɪni bɪˈsaʊ/ | Guinean /ˈgɪniən/ |
| Guyana /gaɪˈænə/ | Guyanese /ˌgaɪəˈniz/ |
| Haiti /ˈheɪt̬i/ | Haitian /ˈheɪʃn/ |
| Holland /ˈhɑlənd/ → (the) Netherlands | |
| Honduras /hɑnˈdʊrəs/ | Honduran /hɑnˈdʊrən/ |
| Hungary /ˈhʌŋgəri/ | Hungarian /hʌŋˈgɛriən/ |
| Iceland /ˈaɪslənd/ | Icelandic /aɪsˈlændɪk/, an Icelander /ˈaɪslændər/ |
| India /ˈɪndiə/ | Indian /ˈɪndiən/ |
| Indonesia /ˌɪndəˈniʒə/ | Indonesian /ˌɪndəˈniʒn/ |
| Iran /ɪˈrɑn; ɪˈræn/ | Iranian /ɪˈreɪniən/ |
| Iraq /ɪˈrɑk; ɪˈræk/ | Iraqi /ɪˈrɑki; ɪˈræki/ |
| Ireland /ˈaɪərlənd/ | Irish /ˈaɪrɪʃ/, an Irishman, /ˈaɪrɪʃmən/, an Irishwoman /ˈaɪrɪʃˌwʊmən/ |
| Israel /ˈɪzreɪl; ˈɪzriəl/ | Israeli /ɪzˈreɪli/ |
| Italy /ˈɪt̬l·i/ | Italian /ɪˈtælyən/ |
| (the) Ivory Coast /ˌaɪvri ˈkoʊst; ˌaɪvəri-/ → Côte d'Ivoire | |

| Noun | Adjective; Person |
|---|---|
| Jamaica /dʒə'meɪkə/ | Jamaican /dʒə'meɪkən/ |
| Japan /dʒə'pæn/ | Japanese /ˌdʒæpə'niz/ |
| Jordan /'dʒɔrdn/ | Jordanian /dʒɔr'demiən/ |
| Kazakhstan /ˌkɑzɑk'stɑn; ˌkæzæk'stæn/ | Kazakh /kə'zɑk; -'zæk/ |
| Kenya /'kɛnyə; 'kin-/ | Kenyan /'kɛnyən; 'kin-/ |
| Kiribati /'kɪrəbæs/ | Kiribati /'kɪrəbæs/ |
| Korea, North /ˌnɔrθ kə'rɪə/ | North Korean /ˌnɔrθ kə'riən/ |
| Korea, South /ˌsaʊθ kə'rɪə/ | South Korean /ˌsaʊθ kə'riən/ |
| Kuwait /ku'weɪt/ | Kuwaiti /ku'weɪt̬i/ |
| Kyrgyzstan /ˌkɪrgɪ'stɑn/ | Kyrgyz /'kɪrgiz/ |
| Laos /laʊs; 'lɑoʊs/ | Laotian /leɪ'oʊʃn/ |
| Latvia /'lætviə/ | Latvian /'lætviən/ |
| Lebanon /'lɛbənɑn; -nən/ | Lebanese /ˌlɛbə'niz/ |
| Lesotho /lə'soʊtoʊ; lə'sutu/ | Sotho /'soʊtoʊ; 'sutu/, person: Mosotho /mə'soʊtoʊ; -sutu/, people: Basotho /bə'soʊtoʊ; -sutu/ |
| Liberia /laɪ'bɪriə/ | Liberian /laɪ'bɪriən/ |
| Libya /'lɪbiə/ | Libyan /'lɪbiən/ |
| Liechtenstein /'lɪktənstaɪn; -ʃtaɪn/ | Liechtenstein, a Liechtensteiner /'lɪktənstaɪnər/ |
| Lithuania /ˌlɪθu'eɪniə/ | Lithuanian /ˌlɪθu'eɪniən/ |
| Luxembourg /'lʌksəmbərg/ | Luxembourg, a Luxembourger /'lʌksəmbərgər/ |
| Madagascar /ˌmædə'gæskər/ | Madagascan /ˌmædə'gæskən/, a Malagasy /ˌmælə'gæsi/ |
| Malawi /mə'lɑwi/ | Malawian /mə'lɑwiən/ |
| Malaysia /mə'leɪʒə/ | Malaysian /mə'leɪʒn/ |
| (the) Maldives /'mɔldivz; -daɪvz/ | Maldivian /mɔl'dɪviən/ |
| Mali /'mɑli/ | Malian /'mɑliən/ |
| Malta /'mɔltə/ | Maltese /ˌmɔl'tiz/ |
| Mauritania /ˌmɔrə'teɪniə/ | Mauritanian /ˌmɔrə'teɪniən/ |
| Mauritius /mɔ'rɪʃəs/ | Mauritian /mɔ'rɪʃn/ |
| Mexico /'mɛksɪkoʊ/ | Mexican /'mɛksɪkən/ |
| Moldova /mɑl'doʊvə; mɔl-/ | Moldovan /mɑl'doʊvn, mɔl-/ |
| Mongolia /mɑŋ'goʊliə/ | Mongolian /mɑŋ'goʊliən/, a Mongol /'mɑŋgəl; -goʊl/ |
| Morocco /mə'rɑkoʊ/ | Moroccan /mə'rɑkən/ |
| Mozambique /ˌmoʊzæm'bik; -zəm-/ | Mozambican /ˌmoʊzæm'bikən; -zəm-/ |
| Myanmar /'myɑnmɑr/ → Burma | |
| Namibia /nə'mɪbiə/ | Namibian /nə'mɪbiən/ |
| Nauru /nɑ'uru/ | Nauruan /nɑ'uruən/ |
| Nepal /nə'pɔl, nə'pɑl/ | Nepalese /ˌnɛpə'liz/ |
| (the) Netherlands /'nɛðərləndz/ | Dutch /dʌtʃ/, a Dutchman /'dʌtʃmən/, a Dutchwoman /'dʌtʃˌwʊmən/ |
| New Zealand /ˌnu 'zilənd/ | New Zealand, a New Zealander /ˌnu 'ziləndər/ |
| Nicaragua /ˌnɪkə'rɑgwə/ | Nicaraguan /ˌnɪkə'rɑgwən/ |
| Niger /'naɪdʒər; ni'ʒɛr/ | Nigerien /naɪˌdʒɪri'ɛn; ni'ʒeriən/ |
| Nigeria /naɪ'dʒɪriə/ | Nigerian /naɪ'dʒɪriən/ |
| Northern Ireland /ˌnɔrðərn 'aɪərlənd/ | Northern Irish /ˌnɔrðərn 'aɪrɪʃ/, a Northern Irishman /- 'aɪrɪʃmən/, a Northern Irishwoman /- 'aɪrɪʃˌwʊmən/ |
| Norway /'nɔrweɪ/ | Norwegian /nɔr'widʒən/ |
| Oceania /ˌoʊʃi'æniə/ | Oceanian /ˌoʊʃi'æniən/ |
| Oman /oʊ'mɑn/ | Omani /oʊ'mɑni/ |
| Pakistan /'pækəstæn/ | Pakistani /ˌpækə'stæni/ |
| Panama /'pænəmɑ/ | Panamanian /ˌpænə'meɪniən/ |
| Papua New Guinea /ˌpæpyuə nu 'gɪni/ | Papuan /'pæpyuən/ |
| Paraguay /'pærəgwaɪ; -gweɪ/ | Paraguayan /ˌpærə'gwaɪən; -'gweɪ-/ |
| Peru /pə'ru/ | Peruvian /pə'ruviən/ |
| (the) Philippines /'fɪləpinz; ˌfɪlə'pinz/ | Philippine /'fɪləpin/, a Filipino /ˌfɪlə'pinoʊ/ |
| Poland /'poʊlənd/ | Polish /'poʊlɪʃ/, a Pole /poʊl/ |
| Portugal /'pɔrtʃəgl/ | Portuguese /ˌpɔrtʃə'giz; 'pɔrtʃəgiz/ |
| Qatar /'kɑtɑr/ | Qatari /kə'tɑri/ |
| Romania /rʊ'meɪniə; roʊ-/ | Romanian /rʊ'meɪniən; roʊ-/ |
| Russia /'rʌʃə/ | Russian /'rʌʃn/ |

| Noun | Adjective; Person |
|---|---|
| Rwanda /ru'ɑndə/ | Rwandan /ru'ɑndən/ |
| Samoa /sə'moʊə/ | Samoan /sə'moʊen/ |
| San Marino /ˌsæn mə'rinoʊ/ | San Marinese /ˌsæn ˌmærə'niz/ |
| São Tomé and Principe /ˌsaʊ tə'meɪ ən 'prɪnsəpi; ˌsaʊn-/ | São Tomean /ˌsaʊ tə'meɪən; ˌsaʊn-/ |
| Saudi Arabia /ˌsaʊdi ə'reɪbiə; ˌsɔdi-/ | Saudi /'saʊdi; 'sɔdi/, Saudi Arabian /ˌsaʊdi ə'reɪbiən; ˌsɔdi-/ |
| Scandinavia /ˌskændə'neɪviə/ | Scandinavian /ˌskændə'neɪviən/ |
| Scotland /'skɑtlənd/ | Scottish /'skɑtɪʃ/, Scots /skɑts/, a Scot /skɑt/, a Scotsman /'skɑtsmən/, a Scotswoman /'skɑtsˌwʊmən/ |
| Senegal /ˌsɛnə'gɔl; -'gɑl/ | Senegalese /ˌsɛnəgə'liz/ |
| Serbia and Montenegro /ˌsərbiə ən mɑntə'nɛgroʊ; -'nigroʊ/ | Serbian /'sərbiən/, a Serb /sərb/, Montenegrin /ˌmɑntə'nɛgrən; -'nigrən/ |
| (the) Seychelles /seɪ'ʃɛlz; -ʃɛl/ | Seychellois /ˌseɪʃɛl'wɑ/ |
| Sierra Leone /siˌɛrə li'oʊn/ | Sierra Leonean /siˌɛrə li'oʊniən/ |
| Singapore /'sɪŋəpɔr; 'sɪŋgə-/ | Singaporean /ˌsɪŋə'pɔriən; ˌsɪŋgə-/ |
| Slovakia /sloʊ'vɑkiə; -'væk-/ | Slovak /'sloʊvɑk; -væk/ |
| Slovenia /sloʊ'viniə/ | Slovene /'sloʊvin/, Slovenian /sloʊ'viniən/ |
| (the) Solomon Islands /ˌsɑləmən 'aɪləndz/ | Solomon Islander /ˌsɑləmən 'aɪləndər/ |
| Somalia /sə'mɑliə/ | Somali /sə'mɑli/ |
| South Africa /ˌsaʊθ 'æfrɪkə/ | South African /ˌsaʊθ 'æfrɪkən/ |
| Spain /speɪn/ | Spanish /'spænɪʃ/, a Spaniard /'spænyərd/ |
| Sri Lanka /ˌsri 'lɑŋkə; ˌʃri-/ | Sri Lankan /ˌsri 'lɑŋkən; ˌʃri-/ |
| St Kitts and Nevis /seɪnt ˌkɪts ən 'nivəs/ | Kittitian /kə'tɪʃn/, Nevisian /nə'vɪʒn/ |
| St Lucia /seɪnt 'luʃə/ | St Lucian /seɪnt 'luʃən/ |
| St Vincent and the Grenadines /seɪnt 'vɪnsnt ən ðə 'grɛnədinz/ | Vincentian /vɪn'sɛnʃn/ |
| Sudan /su'dæn/ | Sudanese /ˌsudn'iz/ |
| Suriname /ˌsʊrə'nɑmə/ | Surinamese /ˌsʊrənə'miz/ |
| Swaziland /'swɑzilænd/ | Swazi /'swɑzi/ |
| Sweden /'swidn/ | Swedish /'swidɪʃ/, a Swede /swid/ |
| Switzerland /'swɪtsərlənd/ | Swiss /swɪs/ |
| Syria /'sɪriə/ | Syrian /'sɪriən/ |
| Taiwan /ˌtaɪ'wɑn/ | Taiwanese /ˌtaɪwɑ'niz/ |
| Tajikistan /tɑˌdʒɪkə'stɑn; -'stæn-; -ˌdʒik-/ | Tajik /tɑ'dʒɪk; tɑ'dʒik/ |
| Tanzania /ˌtænzə'niə/ | Tanzanian /ˌtænzə'niən/ |
| Thailand /'taɪlænd/ | Thai /taɪ/ |
| Togo /'toʊgoʊ/ | Togolese /ˌtoʊgə'liz/ |
| Tonga /'tɑŋgə/ | Tongan /'tɑŋgən/ |
| Trinidad and Tobago /ˌtrɪnədæd ən tə'beɪgoʊ/ | Trinidadian /ˌtrɪnə'dædiən; -'deɪd-/, Tobagonian /ˌtoʊbə'goʊniən/ |
| Tunisia /tu'niʒə/ | Tunisian /tu'niʒn/ |
| Turkey /'tərki/ | Turkish /'tərkɪʃ/; a Turk /tərk/ |
| Turkmenistan /tərkˌmɛnə'stɑn; -'stæn-/ | Turkmen /'tərkmɛn; -mən/ |
| Tuvalu /tu'vɑlu/ | Tuvaluan /tu'vɑluən/ |
| Uganda /yu'gændə/ | Ugandan /yu'gændən/ |
| Ukraine /yu'kreɪn; 'yukreɪn/ | Ukrainian /yu'kreɪniən/ |
| (the) United Arab Emirates /yuˌnaɪt̬əd ˌærəb 'ɛmərəts/ | Emirian /ɛ'mɪriən; ɪ-/ |
| (the) United Kingdom /yuˌnaɪt̬əd 'kɪŋdəm/ | British /'brɪt̬ɪʃ/, a Briton /'brɪtn/ |
| (the) United States of America /yuˌnaɪt̬əd ˌsteɪts əv ə'mɛrɪkə/ | American /ə'mɛrɪkən/ |
| Uruguay /'yʊrəgwaɪ; -gweɪ/ | Uruguayan /ˌyʊrə'gwaɪən; -'gweɪ-/ |
| Uzbekistan /ʊzˌbɛkə'stɑn; -'stæn/ | Uzbek /'ʊzbɛk/ |
| Vanuatu /ˌvænu'ɑtu; ˌvænwɑ'tu; ˌvɑn-/ | Vanuatan /ˌvænuɑ'tuən; ˌvænwɑ'tu; ˌvɑn-/ |
| Venezuela /ˌvɛnə'zweɪlə/ | Venezuelan /ˌvɛnə'zweɪlən/ |
| Vietnam /ˌviɛt'nɑm; -'næm/ | Vietnamese /ˌviətnə'miz; viˌɛt-/ |
| Wales /weɪlz/ | Welsh /wɛlʃ/, a Welshman /'wɛlʃmən/, a Welshwoman /'wɛlʃˌwʊmən/ |
| (the) West Indies /ˌwɛst 'ɪndiz/ | West Indian /ˌwɛst 'ɪndiən/ |
| (the) Yemen Republic /ˌyɛmən rɪ'pʌblɪk/ | Yemeni /'yɛməni/ |
| Zambia /'zæmbiə/ | Zambian /'zæmbiən/ |
| Zimbabwe /zɪm'bɑbweɪ; -wi/ | Zimbabwean /zɪm'bɑbweɪən; -wien/ |

# Key to study pages

## Words that go together (A2–A3)

**EXERCISE 1**

make a mistake, enter a contest, open an account, play a trick, do a favor, take a picture, break a promise

**EXERCISE 2**

a a low salary
b a narrow street
c the wrong answer
d an odd number
e a minor offense

**EXERCISE 3**

1 a sharp increase
2 a wild guess
3 a heavy fine
4 fierce competition
5 full responsibility

**EXERCISE 4**

a at
b with
c to
d from
e in
f to, for
g of
h to

**EXERCISE 5**

1. broke his promise
2. caught fire
3. formed a line
4. achieved her ambition
5 tell the difference
6 committed suicide
7 drives me crazy
8 draw the curtains

**EXERCISE 6**

a cleaning
b calling
c to come
d making
e to smoke
f to loan

## Phrasal verbs (A4–A5)

**EXERCISE 1**

a off
b for
c out
d across
e up
f down
g of
h down

**EXERCISE 2**

a take it off
b look it up
c get over it
d get around to it
e threw it away
f put it off

## Word Formation (A6–A7)

1 eight
2 1776
3 but
4 no
5 after
6 before
7 because you have to write it again
8 supersonic
9 very small
10 very full
11 incorrect uncertain impossible irregular unsure illegal invalid irrelevant impatient illegible
12 no
13 yes
14 a road that links two or more states
15 development kindness arrangement imagination happiness organization (the "y" of "happy" becomes an "i")
16 actor teacher conductor explorer
17 magnetize beautify sharpen generalize loosen purify
18 useful friendless noticeable thirsty

## Writing a paper (A12–A14)

**EXERCISE 1**

**paragraph 1** nowadays, recently
**paragraph 2** as a result, consequently, therefore
**paragraph 3** furthermore, in addition, moreover
**paragraph 4** nevertheless, on the other hand, while, however
**paragraph 5** in conclusion, to sum up, finally

**EXERCISE 2**

compared with = in comparison with
obviously = clearly
affect sth drastically = have a devastating impact on sth
in particular = especially
appreciate = value
moreover = furthermore
whereas = while
is a significant factor = plays an important role
in contrast = on the other hand
a cross section = a representative group
as a result = consequently
grave difficulties = serious problems

**EXERCISE 3**

**suggested plan:**

**paragraph 1**
— recent advances in science – new possibilities
**paragraph 2**
— unknown dangers
— interfering with nature
— can't go back
**paragraph 3**
— religious concerns
— designer babies
— cloning humans – political purposes
**paragraph 4**
— new cures for illnesses
— banning impractical – impossible to regulate

**EXERCISE 4**

Recently On the other hand Furthermore
As a result In conclusion

## Interpreting Graphs (A15–A17)

**EXERCISE 1**

1 peaked
2 1994 and 1996
3 plummeted
4 January and August

5 leveled out
6 1996
7 increased/rose
8 declined/decreased/dropped/fell

**EXERCISE 2**

1 Sales increased/rose dramatically/sharply.
2 Sales decreased rapidly.
3 Sales increased gradually.
4 Sales fell steadily.
5 Sales rose moderately.
6 Sales increased slightly.

1 There was a dramatic increase in sales from 1994 to 1996.
2 There was a rapid decrease in sales from 1996 to 1998.
3 There was a gradual increase in sales between 1998 and 2001.
4 There was a steady fall in sales from 2001 to 2003.
5 Between July and August 2003 there was a moderate rise in sales.
6 There was a slight increase in sales from November to December 2003.

**EXERCISE 3**

| | | |
|---|---|---|
| 1 of | 3 at, in, to | 5 at, of |
| 2 From, to, to | 4 at, of | 6 by, by |

**EXERCISE 4**

well over ↑
just over
exactly — 10 000
almost/nearly — half
just under
well under ↓

**EXERCISE 5**

text with suggested corrections:
Family A's biggest expenditure each month is the mortgage. Family A spends far more on their mortgage than they do on anything else (32%). This is exactly **double** what they spend on entertainment each month. Their food budget (19%) is **slightly higher** than their entertainment budget, while they spend **just under** 10% each month on clothes. Family B's clothes budget is a **little** less (5%). Family B's entertainment budget in **considerably** less than Family A's, at just 9%. In contrast, Family B spends much more on bills each month, **nearly** a quarter of the whole monthly budget. This is compensated for by their mortgage, which is **much** less than Family A's, at only 24%. **Just under** 15% of their monthly budget goes on the car, significantly more than the 9% that Family A spends each month. In general Family B spends more on necessary items such as bills, food and the car, while Family A allows **significantly** more money for entertainment and clothes.

## Letter writing (A18–A21)

**EXERCISE 1**

| | | | |
|---|---|---|---|
| a 6 | e 12 | i 11 | m 1 |
| b 9 | f 8 | j 5 | n 7 |
| c 14 | g 13 | k 4 | |
| d 3 | h 2 | l 10 | |

**EXERCISE 2**

| | | |
|---|---|---|
| 1 d | 3 f | 5 a |
| 2 e | 4 b | 6 c |

**EXERCISE 3**

| | | |
|---|---|---|
| 1 d | 4 f | 7 a |
| 2 h | 5 b | 8 e |
| 3 c | 6 I | 9 g |

## TOEIC and TOEFL practice tests (A22–A23)

**EXERCISE 1**

1C, 2B, 3A, 4A, 5D, 6D, 7B, 8A, 9C, 10B, 11D, 12A, 13B, 14A

**EXERCISE 2**

| | | | |
|---|---|---|---|
| 1 B | 4 D | 7 A | 10 B |
| 2 C | 5 A | 8 C | 11 A |
| 3 D | 6 B | 9 D | 12 D |

## Taking notes (A24–A25)

**EXERCISE 1**

| | | |
|---|---|---|
| 1 | * | this is an important point |
| 2 | ≈ | is approximately equal to |
| 3 | ≠ | is not, does not equal to |
| 4 | + | and, plus |
| 5 | = | equals, is |
| 6 | @ | at |
| 7 | > | is more than |
| 8 | < | is less than |
| 9 | ♂ | male |
| 10 | ♀ | female |
| 11 | & | and |
| 12 | " | the same word as above |

**EXERCISE 2**

| | |
|---|---|
| vol. | volume |
| ex. | example |
| usu. | usually |
| diffs. | differences |
| sing. | singular |
| approx. | approximately |
| incl. | including, inclusive |

**EXERCISE 3**

| | |
|---|---|
| i.e. | that is |
| e.g. | for example |
| c. | cups(s); century; about, approximately |
| pp. | pages |

**EXERCISE 5**

suggested notes:

*Energy*
*Most energy for heat, light, machs. etc. fossil fuels. Will run out.*
*a) need altern. srcs – e.g. wind, solar pwr.*
*Renew.; not poll. air.*
*b) don't waste:*
*– use less elec. + wtr.*
*– insul. houses.*

# Pronunciation

If more than one pronunciation is given for a word, they are all acceptable. The first form given is considered the most common. Not all possible American pronunciations and dialects are shown in this dictionary. For example, some speakers only use /ɔ/ when it is followed by /r/ (as in the word **horse** /hɔrs/) and use /ɑ/ in all other words which are shown with /ɔ/ in this dictionary, so that they pronounce both **caught** and **cot** as /kɑt/.

/ - / A hyphen is used to show another possible pronunciation when only part of the pronunciation changes. The part that remains the same is replaced by the hyphen.

**project** /ˈprɑdʒɛkt, -dʒɪkt/

/ ˈ / This mark shows that the syllable after it is said with more force (stress) than the other syllables in the word or group of words. For example, **any** /ˈɛni/ has a stress on the first syllable; **depend** /dɪˈpɛnd/ has a stress on the second syllable.

/ ˌ / This mark shows that the syllable is said with more force than other syllables in a word, but with a stress that is not as strong as for those syllables marked / ˈ /. So in the word **pronunciation** /prəˌnʌnsiˈeɪʃn/, the main stress is on the syllable /ˈeɪ/, and the secondary stress is on the syllable /ˌnʌn/.

/t̬/ American speakers use this sound, which is like a quick /d/, in many words spelled with *-t-* or *-tt-*. It is used in words after a vowel or /r/ and before an unstressed vowel or syllabic /l/.

city /ˈsɪt̬i/; parting /ˈpɑrt̬ɪŋ/; little /ˈlɪt̬l/

/t̬/ also occurs in the *-ed* and *-ing* forms of verbs whose stem ends in /t/ after a vowel or /r/, e.g. **patting** /ˈpæt̬ɪŋ/; **patted** /ˈpæt̬əd/ and in the comparative and superlative forms of adjectives which end in /t/ after a vowel or /r/, e.g. **smarter** /ˈsmɑrt̬ər/; **smartest** /ˈsmɑt̬əst/.

## Strong and weak forms

Some very common words, e.g. **an**, **as**, **that**, and **of**, have two or more pronunciations: a strong form and one or more weak forms. In speech, the weak forms are more common. For example, **for** is /fər/ in the sentence *It's for you*. The strong form occurs when the word comes at the end of a sentence or when it is given special emphasis. For example, **for** is /fɔr/ in *Who's it for?* and *The present's not ˈfrom Ann, it's ˈfor her.*

## Pronunciation in derivative and compound words

Many **derivatives** are formed by adding a common suffix to the end of a word. These are pronounced by simply saying the suffix after the word. For example, **safely** /ˈseɪfli/ is said by joining the suffix *-ly* /li/ to the word *safe* /seɪf/.

In **compounds** (made up of two or more words which are separated by a space or hyphen), the pronunciation of the individual words is not repeated. The dictionary shows how the compound is stressed by using the marks / ˈ / and / ˌ /. In **ˈhot dog**, the stress is on the first word. In **ˌcivil ˈrights**, the secondary stress is on the first syllable of *civil* and the main stress is on *rights*.